P9-CDX-146

THE NEW-YORK HISTORICAL SOCIETY'S DICTIONARY OF ARTISTS IN AMERICA

1564-1860

THE NEW-YORK HISTORICAL SOCIETY'S DICTIONARY OF ARTISTS IN AMERICA

1564-1860

BY GEORGE C. GROCE

AND DAVID H. WALLACE

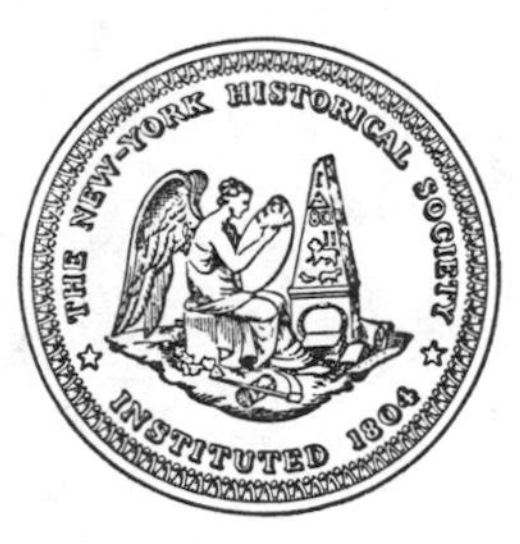

New Haven and London: YALE UNIVERSITY PRESS

Printed in the United States of America by
The Murray Printing Company, Westford, Mass.
Library of Congress catalog card number: 57–6338.

ISBN 0–300–00519–9

15 14 13 12 11 10 9 8

CONTENTS

Introduction vii

Acknowledgments xx

Abbreviations xxvii

Dictionary 1

Key to Citations of Sources 713

INTRODUCTION

THE PAST THIRTY-FIVE YEARS have seen the growth of a lively interest in early American art, an interest expressed in avid private and public collecting and in a deluge of publications. There are several reasons for this phenomenon, among them the emergence of the picture as a serious rival to the printed word, the European-inspired "cult of the primitive," a general awakening of interest in social history, and the widespread search for national roots in an age of international anxiety. In attempting to keep up with the demand for information, however, scholarship has been hampered in recent years not so much by a lack of material as by the lack of a convenient guide to it. What biographical compendia we have had in the field, such as Smith's *Biographical Index of American Artists, Mallett's Index of Artists,* and Fielding's *Dictionary of American Painters, Sculptors, and Engravers,* are out-of-date or otherwise inadequate, while the most comprehensive listing of artists associated with America, strangely enough, is scattered through the many volumes of Thieme and Becker's *Allgemeines Lexikon der bildenden Künstler,* available in few American libraries and then only to those who can read German. What is needed is a comprehensive, documented biographical dictionary summarizing a generation's research on the artists of early America. *The New-York Historical Society's Dictionary of Artists in America, 1564–1860* is designed to meet that need.*

SCOPE OF THE DICTIONARY

This is a purely biographical dictionary, arranged alphabetically by artist. The aim has been to give for every artist as much as possible of the following information: full name, dates and places of birth and death, media and subject matter of his work, chronology of residences and exhibitions, pupils, and in some instances locations and reproductions of representative works. It should be noted that the length of an entry does not indicate the relative importance of the subject. Some minor artists whose lives have not hitherto been recorded will be found to have entries much longer and more detailed than those dealing with better-known artists. Similarly an effort has been made by the authors not to impinge on the domain of the art critics by

* A brief account of the history of the *Dictionary* will be found in the Acknowledgments.

attempting to judge the merits of particular artists. What has been aimed at is an objective setting down of the essential facts in the lives of those men and women who played a part, however humble, in the art life of early America.

All entries are documented, the source references being separated from the text in each instance by the symbol ¶. An analysis of the major categories of sources used will be found in the next section of the Introduction and a Key to Citations follows the main body of the *Dictionary*.

Although indicated in the title *Artists in America, 1564–1860,* a more precise statement of the *Dictionary*'s scope will be helpful.

The term "artist" is here understood to include persons or firms engaged in any of the following categories of artistic activity: PAINTING, including portrait, miniature, figure, landscape, historical, religious, still life, allegorical, and heraldic painting in oils or water colors, theorem or poonah painting, representational sign and banner painting, but *not* including house painting and related crafts; DRAWING and SKETCHING, including work in pen-and-ink, pencil, charcoal, and pastels, but *not* including mechanical drawing, map drawing, and print making; SCULPTURE, including modeling in clay and wax, carving in stone or wood where the intention was to represent natural objects, cameo-cutting, and the making of plaster busts and figures (image-making); ENGRAVING on steel, copper, and wood, etching, seal-cutting or engraving, and the cutting of dies for coins and medals; LITHOGRAPHY; and SILHOUETTE CUTTING. Architects, photographers, and craftsmen, as such, are not included unless they are known to have done artistic work as defined above. Persons listed simply as "artist" in census or other records have been included unless found, through other evidence, to have been actors, musicians, photographers, or otherwise ineligible for inclusion in a dictionary of artists as here interpreted.

The phrase "in America" has been used to indicate that coverage includes not only artists who were born in or spent most of their lives in what is now the continental United States, but also foreign artists, amateur or professional, who visited the country during the period covered. Conversely, artists who were born in America but spent most of their lives abroad also are included. The criterion of selection is simply that the artist must have been active in the present area of the continental United States in 1860 or before.

The span of years covered by the *Dictionary* is approximately three centuries, from 1564 to 1860. The earlier date was determined by the fact that no artist is now known to have worked in America before the arrival of the Frenchman Jacques Le Moyne in Florida in that year. Only one other artist is known to have been in America in the 16th century, John White, Governor of Raleigh's colony on Roanoke Island. From the 17th century only a handful of names have come down to us. The number of artists increases slowly through the Colonial period, then burgeons after the Revolution until by the middle of the 19th century the whole country appears to swarm with artists in every medium and of every degree of merit. The year 1860 was arbitrarily selected as the terminal date for the *Dictionary* primarily because it has long been accepted as a convenient date for the end of the "Early American" period. Practical considerations also influenced the decision, for the addition of ten or twenty years would have increased the bulk of the volume to wholly unmanageable proportions.

In applying the terminal date of 1860 to the selection of artists, the procedure has been to include only persons known to have been engaged in artistic activity before 1861. Unless there is evidence of such activity before 1861, artists born in 1841 or later have been excluded on the assumption that their active careers would have begun after 1860.

To summarize, *The New-York Historical Society's Dictionary of Artists in America, 1564–1860* is a documented biographical dictionary of painters, draftsmen, sculptors, engravers, lithographers, and allied artists, either amateur or professional, native or foreign-born, who worked within the present continental limits of the United States between the years 1564 and 1860, inclusive.

Sources

Following the example of the *Dictionary of American Biography,* the *Dictionary of National Biography,* and Thieme and Becker's *Allgemeines Lexikon der bildenden Künstler,* this *Dictionary* provides documentation for each entry, including the authors' sources, additional references, and in many cases references to reproductions and the location of works. The symbol ¶ has been used to separate the biographical information from source references in each entry. Books, pamphlets, periodicals, and newspapers are cited in italics; articles in periodicals, and unpublished manuscripts, within quotation marks. A complete Key to Citations will be found at the end of the volume. This Key, it should be emphasized, does not pretend to be a working bibliography of American art, since it contains only titles cited in the documentation of the *Dictionary*. Information supplied directly by correspondents is cited as "Information courtesy of [name]" and the names and addresses of these correspondents are given in the Acknowledgments. Abbreviations used are explained in the list of Abbreviations.

From the Key to Citations it will readily be seen that a wide variety of source material has been tapped in the research for this *Dictionary*. Among the important groups of primary sources (*i.e.*, published or unpublished materials contemporary with the period covered by the *Dictionary*) are city and regional directories, census records, exhibition catalogues, autobiographies and memoirs, signed and dated works of art, collections of vital statistics, newspapers, and periodicals. Major groups of secondary materials (not contemporary with the early period) include biographical dictionaries, local histories, genealogies, and the all-important books, monographs, and articles on art and artists. The use made of each of these types of sources in preparing *The New-York Historical Society's Dictionary of Artists in America, 1564–1860* will be described in some detail, both as an aid for evaluating this work and as a guide to others working in the same field.

Primary Sources

Directories. Probably no single type of source has provided more artists' names than the directories of towns, cities, counties, states, and regions, of which the first appeared in Boston, New York, and Philadelphia shortly before the end of the 18th century. In some cases directories provide the only information we have, while in others they provide a fairly reliable chronological and geographical framework on which to hang otherwise unrelated information from other sources.

Directories generally are of two types: the City Directory (cited as CD with place and date), in which all the names are thrown together in one alphabetical list, and the Business Directory (BD), in which individuals are classified according to trade or profession. Sometimes both are contained in the same volume, as in the Philadelphia directories for 1854–60, but more often they were published separately. Business directories came in later than the city directories, few appearing before 1840.

The City Directory, potentially the richest field for the gleaner of artists' names, has in this work been used chiefly to supplement information on artists already known by name. The reason is, simply, that the labor of reading through these directories name by name in search of artists would consume more time than the result would justify in a project of this magnitude. Pioneer work in this field has been done and published, however (for example, H. Glenn Brown and Maude O. Brown, *A Directory of the Book-Arts and Book Trade in Philadelphia to 1820, Including Painters and Engravers,* New York Public Library, 1950, and George L. McKay, "A Register of Artists, Booksellers, Printers, and Publishers in New York City [1781–1820]," *New York Public Library Bulletin,* XLIII–XLV, 1939–41), and the artists so uncovered incorporated in the *Dictionary*. But the systematic searching of the thousands of pre-Civil War directories published in the United States has scarcely begun. This is a project which could well be undertaken by individuals or societies interested in the art of particular localities or regions.

Business Directories, since they are conveniently classified by trades, yield their treasures far more readily. The art researcher need only look up "Artists," "Painters," "Engravers," "Lithographers," "Sculptors," and extract the names listed under those headings. Knowing the names, it is then a simple, if time-consuming, matter to follow them through the usually more complete City Directories. This is the method which was followed by the compilers of this work.

Business and City Directories cited in the *Dictionary* are available for reference at the Library of Congress, New York Public Library, or New-York Historical Society. A list of cities, etc., whose directories have been consulted will be found on p. 713 of the Key to Citations.

Census Records. An important primary source which has yielded much information on known artists, as well as many new names, is the collection of manuscript United States Census reports in the National Archives, Washington, D.C. No more than a sampling could be made among the thousands of volumes in this collection, and the *Dictionary* accordingly incorporates the results of a search of the following: Baltimore, Md., 1850, 1860; Boston, Mass., 1850, 1860; Charleston, S.C., 1850; Detroit, Mich., 1860; District of Columbia, 1850, 1860; Litchfield, Conn., 1850; Louisville, Ky., 1850; New Haven and New London, Conn., 1850; New Orleans, La., 1850, 1860; New York, N.Y., 1850, 1860; Ohio, 1850; Philadelphia, Pa., 1850, 1860; Pittsburgh, Pa., 1860; San Francisco, Cal., 1860; Vermont, 1850.

Useful though they undoubtedly are, census records must be used with caution. Difficult handwriting and erratic spelling often make it impossible to make out what names were intended. Dr. Groce, who initiated and carried out all the census research, estimates that more than half of the artists listed in the New York City census, 1850 and 1860, had to be left out because the names could not be deciphered. Another danger inherent in the use of census records lies in the unreliability of their statements concerning ages. Too often, it seems, the information given in a census report represents merely a guess on the part of the census-taker or boarding-house keeper. When birth dates are already known from other sources, they seldom correspond to the age given in the census; similarly, when the same name appears in both the 1850 and 1860 census, the age in 1860 may be anywhere from three to fifteen years more than in 1850, and only rarely the expected ten. For this reason, birth dates or ages derived from census records must be considered only approximations. Still another peculiarity of the census, which it shares to a certain degree with the directories, is the use of the vague term "artist" as an occupational category. The art researcher must be wary of these "artists," since the term has been found to cover not only artists in the sense here understood but also at times musicians, actors, and photographers, and, it is suspected, even prostitutes. Where such "artists" have been found, through other evidence, to be inadmissible, they have been omitted; otherwise, they have been included.

Despite these limitations, the census records contain undeniably useful information on many legitimate artists. From the test samples made in our research, two thousand artists were picked up, of whom about one quarter were already known. Of the new artists thus added to the *Dictionary,* a sizeable, though undetermined, proportion were subsequently found in city directories.

Exhibition Catalogues. Qualitatively, the most valuable type of primary source material reposes in the catalogues of public exhibitions held in major cities from 1795 to the end of the early period. Access to most of these catalogues, some of them very rare, has been made much easier in recent years through the publication of indexes or cumulative exhibition records, alphabetized by artist, and in most cases our citations are to these volumes, although much of our research was done in the catalogues themselves. The galleries whose exhibition records have thus been made easily accessible are as follows:

Pennsylvania Academy of Fine Arts, Society of Artists, and Artists' Fund Society, Philadelphia, 1811–70, compiled by Anna Wells Rutledge (Philadelphia, American Philosophical Society, 1955)

American Academy of Fine Arts, Apollo Gallery and Association, and American Art-Union, New York, 1816–52, compiled by Mary Bartlett Cowdrey (New York, New-York Historical Society, 1954)

National Academy of Design, New York, 1826–60, compiled by Mary Bartlett Cowdrey (New York, New-York Historical Society, 1943)

Athenaeum Gallery, Boston, 1827–73, compiled by Mabel Munson Swan (Boston, Boston Athenaeum, 1940)

Galleries whose exhibition records have been compiled but not published are Maryland Historical Society, 1848–1907, by Anna Wells Rutledge, and National Academy of Design, 1861–90, by Mary Bartlett Cowdrey. Available catalogues of the Washington (D.C.) Art Association, 1857–60, and the American Institute of the City of New York, 1842, 1844–51, 1856, have also been searched.

Autobiographies, etc. Autobiographical writings, contemporary memoirs, diaries, letters, and other published or manuscript contemporary records are, of course, among the most valuable sources of information on early artists. Much has been located through guides to published writings on American history and art, but still more undoubtedly remains unused. Future work in this field will be much aided by the comprehensive program of locating, acquiring, and microfilming records of artists now being carried on by the Archives of American Art, Detroit, Michigan.

Signed and Dated Works of Art. Quite a number of minor artists, particularly 19th century "primitives," are known only through signed and dated examples of their work. Even though some of these signatures may eventually prove to be incorrectly transcribed or fraudulent, these names have been included here in the hope that publication may lead to further information.

Vital Statistics. For artists born in Massachusetts before 1850, it is frequently possible to establish the date and place of birth, marriage, and even death through the published lists of vital records which are available for nearly every town in the Commonwealth. Similar lists are available for some towns and cities outside Massachusetts, notably Providence, R.I. The bulk of such records, however, remain unpublished.

Newspapers. Much valuable information on the lives and work of early artists is hidden away in the columns of early newspapers. No attempt has been made by the compilers of the *Dictionary* to go through any newspapers page by page in search of such material. Some of this material has been utilized, however, through the aid of several useful compilations of extracts from newspapers. Notable among these are the following: George Francis

Dow, *The Arts and Crafts in New England, 1704–1775* (Topsfield, Mass., 1927); Rita S. Gottesman, *The Arts and Crafts in New York, 1726–1799* (New York, New-York Historical Society, 1938 and 1954); William Kelby, *Notes on American Artists, 1754–1820* (New York, New-York Historical Society, 1922); and Alfred Coxe Prime, *The Arts and Crafts in Philadelphia, Maryland, and South Carolina, 1721–1800* (Topsfield, Mass., Walpole Society, 1929–32).

Much other information from contemporary newspapers has been gleaned from the unpublished notes of the Delgado Art Museum Project, W.P.A., and a number of state Historical Records Surveys conducted by the W.P.A.

Obituaries of a number of artists have been located through the help of indexes to the obituaries in the *Boston Transcript,* [New York] *Evening Post,* and [New York] *Christian Intelligencer.*

Periodicals. Early magazines, like the newspapers, often contained notices of artists. Systematic searching of these has been limited to the illustrations in *Port Folio* and *Analectic Magazine* and to obituaries in *American Art Review,* 1880–81, and *American Art Annual,* 1898–1919, 1925. Other early periodicals such as *The Crayon, The* [London] *Art Journal,* and *Harper's Weekly* and *Monthly* have been consulted in following leads from other sources.

Secondary Sources

Biographical Dictionaries. Of special value to this work have been the *Dictionary of American Biography,* the *Dictionary of National Biography, Appleton's Cyclopaedia of American Biography,* Walter G. Strickland's *Dictionary of Irish Artists,* Samuel Redgrave's *Dictionary of Artists of the English School,* Clara E. Clement's and Laurence Hutton's *Artists of the Nineteenth Century,* Emmanuel Bénézit's *Dictionnaire Critique et Documentaire des Peintres, Sculpteurs, Dessinateurs, et Graveurs,* and Algernon Graves's *Dictionary of Artists Who Have Exhibited Works in the Principal London Exhibitions of Oil Paintings from 1760 to 1880.* Most valuable of all, however, has been Ulrich Thieme and Felix Becker's *Allgemeines Lexikon der bildenden Künstler,* which stands without a peer among artist dictionaries for comprehensiveness and excellence.

Local histories. Much useful and otherwise unavailable information on artists of local note has been found in the numerous histories of towns, cities, counties, and states which began to appear about the 1870's. These accounts, though seldom documented and often based on memory rather than research, often provide the only clues to the identification of obscure artists, both professional and amateur. A systematic search for such material has not been attempted.

Genealogies. Genealogies and family histories in the large collection at the New-York Historical Society have frequently proved useful in identifying artists known only through signed works, exhibition records, or directory listings. They are particularly helpful for artists of English, Dutch, or French Huguenot descent whose forbears settled in New England and New York before 1800.

Books, Monographs, and Articles on Art and Artists. Of all secondary sources, the most numerous and most important are the studies by amateur and professional art historians. This group includes general studies from William Dunlap and Henry T. Tuckerman to Virgil Barker, James T. Flexner, and Oliver W. Larkin; regional studies such as French's *Art and Artists in Connecticut,* Butts' *Art in Wisconsin,* and Peat's *Pioneer Painters of Indiana;* * topical works like Taft's *History of American Sculpture,* Bolton's *Early American Portrait Painters in Miniature,* Peters' *America on Stone,* and Stauffer's *American Engravers;* and countless books, monographs, and articles on individual artists from "The Late Frederick S. Agate," by Francis W. Edmonds, in *The Knickerbocker, or New-York Monthly Magazine,* August 1844, to Eliot C. Clark's *Alexander Wyant* (New York, 1916).

As yet there is no adequate bibliographical guide to the voluminous literature on American art. Use of the *Art Index* (1944–48) and Griffin's *Writings in American History* (1906–40) has made easier the task of locating many articles and books, while the Union Catalogue, Library of Congress, has been helpful in finding illustrated books of travel in the United States. A number of specialized periodicals have also been searched for pertinent articles: *American Collector,* Vols. 1–17; *Antiques,* Vols. 1–55; *Art in America,* Vols. 1–39; *Art Digest,* Vols. 1–14; *Art Quarterly,* Vols. 1–14; *Magazine of Art,* Vols. 30–40; *Panorama,* Vols. 1–4.

The value, in sum, of all this secondary material is immeasurable, but the value of individual works varies greatly and can only be judged through intensive study of original sources. In general it has been the policy of the

* Edna T. Whitley's *Kentucky Ante-Bellum Portraiture,* unfortunately, was published after the *Dictionary* had gone to press, but Mrs. Whitley had earlier made available many of her then-unpublished notes.

authors of the *Dictionary* to rely on the accuracy of documented studies. Wherever practicable, undocumented work has been supplemented or corrected by additional research.

Uses of the Dictionary

The total number of artists listed in *The New-York Historical Society's Dictionary of Artists in America, 1564–1860* is between ten and eleven thousand. By way of comparison, Dunlap's *History of the Rise and Progress of the Arts of Design in the United States,* published in 1834, recorded about five hundred artists. Later compilers such as Mantle Fielding and Ralph Clifton Smith had added by 1930 about another thousand names, thus bringing to approximately fifteen hundred the total of recorded artists in America who were active in 1860 or before. In short, the users of the *Dictionary* will have at their fingertips information about seven times as many artists as have been recorded hitherto in a single volume.

Although the *Dictionary* will be used primarily by students interested in particular artists and is therefore arranged alphabetically by artist, it can also be used in other ways. For example, statistical studies might be made of the several categories of artist or subject matter, and artists active in a particular city or region might be listed through a cover-to-cover search of the *Dictionary*. Such studies could form the bases for some very interesting contributions to cultural history. Other unexplored areas include the work of the artists who accompanied American exploring expeditions in foreign waters, and the artistic contributions of French, Dutch, Irish, and other national stocks to American art.

The hundreds of requests for information which have been answered while the work has been in progress have shown that the *Dictionary* will be useful not only to art historians, as such, but to many others as well. Authors and editors seeking illustrations and caption copy; descendants in search of artist ancestors; owners and dealers anxious to identify the artists of particular works; art museums, historical societies, and other institutions preparing catalogues of special exhibitions or permanent collections; library cataloguers seeking information on illustrators, engravers, and lithographers; reference librarians who can ill afford time-consuming research for all of these—these are some of the people this *Dictionary* is designed to serve.

The reader who is making a special study of an artist or group of artists will find the *Dictionary* useful chiefly as a starting point for intensive research. By consulting the sources cited and following up clues provided by an artist's chronology and exhibition record, the researcher in many cases will be able to supplement the *Dictionary*'s information. The majority of readers, however, will find most of what they need to know about particular artists—when and where they were born, worked, and died, and what sort of work they did—within the pages of this volume.

Among the thousands of artists here gathered together for the first time, there are many, of course, about whom next to nothing is known. Some are known only through extant, signed works; others through isolated directory or census listings. Some of these undoubtedly will remain forever mere names, but further identification of many others will come in time, through systematic research or by chance. A few sample entries dealing with hitherto unrecorded or misrecorded artists will illustrate the possibilities. The following entry, for example, records the activity of an artist overlooked by earlier American art dictionaries:

> ROSS, GEORGE GATES (1814–1856). Portrait painter, born April 10, 1814, at Springfield (N.J.); active in Newark (N.J.) from 1835 to 1856; exhibited at National Academy and Apollo Association; died in Newark August 17, 1856. ¶ Information courtesy Mrs. Grace P. Smith of Maplewood (N.J.), who cites *Newarker,* April 1936, and Newark *Daily Advertiser,* April 5, 1847, June 5, 1850, Dec. 3, 1852, Dec. 11, 1854, August 18 and 19, 1856; Newark CD 1835–56; Cowdrey, NAD; Cowdrey, AA & AAU; repros., *American Collector,* XVI (Jan. 1948), 6–7.

We have had scholarly studies of great portraitists like Stuart, Copley, and Sully. Recently, itinerant and "primitive" painters have come into the public eye. George G. Ross was neither a great master nor an itinerant jack-of-all-trades, but he and thousands like him were the backbone of the pre-photographic portrait industry in the United States and important indicators of American achievement and taste in the 19th century. In the past these men have been ignored wholesale. This should not be the case in the future.

Important also, and equally victims of previous oversight or caprice, are the host of European artists who have left first-hand pictorial impressions of the early American scene. American art history, aside from the anonymous work of the Indians, begins with such foreign visitors, and their numbers increased until by the 19th century hardly a picturesque spot in the country had escaped being recorded in the sketchbook of some talented amateur or professional from Europe. To cite but one example, the Bordentown (N.J.) estate of Joseph Bonaparte, Count de Survilliers and brother of Napoleon, was the home of one alien artist and was pictured by at least two others. The resident was Joseph's daughter Charlotte Julie (1802–1839), who exhibited landscapes and flower pieces at the Pennsylvania Academy in 1822–24; the visitors who recorded their visual impressions of the estate were Captain Basil Hall, the English traveler who toured America in 1827–28, and Karl Bodmer, the Swiss painter whose work has recently come into deserved prominence. No earlier dictionary of American artists has listed these three, or hundreds of other pictorial reporters from the other side of the Atlantic.

If thousands of artists who did exist have been forgotten, it is unfortunately true that some who never existed have been recorded. Dunlap's inadvertencies, such as listing Justus Englehardt Kühn as "Cain" and Henry Benbridge as "Bembridge," have created typographical "ghosts" which continue to haunt many an otherwise erudite page. The misreading of William Jennys' signature created another ghost, J. William Jennys. And the whimsical John Wesley Jarvis probably was himself responsible for the crediting of his "Musidora" at the 1814 exhibition of the Society of Artists to a mysterious J. Sivraj! The *Dictionary* aims to lay as many of these ghosts as possible.

In addition to the omitted artist and the "ghost," there is the very real artist whose identity has been lost through confusion of names. "Alphabet" Burnham, painter of a celebrated 1837 Michigan election scene, is a case in point. The artist's real name was Thomas Mickell Burnham, but a historian's faulty memory or the misreading of the abbreviation "Thos." transmuted this in later years to T. H. O. P. Burnham, whence arose the nickname "Alphabet." More recently the initials were reshuffled, by analogy with the name of the popular War of 1812 hero Thomas Oliver Hazard Perry, to read T. O. H. P., and the artist then was tentatively identified with an eccentric, though not artistic, Boston bookseller named Thomas Oliver Hazard Perry Burnham. Research for the *Dictionary* restored to the original artist his rightful distinction and corrected a long-lived error.

Although the *Dictionary* aims to give for every artist, great or small, the full name, dates and places of birth, residence, exhibition, and death, and the media and subject matter of his work, in most instances some of the desiderata have not been found. There were some cases, however, where tiny fragments gathered as research went forward fell into place, mosaic-like, to produce a comparatively full record of lives that long had been forgotten. In 1833, for instance, William Dunlap asked in his diary, "Who is Bowman?" Readers of the *Dictionary* will learn, what Dunlap could not, that James Bowman of Mercer (Pa.) had gone to London in the early 1820's riding the crest of a wave of local prestige only to return in 1829 and, unlike his good friend Chester Harding, spend the rest of his life as an obscure itinerant portrait painter. George Cooke, to cite one other example, puzzled Fielding and Stauffer and confused Smith. The place and circumstances of his death were a mystery. The dragnet of research not only disclosed that Cooke died of cholera in New Orleans on March 26, 1849, but also made possible a reasonably detailed account of his wandering life and brought to light some of his paintings, published writings, and manuscript letters.

In conclusion, let it be said that the authors of this work are under no illusions as to its completeness. An undertaking of this nature can never be said to be definitive. It is hoped, however, that at some future time the work may be revised and brought up to date. In order to prevent the repetition of errors and to insure the inclusion of all possible new material, users of the *Dictionary* are requested to send suggestions and documented contributions to The New-York Historical Society, 170 Central Park West, New York 24, N.Y.

GEORGE C. GROCE
DAVID H. WALLACE

July 10, 1956

ACKNOWLEDGMENTS

THE COLLABORATIVE EFFORTS which have gone into the making of *The New-York Historical Society's Dictionary of Artists in America, 1564–1860,* embrace far more than those of the two principal authors, George C. Groce and David H. Wallace. In every stage of its preparation, the work has benefited by the aid of many institutions and individuals.

The *Dictionary* had its inception in a project of the New Jersey Historical Records Survey of the Works Progress Administration. Under the direction of Dr. Groce, the Survey compiled and published in December 1940 *1440 Early American Portrait Artists,* a documented biographical record of portraitists in all media active in America in or before 1860 which owed much, both in form and content, to three pioneer works by Theodore Bolton, Librarian of the Century Association: *Early American Portrait Painters in Miniature* (New York, 1921), *Early American Portrait Draughtsmen in Crayons* (New York, 1923), and "Early American Portrait Painters in Oils," the unpublished manuscript of which is now at the New-York Historical Society.

In 1941 Dr. Groce, with assistance from the New York City Art Project and Historical Records Surveys in several states, undertook a revision of this preliminary list which resulted in expansion of the work to include a total of about 3,000 portrait artists. This expanded manuscript, completed but not published before the demise of the sponsoring Works Progress Administration in 1942, was turned over to the New-York Historical Society for final editing and eventual publication.

Work on the *Dictionary,* suspended during the war, was resumed in 1945 under the joint direction of Dr. Groce and Charles E. Baker, Editor of the Society. In the meantime, at the suggestion of Mr. Baker, it had been decided to extend its scope to include not only portraitists but all artists (as defined in the Introduction to the present volume) active within the present continental limits of the United States in or before 1860. Additional research required by the new plan was carried on from 1945 to 1952 by Dr. Groce at the Library of Congress and National Archives in Washington and by staff members of the Society, especially Mr. Baker, his assistants, Miss Elizabeth Marting and Miss Roberta Leighton, and Miss E. Marie Becker, Reference Librarian.

In September 1952 major responsibility for completion of the *Dictionary* was entrusted to David H. Wallace, Assistant Editor of the Society, while Dr. Groce continued his research in Washington, notably in the 1850 and 1860 census records. In Mr. Wallace's hands, the *Dictionary* gradually took final shape. The task of consolidating information previously gathered, reconciling wherever possible conflicting statements of fact, carrying out extensive research for new material in directories, genealogies, and local histories, and writing the thousands of entries, a complicated and slow process, was finally completed by Mr. Wallace in June 1956.

In expressing their profound gratitude to the many individuals and institutions whose assistance has immeasurably eased their burden, the authors wish first to pay tribute to the officers and trustees of the New-York Historical Society. Without their unflagging faith and generous cooperation this work could not have been carried through to its present fruition. To many present and former members of the Society's staff, besides those already mentioned, the authors are likewise deeply indebted for information and assistance freely given. This is, in a very real sense, the New-York Historical Society's dictionary.

Among the many other institutions which generously aided their research, the authors wish particularly to thank the Frick Art Reference Library, the Library of Congress, and the New York Public Library.

A large measure of gratitude is due also to the staffs, long since dissolved, of the New York City Art Project, Delgado Museum [New Orleans] Art Project, the Historical Records Surveys of Alabama, Arkansas, District of Columbia, Illinois, Massachusetts, New Hampshire, New Jersey, South Carolina, Texas, and Vermont, and to the administrative officers of the Works Progress Administration in New Jersey, New York, and Washington, D.C.

Finally, the authors wish to take this opportunity of acknowledging publicly their particular indebtedness to the following persons and institutions for information of value to the *Dictionary:*

Mrs. Helen Adams, New York City; Adjutant-General's Office, Department of the Army; Alabama Department of Archives and History; Edward P. Alexander, Colonial Williamsburg; Harry M. Allice, Montreal; Anne Allison, former Curator of Maps and Prints, New-York Historical Society; Russell H. Anderson, former Director, Western Reserve Historical Society; Paul M. Angle, Director, Chicago Historical Society; J. Earl Arrington, Hollis, N.Y.

Margaret L. Bailey, Philadelphia; Hazel M. Ball, Society of California Pioneers; the late James Lenox Banks; Muriel F. Baldwin, New York Public Library; Richard E. Banta, Crawfordsville, Ind.; Dorothy C. Barck, former Librarian of The New-York Historical Society, now of the New York State Historical Association; Mrs. Laurence Barrington, Worcester, Mass.; John I. H. Baur, Whitney Museum of American Art; the late Waldron Phoenix Belknap, Jr.; Rudolph Berliner, Museum of Art, Rhode Island School of Design; Mrs. Josephine M. Bever, Washington, D.C.; Francis W. Bilodeau, Supervisor of Education, New-York Historical Society; Henry B. Binsse, Washington, D.C.; Edith Bishop, Newark [N.J.] Museum; Harry MacNeill Bland, New York City; the late Charles Knowles Bolton; Theodore Bolton, Librarian, The Century Association, New York City; the late Wolfgang Born; Harold Bowditch, Brookline, Mass.; Carl Bridenbaugh, University of California, Berkeley; Martha von Briesen, Sweet Briar College, Sweet Briar, Va.; Clarence S. Brigham, Director, American Antiquarian Society; Sigmund Broda, formerly of the New York City Art Project; Henry D. Brown, Director, Detroit Historical Commission; Mrs. Yves Henry Buhler, Museum of Fine Arts, Boston; Mrs. Helen Duprey Bullock, National Trust for Historic Preservation; Mary E. Bunce, Bayonne, N.J.; John Kenneth Byard, Silvermine, Conn.

Robert B. Campbell, Boston; William P. Campbell, National Gallery of Art; John T. Carey, Columbus, Ohio; Arthur B. Carlson, Curator of Maps and Prints, New-York Historical Society; Mrs. Carrie R. Carns, Cataloguer of Maps and Prints, New-York Historical Society; Mrs. Joseph B. Carson, Philadelphia; David Carter, Metropolitan Museum of Art, New York City; Edward C. Caswell, New York City; Mrs. Ralph Catterall, Valentine Museum, Richmond, Va.; Mrs. Robert S. Chamberlain, Alexandria, Va.; Eliot C. Clark, President, National Academy of Design; Katherine Coffey, Director, Newark [N.J.] Museum; Mrs. Wendell P. Colton, New York City; Mrs. Frank Commanday, Yonkers, N.Y.; Helen Comstock, New York City; Charlotte D. Conover, New Hampshire Historical Society; Cooper Union for the Advancement of Science and Art, New York City; Mrs. George B. Cortelyou, Rumson, N.J.; Mrs. Edith M. Coulter, Bancroft Library, University of California, Berkeley; Mary Bartlett Cowdrey, former Curator of Maps and Prints of the New-York Historical Society, now New York representative of the Archives of American Art; Christopher Crittenden, North Carolina Department of Archives and History; Mary Crockett, Roanoke, Va.; Mrs. Rowland M. Cross, New York City; Mrs. William T.

Cross, Menlo Park, Cal.; Charles C. Cunningham, Director, Wadsworth Athenaeum, Hartford, Conn.; Mrs. Arline Custer, Archives of American Art, Detroit.

Marshall B. Davidson, Metropolitan Museum of Art, New York City; Ruth Davidson, New York City; Curtis Carroll Davis, Baltimore, Md.; General John Ross Delafield, New York City; Mrs. Clara Louise Dentler, Florence, Italy; Mildred Deyo, Newburgh, N.Y.; Harold E. Dickson, Pennsylvania State University; Howard N. Doughty, Ipswich, Mass.; the late Carl W. Drepperd; Louisa Dresser, Worcester [Mass.] Art Museum; Rev. Fred W. Druckenmiller, Union, N.J.; Henry J. Dubester, Library of Congress; Arthur L. Dunham, University of Michigan; David C. Duniway, State Archivist, Oregon State Library; Orrin E. Dunlap, Great Neck, N.Y.; Edward H. Dwight, formerly of the Cincinnati Art Museum, now Director, Milwaukee Art Institute.

Mrs. Margaret F. Eden, San Diego, Cal.; Mrs. Leonard W. Edwards, Wilmington, Del.; Helen H. Ellis, Burton Historical Collection, Detroit Public Library; Mrs. Linns M. Ellis, Washington, Ga.; Edith Emerson, Woodmere Art Gallery, Germantown, Pa.; Helmut H. von Erffa, Rutgers University; Elliott A. P. Evans, Santa Barbara [Cal.] College; Mrs. Alice E. Ferris, Watertown, Mass.; James Thomas Flexner, New York City; Hugh M. Flick, Motion Picture Division, New York State Education Department; I. T. Frary, Chagrin Falls, Ohio; Albert Ten Eyck Gardner, Metropolitan Museum of Art, New York City; Joseph Gavit, Delmar, N.Y.; William H. Gerdts, Newark [N.J.] Museum; Mrs. B. B. Glen, Panama City, Fla.; J. H. Granbury, New York City; W. E. Groves, New Orleans; Prosper Guerry, New York City.

Mrs. Martha K. Hall, Huntington [N.Y.] Historical Society; Virginius C. Hall, Director, Historical and Philosophical Society of Ohio; Sinclair Hamilton, New York City; William J. Hamilton, Dayton [O.] Public Library; Dorothy Hammell, Providence, R.I.; George P. Hammond, Bancroft Library, University of California, Berkeley; Louise Hardenbrook, Columbia County Historical Society, Valatie, N.Y.; W. J. Harrison; Daniel C. Haskell, Cataloguer, New-York Historical Society; Ira J. Haskell, Lynn, Mass.; Katharine Hastings, Santa Barbara [Cal.] Historical Society; John Davis Hatch, Jr., Director, Norfolk [Va.] Museum; Bertha L. Heilbron, Minnesota Historical Society; Heraldic Branch, Office of the Quartermaster General, U. S. Army, Washington, D.C.; Mrs. Edith Jewett Marvin Herrmann, Brooklyn, N.Y.; Sidney Hill, New York City; Albert Hise, Massillon [O.] Museum; the late Franklin F. Holbrook, Historical Society of Western Pennsylvania; H. Maxson Holloway, Director, Saginaw (Mich.) Museum; Ruth C. Holum, Quincy, Ill.; Emmet Field Horine, Brooks, Ky.; Mrs. Henry W. Howell, Jr., Frick Art Reference Library; Robert A. Hug, New York Public Library; Henry E. Huntington Library, San Marino, Cal.; Ethel Hutson, Southern States Art League, New Orleans.

Sidney Janis, New York City; Mrs. Frances S. Janney, Rancocas, N.J.; Ellen Johnson, Oberlin College; Louis C. Jones, Director, New York State Historical Association; Lucile Kane, Minnesota Historical Society; R. Erskine Kerr, Lake Charles, La.; Mrs. Katharine McCook Knox, Washington, D.C.; Richard J. Koke, Curator of the Museum, New-York Historical Society; Mrs. Bella C. Landauer, Honorary Curator of the Bella C. Landauer Business and Professional Collection, New-York Historical Society; T. A. Larremore, Jamaica, N.Y.; C. C. Leach, Brookline, Mass.; Cuthbert Lee, Asheville, N.C.; B. H. Leffingwell, Rochester, N.Y.; Virginia E. Lewis, University of Pittsburgh, Pa.; Theodore A. Liebler, Jr.; Mrs. Jean Lipman, Cannondale, Conn.; Mrs. Nina Fletcher Little, Brookline, Mass.; Clifford L. Lord, Director, State Historical Society of Wisconsin.

Elizabeth McCausland, New York City; Gilbert S. McClintock, Wilkes-Barre, Pa.; Janet R. MacFarlane, Director, Albany [N.Y.] Institute of History and Art; Helen McKearin, New York City; Blake McKelvey, Rochester, N.Y.; Donald MacKenzie, College of Wooster, Ohio; Ethelwynn Manning, Frick Art Reference Library; James R. Masterson, National Archives; Hope Mathewson, Frick Art Reference Library; the late J. H. F. Mayo, Washington, D.C., and Bethesda, Md.; Mrs. Charles P. Maxwell, Easton, Pa.; John Mayfield, Washington, D.C.; Howard S. Merritt, University of Rochester, N.Y.; Frank Miles, London, England; Mrs. W. H. Miller, New Carlisle, O.; Douglas Maxwell Moffat, New York City; Clifford P. Monahon, Rhode Island Historical Society; Maurice A. Mook, Pennsylvania State University; Rev. Leo C. Mooney, Rochester, N.Y.; Donald W. Moreland, Cambridge, Mass.; John F. Morman, Bethlehem, Pa.; Mrs. John S. Moses, Andover, Mass.; Howard S. Mott, New York City.

Mrs. T. Webster Nock, New York City; Paul H. North, Jr., Columbus, O.; Mrs. Wilson Noyes, Savannah, Ga.; Norris S. Oliver, East Orange, N.J.; Georgia M. Palmer, West Chester, Pa.; Mrs. Barbara N. Parker, Museum of Fine Arts, Boston; Cullen W. Parmelee, Urbana, Ill.; Wilbur D. Peat, Director, John Herron Art Institute, Indianapolis, Ind.; Ralph D. Phillips,

New York City; J. Hall Pleasants, Baltimore, Md.; Waldron Kintzing Post, New York City; M. L. Pringle.

Wilhelmine Rall, formerly of the New York City Art Project; Claude J. Ranney, Malvern, Pa.; Fordan Ransom, Washingtonville, N.Y.; Perry T. Rathbone, Director, Museum of Fine Arts, Boston; Helen Fleming Reed, Sharon, Pa.; Foster W. Rice, Rowayton, Conn.; Howard C. Rice, Jr., Princeton University Library; E. P. Richardson, Director, Detroit Institute of Arts; Milton Rickels, Los Angeles, Cal.; Francis W. Robinson, Detroit Institute of Arts; Mary V. Rogers, Historical Society of Newburgh Bay and the Highlands, Newburgh, N.Y.; Anna Wells Rutledge, Charleston, S.C.

Israel Sack, New York City; Mrs. Susan C. Sawitzky, New Haven, Conn.; the late William Sawitzky, former Advisory Curator of American Art, New-York Historical Society; Frederick B. Schell, New York City; Heinrich Schwarz, Davison Art Center, Wesleyan College, Middletown, Conn.; Morgan H. Seacord, New Rochelle, N.Y.; Clara Endicott Sears, Harvard, Mass.; Charles Coleman Sellers, Dickinson College; Donald A. Shelley, Director, Henry Ford Museum and Greenfield Village, Dearborn, Mich., formerly Curator of Paintings and Sculpture, New-York Historical Society; Mrs. Harold M. Sill, Philadelphia; Donald A. Sinclair, Rutgers University; John R. Sinnot, U. S. Mint; Edgar Sittig, Shawnee-on-the-Delaware, Pa.; Theodore Sizer, Yale University; Mrs. Grace P. Smith, Maplewood, N.J.; Julian Denton Smith, Wantagh, N.Y.; Smithsonian Institution, Washington, D.C.; Charles F. Snyder, Northumberland County Historical Society, Sunbury, Pa.; Mrs. Victor Spark; Mrs. Pierre Spencer; Frank O. Spinney, Director, Old Sturbridge Village, Sturbridge, Mass.; Mildred Steinbach, Frick Art Reference Library; Stephen DeWitt Stephens, Newark Colleges, Rutgers University; Odille D. Stewart, City Art Museum of St. Louis; the late Harry Stone, New York City; Nancy V. Stone, Parkersburg, W. Va.; Mrs. Elleine H. Stones, Burton Historical Collection, Detroit Public Library; Mrs. Raymond M. Stowell, Mattapoisett, Mass.

Robert Taft, University of Kansas; Thomas Thorne, William and Mary College; the late Ruel P. Tolman; Prudence B. Trimble, Historical Society of Western Pennsylvania; Tulane University; R. W. G. Vail, Director of The New-York Historical Society; James G. Van Derpool, Avery Library, Columbia University; Mrs. J. J. Van Nostrand, Berkeley, Cal.; Robert C. Vose, Jr., Boston.

The late Alexander J. Wall, formerly Director, New-York Historical Society; Alexander J. Wall, Jr., Old Sturbridge Village, Sturbridge, Mass., former Assistant Director and Supervisor of Education and Public Relations, New-York Historical Society; H. T. Watlington, Hamilton, Bermuda; Mrs. John D. Watson, Anchorage, Alaska; Alexander W. Weddell, late President, Virginia Historical Society; Harry B. Wehle, formerly of the Metropolitan Museum of Art; Frank Weitenkampf, formerly of the New York Public Library; Mrs. Harry Hall White, Detroit, Mich.; Philip B. Whitehead, Beloit College, Beloit, Wis.; Mrs. Edna T. Whitley, Paris, Ky.; Benton H. Wilcox, State Historical Society of Wisconsin; Arthur B. Wilder, Woodstock, Vt.; William J. Wilgus, Claremont, N.H.; Ruth Kimball Wilkie, Boston; Hermann W. Williams, Jr., Director, Corcoran Gallery of Art, Washington, D.C.; R. Norris Williams, 2nd, Director, Historical Society of Pennsylvania; Thomas D. Williams, Litchfield, Conn.; Katharine Woodward, Middleburg, Va.; Richardson Wright, New York City; Henry J. Young, Pennsylvania Historical and Museum Commission, Harrisburg, Pa.; Mahonri S. Young, Director, Columbus [O.] Gallery of Fine Arts.

ABBREVIATIONS

For the convenience of the reader, abbreviations have been used sparingly. Aside from the usual abbreviations of names of states and provinces, the following appear in the *Dictionary:*

AA & AAU	American Academy and American Art-Union
Adv.	advertisement
Am.	American
Am. Inst.	American Institute of the City of New York
A.N.A.	Associate Member, National Academy of Design
BA	Boston Athenaeum
BD	Business Directory [with date]
c.	about [with date]
CAB	*Appleton's Cyclopaedia of American Biography*
Cat.	Catalogue
CD	City Directory
Cf.	compare
DAB	*Dictionary of American Biography*
DNB	*Dictionary of National Biography*
FARL	Frick Art Reference Library
LC	Library of Congress
Met. Mus.	Metropolitan Museum of Art, New York City
MHS	Maryland Historical Society
N.A.	Member, National Academy of Design
NAD	National Academy of Design
NYBD	New York City Business Directory
NYC	New York City
NYCD	New York City Directory
NYHS	New-York Historical Society
NYPL	New York Public Library
Obit.	obituary
PA	Pennsylvania Academy of the Fine Arts
Phila.	Philadelphia
RA	Royal Academy, London
Repro.	reproduction

DICTIONARY

A

AAMOND or AAMAND, see AMENDT.

ABEL, HENRY C. Engraver, NYC, 1859–60 and after. ¶ NYCD 1859–60+.

ABERNETHIE, THOMAS. Engraver. A native of Scotland, working in Charleston (S.C.) from 1785 to 1796. He died sometime before September 5, 1796, when part of his estate was advertised for sale. ¶ Prime, I, 15, and II, 64–65; Rutledge, *Artists in the Life of Charleston,* 183; Stauffer.

ABERT, JAMES WILLIAM (1820–1871). Topographical artist. Born November 18, 1820, at Mt. Holly (N.J.); graduated from West Point in 1842. During his service with the corps of topographical engineers, he made several expeditions into the West, the reports of which were illustrated by his own sketches. In 1848–50 Abert was assistant in drawing at West Point. During the fifties he worked on the improvement of western rivers. He was wounded in the Civil War and retired with the rank of colonel in 1864. After the war he became professor of mathematics and drawing at the University of Missouri. ¶ CAB; Heitman, *Historical Register;* Wagner and Camp, *The Plains and the Rockies,* nos. 120, 143. Original watercolors by Abert are owned by Fred Rosenstock of Denver and Thomas W. Streeter of Morristown (N.J.).

ABRAHAM, SOLOMON. Engraver and limner, Baltimore, 1787. ¶ Prime, I, 65.

ABRAMSE, ELIZA (1776–1865). Amateur artist who married ARCHIBALD ROBERTSON, the Scottish-American artist, in NYC in December 1794. Several of her pen-and-ink sketches of Shakespearean subjects have been preserved. ¶ Stillwell, "Archibald Robertson, Miniaturist," 2, 20, 23, 25.

ACHESON, HENRY. Engraver and lithographer, Chicago, 1853–56; of ACHESON & RODWAY in 1853. ¶ Chicago BD 1853–56; CD 1854.

ACHESON & RODWAY. Engravers and lithographers, Chicago, 1853; HENRY ACHESON and —— RODWAY. ¶ Chicago BD 1853.

ACKERMAN, EMIL (1840–?). Lithographer; born in Dresden (Germany); came to the U.S. with his father in 1848. He was apprenticed about 1856 to MAX ROSENTHAL of Philadelphia and later worked in Boston. ¶ Peters, *America on Stone.*

ACKERMAN, JAMES. Lithographer; born in New York about 1813. A partner in ACKERMAN & MILLER, sign and banner painters of NYC, 1838–65, he exhibited colored lithographs at the American Institute in 1845 and 1847. A number of his hand-colored lithographs of flowers appeared as book illustrations. ¶ NYCD 1838–62, 1864–65; 7 Census (1850), N.Y., XLVII, 298; Peters, *California on Stone;* Am. Inst. Cat., 1845, 1847; McClinton, "American Flower Lithographs."

ACKERMAN & MILLER. Sign and banner painters, block letter makers, NYC, 1838–65. The partners were JAMES ACKERMAN and EDWARD A. MILLER. The firm was listed 1841–46 and 1851–62; Miller and Ackerman were listed separately but at the same address in 1838–40, 1847–49, and 1864; Ackerman, "late of Ackerman & Miller," in 1846; Miller only, in 1832–37, 1863–64, and 1866–74. ¶ NYCD 1832–74.

ACKERMAN, ROBERT. Wood engraver, 48, a native of Canada, living with his wife Celeste in NYC in August 1860. ¶ 8 Census (1860), N.Y., XLIX, 723.

ACKERMAN, SAMUEL. Engraver, NYC, 1829–48; 1829–36, of Samuel Ackerman & Co. ¶ NYCD 1829, 1831–44, 1846–48; Peters, *America on Stone.*

ACKERS, see AKERS.

ADAMS, CHARLES. Ohio-born artist, 34, at NYC in August 1850. ¶ 7 Census (1850), N.Y., XLVIII, 554.

ADAMS, CHRISTOPHER. Portrait painter, NYC, 1850. ¶ NYCD 1850.

ADAMS (Adems), DUNLAP. Engraver and writing master; in NYC in 1763, offering his services as writing master and engraver, and in Philadelphia in 1764, advertising as an engraver on gold, silver, copper, brass, and ivory and as a piercer of gold and silver medals, and announcing his intention of opening a writing school. ¶ Gottesman, I, cites *N. Y. Mercury* for Jan. 10, 1763 and *N. Y. Gazette & Weekly Post Boy* for June 23, 1763; for Phila., see *Pennsylvania Gazette,* Sept. 6, 1764; Stauffer.

ADAMS, GEORGE E. (1814–1885). Portrait, landscape, and sign painter; born at

Harpers Ferry (Va.); moved to Logansport (Ind.) after 1836 and worked there until his death. ¶ Peat, *Pioneer Painters of Indiana,* 117.

ADAMS, Mrs. J. G. Portrait painter at Boston in 1856, at Indianapolis 1859–60. ¶ Boston BD 1856; Indianapolis CD 1859–60.

ADAMS, JOHN ALEXANDER, see JOSEPH ALEXANDER ADAMS.

ADAMS, Rev. JOSEPH (1689–1783). Landscape and portrait painter; born in Massachusetts; died at Newington (N.H.), May 26, 1783. ¶ WPA (N.H.); WPA (Mass.), *Portraits Found in N.H.,* records his portrait of Mrs. Joseph Adams (1689–1757), at the Portsmouth (N.H.) Athenaeum.

ADAMS, JOSEPH ALEXANDER (*c.* 1803–1880). A.N.A. Wood engraver. Born *c.* 1803 at New Germantown (N.J.), Adams was apprenticed to a printer and followed that trade for a short time after his removal to NYC *c.* 1825. He taught himself wood engraving, with encouragement from ALEXANDER ANDERSON, and enjoyed considerable success as an illustrator. His best known work was the set of 1,600 illustrations for Harper's *Illuminated Bible* (1843). He worked in NYC until 1847, and died at Morristown (N.J.), September 16, 1880. ¶ DAB; N. Y. *Herald,* Sept. 17, 1880, obit., gives his age at death as 76; *Am. Art Review,* I (1880), obit., 238–42, 551; Cowdrey, NAD; NYCD 1826, 1828–47 (listed as J. A. Adams 1828–30, as John A. Adams 1831–32, otherwise as Joseph A. Adams; in 1847 listed as "late engraver" and his name does not appear thereafter in NYCD).

ADAMS, M. B. Portrait painter, New England, 1839. This artist was identified by the late William Sawitzky, who owned two canvases portraying members of one family group, one of which bears the inscription: "M. B. Adams/Betsy F. Bolster/Aged 30/March 1839"; the second is inscribed: "Betsy Knight/Aged 62/March 1839." ¶ Courtesy the late William Sawitzky.

ADAMS, THOMAS W. Designer and engraver, of TAYLOR & ADAMS, Boston, 1850–60 and after. ¶ Boston BD 1850–60+.

ADAMS, WILLIAM ALTHORPE (Apthorp) (1797–1878). Jurist and amateur painter. Born in Boston, July 3, 1797, Adams opened a law office at Cincinnati in 1840. He was also "well known as a critical judge of art and he painted some pieces, among them some portraits," and exhibited pen-and-ink sketches at the National Academy, of which he was an Honorary Member. He died at his home in Newport (Ky.), December 25, 1878. ¶ Boston *Advertiser,* Jan. 1, 1879; Cow-

ADAMS, WILLIAM B. Portrait painter, Brooklyn (N.Y.), 1841–42. He exhibited at the Apollo Association and the National Academy. ¶ Brooklyn CD 1842/43; Cowdrey, NAD; Cowdrey, AA & AAU.

ADAMS, WILLIAM H. Engraver, of BALDWIN, ADAMS & Co., NYC, 1851–54. ¶ NYCD 1851–54.

ADDELSTERREN, Mrs. L. E. Artist of Cincinnati, active from 1830. ¶ Information courtesy Edward H. Dwight, Cincinnati Art Museum.

ADDY, JAMES, see JAMES EDDY.

ADELUNG, ERNST. Lithographer; born *c.* 1824 in Württemberg (Germany); at Philadelphia in 1860. ¶ 8 Census (1860), Pa., LII, 951.

ADEMS, DUNLAP, see DUNLAP ADAMS.

AFFICK, WILLIAM H. Engraver, NYC, 1854. ¶ NYBD 1854.

AGATE, ALFRED T. (1812–1846). A.N.A. Painter in oils, miniaturist, and illustrator. Born February 14, 1812, probably at Sparta (N.Y.), Alfred T. Agate was a younger brother of FREDERICK S. AGATE. He studied under his brother and T. S. CUMMINGS, and first exhibited at the National Academy in 1831. He worked in NYC from 1831 to 1838, when he joined the around-the-world exploring expedition of Charles Wilkes. On his return in 1842, Agate took up residence at Washington, where he prepared for publication the numerous sketches and paintings he had made on the expedition. He became an Associate of the National Academy in 1832 and an Honorary Member, Professional, in 1840. He died in Washington, January 5, 1846. ¶ The 1812 birth date is given in DAB; obits. in Washington *Intelligencer* (Jan. 6, 1846) and N. Y. *Evening Post* (Jan. 8, Jan. 9, 1846) give his age at death as 28, thus placing his birth in 1817 or 1818. The latter dates seem doubtful, since they would make Agate only 13 when he first exhibited at the National Academy. Cowdrey, NAD; Cummings, *Historic Annals,* 190; NYCD 1833–35. Examples of Agate's work are reproduced in Wilkes,

U. S. Exploring Expedition (1844–74) and Met. Mus. *Bulletin* (May 1952), 251.

AGATE, FREDERICK STYLE(S) (1807–1844). N.A. Portrait and historical painter. Born in 1807, at Sparta (N.Y.), Agate studied under JOHN RUBENS SMITH and SAMUEL F. B. MORSE. He was in NYC 1826–34, went to Europe in 1834 and returned to NYC in 1836, remaining there until the spring of 1844, when he went back to his mother's home at Sparta and there died May 1, 1844. One of the founding members of the National Academy of Design, Agate exhibited there and at the Pennsylvania Academy, Artists' Fund Society, and Apollo Association. ¶ Edmonds, "The Late Frederick S. Agate," a contemporary estimate by a fellow artist, gives the above dates; the DAB gives Jan. 29, 1803, and May 1, 1844, NYC. See also CAB; NYCD 1834; Cowdrey, NAD; Cowdrey, AA & AAU; Rutledge, PA.

AGATE, Miss H. Landscape painter, exhibited "View near Sleepy Hollow" at National Academy in 1833. ¶ Cowdrey, NAD.

AGUR, HEZEKIAH, see HEZEKIAH AUGUR.

AHERN, ANDREW. Lithographer; born *c.* 1827 in Massachusetts; working at Boston in 1860. ¶ 8 Census (1860), Mass., XXVII, 462.

AHERN, MARTIN. Engraver, born in Ireland about 1817. He left Ireland and came to NYC sometime between 1843 and 1846 and was living there in 1860 with his wife and five children. His daughter Ann, 17, also was listed as an engraver. In 1863 Martin was listed as keeper of a boarding house. ¶ 8 Census (1860), N.Y., XLII, 367; NYCD 1863.

AHRENS, HERMANN. Engraver from Germany, aged 28, at NYC in 1850. ¶ NYCD 1850; 7 Census (1850), N.Y., XLVI, 184 [as Herman Ahrenz].

AIKEN & HARRISON. Engravers and publishers, Philadelphia, 1800. The partners were JAMES AKIN and WILLIAM HARRISON, JR. ¶ Prime, II, 65; Brown and Brown.

AIKMAN, WALTER M. Engraver of view of Collect Pond, NYC, *c.* 1798: ¶ Stokes, *Hist. Prints,* pl. 34-B.

AIRY, JOHN. Early sculptor of Cincinnati. ¶ Information courtesy Edward H. Dwight, Cincinnati Art Museum.

AITKEN, JAMES, see JAMES AKIN.

AITKEN, ROBERT (1734–1802). Engraver, printer, stationer, etc. Born in 1734 at Dalkeith (Scotland); worked in Philadelphia from 1769 to 1802. He died July 15, 1802. ¶ DAB; Brown and Brown; Prime; *Portfolio* (Feb. 1954), 125, repro.

AITKIN, THOMAS. Scottish engraver, 40, at NYC in June 1860. ¶ 8 Census (1860), N.Y., LI, 97.

AKERS, BENJAMIN PAUL (1825–1861). Sculptor, painter, and author; born July 10, 1825, in Sacoarapa, Westbrook (Me.). He studied casting under JOSEPH CAREW at Boston in 1849 and was living in Portland (Me.) in 1850. In December 1852 he made the first of three visits to Europe, and is said to have studied under HIRAM POWERS at this time. On his second visit, 1855–57, he traveled in Italy, Switzerland, France, and England. After a third trip in 1859, he returned to America in poor health and died at Philadelphia on May 21, 1861. Paul Akers, as he signed himself, was a contributor to various magazines and newspapers. ¶ CAB; DAB; 7 Census (1850), Me., IV (3), 86; Fairman, *Art and Artists of the Capitol,* 371–72; "Maine Artists"; Gardner, *Yankee Stonecutters,* 60; Cowrey, NAD; Rutledge, PA; represented in Supreme Court Building, Washington.

AKERS, CHARLES (1835/36–1906). Sculptor and crayon portraitist; born October 15, 1835 or 1836, near Hollis (Me.). He studied with his brother, BENJAMIN PAUL AKERS, in Rome about 1855, worked in NYC during the sixties, and had a studio at Waterbury (Conn.) in 1875. He died September 16, 1906, in NYC. ¶ *Art Annual,* VI (1907/08), 106; *Art News,* Oct. 20, 1906; Bolton, *Crayon Draftsmen;* French, *Art and Artists in Conn.*

AKIN or AITKEN, JAMES (*c.* 1773–1846). Copperplate and wood engraver, miniaturist, caricaturist, profilist, and designer. Born in Charleston (S.C.), he spent most of his life, *c.* 1790–1846, in Philadelphia, where he died July 18, 1846. He also worked in Salem and Newburyport (Mass.), 1804–08 (see Mrs. [JAMES] AKIN). He exhibited at the Artists' Fund Society in 1841 and at the Pennsylvania Academy in 1853 (posthumously). ¶ Stauffer; Sanborn, "Thomas Leavitt and James Akin"; Phila. CD 1811–46; Peters, *America on Stone;* Brown and Brown; Bolton, *Miniature Painters;* Rutledge, PA; Middlebrook, "A Few of the New England Engravers," 359.

AKIN, Mrs. [JAMES]. Engraver, Newburyport (Mass.); thought to have been the wife of JAMES AKIN, who was working as an engraver at Newburyport in 1808. ¶ Stauffer.

AKINS, JOHN. Artist; born *c.* 1827 in Massachusetts; working in Phildelphia in 1850. ¶ 7 Census (1850), Pa., LII, 406.

ALBAN, ——. Cartoonist, NYC, 1849. ¶ Vail, *Gold Fever,* repro. of "Forty-niner" cartoon.

ALBRIGHT, DANIEL K. Teacher of "monochromatic landscape drawing," Charleston (S.C.), 1847. ¶ Rutledge, *Artists in the Life of Charleston,* 183.

ALBRIGHT, WILLIAM, see ALLBRIGHT.

ALBRO, JOHN. Lithographer; born *c.* 1824, Massachusetts; working at Boston in 1860. ¶ 8 Census (1860), Mass., XXVII, 479.

ALCOTT, [ABIGAIL] MAY. Landscape and still life painter, illustrator. Born at Concord (Mass.), July 26, 1840, May Alcott studied painting in Boston, London, and Paris with financial assistance from her elder sister, Louisa May Alcott, many of whose books she illustrated. She died in Paris in 1879, a year after her marriage to Ernest Nieriker, a Swiss artist. ¶ Clement and Hutton; Stern, *Louisa May Alcott;* Cheney, *Life and Letters of Louisa May Alcott.*

ALDEN, JAMES (1810–1877). Naval officer, amateur water colorist. Born March 31, 1810, at Portland (Me.), Alden entered the U. S. Navy in 1828. Accompanying Wilkes on his exploring expedition of 1838–42, he helped to survey and chart the Sacramento River. From 1848 to 1860 he commanded the party surveying the west coast from Mexico to Canada. After service in both the Mexican and Civil Wars, Alden retired from the Navy in 1873 and lived in San Francisco until his death, February 6, 1877. ¶ DAB; Van Nostrand and Coulter, *California Pictorial,* 144–45, with repro. of Alden's view of Crescent City in 1859.

ALDEN, JAMES MADISON. Amateur artist. A nephew of JAMES ALDEN, with whom he lived and worked in California *c.* 1860. ¶ Van Nostrand and Coulter, *California Pictorial,* 144.

ALDEN, WILLIAM C. Lithographer, Hartford (Conn.), 1849. ¶ New England BD 1849.

ALDERTON, WILLIAM. Engraver and die sinker, NYC, 1850–51. ¶ NYBD 1850–51.

ALDWORTH, Mr. ——. Miniaturist and teacher; advertised in Charleston (S.C.), December 31, 1778, as "late from London." ¶ Prime, I, 1.

ALEXANDER, ——. Portrait painter, Jefferson Co. (Va., now W.Va.), 1850–60. ¶ Willis, "Jefferson County Portraits."

ALEXANDER, ——. Panoramic artist. In 1850 he exhibited in Louisville (Ky.) a panorama of a voyage to California via Capetown and a diorama of the gold diggings. In 1851 he showed in Charleston and Baltimore a panorama of the antediluvian world, with the Last Supper and Resurrection. ¶ Courtesy J. Earl Arrington who cites: Louisville *Morning Courier,* Jan. 1, 1850; Charleston *Courier,* June 16, 1851; Baltimore *Sun,* Nov. 25, 1851.

ALEXANDER, COSMO (*or* Cosmo John, *or* Cosmus). Portrait painter. Born *c.* 1724 in Scotland, Alexander was a portrait painter in Edinburgh in 1765, when he exhibited at the London Society of Artists. A few years later he came to America, working in NYC (1768), Burlington, N.J. (1768–69), Newport, R.I. (1769–70), the South (1770 or 1771), and Philadelphia (1770–71). While at Newport he was GILBERT STUART's first instructor. Alexander returned to Edinburgh with Stuart *c.* 1771 and died there August 25, 1772. ¶ Information courtesy the late William Sawitzky; Graves *Dictionary;* Whitley, *Gilbert Stuart,* 7–9; *Pa. Mag.*, XXV (Oct. 1911), 140 (citation courtesy Theodore Bolton); Brown and Brown. Examples of his work are reproduced in *Portraits in Delaware,* 105, in *Art Digest,* X (Aug. 1, 1936), 21; and in Flexner, "Gilbert Stuart, 'Primitive.' "

ALEXANDER, FRANCESCA (1837–1917). Genre painter and author. Esther Frances, daughter of FRANCIS ALEXANDER (1800–1880), was born at Boston, February 27, 1837. She exhibited at the Boston Athenaeum in 1869, but it was in Italy that she made her reputation as a painter of peasant life and as the author of several volumes of prose and poetry on Italian life, under the name Francesca Alexander. She died at Florence, January 21, 1917. ¶ Alexander, *Francesca Alexander;* Spielman, "Francesca Alexander and 'The Roadside Songs of Tuscany,'" with repros.; Swan, BA, 195; Pierce, "Francis Alexander."

ALEXANDER, FRANCIS (1800–1880). Portrait, genre, and still life painter; lithographer. Born February 3, 1800, in Killingly (Conn.), he studied briefly in NYC with ALEXANDER ROBERTSON and began his career in Killingly and Providence (R.I.) in the early twenties. He settled in Boston about 1827 and lived there until 1853, except for a visit to Washington in 1830 and a two-year visit to Italy from 1831 to 1833. During the thirties and forties he was one of Boston's most successful portrait painters and in 1840 he was made an Honorary Member of the National Academy. In 1853 Alexander went to Europe with his family and settled in Florence where he remained for the rest of his life, revisiting the United States only once, in 1868–69. He did little painting in Italy, but instructed his daughter Esther Frances, better known as FRANCESCA ALEXANDER, and collected Italian primitives. He died in Florence on March 27, 1880. ¶ Pierce, "Francis Alexander," nine repros., photo., checklist; DAB; Alexander, *Francesca Alexander;* Peters, *America on Stone;* French, *Art and Artists in Connecticut;* Sears, *Some American Primitives,* 266; 7 Census (1850), Mass., XXII, 849; Boston CD 1835–53; Swan, BA; Rutledge, PA; Cowdrey, NAD; Cowdrey, AA & AAU.

ALEXANDER, J. B. Miniaturist, Charleston (S.C.), 1839. ¶ Carolina Art Assoc. *Cat.* 1935.

ALEXANDER, MICHAEL. Portrait painter, NYC, 1857–60. He was born in Prussia about 1807. ¶ NYCD 1857; 8 Census (1860), N.Y., XLIV, 219.

ALEXANDER, PETER. Lithographer, 25, a native of New York State, at NYC in June 1860. Peter Alexander, engineer, was listed in 1863. ¶ 8 Census (1860), N.Y., XLIII, 606; NYCD 1863.

ALI, BEN, see BEN.

ALLAN, J. MCGREGOR. Portrait painter, NYC, exhibited at National Academy in 1852. ¶ Cowdrey, NAD. A London portrait painter of the same name exhibited at the Royal Academy, 1854–56 (Graves, *Dictionary*).

ALLANSON, JOHN (1800–1859). Wood engraver, NYC, 1836. ¶ Cowdrey, NAD.

ALLARDICE (Allerdice), SAMUEL. Engraver and copperplate printer. First a pupil, then a partner, of ROBERT SCOTT, Allardice worked in Philadelphia in the 1790's. He died August 24, 1798. ¶ Stauffer, I, 8; Phila. CD 1796, 1798; Prime, II, 65.

ALLBRIGHT (Albright), WILLIAM. Landscape painter, limner, drawing teacher. Born *c.* 1795 in Pennsylvania, Allbright worked in Philadelphia (1818–20, 1830, 1832, 1850) and Baltimore (1824, 1829). He may have been the W. Allbright who did colored lithographs for *The Floral Magazine and Botanical Repository*. (Phila. 1832). ¶ 7 Census (1850), Penna., LI, 58; Scharf and Westcott; Rutledge, PA; Brown and Brown; Lafferty; McClinton, "American Flower Lithographs," 361.

ALLEGRI, JOSEPH. Italian artist, 32, living with NICOLINO CALYO in NYC in 1850. ¶ 7 Census (1850), N.Y., LVI, 1; NYCD 1850.

ALLEN, Miss ——. Crayon portraitist, Philadelphia, 1850. *Cf.* SARAH LOCKHART ALLEN. ¶ Phila. BD 1850.

ALLEN, BENJAMIN. Wood engraver and printer, Boston, 1845–60 and after. ¶ Boston BD 1848–57; CD 1845–47, 1858–60+.

ALLEN, CHRISTOPHER. Lithographer. Born in Ireland *c.* 1838, Allen was living in Philadelphia July 7, 1860, with an Irish-born wife (aged 21) and five Pennsylvania-born children (aged 1 to 5), and personal property valued at $100. ¶ 8 Census (1860), Pa., L, 652.

ALLEN, EZRA T. Engraver, Boston, 1856–60 (of CARPENTER & ALLEN from 1860). ¶ Boston CD 1856–60+.

ALLEN, G. Gravestone sculptor and writing master, Boston, 1716. *Cf.* GEORGE ALLEN. ¶ Forbes, "Early Portrait Sculpture in New England."

ALLEN & GAW. Engravers, early 19th century. See R. M. GAW. ¶ Stauffer.

ALLEN, GEORGE. Gravestone sculptor, Charleston (S.C.), 1787, 1795. ¶ Rutledge, *Artists in the Life of Charleston,* 183, cites adv. of 1787; Ravenel, "Here Lyes Buried," 194, cites a gravestone dated 1795.

ALLEN & HOYT. Engravers, Providence (R.I.), 1854. The partners were RICHMOND ALLEN and WILLIAM S. HOYT. ¶ Providence CD 1854/55.

ALLEN, JAMES H. Engraver. Born *c.* 1810 in Pennsylvania, Allen lived in Philadelphia at least from 1850 to 1860; the 1860 census records that he was unmarried and owned $4,500 in personalty on July 19, 1860. ¶ 7 Census (1850), Pa., LV, 671; 8 Census (1860), Pa., LV, 816; Phila. CD 1850, 1852.

ALLEN, JOEL KNOTT (1755–1825). Miniaturist and engraver, born in Farmington, now Southington (Conn.), in 1755. He lived and worked mainly in Middletown (Conn.) and died there in 1825. The city seals of Middletown are thought to have been cut by him. ¶ Stauffer; Middlebrook, "A Few of the New England Engravers," 359.

ALLEN, JOHN. Copper engraver, NYC, Boston, and Philadelphia, *c.* 1792. ¶ Thieme-Becker; Bénézit.

ALLEN, JOHN. Sculptor, 25, born in Maryland, at NYC in June 1860. ¶ 8 Census (1860), N.Y., L, 12.

ALLEN, JOHN C. Engraver, 23, from Ireland, living in NYC in 1860. His brother William G. Allen, 22, was also an engraver. ¶ 8 Census (1860), N.Y., LXII, 302; NYCD 1862.

ALLEN, JOHN N. Engraver, Boston, 1854–60 and after. ¶ Boston CD 1854–60 and after.

ALLEN, JOSEPH. Watchmaker, engraver, and limner, New England, *c.* 1684–*c.* 1728. ¶ Mass. Hist. Soc. *Collections* (1868), Ser. 4, VIII, 52, contains a letter by and about Allen; Mass. Hist. Soc. *Proceedings,* X (1867–69); Barker, *American Painting,* 21–22; Lee, "John Smibert," 119.

ALLEN, L. Engraver of a view of Newport (R.I.), 1795, and a portrait of Rev. Stephen Williams of Longmarsh (Mass.). ¶ Stokes, *Hist. Prints,* pl. 32; Stauffer, I, 7, and II, no. 40.

ALLEN, LUTHER (1780–1821). Engraver, portrait painter, musician. Born at Enfield (Conn.), June 11, 1780, Allen settled in Ithaca (N.Y.) after 1802 and died there, November 27, 1821. ¶ Fielding, *Supplement to Stauffer.*

ALLEN, MARIA W. Winner of 1st prize at Illinois State Fair, 1855, for monochromatic painting and crayon drawing. ¶ Chicago *Daily Press,* Oct. 15, 1855.

ALLEN, MARIE. Artist. Born in France *c.* 1815; boarding in Philadelphia, June 14, 1860, with personalty valued at $1,000. ¶ 8 Census (1860), Pa., LIII, 90.

ALLEN, ORVILLE. Engraver. Born in Michigan *c.* 1842; living in Detroit, June 20, 1860. ¶ 8 Census (1860), Mich., XX, 53.

ALLEN, RICHMOND. Engraver, Providence (R.I.), 1853–58; of ALLEN & HOYT in 1854. ¶ Providence CD 1853–58.

ALLEN, SARAH LOCKHART (1793–1877). Miniaturist and crayon portraitist. Born at Salem (Mass.), August 12, 1793; working in Salem as early as 1820; died there July 11, 1877. ¶ Belknap, *Artists and Craftsmen of Essex County,* 6; Bolton, *Miniature Painters,* and *Crayon Draftsmen; cf.* Miss —— ALLEN.

ALLEN, THOMAS. Portrait painter, at Louisville (Ky.) in 1843, at Philadelphia in 1860. ¶ Louisville CD 1843; Phila. CD 1860.

ALLEN, VALENTINE R. Engraver and stencil cutter, Cincinnati, 1850–57. ¶ Cincinnati BD 1850, 1853; CD 1851, 1853, 1856–57.

ALLEN, WILLIAM. Engraver, Philadelphia, 1818. ¶ Brown and Brown.

ALLEN, WILLIAM B. Engraver. Born *c.* 1834 at Philadelphia; living there on July 27, 1860, with wife Mary (aged 25, from Lancaster County) and daughter Rebecca (aged 2, born Philadelphia); his personal property valued at $400. ¶ 8 Census (1860), Pa., XLIX, 532.

ALLEN or ALLAN, WILLIAM C. Artist of Louisville (Ky.) in 1841 and 1848. ¶ Information courtesy Edward H. Dwight, Cincinnati Art Museum; Louisville CD 1848.

ALLEN, WILLIAM G., see JOHN C. ALLEN.

ALLERDICE, see ALLARDICE.

ALLISON, JOSEPH B. Artist and photographer. Born in Pennsylvania *c.* 1837; listed in Philadelphia in 1860 as an artist and in 1871 as a photographer. ¶ 8 Census (1860), Pa., LX, 1078; Phila. CD 1871.

ALLSTON, WASHINGTON (1779–1843). Portrait, historical, religious, and allegorical painter. Born at Georgetown (S.C.) November 5, 1779, Allston graduated from Harvard College in 1800 and went to Europe to study art. He returned to America in 1808, spent the next three years at Boston, and then went back to Europe in 1811, remaining there until 1818. The rest of his life he spent mainly in Boston and Cambridge, producing little himself but exerting a strong influence upon the romantic painters of the time. He died at Cambridgeport (Mass.), July 9, 1843. ¶ The authoritative study is E. P. Richardson's *Washington Allston,* which contains a catalogue of the artist's works, many reproductions and an extensive bibliography. See also Flexner, *The Light of Distant Skies;* Barker, *American Painting;* DAB.

ALLWELL, WILLIAM. Engraver, 17, from Ireland, at NYC in August 1850. ¶ 7 Census (1850), N.Y., LIV, 161.

ALLWOOD, JOHN. Fancy painter. Painted and gilded an altar piece for St. Michael's Church, Charleston (S.C.), in 1772; advertised again in 1773, offering for sale his Negro assistants. ¶ Rutledge, *Artists in the Life of Charleston,* 121.

ALMAINE, GEORGE D., see GEORGE D'ALMAINE.

ALMY, OSCAR. Scenic and panoramic painter, born in the West Indies about 1818. He was working in NYC in 1850 and 1859, in the latter year painting a panorama of the Nile for the production of *Anthony and Cleopatra* at the Broadway Theatre. ¶ 7 Census (1850), N.Y., XLVI, 139; N. Y. State BD 1859; N. Y. *Herald,* March 10, 1859 (courtesy J. Earl Arrington).

ALSHUCH, MARTIN. Lithographer. Born in Germany *c.* 1832; living in Philadelphia in June 1860 with three dependents and personal property valued at $50. ¶ 8 Census (1860), Pa., LIV, 515.

AMANS, JACQUES (1801–1888). Portrait painter who exhibited at the Salon in Paris 1831–37, "returning" in the latter year to New Orleans, where he was working during the forties and fifties. He died in Paris in 1888. ¶ Thieme-Becker; Delgado-WPA, cites New Orleans *Bee,* Dec. 2, 1837, Nov. 23, 1840, and Dec. 27, 1844; New Orleans CD 1842, 1846, 1852–56; Cline, "Art and Artists in New Orleans," 33; Barker, *American Painting.*

AMENCH, see AMENDT.

AMENDT, PHILIP. Lithographer, New Orleans, 1851–61. The name is variously spelt in the directories: Aamond or Aamand 1851–54, Amendt, Amench, or Amerdt 1853–61. ¶ New Orleans CD 1851–54, 1858–61. *Cf.* HERMANDT.

AMERICAN BANK NOTE COMPANY. Banknote engravers of NYC and Philadelphia, organized in 1858 and still in existence. Although the name was sometimes used by JOCELYN, DRAPER, WELSH & CO. from 1854 to 1858, the present company was formed in 1858 at New York by a merger of the leading bank note firms of the east, *viz.:* TOPPAN, CARPENTER & CO.; RAWDON, WRIGHT, HATCH & EDSON; DANFORTH, PERKINS & CO.; JOCELYN, DRAPER, WELSH & CO.; WELLSTOOD, HAY & WHITING; BALD, COUSLAND & CO.; and JOHN E. GAVITT of Albany. ¶ NYCD 1854–60; Phila. CD 1858–60; Toppan, *A Hundred Years of Bank Note Engraving.*

AMES, ALEXANDER. Wood carver, near Buffalo (N.Y.), 1847. His known works are a "Head of a Child" in polychromed oak and a "Head of a Boy." ¶ Lipman, *American Folk Art,* 22, repro. 181; *Art in America* (April 1950), repro. 121.

AMES, DANIEL. Artist and wood engraver, NYC, 1846. ¶ NYBD 1846/47, as wood engraver; NYCD 1846/47, as artist.

AMES, DANIEL F. Portrait and miniature painter; at NYC *c.* 1837–50; at Canarsie (N.Y.) in 1858. ¶ NYCD 1839, 1841, 1846; NYBD 1848, 1850; Cowdrey, NAD; Cowdrey, AA & AAU.

AMES, EZRA (1768–1836). Portrait, miniature, landscape, sign, and fancy painter. Born at Framingham (Mass.), May 5, 1768, Ames first worked as an artist at Worcester (Mass.), 1790–93, but moved in 1793 to Albany (N.Y.), where he lived until his death, February 23, 1836. He achieved a national reputation in 1812 with his portrait of George Clinton, exhibited at and bought by the Pennsylvania Academy. A prolific artist (nearly 500 works are recorded), Ames was also a prominent Mason and banker. ¶ The authoritative study. is Bolton and Cortelyou's *Ezra Ames of Albany,* with extracts from his account books, a checklist of his works, and many illustrations. Ames's manuscript account books, expense books, letters, and family records are at the Albany Institute of History and Art and the New-York Historical Society.

AMES, JOSEPH ALEXANDER (1816–1872). N.A. Portrait and genre painter. Born at Roxbury (Mass.), in 1816, Ames worked in Boston 1841–47, then went to Italy (1848), where he painted a portrait of Pope Pius IX, and on his return worked mainly in Boston, though he visited NYC in 1850. He was in Baltimore in 1870, and thereafter in NYC, where he died October 30, 1872. He exhibited frequently at the Boston Athenaeum from 1845 to his death, at the Maryland Historical Society (1848–50), at the National Academy (1850, 1869–72), and at the Pennsylvania Academy and the Washington Art Association (1859). His wife, SARAH FISHER AMES, was a sculptress. ¶ DAB; N. Y. *Evening Post* (semi-weekly), Nov. 5, 1872, obit.; Boston BD 1841–42, 1844–47, 1849, 1850–58; Boston CD 1849, 1859–60 and after (in 1859–60 as of Boston and Newport, R.I.); Boston *Evening Transcript,* Dec. 28, 1848 (cited by Arrington); Cowdrey, NAD; Swan, BA; Rutledge, MHS; Rutledge, PA; Washington Art Assoc. Cat. 1859; Peters, *America on Stone;* Clement and Hutton; Cowdrey, AA & AAU; 8 Census (1860), Mass., XXVI, 687.

AMES, JULIUS RUBENS (1801–1850). Miniature painter. Born January 1 or May 1, 1801, at Albany (N.Y.), a son of EZRA AMES, he worked as a miniaturist in Albany from *c.* 1820 probably until his death there June 5, 1850. He was also the author of a pamphlet, *Liberty,* published in 1839 by the American Anti-Slavery Society. ¶ Bolton and Cortelyou, *Ezra Ames of Albany,* 35, 129–31, 133, 314–15; Bolton, *Miniature Painters;* Albany CD 1835, 1837–38, 1840; repro. in *Antiques* (Jan. 1933), 14.

AMES, MARIA. Artist. Born *c.* 1836 in Delaware, living in Philadelphia, June 26, 1860. ¶ 8 Census (1860), Pa., LIV, 170.

AMES, Mrs. SARAH FISHER, *née* Clampitt (1817–1901). Sculptress. Born at Lewes (Del.), August 13, 1817, Miss Clampitt, later the wife of the painter JOSEPH ALEXANDER AMES, studied in Boston and Rome and executed busts of many notables of the day, including one of Lincoln which now stands in the Capitol at Washington. She was prominent in antislavery circles and served as a nurse during the Civil War. She died in Washington, March 8, 1901. ¶ Fairman, *Art and Artists;* Wilson, *Lincoln in Portraiture;* Gardner, *Yankee Stonecutters;* Rutledge, PA; NAD Cat. 1868/69 (courtesy Mary Bartlett Cowdrey).

AMEY, HENRY. Lithographer. Born *c.* 1831 in Baden (Germany), Amey was living in Baltimore July 18, 1860, with his wife Josephine (aged 21, born in Baden); his personal property was valued at $100. ¶ 8 Census (1860), Md., IV, 207.

AMSTEAD (Armstead?), WILLIAM. Engraver. Born *c.* 1831 at Philadelphia; living there July 2, 1860, with his wife Ann. ¶ 8 Census (1860), Pa., LVIII, 61.

ANCORA, PIETRO. Drawing master, religious & still life painter, proprietor of art gallery. Ancora came to Philadelphia from Italy *c.* 1800, was associated with BELL & ANCORA's art gallery in 1819. His pupils included JOHN NEAGLE and D. H. STROTHER. He exhibited at the Pennsylvania Academy and Artists' Fund Society, 1829–43. ¶ Brown and Brown; Rutledge, PA; Phila. CD 1830; Phila. BD 1838 Thieme-Becker states that Ancora was at Naples in 1805, but he is listed in the Phila. CD that year.

ANDERSON, ALEXANDER (1775–1870). N.A. Wood engraver, miniaturist, physician. Born April 21, 1775, in NYC, Anderson began wood engraving about 1793, and was the first known engraver (as distinguished from cutter) on wood in the U. S. He lived in NYC until 1866, then moved to Jersey City, where he died in January 1870. He was a frequent exhibitor at the American Academy, Society of Artists, and National Academy, and a founder of the last. ¶ Birth and death dates from DAB and N. Y. *Herald,* Jan. 18, 1870, obit.; Miss Helen M. Knubel, who is writing "The Life and Work of Alexander Anderson, with Notes on the Publishers for Whom He Worked," cites engravings listed in Anderson's "Diary" and signed published engravings to show that he was working in NYC as early as 1793; NYCD 1800–60 and after; Cowdrey, AA & AAU; Cowdrey, NAD; Rutledge, PA; N. Y. Public Library *Bulletin* (Oct. 1939), 715; Burr, *Life of Alexander Anderson;* Knubel, "Alexander Anderson: A Self-portrait"; eight scrapbooks at N. Y. Public Library believed to contain proofs of Anderson's engravings; Hamilton, 82–110, lists 122 books with Anderson illustrations; CAB; Bolton, *Miniature Painters; American Collector* (Oct. 1947), 38, repro.

ANDERSON, ANDREW. Pennsylvania-born artist, 30, living in NYC in 1860. His wife Maria and son George (11) were born in Pennsylvania, but his four-year-old daughter Sarah was born in New York State. ¶ 8 Census (1860), N.Y., LX, 837.

ANDERSON, ANN, see ANN MAVERICK.

ANDERSON, EMMELINE, see Mrs. EMMELINE MAYBE.

ANDERSON, HUGH. Engraver who worked in Philadelphia from 1811 to 1834 and thereafter at St. Clairsville (Ohio) at least until 1853. In Ohio he became acquainted with the young historical painter SYLVESTER GENIN, a number of whose paintings he engraved for *Selections from the Works of the Late Sylvester Genin . . .* (1855). Anderson also engraved a map of the ancient world, showing modern place names and boundaries. ¶ Stauffer; Brown and Brown; [Genin,] *Selections.*

ANDERSON, J. Executed drawings of Trinity Church, Columbia College, St. Paul's Chapel, and Belvedere House, NYC, 1789–90, *c.* 1794–95. ¶ Stokes, *Iconography,* I, 413–15, pl. 53a, 54b, 54c, 60a.

ANDERSON, J. B. Profilist, Richmond (Va.), 1807. ¶ *Richmond Portraits,* 241, cites Richmond *Enquirer,* May 5–22, 1807.

ANDERSON, J. S., & SON, see JACOB S. ANDERSON and JOHN W. ANDERSON.

ANDERSON, JACOB S. Figurehead carver, NYC, 1830–57. Partner in Jacob Anderson & Co. 1830–33, in DODGE & ANDERSON 1845, in J. S. Anderson & Son (with JOHN W. ANDERSON) 1856–57; died probably in 1857. ¶ NYCD 1830–57; NYBD 1856/57; NYBD 1857–58 list Anderson's widow; Pinckney, *American Figureheads,*

186, and pl. XXIII, repro. of figure of Davy Crockett.

ANDERSON, JAMES M. Engraver, Baltimore, 1842–60; of James M. Anderson & Son (with WINFIELD SCOTT ANDERSON), 1858–60. ¶ Baltimore BD 1842, 1859–60; Baltimore CD 1856, 1858, 1860.

ANDERSON, JOHN W. Carver, NYC, 1855–1903; of J[acob] S. Anderson & Son 1858–60. ¶ Pinckney, *American Figureheads,* 132, 187; NYCD 1855–1903.

ANDERSON, P. Executed a drawing, "View of Worcester, Mass.," *c.* 1837/38. *Cf.* PETER ANDERSON. ¶ Stokes, *Hist. Prints,* pl. 60b.

ANDERSON, PETER. Painter of water colors, ships, and a townscape; at Lowell (Mass.) in 1835. *Cf.* P. ANDERSON. ¶ Lipman and Winchester, 168.

ANDERSON, Mrs. SOPHIE (*née* Gengembre). Portrait and landscape painter. A daughter of the French architect and engineer, CHARLES A. C. GENGEMBRE, she accompanied her parents to America in 1849. The family first settled in Cincinnati, where Miss. S. Gengembre painted portraits and contributed five illustrations to Henry Howe's *Historical Collections of the Great West* (1851). Within a few years the Gengembres moved eastward to Manchester, a small town near Pittsburgh (Pa.). At about this same time Sophie Gengembre married the artist WALTER ANDERSON, with whom she was to spend many years in Europe, living chiefly on the isle of Capri and in London, where both husband and wife were frequent exhibitors from 1856 to 1890. They returned to America at least once, in 1860, when they both exhibited at the National Academy as residents of Manchester (Pa.). Sophie Anderson is said to have painted portraits of many of Pittsburgh's early citizens. *Cf.* Mrs. SOPHIE WEST. ¶ McCreery, "The French Architect of the Allegheny City Hall," 238–39; Cist, *Cincinnati in 1851;* Hamilton, 265; Graves, *Dictionary;* Cowdrey, NAD.

ANDERSON, WALTER. Landscape painter. Walter Anderson and his wife, SOPHIE (GENGEMBRE) ANDERSON, lived for many years in Europe, partly in Italy but mainly in England, where both exhibited frequently from 1856 to 1886, and Mrs. Anderson until 1890. They appear to have made at least one visit to the United States, in 1860, when they both exhibited at the National Academy as residents of Manchester (Pa.), the home of Sophie's parents. Anderson's home before his marriage was probably in or near Pittsburgh, or possibly Cincinnati. ¶ Graves, *Dictionary;* McCreery, "The French Architect of the Allegheny City Hall," 238–39; Cowdrey, NAD.

ANDERSON, WALTER W. Engraver and lithographer, Cincinnati, 1850–53. ¶ Cincinnati BD 1850–51; Cincinnati CD 1851; Ohio BD 1853.

ANDERSON, WILLIAM. Artist. Born *c.* 1818 in England, Anderson worked in Pennsylvania *c.* 1842–48 and was living in Dayton (Ohio), October 13, 1850, with real property valued at $300. His wife Rebecca (33) and children, William H. (7) and Amelia (2), were all born in Pennsylvania. ¶ 7 Census (1850), Ohio, XXXV, 460.

ANDERSON, WILLIAM. Engraver of portraits and landscapes. Born *c.* 1834 in Indiana, Anderson was working for the engravers C[HARLES] A. JEWETT & Co. of Cincinnati *c.* 1855. In 1860 he was living in Cincinnati with his wife Mary (aged 19, from Delaware) and two children, aged two. ¶ Stauffer; 8 Census (1860), Ohio, XX, 925.

ANDERSON, WINFIELD SCOTT. Engraver, Baltimore, 1859–60. Son and partner of JAMES M. ANDERSON. ¶ Baltimore BD 1859–60.

ANDERTON, G. Engraver of portraits in stipple and mezzotint. Born *c.* 1825 in London; working in Philadelphia, September 14, 1850; died *c.* 1890. ¶ 7 Census (1850), Pa., LIII, 967; Stauffer gives *c.* 1828–1890.

ANDRÉ, JOHN (1751–1780). Amateur artist. Born in London in 1751, André served in the British Army during the American Revolution, was caught and hanged as a spy, October 2, 1780, at Tappan (N.Y.). As an artist, he is best known for his self-portrait, drawn on the eve of his execution and now in the Yale University Art Gallery. ¶ DNB; Runyan, "John André, the Artist," 5, repro.; *Album of American Battle Art,* 45–47, repro. p. 66. A pencil drawing by André (1776) was exhibited at the Pennsylvania Academy in 1812 (Rutledge, PA).

ANDREI, GIOVANNI (1770–1824). Sculptor. Born at Carrara (Italy) in 1770, Andrei worked with GIUSEPPE FRANZONI on the Capitol at Washington and at Baltimore, 1806–*c.* 1815. Returned to Italy *c.* 1815, but died at Washington, October 21, 1824. ¶ Fairman, *Art and Artists,* 5, 47; Thieme-

Becker; Borneman, "Franzoni and Andrei."

ANDREW & FILMER. Wood engravers, Boston, 1858–60 and after. The partners were JOHN ANDREW and JOHN FILMER. ¶ Boston BD 1860 and after; Hamilton, 318–19, cites examples of their work in Holmes' *The Autocrat of the Breakfast Table* (Boston, 1858) and in *Arabian Days' Entertainments* (Boston, 1858).

ANDREW, JOHN (1815–1875). Wood engraver and designer. Born at Hull (England) in 1815, Andrew was at Boston by 1851, when he exhibited a wood engraving at the Annual Fair of the American Institute in NYC. He remained at Boston apparently until his death there in 1875. In 1853/54 he was a partner in BAKER & ANDREW and from 1858 in ANDEW & FILMER. He had a son John who also did wood engraving. ¶ Smith; Am. Inst. Cat. 1851, no. 983; Boston BD 1854–60 and after; Boston CD 1853–55; Cowdrey, *Winslow Homer: Illustrator.*

ANDREWS, ——. Landscape painter; exhibited at the National Academy in 1843, giving as his address the Park Theatre, NYC. This might be the Andrews who exhibited a panorama of the Great West in Philadelphia and other cities in 1856. ¶ Cowdrey, NAD; J. Earl Arrington cites Phila. *Public Ledger,* May 9, 1856.

ANDREWS, AMBROSE. Itinerant portrait, miniature, and landscape painter, active 1824–59. He was working in Schuylerville (N.Y.) in 1824; Troy (N.Y.), 1829–31; Stockbridge (Mass.), 1836; New Haven (Conn.), 1837; New Orleans, 1841–42; NYC, 1847–53 (during this time he exhibited at the American Art-Union several views of Montreal, Vermont, and Connecticut); Buffalo, 1856–59; and St. Louis. His portrait of Henry Clay was shown at the American Institute in 1856; he also exhibited at the Royal Academy in 1859, the National and Pennsylvania Academies, and the American Art-Union. ¶ NYHS owns a water color portrait of Philip Schuyler and family of Schuylerville, 1824; Bolton, *Miniature Painters;* Cowdrey, NAD; Cowdrey, AA & AAU; Delgado-WPA cites New Orleans *Picayune,* June 24 and Aug. 17, 1841, and Aug. 12, 1842; NYBD 1849–52; Buffalo BD 1856–58; N. Y. State BD 1859; Graves, *Dictionary;* Am. Inst. Cat., 1856; Rutledge, PA; *American Collector* (Jan. 1935), 2, repro.; *American Primitive Painting,* repro.; *Antiques* (Nov. 1950), 393, repro. Andrews' presence in Stockbridge in 1836 suggests the possibility that he was the Ambrose Andrus born at West Stockbridge, July 19, 1801 (*West Stockbridge Vital Statistics,* 9).

ANDREWS, CHARLES. Lithographer; born in Pennsylvania about 1841; working in Philadelphia in June 1860. He owned property valued at $2,500 and lived in the home of Mary Anderson, 25, a native of Prussia. Charles Y. Andrews, listed as an engraver in 1871, may be the same man. ¶ 8 Census (1860), Pa., LVI, 850; Phila. CD 1871.

ANDREWS, CHARLES D. Lithographer and plate printer, Boston, 1856–after 1860. ¶ Boston CD 1856–57; BD 1858–60+.

ANDREWS, DAVID. Artist, NYC, 1851–52. ¶ NYCD 1851–52.

ANDREWS, ELIPHALET FRAZER (1835–1915). Portrait painter. Born at Steubenville (Ohio), June 11, 1835, Andrews studied painting in Paris under Bonnat and at the Düsseldorf Academy in Germany. On his return to the U.S. he settled in Washington, eventually becoming Director of the Corcoran School of Art. He died at Washington, March 19 or 20, 1915. ¶ Thieme-Becker; *Art Annual,* XII (1915), 255, gives March 19 as date of death, while *Art News,* March 27, 1915, gives March 20; *Artists Year Book,* 4; NAD Cat. 1864–1887 (courtesy Mary Bartlett Cowdrey).

ANDREWS, EMANUEL. Portrait painter, 24, from Massachusetts, at NYC in August 1850. ¶ 7 Census (1850), N.Y., XLIV, 525.

ANDREWS, F. Engraver of a view of Yellow Springs (Pa.), 1810. ¶ *Port Folio,* IV (July 1810), opp. p. 45.

ANDREWS, GEORGE. Manufacturer of statuary and composition ornaments, NYC, 1796. ¶ McKay cites NYCD 1796.

ANDREWS, JOSEPH (*c.* 1805–1873). Wood and line engraver. Born *c.* 1805 in Massachusetts, Andrews served his apprenticeship under the engraver ABEL BOWEN of Boston, worked also with WILLIAM HOOGLAND, and from *c.* 1827 to 1833 was a partner in CARTER, ANDREWS & Co. of Lancaster (Mass.). He made three visits to Europe to study and practice engraving (1835, 1840–41, 1853); the rest of his time was spent in Boston. He excelled in portrait engraving, though his best-known work is "Plymouth Rock, 1620," after ROTHERMEL. ¶ DAB; Boston BD 1844–57.

ANDREWS, JOSHUA P. Portrait painter, NYC, 1850; born in Pennsylvania about 1800. ¶ NYCD 1850; 7 Census (1850), N.Y., XLVI, 133.

ANDREWS, ROBERT. Lithographer and copperplate painter, Boston, 1833–56; in partnership with T. D. Andrews in 1833. He died in 1856 or 1857. ¶ Boston CD 1833–35, 1837–46, 1850–57; Boston BD 1847–49, 1856; Boston CD 1857 lists Mrs. Robert Andrews, widow.

ANDREWS, T. D., see ROBERT ANDREWS.

ANDRIEU, ADOLPH. Lithographer, New Orleans, 1846, spoken of as "a young artist." ¶ Delgado-WPA cites New Orleans *Courier,* April 7, 1846.

ANDRIEU, C. Portrait painter, New Orleans, 1841. ¶ New Orleans CD 1841.

ANDRIEU, MATHUREN ARTHUR (?–1896). Portrait, landscape, scenery, and panorama painter. A native of France and student at the French Royal Academy, Andrieu was working in New Orleans as early as 1840. He is next heard of in the fall of 1851 at Charleston (S.C.), when he exhibited a series of dissolving views of London, the Crystal Palace, and New Orleans. In the spring of 1853 he was at St. Louis exhibiting panoramas of St. Louis and "Southern Life." He was at Macon (Ga.) in 1855. In 1862 he settled in Providence (R.I.) where he lived until his death in 1896. ¶ Arnold, *Art and Artists in Rhode Island;* New Orleans *Picayune,* April 22, 1840 (courtesy Delgado-WPA); Rutledge, *Artists in the Life of Charleston;* Charleston *Courier,* Sept. 8, 1851, St. Louis *Missouri Republican,* April 22, May 5, and June 12, 1853 (citations courtesy J. Earl Arrington); WPA Guide, *Maine,* repro.

ANDY, JOHN BAPTIST. Portrait painter, NYC, 1844–45. ¶ NYCD 1844/45; Am. Inst. Cat. 1845.

ANELLI, FRANCISCO (or Francis Annellio). Portrait, miniature, and historical painter, born in Italy about 1805. He came to NYC from Milan about 1835 and was active there until 1878. His religious paintings, especially "The Opening of the Sixth Seal, or The End of the World," were widely exhibited between 1845 and 1856. Anelli also exhibited at the National Academy and the Boston Athenaeum. His diary is at the Frick Art Reference Library. ¶ 7 Census (1850), N.Y., XLVI, 282; NYBD 1841–60+; Bolton, *Miniature Painters;* Cowdrey, NAD; Swan, BA; N. Y. *Herald,* April 5, 1845, Phila. *Public Ledger,* Nov. 12, 1845, New Orleans *Picayune,* March 26, 1847, Baltimore *Sun,* July 27 and Aug. 7, 1853, Phila. *Public Ledger,* April 30, 1856 (citations courtesy J. Earl Arrington).

ANET, L. Cameo portrait engraver, New Orleans, 1849. ¶ Delgado-WPA, cites New Orleans *Bee,* April 21, 1849.

ANGELAIN, ANTOINE. Portrait and miniature painter, New Orleans, 1841–46. ¶ New Orleans CD 1841–42, 1846.

ANNIBALE, GEORGE OLIVER (*c.* 1829–1887). Portrait sculptor in marble and cameo. Born *c.* 1829 [at Providence, R.I.?], Annibale studied under Mrs. JANE (VALUE) CHAPIN and in Europe for four years. He was working in Providence in 1859 and was awarded several medals for cameos and busts by the Rhode Island Society for the Encouragement of Domestic Industry. He died April 22, 1887, in Brooklyn (N.Y.). ¶ Chapin, "George Oliver Annibale," with 10 repros.; Gardner, *Yankee Stonecutters;* Providence CD 1859; Cowdrey, NAD; Arnold, *Art in Rhode Island;* Cole, "Some American Cameo Portraitists," 171.

ANNESS, SAMUEL. Engraver, Philadelphia, 1818. ¶ Brown and Brown.

ANNIN, PHINEAS F. Wood engraver and illustrator, NYC, 1852–58. He was a partner in WHITNEY & ANNIN (1852), WHITNEY, JOCELYN & ANNIN (1853–55), and LOOMIS & ANNIN (1858), all wood-engraving firms. ¶ NYBD 1852, 1854, 1858; NYCD 1853–58.

ANNIN & SMITH. Engravers, Boston, 1820–23, 1826–33. The partners were WILLIAM B. ANNIN and GEORGE G. SMITH. ¶ Boston BD 1820–23, 1826–33; *Portfolio,* II (April 1943), 179.

ANNIN, WILLIAM B. Engraver of portraits, views, and maps, Boston, 1813–39. Worked under ABEL BOWEN *c.* 1813; engraved maps for Morse's *American Geography;* partner in ANNIN & SMITH (1820–23, 1826–33). ¶ Whitmore, "Abel Bowen," 41; Hamilton, 187, cites two illustrations by Annin for *The Naval Monument* (Boston, 1816); Boston CD 1818, 1820–23, 1826–39; *Antiques,* XLVII (June 1945), 332, repro. of Annin's "Second View of Comm. Perry's Victory."

ANNUS [?], BERNARD. English artist, 34, at NYC in 1860. He left England with his wife and one child sometime between 1847 and 1850. ¶ 8 Census (1860), N.Y., XLIV, 471.

ANSON, WILLIAM. Portrait and miniature

painter, advertised in Augusta (Ga.), April 7, 1792, as from London. ¶ WPA Guide, *Georgia,* 175.

ANTHONY, ANDREW VARICK STOUT (1835–1906). Wood engraver. Born in NYC, December 4, 1835, Anthony went to California *c.* 1853 and there established the firm of ANTHONY & BAKER. He was back in NYC 1855–58, and in 1878 he executed four illustrations for Lowell's *The Rose* (Boston, 1878). He died at West Newton (Mass.), July 2, 1906. ¶ DAB; Hamilton, 238; NYCD 1855–58; NYBD 1857–58; Benjamin, *Our Artists;* CAB.

ANTHONY & BAKER. Wood engravers, California, 1853–54. The senior partner was ANDREW VARICK STOUT ANTHONY, but Baker's identity has not been established. ¶ Hamilton, 238, cites illustrations for *The Miner's Ten Commandments* (San Francisco, 1853) and a broadside of 1854, "Hutching's California Scenes: the Mammoth Tree," signed Anthony & Baker.

ANTOGNILLI, DAVID. Sculptor, New Orleans, 1853. ¶ New Orleans CD 1853.

ANTONIA, AMANDA [sic]. Engraver (male), 20, from Italy, at NYC in July 1860. ¶ 8 Census (1860), N.Y., XLII, 422.

ANTROBUS, JOHN (1837–1907). Portrait, landscape, and genre painter, poet, and journalist. Born *c.* 1837 in Warwickshire (England), Antrobus came to the U.S. before 1855, when he advertised as a portrait painter at Montgomery (Ala.). He was at New Orleans by 1860, as a poet and genre painter; in April of that year he withdrew from the city to paint scenes of plantation life. On the outbreak of the Civil War Antrobus was commissioned lieutenant in the Delhi Southrons and he left for the seat of war in Virginia in July 1861. After the war Antrobus married Miss Jeannie Watts of New Orleans, lived for some years in Chicago and Washington, and settled in Detroit *c.* 1875, becoming the leading portrait and landscape painter of that city and a frequent contributor to the local newspapers. He died in Detroit, October 18, 1907. ¶ Detroit *Free Press,* Oct. 19, 1907, obit.; *Art Annual,* VI (1907/08), 106, obit; WPA (Ala.) cites *Weekly Montgomery Mail,* June 14, 1855; Delgado-WPA cites *True Delta,* April 29, 1860, and *Picayune,* July 9, 1861. Loubat, *Medallic History of the U.S.,* 370–71, lists an Antrobus who designed the U. S. Grant medal of 1863 and was living in Iowa in 1870.

ANTZ, G. Engraver, of LUND & ANTZ, New Orleans, 1852–56. ¶ New Orleans CD 1852–56.

ANYON, JAMES. Engraver and die sinker, NYC, 1841–54. ¶ NYBD 1841, 1844, 1846, 1854, as engraver and die sinker; NYCD lists him mainly as die sinker.

APFEL, HENRY (1838–?). Portrait and landscape painter, photographer. Born April 1, 1838, in Soultz (France), Apfel was brought to the U.S. in 1841. He began painting as a child, studied for two years in Chicago, and visited Europe in 1861. After his return he took up photography, working at Waverley (Iowa) in 1865, and later at Shell Rock (Iowa). Most of his paintings were destroyed in the Chicago fire. ¶ Ness and Orwig, *Iowa Artists,* 17.

APPLETON, GEORGE WASHINGTON (1805–1831). Portrait painter and engraver, Boston, 1830–31. In 1829 he painted a portrait of John Neal of Portland (Me.). ¶ Maine Hist. Soc., *Cat.;* Swan, BA, 197; Boston CD 1830–31; WPA (Mass.), *Portraits Found in Maine,* no. 166.

APPLETON, THOMAS GOLD (1812–1884). Amateur painter. Born at Boston, March 31, 1812, Appleton was educated at Harvard, traveled widely in Europe and the Near East, and became a well known essayist and poet, as well as an amateur and patron of art in Boston. He died in NYC on a visit, April 17, 1884. ¶ Hale, *Thomas Gold Appleton,* 7–13; DAB; CAB.

ARBESSIER, F. Lithographer, St. Louis, 1859. ¶ St. Louis BD 1859.

ARCHER, JAMES. Engraver; born *c.* 1800 in England; living in Philadelphia, June 28, 1860. *Cf.* JAMES ARCHER, below. ¶ 8 Census (1860), Pa., LII, 821.

ARCHER, JAMES. Engraver, at Boston 1835–49, at Cincinnati 1850–51, 1856–57. Stauffer suggests he was the James Archer who engraved for publishers in London in 1832. *Cf.* JAMES ARCHER, above. ¶ Boston BD 1841–42, 1844–49; Boston CD 1835–40, 1843; Cincinnati CD 1850–51, 1856–57; Stauffer.

ARCHER, JOHN. Engraver, NYC, 1849. ¶ NYBD 1849.

ARDENOND or ARDENAUD, ——. French showman who brought his "Mechanical and Picturesque Theatre," consisting of views with mechanical props, from London to NYC and showed it at 141 Broadway from September to November 1818. ¶ N. Y. *Evening Post,* Sept. 21, Oct. 6, Nov. 14, 1818 (courtesy J. Earl Arrington).

ARDRIEN, JAMES. Engraver; born in England *c.* 1815; living in Frankford (Pa.) in 1850, with his Pennsylvania-born wife Ann (24) and two children—Joseph (6) and Lavinia (2). ¶ 7 Census (1850), Pa., LVI, 344.

ARMAND, G. "Artist of the Theatre," New Orleans, 1822. ¶ New Orleans CD 1822.

ARMAND, POLERMO. Engraver; born *c.* 1842 in France; living in San Francisco July 5, 1860, with his parents. ¶ 8 Census (1860), Calif. VII, 1413.

ARMANDO, JOHN. "Artiste in plaster [of] paris," New Orleans, 1823–24. ¶ Delgado-WPA, cites New Orleans CD 1823–24.

ARMBRUSTER, ANTHONY. Engraver, Philadelphia, 1759, 1763. ¶ Prime, I, 15.

ARMOR, SAMUEL. Miniaturist, Baltimore, 1840. ¶ Lafferty.

ARMSTEAD, see AMSTEAD.

ARMSTRONG, ARTHUR (1798–1851). Portrait, landscape, and historical painter. Born in 1798 at Lancaster (Pa.), Armstrong worked for several years at Marietta (Pa.), in Virginia and Kentucky, and at Lancaster (*c.* 1849). He died June 18, 1851. ¶ Lancaster County Hist. Soc., *Papers and Addresses,* XVI (Sept. 6, 1912), 186–91; *American Collector,* XVII (May 1948), repro. on reverse of cover.

ARMSTRONG, CHRISTOPHER. Wood engraver, San Francisco, 1856–58. ¶ San Francisco CD 1856; BD 1858.

ARMSTRONG, DAVID MAITLAND (1836–1918). A.N.A. Painter and glass stainer. Born April 15, 1836, at Danskammer, near Newburgh (N.Y.), Armstrong graduated from Trinity College in 1858 and visited Europe the following year. He studied law in NYC and was admitted to the bar in 1862, but soon after gave up the practice of law for a career as an artist. From 1869 to 1873 he was U. S. Consul at Rome. He is best known for his work in stained glass. ¶ Armstrong, *Day Before Yesterday;* DAB; *Art Annual,* XV, obit.; NAD Cats. 1863–82 (courtesy Mary Bartlett Cowdrey).

ARMSTRONG, Mrs. JAMES, see HANNAH CROWNINSHIELD.

ARMSTRONG, THOMAS. Wood engraver, San Francisco, 1849–57. ¶ Peters, *California on Stone.*

ARMSTRONG, WILLIAM G. (1823–1890). Engraver, portrait draftsman, and painter. Born 1823 in Montgomery County (Pa.), Armstrong was working in Philadelphia 1840–60 and after. He died in 1890. ¶ Stauffer; Phila. CD 1840–60 and after; Bolton, *Miniature Painters;* 8 Census (1860), Pa., LII, 86.

ARNOLD, BERNARD. Sculptor, San Francisco, 1858. ¶ San Francisco BD 1858.

ARNOLD, EDWARD. Portrait, landscape, historical, marine, and sign painter. He was working at New Orleans 1850–1860 and painted the Battle of Port Hudson (La.), March 14, 1863. He also worked with J. G. EVANS. ¶ Delgado-WPA, cites *Orleanian,* Sept. 22, 1850, and March 14, 1851; New Orleans CD 1852–56, 1860; *American Processional,* 246, repro. p. 173; Met. Museum, *Life in America.*

ARNOLD, GEORGE. Ornamental and figure painter, Rochester, N.Y., *c.* 1820. ¶ Ulp, "Art and Artists in Rochester."

ARNOLD, GEORGE G. Painter, NYC, 1854–56; exhibitor at the National Academy. ¶ Cowdrey, NAD.

ARNOLD, J. Engraver. Born *c.* 1827 in the District of Columbia, Arnold was working in Washington, July 8, 1850, aged 23. ¶ 7 Census (1850), D.C., I, 315.

ARNOLD, J. J. G. Portrait painter, Jefferson County (Va.), 1849. *Cf.* JOHN JAMES TRUMBULL ARNOLD. ¶ Willis, "Jefferson Co. Portraits."

ARNOLD, JOHN JAMES TRUMBULL (or John T.). Portrait painter who worked in and around York Springs (Pa.) from about 1846 until shortly after the Civil War. He is said to have been born in 1812 and to have "drunk himself into an early grave." Several examples of his work are owned in York Springs. ¶ Information courtesy FARL, from letters of Mrs. Maude Wierman Kennedy of York Springs and Mr. Albert Cook Myers. *Cf.* J. J. G. ARNOLD.

ARNOLD, JOHN KNOWLTON (1834–1909). Portrait painter. Born in 1834, Arnold painted portraits of many citizens of Rhode Island. He died in Providence, May 31, 1909. ¶ *Art Annual,* VII (1909/10), 73, obit.; Fielding. Exhibited NAD 1868–73 (courtesy Mary Bartlett Cowdrey).

ARNOT, DAVID H. Architect and artist, NYC, 1845–49. His drawing of the entrance to the First Congregational Church, Broadway, NYC, was published. He exhibited views and architectural drawings at the National Academy, 1847–49. ¶ NYCD 1845–49; Peters, *America on Stone;* Cowdrey, NAD.

ARRIOLA, FORTUNATO. Portrait painter, San Francisco, 1858–59. Exhibited at the National Academy in 1872. ¶ San Francisco

BD and CD. 1858–59; NAD Cat. 1872 (Courtesy Mary Bartlett Cowdrey).

ARTHUR, JOHN H. V. Painter of Welsh scenes, living at Hoboken (N.J.) in 1855. ¶ Rutledge, PA.

ARTHUR, W. H., & COMPANY. Lithographers, NYC, 1856–57. William H. Arthur, head of the company, was a stationer in NYC from 1849 to the 1880's. ¶ NYBD 1856–57; NYCD 1849–80 and after.

ARTOIS, Mr. ——. Drawing teacher and schoolmaster, Charleston, 1842. ¶ Rutledge, *Artists in the Life of Charleston,* cites Charleston *Courier,* May 30 and October 22, 1842.

ARY, HENRY. Portrait and landscape painter of the "Hudson River school," born in Rhode Island, 1802 (Minick), or at Hudson (N.Y.), 1807 (Hardenburg). He advertised as a portrait painter in Albany 1831–32, then moved to Catskill, where he came under the influence of THOMAS COLE. After his return to Hudson in 1844, Ary devoted himself mainly to painting Hudson River landscapes and was noted for his engaging disposition and personal charm. He exhibited landscapes at the National Academy in 1845, 1853, 1858 and at the American Art-Union from 1846 to 1853. He died on January 28 (Minick) or in February, 1859 (*Crayon*). ¶ Minick, "Henry Ary," with repros. and checklist, cites 7 Census (1850) for date and place of birth; information courtesy Louise Hardenbrook of the Columbia [County, N.Y.] Historical Society; Albany CD 1831/32 (adv. p. 198), 1832/33; *Crayon,* VI (1859), 132, obit; Bradbury, *History of the City of Hudson,* 209; Cowdrey, NAD; Cowdrey, AA & AAU.

ASHE, WILLIAM A. Portrait, historical, and commercial painter, NYC, 1846–51. ¶ NYCD 1846–51.

ASHLEY, SOLOMON. Gravestone portrait sculptor, Deerfield (Mass.), 1792. His portrait in marble of Col. Oliver Partridge is at Hatfield (Mass.). ¶ Lipman, *American Folk Art,* 22, repro. p. 177.

ASHTON, AUTO [?]. English engraver, 37, at NYC in August 1850. ¶ 7 Census (1850), N.Y., LIII, 181.

ASHTON, THOMAS B. Landscape and genre painter, wood engraver, and dealer in artists' supplies, Philadelphia, 1835–44. Although listed as a landscape painter in the 1835 directory, Ashton was subsequently listed as a merchant, of Ashton & Browning, dealers in artists' materials. He exhibited frequently at the Artists' Fund Society (1835–45), the Pennsylvania Academy (1843–52), the National Academy (1837), the Boston Athenaeum (1837–49), the Apollo Association and American Art-Union (1838–52). Ashton left Philadelphia about 1844 and was in Italy from 1845 at least until 1852. ¶ Thieme-Becker; Rutledge, PA; Cowdrey, NAD; Cowdrey, AA & AAU; Swan, BA.

ASHTON, WILLIAM H. Lithographer, NYC, 1857. ¶ NYBD 1857.

ASPELL, R. C. Engraver, Philadelphia, 1813–14. ¶ Brown and Brown.

ASPINWALL, HORATIO G. Engraver, seal and die cutter, Charleston, 1823. ¶ Rutledge, *Artists in the Life of Charleston,* cites Charleston *Courier,* Dec. 29, 1823.

ATHERTON, EZRA. Portrait and miniature painter, wood engraver, Boston, 1830–42. ¶ Bolton, *Miniature Painters;* Swan, BA; Boston BD 1841.

ATKENSON, PETER. Artist whose drawing of "The Retreat" near NYC was engraved by J. KENNEDY (active 1797–1812). *Cf.* —— ATKINSON. ¶ Stauffer.

ATKIN, JAMES. General engraver, NYC, 1855–60 and after. He was an Englishman, born about 1832. ¶ NYCD 1855–60+; 8 Census (1860), N.Y., LI, 697.

ATKINS, THOMAS. Irish engraver, 50, at NYC in July 1860. ¶ 8 Census (1860), N.Y., XLVI, 450.

ATKINSON, Mr. ——. Artist whose view of Petersburg (Va.) was engraved by JOHN BOYD (active 1811–27) of Philadelphia. *Cf.* PETER ATKENSON. ¶ Stauffer.

ATKINSON, MARY B. Artist. Born *c.* 1830 in Pennsylvania; living with her parents—a scholarly family—in Philadelphia, July 9, 1860, aged 30. ¶ 8 Census (1860), Pa., LII, 45.

ATKINSON, R. M. Artist, NYC, 1843–44. Exhibited at the National Academy and the American Institute. ¶ Cowdrey, NAD; Am. Inst. Cat. 1844.

ATTWOOD, Miss E. H. Watercolor painter, NYC, 1845. ¶ Am. Inst. Cat. 1845.

ATWOOD, J. Map engraver, Philadelphia, *c.* 1840. *Cf.* JOHN M. ATWOOD. ¶ Stauffer.

ATWOOD, JESSE. Itinerant portrait painter, *c.* 1828–54. Born in New Hampshire *c.* 1802, Atwood appears to have married in Rhode Island, where his wife Anna and their first child, George, were born, the latter about 1828. The family moved to Pennsylvania, where a daughter, Mary, was born *c.* 1830. During the next decade Atwood is known to have worked at Deerfield (Mass.) in 1832, at Richmond (Va.) in 1841, and at Philadelphia in 1841 and 1843. In 1847 he was at Monterey (Mexico), where he painted a portrait of Gen. Zachary Taylor now owned by the Historical Society of Pennsylvania. Atwood was again in Philadelphia 1849–54, where his wife owned real property valued at $6,000 in the 1850 Census. ¶ 7 Census (1850), Pa., LIII, 315; letter of Mrs. George Spencer Fuller to Frick Art Reference Library, June 25, 1943; *Richmond Portraits,* cites *Richmond Whig,* Feb. 15, 1841; Phila. CD 1841, 1843, 1849, 1851–54; Rutledge, PA; Sawitzky, *Hist. Soc. of Penna. Cat.* A hand-bill advertising J. Atwood, itinerant portrait painter, is reproduced in "Somebody's Ancestors," cat. of exhibition at Springfield (Mass.) Museum, Feb.–March 1942.

ATWOOD, JOHN M. Engraver; born in Washington (D.C.) about 1818; active in NYC from 1838 to 1852. In 1844 he was with STORY & ATWOOD. *Cf.* J. ATWOOD. ¶ 7 Census (1850), N.Y., XLIII, 489; NYCD 1838–52; NYBD 1844.

ATWOOD, WILLIAM C. Portrait painter, Boston, 1859–60. ¶ Boston BD 1859–60.

ATWOOD (Attwood), WILLIAM F. (or T.). Portrait painter, NYC, 1858–60. Exhibited at the National Academy, and painted a portrait of Mr. and Mrs. George S. Brown driving a tandem into their estate near Baltimore, signed "W. F. [or T.] Attwood, N.Y. '60." ¶ Cowdrey, NAD; information courtesy FARL.

AUB (Aube, Aul), JACOB. Lithographer, Philadelphia, 1850–60 and after; of FRIEND & AUB from 1852. ¶ Phila. CD 1850–52, 1854–56, 1858–60 and after.

AUBANEL, see Mrs. CHARLES LAVENDER.

AUBE, see AUB.

AUBERG, JOHN, see JEAN AUBERY.

AUBERT, CHARLES J. Engraver and die sinker, NYC, 1856–60 and after. ¶ NYCD 1856–60 and after.

AUBERT, Mrs. PAUL. Portrait and "water-painter," San Francisco, 1860; her husband was a jeweler. ¶ San Francisco BD & CD 1860.

AUBERY, JEAN (1810–1893). Portrait and religious painter. Born August 13, 1810, at Kassel (Germany), Aubery worked in Paris 1838–48, came to the U.S., and was settled in Cincinnati by 1853. ¶ Thieme-Becker; Swan, BA, 199; Cincinnati BD 1853, 1856, 1859–60; NAD Cat. 1860, BA Cat. 1860. John Auberg, listed in the Ohio BD 1859 as of Cincinnati, was probably the same as Jean Aubery.

AUBINEAU, LEWIS. Miniaturist, NYC, 1799–1814. ¶ McKay, cites NYCD 1799–1801, 1803, 1813–14; H. W. Williams, Jr., of the Corcoran Gallery reports a signed miniature owned in Halifax, N.S. Lewis Obeno, listed in NYCD 1806 and 1808, was presumably the same man.

AUBRY, ——. Executed a sepia wash drawing of "Napoleonic Emigrés in Texas (Le Champ d'Asile)," 1818, now owned by the Musée National de la Coopération Franco-Américaine, Blérancourt (France). ¶ *American Processional,* 28, 240.

AUBRY, ADOLPHE. Engraver, NYC, 1856–58. ¶ NYCD 1856–58; NYBD 1856, 1858. In NYCD 1856 an Andrew Aubry is listed at the address given for Adolphe Aubry in NYBD 1856.

AUDEBERT, WILLIAM A. Drawing teacher, New Orleans, 1809. ¶ Delgado-WPA, cites *Moniteur,* July 5, 1809.

AUDIBERT, LOUIS. Portrait painter; born *c.* 1818 in France; working in New Orleans, August 2, 1850, aged 32. ¶ 7 Census (1850), La., V, 169.

AUDIN, ——. Theatrical scene painter from Paris, working in Charleston (S.C.) and in Virginia, 1795–96. ¶ Prime, II, 33; Rutledge, *Artists in the Life of Charleston,* cites E. Willis, *The Charleston Stage in the 18th Century,* 276, 306–07.

AUDIN, ——, JR. Theatrical painter and mechanic, Charleston, 1795. Presumably a son of the above. ¶ Rutledge, *Artists in the Life of Charleston,* cites Willis, *The Charleston Stage,* 306–07.

AUDUBON, JOHN JAMES (1785–1851). America's foremost painter of wild-life, best known for his great series of *Birds of America;* in early life a portrait painter. Born at Les Cayes (Haiti), April 26, 1785, Audubon was brought up in Revolutionary France, but settled in the U.S. in 1806. After the failure of a store he owned in Kentucky for a number of years, he turned to portrait painting. His real interest, however, was in natural history and from about 1820 until his death he devoted himself to painting and writing on the birds and mammals of America. Audubon traveled widely in the U.S. and Canada in search of specimens and the results of his study and artistic work were embodied in *Birds of America, Quadrupeds of America,* and *Ornithological Biographies,* all first published in Great Britain where he spent much of his time between 1826 and 1839. His last years were spent in or near NYC, where he died January 27, 1851. From about 1832 until his death Audubon was assisted in his work by his sons, JOHN WOODHOUSE AUDUBON and VICTOR GIFFORD AUDUBON. He became an Honorary Member, Professional, of the National Academy in 1833. ¶ Among the many works on Audubon, the best is Herrick's *Audubon the Artist* (1917), a two-volume life with an extensive bibliography. Other sources include: Graves, *Dictionary;* Cowdrey, NAD; Alabama Dep't. of Archives and History; NYCD 1843–49; McDermott, "Likeness by Audubon"; Flexner, *The Light of Distant Skies,* biblio., 257.

AUDUBON, JOHN WOODHOUSE (1812–1862). A.N.A. Portrait and wild-life painter, younger son of JOHN JAMES AUDUBON; born at Henderson (Ky.), November 30, 1812. With his older brother, VICTOR GIFFORD AUDUBON, he was trained by his father to assist in the latter's work on American birds and mammals. As early as 1833 he accompanied his father on a trip to Labrador and in 1834 to England, where he remained until 1836. On his return to America he married Maria, the eldest daughter of the Charleston naturalist, Dr. John Bachman. From 1839 John W. Audubon made his home in NYC, exhibiting frequently at the Apollo Association and American Art-Union and the National Academy. Continuing to help his father, he made trips to Texas (1845–46) and to England (1846–47). In 1849 he joined a gold-rush expedition to California, but returned to NYC the following year. For the rest of his life he worked mainly in New York, painting nearly half the plates for *Quadrupeds of America* and later reducing all the pictures for the smaller edition of both the *Birds* and the *Quadrupeds.* He died at his home a few miles north of NYC on February 18 or February 21, 1862. ¶ Herrick, *Audubon the Naturalist;* Cowdrey, AA & AAU; Cowdrey, NAD; Am. Inst. Cat., 1851; Audubon, *Western Journals;* 8 Census (1860), N.Y., XLIX, 1052; NYHS *Quarterly* (April 1946), 71; represented at South-West Museum, Los Angeles.

AUDUBON, VICTOR GIFFORD (1809–1860). N.A. Wildlife and landscape painter, miniaturist, elder son of JOHN JAMES AUDUBON; born at Louisville (Ky.), June 12 (Herrick) or June 29 (*Crayon*), 1809. He studied painting under his father, but for a number of years worked as a clerk in a commercial house in Louisville. In 1832, however, he went to England to arrange for the publication of his father's *Birds of America.* While in England he exhibited a number of times at the Royal Academy, though his chief activity then and later was as secretary and agent for his father. Returning to America in 1839, Victor married Mary Eliza Bachman, sister of JOHN WOODHOUSE AUDUBON'S first wife, and settled in NYC in 1840, where he worked with his father and brother. He exhibited at the National Academy, of which he was elected a Member, and at the Apollo Association and the American Art-Union. After their father's death in 1851, the two brothers continued to collaborate on new editions of his works on American birds and quadrupeds. Victor G. Audubon died after a long illness at his home on upper Manhattan Island, August 17 (*Crayon*) or 18 (Herrick), 1860. ¶ Herrick, *Audubon the Naturalist;* obituary by "a friend" in *Crayon,* VII (1860), 269; Graves, *Dictionary;* Cowdrey, NAD; Cowdrey, AA & AAU; 8 Census (1860), N.Y., XLIX, 1052. His miniature of his father was shown at the Carolina Art Assoc. in 1936.

AUDY, ROY. Portrait painter, Rochester (N.Y.), *c.* 1834–37. ¶ Ulp, "Art and Artists of Rochester," 32.

AUGER, see AUGUR.

AUGERO, FRANCESCO. Portrait painter, NYC, 1854–70. ¶ NYBD 1854–57, 1859; Cowdrey, NAD.

AUGUR, HEZEKIAH (1791–1858). Sculptor, wood carver. Born February 21, 1791, at New Haven (Conn.), Augur exhibited at the National Academy (1827–28), the Pennsylvania Academy (1831), and the Boston Athenaeum (1832). He was also the inventor of a wood carving machine. He died at New Haven, January 10, 1858. ¶ DAB; 7 Census (1850), Conn., VIII, 273 (gives Ireland as his birthplace); Fairman, *Art and Artists of the Capitol,* 75; Cowdrey, NAD; Rutledge, PA; Swan, BA; French, *Art and Artists in Conn.;* represented at Yale School of Fine Arts and U. S. Supreme Court.

AUGUST, WILLIAM P. Engraver. Born *c.* 1842 in England, August was working in Boston, August 3, 1860, aged 18. ¶ 8 Census (1860), Mass., XXVII, 269.

AUL, see AUB.

AULD, WILBERFORCE. Carver and cameo-cutter, NYC, 1834–47. ¶ Pinckney, 187 (as carver, 1834); NYCD 1835–37, 1841–43 (as cameo-cutter), 1845–47.

AURAY, Mr. ——. Teacher of drawing and French, Charleston (S.C.), 1850. ¶ Rutledge, *Artists in the Life of Charleston,* 185.

AUSTEN, R. Wood engraver, *c.* 1801. ¶ Hamilton, cites *The Farmer's Boy* (Robert Bloomfield, 4th American edition, N.Y., 1801), for which Austen did 3 cuts and ALEXANDER ANDERSON some others, and Bewick's *Quadrupeds* (1st American edition), in which appears one engraving by Austen.

AUSTIN, ALEXANDER. Engraver, Philadelphia, 1803. ¶ Brown and Brown.

AUTENRIETH (Autenreith), CHARLES. Executed drawings of Castle Garden and the Custom House, New York University, City Hall and Croton Reservoir, NYC, for HOFF's *Views of New York* (1850). ¶ Peters, *America on Stone; Portfolio,* I (Sept. 1941), 5 and 7; *Ibid.,* III (March 1944), 156–57.

AUTENRIETH (Autenreith), LUDWIG (Louis). Engraver and die sinker; born *c.* 1832 in Germany; working in Cincinnati 1850–60, his father having come from Germany with a large family not before 1843. ¶ 7 Census (1850), Ohio, XXI, 460 and 861; Cincinnati CD 1853, 1856, 1858–59; Cincinnati BD 1853, 1856, 1859–60.

AVERILL, ——. Proprietor and/or artist of a panorama of the Crimean War and a voyage from England to the Crimea, shown in Davenport (Iowa) in January 1856. ¶ Schenck, *The Early Theater in Eastern Iowa* (courtesy J. Earl Arrington).

AVERY, JOHN. Mural painter "of some local renown," painted murals for Wolfeboro (N.H.) meetinghouse, *c.* 1818; also worked in Middleton (N.H.). ¶ *Antiques,* XXIII (June 1938), repro. frontispiece, and 319; *Art in America,* Oct. 1950, 167.

AVERY, SAMUEL PUTNAM (1822–1904). Copper and wood engraver, connoisseur and art dealer. Born March 17, 1822, in NYC, Avery first worked as a copper engraver, then turned to wood engraving, and eventually became a collector and dealer. A founder of the Metropolitan Museum, Avery also gave valuable collections of art and art books to the New York Public Library and Columbia University. He died in NYC, August 11, 1904. ¶ DAB; *Art Annual,* V (1905/06), 118, obit.; NYCD 1843–60 and after; American Institute Cats. 1847–49; Cowdrey, NAD. There is an unpublished Master's Essay on Avery on deposit at Columbia University: *Samuel Putnam Avery (1822–1904), Engraver on Wood: a Bio-Bibliographical Study,* by Ruth Sieben-Morgen (1942).

AVERY, WILLIAM. Engraver, 26, at NYC in June 1860. Avery, his wife Elizabeth, and their two-year-old daughter Caroline were all born in Pennsylvania. ¶ 8 Census (1860), N.Y., LVII, 904.

AVIGNON, see D'AVIGNON.

AVIGNONE, ANTONIO. Artist; born *c.* 1814 in Milan (Italy), working at Philadelphia, September 11, 1850, aged 36. ¶ 7 Census (1850), Pa., L, 25.

AYER, CHARLES. Engraver; born *c.* 1841 in Massachusetts, working in Boston, aged 19, June 15, 1860. ¶ 8 Census (1860), Mass., XXVI, 757.

AYER, L. Painter of a fire engine panel, "Howard Giving Aid to the Sick," NYC, *c.* 1823. ¶ Smith, "Painted Fire Engine Panels," 247, with repro.

AYERS, CHARLES. Artist at Cincinnati in 1841. ¶ Information courtesy Edward H. Dwight, Cincinnati Art Museum.

AYME, FRANCIS. Miniaturist, Philadelphia, 1805–08. ¶ Brown and Brown.

AYR, JOHN F. Sketched in Kansas before 1861. ¶ WPA Guide, *Kansas.*

AYRES, CLARENCE L. Portrait painter, NYC, 1858. ¶ NYBD 1858.

AYRES, THOMAS A. (?–1858). Landscape painter. A native of New Jersey, Ayres went west in 1849 and spent the next seven years in California. He traveled widely throughout the state and in 1855 was with the first party to visit the Yosemite Valley, of which he sketched the earliest known views. He also painted a panorama which had a long run at McNulty's Hall in Sacramento. Returning to the East in 1857, Ayres exhibited in NYC and was engaged by *Harpers* to illustrate a series of articles on California. During the early part of 1858 he made a sketching tour in southern California, but on his way back to San Francisco was drowned in the sinking of the *Laura Bevan,* April 26, 1858. ¶ Van Nostrand, "Thomas A. Ayres: Artist-Argonaut of California"; Van Nostrand and Coulter, with 3 repros.; Peters, *America on Stone,* pl. 22; *Portfolio,* Sept. 1942, frontis.; Howell, "Pictorial Californiana," 63–64, two repros. of drawings now in Yosemite Museum.

B

B——, G. S. Artist of a lithographic cartoon, "Pork and Beans in the Gold Diggins," published by Robert H. Elton of NYC about 1849. ¶ Copy in Map and Print Room, NYHS.

Babb, Robert [B.]. Lithographer. Born *c.* 1839 in Pennsylvania, living with William F. Babb, chairmaker, in Philadelphia, 1860. ¶ 8 Census (1860), Pa., LIX, 235.

Babcock, Amory L. Still life painter, Rhode Island [?], 1857. ¶ *Portfolio,* I (Oct. 1941), 24, repro. of painting of fruit and flowers, reported to have come from Providence.

Babcock, William P. (1826–1899). Portrait painter. Born January 17, 1826, at Boston; exhibited at Boston Athenaeum 1853–56, 1859, 1864, 1869–70, and National Academy 1863; died at Bois d'Arcy (France) in 1899. ¶ Thieme-Becker; Bénézit; Swan, BA; NAD Cat. 1863 (courtesy Mary Bartlett Cowdrey).

Babson, R. Stipple engraver, Boston, 1860; engraved plates for Joseph Andrews. *Cf.* Robert E. Babson. ¶ Stauffer; Thieme-Becker.

Babson, Robert E. Carver and engraver, Boston, 1854–57. ¶ Boston CD 1854–56; Boston BD 1857; Hinton, *History and Topography,* repro.

Bache, William (1771–1845). Profilist and silhouettist. Born December 22, 1771, at Broomsgrove (Worcestershire), Bache was working in Philadelphia as early as 1793. He was at Richmond (Va.), in 1804; at Salem (Mass.) and probably Hartford and New Haven (Conn.) in 1810; and is thought to have worked in Louisiana and the West Indies as well. In 1812 he was again in Philadelphia, shading profile likenesses, reducing profiles, and re-shading old profiles, but the same year he moved to Wellsboro in northwestern Pennsylvania. After the loss of his right arm, Bache kept a general store and he also served as postmaster of Wellsboro from 1822 to 1845. His work is represented at the Connecticut Historical Society and the Rhode Island Historical Society. ¶ Carrick, "The Profiles of William Bache," with repros.; *Richmond Portraits,* 241, cites advs. in *Va. Gazette,* Jan. 28, 1804, and *Argus,* March 14, 1804; *U. S. Gazette,* Jan. 25 and March 7, 1812, cited in Brown and Brown.

Bachelder (Batchelder), John Badger (1825–1894). Portrait and landscape painter, historian. Born in September 1825 at Gilmanton (N.H.), Bachelder painted a view of Manchester (N.H.) in 1854 and at about the same time a view of New Jersey from the Lycoming County (Pa.) side of the Delaware. He is thought to have been at Providence (R.I.) and NYC in 1858, and the following year he painted a picture of the firemen's muster at Manchester. From 1863 to 1865 he was listed as a print publisher at Boston. An oil painting, "The Death of Lincoln," now at Brown University, is inscribed "Jno. B. Bachelder/Designer 1865" and "A. Chappel 1868." Bachelder also painted views of Haverhill, Salem, and Worcester (Mass.), and Providence (R.I.). He died at Hyde Park (Mass.), December 22, 1894. ¶ "Art and Artists in Manchester," 117; Manchester Hist. Assoc., *Collections,* III (Oct.–Dec. 1902), frontis.; *Portfolio* (Nov. 1944), 71; Peters, *America on Stone;* Boston CD 1863–65; Met. Mus., *Life in America; American Processional;* Childs Gallery, *Bulletin* (Oct. 1951), 2.

Bachman(n), C. Landscape draftsman and lithographer, executed views of City Hall and Union Square, NYC, *c.* 1849. ¶ Stokes, *Historical Prints,* pl. 66-b; Stokes, *Iconography,* III, 702, and pl. 135.

Bachman, Henry. Sculptor and engraver. Born *c.* 1838 in Germany, working in Philadelphia June 1, 1860, aged 22. Exhibited a "Silenus" (in ivory) at the Pennsylvania Academy 1861–63. ¶ 8 Census (1860), Pa., LIX, 792; Rutledge, PA.

Bachman(n), John. Landscape draftsman and lithographer, 1850–77. Executed a view of NYC in 1850; at New Orleans in 1851; working in NYC in 1851–52, 1855, in Brooklyn in 1858, and Hoboken (N.J.) in 1859. He executed a lithograph showing the seat of war in Virginia in 1861 and a view of NYC in 1877. ¶ *Portfolio,* I (June 1942), 1 and 20; *ibid.,* VII (March 1948), 156–57, view of NYC with airplane; NYCD 1851–52; Stokes, *Historical Prints,* pl. 80, pl. 95-b, pl. P 1859 G57, pl. 100-f.

Backofen, Charles. Portrait painter; born in Germany about 1801; active in NYC from 1850 to 1860. He exhibited at the National Academy and is represented in the Brooklyn Museum. ¶ 7 Census (1850), N.Y., XLVIII, 3; NYCD 1851–60; Cowdrey, NAD; information courtesy John I. H. Baur.

BACON, E. F., see BACON & ELLIS.

BACON & ELLIS. Engravers, Chicago, 1856. The partners were probably E. F. Bacon and WILLIAM C. ELLIS. The firm of DAYE & ELLIS was listed in 1858 as successor to E. F. Bacon. ¶ Chicago BD 1856; Chicago CD 1858.

BACON, GEORGE. Music engraver and publisher, Philadelphia, 1814–20. ¶ Brown and Brown.

BACON, HENRY (1839–1912). Painter and illustrator. Born in 1839 at Haverhill (Mass.), Bacon enlisted in the U. S. Army at 18 and served as field artist for *Leslie's Weekly* during the Civil War. He later studied art in Europe, settling in Paris. Noted especially for his watercolors of Normandy and Egypt, he exhibited at the Boston Athenaeum, National Academy, and the Paris Salon. He died at Cairo (Egypt), March 13, 1912. ¶ *Art Annual,* X, 75, obit.; Swan, BA; *Panorama,* I (May 1946), 95, repro.; NAD Cat. 1871–83 (courtesy Mary Bartlett Cowdrey).

BACON, JOHN E. NYC, 1856–60, "decorative and mercantile painter, designer and engraver for all the principal circuses, menageries and traveling exhibitions throughout the United States, England, California, Canada &c." ¶ NYCD 1856–60. An iron merchant is listed at the same address in 1844–55. NYBD 1858/59 lists Bacon as a wood engraver.

BACON, LOUIS. Sculptor, San Francisco, 1856, 1860. ¶ San Francisco CD 1856; BD 1860.

BACON, MARY ANN (Mrs. Chauncey Whittlesey). Views in watercolor. Born February 9, 1787, she went to school in Litchfield (Conn.). Two watercolor views of Quebec painted by her are in the Litchfield Historical Society. ¶ Vanderpoel, *Chronicles of a Pioneer School,* 66–79, repros. opp. 176 and 192; Barker, *American Painting,* 378.

BADEAU & BROTHER. Wood engravers, NYC, 1850; ISAAC BADEAU and JONATHAN F. BADEAU. ¶ NYBD and NYCD 1850.

BADEAU, ISAAC. Engraver, of BADEAU & BROTHER, NYC, 1850. ¶ NYCD 1850. Isaac Badeau, perfumer, was listed in 1848.

BADEAU, JONATHAN F. Wood engraver, NYC and Brooklyn, 1849–53. Exhibited at American Institute in 1849 and 1850; partner in BADEAU & BROTHER in 1850. ¶ NYCD 1849–53; NYBD 1851; Am. Inst. Cats. 1849, 1850.

BADGER, JAMES W. Portrait painter and miniaturist at Richmond in 1836 and Boston 1845–46. ¶ *Richmond Portraits,* 241, cites Richmond *Compiler,* Dec. 7–18, 1836; Boston BD 1845–46.

BADGER, JOHN C. Artist and crayon portraitist. Born *c.* 1822 in New Hampshire; living in Philadelphia, September 19, 1850, with wife Mary (born *c.* 1825, Vermont). Exhibited at the Pennsylvania Academy in 1852 and 1854. ¶ 7 Census (1850), Pa., LII, 988; Phila. CD 1852–54; Phila. BD 1853; Penna. BD 1854/55; Rutledge, PA.

BADGER, JONATHAN. Music engraver, Charleston, 1752. ¶ Rutledge, *Artists in the Life of Charleston,* cites *South Carolina Gazette,* Nov. 13, 1752.

BADGER, JOSEPH (1708–1765). Portrait painter. Born March 14, 1708, at Charlestown (Mass.), moved to Boston *c.* 1733. He was the principal portrait painter of Boston between SMIBERT and COPLEY. He died in the summer of 1765, presumably in Boston. ¶ DAB; represented at American Antiquarian Society (Weis, *Check List*) and at Maryland Historical Society (Rutledge, MHS); Park, "Joseph Badger"; Park, "Joseph Badger and His Portraits of Children"; Barker, *American Painting,* 125, repro.; *American Processional,* 39, repro.; Dow, *Arts and Crafts;* Met. Mus., *Life in America.*

BADGER, JOSEPH W. Portrait and miniature painter, NYC, 1832–37; exhibited at the National Academy and American Academy. ¶ NYCD 1833–36; Cowdrey, NAD; Cowdrey, AA & AAU; Stauffer, nos. 2488, 2597; Bolton, *Miniature Painters.*

BADGER, Mrs. MILTON, see CLARISSA MUNGER.

BADGER, S. Portrait painter, Boston, 1834, 1840; possibly THOMAS BADGER (1792–1868). ¶ Boston Athenaeum Cats. 1834 (no. 158) and 1840; Swan, BA, 198.

BADGER, S. W. Miniature and portrait painter, 1836. Possibly the same as JOSEPH W. BADGER. ¶ Cowdrey, NAD.

BADGER, THOMAS (1792–1868). Portrait painter, miniaturist, and lithographer. Born December 25, 1792, at South Reading, now Wakefield (Mass.), Thomas Badger began painting portraits in Boston in 1814 and continued working there at least until 1859, with occasional professional trips to Maine *c.* 1832 and 1858. He exhibited at the Boston Athenaeum, the National Academy, and the American Academy. He died at Cambridge (Mass.), February 3, 1868. ¶ *Old Family Portraits of Kennebunk* gives 1792 birth date; Swan, BA, 198, gives *c.* 1793; 7 Census (1850), Mass., XXV, 555, gives his age in 1850 as 60 years, implying a birth date in 1790 or 1791. Boston Athenaeum Cats. 1830, 1837; Boston BD 1841–42, 1844–51; Cowdrey, NAD; Cowdrey, AA & AAU; WPA (Mass.), *Portraits Found in Maine*. Represented at the Maine Historical Society and Bowdoin College.

BADGER, THOMAS H. Portrait painter and lithographer, Boston, 1849. ¶ Boston BD 1849/50 (THOMAS BADGER listed separately at same address); Thieme-Becker.

BADGER, WILLIAM. Miniaturist, New Haven (Conn.), *c.* 1838–40. The Wadsworth Athenaeum, Hartford, owns six miniatures ascribed to William Badger by the donor, Mrs. Susan T. Darling. Three are on ivory and three on paper; the subjects are members of the families of Dr. Charles Steele Thomson and his wife, née Susan Coit Belcher. ¶ Courtesy of C. C. Cunningham, Wadsworth Athenaeum, Hartford (Conn.).

BADLAM, ——. Teacher of painting and and drawing at Kennebunk (Maine), 1835: possibly Stephen Badlam of Dorchester. ¶ *Old Family Portraits of Kennebunk.*

BAER, ——. Portrait painter, NYC, *c.* 1846. Painted a portraint of Israel Bear Kurscheedt (1776–1852) of NYC, owned by the Misses Kurscheedt of NYC (1938). ¶ Reid, *Masonic Publication,* 167, repro.; London, *Portraits of Jews,* 63; WPA (Mass.), *Portraits Found in N.Y.*

BAERER, HENRY (1837–1908). Sculptor. Born in 1837 at Kircheim (Hesse-Kassell, Germany), Baerer came to the U.S. in 1854 upon completition of his university course. He was a portrait sculptor, and several of his statues stand in New York City parks. He died in The Bronx, NYC, December 7, 1908. ¶ *Art Annual,* VIII, 397, obit.; Thieme-Becker; NYHS *Cat.* 1941 lists two examples of his work at the Society; Rutledge, PA; NAD Cats. 1866–89 (courtesy Mary Bartlett Cowdrey).

BAGETT, A., see ALFRED DAGGETT.

BAHIN, LOUIS JOSEPH. Portrait artist from France, at Natchez (Miss.) *c.* 1850. ¶ Barker, *American Painting,* 522, 525; represented in Rockefeller Folk Art Collection. Williamsburg.

BÄHR, C. O. Executed drawing of Galveston, Texas, *c.* 1855. ¶ Stokes, *Historical Prints,* pl. 91-b.

BAIL (Bale), LOUIS (Lewis). Crayon, pencil, and medallion portrait artist, art teacher, and author. Bail was working in NYC 1850–54 and exhibited at the National Academy and the American Institute. He was at New Haven 1855–63 as professor of art and was the author of *The Teacher's Guide* (New Haven, 1858) and *Bale's Drawing System* (New Haven, 1859, with plates). ¶ Cowdrey, NAD; Am. Inst. Cats. 1850, 1851; NYBD 1854; New Haven CD 1855–58, 1861–63.

BAILEY, A., see JOSEPH ALEXIS BAILLY.

BAILEY, ADOLPH. Sculptor. Born *c.* 1822 in France; living in Philadelphia, July 16, 1860, aged 38, with wife, aged 34, and four children between the ages of 3 and 14, all born in France; personal property valued at $500. ¶ 8 Census (1860), Pa., LIV, 301.

BAILEY, ALFRED. Artist. Born March 15, 1823, at Amesbury, Mass; active in 1844. ¶ Belknap, *Artists and Craftsmen of Essex County.*

BAILEY, BENJAMIN. Engraver, Boston, 1834–50. ¶ Boston CD 1834–35; Boston BD 1841–44, 1846–50.

BAILEY, FRANCIS. Engraver, printer, publisher, and typefounder, Philadelphia, 1778–1817. ¶ Brown and Brown.

BAILEY, FRANCISCO. Portrait painter. Born *c.* 1817 in France; living in San Francisco, June 29, 1860, with his family, Pancha (aged 27) and Lagurda (aged 10), both born in Mexico, and Mr. and Mrs. EDWARD JUMP. ¶ 8 Census (1860), Cal., VII, 717.

BAILEY, GEORGE M. India ink draftsman, Williamsburgh (N.Y.), 1850. ¶ Am. Inst. Cat. 1850.

BAILEY, JAMES. English artist, 44, at NYC in 1850. Other artist members of his household were JAMES CANTWELL, JAMES GARROW, and WILLIAM MORLEY. Possibly the same as JAMES S. BAILLIE, lithographer and colorer for CURRIER & IVES. ¶ 7 Census (1850), N.Y., L, 81.

BAILEY & MATTHEWSON. Engravers and diesinkers, NYC, 1849. ¶ NYBD 1849.

BAILEY, TILLINGHAST. Lithographer. Born *c.* 1823 in Massachusetts; working in Boston, June 26, 1860. ¶ 8 Census (1860), Mass., XXVIII, 112.

BAILEY, WALTER C. Engraver, Boston, 1857–60 and after. ¶ Boston BD 1859–60; Boston CD 1857–58, 1860 and after.

BAILEY, WILLIAM A. Engraver active in NYC from 1848 to 1858. He was a native of New York State, born about 1827. ¶ NYCD 1848–58; 7 Census (1850), N.Y., XLVI, 201.

BAILIE, JAMES. Portrait painter, NYC, 1807–09. ¶ NYCD 1807–09; Stauffer, no. 1805, engraving after portrait by Bailie.

BAILLIE, JAMES S. Artist, colorer of prints, and lithographer, NYC, 1838–55. The City Directory lists James or James S. Baillie as picture framer (1838–39), artist (1841–43), colorer of prints (1843–47), lithographer (1847–49, 1853), and painter (1854–55). He was a colorer for CURRIER & IVES and a well-known lithographer in his own right. Possibly the same as JAMES BAILEY. ¶ NYCD 1838–39, 1841–49, 1854; Peters, *America on Stone,* 84–85 and pl. 10; *American Collector,* XVI (Jan. 1948), 19, repro.; Davidson, II, 33, repro.

BAILLY, A., see JOSEPH ALEXIS BAILLY.

BAILLY, ALEXIS J., see JOSEPH ALEXIS BAILLY.

BAILLY, JOSEPH ALEXIS (1825–1883). Wood carver and sculptor. Born January 21, 1825, in Paris, Bailly lived there until 1848, when he came to America. After brief residences in New Orleans, NYC, Philadelphia, and Buenos Ayres, he married and settled in Philadelphia in 1850. At first a wood carver & wax modeler, he turned to portrait sculpture, his works including a bust of Washington now in Independence Hall. Elected an Academician of the Pennsylvania Academy in 1856, Bailly served as instructor at the Academy in 1876 and 1877. He died at Philadelphia, June 15, 1883. ¶ DAB; Gardner, *Yankee Stonecutters,* 60; 8 Census (1860), Pa., LV, 754–55; Rutledge, PA; Taft, *American Sculpture.* His work is represented at the Maryland Hist. Soc. (Rutledge, MHS) and Princeton University (Egbert, *Princeton Portraits*). Delgado-WPA records an A. Bailly, sculptor, in New Orleans CD 1850; Pinckney, 187, records an Alexis J. Bailly, carver, in NYC, 1855—both are probably the same as Joseph Alexis Bailly.

BAILY, A. Artist, Philadelphia, 1811. ¶ Brown and Brown.

BAILY, JULIUS T. Sculptor, NYC, 1858. ¶ NYBD 1858.

BAILY, WILLIAM A., see WILLIAM A. BAILEY.

BAINBOROUGH, WILLIAM, see WILLIAM BAMBOROUGH.

BAINBRIDGE, HENRY. Landscape draftsman, worked in collaboration with GEORGE W. CASILEAR on views of San Francisco and Sacramento, *c.* 1851. Possibly the same as Henry Bainbridge, clerk, listed in 1852 Directory of San Francisco. ¶ Peters, *California on Stone; Portfolio,* X (May 1951), 209, repro.; San Francisco CD 1852.

BAINBRIGGS, PHILIP. Executed a watercolor drawing of Montpelier (Vt.) in 1841. ¶ Stokes, *Historical Prints,* 151.

BAKER, ALFRED E. Lithographer, artist, police officer, NYC. Listed as a lithographer 1833–42, as city marshall, police officer, fire marshall, or reporter from 1843 through 1860. He exhibited a sketch of the steamship *Great Britain* at the 1845 Fair of the American Institute. ¶ NYCD 1833–60; Am. Inst. Cat. 1845; Davidson, I, 521, repro.

BAKER, ALVIN H. Artist. Born *c.* 1808 in Vermont; living at Enosburgh (Vt.), September 9, 1850, with wife, aged 30, and Charles, aged 5, and property valued at $1,000. ¶ 7 Census (1850), Vt., V, 354.

BAKER & ANDREW. Engravers, Boston, 1854. Partnership between WILLIAM JAY BAKER and JOHN ANDREW, after the dissolution of BAKER, SMITH & ANDREW. ¶ Boston CD 1854; Boston BD 1854.

BAKER, CHARLES. Landscape painter, NYC, 1839–88. Baker exhibited at the National Academy from 1839 to 1873 and at the American Art-Union in 1847, and was still living in 1888. ¶ Cowdrey, NAD; Cowdrey, AA & AAU; Thieme-Becker.

BAKER, GEORGE AUGUSTUS. Miniaturist. Born in 1760 at Strasbourg (France), Baker was working in NYC by 1819 and died after 1830. He was the father of the better-known artist, GEORGE AUGUSTUS BAKER, JR. ¶ Bolton, *Miniature Painters;* McKay, cites NYCD 1819.

BAKER, GEORGE AUGUSTUS, JR. (1821–1880). N.A. Portrait and miniature painter. Born in March 1821 in NYC, George A. Baker, Jr., spent almost his entire life there, except for a trip to Italy *c.* 1846. He exhibited frequently at the National Academy, of which he was an Associate from 1844 and an Academician from 1852 to his death. Baker also exhibited at the Maryland Historical Society, the Pennsylvania Academy, the Artists' Fund Society, and the American Art-Union. He died in NYC, April 2, 1880. ¶ DAB; CAB; *American Art Review,* I (1880), 320–21, obit.; Cowdrey, NAD; NAD Cat., 1861–79; Rutledge, MHS; Rutledge, PA; French, *Art and Artists in Conn.*

BAKER, GEORGE HOLBROOK. Artist, lithographer, and publisher. Born March 9, 1827, at Boston or East Medway (Mass.), Baker studied at the National Academy in 1848, but joined the gold rush to California, arriving at San Francisco in May 1849. He worked at Sacramento from 1852 to 1862 as a publisher and lithographer and made many sketches of mining camps. He moved to San Francisco in 1862, remaining there until his death, January 1906. ¶ George H. Baker, "Records of a California Journey" and "Records of a California Residence"; Van Nostrand and Coulter, *California Pictorial,* 84–85, 158–59, with repros. (the reference on p. 130 to George A. Baker seems actually to refer to George Holbrook Baker); Peters, *California on Stone,* like Van Nostrand and Coulter, gives East Medway as Baker's birthplace; Cowdrey, NAD; NYCD 1848.

BAKER, GEORGE J. Lithographer, of SNELL & BAKER, New Orleans, 1841. ¶ New Orleans CD 1841.

BAKER, HENRY M. (1810–1874). Portrait painter, Frederick County (Va.). ¶ Willis, "Jefferson County Portraits."

BAKER, HORACE (1833–1918). Wood engraver. Born November 12, 1833, at North Salem (N.Y.), he was trained in his brother's firm at Boston (WILLIAM JAY BAKER of BAKER & ANDREWS?) and later worked in the engraving departments of *Harper's Monthly* and the Frank Leslie publications. He died March 2, 1918, at his home in Great Neck, Long Island (N.Y.). ¶ *Art Annual,* XV, obit.; Thieme-Becker.

BAKER, I. H. Stipple engraver, Boston, *c.* 1860. ¶ Stauffer, I, 13.

BAKER, ISAAC C. Portrait painter, Albany (N.Y.), 1835–37. ¶ Albany CD 1835, 1837.

BAKER, J. F. Wood engraver, NYC, exhibited at American Institute in 1845. *Cf.* SAMUEL F. BAKER. ¶ Am. Inst. Cat., 1845.

BAKER, JAMES. Painter in oils, NYC, exhibited at American Institute in 1846. ¶ Am. Inst. Cat., 1846.

BAKER, JOHN. Artist, engraver, and etcher, NYC, 1831–41. Known for engravings of "Battle of Lexington" and "Washington Crossing the Delaware." ¶ NYCD 1831–32, 1834–39, 1841; Stauffer.

BAKER, JOHN. Engraver, 21, a native of New York State, at NYC in 1860. ¶ 8 Census (1860), N.Y., XLVI, 448.

BAKER, JOHN S. Artist, 20, born in New York State, at NYC in 1850. ¶ 7 Census (1850), N.Y., XLVIII, 423.

BAKER, JOSEPH E. Lithographer and pencil portraitist. Baker was a fellow-apprentice with WINSLOW HOMER in BUFFORD'S lithographic establishment at Boston, 1857. He was working in NYC in 1860 and 1867, and is said to have done some Civil War cartoons. ¶ Downes, *Winslow Homer,* with repro. of Baker's pencil portrait of Homer opp. p. 8; Fielding.

BAKER, M. A. Portrait painter, NYC, 1852. Probably the same as M. A. Barker. ¶ NYBD 1852.

BAKER, NATHAN F. Sculptor. Born *c.* 1822 in Ohio, the son of John Baker, a wealthy Cincinnatian whose property was valued in 1850 at $265,000. Nathan was working in Cincinnati 1841–50, and exhibited at the National Academy and the Boston Athenaeum in 1847. ¶ 7 Census (1850), Ohio, XX, 316–17; *Cincinnati Miscellany,* April 1845, 218–19; Cowdrey, NAD; Swan, BA; information courtesy Edward H. Dwight, Cincinnati Art Museum.

BAKER, SAMUEL F. Wood engraver, NYC, 1846–56. *Cf.* J. F. BAKER. ¶ NYCD 1846–50, 1856; NYBD 1850; Thieme-Becker.

BAKER & SMITH. Engravers, Boston, 1852. The partners were WILLIAM JAY BAKER and DANIEL T. SMITH. In 1853 the name was changed to BAKER, SMITH & ANDREW, the original partners having been joined by JOHN ANDREW. ¶ Boston CD and BD 1852–53.

BAKER, SMITH & ANDREW. Engravers, Boston, 1853–54. The partners were WILLIAM JAY BAKER, DANIEL T. SMITH, and JOHN ANDREW. Baker, Smith & Andrew succeeded the firm of BAKER & SMITH and was in turn succeeded by BAKER & ANDREW. ¶ Boston CD and BD 1853–54.

BAKER, WILLIAM D. Wood engraver at Philadelphia 1851–56 and at Chicago 1858–59. ¶ Phila. CD 1851–56; Chicago BD 1858–59.

BAKER, WILLIAM H. (1825–1875). Portrait painter and teacher. Born in 1825, William H. Baker's home in the 1850's was in New Orleans. In 1854 it was noted that he had returned to New Orleans after a residence in the North, where he had been warmly received, and in 1858 it was stated that he had for several years been residing in New Orleans only in the winter and spring. From 1865 he seems to have lived in NYC or Brooklyn, and he served as principal of the Brooklyn Art Association from 1869. He died in Brooklyn, March 29, 1875. ¶ CAB; Delgado-WPA, cites New Orleans *Mercantile Advertiser,* Dec. 17, 1851, *Picayune,* Dec. 16, 1854, and Nov. 14, 1858, *Crescent,* Nov. 26, 1855; New Orleans CD 1852–56; New Orleans BD 1859; Thieme-Becker, cites obit. in *L'Art,* III, 24; Clement and Hutton; NAD Cats. 1866–71 (courtesy Mary Bartlett Cowdrey).

BAKER, WILLIAM JAY (or J.). Engraver. William J. Baker was working in NYC in 1847 and 1848 and exhibited at the American Institute in 1847. In 1850 he was working at Portland (Maine) and from 1851 to 1855 at Boston, as a partner in the engraving firms of BAKER & SMITH; BAKER, SMITH & ANDREW; and BAKER & ANDREW. He was probably the brother of HORACE BAKER, also an engraver. ¶ NYCD 1847–48, address Jersey City; Am. Inst. Cat. 1847; New England BD 1850/51; Boston BD 1851–52; Boston CD 1851–55.

BAKEWELL, ROBERT. Drawing master. Born *c.* 1790 in England, living in New Haven (Conn.), October 2, 1850. ¶ 7 Census (1850), Conn., VIII, 524.

BALCH & CO. Engravers and copperplate printers, NYC, 1833. The senior partner was VISTUS BALCH. ¶ NYCD 1833.

BALCH, EUGENE. Artist, 20, born in Massachusetts, living in NYC in 1860. He was a son of Mrs. Leland Balch, Sr., and brother of LELAND BALCH, JR. ¶ 8 Census (1860), N.Y., XLIV, 416.

BALCH, LELAND, JR. Artist, 26, born in Vermont, son of Leland and Eliza Balch. He was living in NYC in 1860 with his widowed mother and his younger brother EUGENE, also an artist. Mrs. Balch was a daguerreotypist. ¶ 8 Census (1860), N.Y., XLIV, 416.

BALCH, RAWDON & CO. Engravers, Albany (N.Y.), 1822. The partners were VISTUS BALCH and RALPH RAWDON. ¶ Albany CD 1822, with full page adv.

BALCH, STILES & CO. Engravers, NYC and Utica (N.Y.), 1828–30. The senior partners were VISTUS BALCH and SAMUEL STILES; WILLIAM WILLIAMS was with the Utica branch in 1828. N. & S. S. JOCELYN did work for Balch, Stiles & Co. in New Haven (Conn.), 1829–30. ¶ NYCD 1828–30; Utica CD 1828–29; Williams, *An Oneida County Printer,* 120; Rice, "Life of Nathaniel Jocelyn," unpublished Ms., courtesy of the author.

BALCH, STILES, WRIGHT & CO. Engravers, NYC and Utica (N.Y.), 1831–32. The partners were VISTUS BALCH, SAMUEL STILES and NEZIAH WRIGHT. ¶ NYCD 1831–32; Utica CD 1832.

BALCH, VISTUS (1799–1884). Engraver and portrait draftsman on stone. Born February 18, 1799, at Williamstown (Mass.), Balch was working at Albany (N.Y.) in 1822 as senior partner in the engraving firm of BALCH, RAWDON & CO. From 1826 to 1833 he headed a number of engraving firms with headquarters in NYC and a branch at Utica: BALCH, STILES & CO. (1828–30); BALCH, STILES, WRIGHT & CO. (1831–32); BALCH & CO. (1833). He died at Johnstown (N.Y.), October 25, 1884. ¶ Thieme-Becker; Albany CD 1822; NYCD 1826–33; Utica CD 1828–29, 1832; Peters, *America on Stone.*

BALD, COUSLAND & CO. Banknote engravers, 1854–60. A Philadelphia firm, headed by J. DORSEY BALD and WILLIAM COUSLAND; there was also a branch in NYC 1855–58 (under the name of BALDWIN, BALD & COUSLAND in 1856–57). Bald, Cousland & Co. was one of the group of banknote engraving firms which merged in 1858 to form the powerful AMERICAN BANK NOTE CO. ¶ Phila. CD 1854–60; NYCD 1855–58; Toppan, *100 Years of Bank Note Engraving,* 12.

BALD, J. DORSEY (*c.* 1826–*c.* 1878). Lawyer and banknote engraver, Philadelphia, 1849–78. Born *c.* 1826, a son of the engraver ROBERT BALD and brother of ROBERT L. BALD. J. Dorsey Bald began his career as a lawyer and counsellor *c.* 1849, but appears to have taken charge of the family engraving interests in 1854, probably after the death of his brother ROBERT L. BALD. From 1854 to 1860 he was senior partner in the engraving firm of BALD, COUSLAND & CO. of Philadelphia and NYC, and in 1858 participated in the formation of the AMERICAN BANK NOTE CO. He is listed as an engraver in the Philadelphia Directories until 1878. ¶ 7 Census (1850), Penna., LI, 101; Phila.

CD 1854–78; NYCD 1855–56, 1858, address Phila.

BALD, ROBERT (*c.* 1793–*c.* 1856). Engraver. Born *c.* 1793 in Scotland, Robert Bald came to Philadelphia *c.* 1823 and worked there as an engraver from 1825 to 1848. He was a partner in a number of banknote engraving firms, including UNDERWOOD, BALD & SPENCER (NYC and Phila., 1835–36); UNDERWOOD, BALD, SPENCER & HUFTY (NYC and Phila., 1837–43); and DANFORTH, BALD, SPENCER & HUFTY (NYC 1843). He appears to have retired *c.* 1848/49, as he is listed as "gentleman" in the Philadelphia Directories from 1849 to 1856. His sons, ROBERT L. BALD and J. DORSEY BALD, carried on the family business. ¶ 7 Census (1850), Penna., LI, 101; Phila. CD 1825–56; NYCD 1835–38, 1843.

BALD, ROBERT L. (*c.* 1826–*c.* 1853?). Banknote engraver and printer. Born at Philadelphia *c.* 1826, Robert L. Bald was a son of the engraver, ROBERT BALD. On his father's retirement about 1848 he took over the family engraving business, entering into partnership with MOSELY I. and EDWARD J. DANFORTH of NYC, under the name of DANFORTH, BALD & Co. The company had offices in NYC, Boston, Philadelphia and Cincinnati from 1850 to 1853. Robert L. Bald's name disappears from the Philadelphia Directory after 1853, and it seems likely that he died in that year, as the Bald engraving interests were thereafter managed by his brother, J. DORSEY BALD. ¶ 7 Census (1850), Penna., LI, 101; Phila. CD 1850–53; NYCD 1850–53.

BALDWIN, ADAMS & CO. Banknote engravers, NYC, 1851–54. The partners were GEORGE D. BALDWIN and WILLIAM H. ADAMS. The firm was succeeded in 1855 by BALDWIN, BALD & COUSLAND. ¶ NYCD 1851–55.

BALDWIN, ALMON. Portrait, landscape, and sign painter, Cincinnati, 1838–53. Baldwin is listed variously as a painter of portraits and landscapes (1838–41), as a pictorial and sign painter (1842–43), as senior partner in the firm of BALDWIN & WILLIAMS, artists (1853), as artist (1856–58), and as curator of the Gallery of the Art Union of Cincinnati (1849, 1853). ¶ Cist. *Cincinnati in 1841;* Cincinnati CD 1842–58; Ohio BD 1853/54.

BALDWIN, BALD & COUSLAND. Banknote engravers, NYC, 1855–58. In 1854 or 1855 GEORGE D. BALDWIN, formerly of BALDWIN, ADAMS & CO., joined with J. DORSEY BALD and WILLIAM COUSLAND of Philadelphia under the firm name of Baldwin, Bald & Cousland. The company operated under that name until 1858, when Baldwin withdrew and the firm took the name of BALD, COUSLAND & CO. ¶ NYCD 1855–58.

BALDWIN & DUNNEL. Engravers, NYC, 1847. The partners were ENOS B. BALDWIN and WILLIAM N. DUNNEL. ¶ NYCD 1847.

BALDWIN, ENOS. Wood engraver, NYC, 1847–60 and after. In 1847 he was senior partner of BALDWIN & DUNNEL. ¶ NYCD 1847–48, 1853–60 and after; NYBD 1859.

BALDWIN, GEORGE C. Portrait painter, working mainly at Thompson (Conn.) where he was born *c.* 1818. An oil portrait of a child, signed "G. C. Baldwin," is owned by James Thomas Flexner of NYC. Baldwin died after 1879. ¶ French, *Art and Artists in Conn.;* information courtesy James Thomas Flexner.

BALDWIN, GEORGE D. Banknote engraver, NYC, 1848–72; listed as a merchant from 1830 to 1846 and as a plate printer in 1847. He was associated with the following firms: DURAND, BALDWIN & CO. (1848–50); BALDWIN, ADAMS & CO. (1851–54); and BALDWIN, BALD & COUSLAND (1855–58). From 1858 to 1872 he was in business independently. George Baldwin, engraver, was listed in the 1850 Census as 46 years old, born in New Jersey. *Cf.*, GEORGE D. BALDWIN, artist. ¶ NYCD 1830–72; 7 Census (1850), N.Y., LII, 272.

BALDWIN, GEORGE D. Artist from Connecticut, aged 41, at NYC in July 1860 with his wife Rebecca G., also a native of Connecticut. He owned personalty valued at $2,000. *Cf.* GEORGE D. BALDWIN, engraver. ¶ 8 Census (1860), N.Y., LVII, 372.

BALDWIN, J. G. Crayon draftsman, NYC, exhibited at the American Institute, 1844. ¶ Am. Inst. Cat., 1844. The address given is the same as that of Nehemiah Baldwin, chemist, in NYCD 1844.

BALDWIN, J. L. Watercolor painter and pencil draftsman, Newark (N.J.); exhibited at the American Institute, 1856. ¶ Am. Inst. Cat., 1856.

BALDWIN, JAMES. Engraver, 30, a native of New York State, at NYC in 1860. ¶ 8 Census (1860), N.Y., XLVI, 287.

BALDWIN, WILLIAM. Connecticut-born portrait painter, 35, at NYC in 1850. ¶ 7 Census (1850), N.Y., XLV, 145.

BALDWIN, WILLIAM. Miniaturist and portrait painter, born in Louisiana *c.* 1808 and working in New Orleans *c.* 1827–50. ¶ 7 Census (1850), La., IV, 378; New Orleans CD 1843; Bolton, *Miniature Painters;* Fielding.

BALDWIN & WILLIAMS. Artists, Cincinnati, 1853. The partners were ALMON BALDWIN and G. INSCO WILLIAMS. ¶ Cincinnati CD 1853.

BALE, JAMES. Engraver and die-sinker, NYC, 1829–51. Bale was a partner in various engraving and die-sinking firms: WRIGHT & BALE (1829–33), with CHARLES C. WRIGHT; BALE & SMITH (1835–47), with FREDERICK B. SMITH; BALE & MAY (1848–51), with GEORGE W. MAY. His name does not appear in the directories after 1851. ¶ NYCD 1829–51.

BALE, LOUIS, see LOUIS BAIL.

BALE & MAY. Engravers and die-sinkers, NYC, 1848–51. On the dissolution of BALE & SMITH in 1847, JAMES BALE took into partnership GEORGE W. MAY, who had been with the earlier company from 1843. Bale & May operated from 1848 to 1851, when Bale died or left NYC. May carried on alone during 1852, but entered into partnership with GEORGE J. GLAUBRECHT in 1853, under the name of MAY & GLAUBRECHT. ¶ NYCD 1848–53.

BALE & SMITH. Engravers and die-sinkers, NYC, 1835–47. This partnership between JAMES BALE and FREDERICK B. SMITH was the successor to WRIGHT & BALE; in 1847 it was dissolved, to be succeeded the next year by BALE & MAY. ¶ NYCD 1835–47.

BALIGNANT, ——. Teacher of flower and landscape painting, New Orleans, 1808. ¶ Delgado-WPA, cites *Moniteur,* Aug. 10 and Nov. 30, 1808.

BALIS, C. Portrait painter, probably at New Hartford (N.Y.), 1846–50. ¶ Repros. and notes at FARL; letter, E. Manning to G. C. Groce, Sept. 15, 1947.

BALL, EZRA H. Engraver, born in Massachusetts *c.* 1824; living in Boston, August 2, 1850, with wife Betsy (born *c.* 1826 in Massachusetts) and a daughter. He is listed as a plate printer in the directories 1846–51; of BALL & POLLARD, 1849. ¶ 7 Census (1850), Mass., XXV, 618; Boston CD 1846–51.

BALL, FRANKLIN. Painter, Brooklyn (N.Y.); exhibited at the American Institute, 1849. ¶ Am. Inst. Cat., 1849.

BALL, HUGH SWINTON. Amateur painter, patron of art, and Honorary Member of the National Academy of Design, 1838. He died in South Carolina, June 16, 1838. ¶ Cummings, *Historic Annals,* 152; Cowdrey, NAD.

BALL, LIBERTY P. Portrait painter who was at Utica (N.Y.) in 1839 and at NYC between 1844 and 1858. He exhibited at the National Academy. ¶ Utica CD 1839; NYBD 1844, 1854, 1857–58; Cowdrey, NAD.

BALL, LUTHER. Engraver, born *c.* 1827 in Connecticut and working at New Haven in 1850. ¶ 7 Census (1850), Conn., VIII, 329.

BALL, Mrs. MARGARET. Watercolor painter, Onondago County (N.Y.); exhibited at the American Institute in 1845. ¶ Am. Inst. Cat., 1845.

BALL & POLLARD. Plate printers, Boston, 1849. The senior partner, EZRA H. BALL, was an engraver. ¶ Boston CD 1849.

BALL, S. Amateur artist, Brooklyn (N.Y.); exhibited drawings at the American Institute, 1849. ¶ Am. Inst. Cat., 1849.

BALL, SOPHIA. Amateur artist, Marcellus (N.Y.); exhibited drawing at American Institute, 1842. ¶ Am. Inst. Cat., 1842.

BALL, THOMAS (1819–1911). Sculptor, miniature, and portrait painter, musician. Ball was born June 3, 1819, at Charlestown (Mass.), the son of a house and sign painter. After a brief apprenticeship to the wood engraver ABEL BOWEN, he set up in Boston as a miniature and portrait painter, supplementing his income by singing. From 1837 to 1853 Ball maintained a studio in Boston; from 1854 to 1857 he was in Italy, where he studied sculpture. On his return to Boston in 1857, he executed a statue of Washington, his best-known work. Ball remained in Boston until 1864, then returned to Italy, where he passed most of his remaining years as an artist, though he made frequent visits to the U.S. He finally returned to America in 1897, settling at Montclair (N.J.), where he died December 11, 1911. His autobiography, *My Threescore Years and Ten,* appeared in 1892. ¶ DAB; Boston CD 1837–53; 1857–64; Swan, BA; Washington Art Assoc. Cats., 1857, 1859; Cowdrey, AA & AAU; Lee, *Familiar Sketches,* 212–13; Gardner, *Yankee Stonecutters;* Bolton, *Miniature Painters.*

BALL, W. Lithographer, known for set of presidential portraits, *c.* 1830. ¶ Peters, *America on Stone.*

BALL, WILLIAM, JR. (1794?–1813). Amateur engraver who executed a few plates while clerking in a store at Winchester (Va.) in 1812–13. He was accepted as a pupil by the Philadelphia engraver GEORGE MURRAY but was called up with his militia regiment before he could begin his studies. On May 24, 1813, while on duty at Fort Nelson, he was shot and killed by an over-zealous sentry. Ball was then in his twentieth year. ¶ *Port Folio,* Third Series, Vol. II (July 1813), 84–93.

BALLARD, GEORGE. English engraver, 26, at NYC in July 1850. ¶ 7 Census (1850), N.Y., XLII, 350.

BALLARD, OTIS A., see OTIS A. BULLARD.

BALLIN, J., see JOHN T. BATTIN.

BALLING, OLE PETER HANSEN (1823–1906). Portrait painter. Born at Christiania (now Oslo), Norway, on April 13, 1823, Balling came to NYC in 1856. He is best known for his Civil War canvas depicting Gen. U. S. Grant and twenty-six of his generals, owned by the Smithsonian Institution at Washington. The artist died May 1, 1906. He exhibited at the National Academy 1863–80 as H. Balling. ¶ Thieme-Becker; Bénézit; Mayo, cites Washington *Sunday Star,* Sept. 27, 1931; Rutledge, PA; NAD Cats. 1863–80 (courtesy Mary Bartlett Cowdrey).

BALLOU, GIDDINGS HYDE (1820–1886). Portrait and landscape painter. Born November 10, 1820, at Stafford (Conn.), Ballou was the son of a former president of Tufts College. During the Civil War he edited the *Gospel Banner* and he later worked for eight years in the Agricultural Bureau at Washington. He died June 8, 1886, at Chatham (Mass.). ¶ Ballou, *Ballou Genealogy,* 758–59; Boston *Transcript,* June 14, 1886.

BALMANNO, Mrs. ROBERT. Still life painter, Brooklyn (N.Y.); exhibited at the National Academy in 1843 and at the American Institute in 1851. Mr. Balmanno was a clerk at the customhouse. ¶ Cowdrey, NAD; Am. Inst. Cat., 1851.

BAMBOROUGH, WILLIAM (1792–1860). Portrait painter. Born at Durham (England), Bamborough came to the U.S. and settled at Columbus (Ohio) in 1819. He was a friend of J. J. AUDUBON and traveled with him in the South between 1824 and 1832. He is said to have been at Shippenport (Ohio) in 1830 and he appears to have worked at Louisville (Ky.) in 1832. On September 19, 1850, he was living at Columbus with his wife Lucy (born *c.* 1811 in Pennsylvania) and a daughter Mary (born *c.* 1844 in Ohio); his real property was valued at $4,000. ¶ Clark, *Ohio Art and Artists,* 113; Dunlap, *History,* II, 471; Louisville CD 1832 (courtesy Mrs. W. H. Whitley of Paris, Ky.); 7 Census (1850), Ohio, XV, 659; *Ohio State Journal,* Oct. 26, 1911 (courtesy Donald MacKenzie, Wooster College).

BANGS, FRANCIS A. Artist. Born *c.* 1836 in Virginia, working at Washington (D.C.), June 20, 1860, with personal property valued at $150. ¶ 8 Census (1860), D.C., I, 698.

BANKER, HEZEKIAH. Wood engraver, 29, born in New York State, at NYC in 1860. ¶ 8 Census (1860), N.Y., XLV, 37.

BANKS, JAMES. Engraver, Philadelphia, 1850–71? J. Bank, engraver, aged 21, born in Virginia, was recorded in the Philadelphia Census of 1850. James Banks, aged 28, born in Virginia, was listed as an engraver in the Census of 1860; he was then living with his wife and one child, with property valued at $2,300. James O. H. Banks, engraver, was listed in the Directory for 1871. ¶ 7 Census (1850), Penna., LII, 227; 8 Census (1860), Penna., LVIII, 71; Phila. CD 1871.

BANN, CHARLES. Engraver. Born *c.* 1826 in France, working at Philadelphia, August 2, 1850. ¶ 7 Census (1850), Penna., L, 589.

BANNERMAN, JAMES. Engraver, NYC, 1797. ¶ McKay, cites NYCD 1797.

BANNERMAN, JOHN. Engraver, Baltimore, *c.* 1800–07. J. Bannerman engraved portraits for books published at Huntingdon (Pa.) and Baltimore *c.* 1800–02. He is probably identical with the John Bannerman listed in the Baltimore Directory for 1807. ¶ Stauffer, I, 14; Fielding; Baltimore CD 1807.

BANNERMAN, JOHN B. Engraver, probably the son of WILLIAM W. BANNERMAN, engraver of Baltimore. He was working in Baltimore 1849–53 and in San Francisco 1856–60. ¶ Baltimore BD 1849, 1851, 1853; San Francisco BD and CD, 1856, 1858–60.

BANNERMAN, WILLIAM W. Engraver. William Bannerman was a partner in the Baltimore firm of MEDAIRY & BANNERMAN *c.* 1827–31; he appears to have worked on his own in Baltimore after that, his best known work being a series of engraved portraits of American statesmen for the *U. S. Magazine and Democratic Review,* 1840–45. Bannerman died about 1845/46, leaving his widow, who kept a fancy and household goods store for some years, and a son[?], JOHN B. BANNERMAN, who carried on the engraving business at the same address. ¶ Baltimore CD 1827–51; Stauffer, I, 14.

BANNING, WILLIAM J. or T. (1810–1856). Portrait painter, born at Lyme (Conn.); worked in Connecticut and Long Island; exhibited at the National Academy in 1841 and 1842. ¶ Thieme-Becker; Cowdrey, NAD; Fielding.

BANNISTER, EDWARD M. (1833–1901). Portrait painter; born at St. Andrews (N.B.); worked at Boston from 1858 to *c.* 1871; moved to Providence (R.I.) in 1871 and died there January 9, 1901. ¶ Smith; Providence *Journal,* Jan. 11, 1901; Boston CD and BD 1858–60 and after; CAB; NAD Cat. 1879 (courtesy Mary Bartlett Cowdrey).

BANNISTER, EDWIN. Artist. Born in Virginia *c.* 1823; working in Boston July 7, 1860, boarding there with his wife Christiana, aged 30; he owned personal property valued at $200. ¶ 8 Census (1860), Mass., XXVI, 894.

BANNISTER, JAMES (1821–1901). Banknote and general engraver. Bannister was born in England in 1821, but came to NYC before 1846. His earlier work, which is signed, consisted chiefly of portraits and book illustrations. He exhibited at the National Academy in 1858. He died October 11, 1901, in Brooklyn (N.Y.). ¶ Stauffer; *Art Annual,* IV, 136, obit.; NYBD 1846; NYCD 1850; Cowdrey, NAD; 8 Census (1860), N.Y., LVII, 882.

BANONI, see BONANNI.

BANTA, THEODORE M. Amateur artist, aged 15, who exhibited pencil and crayon drawings at the American Institute in 1850. He lived in NYC. ¶ Am. Inst. Cat., 1850.

BANTA, WEART. Portrait painter, NYC, 1858–60 and after. Exhibited at the National Academy in 1878. ¶ NYCD 1858–60 and after; NAD Cat. 1878 (courtesy Mary Bartlett Cowdrey).

BANTON, J. Profilist, Portsmouth (N.H.), 1825. He advertised that his profiles "shall be perfect if the sobriety of the person admits, or no pay for them." ¶ Little, "Itinerant Painting in America," 212. *Cf.* T. S. BANTON.

BANTON, T. S. Silhouettist, New England, early 19th century. *Cf.* J. BANTON. ¶ Jackson, *Silhouette,* 79.

BANVARD, JOHN (1815–1891). Panorama, landscape, and portrait painter. Born and brought up in NYC, he left home at 15 and went to Louisville (Ky.) where he worked in a store for a short time before turning itinerant portraitist. During the 1830's he worked along the Ohio and Mississippi Rivers from Cincinnati to New Orleans. In 1840 he began work on a mammoth panorama of the Mississippi, making hundreds of on-the-spot sketches which he later transferred to canvas in a makeshift studio at Louisville. On its completion in 1846 Banvard took the panorama on a highly successful tour of the United States, followed by an equally triumphant tour of Europe and North Africa. Later he traveled widely in Europe, Africa, and Asia, and painted scenes in Palestine and a panorama of the Nile. He was also a prolific writer of verse, plays, novels, and travel books. In 1880 he settled with his family in Watertown (S.D.) where he died May 17, 1891. He exhibited at the Boston Athenaeum and National Academy. ¶ DAB; *Banvard, or, the Adventures of an Artist;* Boston *Transcript,* May 19, 1891, obit.; Swan, BA; Cowdrey, NAD; CAB; McCracken, *Portrait of the Old West,* 218; information courtesy J. Earl Arrington.

BAR, see DE BAR.

BARBAUD, AUGUSTE. Portrait painter, Philadelphia, 1818. *Cf.* J. J. A. BARBAUD. ¶ Phila. CD 1818.

BARBAUD, J. J. A. Portrait painter, Philadelphia, 1820. *Cf.* AUGUSTE BARBAUD. ¶ Phila. CD 1820.

BARBEE, T. R., is WILLIAM RANDOLPH BARBEE.

BARBEE, WILLIAM RANDOLPH (1818–1868). Sculptor. Born on January 17, 1818, near Luray (Va.), W. R. Barbee studied law and was admitted to the bar in 1843. For over ten years he practised in Luray until he was able to give up the law for his real interest, sculpture. He spent two years in Italy, working with HART and POWERS, whose influence was seen in his principal works, "The Coquette" and "The Fisher Girl," which were exhibited successfully in Richmond, Baltimore, and New York in 1858 and 1859. Though he had failed to secure a commission for work on the U. S. Capitol in 1857, Barbee later won official patronage and had a studio in the Capitol before and after the Civil War. His plaster bust of Speaker Orr was exhibited at the Pennsylvania Academy in 1859–60, when the artist was resident in Washington. He died at "Barbee Bower," near Luray on June 16,

1868. His son, Herbert Barbee, born in 1848, also was a sculptor. ¶ Wayland, *Shenandoah County,* 524–25, 582–83; Fairman, *Art and Artists,* 164–65; Gardner, *Yankee Stonecutters,* 61; Rutledge, PA; Richmond *Enquirer,* Oct. 1–12, 1858, June 19, 1868 (obit.); Mayo, cites Smithsonian Morgue; Thieme-Becker. Mallett and Smith erroneously give 1868 as Barbee's year of birth.

BARBER, ——. Limner and drawing master, of HAND & BARBER, Baltimore, 1795–99. ¶ Prime, II, 50; Mayo, cites Baltimore CD 1796, 1799; Lafferty.

BARBER, EDMUND L. Wood engraver, Hartford or New Haven (Conn.), 1831–39. ¶ *American Advertising Directory* (1831), 53; Hamilton notes two cuts by Barber in *Historical Collections . . . of Every Town in Massachusetts* (Worcester, 1839), opp. pp. 404, 457.

BARBER, JAMES. Copperplate engraver. Born *c.* 1825 in Connecticut, Barber was living in New Haven on September 30, 1850, with his wife Charity (born *c.* 1822 in Connecticut). ¶ 7 Census (1850), Conn., VII, 501.

BARBER, JOHN JAY (1840–after 1905). Landscape and animal painter, lawyer. Born April or September 21, 1840, at Sandusky (Ohio), Barber studied law and was admitted to practice in 1862. The following year he joined the Ohio volunteers for Civil War duty. In 1864 he opened a studio in Columbus (Ohio). He exhibited at the National Academy in the 1880's and was still living in Columbus in 1905. ¶ Clark, *Ohio Art and Artists,* gives the April birth date, while the CAB and *Artists Year Book* (1905–06) both give September 21, 1840; National Academy Cat. 1881–87 (courtesy Mary Bartlett Cowdrey).

BARBER, JOHN WARNER (1798–1885). Engraver, topographical draftsman, and historian. Born February 2, 1798, at East Windsor (Conn.), J. W. Barber served his apprenticeship under ABNER REED, engraver of East Windsor. He established his own engraving business in New Haven in 1823, but soon was devoting himself to history. He traveled widely over the eastern United States, gathering historical information for the many books he published and for the hundreds of engravings with which he embellished them. Barber died at his home in New Haven, June 22, 1885. ¶ DAB; Linton; CAB; Stokes, *Historical Prints;* Davidson, I, 342, repro.; Larsen, "Historical Views on Staffordshire China"; original sketches for his *History of Connecticut* are at Conn. Hist. Soc., Hartford.

BARBER, WILLIAM (1807–1879). Engraver. Born May 2, 1807, in London, Barber was brought to America by his father, John Barber, from whom he learned to engrave on silver. William Barber worked for about ten years in Boston, but from 1865 until his death served at the U. S. Mint in Philadelphia as assistant and chief engraver. He died in Philadelphia August 31, 1879, and was succeeded as chief engraver by his son, Charles E. Barber (1842–1917). ¶ Stauffer; Thieme-Becker; Rutledge, PA.

BARBER, WILLIAM. Engraver, 49, at NYC in 1860. He was a native of New York State, as were his wife Rosina and their three children. ¶ 8 Census (1860), N.Y., LXII, 408.

BARBIER, ——. "Young" theatrical scene painter at New Orleans in 1819–20. He may have been the Barbier who exhibited at the Pennsylvania Academy in 1811 and 1813 a landscape and a portrait of "Miss Farren" as Juliet. ¶ Delgado-WPA cites New Orleans *Courier,* Nov. 19, 1819, and *Gazette,* June 5, 1820; Rutledge, PA.

BARBIER-WALBONNE (Barbierre-Walbonne), JACQUES LUC (1769–1860). Miniaturist, portrait, and historical painter. Born at Nimes (France) in 1769, Barbier-Walbonne was sent to the United States by Louis XVI to paint a portrait of George Washington. He died at Passy (France) in 1860. ¶ Bénézit; Thieme-Becker; Bolton, *Miniature Painters.*

BARBIERI, LEONARDO. Italian portrait painter who went to California in 1847 and painted many prominent citizens, including the members of the Constitutional Convention of 1849. ¶ *Antiques* (Nov. 1953), 373.

BARBOUR, F. Historical painter, NYC, exhibited at the National Academy, 1835–36. ¶ Cowdrey, NAD.

BARCLAY, WILLIAM KENEDY. Portrait painter, Charleston (S.C.), 1831, 1846; he painted a portrait of John C. Calhoun and had been a pupil of SULLY. ¶ Rutledge, *Artists in the Life of Charleston.*

BARD, JAMES (1815–1897). Marine artist. James Bard was born in 1815 at Chelsea, now part of NYC. He and his twin brother, JOHN BARD, were self-taught artists who specialized in portraying the steamboats and small sailing vessels of

NYC and the Hudson River. Over three hundred of their pictures have been recorded. James Bard died at White Plains (N.Y.) on March 26, 1897. ¶ Sniffen, "James and John Bard," in *Art in America* (April 1949), with checklist and repros.; chapter by Sniffen in Lipman and Winchester; repros. in NYHS *Quarterly Bulletin,* VIII (Oct. 1924), 61–68, and XX (Oct. 1936), cover; Karolik Coll. Cat., 70–73, with repros. The Bards' work is represented in the collections of NYHS and the Mariners' Museum, Norfolk, Va.

BARD, JOHN (1815–1856). Marine artist. John Bard, twin brother of JAMES BARD, was born in 1815 at Chelsea (N.Y.) and died in NYC in 1856. He and his brother worked in close collaboration, and it is often difficult to differentiate between their work, since both seem to have used the signature "J. Bard" at times. ¶ Sniffen, "James and John Bard." For further references, see note to JAMES BARD.

BARDET, see BOUDET.

BARELET, see BARRALET.

BARINCOU, J. Portrait painter, Philadelphia, 1839. *Cf.* F. BARINSOU. ¶ Phila. CD 1839.

BARINSOU, F. Lithographer, *c.* 1835, who executed many of the lithographs in JAMES OTTO LEWIS's *Aboriginal Portfolio. Cf.* J. BARINCOU. ¶ Lewis, *Aboriginal Portfolio* (Philadelphia, 1835).

BARKENBURG, JOHN. Lithographer, NYC, 1854. ¶ NYBD 1854.

BARKER, DAVID R. (1806–1881). Portrait and miniature painter. Born in 1806 in Westchester County (N.Y.), D. R. Barker turned to portrait painting after working as a grocery clerk and penmanship instructor. From 1836 to 1848 he worked in NYC and exhibited at the National Academy and Apollo Association. He was in Charleston (S.C.) from December 1848 to February 1849, painting portraits and miniatures. Returning to NYC in 1849 he continued to paint portraits, gaining a considerable local reputation and exhibiting at the American Institute and the National Academy. From 1856 to 1871 he maintained an auction house in NYC. Barker died March 14 or 15, 1881, in NYC. ¶ N. Y. *Tribune,* March 17, 1881, obit., gives March 14 as date of death; *Art Review,* II (1881), 256, obit., gives March 15; NYCD 1836–52; Cowdrey, NAD; Cowdrey, AA & AAU; Am. Inst. Cat., 1851; Rutledge, *Artists in the Life of Charleston.*

BARKER & DRESSER. Lithographers, Philadelphia, 1859. Barker, otherwise unidentified, may be the same as WILLIAM J. BARKER, lithographer of Philadelphia in 1859, though the business addresses are different. The other member of the firm was WILLIAM DRESER. ¶ Phila. BD 1859.

BARKER, Miss E. J. Watercolor artist, Brooklyn (N.Y.); exhibited at the American Institute in 1850. ¶ Am. Inst. Cat., 1850.

BARKER, EDWARD. Engraver, 29, at NYC in 1860. He was born in Connecticut but his wife and two children, ages 1 and 2 years, were born in New York. ¶ 8 Census (1860), N.Y., XLIV, 872.

BARKER, J. J. Lithographer, [Philadelphia?], 1832. ¶ Peters, *America on Stone. Cf.* JOHN JESSE BARKER, below.

BARKER, JOHN JESSE. Portrait, landscape, and animal painter and drawing master of New Brunswick (N.J.), active 1815–60. He exhibited at the Apollo Association in NYC in 1839. *Cf.* J. J. BARKER. ¶ New Brunswick *Fredonian,* May 25, 1815 (courtesy Mrs. George B. Cortelyou, Jr.); Cowdrey, AA & AAU; New Brunswick CD 1855; N.J. BD 1860; information courtesy Donald A. Sinclair, Rutgers University.

BARKER, JOSEPH. Massachusetts-born engraver, 24, at NYC in 1860. ¶ 8 Census (1860), N.Y., XLIII, 276.

BARKER, M. Miniaturist, NYC, *c.* 1820. ¶ Bolton, *Miniature Painters.*

BARKER, Miss M. A. Landscape, still life, and portrait painter. The Miss M. A. Barker who exhibited at the National Academy 1851–53 as a resident of Brooklyn and NYC is probably the same as the Miss M. A. Barker who exhibited landscapes in England 1820–22 as a resident of Bath. The Barkers were an artistic family of Bath, of whom Thomas Barker (1769–1847) was the best-known. Paintings by Thomas Barker were exhibited at the American Academy in 1820 and at the National Academy in 1853. Miss M. A. Barker may have been a daughter of Thomas Barker. ¶ Graves, *Dictionary;* Cowdrey, NAD; Cowdrey, AA & AAU; NYCD 1852.

BARKER, WILLIAM. Engraver, Philadelphia, 1795–1803. ¶ Brown and Brown, cites Phila. CD 1795–96, 1800–03; Stauffer; Stokes, *Historical Prints,* 40–41.

BARKER, WILLIAM J. Lithographer and map publisher, Philadelphia, 1859. Possibly a member of the firm of BARKER & DRESSER, Philadelphia lithographers. ¶ Phila. CD 1859.

BARLOW, EDWARD. Banknote engraver. Born *c.* 1832 at sea, Barlow was living in Philadelphia 1859–60 with his wife Emma (born *c.* 1841 in Pennsylvania). ¶ 8 Census (1860), Penna., LI, 719; Phila. CD 1859–60.

BARLOW, HENRY N. (1824–1884). Painter, picture liner, and restorer. Barlow was working in Philadelphia from 1856 to after 1860, and died at Washington (D.C.), August 31, 1884. ¶ Boston *Transcript,* Sept. 1, 1884, obit.; Phila. CD 1856–60 and after.

BARNARD & DICK. Engravers, NYC, *c.* 1831. The partners probably were WILLIAM S. BARNARD and ARCHIBALD DICK, though the company is not listed in the NYC directories. ¶ Fay, *Views of New York,* title page vignette and pl. 3 and 4.

BARNARD, HENRY S. Engraver. Barnard was born in England *c.* 1818, married there and came to the U.S. after 1850, all his children having been born in England. He was working in Washington (D.C.) by 1858; in 1860 he was living there with his wife Matilda (born *c.* 1818 in England) and three daughters (ages 10 to 18), with personal property valued at $1,000. He was employed as an engraver in the Coast Survey from 1858 to 1869. ¶ 8 Census (1860), D.C., II, 428; Washington CD 1858–69.

BARNARD, JAMES. Engraver. James Barnard was born in Maryland *c.* 1820. He was working in Philadelphia 1850–52. His wife Rebecca was born in Delaware *c.* 1827. ¶ 7 Census (1850), Penna., LII, 525; Phila. CD 1850–52.

BARNARD, S. Painter of a view of Charleston (S.C.) in 1831, now owned by Yale University. ¶ Davidson, II, 116, repro.

BARNARD, WILLIAM. Amateur painter in oils, NYC; exhibited at the American Institute, 1845. ¶ Am. Inst. Cat., 1845.

BARNARD, WILLIAM S. Engraver and illustrator; born in Connecticut about 1809; active in NYC from 1830. He was with BARNARD & DICK in 1831. ¶ 7 Census (1850), N.Y., LV, 853; NYCD 1830–39, 1844–60+; Stauffer.

BARNES, ——. Painter of "The History of the United States," a "great Historical Mirror of America" covering 20,000 square feet of canvas, shown in Boston in June 1852. ¶ Boston *Evening Transcript,* June 29, 1852 (cited by J. E. Arrington).

BARNES, ALBERT. Engraver and silversmith; born *c.* 1839, working in Boston July 30, 1860, and after. ¶ 8 Census (1860), Mass., XXVI, 610, lists him as engraver; Boston CD 1860 and after lists Albert Barnes, silversmith.

BARNES, Mrs. PENELOPE BIRCH. Still life painter, Philadelphia, 1812–40. Mrs. Barnes exhibited frequently at the Society of Artists, the Pennsylvania Academy, and the Artists' Fund Society. In 1813 and 1814 she was living at "Springland," the home of her father, WILLIAM BIRCH, near Bristol (Pa.); from 1829 her address was Philadelphia. ¶ Rutledge, PA.

BARNET & DOOLITTLE. First lithographic firm in the United States, established in NYC *c.* 1821–22 by WILLIAM ARMAND BARNET and ISAAC DOOLITTLE. ¶ Peters, *America on Stone;* McClinton, "American Flower Lithographs," 361.

BARNET, W. A. Engraver from Connecticut, 51, living in NYC in 1860 with his wife, Susan J., a native of New York State. ¶ 8 Census (1860), N.Y., XLVI, 790.

BARNET, WILLIAM ARMAND. Lithographer. The son of Isaac Cox Barnet, U. S. Consul at Paris from 1816 to 1833, he studied in Paris and in 1818 he and ISAAC DOOLITTLE applied from Paris for American patents on certain improvements on steamboats. In 1821 the two men established in NYC the first lithographic house in the United States, under the name of BARNET & DOOLITTLE. Nothing is known of Barnet's later career. ¶ Peters, *America on Stone;* McClinton, "American Flower Lithographs," 361.

BARNETT, ——. Of DUGAN & BARNETT, engravers, NYC, 1844. ¶ NYBD 1844.

BAROLET, see BARRALET.

BARON, CLEMIRE. Engraver, New Orleans, 1835. ¶ Delgado-WPA, cites New Orleans CD 1835.

BARONTO, LOUIS. Portrait and religious painter, carver in alabaster, NYC, 1844–45. ¶ NYCD 1844–45; NYBD 1844; Am. Inst. Cat., 1844.

BARR, W. Landscape artist, known for a view of Hell Gate, NYC, drawn *c.* 1790. ¶ Stauffer.

BARRAC, see DE BARRAC.

BARRALET, JOHN JAMES (*c.* 1747–1815). Painter, designer, and engraver, born *c.* 1747 in Dublin (Ireland). After a successful career as a painter of portraits and landscapes, book illustrator, and drawing master in Dublin and London, Barralet came to the United States in 1795. Settling in Philadelphia, he found employment as a book illustrator, working for a time in association with the engraver, ALEXANDER LAWSON. Barralet also invented a ruling machine for the use of engravers and made improvements in the ink used in copperplate printing. He exhibited many paintings at the Society of Artists and the Pennsylvania Academy. He died in Philadelphia, January 16, 1815. ¶ Strickland, *Dictionary of Irish Artists;* Graves, *Dictionary;* Phila. CD 1797–98, 1800, 1802–03, 1805–07; Rutledge, PA; *Port Folio,* June 1809, frontis.; Bolton, *Miniature Painters;* Snow, "Delineators of the Adams-Jackson American Views," 18; Smith, *British Mezzotint Portraits,* IV, Part I; Davidson, I, 487, repro.

BARRALETT, see BARRALET.

BARRATT, HENRY. Portrait painter, Philadelphia; exhibited at the Artists' Fund Society, 1840. ¶ Rutledge, PA.

BARRATT, THOMAS E. [erroneously E. Thomas]. Miniaturist and portrait painter, born *c.* 1814, England. Barratt came to the United States after 1833 and settled in Philadelphia where he remained at least until 1854. On September 13, 1850, he was living there with his wife Elizabeth (born *c.* 1810 in England) and his daughter Elizabeth (born *c.* 1833 in England). He exhibited frequently at the Artists' Fund Society and Pennsylvania Academy 1837–48. ¶ 7 Census (1850), Penna., LII, 964; Phila. CD 1837, 1839–54; Phila. BD 1838; Rutledge, PA.

BARRE, see DE BARRE.

BARRET, ANTHONY. Sculptor and marble cutter, New Orleans, 1850–56. He was a partner in JUNJEL & BARRET, marble sculptors, 1850–51. ¶ New Orleans CD 1850–56.

BARRETT, ALEXANDER. Lithographer, born *c.* 1833 in Ireland, working in Boston June 28, 1860. ¶ 8 Census (1860), Mass., XXVIII, 421.

BARRITT, WILLIAM. Wood engraver; born in New York State about 1822; active in NYC from about 1845 to 1869. He was the partner of BENSON J. LOSSING from 1847. ¶ 7 Census (1850), N.Y., LVI, 2; NYCD 1845–69; Hamilton, *Early American Book Illustrators and Wood Engravers,* 525.

BARROETA, ——. Miniaturist, painted miniature portrait of Isaiah Thompson, 1835. ¶ Frick Art Reference Library, repro.

BARRON, JOHN W. Engraver and lithographer, born *c.* 1826 in Massachusetts. He was working in Boston from 1850 to 1865 and after. ¶ 7 Census (1850), Mass., XXIII, 598; Boston BD 1856–57, 1859–65 and after; Boston CD 1858.

BARROW, JOHN DOBSON (1823–1907). Portrait and landscape painter who was living in NYC in 1858–60 when he exhibited at the National Academy and the Washington Art Association (as J. L. Barrow). He also worked in Skaneateles (N.Y.) and exhibited at the Boston Athenaeum and the Pennsylvania Academy. ¶ Dates from Swan, BA; Cowdrey, NAD; Washington Art Assoc. Cat., 1859; Tuckerman, *Book of the Artists,* 479; Rutledge, PA.

BARROW, J. L., see JOHN DOBSON BARROW.

BARROW, THOMAS. Artist, NYC, 1780; known only by his view of the ruins of Trinity Church. ¶ Stokes, *Historical Prints.*

BARRY, CHARLES. Artist, born *c.* 1820 in Massachusetts, working in Boston, September 4, 1850. Although the dates of birth differ, this artist and CHARLES A. BARRY may be the same person. ¶ 7 Census (1850), Mass., XXVI, 255.

BARRY, CHARLES A. (1830–1892). A.N.A. Portrait and genre painter, crayon portraitist, born July 14, 1830, at Boston. He was working as an artist in Boston 1850–59, in NYC 1860, and from about 1865 to 1877 in Boston, as a teacher of art in the public schools. During the Civil War the Boston Directories list a Charles A. Barry, coastwise clerk in the Customhouse, possibly the same person. The artist exhibited at the Boston Athenaeum and the National Academy. *Cf.* CHARLES BARRY. ¶ Thieme-Becker; Swan, BA, 199; Boston CD 1850–59, 1861–64, 1866–77; Boston BD 1851–53, 1855, 1858–59; New England BD 1856; Cowdrey, NAD; information courtesy of Charles Knowles Bolton.

BARRY, DANIEL. Lithographer, born in Ireland *c.* 1824. He appears to have been brought to Boston before 1834, when his brother THOMAS J. BARRY was born there. He was living in Boston, September 16, 1850, along with his 16-year-old brother and COMRI and J. T. POWELL. ¶ 7 Census (1850), Mass., XXV, 311.

BARRY, DAVID J. Lithographer, Boston, 1857. Barry's address was the same as that of John H. Barry, grocer; others living at the same address in 1857 were: Daniel Barry, laborer; John Barry, currier; and THOMAS J. BARRY, lithographer. ¶ Boston CD 1857.

BARRY, THEODORE. Lithographer, Boston, 1848–49. ¶ Boston CD 1848–49.

BARRY, THOMAS J. Lithographer, born *c.* 1834 in Boston, of Irish parents. In 1850 Thomas Barry was living in Boston with his parents and brother, DANIEL BARRY. He is listed in the Boston directories 1857–62 as a lithographer, residing with John H. Barry, grocer; the 1860 Census records that he was living with his parents and owned $150 personal property. DAVID J. BARRY may have been another brother. ¶ 7 Census (1850), Mass., XXV, 311; 8 Census (1860), Mass., XXVII, 350; Boston CD 1857, 1859, 1860, 1862.

BARRY, TIMOTHY. Painter of a view of Plymouth (Mass.), 1845. This may be the Timothy Barry, book agent of Boston, whose home was at Plymouth, as recorded in the Boston Directory for 1855; or it may be Timothy Barry, painter in Boston 1851–57. ¶ Stokes, *Historical Prints,* pl. 83-A; Boston CD 1851–52, 1855, 1857.

BARSHAM, J. W. Artist, Buffalo (N.Y.), 1858–60. ¶ Buffalo BD 1858–60.

BARSOTTE, FRANCISCO. Artist and plaster image maker, born in Lombardy, working in Philadelphia with LORENZO HARDIE, June 11, 1860. ¶ 8 Census (1860), Pa., LXII, 106.

BARSTOW, Miss S. M. Landscape painter, NYC, exhibited at the National Academy 1858–59, 1861–89, and at the Pennsylvania Academy 1867–69. Possibly the same as Salome Barstow, still life painter on velvet, recorded in Lipman and Winchester. ¶ Cowdrey, NAD; Rutledge, PA; Lipman and Winchester, 169.

BARTELL, SARAH. Portrait painter in water colors. Her portraits of Mr. and Mrs. John Converse of Brimfield (Mass.), painted in 1790, were owned in 1941 by the Rev. Morgan Ashley of Rutland (Vt.). ¶ WPA (Mass.), *Portraits Found in Vt.*

BARTELLE, D. W. C., see DE WITT CLINTON BOUTELLE.

BARTELLO, ——. Young portrait painter from Italy at Philadelphia in 1796. ¶ Scharf and Westcott, II, 1045.

BARTELS, LOUISA M. Artist, 25, from Germany, living in NYC in 1860. ¶ 8 Census (1860), N.Y., LI, 699; NYCD 1863.

BARTH, FREDERICK. Engraver, die-sinker, and jeweler, Cincinnati, 1850–59. Barth was born in Germany *c.* 1804 and came to the United States before 1850, when he was working as a watchmaker in Cincinnati. During the 1850's he was recorded in the directories variously, as watchmaker, xylographer and engraver, tool engraver and die-sinker, and as the proprietor of a jewelry store. S. Barth and E. Barth, engravers listed in the directories for 1853 and 1856, respectively, are probably misprints for F. Barth. ¶ 7 Census (1850), Ohio, XXII, 121; Cincinnati BD 1851, 1856; Cincinnati CD 1850–51, 1853, 1856–59; Ohio BD 1853.

BARTH, RUDOLPH F. Engraver, born *c.* 1836 in Virginia, working in Washington (D.C.), June 12, 1860, in the firm of SAVINE & BARTH. ¶ 8 Census (1860), D.C., II, 734.

BARTH, VALENTINE. Sculptor, 23, a native of Bremen (Germany), at NYC in 1860. His wife and one son were born in Waldeck (Germany) and a younger son in NYC. ¶ 8 Census (1860), N.Y., LV, 801.

BARTHOLOMEW, EDWARD SHEFFIELD (1822–1858). Sculptor and painter; born July 8, 1822, at Colchester (Conn.); moved to Hartford about 1836. He studied painting for a year at the National Academy, but, discovering that he was color blind, turned to sculpture. He worked at Hartford in the 1840's, exhibiting at the National Academy and the Boston Athenaeum. In 1850, after another year of study at the National Academy, Bartholomew went to Italy, where he remained, except for two brief visits to America, until his death in Naples in May 1858. Although Bartholomew did some portrait sculpture, most of his work was classical in theme. His work was exhibited at the Pennsylvania Academy in 1859, 1863 and 1869. ¶ DAB; *Crayon,* V (1858), 211, obit.; Gardner, *Yankee Stonecutters;* French, *Art and Artists in Conn.;* Taft, *History of American Sculpture;* Cowdrey, NAD; Swan, BA; Rutledge, PA; Rutledge, MHS; Peabody Institute, *Works of Art.*

BARTHOLOMEW, TRUMAN C. (1809–1867). Scenic artist of Boston from the early thirties until his death. He was born December 15, 1809, in Vershire (Vt.), the eldest son of the inventor Erastus Bartholomew. His entire career was spent in Boston where he painted theater scenery and panoramic views. He was associated with MINARD LEWIS from 1838 to 1841 and in 1858 collaborated with him on scenery for a play based on Kane's Arctic voyages. His view of Jerusalem was shown in Charleston (S.C.) in 1847. He died December 7, 1867, at Melrose (Mass.). WILLIAM N. BARTHOLO-

MEW was his half-brother. ¶ Bartholomew, *Record of the Bartholomew Family*, 274–75; Boston *Evening Transcript*, Dec. 8, 1838, Dec. 10, 1840, April 25, 1841, and Feb. 17, 1858, and Charleston *Courier*, Dec. 10, 1847 (citations courtesy J. Earl Arrington).

BARTHOLOMEW, WILLIAM NEWTON (1822–1898). Drawing teacher and landscape painter. Born in Boston on February 13, 1822, he was a son of Erastus and half-brother of TRUMAN C. BARTHOLOMEW. Though trained to be a cabinetmaker, he gave up that trade to become an artist. In 1850 he went to California with J. Wesley Jones, the daguerreotypist. In 1852 he introduced systematic instruction in drawing in several Boston schools and soon after was put in charge of drawing instruction in all the Boston High Schools, a position he held until 1871. He also published a series of popular drawing books. After his retirement he made his home at Newton Centre (Mass.) where he died in 1898. ¶ Bartholomew, *Record of the Bartholomew Family*, 275–76 (photo. on 175); Van Nostrand and Coulter, *California Pictorial*, 106; Boston CD 1855–65; Swan, BA; Union Catalogue, Library of Congress.

BARTLETT, JASON ROBBINS. Portrait and miniature painter, 1811–32. He was at Philadelphia in 1811, when he exhibited at the Society of Artists, and in NYC 1829–30, 1832, when he exhibited at the National Academy. ¶ Rutledge, PA; Cowdrey, NAD; NYCD 1830–31; Stauffer, no. 3386, portrait of Alden Partridge by A. Willard after Bartlett.

BARTLETT, JOHN RUSSELL (1805–1886). Eminent historian, ethnologist, and bibliographer, born October 23, 1805, at Providence (R.I.). A number of his own sketches illustrate his *Personal Narrative of Explorations and Incidents in Texas, New Mexico, California, Sonora and Chihuahua* (N.Y. 1854). Bartlett died at Providence on May 28, 1886. ¶ DAB; CAB; Library of Congress; repros. from *Personal Narrative* are in Jackson, *Gold Rush Album*, pp. 3, 5, 80, 83, 85, 89, 90, 121, 172, and in Davidson, I, 227.

BARTLETT, TRUMAN HOWE (1835–1923). Portrait and monumental sculptor, born at Dorset (Vt.). He studied under LAUNITZ in NYC, and later studied in Paris, Rome, and Perugia. He worked after 1860 at Hartford, Waterbury, and New Haven (Conn.) and in NYC, exhibited at the National Academy 1866–80, and was for 23 years instructor in modelling at the Massachusetts Institute of Technology. Paul Wayland Bartlett (1865–1925), the sculptor, was his son. ¶ Clement and Hutton; Mallett; DAB (under Paul Wayland Bartlett); French, *Art and Artists in Conn.;* Cowdrey, NAD.

BARTLETT, WILLIAM HENRY (1809–1854). Landscape artist. Born March 26, 1809, in Kentishtown, London, Bartlett made four visits to the United States between 1836 and 1852. From the earlier of these visits resulted a series of views which were published *c.* 1840 as *American Scenery*, with a text by Nathaniel P. Willis. Bartlett died September 13, 1854, on board a French ship returning from a voyage to the Orient. Engravings based on Bartlett's views were later used in his posthumous *History of the United States of North America*, continued by B. B. Woodward and published *c.* 1856. A diorama "Jerusalem and the Holy Land," based on drawings made by Bartlett on several visits to the Near East, was exhibited in London and then in Boston in 1856. ¶ Cowdrey, "William Henry Bartlett"; DNB; *Antiques*, XXII (Aug. 1932), 54; Boston *Evening Transcript*, March 27, 1856, cited by Arrington.

BARTLETTE, Mrs. ——. Drawing teacher, Charleston (S.C.), 1831. Mrs. Bartlette advertised that she taught "drawing from nature by the rules of perspective simplified," "imitation of oil painting in the style of Harding," as well as japanning, bronzing, and gilding. ¶ Rutledge, *Artists in the Life of Charleston*.

BARTNEY, JOHN. Artist, New Orleans, 1860. ¶ Delgado-WPA, cites New Orleans CD 1860.

BARTOLARCHI, SEBASTIAN. Sicilian artist, 33, at NYC in 1860. His wife Frances was from Massachusetts and they had an infant son, George H., born in NYC. ¶ 8 Census (1860), N.Y., LIV, 593.

BARTOLI, F. or J. Portrait painter. Bartoli exhibited at the Royal Academy, London, in 1783. He appears to have come to New York before 1796, the date of his portrait of the Seneca chief, Cornplanter, now at the New-York Historical Society. He is also known to have painted a portrait of George Washington about the same time. ¶ Graves, *Dictionary;* NYHS *Cat.* (1941); Stauffer, nos. 905, 1024; Fielding; Thieme-Becker.

BARTOLL, SAMUEL (*c.* 1765–1835). Landscape, marine, mural, sign, and house painter, whose early career seems to have been passed in Marblehead (Mass.), where he married Mercy Northey in 1785. Their first child was born there the following year. He later moved to Salem, where he was working in 1814 and 1825, and he died there on January 22, 1835, at the age of 70. ¶ Belknap, *Artists and Craftsmen of Essex County,* 6; *Vital Records of Marblehead:* (Marriages), 27, and (Births), 33; Robinson and Dow, I, 61.

BARTOLL, WILLIAM THOMPSON (1817–1859?). Portrait and mural painter of Marblehead (Mass.), son of John and Rebecca Bartoll, baptized in Marblehead on June 22, 1817. He married Sally L. Selman in April 1835. Bartoll exhibited at the Boston Athenaeum between 1841 and 1855, and is said to have died in Marblehead in 1859. ¶ *Vital Records of Marblehead* (Births), 34, and (Marriages), 27; New England BD 1856; Swan, BA; Lipman and Winchester, 169.

BARTON & BOERUM. Wood engravers, Philadelphia, 1857. The second partner was SIMEON BOERUM, but the identity of Barton is uncertain. He may have been either EDGAR F. BATON (or Barton) or HENRY C. BATON, both listed as engravers in the 1857 directory, though not at the same address as Barton & Boerum. No other engraver named Barton is listed. ¶ Phila. CD and BD 1857.

BARTON, Mrs. CALEB D., see EMMA CLARA PEALE.

BARTON, CHARLES C. Marine artist and naval officer. Commissioned midshipman in 1824 and lieutenant in 1841, Barton served during the Mexican War and died in 1851. His known work includes a number of drawings of naval actions of the war with Mexico. ¶ *Album of American Battle Art,* 134, and plates 60–61.

BARTON, EDGAR F., see EDGAR F. BATON.

BARTON, JAMES PIERCE (1817–1891). Portrait and landscape painter of Zanesville (Ohio), 1845 and after. He exhibited at the American Art-Union in 1848 and at the National Academy in 1852. ¶ *Antiques,* XXI (March 1932), 152; Ohio BD 1859; Cowdrey, NAD; Cowdrey, AA & AAU; full name and dates courtesy Donald MacKenzie, Wooster College.

BARTON, L. H. Wood engraver, Buffalo N.Y.), 1850–after 1860; of VAN DUZEE & BARTON, 1853–59. ¶ Buffalo CD 1850–60+.

BARTON, M. Landscape and animal painter, exhibited at the Pennsylvania Academy in 1812 (painting of a dog) and 1813 (view of the Susquehanna River). ¶ Rutledge, PA.

BARTON, PETER and SAMUEL. Lithographers, living together in a Philadelphia hotel in July 1860. Both were native Pennsylvanians; Peter was 44 years old and Samuel 29. ¶ 8 Census (1860), Pa., LII, 849.

BARTON, WILLIAM P. C. (1786–1856). Surgeon, botanist, and botanical artist, born in Philadelphia on November 17, 1786. In 1815 he succeeded his uncle, Benjamin Smith Barton, as Professor of Botany at the University of Pennsylvania. His *Vegetable Materia Medica of the United States,* illustrated by himself, was published in 1817–18, to be followed a few years later by his *Flora of North America,* with plates drawn by Barton and colored by his wife. After serving as the first chief of the U. S. Navy Medical Bureau (from 1842), Barton died in Philadelphia on February 29, 1856. ¶ Harshberger, *Botanists of Philadelphia,* 159–62; Scribner's Cat. 138, "Rare Books in Science and Thought, 1490–1940."

BARTRAM, JOHN (1699–1777). Although he is best known as America's first great botanist and as the father of the noted traveler and naturalist, WILLIAM BARTRAM, the elder Bartram's "View of William and Mary College," first published in 1740, has since been frequently reproduced. ¶ DAB; *American Processional,* 234; Davidson, I, 58.

BARTRAM, WILLIAM (1739–1823). A noted traveler and naturalist, and painter of American flora and fauna. The son of the botanist JOHN BARTRAM, William was born at Kingsessing, near Philadelphia, February 9, 1739. Although he was one of the best natural-history artists working before AUDUBON, Bartram's artistic work has met with undeserved neglect. He began sketching botanical specimens for his father in 1755, at the age of 16. Two of his early watercolors of birds were reproduced in color in George Edward's *Gleanings from Natural History,* published at London in 1758. From 1773 to 1777 William Bartram traveled through the southeastern colonies, under the sponsorship of Dr. John Fothergill, who had much admired his "elegant performances." During these travels Bartram collected specimens, kept a journal of his observations, and made many drawings from life. These drawings are now in the British Museum (Natural History) at South Kensington; they consist of 16 colored representations of snakes, birds, and flowers, and 64 black and white sketches of birds, flowers, alligators, and marine life. A set of photographs and slides of these drawings and watercolors is to be found in the Institute of Early American History and Culture, Williamsburg (Va.); the Historical Society of Pennsylvania also has photostats of the same collection. Bartram made a large number of botanical drawings for Benjamin Smith Barton's *Elements of Botany* (1803), which are now in the Delafield Collection, New York, as are a few drawings apparently made for a quarto edition of Bartram's *Travels* which was never published. William Bartram died at his home at Kingsessing (Pa.), July 22, 1823. ¶ DAB; Darlington, *Memorials of John Bartram and Humphry Marshall,* 199; Bridenbaugh, *Rebels and Gentlemen,* 58, 168; Dr. Lionel Chalmers to John Bartram, April 1773, letter in Gratz Coll., Hist. Soc. of Pa. All data courtesy Carl Bridenbaugh. University of California.

BASCOM, ANDREW J. Portrait and miniature painter, working at Lowell (Mass.) in 1833 and at Lawrence (Mass.), 1857–60. ¶ Belknap, *Artists and Craftsmen of Essex County;* Lawrence BD 1857, 1859; Lawrence CD 1859; New England BD 1860.

BASCOM, Mrs. RUTH HENSHAW MILES, known as "Aunt Ruth" (1772–1848). Primitive crayon portraitist. Ruth Henshaw was born December 15, 1772, at Leicester (Mass.), the daughter of Col. William Henshaw. Her first husband, whom she married in 1804, was Dr. Asa Miles, a teacher at Dartmouth College. On his death in 1806, she married Ezekiel Lysander Bascom. Mrs. Bascom was living at Gill (Mass.) in the 1830's and died at Ashby (Mass.), February 19, 1848. Her diaries are at the American Antiquarian Society. ¶ Harris, *Genealogical Record of Thomas Bascom and His Descendants,* 44; Dods, "Connecticut Valley Painters," 208–09; Dods, "Ruth Henshaw Bascom," in Lipman and Winchester, 31–38, with repros.; WPA (Mass.), *Portraits Found in Massachusetts;* Sears, *Some American Primitives,* 118–26.

BASHAM, FREDERICK. Modeller, plaster-worker, architect, draftsman. Basham was in NYC 1837–52, exhibited a model of the Parthenon at the Apollo Association 1840, and a drawing [?] "Origin of the Corinthian Capital" at the National Academy in 1842. ¶ NYCD 1837–52; Cowdrey, AA & AAU; Cowdrey, NAD.

BASS, EDWARD (*c.* 1760–1847). Heraldic and house painter, Newburyport (Mass.). The successor and perhaps partner of the heraldic painter GEORGE SEARLE. Two coats of arms by Bass are known: the Peirce arms, *c.* 1800 (Collection of Dr. James Lincoln, Huntington) and the Teel arms, *c.* 1800 (Historical Society of Old Newbury). He died at Newburyport in 1847. ¶ Bowditch, "Heraldry and the American Collector," 540; Bowditch, "Early Water-Color Paintings of New England Coats of Arms," 187–88.

BASS, EDWARD. Engraver, Newburyport (Mass.), 1850–51, 1858. ¶ Belknap, *Artists and Craftsmen of Essex County,* 2.

BASSETT, IONA H. Artist, born *c.* 1829 in Vermont, living in Castleborough (Vt.), August 28, 1850. ¶ 7 Census (1850), Vt., IX, 361.

BASSETT, W. H. Engraver of plates for Trumbull's *Poetical Works* (Hartford, 1820). ¶ Stauffer.

BASSIE, Mme. ADELE. Portrait painter, NYC, exhibited at the National Academy 1857–72. ¶ Cowdrey, NAD.

BASTEROT, ——. Portrait and religious painter and teacher of painting and drawing. A religious painting by Basterot in the Church of St. Genevieve. St. Louis, was unveiled in 1820. The following year Basterot advertised in New Orleans as a portrait painter and teacher of painting and drawing, describing himself as a "pupil of the French School." He was still in New Orleans in 1823. ¶ WPA Guide, *Missouri;* Delgado-WPA, cites New Orleans *Courier,* October 24, 1821, and New Orleans CD 1823.

BASTIAN, JOHN. Lithographer, born *c.* 1832 in Pennsylvania, living in Philadelphia, June 29, 1860, with his wife and three children. ¶ 8 Census (1860), Pa., XL, 249.

BATCHELDER, see JOHN BADGER BACHELDER.

BATCHELLER, FREDERICK S. (1837–1889). Still life and landscape painter, sculptor. Although Batcheller started as a marble cutter in Providence (R.I.) *c.* 1857 and later produced a few marble busts, he apparently devoted most of his time from 1860 to painting. He died in Providence, March 17, 1889. ¶ Boston *Transcript,* March 18, 1889, obit.; Providence CD

1857, 1859–61, 1864–67; New England BD 1860; Gardner, *Yankee Stonecutters.*

BATEMAN, CHARLES E. Presumably an amateur, known for his pencil drawings of ships at Newburyport (Mass.) in 1853. ¶ Robinson and Dow, I, 61.

BATEMAN, WILLIAM. Stone and seal engraver, NYC, 1774. ¶ Kelby, *Notes on American Artists;* Stauffer; Thieme-Becker.

BATES, ——. Portrait and landscape painter, of ROBINSON & BATES, Bellefontaine (Ohio), 1859. ¶ Ohio BD 1859.

BATHER, GEORGE. Portrait engraver; born in England about 1826; working in NYC in 1850 and in Brooklyn from 1854 until 1890. ¶ 7 Census (1850), N.Y., XLVI, 514; Stauffer; Brooklyn CD 1854–90; 7 Census (1850), N.Y., XLI, 41.

BATHIER (Battier), Mme. ——. Miniaturist and teacher, New Orleans, 1851–55. ¶ Delgado-WPA, cites *Bee* of Nov. 5, 1851, and *Picayune,* Nov. 29, 1854, and March 17, 1855.

BATON or BARTON, EDGAR F. General engraver and jeweler, born *c.* 1832 in Pennsylvania. Baton was in Philadelphia 1850–60 and after. He was the brother of HENRY C. BATON. ¶ 7 Census (1850), Pa., LV, 569; Phila. CD 1855–60 and after; in the Phila. BD at the same period the name is sometimes spelled Barton.

BATON or BARTON, HENRY C. Jeweler and general engraver, born *c.* 1834 in Pennsylvania, younger brother of EDGAR F. BATON. On August 7, 1850, he was living in Philadelphia with his mother, Mrs. Elizabeth Baton (born *c.* 1805, Pennsylvania), and brother. His occupation at this time was jeweler, though later directories indicate that he also was a general engraver. ¶ 7 Census (1850), Pa., LV, 569; Phila. CD and BD 1856–60 and after.

BATSON, MELVINA HOBSON (Mrs. Andrew Batson). Portrait painter, born in 1826 at New Castle (Ind.); died there in February 1853. After studying briefly at Cincinnati, Mrs. Batson painted at New Castle and La Porte (Ind.) Her portraits of Mr. and Mrs. James Peed and Mr. and Mrs. Abraham Elliott are now in the Henry County Historical Museum, New Castle. ¶ Peat, *Pioneer Painters of Indiana,* 102–03.

BATTEE, JOHN O. Artist, Baltimore, 1856–57. ¶ *Baltimore* CD 1856–57.

BATTERSON, JAMES. Sculptor, from Hartford (Conn.), at Cleveland (Ohio) in December 1850. He specialized in mantles, monuments, and fountains. ¶ WPA (Ohio), *Annals of Cleveland.*

BATTERTON, J. Portrait painter, Philadelphia, 1857. ¶ Phila. BD 1857.

BATTIER, see BATHIER.

BATTIN (Batton, Ballin), JOHN T. Sculptor, born *c.* 1805 in England. J. Battin exhibited at the Artists' Fund Society in 1840, and was working in NYC 1841–45, during which time he executed a bust of Philip Hone's daughter and exhibited at the National Academy, both under the name T. Battin. He moved to Philadelphia about 1847 and remained there until after 1860. His household in 1850 included P. Battin (born *c.* 1820 in Delaware, possibly a brother), George (born *c.* 1834 in NYC), Augustus (born *c.* 1841 in NYC), and S. Battin (born *c.* 1848 in Pennsylvania), probably John Battin's sons. In 1860 he owned personal property valued at $300. ¶ 7 Census (1850), Pa., LIV, 513; 8 Census (1860), Pa., LI, 27; NYCD 1841–45; Cowdrey, NAD; Phila. CD 1847–51, 1853–54, 1857–60 and after; Rutledge, PA; Gardner, *Yankee Stonecutters,* 61. National Academy Cat. 1842 lists J. Ballin, sculptor, and in 1843 T. Battin, sculptor; both entries refer to John T. Battin.

BATTIN, T., see JOHN T. BATTIN.

BATTLE, MILAN. Artist, Albany (N.Y.), 1827–28. ¶ Albany CD 1827–28.

BATTLEWAY, JAMES. Artist, 32, from Scotland, at NYC in 1860. ¶ 8 Census (1860), N.Y., LIII, 475.

BATTON, see BATTIN.

BATURONE, JOSE. Young Cuban artist who contributed 6 sketches to *Album Californiano,* a set of 12 studies of California miners published at Havana *c.* 1849–50. Baturone's collaborator was AUGUSTO FERRAN. ¶ Vail, *Gold Fever,* description of the *Album,* with 2 repros.; Jackson, *Gold Rush Album,* repros, pp. 69, 136, 139–42, 144[?].

BATZ, A. DE. French traveler who visited Louisiana about 1732 and made some crude drawings of Indians. ¶ Van Ravenswaay, "The Forgotten Arts and Crafts of Colonial Louisiana," 195.

BAUCHMAN, EDWARD. Engraver, 53, from Switzerland, at NYC in 1860 with his wife and 8 children, all born in Switzerland before 1853. The eldest son, Leopold, age 23, was also an engraver. ¶ 8 Census (1860), N.Y., XLIV, 862.

BAUDIER, ALEXANDER. Lithographer at New Orleans in 1849, described as young and self-taught. He is perhaps the Alexander Baudier listed as a clerk in the 1852 directory. ¶ Delgado-WPA, cites New Orleans *Bee,* Oct. 29, 1849; New Orleans CD 1852.

BAUER, FREDERICK. Lithographer, Louisville (Ky.), 1848. ¶ Louisville CD 1848.

BAUERLE, CHARLES B. Wood engraver, designer, and draftsman, Cincinnati. Bauerle was a partner in the firms of LOVIE & BAUERLE (1856) and LOVIE, BAUERLE & BRUEN (1857). ¶ Cincinnati BD and CD 1856–57.

BAULT, see DE BAULT.

BAULY, WILLIAM. Painter, NYC, exhibited at the National Academy 1859. ¶ Cowdrey, NAD.

BAUMGARTEN, Dr. GUSTAVUS E. (1837–1910). Physician and amateur artist. Born June 1, 1837, at Clausthal (Germany), Baumgarten was brought to the United States *c.* 1846. After a short residence in Galveston (Texas) the family moved in 1849 to St. Louis, where Gustav graduated from the Medical College in 1856. After a number of years' study in Europe and service in the U. S. Navy during the Civil War, Dr. Baumgarten settled again in St. Louis where he practiced and taught medicine until his death, September 20, 1910. During the 1850's and 1870's he made a number of sketches of St. Louis scenes, some of which have been reproduced. ¶ Missouri Hist. Soc. *Bulletin,* VI, Oct. 1949, 57–58, notes on Baumgarten followed by 7 repros., full size.

BAUMGARTEN, JULIUS. Engraver, born *c.* 1835 in Germany. In 1860 Baumgarten was living in Washington with his wife Elizabeth (born *c.* 1841 in Maryland, a dressmaker), a son Henry (born in Washington 1859), one domestic servant, and personal property valued at $500. ¶ 8 Census (1860), D.C., I, 699; Washington CD 1860.

BAUMGARTNER, N. A. Artist, New Orleans, 1860. ¶ Delgado-WPA, cites New Orleans CD 1860.

BAUMGRAS, PETER (1827–1904). Portrait painter; born in Bavaria; came to the United States in 1853; was in Washington in 1859, when he exhibited at the Washington Art Association; painted a portrait of Lincoln in 1865; exhibited at the National Academy in 1868; and became a professor at the University of Illinois in 1877. He died at Chicago in 1904. ¶ Pratt, *A Forgotten American Painter: Peter Baumgras* (citation courtesy of Mary Bartlett Cowdrey); *Art Annual,* V (1905–06), 118, obit.; Washington Art Assoc. Cat., 1859; Cowdrey, NAD.

BAUNACH, CHARLES. Lithographer, NYC, 1858. ¶ NYCD 1858.

BAUR, GEORGE A. Wood and general engraver, St. Louis, 1854, 1859. ¶ St. Louis BD 1854, 1859; St. Louis CD 1854.

BAXTER, DE WITT C. General and wood engraver, born *c.* 1829 in Massachusetts, working in Philadelphia 1850–60 and after. From 1858 to 1860 he was a partner in the engraving firm of BAXTER & HARLEY. In 1860 he was living with his wife Susan (born *c.* 1830 in Pennsylvania) and three children, from one to eleven years old, and at that time he owned personal property valued at $10,000. After 1863 Baxter seems to have given up engraving; he is listed as Colonel in the U. S. Army 1864–66, as naval officer at the Custom House 1868–71, as of the Keystone Portable Forge Co. 1873–78, and finally in 1881 as a watchman. ¶ 7 Census (1850), Pa., LIV, 881; 8 Census (1860), Pa., LVI, 641; Phila. CD 1850–81. *Annals of San Francisco* (1854) contains examples of his work.

BAXTER, EDGAR. Ship-chandler and amateur artist, NYC, exhibited at the American Institute in 1851. Baxter was the son of John C. Baxter and from 1858 to 1870 a junior partner in his father's ship-chandlery firm, John C. Baxter & Sons. ¶ Am. Inst. Cat., 1851; NYCD 1858–70.

BAXTER & HARLEY. Wood engravers, Philadelphia, 1858–60; the partners were DE WITT C. BAXTER and JOSEPH S. HARLEY. ¶ Phila. CD 1858–60.

BAXTER, W. H. Artist who depicted the fire in Nevada City (Cal.), March 12, 1851. ¶ Peters, *California on Stone.*

BAYER, JANE. Portrait painter, NYC, 1849. ¶ NYBD 1849/50.

BAYER, JUSTIN. German portrait painter, 38, at NYC in July 1850. ¶ 7 Census (1850), N.Y., LIII, 75.

BAYLAT, ——. Portrait painter in oils and pastels, miniaturist, and engineeer. A former pupil of David at Paris, Baylat advertised in New Orleans in May 1817. ¶ Delgado-WPA, cites *Louisiana Courier,* May 30, 1817.

BAYLESS (or Baylies), WILLIAM HENRY. Architect and artist; exhibited architectural drawings at the National Academy in 1841 and 1842; professor of perspective at the Academy from 1844 to 1852. ¶ Cowdrey, NAD.

BAYLEY, WILLIAM. Landscape painter, NYC, exhibited at the National Academy 1832, 1834, 1843–48, and at the American Art-Union 1841–43. ¶ Cowdrey, NAD; Cowdrey, AA & AAU.

BAYLIS, RICHARD. Stone and wood carver, Charleston (S.C.), 1739. ¶ Rutledge, *Artists in the Life of Charleston.*

BAYNE, Miss ELIZA. Miniaturist, living with her mother, Mrs. Arabella Bayne, in Washington (D.C.) when her silhouette was cut by AUGUST EDOUART on May 3, 1841. ¶ Jackson, *Ancestors in Silhouette,* 193.

BAYNE, WALTER MCPHERSON (1795–1859). Landscape and panorama painter. A British artist, who exhibited in London galleries between 1833 and 1858, Bayne exhibited at the Boston Athenaeum from 1837 to 1846 and was listed as a resident of Boston in 1848 when he exhibited at the Pennsylvania Academy. His panorama of a voyage to Europe was shown in Boston, Philadelphia, NYC, Baltimore, Charleston, and St. Louis between 1847 and 1856. ¶ Swan, BA; Graves, *Dictionary;* Rutledge, PA; information courtesy J. Earl Arrington, who cites *Description of Bayne's Gigantic Panorama of a Voyage to Europe* (Phila. 1849) and contemporary newspaper notices.

BEALE & CRAVEN. Artists (?) and proprietors of a panorama of a trip from Charleston to California, shown in Baltimore in April 1850. ¶ Baltimore *Sun,* April 23 and 25, 1850 (courtesy J. Earl Arrington).

BEALE, Dr. G. D. Artist (?) and proprietor of a panorama of Italy exhibited at Savannah (Ga.) in January 1858. ¶ Savannah *Daily Republican,* Jan. 20, 1858 (courtesy J. Earl Arrington).

BEALS, CARRIE. Amateur crayon portraitist, Brattleboro (Vt.), *c.* 1855. Her portrait of a 10-year old girl was owned in 1941 by Mrs. James B. M'Leod of Barre (Vt.). ¶ WPA (Mass.), *Portraits Found in Vt.*

BEAMAN, see BEMAN.

BEARD, GEORGE. Miniaturist, Cincinnati, 1840. ¶ Clark, *Ohio Art and Artists,* 442; Bolton, *Miniature Painters.*

BEARD, JAMES CARTER (1837–1913). Illustrator and journalist; born at Cincinnati on June 6, 1837, a son of the painter, JAMES HENRY BEARD. After studying law and service in the Civil War, he turned to art, becoming a well-known illustrator of books and articles on nature. He lived for many years in Brooklyn and died November 15, 1913, at New Orleans. ¶ DAB; Smith; Davidson, I, 261.

BEARD, JAMES HENRY (1812–1893). N.A. Portrait, animal, and genre painter, born May 20, 1812, in Buffalo (N.Y.). In 1823 the family moved to Painesville (Ohio) where James's brother, WILLIAM HOLBROOK BEARD, was born the following year. James became an itinerant painter at 17 and worked in Pittsburgh, Cincinnati, Louisville, New Orleans, and other Southern cities before he settled in Cincinnati about 1834. Except for a brief residence in NYC (1846–47) and his service in the Civil War, Beard made his home in Cincinnati until 1870, after which he lived in NYC and Flushing, Long Island. He was particularly successful as a portraitist of children, but later he turned more to genre and animal painting. He was made a National Academician in 1872. His children all showed artistic talent, including JAMES CARTER BEARD and Daniel Carter Beard, the great Boy Scout leader. ¶ Smith, "James Henry Beard"; DAB; Cist, *Cincinnati in 1841;* Cowdrey, AA & AAU; Cowdrey, NAD; Cincinnati CD 1850–51, BD 1853–60; *American Processional,* 133.

BEARD, WILLIAM HOLBROOK (1824–1900). N.A. Portrait and animal painter, brother of JAMES HENRY BEARD. Born April 13, 1824, at Painesville (Ohio), he worked for a short time as a portrait painter in Ohio, then in 1845 moved to NYC. He opened a studio in Buffalo in 1850 where he remained until 1856, when he went to Europe. On his return in 1858, Beard lived for two more years in Buffalo, but in 1860 settled in NYC. There he married the daughter of the portrait painter, THOMAS LE CLEAR. Beard was best known for his humorous story-pictures of animals. He died in NYC February 20, 1900. ¶ DAB; Buffalo BD 1855–56, 1858–60; Cowdrey, AA & AAU; Cowdrey, NAD; Rutledge, PA; Rutledge, MHS; CAB; Clement and Hutton; *Portfolio* (Jan. 1954), 120, repro.

BEARDSLEY, JEFFERSON. Genre painter, Ithaca (N.Y.), exhibited at the National Academy in 1859. ¶ Cowdrey, NAD.

BEASTALL, ——. Miniature painter, advertised at Portsmouth (N.H.) in August 1795. ¶ *Antiques,* XLVI (Sept. 1944), 158.

BEATSON, HELENA. Teacher of "The Art of

Painting Portraits in Crayons," Charleston (S.C.), 1772. ¶ Rutledge, *Artists in the Life of Charleston,* 185.

BEAU, JOHN ANTHONY. Drawing teacher and engraver, NYC, 1770. ¶ Gottesman, I, 8, 42–43; Stauffer, I, 19.

BEAUCE, ——. Artist of the Orleans Theatre, New Orleans, 1842. ¶ New Orleans CD 1842.

BEAUCOURT, [FRANCOIS?]. Portrait and historical painter, formerly of Bordeaux, Paris, St. Petersburg, and Nantes, working in Philadelphia in 1792. ¶ Prime, II, 3; *Art News,* Jan. 15, 1946, p. 7, repro.

BEAUDIEKAMP, B. S. Exhibited "Swamp near New Orleans" at the Pennsylvania Academy in 1859. ¶ Rutledge, PA.

BEAUGUREAU, ——. Lithographer working for P. S. DUVAL, Philadelphia, 1845. He was probably of the same family as Jean and Philibert Beaugureau, teachers in Philadelphia 1845–54, and A. Bougereau, teacher of French and drawing in Philadelphia 1857–61. ¶ Peters, *America on Stone;* Phila. CD 1845–54, 1857–61.

BEAUGUREAU, P. H., JR. Artist in crayon, Philadelphia; exhibited at the Pennsylvania Academy in 1848, 1850, and 1856. Possibly Philibert Beaugureau, teacher in Philadelphia from 1847 to 1854. ¶ Rutledge, PA; Phila. CD 1847–54.

BEAUJOLAIS, LOUIS CHARLES D'ORLEANS, Comte de (1779–1808). Amateur artist. A prince of the House of Orleans, the Count de Beaujolais came to the U.S. in 1797 with his brother Louis Philippe, later King of the French. During a three year stay, Beaujolais travelled widely in the U.S. and made drawings and paintings from nature, among them an oil painting of Genesee Falls (N.Y.) now at the New-York Historical Society. Having returned to Europe in 1800, the Count de Beaujolais died in Malta in 1808. ¶ Taylor, *Memoirs of the House of Orleans; Encyclopaedia Britannica* (11th edition); Rochester Hist. Soc. *Scrapbook,* 1950, 1–2; Museum Dep't., NYHS.

BEAULIEU, EMILE F. Designer, wood engraver, and landscape painter. Beaulieu (or Bealieu) was working in Philadelphia as an artist and designer from 1852 to 1857, exhibiting in the latter year at the Pennsylvania Academy. From 1858 to 1860 and after, he worked in NYC as a wood engraver and he exhibited landscapes at the National Academy 1859–62. ¶ Phila. CD 1852–57; Pa. Academy Cat. 1857; NYCD 1858, 1860 and after; Cowdrey, NAD; *Portfolio,* I (Nov. 1941), 13, 18 (repros.).

BEAUMONT, CHARLES. Portrait painter, Boston, 1831–34; exhibited at the Boston Athenaeum 1834 and 1856. His wife, born LAURANA RICHARDS BREWER, was also an artist, as was their son, JOHN P. BEAUMONT. ¶ Swan, BA, 90, 98, 200.

BEAUMONT, Mrs. CHARLES, see LAURANA RICHARDS BREWER.

BEAUMONT, JOHN P. Portrait and landscape painter and art dealer, active *c.* 1831–1876. He was a son of CHARLES BEAUMONT of Boston but worked mainly in NYC from 1833 to 1860 and after, exhibiting frequently at the National Academy and the Apollo Association. In 1834 he exhibited at the Boston Athenaeum a Portrait of Black Hawk "sketched at the request of . . . James Herring, the engraver, while under government escort to Green Bay." ¶ Swan, BA, 90, 200; NYCD 1833–54, 1856–60; NYBD 1837, 1857–60; Cowdrey, NAD; Cowdrey, AA & AAU; BA Cat., 1834.

BEAUPOIL DE SAINT AULAIRE, see SAINT AULAIRE.

BEBIE or BEBEE, HENRY (or Hans Heinrich). Miniaturist, painter of cabinet portraits and conversation pieces. Born *c.* 1824 in Switzerland, Bebie was at Richmond (Va.) as early as 1842. After a brief stay in the western part of Virginia he seems to have settled in Baltimore *c.* 1846, remaining there at least until 1877 and probably until his death in 1888. He exhibited at the Maryland Historical Society. *Cf.* HENRY BRABY. ¶ 7 Census (1850), Md., V, 143; date of death courtesy of Dr. H. W. Williams, Jr., of the Corcoran Gallery; Baltimore CD 1853, 1858, 1860, 1865, 1867, 1874, 1877; Lafferty, cites Baltimore CD 1873–75, 1877, for Henry Bebee; Rutledge, MHS; Pleasants, *250 Years of Painting in Md.,* 47–48 with repro.

BEBIE, W. Portrait and landscape painter, *c.* 1845, represented at the Minneapolis Institute of Art. ¶ Fielding; Bénézit.

BECHER, CLARENCE. Engraver, Philadelphia, 1860. Born *c.* 1840, the son of GEORGE T. BECHER, professor of drawing at Girard College. ¶ 8 Census (1860), Pa., LXII, 379.

BECHER, GEORGE T. Professor of drawing at Girard College, Philadelphia, in 1860. Becher was born in Bavaria *c.* 1817 and came to Pennsylvania before 1840, when his son, CLARENCE BECHER, was born there. ¶ 8 Census (1860), Pa., LXII, 379.

Bechet, F. L. Portrait painter, NYC, 1859. ¶ NYBD 1859.

Bechler, Christian. Engraver at Philadelphia, July 13, 1860, with William Bracher. He was born *c.* 1828 in Saxony. ¶ 8 Census (1860), Pa., LXII, 300.

Bechtel, David B. Portrait painter, Philadelphia, 1855–60 and after. ¶ Phila. CD 1855, 1857–60 and after; Rutledge, PA.

Beck, C. H. Reputed painter of a Colorado landscape in 1813. *Cf.* Von Beckh. ¶ Sherman, "Unrecorded Early American Painters" (1943), 208.

Beck, George (1748 or 1750–1812). Landscape painter and teacher, born in Ellford (England). After some years in London, where he exhibited in the early 1790's, he emigrated to America, arriving at Norfolk (Va.) in 1795. During the next decade he worked mainly in Baltimore, *c.* 1795–97, and Philadelphia, 1798–1807. In 1804 he toured the western part of the country and painted a view of Niagara Falls. He is thought to have worked in Pittsburgh (Pa.) from 1804 to 1806 and he painted a view of the town in the latter year. He was listed in Philadelphia directories from 1805 to 1807 and in the Lexington (Ky.) directory in 1806. In 1808 he painted a view of Wright's Ferry on the Susquehanna in Pennsylvania. Thereafter he made his home in Lexington (Ky.) where he died December 14, 1812. His widow (see Mrs. George Beck), was also an artist. Beck's work was shown at the Society of Artists in Philadelphia, 1811–14. ¶ Pleasants, "George Beck" and "Four Late Eighteenth Century Anglo-American Landscape Painters," the latter with checklist and 3 repros.; Phila. CD 1798, 1800, 1802–03, 1805–07; Prime, II, 44; Graves, *Dictionary;* Stokes, *Historical Prints;* Mulkearn, "Pittsburgh in 1806"; Dunlap, *History,* II, 226; Davidson, I, 385; Rutledge, PA; Flexner, *The Light of Distant Skies,* biblio., 258. Listed erroneously as George Jacob Beck in Clark, *Ohio Art and Artists,* and Knittle, *Early Ohio Taverns.*

Beck, Mrs. George. Landscape painter and teacher. Mary Beck was the wife of the landscape painter, George Beck, whom she married in England in 1786. On their emigration to America in 1795, Mrs. Beck conducted schools for girls at Baltimore and Philadelphia, and after 1808 at Cincinnati and Lexington (Ky.). She died in 1833. Although primarily a teacher, Mrs. Beck is also spoken of as a landscape painter. ¶ Pleasants, "Four Late Eighteenth Century American Landscape Painters," 205–06; Dunlap *History,* II, 226; Price, *Old Masters of the Bluegrass;* Van Ravenswaay, "Anna Maria von Phul," 369, 383; Cincinnati CD 1829.

Beck, George Jacob, see George Beck.

Beck, J. Augustus. Sculptor, portrait and landscape painter. Born at Lititz (Pa.) in 1831, Beck studied under Hiram Powers and Thomas Crawford in Italy. He was at Philadelphia in 1856 and at Lancaster in 1858, but settled permanently at Harrisburg in 1861. After 1860 Beck apparently turned from sculpture to painting portraits and landscapes. He was still living in 1912, but Sawitzky states that he died before 1918. ¶ Birth and death dates courtesy of the late William Sawitzky; Lancaster County Hist. Soc., *Portraiture in Lancaster Co.,* 114 and repro.; Rutledge, PA; Fielding, listed erroneously as Augustus J. Beck; Cowdrey, NAD (1873).

Beck, Mary, see Mrs. George Beck.

Beck, Samuel M. Wood engraver; born in the District of Columbia about 1827; active in NYC from 1845 to 1850. He exhibited at the American Institute. ¶ 7 Census (1850), N.Y., XLIII, 106; NYBD 1848; Am. Inst. Cat. 1845.

Becker, August. Mural painter. Born in 1840 in Germany, Becker was brought to St. Louis in 1843. He studied under Leon Pomarede, and in 1861 assisted his half-brother, Charles Wimar, in painting the new dome of the St. Louis Courthouse. He may also have worked at New Orleans with P. Snell. ¶ Rathbone, "Charles Wimar," in City Art Museum of St. Louis, *Catalogue, Charles Wimar* (1946).

Beckett, Charles E. Landscape painter, Portland (Me.); exhibited at the American Art-Union 1847, 1849–50. ¶ Cowdrey, AA & AAU.

Beckh, Frederick. Artist; born in Württemberg about 1814; married in Germany and emigrated to America after the birth of his son John about 1842. He was living in Baltimore in 1850 and in NYC in 1860. ¶ 7 Census (1850), Md., VI, 223; 8 Census (1860), N.Y., LIV, 908.

Beckh, H. V. A. V., see Von Beckh.

Beckman & Brothers. Portrait painters, NYC, 1851. Rudolph Beckman, phototypist, worked at the same address in 1851. ¶ NYBD 1851; NYCD 1851.

BECKWITH, HENRY. Engraver and landscape artist. Born in England, Beckwith achieved considerable reputation there for his engravings after Landseer before his coming to NYC *c.* 1842. He worked in NYC 1842–43 with the engraver ALFRED JONES. A view of NYC from Staten Island, drawn and engraved by Beckwith, and three landscapes engraved by him appeared in *Home Book of the Picturesque* (1852); five of his engravings also appeared in *Home Authors. . . .* (1857). ¶ Stauffer, I, 19; NYCD 1851–52, 1854; *Home Book of the Picturesque; Home Authors and Home Artists.*

BECKWITH, JOHN. Portrait painter, NYC, 1842–45. ¶ NYCD 1842, 1844–45.

BEDWELL, THOMAS. Miniaturist and engraver of Philadelphia, 1779–95. He was associated with JOHN NORMAN in 1779 and with JOHN WALTERS in 1782 and 1788. He was probably the Bedwell whose "View of a Pass over the South Mountain from York Town to Carlisle [Pa.]" was published in the *Columbian Magazine* in 1788. He advertised as a drawing master in 1795, as Thomas Bidwell. ¶ Prime, I, 11–12, 26, 30–31; Prime, II, 44–45; Stauffer.

BEECHER, AMARIAH DWIGHT (1839–?). Portrait and genre painter, born at Avon Springs (N.Y.) in 1839. Beecher turned from the study of law to art in 1854, and for the next three years studied under COLBY KIMBLE of Rochester (N.Y.). For a few years he had a studio at Avon Springs, a popular summer resort, but in 1865 he opened a studio in Rochester. Beecher moved to Chicago in 1870, but, losing heavily in the fire of 1871, soon moved to Geneva (Ill.) and subsequently to NYC. In 1877 he returned to Chicago, where he remained at least until 1892 and won considerable local reputation. He exhibited at the National Academy in the 1860's. ¶ Andreas, *History of Chicago,* II, 562 (citation courtesy of H. Maxson Holloway); Ulp, "Art and Artists in Rochester," 32; Rochester CD 1867; Chicago CD 1885–92; Cowdrey, NAD.

BEECHER, LABAN S. Figurehead carver, Boston, *c.* 1822–39. Born *c.* 1805, Beecher went to Boston in 1822 at the age of 17. He became a prominent carver and was commissioned in 1834 to carve the Andrew Jackson figurehead for the *Constitution.* Beecher seems to have given up carving about 1839, and gone into the leather business for a short time, but *c.* 1843 he left Boston for the West, becoming a prosperous landowner near Sharon (Wis.). ¶ Pinckney, 99–100, 187, and pl. XIV; Boston CD 1826–43; NYHS *Quarterly,* XXX (Jan. 1946), 14.

BEECHER, PHILIP. Artist, Philadelphia, 1860. Born *c.* 1835 in NYC; boarding in Philadelphia, July 23, 1860. He may have been the Philip Beecher listed as "dry goods" in 1865. ¶ 8 Census (1860), Pa., LIV, 335; Phila. CD 1865.

BEECHER, ROXANA (FOOTE). Amateur miniaturist, wife of the Rev. Lyman Beecher. Mrs. Beecher was born January 10, 1775, in Guilford (Conn.); lived at Easthampton, Long Island, 1799–1805, and probably at Litchfield (Conn.), 1810–16; and died September 25, 1816. ¶ Letter of Mr. Lyman Beecher Stowe to Mr. F. F. Sherman, Sept. 26, 1933; Lyman Beecher Stowe, "The First of the Beechers," in *Atlantic Monthly,* August 1933, p. 214. (citations courtesy of Mrs. Henry W. Howell, Jr., Frick Art Reference Library).

BEEHAN, see BEHAN.

BEELER, CHARLES H. [JR.]. Wood engraver, Philadelphia, 1851–56, 1859–72. The name appears as Charles H. Beeler until 1856; in 1859 it is C. H. Beeler, Jr., and thereafter varies, so that it is difficult to tell whether or not there were two Beelers. Beeler's home in the 1870's was in Camden (N.J.). ¶ Phila. CD 1851–56, 1859–72.

BEERS, Mrs. JULIE HART, see Mrs. JULIE HART KEMPSON.

BEERS, N. P. Child artist, NYC, exhibited at the American Institute in 1849 along with FRANCIS SILVA and HENRY HAYS, who later became professional artists. ¶ Am. Inst. Cat., 1849.

BEESE, H., see HENRY BOESE.

BEEST, ALBERT VAN (1820–1860). Marine and landscape painter and teacher, born in Rotterdam (Holland), June 11, 1820. After serving in the Dutch Navy, Van Beest came to the United States *c.* 1855. He appears to have divided his time between New Bedford (Mass.), where he was in October 1855 and again in 1857, and NYC, where he lived in 1856 and from 1858 until his death October 8, 1860. While at New Bedford in 1857, Van Beest shared a studio with his pupil, WILLIAM BRADFORD. He exhibited at the Boston Athenaeum in 1857 and posthumously in 1861. ¶ CAB; Thomas, "The American Career of Albert Van Beest," with 10 repros. and bibliography which cites A. J. Barnouw, "A Life of Albertus Van Beest" in the *Rotterdam Year Book* for 1919; NYCD 1856, 1858–60; Swan, BA, 200; Tuckerman, *Book of the Artists.*

BEET, CORNELIUS DE. Landscape and still life painter, born *c.* 1772 in Germany. Beet worked in Baltimore and Philadelphia in 1812 and in Baltimore 1813–14 and 1832. He exhibited at the Society of Artists and the Pennsylvania Academy, and is said to have died in 1840. ¶ Thieme-Becker; Dunlap, *History* II, 254; Rutledge, PA.

BEGODEN, ACHILLES (*c.* 1816–1899). Importer and commission merchant of NYC who painted watercolor views of NYC and vicinity, a number of which are at the NYHS. He was a native of France, but lived in NYC from about 1840 to 1885 and died at Northport, Long Island, on October 15, 1899, at the age of 83. ¶ NYHS Museum Dep't.

BEHAN, THOMAS. Portrait and miniature painter and teacher, 1805–15. Behan was working in NYC in 1805 and 1807, in the latter year apparently in partnership with an artist named LYMAN (a print of Paterson Falls on the Passaic River (N.J.), was "drawn and published" by Behan & Lyman). Behan was working as a portrait painter in Philadelphia in 1810 and 1811, and again in NYC in 1815. ¶ NYCD 1805 (as Beehan), 1815; N. Y. *Evening Post,* Jan. 2, 1805 (cited by McKay); Brown and Brown, cites Phila. CD 1810–11; Fielding, *Supplement to Stauffer,* nos. 192 and 985.

BEHNE, GUSTAVUS ADOLPHUS (1828–1895). Religious and landscape painter, working at Reading (Pa.) in 1855 and at Philadelphia in 1857, when he exhibited a haymaking scene in Berks County. ¶ Rutledge, PA.

BEHRENS, L. Landscape artist, known only for a view of West Point (N.Y.), 1850. ¶ Stokes, *Historical Prints,* pl. 94-B.

BEIGEL, JOHN. Still life painter active 1855, known only through a single canvas, "Field Flowers," in the collection of Paul Magriel. ¶ McCausland, "American Still-life Paintings," repro.

BEITOLDI, J. Engraver, Philadelphia, 1859. ¶ Phila. BD 1859.

BELANGER, F. J. Drawing teacher, hairworker, and profile painter in watercolor, Charleston (S.C.), 1806. ¶ Rutledge, *Artists in the Life of Charleston,* 185–86.

BELAUME or BELLAUME, J. General and seal engraver, New Orleans, 1826. ¶ Delgado-WPA, cites New Orleans *Argus,* June 20, 1826; Fielding, *Supplement to Stauffer,* 5, gives 1825.

BELEY, MAXIMILIAN. Engraver, born *c.* 1821 in France; at Philadelphia in 1850. ¶ 7 Census (1850), Pa., L, 932.

BELKNAP, ZEDEKIAH (1781–1858). Portrait painter, born at Weathersfield (Vt.), March 8, 1781. Belknap worked at Springfield (Vt.); in Massachusetts as early as 1810; and in NYC. He died at Weathersfield in April 1858. ¶ Baker, *Folklore of Springfield,* 67; Dunlap, *History* (1918), III, 283; Fielding. Belknap's work is represented at the American Antiquarian Society (Weis, *Check List*) and at Dartmouth College (General Catalogue, 143); there is a repro. in Sears, *Some American Primitives,* 177.

BELL & ANCORA. Proprietors of an art gallery in Philadelphia, 1819. The partners were the artist PIETRO ANCORA and, probably, the bookseller Charles Bell. ¶ Brown & Brown, cites the *Aurora,* May 1, 1819.

BELL, JAMES. Portrait painter, Philadelphia, 1854–55. ¶ Penna. BD 1854/55; Phila. CD 1854–55.

BELL, JOHN C. Portrait and landscape painter, Baltimore, 1810–16, worked with THOMAS BELL. His sepia portrait of John Gray (1785–1823) is at the Maryland Historical Society. ¶ Mayo, cites Baltimore CD, 1810, 1812, 1814, 1816; Lafferty; Rutledge, "Handlist of Miniatures."

BELL, THOMAS. Miniaturist, Baltimore, 1810–18, worked with JOHN BELL. ¶ Mayo, cites Baltimore CD 1810, 1812, 1814, 1816–18.

BELLAMY, JOHN HALEY (1836–1914). Wood carver, creator of the "Bellamy" or "Portsmouth eagles." Born April 16, 1836, at Kittery Point (Me.), Bellamy studied art in Boston and NYC and served his apprenticeship as a wood carver in Boston. Most of his work was done for the Boston and Portsmouth Navy Yards, though he also did some commercial ship carving and decorative work for public buildings and private homes. He was best known, however, for his carvings of eagles. Bellamy was also an amateur poet and inventor. He died at Portsmouth (N.H.), April 5, 1914. ¶ Safford, "John Haley Bellamy, the Woodcarver of Kittery Point," with repros.; Hill, "Bellamy's Greatest Eagle," with repro.; Pinckney, 161–62, 187, and pl. XXVII. Bellamy's work and some of his tools are represented in the Mariners' Museum, Newport News (Va.).

BELLARD, MAXIM. Lithographer. A Canadian, born *c.* 1830, Bellard was working in Philadelphia in July 1860. His wife Sarah, also a Canadian, was born *c.* 1823. ¶ 8 Census (1860), Pa., LII, 709.

BELLENOT (Bellenet), CHARLES. Engraver, New Orleans, 1852–56. ¶ New Orleans CD 1852–56.

BELLER, AUGUSTUS G. Amateur artist, Weston (Mo.). Born February 14, 1830, in Baden (Germany), Beller came to Weston with his family in 1841 or 1846. He had a varied career as blacksmith, lawyer, judge, postmaster of Weston, mayor of Weston (1863), editor of the *Border Times* (1864–1871), and in his later years as a Baptist minister. Only one painting by Beller is known, a view of Weston, now owned by the State Historical Society of Missouri. ¶ "Special Acquisitions of the Society," in *Missouri Hist. Review,* XLIV (Jan. 1950), 109–12, and repro. on cover. Sources cited are Paxton's *Annals of Platte County* (1897) and a *History of Clay and Platte Counties, Missouri* (St. Louis, 1885).

BELLEW, FRANK HENRY TEMPLE (1828–1888). Caricaturist, cartoonist, and comic illustrator. Born in Cawnpore (India), April 18, 1828, Bellew lived for some years in France and England before coming to America in 1850. He settled in NYC, where he remained until his death June 29, 1888. He was a popular contributor to many comic journals and books. ¶ DAB; Smith; NYBD 1852; Cowdrey, NAD.

BELLI, AMATO. Plaster image maker, Philadelphia, 1860. Born in Tuscany *c.* 1836, Belli was living with DOMINICA and MICHAEL BELLI in the home of L. HARDIE. ¶ 8 Census (1860), Pa., LII, 106.

BELLI, DOMINICA. Plaster image maker, Philadelphia 1860. Born in Tuscany *c.* 1835, probably the sister of AMATO and MICHAEL BELLI. ¶ 8 Census (1860), Pa., LII, 106.

BELLI, MICHAEL. Plaster image maker, Philadelphia, 1860. Born in Tuscany, probably the brother of AMATO and DOMINICA BELLI. ¶ 8 Census (1860), Pa., LII, 106.

BELLMAN, EDWIN. Engraver, NYC and Brooklyn, 1851–1895. Bellman seems to have retired *c.* 1895 and died *c.* 1900. His home was in Brooklyn. ¶ NYCD 1851–1900; listed in 1858 as Edward Bellman.

BELLOWS, ALBERT FITCH (1829–1883). N.A. Landscape and genre painter in oils and watercolors, etcher. He was born November 29, 1829, at Milford (Mass.) and took up the study of painting in Boston. He was principal of the New England School of Design in 1850–56. Resigning this position, Bellows visited Europe, studying at Paris and Antwerp. On his return to America he settled in NYC, where he remained until a second visit to Europe in 1867–68. Shortly after his return, he moved to Boston, but, suffering heavily in the fire of 1872, he returned to NYC. He took up etching late in his career. He died at Auburndale (Mass.), November 24, 1883. ¶ DAB; Clement and Hutton; NYCD 1858–60. Bellows exhibited at the Washington Art Assoc. (Cat. 1857), the National Academy (Cowdrey, 1857–83), the Penna. Academy (Rutledge), and the Boston Athenaeum, 1858–73 (Swan).

BELUCAN, C. Engraver, New Orleans, July 1850. Belucan was French, born *c.* 1822; his wife was English, born *c.* 1824. ¶ 7 Census (1850), La., V, 10.

BELZONS, JEAN, known also as "Zolbius." Miniaturist, drawing teacher, scene painter. Belzons was the brother-in-law and first teacher of THOMAS SULLY, whose sister he married in Charleston in 1794. He was French and claimed to have studied under David. He worked in Charleston from about 1794 to 1812, painting miniatures, portraits, scenery, and transparencies, as well as teaching. In 1796 he visited Savannah (Ga.) and in 1798 Georgetown and Camden (S.C.). ¶ Rutledge, *Artists in the Life of Charleston,* 126, 147, 153, 186; Prime, II, 3–4; Biddle and Fielding, *Life of Sully,* 4; Dunlap, *History* (1918), II, 114, 238–39.

BEMAN, ALLEN C. Engraver, Chicago, 1856–57, in the latter year as Beaman. ¶ Chicago BD 1856; CD 1857/58.

BEMENT, GEORGE. Artist, 40, from Connecticut, at NYC in 1860. ¶ 8 Census (1860), N.Y., XLIII, 520.

BEMIS, ——. Portrait and landscape painter, vicinity of Worcester (Mass.), *c.* 1850. ¶ Fielding.

BEN, ALI. Profile painter, NYC, 1806. ¶ McKay, cites NYCD 1806.

BENADE & DEVLAN. "Landscape and Cattle," the joint work of these artists, was exhibited at the Pennsylvania Academy in 1853. The artists were JAMES A. BENADE, landscape painter, and his pupil, F. D. DEVLAN, who is said to have provided the animals for a number of his teacher's landscapes. ¶ Rutledge, PA; Montgomery, *Berks County,* 809.

BENADE, JAMES ARTHUR (1823–1853). Landscape painter. James A. Benade, son of Bishop Andrew Benade of the Moravian Church, was born at Bethlehem (Pa.) in 1823. He studied for a time with the painter, GUSTAVUS GRUNEWALD, and exhibited as early as 1838 at the Artists' Fund Society in Philadelphia. A few years later young Benade established himself at Reading (Pa.) where he spent the rest of his brief career. He exhibited two landscapes at the Pennsylvania Academy in 1848. Shortly before his death, Benade took as a pupil F. D. DEVLAN, with whom he collaborated on "Landscape and Cattle," exhibited at the Pennsylvania Academy in 1853 as their joint work. He died at Reading on February 2, 1853. ¶ Montgomery, *Berks County,* 808–09; Rutledge, PA. Stokes, *Hist. Prints,* lists and reproduces a view of Lancaster (Pa.), drawn on stone by Jas. A. Benade. The date assigned, *c.* 1835, is probably several years too early, as Benade would then have been only 12 years of age.

BENBRIDGE, HENRY (1743–1812). Portrait and historical painter, miniaturist. Benbridge was born in Philadelphia probably in November 1743, as he was seven months old at the time of his baptism May 27, 1744. His early interest in art was encouraged by his wealthy stepfather, who enabled him to go to Italy to study in 1764. By 1769 he was in London, where he won some attention by a portrait of the Corsican patriot Paoli, but the following year he returned to Philadelphia. After his marriage in 1771 to Letitia Sage of Philadelphia, herself an accomplished miniaturist, Benbridge moved to Charleston, where he succeeded JEREMIAH THEUS as the most popular portrait painter of South Carolina. Dunlap states that he was a British prisoner during the Revolution and returned to Charleston in 1784. About 1800 he moved to Norfolk (Va.) where he was one of THOMAS SULLY's early instructors. He died late in 1811 or early in 1812, and was buried at Christ Church, Philadelphia, January 25, 1812. ¶ Hildeburn, "Records of Christ Church, Phila., Baptisms 1709–1760," 237; DAB; Rutledge, "Henry Benbridge (1743–1812?) American Portrait Painter," with 15 repros. and tentative lists of oil portraits by Benbridge and miniatures probably by Mrs. Benbridge; Rutledge, *Artists in the Life of Charleston,* repro. 174; Dunlap, *History,* I, 142–44; Burial Records of Board of Health 1807–1814, in Geneal. Soc. of Pa., p. 335; Records of Christ Church Burials 1785–1900, in Geneal. Soc. of Pa., p. 3691 (citation courtesy of R. N. Williams, Hist. Soc. of Pa., and Miss Anna W. Rutledge); Flexner, *The Light of Distant Skies,* biblio., 258.

BENBRIDGE, Mrs. HENRY, born Letitia Sage. Miniaturist. Letitia Sage of Philadelphia, a pupil of CHARLES WILLSON PEALE, married the portrait painter HENRY BENBRIDGE in 1771. From 1773 they lived in Charleston (S.C.). None of the miniatures attributed to her are dated later than 1780. ¶ Rutledge, *Artists in the Life of Charleston,* 178, with repro.; Rutledge, "Henry Benbridge," tentative list of miniatures probably by Mrs. Benbridge.

BENDANN, DAVID. Portrait painter. David Bendann and a brother painted many portraits and founded Bendann's Picture Shop in Baltimore, 1859. ¶ Lancaster Co. Hist. Soc., *Portraiture in Lancaster County,* 114–15 and 3 repros.

BENDER, FREDERICK. Portrait painter, NYC, 1857. ¶ NYBD 1857.

BENECKE, THOMAS. Lithographer, NYC, 1855–56. ¶ Peters, *America on Stone,* pl. 12; *Portfolio,* II (April 1943), 192.

BENEWORTH, JAMES C. An English engraver who arrived in America in 1843 and was working at Madison (Wis.) *c.* 1869. ¶ *Wisconsin Mag. of Hist.,* March 1947.

BENGOUGH, RICHARD. Panoramist and theatrical scene painter, NYC, 1836–1850. In 1836 Bengough was working for the HANINGTONS in NYC as a painter of drop scenes and dioramas. The next year he painted scenery for the National Theater. He is listed in city directories for 1842–44 and 1847–48. In 1848 his panorama of Broadway was shown in NYC, and at about the same time he collaborated with HILLYARD and others on a panorama of the Hudson River. His panorama of Broadway, described as his "last work," was offered for sale in NYC, and in 1852 his widow, Elizabeth Bengough, was listed in the city directory. ¶ N. Y. *Herald,* Dec. 7 and 22, 1836; March 28, 1837; Aug. 21, 1850; Odell, V, 469; Boston *Evening Transcript,* July 18, 1838; Cincinnati *Daily Gazette,* July 12, 1839; Phila. *Public Ledger,* Aug. 30, 1851 (citations courtesy of J. E. Arrington); NYCD 1842–44, 1847–48, 1852.

BENITO, F. Artist, New Orleans, 1849. ¶ Delgado-WPA, cites New Orleans CD 1849.

BENJAMIN, M. Portrait painter, NYC, 1859–60. ¶ NYBD 1859–60; NYCD 1859–60.

BENJAMIN, SAMUEL GREEN WHEELER (1837–1914). Painter, illustrator, author, and diplomat. The son of a missionary, Benjamin was born February 13, 1837, at Argos (Greece) and spent his first 18 years in Greece and the Levant. He made his first visit to America in 1847–48 and returned in 1855 on the death of his father. He had studied drawing in Europe and sent pictures of the Crimean War to the *Illustrated London News.* After graduation from Williams College in 1859, Benjamin taught school for a short time and served as an assistant in the New York State Library at Albany (1861–64). Thereafter he lived at Brookfield (Mass.), Boston, and NYC. He published many volumes of poetry, fiction, and art history from 1860, and established himself as a marine painter in Boston about 1870. He served as first U. S. Minister to Persia 1883–1885. On his return Benjamin lived quietly on Staten Island and in Washington (D.C.), and died at Burlington (Vt.), July 19, 1914. ¶ DAB; *Harpers Magazine,* XLIX (1879), 241, 481, 673; *Art Annual,* XI; Clement and Hutton; Cowdrey, NAD (1878–82).

BENNER, HENRY C. Engraver, Washington (D.C.), 1855–60. ¶ Washington CD 1855, 1858, 1860.

BENNETT, DANIEL S. Drawing teacher. Born *c.* 1829 in Michigan; living in Baltimore in 1850 with his brother [?] JAMES A. T. BENNETT and his father [?] James C. Bennett, teacher of grammar. ¶ 7 Census (1850), Md., VI, 151.

BENNETT, JAMES A. T. Drawing teacher. Born *c.* 1833 in NYC; living in Baltimore in 1850 with his brother [?] DANIEL S. BENNETT and father [?] James C. Bennett, grammar teacher. ¶ 7 Census (1850), Md., VI, 151.

BENNETT, WILLIAM JAMES (1787–1844). N.A. Water color landscape painter, aquatint engraver, and etcher. A native of England, Bennett exhibited in London galleries from 1808 to 1825. By 1826 he was in NYC, where he painted and engraved a view of Bowling Green, and NYC remained his home until 1843, when he apparently moved to Nyack (N.Y.). He made a number of sketching trips through the States, in 1830 to Boston, West Point, and Baltimore, in 1834 and 1835 to Buffalo and Detroit. He died in NYC in May 1844. ¶ Thieme-Becker; Graves, *Dictionary;* Stokes, *Historical Prints;* Cowdrey, NAD; Grant, *Dictionary;* NYCD 1834, 1836, 1838, 1840–43; American Art-Union *Trans.* 1844; Davidson, I, 169, 189, 327 and II, 137, 146, 221, 223, repros.; Stauffer.

BENONI, ——. Theatre scene painter, New Orleans, 1830. ¶ Delgado-WPA, cites *La. Courier,* Jan. 28, 1830.

BENSADON, J. Marble sculptor, New Orleans, 1852. ¶ New Orleans CD 1852.

BENSELL, GEORGE FREDERICK (1837–1879). Portrait, genre, and historical painter in oils and crayon; poet. Bensell was born in Philadelphia in 1837 and exhibited annually at the Pennsylvania Academy from 1856 to 1868. A 22 page poem, "The Artist's Dream," written in 1867 by Bensell and Samuel Diffield, is at the Historical Society of Pennsylvania. The artist Edmund Birckhead Bensell, born 1842, was probably his brother. ¶ Thieme-Becker; Rutledge, PA; Bensell's poem is recorded in the Union Catalogue, Library of Congress.

BENSON, BENJAMIN W. Of WELLSTOOD, BENSON & HANKS, banknote engravers, NYC, 1848–51. ¶ NYCD 1848–51.

BENSON & BROTHER. House, sign, and ornamental painters, New Orleans, 1856–60. This firm, composed of John and Joseph Benson, painted murals for St. Joseph's Roman Catholic Church, New Orleans, in 1856. ¶ Delgado-WPA, cites *Delta,* July 6, 1856; New Orleans CD 1856, 1858, 1860.

BENSON, EUGENE (1839–1908). A.N.A. Portrait and genre painter, art critic. Born November 1, 1839, at Hyde Park (N.Y.), Benson studied at the National Academy in 1856 and with J. H. WRIGHT. A frequent exhibitor at the Academy from 1858 to 1870, he moved in 1869 to New Haven. He went to Italy in 1873 and remained there until his death at Venice, February 28, 1908. He was an Associate of the National Academy. ¶ DAB; Cowdrey, NAD (1858–84); CAB; Clement and Hutton. Benson also exhibited in London (Graves); at the Boston Athenaeum (Swan); and at the Maryland Hist. Soc. (Rutledge).

BENSON, JOHN, see BENSON & BROTHER.

BENSON, JOSEPH, see BENSON & BROTHER.

hibited at the Athenaeum five times from 1857 to 1860. He painted portraits of Lincoln and Horace Mann. He died April 23, 1915, at Malden (Mass.). ¶ *Art Annual,* XII, obit.; Boston BD 1857–60; 8 Census (1860), Mass., XXVI, 723, shows that Bicknell's father was a prosperous grocer; Swan, BA; *Panorama* (Oct. 1945), 9, repro.; Cowdrey, NAD (1868).

BIDDLE, ROBERT STONE. Miniature profilist on cardboard. A native of Wotton-under-Edge (Gloucestershire, England), Biddle was at Philadelphia as early as 1834 and appears to have lived there until his death in 1857 or early 1858. In 1839 and 1845–46 he was listed as a portrait painter, in 1848 as a druggist, and in 1852 as "China Store." ¶ Stillwell, "Some 19th Century Painters"; Gillingham, "Notes on Philadelphia Profilists," 516–18 with repro.; represented at NYHS.

BIDWELL, Miss MARY W. Portrait painter and modeller in clay. A native of East Hartford (Conn.), Mary Bidwell had her first drawing lessons there about 1858. Later she studied with F. S. JEWETT, maintained a studio in Hartford, and spent her winters in Brooklyn, where she exhibited her work. ¶ French, *Art and Artists in Connecticut,* 162.

BIDWELL, THOMAS. Drawing master, Philadelphia, 1795. Probably the same as THOMAS BEDWELL. ¶ Prime, II, 44–45.

BIEN, JULIUS (1826–1909). Lithographer, cartographer, and portrait painter. Born at Cassel (Germany) September 27, 1826, Bien emigrated to the U.S. in 1849, having been a participant in the revolution of the previous year. He established himself in NYC as a lithographer and mapmaker. His work as a cartographer, much of it for the U. S. Government, was of the highest quality and earned him the reputation of being the finest American cartographer of the century. He died December 21, 1909. ¶ DAB: *Who's Who in America,* 1901/02; NYCD 1850–60 and after; Stokes, *Historical Prints,* repro.; Peters, *America on Stone;* National Academy Cat. 1866.

BIERSTADT, ALBERT (1830–1902). N.A. Landscape and animal painter. Born at Solingen, near Düsseldorf (Germany), January 7, 1830, Bierstadt was brought to America as a baby and grew up at New Bedford (Mass.). He returned to Düsseldorf at the age of 23 and studied painting there and at Rome until 1857. In 1858 he made a trip to the American West, settled in NYC in 1860, and was made a National Academician the same year. For a number of years he had a studio at Irvington-on-the-Hudson, but after 1882 he lived in NYC. Bierstadt revisited Europe in 1867, 1878, and 1883. Although his reputation was made by his vast landscapes of Western scenes, in later years Bierstadt also painted wild animals of North America. He died in NYC February 18, 1902. ¶ DAB; Cowdrey, NAD; Rutledge, MHS; Washington Art Assoc. Cat., 1859; Rutledge, PA, 1859–67; Graves, *Dictionary* (Royal Academy 1869–79); Corcoran Gallery Cat.; Karolik Cat., 74–107, with 19 repros. and chronology; Davidson, I, 292, 293, repros.; Spieler, "A Noted Artist in Early Colorado; the Story of Albert Bierstadt."

BIESTER, ANTHONY (1840–1917). Portrait and landscape painter. Biester was born August 26, 1840, at Cleves (Germany) and died at Madisonville (Ohio) March 26, 1917. He was living at Cincinnati in 1905. ¶ *Artists Year Book* (1905), 14, gives the 1840 birth date, while *Art Annual,* XIV, gives 1837; Thieme-Becker cites *Cleveland Commercial Tribune,* Aug. 9, 1903.

BIFELT, see BILFELDT.

BIGELOW, DANIEL FOLGER (1823–1910). Landscape and still life painter. Born at Peru, Clinton County (N.Y.), July 22, 1823, Bigelow is said to have received his first instruction in art from a cousin of HIRAM POWERS. He moved to Chicago in 1858, there winning considerable reputation as a landscape painter and becoming one of the associates of G. P. A. HEALY and the group of artists who founded the Chicago Academy of Design. Bigelow died in Chicago in July 1910. ¶ Gilman Bigelow Howe, *Genealogy of the Bigelow Family of America,* 477; Andreas, *History of Chicago,* II, 561; *Art News,* Sept. 17, 1910, obit.; *Art Annual,* VIII (1910/11), 397, obit., erroneously states that Bigelow was born at Peru (Ind.), and the error is repeated in Burnet, *Art and Artists of Indiana,* in Smith, and in Mallet. Represented at the Chicago Hist. Soc., information courtesy of H. Maxson Holloway.

BIGELOW, JAMES W. (or I. W.). Portrait painter. Fielding states that I. W. Bigelow painted a portrait at White Plains (N.Y.) *c.* 1840. James W. Bigelow appears in the Brooklyn directories as printer (1852), ferry master or ferryman (1853–

54, 1856), artist (1855, 1858), and clerk (1857). SOPHIA B. BIGELOW, portrait painter, was apparently his wife. ¶ Fielding; Brooklyn CD 1852–58.

BIGELOW, Mrs. JAMES W., see SOPHIA B. BIGELOW.

BIGELOW, SAMUEL. Lithographer, 23, a native of New York State, at NYC in 1850. ¶ 7 Census (1850), N.Y., XLIV, 369.

BIGELOW, SOPHIA B. Portrait painter. As Sophia B. or Mrs. J. W. Bigelow, she was active in Brooklyn from 1852 to 1857. She was the wife of JAMES W. BIGELOW, artist and ferrymaster. ¶ Brooklyn CD 1852–54, 1856–57; Frick Art Reference Library.

BIGGINS, HENRY. Modeller, chaser, and die-sinker, NYC. Biggins is listed as chaser, of Batchelor & Biggins, 1844–45; as modeller, 1846–52; as die-sinker in 1852 and as wellsinker in 1850. ¶ NYCD 1844–52.

BIGOT, ALPHONSE (*c.* 1828–*c.* 1873). Lithographer; born in France about 1828, probably the son of FRANCIS BIGOT. He came to Philadelphia before 1854 and worked there until his death in 1872 or 1873. His household in 1860 included, besides his wife and three children, FRANCIS BIGOT and FRANCIS ROUX, both lithographers. ¶ 8 Census (1860), Pa., LVIII, 375; Phila. CD 1855–72.

BIGOT, FRANCIS. French lithographer, 55, living in Philadelphia in 1860 in the household of ALPHONSE BIGOT, probably his son. ¶ 8 Census (1860), Pa., LVIII, 375.

BIGOT, TOUSSAINT FRANÇOIS (*c.* 1794–1869). Landscape, historical, and portrait painter and drawing master, New Orleans, *c.* 1816–69. Bigot was a native of Rennes (France). After studying in the "first schools" of France, he came to New Orleans *c.* 1816 and remained there for over forty years as a painter and drawing master. His wife appears to have been a teacher also. The F. Bigot listed in the directories after 1850 is probably the same as Toussaint Francois, who died at New Orleans on March 14, 1869. ¶ Delgado-WPA, cites *Bee,* March 17, 1869 (obit.), *Argus,* March 20 and June 1, 1826, and March 13, 1827; New Orleans CD 1830, 1832, 1841–43, 1851–54, 1858.

BILFELDT (Bilfelat, Bilfield, or Bifelt), JOHN JOSEPH (1793–*c.* 1849). French portrait and miniature painter, born at Avignon in 1793, died at Paris *c.* 1849. He was probably the Mr. Bilfield, portrait and miniature painter, who "returned" to New Orleans from France in 1837, appeared in the 1838 directory as Mr. Bilfelat, advertised in 1841 as Mr. Bilfield, and was listed in the 1842 directory as Bifelt. ¶ Thieme-Becker; Delgado-WPA, cites *Bee,* Nov. 17, 1837, and *Commercial Advertiser,* Dec. 18, 1841; New Orleans CD 1838, 1842.

BILFIELD, see BILFELDT.

BILLINGS, A. Engraver. One signed example of his work is known—the bookplate of Richard Varick. Stauffer states that Billings instructed ABRAHAM GODWIN *c.* 1782. ¶ Stauffer, I, 20.

BILLINGS, E. A portrait of Ichabod Goodwin (1794–1882) by this artist is in the State House, Concord (N.H.). *Cf.* EDWIN T. BILLINGS. ¶ WPA (Mass.), *Portraits Found in N. H.,* 9.

BILLINGS, EDWIN (or Edward) T. (1824–1893). Portrait painter. Born in 1824, Billings was at the Leicester (Mass.) Academy in 1853–54, when he made a copy of JOHN GREENWOOD's portrait of ISAIAH THOMAS. He was in Alabama in 1857 and the following year at Worcester (Mass.). From *c.* 1865 he lived as a recluse in Boston. Billings died October 19, 1893, at Dorchester (Mass.). *Cf.* E. BILLINGS. ¶ Smith; *New York Tribune,* Oct. 21, 1893, obit.; Brigham, "Notes on the Thomas Family Portraits," 50; WPA (Ala.), HRS, cites Alabama Dept. of Archives and History; Cowdrey, NAD; Billings' work is represented at the American Antiquarian Society (Weis).

BILLINGS, HAMMATT (1816–1874). Artist, designer, architect, illustrator, watercolor painter. He was born at Milton (Mass.) but the family apparently moved to Boston before 1828. His father, a clerk, died *c.* 1836, leaving a widow and several sons who established themselves as architects *c.* 1843. Hammatt continued to work in Boston until his death, November 14, 1874. In 1860 he lived at 13 Tremont Row, owned $6,000 in personal property. Among his boarders was the wood engraver, E. N. TARBELL. He exhibited at the Boston Athenaeum in 1859 and 1873, and was well-known as an architect and designer of monuments. ¶ Thieme-Becker; Boston CD 1828–50; 7 Census (1850), Mass., XXVI, 180; 8 Census (1860), Mass., XXVIII, 645; Boston CD 1860; Swan, BA; WPA (Mass.), *Portraits*

Found in N. H., 17, 20; Gage; Hinton; Rutledge, PA.

BILLINGS, JOSEPH. Engraver, *c.* 1770. A proclamation of Lt. Gov. John Penn of Pennsylvania, January 15, 1770, denounced Billings as a forger of colonial paper currency. No examples of his engraving are known to be extant. ¶ Stauffer, I, 20–21.

BILLINGS, MOSES (1809–1884). Portrait painter. Billings settled at Erie (Pa.) in 1829. He had a studio in Cleveland (Ohio) 1833–34, but was back in Erie in 1848 when he encouraged and perhaps instructed JUNIUS R. SLOAN. ¶ Webster, "Junius R. Sloan," 104.

BILLINGS, RICHARDSON. Portrait painter, Guilford (Vt.), 1815–47. Two of his portraits are on wooden panels. A portrait of TRYPHENA GOLDSBURY SMITH has been attributed to him. ¶ Dods, "Connecticut Valley Painters," 209.

BILMER, COLBY, see COLBY KIMBLE.

BINDING, SOLOMON GOTLIP. Miniaturist and engraver on glass. Binding was advertised for in Baltimore in 1791 as a fugitive indentured servant, age 21, who could draw miniatures and engrave on glass with glass. ¶ Prime, II, 4.

BINGHAM & BREOBEY, see THOMAS T. BINGHAM.

BINGHAM & DODD (or Bingham, Dodd & Co.). Lithographers, Hartford (Conn.), 1860–83. The partners in 1860 were JOHN H. BINGHAM and WILLIAM HENRY DODD. ¶ Hartford CD 1860–83.

BINGHAM, GEORGE CALEB (1811–1879). Genre, portrait and, occasionally, landscape painter. Bingham was born in Augusta County (Va.), March 20, 1811, but moved with his family in 1819 to Missouri, where he spent most of his life. He studied art at the Pennsylvania Academy in 1837, lived in Washington from 1840 to 1844, and studied at Düsseldorf (Germany) 1856–58 and again in 1859. Thereafter Bingham lived in Missouri, where he was prominent as a politician and as a painter of portraits and genre scenes, particularly of political subjects. Bingham exhibited at the Pennsylvania Academy, the National Academy, and the Washington Art Association. He died at Kansas City (Mo.), July 7, 1879. ¶ Rusk, *George Caleb Bingham, The Missouri Artist;* DAB; Christ-Janer, *George Caleb Bingham of Missouri;* [Bingham,] "Letters of George Caleb Bingham"; Rutledge, PA; Cowdrey, NAD; Cowdrey, AA & AAU; Washington Art Assoc. Cat., 1859; Met. Mus., *Life in America;* Sweet, *Hudson River School;* Karolik Cat.; Davidson, I, 109, 188, 191, and II, 331, 334, repros.; Shapley, "Bingham's 'Jolly Flatboatmen.' "

BINGHAM, HIRAM (1789–1869). Engraver of Boston and a leader of the first American missionary group in Hawaii in 1820. Bingham apparently served as printer to the group in Honolulu and engraved some woodcuts for their religious publications. ¶ Hamilton, 136–37.

BINGHAM, JOHN H. Lithographer, Hartford (Conn.), 1855–84. In 1857–58 Bingham was associated with JOSEPH KELLEY in the lithographic firm of BINGHAM & KELLEY, and from 1860 to 1883 with WILLIAM HENRY DODD in the firm of BINGHAM & DODD (or Bingham, Dodd & Co.). In 1884 he was listed as working in NYC but living in Hartford. ¶ Hartford CD 1855–84.

BINGHAM & KELLEY. Lithographers, Hartford (Conn.), 1857–58. The partners were JOHN H. BINGHAM and JOSEPH KELLEY. ¶ Hartford CD 1857–58.

BINGHAM, LUTHER. Portrait painter, NYC, 1838–42; exhibited at the National Academy in 1838. ¶ Cowdrey, NAD; NYCD 1838, 1842.

BINGHAM, SAMUEL. Lithographer, 26, a native of New York State, living in NYC in 1850. His wife was English and they had one child, aged two, born in Pennsylvania. ¶ 7 Census (1850), N.Y., LIV, 166; NYCD 1850.

BINGHAM, THOMAS T. Engraver, die-sinker, and letter-cutter, Philadelphia, 1797–1805, 1809–11; of Bingham & Breobey, engravers, in 1800. ¶ Brown and Brown, cite Phila. CD 1797–1805, 1809–11; Prime, II, 66.

BINGHAM, WILLIAM. Portrait painter at Cincinnati in 1843–44. ¶ Cincinnati CD 1843–44 (courtesy Edward H. Dwight, Cincinnati Art Museum).

BINGLEY, GEORGE. Engraver, born in England *c.* 1813, living in Boston in August 1850. ¶ 7 Census (1850), Mass., XXV, 646; not listed in directories.

BINGLEY, JOSEPH. Engraver, born in England *c.* 1805, living in Philadelphia from 1850 to 1865. This is probably the same Joseph Bingley listed as an engraver in NYC 1839–40 and in Brooklyn 1841–48. Bingley was associated with CHARLES WHITAKER in NYC in the engraving firm of BINGLEY & WHITAKER. ¶ 7 Census (1850),

Penna., LII, 867; Phila. CD 1851, 1854 (as Binkley), 1856–65; NYCD 1839–40, 1842; Brooklyn CD 1841 (as engineer), 1842, 1844, 1845, 1847, 1848.

BINGLEY, THOMAS. Engraver, NYC, 1838. ¶ NYCD 1838 (at the address given for JOSEPH BINGLEY in 1839).

BINGLEY & WHITAKER. Engravers, NYC, 1842. The partners were JOSEPH BINGLEY and CHARLES WHITAKER. ¶ NYCD 1842.

BININGER, W. B. Portrait painter, NYC; exhibited at the Apollo Association in 1839 and 1840 and at the National Academy in 1840. ¶ Cowdrey, AA & AAU; Cowdrey, NAD; NYCD and NYBD 1840.

BINON, J. B. A French sculptor who worked in Boston *c.* 1820 and was one of the early instructors of HORATIO GREENOUGH. He was best known for a bust of John Adams. ¶ Dunlap, *History,* II, 378; Swan, BA.

BINSSE (Binse), LOUIS FRANCIS DE PAUL (1774–1844). Portrait and miniature painter. Binsse was born in France in 1774 and held an official position in Haiti under the Vicomte de Rochambeau until forced to flee from the native uprising. He settled in NYC about 1805 and remained there until his death. From 1806 to 1809 his occupation was given as portrait or miniature painter, but thereafter the directories list no occupation for Binsse until 1842–44 when he is listed simply as "school." At his death, December 24, 1844, Binsse was survived by his widow, Victoria, and a son, Lewis B. Binsse, who had a fancy goods store. ¶ N. Y. *Commercial Advertiser,* Dec. 26, 1844, obit.; letters of Henry B. Binsse (grandson of the artist) to T. Bolton, at NYHS; NYCD 1805–09, 1812, 1814–44, 1845 (Victoria Binsse). Represented at NYHS by a signed miniature.

BIRCH, ——. Line engraver, known for portrait frontispiece to Thomas Sarjeant's *An Easy and Compendious System of Short Hand* (Phila., Dobson & Lang, 1789). *Cf.* B. BIRCH. ¶ Stauffer, I, 21.

BIRCH, B. Crayon portraitist, miniaturist, engraver, and watchmaker from London, in NYC, 1784. *Cf.* —— BIRCH. ¶ Kelby, *Notes on American Artists,* 22; Bolton, *Crayon Draftsmen* and *Miniature Painters;* Fielding.

BIRCH, GEORGE. Landscape painter, Philadelphia, 1807–10. ¶ Brown and Brown, cite Phila. CD 1807–10.

BIRCH, J. Landscape and marine painter, Philadelphia, 1839. Cowdrey identifies this artist with THOMAS BIRCH. ¶ Apollo Association *Transactions,* 1839; Cowdrey, AA & AAU.

BIRCH, THOMAS (1779–1851). Marine, landscape, portrait, and miniature painter, son of the artist WILLIAM RUSSELL BIRCH. He was born in England in 1779 and came to Philadelphia in 1794 with his father. The two were working together 1799–1800 as William Birch & Son, designing, engraving, and publishing views of Philadelphia. Thomas Birch continued to work in Philadelphia until his death on January 14, 1851. He was especially noted for his marine and winter scenes and his paintings of naval battles of the War of 1812. His work was exhibited frequently at the Society of Artists and Pennsylvania Academy (1811–61), the Artists' Fund Society (1835–45), the National Academy (1832–45), the Maryland Historical Society (1848–58), the American Academy (1833–35), and the Apollo Association and American Art-Union (1838–50). He was an Honorary Member, Professional, of the National Academy. ¶ DAB: CAB: Stokes, *Historical Prints;* Brown and Brown; Phila. CD 1802–51; Rutledge, PA; Rutledge, MHS; Cowdrey, NAD; Cowdrey, AA & AAU; Cummings, *Historic Annals,* 226; Sartain, *Reminiscences,* 143, 180; Karolik Cat., 111–23, eight repros.; Flexner, *The Light of Distant Skies,* biblio., 258.

BIRCH, WILLIAM RUSSELL (1755–1834). Miniaturist, enamel painter, engraver, and etcher; born April 9, 1755, in Warwickshire (England). He studied at Bristol and London and exhibited frequently in London from 1775 to 1794. In the latter year he emigrated to America with his son, THOMAS BIRCH, settling in Philadelphia. He achieved considerable reputation for his miniatures and enamel portraits, and worked with his son on a series of *Views of Philadelphia,* published in 1800. Birch published two views of NYC in 1802 and one of Mt. Vernon the following year. He apparently lived in Philadelphia until about 1812, when he moved to a country estate, "Springland," near Bristol (Pa.). Returning to Philadelphia in 1828, he resided in the city until his death on August 7, 1834. He had been a frequent exhibitor at Philadelphia galleries, including the Columbianum in 1795, the Society of Artists, the Pennsylvania Academy, and the Artists' Fund Society, and at the Maryland Historical

Society in Baltimore and the American Academy and Apollo Association in NYC. ¶ DAB; DNB; Graves, *Dictionary;* Prime, II, repro. of adv.; Stokes, *Iconography,* I, 468, plates 76 and 77; Stokes, *Historical Prints,* 48; Brown and Brown; Phila. CD 1828–31, 1833; Columbianum Cat., 1795; Rutledge, PA; Rutledge, MHS; Cowdrey, AA & AAU; Ross, "William Birch"; Davidson, I, 389, repro.; Flexner, *The Light of Distant Skies,* biblio., 258.

BIRD, ALBERT G. Engraver, Philadelphia, 1829–58. Bird was born in Pennsylvania *c.* 1800 and worked as an engraver in Philadelphia as early as 1829. In August 1850 he was living there with his wife Lydia, aged 48, and seven children, all born in Pennsylvania. One son was a seaman and another a carpenter. Bird's name appears in the directories as late as 1858. ¶ 7 Census (1850), Pa., LII, 821; Phila. CD 1829–58.

BIRD, FREDERICK. Portrait painter, Brooklyn (N.Y.), 1856–57. ¶ Brooklyn CD 1856; BD 1857.

BIRD, HORATIO G. Engraver and lithographic printer, Boston, 1846–80. Bird was born in Massachusetts *c.* 1824 and was working in Boston as a lithographic printer by 1846. From 1848 to 1857 he was listed in the directories merely as printer, but in the 1850 Census he gave his occupation as engraver. His wife Rebecca and their two daughters, 5 and 7 years old, were also born in Massachusetts. Bird continued to be listed in the directories as printer and lithographic printer until after 1880. ¶ 7 Census (1850), Mass., XXV, 49; Boston CD 1846, 1848–57, 1859–80.

BIRD, JOHN. Sculptor, 39, a native of New York State, living in NYC in August 1850. ¶ 7 Census (1850), N.Y., LII, 374.

BISBEE, EZRA. Portrait painter and lithographer, NYC and Brooklyn, 1820–56. ¶ NYCD 1820; Peters, *America on Stone;* Brooklyn CD 1844, 1851–52, 1855–56.

BISBEE, JOHN. Portrait painter, lithographer, and publisher, NYC, 1821–40. Bisbee exhibited at the American Academy in 1821 and 1824 and was an Associate Member of the Academy 1825–28. He was listed in the directories 1824–1837, usually as portrait painter, though Dunlap speaks of him as a lithographer. Peters states that he did lithographic work for ENDICOTT & SWETT. The 1838 edition of *New York As It Is* lists him as lithographer and publisher. The last record of Bisbee is in the 1840 Brooklyn directory, as portrait painter. ¶ NYCD 1824–37; Cowdrey, AA & AAU; *New York As It Is* (1838); Dunlap, *History,* II, 454; Peters, *America on Stone;* Brooklyn CD 1840.

BISCHEBOU, ——. Lithographer, Boston, *c.* 1826. *Cf.* AUGUST BISHOPBOIS. ¶ Peters, *America on Stone.*

BISCHOFF, FREDERICK CHRISTOPHER (1771–1834). Portrait, miniature, and butterfly painter. Born February 18, 1771, at Stadtilm (Germany), Bischoff came to America between 1796 and 1799 and settled in Reading (Pa.), where he worked as a painter of portraits, miniatures, and profiles for over thirty years, apparently until his death on June 3, 1834. The Historical Society of Berks County owns a volume of paintings of butterflies, painted by Bischoff *c.* 1800–17, and examples of his portrait work are still owned by private families in Reading. ¶ Shoemaker, "Reading's First Artist, A Painter of Butterflies."

BISDORF, PETER J. Engraver, of CAMMEYER & BISDORF, NYC, 1856–57. ¶ NYCD 1856–57.

BISHABOY and BISHBOY, see BISHOPBOIS.

BISHOP, ——. Portrait and genre painter, *c.* 1850. ¶ Fielding.

BISHOP, ANGELICA. Portrait and miniature painter, Philadelphia, 1835–44. Miss Bishop resided with THOMAS BISHOP, probably her father, until his death *c.* 1840. She exhibited at the Artists' Fund Society from 1835 to 1844 (except 1839). In 1844 she was living in Washington (D.C.). ¶ Rutledge, PA; Cowdrey, NAD; Phila. CD 1837–42.

BISHOP, ANNETTE. Genre painter, exhibited at the National Academy in 1859 as of New Russia, Essex County (N.J.?) and from 1864 to 1867 at the National Academy and the Pennsylvania Academy as of NYC. ¶ Cowdrey, NAD; Rutledge, PA.

BISHOP, THOMAS (*c.* 1753–*c.* 1840). Miniaturist. Bishop was a native of London, where he also received his early training and exhibited in 1787. About 1789 he made a visit to France, was exhibiting in London again in 1798, and was in Portugal about 1808. He emigrated to America in 1811, settling in Philadelphia, where he spent most of the rest of his life. A leader in the formative period of the Pennsylvania Academy, Bishop turned his attention in his last years almost exclusively to the Artists' Fund Society, and exhibited frequently at both from 1811 to 1841 (in the latter year as "deceased"). ANGELICA BISHOP, Philadelphia portrait painter, was his daughter. ¶ Sartain, *Reminiscences,* 71–74; Graves, *Dictionary;* Rutledge, PA; Brown and Brown; Phila. CD 1830–40; Dunlap, *History,* II, 263; represented at NYHS.

BISHOP, THOMAS. Landscape and marine painter, musician, Philadelphia, 1858–83. Listed in Philadelphia directories as a musician or professor of music (1858–81) and as an artist (1882–83), Thomas Bishop exhibited many landscapes at the Pennsylvania Academy from 1860 to 1869. The subjects of some of these suggest that Bishop either came from or had visited England. ¶ Rutledge, PA; Phila. CD 1858–83.

BISHOPBOIS, AUGUST. Lithographer and printer. Born in France *c.* 1814, Bishopbois was in Boston 1838–40, as Augustus Bishboy. He moved with his family to Philadelphia, where he was listed as a printer from 1844 to 1848, under the name A. Bishaboy. In 1850 Bishopbois was recorded in the Philadelphia Census as a lithographer, occupying a separate dwelling with his wife (aged 30, born in Virginia) and four children, Virginia (aged 12, born in Massachusetts), Henry (aged 10, born in Massachusetts), Lavinia (aged 5, born in Pennsylvania), and Julia (aged 6 months, born in Pennsylvania). *Cf.* BISCHEBOU. ¶ 7 Census (1850), Pa., LII, 933; Boston CD (Bishboy), 1838–40; Phila. CD (Bishaboy), 1844–48.

BISSELL, GEORGE EDWIN (1839–1920). Sculptor, born February 16, 1839, in New Preston (Conn.), the son of a stonecutter. It was not until after the Civil War that he joined his father in the marble business and began to study sculpture. In 1875, having filled several commissions in Poughkeepsie (N.Y.), he went to Europe for two years of study and thereafter he divided his time between America and Europe. In 1896 he settled in Mt. Vernon (N.Y.) where he died August 30, 1920. ¶ DAB; Mallett; represented at NYHS.

BISSY, ——. Drawing and music academy, Philadelphia, 1798–99. ¶ Brown and Brown.

BISSY, A. Miniature painter, Philadelphia, 1809–11. ¶ Brown and Brown.

BITTERS, NEZIAH WRIGHT (*c.* 1840–*c.* 1882). Artist, painter, and sign painter, Philadelphia, 1860–*c.* 1882. Bitters was born in Pennsylvania, the son of Lorenzo C. Bitters, cordwainer in Philadelphia. The 1860 census lists Neziah W. Bitters' occupation as artist; the directories from 1862 to 1881 list him variously as Neziah W., N. W., and N. Wright Bitters, painter, artist, or signpainter. He died about 1882, leaving a widow, Ruth Bitters. ¶ 8 Census (1860), Pa., LVI, 120; Phila. CD 1862–83.

BLACK, Miss ——. Landscape painter, Bethlehem (Pa.), exhibited at the National Academy in 1837. ¶ Cowdrey, NAD.

BLACK, JAMES. Lithographer; born in New York State about 1814; active in NYC from about 1850 until after 1880. He was with the firms SNYDER & BLACK and SNYDER, BLACK & STURN. In 1860 his real and personal property were valued at $20,000. ¶ 7 Census (1850), N.Y., XLIII, 3; NYCD 1850–80+; 8 Census (1860), N.Y., LVII, 320.

BLACK, MARY. Artist. Born in Pennsylvania *c.* 1842, Miss Black lived in Philadelphia in 1860 with her father, James R. Black, aged 44, born in Pennsylvania, a photographer. ¶ 8 Census (1860), Pa., L, 176.

BLACK, THURSTON W. Crayon portraitist, pastellist, and portrait painter. Better known as William T. or William Thurston Black, he was born in New Jersey *c.* 1810. He exhibited at the National Academy in 1845, address not given. In 1850 and 1851 he was living in Philadelphia with his wife Eliza (aged 37, born in New Jersey), and in 1850 he exhibited at the Pennsylvania Academy. Black apparently moved in 1851 to NYC, where he resided at least until 1860, exhibiting at the National Academy in 1851 and 1852. ¶ 7 Census (1850), Pa., L, 356; Phila. CD 1851; NYCD 1851, 1855, 1857, 1859–60; Cowdrey, NAD; Rutledge, PA.

BLACK, WILLIAM H. H. Scenic artist who painted for M. R. Cook a panorama of the workings of American Slavery. ¶ Indianapolis *Daily Indiana State Sentinel,* April 27, 1854 (courtesy J. Earl Arrington).

BLACK, WILLIAM THURSTON, see THURSTON W. BLACK

BLACKBURN, JOSEPH. Portrait painter. Presumably an English artist, Blackburn is known to have worked in Bermuda from

October 1752 into the next year and then to have come to New England. He was probably at Providence (R.I.) in 1754, but his main American work was done at Boston from 1755 to 1760. He was at Portsmouth (N.H.) in 1760 and appears to have divided his time between that town and Boston from 1761 to 1763. By January 1764 Blackburn was in London, where he is thought to have been again in 1778. The artist's name has been given erroneously as Jonathan B. Blackburn. ¶ Baker, "Notes on Joseph Blackburn and Nathaniel Dance," includes a chronological list of Blackburn's portraits (citation courtesy of T. Bolton); Morgan and Foote, "Joseph Blackburn"; Park, "Two Portraits by Blackburn"; Robie, "Waldo Portraits by Smibert and Blackburn"; DAB; Bolton, *Crayon Draftsmen.* Repros.: *Panorama,* V (Oct–Nov. 1949), cover; Met. Mus., *Life in America; Art Digest,* IV (Feb. 15, 1930), cover and p. 13; *Antiques,* LIX (March 1951), 224.

BLACKWELL, S. ELLEN. Genre painter, NYC, exhibited at the National Academy 1860–67 and at the Pennsylvania Academy in 1861. ¶ Cowdrey, NAD; Rutledge, PA.

BLADA, V., pseudonym of ADALBERT J. VOLCK.

BLADES, MARY. Watercolor artist, painted view of "Woodbury," St. Mary's County (Md.) before 1840. Miss Blades was governess of the Leigh children at "Woodbury" and later married Richard Miles. ¶ *Antiques,* LV (Feb. 1949), 134–35.

BLAIR, ——. Painter of "The Reception of Gen. Taylor at New Orleans," exhibited in March 1848 at New Orleans, and of a panorama of geology and biblical history, shown in St. Louis and Milwaukee in 1852. ¶ New Orleans *Picayune,* March 23, 1848, and St. Louis *Missouri Republican,* Jan. 20, 1852 (citations courtesy J. Earl Arrington); Butts, *Art in Wisconsin,* 53–54.

BLAIR, MARION (1824–1901). Portrait painter, Indiana. Born January 22, 1824, at Bloomington (Ind.), Blair spent most of his life in his native town, though he also worked in Indianapolis. He died at Bloomington in 1901. His portrait of Oliver P. Morton (*c.* 1862) is now owned by the Indiana State Library. ¶ Peat, *Pioneer Painters of Indiana,* 76–77.

BLAKE & CO. Engravers and printers, NYC, 1841. The head of the firm was WILLIAM W. BLAKE. ¶ NYCD 1841.

BLAKE, E. W. Itinerant portrait painter, at Philadelphia in 1860, also worked in New England. ¶ Penna. BD 1860; Sears, *Some American Primitives,* 287.

BLAKE, WILLIAM PHIPPS (1825–1910). Geologist and mining engineer, illustrator of his own geological writings. Blake was born in NYC June 21, 1825, trained as a mineralogist and chemist, and during a long career became one of the leading geologists of the country. His work as an artist was chiefly in connection with the Pacific Railroad surveys, 1854–56, his drawings being reproduced in *Report of a Geological Reconaissance in California* (N.Y. 1858) and in *U. S. Exploring Expeditions, V,* opp. p. 258. Blake died May 22, 1910. ¶ DAB; Union Catalogue, Library of Congress.

BLAKE, WILLIAM W. Engraver, NYC, 1841–50. In 1841 he was senior partner in the engraving and printing firm of BLAKE & CO. ¶ NYBD 1841; NYCD 1842–50; Stauffer.

BLANC, ANTHONY. Profile painter, Philadelphia, 1805. ¶ Brown and Brown; Fielding.

BLANCHARD, ALONZO. Sculptor, secured the first patent for a piece of sculpture under Patent Act of 1842. ¶ Gardner, *Yankee Stonecutters.*

BLANCHARD, CHARLES. Portrait painter, known only by his portrait of William Glover, owned in Maine. ¶ WPA (Mass.), *Portraits Found in Maine,* no. 881.

BLANCHARD, Mrs. ELIZA H. Portrait and miniature painter, Providence (R.I.), 1843–49. ¶ Providence *Almanac,* 1843, 1845, 1847, 1849; Bolton, *Miniature Painters.*

BLANCHARD, ELIZABETH. Art and Latin teacher at Mt. Holyoke College, of which she was a graduate, Class of 1850. She died November 29, 1891 at Springfield (Mass.). ¶ Boston *Transcript,* Nov. 30, 1891.

BLANCHARD, THOMAS. Sculptor, Boston. Asked permission in 1847 to make casts of busts in the Library of Congress at Washington, and in the same year exhibited two marble busts at the American Institute. ¶ Fairman, *Art and Artists,* 107; Am. Inst. Cat., 1847.

BLANCHARD, WASHINGTON (1808–?) Miniaturist of Boston, active 1831–49. He exhibited at the Athenaeum Gallery in 1835 and 1836. He visited Richmond (Va.) in the winter of 1838–39, Philadelphia in 1841, and Charleston (S.C.) in January

1844. In 1849, when he donated to the New-York Historical Society his miniature of Alexander Hill Everett, he was living in Boston. ¶ Swan, BA; Bolton, *Miniature Painters; Richmond Portraits,* 241; Rutledge, *Artists in the Life of Charleston;* Boston CD 1831–36; Rutledge, PA; NYHS Cat. (1941).

BLANCHETT, ——. Painter of watercolor miniatures about 1812. ¶ Information courtesy Mrs. W. H. Whitley of Paris (Ky.).

BLAUEL, CHARLES. Lithographer of Milwaukee (Wis.) in the late 1850's. ¶ Kent, "Early Commercial Lithography in Wisconsin," 249.

BLAUTEAU, E. Artist, Philadelphia, 1855–56. ¶ Phila. CD 1855–56.

BLAUVELT, CHARLES F. (1824–1900). N.A. Portrait and genre painter. Born in NYC, he worked there from 1847 to about 1862 when he moved to Philadelphia. He returned to NYC in 1867, was living in Yonkers in 1869, and later joined the faculty of the Naval Academy at Annapolis (Md.). He exhibited at the Washington Art Association, the Boston Athenaeum, the American Art-Union, the National Academy, and the Pennsylvania Academy. He died at Greenwich (Conn.) on April 16, 1900. ¶ *Art Annual,* III, obit.; Thieme-Becker; Cowdrey, NAD; NYBD 1851–57; *Who's Who in America,* 1900; Washington Art Assoc. Cat., 1857; Swan, BA; Cowdrey, AA & AAU; Rutledge, PA; 8 Census (1860), N.Y., LIII, 517.

BLECH, Miss C. Exhibited a drawing, "William Tell's Chapel," at the Artists' Fund Society in 1836. She was then a resident of Bethlehem (Pa.). This is probably Caroline Bleck, tutoress at the Moravian Seminary for Young Ladies, Bethlehem, from 1828 to 1845, living at Dover (Ohio) in 1874. ¶ Rutledge, PA; Reichel, *Moravian Seminary,* 314.

BLEECKER, JOHN R. Landscape and genre painter, exhibited at the National Academy 1837–42 and 1845, at the Apollo Association 1838–39. His address in 1838, 1841–42, and 1845 was NYC. ¶ Cowdrey, NAD; Cowdrey, AA & AAU.

BLENER or BEEMER, JAMES. Lithographer, born in Pennsylvania *c.* 1834, living in Philadelphia in 1860, with wife Catherine (aged 22, born Pa.), and two sons (ages 3 years and nine months, both born in Philadelphia). ¶ 8 Census (1860), Pa., LIX, 188.

BLICKER, GEORGE. Lithographer, Philadelphia, 1860. Blicker was born in Hannover (Germany) *c.* 1833; his wife Madelin was born in Bavaria *c.* 1833. They appear to have come to Philadelphia before 1855, since their three daughters were born in Pennsylvania between 1855 and 1859. ¶ 8 Census (1860), Pa., LII, 444.

BLISH, H. A. Engraver, Hampton (Pa.), 1860. ¶ Penna. BD 1860.

BLISS, EBERHARD & FESTNER. Booksellers and stationers, printsellers and metal engravers, Madison (Wis.), 1858. The partners were HORACE G. BLISS, JOHN EBERHARD, and FREDERICK C. FESTNER. ¶ Madison CD and BD 1858.

BLISS, HORACE G. Bookseller, stationer, and engraver [?], of BLISS, EBERHARD & FESTNER, Madison (Wis.), 1858. ¶ Madison CD 1858.

BLIVEN, Miss M. A. Still life painter, NYC, exhibited at the National Academy 1860, 1862–67. ¶ Cowdrey, NAD.

BLOCK, H. or J. P. Engraver, born in Maryland *c.* 1835, boarding in Washington (D.C.) in 1860. ¶ 8 Census (1860), D.C., I, 660.

BLOCK, LAURENS. Dutch artist of a view of New Amsterdam (now NYC) *c.* 1650. ¶ Stokes, *Iconography,* I, 138–39 and pl. 4; *Magazine of Art,* XL (April 1947), 141, repro.; Davidson, I, 37, repro.

BLODGET, SAMUEL. A Boston (Mass.) sutler, drew "A Prospective Plan of the Battle Fought Near Lake George" September 8, 1755, engraved by THOMAS JOHNSTON. ¶ Stauffer; *American Processional,* 24 and repro. p. 51; *Album of American Battle Art,* repro.; Davidson, I, 102–03, repro.

BLON, E. VAN. Landscape and marine artist. A series of views of the Susquehanna River, the vicinity of Baltimore, the Highlands of the Hudson, and a Mississippi River pilot station were drawn and colored by Blon for a *Progressive Drawing Book,* published at Baltimore in 1827. ¶ Drepperd, "Rare American Prints," reproduces four of Blon's views, from JOHN HILL's engravings in *Progressive Drawing Book* (Baltimore, F. Lucas, Jr., *c.* 1827).

BLONDE, ADOLPH. Engraver, Washington (D.C.), 1860. Blonde was born in France *c.* 1812. His Washington household included Edith Blonde (French, aged 50), GESTON BLONDE (French, aged 21), and an Irish servant-girl, aged 18. ¶ 8 Census (1860), D.C., II, 551.

BLONDE, GESTON. Engraver, Washington

(D.C.), 1860. Geston (probably an error for Gaston) Blonde was born in France *c.* 1839, probably the son of ADOLPH BLONDE, with whom he lived in Washington in 1860. ¶ 8 Census (1860), D.C., II, 551.

BLONDEL or BLONDELL, JACOB D. (1817–1877). A.N.A. Portrait, genre, religious, and landscape painter. A native of NYC and a pupil there of WILLIAM PAGE, Blondel first exhibited at the Apollo Association in 1839 and thereafter was a frequent exhibitor at the Apollo Association (1839–41), the American Art-Union (1847), the National Academy (1840–72), the Boston Athenaeum (1860, 1863), and the Washington Art Association (1857). Except for a brief residence in Washington in 1847–48, Blondel made his home in NYC. His last years were spent in poverty and he is said to have starved to death in his studio. ¶ Clement and Hutton; Cowdrey, AA & AAU; Cowdrey, NAD; Swan, BA; Washington Art Assoc. Cat., 1857; 7 Census (1850), N.Y., LII, 89; 8 Census (1860), N.Y., LVII, 362; Fielding.

BLOOD & EVANS. Lithographic printers, Boston, 1857–58. The partners were JOHN H. BLOOD and CHARLES A. EVANS. ¶ Boston CD 1857; Boston BD 1857 (as Blood, Evans & Co.); *Boston Almanac,* 1858.

BLOOD, JOHN H. Lithographer, of BLOOD & EVANS, Boston, 1857–58. ¶ Boston CD 1857; *Boston Almanac* 1858.

BLOOME, ROBERT. German engraver, 29, at NYC in 1850. His wife was also German; one child, aged one year, was born in England; a second child, aged 5 months, was born in NYC. ¶ 7 Census (1850), N.Y., LI, 137.

BLOOMER, EDWARD. Engraver, 22, born in New York State, at NYC in 1860. ¶ 8 Census (1860), N.Y., LI, 244.

BLOSS, MICHAEL. Wood engraver from Bavaria, aged 31, at NYC in 1860. His wife Laura was a native of Prussia; their two older children, ages 2 and 4, were born in Wisconsin; the youngest child, aged 7 months, was born in New York. Bloss was listed as a carver in 1863. ¶ 8 Census (1860), N.Y., LVII, 463; NYCD 1863.

BLUCHER, JOSEPH. Lithographer, Philadelphia, 1850. Blucher was born in France *c.* 1810. His wife Mary, also French, was born *c.* 1795. They came to Pennsylvania before 1844, their two daughters, Mary and Catherine, being born there *c.* 1844 and 1847. ¶ 7 Census (1850), Pa., L, 593.

BLUCHER, XAVIER. Lithographer, Philadelphia, 1853–55. ¶ Phila. CD 1853–55.

BLUM & DAVIS. Copperplate and steel engravers, Philadelphia, 1857. The senior partner may have been ROBERT D. BLUM, though he is listed in the City Directory for the same year as senior partner in the engraving firm of BLUM & JEFFRAYS. Davis has not been identified. ¶ Phila. CD (business section) 1857, address 116 Chestnut St.

BLUM & JEFFRAYS. Engravers, Philadelphia, 1857. The senior partner was ROBERT D. BLUM, but Jeffrays has not been identified. The firm was located at 106 Chestnut Street (cf. BLUM & DAVIS). ¶ Phila. CD 1857.

BLUM, ROBERT D. Engraver. Blum was senior partner in the firm of BLUM & JEFFRAYS, Philadelphia, 1857, and probably of BLUM & DAVIS, Philadelphia, 1857. He seems to have moved to Nashville (Tenn.) where R. D. Blum, engraver, was listed in the 1859–60 directories. ¶ Phila. CD 1857; Phila. BD 1857; Nashville CD 1859, 1860.

BLUMNER, FREDERICK. Portrait and landscape painter, lithographer. Blumner worked in NYC in 1856 and 1859, in Brooklyn in 1859. His "Winter Scene in the Country" was published *c.* 1865. ¶ NYBD 1856, 1859; Peters, *America on Stone,* pl. 13; *Portfolio,* XI (Jan. 1952), 103, repro.

BLUNT, EDMUND. Engraver, NYC, 1819–20. ¶ NYCD 1819–20.

BLUNT, JOHN S. (1798–1835). Landscape and marine, portrait and miniature painter. Blunt was born in 1798, probably at Portsmouth (N.H.) where he spent most of his life. In 1821 he was listed in the Portsmouth business directory as an ornamental and portrait painter and in the same year he married in Boston. Blunt advertised in 1822 that he did "profiles, profile miniature pictures, landscapes and ornamental painting" and in 1825 that he proposed opening a drawing academy in Portsmouth. He may have visited NYC about 1823, when he painted "Picknick on Long Island." Blunt exhibited at the Boston Athenaeum in 1829 (mistakenly listed as Joseph S. Blunt) and 1831, and appears to have been working in Boston in 1830. He died at the age of 37 on a ship traveling between New Orleans and Boston. ¶ Little, "J. S. Blunt, New England Landscape Painter," eight repros.; Swan, BA (under Joseph S. Blunt); C. K.

Bolton, "Workers with Line and Color"; Karolik Cat., 124–27.

BLUNT, JOSEPH S., see JOHN S. BLUNT.

BLUNT, SIMON F. Landscape artist. Lieutenant Blunt, U.S.N., accompanied Commander Cadwalader Ringgold on a surveying expedition to California in 1849–50 and there made several sketches of the California coast which were reproduced in Ringgold's *A Series of Charts, with Sailing Directions,* 1852. ¶ Peters, *California on Stone.*

BLYDENBURG, S. Sign and ornamental painter, gilder, and paper hanger, Hartford (Conn.), 1799. Blydenburg advertised in May 1799 in the *Connecticut Courant* as a sign painter accomplished in "other branches of PAINTING," and in July advertised for an "Active ingenious lad as an apprentice." ¶ [Hartford] *Connecticut Courant,* May 20–27 and July 15, 1799.

BLYTH (Blythe), BENJAMIN. Portraitist in oils, crayons, and miniature; engraver and ornamental painter. The brother (?) of the Salem portrait painter SAMUEL BLYTH, Benjamin was baptized in Salem May 18, 1746. He advertised in the *Salem Gazette* May 10–17, 1769, and is reported to have been living there as late as 1787. In July and August 1786, however, he was in Richmond (Va.) where he advertised as a limner, gilder, and ornamental painter. Stauffer states that Blyth was born in 1740, married in 1769, admitted to the Essex Lodge in 1781, and did portraits of George and Martha Washington which were engraved by JOHN NORMAN and published in Boston in 1780 and 1782. An allegorical engraving by "Blyth" has been ascribed to him. ¶ Belknap, *Artists and Craftsmen of Essex County,* 3, 6; [Richmond] *Virginia Gazette,* July 18–August 16, 1786; Stauffer, I, 23–24, and II, nos. 2351, 2356; Bolton, *Crayon Draftsmen;* Essex Institute *Hist. Coll.,* LXXIX (Oct. 1943), 370; *Art in America,* XXXIII (Oct. 1945), 198, two repros.; *Antiques Journal* (Jan. 1954), 14, repro.

BLYTH (Blythe), SAMUEL. Heraldic and portrait painter, Salem (Mass.). This artist, possibly a brother of BENJAMIN BLYTH, was baptized at Salem in 1744. His father, Samuel Blyth, was a sailmaker. The younger Samuel became a painter, married Abigail Massey, and died in 1795. He is known to have painted a house in July 1782. Belknap, however, combines the two into one Samuel Blyth, sailmaker and painter, 1721–1774, who married Abigail Massey and was the father of BENJAMIN and William Blyth. ¶ Perley, *History of Salem,* III, 369; Essex Institute *Hist. Coll.,* LXXVI, 45; Belknap, *Artists and Craftsmen of Essex County,* 6; WPA (Mass.), *Portraits Found in Maine,* II, 523.

BLYTHE, DAVID GILMOUR (1815–1865). Portrait and genre painter, sculptor and carver, panoramist, illustrator, and poet. Blythe was born May 9, 1815, near East Liverpool (Ohio) and was apprenticed to a Pittsburgh (Pa.) wood carver 1832–35. He worked as a carpenter and house painter at Pittsburgh 1835–36, but in the latter year went to New Orleans. From 1837 to 1840 Blythe served in the U. S. Navy as a ship's carpenter, cruising to Boston and the West Indies, etc. On his release from the Navy, he became an itinerant portrait painter in western Pennsylvania and eastern Ohio (1841–45), settled at Uniontown (Pa.) 1846–51, and toured with a panorama to Cumberland and Baltimore (Md.), Pittsburgh (Pa.), and Cincinnati and East Liverpool (Ohio). While in Uniontown he carved a statue of Lafayette for the County Courthouse. From 1852 to 1855 he continued to paint portraits in western Pennsylvania, and in 1853 he visited Indiana. His last years, from 1855 to 1865, were spent in Pittsburgh. He died May 15, 1865, in the Passavant Hospital, Pittsburgh, and was buried at East Liverpool (Ohio). ¶ Miller, *The Life and Work of David G. Blythe,* with checklist and 21 repros.; Abraham, "David G. Blythe"; O'Connor, "David G. Blythe"; Rutledge, PA; Cincinnati *Daily Gazette,* Feb. 26, 1852 (courtesy J. Earl Arrington). Represented at Carnegie Institute, Rochester Museum, Brooklyn Museum, and National Baseball Museum, Cooperstown (N.Y.). Special exhibitions at Carnegie Institute (1932–33) and Whitney Museum (1936).

BOAL, JAMES MCC. (1800?–1862). Known only for painting of Fort Snelling (Minn.), owned by the Minnesota Historical Society. ¶ Courtesy of Bertha Heilbron, Minn. Hist. Soc.; *American Heritage,* II (Autumn 1950), 42, repro.

BOARDLEY, B., see JOHN BEALE BORDLEY.

BOARDLEY, PEALE, see JOHN BEALE BORDLEY.

BOARDLEY, THOMAS. Engraver, Boston, 1842–50. Boardley was born in England *c.* 1813 and emigrated to America between 1840 and 1842, judging from the dates and places of birth of his five children. ¶ 7 Census (1850), Mass., I (part 1), 326.

BOARDLEY, WILLIAM. Engraver, Boston, 1851. ¶ Boston CD 1851.

BOARDMAN, Mrs. G. A. Crayon portraitist, Binghamton (N.Y.), exhibited at the National Academy in 1860. ¶ Cowdrey, NAD.

BOARDMAN, WILLIAM G. Landscape, portrait, and miniature painter. He was born in Cazenovia (N.Y.), probably about 1815, and entered Cazenovia Seminary in 1830. He was launched on his artistic career by 1841, when he was at Cleveland (Ohio). He worked in New Haven (Conn.) in 1846 and Charlestown (Mass.) in 1847, but from 1848 into the sixties he had his studio in NYC. He was a frequent exhibitor at the National Academy, American Art-Union, and Boston Athenaeum. From 1868 to 1871 he was at Providence (R.I.) and from 1874 to 1877 in Boston. He is said to have died in Providence at the age of 80. ¶ Miner, *Angell's Lane,* App. B, vi; *First Fifty Years of Cazenovia Seminary,* 409; *Annals of Cleveland,* July 1841; Cowdrey, NAD; Cowdrey, AA & AAU; Swan, BA; NYCD 1857–60; Providence CD 1868–71; Boston CD 1874, 1877; Phila. *Public Ledger,* April 13 and 28, May 1, 1854 (courtesy J. Earl Arrington).

BOARDMAN, WILLIAM H. Engraver, of DAVIES & BOARDMAN, Boston, 1860. ¶ Boston CD 1860.

BOBBETT, ALBERT or ALFRED. Wood engraver; born in England about 1824; active in NYC and Brooklyn, 1848–88. Bobbett was a partner in BOBBETT & EDMONDS (1848–54). In 1855 he and EDWARD HOOPER had the same business address, though the firm of BOBBETT & HOOPER was not listed in the directory until the following year. Bobbett & Hooper continued to operate as wood engravers in NYC until 1865; in 1867 they were listed in Brooklyn as printers and from 1868 to 1870 as "chromos." After the break-up of this partnership, Bobbett returned to NYC and worked there as an engraver from 1871 until his death in 1888 or 1889. At his death Bobbett left a widow, Marian, and a son, Walter, who was an artist. Albert Bobbett was an Honorary Member of the American Society of Painters in Water Colors, 1867–73. ¶ NYCD 1848–65, 1871–79, 1883–89; Brooklyn CD 1867–70. Smith, citing Thieme-Becker, gives the name as Alfred Bobbett and his dates as *c.* 1840–88; 7 Census (1850), N.Y., LII, 205 [as Alfred Bobbets]; information courtesy Mary Bartlett Cowdrey.

BOBBETT, ALFRED, see ALBERT BOBBETT.

BOBBETT & EDMONDS. Wood engravers, NYC, 1848–54. The partners were ALBERT BOBBETT and CHARLES EDMONDS. ¶ NYCD 1848–54; NYBD 1854.

BOBBETT & HOOPER. Wood engravers, NYC, 1855–65. The partners were ALBERT BOBBETT and EDWARD HOOPER. Though the firm was not listed before 1856, Bobbett and Hooper were working at the same address in 1855. They were also listed in the Brooklyn directory in 1867 as printers and in 1868–70 as "chromos." They exhibited at the National Academy in 1869. ¶ NYCD 1855–65; Brooklyn CD 1867–70; Hamilton, 213, records engravings by Bobbett & Hooper in *Ten Years Among the Mail Bags* (Phila., 1855); Cowdrey, NAD (1869).

BOCHLER, see BOEHLER.

BODEN, EDWARD. Artist, Philadelphia, 1860. Boden (aged 33) and his wife Clementia (milliner, aged 35) were both born in France, as were two children (aged 7 and 9). A third child, Emily (aged 5), was born in N.Y., which suggests that the Bodens came to NYC shortly before 1855 and settled in Philadelphia before 1860. ¶ 8 Census (1860), Pa., LV, 126.

BODIN, LOUIS. Artist and cleaner of old engravings, Philadelphia, 1808–09, 1811, 1813. ¶ Brown and Brown.

BODMER, KARL (or Charles) (1809–1893). Lithographer, engraver, painter of American Indians and landscapes; born February 6, 1809, at Riesbach (Switzerland); died October 30, 1893, at Barbizon (France). In 1832–34 Bodmer accompanied Maximilian, Prince of Wied-Neuwied, on a tour of the United States, which took them to Massachusetts, Rhode Island, New York, New Jersey, Pennsylvania, Ohio, Indiana, Illinois, Missouri, Nebraska, North and South Dakota, and Montana. The 81 plates in Maximilian's *Travels* are based on sketches made by Bodmer, including landscapes, views of towns, portraits, studies of equipment, and numerous Indian studies. ¶ Thieme-Becker; Wied-Neuwied, *Travels in the Interior of North America, 1832–34;* De Voto, *Across the*

Wide Missouri; Draper, "American Indians—Barbizon Style—The Collaborative Paintings of Millet and Bodmer"; Draper, "Karl Bodmer—An Artist among the Indians"; Weitenkampf, "A Swiss Artist Among the Indians"; *Ladies Garland,* III (1849), repros. opp. 37, 166; Davidson, I, 168, 194, 196, 208–09 and II, 241, repros.; Smithsonian Institution, "Carl Bodmer Paints the Indian Frontier."

BODSTEIN, HERMAN. Engraver, Chicago, 1856. ¶ Chicago BD 1856.

BOEHLER, JOHN E. Lithographer, New Orleans, 1841–70. Boehler was born in Baden (Germany) *c.* 1811. He was working in New Orleans as early as 1841. In 1845 and 1846 the directories list him as J. E. Bockler and J. E. Bochler, respectively. In 1850 Boehler was living in New Orleans with his wife and two daughters. He made a lithograph of St. Paul's Church in 1854 and was still working in New Orleans as late as 1870. ¶ 7 Census (1850), La., V, 84; New Orleans CD 1841, 1845–46, 1850–56, 1859–61, 1867, 1870; Delgado-WPA, cites *Bee,* May 27, 1854.

BOEHMORE, FRANCIS. Engraver, Philadelphia, 1850. Boehmore was born in Pennsylvania *c.* 1828 and was living at Southwark (Philadelphia County) in 1850. ¶ 7 Census (1850), Pa., LV, 655.

BOELL & LEWIS. Lithographers, NYC, 1855. The partners were WILLIAM BOELL and GEORGE W. LEWIS. ¶ NYCD 1855.

BOELL & MICHELIN. Lithographers, NYC, 1856–58; FRANCIS MICHELIN and WILLIAM BOELL. ¶ NYCD 1856–58.

BOELL (Boele), WILLIAM. Lithographer, NYC (1854–57) and Philadelphia (1859–60 and after). In 1855 he was in the firm of BOELL & LEWIS, lithographers of NYC; in 1856–58, with BOELL & MICHELIN. ¶ NYCD 1854–58; Phila. CD 1859–61; Peters, *America on Stone.*

BOERUM, SIMEON. Wood engraver and printer, Philadelphia, 1856–60 and after. Boerum was listed as an engraver in 1856 and 1858 at different addresses, but in 1857 the engraving firm of BARTON & BOERUM was listed at the address given for Simeon Boerum in 1858. S. Boerum, cigar store, was also listed at this address in 1856–57. ¶ Phila. CD 1856–60 and after.

BOESE, HENRY. Landscape and portrait painter, NYC, 1844–63. Exhibited at the National Academy in 1847, 1857, 1859, and 1863. In the 1860 Census he was listed as a native New Yorker, aged 36; his wife Charlotte and their three children, ages six to one year, were also born in New York. ¶ NYCD, 1844–54, 1856; NYBD 1857–60; Cowdrey, NAD; 8 Census (1860), N.Y., LX, 77; *American Processional,* 244, repro. 145; Sherman, "Unrecorded Early American Painters" (1943), 208, as H. Beese.

BOESSER, H. Wood engraver, Louisville (Ky.), 1850. Boesser was born in Germany *c.* 1820. ¶ 7 Census (1850), Ky., XI, 488.

BOETTGER (Bottger), ADOLPH. Lithographer (1856), painter (1857), artist (1858), Buffalo (N.Y.). ¶ Buffalo CD 1856–58.

BOETTICHER, OTTO (*c.* 1816–?). Military artist and lithographer. Probably a Prussian by birth, for he served in the Prussian Army, Boetticher came to America about 1850 and had a studio in NYC from 1851 to 1858. In 1851 he was in partnership with CHARLES GILDEMEISTER. During the fifties Boetticher produced a number of lithographs of military subjects, including the 1855 encampment of the 7th Regiment, N. Y. National Guard, and the 8th Regiment on duty at the Quarantine Station on Staten Island. From 1861 to 1864 he was an officer of the 68th N. Y. Volunteers. He was captured in March 1862 and while a prisoner at Salisbury (N.C.) he made a well-known drawing of a baseball game among the prisoners. Boetticher was brevetted lieutenant-colonel in 1865 "for gallant and meritorious conduct" during the war. Of his later career nothing is known. ¶ Information courtesy Major John V. Gallagher, Office of the Adjutant General, Albany (N.Y.), August 30, 1954; *Album of American Battle Art;* Stokes, *Iconography,* III, 708 [the 1855 7th Regiment print misdated 1835]; NYCD 1851–58; *Portfolio* (Oct. 1941), 23; *Antiques* (May 1936), 202; Davidson, II, 58–59.

BOGARDUS, ABRAM. Painter, exhibited at American Institute in 1845. Rutgers University owns a pastel portrait of Thomas DeWitt inscribed "A. Bogardus, New York, B'Way and 27th St." Abraham Bogardus, daguerreotypist and photographer, is listed in NYC directories from 1847 to 1860. ¶ Am. Inst. Cat., 1845; WPA (N.J.), Hist. Records Survey; NYCD 1847–60.

BOGARDUS, JAMES (1800–1874). Engraver, diesinker, inventor; born March 14, 1800, at Catskill (N.Y.); died April 13, 1874, in NYC. Stauffer states that Bogardus learned engraving while apprenticed to a watchmaker *c.* 1814, but he was best known in his own day as a machinist and inventor. His name was especially associated with the eccentric mill (1829), a number of improved machines for engraving, and the introduction of cast-iron buildings. Bogardus was in England *c.* 1836–39, with his wife (see Mrs. JAMES BOGARDUS), a miniaturist, and there engraved portraits of Queen Victoria and Sir Robert Peel, as well as winning a competition to furnish the British Government with a plan for the manufacture of the first postage stamps. After visiting France and Italy, Bogardus returned to NYC in 1840 and worked there as a machinist, manufacturer of eccentric mills, and architect in cast-iron until his death. ¶ Dunlap, *History* (1918), III, 284; Stauffer, I, 24; N. Y. *Evening Post* (Semi-Weekly), April 17, 1874, obit.; NYCD 1842–74.

BOGARDUS, Mrs. JAMES (née Margaret Maclay) (1804–1878). A.N.A. Portrait and miniature painter; daughter of Archibald Maclay, D.D.; married the inventor-engraver JAMES BOGARDUS, and accompanied him to England in the 1830's. She exhibited at the Royal Academy in 1839. On her return to NYC Mrs. Bogardus exhibited at the National Academy 1842–43, 1845–46, 1868/69. She was made an Associate of the Academy. She has been listed as Mrs. M. Bogardus (Smith) and as Mrs. William Bogardus (Mallett, and Bolton). ¶ Cowdrey, NAD; Graves, *Dictionary;* Smith; Mallett; Bolton, *Miniature Painters.*

BOGARDUS, JOHN D. Lithographer, of BOGARDUS & LEWIS, Buffalo (N.Y.), 1857. There was a John D. Bogardus, bookkeeper, listed in 1854, probably the same. ¶ Buffalo CD 1854, 1857.

BOGARDUS & LEWIS. Lithographers, Buffalo (N.Y.), 1857. The partners were JOHN D. BOGARDUS and C. E. LEWIS. ¶ Buffalo CD 1857.

BOGARDUS, WILLIAM. Listed as an engraver and die-sinker and/or miniaturist in Bolton, *Miniature Painters,* in Fielding, in Mallett, and in Smith. Although there was a William Bogardus, house painter, in NYC 1844–60, the information given by the above authors indicates that his name has been inadvertently applied to the work of JAMES BOGARDUS, engraver and die-sinker, and Mrs. JAMES BOGARDUS, miniaturist. There is no evidence that William Bogardus was an artist. ¶ Bolton, *Miniature Painters;* Fielding; Smith; Mallett; NYCD 1844–60.

BOGARDUS, Mrs. WILLIAM, see Mrs. JAMES BOGARDUS.

BOGART, ROBERT M. Wood engraver, of BROSS & BOGART, NYC, 1856–57. ¶ NYBD 1856; NYCD 1857.

BOGERT & BROWN. Wood engravers, NYC, 1850. The partners were J. AUGUSTUS BOGERT and CHARLES F. BROWN. ¶ NYCD and NYBD 1850.

BOGERT, CHARLES. Engraver, 22, born in New York State, living in NYC in 1850. ¶ 7 Census (1850), N.Y., XLVII, 827.

BOGERT, DAVID. Wood engraver, 22, living in NYC in 1860. He was born in New York State, the son of John D. and Caroline Bogert. ¶ 8 Census (1860), N.Y., XLVI, 404.

BOGERT, J. AUGUSTUS. Wood engraver, active 1850–81. He was listed in NYC directories in 1850. The 1850 Census lists an Augustus Bogart, engraver, at NYC in 1850; his age was 53 and he was a native New Yorker. ¶ NYBD and NYCD 1850; 7 Census (1850), N.Y., XLVI, 752; Hamilton, *Early American Book Illustrators and Wood Engravers.*

BOGGS, ROBERT R. Portrait, genre, and landscape painter. Boggs exhibited at the National Academy in 1851 and 1859, the latter year two Italian scenes. In 1857 R. Boggs of Augusta (Ga.) exhibited at the Washington Art Association. Robert R. Boggs was working as a portrait and landscape painter at Mobile (Ala.) in 1859 and in 1870. ¶ Cowdrey, NAD; Washington Art Assoc. Cat., 1857; WPA (Ala.), Hist. Records Survey, cites *Mobile Advertiser and Register,* Nov. 3, 1859; Mobile CD 1870.

BOGGS, WILLIAM BRENTON. A.N.A. Landscape artist in oils, water colors, and pencil, born July 2, 1809, New Brunswick (N.J.); died March 11, 1875, Georgetown (D.C.). Boggs was educated at Captain Partridge's Military School, Middletown (Conn.) and later was employed by the Phoenix Bank of NYC. He exhibited landscapes of New York, New Jersey, and New Hampshire at the National Academy 1839–41 and 1844, and was an Associate of the Academy from 1842 to 1845. In 1842 he became a civilian clerk in the Navy Department at Washington and married Eleanor Carter, daughter of Charles Beale Carter of

"Sabine Hall" (Va.). He was commissioned Purser in the U. S. Navy on November 30, 1852, serving for the next four years with the Pacific Surveying Expedition on the U.S.S. *Vincennes,* under Commodore Cadwalader Ringgold and Commander John Rodgers. Boggs was spoken of as an artist of the expedition and certainly made some pencil landscapes at this time. In 1856 Boggs was on special duty in Washington; from 1857 to 1859 with the U.S.S. *Plymouth*; from 1859 to 1861 with the U.S.S. *Wyoming* in the Pacific Squadron; in 1862 with the Bureau of Provisions; from 1862 to 1864 with the Mississippi Squadron, Western Flotilla, as Purchasing Pay Master with special duty. Boggs was injured in 1864 while rescuing books and papers from a fire on board the S.S. *Mound City*. He was stationed in Washington from 1864 to 1873, as Pay Director from 1871. He retired in 1873 and died two years later. He had exhibited at the First Annual Exhibition, Washington Art Association in 1857, as well as at the National Academy. His work is represented at the Corcoran Gallery, Washington. ¶ Boggs, *Genealogical Record of the Boggs Family,* 28; [Washington] *Evening Star,* March 11, 1875, obit.; Cowdrey, NAD and letter from the Secretary of the National Academy, Jan. 15, 1948; transcript of naval orders to Pay Director William Brenton Boggs, prepared by Bureau of Naval Personnel and sent Sept. 18, 1947, by Office of Naval Records and Library; Knox, *History of the U. S. Navy,* 182; Order No. 6, issued by Commodore Ringgold, dated June 23, 1853, and quoted in letter from Director, Naval Records and Library, Sept. 18, 1947; two dated pencil landscapes, acquired by Corcoran Gallery Jan. 23, 1948, prove that Boggs worked as an artist while on the Expedition; two watercolor landscapes, acquired by the Corcoran Gallery at the same time, show that Boggs worked in water colors and, though undated, the subjects suggest that they may also have been done on this expedition; *Navy Register,* Vol. 11, 1859–61, p. 96 of 1861 section; Washington Art Assoc. Cat. 1857, nos. 39, 40, and 41; *American Paintings in The Corcoran Gallery of Art,* 30, landscape in oils. [All information courtesy Josephine Morton Bever.]

BOGLE, JAMES (*c.* 1817–1873). N.A. Portrait, genre, and fancy painter. The twin brother of ROBERT BOGLE, he was born in Georgetown (S.C.) between 1817 (CAB) and 1820 (1860 Census, under Robert Bogle). James and Robert were both working in Charleston in 1840–41, in Baltimore in 1842 and again in Charleston in 1843. In 1843 James moved to NYC and he remained there, except for at least one visit to Charleston in 1849, until his death in Brooklyn on October 12, 1873. He exhibited at the National Academy, of which he was made an Academician in 1861, and at the Washington Art Association. ¶ CAB; 8 Census (1860), D.C., I, 49 [Robert Bogle]; Rutledge, *Artists in the Life of Charleston,* 186–87; Baltimore CD 1842; NYBD 1844; NYCD 1846+ [sometimes as Boyle]; Cowdrey, NAD; Washington Art Assoc. Cats., 1857, 1859; Stauffer, nos. 305, 2561; Fielding, Supplement to Stauffer, no. 1228; repro., *NYHS Quarterly,* Oct. 1944, 160; represented: NYHS.

BOGLE, ROBERT (*c.* 1817–?). Portrait and fancy painter. The twin brother of JAMES BOGLE, he was born in Georgetown (S.C.) between 1817 (CAB) and 1820 (1860 Census). He was working with his brother in Charleston in 1840–41, in Baltimore 1842, and again in Charleston in 1843. The brothers then separated, James going to NYC and Robert to New Orleans, where he was in January 1844. Robert married Adelaide Bailey, a wealthy heiress, in 1845, and his eldest daughter, Ada, was born in South Carolina *c.* 1846. A son, Robert, was born *c.* 1848 in Italy and a second son, Harry, in Maryland *c.* 1850. Robert Bogle may have exhibited at the Washington Art Association in 1857 and 1859. He was living in Baltimore in 1859–60, but at the time of the 1860 Census (June 6) he was living in Georgetown (D.C.) with his wife, three sons, and two daughters; at that time he owned $5,000 in real and $10,000 in personal property. In November 1860 Bogle was in Charleston again, advertising as a portrait painter. Of his subsequent career nothing is known. ¶ 8 Census (1860), D.C., I, 49; Rutledge, *Artists in the Life of Charleston;* Baltimore CD 1842, 1859–60; Delgado-WPA, cites *Picayune,* Jan. 7 and 9, 1844.

BÖHM, G. Lithographer, of LEWIS & BÖHM, San Francisco, 1857. ¶ Peters, *California on Stone.*

BOHN, C. Artist of an elaborate view of the

University of Virginia, drawn in 1856. ¶ Reproduced in *American Collector,* XIII (March 1944), 3.

BOHURD (or Bohhurd), G. A. Lithographer, New Orleans, *c.* 1844–60. Bohurd was born in Baden (Germany) *c.* 1810, married there, and had a daughter Emilia born in Baden *c.* 1840. Bohurd brought his family to America between 1840 and 1844, his son Julius being born at New Orleans in the latter year. A second son, Emile Bohurd (listed as an engraver in 1860), was born at New Orleans *c.* 1846 and a third, John, *c.* 1856. Bohurd, his wife, and their four children were living together in New Orleans in June 1860. He is not listed in the directories for 1858 and 1870. ¶ 8 Census (1860), La., VIII, 15.

BOILEAU, JAMES G. Artist, born *c.* 1840 in Pennsylvania, working in Philadelphia on July 23, 1860. The Philadelphia directories list James G. Boileau as clerk (1861) and conductor (1862–63). ¶ 8 Census (1860), Pa., LII, 696; Phila. CD 1861–63.

BOILLY, ——. Stipple engraver who worked for ASHER B. DURAND in NYC during the 1820's. He was the son of a French painter. ¶ Durand, *Life and Times of Asher B. Durand,* 90.

BOISSEAU, ALFRED (1823–?) Portrait and genre painter, drawing and painting teacher, and art dealer. Boisseau was born in 1823 in Paris and exhibited at the Salon in 1842. He was in New Orleans in 1845 and 1846, and in NYC in 1849 and 1852, when he exhibited at the National Academy and American Art-Union, respectively. He apparently moved to Cleveland (Ohio) late in 1852, advertising there in December 1852 and January 1853 as a portrait and landscape painter, teacher of drawing and painting, and art dealer. He was in Cleveland as late as 1859. ¶ Bénézit; Delgado-WPA, cites *Bee,* Jan. 3, 1845; New Orleans CD 1846; Cowdrey, NAD; Cowdrey, AA & AAU; WPA (Ohio), *Annals of Cleveland;* Cleveland CD 1853, 1859; Seebold, *Old Louisiana Plantation Homes and Family Trees,* I, opp. p. 22; Cleveland CD 1857.

BOISSEAU, S. D. Artist, portrait painter, and daguerreotypist, Cleveland, 1857. Probably the same as ALFRED BOISSEAU, who was listed in 1856 as portrait painter and daguerreotypist. ¶ Cleveland CD 1856–57; BD 1857.

BOIT, EDWARD DARLING (or Darley). Painter, noted mainly for his watercolors. He was born in 1840 in Boston, and died April 22, 1916, in Rome. ¶ *Art Annual,* XIV, 313; Clement and Hutton; Mallett.

BOLEN, JOHN GEORGE. Engraver, printer, and gunsmith. Bolen was thus listed in NYC from 1834 to 1846, in NYC and Brooklyn from 1847 to 1850. From 1851 to 1857 he was listed only as gunsmith or seller of guns and pistols. ¶ NYCD 1834–57; Stauffer, I, 25, as J. G. Bolen.

BOLLES, FRANK, JR. Wood engraver, Hartford (Conn.), 1859–60. ¶ Hartford CD 1859–60.

BOLLES, JESSE. H. Artist, daguerreotypist, and photographer, Charleston (S.C.), 1857 and 1859. In 1857 he was a partner in WENDEROTH & BOLLES. ¶ Rutledge, *Artists in the Life of Charleston.*

BOLLET, CHARLES. Swiss engraver, aged 40, living in Philadelphia in 1860 with his wife and month-old daughter. EDWARD HEGUERIN boarded with them. ¶ 8 Census (1860), Pa., L, 526.

BOLLMAN or BOLMAN, CAROLINE. Philadelphia miniaturist who exhibited at the Pennsylvania Academy in 1823 and 1827. ¶ Rutledge, PA; Bolton, *Miniature Painters;* Fielding.

BOLTON, ABBY (1827–1849). Exhibited a flower painting at the National Academy in 1845. A daughter of the Rev. Robert Bolton (1788–1857), she was born February 3, 1827, at Henley-on-Thames (England); came to America with her family in 1836; lived at Pelham (N.Y.) from 1838 until her death on June 16, 1849. She was a sister of ADELAIDE, JOHN, and WILLIAM JAY BOLTON. The Abby Bolton of Pelham who exhibited flower paintings at the National Academy in 1871 and 1872 may have been her niece (1849–1885), daughter of the Rev. JOHN BOLTON of West Chester (Pa.). ¶ Bolton, *The Family of Bolton,* 385; Cowdrey, NAD. An account of her life, *The Lighted Valley; or the Closing Scenes of the Life of Abby Bolton* (New York, 1850), was written by her sister, Anne (Nannette) Bolton.

BOLTON, ADELAIDE (1830–?). Flower painter who exhibited at the National Academy in 1870 as a resident of Brighton (England). One of the daughters of the Rev. Robert Bolton (1788–1857), she was born March 5, 1830, at Henley-on-Thames (England); lived at Pelham (N.Y.) from 1838 to 1850; and spent the rest of her life in England. She was a sister of ABBY, JOHN, and WILLIAM JAY BOLTON. ¶ Bolton, *The Family of Bolton,* 386; Cowdrey, NAD.

BOLTON, JOHN (1818–1898). Architect, glass stainer, and wood carver. Born February 7, 1818, at Bath (England), a son of the Rev. Robert Bolton (1788–1857). He came to America with his parents in 1836 and became an architect, but in 1862 he took orders in the Episcopal Church. From 1864 to 1891 he was Rector of the Church of the Holy Trinity in West Chester (Pa.) and from 1891 until his death Dean of Chester. Examples of his stained glass and wood carvings, done in collaboration with his brother WILLIAM JAY BOLTON, are in Christ Church and Pelham Priory (Pelham, N.Y.) and the Church of the Holy Trinity (Brooklyn, N.Y.). John Bolton had a daughter Abby (1849–1885) who may have been the ABBY BOLTON who exhibited at the National Academy in 1871–72. ¶ Bolton, *The Family of Bolton,* 373–75; *Christ Church, at Pelham, Pelham Manor, New York* (1943), 17–18, 22, 31, 69.

BOLTON, WILLIAM JAY (1816–1884). A.N.A. Portrait, landscape, and historical painter; designer and maker of stained glass. Born at Bath (England) August 31, 1816, a son of the Rev. Robert Bolton (1788–1857). He came to America in 1836 with his parents who settled at Pelham (N.Y.). He studied painting at the National Academy under MORSE and became an Associate Member of the Academy, but he soon turned to designing and making stained glass. Examples of his work are in Christ Church and Pelham Priory (Pelham, N.Y.) and the Church of the Holy Trinity (Brooklyn, N.Y.). In the mid-forties Bolton went to England and opened a glass-staining studio at Cambridge. He entered the University in 1849 and was ordained to the Anglican ministry about 1853. After holding several curacies he was vicar of Stratford East, London, from 1866 to 1881 and of St. James's, Bath, from 1881 until his death in 1884. He was a brother of ABBY, ADELAIDE, and JOHN BOLTON. ¶ Reginald P. Bolton, "William Jay Bolton . . . ," *Quarterly Bulletin of the Westchester County Historical Society,* IX (April 1933), 25–32 and frontis.; Roscoe C. E. Brown, *Church of the Holy Trinity, Brooklyn Heights* (N.Y., 1922), 21, repros. 13, 16–24; *Christ Church, at Pelham, Pelham Manor, New York* (1943), 16–18, 22, 30–31.

BONANNI, PIETRO (1789–1821). Mural painter. Born in 1789 at Carrara (Italy), Bonanni studied in Paris from 1812 to 1814, worked for a few years in Rome and Carrara, and *c.* 1817 came to America, where he decorated the ceiling of the old House of Representatives at Washington. He exhibited at the Pennsylvania Academy in 1819 and died at Washington June 15, 1821. ¶ Fairman, *Art and Artists of the Capitol,* 476, repros. of self-portrait (p. 477) and portrait of CARLO FRANZONI (p. 26); Rutledge, PA.

BONA PARTE. A fictitious signature, probably of JAMES AKIN, portrait engraver. ¶ Stauffer, and Fielding's *Supplement to Stauffer.*

BONAPARTE, CHARLOTTE JULIE, Comtesse de Survilliers (1802–1839). Portrait, landscape, and flower painter. The daughter of Joseph Bonaparte, Comte de Survilliers and ex-King of Spain, she lived with her father on his estate near Bordentown (N.J.) from about 1819 to about 1828, and exhibited at the Pennsylvania Academy in 1822, 1823, and 1824. She is said to have designed eleven views which appeared in Joubert's *Picturesque Views of American Scenery.* Her portrait of Cora Monges, painted in 1822, is owned by the Historical Society of Pennsylvania. ¶ Wharton, *Salons Colonial and Republican,* 244–45; *American Collector,* XVI (Jan. 1948), 16 and repro. of Cora Monges portrait; Rutledge, PA; Scharf and Westcott, *History of Phila.,* 1054.

BONAR & CUMMING. Lithographers, NYC, 1847. The senior partner was THOMAS BONAR but Cumming has not been identified. ¶ NYCD 1847; NYBD 1847; Peters, *America on Stone.*

BONAR, THOMAS. Lithographer and engraver, NYC, 1847–60 and after. In 1847 he was a partner in the lithographic firm of BONAR & CUMMING, but he seems to have worked independently thereafter. He was listed as engraver only in 1852–54 and 1860. Though his business was in NYC, Bonar's home address was variously Williamsburg (1847–55), Brooklyn (1857–58), Long Island (1859), Brooklyn (1860 and after). ¶ NYCD 1847–55, 1857–60 and after; Peters, *America on Stone.*

BONAR, WILLIAM. Limner, Philadelphia, 1800. ¶ Brown and Brown.

BOND, CHARLES V. Portrait and landscape painter, active 1846–64. Bond was at Detroit in 1833 and 1846; at Boston in 1846, 1849–50; in Brooklyn (N.Y.) in 1852 when he painted a portrait of a Professor Ayres. He was again in Detroit 1852–53, but moved on to Chicago, where in 1855 he exhibited portraits and landscapes at the Illinois State Fair. He was still in Chicago in 1857. The last record of his activity is for 1864, when he was at Louisville (Ky.). ¶ Burroughs, "Painting and Sculpture in Michigan," 397; Boston BD 1846, 1849–50; *Art in America,* XXIII (March 1935), 82; Detroit CD 1852–53; Chicago CD 1855, 1857; [Chicago] *Daily Press,* Oct. 11, 1855; Mrs. W. H. Whitley, cites Louisville CD 1864. Represented at Chicago Hist. Soc.

BOND, HENRY. Engraver, 23, born in New York State, at NYC in 1860. ¶ 8 Census (1860), N.Y., XLIV, 747.

BOND, MARIA. Teacher of painting, drawing, and music in Brooklyn for many years. She came from Leicester (England) in the 1840's with her brother ROBERT and sister MRS. FRANCES FLORA BOND PALMER. Miss Bond may have assisted her sister on work for CURRIER & IVES. ¶ Peters, *Currier & Ives,* 111–15.

BOND, MARSHALL S. P. Designer and wood engraver, Boston, 1856–60 and after. ¶ Boston CD 1856–59; Boston BD 1860.

BOND, ROBERT. Still life and landscape painter, architectural draftsman, and music teacher in NYC for many years. He was the brother of MARIA BOND and Mrs. FRANCES FLORA BOND PALMER and came to NYC with them in the 1840's from Leicester (England). He was best known as a still life artist, but may also have done work for CURRIER & IVES in collaboration with his sister, Mrs. Palmer. ¶ Peters, *Currier & Ives,* 111–15; Stokes, *Iconography,* III, 708–09, and repro. pl. 140; *American Collector,* XIV (March 1945), 3, repro.; *Portfolio,* II (Feb. 1945), 142, repro.

BONDET, see BOUDET.

BONEAU, ——. Painter (?) and exhibitor of a panorama of Australia, China, and Perry's expedition to Japan, shown at St. Louis in 1855 and Baltimore in 1858. ¶ St. Louis *Missouri Daily Democrat,* Feb. 17, March 1 and 21, 1855, and Baltimore *Sun,* April 26, 1858 (citations courtesy J. Earl Arrington).

BONEY, JOHN. English artist, 40, at NYC in July 1860. His wife and daughter, aged 14, were also English by birth. ¶ 8 Census (1860), N.Y., XLIII, 465.

BONFIELD, GEORGE R. (1802–1898). Marine and landscape painter. A native of Portsmouth (England), he came to America about 1836 and settled in Philadelphia where he made his home until his death, except for brief residences in Beverly, Bordentown, and Burlington (N.J.) in the 1850's. He was a frequent exhibitor at the Artists' Fund Society (1836–45), the Pennsylvania Academy (1847–67), the National Academy (1837–44), the Apollo Association and American Art-Union (1838–49), and the Maryland Historical Society in 1848, and was an Honorary Member of the National Academy. ¶ Smith; Tuckerman, *Book of the Artists;* Rutledge, PA; Phila. CD 1845–53; BD 1859–60; Cowdrey, NAD; Cowdrey, AA & AAU; Rutledge, MHS; *Panorama* (Aug.–Sept. 1948), 8.

BONFIELD, WILLIAM VAN DE VELDE. Landscape painter, Philadelphia, 1860 and after. He was probably a son of GEORGE BONFIELD, as they were living at the same address in 1864. William V. de V. Bonfield exhibited at the Pennsylvania Academy 1861–69. ¶ Phila. CD 1860–64 and after; Rutledge, PA.

BONHAM, HORACE. Genre painter; born 1835 at West Manchester (Pa.); died 1892. His work is represented at the Corcoran Gallery, Washington, by "Nearing the Issue at the Cockpit," signed "Horace Bonham '70." He exhibited at National Academy 1879–86. ¶ Fielding; Smith; Corcoran Cat., 1947; Met. Mus., *Life in America;* Cowdrey, NAD.

BONNELL, WILLIAM. Portrait painter, known for portrait of Mary Wolverton Bray, inscribed "William Bonnell, Feb. 9, 1825, Painter," now owned by Historical Society of Hunterdon Co., Flemington (N.J.). ¶ WPA (N.J.), Hist. Records Survey.

BONNER, A. W. Portrait painter, known for portrait of John Stark, painted in 1811 and owned in 1941 by Andrew Oatman of North Bennington (Vt.). ¶ WPA (Mass.), *Portraits Found in Vt.*

BONNO, PIERRE. Sculptor, New Orleans, 1830–35. ¶ Delgado-WPA, cites CD 1830, 1832, 1834–35.

BONTE, A. P. Landscape painter, Cincinnati, 1851. ¶ Cist, *Cincinnati in 1851.*

BONVILLE, CHARLES. Lithographer, born *c.* 1836 in Maryland, living in Philadelphia,

July 18, 1860. ¶ 8 Census (1860), Pa., LII, 87.

BOOKHOUT, EDWARD. Wood engraver and designer, NYC, 1842–60, exhibited at the American Institute in 1851. ¶ NYCD 1842–43, 1845, 1847–51; NYBD 1844, 1846, 1850–54, 1858–60; Am. Inst. Cat., 1851; Thieme-Becker.

BOOTH, GEORGE N. Portrait painter, Boston, 1851. ¶ Boston BD 1851.

BOOTH, T. DWIGHT. Engraver, active 1830–57. Stauffer states that Booth was apprenticed to a NYC engraver in 1830 and that he returned to NYC in 1857 after working in Cincinnati and Chicago. He is listed in the Cincinnati directories for 1849–50, 1853 (as a resident of Newport, Ky.) and 1855, but does not appear in either the Chicago or NYC directories. ¶ Stauffer; Cincinnati CD 1849–50, 1853, 1855; Thieme-Becker.

BOQUETA DE WOISERI, J. L. Landscape painter in aquatint and watercolors, engraver. Davidson reproduces his views of New Orleans (1803) and Boston (*c.* 1810). This is presumably the same as the I. L. Boqutea listed as a painter and engraver in the NYC directories 1807–11. ¶ Davidson, II, 110, 117; NYCD 1807–11; Stokes, *Historical Prints* and *Iconography* reproduce views of Phila., NYC, Baltimore, Boston, Richmond, and Charleston; Rathbone, *Mississippi Panorama,* 52.

BOQUTEA, I. L., see J. L. BOQUETA.

BORCHARD, Miss H., see HERMINIA DASSEL.

BORDLEY, Judge JOHN BEALE (1727–1804). Jurist, agricultural experimenter and publicist, founder of the Philadelphia Society for Promoting Agriculture, amateur artist. Bordley was born at Annapolis (Md.) February 11, 1727, and spent the greater part of his life in Maryland. He was an early patron of CHARLES WILLSON PEALE, and shared a painting-room in Phila. with him in 1776. In 1791 he moved to Philadelphia, where he was prominent as a promoter of agricultural improvements. He died on January 26, 1804. His drawing of wheat-harvesting in Maryland in 1787 is owned by the Philadelphia Society for Promoting Agriculture. ¶ DAB; Davidson, I, 387, repro.; [T. Bolton], *Peale Family Exhibition, Century Assoc., 1953.*

BORDLEY, JOHN BEALE (1800–1882). Portrait painter. A grandson of Judge BORDLEY (above), he was born at "Wye Island," Talbot County (Md.) in 1800. After a period of legal study in Philadelphia, Bordley took up painting. He worked in Baltimore from *c.* 1834 to 1851, appearing in the directories variously as John Beale Bordley, Beale Boardley, and Peale Boardley. He exhibited at the National Academy in 1843 as B. Boardley, and at the Pennsylvania Academy in 1832. After 1851 Bordley retired to a farm in Harford County (Md.) where he continued to paint. He later moved to Bel Air and then to Baltimore, where he died in 1882. ¶ Pleasants, *250 Years of Painting in Md.,* 49–50; Baltimore CD 1835/36, 1837/38, 1840, 1842, 1845, 1851; Cowdrey, NAD; Rutledge, PA; represented at the Md. Hist. Soc. (Rutledge, "Portraits Painted before 1900") and at the Peabody Institute (*Works of Art in the Collection of the Peabody Institute,* 1949).

BORDLEY, MARGARET C. Portrait painter, Margaret (or Margaretta, as she is listed in the 1860 Census) Bordley was born in Maryland *c.* 1822 and worked as a portrait painter in Baltimore from 1849 to 1860. In the latter year she occupied a separate dwelling, but owned no real estate and only $100 in personal property. In the same house lived Jose A[ntonio] Pizaro, Consul of Spain and Mexico. ¶ 8 Census (1860), Md., V, 17; Baltimore CD 1849, 1851, 1853, 1855–56, 1859–60.

BORGMAN, JOHN. Artist, born in Germany *c.* 1834; boarding in Baltimore on October 27, 1860. ¶ 8 Census (1860), Md., III, 981.

BORLAND, ——. Portrait painter working at Baltimore or Louisville about 1830–35. ¶ Information courtesy Mrs. W. H. Whitley of Paris (Ky.).

BORNEMAN, F. W. Sculptor of a "miniature statue," Charleston, 1851. ¶ Rutledge, *Artists in the Life of Charleston,* 187.

BORNET, J. Townscape artist and lithographer, NYC, 1850–55. Best known for his 18 small NYC views (1850) and a view of NYC from the Battery (*c.* 1851). Bornet was listed as a lithographer in Wilson's 1852 Directory and as an artist in Trow's 1855 Directory. ¶ Stokes, *Historical Prints;* Peters, *America on Stone,* 201; Comstock, "The Hoff Views of New York"; Stokes, *Iconography,* III, 705, and pl. 137; NYCD 1852, 1855.

BORRELL, PHILIP. Engraver, NYC, 1840. ¶ NYCD 1840.

BORRON, J. H. (or J. A.). Landscape painter, NYC, 1839–40. He exhibited Welsh, Sicilian, and Scottish landscapes at the Apollo Association. ¶ Cowdrey, AA & AAU.

BORTHWICK, ——. Portrait and landscape painter, Philadelphia, 1821. ¶ Scharf and Westcott, *History of Phila.*, II, 1054.

BORTHWICK, JOHN DAVID. Artist, author of *Three Years in California . . . with Eight Illustrations by the Author* (1857). Borthwick was born and educated in Edinburgh (Scotland), but came to America some time after 1840. After a brief stay in NYC the young artist went to California in September 1851, remaining there as a gold seeker and artist until 1854, when he left for Australia. His California experiences were recorded in the book cited above and in drawings published in the *Illustrated London News*. He was back in England by 1860 and during the next seven years exhibited at English galleries, including the Royal Academy, of which he was a member. ¶ Borthwick, *Three Years in California . . . with Eight Illustrations by the Author* (London: Blackwood, 1857); Van Nostrand and Coulter, *California Pictorial*, 104, 120, with repros.; Graves, *Dictionary;* Jackson, *Gold Rush Album*, 68, 71–72, 103, 150–51, 181, 191, repros.; Davidson, I, 257, repro.

BOSON, ADOLPHE. Artist, at Mormon Island (Cal.) in January, 1850. ¶ Van Nostrand and Coulter, *California Pictorial*, 124–25.

BOSQUI, EDWARD (1832–1917). Printer and amateur landscape painter, born in Montreal (Quebec) July 23, 1832. Bosqui went to California in 1850 and established one of San Francisco's largest printing houses, the Bosqui Engraving and Printing Co. He was a patron of artists and examples of his own work have been preserved. He died in San Francisco December 8, 1917. ¶ Van Nostrand and Coulter, *California Pictorial*, 82–83; Peters, *California on Stone*.

BOSS, E. H. Known only for a view of Chicago, drawn *c.* 1849. ¶ Stokes, *Historical Prints*, pl. 77-b.

BOSS, PHILIP. Portrait painter, Rochester (N.Y.), 1827–38. ¶ Ulp, "Art and Artists in Rochester," 30; Rochester CD 1834, 1838, 1841 (as watchmaker & jeweler).

BOSSUET, ——. Panoramist and scene-painter. He assisted DELAMANO in the painting of a moving picture of the Crystal Palace, first shown in NYC in December 1851. ¶ N. Y. *Herald*, Dec. 2, 1851 (cited by J. E. Arrington).

BOSTON BANK NOTE COMPANY. Bank note engravers, Boston, 1841–42. This company was probably formed by OLIVER PELTON and EBENEZER TAPPAN, who were listed in the city directories in 1840, 1842 and 1843 at the same address as that given for the Company in the 1841–42 business directories. ¶ *Boston Almanac* and BD 1841–42; Boston CD 1840, 1842–43.

BOSTON BEWICK COMPANY. Engravers and printers, Boston, 1834–37[?]. The company was established "for the purpose of employing, improving, and extending the art of engraving, polytyping, embossing, and printing." Its personnel included ABEL BOWEN, ALONZO HARTWELL, JOHN H. HALL, WILLIAM CROOME, GEORGE W. BOYNTON, JOHN C. CROSSMAN, DANIEL H. CRAIG, and N. B. DEVEREUX, JR. The Boston Bewick Co. was the publisher of *The American Magazine* (1835–Sept. 1837), except for the last volume. ¶ Whitmore, "Abel Bowen," 44–45, with check list of illustrations in *The American Magazine*, 45–46; Boston CD 1834.

BOSWORTH, SALA (1805–1890). Portrait and landscape painter, illustrator. Born in Halifax (Mass.) in 1805, he moved in childhood to a farm near Marietta (Ohio). After a year of study at the Pennsylvania Academy, he set up in Marietta as a portrait painter about 1827. He illustrated Hildreth's *Pioneer Histories* and also painted some landscapes and mural decorations. He moved to Cincinnati in 1882 and died there eight years later. ¶ Reiter, "Sala Bosworth"; Clark, *Ohio Art and Artists*, 103–04; Lipman and Winchester, 169; Ford, *Pictorial Folk Art*, 70; represented at Ohio State Archaeological and Historical Society.

BOTELER, HENRY (1817–?). Portrait painter, born December 31, 1817, probably in Sheperdstown (Va., now W. Va.), where his brother, Alexander Robinson Boteler (1815–1892), later a Confederate officer and U. S. Congressman, was born. On his mother's side, he was a great-grandson of CHARLES WILLSON PEALE. Boteler worked in Jefferson County before and after the Civil War and made life sketches of John Brown and several Confederate generals. ¶ Willis, "Jefferson County Portraits"; Sellers, *Charles Willson Peale*, II, 417.

BOTICHER, see BOETTICHER.

BOTT, EMIL. Portrait and landscape painter, Cincinnati, 1853–59, and Pittsburgh, 1864, 1868. ¶ Ohio BD 1853, 1859; Cincinnati CD 1857, 1859, BD 1859; Pittsburgh CD 1864, BD 1868.

BOTTCHER, JOHN A. Art teacher, New Orleans, 1823. ¶ Delgado-WPA, cites *Gazette,* Dec. 25, 1823.

BOTTICHER & GILDEMEISTER. Portrait painters, NYC, 1851. The artists were OTTO BOETTICHER and CHARLES GILDEMEISTER. ¶ NYCD and BD 1851.

BOTTICHER, see BOETTICHER.

BOTTIGER, see BOETTICHER.

BOTTLES, JOSEPH. Lithographer; born in New Jersey *c.* 1825; living in Southwark, Philadelphia County (Pa.) September 10, 1850. ¶ 7 Census (1850), Pa., LV, 698.

BOTTS, GEORGE. Artist. He was born *c.* 1829 in Germany, and on July 30, 1860, was boarding in Philadelphia, unmarried. ¶ 8 Census (1860), Pa., LVII, 645.

BOTTUME, GEORGE F. Portrait painter. Bottume was born in July 1828 at Baltic (Conn.), and took up the study of painting about 1841. About 1844–45 he was in NYC, a pupil of SOLOMON FANNING, but he shortly returned to Connecticut, working as a portrait painter for several years in Norwich, then moving about the state until he finally settled in Springfield (Mass.) where he was still living in 1878. ¶ French, *Art and Artists in Connecticut,* 136; Smith erroneously states that Bottume died at Norwich in 1846.

BOUCHARD, ADOLPH. Sculptor, New Orleans, 1857–59. ¶ Delgado-WPA, cites CD 1857, 1859.

BOUCHÉ, ——. Portrait painter and drawing teacher, Maryland, active 1794–95. In 1794 Bouché painted a portrait of the daughters of James Murray of Annapolis, and in the following year advertised in Baltimore that he and M. de VALDENUIT were opening a drawing school in that city. ¶ Pleasants, *250 Years of Painting in Md.,* 31–32.

BOUDEN, see BOUDON.

BOUDET, Miss ——. Portrait painter, daughter of the artist NICHOLAS VINCENT BOUDET. She proposed to open a drawing academy for young ladies in Baltimore in 1810. ¶ Courtesy of Dr. J. H. Pleasants, who cites [Baltimore] *American,* May 22, 1810.

BOUDET, DOMINIC W. (?–1845). Portrait, miniature, and historical painter, active 1805–45. Dominic W. was the son of NICHOLAS VINCENT BOUDET, with whom he appears to have worked much of the time from 1805 to 1820. The two Boudets were at Richmond in 1805 (Dominic as dancing master), at Baltimore in 1807–08, and at Washington in 1810. Dominic was in Virginia in 1811, copying portraits by JOHN HESSELIUS on the estate of John Mason (1767–1849). Father and son were in Philadelphia in 1814, and in 1819–20 they were working together in Baltimore on a huge painting of the "Battle of North Point" for the city, a project which brought the elder Boudet to bankruptcy in February 1820. Dominic Boudet was at Charleston (S.C.) later in 1820, and in NYC in 1825, 1827–28, 1830–33, and 1837. In August 1833, he exhibited "The Raising of Lazarus" at the Frederick (Md.) City Hall and in December of the same year he exhibited "La Belle Nature" at New Orleans. D. W. Boudet was working in Charleston in 1838, chiefly as a portrait and miniature painter. He exhibited "La Belle Nature" at Baltimore about October 20, 1845, and died there by October 29th. He exhibited at the National Academy in 1831. *Cf.* WILLIAM BOUDET. ¶ Richmond *Enquirer,* March 21, 1805; Baltimore CD 1807–08; Washington *National Intelligencer,* Oct. 10, 1810 (courtesy Dr. J. Hall Pleasants); Rutledge, MHS; Corcoran Gallery, *150th Anniversary of the Formation of the Constitution,* nos. 4 and 123; Brown and Brown; Boudet transcripts made by Dr. Pleasants; Carolina Art Assoc. MS on miniatures; N. Y. *Evening Post,* Sept. 19, 1825; NYCD 1827–28, 1830–33, 1837; Frederick *Herald,* August 31, 1833 (courtesy Dr. Pleasants); New Orleans *Courier,* Dec. 24 and 27, 1833; Rutledge, *Artists in the Life of Charleston,* 125, 239, 242–43; Baltimore *American,* Oct. 20 and 29, 1845; Cowdrey, NAD; represented at NYHS.

BOUDET, NICHOLAS VINCENT. Portrait, miniature, and historical painter, active 1793–1820. Boudet (or Bondit, Bondet, Bardet) was at Philadelphia in 1793 and at Charleston in 1803. In 1805, he was at Richmond (Va.) with his son DOMINIC W. BOUDET, a dancing master. Father and son were both at Baltimore in 1807–08, probably at Washington and Baltimore in 1810, and at Philadelphia in 1814. The Boudets collaborated on a large painting of the "Battle of North Point" for the City of Baltimore in 1819, but the project brought the elder Boudet to bankruptcy by February 1820, and his subsequent history is not known. Besides his son Dominic, Nicholas Boudet had a daughter, Miss —— BOUDET, who advertised the opening of a drawing school for young ladies in Baltimore in 1810. ¶ Brown and Brown; Carolina Art Assoc., MS on miniatures; Richmond *Enquirer,* March 21, 1805; Baltimore CD 1807–08; Dr. J. Hall Pleasants, Boudet transcripts.

BOUDET, WILLIAM. Miniaturist, portrait painter, and drawing master, who advertised in Charleston (S.C.) in 1801–02 as a native of Bremen (Germany). This may have been DOMINIC (or D. W.) BOUDET. ¶ Rutledge, *Artists in the Life of Charleston,* 126, 187.

BOUDIER, J. J. (or I. I.). Engraver and physiognotrace artist. Boudier worked in Philadelphia in 1796–97, in the latter year advertising a special ink for making copies of letters. At this time he engraved a portrait of "Buonaparte," signed "Boudier, sculpt, Philada." He was in NYC in 1816. ¶ Prime, II, 66–67; Stauffer, I, 26 and II, 209; Phila. *Aurora,* March 28, 1797; McKay cites NYCD 1816.

BOUDIT, see BOUDET.

BOUDON, DAVID. Miniaturist at Philadelphia in 1797 and at Chillicothe (Ohio) in 1816. Boudon was from Geneva (Switzerland) and painted watercolor profiles on vellum (at $6) and miniatures on ivory. *Cf.* DAVID BOURDON. ¶ [Phila.] *Aurora,* Dec. 8, 1797; Prime, II, 5; [Chillicothe] *Scioto Gazette,* Nov. 28, 1816 (Courtesy Donald MacKenzie, Wooster College). Brown and Brown gives the name as Bouden.

BOUDON, see BOUTON.

BOUGHTON, GEORGE HENRY (1833–1905). N.A., R.A. Portrait, genre, and landscape painter. Born December 4, 1833, at Norwich (England), Boughton was brought to America in 1839 and grew up at Albany (N.Y.). At the age of 19 (1852) he was listed as a landscape painter in Albany and he continued to make his home there until 1858, except for a visit to Scotland in 1856. He worked in NYC in 1859–60, but left the United States in 1861 to study in Paris. He settled in London, where he apparently remained until his death on January 19, 1905. Boughton exhibited at the National Academy in 1853 and from 1856 to 1876; was an Honorary Member, Professional, 1859–60, and a Member of the Academy from 1871 to 1905. He was elected an Associate of the Royal Academy in 1879 and a Member in 1896. Boughton also exhibited at the American Art-Union in 1852, at the Washington Art Association in 1857, and at the Maryland Historical Society in 1868. He was best known in America for his subject-pictures, especially the familiar "Pilgrims Going to Church," now at the New-York Historical Society. ¶ Thieme-Becker; *Encyclopaedia Britannica* (11th ed.); Albany CD 1852, 1855–58; Cowdrey, NAD; Cowdrey, AA & AAU; Graves, *Dictionary;* Washington Art Assoc. Cat., 1857; Rutledge, MHS.

BOUGUEREAU, ELIZABETH JANE GARDNER. Painter. Elizabeth Jane Gardner was born at Exeter (N.H.) in 1837. She married the famous French artist, William Adolphe Bouguereau (1825–1905), and died at St. Cloud (France) in January 1922. ¶ *Art Annual,* XIX (1922), obit.

BOUGUEREAU, P. H., JR., see BEAUGUREAU.

BOUILLER, JULE[s]. Lithographer. Born in France *c.* 1841, he was living with his parents in San Francisco on June 27, 1860. ¶ 8 Census (1860), Cal., VII, 1370.

BOULET, ALEX. Artist, painter, New Orleans, 1850. Born in Italy *c.* 1818, Boulet was living in New Orleans on August 1, 1850, with his wife Marie, born in France. ¶ 7 Census (1850), La., V, 82.

BOULTON, G[ILES?] Amateur artist, designer of a view of Rochester (N.Y.) published as frontispiece of *The Monthly Repository and Library of Entertaining Knowledge* (N.Y., Oct. 1831). G. Boulton, the artist, was described as "an intelligent gentleman of Rochester," and was probably Giles Boulton, merchant of Rochester, who died *c.* 1833. ¶ Hamilton, 96, 140; Rochester CD 1827, 1834 (as late merchant).

BOUNETHEAU, HENRY BREINTNALL (or Brintnell) (1797–1877). Painter of miniatures and crayon portraits, Charleston. Bounetheau was born at Charleston, December 14, 1797, and died there January 31, 1877. He had early art training and for a time supported himself by painting miniatures, but for most of his life was an accountant. Bounetheau's work as a miniaturist was mentioned in the Charleston papers in 1835, 1845, and 1849. His wife, born JULIA CLARKSON DUPRÉ, was also an artist of note, and in 1855 Mr. and Mrs. Bounetheau were offering classes in drawing and oil painting at the Charleston Academy of Design. ¶ DAB; Rutledge, "Henry Bounetheau (1797–

1877), Charleston, S.C., Miniaturist," with 6 repros.; Rutledge, *Artists in the Life of Charleston,* 160, 179 (repro.), 187.

BOUNETHEAU, Mrs. H. B. or J. C., see JULIA CLARKSON DUPRÉ.

BOUQUET, see BOQUETA.

BOURDON, DAVID. Painter, musician, and dancing master. A French refugee, Bourdon painted "small portraits in an indifferent manner" (Dunlap) at Pittsburgh (Pa.) *c.* 1810. A portrait inscribed "Done by David Bourdon, painter" and dated "7 October 1813" was discovered by Miss J. L. Brockway in the hands of a private owner at Annapolis (Md.). DAVID BOUDON may have been the same man. ¶ Dunlap, *History,* II, 227; *Antiques,* XXI (Jan. 1932), 12, repro.

BOURGEOIS, FRANCIS. Engraver and enameller from Paris, at Philadelphia in 1796 and 1799. ¶ Prime, II, 67; Brown and Brown, cites Phila. CD 1799.

BOURGOIN, JOSEPH. Miniaturist, NYC, 1806–07. A Francis Joseph Burgoin worked as a miniaturist in Paris (France) from 1760–86. ¶ McKay, cites NYCD 1806–07; Thieme-Becker.

BOURKE & SMITH. Engravers, NYC, 1857. The partners were THOMAS BOURKE and CHARLES W. SMITH. ¶ NYBD 1857.

BOURKE, THOMAS. Engraver and printer, NYC, 1857–60. He was a partner in BOURKE & SMITH, engravers, 1857. ¶ NYBD 1857–58; NYCD 1858–60.

BOURLIER, ALFRED J. B. Sculptor, NYC, 1853–60 and after. In 1854 he was with LARMANDE & BOURLIER and in 1859 with GORI & BOURLIER. ¶ NYCD 1853–60 and after.

BOURQUIN, CHARLES F. Lithographer and lithographic printer, Philadelphia, 1844–61. Bourquin was born in Switzerland *c.* 1800 and came to America some time before 1844, when he was first listed in the Philadelphia directory. It is possible that he was in NYC before this, since his wife, Eliza C. Bourquin, was born there *c.* 1820 and his brother [?], FREDERICK BOURQUIN, lived there for a number of years before coming to Philadelphia *c.* 1843. In 1850 Charles and Frederick Bourquin lived in adjoining houses in Philadelphia. Charles Bourquin's household included his wife, and their daughter, Margaret E., aged 7 and a native of Pennsylvania. Bourquin was living in Philadelphia as late as 1861. ¶ 7 Census (1850), Pa., LII, 869; Phila. CD 1844–53, 1855–59, 1861.

BOURQUIN & COMPANY. Lithographers, Philadelphia, 1858–60 and after. The firm consisted of FREDERICK BOURQUIN and R. P. SMITH. The latter may have been the Philadelphia map publisher, Robert Pearsall Smith, though his address during these years was different from that of Bourquin & Co. ¶ Phila. BD 1858; BD and CD (as Borquin & Co. or F. Bourquin & Co.) 1859–60 and after.

BOURQUIN, FREDERICK. Lithographer, Philadelphia, 1843–60 and after. Bourquin was born at Geneva (Switzerland) in 1808, probably a younger brother of CHARLES F. BOURQUIN, also a lithographer. Frederick came to America before 1838 and first settled in NYC, where he married. Two sons were born to the Bourquins in New York: Frederick W., *c.* 1838 and Gordon M., *c.* 1840. By 1843 they had moved to Philadelphia, where Frederick and Charles Bourquin lived in adjoining houses and followed the same trade. By 1850 two more children had been born: David L., *c.* 1843, and Mary B., *c.* 1846. Frederick Bourquin continued as a lithographer in Philadelphia at least until the 1860's, and from 1858 to *c.* 1863 headed the firm of F. BOURQUIN & CO. According to Peters, he was still living in 1872. ¶ Peters, *America on Stone;* 7 Census (1850), Pa., LII, 869; Phila. CD 1843–52, 1855–60 and after; Thieme-Becker.

BOUTELLE, DE WITT CLINTON (1820–1884). A.N.A. Portrait and landscape painter, born in Troy (N.Y.) on April 6, 1820. He worked in NYC in 1846; in Baskingridge (N.J.) in 1848; in NYC, 1851–55; in Philadelphia, 1855–57; and in Bethlehem (Pa.), 1858 and after. He died November 5, 1884. An Associate of the National Academy from 1851, he exhibited there (1846–74), as well as at the Pennsylvania Academy (1854–69), the Boston Athenaeum (1854–61), the Washington Art Association (1857–59), and the American Art-Union (1845–52). His son, Edward C. Boutelle, was also an artist. ¶ CAB (rev. ed.); Cowdrey, NAD; Rutledge, PA; Swan, BA; Washington Art Assoc. Cat., 1857, 1859; Cowdrey, AA & AAU; information courtesy of John F. Morman, Bethlehem (Pa.); represented in the Karolik Collection (Cat., 137–39) and in the Moravian Archives, Bethlehem. A landscape of 1865 is repro. in *Antiques* (May 1947), 307. Boutelle was listed as Bartelle in Phila. CD 1857.

BOUTON, G. B. or JEAN B. Sculptor, NYC,

1850. G. B. Bouton exhibited a wood "Statue of St. Mary" at the American Institute in 1850, and in the same year Jean B. Boudon, sculptor, was listed in the City Directory at the same address. ¶ Am. Inst. Cat., 1850; NYCD 1850.

BOUVÉ, ELISHA W. Lithographer, Boston, 1847–49. ¶ Boston CD 1847–49.

BOUVÉ, EPHRAIM. Engraver and lithographer. Bouvé was born in Boston in 1817, and died there April 13, 1897. He was working as a lithographer in Boston as early as 1839, and at his death was said to be the oldest engraver in the city. From 1843 to 1845 Bouvé was associated with WILLIAM SHARP in the firm of BOUVÉ & SHARP. ¶ Boston *Transcript,* April 15, 1897, obit.; Boston CD 1839–40, BD 1841–42, CD 1843, BD 1844–48, 1851–60 and after.

BOUVÉ & SHARP. Engravers and lithographers, Boston, 1843–45. The partnership of EPHRAIM W. BOUVÉ and WILLIAM SHARP was dissolved in 1845, Bouvé continuing independently at the same address and Sharp carrying on at another address as WILLIAM SHARP & CO. ¶ Boston CD 1843–44, BD 1844–45.

BOVELL, THOMAS W. Lithographer, of DALSTON & BOVELL, NYC, 1859–60. ¶ NYBD 1859; NYCD 1860.

BOVETT (Bovet), AMI. Engraver, Philadelphia, 1860. Bovet was born in Europe *c.* 1818 and settled in Pennsylvania sometime before 1835. His 1860 household included his wife (aged 29) and four children (ages 15 to 6), all born in Pennsylvania. ¶ 8 Census (1860), Pa., L, 528; Phila. CD 1860 (as Bovet).

BOWA, PETER. Artist in plaster of Paris, at New Orleans, 1823. ¶ Delgado-WPA, cites CD 1823.

BOWDISH, NELSON S. Landscape painter; born at New Lisbon (N.Y.) in 1831; died at Skaneateles (N.Y.) April 3, 1916. ¶ *Art Annual,* XIII, obit.

BOWEN, ABEL (1790–1850). Copperplate and wood engraver, lithographer, publisher, and antiquarian. Bowen was born at Sand Lake Village, Greenbush (N.Y.) on December 23, 1790. He made his first woodcut in Boston in 1805 and soon became a leading engraver in that city and the instructor of at least 25 other engravers. In 1816 he published *The Naval Monument,* with many War of 1812 scenes engraved by himself. Bowen was associated for a short time (*c.* 1821) with ALEXANDER MCKENZIE, in 1825–26 with WILLIAM S. PENDLETON, and in 1834 he helped to organize the BOSTON BEWICK COMPANY. Sinclair Hamilton lists 27 books containing examples of his work. Bowen died on March 11, 1850. ¶ Whitmore, "Abel Bowen," with 63 repros.; Stauffer; DAB (date of birth given erroneously as Dec. 3, 1790); Grolier Club, "The U. S. Navy"; Dunlap, *History;* Hamilton.

BOWEN, CHARLES C. Engraver; born in Pennsylvania *c.* 1839; working in Philadelphia in 1860 and 1871. ¶ 8 Census (1860), Pa., LVII, 351; Phila. CD 1871.

BOWEN & COMPANY. Lithographers and colorists, Philadelphia, 1859–60 and after. The firm was composed of Mrs. LAVINIA BOWEN and JOHN CASSIN. ¶ Phila. CD 1859–60 and after.

BOWEN, DANIEL (*c.* 1760–1856). Wax modeler and showman. Though he is known to have modeled wax portraits of Franklin and Washington, Bowen is best known as one of the first American museum proprietors. His museum and waxworks was advertised in NYC in 1789, Philadelphia in 1790, Boston in 1791, Philadelphia 1793–94, NYC 1794. In 1795 he opened the Columbian Museum in Boston and he remained there until 1807 when the museum burned down for the second time in four years. He was still active in 1818 when he showed in Philadelphia a panorama of New Haven, and he died in Philadelphia on February 29, 1856, at the age of 96. ABEL BOWEN, the engraver, was his nephew. ¶ Wall, "Wax Portraiture"; E. S. Bolton, *American Wax Portraits,* 15, 19, 35; Prime, II, 54–55; NYCD 1794; Gottesman, II, nos. 1275–77, 1280, 1282–83, 1285. A portrait of Daniel Bowen by JOSEPH KYLE is reproduced in *Bostonian Society Publications,* I, 32.

BOWEN, GEORGE P. Of WALKER & BOWEN, portrait painters at Boston, 1845–46. ¶ Boston CD 1845, BD 1846.

BOWEN, GEORGE W. Engraver; born in Massachusetts *c.* 1821; living in Boston in 1850. ¶ 7 Census (1850), Mass., XXIII, 20.

BOWEN, H[ENRY] M. Portrait painter, at Charleston (S.C.) in 1844 and in Jefferson County ([W.] Va.) in 1847, 1849. ¶ Rutledge, *Artists in the Life of Charleston,* 187; Willis, "Jefferson County Portraits."

BOWEN, JOHN, see JOHN BOWER.

BOWEN, JOHN T. Artist and lithographer.

Born in England *c.* 1801, Bowen was working in NYC from 1834 to 1838, and in Philadelphia from 1839 to 1856. He published a drawing book in 1839 and exhibited a color print at the Pennsylvania Academy in 1850. His wife, LAVINIA BOWEN, whom he married before 1850, was a colorist and appears to have carried on her husband's lithography business after his death, probably in 1856. ¶ 7 Census (1850), Pa., LI, 80; Peters, *America on Stone;* Phila. CD 1839–56; Bowen, *The United States Drawing Book* (Phila., T. Wardle, 1839, 24 pp., 36 plates); PA Cat. 1850; *Antiques,* XVII (Jan. 1930), 18, repro. of "The Great Fire of New York City, 16 December 1835," drawn by A. HOFFY, lithograph by J. T. Bowen.

BOWEN, LAVINIA (Mrs. John T.). Colorist and lithographer. Mrs. Bowen was born in Maine *c.* 1820 and married JOHN T. BOWEN some time before 1850, when they were living in Philadelphia. Her husband dying apparently in 1856, Lavinia Bowen carried on his lithographic business at the same address. In 1859 she joined with JOHN CASSIN to form the firm of BOWEN & COMPANY which continued into the 1860's. ¶ 7 Census (1850), Pa., LI, 180; Phila. CD 1857, 1859–60 and after.

BOWEN, THOMAS. Fielding lists a portrait painter of this name with the death date 1790. No further information has been found to establish him as an American artist. He may be the Thomas Bowen listed in Thieme-Becker as an English engraver who died in London, March 3, 1790. ¶ Fielding; Thieme-Becker.

BOWER, JOHN. Engraver of maps and portraits, book illustrator, Philadelphia, 1809–19. ¶ Brown and Brown; Stauffer; Fielding (erroneously as John Bowen); *American Collector,* XIV (Aug. 1945), 3, repro.; *Antiques,* XLVIII (July 1945), 19, repro.

BOWER, WILLIAM. Engraver and die sinker, stamp-cutter, NYC, 1848–60. ¶ NYBD (as stamp-cutter) 1848, 1850–52, 1854, 1856–60; NYCD (as engraver and die sinker) 1850–54, 1856–60.

BOWERS, EDWARD. A.N.A. Portrait, genre, and still life painter, crayon portraitist. He was born in Maryland *c.* 1822 and worked in Baltimore as early as 1850–52. He was in Philadelphia 1854–59 (as E. Bowers, artist), in NYC 1859, and in Baltimore from 1860 to 1870, though he apparently spent some time in Detroit in 1865. Bowers exhibited at the Maryland Historical Society in 1850, the Pennsylvania Academy (1854–58, 1860), the National Academy (1856, 1859–61), and the Washington Art Association (1857, 1859). ¶ 7 Census (1850), Md., IV, 780; Baltimore CD 1852, 1860; Lafferty, cites CD 1860–70; Phila. CD 1855–59; NYBD 1859; *Antiques,* L (Sept. 1946), 159; Karolik Cat., 140–41, repro. of "Fruit and Wine," signed and dated "E. Bowers, Detroit, 1865"; Rutledge, MHS; Washington Art Assoc. Cats., 1857, 1859; Rutledge, PA; Cowdrey, NAD; Bolton, *Crayon Draftsmen.*

BOWERY, THOMAS. Engraver, 20, a native of New York State, living with WILLIAM EVERDELL in NYC in August 1850. ¶ 7 Census (1850), N.Y., XLI, 535.

BOWES, CHARLES E. Portrait and landscape painter, NYC, exhibited at the National Academy 1839–40. ¶ Cowdrey, NAD.

BOWES, JOSEPH. Architect and engraver, who arrived in Philadelphia in 1794 and was there in 1796–98. ¶ Brown and Brown, cites *Aurora,* Oct. 15, 1794; Phila. CD 1796–98; Stauffer.

BOWLER, JOSHUA SOULE. Engraver. Born June 10, 1818, at Lynn (Mass.); died August 23, 1847, at Boston [?]. His wife, SOPHIA A. BOWLER, née Sawyer, was also an artist. They were living in Boston in 1846–47. ¶ Belknap, *Artists and Craftsmen of Essex County,* 3; Boston CD 1846–47.

BOWLER, Mrs. SOPHIA A. Portrait and miniature painter. Sophia A. Sawyer of Portland (Maine) married the engraver, JOSHUA SOULE BOWLER, on July 15, 1838. She was listed in the Boston directories for 1847 and 1848 as a portrait painter and miniature painter, respectively. Her husband died in 1847. ¶ Belknap, *Artists and Craftsmen of Essex County,* 3; Boston CD 1847–48.

BOWLES, JOSHUA. Carver, of BOWLES & LUCKIS (Lucus), Boston, *c.* 1760–68. ¶ Swan, "Boston's Carvers and Joiners, Part I," 199.

BOWLES & LUCKIS. Carvers, Boston, 1760–68. The partners were JOSHUA BOWLES and THOMAS LUCUS. Their work included a female head. ¶ Swan, "Boston's Carvers and Joiners, Part I," 199.

BOWLEY, CHARLES G. Engraver; born in England about 1815; left England between 1841 and 1843, when his son was born in Alabama; living in NYC from

1845 to 1852 and in Cincinnati from 1855 to 1857. ¶ 7 Census (1850), N.Y., XLVI, 5; NYCD 1845–52; Cincinnati CD 1855–57.

BOWMAN, ALEXANDER. Designer. Born *c.* 1823, Bowman worked in Boston as a designer from 1849 to 1852 and as a die sinker in 1857. He was listed in the 1850 Census as "Mr. Bowman" and was then unmarried. ¶ 7 Census (1850), Mass., XXV, 21; Boston CD 1849–52, 1857.

BOWMAN, JAMES (1793–1842). Portrait painter, born in Alleghany County and brought up in Mercer County (Pa.). While working as a carpenter at Chillicothe (Ohio) about 1816, he learned the rudiments of painting from a Mr. Turner (probably J. T. TURNER) and soon after became an itinerant portraitist, plying his new trade with encouraging success in Pittsburgh, Philadelphia, Washington, and smaller towns until about 1822 when he was enabled to go abroad for further study. After five or six years in London, Paris, and Rome, he returned to America and opened a short-lived gallery in Pittsburgh in 1829. During the winters of 1829/30 and 1830/31 he was in Charleston and later in 1831 he went to Boston. In the fall of 1835, after a season of painting in Montreal, Bowman turned up in Detroit where he was married the following year to Julia M. Chew. In 1836 he also painted a portrait of Governor Henry Dodge of Wisconsin Territory at Green Bay. During the next few years he appears to have worked as an itinerant in western Pennsylvania and New York, returning occasionally to his family at Mercer (Pa.). He opened a studio in Rochester (N.Y.) in October 1841 and was prospering there when he died suddenly on May 18, 1842. Most of his work has disappeared, including portraits of Lafayette and his daughters, James Fenimore Cooper, Albert Thorwaldsen, and Justice Henry Baldwin, but his portrait of Gov. Dodge is at the State Historical Society of Wisconsin. His only known pupils were GEORGE W. FLAGG and JOHN MIX STANLEY. ¶ Brief accounts of Bowman's career appear in Wilson, *Standard History of Pittsburgh,* 862–63 (citation courtesy Prudence Trimble, Hist. Soc. of Western Pa.); *History of Monroe County, N.Y.,* 141; Ross, *Detroit in 1837,* 16 (citation courtesy Burton Hist. Coll., Detroit Public Library); *Rochester Daily Democrat,* June 1, 1842 (citation courtesy Rev. Leo C. Mooney, St. Patrick's Rectory, Rochester); *Rochester Evening Post,* May 18, 1842; *Rochester Daily Advertiser,* May 19, 1842 (citation courtesy Blake McKelvey, Rochester City Historian). See also: Rutledge, PA; Chester Harding, *My Egotistography;* Dickson, *Selections from the Writings of John Neal;* Rutledge, *Artists in the Life of Charleston;* BA Cat. 1831; Dunlap, *History,* II, 448, 471; Dunlap, *Diary,* III, 696, 765–66; State Historical Society of Wisconsin, *Second Triennial Cat. of Portrait Gallery* (1892); *Detroit Free Press Digest, 1835–37,* 74, 130, 172, 268, and *Detroit Advertiser Digest, 1836–37,* 115–16 (citations courtesy Burton Hist. Coll., Detroit Public Library).

BOWNE, A. Exhibited a wood-engraving at the American Institute in 1848; a resident of NYC. ¶ Am. Inst. Cat. 1848.

BOWNE, J. C. Engraver, Philadelphia, *c.* 1854; engraved plates for *Peterson's Magazine. Cf.* JOHN T. BOWEN. ¶ Fielding; Smith.

BOWSER, DAVID BUSTILLE. Negro portrait, marine, and banner painter; born in Philadelphia January 16, 1820; died June 30, 1900. In 1860 Bowser was living in Philadelphia with his wife, Elizabeth H. Bowser, aged 27, and two children: Mary S., aged 3, and Raphael, aged 2. The whole family were listed as mulattos, born in Pennsylvania. In 1871 Bowser was listed in the City Directory as an artist, and his wife "Lizzie" as a dressmaker. The 1860 Census lists Bowser's assets as $5,000 in realty and $500 in personality. ¶ Porter, *Modern Negro Art,* 39–42; 8 Census (1860), Pa., LVI, 117; Phila. CD 1871.

BOWYER (Boyer), MICHAEL H. Writing and drawing master, NYC, 1813–15. ¶ McKay cites NYCD 1813–15.

BOYD, BENJAMIN E. Banknote engraver, Cincinnati, 1857–60. ¶ Cincinnati CD 1857–59; BD 1860.

BOYD, JOHN. Engraver, Philadelphia, 1810–1825. Boyd was an associate of the Columbian Society of Artists from 1811 to 1814. ¶ Brown and Brown; Phila. CD 1816–19, 1823–25; Society of Artists Cats., 1811–14; Stauffer; Dunlap.

BOYD, SAMUEL. Engraver; born *c.* 1836 in Delaware; living unmarried in Philadelphia, July 12, 1860. ¶ 8 Census (1860), Pa., LIV, 275.

BOYD, THEODORE C. Wood engraver, NYC, 1850–1852. ¶ NYCD and NYBD 1850–1852.

BOYD, THOMAS C. Wood engraver of portraits and views, San Francisco, 1856–60. ¶ San Francisco BD 1856, 1858–1860; view of Sacramento repro., *Portfolio,* VII (Nov. 1948), 61.

BOYER, MICHAEL, see MICHAEL BOWYER.

BOYERS, E. Artist, Philadelphia, 1855. ¶ Phila. CD 1855.

BOYLE, CALEB. Portrait painter active *c.* 1800–1815. Boyle worked as a carriage maker and painter and as a portrait painter in NYC, 1800 to 1805. In 1807 he was painting portraits in Baltimore, but he moved on to Washington the next year, remaining there until 1811. In Washington, Boyle had his studio and museum in a studio built for GILBERT STUART by the architect BENJAMIN LATROBE. On leaving Washington, Boyle probably returned directly to Baltimore, where he certainly was in 1814 and 1815. Of his work little is known, though portraits of Thomas Jefferson and John Jay have been attributed to him. He was doing "encaustic portrait painting" at New Brunswick (N.J.) in the fall of 1822. ¶ The pioneer work on Caleb Boyle has been done by John Jay Ide in his *Portraits of John Jay* and in his "A Discovery in Early American Portraiture." Other information is derived from: NYCD 1800–1805; manuscript notes of Dr. J. Hall Pleasants; Baltimore CD 1814–15; *The Times and New Brunswick Advertiser,* Nov. 14, 1822 (Courtesy Donald A. Sinclair. Rutgers University).

BOYLE, FERDINAND THOMAS LEE A.N.A. Portrait and miniature painter, art teacher; born at Ringwood (England), 1820; died in Brooklyn (N.Y.), December 2, 1906. Brought to America as a child, F. T. L. Boyle studied under HENRY INMAN. He lived in New Rochelle (N.Y.) in 1843, and in NYC from 1844 to 1855. In the latter year he moved to St. Louis, where he was one of the founders of the Western Academy of Art. Returning to NYC in 1866, Boyle served for many years as Professor of Art in the Brooklyn Institute and as head of the Art Department of Adelphi College. His home in later years was in Brooklyn. Among his works were portraits of Lincoln (reproduced in *Portfolio,* Feb. 1945, p. 144), Grant (owned by the Union League Club), Archbishop Bailey of New Jersey, and Charles Dickens. He was an Associate of the National Academy from 1849. ¶ *Art Annual,* VI; Cowdrey, NAD; Cowdrey, AA & AAU; NYBD 1846, 1854–55; NYCD 1850; St. Louis BD 1859, 1865; Brooklyn CD 1898; Met. Mus., *Life in America;* Sears, *Some American Primitives,* 87; Kende Galleries Cat. 228, p. 10; *Portfolio* Feb. 1945, p. 144; Clement and Hutton.

BOYLE, JAMES. Portrait painter. So listed in NYBD 1844, 1849–51, 1854, 1856, this appears to be the same man as JAMES BOGLE, portrait painter, listed in the NYCD at the same address. ¶ NYBD and NYCD 1844–56.

BOYLE, JAMES A. Lithographer, NYC, 1850–60. From 1851 Boyle worked with PETER MILLER, under the name of MILLER & BOYLE. ¶ NYCD 1851–59; NYBD 1850–60.

BOYLE, JOHN C. Sculptor; born in Ireland about 1815; working in NYC from the mid-forties until after 1860. He was in partnership with JAMES LAUDER, JR., from 1847 to 1859. ¶ 7 Census (1850), N.Y., LVI, 32; NYCD 1847–60+.

BOYLE & LAUDER. "Artificers in Marble, Statuary, Monuments, and Mantel Pieces," NYC, 1847–59. The partners were JOHN C. BOYLE and JAMES LAUDER, JR. ¶ NYCD 1847–59; NYBD 1850–52.

BOYLE, M. Primitive painter in oil of a historical scene and a still life, Carlisle (Pa.) *c.* 1850. ¶ Lipman and Winchester, 169.

BOYLE, Mrs. M. C. Teacher of painting and drawing, Charleston (S.C.), 1834. ¶ Rutledge, *Artists in the Life of Charleston,* 187.

BOYLE, THOMAS. Engraver; born in Pennsylvania *c.* 1827; living in Philadelphia August 1, 1850. ¶ 7 Census (1850), Pa., LIII, 551.

BOYLE, WILLIAM. One, or perhaps several, artists of this name worked in Philadelphia *c.* 1852–69. William W. Boyle of Philadelphia exhibited landscapes at the Pennsylvania Academy (1852–54, 1856–57, 1869), the subjects being scenes in Ohio, western Pennsylvania, and the Philadelphia area. William W. Boyle, artist, is listed in the 1856 City Directory, at the same address as the W. H. Boyle listed in the 1855 and 1856 Business Directories. Later directories list: William Boyle, painter (1859), William Boyle, engraver (1860), and William Boyle, artist

(1861)—all at different addresses. ¶ Rutledge, PA; Phila. BD 1855–56; CD 1856, 1859–61.

BOYNTON, G. W. & Co. Engravers, Boston, 1833. The firm was headed by GEORGE W. BOYNTON. ¶ Boston CD 1833.

BOYNTON, GEORGE W. Engraver, Boston, 1831–60 and after. Stauffer lists Boynton as a map engraver, and he was probably the G. Boynton who engraved a map of New York State for Peter Parley's *Tales about the State and City of New York* (1832). The Boston directories list him as a plate engraver. In 1833 Boynton headed the firm of G. W. BOYNTON & Co., and in 1834 he was a member of the BOSTON BEWICK COMPANY. Since his home address in 1850 was Dorchester (Mass.), Boynton the engraver was probably the same as the George W. Boynton, inventor of a bell diving apparatus, who died in Dorchester on June 20, 1884. ¶ Boston CD 1831–60 and after; Stauffer; Whitmore, "Abel Bowen," 44; Boston *Transcript,* June 21, 1884.

BRAAN, EDWARD. Lithographer; born in Hesse-Darmstadt (Germany) *c.* 1839, and came to America before 1858. On July 20, 1860, he was living in Baltimore, with his wife, Catherine, aged 21, and two children—Edward, aged 2, and Louisa, aged 10 months—all born in Maryland. Braan's personal property was valued at $1,500. ¶ 8 Census (1860), Md., LV, 920.

BRABY, HENRY. Portrait painter, Baltimore, 1842; possibly the same as HENRY BEBIE. ¶ Baltimore CD 1842.

BRACHER, WILLIAM. Engraver and lithographer, Philadelphia, 1857–60 and after. Bracher was born in Württemburg (Germany) *c.* 1828, and came to America *c.* 1857. He worked in Philadelphia as a lithographer, from 1859 as a member of the firm of WORLEY, BRACHER & MATTHIAS. In July 1860 he owned realty valued at $2,000 and personalty valued at $600. His household in 1860 included his German-born wife Emily, aged 24; his son, Emil, aged 1; two boarders, one of whom, CHRISTIAN BECHLER, age 32, was a native of Saxony; and a German maid. ¶ 8 Census (1860), Pa., LXII, 300; Phila. CD 1857–60 and after. Bracher is variously misspelled as Beacher, or Brorher.

BRACKENRIDGE, A. Designer of a view of Dickinson College (Carlisle, Pa.), published in 1811. ¶ *Port Folio,* XVI (1811), 241.

BRACKETT, CHRISTOPHER C. Sculptor at Cincinnati in 1838. ¶ Information courtesy Edward H. Dwight, Cincinnati Art Museum.

BRACKETT, EDWARD AUGUSTUS (Edwin C. or E.). Portrait sculptor; born at Vassalboro (Maine), October 1, 1818; died March 15, 1908, at Winchester (Mass.). Brackett worked in Cincinnati *c.* 1841 and in the same year exhibited at the National Academy as a resident of NYC. From 1842 to 1860 and after he lived in Boston, where he exhibited many times at the Athenaeum Gallery between 1843 and 1866. Brackett also exhibited at the Apollo Association (1840–41) and the National Academy (1841, 1850, 1866). He was an older brother of the portrait painter, WALTER M. BRACKETT. ¶ DAB; Cist, *Cincinnati in 1841;* Cowdrey, NAD; NYBD 1841; Boston BD 1844–53, 1855–60; Swan, BA, 205; Cowdrey, AA & AAU; Gardner, *Yankee Stonecutters;* Lee, *Familiar Sketches,* 194–202; Met. Mus. *Bulletin,* III (Oct. 1944), 57, repro.; represented at NYHS.

BRACKETT, Miss H. V. One of the earliest recorded women engravers on copper in America. Her etching of "Ruth and Boaz" was published in NYC *c.* 1816. ¶ Stauffer, I, 28–29.

BRACKETT, WALTER M. Portrait painter; born at Unity (Maine), June 14, 1823; died at Boston (Mass.), March 8, 1919. A younger brother of the sculptor, EDWARD A. BRACKETT, he seems to have passed his entire professional career in Boston. In 1860 he was living in Tremont Row with his wife, Maria L., age 32, and their son, Arthur C., age 4, both natives of Massachusetts. Brackett exhibited a number of times at the Boston Athenaeum from 1846 to 1869, at the Apollo Association in 1852, and at the National Academy in 1860 and 1865. ¶ "Maine Artists," 5; *Art Annual,* XXV (1928), 379; Boston BD 1845–59; 8 Census (1860), Mass., XXVIII, 189; Swan, BA; Cowdrey, AA & AAU; Cowdrey, NAD; DAB; Tuckerman, *Book of the Artists.*

BRACKMAN, JOHN. Exhibited lithographic view of New York at the American Institute, NYC, 1849. ¶ Am. Inst. Cat., 1849.

BRADBURY, EDWARD. Engraver and metal-turner, Philadelphia, 1819–20. ¶ Brown and Brown, cites CD 1819–20.

BRADFORD, ——. Lithographer, age 26, living with LODOWICK H. BRADFORD in Boston, 1850. ¶ 7 Census (1850), Mass., XXV, 582.

BRADFORD, HENRY. Engraver, NYC, 1815–20. ¶ McKay, cites NYCD 1815–17, 1819–20.

BRADFORD, L. H., & Co. Engravers and lithographers, Boston, 1854–1859. This firm, headed by LODOWICK H. BRADFORD, was the successor to TAPPAN & BRADFORD. ¶ Boston CD 1854–59.

BRADFORD, LODOWICK H. Lithographer; born in Massachusetts *c.* 1815; working in Boston 1845–1859. From 1849 to 1854 Bradford was associated with the engraver, EBENEZER TAPPAN, in the engraving and lithographic firm of TAPPAN & BRADFORD, and from 1854 to 1859 he headed the firm of L. H. BRADFORD & Co. In 1850 Lodowick H. Bradford was boarding in Ward 9 along with —— BRADFORD, age 26, possibly a younger brother. ¶ 7 Census (1850), Mass., XXV, 582; Boston CD 1845–1859; Peters, *America on Stone;* Belknap, *Artists and Craftsmen of Essex County,* lists him as an artist.

BRADFORD, WILLIAM (1823–1892). A.N.A. Painter of Arctic scenes, photographer, lecturer; born at Fairhaven, near New Bedford (Mass.) April 30, 1823; died in NYC, April 25, 1892. In 1857 Bradford turned from business to art, studying under VAN BEEST. He first exhibited at the National Academy in 1860. From 1861 to 1867 he made annual trips to Labrador and became celebrated both in America and in England for his Arctic scenes. Bradford exhibited at the National Academy (1860–90), the Boston Athenaeum (1857, 1859, 1862, 1864–65, 1871), and at the Royal Academy in London in 1875, when he was listed as of NYC. His home was at Fairhaven (Mass.), though he died in NYC in 1892 while on a lecture visit. He was an Associate of the National Academy. ¶ DAB; Wood, "William Bradford"; CAB (gives birth date as 1827); obit., N. Y. *Times,* April 25, 1892; Cowdrey, NAD; Swan, BA; Graves, *Dictionary;* Clement and Hutton; Champlin and Perkins; Thieme-Becker.

BRADISH, ALVAH. Portrait painter, professor of art; born at Sherburne (N.Y.), September 4, 1806; died at Detroit (Mich.), April 2, 1901. Bradish was working in Rochester (N.Y.) during the decade from 1837 to 1847, though he seems to have made several trips to the West during those years, to Detroit as early as 1837 and to Cleveland in 1840. He exhibited at the National Academy in 1846–47 as a resident of Fredonia (N.Y.) and in 1851 as of Detroit. From 1852 to 1863 he served as Professor of Art in the University of Michigan and for many years he was one of Detroit's most successful portrait painters. ¶ *Art Annual,* IV (1903), 137; Ulp, "Art and Artists in Rochester," 32; Cowdrey, NAD; Burroughs, "Painting and Sculpture in Michigan," 398; WPA (Ohio), *Annals of Cleveland,* June 1840; repro., Detroit Hist. Soc. *Bulletin,* April 1949, 7.

BRADLEY, H. W. Artist, San Francisco, 1850. He was listed as a daguerreotypist in 1852. ¶ San Francisco CD 1850, 1852.

BRADLEY, I. J. H. Itinerant portrait painter, *c.* 1830–1840. He is known to have painted portraits at Rhinebeck (N.Y.) in 1832, and at Kingston (N.Y.) and Kent (Conn.) in 1836, and may be the same as JOHN BRADLEY, portrait painter in NYC from 1837 to 1845. ¶ Lipman, "I. J. H. Bradley"; Stechow, "Another Signed Bradley Portrait"; repro., *Antiques,* LI (Feb. 1947), 102.

BRADLEY, JOHN. Portrait and miniature painter, NYC, 1837–1845. Miss Marion Stephens, of Closter (N.J.), who owns a portrait by this artist, states that it bears no resemblance to the work of I. J. H. BRADLEY, the itinerant primitive portrait painter. ¶ NYCD 1837–45; information courtesy Miss Mary Bartlett Cowdrey.

BRADLEY, LEWIS. Landscape painter and draughtsman, Utica (N.Y.), 1832–73. He was listed as a lithographer and drawing master in Utica directories for 1832 and 1833; exhibited landscape and still life paintings at the National Academy in 1838 and 1839; was listed as an artisan in the directories 1846 to 1851, and from 1852 to 1873 as a landscape painter and draughtsman. His view of Syracuse *c.* 1850 has been reproduced. ¶ Utica CD 1832–33, 1839, 1844, 1846–59, 1861–73; Cowdrey, NAD; Stokes, *Hist. Prints,* 109; repro., Peters, *America on Stone,* pl. 100.

BRADLEY, RELINS (or Relius). Artist; born in Pennsylvania *c.* 1831; living in Philadelphia, 1860, with his wife, age 23, and daughter Kate, age 7, both natives of Pennsylvania. ¶ 8 Census (1860), Pa., LI, 187.

BRADLEY, THOMAS. Artist; born in England *c.* 1838; living in Philadelphia, June 16,

1860. ¶ 8 Census (1860), Pa., LV, 489.

BRADSHAW, JOHN H. Engraver, Boston, 1860. ¶ New England BD 1860.

BRADWOOD, JOHN. Engraver; born in Scotland *c.* 1824; living in Philadelphia with THOMAS BRADWOOD in September 1850. ¶ 7 Census (1850), Pa., LII, 946.

BRADWOOD (Braidwood), THOMAS W. Engraver and drawing teacher, Philadelphia, 1850–61. Born in Scotland *c.* 1814–15, Thomas Bradwood was working as an engraver in Philadelphia in 1850, when he lived with JOHN BRADWOOD, also an engraver and probably a younger brother. Thomas W. Braidwood, artist, appears in the Philadelphia directories for 1856–1858. In 1860 he was recorded in the Census as Mr. Bradwood, teacher of drawing, age 46. The following year Thomas W. Braidwood was listed in the directory as president of the Philadelphia School of Design for Women. ¶ 7 Census (1850), Pa., LII, 946; 8 Census (1860), Pa., LX, 638; Phila. CD 1856–58, 1861.

BRADY, ——. Painter of a portrait of Mark Twain at St. Louis, 1859. ¶ FARL question file.

BRADY, JAMES. Engraver and die sinker, NYC, 1849. ¶ NYBD 1849.

BRADY, JAMES. Artist; born in Pennsylvania *c.* 1839; living in Philadelphia with his mother, Mary Brady, age 40, a native Pennsylvanian, and his sister, Annie. ¶ 8 Census (1860), Pa., LIV, 266.

BRADY, MATHEW B. Pioneer photographer, artist and lithographer; born in Warren County (N.Y.), *c.* 1823; died in NYC, January 16, 1896. Though Brady's name is associated primarily with his magnificent photographic record of the Civil War, he made his start as an artist and lithographer. His early instructors were WILLIAM PAGE of Saratoga (N.Y.) and SAMUEL F. B. MORSE of NYC. He was already practising as a daguerreotypist in NYC in 1849 when he exhibited a lithograph of President Taylor and his Cabinet. Brady's career as a photographer was spent mainly in NYC and Washington and in the Civil War theaters of operations, and the most important collections of his photographs are in the Library of Congress and the National Archives. ¶ DAB; Peters, *America on Stone;* NYCD 1848–49; Am. Inst. Cat. 1849. See Meredith, *Mr. Lincoln's Camera Man: The Story of Mathew Brady,* for an extended treatment of Brady's career.

BRAEKELEER, see DE BRAEKELEER.

BRAHM, JOHN. Engraver, 29, from Bavaria, at NYC in June 1860 with his wife Mary and one-month-old son Charles. ¶ 8 Census (1860), N.Y., LI, 671.

BRAIDWOOD, THOMAS W., see THOMAS W. BRADWOOD.

BRAINARD & BURRIDGE. Wood and general engravers and lithographers, Cleveland, 1853–59. The partners were JEHU BRAINARD and W. H. BURRIDGE. ¶ Ohio BD 1853, 1857, 1859; Cleveland CD 1853, 1857.

BRAINARD (Brainerd), JEHU (or John). Engraver and drawing teacher, Cleveland, 1849–59. In 1849 Jehu Brainard, teacher of perspective drawing, lectured in Cleveland on geology and was active in the Free Soil party. John Brainerd was listed in the 1850 Census as an engraver, age 46, living in Cleveland with his wife, Lucy, age 38, and daughter Lucy, age 10; all were natives of Ohio. From 1853 to 1859 Jehu Brainard was a member of the engraving firm of BRAINARD & BURRIDGE. ¶ WPA (Ohio), *Annals of Cleveland,* 1849; 7 Census (1850), Ohio, XI, 450; Ohio BD 1853, 1857, 1859; Cleveland CD 1853, 1857.

BRAINERD, Miss ——. Teacher of painting in oils and watercolors, of perspective drawing, and of the use of crayons, Charleston (S.C.), 1824–25. ¶ Rutledge, *Artists in the Life of Charleston,* 188.

BRALLY, JAMES. Engraver; born in Ireland *c.* 1822; came to America between 1848 and 1851; living in Philadelphia in July 1860. Brally's wife Margaret, age 36, and four sons, ages 17 to 12, were born in Ireland; a daughter, Margaret, age 9, was born in New Jersey; and the three youngest children, ages 7 to 1, were born in Pennsylvania. ¶ 8 Census (1860), Pa., XLIX, 322.

BRAMMER, JOSEPH. American artist; born 1833; died 1904. He exhibited at the Boston Athenaeum in 1859. ¶ Swan, BA, 206.

BRAMMER, ROBERT (?–1853). Portrait and landscape painter, of Louisville and New Orleans, active 1839 to 1853. He was at Louisville in 1839 and 1841. He was a member of the firm of BRAMMER & VON SMITH, portrait painters in New Orleans, 1842. He was again in New Orleans in November 1847, just returned from the North and spoken of as a landscape painter. He was working in New Orleans again in June 1853, but died the same month at his summer home in Biloxi

(Miss.). ¶ New Orleans CD 1842; Delgado-WPA, cites *Commercial Times,* Nov. 25, 1847, *Orleanian,* June 11 and 16, and Aug. 6, 1853; information courtesy Edward H. Dwight, Cincinnati Art Museum.

BRAMMER & VON SMITH. Portrait painters, New Orleans, 1842. The partners were ROBERT BRAMMER and —— VON SMITH. ¶ New Orleans CD 1842.

BRAMSON, ——. Painter of a miniature, signed and dated 1829. ¶ Courtesy of Dr. H. W. Williams, Corcoran Gallery.

BRANDES, see VON BRANDES.

BRANDT, CARL LUDWIG (1831–1905). N.A. Portrait, landscape, and historical painter; born in Hamburg (Germany), September 22, 1831; died in Savannah (Ga.), January 20, 1905. Brandt came to America in 1852, settling in NYC, where he exhibited at the National Academy in 1855, 1860, and 1862–1884. He was elected to the Academy in 1872. He was at one time Director of the Telfair Academy in Savannah. ¶ Thieme-Becker; *Art Annual,* V, obit.; Cowdrey, NAD; *Artists Year Book,* 1905, 20; N. Y. State Hist. Assoc. "Checklist of Paintings," Feb. 1950. Smith gives Holstein (Germany) as Brandt's birthplace.

BRANNAN, WILLIAM PENN (?–1866). Portrait painter and author. Brannan worked in Cincinnati *c.* 1841–47, in the latter year exhibiting at the National Academy. In 1859 he was working in Louisville, but he later returned to Cincinnati, where he died August 9, 1866. His writings included "Vagaries of Vandyck Brown" and "Harps of a Thousand Strings." ¶ Cist, *Cincinnati in 1841,* 140; Cowdrey, NAD; Cincinnati BD 1844; New Orleans CD 1853; Louisville CD 1859; CAB.

BRANO, JOSEPH. Artist and naturalist. Joseph Brano worked in Philadelphia from 1829 to 1840 as a preparer of natural curiosities; in 1844 he was listed as a naturalist; in 1849, 1850, 1855–1857, 1862, 1867–1868, and 1871 as an artist; and in 1866 as a taxidermist. Possibly the same Joseph Brano worked in NYC as a teacher (1844–1845), sculptor (1846) and professor (1851). ¶ Phila. CD 1829–1871; NYCD 1844–45, 1851; NYBD 1846.

BRANTZ, LEWIS. Landscape artist who sketched the first known view of Pittsburgh (Pa.) in 1790. ¶ Stokes, *Hist. Prints,* 42; N. Y. Public Library *Bulletin,* Oct. 1917, frontis.; *Antiques,* XL (Nov. 1941), 311.

BRASHER, JOHN H. Engraver; born in New York *c.* 1827; died in Boston *c.* 1869. John H. Brasher was listed as an engraver in NYC directories from 1847 to 1853, and in Boston from 1856 to 1869. In the 1860 Census, however, he appears as James H. Brasher. This is certainly the same man, since "James" lived in NYC at least until 1853, when his fourth child was born, and was in Boston by 1855, when the next child came. His household in 1860 included his English wife Jane, age 32; four children born in N.Y.—James H., age 13, George, age 10, Jane, age 9, and Frances, age 7; and three children born in Massachusetts—Clara, age 5, Ida, age 2, and Estelle, age 5 months. Further proof of the identity of John H. and "James H." Brasher is found in the 1865 Boston Directory, where James H. and George T. Brasher are listed as boarding in the house of John H. Brasher; at this time all three were serving in the Union armies. James H. continued to live with his father until 1870, when the house is listed in the name of Mrs. John H. Brasher, presumably his widow. ¶ 8 Census (1860), Mass., XXV, 801; NYCD 1847, 1850–1853; Boston CD 1856, 1859–69.

BRATT, ADOLPH. Artist, Philadelphia, 1857. ¶ Phila. CD 1857.

BRATTON, FRANKLIN. Engraver, age 17, living in Philadelphia in 1860, with his mother, an embroiderer. ¶ 8 Census (1860), Pa., LIII, 111.

BRAUN, JOHN. German artist, 26, at NYC in August 1850. ¶ 7 Census (1850), N.Y., LV, 643.

BRAUN, L. German religious painter, refugee from the Revolution of 1848, exhibited "The Saviour Rising from the Sepulcher" at Pittsburgh (Pa.) *c.* 1850. ¶ Fleming, *History of Pittsburgh,* III, 626.

BRAY, JOB F. Landscape painter; born in Wales *c.* 1805; living in Philadelphia in 1860. Bray and his Welsh wife were in Pennsylvania as early as 1837 when their eldest child was born, though Bray's name does not appear in the directories until 1857. In 1860 he lived with his wife, age 48, and children, ages 14 to 23, including John Bray, age 17, engraver. ¶ 8 Census (1860), Pa., LII, 98; Phila. CD 1857–60.

BRAY, JOSEPH W. Sculptor, NYC, 1859–60. ¶ NYBD 1859–60.

BRECHEMIN & CAMP. Lithographers, Philadelphia, 1848. The partners were LEWIS BRECHEMIN and HENRY CAMP. ¶ Phila. CD 1848.

BRECHEMIN, LEWIS. Jeweler and lithographer, Philadelphia, 1825–1866. In 1848 Lewis Brechemin, jeweler, was associated with HENRY CAMP, lithographer, in the firm of BRECHEMIN & CAMP, lithographers; in the same year Brechemin lithographed a portrait of David R. Porter, governor of Pennsylvania, at Philadelphia. ¶ Phila. CD 1825–1866; Peters, *America on Stone*.

BRECK, ALPHONSE, see ALPHONSE BRETT.

BREFLCHL [sic], ——. Engraver, New Orleans, 1830–32. ¶ Delgado-WPA, cites CD 1830, 1832.

BREHAN, MARQUISE DE. Amateur profilist and landscape painter. A sister of the Comte de Moustier, French Minister to the United States, the Marquise arrived in America in February 1788. In November of that year she visited Mount Vernon, where she did a profile of Washington. In the fall of 1789 she was living in NYC and executed another Washington profile and a watercolor view of NYC from her window near Bowling Green. ¶ Eisen, "A Houdon Medallion"; *Washington Diaries,* III, 441, IV, 14, 17; Stokes, *Historical Prints,* 35; Stokes, *Iconography,* V, 1255, VI, pl. 90a; Morgan and Fielding, *Life Portraits of Washington,* 143–49.

BRENNAN, JAMES. Portrait, landscape, and animal painter, working in NYC from 1837 to 1866. Since he exhibited several Irish views at the National Academy in 1837–38, he may have been the Irish artist of the same name who was born in Dublin before 1802, studied at the School of the Dublin Society, and exhibited from 1826 to 1834 at the Royal Hibernian Academy. ¶ Cowdrey, NAD; Peters, *America on Stone;* Strickland, *Dictionary of Irish Artists.*

BRENNAN, JOHN, see JOHN BRYNAN.

BRENT, HENRY. A "native" artist, just returned from Europe, at New Orleans, 1845. *Cf.* HENRY JOHNSON BRENT. ¶ Delgado-WPA, cites *Bee,* June 3, 1845.

BRENT, HENRY JOHNSON (1811–1880). Landscape painter. Brent was living in NYC 1848–49, in Brooklyn 1851, in NYC and Rochester (N.Y.) 1857. He exhibited in 1851 at the National Academy, of which he was an Honorary Member, Professional. He also exhibited at the American Art-Union (1848–1852) and at the Washington Art Association (1857). At least two of his landscapes were British scenes, and one was owned in New Orleans, so he may be the same as HENRY BRENT above. ¶ Cowdrey, NAD; Cowdrey, AA & AAU; Washington Art Assoc. Cat., 1857.

BREOBEY, see BINGHAM & BREOBEY.

BRESLAW, ——. Heraldic painter, Boston 1850. Breslaw worked with CHARLES HOPPS. ¶ Bowditch, "Early Water-Color Paintings of New England Coats of Arms," 205; *Heraldic Journal,* IV (1868), 192.

BRETON, W. L. Painter of ships and views, Philadelphia, *c.* 1830–1839. In 1838 a number of his views of ships, including one of the departure of the steamship *Great Western* from NYC in 1838, were on exhibition in Philadelphia. The frontispiece of *A History of Philadelphia* (Phila., 1839), designed by "Breton," was probably the work of W. L. Breton. ¶ Peters, *America on Stone;* Phila. *Public Ledger,* May 2, 1838, cited by J. E. Arrington; Hamilton, 149.

BRETT, ALPHONSE. Lithographer, Philadelphia, 1848–59; NYC, 1860. Alphonse Brett, or Brette, lithographer, was listed in Philadelphia directories in 1848, 1852–56, 1858–59. This is probably the same man as Alphonse Breck, lithographer, listed in the 1850 Census as a native of France, age 28. In 1853 Brett headed the firm of Alphonse Brett & Co., lithographers. By August 1860 he had moved to NYC. ¶ Phila. CD 1848, 1852–56, 1858–59; 7 Census (1850), Pa., L, 874; Peters, *America on Stone;* repros., *Portfolio,* V (Oct. 1945), 47; 8 Census (1860), N.Y., LIV, 418.

BRETTE, Professor ——. Landscape painter and teacher, New Orleans, 1853. ¶ Delgado-WPA, cites *Picayune,* January 9, 1853.

BREUGGER, CHRISTIAN. Amateur painter; born in Canton Curwaldo (Switzerland), November 22, 1822; died in Nauvoo (Ill.), July 1895. Breugger came to America in the 1840's and lived for a time in Wisconsin before finally settling at Nauvoo in 1848. Shortly after coming to Nauvoo he made an oil painting of the famous Nauvoo Temple. ¶ Arrington, *Nauvoo Temple,* Chap. 8.

BREUL, H. Lithographer, NYC, 1825. A

lithograph of a New York "beer garden" by Breul is owned by the American Antiquarian Society. ¶ Davidson, II, 167, repro.

BREUNIG, JOSEPH (or Charles). Joseph Breunig, artist, was listed in the Buffalo directory in 1858, at the same address as Joseph Breunig, no occupation given, in 1855 and Charles Breunig, ornamental painter, in 1857. He was also a partner in STANSFIELD & BREUNIG, fresco and ornamental painters, in 1856. ¶ Buffalo CD 1855–1858.

BREVOORT, JAMES RENWICK (1832–1918). N.A. Landscape painter; born in Yonkers Township (N.Y.), July 20, 1832; died at Yonkers, December 15, 1918. Brevoort's work was exhibited at the National Academy (1856–90) and at the Boston Athenaeum (1858). His home in 1856–57 was Fordham (N.Y.) and from 1858 to 1860 in NYC. Brevoort was a cousin of the architect, James Renwick; his second wife, Marie Louise Bascom, was also an artist and first medallist of the National Academy school. ¶ DAB; Cowdrey, NAD; Swan, BA; *Art Annual,* XVI; Clement and Hutton.

BREWER, GEORGE ST. P. (1814–1852). Panoramist; born in England in March 1814; died in St. Louis, December 26, 1852. Brewer came to America probably some time in the 1830's and married a Georgia girl, born *c.* 1818. Their first son, George, was born in Illinois *c.* 1840; a daughter, Georgiann, was born in Missouri *c.* 1844; and a second son, George R., was born in Kentucky *c.* 1848. Brewer's most popular work, a panorama of Mammoth Cave and other "natural curiosities of North America," was shown in Louisville, Philadelphia, New Orleans, Cincinnati and Boston from 1848 to 1851. The family was living in Louisville (Ky.) in August 1850. Brewer died in St. Louis in 1852, but his last panorama, "Grand View of the Torrid, Temperate and Frigid Zones," as well as the "Mammoth Cave," continued to be shown after his death as late as 1859. The name was sometimes given as Brewster. ¶ *Missouri Republican,* December 28, 1852; 7 Census (1850), Ky., XI, 347; J. E. Arrington cites: Louisville *Daily Democrat* (July 19 and Nov. 9, 1848), Phila. *Public Ledger* (June 18, 1849), New Orleans *Daily Picayune* (Jan. 20, 1850), Cincinnati *Daily Gazette* (Apr. 23, 1850), Boston *Evening Transcript* (Aug. 8 and Sept. 18, 1850, and Feb. 12, 1851), N. Y. *Herald* (July 4 and 18, 1853), Cincinnati *Daily Gazette* (March 15, 1854), and New Orleans *Daily Picayune* (March 19, April 5, 1859).

BREWER, JOHN S. Portrait painter; born in Canada about 1824; at NYC in 1850; also worked in New Hampshire and Vermont. ¶ 7 Census (1850), N.Y., XLVI, 295; NYBD 1850; Sears, *Some American Primitives.*

BREWER, LAURANA RICHARDS. Painter; born in 1808; died in 1843. She was the wife of CHARLES BEAUMONT, Boston portrait painter, and exhibited at the Boston Athenaeum in 1832. ¶ Swan, BA, 206.

BREWERTON, GEORGE DOUGLAS. Landscape painter; born *c.* 1820; died in 1901. He was at Brooklyn (N.Y.) in 1854, and exhibited western views at the National Academy in 1854 and 1855. *Cf.* G. D. BREWSTER. ¶ Cowrey, NAD.

BREWSTER, ——, see GEORGE ST. P. BREWER.

BREWSTER, EDMUND. Portrait and landscape painter, engraver, active 1818–39. Brewster was living in Philadelphia in 1818, when he exhibited a self-portrait at the Pennsylvania Academy, but the following year he arrived in New Orleans, where he was spoken of as a very young artist of unusual merit. He was again in New Orleans from 1822 to 1824, working as an engraver and portrait and landscape painter. By 1828 Brewster had returned to Philadelphia where he seems to have remained until 1839. ¶ Rutledge, PA; Delgado-WPA, cites *Louisiana Gazette,* April 6 and 10, 1819, and March 13, 1824; New Orleans CD 1822–23; Phila. CD 1828–31, 1833, 1835, 1837 (as Edward Brewster), 1839; Gillingham, "Notes on Phila. Profilists"; Peters, *America on Stone;* Thomas Thompson, *Louisiana Writers,* gives the name as Edmund Bruster.

BREWSTER, G. D. Artist of Newport (R.I.) who exhibited Western landscapes at the Pennsylvania Academy in 1859. This was probably GEORGE DOUGLAS BREWERTON. ¶ Rutledge, PA.

BREWSTER, JOHN. Portrait and miniature painter; born at Hampton (Conn.), May 30/31, 1766; still living in 1846. A deaf mute from birth, John Brewster painted portraits and miniatures in Boston in 1802, at Salem in 1809, and at Portland (Me.) *c.* 1830. ¶ Jones, *Brewster Geneaolgy,* I, 189; *Boston Citizen,* Dec. 28,

1802; Belknap, *Artists and Craftsmen of Essex County;* Lipman and Winchester, 169; Dunlap, *History* (1918), III, 284; Karolik Cat., 143, repro.; Bolton, *Miniature Painters.*

BREYMAN, WILLIAM. Artist of pre-Civil War Kansas. ¶ WPA Guide, *Kansas,* 137–38.

BRIAN, JULIUS. German-born lithographer, 34, living in NYC in 1860. His wife was also German-born but their three children were born in New York between 1854 and 1858. Brian owned realty valued at $8,000 and kept two servants. ¶ 8 Census (1860), N.Y., XLVIII, 1107.

BRICHER, ALFRED THOMPSON (or Albert T.) (1837–1908). A.N.A. Marine and landscape painter; born in Portsmouth (N.H.), April 10, 1837; died in New Dorp, Staten Island (N.Y.), September 30, 1908. Bricher studied art in his leisure time while employed in business in Boston from 1851 until he became a professional artist in 1858. He worked in Boston and Newburyport (Mass.) until 1868 when he moved to New York. He exhibited after 1860 at the Boston Athenaeum and at the National Academy, of which he was elected an Associate Member in 1879. ¶ *Art Annual,* VII; CAB; Clement and Hutton; New England BD 1860; Swan, BA; Belknap, *Artists and Craftsmen of Essex County;* Thieme-Becker; NAD Cats. 1868–1890.

BRICHER & DAMOREAU. Engravers, Boston, 1856. The partners were HENRY BRICHER and CHARLES F. DAMOREAU. ¶ Boston CD 1856.

BRICHER, HENRY. Engraver on wood, designer; born in England *c.* 1817; working in Boston 1847–60 and after. Engravings by Bricher appeared in books published in 1847 and 1848; from 1849 he was listed in the Boston directories. In 1856 he was associated with CHARLES F. DAMOREAU in the engraving firm of BRICHER & DAMOREAU, and in 1860 with STEPHEN S. C. RUSSELL as BRICHER & RUSSELL. ¶ 8 Census (1860), Mass., XXVIII, 928; Hamilton, 192–93, 230, Boston CD 1849–50, 1853–54, 1856, 1858–60 and after.

BRICHER & RUSSELL. Designers, photographers, and engravers, Boston 1859–60 and after. The partners were HENRY BRICHER and STEPHEN S. C. RUSSELL. ¶ Boston CD 1859–60 and after.

BRICKEY, W. J. Portrait painter, St. Louis, 1851. A portrait by Brickey was owned in 1943 by the Kinney family of New Franklin (Mo.). ¶ Information courtesy St. Louis City Art Museum and Frick Art Reference Library.

BRIDGENS, CHARLES. Engraver, die-sinker, letter-cutter, NYC, 1833. ¶ NYCD 1833.

BRIDGENS, HENRY and ROBERT. Lithographers, Philadelphia, 1850. Henry was 25 and Robert 30 years old and both were born in Pennsylvania. ¶ 7 Census (1850), Pa., XLIX, 480.

BRIDGENS, WILLIAM HENRY. Engraver, die-sinker, NYC, 1829–1857. In 1829 he was listed as Henry Bridgens, tool-cutter, and in 1832 as H. Bridgens, copper engraver. ¶ NYCD 1829–53; NYBD 1840–57; *Am. Adv. Directory* 1832, p. 96.

BRIDGES, CHARLES. Portrait painter, working in Virginia *c.* 1735–40, returned to England by 1746. ¶ Foote, "Charles Bridges"; repros. *Connoisseur* (June 1947), 129, and *Antiques* (Feb. 1945), 101 and (March 1951), 204.

BRIDGES, E. W. Landscape painter, exhibited "View of the Exchange at Baltimore" at the National Academy in 1826. ¶ Cowdrey, NAD.

BRIDGES, EARL. Portrait painter, Albany (N.Y.), 1835–46. In 1847 his widow was listed. ¶ Albany CD 1835, 1837–38, 1840–47.

BRIDGES, FIDELIA (1835–1923). A.N.A. Landscape, marine, and nature painter; born at Salem (Mass.), May 19, 1835; died at Canaan (Conn.), May 1923. Miss Bridges was a pupil of W. T. RICHARDS. She moved to Brooklyn (N.Y.) in 1854, lived in Philadelphia in 1859 and 1862–63, visited Europe in 1865–66, was again in Philadelphia in 1879–80, and spent her later years in Connecticut. She exhibited at the Pennsylvania Academy (1862–63, 1865–66) and the National Academy (1863–89), and became an Associate Member of the latter. ¶ CAB; *Who's Who in America,* 1922–23 and 1924–25; Randall, "Conn. Artists and Their Work," 583–88 with 7 repros.; Belknap, *Artists and Craftsmen of Essex County; Art Annual,* XXI; Cowdrey, NAD; Rutledge, PA; Graves, *Dictionary.*

BRIDGES, WELLINGTON E. Wood engraver, NYC, 1850–52. ¶ NYBD 1850–52.

BRIDPORT, GEORGE. Decorative painter and drawing master. In 1808 he decorated the ceiling of the House of Representatives in Washington, but his work was destroyed in the fire of 1814. From 1811 to 1819 he lived in Philadelphia, where he and his brother, HUGH BRIDPORT, had a drawing academy in 1816–17. ¶ Fairman, *Art and Artists of the Capitol,* 16; Brown and Brown, cites Phila. CD 1811, 1813, 1816–19 and *Aurora,* Nov. 22, 1817.

BRIDPORT, HUGH (1794–*c.* 1868). Portrait and landscape painter, miniaturist, engraver, lithographer, and architect; born in London, 1794; died in Philadelphia [?], *c.* 1868. Bridport began his artistic career in England and exhibited three miniatures at the Royal Academy in 1813, but he followed his brother, GEORGE BRIDPORT, to America *c.* 1816 and settled in Philadelphia where they had a drawing academy in 1816–17. He made professional visits to Massachusetts in 1820 and Troy (N.Y.) in 1822, but made his home in Philadelphia until his death. He exhibited many times at the Pennsylvania Academy from 1817 to 1843 and at the Artists' Fund Society in 1844–45. After 1848 he was listed in the Philadelphia directories as "gentleman." ¶ Smith; Graves, *Dictionary;* Brown and Brown; Lipman and Winchester, 169; Troy *Post,* Oct. 8, 15 and 22, 1822, cited by Joseph Gavit (letter to R. W. G. Vail, April 1952); Phila. CD 1825–68; Stauffer, nos. 278, 2321–22, 3038; Rutledge, PA.

BRIEN, JOSEPH. Lithographer; born in Ireland *c.* 1841; working in Boston in July 1860. ¶ 8 Census (1860), Mass., XXVII, 528.

BRIGGS, L. A. Primitive painter of ship pictures in watercolors, Boston, *c.* 1850. ¶ Lipman and Winchester, 169.

BRIGGS, R. W. Portrait painter, known only for his portrait of the Rev. John Leland, 1837, owned in 1941 by Misses May and Kate Cummings of Vermont. ¶ WPA (Mass.), *Portraits Found in Vermont.*

BRIGHAM, F. Landscape painter, Minneapolis, 1857. His only recorded work is a view of St. Anthony's Falls with the first building of the University of Minnesota in the background. ¶ *American Collector,* X (May 1941), 3, repro.

BRIGHAM, WILLIAM H. Portrait painter, Boston, 1858–59; exhibited at the National Academy in 1863. ¶ Boston BD 1858–59; Cowdrey, NAD.

BRIGHTLY, HENRY. Engraver and machinist, Philadelphia, 1850–51. He was born in England *c.* 1822, the son of HENRY A. BRIGHTLY, engraver, with whom he lived in Philadelphia in 1850. Though listed as an engraver in the 1850 Census, Henry Brightly is listed in city directories in 1850–51 as a machinist. ¶ 7 Census (1850), Pa., LIII, 94; Phila. CD 1850–51.

BRIGHTLY, HENRY A. Engraver; born in England *c.* 1791; living in Philadelphia, 1835–58. Brightly came to America sometime between 1825 and 1835 and established himself as a printer and wood engraver. In 1850 his household included his wife Emily, age 64, and three children—Harriett, age 30, Henry, age 28, May, age 25—all born in England. HENRY BRIGHTLY, the son, was listed as an engraver. JOSEPH H. BRIGHTLY, also a Philadelphia engraver in 1850, was probably another son of Henry A. Brightly. ¶ 7 Census (1850), Pa., LIII, 94; Phila. CD 1835, 1837, 1840–54, 1856–58.

BRIGHTLY, JOSEPH H. Wood engraver; born in England *c.* 1818; living in Philadelphia and NYC 1841–58. Probably a son of HENRY A. BRIGHTLY, engraver in Philadelphia *c.* 1835–58, Joseph H. Brightly (or Brightley) was listed in city directories from 1841 to 1858. In 1850 his household in the Spring Garden Ward of Philadelphia included his New Jersey born wife Harriet, age 35, and five children, from 9 to 2 years of age, all born in Pennsylvania. Brightly moved about 1858 to NYC, where he headed the wood-engraving firm of BRIGHTLY, WATERS & Co. ¶ 7 Census (1850), Pa., Phila. County, Spring Garden Ward, July 13, 1850; Phila. CD 1841–54; NYCD and NYBD 1858; Hamilton, 151, lists two books with engravings by Brightly; represented in Map Division, Library of Congress.

BRIGHTLY, WATERS & CO. Wood engravers, NYC, 1858. The partners were JOSEPH H. BRIGHTLY and CHARLES J. B. WATERS. ¶ NYBD and NYCD 1858.

BRINGHARD, MIKE. Engraver, New Orleans, 1857. ¶ Delgado-WPA, cites CD 1857.

BRISCOE, A. H. Dentist, exhibited portrait busts and medallions in clay at the Pennsylvania Academy in 1850, 1852, 1853, and 1859. ¶ Phila. CD 1852–60; Rutledge, PA.

BRISCOE, DANIEL. Engraver; born in Ireland *c.* 1825; died at South Boston in 1883. Briscoe was in Boston by 1850, with his Irish-born wife Hannah, age 25. Ten years later he owned real property worth $6,000 and personal property worth $1,500. ¶ 7 Census (1850), Mass., XXV (Suffolk County, Part 2), 16; 8 Census (1860), Mass., XXIX, 26; Smith; Boston BD 1850–60, CD 1851–60.

BRISSET, EUGENE. Drawing teacher and lithographer, New Orleans, 1821–22. He advertised in 1821 as a drawing teacher to colored children. ¶ Delgado-WPA, cites *La. Gazette,* Dec. 14, 1821; New Orleans CD 1822.

BRISTOL, JOHN BUNYAN. N.A. Landscape painter; born at Hillsdale (N.Y.), April 14, 1826; died in NYC, August 31, 1909. Largely self-taught, except for a few lessons from HENRY ARY, Bristol was exhibiting at the National Academy by 1858. He was elected an Associate in 1860 and a member in 1875. From about 1860 Bristol made his home in NYC, but spent most of his summers in New England, where he found inspiration for some of his best landscapes. ¶ DAB; Cowdrey, NAD; CAB; Clement and Hutton; *Art Annual* VI; French; *Art Journal* (1879), 110–11, cited by Thieme-Becker. His work is represented in the Peabody Institute, Baltimore ("List of Works of Art . . . ," 1949).

BRITT, PETER (1819–?). Portrait and landscape painter, photographer; born at Obstalden, Glarus (Switzerland), March 11, 1819; came to America in 1845. In 1847 Britt was working as a photographer at Highland (Ill.), but in 1852 he moved with his family to Oregon, where he set up a photographic business at Jacksonville, the first in the territory. His gallery included a number of his own oil portraits and Oregon landscapes. He was spoken of in 1939 as "dead for 30 years." ¶ Rasmussen, "Art and Artists of Oregon"; Hines, *History of Oregon,* 420; *Portrait and Biographical Record of Western Oregon,* 906–07; *Oregon Journal,* March 5, 1939, Mag. Sec., p. 1; *Oregon Historical Quarterly,* XXXV (Dec. 1934), 385; Lockley, *Oregon Trail Blazers,* 15–16.

BRITT, WILLIAM W. Wood engraver; born in New York State about 1820; working in NYC from 1844 to 1850. ¶ 7 Census (1850), N.Y., L, 320; NYBD 1844–46; NYCD 1850.

BRITTON & CO. Lithographers, San Francisco, 1859–66. The firm was headed by JOSEPH BRITTON, assisted by HENRY STEINEGGER and X. VAN DE CASTEELE. ¶ San Francisco BD 1858–60; Peters, *Calif. on Stone.*

BRITTON, ISAAC W. Wood engraver, NYC, *c.* 1858–60. Britton was special artist for *The New York Coach-Maker's Magazine,* for which he executed many illustrations of coaches and carriages. ¶ Hamilton, 152.

BRITTON, JOHN. Landscape painter, exhibited a view of NYC from Hoboken at the American Art-Union in 1848. ¶ Cowdrey, AA & AAU.

BRITTON, JOSEPH. Lithographer; born in Yorkshire (England), 1825; died in San Francisco, 1901. Britton was brought to America at the age of ten and was established as a lithographer in NYC by 1847. Two years later he went to California, settling in San Francisco. He was for a time a partner in the lithographic firm of POLLARD & BRITTON (1852), but soon established his own business in association with his brother-in-law, JACQUES J. REY, first as BRITTON & REY, lithographers (1852–1858), then as Britton, Rey & O'Brien, plumbers and gas-fitters (1859–1861). Britton continued his interest in lithography after 1858, forming a new company, BRITTON & CO. (1859–1866) in which he was assisted by the lithographers, HENRY STEINEGGER and X. VAN DE CASTELLE. In 1860 Britton lived in the home of JACQUES J. REY with Jane Britton, age 65, presumably his mother; at that time he owned realty valued at $5,000 and personalty valued at $4,000. He is said to have been active in public affairs in San Francisco. ¶ Peters, *Calif. on Stone;* San Francisco CD 1852, BD 1856, 1858–60; 8 Census (1860), Calif., VII, 587.

BRITTON & REY. Lithographers, San Francisco, 1852–1858. The partners were JOSEPH BRITTON and JACQUES J. REY. After 1858 they seem to have abandoned lithography for plumbing, though Britton kept his hand in by establishing the lithographic firm of BRITTON & CO., at the same time that he set up the plumbing and gas-fitting of Britton, Rey & O'Brien. ¶ Peters, *Calif. on Stone;* San Francisco BD 1856, 1858.

BROADBENT, Dr. SAMUEL. Portrait painter of Wethersfield (Conn.); born March 29, 1759; died April 2, 1828. ¶ Stiles, *Ancient Wethersfield,* II, 135.

BROAR, BENJAMIN. Engraver, 20, born in New York State, at NYC in September 1850. ¶ 7 Census (1850), N.Y., LI, 401.

BROBST, see PROBST.

BROCARD (or Brocadd), A. Artist, New Orleans, 1849–52. ¶ Delgado-WPA, cites New Orelans CD 1849, 1850; New Orleans CD 1852.

BRODEAU, ANNA MARIA. Miniaturist; born in Philadelphia, 1775; married Dr. WILLIAM THORNTON in Philadelphia, 1790; died in Washington (D.C.) in August

1865. ¶ Bolton, *Miniature Painters;* Fielding.

BROMSTEAD, HENRY. Lithographer; born in Germany *c.* 1806; living in Washington (D.C.) in July 1850. ¶ 7 Census (1850), D.C., I, 185.

BRONSON, D. Portrait painter, NYC, 1839–43, exhibited at the National Academy. ¶ Cowdrey, NAD.

BROOKES, SAMUEL MARSDON (1816–1892). Portrait, miniature, and landscape painter; born in Newington Green, Middlesex (England), April 8, 1816; died in San Francisco, January 31, 1892. Brookes came with his parents to Chicago in 1832 and commenced painting in 1841. The following year he moved to Milwaukee and in 1845, having sold his paintings by lottery, he returned to England to further his artistic training. On his return to America in 1847, Brookes revisited Chicago, where his work was well received. From 1847 to 1862 he worked in Milwaukee, for some time after 1855 in association with THOMAS H. STEVENSON. Brookes finally left Wisconsin in 1862 to settle permanently in San Francisco, where he became prominent in artistic circles as a founder of the San Francisco Art Association and the Bohemian Club. In later years he was best known as a painter of fish. Many of his portraits and Indian studies are preserved in Wisconsin. ¶ Ely, "Art and Artists of Milwaukee," 72; Butts, *Art in Wisconsin,* 70–75, with 3 repros.; Pierce, *A History of Chicago,* I, 314–15.

BROOKS, ——. Engraver of a book plate for Dr. J. Dove of Richmond (Va.), *c.* 1800. ¶ Stauffer.

BROOKS, ——. Miniaturist and painting teacher, visited Fredericksburg (Va.) in April 1829. ¶ Fredericksburg *Political Arena,* April 28, 1829.

BROOKS, ALDEN FINNEY. Portrait painter; born at West Williamsfield (Ohio), April 3, 1840; living in Chicago in 1931. ¶ *Art Annual,* XXX.

BROOKS, CAROLINE SHAWK. Sculptor in marble, plaster, and butter; born in Cincinnati, April 28, 1840; working at Washington (D.C.) and NYC in 1878; still living in 1900. ¶ CAB; Mallett.

BROOKS, NEWTON. Portrait painter, primitive, worked in Massachusetts and at New Ipswich (N.H.). ¶ Sears, *Some American Primitives,* 291; Lipman and Winchester, 169.

BROOKS, NOAH. Landscape painter, stylistically of the "Hudson River School," known for a view, "On the Susquehanna," signed and dated 1854. ¶ Courtesy of Miss Ruth Davidson of *Antiques.*

BROOKS, SAMUEL [E.]. Medallist, miniature and profile painter, working in Boston, September 1790, with JOSEPH WRIGHT. He probably worked also in the Carolinas. ¶ Bolton, *Miniature Painters;* Ford, *Broadsides,* no. 2567; Storer, "The Manly Washington Medal"; Thieme-Becker, cites Forrer's *Dictionary of Medallists.*

BROOME, ISAAC. Sculptor, expert on ceramics; born in Valcartier (Canada), May 16, 1835; died in Trenton (N.J.), May 4, 1922. Broome was working in Philadelphia from 1855 to 1860, and exhibited at the Pennsylvania Academy (1855, 1859) and the Washington Art Association (1857). ¶ Thieme-Becker; N. Y. *Times,* May 5, 1922; Rutledge, PA; Phila. CD 1857–60; Fielding; Washington Art Assoc., 1857; Taft, *History of American Sculpture; Who's Who in America* (1910); *American Collector,* XV (Aug. 1946), 17, repro.

BROSS & BOGART. Wood engravers, NYC, 1856–1857. The partners were ROBERT S. BROSS and ROBERT M. BOGART. ¶ NYBD 1856; NYCD 1857.

BROSS, ROBERT S. Wood engraver; born in New Jersey about 1831; active in NYC from 1856 to 1860. His wife Susan and son Robert B. were both born in New York. ¶ 8 Census (1860), N.Y., LVII, 719; NYBD 1856; NYCD 1857, 1859; Cowdrey, *Winslow Homer: Illustrator.*

BROSS, SAMUEL. Pennsylvania-born engraver, 30, at NYC in 1850. ¶ 7 Census (1850), N.Y., XLI, 74.

BROTHERHEAD, ——. Wood engraver, active 1849. He engraved four of HENRY WILLIAM HERBERT's drawings of game birds and animals to illustrate *Frank Forester's Field Sports of the United States and British Provinces of North America* (N.Y., 1849). Other engravings in the same volume were done by JOSEPH H. BRIGHTLY, and Brotherhead may have been, like Brightly, a Philadelphian. ¶ Hamilton, 296.

BROTZE, RUDOLPH. Engraver; born in Germany *c.* 1820; living in Philadelphia in August 1850. ¶ 7 Census (1850), Pa., LII, 147.

BROUGHAM, J. Historical painter. His work is known only through an engraving by THOMAS KELLY (1795–1841) after Brougham's painting of General Joseph

Warren taking leave of his wife on the eve of the Battle of Bunker Hill. ¶ Stauffer, no. 1629.

BROWER, FRANCIS M. Artist and actor; born in Maryland *c.* 1823; living in Philadelphia in 1860. Brower owned real estate valued at $3,000 and personal property valued at $1,500. His wife, Louisa, was born in Maryland *c.* 1822. ¶ 8 Census (1860), Pa., LIII, 104.

BROWERE, ALBERTUS D. O. (or Albertis del Orient) (1814–1887). Landscape, genre, and still life painter; born at Tarrytown (N.Y.), March 17, 1814; died at Catskill (N.Y.), February 17, 1887; son of JOHN HENRI ISAAC BROWERE, noted sculptor and taker of life masks. The younger Browere turned to painting rather than sculpture, and exhibited for the first time at the National Academy in 1831. He moved from NYC to Catskill in 1834 and supported himself by clerking in a drug store and painting in his free time. In 1852 he sailed for California where he remained for almost four years, returning to Catskill in 1856. Two years later he again went to California and he remained in San Francisco until 1861, when he settled permanently in New York State. Browere was noted primarily as a painter of genre pictures of American life. He exhibited at the National Academy from 1831 to 1846 and at the American Academy, the Apollo Association, and the American Art-Union from 1833 to 1848. ¶ Bolton, *Miniature Painters;* Cowdrey, NAD; Van Nostrand and Coulter, *California Pictorial;* Cowdrey, AA & AAU; Sweet, *Hudson River School;* Met. Mus., *Life in America;* Stokes, *Iconography;* Davidson, *Life in America;* Howell, "Pictorial Californiana," 64–65; represented at N. Y. State Hist. Assoc. ("List of Paintings," 1950).

BROWERE, JOHN HENRI ISAAC (1790–1834). Sculptor, taker of life masks, painter in oils; born in NYC, November 18, 1790; died in NYC, September 10, 1834. Browere studied in NYC with ARCHIBALD ROBERTSON and continued his studies, especially of sculpture, during a two-year residence in Europe (1816–17). During the remainder of his life Browere made his home in NYC but traveled over the country taking life masks of distinguished Americans by an improved method of his own invention. This collection, bequeathed to his family and still extant, is an authentic and very valuable historical record of Browere's famous contemporaries, including Jefferson, Lafayette and others. ¶ MS records of First German Reformed Church, NYC, at NYHS; DAB, gives birth date as 1792; McKay, cites NYCD 1811–15, 1817–19; C. H. Hart, *Browere's Life Masks of Great Americans;* Bennett, *The Mask of Fame;* C. H. Hart, "Unknown Life Masks of Great Americans"; M. Knoedler & Co., *Life Masks of Noted Americans;* N. Y. State Hist. Assoc., *Life Masks of Noted Americans;* Millard, "The Browere Life Masks"; MSS of Browere and examples of his work at N. Y. State Hist. Assoc., Cooperstown; represented at NYHS.

BROWN, ABBY MASON. Miniaturist, active 1800–22, probably in New England. ¶ Bolton, *Miniature Painters,* lists a miniature of Lewis Herreshoff, owned in 1920 by a descendant in Newport (R.I.); Fielding.

BROWN, ALICE. Of Brooklyn (N.Y.), exhibited an oil painting at the American Institute in 1848. ¶ Am. Inst. Cat., 1848.

BROWN, ARTHUR. Lithographer, NYC, 1854–59. ¶ NYBD, 1854, 1857, 1859.

BROWN, BENJAMIN. Engraver and printer of book-plates, maps, and cards, NYC, 1817–19. ¶ Stauffer; McKay, cites NYCD 1817–19.

BROWN, BENJAMIN H. Engraver, 19, born in New York State, at NYC in 1850. ¶ 7 Census (1850), N.Y., L, 381.

BROWN, CHARLES. Sculptor; born in Connecticut *c.* 1825; living in Columbus (Ohio) in October 1850. ¶ 7 Census (1850), Ohio, XV, 485.

BROWN, CHARLES F. Wood engraver, NYC, 1848–50. In 1848 he exhibited a wood engraving at the American Institute, under the name of C. F. Brown; his address was at that time the same as that of WILLIAM ROBERTS, engraver. In 1850 Brown was in partnership with J. AUGUSTUS BOGERT under the firm name, BOGERT & BROWN. ¶ Am. Inst. Cat., 1848; NYBD and NYCD 1850.

BROWN, "CLAUDE," see GEORGE LORING BROWN.

BROWN, CRAWFORD F. Engraver, Boston, 1858–60 and after. ¶ Boston CD 1858–60 and after.

BROWN, DAVID. Landscape painter; born in Scotland *c.* 1830; living in Boston, unmarried, in 1860. ¶ 8 Census (1860), Mass., XXVII, 551.

BROWN, DAVID. Portrait painter, 56, from Vermont, living in NYC in July 1850.

¶ 7 Census (1850), N.Y., XLVII, 422. *Cf.* DAVID L. BROWN.

BROWN, DAVID L. Drawing teacher and painter, Boston, 1818–35. He exhibited three miniature landscapes at the Boston Athenaeum in 1828, including "On the Banks of the Tweed." DAVID BROWN, above, may be the same. ¶ Swan, BA, 180, 207.

BROWN, EDMUND (or Edward). Engraver, Utica (N.Y.), 1857–61. He was listed as Edward in 1857–58, and as Edmund from 1859. ¶ Utica CD 1857–61; Rome CD 1859, adv. p. 7.

BROWN, EDWARD. Artist; born in Maine *c.* 1835; living in Dallas, Wasco County (Oregon) in 1860. ¶ 8 Census (1860), Oregon, info. courtesy of David C. Duniway, Oregon State Archivist.

BROWN, E. & J. Lithographers, NYC, 1846–48; exhibited 2 lithographs at the American Institute in 1846 and lithographed portraits, marine, and town scenes in 1848. The partners were ELIPHALET M. BROWN, JR. and, presumably, a brother, not otherwise identified. ¶ Am. Inst. Cat., 1846; Peters, *America on Stone,* 114.

BROWN, ELIPHALET M., JR. (1816–1886). Lithographer, portrait, historical, and marine artist; born in Newburyport (Mass.) in 1816; died in NYC, January 23, 1886. He was working in NYC by 1839 when his lithograph of "Boz" after D. Lawrence, drawn for CURRIER & IVES, was published. He remained in NYC until 1852, working alone and with others (E. & J. BROWN, 1846, 1848; BROWN & SEVERYN, 1851; CURRIER & IVES, 1852). From 1852 to 1854 Brown was attached to Commodore Perry's expedition to Japan as daguerreotypist and artist. On his return he received permission from Perry to publish sketches of the "landing in Japan" under his own supervision and at his own expense; and under this arrangement a series of four large folios appeared, with lithography by SARONY & Co. From about 1855 to 1875 Brown was connected with the U. S. Navy almost constantly, serving during the Civil War as Master and Ensign and afterwards as Admiral's secretary for some years in the Mediterranean Squadron. He married about 1875 and retired from the Navy. He exhibited at the National Academy in 1841. His work is represented in the Library of Congress, the New York Public Library, and the Museum of the City of New York. He signed his work "E. Brown, Jr." ¶ N. Y. *Times,* Jan. 24, 1886, obit.; Peters, *Currier & Ives,* II, 200; Cowdrey, NAD; Am. Inst. Cat., 1846; Peters, *America on Stone;* Peters, *Clipper Ship Prints,* 12; Perry, *Expedition to Japan* (1856), I, contains many illustrations by Brown. [All information courtesy Josephine M. Bever.]

BROWN, EPHRAIM. Portrait painter, Indianapolis, 1837–40. ¶ Peat, *Pioneer Painters of Indiana,* 150–51.

BROWN, F. H., & Co. Engravers, Chicago, 1856. ¶ Chicago BD 1856.

BROWN, G. Two miniatures by this artist were exhibited at the Pennsylvania Academy in 1847. This may be the G. Brown, Jr., whose "Ariadne" was in the American Art-Union Sale in 1852. *Cf.* G. B. BROWN and GEORGE LORING BROWN. ¶ Rutledge, PA; Cowdrey, AA & AAU.

BROWN, G. B. Miniature and portrait painter, NYC, 1817–25. This artist was a Member of the American Academy from 1817 to 1825 and exhibited there in 1816, 1817, 1820, and 1824. He was listed in the 1817 NYCD as G. Brown, miniature painter. He was probably the "Brown" who exhibited a miniature at the Pennsylvania Academy in 1823 and may have been the George or G. Brown who exhibited portraits at the Royal Academy in London from 1825 to 1839. *Cf.* also G. BROWN, above. ¶ Cowdrey, AA & AAU; Rutledge, PA; NYCD 1817; Graves, *Dictionary.*

BROWN, GEORGE. Artist, 34, a native of New York State, at NYC in June 1860. ¶ 8 Census (1860), N.Y., XLIII, 245.

BROWN, GEORGE. Engraver, 17, born in New York State, at NYC in 1850. ¶ 7 Census (1850), N.Y., L, 393.

BROWN, GEORGE LORING (or "Claude" Brown) (1814–1889). Landscape, portrait, and miniature painter, lithographer, etcher, and wood engraver; born in Boston, February 2, 1814; died in Malden (Mass.), June 25, 1889. He was working in Boston from 1834 to 1836, in NYC in 1837, and in Shrewsbury, Worcester and Boston (Mass.) in 1838. From about 1839 to 1859 Brown was in Europe, particularly in Florence and Rome. He returned to America in 1859 and was working in NYC in 1862 and in Boston in 1864. He was a frequent exhibitor at the Boston Athenaeum (1834 to 1874), the National Academy (1837–1866), the Apollo Association and American Art-Union (1839–1852), the Pennsylvania

Academy and Artists' Fund Society (1836–1864) and the Maryland Historical Society (1848–1853). ¶ Bolton, *Miniature Painters;* Karolik Cat., 145–153; Clement and Hutton; CAB; Swan, BA; NYBD 1837; Rutledge, PA; Cowdrey, NAD; Cowdrey, AA & AAU; Stauffer; Sweet, *Hudson River School; Portfolio* (Nov. 1942), and *Panorama* (Jan. 1947), repros.

BROWN, GRAFTON T. Artist and lithographer, active 1856–77. In the 1850's and early 1860's Brown designed views of several western towns, including Virginia City (Nev.), for the San Francisco lithographers, KUCHEL & DRESEL. He established his own lithographic business, as Brown & Co., in San Francisco in 1872 and was still active in 1877. ¶ Peters, *California on Stone,* 89–90, 147; Stokes, *Hist. Prints,* pl. 98-b.

BROWN, H. E. Painter of a portrait of John Christian Till, organist in Bethlehem (Pa.) early in the 19th century. ¶ Levering, *History of Bethlehem,* 710.

BROWN, H. I. Miniature painter, Boston, 1844–51. ¶ Boston BD 1844, 1850–51; Bolton, *Miniature Painters.*

BROWN, HARRISON B. (sometimes as Harry or Henry B.) (1831–1915). Marine and landscape painter; born at Portland (Maine) in 1831; died in London, March 10, 1915. Brown began his career with a sign and banner painter in Portland, but was exhibiting landscapes at the National Academy by 1858. He settled in England in 1892. ¶ "Maine Artists," *Art Annual,* XII, obit., and *Art News,* March 27, 1915, obit., all give the name as Harrison B. Brown; NAD Cats. 1858–1875 list him as Harry, while Thieme-Becker and Clement and Hutton call him Henry B. Brown; in the Providence *Daily Journal,* Aug. 5, 1850, he was spoken of as Henry Box Brown (courtesy J. Earl Arrington).

BROWN, HENRY B., see HARRISON B. BROWN.

BROWN, HENRY JAMES (1811–1855). Portrait painter, born October 12, 1811, at Woodlawn Plantation, Cumberland County, Va. As a young man he met and studied under GEORGE CALEB BINGHAM in Missouri and he also studied with THOMAS SULLY in Philadelphia in 1845. Most of his painting was done in eastern and southern Virginia, where he was also a Methodist clergyman and farmer. He died April 9, 1855, at Buckingham Female Seminary in Virginia. He was married to Susan Ann Hobson and most of his known works are owned by their descendants in and near Lynchburg (Va.). ¶ Information courtesy Miss Martha von Briesen, Sweet Briar College (Va.); and FARL, citing Mount Lynchburg (Va.) *News,* Oct. 16, 1941.

BROWN, HENRY KIRKE (1814–1886). N.A. Sculptor and portrait painter; born at Leyden (Mass.), February 24, 1814; died at Newburgh (N.Y.), July 10, 1886. Brown was working in NYC in 1833; in Cincinnati in 1836–37, and in Albany and Troy (N.Y.) from 1839 to 1842. In the latter year he left for a four-year stay in Europe, after which he lived in NYC and Brooklyn from 1849 to 1856. In 1856 was unveiled his greatest work, the equestrian statue of Washington in Union Square, NYC. Brown was in Washington (D.C.) in 1859. His home after 1861 was in Newburgh. Brown exhibited at the National Academy, the Boston Athenaeum, the Pennsylvania Academy and the Washington Art Association. ¶ DAB; Cist, *Cincinnati in 1841,* 141; NYCD 1847–48; Brooklyn CD 1849–50, 1853–56; Cowdrey, NAD; Swan, BA; Rutledge, PA; Washington Art Assoc. Cat., 1859; Lee, *Familiar Sketches,* 203–12; Fairman, *Art and Artists;* Stokes, *Icon.;* Taft, *History of American Sculpture;* Boston *Transcript,* July 12, 1886, obit.; Gardner, *Yankee Stonecutters.*

BROWN, J. One or more artists of this name worked in Massachusetts between 1802 and 1835: J. Brown, profilist at Salem in 1802; J. Brown, watercolor portrait painter at Salem in 1810; and J. Brown, miniaturist at Lowell in 1835. ¶ Jackson, *Silhouette,* 86; Lipman and Winchester, 169; Belknap, *Artists and Craftsmen of Essex County,* 7.

BROWN, JAMES. Landscape, marine, genre, and portrait painter; born in New York State about 1820; at NYC, 1844–55; St. Louis, 1859. A portrait painter, J. Brown, is listed in NYBD 1844; James Brown appears in NYCD 1850 as artist, and exhibited at the American Art-Union (1850) and National Academy (1850–55). ¶ 7 Census (1850), N.Y., XLIII, 67; NYBD 1844; NYCD 1850; Cowdrey, NAD; Cowdrey, AA & AAU; St. Louis BD 1859; repros., Davidson, 21, 131.

BROWN, JAMES W. Engraver, Philadelphia, 1856. ¶ Phila. BD 1856.

BROWN, JAMES W. Artist; born in Maryland *c.* 1838; living in Baltimore in August 1860. ¶ 8 Census (1860), Md., IV, 930.

BROWN, JOHN. Ship figurehead carver, Philadelphia, 1798. A pupil of WILLIAM RUSH, Brown carved figureheads for the ships *Maryland* and *Eagle*. ¶ Pinckney, 81, 188.

BROWN, JOHN. Engraver, Philadelphia, 1860. Born in Pennsylvania *c.* 1837, John was the son of Robert Brown, a Scottish carpenter who had come to America before 1835 and in 1860 owned property valued at $1,100. ¶ 8 Census (1860), Pa., LIII, 778.

BROWN, JOHN. Engraver, Baltimore, 1860. Born in Maryland *c.* 1839, he was the son of Robert Brown, a native of Ireland, who was a dealer in fine watches and jewellery. The father's property was valued at $8,000 in realty and $20,000 in personalty. ¶ 8 Census (1860), Md., V, 269.

BROWN, JOHN GEORGE (1831–1913). N.A. Genre painter; born in Durham [?], England, November 11, 1831; died in NYC, February 8, 1913. Brown was working in Brooklyn as early as 1855 and first exhibited at the National Academy in 1858. His paintings of street urchins achieved great popularity and Brown exhibited frequently at the National Academy, the Boston Athenaeum, and the Pennsylvania Academy. ¶ DAB; Brooklyn CD 1855–58; Cowdrey, NAD; Swan, BA; Clement and Hutton; Peters, *America on Stone;* repros. in Met. Mus., *Life in America; Portfolio* (May 1946); *Art Digest* (March 15, 1945); *American Collector* (May 1946); *Panorama* (May 1946), and Davidson. His work is represented at the Corcoran Gallery (Cat. 1947) and the Peabody Institute ("List of Works of Art," 1949).

BROWN, JOHN HENRY (1818–1891). Portrait painter and miniaturist; born in Lancaster (Pa.), August 21, 1818; died in Philadelphia [?], April 3, 1891. While working as a clerk in the Recorder's Office in Lancaster, Brown began to study painting in 1836 under ARTHUR ARMSTRONG. He became a professional portrait painter in Lancaster in 1839, but from about 1844 seems to have painted only miniatures. He moved in 1845 to Philadelphia where he remained until his death. In 1860 Brown painted a miniature of Lincoln at Springfield (Ill.). He was a frequent exhibitor at the Pennsylvania Academy between 1844 and 1864 and exhibited at the National Academy in 1875. ¶ Lancaster County Hist. Soc., *Portraiture in Lancaster County*, 116–17, repro.; Bolton, *Miniature Painters; Antiques* (Nov. 1943), 210, 212; Phila. CD 1849, BD 1850, 1852–53; Wilson, *Lincoln in Portraiture;* Rutledge, PA; Clement and Hutton; 7 Census (1850), Pa., LI, 312; Cowdrey, NAD.

BROWN, JOHN R. Lithographer; born in Scotland *c.* 1836; living in Baltimore in October 1860. ¶ 8 Census (1860), Md., III, 981.

BROWN, LAURENCE. "Limner," Boston, 1701. ¶ Dunlap, *History* (1918); Thieme-Becker.

BROWN, M., JR., see WILLIAM GARL BROWN.

BROWN, M. E. D. Lithographer; historical, portrait, and genre painter, active 1832 to 1896. One of the best of the early lithographers, Brown worked in Philadelphia 1832 to 1834. NATHANIEL CURRIER worked for him in 1833 and the following year a lithograph by M. E. D. Brown was the first known work to issue from Currier's press in NYC. Brown was in Boston in 1835, when he exhibited at the Artists' Fund Society of Philadelphia. He exhibited, without address, at the National Academy in 1845 and as of Utica (N.Y.) in 1850. His name appears in Utica directories, as "artist," from 1849 to 1896. ¶ Peters, *America on Stone;* Peters, *Currier and Ives;* PA Cat., 1832; Artists' Fund Soc. Cat., 1835; Cowdrey, NAD; Utica CD 1849–1896; McClinton, "American Flower Lithographs"; repros. in *Antiques* (Feb. 1927), 110.

BROWN, Miss M. P. Landscape painter, exhibited at the National Academy in 1852. ¶ Cowdrey, NAD.

BROWN, MARTIN S. Engraver; born in Virginia *c.* 1805; working in Baltimore as early as 1842, but seems to have returned to Virginia, where his younger child was born *c.* 1844. He was again in Baltimore in 1845 and in 1850, when he was living there with his wife and two children, all natives of Virginia, and was still in Baltimore as late as 1858–60. ¶ 7 Census (1850), Md., V, 462; Baltimore CD 1842, 1845, 1858–60.

BROWN (Browne), MARY ANN. Still life, genre, and landscape painter. Miss Brown, who exhibited at the National Academy in 1837 as of NYC and in 1858–1859 as of Hoboken (N.J.), was a daughter of WILLIAM G. BROWN, SR., and sister of WILLIAM GARL BROWN. M. A. Brown, who exhibited a watercolor still life at the

National Academy in 1867 as of NYC, may have been the same artist. From 1868 to 1873 she exhibited as Mrs. Chaney. ¶ Cowdrey, NAD.

BROWN, MATHER (1761–1831). Portrait and miniature painter; born in Boston, October 7, 1761; died in London, May 25, 1831. Mather Brown was an itinerant portrait painter and wine merchant at Peekskill (N.Y.) and Worcester and Springfield (Mass.) from 1777. He went to Europe about 1780, first to Paris, then to London where he made his home from 1781 to his death. He exhibited over a hundred portraits in London galleries. ¶ DAB; Graves, *Dictionary;* Morgan, *Gilbert Stuart and His Pupils;* Bolton, *Miniature Painters;* Swan, BA; Thieme-Becker. He is represented at the American Antiquarian Society (Weis, *Cat. of Portraits,* 1946). See also: Coburn, "Mather Brown," and Hart, "Portrait of Thomas Dawson, Viscount Cremorne," repro. in *Portraits in Delaware,* 111, and biblio. in Flexner, *The Light of Distant Skies,* 258–59.

BROWN, "MYSTERIOUS." This artist, an experienced miniaturist of about 50, came to NYC from England in the first decade of the 19th century and remained for about 12 years, according to WILLIAM DUNLAP. He was one of the teachers of NATHANIEL ROGERS. Dunlap, who believed that Brown was an assumed name, called him "mysterious Brown." He may, however, have been the URIAH BROWN working as a portrait and miniature painter in NYC in 1808. ¶ Dunlap, *History,* II, 253–54; NYCD 1808; Bolton, *Crayon Draftsmen;* Bolton, *Miniature Painters.*

BROWN, NATHAN. Wood engraver, Boston, 1847–53. This was probably the N. Brown who engraved on wood two illustrations for *Life and Sayings of Mrs. Partington, and Others of the Family* (N.Y., 1854). ¶ Boston BD 1847–52, CD 1853 (as designer); Hamilton, 160.

BROWN, PAUL. Portrait painter, Washington, 1860. *Cf.* WILLIAM P. BROWN. ¶ Washington and Georgetown CD 1860.

BROWN, ROBERT (*c.* 1812–1832) Portrait and figure painter. A native of Pittsburgh (Pa.) who, while still in his teens, won local praise for his painting, engraving, and mechanical skill. He studied painting in Philadelphia for a short time but contracted tuberculosis and returned to Pittsburgh, where he died July 22, 1832, in his twentieth year. ¶ *Hazard's Register of Pennsylvania,* X, Sept. 1832, 199–200.

BROWN, SAMUEL E. Wood engraver, Boston, 1840–60. The engraving firms with which he was associated were: DEVEREUX & BROWN (1842–44), BROWN & WORCESTER (1846–47), SAMUEL E. BROWN & Co. (1848), and MANNING & BROWN (1856). Brown probably died *c.* 1860, when his name disappears from the directories. His widow died in Boston, May 23, 1893, age 72. ¶ Boston BD 1841–42, 1847–60, CD 1841–44, 1846, 1851–59; Boston *Transcript,* May 25, 1893, obit.

BROWN, SAMUEL E., & Co. Wood engravers, Boston, 1848. ¶ Boston CD 1848.

BROWN & SEVERYN. Lithographers, NYC, 1851–53; ELIPHALET M. BROWN, JR., and CHARLES SEVERYN. ¶ Peters, *America on Stone.*

BROWN, SOLYMAN (1790–1876). Portrait painter and sculptor; born at Litchfield (Conn.), November 17, 1790; died at Dodge Center (Minn.), February 13, 1876. Though noted primarily as a pioneer in dentistry, as "Poet Laureate of the Dental Profession," and as a Swedenborgian preacher, Solyman Brown was also an amateur artist, his best known works being a bust and portrait of Eleazar Parmly, a New York dentist. He exhibited four busts at the National Academy in 1842, one of them executed in collaboration with J. BALLIN. ¶ DAB; Cowdrey, NAD.

BROWN, THEOPHILUS B. (?–1834). Amateur artist. He entered the U. S. Military Academy in 1822 and was commissioned Lieutenant of Artillery in 1826. His view of West Point was engraved by J. F. E. PRUDHOMME *c.* 1830. Lt. Brown died September 14, 1834. ¶ Heitman, *Historical Register;* Stauffer.

BROWN, THOMAS. Stone seal engraver, NYC, 1800–50. Brown cut a cornelian seal with the head of Joseph Smith in 1843 and in 1848 he exhibited a stone seal engraving, "Head of Washington," at the American Institute. ¶ NYCD 1800–11, 1814–50; Arrington, *Nauvoo Temple,* Chap. 8; Am. Inst. Cat., 1848.

BROWN, URIAH (or Uriel). Portrait and miniature painter, working at Salem (Mass.) in 1805 and at NYC in 1808. It is possible this is the artist referred to by Dunlap as "MYSTERIOUS" BROWN. ¶ Belknap, *Artists and Craftsmen of Essex County,* 7; McKay, cites NYCD 1808.

BROWN, W. Miniaturist, Philadelphia, exhibited at the Pennsylvania Academy in 1819. ¶ Rutledge, PA.

BROWN, WALTER. Amateur artist and collector; died at Burlington (Vt.), April 30, 1879. A wealthy woolen merchant of Philadelphia and NYC, Walter Brown was "known for years as the friend and helper of struggling artists." He was a member of the art committee of the Union League Club, a member of the American Watercolor Society, and a noted collector of "old masters." Several of his own works were exhibited at the National Academy in 1860 and 1867–73, and at the Pennsylvania Academy in 1867. ¶ Boston *Advertiser,* May 7, 1879; Cowdrey, NAD; Rutledge, PA.

BROWN, WILLIAM. Engraver and lithographer, Buffalo (N.Y.), 1858–62. ¶ Buffalo CD 1858–62.

BROWN (or Browne), WILLIAM G., [SR.]. English landscape and genre painter, working in America from 1837 to *c.* 1861. W. G. Brown of Leicester exhibited a "domestic" scene at the Royal Academy in 1835. The following year he brought his family to America and settled in Brooklyn. For the next ten years, as William or William G. Brown he worked in Brooklyn and NYC, and exhibited genre paintings at the National Academy (1838, 1847, 1848), the Apollo Association (1838, 1841), and the American Art-Union (1847). Two of his children, WILLIAM GARL BROWN and MARY ANN BROWN, also exhibited at this time. From 1856 to 1861 the elder Brown and his daughter Mary Ann lived in Hoboken (N.J.), while William, Jr., apparently made his home in NYC. Mary Ann moved to NYC in 1864 or 1865, possibly an indication that the father had died. He exhibited for the last time at the National Academy in 1859, a painting of "The Last Day of the N. Y. State Fair, Buffalo, 1857." ¶ Graves, *Dictionary;* NYCD 1837–42, 1847, 1856–65; Brooklyn CD 1837–45; Cowdrey, NAD; Cowdrey, AA & AAU; Jersey City and Hoboken CD 1856, 1858–61. He may have been in Baltimore in 1856 (*cf.* WILLIAM GARL BROWN).

BROWN (or Browne), WILLIAM GARL, [JR.] (1823–1894). Portrait painter; born in England, October 1823, the son of WILLIAM G. BROWN, [SR.], landscape painter of Leicester; died in Buffalo (N.Y.), July 28, 1894. Within a few years of his arrival in America in 1837, the younger Brown exhibited a portrait at the National Academy (1840). By 1846 he had gone to Virginia, where he established himself as a portrait painter in Richmond. In 1847 he made a trip to Mexico to paint portraits of Zachary Taylor and other heroes of the Mexican War which he exhibited in Richmond and Philadelphia in the fall of the same year. During the 1850's he probably traveled in the South, painting numerous portraits in North Carolina and possibly in Maryland, though he seems to have made his home in NYC from 1856 to 1865. In the latter year he was joined in NYC by his artist sister, MARY ANN BROWN, who had been living in Hoboken (N.J.) with their father. After the war William Garl Brown again visited the South, painting the portraits of many North Carolinians and Virginians. In 1876 he married Mary McFeely of Charleston (S.C.), and they made their home in Richmond during the 1880's and until 1894, when Brown died on a visit to his sister in Buffalo (N.Y.). ¶ Information courtesy V. L. Thompson, Forest Lawn Cemetery, Buffalo; Cowdrey, NAD (it may also have been this artist who, with Miss A. Brown, exhibited four vignettes and broach at the National Academy in 1838); NYCD, 1837–42, lists William or W. G. Brown, portrait painter or artist (this could be either father or son, though it is likely that both lived in Brooklyn, see CD 1837–45, and shared a studio in NYC until *c.* 1842); *Richmond Portraits;* Information courtesy Christopher Crittenden, Director, North Carolina Dep't. of Archives and History; Baltimore CD 1856 lists a "William Brown, artist," and a "W. Brown" exhibited a landscape at the Md. Hist. Soc. the same year (this could be either W. G. Brown, Sr., or Jr., or possibly a different artist altogether); NYCD 1856–60, 1862–63, 1865; represented at the Virginia Military Institute, the Virginia Historical Society, the Corcoran Gallery, the University of North Carolina, Wake Forrest College, and in various State buildings at Raleigh (N.C.).

BROWN (or Browne), WILLIAM H. Wood engraver, active 1848–55. Four examples of his work are found in *A Pictorial Description of the United States* (N.Y., 1855). ¶ NYCD and NYBD 1848; Hamilton, 109.

BROWN, WILLIAM H. Amateur landscape painter; an employee of the New York

City Custom House, living in NYC 1846–48 and in Brooklyn 1851–53. He exhibited two landscapes at the National Academy in 1851. ¶ NYCD 1846–48; Brooklyn CD 1851–53; Cowdrey, NAD.

BROWN, WILLIAM HENRY (1808–1883). Silhouettist; born in Charleston (S.C.), May 22, 1808; died there September 16, 1883. Brown first worked as an engineer in Philadelphia where he made his home from 1824 at least until 1841 and probably later. His career as an artist began early in the 1830's and continued until 1859. Working first in New England, he later travelled widely in the South, visiting Charleston in 1839, 1842, 1846 and 1849, as well as St. Louis, New Orleans, Natchez, and Blue Lick Springs (Ky.). His best known work, *Portrait Gallery of Distinguished Americans,* a collection of full-length silhouettes with biographical sketches and facsimile letters of the subjects, was published in Hartford in 1846 by the noted lithographers, E. B. & E. C. KELLOGG. The 1850 Census for Philadelphia indicates that Brown was then living in North Mulberry Ward with his wife Emaline, age 39, and two sons, all born in Pennsylvania. Brown himself was, however, apparently visiting in Charleston at this time, since he is listed alone in the Charleston Census less than two weeks after the taking of the Philadelphia count. After abandoning his artistic career in 1859, Brown continued to work as an engineer in Pennsylvania until his return to Charleston in his last years. ¶ Rutledge, "William Henry Brown of Charleston"; Hart, "The Last of the Silhouettists"; Jackson, *Silhouette,* 86; Carrick, *Shades; Richmond Portraits;* Rutledge, *Artists in the Life of Charleston;* 7 Census (1850), Pa., L, 684 (Aug. 1); 7 Census (1850), S.C., II, 216 (Aug. 13); repros. in *Rhode Island History* (July 1948, cover) and (Jan. 1949, 26–27), and in *Antiques* (Aug. 1924, 88). The *Portrait Gallery* has been reissued twice within recent years: at Troy (N.Y.) in 1925, and by G. A. Baker in NYC in 1931.

BROWN, WILLIAM K. Of LEWIS & BROWN, lithographers, NYC, 1844–48. ¶ NYCD 1844–48; NYBD 1846, 1848.

BROWN, WILLIAM M. Portrait painter, miniaturist, and designer of transparencies, advertised in Charleston (S.C.) in 1825 and at Richmond (Va.) in 1829. Mrs. Brown also advertised in Charleston as a teacher of painting on velvet and satin, without theorems. ¶ Rutledge, *Artists in the Life of Charleston,* 158 (on p. 188 as William Mason Brown); *Richmond Portraits,* 241.

BROWN, WILLIAM MASON (1828–1898). Landscape painter; born at Troy (N.Y.) in 1828; died in Brooklyn, September 6, 1898. Brown was in NYC by 1859, and exhibited at the National Academy annually from 1859 to 1890. At the time of his death he was a resident of Brooklyn. ¶ *Art Annual,* I, obit.; Brooklyn *Eagle,* Sept. 6, 1898, obit.; NAD Cats. 1859–70; NYBD 1859; Brooklyn CD 1898. A still life in the Peabody Institute, signed W. M. Brown, is ascribed to this artist, as Wm. Mason Brown, 1830–1895 ("List of Works of Art," 1949).

BROWN, WILLIAM PAUL. Artist, Baltimore, 1856, 1860. Listed as William P. Brown in the 1860 Census and as William Paul Brown in the 1856 directory. The Baltimore 1860 Census records that William P. Brown (age 35, born in N.Y.) lived with his mother, Harriet (age 62, born in N.Y.), his wife, Clara (age 29, born in Vermont), and one child, Frank (age 1, born in the District of Columbia). Since the Browns were evidently living in the Washington area in 1859, it is possible that William Paul Brown was the same as PAUL BROWN, listed as portrait painter in the 1860 Washington and Georgetown Directory. ¶ Baltimore CD 1856; 8 Census (1860), Md., V, 391; Washington and Georgetown CD 1860.

BROWN & WORCESTER. Wood engravers, Boston, 1846–1847. The partners were SAMUEL E. BROWN and FERNANDO WORCESTER. ¶ Boston BD 1846–47; CD 1846.

BROWNE, O. E. Wood engraver whose work appeared in *A Pictorial Geography of the World* . . . (Boston, 1847). ¶ Hamilton, 192.

BROWNE, WILLIAM R. Lithographer, NYC, 1833–1837; from 1833 to 1835 as a partner of CHARLES RISSO. ¶ NYCD 1833–37.

BROWNELL, CHARLES DE WOLF (1822–1909). Landscape and still life painter; born in Providence (R.I.) in 1822; living at Bristol (R.I.) in 1878. A resident of East Hartford (Conn.) from 1824 to 1860, Brownell gave up a law career in 1853 to devote himself to landscape painting. He studied in Hartford under JULIUS BUSCH and JOSEPH ROPES, and spent seven consecutive winters in Cuba, where he made many studies of tropical scenery. He lived in NYC 1860–65 and spent the next six years in Europe. His best known work was a painting of the Connecticut Charter Oak. ¶ French, *Art and Artists in Conn.;* Clement and Hutton; repro. in *Antiques,* XV (April 1929), 325; Cowdrey, NAD. Miss Dorothy Hammell cites an article by Robert L. Sheeler, "The Strange and Cryptic Picture Diary of Charles De Wolf Brownell," in Providence *Sunday Journal,* June 8, 1947.

BROWNELL, WILLIAM V. Engraver, 17, born in New York, at NYC in 1850. ¶ 7 Census (1850), N.Y., L, 528.

BROWNING, Mrs. H. Miniaturist, 1839–42. In 1839 she was living in NYC and exhibited at the National Academy. ¶ Bolton, *Miniature Painters;* Cowdrey, NAD.

BROWNSON, LEMUEL. Engraver; born in Connecticut *c.* 1806; living in Cincinnati in August 1850. Brownson's real property was valued at $1,700. His wife, Phoebe, age 43, and seven children, ages 7 to 21, were all born in Connecticut. ¶ 7 Census (1850), Ohio, XX, 735.

BROWNSON, WILLIAM M. Xylographic engraver and printer, NYC, 1841–44. In 1843–44 he headed the firm of William Brownson & Co. ¶ NYCD 1841–44.

BRUCCINI (Brucciani), NICOLAO. Modeler in plaster, NYC, 1844; exhibited four plaster figures at the American Institute. ¶ NYCD 1844; Am. Inst. Cat., 1844.

BRUCE, EDWARD CALEDON. Portrait and genre painter, active *c.* 1840–77. During the 1840's Bruce was working in Richmond (Va.). In 1849 he exhibited, without address, at the American Art-Union. From 1854 to 1857 he was at Charlestown ([W.]Va.), during the 1860's again at Richmond, and from 1875 to 1877 again at Charlestown. ¶ Info. courtesy of Mrs. Ralph Catterall, Valentine Museum; Cowdrey, AA & AAU; Willis, "Jefferson County Portraits."

BRUCE, JOSEPH A. Panoramic artist and interior decorator, NYC, 1852–71, thereafter in Brooklyn. Bruce apparently came to America from England about 1852. In 1856 he advertised for sale "Bruce's Gigantic Illustration of the Russian War." His name appears in NYC directories until 1871 and in Brooklyn from 1870 to at least 1895. The Joseph Bruce, fruit and flower painter, who died in Brooklyn on June 8, 1909, age 70, can hardly have been the same man, though he may have been a son of Joseph A. Bruce. ¶ NYCD 1852–71; Brooklyn CD 1870–95, 1904; J. Earl Arrington cites N. Y. *Herald,* June 9 and June 20, 1856; *Art Annual,* VII, obit. of Joseph Bruce (1839–1909).

BRUCE, ROBERT J. Portrait painter; born in 1754; died 1826. ¶ FARL question file.

BRUCKNER, HENRY. Lithographer, NYC, 1859 and after. ¶ Peters, *America on Stone; Portfolio* (Feb. 1954), 126, repro.

BRUDER, CHARLES. Lithographer; born in Baden (Germany) *c.* 1811; working in Louisville (Ky.), 1848–52. He was a partner in the firm of MILNE & BRUDER. He was living in 1850 with his wife, Marie, 35, born in Switzerland, and four children—Frederick, 10, born in Basle (Switzerland); Mariana and William, 8, and Mary-Augusta, 6, born in Baden; and Charles, 2, born in Kentucky. ¶ 7 Census (1850), Ky., XI, 275; Louisville CD 1848, 1852; BD 1850.

BRUEN, JOHN C. Wood engraver; at Cincinnati in 1857, as a partner in the firm of LOVIE, BAUERLE & BRUEN; at NYC in 1860. ¶ Cincinnati BD and CD 1857; NYBD 1860.

BRUEN, ROBERT C. Engraver, probably in NYC, *c.* 1820. He was apprenticed to PETER MAVERICK at the same time as A. B. DURAND. ¶ Dunlap, *History,* II, 299.

BRUENING, EDWARD and JOSEPH. Artists and photographers, Indianapolis, 1860. Joseph Bruening, clerk, appears in the 1855 directory. In 1861 Edward Bruening, of E. & J. Bruening, photographers, advertised himself as an artist from Düsseldorf (Germany). They were probably brothers. ¶ Indianapolis CD 1855, 1860, 1861 (adv.).

BRUFF, J. Artist, Baltimore, 1808. ¶ Lafferty, cites Baltimore *Evening Post,* Dec. 1, 1808.

BRUFF, JOSEPH GOLDSBOROUGH (1804–1889). Topographical draftsman and amateur artist; born in Washington (D.C.), October 2, 1804; died April 14, 1889. A graduate of West Point, Bruff was in 1849 employed in the U. S. Bureau of Topographical Engineers. He organized the Washington City and California Mining Association, and during a trip to the gold fields kept a journal of his experiences, illustrated by many pen sketches. The journal was published in 1944. From 1876 until his death Bruff was in the Office of the Supervising Architect, Treasury Department, Washington. He exhibited at the Washington Art Association in 1859. ¶ Read and Gaines, *Gold Rush: The Journals, Drawings, and Other Papers of J. Goldsborough Bruff . . .* , Introduction; Washington Art Assoc. Cat., 1859; repros. in Jackson, *Gold Rush Album,* pp. 27, 30, 44, 57–59, 186–87, and in Davidson.

BRUFF, W. Silhouettist of Baltimore. ¶ Jackson, *Silhouette,* 87; Carrick, *Shades,* 121.

BRUHL, see DE BRUHL.

BRULS, see DE BRULS.

BRUM (or Bruon), CHARLES. Engraver; born in Pennsylvania *c.* 1815; living in Philadelphia in 1850. ¶ 7 Census (1850), Pa., LII, 580.

BRUMIDI, CONSTANTINO (1805–1880). Fresco, mural, and portrait painter; born in Rome, July 26, 1805; died in Washington (D.C.), February 19, 1880. Brumidi came to America in 1852 after a successful career in Italy, which had been interrupted by his participation in the revolutionary troubles of 1848–49. He spent a short time in Mexico City, but settled about 1855 in Washington, where for the next twenty-five years he was almost constantly employed in decorating the U. S. Capitol. ¶ DAB; Fairman, *Art and Artists of the Capitol;* Thieme-Becker; *Am. Art Review,* I (1880), 227, obit.

BRUNDAGE, EBENEZER F. Portrait painter, NYC, 1843–67. He was listed as portrait painter, painter, or artist from 1843 to 1847; as coffee [seller], 1848–54; with no occupation, 1854–56; thereafter as painter or artist. He exhibited a bust of Silas Wright at the American Institute in 1847. ¶ NYCD 1843–67; NYBD 1846; Am. Inst. Cat., 1847.

BRUNDIGE, WILLIAM. Artist from Connecticut, aged 24, at NYC in 1850. ¶ 7 Census (1850), N.Y., L, 706.

BRUNS, THOMAS. Engraver; born in New York State about 1830; active in NYC from 1851 to 1860. ¶ 8 Census (1860), N.Y., LVII, 911; NYBD 1851–58.

BRUNSWICK, HYMAN. Artist in wax, manufacturer of composition figures and artificial noses, NYC, 1844–68. Brunswick exhibited at the American Institute in 1844, 1845, 1848–1851. Probably the father of THOMAS M. BRUNSWICK. ¶ NYCD 1844–68; Am. Inst. Cats., 1844–45, 1848–51.

BRUNSWICK, THOMAS M. Artist in wax, exhibited a crucifixion and six wax dolls at the American Institute in 1849 and 1851. He was probably the son of HYMAN BRUNSWICK and his successor in 1869 in the manufacture of composition figures. ¶ Am. Inst. Cats., 1849, 1851; NYCD 1868–69.

BRUNTON, RICHARD (?–1832). Engraver. Brunton's earliest known engraving is a bust portrait of Washington, published in 1781. He is thought to have been a deserter from the British army during the Revolution. During the 1790's he worked in various towns of Connecticut, served several jail terms for counterfeiting, and worked as engraver on silver, bookplate engraver, designer of woodcuts for textile printing, etc. By 1815 he was a public charge in Groton, and he died in the Groton Poor House on September 8, 1832. ¶ Warren, "Richard Brunton"; Bates, *An Early Connecticut Engraver;* Terry, *Allen Hyde of Ellington;* repro. in Davidson.

BRUSH, CHARLOTTE T. Amateur artist, exhibited jointly with SOPHIA E. BRUSH at the American Institute in 1845. They were probably sisters of JOHN Y. BRUSH, with whom they lived in NYC. ¶ Am. Inst. Cat., 1845.

BRUSH, JOHN Y. Portrait painter; born in New York State about 1826; active in NYC from 1844 to 1857. He exhibited at the National Academy and the American Institute. He was probably a brother of CHARLOTTE, RODMAN, and SOPHIA BRUSH. ¶ 7 Census (1850), N.Y., XLV, 485; Am. Inst. Cat., 1844–45; NYCD 1846–47, 1851–57; NYBD 1854–57; Cowdrey, NAD.

BRUSH, RODMAN. Amateur painter, exhibited an oil painting at the American Institute in 1851. He was probably a brother of JOHN Y. BRUSH, portrait painter at the same NYC address. In 1857 he was listed as a dentist. ¶ Am. Inst. Cat., 1851; NYCD 1857.

BRUSH, SOPHIA E. Amateur painter, exhibited an oil painting and pencil drawing jointly with CHARLOTTE T. BRUSH at the American Institute in 1845. The address given was the same as that of JOHN Y. BRUSH, probably their brother. ¶ Am. Inst. Cat., 1845.

BRUSH, WILLIAM. Engraver, 36, a native of New York State, at NYC in 1860. He was married and had seven children, ages 1 month to 11 years, all born in New York State. ¶ 8 Census (1860), N.Y., LVI, 975.

BRUSHMAN, CHARLES. Lithographer; born in Pennsylvania *c.* 1825; living in Philadelphia in 1850. ¶ 7 Census (1850), Pa., LII, 932.

BRUSTER, EDMUND, see EDMUND BREWSTER.

BRYAN, CHARLES. Engraver; born in Germany *c.* 1828; living in Philadelphia in 1850. ¶ 7 Census (1850), Pa., L, 862.

BRYAN, EDWARD B. Figure painter in watercolors, Charleston (S.C.), 1849. ¶ Rutledge, *Artists in the Life of Charleston,* 188.

BRYANT, HENRY (1812–1881). A.N.A. Portrait and landscape painter, engraver, pioneer daguerreotypist; born at Manchester Green, East Hartford (Conn.) in 1812; died at East Hartford, December 7, 1881. First apprenticed to an engraver, Bryant became an itinerant portrait painter about 1832. After a brief stay in Albany (N.Y.), 1834–35, he went to NYC, where he remained until about 1840. Elected an Associate of the National Academy in 1837, Bryant exhibited there from 1837 to 1840, as well as at the Apollo Association in 1838–39. After returning to Hartford, Bryant was one of the first artists to take up daguerreotyping, which he practised in Virginia from 1844 to 1846. About 1850 he began to specialize in landscape painting. He exhibited at the National Academy again in 1852–54, and made his home in East Hartford from about 1850. ¶ Boston *Transcript,* Dec. 8, 1881, obit.; French, *Art and Artists in Conn.;* Albany CD 1834–35; Cowdrey, NAD; Cowdrey, AA & AAU; *Richmond Portraits,* 241; Hartford BD 1851, CD 1855–58; Clement and Hutton.

BRYANT, JULIAN. Art Student who came to NYC in December 1857 from Princeton (Ill.) with JUNIUS R. SLOAN. He was a nephew of the editor-poet, William Cullen Bryant. ¶ Webster, "Junius R. Sloan," 108.

BRYNAN, JOHN. Copperplate, steel, and banknote engraver; born in Pennsylvania *c.* 1828; working in Philadelphia 1859 and after. John Brynan (spelled Brennan in 1860 Census) was the son of John and Mary Brynan, umbrella merchants. In 1860 he was living in Philadelphia with his widowed mother (age 56, born in Pennsylvania), his brother Edward, a commission merchant (age 35), and a mute sister (age 25). The mother owned $5,000 in realty and $10,000 in personalty. ¶ 8 Census (1860), Pa., LII, 221 (as Brennan); Phila. CD 1854–62.

BRYSON, EDWARD A. Engraver, Lexington (Ky.), 1848. ¶ Louisville CD 1848.

BUAT, JOSEPH. Lithographer, Hartford (Conn.), 1859–60 and after. ¶ Hartford CD 1859–61.

BUBERI or BUBERL, CASPAR (1834–1899). Sculptor; born in Bohemia; came to America in 1854. He exhibited at the National Academy in the 1860's and 1870's. He died in NYC August 22, 1899. ¶ *Art Annual,* I, obit.; Thieme-Becker; 8 Census (1860), N.Y., LIV, 966 [as Caspar Bubel]; Cowdrey, NAD.

BUCHANAN, [ANDREW], & Co. Lithographers, NYC, 1849–50. The company did 46 colored lithographs for *The Floral Keepsake* (1850). Andrew Buchanan appears in the directories as a lithographer in 1849–50 and as a draughtsman 1853–54. ¶ McClinton, "American Flower Lithographs"; NYCD 1849–50, 1853–54.

BUCHESNE, T. Exhibited views of sugar plantations, a view in South Wales, and a model of Boston at NYC in January 1818. ¶ N. Y. *Evening Post,* Jan. 3, 1818 (courtesy J. Earl Arrington).

BUCHOLAER, H. Cartoonist. His work, published by James Baillie of NYC between 1843 and 1847, included pro- and anti-Clay, pro-Polk and anti-Van Buren cartoons. Apparently of foreign origin, he is said to have failed to capture the American spirit with his conception of Uncle Sam as an elderly gentleman in short coat and low broad hat. ¶ Information courtesy of Frank Weitenkampf, NYPL.

BUCHWEILER, S. Lithographer, NYC, 1859. ¶ NYBD 1859/60.

BUCKLEY, ISABELLA. Painter of "Falls of Niagara," exhibited at the Pennsylvania Academy in 1855. ¶ Rutledge, PA.

BUCKLIN, BRADLEY A. (1824–1915). Painter; born at Little Falls (N.Y.) in 1824; died at Troy (N.Y.), April 24, 1915. Bucklin was working in Troy as early as 1859, and exhibited at the National Academy in 1865. ¶ *Art Annual,* XII (1915), 256; N. Y. State BD 1859; NAD Cat. 1865.

BUCKMAN, HENRY and JOHN. German lithographers, aged 27 and 26 respectively, living in NYC in 1850. ¶ 7 Census (1850), N.Y., XLII, 109.

BUCKNER, HENRY. German portrait painter, 28, at NYC in September 1850. ¶ 7 Census (1850), N.Y., XLIV, 530.

BUDDINGTON, JONATHAN. Portrait painter, NYC, *c.* 1798–1812. His portrait of a little girl, signed and dated "J. Buddington pinxt 1800," is owned by Mrs. Bertram K. Little of Brookline (Mass.). ¶ Dunlap, *History,* II, 470; NYCD 1800–1805, 1809–1812; *Panorama,* IV (April 1949), 88; information courtesy Mrs. B. K. Little.

BUDDY, WILLIAM M. Engraver; born in Pennsylvania *c.* 1839; living with his parents in Philadelphia in June 1860. ¶ 8 Census (1860), Pa., LIV, 573.

BUDIE(?), ANDREW. Artist; born in Cincinnati *c.* 1837; living there in June 1860. ¶ 8 Census (1860), Ohio, XXV, 250.

BUECHNER, ——. Of WEGNER & BUECHNER, lithographers at Pittsburgh (Pa.) before 1859. ¶ Drepperd, "Pictures with a Past," 96.

BUELL, ABEL (1741/42–1822), Engraver, type-founder, silversmith, lapidary, mechanic, etc.; born at Killingworth (Conn.), February 1, 1741/42; died in New Haven, March 10, 1822. A jack-of-all-trades, Buell was particularly noted as the first American type-founder and the engraver of a large wall map of the territories of the United States in 1784. He worked mainly in New Haven and is said to have cut the Colonial Seal of Connecticut. ¶ The standard work on Buell is Wroth's *Abel Buell . . .* (New Haven, 1926). See also: DAB; Stauffer.

BUELL, CHARLES W. Lithographer, Buffalo, 1852–57. Buell was a partner in the following firms: MOONEY & BUELL (1852) and WARREN & BUELL (1856). ¶ Buffalo CD 1852, 1856; BD 1855, 1857.

BUFFORD, JAMES A. Engraver, Boston, 1850 and later. *Cf.* JOHN H. BUFFORD. ¶ Fielding's *Supplement to Stauffer.*

BUFFORD, JOHN H. Lithographer, publisher of prints, active 1835–71. Bufford worked in NYC from 1835 to 1839 and thereafter in Boston, where he was for some years associated with B. W. THAYER & Co. (1841–44). From 1845 to 1852 he headed the firm of J. H. Bufford & Co., and a print of 1865 bears the name of J. H. Bufford & Sons. His known work includes a rare view of Princeton University in 1836 and numerous town views in New York and New England. *Cf.* JAMES A. BUFFORD. ¶ NYCD 1835–39; Boston CD 1840–60 and after; Stokes, *Hist. Prints;* Stokes, *Icon.,* III, 879 and pl. A22-b; Peters, *America on Stone,* pl. 54; Peters, *Calif.;* repro. in *American Collector,* XIV (Sept. 1947), 205.

BUHLE, NICHOLAS A. Engraver, NYC, 1859–60; in 1859 of Buhle & Co. ¶ NYCD 1859–60; NYBD 1859.

BUHLER, GASPAR. Engraver, Newark (N.J.), 1860. ¶ New Jersey BD 1860.

BUJAC, ALFRED. Artist, Jefferson Parish (La.), 1850's. ¶ Delgado-WPA, cites New Orleans CD 1857.

BULFINCH, CHARLES (1763–1844). Architect and draftsman; born in Boston, August 8, 1763; died there April 4, 1844. Bulfinch did most of his work in Boston. Engravings were made from his drawings of the Hollis Street Church, Boston, and his views of the U. S. Capitol, of which he was supervising architect for a number of years. ¶ DAB; Stauffer.

BULGER, THOMAS J. Apprentice lithographer; born in Massachusetts *c.* 1844; living in Boston in August 1860. Bulger's mother, born in Ireland *c.* 1810, kept a grocery; she owned realty valued at $5,000 and personal property valued at $800. ¶ 8 Census (1860), Mass., XXVII, 271; Boston CD 1860.

BULL, ——. Proprietor and/or painter of a panorama of the New Testament, shown at Louisville in March 1858. ¶ Louisville *Daily Democrat,* March 6, 1858 (courtesy J. Earl Arrington).

BULL, JOHN. Tombstone engraver, Charleston (S.C.), 1773. ¶ Rutledge, *Artists in the Life of Charleston,* 188.

BULL, MARTIN. Goldsmith and engraver of Farmington (Conn.); born December 3, 1744; died March 24, 1825. ¶ Stauffer.

BULLARD, A. Painter of portraits in pastels, Westerly (R.I.), *c.* 1850. ¶ Lipman and Winchester, 170.

BULLARD, CHARLES. Ornamental painter, Boston, 1820–44. A pupil of JOHN RITTO PENNIMAN, Bullard is said to have enjoyed a successful career in Boston as an ornamental painter. Lipman and Winchester record a C. Bullard, primitive painter on velvet, possibly the same artist. ¶ Boston CD 1820, 1822, 1826, 1828–1844; Swan, "John Ritto Penniman," 247; Lipman and Winchester, 170.

BULLARD, OTIS A. (1816–1853). Portrait, genre, historical, and panoramic painter; born at Howard (N.Y.), February 25, 1816; died in NYC, October 13, 1853. Apprenticed at 14 to a sign and wagon painter, Bullard later received instruction in portrait painting from the Hartford artist, PHILIP HEWINS. In 1840 he was at Amherst (Mass.), painting portraits of the family of Emily Dickinson. The following year the artist returned to Howard (N.Y.), where he married the daughter of his first master, and in 1842 he settled in NYC. Bullard exhibited at the National Academy (1842–53) and at the American Art-Union (1847–48), but his chief work was a panorama of New York City, painted with the assistance of several other artists between 1846 and 1850. Bullard showed this panorama throughout New York State and after his death it was shown in Baltimore, Cincinnati, and Davenport (Iowa). Of over 900 portraits he is said to have painted, only eight have been located. ¶ Parker, "The Dickinson Portraits by Otis A. Bullard"; 7 Census (1850), N.Y., XLVI, 154; Cowdrey, NAD; Cowdrey, AA & AAU; information courtesy J. Earl Arrington who cites Baltimore *Sun,* Oct. 20, 1854, Cincinnati *Gazette,* Dec. 11, 1855, and Schick, *The Early Theater in Eastern Iowa,* 257–58.

BULLEN, Mrs. WILLIAM, see MARY S. LEGARÉ.

BULLET, CHARLES. Sculptor. Bullet was living in Brooklyn in 1849, when he exhibited at the National Academy and at the American Institute, but from 1850 to 1860 his home was in Cincinnati. ¶ Cowdrey, NAD; Cincinnati BD 1851, 1859–60; CD 1850–59; Clark, *Ohio Art and Artists.*

BUNCE, WILLIAM GEDNEY (1840–1916). N.A. Marine and landscape painter; born in Hartford (Conn.), September 19, 1840; died there November 5, 1916. Though Bunce took drawing lessons under JULIUS BUSCH as early as 1856, it was not until 1863 that he seriously began to study painting in NYC. After the Civil War he went to Europe for further study and remained there for many years. He was made a National Academician in 1907. ¶ *Art Annual,* XIV; DAB; CAB; Clement and Hutton; French, *Art and Artists in Conn.;* Thieme-Becker; *Who's Who in America,* 1916/17 and 1918/19.

BUNCHER, HENRY. Steel and copperplate engraver, Lowell (Mass.), 1858. ¶ Lowell BD 1858.

BUNDY, HORACE (1814–1883). Portrait and landscape painter, born July 22, 1814, in Hardwick (Vt.). He worked as an itinerant artist in New Hampshire and Vermont during the 1840's and 1850's and was also a licensed Adventist preacher. For many years he spent a part of each year at North Springfield (Vt.); in 1846 he was at Claremont (N.H.) and in 1850 at Hancock (N.H.). He died in Concord (N.H.) on June 15, 1883, a few weeks after his return from a trip to Jamaica. ¶ Boston *Evening Transcript,* June 16, 1883, obit. (courtesy Henry J. Dubester, Library of Congress); Baker, *Folklore of Springfield, Vt.,* 71; *Art in America* (March 1935), repro., 82; New England BD 1849; Sears, *Some American Primitives,* 71, 87; repro., Garbisch Collection, Catalogue, 91.

BUNSE, AUGUSTUS. Marine artist. In 1856 Bunse and JOHN FULLER drew a marine view of the U. S. Frigate "Savannah" in trouble off Rio de Janeiro. It was published in NYC by Hall & Maigne. ¶ *Portfolio,* Nov. 1952, 68.

BUNTEN, ALONZO. Wood engraver at Manchester (N.H.) in 1858 and Laconia N.H.) in 1860. ¶ Manchester BD 1858; New England BD 1860.

BURBANK, ——. Watercolor painter, whose "Daniel in the Den of Lions" was exhibited in New Orleans in 1851. ¶ Arrington, cites *Picayune,* Feb. 23, 1851.

BURBANK, CALEB. Painter living at North Salem (Mass.) in 1837. ¶ *Essex Inst. Hist. Coll.,* LXXXV (Oct. 1949), 348.

BURBANK, J. MAZE. Caricaturist. His "Interior of an American Bar Room" and "Rocking, a Favorite Amusement with the American Ladies" were lithographed about 1840 by FREDERICK SWINTON. In 1858 Burbank exhibited "Wallace, the Lion, from Life" at the National Academy. ¶ *Portfolio* (Jan. 1954), 104; Cowdrey, NAD.

BURBANK, T. L. Artist; born in Pennsylvania *c.* 1814; living in Independence, Polk County (Oregon) in 1860. ¶ 8 Census (1860), citation courtesy of David C. Duniway, Oregon State Archivist.

BURCH, THOMAS. Engraver, Newark (N.J.), 1860. ¶ N.J. BD 1860.

BURD, ELIZA HOWARD. Watercolor painter, Philadelphia, *c.* 1840. ¶ Lipman and Winchester, 170.

BURFIELD, GEORGE. Marine painter; born in England *c.* 1805; living in Spring Garden, Philadelphia County (Pa.) in August 1850. Burfield's wife, Mary E., age 45, and children, ages 5 to 17, were all born in Pennsylvania. His eldest son, Silvester Burfield, born about 1833, was a wood engraver. ¶ 7 Census (1850), Pa., LIV, 870.

BURFORD, JOHN. Landscape, genre, portrait, and animal painter, active 1812–50. An English artist, Burford exhibited landscapes at London galleries from 1812 to 1829. He was in NYC by 1829 when he first exhibited at the National Academy and apparently remained there until about 1850, except for a brief residence in New Haven *c.* 1841. He exhibited frequently at the National Academy from 1829 to 1846 and at the American Art-Union from 1844 to 1850, his subjects including landscapes, paintings of animals, and a few portraits. ¶ Graves *Dictionary;* Cowdrey, NAD; Cowdrey, AA & AAU; 7 Census (1850), N.Y., XLIII, 210.

BURG, LOUIS. French portrait painter, born about 1820, at NYC from 1857 to 1860. His wife Caroline was a dressmaker. ¶ 8 Census (1860), N.Y., XLIV, 997; NYBD 1857–58.

BURGER, CHARLES F., see CHARLES F. BERGER.

BURGER & DIX. Lithographers, Detroit, 1853. The partners were ROBERT BURGER and CUNO DIX. ¶ Detroit CD 1853/54.

BURGER, ROBERT. Lithographer, of BURGER & DIX, Detroit, 1853. ¶ Detroit CD 1853/54.

BURGES, BARTHOLOMEW. Designer of an astronomical chart engraved *c.* 1789 by JOHN NORMAN. ¶ Stauffer.

BURGESS, GEORGE. Engraver; born in London (England) in 1831; working in San Francisco 1856–58. ¶ Peters, *Calif.;* San Francisco BD 1856, CD 1858.

BURGIS, WILLIAM. Designer and engraver of views, active *c.* 1716–31. The known views by Burgis include New York Harbor (*c.* 1718), Boston Harbor (*c.* 1716–22), Harvard College (*c.* 1725–26), New York (*c.* 1729–31) and New York (*c.* 1731). ¶ Stokes, *Icon.,* I, 239, pl. 25 and 28; Stokes, *Hist. Prints,* pl. 10a, 10b, and 11b; *Portfolio,* VIII (Dec. 1948), frontis.; Dow, *Arts and Crafts,* 16, 20; DAB; Stauffer.

BURGUM, JOHN (1826–1907). Portrait and carriage painter; born in Birmingham (England) in 1826; died in 1907. Burgum came to Concord (N.H.) in 1850, and his portrait of David A. Ward was presented to the State House at Concord in 1876. ¶ WPA (N.H.), HRS; C. K. Bolton, "Workers with Line and Color in New England."

"BURINE." The signature "Burine sc." appears on a large plate of shells engraved for S. F. Bradford's edition of *Ree's Encyclopedia* (Philadelphia, 1805–1818). It is probably a pseudonym derived from the word burin. ¶ Fielding, *Supplement to Stauffer.*

BURKE, G. Engraver, New Orleans, 1838. ¶ Delgado-WPA, cites *Picayune,* Oct. 7, 1838.

BURKE, JEREMIAH. Apprentice lithographer; born in Massachusetts *c.* 1843; living in Boston with his widowed mother, Margaret Burke, July 1860. ¶ 8 Census (1860), Mass., XXVII, 207.

BURLIN, RICHARD. Portrait, miniature, and landscape painter, NYC, 1834–60 and after. ¶ *N. Y. As It Is* (1837); NYCD 1834–44, 1847–57, 1860 and after; NYBD 1846, 1858–59; Bolton, *Miniature Painters.*

BURMAN, RUSSELL. Engraver, 25, at NYC in 1860 with his wife Caroline. ¶ 8 Census (1860), N.Y., XLV, 863.

BURNAP, DANIEL. Engraver of brass clock faces, East Windsor (Conn.), before 1800. ¶ Stauffer.

BURNARD, WILLIAM S. Portrait, historical and landscape painter, NYC, 1854. ¶ NYBD 1854.

BURNES, E. P. Artist of NYC, principal painter of "Great Historical Mirror of America." ¶ Bangor *Daily Whig & Courier,* July 8, 1852 (courtesy J. Earl Arrington).

BURNET, JOHN M. Lithographer, NYC, 1859. ¶ NYBD 1859.

BURNETT, Mrs. WALTER D. Pastel portraitist, Newark (N.J.), exhibited at the American Institute in 1856. ¶ Am. Inst. Cat., 1856.

BURNHAM, ——. Painter of a "Grand Tableaux of the Life of Christ," exhibited in Bangor (Me.) and Worcester (Mass.) in 1859–60. *Cf.* THOMAS M. BURNHAM. ¶ Bangor *Daily Whig & Courier,* March 21, 1859, and Worcester *Daily Spy,* March 19, 1860 (courtesy J. Earl Arrington).

BURNHAM, THOMAS MICKELL (1818–1866). Genre, portrait, and landscape painter. A native of Boston, he went out to Detroit about 1836 and found work as a sign painter. In 1838 he opened a studio where he painted portraits and genre works, including the satirical "State Election of 1837," a portrait of Governor Stevens Mason, and "The Burning of the Steamboat *Great Western.*" After a brief trip to Scotland in 1839, Burnham returned to Boston in 1840. During the next three or four years he exhibited at the Boston Athenaeum, the National Academy, and the Apollo Association, and the Athenaeum bought one of his paintings. In 1852 he was at Melrose (Mass.), employed with other artists in transferring to canvas J. Wesley Jones's daguerreotype views of California. Burnham lived in Boston until his death in 1866. *Cf.* —— BURNHAM, above. ¶ Burnham, *The Burnham Family,* 211–212; BA Cat., 1840–72; Swan, BA, 125, 208; Cowdrey, NAD; Cowdrey, AA & AAU; Boston CD 1840–67; Boston *Almanac,* 1840–67; 8 Census (1860), Mass., XXVII, 483; information courtesy Francis W. Robinson, Detroit Institute of Arts; "Jones' Pantoscope of California," 111.

BURNHAM, T. H. O. P. or "Alphabet." Supposed artist of "State Election of 1837," a Detroit scene now at the Detroit Institute of Arts. The artist was really THOMAS MICKELL BURNHAM. ¶ Farmer, *History of Detroit and Michigan,* 112–13; Burroughs, "Painting and Sculpture in Michigan," 396–97; information courtesy Francis W. Robinson, Detroit Institute of Arts.

BURNS, CHARLES MARQUADANT, JR. Genre painter; born in Pennsylvania about 1834; active in Philadelphia and Germantown (Pa.), 1858 to 1860 and after. The son of a prominent Philadelphia publisher and bookseller, Burns exhibited several genre paintings on literary and religious subjects at the Pennsylvania Academy from 1858 to 1863, and the National Academy 1876–78. He was by profession an architect. ¶ Rutledge, PA; Phila. CD 1861; 8 Census (1860), Pa., LV, 810; Cowdrey, NAD.

BURNS, GEORGE. Sculptor, NYC, 1850. ¶ NYBD 1850.

BURNS, JAMES. Portrait and historical painter; born in Scotland about 1810; active in NYC, 1840–60; exhibited at the National Academy. ¶ 7 Census (1850), N.Y., XLVI, 280; NYCD 1840–60; Cowdrey, NAD.

BURR, ——. Panoramist. Burr's "Seven Mile Mirror" of the Great Lakes, Niagara Falls, the St. Lawrence and Saguenay rivers was exhibited in NYC, Boston, Baltimore, and Philadelphia from 1849 to 1852. ¶ Arrington cites N. Y. *Herald* (Sept. 17 and Oct. 3, 1849), Boston *Evening Transcript* (Mar. 8, 1850), Phila. *Public Ledger* (April 29 and July 29, 1852).

BURR, AUGUSTUS. Miniature painter, New York State, *c.* 1825; known only by miniature portraits of Joseph and Mathilda Scarrett. ¶ *Antiques,* Dec. 1941, repros.

BURR, CHRISTOPHER. Engraver, Providence (R.I.), 1849–60. ¶ New England BD 1849, 1860; Providence CD 1856, 1859.

BURR, ELIZA J. Watercolor painter. In 1823 Miss E. J. Burr of Sunbury (Pa.) exhibited two watercolors of flowers at the Pennsylvania Academy. The same paintings were exhibited at the Academy in 1824, 1829, and 1830, and at Special Exhibitions in 1836–38 and 1840. Eliza J. Burr of NYC exhibited two watercolor paintings at the American Institute in 1842. It is assumed that the two artists were the same. ¶ Rutledge, PA; Am. Inst. Cat., 1842.

BURR, HIPPOLYTE. Portrait painter, reputedly a grandson of Aaron Burr. His copy of VANDERLYN's portrait of the former Vice-President is now owned by Princeton University. ¶ Egbert, *Princeton Portraits,* 259.

BURR, Mrs. L. E. Landscape painter, Buffalo (N.Y.), 1855. ¶ Buffalo BD 1855.

BURR, LEONARD U. Portrait painter, Massachusetts, 1840. ¶ Sears, *Some American Primitives,* 149, and repro. 139.

BURR, WILLIAM HENRY. Portrait and genre painter, active 1841–59. Except for a brief residence in Syracuse (N.Y.) around 1846, the artist lived in NYC. He exhibited at the National Academy from 1841 to 1859, at the American Art-Union in 1848, and at the Pennsylvania Academy in 1847. ¶ NYCD 1844, 1856; Cowdrey, NAD; Cowdrey, AA & AAU; Rutledge, PA.

BURRELL (or Burell), ——, see R. BURRILL.

BURRELL, A. M. Portrait painter, Quincy (Mass.), 1849. ¶ New England BD 1849.

BURRIDGE, CHARLES. Portrait painter, NYC, 1857–60. ¶ NYBD 1857–58, 1860.

BURRIDGE, THOMAS H. Landscape and marine artist, draughtsman, machinist, active 1843–84. As a machinist in NYC 1843–45, Burridge exhibited a Dutch landscape and marine view at the National Academy in 1844. After 1860 he worked in St. Louis (Mo.) as a draftsman, engineer, and machinist. His view of Ticonderoga (N.Y.) has been reproduced. ¶ NYCD 1843–45; Cowdrey, NAD; St. Louis CD 1865, 1867, 1869, 1871–72, 1874–75, 1878–79, 1881–84; information courtesy of Miss Janet R. MacFarlane; *Art Digest,* XXII (Aug. 1948), 6.

BURRIDGE, WILLIAM H. Partner in BRAINARD & BURRIDGE, engravers and lithographers, Cleveland (Ohio), 1853–59. ¶ Ohio BD 1853, 1857, 1859; Cleveland BD 1853, 1857.

BURRILL, EDWARD. Lithographer, Boston, 1860 and after. ¶ Peters, *America on Stone;* Boston CD 1861.

BURRILL, JOHN Q. Lithographer and designer; born in Massachusetts *c.* 1841; living in Boston in 1860. Burrill was the son of John T. Burrill, a Protestant Episcopal clergyman, born in Massachusetts *c.* 1800. ¶ 8 Census (1860), Mass., XXIX, 87; Boston CD 1860.

BURRILL, R. Cameo-carver; exhibited cameo portraits at the American Institute in 1849, giving a NYC address. It was probably the same man who was employed by F. A. WENDEROTH as a cameo-carver in Charleston (S.C.) in 1859, under the name of "Mr. Burrell" or "Burell." ¶ Am. Inst. Cat., 1849; Rutledge, *Artists in the Life of Charleston,* 165, 231.

BURROUGHS, SARAH A. Landscape painter, Norwich (Conn.), *c.* 1830. Her "Ruins of an Old Mill, Norwich, Connecticut" has been reproduced. ¶ Lipman and Winchester, 170; *Art in America* (Feb. 1951), 21.

BURROWS, HENRY. Engraver, age 17, living in Philadelphia in August 1850. ¶ 7 Census (1850), Pa., LI, 778.

BURRY, LOUIS. Engraver, NYC, 1851. ¶ NYBD 1851.

BURT, CHARLES KENNEDY (1823–1892). Portrait, historical, and landscape engraver; born in Edinburgh (Scotland), November 8, 1823; died in Brooklyn (N.Y.), March 25, 1892. Burt was working in NYC at least by 1850. At the time of his death it was stated that "a head of Queen Victoria, executed by Mr. Burt for the Canadian government for a postage stamp, was on its issue rated by philatelists as 'the queen of stamps.'" ¶ Obit., Boston *Transcript,* March 28, 1892; Stauffer; NYBD 1850–51; repro. in *American Collector,* XVI (Sept. 1947), 18–19. Four of Burt's steel engravings after famous artists were included in the American Art-Union sale of 1852 (Cowdrey, AA & AAU).

BURT, JAMES. Portrait and landscape painter, active 1835–49. A view of "Trenton Falls, Mohawk River, N.Y.," signed "J. Burt" and dated 1835, is owned (1948) by Donald W. Moreland of Cambridge (Mass.). Burt worked in Boston from about 1841 to 1849, exhibiting at the Athenaeum in 1841 and 1848. ¶ Information courtesy of Donald W. Moreland; Boston BD 1842, 1844–45; Swan, BA, 208.

BURTON, Miss A. M. H. Watercolor artist of NYC, exhibited at the American Institute in 1851. ¶ Am. Inst. Cat., 1851.

BURTON, CHARLES (or C.). Draftsman, landscape, and portrait painter. Best known for his miniature views of New York City and Philadelphia published in 1831, C. Burton was apparently an English artist who worked in America from about 1819 to 1842. JAMES HERRING, meeting Charles Burton, a drawing teacher, at Wilmington (Del.) in 1836, recalled that he had known him in London as early as 1802, when Burton was a painter on glass for magic-lanterns and transparencies and his brother William was a printer in Fetterlane. It may have been the same artist who exhibited "church" subjects at the Royal Academy in 1800–02, under the name of C. Burton. Burton's name first appears in an American context in 1819, when C. Burton of NYC exhibited two landscapes at the American Academy. In 1820 he painted a view of the Battery, NYC, and in 1824 a view of the U. S. Capitol at Washington. He is also said to have painted a series of NYC views for presentation to Lafayette by the City of New York in 1824. As Charles Burton, draftsman, he was listed in NYC directories from 1828 to 1831. It was during these years that he prepared the series of NYC and Philadelphia views for which he is chiefly remembered. If Herring's Charles Burton and the C. Burton of the 1831 views were identical, then Burton apparently went south after 1831, working as a teacher of drawing and painting in Wilmington (Del.) about 1836 and as a portrait painter in Jefferson County (Va., now W. Va.) and Baltimore (Md.) in 1838–39. This identification appears to be confirmed by the Baltimore directory for 1842, which lists Charles Burton as a scientific draftsman. Of his later career nothing is known, though a C. Burton exhibited architectural subjects at the Royal Academy, London, in 1845–46. CHARLES W. BURTON, who appeared in NYC in 1849, is not known to have been related. ¶ Stokes, *Icon.,* III, 594–98, pl. 101a and 101b; Stokes, *Hist. Prints,* 71; James Herring, MS autobiography; Graves, *Dictionary;* Cowdrey, AA & AAU; Snow, "Delineators of the Adams-Jackson American Views—Part III"; *American Processional,* 103 (repro.), 240; NYCD 1828–31; Willis, "Jefferson County

Portraits"; Lafferty, cites Baltimore *Sun,* March 12, 1839; Baltimore CD 1842; represented at NYHS.

BURTON, CHARLES W. Lithographer, artist, and engraver. Listed in the 1849 NYC directory as a lithographer, Charles W. Burton drew and lithographed in that year a view of the Bay and City of New York with Brooklyn and Jersey City, and he also exhibited engravings in imitation of mezzotint at the American Institute in the same year. In 1850 a Charles Burton, artist, was listed in the Boston Census as a native of England, age 43(?). Since the latter had a two-year-old son, born in New York, it seems likely that he was the same man as Charles W. Burton of NYC in 1849. The Boston artist's wife and daughter Margaret (age 18) were also born in England. It is not known that he was related to CHARLES (or C.) BURTON, with whom he has been confused. ¶ NYCD 1849; Stokes, *Icon.,* III, 701, pl. 134; Peters, *America on Stone;* Am. Inst. Cat., 1849; 7 Census (1850), Mass., XXV, 17.

BURTON, GURLEY & EDMONDS. Engravers, NYC, 1837. The firm was composed of JAMES R. BURTON, ROYAL GURLEY, and WILLIAM EDMONDS. By 1838 Edmonds had apparently dropped out and the firm was listed that year as Burton & Gurley. ¶ NYBD 1837; NYCD 1837–38.

BURTON, JAMES R. Copperplate printer and engraver, NYC, 1821–47. Listed in the directories as a copperplate printer before 1842, Burton headed the engraving firm of BURTON, GURLEY & EDMONDS. In 1837–38 and from 1842 to 1847 was listed as an engraver. ¶ NYCD 1821, 1824, 1827–39, 1841–47.

BURTON, NATHAN. English engraver, 31, at NYC in June 1860. ¶ 8 Census (1860), N.Y., LIV, 28.

BURY, JOHN JACOB. Engraver "lately from Europe," at Philadelphia in 1794. ¶ Prime, II, 67–68.

BUSBY, CHARLES A. Architectural draftsman. An architect of London, Busby exhibited frequently at the Royal Academy from 1801 to 1830. He worked in NYC as an architect and engineer from 1817 to 1819, exhibiting in those years at the American Academy, to which he later presented two of his architectural drawings (1826). His views of City Hall and the State Prison are known from engravings by WILLIAM HOOKER. ¶ Graves, *Dictionary;* NYCD 1818; Cowdrey, AA & AAU; Gage.

BUSCH, JULIUS THEODORE (1821–1858). Artist and teacher of drawing. Born in Dresden (Germany) in 1821, Busch came to America *c.* 1848. After two years in NYC, he moved to Hartford (Conn.) where he made his home until his death at sea in 1858. A popular teacher of drawing, Busch himself worked in various media and exhibited at the American Institute in 1848 and 1849. ¶ French, *Art and Artists in Conn.;* NYCD 1848–49; Hartford BD 1851, CD 1856–58; Am. Inst. Cats., 1848–49.

BUSH, JOSEPH HENRY (?–1865). Portrait painter; born at Frankfort (Ky.) between 1794 and 1800, son of PHILIP BUSH; died at the home of his brother in Lexington (Ky.), January 11, 1865. Bush went to Philadelphia at the age of 17, studying for two years under THOMAS SULLY and exhibiting in 1815 at the Pennsylvania Academy. On his return to Kentucky, he worked in Frankfort, Lexington, and Louisville, and spent many of his winters before the Civil War painting portraits for Louisiana and Mississippi planters. He was recorded in the 1850 Census as living in a hotel at Louisville (Ky.), with real property valued at $1,600. ¶ Price, *Old Masters of the Blue Grass* (birth date given as 1794); 7 Census (1850), Ky., XI, 301 (age given as 50, indicating birth date *c.* 1800); Louisville *Kentucky Herald,* June 9, 1819, cited by Dr. Clarence H. Brigham; New Orleans *Bee,* Dec. 9, 1831, and *Picayune,* Jan. 28, 1845, cited by Delgado-WPA; Rutledge, PA.

BUSH, NORTON. Landscape and portrait painter; born at Rochester (N.Y.), February 22, 1834; died at San Francisco (Cal.) in 1894. Bush studied under JAMES HARRIS in Rochester before going to NYC in 1852 for further study under J. F. CROPSEY. His favorite subject was tropical landscape, which he studied during three visits to South and Central America. The greater part of his artistic career was spent in San Francisco. He exhibited at the National Academy in 1852 and 1871. ¶ Clement and Hutton; Barker, *American Painting,* 456; Cowdrey, NAD; CAB.

BUSH, PHILIP. Amateur portrait painter and hotel-keeper of Winchester (Va.) and Frankfort (Ky.) in the 1790's. He was the father of the portrait painter, JOSEPH

H. Bush. ¶ Price, *Old Masters of the Blue Grass,* 71–73.

Bushby, Asa (1834–1897). Portrait painter; born at Danvers (Mass.), June 9, 1834; died at Tacoma (Wash.), June 31, 1897. Largely self-taught, Bushby was painting portraits around Danvers as early as 1856. After the Civil War he went into photography at Lynn (Mass.) and later at Boston. He settled in Tacoma toward the end of the 1880's. ¶ Danvers Hist. Soc. *Collections,* XXIV (1936), 1–20, including check list of his work; Sears, *Some American Primitives,* 291.

Busher, Charles. Sculptor, Philadelphia, 1857–58. ¶ Phila. CD 1857–58.

Bushnell, E. L. Engraver, NYC, 1854. ¶ NYBD 1854.

Bushwry, Francis. Engraver and enamel painter, Philadelphia, 1798. ¶ Phila. CD 1798, cited by Brown and Brown.

Buskirk, John A. Engraver, NYC, 1854–58. ¶ NYBD 1854, 1856, 1858.

Buss, C. G. A crayon portrait by this artist of Daniel Bowen Bishop (1764–1844) was owned in 1941 by John Casey of Essex Junction (Vt.). ¶ WPA (Mass.), *Portraits Found in Vt.*

Busse, Herman. German wood engraver, 25, at NYC in June 1860. ¶ 8 Census (1860), N.Y., XLIV, 490.

Butaud, Isaac. Engraver, hair worker, and taker of portraits by the physiognotrace, Philadelphia, 1811–18. ¶ Phila. CD 1811, 1813–14, 1817–18, and *Aurora,* Apr. 15, 1811, cited by Brown and Brown.

Butet, John Francis. Drawing master, Charleston (S.C.), 1761. ¶ Bowes, *Culture of Early Charleston,* cites *S. C. Gazette,* Nov. 28, 1761.

Butler, ——. Engraver of a plate of a lion and man, Baltimore, before 1835. ¶ Stauffer, I, 38.

Butler, B. D. Artist; born in North Carolina *c.* 1821; living in Polk County (Ore.) in 1860. ¶ 8 Census (1860), Oregon, cited by David C. Duniway, Oregon State Archivist.

Butler, Benjamin F. Lithographer; in New Orleans, 1841; in NYC, 1846–48; in San Francisco, 1852–59. *Cf.* F. P. Butler, and Gihon & Butler. ¶ New Orleans CD 1841; NYBD 1846, 1848; San Francisco BD 1852, 1858–59; Peters, *Calif.*

Butler & Brown. Wood engravers, 1 Spruce St., NYC; exhibited at the American Institute in 1850. Warren C. Butler was listed at this address in 1849–50, but Brown has not been identified. ¶ Am. Inst. Cat., 1850; NYCD 1849–50.

Butler, Esteria. Miniaturist and landscape painter, Kennebec County (Maine) before 1850. Esteria Butler, painter of portraits of Jonathan Pullen (1775–1828) and Mrs. Jonathan Pullen (d. 1847), is presumed to be the same as E. Butler, whose view of Waterville College was lithographed by [Emery] Moore of Boston (1842–60). ¶ Stackpole, *History of Winthrop, Maine,* 561; *Portfolio,* V (May 1946), 206.

Butler, F. P. Lithographer, San Francisco, 1856. Peters suggests that this is an error for Benjamin F. Butler. ¶ San Francisco CD 1856; Peters, *Calif.*

Butler, George Bernard, Jr. (1838–1907). N.A. Portrait, genre, animal, and still life painter; born in NYC, February 8, 1838; died near Croton Falls (N.Y.), May 4, 1907. After study with Thomas Hicks in NYC, Butler went to Paris in 1859 for further study under Couture. After the Civil War, in which he lost his right arm, Butler worked in NYC and San Francisco. He was elected a National Academician in 1873, and in 1875 he went to Italy, where he remained for a number of years. He was best known for his paintings of animals. ¶ *Art Annual,* VI (1907/08), 106; *Who's Who in America* (1899–1900); Clement and Hutton; Cowdrey, NAD.

Butler, J. B. (or I. B.). His portrait of Winfield Scott was published *c.* 1856 by R. Magee of Philadelphia. ¶ Peters, *America on Stone,* pl. 94.

Butler, John M. Engraver, copperplate printer, and publisher, Philadelphia, 1841–60 and after. Before 1855 Butler was listed in the directories as a copperplate printer, but thereafter he was also listed as an engraver. He appears to have been a portrait painter as well, exhibiting a portrait of Isaac A. Pennypacker at the Pennsylvania Academy in 1855. ¶ Phila. CD 1841–42, 1844–60 and after; Stauffer, I, 38; Rutledge, PA.

Butler, Joline J. Wood engraver, NYC, 1841–45. He was probably the father or brother of Warren C. Butler, whose eldest son, born *c.* 1847, was called Joline. Thomas W. Butler may have been another son of Joline J. ¶ NYCD 1841–45.

Butler & Roberts. Engravers, NYC, 1846. The junior partner was William Roberts, but the identity of Butler is not known, though it was probably one of the family which included JOLINE J., THOMAS W., and WARREN C. BUTLER. ¶ NYBD 1846; NYCD 1846.

BUTLER & STRYPE. Wood engravers, NYC, 1847–48. In 1847 the firm included THOMAS W. and WARREN C. BUTLER and FREDERICK C. STRYPE; by the following year Thomas Butler had apparently dropped out. ¶ NYCD 1847; NYBD 1848.

BUTLER, THOMAS R. Engraver, Philadelphia, 1820. ¶ Brown and Brown.

BUTLER, THOMAS W. Engraver, NYC, 1847. Probably a brother of WARREN C. BUTLER, with whom he was associated in the firm of BUTLER & STRYPE. ¶ NYCD 1847.

BUTLER, WARREN C. (1826–1878). Wood engraver; born in NYC in 1826; died in San Francisco [?] in 1878. Warren C. Butler worked as an engraver in NYC from 1847 to 1854, for the first two years as a partner in the firm of BUTLER & STRYPE. He was probably the son of JOLINE J. BUTLER and brother of THOMAS W. BUTLER. He moved to San Francisco about 1855 and worked there until 1860 and after. The 1860 Census records that Butler owned personal property valued at $500, and that his household included his wife Margaret (born in N. Y. *c.* 1826) and four children—Joline, 13; Henry Clay, 7; Theodore, 6; and Emma, 2. ¶ Smith; 8 Census (1860), Cal., VII, 715; NYBD 1848; NYCD 1847, 1840–54; San Francisco BD 1856, 1858–61.

BUTMAN, FREDERICK A. Landscape painter, San Francisco, 1859–71; exhibited at the National Academy in 1867 and the Pennsylvania Academy in 1868. ¶ San Francisco CD 1859–60, 1862–65, 1871; Cowdrey, NAD; Rutledge, PA.

BUTT, FREDERICK. Ornamental and portrait painter, Cincinnati (Ohio), 1857–68. He was probably the artist or proprietor of Butt's Panorama of the New Testament, exhibited in Cincinnati in December 1857 and in Detroit in 1863. ¶ Cincinnati CD 1857–68; Cincinnati *Daily Gazette,* Dec. 23, 1857, and Detroit *Free Press,* Aug. 19, 1863, cited by J. E. Arrington.

BUTTERTON, JOHN. Portrait painter, Philadelphia, 1856. Butterton exhibited two English portrait subjects at the Pennsylvania Academy in 1856. It is probable that he was the London artist who exhibited at the Royal Academy in 1847, under the name of J. Butterton. ¶ Rutledge, PA; Graves, *Dictionary.*

BUTTERSWORTH, JAMES E. (1817–1894). Marine, landscape, and portrait painter; born on the Isle of Wight (England) in 1817; died in West Hoboken (N.J.) in 1894. One of the best known of the mid-19th century painters of ships, Buttersworth came to America about 1850. Many of his ship pictures were published by CURRIER & IVES. He exhibited a number of landscapes and marine pictures at the American Art-Union (1850–52). Thomas Buttersworth of London, who exhibited "sea pieces" at London galleries from 1813 to 1827, may have been a relative of James E. Buttersworth. ¶ Cowdrey, AA & AAU, cites obit. in NYPL Art Room; Peters, *Clipper Ship Prints;* Peters, *Currier and Ives,* pl. 148; Crouse, *Mr. Currier and Mr. Ives,* opp. 92; *Panorama,* I (1946), 71, 108; Whitehill, "Portraits of American Ships," 7; represented in N. Y. State Hist. Assoc. (Cat. 1950).

BUTTERWORTH, A. H. Engraver of frontispiece and vignette title page of *The Life and Adventures of Robinson Crusoe,* published at Hartford (N.J.) about 1828. ¶ Fielding; Fielding, *Supplement to Stauffer.*

BUTTI, GUIDO. Sculptor and modeler, working in NYC in 1853, and at Washington (D.C.) *c.* 1856–64. Butti's original model for the sculptured decorations over the entrance to the General Post-Office at Washington was exhibited at the Pennsylvania Academy from 1856 to 1870. ¶ Cowdrey, NAD; Rutledge, PA.

BUTTON, JOSEPH J. Wood engraver and landscape painter; born in New York State about 1822; active in NYC, 1842–50. He was an engraver by trade, but exhibited several paintings at the American Institute. ¶ 7 Census (1850), N.Y., LV, 412; Am. Inst. Cat., 1842, 1845–47; NYCD 1846.

BUTTRE, JOHN CHESTER (1821–1893). Wood engraver, portrait painter, publisher; born at Auburn (N.Y.), June 10, 1821; died at Ridgewood (N.J.), December 2, 1893. Buttre received his first lessons in art at Auburn from a Polish exile named HULANSKI, and was working as an engraver in NYC as early as 1847. From 1848 to 1850 he was a partner in the firm of RICE & BUTTRE. He is chiefly noted as publisher of *The American Portrait Gallery* (3 vols., NYC, 1880–81). ¶ CAB; NYCD 1847–49, 1851–60 and after; Am. Inst. Cat., 1856; Stauffer; Peters, *America on Stone; Antiques,* LIII

(June 1948), 442, repro.; 8 Census (1860), N.Y., XLIV, 207.

BUTTS, RALPH. Landscape and portrait painter at Cincinnati in 1851. ¶ Information courtesy Edward H. Dwight, Cincinnati Art Museum.

BUTTS, RICHARD. Lithographer, surveyor, and architect, Brooklyn (N.Y.), 1845. ¶ Brooklyn CD 1845.

BUXTON, CHARLES. A NYC physician who drew an emblematical picture of George Washington and the British evacuation of New York in 1783, engraved by CORNELIUS TIEBOUT and published in 1798. ¶ Stokes, *Icon.*, I, 413 and pl. 52; *Antiques,* LV (Feb. 1949), 138, repro.; NYCD 1792–94.

BYER, see BEYER.

BYERS, WILLIAM. Engraver; born in Pennsylvania *c.* 1834; living in Philadelphia in August 1850, age 16. ¶ 7 Census (1850), Pa., LI, 567.

BYFIELD, N. Portrait painter. His only known work is a portrait of Richard Middlecott(?), signed and dated 1713. The artist may have been Judge Nathaniel Byfield (born in Boston, November 14, 1677), though there is no other evidence that the Judge was artistically inclined. ¶ The problem is discussed in C. K. Bolton's *Portraits of the Founders,* Vol. II (1919), 425, and (1926), 423; Burroughs, *Limners and Likenesses,* 21–22 and pl. 16; WPA (Mass.), *Portraits Found in Mass.*, no. 1438, with bibliography. [All references courtesy Theodore Bolton].

BYNAM, BENJAMIN. Portrait painter, Greenville (S.C.), 1835. ¶ Information courtesy Miss Anna Wells Rutledge.

BYRAM, JOSEPH H. Wood engraver, Philadelphia, 1853–60 and after. ¶ Phila. CD 1853–60 and after; in 1853 as Joseph Byran.

BYRD, FREDERICK. Painter, NYC, 1842–45; exhibited a portrait and a painting at the American Institute in 1842 and 1844, respectively. ¶ NYCD 1842–45; Am. Inst. Cats., 1842, 1844.

BYRD, [JOHN] HENRY. Portrait painter, active 1840–83. Henry Byrd was working in New Orleans 1841–42 and at Huntsville (Ala.) in 1846. John Henry Byrd is stated to have been at Little Rock (Ark.) as early as 1840, and to have worked in Arkansas, Mississippi, and Louisiana between 1842 and 1857. Henry Byrd was listed in New Orleans directories again from 1867 to 1883. The two men are assumed to be identical. ¶ New Orleans *Picayune,* March 18, 1841, cited by Delgado-WPA; New Orleans CD 1842, 1867–83; Huntsville *Southern Advocate,* April 3, 1846, cited in WPA (Ala.), Hist. Rec. Survey; Little Rock *Arkansas Gazette,* July 2, Sept. 2, Nov. 12, Dec. 3, 1933; WPA Guide, *Arkansas.*

BYRNE, ——. Artist, Pittsburgh (Pa.), *c.* 1828. ¶ Anderson, "Intellectual Life of Pittsburgh: Painting," 291.

BYRON, HENRY. Engraver, 23, born in New York State, at NYC in August 1850. ¶ 7 Census (1850), N.Y., XLVIII, 232.

C

C——, H. Painter of a "View of New-York, Taken from South Brooklyn Wharf," exhibited at the National Academy, 1842. ¶ Cowdrey, NAD.

C——, H., see HENRY CONOVER.

CABOT, EDWARD CLARKE (1818–1901). Architect and watercolor painter; born in Boston, April 1818; died January 1901. Cabot first exhibited at the Boston Athenaeum in 1856, and was for many years a member of the Boston Art Club and the Boston Water Color Society, and an Honorary Member, American Society of Painters in Water Color. ¶ *Art Annual* (1903); Swan, BA, 208; Thieme-Becker; Cowdrey, NAD.

CACADE, GEORGE. Irish engraver, 26, at NYC in September 1850. ¶ 7 Census (1850), N.Y., LI, 209.

CADEN, WILLIAM C. Engraver, 26, born in New York State, at NYC in 1860. ¶ 8 Census (1860), N.Y., XLV, 857.

CADMUS, A. Ceramic modeller, apparently working at the Congress Pottery, South Amboy (N.J.), *c.* 1850. His "Bull Calf" has been reproduced. ¶ *Antiques,* XXV (May 1934), frontis.

CADOUX, LOUIS. Lithographer; born in France *c.* 1834; living in "marine barracks," Washington (D.C.), July 1860. ¶ 8 Census (1860), D.C., II, 700.

CADY, EMMA. Primitive painter of still life in watercolor, New Lebanon (N.Y.), *c.* 1820. ¶ Lipman and Winchester, 170; repro. in *Art in America,* XXXIII (Oct. 1945), 248.

CAFFERTY, JAMES H. (1819–1869). N.A. Portrait, landscape, and genre painter; born in Albany (N.Y.), 1819; died in NYC, September 7, 1869. He came to NYC in the early 1840's and was a frequent exhibitor there at both the American Academy and the National Academy, becoming an Associate of the latter in 1850 and a Member in 1853. He also exhibited at the Boston Athenaeum, the Washington Art Association, and the Pennsylvania Academy. ¶ CAB; obit., *N. Y. Herald,* Sept. 8, 1869; NYCD 1844–60; Cowdrey, NAD; Cowdrey, AA & AAU; Swan, BA; Washington Art Assoc. Cat., 1857; Rutledge, PA; represented at the Museum of the City of New York (*American Processional,* 161, 245) and NYHS (Cat. 1941).

CAFFREY, T. or F. German-born lithographer, 39, living in NYC in 1860 with his German-born wife and six children, all born in New York State after 1854. ¶ 8 Census (1860), N.Y., XLIII, 701.

CAIN, ——. Painter in Maryland *c.* 1760, probably the same as JUSTUS ENGLEHARDT KUHN. ¶ Dunlap, *History,* I, 130; Fielding.

CAKER, THOMAS. Artist; born in Pennsylvania *c.* 1825; living in Philadelphia in August 1860. ¶ 8 Census (1860), Pa., LII, 136.

CALAME, JUSTIN L. Engraver, Newark (N.J.), 1860. ¶ N.J. BD 1860.

CALDER, MAY. Landscape painter and teacher of art at Muncy (Pa.) Seminary, 1858. Her work is represented at the Muncy Hist. Soc. ¶ *Now and Then,* Jan. 1948, cover.

CALDWELL, Dr. ——. Professor at the University of South Carolina and, in 1813, artist to the South Carolina boundary commission. ¶ Rutledge, *Artists in the Life of Charleston,* 188.

CALDWELL, W. D. Portrait painter, Philadelphia, 1838, when he exhibited at the Artists' Fund Society. ¶ Rutledge, PA.

CALDWELL, WILLIAM H. (1837–1899). Illustrator, art editor of the *Daily Graphic;* born in Rochester (N.Y.), 1837; died in NYC, May 22, 1899. ¶ *Art Annual* (1899, supp.), obit.

CALLAS, see COLLAS.

CALLAWAY, GEORGE. Portrait painter, NYC, 1843, when he exhibited at the National Academy. ¶ Cowdrey, NAD.

CALLENDER, BENJAMIN [JR.] (1773–1856). Engraver, chiefly of maps and charts. Born in Boston, March 16, 1773, Callender moved in 1798 to Northfield (Mass.), where he lived until his death on February 22, 1856. ¶ Stauffer; Thieme-Becker, cites H. W. Fincham, *English and American Book Plates.*

CALLENDER, JOSEPH (1751–1821). Engraver of portraits, etc.; born in Boston (Mass.), May 6, 1751; working there in 1789; buried in Old Granary Burying Ground, Boston, November 10, 1821. He studied with PAUL REVERE and was a die-sinker for the Massachusetts Mint. ¶ Stauffer, I, 40; Boston CD 1789; Fielding; Thieme-Becker; Middlebrook, "A Few of the New England Engravers," 360.

CALLICOT (or Callico), J. P. Marble sculptor, New Orleans, 1855. ¶ *Journal du Soir,* Oct. 1, 1855, cited by Delgado-WPA.

CALM (or Cahn), FILEN(?). Theatrical scene-painter; born in France *c.* 1831; living in Louisville (Ky.) in 1850, age 19. There was a Charles J. Calm, clerk, in Louisville at this time, possibly related to the young artist. ¶ 7 Census (1850), Ky., XI, 500; Louisville CD 1850.

CALVERLEY, CHARLES (1833–1914). N.A. Sculptor; born in Albany (N.Y.), November 1, 1833; died in Essex Falls (N.J.), February 24, 1914. For fourteen years an assistant of ERASTUS DOW PALMER in Albany, Calverley moved to NYC in the late 1860's. Elected to the National Academy in 1874, he executed busts of many well-known men, including Peter Cooper, Horace Greeley, Elias Howe, Lafayette S. Foster (now in the U. S. Capitol) and CHARLES LORING ELLIOTT (now at the National Academy). ¶ DAB; NAD, Cat. of Permanent Collection (1911); Fairman, *Art and Artists of the Capitol,* 345; Egbert, *Princeton Portraits,* 61–63; Taft, *History of American Sculpture; Art Annual,* XI; Cowdrey, NAD.

CALVERT & Co., see THOMAS B. CALVERT.

CALVERT, RICHARD. Engraver, Philadelphia, 1855–60; listed in 1856–57 as Richard S. and in 1858–59 as Richard T. ¶ Phila. CD 1855–60.

CALVERT, THOMAS B. Copper, steel, and wood engraver, envelope manufacturer, Philadelphia, 1853–56. Head of T. B. Calvert & Co. in 1854–56. ¶ Phila. CD 1853–56 (envelope maker); Phila. BD 1854–56 (engraver).

CALYO, HANNIBAL W. Artist, son of NICOLINO CALYO. He was born in Maryland about 1835 and was living with his father in NYC in 1850 and 1863. ¶ 7 Census (1850), N.Y., LVI, 1; NYCD 1863.

CALYO, JOHN A. (*c.* 1818–1893). Historical and landscape painter, teacher of painting; born in Italy about 1818. He was the son of NICOLINO CALYO, with whom he was working in NYC in 1848 as N. Calyo & Son, historical painters and teachers. J. A. Calyo of Richmond (Va.) exhibited an Italian landscape at the Washington Art Association in 1857 and at the National Academy 1867–68. He died June 8, 1893. ¶ NYCD 1848; Washington Art Assoc. Cat., 1857; Boston *Transcript,* June 15, 1893; 7 Census (1850), N.Y., LVI, 1; Cowdrey, NAD.

CALYO, NICOLINO (1799–1884). Portrait, landscape, historical, miniature, and panoramic painter; born in Naples. Calyo studied at the Naples Academy and lived for some time in Malta before coming to America in the early 1830's. He was working in Baltimore in 1835, but came to NYC in time to paint the great fire of December 16 and 17 of the same year. He stayed in NYC until at least 1850, when he and his sons, JOHN A. and HANNIBAL, were listed as artists in the U. S. Census. From 1847 to 1852 Calyo's scenes from the Mexican War and a panorama of the Connecticut River were exhibited in NYC, Philadelphia, Boston, and New Orleans. Calyo is said later to have worked in Spain, returning to America in 1874, presumably to NYC, where he died ten years later, December 9, 1884. ¶ Boston *Transcript,* Dec. 11, 1884; Baltimore CD 1835 and Baltimore *Republican,* June 16, 1835, cited by Lafferty; Stokes, *Icon.,* III, 617–18 and pl. 114, a and b; *Antiques,* XLVI (Dec. 1944), 352; *Antiques,* LXIII (April 1953), 310; NYBD 1844, 1846, 1848; Arrington cites: New York *Herald,* June 15, 1847, and Dec. 16, Dec. 24, 1850, Phila. *Public Ledger,* Aug. 14, 1847, Boston *Evening Transcript,* April 22, 1850, and New Orleans *Picayune,* Nov. 11–12, 1852; *Antiques* (Jan. 1954), 33, repro.; 7 Census (1850), N.Y., LVI, 1; Cowdrey, NAD, 1867–68.

CAMBELL, GEORGE. Engraver; born in Massachusetts *c.* 1838; living in Boston in 1860. ¶ 8 Census (1860), Mass., XXVII, 891.

CAMBELL, see CAMPBELL.

CAMERER, EUGENE. Landscape artist, California, late 1850's. His views of Mt. Shasta, Stockton, and San Francisco were lithographed by KUCHEL & DRESEL and published between 1856 and 1859. ¶ Peters, *Calif. on Stone;* Watson, *Calif. in the Fifties,* repros.

CAMERON, EMMA. Artist. A native of Philadelphia, she was living there in 1850 with her artist-husband, JAMES CAMERON. ¶ 7 Census (1850), Pa., LI, 96.

CAMERON, JAMES. Portrait and landscape painter. Born in Scotland *c.* 1816, Cameron apparently came to America before 1839, when he is reported to have been working in Indianapolis (Ind.). By 1849 he was in Philadelphia, where he married (see EMMA CAMERON) and was living there with his wife and mother in 1850, his property at that time being valued at $11,000. James Cameron exhibited at the Pennsylvania Academy in 1849 and 1851, and since those exhibitions of his work included two Italian subjects, it is probable that he was the J. Cameron who exhibited at the American Art-Union in 1848 as a resident of Rome, where he was presumably a student. ¶ 7 Census (1850), Pa., LI, 96; Peat, *Pioneer Painters of Indiana,* 151; Phila. CD 1849, BD 1850; Rutledge, PA; Cowdrey, AA & AAU.

CAMERON, JOHN. Lithographer, NYC, 1848–62; born in Scotland about 1828. A hunchback, Cameron was for many years associated with CURRIER & IVES, specializing in horse prints, comics, and caricatures. He also worked independently, doing a series of plates for Letts' *Pictorial View of California* (N.Y., 1853), as well as forming two short-lived partnerships in 1859–60 (LAWRENCE & CAMERON and CAMERON & WALSH). ¶ Peters, *America;* Peters, *Currier and Ives,* 13; Peters, *Calif.;* Fred Peters, *American Clipper Ship Prints;* Am. Inst. Cat., 1848; NYCD 1854, 1857–60; 7 Census (1850), N.Y., XLIII, 144.

CAMERON, JOHN B. Artist; born in Nova Scotia *c.* 1830; boarding in Boston in 1860. ¶ 8 Census (1860), Mass., XXVIII, 59; Boston CD 1860.

CAMERON & WALSH. Lithographers, NYC, 1859–60. The partners were JOHN CAMERON and JOSEPH WALSH. ¶ NYBD 1859–60.

CAMMEYER, AUGUSTUS F. Engraver and die sinker, NYC, 1851–56. He was the son of Augustus F. Cammeyer, looking-glass maker of NYC, 1828–51. The younger Cammeyer was listed in 1851–52 as a wood engraver, in 1853 as a clerk, and in 1856 as an engraver and die-sinker. ¶ NYBD 1851–52, 1856; NYCD 1828–49, 1851–53, 1856.

CAMMEYER & BISDORF. Engravers, NYC, 1857. The partners were DEWITT C. CAMMEYER and PETER J. BISDORF. ¶ NYCD 1857.

CAMMEYER & CLARK. Engravers, NYC, 1834–36. The partners were WILLIAM CAMMEYER [JR.] and JAMES CLARK. ¶ NYCD 1834–36.

CAMMEYER & CO., see DEWITT C. CAMMEYER.

CAMMEYER, DEWITT C. Wood engraver, NYC, 1844–86; born in New York State about 1828. Probably serving his apprenticeship under the noted wood engraver, BENSON J. LOSSING, in 1844 when he exhibited a case of specimens of wood engravings at the American Institute, giving as his address that of Lossing's establishment in Chambers Street. He went into business under the name of Cammeyer & Co. in 1850 and continued until at least 1886. He was associated in 1857 with PETER J. BISDORF in the firm of CAMMEYER & BISDORF. ¶ Am. Inst. Cat., 1844; NYCD 1850–54, 1857, 1860–86; 7 Census (1850), N.Y., XLI, 617.

CAMMEYER, WILLIAM [SR.]. Engraver, Albany (N.Y.), *c.* 1812. ¶ Dunlap, *History* (1918), III, 287.

CAMMEYER, WILLIAM [JR.]. Engraver and copperplate printer, active 1817–41. Presumably the son of the Albany engraver, WILLIAM CAMMEYER, [SR.], the younger Cammeyer was working in Philadelphia 1817–21 as a copperplate printer, in NYC 1825, in Albany 1828–33 as an engraver and copperplate printer, and again in NYC 1830–41 as an engraver. He was senior partner in CAMMEYER & CLARK in 1834–35. ¶ Phila. CD 1817–21; NYCD 1825, 1830–36, 1838–41; Albany CD 1828, 1831–32 (courtesy Miss Mary Bartlett Cowdrey).

CAMP, JOHN HENRY (1822–1881). Lithographer. Born in Prussia; came to America some time in the 1840's, settling in Philadelphia, where he was listed in the directories from 1847 to 1851 as Henry Camp and thereafter as John Henry Camp. His wife was a native of Strasbourg (France), born *c.* 1823, but their three children were all born in Pennsylvania between 1847 and 1855. In 1860 Camp owned realty valued at $2,000 and personalty valued at $5,000. He died in Philadelphia. ¶ Peters, *America on Stone;* 7 Census (1850), Pa., XLIX, 257 (as Henry Camp); 8 Census (1860), Pa., LIV, 830; Phila. CD 1847–60 and after.

CAMPBELL, see CAMBELL.

CAMPBELL, A. G. and J. K. Engravers, NYC, *c.* 1860. ¶ Stauffer.

CAMPBELL, ALBERT H. (1826–1899). Civil engineer, landscape artist; born in Charlestown (Va., now W. Va.), October 23, 1826; died in Ravenswood (W. Va.), February 23, 1899. A graduate of Brown University (1847), Campbell served as engineer and surveyor with several railroad surveys in the Southwest during the 1850's, a number of his views later appearing in the reports of these expeditions. During the Civil War he was Chief of the Topographic Bureau, C. S. A., and his maps played an important part in Confederate military tactics, according to Freeman. Campbell's later life was spent in West Virginia, where he was chief engineer for a number of railroads. ¶ Taft, *Artists and Illustrators of the Old West,* 264–66.

CAMPBELL, ALEXANDER. A number of prints of Washington on horseback are inscribed "Drawn from life by Alex^r Campbell." One of these, issued by C. Shepherd in September 1775, was presented to Mrs. Washington by Joseph Reed; and Washington in a letter to Reed, dated Cambridge (Mass.), January 31, 1776, wrote: "Mrs. Washington desires I will thank you for the picture sent her. Mr. Campbell, whom I never saw to my knowledge, has made a very formidable figure of the commander-in-chief, giving him a sufficient portion of terror in his countenance." Though Morgan and Fielding point out that the sketch might have been made from life without Washington's knowledge, it has been generally assumed that Alexander Campbell was a fictitious name. ¶ W. S. Baker, *The Engraved Portraits of Washington;* Morgan and Fielding, *Life Portraits of Washington.*

CAMPBELL & BROTHER, see J. ALAN and THOMAS CAMPBELL.

CAMPBELL, DONALD. Engraver, NYC, 1840–47. Though Donald Campbell was listed in the directories only from 1840 to 1843, he was probably the D. Campbell who exhibited wood engravings at the American Institute in 1847. ¶ NYCD 1840–43, in the last year on Gold Street; Am. Inst. Cat., 1847, address: 56 Gold Street.

CAMPBELL, DANIEL A. Designer and engraver, Damariscotta (Maine), 1855–56. ¶ *Maine Register,* 1855–56. *Cf.* JOHN CAMPBELL.

CAMPBELL, EDWARD R. Portrait painter; born in England *c.* 1820; living in Freehold Township (N.J.) in 1850, with his wife Susan (30), a native of New Jersey. ¶ 7 Census (1850), N.J., XI, 157.

CAMPBELL, HAMILTON. Artist; born in Virginia *c.* 1813; living in San Francisco in 1860, with personal property valued at $600. His wife, Harriet B. Campbell, was born in Virginia *c.* 1817; their eldest daughter, age 21, in Illinois; and the remaining children, ranging from 1 year to 18 years in age, in Oregon. The 1861 directory listed Campbell as "artist with William Davis." ¶ 8 Census (1860), Cal., VII, 92; San Francisco CD 1861.

CAMPBELL, J. Portrait painter, Cincinnati, 1853. ¶ Ohio BD 1853/54.

CAMPBELL, J. ALAN. Sculptor, of CAMPBELL & BROTHER, Louisville (Ky.), 1859. See THOMAS E. CAMPBELL. ¶ Louisville CD 1859.

CAMPBELL, J. K., see A. G. and J. K. CAMPBELL.

CAMPBELL, JOHN. Designer and engraver, Damariscotta (Maine), 1855–56. *Cf.* DANIEL A. CAMPBELL. ¶ *Maine Register,* 1855–56.

CAMPBELL, ORSON. Author and, presumably, illustrator of *Treatise on Carriage, Sign and Ornamental Painting,* published in 1841 at De Ruyter (N.Y.). ¶ Library of Congress.

CAMPBELL, PATRICK. British traveler, whose sketches of the American wilderness appeared as illustrations in his *Travels in the Interior Inhabited Parts of North America in the Years 1791 and 1792* (Edinburgh, 1793). ¶ Library of Congress.

CAMPBELL, PRYSE. Primitive portrait painter, *c.* 1770–84. ¶ Lipman and Winchester, 170; *Am. Provincial Painting,* nos. 21 and 22.

CAMPBELL, ROBERT. Engraver, Philadelphia, 1806–31. Campbell engraved plates for Bradford's *Encyclopedia* between 1806 and 1813 and did portrait and general engraving in line and stipple from 1822 to 1831. ¶ Brown and Brown; Stauffer, I, 41; Fielding.

CAMPBELL, ROBERT L. Artist, St. Louis (Mo.), 1848. ¶ St. Louis CD 1848.

CAMPBELL, THOMAS. Irish lithographer, 27, at NYC in 1860 with his wife and one child, aged one year. ¶ 8 Census (1860), N.Y., XLII, 385.

CAMPBELL, THOMAS (1790–1858). Portrait and miniature painter, lithographer. He worked in Baltimore in 1833 (as an artist) and 1835 (as "artist, lithog. and agent for Hygein Medicine"); in Cincinnati, 1840–44; and in Louisville (Ky.), 1845. *Cf.* THOMAS E. CAMPBELL, possibly a son. ¶ Baltimore CD 1833, 1835; Cist, *Cincinnati in 1841,* 141; Louisville CD 1845; information courtesy Edward H.

Dwight, Cincinnati Art Museum; birth and death dates courtesy Donald MacKenzie, Wooster College.

CAMPBELL, THOMAS E. (or F.). Sculptor and stone engraver, Louisville (Ky.), 1850–59. Born in Maryland *c.* 1833, Thomas F. Campbell was working as a stone engraver in Louisville at the age of 17. The four other children of the family, probably including J. ALAN CAMPBELL, were born in Kentucky between 1838 and 1846. Their father may well have been the artist THOMAS CAMPBELL, who was in Maryland in 1833 and in Louisville or its vicinity from at least as early as 1840. In 1859 Thomas E. and J. Alan Campbell were listed in the 1859 directory as sculptors in Louisville. ¶ 7 Census (1850), Ky., XI, 685; Louisville CD 1859.

CAMPBELL, WILLIAM. Engraver; born in England *c.* 1826; living in Philadelphia in 1850–51, with his Maryland-born wife, Louisa, age 20, and two daughters, ages 5 and 2, born in Pennsylvania. ¶ 7 Census (1850), Pa., LIII, 747; Phila. CD 1850–51.

CAMPBELL, WILLIAM. Engraver; born in Ireland *c.* 1833; living in Philadelphia in August 1850. ¶ 7 Census (1850), Pa., LIII, 831.

CAMPBELL, WILLIAM B. Artist of Brooklyn (N.Y.) who exhibited six paintings at the American Institute in 1849. W. B. Campbell, of 111 Front Street, NYC, who exhibited 2 oil paintings at the same exhibition, may have been the same man. ¶ Am. Inst. Cat., 1849.

CANDEE, GEORGE EDWARD (1838–?). Portrait, landscape, and still life painter in watercolors and oils. Born in New Haven (Conn.), December 24, 1838, Candee studied there briefly under JOSEPH KYLE. He moved to NYC in 1865 and visited Europe in the early 1870's. He was working in New Haven as late as 1878. ¶ French, *Art and Artists in Conn.,* 146; Fielding; Cowdrey, NAD.

CANFIELD, ABIJAH (1769–1830). Farmer and primitive portrait painter; born at Chusetown, now Humphreysville (Conn.), September 9, 1769; died there August 14, 1830. His portraits of Hiram and Sarah Upson, painted in 1820 in settlement of a debt, are now (1951) owned by Miss Grace Rogers of Newark (N.J.). ¶ Scott, "Abijah Canfield of Connecticut," repros.

CANNON (or Cannan), HUGH. Sculptor; born in Pennsylvania *c.* 1814; living in Philadelphia 1840–57. Listed in city directories variously as marble mason (1840–45), sculptor (1846–53), and carver (1854–57), Cannon was an exhibitor at the Artists' Fund Society (1840, bust of Chief Justice Marshall), the Apollo Association (1841, busts of Henry Clay and Edwin Forrest), and the Pennsylvania Academy (1851, 1855–56, busts of Clay, Nicholas Biddle, the artist, and others). ¶ 7 Census (1850), Pa., L, p. 345 (stamped, 200); Fielding (birthplace given as Ireland); Phila. CD 1840–57; Rutledge, PA; Cowdrey, AA & AAU; Taft, *History of American Sculpture;* represented at the Penna. Academy and the Md. Hist. Soc.

CANOVA, DOMINICO. Lithographer, portrait painter, teacher of painting and drawing. In 1825 Dominico Canova was working in NYC for the lithographer ANTHONY IMBERT and prepared several of the illustrations for Cadwallader D. Colden's *Memoir* of the Erie Canal celebrations. This may be the D. Canova who "returned" to New Orleans in 1840 after three years teaching at Jefferson College and who was active in New Orleans as a painter and teacher in the forties, fifties, and sixties. ¶ Colden, *Memoir Prepared at the Request of the Committee of the Common Council of the City of New York,* 362, 379, 389, 393 (illus. opp. pp. 262, 343, 378, 388); New Orleans *Bee,* Jan. 8 and March 1, 1840 (cited by Delgado-WPA); New Orleans CD 1841, 1850–56, 1860–61, 1866.

CANTER, JOHN (*c.* 1782–1823). "An artist of no inferior standing" who died in Charleston (S.C.) in 1823, age 41. He was the son of Jacob and Rebecca Canter, and a relative of JOSHUA CANTER. ¶ Rutledge, *Artists in the Life of Charleston,* 124, 188.

CANTER, JOSHUA (?–1826), also known as J. Canterson or Cantir. Canter was a Danish Jew who studied painting in Copenhagen and came to America *c.* 1788, when he first advertised at Charleston (S.C.) as a portrait and landscape painter who would take likenesses from life, designs from fancy or copies from nature, as well as teach drawing after the "academical" style. He was prominent in Charleston's artistic life until the 1820's, serving as one of the original Directors of the South Carolina Academy of Fine Arts. Some time after 1819 Canter moved to NYC, where he died on November 1st, 1826. ¶ Rutledge, *Artists in the Life of Charleston,* 124, 152, 188; Dunlap, *History,* I, 426; Charleston CD 1819; NYCD 1826 (date of death inserted in ink—NYHS).

CANTERSON, J., see JOSHUA CANTER.

CANTIR, see CANTER.

CANTON, THOMAS. Artist; born in Tennessee *c.* 1815; living at the Tremont Hotel, New Orleans, 1850, with his 12-year-old son, Richard, also listed as an artist. ¶ 7 Census (1850), La., IV (1), 615.

CANTWELL, EDWIN. Lithographer; born in Ireland *c.* 1834; living in Philadelphia in 1860, with his Pennsylvania-born wife, Margaret, age 19, and three children, of whom the eldest was two years old. Cantwell's personal property was valued at only $200. ¶ 8 Census (1860), Pa., LI, 69.

CANTWELL, JAMES. Irish artist, 24, living in NYC in 1850 with JAMES BAILEY. ¶ 7 Census (1850), N.Y., L, 81.

CANY, HARRIET, see Mrs. REMBRANDT PEALE.

CAPELLANO, ANTONIO. Italian sculptor, working in America from 1815 to 1827. Employed to work on the U. S. Capitol in Washington, Capellano also spent some time in Baltimore and NYC in 1815–17. In 1816 he exhibited "The Peace of Ghent," presumably a clay group, at the American Academy, and in 1824 a marble bust, "Chloris," at the Pennsylvania Academy. He returned to Italy in 1827, so prosperous after his years in America, it was said, that he retired to "uno piccolo pallazzo" in Florence, where Rembrandt Peale met him in 1830. His work is represented in the U. S. Capitol by a relief of Pocahontas and John Smith. ¶ Fairman, *Art and Artists of the Capitol,* 27, 30, 39; Dunlap, *History,* II, 468.

CAPEN, AZEL. Portrait painter, working at Stoughton (Mass.) in September 1839. ¶ WPA (Mass.), *Portraits Found in Maine,* no. 331; Lipman and Winchester, 170.

CAPEWELL & KIMMEL. Portrait and historical engravers, printers, NYC, 1853–60 and after. The partners were SAMUEL CAPEWELL, letter engraver, and CHRISTOPHER KIMMEL, engraver, lithographer and printer. Stauffer states that plates signed by the firm name were generally the work of employed engravers. Samuel Capewell's name disappears from the directories after 1862, though Stauffer states that the firm was still in existence in 1907. ¶ NYCD 1853–60 and after; Stauffer, I, 41; repro. in *Antiques,* LIX (Apr. 1951), 301.

CAPEWELL, SAMUEL. English engraver, 24, at NYC in 1850. From 1853 to 1862 he was with the firm of CAPEWELL & KIMMEL, engravers and printers. He was primarily a letter engraver. ¶ 7 Census (1850), N.Y., XLI, 416; NYCD 1853–62; Stauffer.

CAPPELLI, ——. Painter of frescoes at Castle Garden, NYC, 1846–47. ¶ N. Y. *Herald,* April 24, 1847 (courtesy J. E. Arrington).

CARADEUC, JAMES ACHILLE DE. Flower painter in watercolors and teacher of drawing and painting, Charleston, 1840 and 1849. In November 1840 he married Elizabeth Ann, eldest daughter of Mr. A. Della Torre, of Charleston. In 1849 he exhibited an "Adam and Eve" at the First South Carolina Institute Fair. ¶ Rutledge, *Artists in the Life of Charleston,* 160, 188.

CARDELLA, LIBERATO or LIBERTO. Portrait painter and drawing master. In May 1831 he was listed as instructor in Italian, music, and drawing at the Mt. Pleasant Classical Institute, Amherst (Mass.). He also exhibited at the Boston Athenaeum in 1831. He was at Hartford (Conn.) in 1841; at Boston in 1846; and again at Hartford 1848–52. ¶ *Boston Daily Advertiser,* May 9, 1831, p. 2, col. 6; Swan, BA; Hartford CD, 1841, 1848–52; Boston CD 1846.

CARDELLI, GEORGIO. Sculptor and itinerant portrait painter. Born in Florence (Italy) in 1791, Cardelli came to America *c.* 1816, worked first as a sculptor in NYC and Washington, where he was employed as a carver at the U. S. Capitol, *c.* 1819, and later as an itinerant portrait painter. In the latter capacity Cardelli visited Hartford (Conn.) in 1820. *Cf.* PIETRO CARDELLI. ¶ French, *Art and Artists in Conn.;* Fairman, *Art and Artists of the Capitol.*

CARDELLI, PIETRO (?–1822). Portrait and decorative sculptor, architect, and professor of design. Presumably a native of Italy, Pietro Cardelli worked in Paris from 1806 to 1810, and in London in 1815–16. By 1818 he was in Washington (D.C.), where he did some decorative carving for the U. S. Capitol, as well as portrait busts for a number of distinguished Americans, including Jefferson and Madison. He left for New Orleans probably in 1820 and remained there, as professor of design at the "Establishment" and as architect of the facade of the City Hall, until his death in October 1822. Fairman suggests that Pietro and GEORGIO CARDELLI may be the same man. ¶ New Orleans *Gazette,* July 25, 1821, and obituary, Oct. 7, 1822 (cited by Delgado-WPA); Thieme-Becker; Fairman, *Art and Artists of the Capitol,* 46; New Orleans CD 1822.

CARDERO, see CORDERO.

CARDWELL, BYRON. Artist; born in Illinois *c.* 1833; living in Multnomah County (Oregon) in 1860. ¶ 8 Census (1860), Oregon (citation courtesy of David C. Duniway, Oregon State Archivist).

CAREW & BROTHER, see JOSEPH CAREW and THOMAS A. CAREW.

CAREW, JOHN. Sculptor; born in England *c.* 1820; living in Boston (Mass.), August 1850. He was listed in the 1850 directory, but the following year only Ellen Carew, widow, was listed at the same address. ¶ 7 Census (1850), Mass., XXVI, 62; Boston CD 1850–51. *Cf.* John E. Carew, sculptor of London, exhibited at London galleries 1812–1845, possibly his father (Graves).

CAREW, JOSEPH (?–1870). Sculptor, Boston, 1843–70. From 1844 to 1851, and again in 1854, Joseph and THOMAS A. CAREW were associated in the firm of Carew & Brother. Joseph exhibited at the Boston Athenaeum in 1843, 1845, and 1847. ¶ Boston CD 1843–60 and after; Boston BD 1844–51, 1854; Swan, BA, 209.

CAREW, THOMAS A. Sculptor, Boston, 1843–59, and Cambridge (Mass.), 1860. Thomas A. and JOSEPH CAREW worked together from 1844 to 1851, and in 1854, as Carew & Brother. He exhibited at the Boston Athenaeum in 1853, 1859 and 1860. ¶ Boston CD 1843–51, 1853–59; New England BD 1860; Swan, BA, 209.

CAREY, JOHN B. Lithographer and "manufacturer of fancy show cards," NYC, 1847. ¶ NYBD 1847.

CAREY, JOSEPH. Painter of a primitive scene on wood, Salem (Mass.), 1785. ¶ Lipman and Winchester, 170.

CAREY, PEYTON. Designed and engraved the seal of the University of Georgia, of which he was a graduate, Class of 1810. ¶ Stauffer.

CARLIN, ANDREW B. Portrait, miniature, and historical painter. A deaf-mute, born in Pennsylvania *c.* 1816, Andrew B. Carlin was a younger brother of the artist JOHN CARLIN, also a deaf-mute. Andrew worked in Philadelphia as an artist from 1839 until after 1860, when he became a professional photographer. He exhibited three paintings at the Artists' Fund Society in 1840. In 1860 Andrew B. Carlin and his deaf-mute wife, Anna Maria (age 33, b. Mass.), had five children, ages 3 to 15, all born in Pennsylvania; no property was listed. The only painting by Carlin known to be extant is "Sherman's March Through Georgia, 1864," painted in 1871, owned by Mrs. Katharine McCook Knox of Washington (D.C.). ¶ 8 Census (1860), Pa., LII, 220; Phila. CD 1839–40, 1842, 1847–48, 1860–61; Rutledge, PA; *American Processional,* p. 185. [All information courtesy George C. Groce.]

CARLIN, DANIEL. Lithographer. Born in Pennsylvania *c.* 1826, Daniel Carlin was working in Philadelphia in 1850 and 1861. His household in 1850 included Sarah (age 23, b. Delaware) and Charles (age 7 months, b. Penna.); no property was recorded. ¶ 7 Census (1850), Pa., LV, 571; Phila. CD 1861.

CARLIN, JOHN (1813–1891). Miniaturist; portrait, genre, and landscape painter; writer; born in Philadelphia, June 15, 1813; died in NYC, April 23, 1891. A deaf-mute, John Carlin studied at the Pennsylvania Institute for the Deaf and Dumb from 1821 to 1825. He studied drawing under JOHN RUBENS SMITH and portrait painting under JOHN NEAGLE in 1833–34, and exhibited, as a resident of Philadelphia, at the Artists' Fund Society from 1835 to 1838. He spent the next few years in Europe, studying at the British Museum in London and under Paul Delaroche in Paris. On his return to America the artist settled in NYC where he made his home until his death almost fifty years later.

Carlin exhibited widely: at the National Academy (1847–86), the American Institute (1849), the American Art-Union (1848, 1850), the Artists' Fund Society (1835–42), the Maryland Historical Society (1856), and the Pennsylvania Academy (1864, 1868). After the introduction of photography, which cut heavily into the market for miniatures, he devoted himself mainly to genre and landscape painting.

As a writer, John Carlin was best known for *The Scratchside Family* (N.Y., 1861) and his poem, "The Mute's Lament," which begins with the line, "I move a silent exile on this earth." Despite his handicap, which his wife, though not his children, shared, Carlin won many friends through his profession, among them William H. Seward, Thurlow Weed, Hamilton Fish and Horace Greeley. The New York *Tribune,* at the time of Carlin's death in his seventy-eighth year, quoted the following lines on death from his "Mute's Lament":

"My ears shall be unsealed and I shall hear;
My tongue shall be unbound and I shall speak."

¶ CAB; obit., N. Y. *Times,* April 24, 1891; Rutledge, PA; Phila. CD 1837; NYBD 1844; NYCD 1845–50, 1856–58; 8 Census (1860), N.Y., LIII, 895; Cowdrey, NAD; Am. Inst. Cat., 1849; Cowdrey, AA & AAU; Rutledge, MHS; obit., N. Y. *Tribune,* April 24, 1891. Examples of Carlin's work are at the New-York Historical Society and in the collection of Mrs. Wendell P. Colton of New York City. FARL records 57 miniatures, 2 oil portraits and a fishing scene in oil (FARL to undersigned, Oct. 7, 1952). Other works by Carlin are owned by his grandsons, Francis Wayland Carlin and Phillips Carlin. [All information courtesy George C. Groce.]

CARLING, JOHN (1800–1855). Wood carver who made the pattern for the oxen to support the wooden baptismal font of the Mormon Temple, Nauvoo (Ill.) in the 1840's. He was born September 11, 1800, in Kingston (N.Y.); went to Nauvoo in 1840; later moved to Utah and settled at Fillmore, where he died April 2, 1855. ¶ Arrington, *Nauvoo Temple.*

CARLO, WILLIAM. English artist, 37, at NYC in July 1850. He came to NYC about 1847, before the birth of the two youngest of his five children. ¶ 7 Census (1850), N.Y., LI, 54.

CARLSON, EDWARD. Engraver, book-binder, and toolcutter, Cincinnati, 1859–60. ¶ Cincinnati CD 1859–60.

CARLTON, WILLIAM TOLMAN (1816–1888). Portrait and genre painter. Though not listed in Boston directories until 1850, Carlton exhibited at the Boston Athenaeum as early as 1836 and 1842, as well as in 1855. He also exhibited a genre painting at the American Art-Union in NYC in 1850. ¶ Boston CD 1850, 1852–60 and after; New England BD 1856, 1858; Swan, BA, 209; Cowdrey, AA & AAU; represented in the collections of the N. Y. State Hist. Assoc., Cooperstown (Cat., 1950).

CARMAN, J. Portrait painter, NYC, 1817. Carman exhibited a "Portrait of a Gentleman" at the American Academy in 1817 and 1819, and painted a portrait of Captain James Riley (1777–1840) in or before 1818. ¶ Cowdrey, AA & AAU; Stauffer, no. 1086.

CARMAN, RADCLIFF. Lithographer, NYC, 1852. Earlier directories list him as a painter or paint-seller. Miss P. J. Carman, at the same address, exhibited a watercolor painting at the American Institute in 1844. ¶ NYBD 1852; NYCD 1836, 1844; Am. Inst. Cat., 1844.

CARMICHAEL, J. W. Painter of "Niagara Falls with Half-breed Voyageurs" in 1837. The artist may have been James Wilson Carmichael (1800–1868), the English marine artist. Though the latter is not known to have worked in America, his "Wreck Ashore" was exhibited at the Artists' Fund Society in Philadelphia in 1838. ¶ Repro. in *Connoisseur* (April 1953), lxxvi; Rutledge, PA; DNB.

CARMICHAEL, T. J. Landscape painter. He was working in NYC as an architect and draftsman in 1836, but in 1841–42 he exhibited at the National Academy as a resident of Sing Sing (N.Y.). ¶ Cowdrey, NAD; NYCD 1836.

CARMIENCKE, JOHANN HERMANN (1810–1867). Landscape painter, born February 9, 1810, in Hamburg (Germany). After studying in Dresden, Copenhagen, and Leipzig in the 1830's, he travelled in Sweden, Germany, and Italy. From 1846 to 1851 he was court painter at Copenhagen. He came to America in 1851 and worked in NYC until his death, in Brooklyn, on June 15, 1867. He exhibited at the National Academy, Pennsylvania Academy, and Maryland Historical Society. ¶ Thieme-Becker; Bryan, *Dictionary;* CAB; Cowdrey, NAD; Rutledge, PA; Rutledge, MHS.

CARNAHAN, CHARLES. Lithographer, of TOLTI & CARNAHAN, New Orleans, 1856–59. ¶ New Orleans CD 1856, 1858–59, BD 1859 (cited by Delgado-WPA).

CARNES, JAMES. Scottish lithographer, 23, at NYC in July 1850. ¶ 7 Census (1850), N.Y., XLIV, 351.

CARP, ROBERT. Irish engraver, 35, at NYC in October 1850. Of his three children two were born in Ireland before 1849 and one in NYC in 1850. ¶ 7 Census (1850), N.Y., XLIX, 1008.

CARPEAUX, CHARLES. French artist, 25, at NYC in September 1850. ¶ 7 Census (1850), N.Y., LI, 549.

CARPENTER, A. Resident of Philadelphia, exhibited an oil painting, "The Unwelcome Visitor," at the Washington Art Association in 1857. ¶ Washington Art Assoc. Cat., 1857.

CARPENTER & ALLEN, see REUBEN CARPENTER and EZRA T. ALLEN.

CARPENTER, B. Line engraver of landscapes and buildings, Boston, *c.* 1855. *Cf.* REUBEN CARPENTER. ¶ Stauffer.

CARPENTER, COMMANDER BENJAMIN. His sketch of Boston (Mass.) Light House, drawn in 1792, is now owned by the Essex Institute. No American officer of this name and rank is recorded in Hamersley. ¶ Repro. in Brown, *Mirror for Americans;* Hamersley, *Naval Register.*

CARPENTER, BENJAMIN F. Portrait painter, NYC, 1855. ¶ NYBD 1855.

CARPENTER, ELLEN MARIA (1836–*c.* 1909). Landscape and portrait painter and teacher of art; born in Killingly (Conn.), November 23, 1836. A student of THOMAS EDWARDS and at the Lowell Institute in Boston, where she made her home from 1858. She studied in Europe in 1867 and in 1873, and became a popular landscape painter and teacher of art in Boston, where she died about 1909. ¶ *Who's Who in America* (1906/07) contains an autobiographical sketch, with the date of birth as above, while CAB and Clement and Hutton give 1830 and 1831, respectively; date of death is inferred from the disappearance of the name from Boston CD after 1909.

CARPENTER, FRANCIS BICKNELL (1830–1900). A.N.A. Portrait painter; born in Homer (N.Y.), August 6, 1830; died in NYC, May 23, 1900. Best known for his "First Reading of the Emancipation Proclamation" and his book, *Six Months in the White House,* Carpenter spent most of his career in Homer (until 1852) and NYC (1852–60 and after), with professional visits to Washington in 1855 and 1864. He exhibited widely: at the National Academy, American Art-Union, Brooklyn Athenaeum, Brooklyn Art Association, Washington Art Association, and the Boston Athenaeum. ¶ Goodwin, *Pioneer History,* 415–19; obits. in N. Y. *Herald,* N. Y. *Evening Post,* N. Y. *Sun,* May 24, 1900, and *Sun,* May 25, 1900, and June 22, 1945; Fairman, *Art and Artists of the Capitol,* repro. 306; NAD Cats. 1848, 1851, 1855–60, 1865, 1868–71, 1876–77, 1879, 1884, 1886, 1889–90, 1896; American Art-Union *Transactions* and *Bulletins,* 1848–51; Brooklyn Athenaeum Cat. 1856; Brooklyn Art Assoc. Cat. 1861–63, 1872; Washington Art Assoc. Cat. 1859; Swan, BA, 209. Represented in the U. S. Capitol (Fairman), the New-York Historical Society (Cat., 1941), and the American Antiquarian Society (Weis). See also: DAB; CAB; Bénézit; Fielding; Thieme-Becker; Clement and Hutton. There is a collection of material on Carpenter at the Cortland County Historical Society, presented by M. B. Cowdrey. [All information courtesy Mary Bartlett Cowdrey.]

CARPENTER, J. W. Engraver, probably employed by the Philadelphia firm of MURRAY, DRAPER & FAIRMAN in 1819, when he went to England with JACOB PERKINS, GIDEON FAIRMAN, CHARLES TOPPAN and ASA SPENCER. Possibly the Carpenter who was working with CEPHAS CHILDS in 1822. ¶ Bathe, *Jacob Perkins,* 72; Stauffer.

CARPENTER, R. R. Engraver, Chicago, 1854. ¶ Chicago CD 1854.

CARPENTER, REUBEN. Engraver; born in England *c.* 1827; living in Boston in 1860 with his wife, Martha (Vt., *c.* 1839) and daughter (Mass., *c.* 1859); personal property valued at $500. Carpenter was working in Boston from 1857, and in 1860 was a partner in the firm of CARPENTER & ALLEN. ¶ 8 Census (1860), Mass., XXIX, 577; Boston CD 1857–60, BD 1858–60.

CARPENTER, SAMUEL H. Engraver; born in New Jersey (7 Census) or Pennsylvania (8 Census), *c.* 1798–99; working in Philadelphia at least from 1846 to 1860. From 1846 to 1859 Carpenter was a partner in the banknote engraving firm of TOPPAN, CARPENTER, [CASILEAR] & CO., which merged in 1858 with the AMERICAN BANK NOTE CO. In the 1850 Census he was listed as the owner of real estate valued at $7,500, while ten years later his property was estimated at $30,000 in realty and $40,000 in personalty. Carpenter's wife, Ann, and three children—Emily, Joseph and SAMUEL H., JR.—were all born in Pennsylvania. ¶ 7 Census (1850), Pa., LI, 248; 8 Census (1860), Pa., LIV, 441; Phila. CD 1846–47, 1849–59.

CARPENTER, SAMUEL H., JR. Engraver; born in Pennsylvania *c.* 1832; working in Philadelphia 1859–60 and after. See SAMUEL H. CARPENTER, above, his father. ¶ 7 Census (1850), Pa., LI, 248; Phila. CD 1859–61.

CARR, JOHN (?–1837). Landscape painter of Philadelphia who married a daughter of RAPHAELLE PEALE in 1829. He died in April 1837. Local views by him were exhibited at the Artists' Fund Society in 1837–38. ¶ Sellers, *Charles Willson Peale,* II, 417; Rutledge, PA.

CARR, RICHARD. Lithographer; born in England *c.* 1801; living in Philadelphia in 1860 with his wife Kiziah (age 59, b. England) and three children—William J. (age 25, b. N.Y., gas fitter), Julia (age 19, b. Pa., tailoress), and John E. (age 17, b. N.Y., carpenter's apprentice); personal property valued at $300. ¶ 8 Census (1860), Pa., XLIX, 202.

CARR, WILLIAM. Engraver; born in England *c.* 1772; living in Philadelphia 1800–1851. Carr was listed in Philadelphia directories from 1800 to 1819 as engraver, bright engraver, umbrella maker and, in 1809–10, as a partner of JOHN DRAPER in the firm of Carr & Draper, copperplate printers. Since he was still living in Philadelphia in 1851, it is possible that he was also the William Carr who in 1833 painted a "Harbor Scene with Fish Market near Philadelphia." The 1850 Census lists William Carr, engraver, age 78, and his wife Mary, age 40 (b. Pa.); Carr's real property was at that time valued at $7,500. ¶ 7 Census (1850), Pa., L, 553; Phila. CD 1800–07, 1809–11, 1813–14, 1817–19 (cited by Brown and Brown); repro. in *American Processional,* 117; Phila. CD 1850–51.

CARR, WILLIAM. Sculptor; born in Pennsylvania *c.* 1823. In July 1850 he was employed at the marble works of Jacob Neable (age 26, German) at Chillicothe (Ohio). ¶ 7 Census (1850), Ohio, XL, 95.

CARRACROSS, Miss ——. Advertised to do monochromatic or Grecian painting, Richmond (Va.), November 1850. ¶ *Richmond Portraits,* cites *Times,* Nov. 27, 1850.

CARRIERE, LEOPOLD. Artist, New Orleans, 1852–56. ¶ New Orleans CD 1852–56.

CARROLL, J. R. Portrait painter, opened a studio at Pittsburgh (Pa.) in 1812. He was a teacher of freehand drawing, crayon work, watercolors, and landscapes. ¶ Fleming, *History of Pittsburgh,* III, 625.

CARROLL, JOHN. Portrait painter at Cincinnati in 1814. He was from England. ¶ Information courtesy Edward H. Dwight, Cincinnati Art Museum.

CARROLL, JOHN CHARLES. Portrait and marine painter, NYC and Brooklyn, 1843–45. In NYC 1843 as John C. Carroll, portrait painter; in 1844 exhibited oil painting of U. S. Brig "Somers" at American Institute, giving his address as U. S. Navy-Yard, Brooklyn; listed in NYC 1845 merely as artist. ¶ NYCD 1843, 1845; Am. Inst. Cat., 1844.

CARSON, Mrs. ANN. Teacher of drawing and painting, Philadelphia, 1823–24. She exhibited several watercolor still lifes at the Pennsylvania Academy. ¶ Rutledge, PA.

CARSON, BERNARD. Engraver; born in Ireland *c.* 1820; working in San Francisco 1856–60 and after. Carson's family included in 1860: his wife, Rebecca (38) and four children (8 to 17), all born in Ireland, and two children (1 year and 2 months) born in California. ¶ 8 Census (1860), Cal., VII, 485–86; San Francisco BD 1856, 1858–60; CD 1861.

CARSON, C. W. Line engraver of maps and vignettes, Albany (N.Y.), 1843. ¶ Stauffer.

CARSON, R. H. Wood engraver; at NYC in 1847; at Albany (N.Y.) in 1852. ¶ NYBD 1847/48; Troy and Albany Directory 1852.

CARSON, Mrs. WILLIAM A., see CAROLINE PETIGRU.

CARTEL, JOHN. Artist, Newark (N.J.), 1850. ¶ N. J. BD 1850/51.

CARTER, ——. Eleven-year-old artist of Washington (D.C.), who in 1850 exhibited at the Maryland Historical Society a painting of "Daniel Boone discovering the Valley of the Mississippi." ¶ Rutledge, MHS.

CARTER, ANDREWS & CO. Printers, engravers, and publishers of Lancaster (Mass.) in the 1830's. JOSEPH ANDREWS, the engraver, was one of the partners in this large establishment which employed a number of other wood and steel engravers, including JOHN H. HALL. ¶ Linton, *History of Wood Engraving,* 17–18; Marvin, *History of the Town of Lancaster,* 607–09; DAB (under Joseph Andrews); Hamilton, *Early American Book Illustrators and Wood Engravers,* 276–79.

CARTER, CHARLES. Engraver; born in Massachusetts *c.* 1830; working in Boston in 1850. His father, J. B. Carter (b. Mass., *c.* 1805), was the keeper of a public house; a younger brother, George Carter, aged 16, was also listed as an engraver. ¶ 7 Census (1850), Mass., XXIII, 357.

CARTER, CHARLES P. Engraver, Ware (Mass.), 1856, 1860. ¶ New England BD 1856, 1860.

CARTER, DENNIS MALONE (1818 or 1820–1881). Portrait and figure painter, born in Ireland, who came to America in 1839. Except for a brief residence in New Orleans in 1845–46 he seems to have spent the rest of his life in NYC. He exhibited at the National Academy (1848–82), Pennsylvania Academy (1855–67), American Art-Union (1848–49), Boston Athenaeum (1857–61), and Washington Art Association (1857). He died in NYC on July 6, 1881. ¶ *American Art Review,* II (1881), 175; N. Y. *Daily Tribune,* July 9, 1881 (citation courtesy H. Maxson Holloway); New Orleans CD 1845–46; Cowdrey, NAD; NAD Cat. 1861–82 (courtesy Mary Bartlett Cowdrey); Rutledge, PA; Cowdrey, AA & AAU; Swan, BA; Wash. Art Assoc. Cat. 1857; Clement and Hutton; Fielding. Represented at Chicago Hist. Soc.

CARTER, FRANKLIN N. Lithographer; born in Massachusetts *c.* 1827; boarding in Boston in 1860 with his wife Eliza (age 30) and daughter Annie F. (age 1), both born in Massachusetts. ¶ 8 Census (1860), Mass., XXVI, 577.

CARTER, GEORGE, see CHARLES CARTER.

CARTER, HENRY, see FRANK LESLIE.

CARTER, Mrs. ROBERT. Amateur painter, living at Troy (N.Y.) in the 1830's. Her "Napoleon's Army Crossing the Alps," now in the Karolik Collection, bears the following inscription: "Painted by Mrs. Robert Carter, and presented to her/ husband as an expression of her love and duty to him./ Troy. Febuary [sic] 17/ 1833." ¶ Karolik Cat., 154–55.

CARTEREAU, PETER. Wood carver, NYC, *c.* 1847–49. Apparently a dealer in mahogany, Cartereau exhibited specimens of carving at the American Instiute in 1847 (as P. Castireau) and 1848 (as P. Cartereau). ¶ NYCD 1847–49; Am. Inst. Cat., 1847–48.

CARTWRIGHT, J. Active *c.* 1789–1829, painter of "H. M. Sloop Little Belt and the U. S. Frigate President off Sandy Hook, May 16, 1811," owned by the U. S. Naval Academy, Annapolis (Md.). ¶ *American Processional,* 239.

CARTWRIGHT, T. Engraver of GEORGE BECK's "George Town and Federal City or City of Washington." ¶ *Antiques* (Feb. 1954), 105, repro.

CARTY, MARTIN. Engraver and die sinker, NYC, 1860. ¶ NYBD 1860.

CARVALHO, SOLOMON NUNES (1815–1894). Portrait and landscape painter, daguerreotypist, and photographer; born in Charleston (S.C.), April 27, 1815. The artist's father, David N. Carvalho (1784–1860), a watchmaker and merchant in Charleston for many years, moved in 1828 to Baltimore, where he established a marble paper manufactory. The family moved again in 1835, to Philadelphia, where they remained for the next fifteen years. Solomon's career as an artist began in Philadelphia about 1838 and centred there for the next decade, though he also worked in Charleston and Washington in the early 1840's. S. N. Carvalho was again in Philadelphia in 1849, when he exhibited at the Pennsylvania Academy, but the following year the whole family, including Solomon's wife and two-year-old son David, moved to Baltimore, where they made their home until the elder Carvalho's death in 1860. In 1851–52 Solomon again paid a professional visit to Charleston. His next professional venture was his two-year service as artist-photographer with John C. Fremont's expedition to the Far West (1853–54), Carvalho's own account of which was published in 1857. During the latter half of the 1850's the artist worked in Baltimore, but soon after his father's death he moved to NYC, accompanied by his wife and four sons—David, Jerrite, Jacob, and Solomon (ages 12, 10, 8 and 4, respectively, in 1860). Carvalho was listed as an artist or photographer in NYC directories until about 1880 and thereafter as president of the Carvalho Heating and Super-heating Co. or simply as inventor. He died in NYC in 1894. ¶ Markens, 203; Elzas, 187; London, *Shades of My Forefathers;* Reznikoff and Engelman, 109; Baltimore CD 1831, 1851–60; Phila. CD 1835–50; Rutledge, *Artists in the Life of Charleston;* Jackson, *Ancestors,* mentions a silhouette of Carvalho, cut by EDOUART in Washington, March 20, 1841; Rutledge, PA; 7 Census (1850), Md., V, 103; Carvalho, *Incidents of Travel and Adventure in the Far West* (N.Y., 1857); *Portfolio* (Feb. 1952), 123–129, repro.; 8 Census (1860), Md., IV, 939; NAD Cat. 1862–64; NYCD 1864–1893. Carvalho's work was exhibited at the Maryland Historical Society in

1850 and 1856 (Rutledge, MHS) and is represented there (Rutledge, "Portraits in the Md. Hist. Soc.").

CARVER, JOHN E. Architect and draftsman, Philadelphia, exhibited water colors at the Artists' Fund Society in 1840 and 1841. ¶ Rutledge, PA; Phila. CD 1841.

CARY, ISAAC. Banknote engraver and copperplate printer, Boston, 1828–60 and after. In 1848–49 he was an agent for the NEW ENGLAND BANK NOTE CO. ¶ Boston CD 1828–60 and after; Boston BD 1852–57.

CARY, WILLIAM DE LA MONTAGNE (1840–1922). Painter of Western scenes. At the age of 21, Cary and two friends left NYC on a trip through the Far West. Cary's sketches made during this trip and a later one in 1874 provided the basis for a long career as a painter and illustrator of Indian and other Western scenes. His work was often reproduced in the late 1860's and 1870's. He died at Brookline (Mass.) on January 7, 1922. ¶ Taft, *Artists and Illustrators of the Old West,* 52–53, 292; McCracken, *Portrait of the Old West; Art Digest* (Feb. 1, 1937), 17, 2 repros.; *American Museum Journal* (May, 1917), 332–340, nine repros.; *Antiques* (June 1935), 229, repro.; represented in the Gilcrease Foundation Collection, Tulsa (Okla.).

CASE & GREEN, see LUCIUS CASE and WILLIAM GREEN.

CASE, JOSIAH. A New Yorker, exhibited wood engravings at the American Institute in 1844. ¶ Am. Inst. Cat., 1844.

CASE, LUCIUS. Lithographer and copperplate printer, Hartford (Conn.), *c.* 1838–56. Though primarily a printer, Case was from 1849 to 1852 senior partner in the lithographic firm of CASE & GREEN. ¶ Hartford CD 1831–56, and later as Case, Lockwood & Co., printers.

CASHEN, ——. Portrait painter, Cincinnati (Ohio), 1853; possibly the same as J. Cashin, a watercolor painter in England in 1825. ¶ Ohio BD 1853/54; Thieme-Becker.

CASHMAN, G. H. Portrait painter, Philadelphia, 1850. ¶ Phila. BD 1850.

CASILEAR, GEORGE W. Engraver and landscape artist, NYC, 1847–52. Brother of JOHN W. CASILEAR, with whom he was working as an engraver in NYC in 1847–48. A view of San Francisco, drawn by G. W. Casilear and HENRY BAINBRIDGE, was published by SARONY & MAJOR in 1851, while a view of Sacramento by Casilear was lithographed about the same time by N. SARONY. The frontispiece of Lett's *Pictorial View of California* was drawn by G. V. COOPER from a sketch by G. W. Casilear. From 1852 to 1857 he worked as an editor, secretary, and solicitor of patents. ¶ NYCD 1847–1857; Peters, *Calif.; Portfolio* (May 1951), 209, repro.

CASILEAR, J. H. [sic] & G. W. Portrait, historical, and landscape engravers, NYC, 1847–48. The partners were JOHN WILLIAM and GEORGE W. CASILEAR. ¶ NYCD 1847–48.

CASILEAR, JOHN WILLIAM (1811–1893). N.A. Engraver and landscape painter of the Hudson River school; born in NYC, June 25, 1811; died in Saratoga (N.Y.), August 17, 1893. Casilear served his apprenticeship under PETER MAVERICK and studied also with A. B. DURAND. Except for two trips to Europe, in 1840–43 and in 1857–58, his professional life was spent mainly in NYC, where he became a prominent banknote engraver and member of the National Academy. His summers were spent in up-state New York and Vermont and provided the subjects for the many landscapes he exhibited at a number of galleries: National Academy (1833–90), Apollo Association (1838–43), American Art-Union (1847–51), and Pennsylvania Academy (1855–65), as well as occasionally at the Washington Art Association and the Maryland Historical Society. As an engraver, Casilear worked with several firms, including TAPPAN, CARPENTER, CASILEAR & CO., and in 1847–48 with his brother, GEORGE W. CASILEAR. ¶ DAB; Cowdrey, NAD; NYCD 1833–36, 1838, 1846–54, 1856–60 and after; Stauffer; Cowdrey, AA & AAU; Rutledge, PA; Rutledge, MHS; Washington Art Assoc. Cat., 1857. Mrs. Charles P. Rogers, the artist's granddaughter, owns many of his sketches and papers. His work is also represented at the Metropolitan Museum, NYHS, Corcoran Gallery (Cat.), and Peabody Institute (List of Works of Art, 1949).

CASILEAR, PAUL. Banknote engraver, 42, at NYC in 1860. He and his whole family were native New Yorkers. ¶ 8 Census (1860), N.Y., XLV, 50.

CASS, GEORGE NELSON (1831/32–1882). Landscape painter. Born in 1831 or 1832; lived for many years at Boston (Mass.), where he died in 1882. He exhibited at the American Art-Union in 1849, the

Boston Athenaeum in 1863 and 1865, and the National Academy in 1867. He was a pupil of INNESS. ¶ Smith; Clement and Hutton; Cowdrey, AA & AAU; Swan, BA, 210; CAB; Thieme-Becker; Cowdrey, NAD.

CASSE, ALFRED. Portrait and miniature painter, Newark (N.J.), 1835–37. Possibly the same as A. Casse of Philadelphia who exhibited "Alpine Sunrise" at the Pennsylvania Academy in 1862. ¶ Newark CD 1835–37; Rutledge, PA.

CASSIDY, GEORGE W. Panorama painter who collaborated with SAMUEL A. HUDSON on panoramas of the Ohio and Mississippi Rivers, about 1847–48. Cassidy was exhibiting a similar panorama in New England in the spring of 1849 and by 1850 was in Germany, exhibiting his panorama in Leipzig and Hamburg. ¶ Arrington, "Samuel A. Hudson's Panorama of the Ohio and Mississippi Rivers."

CASSIN, JOHN. Lithographer, Philadelphia, from 1859 as a partner in BOWEN & CO. ¶ Phila. CD 1859–60 and after.

CASTELLE, see VAN DE CASTELLE.

CASTELNAU, FRANCIS. French traveler and lithographer, who visited America *c.* 1838–40 and on his return to France published *Vues de l'Amerique du Nord* (Paris, 1842). ¶ *Portfolio* (March 1950), 154–157, eight repros.

CASTEREAN, ALPHONSE. Artist, Baltimore (Md.), 1858. ¶ Baltimore CD 1858/59.

CASTLE, ARTHUR S. Marine painter of NYC, exhibited at the National Academy in 1860. ¶ Cowdrey, NAD.

CASTLE, LYDIA. Engraver; born in New York *c.* 1840; working in Philadelphia in 1860. ¶ 8 Census (1860), Pa., LIV, 508.

CASTLEMAN, P. F. Artist; born in Kentucky *c.* 1827; living in Eugene City (Ore.) in 1860. ¶ 8 Census (1860), Ore., cited by David C. Duniway, Oregon State Archivist.

CATESBY, MARK (*c.* 1679–1749). English naturalist and etcher. Catesby made two visits to America, spending the years 1712 to 1719 with relatives in Virginia and on the second trip, 1722–1725, traveling through the Carolinas, Georgia, and Florida and spending some time in the Bahamas before his return to England in 1726. The result of his American residences was the important *Natural History of Carolina, Florida and the Bahama Islands* (London, 1731–1743), for which Catesby etched upward of 100 plates, the first set of which he also colored himself. In recognition of his scientific work Catesby was elected to the Royal Society in 1733. A posthumously published volume, *Hortus Britanno-Americanus,* also contained a number of Catesby's etchings of American trees and shrubs, many of which he had himself introduced to English horticulturalists. He died in London, December 23, 1749. ¶ DAB and DNB; Comstock, "An 18th Century Audubon"; repro. *Art News* (Aug. 1947), 1; *Connoisseur* (March 1948), 47–52. A copy of Catesby's *Natural History* is in the Rare Book Room, Library of Congress.

CATHERWOOD, FREDERICK (1799–1854). Architect, historical, and panoramic painter, archaeologist; born in London, February 27, 1799. 1815–20, apprentice architect, London; 1820, exhibited at the Royal Academy; 1821–25, Italy, Greece, and Egypt; 1826–28, London; 1829–34, the Levant, Greece, and Egypt; 1835–36, London; 1836–39, NYC; 1839–40, Central America, with John Lloyd Stephens; 1840–41, NYC; 1841–42, Yucatan; 1842–43, NYC; 1843–44, London; 1844–45, NYC; 1846–49, British Guiana; 1850, Panama; 1851–53; California; 1854, to England via Mexico; September 27, 1854, lost in the sinking of the steamship *Arctic* en route to NYC. Catherwood's most important work was his series of illustrations of the Maya ruins of Yucatan and Guatemala. ¶ The standard life is Von Hagen's *Frederick Catherwood, Archt.* (N.Y., 1950), with biblio. and many illustrations. See also: Von Hagen, "F. Catherwood, Archt.," in NYHS *Quarterly* (Jan. 1946), 17–29; NYCD 1838–43, 1845; Cowdrey, NAD; Cowdrey, AA & AAU; Stokes, *Icon.,* III, 697–98 and pl. 131; *Valentine's Manual* (1860), frontis.; Lancour, no. 26.

CATLIN, GEORGE (1796–1872). N.A. Portrait painter and miniaturist, best known for his paintings of the American Indian; born in Wilkes-Barre (Pa.), July 26, 1796. After studying law, Catlin in 1820 set up as a miniaturist in Philadelphia, where he worked until 1825. He worked in New York State from 1825 to 1829, when he moved to Richmond (Va.). In 1830 he made his first visit to the West and began the major work of his life, the portrayal of the American Indians and their customs. After about eight years of travel and painting in the American West, Catlin in 1839 took his collections to Europe, where he was to spend the next thirty years, except for several years in South America (1852–57). He returned to America in 1870 and died in Jersey City (N.J.) two years later, on December 23, 1872. ¶ The most recent biography is Haberly's *Pursuit of the Horizon: A Life of George Catlin, Painter and Recorder of the American Indian* (N.Y., 1948). See also: Catlin, *Letters and Notes;* DAB; Phila. CD 1823–25; *Richmond Portraits,* 241; Vail, "The Last Meeting of the Giants"; New Orleans *Bee,* March 24, 1835, and *Courier,* April 2, 1835 (cited by Delgado-WPA); Rutledge, *Artists in the Life of Charleston,* 188; Rutledge, PA; Cowdrey, AA & AAU; Thomas, "George Catlin, Portrait Painter," repros.; De Voto, *Across the Wide Missouri,* repros.; Colden, *Memoir;* represented in the Smithsonian Institution and NYHS.

CATLIN, THEODORE BURR. Portrait painter. Nephew of GEORGE CATLIN, with whom he studied *c.* 1839 and whom he assisted in the management of Catlin's Indian Gallery. He moved to Green Bay (Wis.) before the Civil War, in which he served as a Lieutenant Colonel. After the war he worked in Green Bay as a fresco and ornamental painter. He was the teacher of FRANK PEBBLES. ¶ NYBD 1846, 1849; Butts, *Art in Wisconsin,* 44, 46; Am. Inst. Cat., 1849.

CATTON, CHARLES, JR. (1756–1819). Landscape and animal painter; born in London, December 30, 1756. A pupil of his father, who was a Royal Academician and heraldic painter to George III, the younger Charles Catton exhibited frequently at the Royal Academy from 1776 to 1800, and in 1789 published a set of 36 "Animals Drawn from Nature, and Engraved in Acquatinta." He emigrated to America *c.* 1802 and settled on a farm at New Paltz in Ulster County (N.Y.), where he remained until his death, April 24, 1819. Though he is said to have painted little after his arrival in America, Catton's work was shown at the American Academy in 1816, 1818–1822 and 1827. ¶ DNB; obit., N. Y. *Commercial Advertiser,* May 5, 1819 (citation courtesy of Miss E. Marie Becker); Thieme-Becker; Edwards, *Anecdotes of Painters* (1808), 260; Graves, *Dictionary;* Dunlap, *History,* II, 208–11; Cowdrey, AA & AAU; Flexner, *The Light of Distant Skies,* biblio., 259.

CAUGHEY (or Coughey), JOHN. Wood engraver, NYC, 1845–56; in 1852 of Caughey & Momberger. J. Caughey exhibited wood engravings at the American Institute in 1847 and 1848, and G. Caughey in 1849. ¶ NYCD 1845–56; Am. Inst. Cats., 1847–49.

CAUGHEY & MOMBERGER, see JOHN CAUGHEY and WILLIAM MOMBERGER.

CAUGHEY, WILLIAM. Wood engraver, NYC, 1848–63. He was apparently working with JOHN CAUGHEY in 1848, when he exhibited at the American Institute. ¶ Am. Inst. Cat., 1848; NYCD 1855–63.

CAUSICI, ENRICO. Sculptor. A native of Verona (Italy), Causici claimed to be a pupil of Canova. He was working in America as early as 1822 and until *c.* 1832. His most ambitious work was the statue of Washington for the Monument at Baltimore; he also worked on the U. S. Capitol at Washington *c.* 1823–25 and in NYC. He died at Havana (Cuba). ¶ Fairman, *Art and Artists of the Capitol,* 48–52; Dunlap, *History,* II, 468; Stokes, *Icon.*

CAUSSE, Mrs. M. S. Teacher of drawing, "flourishing work," painting on velvet, reading, and writing, etc., at Charleston (S.C.), 1823. ¶ Rutledge, *Artists in the Life of Charleston,* 189.

CAVALER, PAUL. Lithographer, New Orleans, 1846–56. ¶ New Orleans CD 1846, 1852–56.

CAVALHO, see CARVALHO.

CAVANAUGH (or Cavanagh), JOHN. Sculptor in marble, New Orleans, 1852–56. ¶ New Orleans CD 1852–56.

CAVANAUGH, MICHAEL. Engraver; born in Pennsylvania, *c.* 1834; living in Southwark (Philadelphia County, Pa.), September 1850. ¶ 7 Census (1850), Pa., LV, 269.

CAVANAUGH (Cavenaugh or Cavanagh), WILLIAM F. (or J.). William F. Cavanaugh was listed in Philadelphia directories from 1850 to 1860 as an engraver or jewelry engraver, in 1850 of DOYLE & CAVANAUGH. This is probably the same as William J. Cavanagh, engraver, in the 1860 Census. The latter was 33 years old in 1860, owned $100 in personalty, and had three children, ages 4 to 7; all the family were born in Pennsylvania. ¶ Phila. CD 1850–60 and after; 8 Census (1860), Pa., XLIX, 301.

CAVE, C. Engraver of Boston, active 1805. ¶ Information courtesy Miss Helen Comstock.

CAZENOVA, EDWARD. German engraver, 30,

at NYC in August 1850. ¶ 7 Census (1850), N.Y., XLII, 91.

CECOIN, MICHAEL. Engraver, Philadelphia, 1818. ¶ Phila. CD 1818 (cited by Brown and Brown).

CERACCHI (or Ceracci), GIUSEPPE (1751–1802). Sculptor; born in Corsica, July 1751. After study under Rhigi in Rome, Ceracchi went to England, exhibiting at the Royal Academy from 1776 to 1779, but returned to Rome, where he remained until c. 1790. He made two visits to America, *c.* 1790 and in 1793, and there executed busts of Washington, Jefferson, Franklin, Adams, and Hamilton. He was executed in Paris, January 30, 1802 for his part in a conspiracy against Napoleon. ¶ Thieme-Becker; *La Grande Encyclopedie;* Morgan and Fielding, *Life Portraits of Washington;* Graves, *Dictionary;* J. I. Smith, "Ceracchi and His American Visit," repro.; Gardner, "Fragment of a Lost Monument"; Fielding; represented at the National Academy, Maryland Historical Society, Peabody Institute, and the New-York Historical Society.

CERESA & PINOLI. Portrait painters, New Orleans, 1838. See A. PINOLI. ¶ New Orleans CD 1838 (cited by Delgado-WPA).

CERTIER, GEORGE. Lithographer; born in France, *c.* 1831; living in Philadelphia with his parents in 1850. The directories for 1850–51 list a Geo. Certier, watch spring manufacturer. ¶ 7 Census (1850), Pa., L, 932; Phila. CD 1850–51.

CETTI, LEWIS, see LOUIS CITTI.

CHADWICK, ——. Painter, possibly American, of "Placer Mining," 1854. ¶ Met. Mus., *Life in America,* no. 144, repro.

CHADWICK, JOSH. Delineator of a 1768 view of Harvard College, Cambridge (Mass.). ¶ Stokes, *Hist. Prints.*

CHADWICK, WILLIAM F. Artist; born in Maine, *c.* 1828; living in Portland (Me.) in 1850, in the home of his father, Samuel Chadwick, merchant, whose real property was valued at $25,000. ¶ 7 Census (1850), Maine, IV(3), 260.

CHAFFEREAU, PETER. Itinerant artist, South Carolina, 1734. ¶ *Connoisseur,* CXXXI (April 1953), 67.

CHALL, ALFRED. Artist of the French Theatre, New Orleans, 1850. Chall, age 24, and his wife Henrietta, age 25, were both natives of France. ¶ 7 Census (1850), La., V, 548.

CHAMBAUD, T. Miniaturist, New Orleans, 1827. ¶ New Orleans CD 1827 (cited by Delgado-WPA).

CHAMBERLAIN, BENJAMIN B. Wood engraver, born in New York about 1833. In 1851, as an apprentice or employee of DURAND & MOORE, he exhibited at the American Institute. He was working in NYC in 1860. ¶ 8 Census (1860), N.Y., XLV, 187; Am. Inst. Cat., 1851; NYBD 1851.

CHAMBERLAIN, WILLIAM (1790–?). Silhouettist. Born at Loudon (N.H.) in April 1790, Chamberlain made a tour of New England (particularly New Hampshire and Massachusetts) and New York *c.* 1820, cutting profiles, of which 89 are owned by the American Antiquarian Society. ¶ Carrick, *Shades,* 121; Carrick, "Novelties in Old American Profiles"; N. H. Vital Records (cited by Miss Charlotte D. Conover, Librarian, N. H. Hist. Soc.).

CHAMBERS, ——. Painter who came to NYC from London in 1725 and remained for nine years before returning to England. He was a Scot, studied in Edinburgh under Sir John Medina, served in the Spanish war (1709), and worked in London as an assistant to the artists Gouge and William Aikman before coming to America. In September 1735 he was employed in copying, cleaning, and lettering pictures for Lord Egmont. ¶ Whitley, *Artists and Their Friends in England,* I, 67.

CHAMBERS, BENJAMIN. Engraver, Washington (D.C.), 1843–60. He was born in Virginia *c.* 1800; his son, B. Chambers, was born in the District of Columbia *c.* 1841. ¶ Washington and Georgetown CD 1843, 1853, 1855, 1858, 1860; 7 Census (D.C.), I, 310.

CHAMBERS, JOSEPH T. Artist, Chicago (Ill.), 1858. ¶ Chicago CD 1858.

CHAMBERS, R. Engraver, Washington, 1820–26. ¶ Stauffer; Fielding, *Supplement to Stauffer.*

CHAMBERS, SUSAN. Amateur artist, probably of Chambersburg (Pa.). Her view of The Church of the Falling Spring at Chambersburg has been reproduced. ¶ *Penna. History* (July 1953), 286, repro.

CHAMBERS, THOMAS (*c.* 1808–?). Marine, landscape, portrait, and ornamental painter. An Englishman, Chambers came to America in 1832 and became a citizen by naturalization. From 1834 to 1840 he was living in NYC, from 1843 to 1851 in Boston, 1852–57 in Albany (N.Y.), and 1858–59, 1861–66 in NYC. ¶ Information courtesy Howard S. Merritt, University of Rochester, who cites New York State Census, 1855, Albany County, and Albany CD 1852–57; 7 Census (1850), Mass., XXIV, 473; NYCD 1834–39, 1858–59, 1861–66; Little, "T. Chambers, Man or Myth" and "Earliest Signed Picture by T. Chambers"; Ford, *Pictorial Folk Art,* repros.; *Panorama,* IV (Aug. 1948), 4–5, repros.; *American Collector* (May 1946) and (May 1948), repros.; Lipman and Winchester, 106–12.

CHAMBERS, WILLIAM B. Portrait and genre painter. Possibly related to THOMAS CHAMBERS, William B. Chambers was working in NYC at the same time, 1834–41. He exhibited at the Apollo Association in 1839 watercolor copies of European masters. From 1848 to 1857 he was a resident of Philadelphia, where he exhibited portraits and Italian genre studies at the Pennsylvania Academy from 1848 to 1856. ¶ Little, "T. Chambers, Man or Myth?"; Cowdrey, AA & AAU; Phila. CD 1851–57, BD 1850, 1853; Rutledge, PA.

CHAMPAGNE, GEORGE. A crayon portrait of Mary Elizabeth Germain, drawn by this artist in 1858, was owned in 1941 by R. W. Jermaine of Jonesville (Vt.) ¶ WPA (Mass.), *Portraits Found in Vt.*

CHAMPLAIN, SAMUEL, Sieur de (*c.* 1567–1635). French explorer and colonial administrator who illustrated his numerous works on North America with his own sketches. Born at Brouage, near Rochefort on the Bay of Biscay, Champlain served in the army and navy of Henry of Navarre and in 1599–1601 visited New Spain, drawing up an illustrated report to King Henry IV of France, the original of which is now in the John Carter Brown Library, Providence (R.I.). He first visited Canada in 1603 and in 1608 he founded Quebec. In 1615–16 he explored the Great Lakes region and visited what is now upper New York State. He died in Quebec on Christmas Day, 1635. ¶ DAB, lists several biographies and editions of his writings.

CHAMPNEY, BENJAMIN (1817–1907). Landscape, panoramic, and portrait painter; born in New Ipswich (N.H.), November 17, 1817. Apprenticed to a lithographer in Boston, Champney took drawing lessons from ROBERT COOKE and before 1841 went into business with him as a portrait painter. Champney and Cooke went to France in 1841. Champney returned to Boston in 1846, but went back to Europe almost at once to paint a panorama of the Rhine. Interrupted by the Revolution of 1848, scenes from which he also painted, Champney returned to America in 1848 and during the next few years he exhibited his panoramas in Boston and NYC. About 1850 he turned to landscape painting, making his summer headquarters on the Saco River at North Conway (N.H.) and wintering at Woburn (Mass.), where he died December 11, 1907. He was a founder of the Boston Arts Club and a frequent exhibitor there and at the Boston Athenaeum, as well as at the American Art-Union, the National Academy, and the Pennsylvania Academy. His autobiography, *Sixty Years' Memories of Art and Artists,* was published in 1900. His son, J. Wells Champney (1843–1903) was a well-known genre painter. ¶ DAB; Boston BD 1850, 1853–58; Cowdrey, NAD; Cowdrey, AA & AAU; Swan, BA; Rutledge, PA; Boston *Evening Transcript,* Nov. 25 and Dec. 29, 1848, and March 14, 1849, and N. Y. *Herald,* March 3, 1850 (cited by J. E. Arrington).

CHAMPNEY, W. L. Illustrator, whose earliest known work is a set of four illustrations for *Minnie, or The Little Woman* (Boston, 1857). Other illustrations by W. L. Champney appeared in the *Riverside Magazine for Young People,* Vols. I and II (1867–68). ¶ Hamilton, 167.

CHANDLER & CO., see SAMUEL W. CHANDLER and JOHN G. CHANDLER.

CHANDLER & DURAN, see VICTOR L. L. CHANDLER and JOHN DURAN.

CHANDLER, G. L. Portrait sculptor, Boston, exhibited at the Boston Athenaeum in 1842 and 1853. ¶ Swan, BA.

CHANDLER, ISAAC N. Engraver, Newark (N.J.), 1859. ¶ Essex, Hudson & Union Counties BD 1859.

CHANDLER, JOHN GREENE (1815–1879). General and wood engraver; born at "Deer Farm," Petersham (Mass.), December 18, 1815. Chandler was living in Boston as early as 1828. From 1836 to 1839 he was a partner in the wood-engraving firm of CHANDLER, WRIGHT & MALLORY. He illustrated, and possibly wrote, *The Remarkable Story of Chicken Little,* published in Boston in 1840. He married in 1850 SARAH ANN GUILD. John G. Chandler and his brother, SAMUEL W. CHANDLER, a Custom House inspector, worked together 1854–55 as CHANDLER & CO. or SAMUEL W. CHANDLER & BROTHER, successors to B. W. THAYER & CO. After 1857 John G. Chandler moved to Lancaster (Mass.), where he died

September 11, 1879. Besides his engraving and lithographic work, he manufactured paper dolls and cut-outs, a toy circus, and games. ¶ Hosmer, "John G. Chandler," with three repros.; Boston CD 1835–57; Stokes, *Hist. Prints* (under Chandler & Co.).

CHANDLER, Mrs. JOHN GREENE, see SARAH ANN GUILD.

CHANDLER, JOSEPH GOODHUE (1813–1880?). Itinerant portrait painter; born in South Hadley (Mass.), October 3, 1813. Trained as a cabinetmaker, J. G. Chandler later turned to portrait painting, studying under WILLIAM COLLINS of Albany (N.Y.). Most of his work was done during the 1840's and 1850's, including a portrait of Daniel Webster now owned by the New-York Historical Society. From 1852 to 1860 Chandler worked in Boston. His wife, see below, was also an artist. He died in Hubbardstown (Mass.), probably in 1880. ¶ Dods, "Connecticut Valley Painters," 209; Boston BD 1852, 1855–59; Sears, *Some American Primitives,* 81, repro. p. 66.

CHANDLER, Mrs. JOSEPH GOODHUE, née Lucretia Ann Waite (1820–1868). Painter and drawing teacher. Miss Waite was already known as a painter in Hubbardstown (Mass.) when she married the itinerant artist, JOSEPH GOODHUE CHANDLER, in 1840. While they were living in Boston she exhibited at the Boston Athenaeum in 1856 and later she taught drawing at the Willston Academy, Easthampton (Mass.). ¶ Swan, BA, 211; Dods, "Connecticut Valley Painters," 209, repro.

CHANDLER, SAMUEL W. (1803–1900). Lithographer and engraver, Boston, 1854–55. A graduate of Harvard (1822), Chandler served as an inspector in the Custom House at Boston from 1844 to 1853, then went into business with his brother, JOHN GREENE CHANDLER, as lithographer and engraver until 1856. Their establishment, known as CHANDLER & Co. and SAMUEL W. CHANDLER & BROTHER, specialized in children's books and cut-outs. After 1856 Samuel seems to have given up lithography and moved to Taunton (Mass.) where he was a manufacturer; he later moved to Philadelphia where he was in the junk trade. ¶ Hosmer, "John G. Chandler"; Peters, *America on Stone;* Boston CD 1844–55; Chandler, *The Chandler Family.*

CHANDLER, VICTOR L. L. Wood engraver; born in Massachusetts *c.* 1836; living in Boston in 1860 in the home of his father, Thomas H. Chandler, dentist. He was listed in the directories from 1857 to 1860 and after, in 1859–60 as a member of the firm of CHANDLER & DURAN. ¶ 8 Census (1860), Mass., XXVIII, 878; Boston CD 1857–60 and after; Hamilton, 312 (as Chadler-Duran).

CHANDLER, WINFIELD. Engraver; born in Philadelphia *c.* 1841; living there in July 1860. ¶ 8 Census (1860), Pa., LIV, 1098.

CHANDLER, WINTHROP (1747–1790). Portrait and landscape painter; born at "Chandler Hill," Woodstock (Conn.) April 6, 1747; died at Woodstock (Conn.), July 29, 1790. His work was done mainly at Woodstock and Thompson (Conn.) and Worcester (Mass.). ¶ Little, "Winthrop Chandler," with biblio., catalogue, and many repros.; Little, "Recently Discovered Paintings by Winthrop Chandler," seven repros. and suppl. catalogue; Flexner, "18th Century Artisan Painter"; Chandler, *The Chandler Family,* 128, 277–78; Ford, *Pictorial Folk Art,* 57; represented at the American Antiquarian Society (Weis), and the Ohio State Archaeological Society (Ford, *op. cit.*).

CHANDLER, WRIGHT & MALLORY, see JOHN GREENE CHANDLER, EDWARD WRIGHT, and RICHARD P. MALLORY; also WRIGHT & MALLORY.

CHANEY, Mrs. MARY ANN BROWNE, see BROWNE.

CHANOU & DESOBRY, see PROSPER DESOBRY.

CHAPIN, ALPHEUS (*c.* 1787–1870). Portrait painter; born in Massachusetts *c.* 1787; died in Boston on March 4, 1870. He was living in Boston in 1850 with his wife Beulah, a native of Vermont, and he worked there at least until 1860. He is also known to have worked in Benson and Bennington (Vt.) and in NYC. ¶ C. K. Bolton, "Workers with Line and Color in New England"; 7 Census (1850), Mass., XXV, 109; Boston CD 1851, 1860; BD 1857, 1860; New England BD 1856; WPA (Vt.).

CHAPIN, BENJAMIN M. Portrait painter, NYC, 1857–60; exhibitor at the National Academy. ¶ Cowdrey, NAD; NYBD 1860.

CHAPIN, Mrs. JANE CATHERINE LOUISE VALUE (1814–1891). Miniaturist and portrait painter, who also painted on velvet, taught drawing and painting, drew views for engraving, and colored photographs. She was born at Hartford (Conn.), September 10, 1814; attended school in NYC in 1826; visited Providence (R.I.) in 1829. Though she later made her home in New Haven (Conn.), Mrs. Chapin often wintered in the South, at Richmond (Va.), Charleston, and Columbia (S.C.). During one of her southern visits she painted a life portrait of Chief Justice John Marshall. She died November 29, 1891, probably at Providence. ¶ *Antiques,* VIII (Aug. 1925), 97, with repros.

CHAPIN, JOHN R. (1823–?). Designer and illustrator, painter of battle scenes; born in Providence (R.I.), January 2, 1823. He worked as a designer in NYC from 1844 to 1860 and after, and exhibited there at the 1849 American Institute Fair. In 1859 he was living in Rahway (N.J.). He was still living in 1907, at Buffalo (N.Y.). ¶ *Art Annual,* VI (1907/08), 328; NYCD 1844–1854; Am. Inst. Cat., 1849; Essex, Hudson and Union Counties BD 1859; Peters, *America on Stone,* pl. 172; Thieme-Becker; Bénézit.

CHAPIN, WILLIAM (1802–1888). Engraver; born in Philadelphia, October 17, 1802; died there, September 20, 1888. Chapin worked mainly in Philadelphia and NYC before 1840. He exhibited engravings of machines at the National Academy in 1826. ¶ Stauffer; Cowdrey, NAD; *Am. Advt. Directory,* 1832, 188 (NYC); Fielding.

CHAPMAN, ALVA R. Miniaturist and silhouettist, Cleveland (Ohio), 1826. ¶ *Antiques,* XXI (March 1932), 152.

CHAPMAN, FREDERIC A. (1818–1891). Portrait, historical and landscape painter, stained glass designer; born in 1818, in Connecticut. About 1850 he painted historical scenes of Boston, and in 1850 he exhibited landscape and historical paintings at the American Art-Union. In August 1850 he was at NYC and he soon after settled in Brooklyn (N.Y.), remaining there until after 1860. He was the first president of the Brooklyn Art Association, and his oils, especially a series of Civil War scenes, attracted much attention in the 1860's. He died January 26, 1891. ¶ Obit., Boston *Transcript,* Jan. 27, 1891; 7 Census (1850) N.Y., XLVII, 81; Kende Gallery Cat. (1946), 229; Cowdrey, NAD; Cowdrey, AA & AAU; *Portfolio* (Feb. 1954), 127, repro.

CHAPMAN, JOHN GADSBY (1808–1889). N.A. Landscape, historical and portrait painter, wood engraver, etcher and illustrator; born in Alexandria (D.C.), December 8, 1808; died in Brooklyn (N.Y.), November 28, 1889. A pupil of GEORGE COOKE and C. B. KING, Chapman established himself as a professional artist in 1827, when he visited Winchester (Va.). After a brief period of study at the Pennsylvania Academy, he went to Europe, studying in Rome and Florence until 1831. On his return to America he enjoyed success as a portrait and historical painter, dividing his time between NYC and the District of Columbia. He was elected a full member of the National Academy in 1836, and in 1838 was one of the founders of the Apollo Gallery. His *American Drawing Book,* published in 1847, and his illustrations for the Harpers *Bible,* as well as landscapes and historical paintings, such as the "Pocahontas" in the U. S. Capitol, were widely known in his day. Chapman returned to Europe in 1848, and remained there for many years. His works were frequently exhibited in American galleries: National Academy, Boston Athenaeum, Pennsylvania Academy, American Academy, Apollo Gallery and Association, American Art-Union, Artists' Fund Society, and the Maryland Historical Society. ¶ DAB; Stauffer; Clement and Hutton; Dunlap, *History,* II, 436–38; Dunlap, *Diary;* Fairman, *Art and Artists of the Capitol;* Cowdrey, NAD; Swan, BA; Rutledge, PA; Cowdrey, AA & AAU; Rutledge, MHS. The Library of Congress Union Catalogue contains over 30 cards on Chapman, including his *American Drawing Book* (N.Y., 1847), *Elements of Art* (London, 1848) and *Elementary Drawing Book* (N.Y. and Chicago, 1872). Chapman's scrapbook of designs on wood is at the Virginia State Library, Richmond.

CHAPMAN, MOSES (1783–1821). Itinerant silhouettist of eastern Massachusetts. ¶ Jackson, *Silhouette,* 89; Carrick, *Shades.*

CHAPMAN, WILLIAM. Engraver, NYC, 1859. ¶ NYBD 1859.

CHAPPEL, ALONZO (1828–1887). Portrait, historical, landscape, and figure painter and illustrator; born in NYC, March 1, 1828. Chappel is said to have studied at the National Academy as early as 1836, and he had exhibited twice at the American Institute before he was seventeen. Though only 16 in 1844, Alonzo Chappel was listed in the NYC directory for that year. The following year he moved with his family to Brooklyn, where he was listed as an artist from 1848 to 1868. His later years were spent on Middle Island, Long Island, where he devoted himself mainly to illustrating historical books. He died there December 4, 1887. ¶ Diers, "The Strange Case of Alonzo Chappel," with repros., and partial listing of paintings and illustrations by Chappel; Lewis, "Alonzo Chappel and His Naval Paintings"; Stiles, *History of King's County,* II, 1147–48; Cowdrey, NAD; *Museum Notes,* II (Feb. 1944); *Chicago History,* I (Spring 1947), 185–187; Am. Inst. Cat., 1842, 1844; historical data in the Heraldic Branch, Office of the Quartermaster General, U. S. Army, Washington (D.C.), and in the New York Public Library. Chappel's work is represented in the New-York and Chicago Historical Societies.

CHAPPEL, WILLIAM. Painter of NYC street scenes in oils and watercolors. A set of ten small oils, showing street criers of fruit, vegetables, and water from the "Tea Water Pump," were painted by him between 1806 and 1813. Stokes reproduces four views dating from 1807 to 1812. ¶ The street criers were on exhibit at the Museum of the City of New York in 1936 (*American Collector,* V, March 1936, 17); Stokes, *Icon.,* III, pl. A14-a and -b, and VI, pl. 92-a and -b.

CHAPPELSMITH, JOHN (*c.* 1807–after 1883). Engraver and scientific draftsman, Chappelsmith was a wealthy Englishman who assisted Robert Owen in the founding of New Harmony (Ind.) in 1826. As a resident of New Harmony, he made cuts of many fossils for government geological reports, drew maps, and made many drawings which are now in the New Harmony Library. He returned to England about 1883 and died there a few years later. ¶ Peat, *Pioneer Painters of Indiana,* 29; Burnet, *Art and Artists of Indiana,* 23–24.

CHARLES, ——. A watercolor, shadowgraph, bust portrait of David Johnstone (1724–1809) of NYC and New Jersey is signed "Charles." On the reverse of the portrait is pasted a printed note: "The original inventor on Glass and the only one who can take them in whole length by a pentgraph." ¶ Information from FARL.

CHARLES, H. Engraver of a set of plates illustrating a book of poems published in Philadelphia in 1810. This was probably Henry Charles, copperplate printer in Philadelphia from 1809 to 1824. He may have been a brother of the caricaturist, WILLIAM CHARLES, one of whose cartoons was published in 1806 by W. & H. Charles. ¶ Fielding's *Supplement to Stauffer;* Phila. CD 1809–24; Weitenkampf, "Political Caricature in the U. S."

CHARLES, MAURICE. Wood engraver, NYC, 1848–56. ¶ NYBD 1848, 1850, 1854, 1856.

CHARLES, S. M. A miniature of Andrew Jackson is said to have been inscribed "S. M. Charles, 1836." The earliest known reference to this miniature appears in the late Charles Henry Hart's article on Jackson's life portraits. The portrait is said to have been owned by Col. Wright Rives (or Reeves), USA (Ret.), who was living *c.* 1900 on a farm near Bladensburg (Md.). Theodore Bolton referred to the Hart citation in his book on miniaturists published nearly thirty years ago. In 1934 the late F. F. Sherman listed and reproduced a self-portrait in oils, inscribed on the back, "Painted by S. M. Charles at Washington 1840"; Sherman gives the Christian name as Samuel. No reference to the artist has been found in Bassett's edition of Jackson's papers, in Washington directories of the period, or at the Frick Art Reference Library. No evidence has been found to substantiate the assertions of Hart and Sherman. ¶ George C. Groce, who cites: Hart, "Life Portraits of Jackson"; Cullum, *Register of West Point Graduates;* Bolton, *Miniature Painters;* Sherman, "Some Unrecorded Early American Painters" (1934), 145 and repro. 147; Bassett, *Writings of Andrew Jackson;* postcard, FARL to Groce, 18 Jan. 1950.

CHARLES, WILLIAM (1776–1820). Cartoonist, etcher, and engraver; born in Edinburgh (Scotland), 1776. Charles left Great Britain *c.* 1805, reputedly to escape trouble over some of his political cartoons. He worked in NYC from 1806 to 1814, then moved to Philadelphia, where he remained until his death, August 29, 1820. Best known as a cartoonist of the War of 1812, Charles also illustrated and published chap-books and novels. His associates at various time included H. CHARLES (possibly a brother), JOSEPH YEAGER, and S. KENNEDY. ¶ DAB; Stauffer; Phila. CD 1816–20; Weitenkampf, "Political Caricature in the U. S.," 107–118 lists a large number of Charles's cartoons; *American Processional* reproduces on p. 98 Charles's colored engraving of "Admiral Cockburn Burning and Plundering Havre de Grace, May 3, 1813," owned by the Md. Hist. Soc.

CHARMAILLE, J. B. (also known as J. B. Charmailley, or F. B. Charmaille). Landscape painter, NYC, 1842–1852. He exhibited Italian landscapes and views of NYC and West Hoboken (N.J.) at the National Academy (1849–52) and the American Art-Union (1851–52). ¶ Cowdrey, NAD; Cowdrey, AA & AAU.

CHARRAUD, JOHN J. Artist, 66, a native of Santo Domingo, at NYC in 1860. He owned real estate valued at $40,000 and his wife, Louisa M. Charraud, owned real and personal property valued at $9,000. ¶ 8 Census (1860), N.Y., LVI, 212.

CHASE, BEVERLEY. Engraver of portraits, views, etc., on copper, steel, or wood; advertised in Syracuse (N.Y.) in 1851; listed as a resident of Rochester in 1859. ¶ Syracuse CD 1851; N. Y. State BD 1859.

CHASE, DARIUS. Artist and restorer of oil paintings. Chase was born in Massachusetts *c.* 1808 and worked in Boston as a restorer from 1844 to 1848. In 1850 he was living in Philadelphia, with his three children—Charles H. (13), Eliza L. (11) and Mary E. (6)—and owned realty valued at $3,000. In 1851 his name appears in the Philadelphia directory as an artist, while at a different address there is listed a D. Chase, restorer of oil paintings. The two are probably identical. Chase apparently moved again in the 1850's, for his advertisements appeared in Charleston (S.C.) papers in 1857 and 1859, chiefly as a restorer, though he was also spoken of as a professional artist. ¶ 7 Census (1850), Pa., LIII, 8; Boston CD 1844–48; Phila. CD 1851; Rutledge, *Artists in the Life of Charleston,* 189.

CHASE, GEORGE L. Artist, Buffalo (N.Y.), 1860. ¶ Buffalo BD 1860.

CHASE, JANE. Artist, Buffalo (N.Y.), 1858. ¶ Buffalo BD 1858.

CHASE, THOMAS G. An exhibitor of landscapes and figure pieces at the Pennsylvania Academy in 1832, Chase was from 1835 to 1844 the proprietor of a library and music store in Philadelphia. ¶ Rutledge, PA; Phila. CD 1835–44.

CHASSEREAU, PETER. Though primarily a surveyor and map-maker, Chassereau also drew views of buildings and taught drawing at Charleston (S.C.) in January 1734/35. ¶ Rutledge, *Artists in the Life of Charleston,* 189.

CHASTAINER, Mlle. L. Portrait and still life painter of Philadelphia, exhibited at the Pennsylvania Academy in 1852–53. ¶ Rutledge, PA.

CHATAIGNER, ——. A portrait of Andrew Jackson, made after 1815, was drawn by Chataigner and engraved by LENEY. *Cf.* Alexis Chataigner (1772–1817), a prolific French engraver. ¶ Fielding's *Supplement to Stauffer,* no. 964; Thieme-Becker.

CHATILLON, AUGUSTE DE. Portrait and historical painter at New Orleans in 1846 and 1847. In November 1847 he exhibited a painting of the Battle of Resaca de la Palma. ¶ Delgado-WPA cites New Orleans CD 1846 and *Bee,* Jan. 23, 1846; Arrington cites *Picayune,* Nov. 28, 1847.

CHAVIN, FRANCOIS. Lithographic printer, New Orleans, 1849–50. ¶ New Orleans CD 1849–50 (cited by Delgado-WPA).

CHEESEBOROUGH, MARY HUGGER [Huger?] (1824–1902). Miniature painter; born in Charleston (S.C.)?, 1824; died in Saratoga (N.Y.), July 8, 1902. Her home was at Charleston. ¶ *Art Annual,* IV (1903/04), 138; Smith.

CHEFDEBIEN, LEWIS (or Mr. Chesdebien). Miniature painter, advertised at Williamsburg (Va.) in November 1779, at Baltimore (Md.) in November 1783, and at Richmond (Va.) in April 1792. ¶ [Williamsburg] *Virginia Gazette,* Nov. 20, 1779; *Maryland Gazette and Baltimore Advertiser,* Nov. 7, 1783 (cited by Prime, I, 1); [Richmond] *Virginia Gazette and General Advertiser,* April 4, 1792 (citation courtesy of Mrs. Ralph Catterall); Bolton, *Miniature Painters;* Fielding; Lafferty.

CHENARD, ANTHONY F. Lithographer, NYC. Peters states that Chenard worked in NYC from 1826 to 1828 and 1831 to 1839. Longworth's City Directories list him as "dry goods" in 1828, as lithographer in 1831, and without occupation from 1834 to 1838. ¶ Peters, *America on Stone;* NYCD 1828, 1831, 1834–38.

CHENEY, C. L. Artist of Hartford and East Hartford (Conn.) in 1860. This was Cornelius Lyman Cheney (1829–1897), a native of Manchester (Conn.), who was an optician by profession and worked in Hartford, Glastonbury, and Meriden (Conn.) until 1882 when he moved to Florida. He became mayor of Orange Park and a church leader there. He died at Orange Park, June 23, 1897. ¶ Hartford CD 1860; Charles Henry Pope, *The Cheney Genealogy* (Boston, 1897), 484.

CHENEY, Mrs. HARRIET ELIZABETH CHENEY (1838–1913). Portrait painter; born in Middletown (Conn.) June 23, 1838; married her cousin James Woodbridge

Cheney (1838–?), nephew of the artists JOHN and SETH WELLS CHENEY. Mrs. Cheney exhibited at the Boston Athenaeum in 1860 and at the National Academy in 1861–66. She died December 14, 1913. ¶ C. K. Bolton, "Workers in Line and Color"; Swan, BA; Cowdrey, NAD; Charles Henry Pope, *The Cheney Genealogy* (Boston, 1897), 408, 486.

CHENEY, JOHN (1801–1885). Engraver and lithographer, portrait painter; born in South Manchester (Conn.), October 20, 1801; died there, August 20, 1885. Cheney received his training under ASAPH WILLARD at Hartford (Conn.) *c.* 1820 and at PENDLETON's engraving establishment in Boston in 1826. He worked in NYC in 1829, and the following year went to Europe where he remained until 1834. After his return, Cheney worked in Philadelphia, where he exhibited at the Artists' Fund Society in 1837, and in Boston. He gave up engraving after 1857, and spent much of his time in travel both in Europe and America. John was the brother of SETH WELLS CHENEY. ¶ DAB; Owen, "John Cheney, Connecticut Engraver," with repros. and check list; Artists' Fund Soc. Cat., 1837; Boston BD 1840; CAB. See also the *Memoir of John Cheney* (1889) by his sister-in-law, Ednah D. Cheney, and Koehler, *Catalogue.*

CHENEY, SETH WELLS (1810–1856). A.N.A. Crayon portrait artist, engraver, occasional painter in oils and modeller in clay; born in South Manchester (Conn.), November 26, 1810. Seth Wells Cheney began his artistic career by studying engraving with his elder brother, JOHN CHENEY. He also studied briefly in Europe in 1834. Ill health and family business interests took him to Europe again from 1837 to 1840, and on his return he moved to Boston, where he turned from engraving to the drawing of crayon portraits, in which he enjoyed considerable success before ill health forced the artist to give up his work. He made two more trips to Europe before his death, studying in Rome in 1843–44 and traveling with his family in 1854. He died in South Manchester (Conn.), September 10, 1856. ¶ DAB; obit., *Crayon,* III (1856), 312; Boston CD 1843, 1845–46; Cowdrey, NAD; Swan, BA; Rutledge, PA; French; CAB. See also the *Memoir of Seth Wells Cheney* by his widow, Ednah D. Cheney (1881), and Koehler, *Catalogue.* His work has been reproduced in the Wadsworth Athenaeum *Bulletin,* April 1945, [p. 2], and *Antiques,* Jan. 1954, 61, and is represented in the collections of NYHS.

CHERRILL, ADOLPHUS (1808–?). Amateur watercolor painter and cartographer. Born in London (England) in 1808, Cherrill married there in 1835 and brought his family to America in 1838. He settled in Illinois as a merchant, first at Jacksonville, then at Augusta in 1842, and finally at Carthage in 1847. His map of Hancock County, with vignettes of local scenes, was published in Chicago in 1859. ¶ Arrington, *Nauvoo Temple.*

CHÉRY, LOUIS. Engraver; born in France *c.* 1829; living in New Orleans in 1860, with his wife, Christina (born in Mayence, Germany, *c.* 1834), and daughter, Clémence (New Orleans, age 2). ¶ 8 Census (1860), La., VIII, 101.

CHESNER, WILLIAM. German portrait painter, 28, at NYC in August 1850. ¶ 7 Census (1850), N.Y., XLV, 189.

CHESS, WILLIAM. Lithographer; born in Germany *c.* 1828; living in Baltimore (Md.) in 1860, with his German wife Barbara (age 25) and three daughters (ages 1 to 4 years, all born in Maryland); his personal property valued at $400. ¶ 8 Census (1860), Md., VI, 31.

CHESSITO, or CHESSITI, ——. Scene and panorama painter, assistant to WILLIAM DELAMANO in the painting of a panorama of the London Crystal Palace Exposition of 1851, which was shown in NYC and Boston in 1851 and 1852. ¶ N. Y. *Herald,* Dec. 2, 1851 (citation courtesy J. E. Arrington).

CHESSMAN, FREDERICK. Artist; born in Massachusetts *c.* 1838; boarding in Boston in July 1860. ¶ 8 Census (1860), Mass., XXV, 813.

CHEVALIER, ABRAHAM. Sculptor and wood carver. Working in Baltimore from 1805 to 1825 and in Philadelphia from 1825 to 1827. He exhibited at the Pennsylvania Academy in 1827 and is represented at the Maryland Historical Society. ¶ Scharf and Westcott, *History of Phila.,* 1067; Rutledge, PA; Rutledge, "Portraits in Varied Media."

CHEVALIER, ALEXANDER. Limner, Philadelphia, 1793. ¶ Phila. CD 1793 (cited by Brown and Brown).

CHEVALIER, AUGUSTIN. Sculptor, Baltimore, *c.* 1820–30. *Cf.* ABRAHAM CHEVALIER. ¶ Gardner, *Yankee Stonecutters,* 59.

CHEVALIER, J. B. Lithographer, Philadelphia,

1838–41. In 1838–39 he was a partner of John Caspar Wild (see Wild & Chevalier). ¶ Phila. CD 1839–41; *Portfolio* (Jan. 1946), 120.

Chevalier, Leonard F. Lithographer; born in France *c.* 1820; living in Southwark (Philadelphia County, Pa.) in 1850, with his wife Susan (age 21, born in Delaware). He was listed in the 1852 directory of Philadelphia. ¶ 7 Census (1850), Pa., LV, 558; Phila. CD 1852.

Chevet, F. Drawing master, New Orleans (La.), 1841. ¶ [New Orleans] *Bee,* March 12, 1841 (cited by Delgado-WPA).

Chichowski, Severin. His lithograph of the Macon (Ga.) Volunteers was published in the *U. S. Military Magazine,* Vol. III (Philadelphia, 1842). ¶ Todd, "Huddy & Duval Prints"; Peters, *America on Stone.*

Chidsey, D. M. Engraver, Bristol (Conn.), 1856. ¶ New England BD 1856.

Child, Mrs. ——. Drawing teacher, Cincinnati (Ohio), September 1841. ¶ WPA (Ohio), *Annals of Cleveland.*

Child, Isaac (1792–1885). Heraldic painter; born in Roxbury (Mass.)[?], 1792; died in Boston[?], December 23, 1885. Shortly after 1810 he made a copy of the *Irish Compendium,* in which, it is said, "it is hard to tell the work of the quill pen from an engraving." His copy of the "Gore Roll of Arms," painted *c.* 1847, is owned by the New England Historical and Genealogical Society. ¶ Bowditch, "Early Water-Color Paintings of New England Coats of Arms," 199–200, repro. fig. 17.

Child, J. M. Artist of Sandwich (Mass.) who exhibited at the Boston Athenaeum in 1831. *Cf.* the J. M. Child of Dudley (England) who exhibited flower paintings at the Royal Academy in 1827. ¶ Swan, BA, 212; Graves, *Dictionary.*

Child, John, see John Childs.

Child, Lewis (*c.* 1781–1829). Portrait and sign painter, glazier; born possibly at Wincanton (Somerset, England), *c.* 1781; died in NYC, May 14, 1829. He came to NYC in 1802 and the following year married Elizabeth, sister of John Wesley Jarvis. He was the teacher of Henry Smith Mount. ¶ Obit., N. Y. *Evening Post,* May 15, 1829; Fielding; Buffet, "William Sidney Mount"; Met. Mus., Mount Exhib. Cat. (1945), no. 61; Winn, *Winn-Jarvis Genealogy,* 52; Dickson, *John Wesley Jarvis,* 63, 80; Cowdrey and Williams, *William Sidney Mount,* 2.

Child, Thomas (?–1706). Painter-stainer and possibly limner; born in England, mid-17th century; died in Boston[?], November 10, 1706. Judge Samuel Sewall noted under the above date in his diary:

"This morning, Tom Child, the Painter, died.
Tom Child had often painted Death
But never to the Life, before:
Doing it now he's out of Breath:
He paints it once and paints no more."

Child was apprentice to a member of the London Company of Painter-Stainers from 1671 to 1679. Admitted to the Company in 1679, he married and came to America before April 1688. Although Frederic W. Coburn has attributed a portrait of Sir William Phipps to Child, the late William Sawitzky interpreted Sewall's doggerel obituary of Child to mean that Child was a painter of hatchments (heraldic devices) on coffins, rather than a limner of the living. ¶ Sewall, "Diary," Mass. Hist. Soc. *Collections,* Ser. 5, Vol. 6, p. 170; Barker, *American Painting,* 16–20; information from William Sawitzky; Coburn, "Thomas Child."

Child, Mrs. Willard. At Castleton (Vt.) *c.* 1858 Mrs. Child drew crayon portraits of Mr. and Mrs. Erastus Higley, owned in 1941 by Miss Edna Higley, of Castleton. ¶ WPA (Mass.), *Portraits Found in Vt.*

Childs, Benjamin F. (1814–1863). Wood engraver; born in Cambridgeport (Mass.) in 1814. He was probably a younger brother of Shubael D. Childs, with whom he studied engraving along with Henry Kinnersley and Joseph W. Morse, either in Boston or in NYC. Shubael was in NYC by 1831, but Benjamin's name does not appear in the directories until 1835. In 1836 both were working at the same address, but the following year the elder went west to Chicago and Benjamin remained in NYC. Linton states that in 1850 Benjamin F. Childs succeeded R. Roberts as superintendent of engraving for the American Tract Society. From *c.* 1858 to his death he seems to have published *The Childs' Paper* in NYC. See Childs & Jocelyn. ¶ Thieme-Becker; Linton, 24–25; NYCD 1835–40; NYBD 1840–50; NYCD 1858–60. Hamilton calls Benjamin F. Childs a pupil of Abel Bowen as early as 1827 but this was probably Shubael D. Childs.

Childs & Carpenter, see Cephas G. Childs and J. W. Carpenter.

Childs, Cephas Grier (1793–1871). Engraver, pioneer lithographer, editor, and publisher; born in Plumstead Township (Bucks County, Pa.), September 8, 1793. Apprenticed to the engraver GIDEON FAIRMAN in 1812, Childs set up his own business in Philadelphia in 1818, but worked occasionally, with Fairman, as well as with STEPHEN GIMBER and one Carpenter (possibly J. W. CARPENTER). He exhibited at the Pennsylvania Academy in 1824–25 and 1829–30. Childs was a member of the pioneer lithographic firm of PENDLETON, KEARNEY & CHILD in 1829, but the following year joined with the portrait painter HENRY INMAN, under the name of CHILDS & INMAN. This partnership continued until 1833, when Inman withdrew, and was succeeded by CHILDS & LEHMAN. Injuries received during a trip to Europe in 1830–31 forced Childs to give up much of his work as an engraver and lithographer thereafter, though he was listed as such in the directories until 1845. His later career was chiefly in commercial journalism and finance. He died in Philadelphia, July 7, 1871. ¶ DAB; Phila. CD 1818–20, 1823–25, 1828–31, 1833, 1835–60 and after; Pa. Acad. Cats. 1824–25, 1829–30; Stauffer; Linton.

CHILDS, F. Painter of a view of Nassau Hall, Princeton (N.J.), in 1860. ¶ *Portfolio,* I (Sept. 1941), 6, 8.

CHILDS & GIMBER, see CEPHAS G. CHILDS and STEPHEN GIMBER.

CHILDS & HAMMOND, see JOHN V. CHILDS and JOHN T. HAMMOND.

CHILDS & INMAN. Lithographers, Philadelphia, 1830–33. The partners were CEPHAS G. CHILDS, engraver-lithographer, and HENRY INMAN, portrait painter. Inman withdrew in 1833, but Childs continued the business with GEORGE LEHMAN under the name of CHILDS & LEHMAN. Childs & Inman are said to have been instrumental in bringing P. S. DUVAL to Philadelphia from Europe. ALBERT NEWSAM was also employed by this company. ¶ Phila. CD 1831, 1833; *American Advt. Directory,* 1832, 180; Peters, *America on Stone;* Stauffer; DAB (under Childs).

CHILDS & JOCELYN. Wood engravers, NYC, 1849–50. During these years BENJAMIN F. CHILDS and ALBERT H. JOCELYN were working together, though the firm itself is not listed in the directories. An example of their work has been found in Darley's illustrated edition of Irving's *Knickerbocker History of New York* (1850). ¶ NYCD 1849–50; Hamilton, 209.

CHILDS, JOHN. Lithographer, engraver, painter in oils and watercolors. Childs' earliest lithograph is dated 1830. John and John C. Childs, engraver and colorist respectively, appear at different addresses in the 1834 NYC directory. John C. Childs, colorist, is listed also in 1835, 1836, and 1838. The identity of these two seems probable, however, since John Childs' lithographs of 1839 bear the same address as that given for the colorist the year before. Only John Childs, lithographer, appears in the NYC directories from 1840 to 1844. In 1845 he was in Boston, but an oil painting by him was exhibited by John Ingram at the [NYC] American Institute in the same year. Childs had moved to Philadelphia by 1847, when he exhibited two drawings at the Pennsylvania Academy, and he remained there until after 1860. ¶ Peters, *America on Stone;* NYCD 1834–44; Boston CD 1845; Am. Inst. Cat., 1845; Rutledge, PA; Phila. CD 1848–60 and after. The 1856 Phila. CD lists a John Child, lithographic engraver, as well as John Childs, lithographer, at different addresses, but this may be an error.

CHILDS & LEHMAN, lithographers, see CEPHAS G. CHILDS and GEORGE LEHMAN.

CHILDS, SHUBAEL D. Wood engraver, seal-cutter, and die-sinker. In 1821 Shubael D. Childs was working in Boston with ABEL BOWEN. He worked independently in Boston at least until 1826, and in NYC from 1831 to 1837. His younger brother, BENJAMIN F. CHILDS, as well as HENRY KINNERSLEY and JOSEPH W. MORSE, are said to have learned engraving from him. Benjamin F. and Shubael D. Childs were working together in NYC in 1836, but the following year Shubael left for Chicago, where he continued in the engraving, seal-cutting, and die-sinking business until about 1864. He was assisted from about 1851 by his son, SHUBAEL D. CHILDS, JR. ¶ Boston CD 1821–22, 1826; NYCD 1831–37; Linton, 24–25 (only as brother of Benjamin F. Childs); Chicago CD 1844–64 (advt. in 1858 states that the business was established in 1837).

CHILDS, SHUBAEL D., JR. Engraver, Chicago, 1852–64 and after. He was the son of and partner of SHUBAEL D. CHILDS, above. ¶ Chicago BD 1852–53, 1856; CD 1854, 1859, 1864, 1866.

CHILLAS (or Chilas), DAVID. Lithographer, Philadelphia, 1852–59. In 1853 he was listed as a merchant. ¶ Phila. CD 1853–59; *Portfolio* (Feb. 1954), 131, repro.

CHILLER, GODFREY. Engraver, Newark (N.J.), 1859. ¶ Essex, Hudson, and Union Counties BD 1859.

CHINERY, ISAAC. Artist, 21, a native of New York State, at NYC in 1860. In 1863 he was listed as a printer. ¶ 8 Census (1860), N.Y., XLV, 503.

CHINERY, JAMES. Listed in the American Advertising Directory for 1832 as a NYC engraver, but the NYC directories for 1828–29 and 1831–39 list him as a letter and tool cutter and in 1840 as a tavern keeper. ¶ *Am. Adv. Directory,* 1832; NYCD 1828–40.

CHIPMAN, ——. Primitive still life painter, *c.* 1840–*c.* 1850. His known work consists of a still life fruit with simulated wood border, with an inscription on the back of the canvas which states that the painting was done in the winter from memory. ¶ Repro., *Panorama,* I (April 1946), 76; Lipman and Winchester, 170.

CHIQUET, ——. Engraver, NYC, *c.* 1814. ¶ Stauffer; Fielding's *Supplement.*

CHIZZOLA, GIOVANNI. Decorative and theatre scene painter. Chizzola was in NYC in 1837, when he exhibited an "Arabesque Ornament, Frieze in Chiaro Scuro" at the National Academy. From there he went to Charleston (S.C.), where during 1837–39 he painted drop scenes for the Charleston theatre and decorations for the French Church and Roman Catholic Cathedral of Charleston. ¶ Cowdrey, NAD; Rutledge, *Artists in the Life of Charleston,* 189.

CHOL, A. Artist, New Orleans, 1852–56. *Cf.* A. COLON. ¶ New Orleans CD 1852–56.

CHOPMANN, see COPMANN.

CHORIS, LUDOVIK (Ludwig or Louis) (1795–1828). Russian artist, born March 22, 1795. Trained in Moscow, Choris made drawings of botanical specimens for the naturalist F. A. Marschall von Bieberstein in the Caucasus, and in 1815 joined the South Sea expedition of Otto von Kotzebue as official artist. When the Kotzebue expedition visited California in 1816, Choris made water color sketches of the Presidio at San Francisco and of the natives, which appeared in his *Voyage Pittoresque Autour du Monde* (Paris, 1822). Choris' second book, published in 1826, was entitled *Vues et Paysages des Regions Equinoxialles.* . . . He was killed near Vera Cruz, Mexico, March 22, 1828, on a later visit to the Western Hemisphere ¶ Peters, *Calif.;* Van Nostrand and Coulter, *California Pictorial,* repros. 16, 18.; Stokes, *Hist. Prints,* pl. 44a.

CHORLEY, JOHN. Engraver and lithographer. Stauffer states that Chorley was working in Boston as early as 1825, though his name does not appear in the directories until 1830, when he was a member of the SENEFELDER LITHOGRAPHIC COMPANY. He is listed as engraver from 1831 to 1834, but thereafter until 1860 as a bank clerk or book-keeper. In 1825 Chorley married MARGARET BYRON DOYLE, portrait painter and daughter of the artist-proprietor of the Columbian Museum in Boston, WILLIAM M. S. DOYLE. ¶ Stauffer, I, 48; Boston CD 1830 (advt. of Senefelder Lith. Co.), 1831–60; Whitmore, "Abel Bowen," 41.

CHORLEY, Mrs. JOHN, see MARGARET BYRON DOYLE.

CHORMAN, ERNEST C. (or Chormann, Ernest G.). Die-sinker, copperplate and steel engraver, Philadelphia, 1853–59 and after 1860. He was first listed as an engraver in 1857. ¶ Phila. CD 1853–59 and after 1860.

CHOUQUET, GUSTAVE. Artist of NYC who exhibited "Sketch from Nature" at the National Academy in 1847. ¶ Cowdrey, NAD.

CHOWING, HENRY C., JR. Partner in MOONEY & CHOWING, wood engravers, Buffalo (N.Y.), 1856–57. ¶ Buffalo CD and BD 1856–57.

CHRIST, BERNHARD. Engraver and die-sinker, NYC, 1858–59. ¶ NYBD 1858–59.

CHRIST, HENRY. Fresco painter; born in Nassau (Germany ?), *c.* 1824; boarding in Philadelphia in June 1860. ¶ 8 Census (1860), Pa., LIV, 968.

CHRISTIAN, J. H. Engraver, NYC, 1856. ¶ NYBD 1856.

CHRISTIANIA, JOSEPH. Swiss engraver, 29, at NYC in 1850. His wife was also Swiss, but they had one child born in New York in 1849. This may be the J. H. Christian listed in the 1856 business directory. ¶ 7 Census (1850), N.Y., XLI, 661; NYBD 1856.

CHRISTIE, ALEXANDER. Drawing master, coach, sign, and heraldic painter, Philadelphia, 1785–86. ¶ Brown and Brown; Prime, II, 45.

CHRISTY, ALEXANDER. Engraver, Philadelphia, 1860. Both Christy, age 64, and his wife Margaret, age 70, were natives of Scotland; their personal property was valued at only $75. ¶ 8 Census (1860), Pa., LIII, 775.

CHRONISTER, D. J. Engraver, Hampton (Pa.), 1860. ¶ Penna. BD 1860.

CHUBB, FREDERICK Y. Artist and engraver, NYC, 1856 and after; born in New York about 1838. An exhibitor at the American Institute in 1856, Chubb was then living with his mother, the widow of Thomas Yours Chubb, professor of music in NYC from 1837 to 1845. Frederick Y. Chubb is listed in NYC directories from 1862 to 1866 as an artist, and from 1868 into the 1880's as an engraver. He exhibited at the National Academy, 1865–75. It seems probable that the engraver listed as T. Y. Chubb by Stauffer and Fielding is really F. Y. Chubb. ¶ 8 Census (1860), N.Y., LX, 858; Am. Inst. Cat., 1856; NYCD 1837–45; NYCD 1862–80's; Cowdrey, NAD.

CHUBBUCK, THOMAS (?–1888). Engraver. Born in Boston and trained there as an engraver, Chubbuck moved in 1846 to Brattleboro (Vt.), where he engraved the Brattleboro "postmaster's provisional" postage stamp of 1846, now a valuable philatelic rarity. In 1849 he moved to Springfield (Mass.), where he remained until his death on January 10, 1888. Stokes has reproduced a view of Mt. Holyoke Seminary, South Hadley (Mass.), drawn and engraved by Chubbuck in 1860. ¶ Obit., Boston *Transcript,* Jan. 11, 1888; New England BD 1849; New England BD 1856, 1860; Springfield CD 1855, 1859; Stokes, *Hist. Prints;* Stauffer.

CHUPIEN, T. Carver in ivory, Charleston (S.C.), 1849. ¶ Rutledge, *Artists in the Life of Charleston,* 189.

CHURCH, DWIGHT. Artist, 22, a native of New York State, at NYC in 1860. ¶ 8 Census (1860), N.Y., LVIII, 259.

CHURCH, FREDERIC EDWIN (1826–1900). N.A. Landscape painter; born in Hartford (Conn.), May 4, 1826. Church received his first instruction in Hartford from BENJAMIN A. COE and A. H. EMMONS, but his real master was THOMAS COLE, with whom he studied and lived from 1844 to 1848. He first exhibited at the National Academy in 1845, was elected an Associate in 1848 and a full Member in 1849. He also exhibited at the American Art-Union from 1847 to 1852, while he was in NYC. In 1853 and again in 1857 Church visited Ecuador and Colombia, where he found inspiration for his most characteristic landscapes. He later made visits to the coast of Labrador, the West Indies, Europe, and the Near East in search of romantic subjects. After 1877 Church was crippled by rheumatism and the last twenty years of his life were spent in enforced idleness at his oriental villa on the Hudson. He died April 7, 1900, in NYC. ¶ DAB; Cowdrey, NAD; Cowdrey, AA & AAU; Karolik Cat., 160–65, three repros.; Bolton, *Miniature Painters;* Rutledge, PA; Washington Art Assoc. Cat., 1857; French; Clement and Hutton; Tuckerman; CAB.

CHURCH, HENRY (1836–1908). Self-taught painter and sculptor of Chagrin Falls (Ohio). His work included a great bas-relief carved in a rock over the Chagrin River, depicting a female nude encircled by a snake and symbolizing the rape of Indian America by the white man. Some of his smaller works, including a "Group of Owls" in stone and a "Greyhound" in cast iron, as well as several paintings, have been exhibited at the Museum of Modern Art. ¶ *Antiques,* LX (Sept. 1951), 207, 209, two repros.; Lipman and Winchester, 170.

CHURCHILL & CO., see H. W. CHURCHILL.

CHURCHILL, H. W. Wood engraver, Albany (N.Y.), 1854–60 and after. In 1860 he headed the firm of Churchill & Co. ¶ Albany CD 1854–60 and after.

CHURCHILL, J. EDWIN. Portrait painter, Philadelphia, 1860. ¶ Phila. CD 1860.

CICERI, ——. Scene painter at the New Theatre, NYC, in 1799. Listed in NYC directories from 1801 to 1806. Painter of an interior of Cologne Cathedral for HANINGTON'S Moving Dioramas, 1837. ¶ N. Y. *Commercial Advertiser,* Jan. 9 and July 2, 1799 (courtesy J. Earl Arrington); NYCD 1801–06 (McKay); *Guide to Hanington's Moving Dioramas* (courtesy J. Earl Arrington).

CICERONG, ——. Painter of a portrait of Col. James Jameson, formerly of George Washington's staff, [Virginia ?], *c.* 1809. ¶ Willis, "Jefferson County Portraits."

CIL, MANUEL. Spanish miniaturist and drawing teacher, who studied in Madrid and Barcelona, and was working in Charleston (S.C.) in 1825. ¶ Rutledge, *Artists in the Life of Charleston,* 133, 153, 189; Carolina Art Assoc. *Cat.,* 1935.

CINCANON, see CONCANNON.

CIST, JACOB (1782–1825). Amateur artist in oils and watercolors, naturalist, and businessman; born in Philadelphia, March 13, 1782. After working as a printer and government clerk in Philadelphia and Washington for a decade, Cist settled in 1808 at Wilkes-Barre (Pa.), where he served as postmaster until his death, December 30, 1825. He was an amateur geologist, a pioneer promoter of anthracite mining, and an entomologist of more than local note, as well as a painter of portraits, miniatures, and entomological subjects. ¶ DAB, and information courtesy of Gilbert L. McClintock of Wilkes-Barre, a descendant of Jacob Cist and owner of a collection of Cist's drawings, paintings, and manuscripts.

CITAROTO (or Citarrato), JOHN. Sculptor and wax-modeler, NYC; exhibited a wax model of "Tarquin the Proud and the Roman Lucretia" and a casting of a figure of Washington, at the American Institute in 1856 ¶ Am. Inst. Cat., 1856.

CITTI, JOHN. Image-maker, Philadelphia, 1850–55; portrait painter, NYC, 1856. ¶ Phila. CD 1850–55; NYBD 1856.

CITTI, LOUIS. Lithographer, born in Pennsylvania about 1827, working in Philadelphia 1850–53. In 1850 of HALLMAN & CITTI. ¶ 7 Census (1850), Pa., LV, 643 [as Cetti]; Phila. BD 1850, CD 1850–53.

CITTI, ORELIUS. Lithographer, Philadelphia, 1855. ¶ Phila. CD 1855.

CLAGUE, RICHARD (1816–1878). Artist, teacher, and landscape painter. He advertised in New Orleans in 1851 as an artist and teacher and was listed there in the directories for 1854–55 without occupation. In 1861 he was an officer of the New Orleans Blues, and was also said to have been a member of an expedition to discover the source of the Nile. In 1867 he exhibited two local views in New Orleans, and he exhibited again in 1871. He died in New Orleans in 1878. ¶ Smith; New Orleans *Bee,* April 15, 1851 (cited by Delgado-WPA); New Orleans CD 1854–55; *Bee,* June 21, 1861 and *Picayune,* Feb. 20, 1867, March 23, 1867, and Nov. 6, 1871 (cited by Delgado-WPA); Seebold, *Old Louisiana Plantation Homes,* I, 25.

CLAIRVILLE, WILLIAM H. Engraver and die-sinker, NYC, 1860. ¶ NYBD 1860.

CLANCY, PETER. Lithographer; born in Pennsylvania *c.* 1841; boarding in Philadelphia in July 1860. ¶ 8 Census (1860), Pa., LIV, 1051.

CLAP, Miss ——. Exhibited American views at Boston Athenaeum, 1827–28. ¶ Swan, BA, 212.

CLAPP, H. Of SHARP, PEIRCE & CO., Boston lithographers, 1846–48. ¶ Boston CD; Peters, *America on Stone.*

CLAPP, JAMES C. Delineator of views of Key West (Fla.) *c.* 1855 and of Pittsfield (Mass.) *c.* 1854–60. ¶ Repro., *Portfolio,* I (Feb. 1942), 18; Stokes, *Hist. Prints,* 117.

CLAPPERTON, WILLIAM R. Landscape, heraldic, and ornamental painter. Clapperton apparently came to America from England in the 1840's, settling for a time in NYC. He was listed there as a painter from 1849 to 1851, during which time he exhibited an oil painting (1849), six heraldic paintings (1850), and several watercolor paintings (1851) at the American Institute. By 1853 he had moved to Chicago, where he was employed as an ornamental painter at the American Car Company works, but he died apparently before 1854, when only Mrs. William Clapperton was listed in the directory. Clapperton's widow advertised in March 1855 that she was anxious to sell her late husband's paintings in order to return to England. ¶ NYCD 1849–51; Am. Inst. Cat., 1849–51; Chicago CD 1853–55; [Chicago] *Daily Press,* March 10, 1855.

CLARK, ——. Of GRIER & CLARK, wood engravers, Philadelphia, 1856. ¶ Phila. BD 1856.

CLARK, ——. Of SWAIM & CLARK, portrait painters, South Bend (Ind.), 1860. ¶ Indiana BD 1860.

CLARK, ALVAN (1804–1887). Engraver, portrait and miniature painter; born in Ashfield (Mass.), March 8, 1804. Clark taught himself engraving *c.* 1824–25, and followed that career for a few years in Boston, Providence, NYC, and Fall River (Mass.). About 1835 he gave up engraving for painting portraits and miniatures and opened a studio in Boston. He exhibited at the National Academy, the Apollo Gallery, and the Boston Athenaeum. About 1844 he became interested in optics and with his son developed the manufacture of telescopes with which his name is generally associated. He died in Cambridge (Mass.), August 19, 1887. ¶ DAB, cites "Autobiography" in *New England Hist. and Geneal. Reg.,* Jan.–July 1889; Boston BD 1841–42, 1844–59; Swan, BA, 181; Cowdrey, NAD; Cowdrey, AA & AAU; Dunlap, *History* (1918), III, 290; CAB; Wehle and Bolton; Bolton, *Miniature Painters;* Tuckerman; represented at the Essex Institute ("Additions to the Cat. of Portraits in the Essex Inst.").

CLARK, ASAHEL. Engraver, said to have been a native of Cooperstown (N.Y.). He worked in Albany (N.Y.) from about 1825 to 1834, as RALPH RAWDON's partner in RAWDON, CLARK & CO., the forerunner of the important banknote engraving firm of RAWDON, WRIGHT, HATCH & EDSON. Dunlap, writing *c.* 1834, said that Clark was then working in NYC. His name appears erroneously as Abraham Clark in Dunlap (1918) and in Smith. ¶ Dunlap, *History,* II, 470; Dunlap, *History* (1918), III, 290; Stauffer; Albany CD 1826, 1828, 1831–34; NYCD 1834; Smith.

CLARK, CHARLES W. Engraver, Hartford (Conn.), 1860. ¶ New England BD 1860.

CLARK, CHESTER. Scene painter; born in New York, *c.* 1828; living in Cincinnati in 1850, with his wife Rebecca (age 22, b. Ohio). ¶ 7 Census (1850), Ohio, XX, 125.

CLARK, EDWARD. Landscape painter in water colors, Philadelphia; exhibited at the Artists' Fund Society in 1841. ¶ Rutledge, PA.

CLARK, G. W. Portrait painter, Chicago, 1855. ¶ Chicago *Almanac,* 1855.

CLARK, GEORGE. Portrait painter, advertised in Charleston (S.C.), 1831. ¶ Rutledge, *Artists in the Life of Charleston,* 189.

CLARK, HARRY A. Crayon artist, prize winner at the Illinois State Fair in 1855. ¶ Chicago *Daily Press,* October 15, 1855.

CLARK, J. R. Note engraver, New Orleans, 1842. ¶ New Orleans CD 1842.

CLARK, JACOB. Artist; born in Pennsylvania *c.* 1819; living in Philadelphia in 1860, with wife Emma (age 38) and son Edwin H. (age 17), both born in Pennsylvania. ¶ 8 Census (1860), Pa., LV, 954.

CLARK, JAMES. Engraver and printer, born in Ireland about 1816, working in NYC from 1834 to 1860. Partner in CAMMEYER & CLARK in 1834–36. His wife and three children, born between 1841 and 1844, were born in New Brunswick. ¶ 7 Census (1850), N.Y., XLV, 429; NYCD 1834–60.

CLARK, JOHN. Artist, NYC, 1841–42; seller of paintings, 1844–46. ¶ NYCD 1841–46.

CLARK, JOHN W. Of GUNNING & CLARK, carvers, who exhibited "Carved eagles, festoon & wreath" at the American Institute in 1856. ¶ Am. Inst. Cat., 1856; NYCD 1856; Pinckney, 189.

CLARK, LOUISA. Miniaturist at Philadelphia, exhibited at the Artists' Fund Society in 1844. Possibly the same as Miss Louisa Campbell Clark of London who exhibited miniatures at the Royal Academy in 1887–91. ¶ Rutledge, PA; Graves, *Dictionary.*

CLARK, M. M. Portrait painter, Cleveland (Ohio), 1826; said to have come from NYC. Sherman stated that this artist painted a portrait of the Kentucky poetess, Rosa Jeffrey, in 1853. ¶ Knittle, *Early Ohio Taverns;* Sherman, "Newly Discovered American Portrait Painters."

CLARK, MATTHEW. Designer; born in Scotland *c.* 1810; living in Boston in 1850. ¶ 7 Census (1850), Mass., XXV, 731.

CLARK (Clarke), PETER. Engraver, born in Scotland *c.* 1796. Clark was in America by about 1840, his only child being born in Ohio *c.* 1841. In 1850 he was listed in the Cincinnati census as an engraver, with real property valued at $4,000. His name appears in city directories from 1850 to 1860 as a general and seal engraver. ¶ 7 Census (1850), Ohio, XX, 827; Cincinnati BD 1850, 1860; Cincinnati CD 1851, 1853, 1856–59; Ohio BD 1859.

CLARK (Clarke), RICHARD T. Portrait painter, working in Baltimore from 1851 to 1858; probably the same as Richard T. Clarke, artist, working in Louisville (Ky.) in 1859 and 1865. ¶ Lafferty; Baltimore CD 1858; Louisville CD 1859, 1865.

CLARK, Miss S. D., see SARA ANN CLARKE.

CLARK, SAMUEL C. Engraver, NYC, 1846–60. ¶ NYCD 1846–60.

CLARK, SETH A. Engraver, 21, a native of New York, at NYC in 1850 with his wife (?) Mary B. Clark, aged 34. ¶ 7 Census (1850), N.Y., XLIII, 57.

CLARK, SETH H. Hartford (Conn.) engraver, 1849–60. ¶ New England BD 1849; Hartford BD 1851, CD 1855–60).

CLARK, SILAS C. Master engraver, 38, a native of New York State, living in NYC in 1860 with the engraver WILLIAM J. COCHRAN. ¶ 8 Census (1860), N.Y., XLVI, 790.

CLARKE, COLLINS. Engraver; born in Nova Scotia *c.* 1842; living in Boston in 1860 with his parents. ¶ 8 Census (1860), Mass., XXVIII, 944.

CLARKE, ROBERT A. Painter of animals; born in Ireland *c.* 1817. He had settled in NYC by 1843 when his first child was born; his wife Mary was a native of New Jersey, born *c.* 1821. Clarke stayed in NYC until 1849, and exhibited a number of times at the National Academy and the American Art-Union. By August 1850 he had moved to Philadelphia with his wife and two children (ages 4 and 7), and there he remained until 1854, exhibiting several times at the Pennsylvania Academy. ¶ 7 Census (1850), Pa., LIII, 710; NYCD 1846, 1849; Cowdrey, NAD; Cowdrey, AA & AAU; Phila. CD 1851 (as R. E. Clarke), 1853–54; Rutledge, PA; repro., Peters, *America on Stone,* pl. 92.

CLARKE, SARA ANN (1808–after 1888). Landscape painter. A resident of Boston (Mass.) during the 1840's, Miss Clarke exhibited scenes from Kentucky, Illinois, and Italy at the Boston Athenaeum, the Apollo Association, and the American Art-Union. In 1860 she exhibited at the Boston Athenaeum a portrait of Charles Kemble as Cromwell. ¶ Swan, BA, 213; BA Cat. 1841, 1860; Cowdrey, AA & AAU. The Miss S. D. Clark who exhibited at the Boston Athenaeum in 1846 and 1848 was probably the same artist.

CLARKE, THOMAS. Engraver, Philadelphia, 1797; NYC, 1799–1800. ¶ Brown and Brown; Stauffer, I, 49–50; Groce, "New York Painting before 1800"; NYCD 1799–1800.

CLARKE (Clark), WILLIAM. Portrait and miniature painter. He was painting portraits in Lancaster County (Pa.) as early as 1785, worked in Delaware and Baltimore (Md.) in the 1790's, but from at least 1796 to 1806 seems to have worked primarily in Philadelphia, where he was associated with JEREMIAH PAUL, MATTHEW PRATT, and GEORGE RUTTER, *c.* 1796. ¶ Bolton, *Miniature Painters;* Lancaster Co. Hist. Soc., *Portraiture in Lancaster Co.,* 118; Pleasants, *250 Years of Painting in Md.,* 28–29, repro.; *Portraits in Delaware,* 32; Prime, II, 5, 31; Dickson, "A Note on Jeremiah Paul"; Brown and Brown.

CLARKSON, CHARLES. Artist; born in Pennsylvania *c.* 1825; boarding with wife and four children (3 months to 4 years) in Philadelphia in 1860. ¶ 8 Census (1860), Pa., LIV, 265.

CLARKSON, EDWARD. Wood engraver, Philadelphia, 1849–57. Possibly the same as, though more likely the father of, EDWARD CLARKSON, animal painter. ¶ Phila. CD 1849–1857.

CLARKSON, EDWARD. Painter of animals, Philadelphia, 1855–59 and after 1860. He exhibited at the Pennsylvania Academy in 1855 and 1856. The painter may have been the same as EDWARD CLARKSON, engraver at the same address in 1855, but it is also possible that they were father and son. The 1856 and 1857 directories list them at different addresses, but after 1857 only the artist is listed, suggesting that the engraver had moved away or died. ¶ Phila. CD 1856–59 and after 1860; Rutledge, PA.

CLARKSON, JOHN. Carver and modeller, Charleston (S.C.), 1847. This amateur's work included portrait busts and heads in wood, plaster of paris, and clay. ¶ Rutledge, *Artists in the Life of Charleston,* 189.

CLARY, LETILLIER DU, see LEPELLETIER DUCLARY.

CLASEBULL, JOSEPH H. English engraver, 24, at NYC in October 1850. ¶ 7 Census (1850), N.Y., LII, 205.

CLASSEN & FORSYTH, engravers, see WILLIAM M. CLASSEN and ROBERT FORSYTH.

CLASSEN, JAMES M. Engraver; working in New Orleans, 1843; in NYC from 1844 to 1850. He was probably the Classen of LEE & CLASSEN, engravers in NYC in 1844. ¶ New Orleans *Picayune,* March 8, 1843 (cited by Delgado-WPA); NYCD 1844–50; NYBD 1844, 1846, 1849.

CLASSEN, WILLIAM M. (or H.). Portrait, historical, and landscape engraver, NYC, 1842–49. In 1843 he was a partner in CLASSEN & FORSYTH. He was listed in the 1849 CD as William M. Classet. ¶ NYCD 1842–43; NYBD 1844; NYCD 1849; Smith; Stauffer.

CLAUSEN, PETER (1830–1924). Early Minnesota artist whose "Break in St. Anthony's Falls," in three sections, is owned by the Minnesota Historical Society. ¶ *Historic Minnesota.*

CLAVEAU, ANTOINE. Landscape and portrait painter at San Francisco, 1857–59. In 1857 he first exhibited his panorama of Yosemite Valley. ¶ San Francisco *Evening Bulletin,* Oct. 26, 1857, December 11–17, 1858 (courtesy J. Earl Arrington); San Francisco CD and BD 1859.

CLAXTON, ALEXANDER (?–1841). An officer in the U. S. Navy from his appointment as midshipman in 1806 until his death, March 7, 1841. He was also an amateur painter, and his view of the engagement between the *Wasp* and *Frolic,* October 8, 1813, was later engraved. ¶ Hamersley; Gage; *Portfolio* (Feb. 1955), repro.

CLAY, CECIL. Landscape painter, Philadelphia; exhibitor at the Pennsylvania Academy in 1860. ¶ Rutledge, PA.

CLAY, EDWARD WILLIAMS (1799–1857). Caricaturist, engraver and lithographer, etcher, portrait painter; born in Philadelphia, April 19, 1799. Clay studied law and was admitted to the Philadelphia Bar about 1825, but he soon abandoned law for art and achieved considerable notoriety in Philadelphia for his biting caricatures. He left Philadelphia for NYC in 1837 and shortly after went to Europe for further art study, but his eyesight failed and he was obliged to give up his artistic career. In his last years he held a minor public office in Delaware. He died December 31, 1857, in NYC. ¶ DAB; Stauffer and Scharff and Westcott give the date of birth as 1792; Stokes, *Hist. Prints;* Peters, *America on Stone,* Nevins and Weitenkampf; repros. in *Amer. Collector* (Aug. 1936), 11; *Antiques* (April 1951), 300; *Portfolio* (Feb. 1951), 127, (Feb. 1952), 132, (Jan. 1955), 115.

CLAY, SAMUEL. Lithographer; born in Pennsylvania *c.* 1840; boarding in Philadelphia in 1860. ¶ 8 Census (1860), Pa., LVI, 513.

CLAYPOOLE, JAMES. Engraver and portrait painter. One of Pennsylvania's earliest artists, Claypoole was active in Philadelphia in 1762, when his work was seen by CHARLES WILLSON PEALE. Claypoole's father was a house painter and glazier, born in 1720, died *c.* 1784. The artist was also the uncle and teacher of MATTHEW PRATT. The latter part of his life was spent on the island of Jamaica, where he is said to have died about 1796. ¶ Sellers, "James Claypoole"; Sawitzky, "The American Work of Benjamin West," 441, no. 12; Stauffer, I, 51–52; Sartain, *Reminiscences,* 148; Dunlap, *History,* I, 98.

CLAYTON, CHARLES O. Canadian engraver, born about 1830, at NYC in 1850 and 1860. ¶ 7 Census (1850), N.Y., XLIII, 224; 8 Census (1860), N.Y., XLVII, 311; NYCD 1863.

CLEMENS, ISAAC. Engraver, NYC, 1776. ¶ Gottesman, *Arts and Crafts,* I, 8.

CLEMENT, DANIEL B. Portrait painter, Boston, 1859. ¶ Boston BD 1859.

CLEMENTS, ALEXANDER H. (1818–after 1879). Landscape painter; born in Georgetown (D.C.), June 1, 1818; living in 1879. Clements painted a view of Washington in 1848 and the same year exhibited at the American Art-Union. He was a resident of Washington in 1860. His work is represented in the Corcoran Gallery by his oil, "The Source of the Potomac," and in the National Gallery by the 1848 view of Washington. ¶ Records of artists at the Corcoran Gallery of Art, Washington (D.C.); Cowdrey, AA & AAU; Washington and Georgetown CD 1860.

CLEMENTS, JOHN. Lithographer; born in Holland *c.* 1832; boarding in Philadelphia in 1860. ¶ 8 Census (1860), Pa., LII, 670.

CLEPHAN, LEWIS. Miniaturist, portrait painter, and hair-worker, advertised in NYC in 1787. ¶ Kelby, *Notes,* 31.

CLERK, HENRY H. Connecticut-born artist, age 25, living in Baltimore in 1850, with Mary (age 23) and Sarah L. Clerk (age 6), both also from Connecticut. ¶ 7 Census (1850), Md., IV, 145.

CLEVELAND, JAMES A. (1811–after 1859). Landscape, portrait, and miniature painter; born in 1811, the son of Capt. William Cleveland of Salem (Mass.). He exhibited at the Boston Athenaeum in 1834 and 1835, but moved away from Salem after 1837. He apparently went to Ohio, married there, and had a son, born about 1840. He next appears as a landscape and miniature painter in Rochester (N.Y.) in 1844 and 1845, but may have been in NYC *c.* 1839, since J. A. Cleveland drew ten plates for John Delafield's *Inquiry into the Origins of the Antiquities of America,* published in NYC 1839. Cleveland was working in NYC from 1847 to 1852, in Tarrytown (N.Y.) from 1854 to 1857, and again in NYC in 1858. ¶ Swan, BA, 213; Belknap, *Artists and Craftsmen,* 7; BA Cat. 1834–35; Cowdrey, NAD; Boston CD 1835; 7 Census (1850), N.Y., XLVII, 330; Rochester CD 1844–45; Ulp; NYBD 1851–52; *Portfolio* (Sept. 1942), 7, repro.

CLEVELAND, Mrs. J. R. The lady who exhibited a pencil drawing at the 1847 American Institute under this name lived at the same address as JAMES A. CLEVELAND. ¶ Am. Inst. Cat., 1847; NYCD 1847.

CLEVELAND, WILLIAM (1777–1845). Painter of ship portraits at Salem (Mass.). ¶ Robinson and Dow, I, 61.

CLEVELEY, JOHN (1747–1786). English marine and landscape painter; born at Deptford, December 25, 1747; died there, June 25, 1786. Though most of his career was spent in England. Cleveley served as draughtsman on two expeditions in the

North Seas in the 1770's. A "View of New York in 1775" suggests that he may have visited America. ¶ DNB; Graves, *Dictionary;* Met. Mus., *Life in America.*

CLEVENGER, SHOBAL VAIL (1812–1843). Sculptor; born near Middletown (Ohio), October 22, 1812. He learned the rudiments of stone-cutting from DAVID GUION in Cincinnati in the early 1830's, and from about 1836 to 1840 he enjoyed great success as a portrait sculptor, visiting Philadelphia, Washington, Boston, and NYC and executing busts of the nation's most distinguished men. In 1840, under the patronage of Nicholas Longworth, he went to Europe for further study in Paris and Florence, but within a short time he had developed consumption. He died at sea as he was returning to America with his family in September 1843. ¶ DAB; Cist, *Cincinnati in 1841;* Swan, BA; CAB; repro. *American Collector,* XV (May 1946), 13. His work is at MHS and NYHS.

CLIFFORD, R. A. Portrait painter and photographer, Milwaukee (Wis.) in the 1850's. ¶ Butts, *Art in Wisconsin,* 97.

CLINTON, DEWITT. Pennsylvania-born artist, 32, at NYC in 1860. ¶ 8 Census (1860), N.Y., LVI, 247.

CLIREHUGH, W. S. Wigmaker and amateur painter of NYC, exhibited "Royal Family of Scotland" at the American Institute in 1850. ¶ Am. Inst. Cat., 1850; NYCD 1850.

CLONNEY, JAMES GOODWYN (1812–1867). A.N.A. Genre and miniature painter; born in Liverpool (England), January 28, 1812; Clonney came to America as a young man, establishing himself as a miniature painter in NYC as early as 1834. From about 1841 he devoted himself mainly to genre painting. His home from 1842 to 1852 was at New Rochelle (N.Y.), and thereafter at Cooperstown (N.Y.). He died in Binghamton (N.Y.), October 7, 1867. A frequent exhibitor at the National Academy, the Apollo Association and American Art-Union, and the Pennsylvania Academy. ¶ Bolton, *Miniature Painters; Panorama,* III (Dec. 1947), 44, repro.; Cowdrey, NAD; Cowdrey, AA & AAU; Rutledge, PA; NYCD 1834; Karolik Cat., 166–185, with 14 repros.; information from Mr. Morgan H. Seacord of New Rochelle, who owns a portrait of Virginia T. Seacord painted after her death in 1847.

CLORIVIÈRE, JOSEPH-PIERRE PICOT DE LIMOËLAN DE (1768–1826). Miniature painter, born November 4, 1768, in Broons, Brittany. Charged with an attempted assassination of Napoleon, he escaped to America in 1803 and found employment as a miniaturist in Savannah (1803–06), Baltimore (1806–12), Charleston (1812–18). He spent his last years in the Jesuit Monastery of the Visitation at Georgetown (D.C.), where he died September 29, 1826. His work was variously signed: de Clorivière, Picot, or Guitry. ¶ Rutledge, "A French Priest, Painter and Architect in the United States: Joseph-Pierre Picot de Limoëlan de Clorivière"; Carolina Art Assoc., *Cat.,* 1936.

CLOUDMAN, JOHN J. Portrait painter, Portland (Me.), 1856–59. ¶ New England BD 1856; Portland CD 1856, 1859.

CLOUGH, GEORGE L. (1824–1901). Portrait and landscape painter; born in Auburn (N.Y.), September 18, 1824. About 1844 Clough met the portrait painter, CHARLES LORING ELLIOTT, with whom he studied for some years, both at Auburn and in NYC. He exhibited at the National Academy in 1848 and 1850, and in the latter year went to Europe for further study. After his return he is said to have lived near New York. He died at Auburn, February 20, 1901. ¶ CAB; *Art Annual,* IV (1903/04), 138; Cowdrey, NAD, Thieme-Becker.

CLOVER, LEWIS P., JR. (1819–1896). A.N.A. Portrait, landscape, and genre painter, engraver; born in NYC, February 20, 1819. After training as an engraver under ASHER B. DURAND, Clover turned to painting and was successful in NYC and Baltimore during the 1840's. He exhibited at the National Academy, the American Academy, the Apollo Association, the Artists' Fund Society, and the Boston Athenaeum, and was elected an Associate of the National Academy in 1840. He gave up his artistic career after 1850 to enter the Episcopalian ministry, and served parishes in Lexington (Va.), Springfield (Ill.) and elsewhere. He painted a portrait of Lincoln in 1860, presumably at Springfield. He died in NYC on November 9, 1896. ¶ Thieme-Becker; CAB; Cowdrey, AA & AAU; Cowdrey, NAD; Swan, BA; Rutledge, PA; Lafferty; *Appleton's Journal,* March 25, 1872, 573; Stauffer; repro. in *International Studio,* LIII (Aug. 1914), opp. xxix.

CLOVER, PHILIP (1832–1905). Portrait painter. He painted portraits of Chicago politicians and lived for a time in Columbus (Ohio). ¶ *Art Annual,* V (1905–06), 119; Smith.

Clover, William C. Amateur painter, NYC, exhibited at the American Institute in 1844. Apparently a brother of Lewis P. Clover, Jr., he was listed in the 1848 directory as proprietor of a bonded warehouse. ¶ Am. Inst. Cat., 1844; NYCD 1844, 1848.

Clows, John. English engraver, 60, at NYC in 1850. ¶ 7 Census (1850), N.Y., XLI, 769.

Cloyes, Frederick. Engraver; born in Massachusetts *c.* 1828; living in Boston in 1850. ¶ 7 Census (1850), Mass., XXV, 52.

Clozel, Mr. and Mrs. Artists, New Orleans, 1841–42. He was employed at the New Orleans Theatre. ¶ New Orleans CD 1841–42.

Cluff, William. Engraver, NYC, 1858. ¶ NYBD 1858.

Clules, John. Lithographer, Philadelphia, 1854. ¶ Penna. BD 1854.

Clute, Edward C. Sculptor who came to Rochester (N.Y.) in 1854 and was the first artist there to execute a life-size bust in marble. ¶ Ulp, "Art and Artists in Rochester," 33.

Coate, S. Engraver of a portrait of John Wesley, 1803, which Fielding thought was American in workmanship. The artist may, however, have been the S. Coate of London who exhibited drawings at the Royal Academy in 1812. ¶ Fielding, *Supplement to Stauffer,* 9; Graves, *Dictionary.*

Coates, E. C. Landscape and historical painter, active 1837–57. As Edmund C., Edmund F., or Edward Coates, he was listed in NYC directories in 1837, 1841–43, and as E. C. Coates he exhibited at the Apollo Gallery and Association in 1839–40 and at the National Academy in 1841. His landscapes were chiefly of Italian and New York State scenes, though he also worked in Canada. ¶ NYCD 1837, 1841–43; Cowdrey, AA & AAU; Cowdrey, NAD; Sweet, *Hudson River School,* 70–71; repros. in *Art Digest,* March 1, 1945, 5; *Antiques,* July 1944, 13; *Panorama,* March 1947, 76.

Coates, Frederick. Landscape painter and teacher, NYC; exhibited at the Apollo Gallery in 1838 and 1839. ¶ Cowdrey, AA & AAU.

Coates, Nancy. Artist; born in England *c.* 1805; living in Allegheny County (Pa.) in 1860. ¶ 8 Census (1860), Pa., IV, 692.

Cobb, Mrs. C. S. Landscape painter of East New York (N.Y.), who exhibited at the National Academy in 1855. ¶ Cowdrey, NAD.

Cobb, Cyrus (1834–1903). Portrait painter and sculptor; born in Malden (Mass.), August 6, 1834; died in Allston (Mass.), January 29, 1903; twin brother of Darius Cobb. The brothers worked together in Boston from the mid-1850's, painting portraits and collaborating on large historical and religious paintings. Cyrus also studied and practised law in Boston from 1869 to 1879 and was active in musical and literary circles in Boston. ¶ *Art Annual,* IV (1903/04), 138; CAB (under Sylvanus Cobb); Boston BD 1855–59; Swan, BA; Fielding; Gardner, *Yankee Stonecutters.*

Cobb, Darius (1834–1919). Portrait and landscape painter; born in Malden (Mass.), August 6, 1834; died in Newton Upper Falls (Mass.), April 23, 1919; twin brother of Cyrus Cobb. Primarily a portrait painter, Darius Cobb collaborated with his brother on a number of large historical and religious paintings and also painted some landscapes. Like his brother, he spent the greater part of his career in Boston. ¶ *Art Annual,* XVI (1919); CAB (under Sylvanus Cobb); Swan, BA; Boston BD 1855; Mallett; Thieme-Becker, cites *New England Mag.,* May 1910.

Cobb, E. D. Teacher of art, lectured on Chinese or flower painting and mezzotint engraving at Cincinnati, August 1840. ¶ WPA (Ohio), *Annals of Cleveland.*

Cobb, Gershom (*c.* 1780–1824). Writing master and wood engraver; born [in or near Boston, Mass. ?] *c.* 1780; died in Dorchester (Mass.), October 3, 1824. Cobb was married in Boston, October 21, 1807, to Sarah Boyd of Weston. He was a writing master and bank clerk in Boston and, according to Abel Bowen, an occasional engraver on wood. Dunlap and Stauffer list him as G. Cobb. ¶ *Dorchester Births, Marriages and Deaths to 1825,* p. 371; *Boston Marriages, 1752–1809;* Whitmore, "Abel Bowen," 34; Boston CD 1819–22; Stauffer.

Cobb, George T. Engraver; born in Pennsylvania *c.* 1828; living in Philadelphia in 1850 and 1860. ¶ 7 Census (1850), Pa., XLIX, 884; 8 Census (1860), LVI, 408.

Cobb, Zenas. Artist, Albany (N.Y.), 1822, 1826–28. Also listed as printer, 1815–16, 1831, and as artizan, 1832–45. ¶ Albany CD 1815–45.

Cobden, Frederick. Artist; born in England

c. 1833; living with his family in Philadelphia in 1860. His family appears to have come to America after 1846. ¶ 8 Census (1860), Pa., L, 332.

COCCHI, JACINT. Venetian painter who came to Philadelphia from Rome in 1795. He advertised with JOSEPH PEROVANI in September 1795; his specialty was perspective painting and decoration of interiors in the Italian manner. ¶ Prime, II, 26.

COCHARD, JOHN. Lithographer, NYC, 1854. ¶ NYCD 1854.

COCHEU & CO. Wood engravers, Cincinnati, 1858–60. The partners were HENRY COCHEU and JOSEPH W. HART. Their work appeared in *Now-A-Days* (N.Y., 1854) and in *Annals of San Francisco* (N.Y., 1855). ¶ Cincinnati CD 1858–60; Hamilton, 199, 474.

COCHEU, HENRY. Wood engraver and designer, NYC, 1851–54, and Cincinnati, 1856–60. In 1851 H. Cochue [sic] exhibited a wood engraving at the American Institute, and in 1854 he headed the engraving firm of COCHEU & THATCHER. In Cincinnati Cocheu was in business as a showman as well as an engraver, exhibiting in 1859 "Cocheu's Historical Living Tableaux." The artist described himself at that time as "favorably known as a delineator of animate nature." From 1858 to 1860 he headed the engraving firm of COCHEU & CO. ¶ Am. Inst. Cat., 1851; NYCD 1852; NYBD 1854; Cincinnati CD 1856–60; Cincinnati *Gazette,* Oct. 14, 1859 (cited by J. E. Arrington).

COCHEU & THATCHER, wood engravers, see HENRY COCHEU and GEORGE W. THATCHER.

COCHRAN, Mrs. ELIZA (TORRANS). Landscape painter, Charleston (S.C.), active *c.* 1800–1810. Ramsay's *History of South Carolina* (1809) describes Mrs. Eliza Cochran and her sister, ROSELLA TORRANS, as the best of the female artists of Charleston. She was married to Thomas Cochran, Jr., in 1799. ¶ Rutledge, *Artists in the Life of Charleston,* 127; Torrence, *Torrence and Allied Families,* 179.

COCHRAN, WILLIAM J. Engraver; born in New York about 1820; working in NYC in the 1850's and 1860's. ¶ 7 Census (1850), N.Y., XLIII, 129; 8 Census (1860), N.Y., XLVI, 790; NYCD 1850, 1863.

COCKBURN, JAMES PATTISON (*c.* 1779–1847). Amateur landscape painter in watercolors. A British artillery officer, who published several illustrated books of European travels, Cockburn was stationed at Quebec from 1826 to 1836. During this time he sketched along the St. Lawrence and Lake Ontario and on the Passaic River in New Jersey. After his return to England he was made Director of the Royal Laboratory at Woolwich. He was appointed Major-General four months before his death in 1847. ¶ Spendlove, "The Canadian Watercolours of James Pattison Cockburn."

COCKER, GEORGE. Engraver, Lowell (Mass.), 1848. ¶ Lowell BD 1848.

CODMAN, CHARLES (1800–1842). Landscape, marine, and sign painter; born in Portland (Me.), 1800; died there [?] in 1842. Codman was working as a limner in Portland as early as 1823, but his recognition as a landscape painter came after 1828, when JOHN NEAL "discovered" him. Thereafter he exhibited at the Boston Athenaeum (1828–34), the National Academy (1832 and 1838), and the Apollo Gallery (1839). He may have been a son of WILLIAM P. CODMAN, since the Boston directories for 1822 and 1823 list William P. and Charles Codman together as portrait painters. ¶ "Maine Artists," represented in Portland Art Museum; Portland CD 1823, 1827, 1831, 1834, 1841; Dickson, *Observations on Art from the Writings of John Neal,* 90–91, 96; Boston CD 1822–23; Swan, BA; Cowdrey, NAD; Cowdrey, AA & AAU (under John Amory Codman, 1839); repros. in *American Processional,* 116, 241; Karolik Cat., 186–188.

CODMAN, JOHN AMORY (1824–1886). Portrait and marine painter; worked in Boston from 1849 to 1860 and after, exhibiting at the American Art-Union in 1849 and at the Boston Athenaeum in 1856. ¶ Boston CD 1849–55 as artist, thereafter without occupation; Cowdrey, AA & AAU; Swan, BA.

CODMAN, WILLIAM P. Portrait painter, active 1805–31; married Susannah Coffin of Portland (Me.) at Boston, September 27, 1791. He painted a portrait at Hallowell (Me.) in 1805, and was listed in Boston directories from 1820 to 1831. In 1832 his widow, Susan Codman, was listed. William P. may have been the father of CHARLES CODMAN, since the 1822 and 1823 directories list them together as portrait painters. ¶ *Boston Marriages 1752–1809,* p. 462; Sears, *Some American Primitives,* 156, and repro. 166; Boston CD 1820–32; *Art in America,* XXIII

(March 1935), 82; Boston *Agricultural Intelligencer,* Feb. 18, 1820, advt. (citation courtesy of Clarence S. Brigham).

CODNER, WILLIAM (1709–1769). Gravestone sculptor; born in Boston, July 24, 1709; died there, September 12, 1769. A popular gravestone artist of Boston for many years, Codner was one of the first to introduce portraits in American mortuary art. His sons, Abraham and John Codner, also were gravestone sculptors. ¶ Forbes, "Early Portrait Sculpture," 59–61; Lipman, *American Folk Art,* 21, ill. 170; Ravenel, "Here Lyes Buried," 193–94.

COE, BENJAMIN HUTCHINS (1799–after 1883). Drawing teacher and landscape painter; born in Hartford (Conn.), October 8, 1799. Coe was the first teacher of FREDERIC EDWIN CHURCH and E. S. BARTHOLOMEW, and for many years taught drawing in NYC and other cities of the north-eastern United States. In 1854 he settled permanently in New Haven and *c.* 1864 he gave up teaching to devote himself to temperance work. He published a number of drawing books: *Easy Lessons in Landscape Drawing* (Hartford, 1840); *A New Drawing Book of American Scenery* (N.Y., 1845); *Drawing Book of Trees* (New Haven, 1841), and others. He exhibited at the National Academy from 1846 to 1863. ¶ French, *Art and Artists in Conn.,* 61; New Haven CD 1883; Library of Congress Cat.; 7 Census (1850), N.Y., LII, 264.

COFFEE & GIBSON, sculptors, see THOMAS COFFEE and RICHARD P. GIBSON.

COFFEE, THOMAS. Sculptor, NYC, 1830–69; born in England about 1800. Thomas Coffee exhibited a bust of Judge Hitchcock of Mobile (Ala.) at the Apollo Gallery in 1839, several busts, including one of Osceola, at the National Academy in 1841–42, a statue of Henry Clay at the American Institute in 1844, and four plaster busts at the American Institute in 1856. In the latter year he was in partnership with RICHARD P. GIBSON. His son THOMAS was also a sculptor. ¶ NYCD 1830–69; Cowdrey, AA & AAU; Cowdrey, NAD; Am. Inst. Cat., 1844, 1856; 7 Census (1850), N.Y., XLIII, 7; 8 Census (1860), N.Y., LIII, 612.

COFFEE, THOMAS, JR. Sculptor, son of THOMAS COFFEE; born in NYC about 1839 and working with his father in 1860. ¶ 8 Census (1860), N.Y., LIII, 612.

COFFEE, WILLIAM J. (*c.* 1774–*c.* 1846). English sculptor, still life, and portrait painter; born *c.* 1774; died probably at Albany (N.Y.), *c.* 1846. From 1795 to 1816 Coffee worked as a sculptor in terra cotta in Derby and London and he exhibited a number of times at the Royal Academy. He came to America in 1816, settling in NYC for the next decade. In 1816 he executed a bust of Hugh Williamson, now at the New-York Historical Society. In 1817 he exhibited at the American Academy two terra cotta animals, an "Infant Morpheus in Terra Cotta," and several paintings of animals and dead game. In April 1818 he executed busts of Thomas Jefferson, his daughter, and grand-daughter, and he corresponded frequently with Jefferson thereafter. Coffee was listed in New York directories as a sculptor in 1821–22 and as a portrait painter from 1821 to 1826, though he also visited Charleston (S.C.) in 1821 and was in Newark (N.J.) in 1824. From 1827 to 1845 he lived in Albany (N.Y.), where he executed several bas-reliefs for the City Hall. He exhibited at the National Academy in 1833 as J. Coffee, and at the Apollo Gallery in 1839. ¶ Solon, *Hist. of Old English Pottery; Apollo,* XLV (Feb. 1947), 51, repro.; Groce, "Long-lost Sculptor"; Rutledge, "William John Coffee as a Portrait Sculptor"; Graves, *Dictionary;* NYHS Cat. (1941); Cowdrey, AA & AAU; Hart, "Life Portraits of Jefferson"; NYCD 1819–22, 1824–26; Albany CD 1827–29, 1831, 1833–35, 1838, 1840–45; Munsell, *Annals,* V, 259; Rutledge, *Artists in the Life of Charleston;* Stauffer, no. 569; Dunlap, *History,* II, 308; represented at NYHS. A terra cotta bust of an unidentified man, inscribed "William J. Coffee, Fecit/Newark/Oct. 23, 1824," was owned in 1941 by Harry MacNeill Bland of NYC.

COFFIN, FREDERICK M. Illustrator, active during the 1850's. He worked for *Harper's Magazine,* as well as in the book trade. Hamilton lists 14 books illustrated by him. ¶ Weitenkampf, *American Graphic Art;* Hamilton, 178–181.

COFFIN, S. C. Portrait painter at Pittsburgh (Pa.) in 1850. Coffin, a native of Massachusetts, was 36 years old in 1850. His family included Nancy R. (b. N.Y., age 28), Helen V. (b. Va., age 4), and Ira D. (b. Pa., age 3). ¶ 7 Census (1850), Pa., III (part 2), 144; Pittsburgh CD 1850.

COFFIN, W. H. Painter of a ship portrait entitled "View of brig Ceylon of Duxbury, Wrecked on the South Side of Nantucket, April 8, 1837." ¶ Taylor Coll. of Ship Portraits in the Peabody Museum, *Catalogue,* 5.

COFFIN, WILLIAM A. Primitive portrait painter, *c.* 1850. ¶ Information courtesy Mrs. Jean Lipman.

COGDELL, JOHN STEVENS or STEPHANO (1778–1847). Amateur sculptor and painter; born in South Carolina, September 19, 1778. A lawyer by profession, Cogdell took up painting after a visit to Italy in 1800. About 1825 he began modelling in clay and he later worked in plaster and marble. He exhibited at the National Academy (of which he was an Honorary Member), the Pennsylvania Academy, the Artists' Fund Society, the Boston Athenaeum, and the American Academy. In his later years Cogdell held a number of public offices in Charleston and served as a bank president. He died in Charleston, February 25, 1847. ¶ DAB; Rutledge, "Cogdell and Mills, Charleston Sculptors," with check list of his work; Rutledge, *Artists in the Life of Charleston;* Cowdrey, NAD; Cowdrey, AA & AAU; Rutledge, PA; Swan, BA.

COGGESWELL, WILLIAM (*c.* 1824–1906). Painter and musician. A resident of Beverly (R.I.), Coggeswell died at Amityville (Long Island, N.Y.) on August 7, 1906, at the age of 82. The obituary in the 1907/08 *Art Annual* mistakenly attributes to him the White House portrait of Lincoln painted by WILLIAM F. COGSWELL. ¶ *Art Annual,* VI (1907/08), 107; information courtesy of FARL.

COGGER, EDWARD P. Wood engraver, NYC, 1856–59. In 1858 he was also listed as Edwin P. Cogger. ¶ NYBD 1856, 1858; NYCD 1857–59.

COGGINS, EDWARD H. Engraver, Philadelphia, 1858–60; in 1859–60, of Coggins & Harbach. ¶ Phila. CD 1858–59; BD 1860.

COGGINS & HARBACH, engravers, see EDWARD H. COGGINS and HORATIO M. HARBACH.

COGSWELL, JOHN. Engraver and copperplate printer, Lowell (Mass.), 1859. ¶ Lowell CD 1859, p. 254.

COGSWELL, WILLIAM F. (1819–1903). Portrait and genre painter; born in Sandusky (N.Y.), July 15, 1819. Cogswell taught himself portrait painting in the 1830's while working in a color factory at Buffalo (N.Y.), and worked as a professional artist in NYC during the 1840's. He exhibited at the National Academy and the American Art-Union. In 1849 he went to California, but he soon returned to NYC. During the next twenty-five years Cogswell worked in NYC, St. Louis, and Washington. His best-known work was the portrait of Lincoln which now hangs in the White House. In 1873 he moved to California, where he spent the rest of his life. He died at South Pasadena, December 24, 1903. ¶ Obit., Pasadena *Evening Star,* December 26, 1903 (quoted in a letter from the Pasadena Public Library to FARL, June 10, 1941); Bolton, *Portrait Painters in Oil;* Fielding; Cowdrey, NAD; Cowdrey, AA & AAU. His work is represented in the Pasadena City Auditorium, as well as the White House.

COHEIL, CHARLES or JOHN S. Portrait painter, Charleston (S.C.), January, 1844. *Cf.* CHARLES COHILL. ¶ Rutledge, *Artists in the Life of Charleston,* 190 (as Charles), 235 (as John S.).

COHEN, ALFRED. Primitive mural painter of Kentucky. A native of Bordeaux (France), Cohen settled in Kentucky before he was twenty. During the 1830's he is thought to have painted landscape murals in three houses of Woodford County, and he shortly after moved to Lawrenceburg (Ky.). A photograph taken at Danville (Ky.) in 1867 shows Cohen at about the age of 50. ¶ Lancaster, "Primitive Mural Painter of Kentucky: Alfred Cohen," with 8 repros.

COHEN, FREDERICK E. Portrait and genre painter. An English Jew, Cohen came to Detroit from Woodstock (Upper Canada) during the Canadian Rebellion of 1837. He was the teacher of LEWIS F. IVES and ROBERT HOPKIN and exhibited in 1848 at the American Art-Union. In 1855 he moved from Detroit to Oberlin (Ohio). ¶ Katz, "Jews in Detroit," 7, repro. of self-portrait; Burroughs, "Painting and Sculpture in Michigan"; Detroit CD 1846, 1850; Cowdrey, AA & AAU; WPA Guide, *Michigan.*

COHEN, GEORGE. Engraver, 21, born in New York State, at NYC in 1860. ¶ 8 Census (1860), N.Y., LIII, 858.

COHEN, LAWRENCE L. Portrait painter. In 1849, at the age of 13, Cohen was already attracting attention as an artist in Charleston (S.C.). He went to Düsseldorf (Germany) for further study in 1855–56, returned to Charleston, and went off to war in 1861. ¶ Rutledge, *Artists in the Life of Charleston,* 169, 190.

COHILL, CHARLES. Portrait painter; born in Pennsylvania *c.* 1812; working in Philadelphia from 1835 to 1860. A pupil of JOHN NEAGLE, Cohill exhibited at the Artists' Fund Society in 1838, 1840, and 1841. He may have visited Charleston (S.C.) in 1844 [see CHARLES COHEIL]. In 1860 he was living in Philadelphia with his wife Ann (age 46, born in New Jersey) and six children (ages 5 to 24, all born in Pennsylvania). ¶ 7 Census (1850), Pa., LIII, 42; 8 Census (1860), Pa., LVI, 734; Phila. CD 1835, 1839–60; Rutledge, PA.

COIT, DANIEL WADSWORTH. Merchant, NYC, exhibited "Drawings from the Sketchbook of an Amateur" at the National Academy in 1841. He was an Honorary Member. ¶ NYCD 1837; Cowdrey, NAD.

COKE, EDWARD THOMAS (1807–1888). Amateur artist. An English army officer who visited North America in 1832 and on his return to England published an account of his travels, *A Subaltern's Furlough* (London, 1833). The book was illustrated with thirteen views of American scenes lithographed from Coke's own sketches. ¶ Coke, *A Subaltern's Furlough.*

COKER, THOMAS. Irish engraver, 20, at NYC in 1850. ¶ 7 Census (1850), N.Y., XLVI, 546.

COLAC, DENIS. Marble sculptor, New Orleans, 1841–42. ¶ New Orleans CD 1841–42.

COLBERT, EDOUARD-CHARLES-VICTURNIEN, Comte de Maulevrier (1758–1820). Amateur. A French naval officer who served under de Grasse in America, the Comte de Maulevrier visited America again in the late 1790's as an emigré. He made his headquarters in Philadelphia, but spent much of his time traveling in Pennsylvania, New York, and Quebec. His journals and many sketches and watercolors of American scenes have been preserved. After his return to France in 1799, de Maulevrier lived quietly until the Bourbon Restoration, when he returned to naval service. He died February 2, 1820. ¶ Colbert, *Voyage dans l'Intérieur des Etats-Unis et au Canada* (Baltimore, 1935), v-xx, and 20 repros.; *Penna. History,* XX (April 1953), 140–141, two repros.; Clarke, *Emigrés in the Wilderness,* 62, repro.

COLBORN, WILLIAM. Lithographer; born in Connecticut *c.* 1828; boarding in Philadelphia in 1860. ¶ 8 Census (1860), Pa., LVI, 916.

COLBURN, CHARLES H. Lithographer; born in Connecticut *c.* 1822; working in Boston between 1852 and 1860. In 1853 he was a partner in UPHAM & COLBURN. In 1860 his family included: Martha A. (38, born in Conn.); Charles H., clerk (15, Pa.); Clarence S. (13, Conn.); Mary H. (10, Pa.); Eugene M. (8, Mass.); Hattie B. (2, Mass.); and Willis (9 months, Mass.). ¶ 8 Census (1860), Mass., XXVIII, 413; Boston CD 1852–55, 1857–59, and after 1860; Peters, *America on Stone.*

COLBURN, LUKE. Engraver and copperplate printer, Boston, 1837. Earlier he was listed as a comb-maker. Peters links him with DANIEL S. JENKINS in the lithographic firm of JENKINS & COLBURN, 1836–37, 1840. ¶ Boston CD 1834–37; Peters, *America on Stone.*

COLBY, JAMES [T.?]. Engraver; born in Massachusetts *c.* 1822; living in San Francisco in 1860. His family, all born in Massachusetts, consisted of: Lydia (23), Sarah (17), Rebecca (15), William (6), and Mary (1); he owned personal property valued at $175. ¶ 8 Census (1860), Cal., VII, 1241.

COLE, A. Painter of a portrait of Henry Kemble Oliver (1800–1885), owned by Dartmouth College, Hanover (N.H.). ¶ WPA (Mass.), *Portraits Found in N.H.,* p. 16.

COLE, CHARLES OCTAVIUS (1814–?). Portrait painter; born in Newburyport (Mass.), July 1, 1814; son of MOSES DUPRÉ COLE, and brother of JOSEPH GREENLEAF and LYMAN EMERSON COLE. He worked in New Orleans in 1838 and 1841, but eventually settled in Portland (Me.), where he was from at least 1850 to 1856. In 1850 his household included his wife, Marie B. Cole (31) and three children (2 months to 11 years), all born in Maine; his real property was then valued at $3,300. Several portraits of Portland and Newcastle residents were painted by Cole in the 1840's. A portrait of Benjamin Foster, of Gloucester (Mass.), credited to W. O. Cole of Newburyport, may have been the work of C. O. Cole. ¶ Belknap, *Artists and Craftsmen,* 7; *Vital Records of Newburyport;* 7 Census (1850), Maine, IV, 244; New Orleans CD 1838, 1841; Portland CD 1852, 1856; *Maine Register,* 1855; New England BD 1856; WPA (Mass.), *Portraits*

Found in Maine; WPA (Mass.), *Portraits Found in Mass.,* no. 785.

COLE, ISAAC P. Engraver, Philadelphia, 1814. ¶ Brown and Brown.

COLE, JOSEPH FOXCROFT (1837–1892). Landscape painter; born in Jay (Me.), November 9, 1837. After his apprenticeship as a lithographer at J. H. BUFFORD's establishment in Boston, Cole went to Europe in 1860 to study painting. During the next seventeen years he divided his time between Europe and America, exhibiting in Paris and London as well as at the Boston Athenaeum, the National Academy, and the Pennsylvania Academy. In 1877 he settled at Winchester (Mass.), where, except for brief visits to Europe and California, he spent the rest of his life; he died there May 2, 1892. He was influential in introducing French painting in America. His daughter, Adelaide (Cole) Chase, became a well-known portrait painter in Boston. ¶ DAB; Boston BD 1858–60; "Maine Artists"; Graves, *Dictionary;* Stokes, *Hist. Prints;* Swan, BA; Cowdrey, NAD; represented in the Walker Art Museum at Bowdoin (Maine).

COLE, JOSEPH GREENLEAF (1806–1858). Portrait painter; born in Newburyport (Mass.), April 10, 1806; son of MOSES DUPRÉ COLE, and brother of CHARLES OCTAVIUS and LYMAN EMERSON COLE. He worked in Boston from 1836 to 1847 and from 1855 to 1858, and exhibited at the Boston Athenaeum, the National Academy, and the Apollo Gallery. ¶ Belknap, *Artists and Craftsmen,* 7; *Vital Records of Newburyport;* Boston CD 1836–47, 1855–59; Swan, BA; Cowdrey, NAD; Cowdrey, AA & AAU; WPA (Mass.), *Portraits Found in N.H.,* pp. 1, 20; WPA (Mass.), *Portraits Found in Maine;* WPA (Mass.), *Portraits Found in Mass.;* repros. in Sears, *Some American Primitives,* 178, 255–57, 260; *Art in America,* XXXVIII (Feb. 1950), 10–11, 13.

COLE, LYMAN EMERSON (1812–*c.* 1878). Portrait painter; born in Newburyport (Mass.), May 28, 1812; son of MOSES DUPRÉ COLE, brother of CHARLES OCTAVIUS and JOSEPH GREENLEAF COLE. He was working in Lowell (Mass.) in 1833, and in 1849 apparently at Amesbury (Mass.), where his son was born. He was at Bath (Maine) in 1855. From 1860 until 1877 his name appears in the Newburyport directories. ¶ Belknap, *Artists and Craftsmen,* 7; *Vital Records of Newburyport;* Lowell CD 1833; *Vital Records of Amesbury; Maine Register,* 1855; Newburyport CD 1860–77.

COLE, Major. Painter of a portrait of Dr. Benjamin Page (1746–1824) of Hallowell (Maine) in 1812. *Cf.* MOSES DUPRÉ COLE. ¶ WPA (Mass.), *Portraits Found in Maine,* no. 175.

COLE, MOSES DUPRÉ, born Jacques Moyse Dupré (1783–1849). Sign and portrait painter; born in Bordeaux (France), in 1783; died in Newburyport (Mass.), September 18, 1849. He was the illegitimate son of Nicholas Cools Godefroy, a French West Indian planter, who came to Newburyport in 1795 and died the same year. After his father's death young Dupré changed his name to Moses Dupré Cole. He married in 1802 and had a sign-painting business until the Newburyport fire of 1811, after which he set up as a portrait painter. His three sons, CHARLES OCTAVIUS, JOSEPH GREENLEAF, and LYMAN EMERSON COLE, were also portrait painters. ¶ Belknap, *Artists and Craftsmen,* 8; *Vital Records of Newburyport;* Currier, *History of Newburyport,* II, 349–50; *Art in America,* XXXVIII (Feb. 1950), 13.

COLE, SARAH. Landscape painter; sister of THOMAS COLE. Miss Cole, of Catskill (N.Y.), exhibited at the National Academy in 1848, 1850–52, at the Maryland Historical Society in 1849, and at the American Art-Union 1848–52. ¶ DAB (under Thomas Cole); Cowdrey, NAD; Rutledge, MHS; Cowdrey, AA & AAU.

COLE, T. Portrait painter, whose portraits of Mr. and Mrs. Nathan Lord are owned by Dartmouth College, and one of Mrs. Jacob Sheafe (1751–1833) by the Portsmouth (N.H.) Athenaeum. ¶ WPA (Mass.), *Portraits Found in N.H.,* pp. 12, 14, 20.

COLE, THOMAS (1801–1848). N.A. Landscape, portrait, and religious painter, pioneer of the Hudson River School; born in Bolton-le-Moor (Lancashire, England), February 1, 1801. He came to America with his parents in 1819; visited the West Indies in 1820; worked as a block engraver in Steubenville (Ohio), 1820–22; took up portrait painting in 1822. After a winter in Philadelphia, he went to NYC, where he quickly won recognition as a portrait and landscape painter and was a founder of the National Academy. From 1829 to 1832 he was in

England and on the Continent. On his return he worked for a few years in NYC, then married and settled at Catskill. His most ambitious works, the two allegorical series: *The Course of Empire* and *The Voyage of Life,* were painted during the late 1830's. He visited Europe again in 1841–42, and was working on *The Cross and the World* at the time of his death, February 11 or 12, 1848, at Catskill. ¶ The only biography of Cole is Louis L. Noble's *Life and Works of Thomas Cole,* published shortly after the artist's death. He receives extended mention in DAB; Tuckerman; CAB; Bénézit; Fielding; and Thieme-Becker. Other sources include: French; Sweet, *Hudson River School;* Cowdrey, NAD; Rutledge, PA; Rutledge, MHS; Cowdrey, AA & AAU; *Albany Argus* (semi-weekly), Feb. 18, 1848; Graves, *Dictionary;* Karolik Cat.; Corcoran Gallery Cat.; Am. Inst. Cat., 1856. Pertinent magazine articles include: E. P. Lesley, "Some Clues to Thomas Cole"; E. E. Hale, "The Early Art of Thomas Cole"; Sydney Kellner, "The Beginnings of Landscape Painting in America"; E. P. Lesley, "Thomas Cole and the Romantic Sensibility"; and Evelyn Schmitt, "Two American Romantics—Thomas Cole and William Cullen Bryant."

COLE, W. O., see CHARLES OCTAVIUS COLE.

COLEHANDLER, GEORGE A. Fancy painter; born in New York *c.* 1825; living in Boston in 1850 with Elizabeth H. (72) and his wife, both born in Maine. ¶ 7 Census (1850), Mass., XXIII, 49.

COLEMAN, CHARLES. Artist; born in Massachusetts *c.* 1838; living in Boston in 1860 with his wife Emma, age 23. Coleman does not appear in the city directories, but Emma Coleman, widow, appears in 1865. ¶ 8 Census (1860), Mass., XXVI, 213; Boston CD 1865.

COLEMAN, CHARLES (?–1874). American landscape painter, who exhibited at the National Academy in 1857, as a resident of Rome (Italy). ¶ Thieme-Becker; Cowdrey, NAD.

COLEMAN, CHARLES CARYL (1840–1928). A.N.A. Landscape, portrait, and figure painter; born in Buffalo (N.Y.), April 25, 1840; died in Capri (Italy), December 4, 1928. After studying in Buffalo under WILLIAM H. BEARD, he went to Paris in 1859. He returned in 1862 to serve in the Civil War, but in 1866 he went back to Europe with his artist friends, WILLIAM HUNT and ELIHU VEDDER. Coleman eventually made his home in Capri and remained there for the rest of his life. He exhibited at the Boston Athenaeum and at the National Academy, as well as at galleries in England between 1878 and 1891. ¶ DAB; Swan, BA; Cowdrey, NAD, 1864–90; Clement and Hutton; Graves, *Dictionary.*

COLEMAN, EDWARD A. Engraver, 24, born in New York State, at NYC in 1860. ¶ 8 Census (1860), N.Y., XLVI, 923.

COLEMAN, SILAS A. Landscape and genre painter, of Philadelphia in 1858 and 1864–65, of Bordentown (N.J.) in 1859. He exhibited at the Pennsylvania Academy. ¶ Rutledge, PA.

COLEMAN, see also COLMAN.

COLEN, JOHN H. Lithographer, NYC, 1853–54. His views of Salem (Mass.) and Buffalo (N.Y.) in 1853 have been reproduced. ¶ NYBD 1854; Stokes, *Hist. Prints.; Portfolio* (Jan. 1954), 98.

COLES, JOHN, SR. (*c.* 1749–1809). Heraldic painter; died at Boston, September 16, 1809, aged 59. In the 1780's Coles worked with JOHN NORMAN, whose engravings after BENJAMIN BLYTH's portraits of George and Martha Washington were published by Coles in 1782. Coles first appears in the Boston directories in 1796 as a heraldry painter. His son, JOHN COLES, JR., was also a portrait and heraldic painter. ¶ Bowditch, "Early Water-Color Paintings of New England Coats of Arms," 190–195 and fig. 11, 12, 13; Watkins, "John Coles, Heraldic Painter."

COLES, JOHN, JR. (1776 or 1780–1854). Portrait, miniature, and heraldic painter; born in Massachusetts, 1776 (Swan) or 1780 (French); died in Charlestown (Mass.), September 6, 1854, aged 78. The younger Coles was first listed as a miniature and portrait painter in 1803 at Boston, where his father, JOHN COLES, SR., was a heraldic painter until 1809. John, Jr., was listed in Boston directories until 1825. He exhibited at the Boston Athenaeum in 1829 as of Providence (R.I.) and in 1830 as of Boston. From 1831 to 1848 he had a studio in Hartford (Conn.) in the winter and a summer home at Durham (Conn.). In 1849 he was again in Providence, but shortly after he moved to Worcester (Mass.). He was a close friend of JAMES FROTHINGHAM, with whom he is said to have studied under GILBERT STUART. ¶ Swan, BA; French, 43–44; Bowditch, "Early Water-Color Paintings of New

England Coats of Arms," 196–97; Stauffer; *Antiques* (Feb. 1956).

COLLARD, JOHN. English engraver, 35, in the NYC Almshouse in July, 1860. ¶ 8 Census (1860), N.Y., LXI, 143.

COLLARD, W. Line engraver of portraits for American magazines, *c.* 1840–45. ¶ Stauffer, I, 53.

COLLAS, LOUIS ANTOINE (1775–?), also known as Louis Augustin Collas or Lewis Collers. Miniature painter, born in Bordeaux (France) in 1775. After studying under the French artist Vincent, he worked in St. Petersburg (Russia) from 1808 to 1811. In 1816 he was listed in the New York City directory as Lewis Collers, portrait painter; he also visited Charleston (S.C.) in December 1816. He exhibited at the American Academy in 1816 and 1820 as a resident of NYC. Collas was in New Orleans from 1822 to 1824, and returned there in 1826 and 1829. ¶ Thieme-Becker; NYCD 1816; Rutledge, *Artists in the Life of Charleston,* repro., 178; Cowdrey, AA & AAU; Delgado-WPA cites New Orleans CD 1822–24, *Louisiana Gazette* (Jan. 20, 1823, and Jan. 28, 1824), and New Orleans *Courrier* (April 24, 1826, and March 7, 1829).

COLLERS, LEWIS, see LOUIS ANTOINE COLLAS.

COLLES, JOHN (1751–1807). Miniature profile painter and paperhanger; born in 1751; died in 1807. Colles painted miniatures in NYC in 1778 and 1780, and advertised in Philadelphia in 1783 as a paperhanger as well as miniaturist. He had previously worked in England and Ireland. ¶ Bolton, *Miniature Painters;* Fielding; Jackson, *Silhouette,* 91; Prime, I, 1.

COLLET, LOUIS. Engraver; born in France *c.* 1814; living in Philadelphia in 1860, with his Irish-born wife, Bridget (40), and two sons (3 and 6), both born in Pennsylvania. ¶ 8 Census (1860), Pa., LII, 204.

COLLIER, see also COLYER.

COLLIER, CHARLES MYLES (1836–1908). Marine painter; born in Hampton (Va.). He lived for many years in Memphis (Tenn.) and later had a studio in NYC. He died at Gloucester (Mass.), September 14, 1908. ¶ *Art Annual,* VII, obit.; Fielding.

COLLIER, J. HOWARD (?–1900). Crayon portrait draftsman; working in Boston in the 1850's. He exhibited at the Boston Athenaeum in 1856 and probably at the Pennsylvania Academy in 1850 (as —— Collier, address: Philadelphia). ¶ Boston CD 1850, 1859, 1861; BD 1856–57, 1860; Swan, BA; Rutledge, PA.

COLLIERE, LUCIEN C. Artist in Kentucky in 1855. ¶ Information courtesy Edward H. Dwight, Cincinnati Art Museum.

COLLIN [?], ——. A wood engraving bearing this name appears in the 1850 edition of Irving's *Knickerbocker's History of New York. Cf.* JOHN H. COLLINS. ¶ Hamilton, 209.

COLLIN, JOHN. Artist, 37, born in New York, at NYC in 1850. *Cf.* JOHN H. COLLINS. ¶ 7 Census (1850), N.Y., XLVII, 597.

COLLINS, Mr. ——. Miniaturist, advertised in Fredericksburg (Va.) in June 1829. *Cf.* FELIX COLLINS and W. P. COLLINS. ¶ [Fredericksburg, Va.] *Political Arena,* June 9, 1829.

COLLINS, ARNOLD. Silversmith of Newport (R.I.) who, in 1690, cut the seal of Rhode Island Colony. ¶ Bowditch, Ms. notes.

COLLINS, CHARLES. Copperplate engraver, of SHIELDS & COLLINS, New Orleans, 1842. ¶ New Orleans CD 1842.

COLLINS, FELIX. Miniaturist, NYC, 1814. *Cf.* Mr. —— COLLINS. ¶ NYCD 1814 (cited by McKay).

COLLINS, GEORGE T. An oil portrait by this artist, dated 1860, was owned in 1941 by Berney C. Batcheller of Wallingford (Vt.). ¶ WPA (Mass.), *Portraits Found in Vt.*

COLLINS, JEREMIAH. Irish lithographer, 21, at NYC in 1860. ¶ 8 Census (1860), N.Y., XLII, 322.

COLLINS, JOHN. Lithographer and watercolor artist, active 1833–69. His work included views of Philadelphia (Pa.), Burlington (N.J.), and Newport (R.I.). He was listed in the Philadelphia directories 1838–40 and worked for some years with the Philadelphia lithographer, THOMAS SINCLAIR. ¶ Peters, *America on Stone;* Phila. BD 1838; Phila. CD 1839–40; repros. in *Portfolio,* II (May 1943), 202–203.

COLLINS, JOHN H. Engraver, NYC, 1849–60. *Cf.* —— COLLIN. ¶ NYCD 1849–60; NYBD 1850–59.

COLLINS, W. P. Portrait or miniature painter, advertised in Salem (Mass.) in 1826. *Cf.* —— COLLINS and WILLIAM COLLINS. ¶ Belknap, *Artists and Craftsmen, Essex County,* 8.

COLLINS, WALTER P. Irish engraver, 25, at NYC in 1850. ¶ 7 Census (1850), N.Y., LVI, 368; NYCD 1850.

COLLINS, WILLIAM. Portrait painter, Albany (N.Y.), 1827–32. His portrait of Gen. Pierre Van Cortlandt II (1762–1848) is owned by the New-York Historical Society. ¶ Albany CD 1827–1832; NYHS Cat. (1941), repro.

COLLINSON, Capt. ——. British army or naval officer, whose view of San Francisco from Signal Hill was published in London in 1851. *Cf.* Commander Richard Collinson, R.N. (1811–1883), from 1849 to 1854 in command of the expedition to relieve Sir John Franklin. Commander Collinson had done coast surveying earlier in China and may have made this view of San Francisco and its harbor while on his way up the Pacific coast to Point Barrow (Alaska) in 1849–50. ¶ Peters, *Calif. on Stone* (under Hanhart, M. & N.); DNB.

COLLIS, GEORGE S. Artist, Chicago, 1858. ¶ Andreas, *History of Chicago,* II, 556 (cited by H. Maxson Holloway).

COLLMAN, GIDEON. Artist. Born *c.* 1831 in Hesse-Cassel (Germany); living in Philadelphia in 1860, aged 29. ¶ 8 Census (1860), Pa., LVI, 834.

COLLOT, GEORGE HENRI VICTOR (*c.* 1751–1805). French explorer and soldier, amateur artist, who served with Rochambeau in America and later was governor of Guadeloupe. During a visit to America in 1796, he made a map of Detroit and watercolor sketches of various American scenes, including a view of Pittsburgh (Pa.). He died in Paris in July 1805. Some of Collot's sketches appeared in his *Voyage dans l'Amerique* (Paris, 1826). ¶ CAB; *Antiques,* XX (Dec. 1931), 337, repro.

COLLUM, JOHN. Engraver, Washington (D.C.), 1858. ¶ Washington and Georgetown CD 1858.

COLMAN, CHARLES. Lithographer, with his brother WILLIAM COLMAN, Boston, 1850. He was born in Pennsylvania *c.* 1818. ¶ 7 Census (1850), Mass., XXV, 880.

COLMAN or COLEMAN, SAMUEL (1832–1920). N.A. Landscape and genre painter, etcher and watercolorist; born in Portland (Me.), March 4, 1832, the son of Samuel Colman, Sr., a bookseller and publisher of Portland, who moved to NYC, where his son studied painting under ASHER B. DURAND. Elected an Associate of the National Academy in 1855 and Academician in 1862, Samuel, Jr., exhibited at the Boston Athenaeum, the Maryland Historical Society, the Pennsylvania Academy, as well as at the National Academy. He went to Europe to study in 1860 and again in 1871. In later years he lived at Newport (R.I.), though he died in NYC, March 26, 1920. From 1867 to 1871 he was president of the American Society of Painters in Water Colors. ¶ DAB; Clement and Hutton; *Art News,* April 3, 1920, obit.; Cowdrey, NAD; Swan, BA; Rutledge, Pa; Rutledge, MHS; Met. Mus., *Life in America; Mag. of Art,* XXXII (April 1939), 292.

COLMAN, WILLIAM. Lithographer; born *c.* 1822 in Pennsylvania; living with his brother, CHARLES COLMAN, in Boston in 1850. ¶ 7 Census (1850), Mass., XXV, 880.

COLOMB, CHRISTOPHE. Landscape artist, working in Louisiana *c.* 1790; known only through his gouache of "White Hall Plantation." ¶ *American Processional,* 83; Rathbone, *Mississippi Panorama,* 84–85, repro.

COLOMBARA, C. Sculptor, working in Charleston (S.C.) in 1855. ¶ Rutledge, *Artists in the Life of Charleston.*

COLON, A. Artist, New Orleans, 1849. *Cf.* A. CHOL. ¶ New Orleans CD 1849 (cited by Delgado-WPA).

COLQUHOUN, ——. His portrait of George Ross was engraved by LENEY and published in NYC, 1809. ¶ Fielding's *Supplement to Stauffer,* no. 968.

COLT, MARY. Her pencil portrait of Thomas Oliver (1802–1848) of Baltimore is owned by the Maryland Historical Society. ¶ Rutledge, "Portraits in Varied Media."

COLTON, WALTER (1797–1851). Amateur landscape artist, born in Rutland County (Vt.), May 9, 1797. Ordained in 1825, he taught at Middletown (Conn.) Academy for four years, then served as editor of the [Washington, D.C.] *American Spectator and Washington City Chronicle* in 1829–30. In 1830 he was appointed a naval chaplain and from 1831 to 1834 he served with the Mediterranean squadron. During the next decade he lived in Philadelphia, devoting most of his time to journalism and writing travel books. In 1845 he went to California, where he remained until 1849, as alcalde of Monterey. He returned in 1849 to Philadelphia, where he died, January 22, 1851. Some of his sketches made in California were used by GEORGE HEILGE for a "Panorama of the Route to California," shown in Philadelphia in October 1849. ¶ Colton,

Three Years in California, ed. by Marguerite Eyer Wilbur; Hamersley, *Naval Register;* Phila. *Public Ledger,* Oct. 8 and 17, 1849 (cited by J. E. Arrington).

COLVINE, A. H., see AARON H. CORWINE.

COLYER, JOEL. Lithographer, 20, a native of New York State, at NYC in 1850. ¶ 7 Census (1850), N.Y., L, 721.

COLYER, VINCENT (1825–1888). A.N.A. Crayon portraitist, landscape painter, and lithographer; born in Bloomingdale (N.Y.), 1825; died on Contentment Island, near Darien (Conn.), July 12, 1888. Colyer (or Collier) studied with JOHN R. SMITH in NYC from 1844 to 1848, was elected an Associate of the National Academy in 1849, and worked as a crayon portraitist in NYC until the Civil War. During the war he worked with the sick and wounded and after the war devoted many years to work among the western Indians. In 1866 he settled near Darien (Conn.) and enlarged some of the many watercolor sketches he had made during his years in the West. His work was shown at the National Academy, the American Art-Union, the Boston Athenaeum, the Pennsylvania Academy, and the Maryland Historical Society. ¶ Clement and Hutton; Bolton, *Crayon Draftsmen;*. French; Cowdrey, NAD; Cowdrey, AA & AAU; Swan, BA; Rutledge, PA; Rutledge, MHS; N. Y. *Herald,* Oct. 31, 1856 (cited by J. E. Arrington). According to 7 Census (1850), N.Y., LII, 295, he was born in France about 1822.

COMAN, Mrs. CHARLOTTE BUELL (1833–1924). A.N.A. Landscape painter, born in Waterville, Oneida County (N.Y.) where her father, Chauncey Buell, had a tannery and shoe factory. She married and went out to Iowa as a pioneer wife, but her husband died in a few years and she returned to Waterville. She was nearly forty when she began painting. Her first instructor was JAMES R. BREVOORT of NYC and she also studied for several years in France and Holland. She began exhibiting at the National Academy in 1875 and was made an Associate Member in 1910. She died in a rest home in Yonkers (N.Y.) on November 11, 1924. ¶ *Art News,* Nov. 15 and Nov. 22, 1924; Cowdrey, NAD; NYCD 1875–76; Graves, *Dictionary;* Clement and Hutton; Champlyn and Perkins; Thieme-Becker; Ness and Orwig, *Iowa Artists,* 48.

COMEGYS, GEORGE H. Genre, portrait, and historical painter. Fielding states that Comegys was born in Maryland and died in the Pennsylvania Hospital for the Insane at Philadelphia. As a youth in Philadelphia in the 1830's he studied under JOHN NEAGLE, his earliest known work being dated 1836. Comegys was an exhibitor at the Artists' Fund Society from 1837 to 1841, at the Pennsylvania Academy from 1843 to 1852, at the National Academy in 1843, and at the Apollo Gallery and Association from 1838 to 1841. In 1845 he was a member of the board of the Artists' Fund Society. ¶ Fielding; *Panorama,* June–July 1946, 106–107, repros.; *Portfolio,* Oct. 1943, 33, repro.; Rutledge, PA; Cowdrey, NAD; Cowdrey, AA & AAU.

COMGMACKER [*sic*], AUGUST. Engraver; born *c.* 1825 in Germany; living in a Philadelphia boarding house in September 1850. ¶ 7 Census (1850), Pa., L, 898.

COMLY, ETHAN. A resident of Philadelphia in 1825; exhibited at the Pennsylvania Academy from 1824 to 1828 a drawing entitled "The Woodlands," which was described as "drawn in India ink whilst lying in bed." ¶ Rutledge, PA.

COMLY, THOMAS. Engraver; born *c.* 1826 in Pennsylvania; living in Philadelphia in 1850. He was the third son of Samuel (61) and Mary (52) Comly. The father was an auctioneer and the mother owned realty valued at $7,000. Thomas J. Comly was listed in the 1850 directory as a printer. ¶ 7 Census (1850), Pa., LIII, 716; Phila. CD 1850.

COMPTON & GIBSON, engravers, see JAMES H. COMPTON and C. H. GIBSON.

COMPTON, JAMES H. Engraver and lithographer, Buffalo (N.Y.), 1853–55. He was associated with Compton & Co. in 1853, with COMPTON & GIBSON in 1854, and with RICHARD J. COMPTON in 1855. ¶ Buffalo CD 1853–55.

COMPTON, RICHARD J. Engraver and lithographer at Buffalo (N.Y.) from 1851 to 1856, at St. Louis (Mo.) from 1859. In 1855 he was associated with JAMES H. COMPTON. By 1865 he had become a piano manufacturer. ¶ Buffalo CD 1851–56; St. Louis BD 1859; St. Louis CD 1865.

COMRI or CAMORE, ——. Lithographer; born in Ireland *c.* 1815; living with DANIEL BARRY in Boston in 1850. ¶ 7 Census (1850), Mass., XXV, 311.

COMSTOCK, JOHN C. Lithographer; lived in Hartford (Conn.) from 1847 to 1858. From 1848 to 1850 he was associated with the firm of KELLOGGS & COMSTOCK, of Hartford and NYC, but he later opened a law office in Hartford. ¶ Hartford CD 1847–58; NYCD 1850; Conn. Hist. Soc., *Cat. of Exhib. of Kellogg Prints* (1952).

COMSTOCK, SAMUEL S. Portrait painter, NYC, 1844–46; National Academy exhibitor. ¶ *The Gem* (NYBD), 1844, 1846; Cowdrey, NAD.

CONANT, A. A view of Newburyport from Salisbury (Mass.), drawn by A. Conant, was lithographed in color by LANE & SCOTT and published in Boston by A. Conant, *c.* 1846–48. ¶ Stokes, *Historical Prints.*

CONANT, ALBAN JASPER (1821–1915). Portrait painter and archaeologist; born in Chelsea (Vt.), September 24, 1821. Conant went to NYC in 1844 and shortly after settled at Troy (N.Y.), where he lived until 1857. In 1857 he moved to St. Louis (Mo.), where he became a founder of the Western Academy of Art. During the 1860's he visited Springfield (Ill.) and Washington (D.C.), painting portraits of leading statesmen, including Abraham Lincoln. After 1885 he lived in NYC, and he died there February 3, 1915. ¶ DAB, CAB; Fielding; Troy BD 1852, 1857; Cowdrey, NAD, 1886–87.

CONANT, EDWIN A. Portrait and miniature painter, Boston, 1838–46. ¶ Boston CD 1838–45; BD 1841–42, 1844, 1846.

CONANT, MARIA. Portrait painter and teacher, Cambridge (N.Y.), 1843. ¶ *American Provincial Painting,* no. 54.

CONARROE, GEORGE W. (1803–1882 or 1884). Portrait and genre painter; born in Delaware, 1803; died in Philadelphia, 1882 (Smith) or 1884 (Mallett). In 1829 Conarroe was a resident of Salem (N.J.), but from 1831 until his death he appears to have made his home in Philadelphia. In 1850 he was living there with his wife Charlotte (age 46, born in New Jersey) and their three children—George (18), Maria (15), and Ellen (11); he owned realty valued at $25,000. Conarroe was a frequent exhibitor at the Artists' Fund Society and the Pennsylvania Academy, and also exhibited at the Boston Athenaeum, the Apollo Gallery, the Maryland Historical Society, and the Washington Art Association. ¶ Mallett; Smith; Rutledge, PA; 7 Census (1850), Pa., LI, 817; Swan, BA; Cowdrey, AA & AAU; Rutledge, MHS; Washington Art Assoc. Cat., 1859; Stauffer, no. 2101; *Portraits in Delaware 1700–1850,* 149.

CONCANNON, THOMAS. Lithographer and printer; born in Ireland *c.* 1841; living in Philadelphia in 1860. ¶ 8 Census (1860), Pa., LII, 289 (as lithographer); Phila. CD 1861 (as printer).

CONCKLIN, JEREMIAH. English wood engraver, 16, at NYC in 1850. ¶ 7 Census (1850), N.Y., LII, 131.

CONDON, JAMES. Engraver, 21, a native of New York State, at NYC in 1850. ¶ 7 Census (1850), N.Y., L, 723.

CONDON, WILLIAM. Artist, 17, a native of New York State, at NYC in 1850. ¶ 7 Census (1850), N.Y., L, 799.

CONE, GEORGE M. English engraver, 35, at NYC in 1850. ¶ 7 Census (1850), N.Y., XLI, 709.

CONE, JOSEPH. Engraver in line and stipple. After working in Philadelphia from 1814 to 1824, Cone apparently moved to Baltimore, where during the next few years he prepared the plates for two drawing books: *Progressive Drawing Book* (Baltimore, 1827–28) and *Practical Perspective* (Baltimore, *c.* 1827). ¶ Stauffer; Dreppred, "Rare American Prints," repro.

CONELY, WILLIAM B. (1830–1911). Portrait painter; born in NYC, December 15, 1830; died in Detroit (Mich.), October 12, 1911. Exhibited, National Academy, 1882–88. ¶ Burroughs, "Painting and Sculpture in Michigan"; Cowdrey, NAD.

CONEY (Cony or Conny), JOHN (1655–1722). Engraver, gold- and silversmith; born in Boston, 1655; died there, 1722. Besides his engraving on gold and silver, Coney engraved bills of credit for the Province of Massachusetts in 1703. ¶ Stauffer; Fielding; Toppan, *100 Years of Bank Note Engraving,* 4–5; *Yale Associates Bulletin,* XVI (July 1948), repro.

CONGDON, SAMUEL B. Engraver and die sinker, Worcester (Mass.), 1851–60. ¶ New England BD 1856, 1860; Worcester CD 1851, 1853–54, 1857–60.

CONKEY, SAMUEL (1830–1904). Sculptor and landscape painter; born in NYC, 1830; died in Brooklyn, December 2, 1904. Conkey lived for a time in Chicago, but returned to the East after the loss of his property in the Chicago Fire of 1871. He exhibited at the National Academy, 1867–90. ¶ *Art Annual,* V; Smith; Thieme-Becker; Cowdrey, NAD.

CONKLIN, G. P. Engraver, Detroit (Mich.), 1855–60; born in New York *c.* 1830. ¶ Detroit BD 1855; 8 Census (1860), Mich., XX, 441.

CONLIN, JOHN S. Lithographer, 29, at NYC

in 1860. He, his wife, and two children (8 and 7) were born in Ireland; two younger children (4 and 2) were born in New York. ¶ 8 Census (1860), N.Y., XLVI, 929.

CONN, JAMES. Engraver and writing master, Elizabethtown (N.J.), 1771. ¶ Fielding.

CONNAROE, see CONARROE.

CONNELY, PIERCE FRANCIS (*c.* 1840–?). Sculptor and landscape painter, born in the American South, but brought up in England. He studied art in Paris and Rome and took a studio as a sculptor in Rome about 1860. He visited the U.S. in 1876 and then went to New Zealand where he became a well-known mountain climber and landscape painter. ¶ CAB; Gardner, *Yankee Stonecutters,* 74; Rutledge, PA.

CONNELLY, WILLIAM. Lithographer; born in Ireland *c.* 1839; living in Boston in 1860. ¶ 8 Census (1860), Mass., XXVII, 345.

CONNER, DENNIS M. Irish artist, 32, at NYC in 1850. *Cf.* DENNIS MALONE CARTER. ¶ 7 Census (1850), N.Y., XLIII, 294.

CONNER, JAMES L. Portrait and landscape painter. Born at Northfield (N.H.), Conner was working in Lynn (Mass.) in 1849. By 1858 he was living in Brooklyn (N.Y.); he exhibited at the National Academy in 1858 and 1869. In 1859 he was at Taunton (Mass.). ¶ Belknap, *Artists and Craftsmen;* Cowdrey, NAD; Taunton CD 1859.

CONNER (Connor), RICHARD. Engraver, St. Louis (Mo.), 1854–59. In 1859 he was probably the senior partner in CONNOR & HUSSEY. ¶ St. Louis CD 1854, BD 1859.

CONNER, ROBERT. Artist and designer, working at Salem (Mass.) in 1846, and at Cincinnati (Ohio) from 1853 to 1858 (in 1857–58 at the "Academy of Design"). ¶ Belknap, *Artists and Craftsmen;* Cincinnati BD 1853, CD 1857–58.

CONNOR & HUSSEY, engravers, see RICHARD CONNER and E. C. HUSSEY.

CONNORS, THOMAS. Lithographer; born in Ireland *c.* 1836; boarding in Boston in 1860 in the household of THOMAS J. BULGER. ¶ 8 Census (1860), Mass., XXVII, 271.

CONNY, see CONEY.

CONOVER, ——. Assistant to the panoramist, BENGOUGH, in the painting of a panorama of Broadway which was shown in NYC in 1848. ¶ Odell, *Annals,* V, 469 (cited by J. E. Arrington).

CONOVER, HENRY. Subject, not artist as has been stated, of a pastel portrait drawn at Freehold (N.J.) in 1819. The artist was —— WILLIAMS. ¶ Cortelyou, "Henry Conover: Sitter, Not Artist."

CONRAD, AUGUSTUS. Engraver; born in Brunswick (Germany) *c.* 1842; living in Philadelphia in 1860. ¶ 8 Census (1860), Pa., LVI, 885.

CONRAD, P. Wood engraver, Philadelphia, 1854. ¶ Penna. BD 1854/55.

CONRAD, TIMOTHY A. Naturalist-artist, lithographer. He did the illustrations for "The Geology and Organic Remains of a Part of the Peninsula of Maryland," in the *Journal* of the Academy of Natural Sciences, May 20 and June 15, 1830. ¶ Eckhardt, "Early Lithography in Phila.," 249–50.

CONRADT, CHARLES. Engraver and chaser, Philadelphia, 1860. ¶ Phila. CD 1860.

CONROW, J. Portrait painter, Providence (R.I.), 1849. ¶ New England BD 1849.

CONROY, J. Exhibitor, with W. CUINER, of a "Bust of Washington" at the American Institute in 1845. This may have been John Conroy, brassfounder of NYC. ¶ Am. Inst. Cat., 1845; NYCD 1845.

CONVERSE, JESSE. Painter of portraits of William Myrick and wife, now owned by the Sheldon Museum, Middlebury (Vt.). ¶ WPA (Mass.), *Portraits Found in Vt.*

CONY, see CONEY.

COOK, ——. Portrait painter at Montgomery (Ala.) in 1860. ¶ WPA (Ala.), Hist. Records Survey cites *Montgomery Daily Mail,* April 12, 1860.

COOK, CHARLES. Lithographer and engraver, Boston, 1843–54. Cook was born in Massachusetts *c.* 1810; his wife Lena in Maine *c.* 1822; and their son Willy in Massachusetts *c.* 1849. Cook's work appeared in C. T. Jackson's *Scenery and Geology of New Hampshire.* ¶ Boston BD 1844–54; 7 Census (1850), Mass., XXIV, 451; Jackson, *op. cit.*

COOK, CLARENCE CHATHAM (1828–1900). Artist and art critic; born in Dorchester (Mass.), September 8, 1828; died in Fishkill (N.Y.), June 1 or 2, 1900. After graduation from Harvard in 1849, Cook studied architecture in Newburgh (N.Y.), but soon gave it up to become a teacher and journalist. From about 1863 he was a leading art critic, working for some years on the N. Y. *Tribune,* and later as editor of *The Studio.* His *Art and Artists of Our Time* was published in 1888. ¶ DAB; *Art Annual,* II.

COOK, G. W. E. Winner of a prize for pencil drawing at the Illinois State Fair in 1855. His home was at Lacon, Marshall County (Ill.). ¶ Chicago *Daily Press,* Oct. 15, 1855.

COOK, GEORGE. Engraver; born in England *c.* 1825; living in Philadelphia in 1850. ¶ 7 Census (1850), Pa., LII, 406.

COOK, GEORGE, see GEORGE COOKE.

COOK, J. M. Portrait painter, Boston, 1846. ¶ Boston BD 1846.

COOK, JANE A. Amateur artist, NYC, 1842–56. She exhibited specimens of drawing and rice painting at the American Institute in 1842, 1845, 1846, 1849, and 1856. She was probably a daughter of SARAH A. COOK. ¶ Am. Inst. Cat., 1842, 1845, 1846, 1849, 1856.

COOK, JOHN. Enameller and engraver, NYC, 1794–96. ¶ NYCD 1794–96 (cited by McKay).

COOK, MEHITABEL JONES (1809–?). Portrait painter and teacher working at Fryeburg (Maine) *c.* 1836. ¶ WPA (Mass.), *Portraits Found in Maine,* no. 50.

COOK, NELSON (1817–1892). Portrait painter; working at Saratoga Springs (N.Y.) from 1841 to 1844, at Rochester (N.Y.) in 1852 and 1856, and again at Saratoga Springs from 1857 to 1859. The *Boston Transcript* obituary, July 29, 1892, called him a well-known artist, poet, and portrait painter. He exhibited at the National Academy. ¶ *Boston Transcript,* July 29, 1892, obit.; Jackson, *Ancestors in Silhouette,* 199; Cowdrey, NAD; N. Y. State BD 1859.

COOK (Cooke), ROBERT. Portrait painter and lithographic draftsman. During the 1830's he was chief draftsman at MOORE's lithographic establishment in Boston. A few years before 1841 he went into business as a portrait painter with his former pupil, BENJAMIN CHAMPNEY, and in 1841 he and Champney visited Europe together. ¶ DAB (under Champney); Boston BD 1841.

COOK, Mrs. SARAH A. Amateur artist, NYC, 1840's. A widow, Mrs. Cook ran a boarding house in NYC, and she exhibited at the American Institute in 1846 and 1848. Miss JANE A. COOK, probably her daughter, also exhibited at the Institute. ¶ Am. Inst. Cat., 1846, 1848; NYCD 1840's.

COOK, T. B. Stipple engraver for NYC publishers, active from 1809 to 1816. ¶ Stauffer, I, 55; Fielding; Thieme-Becker.

COOK, VICTOR. Portrait painter, Kingston (N.Y.), 1859. ¶ N. Y. State BD 1859.

COOK, WESLEY. Artist, 35, a native of New York State, at NYC in 1850. ¶ 7 Census (1850), N.Y., XLVI, 139.

COOK, WILLIAM (Reverend "Willy") (1807–?). Amateur artist and wood engraver. Cook was a well-educated, eccentric "character" of Salem (Mass.), born March 7, 1807, and still active in 1876. His paintings, though usually of religious subjects, also included landscapes and portraits, which he exhibited in his own home. He also made wood-cuts to illustrate his numerous pamphlets. ¶ Jenkins, "William Cook of Salem, Mass."; Hamilton, 184–185.

COOKE & COMPANY. Miniature painters and jewelers from London who advertised at Philadelphia and in Maryland in 1784. ¶ Prime, I, 2.

COOKE (Cook), GEORGE (1793–1849). A.N.A. Portrait, historical, and landscape painter; author; born in St. Mary's County (Md.), March 17, 1793; died in New Orleans (La.), March 26, 1849. Chronology: 1810, merchant in native county; 1812, in grocery and china business, Georgetown (D.C.); 1816, March 26, married Maria (baptized Mary Ann), daughter of John Heath (1761–1810) of Richmond (Va.); 1818, failed in business and went west; 1819–20, began painting professionally; painted 130 portraits in 28 months before 1825; 1824–26, in Richmond (Va.); July 1826–August 1831, study in Italy and France; 1833, in the Catskills (N.Y.), New York City, Washington (D.C.), and probably Richmond (Va.); 1834, Washington and New York City; 1836, January–March, advertised in Charleston (S.C.); 1837 and 1839, in Washington; 1840, Habersham County, Dahlonega, and Athens (Ga.); 1841–42, New Orleans, Athens, Augusta, and Columbus (Ga.); 1843, autumn, Pittsburgh (Pa.); 1844, Memphis (Tenn.) and Athens (Ga.); 1845–47, New Orleans; June 1848, Pittsburgh; July 1848, Washington; 1849, Athens (Ga.) and New Orleans. He was buried in Prattville (Ala.), where his patron Daniel Pratt had built a gallery to display Cooke's paintings. Cooke exhibited at the Boston Athenaeum, National Academy, Pennsylvania Academy, American Academy, Apollo Gallery and Association, and at Richmond (Va.). ¶ "Descriptive Catalogue of Paintings . . . with a Memoir of George Cooke," 1853; George Cooke MSS owned by Dr. J. Hall Pleasants, Baltimore; George Cooke MSS owned by Valentine Museum, Richmond, including extracts from letters by Cooke published in part in *Richmond Standard,* Oct. 1 and 8, 1881; Dunlap, *History,* II, 346–47; Am. Acad. Cat., 1833, as Cook; Stokes, *Historical Prints;* Rutledge, *Artists in the Life of Charleston,* lists five works [use of middle initial E. found only in this source]; *New York As It Is* (1834); NAD Cat., 1833–34; G[eorge] C[ooke]. "Sketches of Georgia," *Southern Literary Messenger,* VI (1840), 775–77; New Orleans CD 1846; PA Cat., 1849; BA Cat., 1835; Swan, BA, 215; Am. Art-Union *Trans.,* 1839. Stauffer lists five engravings; *American Collector,* XVI (Jan. 1948), 8, two repros.; other repros. in William Burke, *Mineral Springs of Western Virginia; Richmond Portraits;* Alexander Brown, *The Cabells and Their Kin,* 340, 388; *Emory University Quarterly,* Dec. 1946; Valentine, *Dawn to Twilight.* Cooke's oil, "A View of Athens, Georgia," painted about 1845, is owned by the University of Georgia and is repro. in *American Processional,* 242. Cooke's view of West Point in *Connoisseur,* Sept. 1944, 47, is erroneously attributed in *Art Index* (Oct. 1944–Sept. 1945) to the English engraver George Cooke (1781–1834).

COOKE, RICHARD CLARKE. Painter and limner, NYC, 1744. ¶ NYHS *Collections,* XVIII (1885), 150.

COOKINS, JAMES, see JAMES F. GOOKINS.

COOMB, WILLIAM. Artist in Philadelphia, 1850. Coomb, age 38, was a native of England, while his wife Rosanna (30) and their two children (2 and 4) were all born in Pennsylvania. ¶ 7 Census (1850), Pa., LIV, 781.

COON, DANIEL M. Artist, living in Buffalo (N.Y.), 1858–59. ¶ Buffalo CD 1858–59.

COON, FREDERICK. German engraver, 44, at NYC in 1860 with his wife and one son. ¶ 8 Census (1860), N.Y., L, 471.

COON, S. Portrait painter, Oswego (N.Y.), 1859. ¶ Oswego CD 1859; N.Y. State BD 1859.

COOPER, B. S. Transparency painter, NYC; exhibited india ink drawing at the American Institute in 1844. William Cooper, at the same address, exhibited engravings at the same time. ¶ Am. Inst. Cat., 1844; NYCD 1843 (STANFIELD & COOPER).

COOPER, CASPER. Artist; born in New Jersey *c.* 1837; living in Philadelphia in 1860. ¶ 8 Census (1860), Pa., LIII, 165.

COOPER, CORNELIUS V. (or C. Cooper). Portrait painter, NYC, 1813–19. A portrait by "C. Cooper" of a Catskill (N.Y.) innkeeper, painted *c.* 1815, is thought to have been the work of this artist. C. Cooper of NYC also exhibited a portrait at the American Academy in 1817. ¶ NYCD 1813–19; *Panorama,* II (March 1947), 79, repro.; Cowdrey, AA & AAU.

COOPER, DAVID M. Engraver, 43, a native of New York State, at NYC in 1860. His wife Georgiana and their three children were also born in New York. ¶ 8 Census (1860), N.Y., LVII, 783.

COOPER, GEORGE VICTOR (1810–1878). Portrait and landscape painter, lithographer, cameo cutter and sculptor; born in Hanover (N.J.), January 12, 1810; died in NYC, November 12, 1878. G. V. Cooper was working in NYC as early as 1835–36, and was probably the same as "C. V. Cooper" who exhibited portraits at the Apollo Association and the National Academy in 1839. He continued to work in NYC until 1849, when he left for California. He apparently worked with J. M. Lett, for whose *California Illustrated* (N.Y., 1853) Cooper provided all the illustrations. Cooper was back in NYC again by 1851 and worked there until his death. In 1865 he painted a portrait of Abraham Lincoln. ¶ Peters, *Calif. on Stone;* NYCD 1835–36, 1838–39 (as C. V. Cooper), 1841, 1847–48, 1851–53; Cowdrey, AA & AAU; Cowdrey, NAD; Stokes, *Hist. Prints,* pl. 77a; Am. Inst. Cat., 1847; Wilson, *Lincoln in Portraiture.*

COOPER, J. (*c.* 1695–living 1754?). Portrait painter. Although many of his works have been found in America and he has sometimes been called an American artist, all the available evidence indicates that this artist worked only in England. ¶ George C. Groce, "Who Was J[ohn?] Cooper."

COOPER, JAMES. Miniaturist, Philadelphia, 1855, exhibitor at the Pennsylvania Academy. ¶ Bolton, *Miniature Painters;* Fielding; Rutledge, PA.

COOPER, JAMES GRAHAM (1830–1902). Naturalist and illustrator; born in NYC, June 19, 1830; died in Hayward, Cal., July 19, 1902. After graduation from the College of Physicians and Surgeons in NYC and two years of medical practice, Cooper joined the 1853–55 Survey of the route for the western railway. It was during this period that he painted the view of Mt. Rainier which has been reproduced. Cooper settled in California and became prominent as an ornithologist and zoologist. ¶ DAB; *U. S. Exploring Expeditions,* XII; Taft, *Artists and Illustrators of the Old West,* 256–57.

COOPER, JOHN. Engraver, Philadelphia, 1850. Cooper (31), his wife (22) and their daughter (3) were all natives of Philadelphia. ¶ 7 Census (1850), Pa., LI, 376; Phila. CD 1851.

COOPER, NATHANIEL M. Engraver, 23, a native of New York State, at NYC in 1850. He was the son of William Cooper, printer. ¶ 7 Census (1850), N.Y., LI, 224.

COOPER, PEREGRINE F. (Pere, Pierre or P. F. Cooper). Portrait and animal painter, miniaturist, and pastel portraitist, who worked in Philadelphia from 1840 to 1890. In 1863 he published *The Art of Making and Coloring Ivory Types, Photographs, Talbotypes and Miniature Painting on Ivory.* He exhibited at the Pennsylvania Academy in 1849–50, 1856. ¶ Bolton, *Crayon Draftsmen;* Phila. CD 1843–48, 1850, 1852–58, 1860 and after; Rutledge, PA.

COOPER, PETER. Painter of a view of Philadelphia from the south-east, about 1720. He was admitted a freeman of Philadelphia in May 1717. ¶ Scharff and Westcott, *History of Phila.,* 1029; *American Processional,* 45, repro.

COOPER, WASHINGTON BOGART (1802–1889). Portrait painter; born near Jonesboro (Tenn.) in 1802; died in Nashville (Tenn.), April 19, 1889. He worked in Memphis, Chattanooga, and Knoxville (Tenn.), and made at least one painting tour down the Mississippi to Natchez (Miss.) and New Orleans. His younger brother, WILLIAM BROWN COOPER, was also a portrait painter, and since both often signed their work "W. B. Cooper" and were so listed in directories, it is difficult to distinguish between them. ¶ WPA (Ala.), Hist. Records Survey, quotes Mrs. John Trotwood Moore, State Archivist, Nashville (Tenn.); Delgado-WPA, cites New Orleans *Picayune,* Jan. 9, 1839. The "Cooper" mentioned in the *Arkansas Gazette* of May 5, 1935, as a portrait painter from Louisville (Ky.) may have been one of the Cooper brothers (WPA, Ark. Hist. Records Survey).

COOPER, WILLIAM BROWN (1811–1900). Portrait painter; born in Smith County (Tenn.); died in Chattanooga (Tenn.). He worked with his elder brother, WASHINGTON BOGART COOPER, in Memphis, Chattanooga, and Knoxville (Tenn.), Natchez (Miss.), and New Orleans (La.). In 1860 he was working in Nashville, where he was the teacher of WILLIAM D. MURPHY. Since both brothers signed their work "W. B. Cooper," it is difficult to distinguish between them. ¶ WPA (Ala.), Hist. Records Survey, quotes Mrs. John Trotwood Moore, State Archivist, Nashville (Tenn.); Fairman, *Art and Artists,* 460; Nashville CD 1860 (as W. B. Cooper).

COPE, THOMAS. Artist, Philadelphia, 1850. Cope (45), his wife Mary (34), and their four children (1 to 10) were all natives of Pennsylvania. ¶ 7 Census (1850), Pa., LIV, 961.

COPELAND, Mr. ——. Portrait painter, exhibited his painting of the death of John Wesley at Richmond (Va.) in 1850. ¶ *Richmond Portraits,* 241; information courtesy Mrs. Ralph Catterall.

COPELAND, ALFRED BRYANT (1840–1909). Landscape painter; born in Boston in 1840; died there, January 30, 1909. Copeland studied at Antwerp (Belgium), served as professor of art at the University of St. Louis (Mo.), and in 1877 opened a studio in Paris. ¶ *Art Annual,* VIII; CAB; Clement and Hutton.

COPESTICK, ALFRED. Landscape painter, NYC, 1858. In 1859 he exhibited "Headwaters of the Juniata" (Pa.) at the National Academy. ¶ NYBD 1858; Cowdrey, NAD.

COPLEY, CHARLES. Engraver and map publisher, NYC, 1847–51. In 1848 he exhibited an engraved map of the world at the American Institute. ¶ NYCD 1847–48; NYBD 1851; Am. Inst. Cat., 1848.

COPLEY, FREDERICK S. Portrait, genre, and landscape painter, Brooklyn (N.Y.); exhibited at the National Academy 1855–70. ¶ Cowdrey, NAD.

COPLEY, JOHN SINGLETON (1738–1815). Portrait and historical painter; born in or near Boston, July 3, 1738; died in London, September 9, 1815. Copley spent the early part of his life in Boston and began painting there as early as 1753. He made painting trips to Philadelphia and NYC in 1771–72. In 1774 he left for Europe, settling the following year in London, where he remained for the rest of his life. He was elected an Associate of the Royal Academy in 1776 and a full Member in 1783. PETER PELHAM was his stepfather and HENRY PELHAM, his half-brother. ¶ The standard studies are Flexner's *John Singleton Copley* (1948) and Parker and Wheeler's *John Singleton Copley: American Portraits* (1938). See also, Copley, *Letters.*

COPMANN, P. (Pierce or Peter). Danish or North German portrait and landscape painter in oils and pastels. After working and exhibiting at Copenhagen in 1832, Copmann came to America and was at Brooklyn (N.Y.) when he exhibited at the National Academy (as Pierce Chopmann) in 1834, but later the same year he turned up in Charleston (S.C.), where he seems to have remained at least until July 1835. Later mention of him indicates that he was working in New Orleans in 1837 and in Louisville (Ky.) in 1848. He was also the inventor of a fixative for pastel pictures. ¶ Rutledge, *Artists in the Life of Charleston,* 154, 177; Cowdrey, NAD; New Orleans CD 1837 (cited by Delgado-WPA); Louisville CD 1848; Charleston (S.C.) CD 1835.

COPPER, JOHN C. Engraver, Philadelphia, 1839–60. In 1850 Copper (34, born Pennsylvania), his wife Mary F. (born New Jersey), and their son Noris (6) were living in Spring Garden Ward, Philadelphia. ¶ 7 Census (1850), Pa., LIV, 787; Phila. CD 1839–60.

COQUARDON, A. Painter of a view of the procession celebrating the admission of California to the Union in 1850 and a view of Weaverville (Cal.), lithographed by BRITTON & REY before 1856. ¶ Peters, *Calif. on Stone; Portfolio,* VIII (Nov. 1948), 57, repro.

CORADI, L. Artist, New Orleans, 1850. Coradi (37), his wife (40), and two children were born in France. They lived in the same house as C. and E. BERTON. ¶ 7 Census (1850), La., V, 227.

CORAM, THOMAS (1757–1811). Portrait and landscape painter, engraver; born in Bristol (England), April 25, 1757; died in Charleston (S.C.), May 2, 1811. Coram came to Charleston in 1769 and worked there presumably until his death. He took up engraving after 1770 and engraved bills of credit for the State of South Carolina during the Revolution. In 1784 he advertised as a drawing master. ¶ Pringle, "Thomas Coram's Bible"; Rutledge, *Artists in the Life of Charleston;* Middleton, "Thomas Coram, Engraver and Painter," repros.; Prime, I, 2, 17–18; Wilson, "Art and Artists of Provincial S.C."; Stauffer. Erroneously listed as Thomas Goram (1756–1810) in Neuhaus, *History and Ideals of American Art,* 14.

CORBETT, GEORGE. Portrait, historical, and landscape engraver, NYC, 1851–60. ¶ NYBD 1851, 1852, 1856, 1858, 1860.

CORBETT, THOMAS H. Engraver, NYC, 1856, 1859. ¶ NYBD 1856, 1859.

CORBIN, ——. Amateur carver, Centerville (Ind.), who carved a statue of Henry Ward Beecher about 1850, when Beecher visited Corbin's farm. ¶ Lipman, *American Folk Art,* 178, repro. 183.

CORDANO, ——, see GARIBALDI & CORDANO.

CORDELL, L. C. (1808–1870). A physician in Jefferson County (W. Va.) who painted landscapes and portraits. ¶ Willis, "Jefferson County Portraits."

CORDERO or CARDERO, JOSÉ. Artist with the Galiano-Valdés expedition to California in 1792. His sketch of the Mission of San Carlos at Carmel is now in the Museo Naval, Madrid, as is a sketch of the Presidio of Monterey which has been attributed both to Cordero and to TOMAS SURIA. ¶ Van Nostrand and Coulter, *California Pictorial,* 6; *Antiques* (Nov. 1953), 371.

CORDES, H. T. A. Artist, Hartford (Conn.), 1860. ¶ Hartford CD 1860.

CORKERY, DANIEL. Irish lithographer, 50, at NYC in 1860. His sons, Daniel, Jr. (20) and Michael (22), both born in Ireland, were also lithographers. ¶ 8 Census (1860), N.Y., XLII, 780.

CORLIES, BENJAMIN F. Engraver and lithographer, NYC, 1859. ¶ NYBD 1859.

CORNÉ, MICHEL FELICE (*c.* 1752–1845). Marine, landscape, portrait, panorama, and mural painter; born on the island of Elba (Italy), probably in 1752. He was brought to America in 1799 by the Salem merchant Elias Hasket Derby, Jr., and worked in Salem until 1806, occasionally in association with SAMUEL MCINTIRE and WILLIAM KING. From 1807 to 1822 he lived in Boston, where he became particularly noted for his paintings of ships and naval battles of the War of 1812, many of which were engraved for ABEL BOWEN'S *The Naval Monument* (1816). After 1822 Corné made his home in Newport (R.I.), where some fine examples of his wall paintings are preserved in the Sullivan Dorr house. He died in Newport on July 10, 1845, at the age of 93. Among his pupils were GEORGE ROPES, HANNAH CROWNINSHIELD, and ANSTIS STONE. Corné is also remembered for introducing the tomato to the American table. ¶ Dates of birth and death from Corné's tombstone in Newport (courtesy Mrs. Katharine McCook Knox, Washington, D.C.); Nerney, "An Italian Painter Comes to Rhode Island"; Knox, "A Note on Michel Felice Corné"; Swan and Kerr, "Early Marine Painters of Salem"; Bentley, *Diary;* Mason, *Reminiscences of Newport;* Allen, *Early American Wall Painting;* Little, *American Decorative Wall Painting;* Robinson and Dow, *Sailing Ships of New England,* Vol. I.

CORNELL, JAMES E. Of HYATT & CORNELL, engravers, NYC, 1851. ¶ NYBD and NYCD 1851.

CORNELL, JOHN V. Landscape painter, NYC, 1838–49. In 1838 he painted a view of the Hudson River Highlands from Newburgh (N.Y.), now owned by the New-York Historical Society. He was listed in NYC directories from 1843 to 1847, and exhibited at the National Academy in 1844 and American Institute in 1844, 1845 and 1847. He was GEORGE HEISTER's assistant in the painting of a Hudson River panorama, shown in NYC in December 1849. ¶ NYHS files; NYCD 1843–47; Cowdrey, NAD; Am. Inst. Cats.; N. Y. *Herald,* Dec. 12, 1849 (cited by J. E. Arrington).

CORNER & MCKONKEY. Decorative and scene painters, Charleston (S.C.), 1849. ¶ Rutledge, *Artists in the Life of Charleston.*

CORNISH, CHARLES L. Amateur artist; bookseller and publisher in NYC during the 1850's. In 1856 he exhibited 13 oil paintings at the American Institute. ¶ NYCD 1850–56; Am. Inst. Cat., 1856.

CORNISH, JOHN. An English portrait painter who painted the American, Charles Paxton (1707/08–1788), in England in 1751. Listed here only because he has several times been recorded as an American artist. ¶ Weis, *Am. Antiq. Soc. Cat.;* Dunlap, *History* (1918), III, 293; Mallett; Fielding.

CORRA, FRANCIS. Italian decorative and scene painter in oils and fresco, who went into exile in 1848, settling first at Savannah (Ga.) and in 1854 at Charleston (S.C.). ¶ Rutledge, *Artists in the Life of Charleston.*

CORRADI, NESTOR (Nester or Nestore). Portrait and miniature painter, working at New Orleans in 1837, at NYC 1854–60. ¶ New Orleans *Bee,* Aug. 31, 1837 (cited by Delgado-WPA); NYCD 1854, 1857–60; NYBD 1854, 1856.

CORRISE, JEAN. Lithographer; born in France *c.* 1834; living in San Francisco in 1860. ¶ 8 Census (1860), Calif., VII, 724.

CORSON, RUFUS C. (T.). Engraver; born in Ireland *c.* 1826; living in Frankford Borough, Philadelphia County (Pa.) in 1850. ¶ 7 Census (1850), Pa., LVI, 229.

CORTWRIGHT, J. D. Portrait painter, possibly at Lowell (Mass.) in 1838. ¶ *American Provincial Painting,* no. 40.

CORWINE, AARON H. (1802–1830). Portrait painter, born August 31, 1802, near Maysville (Ky.). At the age of fifteen he received some instruction from an itinerant artist named Turner (possibly J. T. TURNER) and in 1818, after a brief visit to Cincinnati, he went to Philadelphia to study for two years with THOMAS SULLY. From 1820 to 1829 he was a successful portrait painter in Cincinnati, his sitters including Jackson and Lafayette. In 1829 he went to England for further study and for his health, but he returned to America the following year and died in Philadelphia on the 4th of July. ¶ Dwight, "Aaron H. Corwine"; Clark, *Ohio Art and Artists,* 73; Cist, *Cincinnati in 1841,* 139; Rutledge, PA; Cowdrey, NAD.

COSGROVE, B. G. Artist of Fort Wayne (Ind.) before 1850. ¶ Peat, *Pioneer Painters of Indiana,* 228.

COSLER, WILLIAM. Engraver; born in Pennsylvania *c.* 1825; living in Philadelphia in 1850. ¶ 7 Census (1850), Pa., L, 494.

COSTAGNI, PHILIPPO (1839–1904). Painter in oils; born in Italy, 1839; worked in NYC, Philadelphia, Baltimore, and Washington; died in Maryland, April 15, 1904. ¶ *Art Annual,* V; Fielding.

COSTAR (or Coster), GEORGE. Lithographer; born in Pennsylvania *c.* 1839; living with his parents in Philadelphia in 1860. A George Coster, goldbeater, in the Philadelphia directory for 1871 may be the same man. ¶ 8 Census (1860), Pa., LIX, 427.

COSTELLO, JOSEPH G. Engraver; born in Pennsylvania *c.* 1836; boarding in Philadelphia in 1860. ¶ 8 Census (1860), Pa., LV, 700.

COSTELLO, MICHAEL. Engraver and die sinker, Philadelphia, 1860. ¶ Phila. CD 1860.

COSTELLO, WILLIAM. Spanish artist, 52, at NYC in 1860. By his Spanish wife he had three children of whom the eldest, aged 20, was born in Louisiana, and the younger, aged 13 and 11, in New York. ¶ 8 Census (1860), N.Y., XLVIII, 804.

COSTIGAN, DANIEL. Engraver, 45, a native of New York State, at NYC in 1860. ¶ 8 Census (1860), N.Y., LI, 273.

COTTERELL, WILLIAM. Engraver; born in Maryland *c.* 1835; living with his mother and three other children, all born in Maryland, in Philadelphia in 1850. ¶ 7 Census (1850), Pa., LI, 1.

COTTON, Lieut. J. S. Contributed 7 illustrations to *The New Tale of a Tub,* by F. W. M. Bayley (N.Y., 1854). ¶ Hamilton, *Early American Book Illustrators,* 188.

COTTU, Mr. ——. Miniaturist and profilist, Providence (R.I.), 1811. ¶ Carrick, *Shades of Our Ancestors,* 118.

COUGHLAN, JEREMIAH. Apprentice lithographer (age 19). A native of Massachusetts, Coughlan was living in Boston in 1860 with his family, of which William Coughlan (40), a native of Ireland, was the head. ¶ 8 Census (1860), Mass., XXVII, 265.

COUGHLAN, JEREMIAH A. Wood engraver, NYC. As an apprentice he exhibited at the American Institute in 1849. He was listed in the 1858/59 business directory. ¶ Am. Inst. Cat., 1849; NYBD 1858/59.

COULLON, JOHN. Seal engraver, Boston (Mass.), 1850. Coullon and his wife Mary, both aged 50, were natives of Ireland. ¶ 7 Census (1850), Mass., XXV, 509.

COULON, GEORGE DAVID (*c.* 1823–*c.* 1904). Portrait painter. Born in France about 1823, Coulon was working in New Orleans (La.) as early as 1846, and died there about 1904. ¶ 7 Census (1850), La., V, 555; New Orleans CD 1846, 1852–56; Cline, 38; Fielding.

COUNCE, HARVEY (1821–?). Figurehead carver; born in Thomaston (Maine), August 19, 1821. Counce was working as a cabinet maker and carver as early as 1840, but his known figureheads date from the 1860's and 1870's. He worked in Thomaston and Rockport (Maine) until the 1880's, and examples of his work are extant in Thomaston. ¶ Cyrus Eaton, *History of Thomaston, Rockland, and South Thomaston, Maine,* II, 188, gives his full name as Rufus Harvey Counce; Pinckney, 138–139, refers to Harvey P. Counce and R. H. Counce in the same context.

COURSEN, A. B. Portrait painter, NYC, 1812. ¶ NYBD 1812 (cited by McKay).

COURTAULD, Miss or Mrs. S. L. A drawing mistress who exhibited a still life at the Pennsylvania Academy in 1829. Possibly the Sarah Courtauld (Courfaule or Couteau), widow, listed in Philadelphia directories from 1829 to 1835. ¶ Rutledge, PA; Phila. CD 1829–35.

COURTENAY, T. E. Associate of LEON POMAREDE, panoramic painter, at St. Louis (Mo.) in the 1840's. In 1843 Pomarede and Courtenay advertised to do portrait, landscape, and scenic painting, as well as signs, transparencies, banners, and plain wall painting. ¶ McDermott, "Leon Pomarede," 10, 13.

COURTNEY, ROBERT. Engraver; born in London *c.* 1829. The birthplaces and dates of his children indicate that Courtney married in London before 1851, was in Ireland in 1854 and 1856, and in Washington (D.C.) by 1860. ¶ 8 Census (1860), D.C., II, 539.

COURVOISIER, HENRY. Engraver, NYC, 1852. ¶ NYBD 1852.

COUSLAND, WILLIAM. Bank note engraver; born in Pennsylvania *c.* 1825; working in Philadelphia 1847–60. Cousland was a member of the Philadelphia firm of BALD, COUSLAND & CO. from 1854 to 1860, and of its NYC branch BALDWIN, BALD & COUSLAND (later, Bald, Cousland & Co.) from 1855 to 1858. His household in 1860 included his wife Sarah A. (32), William (5), Mary M. (7), and Ann M. (3), all born in Pennsylvania; Cousland owned personal property valued at $1,000. ¶ 8 Census (1860), Pa., LIII, 526; Phila. CD 1847 (as Cousland & Co.), 1851, 1853–59.

COUSSIN, Mr. ——. Landscape painter and drawing master, Charleston (S.C.), 1801. ¶ Rutledge, *Artists in the Life of Charleston.*

COUTANT, W. H. Miniaturist, New Orleans, 1832. ¶ New Orleans *Courier,* Nov. 14, 1832 (cited by Delgado-WPA).

COUTHOUY, J. P. Artist-naturalist, who provided some of the illustrations in *Narrative of the U. S. Exploring Expedition* (5 vols., 1844). ¶ Rasmussen, "Artists of the Explorations Overland, 1840–1860," 58.

COUTURIER, HENDRICK (Cousturier, Coutourier, Coutrie, or Coettrier). Portrait painter and merchant of New Netherlands. So far as is known today Couturier was the first European-trained artist to practise in this country. Probably a native of Leyden (Holland), Couturier was married in Leyden in 1648 and studied there briefly at St. Luke's Guild art school the same year. In 1649 he moved to Amsterdam. By 1661, possibly earlier, Couturier had emigrated to America, settling at New Amstel on the Delaware River, where he was a trader and public official. He also spent much time in New Amsterdam itself and obtained the burgher right of the city by 1663 by painting a portrait of Governor Stuyvesant, and making drawings of his sons. He is said to have moved to England in 1674 and to have died there about ten years later. Although several portraits have been attributed to Couturier by Harris, including those of Peter and Nicholas William Stuyvesant and Cornelis Steenwyck (at the New-York Historical Society) and that of Jacobus G. Strycker (at the Metropolitan Museum of Art), none can be definitively assigned to his brush. ¶ Stokes, *Icon.*, IV, 225 (under date of June 12, 1663); Harris, "Henri Couturier"; *N. Y. Col. Docs.*, XI, 487, XII, 467; NYHS Cat. (1941), with views of the late William Sawitzky on the Couturier question; letter of E. P. Richardson to George C. Groce, Sept. 27, 1948, confirming Sawitzky's attribution of the two Stuyvesant portraits and that of Steenwyck to one hand, and suggesting that the Strycker portrait was also by the same artist.

COVERT, LEWIS B. Engraver, NYC, 1859. ¶ NYBD 1859.

COWAN, GEORGE. Engraver, NYC, 1859. ¶ NYBD 1859.

COWAN, ROBERT (?–1846). Ornamental painter from Scotland who settled in Salem (Mass.) before 1782 and worked there until his death in 1846. He painted chimney boards, carpets, sleighs, chairs, and ship decorations, including work on the Derby ship *Grand Turk.* ¶ Information courtesy Mrs. Nina Fletcher Little and Dr. Harold K. Bowditch, Brookline (Mass.).

COWELL, JOSEPH LEATHLEY (1792–1863). Actor, author and painter; born near Torquay (England), August 7, 1792; died in London, November 13, 1863. Cowell took up portrait painting after several years with the British Navy during the Napoleonic Wars, but gave it up for the stage in 1812, making his debut in NYC. Returning to England, he worked there until 1821 as an actor and scene-painter in London and the North Country. He returned in 1821 to America, where he remained almost until the end of his life. He was very successful in low comedy, and played at Charleston, Philadelphia, Wilmington, and Boston, as well as in NYC. In 1829, while in Boston, Cowell exhibited several English landscapes and marine views at the National Academy, as he had the year before at the Pennsylvania Academy. His autobiography, *Thirty Years of Theatrical Life,* appeared in 1844. One of his sons, Joseph, was a scene-painter, but died young. ¶ DNB; Cowdrey, NAD; Rutledge, PA.

COWELL, JOSEPH S. Landscape painter at St. Louis in 1839 and 1841, and in Alabama in 1842. Possibly JOSEPH L. COWELL or his son (see above). ¶ Information courtesy Edward H. Dwight, Cincinnati Art Museum.

COWELL, THOMAS J. Though primarily a copperplate printer, Cowell was also, in 1859–60, a partner in GAVIT & COWELL, banknote, wood, steel, and seal engravers and lithographers of Albany (N.Y.). ¶ Albany CD 1853–60.

COX, CHARLES HUDSON (1829–1901). Landscape painter, watercolorist. Born in Liverpool (England), January 28, 1829, Cox studied in England and was a member of the Liverpool Watercolor Society. He was a cotton broker by trade. He later moved to Waco (Texas), where he continued in the cotton business and became a director of the Waco Art League. He died in Waco, August 7, 1901. ¶ *Art Annual,* IV; Smith; Thieme-Becker; Bénézit.

COX, H. F. Delineator of a view of the Center Post Office of San Francisco in 1849. ¶ Stokes, *Hist. Prints,* pl. 76-b.

COX, JACOB (1810–1892). Portrait and landscape painter; born in Philadelphia, November 9, 1810; died in Indianapolis (Ind.), January 2, 1892. Jacob Cox came to Indianapolis from western Pennsylvania in 1833. A tinsmith by trade, he took up portrait painting about 1840, and except for a few professional visits to Cincinnati and NYC he devoted the rest of his life to painting in Indianapolis. He was a frequent exhibitor at the Cincinnati Art Union, but little known in the East. In 1853–54 he collaborated with HENRY WAUGH on a temporance panorama. Among his many pupils were JOSEPH O. EATON, JOHN HENRY NIEMEYER, and JAMES F. HARRIS. ¶ Burnet, *Art and Artists of Indiana,* 78–112, repros.; Peat, *Pioneer Painters of Indiana;* Indiana BD 1858; Indianapolis BD 1857, 1859–60.

COX, JAMES (1751–1834). Philadelphia drawing master; born in England; died in Philadelphia. He advertised in Philadelphia as early as 1790. His valuable collection of books on art was sold to the Library Company of Philadelphia before his death. ¶ CAB; Prime, II, 45–46; Brown and Brown.

COX, JAMES. Engraver; born in Pennsylvania *c.* 1838, the son of Henry Cox, chairmaker; living in Philadelphia in 1860. ¶ 8 Census (1860), Pa., LII, 984.

COX, ROBERT. English heraldic painter who was in NYC about 1818 when he gave lessons in painting to ROBERT W. WEIR. ¶ DAB, under Weir.

COX, THOMAS, JR. Wood engraver, NYC, 1850–60; born in New York about 1831. He was apparently the son of Thomas Cox, marble-cutter. The younger Cox was associated with the engraving firm of RICHARDSON & COX, who illustrated many books. ¶ NYCD 1853–54, 1857–60; 7 Census (1850), N.Y., XLVII, 536; Hamilton, *Early American Book Illustrators and Wood Engravers.*

COX, W. R. (1829–1873). Artist; born in Kentucky. ¶ Information courtesy Mrs. W. H. Whitley, Paris (Ky.) through Edward H. Dwight, Cincinnati Art Museum.

COY, WILLIAM. Engraver, 26, a native of New York State, at NYC in 1850. ¶ 7 Census (1850), N.Y., XLVIII, 45.

COYLE, JAMES (1798–1828). N.A. Theatrical scene painter; born in England; came to NYC in 1824; a founding Member of the National Academy in 1826; died in NYC [?] July 22, 1828. He was at the New York Theatre in 1824. ¶ Cummings, *Historic Annals,* 114; Dunlap, *History,* II, 470; N. Y. *Evening Post,* Sept. 1, 1824 (courtesy J. Earl Arrington).

CRAFT (Crafft), R. B. Indiana portrait painter. His works included portraits of the Miami chief, La Fountain, and a portrait of Robert Filson, painted at Fort Wayne in 1839. ¶ Burnet, *Art and Artists of Indiana,* 364; Peat, *Pioneer Painters of Indiana;* repro. in *Antiques,* LVIII (Nov. 1950), 383.

CRAFTS, FREDERICK, JR. Lithographer, age 15, living in Boston in 1850 with his father, who was master of the Bigelow School. Both were natives of Massachusetts. ¶ 7 Census (1850), Mass., XXV, 576.

CRAIG, ISAAC (or J.) EUGENE (1830–?). Portrait, religious, and historical painter, born near Pittsburgh (Pa.) in 1830. Craig's exhibition record at the Pennsylvania and National Academies shows that he was in Pittsburgh in 1848, in Europe [1853 to] 1855, Philadelphia 1856, Pittsburgh 1857–58, College of St. James (Md.) 1860, New Brighton (Pa.) 1861, and Pittsburgh 1864. Returning to Europe, he spent a year at Munich and then settled in Florence, where he was still working in 1878. ¶ Rutledge, PA; Cowdrey, NAD; Clement and Hutton; Smith.

CRAIG, SAMUEL. Engraver, age 23, working in Philadelphia in 1850. Craig lived with his mother Catherine Craig (41) and seven brothers and sisters (4 to 21); all were natives of Pennsylvania. ¶ 7 Census (1850), Pa., LIII, 275; Phila. CD 1850.

CRAIK, WILLIAM. Sculptor; born in Ireland *c.* 1829; working in Castleton (Vt.) in 1850. ¶ 7 Census (1850), Vt., IX, 363.

CRANCH, CHRISTOPHER PEARSE (1813–1892). N.A. Portrait, landscape, and still life painter; born in Alexandria (D.C.), March 8, 1813; died in Cambridge (Mass.), January 20, 1892; brother of JOHN CRANCH. After graduation from Harvard in 1831, C. P. Cranch went into the Unitarian ministry, during the following decade serving congregations in Maine, Richmond, Washington, St. Louis, Cincinnati, Louisville, and finally Boston. After 1840, however, he gave up the ministry for painting, and after a few years in NYC he left for Italy with his wife in 1846. They returned to NYC in 1849, but again left for Europe in 1853, this time spending ten years in Paris. From 1863 to 1873 Cranch lived on Staten Island (N.Y.), and from 1873 until his death his home was in Cambridge (Mass.) C. P. Cranch exhibited at the National Academy (of which he was a Member from 1864), the Boston Athenaeum, the Pennsylvania Academy, and the American Art-Union. ¶ Miller, *Christopher Pearse Cranch;* DAB; Barker, *American Painting,* 536, cites Donora Cranch Scott's *Life and Letters of C. P. Cranch;* Cowdrey, NAD; Rutledge, PA; Swan, BA, 26; Cowdrey, AA & AAU; Clement and Hutton; represented at the Corcoran Gallery.

CRANCH, JOHN (1807–1891). A.N.A. Portrait painter; born in Washington (D.C.), February 2, 1807; died in Urbana (Ohio), January 1, 1891; elder brother of CHRISTOPHER PEARSE CRANCH. John Cranch was in Italy from 1830 to 1834, worked in NYC in 1838–39, when he first exhibited at the National Academy (of which he later became an Associate), at Cincinnati from 1839 to 1844, in NYC again from 1848 to 1854, and from 1857 at least to 1878 in Washington (D.C.). He exhibited at the National Academy, the Apollo Association, the Boston Athenaeum, the American Art-Union, and the Washington Art Association. ¶ Bolton, *Crayon Draftsmen;* Cist, *Cincinnati in 1841,* 140; Clement and Hutton; Cowdrey, NAD; Cowdrey, AA & AAU; Swan, BA; Washington Art Assoc. Cat., 1857; Washington and Georgetown CD 1860.

CRANCH, JERE[MIAH]. Engraver; born in Pennsylvania *c.* 1821; working in Cincinnati in 1850. ¶ 7 Census (1850), Ohio, XX, 786.

CRANDALL, E. Monochromatic painter at Cleveland (Ohio) in August 1851. ¶ WPA (Ohio), *Annals of Cleveland.*

CRANE, W. T. Illustrator for *Frank Leslie's Weekly* during the Civil War. Possibly the same as William T. Crane, artist-designer, of Rahway (N.J.) in 1859. ¶ Taft, *Artists and Illustrators of the Old West,* 296; Essex, Hudson and Union Counties (N.J.) BD 1859.

CRANSTONE, LEFEVRE F. English artist who traveled in the United States in 1859–60, and made hundreds of ink and wash drawings of scenes in the East and Midwest, many of which are now owned by the Indiana Univ. Library, Indiana Hist. Soc., and Karolik Collection. ¶ Peat, *Pioneer Painters of Indiana,* 12–13.

CRAP, CHARLES F. Wood engraver, Philadelphia, 1850–60. Born in Pennsylvania *c.* 1828, the son of George Crap, tinworker, Charles F. Crap owned $400 in personal property in 1860, was married and had two children. In 1852 he had been in the engraving firm of MCCARTHY & CRAP. His younger brother, WILLIAM CRAP, also was an engraver. ¶ 7 Census (1850), Pa., LV, 403; 8 Census (1860), Pa., L, 595; Phila. CD 1850–60.

CRAP, WILLIAM. Engraver; born in Pennsylvania *c.* 1832; living in Southwark (Philadelphia County, Pa.) in 1850, with his father, George (tinworker), and brother, CHARLES F. (engraver). ¶ 7 Census (1850), Pa., LV, 403.

CRASKE, CHARLES. Engraver, NYC, 1850–58. In 1851 he and JOHN REYNOLDS exhibited jointly several specimens of a new process of seal engraving at the American Institute. ¶ NYBD 1850–51, 1854, 1856, 1858; NYCD 1852 (as Craske & Reynolds); Am. Inst. Cat., 1851.

CRASKE & REYNOLDS, engravers, see CHARLES CRASKE and JOHN REYNOLDS.

CRAWFORD, ALEXANDER (?–1809). House and sign painter, Charleston (S.C.) in 1788. He died at St. Mary's (S.C.) in February 1809. ¶ Rutledge, *Artists in the Life of Charleston.*

CRAWFORD, JOHN. Artist; born in Ohio *c.* 1838; working in Philadelphia in 1860. Exhibited "Girl and Dove" at Pennsylvania Academy, 1862. ¶ 8 Census (1860), Pa., LIV, 60; Rutledge, PA.

CRAWFORD, THOMAS (1814–1857). Sculptor; born in NYC, March 22, 1814; died in London, October 10, 1857. After serving his apprenticeship in NYC under FRAZEE and LAUNITZ, Crawford went to Italy in 1835 for further study with the great Danish sculptor, Thorwaldsen. He returned to NYC briefly in 1844 for his marriage, and again in 1849 and 1856. His reputation rivalled those of POWERS and GREENOUGH. Among his works are several at the U. S. Capitol in Washington, including the bronze figure of Liberty which surmounts the dome. ¶ Hillard, "Thomas Crawford, A Eulogy"; DAB, which cites evidence for Ireland as his birthplace and 1813 as the year of his birth; Cowdrey, NAD; Fairman, *Art and Atists of the Capitol;* Swan, BA; Lee, *Familiar Sketches,* 173–77; *Art Journal* (1857), 322; *Crayon* (1857), 380; Taft, *History of American Sculpture.*

CRAWLEY, JOHN (1784–?). Portrait painter. Born in England in 1784, Crawley spent his early years at Newark (N.J.). From 1811 to 1814 he worked in Philadelphia, where he was an exhibitor at the Society of Artists and the Pennsylvania Academy. He was in Pittsburgh in November 1814, at Charleston (S.C.) in January 1817, at Norfolk (Va.) in 1820 and 1838, and at Richmond (Va.) in January 1842. His son, JOHN, JR., was a lithographer. ¶ Fielding; Rutledge, PA; Anderson, "Intellectual Life of Pittsburgh: VIII, Painting," 288; Rutledge, *Artists in the Life of Charleston; Richmond Portraits;* Cowdrey, AA & AAU; Stauffer, and Fielding's *Supplement;* Dunlap, *History,* II, 233–34.

CRAWLEY, JOHN R., JR. Lithographer, working for ENDICOTT & SWETT at NYC, 1834. He was the son of the foregoing. ¶ Dunlap, *History,* II, 234; Peters, *America on Stone.*

CREBASSOL, PROSPER. Portrait painter, NYC, 1850–52; exhibitor, National Academy. ¶ Cowdrey, NAD; NYBD 1851–52.

CREED, WILLIAM. Engraver from London working at Baltimore in 1792. ¶ Prime, II, 68.

CREHEN, CHARLES G. (1829–?). Lithographer and portrait painter; born in Paris in 1829; still living in 1891. He came to America in 1848 and worked in NYC from 1848 to 1860, as well as in most of the major cities of the country. His original painting, "America," now owned by the New-York Historical Society, was engraved by Lafosse and published in 1850. Crehen exhibited at the American Institute in 1849 as C. G. Creker. ¶ Peters, *America on Stone;* NYCD 1848–63; Cowdrey and Williams, *W. S. Mount;* Am. Inst. Cat., 1849; 7 Census (1850), N.Y., XLII, 344; 8 Census (1860), N.Y., LI, 418.

CREHEN, E. Lithographer, working at Richmond (Va.) in 1860. He also executed 14 plates in 1861 for *Uniform and Dress of the Army of the Confederate States. Cf.* CHARLES G. and LEWIS E. CREHEN. ¶ Peters, *America on Stone;* Library of Congress Cat.

CREHEN, LEWIS E. Artist, 18, living in NYC in 1850 with CHARLES G. CREHEN. Both were natives of Paris. ¶ 7 Census (1850), N.Y., XLII, 344.

CREIFIELD, ——. Of MICHELIN & CREIFIELD, lithographers, NYC, 1844. ¶ Peters, *America on Stone,* under Michelin.

CREIGHTON, W. Portrait painter, NYC, 1838–40; exhibitor, National Academy. ¶ Cowdrey, NAD.

CREKER, see CREHEN.

CREPSON, LEONARD. Artist; born in France *c.* 1837; came to America between 1853 and 1858; living in Philadelphia in 1860. ¶ 8 Census (1860), Pa., LIV, 76.

CRESIND, see CRISAND.

CRESSY, JOSIAH PERKINS (1814–?). Amateur artist. Born in 1814, Cressy was a master mariner of Marblehead (Mass.). He was master of the clipper ship *Flying Cloud* on its record-breaking maiden voyage to San Francisco. He painted a view of Stockton (Cal.) in 1849. ¶ Van Nostrand and Coulter, *California Pictorial,* 86–87.

CRIDLAND, CHARLES E. Portrait painter. In March 1855 Charles E. Cridland, a "young artist of much promise," arrived in Cleveland (Ohio) from Cincinnati. This was presumably the artist listed in Cincinnati directories in 1852–53 and in Cist (1851) as Edward Cridland. Later in 1855 C. E. Cridland appeared in the Chicago directory and exhibited at the Illinois State Fair (as C. E. Cridland of Chicago, and as J. C. Cridland of Cincinnati). Charles E. Cridland was back in Cincinnati by 1858 and worked there until after 1860. ¶ WPA (Ohio), *Annals of Cleveland;* Cincinnati CD 1852–53; Cist, *Cincinnati in 1851;* Chicago CD 1855; [Chicago] *Daily Press,* Oct. 11 and 15, 1855; Cincinnati CD 1858–61. C. M. Cridland, who exhibited chemical paintings of religious and historical subjects in Cincinnati in 1845, may have been a relative (Cincinnati *Daily Gazette,* Nov. 29, 1845, cited by J. E. Arrington).

CRIDLAND, LEANDER, JR. Lithographer; born in Pennsylvania *c.* 1841; living in Philadelphia in 1860 with his father, a carpenter. ¶ 8 Census (1860), Pa., LVII, 214.

CRISAND, EMIL. Lithographer, New Haven (Conn.), 1858–60 and after. Listed as Emil Cresind in 1858–59 and as E. Crisand, of PUNDERSON & CRISAND, 1860 and after. Several prints by Crisand or Punderson & Crisand are known. ¶ New Haven CD 1858–60; *Portfolio* (Aug.–Sept. 1952), 21, repros.

CRISTY, JOSEPH H. French engraver, 39, at NYC in 1860. His wife Susan and son Henry (9) were also born in France, but the younger children (8 to 3) were born in America. ¶ 8 Census (1860), N.Y., XLIII, 12.

CROCKER, Mr. and Mrs. Teachers of drawing and painting on velvet, Charleston (S.C.), 1822. ¶ Rutledge, *Artists in the Life of Charleston.*

CROCKER, J. DENISON (1823–?). Portrait and landscape painter; born in Salem (Conn.), November 25, 1823. A silversmith by trade, he took up portrait painting about 1840, but later devoted himself mainly to landscape painting. He was a resident of Norwich (Conn.) in 1879. ¶ French, *Art and Artists in Conn.,* 121; Stokes, *Hist. Prints;* New England BD 1856, 1860; Norwich BD 1857, 1860.

CROCKER, JOHN W. Artist, 25, from Connecticut, at NYC in 1850. He lived in the same house as JOSEPH DUNN and A. MILLER. ¶ 7 Census (1850), N.Y., XLVIII, 351.

CROCKETT, SAMUEL LANE (1822–1855). Portrait and landscape painter; born in Boston, January 9, 1822; died June 9, 1855. He was an invalid and spent almost the whole of his life in Boston. Among his works were portraits of Lyman Beecher and Lowell Mason. ¶ Runnels, *History of Sanbornton (N.H.),* II, 194; Boston CD 1842–55.

CROGAN, ANDREW. Engraver, 20, a native of New York State, at NYC in 1860. ¶ 8 Census (1860), N.Y., LX, 249.

CROMWELL, ——. Portrait and miniature painter and profilist, working at Charleston (S.C.) in 1811. ¶ Rutledge, *Artists in the Life of Charleston.*

CROMWELL, GEORGE R. Still life painter of NYC who exhibited at the National Academy in 1859 and 1861. ¶ Cowdrey, NAD: 1859 (no address), 1861 (NYC).

CROMWELL, JOHN L. Carver, NYC, 1838–55. He was associated with HERON & CROMWELL in 1838–41. One example of his work, a cigar-store Indian of polychromed wood, has been identified. ¶ Lipman, *American Folk Art;* NYCD 1838–55.

CRONIN, DAVID EDWARD (1839–1925). Illustrator, portrait painter, and political cartoonist; born in Greenwich (Washington County, N.Y.), July 12, 1839; died in Philadelphia, June 9, 1925. Cronin came to NYC in 1855, after studying art in Troy (N.Y.) with ALBAN CONANT. He spent three years in Europe before the Civil War, returning in 1860 to join the army and serve as staff artist for *Harper's Weekly.* After the war he worked as a journalist in Binghamton (N.Y.), as a lawyer in NYC, and as a railroad promoter in Texas, before settling in NYC in the late 1870's. From 1879 to 1903 he devoted himself to the hand-illustration of books and for a few years as a political cartoonist. He moved to Philadelphia in 1890 and resided there until his death. ¶ Washbourn, "The Work of David E. Cronin"; *Artists Year Book,* 42; represented at NYHS.

CROOME, GEORGE L. Wood engraver and designer, working at Cincinnati in 1850, and at Dayton (Ohio) in 1853. ¶ Cincinnati CD 1850; Ohio BD 1853.

CROOME, MEIGNELLE & MINOT, engravers, see WILLIAM CROOME; MEIGNELLE; MINOT.

CROOME, WILLIAM (1790–1860). Designer and engraver on wood, steel, and copper. Croome was one of the organizers of the BOSTON BEWICK CO. of Boston (Mass.) in 1834. He worked in Philadelphia during the 1840's and 1850's; in 1841–42 as a member of the engraving firms of CROOME, MEIGNELLE & MINOT and CROOME & MINOT. ¶ Hamilton, 191–196; Mallett; Whitmore, "Abel Bowen," 44; Phila. CD 1841–52, 1854; Hinton, *History and Topography,* repro.; Fielding; Thieme-Becker.

CROPSEY, JASPER FRANCIS (1823–1900). N.A. Landscape painter and architect; born in Rossville (N.Y.), February 18, 1823; died in Hastings-on-Hudson (N.Y.), June 22, 1900. After five years of study in the office of the architect Joseph Trench, Cropsey turned to the study of landscape painting. He went to Europe in 1847, staying for three years, and again in 1857, this time remaining in London until 1863. After his second return to America he devoted himself mainly to the painting of autumn scenes. Cropsey was elected a Member of the National Academy in 1851, having exhibited there as early as 1843, and he was also an exhibitor at the Royal Academy, the Apollo Association and American Art-Union, the Pennsylvania Academy, the Maryland Historical Society, and the Boston Athenaeum. ¶ DAB; Cowdrey, "Jasper F. Cropsey, 1823–1900, the Colorist of the Hudson River School"; Cowdrey, NAD; Cowdrey, AA & AAU; Graves; Rutledge, PA; Rutledge, MHS; Swan, BA; Sweet, *Hudson River School;* Clement and Hutton; CAB; obit., N. Y. *Times,* June 24, 1900; represented at the NYHS, the Peabody Institute, and in the Karolik Collection.

CROSBY, CHARLES H. (1819–1896). Engraver, lithographer, and printer. Listed as a printer in Boston as early as 1847, Crosby joined the engraving and lithographic firm of MOORE & CROSBY in 1852. After the firm's dissolution in 1856, he continued as an engraver in Boston until after 1860. He died in Roxbury, July 9, 1896. ¶ Boston *Transcript,* July 9, 1896, obit.; Boston CD 1847–60; Peters, *America on Stone.*

CROSBY, JAMES L. Of THOMPSON & CROSBY, wood engravers, Providence (R.I.), 1852–54. ¶ Providence CD 1852, 1854.

CROSBY, MARIA. Drawing teacher, Cleveland (Ohio), 1848–49. ¶ WPA (Ohio), *Annals of Cleveland;* Cleveland CD 1848–49.

CROSS, A. B. Engraver, 1840. A pupil of A. L. DICK, Cross is said to have given up engraving early in his career. ¶ Fielding.

CROSS, GEORGE. Artist. Born in Virginia *c.* 1838, Cross was living in Baltimore in 1860, in the home of JOHN SPATES. With him were Martha (25), Margaret (23), Maria (17) and Albert Cross (9), all natives of Virginia. ¶ 8 Census (1860), Md., VII, 189.

CROSS, HENRY H. (1837–1918). Painter of Indian portraits; born in Flemingville

(N.Y.), November 23, 1837; died in Chicago, April 2, 1918. After working with a traveling circus in 1852, Cross studied painting in France in 1853–55. After his return to America he again traveled with a circus and painted Indians. He settled in Chicago in 1860, but made several trips into the Indian country where he continued his artistic work. There is a collection of his works at the Walker Art Gallery in Minneapolis (Minn.). ¶ Walker Art Center, *Illustrated Catalogue of Indian Portraits, All Painted by Henry H. Cross* (1927); *Art Annual,* XV (1918), 279; Turner, "Early Artists."

CROSS, HIRAM. Artist, Buffalo (N.Y.), 1855. ¶ Buffalo BD 1855.

CROSS, MAJOR OSBORNE. Quartermaster of the Mounted Rifle Regiment which reached Oregon in 1849, he kept a journal which was published in 1851. The drawings illustrating his book, done probably by GEORGE GIBBS and Lt. ANDREW J. LINDSAY, have sometimes been misattributed to Major Cross (*cf.* J. B. Brown, *Fort Hall on the Oregon Trail,* 148, 231; W. J. Ghent, *The Road to Oregon,* 38, 80, 132, 136, 142, 148; Parrish, *Historic Oregon,* 146, 148). ¶ Schafer, "Trailing a Trail Artist of 1849"; Rasmussen, "Art and Artists in Oregon" (information courtesy of David C. Duniway, Oregon State Archivist).

CROSS, PETER F. Engraver; born in New York *c.* 1820; working in Philadelphia 1855–60 and after. Cross was listed in NYC directories from 1846 to 1848 as "late engraver." By 1855 he was working at the United States Mint in Philadelphia. His household in 1860 included Harriet (38), Maria (16), Hannah (14), William E. (10), and Edward (2), all born in New York except the last; his personal property was valued at $200. Loubat reproduces a medal struck in 1853, of which P. F. Cross was the sculptor, and states that Cross was a native of Sheffield (England) and died in Philadelphia in 1856; this might be the father of Peter F. Cross. ¶ 8 Census (1860), Pa., LXII, 465; NYCD 1846–48; Phila. CD 1855–60; Loubat, pl. 68.

CROSSCUP, DANIEL L. Sculptor; born in Pennsylvania *c.* 1841; working in Philadelphia in 1860 and 1871 (as designer). He was a brother of GEORGE W. CROSSCUP, and son of Albert Crosscup, shoemaker. ¶ 8 Census (1860), LXII, 270; Phila. CD 1871.

CROSSCUP, GEORGE W. Engraver; born in Pennsylvania *c.* 1843; working in Philadelphia in 1860 and 1871 (as wood engraver). He was a brother of DANIEL L. CROSSCUP and son of Albert Crosscup, shoemaker. In 1871 he was a partner of William R. West, wood engraver. ¶ 8 Census (1860), Pa., LXII, 270; Phila. CD 1871.

CROSSETT, ALEXANDER. Portrait painter. A policeman by profession, Crossett exhibited at the American Institute in 1847 a portrait of Ephraim L. Snow, Clerk of the 1st District Police Court, NYC. ¶ Am. Inst. Cat., 1847; NYCD 1847.

CROSSMAN, CHARLES. Engraver, with JOHN CROSSMAN, at Boston in 1851. ¶ Boston CD 1851.

CROSSMAN, JOHN. Portrait painter from New York at Cincinnati in 1840. ¶ Cincinnati CD 1840 (courtesy Edward H. Dwight, Cincinnati Art Museum).

CROSSMAN, JOHN C. Engraver; born in Rhode Island *c.* 1806. A pupil of ABEL BOWEN, Crossman (or Crosman) was working with Bowen in Boston by 1830, with ALONZO HARTWELL in 1833, and joined the BOSTON BEWICK CO. in 1834. He continued to work as a wood engraver in Boston at least until 1859. ¶ 7 Census (1850), Mass., XXV, 125; Hamilton, 145, 277; Whitmore, "Abel Bowen," 44; Boston CD 1834, 1844–59; Linton; Thieme-Becker.

CROTHERS, JOHN H. Engraver, Yardleyville (Pa.), 1860. ¶ Penna. BD 1860.

CROUSE, LEWIS. Lithographer; born in Cassel (Germany) *c.* 1830; living in Philadelphia in 1860 with his German-born wife and one child, born in Pennsylvania *c.* 1858. ¶ 8 Census (1860), Pa., LII, 518.

CROUTA, JOHN. Artist and actor; born in Pennsylvania *c.* 1805. Listed as John Crouter, comedian, in the 1839 Philadelphia directory; as John Crouta, artist, in NYC directories 1841 to 1846; as John Crouta, artist, in Boston census, 1850; as John Crouta, artist, in NYC 1852–53; as John Crouta, comedian, in NYC directory for 1856. Numerous references to his work as an actor are to be found in Odell's *Annals of the New York Stage,* Vols. IV to VI. ¶ 7 Census (1850), Mass., [XXV ?], 797; Phila. CD 1839; NYCD 1841–46, 1852–53, 1856; Odell, *Annals of the New York Stage.*

CROW, WILLIAM. Irish engraver, 30, at NYC in 1860. His wife was also a native of Ireland, but their five children (6 years to 11 months) were born in New York. ¶ 8 Census (1860), N.Y., LXII, 499.

CROWE, EYRE (1824–1910). Painter. After study in Paris under Paul Delaroche, Crowe became secretary to William Makepeace Thackeray, whom he accompanied to America in 1852–53. His account of this trip was published in 1893 as *With Thackeray in America.* His "A Slave Market, Richmond, Virginia, about 1853," was shown in the "American Processional" exhibition at the Corcoran Gallery in 1950. Crowe was an Associate of the Royal Academy, where he exhibited from 1846 to 1904. ¶ DNB; *American Processional,* 28, 245, repro. 156.

CROWLEY, WILLIAM. Panoramist. An Englishman, Crowley studied at the Royal Academy and painted a panorama of China from drawings at the British Museum, which was shown in Boston (Mass.) in 1850 and the following year offered for sale by the artist in NYC. His address in 1851 was the same as that of William Crowley and Son, manufacturers of needles and fish-hooks in NYC from 1836 to 1860. ¶ Boston *Evening Transcript,* July 1, 1850, and N. Y. *Herald,* April 22, 1851 (citations courtesy of J. E. Arrington); NYCD 1836–60.

CROWLEY, WILLIAM M. Historical and genre painter, Philadelphia; exhibitor, Artists' Fund Society, 1835 and 1841, National Academy, 1848. ¶ Rutledge, PA.; Cowdrey, NAD.

CROWNINSHIELD, HANNAH (1789–1834). Portrait painter and draftsman; baptized at Salem (Mass.), June 28, 1789; married Lt. James Armstrong, U.S.N., March 29, 1819; died May 4, 1834. She was a pupil of MICHEL FELICE CORNÉ. ¶ Belknap, 8; WPA (Mass.), *Portraits Found in Mass.,* no. 2027; WPA (Mass.), *Portraits Found in N.H.,* p. 21.

CROWTHER[s], GEORGE H. Of MORRISON & CROWTHER, engravers and silverplaters, Cincinnati (Ohio), 1855–1860. ¶ Cincinnati CD 1855–60.

CROWTHER[s], HENRY. Of MORRISON & CROWTHER, engravers and silverplaters, Cincinnati (Ohio), 1853, 1856. ¶ Cincinnati CD 1853, 1856.

CROYEAU, AUGUSTIN. Panoramist at Baltimore in October 1851, recently arrived from Europe with small moving panoramas of the Crystal Palace. ¶ Baltimore *Sun,* Oct. 22, 1851 (courtesy J. Earl Arrington).

CRUISIN, C. Engraver; born in Virginia *c.* 1812; living in New Orleans in 1860. His household included his wife Mathilde (46), three children born in Virginia (18 to 22) and five children born in New Orleans (9 to 14); he owned real estate valued at $4,500 and personalty valued at $6,000. ¶ 8 Census (1860), La., VIII, 227.

CRUMBIE, W. D. Amateur modeller. A druggist of NYC, Crumbie exhibited a plaster cast, "Dentist and Patient," at the American Institute in 1845. ¶ Am. Inst. Cat., 1845; NYCD 1845.

CRUMP, RICHARD. Portrait painter; born in Virginia *c.* 1805; living in Louisville (Ky.) in 1850, with realty valued at $1,100. ¶ 7 Census (1850), Ky., XI, 813.

CRUMP, ROBERT. Of STILLMAN & CRUMP, engravers of Cincinnati (Ohio), 1859. It may have been this Crump who did some engravings for *The Encyclopedia of Wit and Humor* (N.Y., 1858). ¶ Cincinnati CD 1859; Ohio BD 1859; Hamilton, 464.

CRUMP, SAMUEL. Xylographic (wood) engraver, NYC, 1841. ¶ NYBD 1841/42.

CRUSE, EDWARD. Engraver. Cruse (32), his wife Elizabeth (29) and their four daughters (3 to 10), were all natives of Pennsylvania, and lived in Philadelphia in 1860. ¶ 8 Census (1860), Pa., LIX, 379.

CUINER, W. Amateur sculptor of NYC, exhibited, with J. CONROY, a bust of Washington at the American Institute 1845. ¶ Am. Inst. Cat., 1845.

CUIPERS, PETER. Of MICHELIN & CUIPERS, lithographers, NYC, 1844. ¶ NYCD 1844.

CULBERT, SAMUEL L. Panorama and portrait painter; born in New York about 1822; active in NYC from 1845 to 1860. He painted a panorama of Rhodes, the Mediterranean, and the Holy Land, and with T. R. JEFFEREYS a series of views of views of ancient Babylon. In 1859–60 he was listed as a portrait painter. ¶ 7 Census (1850), N.Y., LII, 425; NYCD 1845–60; N. Y. *Herald,* April 8, 1850, and Baltimore *Sun,* Dec. 29, 1854 (courtesy J. Earl Arrington).

CULLBURG, EDWIN. An officer in the Hydrotechnic Corps of the Swedish Navy, who was with Ringgold's survey of California waters, 1849–50. A number of his sketches of California scenes were reproduced in Ringgold's *A Series of Charts, with Sailing Directions* (1852). ¶ Peters, *Calif. on Stone.*

CULLEN, JOHN. Engraver; born in Kentucky *c.* 1837; living in Cincinnati (Ohio) in 1860. ¶ 8 Census (1860), Ohio, XXV, 251.

CULLIN, CHARLES. Irish engraver, 23, at NYC in 1860. ¶ 8 Census (1860), N.Y., XLVIII, 1009.

CULLOM or CULLUM, JOHN. Engraver and copperplate printer, born in England *c.* 1798. He worked in Boston (Mass.) from 1826 to 1832, at Portland (Maine) in 1834, and in Washington (D.C.) from 1846 to 1853. ¶ 7 Census (1850), D.C., I, 167; Boston CD 1826–32; Portland CD 1834; Washington CD 1846, 1850, 1853.

CULVERHOUSE, JOHANN MONGLES. Landscape painter. A native of Rotterdam (Holland), Culverhouse worked in America from about 1849 to 1891, chiefly in NYC. He was an occasional exhibitor at the National Academy, the American Art-Union, the Boston Athenaeum, and the Pennsylvania Academy. ¶ Swan, 217; Thieme-Becker; Bénézit; Cowdrey, NAD; Cowdrey, AA & AAU; Rutledge, PA; repros. in *Panorama,* II (Dec. 1946), 44; *ibid.,* IV (Aug.–Sept. 1948), 2 and back cover; *Portfolio,* I (April 1942), 19.

CUME, JUAN. Portrait and landscape painter, Philadelphia, 1853. Probably the same as JUAN CURRIE. ¶ Phila. BD 1853.

CUMMING, ——. Of BONAR & CUMMING, lithographers, NYC, 1847–48. ¶ NYCD 1847; NYBD 1848.

CUMMINGS, CHARLES. Wood engraver, 17, a native of New York, at NYC in 1850. He was a son of the well known artist, THOMAS SEIR CUMMINGS. ¶ 7 Census (1850), N.Y., LII, 333.

CUMMINGS, THOMAS AUGUSTUS (or Thomas, JR.) (1823–1859). A.N.A. Portrait painter and miniaturist; born July 27, 1823; died February 14, 1859. A son of THOMAS SEIR CUMMINGS, he first exhibited in 1842, at the American Institute and the National Academy; he began exhibiting at the American Art-Union in 1845. His entire professional life appears to have been spent in NYC. His father later wrote of him: "Dying young, his works are not numerous, or generally known." ¶ Birth date courtesy of FARL; Cummings, *Historic Annals,* 271; Cowdrey, NAD; Cowdrey, AA & AAU; Am. Inst. Cat., 1842; NYCD 1845–48.

CUMMINGS, THOMAS SEIR (1804–1894). N.A. Miniaturist and portrait painter; born in Bath (England), August 26, 1804; died in Hackensack (N.J.), September 24 or 25, 1894. Brought to NYC as a child, Cummings lived there until his retirement in 1866. He studied under AUGUSTUS EARL, JOHN RUBENS SMITH, and HENRY INMAN, with the last of whom he formed a partnership for a number of years. Cummings was one of the founders of the National Academy of Design, of which he was Treasurer for forty years and Vice-President from 1852 to 1859. In 1865 he published his *Historic Annals of the National Academy of Design.* On retiring in 1866, Cummings moved to Mansfield (Conn.) and in 1889 to Hackensack (N.J.), where he died five years later. CHARLES and THOMAS AUGUSTUS CUMMINGS were his sons. His wife, Mrs. Rebecca S. Cummings, an amateur artist, exhibited at the American Institute in 1847. ¶ DAB; N. Y. *Daily Tribune,* Sept. 26, 1894, p. 7, obit.; NYCD 1825–51; 7 Census (1850), N.Y., LII, 333; Lossing. "The National Academy of the Arts of Design and Its Surviving Founders"; Cowdrey, NAD; Cummings, *Historic Annals,* 271; Am. Inst. Cat., 1847; Bolton, *Miniature Painters;* Swan, BA; Fielding; Isham, *History of American Painting;* Wehle and Bolton; repros. in NYHS *Quarterly,* XXXI (Oct. 1947), 215. [All citations courtesy Miss Hope Mathewson.]

CUNNINGHAM, Mrs. ——. Drawing mistress, proprietor of a ladies' seminary at Charleston (S.C.) in 1849. ¶ Rutledge, *Artists in the Life of Charleston.*

CUNNINGHAM, ANTHONY W. Banknote and general engraver, NYC, 1854, 1858. ¶ NYBD 1854, 1858.

CURAM, GEORGE. Designer; born in Pennsylvania *c.* 1818; living in Philadelphia in 1850. ¶ 7 Census (1850), Pa., LVI, 323.

CURRIE (Curry), JOHN A. Artist, picture restorer, and stationer, working in Philadelphia, 1848–60. Possibly the same as JUAN CURRIE, although both names appear concurrently at different addresses in 1852–54. ¶ Phila. CD 1848, 1850–56, 1857 (as Jean Curry), 1858 (as J. Curry), 1860 (as John Curry and John A. Currie).

CURRIE, JUAN. Portrait, and animal painter, Philadelphia, 1852–67. Exhibited at the Pennsylvania Academy in 1852, 1854–58, and 1867. He may have been the same as JOHN A. CURRIE, although both names appear concurrently in the directories for 1852–54, at different addresses. *Cf.* also

JUAN CUME. ¶ Rutledge, PA; Phila. CD 1852–54.

CURRIE (Curry), WILLIAM. Portrait painter and talbotypist. Listed in Philadelphia directories as follows: Mr. and Mrs. William Currie, talbotypists, 1854–55; William Curry, portrait painter, and William Currie & Co., artists, 1856; William Currie & Co., artists, 1857. ¶ Phila. CD 1854–57.

CURRIER, CHARLES (1818–1887). Lithographer; born in Roxbury, Mass. [?], 1818; died January 4, 1887. For many years associated in NYC with his brother, NATHANIEL CURRIER, and his brother-in-law, JAMES M. IVES, Charles Currier also conducted his own lithographic and publishing business in NYC. He was the inventor of a special lithographic crayon used by CURRIER & IVES. ¶ Peters, *Currier & Ives;* NYBD 1848, 1850–52, 1854, 1857, 1859; repro. in *Portfolio* (March 1945), 161.

CURRIER & IVES. Lithographers, NYC, 1857–1907. See NATHANIEL CURRIER and JAMES M. IVES. See also: LOUIS MAURER, FANNY PALMER, THOMAS WORTH, ARTHUR FITZWILLIAM TAIT, GEORGE HENRY DURRIE, CHARLES PARSONS, JAMES E. BUTTERSWORTH, all artists who worked for Currier & Ives; among the lithographers employed by the company were OTTO KNIRSCH, FRANZ VENINO, JOHN CAMERON, C. SEVERYN, J. SCHULTZ, and NAPOLEON SARONY. ¶ The standard work is Peters' *Currier & Ives: Printmakers to the American People* (N.Y., 1931). Many of the prints are repro. in color in Simkin, *Currier & Ives' America.*

CURRIER, NATHANIEL (1813–1888). Lithographer; born in Roxbury (Mass.), March 27, 1813; died in NYC, November 20, 1888. After serving his apprenticeship in Boston with WILLIAM S. and JOHN PENDLETON, 1828–33, Currier worked with M. E. D. BROWN in Philadelphia for a year before going to NYC in 1834. He entered into partnership there with ADAM STODART, but on the dissolution of Currier & Stodart in 1835, Currier set up in business on his own. In 1857 N. Currier joined with JAMES M. IVES in the famous partnership of CURRIER & IVES, which was to flourish until 1907. Currier himself retired in 1880, and Ives a few years later, but the business was carried on by their sons. ¶ Peters, *Currier & Ives;* DAB; Simkin, *Currier & Ives' America.*

CURRY, JOHN. Irish engraver, 17, at NYC in 1850. ¶ 7 Census (1850), N.Y., XLIX, 953.

CURRY, JOHN J. Sculptor, 21, a native of New York, at NYC in 1850. ¶ 7 Census (1850), N.Y., LIV, 149.

CURRY, WILLIAM. English artist, 36, at NYC in 1860. ¶ 8 Census (1860), N.Y., LXII, 22.

CURTES, HENRY. Engraver; born in Connecticut *c.* 1831; boarding in Philadelphia in 1850. ¶ 7 Census (1850), Pa., LII, 604.

CURTIS, BENJAMIN B. Artist. Born in Massachusetts *c.* 1795; worked in Boston as an ornamental painter from 1818 to 1827, in NYC as a signpainter and artist 1831 and 1841, in Philadelphia as an ornamental painter in 1845 and as an artist in 1860. He may have been related to CHARLES CURTIS, portrait painter, who lived next door to Benjamin B. Curtis in Boston in 1823. ¶ 8 Census (1860), Pa., LIV, 147; Boston CD 1818, 1820, 1822–23, 1827; NYCD 1831; NYBD 1841; Phila. CD 1845.

CURTIS, CALVIN (1822–1893). Portrait and landscape painter. Born at Stratford (Conn.), July 5, 1822, Calvin Curtis began his formal studies under DANIEL HUNTINGTON in December 1841. He had a studio in NYC from 1843 to 1847, worked in Birmingham and Waterbury (Conn.) *c.* 1849, and then settled in Bridgeport (Conn.), where he was living in 1878. He died in 1893. ¶ French; Smith; Cowdrey, NAD; NYBD 1844–48; Clement and Hutton; Boston BD 1847; Fielding; Thieme-Becker.

CURTIS, CHARLES. Portrait and miniature painter; working in Boston in 1821–23, in the latter year next door to BENJAMIN B. CURTIS, possibly his brother. He was at Worcester (Mass.) in August 1824, probably at Baltimore (Md.) in 1829, in NYC 1832–36, and again in Boston from 1846 to 1860. ¶ Boston CD 1821–23; Sears, *Some American Primitives,* 289; Lafferty; NYCD 1832, 1835–36; Boston CD 1846–47, 1849–55, 1858–60 and after.

CURTIS, GEORGE (1826–1881). Marine artist; died at Chelsea (Mass.), May 22, 1881. Curtis exhibited at the Boston Athenaeum in 1848, 1857, 1863–67, and 1869. In 1857 he and MINARD LEWIS designed scenery for a Boston production of a play based on Kane's voyages in the Arctic. ¶ *Am. Art Review,* II, 2 (1881), 90, obit.; Swan, BA; Boston *Evening Transcript,* Oct. 12, 1857 (cited by J. E. Arrington).

CURTIS, ROBERT J. Portrait painter, born in Germany *c.* 1816. He must have come to America in childhood, for he advertised in Charleston (S.C.) as early as 1833. Two years later he was spoken of in Charleston as "a native artist" who had just completed a course of study under NEAGLE of Philadelphia. Curtis continued to work in Charleston until 1867, but made at least one visit to Mobile (Ala.) in 1847. He exhibited at the Artists' Fund Society in 1836–37 and at the Apollo Gallery in 1838. In 1836 he produced a decorative work entitled "The Witch of the Alps." ¶ 7 Census (1850), S.C., II, 724; Rutledge, *Artists in the Life of Charleston;* WPA (Ala.) cites Mobile *Commercial Register & Patriot,* May 6, 1847; Rutledge, PA; Cowdrey, AA & AAU.

CUSHING, W. T. Artist, NYC, exhibitor of "A Calm Morning" at the National Academy in 1860. At the address given resided Tileston Cushing, importer, possibly the father of the artist. William Cushing of NYC exhibited at the National Academy in 1867. ¶ Cowdrey, NAD; NYCD 1860.

CUSHMAN, ALONZO C. Artist, Philadelphia, 1860. ¶ Phila. BD 1860.

CUSHMAN, GEORGE HEWITT (1814–1876). Portrait and miniature painter, engraver; born in Windham (Conn.), June 5, 1814; died in Jersey City Heights (N.J.), August 3, 1876. After instruction in drawing from WASHINGTON ALLSTON, Cushman took up engraving, at first under ASAPH WILLARD of Hartford, then with the CHENEY brothers of Boston. About 1842 he moved to Philadelphia where for the next twenty years he was a banknote engraver. During this period Cushman also did some engraving for the book trade, including a large number of F. O. C. DARLEY's illustrations of Cooper and Dickens. Having begun to paint miniatures as early as 1842, when he first exhibited at the Artists' Fund Society, Cushman devoted his later years, from about the time of his removal to NYC in 1862, to portraiture instead of engraving. ¶ DAB; Rutledge, PA; Phila. CD 1843–62; Fielding; Wharton, *Heirlooms in Miniatures;* Bolton, *Miniature Painters;* Stauffer.

CUSHMAN, THOMAS HASTINGS (1815–1841). Banknote and general engraver; born in Albany (N.Y.), June 6, 1815; died there, November 17, 1841. A member of the Albany banknote engraving firm of HALL, PACKARD & CUSHMAN in 1838–39, Cushman exhibited an engraving at the National Academy in 1838. He was working in NYC in 1840, but died in Albany the following year. ¶ Fielding's *Supplement to Stauffer;* Cowdrey, NAD; Albany CD 1838, 1841.

CUSTER, EDWARD L. (1837–1881). Portrait, animal and landscape painter; born in Basel (Switzerland), January 24, 1837; died in Boston (Mass.), January 8, 1881. Custer came to America in 1846 or 1847 with his father, who became a doctor in Manchester (N.H.). Edward Custer exhibited at the Boston Athenaeum from 1848 to 1869. He went to Germany to study in 1860 and again in the 1870's. In his later years Custer was best known for his studies of cattle. ¶ *American Art Review,* II (1881), 169, *obit.;* Manchester (N.H.) Hist. Assoc. *Collections,* IV, 116; Swan, BA; Thieme-Becker.

CUSTIS, ELEANOR PARKE (1779–1852). Amateur silhouettist and landscape painter; born in Abingdon (Va.), 1779; died in Audley (Va.), 1852. She was a stepdaughter of George Washington. In 1798 she made silhouettes of George and Martha Washington and she also painted landscapes which were seen in 1799 by the English visitor, Joshua Brookes. She later became Mrs. Lawrence Lewis. ¶ Jackson, *Silhouette,* 92; Carrick, *Shades of our Ancestors;* Vail, "A Dinner at Mount Vernon," 78.

CUTBUSH, EDWARD and SAMUEL. Ship carvers from London, working in Philadelphia in 1783. Edward was the teacher of the noted American carver, WILLIAM RUSH. ¶ Pinckney, 57, 190.

CUTLER, GEORGE YOUNGLOVE. Amateur artist. Born in Watertown (Conn.), Cutler became a lawyer. His journal contains some pen-and-ink drawings which have been reproduced. He died at Nauvoo (Ill.) September 3, 1834. ¶ Vanderpoel, *Chronicles of a Pioneer School from 1792–1833,* 192–207, three repros.

CUTLER, JERVIS (1768–1846). Engraver; born on Martha's Vineyard (Mass.), September 19, 1768; died Evansville (Ind.), June 25, 1846. After working in Boston and a brief trip to Europe, Cutler emigrated in 1788 to the new settlement in Ohio at Marietta. He lived in Ohio until 1809, when he removed on military service to New Orleans. He stayed in Louisiana for eight years and published an account of the country. Later he lived for a time in Nashville (Tenn.) and in Evansville (Ind.), where he died in 1846. ¶ Fielding's *Supplement to Stauffer;* Smith.

CUTTS, JOHN. "Figurist"; born in Italy *c.* 1794; living in Philadelphia in 1850. His household included Fortunia (37), Orillio (21, lithographer), John (19, lithographer), Theodore (17) and three daughters (11 to 14)—all born in Italy. ¶ 7 Census (1850), Pa., LV, 84.

CUTTS, JOHN, JR., lithographer, see JOHN CUTTS.

CUTTS, LOVE PICKMAN (?–1873). Pastel portraitist who died at Salem (Mass.) in 1873. His portrait of Peter Frye (1723–1820) is owned by the Essex Institute. ¶ WPA (Mass.), *Portraits Found in Mass.*, no. 827 and v. 2, p. 575; the portrait is reproduced in Essex Institute, *Catalogue of Portraits.*

CUTTS, ORILLIO, lithographer, see JOHN CUTTS.

CUYPERS, F. H. or FRANCIS A. Portrait painter working at Newark (N.J.) in 1859. It was probably the same artist who exhibited an oil painting at the American Institute in 1848, as F. Cuypeers of NYC. ¶ *The Museum,* I (July 1949), 9; Essex, Hudson, and Union Counties BD 1859; Am. Inst. Cat., 1848.

D

Dacre, Henry. Lithographer; born in England *c.* 1820; working for the lithographer P. S. Duval in Philadelphia, 1847–50. ¶ 7 Census (1850), Pa., L, 918; Peters, *America on Stone.*

Daggett, Alfred (1799–1872). Portrait and banknote engraver of New Haven (Conn.), where he was born September 30, 1799, and died January 27, 1872. He was the uncle and first teacher of the painter John Frederick Kensett and was associated with the firms of Daggett & Ely (1831–32) and Daggett, Hinman & Co. (1840), both of New Haven. ¶ Fielding, *Supplement;* Dunlap, *History* (1918), III, 293; *Am. Adv. Directory,* 1831, p. 75, and 1832, p. 42; New Haven CD 1840; Hamilton, 99 (as Bagett).

Daggett & Ely. Engravers, New Haven (Conn.), 1831–36; Alfred Daggett and —— Ely. ¶ *Am. Adv. Directory,* 1831, p. 75, and 1832, p. 42; Hamilton, 99 (as Doggett & Ely).

Daggett, Hinman & Co. Engravers, New Haven (Conn.), 1840; Alfred Daggett and David C. Hinman. ¶ New Haven CD 1840.

Dainty, S. Landscape engraver, working in Philadelphia *c.* 1840; possibly a son of John Dainty, copperplate printer of Philadelphia *c.* 1817. ¶ Stauffer; Thieme-Becker.

Dajety, F. Two portraits by this artist were shown at the National Academy in 1830. ¶ Cowdrey, NAD.

Dakin, James H. (1806–?). Architect and draftsman. Born August 24, 1806, Dakin worked in NYC during the 1830's as an associate of Ithiel Town and Alexander Jackson Davis. He also drew several NYC views, one of which was engraved for Theodore Fay's *Views in New York and Its Environs* (1831–34). ¶ *Architect and Engineer* (Aug. 1938), 24, cites Dakin's diary, found in New Orleans; NYCD 1831–36; Stokes, *Icon.,* III, 605, and pl. 103-b; *Connoisseur* (Dec. 1945), 117, repro.

Dalbey, A. L. Portrait painter in Pittsburgh (Pa.) *c.* 1832. ¶ Anderson, "Intellectual Life of Pittsburgh: Painting," 289.

Dale, George Edward (1840–1873). Painter. Born at Bangor (Me.), March 22, 1840, Dale was considered a painter of promise but died before he had completed his studies abroad. His death occurred June 25, 1873, probably at Antwerp (Belgium). ¶ Simpson, *Leaflets of Artists;* Cowdrey, NAD, 1867–68.

Dale, John B. (?–1848). Naval officer and artist. Appointed midshipman in 1829, Dale had advanced to lieutenant by 1845. From 1838 to 1842 he was a member of Wilkes' U. S. Exploring Expedition, and the *Narrative* of the expedition contains some illustrations from his pen. He died July 24, 1848. ¶ Hamersley, *Naval Register;* Rasmussen, "Artists of the Explorations Overland, 1840–1860," 58.

Dale, Wilton. Artist; born in England *c.* 1818; living in Philadelphia in September 1850. He may have been a scene painter, as there were a number of actors living in his immediate neighborhood. ¶ 7 Census (1850), Pa., LI, 169.

Dallas, Jacob A. (1825–1857). A.N.A. Painter and book illustrator; born in Philadelphia, 1825; died in NYC, September 9, 1857. The son of a wealthy Philadelphia merchant, Dallas moved to Missouri in 1833 with his family. On graduating from Ames College *c.* 1843, he returned to Philadelphia to study painting with Bass Otis at the Pennsylvania Academy. From *c.* 1850 until his death Dallas lived in NYC, where he worked with Daniel Huntington, Charles Lehr, George R. West, William Heine and others on a number of large panoramas. ¶ *Crayon* (Oct. 1857), 317, obit.; N. Y. *Tribune,* Sept. 12, 1857, obit.; Thieme-Becker; Cowdrey, NAD; NYCD 1857; 7 Census (1850), Pa., LV, 453; Phila. *Public Ledger,* Aug. 30, 1851, and April 12, 1852, New Orleans *Daily Picayune,* April 13, 1855, and N. Y. *Herald,* Jan. 27, 1856, cited by J. E. Arrington.

D'Almaine, George (?–1893). Portrait painter, silhouettist, crayon, and wash drawing portraitist. D'Almaine was an Englishman who came to America before 1848. He worked mainly in Baltimore from 1855 to 1884, but did some painting in Boston, Pittsburgh (Pa.), Illinois, and New York. During the 1880's he went west, probably to Peoria (Ill.). He died in 1893. ¶ *Pageant of America,* IV, 201, repro. of portrait published in *Democratic Review* (1848); Baltimore CD 1855, 1858, 1860, 1864–75, 1878–80; Pleasants, *250*

Years of Painting in Maryland, 59; Lafferty; Rutledge, MHS; Rutledge, "Portraits in Varied Media"; information courtesy Miss Mary Bartlett Cowdrey.

DALSTON, ALFRED. Lithographer, 20, a native of New York, at NYC in 1860. ¶ 8 Census (1860), N.Y., XLVI, 452.

DALSTON & BOVELL. Lithographers, NYC, 1859–60. See WILLIAM B. DALSTON and THOMAS W. BOVELL. ¶ NYBD 1859; CD 1860.

DALSTON, WILLIAM B. Lithographer, of DALSTON & BOVELL, NYC, 1859–60. ¶ NYBD 1859; CD 1860.

DALTON, E. Miniaturist and portrait painter, living in Philadelphia in 1827, when he exhibited at the Pennsylvania Academy. This may well be the Edwin Dalton of London (England) who exhibited portraits at the Royal Academy from 1818 to 1844. Mrs. Edwin Dalton (née Magdalene Ross) exhibited miniatures at the Royal Academy between 1820 and 1856. *Cf.* Miss M. Ross. ¶ Rutledge, PA; Graves *Dictionary.*

DALTON, JAMES. Artist, NYC, 1835. ¶ NYCD 1835.

DAMOREAU, CHARLES F. Engraver, working in Boston (Mass.) from 1856 to 1860. He was a member of the firms of BRICHER & DAMOREAU (1856) and SMITH & DAMOREAU (1859/60). He engraved some of WINSLOW HOMER's early work for *Ballou's Pictorial,* 1857–59. ¶ Boston CD and BD 1856–59; Boston *Almanac* 1860; Cowdrey, *Winslow Homer, Illustrator.*

DANA, EDMUND TROWBRIDGE (1779–1859). Exhibited at the Boston Athenaeum in 1828. ¶ Swan, BA, 217.

DANA, J. F. New England artist, active about 1823, when he executed views of Dartmouth College and the White Mountains of New Hampshire, both of which were engraved by ABEL BOWEN. ¶ Stauffer.

DANA, JAMES DWIGHT (1813–1895). Eminent geologist and zoologist, draftsman; born in Utica (N.Y.), February 12, 1813; died in New Haven (Conn.), April 14, 1895. As a scientist attached to Wilkes' South Seas explorations (1838–42), Dana made many important additions to scientific knowledge and executed many fine drawings to illustrate his reports, which were in preparation from 1842 to 1855. In 1855 he became Professor of natural history at Yale, succeeding his father-in-law, Benjamin Silliman. He retired in 1890. ¶ DAB; CAB; Wilkes, *U. S. Exploring Expedition.*

DANA, WILLIAM PARSONS WINCHESTER (1833–1927). N.A. Portrait and genre painter; born in Boston (Mass.), February 18, 1833; died in London, April 8, 1927. He was working as an artist in Boston as early as 1852 and went to France for further study by 1857. During the 1860's he lived in France and in NYC, where he exhibited at the National Academy, of which he became a member in 1863. He was also an exhibitor at the Boston Athenaeum between 1857 and 1871, and at the Pennsylvania Academy in the 1860's. ¶ Thieme-Becker; *Art Annual* (1928), 384; Boston BD 1852; NYBD 1859; Cowdrey, NAD; Swan, BA; Rutledge, PA; Graves, *Dictionary;* Fielding.

DANCKAERTS, JASPER. Amateur artist who sketched several views of New York City and Manhattan Island in 1679–80. He was one of the leaders of the Dutch sect known as Labadists, who settled in the 1680's at the head of Chesapeake Bay. Danckaerts' views were sketched during his first visit to America and inserted in his journal, which was discovered and published in the 19th century. After settling in Maryland, Danckaerts returned to Holland, where he was living as late as 1693. ¶ Murphy, ed., *Journal of a Voyage to New York . . . by Jasper Dankers and Peter Sluyter,* Introduction; Stokes, *Icon.,* I, 224–31, plates 17–19. The MS of Danckaert's *Journal* is at the Long Island Hist. Soc.

DANEY, T., see THOMAS DONEY.

DANFORTH, BALD & CO. Banknote engravers of Boston, Cincinnati, Philadelphia, and NYC, 1850–53. See MOSELEY I. DANFORTH, EDWARD J. DANFORTH, and ROBERT L. BALD. ¶ Boston CD 1851–52, CD 1852–53; Cincinnati BD 1850–51; Phila. CD 1850–53; NYCD 1850–52.

DANFORTH, BALD, SPENCER & HUFTY. Banknote engravers of NYC, 1843/44. See MOSELEY I. DANFORTH, ROBERT BALD, ASA SPENCER, and SAMUEL HUFTY. ¶ NYCD 1843.

DANFORTH, EDWARD J. Banknote engraver, NYC, 1850–59. In 1850–53 he was associated with the firm of DANFORTH, BALD & CO. ¶ NYCD 1850–52; NYBD 1859.

DANFORTH & HUFTY. Banknote engravers of NYC (1847–49) and Philadelphia (1848–51, as Hufty & Danforth). See MOSELEY I. DANFORTH and SAMUEL

HUFTY. ¶ NYCD 1847–49; Phila. CD 1848–51.

DANFORTH, J. B. A print of the Richmond (Va.) Light Infantry, drawn by this artist, was published in the *U. S. Military Magazine* (Oct. 1841). ¶ Todd, "Huddy & Duval Prints."

DANFORTH, MOSELEY (or Mosely) ISAAC (1800–1862). N.A. Engraver and painter in oils and watercolors; born in Hartford (Conn.), December 7 [Stauffer] or December 11 [DAB], 1800; died in NYC, January 19, 1862. Danforth's first instructor in engraving was ASAPH WILLARD of the HARTFORD GRAPHIC & BANK NOTE ENGRAVING CO., where Danforth was enrolled as an apprentice in 1818. In 1821 he moved to New Haven (Conn.), and thence to NYC in 1825. During his three years in NYC, Danforth played a part in the organization of the New York Drawing Association (1825) and the National Academy of Design (1826). He was a Founding Member of the Academy in 1826–27 and an Honorary Member, Professional, 1828–60. In 1827 or 1828, he went to London to continue his artistic studies, remaining there until about 1840. On his return to NYC he turned his attention to banknote engraving. For the next twenty years Danforth headed a number of firms with branches in the larger cities: DANFORTH, UNDERWOOD & CO. (1839–43); DANFORTH, BALD, SPENCER & HUFTY (1843); DANFORTH, SPENCER & HUFTY (1844–46); DANFORTH & HUFTY (1847–49); DANFORTH, BALD & CO. (1850–52); DANFORTH, WRIGHT & CO. (1856–58); and DANFORTH, PERKINS & CO. (1858–59). In 1858 he was one of the chief engineers of the important merger of banknote engraving companies into the AMERICAN BANK NOTE COMPANY, of which he became Vice-president. Though best known as an engraver, he also received praise for his work in watercolors and his copies from the Italian Masters. ¶ DAB; CAB; French; Clement and Hutton; Stauffer; Rice, "Life of Nathaniel Jocelyn"; Cowdrey, NAD; Cowdrey, AA & AAU; NYCD 1840–58.

DANFORTH, PERKINS & CO. Banknote engravers of NYC and Philadelphia, 1858–59. This firm, composed of MOSELEY I. and EDWARD J. DANFORTH and HENRY PERKINS, was one of those which combined to form the AMERICAN BANK NOTE COMPANY in 1858. ¶ NYCD 1858; Phila. CD 1859; Toppan, *100 Years of Bank Note Engraving,* 12.

DANFORTH, SPENCER & HUFTY. Banknote engravers of NYC, 1844–1846; as SPENCER, HUFTY & DANFORTH in Philadelphia, 1844–47. See MOSELEY I. DANFORTH, ASA SPENCER, and SAMUEL HUFTY. ¶ NYCD 1844–46; Phila. CD 1844–47.

DANFORTH, UNDERWOOD & CO. Banknote engravers of NYC, 1839–42. See MOSELEY I. DANFORTH and THOMAS UNDERWOOD. ¶ NYCD 1839–42.

DANFORTH, WRIGHT & CO. Banknote engravers of Boston, Cincinnati, Philadelphia, and NYC, 1853–59. See MOSELEY I. and EDWARD J. DANFORTH and JAMES WRIGHT. Samuel B. Munson was Cincinnati agent for the firm 1856–58. ¶ Boston CD 1853–58; Cincinnati BD 1853, 1856–57, CD 1856–58; Phila. CD 1854–59; NYCD 1853–58.

DANGERFIELD, A. D. Engraver, NYC, 1850. ¶ NYBD 1850.

DANIEL, HOLY. Primitive landscape painter in watercolors, Illinois, *c.* 1850. ¶ Lipman and Winchester, 171.

DANIEL, J. Engraver; born in Massachusetts *c.* 1835; boarding in Boston in 1860. *Cf.* JOHN H. DANIELS. ¶ 8 Census (1860), Mass., XXVIII, 645; Boston CD 1860.

DANIELS, ANSON (1813–1884). Portrait painter; born at East Medway (now Millis, Mass.), July 8, 1813; died at Medway (Mass.), November 6, 1884. An itinerant painter, Daniels worked in Massachusetts, New York, New Jersey, Pennsylvania, and elsewhere. At least 37 portraits by him have been located, including a self portrait. ¶ Information courtesy Charles K. Bolton.

DANIELS, CHARLES H. Jeweler and engraver of Boston (Mass.), listed as engraver in the 1855 and 1856 business directories. ¶ Boston BD 1855–56.

DANIELS, JOHN H. Engraver and copperplate printer at Boston (Mass.) in the 1850's and 1860's. From about 1855 to 1858 he was a partner in the firm of Wilson & Daniels. *Cf.* J. DANIEL. ¶ Boston CD 1855–61.

DANIELS, GEORGE FISHER (1821–?). American artist, born in 1821, died after 1879. He exhibited at the Boston Athenaeum in 1866 and 1878, and at the National Academy, 1867–68, as G. F. Daniell. ¶ Swan, BA; Cowdrey, NAD.

DANIELS, WALTER. Artist working at Baltimore (Md.) in 1856–57. ¶ Lafferty.

DANKWORTH, FREDERICK. Engraver, born in

Pennsylvania *c.* 1804. In 1850 he was living in Washington (D.C.) with his wife and a seven-year-old daughter, both natives of the District of Columbia. ¶ 7 Census (1850), D.C., II, 198.

DANNEMAN (or Denneman), L. Sculptor working in New Orleans (La.) from 1849 to 1851. The name appears as Denneman only in 1849. ¶ New Orleans CD 1849–51 (cited by Delgado-WPA).

DANNER, ADAM or J. A. Probably one artist, J. A. and Adam Danner are recorded as painting portraits in Lancaster (Pa.) in 1836 and 1837, respectively. ¶ Lancaster County Hist. Soc., *Portraiture in Lancaster County,* 118.

DANTONET, A. Artist of New Orleans (La.), 1857. ¶ New Orleans CD 1857 (cited by Delgado-WPA).

DARBY, HENRY F. (*c.* 1831–?). Portrait painter. Born about 1831, Darby was working in Washington (D.C.) as early as 1849, when he made studies for the life portraits of Henry Clay and John C. Calhoun now hanging in the U.S. Capitol. From 1853 to 1860 he lived in NYC and Brooklyn and exhibited at the National Academy. He shared a studio with SAMUEL COLMAN. After his wife's death about 1859, Darby went to England where he became a clergyman of the Church of England. He visited Colman in New York in 1878, but nothing further is known of him, unless he was the Rev. Henry Darby who exhibited at the National Academy, 1875–84. ¶ Fairman, *Art and Artists of the Capitol,* 321; Cowdrey, NAD; NYBD 1854–55, 1857; Fielding; repros. in Kende Gallery Cat. 229 (1946) and Fairman.

DARBY, J. G. Engraver on steel, copper, and wood. He was working at Buffalo (N.Y.) in 1838, when he engraved a view of Niagara Falls and a map of the Falls region. In 1853 he was living in Detroit (Mich.). ¶ Stauffer; Detroit BD 1853.

DARLEY, E. H. Portrait painter, brother of F. O. C. DARLEY. Variously listed as H., E. H., Edward H., Edmund H., and Edwin Darley or Darly, he was working in Philadelphia from about 1828 to 1835 and again in 1840, and in Claymont (Del.) from 1860 to about 1868. An exhibitor at the Pennsylvania Academy from 1828 to 1868, E. H. Darley painted portraits of Edgar A. Poe and N. P. Willis. ¶ Phila. CD 1828–31, 1833, 1835, 1840; Rutledge, PA; Dunlap, *History* (1918), III, 294; Fielding.

DARLEY, FELIX OCTAVIUS CARR (1822–1888). N.A. Illustrator. Born June 23, 1822, in Philadelphia (Pa.), the son of John Darley or Darly, an English comic actor; began his notable career as an illustrator in Philadelphia about 1842. Moving to NYC in 1848, he won wide popularity through his illustrations for the works of Washington Irving and James Fenimore Cooper during the 1850's. After his marriage in 1859, he moved to Claymont (Del.), where he made his home until his death on March 27, 1888. An exhibitor at the National Academy from 1845 and a Member from 1852, Darley was not only a book and magazine illustrator, but also a designer of bank-note vignettes for TOPPAN, CARPENTER & CO. His brother, E. H. DARLEY, and his sister-in-law, JANE COOPER (SULLY) DARLEY, were also artists. ¶ Bolton, "The Book Illustrations of F. O. C. Darley," life and checklist; DAB; Fielding; Cowdrey, NAD; Cowdrey, AA & AAU; Swan, BA; Weitenkampf, "F. O. C. Darley, American Illustrator"; Toppan, *100 Years of Bank Note Engraving,* 12; *Antiques* (July 1946), 42; *American Collector* (April 1943), cover; *Portfolio* (Feb. 1944), 141, (Jan. 1954), 108–09; 7 Census (1850), N.Y., XLVII, 589.

DARLEY, JANE COOPER (SULLY), Mrs. W. H. W. Darley (1807–1877). Portrait painter, born in New York, January 14, 1807, a daughter of THOMAS SULLY; died in Philadelphia, March 3, 1877. As Miss J. C. Sully and later as Mrs. W. H. W. Darley, she exhibited frequently at the Pennsylvania Academy and the Artists' Fund Society from 1825 to 1869. Her husband, a professor of music in Philadelphia, was an older brother of the illustrator, F. O. C. DARLEY. She also exhibited at the National Academy, the Boston Athenaeum, and the Maryland Historical Society. ¶ Swan, BA; 8 Census (1860), Pa., LV, 267; Rutledge, PA; Phila. CD 1837–60; Cowdrey, NAD; Rutledge, MHS; Dunlap, *History* (1918), III, 336.

DARLEY, JOHN CLARENDON. Portrait painter. Born about 1808, possibly of the same family as E. H. and F. O. C. DARLEY, this artist was working in Philadelphia in 1826, in Baltimore from 1829 to 1834, again in Philadelphia in 1840, and in Pittsburgh (Pa.) in 1850. He exhibited at the Pennsylvania Academy in 1822, 1825, and 1826, and at the Artists' Fund Society in 1840. ¶ 7 Census (1850), Pa. III (Part 2), 474; Rutledge, PA: Baltimore CD 1829, 1831 (cited by Dr. J. Hall Pleasants); Stauffer lists two engravings after portraits by him; Anderson, "Intellectual Life of Pittsburgh: Painting," 289.

DARLEY, Mrs. W. H. W., see JANE COOPER (SULLY) DARLEY.

DARLING, J. Portrait painter who advertised in Charleston (S. C.) in September 1829 and again in the early part of 1837. In the latter year he and ABEL NICHOLS advertised as pupils of CHESTER HARDING and CHARLES OSGOOD. Darling probably came from Massachusetts and may have been the John Darling listed as a "painter" in the Boston directories from 1827 to 1830. ¶ Rutledge, *Artists in the Life of Charleston,* 152–53, 192; Boston CD 1827–30.

DARRAGH, JOHN. Engraver working in Philadelphia in 1783. ¶ Prime, I, 18.

DARRAH, ANN SOPHIA TOWNE, Mrs. Robert K. Darrah (1819–1881). Pastel portraitist, landscape and marine painter; born in Philadelphia, September 30, 1819; died in Boston in 1881. Mrs. Darrah exhibited regularly at the Boston Athenaeum from 1855 to 1865, as well as at the Pennsylvania Academy. The catalogues of the latter institution list her in 1856 as a resident of Philadelphia, in 1858 as of South Charleston (N.H.), and in 1867 as of Boston. Her husband was for many years in the U. S. Appraiser's Office at Boston. ROSALBA M. TOWNE was her sister. ¶ Clement and Hutton; Thieme-Becker; Boston CD 1859–1881; Towne, *The Descendants of William Towne,* 107; Rutledge, PA; Swan, BA; Cowdrey, NAD, 1871/72.

DARROW, T. H. In 1853 E. C. Kellog published a view of New Haven (Conn.), drawn by this artist. ¶ *Portfolio* (June–July 1945), 232, repro.

DART, FREDERICK. Engraver of Hartford (Conn.), 1860. ¶ New England BD 1860.

DARVIN, ERASMUS. Portrait painter of NYC, who exhibited at the National Academy in 1847. ¶ Cowdrey, NAD.

DASSEL, Mrs. HERMINIA BORCHARD (?–1857). Genre and portrait painter. A native of Koenigsberg (Prussia), where her father was a banker, Miss Borchard studied painting under Sohn at Düsseldorf and spent several years in Italy. She came to NYC in 1849 and soon after married. As Miss H. Borchard and as Mme. Dassel she was a regular exhibitor at the American Art-Union (1849 to 1851) and at the National Academy, of which she was an Honorary Member, Professional, from 1850 until her death on December 7, 1857. Mme. Dassel was best known for her portraits of children and her Italian genre scenes. ¶ *Crayon,* V (1858), 26–27; Cummings, 271; Cowdrey, NAD; Cowdrey, AA & AAU; Swan, BA; Rutledge, PA; Washington Art Assoc. Cat., 1857.

DAVENPORT, JOHN. Engraver. A native of Pennsylvania, age 24, Davenport was living in Philadelphia in 1860 in the home of JOSEPH ELDER, also an engraver. ¶ 8 Census (1860), Pa., LX, 235.

DAVENPORT, JOHN D. Engraver, working in Cincinnati (Ohio), 1856–60; in 1859–60 a partner in the firm of DAVENPORT & THOMSON. ¶ Cincinnati CD 1856–59; BD 1860.

DAVENPORT, PATRICK HENRY (1803–1890). Itinerant portrait painter. Born in Danville (Ky.), November 3, 1803; lived in Danville until 1840; subsequently worked in Sumner (Ill.) and in Indiana (*c.* 1857–73); died in Sumner (Ill.), May 13, 1890. ¶ Peat, *Pioneer Painters of Indiana,* 71–72, 228.

DAVENPORT, THOMAS. Engraver; born in England *c.* 1805; living in Frankford (Pa.) in 1850. ¶ 7 Census (1850), Pa., LVI, 318.

DAVENPORT & THOMSON. Engravers of Cincinnati (Ohio), 1859–60. See JOHN D. DAVENPORT and JAMES P. THOMSON. ¶ Cincinnati BD 1859–60.

DAVEY, GEORGE WILLIAM. Engraver, Albany (N.Y.), 1858. The Albany directories for 1859 and 1860 list Davey as a partner in the firm of Cook & Davey, fancy goods. ¶ Albany CD 1857–60.

DAVID, L. Portrait painter, working in Montgomery (Ala.) in June 1860 and in 1878. ¶ *Montgomery Daily Advertiser,* June 11, 1860 (cited by WPA (Ala.), Hist. Records Survey); Montgomery CD 1878.

DAVID, LOUIS P. Commercial artist, portrait painter, drawing master, and daguerreotypist, working in New Orleans *c.* 1838–66. A sign and ornamental painter during the late 1830's and 1840's, David turned to portrait painting and teaching about 1850. From about 1855 he appears to have devoted himself chiefly to daguerreotype work, although he was listed in 1866 as "painter." ¶ New Orleans CD 1838–66.

DAVID, S. S. Landscape painter. He exhibited at the National Academy in 1859 a painting entitled "Coal Rock." In the same year he was listed in the NYC Business Directory as a landscape painter at the same address as WILLIAM INGRAM, also a landscape painter. ¶ Cowdrey, NAD; NYBD 1859/60.

DAVIDS, A. J. Banner painter, at Charleston (S.C.), November 1849. ¶ Rutledge, *Artists in the Life of Charleston.*

DAVIDSON, GEORGE (?–1800). Amateur artist and job-painter. A resident of Charlestown (Mass.), Davidson served as ship-painter on board the ship *Columbia* during its famous voyage to the Pacific North-West (1790–1793) under the command of Captain Robert Gray. He made a number of sketches of scenes along the coasts of the present states of Washington and Oregon, some of which have been reproduced. He died somewhere in the Pacific in 1800. ¶ Porter, "The Ship Columbia and the Discovery of Oregon," 480–86, with 6 repros.; *American Processional,* 26, 238.

DAVIES & BOARDMAN. Engravers, Boston (Mass.), 1860 and after. See DAVID L. DAVIES and WILLIAM H. BOARDMAN. ¶ Boston CD 1860; BD 1861.

DAVIES, DAVID L. Engraver, working in Boston (Mass.) from 1855 to 1860 and after; in 1859 as a partner in DAVIES & HARVEY, in 1860 and after as of DAVIES & BOARDMAN. ¶ Boston CD 1855–60; *Boston Almanac* 1859–60.

DAVIES & HARVEY. Engravers, Boston, 1859. See DAVID L. DAVIES and —— HARVEY. ¶ *Boston Almanac* 1859.

DAVIES, HENRY F. (1822–1884/85). Itinerant portrait painter, working mainly in the Housatonic Valley of Connecticut. He was born June 18, 1822, and died in an asylum at Elmira (N.Y.) in 1884 or 1885. ¶ Sherman, "Unrecorded Early American Painters" (1934).

DAVIES, THOMAS. Watercolor artist. A British artillery officer, who eventually attained the rank of major-general, Davies was in America as early as 1759, when he painted a view of Fort Ticonderoga, now at the NYHS. Other watercolors by him include several views in New York and New Jersey in 1766 and several Revolutionary scenes in the neighborhood of NYC, done in 1776 and 1778. ¶ Information courtesy Dr. R. W. G. Vail, NYHS; information courtesy Dr. James R. Masterson, who cites plates after Davies in the Rev. Andrew Burnaby's *Travels* (3d ed., London, 1798); Ford, *British Officers;* Stokes, *Iconography;* Stokes, *Historical Prints; Antiques* (March 1948), 229–30; *American Processional,* 24–25; *Portfolio* (May 1955), 200–01; represented at NYPL, NYHS, and Winterthur Museum.

D'AVIGNON, FRANCIS. Lithographer and engraver, portrait painter; born about 1814. He is said to have been born in St. Petersburg (Russia) of French parents [Thieme-Becker], but the 1850 Census gives his birthplace as France. He came to America in the early 1840's and worked principally in NYC (1844–59) and Boston (1859–60). His eldest child was born in Germany about 1843; others were born in New York (about 1844 and 1848), Pennsylvania (about 1846), and Connecticut (about 1849). ¶ 7 Census (1850), N.Y., LVII, 127; Thieme-Becker; NYBD and NYCD 1844–58; Boston CD 1859–60; Peters, *America on Stone; American Collector* (March 1948), 11; Coffin, *History of Boscawen and Webster, N.H.,* plate opp. 447.

DAVIS, ——, see BLUM & DAVIS.

DAVIS, ALEXANDER JACKSON (1803–1892). A.N.A. Architect, draftsman, and lithographer. Born in NYC on July 24, 1803, A. J. Davis was first trained as a draftsman and lithographer and produced some excellent views of NYC and Boston buildings in the 1820's. Turning his attention to architecture, he entered into partnership with Ithiel Town in 1829. After 1843 he continued alone for thirty years, occupying a dominant position in American architecture. Many of Davis's architectural drawings were shown at the National Academy and at the American Academy and the American Art-Union; a large number are now owned by the Metropolitan Museum of Art and the New-York Historical Society. He died at West Orange (N.J.), January 14, 1892. ¶ DAB; Snow, "Delineators of the Adams-Jackson American Views, Part II—A. J. Davis"; Cowdrey, NAD; Cowdrey, AA & AAU; Stokes, *Icon.*; Fay, *Views of New York,* repros.

DAVIS, CATHERINE. Painter of two oils showing Boston Common and the State House, Boston (Mass.) in 1827. ¶ *American Collector* (April 1942), frontis.; *Portfolio* (January 1945), repro.

DAVIS, CALEB F. Commercial artist, Detroit (Mich.), *c.* 1834–70; delineator of an 1834 view of Detroit. ¶ Information courtesy Francis W. Robinson, Detroit Institute of Arts; Stokes, *Hist. Prints,* pl. 53.

DAVIS, DAVID. Sculptor. Dr. Davis's bust of John Belton O'Neall was mentioned in the Charleston (S.C.) *Courier* of May 27, 1845. ¶ Rutledge, *Artists in the Life of Charleston.*

DAVIS, EBEN. Watercolor portraitist working in Massachusetts about 1850. ¶ *American Folk Art,* no. 76, repro. p. 25.

DAVIS, ELIAKIM. Portrait painter, Lowell (Mass.), 1837. ¶ Belknap, *Artists and Craftsmen of Essex County,* 9.

DAVIS, J. M. Wood engraver, Portland (Me.), 1860. ¶ Portland BD 1860.

DAVIS, JOHN PARKER (1832–1910). Wood engraver; born at Meredith Bridge (N.H.), March 17, 1832; died at Elmhurst, Long Island (N.Y.), January 19, 1910. He studied wood engraving in Philadelphia, came to NYC in the 1850's, lived for a time in Schenectady (N.Y.), but returned to NYC in 1875. He was also a landscape painter, lecturer, and writer. ¶ *Art Annual,* VIII, obit.; Thieme-Becker; *Artists Year Book,* 50; 8 Census (1860), N.Y., LVII, 904.

DAVIS, JOSEPH B. Portrait and landscape painter, located at New Haven (Conn.) in 1856. This may have been the J. B. Davis who exhibited "Play Fellows, Boy and Dog" at the Maryland Historical Society in 1856. ¶ New England BD 1856; Rutledge, MHS.

DAVIS, JOSEPH D. Artist, Philadelphia, 1857–60 and after. In 1860 he was associated with his father, Solomon Davis, in the cigar business. ¶ Phila. CD 1857, 1859–61.

DAVIS, JOSEPH H. "Left hand painter" of watercolor portraits, working in rural New Hampshire and Maine from 1832 to 1837. Over one-hundred silhouette-like portraits, three of them signed, have been attributed to this prolific primitive painter. ¶ Spinney, "Joseph H. Davis," in Lipman and Winchester, 97–105, with 4 repros.; Spinney, "Joseph H. Davis," in *Antiques* (Oct. 1943), 177–180; Spinney, "The Method of Joseph H. Davis," in *Antiques* (Aug. 1944), 73.

DAVIS, KEENE WEST. Portrait painter whose portrait of Mr. and Mrs. Nathaniel Jillson, painted in 1844, was owned in 1941 by Mrs. Frank E. Craddock of Barre (Vt.). ¶ WPA (Mass.), *Portraits Found in Vt.*

DAVIS, OAKLEY. Connecticut-born artist, 19, at NYC in 1850. ¶ 7 Census (1850), NY., L, 663.

DAVIS, OSCAR. Sculptor. A native Vermonter, age 17, he was living in Brattleboro (Vt.) in September 1850. ¶ 7 Census (1850), Vt., XI, 310.

DAVIS, THEODORE RUSSELL (1840–1894). Illustrator and artist-correspondent for *Harper's Weekly c.* 1861–84. Born in Boston (Mass.), Davis apparently moved to Brooklyn (N.Y.) at about the age of 15. He is said to have had some training in drawing from one Herrick, possibly HENRY W. HERRICK, wood engraver and designer, who was living in Brooklyn in 1856. Davis exhibited in that year at the American Institute a crayon drawing, "Washington." He joined the staff of *Harper's* in 1861, was twice wounded during the Civil War, and afterwards traveled for *Harper's* throughout the conquered South and the mining districts of the Far West. Best known for his illustrations of western life, Davis continued to draw for *Harper's* until about 1884, when he retired to Asbury Park (N.J.) to do free-lance work. He died there on November 10, 1894. ¶ Taft, *Artists and Illustrators of the Old West,* 62 *et seq.;* Am. Inst. Cat., 1856.

DAVIS, WILLIAM. Engraver, working in Lowell (Mass.) from 1834 to 1838. ¶ Lowell CD 1834, 1836–38; Belknap, *Artists and Craftsmen,* 3.

DAVIS, WILLIAM J. Engraver, working in NYC from 1846 to 1854. ¶ NYCD 1846, 1848–50, 1852–54; NYBD 1846.

DAWES, H. M. Engraver of the bookplate of Rev. William Emerson (1796–1811) of Boston. ¶ Stauffer; Fielding.

DAWKINS, HENRY. English copper engraver who came to America *c.* 1753. After a few years in NYC, where he did some bookplate engraving, he settled in 1757 in Philadelphia. He worked at first as assistant to JAMES TURNER, engraver, but in 1758 went into business on his own. In addition to general engraving, Dawkins did caricatures and some book illustrations. In May 1776 he was arrested in NYC on suspicion of counterfeiting, but was apparently released after some time in prison, for in 1780 he was paid by the Continental Congress for engraving bills of credit for the government. Although nothing further is known of his later career, Dawkins may have died in 1786, as his plates were advertised for sale in May of that year. ¶ DAB; Decatur, "The Conflicting History of Henry Dawkins"; Reid, "Some Early Masonic Engravers in America," 100–103; Stauffer; Stokes, *Hist. Prints;* Gottesman, I, 8–9; *American Collector* (Feb. 1945), 6, repro.

DAWSON, THOMAS. Miniaturist. Born in Ireland *c.* 1800; working in Cincinnati (Ohio) as early as 1825, and appears to have lived there at least until 1850. In the latter year his household in Cincinnati included his wife Eliza, a native of Pennsylvania, and two children, ages 17 and 14, both born in Ohio. ¶ 7 Census (1850), Ohio, XXI, 285; Cist, *Cincinnati in 1841,* 141.

DAY, AARON. Portrait painter at Cincinnati in 1829. ¶ Cincinnati CD 1829 (courtesy Edward H. Dwight, Cincinnati Art Museum).

DAY, AUGUSTUS. Carver and gilder of Philadelphia who also did profiles and silhouettes. He advertised as a physiognotrace profilist in Charleston (S.C.) in 1804, and is known to have painted several profiles in Philadelphia in 1834. In the Philadelphia directories he was listed as carver and gilder (1800–06, 1814–21), looking glass maker (1823–25), and painter (1829–33). ¶ Gillingham, "Notes on Philadelphia Profilists," 518; Jackson, *Silhouette,* 93; Carrick, *Shades;* Rutledge, *Artists in the Life of Charleston;* Phila. CD 1800–33.

DAY, BENJAMIN. Sculptor. Major Benjamin Day is listed in Lowell (Mass.) directories as a stonecutter (1832–33), sculptor (1834–40), gravestone manufacturer (1841–47), and proprietor of a marble yard (1842–55). ¶ Lowell CD 1832–55; Belknap, *Artists and Craftsmen,* 18.

DAY, BENJAMIN H., JR. (1838–1916). Artist, illustrator, and inventor; born in NYC in 1838, the son of Benjamin H. Day, publisher. During the 1860's the younger Day worked as a designer in his father's publishing house at 48 Beekman Street, NYC. He exhibited at the National Academy in 1885. He died at Summit (N.J.), August 30, 1916. ¶ *Art Annual,* XIII, obit.; NYCD 1863–65; Cowdrey, NAD.

DAY, CHARLES WILLIAM. An English miniaturist, who exhibited at the Royal Academy from 1821 to 1854, Day was in Boston (Mass.) in 1844. In that year he exhibited seven miniatures at the Boston Athenaeum and was listed in the city directory as William Day, artist. ¶ Swan, BA, 181; Boston CD 1844.

DAY, EMILY. Portrait painter, 21, a native of New York, at NYC in 1860. ¶ 8 Census (1860), N.Y., XLVI, 680.

DAY, HENRY. Drawing teacher, painter in bronze on papier maché. He was living in NYC in 1847 when he first exhibited at the American Institute, but by the following year had moved to Boston where he taught drawing at least until 1860. ¶ Am. Inst. Cat., 1847, 1848; Boston CD 1848, 1851–60.

DAY, HENRY E. Engraver and lithographer; born in New York about 1820. Listed as an engraver and lithographer in NYC directories for 1849–50; exhibited at the American Institute in 1850 a wood engraving done by machinery. He seems to have given up engraving, however, and gone into the publishing business with Benjamin H. Day *c.* 1853. From 1856 he was listed in the directories as a banker. ¶ NYCD 1849–60; Am. Inst. Cat., 1850; 7 Census (1850), N.Y., XLVII, 906.

DAY, MALVINA (1826–?). Painter of a primitive view of Mount Vernon, based on the Robinson-Jukes aquatint; it is now in the collection of Mrs. C. Braxton Valentine. ¶ *Antiques* (Jan. 1952), repro. and information from Marshall Davidson.

DAY, MARION M. Amateur artist of NYC who exhibited three crayon drawings at the American Institute in 1849; possibly a member of the same family as BENJAMIN H. DAY and HENRY E. DAY of NYC. ¶ Am. Inst. Cat., 1849.

DAYE & ELLIS. Engravers, Chicago, 1858. See THOMAS J. DAYE and WILLIAM C. ELLIS; also BACON & ELLIS. ¶ Chicago CD 1858.

DAYE, THOMAS J. Engraver, Chicago (Ill.), 1858–59; in 1858 a partner in DAYE & ELLIS. ¶ Chicago CD 1858–59.

DEAN, BENJAMIN (*c.* 1794–1866). Engraver. He was living in Lowell (Mass.) as early as 1831, when his daughter was born there, and worked in Lowell as an engraver until about 1844. By 1847 he had moved to Providence (R.I.), where he remained until his death on November 18, 1866. In Providence he worked with his sons JAMES and JOHN DEAN, and his brother SAGAR DEAN. ¶ *Providence, Births, Marriages and Deaths: II, Deaths from 1851 to 1870; Lowell Vital Statistics: I, Births;* Lowell CD 1838–44; Providence CD 1847–65.

DEAN, JAMES. Engraver and calico printer, Providence (R.I.), 1847–55. In 1854–55 he was associated with his father, BENJAMIN DEAN, in the firm of B. Dean & Son, engravers and calico printers. ¶ Providence CD 1847–55.

DEAN, JOHN. Engraver, Providence (R.I.), 1847–57. In 1847 and in 1857 he was associated with his father, BENJAMIN

DEAN, in the firms of Dean, Brother & Son and B. Dean & Son, respectively. ¶ Providence CD 1847, 1854–57.

DEAN, ORVILLE B. Engraver, Providence (R.I.), 1860. ¶ Providence CD 1860.

DEAN, REUBEN. Engraver, Providence (R.I.), 1850, as a partner in the firm of [Benjamin] Dean, Brother & Son. ¶ Providence CD 1850.

DEAN, SAGAR (*c.* 1805–1874). Engraver; a younger brother of the engraver BENJAMIN DEAN, with whom he worked both in Lowell (Mass.) and in Providence (R.I.). He was married in Lowell in 1838 and lived there until about 1845. From about 1847 the Deans lived in Providence, where they established the firm of Dean, Brother & Son (1847–50). After 1860 Sagar Dean became a toy merchant. He died in Providence on July 19, 1874, at the age of 69. ¶ *Providence, Births, Marriages and Deaths: VII, Deaths from 1871 to 1880; Lowell Vital Statistics: II, Marriages;* Lowell CD 1839–44; Providence CD 1847–67.

DEANE, E. Miniaturist, advertised at Richmond (Va.) in May 1807. ¶ *Richmond Portraits.*

DEARBORN, NATHANIEL (1786–1852). Wood engraver, copperplate printer. Born in Massachusetts, he took up wood engraving in Boston about 1811, and for over forty years was one of the city's leading engravers. He died at South Reading (Mass.) on November 7, 1852. His son, NATHANIEL S. DEARBORN, also was an engraver and plate printer; the two worked together from 1836 to 1838 as Nathaniel Dearborn & Son. ¶ Stauffer; 7 Census (1850), Mass., XXV, 339; Whitmore, "Abel Bowen," 34; Boston CD 1816, 1820–23, 1826–52.

DEARBORN, NATHANIEL S. Engraver and plate printer, son of NATHANIEL DEARBORN (1786–1852). The younger Dearborn entered the engraving business as his father's partner in the Boston firm of Nathaniel Dearborn & Son (1836–38). He continued to work as an engraver and plate printer in Boston until after 1860. ¶ Boston CD 1836–38, 1841–60 and after.

DEARBORN, SAMUEL H. Portrait painter; son of Benjamin Dearborn, school teacher and manufacturer of balances at Boston. Worked as a portrait painter and musician in Pittsburgh (Pa.) about 1804–06 and in Cleveland (Ohio) about 1807–09. He had returned to Boston by 1818 and was listed there as a portrait painter from 1820 to 1823. ¶ Anderson, "Intellectual Life of Pittsburgh: VI, The Theatre" (226), and "VII, Music" (233); Cuming, "Sketches of a Tour to the Western Country," 81; Boston CD 1818, 1820–23.

DEARING, WILLIAM. Ship carver. During the 1790's Dearing (or Deering) worked at Kittery (Me.) and Portsmouth (N.H.). In 1798 he went to Newburyport (Mass.), where he carved a figurehead for the *Merrimac,* and the following year to Salisbury (Mass.) to carve a figurehead (now in the Old State House, Boston) for the *Warren.* ¶ Swan, "Ship Carvers of Newburyport," 79; Pinckney, 78–79, 190, plate vi.

DEAS, CHARLES (1818–1867). A.N.A. Genre, landscape, and portrait painter, best known for his scenes of frontier and Indian life on the Great Plains. Born in Philadelphia, Deas spent his early years there and in the Hudson Valley. He decided to become a painter about 1836, after failing to win an appointment to West Point, and studied briefly in NYC. In 1838 he exhibited for the first time at the National Academy, of which he was elected an Associate Member the following year. In 1840 he visited his brother at Fort Crawford, Prairie du Chien (Wis.) and became so fascinated with the life of the Plains that he stayed in the West for seven years. He made his headquarters at St. Louis (Mo.) and spent several months each year sketching among the Indians west of the Mississippi. His colorful paintings of Indian and frontier life were shown with considerable success at many exhibitions of the National Academy, the American Art-Union, the Pennsylvania Academy, the Artists' Fund Society, and the Boston Athenaeum. Deas returned to NYC in 1847 but a few years later suffered a mental breakdown from which he never recovered. He died in an asylum in 1867. ¶ McDermott, "Charles Deas: Painter of the Frontier"; Tuckerman; Baur, "Unknown American Painters of the 19th Century," 277–282; Cowdrey, NAD; Cowdrey, AA & AAU; Rutledge, PA; Swan, BA; Turner, "Early Artists"; American Art-Union, *Circular,* 1844–45.

DEAS, R. H. Amateur artist. In October 1843 the Charleston (S.C.) *Courier* noted three crayon views of English subjects and a copy of a portrait of Benjamin Franklin, all by R. H. Deas. The Franklin was described as his first attempt in oil. ¶ Rutledge, *Artists in the Life of Charleston.*

DEAVES, EDWIN F. Engraver and scenic artist working as an artist in New Orleans in February 1850. From 1856 to 1860 he was in San Francisco (Cal.), where he was variously listed as wood engraver, minstrel, scenic artist, and vocalist. ¶ New Orleans *Crescent,* Feb. 28, 1850 (cited by Delgado-WPA); San Francisco BD 1856, 1858; CD 1859–60.

DEBAR, B. Artist; born in England *c.* 1814; living in New Orleans in 1850 with his wife Harriet (age 23, born in Pennsylvania) and a Polish artist A. ZAVYTOWSKY. This may be the Benjamin DeBar listed in the 1858–61 New Orleans directories as lessee of the St. Charles Theatre. ¶ 7 Census (1850), La., IV(1), 465; New Orleans CD 1858–61.

DE BARRAC, HENRY (?–1800). Miniaturist. A native of Guyenne (France), De Barrac fled from the French Revolution and settled in Charleston (S.C.), where he supported himself during the latter part of the 1790's by miniature painting. He died there September 3, 1800. ¶ Sherman, "Some Recently Discovered Early American Portrait Miniaturists"; *not* listed in Rutledge, *Artists in the Life of Charleston.*

DE BARRE, JOSEPH. Engraver. De Barre, born *c.* 1806, and his wife Harriett were both natives of Ireland; they left for America sometime after 1842 and were settled in Maryland by 1848. In 1860 De Barre was living in Baltimore with his wife and five children and owned personalty valued at $400. The oldest son John, born in Ireland *c.* 1842, was an apprentice engraver in 1860; Joseph (12), Harriett (6), and Emma (5) were all born in Maryland, while Julia (3) was born in New Jersey. ¶ 8 Census (1860), Md., VI, 840.

DE BATZ, see BATZ.

DE BAULT, CHARLES. Crayon portraitist. While in Nauvoo (Ill.) in 1853, he made a crayon copy of an oil portrait of the Mormon Prophet, Joseph Smith. ¶ Josephson, "What Did the Prophet Joseph Smith Look Like?", 313, repro.

DEBEERSKI, JOHN. Miniaturist and painter, NYC, 1859–60. ¶ NYCD and BD 1859–60.

DE BIBORY, see BIBEROY.

DEBLOIS, Miss L. Flower painter, who exhibited at the Boston Athenaeum in 1859. She may have been related to François B. Deblois (*c.* 1829–1913), a Canadian-American artist who exhibited at the Athenaeum in 1867 and 1873. ¶ Swan, BA.

DE BRAEKELEER, FERDINAND, JR. (1828–1857). Genre and portrait painter born in Antwerp (Belgium), eldest son of the Belgian artist, Ferdinand de Braekeleer (1792–1883). In 1853–54 he was in NYC as agent for the artists of Belgium and in 1853 he exhibited at the National Academy. By 1856 he was back in Europe and he died the following year. ¶ Thieme-Becker; NYCD 1853–54; Cowdrey, NAD.

DE BRUHL, MICHAEL SAMUEL. Miniaturist, jeweler, and watchmaker, "late from London," at Charleston (S.C.) in August 1798. ¶ Prime, II, 5–6; Rutledge, *Artists in the Life of Charleston.*

DE BRULS, MICHAEL (or Michelson Godhart). Landscape and map engraver who was working in NYC between 1757 and 1763. He engraved at least two NYC views and a map of the region around Fort Niagara. ¶ Gottesman, *Arts and Crafts in New York,* I, 9–12; Dow, *Arts and Crafts in New England;* Stauffer.

DE CHATILLON, see CHATILLON.

DECKER, ERNEST G. Portrait painter, NYC, 1859. ¶ NYBD 1859.

DE CLORIVIÈRE, see CLORIVIÈRE.

DECOMBES, J. MC. Lithographer, New Orleans (La.), 1852–53. ¶ New Orleans CD 1852–53.

DECOMBES, see also DES COMBES.

DEELEY, CALEB. Engraver and lithographer, working in Boston (Mass.) from 1838 to 1854. Mary Deeley, widow, was listed at the same address in 1855. ¶ Boston CD 1838–55; Stauffer; Thieme-Becker.

DE ENZLING, see ENZLING.

DEFAN, ——. Drawing teacher at the [New Orleans] Louisiana Academy in 1825. He was a former pupil of the Academy. ¶ *Louisiana Courier*, Oct. 31, 1825 (cited by Delgado-WPA).

DE FERRIT, see FERRIT.

DE FLORAT, see FLORAT.

DE FRANÇA OR DE FRANCIA, see FRANÇA.

DEFRASSE, AUGUSTE. Sculptor. Born in France *c.* 1821, he worked in New Orleans (La.) from 1854 to 1860. In the latter year his family included his wife Mathilde (29, born in France) and three children —Virginia (8), Charles (6), and Louise (3), all born in Louisiana. His personal property was valued in 1860 at $500. ¶ 8 Census (1860), La., VI, 475; New Orleans BD 1854–56, CD 1856–58, 1860.

DE GERSDORFF, ERNEST BRUNO VON. Amateur artist. A physician, De Gersdorff came from Germany and settled in Salem (Mass.) before 1849. His letters were often illustrated with humorous pen sketches, some of which have been published. ¶ *Essex Institute Historical Collections,* LXXIX (April 1943), 134–52, repros. of 15 of De Gersdorff's sketches.

DEGOUT, MICHEL. "Master sculptor of Paris" who settled at Nachitoches (La.) in the mid-18th century and is remembered for a murder committed by him in 1760 with a sculptor's chisel. ¶ Van Ravenswaay, "The Forgotten Arts and Crafts of Colonial Louisiana," 195.

DE GRAILLY, VICTOR. French landscape painter whose work included many American views, most of them derived from the engravings after WILLIAM HENRY BARTLETT in *American Scenery* (London, 1840). Although it has been asserted (Sears) that De Grailly came to this country about 1840 and returned to France in 1870, no evidence has been found to confirm this statement. ¶ Sears, *Highlights Among the Hudson River Artists,* 1–2, pl. 16–19; *Portfolio* (April 1942), 17, (Aug.–Sept. 1952), 7, (Jan. 1955), 119, repros.; Cowdrey, "William Henry Bartlett and the American Scene."

DE GROOT, JOHN. Engraver, 19, a native of New York, at NYC in 1850. ¶ 7 Census (1850), N.Y., XLIII, 460.

DE GROSS, JOHN. Engraver; born in Kentucky *c.* 1828; working in Cincinnati (Ohio) in 1850. ¶ 7 Census (1850), Ohio, XXI, 286.

DE HAAS, MAURITZ FREDERIK HENDRIK (1832–1895). N.A. Marine painter, born in 1832 in Rotterdam (Holland). He studied in his native city and The Hague and served as Artist to the Dutch Navy before coming to NYC in 1859. He painted a number of naval scenes for Admiral Farragut during the Civil War and also won considerable attention by his coastal scenes. He exhibited at the Boston Athenaeum, the National Academy, and the Maryland Historical Society. He died in NYC in November 1895. WILLIAM FREDERICK DE HAAS was his brother. ¶ Clement and Hutton; Thieme-Becker; Cowdrey, NAD; Swan, BA; Rutledge, MHS; Benjamin, "Fifty Years of American Art," 678, repro.; *Antiques* (June 1944), 286, repro.

DE HAAS, WILLIAM FREDERICK (1830–1880). Marine painter, brother of MAURITZ FREDERIK HENDRIK DE HAAS. Born in 1830 in Rotterdam (Holland), he studied there and at The Hague before coming to America in 1854. He settled in NYC and was a frequent exhibitor at the National Academy after 1865. He was best known for his coastal scenes. He died at Fayal in the Azores, July 16, 1880. ¶ *American Art Review,* I (1880), 551, obit.; CAB; Clement and Hutton; Champlin and Perkins; Bénézit; Thieme-Becker.

DE HART, SARAH. Silhouettist. A resident of Elizabethtown (N.J.), she cut George Washington's silhouette at Philadelphia (Pa.) in 1783. ¶ Jackson, *Silhouette,* 93; Carrick, *Shades,* 18.

DE HOLLOSY, A. Artist working for the ENDICOTTS, NYC lithographers, *c.* 1835. ¶ Peters, *America on Stone.*

DEIERLEIN, FREDERICK. Painter, working in Cincinnati (Ohio) from 1849 to about 1855; he was listed as a portrait painter in 1850. The name appears in the directories variously as Deierlein, Dierlin, and Dierlier. ¶ Cincinnati CD 1849–55.

DEITZ, see DIETZ.

DE KRAFT, CHARLES. Drawing master, Philadelphia (Pa.), 1788. ¶ Prime, II, 46.

DELACROIX, JOSEPH C. or C. I. Exhibitor of transparencies and fireworks at Vauxhall Gardens, NYC, between 1802 and 1815. ¶ Information courtesy J. Earl Arrington, from newspaper advertisements.

DELAMANO, WILLIAM. Painter of stage scenery and panoramas. Listed as an artist in NYC directories from 1843 to 1860, Delamano was employed in the early 1850's as principal artist at P. T. Barnum's American Museum. In 1851 he produced for Barnum a moving panorama of the London Crystal Palace Exhibition of that year. His panorama of the Hudson River was shown in NYC in 1858. ¶ NYCD 1843–60; N. Y. *Herald,* Dec. 2, 1851, June 4 and June 21, 1858. The N. Y. *Herald,* Nov. 7, 1853, mentions a Delamere as painter of scenery for Barnum's production of *Uncle Tom's Cabin* in NYC; this may have been Delamano, since no Delamere appears in NYCD. (*Herald* citations courtesy of J. E. Arrington.)

DELAMERE, see DELAMANO.

DELANEY, JAMES. Portrait, historical, and landscape engraver, NYC, 1846. This may be the J. E. Delaney listed by Stauffer as a portrait and landscape engraver who worked for the magazines about 1850. ¶ NYBD 1846; Stauffer, I, 63.

DELANEY, J. E., see JAMES DELANEY.

DE LANNOY, see DELAUNAY.

DELANOY, ABRAHAM, JR. (1742–1795). Portrait painter. A native of NYC, Delanoy studied under BENJAMIN WEST in London about 1766. On his return in 1767, he set up as a portrait painter in NYC, but the following year he visited Charleston, probably en route to the West Indies. He was back in NYC by 1771 and appears to have remained there until his death. DUNLAP speaks of having known Delanoy in the 1780's, when he was poor and consumptive and his only employment sign-painting. Toward the end of his life he painted portraits in and near New Haven (Conn.). He died in Westchester County (N.Y.) in 1795. ¶ Information courtesy Mrs. William Sawitzky; Stokes, *Icon.;* Sellers, *Charles Willson Peale,* I, 71–73; Gottesman, I; Prime, I; Kelby; Dunlap, *History,* I, 161; Groce, "New York Painting before 1800," repro.; represented at NYHS.

DELAQUIERT, JULES. Artist, New Orleans (La.), 1852–53. ¶ New Orleans CD 1852–53.

DE LARA, ——. Panoramist. Signor De Lara assisted WILLIAM DELAMANO in painting a "grand moving picture of the Crystal Palace [London]," first exhibited in NYC in December 1851. He may have been the William Laragh listed as a painter in the NYC directory for 1851. ¶ N. Y. *Herald,* Dec. 2, 1851 (cited by J. E. Arrington).

DE LAS RIOS, ——. Teacher of "poonah painting" at New Orleans in 1834. ¶ Delgado-WPA cites *Bee,* Sept. 29 and Oct. 18, 1834.

DE LATOUR, see LATOUR.

DELATTRE (or De Latre), HENRI (1801/02–1867). Portrait and animal painter; born in St. Omer (France) in 1801 or 1802; spent most of his life in France. He was in Philadelphia, however, from 1850 to 1855, and during that time exhibited at the Pennsylvania Academy, the National Academy, and the Maryland Historical Society. In 1850 he painted a portrait of President Zachary Taylor on his horse "Mac." He died in Paris in June 1867. ¶ Thieme-Becker; Bénézit; Rutledge, PA; Cowdrey, NAD; Rutledge, MHS; Met. Mus., *Life in America; Antiques,* LII (Nov. 1947), 348–49, repro.

DELAUNAY, JULES. Teacher of drawing and painting, as well as French and Latin, in Charleston (S.C.) from 1848 to 1856. In 1849 he was spoken of as Rev. J. Delaunay; in 1852 as J. P. Delaunay, professor; and in 1856 as Prof. De Lannoy. This may be the Jules Delannay whose silhouette was cut at New Orleans in 1844 by AUGUSTE EDOUART. ¶ Rutledge, *Artists in the Life of Charleston;* Charleston CD 1852; Jackson, *Ancestors in Silhouette,* 105 and 201, identifies Jules Delannay of New Orleans with the French artist, Jules Elie Delaunay (1828–1891).

DE LAUNY, see DELANOY.

DELESSARD (Dellesard), AUGUSTE JOSEPH (1827–?). Painter of portraits, landscapes and interiors. Born in Paris, April 6, 1827, Delessard was working in NYC in 1851 and from 1858 into the 1860's. He exhibited at the National Academy during these years, and also at the American Art-Union from 1849 to 1852. He died after 1891. ¶ Thieme-Becker; Cowdrey, NAD; Cowdrey, AA & AAU; NYCD 1863.

DELEVANNE, ——. Drawing master, working with AUGUSTE DEMILLIÈRE at Philadelphia (Pa.) in 1797. ¶ Prime, II, 6.

DELITISCH, B. Portrait and/or landscape painter, of GROENLAND & DELITISCH, Cleveland (Ohio), 1857. ¶ Cleveland CD 1857.

DELLEKER (Delliker, Dellaker, Deleker), GEORGE. Miniaturist and engraver, Philadelphia, 1817–24. With WILLIAM KNEASS in 1817. With J. H. YOUNG he formed the engraving company of DELLEKER & YOUNG. The New-York Historical Society owns a miniature, signed "G. D." and dated 1805, which is thought to be the work of Delleker. ¶ Stauffer; Fielding; *The United States Navy, 1776–1815,* 125.

DELLEKER & YOUNG, see GEORGE DELLEKER and JAMES H. YOUNG.

DELNOCE, LOUIS (Lewis or Luigi). Engraver, painter of landscapes, portraits, and bank-note vignettes. A native of Italy, Delnoce worked in NYC from 1849 to 1860 and probably until his death about 1888. He exhibited at the National Academy. ¶ Stauffer; NYCD 1849; Cowdrey, NAD.

DE LOUTHERBOURG, see LOUTHERBOURG.

DEMANE, JOHN. Engraver. A native of the District of Columbia, age 24, Demane was in 1860 an inmate of the District Penitentiary, having been committed for larceny in 1856. ¶ 8 Census (1860), D.C., II, 538.

DE MARE, JOHN. Belgian engraver who came to NYC about 1850 and returned to Europe about 1861. His engraving of C. W. PEALE's miniature of George Washington was published in Irving's *Life of Washington* (1855). ¶ Stauffer; *Antiques* (May 1932), 211–12; Morgan and Fielding, *Life Portraits of Washington,* 51–52.

DEMAREST, ABRAHAM. Engraver, die-sinker

and seal engraver, NYC, 1850–59. ¶ NYBD 1850–51, 1854, 1856–59.

DEMAREST, ALEX. Engraver, 28, a native of New York, at NYC in 1850. ¶ 7 Census (1850), N. Y., XLVII, 752.

DEMAREST, ANDREW J. Amateur artist. In 1844 and 1845 Andrew J. Demarest of NYC exhibited portraits of steamboats, including one of the *Troy,* at the American Institute. He was probably a relative of James B. Demarest, tailor, of the same address. ¶ Am. Inst. Cat., 1844–45; NYCD 1845.

DEMILLIÈRE, ANN. Teacher of drawing and painting; wife of AUGUSTE DEMILLIÈRE. She arrived from France with her husband in January 1797, and, after a short time in NYC and Philadelphia, settled in Charleston (S.C.), where she was still living in 1807. ¶ *New York Diary,* Jan. 28, 1797; Rutledge, *Artists in the Life of Charleston.*

DEMILLIÈRE, AUGUSTE. Miniaturist, profilist, and drawing master, who arrived in NYC from Paris in January 1797, accompanied by his wife, ANN DEMILLIÈRE, and presumably their son, AUGUSTE, JR. Later that year the elder Demillière opened a drawing academy in Philadelphia, in association with DELEVANNE. By 1802 he had moved again, to Charleston (S.C.), where he remained until 1807, except for a trip to France in 1806. In 1807 he and his son were working together as Demillière and Son, portrait and miniature painters and profilists. In 1816 his home was at Baton Rouge (La.). ¶ *New York Diary,* Jan. 28, 1797; Prime, II, 6; Rutledge, *Artists in the Life of Charleston; L'Ami des Lois et Journal du Soir,* May 14, 1816 (cited by Delgado-WPA).

DEMILLIÈRE, AUGUSTE, JR. Miniaturist, portrait painter, and profilist; son of AUGUSTE and ANN DEMILLIÈRE. He appears to have begun his artistic career in Charleston (S.C.) about 1807, when he was working with his father as Demillière & Son, portrait and miniature painters and profilists. Nothing further is known of him until 1816 when it was announced in a New Orleans newspaper that, his mind deranged, the young miniaturist had left his wife and home in New Orleans on May 4, apparently intending to rejoin his father who was then living at Baton Rouge (La.). ¶ Rutledge, *Artists in the Life of Charleston; L'Ami des Lois et Journal du Soir,* May 14, 1816 (cited by Delgado-WPA). *Cf.* DOUVILLIER.

DEMING (Denning), Miss CHARLOTTE. Miniature and portrait painter who exhibited at the National Academy in 1833 as a resident of Plattsburg (N.Y.), in 1834 without address, and from 1856 to 1874 as a resident of NYC. Her miniature of E. Corwin, painted in 1833, was engraved by W. D. SMITH. Dunlap lists her as Denning, but the National Academy catalogues consistently list her as Deming. ¶ Cowdrey, NAD; Dunlap, *History,* II, 470; Stauffer, no. 2949.

DEMME, WILLIAM. Lithographer, Philadelphia (Pa.), 1856–57. In the latter year he was a partner in the firm of Schnabel, Finkeldey & Demme (see under SCHNABEL & FINKELDEY). ¶ Phila. CD 1856–57.

DE MONTPREVILLE, see MONTPREVILLE.

DE MONTULÉ, see MONTULÉ.

DEMPSEY, JOHN. Engraver, working in NYC from 1850 to 1860. ¶ NYBD 1850–60.

DEMPSEY & O'TOOLE, see WILLIAM H. DEMPSEY and LAURENCE J. O'TOOLE.

DEMPSEY, WILLIAM H. Engraver, working in Washington (D.C.) from 1858 to 1860, in the latter year as a partner in the firm of DEMPSEY & O'TOOLE. ¶ Washington CD 1858, 1860.

DEMUTH, JOHN (*c.* 1770–1820). Portrait and miniature painter, carver. A life-long resident of Lancaster (Pa.), Demuth painted portraits of his family and carved a wooden figure, "The Snuff Taker of Revolutionary Days," which was still in the possession of his descendants in 1912. ¶ Lancaster County Hist. Soc., *Portraiture in Lancaster County,* 119.

DENECHAUD, CELESTA. Artist. A native of France, living in New Orleans in 1860, age 37, with her brother Edward and his family. They had apparently come to New Orleans before 1856/57, when Edward's elder son was born there. ¶ 8 Census (1860), La., VIII, 138; New Orleans CD 1858.

DENEGAN, SAMUEL. Sculptor, New Orleans (La.), 1841–42. ¶ New Orleans CD 1841–42.

DENHAM, LOUIS W. Engraver, age 16, living in Washington (D.C.) in August 1850. ¶ 7 Census (1850), D.C., I, 83.

DENIS (Dennis), JULIAN N. Engraver, Cincinnati (Ohio), 1850–53; born in Ohio *c.* 1829, the son of Julian C. Denis, a French merchant. Julian N. Denis was a partner in the firm of FRAZER & DENNIS, wood engravers. ¶ 7 Census (1850), Ohio, XX, 150; Cincinnati CD 1850–51, 1853.

DENISE, IRA CONDIT. Artist; born in Franklin (Ohio) in 1840; exhibited in Cincinnati in 1863 and 1866. ¶ Information courtesy Edward H. Dwight, Cincinnati Art Museum.

DENISON (Dennison), Mrs. M. A. A resident of Brooklyn (N.Y.), who exhibited a snow scene at the National Academy in 1855. ¶ Cowdrey, NAD.

DENNEMAN, see DANNEMAN.

DENNETT, Miss A. H. Artist, Boston (Mass.), 1860. She worked in partnership with Miss H. M. TWOMBLY. ¶ Boston BD 1860.

DENNING, see DEMING.

DENNIS, EDGAR. Sixteen-year-old artist at New London (Conn.) in August 1850. ¶ 7 Census (1850), Conn., X, 305.

DENNIS, JAMES M. (1840–?). Portrait and landscape painter. Born in Dublin (Ind.) in 1840, Dennis went to Cincinnati at the age of 18 to study art. He took a studio with ALEXANDER WYANT, studied portraiture under JOSEPH O. EATON, and also painted landscapes. He was in Indianapolis (Ind.) in 1865, in NYC in 1873, and worked for a time in the South before settling in Indianapolis for 20 years. In later years he worked chiefly in pastels. ¶ Burnet, *Art and Artists of Indiana,* 109–112; Cincinnati BD 1860; Peat, *Pioneer Painters of Indiana.*

DENNIS, see DENIS.

DENNISON, see DENISON.

DE NOON, CHARLES. A seaman in the U. S. Navy, De Noon made a sketch of the destruction of the U. S. S. *Philadelphia* at Tripoli in 1803. ¶ *Album of American Battle Art,* pl. 78; *American Collector,* IX (July 1940), cover.

DENYER, ROBERT J. Engraver and die-sinker, NYC, 1848–50. ¶ NYBD 1848–50.

DEPESSEVILLE, ——. Teacher of landscape and architectural drawing, Charleston (S.C.), 1797–98. ¶ Rutledge, *Artists in the Life of Charleston;* Prime II, 6.

DEPEYSTER, GERARD BEEKMAN (1834–1870). Portrait painter; born September 21, 1834, son of William A. DePeyster of NYC. He exhibited at the National Academy in 1863 and 1865, and one portrait by him is owned by the New-York Historical Society, of which he was a member. He died in NYC on June 4, 1870. ¶ NYHS files; Cowdrey, NAD; 8 Census (1860), N.Y., LX, 83.

DE PONTELLI, see PONTELLI.

DERBY, MARY (1814–1900). Portrait painter; born June 17, 1814, in Salem (Mass.); died there January 19, 1900. She was active in Salem during the 1850's and later. Her portrait, painted in 1840 in Louisville (Ky.) by PETER MARSH, is owned by the Essex Institute. ¶ Essex Institute, *Catalogue of Portraits,* 50–51; Belknap, *Artists and Craftsmen of Essex County,* 9; Salem BD 1859, 1861.

DERBY, MARY JANE (1807–1892). Amateur artist and lithographer, born in Salem (Mass.) January 30, 1807. As a girl she did a great deal of drawing, chiefly views, and a lithograph of her father's house in Salem. After her marriage to the Rev. Ephraim Peabody in 1831 she had to give up drawing because of eye trouble. At the time of his death in 1856 Mr. Peabody was minister of King's Chapel, Boston. JOHN ROGERS, the sculptor, was her nephew. ¶ Peabody, *A New England Romance: The Story of Ephraim and Mary Jane Peabody.*

DERBY, PERLEY (1823–1896). Portrait painter. Born at Murfreesboro (Tenn.) in June 1823, Derby came to Salem (Mass.) in 1837, took lessons in painting from CHARLES OSGOOD, and painted portraits of many residents of the town. After the Civil War, he worked in Salem as a genealogist. He died there on March 28, 1896. ¶ Boston *Transcript,* March 29, 1896; Bolton, "Workers with Line and Color in New England."

DERMITT, GRANVILLE. Artist, Boston (Mass.), 1860. He was born in New Hampshire *c.* 1830; his wife Mary E. Dermitt, age 30, was a native of Massachusetts. ¶ 8 Census (1860), Mass., XXVII, 955.

DEROSE, ANTHONY LEWIS (1803–1836). N.A. Portrait, historical, and miniature painter. Born in NYC in 1803, DeRose exhibited at the American Academy in 1823–24 and 1833, and at the National Academy from 1829 to 1835. His portrait of Davy Crockett, the original of which is at NYHS, was engraved by A. B. DURAND. He died in NYC in 1836. ¶ Fielding; Cowdrey, AA & AAU; Cowdrey, NAD; Stauffer, no. 577; NYHS *Quarterly,* Oct. 1955, frontis.

DERRICK, PHILIP (1772–1819). Painter and printer. Born in 1772 at Philadelphia (Pa.); settled in West Chester (Pa.) in 1793; buried there on April 21, 1819. ¶ Pleasants, *Yesterday in Chester County Art.*

DESAIGNES, ——. Portrait and miniature

painter, Philadelphia (Pa.), 1792. ¶ Prime, II, 6–7.

DE SAINT-AULAIRE, see SAINT-AULAIRE.

DE SAINT-MÉMIN, see SAINT-MÉMIN.

DE SAINT REMY, see SAINT REMY.

DE SALAZAR, see SALAZAR.

DESCHAUM, ED. Artist, NYC, 1834. ¶ Information courtesy Mrs. W. H. Whitley, Paris (Ky.).

DES COMBES, ——. German portrait painter with whom THOMAS COLE competed at St. Clairsville (Ohio), 1820. ¶ Dunlap, *History,* II, 354–55.

DES ESSARTS, D. D. Teacher of art, New Orleans (La.), 1808. ¶ *Moniteur,* March 19, 1808 (cited by Delgado-WPA).

DES GENTILS, see MARCHAIS.

DESHON, MOSES. Carver of Boston (Mass.), active *c.* 1742–52. Carved the Faneuil coat of arms for Faneuil Hall (1742) and the arms of the colony for the House of Representatives (1752). ¶ Swan, "Boston's Carvers and Joiners, Part I," 199 and 201.

DESOBRY, PROSPER. Lithographer, working in NYC from 1824 to 1844. In 1824 he was with CHANOU & DESOBRY. ¶ Peters, *America on Stone;* NYCD 1829–43.

DESPORTES, HENRIETTA, see Mrs. HENRY MARTYN FIELD.

DESSARTS, C. Artist of a lithograph by A. IMBERT, NYC, 1835. ¶ Peters, *America on Stone.*

DESSAUR, FERDINAND. Portrait painter, NYC, 1858–59. ¶ NYBD 1858–59.

DE SURÍA, TOMÁS. Topographic artist. A Spaniard, de Suría went to Mexico in 1778. In 1790 or 1791 he accompanied the Malaspina expedition to California as official artist. Six engravings from his paintings were reproduced in the report of the expedition, published in Madrid in 1885 under the title *Viaje politico-cientifico abrededor del mundo por las corbetas Descubierta y Atrevida.* Van Nostrand and Coulter reproduce a watercolor, "View of the Presidio of Monterey, 1791," which is attributed to de Suría or JOSE CORDERO. ¶ Van Nostrand and Coulter, *California Pictorial,* 6–7.

DE TEJADA, see TEJADA.

DETTRITH (or Detirth), WILLIAM. Engraver. A native of Germany, age 24, living in a Philadelphia (Pa.) hotel in September 1850. ¶ 7 Census (1850), Pa., L, 894.

DEUCHEN, ROBERT. Scottish engraver, 26, at NYC in 1850. ¶ 7 Census (1850), N.Y., XLI, 546.

DEVANNIE, FRANCIS. Italian-born sculptor, age 25, living in Philadelphia (Pa.) in 1860. Other boarders in the same house were three young lithographers—NICHOLAS SHIPS, CHARLES SCHILCOCK, and ADOLPHE LABORN. ¶ 8 Census (1860), Pa., LII, 432.

DE VAUDRICOURT, see VAUDRICOURT.

DEVEAUX, DAVID H. Decorative and scenic painter, Charleston (S.C.), 1846 to 1849. Though primarily a commercial artist, Deveaux's work included a miniature painting of "The Fire on Magwood's Wharf" (1846), as well as scenery, transparencies, Masonic aprons, banners, and "The Decorations of the Webster Ball" (May 1847). ¶ Rutledge, *Artists in the Life of Charleston.*

DEVEAUX, JACQUES MARTIAL (1825–1891). Portrait painter. ¶ Fielding.

DEVEAUX, JAMES (1812–1844). Portrait painter. Born in Charleston (S.C.) on September 12, 1812, Deveaux studied painting in Philadelphia *c.* 1830 under JOHN R. SMITH, HENRY INMAN, and THOMAS SULLY. He returned to South Carolina *c.* 1832, and during the next three years worked in Charleston, Columbia, and Camden. From 1836 to May 1838 he was in Europe. Returning to South Carolina in the latter year, he worked there and in Virginia, and possibly at New Orleans, until September 1841, when he again left for Europe. He died in Rome on April 28, 1844. ¶ Gibbes, *Memoir of James Deveaux;* Rutledge, *Artists in the Life of Charleston;* New Orleans *Bee,* July 2, 1844 (cited by Delgado-WPA); Cummings, *Historic Annals,* 178; Cowdrey, NAD; Rutledge, PA.

DEVELLE (Deville), J. Scene painter and teacher. As a young man Develle was employed to paint decorations in the Cathedral at Rheims (France) for the coronation of Charles X (1824). For several years thereafter he was scene-painter for the theater at Le Havre. About 1829 he accepted an invitation to come to New Orleans as a scene-painter and he seems to have remained there at least until 1846. Among his pupils was the panoramist, LEON POMAREDE (*c.* 1830). ¶ *Revue Louisianaise,* I (1846), 22–23, citation courtesy Tulane University; Delgado-WPA cites *Louisiana Courier,* March 24, 1829, Feb. 26, 1833, and Dec. 12, 1842, New Orleans *Bee,* Nov. 18, 1830, July 30, 1836, and New Orleans CD 1830, 1832, 1835, 1837, 1843, 1846;

Arrington, *Nauvoo Temple,* Chap. 8 (MS).

DE VERE, J. Lithographer of two letterhead views of the San Francisco (Cal.) fire of June 22, 1851. ¶ Peters, *California on Stone.*

DEVEREUX & BROWN, see GEORGE T. DEVEREUX and SAMUEL E. BROWN.

DEVEREUX & CO., see NICHOLSON B. DEVEREUX.

DEVEREUX, GEORGE T. Engraver. Born in Massachusetts *c.* 1810–1814, George T. Devereux worked as an engraver in Boston from 1837 to 1844, and then moved to Philadelphia, where he was listed as an artist or engraver from 1847 to 1850 and 1855 to 1860. In Boston he had been a partner in the firm of DEVEREUX & BROWN. In 1860 his household included his wife Sarah (age 44, a native of Pennsylvania) and his brother NICHOLSON B. DEVEREUX, also an engraver; his personal property was valued at $3,000. ¶ 7 Census (1850), Pa., LI, 126; 8 Census (1860), Pa., LX, 550; Boston CD 1837–44; Phila. CD 1847–48, 1845–59; Linton, 19, repro.

DEVEREUX, JOHN. Artist. Born in Ireland *c.* 1817; living in Boston in 1850 with his wife Anastasia (33) and six children, all natives of Massachusetts. ¶ 7 Census (1850), Mass., XXVI, 77.

DEVEREUX, NICHOLSON (or Nicholas) B. Wood engraver. Born in Massachusetts *c.* 1813, apparently an older brother of GEORGE T. DEVEREUX. A member of the BOSTON BEWICK CO. in 1834, he worked in Boston until 1842, and then moved to Philadelphia, where he was listed as Nicholson (or Nicholas) B. Devereux, wood engraver, from 1849 to 1860. From 1858 to 1860 he headed the firm of Devereux & Co., and in 1860 he was living in Philadelphia with his brother and sister-in-law. ¶ 8 Census (1860), Pa., LX, 550; Whitmore, "Abel Bowen," 44; Boston CD 1834–42; Phila. CD 1849–60.

DEVILLE, FELIX. Artist. Born in Florida *c.* 1820, Deville was in 1860 a resident of New Orleans (La.). Though living in a predominantly white neighborhood, Deville's household consisted of Rosida (25) and George (11), both mulattoes, and two mulatto boarders. Deville himself was not listed as a mulatto. ¶ 8 Census (1860), La., VII, 76.

DEVILLE, J., see J. DEVELLE.

DEVLAN (Devlin), FRANCIS DANIEL (1835–1870). Landscape painter; born in Paterson (N.J.), December 15, 1835; died June 6, 1870. Devlan grew up in Reading (Pa.), where at 17 he became a pupil of JAMES A. BENADE. In 1853 teacher and pupil collaborated on a "Landscape with Cattle" exhibited at the Pennsylvania Academy, Benade painting the landscape and Devlan the cattle. Devlan continued to exhibit at the Academy until 1866. During the Civil War he was a cartoonist for *Leslie's Illustrated News.* ¶ Montgomery, *Berks County,* 809–810; Rutledge, PA.

DEVRIES, JOSEPH C. Portrait painter. Devries and his wife Fanny were both born in Holland about 1820, were living in NYC in 1855–56, and in Boston (Mass.) in 1859–60. ¶ 8 Census (1860), Mass., XXVII, 900; NYCD 1855–56; Boston BD 1859–60. NYBD 1856 gives the name as Jacob C. Devries.

DEWEY, JULIUS E. Artist. Born in New York *c.* 1831, Dewey apparently moved to Kentucky sometime before 1850, since his first child was born in that state *c.* 1851. His wife Virginia was also a native of Kentucky. A second child was born to the Deweys in Indiana *c.* 1855. By 1857 they had settled in Cincinnati (Ohio), where a third child was born *c.* 1858. Though listed as an artist in 1857, Dewey was thereafter listed in the directories as a photographer or ambrotypist; the 1860 census records him as artist. ¶ 8 Census (1860), Ohio, XXV, 234; Cincinnati CD 1857–60.

DEWEY, SILAS. Portrait and miniature painter, silhouettist and engraver. He advertised as a portrait painter at Charleston (S.C.) in January 1807, having come there from NYC. He advertised in Baltimore (Md.) in 1810 and was listed in Baltimore directories from 1814 to 1818, although he was in Charleston again in 1816. ¶ Rutledge, *Artists in the Life of Charleston;* Lafferty; Mayo; Bolton, *Miniature Painters;* Dunlap, *History* (1918), III, 294.

DEWING, FRANCIS. Copperplate engraver and printer who worked in Boston from 1716 to 1723. He engraved a number of maps and coats of arms. He was an Englishman and returned to England after 1723, possibly by way of St. Lucia, and was active as late as 1745. ¶ DAB; Stauffer; Middlebrook, "A Few of the New England Engravers"; Dexter, *Memorial History of Boston,* IV, Chap. 6 (courtesy Harold K. Bowditch).

DEWITT, C. Engraver, Philadelphia, 1860. ¶ Phila. BD 1860.

DEWITT, HENRY. Artist, Buffalo (N.Y.), 1856. ¶ Buffalo BD 1856.

DEXTER, FRANKLIN (1793–1857). A prominent Boston lawyer who not only patronized artists but was himself an avid painter. He was born in Charlestown (Mass.), November 5, 1793, and died in Beverly (Mass.), August 13, 1857. ¶ Dexter, *Dexter Genealogy,* 135–137; *Art in America* (Feb. 1950), 21.

DEXTER, HENRY (1806–1876). Portrait painter and sculptor. Born October 11, 1806, in Nelson (N.Y.); spent his early years there and in Pomfret (Conn.), where he was apprenticed to a blacksmith. Taught himself to paint, with encouragement from his wife's uncle, the artist FRANCIS ALEXANDER, and first exhibited at the Boston Athenaeum in 1834. Moved to Boston in 1836 and largely abandoned painting for portrait sculpture. His most ambitious work was a series of busts of the governors of the states, executed in 1859–60. He died in Boston on June 23, 1876. ¶ DAB; Lee, *Familiar Sketches;* Taft, *History of American Sculpture;* Clement and Hutton; Swan, BA; Boston BD 1844–56; Rutledge, MHS; Cowdrey, AA & AAU; Albee, *Henry Dexter, A Memorial.*

DE YOUNG, J. R. Portrait painter and picture restorer, Philadelphia, 1854–60. ¶ Phila. CD 1854–60.

DEZYICK, ALBERT. Engraver. Born in Hungary *c.* 1825; living in Washington (D.C.) in 1860. His wife Elizabeth (35) was a native of the District of Columbia and owned real and personal property valued at $6,800. There were three children: Oliver Whittlesey (10), born in the District of Columbia and possibly Mrs. Dezyick's son by a former marriage; and Albert and Elker Dezyick, both two years old and born in "Ioway." ¶ 8 Census (1860), D.C., II, 421.

DIAZ, CRISTOBAL. Chaplain of the Spanish ship *San Carlos* and painter of a view of the Mission San Carlos Borromeo at Monterey (Cal.) in the late 18th century. This painting, formerly owned by the Society of California Pioneers, was destroyed in the San Francisco fire of 1906. ¶ Van Nostrand and Coulter, *California Pictorial,* 4.

DICK, ARCHIBALD L. (*c.* 1805–*c.* 1855). Engraver. Born in Scotland; studied engraving in Edinburgh and came to America in the early 1830's. He was a partner in the NYC firms of BARNARD & DICK (*c.* 1831) and GIMBER & DICK (1833), but later established his own business. His home from 1839 to 1855 was in Brooklyn. Although Stauffer gives 1865 as his death date, Archibald L. Dick is not listed in Brooklyn or NYC directories after 1855. Mrs. A. L. Dick, widow, is listed in 1857 and 1865, at the same address as ARCHIBALD R. DICK (engraver) and JAMES L. DICK (portrait painter), presumably sons of Archibald L. Dick. ¶ Stauffer; NYCD 1832–40, NYBD 1837–50; Brooklyn CD 1839–68; Cowdrey, NAD; Cowdrey, AA & AAU. Dick's work has been reproduced in Fay, *Views of New York;* Stokes, *Historic Prints; Ladies' Garland* (1849), opp. 133; *Connoisseur* (Dec. 1945), 118–119; *Portfolio* (March 1946), 151.

DICK, ARCHIBALD R. Engraver. Listed in the brooklyn directories for 1856–58 and again in 1868; presumably a son of ARCHIBALD L. DICK and brother of JAMES L. DICK. In 1857 he was living with Mrs. A. L. Dick, widow. ¶ Brooklyn CD 1856–68.

DICK, GEORGE. Scottish engraver, 30, at NYC in 1860. ¶ 8 Census (1860), N.Y., XLV, 50.

DICK, JAMES L. (1834–1868). Portrait painter. Born in NYC in 1834, son of the engraver ARCHIBALD L. DICK. He was a resident of Brooklyn from about 1839 until his death on January 19, 1868. He exhibited at the National Academy from 1855 to 1867. ¶ Stauffer (as James T. Dick, engraver); Brooklyn CD 1855–67; Cowdrey, NAD.

DICKERMAN, SUMNER, see under JOHN MIX STANLEY.

DICKERMAN, WYATT. Portrait painter, Boston, 1844–45. ¶ Boston BD 1844–45.

DICKERSON, DANIEL, see DANIEL DICKINSON.

DICKESON, MONTROVILLE WILSON (1810–1882). Archaeologist and topographical artist. A native of Philadelphia, Dr. Dickeson spent much time in the Mississippi Valley between 1837 and 1844, investigating Indian antiquities. His sketches were elaborated in a moving diorama by J. J. EGAN in 1851, with which Dickeson illustrated his lectures on the subject. ¶ Mason, "Grand Moving Diorama"; Phila. *Public Ledger,* Dec. 31, 1851 (courtesy J. Earl Arrington).

DICKEY, S. Artist. Born in Missouri *c.* 1840, Dickey was living in Coast Fork Precinct, Lane County (Ore.) in 1860.

¶ 8 Census (1860), Oregon (courtesy David C. Duniway, Oregon State Archivist).

DICKHOUT, GEORGE. Artist. Born in Hesse-Cassel (Germany) *c.* 1836, boarding in Philadelphia (Pa.) in June 1860. ¶ 8 Census (1860), Pa. LVI, 834.

DICKINSON, ANSON (1779–1852). Miniature painter, born in Milton, near Litchfield (Conn.), April 19, 1779, a son of OLIVER DICKINSON, JR., and elder brother of DANIEL DICKINSON. He took up miniature painting in Litchfield about 1803, and the following year established his headquarters in NYC. During the next twenty years he travelled widely in New York State and Connecticut, as well as to Charleston, Baltimore, Washington, Philadelphia, Boston, Montreal, and Quebec. One of the most successful miniaturists of his day, Dickinson exhibited at the American Academy, the National Academy, the Pennsylvania Academy and the Boston Athenaeum. After 1825 he worked mainly in NYC, Washington, and in Connecticut. He died in Litchfield March 8, 1852. ¶ Kidder, *Miniatures by Anson Dickinson;* DAB; Cowdrey, AA & AAU; Cowdrey, NAD; Rutledge, PA; Swan, BA; Rutledge, *Artists in the Life of Charleston;* French; Weaks, "A Miniature of Herman Melville's Mother"; *Art in America* (July 1940), 120, repros.; Dunlap, *History,* II, 217; 7 Census (1850), Conn., V, 531.

DICKINSON (Dickerson), DANIEL (1795–?). Miniature and portrait painter; born at Litchfield (Conn.) in 1795, a son of OLIVER DICKINSON, JR., and younger brother of the more famous miniaturist ANSON DICKINSON. He is said to have studied for a time in New Haven (*c.* 1812). About 1818 he settled in Philadelphia, where he worked as a portrait and miniature painter until 1846. From 1847 until at least 1866, Dickinson lived in Camden (N.J.), where he seems to have gradually abandoned portrait painting for horticulture. He is said to have died in Litchfield [Smith]. ¶ Bolton, *Miniature Painters;* French; Phila. CD 1818–46, [Camden section] 1847–61; Camden CD 1865–66 (as Daniel Dickerson); Rutledge, PA; Cowdrey, NAD; Cowdrey, AA & AAU; Smith.

DICKINSON, LOFTUS A. Wood engraver, NYC, 1852–60; born in New York about 1830. As L. A. Dickinson he exhibited a wood engraving at the American Institute in 1856. ¶ NYBD 1852–60; Am. Inst. Cat., 1856; 8 Census (1860), N.Y., XLIV, 505.

DICKINSON, OBADIAH (1812–1850). Portrait and genre painter. Born in Haddam (Conn.) in March 1812; working in NYC in 1839–40 and at Hartford (Conn.) in 1847. He exhibited at the National Academy from 1839 to 1844. C. K. Bolton states that he died in 1850. ¶ Stiles, *Ancient Wethersfield,* II, 291; NYCD 1839–40; Hartford CD 1847; Cowdrey, NAD; C. K. Bolton, "Workers with Line and Color in New England." [All citations courtesy Muriel Baldwin].

DICKINSON, OLIVER, JR. (1757–1847). Amateur portrait painter; born at Litchfield (Conn.), July 10, 1757; died there, March 23, 1847. Though himself an artist of sorts, Oliver Dickinson is chiefly noted as the father of the miniaturists ANSON and DANIEL DICKINSON. ¶ C. K. Bolton, "Workers with Line and Color in New England"; repro. in *Art in America* (April 1925), 156.

DICKINSON, WILLIAM. Miniaturist? The Cleveland (Ohio) Museum of Art owns a miniature portrait on ivory of an unidentified man painted at Troy (N.Y.) in 1836. The almost illegible signature was read by Lawrence Park as "Wm. Dickinson" and was so recorded by Sherman. The Museum, however, lists the miniature as by an anonymous miniaturist of the 19th century. ¶ Letter of Henry S. Francis, Curator of Paintings and Prints, Cleveland Museum, to George C. Groce, Oct. 5, 1954; Sherman, "Some Recently Discovered Early American Portrait Miniaturists," 293–94.

DICKMAN, W. Artist. Born in Pennsylvania *c.* 1824; living in Sacramento (Cal.) in June 1860, with personal property valued at $500. ¶ 8 Census (1860), Cal., V, 22.

DIDDELL, GEORGE. English artist, 30, at NYC in 1860. The 1863 directory lists a George H. Diddell, barber. ¶ 8 Census (1860), N.Y., XLIII, 127; NYCD 1863.

DIDIER, E. Watercolorist and painter of French scenes. A resident of NYC, Didier exhibited at the National Academy 1843–1845, 1870/71. The artist was probably Eugene Didier, a commission merchant from Paris, who was in business in NYC from 1846 to 1860. *Cf.* also Mme. Elizabeth Didier (1803–1877), porcelain painter of Paris, listed by Thieme-Becker. ¶ Cowdrey, NAD; NYCD 1846–60; Thieme-Becker.

DIEMAR, RICHARD. Engraver and gunsmith, Taunton (Mass.), 1856–60. ¶ New England BD 1856, 1860; Taunton CD 1857, 1859.

DIETZ, AUGUST. Prussian lithographer, 24, at NYC in 1860. ¶ 8 Census (1860), N.Y., XLVIII, 978.

DIETZ, JOSEPH J. Artist. Born about 1790; worked in Philadelphia from 1813 to 1860. Sometime before 1833 he is known to have painted a view of "Milford," birthplace of Jonathan Jones Wheeler, at North Wales (Pa.). In 1850 he was living in Philadelphia with his wife Ann (born in Ireland *c.* 1800) and three daughters (born in Pennsylvania between 1822 and 1830); Mrs. Dietz owned $1,400 in realty. ¶ 7 Census (1850), Pa., LIII, 390; Phila. CD 1813–60; Karolik Cat., 216–217 (repro.).

DILL, JAMES E. Engraver, NYC, 1856. ¶ NYBD 1856.

DILLAWAY, GEORGE W., see DILLOWAY.

DILLE, J. H. (1820–?). Portrait painter. Born in Ohio in 1820, Dille was working in Goshen (Ind.) in the late 1850's and was the teacher of ALEXANDER WYANT. ¶ Indiana BD 1860; Peat, *Pioneer Painters of Indiana*, 137–38, 229.

DILLINGHAM, JOHN E. Winner of a prize for pencil drawing at the Illinois State Fair, Chicago, 1855. ¶ Chicago *Daily Press*, Oct. 15, 1855.

DILLON, CHARLOTTE E. Portrait and landscape painter, Cleveland (Ohio), 1857–59. ¶ Ohio BD 1857–59.

DILLON, JOHN B. Irish artist, 39, at NYC in 1850. ¶ 7 Census (1850), N.Y., XLIII, 39.

DILLOWAY, GEORGE W. Sculptor, 40, at NYC in 1850. He was born in Massachusetts; his wife Rebecca and four children, ages 15 to 7, were born in Pennsylvania; the two youngest children, ages 5 and 2, were born in New Jersey. ¶ 7 Census (1850), N.Y., LVI, 39; NYBD 1850–52, as Dillaway.

DIMECK, VICTOR M. Marble engraver. A native of Vermont, living at St. Johnsbury (Vt.) in August 1850, age 37. ¶ 7 Census (1850), Vt., III, 119.

DIMOND, Miss M. Flower painter, NYC. She won a diploma for the best flower painting at the American Institute in 1847. ¶ Am. Inst. Cat., 1847.

DIONIS, SIMON, see SIMON.

DISBROW, JOHN B. Painter. Listed as a painter in NYC directories from 1833 to 1842; exhibited two Mohawk Valley views at the National Academy in 1843. ¶ NYCD 1833–42; Cowdrey, NAD.

DISDORF, PETER J. Engraver and die-sinker, NYC, 1856. ¶ NYBD 1856.

DIX, CHARLES TEMPLE (1840–1873). A.N.A. Landscape painter. A son of General John A. Dix, he was born in Albany (N.Y.) in 1840 and graduated from Union College in 1858. He studied painting in NYC until the outbreak of the Civil War, in which he served as an officer, and after the war continued his studies in Europe. He exhibited at the National Academy, of which he was an Associate, and the Royal Academy. He died in 1873 in Rome. ¶ Clement and Hutton; Thieme-Becker (gives birth date as 1838); NYBD 1858–59, CD 1860; Graves, *Dictionary;* Cowdrey, NAD.

DIX, CUNO. Lithographer, of BURGER & DIX, Detroit (Mich.), 1853. ¶ Detroit CD 1853.

DIXEY, GEORGE (?–*c.* 1853). Sculptor and carver, son of the Irish-American sculptor, JOHN DIXEY, and brother of the landscape painter, JOHN V. DIXEY. He exhibited at the American Academy (1817–20) and the Pennsylvania Academy (1818), and succeeded his father in the carving and gilding business in NYC (1821–32). He continued to live in NYC, with no recorded occupation, until 1853. He died probably in 1853 or 1854, since only his widow was listed from 1854. ¶ DNB (under John Dixey); Cowdrey, AA & AAU; PA Cat. 1818; NYCD 1821–54; Gardner, *Yankee Stonecutters;* Dunlap, *History,* II, 299.

DIXEY, JOHN (?–1820). Sculptor and carver. Born in Dublin (Ireland), probably between 1760 and 1770, John Dixey went to London as a youth to study at the Royal Academy. He exhibited at the Academy in 1788 and is said to have been selected to go to Italy in 1789 for further study. In that year, however, he came to America. He worked for a time in Philadelphia, but by 1801 was established in NYC as a carver and gilder. Though chiefly an ornamental sculptor, Dixey exhibited at the American Academy and the Pennsylvania Academy. His copy of CERACCHI's bust of Alexander Hamilton is owned by the New-York Historical Society. He also executed the statues of Justice for the City Hall (NYC) and the State House (Albany, N.Y.). He died in NYC in 1820, leaving two sons—GEORGE DIXEY, carver and sculptor, and JOHN V. DIXEY, landscape painter. ¶ Strickland,

Dictionary of Irish Artists; DNB; RA Cat. 1788, no. 538; Lee, *Familiar Sketches,* II, 122–23; Dunlap, *History,* I, 329–30; NYHS Cat. (1941); Taft, *History of American Sculpture;* Redgrave, *Dictionary;* Rutledge, PA; Cowdrey, AA & AAU; NYCD 1801–20.

DIXEY, JOHN V. Landscape painter. A son of the sculptor JOHN DIXEY, he first exhibited at the American Academy in 1819, when he showed a bas-relief and six colored drawings. Apparently abandoning sculpture, he later (1827–41) exhibited landscapes at the American Academy, the Apollo Association, and the National Academy. Listed in NYC directories from 1827 to 1850 without occupation, as a lawyer from 1853 to 1863. GEORGE DIXEY was his brother. ¶ DNB; Gardner, *Yankee Stonecutters;* NYCD 1827–63; Cowdrey, NAD; Cowdrey, AA & AAU.

DIXON, ——. Of MACK, DIXON & Co., book illustrators and/or lithographers of New Bedford (Mass.) *c.* 1834. ¶ Peters, *America on Stone.*

DIXON, ELIJAH. Engraver and die-sinker, NYC, 1848. ¶ NYBD 1848.

DIXON, GEORGE. Amateur artist. Captain Dixon visited the northwest coast of North America during a voyage around the world, with Captain Nathaniel Portlock from 1785 to 1788. Several of his sketches were used to illustrate the published account of the voyage, *A Voyage Round the World; but more particularly to the North West Coast of America . . .* (2d ed., London: 1789), opposite pages 192, 205, and 226. ¶ Rasmussen, "Art and Artists in Oregon" (cited by David C. Duniway, Oregon State Archivist).

DMOCHOWSKI, see HENRY DMOCHOWSKI SAUNDERS.

DOBBINS, ——. Painter of a watercolor view of the State House and the Common, Boston (Mass.), 1804, upon which were based several Staffordshireware designs. ¶ Keyes, "The Boston State House in Blue Staffordshire"; Larsen, *American Historical Views on Staffordshire China.*

DOBSON, ——. Itinerant portrait painter of Massachusetts *c.* 1845. His portrait of Miss Wyman of Winchendon (Mass.), painted in 1845, is reproduced in Sears. ¶ Sears, *Some American Primitives,* 183–84, repro. p. 198.

DODD, SAMUEL (1797–1862). Engraver; born in Bloomfield (N.J.), April 7, 1797, and died there August 1, 1862. His engraving business was in Newark. Dodd was active from before 1820 to about 1860. From 1853 he was in partnership with his son, WILLIAM H. C. DODD. ¶ Fielding, *Supplement,* 13; Newark CD 1849–62.

DODD, WILLIAM H. C. Engraver, Newark (N.J.), 1853–60 and after. He was the son and partner of SAMUEL DODD. ¶ Newark CD 1853–60.

DODD, WILLIAM HENRY. Engraver, Hartford (Conn.), 1849–83. He was a partner in BINGHAM & DODD (or Bingham, Dodd & Co.) from 1860 to 1883. ¶ Hartford CD 1849–83; New England BD 1849, 1860.

DODGE & ANDERSON. Ship carvers, NYC, 1845. The partners were CHARLES J. DODGE and JACOB S. ANDERSON. ¶ Pinckney, 190; NYCD 1845.

DODGE, C. Painter of a "still life with melons," signed "C. Dodge, pinxt, Hartford, Conn., 1828." The artist may have been Clarissa Dodge, listed in the Hartford directory for that year. ¶ *American Collector* (July 1947), 17, repro.; Hartford CD 1828.

DODGE, CHARLES J. (1806–1886). Ship and figurehead carver of NYC, in business with his father JEREMIAH from 1828 to 1838. Later he carried on the carving business by himself, and took an active part in civic affairs as school trustee, tax commissioner, alderman, Colonel of Militia, and Mason. His best work as a carver was a bust of his father, now owned by the New-York Historical Society. ¶ [Vail,] "Report of the Board of Trustees," NYHS *Annual Report,* 1952, 16–21; Pinckney, 92, 101, 192; NYCD 1828–70.

DODGE, EDWARD SAMUEL (1816–1857). Miniaturist; born July 8, 1816; died April 6, 1857. He was working in NYC in 1836 and in Poughkeepsie (N.Y.) from 1837 to 1842, and advertised in Richmond (Va.) in 1844. He exhibited miniatures at the National Academy and the American Institute. ¶ Bolton, *Miniature Painters;* Cowdrey, NAD; Am. Inst. Cat., 1842; *Richmond Portraits.*

DODGE, JEREMIAH (1781–1860). Ship and figurehead carver of NYC. He studied ship carving with SIMEON SKILLIN as early as 1798 and was his partner from 1806 to 1811 (SKILLIN & DODGE). After a brief period on his own, he formed a partnership with CORNELIUS N. SHARPE (DODGE & SHARPE, 1815–28). On Sharpe's death, Dodge took into the partnership his son, CHARLES J. DODGE, with whom he worked until 1838. Among the figureheads Jeremiah Dodge is known to have carved were a "Hercules" for the U.S.S. *Ohio* (1820), heads for the *Lexington* and the *Vincennes* (1825), and the well-known "Andrew Jackson" for the U.S.S. *Constitution* (1835). From 1844 to 1849 he was an employee in the U. S. Customs House at NYC. ¶ [Vail,] "Report of the Board of Trustees," NYHS *Annual Report,* 1952, 16–21; Pinckney, 92, 101, 190, repro. opp. 65.

DODGE, JOHN WOOD (1807–1893). A.N.A. Miniaturist and dioramist. Born November 4, 1807 in NYC, worked there as a miniaturist from 1830 to 1844, and exhibited at the National Academy and the Apollo Gallery. In 1848 and 1849 he was in New Orleans (La.), exhibiting a series of dioramas, such as "View of New York," "The Opening of the Sixth Seal," "Interior of St. Peter's Church at Rome," and "The Departure of the Israelites from Egypt." Of his later career little is known, except that he was at Huntsville (Ala.) in 1854, exhibited at the National Academy in 1862, and died December 16, 1893. ¶ Bolton, *Miniature Painters;* NYCD 1830; Cowdrey, NAD; NYBD 1844; Delgado-WPA cites New Orleans *Commercial Bulletin* (Feb. 28, 1848) and *Delta* (Feb. 23, 1849); J. E. Arrington cites *Picayune* (Feb. 22 and March 2, 1849); WPA (Ala.), Hist. Rec. Survey cites Huntsville *Southern Advocate* (March 15, 1854); Dunlap, *History,* II, 444–45.

DODGE, SAMUEL. Artist, 42, a native of New York, at NYC in 1850. The directory for that year lists Samuel N. Dodge, paints. ¶ 7 Census (1850), N.Y., LII, 495; NYCD 1850.

DODGE & SHARPE. Ship carvers, NYC, 1815–28. The partners were JEREMIAH DODGE and CORNELIUS N. SHARPE. On Sharpe's death in 1828 his place was taken by CHARLES J. DODGE and the name of the firm changed to Dodge & Son. ¶ Pinckney, 92, 190.

DODGE & SON, see JEREMIAH DODGE and CHARLES J. DODGE, shipcarvers.

DODSON, RICHARD W. (1812–1867). Engraver, illustrator, portrait artist; born in Cambridge (Md.) February 5, 1812; died at Cape May (N.J.) July 25, 1867. His professional career was spent in Philadelphia. Dodson did a few portraits in sepia which he exhibited at the Artists' Fund Society in Philadelphia and at the Apollo Gallery in NYC (1837–43). ¶ Thieme-Becker; Rutledge, PA; Cowdrey, AA & AAU; Baker, *American Engravers;* Rasmussen, "Artists of the Explorations Overland, 1840–1860," 58, repro. of portrait of Lt. Charles Wilkes, engraved by Dodson after T. Sully.

DOE, JOHN. English engraver, 30, at NYC in 1860. His wife Margery was Irish and their two children were born in New York in 1857 and 1859. ¶ 8 Census (1860), N.Y., LV, 573.

DOEPLER, CARL EMIL (1824–1905). Painter and illustrator; born in Warsaw (Poland), March 8, 1824; came to America in 1849. He worked in NYC from 1849 to 1855, as an illustrator for Harper's and Putnam's. In 1849 and 1850 he sold two European landscapes to the American Art-Union. He died in Berlin (Germany), August 20, 1905. ¶ Thieme-Becker; NYCD 1850–55; Cowdrey, AA & AAU; Cowdrey, NAD; Peters, *America on Stone.*

DOFLEIN, PHILIP. Engraver and die-sinker, Philadelphia, 1859. ¶ Phila. BD 1859.

DOGGETT & ELY, see DAGGETT & ELY.

DOHERTY, ——. Miniature painter. Doherty was a young Irishman whom WILLIAM DUNLAP employed from 1822 to 1824 to exhibit his "Christ Rejected" in Norfolk (Va.), Philadelphia, Boston, Utica (N.Y.), and Washington (D.C.). His own work is represented by a miniature of Samuel Munro Wilson (1805–1832), signed and dated "Doherty 1826" and owned in 1935 by Miss Elizabeth P. Ravenel of Charleston (S.C.). ¶ Dunlap, *History* (1918), I, 341–42, 344–45, 348; Carolina Art Assoc. *Cat.,* 1935.

DOIG, GEORGE. Heraldic painter from London working in Portsmouth (N.H.) in 1775. ¶ Bowditch, "Early Water-color Paintings of New England Coats of Arms," 205.

DOLAN, THOMAS. Artist, 21, a native of New York, at NYC in 1860. ¶ 8 Census (1860), N.Y., XLIV, 911.

DOLANOWSKI, RUDOLPH. Lithographer, of WYSZYNSKI & DOLANOWSKI, NYC, 1845–46. ¶ NYCD 1845; NYBD 1846.

DOLL, CHARLES W. Engraver, 38, a native of Württemberg, at NYC in 1860. His wife also was from Germany but their two children, ages 9 and 5, were born in New York. ¶ 8 Census (1860), N.Y., LIV, 993.

DOLL, FREDERICK W. German-born engraver, 25, at NYC in 1850. ¶ 7 Census (1850), N.Y., XLIII, 39.

DOLPH, JOHN HENRY (1835–1903). N.A. Portrait, genre, and animal painter; born at Fort Ann (N.Y.), April 18, 1835. He began his career as a portrait painter in

Detroit (Mich.), where he was living in 1860. He was working in NYC by 1865, but later studied for five years in Antwerp and Paris. He was well-known after 1875 as a painter of cats and dogs. He died in NYC, September 28, 1903. ¶ *Art Annual* (1903), obit.; CAB; Clement and Hutton; 8 Census (1860), Mich., XX, 104; Wehle and Bolton; Bolton, *Miniature Painters;* Champlin and Perkins; Swan, BA; Cowdrey, NAD.

DONAGHY, JOHN (1838–1931). Genre and landscape painter, newspaper artist during the Civil War. He was born May 4, 1838, in Hollidaysburg (Pa.). He enlisted as a private in the Pa. Volunteers in December 1861, and rose to the rank of captain, and received a disability discharge in December 1864, having been wounded, captured, and imprisoned at Andersonville Prison, from which he escaped in April 1864. He later became a well known genre painter and worked mainly in Pittsburgh (Pa.) and NYC. ¶ *Panorama* (Nov. 1946), 29; *Artists Year Book,* 54; MS Military and Pension Records at National Archives, disability discharge, Dec. 19, 1864; Rutledge, PA; Cowdrey, NAD.

DONALDSON, AUGUSTINE. Artist; born in Philadelphia *c.* 1843, the daughter of DAVID L. DONALDSON, Philadelphia portrait painter, with whom she resided in 1860. In 1864 she was listed in the city directory merely as gentlewoman. ¶ 8 Census (1860), Pa., L, 428; Phila. CD 1860.

DONALDSON, DAVID L. Portrait painter, born in Pennsylvania *c.* 1809. He is listed in city directories as a portrait painter (1837–45), alderman (1846–55), artist (1857–60, 1862), and ambrotypist (1861). He owned realty valued at $3,800 in 1860, when he was living in Philadelphia with his wife and four children, all native Pennsylvanians. His son, Washington, age 20, was a magician, and his eldest daughter, AUGUSTINE, was an artist. ¶ 8 Census (1860), Pa., L, 428; Phila. CD 1835–1862.

DONALDSON, SIDNOR. Artist. Born in Switzerland *c.* 1813, Sidnor (Sidner S., Sydnor S., or S. S.) Donaldson worked in Baltimore as a carpenter (1842, 1845) and as an artist (1847, 1860, 1864). ¶ 8 Census (1860), Md., III, 911; Baltimore CD 1842, 1845, 1847, 1860, 1864; Lafferty.

DONAVAN'S, ——. Jewelers, silversmiths, and miniature painters, working in Philadelphia (Pa.) in 1785 and 1786. ¶ Brown and Brown.

DONEY, THOMAS. Engraver of mezzotint portraits. A native of France, he came to NYC about 1844, after having worked in Canada, Illinois, and Ohio. He exhibited a frame of engravings at the American Institute in 1844 and his name appears in NYC directories until 1849. He was also represented in the 1852 sale of the American Art-Union holdings. ¶ Stauffer; Am. Inst. Cat., 1844; Cowdrey, AA & AAU; NYCD 1845–49; *Richmond Portraits,* repro.; *Antiques* (April 1932), frontis.

DONNAVAN, C. Painter of a panorama of Mexico showing scenes on the invasion routes of the American armies. The panorama was produced and first exhibited in Cincinnati in 1848, and later shown in Boston and NYC. ¶ Boston *Evening Transcript* (Sept. 12, 1848), and N. Y. *Herald* (Feb. 1, 1849), citations courtesy of J. E. Arrington.

DONNELL, S. H. Artist of a view of Madison (Wis.) in 1855. ¶ Stokes, *Historic Prints,* pl. 94-a.

DONNELLY, T. J. Portrait painter, San Francisco, 1858. ¶ San Francisco BD and CD 1858.

DONNELSON, J. L. Modeller of a plaster bust of Dr. Stone of Carrollton (La.), 1852. ¶ New Orleans *Picayune,* March 16, 1852 (cited by Delgado-WPA).

DONOVAN, MICHAEL R. O. Lithographer and locksmith, Philadelphia, 1859. ¶ Phila. BD and CD 1859.

DOOLITTLE, A. B. Miniaturist, profilist, engraver, etcher on glass, and jeweler. A. B. Doolittle first appears as a maker of physiognotrace portraits in Philadelphia in 1804. Two years later he set up shop in New Haven (Conn.) as a jeweler, miniaturist and profilist. In 1807 he drew and engraved a view of Yale College, which was published by A. Doolittle & Son. A profile of John Adams, etched in gold on glass, dates from about the same time. His relationship to AMOS DOOLITTLE is not known. ¶ Brown and Brown cite *U. S. Gazette,* Feb. 29, 1804; Beardsley, "An Old New England Engraver and His Work: Amos Doolittle"; *Antiques* (Oct. 1928), 323–324, repro.; Jackson, *Silhouette,* 95; Carrick, *Shades;* Weis, *Check List. Cf.* Owen, "America's Youngest Engraver," in which it is suggested that A. B. Doolittle was *not* the son of Amos Doolittle.

DOOLITTLE, AMOS (1754–1832). Engraver. Amos Doolittle, one of the earliest American engravers on copper, was born at

Cheshire (Conn.) on May 18, 1754. Trained as a jeweler and silversmith, he taught himself engraving. His most famous work was a series of four engravings of the Battles of Lexington and Concord, drawn by RALPH EARL, engraved and published by Doolittle in 1775. Doolittle also engraved bookplates, portraits, and biblical illustrations. In 1807 he and a son, possibly A. B. DOOLITTLE, were in business together in New Haven. Another son, HORACE DOOLITTLE, was producing engravings as early as 1804. Amos Doolittle died in New Haven, January 30, 1832 (DAB, but New Haven Vital Records gives February 2, 1832). ¶ DAB; Doolittle, *The Doolittle Family in America,* III, 239 ff.; New Haven Vital Records, II, 663; Stauffer; Beardsley, "An Old New England Engraver and His Work: Amos Doolittle"; Stokes, *Historic Prints,* pl. 80. Owen, "America's Youngest Engraver," suggests that A. B. Doolittle was *not* a son of Amos.

DOOLITTLE, CURTIS M. Engraver, of DOOLITTLE & MUNSON, Cincinnati (Ohio), 1831–49. A native of Connecticut, he may have been related to AMOS DOOLITTLE. ¶ Stauffer; Cincinnati CD 1831–49.

DOOLITTLE, HORACE (1792–?). Engraver, who in 1804 made two small engravings for a manuscript by a Rebecca W. Hillhouse. He was 12 years old at the time, according to the signature of one of the engravings. A third engraving for Miss Hillhouse's work was done by AMOS DOOLITTLE, presumably Horace's father. He is thought to have died before reaching maturity. ¶ Owen, "America's Youngest Engraver."

DOOLITTLE, ISAAC. Lithographer, of BARNET & DOOLITTLE, in NYC *c.* 1821–22. Barnet and Doolittle had studied lithography in Paris and were among the earliest practitioners of the new art in America. They had earlier been interested in patents for improvements in steamboats. ¶ McClinton, "American Flower Lithographs," 361, repro.

DOOLITTLE & MUNSON. Engravers specializing in banknote work, Cincinnati, 1831–49. The partners, both from Connecticut, were CURTIS M. DOOLITTLE and SAMUEL B. MUNSON. ¶ Cincinnati CD 1831–49; Stauffer.

DOOLITTLE, SAMUEL. Engraver. A bookplate signed "S. D. Sct. 1804" has been attributed to Samuel Doolittle of Boston. ¶ Stauffer.

DOOLITTLE, S. C. Silhouette cutter, Charleston (S.C.), *c.* 1800–10. ¶ Jackson, *Silhouette,* 95.

DORAN, JAMES. Irish artist, 45, at NYC in 1850. His wife Mary was also Irish but their daughter Margaret, aged 15, was born in Rhode Island. He was listed as a designer in the directory. ¶ 7 Census (1850), N.Y., XLIII, 460; NYCD 1850.

DORAN, JOHN C. Engraver. Born in Rhode Island *c.* 1826; married and living in Philadelphia (Pa.) in August 1850. ¶ 7 Census (1850), Pa., XLVII, 244.

DORATT (Dorratt), CHARLES. Portrait painter, NYC, 1838–39. In 1839 he exhibited at the National Academy. He exhibited in Cincinnati in 1841. ¶ NYCD 1838–39; Cowdrey, NAD; information courtesy Edward H. Dwight.

DORIVAL, JOHN. Lithographer, NYC, 1826–38. During part of this time he was listed merely as "fine arts" and later as "merchant." ¶ Peters, *America on Stone;* NYCD 1826–38.

D'ORLEANS, ANTOINE PHILIPPE, see MONTPENSIER.

D'ORLEANS, LOUIS CHARLES, see BEAUJOLAIS.

DORNS, FRANCIS. Engraver. Born in "Bohama" [Bahama?] *c.* 1815; boarding in Baltimore (Md.) in September 1860. ¶ 8 Census (1860), Md., V, 229.

DORRANCE, W. H. Portrait painter of NYC, exhibitor at the National Academy in 1837. ¶ Cowdrey, NAD.

DORSEY, JOHN. Apprentice lithographer, age 16, living in the home of his father, James H. Dorsey (porter), in Boston, July 1860. ¶ 8 Census (1860), Mass., XXVII, 229; Boston CD 1860.

DORSEY, JOHN. Artist, 33, a native of Nova Scotia, at NYC in 1860. ¶ 8 Census (1860), N.Y., LVI, 165.

DORSEY, JOHN SYNG (1783–1818). Medical artist, born in Philadelphia, December 23, 1783. After studying in Philadelphia, London, and Paris, he began the practise of medicine in Philadelphia in 1804. An amateur artist of considerable skill, he provided many of the illustrations for his own *Elements of Surgery* (1813). He also painted some portraits and did engraving and etching. He died at Philadelphia, November 12, 1818, at the age of 35. ¶ DAB; Fielding; Fielding, *Supplement.*

DORSEY, THOMAS. Engraver. A native of France, living in Philadelphia (Pa.) in July 1860. He was then 27 years old and owned personal property valued at $2,000. ¶ 8 Census (1860), Pa., LII, 899.

D'Othon, A. H. Landscape painter, NYC, 1859. ¶ NYBD 1859.

Doty & Bergen. Engravers and lithographers, NYC, 1846–59; Warren S. Doty and Peter G. Bergen. They were listed as lithographers only in 1859. ¶ NYCD 1846–49; NYBD 1846–59.

Doty & Jones. Engravers, NYC, 1844–45; Warren S. Doty and George Jones. ¶ NYCD 1844–45.

Doty, Warren S. Engraver, NYC, 1840–59. From 1834 to 1839 he was listed as a map-mounter; in 1840 as engraver; in 1841, of Pollock & Doty, engravers; 1844–45, of Doty & Jones, engravers; 1846–59, of Doty & Bergen, engravers. ¶ NYCD 1834–49; NYBD 1846–59.

Dougal, William H. (1822–1895). Engraver and draftsman. Born in New Haven (Conn.), January 30, 1822, he was apprenticed at 15 to the NYC engravers, Sherman & Smith. By 1844 he was working independently in Washington (D.C.), his first important commission being the engraving of plates for the reports of the Wilkes expedition. During 1849 and 1850 he was in California, where he made numerous sketches (reproduced in Stanger). Returning to Washington toward the end of 1850, Dougal married there the following year and continued to work as an engraver for government publications, banks, and publishers until his death in 1895. He exhibited at the Washington Art Association in 1857. In 1860 his household included his wife and three children, all born in Washington; Dougal then owned $10,000 in realty and $7,000 in personalty, while his wife owned realty valued at $2,500. Gilbert Manger lived with the Dougals. ¶ Stanger, ed., *Off for California;* 8 Census (1860), D.C., II, 28; Cal. Hist. Soc. *Quarterly* (Sept. 1943), 235–252, letters and repros.; Washington Art Assoc. Cat., 1857; Stauffer. Plates by Dougal appeared in Wilkes, *United States Exploring Expedition;* Marcy's *Exploration of the Red River of Louisiana.*

Dougherty, Hugh. Lithographer. Born in Pennsylvania *c.* 1843; boarding in Philadelphia in June 1860. ¶ 8 Census (1860), Pa. LIV, 383.

Dougherty, James. Engraver. Born in Ireland *c.* 1841; living in Philadelphia in 1860–61, in the home of Jane, widow of William (or Francis) Dougherty. ¶ 8 Census (1860), Pa., LVII, 516; Phila. CD 1861.

Dougherty, William. Engraver. Born in Pennsylvania *c.* 1832; living in Philadelphia in 1850, with his mother, Jane Dougherty (45), and listed in city directories for 1859–61. ¶ 7 Census (1850), Pa., LIII, 567; Phila. CD 1859–61.

Doughty, Edmund. Engraver, 21, a native of New York, at NYC in 1860. ¶ 8 Census (1860), N.Y., XLIV, 889.

Doughty, Thomas (1793–1856). Landscape painter and lithographer. Born in Philadelphia on July 19, 1793, he was apprenticed to a leather merchant and worked as a leather currier in Philadelphia until 1820 when he abandoned his trade for the profession of landscape painting. One of the first American artists to devote himself primarily to the genre, Doughty quickly won critical acclaim for his quiet landscapes of the rivers and mountains of Pennsylvania, New York, and New England. He was elected a Member of the Pennsylvania Academy in 1824 and an Honorary Member, Professional, of the National Academy in 1827. Though he spent much time in Baltimore, Washington, Boston, and NYC, Doughty continued to make his home in Philadelphia until 1832 when he moved to Boston. After five years in Boston, he went to England for two years. On his return to America in 1838, Doughty lived for a time in NYC, but in 1839–40 he was at Newburgh (N.Y.) on the Hudson River. He returned in 1841 to NYC, where he remained, except for a second trip to Europe (1845–46) and a brief residence in western New York (1852–54), until his death on July 22, 1856. A prolific artist, Doughty exhibited frequently at the Pennsylvania Academy, Boston Athenaeum, American Academy, National Academy, Maryland Historical Society, and several British and French galleries, and he sold many paintings to the Apollo Association and American Art-Union. As a lithographer he is best known for a series of rural scenes published in the *Cabinet of Natural History and American Rural Sports,* a periodical published in Philadelphia (1830–34) by the brothers, John and Thomas (J. & T.) Doughty. ¶ The most complete record of Doughty's life is Howard N. Doughty's manuscript "Life and Works of Thomas Doughty," given by the author to the New-York Historical Society. See also: DAB; Clement and Hutton; Peters, *America on Stone;* Cowdrey, NAD; Cowdrey, AA & AAU; Rutledge, PA; Rutledge, MHS;

Swan, BA; Graves, *Dictionary*. Doughty's work is represented in the Metropolitan Museum, Pennsylvania Academy, Brooklyn Museum, Corcoran Gallery, Peabody Institute, the New-York Historical Society, and elsewhere.

DOUGHTY, THOMAS, JR. Genre and landscape painter. A son of the noted landscape painter, he submitted paintings to the American Art-Union in 1849 and 1850. In 1850 his "Sporting Scene—Long Island," was bought by the Art-Union. ¶ Doughty, "Thomas Doughty," 72, 73; Cowdrey, AA & AAU, under Thomas Doughty (1793–1856).

DOUGLAS, JOHN. Engraver and lithographer, New Orleans. Born in Ireland *c.* 1826; working in New Orleans from 1854 to 1870, as successor to T. H. SHIELDS. In 1860 his household included his wife Mary (Irish, age 22) and their two-months-old son John; his property was valued at $20,000 in realty and $3,500 in personalty. ¶ 8 Census (1860), La., V, 529; New Orleans CD 1854–56, 1870.

DOUGLAS, LUCY. Primitive watercolorist, active *c.* 1810. Her painting, "The Royal Psalmist," was shown at the Stone Gallery, NYC, in 1942. ¶ Lipman, *American Primitive Painting,* repro.; *Art in America* (July 1942), 202.

DOUGLAS, ROBERT, see ROBERT DOUGLASS.

DOUGLASS, ——. Portrait painter. Stauffer lists an engraving (1826) after his portrait of Rev. Henry Kollock of Savannah (Ga.). ¶ Stauffer, nos. 2031–32.

DOUGLASS, ALONZO (*c.* 1815–1886). Portrait painter. A native of the District of Columbia, working in Cincinnati as a portrait painter from 1828 to 1831 and from 1842 to 1846. In 1840 and after 1848 he was employed as a bank clerk. An obituary notice in the Boston *Transcript,* April 5, 1886, states that Douglass—a ripe scholar, accomplished musician, and excellent painter—died "last week" in Louisville (Ky.) at the age of 71. ¶ Cincinnati CD 1829–65; Cist, *Cincinnati in 1841,* 139; Boston *Transcript,* April 5, 1886.

DOUGLASS, CAROLINE. Drawing teacher. A native of Pennsylvania, age 22, living in Philadelphia in 1860, with her father John Douglass, shoemaker. ¶ 8 Census (1860), Pa., LIII, 513.

DOUGLASS, DAVID BATES (?–1849). Amateur artist; officer in the Corps of Engineers, U. S. Army. Appointed 2d Lieutenant in 1813, he served at Fort Erie, and in 1815 was present at the Battle of New Orleans, of which he made a sketch, later engraved by J. VALLANCE. He was on the faculty of West Point from 1820 to 1831, and died October 19, 1849. ¶ Heitman, *Historical Register;* Stauffer (under Vallance).

DOUGLASS, ROBERT M. J. (1809–1887). Portrait, sign, and ornamental painter, lithographer. A Negro, born in Philadelphia, February 8, 1809, Robert Douglass studied under THOMAS SULLY. Except for visits to Haiti and England, he seems to have worked almost exclusively in Philadelphia. He exhibited one portrait at the Pennsylvania Academy in 1834. He was recorded in the 1850 Census as Robert Douglass, engraver, age 37, mulatto, owning realty valued at $1,000; others in the house were his wife Sarah, age 21, mulatto, $1,000 in realty; and James F. Douglass, age 35, hairdresser, $1,000 in realty. The artist died, probably in Philadelphia, on October 26, 1887. ¶ J. A. Porter, *Modern Negro Art,* 30–35; Phila. CD 1833–87; Rutledge, PA; 7 Census (1850), Pa., LII, 351.

DOUGLASS, RUSH. French engraver, 34, at NYC in 1860. His wife was also French but their two children were born in New York in 1857 and 1859. ¶ 8 Census (1860), N.Y., XLVI, 85.

DOURITCH (possibly Danrith or Denrith), FRANCIS. Lithographer; born in Germany about 1825; working in Pittsburgh (Pa.) in August 1850. ¶ 7 Census (1850), Pa., III(2), 156.

DOUVILLIER, ——. Scene painter at a New Orleans theatre in 1813. ¶ New Orleans *Moniteur,* March 20, 1813 (cited by Delgado-WPA). *Cf.* AUGUSTE DEMILLIÈRE, JR.

DOVE, Mrs. ——. Miniaturist, working in Charleston (S.C.) in 1844. ¶ Rutledge, *Artists in the Life of Charleston;* Carolina Art Assoc., MS on miniaturists.

DOWN, FREDERICK. Painter, NYC, 1840's. Listed merely as "painter" in the directories, Down exhibited three paintings at the American Institute in 1844. ¶ NYCD 1843–44; Am. Inst. Cat., 1844.

DOWNES, J. Engraver and designer of Worcester (Mass.), *c.* 1834–50; designed cuts for many books during this period, and contributed to *The American Magazine of Useful and Entertaining Knowledge* (Boston, 1835). ¶ Hamilton, *Early American Book Illustrators.*

Downey, Sabien B., sculptress, see S. Boardman Downing.

Downing, S. Boardman (or Sabien B. Downey). Sculptor. S. Boardman Downing, listed as artist or sculptor in Philadelphia directories from 1860 to 1864, exhibited portrait busts in plaster and marble at the Pennsylvania Academy from 1858 to 1868. Sabien B. Downey, recorded in the 1860 census as a sculptress, age 20, native of Pennsylvania, is undoubtedly the same, since both are recorded as residing with Delia Downing or Downey (a native of Massachusetts, age 48, $1,000 in personalty). ¶ Rutledge, PA; Phila. CD 1860–64; 8 Census (1860), Pa., LV, 102.

Doyle & Cavanaugh. Engravers, Philadelphia, 1850; probably William Doyle and William Cavanaugh. ¶ Phila. BD 1850.

Doyle, Margaret Byron (Mrs. John Chorley). Portrait and miniature painter; daughter of William M. S. Doyle, portrait and miniature painter, and the wife of John Chorley, engraver. She exhibited at the Boston Athenaeum in 1828 and 1829. ¶ Swan, BA; Smith; Stauffer, nos. 97, 104, 1415 (as Maria Byron Doyle).

Doyle, William. Engraver, of Philadelphia, 1849; probably a partner in Doyle & Cavanaugh, 1850. ¶ Phila. CD 1849; BD 1850.

Doyle, William M. S. (1769–1828). Portrait and miniature painter, pastel and crayon portraitist, silhouettist. Doyle was born in Boston, worked there, and died there in May 1828. He was the father of Margaret Byron Doyle. ¶ Bolton, *Miniature Painters;* Bolton, *Crayon Draftsmen;* Stauffer, nos. 78, 838, 2636, 2931; Jackson, *Silhouette,* 95; Sears, *Some American Primitives,* repro. 133–34; Brigham, "Notes on the Thomas Family Portraits"; *Antiques* (Feb. 1934), 76, and (Oct. 1942), 171, repros.; represented in the American Antiquarian Society (Weis).

Drach, S. Portrait painter, NYC, 1820. *Cf.* Simon Drach, German miniaturist. ¶ NYCD 1820; Rosette Drach or Dracht, widow, was listed in NYCD 1829–35; Thieme-Becker.

Draddy, John G. (1833–1904). Sculptor. In 1859–60 he was working in Cincinnati, in the latter year as a partner in the firm of Draddy & O'Brien. He later worked in NYC with his brothers Daniel and James. Examples of his work are in St. Patrick's Cathedral, NYC. ¶ Thieme-Becker; Cincinnati CD 1859, BD 1860; NYCD 1865, 1868 (the Draddy brothers were sons of Daniel Draddy, stonecutter, NYCD 1858).

Draddy & O'Brien. Sculptors, Cincinnati, 1860; John G. Draddy and Daniel O'Brien. ¶ Cincinnati BD 1860.

Drake, John Poad (1794–1883). Historical painter, naval architect, and inventor; baptized July 20, 1794, in the village of Stoke Damerel (Devon, England). An accomplished draftsman, he designed a number of improvements in naval construction and ordnance. Seeing Napoleon on board H.M.S. *Bellerophon* in 1815, he made a painting of the scene, which he shortly after brought to America. First visiting Nova Scotia and Montreal, where he painted a few portraits, he came to NYC in 1821 and there exhibited his painting of Napoleon. After his return to England in 1827, he worked chiefly as a naval designer and inventor until his death on February 26, 1883, at Fowey (Cornwall). ¶ DNB; Piers, "Artists in Nova Scotia," 121–22; Dunlap, *History,* II, 471; Thieme-Becker.

Drake, William. Irish engraver, 29, at NYC in 1860. ¶ 8 Census (1860), N.Y., LXII, 537.

Draper & Company. Banknote engravers, Philadelphia, 1845–1850. This firm, composed of John, Robert, and William Draper, was successor to Draper, Toppan & Co. and was followed by Draper, Welsh & Co. ¶ Phila. CD 1845–50.

Draper, John. Banknote engraver. A native Pennsylvanian, Draper studied engraving under Robert Scott of Philadelphia. Starting in the mid-1790's, he continued in the engraving business over 50 years. He was a partner in the following firms: Murray, Draper, Fairman & Co. (1814–17); Fairman, Draper & Co. (1823–24); Fairman, Draper, Underwood & Co. (1825); Draper, Underwood & Co. (1828–31); Draper, Underwood, Bald & Spencer (1833); Draper, Toppan, Longacre & Co. (1835–39); Draper, Toppan & Co. (1840–44); and Draper & Co. (1845–46). He reappears in 1851 as a partner in Draper, Welsh & Co. John Draper was the father of Robert and William Draper, who joined him in 1845 in Draper & Co. ¶ Toppan, *100 Years of Bank Note Engraving,* 7; Stauffer; Phila. CD 1805–1851; Brown and Brown.

Draper, Robert. Banknote engraver; born about 1820 in Pennsylvania, probably in

Philadelphia where his father, JOHN DRAPER, was a banknote engraver. He and his brother, WILLIAM DRAPER, were taken into partnership by their father in 1845, under the name of DRAPER & Co. On the dissolution of this partnership in 1850/51, Robert Draper established the firm of DRAPER, WELSH & Co. which flourished until its merger in 1858 with the newly-formed AMERICAN BANK NOTE COMPANY, of which Draper was manager in 1863–64. In 1860 he was living, unmarried, in Philadelphia, with personal estate valued at $25,000. His name appears in the directories from 1865 to 1889 without occupation. ¶ 8 Census (1860), Pa., LII, 489; Phila. CD 1845–1889.

DRAPER, TOPPAN & COMPANY. Banknote engravers. This firm, successor to DRAPER, TOPPAN, LONGACRE & Co., was established in 1840 by JOHN DRAPER and CHARLES TOPPAN. Its main office was at Philadelphia, while subsidiary branches were maintained in NYC and Boston. In 1844/45 Toppan withdrew, and Draper took his own sons into partnership as DRAPER & Co. ¶ Phila. CD 1840–44; NYBD 1840–41, 1844; Boston BD 1843, CD 1844.

DRAPER, TOPPAN, LONGACRE & COMPANY. Banknote engravers. Established in Philadelphia in 1834 or 1835 by JOHN DRAPER, CHARLES TOPPAN, and JAMES B. LONGACRE, the firm continued under this name until 1839/40, when Longacre withdrew and the name changed to DRAPER, TOPPAN & COMPANY. ¶ Phila. CD 1835–40.

DRAPER, UNDERWOOD, BALD & SPENCER. Banknote engravers. This short-lived firm, successor to DRAPER, UNDERWOOD & Co., was established in Philadelphia in 1832/33 and lasted only a year or two. The partners were JOHN DRAPER, THOMAS UNDERWOOD, ROBERT BALD, and ASA SPENCER. A branch in New Haven (Conn.) was operated by NATHANIEL and SIMEON S. JOCELYN. By 1835 the firm had split into DRAPER, TOPPAN, LONGACRE & COMPANY and UNDERWOOD, BALD & SPENCER. ¶ Phila. CD 1833–35; Rice, "Life of Nathaniel Jocelyn."

DRAPER, UNDERWOOD & COMPANY. Banknote engravers. Following the dissolution of FAIRMAN, DRAPER, UNDERWOOD & Co. (*c.* 1827), JOHN DRAPER and THOMAS UNDERWOOD carried on under this name until about 1833, when it became DRAPER, UNDERWOOD, BALD & SPENCER. The firm was represented in the Pennsylvania Academy exhibition of 1831. ¶ Phila. CD 1828–31; *Am. Adv. Directory* 1832; Pa. Acad. Cat., 1831.

DRAPER, WELSH & COMPANY. Banknote engravers. Established in 1851 by JOHN and ROBERT DRAPER and CHARLES WELSH, this Philadelphia firm was active in Phildelphia until the formation of the great AMERICAN BANK NOTE COMPANY in 1858. A branch in NYC was known as JOCELYN, DRAPER, WELSH & Co. (1854–58). ¶ Phila. CD 1851–59; Rice, "Life of Nathaniel Jocelyn."

DRAPER, WILLIAM. Banknote engraver, Philadelphia, 1845–1850. William, son of JOHN and brother of ROBERT DRAPER, was a partner in the family firm of DRAPER & Co. ¶ Phila. CD 1845–50.

DRAYTON, J. (in Stauffer), see JOSEPH DRAYTON.

DRAYTON, JOHN (in Smith), see JOSEPH DRAYTON.

DRAYTON, JOHN (1766–1822). Amateur artist and illustrator. Born at "Drayton Hall," near Charleston (S.C.), June 22, 1766, Drayton became a prominent legislator and jurist and served two terms as governor of his native state. He was also the author of several books, including *Letters Written during a Tour through the Northern and Eastern States of America* (1794); a translation of Thomas Walter's *Flora Caroliniana* (1798); and *A View of South Carolina, as Respects Her Natural and Civil Concerns* (1802). The manuscripts of the last two, with watercolor illustrations by Drayton, are now owned by the Charleston Library Society. Drayton died in Charleston November 27, 1822. ¶ DAB; Rutledge, *Artists in the Life of Charleston,* 127; [Drayton], *The Carolina Florist of Governor John Drayton of South Carolina . . . with Water-color Illustrations from the Author's Original Manuscript* (Columbia, S.C., 1943).

DRAYTON, JOSEPH. Engraver, portrait painter, and artist to the Wilkes expedition; working in Philadelphia as an engraver as early as 1819 when his engraving of a Scottish landscape by CAROLINE SCHETKY was published in the *Analectic Magazine.* Other engravings by Drayton appeared in the *Analectic* the following year. He continued to work in Philadelphia until about 1838, when he joined the Wilkes exploring expedition as artist. On the conclusion of the expedition in 1842, Drayton may have gone to Washington to work on the illustrations for the Wilkes reports. ¶ *Analectic Magazine,* XIV–XV (1819–20); Phila. CD 1820–35; Wilkes, *U. S. Exploring Expedition.* Stauffer lists him as J. Drayton, and Smith erroneously as John Drayton.

DREHER, E. Engraver, Rockport (Ind.), 1860. ¶ Indiana BD 1860/61.

DREKA, LOUIS. Steel engraver. Born in Pennsylvania *c.* 1839, was the son of a German piano-maker of the same name and his German wife Caroline. The younger Dreka was working as an engraver in Philadelphia in 1860 and after. ¶ 8 Census (1860), Pa., LX, 827; Phila. CD 1871.

DRESEL (Dressel), EMIL. Lithographer; worked mainly in San Francisco (Cal.) from 1853 to 1859, after 1855 as a partner in the firm of KUCHEL & DRESEL. He also travelled in Oregon and made views there during the 1850's. ¶ Peters, *California on Stone;* San Francisco CD 1856–59; Rasmussen, "Art and Artists in Oregon," (cited by David C. Duniway, Oregon State Archivist).

DRESER & ROBYN. Lithographers, Philadelphia, 1849–50. See WILLIAM DRESER and EDWARD ROBYN. ¶ Phila. BD 1849–50.

DRESER, WILLIAM. Lithographer; born in Germany about 1820; at Philadelphia, 1847–60, and NYC, 1860. In 1849–50 he was a partner in DRESER & ROBYN, Philadelphia, in 1859 of BARKER & DRESSER, and in 1860 of DRESER & WISSLER, NYC. ¶ Phila. CD 1847–60; NYCD and BD 1860; 8 Census (1860), N.Y., LIV, 969.

DRESER & WISSLER. Lithographers, NYC, 1860; WILLIAM DRESER and JAMES WISSLER. ¶ NYBD and CD 1860.

DREW, CLEMENT. Marine painter, figurehead carver, photographer, and art dealer. Born in Boston (FARL) or Kingston (Robinson and Dow), Mass., in 1807 (FARL) or 1810 (1860 Census), Drew worked in Boston from 1841 at least until 1860. In the latter year he was living there with his English wife Elizabeth (45) and three children: GEORGE H. (artist, 27, born in Massachusetts), Clara B. (25, born in England), and Ella H. (3, born in Massachusetts); Drew owned realty valued at $6,000 and personalty valued at $500. He was working in and around Gloucester (Mass.) in the 1880's and is said to have been living in Maine as late as 1889. ¶ Information courtesy Frick Art Reference Library and Mrs. Nina Fletcher Little; Robinson and Dow, *The Sailing Ships of New England,* I, 61; Boston CD 1841, BD 1842–60 and after; 8 Census (1860), Mass., XXVII, 494; repros. in Peters, *America on Stone,* pl. 28, and in *Portfolio* (Aug.–Sept. 1944), 20.

DREW, EDWARD. Wood engraver, Buffalo (N.Y.), 1859–60. ¶ Buffalo BD 1859–60.

DREW, GEORGE H. Artist; born in Massachusetts about 1833, son of the painter CLEMENT DREW. In 1860 he was associated with his father in Boston, where they had a shop dealing in paintings, engravings, and artists' materials. ¶ 8 Census (1860), Mass., XXVII, 494; Boston CD 1860.

DREW, LEWIS. Lithographer. A native of Pennsylvania, age 20, living with his father (42, born in Delaware) in Philadelphia in 1860. ¶ 8 Census (1860), Pa., LV, 750.

DREXEL, ANTHONY or ANTONY. Primitive portrait painter. His portrait of a little girl in white, signed and dated 1828, has been reproduced. He is said to have worked in Massachusetts *c.* 1830. ¶ Repro., *Art Digest* (Feb. 1, 1939), 23; *American Folk Art,* no. 6; represented in Rockefeller Folk Art Collection, Williamsburg (Va.); Sherman, "Newly Discovered American Portrait Painters."

DREXEL, FRANCIS MARTIN (1792–1863). Portrait painter. Born in Dornbirn (Tyrol, Austria) on April 7, 1792, Drexel painted portraits in several European countries before emigrating to America in 1817. He settled in Philadelphia and plied his trade as portrait painter there until 1837, except for several years spent in South America and Mexico. He exhibited frequently at the Pennsylvania Academy from 1818 to 1825. In 1837 he gave up painting to open a brokerage office in Louisville (Ky.) which he transferred the following year to Philadelphia. The house of Drexel & Co. became one of the most important banking concerns in the country before its founder's death on June 5, 1863. ¶ DAB; Scharf and Westcott, II, 1053; Phila. CD 1818–1837; Rutledge, PA; *Portraits in Delaware 1700–1850,* with two repros.

DRINKER, JOHN. Miniaturist, portrait painter, and drawing master, who advertised in 1787 that he was opening a drawing school in Philadelphia with the assistance of MATTHEW PRATT. He was listed as a portrait painter or limner in Philadelphia directories in 1801–02. Two portraits by him are listed by FARL. ¶ Prime II, 46–47; Brown and Brown; information courtesy FARL.

DRISCOLL, H. Engraver. Born in Maryland *c.* 1819; living in Boston in 1850. ¶ 7 Census (1850), Mass., XXV, 73.

DROUAILLET, GUSTAV. Lithographer; worked in San Francisco in 1860 and after. In 1868 he was also president of the French Savings and Loan Association of that city. ¶ Peters, *Calif. on Stone;* San Francisco CD 1868.

DROWNE, SHEM (1683–1774). Maker of weather vanes, carver of figureheads and ornamental pieces. Born in Kittery (Maine), "Deacon" Drowne spent most of his long life in Boston, where he is buried. Several of his imaginative copper weather vanes still exist. ¶ Averill, "Early Weathervanes Made in Many Styles and Forms"; Lipman, *American Folk Art,* 13, repros. pp. 25 and 30; Pinckney, 49–50, 191. *Cf.* "Drowne's Wooden Image" in Hawthorne's *Mosses from an Old Manse.*

DROZ, A. Engraver, of ZIMMER & DROZ, New Orleans, 1833. ¶ New Orleans *Courier,* Jan. 25, 1833 (cited by Delgado-WPA).

DRUCEZ, P. J. Portrait and miniature painter from Antwerp (Belgium), advertised in NYC in 1805. ¶ Dunlap, *History* (1918), III, 296; Fielding.

DRURY, JOHN H. (1816–?). Landscape, figure, and cattle painter. Born in Washington (D.C.), June 30, 1816, Drury first studied under THOMAS DOUGHTY. From 1856 to 1859 he was in Europe, where he studied with Couturier. He settled about 1863/64 in Chicago (Ill.), where he was living as late as 1905. ¶ Andreas, *History of Chicago,* II, 560 (cited by H. Maxson Holloway); Chicago CD 1864–1904; represented in the Chicago Historical Society.

DUANE, JAMES. Canadian engraver, 40, at NYC in 1850. His wife was also a Canadian, but their four children, ages 14 to 6, were born in New York. ¶ 7 Census (1850), N.Y., XLVII, 800.

DUBOIS, ALBERT. Lithographer. Born in Germany *c.* 1831; living in Philadelphia with his father, GEORGE DUBOIS, in 1850–51. ¶ 7 Census (1850), Pa., XLIX, 399; Phila. CD 1851.

DUBOIS, Mrs. CORNELIUS, see MARY ANN DELAFIELD DUBOIS.

DUBOIS, DANIEL N. (*c.* 1802–1846). Portrait painter of NYC, 1830–46. His death at the age of 44 occurred on Friday, November 13, 1846. ¶ Barber, "Deaths taken from the New York Evening Post," XXIII, 6; NYCD 1830–36, 1840–46; Dunlap, *History* (1834), II, 471.

DUBOIS, GEORGE. Lithographer. A native of Germany, who came to Philadelphia in 1850 and worked there for at least two years. The 1850 Census recorded George and Charlotte DuBois, ages 39 and 37, and eight children ranging from 19 years to 9 months, all born in Germany. The eldest son, ALBERT DUBOIS, also was listed as a lithographer. ¶ 7 Census (1850), Pa., XLIX, 399; Phila. CD 1850–52. Peters, *America on Stone,* reproduces a print by G. DuBois, probably the same man.

DUBOIS, H. W. Lithographer of Fall River (Mass.) *c.* 1850. ¶ Peters, *America on Stone.*

DUBOIS, MARY ANN DELAFIELD (1813–1888). A.N.A. Amateur sculptor and cameo-cutter. Born in NYC on November 6, 1813, daughter of John Delafield; married Cornelius DuBois, merchant of NYC, in 1832. She took up sculpture about 1842 and produced a number of busts, ideal figures, and cameos before ill health forced her to give up her modeling about ten years later. Her cameo self-portrait is reproduced in the Delafield family history. Mrs. DuBois died October 27, 1888. ¶ Delafield, *Delafield, The Family History,* I, 252, illus. opp. 246, 270; Lee, *Familiar Sketches,* 218–221; Gardner, *Yankee Stonecutters* [as Mrs. Cornelia DuBois].

DUBOIS, R. P. Painter of a conversation piece shown at the Pennsylvania Academy in 1831. This was probably Robert P. DuBois, brother of SAMUEL F. DUBOIS. He was a teacher in the Academy at Dolyestown (Pa.) and later served for many years as pastor of a church at New London (Pa.). ¶ Rutledge, PA; Davis, *Doylestown Old and New.*

DUBOIS, SAMUEL F. (1805–1889). Portrait painter, son of the Rev. Uriah DuBois; born in Doylestown (Pa.) in 1805. After studying under THOMAS SULLY, he painted portraits around Doylestown and Philadelphia. Much of his work was hung in the U. S. Mint at Philadelphia, the director of which (Dr. Robert M. Patterson) was a friend of DuBois' family. For several years the artist divided his time between Doylestown and Wilkes-Barre (Pa.), but the last twenty-five years of his life were spent in Doylestown, where he died on October 20, 1889. DuBois exhibited at the Artists' Fund Society in 1836–37 and at the Pennsylvania Academy in 1855–56. See R. P. DuBois. ¶ Davis, *Doylestown Old and New,* 267–268; Rutledge, PA; Phila. CD 1837, 1839; *Antiques* (Aug. 1931), 108, repro. of self-portrait dated 1830.

DUBOURJAL, SAVINIEN EDMÉ or EDMÉ SAVINIEN (1795–1865). Portrait and miniature painter in oil, portrait draftsman in pencil. Born in Paris, February 12, 1795, Dubourjal studied there and first exhibited at the Salon in 1814. His work was shown at the Pennsylvania Academy as early as 1824 and at the National in 1832. About 1835 he became a close friend of the American portrait painter G. P. A. HEALY, then studying in Paris. Dubourjal visited America in 1844 and the following year he settled there, living for a year in Boston and from 1847 to 1848 in NYC. During this period he exhibited at the Pennsylvania Academy, the National Academy, the Boston Athenaeum, and the American Art-Union. After his return to France in 1848, his health failed and he was supported during his last years by Healy. Though Bolton and others have given 1853 as the year of Dubourjal's death, Healy's latest biographer (De Mare) states that he died in Paris December 8, 1865. ¶ Bolton, *Crayon Draftsmen;* De Mare, *G. P. A. Healy;* Bigot, *Life of George P. A. Healy,* 17–18; Rutledge, PA; Cowdrey, NAD; Healy, *Reminiscences,* 43–45; Swan, BA; Cowdrey, AA & AAU; Hinton, repro.; Met. Mus. *Bulletin* (Nov. 1947), 106, repro.; Thieme-Becker; Bénézit.

DUBOUSQUET, EUGENE. Engraver, New Orleans, 1834. ¶ New Orleans CD 1834 (cited by Delgado-WPA).

DUBUFE, CLAUDE MARIE (1790–1864). Portrait painter; born in Paris in 1790; died in St. Cloud (France), October 1864. One of the last pupils of David, Dubufe had a successful career in France as a fashionable portrait painter. Although Fielding states that Dubufe had a studio in New Orleans (La.) about 1837 and painted portraits of many wealthy Creoles, no evidence has been found to support the assertion. A number of Dubufe's paintings were exhibited in New Orleans in 1835, but contemporary newspaper accounts do not mention the artist's presence in the city at that time. ¶ Thieme-Becker; Fielding; *Louisiana Courier,* Jan. 10, 12, and 20, Feb. 25, 1835 (cited by Delgado-WPA). Clement and Hutton lists among Dubufe's most popular genre paintings one entitled "The Slave-Merchant"; if done from life, this may indicate that the artist did visit the American South.

DUCHASSEY, M. J. Professor of drawing at Spring Hill College, New Orleans (La.), 1840. ¶ New Orleans *Bee,* Dec. 12, 1840 (cited by Delgado-WPA).

DUCHÉ, THOMAS SPENCE, JR. (1763–1790). Portrait and allegorical painter, son of the Rev. Jacob Duché; born in Philadelphia, September 15, 1763. He was taken to England in 1777, his father being a Loyalist, and became a pupil of BENJAMIN WEST. He painted a few portraits and allegorical subjects before his death in London at the age of 26 on March 31, 1790. ¶ Gegenheimer, "Artist in Exile: The Story of Thomas Spence Duché"; Bennett, "The Story of Two Old Prints"; Roberts, "Thomas Spence Duché"; repro. NYHS *Quarterly* (April 1947), 93.

DUCHÉ DE VANCY, GASPARD (?–1788). Painter, draftsman, and engraver. A native of France, Duché de Vancy was living in London in 1784 when he exhibited at the Royal Academy. Shortly thereafter he joined the La Pérouse expedition as artist. When the expedition reached California in 1786, Duché de Vancy painted the scene of La Pérouse's reception at the Carmel Mission, now known only through early copies. The artist lost his life in the Pacific in 1788. ¶ Van Nostrand and Coulter, *California Pictorial,* 4–5, repro.; Roberts, "Thomas Spence Duché," 273, cites an essay on Duché de Vancy by Emile Delignières in *Journal des Arts,* Jan. 1, 1911.

DUCHESNE, Mrs. ——. Landscape painter. In 1838 she announced that, since her arrival in Charleston (S.C.), she had executed a painting of a large plantation on the island of Santo Domingo. ¶ Rutledge, *Artists in the Life of Charleston,* 158–159.

DUCLARY, LEPELLETIER. Portrait painter. Born in Martinique *c.* 1824, Duclary or du Clary came to New Orleans from Santo Domingo about 1849 and apparently returned to Santo Domingo about 1852. ¶ 7 Census (1850), La., V, 70; New Orleans CD 1849 and New Orleans *Bee,* May 29, 1852 (cited by Delgado-WPA).

DUDENSING, RICHARD (?–1899). Portrait and landscape engraver, book publisher. A native of Germany, Dudensing came to the

United States about 1857. He died in NYC on September 4, 1899. ¶ Thieme-Becker, cites *Art Annual* (1899), 82; Stauffer, I, 70.

DUFF, JOHN T. Artist, Louisville (Ky.), 1848. This may be the Ned Duff, artist, age 23, recorded in the Louisville (Ky.) census of 1850. ¶ Louisville CD 1848; 7 Census (1850), Ky., XI, 573.

DUFF, NED, see JOHN T. DUFF.

DUFFIELD, EDWARD. Engraver of medals, Philadelphia, 1756, 1762. He was also a die-sinker and watch- and clock-maker. ¶ Stauffer.

DUFFY, RICHARD. Lithographer. Born in Ireland *c.* 1832–34, but brought to America as an infant. In 1850, at the age of 16, he was recorded in the census as a lithographer, residing with his mother Ellen Duffy (49), his brother WILLIAM DUFFY (20), and two younger sisters. By 1860 he was married and had a three-year-old son, Francis; he was still working as a lithographer in Philadelphia at that time. ¶ 7 Census (1850), Pa., L, 273; 8 Census (1860), Pa., XLIX, 295.

DUFFY, WILLIAM. Lithographer. William, elder brother of RICHARD DUFFY, was born in Ireland *c.* 1830. He was brought to America about 1835 and in 1850 was working as a lithographer in Philadelphia; he made his home with his mother, brother and two younger sisters. ¶ 7 Census (1850), Pa., L, 273.

DUFRENE, EDWARD. Artist, working in Philadelphia from 1851 to 1861. He was recorded in the 1860 census as a native of Belgium, age 24. The city directories for 1860 and 1861 list him as a manufacturer of statuary and imitation marble. ¶ Phila. CD 1851–61; 8 Census (1860), Pa., LIV, 280.

DUFRENE, THOMAS. Sculptor. A native of England, Dufrene worked in Philadelphia from 1841 to 1853, from 1849 as proprietor of an ornament works. His household in 1850 included the artist (57), his wife (47, English), Thomas, Jr. (14, born in Canada), and John (7, born in Philadelphia). ¶ 7 Census (1850), Pa., L, 225; Phila. CD 1841–53.

DUGAN, AUGUSTINE A. Engraver. He worked in NYC from 1840 to 1849 (in 1844 as a partner in DUGAN & BARNETT) and in Philadelphia from 1851 to 1860. ¶ NYCD 1840–49; NYBD 1840–46; Phila. CD 1851–53, 1856–60.

DUGAN & BARNETT. Engravers, NYC, 1844; AUGUSTINE A. DUGAN and —— BARNETT. ¶ NYBD 1844.

DUGARY (or Duggary), ——. Drawing master, New Orleans (La.), 1826, 1829, 1834. ¶ New Orleans *Argus,* Feb. 15, 1826, and March 2, 1829, *Bee,* Nov. 7, 1834 (cited by Delgado-WPA).

DUGGAN, PETER PAUL or PAUL PETER (?–1861). N.A. Portrait artist, chiefly in crayon, and designer of medals. Born in Ireland, he is said to have been brought to America as a child about 1810. His career in NYC extended only from about 1844 to about 1856 when ill health obliged him to retire. He was a frequent exhibitor at the National Academy, of which he was a member, and designed several medals for distribution by the American Art-Union. After retiring, Duggan lived for a time in London and then in Paris, where he died, October 15, 1861. ¶ CAB; Clement and Hutton; NYCD 1845–56; Bolton, *Crayon Draftsmen;* Strickland, *Dictionary of Irish Artists;* Cowdrey, NAD; Cowdrey, AA & AAU; Swan, BA.

DU HAUTCILLY, see BERNARD.

DUKES, J. Miniature painter, at Easton (Md.) in August 1801. ¶ *Maryland Herald,* Aug. 11, 1801.

DULONGPRÉ, LOUIS (1754–1843). Portrait painter. Born in St. Denis (near Paris), April 16, 1754, Dulongpré came to America with Rochambeau during the American Revolution. After the war he settled for a time in Albany (N.Y.), but eventually he moved to Canada. He died at St. Hyacinthe (Que.) in 1843. ¶ *Récherches Historique,* VIII (1902), 119–20, 150–51.

DULUC, ANDREW. Battle artist. A resident of Baltimore, this soldier-artist drew and engraved a view of the Battle of Patapsco Neck, Sept. 12, 1814, in which he had participated. ¶ Hunter, "The Battle of Baltimore Illustrated," repro.

DUMAS, VALSIN (or Valsain). Marble sculptor, New Orleans (La.) 1841–42. ¶ New Orleans CD 1841–42.

DUMCKE (Dumke), JOHN D. Lithographer, NYC, 1856–58. In 1856–57 he was a member of the firm of DUMCKE & KEIL. ¶ NYCD 1856–58.

DUMCKE & KEIL. Lithographers, NYC, 1856–57; JOHN D. DUMCKE and VALENTINE KEIL. ¶ NYCD 1856–57; Peters, *America on Stone.*

DUMKE, see DUMCKE.

DUMMER, JEREMIAH (1645–1718). Silversmith, magistrate, and alleged portrait painter; born in Newbury (Mass.), September 14, 1645; died in Boston, May 25, 1718. Considerable controversy has arisen over the question whether Dummer was a portrait painter. The claim was first made in 1921 by F. W. Bayley who claimed to have discovered two signed portraits by Dummer. More recent scholarship, notably that of H. W. Foote and Alan Burroughs, has tended to discredit the Dummer attributions. Except for the signatures, which have been under suspicion, there is no documentary evidence to support the theory that Jeremiah Dummer was a painter. ¶ Information courtesy Theodore Bolton, who cites: Clarke and Foote, *Jeremiah Dummer;* Dresser, *XVIIth Century Painting in New England,* contains Burroughs' report on the disputed signatures; Burroughs, *Limners and Likenesses;* DAB; Bayley, "An Early New England Limner"; *Harvard Tercentenary Exhibition Catalogue* (1936), 101.

DUMONT, CONRAD. French lithographer, 28, at NYC in 1850. ¶ 7 Census (1850), N.Y., XLII, 72.

DUMONT DE MONTIGNY, LOUIS-FRANÇOIS-BENJAMIN. Amateur artist who served as an infantry officer in Louisiana from *c.* 1715 to *c.* 1740. While in the colony he made numerous maps and sketches of Indians and flora and fauna of the Mississippi Valley. These later served to illustrate his *Mémoires* (Paris, 1753) and his "Poeme en Vers Touchant l'Establissement de la Province de la Louisianne." ¶ Dumont de Montigny, works cited.

DUNBAR, Miss F. J. Portrait painter, Tuskegee (Ala.), 1860. ¶ [Tuskegee] *Southwestern Baptist,* Feb. 9, 1860 (cited by WPA (Ala.), Hist. Records Survey).

DUNBAR, GEORGE, SR. Portrait, sign, and ornamental painter of Canton (Ohio), 1817–23. Represented in the Massilon (Ohio) Museum. ¶ Knittle, *Early Ohio Taverns;* information courtesy of Albert Hise, Massilon Museum.

DUNBAR, GEORGE, JR. Sign and ornamental painter, Canton (Ohio), 1833. Son of the above. ¶ Knittle, *Early Ohio Taverns.*

DUNCAN, GEORGE. Irish engraver, 30, at NYC in 1860. His wife Martha and son William, age 12, were also born in Ireland, but four younger children were born in New York. ¶ 8 Census (1860), N.Y., LXII, 382.

DUNCAN, JOSEPH. Artist. A native of Scotland, age 25, boarding in New Orleans (La.) in October 1850. ¶ 7 Census (1850), La., IV (1), 596.

DUNCAN, OLIVER. Canadian lithographer, 25, at NYC in 1850. His wife and one child were born in New York. ¶ 7 Census (1850), N.Y., XLI, 113.

DUNCAN, THOMAS. Miniaturist. A native of Ireland; in 1850 a resident of Cincinnati (Ohio), where he owned realty worth $5,000. The household included Thomas (50), Eliza (45, of Pennsylvania), and two children (14 and 17, both born in Ohio). ¶ 7 Census (1850), Ohio, XXI, 285; Cincinnati CD 1849 (as painter).

DUNCAN, Mrs. WILLIAM, see ANNA CLAYPOOLE PEALE.

DUNCANSON, ROBERT S. (1817–22 to 1872). Portrait, landscape, and genre painter born in New York State between 1817 (Porter) and 1822 (1860 Census), of a Negro mother and a Scotch-Canadian father. After spending his childhood in Canada, Duncanson joined his mother at Mount Holly, near Cincinnati, in 1841. The following year he exhibited for the first time in Cincinnati. His first important commission was for a series of mural landscapes for "Belmont," the home of Nicholas Longworth (now the Taft Museum). He made two visits to Europe, to Italy in 1853 and to Britain 1863–66, and possibly a third, to Scotland, in 1870–71. During most of his career, Duncanson's home was in Cincinnati, but he also made a number of visits to Detroit and it was there he died, December 21, 1872, after a mental and physical breakdown. ¶ Dwight, "Robert S. Duncanson"; Porter, "Robert S. Duncanson, Midwestern Romantic-Realist" (with checklist and 26 repros.). See also *Bulletin of the Detroit Institute of Arts,* 33 (1950–51), 21–25; 8 Census (1860), Ohio XXV, 255; Cist, *Cincinnati in 1851;* Cincinnati CD 1853, 1856–60; Webster, "Junius R. Sloan," 107; Swan, BA; Cowdrey, AA & AAU; Park, *Mural Painters in America;* Locke, *The Negro in Art.*

DUNCKERLEY, see DUNKERLEY.

DUNHAM, DAVID R. Engraver, NYC, 1851–56. ¶ NYBD 1851–56.

DUNHAM, J. Artist whose view of Dartmouth College, Hanover (N.H.), was engraved *c.* 1793 by SAMUEL HILL. ¶ Stauffer; *American Collector* (Oct. 1937), 7, repro.

DUNHAM, THOMAS. English engraver, age 26, living with his English wife Mary, age 20, in East Boston (Mass.) in August 1850. ¶ 7 Census (1850), Mass., XXIV, 33.

DUNHAM, WILLIAM S. Banknote engraver, NYC, 1852. ¶ NYBD 1852.

DUNKERLEY, JOSEPH. Miniaturist. Dunkerley (or Dunckerley) was working in Boston (Mass.) in 1784–85, in the latter year advertising his intention of opening a drawing school in association with JOHN HAZLITT. He was still working in the United States as late as 1787, but later went to Jamaica. ¶ Wehle and Bolton, 27, repro. pl. X; information courtesy Richardson Wright.

DUNLAP, JAMES BOLIVER (1825–1864). Portrait sculptor and painter, lithographer, wood engraver, cartoonist; born in Indianapolis (Ind.), May 7, 1825. At the age of 25 he went to California by way of New Orleans and opened a studio in San Francisco, where he executed a marble bust of John Sutter. He was back in the East by 1860, when he made a bust of Lincoln. Dunlap also painted portraits and landscapes, and drew cartoons for the Indianapolis *Locomotive.* He died in Indianapolis on September 4, 1864. ¶ Burnet, 66–68; Peat, *Pioneer Painters;* Gardner; 7 Census (1850), La., IV, 701; Peters, *California on Stone;* Rasmussen, "Art and Artists in Oregon," (cited by David C. Duniway).

DUNLAP, JOSEPH. Engraver, age 23. A native of Philadelphia, living there in 1860 with his father, James Dunlap, and a brother William, who was a watch case maker. ¶ 8 Census (1860), Pa., LVIII, 230; Phila. CD 1871.

DUNLAP, WILLIAM (1766–1839). N.A. Artist, playwright, historian; born in Perth Amboy (N.J.), February 18, 1766. Showing an interest in painting, he was sent to England in 1784 to study under BENJAMIN WEST. For a few years after his return in 1787 he did some portrait painting, but his interest soon shifted to writing and the theatre and from about 1793 until 1811 he was active as both writer and manager. In 1805–06 and again in 1811–13 he worked as an itinerant miniaturist, but after 1813 his painting was limited mainly to oil portraits and large religious show-pieces which were exhibited throughout the East. Appointed Librarian and Keeper of the American Academy in 1817, Dunlap left that organization in 1826 to help found the rival National Academy of which he became Treasurer and later Vice-President. His last years were spent in poverty and ill-health in NYC, but Dunlap devoted them to the writing of his notable histories of the American Theatre (1832) and of the arts of design in America (1834). He died in NYC on September 28, 1839. ¶ The fullest biographical account of Dunlap is Oral Sumner Coad's *William Dunlap, a Study of his Life and Works and of his Place in Contemporary Culture* (N.Y., 1917). Dunlap's own two-volume *History of the American Theatre* (N.Y., 1832) and two-volume *History of the Rise and Progress of the Arts of Design in the United States* (N.Y., 1834; rev. ed., 1918) contain much autobiographical material, as do his published diaries, three volumes, edited by Dorothy C. Barck and published in 1930 by the New-York Historical Society. See also: DAB; CAB; Wehle and Bolton; Cowdrey, AA & AAU; Cowdrey, NAD; NYCD 1789–1839; Johnson, "William Dunlap and His Times"; Woolsey, Theodore, "The American Vasari."

DUNN, ALEXANDER GORDON (1815–1887). Landscape painter. Born December 16, 1815, in Glasgow (Scotland); became a pattern designer and worked there until 1854, when he came to NYC. Returned to Scotland before his wife's death in 1858 and stayed there until 1867, when he permanently settled in the U.S. Lived in Brooklyn (N.Y.) until about 1885, then moved to Holton (Kans.) where he died October 2, 1887. Most of his painting was done in Scotland, but he did some while in Brooklyn and exhibited at the Watercolor Society in the 1870's. ¶ Information courtesy Mary Bartlett Cowdrey, who cites obituary in a Holton (Kans.) paper; an article by Bertha Havens in *The Holton Signal,* May 5, 1910; and a letter of Mrs. E. C. Starin, Holton, to J. Canfield Howe, Passaic (N.J.), Feb. 14, 1954.

DUNN, CHARLES FREDERIC (1810–1882). Primitive watercolorist. Born in Boston; settled in Maine in 1841. He was a farmer, scholar, and poet, as well as a painter of watercolor townscapes. ¶ Lipman, "American Townscapes," 341, two repros.

DUNN, DANIEL. Irish artist, 26, at NYC in 1860. ¶ 8 Census (1860), N.Y., XLV, 514.

DUNN, EDWARD W. Engraver, NYC, 1859. ¶ NYBD 1859.

DUNN, GEORGE. Lithographer, age 19, living in Philadelphia in June 1860. He was a native of Pennsylvania. ¶ 8 Census (1860), Pa., L, 567.

DUNN, JOHN GIBSON (*c.* 1826–*c.* 1858). Genre painter, born in Lawrenceburg

(Ind.) about 1826; came to Indianapolis about 1840 from Lawrenceburg. For a few months he shared a studio with JACOB COX in Cincinnati. A physician by profession, he was considered something of an eccentric genius. His only known painting, "Temperance," is owned by the John Herron Art Institute of Indianapolis. When he visited New Orleans in 1850, Dunn was also mentioned as the author of a poem entitled "The Angel Who Paints in the West." He died at New Orleans about 1858. ¶ Burnet, 62–63, repro. opp. 65; New Orleans *Delta,* April 1, 1850 (cited by Delgado-WPA); Peat, *Pioneer Painters of Indiana.*

DUNN, JOSEPH. English artist, 26, at NYC in 1850 in the home of JOHN W. CROCKER. ¶ 7 Census (1850), N.Y., XLVIII, 351.

DUNN, LEVERETT H. Stencil plate engraver, of NEWTON & DUNN, NYC, 1852. ¶ NYCD 1852.

DUNN, THOMAS W. Lithographer, 24, from Newfoundland, at NYC in 1860. ¶ 8 Census (1860), N.Y., LI, 485; NYCD 1863.

DUNNELL, ELBRIDGE G. Engraver, NYC, 1842–54. The name is also spelled Dunnel. ¶ NYCD 1842–54; Stauffer.

DUNNELL, JOHN HENRY (1813–1904). Amateur landscape painter. Born in Millbury (Mass.), Dunnell was a business man, probably in the New York area, before going to California in 1849. He exhibited New York and New Jersey views at the National Academy in 1847–48. From 1849 to 1851 he was in business in Coloma (Cal.), and at this time he made three views of Sutter's Mill. Dunnell returned to NYC in 1851 and became active in Republican politics, especially in the election of 1856. In 1857 he returned to California for three years, as agent for the Singer Manufacturing Company. From 1860 until his death, January 25, 1904, he was a resident of NYC. ¶ Van Nostrand and Coulter, *California Pictorial,* 62; *Art Annual,* V; Cowdrey, NAD; Cowdrey, AA & AAU.

DUNNELL, JOHN H. Artist, age 11, exhibited crayon drawing at the American Institute in 1856. He was apparently the son of the foregoing JOHN HENRY DUNNELL. ¶ Am. Inst. Cat., 1856.

DUNNELL (Dunnel), WILLIAM N. Engraver and illustrator, NYC, 1847–58. He was a partner in the firm of BALDWIN & DUNNEL in 1847/48. In 1849 he exhibited a wood engraving and a steel line engraving at the American Institute. His name is absent from NYC directories from 1849 to 1856. Stauffer states that Dunnell "contracted bad habits and disappeared." ¶ NYCD 1847–49; NYBD 1848, 1856–58; Stauffer; Am. Inst. Cat., 1849; Thieme-Becker; Cowdrey, NAD.

DUNNING, ROBERT S. (1829–1905). Portrait and genre painter. A native of Brunswick (Maine), Dunning exhibited at the National Academy 1850–80 and the American Art-Union in 1850. In the late 1850's he was living in Fall River (Mass.), where in 1859 he was a partner in the firm of GROUARD & DUNNING, artists. He died at Westport Harbor (Mass.), August 12, 1905. ¶ *Art Annual,* V; Cowdrey, NAD; Cowdrey, AA & AAU; Fall River BD 1857, 1859.

DUNPHY, RICHARD L. Sculptor. At the age of 13 Dunphy, the son of a NYC cabinetmaker, exhibited a case of cameos and busts at the American Institute for which he was awarded a silver medal. A New Orleans newspaper the same year commented on his busts of Zachary Taylor, William B. Townsend, and James Webb. After 1856 he was listed as a sculptor in NYC directories. The name was sometimes spelled Dumphy or Durphy. URIAH DUNPHY was presumably a brother. ¶ Am. Inst. Cat., 1847; New Orleans *Delta,* Oct. 26, 1847 (cited by Delgado-WPA); NYCD 1857–60.

DUNPHY, URIAH. Pencil draftsman and carver, NYC, 1847–60. Presumably a brother of RICHARD L. DUNPHY, Uriah exhibited crayon drawings at the American Institute in 1847 and the following year won $3.00 and a certificate for a pencil drawing shown at the Institute fair. From 1857 to 1860 he was listed in the directories as a carver. ¶ Am. Inst. Cat., 1847–48; NYCD 1857–60.

DUPALAIS, VIRGINIA POULLARD (1804–1864), Mrs. William Albert Twigg. Portrait artist in pen and pencil. Born in Philadelphia, March 20, 1804, Virginia Dupalais and a brother accompanied their uncle CHARLES A. LESUEUR, in the famous "Boatload of Knowledge" to New Harmony (Ind.) in 1826. After her marriage to Mr. Twigg, Lesueur resided with his niece until his departure from New Harmony in the 1840's. She was an amateur artist whose work included a pencil portrait of Maximilian, Prince of Wied, who visited New Harmony in 1842. Mrs. Twigg died in New Harmony, January 8, 1864. ¶ Peat, *Pio-*

neer Painters of Indiana, 30, 229; Burnet, 31.

DUPERLY, ARMAND. Lithographer, New Orleans, 1857–60. ¶ New Orleans *Bee,* April 17, 1857, and CD 1860 (cited by Delgado-WPA).

DUPONCHEL, FELIX. Artist of several upstate New York views, about 1825, published in Colden's *Memoir* prepared at the time of the Erie Canal opening. ¶ Colden, *Memoir.*

DU PONT, SAMUEL FRANCIS (1803–1865). Amateur artist. Entering the U. S. Navy as a midshipman in 1815, Du Pont rose to the rank of rear admiral before his death. During the Mexican War he was in command of a ship in the Pacific squadron and participated in the capture of San Diego (Cal.) and La Paz (Lower Cal.). Sketches by Du Pont were later used by GEORGE HEILGE in the painting of his panorma of a voyage to California (1849). Du Pont played an important role in the naval operations of the first years of the Civil War. ¶ CAB; Hamersley; Phila. *Public Ledger,* March 28, 1851 (cited by J. E. Arrington).

DU PORTAIL, see PONTEL.

DUPOUY, A. L. Teacher of drawing and painting, Richmond (Va.), 1831. ¶ *Richmond Portraits.*

DU PRATZ, ANTOINE SIMON LE PAGE (*c.* 1689/90–1775). French explorer who is believed to have made the drawings illustrating his *Histoire de la Louisiane* (Paris, 1758). He settled in Louisiana in 1718 and stayed until 1734 when he returned to France. ¶ DAB.

DUPRÉ, AUGUSTIN. A crayon drawing by this artist, entitled "The Battle of the Cowpens, January 17, 1781," is owned by the Musée de la Coopération Franco-Américaine, Blérancourt (France). It is assumed that Dupré was present at the battle. ¶ *American Processional,* 237 (no. 71).

DUPRÉ, EUGENE CHARLES. Lithographer from Paris, who settled in St. Louis (Mo.) in the mid-1830's and married a local girl. From 1837 to 1840 he ran a lithographic shop and subsequently he opened a haberdashery. He was arrested and imprisoned on a morals charge in 1845, escaped and was again imprisoned in 1847. Nothing is known of him after the seizure of his property in 1849 by court order. ¶ *Missouri Historical Society Bulletin,* Oct. 1955, cover, 5–7; Stokes, *Historical Prints,* pl. 68.

DUPRÉ, JULIA CLARKSON (Mrs. Henry B. Bounetheau). Portrait and landscape painter, pastellist, teacher of drawing and painting. A relative of WASHINGTON ALLSTON, Miss Dupré studied for a few years in Paris before 1841. Her home was in Charleston (S.C.), where she won considerable acclaim as an artist and musician. In 1844 she married the miniaturist, HENRY B. BOUNETHEAU. She continued to paint and teach in Charleston until the Civil War, except for a period of study in France *c.* 1856. During the latter part of the Civil War the Bounetheau family took refuge in Aiken (S.C.). ¶ Rutledge, *Artists in the Life of Charleston,* 160; Rutledge, "Henry Bounetheau," lists several of Mrs. Bounetheau's works.

DUQUEMY, JOHN (Jean) D. Sculptor and carver, San Francisco, 1858–60. ¶ San Francisco BD 1858, CD 1860.

DURAN, JOHN. Wood engraver, Boston (Mass.), 1857–60. He was a partner in the firm of CHANDLER & DURAN (1859–60). ¶ Boston CD 1857–60.

DURAND, ALBERT G. Engraver, probably a son of CYRUS DURAND; listed in NYC directories from 1834 to 1841 as a machinist, in 1848–49 as an engraver, and in 1861 as an artist. In 1849 he appears to have been in the banknote engraving firm of DURAND, BALDWIN & CO. ¶ NYCD 1834–41, 1848–49, 1861, usually at the same address as that of Cyrus Durand.

DURAND, ALFRED B. Artist, born in Pennsylvania *c.* 1826. In June 1860 Durand (34) and his wife Marie (24), a native of Maryland, were living in Philadelphia (Pa.) with Durand's parents, Elias B. and Mary Durand. ¶ 8 Census (1860), Pa., LIV, 165.

DURAND, ASHER BROWN (1796–1886). N.A. Engraver; landscape, figure, and portrait painter. Born in Jefferson Village (now Maplewood, N.J.), August 21, 1796, he served his apprenticeship under the noted engraver PETER MAVERICK from 1812 to 1817 and worked in partnership with his former master for three more years. His reputation as an engraver was established in 1823 when he completed the plate of TRUMBULL's "Declaration of Independence," upon which the young engraver had spent the better part of three years. From this time until about 1835, Durand was one of the foremost engravers of the country, with portraits, landscapes, and banknote vignettes his special province. During this time Durand headed several companies: A. B. & C. DURAND (1824);

A. B. DURAND & C. WRIGHT & CO. (1826–27); and DURAND, PERKINS & CO. (1828–31). He also had many pupils, including JOHN W. CASILEAR, GEORGE W. HATCH, J. W. PARADISE, and LEWIS P. CLOVER. By 1835 Durand's interest in painting had led him to give up engraving almost completely. At first a painter of portraits, he soon became identified with the "Hudson River school" of landscape painting, of which he was one of the most accomplished exponents. Durand made the customary pilgrimage of study to the art centers of Europe in 1840–41, and from 1845 to 1861 served as president of the National Academy of Design, of which he had been a founder in 1826. Durand retired in 1869 to his childhood home in New Jersey and died there at the age of 90 on September 17, 1886. ¶ John Durand, *Life and Times of Asher B. Durand,* is the standard life, but see also: Sweet, "Asher B. Durand"; DAB; NYCD 1818–69; Cowdrey, NAD; Cowdrey, AA & AAU; Rutledge, PA; Swan, BA; Rutledge, MHS; Sherman, "Asher B. Durand as a Portrait Painter"; Kellner, "The Beginnings of Landscape Painting in America"; Cowdrey, "Asher Brown Durand"; Blanchard, "The Durand Engraving Companies."

DURAND, BALDWIN & COMPANY. Banknote engravers, NYC, 1849–1850. The company was composed of CYRUS DURAND, GEORGE D. BALDWIN, and probably ALBERT G. DURAND. ¶ NYC 1849–50.

DURAND, CYRUS (1787–1868). Banknote engraver and inventor, elder brother of ASHER BROWN DURAND; born at Jefferson (N.J.), February 27, 1787. Though listed as an engraver in NYC directories from 1826 to 1858, Cyrus Durand appears to have been more mechanic than artist. He was especially noted as the inventor of a geometric lathe for use in banknote engraving. Cyrus Durand worked with his brother Asher from about 1824 to 1831, and later established his own company (Cyrus Durand & Co., 1839–1842), as well as DURAND, BALDWIN & CO. (1849–50). ALBERT G., ELIAS W., WILLIAM and SILAS DURAND probably were sons of Cyrus. From about 1848 Cyrus Durand made his home in New Jersey; he was living at Irvington at the time of his death, September 18, 1868. ¶ Stauffer; NYCD 1826–35, 1839–42, 1848–58; Blanchard, "The Durand Engraving Companies."

DURAND, ELIAS W. Engraver and landscape painter, probably the son of CYRUS and brother of ALBERT G., SILAS and WILLIAM DURAND; listed as an engraver in NYC 1846–49, and as a landscape painter in NYC and New Jersey 1852–57. He was an exhibitor at the National Academy. ¶ NYCD 1846–49, 1857; NYBD 1857; Cowdrey, NAD.

DURAND, EUGENE. Artist, NYC, 1850. ¶ NYCD 1850.

DURAND, JOHN. Portrait and figure painter; teacher of drawing and watercolor painting; active between 1766 and 1782. Probably of French birth or parentage (the name appears occasionally as Duran), he is first heard of in 1766 when he painted portraits of the six children of James Beekman of NYC. In 1767–68 he advertised in NYC as a drawing and painting teacher and sought patronage for a projected series of historical paintings. About this time he painted the Rapalje children (now at NYHS) and the Rays (Museum of the City of New York). After a brief visit to Connecticut, he went to Virginia (June 1770). In 1777–78 one John Durand of London exhibited landscapes at the Royal Academy; this may be the same artist, although the American Durand is not known to have painted landscapes. By 1781 Durand was again in Virginia painting "immense numbers" of portraits which, though "hard and dry," appear to have been "strong likenesses" (Dunlap). He was still in Virginia in 1782 but of his later career nothing is known. ¶ White, *The Beekmans of New York;* Kelby; Gottesman, I; *Antiques,* LI (1947), 174–75, repro.; Oberlin College, *Allen Memorial Art Museum Bulletin,* III (1946), 69; *Virginia Gazette,* June 7 and 21, 1770; *William and Mary Quarterly,* II (1893/94), 31; Graves, *Dictionary; William and Mary Quarterly* (1929), 215–16; Dunlap, *History,* I, 144; Flexner, *The Light of Distant Skies;* Thorne, "America's Earliest Nude?"; represented at NYHS, Museum of the City of New York, New Haven Colony Hist. Soc., Baltimore Museum of Art, and William and Mary College.

DURAND, JOHN. Engraver. A younger brother of ASHER BROWN DURAND and CYRUS DURAND, John worked with the former in NYC from 1820 to 1822, but his career was cut short by his death at the age of 28. ¶ NYCD 1820–22; Stauffer.

DURAND & MOORE. Ornamental engravers, NYC 1850–52; probably WILLIAM DU-

RAND and WILLIAM MOORE. ELIAS W. DURAND was at the same address from 1847 to 1849. ¶ NYBD 1850–52; NYCD 1847–49.

DURAND, PERKINS & COMPANY. Banknote engravers, NYC, 1828–31; ASHER BROWN DURAND, CYRUS DURAND, JOSEPH PERKINS, and ELIAS WADE, JR. ¶ NYCD 1828–31; Stauffer; Blanchard, "The Durand Engraving Companies."

DURAND, SILAS. Engraver, NYC, 1834, at same address as CYRUS DURAND. ¶ NYCD 1834.

DURAND, THEODORE. Engraver, NYC, 1833–36. His widow was listed in 1837. ¶ NYCD 1833–37; Blanchard, "The Durand Engraving Companies."

DURAND, WILLIAM. Engraver and portrait painter. Probably a son of CYRUS DURAND, William was a partner in DURAND & MOORE, ornamental engravers, 1850–52, and made his home with ASHER BROWN DURAND, his uncle. He was listed as a portrait painter in NYC in 1855 and exhibited as such at the Washington Art Association exhibition of 1857. ¶ NYCD 1850–53, 1855; NYBD 1855, 1857; Washington Art Assoc. Cat., 1857; Stauffer.

DURAND & WRIGHT & COMPANY. Engravers, NYC, 1823–27; ASHER BROWN DURAND, CYRUS DURAND and CHARLES CUSHING WRIGHT. ¶ NYCD 1826–27; Dunlap, *History* (1918), III, 250–251; Blanchard, "The Durand Engraving Companies."

DURANG, E. F. Panoramic and scenery painter. In 1848–49 Durang was at Cincinnati (Ohio), painting theater scenery and assisting HENRY LEWIS with his Mississippi panorama. Durang's panoramas of the Old and New Testaments and of American history were shown in Louisville in 1849 and in Philadelphia in 1851. ¶ Arrington, *Nauvoo Temple,* VIII; Louisville *Morning Courier,* June 8 and Aug. 29, 1849, Phila. *Public Ledger,* Feb. 4 and March 13, 1851 (cited by J. E. Arrington).

DURANT, CHARLES F. Engraver, lithographer and printer, NYC, 1839–60. ¶ NYCD 1839–60 and after.

DURANT, JOHN WALDO (*c.* 1774–1832). Portrait painter; born on the island of St. Croix (W.I.); died in Philadelphia (Pa.), 1832. He appears to have been educated in Boston (Mass.) and painted a few portraits in Massachusetts and Maine. During the last few years of his life he was inspector of customs at Philadelphia. ¶ Dunlap, *History* (1918), III, 297; Fielding; Phila. CD 1828–31; WPA (Mass.), *Portraits Found in Mass.,* no. 2246.

DURAT, ——. Painter of "Cupid blowing soap-bubbles," a "Nativity," and a "Study from Nature," all exhibited at the American Academy in 1835. The artist was listed as residing on Grand Street, NYC. ¶ Cowdrey, AA & AAU.

DURFEE, CHARLES (1793–1849). Portrait painter; born near Tiverton (R.I.), February 26, 1793; died there (?), October 7, 1849. ¶ Arnold, *Art and Artists in R.I.,* 14–15.

DURHAM, THOMAS. Engraver, Boston, 1850. Durham (28) and his wife Emma (22) were both natives of England. ¶ 7 Census (1850), Mass., XXV, 431.

DURHAM, TYLER. Engraver, Washington (D.C.), 1860. Durham, age 18, was a native of New York State and lived with his father, James H. Durham, in Washington. ¶ 8 Census (1860), D.C., II, 443.

DURHOLZ, AUGUSTE. Engraver, NYC, 1854. ¶ NYBD 1854.

DURRIE, GEORGE HENRY (1820–1863). Landscape, genre, and portrait painter, best known for rural winter scenes; born in Hartford (Conn.), June 6, 1820. In 1839 he and his elder brother, JOHN DURRIE, received instruction from NATHANIEL JOCELYN, though George was already painting portraits around New Haven and Bethany (Conn.). From 1840 to 1842 he divided his time between Connecticut and New Jersey, but he finally settled in New Haven, where he remained, except for occasional professional trips to New Jersey, New York, and Virginia, until his death, October 15, 1863. At first a portrait painter, he turned about 1850 to the rural genre and winter landscapes for which he is remembered, largely through the CURRIER & IVES prints of the 1860's. ¶ Cowdrey, "George H. Durrie," in *Catalogue of the Durrie Exhibition,* Wadsworth Athenaeum, Hartford, 1947; Cowdrey, NAD; French; Swan, BA; New Haven CD 1843–60; 7 Census (1850), Conn., VIII, 535; Durrie, "George H. Durrie, Artist"; Peters, "George Henry Durrie, 1820–1863"; Karolik Cat.; represented at NYHS and Wadsworth Athenaeum.

DURRIE, JOHN (1818–?). Landscape, still life, and portrait painter; elder brother of GEORGE HENRY DURRIE; born in Hartford (Conn.) in 1818 and still living there in 1879. Though he studied briefly with NATHANIEL JOCELYN in 1839, John Durrie never equalled his brother's achievement as an artist. ¶ French; Cowdrey, "George H. Durrie."

DURWARD, BERNARD ISAAC (1817–1902). Portrait and religious painter. A native of Montrose (Scotland), Durward was a self-taught artist who made a name for himself in Scotland and England before emigrating in 1845 to the United States. He settled in Wisconsin, where he became a convert to Roman Catholicism and devoted his life to teaching, painting, and writing poetry. ¶ Butts, *Art in Wisconsin,* 76–80, two repros.

DURY, GEORGE (1817–1894). Portrait painter; came to Watburg (Tenn.) from Munich (Germany) in 1849. Among his portraits is that of Mrs. James Knox Polk, which hangs in the White House. Dury also painted Abraham Lincoln and Robert E. Lee. He made his home in Nashville (Tenn.), where he died in 1894. Some of his paintings are in the State Library at Nashville. ¶ WPA Guide, *Tennessee,* 171; Nashville CD 1860; Egbert, *Princeton Portraits.*

DU SIMITIERE, PIERRE EUGENE (*c.* 1736–1784). Portrait painter. A native of Geneva (Switzerland), Du Simitiere came to the American colonies in 1765 after spending several years in the West Indies collecting natural history specimens. From 1765 to 1770 he worked for brief periods in NYC, Philadelphia, Burlington (N.J.), and Boston, but from *c.* 1770 he was a resident of Philadelphia. There he painted portraits, served as curator of the American Philosophical Society, set up a natural history museum, and gathered a valuable collection of Revolutionary War ephemera and literature which went to the Library Company of Philadelphia. He died in Philadelphia and was buried there in October 1784. ¶ DAB; Morgan and Fielding, *Life Portraits of Washington.* Some of Du Simitiere's papers are in the Library of Congress; others are in the possession of the Library Company of Philadelphia. See WPA Hist. Records Survey (Pa.), *Descriptive Catalogue of the Du Simitière Papers in the Library Company of Philadelphia.*

DUSTAN, Captain ISAAC K. Amateur painter who exhibited an oil painting of the steamboat *Atlantic* at the American Institute in 1846. ¶ Am. Inst. Cat., 1846.

DU SUAW, ——. Portrait and miniature painter, profilist and drawing master, who arrived in Charleston (S.C.) from Santo Domingo in 1794. ¶ Rutledge, *Artists in the Life of Charleston;* Prime, II, 7.

DUTHIE, JAMES. Steel and copper engraver; lithographer. An Englishman, he was working in NYC *c.* 1850–55 and at Albany in 1859. He is presumably the J. D. Duthie who engraved one plate for *Homes of American Authors* (N.Y., 1853). ¶ Stauffer; Albany CD 1859; Linton, *History of Wood-Engraving,* repro.; Hamilton, *Early American Book Illustrators and Wood Engravers,* 394.

DUTTON, THOMAS. Artist, Baltimore, 1860. ¶ Baltimore BD 1860.

DUTZER, FREDERICK. German engraver, 32, at NYC in 1860. ¶ 8 Census (1860), N.Y., XLII, 430.

DUVAL, AMBROSE. Portrait and miniature painter, drawing master; first appeared in New Orleans in 1803 and worked there during the 1820's and 1830's. ¶ Van Ravenswaay, "The Forgotten Arts and Crafts in Colonial Louisiana," 195; New Orleans CD 1823–24, 1827, 1830, 1832, 1834–35 (cited by Delgado-WPA); Bolton, *Miniature Painters;* Stauffer; Cline, "Art and Artists in N.O."

DUVAL, E. Painter, drawing master and naturalist, Charleston (S.C.), 1837. He advertised to do portraits and miniatures, as well as fruits, flowers, and landscapes. ¶ Rutledge, *Artists in the Life of Charleston.*

DUVAL, J. Drawing teacher, New Orleans. He was mentioned in 1819 as J. Duval, Jr., and in 1837 as J. Duval and lady. These may have been different persons. *Cf.* JOHN DUVAL. ¶ Delgado-WPA cites *Louisiana Courrier,* June 14, 1819, and New Orleans CD 1837.

DUVAL, JOHN. Miniaturist, Philadelphia, 1794. ¶ Prime, II, 7.

DUVAL, PETER S. Lithographer. In 1831 Duval, a French lithographer in his early twenties, was hired by CEPHAS G. CHILDS to come to Philadelphia to work for the firm of CHILDS & INMAN. A few years later Duval and GEORGE LEHMAN established the firm of LEHMAN & DUVAL (1835–37) as successor to Childs & Inman. From 1839 to 1843 Duval was associated with WILLIAM W. HUDDY in the lithographic and publishing house of HUDDY & DUVAL. Thereafter Duval had his own lithographic establishment in Philadelphia, in which he was joined in 1858 by his son STEPHEN ORR DUVAL. P. S. Duval was one of the leading lithographers of the country until his retirement in 1879. ¶ Peters, *America on Stone;* Eckhardt, "Early Lithography in Philadelphia," 252; Phila. CD 1835–60 and after; 7 Census (1850), Pa., L, 277; 8 Census (1860), Pa., LIV, 128; Am. Inst. Cat., 1850; Todd, "Huddy & Duval Prints."

DUVAL, P. S., & SON. Lithographers, Philadelphia, 1858–60 and after; PETER S. DUVAL and STEPHEN ORR DUVAL. ¶ Phila. CD 1858–60 and after; Peters, *America on Stone.*

DUVAL, STEPHEN. Engraver, Philadelphia, 1835. Possibly PETER S. DUVAL. ¶ Phila. CD 1835.

DUVAL, STEPHEN ORR. Lithographer, son of PETER S. DUVAL; born in Philadelphia *c.* 1832; learned lithography in his father's shop. He became a partner in the firm of P. S. DUVAL SON in 1858. ¶ 7 Census (1850), Pa., L, 277; 8 Census (1860), Pa., LIV, 128; Phila. CD 1858–60 and after.

DUVERGER, PAUL. Artist, New Orleans, 1857. ¶ New Orleans CD 1857 (cited by Delgado-WPA).

DUVIVIER & SON. Teachers of drawing, Philadelphia, 1796–97. The elder Duvivier claimed membership in the Royal Academy at Paris. Both advertised themselves as skilled in drawing portraits, landscapes, still lifes, etc. One of them was still in Philadelphia in 1798. ¶ Prime, II, 47–48; Bolton, *Miniature Painters;* Bolton, *Crayon Draftsmen;* Brown and Brown.

DUYCKINCK, EVERT (the First) (1621–1702). Limner and glazier. Born in Holland in 1621, he came to New Amsterdam (New York) in 1638 and lived there until his death in 1702. He was the father of GERRIT DUYCKINCK and grandfather of EVERT DUYCKINCK (the Third) and GERARDUS DUYCKINCK (the First). ¶ Vail, "Storied Windows Richly Dight"; Fielding; NYHS *Collections* (1885), 21.

DUYCKINCK, EVERT (the Third) (*c.* 1677–1727). Portrait painter. Born in NYC *c.* 1677, Evert Duyckinck III learned to paint in the workshop of his grandfather, EVERT DUYCKINCK I. Evert III was admitted a freeman of NYC in 1698, and at least nine portraits have been attributed to him. ¶ Vail, "Storied Windows Richly Dight," 150; NYHS *Collections* (1885), 72; Fielding; repro., NYHS *Quarterly* (Oct. 1947), 192.

DUYCKINCK, GERARDUS (the First) (1695–1746?). Limner, painter, and glazier. Gerardus, son of GERRIT and grandson of EVERT DUYCKINCK (the First), was baptized in NYC in 1695. Made a freeman of NYC in 1731, he carried on a painting and glazing business at the sign of the Two Cupids until his death, which probably occurred some time in 1746, for on August 18 of that year his son, GERARDUS DUYCKINCK II, advertised that he was carrying on the business of his "late father, deceas'd." The elder Gerardus's will, dated 1741, was not proved until 1756. ¶ Information courtesy the late Waldron Phoenix Belknap who cited: "Baptisms, Dutch Church in N.Y., 1639–1730," *N. Y. Genealogical and Biographical Society Collections,* II (1901), 228; NYHS *Collections* (1885), 117; Gottesman, I, 129–30; NYHS *Collections* (1896), 94, and (1907), 204.

DUYCKINCK, GERARDUS (the Second) (1723–1797). Limner; teacher of drawing and painting on glass; dealer in glass, maps and prints, and painting materials. Gerardus II, son of GERARDUS DUYCKINCK (the First), was baptized in NYC in 1723, and died there in 1797. After the death of his father in 1746, Gerardus II carried on the family business at least until 1773 and probably later. He was admitted a freeman of NYC in 1748. His portrait is at the NYHS. ¶ Information courtesy the late Waldron Phoenix Belknap, who cited: "Baptisms, Dutch Church in N.Y., 1639–1730," *N. Y. Genealogical and Biographical Society Collections,* II (1901), 440; "Burials in the Dutch Church, N.Y.," *Holland Society Year Book 1899,* 161; NYHS *Collections* (1906), 56; Gottesman I, 15, 21, 24–25, 97, 130, 354; NYHS *Collections* (1885), 163.

DUYCKINCK, GERRIT (1660–*c.* 1710). Limner, glazier, and glass stainer. Gerrit, son of EVERT DUYCKINCK (the First), was baptized in New Amsterdam (NYC) in April 1660, admitted freeman of the city in February 1698/99, and died there *c.* 1710. As early as 1680 he was assisting his father in the making and painting of glass for churches and private homes of the Dutch towns from New York to Kingston. A number of oil portraits have also been attributed to Gerrit Duyckinck. ¶ Morgan, *Early American Painters;* Vail, "Storied Windows Richly Dight," 150, 159; NYHS *Collections* (1885), 73; repros., *Portraits in Delaware 1700–1850,* 40; *American Collector* (Nov. 1943), cover; *Portfolio* (Oct. 1943), 47, back cover.

DUZDEIN [?], JOHN A. Engraver, 45, a native of South Carolina, at New Orleans in 1860. By his Georgia-born wife Mary he had five children; the two oldest, 16 and 14, were born in Alabama; the rest, in Louisiana. ¶ 8 Census (1860), La., V, 752.

DWIGHT, Miss ——. An amateur artist of Boston who exhibited copies of paintings by Carlo Dolci and Both at the Apollo Gallery in 1839. ¶ Cowdrey, AA & AAU.

DWIGHT, N. W. Sculptor, Fall River (Mass.), 1860. ¶ New England BD 1860.

DWIGHT, STEPHEN. Portrait and historical painter, teacher of drawing, carver. Dwight first advertised in NYC in 1755 as a carver, late apprentice to Henry Hardcastle of NYC. In 1762 and 1774 he advertised both as a carver and as a painter of portraits and historical scenes and offered to teach drawing. ¶ Gottesman I, 3, 127; Pinckney, 191.

DYER, RICHARD. Engraver, Boston, 1860. Aged 23, he was a native of Massachusetts and was living with his parents; his father, David Y. Dyer, was a seaman. ¶ 8 Census (1860), Mass., XXV, 642.

DYKE, SAMUEL P. Landscape painter of Philadelphia, active 1856 to 1869. He exhibited several times at the Pennsylvania Academy, chiefly central Pennsylvania and West Virginia scenes. ¶ Rutledge, PA; Phila. CD 1857–60.

DYSART, THOMAS. Portrait and landscape painter. He was living in Lancaster (Pa.) in 1859, and in Philadelphia in 1860. ¶ Lancaster County BD 1859; Penna. BD 1860.

E

Eaches, Hector (1840–1873). Portrait painter. A son of Mayor Joseph Eaches of Alexandria (Va.) and younger brother of James Eaches, he was a pupil of Christopher P. Cranch before going to Kentucky in his teens and opening a studio in Louisville. He returned to Alexandria on the outbreak of the Civil War and joined the Confederate Army. Severely wounded, he retired from active service to become a government draftsman in Richmond. After the war he went to NYC and had a studio there till his death in 1873. He was best known for his portraits of Gen. Robert E. Lee. ¶ Information courtesy Mrs. Una Franklin Carter, President, Alexandria Association; represented in exhibition of Portraits of Early Alexandrians, April 1956.

Eaches, James [M.?] (1817–1847). Portrait painter, Alexandria (Va.). He was a son of Mayor Joseph Eaches and the older brother of Hector Eaches. Painted a self-portrait at the age of 17. In February 1842 he was at New Orleans. Exhibited at National Academy in 1838. ¶ Information courtesy Mrs. Una Franklin Carter, President, Alexandria Association; represented in exhibition of Portraits of Early Alexandrians, April 1956; New Orleans CD 1842; New Orleans *Picayune,* Feb. 2, 1842 (courtesy Delgado-WPA); Cowdrey, NAD.

Eager, Frank S. Engraver, Newburgh (N.Y.), 1859. ¶ N. Y. State BD 1859.

Eald, Peter. Wood engraver, age 45, living in Philadelphia in 1860. A native of England, he lived next-door to the wood engraver John Thompson. His family included Ellen (22, Ireland), John (16, Pa.), and Thomas (10, Pa.). ¶ 8 Census (1860), Pa., LX, 643.

Eames, see Ames.

Earl, Augustus (1793–*c.* 1833). Portrait painter, scenic and scientific draftsman; son of James Earl; born in England, studied at the Royal Academy (*c.* 1813), and spent several years in the Mediterranean area. He came to the United States in March 1818, spent some time in NYC and Philadelphia (where he exhibited at the Pennsylvania Academy), and visited many parts of the country before his departure for South America early in 1820. During the next decade Earl, who was known as "the wandering painter," painted and travelled in South America, the South Seas and Australasia, the East Indies and India. Returning to England, where many of his sketches were used for Burford's panoramas, Earl soon after (1832) accepted the post of draftsman on H.M.S. *Beagle,* on the South American expedition in which Charles Darwin served as naturalist, but he is said to have died before the end of the four-year voyage. ¶ Earle, *The Earle Family,* 91–93; CAB; Rutledge, PA; Dunlap, *History,* II, 322–25.

Earl, George W. Historical painter at NYC, 1858–59. Possibly the George Earle listed in the 1850 Census of NYC. The latter was 33 years old in 1850, an Englishman whose wife and six children, ages 16 to 6, were also born in England. ¶ NYBD 1858–59; 7 Census (1850), N.Y., XLII, 323.

Earl, James (1761–1796). Portrait and miniature painter; brother of Ralph Earl and father of Augustus Earl; born May 1, 1761, in that part of Leicester (Mass.) now known as Paxton. He went to England as a young man, studied in London, and exhibited at the Royal Academy. Returning to America in 1794, he painted a number of portraits in Charleston (S.C.) and intended settling there, but his career was cut short by an attack of yellow fever from which he died in Charleston on August 18, 1796. ¶ DAB; Prime, II, 7; Rutledge, *Artists in the Life of Charleston,* 174, repro.; *Art Digest* (Feb. 15, 1938), 11, repros.; Dunlap, *History,* I, 427; Bolton, *Miniature Painters.*

Earl, Ralph (1751–1801). Portrait and landscape painter. Ralph Earl (or Earle), one of the leading American portrait painters of the last quarter of the 18th century, was born in Worcester County (Mass.) on May 11, 1751. He set up as a painter in New Haven (Conn.) just before the Revolution, but was forced to flee to England early in 1778 because of his Loyalist sympathies. During the seven years he spent in England, Earl painted portraits in London and in the County of Norfolk and exhibited at the Royal Academy. After his return to America in the fall of 1785, he painted portraits and a few landscapes through Connecticut and neighboring states until his death at

Bolton (Conn.), August 16, 1801. He was the brother of JAMES EARL and father of RALPH E. W. EARL. ¶ Sawitzky, *Ralph Earl 1751–1801;* Phillips, "Ralph Earl, Loyalist"; DAB; Graves; Gottesman, II, [7]; Cowdrey, "The Stryker Sisters by Ralph Earl"; Reese, "A Newly Discovered Landscape by Ralph Earl"; Yale University Gallery of Fine Arts, *Connecticut Portraits by Ralph Earl,* foreword by William Sawitzky; Goodrich, "Ralph Earl"; Flexner, *The Light of Distant Skies.*

EARL, RALPH ELEASER WHITESIDE (*c.* 1785–1838). Portrait painter; son of RALPH EARL by his second wife; born in England before 1785 and probably brought to America by his father as a child, for they were working together in Connecticut as early as 1800. The younger Earl went to England in 1809, spent four years in Norwich, then visited France and returned to the United States in 1815. As an itinerant artist he worked during the next few years in Georgia, Alabama, Tennessee, and along the Mississippi. Through his marriage in 1818 to a niece of Mrs. Andrew Jackson, Earl became an intimate of the Jacksons and after Mrs. Jackson's death in 1828 the artist became a member of General Jackson's household. For the rest of his life Earl devoted himself to painting portraits of Jackson for the president's friends. When Jackson left the White House in 1837, Earl accompanied him to "The Hermitage," near Nashville (Tenn.), where he died on September 16, 1838. Because of his position in Andrew Jackson's entourage in Washington, R. E. W. Earl was jocularly known as "The King's Painter." ¶ Hart, "Life Portraits of Andrew Jackson"; Bolton, *Miniature Painters;* Alabama Dept. of Archives and History (cited by WPA (Ala.), Historic Records Survey); *Knoxville* (Tenn.) *Gazette,* July 28, 1818 (cited by Dr. C. S. Brigham); Sawitzky, *Ralph Earl 1751–1801;* Bassett, *Correspondence of Andrew Jackson.*

EARL, S. F. Portrait painter, whose portrait of George Lippard (1822–1854) of Philadelphia, signed and dated 1846, is owned by the Historical Society of Pennsylvania. ¶ Sawitzky, *Hist. Soc. of Pa. Cat.*

EARLE, see also EARL, EARLL.

EARLE, ELSIE. Portrait, figure, and marine painter, who exhibited at the American Institute in 1856 two oils, "Shipwreck" and "Figure Piece," and was listed as a portrait painter in NYC from 1858 to 1860. She lived at the same address as Edward I. Earle, policeman, and John E. Earle, engineer. ¶ Am. Inst. Cat., 1856; NYBD 1858, 1860.

EARLE, HENRY. Engraver, age 23, living in Philadelphia in 1850 with his tailor-father and his brother William Earle, age 18, also an engraver. Both sons were born in Pennsylvania, the father in England. ¶ 7 Census (1850), Pa., L, 646.

EARLE (or Earles), JOSEPH. Portrait painter. Working in Brooklyn (N.Y.) 1842–43, in NYC 1846–52. ¶ Brooklyn CD 1842–43; NYBD 1846, 1848, 1851, 1852.

EARLE, WILLIAM, see HENRY EARLE.

EARLE, Mrs. WILLIAM. The widow Earle had a drawing academy in NYC in 1808–09. She was presumably the widow of William Earle, listed at the same address in 1806. ¶ NYCD 1806–09.

EARLL, JOHN. Portrait, landscape, and heraldic painter who advertised in July 1774 his intention of carrying on his trade in New Haven (Conn.). ¶ *The Connecticut Journal and New-Haven Post Boy,* July 8, 15, and 22, 1774.

EASTMAN, HARRISON. Wood engraver and lithographic designer. Born in New Hampshire *c.* 1823, Eastman went to California *c.* 1853, worked for several San Francisco lithographers from 1854 to 1858, and in 1859/60 established the engraving firm of EASTMAN & LOOMIS. In 1860 he owned property valued at $9,000 in realty and $1,200 in personalty. His wife Sophia was from New Hampshire, but their three children, ages 1 to 6, were born in California. ¶ 8 Census (1860), Cal. VII, 408; Peters, *California on Stone;* San Francisco CD 1856, 1858, BD 1858–60.

EASTMAN, J. FREDERICK. Engraver, Boston, 1856 and after; from 1859 as partner in EASTMAN & LOWELL. He was born in Maine (?) about 1833. ¶ Boston CD 1856–60; 8 Census (1860), Mass., XXVI, 573.

EASTMAN & LOOMIS. Engravers of San Francisco, 1860 and after; HARRISON EASTMAN and PASCAL LOOMIS. ¶ San Francisco BD 1860.

EASTMAN & LOWELL. Engravers of Boston (Mass.), 1859 and after; J. FREDERICK EASTMAN and JOHN ADAMS LOWELL. ¶ Boston CD 1859–60 and after.

EASTMAN, SETH (1808–1875). Army officer, topographical draftsman, and painter, especially of Indian life. Born at Brunswick (Maine), January 24, 1808, attended West Point from 1824 to 1829, and served four years at Fort Crawford (Wis.) and Fort Snelling (Minn.). From 1831 to 1833 he was on topographical duty and from 1833 to 1840 he was assistant teacher of drawing at West Point. After service in the Florida War (1840–41) he returned to Fort Snelling, where he remained until 1848. In 1848–49 he went to Texas. From 1850 to 1855 he worked on illustrations for Henry R. Schoolcraft's *History and Statistical Information Respecting the . . . Indian Tribes of the United States* (6 vols., 1853–56). He served in Texas again in 1855–56 and in the office of the Quartermaster General, Washington (D.C.), in 1857–58. Placed on the retired list in 1863, Colonel Eastman was brevetted Brigadier General in 1866. From 1867 until after 1870 he was engaged in painting Indian scenes and views of western forts for the Capitol. He died in Washington, August 31, 1875. ¶ Bushnell, "Seth Eastman," repros.; Cowdrey, "Seth Eastman," repros.; Fairman, 239–40; Cowdrey, NAD; Eastman, *American Aboriginal Portfolio* (1853), 26 plates; Cullum; Butts; Sweet, *Hudson River School;* Cowdrey, AA & AAU; Karolik Cat.; CAB; Heilbron, "Seth Eastman's Water Colors." Represented Corcoran Gallery, U.S. Capitol, and Minneapolis Institute of Arts.

EASTON, W. W. Portrait painter, NYC, 1846. ¶ NYBD 1846.

EATON, CHARLES W. Engraver, age 17, living in Boston in August 1850. ¶ 7 Census (1850), Mass., XXIII, 2.

EATON, J. N. Portrait and figure painter, Greene (N.Y.), *c.* 1800. ¶ *American Provincial Painting,* no. 4; Lipman and Winchester, 172; repro., *Antiques* (Sept. 1941), 143.

EATON, JOSEPH HORACE (1815–1896). Portrait and landscape painter in oils and watercolors; born in Salem (Mass.), October 12, 1815; graduated from West Point in 1835. After service in Louisiana, where he mapped the Sabine River, he was instructor in tactics at West Point from 1839 to 1843. In 1845 he became aide to General Zachary Taylor, with whom he served in the Mexican War and whose portrait he painted. From 1848 to 1856 Captain Eaton was stationed at Fort Defiance (N.M.), where he made many drawings of the Zuni and Navajo, studied their languages, and contributed an article on them to Schoolcraft's *History.* He resigned from the army in 1856 to supervise the construction of the Chicago Customs House, but served again during the Civil War. Eaton went to Oregon in 1874 and lived there until his death at Portland, January 20, 1896. ¶ Association of Graduates, U. S. Military Academy, Annual Reunion, 1896, pp. 90–96; Schoolcraft, *History,* II, 216–221; *Album of American Battle Art,* pl. 57; National Gallery of Art, *American Battle Painting, 1776–1918,* color pl. opp. 4.

EATON, JOSEPH ORIEL (1829–1875). Portrait, genre, and landscape painter. Born in Newark (Ohio), February 8, 1829, he studied in NYC but worked mainly in the Midwest. He was in Indianapolis (Ind.) 1846–48; in Cincinnati, 1850, 1853, and 1857–60; and in New Orleans before 1857. During the latter part of his career he was a successful painter of children's portraits in NYC and an Associate of the National Academy. He died at his home in Yonkers (N.Y.), February 7, 1875. ¶ DAB; Peat, *Pioneer Painters of Indiana;* CAB; Clement and Hutton; Champlin and Perkins; Cowdrey, NAD; Cowdrey, AA & AAU; Lancaster County Hist. Soc., *Portraiture in Lancaster County;* New Orleans *Crescent,* Jan. 29, 1857 (cited by Delgado-WPA); Cincinnati CD 1853, 1857–60; repro. of landscape in *Princeton Museum Record,* IV (1945), no. 1, p. 5; Rutledge, PA.

EATON, SERANA(?) D. Engraver, age 27, born in Massachusetts, living in Boston in August 1850. ¶ 7 Census (1850), Mass., XXV, 418.

EATON, WILLIAM BRADLEY (1836–1896). Artist. Presumably a native of Salem (Mass.), where he was baptized July 31, 1836, Eaton worked in Salem as a carpenter from 1855 to 1859. Changing his occupation to that of "artist," he had a studio in Salem from 1861 and was active as late as 1884. He died in 1896. ¶ Belknap, 9; Robinson and Dow, I, 61.

EAVES, JOHN. Portrait, miniature, and landscape painter at Philadelphia in 1809. ¶ Phila. *Aurora,* Nov. 3, 1809 (cited by Brown and Brown).

EAVES, WILLIAM. Engraver and die-sinker, NYC, 1857–60. ¶ NYBD 1857–60.

EBERHARD, JOHN. Engraver, of BLISS, EBERHARD & FESTNER, Madison (Wis.), 1858. ¶ Madison BD 1858.

EBERT, CAROLINE. Artist from Trinidad, aged 48, living in NYC in 1860. She was the wife of Otterman Ebert, paperhanger, and the mother of three children born in

France between 1837 and 1848. The eldest, Gustavus (23), was an engraver. ¶ 8 Census (1860), N.Y., XLIX, 1011.

ECK, WILLIAM. Engraver and die-sinker, NYC, 1856 and after. He was born in Prussia about 1824. ¶ NYBD 1856–60; 8 Census (1860), N.Y., XLIV, 981.

ECKEL, J. L. In 1851 this 14-year-old artist of NYC won $5.00 and a certificate for crayon drawings exhibited at the American Institute. ¶ Am. Inst. *Cat.* and *List of Premiums,* 1851.

ECKENDORF, GEORGE. Apprentice wood engraver, age 18, at Philadelphia in June 1860. A native of Pennsylvania, he was a son of Gustavus Eckendorf, master gilder. ¶ 8 Census (1860), Pa., LX, 706.

ECKHART, FRANCIS. German lithographer, 30, at NYC in 1850. ¶ 7 Census (1850), N.Y., XLII, 148.

ECKHART, OTTO. Prussian portrait painter, 32, living in NYC in 1860 with his wife Matilda. ¶ 8 Census (1860), N.Y., XLIX, 443.

ECKHART, WILLIAM. German sculptor, 25, at NYC in 1860. ¶ 8 Census (1860), N.Y., XLVI, 177.

ECKLEY, Mrs. SOPHIA MAY (TUCKERMAN) (*c.* 1825–1874). Sculptor; exhibited at the Boston Athenaeum 1864–67. ¶ Swan, BA.

ECKSTEIN, FREDERICK (*c.* 1775–1852). Sculptor and drawing master; son of JOHANN ECKSTEIN; probably born in Berlin (Prussia), where his father was employed as a sculptor by Frederick the Great. After study at the Academy in Berlin, he accompanied his father to America in 1794, settling in Philadelphia, where he worked with his father and with him helped found the Pennsylvania Academy. After the death of the elder Eckstein in 1817 the son left Philadelphia to become a school teacher, first at Harmony (Pa.) and subsequently at Wheeling and Charleston (Va., now W. Va.). Settling in Cincinnati in December 1823, he continued to teach school and resumed his artistic work. His heads of Jackson and Lafayette (1825) attracted much attention and encouraged Eckstein to found the short-lived Cincinnati Academy of Fine Arts. In 1828 he also collaborated briefly with Mrs. Trollope's artist-protege, AUGUSTE HERVIEU, in a school-teaching venture. From 1830 to 1838 Eckstein taught school in Frankfort, Millersburg, and Augusta (Ky.), from 1838 to 1840 in Cincinnati, and from 1840 until his retirement in Louisville (Ky.). He spent his last years in Cincinnati, where he died in his 77th year, February 10, 1852. His pupils included the noted sculptors HIRAM POWERS and SHOBAL CLEVENGER. ¶ Ophia D. Smith, "Frederick Eckstein, the Father of Cincinnati Art"; Clark, *Ohio Art and Artists,* 74; Gardner, *Yankee Stonecutters.*

ECKSTEIN, JOHANN (*c.* 1736–1817). Portrait and historical painter, modeler in wax, sculptor, and engraver. Probably born in Mecklenburg (Germany), Eckstein was employed by the Prussian court as a historical painter and sculptor from *c.* 1772 to 1794. Especially noted as a modeller in wax, he executed a death mask and plaster bust of Frederick the Great in 1786. Many of his works were exhibited at the Royal Academy (London). In 1794 he emigrated to the United States and settled in Philadelphia, where he worked as a limner and "statuary" with his son, FREDERICK ECKSTEIN. One of the organizers of the Columbian Society of Artists (1795), the Pennsylvania Academy (1805), and the Society of Artists (1810), the elder Eckstein exhibited at the latter in 1811–12 a design for an equestrian statue of Washington in Roman costume. He died at the age of 81 in Havana, Cuba, June 27, 1817. ¶ Ophia D. Smith, "Frederick Eckstein"; DAB; Graves; *Columbianum* 1795; Prime, II, 7–8; Rutledge, PA; Stauffer; repro., *Portfolio* (Jan. 1952), 103.

EDDY, BENJAMIN F. Portrait painter, Brooklyn (N.Y.), 1837; exhibitor, National Academy. ¶ Cowdrey, NAD.

EDDY, C. F., see OLIVER TARBELL EDDY.

EDDY, ISAAC (1777–1847). Copperplate engraver, printer, and possibly portrait painter. Born February 17, 1777, in Weathersfield (Vt.); worked there as an engraver and printer until 1826. In 1812 he engraved plates for the first Vermont Bible and from 1814 to 1816 he operated a printing establishment in which he used the famous Stephen Daye press. In 1826 he moved to Troy (N.Y.), where he made a modest fortune as a manufacturer of printer's ink. He died in Waterford, near Troy, July 25, 1847. OLIVER TARBELL EDDY, the portrait painter, was his son. ¶ Bishop, *Oliver Tarbell Eddy,* 7–9; Fielding, *Supplement.*

EDDY, JAMES (1806–1888). Engraver, portrait painter, art dealer. Born in Providence (R.I.), May 29, 1806, he studied engraving in Boston and then established himself in NYC as a portrait painter and importer of old masters, largely made-to-order copies. After his marriage at the age of 40, Eddy resided for some years in Boston, but he later returned to Providence, where he died May 18, 1888. ¶ *James Eddy . . . Biographical Sketch* (Providence, 1889); Stauffer; 7 Census (1850), Mass., XXV, 667; NYBD 1844 (as James Addy); Boston BD 1855–57; *Boston Transcript,* May 19, 1888; *Providence Journal,* May 19, 1888.

EDDY, OLIVER TARBELL (1799–1868). Portrait painter and engraver. A son of ISAAC EDDY, he was born in Greenbush (Vt.), November 14, 1799, and began engraving under his father's instruction as early as 1814. He left Vermont sometime before November 1822, when he was married at Newburgh (N.Y.). From 1826 to 1829 he was in NYC, where he exhibited at the National Academy (1827); from 1831 to 1835, in Elizabeth (N.J.); from 1835 to 1840, in Newark (N.J.); from 1842 to 1850, in Baltimore (Md.); and from 1850 until his death, in Philadelphia. He was an inventor as well as an artist, having patented among other things a forerunner of the typewriter. He died in Philadelphia, October 8, 1868. ¶ Bishop, *Oliver Tarbell Eddy,* biographical sketch and catalogue, with 30 repros.; 7 Census (1850), Pa., L, 869; Rutledge, PA; Cowdrey, NAD. C. F. Eddy, artist, 258 Chestnut St., Phila. (BD 1857) is probably the same as O. T. Eddy, 260 Chestnut St. (CD 1857). Represented at Newark Museum and Maryland Historical Society.

EDES, JONATHAN W. Marine and landscape artist. His "Boston Lighthouse" *c.* 1787 and "Eden Vale, Waltham, Mass." *c.* 1793 were engraved by SAMUEL HILL. ¶ Gage (as J. Edes); *Connoisseur* (Apr. 1953), 67, as Jonathan W. Edes.

EDGAR, ——. Portrait painter, working at Vergennes (Vt.) in 1800. His portrait of Noah Smith is at the Masonic Grand Lodge, Burlington (Vt.). ¶ FARL question file.

EDGAR, Mrs. C. H. A portrait inscribed "by Mrs. C. H. Edgar 1843" is listed by FARL. ¶ FARL photo.

EDMONDS, CHARLES. Wood engraver, designer, and artist, NYC, 1848–1860. From 1848 to 1854 he was a partner in the firm of BOBBETT & EDMONDS. He was born in England about 1823. ¶ NYCD 1847–61; NYBD 1854–60; 7 Census (1850), N.Y., LII, 205.

EDMONDS, FRANCIS WILLIAM (1806–1863). N.A. Genre and portrait painter; born at Hudson (N.Y.), November 22, 1806. Though he made his career in banking, he devoted much time to painting and was an officer in both the National Academy and the American Art-Union. He was a frequent exhibitor at the National Academy (in 1836, 1837 and 1838 under the name of "E. F. Williams"), as well as at the Apollo Association, American Art-Union, Boston Athenaeum, Maryland Historical Society, Pennsylvania Academy, and Royal Academy. He died at his country home, "Crow's Nest," on the Bronx River (N.Y.), February 7, 1863. ¶ DAB; Cummings, *Historic Annals,* 317–320; Cowdrey, NAD; Cowdrey, AA & AAU; Swan, BA; Rutledge, MHS; Rutledge, PA; Graves; *American Collector* (Sept. 1947), 19, repro.; *Antiques* (Aug. 1932), frontis.

EDMONDS, WILLIAM. Engraver, NYC, 1835–37. In 1837 he was one of the partners in BURTON, GURLEY & EDMONDS, banknote engravers. ¶ NYCD 1835–37; NYBD 1837.

EDMONDSON, EDWARD, JR. Portrait or landscape painter, Dayton (Ohio), 1859. ¶ Ohio BD 1859.

EDMUND, JOHN H. Engraver. Edmund (29) and his wife (24), both German, were living in Philadelphia in 1850. Their two-year-old son was born in Pennsylvania. ¶ 7 Census (1850), Pa., LII, 737.

EDOUART, ALEXANDER (1818–1892). Portrait and landscape painter, photographer. Son of the noted silhouettist AUGUSTE EDOUART, Alexander was born in London on November 5, 1818, was educated at Edinburgh, and studied art in Italy. He was living in NYC in 1848–50 and exhibited at the National Academy and American Art-Union. About 1852 he went out to California where he spent the rest of his life, except for a brief trip to Europe about 1859. Though he painted some California landscapes, he was best known as a photographer in San Francisco. In 1889 or 1890 he moved to Los Angeles, where he died in 1892. *Cf.* ALEXANDER EDWARD. ¶ Van Nostrand and Coulter, *California Pictorial,* 142–43; Howell, "Pictorial Californiana," 63 (repro.), 64–65; Cowdrey, NAD; Cowdrey, AA & AAU; 8 Census (1860), Cal., VII, 515; NYBD 1850; San Francisco BD 1858–60, CD 1862–87.

EDOUART, AUGUSTE (Augustin-Amant-Constan-Fidèle) (1789–1861). Silhouettist. A native of Dunquerque (France), Edouart served in the French army until about 1813 when he went to England. Supporting himself at first by teaching, he began to make hair devices and landscapes and painted some animal portraits which were exhibited at the Royal Academy in 1815–16. In 1825 he commenced his phenomenal career as a silhouettist. In 1830 he went to Scotland and thence in 1833 to Ireland, where he stayed for six years. In 1839 he came to the United States and during the next decade he cut silhouettes all over the country, among the places he visited being Boston, Washington (D.C.) 1841, Cambridge (Mass.) and New Orleans 1842, Philadelphia 1843, New Orleans 1844, Charleston (S.C.) 1845 and 1847, and NYC 1849. Returning to France in 1849, he lost most of his duplicates, said to have numbered over 50,000, in a shipwreck off the island of Guernsey, and the loss so affected him that he never resumed his profession. He died at Guînes, near Calais, in 1861. ¶ Jackson, *Ancestors in Silhouette;* Strickland; Carrick, "Silhouettes"; New Orleans *Picayune,* March 21, 1844 (cited by Delgado-WPA); Graves, *Dictionary;* Rutledge, *Artists in the Life of Charleston.*

EDSON, TRACY R. (1809–1881). Banknote engraver. Born in Otsego County (N.Y.), Edson worked as an engraver in NYC from 1834 to 1837, in New Orleans in 1841–42, and again in NYC from 1847 until after 1860. He was a member of the well-known firm of RAWDON, WRIGHT, HATCH & EDSON in 1835 and from 1847 to 1858, when the firm merged with others to form the AMERICAN BANK NOTE COMPANY. Edson was president of the latter from 1860 to 1863. He died on November 29th, 1881. ¶ Boston *Transcript,* Nov. 30, 1881, obit.; 7 Census (1850), N.Y., LII, 535; NYCD 1834–37, 1847–60; New Orleans CD 1841–42; Toppan, *100 Years of Bank Note Engraving,* 13.

EDWARD, ALEXANDER. Artist, 25, born in England, at NYC in 1850. *Cf.* ALEXANDER EDOUART. ¶ 7 Census (1850), N.Y., XLIV, 275.

EDWARDS, CHARLES (1797–1868). Amateur artist, Honorary Member (Amateur) of the National Academy, 1833–68. Edwards was born in Norwich (England), March 17, 1797, received his education at Cambridge, and emigrated to America soon after. He studied law, served for twenty-five years as counsel to the British consulate-general in NYC, and was a well-known writer on legal and literary subjects. In 1831 he exhibited a pen drawing, "Vue du Tombeau d'Archimede" at the National Academy and during the same decade he several times lectured at the Academy on antique statues. He died in NYC, May 30, 1868. ¶ DAB; Cowdrey, NAD; Cummings, *Historic Annals.*

EDWARDS, CLEMENT R. Portrait painter, Cincinnati (Ohio), 1842–53. He was a native of New Jersey, born about 1820. ¶ 7 Census (1850), Ohio, XXI, 504; Ohio BD 1853; information courtesy Edward H. Dwight, Cincinnati Art Museum.

EDWARDS, THOMAS. Portrait and miniature painter, silhouettist, teacher, and lithographer of Boston, 1822–56. He exhibited portraits and miniatures at the Boston Athenaeum between 1827 and 1846. He was working as a lithographer as early as 1825, and in 1830 was with the SENEFELDER LITHOGRAPHIC COMPANY. His *Juvenile Drawing Book or Instructions in Landscape Drawing and Painting in Water-Colors* was published in 1844. ¶ Swan, BA; Boston BD 1846–56; Bodley Book Shop Cat. No. 80 (1945), no. 12a; Carrick, *Shades;* Jackson, *Silhouette;* Peters, *America on Stone;* Stauffer; Thieme-Becker; *Antiques* (Oct. 1928), 323.

EDWARDS, W. Etcher of D. ROGERS' portraits of Joseph and Hyrum Smith, Nauvoo (Ill.), 1842. ¶ Josephson, "What Did the Prophet Joseph Smith Look Like?" 314, repro.

EDWIN, DAVID (1776–1841). Stipple engraver. Born in Bath (England) in December 1776, studied engraving in England and Holland, and came to the United States in December 1797. At first employed by the Philadelphia publisher, J. B. Freeman, early in 1798 he entered the workshop of EDWARD SAVAGE with whom he was associated until 1801. He made an independent reputation shortly after leaving Savage by his engravings of several portraits by GILBERT STUART. Edwin continued to engrave, chiefly in Philadelphia, until about 1831. During the last six years of his life he served as treasurer of the Artists' Fund Society. He died in Philadelphia, February 22, 1841. ¶ DAB; Stauffer; Dickson, "The Case against Edward Savage"; Dickson, "A Misdated Episode in Dunlap"; Society of Artists Cat. 1813–14; Penna. Academy Cat. 1818–20, 1823–

24; Artists' Fund Soc. Cat. 1835; Fielding, *Engravings of David Edwin.*

EECKHOUT, Dr. JAN. Modeler of a wax portrait of Dr. Abraham Chovet of Philadelphia, 1784. ¶ E. S. Bolton, *American Wax Portraits,* 35–36.

EFFIE (or Eiffe), WILLIAM. Portrait, genre, landscape, and religious painter; at NYC in 1833, at Lancaster (Pa.) in 1835, at NYC in 1836–40, at Philadelphia in 1840, and at NYC in 1846–48. ¶ Cowdrey, NAD; Cowdrey, AA & AAU; Rutledge, PA; NYBD 1846–48.

EGAN, JOHN J. Panoramist and landscape painter, Philadelphia, *c.* 1850–51. Egan was the painter of a panorama of Ireland, shown in Philadelphia in December 1850; of two views in Ireland and England, exhibited at the Pennsylvania Academy in 1850; and of a moving diorama of the Mississippi based on sketches by M. W. DICKESON, shown in Philadelphia in December 1851 and now owned by the City Art Museum of St. Louis. He may have been the Irish artist, J. Egan, whose views of Kilkenny and neighborhood were engraved and published in Hall's *Ireland, Its Scenery and Character* (1841). ¶ Phila. *Public Ledger,* Dec. 13, 1850, and Dec. 31, 1851 (cited by J. E. Arrington); Rutledge, PA; Strickland; Mason, "Grand Moving Diorama."

EGAN, THOMAS H. Portrait and religious painter, Charleston (S.C.), 1850–57. His painting of St. Paul was shown in Charleston in 1851. ¶ Rutledge, *Artists in the Life of Charleston.*

EGBERT, HENRY (1826–1900). Illustrator. This was presumably the Henry Egbert, Jr., who in 1846 won a diploma for crayon drawing at the American Institute. Henry Egbert, Sr., was a printer. The artist died in Brooklyn (N.Y.), March 12, 1900. ¶ *Art Annual,* II, obit.; Am. Inst., *5th Annual Report,* 1846.

EGLAN or EGLAU, MAX. As Max Eglan, exhibitor of a study after nature at the National Academy, 1860. As Max Eglau in the 1860 Census, aged 35, a native of Bavaria. ¶ Cowdrey, NAD; 8 Census (1860), N.Y., LIV, 926.

EGLER, AMMIEL. Engraver, 34, a native of Philadelphia, at NYC in 1860 with his German-born wife Emily. ¶ 8 Census (1860), N.Y., L, 679.

EGLOFFSTEIN, F. W. VON (*c.* 1824–1898). Topographical draftsman. A native of Prussia, von Egloffstein came to America sometime before 1853 and remained for at least twenty years. He served as artist to several Western exploring expeditions and surveys, including Frémont's last expedition to the Rockies (1853–54), Beckwith's Utah-to-California railroad survey (1854), and Ives's Colorado River expedition (1857–58), his drawings being reproduced in the reports of these expeditions. During the Civil War von Egloffstein served with the 103d Regiment, New York Volunteers, and was brevetted out as Brigadier General in 1865. From 1864 to 1873 he lived in NYC, where he was engaged in development of the half-tone process of engraving. His *New Style of Topographical Drawing* was published in Washington in 1857. According to the recollection of his grandson, von Egloffstein died in London in 1898. ¶ Taft, *Artists and Illustrators of the Old West,* 264.

EHLARS, JOHN D. Engraver, Baltimore, 1860. ¶ Baltimore BD 1860.

EHNINGER, JOHN WHETTEN (1827–1889). N.A. Genre and portrait painter, illustrator; born in NYC, July 22, 1827. After graduation from Columbia College in 1847, he went abroad to study in France, Germany, and Italy until about 1853. On his return he settled in NYC and for the next six years he was a frequent exhibitor at many of the Eastern galleries, including the National Academy of which he became a Member in 1860. After another visit to Europe, he settled briefly in Newport (R.I.), married, and about 1872 moved to Saratoga (N.Y.), where he lived until his death, January 22, 1889. ¶ DAB; CAB; Cowdrey, NAD; Cowdrey, AA & AAU; Swan, BA; Rutledge, PA; Washington Art Assoc. Cat., 1857; Karolik Cat.; *Portfolio* (Oct. 1943), 30–31.

EHRET, ADOLPH. German lithographer, 29, at NYC in 1860. ¶ 8 Census (1860), N.Y., XLIV, 207.

EHRGOTT & FORBRIGER. Lithographers of Cincinnati (Ohio), 1857 and after; PETER EHRGOTT and ADOLF FORBRIGER. ¶ Ohio BD 1857, 1859; Cincinnati BD 1859–60, CD 1858–59; examples of their work in Cist, *Cincinnati in 1859.*

EHRGOTT, PETER. Lithographer. A native of Germany, Ehrgott was working in Cincinnati (Ohio) as early as 1850, when he was 24. He continued to work there at least until 1860, from 1857 as a member of the firm of EHRGOTT & FORBRIGER. ¶ 7 Census (1850), Ohio, XX, 345; Cincinnati CD 1853–59, BD 1851, 1859–60; Ohio BD 1857, 1859.

EICHBAUM, GEORGE CALDER (1837–1919). Portrait painter. Born in Bowling Green (Ky.) in 1837, Eichbaum studied in Pittsburgh (Pa.) under DAVID R. SMITH. His work was shown at the National Academy, where he maintained a studio for some time, though his home after 1859 was in St. Louis (Mo.). He died in St. Louis in the spring of 1919. ¶ *Art Annual,* XVI, 220, obit.; *American Art News* (May 24, 1919), 4. Both citations courtesy Theodore Bolton.

EICHBERG, SOLOMON. German engraver, 45, living in NYC in 1850. His wife Clara and four children were born in Germany before 1839; one child was born in Brussels (Belgium) about 1843, and the two youngest in France about 1845–47. Mrs. Eichberg was listed as a widow in 1863. One son, Theodore, aged 15, was listed as an engraver in 1850. ¶ 7 Census (1850), N.Y., LV, 325; NYCD 1863.

EICHHOLTZ, JACOB (1776–1842). Portrait, landscape, and historical painter. Eichholtz was born in Lancaster (Pa.), November 2, 1776 and commenced his career there as a coppersmith. Though he had lessons from THOMAS SULLY in Lancaster as early as 1808, it was not until about 1811, when he was 35, that Eichholtz was able to devote himself wholly to painting. In 1812 he went to Boston to study briefly under GILBERT STUART. A regular exhibitor at the Society of Artists (1811–14) and the Pennsylvania Academy (1823–42), he spent most of his career in Lancaster and Philadelphia, though he also made visits to Baltimore and Washington. He died in Lancaster, May 11, 1842. ¶ DAB; Richardson, "Jacob Eichholtz," 6 repros.; Hensel, "Jacob Eichholtz, Painter," with catalogue; Hensel, "An Artistic Aftermath"; Rutledge, PA; Karolik Cat.; Pleasants, *250 Years of Painting in Md.;* Lancaster Co. Hist. Soc., *Portraiture in Lancaster County,* 7 repros.; *Antiques* (Jan. 1954), 22, repro.

EIFFE or EIFFEE, WILLIAM, see WILLIAM EFFIE.

EIGHTS, JAMES (1798–1882). Topographical and scientific draftsman. Eights was born in Albany (N.Y.) and spent most of his life there, though he died at Ballston (N.Y.). Best known for his series of views of Albany as it was in 1805 (first published *c.* 1847–54), he was also a naturalist, physician, explorer, and scientific artist for the Erie Canal geological survey and for Emmons' geological report on New York. ¶ Cassiter, "James Eights and His Albany Views," 8 repros.; *Portfolio* (Nov. 1952), 64; Stokes, *Historic Prints,* pl. 37b; Colden, *Memoir;* Albany CD 1832–44.

EIMERMANN, GEORGE MICKLE. Portrait painter, Camden (N.J.), 1860. ¶ N. J. BD 1860, p. 358.

EISEMAN, PAUL. German lithographer, 31, at NYC in 1850. ¶ 7 Census (1850), N.Y., XLI, 495.

ELDER, JOHN ADAMS (1833–1895). Portrait, genre, landscape, and battle painter. Born in Fredericksburg (Va.), February 3, 1833, Elder went to NYC at the age of 17 to study under DANIEL HUNTINGTON and the following year he went to Düsseldorf (Germany) with EMANUEL LEUTZE. After five years abroad, he worked for several years in NYC, returning to Fredericksburg shortly before the outbreak of the Civil War. He fought in the Confederate Army, and after the war he remained in Virginia, working mainly in Richmond. Incapacitated by illness, Elder spent the last five years of his life in Fredericksburg and died there on February 24, 1895. ¶ Davis, "A Retrospective Exhibition of the Work of John Adams Elder," catalogue, bibliography, and 10 repros.; *Richmond Portraits;* Fielding.

ELDER, JOSEPH. Engraver. A native of Ireland, age 26, living in Philadelphia in 1860 with his wife Eliza (17, Pa.) and the engraver JOHN DAVENPORT. ¶ 8 Census (1860), Pa., LX, 235.

ELDRIDGE, CHARLES WILLIAM (1811–1883). Miniaturist. Born in New London (Conn.) in November 1811, Eldridge studied for a year with THOMAS H. PARKER and then entered into partnership with him. For nine years they worked together in NYC, Vermont (1833) and in the South, until Parker was obliged by ill health to retire. Eldridge remained three years longer in the South until he, too, was forced by failing eyesight and competition from the daguerreotypists to give up painting. He settled in Hartford (Conn.) and died there in 1883. ¶ French, 78; Eldridge, "Journal of a Tour through Vermont to Montreal and Quebec in 1833"; Bolton, *Miniature Painters.*

ELDRIDGE, J. Painter of children, Philadelphia, 1841; exhibited at the Artists' Fund Society. ¶ Rutledge, PA.

ELENA, LUIGI. Artist. An Italian by birth, living in Philadelphia in 1850; he was then only 19 years of age. ¶ 7 Census (1850), Pa., LII, 956.

ELINGHAM [sic], ROBERT. Artist, 21, a native of New York, at NYC in 1850. ¶ 7 Census (1850), N.Y., XLVIII, 380.

ELLENWOOD, CHARLES. Painter, born in Massachusetts *c.* 1825. In 1850, at the age of 25, he was living in Boston, where he was listed in the census of that year as a fancy painter and in the city directory as a shade painter (in partnership with WILLIAM N. WEBB). In 1860 he was working as a portrait or landscape painter in Rutland (Vt.). ¶ 7 Census (1850), Mass., XXV, 87; Boston CD 1850; New England BD 1860.

ELLIOT, GEORGE (1776–1852). Portrait painter, probably working in Connecticut. ¶ Fielding.

ELLIOT, W. P. A drawing by this artist, depicting the First Presbyterian Church in Washington (D.C.), was engraved *c.* 1819. ¶ Stauffer.

ELLIOTT, BENJAMIN F. (1829–1870). Portrait and landscape painter. He was born in Middletown (Conn.), September 26, 1829, and opened a studio there in 1860. He did a number of portraits for KELLOGG BROTHERS of Hartford. He died in Middletown, September 6, 1870. ¶ French; Fielding.

ELLIOTT, CHARLES LORING (1812–1868). N.A. Portrait painter; born October 12, 1812, at Scipio, Cayuga County (N.Y.). By 1829 he was studying in NYC under JOHN QUIDOR; during the next ten years he was an itinerant portrait painter throughout central New York State. He worked chiefly in NYC after 1840 and became a very popular portraitist. A frequent exhibitor at various galleries, he was elected a Member of the National Academy in 1846. He died in Albany (N.Y.), August 25, 1868. ¶ Information courtesy Theodore Bolton, who cites: *Harper's Weekly* (Sept. 12, 1868), obit.; C. E. L[ester], "Charles Loring Elliott," *Harper's New Monthly Magazine* (Dec. 1868), 42–50; T. B. Thorpe, "Reminiscences of Charles L. Elliott, Artist," N. Y. *Evening Post* (Sept. 30, Oct. 1, 1868); DAB; Tuckerman, 300–305; Cowdrey, NAD; Cowdrey, AA & AAU; Swan, BA; Rutledge, PA; Washington Art Assoc. Cat., 1857, 1859; Karolik Cat.; 7 Census (1850), N.Y., XLIV, 308; checklist of his work in Bolton, "Charles Loring Elliott."

ELLIOTT, JAMES. Scottish lithographer, 19, at NYC in 1850. ¶ 7 Census (1850), N.Y., XLIII, 30.

ELLIOTT, LEO (or Lee) (*c.* 1814–?). Panoramist and historical painter. A native of France, the 36-year-old Elliott was living in Philadelphia in 1850. He collaborated with EDWARD BEYER on a panoramic painting of the Wars for Liberty in Hungary, Upper Italy and Rome (*i.e.*, the revolutions of 1848) which was exhibited in Philadelphia in December 1850 and in NYC the following April. Lee and Sophia Elliott lived in Philadelphia with the lithographer CHARLES REEN. ¶ 7 Census (1850), Pa., LI, 657; Phila. *Public Ledger,* Dec. 9, 1850, and N. Y. *Herald,* Mar. 29 and April 13, 1851 (citations courtesy of J. E. Arrington).

ELLIOTT, Lt. W. Artist and engraver of "Representation of the Action off Mud Fort in the River Delaware . . . 15th Novr. 1777," a rare naval print published by W. Elliott in Philadelphia, 1787. ¶ Stokes, *Historic Prints,* 31, and pl. 25b.

ELLIS, EDWIN M. Engraver, Philadelphia, 1844. ¶ Stauffer.

ELLIS, GEORGE B. Engraver of Philadelphia, active 1821–38; exhibited several times at the Pennsylvania Academy. He was a pupil of FRANCIS KEARNEY. ¶ Penna. Acad. Cat. 1821–22, 1824–27, 1832; *Am. Adv. Directory* 1832; Stauffer; repros. in *Art Quarterly* (1945), 47; *Antiques* (July 1947), 56; *American Collector* (Sept. 1947), 20.

ELLIS, JOHN D. Wood engraver, Baltimore, 1859–60. ¶ Baltimore BD 1859, CD 1860.

ELLIS, SALATHIEL (1860–?). Cameo portraitist, sculptor, and designer of medals. Born in Vermont (some sources say Toronto, Canada), he moved with his parents to St. Lawrence County (N.Y.) where he began his career as a cameo-cutter. He went to NYC in 1842 and worked there until 1864, possibly later. After 1856 his home was in Rye (N.Y.). Between 1848 and 1862 Ellis executed a number of medals for the U. S. Mint and in 1864 he contributed two medallions to the Metropolitan Fair. ¶ Chamberlain, "Salathiel Ellis"; Chamberlain, "Bas-Relief Portraits by Salathiel Ellis"; Gardner, *Yankee Stonecutters;* Thieme-Becker; Loubat, *Medallic History;* NYHS Cat. (1941); Cowdrey, NAD; Cowdrey, AA & AAU; Am. Inst. Cat., 1844, 1848; NYBD 1848–59.

ELLIS, WILLIAM C. Engraver, Chicago, *c.*

1856–58. He appears to have been connected with the firms of BACON & ELLIS (1856) and DAYE & ELLIS (1858). ¶ Chicago CD 1856, 1858.

ELLIS, WILLIAM H. Engraver, Philadelphia, 1845–47. ¶ Stauffer.

ELLMORE, RICHARD H. Artist, 23, a native of New York, at NYC in 1860. Richard H. Elmore, driver, was listed in 1863. ¶ 8 Census (1860), N.Y., L, 486; NYCD 1863.

ELLMS, CHARLES. Illustrator. Ellms was the author of *Robinson Crusoe's Own Book* (Boston, 1843), which he illustrated himself, as well as of *Shipwrecks and Disasters at Sea* and *The Tragedy of the Seas.* ¶ Hamilton, 242; Library of Congress Cat.

ELLSWORTH, GEORGE CANNING. Painter, *c.* 1860, of an oil portrait of Stephen Royce, now in the Executive Chamber of the State Capitol, Montpelier (Vt.). ¶ WPA (Mass.), *Portraits Found in Vermont.*

ELLSWORTH, JAMES SANFORD (1802–1874). Silhouettist, portrait, and miniature painter. A native of Windsor (Conn.), Ellsworth painted miniatures on paper, mainly of Massachusetts and Connecticut farmers and their families, though he is believed to have worked as far west as Louisville (Ky.) and St. Louis (Mo.). He made a trip from Connecticut to Ohio and back through Pennsylvania and New York in 1861. He died in Pittsburgh (Pa.) in 1874. ¶ Mitchell, "James Sanford Ellsworth," repros. and catalogue; French, 72–73; Jackson, *Silhouette,* 102; Carrick, *Shades;* Snow, "King *vs* Ellsworth," 3 repros.; Sherman, "James Sanford Ellsworth," in Lipman and Winchester, 67–71.

ELMENDORF, A. A. Wood engraver, NYC, 1850. ¶ NYBD 1850.

ELOUIS, JEAN PIERRE HENRI (1755–1840). Portrait and miniature painter; born in Caen (France), January 20, 1755; died there December 23, 1840. In 1791 he came to Baltimore, after having worked for a time in Alexandria (Va.) and Annapolis (Md.), and he was working in Philadelphia from 1792 to 1794. ¶ Wehle and Bolton; Prime, II, 8–9; Bolton, *Miniature Painters;* Thieme-Becker; *American Collector* (July 1937), 3, repro.; represented at the Maryland Historical Society (Rutledge).

ELTON, ROBERT H. Engraver, lithographer, and publisher, NYC, 1828–53. Though listed in the NYC directories as a book- and printseller and publisher from 1828, Elton's period of activity as an engraver and lithographer seems to have been from about 1840 to 1850. Several gold rush cartoons by him are known. ¶ NYCD 1828–53; NYBD 1840, 1844, 1845; Peters, *America on Stone;* Peters, *California on Stone,* repro.; Jackson, *Gold Rush Album,* 14–15, repro.

ELVERT, LEWIS. Swiss engraver, age 21, living in Philadelphia, July 1860. ¶ 8 Census (1860), Pa., LII, 90.

ELWELL, WILLIAM S. (1810–1881). Portrait painter. Born in 1810, Elwell exhibited at the National Academy in 1840, was working in Richmond (Va.) in 1847, and apparently settled in Washington (D.C.), where he was a government clerk. He suffered a paralytic stroke about 1855, but continued to do some painting. He died in Springfield (Mass.), August 12, 1881. ¶ *American Art Review* (1881), part 2, 214; Cowdrey, NAD; *Richmond Portraits;* Sears, *Some American Primitives,* 64, repro.

ELY, A. Engraver, working in Connecticut *c.* 1800–32. In 1831–32, of DAGGETT & ELY, New Haven. ¶ Dunlap, *History* (1918), III, 298; *Am. Adv. Directory* (1831), 75, and (1832), 42.

ELY, Mrs. LYDIA (?–1914). Water color artist. Mrs. Ely was taken to Milwaukee (Wis.) in 1840 as a child. She studied drawing under HENRY VANE THORNE and painting under ALEXANDER MARQUIS. During the 1870's, 1880's and 1890's she made a number of sketching tours in the Far West, in Florida, and in Europe. She was the author of the chapter on art and artists of Milwaukee in Conrad's *History of Milwaukee County* (1898) and an active patron of art until her death in 1914. ¶ Butts, *Art in Wisconsin,* 129–30, 170, 179.

EMBLER, A. H. Sculptor, NYC. In 1858 he exhibited two bas-relief portraits at the National Academy. ¶ Cowdrey, NAD.

EMERSON, J. Contributed one illustration to *The Rough and Ready Annual* (N.Y., 1848). ¶ Hamilton, 243.

EMERT (Emmert), PAUL. Panoramic artist, NYC, 1845–49. Listed as a painter in 1845, as an artist in 1848–49, and was probably one of the artists of Emmert & Penfield's "Original Panorama of the Gold Mines," shown in NYC and elsewhere in 1850–51. ¶ NYCD 1845, 1848–49; N. Y. *Herald,* March 10, 1850, St. Louis *Intelligencer,* Dec. 28, 1850, July 17, 1851 (courtesy J. Earl Arrington).

EMERY, DAVID F. Engraver; born in Massachusetts *c.* 1828; working in Philadelphia in 1850. ¶ 7 Census (1850), Pa., LIV, 709.

EMERY, ELIZA. Portrait painter, Boston, 1855–56; exhibited at the Boston Athenaeum. ¶ Swan, BA; Boston BD 1856.

EMERY, RUFUS H. Engraver, Bucksport (Maine), 1855–56. ¶ *Maine Register* 1855–56.

EMERY, WILLIAM B. Engraver, Boston, 1844–46. ¶ Boston CD 1844–46.

EMMERT, see EMERT.

EMMERTON, WILLIAM HENRY (1828–?). Painter. Born in Salem (Mass.), June 18, 1828; active in Salem from 1853 to 1864, in the firm of Emmerton & Foster, architects and engineers. ¶ Belknap, *Artists and Craftsmen of Essex County,* 9.

EMMES, HENRY. Gravestone-portrait sculptor, working in Boston *c.* 1740–57. He probably learned stone-cutting from his father, Nathaniel Emmes, the teacher of WILLIAM CODNER, whose niece Henry Emmes married. ¶ Ravenel, "Here Lyes Buried," 193–95, repro.

EMMES, THOMAS. Engraver, Boston, late 17th and early 18th century. His portrait of Increase Mather, *c.* 1701, is the earliest known portrait engraving on copper by an American. ¶ Stauffer, I, 78–80; Middlebrook, "A Few of the New England Engravers," 361.

EMMET, ELIZABETH, see Mrs. ELIZABETH EMMET LEROY.

EMMET, JOHN M. Engraver, working in NYC from 1830 to 1870. He was born in New York about 1811. ¶ NYCD 1830–70; 7 Census (1850), N.Y., XLVI, 414.

EMMET, JOHN PATTEN (1797–1842). Amateur painter and sculptor. A son of the noted Irish patriot Thomas Addis Emmet (1764–1827), he was born in Dublin, April 8, 1797, and accompanied his father to America in 1804. After several years at West Point, he went to Italy for a year to learn the language and study art and music, then returned to NYC, where he took his degree in medicine. After practising in Charleston (S.C.) from 1822 to 1824, he was appointed to the chair of chemistry in the University of Virginia, a position which he held until shortly before his death. Emmet did many sketches, as well as a few oil paintings and marble busts. He died in NYC, August 13, 1842. ¶ CAB; T. A. Emmet, *The Emmet Family.*

EMMETT (Emmott), JOHN (*c.* 1804–1853). Engraver at Lowell (Mass.) as early as 1830, when he married Mary Ann Dugdale. Worked there until his death in November 1853, at the age of 49. His business was apparently carried on by his son JOHN, who was born in Lowell in 1834. ¶ *Lowell Vital Records; Parish Register of St. Anne's Church, Lowell, Mass.,* under Burials, Nov. 27, 1853; Lowell CD 1834–37, 1844–51, 1855–61.

EMMETT, JOHN (1834–?). Engraver of Lowell (Mass.). A son of the above JOHN EMMETT, he was born in Lowell in 1834 and took over his father's business after the latter's death in 1853. He was still in Lowell in 1861. ¶ *Lowell Vital Records: Births;* Lowell CD 1855–61.

EMMONS, ALEXANDER HAMILTON (1816–?). Portrait, miniature, and landscape painter; born at East Haddam (Conn.), December 12, 1816. A house painter by trade, he married at 20 and moved to Norwich (Conn.), where he soon turned to the painting of portraits. In 1843 he opened a studio in Hartford, but five years later he returned to Norwich where, except for an extended visit to Europe, he spent the rest of his career. ¶ French, 90–91; Cowdrey, NAD; New England BD 1856; Sears, *Some American Primitives,* 233; Bolton, *Miniature Painters;* Sherman, "Three New England Miniatures," 275–276, repros.; *Antiques* (May 1930), 424, repro.; *Art in America* (April 1936), 81, repro.

EMMONS, EBENEZER, JR. One of several artists who did views and technical illustrations for R. H. PEASE, engraver and lithographer of Albany (N.Y.), *c.* 1848–54. He was a son of the eminent geologist, Ebenezer Emmons (1799–1863). The Albany Institute owns two portraits of JAMES EIGHTS by Ebenezer Emmons (information courtesy of the late William Sawitzky); whether these are the work of the younger Emmons or of his father, who was an intimate associate of Eights in geological work, is not stated. ¶ Peters, *America on Stone;* DAB; information courtesy the late William Sawitzky.

EMMONS, GEORGE. Wood engraver, Boston, 1841–48. In 1842 he was in the firm of FOSTER & EMMONS. ¶ Boston BD 1841–48.

EMMONS, NATHANIEL (1704–1740). Portrait and landscape painter; born in Boston in 1704; worked in Boston and died there, May 19, 1740. ¶ Dow, 1–2, obit.; Fielding; *Antiques* (February 1947), 110, repro.

EMMONS, WILLIAM. Lithographer, known only for an 1833 print of the Battle of the Thames and death of Tecumseh. ¶ Peters, *America on Stone.*

ENDE, LOUIS. Wood engraver, NYC, 1846–49. He was listed as a publisher, of Ende & Walsh, in 1844–45. In 1847 he exhibited at the American Institute wood engravings and a landscape painting. He died before 1855, when his widow, Sarah Ende, was listed. ¶ NYCD 1844–45; Am. Inst. Cat., 1847.

ENDICOTT & COMPANY. Lithographers, NYC, 1852–86. One of the leading lithographic firms of the mid-19th century, Endicott & Company was formed in 1852 as the successor to WILLIAM ENDICOTT & COMPANY. The original partners were SARAH L. ENDICOTT and CHARLES MILLS, but from 1853 the senior partner was FRANCIS ENDICOTT. The company frequently did work for CURRIER & IVES and for many years employed the well-known artist CHARLES PARSONS. In 1856 Endicott & Company was awarded a diploma for the best specimen of lithography at the 28th Annual Fair of the American Institute. ¶ NYCD 1852–60 and after; Peters, *America on Stone,* repros.; Am. Inst. *Transactions,* 1856.

ENDICOTT, FRANCIS. Lithographer, of ENDICOTT & COMPANY, NYC, 1853–86. He was born about 1832, a son of GEORGE and SARAH ENDICOTT. ¶ Peters, *America on Stone;* NYCD 1853 and after; 8 Census (1860), N.Y., XLVII, 28.

ENDICOTT, G. & W. Lithographers, NYC, 1845–48. The firm was composed of GEORGE ENDICOTT and his younger brother, WILLIAM ENDICOTT, who carried it on under his own name after George's death in 1848. The firm exhibited specimens of lithography at the American Institute in 1845, 1846, and 1847, and was twice cited for its excellent work. ¶ NYCD 1845–48; Peters, *America on Stone;* Am. Inst. Cat., 1845–47; Am. Inst., *Transactions,* 1846, 1847.

ENDICOTT, GEORGE (1802–1848). Lithographer. Born in Canton (Mass.), June 14, 1802; working as an ornamental painter in Baltimore (Md.) *c.* 1828, when he first took up lithography. The firm of ENDICOTT & SWETT was formed in Baltimore by April 1830 and moved to NYC in December 1831. Swett left the partnership *c.* 1834 and Endicott carried on alone until 1845 when he was joined by his younger brother, WILLIAM ENDICOTT. The firm of G. & W. ENDICOTT lasted until George's death, August 21, 1848, after which the name changed to WILLIAM ENDICOTT & CO. ¶ Endicott, *Record of Births, Marriages and Deaths in . . . Stoughton, Canton and Dorchester; Antiques* (Nov. 1932), 167–168; Peters, *America on Stone;* NYCD 1832–48; N. Y. *Evening Post,* August 27, 1848, obit.

ENDICOTT, ISRAEL. Portrait painter, Manchester (N.H.), 1842. ¶ Manchester Hist. Assoc., *Collections,* IV, 111.

ENDICOTT, SARAH L. Lithographer, NYC, 1852–54. The widow of the prominent NYC lithographer, GEORGE ENDICOTT, Sarah Endicott was apparently the organizer in 1852 of the firm of ENDICOTT & CO., which succeeded the firm of WILLIAM ENDICOTT & CO., established in 1849 by her brother-in-law. Mrs. Endicott's place in the firm was taken by her son, FRANCIS ENDICOTT, from 1853, though she may have retained an interest in it. Whether or not Mrs. Endicott was herself a lithographic artist is not known. In 1860 her property was valued at $55,000 (real) and $8,500 (personal). ¶ NYCD 1852, 1854; 8 Census (1860), N.Y., XLVII, 28.

ENDICOTT & SWETT. Lithographers of Baltimore, 1830–31, and of NYC, 1831–34. The partners were GEORGE ENDICOTT and MOSES SWETT. Among their employees were JOHN BISBEE and JOHN R. CRAWLEY, JR. After the dissolution of the partnership *c.* 1834, Endicott carried on alone in NYC and Swett apparently went to Washington (D.C.). ¶ NYCD 1832–34; Peters, *America on Stone;* Stokes, *Historic Prints; Antiques* (Nov. 1932), 167.

ENDICOTT, WILLIAM (1816–1851). Lithographer. William, younger brother of GEORGE ENDICOTT, was born in Canton (Mass.), August 20, 1816. He joined his brother in NYC *c.* 1841 and was in partnership with him, as G. & W. ENDICOTT, from 1845 to 1848. After George's death in 1848, William carried on the business under the name of WILLIAM ENDICOTT & CO. until his death, October 18, 1851, at Canton (Mass.). In 1848 he was awarded a diploma for 8 specimens of lithography shown at the Annual Fair of the American Institute. ¶ Endicott, *Record of Births, Marriages and Deaths in . . . Stoughton, Canton and Dorchester;* NYCD 1841–51; Peters, *America on Stone;* Am. Inst., *Transactions,* 1848; N. Y. *Evening Post,* Oct. 21, 1851, obit.

ENDICOTT, WILLIAM, & COMPANY. Lithographers, NYC, 1849–51. The firm was organized by WILLIAM ENDICOTT (1816–1851) in 1849, after the death of his brother GEORGE ENDICOTT and the dissolution of the firm of G. & W. ENDICOTT. After William's death in 1851, the name was again changed to ENDICOTT & COMPANY (1852–86). William Endicott & Co. exhibited at the American Institute in 1849 and 1850, but won no awards. ¶ NYCD 1849–51; Am. Inst. *Cat.* and *Transactions,* 1849–50.

ENGEL, WILLIAM. Lithographer, Roxbury (Mass.), 1853. ¶ Mass. BD 1853.

ENGELMANN, C. F. Engraver, near Reading (Pa.), *c.* 1814. Stauffer records him as the engraver of an "elaborate, curiously designed, and crudely engraved Birth and Baptismal certificate." ¶ Stauffer.

ENGLEKEN, JACOB. Lithographer, Philadelphia, 1850. He was a native of Germany, aged 46. ¶ 7 Census (1850), Pa., LII, 869.

ENGLISH, J. Artist, New Orleans, 1853. ¶ New Orleans CD 1853.

ENGSTROM, A. B. Still life and landscape painter, active in Philadelphia from 1829 to 1846. He exhibited at the Pennsylvania Academy, the Artists' Fund Society and the National Academy. ¶ Rutledge, PA; Cowdrey, NAD; Phila. BD 1838, CD 1839.

ENKE, LUDWIG. Artist, Baltimore, 1858 and after. ¶ Baltimore CD 1858–60; Lafferty (to 1879).

ENNIS, GEORGE. Artist, 25, a native of New York, at NYC in 1850. ¶ 7 Census (1850), N.Y., XLVII, 545.

ENSIGN, EDWARD. Lithographer? Though listed as a lithographer by Peters, Edward Ensign appears in NYC directories from 1841 to 1860 and after as a map and book publisher. From 1841 to 1848 he was associated with TIMOTHY ENSIGN and thereafter with Ensign & Thayer (1849–51) and Ensign, Bridgman & Fanning (from 1854). ¶ NYCD 1841–60 and after; Peters, *America on Stone.*

ENSIGN, TIMOTHY (*c.* 1795–1849). Lithographer. Timothy Ensign was active in NYC as a map publisher and, according to Peters, lithographer from 1835 to 1848. EDWARD ENSIGN, probably his son or his brother, was in business with him from 1841. Timothy died in Windsor (Conn.), September 16, 1849, at the age of 54. ¶ NYCD 1835–48; Peters, *America on Stone;* N. Y. *Evening Post,* Sept. 19, 1849, obit.

ENZING-MÜLLER, JOHANN MICHAEL (1804–1888). Religious painter, portrait engraver, and designer. A native of Nuremberg (Germany); came to America *c.* 1848. In 1848–49 he was in NYC and exhibited at both the American Art-Union and the National Academy. He also worked as an engraver in Philadelphia and in Newark (N.J.). ¶ Thieme-Becker; Stauffer; Cowdrey, NAD; Cowdrey, AA & AAU; N. J. BD 1860.

ENZLING, Mons. DE. Miniaturist, at Huntsville (Ala.) in 1856. ¶ [Huntsville] *Southern Advocate,* Aug. 7, 1856 (cited by WPA, (Ala.), Hist. Records Survey).

ERBA, GASPAR. Sculptor and plaster modeller, San Francisco, 1856 and after. ¶ San Francisco BD 1856, 1858, CD 1860.

ERICSON, MAURITZ A. (1836–1912). Sculptor; died at Pelham (N.Y.), October 24, 1912. ¶ *Art Annual,* X, obit.

ERNEST or ERNST, JULIUS. Lithographer, NYC, 1854–60; born in Darmstadt (Germany) about 1831. ¶ NYBD 1854, 1857; 8 Census (1860), N.Y., XLIV, 305.

ERNST, FR. Painter of a watercolor view of Kips Bay, Manhattan Island (N.Y.), 1830. ¶ Stokes, *Icon.,* III, 610 and pl. 107.

ERNST, THOMAS J. Wood engraver, designer, and stencil-plate cutter, Cincinnati, 1850–57. He was born in Ohio *c.* 1829 of German parents. ¶ 7 Census (1850), Ohio, XXII, 721; Cincinnati CD 1850, 1856–57.

ERUS, JOHN, see JOHN EVERS.

ERWIN, BENONI. Portrait painter, *c.* 1850, whose portrait of Mrs. David Sherman Boardman is owned by the New Milford (Conn.) Historical Society. ¶ Sherman, "Unrecorded Early American Portrait Painters" (1933).

ESCHERICK, A. W. Engraver, NYC, 1852. ¶ NYBD 1852.

ESHLEMAN, AARON (1827–?). Portrait and landscape painter; born in Lancaster (Pa.) in 1827. The son of an innkeeper, he also kept an inn in Lancaster until 1857, when he went to Kentucky and disappeared. ¶ Demuth, "Aaron Eshleman"; Lancaster County Hist. Soc., *Portraiture in Lancaster County,* 120.

ESCOFFIER, JOHN. Portrait painter, New Orleans, 1837. ¶ New Orleans CD 1837 (cited by Delgado-WPA).

ESSIG, GEORGE EMERICK (1838–?). Marine and landscape painter, illustrator. Born in Philadelphia, September 2, 1838, he studied there under EDWARD MORAN and exhibited many times at the Pennsylvania Academy. He later moved to Atlantic City (N.J.), where he was still living in 1925. ¶ *Art Annual* (1925); *Artists Year Book,* 60.

ESTABROOKS, JOHN F. Portrait and landscape painter, Brandon (Vt.), 1860. ¶ New England BD 1860.

ESTES, THOMAS. Portrait painter, NYC, 1854–57. ¶ NYBD 1854–55, 1857.

ESTHEHAM, ANDREW. Portrait painter, Pittsburgh (Pa.), 1850. He was then 25 years of age, a native Pennsylvanian. ¶ 7 Census (1850), Pa., III(2), 57.

ETHRIDGE, W. B. Portrait painter, Dallas (Ala.), 1850. ¶ 7 Census (1850), Ala., Dallas County (cited by WPA, (Ala.), Hist. Records Survey).

ETRANGER & GRAINES. Painters of panoramas of Adam and Eve, the Hudson River, and Virginia scenes. Graines was PETER GRAIN. ¶ Washington *Daily National Intelligencer,* May 25, 1850 (courtesy J. Earl Arrington).

ETTER, DAVID RENT (1807–1881). Portrait copyist and ornamental painter. He was a native of Philadelphia and apparently spent his entire life there. Several fire-engine panels by him are extant. ¶ Fielding; J. I. Smith, "Painted Fire Engine Panels."

EULER, CHARLES (or Karl) (1815–?). Landscape painter, lithographer; born in Kassel (Germany), March 9, 1815, came to the United States probably in the late 1850's. He settled in Philadelphia and there exhibited European landscapes at the Pennsylvania Academy shows of 1859–61. ¶ Thieme-Becker; Rutledge, PA.

EVANS & ARNOLD. Marine artists, New Orleans, *c.* 1850; J. G. EVANS and EDWARD ARNOLD. ¶ Robinson and Dow, I, 61.

EVANS, BERNARD. Engraver, New Orleans, 1834–35. ¶ New Orleans CD 1834–35 (cited by Delgado-WPA).

EVANS, B. R. Delineator of a Philadelphia street scene, 1851. ¶ Gillingham, "Notes on Phila. Profilists," 517–18, repro.

EVANS, CHARLES A. Lithographer, Boston, 1856 and after. In 1857–58 he was in the firm of BLOOD & EVANS. ¶ Boston CD 1856–60.

EVANS & COMPANY. Engravers and printers, Boston, 1856 and after. This firm, of which NATHANIEL EVANS, JR., was the head, was successor to EVANS & PLUMER. ¶ Boston CD 1856–60 and after.

EVANS, E. S. Portrait painter, Sandusky (Ohio), 1858. ¶ Sandusky BD and CD 1858.

EVANS, HANNAH (SLAYMAKER) (1801–1860). Portrait and miniature painter of Lancaster (Pa.). ¶ Lancaster Co. Hist. Soc., *Portraiture in Lancaster County,* 123.

EVANS, J. G. Marine and historical painter, active *c.* 1840–59. Working with EDWARD ARNOLD in New Orleans in 1850. His known canvasses include "Hurricane and Bombardment at Vera Cruz, 1847" and "Commodore Perry Carrying the Gospel of God to the Heathen, 1853." He was probably also the J. Evans whose marine views appeared in the *U. S. Military Magazine,* July–October 1840. ¶ *American Processional,* no. 193; [New Orleans] *Orleanian,* Sept. 22, 1850 (cited by Delgado-WPA); Peters, *America on Stone; Portfolio* (Aug.–Sept. 1952), 12–13, repro.

EVANS, J. M. Primitive landscape painter, Poughkeepsie (N.Y.), *c.* 1850. ¶ Lipman and Winchester, 172.

EVANS, JAMES. Profilist and silhouettist, Charleston (S.C.), 1803. ¶ Rutledge, *Artists in the Life of Charleston.*

EVANS, JAMES B. Engraver; born in Pennsylvania *c.* 1829; living in Cincinnati in September 1850. ¶ 7 Census (1850), Ohio XX, 258.

EVANS, JOHN. Artist, 52, a native of New York, at NYC in 1850. *Cf.* JOHN EVERS. ¶ 7 Census (1850), N.Y., LII, 297.

EVANS, JOHN T. Portrait and landscape painter in watercolors, Philadelphia, 1809. ¶ Bolton, *Miniature Painters;* Dunlap, *History* (1918), III, 299–300.

EVANS, JOHN W. Portrait painter, Schenectady (N.Y.), 1860. ¶ Schenectady BD 1860.

EVANS, NATHANIEL, JR. Engraver and printer, Boston, 1855 and after. He was associated with the firms of EVANS & PLUMER (1855–56) and with EVANS & CO. from 1856 into the 1860's. ¶ Boston CD 1855–60 and after.

EVANS & PLUMER. Engravers, Boston, 1855–56; NATHANIEL EVANS, JR., and JACOB P. PLUMER. ¶ Boston CD 1855–56.

EVANS, THOMAS. Engraver, Philadelphia, 1860. Thomas (34) and Sophia Evans (31) were both from Massachusetts, but their son Frank (5) was born in Pennsylvania. Thomas Evans owned personalty valued at $200. ¶ 8 Census (1860), Pa., XLIX, 276.

EVANS, WALTER. Engraver, Philadelphia,

1860. A native of Philadelphia, age 33, he lived with his parents, Mr. and Mrs. Benjamin M. Evans. ¶ 8 Census (1860), Pa., LI, 1001.

EVANS, WILLIAM. Engraver, Frankford (Pa.), 1850. Evans (45), his wife and the three eldest children (15 to 5) were born in England; the youngest, age one month, was born in Pennsylvania. ¶ 7 Census (1850), Pa., LVI, 337.

EVAREST, H. G. Engraver and jeweler, Philadelphia, 1849–56. ¶ Phila. BD 1849, 1856.

EVEN, LOUIS. Artist. He appears in New Orleans directories as follows: 1837, Ls. Even, artist; 1838, L. Even, professor of music; 1843, 1854, 1858, Louis Even; 1860, Louis Even, mustard works. In the 1850 census he was listed as L. Even, artist, age 53, born in France. ¶ New Orleans CD as cited; 7 Census (1850), La., V, 197.

EVEN, LUCAS. Lithographer. So listed in New Orleans directory for 1858, but in the following years as a telegrapher. He lived at the same address as LOUIS EVEN. ¶ New Orleans CD 1858–60.

EVENS, PLATT, JR. Seal engraver, Cincinnati (Ohio), 1854 and after. His specialty was the manufacture of seal presses, for which he took out a patent in 1854. ¶ Cincinnati CD 1853 (as manuf. of philosophical instruments), 1855–60; a sample seal is affixed to his adv. in 1858 CD, p. 66.

EVENS, THEODORE A. Engraver, Cincinnati (Ohio), 1859–60. ¶ Cincinnati CD and BD 1859–60.

EVERDELL, CHARLES. Engraver, NYC, 1849–63. His home in 1859 was at Morrisania (N.Y.). ¶ NYCD 1849–63.

EVERDELL, FRANK. Engraver, 21, a native of New York, living in NYC in 1860 with his father, MARTIN (probably the same as WILLIAM) EVERDELL, engraver. In 1863 he was listed as a printer. ¶ 8 Census (1860), N.Y., LVI, 284; NYCD 1863.

EVERDELL, GEORGE. Engraver, NYC, 1854. ¶ NYBD 1854.

EVERDELL, HENRY. Engraver, NYC, 1859 and after, at the same address as WILLIAM EVERDELL. ¶ NYCD 1859–60 and after.

EVERDELL, JAMES. Engraver, NYC, 1843–1860 and after, part of the time at the same address as WILLIAM EVERDELL and WILLIAM EVERDELL, JR. He was born in New York about 1819. ¶ NYCD 1843–60 and after; 7 Census (1850), N.Y., LII, 330.

EVERDELL, MARTIN. Engraver, 60, a native of New York, at NYC in 1860. He lived with his wife Mary and five children, including FRANK, also an engraver. Since WILLIAM EVERDELL had a wife named Mary and a son named Francis and was about the same age, it seems probable that the name Martin was an error for William in the census return. ¶ 8 Census (1860), N.Y., LVI, 283.

EVERDELL, WILLIAM. Artist, NYC, 1820–21. He is apparently to be distinguished from the engraver of the same name, who was working in NYC at the same time but at a different address. ¶ NYCD 1820–21.

EVERDELL, WILLIAM. Engraver and printer; born in New York about 1799; active in NYC from 1820 until after 1860. From 1844 he was in partnership with his son, WILLIAM, JR. *Cf.* WILLIAM EVERDELL, above. The MARTIN EVERDELL, engraver, listed in the 1860 Census may very well be the same man; their ages correspond, and both had wives named Mary and sons named Francis. ¶ 7 Census (1850), N.Y., XLI, 535; NYCD 1820–60+.

EVERDELL, WILLIAM, JR. Engraver, NYC and Brooklyn (N.Y.), 1844–60 and after; son of the above. ¶ NYCD 1844–60 and after.

EVERETT, EDWARD (1818–after 1900). Amateur draftsman. Edward Everett, nephew of the famous orator, was born in London, March 31, 1818. Educated in England, he visited Boston (Mass.) in 1834–36, but continued to make his home in England until 1840. Soon after 1840, however, he returned to America and settled in Quincy (Ill.). During a visit to the Mormon town of Nauvoo (Ill.) in 1846 he made a sketch of the Temple, which is now at the Illinois Historical Society. A few years later he served with the army in Texas and was assigned to sketch buildings and objects of military interest, including the Alamo and the San Jose Mission. After the Mexican War he returned to Quincy, but he moved to Springfield (Ill.) during the Civil War. After 1865 he moved to Sing Sing (N.Y.), where he remained until 1899. His last years were spent at Roxbury (Mass.). ¶ Arrington, *Nauvoo Temple,* Chap. 8.

EVERITE, G. Artist, age 22, at New Orleans in October 1850; he was English by birth. ¶ 7 Census (1850), La., IV (1), 596.

EVERLY, MORTON. Engraver, age 25, born in Pennsylvania, living in Philadelphia in 1860. His brother Rufus was a carver. ¶ 8 Census (1860), Pa., L, 251.

EVERS, JOHN (1797–1884). N.A. Miniature, landscape, and theatrical scene painter. Born at Newtown, Long Island (N.Y.), August 17, 1797, John Evers began his artistic career about 1816, when he first exhibited architectural drawings at the American Academy. In 1818 he appears to have become a pupil of JOHN J. HOLLAND, scene-painter at the old Park Theatre, with which Evers was associated until at least 1839. During the 1840's and 1850's he was active as a panorama painter in NYC, and he continued to be listed in the directory until 1864. He was a founder of and a frequent exhibitor at the National Academy. He died May 3, 1884, in Hempstead, Long Island, at the age of 86. ¶ Bolton, *Miniature Painters;* Boston *Transcript,* May 5, 1884 (obit. of John Erus [*sic*]); Cowdrey, AA & AAU; N. Y. *Herald,* March 21, 1839; NYCD 1821–64; Odell, *Annals of the N. Y. Stage,* II; Cowdrey, NAD; N. Y. *Herald,* Nov. 8, 1849; Cincinnati *Gazette,* July 12, 1839; Phila. *Public Ledger,* Aug. 30, 1851 (newspaper citations courtesy of J. E. Arrington); Stokes, *Icon.,* III, 868, and pl. A8, repro. of Evers' drawing of ruins of Trinity Church, NYC, as they were in 1780; 8 Census (1860), N.Y., LVI, 98.

EVERS & KIENTZLE (or Kientyle). Portrait painters, Philadelphia, 1860; THEODORE EVERS and ALEXANDER KINSLER (Kientzle). Listed in 1861 as "photographers." ¶ Phila. BD and CD 1860, CD 1861.

EVERS, THEODORE. Portrait painter, of EVERS & KIENTZLE, Philadelphia, 1858–60. He was listed the following year as a photographer. ¶ Phila. CD 1858–61.

EWBANK, JAMES L. Engraver, 22, a native of New York, at NYC in 1850. ¶ 7 Census (1850), N.Y., LI, 208.

EWING, MARTIN B. Engraver or lithographer, Cincinnati, 1858–59. He was an employee of MIDDLETON, WALLACE & Co. in 1858, and of MIDDLETON, STROBRIDGE & Co. in 1859. ¶ Cincinnati CD 1858–59.

EXILIOUS, JOHN G. Engraver and landscape artist, Philadelphia, 1810–14. He exhibited landscapes at the Pennsylvania Academy in 1812–1813. ¶ Stauffer; Scharf and Westcott; Rutledge, PA.

EXNER, CARL. Fresco painter, Washington (D.C.), 1850. Exner (38) and his wife Whilhelmina (25) were both German; their daughter Matilda (2) was born in New York, and a 5-month-old son was born in Washington. ¶ 7 Census (1850), D.C., II, 145.

EYTINGE, CLARENCE. Lithographer, NYC, 1853–58. ¶ NYCD 1853–58; Peters, *America on Stone.*

EYTINGE, ROBERT. Lithographer, NYC, 1854–56. ¶ NYCD 1854, 1856; Peters, *America on Stone.*

EYTINGE, SOLOMON (1833–1905). Genre painter and illustrator; probably a son of the actor of the same name. Eytinge was for many years on the staff of *Harper's Weekly* and was also well known for his genre paintings of Negro life in the South. He died in Bayonne (N.J.), March 25, 1905. ¶ *Art Annual* (1905–06), obit., 120; Thieme-Becker; Hamilton, 244–247.

F

FABER, HARMAN (1832–1913). Portrait painter and medical illustrator. A native of Germany; came to the United States in 1854 and worked during the Civil War as an illustrator for the Surgeon General's medical record of the war. He died in Philadelphia, December 10, 1913. ¶ *Art Annual,* XI, obit.

FABRE, LUCIAN. Artist, Buffalo (N.Y.), 1860. ¶ Buffalo BD 1860.

FABRI, LUDOVICK. Italian figure-maker, 50, at NYC in 1850. His wife and five children, ages 14 to 2, were born in New York. ¶ 7 Census (1850), N.Y., XLVIII, 178.

FABRONI, FABIAN. Portrait painter, NYC, 1850–68; born in Italy about 1800. ¶ NYBD 1850, 1854–68; his widow was listed in 1872; 7 Census (1850), N.Y., XLVIII, 508.

FABRONIUS, CHRISTIAN. Lithographer; born in Germany about 1804; working in NYC in 1850 and in Cincinnati from 1858 to 1873. In 1859 both Christian and DOMINIQUE C. FABRONIUS were employed by MIDDLETON, STROBRIDGE & Co. of Cincinnati. ¶ 7 Census (1850), N.Y., L, 72; Cincinnati CD 1858–73.

FABRONIUS, DOMINIQUE C. Lithographer, watercolor and crayon portraitist. The son of a Belgian lithographer and publisher, he went to England early in his career and is said to have won the patronage of the Prince Consort and many of the English nobility. He came to America probably in the 1850's, worked for a Philadelphia firm, and in 1859 was employed by MIDDLETON, STROBRIDGE & Co. in Cincinnati, where CHRISTIAN FABRONIUS, presumably a relative, also was located. From 1861 to 1864 Dominique was in Boston and from 1865 to 1872 he was working in NYC. Later he turned to painting water color portraits in Philadelphia (1888) and he is said also to have had a studio in NYC where in old age he drew crayon portraits and taught lithography and drawing. ¶ Peters, *America on Stone;* Cincinnati CD 1859; Boston CD 1861, 1863–64; NYCD 1865–72; Swan, BA; Rutledge, PA.

FAEFFERD, EDMUND. Engraver, New Orleans, 1841–42. ¶ New Orleans CD 1841–42.

FAGAN, LAWRENCE. Artist, Philadelphia, 1860. A native of Ireland, he was 35 years of age and owned $3,000 in realty. ¶ 8 Census (1860), Pa., LIX, 256.

FAGIN, I. Portrait silhouettist, working in America *c.* 1830. ¶ Martin, "Early American Profiles on Glass," repro.

FAGLER, AMEL. Artist, Baltimore, 1860. A native of Massachusetts, Fagler was 26 years of age and lived with his parents in the home of ERNEST RUDOLPH, artist. ¶ 8 Census (1860), Md., VII, 193.

FAGNANI, GIUSEPPE or JOSEPH (1819–1873). Portrait and figure painter, sculptor, and crayon portraitist; born in Naples, December 24, 1819. He was working in Naples in 1840, in Paris 1842–44, in Spain 1846, in Paris 1847. By 1849 he had emigrated to the United States and was working in Washington (D.C.). From 1852 to 1857 he was in NYC, where he settled permanently in 1865, after several years in Europe. He died in NYC, May 22, 1873. He exhibited at the National Academy, Boston Athenaeum, and Pennsylvania Academy. ¶ Fagnani, *The Art Life of a 19th Century Portrait Painter, Joseph Fagnani,* five plates and catalogue; Cowdrey, NAD; Swan, BA; Rutledge, PA; Thieme-Becker.

FAHNESTOCK, JOHN. Engraver and lithographer, Indianapolis, 1857 and after. ¶ Indiana BD 1858–60; Indianapolis BD 1857–60.

FAHRENBERG, ALBERT. Portrait painter. A native of Cologne (Germany), he came to NYC about 1850 and worked there as an artist and cigar-maker until about 1858. By 1859 he was in Louisville (Ky.) and a year later in New Orleans. In the 1860 census he was listed as a portrait painter, age 35, with personal property valued at $600. Living with him were his wife Emma (28, Prussia) and their three children: Oscar (6, N.Y.), Lena (2, N.Y.), and Albert (3 months, La.). ¶ NYCD 1851–55; Louisville CD 1859; 8 Census (1860), La., VII, 909.

FAIRBANKS, Mrs. FRANCIS J. (*c.* 1835–1913). Painter who died February 24, 1913, at the age of 78, in Paterson (N.J.). ¶ *Art Annual,* XI, obit.

FAIRCHILD, JOHN W., see FAIRCHILDS.

FAIRCHILD, LEWIS. Engraver and miniature painter, born in Farmington (Conn.) about 1801. He studied engraving with ASAPH WILLARD at New Haven and worked as draftsman with the HARTFORD GRAPHIC & BANK NOTE CO. At about the same time, the early 1820's, he did some miniature painting. He left Hartford and went to Providence (R.I.) between 1828 and 1838 and remained in Providence until about 1855. Sometime during this period he also did some engraving on wood and copper for Joseph Knowles of Boston. In 1880 Fairchild was described as "late of this city [Boston]." ¶ French, *Art and Artists of Connecticut,* 66; Stauffer; *American Art Review,* I (1880), 455; Hartford *Pocket Register,* 1825; Hartford CD 1828; Providence CD 1838–54; Sherman, "American Miniaturists of the Early 19th Century," repro.; Bolton, *Miniature Painters.*

FAIRCHILDS or FAIRCHILD, JOHN W. Scenic artist working in Boston in 1847–48 and in San Francisco in 1854 and 1856. In 1856 he was associated with CHARLES ROGERS in work on a panorama of the activities of the Vigilance Committee. D. W. Fairchilds, who exhibited at the Boston Athenaeum in 1848, was probably the same man. ¶ Boston CD 1847–48; San Francisco CD 1854+; MacMinn, *The Theatre of the Golden Era in California,* 226 (courtesy J. Earl Arrington); Swan, BA.

FAIRFAX, D. R. Portrait painter. Known only for his portrait of Johnston Blakeley (1781–1814), American naval hero of the War of 1812, now at Independence Hall, Philadelphia (Pa.). It is assumed that Fairfax was an American artist, possibly of North Carolina, Blakeley's home state. ¶ Fielding.

FAIRFAX, FERDINAND. Painter of a water color portrait of Elizabeth Gibson (1800–1816) of Charleston (Va., now W. Va.). ¶ Willis, "Jefferson County Portraits."

FAIRFAX, W. H. Portrait painter of Fredericksburg (Va.), who exhibited in 1834 at the Pennsylvania Academy. ¶ Rutledge, PA.

FAIRFIELD, Miss HANNAH T. Portrait painter, NYC, 1836–39; exhibitor, National Academy, 1836–38. ¶ Cowdrey, NAD; NYCD 1837, 1839.

FAIRIES, JOHN. Limner at Philadelphia, August 1770. ¶ Brown and Brown, cite *Pa. Gazette,* Aug. 2, 1770.

FAIRMAN, DAVID (1782–1815). Engraver. David, brother of GIDEON and RICHARD FAIRMAN, was born in 1782, probably in Fairfield County (Conn.). In 1810 he was working in Newburyport (Mass.), but shortly thereafter he moved to Philadelphia, where his brothers were established. He died there August 19, 1815. ¶ Belknap, 3; Stauffer.

FAIRMAN, DRAPER & COMPANY. Banknote engravers, Philadelphia, 1823–24; successors to MURRAY, FAIRMAN & CO. The partners were GIDEON FAIRMAN and JOHN DRAPER. THOMAS UNDERWOOD joined the firm about 1825 and it was known thereafter as FAIRMAN, DRAPER, UNDERWOOD & CO. ¶ Phila. CD 1823–25.

FAIRMAN, DRAPER, UNDERWOOD & COMPANY. Banknote engravers, Philadelphia, 1825–27. Formed in 1825 when THOMAS UNDERWOOD joined the firm of FAIRMAN, DRAPER & CO., this firm lasted until Fairman's death in 1827 when it became DRAPER, UNDERWOOD & CO. There were branches in NYC and New Haven (Conn.). ¶ Phila. CD 1825–27; Rice, "Life of Nathaniel Jocelyn."

FAIRMAN, GIDEON (1774–1827). Banknote engraver and portrait painter; born in Newtown, Fairfield County (Conn.), June 26, 1774. He was apprenticed to a blacksmith but was encouraged to take up engraving by an itinerant engraver, probably RICHARD BRUNTON. After working in Albany (N.Y.) for a time, he moved to Philadelphia in 1810 and there became a prominent engraver of banknote vignettes. From 1814 to 1818 he was with the firm of MURRAY, DRAPER, FAIRMAN & CO. In 1819 he went to England with JACOB PERKINS to compete for a banknote-engraving contract from the Bank of England. The effort proving unsuccessful, Fairman returned to Philadelphia in 1822 and established the firm of FAIRMAN, DRAPER & CO. (later FAIRMAN, DRAPER, UNDERWOOD & CO.). He died there March 18, 1827. In addition to his engraving, Fairman painted some portraits. He was a frequent exhibitor at the Society of Artists and the Pennsylvania Academy. ¶ CAB; Phila. *Democratic Press,* March 19, 1827; Stauffer; French; Soc. of Artists Cat. 1811–14; Penna. Acad. Cat. 1817–26; Toppan, *100 Years of Bank Note Engraving,* 3, 8–10; Phila. CD 1811–27.

FAIRMAN, JAMES (1826–1904). Landscape painter; born in Glasgow (Scotland) in 1826 and brought to the United States at the age of 6. He entered the National Academy as a student in 1842 and in 1844 exhibited drawings at the American Institute (as J. Fairman). He was in England in 1851. After two years service in the Civil War, he set up a studio in NYC where he remained until 1871. In 1871 he left for Europe and spent the next ten years studying in Italy, France, Germany, and England. After his return to America in the 1880's he became a prominent critic and lecturer and taught at Olivet College. He died in NYC March 12, 1904. ¶ *Art Journal* (1880), 229–231; *Art Annual,* V, obit.; Am. Inst. Cat., 1844; Rutledge, PA; Thieme-Becker also cites *Art Journal* (1879), 118 ff.

FAIRMAN, RICHARD (1788–1821). Line engraver. Presumably a native of Connecticut, since he was a brother of GIDEON and DAVID FAIRMAN. He settled with his brothers in Philadelphia about 1810 and worked there until his death in 1821. ¶ Stauffer; Brown and Brown; Phila. CD 1820; CAB (under Gideon Fairman).

FAIRTHORNE, WILLIAM. Copperplate engraver and printer; born in England about 1811; working at Albany (N.Y.) in 1835, and at NYC from about 1839 to 1853. ¶ Albany CD 1835; NYCD 1839, 1844, 1849–53; 7 Census (1850), N.Y., LI, 128.

FALCONER, JOHN M. (1820–1903). Portrait, landscape and genre painter, enameller, etcher, and watercolorist. Born May 22, 1820, in Edinburgh (Scotland), he came to NYC about 1848 and lived there, except for painting trips to Canada and the Midwest, until his death, March 12, 1903. He exhibited at the American Art-Union, National Academy, Pennsylvania Academy, and Boston Athenaeum, and was an Honorary Member, Professional, of the National Academy. ¶ *Art Annual,* IV, obit.; Thieme-Becker; Cowdrey, AA & AAU; Cowdrey, NAD; Rutledge, PA; Swan, BA; *Portfolio* (March 1945), 168, repro.; represented at NYHS.

FALINSKI, F. Portrait painter, NYC, exhibited at the National Academy in 1841. ¶ Cowdrey, NAD.

FALIZE, CLAUDIUS. Drawing master, Philadelphia, 1793–95. ¶ Prime, II, 48–49.

FALK, FREDERICK. Lithographer, Philadelphia, 1860. Falk (29, Bavaria) and his wife Sophia (29, Wittenberg, Germany) had three children, ages 4 years to 3 months, all born in Pennsylvania. ¶ 8 Census (1860), Pa., LIV, 961.

FALKER, FLETISS(?). Engraver, New Orleans, 1850. Falker, age 20, lived with his parents; all the family were born in Germany except the youngest child, age 1, born in Louisiana. ¶ 7 Census (1850), La., V, 236.

FALL, GEORGE. Portrait painter at Fayette (Mo.) in 1846. ¶ WPA Guide, *Missouri.*

FALLER, CLÉMENT (1819–1901). Landscape, portrait, and figure painter in oils and watercolors; born June 1, 1819, at Habsheim (Alsace). The greater part of his career was spent in France. He came to America about 1850, worked in St. Louis (Mo.) in 1851–52 and in NYC from 1853 to 1856, and exhibited at the National Academy in 1853. By 1858 he had returned to Alsace. He died in Paris, February 27, 1901. ¶ Girodie, *Une Peintre Alsacienne de Transition: Clément Faller,* with catalogue and 23 plates; Cowdrey, NAD.

FANNING, SOLOMON (1807–?). Portrait and ornamental painter, born in Preston (Conn.) in 1807. He went to NYC in 1833 to study portrait painting, worked in Norwich (Conn.) as a portrait painter from 1840 to 1844 and in NYC in 1846. About 1850 he gave up portraiture for the more lucrative branch of ornamental painting. He was a resident of Norwich in 1878. ¶ French, 72; NYBD 1846; Fielding.

FANSHAW, SAMUEL RAYMOND (1814–1888). A.N.A. Miniature and portrait painter, born in NYC December 21, 1814, died there December 15, 1888. A life-long resident of NYC, Fanshaw was a frequent exhibitor at and Associate Member of the National Academy. He also exhibited in 1844 at the American Institute. ¶ Bolton, *Miniature Painters;* Cowdrey, NAD; NYCD 1839–88; Am. Inst. Cat., 1844.

FARIS, HIRAM or HYRAM (1769–1800). Miniaturist. Hiram, son of WILLIAM FARIS, was born in Annapolis (Md.), January 18, 1769 and died at sea, August 30, 1800. Brought up to his father's trade of watchmaker and silversmith, he also painted miniatures, including one of his brother St. John Faris (1771–1796), now owned by the Maryland Historical Society. ¶ Pleasants and Sill, *Maryland Silversmiths 1715–1830,* 266, 270, plates 54–55; Rutledge, "Handlist of Miniatures."

FARIS, WILLIAM. Portrait painter. Well known as a watchmaker and silversmith of Annapolis (Md.) in the mid-18th century, William Faris is reputed to have painted a portrait of his mother, Abigail Faris. He was the father of HIRAM FARIS. ¶ Pleasants and Sill, *Maryland Silversmiths 1715–1830,* 269; Barker, *American*

Painting; Barr, "William Faris, Annapolis Clockmaker."

FARLEY, JOHN. Lithographer, San Francisco, 1858. ¶ San Francisco BD 1858.

FARLEY, SIMON. Scottish engraver, 45, at NYC in 1860 with his wife Bridget. ¶ 8 Census (1860), N.Y., XLVI, 284.

FARMER, JOHN (1798–1859). Engraver; born in Half Moon (N.Y.), February 9, 1798; moved to Michigan in 1821; died in Detroit, March 24, 1859. ¶ Stauffer.

FARRAR, A. E. Delineator of a view of Lowell (Mass.) in 1833, lithographed by PENDLETON of Boston. ¶ Stokes, *Historic Prints.*

FARRAS, ——. Fresco, portrait, and ornamental painter, working in partnership with MECHAU at Richmond (Va.) in 1847. ¶ *Richmond Portraits.*

FARRELL, GEORGE L. Engraver and stencil cutter, Philadelphia, 1850 and after. Farrell was born in Pennsylvania *c.* 1824. He was listed as an engraver in the 1850 census and in city directories for 1852 and 1853; otherwise he appears as a stencil cutter. ¶ 7 Census (1850), Pa., LII, 584; Phila. CD 1851–60 and after.

FARRER, THOMAS CHARLES (*c.* 1840–1891). Landscape and genre painter and etcher; born in London; died, probably in England, in 1891. He apparently began his career in NYC *c.* 1860 and lived there until his return to England in 1872. He exhibited at the Pennsylvania Academy in 1862 and 1868. ¶ Bénézit; Thieme-Becker; Rutledge, PA.

FARRINGTON, DAVID. Engraver, 25, a native of New York, at NYC in 1860. ¶ 8 Census (1860), N.Y., L, 719; NYCD 1863.

FARWELL, PURCELL & COMPANY. Designers, engravers, and printers of circus, menagerie, and travelling exhibition posters and bills. Founded by William W. Farwell, printer, and EDWARD PURCELL, engraver, the firm operated in NYC in the late 1850's. ¶ NYCD 1855–57; NYBD 1856.

FASEL, GEORGE WILHELM. Portrait, historical, and religious painter; lithographer; born in Germany. He began his career in Karlsruhe (Germany) about 1829, visited Rome in 1837–38, and then returned to Karlsruhe where he worked apparently until 1848. By 1850 he was in NYC, exhibiting two religious paintings at the American Art-Union, and he worked there until at least 1865. In 1862 he did some lithographic work with EDWARD VALOIS. ¶ Thieme-Becker; Cowdrey, AA & AAU; NYCD 1852–65; Peters, *America on Stone; Portfolio* (May 1947), 211–213, four repros.; *Album of American Battle Art,* plates 21–22; 8 Census (1860), N.Y., LIII, 511.

FASSETT, CORNELIA ADÈLE (STRONG) (1831–1898). Portrait and figure painter, miniaturist. Born in Owasco, Cayuga County (N.Y.), November 9, 1831, Cornelia Adèle Strong was married in 1851 to SAMUEL MONTAGUE FASSETT, photographer and artist of Chicago. She studied in NYC under the English painter J. B. WANDESFORDE and later spent three years studying in Paris and Rome. After twenty years in Chicago, Mrs. Fassett moved to Washington (D.C.) in 1875. She painted portraits of many prominent public officials, as well as group portraits of the Supreme Court of 1876 and the Electoral Commission of 1877. She died in Washington, January 4, 1898. ¶ DAB; Fairman, *Art and Artists of the Capitol;* CAB; *Art Annual,* I, obit.

FASSILAT, HENRY. Engraver (26, Swiss), Philadelphia, 1850. ¶ 7 Census (1850), Pa., LII, 892.

FATZER, CONRAD. Lithographer, NYC, 1857–59. ¶ NYBD 1857–59.

FAUGERE, Monsieur. French portraitist and miniaturist in oils and black lead, working at Baltimore, 1792. ¶ Prime, II, 9.

FAUST, WILLIAM. Lithographer, NYC, 1856–65. In 1856 he exhibited "specimen pictures, cut with scissors," at the American Institute. ¶ NYCD and NYBD 1856–65; Am. Inst. Cat., 1856.

FAXON, ELIHU J. Wood engraver, of FAXON & MYER, Buffalo (N.Y.), 1858–59. ¶ Buffalo BD 1858–59.

FAXON & MYER. Wood engravers, Buffalo (N.Y.), 1858–59; ELIHU J. FAXON and H. E. MYER. ¶ Buffalo BD 1858–59.

FAY, see FOY.

FAY, AUGUSTUS. Wood engraver and lithographer, illustrator; born in New York about 1824. He was listed as an engraver in NYC directories from 1848 to 1860, in 1852–53 as of SWINTON & FAY. This man is probably the same as A. Fay, illustrator of Stansbury's *Exploration and Survey of the Valley of the Great Salt Lake of Utah* (Phila., 1852, lithography by JAMES ACKERMAN of NYC), and A. Fay, lithographer at Hoboken (N.J.) in 1854 (listed by Peters). ¶ NYBD 1848–60; NYCD 1849–56; 7 Census (1850), N.Y., XLIII, 500; Peters, plate 53; Stansbury, *op. cit.;* Comstock, "The Hoff Views of New York."

FEELY, JOHN. Engraver and die-sinker, NYC, 1846–60. ¶ NYBD and NYCD 1846–60.

FEKE, ROBERT. Portrait painter, active *c.* 1741–50. One of the best of the colonial limners, Feke is thought to have been born between 1705 and 1710 at Oyster Bay, Long Island (N.Y.). Of his early career nothing certain is known, though family tradition states that he was a mariner and made a number of trips to England and the Continent. By 1741, however, he was established as a portrait painter in Boston. In 1742 he was married in Newport (R.I.) where he made his home until 1750. Feke made professional visits to Philadelphia in 1746 and 1750 and to Boston in 1748. Nothing is known of him after 1750 and family tradition states that he died shortly after in Bermuda or Barbados. ¶ Foote, *Robert Feke;* Belknap, "The Identity of Robert Feke"; Parker, "The Identity of Robert Feke Reconsidered"; Goodrich, "Robert Feke"; T. Bolton and H. L. Binsse, "Robert Feke."

FELCH, J. Itinerant artist of western New York in the 1830's. In 1836 or 1839 he was associated with HENRY WALTON at Ithaca. ¶ *Portfolio* (Oct. 1945), 41.

FELCH, JOHN H. Engraver, Columbus (Ohio), 1850–57. In 1850 Felch, a native of Connecticut, age 28, was living with his family who were from New York and New Jersey. In 1856–57 he was a partner in FELCH & RICHES. ¶ Columbus CD 1850, BD 1856; Ohio BD 1857; 7 Census (1850), Ohio, XV, 625.

FELCH & RICHES. Copper, steel, and seal engravers, Columbus (Ohio), 1856–57; JOHN H. FELCH and [W.?] RICHES. ¶ Columbus BD 1856; Ohio BD 1857.

FELLOWES, FRANK WAYLAND (1833–1900). Painter; died in New Haven (Conn.), June 16, 1900. ¶ *Art Annual,* II, obit.

FELTER, JOHN D. Wood engraver, NYC, 1847–60; exhibited at the American Institute in 1847. He was born in New York about 1825. ¶ NYCD and NYBD 1847–60; Am. Inst. Cat., 1847; 7 Census (1850), N.Y., XLVII, 397.

FELTMAN, BERNHARD. Designer, Philadelphia, 1860. A Prussian, Feltman was 33 years old and owned personalty valued at $7,000. ¶ 8 Census (1860), Pa., LVI, 512.

FELTON, CHARLES B. Lithographer and artist, born in England about 1793. He had two sons born in Canada between 1837 and 1840. He was living in NYC from 1850 to 1863. One son, Frederick, born about 1840, was also listed as an artist in the 1860 census. ¶ 7 Census (1850), N.Y., LIV, 578; 8 Census (1860), N.Y., XLVII, 626; Peters, *America on Stone.*

FELTON (or Fenton), ROBERT. Seal cutter, Philadelphia, 1683. Felton or Fenton, a servant, was convicted of counterfeiting Spanish coins in August 1683. ¶ *Minutes of the Provincial Council of Penna.,* I, 84–85, 88. Weiss, "The Growth of the Graphic Arts in Philadelphia 1663–1820," and Brown and Brown, following Fielding's *Supplement to Stauffer's American Engraving on Copper and Steel,* erroneously date this incident to 1663, almost two decades before the founding of Philadelphia.

FENDERICH, CHARLES. Portrait painter and lithographer. Fenderich was a native of Baden (Germany) who came to the United States probably about 1830. He worked in Philadelphia with JOHN CASPAR WILD (1833–34) and did many portraits there for LEHMAN & DUVAL (1835–37) and for P. S. DUVAL. He then moved to Washington (D.C.) where he brought out a number of political portraits between 1837 and 1843. He may also have been in Baltimore about this time, since Peters credits him with portraits, and military and naval views done for EDWARD WEBER. Two of his crayon portraits were shown at the Apollo Association in 1838 and 1839. Nothing further is heard of him until the 1850's when he apparently settled in San Francisco, to remain there until after 1870. He was recorded in the 1860 census as C. Fenrick, portrait painter, age 44, with $250 in personalty. *Cf.* CHARLES H. B. FENWICK. ¶ 8 Census (1860), Cal., VII, 467; Peters, *America on Stone;* Washington CD 1843; Todd; "Huddy & Duval Prints"; Cowdrey, AA & AAU; San Francisco BD 1856, CD 1858–72; *Portfolio* (Nov. 1945), 55, repro.

FENIMORE, JAMES S. Engraver, Philadelphia, 1860 and after. The 1860 census lists him as James S. Fennamore, age 23, born in New Jersey; he appears in city directories variously as James S. Fenimore, toolcutter (1859), James Fenimore, engraver (1861), and James L. Fennemore, engraver (also 1861). ¶ Phila. CD 1859–65; 8 Census (1860), Pa., LV, 964.

FENN, FREDERICK C. M. Engraver, San Francisco, 1852 and after. ¶ San Francisco CD 1852, 1856, 1858–60.

FENNAMORE and FENNEMORE, see FENIMORE.

FENNEY, WILLIAM H. Painter of English scenes, Philadelphia, 1855. ¶ Rutledge, PA.

FENNO, CHARLES HORACE. Engraver, Boston, 1842–60 and after. ¶ Boston CD and BD 1842–60.

FENTON, CHARLES L. (*c.* 1808–1877). Portrait painter, Boston (Mass.), 1832–58. He is reported to have been working in Dover (N.H.) in 1850. He exhibited at the Boston Athenaeum. ¶ Swan, BA; Boston BD 1844–58; Lipman and Winchester, 172.

FENTON, ROBERT, see ROBERT FELTON.

FENWICK, CHARLES H. B. Lithographer (1852) and engraver (1856), San Francisco (Cal.). *Cf.* CHARLES FENDERICH. ¶ San Francisco CD 1852, BD 1856.

FERAUD, THOMAS, JR. Drawing master at Charleston (S.C.), 1803. He was spoken of as a former student at the Paris Academy. ¶ Rutledge, *Artists in the Life of Charleston.*

FERENTO, AUGUST. Lithographer, 29, a native of New York, at NYC in 1850. One of his children, aged 8, was born in Massachusetts. ¶ 7 Census (1850), N.Y., XLVIII, 314.

FERGUSON, DUNCAN. A.N.A. Portrait painter, NYC, 1832–36. He exhibited in 1832–33 at the National Academy, of which he was an Associate Member 1832–36. ¶ Cowdrey, NAD.

FERGUSON, HIRAM. Wood engraver, Albany (N.Y.), 1855 and after. ¶ Albany CD 1855–60 and after.

FERGUSON, JAMES. Lithographer, Philadelphia, 1860 and after. He was born in Pennsylvania *c.* 1834; his wife Mary, born *c.* 1840, was from Massachusetts. ¶ 8 Census (1860), Pa., LXI, 772; Phila. CD 1871.

FERGUSON, JOHN. Engraver, 51, a native of Delaware, at NYC in 1850. ¶ 7 Census (1850), N.Y., LI, 187.

FERGUSON, JOHN. Engraver, 22, a native of New York, at NYC in 1860. ¶ 8 Census (1860), N.Y., LVIII, 112.

FERGUSON, WILLIAM. Artist, working in NYC 1805–20. ¶ NYCD 1805–20.

FERGUSON, WILLIAM. Irish lithographer, 35, at NYC in 1850. ¶ 7 Census (1850), N.Y., XLI, 765.

FERGUSON, WILLIAM K. Engraver, age 28, Philadelphia, 1860. Ferguson and his wife Martha (26) were both native Pennsylvanians. ¶ 8 Census (1860), Pa., LIV, 304.

FERGUSON, WILLIAM P. Artist, age 32, Washington (D.C.), 1850. Though the artist was born in the District of Columbia, his wife and their oldest child (12) were born in Maryland; the younger children (10 to 4) were born in the District. ¶ 7 Census (1850), D.C., II, 80.

FERNAN, T. S. Portrait painter, Philadelphia, 1842; exhibitor, Artists' Fund Society. ¶ Rutledge, PA.

FERNAU, FREDERICK. Portrait painter, NYC, 1850–51. ¶ NYBD 1850–51.

FERNORO, THOMAS B. Artist, age 25, Kensington (Pa.), 1850. He was a native Pennsylvanian. ¶ 7 Census (1850), Pa., XLIX, 85.

FERRAN, AUGUSTO. Cuban artist who collaborated with J. BATURONE on *Album Californiano,* a set of sketches of California miners lithographed and published in Havana *c.* 1849. ¶ Vail, *Gold Fever,* 7–11, repros.; Peters, *California on Stone;* Jackson, *Gold Rush Album.*

FERRANA, JOSEPH. Plaster figure maker, Baltimore, 1860. Born in Italy *c.* 1800, he lived in Baltimore with his Irish wife Margaret (48) and his son PILARENE, age 19, born in Tuscany. ¶ 8 Census (1860), Md., IV, 572.

FERRANA, PILARENE. Plaster figure maker, Baltimore, 1860. He was born in Tuscany *c.* 1841 and lived in Baltimore with his father, JOSEPH FERRANA. ¶ 8 Census (1860), Md., IV, 572.

FERRETA, JOHN. Italian artist, age 28, Baltimore, 1850. ¶ 7 Census (1850), Md., IV, 81.

FERRIS, STEPHEN JAMES (1835–1915). Portrait painter and etcher. Born January 25 (Baker) or December 25, 1835 (*Art Annual*) in Plattsburg (N.Y.); went to Philadelphia about 1846 to study at the Pennsylvania Academy under SARTAIN and others. He also studied and exhibited in Europe, winning the Fortuny prize in Rome in 1876. A popular portrait painter and etcher, he was a resident of Philadelphia until his death, July 9, 1915. ¶ Baker, *American Engravers,* 63–65; *Art Annual,* XII (1915), 258, obit.; Bolton, *Crayon Draftsmen; American Art Review* (1880), 104; Rutledge, PA; Phila. CD 1858 and after; 8 Census (1860), Pa., LIV, 260; *Antiques* (Apr. 1929), repro.

FERRIT, Madame DE. Watercolor portraitist. About 1815 she painted a portrait of Vincent Le Roy de Chaumont (1792–1866) at Le Raysville (N.Y.), now owned by the Jefferson County Historical Society,

Watertown (N.Y.). ¶ WPA (Mass.), *Portraits Found in N.Y.*

FERRY, FRANCIS. Engraver, age 40, Philadelphia, 1860. Ferry was a native of Maryland, but his wife Annie (40) and their two children (5 and 2) were born in Pennsylvania. ¶ 8 Census (1860), Pa., LIV, 305.

FESSENDEN, BENJAMIN. Artist, Boston, 1850's. Fessenden was born in Westminster (Mass.) *c.* 1809; his wife Elizabeth was born in Dover (N.H.) *c.* 1809; and their three children (16, 14, and 12) were born in Boston. In 1860 Fessenden owned $7,000 in realty and $500 in personalty. ¶ 8 Census (1860), Mass., XXV, 231; Boston CD 1851, 1860.

FEST, ADAM. Engraver, age 15, Philadelphia, 1850. He was a native of Germany. ¶ 7 Census (1850), Pa., LII, 341.

FESTNER, FREDERICK C. Engraver, of BLISS, EBERHARD & FESTNER, Madison (Wis.), 1858. ¶ Madison CD 1858.

FETERS, W. T. Engraver of portrait of Rev. John Davenport of Connecticut *c.* 1820. Stauffer suggests this may be W. T. PETERS. ¶ Stauffer.

FETSCH, see PFETSCH.

FETTE, HENRY GERHARD. Portrait and miniature painter. He was working in Boston from 1842 to 1847, exhibited at the Boston Athenaeum in 1851, and did at least one miniature in St. Louis (Mo.). ¶ Boston BD 1842–47; Swan, BA; information courtesy Dr. H. W. Williams, Jr., Corcoran Gallery.

FETTER, GEORGE. Portrait and landscape painter. A Moravian, Fetter painted a view of Bethlehem (Pa.) in 1797 and a watercolor portrait of Sister Thomas, both now in the Moravian Archives, Bethlehem. Fetter and his wife are said to have taught in the Bethlehem school and to have moved to Lancaster (Pa.) in 1830. ¶ Levering, *History of Bethlehem*, 654, 709.

FEUILLE, J. F. Engraver, miniature and portrait painter, New Orleans, 1835–41. The name appears as J. F. Fenille in the 1837 directory. ¶ New Orleans *Bee,* March 5, 1835, and New Orleans CD 1837 (both citations in Delgado-WPA); New Orleans CD 1838, 1841.

FEWSMITH, HENRY (1821–1846). Portrait and figure painter. Born in Philadelphia, September 28, 1821, FewSmith [sic] studied in Philadelphia under JOHN NEAGLE for two years, and then spent four years (1842–46) in Europe, studying at Düsseldorf, Munich, Paris, and Rome. Shortly after his return to Philadelphia, the young artist died in his studio, October 22, 1846. ¶ Cramer, "Henry FewSmith, Philadelphia Artist, 1821–1846."

FEY, CHARLES. German-born engraver, age 19, living in Cleveland (Ohio) in August 1850. ¶ 7 Census (1850), Ohio, XI, 487.

FIBICH, R. Painter of "York Springs (Pa.) Graveyard," *c.* 1850–60, owned by N. Y. State Historical Association. ¶ Lipman and Winchester, 172; *American Primitive Painting; Art in America* (July 1942), 202.

FICHT, HARTMAN. Artist, NYC, 1844–46; probably a brother of OTTO C. FICHT and possibly the same as JOHN H. FICHT. ¶ NYCD 1844–46.

FICHT, JOHN H. Artist, NYC, 1846–52; probably a brother of OTTO C. FICHT and possibly the same as HARTMAN FICHT. He is listed in directories from 1857 to after 1860, but without occupation. ¶ NYCD 1846–65.

FICHT, OTTO C. Artist, painter and fresco painter, NYC, 1844–after 1860. Otto was probably a brother of HARTMAN and JOHN H. FICHT, with whom he worked at various times between 1844 and 1852. From 1857 to 1860 he was a member of the firm of FINKENAUER & FICHT, fresco painters and artists' suppliers. Otto C. Ficht exhibited a "view near Tarrytown" at the National Academy in 1851. ¶ NYCD 1844–65; Cowdrey, NAD.

FICKES, FRANK B. Artist, Buffalo (N.Y.), 1857. ¶ Buffalo BD 1857.

FIELD, Mrs. CHARLOTTE E. (1838–1920). Miniaturist; died April 8, 1920, in Brooklyn (N.Y.). She was for several years president of the Brooklyn Society of Miniature Painters. ¶ *Art Annual,* XVII (1920), 267, obit.; Fielding.

FIELD, EDWARD R. Artist and designer on wood. A resident of Brooklyn (N.Y.), he exhibited a pen drawing at the 1844 Fair of the American Institute, and in 1850–52 was listed in the NYC directory as "artist and designer on wood." ¶ Am. Inst. Cat., 1844; NYCD 1850–52.

FIELD, ERASTUS SALISBURY (1805–1900). Primitive painter; born in Leverett (Mass.), May 19, 1805. Largely self-taught, except for three months under S. F. B. MORSE in 1824–25, he was primarily a portrait painter, though now remembered chiefly for his scenes from classical mythology and Biblical history and for his grandiose "Historical Monument of the American Republic" (*c.* 1875 and later). In 1831 he married Phebe Gilmore of Ware (Mass.) who, as Mrs. P. G. FIELD, later exhibited several paintings at the American Institute in NYC. The Fields lived first in Hartford (Conn.), then in Monson and Palmer (Mass.) from about 1832 to 1842. From 1842 to 1848 they lived in NYC. Returning in 1848 to Massachusetts, they lived for a time in Leverett and then Palmer before finally settling in Sunderland in 1859, the year of Mrs. Field's death. Field continued to paint until after 1876 and lived on in Sunderland until his death in 1900 at the age of 95. ¶ Robinson, "Erastus Salisbury Field," in Lipman and Winchester, 72–79; Robinson, "Erastus Salisbury Field," *Art in America* (Oct. 1942), 244–253; Dods, checklist of Field's portraits in *Art in America* (Jan. 1944); NYCD 1842–48; Am. Inst. Cat., 1845, 1847; Karolik Cat., 255–257.

FIELD, Mrs. ERASTUS SALISBURY, see Mrs. P. G. FIELD.

FIELD, Mrs. HENRY MARTYN (née Henriette Des Portes) (*c.* 1813–1875). Crayon draftsman. Born in Paris, Mlle. Des Portes became a governess and in 1847 was involved in the Choiseul-Praslin tragedy. She emigrated to America soon after and in 1851 married the noted clergyman and author Henry Martyn Field. Mrs. Field exhibited at the National Academy in 1858. She died in 1875. Her life formed the basis for Rachel Field's popular novel, *All This and Heaven Too* (1938). ¶ DAB (under Henry Martyn Field; her Christian name is there given as Laure Desportes); Cowdrey, NAD.

FIELD, J. A. Amateur artist who made a pen-and-ink sketch of the Mormon Temple, Nauvoo (Ill.), in 1851. ¶ Arrington, *Nauvoo Temple,* Chapter 8.

FIELD, JULIA A. Amateur artist of NYC who in 1850 exhibited a watercolor landscape at the American Institute. ¶ Am. Inst. Cat., 1850.

FIELD, MARRIOTT. Portrait and miniature painter. A frequent exhibitor at the National Academy between 1839 and 1853, Field was in NYC in 1839, in Charleston (S.C.) during the winter of 1841–42, and again in NYC in 1852–57. The Wadsworth Athenaeum, Hartford (Conn.), has a portfolio of watercolor sketches made by him "in America 1850–1860." ¶ Cowdrey, NAD; Rutledge, *Artists in the Life of Charleston;* NYBD 1854–57; information courtesy Wadsworth Athenaeum.

FIELD, Mrs. P. G. (?–1859). Amateur artist. Phebe Gilmore of Ware (Mass.) married the painter ERASTUS SALISBURY FIELD in 1831. During their residence in NYC between 1842 and 1848, Mrs. Field exhibited several sketches and paintings at the American Institute. She died in 1859, shortly after they settled in Sunderland (Mass.). ¶ Robinson, "Erastus Salisbury Field," in Lipman and Winchester, 72; Am. Inst. Cat., 1844, 1845, 1847.

FIELD, ROBERT (*c.* 1769–1819). Miniature and portrait painter, engraver. Born in England, possibly in Gloucestershire, Field studied engraving at the Royal Academy school in London in the early 1790's. In 1794 he emigrated to America, spending a few months in Baltimore before settling in Philadelphia. A good engraver, he also became a leading painter of miniatures in the then capital of the United States. In 1800 he moved to the new capital at Washington and worked there, at Georgetown, and in the State of Maryland until 1805, when he moved to Boston. Leaving Boston in 1808, Field moved to Halifax (N.S.) where he had a successful career as portrait and miniature painter until 1816. In that year he moved to the island of Jamaica and three years later, on August 9, 1819, he died of yellow fever in Kingston. ¶ Piers, *Robert Field;* Bolton, *Crayon Draftsmen;* Wehle and Bolton; Prime, II, 9; Sherman, "Two Newly Discovered Watercolor Portraits by Robert Field."

FIELD, WILLIAM. Engraver and watercolorist, NYC, 1840–44. Listed as engraver in the directories, he exhibited a watercolor painting at the American Institute in 1844. ¶ NYBD 1840–41; NYCD 1843–44; Am. Inst. Cat., 1844.

FIELDER, JOHN W. Engraver and die-sinker, Boston, 1859 and after. ¶ Boston CD 1859 and after.

FIELDING, E. M. Portrait painter, Rochester (N.Y.), 1858. ¶ N. Y. State BD 1858.

FIENZES, F. French artist, age 42, boarding in New Orleans, 1860. ¶ 8 Census (1860), La., VII, 33.

FILLMORE, WILLIAM. Artist, 36, born in the United States, at NYC in 1850. ¶ 7 Census (1850), N.Y., XLIII, 128.

FILLOT, ADOLPHE. French artist, living in

Philadelphia, 1849–60. In 1850 he was 33, married, with a son George, age 1 year. ¶ Phila. CD 1849–56, 1859–60; 7 Census (1850), Pa., LI, 229 (as Albert Fillot, artist).

FILMER, JOHN. Wood engraver, Boston, 1858 and after. In 1860 he was a partner in ANDREW & FILMER. ¶ Boston CD 1858–60 and after; Smith; *Portfolio* (Jan. 1943), 102.

FILMER, JOHN. English wood engraver, 25, at NYC in 1860; still there in 1863. ¶ 8 Census (1860), N.Y., XLV, 485.

FINCH, E. E. Portrait artist in oils and pen-and-ink, working probably in Maine, 1833–50. ¶ WPA (Mass.), *Portraits Found in Maine,* nos. 74–78, 149; Lipman and Winchester, 172.

FINK, FREDERICK (1817–1849). Portrait, miniature, and figure painter; born December 28, 1817, at Little Falls (N.Y.). He studied under S. F. B. MORSE in NYC in 1835–36, and thereafter worked in Albany (N.Y.), where he died January 23, 1849. He was a frequent exhibitor at the National Academy, the Apollo Association, the Pennsylvania Academy, and the Boston Athenaeum, and he was an Honorary Member, Professional, of the National Academy from 1840. ¶ Cummings, *Historic Annals,* 211–212; Cowdrey, NAD; Cowdrey, AA & AAU; Rutledge, PA; Swan, BA.

FINKELDEY, JOHN FREDERICK. Lithographer, Philadelphia, 1850–60. A native of Hesse (Germany), he was listed in the 1850 census as 27 years of age and unmarried; ten years later he was listed as 39 years old, with a Hessian wife and a five-months-old daughter. With TRAUBEL, SCHNABEL & FINKELDEY in 1850; with SCHNABEL & FINKELDEY from 1857. ¶ 7 Census (1850), Pa., L, 861; 8 Census (1860), Pa., LIII, 539; Peters, *America on Stone;* Phila. CD 1854–60 and after.

FINKENAUER & FICHT. Fresco painters, NYC, 1856–60; GEORGE FINKENAUER and OTTO C. FICHT. In 1856 they exhibited at the American Institute a specimen of waterproof fresco painting. From 1858 they were listed as dealers in artists' supplies. ¶ Am. Inst. Cat., 1856; NYCD 1857–60.

FINKENAUER, GEORGE. Fresco painter, of FINKENAUER & FICHT, NYC, 1856–60. ¶ NYCD 1857–60; Am. Inst. Cat., 1856.

FINKERNAGEL, ERNEST. Landscape painter, NYC, 1851; exhibitor, National Academy. ¶ NYCD and NYBD 1851; Cowdrey, NAD.

FINLEY, ANTHONY. Map engraver, Philadelphia, 1831. ¶ *Am. Adv. Directory,* 1831, 101.

FINN, HENRY JAMES WILLIAM (1787–1840). Miniaturist. Born in Sydney (N.S.), June 17, 1787, Finn was brought up in NYC and studied law there. On a visit to England about 1811 he became an actor and thereafter he devoted his life chiefly to the theater both in England and America. He made his American debut in Philadelphia in 1817, played in NYC in 1818, and spent several years in Savannah (Ga.). In 1821 he was again in England, painting miniatures and acting, but the following year he settled in Boston (Mass.). During the rest of his life Finn had a highly successful career as a comic actor in Boston and elsewhere and continued to paint miniatures, exhibiting at the Boston Athenaeum 1830–33. He died in the burning of the steamer *Lexington* in Long Island Sound, January 13, 1840. ¶ DAB; Swan, BA; CAB; Bolton, *Miniature Painters.*

FINN, MATTHEW D. Author and presumably illustrator of *Theoremetical System of Painting* (N.Y., 1830). Finn was a teacher and lecturer on bookkeeping in NYC from about 1828 to 1848. ¶ Library of Congress; NYCD 1828–48.

FINNEGAN, JOHN. Irish engraver, 29, at NYC in 1860. ¶ 8 Census (1860), N.Y., LXII, 391.

FIRKS, HENRY. Painter of the Firks view of San Francisco in 1849, lithographic prints of which were published in NYC and San Francisco the same year. ¶ Peters, *California on Stone; Portfolio* (Nov. 1948), 60–61, and (May 1951), 208; Stokes, *Historic Prints,* pl. 76a; Jackson, *Gold Rush Album,* 174–175.

FISCHER, ——. Mr. Fischer or Fisher, lately from Europe, advertised in NYC and Philadelphia in 1828 his "perspective transparent" views of European cities and Swiss scenery. *Cf.* —— FISHER, who exhibited his "Theatre Mundi," scenes in India, America and Europe, in Philadelphia in April 1837. ¶ J. E. Arrington cites N. Y. *Evening Post,* June 6 and 20, 1828, Phila. *Ariel,* Nov. 15, 1828, and Phila. *Public Ledger,* April 4, 1837.

FISCHER, CHARLES. Engraver, of FISCHER & KELLER, NYC, 1857–58. ¶ NYCD 1857; NYBD 1858.

FISCHER, CHARLES HENRY. Painter of scenes in oil, Newark (N.J.), 1860. ¶ Lipman and Winchester, 172.

FISCHER, ERNST (or Ernest) GEORG (1815–1874). Portrait and genre painter; born November 6, 1815, in Coburg (Germany). He came to the United States *c.* 1848 and settled in Baltimore where he lived until about 1858. He returned to Germany and died in Coburg September 22, 1874. During his residence in Baltimore Fischer exhibited at the Maryland Historical Society, as well as at the National Academy, American Art-Union, and Washington Art Association. FRANK B. MAYER received instruction in painting from him. ¶ Thieme-Becker; Rutledge, MHS; 7 Census (1850), Md., V, 63; Baltimore CD 1849–54; Lafferty; Cowdrey, NAD; Cowdrey, AA & AAU; Washington Art Assoc. Cat., 1857; Mayer, *Diary;* Pleasants, *250 Years of Painting in Md.,* 57, 59 (repro.).

FISCHER, FREDERICK. Artist, 50, a native of Saxony, at NYC in 1860. His wife and daughter were both cloakmakers. ¶ 8 Census (1860), N.Y., LI, 441.

FISCHER, J. F. Listed by Fielding as the painter of a portrait of Albert Pike (1809–1891), former Confederate General living in Washington (D.C.) from 1868. The artist was probably FLAVIUS J. FISHER (1832–1905) who painted many portraits in Washington after the Civil War. ¶ Fielding; *Art Annual,* V, obit. of Flavius J. Fisher.

FISCHER, JOHN (1736–1808). Portrait painter? A clockmaker by trade and an amateur wood-carver and painter, John Fischer was born June 4, 1736, in Pfeffing, Swabia (Germany), came to America in 1749, and settled in 1756 in York (Pa.), where he lived until his death, December 8, 1808. He was probably the "Fisher" whose portrait of the Rev. Jacob Goering (1755–1807) of York was engraved by WILLIAM WAGNER of York in the 1820's or 1830's. ¶ Beers' *History of York County,* II, 111; Fielding, *Supplement to Stauffer,* no. 1729.

FISCHER, JOHN G. Lithographer, Philadelphia, 1860. Fischer, age 29, was a native of Baden (Germany); his wife Maria, age 26, of Prussia; and their sons Joseph, age 2, and John, age 11 months, of Pennsylvania. His personal property was valued at $300. ¶ 8 Census (1860), Pa., LX, 420.

FISCHER & KELLER. Engravers, NYC, 1857–58; CHARLES and PHILIP FISCHER and ADAM KELLER. ¶ NYCD 1857; NYBD 1858.

FISCHER, LEWIS. German fresco painter, age 25, living in Boston in August 1850. ¶ 7 Census (1850), Mass., XXV, 632.

FISCHER, PHILIP. Engraver, of FISCHER & KELLER, NYC, 1857–58. ¶ NYCD 1857; NYBD 1858.

FISH, CHARLES. Engraver, 30, a native of New York, at NYC in 1850. ¶ 7 Census (1850), N.Y., XLI, 602.

FISH, GEORGE G. Portrait and historical painter, crayon portraitist. Possibly a brother of WILLIAM H. FISH. Working in Boston (Mass.) in 1849, and in NYC from 1857 to 1880. Several pastels, signed by him and dated at NYC in 1858–59, were owned in 1939 by Mr. Charles Hefferman of Schenectady (N.Y.). ¶ Boston BD 1849; Cowdrey, NAD; NYCD 1857–80; FARL files.

FISH, J. Portrait painter at Charleston (S.C.) in 1850. ¶ Rutledge, *Artists in the Life of Charleston.*

FISH, WILLIAM H. (1812–1880). Crayon artist. Born in Nantucket (Mass.); apparently worked in Massachusetts before coming to NYC just after the Civil War. In 1865 he was listed at the same address as the artist GEORGE G. FISH, possibly his brother, and he died at the same address July 9, 1880. ¶ *American Art Review* (1880), 455, cites obit. in Boston *Transcript,* July 10, 1880.

FISHBOURNE, R. W. Lithographer. Fishbourne worked with WILLIAM GREEN in NYC 1836 and in New Orleans from 1840 to 1850; he was associated with the firms of GREEN & FISHBOURNE and SNELL & FISHBOURNE. In 1849 or 1850 he went to California and he worked in San Francisco at least until 1862. Peters lists an 1851 print by Fishbourne & Gows and for 1862 he lists the firm of NAGEL, FISHBOURNE & KUCHEL. From 1858 to 1860 he was employed as a draftsman by the U. S. Surveyor General. ¶ NYCD 1836; Delgado-WPA cites New Orleans *Picayune,* Jan. 2, 1841, and New Orleans CD 1842–44, 1846, 1849–50; Peters, *California on Stone;* Peters, *America on Stone.*

FISHER, ——, see JOHN FISCHER.

FISHER, ——. In April 1837 was exhibited in Philadelphia "Fisher's New Exhibition, or Theatre Mundi," consisting of scenes in India, America and Europe with mechanical figures. *Cf.* —— FISCHER or FISHER, whose "perspective transparent" views of European cities and Swiss scenes were shown in NYC and Philadelphia in 1828. ¶ J. E. Arrington cites Phila. *Public Ledger,* April 4, 1837, N. Y. *Evening*

Post, June 6 and 20, 1828, and Phila. *Ariel,* Nov. 15, 1828.

FISHER, ALANSON (1807–1884). A.N.A. Portrait painter. A resident of NYC; exhibited frequently at the National Academy, of which he was an Associate Member from 1843. His self-portrait is owned by the Academy. ¶ Mallett; Cowdrey, NAD; Cowdrey, AA & AAU; NYBD 1848–60 and after; NAD, *Cat. of Permanent Collections;* Washington Art Assoc., 1859; Rutledge, PA.

FISHER, ALVAN (1792–1863). Painter of portraits, landscapes, genre, and animals. One of the pioneers of American genre and landscape painting, Alvan Fisher was born August 9, 1792, in Needham (Mass.) and grew up in Dedham (Mass.). He began to paint about 1812, receiving his first instruction at that time from JOHN RITTO PENNIMAN. At first a portrait painter, he turned to the painting of animals and rural genre scenes about 1815, though after 1819 he returned to portraiture as his chief means of support. He was living in Boston in 1817 when he exhibited at the Pennsylvania and American Academies, but during the next few years he worked in many parts of the country, including Charleston (S.C.) and Hartford (Conn.). In 1825 he visited Europe and studied briefly in Paris. After his return he settled permanently in Boston. He died in Dedham on February 13 (DAB) or 14 (French), 1863. Fisher was a frequent exhibitor at the Boston Athenaeum, National Academy, Pennsylvania Academy, Artists' Fund Society, Apollo Association, and Maryland Historical Society, and an Honorary Member of the National Academy. ¶ DAB; Burroughs, "A Letter from Alvan Fisher"; Dunlap, *History,* II, 264–65; Rutledge, PA; Cowdrey, AA & AAU; Rutledge, *Artists in the Life of Charleston,* 131; Karolik Cat., 258–261; French; Swan, BA; Cowdrey, NAD; Rutledge, MHS; Johnson, "The European Tradition and Alvan Fisher"; Snow, "Delineators of the Adams-Jackson American Views, Part IV," 20; Flexner, *The Light of Distant Skies;* represented at the Am. Antiq. Soc. (Weis) and the Corcoran Gallery.

FISHER, CHARLES. American seaport artist of the packet and clipper era. *Cf.* CHARLES F. (or J.) FISHER. ¶ Peters, "Paintings of the Old 'Wind-Jammer,'" 32.

FISHER, CHARLES F. (or J.) Portrait, historical, and landscape painter, New Orleans, 1852–56. His painting of the Battle of New Orleans was shown in New Orleans in the winter of 1852–53, in Cincinnati in July 1853, and in NYC in September 1853. ¶ New Orleans CD 1852–53; Thompson, *Louisiana Writers;* Delgado-WPA cites New Orleans *Courier,* Jan. 28, 1853; J. E. Arrington cites New Orleans *Picayune* (Nov. 21, 1852), Cincinnati *Daily Gazette* (July 1, 1853), and N. Y. *Herald* (Sept. 9, 1853).

FISHER, FLAVIUS J. (1832–1905). Portrait painter and crayon portraitist. Born in 1832 in Wytheville (Va.), Fisher apparently grew up in eastern Tennessee but returned to Virginia about 1855. He was at Petersburg (Va.) in 1858. He studied in Germany in 1859–60. After his return to America, he apparently settled in Lynchburg (Va.) and worked there until about 1882. From 1882 until his death he had his studio in the Corcoran Building, Washington (D.C.), where he painted the portraits of many prominent men. He died in Washington May 9, 1905. *Cf.* J. F. FISCHER and J. J. FISHER. ¶ *Art Annual,* V, obit.; Rutledge, PA; information courtesy Mrs. Ralph Catterall, Valentine Museum, Richmond (Va.); letter of Mrs. E. A. Watson of Lynchburg to FARL, Jan. 8, 1949, citing Rosa F. Yanley, *Lynchburg and Its Neighbors* (Richmond, 1935) and obituary in Washington *Post,* May 9, 1905.

FISHER, G. B. A painting of Niagara Falls, so signed and dated 1792, is in the Victoria and Albert Museum, London. This may be the G. Fisher who exhibited landscapes at the Royal Academy in 1780–81. Thieme-Becker states that G. B. Fisher was an army officer and amateur artist. ¶ Thieme-Becker; Graves, *Dictionary.*

FISHER, J. J. Crayon portraitist, working in Petersburg (Va.) in 1850. Probably FLAVIUS J. FISHER. ¶ Bolton, *Crayon Draftsmen;* Smith.

FISHER, JOHN KENRICK (1807–?). Portrait and historical painter. An American, born in 1807, he studied in England and exhibited scriptural paintings at the Royal Academy and other London galleries in 1830–32. By 1833 he was in Boston (Mass.), where he exhibited at the Athenaeum. In 1837 and early 1838 he was working in Charleston and thereafter until 1853 in NYC. Fisher exhibited at the National Academy and the American Art-Union, and was the author of a critical article on American art, published in the

Knickerbocker Magazine, June 1839. ¶ Swan, BA, 225; Doughty, "Thomas Doughty," 60–62; Graves, *Dictionary;* Rutledge, *Artists in the Life of Charleston;* Cowdrey, NAD; Cowdrey, AA & AAU; NYBD 1844, 1850.

FISHER, JONATHAN (1768–1847). Wood engraver, portrait, and landscape painter. Jonathan Fisher, born in New Braintree (Mass.) October 7, 1768, graduated from Harvard College in 1792 and from 1796 to 1837 served as pastor of the Blue Hill (Maine) Congregational Church. He was a man of many parts—clergyman, author, poet, linguist, inventor, farmer, surveyor, architect, naturalist, missionary, teacher. His artistic work included a self-portrait, a copy of HENRY DAWKINS' view of Nassau Hall, Princeton (N.J.), a series of wood engravings showing the animals and other creatures of the Bible, and at least twenty canvases now owned by the Howard Collection at Blue Hill. He died in Blue Hill on September 22, 1847. ¶ Chase, *Jonathan Fisher, Maine Parson,* 227–231; Fisher, *The Fisher Genealogy; Bangor Hist. Mag.* (June 1889), 2; *Sprague's Journal of Maine History,* I:5 (Jan. 1914); *Harvard University, Quinquennial Cat.;* repro., *Portfolio* (March 1955), 150.

FISHER, THEODORE (1789–1819). Artist. The son of the rector of St. Peter's Episcopal Church in Salem (Mass.), Theodore Fisher was baptized April 26, 1789, and died in Salem June 23, 1819. He is represented at the Essex Institute by an oil copy after Claude Lorrain. ¶ Belknap, *Artists and Craftsmen,* 9.

FISKE, CHARLES ALBERT (1837–1915). Painter. A native of Alfred (Mass.), he graduated from Dartmouth College, lived in NYC until 1865, and thereafter in Greenwich (Conn.), where he died May 13, 1915. ¶ *Art Annual,* XII, obit.; Fielding.

FISKE, MARIE ANTOINETTE, see Mrs. J. A. KENNICOTT.

FISKE, W. Illustrator for *Vanity Fair* (1859–63) and *Punchinello* (1870–71). ¶ Hamilton, 256.

FISKE, WILLIAM H. Painter of a portrait of GEORGE CATLIN, 1849, now in the U. S. National Museum, Washington (D.C.). ¶ *American Collector* (April 4, 1935), 3, repro.

FITCH, Captain BERIAH. Portrait painter, New England *c.* 1800. Captain Fitch's known works are portraits of Noah Cooke (1749–1829) of Keene (N.H.), painted in 1800, and of Jonathan Cook (1753–1835) of Provincetown (Mass.). His Christian name is given by C. K. Bolton. ¶ WPA (Mass.), *Portraits Found in Mass.,* nos. 481 and 486; C. K. Bolton, "Workers with Line and Color in New England."

FITCH, JOHN (1743–1798). Best known as the inventor of the steamboat, Fitch also did some engraving. He was born in Windsor Township (Conn.) on January 21, 1743; worked as a brass-founder in and around Windsor until 1769 and worked as a brass and silversmith in Trenton (N.J.) until the Revolution. From 1780 to 1785 he was a surveyor in Kentucky and the Northwest Territory, and in 1785 he engraved a map of the latter. From 1785 until his death he was engaged in work on several types of steamboat, none of which was a commercial success. He died July 2, 1798, in Bardstown (Ky.). ¶ DAB; Stauffer.

FITCH, JOHN LEE (1836–1895). A.N.A. Landscape painter, specializing in forest scenes. Born in Hartford (Conn.) in 1836, he studied under JULIUS BUSCH and GEORGE F. WRIGHT in Hartford before going to Europe in 1855. During three years in Europe he studied in Munich and Milan. Returning to Hartford in 1859 he worked there until 1866 when he settled permanently in NYC. In 1860 he exhibited for the first time at the National Academy of which he was elected an Associate Member in 1870. He was also a member of the Artists' Fund Society and the Century Association. He made a second visit to Germany in 1871. ¶ French, 145; Smith; Clement and Hutton; Cowdrey, NAD; Champlin and Perkins; Fielding; Bénézit; Thieme-Becker.

FITZGERALD, D. J. Engraver and die sinker, NYC, 1854. ¶ NYBD 1854.

FITZWILSON, GEORGE W. Portrait painter, advertised in Charleston (S.C.) in December 1846 and July 1847. ¶ Rutledge, *Artists in the Life of Charleston.*

FIX, LOUIS. Engraver and chaser, NYC, 1854–60. In 1854–55 he was a partner in the firm of LIND & FIX. ¶ NYCD 1854–60.

FLAESCHNER, JULIUS. Sculptor. A German artist working in Berlin in 1844 and 1860–62, Flaeschner also worked in NYC *c.* 1854–57. ¶ Thieme-Becker; NYBD 1854–57.

FLAGELLA, VICTOR. Sculptor and "French carver," NYC, 1848–51. In 1849–50 he was with the firm of SENCE & FLAGELLA. ¶ NYCD 1848–51; NYBD 1849–50.

FLAGG, GEORGE WHITING (1816–1897). N.A. Genre and portrait painter. Born in New Haven (Conn.) June 26, 1816, George W. Flagg accompanied his family to Charleston (S.C.) in 1824 and there received his first instruction in painting from JAMES BOWMAN. In 1830 Flagg and Bowman went to Boston, where Flagg studied for a time with his uncle, WASHINGTON ALLSTON. In 1834 he went to Europe for further study in London, Paris, and Italy, under the patronage of Luman Reed. On his return he worked in Boston and New Haven before settling in NYC about 1843. He became a Member of the National Academy in 1851. He exhibited little after 1867 and in 1879 retired to Nantucket (Mass.) where he died January 5, 1897. He was a brother of HENRY COLLINS FLAGG and JARED BRADLEY FLAGG. ¶ DAB; N. G. and L. C. S. Flagg, *Family Records of the Descendants of Gershom Flagg,* 125; Rutledge, *Artists in the Life of Charleston;* Cowdrey, NAD; Swan, BA; Cowdrey, AA & AAU; Rutledge, PA; 7 Census (1850), Conn., VII, 400; Clement and Hutton; French, 91–94; Tuckerman, 404–408.

FLAGG, HENRY COLLINS (1811–1862). Marine and animal painter, caricaturist. The eldest son of Mayor Flagg of New Haven, Henry C. Flagg was born there December 10, 1811. He spent part of his childhood in South Carolina and entered the U. S. Navy in 1827. He returned to New Haven in 1832 and took up painting, especially marine views, but later resumed his naval career. He exhibited views at the National Academy and the Boston Athenaeum. He died in Jamestown (N.Y.) August 23, 1862, just after receiving the rank of Commander. He was a brother of GEORGE W. and JARED BRADLEY FLAGG. ¶ N. G. and L. C. S. Flagg, *Family Records of the Descendants of Gershom Flagg,* 124; French, 81–82; Hamersley; Cowdrey, NAD; Swan, BA; Boston BD 1849; Delgado-WPA cites New Orleans *Courier,* June 21, 1844.

FLAGG, JARED BRADLEY (1820–1899). N.A. Portrait and religious painter. A younger brother of GEORGE W. and HENRY C. FLAGG, Jared B. Flagg was born in New Haven (Conn.) on June 16, 1820. He graduated from Trinity College, Hartford (Conn.) and then took up the study of painting, his first instructor being his brother George. In 1837–38 he was in New Haven, in 1839 in Newark (N.J.), from 1840 to 1849 in Hartford, and thereafter in NYC. About 1850 he began the study of theology, was ordained a priest in the Episcopal church in 1855, and served parishes in Brooklyn until 1863. After 1863 he resumed his career as a professional painter in New Haven and later in NYC. In later life he was one of the organizers of the Yale Art Library and the author of *Life and Letters of Washington Allston.* He became a Member of the National Academy in 1850. He died in NYC September 25, 1899. ¶ DAB; N. G. and L. C. S. Flagg, *Family Records of the Descendants of Gershom Flagg,* 125–126; French, 106–107; Clement and Hutton; Champlin and Perkins; Cowdrey, NAD; Cowdrey, AA & AAU; 7 Census (1850), N.Y., LII, 124.

FLAGG, JOSIAH, JR. Miniaturist, working in Boston in 1783 and in Baltimore in 1784. This may be Josiah Flagg (1763–?), dentist and musician of Boston, son of Josiah Flagg (1737–*c.* 1795) the Boston musician, and father of JOSIAH FOSTER FLAGG (1788–1853), dentist and anatomical artist. ¶ Bolton, *Miniature Painters;* Prime, I, 2–3; DAB (under Josiah Flagg, 1737–*c.* 1795).

FLAGG, JOSIAH FOSTER (1788–1853). Anatomical artist, wood engraver. Born in Boston, January 10, 1788, the son of JOSIAH FLAGG, JR. (1763–?), he studied medicine and surgery in Boston 1811–15 and later practised dentistry in Boston. In 1813 he collaborated with Dr. J. C. Warren on an edition of Haller's *Anatomical Description of the Arteries of the Human Body,* Flagg providing the wood engravings. Flagg was also a founder of the Boston School of Design for Women. He died December 20, 1853. ¶ DAB.

FLAGG, J. P. Portrait painter at Cincinnati (Ohio) in 1840. ¶ Cist, *Cincinnati in 1841,* 141.

FLAMOUR, LE SIEUR. Engraver from Paris who advertised in Philadelphia in 1794 his intention of publishing a print showing the massacre of several hundred French inhabitants of Haiti in 1794. ¶ Prime, II, 68.

FLANNERY, LOT. Sculptor at the National Capitol, Washington, in the 1850's. ¶ Fairman, *Art and Artists of the Capitol,* 168.

FLEETWOOD, ANTHONY. Lithographer. Born in England *c.* 1800, Fleetwood was working in NYC as early as 1827 and until 1847, when he moved to Cincinnati

(Ohio). He was in Cincinnati at least until 1860, heading the firm of FLEETWOOD & SON from 1849 to 1859. His sons CHARLES and CALEB V. FLEETWOOD also were lithographers. ¶ 7 Census (1850), Ohio, XXII, 292; NYCD 1829–1847; Cincinnati CD 1849–60; Stokes, *Historical Prints,* 78 and pl. 53.

FLEETWOOD, CALEB V. Lithographer, born in NYC *c.* 1838, a son of ANTHONY FLEETWOOD. He began his career in Cincinnati (Ohio) in 1858 and the following year was associated with his brother CHARLES FLEETWOOD in the firm of FLEETWOOD & Co. ¶ 7 Census (1850), Ohio, XXII, 292; Cincinnati CD 1858–59.

FLEETWOOD, CHARLES. Lithographer, born in NYC *c.* 1829, the son of ANTHONY FLEETWOOD. He was associated with his father in the Cincinnati firm of FLEETWOOD & SON from 1849 to 1858, and with his brother CALEB V. FLEETWOOD in the firm of FLEETWOOD & Co. in 1859. ¶ 7 Census (1850), Ohio, XXII, 292; Cincinnati CD 1849–59.

FLEETWOOD & COMPANY. Lithographers, Cincinnati (Ohio), 1859; CALEB V. and CHARLES FLEETWOOD. ¶ Cincinnati CD 1859.

FLEETWOOD & SON. Lithographers, Cincinnati (Ohio), 1849–59; ANTHONY and CHARLES FLEETWOOD. ¶ Cincinnati CD 1849–59.

FLEISCHBEIN, FRANÇOIS. Portrait painter, New Orleans, 1833–56. He was born in Germany *c.* 1804 and his wife Eliza in France *c.* 1807. They were in New Orleans as early as 1833 and by 1850 had four children under fourteen, all born in Louisiana. Fleischbein is listed in directories from 1841 to 1856. Fielding states that he worked in New Orleans as late as 1860. ¶ 7 Census (1850), La., VII, 43; Delgado-WPA cites New Orleans *Bee,* July 8, 1833; New Orleans CD 1841–42, 1846, 1852–54, 1856; Fielding. F. Heischbein, portrait painter, New Orleans 1836, listed by Delgado-WPA, is undoubtedly Fleischbein.

FLEISCHMAN, E. Lithographer, 24, a native of Saxony, at NYC in 1860. ¶ 8 Census (1860), N.Y., XLIV, 286.

FLETCHER, AARON DEAN (1817–?). Itinerant portrait painter. He was born September 15, 1817, in Springfield (Vt.), painted a number of portraits there and in Indiana (1855), and later moved to Keeseville (N.Y.) where he died after 1880. ¶ Baker, *Folklore of Springfield, Vt.,* 68–69; Sears, *Some American Primitives,* 285; Fletcher, *Descendants of Robert Fletcher of Concord, Mass.;* Peat, *Pioneer Painters of Indiana,* 144–45.

FLETCHER, BENJAMIN E. Engraver, born in Philadelphia *c.* 1820. He was listed as an engraver in Philadelphia directories from 1844 to 1855, thereafter as a clerk. In the censuses of 1850 and 1860 he is listed as an engraver. His wife Martha was English; there were eight children in 1860, of whom one, Howard M. Fletcher, later became a lithographer. Fletcher owned $200 in personalty in 1860. ¶ 7 Census (1850), Pa., LI, 899; 8 Census (1860), Pa., LI, 362; Phila. CD 1844–70.

FLETCHER, DANIEL W. Portrait painter. So listed in Philadelphia directory of 1855; listed as artist in 1857–58, as poet in 1859. ¶ Phila. CD 1855–59.

FLETCHER, GEORGE (1796–?). Engraver and drawing master; born in Lancaster (Mass.), June 1, 1796; moved to Philadelphia in June 1812. In 1814 he was listed as proprietor of a drawing academy. He married Sophia C. Cunningham in November 1820. He was variously listed in the directories as jeweller (1825–31), machinist and calico engraver (1833–35), machinist (1837–41), engraver (1842–50), refinisher of goods (1855), agent (1856–60), and clerk (1861 and after). ¶ Fletcher, *Descendants of Robert Fletcher,* 77; 7 Census (1850), Pa., XLIX, 886; Phila. CD 1814–70.

FLETCHER, GEORGE C. Artist, Boston, 1858–59. In 1858 he was working with MINARD LEWIS and T. C. BARTHOLOMEW on scenes illustrating Kane's Arctic voyages. ¶ Boston CD 1858–59; Boston *Evening Transcript,* Feb. 17, 1858 (cited by J. E. Arrington).

FLETCHER, JACOB GUPTIL (1825–?). Portrait painter. Born November 22, 1825, he worked as a clerk in Boston during the 1850's and as an "artist" 1860–61, 1866–70. He was in Portland (Me.) in 1875, but had moved to Columbus (Ohio) by 1877 and was still there in 1880. He exhibited at the Boston Athenaeum in 1858 and 1874. ¶ Fletcher, *Descendants of Robert Fletcher,* 266; Boston CD 1850–70; Swan, BA; Columbus CD 1877.

FLETCHER, VERON. Portrait painter, Philadelphia, 1848–70. He was listed in the directories variously as Veron, Vernon, Beron, V., and B. Fletcher. He exhibited at the Pennsylvania Academy from 1848 to 1862. His "Washington and his Staff at

Valley Forge," shown at the Academy in 1855, was lithographed by E. MORAN for HERLINE & HENZEL the same year. ¶ Phila. CD 1850–70; Rutledge, PA; Peters, *America on Stone;* Penna. BD 1854.

FLETCHER, WILLIAM BALDWIN (1837–1907). Sculptor; born August 18, 1837, in Indianapolis. A physician by profession, he was also an amateur sculptor, his chief work being a portrait bust of his father, Calvin Fletcher, now in the Senate Chamber of the Indiana State House. He died in Florida, April 25, 1907. ¶ Information courtesy Wilbur D. Peat.

FLEURY, ELSIE. While a pupil in the Common School of the Icarian Community at Nauvoo (Ill.) in 1855, Elsie Fleury executed a drawing of the ruins of the Mormon Temple in Nauvoo. ¶ Arrington, *Nauvoo Temple,* Chap. 8.

FLICK, LEWIS. Lithographer, age 24, native of Pennsylvania, boarding in Philadelphia in July 1860. ¶ 8 Census (1860), Pa., LVI, 783.

FLICON, HENRY. Lithographer, age 18, a native of Baden (Germany), living in New Orleans in 1860 with BENEDICT SIMON. ¶ 8 Census (1860), La., VIII, 14.

FLORAT, J. A. DE. Portrait and miniature painter at Trenton (N.J.) in January 1784. ¶ Prime, I, 2.

FLORIAN, ——. Teacher of drawing, painting and embroidery at New Orleans in 1814. ¶ Delgado-WPA cites *Courier,* Nov. 18, 1814.

FLORIMONT, AUSTIN. Miniature and crayon portraitist, portrait painter in oils, and drawing master. He announced his arrival in Philadelphia in January 1781, and visited Baltimore in January 1783. ¶ Prime, I, 3.

FLOWER, GEORGE (1787–1862). Amateur watercolorist. A native of Hertfordshire (England), Flower was an intimate friend of Morris Birkbeck with whom he travelled in Europe before they both emigrated with their families to the United States in 1816–17. In 1818 Birkbeck and Flower settled in Illinois, founding there the settlements of Wanborough and Albion. The Chicago Historical Society owns two watercolors by Flower, one showing his home near Hertford (England) and the other his home in Albion (Ill.). Flower and his wife spent the rest of their lives in Illinois and died within a few hours of one another on January 15, 1862, while visiting in Graysville (Ill.). ¶ *History of Edwards, Lawrence and Wabash Counties,* Ill. (1883), 212–214; *American Primitive Painting,* nos. 36–37.

FLOYD, CHARLES RANALDO (*c.* 1796–1845). Miniaturist, portrait painter, and watercolorist. Born at "Fairfield," Camden County (Ga.) late in 1796, Floyd was one of the pioneer settlers of Florida after its purchase by the United States and was active in the war against the Seminoles. He died at "Bellevue," Camden County (Ga.), March 22, 1845, at the age of 48 years, 5 months. Many of his miniatures, drawings, and sketches have been preserved. ¶ Information courtesy Mrs. Wilson Noyes of Savannah (Ga.), 1952; repro., *Antiques* (Oct. 1945), 200.

FOERSTER, EMIL (1822–1906). Portrait painter. A native of Giessen (Germany), during the 1850's he painted portraits in Pittsburgh (Pa.), also some genre and an "Ascension" for the Catholic Church in Pittsburgh. He later worked in Philadelphia and NYC. He is reported to have painted over 600 portraits. ¶ Information courtesy of the late William Sawitzky; Fleming, *History of Pittsburgh,* III, 626; Rutledge, PA.

FOGG, JOSEPH. Engraver, Boston, 1860; age 22, born in Massachusetts. ¶ 8 Census (1860), Mass., XXVII, 486.

FOGLIARDI, J. B. Theatrical scene painter and drawing master in New Orleans, 1821–25. ¶ Delgado-WPA cites *Courier,* May 4, 1821, October 1, 1824, June 13 and Oct. 31, 1825, and *Gazette,* June 1, 1821, Jan. 1, 1821, Jan. 13, 1822, July 21, 1824, June 13, 1825.

FOLEY, JAMES. Lithographer, Boston, 1860; age 25, native of Ireland. ¶ 8 Census (1860), Mass., XXVII, 2.

FOLEY, MARGARET F. (?–1877). Sculptor and cameo portraitist. Probably a native of Vermont, she began carving and modelling while a schoolgirl in Vergennes (Vt.). She worked for a time in a silk factory at Lowell (Mass.) and was a contributor to *The Lowell Offering,* but in 1848 was established in Boston as a cameo portraitist. After teaching school in Westford (Mass.), 1853–54, she returned to Boston and an artistic career. About 1860 she went to Rome, returning to America only once, in 1865, before her death on December 7, 1877, at Meran in the Austrian Tyrol. Her work was exhibited at the Boston Athenaeum, Pennsylvania Academy and National Academy and in the Centennial Exposition at Philadelphia. ¶ Chatterton, "A Vermont Sculptor"; Gardner, *Yankee Stonecutters;* Taft, *History of American Sculpture,* 211; Clement and Hutton; *Art Journal* (1866), 177; Swan, BA; Rutledge, PA; NAD Cats. 1869–71 (courtesy Mary Bartlett Cowdrey); Graves, *Dictionary;* Cole, "Some American Cameo Portraitists," 170. Represented in Bixby Memorial Library, Vergennes (Vt.), J. W. Fletcher Library, Westford (Mass.), and Amherst College, Amherst (Mass.).

FOLEY, NICHOLAS. Primitive landscape painter, working in Connecticut *c.* 1825. ¶ Lipman and Winchester, 172.

FOLGER, EDWIN G. Cincinnati sign painter who exhibited in an art show there in 1841. He may have been the Folger who exhibited a Mexican War panorama there in 1853. ¶ Information courtesy Edward H. Dwight, Cincinnati Art Museum; Cincinnati *Gazette,* Nov. 8, 1853 (courtesy J. Earl Arrington).

FOLGER, L. Portrait painter working in the South *c.* 1837. ¶ Fielding.

FOLGER, WILLIAM B. Engraver, NYC, 1835–51; thereafter listed only as a printer. ¶ NYCD 1835–60.

FOLIE, A. P. "Delineator," Philadelphia, 1794. ¶ Brown and Brown.

FOLINGSBY, GEORGE FREDERICK (1830–1891). Historical and portrait painter. He was born in County Wicklow (Ireland) and at the age of 18 went to Canada and later to NYC. He was employed as a draftsman for *Harper's Magazine* and for a time served as pictorial editor for the American edition of the *Magazine of Art.* After leaving America *c.* 1852 he travelled in Europe and the eastern Mediterranean and settled in Munich where he remained, except for visits to Paris and Belfast, until 1879. In that year he went to Australia, where he was director of the National Gallery of Victoria from 1884 until his death on January 4, 1891, in Melbourne. Both Folingsby and his wife exhibited at the National Academy in NYC in 1859, giving as their address Appleton's, 346 Broadway, though they were probably then living in Munich. ¶ Strickland, *Dictionary of Irish Artists;* NYCD 1852; Cowdrey, NAD; Graves, *Dictionary.*

FOLINGSBY, MRS. GEORGE FREDERICK. Landscape painter. Mrs. Folingsby and her husband both exhibited at the National Academy in 1859, giving as their NYC address, Appleton's 346 Broadway. At that time, however, they were probably residing in Munich (Germany). Mrs. Folingsby may have visited the United States with her husband in the early 1850's or she may have been an American. ¶ Cowdrey, NAD.

FOLKARD, W. Engraver of two illustrations in *Benjamin Franklin: His Autobiography* (N.Y., 1849), pp. 301, 452. ¶ Hamilton, 172.

FOLSOM, ABRAHAM (1805–1886). Portrait painter. Abraham, son of the Honorable Simeon Folsom of Exeter (N.H.), was born September 19, 1805. He took up portrait painting in Dover (N.H.), but soon gave it up to become a dealer in paints and oils and later a manufacturer of oil cloth. After 1865 he lived in Boston. He died February 19, 1886, in Brookline (Mass.). ¶ Folsom, *Genealogy of the Folsom Family,* 534–535; Dover CD 1833–65; Lipman and Winchester, 172 (as Folson).

FOLSOM, C. A., see MRS. ELIZABETH A. FOLSOM.

FOLSOM, MRS. ELIZABETH A. (1812–1899). Miniaturist, NYC, exhibitor at the National Academy in 1837–38. She appears in the National Academy catalogues variously as Mrs. Folsom, Mrs. E. A. Folsom, and C. A. Folsom. Her address is the same as that of Levi Folsom, printer, teacher and grocer. She was probably Eliza A. (Freeman) Folsom, who was born in NYC December 27, 1812, married Levi Folsom November 21, 1830, and died in Westfield (N.J.) in February 1899. ¶ Cowdrey, NAD; Fielding; Bolton, *Miniature Painters;* NYCD 1833–40 (under Levi Folsom); Folsom, *Genealogy of the Folsom Family,* 478.

FOLWELL, G. Teacher of fancy drawing, Philadelphia, 1819. ¶ Brown and Brown.

FOLWELL, SAMUEL (*c.* 1765–68 to 1813). Miniaturist, silhouettist, engraver, and hair worker, who appeared in America in 1788 and during the next three years worked in Philadelphia, Baltimore, NYC, Charleston, and New Hampshire. From 1791 until his death in 1813 he worked mainly in Philadelphia, though he visited Charleston again in 1805. He was one of the exhibitors at the Columbianum in 1795. ¶ DAB; Prime, II, 9–12, 49–51; Morgan and Fielding, *Life Portraits of Washington,* 393; Stauffer; Rutledge, *Artists in the Life of Charleston; Columbianum Cat.,* 1795; repro., *Antiques* (June 1930), 516; represented at NYHS.

FONDE, C. Lithographer, New Orleans,

1848. ¶ Delgado-WPA cites *Bee,* Feb. 22, 1848.

FONTASS, JEAN. Lithographer, New Orleans, 1846. ¶ New Orleans CD 1846.

FONTELLI, L. DE. Parisian portrait painter and teacher at New Orleans, 1842. ¶ Delgado-WPA.

FOOTE, JOHN PARSONS (1783–1865). Amateur artist. Born June 26, 1783, at Guilford (Conn.), Foote went to Cincinnati (Ohio) in 1820, established the Cincinnati Type Foundry, and became editor of the *Literary Gazette.* During the visit of General Lafayette in 1825, he drew a sketch of Lafayette which is now owned by Mrs. Clement Grubb of Harrisburg (Pa.). He later became prominent in charitable, scientific, and educational organizations in Cincinnati and in 1855 published *The Schools of Cincinnati and Its Vicinity,* which included a chapter on the history of the Fine Arts in Cincinnati. He died in Cincinnati July 11, 1865. ¶ Foote, *Foote Family,* 201; Cincinnati CD 1825–53; repro., *Penna. History* (July 1952), 307.

FORA, LOUIS. Sculptor and carver, active in Charleston (S.C.) 1845–61. His work included portrait busts in marble. ¶ Rutledge, *Artists in the Life of Charleston.*

FORBES, EDWIN (1839–1895). Historical painter and etcher. Born in NYC in 1839, Forbes began studying painting at the age of 18 and was a pupil of ARTHUR F. TAIT in 1859. From 1861 to 1865 he was a staff artist for *Frank Leslie's Illustrated Newspaper.* For the rest of his life he drew upon his Civil War sketches for etchings and book illustrations. He died in Brooklyn (N.Y.) March 6, 1895. ¶ DAB; Clement and Hutton; CAB; Champlin and Perkins; *Panorama* (Nov. 1946), 30–32; Swan, BA; Cowdrey, NAD; *Album of American Battle Art,* plates 87–88, 98–99.

FORBES, ELISHA. Wood engraver, working in New Orleans in 1830 and in NYC from 1833 to 1846. ¶ Delgado-WPA cites New Orleans CD 1830; NYCD 1833–39, 1841; woodcut, 1846, NYHS Map and Print Room.

FORBES, HANNAH LUCINDA. Painter of a memorial painting on velvet, *c.* 1825. ¶ Lipman and Winchester, 172.

FORBRIGER, ADOLF or ADOLPHUS. Lithographer, of EHRGOTT & FORBRIGER, Cincinnati (Ohio), 1858–60. ¶ Cincinnati CD 1858–59, BD 1859–60; repros., *Portfolio* (Jan. 1943), 101.

FORD, A. Portrait copyist. In 1858 the Indian Gallery of the Smithsonian Institution at Washington contained seven Indian portraits painted by A. Ford in 1826, after drawings by JAMES OTTO LEWIS. *Cf.* JAMES W. FORD. ¶ McKenney and Hall, *The Indian Tribes of North America,* edited by Frederick Webb Hodge (Edinburgh, 1933), xxxvi, xlvii, xlix, li (citation courtesy Francis W. Robinson, Detroit Institute of Arts).

FORD, HENRY CHAPMAN (1828–1894). Landscape painter. Born in Livonia (N.Y.) in 1828, Ford went to Europe in 1857 for three years of study in Paris and Florence. He served one year in the Civil War and is said to have done work for the illustrated papers. After his discharge, he opened a studio in Chicago. He was a founder of the Chicago Academy of Design and in 1873 its president. In 1866 and 1869 he made trips to Colorado and in 1875 he moved to Santa Barbara (Cal.), where he died February 27, 1894. In 1883 he published *Etchings of the Franciscan Missions of California.* ¶ Taft, *Artists and Illustrators of the Old West,* 294.

FORD, JAMES (?–1781). Heraldic painter. Probably a native of Ireland, he settled in Salem (Mass.) before 1755 when he served in the Essex Regiment. In 1757 he painted the Bartlett arms (now at the Marblehead Hist. Soc.) and in 1758 he drew a plan of Salem (now in the Essex Institute). In 1761 he was working as a carpenter and from 1765 he was master of a writing school. He died June 27, 1781. ¶ Bowditch, "Early Water-Color Paintings of New England Coats of Arms," 182–183, repro.; information courtesy Dr. Harold Bowditch.

FORD, JAMES W. (?–1866). Portrait painter, probably born in Philadelphia. He exhibited at the Pennsylvania Academy in 1815 and 1820. In 1829 he visited Virginia to paint portraits of delegates to the state's constitutional convention and his advertisements appeared in Richmond papers at intervals from then until 1857. In 1850 he portrayed the members of another Virginia Constitutional Convention and from 1851 to 1853 he lived in the home of Elliotte DeJarnette of Spotsylvania County (Va.) while he painted over 20 portraits of DeJarnettes and Colemans. Ford's portrait of Black Hawk, his son, and The Prophet, painted from life in 1833, hangs in the lower lobby of the State Capitol, Richmond. The artist died in 1866 and was buried in Mount Moriah Cemetery, Philadelphia. His second wife was Ann Binney of Philadelphia; the name of his first wife is not known. ¶ Rutledge, PA; *Richmond Portraits;* information from Valentine Museum, Richmond; information from Francis W. Robinson, Detroit Institute of Arts; *Art in America,* Oct. 1934, 145.

FORD, WILLIAM. English artist, 37, at NYC in 1860. His wife was also English, but their son, Frank E., was born in New York about 1858. ¶ 8 Census (1860), N.Y., LVII, 911.

FORDHAM, ELIJAH (1798–1879). Principal wood carver employed on the Mormon Temple at Nauvoo (Ill.) in the mid-1840's. He was born March 8, 1798, in NYC; joined the Mormons in Michigan in 1833; settled in Nauvoo about 1841; moved to Utah in 1850; died in Wellsville, September 9, 1879. ¶ Arrington, *Nauvoo Temple.*

FORDHAM, GEORGE W. A NYC house and sign painter from 1834 to 1879, he exhibited a fruit piece at the American Institute in 1845 and a landscape at the National Academy in 1859. ¶ NYCD 1834–79; Am. Inst. Cat., 1845; Cowdrey, NAD.

FORDHAM, HUBBARD L. Artist. Dunlap listed H. L. Forham [*sic*] as a NYC artist in 1834 and he appears in the NYCD of that year as H. L. Fordham, portrait painter. His portraits of Mr. and Mrs. Alden Spooner of Brooklyn (N.Y.) are owned by the Long Island Historical Society. Fordham also painted portraits in Springfield (Mass.) and was a resident of Sag Harbor, Long Island (N.Y.) in 1869–70. ¶ Dunlap, *History,* II, 471; NYCD 1834; Weld, *Brooklyn Village,* frontis.; information courtesy of Mary Bartlett Cowdrey; Sears, *Some American Primitives,* 289; Long Island CD 1869–70.

FOREMAN, EDGAR W. Architect and draftsman, NYC, 1846–48. In 1848 appeared a view of NYC and environs from Williamsburg, drawn and lithographed by E. W. Foreman and ELIPHALET M. BROWN, JR. ¶ NYCD 1846; Peters, *America on Stone;* Stokes, *Historic Prints.*

FOREMAN, JOSEPH. Artist, age 19, native of Maryland, living in Baltimore in 1860. ¶ 8 Census (1860), Md., III, 329.

FOREMAN, Miss S. N. Exhibited a "composition" at the National Academy in 1854. Her NYC address was the same as that of Jonathan Foreman, hotelkeeper. ¶ Cowdrey, NAD; NYCD 1854.

FORNEY, ——. Portrait painter, Shepherdstown (Va., now W. Va.), *c.* 1840–*c.* 1860. ¶ Willis, "Jefferson County Portraits."

FORESTER, J. J. Engraver, Bangor (Maine), 1860. ¶ New England BD 1860.

FORREST, CHARLES. English engraver, 38, at NYC in 1860. His wife and four children, ages 9 to 2 years, were also born in England. ¶ 8 Census (1860), N.Y., LX, 419; NYCD 1862.

FORREST, JOHN (or Ian) B. (*c.* 1814–1870). Miniature, landscape, genre, and portrait painter, engraver, and etcher. A native of Aberdeenshire (Scotland), Forrest exhibited two engravings at the American Academy in 1833. He was at Philadelphia in 1837–39 when he exhibited at the Artists' Fund Society and at the Apollo Association (NYC). In 1846 he was in NYC. ¶ Smith; Rutledge, PA; Cowdrey, AA & AAU; NYBD 1846; Stauffer.

FORSHEY, W. Sculptor. A New Orleans youth who in 1847 began his artistic career by carving a friend's likeness out of a billiard ball. In 1850 he exhibited a marble piece, "The Offering of Innocence." He was listed as an artist in the 1851–52 directories, but thereafter as a surveyor. ¶ Delgado-WPA cites *Commercial Bulletin,* Nov. 21, 1850, and *Courier,* Dec. 12, 1850; New Orleans CD 1851–55.

FORSYTH, JOHN. Architect and lithographic draftsman, NYC, 1845–49. Listed as architect in the directories, Forsyth exhibited a lithograph at the American Institute in 1847 and in the same year was published his and E. W. MIMEE's print, "Bird's Eye View of Trinity Church, New York." ¶ NYCD 1845–49; Am. Inst. Cat., 1847; Peters, *America on Stone.*

FORSYTH, RAYMOND. Lithographer, age 33, living in Baltimore in 1850. Both he and his wife Sarah were natives of Maryland. He owned property valued at $200. ¶ 7 Census (1850), Md., VII, 626.

FORSYTH, ROBERT. Partner in the firm of CLASSEN & FORSYTH, engravers and printers, NYC, 1843. Forsyth was listed separately as a copperplate printer and WILLIAM M. CLASSEN as an engraver. ¶ NYCD 1843.

FORTINI, CHARLES. Sculptor, NYC, 1848. ¶ NYBD 1848.

FOSSETTE, H. Artist and engraver of NYC views published between 1831 and 1834. ¶ Stokes, *Historic Prints,* p. 71, 74; Fay, *Views in New York;* Stauffer.

FOSTER, CHARLES. Engraver at Cincinnati,

1842–50. ¶ Information courtesy Edward H. Dwight, Cincinnati Art Museum.

FOSTER, CHARLES ANDREW (1817–1886). Portrait, genre, and animal painter. He was born April 29, 1817, in Kingston (Mass.), worked in Boston in the 1840's, and settled in 1850 in Providence (R.I.), where he lived until shortly before his death in 1886 at Kingston (Mass.). ¶ "Brief Notes on Deceased Artists," 111; *Kingston Vital Records, Births;* Swan, BA; Boston CD 1841, 1843; Providence CD 1850–60.

FOSTER & EMMONS. Wood engravers, Boston, 1842; JOHN R. FOSTER and GEORGE EMMONS. ¶ Boston CD 1842.

FOSTER, GIDEON, JR. Portrait painter, active in Essex County (Mass.) in 1824. ¶ Belknap, *Artists and Craftsmen,* 9.

FOSTER, HENRY W. Engraver, age 35, living in Boston in 1860. Foster was a native of Massachusetts and his wife Caroline (37) was from Maine. ¶ 8 Census (1860), Mass., XXVII, 625.

FOSTER, J., see JOHNSON W. FOSTER.

FOSTER, JOHN (1648–1681). Wood block engraver and portrait painter (?). A native of Dorchester (Mass.), Foster graduated from Harvard in 1667, taught school in Dorchester, and in 1675 became Boston's pioneer printer. He took up engraving as early as 1671, his wood block engraving of the Rev. Richard Mather being the earliest portrait engraving known to have been made in America. Foster also engraved a view of Boston and Charlestown and is said to have painted portraits. He died in Dorchester, September 9, 1681, at the age of 33. ¶ The standard life is Samuel Abbot Green's *John Foster, The Earliest American Engraver and the First Boston Printer* (Boston, 1909). See also: DAB; Middlebrook, "A Few of the New England Engravers," 361; Barker, *American Painting,* 29–30, repro. 31; Stauffer, I, 87–90.

FOSTER, JOHN R. Engraver, Boston, 1840–45. He was probably the senior partner in the firm of FOSTER & EMMONS. ¶ Boston CD 1840, 1844; BD 1845.

FOSTER, JOHNSON W. Portrait painter, Boston, 1840–43. He was probably the J. Foster who exhibited at the Boston Athenaeum in 1840. ¶ Boston CD 1840, 1842–43; Swan, BA.

FOSTER, JOSEPH. Artist, Philadelphia, 1846–50. ¶ Phila. CD 1846–50.

FOSTER, SAMUEL B. Portrait painter working in Boston from about 1833 to 1857 and in Concord (N.H.) in 1860. In 1834 he exhibited four portraits at CHESTER HARDING's exhibition hall in Boston, and he also exhibited at the Boston Athenaeum in 1842 and 1846. He was listed as a dealer in fancy goods from 1837 to 1840. ¶ Boston CD 1833–40, 1843, BD 1844, 1853–57; Concord CD 1860; Swan, BA; Doughty, "Thomas Doughty," 49.

FOULQUIER, V. Engraver, with TRICHON; their work appeared in *Faggots for the Fireside* (New York, 1855). ¶ Hamilton, *Early American Book Illustrators and Wood Engravers,* 180.

FOURCADE, ANACHARSIS. Artist, teacher of drawing and painting. A Frenchman, Fourcade taught in Charleston (S.C.) in 1845–46 and in 1850 was living in Louisville (Ky.). In 1850 he was 37 years old; his wife Eliza, age 25, was from Georgia. ¶ Rutledge, *Artists in the Life of Charleston;* 7 Census (1850), Ky., XI, 350.

FOURCADE, JOSEPH. Portrait and miniature painter, teacher of painting, at New Orleans in 1818 and 1820. *Cf.* —— Fourcade, miniaturist working in southern France in 1830. ¶ Delgado-WPA cites *Courier,* Feb. 13, 1818, and *Gazette,* Nov. 7, 1820; Thieme-Becker.

FOURNIER, JOSEPH. Miniaturist and architect, drawing master, at Charleston (S.C.) 1770–72. In 1772 he also visited Georgia. ¶ Prime, I, 3; Rutledge, *Artists in the Life of Charleston;* Bowes, *The Culture of Early Charleston,* 110.

FOWLE, EDWARD A. Engraver, Boston, 1847–56. ¶ Boston BD and CD 1847–56; Stauffer.

FOWLE, ISAAC. Ship carver, Boston, 1806–43. Fowle served his apprenticeship under SIMEON SKILLIN, JR., of Boston and, after the latter's death in 1806, occupied his shop with EDMUND RAYMOND until *c.* 1822. In 1833 Fowle took into partnership his sons JOHN D. and WILLIAM H. FOWLE. Two examples of his work are now in the Old State House, Boston, one the figure of a woman. ¶ Pinckney, 131; Swan, "Boston's Carvers and Joiners, Part II," 283; Harris, "American Ship Figureheads," 11; Lipman, *American Folk Art,* 12.

FOWLE, JOHN D. Ship carver, Boston, 1833–1869. John D. and his brother WILLIAM H. FOWLE entered into partnership with their father ISAAC FOWLE in 1833. After the father's retirement in 1843, the brothers continued the business. Their known work included an eagle and coat of arms of New York for the *Surprise* (1850) and a crowing cock for the *Game Cock* (1851). ¶ Swan, "Boston's Carvers and Joiners, Part II," 283–284; Pinckney, 131.

FOWLE, WILLIAM BENTLEY (1795–1865). Author of several drawing books. One of the pioneers of modern education, William B. Fowle was born in Boston October 17, 1795, and devoted his life to the liberalization of educational methods in Boston. Among his many educational works were the following: *An Introduction to Linear Drawing* (Boston, 1828); *The Eye and the Hand* (Boston, 1847); and *Principles of Linear and Perspective Drawing* (New York, 1866). He died in Medford (Mass.) February 6, 1865. ¶ DAB; CAB; Union Cat., L. C.

FOWLE, WILLIAM H. Ship carver, Boston, 1833–early 1860's. He worked with his father ISAAC and his brother JOHN D. FOWLE, and died in Lexington (Mass.) soon after 1860. ¶ Swan, "Boston's Carvers and Joiners, Part II," 283; Pinckney, 131.

FOWLER, Mrs. Teacher of bird, flower, and fruit painting; at Richmond (Va.) in January 1829 and in Charleston (S.C.) in October 1829. ¶ *Richmond Portraits;* Rutledge, *Artists in the Life of Charleston.*

FOWLER, EDWARD W. Engraver, Boston, 1854–55; in the latter year as a member of the firm of STUART & FOWLER. ¶ Boston CD 1854–55.

FOWLER, GEORGE W. Engraver, Boston, 1852. ¶ Boston CD 1852.

FOWLER, J., see TREVOR THOMAS FOWLER.

FOWLER, TREVOR THOMAS. Portrait and genre painter. He first appears as exhibitor of a portrait at the Royal Academy in 1829. From 1830 to 1835 he exhibited 35 portraits at the Royal Hibernian Academy in Dublin. By 1837 he had come to New York City, where he exhibited at the National Academy 1837–38. In 1840 he did portraits of Harrison and Clay. He then went to New Orleans. Returning to Europe *c.* 1842, Fowler studied in Paris and in 1843 and 1844 exhibited in Dublin. He returned to New Orleans in the fall of 1844 and worked there and in Cincinnati apparently until *c.* 1853. From 1854 to 1869 he lived in Germantown and Philadelphia and was a frequent exhibitor at the Pennsylvania Academy. ¶ Strickland, *Dictionary of Irish Artists;* Graves, *Dictionary;* Cowdrey, NAD; New Orleans *Picayune,* Oct. 16, 1840, *Commercial Bulletin,* Dec. 12, 1840, New Orleans CD 1841 (all cited by Delgado-WPA); Cowdrey, AA & AAU; *Picayune,* Nov. 30, 1844, Feb. 28, 1845, Dec. 27, 1849 (as J. Fowler), Jan. 30, 1852 (all cited by Delgado-WPA); Rutledge, PA; Phila. CD 1856–60; Thieme-Becker; Fielding; information courtesy Edward H. Dwight, Cincinnati Art Museum.

FOX, ADAM. Wood engraver, 27, a native of New York, at NYC in 1860. ¶ 8 Census (1860), N.Y., XLIII, 631.

FOX, B. K. Delineator of views in and near Philadelphia, *c.* 1820, engraved by J. LYBRAND. Listed in Philadelphia directories 1828–35. ¶ Larsen, *American Historical Views;* Phila. CD 1828–35; Stauffer, under Lybrand.

FOX, FREDERICK E. Wood engraver, Boston, 1852 and after. ¶ Boston CD 1852–60 and after.

FOX, GEORGE WALTER. Portrait painter, Boston, 1854. ¶ Boston BD 1854.

FOX, GILBERT (1776–*c.* 1806). Engraver and illustrator; born in London, 1776; came to America *c.* 1793; worked in Philadelphia, NYC (1800–01), and Boston; died *c.* 1806. About 1798 he was listed as a comedian. ¶ DAB; *American Collector* (Nov. 1939), 8 and frontis.; Stauffer; NYCD 1800–01; *Antiques* (Apr. 1946), 201, repro.; Sellers, *Charles Willson Peale,* II, 74–75.

FOX, JUSTUS (1736–?). Engraver. Born in Mannheim (Germany) in 1736, Fox came to Pennsylvania before the Revolution and was apprenticed to Christopher Sower, Jr., printer of Germantown. He later took over Sower's type foundery in Germantown, where he was active until 1805, not only as a type founder and engraver, but also as a physician, farrier, cutler, ink and lampblack maker, and tanner. ¶ Thomas, *History of Printing in America;* Weiss, "The Growth of the Graphic Arts in Philadelphia," 79; Brown and Brown.

FOY, FLORVILLE. Sculptor in marble, New Orleans, 1841–56. ¶ New Orleans CD 1841–42, 1846, 1852–56.

FOY, PROSPER. Marble cutter, sculptor, gilder, gnomist, and engraver, New Orleans, 1825–38. ¶ Delgado-WPA cites *La. Gazette,* Nov. 8, 1825, and *Bee,* Aug. 6, 1835, and New Orleans CD 1830, 1832, 1838; Pinckney, 192.

FRANÇA, MANUEL JOACHIM DE (1808–1865). Portrait, historical, and religious painter. Born either in Funchal (Madeira) or Oporto (Portugal), settled in Philadelphia *c.* 1830, and worked there until *c.* 1842, during which time he exhibited at the Pennsylvania Academy, Artists' Fund Society, Apollo Association, and National Academy. By 1847 he had moved to St. Louis (Mo.) where he remained until his death on August 22, 1865. Among his works was a portrait of Henry Clay. ¶ St. Louis *Daily Democrat,* Aug. 22, 1865; information at FARL from an anonymous acquaintance of de França gives Funchal as birthplace; Sartain, *Reminiscences,* 175–76, gives Oporto as birthplace; Rutledge, PA; Phila. CD 1839–42 (cited by Miss Margaret L. Bailey); Cowdrey, AA & AAU; Cowdrey, NAD; Rutledge, MHS; WPA Guide, *Missouri; Carnegie Magazine* (June 1946), 42, repro.

FRANCIS, ARTHUR W. Seal engraver, NYC, 1845–77; exhibited stone seal engravings at the American Institute in 1850, 1851, and 1856. He was born in England about 1809 and came to America after 1836. ¶ NYCD 1845–77; Am. Inst. Cat., 1850–51, 1856; 7 Census (1850), N.Y., XLI, 758; 8 Census (1860), N.Y., XLVI, 86.

FRANCIS, GEORGE (1790–1873). Portrait and landscape painter. A lifelong resident of Hartford (Conn.), Francis studied under BENJAMIN WEST and WASHINGTON ALLSTON but was obliged to give up his artistic career to carry on the family business of carriage-making. He continued to paint, however, as an amateur. ¶ French, 46–47; Smith.

FRANCIS, JOHN F. (1808–1886). Portrait and still life painter, silhouettist; born in Philadelphia *c.* 1808 and living there in 1840–41 when he first exhibited at the Artists' Fund Society. During the next 25 years he painted in many Pennsylvania towns—Pottstown, Harrisburg, Lewisburg, Bellefonte, Pottsville, Sunbury, Northumberland, and Milton, as well as in Delaware, Washington (D.C.) and Nashville (Tenn.). His last 20 years were spent in Jeffersonville (Pa.), where he died November 15, 1886. His still lifes were of the 17th century Dutch "luncheon piece" type. ¶ Frankenstein, "J. F. Francis," list of portraits and 9 repros.; Frankenstein, *After the Hunt,* 32, 135–137, plates 106, 111; Rutledge, PA; Phila. BD 1850; Karolik Cat.; Richardson, *American Romantic Painting;* Fielding (wrong dates); Washington Art Assoc. Cat., 1857.

FRANCK, JACOB W. Painter, NYC, 1850's. In 1857 he was of the firm of FRANCK & MOELLER, portrait painters. ¶ NYBD 1857; NYCD 1856–58.

FRANCK & MOELLER. Portrait painters, NYC, 1857; see JACOB W. FRANCK and CHARLES MOELLER. ¶ NYBD 1857.

FRANÇOIS, ALEXANDER (1824–1912). Portrait, genre, and landscape painter. A native of Belgium, he settled in NYC in 1841, was still there in 1851, when he exhibited at the National Academy, and later lived in Rochester and Albany (N.Y.). He died March 1, 1912, in Albany. ¶ *Art Annual,* X (1913), 77, obit.; Cowdrey, NAD; Albany CD 1859–60.

FRANK, JAMES. Engraver, Chicago, 1855. ¶ *Chicago Almanac* 1855.

FRANKENSTEIN, ELIZA. Amateur landscape painter. Youngest of the artistic Frankenstein family of Cincinnati and Springfield (Ohio). She often accompanied her brother GODFREY N. FRANKENSTEIN on his sketching trips, including his 1871 visit to New Hampshire. She was still living in Springfield in 1881, an accomplished botanist and musician, as well as landscape painter. ¶ Martin, "The City of Springfield," 494, 496.

FRANKENSTEIN, GEORGE L. Portrait and landscape painter. He was a younger brother of JOHN P. and GODFREY N. FRANKENSTEIN and assisted the latter in painting a panorama of the Falls of Niagara. Probably born in Germany, he grew up in Cincinnati and lived for a number of years in Springfield (Ohio). In 1875 he moved to NYC where he worked for over twenty years as an artist and journalist. He was living as late as 1901. ¶ Martin, "The City of Springfield," 496; N. Y. *Herald,* July 17, 1853 (cited by J. E. Arrington); NYCD 1875–1901; *Biographical Record of Clark County, Ohio,* 818.

FRANKENSTEIN, GODFREY N. (1820–1873). Landscape and portrait painter; born in Germany September 8, 1820, and brought to Cincinnati (Ohio) by his parents in 1831, along with his brothers JOHN P., GEORGE L., and GUSTAVUS, and his sisters MARIE M. C. and ELIZA FRANKENSTEIN, all of whom became artists. Apprenticed to a sign painter in 1832, he set up his own business the following year at the age of 13 and continued as a sign painter until 1839 when he opened a portrait studio in Cincinnati. In 1841 he became the first president of the Cincinnati Academy of Fine Arts. He soon became interested in landscape painting and, after his first visit to Niagara Falls in 1844, devoted himself mainly to paintings of the

Falls, the White Mountains of New Hampshire, and the Ohio countryside. The Frankensteins moved to Springfield (Ohio) in 1849 and there Godfrey, assisted by GEORGE L. and GUSTAVUS, painted his panorama of Niagara Falls which was shown in Philadelphia and NYC in 1853 and the following year in Cincinnati. From 1867 to 1869 Godfrey and Gustavus were in Europe, and in 1871 Godfrey made his last sketching trip to the White Mountains with his sister ELIZA. He died in Springfied on February 24, 1873. ¶ Martin, "The City of Springfield," 493–496; Cist, *Cincinnati in 1841,* 141–142; Rutledge, PA; Cowdrey, AA & AAU; Cowdrey, NAD; Oakes, *Scenery of the White Mountains* (1848), repro.; Cincinnati CD 1840–49; Springfield CD 1852, 1863, 1873; Cist (1851); Cist (1859); N. Y. *Herald,* July 17, 1853 and Aug. 31, 1853, Phila. *Public Ledger,* Dec. 8, 1853, Cincinnati *Daily Gazette,* Oct. 12, 1854 (all cited courtesy J. E. Arrington); *Harper's New Monthly Magazine* (Aug. 1853), 289–305, repros. of Niagara Falls studies; Ford, *History of Cincinnati,* 239; *Ohio State Arch. and Hist. Quarterly* (Jan. 1948), opp. 48.

FRANKENSTEIN, GUSTAVUS. Landscape and marine painter. Gustavus, youngest of the Frankenstein brothers, was probably born in Germany, but grew up in Cincinnati (Ohio). In 1849 he moved with his family to Springfield (Ohio), where he became a teacher in the Female Academy. About 1850 he assisted his brother GODFREY in painting a panorama of Niagara Falls and in 1867 he accompanied Godfrey on a two-year sketching tour in Europe. Better known as a mathematician and scientist, Gustavus was an amateur painter who specialized in seacoast and marine views. Except for a brief residence in NYC *c.* 1876, he spent most of his life in Springfield and in Cincinnati, where he died before 1902. ¶ Martin, "The City of Springfield," 493–496; Springfield CD 1863; N. Y. *Herald,* July 17, 1853 (cited courtesy J. E. Arrington); *Biographical Record of Clark County, Ohio,* 818.

FRANKENSTEIN, JOHN PETER (*c.* 1816–1881). Portrait and historical painter, sculptor. John P., oldest of the Frankenstein family of artists, was born in Germany in 1816 or 1817, came to Cincinnati in 1831 and began to paint portraits at the age of 15. By 1839 he had moved to Philadelphia and during the next five years he exhibited a number of portraits at the Artists' Fund Society and the Apollo Association. By 1847 he had returned to Cincinnati and two years later he moved with his family to Springfield (Ohio). His interest turning from portrait painting to portrait sculpture, he returned to Cincinnati in 1856 and had a studio there until his removal to NYC about 1875. In 1864 he published a long poem, very critical of American art, entitled "American Art, Its Awful Altitude." He spent his last years as an apparently poverty-stricken recluse in East New York (N.Y.) and died there on April 16, 1881. After his death a considerable amount of money was found in his debris-littered rooms, which the *New York Times* described in an article entitled "The Miserable End of the Life of John Frankenstein Artist." ¶ Dwight, "John P. Frankenstein"; N. Y. *Times,* April 17, 1881; Martin, "The City of Springfield," 493–496; Cist (1841); Rutledge, PA; Cowdrey, AA & AAU; Cincinnati CD 1836, 1840, 1845–46, 1856–60; Cowdrey, NAD; Cist (1851), 123–24; Cist (1859); WPA (Ohio), *Annals of Cleveland; American Art Review,* II (1881), pt. 2, 44; Clark, *Ohio Art and Artists;* Taft, *History of American Sculpture;* Gardner, *Yankee Stonecutters.*

FRANKENSTEIN, MARIE M. C. Amateur painter and modeller. Like the rest of the Frankenstein family, Marie was born in Germany and brought to Cincinnati in 1831. A public school teacher there and in Springfield (Ohio), she was also an amateur artist of local reputation. She was still in Springfield in 1881. ¶ Martin, "The City of Springfield," 496; Springfield CD 1873; Cist, *Cincinnati in 1859,* 202.

FRANKLIN, BENJAMIN (1706–1790). American statesman and scientist (see biographies by Carl Van Doren and others). The Corcoran Gallery in Washington owns several of his drawings, classical in subject, one of them dated September 25, 1782, when he was in France as U. S. Minister. ¶ Information courtesy Corcoran Gallery.

FRANKLIN, JAMES M. Engraver, age 16, living in Philadelphia in 1850; a native of Pennsylvania. ¶ 7 Census (1850), Pa., LV, 577.

FRANKLIN, RICHARD. Engraver; born in London about 1831; living in NYC with his wife and one child in 1860. ¶ 8 Census (1860), N.Y., XLVII, 1009.

FRANKS, F. D. Artist at Fairfield (Ore.) in 1860; born in Pennsylvania in 1836. ¶ David C. Duniway cites 1860 Census, Oregon.

FRANKS, FREDERICK. Swedish artist who studied at Dresden and Munich (Germany) before emigrating to America and settling in Cincinnati (Ohio) in the early 1820's. He was listed as a portrait painter in 1825, artist 1829, thereafter as proprietor of a painting gallery and museum. About 1835 Franks took over Dorfeuille's Western Museum, which he conducted until about 1860. Franks was a painter of grotesque scenes such as the "Infernal Regions" for which the Western Museum was noted. He is also said to have been the instructor of a number of Cincinnati artists, including MINER K. KELLOGG, JAMES H. and WILLIAM H. BEARD, and J. R. JOHNSTON. ¶ Cincinnati CD 1825–59; Ford, *History of Cincinnati,* 237–238; Greve, *Centennial History of Cincinnati,* I, 643.

FRANKS, WILLIAM. Miniaturist, NYC, 1795–98. Possibly the same as William Franks of London who exhibited an example of hair work at the Society of Artists in 1776. ¶ NYCD 1795–98; Graves, *Dictionary.*

FRANQUINET, WILLIAM HENDRIK (1785–1854). Portrait and historical painter, lithographer; born in Maestricht (Holland) on Christmas Day, 1785, and passed the early part of his career in Holland, Germany, and France. From 1831 to 1836 he was in London, exhibiting at a number of London galleries, as well as at the Boston (Mass.) Athenaeum in 1834. By 1840 he had come to America and was working in Washington (D.C.). From 1842 to 1846 and 1849 to 1851 he was listed in NYC directories (in *The Gem* of 1844 as J. Franquinet) and he died there December 12, 1854. He exhibited at the Apollo Association and American Art-Union, National Academy, and Pennsylvania Academy. ¶ Thieme-Becker; Graves, *Dictionary;* Cowdrey, AA & AAU; Swan, BA; NYCD 1842–45, 1849–51; NYBD 1846; Cowdrey, NAD; Rutledge, PA; *The Gem* (N.Y., 1844).

FRANQUINET, JAMES. French artist, 54, at NYC in 1850. ¶ 7 Census (1850), N.Y., XLIV, 271.

FRANZET, LOUIS. Artist, NYC, 1850. ¶ NYCD 1850.

FRANZONI, CARLO (1789–1819). Sculptor. A native of Carrara (Italy), he came to the United States to take the place of his deceased brother, GIUSEPPE FRANZONI, as sculptor at the U. S. Capitol in Washington. His chief work there was the "Car of History." He died in Washington May 12, 1819. ¶ Fairman, *Art and Artists of the Capitol,* 26 (portrait), 43 (repro.), 72–74, 476.

FRANZONI, GIUSEPPE (?–1815). Sculptor from Carrara (Italy), where his father was an official of the Art Museum. In 1806 he came to the United States with GIOVANNI ANDREI to undertake the sculptured decorations of the U. S. Capitol in Washington. Franzoni worked in Washington and Baltimore until his death in Washington on April 6, 1815. His place was taken by his brother CARLO FRANZONI who arrived in 1816 along with FRANCISCO IARDELLA, who married the widow of Giuseppe Franzoni. ¶ Borneman, "Franzoni and Andrei: Italian Sculptors in Baltimore, 1808"; Fairman, *Art and Artists of the Capitol,* 5–25, 29, 476.

FRASER, ARCHIBALD. Artist, NYC, 1848. ¶ NYBD 1848.

FRASER, CHARLES (1782–1860). Portrait, miniature, and landscape painter; a lifelong resident of Charleston (S.C.), where he was born August 20, 1782. He studied law and practised from 1807 to 1818, but thereafter devoted himself to painting. He was a good friend of THOMAS SULLY, WASHINGTON ALLSTON, and EDWARD MALBONE and made many summer visits in the northern states. His work was exhibited frequently at the Boston Athenaeum, as well as in Charleston, Philadelphia, and NYC, and some of his landscapes were engraved as early as 1816–18. A one-man show was held in his honor in Charleston in 1857. Fraser died in Charleston October 5, 1860. ¶ The standard works are Smith and Smith, *Charles Fraser* and Carolina Art Assoc., *Short Sketch of Charles Fraser . . .* Other sources include: Tolman, "The Technique of Charles Fraser, Miniaturist"; Rutledge, *Artists in the Life of Charleston;* DAB; Swan, BA; Cowdrey, NAD; Cowdrey, AA & AAU; *Analectic Magazine* (1816), 264, (1817), 88, 176, (1818), frontis. and title-page vignette; Fraser, *Reminiscences of Charleston;* Smith, *A Charleston Sketch Book, 1796–1806;* Bolton, *Miniature Painters;* Wehle and Bolton.

FRASER, J. Engraver and patent agent, Elmira (N.Y.), 1857. ¶ Elmira BD 1857.

FRASER, JOHN. Architectural draftsman,

Philadelphia; exhibited at the Pennsylvania Academy in 1858. ¶ Rutledge, PA.

FRASER, JOHN (1750–1811). Botanical artist. A native of Scotland, Fraser moved to London in 1770 and there had a hosiery and drapery shop. He became interested in botany and between 1780 and 1806 made at least eight trips to America, from Newfoundland to Cuba and including at least two visits to Charleston (S.C.) in 1784–86. He contributed a plate of "the new Auriculated Magnolia" to his friend Thomas Walter's *Flora Caroliniana* (London, 1788). He died in London, April 26, 1811. ¶ DNB; Rutledge, *Artists in the Life of Charleston.*

FRASER, Miss O. H. Wood engraver, Binghamton (N.Y.), 1859. An O. H. Fraser, wood engraver, was also listed at Elmira (N.Y.) the same year. ¶ N. Y. State BD 1859.

FRAUBEL, M. Lithographer, Philadelphia, 1853. ¶ Phila. BD 1853.

FRAUENBERGER, G. Wood engraver, Rochester (N.Y.), 1859. ¶ N. Y. State BD 1859.

FRAZEE, JOHN (1790–1852). N.A. Sculptor. One of the pioneer sculptors of America, John Frazee was born in Rahway (N.J.) July 18, 1790, and took up stonecutting about 1810. After working in Rahway and New Brunswick (N.J.) for several years, he and his brother opened a marble-shop in NYC in 1818. John specialized in funereal sculpture until the 1830's, when he did a number of portrait busts of distinguished Americans, including Webster, Marshall and Story. During the 1830's he worked in partnership with ROBERT E. LAUNITZ. From 1834 to 1841 he was chiefly occupied with the New York Custom House, of which he was the architect. He died in Crompton Mills (R.I.) February 24, 1852. He was a founder of the National Academy. ¶ DAB; Dunlap; Cummings, *Historic Annals;* Cowdrey, NAD; Cowdrey, AA & AAU; Swan, BA; Rutledge, PA; 7 Census (1850), N.Y., XLVI, 196. Frazee's autobiography was published in the *North American Magazine,* April 1835, 395–403, and July 1835, 1–22, and excerpts from it in *American Collector,* Sept. 1946, 15–16, Oct. 1946, 10–11, and Nov. 1946, 12–13; a manuscript copy of the autobiography is in the New Jersey Historical Society. An MA thesis on Frazee by Henry Bryan Caldwell is on file at New York University.

FRAZEE & LAUNITZ. Sculptors and stonecutters, NYC, 1831–*c.* 1837; see JOHN FRAZEE and ROBERT E. LAUNITZ. ¶ NYCD 1831–37; DAB.

FRAZEE, P. F. Portrait painter. Sherman reported a portrait of a young man, found in Bernardsville (N.J.), signed and dated "P. F. Frazee 1834 Painted." ¶ Sherman, "Unrecorded Early American Portrait Painters" (1933), 28.

FRAZER & DENNIS. Wood engravers, Cincinnati (Ohio), 1850–59; EPHRAIM P. FRAZER and JULIAN N. DENNIS. ¶ Cincinnati BD 1850–51, CD 1856–58, BD 1859.

FRAZER, EPHRAIM P. Wood engraver, of FRAZER & DENNIS, Cincinnati (Ohio), 1850–59; born in Ohio about 1829. ¶ Cincinnati BD 1850–51, 1853, 1859, CD 1856–58; 7 Census (1850), Ohio, XXI, 134.

FRAZER, JOHN. Portrait and genre painter, Poughkeepsie (N.Y.); exhibitor at the National Academy and American Art-Union, 1848–50. ¶ Cowdrey, NAD; Cowdrey, AA & AAU.

FRAZER, OLIVER (1808–1864). Portrait painter. Born February 4, 1808, in Fayette County (Ky.), Oliver Frazer received his first instruction in art from MATTHEW JOUETT of Lexington (Ky.) and then went to Philadelphia to study with THOMAS SULLY. In 1834 he went to Europe with G. P. A. HEALY and studied for four years in Paris, Berlin, Florence, and London. On his return to America in 1838, he settled in Lexington (Ky.) where he had a successful career as a portraitist until his death February 9, 1864. ¶ DAB; Price, *Old Masters of the Bluegrass,* 93–124; *Antiques* (Nov. 1947), 347, repro.

FRAZER, THOMAS. Designer, age 22 and a native of Pennsylvania, living in Philadelphia in August 1850. ¶ 7 Census (1850), Pa., LVI, 343.

FRAZIER, ——. In his autobiography CHARLES WILLSON PEALE mentioned an amateur painter, brother of Joshua Frazier, at Norfolk (Va.) in 1763. Peale thought Frazier's landscapes and a portrait "miserably done." ¶ Sellers, *Charles Willson Peale,* I, 49; Dunlap, *History,* I, 131.

FREDENBURG, GEO. American still life painter in water colors, active *c.* 1830. ¶ Lipman and Winchester, 172.

FREDERICK, CHARLES. German lithographer, 32, at NYC in 1850. ¶ 7 Census (1850), N.Y., XLIII, 536.

FREDERICK, JOHN L. Engraver; born in Pennsylvania between 1797 and 1800; active as an engraver and book illustrator in Philadelphia from 1818 until sometime after 1860. His property was valued in 1860 at $10,000 in realty and $1,000 in personalty. He is said to have died about 1880 or 1881. His son, MONTGOMERY L. FREDERICK, also was an engraver. ¶ 7 Census (1850), Pa., LI, 815; 8 Census (1860), Pa., LV, 711; Stauffer; Phila. CD 1818–60.

FREDERICK, MONTGOMERY L. Engraver, Philadelphia, 1849–60 and after. In 1850 he was 24 years of age and lived with his father, JOHN L. FREDERICK, also an engraver. ¶ Phila. CD 1849–60 and after; 7 Census (1850), Pa., LI, 815.

FREDERICKS, ALFRED. A.N.A. Landscape and figure painter, illustrator. A resident of NYC, he exhibited at the National Academy in 1853 and 1856 and at the Pennsylvania Academy from 1862 to 1869. A number of his paintings were drawn from the plays of Shakespeare. Fredericks also contributed comic illustrations to magazines and illustrated many books between 1864 and 1881. ¶ Cowdrey, NAD; Rutledge, PA; Hamilton, 261–264.

FREDERYCKS, KRYN. Sent out to New Amsterdam in 1625 by the West India Company to construct fortifications and houses in the Dutch settlement, Frederycks may have been the delineator of the so-called Hartgers view of Manhattan *c.* 1626–28. ¶ Stokes, *Icon.*, I, 133–135, plate 1.

FREELAND, ANNA C. (1837–1911). Historical painter, represented at the Worcester (Mass.) Art Museum by her "William the Conqueror." ¶ Fielding; Smith.

FREELAND, O. S. Portrait painter, born in New York about 1820. He exhibited a portrait of Henry Clay at the Maryland Historical Society in 1848, was working in Philadelphia in 1848 and also in 1859–60, and exhibited at the Pennsylvania Academy in 1848 and 1859. He also had a studio in Lancaster (Pa.) at some time. He is last heard of in Baltimore in 1879. ¶ 8 Census (1860), Pa., LII, 729; Rutledge, MHS; Rutledge, PA; Lancaster County Hist. Soc., *Portraiture in Lancaster County,* 125; Lafferty.

FREELAND, THEODORE. Engraver, 23, a native of Pennsylvania, at NYC in 1860. ¶ 8 Census (1860), N.Y., XLIII, 382.

FREELY, JOHN. Engraver and die-sinker, NYC, 1850. ¶ NYBD 1850.

FREEMAN, Miss ANNA MARY. Portrait and miniature painter, who exhibited at the National Academy from 1846 to 1859, her address in 1851 and 1855–57 being the same as that of GEORGE FREEMAN, presumably her father. ¶ Cowdrey, NAD; NYCD 1855–57.

FREEMAN, BRADFORD. Artist, Boston, 1860 and after. In 1860 he was 21 years old and resided with his parents, William and Elizabeth Freeman. ¶ 8 Census (1860), Mass., XXVIII, 81; Boston CD 1860–61.

FREEMAN, E. O., see FRANCIS O. FREEMAN.

FREEMAN, FLORENCE (1836–?). Sculptor. Miss Freeman was born in Boston, received her first training under RICHARD S. GREENOUGH, and in 1861 went to Italy with Charlotte Cushman. After a year's study in Florence under HIRAM POWERS she established a studio in Rome, where she specialized in bas-reliefs and chimney-pieces. She died after 1876. ¶ Clement and Hutton; CAB; Thieme-Becker; *Art Journal* (1866), 177.

FREEMAN, FRANCIS O. Line engraver of historical subjects, active in Boston from 1853. ¶ Boston CD 1853–61, BD 1857–60; Stauffer (as E. O. Freeman).

FREEMAN, GEORGE (1789–1868). Portrait and miniature painter; born April 21, 1789 (Bolton gives 1787), at Spring Hill (Conn.). He painted miniatures around Hartford *c.* 1810, but in 1813 left for England, where he spent the next 24 years. His English career is said to have been very successful, his sitters including Queen Victoria and Prince Albert. After his return to America, probably about 1840, Freeman worked in NYC and Philadelphia until his death, which occurred in Hartford (Conn.), March 7, 1868. ANNA MARY FREEMAN, with whom he lived in NYC in the 1850's, probably was his daughter. He exhibited at the National and American Academies, the Artists' Fund Society, and the Boston Athenaeum. ¶ French; Bolton, *Miniature Painters;* Wharton, *Heirlooms in Miniatures,* repros.; Cowdrey, NAD; Cowdrey, AA & AAU; Rutledge, PA; Swan, BA; Phila. CD 1846–48, 1850; NYCD 1842–48, 1855–57, 1863, 1868; *Richmond Portraits.*

FREEMAN, JAMES. English lithographer, 28, at NYC in 1850. ¶ 7 Census (1850), N.Y., XLVI, 823.

FREEMAN, JAMES EDWARD (1808–1884). N.A. Genre and portrait painter. Though born at Indian Island (N.B.), he spent his childhood in Otsego County (N.Y.). In 1826 he entered the National Academy in NYC as a student; he was made an Associate in 1831 and a Member of the Academy in 1833. After painting for a few years in up-state New York, he went to Europe and settled permanently in Italy, though continuing to exhibit at American galleries. From 1840 to 1849 he was American consul at Ancona, though he resided most of the time in Rome and performed his duties by proxy. Freeman published two volumes of memoirs: *Gatherings from an Artist's Portfolio* (1877) and *Gatherings from an Artist's Portfolio in Rome* (1883). He died in Rome November 21, 1884. ¶ DAB; CAB; Clement and Hutton; Champlin and Perkins; Tuckerman; Cowdrey, NAD; Rutledge, PA; Swan, BA; Albany CD 1838–39.

FREEMAN, T. W. Engraver of a mezzotint of the engagement between the *Constitution* and the *Guerriere,* published in Philadelphia in 1813 by Freeman and Pierie. Freeman and Pierie were listed as carvers and gilders in the 1813 Philadelphia directory. ¶ Grolier Club, *The United States Navy, 1776–1815,* 35; Phila. CD 1813.

FREEMAN, WALTER C. Miniaturist at Richmond (Va.) in November 1854. ¶ Information courtesy Mrs. Ralph Catterall, Valentine Museum, Richmond.

FREEMAN, WILLIAM R. (*c.* 1820–*c.* 1906). Portrait painter, born in New York State *c.* 1820. He was working in NYC in 1844, but shortly after went to Indiana, painting many portraits in Vincennes and Terre Haute in 1849 and after. He also worked in Louisville (Ky.), St. Louis (Mo.), and NYC before going to the South sometime before the Civil War. After the war he returned to Indiana and worked in Indianapolis in the early 1870's. In 1875 he moved to San Francisco. He died in St. Louis (Mo.) *c.* 1906. ¶ Burnet, *Art and Artists of Indiana,* 12–13, repro. opp. 16; NYBD 1844; NYCD 1856; Peat, *Pioneer Painters of Indiana.*

FRELINGHUYSEN, C. MARIA. A water color by this NYC amateur, signed and dated November 20, 1793, was owned in 1951 by Edgar Sittig. ¶ Information courtesy Mr. Sittig.

FRÉMONT, JOHN C. (1813–1890). Topographical draftsman. John C. Frémont, noted explorer, Civil War general and twice candidate for the presidency, provided some sketches of his own for use by JOHN SKIRVING in the latter's panorama of Frémont's overland journey to Oregon and California, shown in Boston (Mass.) in 1849. ¶ DAB; Boston *Evening Transcript,* Sept. 26, 1849 (cited by J. E. Arrington).

FRENCH, C. New England portrait painter, *c.* 1810. ¶ Lipman and Winchester, 172; WPA (Mass.), *Portraits Found in Maine,* nos. 207, 209.

FRENCH, DAVID M. (1827–1910). Sculptor. A native of Newmarket (N.H.), French was best known for his life-size statue of William Lloyd Garrison. He died April 19, 1910, in Newburyport (Mass.). ¶ *Art Annual,* VIII (1910/11), 398; Thieme-Becker.

FRENCH, GEORGE R. Engraver and plate-printer, Boston, 1852 and after. ¶ Boston CD 1852–58, BD 1858–60 and after.

FRENCH, J. H. Lithographer, Syracuse (N.Y.), 1859. ¶ N. Y. State BD 1859.

FRENCH, JOHN T. Pennsylvania-born lithographer employed by THOMAS SINCLAIR of Philadelphia. In 1846 he did some illustrations for *The North American Sylva* and during the 1850's he did fashion plates and landscapes. In 1850 he was 27 years old, living in Philadelphia with his wife Sarah and two daughters. ¶ 7 Census (1850), Pa., L, 989; McClinton, "American Flower Lithographs," 362; Peters, *America on Stone;* Phila. CD 1850–52.

FRERE, THOMAS. Engraver, NYC, 1850's. ¶ NYBD 1852, 1854; *American Collector* (Feb. 1948), 13, repro. of comic valentine.

FRERICHS, WILLIAM CHARLES ANTHONY (*c.* 1829–1905). Portrait painter and art teacher; born and educated in Belgium, but emigrated to America about 1852. He settled first in NYC and exhibited at the National Academy in 1852 a portrait of the Cuban filibuster Narciso Lopez. In 1854 he moved to Greensboro (S.C.), where he taught art until 1863. In 1869 he moved to Tottenville, Staten Island (N.Y.) and later to Newark (N.J.) where he conducted an art school. He died in Tottenville March 16, 1905. ¶ *Art Annual,* V (1905/06), 120; Cowdrey, NAD; NYCD 1854; Leng and Davis, *Staten Island and Its People,* V, 139; letter of Mrs. Linns M. Ellis of Washington, Ga., to NYHS, Oct. 6, 1955.

FREUDENBERG, E. G. German lithographer, 27, at NYC in 1860. ¶ 8 Census (1860), N.Y., LI, 441.

FREUND, HENRY. Engraver and die-sinker, NYC, 1851–58. ¶ NYBD 1851 (as Henry Freand); NYCD 1854–58 and NYBD 1856–58 (as Henry Freund).

FREY, HENRY. Lithographer, NYC, 1853–55. ¶ NYCD 1853, 1855; NYBD 1854.

FRIEND & AUB. Lithographers, Philadelphia, 1852 and after; NORMAN FRIEND and JACOB AUB. ¶ Phila. CD 1852–60 and after.

FRIEND, NORMAN. Lithographer, Philadelphia, 1850 and after; born in Denmark *c.* 1815. By 1850 he was married to a New Jersey girl and living in Philadelphia. About 1852 he entered into partnership with JACOB AUB. The firm of FRIEND & AUB continued until after 1860 and Friend was still working in Philadelphia in 1871. ¶ 7 Census (1850), Pa., L, 877; 8 Census (1860), Pa., LVIII, 166; Phila. CD 1850–71.

FRINCK, O. E. S. Portrait and landscape painter of Medford (Mass.), mid-19th century. ¶ Sears, *Some American Primitives,* 188, repro. 200.

FRINK, A. Delineator of a view of Minot's Ledge Lighthouse, near Cohasset (Mass.), of which a lithographic print was published in 1860. ¶ Peters, *America on Stone,* 128 (under E. Burrill).

FRITSCH, F. J. Lithographer, especially of military prints, working in NYC 1843–44. ¶ Peters, *America on Stone.*

FRITZ, JACOB. Pennsylvania potter, active *c.* 1809. His "Man on Horseback" has been reproduced. ¶ Lipman, *American Folk Art,* 21, pl. 157.

FROMHAGEN, FREDERICK N. Hair-work artist, Philadelphia, 1858–59. ¶ Phila. BD 1858–59.

FROMME, FREDERICK W. Lithographer, age 36, from Germany, at Baltimore in 1850. He was listed again at Baltimore in 1858. ¶ 7 Census (1850), Md., III, 681; Baltimore BD 1858.

FROMONT, CHARLES H. Lithographer, NYC, 1857 and after. ¶ NYCD 1857–60.

FROST, C. K. or C. R. Engraver. C. K. Frost was a Philadelphia engraver from 1843 to 1846. He was probably the same as C. R. Frost, engraver from Philadelphia, who was reported to have committed suicide in NYC on July 26, 1847 (New Orleans *Delta,* August 4, 1847). ¶ Phila. CD 1843–46; Delgado-WPA.

FROST, JOHN. Wood engraver. Frost was a teacher in Philadelphia from *c.* 1833 to 1845 and then turned publisher. In 1860 he was also listed as a wood engraver. ¶ Phila. CD 1833–60; BD 1860.

FROST, JOHN. Portrait painter, Brooklyn (N.Y.), 1857. ¶ Brooklyn BD 1857.

FROST, JOSHUA. Portrait painter, Boston, 1835. He exhibited at the Boston Athenaeum. ¶ Boston CD 1835; Swan, BA.

FROTHINGHAM, JAMES (1786–1864). N.A. Portrait painter. Born in Charlestown (Mass.), began his career in Boston, but moved to NYC in 1826. He made his home in Brooklyn (N.Y.) from about 1843 until his death, which occurred January 6, 1864. Best known for his copies of portraits by GILBERT STUART, he exhibited at the Pennsylvania Academy, Boston Athenaeum, National Academy, American Academy, and Apollo Association. He was the father of SARA C. FROTHINGHAM, miniaturist. ¶ CAB; Stokes, *Icon.,* V, 1654; Stauffer; Dunlap, *History;* Rutledge, PA; Swan, BA; Cowdrey, NAD; Cowdrey, AA & AAU; Brooklyn CD 1843, BD 1857; Sears, *Some American Primitives,* 265; Hart, "Life Portraits of Daniel Webster"; represented at Am. Antiq. Soc. (Weis) and Essex Institute (*Collections,* Oct. 1949, 329).

FROTHINGHAM, SARA C. (1821–1861). A.N.A. Miniaturist, daughter of JAMES FROTHINGHAM. She worked mainly in NYC and Brooklyn (N.Y.) between 1837 and 1845, and exhibited at the Boston Athenaeum and the National Academy, becoming an Associate of the latter in 1841. She died in NYC July 20, 1861. ¶ Cummings, *Historic Annals,* 303; Swan, BA; Cowdrey, NAD; Brooklyn CD 1843.

FRUNE, GEORGE W. Artist, Chicago, 1858. ¶ Chicago CD 1858.

FRY, BENJAMIN J. Landscape painter at Cincinnati in 1841. ¶ Information courtesy Edward H. Dwight, Cincinnati Art Museum.

FRY, WILLIAM C. Engraver, born in Pennsylvania *c.* 1822, living in Philadelphia 1850–52. His wife Hannah A. and daughter Mary E. Fry were also Pennsylvanians. ¶ 7 Census (1850), Pa., LIV, 979; Phila. CD 1851–52.

FRY, W. J. Artist from Cincinnati (Ohio) who in November 1856 won, for the third time, the first prize for painting at the Ohio State Fair. ¶ WPA (Ohio), *Annals of Cleveland.*

FRYE, WILLIAM. Portrait painter, about 30 years old, working in Huntsville (Ala.) in March 1852. ¶ WPA (Ala.), Hist. Rec. Survey cites Huntsville *Southern Advocate,* March 24, 1852.

FRYETT, Mrs. Portrait painter, Philadelphia, 1850. ¶ Phila. BD 1850.

FRYMEIER, G. (or Jacob Frymire). Portrait painter, working in the South *c.* 1799–

1806. Sherman lists a portrait found in Maryland, inscribed "Painted by Jacob Frymire/April 1799." The Chicago Historical Society owns two portraits painted in 1806 by G. Frymeier or J. Frymier, found in Galena (Ill.). ¶ Sherman, "Newly Discovered American Portrait Painters," 234; Lipman and Winchester, 173; *American Primitive Painting,* repros.; *Antiques* (Nov. 1950), 392, repros.; information H. Maxson Holloway, Chicago Hist. Soc.

FUCHS, F. Lithographer, Philadelphia, 1856. ¶ Phila. CD 1856; Peters, *America on Stone.*

FUCHS, OTTO (1839–1906). Teacher of drawing and design; born in Germany; brought to America in 1851. After working for a piano-maker and later for an architect-engineer, Fuchs became a teacher of mechanical drawing at Cooper Union, NYC. After further study in all branches of drawing and design, he became professor of drawing at the U. S. Naval Academy, Annapolis (Md.) and later a teacher of art in Boston. He went to Baltimore in 1883 to become head of the Maryland Institute School of Art and Design, a position he held until his death, March 13, 1906, at Baltimore. ¶ *Art Annual,* VI, obit.; Baltimore *Sun,* March 15, 1906, obit. and editorial.

FUCHS, THEO. Lithographer, Philadelphia, 1859. ¶ Phila. CD 1859; Peters, *America on Stone.*

FUECHSEL, HERMANN (1833–1915). Landscape painter. Born in Brunswick (Germany) in August 1833, he studied painting at Düsseldorf before coming to the United States in 1858. He settled in NYC and was a frequent exhibitor at galleries in NYC, Philadelphia, and Boston during the 1860's. He died in NYC September 30, 1915. ¶ *Art Annual,* XII, obit.; Champlin and Perkins; Cowdrey, NAD; Rutledge, PA; Swan, BA; Thieme-Becker; *Antiques* (June 1935), 229, repro.; represented at Walker Art Gallery, Minneapolis (Minn.).

FULLER, ALFRED (1817–1893). Artist; died at Boston, June 30, 1893. In 1860 he was at Walpole (Mass.). ¶ Boston *Transcript,* July 2, 1893, obit.; New England BD 1860.

FULLER, AUGUSTUS (1812–1873). Portrait painter; born at Brighton (Mass.) December 9, 1812, but moved at an early age to Deerfield. He became a deaf-mute in childhood, was educated at the American Asylum in West Brookfield (Conn.), and studied painting briefly with CHESTER HARDING. All his life Augustus Fuller followed the profession of itinerant portrait painter, working mainly in Massachusetts, western New York, New Hampshire, and Vermont. In the early 1840's he was assisted for a time by his younger half-brother GEORGE FULLER. He died at Deerfield August 13, 1873. ¶ Dods, "Connecticut Valley Painters," 207, repros.; information courtesy Clarence S. Brigham, American Antiq. Society; *Somebody's Ancestors,* repros.; *Art in America* (April 1951), 39, opp. 51, repros.

FULLER, CHARLES A. Engraver, age 21, from Maine, living in Boston in 1860. ¶ 8 Census (1860), Mass., XXV, 720; Boston CD 1860.

FULLER, GEORGE (1822–1884). A.N.A. Portrait, landscape, and figure painter; born at Deerfield (Mass.) January 17, 1822, a younger half-brother of the deaf and dumb artist AUGUSTUS FULLER. He took up painting in 1841, after accompanying Augustus on a painting tour through western New York, George returned to Boston in 1842 and worked there for six years. From 1847 to 1859 he studied in NYC and painted portraits in Philadelphia and some southern cities. In 1860 he went to Europe for six months. On his return he took over the family farm at Deerfield and for fifteen years did little painting. Resuming his artistic career in 1875 he went to Boston the following year and enjoyed great success there until his death, which occurred at Brookline (Mass.) March 21, 1884. He exhibited at the American Art-Union, Boston Athenaeum, and National Academy, and was an Associate Member of the last from 1854. ¶ Millet, ed., *George Fuller,* biographical sketch by William Dean Howells; DAB; Downes, "George Fuller's Pictures"; Sherman, "Four Figure Pictures by George Fuller"; Cowdrey, AA & AAU; Cowdrey, NAD; Swan, BA; Thieme-Becker; Champlin and Perkins; *Fine Arts Journal* (1914), 91 ff. Represented at Corcoran Gallery.

FULLER, GEORGE F. Painter of a steamboat racing scene on the Mississippi, 1859. ¶ Peters, *America on Stone.*

FULLER, I. C. or J. C. Miniaturist, NYC, 1812. ¶ McKay.

FULLER, J. Taker of profile likenesses, at Springfield (Mass.), April 1807. ¶ *Antiques* (July 1941), 37.

FULLER, JAMES. Painter of two water colors,

signed and dated 1816, of "Commodore Bainbridge Going to His Boarding House, Boston" and "General Ripley Walking on Fort Erie." ¶ *Antiques* (Dec. 1950), 429.

FULLER, RICHARD HENRY (1822–1871). Portrait artist in oils and crayon; born at Bradford (N.H.); exhibited at the Boston Athenaeum 1863, 1864; died at Chelsea (Mass.). ¶ Fielding; Swan, BA; Thieme-Becker cites *Kunstchronik* (1872), 346 ff.

FULLER, SAMUEL A. Portrait painter, Boston, 1849–50. ¶ Boston CD 1849, BD 1850.

FULLER, SAMUEL W. Landscape painter who exhibited at the National Academy 1838–39 and at the American Art-Union 1849–51. He did several up-state New York views. ¶ Cowdrey, NAD; Cowdrey, AA & AAU.

FULLER, SARAH E. (*c.* 1829–1902). Wood and steel engraver for *Harper's* and other magazines; died at Lynnbrook, Long Island (N.Y.), November 10, 1902. ¶ *Art Annual,* IV, obit; Smith; Bénézit; Mallett.

FULLER, Mrs. SUSAN E. W. (?–1907). Engraver. A student of engraving at the Cooper Union, NYC, before the Civil War, Mrs. Fuller later lived in Washington (D.C.), where she died July 6, 1907. ¶ Washington *Star,* July 7, 1907; *Art Annual,* VI, obit.

FULLERTON, NATHANIEL. A young Bostonian who painted a miniature portrait of George Washington as he appeared when reviewing the American forces on Boston Common in 1776. Fullerton died of tuberculosis a few years later. His Washington portrait was engraved by GEORGE G. SMITH in 1851. ¶ Sherman, "The Portraits of Washington from Life," 156, 157 (repro.).

FULTON, ROBERT (1765–1815). Portrait and miniature painter, born on a farm near Lancaster (Pa.) November 14, 1765. As a youth he went to Philadelphia and there supported himself by painting portraits and miniatures until he left for England in 1786, not to return to America for twenty years. He continued to paint in England for some years, exhibiting at the Society of Artists and the Royal Academy, but after 1793 he did so only for amusement, his main interest having shifted to engineering. During the remainder of his life, Fulton was occupied chiefly with projects for canals, submarines, and steamboats. After his return to the United States in 1806, he settled in NYC where, in association with Robert R. Livingston, he developed the *Clermont,* the first commercially successful steamboat (1809). He died in NYC February 24, 1815. ¶ The latest of the numerous biographies is Dickinson, *Robert Fulton, Engineer and Artist* (1913). See also: Flexner, *Steamboats Come True;* DAB; Fulton, "Robert Fulton as an Artist"; Rosenthal, "Two American Painters: West and Fulton"; Ormsbee, "Robert Fulton, Artist and Inventor"; Graves, *Dictionary;* Prime, II, 12–13; Bolton, *Miniature Painters;* Flexner, *The Light of Distant Skies.*

FULTON, Mrs. ROBERT, see HARRIET LIVINGSTON.

FUNK, JOHN. Portrait painter, born in Lancaster (Pa.) *c.* 1810–20. His portrait of his wife Ann is owned by the Lancaster County Historical Society. ¶ Courtesy the late William Sawitzky.

FURNESS (Furnass), JOHN MASON (1763–1804). Engraver and portrait painter. Born in Boston March 4, 1763; engraving as early as 1783; died in Dedham (Mass.) June 22, 1804. He was a nephew of NATHANIEL HURD. ¶ Bolton *Miniature Painters;* Stauffer; Swan, BA; Vermont, *America Heraldica, Supplement,* 16; Flexner, *The Light of Distant Skies;* represented at Brooklyn Museum.

FURNESS, WILLIAM HENRY, JR. (1827–1867). Portrait painter and crayon draftsman, born 1827 in Pennsylvania, son of William Henry, clergyman, and Anna Furness, both natives of Massachusetts. He worked in Philadelphia 1848–50, in Boston 1850–52, then went to Europe, returning to Philadelphia in 1856. He continued to work in Philadelphia at least until 1863, but died in Cambridge (Mass.) March 4, 1867. Exhibited at the Boston Athenaeum, the Pennsylvania Academy, and the National Academy, of which he was made an Honorary Member, Professional, in 1862. ¶ Swan, BA; 7 Census (1850), Pa., XXIV, 470; Bolton, *Crayon Draftsmen;* Rutledge, PA; Cowdrey, NAD; Boston CD 1850–52; Clement and Hutton; Tuckerman; Phila. CD 1859–60 and after.

FURST, MORITZ (1782–?). Medallist, engraver, and die-sinker. He was born in March 1782 at Bosing, near Presburg (Hungary), and studied die-sinking in Vienna. In 1807 the American consul at Leghorn (Italy) enlisted him as an engraver for the U. S. Mint and the following spring he arrived in Philadelphia, only to find there was no place for him at the Mint. He set up in business as a seal engraver, die-sinker, and steel engraver and remained in Philadelphia until after 1830. During this period he executed many medals for the U. S. Government, including medals honoring heroes of the War of 1812 and the Indian Peace Medals from Monroe to Van Buren. In 1833, the historian WILLIAM DUNLAP stated that Furst had been living in NYC for the past four years; in 1834 he visited Charleston (S.C.). By November 1841 he had returned to Europe. ¶ Chamberlain, "Moritz Furst, Die-sinker and Artist"; Chamberlain, "Medals Made in America by Moritz Furst"; Loubat, *Medallic History,* plates 27–52, 56–57; Thieme-Becker; Dunlap, *History;* Stauffer; Phila. CD 1809–33; Rutledge, PA.

FUSSELL, CHARLES LEWIS (1840–1909). Genre, landscape, and marine painter. Born in Philadelphia October 25, 1840, he began exhibiting at the Pennsylvania Academy in 1863, with a painting of ROTHERMEL's studio. He also exhibited at the National Academy. He was living at Media (Pa.) in 1905. ¶ Rutledge, PA; *Artists Year Book,* 71.

G

GABLE, AMOS (1840–?). Portrait painter, born February 2, 1840, at Reading (Pa.). A barber by trade, he began painting about 1860, studied painting in Germany in 1867, and gave up barbering to become a professional artist in 1875. ¶ Montgomery, *Berks County,* 810.

GACHOT, A. M. Portrait and miniature painter and teacher at New Orleans in 1817; said to have been a pupil of David at Paris. ¶ Delgado-WPA cites New Orleans *L'Ami des Lois et Journal du Soir,* Nov. 15, 1817.

GAGE, BENJAMIN F. Portrait and landscape painter, St. Johnsbury (Vt.), 1860. ¶ New England BD 1860.

GAGE, NANCY (1787–1845). Water color painter of still life, landscape, genre, and memorial pictures; lifelong resident of Bradford (Mass.). ¶ Lipman and Winchester, 173; information courtesy Mrs. Jean Lipman.

GAGLIARDI & GIAMPAOLI. Sculptors, Washington (D.C.), 1860; TOMMASO GAGLIARDI and DOMINICUS GIAMPAOLI. ¶ Washington CD 1860.

GAGLIARDI, TOMMASO (1820–1895). Sculptor. A native of Rome, Gagliardi was employed in the studio of THOMAS CRAWFORD before his emigration to the United States in 1855. From 1855 to 1858 he was employed as a sculptor at the U. S. Capitol in Washington; at this time he executed his bust of Crawford. Returning to Italy about 1860, he was active in the campaigns of Garibaldi during the decade of the sixties. Soon after 1870 he went to Japan, where he founded a school of sculpture in the Royal Academy at Tokyo. Later he went to India and there executed many portrait busts. He spent his last years in a villa near Lucca (Italy). ¶ Fairman, *Art and Artists of the Capitol,* 266–269, repro. p. 141; Washington CD 1860 (as GAGLIARDI & GIAMPAOLI).

GAINS, ——. Painter of a portrait of the Rev. James Honeyman of Newport (R.I.), engraved by S. OKEY and published at Newport in 1774. ¶ Stauffer, no. 2372; Fielding.

GAIRSHOFER, MAURICE. Engraver, NYC, 1854. ¶ NYBD 1854. See MAURICE GEIERSHOFER.

GALE, T. C. Portrait painter, working at Rochester (N.Y.) in 1843. ¶ Ulp, "Art and Artists in Rochester," 32.

GALEPPI, ALEXANDER. Sculptor and engraver, dealer in prints and carvings, at New Orleans, 1849, 1852–56. ¶ New Orleans CD 1849, 1852–56.

GALL, FREDERICK P. Engraver and diesinker, NYC, 1844. Possibly the same as F. Gall, who did one engraving for *Library of American History* (Cincinnati, *c.* 1851). ¶ NYBD 1844; Hamilton, 108.

GALLAGHER, see GULLAGER.

GALLAGHER, FERDINAND H. Engraver and lithographer, NYC; of NORTH & GALLAGHER, engravers, 1838–48; independently as lithographer in 1849. ¶ NYCD 1838–49; BD 1848.

GALLAND, JOHN. Engraver, Philadelphia, 1796–1817. ¶ Stauffer.

GALLARD, GUSTAVE. "French painter in miniature. Lately arrived" in Philadelphia, 1800. ¶ Prime, II, 13.

GALLAUDET, EDWARD (1809–1847). Engraver; born April 30, 1809, in Hartford (Conn.); died there October 11, 1847. Probably apprenticed to one of the Hartford engravers; later worked in Boston with SETH CHENEY and did his best work for the annuals *c.* 1835–40. ¶ Stauffer.

GALLAUDET, ELISHA (*c.* 1730–1805). Engraver. Born in New Rochelle (N.Y.) *c.* 1730, he was married there in 1755 and was working as an engraver in NYC in 1759, 1771, and 1774. He died in NYC in 1805. ¶ Stauffer; Mallett; Gottesman, *Arts and Crafts in New York,* I, 12.

GALLIER, JOHN. Artist, NYC, 1848. ¶ NYBD 1848.

GALT, ALEXANDER (1827–1863). Sculptor; born June 26, 1827, in Norfolk (Va.). Galt went to study in Florence in 1848, returned to Virginia in 1854, but two years later went back to Italy where he remained until 1860. Opening a studio in Richmond (Va.) in 1860, he executed busts of a number of distinguished Americans before and during the Civil War. He served on the Virginia Governor's staff and made many drawings for the Confederate Engineers during the early years of the war, but died of smallpox at Richmond, January 19, 1863. ¶ Fairman, *Art and Artists of the Capitol,* 174–75; Richmond *Dispatch,* Jan. 21, 1863, obit.; Gardner, *Yankee Stonecutters; Fine Arts*

Quarterly Review (1863), 215; Rutledge, PA; Cowdrey, AA & AAU; *Richmond Portraits.*

GALVANI, CHARLES. Portrait painter and restorer, New Orleans, 1850–60. He was born in Italy about 1805. Probably the same as Carlo Galvani, miniaturist and lithographer, working in Venice *c.* 1830. ¶ Delgado-WPA cites New Orleans CD 1850–51, 1855–56, 1858–60 and *Commercial Register,* Feb. 21, 1857; 7 Census (1850), La., IV (1), 475; Thieme-Becker; Thompson, *La. Writers.*

GAMBARDELLA, SPIRIDIONE. Portrait and landscape painter. An Italian artist, who worked in NYC in 1838–39 and exhibited at the National Academy. From 1842 to 1868 he was in London. Paintings by Gambardella were also shown at the Boston Athenaeum and the Pennsylvania Academy. ¶ Cowdrey, NAD; Swan, BA; Rutledge, PA; Graves, *Dictionary; Antiques* (Nov. 1932), frontis.

GAMBEL, W. Artist of some of the flower lithographs in THOMAS SINCLAIR's *The North American Sylva* (1846). ¶ McClinton, "American Flower Lithographs," 362.

GAMBERINI, DOMENICO. Silhouettist and painter from Ravenna (Italy), working in New Orleans in 1848. His art gallery in New Orleans included silhouettes, portraits, drawings, historical and architectural pictures, flower and landscape paintings—all by his hand. Washington, Pope Pius IX, and Zachary Taylor were among his portrait subjects. ¶ *Picayune,* Feb. 1, 1848 (cited by J. E. Arrington); *Bee,* Jan. 27, *Courier,* Feb. 2, 1848 (cited by Delgado-WPA).

GAMBLE, DAVID. Artist, Baltimore, 1839. ¶ Lafferty cites Baltimore *Sun,* April 2, 1839.

GANDOLFI, MAURO (1764–1834). Engraver and watercolorist. A native of Bologna (Italy), he studied in Italy and France, and became one of the leading engravers of Europe. In 1817 he came to NYC under contract to engrave TRUMBULL's "Declaration of Independence," but he returned to Italy almost immediately without carrying out his engagement, and taking with him as a pupil the young New York engraver WILLIAM MAIN. ¶ Thieme-Becker; Stauffer; Dunlap, *History* (as Monro Gondolfi).

GANTER, DANIEL. Portrait painter at Louisville (Ky.) in 1857. See FREDERICK GUNTER. ¶ Louisville *Journal,* Feb. 4, 1857, citation courtesy Dr. H. W. Williams, Jr., Corcoran Gallery.

GARA, MRS. ISAAC B. (born Calista Ingersoll). Portrait painter and teacher of painting in Erie (Pa.) before and after her marriage in 1853 to Isaac B. Gara, editor of the *Erie Gazette.* She exhibited at the Pennsylvania Academy in 1860. In 1898 Mrs. Gara became Vice-president of the newly organized Erie Art Club. ¶ Miller, *A Twentieth-Century History of Erie County, Pa. . . . ,* I, 838–39; *Nelson's Biographical Dictionary and Historical Reference Book of Erie County, Pa. . . . ,* 578; Rutledge, PA.

GARBEILLE, PHILIP. Sculptor. Formerly a student of Thorwaldsen at Rome, he was working at New Orleans from 1842 to 1848, then went to Mexico where he executed a bust of General Zachary Taylor. He was in NYC 1849–50, but had returned to New Orleans, via Havana, by October 1853. ¶ Delgado-WPA cites New Orleans *Courier,* July 11, 1842, May 22, 1844, *Commercial Times,* April 30 and Oct. 10, 1847, New Orleans CD 1846, and *Courier,* Oct. 1, 1853; NYBD 1849–50.

GARCIA, A. M. Theatrical scene-painter, New Orleans, 1852–54. ¶ New Orleans CD 1852–54.

GARCIA, MIGUEL. A Spanish artist who accompanied Bienville to Louisiana early in the 18th century. ¶ Looney, "Historical Sketch of Art in La.," 382.

GARDEN, FRANCIS. Engraver from London who advertised in Charleston (S.C.) in 1741 as an engraver and drawing teacher and in Boston in 1745 as an engraver and heraldic painter. ¶ Rutledge, *Artists in the Life of Charleston;* Prime, I, 19; Stauffer; Middlebrook, "A Few of the New England Engravers," 361; Bowditch, "Early Water-Color Paintings of New England Coats of Arms," 205.

GARDIN, FRANCIS. Engraver, of NICOUD & GARDIN, NYC, 1854; his home was in Hoboken (N.J.). ¶ NYBD 1854.

GARDINER, MRS. S. W. Portrait painter, Boston, 1859. ¶ Boston BD 1859.

GARDNER, B. Portrait painter, Charleston (S.C.), 1827. ¶ Rutledge, *Artists in the Life of Charleston.*

GARDNER, ELIZABETH JANE, see ELIZABETH JANE GARDNER BOUGUEREAU.

GARDNER, JAMES. Scottish artist, age 28, boarding in Washington (D.C.) in June 1860. ¶ 8 Census (1860), D.C., II, 163.

GARDNER, JOSEPH. Engraver and die-sinker;

at NYC in 1846; at Newark (N.J.) in 1850. ¶ NYBD 1846; N. J. BD 1850.

GARDNER, PATRICK. Artist and painter, New Orleans, 1841–42, 1852–56. ¶ New Orleans CD 1841–42, 1852–56.

GARDNER, SALLY. Portrait painter of Nantucket (Mass.) *c.* 1800–*c.* 1830; represented at Nantucket Historical Society. ¶ WPA (Mass.), *Portraits Found in Mass.*, II, 529; Lipman and Winchester, 173.

GARIBALDI & CORDANO. Statuary makers, Boston, 1850–51; PIETRO GARIBALDI and —— Cordano. ¶ Boston CD 1850–51.

GARIBALDI, LUCINDA, see Mrs. PIETRO GARIBALDI.

GARIBALDI, PIETRO A. Statuary maker, Boston, 1850–51. He was a native of Italy, age 32 in 1850. His wife Lucinda (age 28) was from Maine, as was their eldest child (age 7). The second child (age 5) was born in Pennsylvania, while the two youngest (ages 3 and 1) were born in Massachusetts. Garibaldi was assisted in his work by his wife (see below) and also established the firm of GARIBALDI & CORDANO (1850–51). ¶ 7 Census (1850), Mass., XXV, 31; Boston CD 1850–51.

GARIBALDI, Mrs. PIETRO A. (born Lucinda ——). Statuary maker, with her husband, Boston, 1850; she was a native of Maine, born *c.* 1822. ¶ 7 Census (1850), Mass., XXV, 31.

GARLICK, THEODATUS (1805–1884). Sculptor and wax portraitist. Born March 30, 1805, at Middlebury (?) Vt., Garlick worked as a blacksmith and stonecutter in Cleveland (Ohio) before attending the University of Maryland, where he received a medical degree in 1834. He practised surgery in Youngstown (Ohio) for many years, giving his spare time to experiments in breeding fish, inventing surgical instruments, writing, and modelling portraits in wax. He died at Bedford (Ohio), December 9, 1884. ¶ DAB; N. Y. *Tribune,* Dec. 10, 1884, obit.; Western Reserve Historical Society *Publications,* II (1886), Tract 67.

GARNERAY, AMBROSE LOUIS (1783–1857). Born in Paris on February 19, 1783, the son of a French artist, Garneray went to sea at the age of 13 and was captured by the English in 1806. On his return to France in 1814 he was patronized as a marine artist by Louis XVIII. He may later have visited the United States as he drew a number of views of American seaports *c.* 1834–35 and painted an oil of "The Battle of Lake Erie," dated 1822. He died September 11, 1857. ¶ Thieme-Becker; *Portfolio* (Oct. 1941), 3–4, (Aug.–Sept. 1944), 14–15; Stokes, *Icon.*, III, 614; Stokes, *Historic Prints* cites engravings in *Vue des Cotes de France dan l'Ocean et dans la Mediterranée* (Paris, *c.* 1830–35); represented Chicago Hist. Soc. (*American Processional,* 239, repro. 99).

GARNEREY, ——. Miniature painter and drawing master at Charleston (S.C.), 1810. ¶ Rutledge, *Artists in the Life of Charleston.*

GARRETT, ERASTUS R. Artist, NYC, 1858. ¶ NYCD 1858.

GARRETT, GEORGE. Engraver, age 24, at Cincinnati (Ohio) in 1850. His parents were English; George was born in Pennsylvania, Samuel (18) in New York, and six younger children (17 to 2) in Ohio. ¶ 7 Census (1850), Ohio, XX, 885.

GARRETT, JOHN E. Banknote engraver, born about 1817, probably in New York. His wife and four oldest children, born between 1843 and 1851, were born in New York; two children were born in Albany in 1853 and 1855; and the youngest was born in Massachusetts about 1857. In 1860 the family was in NYC, where Garrett owned property valued at over $9,000. ¶ 8 Census (1860), N.Y., LXI, 285; NYCD 1855–60.

GARRETT, JOHN W. B. Portrait painter, who was working in the South *c.* 1852, had a studio in Cincinnati (Ohio) *c.* 1853–55, and then moved to NYC, where he exhibited at the National Academy in 1857–58. ¶ Fielding; Cincinnati CD 1853, 1855; Ohio State BD 1853 (as engraver); NYBD 1856–57; Cowdrey, NAD.

GARRISON, B. Teacher of "landskip" and marine painting in watercolors, at NYC in 1782. ¶ Kelby, *Notes on American Artists.*

GARRISON, NICHOLAS, JR. Amateur artist. The son of a Moravian sea captain, Garrison served with his father on several voyages to America in the 1740's and 1750's and settled there permanently in 1757 on his marriage to Johanna, daughter of William Parsons of Philadelphia. From 1757 to 1762 he lived in Bethlehem, then in Philadelphia and Reading, served as courier among the Moravian settlements in Pennsylvania during the Revolution, and finally settled at Bethlehem in 1780. His work is known only through engravings of his views of Bethlehem, Nazareth, and the Philadelphia Alms House. The French traveller Chastellux, visiting Bethlehem in 1780, described Garrison as "a seaman who imagined he had some talent for drawing, and amused himself with teaching the young people. . . ." ¶ Levering, *History of Bethlehem;* Stokes, *Historical Prints,* 22–23; *Magazine of Art* (April 1939), 222, repro.

GARRITY, JAMES. Irish engraver, 28, at NYC in 1860. ¶ 8 Census (1860), N.Y., LX, 140.

GARROW, JAMES. Irish artist, 18, at NYC in 1850. He was living with JAMES BAILEY. ¶ 7 Census (1850), N.Y., L, 81.

GARSHOU (or Garshoo), M. Portrait painter who exhibited at the Pennsylvania Academy in 1824; he was listed as an American resident. ¶ Rutledge, PA.

GARTON, JOSEPH. Engraver from the West Indies, working in Annapolis (Md.) in November 1753. ¶ Prime, I, 19.

GARVEY, HENRY. Sculptor in plaster who exhibited at Cleveland (Ohio) in 1857. ¶ WPA (Ohio), *Annals of Cleveland.*

GASKINGS, JOHN A. Engraver and die-sinker, NYC, 1851–60. ¶ NYBD and NYCD 1851–60.

GASNER (Gassner), GEORGE (1811–1861). Portrait and miniature painter; born in Germany; working in Lowell (Mass.) by 1848 and in Boston in 1856; died at Chicopee Falls (Mass.). ¶ Sears, *Some American Primitives,* 289; Lowell CD 1848; Boston BD 1856.

GASS, PATRICK (1771–1870). Topographical sketches. Gass was one of the members of the Lewis and Clark expedition 1804–06 and is said to have made some sketches of the western country (Turner). He was born June 12, 1771, at Falling Springs, near Chambersburg (Pa.), served as a soldier for about 20 years, and spent the latter half of his long life at Wellsburg (W. Va.), where he died April 30, 1870. Gass's journal of the Lewis and Clark expedition was first published in 1807 and a life of Gass, by J. G. Jacobs, was published in 1858. ¶ Turner, "Early Artists"; Gass, *Journal* (1904), intro.

GAST, AUGUST (1819–?). Lithographer. Born March 10, 1819, in Belle (Germany), studied at Detmold, and became a lithographer. Shortly after 1848 he and his brother LEOPOLD GAST emigrated to America, working first in NYC for a few months, then in Pittsburgh for over a year, and finally settling in St. Louis (Mo.) in 1852. There they established the lithographic firm of Leopold Gast & Co. In 1866 Leopold left the firm which was known thereafter as August Gast & Co. By 1883 it was one of the largest lithographic houses in the West. ¶ Arrington, "Nauvoo Temple," Chap. 8.

GAST, LEOPOLD. Lithographer. A native of Germany, he emigrated to America shortly after 1848 and, with his brother AUGUST GAST, worked as a lithographer in NYC and Pittsburgh (Pa.) before settling in St. Louis (Mo.) in 1852. From 1852 to 1866 he headed the firm of Leopold Gast & Co. (or Brother). In the latter year he sold out to his brother August. ¶ Arrington, "Nauvoo Temple," Chap. 8; St. Louis BD 1854.

GATES, BENJAMIN F. Engraver, NYC, 1854–58; born in New York about 1821. ¶ NYBD 1854, 1856–58; 7 Census (1850), N.Y., LI, 87.

GATES, ERASTUS. Decorative wall painter active in Vermont *c.* 1822. He is said to have designed and painted with stencils the wall decorations of the Luther Coolidge house in Plymouth (Vt.), built in 1822. ¶ Little, "Itinerant Painting in America, 1750–1850," 209.

GATES, THOMAS G. Religious painter, NYC, 1848–50. He exhibited at the National Academy and the American Art-Union. ¶ Cowdrey, NAD; Cowdrey, AA & AAU; NYCD 1850; NYBD 1850.

GATHIEL, EDWARD. Artist, New Orleans, 1849. ¶ Delgado-WPA cites CD 1849.

GATTEY, HENRY. Artist, mathematical, and philosophical instrument maker, NYC, 1796. ¶ NYCD 1796.

GAUK, JAMES. Engraver, NYC, 1795–1806. ¶ NYCD 1795–1802, 1804–06.

GAUL, FREDERICK. Engraver, age 19, native of Germany, living in Philadelphia in August 1850. *Cf.* Frederick Gaul, brewer, listed in the Philadelphia directory 1850–51. ¶ 7 Census (1850), Pa., L, 877; Phila. CD 1850–51.

GAUNTT, JEFFERSON. Portrait painter. From 1828 to 1832 he exhibited at the Pennsylvania Academy as a resident of Philadelphia. By 1833 he had moved to Brooklyn (N.Y.), where he lived at least until 1857. In NYC he exhibited at the National Academy and the American Academy. ¶ Rutledge, PA; Cowdrey, NAD; Cowdrey, AA & AAU; Brooklyn CD 1843, BD 1857.

GAUTHIER, A. F. Drawing and painting teacher, painter of landscapes and fancy pieces, active in Charleston (S.C.) *c.* 1830–51. ¶ Rutledge, *Artists in the Life of Charleston.*

GAUTREAU, J. B. Sculptor, New Orleans,

1830–32. ¶ Delgado-WPA cites CD 1830, 1832.

GAUX, JULES A. Portrait and miniature painter, New Orleans, 1834–44. ¶ Delgado-WPA cites CD 1834–35, 1837, 1841, 1843–44.

GAVIN, H. Engraver of frontispiece for book published in Newburyport (Mass.) 1796. This may, however, have been the Scottish engraver Hector Gavin, who is not known to have worked in America. ¶ Stauffer; Thieme-Becker.

GAVIT & COMPANY. Engravers, NYC and Albany (N.Y.) 1859 and after. The head of the firm was JOHN E. GAVIT; his associate in NYC was DANIEL E. GAVIT and in Albany THOMAS J. COWELL. The Albany branch was known as GAVIT & COWELL during the 1860's. ¶ NYBD 1859; NYBD 1860; Albany CD 1859–65.

GAVIT & COWELL. Banknote, steel, wood, and seal engravers, lithographers, at Albany (N.Y.) 1859–60's. The firm was established by JOHN E. GAVIT, who moved to NYC shortly after, leaving its management apparently to his junior partner, THOMAS J. COWELL. ¶ Albany CD 1859–65.

GAVIT, DANIEL E. Engraver, of GAVIT & Co., NYC, 1859 and after; born in New York about 1819. In 1860 his property was valued at $9,000. ¶ NYCD 1859–60; 8 Census (1860), N.Y., LVIII, 778.

GAVIT, JOHN E. (1817–1874). Banknote engraver. Born in NYC October 29, 1817, Gavit learned his trade in Albany (N.Y.) and there established an engraving, printing, and lithographic business about 1840. He became a banknote engraver and was one of the founders of the AMERICAN BANK NOTE Co. in 1858. The following year he moved to NYC where he established the engraving firm of GAVIT & Co., with an Albany branch under the name of GAVIT & COWELL. After serving for several years as secretary of the AMERICAN BANK NOTE Co., Gavit became president in 1866 and held office until his death, August 25, 1874, at Stockbridge (Mass.). ¶ Stauffer; Peters, *America on Stone;* Albany CD 1840–60; NYCD 1859–60; Toppan, *100 Years of Bank Note Engraving,* 12–13.

GAVITZ, JAMES. Irish engraver, 21, at NYC in 1850. ¶ 7 Census (1850), N.Y., XLVIII, 171.

GAW, CHAMBER S. Engraver, age 24, native of New York State, living with his parents in Philadelphia in July 1860. His father, ROBERT M. GAW, also was an engraver. ¶ 8 Census (1860), Pa., LVI, 688.

GAW, ROBERT M. Engraver, born *c.* 1805 in New Jersey. He was probably studying under PETER MAVERICK in Newark (N.J.) in 1829. His three children, including CHAMBER S. GAW, were born in New York in the mid-1830's. In July 1860 the Gaw family were living in Philadelphia. ¶ 8 Census (1860), Pa., LVI, 688; Stauffer.

GAY, EDWARD B. (1837–1928). N.A. Landscape painter; born in Dublin (Ireland) April 25, 1837, but brought to Albany (N.Y.) in 1848 and grew up there. He was painting landscapes as early as 1856, became an Associate Member of the National Academy in 1868 and a Member in 1907. During his later life he resided in Mt. Vernon (N.Y.). ¶ Thieme-Becker; Cowdrey, NAD; *Antiques* (Nov. 1953), 400; *Art Annual,* XX; *Artists Year Book,* 72.

GAY, HENRY B. (?–1862). Landscape painter, NYC, 1852–54; Honorary Member, Amateur, of the National Academy. He was a realtor; died at Roseville (N.J.) on June 18, 1862. ¶ Cowdrey, NAD; N. Y. *Evening Post,* June 20, 1862; NYCD 1853.

GAY, JOHN G. Wood engraver, Boston, 1850–52. ¶ Boston CD and BD 1850–52.

GAY, WINCKWORTH ALLAN (W. Allen Gay) (1821–1910). Landscape painter; born August 18, 1821, West Hingham (Mass.); died there February 23, 1910. After study under ROBERT W. WEIR and several years in Europe, Gay opened a studio in Boston in 1850. During the next quarter century he was a frequent exhibitor in Boston, NYC, and Philadelphia, chiefly of New England and European views. ¶ *Art Annual,* VIII, obit.; Cowdrey, NAD (erroneously as William Allen Gay); Swan, BA; Rutledge, PA; Clement and Hutton; CAB; Champlin and Perkins.

GAYLORD, CHARLES SEELY (1811–1862). Landscape and portrait painter; born December 30, 1811, at Gaylordsville (Gaylord's Bridge), Conn. Little is known of his early life except that he entered Yale College but was obliged to return home soon after because of eye trouble. Gaylordsville remained his home until his death, except for brief residences at Catskill (N.Y.) between 1838 and 1841. He was largely self-taught, though a friend of THOMAS COLE, W. S. JEWETT, and JASPER CROPSEY, the last being a frequent visitor at Gaylordsville from 1843 to 1846. He exhibited at the National Academy and the American Art-Union, and two of his works are owned by Mr. Clarence Evans of Gaylordsville. Gaylord died October 26, 1862, of injuries received a week earlier when he was gored by a cow while painting a farm scene. ¶ Information courtesy Dr. Elliot A. P. Evans, who cites: Thompson R. Harlow, Librarian, The Connecticut Historical Society, Hartford, 5 July 1949; Gaillard, *The History and Pedigree of the House of Gaillard (or Gaylord)*; Miss Mary Elsie Hall, New Milford Historical Society, New Milford (Conn.), July 18, 1949; Mr. Hollon A. Farr, Yale University Library, Nov. 7, 1950 (C. S. Gaylord is not listed in any Yale catalogue but may have attended during 2nd or 3rd terms, in which case his name would not have been printed); Mr. E. P. Lesley, Providence (R.I.), July 25, 1949; C. S. Gaylord to Thomas Cole, March 14, 1838, July 12, 1841 (transcripts courtesy of Mr. Lesley); C. S. Gaylord to Elizabeth Jewett (Preston), Oct. 9, 1844 (Ms. in possession of Mrs. Preston's granddaughter); notation by Jeanette Gaylord (?) *c.* 1920 to W. D. Jewett; C. S. Gaylord to J. F. Cropsey, Jan. 30, 1846; Mrs. Constance Mead, Nov. 11, 1952; Cowdrey, NAD; Cowdrey, AA & AAU; Mr. Edward Hendry, Executive Treasurer, National Academy of Design, New York, July 20, 1949; Mr. Clarence Evans, Gaylordsville, July 20, 1949, enclosing photographs; Mr. Clarence Evans, Nov. 14, 1949.

GEAR, JOHN WILLIAM (1806–1866). Crayon portraitist, miniaturist, watercolor painter, and lithographer. An English artist who made theatrical portraits his specialty, J. W. Gear exhibited in London from 1821 to 1852 and then came to America where his father JOSEPH GEAR had been living since 1824. He worked as an artist and restorer in Boston from 1855 until his death in 1866. He exhibited at the Boston Athenaeum in 1855. ¶ Swan, BA, 183, 229; Boston CD 1855–66; Graves, *Dictionary;* many of his portraits listed in Hall's *Catalogue of Dramatic Portraits in the Theatre Collection of the Harvard College Library.*

GEAR, JOSEPH (1768–1853). Marine painter and caricaturist. He was born in England and lived there until 1824, serving as a chorister at St. Paul's Cathedral, London, and exhibiting marine views at the Royal Academy between 1815 and 1821. In 1824 he emigrated to America, apparently leaving in England his son JOHN WILLIAM GEAR, who later became an artist. The elder Gear was prominent in NYC musical activities between 1826 and 1831, but moved to Boston where he was active as an artist and musician from the early 1830's until his death in 1853. He exhibited at the Boston Athenaeum between 1829 and 1837. ¶ Swan, BA, 183, 229; *Portfolio* (Jan. 1946), 117; Kouwenhoven, *Columbia Historical Portrait of N.Y.,* 122; Odell, *Annals of the New York Stage,* III, 540; Graves, *Dictionary;* NYCD 1826–27 (as James Gear, musician), 1828 (as Joseph Gear, musician); Boston CD 1834–46.

GEBHARD, CHARLES E. Portrait painter; born in Leipzig (Germany) *c.* 1810–15; living in Baltimore 1840–60; exhibitor, Maryland Historical Society 1856. ¶ 7 Census (1850), Md., V, 713 (age 35); 8 Census (1860), Md., V, 18 (age 50); Baltimore CD 1840, 1842, 1849–60; Mayo; Lafferty; Rutledge, MHS.

GEBHARD, LOUIS. Engraver; born in Hanover (Germany) *c.* 1826; living in Philadelphia in July 1860. ¶ 8 Census (1860), Pa., LIV, 347.

GEBHARDT, F. Landscape painter at NYC in 1840–41; exhibitor, Boston Athenaeum and Apollo Association. ¶ Cowdrey, AA & AAU; Swan, BA.

GEDDES, JAMES. Engraver, age 40, native of Pennsylvania, living in Philadelphia in 1850. ¶ 7 Census (1850), Pa., LII, 341.

GEERDERTS, JOHN P. Engraver at NYC, 1852. ¶ NYBD 1852.

GEES, J. F. S. Marble sculptor and polisher; engraver on marble, stone, wood, and wax; at New Orleans in 1818. ¶ Delgado-WPA cites *L'Ami des Lois,* March 14, 1818.

GEIB, G. Landscape painter; exhibited view of Catskill Falls (N.Y.) at the National Academy exhibition of 1837. ¶ Cowdrey, NAD.

GEIERSHOFER, MAURICE (Moritz). Engraver, Philadelphia, 1850; age 32, birthplace Germany. He later became a button manufacturer (1859–72). ¶ 7 Census (1850), Pa., L, 932; Phila. CD 1859–72. See MAURICE GAIRSHOFER.

GEISLER, JOSEPH. Austrian artist, 44, at NYC in 1860. His wife and eleven-year-old daughter also were born in Austria. ¶ 8 Census (1860), N.Y., LV, 415.

GEISTLICH, J. C. Modeller in wax, at New

Orleans in 1860. ¶ Delgado-WPA cites CD 1860.

GEMMELL (or Gemmel), JOHN. Lithographer working in Chicago in the late 1850's. His view of Chicago as it was *c.* 1816–20 was published *c.* 1857. ¶ Chicago CD 1858–59; Stokes, *Historical Prints,* 57–58, pl. 44-b.

GENDHART, EDWARD, see JOHN W. GENDHART.

GENDHART, HERMAN, see JOHN W. GENDHART.

GENDHART, JOHN W. German artist, age 49, living in Baltimore in 1850. With him were his artist sons, Edward (22) and Herman (24), and one other child, age 4, born in New York. ¶ 7 Census (1850), Md., IV, 548.

GENERELLY, FLEURY. Painter, decorator, designer, and engraver at New Orleans in 1818. In 1820 he made a trip up the Mississippi to St. Louis, making sketches along the way, some of which have been preserved. ¶ Delgado-WPA cites *L'Ami des Lois,* Sept. 12, 1818; Detroit Institute of Arts, *The French in America, 1520–1880.*

GENGEMBRE, CHARLES ANTOINE COLOMB (1790–1863). Landscape painter, architect, and engineer. Born in Paris in 1790, Gengembre was a practicing architect as early as 1809, studied in Italy, and worked in France until 1848. He emigrated to America with his family in 1849, settling first in Cincinnati (Ohio), later in Manchester and Allegheny City (Pa.), where he spent the rest of his life. He did some landscape painting and designed several buildings, including the Allegheny City Hall. Before his death in 1863 Gengembre changed his name to Hubert. His daughter, Mrs. SOPHIE ANDERSON, became a well-known artist, and his son, Philip Hubert, was an architect in NYC. ¶ McCreery, "The French Architect of the Allegheny City Hall."

GENGEMBRE, Miss S., see Mrs. SOPHIE ANDERSON.

GENIN, SYLVESTER (1822–1850). Historical and portrait painter. Born in St. Clairsville (Ohio) January 22, 1822, Genin showed an early interest in painting which was encouraged by his family and by the engraver HUGH ANDERSON. Though he did some portraits, his chief interest was in historical painting. He made a visit to the eastern cities in 1840–41, but returned to Ohio. His health failing, he travelled in 1848 to Louisiana and in 1849 to the island of Jamaica. He died of consumption on April 4, 1850, in Kingston (Jamaica). Five years later his father, Thomas H. Genin, published *Selections from the Works of the Late Sylvester Genin, Esq., in Poetry, Prose, and Historical Design, with a Biographical Sketch* and 16 engravings after his paintings. ¶ Genin, *op. cit.;* Tuckerman, 493–94; Fielding.

GENOT, SEBASTIAN. Engraver and die sinker, NYC, 1858–59. ¶ NYBD 1858–59.

GENT, Mrs. SOPHIA S. Portrait and genre painter; born in England *c.* 1818 (1860 Census gives her age as 42) or earlier. As Miss S. S. Daniell she exhibited at London galleries from 1826 to 1831, and as Mrs. S. S. Gent from 1832 to 1845. In 1848 she exhibited at the Maryland Historical Society and she was listed in Baltimore in 1849 and 1850. By 1853 she had moved to Philadelphia where she apparently lived at least until 1868 when her "Pussy, Are You Awake?" was shown at the Pennsylvania Academy. ¶ 8 Census (1860), Pa., LVIII, 586; Graves, *Dictionary;* Rutledge, MHS; Lafferty; Baltimore CD 1849; Phila. CD 1853–54, 1856; Rutledge, PA.

GENTILINI, JOSEPH. Sculptor, Boston, 1848–49. ¶ Boston BD 1848–49.

GENTILS, see MARCHAIS.

GENTILZ, THEODORE (*c.* 1820–1906). Portrait and genre painter and art teacher. A native of France, he was among the original settlers of Castroville (Texas) in 1844, but moved to San Antonio in 1846. He revisited France in 1849, married there, and returned to San Antonio, where he made his home until his death. He taught art at St. Mary's College and is remembered for his genre paintings of early life in Texas. ¶ Yanaguana Society, *Exhibition Catalogue,* Dec. 1933; WPA Guide, *Texas,* 143; *Antiques* (June 1948), 454–455, repros.

GEORGE, ARCHIBALD. "Master" George exhibited two crayon drawings at the Maryland Historical Society in 1848; he was a resident of Baltimore, possibly a son of S. K. George, importer and commission merchant. ¶ Rutledge, MHS; Baltimore CD 1847, 1849.

GEORGE, THOMAS. Engraver, age 35, native of Germany; living in Philadelphia in August 1850. ¶ 7 Census (1850), Pa., L, 916.

GEPHART, S. S. Primitive landscape painter

at Pittsburgh (Pa.) *c.* 1860. ¶ Lipman and Winchester, 173.

GERARD, Mme. ——. Drawing teacher at New Orleans, 1816. ¶ Delgado-WPA cites *L'Ami des Lois et Journal du Soir,* Aug. 12, 1816.

GERHARD, GEORGE (1830–1902). Portrait painter, born in Hanau (Germany). He was apparently in the United States by 1860 when he painted a portrait of Patrick Edward Morris, owned in 1940 by Mr. Edward Morris Van Buren, Jr., of Plainfield (N.J.). He died in NYC November 10, 1902. ¶ *Art Annual,* IV (1903), 140; WPA (N.J.), Hist. Rec. Survey; Bénézit; Thieme-Becker.

GERIOT, ACHILLE. French engraver, 24, at NYC in 1860. ¶ 8 Census (1860), N.Y., XLII, 439.

GERKE, JOHANN PHILIP (1811–?). Portrait and historical painter, born July 31, 1811, in Cassel (Germany). He was in NYC in 1837 and exhibited at the National Academy, but by 1844 he had returned to Germany and settled in Hamburg. ¶ Thieme-Becker; Cowdrey, NAD.

GERLACH, HERMAN. Lithographer; working in NYC in 1844; with RICHARD J. COMPTON at Buffalo (N.Y.) *c.* 1860; and in the firm of STROBRIDGE, GERLACH & WAGNER in Cincinnati 1862–66. ¶ NYBD 1844; Peters, *America on Stone.*

GERMAN, CHARLES W. Of THOMAS & GERMAN, lithographers and engravers of Louisville (Ky.) 1859. ¶ Louisville BD 1859.

GERMON, JOHN D. Miniaturist, active 1835–58. In 1835 he was living in Philadelphia and exhibited at the Artists' Fund Society; in 1836–37 he was a resident of NYC and exhibitor at the National Academy. In 1858 he was a resident of Philadelphia. ¶ Rutledge, PA; NYCD 1836–37; Cowdrey, NAD; Phila. CD 1858; Bolton, *Miniature Painters;* Fielding.

GERMON, WASHINGTON L. Engraver, artist, and photographer, Philadelphia, 1845–60 and after. Listed as an engraver 1845–54, as artist 1856–59, and as photographer from 1860. ¶ Phila. CD 1845–60 and after.

GEROSA, GIUSEPPE. Portrait and religious painter; exhibitor, National Academy, 1849, with a NYC address. ¶ Cowdrey, NAD.

GERRISH, WOODBURY. Ship-figurehead carver, working in Portsmouth (N.H.) *c.* 1844–64. His head of Benjamin Franklin is now in the U. S. Naval Academy, Annapolis (Md.). ¶ Pinckney, 86, 169; Lipman, *American Folk Art,* 18, repro. 104.

GERRY, SAMUEL LANCASTER (1813–1891). Portrait and genre, landscape and animal painter. Born in Boston May 10, 1813, Gerry was a largely self-taught artist, though he travelled in Europe for three years before setting up his Boston studio in 1840. He was a frequent exhibitor at the Boston Athenaeum, as well as the Pennsylvania Academy, National Academy, and American Art-Union. His professional career was spent chiefly in or near Boston. ¶ CAB; Bolton, "Portrait Painters in Oil"; Clement and Hutton; *Portfolio* (Oct. 1943), 44, repros.; Boston BD 1841–42, 1854–59; Swan, BA; Rutledge, PA; Cowdrey, NAD; Cowdrey, AA & AAU.

GERY, LOUIS. Engraver and diesinker; born in France *c.* 1830; working in New Orleans 1850–60. ¶ 7 Census (1850), La., V, 210; New Orleans CD 1852–54, 1860; BD 1859.

GESCHEIDT, MORRIS (Moritz). Architectural painter. Moritz Gesheidt was an architectural painter in Rome in 1834–36. Morris Gescheidt, probably the same man, was in NYC in 1838 and exhibited views of two Italian churches at the National Academy. ¶ Thieme-Becker; Cowdrey, NAD.

GESCHWINDT, see GSCHWINDT.

GESLAIN, the younger. Miniaturist, portrait painter, and teacher at Charleston (S.C.), 1796 and 1802. He claimed to be a pupil of David at Paris. ¶ Rutledge, *Artists in the Life of Charleston.*

GESLEUR, CLEMENT. French artist, 30, at NYC in 1860. His wife also was French, but their two children, aged 5 and 6, were born in New York. ¶ 8 Census (1860), N.Y., XLVI, 81.

GETZ, CHARLES S. Landscape painter of Baltimore 1851–80. He exhibited at the Maryland Historical Society in 1856. In 1860 he was recorded in the census as a native of Pennsylvania, age 38, living with his wife Sophia (35, Pa.), and children: SUMMERS (17, Pa.), Mary (11, Md.), William (8, Md.) and Charles (4, Md.); his personal property was valued at $2,000. ¶ 8 Census (1860), Md., VII, 101; Baltimore CD 1851, 1856; Lafferty; Rutledge, MHS.

GETZ, J. S. Theatrical scene painter, at Richmond (Va.) in 1857. ¶ *Richmond Portraits,* 242.

GETZ, SUMMERS. Student artist, age 17, pupil of his father CHARLES S. GETZ at

Baltimore in 1860. He was a native of Pennsylvania. ¶ 8 Census (1860), Md., VII, 110.

GEVELOT, NICHOLAS. Sculptor, employed on the U. S. Capitol, Washington (D.C.), in the 1820's, his chief work there being a bas-relief of Penn's Treaty. He also executed busts of Lafayette and Hamilton and a model for an equestrian statue of Washington (1834), and offered to design a medal in honor of the late President Zachary Taylor (1850). ¶ Stokes, *Icon.*, V, Nov. 8, 1824, May 18, 1826; Fairman, *Art and Artists of the Capitol,* 52–53, 70, 109.

GEYER, FREDERICK. Artist, type-founder, and mathematical instrument maker, who came to Philadelphia after the Revolution. He worked for Franklin & Bache, printers, and in 1794 was employed in the U. S. Treasury. He is said to have gone mad. ¶ Brown and Brown, cites Thomas, *History of Printing in America.*

GEYER, HENRY CHRISTIAN. Stonecutter and plaster caster, Boston, 1768–70; his work included human and animal likenesses. ¶ Forbes, "Early Portrait Sculpture in New England."

GIAMPAOLI, DOMINICUS. Of GAGLIARDI & GIAMPAOLI, sculptors, Washington (D.C.) 1860. ¶ Washington and Georgetown CD 1860.

GIANELLI, FROSTINO. Artist in plaster. A native of Tuscany, he was living in Philadelphia in 1860, in the house of LORENZO HARDIE. ¶ 8 Census (1860), Pa., LXII, 106.

GIANNINI & FOOTE, see JOSEPH GIANNINI.

GIANNINI, JOSEPH. Sculptor, Cincinnati (Ohio), 1856–60. In 1859 he and Charles D. Foote set up a marble, stone, and terra cotta factory in Cincinnati. ¶ Cincinnati CD 1856–60; Ohio BD 1860.

GIBBS, GEORGE (1815–1873). Amateur artist. Born at Sunswick, Long Island (N.Y.) July 17, 1815, Gibbs spent two years in Europe in the early 1830's, studied law at Harvard, and graduated in 1838. From 1842 to 1848 he was librarian of the New-York Historical Society. In 1849 he accompanied the expedition of the Mounted Rifle Regiment to Oregon, became deputy collector of customs at Astoria, and was attached to the Indian Commission. In 1851 he took part in the McKee exploration of northwestern California. Gibbs settled near Ft. Steilacoom (Wash.), where for nearly ten years he devoted himself to the study of Indian ethnology and linguistics. He returned to NYC in 1861, lived for a time in Washington, and died in New Haven (Conn.), April 9, 1873. His ethnological materials and drawings are now in the Smithsonian. ¶ Bushnell, "Drawings by George Gibbs in the Far Northwest, 1849–1851," repros.; Settle, *The March of the Mounted Riflemen,* an edition of the journals of Gibbs and Major OSBORNE CROSS, to whom some of Gibbs' drawings have been misattributed.

GIBBS, JOHN. Painter (?) of funeral escutcheons, Boston, *c.* 1733. ¶ Dr. Harold K. Bowditch and Mrs. Yves Henry Buhler cite the will of Mary Mico of Boston, Jan. 1, 1733.

GIBBS, JOHN, JR. House, sign, and ornamental painter of NYC, 1840's to 1870's. He exhibited an oil painting at the American Institute in 1845 and a sign in 1848. ¶ NYCD 1843–73; Am. Inst. Cat., 1845, 1848.

GIBERT, A. Painter of "Colonel Colt testing a submarine battery in New York Harbor near Staten Island, 1842," exhibited at the Corcoran Gallery in 1950. Possibly the same Gibert who exhibited an oil painting at the American Institute in 1844. *Cf.* A. GILBERT. ¶ *American Processional;* Am. Inst. Cat., 1844.

GIBSON, CAROLINE. Artist; born in Massachusetts *c.* 1836; boarding in San Francisco in 1860. ¶ 8 Census (1860), Cal., VII, 1354.

GIBSON, C. H. Of COMPTON & GIBSON, engravers and lithographers, Buffalo (N.Y.), 1854. ¶ Buffalo CD 1854.

GIBSON & COMPANY. Engravers and lithographers, Cincinnati (Ohio), 1851–60. The firm included at various times GEORGE, JOHN, ROBERT, and STEPHEN GIBSON. ¶ Cincinnati CD and BD 1851, 1853, 1856–60.

GIBSON, GEORGE. Engraver and lithographer, Cincinnati (Ohio), 1850–53. He was born in England *c.* 1810 and emigrated to America *c.* 1848 with his wife and five children. He established the firm of GIBSON & Co. in Cincinnati, in which he was joined by his sons GEORGE, JOHN, and ROBERT GIBSON and STEPHEN GIBSON, presumably also a relative. ¶ 7 Census (1850), Ohio, XXII, 437; Cincinnati CD and BD 1851–1853.

GIBSON, GEORGE [JR.]. Engraver, Cincinnati (Ohio) 1850. He was then only 14 years old and presumably an apprentice of his father, GEORGE GIBSON. ¶ 7 Census (1850), Ohio, XXII, 437.

GIBSON, JAMES. English artist, 36, at NYC in 1860. His wife also was born in England, but their six children, ages 10 to 1, were born in New York. ¶ 8 Census (1860), N.Y., LXI, 715.

GIBSON, JOHN. Lithographer, Cincinnati (Ohio), 1850–60. John, son of GEORGE GIBSON and brother of GEORGE [JR.] and ROBERT GIBSON, was born in England *c.* 1835. Soon after the family's removal to Cincinnati *c.* 1848, he went into his father's engraving and lithography business. During the 1850's he was in the firm of GIBSON & Co. ¶ 7 Census (1850), Ohio, XXII, 437; 8 Census (1860), Ohio, XXV, 57; Cincinnati CD 1856–60.

GIBSON, JOHN BANNISTER (1780–1853). Jurist; amateur artist. He was born in November 1780 in Perry County (Pa.), attended Dickinson College, and became a lawyer in Carlisle (Pa.). After serving in the state legislature and as a Common Pleas judge, he was appointed Chief Justice of the Pennsylvania Supreme Court in 1827 and he filled this office with great credit until 1851. He died in Philadelphia on May 3, 1853. Two of his paintings were given to the Allegheny County law library in Pittsburgh, and a monument to Dr. Charles Nesbit (first president of Dickinson College), designed by Gibson, is in the English Burial Ground at Carlisle (Pa.). ¶ Hain, *History of Perry County, Pa.,* 666–676; Gage.

GIBSON, MARY. Artist, born in England *c.* 1836; boarding in Philadelphia in 1860. ¶ 8 Census (1860), Pa., LIV, 170.

GIBSON, RICHARD P. Sculptor, NYC, 1856–58. In 1856 he exhibited a statue, "Clitoly," at the American Institute. ¶ NYCD 1856–58; Am. Inst. Cat., 1856.

GIBSON, RICHARD R. Artist and art teacher of Washington (D.C.); born in Maryland about 1795; active in Washington from about 1829 to 1855. In 1829 he was advertised as sole artist of a panorama of Quebec. In 1848 he gave lessons to ELEAZER HUTCHINSON MILLER. ¶ 7 Census (1850), D.C., I, 182; Washington CD 1834–55; Washington, *National Intelligencer,* Sept. 14, 1829 (courtesy J. Earl Arrington); Trotter, "E. Hutchinson Miller, the Artist."

GIBSON, ROBERT. Engraver, Cincinnati (Ohio), 1850–60. He was born in England *c.* 1834, a son of GEORGE GIBSON and elder brother of GEORGE [JR.] and JOHN GIBSON. He worked in association with his father and brothers in the firm of GIBSON & Co. ¶ 7 Census (1850), Ohio, XXII, 437; Cincinnati CD and BD 1856–60.

GIBSON, STEPHEN. Of GIBSON & Co., engravers and lithographers, Cincinnati (Ohio), 1856–60. He was probably related to GEORGE GIBSON and his sons ROBERT, JOHN, and GEORGE [JR.], of the same firm, though he is not listed among the sons of George in the 1850 census. ¶ Cincinnati CD and BD 1856–60.

GIBSON, THOMAS (?–1811). Miniature painter, active in NYC in 1793; died there December 23, 1811. ¶ Dunlap, *History* (1918), III, 302, cites N. Y. *Morning Star,* Dec. 27, 1811. Represented at NYHS.

GIDDINGS, C. M. Painter in oils, Cleveland (Ohio), 1840. ¶ Lipman and Winchester, 173.

GIESEKE, FERDINAND. German artist, 35, at NYC in 1860. ¶ 8 Census (1860), N.Y., XLII, 274.

GIFFORD, CHARLES B. Landscape artist, age 30, living in San Francisco in 1860. Gifford was a native of Massachusetts; his wife Josepha, of Nicaragua; and their two children, ages 5 and 4 years, of California. ¶ 8 Census (1860), Cal., VII, 739.

GIFFORD, ROBERT SWAIN (1840–1905). N.A. Landscape painter and etcher. He was born in Naushon (Mass.), December 23, 1840, and received his first instruction from ALBERT VAN BEEST and BENJAMIN RUSSELL at New Bedford (Mass.) in the late 1850's. He opened a studio in Boston in 1864, but two years later moved to NYC. He became an Associate of the National Academy in 1867 and a Member in 1878. He made extended sketching tours of the Far West, Europe, and North Africa in the 1860's and 1870's, and is chiefly noted for his pictures of oriental life. He died in NYC January 15, 1905. ¶ CAB; *Art Annual,* V; Childs, "Thar She Blows"; Thomas, "The American Career of Albert Van Beest," 16, 18; Rutledge, PA; Swan, BA; *American Art Review* (1880), 5 ff., 417–422; Graves, *Dictionary;* Thieme-Becker.

GIFFORD, SANFORD ROBINSON (1823–1880). N.A. Landscape and portrait painter. Born July 10, 1823, at Greenfield, Saratoga County (N.Y.); studied painting in NYC under John Rubens Smith *c.* 1845. In 1846 he made a sketching tour of the Catskills and Berkshires which fixed his interest on landscape painting. He worked in NYC until 1855 when he left for three years of European study. Gifford served briefly in the Civil War and later spent much time in the Far West. He was elected to the National Academy in 1854 and was a popular member of the Century and Union League clubs. He died in NYC, August 24, 1880. ¶ DAB; CAB; *American Art Review* (1880), 226–27, obit.; Sweet, *Hudson River School;* Cowdrey, NAD; Cowdrey, AA & AAU; Swan, BA; Rutledge, PA; Rutledge, MHS; Washington Art Assoc. Cat., 1857; Gardner, "Hudson River Idyll"; *Panorama* (Apr. 1948, 90–91; represented National Gallery of Art, Corcoran Gallery, NYHS, Met. Mus. of Art.

Gignoux, Régis François (1816–1882). N.A. Landscape painter; born in Lyon (France); died in Paris, August 6, 1882. After study in France under Paul Delaroche, Gignoux emigrated to America *c.* 1841 and opened a studio in Brooklyn (N.Y.). He was a frequent exhibitor at galleries in NYC, Boston, and Philadelphia; a Member of the National Academy; and first President of the Brooklyn Academy. He returned to France in 1870 and lived there until his death in 1882. ¶ CAB; Thieme-Becker; Clement and Hutton; Cowdrey, NAD; Cowdrey, AA & AAU; Swan, BA; Rutledge, PA; Washington Art Assoc. Cat., 1859; Stokes, *Historic Prints,* 99; NYBD 1844–57; represented Corcoran Gallery, NYHS, and Karolik Collection (Cat., 267–69).

Gihon & Butler. Lithographers, San Francisco, 1850's. The partners may have been Thomas Gihon and Benjamin F. Butler. ¶ Peters, *California on Stone.*

Gihon, John L. Portrait painter at Philadelphia, 1860. ¶ Phila. CD 1860.

Gihon, Thomas. Steel engraver and lithographer, San Francisco, 1852–60. He probably was a partner in Gihon & Butler. ¶ San Francisco CD 1852, 1860; BD 1856, 1860.

Gihon, William B. Wood engraver, Philadelphia, 1845–60. He was for a number of years associated with Reuben S. Gilbert. ¶ Phila. CD 1845–54, 1856, 1860; Hamilton.

Gilbert, ——. Artist who visited Pittsburgh (Pa.) in 1828. This may have been Grove Sheldon Gilbert, later of Rochester (N.Y.). ¶ Anderson, "Intellectual life of Pittsburgh: Painting," 291.

Gilbert, A. Painter of an oil portrait of Charles Gordon Atherton (1804–1853), now in the State House, Concord (N. H.). *Cf.* A. Gibert. ¶ WPA (Mass.), *Portraits Found in N.H.,* 2.

Gilbert, A. N. Fresco painter, represented in the Knowlton house, Winthrop (Me.), by landscapes painted *c.* 1830. *Cf.* E. J. Gilbert. ¶ Little, *American Decorative Wall Painting,* 20, 128; *Art in America* (Oct. 1950), 166, 193 (repro.).

Gilbert, Charlotte. Painter of portraits of Daniel Gilbert (1839) and Mary (Waters) Gilbert (1836) of eastern Massachusetts, now in the Essex Institute, Salem. ¶ Essex Inst. *Hist. Collections,* LXXXV (Oct. 1949), 333–334.

Gilbert, E. J. Fresco painter, represented by work in the Knowlton house, Winthrop (Me.) *c.* 1830's. *Cf.* A. N. Gilbert. ¶ Little, *American Decorative Wall Painting,* 132; Allen, *Early American Wall Paintings,* 96; Lipman and Winchester, 173.

Gilbert, Edwin M. Artist, 27, a native of New York, at NYC in 1850. ¶ 7 Census (1850), N.Y., XLVI, 139.

Gilbert, Elizabeth, see Elizabeth Gilbert Jerome.

Gilbert, George. Wood engraver of Philadelphia. He was a pupil of William Mason and one of the earliest wood engravers of the city. He exhibited at the Pennsylvania Academy in 1831. ¶ Hamilton, 375, 397; Pa. Acad. Cat., 1831.

Gilbert, George. Lithographer, age 26, of Pennsylvania; living in Philadelphia in 1860. ¶ 8 Census (1860), Pa., LIV, 1028.

Gilbert & Gihon. Wood engravers of Philadelphia, 1846 into the 1850's. The partners were Reuben S. Gilbert and William B. Gihon. They did work for the book trade. ¶ Hamilton, 522; Phila. CD 1846–49.

Gilbert, Grove Sheldon (1805–1885). Portrait painter. He was born in Clinton (N.Y.), August 5, 1805, graduated from Middlebury Academy *c.* 1825, painted and taught school for a few years in LeRoy (N.Y.) and Niagara (Ont.), and finally settled in Rochester (N.Y.) in 1834. He was made an Honorary Member of the National Academy in 1848. He painted a large number of portraits, many of which were exhibited in Rochester shortly after his death, which occurred March 23, 1885. His son, Grove Karl Gilbert (1843–1918) was a noted geologist. ¶ Peck, *Semi-centennial History of Rochester,* 520; Ulp, "Art and Artists in Rochester," 30–32, 54–60; Cowdrey, NAD; "Paintings of Grove S. Gilbert."

GILBERT, J. or I. Itinerant portrait painter from New Bedford (Mass.) who exhibited a portrait at the Boston Athenaeum in 1833. ¶ Swan, BA; Sears, *Some American Primitives,* 286; Sherman, "Unrecorded Early American Painters" (1934), lists a small portrait of a young woman, inscribed "I. Gilbert Pt."

GILBERT, JAMES A. Printer of NYC who exhibited engravings at the American Institute in 1844 and 1847. ¶ Am. Inst. Cat., 1844, 1847; NYCD 1847–48.

GILBERT, LOUIS. French artist, 40, at NYC in 1850. His wife and two children, ages 12 and 8, were also born in France. ¶ 7 Census (1850), N.Y., LII, 131.

GILBERT, REUBEN S. Wood engraver of Philadelphia, *c.* 1830–50. He executed a number of book illustrations, independently and as a member of the firm of GILBERT & GIHON. He also exhibited engravings at the Pennsylvania Academy in 1830–31 and 1834. ¶ Rutledge, PA; Hamilton; Phila. CD 1833–49.

GILCHRIST, ROBERT COGDELL. Landscape painter of Charleston (S.C.) 1843. He was a nephew of JOHN STEVENS COGDELL. ¶ Rutledge, *Artists in the Life of Charleston.*

GILDEMEISTER, KARL or CHARLES (1820–1869). Painter, lithographer, and architect. He was born in Bremen (Germany), October 11, 1820, studied in Italy *c.* 1844–45, and came to America by 1850. He worked as a portrait painter and lithographer in NYC from 1850 to 1858, part of the time in association with OTTO BOETTICHER. By 1860 he had returned to Bremen. He died February 8, 1869. In America he had exhibited at the National Academy and the American Art-Union. ¶ Thieme-Becker; Peters, *America on Stone;* NYCD 1850–58; Cowdrey, NAD; Cowdrey, AA & AAU. The name appears occasionally as Gildermeister or Geldmeister. He was probably the K. G. who did one of HOFF's *Views of New York* (1850).

GILDER, H. Watercolor artist whose "Naval Engagement on Lake Champlain, October 11, 1776," in the Royal collections at Windsor Castle, is supposed to be an eyewitness representation. ¶ *American Processional,* 236; *Connoisseur* (June 1951), 117–118.

GILES, CHARLES T. (1827–?). Line engraver; born August 25, 1827; working in NYC as early as 1847; living in Brooklyn (N.Y.) in 1900. ¶ Stauffer; Smith.

GILES, H. P. Crayon artist whose portrait of Nathaniel Smith Folsom (1806–1890) is owned by Dartmouth College, Hanover (N.H.). ¶ WPA (Mass.), *Portraits Found in N.H.*

GILES, J. B. Pen-prick portraitist. A portrait by this artist, *c.* 1810, is inscribed "Executed/ENTIRELY/with the Pen/by/ J. B. Giles." Lipman and Winchester place him in Vermont *c.* 1850. ¶ Information courtesy Mr. Sidney Janis; Lipman and Winchester, 173.

GILFOYLE, JOHN. Irish lithographer, 25, at NYC in 1860. ¶ 8 Census (1860), N.Y., LX, 364.

GILL, E. W. Painter of cabinet portraits in Massachusetts *c.* 1822. ¶ Sherman, "Newly Discovered American Portrait Painters."

GILL, JOHN. Engraver, born in Delaware *c.* 1831, living in Philadelphia in July 1850. ¶ 7 Census (1850), Pa., LI, 209.

GILL, ROBERT. Landscape, seal, and card engraver at Cleveland (Ohio) in 1857. ¶ Cleveland BD 1857.

GILLESPIE, J. H. or I. H. Miniature profile painter. After working in London, Edinburgh, and Liverpool in the 1820's, Gillespie appeared in Halifax (N.S.) in 1829. In 1837 he turned up in Baltimore and in December 1838 he was in Philadelphia, having just previously been in NYC. His work has been reproduced. ¶ Piers, "Artists in Nova Scotia," 123; Lafferty cites Baltimore *Sun,* Dec. 9, 1837; Gillingham, "Notes on Philadelphia Profilists," 516–518, repros.; *Antiques* (Feb. 1928), 113, repro., and (June 1930), 514, repros.

GILLESPIE, ROBERT L. Artist, age 35, in Corvallis City (Ore.) in 1860. He was a native of Virginia and had two children, one age 8 born in China and the other age 5 born in Michigan. ¶ 8 Census (1860), Oregon, cited by David C. Duniway, Oregon State Archivist.

GILLESPIE, T. Sculptor at Charleston (S.C.) in 1828. ¶ Rutledge, *Artists in the Life of Charleston.*

GILLESPIE, WILLIAM. Engraver, Baltimore, 1850's. He was born in Pennsylvania

c. 1817, married an Ohio woman, and had three children by 1860, all born in Maryland after 1852. He was listed in Baltimore directories from 1856. In 1860 he owned real estate valued at $2,500. ¶ 8 Census (1860), Md., VI, 443; Baltimore CD 1856–60, BD 1859.

GILLET, EDGAR P. Artist at Madison (Ind.) in 1852. ¶ Peat, *Pioneer Painters of Indiana,* 62.

GILLIAMS, JOHN J. Artist at Philadelphia 1850–52. In 1850 he exhibited "Shipwrecked Mariner" at the Pennsylvania Academy. ¶ Rutledge, PA; Phila. CD 1852.

GILLINGHAM, EDWIN D. Engraver at Baltimore, 1856–59. ¶ Baltimore CD 1856, BD 1858–59.

GILSTRAP, W. H. (1840–1914). Painter and art teacher, born in Effingham County (Ill.) April 24, 1840; studied in Chicago; became curator of the Ferry Museum, Tacoma (Wash.); died in Tacoma, August 2, 1914. ¶ *Art Annual,* XII; Smith.

GIMBER, STEPHEN HENRY (c. 1806–1862). A.N.A. Engraver, portrait and miniature painter. A native of England, as was his wife Louisa, Gimber settled in NYC about 1829 and worked there for a time with ARCHIBALD L. DICK. He moved to Philadelphia in 1842 and worked there as an engraver and lithographer until his death. ¶ 7 Census (1850), Pa., LIII, 9; Bolton, *Miniature Painters;* Cowdrey, NAD; Cowdrey, AA & AAU; Graves, *Dictionary;* Stauffer; Peters, *America on Stone;* NYCD 1829–42.

GIMBERMAN[?], FRANÇOIS. Figuremaker from Spain, age 31, living in Philadelphia in 1850. ¶ 7 Census (1850), Pa., L, 894.

GIMBREDE, JOSEPH NAPOLEON (1820–?). Engraver, born 1820 at West Point (N.Y.), while his father, THOMAS GIMBREDE, was instructor of drawing at the U. S. Military Academy. He studied engraving with his uncle, J. F. E. PRUD'HOMME, and worked as an engraver in NYC from 1841 to 1845. He later had a stationery shop in NYC. He was listed as an engraver in the 1860 census [as Joseph Gimbere]. ¶ Stauffer; NYBD 1844, 1848; Fielding; Thieme-Becker; 8 Census (1860), N.Y., LIII, 541.

GIMBREDE, THOMAS (1781–1832). Engraver, portrait and miniature painter, teacher of drawing. Born in France in 1781, Gimbrede came to America in 1802 as a miniaturist but took up engraving as early as 1810. Except for a brief residence in Baltimore in 1810, he worked in NYC from 1802 to 1819. In the latter year he was appointed drawing-master at the U. S. Military Academy, West Point (N.Y.), which position he held until his death, October 25, 1832. He was the father of JOSEPH NAPOLEON GIMBREDE, and the brother-in-law of J. F. E. PRUD'HOMME, who was his pupil in 1814. ¶ Stauffer; Bolton, *Miniature Painters;* Grolier Club, *The United States Navy,* 37; NYCD 1804–19; Mayo cites Baltimore CD 1810; Lafferty; Cowdrey, AA & AAU; *Art in America* (April 1936), 81, repro. Represented Md. Hist. Soc. (Rutledge).

GIMPEY, ——. Limner at Philadelphia in 1802. ¶ Brown and Brown.

GINDHART, FRANCIS XAVIER. Portrait and miniature painter at Baltimore, 1812–24. He was listed as Xaver Gindhart, limner, in 1812; as Francis Gindhart, portrait and miniature painter, 1814–19; and as Francis Gindhart, miniature painter, grocery, and liquor store, 1822–23. It is here assumed that Francis and Xaver Gindhart were one artist. ¶ Mayo cites Baltimore CD 1812, 1814, 1816, 1819, 1822–23; Lafferty also cites CD 1824.

GINENBACK, JOHN V. Engraver, age 18, at Philadelphia in 1850. His father was a saddler from Germany; the young engraver was a native of Pennsylvania. ¶ 7 Census (1850), Pa., LII, 711.

GIRAULT or GIRAUD, LOUIS MATTHIEUX. Miniature and portrait painter in NYC 1795–1801. ¶ NYCD 1795, 1798–1801; Gottesman, *Arts and Crafts in New York,* II, 10–11; Bolton, *Miniature Painters.*

GIRON, MARC. Engraver in San Francisco, 1852, and in 1858 in the firm of VACHON & GIRON. ¶ San Francisco CD 1852, 1858.

GIRSCH, FREDERICK (1821–1895). Engraver, etcher, and portrait painter; born March 31, 1821, in Büdingen, a suburb of Darmstadt (Germany). He began his studies there, but went to Paris in 1848, and a year later left Europe to come to America. He settled in NYC where he found employment as engraver for a German-language newspaper and later as a banknote engraver. He died at his home in Mt. Vernon (N.Y.) December 18, 1895. ¶ DAB; Stauffer; Fielding; NYBD 1852.

GISSLER, F. X. Artist at New Orleans from 1858. ¶ Delgado-WPA cites CD 1858, 1860, BD 1859.

GISTNER, JOHN C. Engraver at Philadelphia, 1793–96. ¶ Brown and Brown.

GITSINGER, the Misses. Instructors in wax-modelling at Charleston (S.C.) 1851. ¶ Rutledge, *Artists in the Life of Charleston.*

GITTENS, MARY LAURENS. Drawing teacher, with NATHANIEL GITTENS, at Charleston (S.C.) in 1744. ¶ Rutledge, *Artists in the Life of Charleston.*

GITTENS, NATHANIEL. Drawing teacher, with MARY LAURENS GITTENS, at Charleston (S.C.) in 1744. ¶ Rutledge, *Artists in the Life of Charleston.*

GITTI, JOSEPH. Artist, NYC, 1850. ¶ NYCD 1850.

GLADDING, BENJAMIN. Primitive genre painter in oils at Providence (R.I.) in 1810. There were many Gladdings in Providence, but the only Benjamin listed in the first directory (1822) was a barber and wigmaker. ¶ Lipman and Winchester, 173; Gladding, *The Gladding Book.*

GLADDING, FREEMAN (1815–1881). Portrait and ornamental painter of Albany (N.Y.), son of TIMOTHY and brother of TIMOTHY ALLEN GLADDING. He joined the family painting business during the 1830's. ¶ Gladding, *The Gladding Book,* under 8th generation; Albany CD 1849, 1852.

GLADDING, TIMOTHY (*c.* 1775–1846). Portrait and decorative painter; born about 1775, probably in Bristol (R.I.). During the Revolution his father moved to Middletown (Conn.). Timothy and his older brother became painters and moved to Albany (N.Y.), where in 1810 they established a house painting and decorating business well-known in Albany until after the Civil War. Timothy also did some portraits and may have been the silhouettist Gladding who cut a profile of Catherine Sanders of Schenectady (N.Y.) in 1808. Two of Gladding's sons, TIMOTHY ALLEN and FREEMAN GLADDING, became artists. Their father died in Albany at the age of 71 on May 2, 1846. ¶ Gladding, *The Gladding Family,* under 7th generation; Munsell, *The Annals of Albany,* X, 371; Albany CD 1815–38; Baker, "The Story of Two Silhouettes," repro.

GLADDING, TIMOTHY ALLEN (1818–1864). Portrait, landscape, and decorative painter of Albany (N.Y.). Timothy A., son of TIMOTHY and younger brother of FREEMAN GLADDING, was born in Albany March 26, 1818. He followed the family career of painter there from about 1840 to 1860 and then apparently joined the army. He saw service during the Civil War and died at City Point (Va.) in November 1864. ¶ Gladding, *The Gladding Family,* under 8th generation; Munsell, *Collections on the History of Albany,* II, 215; Cowdrey, NAD; Albany CD (both as Allen and as Timothy A. or T. A. Gladding) 1840–60.

GLADWELL, THOMAS E. Artist at Hartford (Conn.) 1859. ¶ Hartford CD 1859.

GLASGOW, D. (1834–1858). Artist of NYC who died January 29, 1858, at the age of 24. ¶ Peters, *America on Stone.*

GLASGOW, J. J. Painter of NYC, exhibitor at the National Academy in 1852. ¶ Cowdrey, NAD.

GLASGOW, J. T. Lithographer of NYC, 1850. ¶ Peters, *America on Stone.*

GLASNER, GEORGE. Painter of a portrait, dated 1838, of the Hunter sisters of North Agawam (Mass.). ¶ *Antiques Journal,* X (May 1955), repro. on back cover.

GLASS, JAMES WILLIAM, JR. (*c.* 1825–1855). Historical and portrait painter. Born in Cadiz (Spain) where his father was British Consul, Glass grew up in America and became an engineer in the U. S. Coast Survey and Fortification Service. About 1844 he turned to painting and he studied for a time under DANIEL HUNTINGTON before going to Europe in 1847 or 1848. Having achieved considerable success in England by his equestrian portrait of the Duke of Wellington, as well as his spirited historical compositions, Glass returned to the United States late in 1855. Less than a month later, December 22, 1855, the young artist committed suicide. He was an Honorary Member of the National Academy. ¶ *Crayon,* III (Jan. 1856), 28, obit.; N. Y. *Evening Post,* Jan. 2, 1856; Cummings, *Historic Annals,* 251; Tuckerman, 241–243; Clement and Hutton; Cowdrey, NAD; Cowdrey, AA & AAU; Swan, BA; Graves, *Dictionary; Now and Then,* IX (Jan. 1951), 278, repro. of Glass's "Friend or Foe?"

GLAUBRECHT, GEORGE J. Engraver and die-sinker of NYC, 1852–70. From 1852 to 1860 he was a partner in MAY & GLAUBRECHT. ¶ NYCD 1852–70; NYBD 1854, 1856–59.

GLEASON, WILLIAM B. One of Boston's leading figurehead and ornamental carvers of the mid-19th century. Began his career in 1845 in partnership with his father Samuel W. and brother Benjamin A. Gleason, but his work was said to be much superior to theirs. William B. Gleason is credited with many figureheads, one of the most famous being his "Minnehaha," reproduced in Pinckney (p. 92). He continued to work until the 1870's. ¶ Pickney, *American Figureheads and Their Carvers;* Boston CD 1845–58.

GLEAVE or GLEAVES, JOHN W. Engraver and die-sinker, at Philadelphia 1850–57, at NYC 1860. ¶ Phila. CD 1850–57, BD 1856–57; NYBD 1860.

GLENNIE, J. S. A Scotsman who toured the United States in 1810–11. His illustrated journal is in the de Coppet Collection, Princeton University Library. This may be the J. Glennie whose view of the Catskills with "the Steamboat on the Hudson" was engraved by HEWITT as the frontispiece for the November 1813 issue of *The Port Folio.* ¶ Thomas, *Elias Boudinot's Journey to Boston in 1809,* [v] and repro. p. 34; *Port Folio,* XXI (Nov. 1813), frontis.; *American Collector* (Jan. 1948), 6.

GLENTON, ——. A crayon portrait of Edward Spalding (1813–1895) by this artist is owned by Dartmouth College, Hanover (N.H.). ¶ WPA (Mass.), *Portraits Found in N.H.*

GLENTWORTH, HARVEY. Engraver, age 25, native of Pennsylvania; living in Philadelphia in 1860 with his druggist-father George Glentworth, who owned real estate valued at $7,000. ¶ 8 Census (1860), Pa., LV, 492.

GLESSING, THOMAS B. (1817–1882). Theatrical scene painter, panoramist, and portrait painter. A native of London, Glessing was working in Philadelphia as early as 1846 when he painted scenes from Shakespeare's life and works to decorate the Arch Street Theatre. In 1849 he painted a panorama of a voyage to California from sketches by W. B. MEYERS. He was still in Philadelphia in 1850. When his name next appears, in 1860, he was working in Cincinnati (Ohio). The following year he settled in Indianapolis (Ind.), where he remained until 1873 as principal scenic artist of the Metropolitan Theater. While in Indianapolis he also painted a number of half-historical, half-allegorical pictures for local celebrations. He left Indianapolis in 1873 to become scenic painter at the Boston Museum and he died in Boston in 1882. ¶ Peat, *Pioneer Painters of Indiana;* Burnet, *Art and Artists of Indiana,* 69–72, repro. opp. p. 68; Phila. *Public Ledger,* Aug. 24, 1846, and N. Y. *Herald,* Sept. 12, 1849 (both cited courtesy Mr. J. E. Arrington); Phila. CD 1849–50; 7 Census (1850), Pa., LIII, 157; Cincinnati CD 1860–61.

GLIDDON, ANNA. Crayon artist in NYC, 1858–59. She was the widow of George Robbins Gliddon (1809–1857), noted archaeologist and lecturer on Egyptian antiquities. Mrs. Gliddon exhibited pencil sketches at the National Academy in 1858 and crayon sketches at the Washington Art Association the following year. ¶ Cowdrey, NAD; Washington Art Assoc. Cat., 1859; NYCD 1858; Chamberlain and Strong, *Descendants of Charles Glidden,* 37–38.

GLITCHMAN, A. Lithographer at New Orleans, 1850. ¶ Delgado-WPA cites CD 1850.

GLOGGER, JOHN N. Portrait and landscape painter working in Pittsburgh (Pa.) between 1857 and 1876. He exhibited at the Pennsylvania Academy in 1857 and at the Pittsburgh Art Association in 1859 and 1860. ¶ Letter of Rose Demorest, Carnegie Library of Pittsburgh, to Anna Wells Rutledge, Oct. 31, 1950 (NYHS files); Rutledge, PA; Fleming, *History of Pittsburgh and Environs,* III, 626.

GLOVER, DE LAY (D. L. or Dillaye) (*c.* 1823–*c.* 1863). Engraver and photographer. Born *c.* 1823, he was a student at Cortland Academy, Homer (N.Y.) in 1836–37 and was probably a brother of DE WITT CLINTON GLOVER and LLOYD GLOVER. He worked as an engraver in Boston from 1846 to 1854 and in Syracuse (N.Y.) as an engraver and photographer from 1855 until his death about 1863. ¶ 7 Census (1850), Mass., XXVI, 437; Cortland Academy, *Catalogues,* 1836–37; Boston CD 1846–53, BD 1854; Syracuse CD 1855–62 (his widow listed in 1864).

GLOVER, DE LLOYD GAGE, see LLOYD GLOVER.

GLOVER, DE WITT CLINTON (1817–1836). Engraver; elder brother of LLOYD and DE LAY GLOVER. He was born in De Ruyter, Madison County (N.Y.) and received his education at Cortland Academy in Homer (N.Y.). About 1834 he went to NYC to study engraving under JOHN W. CASILEAR, but he was taken ill the following year and returned home, where he died January 3, 1836, at the age of 19. ¶ Goodwin, *Pioneer History,* 413–415; Fielding.

GLOVER, LLOYD (1826–?). General and banknote engraver. He was born in July 1826 at De Ruyter (N.Y.) and received his education at Cortland Academy,

Homer (N.Y.), where his family lived after 1827. Christened De Lloyd Gage Glover, he changed his name to Lloyd Glover to avoid confusion with his older brothers De Lay Glover and De Witt Clinton Glover, both engravers. Lloyd went to Boston in 1844 and became a successful engraver and businessman. He was for some years head of the Boston branch of Danforth, Wright & Co. and a director of the American Guano Company. He was active in Boston at least until 1859. ¶ Goodwin, *Pioneer History,* 419–428; Cortland Academy, *Catalogue,* 1836; Boston CD 1847–58.

Glück, B. Lithographer of a view of Wilmington (Del.) in 1841. ¶ Stokes, *Historic Prints,* 91–92, pl. 70b.

Goater, John H. Designer, illustrator, and engraver. He was working for the *Illustrated American News* (NYC) in 1851, visited New Orleans about 1855, then returned to his home in Brooklyn (N.Y.). During the late 1850's and early 1860's he did work for *Vanity Fair* and in 1860 for N. P. Willis's *Sacred Poems.* ¶ Hamilton, 269; Delgado-WPA cites *La. State Republican,* Feb. 7, 1855; NYCD 1857–62.

Goble, Conrad. Lithographer from Hesse, aged 32, at NYC in 1860. He had one child, one year old, born in New York. ¶ 8 Census (1860), N.Y., XLIV, 831.

Gobrecht, Christian (1785–1844). Engraver and die-sinker, medallist, and inventor of engraving tools. He was born December 23, 1785, in Hanover (Pa.), served his apprenticeship under a clockmaker at Lancaster (Pa.), and for some years before 1811 worked in Baltimore as an engraver of clock faces and letter-engraver. In 1811 he moved to Philadelphia where he found employment as a general and seal engraver and die-sinker. In 1816 he was with the engraving firm of Murray, Draper, Fairman & Co. In 1834 he was appointed assistant engraver at the U. S. Mint, and in 1840 he became head of the engraving department of the Mint. He also executed a number of medals and invented some engraving tools. He died in Philadelphia, July 23, 1844. ¶ Darrach, "Christian Gobrecht, Artist and Inventor"; DAB; Stauffer; Rutledge, PA; Brown and Brown.

Goddard, Emerson. Portrait painter at Cumberland (R.I.), 1849. ¶ New England BD 1849.

Goddard, George Henry (1817–1906). Artist for lithographers. Born in Bristol (England) and educated at Oxford University, he exhibited flower pieces in London between 1837 and 1844. In 1852 he emigrated to California, establishing himself as a civil engineer at Sacramento. He made many drawings for California lithographers and planned to publish a series of several hundred California views. Goddard's collection of drawings, maps, and other Californiana was entirely destroyed in the San Francisco fire of 1906 and the artist died a few months later at his home in Berkeley. ¶ Peters, *California on Stone;* Van Nostrand and Coulter, *California Pictorial,* 128–129; Graves, *Dictionary;* Jackson, *Gold Rush Album,* repros.

Godden, A. Portrait painter at Newark (Ohio), 1853. ¶ Ohio BD 1853.

Godding, William C., see Gooding.

Godefroid, F. Advertised in New Orleans in 1807 as portrait, historical, landscape, and animal painter in fresco, water color, and pastel, and drawing master. Said to have been in New Orleans in 1830. ¶ Delgado-WPA cites New Orleans *Moniteur,* April 4 and Oct. 24, 1807; Thompson, *Louisiana Writers Native and Resident;* Fielding.

Godefroy, Maximilian (*c.* 1770–*c.* 1837). Landscape painter and architect. A French architect who was imprisoned by Napoleon, Godefroy was freed to come to America about 1805. After a short time in Philadelphia he settled in Baltimore, where he taught at St. Mary's Seminary and designed a number of buildings and monuments. He exhibited many architectural drawings and other sketches at the Society of Artists (Phila.) in 1811 and 1813. Between 1820 and 1824 he exhibited (as P. M. F. Godefroy of Pennsylvania) nine landscapes at the Royal Academy (London). After a few years in London, Godefroy returned to France in 1827. ¶ Pleasants, *250 Years of Painting in Maryland,* no. 72; Rutledge, PA; *Antiques* (Jan. 1945), 39, repro.; Thieme-Becker cites Herberman, *Sulpicians in the United States,* and Scharf, *Chronicles of Baltimore;* Dunlap, *History,* II, 379.

Godefroy, P. M. F., see Maximilian Godefroy.

Godell, Albert. Portrait painter at Madison (Wis.), 1858. ¶ Madison BD 1858.

Godfrey, E. Sculptor at Salem (Mass.), 1792. ¶ Belknap, *Artists and Craftsmen of Essex County,* 18.

GODWIN, ABRAHAM (1763–1835). Engraver. He was born July 16, 1763, at Paterson (N.J.), served throughout the Revolution, and then went to NYC where he was apprenticed to A. BILLINGS, engraver. He was working there independently in 1786. He later returned to Paterson, where he was for many years proprietor of a hotel, and died there October 5, 1835. His son, Parke Godwin, became a noted editor and author. ¶ Stauffer; Kelby, *Notes on American Artists,* 28; Dunlap, *History,* I, 157.

GOELET, RAPHAEL. Limner and glazier of NYC, 1726–47. He was admitted a freeman of the city February 18, 1734/5. ¶ Groce, "New York Painting before 1800"; Kelby, *Notes on American Artists,* 1.

GOFFART, EDWARD. Engraver, NYC, 1854, 1857. ¶ NYBD 1854, 1857.

GOLDBACKER, BARBARA. Lithographer; born in Baden (Germany) *c.* 1826; living in Philadelphia in 1860. The household included her brother (?) ISAAC GOLDBACKER, also a lithographer, and four children born in Pennsylvania since 1850. ¶ 8 Census (1850), Pa., LVI, 222.

GOLDBACKER, ISAAC. Lithographer; born in Baden (Germany) *c.* 1834; living in Philadelphia in 1860 with his sister (?) BARBARA GOLDBACKER, also a lithographer. ¶ 8 Census (1860), Pa., LVI, 222.

GOLDSMITH, DEBORAH (1808–1836). Itinerant portrait and miniature painter in oils and watercolors. Born in North Brookfield (N.Y.) in 1808, she became a professional portrait painter about 1830. For two or three years she travelled about upstate New York (including Toddsville, Cooperstown, Brookfield, Hamilton) painting to support her family. After her marriage in December 1833 to George Addison Throop of Hamilton, she gave up her professional work. She died in Hamilton, March 16, 1836. ¶ Lipman, "Deborah Goldsmith," repro.; Lipman and Winchester, 90–96, three repros.; Little, "Itinerant Painting in America," 213–214; *American Collector* (March 1946), 9, repro.; *Art in America* (Oct. 1934), 145, repro. See also Smith and Throop, *Ancestral Charts of George Addison Throop* [*and*] *Deborah Goldsmith,* which contains their letters and other material, pp. 65–89.

GOLDSMITH, WILLIAM. Engraver at Boston, 1850–51. *Cf.* WILLIAM E. GOLDSMITH. ¶ Boston CD 1850, BD 1851.

GOLDSMITH, WILLIAM E. Steel engraver at San Francisco, 1852 and after. *Cf.* WILLIAM GOLDSMITH. ¶ San Francisco CD 1852–60.

GOLDTHWAIT, G. H. Engraver at Boston in 1842. ¶ Stauffer; Fielding.

GOLL, FREDERICK P., JR. Engraver and diesinker, daguerreotype case maker; active in NYC 1841–60. He was born in Germany. ¶ NYBD 1841–57; NYCD 1842–54; 8 Census (1860), N.Y., XLIX, 1023.

GOLLMANN, JULIUS (?–1898). Portrait painter. A native of Hamburg (Germany), he worked in the United States as early as 1852 and as late as 1872. During the 1850's and 1860's he worked mainly in NYC and exhibited several times at the National Academy. In 1859 and 1872 he was living in Cleveland (Ohio). He later returned to Germany and died in Berlin August 5, 1898. ¶ Thieme-Becker; NYBD 1853, 1856, 1860; Cowdrey, NAD; Ohio BD 1859; Cleveland CD 1872.

GOMER, JOHN R. Portrait painter at New Orleans, 1859–60. ¶ Delgado-WPA cites CD 1859–60.

GONDOLFI, MONRO, see MAURO GANDOLFI.

GOODACRE, WILLIAM. Landscape and still life painter, teacher of drawing. He was listed as a teacher of drawing in NYC from 1829 to 1835. During this period he exhibited several still lifes and English and American views at the American and National Academies. A number of his views of American cities from Boston (Mass.) to Augusta (Ga.) appeared in Hinton's *History and Topography of the United States* (London, 1830) and were utilized for Staffordshireware designs. ¶ Snow, "Delineators of the Adams-Jackson American Views," Part III; Cowdrey, AA & AAU; Cowdrey, NAD.

GOODALL, ALBERT GALLATIN (1826–1887). Banknote engraver. He was born in Montgomery (Ala.) October 31, 1826, saw active service as a midshipman in the Texan navy during the Mexican-Texan war, and then went to Havana (Cuba) in 1844 to learn copperplate engraving. In 1848 he established himself in Philadelphia as a banknote engraver and became associated with one of the companies which later formed part of the AMERICAN BANK NOTE CO. In 1858 and later he visited several European and South American countries to obtain foreign contracts for his firm. From 1874 to 1887 he served as president of the AMERICAN BANK NOTE CO. He died in NYC February 19, 1887. ¶ Stauffer; Fielding; Toppan, *100 Years of Bank Note Engraving,* 13.

GOODELL, IRA (or J.) C. Portrait painter, born in Connecticut about 1810. He was working at Malden Bridge (N.Y.) in 1830, at New Brunswick (N.J.) in 1859–60, and in June 1860 was living in NYC with his wife Mary and two sons, Samuel (17) and Eugene (13). ¶ 8 Census (1860), N.Y., XLVII, 521; Lipman and Winchester, 173; New Brunswick *Fredonian,* Oct. 19, 1859, to April 1860.

GOODES, EDWARD A. Marine and landscape painter at Philadelphia, 1855–68. He exhibited frequently at the Pennsylvania Academy, chiefly landscape and marine views with a few still lifes and one religious painting. ¶ Rutledge, PA; Phila. CD 1855 (as painter).

GOODING, WILLIAM C. (1775–1861). Portrait and miniature painter active in Canandaigua (N.Y.) as early as 1815. He is buried in the pioneer cemetery at Canandaigua. ¶ From records in the Ontario County Hist. Soc., published in the *Ontario County Times,* Aug. 22, 1928 (courtesy R. W. G. Vail); Dunlap, *History* (1918), 303; Fielding; Bolton, *Miniature Painters* (as Godding).

GOODLIFF, JOHN. Lithographer; born in England *c.* 1828; living in Philadelphia 1850–52, with realty valued at $3,000. ¶ 7 Census (1850), Pa., LII, 746; Phila. CD 1852.

GOODMAN, CHARLES (1796–1835). Engraver. A native of Philadelphia, he learned stipple engraving there under DAVID EDWIN. About 1817 he and his fellow-apprentice ROBERT PIGGOT established the firm of GOODMAN & PIGGOT, which flourished until about 1822, when Goodman abandoned engraving for law and Piggot became a clergyman. Goodman died in Philadelphia February 11, 1835. ¶ DAB; Stauffer; Soc. of Artists Cat., 1811; Grolier Club, *The U. S. Navy, 1776–1815,* 134.

GOODMAN, CHRISTIAN. Lithographer from Württemberg (Germany), age 35, at Philadelphia in 1860. ¶ 8 Census (1860), Pa., LVI, 858.

GOODMAN, JOHN. Engraver at Cleveland (Ohio) in 1853. ¶ Ohio BD 1853.

GOODMAN & PIGGOT. Engravers, Philadelphia, 1817–22. The partners were CHARLES GOODMAN and ROBERT PIGGOT, former pupils of DAVID EDWIN. They exhibited prints at the Pennsylvania Academy 1817–20. The partnership was dissolved in 1822 and both men gave up engraving, Goodman to become a lawyer and Piggot a clergyman. ¶ Stauffer; Penna. Acad. Cat., 1817–20; Brown and Brown; *Analectic Magazine,* XVI (1820), 421 (engraving by Goodman & Piggot).

GOODRICH, HENRY O. (1814–1834). Itinerant wall stenciller of Nottingham (N.H.). ¶ Little, *American Decorative Wall Painting,* 101, 133.

GOODRICH, LEVI. Artist for lithographers, San José (Cal.), 1849 and 1858. ¶ Peters, *California on Stone.*

GOODRIDGE, ELIZA (1798–1882). Miniaturist; sister of the better-known miniaturist, SARAH GOODRIDGE. She is represented at the American Antiquarian Society and the Worcester Art Museum. ¶ Worcester Art Museum, Cat., 179; Weis, *Check List of Portraits.*

GOODRIDGE, SARAH (1788–1853). Miniaturist. Born February 5, 1788, in Templeton (Mass.), she spent her youth there and in the neighborhood of Boston. Largely self-taught, she opened a studio in Boston in 1820 and, with informal instruction and encouragement from GILBERT STUART, achieved considerable success. She made professional visits to Washington in 1828–29 and 1841–42, but most of her career was spent in Boston. During her latter years she lived in Reading (Mass.). She died during a Christmas visit to Boston, December 28, 1853. Her sister, ELIZA GOODRIDGE, also painted miniatures. ¶ Dods, "Sarah Goodridge," with checklist; DAB; Cowdrey, AA & AAU; Cowdrey, NAD; Swan, BA; Boston BD 1841–48; Bolton, *Miniature Painters;* Wehle and Bolton; *Antiques* (March 1940), 125, repro. Represented at Am. Antiq. Soc. (Weis) and Worcester Art Museum (Cat.).

GOODWANE, Mrs. ——. Teacher of drawing and painting, Charleston (S.C.), 1843–44. ¶ Rutledge, *Artists in the Life of Charleston.*

GOODWIN, ——. Engraver, active in NYC *c.* 1787. ¶ Prime, II, 69.

GOODWIN, EDWIN WEYBURN (1800–1845). Portrait and miniature painter. During a career of about 15 years Goodwin painted at least 800 portraits in up-state New York. He was at Auburn in 1836 and he made his home in Albany during the last five years of his life, though he died in Ithaca in 1845. His artist-son, RICHARD LA BARRE GOODWIN, was born in Albany in 1840. ¶ *Art in America* (1933), 27; *Antiques* (1944), 159, repro.; Frankenstein, *After the Hunt,* 132; Cowdrey, NAD; *Antiques* (1934), 236, and (March 1951), 224, repros.; *American Provincial Painting,* no. 34 (as F. W. Goodwin).

GOODWIN, F. W., see EDWIN WEYBURN GOODWIN.

GOODWIN, J. B. Portrait painter at Brookville (Ind.) during the summer of 1844. ¶ Peat, *Pioneer Painters of Indiana,* 85–86.

GOODWIN, RICHARD LA BARRE (1840–1910). Still life, portrait and landscape painter. The son of EDWIN WEYBURN GOODWIN, he was born in Albany (N.Y.), March 26, 1840. After studying in NYC, he worked for a quarter century as an itinerant portrait painter in New York State. During the 1880's he was at Syracuse (N.Y.), in the early 1890's in Washington (D.C.), 1893 to 1900 in Chicago (Ill.), 1900–02 in Colorado Springs (Col.), 1902–06 in California, 1906–08 in Portland (Ore.), 1908–10 in Rochester (N.Y.). He died in Orange (N.J.) December 10, 1910. He was best known as a painter of game and fish. ¶ [Orange] *Daily Chronicle,* Dec. 10, 1910 (citation courtesy Dept. of Health, Orange, N.J., through the late Wolfgang Born); Frankenstein, *After the Hunt,* 131–135, plates 69, 114, 115.

GOODWIN, SAMUEL. Painter of NYC, who had a studio in the basement of Peale's Museum in 1844 and exhibited at the American Institute in that year. ¶ NYCD 1843–44; Am. Inst. Cat., 1844.

GOODWIN, THOMAS. Pennsylvania-born artist, 19, at NYC in 1850. ¶ 7 Census (1850), N.Y., LII, 93.

GOOKIN, WILLIAM STOODLEY (1799–?). Portrait and fancy painter; born in 1799, presumably in Portsmouth (N.H.) where he was baptized November 9, 1800, at the age of one year. By 1837 he was established as a portrait and fancy painter in Dover (N.H.) and there he continued to work both as a painter and as a daguerreotypist until the late 1860's. He was still living in 1872. ¶ Spinney, "William S. Gookin," with repros. and checklist; Lipman and Winchester, 182.

GOOKINS, JAMES FARRINGTON (1840–1904). Portrait and landscape painter; born in Terre Haute (Ind.), December 30, 1840. He was active in Terre Haute from 1860 to 1865; in Chicago, 1865–69; studied in Munich, 1870–73; worked in Indianapolis, 1873–80, Terre Haute, 1880–83, Chicago, 1883–1904, and Indianapolis, 1887–89. He died in NYC on May 23, 1904. During the Civil War Gookins was on the staff of General LEW WALLACE and he contributed some war sketches to *Harper's Weekly* in 1861 and 1862. In 1866, in company with several other artists, he toured the West sketching for *Harper's.* ¶ Peat, *Pioneer Painters of Indiana;* Taft, *Artists and Illustrators of the Old West;* Burnet, *Art and Artists of Indiana;* in CAB and Fielding as Cookins.

GORAM, THOMAS, see THOMAS CORAM.

GORBETT, W. B. Portrait painter at Cincinnati (Ohio) in 1860. ¶ Cincinnati CD 1860.

GORDON, ——. Scene painter at the New York Theatre (NYC) in December 1827 and at the Bowery Theatre (NYC) in November 1828 and January 1830. At the latter he designed scenery for WILLIAM DUNLAP's *Trip to Niagara.* ¶ Odell, *Annals of the New York Stage,* III, 336, 407; N. Y. *Evening Post,* Nov. 28, 1828, and Jan. 13, 1830 (citations courtesy J. E. Arrington).

GORDON, ALEXANDER (*c.* 1692–1754). Painter. A native of Aberdeen (Scotland), Gordon came to South Carolina in 1741 as secretary to Governor Glen and remained in Charleston apparently until his death. The inventory of his estate lists a number of paintings and drawings by him, among which were several portraits. He was also a musician, writer, and antiquarian. ¶ Rutledge, *Artists in the Life of Charleston;* Rutledge, "A Cosmopolitan in Carolina"; Wilson, "Art and Artists of Provincial South Carolina," 144; Fielding; Thieme-Becker.

GORDON, JOHN G. Wood engraver of NYC, 1840–46. He is said to have been a pupil of JOSEPH ALEXANDER ADAMS. ¶ NYBD 1840–41, 1844; Hamilton, 78.

GORDON, PETER. Delineator of a view of Savannah (Ga.) in 1734, engraved by P. Fourdinier. This is the earliest known view of Savannah. ¶ Stokes, *Historic Prints,* 14–15, pl. 13b; *American Processional,* 234.

GORE, JOHN (1718–1796). Heraldic and coach painter. Born in Boston December 29, 1718, Gore lived there until 1776 when he fled as a Loyalist to Halifax (N.S.). Pardoned in 1787, he returned to spend the rest of his life in Boston where he died in January 1796. He was the father of SAMUEL GORE, heraldic and coach painter, and Christopher Gore, governor of Massachusetts, and grandfather of JOHN CHRISTOPHER GORE. ¶ Bowditch, "The Gore Roll of Arms," with repros.; Bowditch, "Early Watercolor Paintings of New England Coats of Arms," 181–182, fig. 3.

GORE, JOHN CHRISTOPHER. Landscape painter. Son of John Gore (1769–1817), nephew of SAMUEL GORE, and grandson of JOHN GORE (1718–1796). He exhibited at the Boston Athenaeum in 1828 and shortly after went to Italy, studying in Florence from about 1830 to 1834. In 1836 his sister Louisa married the sculptor HORATIO GREENOUGH. From 1834 to 1860 Gore was an Honorary Member, Professional, of the National Academy and lived in Boston. ¶ Swan, BA; Whitmore, *A Brief Genealogy of the Gore Family,* 7; F. B. Greenough, ed., *Letters of Horatio Greenough to His Brother, Henry Greenough,* 48; Louisville (Ky.) *Focus,* April 15, 1831 (citation courtesy of Mrs. W. H. Whitley, Paris, Ky.); Cowdrey, NAD.

GORE, JOSHUA. Painter of small watercolor portraits and genre pictures in the American South *c.* 1860. ¶ Lipman and Winchester, 173.

GORE, RALPH. Painter of a large watercolor view of Niagara Falls, dated September 27, 1821, owned by the New-York Historical Society. ¶ *Portfolio* (March 1952), 156–157, repro.

GORE, SAMUEL (1750/51–1831). Heraldic and coach painter. Samuel, son of JOHN GORE, was born in Boston January 26, 1750/51. In 1783 he painted coaches and drew coats of arms for John Hancock in Boston. After 1789 he moved to Newburyport (Mass.), where his cousin, GEORGE SEARLE, lived. He died November 23, 1831. His brother Christopher was governor of Massachusetts, and his nephew, JOHN CHRISTOPHER GORE, was a landscape painter in Boston. ¶ Whitmore, *A Brief Genealogy of the Gore Family,* 6–7; information courtesy Dr. Harold Bowditch, Brookline (Mass.).

GORHAM, FRED P. Engraver at New Haven (Conn.), 1856 and after. ¶ New Haven CD 1856–58; New England BD 1856, 1860.

GORI & BOURLIER. Marble sculptors, NYC, 1859; OTTAVIANO GORI and ALFRED J. B. BOURLIER. ¶ NYBD and CD 1859.

GORI, OTTAVIANO. Marble and alabaster sculptor. Signor Gori produced statuary, monuments, mantle pieces, fountains, etc., in NYC from 1841 to 1859 and exhibited an alabaster carving at the American Institute in 1842. In 1859 he was in partnership with ALFRED J. B. BOURLIER, but by 1861 he had moved to San Francisco where he opened a marble yard. ¶ NYBD 1841–57; NYCD 1859; Am. Inst. Cat., 1842; San Francisco CD 1861.

GORMAN, DAVID. Engraver. A native of Pennsylvania, age 23, Gorman resided in Philadelphia in July 1860, with personal property valued at $200. ¶ 8 Census (1860), Pa., LVIII, 575.

GORMAN, JAMES O. Miniaturist at Mobile (Ala.) in 1834 and at Cincinnati (Ohio), 1838–44. ¶ WPA (Ala.), Hist. Records Survey cites Mobile *Commercial Register and Patriot,* Jan. 25, 1834; Cist, *Cincinnati in 1841,* 141; *Antiques* (Oct. 1940), 186; information courtesy Edward H. Dwight, Cincinnati Art Museum.

GORY, EMANUEL G. Engraver, of GORY & MURRAY, Louisville (Ky.), 1859. ¶ Louisville CD 1859.

GORY & MURRAY. Engravers, Louisville (Ky.), 1859; EMANUEL GORY and GEORGE J. MURRAY. ¶ Louisville CD 1859.

GOSZOLER, ——. Image maker at NYC, 1799. ¶ Groce, "New York Painting Before 1800"; NYCD 1799.

GOTBUT, EDWARD. Prussian lithographer, 37, at NYC in 1850. ¶ 7 Census (1850), N.Y., XLII, 6.

GOTT, JOHN (1785–1860). Sculptor living in Albany (N.Y.) in 1856 when he exhibited a bust of General FRÉMONT at the American Institute in NYC. Three years later he was a resident of NYC. ¶ Gardner, *Yankee Stonecutters;* Am. Inst. Cat., 1856; NYBD 1859.

GOTTFRIED, ALEXANDER. Portrait painter at Philadelphia, exhibitor at the Pennsylvania Academy in 1855 and 1856. ¶ Rutledge, PA.

GOULARD, DAVID. Swiss engraver, age 40, living with his wife Maria in Philadelphia in August 1860. ¶ 8 Census (1860), Pa., L, 576.

GOULD, GEORGE. Artist at Buffalo (N.Y.), 1858. ¶ Buffalo BD 1858.

GOULD, THEODORE A. Portrait painter. After about two years in New Orleans (La.), Gould left in August 1848 and went to NYC to publish a book of verse entitled *A Bouquet of Poesy*. He apparently settled in Brooklyn where he was listed as a portrait painter in 1851 and 1856–57. ¶ Delgado-WPA cites New Orleans *Commercial Times,* Aug. 30, 1848; Library of Congress, Union Catalogue; Brooklyn CD 1851, 1855 (as fancy goods), 1856–57.

GOULD, THOMAS RIDGEWAY (1818–1881). Sculptor. Born November 5, 1818, in Boston, Thomas R. Gould went into the drygoods business there and prospered until the Civil War. About 1851 he became interested in sculpture and modelling, received a little instruction from SETH CHENEY, and made it his avocation. After the failure of his business, he became a professional sculptor and was successful. In 1868 he went to Italy and opened a studio in Florence, where he spent the rest of his life, except for brief visits to the United States in 1878 and 1881. He died in Florence November 26, 1881. ¶ DAB; Gardner, *Yankee Stonecutters;* Swan, BA.

GOULD, WALTER (1829–1893). Portrait, miniature, and genre painter. A native of Philadelphia, Gould studied there under J. R. SMITH and THOMAS SULLY. He first exhibited at the Artists' Fund Society in 1843 and during the next few years painted many portraits in Philadelphia and Fredericksburg (Va.). In 1849 he went to Florence (Italy) and there he spent the rest of his life, except for visits to France and Turkey. He was chiefly noted for his oriental scenes. He died in Florence January 18, 1893. ¶ CAB; Clement and Hutton; Rutledge, PA; Phila. CD 1844–47; Graves, *Dictionary;* Rutledge, MHS.

GOURDEN, JEAN. French sculptor, age 42, at San Francisco in 1860. The 1861 San Francisco directory lists a Desire Gourdin, stonecutter in the employ of OTTAVIANO GORI. ¶ 8 Census (1860), Cal., VII, 725; San Francisco CD 1861.

GOUYT, THÉODORE. Artist at New Orleans in 1841–42. ¶ New Orleans CD 1841–42.

GOVE, ELMA MARY. Portrait painter and crayon artist, who exhibited at the National and Pennsylvania Academies and the Boston Athenaeum between 1849 and 1860. From 1849 to 1855 she was listed as living in NYC, in 1858 in Cincinnati (Ohio), in 1859 in Brooklyn (N.Y.), and in 1860 in NYC. ¶ Cowdrey, NAD; Rutledge, PA; Swan, BA.

GOVER, WILLIAM C. Lithographer and policeman of NYC, 1848–58, printer after 1860. Probably the same as William C. Glover of NYC who exhibited a frame of colored engravings at the American Institute in 1845. ¶ NYBD 1851–52, 1854; Am. Inst. Cat., 1845.

GOW, ——. Lithographer, of FISHBOURNE & GOW, San Francisco, 1851. Gow photographed and then drew on stone a view of San Francisco after the fire of 1851. ¶ Peters, *California on Stone.*

GOWAN, ALEXANDER. Portrait painter and printer at NYC, 1795–98. ¶ NYCD 1795, 1797–98 (cited by McKay).

GRACE, J. D. Ohio-born artist, 35, at NYC in 1860. ¶ 8 Census (1860), N.Y., LI, 669.

GRACE, JOHN C. English artist, age 32, living in Cincinnati (Ohio) in October 1850, with his New England-born wife and his daughter, age one year, born in Ohio. ¶ 7 Census (1850), Ohio, XXII, 715.

GRAEFF, CELESTINE. Swiss artist, age 30, living in Philadelphia in July 1860. ¶ 8 Census (1860), Pa., LV, 629.

GRAFF, ——. German lithographer, 28, at NYC in 1860. ¶ 8 Census (1860), N.Y., XLII, 638.

GRAFF, ALEXANDER M. Wood engraver of NYC, 1856–60+; in the latter year, of HICKOK & GRAFF. He also exhibited pencil drawings at the American Institute in 1848. ¶ NYBD 1856; NYCD 1857–60+; Am. Inst. Cat., 1848.

GRAFFENRIED, CHRISTOPH VON (1661–1743). Amateur artist; born November 15, 1661, in Bern (Switzerland). In 1710 he led a group of Swiss and Palatine colonists to North Carolina and there founded the town of New Bern. After three years in America, von Graffenried, now Landgrave of Carolina, returned to Switzerland. His manuscript account of his American experiences and his sketches of American scenes are in the Bibliothèque Municipale at Yverdon (Switz.). He died in 1743 at Worb (Switz.) shortly after his 82nd birthday. ¶ Thomas P. de Graffenried, *History of the de Graffenried Family,* 58–147, with one repro. and translation of the Landgrave's "Relation du Voyage d'Amerique"; Schutz, "Old New York in Switzerland," repro. of view of NYC in 1713; Stokes, *Historic Prints,* 12.

GRAFTON, JOHN. Portrait painter and teacher of drawing at Charleston (S.C.) in 1774 and 1775. He spoke of himself as a pupil of Sir Joshua Reynolds. He died in the summer of 1775. ¶ Prime, I, 4; Rutledge, *Artists in the Life of Charleston,* cites obituary in *South Carolina Gazette and Country Journal,* July 4, 1775; Bowes, *The Culture of Early Charleston.*

GRAHAM, ——. Copied GILBERT STUART's portrait of William Samuel Johnson in

NYC *c.* 1794, then moved to Philadelphia and *c.* 1796 to Boston, where he was still living in 1798. *Cf.* GEORGE GRAHAM. ¶ Beardsley, *Life and Times of William Samuel Johnson,* 156–157. Groce, *William Samuel Johnson, A Maker of the Constitution,* 197, states that Graham's copy of the Stuart portrait was owned by the Misses Carwalt of New Haven (Conn.) in 1937.

GRAHAM, A. W. Engraver who came from England to the United States about 1832. From about 1838 to 1845 he was working in Philadelphia; in 1869 he was working in NYC. ¶ Stauffer; Phila. BD 1838, CD 1839; Fielding.

GRAHAM, CURTIS BURR (1814–1890). Lithographer; born April 11, 1814, at Ossining (N.Y.); moved to NYC as a small child. In 1835 he established a lithographic business with his brother, JOHN REQUA GRAHAM. Two years later John left the business and Curtis went into partnership with JOHN PRICE as GRAHAM & PRICE. In 1842 he moved to Washington (D.C.) where he lived until his death on March 28, 1890. He was for many years lithographer for the Coast Survey. ¶ Carpenter, *The Reverend John Graham . . . and His Descendants,* 465–467; 8 Census (1860), D.C., I, 592; NYCD 1836–39; Washington CD 1853–60; Peters, *America on Stone.*

GRAHAM, GEORGE. Mezzotint and stipple engraver. Stauffer states that he was probably in Philadelphia in 1797, worked for NYC publishers in 1804, designed and engraved the frontispiece for a book published in Boston in 1812, and was again working in Philadelphia in 1813. He is listed in Boston directories in 1798 and 1803, in the latter year as both painter and engraver. It is possible that he was the man who copied STUART's portrait of William Samuel Johnson in NYC *c.* 1794 and later worked in Philadelphia and Boston (see —— GRAHAM). ¶ Stauffer; Boston CD 1798, 1803; Beardsley, *Life and Times of William Samuel Johnson,* 156–157.

GRAHAM, JOHN B., in Peters, *America on Stone,* is JOHN REQUA GRAHAM.

GRAHAM, JOHN REQUA (1818–1909). Lithographer; younger brother of CURTIS BURR GRAHAM, born in Ossining (N.Y.) February 28, 1818. From 1835 to 1837 he and his elder brother were partners in a lithographic establishment in NYC. After 1837 John abandoned lithography, moved to Camden (N.J.), and there for 40 years conducted a number of express, livery, and hotel enterprises. In 1878 he moved to Washington (D.C.) and for the next 17 years served as a clerk in the Navy Department. He died in Washington on June 30, 1909. ¶ Carpenter, *The Reverend John Graham . . . and His Descendants,* 469–471; Peters, *America on Stone,* (as John B. Graham).

GRAHAM, PATRICK. Irish lithographer, 25, at NYC in 1860. ¶ 8 Census (1860), N.Y., LX, 454.

GRAHAM & PRICE. Lithographers of NYC, 1837; probably CURTIS BURR GRAHAM and JOHN PRICE. ¶ NYBD 1837.

GRAHAM, ROBERT A. Virginia-born artist, age 38, boarding in Philadelphia in June 1860. ¶ 8 Census (1860), Pa., LIV, 79.

GRAHAM, WILLIAM. Engraver from New York, working in San Francisco in 1856 and after. In 1860 he was 29 years old and owned personalty valued at $600. ¶ 8 Census (1860), Cal., VII, 408; San Francisco CD 1856, BD 1859.

GRAIN, FREDERICK. A.N.A. Landscape and panorama painter, active 1833–57. Between 1833 and 1848 F. or Frederick Grain showed a number of panoramas in NYC and Boston and exhibited landscapes at the National Academy, Apollo Association, and American Art-Union. He was made an Associate Member of the National Academy in 1837. In 1847 and 1848 he was living in Philadelphia, but he returned to NYC and was listed in the directories there until 1857. ¶ J. E. Arrington cites N. Y. *Evening Post* (Sept. 26 and 30, 1833), Boston *Transcript* (July 18, Aug. 22, Sept. 10 and 19, 1838), and N. Y. *Herald* (Oct. 19, 1848); Cowdrey, NAD; Cowdrey, AA & AAU; Am. Inst. Cat., 1844; NYCD 1843–57; Stokes, *Historic Prints,* 82.

GRAIN, GEORGE. Artist. George, second son of PETER GRAIN, SR., was born in Boston *c.* 1829. In 1850 he was living with his father and family in Philadelphia. ¶ 7 Census (1850), Pa., LI, 317.

GRAIN, PETER, SR. (*c.* 1786–?). Portrait, miniature, landscape, and scene painter. Born in France *c.* 1786, the elder Grain came to America before 1815. His eldest child, PETER GRAIN, JR., was born in Maryland about that year. In 1822 Grain advertised in Richmond (Va.) as a miniature painter and drawing master and in 1823–24 he was at Charleston (S.C.). His daughter Caroline was born in England about 1825, and Ellen the following year in New York. In 1829 and 1830 he was at Boston, where his second son, GEORGE GRAIN, was born. He was in NYC from 1831 to 1836, in the latter year employed by the dioramist HANINGTON. He visited Charleston again in 1837–38 and returned to NYC the same year. Nothing further is heard of him until 1849–50 when he again visited Charleston. By August 1850 he was established in Philadelphia with his family and he was still there in 1853. ¶ 7 Census (1850), Pa., LI, 317; *Richmond Portraits;* Rutledge, *Artists in the Life of Charleston;* Swan, BA; Dunlap, *History,* II, 471; Cowdrey, NAD; Phila. *Public Ledger,* Aug. 30, 1849 (cited by J. E. Arrington); N. Y. *Herald,* Dec. 7 and 22, 1836 (cited by J. E. Arrington); Phila. CD 1850, 1853; Peters, *America on Stone.*

GRAIN, PETER, JR. Artist; eldest son of PETER GRAIN, SR.; born in Maryland about 1815. He was living in Philadelphia 1848–55. ¶ 7 Census (1850), Pa., LI, 317; Rutledge, PA.

GRAIN, ROBERT A. Virginia-born artist, age 38, living in Philadelphia in June 1860. In the same household were URBAN A. (27) and Mary A. Grain (18), both natives of Pennsylvania. ¶ 8 Census (1860), Pa., LIV, 80.

GRAIN, URBAN A. Pennsylvania-born artist, age 27, living in Philadelphia in June 1860, with ROBERT A. GRAIN. ¶ 8 Census (1860), Pa., LIV, 80.

GRAMBAY, E. A. German lithographer, 35, at NYC in 1860. His wife also was German, but their two children, ages 4 and 2, were born in New York. ¶ 8 Census (1860), N.Y., XLIV, 569.

GRANBERY, GEORGE (1794–1815). Portrait and landscape painter. He was born in Norfolk (Va.) in 1794 and studied in Edinburgh (Scotland). He began painting as a young boy and by 1814 had become a professional portrait painter in Virginia. He and his father were drowned August 27 or 28, 1815, on a trip to Bermuda. Several portraits and landscapes by George Granbery remain in the family. HENRIETTA AUGUSTA and VIRGINIA GRANBERY were his nieces. ¶ Information courtesy of J. H. Granbery of NYC, 1950; Mrs. Ralph Catterall, Valentine Museum, Richmond, 1950; *Richmond Portraits.*

GRANBERY, HENRIETTA AUGUSTA (1829–1927). Landscape painter; born October 3, 1829, Norfolk (Va.); at NYC 1860–69; died December 30, 1927. She was the sister of VIRGINIA GRANBERY and niece of GEORGE GRANBERY. ¶ Information courtesy of J. H. Granbery of NYC, 1950; Cowdrey, NAD; Rutledge, PA.

GRANBERY, VIRGINIA (1831–1921). Still life painter and teacher; born August 7, 1831, probably at Norfolk (Va.); at NYC 1860–69; teacher at Packer Institute, NYC; died December 17, 1921. She was the sister of HENRIETTA AUGUSTA GRANBERY and niece of GEORGE GRANBERY. ¶ Information courtesy J. H. Granbery of NYC, 1950; Cowdrey, NAD; Rutledge, PA.

GRAND, THOMAS. Sculptor at New Orleans in 1818. ¶ Delgado-WPA cites *La. Gazette,* July 3, 1818.

GRANDEL, E. Wood engraver working in NYC about 1856. ¶ *Portfolio* (Feb. 1954), 130, repro.

GRANGER, CHARLES H. Portrait painter and townscape draftsman of Saco (Me.) *c.* 1840–60, and at Boston in 1845. His view of the old Congregational Church, Saco, was lithographed and published by J. H. BUFFORD of Boston in 1860. He was also a piano teacher. ¶ Lipman and Winchester, 173; Boston BD 1845; Saco and Biddeford CD 1849; Biddeford and Saco BD 1856; *Portfolio* (May 1942), 19, repro.

GRANGER, FITZ HENRY, see FRANCIS H. GRANGER.

GRANGER, FRANCIS H. Artist at NYC 1848–49. His address was the same as that of Fitz Henry Granger (or Grainger) who exhibited crayon and ink sketches and landscapes in oils at the American Institute 1845–47. He may also be the F. H. Granger whose portraits of Alexander Hill, his wife, and his daughter, painted in 1853, were owned in 1952 by John K. Byard of Norwalk (Conn.). ¶ NYCD 1848–49; Am. Inst. Cat., 1845–47; *Antiques* (March 1952), 207.

GRANGER (or Grainger), HENRY. In 1845 Henry Granger of Public School No. 2, NYC, exhibited two oil paintings at the American Institute; the following year he exhibited one crayon sketch, his address then being the same as that of FITZ HENRY and JAMES GRANGER. In 1850 Henry Grainger, painter, was listed in the NYC directory. The relationship of Henry to FITZ HENRY, FRANCIS H. and JAMES GRANGER is unknown. ¶ Am. Inst. Cat., 1845–46; NYCD 1850.

GRANGER, JAMES. Exhibited crayon sketches

at the American Institute in 1845 and 1847. His address in both years was the same as that of FITZ HENRY, FRANCIS H. and HENRY GRANGER. ¶ Am. Inst. Cat., 1845, 1847.

GRANT, DANIEL. Lithographer at NYC 1850. ¶ NYBD 1850.

GRANT, J. Portrait painter. Dunlap recorded that J. Grant painted portraits in Philadelphia in 1829. This may be the J. Grant whose signed portrait of two children, dated Brooklyn [N.Y.] 1843, is in the Karolik Collection. ¶ Dunlap, *History,* II, 471; Karolik Cat., 272, repro. 273.

GRANT, JAMES. Pennsylvania-born lithographer, 22, at NYC in 1860. ¶ 8 Census (1860), N.Y., XLVI, 879.

GRANT, OWEN. Apprentice engraver, age 17, at New Orleans in 1860. He was a native of Louisiana, but his mother was Irish. ¶ 8 Census (1860), La., VII, 582.

GRANTLEY, CHARLES. Lithographer, age 27, native of Pennsylvania, living in Philadelphia in June 1860. ¶ 8 Census (1860), Pa., LI, 6.

GRANVILLE, CHARLES BECARD DE. Author and illustrator of a manuscript account of the flora and fauna, Indians, and other natural wonders of what is now eastern Canada and northeastern United States at the close of the 17th century. The manuscript was published in Paris, 1930, as *Les Raretés des Indes, "Codex Canadiensis," Album Manuscrit de la Fin du XVIIe Siècle Contenant 180 Dessins . . . ,* by Charles Becard de Granville, with 79 plates. ¶ Granville, *op. cit.*

GRASS, J. D., see JACOB D. GROSS.

GRASSE, AUGUSTUS DE. Drawing master at Charleston (S.C.) in 1800. He advertised as a teacher of designing plans of fortifications as well as architecture and landscapes. ¶ Rutledge, *Artists in the Life of Charleston.*

GRATACAP, GEORGE G. Lithographer. He worked in NYC in 1845–46 and in Hartford (Conn.) with KELLOGG & Co. in 1848. ¶ NYCD 1845–46; Hartford CD 1848; Conn. Hist. Soc., *Cat. of Exhibition of Kellogg Prints,* 1952.

GRATZ, JOHN. Engraver, age 22, from Bavaria, living in Philadelphia in 1860. ¶ 8 Census (1860), Pa., LIX, 249.

GRAY, ——, see GRAY & TODD.

GRAY, A. H. Decorative, sign, and transparency painter at Charleston (S.C.) in 1842. ¶ Rutledge, *Artists in the Life of Charleston.*

GRAY, CHARLES J. Engraver of NYC 1842–50. From 1846 he was associated with his son WILLIAM T. GRAY as C. J. Gray & Son. ¶ NYCD 1842–50; NYBD 1844, 1846.

GRAY, CHARLOTTE. English artist, 36, at NYC in 1860. ¶ 8 Census (1860), N.Y., LX, 320.

GRAY, HENRY (?–1779). Water color painter. He was a lieutenant in the Second South Carolina Regiment, wounded at Charleston (S.C.) in June 6, 1776. He painted two watercolors of the attack on Sullivan's Island at that time, one of which is reproduced in the *Memoirs* of John Drayton. Lt. Gray was killed in action at Savannah (Ga.) in 1779. ¶ Rutledge, *Artists in the Life of Charleston; American Battle Painting* (gives death date as 1824).

GRAY, HENRY PETERS (1819–1877). N.A. Portrait and figure painter. He was born in NYC June 23, 1819, and studied for a year with DANIEL HUNTINGTON before going to Italy in 1839. After his return in 1841, he painted portraits in NYC and Boston for several years and then made a second trip to Europe in 1845–46. From 1846 to 1871 he resided in NYC where he was one of the most popular portrait painters of the day and much praised for his classical and historical figure pieces. Elected a Member of the National Academy in 1842, he served as its president in 1870–71. He went to Italy again in 1871, remaining for four years. He died in NYC November 12, 1877. ¶ DAB; Clement and Hutton; Cowdrey, AA & AAU; Cowdrey, NAD; Swan, BA; Rutledge, Pa; Rutledge, MHS; Washington Art Assoc. Cat., 1859; NYBD 1848–60; *Magazine of Art* (Nov. 1946), 289, repro.; represented NYHS and Corcoran Gallery.

GRAY, J. F. Painter of *Illustrations of Florida,* advertised in Charleston (S.C.) in 1836. ¶ Rutledge, *Artists in the Life of Charleston.*

GRAY, JAMES. Miniaturist at Richmond (Va.) in 1811 and 1819. ¶ *Richmond Portraits,* 242.

GRAY, JAMES. Scottish engraver, age 31, at Frankford (Pa.) in August 1850. His wife and three children born before 1845 were from Scotland, while two younger children were born in Rhode Island. ¶ 7 Census (1850), Pa., LVI, 323–324.

GRAY, KENNEDY. Engraver at Troy (N.Y.) 1857–59. ¶ Troy BD 1857–58; N. Y. State BD 1859.

GRAY & TODD. Engravers of diagrams and script-work at Philadelphia in 1817. Gray is otherwise unknown; Todd may be A. TODD. ¶ Stauffer; Dunlap, *History* (1918) (under Todd).

GRAY, W. Delineator of a view of the Court House, Salem (Mass.), *c.* 1790, known through an engraving by J. HILL. ¶ Stauffer, under Hill.

GRAY, WILLIAM. Irish lithographer, 32, at NYC in 1860. His wife and two children were natives of New York. ¶ 8 Census (1860), N.Y., XLIV, 122.

GRAY, WILLIAM T. Engraver of NYC 1846–50. He was the son of CHARLES J. GRAY and was born in England about 1826. ¶ NYCD 1846–50; NYBD 1848, 1850; 7 Census (1850), N.Y., XLVI, 797.

GRAYDON, ALEXANDER (1752–1818). Amateur painter. Born April 10, 1752, at Bristol (Pa.), Graydon served during the Revolution and in 1785 was elected prothonotary of Dauphin County (Pa.). He made his home in or near Harrisburg from that time until 1816. He moved to Philadelphia, in 1816 and died there on May 2nd, 1818. In his *Memoirs of a Life, Chiefly Passed in Pennsylvania within the Last Sixty Years* (Harrisburg, 1811), Graydon spoke of his fondness for drawing and painting. He is known to have painted on glass, in the contemporary Chinese manner, a copy of GILBERT STUART'S Washington. ¶ DAB; CAB; Fielding.

GREATH (or Groath), ——. Swedish miniaturist working in Philadelphia *c.* 1773–74. ¶ Sartain, *Reminiscences of a Very Old Man,* 151–152, and Bolton, *Miniature Painters,* say Greath, citing CHARLES WILLSON PEALE to REMBRANDT PEALE, Oct. 28, 1812; Sellers, *Charles Willson Peale,* I, 112, says Groath and suggests he may have been the German artist Groth who painted miniatures in London during the reign of George II.

GREATOREX, Mrs. ELIZA (PRATT) (1820–1897). A.N.A. Landscape and cityscape painter and etcher, born December 25, 1820 at Manor Hamilton (Ireland). She came to NYC with her family in 1840 and in 1849 married Henry W. Greatorex (1816–1858), a prominent musician of NYC. After his death in 1858 Mrs. Greatorex became a professional artist, studying in NYC under WILLIAM W. WOTHERSPOON and JAMES M. and WILLIAM HART and later in Paris and Munich. She was best known for her views of NYC. She was elected an Associate Member of the National Academy in 1869. During her later years she spent much of her time in Europe with her two daughters, Kathleen Honora (born 1851) and Elizabeth Eleanor (born 1854), both of whom became artists. Mrs. Greatorex died in Paris on February 9, 1897. ¶ Thieme-Becker; CAB; Clement and Hutton; N. Y. *Daily Tribune,* Feb. 11, 1897, obit.; *American Art Review* (1881), Part II, 12–13; Cowdrey, NAD; Rutledge, PA; Swan, BA; Washington Art Assoc. Cat., 1859; *Portfolio* (Dec. 1942), 87, repro.

GREELEY, MARY ELIZABETH (1836–1924). Artist and teacher; born February 13, 1836, at Foxcroft (Me.); died there December 31, 1924. She lived in Brooklyn (N.Y.) from 1872 to 1885. ¶ "Maine Artists."

GREEN, EDWARD F. Portrait painter. So listed in NYC business directory for 1846, Green was listed at the same address in the city directories 1845–47 as "liquors." *Cf.* E. F. Green of London who exhibited 55 portraits in galleries there between 1824 and 1851. ¶ NYBD 1846; NYCD 1845–47; Graves, *Dictionary.*

GREEN & FISHBOURNE. Lithographers at NYC 1836 (as Greene & Pishbourne); at New Orleans 1840–42; WILLIAM GREEN and R. W. FISHBOURNE. ¶ Peters, *America on Stone;* NYCD 1836; Delgado-WPA cites *Picayune,* Sept. 10, 1840, and New Orleans CD 1841–42.

GREEN, FRANCIS G. Landscape and marine painter of NYC, 1844–60. He exhibited at the American Institute in 1844 and 1845, the American Art-Union 1849–50, and the National Academy 1850–53 and 1860. ¶ Am. Inst. Cat., 1844–45; Cowdrey, AA & AAU; Cowdrey, NAD; NYCD 1851–52.

GREEN, HENRY F., see HENRY F. GREENE.

GREEN, HENRY J. Engraver of Boston, 1851. *Cf.* HENRY F. GREENE. ¶ Boston CD 1851.

GREEN, JASPER (1829–1910). Wood carver and artist-correspondent for *Harper's Weekly* during the Civil War. He was born January 31, 1829, at Columbia (Pa.), and died March 2, 1910, at Philadelphia. ¶ Lancaster Co. Hist. Soc., *Historical Papers* (1912), 276.

GREEN, JOHN (?–1802). Portrait painter. As a young man in the 1750's Green lived for a time in Philadelphia and was a friend of BENJAMIN WEST, whose portrait of him is owned by the Historical

Society of Pennsylvania. About 1765 he settled in Bermuda. In 1774 he went to London to study painting and there renewed his acquaintance with West. Returning to Bermuda probably a year or so later, Green married and apparently gave up painting as a profession to become Collector of Customs at St. George and later Judge of the Court of Vice-Admiralty. He died in Bermuda September 3, 1802. A number of his portraits are still extant in Bermuda and England. ¶ Watlington, "The Incomplete Story of John Green, Artist and Judge," with frontis. by West; Dunlap, I, 32; Fielding.

GREEN (or Greene), WILLIAM. Lithographers of this name were active in NYC, New Orleans, Albany (N.Y.), and Hartford (Conn.) between 1836 and 1856. The Greene of GREENE & PISHBOURNE [sic] in NYC 1836 and of GREENE & MCGOWRAN in NYC 1837 is almost certainly the William Green who did five views of New Orleans for the directory of 1838 and in 1840–41 was with the New Orleans firm of GREEN & FISHBOURNE. William Green next appears as a lithographer and portrait artist at Albany (N.Y.) from 1843 to 1845; as a lithographer in NYC in 1848; and finally as a lithographer at Hartford (Conn.) from 1849 to 1856 (from 1849 to 1852 as a partner in CASE & GREEN). Although no positive connection between them has been established, it seems probable that these various William Greens were the same man. ¶ NYCD 1836–37; New Orleans CD 1838, 1840–41; Albany CD 1843–44; NYCD 1848; Hartford CD 1849–55; New England BD 1856. Peters, *America on Stone,* makes a distinction between William Green of NYC and New Orleans and William Green of Albany.

GREEN, WILLIAM H. Engraver of Meriden (Conn.) 1856–60. ¶ New England BD 1856, 1860.

GREEN, W. T. Engraver of one illustration in *Benjamin Franklin: His Autobiography . . .* (N.Y., 1849). ¶ Hamilton, 172.

GREENE, ——, lithographer, see WILLIAM GREEN (or Greene).

GREENE, EDWARD D. E. (1823–1879). N.A. Portrait and genre painter. A native of Boston, Greene exhibited there for the first time in 1846. He moved to NYC about 1850 and worked there until his death on June 17, 1879. He was elected a Member of the National Academy in 1858 and also exhibited at the Boston Athenaeum, American Art-Union, Pennsylvania Academy, and Washington Art Association. ¶ Swan, BA; Boston BD 1847; Cowdrey, NAD; Cowdrey, AA & AAU; Rutledge, PA; Washington Art Assoc. Cat., 1857, 1859; *American Art Review* (1880), Part I, 46, obit.

GREENE (or Green), HENRY F. Plate and music engraver of Boston, 1850–60. He was born in Massachusetts about 1828. He was with the firm of WELLER & GREEN in 1852 and GREENE & WALKER from 1857. *Cf.* HENRY J. GREEN. ¶ Boston CD 1851–60; BD 1852–53, 1858; 7 Census (1850), Mass., XXV, 61.

GREENE & MCGOWRAN. Lithographers at NYC, 1837. See WILLIAM GREEN. ¶ NYCD 1837; Peters, *America on Stone.*

GREENE, MOSELY. Engraver at St. Louis (Mo.), 1859. In 1865 he was listed as an oil painter. ¶ St. Louis BD 1859; CD 1865.

GREENE, Mrs. N. Painter of "The Great Carbuncle of the White Mountains," shown at the Boston Athenaeum in 1842. ¶ Swan, BA.

GREENE & PISHBOURNE, see GREEN & FISHBOURNE.

GREENE & WALKER. Plate engravers of Boston, 1857–60; HENRY F. GREENE and WILLIAM F. WALKER. ¶ Boston CD 1857–60; BD 1858.

GREENE, WILLIAM C. Engraver at Chicago, 1856–59. ¶ Chicago BD 1856; CD 1859.

GREENLEAF, BENJAMIN (1786–1864). Portrait painter on glass. Born September 25, 1786, at Haverhill (Mass.), Greenleaf took up portrait painting to pay his way through Dartmouth College. After his graduation in 1813, he became a teacher in Haverhill. From 1814 to 1836 he was preceptor of Bradford Academy, Bradford (Mass.) and it was during these years (until about 1825) that he painted most of his known portraits on glass. After three years in the state legislature (1837–39), Greenleaf founded the Bradford Teachers' Seminary which he headed until 1848. His textbooks, particularly in arithmetic, were widely used. He died in Bradford, October 29, 1864. ¶ Lipman, "Benjamin Greenleaf, New England Limner," checklist and 7 repros.; DAB; Lipman and Winchester, 173; WPA (Mass.), *Portraits Found in Massachusetts,* no. 2201. Represented Mass. Medical Society, Boston.

GREENOUGH, ——. Engraver at Peterboro (N.H.) in 1860. ¶ New England BD 1860.

GREENOUGH, BENJAMIN F. Engraver and stereotype founder of Boston in the 1830's. With J. JAMES GREENOUGH he engraved plates for one of the American editions of the *Penny Magazine* (1832–39). ¶ Boston CD 1833; Linton, *History of Wood Engraving in America,* 19.

GREENOUGH, HORATIO (1805–1852). Sculptor. Born in Boston (Mass.), September 6, 1805, Horatio Greenough showed an early interest in carving and modelling. In 1824 he went to Italy to study sculpture for two years. Returning to Italy in 1829, he settled in Florence and lived there for the next two decades. In 1842 he visited Washington (D.C.) to deliver and install his colossal statue of Washington, which had been commissioned by the U. S. Government. Greenough left Italy in 1851 to take up his residence in Newport (R.I.), but the next year he was stricken with brain fever and died in Somerville (Mass.), December 18, 1852. He was the first American sculptor to win international recognition. Two of his brothers, JOHN and RICHARD S. GREENOUGH, also were professional artists. He was an Honorary Member of the National Academy. ¶ The chief works on Greenough are his own *Travels, Observations, and Experiences of a Yankee Stonecutter,* published in 1852 under the pseudonym "Horace Bender"; Frances Boott Greenough, ed., *Letters of Horatio Greenough to His Brother, Henry Greenough;* and Tuckerman, *Memoir of Horatio Greenough* (1853). Shorter notices appear in DAB; Gardner, *Yankee Stonecutters;* Fairman, *Art and Artists of the Capitol;* Taft, *History of American Sculpture;* Tuckerman, *Book of the Artists;* Dunlap; Swan, BA; Rutledge, PA; Cowdrey, AA & AAU; Cowdrey, NAD; Rutledge, MHS; Lee, *Familiar Sketches of Sculpture and Sculptors,* 130–140; Wynne and Newhall, "Horatio Greenough: Herald of Functionalism"; Wright, "Horatio Greenough, Boston Sculptor."

GREENOUGH, J. JAMES. Engraver of Boston in the 1830's. He was associated with BENJAMIN F. GREENOUGH in engraving cuts for the *Penny Magazine* (1832–39). ¶ Boston CD 1833; Linton, *History of Wood Engraving in America,* 19.

GREENOUGH, JOHN (1801–1852). Portrait and landscape painter. John, elder brother of the famous sculptor HORATIO GREENOUGH, was born in Boston in November 1801. He left Harvard College in his senior year to study art in London. During the 1830's he worked in England, then returned to Boston where he was living from 1844 to 1850. He spent some time with Horatio in Florence and died in Paris in November 1852. He exhibited at the Boston Athenaeum and the Royal Academy. ¶ Dunlap, *History* (1918), III, 304; Fielding; F. B. Greenough, ed., *Letters of Horatio Greenough to His Brother, Henry Greenough,* ix; Boston BD 1844–50; Swan, BA; Graves, *Dictionary.*

GREENOUGH, RICHARD SALTONSTALL (1819–1904). Sculptor. Richard, brother of HORATIO and JOHN GREENOUGH, was born in Jamaica Plain (Mass.), April 27, 1819. He made his first trip to Italy in 1837, visiting his brother Horatio at his studio in Florence. Thereafter he divided his time between Europe and America, but spent most of his studio life in Rome where he died April 23, 1904. Most of his American work was done in Boston and Newport (R.I.). ¶ DAB; *Art Annual* (1905/06), 121; CAB; Taft, *History of American Sculpture;* Boston BD 1847–51, 1855–56; Swan, BA; Graves, *Dictionary;* Gardner, *Yankee Stonecutters.*

GREENWALD, see GUSTAVUS GRUNEWALD.

GREENWALT, JOHN. Print engraver, listed as a "colored man," at Philadelphia in 1817. ¶ Brown and Brown.

GREENWOOD, ——. Decorative painter who did "oriental tinting and mezzotinto" at Charleston (S.C.) 1833–34. ¶ Rutledge, *Artists in the Life of Charleston.*

GREENWOOD, ETHAN ALLEN (1779–1856). Portrait painter. He was born in Hubbardstown (Mass.) on May 27, 1779, and began painting about 1801. From then until 1812 he taught school, attended Dartmouth College, and studied law, while his portrait painting continued as a secondary occupation. He received some instruction from EDWARD SAVAGE in NYC in 1806. In June 1812 he opened a studio in Boston where he painted many portraits; in 1818 he also took over Savage's Museum. After his father's death in 1827 Greenwood returned to Hubbardstown and later entered politics. He died there May 3 or 6, 1856. ¶ "A List of Portraits Painted by Ethan Allen Greenwood," *American Antiquarian Society Proceedings* (April 1946), 129–153, lists over 800 works of the artist; Dunlap, *History* (1918), III, 304; Swan, BA; Sears, *Some American Primitives,* 263–264; *An-*

tiques (Nov. 1939), 224, (Oct. 1944), 208, repros.

GREENWOOD, JOHN (1727–1792). Portrait painter and engraver. Born in Boston on December 7, 1727, John Greenwood was apprenticed to the engraver THOMAS JOHNSTON, but about 1745 he turned to the painting of portraits. He left Boston in 1752, at the age of 25, and went to Surinam where he painted over a hundred portraits during the next five and a half years. In 1758 he went to Holland where he specialized in engraving. He finally settled in London in 1762 and established himself as a dealer in art and curios, though he continued to do some painting, including a few landscapes. He died at Margate on September 16, 1792. ¶ Burroughs, *John Greenwood in America;* DNB; Weitenkampf, "John Greenwood; An American-born Artist in Eighteenth Century Europe, with a Checklist of His Etchings and Mezzotints"; Stauffer.

GREGORY, ELIOT. Itinerant portrait painter of south-eastern Pennsylvania. He was working in Churchtown in 1842. ¶ Lancaster Co. Hist. Soc., *Portraiture in Lancaster Co.,* 126.

GREGORY, WILLIAM C. Engraver at Lowell (Mass.) 1834–37. ¶ Belknap, *Artists and Craftsmen of Essex Co.,* 3.

GREGSON, JAMES. Engraver at Cincinnati (Ohio) 1859–60, in the latter year with GREGSON & SAVER. ¶ Cincinnati BD 1859–60.

GREGSON, (or Greyson) JOHN. Lithographer at Cincinnati (Ohio), 1858–60. ¶ Cincinnati CD 1859–60; BD 1858 (as Greyson).

GREGSON & SAVER. Engravers and lithographers, Cincinnati (Ohio), 1860. The partners were JAMES GREGSON and JOHN S. SAVER. ¶ Cincinnati BD 1860.

GREINER, CHRISTOPHER M. (?–1864). Portrait and miniature painter, who worked in Philadelphia and Reading between 1837 and his death in 1864. At the Artists' Fund Society in 1844 he showed a number of enamel paintings. ¶ Bolton, *Miniature Painters;* Rutledge, PA; Phila. BD 1850.

GREWELDT, ——. Artist at Cincinnati in 1842. ¶ Information courtesy Edward H. Dwight, Cincinnati Art Museum.

GREYSON, JOHN, see JOHN GREGSON.

GRIDER, RUFUS ALEXANDER (1817–1900). Landscape, flower, and still life painter in watercolors. He was born April 13, 1817, in Lititz (Pa.) and attended school there. A Moravian, he spent much time in Bethlehem (Pa.) and many sketches and watercolors done there are now in the Moravian Archives. In 1883 he moved to Canajoharie (N.Y.) as an art teacher. There he executed the series of watercolors of old powder horns now at the NYHS. Grider died at Canajoharie on February 7, 1900. ¶ Dickinson, "Rufus Alexander Grider"; Levering, *History of Bethlehem,* 710, 714–15 (citation courtesy Rev. J. F. Morman, Bethlehem); Rutledge, PA.

GRIDLEY, ENOCH G. Portrait and general engraver working in NYC 1803–04, thereafter at Philadelphia until 1818. ¶ Stauffer; NYCD 1803–04; *American Collector* (Feb. 1945), 6, repro.; *Antiques* (Nov. 1947), 332.

GRIER & CLARK. Wood engravers of Philadelphia, 1856. DAVID GRIER may have been the senior partner; Clark's identity is unknown. ¶ Phila. BD 1856.

GRIER, DAVID. Designer and wood engraver at Philadelphia, 1857–59. He may have been with GRIER & CLARK in 1856. ¶ Phila. CD 1857–59.

GRIES, JOHN M. Architect and watercolor artist of Philadelphia who exhibited at the Pennsylvania Academy in 1857. ¶ Rutledge, PA; Phila. CD 1857.

GRIFFEN, HENRY E. Artist, 26, a native of New York, at NYC in 1850. ¶ 7 Census (1850), N.Y., LV, 792.

GRIFFETH, JOHN M. Artist, 40, a native of New York, at NYC in 1850. His wife and a sixteen-year-old son were born in Virginia; six younger children, in New York. ¶ 7 Census (1850), N.Y., XLIX, 975.

GRIFFIN, JOHN B. of GRIFFIN & SPERONI, engravers of NYC, 1860 and after. ¶ NYBD 1860; NYCD 1862.

GRIFFIN & SPERONI. Engravers of NYC 1860 and after; JOHN B. GRIFFIN and JOHN L. SPERONI. ¶ NYBD 1860; NYCD 1862.

GRIFFING, MARTIN (1784–1859). Itinerant painter of color profiles, after 1806 in Vermont and New York State. ¶ Bolton, *Miniature Painters;* Carrick, *Shades of Our Ancestors,* 122; Fielding.

GRIFFITH, JAMES. Scottish engraver, age 28, at Philadelphia in August 1850. ¶ 7 Census (1850), Pa., LVI, 323.

GRIFFITH, JOSIA[H]. Pennsylvania-born portrait painter, age 55, living in Kensington, near Philadelphia in July 1850. ¶ 7 Census (1850), Pa., XLIX, 178.

GRIGGS, ——. Portrait painter at Cincinnati (Ohio), 1853. ¶ Ohio BD 1853.

GRIGGS, SAMUEL W. (?–1898). Landscape painter and architect of Boston active *c.* 1848–98. He was listed as an architect 1848–52 and thereafter as an artist. He exhibited frequently at the Boston Athenaeum. ¶ Swan, BA; Boston CD 1848–59.

GRIMES, JOHN C. (1804–1837). Portrait painter and teacher of drawing and painting. He was born in Lexington (Ky.) in 1804 and studied under MATTHEW HARRIS JOUETT. He is said to have been working in Huntsville (Ala.) as early as 1820. From 1825 to 1827 he was in Philadelphia, but he returned to Kentucky the following year. He worked in Nashville (Tenn.) during the 1830's, and was teaching at Lexington (Ky.) when he died on December 27, 1837. ¶ Information courtesy Mrs. W. H. Whitley, Paris (Ky.); WPA (Ala.), Hist. Records Survey cites Huntsville *Alabama Republican,* Oct. 6, 1820; Rutledge, PA; Hart, "Portrait of John Grimes, Painted by Matthew Harris Jouett," repro.; Lexington *Gazette,* Dec. 28, 1837, obit.

GRIMM, J. P. P. Portrait painter at Green Bay (Wis.) in September 1851. ¶ Butts, *Art in Wisconsin,* 84.

GRIMMONS, CHARLES. Portrait painter at Glastonbury (Conn.) in 1852. He exhibited at the Pennsylvania Academy in that year a copy of Sir Thomas Lawrence's portrait of BENJAMIN WEST. ¶ Rutledge, PA.

GRINNETT or GRINNELL, MAX. German lithographer, 27, at NYC in 1850. ¶ 7 Census (1850), N.Y., XLII, 10.

GRINNIS, CHARLES. Connecticut portrait painter. *Cf.* CHARLES GRIMMONS. ¶ Sears, *Some American Primitives,* 289–290; Lipman and Winchester.

GRIPPEN, Capt. A. W. Designer of a view of Downieville (Cal.) soon after 1850, used as a letter-head. ¶ Van Nostrand and Coulter, *California Pictorial,* 134–135, repro.

GRISEL, LOUIS. Swiss engraver, age 33, living in Philadelphia in June 1860. His wife was French, and his son Louis, age 10, was born in Delaware. Probably the same as LEWIS GUSEL. ¶ 8 Census (1860), Pa., LIV, 61.

GRISHA, HENRY. Lithographer, age 23, living in Kensington, near Philadelphia in July 1850. He was a native of Pennsylvania, but his father was French. ¶ 7 Census (1850), Pa., XLVII, 7.

GRISLEY, CHARLES. English engraver, 44, at NYC in 1850. ¶ 7 Census (1850), N.Y., XLV, 717.

GRIST, FRANKLIN R. Genre painter of New Haven (Conn.), who exhibited at the National Academy in 1848. ¶ Cowdrey, NAD.

GRISWOLD, CASIMIR CLAYTON (1834–1918). N.A. Landscape painter and wood engraver. He was born in Delaware (Ohio) in 1834, studied engraving in Cincinnati, and moved to NYC *c.* 1850. He first exhibited at the National Academy in 1857 and was elected a Member in 1867. During the 1870's and 1880's he lived in Rome. He died in Poughkeepsie (N.Y.) on June 7, 1918. ¶ CAB; *Art Annual,* XV; Clement and Hutton; Champlin and Perkins; Thieme-Becker; Cowdrey, NAD; Rutledge, PA.

GRISWOLD, VICTOR MOREAU (1819–1872). Landscape painter. Born April 14, 1819, at Worthington (Ohio), V. M. Griswold abandoned the study of law in the early 1840's to take up portrait painting. He studied in Columbus (Ohio) under WILLIAM WALCUTT and exhibited at the American Art-Union and National Academy between 1849 and 1858. In 1851 he became a professional photographer at Tiffin and two years later at Lancaster (Ohio). In 1856 he invented the ferrotype plate with the manufacture of which he was concerned in Lancaster and after 1861 in Peekskill (N.Y.). He died in Peekskill on June 18, 1872. ¶ Wiseman, *Centennial History of Lancaster, Ohio,* 248–250; Cowdrey, AA & AAU; Cowdrey, NAD.

GRITTEN, HENRY. English landscape painter. From 1835 to 1849 he exhibited landscapes in various London galleries. By 1850 he had arrived in America and during the next four years he exhibited at the National Academy as a resident of Brooklyn (N.Y.) and NYC. ¶ Graves, *Dictionary;* Cowdrey, NAD; Cowdrey, AA & AAU.

GROATH, see GREATH.

GROB, TRAUTMAN. Artist and drawing master of San Francisco 1856–61. ¶ Peters, *California on Stone;* San Francisco BD 1861.

GROENLAND, HERRMANN. Portrait and landscape painter at Cincinnati (Ohio) 1844–51, 1856–60. He was in partnership with B. DELITISCH in 1857. ¶ Cist, *Cincinnati in 1851;* Cincinnati CD 1850–51, 1856–59; BD 1859–60; Ohio BD 1859.

GROGAN, NATHANIEL (*c.* 1740–1807). Landscape and ornamental painter, comic illustrator, and aquatint engraver; born in Cork (Ireland). Opposed by his parents in his wish to become an artist, he enlisted in the army and served in America and the West Indies. While stationed in Philadelphia in 1777, he advertised as an ornamental painter. After his return to Cork, Grogan enjoyed a fairly successful career as a painter of landscapes and comic genre, an ornamental painter, and an engraver in aquatint. He died in Cork in 1807. ¶ Strickland, *Dictionary of Irish Artists;* Thieme-Becker; Prime, I, 4.

GROOMBRIDGE, Mrs. CATHERINE (*c.* 1760–1837). Landscape painter and wife of WILLIAM GROOMBRIDGE. She conducted a school for girls in Philadelphia from about 1794 to 1804 and a young ladies' academy in Baltimore from 1804 to 1815. An amateur painter, she exhibited one landscape at the Academy of Fine Arts in Philadelphia in 1812. She died in Kingston (Jamaica) on November 20, 1837, at the age of 77. ¶ Pleasants, "Four Late 18th Century Anglo-American Landscape Painters," 32–40; Rutledge, PA.

GROOMBRIDGE, WILLIAM (1748–1811). Landscape, portrait, and miniature painter. Born in Tunbridge, Kent (England) in 1748, Groombridge was active as a landscape and portrait painter in Kent and London from 1773 to about 1790. He arrived in Philadelphia probably in 1794 and made his home there until 1804, when he moved to Baltimore. His wife, Mrs. CATHERINE GROOMBRIDGE, conducted girls' schools in both cities. WILLIAM DUNLAP remembered meeting Groombridge in NYC about 1796, but gave his name erroneously as Groomrich. Groombridge exhibited at the Society of Artists in Philadelphia and posthumously at the Maryland Historical Society. He died in Baltimore on May 24, 1811. ¶ Pleasants, "Four Late 18th Century Anglo-American Landscape Painters," 31–54, with 4 repros.; DNB; Prime, II, 55–56; Phila. CD 1800, 1804; Rutledge, PA; Dunlap, *History* (1918), I, 321, and II, 176–177; Rutledge, MHS; Pleasants, *250 Years of Painting in Md.; Antiques* (March 1951), 216, repro.; Flexner, *The Light of Distant Skies,* biblio., 261.

GROPPI, PEDRO. Italian-born plaster image maker, age 27, living in Boston in June 1860; personal property valued at $1,000. ¶ 8 Census (1860), Mass., XXVI, 402.

GROSH, PETER LEHN (1798–1859). Portrait, sign, and fancy painter of Mechanicsville (Pa.). Most of his portraits were painted in Mechanicsville between 1816 and 1835. In 1857 he moved to Petersburg (Pa.) where he died two years later. Besides his work as a general painter, he had been an instrument maker and fruit and flower grower. ¶ Lancaster Co. Hist. Soc., *Portraiture in Lancaster Co.,* 126, lists six of his portraits; Lancaster Co. Hist. Soc., *Historical Papers,* XVI (Dec. 1912), 285–291.

GROSS, GEORGE. Portrait painter of NYC, 1851. ¶ NYBD 1851.

GROSS, J. Portrait engraver, probably brought to Philadelphia *c.* 1834 by JAMES LONGACRE to work on his *National Portrait Gallery.* Stauffer distinguishes between J. Gross and the later J. D. GROSS, also a Philadelphia engraver. ¶ Stauffer; Fielding.

GROSS, JACOB D. Engraver of Philadelphia 1848–85. He is listed as J. D. Gross until 1860 (as J. D. Grass, 1854) and as Jacob or Jacob D. Gross thereafter. According to Stauffer, to be distinguished from J. GROSS, engraver in Philadelphia *c.* 1834. ¶ Phila. CD 1848–50, 1854–57, 1861, 1863–85; Stauffer.

GROSVENOR, HORACE C. (or G.) Wood engraver of Cincinnati (Ohio) 1842–58. He was in partnership with G. W. THOMPSON in 1850 and with JOHN R. TELFER in 1851. The 1850 Census lists Horace Grosvenor twice: on August 19 as Horace Grosvenor, engraver, age 30, born in Vermont; and on September 30 as Horace G. Grosvenor, wood engraver, age 31, born in Ohio. Both census entries presumably refer to the same man, despite the discrepancies in age and place of birth. ¶ Cincinnati BD 1850–51, 1853; CD 1842–50, 1851, 1853, 1856–58; 7 Census (1850), Ohio, XX, 351 and 726.

GROSVENOR & TELFER. Wood engravers of Cincinnati (Ohio), who executed one illustration for *Historical Collections of the Great West . . . ,* published in Cincinnati in 1851. The partners were probably HORACE C. GROSVENOR and JOHN R. TELFER. ¶ Hamilton, 265.

GROSVENOR & THOMPSON. Wood engravers of Cincinnati (Ohio), 1849–50; HORACE C. GROSVENOR and CHARLES W. THOMPSON. ¶ Cincinnati BD 1850.

GROUARD & DUNNING. Artists of Fall River (Mass.) 1859; JOHN E. GROUARD and

ROBERT S. DUNNING. ¶ Fall River BD 1859.

GROUARD, JOHN E. Artist, of GROUARD & DUNNING, Fall River (Mass.) 1859. ¶ Fall River BD 1859.

GROUSTEIN, WILLIAM. Artist, born in New York *c.* 1824, living in Philadelphia in August 1850. *Cf.* Z. GROUSTINE. ¶ 7 Census (1850), Pa., L, 928.

GROUSTINE (or Groustein), Z. Landscape and figure painter at Philadelphia 1852–57. Several French views were among the paintings he showed at the Pennsylvania Academy during these years. The name appears as Groustein only in 1853. *Cf.* WILLIAM GROUSTEIN. ¶ Rutledge, PA; Phila. BD 1856–57.

GROUT, JOHN H. Portrait painter in Vermont. His oil portrait of Mrs. Albert Griffin, begun in 1833, was owned in 1941 by Mrs. Anna Byington of Charlotte (Vt.). ¶ WPA (Mass.), *Portraits Found in Vt.*

GROVES, HIRAM. Lithographer at New Orleans in 1838. ¶ New Orleans CD 1838.

GROZELIER, LEOPOLD (1830–1865). Portrait painter and lithographic draftsman. Born in France, Grozelier came to this country in the early 1850's and worked as a portrait painter in NYC in 1852 and as a lithographic artist in Boston from 1854 probably until his death in 1865. In 1854 he was working for S. W. CHANDLER & BROTHER of Boston. In 1855 he married Miss Sara Peters, miniaturist (see Mrs. SARA GROZELIER). ¶ Swan, BA; NYBD 1852; Peters, *America on Stone;* 8 Census (1860), Mass., XXVIII, 103; Stokes, *Historic Prints,* pl. 92b; Hosmer, "John G. Chandler," 46–47.

GROZELIER, Mrs. SARA (PETERS) (1821–1907). Miniaturist; born in Andover (Mass.) on May 21, 1821; married LEOPOLD GROZELIER in Boston in 1855. She was listed in Boston directories in 1866 and from 1877 to 1883. She exhibited at the Boston Athenaeum. ¶ Swan, BA, 184, 233.

GRUBE, LOUIS. Still life, portrait, and landscape painter at Poughkeepsie (N.Y.) 1847–51, and at Brooklyn (N.Y.) 1856–60. A Brooklyn view from an 1846 painting by Grube was published by N. CURRIER. Exhibited at the National Academy and the American Art-Union. ¶ Cowdrey, NAD; Cowdrey, AA & AAU; Stokes, *Historic Prints,* 97; represented at NYHS.

GRUEN, CHRISTIAN. Engraver and die-sinker of NYC in 1860. ¶ NYBD 1860.

GRUENER, CHARLES. Artist at Buffalo (N.Y.) 1855–58. *Cf.* C. GRÜNER. ¶ Buffalo BD 1855–56, 1858.

GRÜNER, C. Portrait painter at Terre Haute (Ind.) in 1859. *Cf.* CHARLES GRUENER. ¶ Information courtesy Wilbur D. Peat.

GRUNER, FERDINAND. Seal engraver and die-sinker at San Francisco in 1856. He was listed as a jeweler in 1858. ¶ San Francisco CD and BD 1856, BD 1858.

GRUNEWALD (or Greenwald), GUSTAVUS (1805–1878). Landscape and portrait painter, lithographer, and drawing teacher. Born in Gnadau (Germany), December 10, 1805, Grunewald came to America in 1831 and settled in Bethlehem (Pa.), where he taught drawing and painting in the Young Ladies' Seminary (Moravian) from 1836 to 1866. During this time he was a frequent exhibitor at the Artists' Fund Society and Pennsylvania Academy, the Maryland Historical Society, the National Academy, Apollo Association, and American Art-Union. He returned to Germany in 1868 and died at Gnadenburg on August 1, 1878. ¶ Thieme-Becker; information courtesy Rev. John F. Morman, Bethlehem; Cowdrey, AA & AAU; Cowdrey, NAD; Rutledge, PA; Rutledge, MHS; Peters, *America on Stone; Magazine of Art* (April 1939), 224, repro. Some of Grunewald's work is now in the Moravian Archives and the Girls' Seminary, Bethlehem.

GSCHWINDT (Geschwindt or Schwindt), ROBERT. Austrian portrait painter and restorer, who worked in Paris and Rome in the early 1850's. By 1854 he was in New Orleans where he worked until 1860. Returning to Europe, he was at St. Petersburg (Russia) about 1864 and Paris about 1879. ¶ Thieme-Becker; Delgado-WPA cites New Orleans *Bee* (Dec. 29, 1854, Jan. 27, Feb. 5, 1855, and Nov. 15, 1856), *Orleanian* (Dec. 31, 1854), *Crescent* (March 21, 1859), New Orleans CD 1858–60.

GUALDI, ANTONIO. Panorama and historical painter at New Orleans. An 1847 view of the American occupation of Mexico City, by Antonio Gualdi, is in the Louisiana State Museum. This is presumably the same Gualdi who exhibited a panorama of New Orleans in that city in 1854. ¶ *American Processional,* 243; New Orleans *Picayune,* March 14, 1854 (cited by J. E. Arrington); Delgado-WPA cites New Orleans *Bee,* March 13, 1854.

GUATALA, LOUIS. Artist at New Orleans,

1830-32. ¶ Delgado-WPA cites New Orleans CD 1830, 1832.

GUÉ, DAVID JOHN (1836–1917). Portrait painter. Born January 17, 1836, in Farmington (N.Y.), Gué was best known for his portraits of Lincoln, Grant, and Beecher. He moved to Iowa in 1852. He died May 1, 1917, in Brooklyn (N.Y.). ¶ Thieme-Becker; *Art Annual,* XIV (1917), 323; Fielding; Ness and Orwig, *Iowa Artists,* 92.

GUELPA, JEAN B. (or T. B.). Portrait painter at Boston 1855–60. ¶ Boston BD 1855–60; New England BD 1856–60.

GUÉNARD, H. Portrait painter at New Orleans 1850–57. Guénard was a native of Louisiana, born about 1827; his mother was also a Louisianan, but his grandmother [?], Jane Guénard, was born in France about 1770. ¶ 7 Census (1850), La., VII, 68; Delgado-WPA cites New Orleans CD 1857.

GUGLER, HENRY, SR. (1816–1880). Banknote and portrait engraver, lithographer. A native of Germany, Gugler came to America in 1853. After serving for several years as engraver with a NYC banknote engraving firm, he became (during the Civil War) one of the first vignette engravers employed in the National Note Bureau at Washington. His most important work was a life size steel engraving of President Lincoln. In 1878 he founded the lithographic firm of H. Gugler & Son in Milwaukee. As the Gugler Lithographing Co. (since 1883) this firm has continued to the present. ¶ Kent, "Early Commercial Lithography in Wisconsin," 249.

GUILD, HARRIET. Amateur artist in watercolor, of Roxbury (Mass.). Some of her drawings, dated May 1853, are preserved in the Guild family, along with those of SARAH ANN GUILD. ¶ Hosmer, "John G. Chandler," 46–47.

GUILD, JAMES (1797–1841). Itinerant portrait and miniature painter and silhouettist. Born July 9, 1797, in Halifax (Vt.), he left home in 1818 to make his way as a peddler and jack-of-all-trades. During the course of his wanderings in up-state New York, he took up silhouette-cutting and a little later portrait and miniature painting, and practised them with considerable success there and in NYC, Boston, Baltimore, Norfolk, and Charleston. In the spring of 1825 he went to England to further his artistic career and he is said to have won several medals for his work in Europe. In his last years he lived in the West Indies. He died in NYC in 1841 on his way to his home at Springfield (Vt.). ¶ [A. W. Peach, ed.], "From Tunbridge, Vt., to London, England—The Journal of James Guild, Peddler, Tinker, Schoolmaster, Portrait Painter, from 1818 to 1824"; Rutledge, *Artists in the Life of Charleston.*

GUILD, SARAH ANN (Mrs. John Greene Chandler). Amateur artist of Roxbury (Mass.), of the same family as HARRIET GUILD. She married in 1850 the Boston engraver, JOHN GREENE CHANDLER. Some of her drawings are preserved in the Guild family. ¶ Hosmer, "John G. Chandler," 46–47.

GUILDER, JOSEPH. Artist of Washington (D.C.) in 1860. Joseph H. Guilder was listed as a painter at a different address in 1858. ¶ Washington and Georgetown CD 1858, 1860.

GUILLAUME, LOUIS MATHIEU DIDIER (1816–1892). Portrait and landscape painter. A native of Nantes (France), he studied in Paris under P. Delaroche and exhibited at the Salon of 1837. He came to America about 1855, spent several years in NYC, but settled in Richmond (Va.) about 1857. He appears to have lived in Richmond until at least 1872 and many of his portraits are preserved there. By 1880 he had moved to Washington (D.C.) where he died April 13, 1892. ¶ *Richmond Portraits,* 220; Bénézit; Thieme-Becker; NYBD 1855–57; Cowdrey, NAD; *Pictures* (March 1945), 23, repro.; information courtesy Mrs. Ralph Catterall, Valentine Museum, Richmond.

GUILLET, Mrs. J. or ISIDORE. Miniaturist. Mrs. or Mme. Guillet was at Philadelphia in 1838, in NYC 1838–41, and at Richmond (Va.) in 1842. She exhibited at the National Academy and the Apollo Association. ¶ Phila. BD 1838; Cowdrey, NAD; Cowdrey, AA & AAU; *Richmond Portraits.*

GUILMETTE, CHARLES. Scottish engraver, age 35, at New Orleans in 1850 with his wife, a native of South Carolina. ¶ 7 Census (1850), La., V, 88.

GUINARD, EMILE. Engraver of NYC 1846–48. ¶ NYBD 1846, 1848.

GUION, DAVID. Sculptor of Cincinnati (Ohio) *c.* 1830–40. He was the first teacher of SHOBAL VAIL CLEVENGER. ¶ Gardner, *Yankee Stonecutters;* DAB (under Clevenger).

GUION, SUSAN. Landscape painter of NYC,

exhibitor at the National Academy in 1859. ¶ Cowdrey, NAD.

GUITRY, see CLORIVIÈRE.

GULAGER, CHARLES. Marine painter of Philadelphia, exhibitor at Pennsylvania Academy in 1860. ¶ Rutledge, PA.

GULDAGER, see GULLAGER.

GULICK, DAVID B. Wood engraver; born in New York about 1829; working in NYC in 1850 and in Boston from 1853 to 1856. ¶ 7 Census (1850), N.Y., XLII, 231; Boston CD 1853–56.

GULICK, ELIZABETH MILLIGAN. Painter of a miniature on ivory of Dolly Madison (1768–1849), owned by Princeton University. ¶ Information courtesy Donald Egbert, Princeton Univ.

GULICK, SAMUEL W. Scenic and fresco painter of Indianapolis (Ind.) 1858–61. In 1858 he was scene painter at the Metropolitan Theater in Indianapolis. *Cf.* S. N. GULICK. ¶ Indianapolis CD 1858, 1861; BD 1860; Peat, *Pioneer Painters of Indiana.*

GULICK, S. N. Scenic artist at Columbus (Ohio) in November 1854, about to leave for the East. *Cf.* SAMUEL W. GULICK. ¶ WPA (Ohio), *Annals of Cleveland.*

GULLAGER (Guldager), CHRISTIAN (1759–1826). Portrait and theatrical painter, modeller in plaster. Gullager was born March 1, 1759, in Copenhagen (Denmark) and studied at the Royal Academy there. He emigrated to America between 1782 and 1786. Married at Newburyport (Mass.), May 9, 1786, he shortly moved to Boston where he worked until 1797. After a few months as a theatrical painter in NYC, he settled in Philadelphia in 1798. He stayed there until 1806 when he left his family, sought work in NYC and Charleston (S.C.), and then disappeared entirely until shortly before his death, which occurred in Philadelphia, November 12, 1826, in the home of his son-in-law. Gullager's best known work was a portrait of George Washington, done at Boston in October 1789. ¶ Dresser, "Christian Gullager—An Introduction to His Life and Some Representative Examples of His Work," with 30 repros.; Worcester Art Museum, *Christian Gullager, 1759–1826—An Exhibition of His Paintings;* Boston CD 1789, 1796; N. Y. *Time Piece,* Oct. 11–Nov. 6, Nov. 10–17, 1797; N. Y. *Minerva,* Sept. 8, 1797; Prime, II, 13–14; Morgan and Fielding, *Life Portraits of Washington,* 150–151, repro.; Stokes, *Icon.,* Sept. 1, 1790; Rutledge, *Artists in the Life of Charleston,* as Mr. Gallagher.

GUNGEL, B. Artist at New Orleans in 1857. ¶ Delgado-WPA cites New Orleans CD 1857.

GUNN, THOMAS BUTLER. Author and illustrator, of NYC during the 1850's. Gunn's works included *Physiology of New York Boarding Houses* (1857) and *Mose among the Britishers, or the B'hoy in London* (1850), both illustrated by himself. He also contributed illustrations to *Yankee Notions* (established 1852) and *The Harp of a Thousand Strings* (*c.* 1858). ¶ Hamilton, 272; NYHS catalogue.

GUNNINGTON, ——. Engraver of some illustrations in *The Cyclopedia of Wit and Humor* (N.Y., 1858). ¶ Hamilton, 464.

GUNTER, FREDERICK. Lithographer, age 49, from Bremen (Germany), living in Louisville (Ky.) in 1850. Of Gunter's five children, three were born in Germany between *c.* 1818 and *c.* 1832, and two were born in Ohio between *c.* 1833 and *c.* 1838. See DANIEL GANTER. ¶ 7 Census (1850), Ky., XI, 386.

GURLEY, ROYAL. Engraver of NYC 1837–38. In 1837 he was with BURTON, GURLEY & EDMONDS, banknote engravers, and in 1838 with Burton & Gurley, engravers. In 1839 he was listed as an auctioneer. ¶ NYCD 1837–39; NYBD 1837.

GUSEL, LEWIS. Engraver at Philadelphia in 1850. Probably the same as LOUIS GRISEL. ¶ Phila. BD 1850.

GUSTAVUS, A. O. Engraver from Quebec, age 19, at Philadelphia in September 1850. ¶ 7 Census (1850), Pa., L, 250 (stamped 125).

GUTEKUNST, FREDERICK (1831–1917). Pastel portraitist. ¶ Addison, *Portraits in the University of Pennsylvania.*

GUTTEN, ERNEST. English artist, 33, at NYC in 1860. ¶ 8 Census (1860), N.Y., XLIII, 412.

GUY, FRANCIS (*c.* 1760–1820). Landscape painter. Guy was born in Lorton, near Keswick, in the English Lake District and became a silk dyer in London. Emigrating to America late in 1795, he reached NYC in December, but soon moved to Brooklyn and there established a silk dyeing plant. After about one year in Brooklyn, he moved on to Philadelphia and thence to Baltimore, where he seems to have remained from *c.* 1798 to 1817. Soon after settling in Baltimore, Guy set up as a landscape painter, specializing in views of gentlemen's seats around the city. In 1812 he was commissioned to paint a view of the new Baltimore Cathedral and during the war with England he painted a number of marine battle scenes. In 1817 he returned to Brooklyn (N.Y.) and he made his home there until his death on August 12, 1820. ¶ Pleasants, "Four Late 18th Century Anglo-American Landscape Painters," 55–116, with checklist and 8 repros.; Pleasants, *250 Years of Painting in Md.*, 29–31, one repro.; Pleasants, "Francis Guy—Painter of Gentlemen's Estates," 8 repros.; Flexner, *The Light of Distant Skies;* Stiles, *History of Brooklyn,* II, 102–104; Lafferty; Rutledge, PA; Rutledge, MHS; Stokes, *Icon.*, pl. 69; Stokes, *Historic Prints;* Dunlap, *History,* II, 149. Represented at NYHS, Long Island Hist. Soc., Brooklyn Museum, Md. Hist. Soc., Peabody Institute.

GUY, SEYMOUR JOSEPH (1824–1910). N.A. Portrait and genre painter. Born January 16, 1824, at Greenwich (England); studied painting in London and emigrated to America in 1854. He settled in NYC where he enjoyed a successful career as a painter of children's portraits and genre scenes. He was elected to membership in the National Academy in 1865, and also exhibited at the Boston Athenaeum and the Maryland Historical Society. He died in NYC on December 10, 1910. ¶ DAB; *Art Annual,* XXV (1928), 391; Swan, BA; Cowdrey, NAD; Rutledge, MHS; Clement and Hutton; CAB; Graves; Rutledge, PA.

GUYOL DE GUIRAN, FRANÇOIS M. Portrait and miniature painter, scenic artist. A native of France, he worked in St. Louis from 1812 until after 1820. He also taught drawing in New Orleans in 1822 and 1828. ¶ *Antiques* (Sept. 1953), 195, repro.; *Missouri Gazette,* March 5, 1812; New Orleans CD 1822; Delgado-WPA cites New Orleans *Argus,* May 9, 1828.

GWYNNE (or Gwyne), EDMUND L. Landscape painter. E. L. Gwyne of NYC exhibited at the National Academy in 1848 a picture entitled "Western Log Cabin." He is presumed to be the same as Edmund Gwynne, age 20, listed as an artist in the 1850 census of Columbus (Ohio), and E. L. Gwynne, listed as stock broker in the 1867 Columbus directory. ¶ Cowdrey, NAD; 7 Census (1850), Ohio, XV, 643; Columbus CD 1867.

H

HAAS, see also DE HAAS.

HAAS, P. Lithographer and publisher of Washington (D.C.) between 1837 and 1845. His work included technical prints, portraits, and views of Washington and Mt. Vernon. ¶ Peters, *America on Stone; Antiques* (Feb. 1945), 104, repro.

HAAS, SOLOMON. Apprentice engraver, age 16, at Philadelphia in July 1860. Both he and his father were native Pennsylvanians. In 1871 Solomon Haas was listed as a maker of burglar alarms. ¶ 8 Census (1860), Pa., LIX, 232; Phila. CD 1871.

HABBITT, JAMES. Artist, 30, a native of New York, at NYC in 1860. ¶ 8 Census (1860), N.Y., XLIII, 245.

HABERSHAM, ROBERT W. Portrait painter from Savannah (Ga.) working in Charleston (S.C.) in 1851. His "Eve, or the First Cloud in Eden," shown in Charleston at that time, was one of a projected series illustrating "the contest of good and evil for the soul of man." ¶ Rutledge, *Artists in the Life of Charleston,* 167, 199.

HABICH, WILLIAM. Engraver at Newark (N.J.) in 1859. ¶ Essex, Hudson, and Union Counties BD 1859.

HABICHER, SEBASTIAN (1805–?). Portrait and genre painter; born in 1805 at Haid in the Austrian Tyrol. He came to America *c.* 1848, exhibiting in that year at the National Academy as a resident of NYC. ¶ Thieme-Becker; Cowdrey, NAD; NYCD 1848.

HACKER, THEODORE S. Landscape painter and daguerreotypist, at Philadelphia 1860 and after. Between 1860 and 1864 he exhibited European and American views at the Pennsylvania Academy. ¶ Rutledge, PA; Phila. CD 1860, 1865.

HACKET, JAMES M. Sculptor; a native of Vermont, living in 1850 in Vergennes (Vt.) with his wife and 5 children; his property valued at $1,600. ¶ 7 Census (1850), Vt., I, 470.

HADDOCA (Haddock?), A. Painter of a primitive oil portrait of the Seneca chief Red Jacket, probably about 1830. ¶ Garbisch Collection catalogue, 49, repro.

HADDOCK, ——. Scene painter at the Bowery Theatre, NYC, from 1827 to 1830. ¶ Odell, *Annals of the New York Stage,* III, 271, 407; N. Y. *Evening Post,* Nov. 28, 1828, and Jan. 13, 1830 (courtesy J. Earl Arrington).

HADDON, MICHAEL (?–1750). Limner who died in Charleston in 1750, leaving property in London. ¶ Rutledge, *Artists in the Life of Charleston,* 115.

HADDUCK, A. T. Portrait and still life painter, at New York University, NYC, in 1837, when he exhibited at the National Academy. ¶ Cowdrey, NAD.

HADLEY, SARA. Painter of primitive landscapes in oil, at Wilton (N.H.) in the early 1850's. ¶ Lipman and Winchester, 173.

HADLIN, W. AD. Wax portrait modeller, working in America *c.* 1850. ¶ E. S. Bolton, *American Wax Portraits,* 36.

HAEDDEN, BINGHAM. Portrait painter at Greenville (S.C.), 1835–37. ¶ Information courtesy Miss Anna Wells Rutledge, Charleston (S.C.).

HAEHNLEN, JACOB (1824–?). Lithographer and lithographic printer; born in Harrisburg (Pa.) in 1824 and moved to Philadelphia in 1841. He was listed as a printer there from 1854 to 1859 and as a lithographer from 1860 until 1871. ¶ Peters, *America on Stone;* Phila. CD 1854–70.

HAERING, DAVID. Lithographer at NYC 1846–50. ¶ NYCD 1846, BD 1850.

HAERING, GEORGE. Lithographer at NYC 1846–47. ¶ NYCD 1846, BD 1847.

HAERING, ROBERT. Lithographer at NYC 1846. ¶ NYCD 1846.

HAGEDORN, H. C. Portrait painter at New Orleans in 1842. This may have been Herman Conrad Hagedorn, painter and architect, who worked in Berlin (Germany) from 1828 to 1838. ¶ New Orleans CD 1842; Thieme-Becker.

HAGEMAN, LOUIS. Landscape painter at NYC 1857–58. ¶ NYBD 1857–58.

HAGEN, JOHN C. Portrait and genre painter. He was at Troy (N.Y.) in 1838; by the following year he had settled in NYC where he was active as late as 1882. He exhibited at the National Academy and the Apollo Association. ¶ Cowdrey, NAD; Cowdrey, AA & AAU; NYBD 1841–60; Bolton, "Portrait Painters in Oil."

HAGER, ——. Landscape painter of Burlington (Iowa). As a young man in 1845–46, he painted scenes of the Upper Mississippi Valley, which were exhibited in Burlington in the latter year. At that time it was said that he intended to make a trip to the East. ¶ Arrington, "Nauvoo Temple," Chap. 8.; Shick, *The Early Theater in Eastern Iowa,* 201 (courtesy J. Earl Arrington).

HAGNY (or Hagney), J. Portrait and ornamental painter of Newark (N.J.) 1855–76. His portraits of Gov. William Pennington (1796–1862) and Chief Justice Edward W. Whelpley (1818–1864) are owned by Princeton University. ¶ Newark CD 1855, 1857–60, 1876; Egbert, *Princeton Portraits.*

HAGSNER, JOHN. Portrait painter, age 21, living with his parents in Philadelphia in June 1860; he was a native of Pennsylvania. ¶ 8 Census (1860), Pa., LX, 649.

HAIDT, JOHN VALENTINE (1700–1780). Portrait and religious painter. Haidt was born in Danzig, October 4, 1700, but grew up in Berlin (Germany), where his father was court goldsmith. After studying at the Berlin Academy, he travelled widely in Europe. He joined the Moravian Church in London about 1725 and in 1754 he went to America to join the Moravian community at Bethlehem (Pa.). He painted portraits of many Moravians there and also a large number of religious pictures to decorate Moravian churches in and around Bethlehem. He died in Bethlehem, January 18, 1780. ¶ Howland, "John Valentine Haidt"; Morman, "The Painting Preacher: John Valentine Haidt," with repros.; CAB; repros. in *Art Digest* (May 1, 1949), 9, and *Antiques* (May 1949), 370; *From Colony to Nation* (Art Institute of Chicago, 1949), 46–47, repros. 22, 23.

HAIGHT, AARON R. Wood engraver at NYC 1848–52. ¶ NYBD 1848, 1850–52.

HAILEY, J. K. Artist at Baltimore in 1859. ¶ Baltimore BD 1859.

HAINES, D. Card engraver at Philadelphia in 1820. ¶ Stauffer.

HAINES, GEORGE W. Landscape painter of Philadelphia 1860 and after. Between 1861 and 1866 he exhibited European and American views at the Pennsylvania Academy. ¶ Phila. CD 1860, 1862; Rutledge, PA.

HAINES, WILLIAM (1778–1848). Engraver, portrait and miniature painter; born June 21, 1778, at Bedhampton (Hampshire, England) and brought up in Chichester. He was trained as an engraver in England. In 1800 he went to the Cape of Good Hope and thence in 1802 to Philadelphia. He remained in Philadelphia until 1809, engraving book illustrations and portraits and painting watercolor portraits. Returning to England he gradually turned from engraving to miniature painting and finally enjoyed considerable success in London as a painter of oil portraits. He retired in his last years to East Brixton, where he died July 24, 1848. ¶ DNB; Stauffer; Fielding; Bolton, *Miniature Painters;* Thieme-Becker.

HAKES, GEORGE W. Landscape and portrait painter, at Troy (N.Y.) in 1857, and at Oswego (N.Y.) in 1859. ¶ Troy BD 1857; N. Y. State BD 1859.

HALBERT, AUGUSTUS. Engraver of NYC, 1832–51. Halbert was a nephew of J. F. E. PRUD'HOMME and probably studied under him. He was employed as a line engraver by Harper Bros., publishers, in 1835, and three years later he was working for the banknote engraving firm of RAWDON, WRIGHT & HATCH. ¶ *Am. Adv. Directory* 1832; NYBD 1846–51; Cowdrey, NAD; Stauffer; Fielding.

HALDER, RUDOLPH. Swiss lithographer, age 52, in the Charity Hospital at New Orleans in December 1850. ¶ 7 Census (1850), La., IV, 696.

HALE, B. F. Portrait painter at Rochester (N.Y.) in 1859. ¶ N. Y. State BD 1859.

HALE, H. Portrait painter at Cleveland (Ohio) in July 1846. ¶ WPA (Ohio), *Annals of Cleveland.*

HALE, SUSAN (1834–1910). Landscape painter in watercolors. Born in Boston in 1834 (or 1833, according to Clement and Hutton), Miss Hale spent most of her professional life in Boston, making one trip to Europe in 1871-72 for study in England, France, and Germany. She died September 17, 1910, at Matunuck (R.I.). ¶ *Art Annual,* VIII; Clement and Hutton; Fielding; Thieme-Becker.

HALKETT, A. Known only for a primitive ship drawing in pencil *c.* 1850. ¶ Lipman and Winchester, 173.

HALL, ANN (1792–1863). N.A. Portrait and miniature painter, born May 26, 1792, in Pomfret (Conn.). While still at Pomfret, she exhibited miniatures at the American Academy in NYC in 1817 and 1818. Moving to NYC in the mid-1820's, she was elected Artist of the National Academy in 1827, Associate Member in 1828, and full Member in 1833. She continued to exhibit at the National Academy until 1852 and died in NYC in December 1863. ¶ N. Y. *Herald,* Dec. 14, 1863, obit.; Cowdrey, AA & AAU; Cowdrey, NAD; Swan, BA; Dunlap, *History,* II, 368–70;

Cummings, *Historic Annals of the NAD,* 189–190; Bolton, *Miniature Painters;* Wehle and Bolton.

HALL, BASIL (1788–1844). Landscape draftsman. Captain Basil Hall, R.N., noted British traveller, author, and naval officer, was born December 31, 1788, probably in Scotland, and died September 11, 1844, in London. During his visit to North America in 1827–28, he made many sketches of American and Canadian scenes, some of which were used to illustrate his *Travels in North America in the Years 1827 and 1828* and *Forty Etchings from Sketches Made with the Camera Lucida in North America in the Years 1827 and 1828.* Still more of his sketches were used for a volume of Mrs. Hall's letters, published in 1931 as *The Aristocratic Journey.* Hall was an Honorary Member, Amateur, of the National Academy, 1828–30. ¶ DNB; Rutledge, *Artists in the Life of Charleston;* Cowdrey, NAD.

HALL, CHARLES BRYAN (1840–after 1906). Engraver of portrait and subject plates. A son of HENRY BRYAN HALL, SR., he was born in Camden Town, London, August 18, 1840, and came to NYC with his father in April 1851. He studied for a time with his father, but in 1855 was apprenticed to JAMES DUTHIE of Morrisania (N.Y.). After service in the Civil War, he worked with GEORGE E. PERINE in NYC, but he later joined his father and brothers (including HENRY BRYAN HALL, JR.) in the firm of H. B. Hall & Sons, later H. B. Hall Sons. After 1899 C. B. Hall carried on the business alone. He was living in NYC as late as 1906. ¶ Stauffer; Fielding.

HALL, CHARLES F. General, seal, and banknote engraver at Cincinnati (Ohio) 1853–60. ¶ Cincinnati CD 1853, 1856–59, BD 1860; Ohio BD 1853, 1859.

HALL, CORNELIUS. Two mid-19th century oil portraits by this artist were owned in Wallingford (Vt.) in 1941. ¶ WPA (Mass.), *Portraits Found in Vt.*

HALL & CUSHMAN, see HALL, PACKARD & CUSHMAN.

HALL, E. W. Landscape painter at Newark (N.J.), exhibited at the National Academy 1860–64. ¶ Cowdrey, NAD.

HALL, EDWARD S. Illustrator of *A Christmas Dream,* by James G. Brady (N.Y., 1860). He was born in England about 1840. ¶ Hamilton, 274; 8 Census (1860), N.Y., XLIV, 770; NYCD 1863.

HALL, GEORGE HENRY (1825–1913). N.A. Portrait and genre painter. He was born September 21, 1825, in Manchester (N.H.), but grew up in Boston, where he began to paint about 1842. Leaving Boston for Europe in 1849, he studied for several years at Düsseldorf and Paris and then settled in NYC about 1852. The rest of his life was spent chiefly in NYC, though he made many trips to Europe and North Africa between 1860 and 1895. Elected a Member of the National Academy in 1868, he exhibited often at the chief galleries of NYC, Boston, and Philadelphia. He died in NYC, February 17, 1913. ¶ DAB; *Art Annual,* XI, obit.; *Panorama* (Dec. 1945), 33, repro.; Cowdrey, NAD; Cowdrey, AA & AAU; Swan, BA; Rutledge, PA; Washington Art Assoc. Cat., 1857; *American Collector* (April 1947), cover; 8 Census (1860), N.Y., LVI, 943.

HALL, GEORGE R. (1818–?). Engraver, born 1818 in London. He learned engraving under his brother, HENRY BRYAN HALL, SR., worked in London and in Leipzig (Germany), and in 1854 joined his brother in NYC. Employed for a time by the banknote engravers RAWDON, WRIGHT, HATCH & Co., he later worked for Putnam and other publishers. ¶ Stauffer; NYCD 1863.

HALL, HENRY BRYAN, SR. (1808–1884). Engraver and etcher, portrait and miniature artist in oils and crayon. Born May 11, 1808, in London, he served his apprenticeship to a well known engraver there and later was engaged to execute the portrait work in the plate of Hayter's painting of the Coronation of Queen Victoria. He came to NYC in 1850 and established a successful engraving and publishing business, in which he was joined after 1860 by his sons, HENRY BRYAN HALL, JR., CHARLES BRYAN HALL and Alfred Bryan Hall (1842–after 1900), all of whom had learned engraving from their father. The elder Hall also painted many portraits both in London and NYC and exhibited at the National Academy, 1862–75. He died at his home in Morrisania (N.Y.) April 25, 1884. ¶ DAB; Stauffer; NYBD 1854 and after; Cowdrey, NAD; Bolton, *Miniature Painters;* Bolton, *Crayon Draftsmen.*

HALL, HENRY BRYAN, JR. Engraver, son of HENRY BRYAN HALL, SR. He was born in Camden Town, London, studied engraving with his father, and came to America with him in 1850. He went back to England in 1858 to work under a London engraver for a year. On his return he established his own business in NYC, but was interrupted by the Civil War, in which he served from 1861 to 1864. After the war he joined his father and brothers in the firm of H. B. Hall & Sons. He engraved many Civil War portraits, historical scenes, and subjects after American artists. He retired in 1899 and was living in NYC in 1900. ¶ Stauffer; Bolton, *Crayon Draftsmen.*

HALL, JAMES (?–1823). Gravestone sculptor, working in Charleston (S.C.) in 1803. He died in 1823. Examples of his work have been found in Wilmington (N.C.) and Georgetown (S.C.). ¶ Ravenel, "Here Lyes Buried," 195; Rutledge, *Artists in the Life of Charleston.*

HALL, JAMES D. Artist, 26, a native of New York, at NYC in 1850. ¶ 7 Census (1850), N.Y., XLVI, 227.

HALL, J. F. Engraver at San Francisco in 1860; he was from Maine and 30 years old. J. F. Hall, stencil-plate manufacturer, was listed in the directory for 1861. ¶ 8 Census (1860), Cal., VII, 524; San Francisco CD 1861.

HALL, JOHN. Engraver, probably at Philadelphia, who engraved one of THOMAS DOUGHTY's views, published in 1825. ¶ Doughty, "Thomas Doughty."

HALL, JOHN. Lithographer at Charleston (S.C.) in 1834 and 1837. ¶ Rutledge, *Artists in the Life of Charleston.*

HALL, JOHN H. Wood engraver and lithographer. A native of Cooperstown (N.Y.), Hall was an apprentice at Albany in 1825 when he applied to Dr. ALEXANDER ANDERSON for instruction in wood engraving. After a year with Anderson in NYC, he returned to Albany where he spent most of his time until 1848. In 1830 he was at Lancaster (Mass.) with CARTER, ANDREWS & CO., and in 1834 he was at Boston as one of the founders of the BOSTON BEWICK COMPANY. His best known work was done for Nuttall's *Manual of Ornithology.* He was senior partner in the Albany firms of HALL, PACKARD & CUSHMAN (1838) and HALL & CUSHMAN (1839). He died in California where he had gone during the gold rush of 1849. ¶ Hamilton, 276–279; Linton, *History of Wood Engraving in America,* 17–18; Lossing, *Memoir of Alexander Anderson,* 75–76; Peters, *America on Stone;* Whitmore, "Abel Bowen," 44; Albany CD 1827–48.

HALL, JOHN L. (or S.). Engraver at San Francisco in 1860. He was an Englishman, age 52, but his wife and daughter (age 12) were born in Maryland. ¶ 8 Census (1860), Cal., VII, 113; San Francisco CD 1861 lists only J. S. Hall, with no occupation stated.

HALL, JOHN P. Lithographer of Buffalo (N.Y.) 1839–52. He was for many years associated with the firm of HALL & MOONEY. ¶ Peters, *America on Stone;* Buffalo BD 1851.

HALL & MOONEY. Lithographers, engravers, and copperplate printers of Buffalo (N.Y.) from 1839 to 1850. The partners were JOHN P. HALL and LAWRENCE MOONEY. Hall left the firm about 1850 and Mooney carried on as MOONEY & BUELL. ¶ Peters, *America on Stone.*

HALL, PACKARD & CUSHMAN. Banknote engravers of Albany (N.Y.) in 1838. The firm was composed of JOHN H. HALL, RAWSON PACKARD, and THOMAS H. CUSHMAN. By 1839 Packard had dropped out, but the firm continued during that year under the name of HALL & CUSHMAN. ¶ Albany CD 1838–39; Peters, *America on Stone.*

HALL, PETER (1828–1895). Banknote engraver. A native of Birmingham (England); came to America in 1849 and learned engraving in the AMERICAN BANK NOTE COMPANY's NYC establishment. He established his own business in NYC in 1886. He died in Brooklyn (N.Y.), July 5, 1895. ¶ Stauffer.

HALL, SIDNEY. Engraver, 34, a native of New York, at NYC in 1860. ¶ 8 Census (1860), N.Y., LIII, 354.

HALL, SYLVESTER (1778–?). Itinerant decorative wall painter of Connecticut; born at Wallingford in 1778; working in New Haven in 1804. A landscape panel showing the green at Cheshire, attributed to Hall, is now in the Cheshire Public Library. ¶ Allen, *Early American Wall Paintings,* 17–18, repro.; Little, "Itinerant Painting in America, 1750–1850," 208.

HALL, WILLIAM. Portrait painter at Philadelphia 1837–40. He exhibited portraits and two copies after Wilkie at the Artists' Fund Society. ¶ Rutledge, PA (1840 as J. Hall); Phila. BD 1838; Peters, *America on Stone,* pl. 16.

HALLAM, JOHN. Official engraver to the Governor and Company of Connecticut, working at New London in 1773. His work included some bills of credit. ¶ Information courtesy Dr. Harold Bowditch, Brookline, Mass.

HALLAM, PETER. German artist, 32, at NYC in 1850 with his German wife Rosetta. ¶ 7 Census (1850), N.Y., XLIII, 360.

HALLBERG, ——. Drawing master, of TRENCHARD & HALLBERG, at Baltimore in 1788. ¶ Prime, II, 52–53.

HALLENBACH, J. F. Listed as an American miniaturist in the 1825 catalogue of the Pennsylvania Academy, p. 22. ¶ Rutledge, PA; PA Cat., 1825.

HALLMAN & CITTI. Lithographers at Philadelphia in 1850. The partners were LOUIS CITTI and probably FRANKLIN B. HALLMAN. ¶ Phila. CD and BD 1850.

HALLMAN, FRANKLIN B. Lithographer of Philadelphia during the 1850's. He was probably with HALLMAN & CITTI in 1850. ¶ Phila. CD 1850, 1852–55, 1857.

HALLMAN, JOHN. Engraver at Philadelphia 1859. ¶ Phila. CD 1859.

HALLMAN, WILLIAM A. Engraver at Philadelphia 1855–60. ¶ Phila. CD 1855–60.

HALLOWAY, THOMAS. Portrait engraver at Philadelphia in 1794. ¶ Prime, II, 69.

HALLOWELL, WILLIAM (1801–1890). Amateur pen and ink artist. A Quaker dentist and physician of Norristown (Pa.) who in 1865 made a pen and ink drawing on the subject of "The Peaceable Kingdom." ¶ Lipman, "Peaceable Kingdoms by Three Pennsylvania Painters," repro.; Norristown CD 1880, as dentist; Lipman and Winchester, 173 (as of Norristown, N.J.).

HALLWIG, OSCAR. Painter of Baltimore 1858–80; represented at the Maryland Historical Society. ¶ Baltimore CD 1858–80; Lafferty; Rutledge, MHS.

HALMAN & SETTY, see HALLMAN & CITTI.

HALPIN, FREDERICK W. (1805–1880). Portrait and historical engraver and book illustrator. He was born in Worcester (England) in 1805 and studied under his father, an engraver for one of the Staffordshire potteries. About 1827 he was located in London. He came to NYC about 1842 and was employed for a time by ALFRED JONES. He worked in NYC at least until 1860 and died in Jersey City (N.J.) in February 1880. He was a brother of JOHN HALPIN. ¶ Stauffer; Thieme-Becker; *American Art Review* (1880), 226–227, obit.; Bénézit; NYBD 1848–60; Cowdrey, NAD (1869).

HALPIN, JOHN. Portrait, historical, landscape, and banknote engraver; watercolorist. A brother of FREDERICK HALPIN, John was employed as an engraver in St. Petersburg (Russia) and Halifax (N.S.) before he came to NYC in the late 1840's. He was working in NYC from 1849 at least until 1867 and later was employed by publishers in Cincinnati (Ohio). He exhibited genre paintings at the National Academy in 1850 and 1854 and was a member of the American Society of Painters in Water Colors. ¶ Stauffer; NYCD 1849–60; Cowdrey, NAD; Thieme-Becker.

HALSEY, JOHN. Wood engraver, 23, a native of New York, at NYC in 1860. ¶ 8 Census (1860), N.Y., LIX, 27.

HALSEY, WILLIAM C. (or I.). Portrait and landscape painter, born about 1820. He was painting at Huntsville (Ala.) in April 1847 and later that year exhibited at the National Academy as of Brooklyn (N.Y.). He was listed in NYC directories in 1850–51. ¶ WPA (Ala.) Hist. Records Survey cites Huntsville *Southern Advocate,* April 2, 1847; Cowdrey, NAD; NYBD 1850–51.

HAMBLEN, ELI (*c.* 1804–1839). Painter, probably of portraits. Eli was the brother of JOSEPH G., NATHANIEL, and STURTEVANT J. HAMBLEN and brother-in-law of WILLIAM MATTHEW PRIOR. He worked with his brothers in Portland (Me.) from 1823 to 1839, the year of his death. ¶ Little, "William M. Prior, Traveling Artist, and His In-Laws, the Painting Hamblens."

HAMBLEN, JOSEPH G. or H. (*c.* 1817–?). Portrait painter; born in Maine *c.* 1817. In 1837 he was listed as a painter, living in Portland (Me.) with his brother-in-law, WILLIAM MATTHEW PRIOR. About 1840 Joseph, along with NATHANIEL and STURTEVANT J. HAMBLEN, moved to Boston. He was listed in the 1850 Boston census as a portrait painter, but by 1856 he had gone into business with his brother Sturtevant as a dealer in "gents' furnishings." ¶ 7 Census (1850), Mass., XXIV, Pt. 2, p. 243 (as Joseph H.); Little, "William M. Prior, Traveling Artist, and His In-Laws, the Painting Hamblens" (as Joseph G.).

HAMBLEN, NATHANIEL. Painter, probably of portraits. Nathaniel, like his brothers, lived in Portland (Me.) in the 1830's and moved to Boston about 1840. See ELI, JOSEPH G., and STURTEVANT J. HAMBLEN. ¶ Little, "William M. Prior, Traveling Artist, and His In-Laws, the Painting Hamblens."

HAMBLEN, STURTEVANT J. Portrait painter. He was listed as a painter in 1837 at Portland (Me.), where he resided with his brother-in-law, WILLIAM MATTHEW PRIOR. About 1840 "the painting Hamblens" (see ELI, JOSEPH G. and NATHANIEL HAMBLEN) moved to Boston. Sturtevant was listed as a portrait painter there until 1856, when he and Joseph went into the gents' furnishings business. ¶ Little, "William M. Prior, Traveling Artist, and His In-Laws, the Painting Hamblens"; Boston BD 1842–56; Lipman and Winchester, 173, as L. J. Hamblin.

HAMBLIN, L. J., see STURTEVANT J. HAMBLEN.

HAMEL, ——. Portrait copyist at New Orleans in 1853. ¶ Delgado-WPA cites *Bee,* Feb. 3, 1853.

HAMER, RAWTHMALL. Genre painter at Boston 1859–61. He exhibited at the Boston Athenaeum in 1860. ¶ Swan, BA; Boston CD 1860 (as designer).

HAMILL, WILLIAM. Dutch lithographer, 26, at NYC in 1860. ¶ 8 Census (1860), N.Y., XLV, 463.

HAMILTON, ALEXANDER (1712–1756). Amateur caricaturist. Dr. Hamilton, noted Maryland physician and colonial traveler, was born and educated in Scotland and emigrated to America in 1738. He settled in Annapolis and lived there until his death. Best known for his *Itinerarium* of a trip through the colonies in 1744, he also wrote an unpublished history of the Tuesday Club of Annapolis, profusely illustrated with comic sketches by the author. ¶ Rutledge, "A Humorous Artist in Colonial Maryland," seven repros.; represented Md. Hist. Soc. (Rutledge) and Johns Hopkins University.

HAMILTON, AMOS. Portrait painter. F. F. Sherman reported that in 1939 he found at Lenox (Mass.) a portrait of Gov. William Palmer (1781–1860) of Vermont, painted by this artist. ¶ Sherman, "Newly Discovered American Portrait Painters"; Lipman and Winchester, 173.

HAMILTON, CHARLES. Artist at Washington (D.C.) in June 1860. Hamilton (28), his wife (24), and two children (4 and 3) were born in Pennsylvania, while the youngest child (1) was born in the District of Columbia. The city directory for 1860 and 1862 lists a Charles O. Hamilton, house and sign painter. ¶ 8 Census (1860), D.C., I, 379; Washington CD 1860, 1862.

HAMILTON, GEORGE W. Artist, age 25, at Woodstock (Vt.) in August 1850. He was born in North Carolina (or possibly New Hampshire). ¶ 7 Census (1850), Vt., XII, 102.

HAMILTON, JAMES (1819–1878). Marine and landscape painter; born October 1, 1819, at Entrien, near Belfast (Ireland) and accompanied his parents to Philadelphia at the age of 15. Encouraged by JOHN SARTAIN and others, he established himself as a landscape artist and teacher of drawing in Philadelphia about 1840. He exhibited for the first time in 1840, at the Artists' Fund Society, and subsequently at that and other galleries in Philadelphia, NYC, Boston, Baltimore, and Washington. He was in London in 1854–55. After his return to Philadelphia he was commissioned to illustrate Kane's *Arctic Explorations* and Frémont's *Memoirs.* He died March 10, 1878, in San Francisco while on a trip around the world. ¶ Baur, "A Romantic Impressionist: James Hamilton," eight repros.; Strickland, *Dictionary of Irish Artists;* Clement and Hutton; CAB; *Portfolio* (June–July 1952), 218–220, repro.; Benjamin, "Fifty Years Of American Art," 490, repro.; Rasmussen, "Artists of the Explorations Overland, 1840–1860," 57; Phila. CD 1840–60 and after (in 1857 CD and 1858 BD there are two James Hamiltons, both artists and at different addresses; one is certainly the landscape painter, while the second may be the same or JAMES HAMILTON the engraver); 7 Census (1850), Pa., LV, 392; Rutledge, PA; Cowdrey, AA & AAU; Cowdrey, NAD; Swan, BA; Rutledge, MHS; Washington Art Assoc. Cat., 1859.

HAMILTON, JAMES. Engraver at Frankford, near Philadelphia, 1860 and after. Not to be confused with JAMES HAMILTON, landscape painter, also of Philadelphia and Frankford, but possibly the same as James Hamilton, artist, listed in Philadelphia directories in 1857–58 at different addresses from the landscape painter. ¶ Phila. CD 1857, 1860–67, BD 1858.

HAMILTON, LYDIA. Artist, age 23, at Philadelphia in June 1860. She was a native Pennsylvanian and lived with her father, James Hamilton, bricklayer. ¶ 8 Census (1860), Pa., LV, 375.

HAMILTON, SOPHIE. Painter of a watercolor pastoral scene, New York State, *c.* 1820. ¶ Lipman and Winchester, 173.

HAMILTON, WILLIAM M. or R. A.N.A. Scottish portrait painter, born about 1810, who came to NYC about 1832 and exhibited at the National Academy between

1833 and 1841 as William R. Hamilton. He was elected an Associate Member in 1833. His daughter was born in New York about 1843. His name disappears from the directories after 1840, but reappears as William M. from 1852 to 1863. He was listed in the 1860 Census simply as William. William M. exhibited at the National Academy in 1858. ¶ 8 Census (1860), N.Y., LIII, 752; Dunlap, *History,* II, 470; Cowdrey, NAD; Cowdrey, AA & AAU; NYCD 1835–40, 1852–63.

HAMLIN, Dr. A. C. Landscape painter of Bangor (Me.); exhibited at the National Academy in 1859. ¶ Cowdrey, NAD.

HAMLIN, WILLIAM (1772–1869). Banknote and general engraver. Born October 15, 1772, in Providence (R.I.), by 1795 he was engraving banknotes for most of the Rhode Island banks. In 1809 he went into partnership with his son in the manufacture of navigation instruments, continuing in the business until his death, November 22, 1869, in his ninety-eighth year. His engravings included views of Providence and several portraits of Washington. ¶ Lane, "Rhode Island's Earliest Engraver," with checklist and repros.; DAB; Stauffer.

HAMM, PHINEAS ELDRIDGE (1799–1861). Engraver. A native of Philadelphia; worked there as an engraver *c.* 1825–27. From 1827 to 1839 he was listed as a coal-dealer, and 1840 to 1845 as assistant city treasurer. He died in Philadelphia, January 31, 1861. ¶ Fielding, *Supplement;* Stauffer; Thieme-Becker.

HAMMAR, GEORGE D. Engraver at Philadelphia in 1860. He was a native Philadelphian, aged 25. ¶ 8 Census (1860), Pa., LIX, 133.

HAMMELL, A. H. Portrait painter who exhibited in Cincinnati in 1847, 1848, and 1866. ¶ Information courtesy Edward H. Dwight, Cincinnati Art Museum.

HAMMOND, JOHN A. French engraver, 35, at NYC in 1860. His wife was Irish, but their four children, ages 8 years to 4 months, were born in New York. ¶ 8 Census (1860), N.Y., XLIX, 1016.

HAMMOND, JOHN T. (*c.* 1820–?). Engraver. Born in New York about 1820, by 1839 Hammond was working as a line engraver of landscapes and subject plates at Philadelphia. By 1852 he had settled in New Orleans where he was active at least until 1860. Stauffer states that he also worked in St. Louis. In 1856–57 he was associated with the New Orleans firm of CHILDS & HAMMOND. ¶ 8 Census (1860), La., VII, 581; Stauffer; New Orleans CD 1852–60; Delgado-WPA.

HANBECK, WILLIAM. Portrait painter at Madison (Ind.) in 1846. ¶ Peat, *Pioneer Painters of Indiana,* 58–59.

HANCOCK, NATHANIEL. Miniaturist at Salem (Mass.) in 1792; later at Portsmouth (N.H.); at Boston in 1799; and again at Salem in 1809. ¶ Essex Institute *Historical Collections,* XLVII (April 1921), 147–148; Belknap, *Artists and Craftsmen of Essex Co.,* 10; Boston *Columbian Centinel,* June 8, 1799 (citation courtesy Dr. Clarence H. Brigham, Worcester); Bolton, *Miniature Painters.*

HANCOCK, SARAH. Still life painter on velvet, *c.* 1822. Three of her paintings were owned in 1931 by Mrs. M. A. Frierson, Athens (Ga.). ¶ Karr, "Paintings on Velvet," 165.

HANCOCK, T. Artist of Boston who exhibited miniatures or drawings at the Boston Athenaeum in 1832. ¶ Swan, BA, 184, 234.

HAND & BARBER. Portrait painters and gilders at Baltimore, 1795–99. In 1795 they opened a painting and drawing academy there. ¶ Prime, II, 50; Baltimore CD 1796, 1799 (cited by Mayo); Lafferty.

HAND, JOSEPH. Lithographer, 19, a native of New York, at NYC in 1850. ¶ 7 Census (1850), N.Y., XLV, 60.

HANELTON, PETER. Engraver, 27, a native of New York, at NYC in 1850. ¶ 7 Census (1850), N.Y., L, 632.

HANINGTON, HENRY. Painter of transparencies and moving dioramas, glass-stainer, decorative painter. The brothers HENRY and WILLIAM J. HANINGTON, starting as commercial artists in NYC about 1832, turned out and showed all over the country a large number of spectacular moving dioramas on such subjects as "The Deluge," "Conflagration of Moscow," "New York Fire of Dec. 16, 1835," "Stellar Universe, a moving telescopic diorama," "The Creation," and "Crimean War." The last-named was shown in Cincinnati and New Orleans during the winter of 1855–56, after which the name of Henry Hanington disappears from the record, though his brother was active as late as 1870. ¶ NYCD 1832–45; Am. Inst. Cat., 1845; Rutledge, *Artists in the Life of Charleston;* J. E. Arrington cites advertisements in N. Y. *Evening Post* (Jan. 12, 1832), N. Y. *Herald* (Sept. 4 and 26, 1835; Jan.

8, March 16, Aug. 31, Nov. 30, Dec. 7 and 22, 1836; March 27 and May 15, 1837), Boston *Evening Transcript* (July 18, Aug. 22, Sept. 10 and 19, Nov. 30, 1838), Cincinnati *Daily Gazette* (July 12, Aug. 2 and 7, 1839), Boston *Evening Transcript* (July 13, 1840), N. Y. *Herald* (Dec. 10, 1841, July 3 and Aug. 15, 1848), Boston *Evening Transcript* (Feb. 27, 1849), N. Y. *Herald* (May 20, 1850), Boston *Evening Transcript* (July 7, 1851), Cincinnati *Daily Gazette* (May 25, 1852, Dec. 27, 1855), and New Orleans *Picayune* (March 1, 1856).

HANINGTON, ROBERT. Painter of a large watercolor, "Daniel in the Lion's Den," shown in Charleston (S.C.) in January 1850. ¶ Charleston *Courier,* Jan. 18, 1850 (courtesy J. Earl Arrington).

HANINGTON, WILLIAM J. Painter of transparencies and dioramas, enameler, glass-stainer, and decorative painter. He and his brother, HENRY HANINGTON, produced a great many moving dioramas which were shown in NYC, Philadelphia, Boston, Charleston, New Orleans, Cincinnati, and other cities between 1832 and 1856. During this period, and until 1870, William J. Hanington was listed in NYC as a transparent painter, decorative painter, enameler, or glass-stainer. He exhibited stained glass and mosaic church window patterns at the American Institute in 1856. ¶ NYCD 1836–70; Am. Inst. Cat., 1856; information courtesy J. E. Arrington (see newspaper citations under HENRY HANINGTON).

HANKS, JARVIS (or Jervis) F. (1799–?). Portrait painter, silhouettist, sign and ornamental painter. He was born in 1799 at Pittsford, Otsego County (N.Y.), served in the army during the War of 1812, moved in 1817 to Wheeling (Va., now W. Va.), and there began painting signs and teaching school. He visited Philadelphia in 1823, but returned to the West, working in Cleveland and Cincinnati in 1825 and 1826. At about this time he assumed the title "Master" and devoted himself to silhouette-cutting and portrait painting. In 1827 he moved to NYC where he was listed as a sign-painter, portrait painter, or simply painter until 1834, though during this period he worked as far afield as Charleston (S.C.), Salem (Mass.), and New Orleans. By 1838 "Master" Hanks had returned to Cleveland where he made his home at least until 1852, with occasional winter trips to the South. ¶ Dunlap, *History,* II, 434; Knittle, *Early Ohio Taverns,* gives his date and place of birth as probably Circleville (Chillicothe), Ohio, 1804, but 7 Census (1850), Ohio, XI, 597, indicates he was born in New York State *c.* 1800, thus confirming Dunlap; *Antiques* (March 1938), 149–150; Jackson, *Ancestors in Silhouette,* 113; Carrick, *Shades of Our Ancestors,* 99–108; Cowdrey, NAD; New Orleans *Argus,* Jan. 20, Feb. 2, 1830; *Annals of Cleveland,* 1838–39, 1841, 1845, 1851–52; represented Md. Hist. Soc. (Rutledge).

HANKS, OWEN G. Banknote engraver and landscape painter; born in Troy (N.Y.) about 1815 or 1820. He worked in NYC from 1838, first with RAWDON, WRIGHT & HATCH and later with other firms. In 1860 his property was valued at $14,000. He died about 1865. ¶ Stauffer; 8 Census (1860), N.Y., LVIII, 358; NYCD 1850, 1857, 1863; Fielding; Cowdrey, NAD.

HANLEY, WALTER. Artist at Boston in 1860. ¶ Boston CD 1860.

HANLEY, WILLIAM H. Portrait artist in oil and crayon. A Canadian by birth, Hanley came to the United States in the early 1840's, worked for a time in Nashua and Manchester (N.H.), and finally settled in Boston, where he had a studio from 1848 to 1869. He exhibited at the Athenaeum and at the National Academy. The 1860 Census for Boston lists a William G. Hanley, Canadian artist, age 25; if the age is given correctly, this cannot be William H., but might be a son or younger brother. *Cf.* also WALTER HANLEY. ¶ "Art and Artists in Manchester," 114; Nashua CD 1843; Boston CD 1848, 1850–59, 1861–69, BD 1850–59; Cowdrey, NAD; Swan, BA; Bolton, *Crayon Draftsmen;* 8 Census (1860), Mass., XXVII, 22.

HANLY, GEORGE. German-born lithographer, age 28, at Pittsburgh (Pa.) in August 1850. ¶ 7 Census (1850), Pa., III, 60.

HANNA, R. Portrait painter at Greenville (S.C.) in 1827. ¶ Information courtesy Miss Anna Wells Rutledge, Charleston (S.C.).

HANNAH, EDWIN. Lithographer, 19, a native of New York, living in NYC in 1860. His brother Robert, 17, and sister Sarah, 16, were listed as lithographer and artist, respectively. They were children of Daniel, deceased, and Sarah Hannah. ¶ 8 Census (1860), N.Y., XLV, 89.

HANNAN, JOHN J. Irish sculptor or stonecutter, 22, at NYC in 1860. ¶ 8 Census (1860), N.Y., LX, 210.

HANOWAY, JOHN. Engraver, 23, a native of New York, at NYC in 1860. He was the son of George Hanoway, gentleman. ¶ 8 Census (1860), N.Y., LXII, 587.

HANSEL, Miss H. M. Still life painter and drawing mistress of Philadelphia; exhibitor at the Pennsylvania Academy in 1828 and 1829. ¶ Rutledge, PA.

HANSELL (or Hansel), GEORGE H. Portrait and miniature painter of NYC, active 1842 to 1858. He exhibited at the National Academy and at the American Institute. ¶ Cowdrey, NAD; NYCD 1845–58, BD 1846–57; Bolton, *Miniature Painters;* Am. Inst. Cat., 1844, no. 158 (as Hansell), no. 682 (as Hanson).

HANSEN, JOHN. Lithographer and portrait painter of NYC 1857–60. ¶ NYBD 1857 (as lithographer), 1860 (as portrait painter).

HANSON, PETER (1821–1887). Landscape painter. A native of Denmark; came to the United States *c.* 1847 and settled in Brooklyn (N.Y.), where he died February 22, 1887. He was also a noted authority on tulips. ¶ Boston *Transcript,* Feb. 24, 1887; NYBD 1858.

HANTON, ANDREW. German artist, 30, at NYC in 1860. ¶ 8 Census (1860), N.Y., LIII, 493.

HANTZ, JACOB F. (1831–1887). Landscape painter; born February 21, 1831, at Wrightsville, York County (Pa.); died there (?), January 27, 1887. Five of his landscapes in oil on boards, dated 1885 and 1886, are owned by Mrs. Robert H. MacLawry of Roxbury (N.Y.). ¶ Information courtesy Henry J. Young, Pa. State Historical and Museum Commission.

HAPLACHER, GEORGE I. German engraver, 32, at NYC in 1850. His wife Constance was French, but their daughter Zelia, aged 4, was born in New York. ¶ 7 Census (1850), N.Y., XLI, 635. *Cf.* GEORGE HASSLACHER.

HARAUX, ALFRED. French wood engraver, 30, at NYC in 1860. He was married and had one child, aged 4, born in France. ¶ 8 Census (1860), N.Y., LI, 216.

HARBACH, HORATIO M. Engraver with COGGINS & HARBACH, Philadelphia, 1859–60. ¶ Phila. CD 1859, BD 1860.

HARBESON, JAMES P. Card and seal engraver at Philadelphia 1859 and after. ¶ Phila. CD 1859–60 and after.

HARDIE, FERNANDO. Plaster image maker from Tuscany, age 23, at Philadelphia in June 1860. He was apparently employed by his father, LORENZO HARDIE, SR. ¶ 8 Census (1860), Pa., LXII, 106.

HARDIE, LORENZO, SR. Plaster image maker from Tuscany, age 42, at Philadelphia in June 1860. He employed a number of artists, including his sons, FERNANDO and LORENZO HARDIE, JR., FRANCESCO BARSOTTE, FROSTINO GIANELLI, MICHAEL BELLI, DOMINICA BELLI, ANATO BELLI, ANGELO MATHEDI, LORENZO PERO, GIOVANNI MARCH. ¶ 8 Census (1860), Pa., LXII, 106.

HARDIE, LORENZO, JR. Plaster image maker from Tuscany, age 26, at Philadelphia in June 1860. He was employed by his father, LORENZO HARDIE, SR. ¶ 8 Census (1860), Pa., LXII, 106.

HARDING (Hardy), ALFRED. English portrait painter and miniaturist at Little Rock and Hot Springs (Ark.) *c.* 1830. ¶ WPA (Ark.), Hist. Records Survey cites *Arkansas Gazette,* June 10, 1934, p. 3.

HARDING, CHESTER (1792–1866). Portrait painter. Born September 1, 1792, in Conway (N.H.); took up sign painting in 1817 at Pittsburgh (Pa.). The following year he joined his brother HORACE HARDING, in Paris (Ky.), but soon moved again to St. Louis where he worked until 1821, rapidly developing his talent for portraiture. Returning to the eastern seaboard, he worked in Washington (D.C.) and Boston and Northampton (Mass.) until 1823, when he went to England. During his three years abroad he enjoyed a fashionable success in London, but hard times in 1826 forced him to return to America. He settled in Boston for a few years, then moved to Springfield (Mass.), much of his time however being spent in painting trips to Washington, Richmond, Baltimore, Canada, New Orleans, and Kentucky. He made a second visit to England and Scotland in 1846. He died in Boston, April 1, 1866, shortly after his return from St. Louis, where he had painted a portrait of General Sherman. He was an Honorary Member, Professional, of the National Academy. ¶ The chief sources on Harding's life are his own *My Egotistography* (1866) and Margaret E. White's *A Sketch of Chester Harding, Artist, Drawn by His Own Hand* (Boston, 1890, and Boston, 1929). See also: DAB; New Orleans *Bee,* Feb. 11, 1841, and Feb. 11, 1849 (cited by Delgado-WPA); Swan, BA; Cowdrey, NAD; Cowdrey, AA & AAU; *Richmond*

Portraits; Karolik Cat.; Dunlap, *History;* Flexner, *The Light of Distant Skies.*

HARDING, CHRISTOPHER. Portrait painter at Cincinnati in 1846. ¶ Cincinnati CD 1846 (courtesy Edward H. Dwight, Cincinnati Art Museum).

HARDING, DEXTER (1796–1862). Portrait, ornamental, and sign painter. A younger brother of CHESTER and HORACE HARDING, he was born in Dedham (Mass.) in 1796, served as a drummer boy in the War of 1812, and probably went west with his brothers about 1820. A primitive watercolor portrait painted probably at Vincennes (Ind.) about 1820 and signed "D. H." is probably his work. He lived in Hopkinsville (Ky.) from 1821 to 1850 and in Pine Bluff (Ark.) from 1850 till his death in 1862. He was a miller by trade but painted family portraits. ¶ Peat, *Pioneer Painters of Indiana,* 19–20.

HARDING, HARVEY A. Sculptor and painter at New Orleans in 1836 and 1856–59. ¶ Delgado-WPA cites *True American,* May 3, 1836, *Bee,* Nov. 10, 1856, *Creole,* Jan. 30, 1856, and Jan. 11, 1857, and New Orleans CD 1856, 1858–59.

HARDING, HENRY H. Religious painter, copyist. Possibly a brother of CHESTER HARDING, H. H. Harding exhibited at the Boston Athenaeum from 1829 to 1831. Henry H. Harding was listed in the 1839 directory as a dealer in West India goods. ¶ Swan, BA; Boston CD 1839.

HARDING, HORACE (1794–*c.* 1857). Portrait painter, born in Conway (Mass.) in 1794. A younger brother of CHESTER HARDING, with whom he operated a furniture business in up-state New York about 1815, Horace Harding soon after moved to Paris (Ky.) and took up portrait painting. There he was joined in 1817 by Chester and his family. Horace Harding later (1820) worked in Vincennes (Ind.) and Cincinnati from 1834 to 1850. He died about 1857 in Woodville (Miss.). ¶ Harding, *My Egotistography;* Peat, *Pioneer Painters of Indiana,* 17–21.

HARDING, J. C. Irish portrait painter, 54, at NYC in 1860. *Cf.* JOHN L. HARDING. ¶ 8 Census (1860), N.Y., LX, 35.

HARDING, JEREMIAH (?–1830). Portrait, sign, and ornamental painter from Tewksbury (Mass.), working in Lowell (Mass.) during the 1820's. He died there of consumption on September 4, 1830. Not to be confused with JOHN L. (J. L.) HARDING. ¶ Sears, *Some American Primitives,* 86–87, repros. 69–70; Bowditch, "Early Water-Color Paintings of New England Coats of Arms," 204–205, repro.; *Lowell Vital Records:* II, Marriages, and IV, Deaths; represented in collection of J. R. Taff, Genesee, N.Y. (info. courtesy A. L. Dunham).

HARDING, JOHN L. Portrait painter, sometimes confused with JEREMIAH HARDING. John L. or J. L. Harding worked in Albany (N.Y.) *c.* 1835–38, in Philadelphia 1841–45, and in NYC from 1848 to 1882. He exhibited at the Artists' Fund Society in Philadelphia. *Cf.* J. C. HARDING. ¶ Albany CD 1835, 1837; Rutledge, PA; NYCD 1848–82; Dunlap, *History* (1918), III, 306; represented at NYHS.

HARDING, SPENCER S. Portrait painter. At Boston in 1835, at the same address as his brother, CHESTER HARDING, and he exhibited in that year at the Athenaeum. In December 1839 he visited Charleston (S.C.), the following year he was at NYC exhibiting at the Apollo Association, and in 1844–45 and 1848 he was again in Boston with CHESTER HARDING. Nothing further is known of him except that he was in Frankfort (Ky.) in 1860. ¶ Swan, BA; Boston CD 1835, BD 1844–45, 1848; Rutledge, *Artists in the Life of Charleston;* Cowdrey, AA & AAU; information courtesy Mrs. W. H. Whitley, Paris (Ky.).

HARDY, ALFRED, see ALFRED HARDING.

HARDY, ANNA ELIZA (1839–1934). Portrait and flower painter. Anna E., daughter of JEREMIAH PEARSON HARDY, was born January 26, 1839, at Bangor (Me.), and died December 15, 1934, at South Orrington (Me.). She exhibited at the National Academy in 1876–77. ¶ *Art Annual,* XII (1915), 388; Mallett; letter of Miss Charlotte W. Hardy to FARL, Oct. 26, 1935; Fielding; "Maine Artists"; Cowdrey, NAD.

HARDY, JEREMIAH PEARSON (1800–1887). Portrait, miniature, genre, animal, and still-life painter. Born October 22, 1800, at Pelham (N.H.), J. P. Hardy moved with his parents to Hampden (Me.) in 1811. After study in Boston about 1822, he returned to Hampden, where he married about 1828, and lived there and in Bangor (Me.) until his death, February 9, 1887. ANNA ELIZA HARDY was his daughter and MARY ANN HARDY his sister. ¶ "Maine Artists," 19; Eckstorm, "Jeremiah Pearson Hardy," with 13 repros.; Simpson, *Leaflets of Artists;* Born, "Notes on Still-Life Painting in America," 159; Karolik Cat., 282–288, with 3 repros.

HARDY, MARY ANN (1809–1887). Miniaturist and landscape painter. Mary Ann, sister of JEREMIAH PEARSON HARDY, was born in Pelham (N.H.), September 15, 1809, and learned painting from her brother after their removal to Hampden (Me.). Most of Miss Hardy's work was done in Maine, where she died April 27, 1887. ¶ FARL transcript of Hardy family bible; *Antiques* (Aug. 1925), 96, repro.; Karolik Cat. (repro. of portrait of Mary Ann Hardy by her brother); Simpson, *Leaflets of Artists;* Hardy and Hardy, *Hardy and Hardie, Past and Present,* 502–503, gives year of death as 1884; Warren, "Mary Ann Hardy—An Appreciation."

HARE, D. O. Engraver and die-sinker. He was born in New York State *c.* 1811 and settled in Washington (D.C.), where he was active from 1843 at least until 1860. ¶ 7 Census (1850), D.C., I, 269; Washington CD 1843, 1850–60.

HARE, WILLIAM. Sherman recorded an artist of this name as painter of a picture of the whaling schooner *Mary C. Terbell* of Providence (R.I.) in 1825. *Cf.* WILLIAM HARE, portrait painter. ¶ Sherman, "Unrecorded Early American Painters," (1943).

HARE, WILLIAM. Portrait painter of Baltimore from 1842 to 1859. ¶ Lafferty. *Cf.* WILLIAM HARE, above.

HARGRAVE (or Hargreave), THOMAS. Marble sculptor and stonecutter of Philadelphia from 1837 to 1860 and after. ¶ Phila. CD 1837–60 and after.

HARKINS, ROBERT. Miniaturist at Brooklyn (N.Y.) in 1841–1842. ¶ Bolton, *Miniature Painters;* Fielding.

HARLEY, JAMES KIMBALL (1828–1889). A native of Canada; settled in Baltimore. In 1849, after three years' study in Antwerp (Belgium), he returned to Baltimore where he enjoyed considerable popularity as a fashionable portrait painter after the Civil War. He committed suicide on February 3, 1889. ¶ Pleasants, *250 Years of Painting in Maryland,* 62; Boston *Transcript,* Feb. 5, 1889, obit.; *Richmond Portraits,* 132, repro.; Lafferty; Washington Art Assoc. Cat., 1859; represented Md. Hist. Soc. (Rutledge).

HARLEY, JOSEPH S. Wood engraver, of BAXTER & HARLEY, at Philadelphia 1857 and after. ¶ Phila. CD 1857–60.

HARLINE, see HERLINE.

HARNISCH, ALBERT E. (1843–?). Sculptor, born in Philadelphia, probably the son of CARL HARNISCH, with whom he was living in Philadelphia in 1859. A pupil of JOSEPH A. BAILLY, he exhibited at the Pennsylvania Academy from 1859 to 1869, then went to Rome for eight years of further study. ¶ Rutledge, PA; Clement and Hutton; Fielding.

HARNISCH, CARL (1800–1883). Lithographer, painter of literary and genre pieces. Born in Altenburg (Germany), Harnisch came to Philadelphia before 1843 and lived there until his death in 1883. He exhibited several times at the Pennsylvania Academy, his subjects including scenes from Shakespeare and Goethe, as well as genre and one piece of sculpture. He was probably the father of ALBERT E. HARNISCH. ¶ Thieme-Becker; Rutledge, PA.

HAROLD & RANDOLPH. Ship carvers of Baltimore, known to have carved the *Scotia* figurehead in 1839. See JAMES T. RANDOLPH. ¶ Pinckney, 120, 193.

HARRIMAN, BENJAMIN. Portrait and sign painter at Cincinnati in 1834. ¶ Cincinnati CD 1834 (courtesy Edward H. Dwight, Cincinnati Art Museum).

HARRINGTON, G. Portrait painter. Sherman reported finding portraits of Charles Tufts and his wife, of Massachusetts, signed "G. Harrington" and dated 1839. ¶ Sherman, "Newly Discovered American Portrait Painters," 235.

HARRINGTON, GEORGE (1833–1911). Landscape painter. Harrington became a painter only after a successful career in business. He exhibited at the National Academy in 1885. He died July 11, 1911, at Springfield (Mass.). ¶ *Art Annual,* IX, obit.; Smith; Cowdrey, NAD.

HARRINGTON, JOHN. Engraver, age 18, at Boston in July 1860; a native of Massachusetts. ¶ 8 Census (1860), Mass., XXVII, 891.

HARRINGTON, WILLIAM H. Artist from Pennsylvania, age 40, boarding in Orleans Parish (La.) in November 1850. ¶ 7 Census (1850), La., IV(1), 631.

HARRIS, Mrs. ——. Portrait painter at Charleston (S.C.) in January and February 1819. A Mrs. Harris and her daughter advertised there in December 1830 as teachers of music, languages and drawing. ¶ Rutledge, *Artists in the Life of Charleston.*

HARRIS, BELINDA. Engraver of NYC, 1848–52. ¶ NYBD 1848–52.

HARRIS, BENJAMIN. Engraver, of HARRIS &

McGauran, in NYC, 1858. ¶ NYCD and BD 1858.

Harris, Elbridge. Fresco painter. Born in Massachusetts *c.* 1817; living with his wife and children in Boston in the early 1850's. In 1853 he was listed as machinist. ¶ 7 Census (1850), Mass., XXV, 717; Boston CD 1850–53.

Harris, George. Coach, sign, and ornamental painter at Charleston (S.C.) in 1766. ¶ Rutledge, *Artists in the Life of Charleston.*

Harris, George D. Artist, age 18, at Boston in 1860. He lived with his parents and five other children, ages 8 to 20; all were born in Nova Scotia. Joseph Harris, the father, was a patternmaker. ¶ 8 Census (1860), Mass., XXVIII, 678.

Harris, James (*c.* 1808–1846). Engraver. In 1829 he married Rebecca Martha, daughter of the engraver Samuel Maverick (1789–1845). He was listed as an engraver in NYC from 1830 to 1845 (in 1835 as of Maverick & Harris), and died there August 24, 1846, at the age of 38. ¶ N. Y. *Evening Post,* Aug. 25, 1846; NYCD 1830–45; information courtesy S. D. Stephens; examples of his work in Fay, *Views of New York* (1831–34).

Harris, James. Landscape painter and teacher of painting at Rochester (N.Y.) in the 1840's. Norton Bush was one of his pupils. ¶ Ulp, "Art and Artists in Rochester"; Clement and Hutton (under Norton Bush).

Harris, James F. Panoramist. A student of Jacob Cox of Indianapolis, J. F. Harris painted two large temperance panoramas there in 1853, as well as the Indiana banner for the New York World's Fair of that year. He had his studio in the Capitol at Indianapolis. ¶ Burnet, *Art and Artists of Indiana,* 92–94; Peat, *Pioneer Painters of Indiana,* 58–59, 157–58, 167, 232.

Harris, Joseph T. Portrait painter from Portland (Me.) where he was active as a portrait painter from 1830 to 1834. During this time he exhibited at the Boston Athenaeum and drew a series of three cartoons showing the hazards of 4th of July celebrations (lithographed by Pendletons of Boston). By 1836 he had moved to NYC where he was a frequent exhibitor at the National Academy until 1852 and Associate Member from 1839. ¶ Swan, BA; Portland CD 1831, 1834; Cowdrey, NAD; Cowdrey, AA & AAU; Fielding; *American Collector* (July 1945), 4, repro. (caption gives artist's name as J. F. Harris, but name on print is J. T. Harris).

Harris & McGauran. Engravers of NYC, 1858. The partners were Benjamin Harris and Patrick McGauran. ¶ NYBD 1858.

Harris, Philip Spooner (1824–1884). Portrait painter. A native of Heath (Mass.); working at Bath (Me.) in 1855–56; died at Flatbush, Long Island (N.Y.). He exhibited at the National Academy in 1865. ¶ Mallett; *Maine Register* 1855; New England BD 1856; Cowdrey, NAD.

Harris, Samuel (1783–1810). Portrait draftsman and engraver, born in Boston in May 1783. Apprenticed at an early age to the Boston engraver, Samuel Hill, a relative, Harris published his first portrait in 1806. He showed great talent for languages and entered Harvard College as a junior in 1808, but drowned in the Charles River on July 10, 1810, while he was still a student. The American Antiquarian Society at Worcester owns a number of Harris's portraits in red chalk and charcoal. ¶ Stauffer; Weis, "Portraits in the Library of the Am. Antiq. Soc."; Fielding.

Harrison, Benjamin J. Amateur watercolorist. A turner and chairmaker by trade, Harrison exhibited at the American Institute watercolor views of the Institute Fairs of 1844 and 1845. ¶ Am. Inst. Cat., 1844, 1845, 1856; NYCD 1848 and after.

Harrison, Charles. Engraver of NYC, 1838–60. Some family relationship probably existed between Charles Harrison and David R., Thomas, and William Harrison of NYC. Charles and David R. had a common business address in 1848 and both lived in Morrisania (N.Y.) from 1849 to 1857. Charles and Thomas had the same business address in 1840, while Charles and William had the same business address in 1838 and home address in 1846. ¶ NYCD 1838–60.

Harrison, Charles P. (1783–1854). Engraver. Charles P., son of William Harrison, Sr., was born in England in 1783 and brought to America in 1794. He learned engraving, probably from his father, and was in business in Philadelphia as a copperplate printer and engraver from 1806 to 1823. Moving to NYC, he continued in the engraving business until 1847 and died there in 1854. He also did some portrait painting. One son, Gabriel Harrison, became a well-known actor, author, and amateur painter; another, name unknown, was engraving with his father in 1838 under the firm name of HARRISON & SON at 27 Wall Street. ¶ Stauffer; NYCD 1824–47; year of death courtesy Mr. W. J. Harrison.

HARRISON, CHRISTOPHER (1775–1863). Amateur painter. Born in 1775 at Cambridge (Md.), he was educated at St. John's College and worked for a time as confidential clerk to a Baltimore merchant. About 1808 he moved to Jefferson County (Ind.) and in 1815 to Salem (Ind.), farming and keeping a store and painting for his own amusement. In 1816 he was elected Indiana's first Lieutenant-Governor and in 1820 one of the commissioners to lay out and survey the site of Indianapolis. He returned to Maryland about 1830 and died there in 1863. ¶ Burnet, *Art and Artists of Indiana,* 6–10; Butts, *Art in Wisconsin,* 23; Smith, *History of the State of Indiana,* I, 213–214; Peat, *Pioneer Painters of Indiana.*

HARRISON, DAVID R. Banknote engraver of NYC, 1830–60. Stauffer states that he was long an employee of the AMERICAN BANK NOTE Co. and continued to engrave until nearly 90 years of age. He was probably a brother of CHARLES HARRISON, having the same business address in 1848 and from 1849 to 1857 the same home address (Morrisania, N.Y.). ¶ Stauffer; NYCD 1830–60; Am. Adv. Directory 1832.

HARRISON, GABRIEL (1818–1902). Landscape and portrait painter; born March 25, 1818, in Philadelphia, a son of CHARLES P. and grandson of WILLIAM HARRISON, SR. Growing up in NYC, Gabriel became stage-struck and made his professional debut in Washington (D.C.) in 1838. He was at the Park Theater in NYC in 1845. After moving to Brooklyn (N.Y.) in 1848, he became prominent in dramatic, literary, and artistic circles there. An early experimenter with the daguerreotype, he also painted landscapes and some portraits, including one of Edwin Forrest. He died in Brooklyn, December 15, 1902. ¶ DAB; *Art Annual,* IV (1903/04), 141.

HARRISON, GEORGE (?–1830). Portrait, miniature, sign, and ornamental painter; possibly from Chester County (Pa.) where he was married in 1792. After several years in Wilmington (Del.), he emigrated to Ohio, settling in Ross County in 1800. On the death of his wife in September of the same year, Harrison returned to the east, left his infant daughter with relatives in Baltimore, and set himself up as a merchant in Charleston (S.C.), where he remained until 1811. He then moved to Philadelphia and in 1818 to Washington (Pa.), where he worked as a painter of portraits, signs, and chairs. He died March 22, 1830. His known works include miniatures of his wife and daughter. ¶ Vann and Dixon, *Denny Genealogy,* Second Book, 120–130, repros.; Phila. CD 1823–24, 1828–33.

HARRISON, HENRY. Wood engraver of NYC, 1844–46. His work appeared in books published in NYC in 1846. *The Annals of San Francisco* (N.Y., 1855), also contains examples of his work, though he is not listed in the NYC directories after 1846. ¶ NYCD 1844–46; Hamilton, 204, 238, 379.

HARRISON, J. P. Engraver at Pittsburgh (Pa.) in 1817, said by Dunlap to have been the first to practise west of the Alleghenies. ¶ Dunlap, *History,* II, 469; Fielding.

HARRISON, MARK ROBERT (1819–1894). Historical and religious painter, who also did some portraits and landscapes. He was born in Hovringham, Yorkshire (England) in 1819, accompanied his family to Oneida County (N.Y.) about 1822 and to Hamilton (Ont.) eleven years later. From 1833 to 1838 he studied art in Toronto, under COLBY KIMBLE in Rochester (N.Y.) and under HENRY INMAN in NYC. He then spent three years in England, studying at the Royal Academy and the British Museum. He returned to Hamilton about 1842. In 1849 he moved to Oshkosh (Wis.) and in 1852 he finally settled at Fond du Lac (Wis.), where he lived as a recluse until his death in 1894. His favorite subjects were drawn from biblical and classical history, though he also painted some portraits and Indian scenes. He exhibited at the National Academy in 1871/72 (Winter). ¶ Butts, *Art in Wisconsin,* 82–83; *Portfolio* (Jan. 1948), 93, repro.; WPA Guide, *Wisconsin;* Cowdrey, NAD.

HARRISON, MILTON F. Engraver; born in Philadelphia about 1817, the son of RICHARD G. HARRISON. He worked in Philadelphia as an engraver from 1839 at least to 1860, from 1840 to 1848 in partnership with his brother VIRGIL F. HARRISON. ¶ 7 Census (1850), Pa., LIV, 869; 8 Census (1860), Pa., LVIII, 155; Phila. CD 1839–59.

HARRISON, RICHARD G. General and banknote engraver; possibly a son of WILLIAM HARRISON (died 1803); born in Philadelphia between 1790 and 1796. He was engraving for *Port Folio* and for Lucas & Cushing of Baltimore as early as 1814. He was listed as engraver in Philadelphia directories from 1825 to 1844 and as banknote engraver from 1845 to 1861. He seems to have been the father of MILTON F., RICHARD G., JR., SAMUEL, VIRGIL F., and WILLIAM F. HARRISON, all engravers. ¶ 7 Census (1850), Pa., LIII, 176 (age given as 60); 8 Census (1860), Pa., LVIII, 155 (age given as 64); Stauffer; Phila. CD 1825–62 (CD 1862 lists Anna, widow of Richard at the 1861 address of the engraver, but both census listings give his wife's name as Harriet); *Analectic Mag.* (1818), frontis.

HARRISON, RICHARD G., JR. Engraver, chiefly of portraits, working in Philadelphia during the early 1860's. He was presumably the son of RICHARD G. HARRISON, above. ¶ Stauffer; Phila. CD 1862 and after.

HARRISON, ROBERT A. English engraver, 52, at NYC in 1860. His wife and two children, aged 18 and 3, were born in England. ¶ 8 Census (1860), N.Y., XLVII, 800.

HARRISON, SAMUEL (*c.* 1789–1818). Engraver; son of WILLIAM HARRISON, SR.; presumably born in England and brought to Philadelphia in 1794. He studied engraving under his father and produced a map of Lake Ontario and western New York as early as 1809. He died July 18, 1818, at the age of 29 years. ¶ Stauffer; Fielding; Phila. CD 1813–18 (1819, widow of Samuel, engraver).

HARRISON, SAMUEL. Engraver; son of RICHARD G. HARRISON; born in Philadelphia. In the census of 1850 he was listed as an engraver, age 27, and in 1860 as an auctioneer, age 40, at both times residing with his father. ¶ 7 Census (1850), Pa., LIII, 176; 8 Census (1860), Pa., LVIII, 155.

HARRISON, S. D. Exhibited a view of the Dutch Church, Washington Square (NYC) at the National Academy in 1842. This is presumably Samuel Decatur Harrison, architect, grocer, and commission merchant of NYC and Jersey City. ¶ Cowdrey, NAD; NYCD 1841–43.

HARRISON & SON, see CHARLES P. HARRISON.

HARRISON, THOMAS. Engraver at Philadelphia in 1798. Possibly an error for WILLIAM HARRISON, SR. ¶ Prime, II, 69.

HARRISON, THOMAS. Engraver of NYC, 1839–40. In the latter year his business address was the same as that of CHARLES HARRISON. ¶ NYCD 1839–40.

HARRISON, THOMAS. Engraver of Philadelphia, 1857. ¶ Phila. CD 1857.

HARRISON, THOMAS. Dutch portrait painter, 31, at NYC in 1860. ¶ 8 Census (1860), N.Y., LIV, 93.

HARRISON, V. F. & M. F. Engravers of Philadelphia, 1840–48. The partners were VIRGIL F. and MILTON F. HARRISON. ¶ Phila. CD 1840–48.

HARRISON, VIRGIL F. Engraver; son of RICHARD G. HARRISON; born in Philadelphia *c.* 1817. He worked there as an engraver with his brother MILTON F. HARRISON from 1839 to 1848, as a publisher 1849–59, as proprietor of a portrait gallery and photographer 1860 and after. ¶ 8 Census (1860), Pa., LVIII, 155; Phila. CD 1839–60 and after.

HARRISON, WILLIAM, SR. (?–1803). Banknote, map, and general engraver. He was born in England, learned to engrave in London, and was employed by the Bank of England and the East India Company. He emigrated to the United States in 1794 under engagement to engrave notes for the Bank of Pennsylvania. He died in Philadelphia on October 18, 1803 and was survived by several sons who were also engravers: WILLIAM HARRISON, JR., CHARLES P. HARRISON, SAMUEL HARRISON (1789–1818), and possibly RICHARD G. HARRISON. ¶ Stauffer; Prime, II, 69; Fielding.

HARRISON, WILLIAM, JR. Portrait and banknote engraver in line and stipple. Born in England, the younger William Harrison presumably accompanied his father, WILLIAM HARRISON, SR., to Philadelphia in 1794. He was engraving there as early as 1797 and was listed in the directories from 1802 to 1819. Stauffer suggests that he was probably chiefly employed in banknote engraving. ¶ Stauffer; Phila. CD 1802–19; Fielding.

HARRISON, WILLIAM. Engraver of NYC, 1836–38. In the latter year he had the same business address as CHARLES HARRISON. ¶ NYCD 1836–38.

HARRISON, WILLIAM F. Engraver; son (?) of RICHARD G. HARRISON; born in Pennsylvania *c.* 1812. He worked in NYC from 1831 to 1840, then apparently moved to Ohio, where a child was born *c.* 1846. By 1850 he was back in Philadelphia with his family, living under the same roof as

RICHARD G. HARRISON and family. Stauffer calls him a letter engraver for bank-note companies. ¶ 7 Census (1850), Pa., LIII, 179; NYCD 1836–38; Stauffer.

HARRY, PHILIP. Portrait and landscape painter. He was working in Boston as early as 1843 and during the next four years exhibited at the Athenaeum, the Massachusetts Charitable Mechanic Association, and the American Art-Union in NYC, chiefly Maine and New Hampshire scenes and, in 1847, views of the Michigan copper mines. In 1844 he was a member of the Boston Artists' Association. Of his later career nothing is known, except that he was living in Washington (D.C.) in 1857 and exhibited at the Washington Art Association. ¶ Karolik Cat., 289–91, repro.; Boston BD 1844–45; Swan, BA; Cowdrey, AA & AAU; Washington Art Assoc., 1857.

HART, A. G. Portrait painter at Cincinnati (Ohio) in 1853. ¶ Information courtesy Dr. H. W. Williams, Jr., Corcoran Gallery.

HART, ALFRED. Portrait painter and panoramist. Born March 28, 1816, at Norwich (Conn.), he began his art studies there and continued them in NYC. In 1848 he settled at Hartford (Conn.), where he painted a panorama of Bunyan's *Pilgrim's Progress.* Another panorama by Hart, showing the New Testament and the Holy Land, was exhibited in NYC in 1852. Hart was still living in Hartford in 1860, but soon after moved to the West, where he was active as an artist and inventor at least until 1878. ¶ French, *Art and Artists in Connecticut,* 88; Hartford CD 1849–60; N. Y. *Herald,* Oct. 16, 1852 (citation courtesy J. E. Arrington).

HART, C. O. Artist at Buffalo (N.Y.) in 1859. ¶ Buffalo BD 1859.

HART, ELIZA, see Mrs. H. H. SPALDING.

HART, HENRY. Lithographer, engraver and job printer of Louisville (Ky.). He was senior partner in the firm of HART, MAPOTHER & Co. of Louisville, 1855–70, and of St. Louis, 1858–59. ¶ Louisville CD 1855–70; St. Louis BD 1858 (adv. p. 94), 1859.

HART, HENRY D. English engraver, age 30, in the Charity Hospital, Orleans Parish (La.), in December 1850. ¶ 7 Census (1850), La., IV, 720.

HART, J., & Co., see JOHN HART.

HART, JAMES, JR. Sculptor at NYC in 1858. ¶ NYBD 1858.

HART, JAMES MCDOUGAL (1828–1901). N.A. Landscape, animal, and portrait painter. A younger brother of WILLIAM HART, he was born May 10, 1828, at Kilmarnock (Scotland) and was brought to America as a child of three. Apprenticed to an Albany (N.Y.) sign painter, he developed an interest in painting which led him in 1850 to go to Düsseldorf (Germany) for academic training. On his return three years later, Hart lived for a time in Albany, but in 1857 he settled in NYC. A frequent exhibitor at the chief galleries of NYC, Philadelphia, Boston, and Baltimore, he was elected a Member of the National Academy in 1860 and later served as its Vice President. He married in 1866 Marie Theresa Gorsuch, an amateur painter, and their son, William Gorsuch Hart, also became an artist. He died in Brooklyn (N.Y.) on October 24, 1901. ¶ DAB; Cowdrey, NAD; Cowdrey, AA & AAU; Swan, BA; Rutledge, PA; Rutledge, MHS; NYBD 1857–60; *Art Annual,* VI; *Panorama* (May–June 1949), 104–105, repros.; *Antiques* (June 1945), 316, repro.; represented at Met. Mus. (Cat. 1922–26); Corcoran Gallery (Cat. 1947).

HART, Mrs. JAMES M. (née Marie Theresa Gorsuch) (1829–1921). Amateur painter and wife of the landscape painter, JAMES MCDOUGAL HART. She was born in 1829, married in 1866, and died at Lakeville (Conn.) September 19, 1921. William Gorsuch Hart, her son, also an artist, died in Mexico in 1906. ¶ *Art Annual,* XVIII; DAB (under James M. Hart); Mallett and Smith give her birth date erroneously as 1872.

HART, JOHN. Lithographer, Philadelphia, 1854–57. In 1857 he was head of J. Hart & Company. ¶ Phila. CD 1854, 1857.

HART, JOEL TANNER (1810–1877). Sculptor; born near Winchester (Ky.) on February 10, 1810. While working in a stoneyard at Lexington (Ky.) about 1831, Hart met SHOBAL VAIL CLEVENGER and was inspired to try portrait sculpture, which he did with immediate success. After doing a bust from life of Andrew Jackson at "The Hermitage," he visited the chief cities of the Eastern Seaboard, winning much attention. Commissioned in 1846 to do a bust of Henry Clay, he went abroad about 1848 to supervise its rendering in marble and settled permanently in Florence. He returned to his native country only once, in 1859, and died in Florence on March 2, 1877. Though primarily a portrait sculptor, Hart also executed a number of "ideal" figures. ¶ DAB; Coleman, "Joel T. Hart, Kentucky Sculptor," repro.; Hart, "Life Portraits of Henry Clay"; CAB; Clement and Hutton; Taft, *History of American Sculpture;* Gardner, *Yankee Stonecutters;* represented at MHS (Rutledge) and Corcoran Gallery.

HART, JOSEPH W. Engraver and designer, of COCHEU & Co., Cincinnati, 1854–1860. ¶ Cincinnati CD 1858–59; Hamilton.

HART, JULIE, see Mrs. JULIE HART KEMPSON.

HART, MAPOTHER & COMPANY. Lithographers, engravers, job printers, and civil engineers at Louisville (Ky.) from 1855 to 1870. In 1858 and 1859 they operated a branch at St. Louis. The firm consisted of HENRY HART and DILLON H. MAPOTHER (and in 1859, JOHN MCKITTRICK). ¶ Louisville CD 1855–70, BD 1859; St. Louis BD 1858 (adv. p. 94), 1859.

HART, MARIE THERESA (GORSUCH), see Mrs. JAMES M. HART.

HART, MARX M. Wood engraver of NYC, 1846–47, and Baltimore, 1856–60. ¶ NYCD 1846–47; Baltimore CD 1856, 1860, BD 1857–59.

HART, WILLIAM (1823–1894). Portrait, landscape, and allegorical painter; born in Paisley (Scotland) on March 31, 1823, five years before his brother, JAMES MCDOUGAL HART; accompanied his family to America in 1831. At Albany (N.Y.), where the Harts settled, William was apprenticed to a carriagemaker, but by the time he was 18 years old he had turned from painting carriages to portraits. Leaving Albany soon after 1840, he travelled widely in the United States, painting in Troy (N.Y.), Richmond (Va.), and in Michigan, where he spent three years. After a brief visit to Scotland, he returned to Albany about 1847 and opened a studio in NYC in 1854. He later moved to Brooklyn, where he became first President of the Brooklyn Academy of Design in 1865. His last years were spent in Mt. Vernon (N.Y.), where he died on June 17, 1894. He was elected to full membership in the National Academy in 1858, was a founder and for three years president of the American Watercolor Society, and exhibited frequently in NYC, Philadelphia, Boston, Baltimore, and Washington. ¶ DAB; Clement and Hutton; Stiles, *History of Kings County,* II, 1145–46; CAB; Cowdrey, AA & AAU; Cowdrey, NAD; Rutledge, PA; Rutledge, MHS; Swan, BA; Washington Art. Assoc. Cat., 1857; *Antiques* (Aug. 1943), 85, repro.; Sweet, *Hudson River School,* repro.; information courtesy Mrs. Ralph Catterall, Valentine Museum, Richmond.

HART, WILLIAM. Lithographer of Philadelphia, 1846–60 and after. ¶ Phila. CD 1846–60+.

HARTFORD GRAPHIC & BANK NOTE ENGRAVING COMPANY. Engravers at Hartford (Conn.), 1816–18. The company was established by ELKANAH TISDALE, MOSELEY I. DANFORTH, ASAPH WILLARD, and NATHANIEL JOCELYN. ¶ Rice, "Life of Nathaniel Jocelyn."

HARTING, MARINUS. Landscape painter, probably from Holland, at NYC, 1848–51. Harting exhibited a number of Dutch landscapes at the National Academy, American Art-Union, Pennsylvania Academy, and Maryland Historical Society. ¶ Cowdrey, AA & AAU; Cowdrey, NAD; Rutledge, PA; Rutledge, MHS; NYCD 1850–51.

HARTING, RIAL. Artist at NYC in 1851. ¶ NYCD 1851.

HARTLEY, WILLIAM. Engraver of Lowell (Mass.), 1834–37. ¶ Belknap, *Artists and Craftsmen of Essex County,* 3.

HARTMAN (or Hartmann), ADAM. Lithographer of NYC, 1850–52, 1859–60. He was with the firm of HARTMANN & HEPPENHEIMER in 1851. ¶ NYCD 1850–60.

HARTMAN (or Hartmann), ADOLPH. Engraver of NYC, 1857–58. ¶ NYCD 1857–58.

HARTMAN, A. O. (or A. D.). Portrait painter of NYC, 1858–60. ¶ NYCD 1858–60 (as A. O. Hartman, artist); NYBD 1859 (as A. D. Hartman, portrait painter).

HARTMAN (or Hartmann), CHARLES F. Engraver of NYC, 1856–57. ¶ NYCD 1856–57.

HARTMAN (or Hartmann), CONRAD FRIED. Engraver and artist at Cincinnati in 1853, at NYC from 1855 to 1860. Stauffer states that a C. Hartman worked for print publishers in NYC from 1850 to 1855. ¶ Cincinnati BD 1853; NYCD 1855–56, 1859–60; Stauffer.

HARTMAN, J. W. Artist of a view of the California gold fields, lithographed in 1851. He worked with ALEXANDER ZAKRESKI. ¶ Peters, *California on Stone.*

HARTMAN, MARTIN. German lithographer, age 19, living in Baltimore with AUGUST HOEN, by whom he was presumably employed. ¶ 7 Census (1850), Md., V, 418.

HARTMAN, THEODORE. Wood engraver of

NYC, 1855–60. In 1858 his occupation was described as "wood cuts for embroidery." He was born in Germany about 1822. ¶ NYCD 1855–60; NYBD 1856, 1860; 8 Census (1860), N.Y., LI, 214.

HARTMANN & HEPPENHEIMER. Lithographers of NYC in 1851. The partners were ADAM HARTMAN and FREDERICK HEPPENHEIMER. ¶ NYCD and NYBD 1851.

HARTMANN, HERMAN. Of SMITH & HARTMANN, die sinkers, NYC, 1850–59. ¶ NYCD and NYBD 1850–59.

HARTRATH, JOSEPH. Engraver at New Orleans in 1860. ¶ New Orleans CD 1860 (cited by Delgado-WPA).

HARTWELL, ALONZO (1805–1873). Engraver, portrait painter, and crayon portraitist. He was born in Littleton (Mass.) in 1805 and commenced engraving in Boston about 1826. He worked with JOSEPH ANDREWS at Lancaster (Mass.) in 1827, with JOHN C. CROSSMAN in 1833, and with the BOSTON BEWICK COMPANY in 1834. He continued to engrave until 1851, but after that date he turned to portraiture in crayon and oil. He died at Waltham (Mass.) in 1873. ¶ Bolton, *Crayon Draftsmen;* Hamilton, 286–289; Karolik Cat., 145; Whitmore, "Abel Bowen," 44; Boston CD 1826–34, 1854–60; BD 1850–51, 1854–60; Swan, BA.

HARTWELL, G. G. Portrait painter in oil, *c.* 1850. ¶ Lipman and Winchester, 174.

HARTWICK, GUNTHER. Landscape painter of NYC, 1847–57. He exhibited at the American Art-Union and the National Academy. ¶ NYCD 1847–57; Cowdrey, AA & AAU; Cowdrey, NAD.

HARTWICK, T. B. Landscape painter of NYC, exhibited a view of Rocky Hill (N.J.), at the American Art-Union in 1848. ¶ Cowdrey, AA & AAU.

HARVEY, GEORGE (*c.* 1800/01–1878). A.N.A. Landscape and miniature painter. A native of Tottenham, England; came to the United States at the age of 20 and spent several years in the West (Ohio, Michigan, Upper Canada) before establishing himself as an artist. By 1828, the year of his election as Associate Member of the National Academy, he had settled in Brooklyn (N.Y.), but the following year he moved to Boston, where he painted many miniatures. Soon after, Harvey visited England for study, returning to America about 1833. He built a home near Hastings-on-the-Hudson, close to Washington Irving's "Sunnyside," which Harvey helped to design. It was at Hastings that he commenced his notable series of "atmospheric views" of American scenery in watercolor, intending to have forty of them engraved and published by subscription. For the next decade he shuttled back and forth between England and America, seeking patronage and financial backing for this project, which eventually failed for lack of subscribers. Only four of the views were published; the collection of watercolors was preserved intact until 1940 and almost half of them are now owned by the New-York Historical Society. Harvey's career after 1850 is obscure. He apparently made his home in England, but continued to make painting trips to North America, including Florida and Bermuda, until about two years before his death in England in 1878. ¶ Shelley, "George Harvey and His Atmospheric Landscapes of North America"; Shelley, "George Harvey, English Painter of Atmospheric Landscapes in America," with 8 repros.; Parker, "George Harvey"; Karolik Cat., 297–300, two repros.; *Portfolio* (Oct. 1943), 41–44, three repros.; Cowdrey, NAD; Cowdrey, AA & AAU; Swan, BA; Stokes, *Historic Prints,* pl. 84b; Harvey, *Harvey's Scenes of the Primitive Forest of America* (N.Y., 1841), four colored engravings.

HARVEY, GEORGE (*c.* 1835–after 1920). Landscape and portrait painter, nephew of GEORGE HARVEY (*c.* 1800–1878). The younger Harvey was a pupil of his uncle in Boston, probably during the late 1850's, and was studying under THOMAS HICKS in NYC when the Civil War broke out. He then returned to his family in Burlington (Iowa) and lived there for most of his long life, though he did some painting along the Mississippi and is said to have painted portraits of three governors of Missouri. He was still living in Burlington in 1920, then over 85 years of age. ¶ Ness and Orwig, *Iowa Artists,* 96–97.

HASELTINE, CHARLES FIELD (1840–1915). Landscape painter and art dealer of Philadelphia. A younger brother of JAMES HENRY and WILLIAM STANLEY HASELTINE; born in Philadelphia July 29, 1840, and established there the Haseltine Art Galleries. He died December 5, 1915. ¶ *Art Annual,* XIII; Shinn, *History of the Shinn Family;* DAB (under James Henry Haseltine).

HASELTINE, Mrs. ELIZABETH STANLEY (SHINN). Amateur landscape painter.

Born in Philadelphia, April 22, 1811, Elizabeth Stanley Shinn was married in 1830 to John Haseltine of Philadelphia. Among their children were three artists: CHARLES FIELD, JAMES HENRY, and WILLIAM STANLEY HASELTINE. Mrs. Haseltine herself exhibited at the Pennsylvania Academy in the 1860's. She died June 29, 1882, at Boston. ¶ Shinn, *History of the Shinn Family;* Rutledge, PA.

HASELTINE, JAMES HENRY (1833–1907). Sculptor. A son of Mrs. ELIZABETH STANLEY HASELTINE, he was born November 2, 1833, in Philadelphia and studied sculpture there under JOSEPH A. BAILLY, exhibiting at the Pennsylvania Academy for the first time in 1855. He went to Italy and France for further study about 1857, but returned in 1861 to serve for two years in the Civil War. After the war he again went abroad and spent most of his life in Rome, where he died on November 9, 1907. ¶ DAB; Rutledge, PA; Shinn, *History of the Shinn Family.*

HASELTINE, WILLIAM STANLEY (1835–1900). N.A. Landscape and marine painter; son of ELIZABETH and brother of JAMES HENRY and CHARLES FIELD HASELTINE. He was born June 11, 1835, in Philadelphia and studied there under PAUL WEBER. He went to Düsseldorf in 1854 for further study and in 1856 accompanied LEUTZE, WHITTREDGE, and BIERSTADT on a sketching trip down the Rhine and to Italy. He returned to America in 1858, settled in NYC, and was elected a Member of the National Academy the following year. After his marriage in 1866, he went abroad again, living for a time in Paris and then settling in Rome. He returned to America in 1895, but went back to Rome in 1899 and died there on February 3, 1900. ¶ Plowden, *William Stanley Haseltine* (citation courtesy Theodore Bolton); *Art Annual,* III, obit.; Rutledge, PA; Cowdrey, NAD; Swan, BA; Clement and Hutton; Champlin and Perkins; CAB; Shinn, *History of the Shinn Family;* Washington Art Assoc. Cat., 1857.

HASKELL, HIRAM BETTS (1823–1873). Portrait painter; born in Fredericton (N.B.) on January 17, 1823; worked in Boston 1849–58; lived in Newburyport (Mass.) from 1858 and died there on August 22, 1873. ¶ Belknap, *Artists and Craftsmen of Essex County,* 10; Boston BD 1849, 1857–58; New England BD 1856, 1860; Newburyport CD 1858, 1860.

HASKELL, JOSEPH ALLEN (1808–1894). Portrait painter, born December 8, 1808, in Pittsfield (Mass.). He was painting in Troy (N.Y.) as early as 1829. In 1831 he moved to NYC where he had his studio for twelve years, during which time he exhibited at the National and American Academies. In 1844 he moved to Ann Arbor (Mich.) and in 1846 he was painting at Marshall (Mich.). Later he returned to New York, settling in Syracuse where he died in 1894. ¶ Information courtesy Ira J. Haskell, Lynn (Mass.), filed at FARL.

HASKELL, LYMAN. Metal engraver at Boston 1853 and after. ¶ Boston CD 1853, 1859; BD 1854–58, 1860+.

HASKELL, THOMAS J. Engraver at Boston 1838–49. ¶ Boston CD 1838–47; BD 1842–49.

HASS, BERNARD. Landscape painter at NYC, exhibited at the National Academy in 1855 view of rapids above Niagara Falls. ¶ Cowdrey, NAD.

HASSEN, WILLIAM. German engraver, 36, at NYC in 1860. He came to NYC about 1854. ¶ 8 Census (1860), N.Y., XLII, 368.

HASSLACHER, GEORGE. Engraver at NYC in 1854. ¶ NYBD 1854. *Cf.* GEORGE I. HAPLACHER.

HASTINGS, ——. A crayon portrait of H. S. Putnam (1835–1863) by this artist is in the State House, Concord (N.H.). ¶ WPA (Mass.), *Portraits Found in N.H.,* p. 18.

HASTINGS, DANIEL. Gravestone sculptor, whose portrait on slate of John Holyoke, 1775, is at Newton (Mass.). ¶ Lipman, *American Folk Art,* p. 21, illus. 171.

HASTINGS, MATTHEW (1834–1919). Painter of portraits and Indian scenes, caricaturist, working in Missouri. ¶ WPA Guide, *Missouri.*

HASTINGS, Dr. JAMES, U.S.N. One of the amateur artists whose sketches were used by GEORGE HEILGE for his panorama of the route to California, 1849. ¶ Phila. *Public Ledger,* Oct. 8 and 17, 1849 (citation courtesy J. E. Arrington).

HASWELL, ROBERT. Amateur artist who accompanied Robert Gray to Oregon in 1788 and 1792, as 2nd mate of the *Lady Washington* and 1st mate of the *Columbia.* Sketches from his log book have been reproduced. ¶ Porter, "The Ship Columbia and the Discovery of Oregon"; Lyman, *History of Oregon,* II, facing 92 and 96; Rasmussen, "Art and Artists in Oregon, 1500–1900" (citation courtesy

David C. Duniway, Oregon State Archivist).

HATCH & COMPANY. Lithographers of NYC, 1855 and after. The firm was established by GEORGE W. HATCH, JR. Its work was exhibited at the American Institute in 1856. ¶ NYCD 1855–60+; Am. Inst. Cat., 1856.

HATCH, ELISHA. Portrait painter in watercolor, working at Canaan (N.Y.), *c.* 1835–40. ¶ *American Provincial Painting,* no. 70; Lipman and Winchester, 174.

HATCH, GEORGE W. (1805–1867). Banknote, portrait and landscape engraver. Born in western New York about 1805, Hatch was one of the first students at the National Academy in 1826 and for a time a pupil of ASHER B. DURAND. He was engraving in Albany by 1830 and later in NYC. Though he did some portrait, landscape and subject plates for the "Annuals," Hatch was primarily a banknote engraver, associated with various firms including HATCH & SMILLIE; RAWDON, WRIGHT & HATCH; RAWDON, WRIGHT, HATCH & EDSON; and RAWDON, WRIGHT, HATCH & SMILLIE. In 1858 he became one of the founders of the AMERICAN BANK NOTE COMPANY, of which he was president from 1863 to 1866. He died at Dobbs Ferry (N.Y.) in 1867. GEORGE W. HATCH, JR., and WARNER D. HATCH were probably his sons. ¶ Stauffer; Cowdrey, NAD; Cowdrey, AA & AAU; NYCD 1827–59; Toppan, *100 Years of Bank Note Engraving,* 13.

HATCH, GEORGE W., JR. Lithographer of NYC, 1852 and after. Presumably a son of GEORGE W. HATCH, banknote engraver, the younger Hatch headed the lithographic firms of HATCH & SEVERYN and HATCH & Co. ¶ NYCD 1852–60+.

HATCH, P. H. Artist at Philadelphia in 1857. ¶ Phila. CD 1857; BD 1857 as "show cards."

HATCH & SEVERYN. Lithographers of NYC, 1854. The partners were GEORGE W. HATCH, JR. and CHARLES SEVERYN. ¶ NYCD 1854; *American Collector* (Oct. 1945), frontis.

HATCH, WARNER D. Lithographer of NYC, 1859 and after. Since his home was at Dobbs Ferry (N.Y.), he was probably a son of GEORGE W. HATCH. ¶ NYCD 1859–60.

HATHAWAY, ——. Painter of a scriptural panorama shown at Boston in March 1852. *Cf.* JAMES S. HATHAWAY. ¶ Boston *Evening Transcript,* March 27, 1852 (citation courtesy of J. E. Arrington).

HATHAWAY, JAMES S. Portrait painter. Barker states that J. S. Hathaway worked on Nantucket Island (Mass.) from 1839 to 1848. This was probably the J. S. or James S. Hathaway who was listed in Boston directories 1847 to 1850. ¶ Barker, *American Painting,* 522; Boston CD 1847–48, BD 1850.

HATHAWAY, Dr. JOSEPH. Miniaturist, active in Massachusetts from 1833 to 1838. In 1833 he exhibited at the Boston Athenaeum, as a resident of North Middleborough. ¶ Swan, BA; Bolton, *Miniature Painters;* Smith.

HATHAWAY, RUFUS (1770–1822). Portrait and miniature painter, carver. He was born May 2, 1770, probably at Freetown (Mass.), and began painting portraits at Taunton (Mass.) in 1791. In 1795 he married and settled in Duxbury (Mass.) where he was a practising physician until his death on October 13, 1822. ¶ Little, "Dr. Rufus Hathaway, Physician and Painter of Duxbury, Massachusetts, 1770–1822"; Bolton, *Miniature Painters;* Fielding.

HATHERTY, HENRY. Engraver at Philadelphia in 1805. ¶ Brown and Brown.

HATTAN, MICHAEL, see MICHAEL HADDON.

HAUBISEN, CHRISTOPHER. Portrait painter; born in 1830; died in St. Louis, February 1913. ¶ *Art Annual,* XI, obit; Smith; Mallett.

HAUGG, LOUIS. Lithographer, working at Philadelphia from 1856 to 1894. ¶ Phila. CD 1856–94; Peters, *America on Stone; Portfolio* (Oct. 1945), 46–47.

HAULICK, CHRISTIAN J. Engraver of NYC, 1856–58. ¶ NYBD 1856, 1858.

HAUSMAN, E. C. Prussian engraver, 25, at NYC in 1860. ¶ 8 Census (1860), N.Y., XLIV, 304.

HAVELAND, JOSEPH H. Engraver, 23, a native of New York, at NYC in 1850. ¶ 7 Census (1850), N.Y., LIII, 80.

HAVELL, HENRY AUGUSTUS. Painter and engraver; brother of ROBERT HAVELL, JR., whom he followed to America after 1839. He worked as a print-colorer and engraver in NYC, first as assistant to his brother, then as partner of THOMAS SPEARING. Samples of his print-coloring were shown at the American Institute in 1844. He was still in NYC in 1845, but is said to have returned to Englar after the failure of his NYC enterpris and to have died in London not lo.g after.

¶ Comstock, "The Complete Work of Robert Havell, Jr."; Am. Inst. Cat., 1844; NYCD 1844–45.

HAVELL, ROBERT, JR. (1793–1878). Aquatint engraver and landscape painter; born November 25, 1793, in Reading (England), the son of a well-known English engraver. He is remembered chiefly as the engraver of all but the first ten plates for AUDUBON's *Birds of America,* on which Havell worked in England from 1827 to 1838. On completion of the Audubon plates, the engraver emigrated to America in 1839, resided for a short time with Audubon in NYC, then moved to Sing Sing, now Ossining (N.Y.), in 1842, and in 1857 finally settled at Tarrytown (N.Y.), where he died November 11, 1878. After his removal to America, Havell devoted himself mainly to landscape painting, though he continued to engrave in aquatint. ¶ DAB; Stauffer; Sweet, *The Hudson River School;* Comstock, "The Complete Work of Robert Havell, Jr."; Shelley, "Audubon to Date"; Havell, "Havell's View of the Hudson from Tarrytown Heights," repro.; Cowdrey, NAD; Cowdrey, AA & AAU; Rutledge, PA.

HAVEN, JOSHUA P. Amateur artist of Philadelphia, exhibited "outlines" after Retch or Retche at the Pennsylvania Academy in 1847. ¶ Rutledge, PA.

HAVILAND & BRIDPORT. Drawing academy, specializing in architectural drafting, at Philadelphia, 1818–20. The school was run by JOHN HAVILAND and HUGH BRIDPORT. ¶ Brown and Brown.

HAVILAND, JOHN (1792–1853). Townscape artist and architect, active in Philadelphia from about 1817 to his death, which occurred March 28, 1853. In 1818–20 he was associated with HUGH BRIDPORT in a drawing academy. He exhibited numerous watercolor views of public and private buildings at the Pennsylvania Academy and National Academy, and was an Honorary Member, Professional, of the latter from 1827. ¶ Thieme-Becker; Rutledge, PA; Cowdrey, NAD; Phila. CD 1845.

HAWES, JOSIAH J. Portrait and miniature painter at Boston, 1838–39. He later turned daguerrean (1844–61, of Southworth & Hawes) and then took up photography, continuing active in Boston until 1901. ¶ Boston CD 1838–39, 1844–1901.

HAWES, SARAH E. Amateur painter of memorials in watercolor, Massachusetts, 1810. ¶ Lipman and Winchester, 174.

HAWES, S. P., see SAMUEL P. HOWES.

HAWK, SYDNEY. Amateur crayon artist. A young inmate of the Pennsylvania Institute for the Deaf and Dumb who in 1824 exhibited a crayon drawing, "Warrior's Head," at the Pennsylvania Academy. ALBERT NEWSAM was a fellow pupil at the Deaf and Dumb Institute. ¶ Rutledge, PA.

HAWKES, WILLIAM. German engraver, 21, at NYC in 1850. ¶ 7 Census (1850), N.Y., XLIX, 203.

HAWKINS, EZEKIEL C. Landscape and portrait painter, commercial artist, later a daguerreotypist and photographer. He is said to have been working in Baltimore as early as 1806; as a window-shade painter in Steubenville (Ohio) in 1811; at Wheeling (Va., now W. Va.) in 1829; and at Cincinnati in 1843. A portrait and miniature painter named Hawkins, working in New Orleans in 1834, may have been the same man. Ezekiel C. later worked as a daguerrean artist and is said to have perfected the collodion process in photography. THOMAS and WILLIAM HAWKINS were his brothers. ¶ Knittle, *Early Ohio Taverns,* 42; Delgado-WPA cites *La. Advertiser,* Feb. 28, 1834.

HAWKINS, ISAAC. Silhouette cutter, working in England in 1803, later came to America and assisted CHARLES WILLSON PEALE at his Museum in Philadelphia. ¶ Jackson, *Silhouette,* 64, 114.

HAWKINS, THOMAS. Sign and coach painter, working in Ohio in the early 19th century. He was a brother of EZEKIEL C. and WILLIAM HAWKINS. ¶ Knittle, *Early Ohio Taverns,* 42.

HAWKINS, WILLIAM. Coach and portrait painter. A brother of EZEKIEL C. and THOMAS HAWKINS, William was a musician as well as painter, and made and decorated organs. He was active in Jefferson County, Ohio, in the 1830's. ¶ Knittle, *Early Ohio Taverns,* 42; Hunter, *Pathfinders of Jefferson County* (citation courtesy Donald MacKenzie, Wooster College).

HAWKSETT, S., JR. (or Daniel). Portrait painter at Brooklyn (N.Y.), 1854–55. A portrait painted by S. Hawksett, Jr., at Brooklyn is dated 1855, while the Brooklyn directory for 1854/55 lists Daniel Hawksett, artist and painter. These are probably references to one man, who may have been a son of Samuel Hawksett (1776–1851), portrait painter of Belfast (Ireland). ¶ Information courtesy Dr. H.

W. Williams, Jr., Corcoran Gallery; Brooklyn CD 1854/55; Strickland, *Dictionary of Irish Artists;* Thieme-Becker.

HAWORTH, GEORGE, see GEORGE HOWORTH.

HAWTHORN, CHARLES. English artist, age 46, at Philadelphia in July 1860. Hawthorn's wife was Irish, and the children, ages 8 and 4, were born in Pennsylvania. ¶ 8 Census (1860), Pa., LIV, 244.

HAWTHORNE, Mrs. NATHANIEL, see SOPHIA AMELIA PEABODY.

HAY, DAVID G. Listed as artist in census, painter in directories. Born in New Jersey *c.* 1798, working in Philadelphia as early as 1834, as late as 1863. ¶ 8 Census (1860), Pa., LV, 162 (as David Hay); Phila. CD 1840–63 (as David G. Hay).

HAY, DEWITT CLINTON. Banknote engraver; born in Saratoga (N.Y.) about 1819 and apprenticed before 1850 to RAWDON, WRIGHT, HATCH & SMILLIE of NYC. From about 1852 he was a partner in the firm of WELLSTOOD, HANKS, HAY & WHITING. ¶ Stauffer; Fielding; 8 Census (1860), N.Y., XLVII, 258 [as De Hay].

HAY, WILLIAM. Line-engraver at Philadelphia, 1819–24. Stauffer distinguishes between his work and that of WILLIAM H. HAY. ¶ Stauffer; Fielding.

HAY, WILLIAM H. Line-engraver at Philadelphia who did plates for Childs' *Views of Philadelphia* (1828). On stylistic grounds Stauffer distinguishes between William H. and WILLIAM HAY. ¶ Stauffer.

HAYDEN, Miss ——. Panorama painter who was at Nashville (Tenn.) in October–November 1847, repairing her panoramas of Venice and Jerusalem which had been injured in a boat wreck. ¶ Nashville *Daily Union,* Nov. 4, 1847 (courtesy J. Earl Arrington).

HAYDEN, Mrs. HARRIET CLARK WINSLOW. Flower painter in oils and water colors; born July 20, 1840, in Franklin (Mass.); died March 29, 1906, in Dayton (Ohio). ¶ *Art Annual,* VI, obit.; Smith.

HAYDEN, J. H. Artist from England, age 30, living in Boston in June 1860. Mrs. Hayden was from Nova Scotia, and their son Howard, age 6, was born in Massachusetts. ¶ 8 Census (1860), Mass., XXVIII, 185.

HAYDON, WILLIAM. Drawing master from London at Philadelphia in 1797–98. ¶ Prime, I, 14, and II, 51.

HAYES, GEORGE H. Wood engraver of Boston from 1853; did work for *Ballou's Pictorial.* ¶ Boston BD 1854–60, CD 1853; *Ballou's Pictorial,* Jan. 29, 1859 (citation courtesy Mary Bartlett Cowdrey).

HAYES, JAMES. English artist, 35, at NYC in 1860. *Cf.* JAMES E. HAYES. ¶ 8 Census (1860), N.Y., LVII, 314.

HAYES, JAMES E. Theatrical scene painter. James E., son of JAMES H. HAYES, was born in England *c.* 1827 and worked as a scene painter in Boston from 1847 to 1856. *Cf.* JAMES HAYES, above. ¶ 7 Census (1850), Mass., XXIV, 470; Boston CD 1847–55; Boston *Evening Transcript,* April 14, 1856 (citation courtesy J. E. Arrington).

HAYES, JAMES HENRY. Shade painter. Hayes, his wife, and all their children were born in England, but the family emigrated to America before 1847. From 1847 to 1855 they lived in Boston. He was assisted in his shade-painting business by his son SAMUEL, while another son, JAMES E. HAYES, became a scene painter for the Boston Theatre. James H. Hayes (or Henry, as he was called in the census) was about 56 years old at the time of the 1850 census. ¶ 7 Census (1850), Mass., XXIV, 470; Boston CD 1847–55.

HAYES, SAMUEL H. Shade painter; born in England *c.* 1825; living in Boston in 1850. He was a son of JAMES H. and brother of JAMES E. HAYES. ¶ 7 Census (1850), Mass., XXIV, 470; Boston CD 1848–54 (as artist).

HAYES, WILLIAM H. (1800–1828). Sign, coach, and ornamental painter, profilist; born in Virginia in 1800 and died in New Orleans, September 4, 1828. He was listed as "ornamental, sign, coach, ship and house painter and glazier and paper hanger" in New Orleans in 1822, and in the spring of the same year announced that he was equipped with a machine for taking profiles. *Cf.* WILLIAM H. HAYS. ¶ *La. Courier,* Sept. 4, 1828 (cited by Delgado-WPA); New Orleans CD 1822; *La. Courier,* April 5 and 17, 1822 (cited by Delgado-WPA).

HAYNES, C. YOUNGLOVE. Sculptor, Philadelphia, 1850. His bas-relief portrait of Henry Clay, patented that year, was owned in 1941 by Edward Dewey of Bennington (Vt.). ¶ Gardner, *Yankee Stonecutters,* 66; WPA (Mass.), *Portraits Found in Vt.*

HAYNES, FRANCIS G. Portrait painter at Manchester (N.H.) in 1858. ¶ Manchester BD 1858.

HAYS, BARTON S. (1826–1914). Portrait, landscape, still life, and panorama painter.

Born April 5, 1826, in Greenville (Ohio); moved to northern Indiana in the early 1850's and painted portraits of early citizens of Wingate, Covington, and Attica. An abolitionist, he painted two panoramas of *Uncle Tom's Cabin* shortly after its publication. Moving to Indianapolis, he went into partnership with a photographer but continued to paint portraits and taught painting at McLean's Female Seminary. He moved to Cincinnati in 1870, but soon returned to Indianapolis. In 1882 he moved to Minneapolis where he died March 14, 1914. ¶ Burnet, *Art and Artists of Indiana;* Peat, *Pioneer Painters of Indiana;* information courtesy Mrs. W. H. Whitley, Paris (Ky.); Indiana BD 1858; Indianapolis BD 1859–60.

HAYS, HENRY, SR. Engraver and heraldist. Bayley and Goodspeed state that he was an English bookplate engraver, working in NYC from *c.* 1830 to 1855. Henry Hays is not listed in NYC directories, however, until 1851. He appears first as heraldist, then as painter (1852–53) and engraver (1856–60). From 1854 he was associated in business with his son, HENRY HAYS, JR. It is difficult to disentangle the concurrent careers of father and son, but it appears that Henry Hays, Sr., was active at least until 1865. ¶ Dunlap, *History* (1918), III, 307; NYCD 1851–65; NYBD 1854.

HAYS, HENRY, JR. Engraver and heraldist. Henry Hays, pupil at Public School No. 7, NYC, won a diploma for pen drawings at the American Institute Fair of 1848, again in 1849, and in 1851 a silver medal for "superior steel engraving." By 1854 he was in business as an engraver, in association with his father, HENRY HAYS, SR., heraldist. They appear to have continued in business together until about 1865, after which the younger man carried on alone. In 1870 he was listed as a genealogist and heraldic engraver. ¶ Am. Inst. Cat. and *Trans.*, 1848, 1849, 1851; NYCD 1854–70; NYBD 1856–58.

HAYS, WILLIAM H. Portrait, landscape, coach, sign, and ornamental painter at New Orleans, 1816–18. In the latter year he advertised that he was giving up his business. *Cf.* WILLIAM H. HAYES and William Hays, from Kentucky, who died of measles at New Orleans, in March 1824, age 35. ¶ Delgado-WPA cites *La. Gazette,* Jan. ?, 1816, Jan. 29, 1818, and *La. Courier,* March 11, 1824.

HAYS, WILLIAM JACOB, SR. (1830–1875). A.N.A. Painter, chiefly of animals. He was born in NYC on August 8, 1830, studied with JOHN RUBENS SMITH, first exhibited (at the American Institute) in 1845, and was elected an Associate Member of the National Academy in 1853. His fame rests on his sketches and oil paintings of animals and views on the upper Missouri, made during a trip to the West in 1860. Hays later visited England and made sketching trips to Nova Scotia and the Adirondacks. His studio was in NYC, where he died on March 13, 1875. ¶ DAB; Taft, *Artists and Illustrators of the Old West,* 36–52; Tuckerman; Clement and Hutton; Am. Inst. Cat., 1845; Cowdrey, AA & AAU; Cowdrey, NAD; Rutledge, PA; Rutledge, MHS; Swan, BA; Washington Art Assoc. Cat., 1857.

HAYSE, MARTHA S. Landscape painter in watercolors, Massachusetts, 1810. ¶ Lipman and Winchester, 174.

HAYWARD, DAVID. Genre painter of NYC, exhibited at the National Academy 1844–48. ¶ Cowdrey, NAD.

HAYWARD, GEORGE. Lithographer of NYC, 1834–72. In 1857 he was associated with GEORGE PILLOW. Hayward was born in England about 1800. ¶ Peters, *America on Stone;* NYCD 1836–59; NYBD 1844–59; Stokes, *Historic Prints,* pl. 133a; *Portfolio* (Dec. 1942), 86; 7 Census (1850), N.Y., LIII, 242.

HAYWARD, JOHN B. Lithographer, age 34, at Boston in July 1860. He was a native of Massachusetts and owned $2,000 in personal property. ¶ 8 Census (1860), Mass., XXVII, 456.

HAYWARD, JOSHUA HENSHAW (1797–1856). Portrait painter of Boston. He was an exhibitor at the Boston Athenaeum from 1838 to 1848. ¶ Swan, BA; Boston BD 1841–49; Boston *Evening Transcript,* Sept. 18, 1850 (citation courtesy J. E. Arrington).

HAYWARD & PILLOW. Lithographers of NYC in 1837. The partners were GEORGE HAYWARD and GEORGE PILLOW. ¶ NYBD 1837.

HAZARD, J. T. Map engraver of Philadelphia, 1850. ¶ Phila. BD 1850.

HAZEN, I. or J. Painter of a portrait of Isaac Tichenor, Governor of Vermont 1797–1807, 1808–09. ¶ C. K. Bolton, "Workers with Line and Color in New England."

HAZLITT, JOHN (1767–1837). Portrait and miniature painter. John, older brother of the famous essayist William Hazlitt, was born in Marshfield (England) and baptized July 6, 1767. The Hazlitt family moved to Ireland in 1780 and thence in 1783 to the United States. After a short time in Philadelphia, the family settled in Massachusetts, first in Salem (1784), then in Dorchester (1786). It was at this time that John commenced his career as a miniature painter. The Hazlitt family returned to England in 1787. John Hazlitt exhibited at the Royal Academy annually from 1788 to 1819. He died at Stockport (England) on May 16, 1837. ¶ T. Bolton, "John Hazlitt—Portrait Painter"; Bolton, *Miniature Painters;* Belknap, *Artists and Craftsmen of Essex County,* 10; Fielding; Thieme-Becker.

HEAD, SAMUEL. Sculptor and marble-cutter at New Orleans, 1852–53. ¶ New Orleans CD 1852–53.

HEADE, MARTIN JOHNSON (1819–1904). Landscape, portrait, and still life painter, born August 11, 1819, at Lumberville, Bucks County (Pa.). Received his first art training from THOMAS HICKS and studied in Italy, France, and England *c.* 1837–40. Soon after his return to America, he began exhibiting in the major eastern galleries and during the next two decades worked as a portrait and landscape painter both in the East (NYC, Brooklyn, Philadelphia, Trenton, and Boston) and in the Mid-West (St. Louis, 1852, and Chicago, 1853–54). In 1863–64 Heade visited Brazil, the first of several painting trips which took him to Nicaragua (1866), to Colombia, Porto Rico, and Jamaica (1870) and later to British Columbia, California, and Florida. A resident of Washington (D.C.) and NYC during the early 1880's, he settled permanently at St. Augustine (Fla.) in 1885 and died there September 4, 1904. A naturalist and poet as well as artist, Heade is best known for his paintings of tropical birds and flowers. ¶ The standard biography is Robert G. McIntyre, *Martin Johnson Heade, 1819–1904* (N.Y.: Pantheon Press, 1948). See also: Karolik Cat., 301–349, with 26 repros.; Rutledge, PA; Cowdrey, NAD; Cowdrey, AA & AAU; Swan, BA; Sweet, *The Hudson River School;* CAB; Tuckerman; *Richmond Portraits;* McCausland, "American Still-life Paintings," repro.

HEADE, WILLIAM P. Artist, age 35, born in Ohio and living in Cincinnati in September 1850. ¶ 7 Census (1850), Ohio, XX, 359.

HEADLEY, JOSEPH H., see JOSEPH H. HIDLEY.

HEAFORD, VINCENT. Landscape painter at Albany (N.Y.) in 1852. ¶ Troy and Albany BD 1852.

HEALD, JAMES. English engraver, age 23, living with his Pennsylvanian wife in Philadelphia, July 1850. ¶ 7 Census (1850), Pa., LIII, 539.

HEALS, JOHN. Spanish engraver, age 25, living with ROBERT HEALS in Philadelphia, August 1850. ¶ 7 Census (1850), Pa., LII, 604.

HEALS, ROBERT. Spanish engraver, age 30, living with JOHN HEALS in Philadelphia, August 1850. ¶ 7 Census (1850), Pa., LII, 604.

HEALY, GEORGE PETER ALEXANDER (1813–1894). Portrait and historical painter. G. P. A. Healy, one of the most successful of 19th-century portrait painters, was born in Boston on July 15, 1813. He began his artistic career in Boston at the age of 17 and in 1834 went to France to study under Gros. When he returned to his native country eight years later, he was already internationally known and patronized by the royal families of England and France. From 1844 to 1867 he spent most of his time in the United States filling innumerable commissions in Washington (D.C.), along the eastern seaboard and in the southern states, as well as in Chicago where he made his home from 1854 to 1867. His sitters included most of the prominent statesmen of the time, as well as the leaders of society and business. After the Civil War he returned to Europe, settling first in Rome, then in Paris, but he continued to travel on important commissions which took him to the United States and many European capitals. Returning finally to the United States in 1892, he spent his last years in Chicago and died there on June 24, 1894. ¶ The career of G. P. A. Healy has been the subject of three books: his own *Reminiscences of a Portrait Painter* (Chicago: 1894); *Life of George P. A. Healy, by His Daughter, Mary* [Mme. Charles Bigot] (Chicago: 1913); and a recent study by his grand-daughter, Marie de Mare, entitled *G. P. A. Healy, American Artist* (New York: 1954). See also: DAB; Swan, BA; Cowdrey, NAD; Cowdrey, AA & AAU; Rutledge, PA; *Richmond Portraits;* Karolik Cat.; Rutledge, *Artists in the Life of Charleston;* Washington Art Assoc. Cat., 1857; represented at Essex Institute, Minnesota Hist. Soc., Chicago Hist. Soc., etc.

HEALY, J. P., is G. P. A. HEALY.

HEALY, THOMAS CANTWELL (1820–1873). Portrait painter. A younger brother of G. P. A. HEALY, T. C. Healy was born in 1820 at Albany (N.Y.) but spent his childhood and early manhood in Boston. He was studying art in Paris in 1838, and by 1842 was painting portraits in Lowell (Mass.). During the 1850's he visited his brother in Chicago and he painted portraits in St. Paul (Minn.) in 1857. By 1860 he was established as a portrait painter at Port Gibson (Miss.) and he apparently remained there during the Civil War, possibly until his death in 1873. He exhibited at the Boston Athenaeum and the National Academy between 1832 and 1842. ¶ de Mare, *G. P. A. Healy, American Artist,* 10 ff.; Swan, BA; Bertha L. Heilbron, "Pioneer Homemaker," 96 (repro.), 100; Barker, *American Painting,* 401; Cowdrey, NAD.

HEAP, GEORGE. Drew a view of Philadelphia from the Jersey shore, under the direction of Nicholas Scull, Surveyor-General of Pennsylvania, which was engraved and published in London in 1754. ¶ *Portfolio* (Feb. 1944), 132–133, repro.

HEAP, GWINN HARRIS. Topographical artist who designed the 13 illustrations (lithographed by DUVAL) for *Central Route to the Pacific, from the Valley of the Mississippi to California: Journal of the Expedition of E. F. Beale . . . and Gwinn Harris Heap, from Missouri to California, in 1853* (published 1854). ¶ Peters, *California on Stone.*

HEAPHY, ELIZABETH, see Mrs. ELIZABETH HEAPHY MURRAY.

HEARSEY, JAMES P. Portrait painter at New Orleans, 1827–30. ¶ Delgado-WPA cites New Orleans CD 1827, 1830.

HEATH, WILLIAM H. Engraver of NYC, 1844–60; exhibited engravings at the American Institute in 1847 and 1849. ¶ NYCD 1844–60; Am. Inst. Cat., 1847, 1849.

HEATON, CHARLES M., JR. (1840–1921). Portrait and miniature painter. Born December 17, 1840, at South Bend (Ind.), Heaton spent most of his life as an artist and realtor in Washington (D.C.) and died at Tacoma Park (D.C.) on August 19, 1921. His portrait of his mother, painted in 1870, is in the South Bend Historical Museum. ¶ Peat, *Pioneer Painters of Indiana,* 232.

HECHENTHALL, LOUIS. Artist at Baltimore, 1858–59. ¶ Baltimore CD 1858–59; Lafferty.

HECHSTETTER, JOHN DAVID. Engraver on wood, stone and ivory. He came from Germany to Philadelphia in 1796. ¶ Prime, II, 69.

HECHT, BENJAMIN. Lithographer of NYC, 1850. ¶ NYBD 1850.

HEDGE, FRANKLIN. Wood engraver and designer. Born in New York State about 1830; worked as an engraver in Lowell (Mass.) *c.* 1848–52 and in Boston from 1853 until after 1860. In 1860 he was living in Boston with his wife Abby and daughter Lizzie (age 2) and owned real property valued at $2,500 and personalty at $1,000. ¶ 8 Census (1860), Mass., XXIX, 23; Lowell CD 1848, 1851–52; Boston BD 1853–60 and after.

HEDGES, WILLIAM W. Wood engraver; born in New York about 1835; active in NYC from 1856 to 1860; exhibited at the American Institute in 1856. A William Hedges, possibly the same man, was working as a wood engraver at Cincinnati in 1857. ¶ 8 Census (1860), N.Y., XLVII, 888; NYBD and NYCD 1856; Am. Inst. Cat., 1856; Ohio BD 1857.

HEDINGER, JOHN H. Artist from Germany, age 34, living in Philadelphia in June 1860. ¶ 8 Census (1860), Pa., 772.

HEDLEY, JOSEPH H., see JOSEPH H. HIDLEY.

HEED, J. Painter of a view in Elkhart County (Ind.) in 1837. ¶ *American Primitive Painting,* no. 29; Peat, *Pioneer Painters of Indiana,* 136–37.

HEED, M. J. or J. M., is MARTIN JOHNSON HEADE.

HEELY, EMMA A. Watercolorist and teacher at the Orphan Asylum, Albany (N.Y.). In 1846 she was awarded a diploma by the American Institute for flower painting in water colors from nature, and the following year she exhibited a "book of paintings" at the Institute. ¶ Albany CD 1847; Am. Inst. *Trans.,* 1846; Am. Inst. Cat., 1847.

HEERMANS (Herrman), AUGUSTYN (*c.* 1605–1686). Amateur artist, surveyor, and mapmaker. Born *c.* 1605 in Prague, capital of Bohemia, Heermans served under Wallenstein in the Thirty Years' War but emigrated to America in 1633, settling first at New Amsterdam as agent for a Dutch commercial house. One of the important men of the settlement, Heermans also was known as an artist of some talent and one of his sketches (a view of New Amsterdam *c.* 1656) was sent to Holland in 1660. In 1659 Heermans was employed by the authorities of Maryland to survey and map that colony, receiving in payment a grant of land in Maryland. He moved to his Maryland manor in 1662 and lived there until his death in 1686. ¶ DAB; Innes, *New Amsterdam and Its People,* 281–291. Innes assigns to Heermans the "Visscher view" of New Amsterdam, *c.* 1652, but Stokes (*Icon.,* II, 226) dismisses this claim. See also Stokes, *Icon.,* I, 142.

HEGEMAN, GEORGE. Of STOUT & HEGEMAN, engravers of NYC, 1859–60. ¶ NYBD 1859–60.

HEGER, JOSEPH. Lithographer. Born in Hesse (Germany), January 11, 1835; came to America as a young man and in 1855 enlisted in the U. S. Army. During his five years' service in the Southwest, he sketched many of the towns and natural wonders of Texas and New Mexico. He was living at Goodlettsville (Tenn.) as late as 1897. ¶ Information courtesy George P. Hammond, who cites War Records Division, National Archives, Washington (D.C.).

HEGLER, JOHN JACOB (1812–1856). Portrait painter. A native of Bertzville (Switz.); came to America in 1831; at Fort Wayne (Ind.) in 1845; at Lafayette (Ind.) 1849–53; at Attica (Ind.) from 1853 until his death. ¶ Peat, *Pioneer Painters of Indiana,* 232; *Antiques* (Nov. 1950), 383, repro.

HEIDEMANS, HENRI P. Miniaturist at NYC, 1841–42. ¶ Bolton, *Miniature Painters:* NYBD 1841; NYCD 1842; Fielding.

HEILGE, GEORGE. Landscape, panorama, and theatrical scene painter. In 1838–39 Heilge, spoken of as a native artist, executed decorations for a NYC theater. In 1840 he was employed as scene painter at the American Theatre in Philadelphia, in 1841 at the Walnut Street Theatre there, and in 1846 at the Arch Street Theatre. Between 1844 and 1855 he painted a number of panoramas, including views of Jerusalem, a tour to California, scenes of the Antediluvian World, Kane's Arctic explorations, and the Siege of Sebastopol. ¶ N. Y. *Herald,* Jan. 10, 1839; Rutledge, PA; Phila. *Public Ledger,* Dec. 23, 1841, March 25, 1844, August 24, 1846, October 8 and 17, 1849; N. Y. *Herald,* May 11, 1850, October 12, 1855 (newspaper citations courtesy J. E. Arrington).

HEILL, CARL. German artist, age 21, boarding with his brothers in New Orleans in August 1850. ¶ 7 Census (1850), La., V, 82.

HEILL, GEORGE. German artist, age 27, boarding with his brothers in New Orleans in August 1850. ¶ 7 Census (1850), La., V, 82.

HEILL, JACOB. German artist, age 24, boarding with his brothers in New Orleans in August 1850. ¶ 7 Census (1850), La., V, 82.

HEILL, PHILIP. German artist, age 30, boarding with his brothers in New Orleans in August 1850. ¶ 7 Census (1850), La., V, 82.

HEIMHOLD, GEORGE. Engraver at Philadelphia in 1800. ¶ Prime, II, 70.

HEINE & KUMMER. Landscape painters and teachers of painting, NYC, 1850. The partners were PETER B. W. HEINE and JULIUS H. KUMMER. ¶ NYBD 1850.

HEINE, PETER BERNARD WILLIAM (1827–1885). Landscape painter and teacher, author; born January 30, 1827, in Dresden (Germany); came to the United States in 1849. After a brief residence in NYC, where he was in partnership with JULIUS H. KUMMER, he served from 1852 to 1854 as artist with the Perry expedition to Japan. Heine made his home in NYC until his return to Europe in 1859. He died near Dresden, October 5, 1885. ¶ Thieme-Becker; Cowdrey, NAD; Cowdrey, AA & AAU; Rutledge, PA; Washington Art Assoc. Cat., 1857, 1859; Perry, *Expedition to Japan.* Repros. in *American Collector* (Aug. 1942), cover and p. 6; *Portfolio* (Jan. 1942), 12, (Jan. 1949), frontis. and p. 100.

HEINE, SEBASTIAN. Painter, who advertised a varied repertory of skills at Cleveland (Ohio) between 1839 and 1864. His view of the southwestern section of the public square in Cleveland, painted in 1839, is now at the Western Reserve Historical Society. ¶ Barker, *American Painting,* 521, repro. 519; *Antiques* (June 1951), 481, repro.

HEINE, WILLIAM, see PETER BERNARD WILLIAM HEINE.

HEINMULLER, or HEINMUELLER, WILLIAM. Painter and teacher of NYC, 1853–89. He exhibited five paintings at the American Institute in 1856. ¶ NYCD 1853–89; Am. Inst. Cat., 1856.

HEINRICH, FRANCIS H. Landscape and portrait painter; came to NYC about 1848, having apparently spent some time in Italy as well as Germany. He exhibited at the

American Art-Union and the National Academy from 1849 to 1852. ¶ Cowdrey, NAD; Cowdrey, AA & AAU; *Antiques* (Aug. 1946), 91, repro. of portrait of the Fiedler family of NYC.

HEISCHBEIN, F., see FRANÇOIS FLEISCHBEIN.

HEISS, GEORGE G. Portrait painter. Born in Pennsylvania *c.* 1823; lived in Philadelphia and exhibited at the Artists' Fund Society from 1840 to 1843. He was listed as a lithographer in Philadelphia directories from 1854 into the 1860's. ¶ 7 Census (1850), Pa., XLIX, 425; Rutledge, PA; Phila. CD 1854, 1858 and after.

HEISTER, EDWARD. Artist, 27, a native of New York, at NYC in 1850. ¶ 7 Census (1850), N.Y., LI, 414.

HEISTER, GEORGE. Portrait, genre, panorama, and theatrical scene painter; born in New York *c.* 1822 and active in NYC as a scene and panorama painter from 1840 to 1854. He exhibited at the National Academy in 1840 and 1844. By 1859 he had moved to Philadelphia where he was listed in the 1860 Census with his wife Irene and five children. ¶ 7 Census (1850), N.Y., XLVIII, 433; 8 Census (1860), Pa., LIV, 569; N. Y. *Herald,* June 16, 1840, Dec. 12, 1849, Jan. 1, 1850, Dec. 26, 1853, Dec. 11, 1854 (citations courtesy J. E. Arrington); Cowdrey, NAD.

HEIT, BENJAMIN. Lithographer, 33, a native of Frankfort (Germany), at NYC in 1860. His wife was also from Frankfort, but their children, ages 11 to 2, were born in New York. ¶ 8 Census (1860), N.Y., LIV, 981.

HEITZ, FREDERICK F. Engraver at NYC, 1859. ¶ NYBD and NYCD 1859.

HEKKING, J. ANTONIO. A German landscape painter who exhibited at the National Academy in 1859 as of Cherry Valley (N.Y.) and subsequently worked in Connecticut for many years. ¶ Cowdrey, NAD; French, *Art and Artists in Connecticut,* 162; Hartford CD 1873.

HELE, EDWARD. Engraver, age 24, living with his father, William Hele, in Philadelphia, June 1860. Both father and son were natives of Pennsylvania. ¶ 8 Census (1860), Pa., LVIII, 737.

HELFF (or Helfth), JOSEPH. Landscape and figure painter. In 1850 and 1852 Helff exhibited over 40 paintings on Italian subjects at the American Art-Union, and one Tyrolese scene at the National Academy in 1852, when his address was NYC. In 1855 Joseph Helfth of Rome exhibited a watercolor view at the Pennsylvania Academy. ¶ Cowdrey, AA & AAU; Cowdrey, NAD; Rutledge, PA.

HELLEM, CHARLES B. Portrait painter at NYC 1855–57, at Newark (N.J.) 1860. ¶ NYBD 1855, 1857; Newark CD 1860.

HELLER, Mrs. T. Portrait and figure painter, at the address of JOSEPH VOLMERING in NYC, 1854. Mrs. Heller exhibited at the National Academy that year a portrait of J. Volmering, and studies of a Hindoo girl and an Italian girl. ¶ Cowdrey, NAD; NYCD 1854.

HELLERMAN, ROBERT. Artist, age 30, living in Philadelphia, July 1860, with his wife Hannah and two small children. All were native Pennsylvanians. ¶ 8 Census (1860), Pa., LXII, 363.

HELLGE, GEORGE, see GEORGE HEILGE.

HELM, AUGUSTUS L. Engraver of Cincinnati, 1856–60. ¶ Cincinnati CD 1856, 1859–60; Ohio BD 1859.

HELMUTH, WILLIAM TOD (1833–1902). Medical illustrator; born October 30, 1833, in Philadelphia; graduated from the Homoepathic Medical College there in 1853. After practising for a few years in Philadelphia, he moved to St. Louis where he was a prominent surgeon until 1870. From 1870 Dr. Helmuth practised in NYC, where he died May 15, 1902. He was the author of many works on medicine and surgery, partly illustrated by himself, and also of *Arts in St. Louis* (1864). ¶ DAB; Union Cat., LC.

HEMENWAY, ASA. Primitive watercolorist at Middlebury (Vt.), 1839–40. ¶ Information courtesy Mrs. Jean Lipman, Dec. 6, 1950, correcting erroneous date given in Lipman and Winchester, 174.

HEMENWAY, CHARLES (?–1887). Sculptor of Providence (R.I.); born early in the 19th century, died 1887. Trained at Tingley's stoneyard in Providence, Hemenway executed a number of portrait busts, as well as cemetery monuments. At the time of his death he was an inmate of the Dexter Asylum at Providence. ¶ Gardner, *Yankee Stonecutters,* 66.

HEMMING, H. Engraver from Berlin (Germany), aged 22, at NYC in 1860. His wife was also from Berlin, but their only child, aged 3, was born in New York. ¶ 8 Census (1860), N.Y., L, 267.

HEMMING, RICHARD. Xylographic (wood) engraver at NYC, 1841. ¶ NYBD 1841.

HENARD, CHARLES. French miniaturist, working in London during the 1780's and 1790's and in Paris from 1806 to 1812. Although Henard painted miniatures of Stephen Van Rensselaer and Robert Oliver (1759–1834) of Baltimore, the latter dated 1814 and now in the Maryland Historical Society, there is no direct evidence of his having worked in America. ¶ Thieme-Becker; Fielding, *Supplement to Stauffer,* no. 512; Rutledge, "Handlist of Miniatures in the Md. Hist. Soc.," 131.

HENDERSON, ABIGAIL (Mrs. Alexander). Artist of Newbury (Vt.) who gave lessons to ALONZO SLAFTER about 1830. ¶ Information courtesy Mrs. K. McCook Knox, Washington (D.C.).

HENDERSON, DAVID ENGLISH (1832–1887). Portrait artist in oils, watercolors, and crayon, cartographer, topographical artist. A native of Jefferson County (Va., now W. Va.), Henderson worked in Georgetown (Va.) and NYC, and after the Civil War in Brooklyn (N.Y.). The Princeton University Library owns a copy of Matthew Carey's *General Atlas* (Phila., 1841) containing 15 original pen and wash drawings of scenes in West Virginia and Tennessee, done by Henderson in 1856–57, apparently for engraving. He died in 1887 in Jefferson County (W. Va.). ¶ Willis, "Jefferson County Portraits and Portrait Painters"; *Princeton University Library Chronicle,* Summer 1951, 222.

HENDLEY, CHARLES. Portrait painter at Boston, 1849. ¶ Boston BD 1849.

HENDLEY, JOHN WALTER (1826–1899). Modeller at the Smithsonian Institution, Washington (D.C.). A native of Virginia, he died July 3, 1899 at Washington. ¶ *Art Annual,* I, Supp., 83; Smith.

HENNENBERGER, MARTIN. Lithographer in NYC, 1850–54. ¶ NYBD 1850–54.

HENNESSY, WILLIAM JOHN (1839–1917). N.A. Landscape and genre painter, illustrator. Born July 11, 1839, at Thomastown, County Kilkenny (Ireland), Hennessy was brought to the United States at the age of ten. The family settled in NYC and in 1856 William entered the school of the National Academy, of which he was made a Member in 1863. After his marriage in 1870 he went to England and in 1875 to France. Returning to England in 1893, he made his home first at Brighton, then at Rudgwick, Sussex, where he died December 26, 1917. He was best known as illustrator of many books of poetry. ¶ DAB; Clement and Hutton; Champlin and Perkins; Cowdrey, NAD; Rutledge, PA; Graves, *Dictionary;* Fielding.

HENNING, A. Engraver and die sinker; at Hartford (Conn.) 1855–56; at NYC, 1859–60, with Henning & Eymann, daguerreotype case makers. ¶ Hartford CD 1855–56; NYCD 1859, NYBD 1860.

HENRI, PIERRE (Peter Henri or Henry). Miniaturist, who advertised in NYC in May 1788 as lately arrived from France. Thereafter he advertised in Philadelphia, 1789–90; Charleston (S.C.), 1790–93; NYC, 1794; Philadelphia, 1795, 1799–1802 (exhibited at the Columbianum 1795); Baltimore, 1803–04; Richmond (Va.), May 1804; Philadelphia, 1804; NYC, 1807; Philadelphia, 1808–14; and NYC, 1818. ¶ Sherman, "Pierre Henri's American Miniatures," with 5 repros. and checklist; Kelby, *Notes on American Artists,* 32; Gottesman, *Arts and Crafts in New York,* II, nos. 14–15; Prime, II, 14–16; Columbianum Cat., 1795; Mayo and Lafferty cite Baltimore CD 1803–04; NYCD 1807, 1818; Rutledge, PA; *Richmond Portraits;* Rutledge, *Artists in the Life of Charleston;* Bermuda Hist. Soc., *Loan Exhibition of Portraits, XVII–XIX Centuries,* no. 129; Brown and Brown.

HENRY, ALBERT P. (1836–1872). Sculptor; born January 8, 1836, at Versailles (Ky.). A clerk in an iron works in his youth, Henry taught himself modelling and cast his early pieces in iron to be used as doorstops. He was captured by the Confederates during the War and devoted much of his time in prison to carving in bone. After the war he was named U. S. Consul at Ancona (Italy) and in Italy he studied under HIRAM POWERS and JOEL T. HART. He died at Paris (Ky.), November 6, 1872. His best known works were busts of Henry Clay, now in the U. S. Capitol at Washington, and a life bust of Lincoln at Louisville (Ky.). ¶ Fairman, *Art and Artists of the Capitol,* 456; Fielding.

HENRY, BENJAMIN WEST (1777–1806). Portrait painter; youngest child of William Henry, the early patron and friend of BENJAMIN WEST; born at Lancaster (Pa.), June 8, 1778. He became an artist in Lancaster, painting a portrait of his brother which in 1912 was owned by the Historical Society of Pennsylvania. In 1798 he was also commissioned to paint a Masonic carpet for the Lancaster Lodge of which he was a member and later Worshipful Master. He died in Lancaster,

December 28, 1806. ¶ Steinman, "Benjamin West Henry, A Lancaster Artist," Lancaster Co. Hist. Soc., *Papers,* XVI (1912), 270–272.

HENRY, EDWARD. Scottish landscape painter, 34, at NYC in 1860. His wife was Irish and their five children, the oldest aged 10, were born in New York. ¶ 8 Census (1860), N.Y., LVIII, 401.

HENRY, EDWARD LAMSON (1841–1919). N.A. Genre, landscape, and portrait painter. Born January 12, 1841, at Charleston (S.C.), he was taken to NYC as a child and received his earliest instruction in painting there in 1855 with W. M. ODDIE. Three years later he was enrolled as a student in Philadelphia and in 1860 he left for a two-year visit to Europe. Settling in NYC on his return, Henry quickly received recognition for his work in both European and American genre, winning election to the National Academy in 1869. He again went abroad in 1871, after his marriage in 1875, and for the last time in 1881. From the mid-1880's the Henrys wintered in NYC and spent their summers in Ellenville (N.Y.) where the artist died, May 11, 1919. ¶ McCausland, *Edward Lamson Henry,* contains the only full account of Henry's career, along with a checklist of 1,222 of his works and 262 illus. See also: Cowdrey, "American Genre Painter"; Cowdrey, NAD; Rutledge, PA; Phila. BD and CD 1859–60.

HENRY, ERASTUS. Portrait painter at Wallingford (Conn.), 1849. ¶ New England BD 1849.

HENRY, GEORGE. Pennsylvania-born artist, age 18, boarding in Philadelphia in June 1860. ¶ 8 Census (1860), Pa., LIV, 403.

HENRY, JOHN. Engraver; working in Philadelphia in 1793, in Baltimore in 1818, and in Lancaster (Pa.) in 1828. ¶ Stauffer; Fielding.

HENRY, JOHN B. Landscape painter at Philadelphia, 1855. In that year he exhibited an Italian view at the Pennsylvania Academy. ¶ Rutledge, PA.

HENRY, MORRIS. Wood engraver of NYC, 1854–56. ¶ NYBD 1854, 1856.

HENRY, PETER, see PIERRE HENRI.

HENRY, THOMAS. Dioramist. Described as a member of the National Institute at Paris, he exhibited in person at NYC in 1844 his forty dioramic views of Palestine and other places of historical interest. ¶ N. Y. *Herald,* Dec. 14, 1844 (citation courtesy J. E. Arrington).

HENRY, VINCENT. Engraver at New Orleans, 1838. ¶ New Orleans CD 1838.

HENRY, WILLIAM. Portrait painter, a native of Pennsylvania, age 19, living in Philadelphia in 1850, with his father John Henry, tavern keeper. ¶ 7 Census (1850), Pa., LIII, 630.

HENRY, WILLIAM. Portrait painter, a native of Pennsylvania, age 20, living in Philadelphia in June 1860, with a younger sister and brother. ¶ 8 Census (1860), Pa., LX, 664.

HENSEL, DANIEL. Lithographer; born in Pennsylvania *c.* 1831; working in Philadelphia from 1850; member of the firm of HERLINE & HENSEL 1856 and after. ¶ 7 Census (1850), Pa., XLVII, 477; Phila. CD 1856–60+; Peters, *America on Stone.*

HENSELL, G. H. Portrait painter at NYC, 1857. ¶ NYBD 1857.

HENSON, URWILER. Lithographic engraver at Philadelphia, 1855. ¶ Phila. CD 1855.

HENTEN, WILLIAM. Portrait painter from Maryland, 25, at NYC in 1860. His wife also was a Marylander, but their eight-month-old daughter was born in New York. ¶ 8 Census (1860), N.Y., XLVII, 753.

HENTZ, NICHOLAS MARCELLUS (1797–1856). Miniaturist. Born in France, July 25, 1797; emigrated to America shortly after the fall of Napoleon and settled at Wilkes-barre (Pa.) in April 1816. During the next few years he taught at schools in Philadelphia and Boston and at the Round Hill School in Northampton (Mass.). He exhibited a miniature of a "Creole lady" at the Pennsylvania Academy in 1819. From 1824 to 1830 he was professor of modern languages at the University of North Carolina and from 1830 to 1849 he served as head of a number of Southern academies and female seminaries. Also a pioneer in American entomology, Hentz was a recognized authority on spiders. He died at Mariana (Fla.) in 1856. ¶ Weiss and Ziegler, *Thomas Say, Early American Naturalist,* 178–179.

HENTZELMAN, A. German engraver, 23, at NYC in 1860. ¶ 8 Census (1860), N.Y., XLII, 631.

HEPBURN, WILLIAM (1817–1891). Genre painter; born in Edinburgh (Scotland), studied at the Royal Scottish Academy, and emigrated to the United States in 1847. After 1861 he made his home in Brooklyn (N.Y.), where he was active in the Brooklyn Art Club. He exhibited at the National Academy in 1857. He died in Brooklyn, May 12, 1891. ¶ Boston *Transcript,* May 14, 1891; Cowdrey, NAD.

HEPPENHEIMER, FREDERICK. Lithographer; active in NYC from 1851 into the 1860's; in 1859 as a partner in HARTMANN & HEPPENHEIMER. ¶ NYBD 1851–59; Peters, *America on Stone; Portfolio* (Nov. 1945), 54, repro.; *American Collector* (June 1948), 11, repro.

HEPS, FRANCIS or FREDERICK. Portrait painter in NYC, 1859–60. Francis Heps is listed in 1858 as "liquors" and 1859–60 as "portraits." Frederick Heps is listed only in the 1860 business directory. Probably Francis and Frederick were the same man. ¶ NYCD 1858–60; NYBD 1860.

HERBERT, HENRY WILLIAM (1807–1858), better known as "Frank Forester." Pen-and-ink artist, illustrator of his own books on field sports. Born in London, April 7, 1807, Herbert graduated from Cambridge in 1830 and the following year emigrated to the United States. Settling in NYC, he taught Latin and Greek for several years and from 1833 to 1835 was editor of the *American Monthly Magazine.* He began publishing historical romances in 1835 and four years later published his first book on sports, under the pen-name "Frank Forester." Many of these books were illustrated by Herbert himself. In 1845 he built himself a retreat on the Passaic River near Newark (N.J.), where much of his writing was done. He committed suicide in NYC, May 17, 1858. ¶ DAB; Hamilton, 295–297.

HEREDIN, FRANCISCO. Mexican lithographer, age 21, at the Charity Hospital, Orleans Parish (La.) in December 1850. ¶ 7 Census (1850), La., IV (part 1), 711.

HERING, ——. Portrait painter of New Jersey, active 1785–1817. *Cf.* JAMES HERRING. ¶ Lipman and Winchester, 174.

HERIOT, Miss ——. Instructor in drawing, painting on velvet, and other "fine works" at her mother's school in Charleston (S.C.) in 1823. ¶ Rutledge, *Artists in the Life of Charleston.*

HERIOT, GEORGE (1766–1844). Amateur landscape artist. A native of the island of Jersey, Heriot settled in Canada before 1800, serving for a time as clerk in the Ordinance Depot at Quebec, and later as Deputy Postmaster-General and Postmaster-General of British North America. He was the author of *Travels through the Canadas* (1807) and painted many watercolor views both in Canada and in the northeastern United States. Several of his sketchbooks, *c.* 1815, are now in the New-York Historical Society. ¶ *Panorama* (Feb. 1949), nos. 4–5, 7; NYHS *Annual Report,* 1944, 16–17, 35; *Portfolio* (Aug.–Sept. 1950), 22.

HERKOMER, Mrs. L. Portrait painter at Cleveland (Ohio), 1857. She was probably the wife of LORENZ HERKOMER. ¶ Cleveland BD 1857.

HERKOMER, LORENZ (1815–1888). Wood engraver; working in NYC and Cleveland (Ohio) about 1851. He was the father of Hubert Herkomer, also an artist, and probably the husband of Mrs. L. HERKOMER, above. He died in August 1888. ¶ Boston *Transcript,* Aug. 18, 1888, obit.; Thieme-Becker.

HERLIN, AUGUST. Lithographer from Wurttemburg (Germany), age 22, boarding in Philadelphia in August 1860. ¶ 8 Census (1860), Pa., LII, 138.

HERLINE (or Herrlein), EDWARD. Lithographer and engraver of Philadelphia, 1852–60 and after. From 1856 he was associated with HERLINE & HENSEL. This is undoubtedly the Edward Harline, age 24, a German lithographer listed with his wife Amelia, also German, and baby Amel, at Philadelphia in August 1850. ¶ Phila. CD 1852–60+; 7 Census (1850), Pa., XLIX, 176.

HERLINE & HENSEL. Lithographers of Philadelphia, 1856–60 and after. Known as Herline & Co. in 1856, thereafter as Herline & Hensel, the partners being EDWARD HERLINE and DANIEL HENSEL. ¶ Phila. CD 1856–60+; Peters, *America on Stone.*

HERMANDT, PH. Lithographer, age 35, from Darmstadt (Germany), living with his wife and four children in New Orleans, July 1860. *Cf.* PHILIP AMENDT. ¶ 8 Census (1860), La., VIII, 571.

HERR, GEORGE. Lithographer from Hesse-Cassel (Germany), living in Philadelphia in 1860 and after. In 1860 he was a 17-year-old apprentice. ¶ 8 Census (1860), Pa., LXII, 407; Phila. CD 1871.

HERRICK, HENRY W. (1824–?). Wood engraver and painter. He was born August 23, 1824, at Hopkinton (N.H.), and did wood engraving at Concord and Manchester (N.H.) for several years before moving to NYC about 1848. In NYC he executed commissions for book publishers and banknote companies, and studied painting at the National Academy. He returned to New Hampshire in 1865, settling in Manchester, where he was prominent as an artist and historian during the next forty years. He died in Manchester after 1904. ¶ "Art and Artists in Manchester," 115–116; NYBD 1848–56; Brooklyn CD 1855–56; Hamilton, 298–300, 523; *Portfolio* (Nov. 1941), 17, repro. Bolton, *Miniature Painters,* lists Henry W. Herrick as a miniaturist at Nashville (Tenn.) in 1843.

HERRICK, WILLIAM F. Wood engraver who appears first as an engraver at Manchester (N.H.) in 1846–47, and may have been a brother of HENRY W. HERRICK. He moved to NYC about 1848 and shortly after settled in San Francisco. During the 1850's he was connected with the *Alta California,* of which he became city editor in 1855 and later manager. He subsequently entered the insurance business in which he was active as late as 1900. ¶ "Art and Artists in Manchester," 125–126; NYBD 1848; San Francisco CD 1856–60, BD 1858–59.

HERRING, Mrs. An amateur painter of NYC, who exhibited a still life at the Apollo Association in 1839. She may have been the wife of JAMES HERRING. ¶ Cowdrey, AA & AAU.

HERRING, FREDERICK WILLIAM (1821–1899). Portrait painter, son of JAMES HERRING; born in NYC in 1821, studied with his father, and worked in NYC before and after 1860. He died in NYC August 13, 1899. ¶ CAB; Cowdrey, AA & AAU; Cowdrey, NAD; NYBD 1857–59; death date courtesy Mrs. Helen Adams, his granddaughter.

HERRING, JAMES (1794–1867). Portrait painter, publisher, and gallery proprietor. Born January 12, 1794, in London, he accompanied his family to America in 1805 and spent his early years in New Jersey and NYC. After some years as a school teacher, then as a distiller, he took up profile and portrait painting. Having enjoyed considerable success in northern New Jersey, he opened a studio in NYC in 1822. In 1830 he established a circulating library in NYC. He is remembered chiefly as the publisher of *The National Portrait Gallery* (1834–39) and as the founder of the Apollo Gallery (later the American Art-Union) in 1838. He was also prominent in Masonic activities in New Jersey and NYC. Herring spent his last years in Paris and died there October 8, 1867. He was survived by his son, FREDERICK WILLIAM HERRING, also an artist. ¶ DAB; CAB; NYCD 1816–17; NYBD 1844–58; Brooklyn CD 1843; Cowdrey, AA & AAU; Cowdrey, NAD; Swan, BA; Bolton, *Crayon Draftsmen;* Fielding; N. Y. *Tribune,* Oct. 23, 1867.

HERRING, LOUIS or LEWIS. Portrait painter, residing at the same address in Brooklyn (N.Y.) as JAMES HERRING, 1859–65. He exhibited at the National Academy in 1859. After 1868 Lewis Herring is listed in Brooklyn as a restaurant or saloon keeper. ¶ Cowdrey, NAD; Brooklyn CD 1861–70 +.

HERRINGTON, TIMOTHY A. Portrait painter, working in Jefferson County (W. Va.) and Baltimore *c.* 1845–84. ¶ Willis, "Jefferson County Portraits and Portrait Painters"; Lafferty.

HERRIOTT, J. Philadelphia engraver, 1859. ¶ Phila. CD 1859.

HERRLEIN, EDWARD, see EDWARD HERLINE.

HERRLEIN, GUSTAV. German lithographer, age 23, at Cincinnati in September 1850. ¶ 7 Census (1850), Ohio, XXII, 299.

HERRLEIN, JULIUS. Engraver at Philadelphia, 1860. ¶ Phila. CD 1860.

HERRMAN, AUGUSTINE, see AUGUSTYN HEERMANS.

HERRON, D. Student at Union College, Schenectady (N.Y.), who in 1859 drew a view of the college buildings which was engraved by G. W. Lewis [GEORGE W. LEWIS ?]. ¶ *Portfolio* (March 1955), 150.

HERVE, ——. Teacher of painting and lithography, at New Orleans, 1853. ¶ Delgado-WPA cites *Bee,* June 2, 1853.

HERVÉ, H. Miniaturist at Charleston (S.C.) in January 1820. *Cf.* H. Hervé of London, who exhibited miniatures in England from 1813 to 1843. This may also be the Hervé who exhibited miniatures of Mr. and Mrs. Finn at the Boston Athenaeum in 1828. ¶ Rutledge, *Artists in the Life of Charleston;* Graves; Swan, BA.

HERVÉ, WALTER R. Miniaturist. Between 1805 and 1812 he painted a miniature of Midshipman Thomas ap Catesby Jones (1790–1858), who was stationed at Norfolk (Va.) *c.* 1805–08 and at New Orleans *c.* 1808–15. ¶ Tolman, "Attributing Miniatures," 523 (repro.), 526. *Cf.* the Hervé who exhibited miniatures at the Boston Athenaeum in 1828 (Swan, BA).

HERVIEU, AUGUSTE. Water color artist, genre and humorous subjects. An exhibitor at London galleries from 1819 to 1858 and a Member of the Société des Beaux-Arts at Lille (France) from 1825, Hervieu came to America in 1828 as a political refugee to join Frances Wright's colony at Nashoba (Tenn.). The same year he went with Mrs. Frances Trollope to Cincinnati, where he resided with the Trollopes until March 1830. Returning to England with them in 1830, Hervieu supplied the illustrations for Mrs. Trollope's *Domestic Manners of the Americans* (1832). Of his later career nothing is known except that he was working in Vienna in 1837 and continued to exhibit in London until 1858. ¶ Siple, "A Romantic Episode in Cincinnati," four repros.; Trollope, *Domestic Manners of the Americans* (New York: 1832) contains eight plates after Hervieu; Graves, *Dictionary*.

HESS, B. Landscape painter. Possibly a native of Switzerland, Hess exhibited Swiss and New York State views at the American Art-Union in 1851–52 and at the National Academy in 1857. ¶ Cowdrey, AA & AAU; Cowdrey, NAD; *Portfolio* (Nov. 1951), 58, repro.

HESS, GEORGE (1832–?). Sculptor. Born September 28, 1832, at Pfungstadt (Germany), he was brought to America as a child but returned to Munich for study at the age of 25. He subsequently settled in NYC and did both portrait and genre work in stone. ¶ Thieme-Becker; CAB; Bénézit.

HESSELIUS, GUSTAVUS (1682–1755). Portrait, religious, and figure painter. He was born in 1682 at Falun, Dalecarlia (Sweden), received his artistic training in Europe, and emigrated to America in 1711. After a brief residence in Wilmington (Del.), he settled at Philadelphia where he made his home, except for painting trips into Delaware, Maryland, and Virginia, until his death on May 25, 1755. From 1712 to the middle of the century Gustavus Hesselius was the principal portrait painter of Philadelphia and the middle colonies. His son, JOHN HESSELIUS, followed his father's profession, and a granddaughter married the Swedish-American artist, ADOLPH U. WERTMÜLLER. ¶ Richardson, "Gustavus Hesselius"; Pleasants, *250 Years of Painting in Maryland;* Brinton, "Gustavus Hesselius"; Hart, "The Earliest Painter in America"; Hart, "Gustavus Hesselius"; Keyes, "Doubts Regarding Hesselius"; Tolles, "A Contemporary Comment on Gustavus Hesselius"; *Portraits in Delaware 1700–1850;* Barker, *American Painting;* DAB; Thieme-Becker; represented Md. Hist. Soc., Pennsylvania Academy, Detroit Institute of Fine Arts.

HESSELIUS, JOHN (1728–1778). Portrait painter; son of GUSTAVUS HESSELIUS; born in 1728, probably in Philadelphia or in Maryland. His earliest dated portrait was painted in 1750. After working in Maryland, Virginia, Delaware, and Philadelphia for about a decade, he married and settled at Annapolis (Md.). CHARLES WILLSON PEALE received his first instruction in painting from him at Annapolis about 1762. Hesselius died April 9, 1778, and was buried at "Bellefield," near Annapolis. ¶ Bolton and Groce, "John Hesselius"; Burroughs, "An Inscription by John Hesselius"; Sawitzky, "Further Notes on John Hesselius"; Pleasants, *250 Years of Painting in Maryland;* DAB; Barker, *American Painting*, 129; Met. Mus., *Life in America*, repro.; Detroit Inst. of Arts, *Bulletin* 24 (1944), 22–23, repro.

HESSELS, LOUIS. Prussian lithographer, 48, at NYC in 1860. He was there as early as 1852 when his son was born. ¶ 8 Census (1860), N.Y., XLVI, 873.

HESSELTINE, FRANCIS S. (1833–1916). Painter, lawyer, traveller, orator, lecturer, and poet; died March 1916 at Boston. ¶ *Art Annual*, XIII, obit.

HESTON, JACOB. Portrait painter at Philadelphia in 1802. ¶ Brown and Brown.

HETFIELD, MRS. E. H. Portrait painter at Cleveland (Ohio) in 1857. ¶ Cleveland BD 1857.

HETZEL, GEORGE (1826–1899). Landscape, still life, portrait, and figure painter. A native of Alsace, Hetzel arrived in the United States before 1855 when he began exhibiting at the Pennsylvania Academy. From 1855 to 1869 he exhibited as a resident of Pittsburgh (Pa.). ¶ Thieme-Becker; Rutledge, PA; Fleming, *History of Pittsburgh*, III, 626.

HEULAN, J. J. Drawing teacher, Charleston (S.C.). In 1805 he operated a school where he taught writing, arithmetic, French, and drawing; in 1813 he also taught music and tuned pianos. ¶ Rutledge, *Artists in the Life of Charleston*.

HEWET (or Hewett), H. W. Wood engraver working in NYC in the 1840's and 1850's. He did some book illustrations and was himself a publisher. ¶ NYBD 1844; Hamilton, 200, 301.

HEWET & LOOMIS. Wood engravers of NYC, 1859. Illustrations so signed appear in *Popular Fairy Tales for Little Folks*

(N.Y.: 1859). The engravers were probably H. W. HEWET and PASCAL LOOMIS. ¶ Hamilton, 200; NYCD 1859.

HEWETT, I. Delineator of two views of the storming of Fort Oswego, May 6, 1814, which were engraved and published in London in 1815. The artist may have been Lt. John Hewett of the Royal Marines. ¶ Stokes, *Historic Prints,* 56; *List of the Officers of the Army and Royal Marines,* 1815.

HEWINS, AMASA (1795–1855). Portrait, genre, and landscape painter. A resident of Boston, Hewins first exhibited at the Athenaeum in 1830 and occasionally thereafter until 1846. He studied in Italy, France, and Spain during the early 1830's. In 1848 he exhibited in Boston a panorama of the sea and shores of the Mediterranean. He also exhibited at the National Academy and the Apollo Association. ¶ Hewins, *Hewins's Journal;* Swan, BA; Boston BD 1841–47; Louisville (Ky.) *Focus,* April 15, 1831 (citation courtesy Mrs. W. H. Whitley, Paris, Ky.); Boston *Evening Transcript,* June 16 and Sept. 18, 1848 (citation courtesy J. E. Arrington); Cowdrey, NAD; Cowdrey, AA & AAU; *Antiques* (Nov. 1950), 373, repro.

HEWINS, PHILIP (1806–1850). Portrait and religious painter. Born at Blue Hill (Me.) in July 1806, he was brought up in the neighborhood of Boston and went into the dry goods business. While residing in Albany (N.Y.) he took up portrait painting, studying for a year with REUBEN ROULERY. In 1834 he settled in Hartford (Conn.) where he enoyed considerable success until his death on May 14, 1850. ¶ French, *Art and Artists in Connecticut,* 71–72; Sears, *Some American Primitives,* 197, repro.; Hartford CD 1849–50.

HEWINS, Mrs. SARA. Portrait copyist of Hartford (Conn.) in 1851. She was the widow of PHILIP HEWINS. ¶ Hartford CD 1851.

HEWITT, ——. Line engraver. Hewitt's engravings of scenes on the Hudson and Schuylkill Rivers and on Lake Champlain were published in *Port Folio* from 1812 to 1814. Stauffer states that he was working as late as 1820. ¶ *Port Folio,* Nov. 1812, June and Nov. 1813, Nov. 1814; Stauffer; Fielding; Weitenkampf, "Early American Landscape Prints," 40 (repro.), 55.

HEWITT, FREDERICK F. Engraver of NYC during the 1850's. ¶ NYCD and NYBD 1856–60.

HEWITT, WILLIAM KEESEY (1817–1893). Portrait and figure painter, crayon artist. A native of Philadelphia, W. K. Hewitt was apparently working in NYC in 1840, when he made a sketch of the burning of the steamboat *Lexington,* upon which NATHANIEL CURRIER based his first popular lithograph. After 1843 Hewitt lived in Philadelphia and was a frequent exhibitor at the Pennsylvania Academy. ¶ Smith; Stokes, *Icon.,* III, pl. 125; Peters, *Currier and Ives,* I, pls. 21–22; Phila. CD 1843–60+; Rutledge, PA; Cowdrey, AA & AAU; *Antiques* (March 1948), 208, repro.

HEYD, CONRAD (1837–1912). Portrait and miniature painter. A native of Germany; came to America *c.* 1860, worked for a time in NYC, and then moved to the Middle West in 1868. After two years in Milwaukee (Wis.) he moved to Prairie du Chien, but he returned ten years later to Milwaukee and lived there until his death in 1912. He was considered by his contemporaries the foremost artist of Wisconsin. ¶ Butts, *Art in Wisconsin,* 97–98.

HEYDE, CHARLES L. Landscape painter. Heyde, who married a sister of Walt Whitman, exhibited at the National Academy in 1850 as of Hoboken (N.J.), from 1851 to 1854 as of Brooklyn (N.Y.), and from 1857 as a resident of Vermont. He made his home in Burlington (Vt.) until some time in the 1890's, and was well known locally as a poet as well as landscape painter. ¶ Frances Winwar, *American Giant: Walt Whitman and His Times* (N.Y., 1941), 239; Cowdrey, NAD; Brooklyn CD 1854; Swan, BA; Hemenway, *Vermont Historical Gazetteer,* I, 725–727; Rutledge, PA.

HEYLIGER, JOSEPH. Engraver at Charleston (S.C.) in 1792. ¶ Rutledge, *Artists in the Life of Charleston.*

HEYMAN, CHARLES. Artist at New Orleans in 1837. ¶ Delgado-WPA cites New Orleans CD 1837.

HEYWOOD, GEORGE. Exhibitor of a drawing of "Randel's Elevated Railway" and a "view of Broadway" [NYC] at the 1848 Fair of the American Institute. *Cf.* GEORGE HAYWARD. ¶ Am. Inst. Cat., 1848.

HICKCOX, THOMAS N. Engraver and stencil-cutter of NYC, 1855 and after. ¶ NYCD 1855–60+.

HICKEY, Mr. ——. Crayon portraitist who visited Baltimore in May 1788. ¶ Prime, II, 16.

HICKEY, WILLIAM. Stonecutter of NYC,

1849–52; awarded a diploma for statuary at the American Institute in 1849. ¶ NYCD 1850–52; Am. Inst. *Trans.*, 1849.

HICKOK, FRANCIS. Wood engraver; at Madison (Wis.) in 1856, but by 1859 working with ALEXANDER M. GRAFF in NYC. ¶ Madison CD 1856; NYBD 1860; Hamilton, 367.

HICKOK & GRAFF. Wood engravers of NYC, 1859–60. The partners were FRANCIS HICKOK and ALEXANDER M. GRAFF. ¶ NYBD and NYCD 1860; Hamilton, 367.

HICKS, C. Engraver, 32, at NYC in 1860. He and his wife were from Massachusetts, but their children were born in New York during the 1850's. ¶ 8 Census (1860), N.Y., XLII, 736.

HICKS, CHARLES C. Engraver of NYC, active 1840–52. ¶ NYBD 1840–52.

HICKS, EDWARD (1780–1849). Landscape, religious, and historical painter. Probably the best known of the 19th century American "primitive" painters, Edward Hicks was born at Attleboro, now Langhorne, Bucks County (Pa.) on April 4, 1780, and spent most of his life in Newtown, Bucks County. He was a coach, sign, and ornamental painter by trade, but gave much of his time to painting historical and religious scenes, the best known being "The Peaceable Kingdom," of which he is thought to have painted over 100 examples. Hicks was also a prominent Quaker preacher and played an active part in the Separation led by his distant cousin Elias Hicks. Another cousin, THOMAS HICKS, received his first instruction in painting from Edward Hicks, whose portrait he painted in 1837. Edward Hicks continued to paint almost until his death, which occurred August 23, 1849, at Newtown. ¶ The standard life is Alice Ford's *Edward Hicks, Painter of The Peaceable Kingdom* (Phila., 1952); Hicks' own *Memoirs* (Phila., 1851) deal largely with his religious activities. See also: Bye, "Edward Hicks, Painter-Preacher"; Bye, "Edward Hicks"; Held, "Edward Hicks and the Tradition"; Lipman and Winchester, 39–49.

HICKS, GILBERT. Engraver of NYC, active 1854–59. ¶ NYBD 1854–59.

HICKS, HENRY. Engraver, 22, a native of New York, at NYC in 1860. ¶ 8 Census (1860), N.Y., LX, 69.

HICKS, JOHN. So listed in DAB, for THOMAS HICKS.

HICKS, THOMAS (1823–1890). N.A. Portrait and landscape painter. Thomas, first cousin of EDWARD HICKS, was born October 18, 1823, at Newtown, Bucks County (Pa.). As early as 1836 he received his first instruction in painting from his cousin, whose portrait he painted the following year. After further study at the Pennsylvania Academy and the National Academy, he went abroad in 1845. Continuing his studies in London, Florence, and Rome, he completed his training in the studio of Thomas Couture at Paris and returned to NYC in 1849. During a successful career, Hicks painted many famous Americans including Lincoln. He died at Trenton Falls (N.Y.), October 8, 1890. ¶ DAB (erroneously listed as John Hicks); George A. Hicks, "Thomas Hicks"; Rutledge, PA; Cowdrey, NAD; Cowdrey, AA & AAU; Swan, BA; Rutledge, MHS; CAB; Tuckerman; Fairman, *Art and Artists of the Capitol;* represented NYHS.

HIDDEN, HENRY A. Engraver of Providence (R.I.), active 1847–60 and after. ¶ Providence CD 1847–60; New England BD 1849.

HIDDEN, JAMES E. Engraver of Providence (R.I.), active 1850 and after. ¶ Providence CD 1850–59.

HIDLEY, JOSEPH H. (1830–1872). Townscape and religious painter. Born March 22, 1830; spent his life in and about Poestenkill and Troy (N.Y.); died at Poestenkill September 28, 1872. He is best known for his views of Poestenkill and other New York villages, though he also did some religious paintings, wood carving, wool floral shadow-box pictures, and taxidermy. ¶ MacFarlane, "Hedley, Headley or Hidley, Painter," two repros.; Lipman, "Joseph H. Hidley," in Lipman and Winchester, 132–138, five repros.; Lipman, "Joseph H. Hidley (1830–1872): His New York Townscapes," six repros.; Lipman, "American Townscapes," two repros.

HIERONIMUS, LEONARD. Of HIERONIMUS & REINHOLD, lithographers of NYC, 1859–60. ¶ NYCD 1859–60.

HIERONIMUS & REINHOLD. Lithographers of NYC, 1859–60. The firm was composed of LEONARD HIERONIMUS and RUDOLPH REINHOLD. ¶ NYCD 1859–60; NYBD 1859.

HIGGINBOTTOM, WILLIAM. Artist at NYC, 1816. The following year his widow was listed. ¶ NYCD 1816–17.

HIGGINS, FRANK. Engraver, 23, a native of

Vermont, at NYC in 1860. ¶ 8 Census (1860), N.Y., XLVII, 654.

HIGGINS, GEORGE F. Artist of Boston; exhibited at the Athenaeum 1859–62; still in Boston in 1873 and active, according to Swan, until 1884. ¶ Swan, BA; Boston CD 1873.

HIGH, B. F. Decorative and banner painter, Charleston (S.C.), 1860. ¶ Rutledge, *Artists in the Life of Charleston.*

HIGH, GEORGE. Artist, age 17, native of Maryland, living in Baltimore with his mother in 1860. In 1864 he was listed as a soldier. ¶ 8 Census (1860), Md., VII, 201; Baltimore CD 1864.

HIGHET, WILLIAM W. Wood engraver at NYC, 1850. ¶ NYBD 1850.

HIGHWOOD, CHARLES. Portrait and landscape painter. Highwood's early years were spent in Munich (Germany) where he was for 12 years associated with the Royal Academy of Fine Arts. He came to America in 1848, settling in NYC. He toured the country in 1853 in company with a group of artists. From 1863 he made his home in Chicago where he was still working in 1885. During the 1870's he made several European trips. Originally a portrait painter, Highwood turned to landscape and figure pieces after he settled in Chicago. ¶ Andreas, *History of Chicago,* II, 560 (citation courtesy H. Maxson Holloway); Fielding; Mallett.

HILDRETH, Mrs. RICHARD, see CAROLINE NEGUS.

HILL, A. Illustrator. His work appears in two books published in NYC in 1857. ¶ Hamilton, 303.

HILL, A. Lithographer, age 23, from England, living in a Cincinnati hotel in September 1850. ¶ 7 Census (1850), Ohio, XX, 343.

HILL, Mrs. AMELIA ROBERTSON, see AMELIA R. PATON.

HILL, Mrs. ANNE. Author of *Drawing Book of Flowers & Fruit* (Phila., 1845), with six color plates. ¶ Library of the U. S. Patent Office, listed in LC Union Catalogue.

HILL, Miss C. Flower painter exhibiting at the National Academy in 1829. She was probably a daughter of JOHN HILL, the engraver, at whose address she was listed in the catalogue. ¶ Cowdrey, NAD; NYCD 1829.

HILL, FRANCIS. Engraver. He was born in England *c.* 1842, but came to America with his family before 1860. In the latter year he was an apprentice engraver in Boston, as was his older brother JOHN R. HILL. By 1865 they were in business together and both were working in Boston after 1870. ¶ 8 Census (1860), Mass., XXIX, 241; Boston CD 1865, 1870.

HILL, FRANCIS C. Drawing teacher, portrait and landscape painter, active in Charleston (S.C.) 1808–43. ¶ Rutledge, *Artists in the Life of Charleston.*

HILL, GEORGE W. (1815–1893). Engraver, born in Massachusetts; working in NYC in 1850 and in Boston from 1856. In 1858 he was with SMITH & HILL. He died at Jamaica Plain (Mass.) on June 12, 1893, at the age of 78. ¶ Boston *Transcript,* June 13, 1893; 7 Census (1850), N.Y., XLIII, 275; Boston CD 1856–58.

HILL, I., see JOHN HILL.

HILL, I. W., see JOHN WILLIAM HILL.

HILL, J. Fruit and flower painter at Philadelphia in 1854; exhibitor at the Pennsylvania Academy. ¶ Rutledge, PA.

HILL, JAMES. Engraver of some Bible illustrations published at Charlestown (Mass.) in 1803, as well as of a large plate of the "Resurrection of a Pious Family" after the painting by the English clergyman, William Peters, possibly before 1800. ¶ Stauffer.

HILL, Dr. JAMES S. Portrait, landscape, and genre painter. A Philadelphia physician, Hill exhibited at the Pennsylvania Academy in 1849 and from 1860 to 1869. ¶ Rutledge, PA.

HILL, J. H. Listed under "Engravers and Sculptors" in Burlington (Vt.) in 1849. ¶ New England BD 1849.

HILL, JOHN (1770–1850). Landscape engraver and aquatintist. A native of London, Hill was well established as an engraver there before his emigration to America in 1816. He settled first in Philadelphia and sent for his family in 1819. His first major commission was the engraving of plates for JOSHUA SHAW'S *Picturesque Views of American Scenery* (Phila., 1820–1821). In 1822 he moved to NYC and he continued to work in aquatint there until 1836 when he moved to a farm near West Nyack (N.Y.), to live there in retirement until his death at 80 in 1850. The most important work of his NYC period was a series of aquatint engravings for WILLIAM GUY WALL'S *Hudson River Portfolio* (N.Y., 1820–25). John Hill was the father of the landscape painter JOHN WILLIAM HILL and grandfather of the landscape painter and etcher JOHN HENRY HILL. ¶ Weitenkampf, "John

Hill and American Landscapes in Aquatint"; Stauffer; Drepperd, "Rare American Prints," four repros. from F. Lucas, *Progressive Drawing Book* (Baltimore, 1827), illustrated by Hill; Stokes, *Icon.*, III, 567; Stokes, *Historic Prints;* Flexner, *The Light of Distant Skies.* Hill's day book and account book are owned by NYHS.

HILL, JOHN HENRY (1839–1922). Landscape painter, aquatintist, and etcher. John Henry Hill, son of JOHN WILLIAM HILL and grandson of JOHN HILL, was born in 1839 at West Nyack (N.Y.) and began exhibiting in NYC and Philadelphia in the late 1850's. In 1888 he prepared *An Artist's Memorial* to honor his father, illustrating it with his own etchings after his father's paintings. ¶ Stauffer; Cowdrey, NAD; Rutledge, PA; Fielding; Stokes, *Icon.*, III, 567; Weitenkampf, "John Hill and American Landscapes in Aquatint"; Thieme-Becker; *Panorama* (Aug.–Sept. 1948), 9, repro.

HILL, JOHN R. Engraver. Born in England *c.* 1840, John R. Hill was an apprentice engraver in Boston in June 1860 and later worked there in association with his brother FRANCIS HILL. ¶ 8 Census (1860), Mass., XXIX, 241; Boston CD 1862–70.

HILL, JOHN WILLIAM (1812–1879). A.N.A. Landscape and topographical painter. The son of the aquatint engraver JOHN HILL, J. W. Hill was born in London, January 13, 1812, and was brought to America in 1819. The family moved from Philadelphia to NYC in 1822 and there the younger Hill served his apprenticeship under his father. After 1836 both made their homes near West Nyack (N.Y.). During the early part of his career J. W. Hill was a topographical artist, employed by the New York State Geological Survey and later by Smith Bros. of NYC, for whom he drew views of many American cities for lithographs published by them. He later came under the influence of Ruskin's *Modern Painters* and turned exclusively to the new "naturalism" or "Pre-Raphaelitism," of which he was considered the leading spirit in America. His later work was chiefly pure landscape, as well as some flower and bird studies in watercolors. He died at his home near West Nyack on September 24, 1879. In 1888 his work was honored in *An Artist's Memorial,* written by his son, JOHN HENRY HILL, and illustrated by the son's etchings after his father's landscapes. ¶ J. H. Hill, *An Artist's Memorial;* Stauffer; *American Art Review,* I (1880), 46, obit.; Peters, *America on Stone;* Cowdrey, NAD; Cowdrey, AA & AAU; Swan, BA; Rutledge, PA; Stokes, *Icon.,* reproduces 7 plates; Stokes, *Historic Prints,* reproduces 8 plates and lists 22; represented in the Ayer Collection, Field Museum, Chicago, by 94 watercolors of birds.

HILL, PAMELIA E. (1803–1860). Miniaturist. Born May 9, 1803, at Framingham (Mass.), Miss Hill exhibited at the Boston Athenaeum between 1828 and 1847 and seems to have worked mainly in Boston between 1828 and 1856. She died at Framingham in 1860. ¶ Swan, BA; Boston BD 1841; Bolton, *Miniature Painters.*

HILL, SAMUEL. Engraver and copperplate printer of Boston, active 1789–1803. He did work for magazines and book publishers and had as a pupil his young relative, SAMUEL HARRIS. ¶ Boston CD 1789–1803; Stauffer; Fielding; *Antiques* (Sept. 1924), 138, and (July 1945), 32, repros.; *Portfolio* (Nov. 1941), 9 and 12, repros.

HILL & SHAW. Illustrators and publishers of *Picturesque Views of American Scenery* (Phila., 1820–21). JOSHUA SHAW was the artist and JOHN HILL the engraver in aquatint of these early landscape prints. ¶ Brown and Brown; Stauffer.

HILL, STEPHEN G. Amateur artist, whose view of Monterey (Cal.) in 1846 was lithographed by SILVER & ROWSE of Cincinnati. Hill was a resident of Cincinnati, age 27, at the time of his enlistment in the Ohio Infantry as a musician in June 1846. He was discharged at Monterey the following October. He was listed as a grocer in the Cincinnati directory. ¶ Cincinnati CD 1846; print in the Map Division of LC; information from Office of the Adjutant General, Department of the Army.

HILL, THOMAS (1829–1908). Landscape, portrait, and still life painter; born September 11, 1829, in Birmingham (England); brought to America by his parents about 1841. He grew up in Taunton (Mass.) and began his career as a decorative painter in Boston in 1844. Later moving to Philadelphia, he took up portrait and flower painting, exhibiting with success both in Philadelphia and Baltimore during the 1850's. In 1861 he moved to California and began painting the grandiose landscapes for which he became noted. After a year's study in Paris (1866), he settled in Boston but during the 1870's he returned to California where he resided until his death by suicide, June 30, 1908, at Raymond. His best known work was "The Last Spike," picturing the completion of the Union-Pacific Railroad. ¶ WPA (Calif.), *Introduction to California Art Research,* II; WPA Guide, *California;* DAB; Clement and Hutton; Rutledge, PA; Phila. CD 1855; Rutledge, MHS; Swan, BA; WPA Guide, *N.H.;* Born, *American Landscape Painting,* fig. 46, 71; N. Y. *Evening Post,* July 2, 1908, obit.

HILL, W. Delineator of a view of Cleveland (Ohio) in 1853, engraved by B. F. SMITH and published in NYC by Smith Bros. This may be JOHN WILLIAM HILL, who did other work for the Smiths. ¶ *Antiques* (Jan. 1946), 60, repro.

HILLEN, EDWARD or J. T. E. Artist from Brussels (Belgium), born *c.* 1818, residing in Philadelphia in 1850–51. ¶ 7 Census (1850), Pa., LIII, 284 (as Edward); Phila. CD 1851 (as J. T. E.).

HILLER, Mrs. ——. Exhibited as an American miniaturist at the Pennsylvania Academy in 1825. ¶ Pa. Cat., 1825.

HILLER, JOSEPH, SR. (1748–1814). Portrait engraver and silversmith. He was born March 24, 1748, in Boston and worked in Salem as a silversmith before and after the Revolution. He removed to Lancaster (Mass.) in 1803 and died there February 9, 1814. He is known to have engraved a portrait of John Hancock. JOSEPH HILLER, JR., his son, also was an engraver. ¶ Belknap, *Artists and Craftsmen,* 3, 101; Stauffer; Fielding.

HILLER, JOSEPH, JR. (1777–1795). Engraver. Born June 21, 1777, at Salem (Mass.) where his father, JOSEPH HILLER, SR., was a silversmith. At 17 he engraved a copy of JOSEPH WRIGHT's etching of Washington. On August 22nd, 1795, he was drowned off the Cape of Good Hope. ¶ Belknap, *Artists and Craftsmen,* 3; Stauffer; Fielding.

HILLIARD, HENRY, see HENRY HILLYARD.

HILLIARD, WILLIAM HENRY (1836–1905). Landscape and portrait painter. Born in Auburn (N.Y.), he studied in NYC and painted in the West before going to Britain and France for further study. On his return he had a studio in NYC, then settled permanently in Boston. He was best known for his New England landscapes and marines. He died in April 1905 at Washington (D.C.). ¶ *Art Annual,* V; CAB; Clement and Hutton; Champlin and Perkins; Thieme-Becker; Graves, *Dictionary.*

HILLMAN, RICHARD S. Painter of a horse-racing scene, "Lady Suffolk Trotting in Her 19th Year," 1851. Hillman was a house, sign, and decorative painter of Springfield (Ill.). ¶ *American Collector* (March 1937), 1, repro.; Springfield CD 1855.

HILLS, JAMES H. Engraver, born in Connecticut *c.* 1814; working in Burlington (Vt.) *c.* 1845–50. Stauffer says that he abandoned engraving for lack of business. ¶ 7 Census (1850), Vt., IV, 539; Stauffer.

HILLYARD, HENRY. Panoramist. Hillyard (or Hilliard) was born in England *c.* 1806 and emigrated to America probably *c.* 1840. He lived in NYC and Brooklyn from 1842 to 1863, except for a brief residence in Boston in 1850–51. He exhibited at the National Academy in 1845. ¶ 7 Census (1850), Mass., XXVI, 721; NYCD 1842–45, 1862–63; Brooklyn CD 1846–60; Phila. *Public Ledger,* Aug. 30, 1851, and N. Y. *Herald,* April 11, 1859 (citations courtesy J. E. Arrington).

HILLYARD, J. Painter of dioramas for the HANINGTONS of NYC in 1840. *Cf.* HENRY HILLYARD. ¶ Boston *Evening Transcript,* July 13, 1840 (citation courtesy J. E. Arrington).

HILLYER, HENRY L. Landscape painter of Jersey City (N.J.), active 1859–65. He exhibited at the National Academy in 1859. After 1865 he went into business with his father and brother as a commission merchant in NYC. ¶ Cowdrey, NAD; Jersey City CD 1861–67.

HILLYER, WILLIAM, JR. Portrait and miniature painter, active in NYC 1832–64. He exhibited at the American Academy in 1833, the National Academy in 1835–36, and the American Institute in 1849. After 1845 he was associated with WILLIAM H. MILLER in the portrait firm of MILLER & HILLYER. The firm exhibited 17 portraits at the American Institute Fair of 1846 and was awarded a diploma for the second-best portrait in oil. After 1862 the firm turned to photography. Hillyer's home was at Morrisania. ¶ NYCD 1832–64; NYBD 1846–60; Cowdrey, AA & AAU; Cowdrey, NAD; Am. Inst. Cat., 1846, 1849; Am. Inst. *Trans.,* 1846; Bolton, *Miniature Painters;* Dunlap, *History,* II, 472.

HINCHEY, WILLIAM J. (1829–1893). Painter of an oil entitled "The Dedication of the

Eads Bridge at St. Louis, Mo., July 4, 1874." ¶ *American Professional,* 249.

HINCKLE, CHARLES. Pennsylvania engraver, age 22, living with his father, the Rev. Adam Hinckle, in Philadelphia, June 1860. ¶ 8 Census (1860), Pa., LVI, 861.

HINCKLEY, ——. Portrait and miniature painter, with WILLIAM D. PARISEN, at Charleston (S.C.) in November 1819. ¶ Rutledge, *Artists in the Life of Charleston.*

HINCKLEY, ——. Sculptor whose "first effort," entitled "Reclining Boy," was shown in Cleveland (Ohio) in September 1851. ¶ WPA (Ohio), *Annals of Cleveland.*

HINCKLEY, CORNELIUS T. Wood engraver. Born in Massachusetts *c.* 1820; worked in Philadelphia from 1845 to 1857. He executed 15 plates for *The Theory of Effect, Embracing the Contrast of Light and Shade, of Colour and Harmony* (Phila., 1851). ¶ 7 Census (1850), Pa., L, 567; Phila. CD 1845, 1850–57; Hamilton, 305.

HINCKLEY, F. H., is THOMAS HEWES HINCKLEY.

HINCKLEY, ROBERT (1853–1941). Portrait painter. Although Hinckley's dates place him outside the scope of this work, he is listed here in order to correct an error of Fielding and *1440 Early American Portrait Painters,* in which his birth date is given as 1835.

HINCKLEY, THOMAS HEWES (1813–1896). Animal and landscape painter. Born November 4, 1813, at Milton (Mass.); apprenticed in 1829 to a merchant of Philadelphia. While in Philadelphia he attended drawing classes conducted by one Mason, probably WILLIAM MASON. Returning to Milton, in 1833 he turned professional painter, finding employment first as a sign and fancy painter, then as a portraitist, and finally as a painter of domestic and game animals. He maintained a studio at Milton throughout his career, but made a visit to Europe in 1851 and to California in 1870. He died at Milton, February 15, 1896. During his later years he also painted many landscapes. ¶ CAB; Karolik Cat., 354–356, repro.; Clement and Hutton; Champlin and Perkins; Cowdrey, NAD; Cowdrey, AA & AAU; Swan, BA; *Connoisseur* (1907), 216, repro.; *Antiques* (May 1941), 231, repro.

HINCKMAN, ——. Pastel artist, whose 1793 portrait of Captain Daniel Prior, Postmaster of Amherst (Mass.), is owned by the New Hampshire Historical Society. ¶ Information courtesy the late William Sawitzky.

HINDS, PAUL. Miniaturist at Rochester (N.Y.) in 1820. ¶ Ulp, "Art and Artists in Rochester," 30.

HINE, CHARLES (1827–1871). Portrait and figure painter. A native of Bethany (Conn.), he grew up in New Haven and at 15 began the study of art under GEORGE W. FLAGG. After further study in Hartford under JARED B. FLAGG and two years of painting in Derby (Conn.), Hine returned to New Haven in 1846 and remained there for the next decade. In 1857 he moved to NYC. His nude figure entitled "Sleep" was considered his best work. He died on July 29, 1871, at New Haven. ¶ French, *Art and Artists in Conn.,* 135–136; NYCD 1862; 8 Census (1860), N.Y., LIII, 130.

HINE, SAMUEL P. Landscape painter. A resident of Boston, who exhibited at the Athenaeum in 1832 and almost twenty years later exhibited in the city a serial tableau of a journey over the Alps from Paris to Rome. In 1851 he was described as a "Boston boy," resident of the city for "the last 20 years." ¶ Swan, BA; Boston *Evening Transcript,* May 16, July 1, July 12, July 18, 1851 (citations courtesy J. E. Arrington).

HINGHAM, ——. Exhibitor of a view of the Albany City Hall at the National Academy, 1832. This was probably Robert Higham [sic], architect, who was at Albany in 1831–32 and at NYC in 1833. ¶ Cowdrey, NAD; Albany CD 1831–32; NYCD 1833.

HINKEL, DAVID. Engraver from Pennsylvania, age 24, at Washington (D.C.) in June 1860. ¶ 8 Census (1860), D.C., II, 421.

HINKLEY, ——. Portrait and miniature painter who had a studio on Nantucket Island (Mass.) in 1822. ¶ Information courtesy Helen McKearin who cites *Nantucket Inquirer,* Feb. 7, 1822.

HINKLEY, JAMES. Draughtsman, whose drawing of a steam locomotive built by Hinkley & Drury of Boston was lithographed by THAYER & Co. and published *c.* 1840. Hinkley & Drury later became the Boston Locomotive Works, of which Holmes Hinkley was president and James Hinkley a draughtsman. ¶ Peters, *America on Stone,* pl. 146; Boston CD 1848 and after; *Portfolio* (Jan. 1955), 109.

HINMAN, DAVID C. Stipple engraver, who worked in New Haven (Conn.) in the 1830's and 1840's both under his own name and as a member of the firm of DAGGETT, HINMAN & Co. ¶ Stauffer; Rice, "Life of Nathaniel Jocelyn"; Fielding.

HINSDALE, RICHARD LAW (1826–1856). Portrait, landscape, and genre painter, wood engraver. Born May 8, 1826, at Hartford (Conn.), Hinsdale received brief instruction in art from ALEXANDER H. EMMONS, PHILIP HEWINS, and JARED B. FLAGG. About 1848 he went to NYC where he exhibited at the American Art-Union and took up wood engraving. He apparently worked in Worcester (Mass.) in 1850, returned to Hartford the same year and resumed his easel work. He was at NYC again in 1853–54, exhibiting at this time at the National Academy. He died in Hartford in 1856. ¶ Hamilton, 307; French, *Art and Artists in Connecticut,* 125–126; Cowdrey, AA & AAU; Cowdrey, NAD; Fielding; New England BD 1856.

HINSHELWOOD (or Hinschelwood), ROBERT (1812–after 1875). Engraver and etcher, landscape painter. A native of Edinburgh (Scotland), Hinshelwood studied drawing and engraving there and emigrated to America *c.* 1835. He settled in NYC, working for Harpers and other publishers and later for the Continental Bank Note Co. He married a sister of JAMES SMILLIE. Best known for his landscape engravings. ¶ Stauffer; NYCD 1837–75; Cowdrey, NAD; examples of his engravings in *Art Journal* (1876), 332; Schoolcraft, *Information Respecting the . . . Indian Tribes of the United States; Ladies Garland* (1849), 37; Thieme-Becker.

HINTON, Mrs. HOWARD (1834–1921). Sculptor; studied under LAUNT THOMPSON. She died in NYC, December 19, 1921. ¶ *Art Annual,* XIX; Mallett.

HIPPENHEIMER, see HEPPENHEIMER.

HIRSH, SIEGFRIED. Miniature and portrait painter, who worked in NYC as a miniature painter from 1851 to 1855, then went to Charleston (S.C.). By 1857 he had reappeared in NYC as a portrait painter and he was still there in 1860. ¶ NYBD 1851–60; Rutledge, *Artists in the Life of Charleston.*

HIRT, L. Map lithographer at New Orleans in 1841. ¶ Delgado-WPA cites *Bee,* July 28, 1841.

HISCOX, GARDNER DEXTER. Engraver, NYC, 1850. ¶ NYCD 1850.

HISLOP, THOMAS. Engraver of Troy (N.Y.), 1857–58. ¶ Troy BD 1857–58.

HITCHCOCK, CHARLES. Portrait painter, who was in NYC in 1845 and 1851, and in Brooklyn (N.Y.) in 1852. Exhibited at National Academy. ¶ Cowdrey, NAD; NYBD 1851.

HITCHCOCK, DEWITT C. Illustrator and wood engraver, landscape painter, active 1845–79. He worked in Boston 1847–50, in Cincinnati 1850–51, again in Boston 1852, and in NYC 1858 and after. He did work for Harpers and for the *Illustrated American News.* ¶ Hamilton, 308–310; Boston BD 1848–50, CD 1847, 1852; Cincinnati BD 1850, CD 1851; NYCD 1858–60.

HITCHCOCK, EDWARD. Miniaturist of NYC, 1799–1801. ¶ NYCD 1799–1801.

HITCHCOCK & MARSH. Designers and wood engravers at Boston in 1848. The partners were DEWITT C. HITCHCOCK and HENRY MARSH. ¶ Boston CD 1848.

HITCHCOCK, ORRA WHITE (Mrs. Edward Hitchcock) (1796–?). Landscape painter, illustrator; born in 1796, teaching at Deerfield (Mass.) in 1817, and in 1821 married Edward Hitchcock, President of Amherst College. Her work was reproduced as early as 1818 in *Port Folio,* and later as illustrations for her husband's scientific works, especially his *Report on the Geology of Massachusetts* (1833). She was living in 1851. ¶ Margaret R. Hitchcock, "And There Were Women, Too," 191–194, three repros.

HITCHCOCK, REUBEN. Portrait painter at Ravenna (Ohio) about 1828; teacher of JAMES HENRY BEARD. ¶ Smith, "James Henry Beard," 27.

HITCHCOCK, SAMUEL J. Artist working at New Haven (Conn.) in 1843. ¶ Rice, "Life of Nathaniel Jocelyn."

HITCHCOCK, WILLIAM E. Lithographer. Born *c.* 1823–25; worked in Philadelphia from 1850 into the 1860's and is said to have committed suicide *c.* 1880. He executed drawings of birds for the great naturalist Agassiz, and was for some time employed by THOMAS SINCLAIR, whose son married Hitchcock's daughter. ¶ Peters, *America on Stone;* 7 Census (1850), Pa., LI, 74 (as William Hitchcock, 25, native of Mass.); 8 Census (1860), Pa., LV, 971 (as William E. Hitchcock, 38, native of Pa.); Phila. CD 1854–61; *Antiques* (Feb. 1927), 111, repro.; Perry, *Expedition to Japan,* plates.

HITCHING, WILLIAM R. Portrait and miniature painter at Baltimore in 1832 and

1842. ¶ Lafferty cites *Federal Gazette,* May 22, 1832; Mayo cites Baltimore CD 1842.

HITCHINGS, HENRY (?–1902). Watercolor landscapist who exhibited at the American Art-Union in 1849, at the Boston Athenaeum in 1856–57, and at the National Academy in 1868/69. He died in 1902. ¶ Swan, BA; Cowdrey, AA & AAU; Cowdrey, NAD.

HITE, GEORGE HARRISON (?–*c.* 1880). Portrait and miniature painter. A native of Urbana (Ohio); working in Charleston (S.C.) as early as November 1835, when he was described as a "native and self-taught artist of Kentucky." He also visited New Orleans (1844), Cincinnati, and some parts of the South, though he was a resident of NYC much of the time between 1838 and 1863. ¶ Clark, *Ohio Art and Artists,* 466; Rutledge, *Artists in the Life of Charleston;* Delgado-WPA cites New Orleans *Picayune,* Nov. 30, 1844; Cowdrey, AA & AAU; Cowdrey, NAD; NYBD 1840–60; NYCD 1847–52, 1863; Bolton, *Miniature Painters;* Fielding; *Antiques* (March 1932), 152.

HOAGLAND, W., see WILLIAM HOOGLAND.

HOBART, ELIJAH. Engraver and lithographer. An Englishman who came to America as early as 1843. He was working in Boston with JOSEPH ANDREWS in the mid–1840's, exhibited a pencil drawing at the American Institute (NYC) in 1846, and worked in Albany (N.Y.) during the 1850's. ¶ Boston CD 1843, 1845, BD 1844, 1846–47; Am. Inst. Cat., 1846; Albany CD 1852–60; Stauffer; Thieme-Becker; Fielding.

HOBBS, G. W. Portrait painter and Methodist minister at Baltimore in 1784. ¶ Porter, *Modern Negro Art,* 28.

HOBBS, NATHAN. Listed as a silversmith at Boston from 1818 to 1846, and as an engraver from 1846 to 1860 and after. ¶ Boston CD 1818–48; Boston BD 1846–60+.

HOCHSTEIN, ANTHONY. Miniature painter of NYC, 1859; exhibited, National Academy, 1868–72. *Cf.* ANTON HOHENSTEIN. ¶ NYBD 1859; Cowdrey, NAD.

HODDOCK, see HADDOCK.

HODGES, BENJAMIN K. Portrait and screen painter, born in Pennsylvania *c.* 1814. He was painting portraits at Philadelphia in 1835, and at Baltimore in 1837 and 1841. In 1842 he was listed at Baltimore only as of the firm of B. O. Hodges & Co., "bedding mart." In 1849 and 1850 he was listed as an artist. In the 1850 Census he was recorded as a "screen painter." ¶ 7 Census (1850), Md., V, 161; Rutledge, PA; Baltimore CD 1837–42; Lafferty.

HODGDON, SYLVESTER PHELPS (1830–1906). Painting portraits at Salem (Mass.) in 1855, at Boston in 1856; exhibited at the Boston Athenaeum from 1858 to 1873 and at the National Academy 1864–68. ¶ Swan, BA; Belknap, *Artists and Craftsmen of Essex County,* 10; Boston CD and BD 1856 (as J. P. Hodgdon); Cowdrey, NAD.

HODGSON, CHRISTMAN WILLIAM (1830–1914). Painter who died February 12, 1914, at Grand Rapids (Mich.). ¶ *Art Annual,* XI, obit.

HODING, THOMAS. Landscape painter of Philadelphia, 1819–25. He exhibited at the Pennsylvania Academy in 1823. ¶ Phila. CD 1819–1825; Rutledge, PA.

HOEFER, U. W. C. Portrait painter, Philadelphia, 1858. ¶ Phila. BD 1858.

HOEFFLER, ADOLF (1825–1898). Landscape and portrait painter; a native of Frankfurt-am-Main (Germany) who came to America, via New Orleans, in December 1848 and returned in 1853 to Germany. While in the United States he travelled widely, painting and sketching in the Mississippi Valley in 1849; along the Ohio Valley and the eastern seaboard in 1850; from NYC through the South to Cuba in 1851; and along the upper Mississippi Valley, especially Minnesota, in 1852. ¶ McDermott, "Minnesota 100 Years Ago"; Cowdrey, AA & AAU.

HOEH, GEORGE. Engraver and die sinker, NYC, 1854–55. ¶ NYCD 1854–55.

HOEN, AUGUST. Lithographer; born in Germany about 1825; came to America as a young man, settling in Baltimore, where his uncle, EDWARD WEBER, had established a lithographic establishment in 1835. About 1848 Hoen took over the business, a few years later enlisting the aid of his brothers, ERNEST and HENRY HOEN. A. Hoen & Co., Inc., was still active in 1943, with plants in Baltimore and Richmond. ¶ Peters, *America on Stone; Antiques* (Sept. 1943), 131–132; 7 Census (1850), Md., V, 418; Baltimore CD 1855–60+. See MARTIN HARTMAN.

HOEN, ERNEST. Lithographer, brother of AUGUST HOEN; working at Baltimore, 1858 and after. ¶ Baltimore CD 1858+; Peters, *America on Stone.*

HOEN, HENRY. Lithographer, brother of

August Hoen; working at Baltimore, 1858 and after. ¶ Baltimore CD 1858+.

Hoff, Henry. Lithographer, working in NYC 1850–53. He was the publisher of *Views of New York* (N.Y., 1850), a series of 20 lithographic views by C. Autenrieth, John Bornet, Augustus Fay, and K. G. [probably Karl Gildemeister]. ¶ Comstock, "The Hoff Views of New York," *Antiques* (April 1947), 250–252, illus.; Peters, *America on Stone; Portfolio* (March 1944), 156–157, repros.; NYBD 1851–52.

Hoffay, A. A. Lithographic artist working in NYC during the 1830's. He also did some work for Pendletons of Boston. Peters states that he is not to be confused with Alfred Hoffy. ¶ Peters, *America on Stone;* information courtesy John Carey, Columbus, Ohio.

Hoffman, Abram J. Lithographer and engraver of Albany (N.Y.), 1854 and after. He headed the following firms: Hoffman & Co. (1854); Hoffman & Knickerbocker (1855); Hoffman, Knickerbocker & Co. (1856–57); A. J. Hoffman & Co. (1858–60). ¶ Albany CD 1854–60.

Hoffman, Adolphus, see Gustavus Adolphus Hoffman.

Hoffman & Co., see Abram J. Hoffman.

Hoffman, Charles. Engraver of Philadelphia, 1855–58. ¶ Phila. CD and BD 1855–58.

Hoffman, C. W. Watercolor artist, known only by a painting showing a group of St. Louis firemen in 1859. *Cf.* George W. Hoffman. ¶ *Antiques* (July 1945), 30, repro.; *cf.* Lipman and Winchester, 174.

Hoffman, Charles Frederick. Portrait painter of NYC, 1848–51. ¶ NYBD 1848, 1851.

Hoffman, David. Portrait painter at St. Louis, 1859–65. ¶ St. Louis BD 1859, CD 1865.

Hoffman, Frederick. Engraver of NYC, 1859. ¶ NYBD 1859.

Hoffman, George W. Portrait painter of NYC, 1842–87; born about 1823 in New York State. He exhibited at the American Institute between 1842 and 1851 and at the National Academy in 1843 and 1849. He may also have been the Hoffman who painted several elaborate panels for the Niagara Engine Co. No. 4 in 1853. *Cf.* C. W. Hoffman. ¶ Information courtesy Donald A. Shelley; Am. Inst. Cat., 1842, 1844, 1845, 1850, 1851; Cowdrey, NAD; J. I. Smith, "Painted Fire Engine Panels," *Antiques* (Nov. 1937), 246; 7 Census (1850), N.Y., LV, 136; 8 Census (1860), N.Y., LV, 653.

Hoffman, Gustavus Adolphus. Wood engraver; born in Philadelphia *c.* 1832, the son of Frederick Hoffman, silversmith. From 1853 to 1860 and after he was connected with the wood engraving firm of Louderbach & Hoffman. He was listed variously as Geo. A., G. A., Gus., and Adolphus Hoffman. ¶ 7 Census (1850), Pa., LI, 849; 8 Census (1860), Pa., LVII, 78; Phila. CD 1852–60+.

Hoffman, Jacob. Landscape artist who drew views of scenes around Philadelphia and in New Jersey between 1792 and 1796, several of which appeared as magazine illustrations at the time. ¶ Weitenkampf, "Early American Landscape Prints," 49–50; *Portfolio* (June–July 1946), 232, repro.

Hoffman & Knickerbocker. Wood engravers and lithographers at Albany (N.Y.). The firm was listed as Hoffman & Knickerbocker in 1855 and as Hoffman, Knickerbocker & Co. in 1856–57. The partners were Abram J. Hoffman and Charles Knickerbocker. ¶ Albany CD 1855–57.

Hoffman, Victor. Lithographer of a *c.* 1856 view of Sacramento (Cal.), designed by Thomas Boyd and printed by Britton & Rey. ¶ *Portfolio* (Nov. 1948), 61, repro.

Hoffmann, E. Portrait painter of NYC, 1850. ¶ NYBD 1850.

Hoffmayer, W. Painter of a copy of Henry Inman's portrait of Martin Van Buren. The copy is signed, "W. Hoffmayer, Washington, March 18th, 1838." ¶ Information courtesy the late William Sawitzky.

Hoffy, Alfred M. Lithographer. Hoffy was born in England *c.* 1790 and was working in the United States by 1835 when he drew on stone a view of the NYC fire of December 16th. He continued to work in NYC until about 1838 when he moved to Philadelphia. From 1839 to 1841 he was producing illustrations for the *United States Military Magazine,* published by Huddy & Duval, and from 1841 to 1843 he was editor of *Orchardist's Companion.* He continued to work in Philadelphia until after 1860 in which year he published his *North American Pomologist,* with 36 color plates. He also exhibited at the Artists' Fund Society and the Pennsylvania Academy. ¶ 7 Census (1850), Pa., L, 927; Stokes, *Icon.,* III, 618–19, pl. 115; NYCD 1836–37;

Phila. CD 1840–60+; Todd, "Huddy & Duval Prints"; Union Cat., LC; Peters, *America on Stone,* pl. 70; Bolton, *Crayon Draftsmen; Portfolio* (May 1947), frontis., 196–198; *Portfolio* (Jan. 1954), 116; Rutledge, PA.

HOGAN, THOMAS. Irish lithographer, 21, at NYC in 1860. ¶ 8 Census (1860), N.Y., XLII, 929.

HOGART, GEORGE. Engraver from New York, age 23, living in Cincinnati in August 1850. ¶ 7 Census (1850), Ohio, XX, 789.

HOHENSTEIN, ANTON. Portrait painter, born in Bavaria *c.* 1823. He came to America in the early 1850's and worked in Philadelphia. He painted a portrait of U. S. Grant in 1867. *Cf.* ANTHONY HOCHSTEIN. ¶ 8 Census (1860), Pa., LVI, 512; Peters, *America on Stone;* Cowdrey, NAD; Rutledge, PA; Phila. CD 1856–60+. The name is given as Hostein in the 1860 census.

HOHL, AUGUST. Lithographer from Germany, age 16, at Philadelphia in 1860. He was later employed as a druggist and salesman. ¶ 8 Census (1860), Pa., LVI, 79; Phila. CD 1867–75.

HOIT, ALBERT GALLATIN (1809–1856). Portrait and landscape painter; born December 13, 1809, at Sandwich (N.H.) and graduated from Dartmouth College in 1829. During the 1830's he worked in Portland, Belfast, and Bangor (Maine) and St. John's (N.B.). After 1839 he made his home in Boston. He visited Europe from 1842 to 1844. He died December 18 or 19, 1856, at West Roxbury (Mass.). ¶ CAB; *Crayon,* IV (1857), 29, obit.; Piers, "Artists in Nova Scotia," 147; Swan, BA; Cowdrey, AA & AAU; Boston BD 1841–56.

HOIT, WILLIAM B. Portrait and ornamental painter of Concord (N.H.), active *c.* 1840–76. ¶ WPA (N.H.); Concord CD 1844–76 (the latter year Mrs. William B. Hoit, widow, is listed).

HOLBERTON, WAKEMAN (1839–1898). Sportsman who painted fish and game subjects; born in NYC, September 1, 1839; died January 4, 1898. ¶ *Art Annual,* I (1898), obit.; Thieme-Becker; Bénézit; Cowdrey, NAD (1865–76).

HOLDEN, ANN. Irish engraver, 49, at NYC in 1860. She had real property valued at $3,000. ¶ 8 Census (1860), N.Y., LXII, 357.

HOLDEN, CLIFFORD C. Early American portrait painter, examples of whose work are owned in New Jersey. ¶ WPA (N.J.), *Historical Records Survey.*

HOLDEN, JOHN (or Jean) J. (*c.* 1810–1855). Sculptor in marble. Born in England *c.* 1810; worked in New Orleans from 1852 to 1855. At the time of his death by suicide in October 1855 he was foreman at P. Monsseau's marble yard in New Orleans. ¶ Delgado-WPA cites *Courier,* Oct. 31, 1855; New Orleans CD 1852–54.

HOLGATE, J. F. H. Amateur landscape painter of NYC; exhibited at the National Academy in 1838. This may have been John F. Holgate, hardware merchant, or one of his family. ¶ Cowdrey, NAD; NYCD 1838–39.

HOLLAND, FRANCIS P. Engraver, 31, at NYC in 1860. He and his wife and children were all born in New York. ¶ 8 Census (1860), N.Y., LXI, 324.

HOLLAND, GEORGE, see JOHN JOSEPH HOLLAND.

HOLLAND, JOHN JOSEPH (*c.* 1776–1820). Townscape and theatrical scene painter. A native of England, J. J. Holland came to America in 1796 under engagement as scene painter to the Philadelphia Theatre. He moved to NYC in 1807, designed the New Theatre, and was its principal scene painter until 1813. During the 1813–14 season he was scene painter for the newly-formed Theatrical Commonwealth in NYC, but by the end of 1814 he had returned to the New Theatre as co-manager. At the time of his death, December 15, 1820, he was employed as scene painter at the Park Theatre. Holland was the teacher of HUGH REINAGLE and JOHN EVERS, and also worked in Philadelphia and NYC with C. MILBOURNE. Several of his NYC views in watercolors have been preserved. ¶ Dunlap, *History,* II, 64–65; Scharf and Westcott, *History of Philadelphia;* Odell, *Annals of the New York Stage,* II; NYCD 1807–20; N. Y. *Evening Post,* Dec. 18, 1820, obit.; Stokes, *Icon.,* I, 445–459 and pl. 67 (as George Holland, though J. J. Holland is clearly intended), III, plates 82Ba, 82Bb, 82Bc; Cowdrey, AA & AAU; Society of Artists [Phila.] Cat., 1811–14 (as J. J. Holland in the entries, but as Thomas Holland in the indexes); *American Collector* (Nov. 1939), frontis.; *Portfolio* (Jan. 1946), 113–114.

HOLLAND & STINSON. Engravers, lithographers, and plate printers at Boston, 1856–58. This firm, which succeeded T. R. Holland & Co., was formed in 1855 by THOMAS R. HOLLAND and WILLIAM H.

STINSON. ¶ Boston CD 1855–57; BD 1856–58.

HOLLAND, THOMAS, see JOHN JOSEPH HOLLAND.

HOLLAND, THOMAS R. Engraver of Boston; born *c.* 1816; active 1839–60 and after. He established the firm of T. R. Holland & Co., with O. HOLMES, in 1855; and HOLLAND & STINSON, with WILLIAM H. STINSON, in 1856. ¶ 7 Census (1850), Mass., XXV, 939; Boston CD 1839–60+; Boston BD 1841–60+.

HOLLEN, JOHN E. Still life painter, exhibitor at the American Institute 1856 and the National Academy 1858–62. He was active as a fancy painter and decorator in NYC from 1850 to 1880. ¶ Am. Inst. Cat., 1856; Cowdrey, NAD; NYCD 1850–80.

HOLLINGSWORTH, GEORGE (1813–1882). Portrait and landscape painter. A native of Milton (Mass.); worked in Boston from 1839 until 1853 and exhibited intermittently at the Boston Athenaeum 1839–45. He died at Milton. ¶ Mallett; Fielding; Swan, BA; Boston BD 1841–53.

HOLLIS, CHARLES J. Engraver of Philadelphia; born in Pennsylvania *c.* 1815; working in Philadelphia 1854–71. ¶ 8 Census (1860), Pa., LVIII, 442; Phila. CD 1854–71.

HOLLOWAY, H. E. Wood engraver, employed by J. W. ORR & BROTHER in NYC, 1849. ¶ Am. Inst. Cat., 1849; NYCD 1849.

HOLLYER, SAMUEL (1826–1919). Engraver, etcher, lithographer. Born February 24, 1826, in London and began his career as an engraver there about 1842. In 1851 he emigrated to America, settling in NYC and working for a number of book publishers. He went back to England in 1860 and worked there for six years, returning to the United States in 1866. For many years he made his home at Hudson Heights, near Guttenberg (N.J.), and commuted to NYC. He was particularly noted for his stipple and line portraits, as well as for landscapes, book plates, illustrations, mezzotints, and etchings. In 1904 he published *Prints of Old New York.* He died in NYC December 29, 1919. ¶ DAB; Stauffer; Cowdrey, NAD; Peters, *America on Stone.*

HOLMAN, JONAS W. Portrait painter. Listed as a portrait painter at Boston in 1833, he subsequently appears as a clergyman and physician at Boston 1834–45 and in NYC 1855–60. In 1856 G. W., J. W., and W. O. Holman, all of the same address in NYC, exhibited at the American Institute. ¶ Boston CD 1833–45; NYCD 1855–60; Am. Inst. Cat., 1856; Fielding, *Supplement to Stauffer;* Lipman and Winchester, 174; *Art in America* (Feb. 1951), 12–13, repros.; *Portfolio* (March 1955), 206, repro.

HOLMES, E. W. Engraver, age 30, at Philadelphia in August 1850. ¶ 7 Census (1850), Pa., LII, 347.

HOLMES, GEORGE W. Landscape painter and drawing master from Ireland, born *c.* 1812; working in Philadelphia from 1838 to 1868. He exhibited at the Pennsylvania Academy between 1850 and 1868 and his wife exhibited in 1869. ¶ 7 Census (1850), Pa., LII, 569; Phila. CD 1838–60; Rutledge, PA.

HOLMES, HENRY. Engraver at NYC, 1850–58; born in New York about 1832. In 1850 he was living with RAWSON PACKARD. ¶ NYCD 1858; 7 Census (1850), N.Y., XLVII, 774.

HOLMES, J. D. Artist from New York State, age 50, living in Briggs (Ore.) in 1860. ¶ 8 Census (1860), Oregon (citation courtesy David C. Duniway, Oregon State Archivist).

HOLMES, NATHANIEL, SR. Lithographer, with NATHANIEL HOLMES, JR., at NYC, 1851–54. ¶ NYCD 1851–54.

HOLMES, NATHANIEL, JR. Lithographer, with NATHANIEL HOLMES, SR., at NYC 1851–54. ¶ NYCD 1851–54.

HOLMES, ZACHEUS, JR. Wood engraver born *c.* 1839 in Massachusetts; living in Boston in July 1860. ¶ 8 Census (1860), Mass., XXVI, 539.

HOLSTE (or Holtze), PETER CASPAR. Artist. Born in Germany *c.* 1775; had a drawing and painting academy in Baltimore from 1819 to 1850. ¶ 7 Census (1850), Md., V, 858; Lafferty.

HOLT, CHARLES. Engraver at Lowell (Mass.) in 1837. ¶ Belknap, *Artists and Crafstmen of Essex County,* 4.

HOLT, SAMUEL (1801–?). Portrait and miniature painter, ornamental painter; born in 1801 at Meriden (Conn.); began painting miniatures in the early 1830's. After a few years of this work, his eyes began to fail and Holt was obliged to abandon miniature painting for ornamental work. He was at Brandon (Vt.) in 1860, and in 1879 was living in Hartford (Conn.). ¶ French, *Art and Artists in Connecticut,* 66; New England BD 1860; Fielding.

HOLTON, HENRY. Wood engraver at NYC

1856–60; associated with HOLTON & JARDINE 1856–58. ¶ NYCD 1856–60.

HOLTON & JARDINE. Wood engravers of NYC, 1856–58; the partners were HENRY HOLTON and JOSEPH P. JARDINE. ¶ NYCD 1856–58.

HOLTZE, see HOLSTE.

HOLTZMANN, F. Artist and publisher of six views of the "New Ditch" of the Columbia and Stanislaus River Water Co., at Columbia, Tuolumne (Cal.), *c.* 1858. The views were lithographed by KUCHEL & DRESEL. ¶ Peters, *California on Stone.*

HOLYLAND, C. J. Engraver and printer at NYC in 1837 and 1846. ¶ NYBD 1837, 1846.

HOLYOKE, EDWARD AUGUSTUS, JR. Portrait painter; born August 19, 1827, at Salem (Mass.). He was painting in Boston in 1847, exhibited at the American Art-Union in NYC in 1848 and 1849, and was at Salem in 1850. ¶ Belknap, *Artists and Craftsmen of Essex County,* 10; Boston BD 1847; Cowdrey, AA & AAU.

HOLZWART, F. A. Artist of a view of Reading (Pa.) *c.* 1836. ¶ Stokes, *Historic Prints,* 83.

HOMAN, SAMUEL V. Miniaturist of Boston, 1841–44. ¶ Boston BD 1841, 1844; Bolton, *Miniature Painters;* Fielding.

HOME, Mrs. M. A. Portrait painter of Baltimore, 1859. ¶ Lafferty.

HOMER, Mrs. HENRIETTA MARIA (BENSON) (1809–1884). Flower painter in watercolor. Mrs. Homer, mother of the artist WINSLOW HOMER, was born at Bucksport (Maine) and grew up in Cambridge (Mass.). Instructed as a girl in the genteel art of watercolor painting, she continued to paint after her marriage and throughout her life. During the 1870's she exhibited at the Brooklyn Art Association along with her famous son. She died at Brooklyn, April 27, 1884. ¶ Goodrich, *Winslow Homer,* 2–3, 83.

HOMER, JAMES. Artist, 25, a native of Massachusetts, at NYC in 1860. ¶ 8 Census (1860), N.Y., LVII, 291.

HOMER, WINSLOW (1836–1910). N.A. Marine, genre, and landscape painter in watercolor and oils; illustrator. Winslow Homer, one of the greatest American artists of the latter half of the 19th century, was born February 24, 1836, in Boston and spent his childhood in Cambridge. At the age of 19 he was apprenticed to the Boston lithographer, J. H. BUFFORD, for whom he designed music sheet covers. In 1857 he went into business on his own and began his career as an illustrator for *Ballou's Pictorial* of Boston and *Harper's Weekly* of NYC. Two years later he moved to NYC, continuing his connection with *Harper's* and taking up painting about 1861. In 1866–67 he spent ten months in France. After 1873 Homer devoted himself chiefly to water color painting. After a visit to England in 1881–82, he settled at Prout's Neck, near Scarboro (Maine), where he made his home for the rest of his life, except for frequent visits to Quebec and the Adirondacks in the summer and to the Bahamas, Bermuda, and Florida in the winter. He died at Prout's Neck on September 29, 1910. ¶ The authoritative life is Lloyd Goodrich's *Winslow Homer.* See also: Downes, *The Life and Works of Winslow Homer;* Cox, *Winslow Homer;* Watson, *Winslow Homer;* Goodrich, *American Watercolor and Winslow Homer;* Richardson, "Winslow Homer's Drawings in *Harper's Weekly";* Weller, "A Note on Winslow Homer's Drawings in *Harper's Weekly";* Weitenkampf, "The Intimate Homer, Winslow Homer's Sketches"; Cowdrey, *Winslow Homer: Illustrator.*

HONEYWELL, Miss M. A. Silhouette cutter. Probably born at Lempster (N.H.) about 1787, Miss Honeywell had no hands and only three toes on one foot. Having learned to make paper cut-outs and silhouettes, embroider, and write with her mouth and toes, she enjoyed a long career as a prodigy from 1806 to at least 1848. She was at Salem (Mass.) in 1806 and 1809, at Charleston (S.C.) in 1808, 1834–35, and at Louisville (Ky.) in 1830. ¶ Carrick, *Shades of our Ancestors,* 104–109; Jackson, *Silhouette,* 116; Belknap, *Artists and Craftsmen of Essex County,* 15; Rutledge, *Artists in the Life of Charleston;* Dexter, *Career Women of America,* 75; *Antiques* (May 1931), 360, 379.

HONFLEUR, Mr. and Mrs. Teachers of drawing and painting at Richmond (Va.) in May 1835. ¶ *Richmond Portraits,* 242.

HOOD, Mrs. MATILDA. Drawing teacher at Philadelphia; exhibitor at the Pennsylvania Academy in 1827. ¶ Rutledge, PA.

HOOD, WASHINGTON. Portrait copyist in the U. S. Army at Washington (D.C.) in 1833. ¶ *Art Quarterly,* III, supplement, p. 394, no. 17; Lipman and Winchester, 174.

HOOGLAND, WILLIAM (*c.* 1795–1832). Line

and stipple engraver. He worked in NYC from 1814 to 1821, then moved to Boston where he was for a time associated with ABEL BOWEN and was the teacher of JOHN CHENEY and JOSEPH ANDREWS. He returned to NYC about 1828 and worked there until his death, September 28, 1832, at the age of 32(?). Hoogland was one of the engravers for *The Naval Monument* (Boston, 1816) and also did banknote engraving for the Massachusetts Bank. ¶ Stauffer; Barber, "Deaths Taken from the New York Evening Post," vol. XI; NYCD 1814–21; Boston CD 1822–28; NYCD 1829–32; Cowdrey, NAD; Toppan, *100 Years of Bank Note Engraving,* 10; Hamilton, 187; *Antiques* (June 1945), 332.

HOOKER, CHARLES. Engraver, age 25, born in Pennsylvania, living in Philadelphia in September 1850. ¶ 7 Census (1850), Pa., XLVII, 235.

HOOKER, PHILIP (1766–1836). Architect and topographical artist; born October 28, 1766, at Rutland (Mass.) but moved in childhood to Albany (N.Y.) where he spent the rest of his life. During his career as an architect and builder from 1797 to 1830 he designed many Albany churches, the City Hall, State Capitol, and Albany Academy. Several of his views of Albany buildings were engraved. He died in Albany, January 31, 1836. ¶ Edward W. Root, *Philip Hooker: A Contribution to the Study of the Renaissance in America;* DAB; Thieme-Becker; Stauffer.

HOOKER, WILLIAM. Engraver, particularly of maps and charts. He was at Philadelphia in 1804, then moved to Newburyport (Mass.) where he remained from 1805 to 1810, working there with GIDEON FAIRMAN. He returned to Philadelphia and finally settled in NYC in 1815. He was active there until 1846 as a map engraver, publisher, and printer, and issued a number of pocket plans of the city. ¶ DAB; NYCD 1815–46; Belknap, *Artists and Craftsmen of Essex County,* 4; Stauffer; Fielding; Cowdrey, AA & AAU.

HOOLE, EDMUND. Engraver of NYC, 1849–58. ¶ NYBD and CD 1849–58.

HOOLE, JOHN R. Engraver of NYC, 1840–56. After 1856 he was listed as a wholesale dealer in bookbinders' supplies. In 1852–54 his home was at Elizabethtown (N.J.). ¶ NYBD 1840; NYCD 1841–57.

HOOPER, EDWARD (1829–1870). Wood engraver and watercolor painter. He was born May 24, 1829, in London and received his education there. He came to America in the early 1850's and entered into partnership with ALBERT BOBBETT. Bobbett & Hooper were listed as wood engravers in NYC from 1855 to 1865, as printers in Brooklyn in 1867 and as "Chromos" in Brooklyn 1868–70. Hooper died in Brooklyn, December 13, 1870. He was well-known as a watercolorist and was one of the founders of the American Watercolor Society. ¶ CAB; NYCD 1855–65; Brooklyn CD 1867–70; Fielding.

HOOPER, JOHN. Lithographer, working in NYC in the 1850's, living in Brooklyn. ¶ NYCD 1855–56.

HOOPER, JOHN E. (?–1848). Portrait and miniature painter who was working in Philadelphia in 1844 and died at Richmond (Va.) on June 25, 1848. ¶ Phila. BD 1844; Lafferty.

HOOPER, W. W. Wood engraver of NYC, 1840. ¶ NYBD 1840.

HOPE, J. W. Landscape and portrait painter who exhibited at the American Academy in 1833 and at the National Academy in 1835. In the latter year his address was given as NYC. ¶ Cowdrey, AA & AAU; Cowdrey, NAD.

HOPE, JAMES (1818/19–1892). A.N.A. Portrait, historical, and landscape painter. Born November 29, 1818 or 1819, at Drygrange, Roxboroughshire (Scotland); brought to Canada as a child. He was apprenticed to a wagon-maker at Fairhaven (Vt.) and attended Castleton Seminary for a year, after which he took up portrait painting in West Rutland (Vt.) in 1843. From 1844 to 1846 he painted portraits in Montreal. He then returned to Castleton, taught at the Seminary, and began to paint landscapes. He saw active service during the Civil War and made many studies which he later developed into a series of large battle paintings and exhibited throughout the country after the war. After 1872 Hope made his home at Watkins Glen (N.Y.) and devoted himself to landscape painting. He died there in 1892. ¶ Karolik Cat., 357–365; Hemenway, *Historical Gazetteer,* III, 532; CAB; Cowdrey, NAD; Cowdrey, AA & AAU; Rutledge, PA; NYBD 1858; New England BD 1860; represented Corcoran Gallery; *Portfolio* (Dec. 1951), 86–87.

HOPE, THOMAS. Portrait painter of Philadelphia, 1841–51. ¶ Phila. CD 1841–51.

HOPE, THOMAS W. Portrait painter and

miniaturist of NYC, 1834–65. ¶ NYCD 1834–65; Bolton, *Miniature Painters.*

HOPKIN, ROBERT (1832–1909). Historical, landscape, animal, and scene painter; born January 3, 1832, in Glasgow (Scotland). From 1843 to his death on March 21, 1909, he resided almost continuously in Detroit (Mich.). His best known work, however, was his decorations for the New Orleans Cotton Exchange. ¶ *Art Annual,* VII (1909), 77, obit.; Burroughs, "Painting and Sculpture in Michigan," 402; Fielding.

HOPKINS, I. Silhouette cutter at New Orleans in 1805. He advertised to "cut four complete likenesses for four bits," *i.e.,* fifty cents. ¶ Delgado-WPA cites *La. Gazette,* Oct. 8, 1805.

HOPKINS, JAMES E. Copperplate engraver, lithographer, at Cleveland (Ohio) in 1853. ¶ Cleveland BD 1853.

HOPKINS, JOHN HENRY (1792–1868). Amateur artist. Born January 30, 1792, in Dublin, he came to America with his parents in 1800 and was brought up in Philadelphia. In his early 20's he worked as an iron-master in western Pennsylvania, then studied and practised law in Pittsburgh. He also taught drawing at a Pittsburgh academy for a short time, one of his pupils being the portrait painter, JAMES R. LAMBDIN. In 1823 he was made rector of the Episcopal Church in Pittsburgh and thereafter his career was chiefly in the church. He moved to Boston in 1831 and the following year, having been elected first Protestant Episcopal Bishop of Vermont, he moved to Burlington (Vt.). His continuing interest in the arts was shown by the publication in 1836 of his *Essay on Gothic Architecture* and between 1838 and 1843 of a series of *Vermont Drawing Books,* illustrated with plates of flowers, figures, and landscapes drawn by the Bishop, lithographed by JOHN HENRY HOPKINS, JR., and hand colored by other members of the family. The elder Hopkins was made Presiding Bishop of the Protestant Episcopal Church in 1865 and died at his home in Rock Point (Vt.) on January 9, 1868. ¶ [J. H. Hopkins, Jr.], *The Life of the Late Right Reverend John Henry Hopkins . . .* (N.Y., 1873), contains scattered references to his work as an artist; Hubbard, "The Hopkins Flower Prints"; DAB.

HOPKINS, JOHN HENRY, JR. (1820–1891). Lithographer, designer of church buildings and appointments; born in Pittsburgh (Pa.) on October 28, 1820; son of Bishop JOHN HENRY HOPKINS of Vermont. He graduated from the University of Vermont in 1839 and shortly after learned the processes of lithography in order to assist his father in publishing a series of *Vermont Drawing Books.* After two years of teaching in Savannah (Ga.), he entered the General Theological Seminary in NYC. From 1853 to 1868 he served as editor of the *Church Journal.* From 1868 to 1872 he was engaged in writing the biography of his father. He was rector of the Episcopal Church in Plattsburgh (N.Y.) from 1872 to 1876 and in Williamsport (Pa.) from 1876 to 1887. He died at Troy (N.Y.), August 14, 1891. ¶ Charles F. Sweet, *Champion of the Cross, Being the Life of John Henry Hopkins* (N.Y., 1894); Hubbard, "The Hopkins Flower Prints."

HOPKINS, M. W. Teacher of "Poonah" or theorem painting at Richmond (Va.) in 1829; painting portraits at Cincinnati in 1844. ¶ *Richmond Portraits,* 242; information courtesy Edward H. Dwight, Cincinnati Art Museum.

HOPKINSON, FRANCIS (1737–1791). Amateur portrait painter and heraldic artist. Francis Hopkinson, noted Colonial lawyer, musician, and writer, was born at Philadelphia, October 2, 1737, and spent most of his life there and at Bordentown (N.J.). He was a prominent public official during and after the Revolution, a signer of the Declaration of Independence, and a political satirist. His artistic work included several crayon self-portraits and some heraldic designs for official seals. He died May 9, 1791. ¶ Hastings, *The Life and Works of Francis Hopkinson* (Chicago, 1926), 464–466; DAB; Rutledge, MHS; represented at MHS.

HOPLER (?), Col. WILLIAM C. Artist of a wash drawing of the ruins of Jamestown (Va.), 1860. ¶ Stokes, *Historic Prints,* 125.

HOPPIN, AUGUSTUS (1828–1896). Illustrator. A younger brother of THOMAS F. HOPPIN, he was born at Providence (R.I.), July 13, 1828, received his education at Brown and Harvard Universities, and practised law for a short time in Providence. Early in the 1850's he began his career as an illustrator for magazine and book publishers. His subjects were chiefly humorous, though he also wrote and illustrated several travel books on Europe and Egypt. He died at Flushing, Long Island (N.Y.), April 1, 1896. ¶ DAB; CAB; Clement and

Hutton; Hamilton, 318–324; Cowdrey, NAD; *Antiques* (July 1944), 16.

HOPPIN, THOMAS FREDERICK (1816–1872). Painter, sculptor, and etcher. An elder brother of AUGUSTUS HOPPIN, he was born at Providence (R.I.), August 15, 1816, studied art in Philadelphia and Paris, and worked in NYC during the late 1830's. From 1841 until his death he lived in Providence. His work was shown at the National Academy (of which he was an Honorary Member), the American Art-Union, Boston Athenaeum, and American Institute. He died in Providence, January 21, 1872. ¶ Thieme-Becker; Stauffer; Gardner, *Yankee Stonecutters;* Cowdrey, NAD; Cowdrey, AA & AAU; Swan, BA; Am. Inst. Cat., 1851; Providence CD 1841–72; *Providence (R.I.), Births, Marriages and Deaths in:* Deaths, 1871–1880.

HOPPS, CHARLES. Heraldic and fancy painter of Boston, 1849–50. In the latter year he was a partner of —— BRESLAW. ¶ Bowditch, "Early Water-Color Paintings of New England Coats of Arms," 205.

HOPWOOD, Mrs. WILLIAM. Art teacher from England, at Cincinnati in 1840. ¶ Cincinnati CD 1840 (courtesy Edward H. Dwight, Cincinnati Art Museum).

HORLOR, EDWARD C. Engraver of NYC, 1858; possibly of JONES & HORLOR. ¶ NYCD 1858.

HORLOR, HENRY P. Engraver of NYC, 1854 and after. In 1858 he was associated with JONES & HORLOR and in 1859–60 with HORLOR & VANSAUN. ¶ NYBD 1854–59; NYCD 1858–60.

HORLOR & VANSAUN. Engravers of NYC, 1859–60. The partners were HENRY P. HORLOR and PETER D. VANSAUN. ¶ NYCD 1859–60.

HORN, A., see AUGUST HOEN.

HORN, HENRY J. Portrait and genre painter working in NYC, Brooklyn, and Connecticut from the 1840's to the 1860's. He exhibited at the National Academy. ¶ Cowdrey, NAD; NYBD 1846–54; Brooklyn BD 1857; Sherman, "Newly Discovered American Portrait Painters," 234.

HORNBY, SQUIRE T. Engraver at Philadelphia, 1860–61. He was listed subsequently as a grocer and mattress-maker. ¶ Phila. CD 1860–67.

HORNDY, J. R. Engraver on copper, born in England *c.* 1832; living in Philadelphia in June 1860. His wife was from New York and their two children, aged 5 and 2, were born in Rhode Island. ¶ 8 Census (1860), Pa., LX, 703.

HORNER, Miss ——. Exhibited "The Mother after the early Roman Manner" at the Boston Athenaeum in 1853. Swan lists her as an American artist. ¶ Swan, BA.

HORNER, JAMES B. Lithographer, 21, a native of Massachusetts, at NYC in 1860. ¶ 8 Census (1860), N.Y., XLVIII, 477.

HORNOR, THOMAS. Topographical artist, engraver, and etcher who came from England to NYC shortly before 1828 and executed several views of the city during the following decade. By 1844 he had moved to Sing Sing, now Ossining (N.Y.). Before coming to America he had painted a panorama of London. ¶ Stokes, *Icon.,* III, 625–628, pl. 120, and VI, pl. 98a; Stokes, *Historic Prints,* 79–80, 84, pl. 58; Dunshee, *As You Pass By,* pl. X; NYCD 1834; Stauffer (as T. Horner); Thieme-Becker.

HORNTEN (or Hosten), ROBERT. Wood engraver from Ireland, age 21, living in Philadelphia in July 1860. ¶ 8 Census (1860), Pa., XLIX, 342.

HORSTMAN, HERMAN. Engraver from Holland, age 20, at Philadelphia in 1860 and after. In 1862 he was listed as a jeweller. A younger brother Henry became an engraver during the 1860's. ¶ 8 Census (1860), Pa., LXII, 148; Phila. CD 1861–70.

HORTER, CHARLES D. Engraver of NYC, 1854 and after. In 1856–58 he was associated with LEICHTWEIS & HORTER. ¶ NYCD 1854, 1856–60.

HORTON, CHARLES. Artist of New Orleans, 1859–61. ¶ Delgado-WPA cites New Orleans CD 1859–61.

HORTON, CHARLES C. Engraver at NYC, 1848. ¶ NYBD 1848.

HORTON, JAS. Engraver at Baltimore, 1831. ¶ Baltimore CD 1831.

HORTON, JOHN S. Engraver working in Baltimore from 1837 to 1845 and in NYC from 1846 to 1853. In NYC he was associated in business with TUDOR HORTON. He may have been the Horton listed by Stauffer and Fielding as an engraver at Providence (R.I.) in the 1820's and at Philadelphia and Baltimore in the early 1830's. ¶ Baltimore CD 1837–45; NYCD 1846–53; Stauffer; Fielding, *Supplement to Stauffer.*

HORTON, RICHARD. Engraver at Providence (R.I.) in 1854. ¶ Providence CD 1854.

HORTON, Mrs. M. N. Amateur artist whose sketch of Downieville (Cal.) was lithographed and published in 1852. ¶ Peters, *California on Stone.*

HORTON, TUDOR. Engraver of NYC, 1846–54. He was apparently associated in business with JOHN S. HORTON, with whom he lived. ¶ NYCD 1846–53.

HOSEA, H. N. (Mrs. R. Hosea, Jr.). Miniaturist working in Cincinnati, 1838–41. ¶ Cist, *Cincinnati in 1841,* 141; *Portfolio* (April 1946), 190, repro.

HOSFORD, BRADLEY. Lithographer and draftsman at Springfield (Mass.), 1849–58. ¶ New England BD 1849; Springfield CD 1851–58.

HOSIER, ABRAHAM. Artist working in NYC from 1856 to 1877. In 1856 he exhibited an india ink drawing of Christ at the American Institute. ¶ NYCD 1856–77; Am. Inst. Cat., 1856; represented at NYHS.

HOSKIN (or Hoskins), ROBERT. Portrait, miniature, and landscape painter of Brooklyn (N.Y.), active 1843–50. He exhibited at the National Academy. ¶ Cowdrey, NAD; Brooklyn CD 1843.

HOSKING, P. W. Engraver at Zanesville (Ohio), 1853. ¶ Ohio BD 1853.

HOSKINS, SYDNEY. English lithographer, 21, at NYC in 1860. ¶ 8 Census (1860), N.Y., LI, 675.

HOSMER, HARRIET GOODHUE (1830–1908). Sculptor. Born October 9, 1830, at Watertown (Mass.), Harriet Hosmer spent her childhood in Massachusetts, studied art in Boston and anatomy in the medical department of St. Louis (Mo.) University. In 1852 she went to Rome where she studied for seven years under the English sculptor John Gibson. After 1860 she won an international reputation as the leading woman sculptor of the day. Much of her work was done in Italy and England, as well as in the United States. She died at Watertown February 21, 1908. ¶ DAB; *Art Annual,* VII (1909), 77, obit.; Lee, *Familiar Sketches,* 221–226; Taft, *History of American Sculpture;* Clement and Hutton; Thieme-Becker; Swan, BA; Cowdrey, NAD. See also: Cornelia Carr, ed., *Harriet Hosmer: Letters and Memories* (1912).

HOSMER, LYDIA. Painter in watercolors and on velvet, active in Concord (Mass.) *c.* 1810–20. ¶ Lipman and Winchester, 174; *Antiques* (Sept. 1931), 162.

HOSTETTER, THOMAS. Pennsylvania-born artist, age 35, at Philadelphia in August 1850. ¶ 7 Census (1850), Pa., Phila. vol., p. 119.

HOTCHKISS, MILO (1802–1874). Portrait painter; born October 10, 1802, at Kensington (Conn.). In his early thirties he went to Hartford, studied with PHILIP HEWINS, and had just started a career as a professional artist when his father's death forced him to return to the family farm. He did little painting thereafter. He died at Kensington, October 12, 1874. ¶ French, *Art and Artists in Connecticut,* 66–67.

HOTCHKISS, T. H. (?–1869). Landscape painter living in NYC in 1856–57 and at Catskill (N.Y.) in 1858. He exhibited at the National Academy, of which he was an Associate Member. ¶ Cowdrey, NAD; Clark, *History of the NAD,* 268.

HOTCHKISS, WALES (1826–?). Portrait painter, born at Bethany (Conn.) in 1826. He studied under GEORGE W. FLAGG at New Haven and in NYC. Returning to New Haven in the mid-1840's he painted some portraits and historical pieces in oils, but was predominantly a watercolor artist. He moved to Northampton (Mass.) about 1870 and was still there in 1879. ¶ French, *Art and Artists in Connecticut,* 134–135; New Haven CD 1856–57; 7 Census (1850), Conn., VIII, 532; Cowdrey, NAD (1861).

HOUDON, JEAN ANTOINE (1741–1828). Sculptor. Houdon, one of 18th-century France's greatest sculptors, was born at Versailles on March 20, 1741. After several years of study at the Académie, he won the Grand Prix de Rome in 1761 and from 1764 to 1769 continued his studies in Rome. On his return to France he quickly established himself as a portrait and ideal sculptor of the first rank, his most notable work being a bust of Voltaire executed in 1778. In September 1785 he accompanied Franklin to America for the purpose of taking a life bust of Washington, which he did at Mt. Vernon during the early part of October. By the end of the year he had returned to France, where he spent the rest of his life. After a long and successful career he died in Paris on July 15, 1828. Many of his works, including busts of a number of famous Americans, are in this country. ¶ The authoritative study is Hart and Biddle's *Memoirs of the Life and Works of Jean Antoine Houdon, the Sculptor of Voltaire and of Washington* (Phila., 1911). See also: Chinard, *Houdon in America: A Collection of Documents in the Jefferson Papers in the Library of Congress* (Baltimore, 1930); L. Réau, "Great French Sculptor of the 18th Century," *Connoisseur* (June 1948), 74–77; Thieme-Becker; Bénézit.

HOUGH, E. K. Primitive pastel artist, working in Vermont *c.* 1850. In 1943 James Thomas Flexner owned a copy by Hough of THOMAS COLE's "Voyage of Life." ¶ Lipman and Winchester, 174; *Magazine of Art* (May 1943), 177, repro.

HOUGHTON, DAVID. Portrait painter, aged 45, at NYC in 1850. ¶ 7 Census (1850), N.Y., XLII, 456.

HOUSE, JAMES (*c.* 1775–1834). Portrait painter at Philadelphia 1798–1812. He was an officer in the U. S. Army from 1799 until his death at Georgetown (D.C.) on November 17, 1834, at which time he held the grade of Brevet Brigadier General. ¶ Heitman, *Historical Register;* Dunlap, *History,* II, 141; CAB; represented at Md. Hist. Soc. (Rutledge) and Peabody Inst.

HOUSE, JAMES. Portrait painter at Troy (N.Y.), 1857–59. ¶ Troy BD 1857–58; N. Y. State BD 1859.

HOUSE, TIMOTHY. Banknote and portrait engraver of Newtonville (Mass.), chiefly employed in Boston from about 1836 until his death *c.* 1865. ¶ Stauffer; Boston BD 1841–58; Boston CD 1843–60.

HOUSEKEEPER, CHENEY H. Artist, age 38, born in Pennsylvania, living in Philadelphia in August 1850. ¶ 7 Census (1850), Pa., LII, 922.

HOUSEWORTH, MORTIMER. Wood engraver of NYC, exhibited at the American Institute in 1846–47. In 1847–48 he was listed as a bookbinder. He was born in New York about 1822. ¶ NYCD 1845–48; Am. Inst. Cat., 1846, 1847; 8 Census (1860), N.Y., XLVI, 785.

HOUSTON, A. Portrait painter at Philadelphia in 1859. ¶ Phila. BD 1859.

HOUSTON, H. H. Irish stipple engraver who came to Philadelphia from Dublin in the late 1790's and between 1796 and 1798 engraved several portraits which Stauffer describes as among the earliest really good stipple engravings produced in the United States. ¶ Stauffer; Strickland, *Dictionary of Irish Artists.*

HOUSTON, WILLIAM C. Portrait painter in oils and watercolors, at Charleston (S.C.) in 1853. He advertised himself as of "the British Academy." ¶ Rutledge, *Artists in the Life of Charleston.*

HOVEY, JOHN. Amateur artist. A resident of Salem (Mass.), who left for California in January 1849 and remained there over two years seeking his fortune in the gold fields. His manuscript journal, in the Huntington Library at San Marino (Cal.), contains several sketches of California scenes. ¶ Van Nostrand and Coulter, *California Pictorial,* 64–65, repro.

HOVEY, OTIS. Portrait painter who was born in 1788 in Massachusetts and taken as a child to Oxford (N.Y.). When he showed a talent for drawing he was taken to NYC by a wealthy patron and there executed a few copies in oil. When a plan to send him to Europe fell through, Hovey returned to Oxford where, Dunlap says, he "painted portraits of the neighbours for a time, and then sunk to oblivion." ¶ Dunlap, *History,* II, 220.

HOWARD, B. Amateur landscape artist in pastel, working at Rumford Point (Maine) *c.* 1850. ¶ Lipman and Winchester, 174.

HOWARD, E. D. Portrait painter at Cleveland (Ohio), 1860. ¶ WPA (Ohio), *Annals of Cleveland.*

HOWARD, EMMA. Artist, 26, a native of the District of Columbia, living in NYC in 1860 with JUDSON HOWARD. ¶ 8 Census (1860), N.Y., LIV, 441.

HOWARD, EVERETT. Portrait and miniature painter, silhouettist; working in NYC in 1813 and 1816, and in New England *c.* 1820. ¶ NYBD 1813, 1816 (cited by McKay); Jackson, *Silhouette,* 117; Carrick, *Shades of Our Ancestors.*

HOWARD, JOSEPH. Painter of ship pictures at Salem (Mass.) in 1798. ¶ Robinson and Dow, *The Sailing Ships of New England,* I, 62.

HOWARD, JOSIAH W. English artist, 27, living in NYC in 1850 with JOHN MILBURN and family. ¶ 7 Census (1850), N.Y., LIII, 260.

HOWARD, JUDSON. Artist, 28, a native of the District of Columbia, living in NYC in 1860 with EMMA HOWARD. ¶ 8 Census (1860), N.Y., LIV, 441.

HOWARD, JUSTIN H. Comic illustrator, active 1856–76. ¶ Hamilton, 326–328; Weitenkampf, *American Graphic Art;* Murrell, *A History of American Graphic Humor,* 12.

HOWARD, REBECCA F. Amateur landscape artist in pencil. She was born in Vermont *c.* 1839 and was living in Walpole (N.H.) in 1860 with her father, William Howard, a farmer. ¶ 8 Census (1860), N.H., III, 706; Lipman and Winchester, 174.

HOWARD, SETH. Engraver at Providence (R.I.), 1860. ¶ Providence CD 1860.

HOWDELL, THOMAS. Topographical artist. A captain in the Royal Artillery, Howdell drew several views of NYC in the 1760's. ¶ Stokes, *Icon.*, I, 279–281, 295–296, pl. 37–38; *Portfolio* (June 1942), 18–19.

HOWE, B. D. Portrait painter whose portrait of Titus Brown (1786–1849) hangs in the State House, Concord (N.H.). ¶ WPA (Mass.), *Portraits Found in N.H.*

HOWE, HENRY (1816–1893). Topographical artist and illustrator of his own historical works; born October 11, 1816, at New Haven (Conn.). His first book, *Eminent Americans,* was published in 1839. For his *Historical Collections of the State of New York* (1841) he made many on-the-spot sketches and many of his other books contained illustrations after his own sketches. He lived in Cincinnati from *c.* 1847 to 1877, in New Haven from 1878 to 1885, and thereafter in the West, probably Ohio. He died October 14, 1893. ¶ DAB.

HOWE, JONAS HOLLAND (1821–1898). Landscape painter; born in Petersham (Mass.) and spent his youth in Massachusetts. At 23 he went to Boston with his cousin GEORGE FULLER to study under their aunt CAROLINE NEGUS (Mrs. Richard Hildreth). Later the two set up a portrait studio in Boston. Howe moved to Minnesota before 1860 and became prominent as a farmer and agricultural publicist. He resumed painting in his later years and four of his landscapes are owned by the Hennepin County Historical Society. ¶ Norman A. Geske, "A Pioneer Minnesota Artist," *Minn. Hist.* (June 1950), 99–104, with biblio.

HOWE, JOSEPH C., see ROSE & HOWE.

HOWE, JOSEPH P. Artist, age 20, born in Pennsylvania, living in Philadelphia with his father, a carpenter, August 1850. ¶ 7 Census (1850), Pa., XLIX, 424.

HOWE, ORVILLE. Artist, age 18, born in Ohio, living in Columbus in September 1850. ¶ 7 Census (1850), Ohio, XV, 570.

HOWE, ZADOC. Engraver and portrait painter, at Simsbury (Conn.) *c.* 1797–98. He is said later to have practised medicine at Billerica (Mass.), where he died. ¶ Sherman, "Unrecorded Early American Portrait Painters" (1933), 31; Hamilton, 14, 73.

HOWELL, J. B. Lithographer at San Francisco in the mid-1850's. ¶ Hamilton, 331; Peters, *America on Stone.*

HOWELL, JOSEPH B. Pennsylvania-born painter, active in Philadelphia 1855–65. In 1860 he was 30 years old and owned property valued at $1,400. He exhibited historical, genre, and dramatic pictures at the Pennsylvania Academy. ¶ 8 Census (1860), Pa., L, 477; Rutledge, PA.

HOWELL, P. Miniaturist working in NYC, 1806–07. ¶ NYCD 1806–07 (cited by McKay; Stauffer; *Art in America* (April 1928), 130–131, repro.

HOWES, SAMUEL P. Portrait, miniature, and landscape painter; working in Boston 1829–35 and in Lowell (Mass.) 1837–60. The name occasionally appears as Hawes. ¶ Bolton, *Miniature Painters;* Belknap, *Artists and Craftsmen of Essex County,* 10; Lowell CD 1845–60; Swan, BA.

HOWLAND, ALFRED CORNELIUS (1838–1909). N.A. Landscape and genre painter. He was born February 12, 1838, at Walpole (N.H.), received his first artistic training from a Boston engraver, and then spent several years studying painting in NYC, Düsseldorf, and Paris. Returning to America in the 1860's, he settled in NYC where he lived until he moved to Pasadena (Cal.) a few years before his death, March 17, 1909. He was elected a National Academician in 1882. ¶ DAB; De Kay, *Illustrated Catalogue of Oil Paintings by the Late Alfred Cornelius Howland, N.A.* (1910); *Art Annual,* VII (1909), 77, obit.; Swan, BA; Rutledge, MHS; Clement and Hutton; Champlin and Perkins; CAB.

HOWLAND, ALFRED R. Engraver at NYC, 1844. In 1848 he was listed simply as "clerk." See HOWLAND BROTHERS. ¶ NYCD 1844, 1848.

HOWLAND, B. F. Genre painter who had a studio at New York University in 1853 and exhibited at the National Academy. *Cf.* FRANK HOWLAND. ¶ Cowdrey, NAD.

HOWLAND BROTHERS. Engravers of NYC in the mid-1840's. The firm included, in 1844, ALFRED R., JAMES and WILLIAM HOWLAND. ¶ NYCD 1844; NYBD 1846.

HOWLAND, CHARITY. Painter of a primitive watercolor landscape, *c.* 1825? ¶ Lipman and Winchester, 174.

HOWLAND, FRANK. Portrait and genre painter working in NYC in 1854, in Paris 1860–66, and again in NYC in 1868. He exhibited at the National and Pennsylvania Academies. *Cf.* B. F. HOWLAND and FRENCH HOWLAND. ¶ Cowdrey, NAD; Rutledge, PA.

HOWLAND, FRENCH. Miniature painter from South Carolina, age 27, at Cincinnati in August 1850. *Cf.* FRANK HOWLAND. ¶ 7 Census (1850), Ohio, XX, 749.

HOWLAND, JAMES. Engraver, NYC, 1844,

with HOWLAND BROTHERS. In 1848 he was listed as a bookkeeper. ¶ NYCD 1844, 1848.

HOWLAND, JOSEPH T. Wood engraver of NYC, 1845–58. In 1852 he was associated with WILLIAM HOWLAND. He exhibited frames of wood engravings at the American Institute from 1845 to 1849. ¶ NYCD 1847–58; Am. Inst. Cat., 1845–49.

HOWLAND, WILLIAM. Wood engraver of NYC, 1842–75; apparently the eldest of the HOWLAND BROTHERS. He exhibited at the American Institute from 1842 to 1850 and at the National Academy 1846–48. ¶ Am. Inst. Cat., 1842, 1844, 1845, 1847–50; Cowdrey, NAD; NYCD 1846–54; NYBD 1846–60; Smith.

HOWORTH (or Haworth), GEORGE. Restorer of oil paintings; born in England about 1791; came to America before 1833 when his first child was born in Connecticut. A second son, JOHN HOWORTH, was born in New York about 1836. In 1860 he had been living in Boston for 23 years and owned personal property valued at $12,000. ¶ 8 Census (1860), Mass., XXVII, 404; New England BD 1860, adv. p. 17.

HOWORTH (or Haworth), JOHN. Restorer. A son of GEORGE HOWORTH, he was born in New York about 1836 and in 1860 was working with his father in Boston. ¶ 8 Census (1860), Mass., XXVII, 404; Boston CD 1860.

HOWS, JOHN AUGUSTUS (1832–1874). Landscape painter, wood engraver, and illustrator. A native of NYC, he graduated from Columbia College in 1852 and became a professional artist only after some years of study for the ministry and for the bar. He specialized in wood engraving and illustrated many books during the 1860's and 1870's. He was elected an Associate of the National Academy in 1862. He died in NYC, September 27, 1874. ¶ CAB; Smith; Cowdrey, NAD; Rutledge, PA; Clement and Hutton; Hamilton, 333–334; Thieme-Becker.

HOXIE, STANSBURY. Portrait and landscape painter of NYC, active 1832–60; exhibited at the National Academy. He was born in the United States about 1800. ¶ Cowdrey, NAD; NYBD 1846, 1848; 8 Census (1860), N.Y., XLVII, 7.

HOYLE, RAPHAEL (1804–1838). N.A. Landscape painter; born May 18, 1804, in Birmingham (England); accompanied his family to America probably about 1823 when his father set up a tailoring business in Newburgh (N.Y.). He began exhibiting at the National Academy in 1828; also exhibited at the Boston Athenaeum in 1831 and the American Academy in 1833. He was working in NYC in 1828 and 1829, at Newburgh in 1830, in NYC in 1831, and at Newburgh again in 1836 and 1838. In 1837 he received an appointment as draftsman to an American exploring expedition to the Pacific, but he was taken ill before the expedition sailed and died at Newburgh on August 12, 1838. He became a National Academician in 1831. ¶ A. Elwood Corning, "Washington's Headquarters, Newburgh, N.Y.: A Painting," and the same author's "Hoyle's Painting of Washington's Headquarters"; Cowdrey, NAD; Swan, BA; Cowdrey, AA & AAU.

HOYT, A. G., see ALBERT GALLATIN HOIT.

HOYT, Mrs. E. C. Landscape painter of Philadelphia, exhibitor at the Pennsylvania Academy, 1858–68. ¶ Rutledge, PA.

HOYT, HENRY E. Scene painter for the Metropolitan Opera Company of NYC; born *c.* 1833/34; died at Germantown (Pa.), December 30, 1906. ¶ *Art Annual,* VI, obit.; Mallett.

HOYT, PURDY B. Engraver, NYC, 1850–1854; born in New York about 1829. ¶ NYBD 1852, 1854; 7 Census (1850), N.Y., XLV, 34.

HOYT, THOMAS. Portrait painter at Bangor (Maine), *c.* 1850. ¶ Lipman and Winchester, 174.

HOYT, THOMAS R., JR. Townscape painter in watercolors, working in New Hampshire *c.* 1835–45. ¶ Lipman and Winchester, 174.

HOYT, WILLIAM H. Still life painter of NYC, exhibitor at the National Academy, 1859–60. ¶ Cowdrey, NAD.

HOYT, WILLIAM S. Wood engraver of Providence (R.I.), 1849–60. A partner in ALLEN & HOYT, 1854. ¶ New England BD 1849, 1856, 1860; Providence CD 1852–60.

HUBARD, WILLIAM JAMES (1807–1862). Silhouettist, portrait painter, and sculptor. Born August 20, 1807, at Whitchurch, Shropshire (England), Hubard developed early a talent for cutting likenesses and was exploited as a child prodigy in England before being brought to America by his manager in 1824. After three years in NYC and Boston, young Hubard broke with his manager and under encouragement from GILBERT STUART gave up silhouettes for oil painting. After a visit to

England (1826–28), he spent several years in Philadelphia and Baltimore and soon after 1832 settled in Gloucester County (Va.), where he married. After a second trip to Europe, he moved to Richmond in October 1841 and there spent the rest of his life. During the 1850's he became interested in sculpture and established a foundry in Richmond for casting bronzes. When the Civil War broke out he turned his hand to the production of ammunition for the Confederate government and was fatally injured in an explosion at his foundry. He died on February 15, 1862. ¶ McCormack, *William James Hubard, 1807–1862; Richmond Portraits,* 94–95; Lord, "Some Light on Hubard"; Swan, "Master Hubard, Profilist and Painter"; Swan, "A Neglected Aspect of Hubard"; Jackson, *Silhouette;* Carrick, *Shades of Our Ancestors;* McCormack, "The Hubard Gallery Duplicate Book"; Cowdrey, AA & AAU; Swan, BA; Rutledge, PA; Cowdrey, NAD; Fairman, *Art and Artists of the Capitol,* 234; represented at MHS, U. S. Capitol, and Valentine Museum, Richmond.

HUBBAN, Miss E. A. Winner of 3rd prize for flower painting at the Illinois State Fair, Chicago, 1855. ¶ Chicago *Daily Press,* Oct. 15, 1855.

HUBBARD, CHARLES (1801–1876). Portrait and commercial painter who was working in Boston from the late 1820's until as late as 1869. In 1834 he advertised as a sign and ornamental painter, and painter of military standards and masonic regalia. He may have been the Hubbard who exhibited four landscapes at CHESTER HARDING's gallery in 1834. His standard for the National Lancers of Boston was reproduced in a print published in 1837. ¶ Swan, BA; Boston BD 1841–60; Boston CD 1834, adv.; Peters, *America on Stone,* pl. 101; Stokes, *Historic Prints,* pl. 64a; Doughty, "Thomas Doughty," 49; *Album of American Battle Art,* pl. 52.

HUBBARD, DAVID. Silhouettist at Portsmouth (N.H.) in January 1807. ¶ *N. H. Gazette,* Jan. 27, 1807 (cited in *Antiques,* Sept. 1944, 158).

HUBBARD, RICHARD WILLIAM (1816–1888). N.A. Landscape and portrait painter. He was born in Middletown (Conn.) in October 1816, entered Yale College in 1837, but left the following year to study art in NYC under S. F. B. MORSE and DANIEL HUNTINGTON. After two years of further study in France and England, he settled in Brooklyn (N.Y.) and made his home there and in NYC until his death, December 21, 1888. Elected to membership in the National Academy in 1858, he later served as president of the Brooklyn Art Association and of the Artists' Fund Society. He also exhibited at the Boston Athenaeum, the American Art-Union, the Pennsylvania Academy, Maryland Historical Society, and Washington Art Association. ¶ DAB; CAB; Swan, BA; Cowdrey, NAD; Cowdrey, AA & AAU; Rutledge, PA; Rutledge, MHS; Washington Art Association Cat., 1857, 1859; French, *Art and Artists in Connecticut;* represented Peabody Institute.

HUBBARD, WILLIAM J., see WILLIAM JAMES HUBARD.

HUBER, ——. Itinerant portrait painter who visited Marietta (Ohio) in 1824. ¶ Reiter, "Charles Sullivan," 4.

HUBER, CONRAD. Lithographer in NYC in the mid-1850's. He executed the plates for F. O. C. DARLEY's *Compositions in Outline from Judd's Margaret* (N.Y., *c.* 1856). ¶ NYBD 1857; Cowdrey, NAD; Hamilton, 213.

HUBERT, ——. Exhibited "Cartoon of Young's Night Thoughts" at the National Academy in 1852. His address was Richmond (Va.). This may have been WILLIAM JAMES HUBARD who was then living in Richmond. ¶ Cowdrey, NAD.

HUBERT, CHARLES, see CHARLES A. C. GENGEMBRE.

HUBERT, JOSEPH. Lithographer, 20, a native of New York, at NYC in 1850. ¶ 7 Census (1850), N.Y., XLI, 553.

HUDDY & DUVAL. Lithographers and publishers of *The United States Military Magazine* (Philadelphia: 1839–42). The partners were WILLIAM M. HUDDY and PETER S. DUVAL. ¶ Todd, "Huddy & Duval Prints," *Journal of the American Military Institute,* III (1939), 171–176; Peters, *America on Stone.*

HUDDY, WILLIAM M. Lithographer, Philadelphia, 1837–47. He furnished a number of plates for *The United States Military Magazine,* of which he and PETER S. DUVAL were the publishers, 1839–42. ¶ Todd, "Huddy & Duval Prints"; Peters, *America on Stone;* Phila. CD 1837–47.

HUDSON, G. H. Assistant to SAMUEL H. HUDSON in the painting of the latter's Panorama of the Ohio and Mississippi Rivers, 1847–48. ¶ Arrington, "Samuel A. Hudson's Panorama of the Ohio and Mississippi Rivers," 5.

HUDSON, JOHN BRADLEY (1832–1903). Landscape and ornamental painter. A native of Portland (Maine), he worked there from the late 1850's until the late 1890's, but spent his last years in Weston (Mass.) where he died in 1903. He exhibited at the Boston Athenaeum. ¶ Karolik Cat., 68, 366–367, repro.

HUDSON, JULES or JULIEN. Negro miniaturist and teacher who studied under A. MEUCCI in New Orleans and briefly in Paris, and worked in New Orleans during the 1830's. ¶ Porter, *Modern Negro Art,* 47–48; Delgado-WPA cites New Orleans *Bee* (June 6, 1831), *Courier* (Dec. 3, 1831, and Jan. 10, 1832), and New Orleans CD 1837–38.

HUDSON, SAMUEL ADAMS (1813–?). Landscape and panorama painter. Born in Brimfield (Mass.) on February 13, 1813, he was christened Samuel Adams Hitchcock but later adopted the name of Hudson. Until 1847 he worked in Boston as a tailor, painting only in his spare time, but in 1847 he began work on a panorama of the Ohio and Mississippi Rivers which was shown from St. Louis to Troy (N.Y.) in 1848–49 and destroyed by fire in the spring of 1849. Hudson soon after returned to Boston and resumed his tailoring. He was still there as late as 1894. ¶ Arrington, "Samuel A. Hudson's Panorama of the Ohio and Mississippi Rivers"; *Panorama* (Oct. 1947).

HUDSON, WILLIAM, JR. (1787–?). Portrait, miniature, and landscape painter, apparently active in Virginia as early as 1818. From 1829 to 1856 he lived in Boston and in 1857–58 in Brooklyn (N.Y.). He exhibited at the Boston Athenaeum and the National Academy. ¶ Swan, BA; Fielding; Boston BD 1844–1856; Brooklyn BD 1857; Cowdrey, NAD; *Richmond Portraits,* 54–55, repro.

HÜCK, FERDINAND. Portrait and religious painter who came from Mayence (Germany) to Lancaster (Pa.) in 1729. In 1912 several of his watercolors and two oils were still in existence, the oils being a self-portrait on wood and a painting of the Crucifixion, painted for the Lancaster Catholic Mission in 1741. Hück is said to have spent the latter part of his life in Baltimore. ¶ Lancaster County Historical Society, *Historical Papers and Addresses,* XVII (1913), 92–93.

HUESTIS, CHARLES P. Wood engraver at NYC in 1844 and at San Francisco 1856–59. ¶ NYBD 1844; San Francisco CD 1856, BD 1858–59; *American Collector* (Feb. 1948), 12, repro. of comic Valentine, 1841.

HUFF, G. Engraver in NYC, 1832. ¶ *American Adv. Directory,* 1832, 123.

HUFFMAN, FREDERICK W. Engraver, 33, at NYC in 1860. He and his wife were from Hesse-Cassel (Germany), but their children, ages 6 to 3, were born in New York. ¶ 8 Census (1860), N.Y., LIV, 992.

HUFTY & DANFORTH. Banknote engravers, Philadelphia, 1848–51. This was the Philadelphia branch of DANFORTH & HUFTY. The partners were SAMUEL HUFTY of Philadelphia and MOSELEY I. DANFORTH of NYC. ¶ Phila. CD 1848–51.

HUFTY, JOSEPH. Copperplate and steel engraver and stationer, Philadelphia, 1835–60. ¶ Phila. CD 1835–60.

HUFTY, SAMUEL. Engraver of Philadelphia, 1823–51. From 1843 he was associated with various banknote engraving firms in Philadelphia: DANFORTH, BALD, SPENCER & HUFTY (1843), DANFORTH, SPENCER & HUFTY (1844–1846), and DANFORTH & HUFTY (or HUFTY & DANFORTH), 1848–1851. ¶ Phila. CD 1823–1851.

HUGE, I. F. Painter of ship pictures at Bridgeport (Conn.) in 1845. ¶ Robinson and Dow, *The Sailing Ships of New England,* I, 62.

HUGHES, BALL, see ROBERT BALL HUGHES.

HUGHES, H. P., & Co. Teachers of "a NEW and IMPROVED SYSTEM OF PAINTING" upon satin or paper, at Charleston (S.C.) in 1832. ¶ Rutledge, *Artists in the Life of Charleston.*

HUGHES, PATRICK. Irish engraver, 40, at NYC in 1860. His wife also was Irish but their children, ages 10 to 2, were born in New York. ¶ 8 Census (1860), N.Y., XLII, 937.

HUGHES, ROBERT BALL (1806–1868). Sculptor and wax-portraitist. Born January 19, 1806, in London, Ball Hughes, as he signed himself, came to America in 1829 and lived for several years in NYC, where he executed a number of important sculpture commissions, as well as portraits in wax. In 1830 he was made an Honorary Member of the National Academy. He also worked in Philadelphia before settling permanently in Boston in the early 1840's. During his later years he largely abandoned sculpture for cameo-cutting and burning pictures in wood with a poker. He died at Dorchester (Mass.) on March 5, 1868. ¶ DAB; E. S. Bolton, *American Wax Portraits;* CAB; Clement and Hutton; Thieme-Becker; Swan, BA; Rutledge, PA; Cowdrey, AA & AAU; Cowdrey, NAD; Lovejoy, "Poker Drawings of Ball Hughes."

HUGUERIN, EDWARD. Engraver, age 44, born in Paris; living in Philadelphia in June 1860. ¶ 8 Census (1860), Pa., L, 526.

HUHN, F. Engraver at Chicago, 1859. ¶ Chicago CD 1859.

HULANSKI, ——. Polish refugee artist at Auburn (N.Y.) *c.* 1840, the first instructor of JOHN CHESTER BUTTRE. ¶ CAB (under Buttre).

HULL (or Hall), ASA. Still life painter, who exhibited "Dead Game" at the American Institute in 1847. He was listed in the NYC directory as a hotel keeper. ¶ Am. Inst. Cat., 1847; NYCD 1846–48.

HULME, JOHN J. Heraldic and "general" artist of NYC, 1843–54. ¶ NYCD 1843–54.

HULSE, C. J. or JESSE. Landscape and fancy painter at Cincinnati, 1847–51. ¶ Cist, *Cincinnati in 1851;* Cincinnati CD 1849–50 (courtesy Edward H. Dwight, Cincinnati Art Museum).

HULSEMAN, EDWARD. Engraver at NYC, 1840. ¶ NYBD 1840.

HUMBERT, ADELE. Portrait, genre, historical, and religious painter. A native of Metz (France), Mlle. Humbert exhibited at the Paris Salon in 1846 and 1848 and is represented in the Metz Museum. She was listed as a resident of Brooklyn (N.Y.) when she exhibited at the National Academy in 1853. ¶ Bénézit; Thieme-Becker; Cowdrey, NAD.

HUME, HENRY C. (or J. H. C.). Drawing master and ornamental painter, Baltimore 1837–51. ¶ Lafferty.

HUME, JOHN. Portrait painter at NYC, 1848. ¶ NYBD 1848.

HUMPHREY, JOSIAH. Teacher of drawing and painting, at Cleveland (Ohio), 1855–57. ¶ WPA (Ohio), *Annals of Cleveland.*

HUMPHREY, MARIA HYDE. Theorem painter, at Norwalk (Ohio) Seminary in 1840. ¶ Lipman and Winchester, 174; *Antiques* (Jan. 1946), 35, repro. of landscape.

HUMPHREYS, CHARLES. Painter of an oil portrait of Rachel White, dated August 12, 1854, and owned in 1940 by Mrs. Hanna Grover of Haddonfield (N.J.). ¶ WPA (N.J.), Hist. Records Survey.

HUMPHREYS, FRANCIS. Engraver from Ireland, born *c.* 1815, working in Philadelphia 1840 to 1858. During the 1850's he did work for the Methodist Book Concern of Cincinnati. ¶ 7 Census (1850), Pa., LV, 363; Phila. CD 1840–51; Stauffer; *Antiques* (April 1951), 300, repro.

HUMPHRIES, G. C. Designer of the reverse of the 1848 medal issued in honor of Gen. Winfield Scott's victories in Mexico. SALATHIEL ELLIS designed the obverse, and the medal was struck by CHARLES C. WRIGHT. Loubat states that Humphries died in England. ¶ Loubat, *Medallic History,* 304, pl. 63–64.

HUMPHRYS (or Humphreys), WILLIAM (1794–1865). Engraver. Born in Dublin; came to the United States as a youth and learned engraving from GEORGE MURRAY at Philadelphia. About 1827 he went to England and enjoyed a successful career there as an illustrator for the annuals, a banknote engraver, and engraver of the heads for the earliest English stamps. He was again in America from 1843 to 1845 and exhibited at the Artists' Fund Society of Philadelphia. He went to Italy for his health in 1864 and died there, near Genoa, on January 21, 1865. ¶ DNB; Strickland, *Dictionary of Irish Artists;* Rutledge, PA; Cowdrey, AA & AAU; Thieme-Becker; Stauffer.

HUNCKEL, GEORGE. Lithographer of Baltimore, 1856–60. He was the father and partner of OTTO HUNCKEL. ¶ Baltimore CD 1856–60.

HUNCKEL, OTTO. Lithographer of Baltimore, 1856–60. He was the son and partner of GEORGE HUNCKEL. ¶ Baltimore CD 1856–60.

HUNCKEL & SON. Lithographers at Baltimore, 1856–60; a branch of a lithographic establishment in Bremen (Germany). The firm was headed by GEORGE HUNCKEL and his son, OTTO. ¶ Baltimore CD 1856–60; BD 1859.

HUNE, J. H. C., see HENRY C. HUME.

HUNT, CHARLES D. (1840–1914). Landscape painter. A native of Detroit, he came to NYC in 1858. He died in Brooklyn on September 25, 1914. ¶ *Art Annual,* XI, obit.; Thieme-Becker.

HUNT, HENRY P. New England landscape painter who was working at Boston in the early 1850's; exhibited at the Athenaeum in 1856 and the Maryland Historical Society in 1858. ¶ Boston CD 1853–54; Swan, BA; Rutledge, MHS.

HUNT, JOHN W. Artist, 19, a native of New York, at NYC in 1850. ¶ 7 Census (1850), N.Y., L, 567.

HUNT, SAMUEL VALENTINE (1803–1893). Landscape painter and engraver; born in

Norwich (England) on February 14, 1803, and came to the United States in 1834. He made his home in Bay Ridge, Brooklyn (N.Y.) and worked for NYC and Cincinnati publishers. He exhibited at the Apollo Association and the National Academy. He died in Bay Ridge in 1893. ¶ Stauffer; Cowdrey, NAD; Cowdrey, AA & AAU; NYCD 1850 and after; *Home Authors and Home Artists* (N.Y., 1852).

HUNT, W. Portrait and genre painter at NYC in 1847–48. He exhibited at the American Art-Union, the National Academy, and the American Institute. *Cf.* WILLIAM HUNT, artist, at New Haven (Conn.) in 1850. ¶ Cowdrey, AA & AAU; Cowdrey, NAD; Am. Inst. Cat., 1848; NYBD 1848.

HUNT, WILLIAM. Carver of a "lyon" for the ship *John and Anna,* Philadelphia, 1734. ¶ Pinckney, *American Figureheads and Their Carvers,* 47, 194.

HUNT, Dr. WILLIAM. Delineator and publisher of a view of Mt. Auburn, near Boston, 1834. ¶ Peters, *America on Stone.*

HUNT, WILLIAM. English artist, age 35, at New Haven (Conn.) in 1850. *Cf.* W. HUNT. ¶ 7 Census (1850), Conn., VIII, 548; New Haven CD 1850.

HUNT, WILLIAM MORRIS (1824–1879). A.N.A. Portrait, genre, and mural painter; cameo portraitist. Born March 31, 1824, at Brattleboro (Vt.), Wm. M. Hunt attended Harvard College for a short time but went to Europe before he graduated. After spending some time in France and Italy, he studied for a year at Düsseldorf. In 1846 he entered the studio of Thomas Couture at Paris. During his years in France, Hunt became a close friend of Millet and a disciple of the Barbizon School. He returned to America in 1856, worked for a few years in Newport (R.I.) and Brattleboro (Vt.), and in the Azores, finally settling in Boston in 1862. In 1875 he was commissioned to paint two murals for the State Capitol at Albany (N.Y.), one of which was his well-known "The Flight of Night." Hunt was drowned on the Isle of Shoals, off the New Hampshire coast, on September 8, 1879. ¶ DAB; Knowlton, *The Art Life of William Morris Hunt;* Shannon, *The Boston Days of William Morris Hunt;* Chapin, *Cameo Portraiture in America;* NYBD 1854; Cowdrey, NAD; Swan, BA; Wilson, *Lincoln in Portraiture;* Thieme-Becker, biblio.

HUNTER, A. An artist of New Orleans who exhibited 12 watercolor paintings at the American Institute of NYC in 1845. This was presumably the same Hunter mentioned as a lithographer at New Orleans the preceding year. An Alfred Hunter had a bookstore in New Orleans in 1851. ¶ Am. Inst. Cat., 1845; Delgado-WPA cites *Picayune,* Dec. 15, 1844; New Orleans CD 1851.

HUNTINGTON, DANIEL (1816–1906). N.A. Portrait, historical, and landscape painter. Born October 14, 1816, in NYC, Huntington was a student at Hamilton College, Utica (N.Y.), from 1832 to 1836 and there came in contact with CHARLES LORING ELLIOTT who encouraged him to become an artist. After studying under MORSE and INMAN in NYC, he went to Europe for further study in 1839 and again from 1842 to 1845, spending most of his time in Rome. After establishing his reputation as a portrait painter in NYC, he made at least two more visits to Europe in the 1850's and in 1882. Elected a National Academician in 1840, Huntington served twice as President of the National Academy, 1862–70 and 1877–90. Of his 1,200 known works 1,000 are portraits. He died in NYC on April 18, 1906. ¶ DAB; Cowdrey, NAD; Cowdrey, AA & AAU; Swan, BA; Rutledge, PA; Rutledge, MHS; Karolik Cat.; Fairman, *Art and Artists of the Capitol;* Thieme-Becker, biblio.

HUNTINGTON, ELEAZER. Engraver of Hartford (Conn.) 1828–39. In 1828 he engraved the maps, diagrams, and American views for a school atlas published in NYC. ¶ Stauffer; Fielding.

HUNTINGTON, J. A. Portrait painter in Jefferson County (Va., now W. Va.), 1848. ¶ Willis, "Jefferson County Portraits and Portrait Painters."

HUNTINGTON, J. D. Wood engraver at Watertown (N.Y.), 1859. ¶ N. Y. State BD 1859.

HURD, BENJAMIN (1739–1781). Engraver, heraldic artist, silver- and goldsmith; younger brother of NATHANIEL HURD; born in Boston on May 12, 1739. His father was Jacob Hurd, one of the finest of the early Boston silversmiths. Benjamin worked as a smith and engraver in Boston until his death on June 2, 1781. ¶ French, *Jacob Hurd and His Sons,* 143–144; Bowditch, "Early Water-Color Paintings of New England Coats of Arms," 206.

HURD, E. Line engraver of buildings, working in the United States *c.* 1840. ¶ Stauffer.

HURD, GILDERSLEEVE. Portrait painter and decorator. He came to Detroit soon after 1824 on a visit to his brother, Dr. Ebenezer Hurd, and stayed to open a decorator's studio. Several of his portraits have survived. ¶ Burroughs, "Painting and Sculpture in Michigan," 395–96.

HURD, NATHANIEL (1729–1777). Engraver, heraldic artist, and silversmith; son of Jacob Hurd, the noted Boston silversmith; born in Boston on February 13, 1729, Old Style. His earliest known engraving is dated 1749. In addition to his work as an engraver and silversmith, he cut seals and dies and designed and engraved armorial bookplates. He was the brother of BENJAMIN HURD and the uncle of JOHN MASON FURNASS, to whom he left his printing press and some of his engraving tools. He died in Boston on December 17, 1777. ¶ French, *Jacob Hurd and His Sons,* 57–140; DAB; Stauffer; Thieme-Becker, biblio.

HURLBURT (or Hurlbut), ELIZABETH. Landscape painter, age 22, living with her father, Moses C. Hurlbut, boarding house keeper, in Boston in July 1860. ¶ 8 Census (1860), Mass., XXVII, 549.

HUSSEY, E. C. Engraver of St. Louis, 1857–60. In 1859 he was in the partnership of CONNOR & HUSSEY. ¶ St. Louis CD 1857–60, BD 1859.

HUSTED, THOMAS C. Lithographer at NYC, 1848. ¶ NYBD 1848.

HUTAWA, JULIUS. Lithographer of St. Louis, 1838–72. ¶ St. Louis CD 1838–72; BD 1854.

HUTCHINGS or HUTCHINS, ——. Painter (?) of several panoramas exhibited in the United States between 1849 and 1854, including "California Scenes," biblical scenes, and a "classical panorama of the sea and shores of the Mediterranean." ¶ Information courtesy J. Earl Arrington.

HUTCHINGS, A. B. Portrait painter, born in New York *c.* 1828. He was working at Montgomery (Ala.) in March 1861. ¶ WPA (Ala.), Hist. Records Survey cites *Montgomery Weekly Mail,* March 1, 1861.

HUTCHINGS (or Hutchins), STEPHEN B. Portrait painter working in NYC from 1811 to 1846. Dunlap states that he started painting in 1802, but was distracted by other pursuits. ¶ NYCD 1811–20 (cited by McKay); NYBD 1846; Dunlap, *History,* II, 151.

HUTCHINGS, WILLIAM E. Landscape painter of NYC, 1857–90. He exhibited at the National Academy and the Washington Art Association. ¶ Cowdrey, NAD; Washington Art Assoc. Cat., 1859.

HUTCHINGS, W. H. Artist, age 43, at New Orleans in October 1850. The artist, his wife, and his children were all born in Louisiana. ¶ 7 Census (1850), La., IV (1), 511.

HUTCHINSON (or Hutchingson), CYRUS. Portrait painter in NYC, 1846. ¶ NYBD and NYCD 1846.

HUTCHINSON, ROBERT. Scottish engraver, 35, at NYC in 1860 with his wife, also from Scotland. ¶ 8 Census (1860), N.Y., XLVI, 67.

HUTCHINSON, UPHAM & CO. Engravers at Boston in 1853. ¶ *Boston Almanac,* 1853.

HUTENREITH, L., see LUDWIG AUTENRIETH.

HUTSON, CHARLES (1840–1935). Primitive genre painter of New Orleans. ¶ Lipman and Winchester, 174.

HUTT, JOHN. Copperplate engraver from London, advertised at NYC in 1773 and 1774. In connection with JOHN NORMAN he engraved some diagrams published in Philadelphia in 1775. ¶ Stauffer; Gottesman, *Arts and Crafts in New York,* I, 12–13, 28.

HUTTON, ISAAC (*c.* 1767–1855). Engraver and silversmith of Albany (N.Y.). His earliest engravings date from 1789. Isaac and his brother, George Hutton, were in business in Albany for many years as silversmiths and jewelers. GIDEON FAIRMAN was employed by them about 1795. Isaac died on September 8, 1855, at Stuyvesant Landing, Columbia County (N.Y.). ¶ Hatch, "Isaac Hutton, Silversmith."

HUTTON, WILLIAM RICH. Topographical artist. A member of one of the military or naval forces in California during the Mexican War, he made a number of sketches and watercolors of California scenes, including views of Monterey and Los Angeles. The Huntington Library at San Marino (Cal.) owns a collection of his work. ¶ Van Nostrand and Coulter, *California Pictorial,* 51; Taft, *Artists and Illustrators of the Old West,* 267.

HYATT, AUGUSTUS. Engraver and seal cutter, NYC, 1840–48. ¶ NYBD 1840; NYCD 1841–48.

HYATT & CORNELL. Engravers at NYC, 1851. The partners were WILLIAM W. HYATT and JAMES E. CORNELL. ¶ NYBD and NYCD 1851.

HYATT, JACOB. Card and seal engraver,

NYC, 1850–60; of STOUT & HYATT in 1850–51. ¶ NYBD 1850; NYCD 1851–60.

HYATT, WILLIAM W. Engraver, of HYATT & CORNELL, NYC, 1851; born in New York about 1826. ¶ NYBD and NYCD 1851; 7 Census (1850), N.Y., LI, 537.

HYDE, EDWARD. Sculptor at Brooklyn (N.Y.), 1859. ¶ N. Y. State BD 1859.

HYDE, HENRY. Engraver, age 28, a native of Pennsylvania, living in Philadelphia in July 1860. ¶ 8 Census (1860), Pa., LIV, 347.

HYDE, WARREN G. Engraver of Boston, 1857 and after. ¶ Boston CD 1857–60+.

HYDE DE NEUVILLE, ANNE-MARGUERITE-HENRIETTE, Baroness (*c.* 1779–1849). Amateur artist. Mlle. Rouillé de Marigny married the Baron Hyde de Neuville (1776–1857) in 1794 and in 1807 accompanied him into exile in America. They remained in the United States until 1814, making their home in NYC and New Brunswick (N.J.). During their travels in New York, Connecticut, New Jersey, Pennsylvania, and Tennessee the Baroness made many pencil and watercolor sketches of American scenes and faces. In 1816, two years after their return to France, the Baron was made Minister to the United States and they resided in Washington from 1816 to 1822, during which time the Baroness again made many sketches of American life. She died in France in 1849. Two collections of her watercolors and drawings, totalling over 100 pieçes, are now owned by the New-York Historical Society and the New York Public Library. ¶ Monaghan, "The American Drawings of Baroness Hyde de Neuville"; Andrews, "The Baroness Was Never Bored"; Fenton, "The Hyde de Neuville Portraits of New York Savages in 1807–1808."

HYLE, N. Lithographer from France, age 57, at San Francisco in July 1860. ¶ 8 Census (1860), Cal., VII, 499.

I

IARDELLA (or Jardella), ANDREW B. Sculptor at Philadelphia from 1803 to 1831. In 1811 he exhibited at the Pennsylvania Academy a bust of Alexander Hamilton. ¶ Phila. CD 1803–31; Rutledge, PA.

IARDELLA, FRANCISCO (1793–1831). Sculptor. A native of Carrara (Italy) and a cousin of CARLO and GIUSEPPE FRANZONI; came to the United States in 1816 to work on the U. S. Capitol at Washington. After the death of GIOVANNI ANDREI in 1824, Iardella succeeded to his position in charge of sculpture work on the Capitol. He died in Washington on January 23, 1831. ¶ Fairman, *Art and Artists of the Capitol,* 83–84, 476; Borneman, "Franzoni and Andrei," 108.

IARDELLA (or Jardella), GIUSEPPE. Sculptor who came to Philadelphia from Italy during the late 1790's to execute decorative sculptures for the home of Robert Morris and was subsequently employed by the Philadelphia stonecutter JAMES TRAQUAIR. He was working in Philadelphia at least until 1803. ¶ Kimball, "Joseph Wright and His Portraits of Washington," 37; Phila. CD 1802–03; Gardner, *Yankee Stonecutters,* 59.

IBBETSON (or Ibbotson), ARVAH J. Lithographer. A. Ibbetson was working in Philadelphia as early as 1849–50 (Peters). H. J. Ibbotson, merchant, appears in Philadelphia directories for 1846–48, and Hervey J. Ibbotson, lithographer, in the 1850 directory. Harvey Ibbetson, engraver, age 32, was at Boston in 1850 (Census). Arvah J. Ibbotson or Ibbetson was in Philadelphia directories from 1855 to 1862. It seems likely that all these listings represent the same man. ¶ Phila. CD 1846–50, 1855–62; Peters, *America on Stone;* Peters, *California on Stone;* 7 Census (1850), Mass., XXV, 42. *Cf.* JAMES IBBOTSON.

IBBOTSON, JAMES. Lithographer. He was at Philadelphia in 1849, but by August 1850 had moved to Boston where he was listed as a native of England, age 22, living with his wife Cornelia (from New Jersey) and son Wilfred (age one year, born in Pennsylvania). He may have been related to ARVAH J. IBBETSON. ¶ Phila. CD 1849; 7 Census (1850), Mass., XXV, 709–710.

IBELSHAUSER, JOHN. Wood engraver, 26, at NYC in 1860. He was from Hesse and his wife from Bavaria; their two-year-old son was born in New York. ¶ 8 Census (1860), N.Y., LVII, 464; NYCD 1863 as carver.

ILLIUS, ——. Portrait painter in watercolor, exhibitor at the Artists' Fund Society (Philadelphia) in 1840. This may be Charles Illias, listed as a merchant in Philadelphia 1840–41. ¶ Rutledge, PA; Phila. CD 1840–41.

ILLMAN BROTHERS. Engravers and printers of Philadelphia 1860 and after. The firm included EDWARD, GEORGE, HENRY, and WILLIAM ILLMAN, and was still in existence in 1907. Charles T. Illman, born about 1842, joined his brothers in the firm after 1860. ¶ Phila. CD 1860+; Stauffer.

ILLMAN, EDWARD. Engraver and printer. Edward was one of the sons of THOMAS ILLMAN and was born in NYC about 1833. The family moved to Philadelphia about 1845 and Edward was first listed as an engraver there in 1856. After the death of his father, Edward, along with GEORGE, HENRY, and WILLIAM ILLMAN, established the firm of ILLMAN BROTHERS (1860+). ¶ 8 Census (1860), Pa., LV, 507; Phila. CD 1856–60+.

ILLMAN, GEORGE. Engraver. George, son of THOMAS ILLMAN, was born in England about 1824, shortly before his father's emigration to America. The family moved from NYC to Philadelphia about 1845 and there George Illman began his career as an engraver as his father's partner in ILLMAN & SONS (1845–47). He later joined with his brothers EDWARD, HENRY, and WILLIAM in the firm of ILLMAN BROTHERS (1860 and after). ¶ 7 Census (1850), Pa., LIV, 804; 8 Census (1860), Pa., LV, 507; Phila. CD 1850 and after; Stauffer.

ILLMAN, HENRY. Engraver. One of the sons of THOMAS ILLMAN and a partner in ILLMAN & SONS, Philadelphia, 1845–47. He later was with the firm of ILLMAN BROTHERS, 1860 and after. ¶ Phila. CD 1844–60+; Stauffer.

ILLMAN & PILBROW. Engravers of NYC, 1829–36. The partners were THOMAS ILLMAN and EDWARD PILBROW. ¶ NYCD 1829–33; Stauffer.

ILLMAN & SONS. Engravers and printers of Philadelphia, 1845–47. The firm was composed of THOMAS ILLMAN and his sons

GEORGE, HENRY and WILLIAM. ¶ Phila. CD 1845–47.

ILLMAN, THOMAS (?–1859/60). Engraver in stipple and mezzotint. A native of England, Illman was engraving in London by 1824. He came to the United States about 1829, settled in NYC and established the firm of ILLMAN & PILBROW which was active until 1836. About 1845 he moved to Philadelphia and went into business under the name of ILLMAN & SONS, the latter probably including HENRY, GEORGE, and WILLIAM ILLMAN. He died in Philadelphia in 1859 or 1860, leaving his sons to carry on the family business under the name of ILLMAN BROTHERS. ¶ Stauffer; NYCD 1829–36; Phila. CD 1845–59; 8 Census (1860), Pa., LV, 507, lists only Illman's widow and children.

ILLMAN, WILLIAM. Engraver and printer. One of the sons of THOMAS ILLMAN; apparently commenced his engraving career in Philadelphia in 1845 as a partner in ILLMAN & SONS. He was later (1860 and after) associated with his brothers in the firm of ILLMAN BROTHERS. ¶ Phila. CD 1845–60+.

IMBERT, ANTHONY. Lithographer and marine painter. One of the pioneers of American lithography, Imbert was originally a French naval officer who, during a long imprisonment in England, took up marine painting. Shortly after his arrival in America he was commissioned to prepare lithographic plates for the illustrations of Colden's *Memoir* of the Erie Canal opening celebrations (1825). Imbert also painted an oil of the festivities, now owned by the Museum of the City of New York. He issued many other prints between 1825 and 1834, the most important being a series of NYC views after designs of A. J. DAVIS (*c.* 1826–28). Imbert died before 1838, when his widow Mary Imbert was listed in the city directory. ¶ Peters, *America on Stone;* Stokes, *Icon.*, III, 581–582, pl. 94b; NYCD 1825–38; *Connoisseur* (Sept. 1950), 53–54, repro.; *Antiques* (Sept. 1951), 181, repros.

IMBERT, JOHN CLAUDE. Miniaturist from Nantes (France) at Charleston (S.C.) in 1793. ¶ Prime, II, 16; Rutledge, *Artists in the Life of Charleston.*

INDERWICK, ——. Artist of a view of Long Island Sound, engraved by WILLIAM LENEY before 1831. ¶ Stauffer.

INGALLS, CHARLES. Connecticut-born artist, 26, at NYC in 1860. ¶ 8 Census (1860), N.Y., LIII, 824.

INGALLS, GARDNER (1800–1874). Portrait painter; a native of Sanbornton (N.H.) and an older brother of WALTER INGALLS. He was at Manchester (N.H.) in 1856 and died at Lowell (Mass.) on August 15, 1874. ¶ Runnels, *History of Sanbornton,* II, 390.

INGALLS, WALTER (1805–1874). Portrait, still life, and scene painter. Born February 16, 1805, at Canterbury (N.H.); working *c.* 1828 at Washington (D.C.) and in the South. He was at Boston in 1838, when he exhibited at the Athenaeum, at Chicago in 1855, and at Sanbornton (N.H.) in 1860. He died July 21, 1874, at Oakland (Md.). He was a younger brother of GARDNER INGALLS. ¶ Runnels, *History of Sanbornton,* II, 391; Swan, BA; *Chicago Almanac* 1855; New England BD 1860.

INGER, CHRISTIAN. Lithographer at Philadelphia, 1858 and after. He was the senior partner of INGER & SON. ¶ Phila. CD 1858–61+; Peters, *America on Stone,* pl. 76, repro.

INGER, EDMUND. Lithographer at Boston, 1857–58. ¶ Boston CD 1857; BD 1858.

INGER, EGMONT. Lithographer at Philadelphia, 1859 and after. He was the junior member of INGER & SON in 1859. ¶ Phila. CD 1859–60+.

INGER & SON. Lithographers at Philadelphia, 1859. The partners were CHRISTIAN and EGMONT INGER. ¶ Phila. CD 1859.

INGERSOLL, ——. Painter of a view of the wreck of the steamer *San Francisco,* shown in November 1854 at Indianapolis (Ind.). ¶ *Indiana State Sentinel,* Nov. 4, 1854 (courtesy J. Earl Arrington).

INGERSOLL, JOHN (1788–1815). Amateur watercolor painter. A mariner, he was born at Haverhill (Mass.) and died of yellow fever in Boston Harbor, August 27, 1815. JOHN GAGE INGERSOLL was his posthumous son. He is said to have painted still lifes. ¶ Lipman and Winchester, 175; Avery, *Genealogy of the Ingersoll Family in America,* 62.

INGERSOLL, JOHN GAGE (1815–1889). Amateur watercolor painter; posthumous son of JOHN INGERSOLL. Born at Bradford (Mass.) on November 23, 1815; married at Bradford in 1840, and died in Boston on April 23, 1889. He is said to have painted landscapes. ¶ Lipman and Winchester, 175; Avery, *Genealogy of the Ingersoll Family in America,* 89.

INGERSOLL, RANDALL E. Wood engraver at

Guilford (N.Y.) in 1859. ¶ N. Y. State BD 1859.

INGHAM, CHARLES CROMWELL (1796–1863). N.A. Portrait and miniature painter. He was born in Dublin in 1796 and studied painting there before coming to America with his parents in 1816. He spent the rest of his life in NYC where he enjoyed considerable success as a portrait painter and was active in many organizations, including the Sketch Club, the Century Club, and the National Academy, of which he was a founder and Vice-President. He died in NYC on December 10, 1863. ¶ DAB; Strickland; Gardner, "Ingham in Manhattan"; Cowdrey, AA & AAU; Cowdrey, NAD; Rutledge, PA; Rutledge, MHS; Swan, BA; Bolton, *Miniature Painters;* represented Met. Museum of Art, NYHS, and NAD.

INGHAM, WILLIAM, see WILLIAM INGRAM.

INGRAHAM, Mrs. ELLEN M. (1832–1917). Portrait and miniature painter and teacher. Born August 12, 1832, in New Haven (Conn.), she studied miniature and portrait painting there and in NYC and taught in Indianapolis (Ind.) where she lived after 1865. She died June 2, 1917. ¶ Burnet, *Art and Artists of Indiana,* 377; Peat, *Pioneer Painters of Indiana.*

INGRAHAM, MARY L. Amateur watercolor artist living in Massachusetts in 1810, when she painted a religious scene. ¶ Lipman and Winchester, 175.

INGRAHAM, THOMAS. Portrait painter in NYC, 1817. ¶ NYCD 1817 (cited by McKay).

INGRAM, WILLIAM. Landscape painter in NYC, 1858–60+. He exhibited at the National Academy in 1860 as William Ingham. ¶ NYBD 1858; Cowdrey, NAD; NYCD 1863.

INMAN, HENRY (1801–1846). N.A. Portrait, miniature, genre, and landscape painter. Inman was born in Utica (N.Y.) on October 28, 1801, but moved with his family to NYC in 1812. In 1814 he began a seven-year apprenticeship under JOHN WESLEY JARVIS. He established his own studio in NYC in 1824 and from 1826 to 1828 worked in partnership with his pupil THOMAS S. CUMMINGS. In 1826 he was instrumental in founding the National Academy of Design, of which he was Vice-President from 1826 to 1831. In 1831 he moved to Philadelphia where for four years he was a partner in the lithographic firm of CHILDS & INMAN. Returning to NYC in 1834, he enjoyed considerable success as a portrait painter until his health began to fail in the early 1840's. His last important commission took him to England in 1844–45 to paint portraits of Wordsworth and Macaulay. He died on January 17, 1846, a few months after his return from England, and an exhibition of his works was held in NYC that same year to raise funds for the support of his family. ¶ Bolton, "Henry Inman" and "A Catalogue of the Paintings of Henry Inman," in *The Art Quarterly* (1940), 353–375, 401–418; DAB; Cowdrey, AA & AAU; Cowdrey, NAD; Rutledge, PA; Rutledge, MHS; Dickson, *John Wesley Jarvis; Karolik Cat.; Richmond Portraits,* 144; Cummings, *Historic Annals;* Clark, *History of the NAD.*

INMAN, JOHN O'BRIEN (1828–1896). A.N.A. Portrait and genre painter. Born in NYC on June 10, 1828, studied under his father, HENRY INMAN, was exhibiting at the National Academy by 1853, and later worked in the South and West. In 1866 he went to Europe and spent the next twelve years mostly in Paris and Rome. He returned to NYC in 1878, and died at Fordham on May 28, 1896. ¶ CAB; information courtesy NAD; *Antiques* (Sept. 1950), 197; Cowdrey, NAD; Swan, BA; represented NYHS.

INNES, CHARLES. Sculptor, NYC, 1854–56. In the latter year he exhibited at the American Institute three plaster busts, of Fremont, Hughes, and Brady, for one of which he won third prize. ¶ NYCD 1854–56; Am. Inst. Cat. and *Trans.,* 1856.

INNESS, GEORGE (1825–1894). N.A. Landscape painter. Born May 1, 1825, on a farm near Newburgh (N.Y.), George Inness grew up in NYC and near Newark (N.J.). In 1841 he was apprenticed to Sherman & Smith, map engravers of NYC, but his interest soon shifted to painting. He exhibited for the first time at the National Academy in 1844 and the following year at the American Art-Union. In 1846 he studied briefly under REGIS F. GIGNOUX of Brooklyn and the following year he made the first of several trips to Europe. He was elected a National Academician in 1853. Inness went abroad again in 1850 and 1854; during the 1860's lived in Medfield (Mass.), Eagleswood (N.J.), and Brooklyn (N.Y.); spent the years 1870–74 in Italy and France; and thereafter spent most of his time in NYC and Montclair (N.J.). He died on August 3, 1894, during a visit at Bridge of Allan (Scotland). Inness was one of the best of the 19th-century American landscape artists. ¶ The most recent study of Inness is Elizabeth McCausland's *George Inness, An American Landscape Painter* (Springfield, Mass., 1946). See also: George Inness, Jr., *The Life, Art and Letters of George Inness* (N.Y., 1917); Elliott Daingerfield, *George Inness* (N.Y., 1911); W. Harley Rudkin, "George Inness, American Landscape Painter"; McCausland, "The Early Inness"; DAB; Cowdrey, NAD; Cowdrey, AA & AAU; Swan, BA; Rutledge, MHS; Rutledge, PA; Karolik Cat.

INSLEE, CHARLES T. Sculptor at NYC, 1859–60. ¶ NYBD 1859–60.

INSLEE, WILLIAM. A.N.A. Portrait and genre painter of NYC, 1827–37. ¶ Cowdrey, NAD.

IRISH, T. T. Copperplate engraver at New Orleans in 1849. ¶ Delgado-WPA cites New Orleans CD 1849.

IRVING, JOHN BEAUFAIN, JR. (1825–1877). N.A. Portrait, genre, and historical painter; born November 26, 1825, in Charleston (S.C.). He painted in Charleston as an amateur before going to Europe in 1851 to study at Düsseldorf under LEUTZE. Returning to America in 1858, he painted in Charleston until after the Civil War when he moved to NYC and turned his attention chiefly to genre and historical subjects. He was elected a National Academician in 1872 and died in NYC on April 20, 1877. ¶ DAB; CAB; Clement and Hutton; Rutledge, *Artists in the Life of Charleston;* Thieme-Becker; Cowdrey, NAD; Rutledge, PA.

IRVING, WASHINGTON (1783–1859). Amateur artist. Though best known as America's first internationally popular essayist, historian, and biographer, Washington Irving was also a dabbler in art. During his childhood in NYC he received instruction in drawing at ARCHIBALD ROBERTSON's Columbian Academy, and throughout his life he was active as a patron and friend of many American artists. He was elected to Honorary Membership in the National Academy in 1842. Irving's own artistic efforts consist mainly of numerous sketches and caricatures which are scattered through his journals and literary notebooks. ¶ DAB; Irving, *Journals* (Boston, 1919); H. G. Rowell, "Washington Irving the Artist"; Shelley, "American Painting in Irving's Day."

IRWIN, MRS. LEE FEARN, née Mary E. Brooks (1840–1919). Amateur painter. The daughter of Augustus Brooks (1810–1871) and Mary Elizabeth Everitt or Everett (1816–1878), she was born in Mobile (Ala.) on October 22, 1840. In 1866 she married Lee Fearn Irwin of Mobile. She died in Mobile on August 11, 1919. Her work includes a few still lifes and flowers in oils, watercolor studies of Negro life, and a number of miniatures on ivory, chiefly of members of her family. ¶ Information courtesy Mrs. George B. Cortelyou, Jr. (Irwin Fearn Cortelyou), granddaughter of the artist.

ISAACS, ANDREW. Landscape painter of Philadelphia, 1836–49. He exhibited chiefly copies at the Artists' Fund Society and Pennsylvania Academy, though he did show an original view along the Wissahickon at the latter in 1849. In 1850 he was in NYC where he was listed as an English artist, aged 40 (or 48). ¶ Rutledge, PA; 7 Census (1850), N.Y., LII, 198.

ISHAM, RALPH. Landscape and portrait painter of Hartford (Conn.). Born about 1820, Isham was the first curator of the Wadsworth Athenaeum in Hartford, opened in 1844. French states that he died early in life. ¶ French, *Art and Artists in Connecticut,* 109; Fielding.

ISHERWOOD, HENRY. Theatrical scene painter and panoramist. He was born in NYC and commenced his career as an actor and scene painter at the Park Theatre in 1817. Throughout most of his long career he was associated with NYC theaters, though he is recorded to have been in Baltimore in 1835 and Charleston (S.C.) in 1842. From 1857 until the mid-1870's he was chief scene painter at Wallack's Theatre in NYC and he was listed in the NYC directories until 1885. ¶ Odell, *Annals of the New York Stage,* III–IX; Ireland, *Records of the New York Stage,* I, 442; Lafferty; Rutledge, *Artists in the Life of Charleston;* Phila. *Public Ledger,* Aug. 30, 1851 (citation courtesy J. E. Arrington); Cowdrey, NAD (1867).

ISNARD, JEAN JACQUES. Engraver and marble sculptor of New Orleans, 1818–46. ¶ Delgado-WPA cites *L'Ami des Lois,* March 21, 1818; New Orleans CD 1822, 1841–42, 1846.

IVES, CHAUNCEY BRADLEY (1810–1894). Sculptor. Born December 14, 1910, at Hamden (Conn.); apprenticed to a woodcarver at New Haven and later went to Boston where he began carving in marble. He moved to NYC about 1840 and had a studio there until 1844, when he went to Italy. After seven years in Florence, he settled in Rome where he remained, except for numerous brief visits to the United States, until his death on August 2, 1894. He was primarily a portrait sculptor. ¶ DAB; NYBD 1841; French, *Art and Artists in Connecticut,* 82–83; Cowdrey, NAD; Cowdrey, AA & AAU; Swan, BA; Rutledge, PA. Represented in U. S. Capitol, Washington, and Connecticut State Capitol, Hartford.

IVES, EDWARD. Lithographer at NYC, 1848. ¶ NYBD 1848.

IVES, JAMES MERRITT (1824–1895). Lithographer. A native of NYC, Ives practised lithography there before 1852, when he was hired as a bookkeeper by N. CURRIER. Five years later he was taken into partnership and for nearly forty years he served as business manager of the famous firm of CURRIER & IVES. He died at Rye (N.Y.) on January 3, 1895. ¶ Peters, *Currier & Ives,* 27–28, 59, and pl. 146.

IVES, J. J. Sculptor who exhibited at the National Academy in 1850 a bust of General Scott. This may be CHAUNCEY BRADLEY IVES, who executed a bust of General Winfield Scott about this time. ¶ Cowdrey, NAD; Clement and Hutton.

IVES, JOSEPH CHRISTMAS (?–1868). Topographical draftsman. A native of New York State, he entered West Point in 1848 and was commissioned in July 1852. The following year he was transferred to the Topographical Engineers. In 1857–58 he headed an expedition to explore the Colorado River and at least one of his own sketches was used in illustrating his *Report.* At the outbreak of the Civil War he entered the Confederate Army in which he served throughout the war. He died on November 12, 1868. ¶ Heitman, *Historical Register;* Ives, *Report upon the Colorado River of the West explored in 1857 and 1858* (Washington, 1861), pl. V.

IVES, LOYAL MOSS. Portrait painter who worked in New Haven (Conn.) during the latter 1850's and in NYC from about 1863 into the 1890's. ¶ New Haven CD 1856–58; NYCD 1863–90+.

IVES, L. T. Lawyer at Detroit who turned to portrait painting and had a successful career both before and after the Civil War. He was one of the artists who exhibited in Detroit's first art exhibition in 1852. His son Percy also became a portrait painter. ¶ WPA Guide, *Michigan,* 138.

IWONSKI, CARL G. VON (1830–1922). Portrait painter; born April 23, 1830, in Hildersdorf (Germany). His family were among the first settlers of New Braunfels (Texas). In 1853 they moved to Hortontown and later to San Antonio. Carl, who had studied at Breslau (Germany), painted portraits of some prominent Texans before his return to Germany in 1872. He died at Breslau in 1922. ¶ Yanaguana Society Exhibition *Catalogue,* Dec. 1933; WPA Guide, *Texas,* 143; *American Processional,* 246; *Antiques* (June 1948), 456.

J

Jackman, William G. Engraver in line, stipple, and mezzotint. He was born in England, came to America about 1841, and worked in NYC until after 1860, chiefly for book publishers. ¶ Stauffer; NYCD, 1841–60; Thieme-Becker.

Jackson, ——. Engraver of a line plate entitled "Captain William Mason in the Magazine, Fort Niagara, Sept. 1826." ¶ Stauffer.

Jackson, Charles. Copperplate engraver at Baltimore, 1856 and after. ¶ Baltimore BD 1856–60.

Jackson, Charles Thomas (1805–1880). Topographical draftsman; born June 21, 1805, at Plymouth (Mass.); received his M.D. from Harvard in 1829. After visiting Europe and practising in Boston for several years, he gave up medicine for chemistry and mineralogy. His most notable work was a series of geological surveys which he conducted for Maine, Rhode Island, and New Hampshire between 1837 and 1844. Some of his sketches for this work were reproduced in his *Views and Map Illustrative of the Scenery and Geology of New Hampshire* (1845), as well as in others of the nearly one hundred publications accredited to him. His later life was much taken up with acrimonious controversies aroused by his claims of priority in the discovery of the electric telegraph, of guncotton, and of surgical anesthesia. He became insane in 1873 and died on August 28, 1880, at Somerville (Mass.). ¶ DAB; Union Cat., LC.

Jackson, Edwin W. Miniaturist. E. W. Jackson was at Bath (Me.) in 1825, painting miniatures and profiles. Edwin W. Jackson, presumably the same artist, was in NYC in 1831–32, at Albany (N.Y.) 1833–35, again in NYC 1846–47, and at Brooklyn (N.Y.) in 1857. ¶ Little, "Itinerant Painting in America, 1750–1850," 212; NYCD 1831–32; Albany CD 1833, 1835; NYBD 1846; Bolton, *Miniature Painters;* Brooklyn BD 1857.

Jackson, Henry. Engraver and landscape painter, son of Joseph Jackson; active in Charleston (S.C.) from 1842 to 1850. After his father's death in June 1850, Henry helped his mother carry on the elder Jackson's restoring business. ¶ Rutledge, *Artists in the Life of Charleston.*

Jackson, J. Miniature painter at NYC, exhibitor at the National Academy in 1833. The address given is the same as that of Joseph Jackson in the directory. ¶ Cowdrey, NAD; NYCD 1833.

Jackson, J. Portrait painter at NYC, exhibitor at the American Academy in 1833. His address is the same as that given in the directory for Thomas Jackson. ¶ Cowdrey, AA & AAU; NYCD 1833.

Jackson, J. Artist of a sketch of the Mormon Temple at Nauvoo (Ill.) *c.* 1840. ¶ Arrington, "Nauvoo Temple," Chap. 8.

Jackson, James. Portrait painter at Baltimore in 1837. His portrait of the Rev. Mr. McJilton was engraved. ¶ Baltimore CD 1837; Stauffer, II, no. 2542.

Jackson, John Adams (1825–1879). Sculptor and crayon artist; born November 5, 1825, at Bath (Me.). He studied drawing in Boston under D. C. Johnston and in Paris under Suisse. One of his earliest works in sculpture was a bust of Daniel Webster in 1851. After a second vist to Europe in 1853–54, he spent the rest of the decade in Boston and NYC. In 1860 he removed permanently to Italy, revisiting the United States only once (1867) before his death at Pracchia on August 30, 1879. His work, highly regarded in his day, included nearly a hundred portrait busts, as well as many ideal figures and groups. ¶ DAB; Clement and Hutton; Taft, *History of American Sculpture;* Bolton, *Crayon Draftsmen;* Boston BD 1855–59; Swan, BA; Cowdrey, NAD; Rutledge, PA.

Jackson, Joseph (?–1850). Portrait and miniature painter and restorer, at Charleston (S.C.) from 1834 until his death in June 1850. When he arrived in Charleston in 1834 this artist was referred to as formerly of Oxford (England), which suggests that he may have been the J. Jackson, Jr., of Oxford, who exhibited miniatures at the Royal Academy between 1816 and 1835. He apparently stopped in NYC on his way from England to South Carolina, for he was listed in the city directory for 1833 and also exhibited (as J. Jackson) at the National Academy that year. After his death in 1850, his wife and son, Henry Jackson, carried on his restoring business in Charleston. ¶ Rutledge, *Artists in the Life of Charleston,* 158; Graves, *Dictionary;* NYCD 1833; Cowdrey, NAD.

JACKSON, Mrs. JOSEPH. Painter and restorer. She assisted her husband, JOSEPH JACKSON, in his business at Charleston (S.C.) until his death in 1850, and continued it with assistance from their son, HENRY JACKSON. ¶ Rutledge, *Artists in the Life of Charleston,* 158.

JACKSON, M. D. Artist of Columbus (Ohio) in the early 1850's who designed and painted a panorama of Bunyan's *Pilgrim's Progress* and a panorama of Europe. ¶ Columbus, *Ohio State Journal,* Nov. 21, 1851, Chillicothe, *Daily Scioto* Gazette, Dec. 2, 1851, and Columbus, *Daily Ohio Statesman,* March 29, 1853; Cincinnati *Daily Gazette,* Nov. 12, 1853 (information courtesy J. E. Arrington).

JACKSON, SAMUEL. Drawing master and portrait painter of NYC, 1830–35. ¶ NYCD 1830–35.

JACKSON, T. J. Portrait and landscape painter, teacher of drawing and monochromatic painting; at Charleston (S.C.) in 1847. ¶ Rutledge, *Artists in the Life of Charleston.*

JACKSON, THOMAS J. (?–1842). Portrait painter. Thomas Jackson, portrait painter, was listed in NYC directories 1832–35 and he exhibited (as J. Jackson, but at the same address as Thomas) at the American Academy in 1833. From 1840 to 1842 he was at New Orleans, but he returned to NYC and was found dead in the Hudson River in November 1842. ¶ NYCD 1832–35; Cowdrey, AA & AAU; Delgado-WPA cites New Orleans *Picayune,* Oct. 13, 1840, and Dec. 1, 1842 (obit.); New Orleans CD 1841–42.

JACKSON, WILLIAM F. Engraver, 23, a native of New York, at NYC in 1860. ¶ 8 Census (1860), N.Y., LX, 777; NYCD 1862.

JACKSON, WILLIAM H. (1832–?). Painter of religious pictures. "Captain Jackson," as he signed his paintings, was born August 15, 1832, at Watertown (Mass.) and was living in Boston in 1905. His paintings were exhibited in Philadelphia, Boston, and London. ¶ *Artists Year Book,* 99.

JACOBS, EDMUND. English artist, age 40, with his wife Rachel at New Orleans in October 1850. ¶ 7 Census (1850), La., IV(1), 499.

JACOBS, EMIL (1802–1866). Portrait and historical painter; born August 18, 1802, at Gotha (Germany), where he passed the greater part of his life. Thieme-Becker suggests that he may have visited Philadelphia in 1850. The catalogue of the Pennsylvania Academy for that year shows that Jacobs did exhibit his "Judith and Holofernes" in Philadelphia in 1850, but it also gives his current address as Gotha. The painting was bought by the Academy and placed on permanent exhibition. The artist's address was given in 1855 as Germany, in 1858 as Dresden, and in 1863 as Gotha. He died on January 6, 1866. ¶ Thieme-Becker; Rutledge, PA.

JACOBS, EMIL. Portrait painter, art dealer, and daguerrean artist, at New Orleans in 1854–56. ¶ Delgado-WPA cites New Orleans *Picayune,* Jan. 3, 1855, and *Bee,* Jan. 18, 1856.

JACOBS, HENRY (1801–1874). Portrait painter at Boston, exhibitor at the Athenaeum in 1846 and 1847. He appears as H. Jacobs in the Athenaeum catalogues and as Henry Jacobs in the 1847 city directory. ¶ Swan, BA, 242; Boston CD and BD 1847.

JACOBS, HIRAM. Swiss engraver, 45, at NYC in 1860. His wife and three older children, ages 20 to 14, were born in Switzerland; one child, 14, was born in Germany; the youngest child, 12, was born in New York. ¶ 8 Census (1860), N.Y., LXII, 435.

JACOBS, ISAAC. Lithographer, of JACOBS & JOHNSON, at NYC 1860–61. ¶ NYBD 1860–61; NYCD 1861.

JACOBS & JOHNSON. Lithographers of NYC, 1860–61. The firm was composed of ISAAC JACOBS and JAMES JOHNSON. ¶ NYBD 1860–61; NYCD 1861.

JACOBS, JOSEPH. Italian figure-maker, age 21, with his English wife Margaret at Cincinnati in October 1850. ¶ 7 Census (1850), Ohio, XXI, 897.

JACOBS, L. R. or ROWLEY. Portrait painter living in Brooklyn (N.Y.) 1852–56, in Cincinnati 1859–61, and in Chicago 1866–67. He exhibited at the National Academy in 1852–53. Dr. and Mrs. W. H. Miller of New Carlisle (Ohio) own his 1867 portrait of Lincoln, said to be a replica of his earlier life portrait painted when Jacobs was a neighbor of Lincoln in Springfield (Ill.). ¶ Brooklyn CD 1852–53 [as L. K.], 1856 [as L. R.]; Cowdrey, NAD; Cincinnati CD 1859–60 [as L. R.], 1861 [as L. Rowley]; Chicago CD 1866–

67; letter, Mrs. W. H. Miller, New Carlisle (Ohio), to D. H. Wallace, May 6, 1955.

JACOBUS, PETER H. Engraver, born in Prussia about 1836, working in Philadelphia 1856–71. From 1856 to 1859 he headed the firm of JACOBUS & SCHELL. PHILIP JACOBUS was a younger brother of Peter. ¶ 8 Census (1860), Pa., LIV, 892; Phila. CD 1856–71.

JACOBUS, PHILIP. Prussian-born engraver, age 16, at Philadelphia in 1860 with his elder brother, PETER JACOBUS. He was still in Philadelphia in 1871. ¶ 8 Census (1860), Pa., LIV, 892; Phila. CD 1871.

JACOBUS & SCHELL. Engravers and die-sinkers at Philadelphia, 1856–59. The partners were PETER H. JACOBUS and JOHN J. SCHELL. ¶ Phila. CD 1856–59.

JACOBY (or Jacobey), JAMES. English artist, age 57, at Baltimore in August 1850. ¶ 7 Census (1850), Md., V, 467.

JAGENS, WILLIAM. Sculptor, born in Vermont about 1818, living in Berkshire (Vt.) in September 1850. In the same house was EBEN E. WILL. ¶ 7 Census (1850), Vt., V, 419.

JAHRAUS, JACOB. Engraver, born in Pennsylvania about 1838, living in Philadelphia in 1860–61. ¶ 8 Census (1860), Pa., LI, 557; Phila. CD 1861.

JAHRAUS, J. L. Portrait painter at Philadelphia, exhibited at the Artists' Fund Society in 1840 and 1841. His address is the same as that given in the directory for Jacob Jahraus, baker. ¶ Rutledge, PA; Phila. CD 1840–41.

JAMACIE, LOUIS. Italian figure-maker, age 19, living in the home of SANTONIO TREAGA, Philadelphia, in August 1850. ¶ 7 Census (1850), Pa., L, 859.

JAMES, ——. Portrait painter. In 1834 Dunlap stated that a Mr. James, a native New Yorker, had painted portraits in NYC about 25 years before and later had gone to Quebec. His name appears in the NYC directory for 1812. Portraits by "James" of Bishop Plessis of Quebec, engraved by A. B. DURAND, and of Amos Sutton, Baptist missionary in India, engraved by O. PELTON, may have been painted by this artist. ¶ Dunlap, *History,* II, 471; NYCD 1812 (cited by McKay); Stauffer, II, nos. 638 and 2523. *Cf.* J. JAMES; JOHN JAMES.

JAMES, A. C. Portrait painter at New Orleans in 1859. ¶ New Orleans BD 1859.

JAMES, A. R. Painter of a portrait of Abraham Lincoln, now hanging in the State House, Concord (N.H.). ¶ WPA (Mass.), *Portraits Found in N.H.*

JAMES, HENRY. Painter. So listed in the NYC directories 1855–56, James exhibited three oil paintings at the American Institute in 1856. He gave up painting shortly to go into business as a daguerreotypist and ambrotypist. ¶ NYCD 1855–60; Am. Inst. Cat., 1856.

JAMES, HENRY. Engraver at Trenton (N.J.) in 1860. ¶ N. J. BD 1860.

JAMES, J. Portrait painter at Charleston (S.C.) in February 1803 and January 1804. *Cf.* —— JAMES. ¶ Rutledge, *Artists in the Life of Charleston,* 128, 203.

JAMES, JAMES. Engraver, age 19, born in Pennsylvania; living in Philadelphia in 1860 with his mother Maria and brothers JOHN and THEODORE JAMES. ¶ 8 Census (1860), Pa., LVII, 358.

JAMES, JOHN. Portrait painter at NYC; exhibitor at the National Academy 1843 and 1845. The head in one portrait was stated to have been painted in 1811. *Cf.* —— JAMES and J. JAMES. ¶ Cowdrey, NAD; NYCD 1845.

JAMES, JOHN. Engraver, age 20, born in Pennsylvania; living in Philadelphia in 1860 with his mother Maria and brothers JAMES and THEODORE JAMES ¶ 8 Census (1860), Pa., LVIII, 358.

JAMES, S. C. Sculptor, Cincinnati, 1849. ¶ Cincinnati CD 1849 (courtesy Edward H. Dwight, Cincinnati Art Museum).

JAMES, THEODORE. Engraver, age 17, born in Pennsylvania; living in Philadelphia in 1860 with his mother Maria and brothers JAMES and JOHN JAMES. In 1871 Theodore James was listed as a clerk. ¶ 8 Census (1860), Pa., LVIII, 358; Phila. CD 1871.

JAMISON (or Jameson), GEORGE W. (?–1868). Artist, actor, and playwright. Jamison made his first appearance in NYC as the exhibitor of a frame of "Conchylia portraits" of Andrew Jackson and others at the 1835 National Academy show. For the next three years he was listed in the directories as a sculptor. He made his debut as an actor in 1837 and was a familiar figure on the NYC stage until his death in October 1868, at Yonkers (N.Y.). ¶ Cowdrey, NAD; NYCD 1836–46; Odell, *Annals of the New York Stage,* Vols. IV–VIII; Jameson, *The Jamesons in America,* 541.

JAMISON & JERVIS. Engravers at NYC, 1841.

The partners were JOHN P. JAMISON and WILLIAM JERVIS. ¶ NYBD and CD 1841.

JAMISON (or Jamieson), JOHN P. Engraver and lithographer who worked in NYC from 1841 to 1851 as an engraver, and in Buffalo (N.Y.) from 1855 to 1858 as a lithographer. See JAMISON & JERVIS and JAMISON & SCOTT. He was listed in the NYC census (1860) as a native of New York State, aged 40. ¶ NYCD 1841–48; NYBD 1841, 1851; Buffalo BD 1855–58, CD 1856; 8 Census (1860), N.Y., LXI, 754.

JAMISON & SCOTT. Lithographers at Buffalo (N.Y.), 1856. The firm was composed of JOHN P. JAMISON and JAMES B. SCOTT. ¶ Buffalo CD 1856.

JANET, HENRY. Sculptor at New Orleans in 1856. He was not a native Louisianan. ¶ Delgado-WPA cites *Courier,* Feb. 29, April 8, 1856.

JANVIER, ALBERT WILSON. Portrait painter, crayon artist; a resident of Philadelphia and exhibited at the Pennsylvania Academy from 1856 to 1861. In 1859 he was at Washington (D.C.). ¶ Rutledge, PA; Phila. CD 1857–60; Bolton, *Crayon Draftsmen;* Washington Art Assoc. Cat., 1859.

JANVIER, FRANCIS DE HAES (*c.* 1775–1824). Portrait and coach painter, musician, and poet of Princeton (N.J.), 1807–24. ¶ Woodward and Hageman, *History of Burlington and Mercer Counties, N.J.,* 653.

JAQUET, AUGUSTUS. Engraver of NYC, 1856–59. ¶ NYBD 1856–59.

JARDELLA, see IARDELLA.

JARDINE, JOSEPH P. Wood engraver, of HOLTON & JARDINE, at NYC 1856–58. ¶ NYCD 1856–58.

JARVASS, JACOB. Engraver at Cadiz (Ohio) in 1853. ¶ Ohio BD 1853.

JARVIS, CHARLES WESLEY (1812–1868). Portrait, miniature, and historical painter. The second son of JOHN WESLEY JARVIS, he was born in NYC, probably in 1812, and brought up by his mother's family, the Burtises of Oyster Bay, Long Island. About 1828 he was apprenticed to HENRY INMAN, with whom he worked in NYC and Philadelphia until 1834. Returning to NYC the younger Jarvis established himself as a portrait painter and worked there until his death, which occurred at his home in Newark (N.J.) on February 13, 1868. ¶ Dickson, *John Wesley Jarvis;* Newark *Daily Advertiser,* Feb. 15, 1868, and *Daily Journal,* Feb. 15, 1868 (obits.); NYCD 1835–67; Cowdrey, NAD; Cowdrey, AA & AAU; Wilson, *Lincoln in Portraiture;* represented NY City Hall and Md. Hist. Soc.; 7 Census (1850), N.Y., XLIII, 97.

JARVIS, JOHN WESLEY (1780–1840). Portrait and miniature painter, engraver, and sculptor; born in England in 1780 and baptized the following year at South Shields, near Newcastle-on-Tyne. The family emigrated to America about 1785 and settled in Philadelphia. From 1796 to 1801 John was apprenticed to the engraver EDWARD SAVAGE. At the end of his apprenticeship he moved to NYC where from 1802 to 1810 he painted portraits and miniatures in partnership with JOSEPH WOOD. He moved to Baltimore in 1810, but returned to NYC in 1813 and undertook to paint a series of full-length portraits of heroes of the War of 1812 for the New York City Hall. In 1814 he took as apprentice HENRY INMAN and later JOHN QUIDOR also studied briefly in Jarvis's studio. After 1820 he began to spend his winters in the South, particularly in New Orleans, Richmond, and Washington. Paralyzed in 1834, he spent his remaining years in NYC and died there on January 12, 1840. Jarvis was the foremost portrait painter of New York during the first quarter of the 19th century and was also noted in his day as a wit and raconteur. ¶ Dickson, *John Wesley Jarvis* (N.Y., 1949), is the standard life, with a bibliography, checklist, and many illustrations. See also: Bolton and Groce, "John Wesley Jarvis," with checklist; DAB; Rutledge, PA; Cowdrey, AA & AAU; Cowdrey, NAD; Swan, BA; Karolik Cat.; *Richmond Portraits;* Flexner, *The Light of Distant Skies.*

JARVIS, SAMUEL. Said to have painted a watercolor portrait of his father, Bishop Abraham Jarvis of Connecticut, at Middletown (Conn.), *c.* 1780. ¶ Sherman, "Unrecorded Early American Portrait Painters" (1933).

JARVIS & WOOD. Portrait and miniature painters of NYC, 1802–10. The partners were JOHN WESLEY JARVIS and JOSEPH WOOD. ¶ Dickson, *John Wesley Jarvis,* 64ff.

JAUME, ALEXANDER CHARLES (?–1858). Portrait and miniature painter and teacher, born in France between 1813 and 1816. He came to the United States as a young man and worked in New Orleans from 1838 until his death on January 19, 1858.

¶ New Orleans *Bee,* Jan. 20, 1858, obit. (cited by Delgado-WPA); 7 Census (1850), La., V, 432; New Orleans CD 1838–56; Thompson, *Louisiana Writers, Native and Resident.*

JAUME, J. Artist at New Orleans in 1842. *Cf.* A. C. JAUME, above. ¶ New Orleans CD 1842.

JAY, MARY. Amateur painter of NYC, who exhibited a portrait of Napoleon painted expressly for the American Institute Fair of 1849. ¶ Am. Inst. Cat., 1849.

JAY, ROBERT W. Artist of NYC, 1846–47. ¶ NYCD 1846–47.

JEANNERET, HENRY A. Engraver in NYC, 1855–58. After 1858 he was listed as a watchmaker. ¶ NYCD 1855–60; NYBD 1858.

JEANNERET, ULYSSE. Engraver in NYC, 1850–57; after 1857 as importer. In the 1850 Census as Ulysses Jeannet, Swiss, aged 25. ¶ NYCD 1851–60; NYBD 1854, 1856; 7 Census (1850), N.Y., XLII, 155.

JEANNIN, JEAN BAPTISTE (*c.* 1792–1863). Teacher of drawing and painting, who came from France to the United States in 1818, taught school in Charleston (S.C.) in 1820, and settled in New Orleans by November of that year. By 1838 he was president of Central College in New Orleans. He died in New Orleans on September 8, 1863. ¶ Delgado-WPA cites *La. Gazette,* Nov. 30, 1820, and Dec. 2, 1822, New Orleans CD 1838, and obit. in New Orleans *Bee,* Sept. 9, 1863. He is listed in Rutledge, *Artists in the Life of Charleston,* as T. B. Jeannin.

JEANNIN, T. B., see JEAN BAPTISTE JEANNIN.

JEFFERSON, JOSEPH, 2nd (1774–1832). Scene painter. The son of Joseph Jefferson, an English actor, he was born in 1774 at Plymouth and went on the stage as a child. In 1795 he emigrated to America, played for a year in Boston (Mass.), and then settled in NYC where he acted and painted scenery for the New or Park Theatre until 1803. After 1803 he was associated for many years with the Chestnut Street Theatre in Philadelphia. He died at Harrisburg (Pa.) in 1832. Among his survivors were his son JOSEPH, 3rd, and grandson, JOSEPH, 4th. ¶ Winter, *The Jeffersons,* 49–126; Wilson, *Joseph Jefferson,* 46–47.

JEFFERSON, JOSEPH, 3rd (1804–1842). Scene and sign painter. The third Joseph Jefferson, son of the above, was born in Philadelphia in 1804. He studied architecture and drawing and was for a time a pupil of ROBERT COYLE, an English scene painter in Philadelphia. After acting, managing, and painting for a number of eastern theaters in the 1820's and 1830's, he went west in 1839 and for the next three years worked in Chicago and Springfield (Ill.), Memphis (Tenn.), New Orleans (La.), and Mobile (Ala.). When the theatrical business was slack, he painted signs and ornamental work. He died in Mobile on November 24, 1842, when his famous son, JOSEPH JEFFERSON, 4th, was only thirteen years of age. ¶ Winter, *The Jeffersons,* 137–50; Wilson, *Joseph Jefferson,* 47.

JEFFERSON, JOSEPH, 4th (1829–1905). Landscape painter. Joseph Jefferson, fourth and most famous of the actors of that name, was born in Philadelphia on February 20, 1829. He made his stage debut about 1833 and continued to appear for over seventy years, making his last appearance in 1904. His most memorable characterization was Rip van Winkle. Throughout his life Jefferson was an enthusiastic amateur painter, particularly of landscapes. He exhibited at the Pennsylvania Academy in 1868 and at the National Academy in 1890, and in 1899 he was given a one-man exhibition in Washington (D.C.). He died at Palm Beach (Fla.) on April 23, 1905. ¶ Wilson, *Joseph Jefferson,* Chapter IV, contains much information on Jefferson's activity as an artist; also, Grace B. Agate, "Joseph Jefferson, Painter of the Teche," *National Historical Magazine* (Nov. 1938), 22–25; Rutledge, PA; DAB; CAB; *Art Annual,* V, obit.

JEFFERYS, THOMAS R. Sign, banner, and fancy painter in Baltimore from 1847 to 1865. In 1856 he exhibited "Landscapes and Figures" and "Arabs Dividing Booty" at the Maryland Historical Society. He also did panoramas on Babylon and Grecian mythology. ¶ Baltimore CD 1847–65; Rutledge, MHS; *Antiques* (Jan. 1945), 38–39; Baltimore *Sun,* Dec. 29, 1854, and June 4, 1858 (courtesy J. Earl Arrington).

JEFFRAYS, ——. Partner in the engraving firm of BLUM & JEFFRAYS, Philadelphia, 1857. ¶ Phila. CD 1857.

JEFFREY, BENJAMIN. Artist, age 22, at New Haven (Conn.) in 1850. ¶ 7 Census (1850), Conn., VIII, 551.

JENCKES, JOSEPH (1602–1683). Engraver of the dies for the "Pine tree shilling," 1652. A native of Colbrooke (England), Jenckes came to America in 1642 to establish the first foundry and forge in the colonies, at Lynn (now Saugus, Mass.). He was a versatile craftsman and made a number of machines, including the earliest American fire-engine. He died at Lynn on March 16, 1683. ¶ Belknap, *Artists and Craftsmen of Essex County,* 4; Stauffer; Fielding.

JENKINS, CHARLES WALDO. Portrait painter; born in New York about 1820. He first exhibited at the National Academy in 1842 as a resident of Utica (N.Y.) and thereafter as of NYC. He was listed in the directories until 1895. ¶ Cowdrey, NAD; NYCD 1849–95; Egbert, *Princeton Portraits;* 7 Census (1850), N.Y., LII, 324; 8 Census (1860), N.Y., LVII, 925.

JENKINS & COLBURN. Lithographers of Boston (Mass.), 1836–40. The firm was composed of DANIEL S. JENKINS and LUKE COLBURN. ¶ Peters, *America on Stone;* Drepperd, "Pictures with a Past," 96.

JENKINS, DANIEL S. Lithographer. He was with the Boston firm of JENKINS & COLBURN from 1836 to 1840, and in the latter year apparently moved to NYC. ¶ Peters, *America on Stone;* Boston CD 1837; NYBD 1840.

JENKINS, FRANCIS A. Engraver and lithographer of Boston, 1860 and after. ¶ Boston CD and BD 1860+.

JENKINS, GEORGE WASHINGTON ALLSTON (1816–1907). Portrait and genre painter. G. W. Jenkins and G. Jenkins exhibited at the National Academy between 1842 and 1865 and George W. Jenkins, artist, was listed in the NYC directory for 1850. His "Headless Horseman of Sleepy Hollow" is at Sleepy Hollow Restorations, Tarrytown (N.Y.). ¶ Full name and dates from *Art Index* (Oct. 1947–Sept. 1948), 243; Cowdrey, NAD; NYCD 1850; *American Collector* (Oct. 1947), 10, repro.

JENKINS, HARVEY. Portrait painter whose portrait of Mrs. Daniel Henderson (1782–1859) is owned by the Monmouth County Historical Society, Freehold (N.J.). This may be the H. Jenkins listed as a portrait painter active in 1850 by Lipman and Winchester. ¶ WPA (N.J.), Historical Records Survey; Lipman and Winchester, 175.

JENKINS, JOSEPH. Artist, age 40, living in Northern Liberties of Philadelphia in August 1850. Jenkins, his wife, and four children were born in Pennsylvania. ¶ 7 Census (1850), Pa., XLIX, 123.

JENKINS, J. S., SR. Profile painter. He was at New Orleans in 1840, visited Havana (Cuba) the following year, but returned to New Orleans by December 1841 and was there in 1842. J. S. Jenkins, Jr., was listed as a dentist in 1846. ¶ Delgado-WPA cites *Picayune,* Sept. 20, 1840, Dec. 7, 1841, and Jan. 20, 1842; New Orleans CD 1846.

JENKINS, P. O. Portrait painter, probably in Christian County (Ky.), about 1848. One signed canvas is known. ¶ Information courtesy Mrs. Ruth Davidson of *The Magazine Antiques.*

JENKINS, WALDO C., see CHARLES WALDO JENKINS.

JENKINSON, GEORGE W. Landscape and genre painter who exhibited at the National Academy in 1839. *Cf.* GEORGE W. A. JENKINS. ¶ Cowdrey, NAD.

JENKINSON, JOSEPH. Miniature and house painter of NYC, 1808–10. ¶ NYCD 1808–10 (cited by McKay).

JENKS, ALBERT (1824–1901). Portrait painter. A native of NYC, Col. Jenks died in Los Angeles (Cal.) on July 22, 1901. ¶ *Art Annual,* IV (1903/04), 141, obit.; Thieme-Becker; Bénézit.

JENKS, B. W. Portrait painter at New Orleans, 1843–44. This may well be the Jenks, portrait painter from New Orleans, who about 1840 worked for a short time in Cincinnati (Ohio) and Charleston (W. Va.) with WORTHINGTON WHITTREDGE. Jenks had been working in New Orleans in the winters and at White Sulphur Springs (Va.) in the summers. He was also at Cincinnati in 1842. ¶ New Orleans CD 1843–44; Baur, "Autobiography of Worthington Whittredge," 13; information courtesy Edward H. Dwight, Cincinnati Art Museum.

JENNER, WILLIAM. Landscape painter, awarded a diploma for a landscape exhibited at the American Institute in 1845. This may be William H. Jenner, teacher, listed in the NYC directories during the 1840's. ¶ Am. Inst. Cat. and *Trans.,* 1845; NYCD 1845–48.

JENNINGS, Mr. ——. Teacher of drawing and painting "on scientific principles," at Charleston (S.C.) in 1833. ¶ Rutledge, *Artists in the Life of Charleston.*

JENNINGS, J. S. Landscape painter at New Hudson (N.Y.), 1850. ¶ Lipman and Winchester, 175.

JENNINGS, SAMUEL. Portrait and miniature painter in oils and crayon, allegorical painter. A native of Philadelphia, he worked there from 1787 to about 1792 and then went to London where he engaged in the business of painting copies of the Old Masters for sale as originals. His allegorical painting of "Liberty Displaying the Arts and Sciences," painted in 1792 for the Library Company of Philadelphia, is still owned by the Library. ¶ Prime, II, 16–17; Dunlap, *History* (1918), II, 124–25; Scharf and Westcott, II, 1045; *American Processional,* 238.

JENNINGS, WILLIAM. American portrait painter, active about 1774 (Fielding); probably WILLIAM JENNYS.

JENNY, ——. Painter of a view of Bath (N.Y.), *c.* 1830. ¶ *Antiques* (May 1947), 307, repro.

JENNY (or Yenni), JOHANN HEINRICH. Topographical draftsman from Switzerland. He was in NYC about 1820 and painted a number of views in the city. Dunlap states that he later accompanied Commodore Stewart's expedition to the Pacific as draftsman. ¶ *Portfolio* (March 1945), 148 and frontis.; NYCD 1820 (as Yenni); Cowdrey, AA & AAU (as Yenni); Dunlap, *History,* II, 378 (as Yenni); Thieme-Becker (as Jenny).

JENNY (or Jenney), N. D. Portrait painter at Portland (Me.), *c.* 1850. His portrait of Samuel Wells (1801–1867) is owned by the Maine Historical Society. ¶ Maine Hist. Soc., *Cat.,* at FARL; Lipman and Winchester, 175.

JENNYS, J. WILLIAM, see WILLIAM JENNYS.

JENNYS, RICHARD. Portrait painter and mezzotint engraver, son of Richard Jennys, a Boston notary public who died in 1768. His earliest known work, a mezzotint portrait of Rev. Jonathan Mayhew of Boston, was published in 1766. In 1771 he advertised in Boston as a dealer in dry goods. He next appears at Charleston (S.C.) in 1783–84 as a portrait and miniature painter late of Boston and the West Indies. By 1792, possibly earlier, he was working in Connecticut and he was active there, chiefly around New Milford, until 1799. ¶ Sherman, *Richard Jennys;* Warren, "The Jennys Portraits" (with catalogue of a Jennys exhibition at the Conn. Hist. Soc., Nov. 1955–Jan. 1956); Warren, "A Checklist of Jennys Portraits"; Stauffer; Whitmore, *Notes Concerning Peter Pelham,* 21.

JENNYS, WILLIAM. Portrait painter working in and around New Milford (Conn.) in mid-1790's and at NYC in 1797–98. After 1800 he moved northward along the Connecticut Valley into Central Massachusetts and Vermont and eastward to Portsmouth (N.H.). Portraits once ascribed, through misreading of his signature, to "J. William Jennys" have been shown to be the work of William. ¶ Warren, "The Jennys Portraits" (with catalogue of a Jennys exhibition at the Conn. Hist. Soc., Nov. 1955–Jan. 1956); Warren, "A Checklist of Jennys Portraits"; Sherman, *Richard Jennys,* 65–67; Dods, "Newly Discovered Portraits by J. William Jennys"; Dods, "More About Jennys"; NYCD 1797–98.

JEROLOMEN, WILLIAM. Engraver from New Jersey, 27, at NYC in 1860. ¶ 8 Census (1860), N.Y., XLIV, 561.

JEROME, ELIZABETH GILBERT, Mrs. Benjamin N. (1824–1910). Portrait, figure, and miniature painter and crayon artist, born December 18, 1824, in New Haven (Conn.), the daughter of Hezekiah and Rebecca Driggs Gilbert. She studied in Hartford with JULIUS T. BUSCH about 1851 and in NYC briefly under EMANUEL LEUTZE and at the National Academy and the Springley Institute. She married Mr. Jerome about 1856 and made her home in Hartford for many years. In 1866–75 she exhibited at the National Academy and in 1869 at the Pennsylvania Academy. After the death of a daughter she gave up painting, but at the age of eighty she took up miniature painting. She died in New Haven on April 22, 1910. ¶ Letter of Thompson R. Harlow, Conn. Hist. Soc., to Anna Wells Rutledge, April 5, 1951 (NYHS files); French, *Art and Artists in Connecticut,* 169 (repro. opp.); Hartford CD 1860+; Rutledge, PA; Cowdrey, NAD.

JERVIS, WILLIAM. General and seal engraver of NYC, 1841–50; born in Pennsylvania about 1818. In 1841 he was with the firm of JAMISON & JERVIS. In 1844 he exhibited a frame of card engravings at the American Institute. ¶ NYBD 1841–46; NYCD 1842; Am. Inst. Cat., 1844; 7 Census (1850), N.Y., XLIV, 279.

JESSUP, EBENEZER. Engraver, 60, a native of New York, at NYC in 1860. ¶ 8 Census (1860), N.Y., XLIV, 510.

JESSUP, JARED. Wall and overmantel painter working in Connecticut and Massachusetts *c.* 1804–13. He probably was born in Easthampton, Long Island (N.Y.) and lived in Richmond (Mass.) for a few years before his marriage in 1802 at Guilford (Conn.). He appears to have taken up painting after his wife's death in 1804 and examples of his work have been found in houses at Stonington, Old Lyme, and Northford (Conn.), and at Deerfield and Bernardston (Mass.). ¶ Little, *American Decorative Wall Painting,* 85–93, repros.

JEWETT, CHARLES A. (1816–1878). Line engraver of subject plates. He was born at Lancaster (Mass.) in 1816 and commenced engraving in NYC about 1838. From 1850 to 1857 he worked in Cincinnati, part of the time as an employee of TOPPAN, CASILEAR & Co. By 1860 he had returned to NYC where he died in 1878. ¶ Stauffer; NYBD 1844; Cincinnati BD 1850–53, CD 1856–57.

JEWETT, FREDERICK STILES (1819–1864). Marine and landscape painter, drawing teacher; born February 26, 1819, at Simsbury (Conn.). At sixteen he went on a two-year whaling voyage, after which he settled in Hartford (Conn.), where he was for a short time editor of the *New England Weekly Review*. From *c.* 1841 to 1853/54 he lived in the West Indies where he is reported to have worked as a journalist. Ill health forced his return to Hartford. There he worked as an insurance agent and in his spare time took up marine and landscape painting. In 1856 he was listed in the Hartford directory as "Artist and Instructor in all the branches of Drawing and Painting." His work, highly regarded locally, was shown at the Wadsworth Athenaeum, the Yale University Art Gallery (1858), and the National Academy (1859–63). In 1864 he moved to Cleveland (Ohio) as western representative of the Connecticut Insurance Company. He died there after a three-months illness on December 26, 1864, and was buried in Simsbury (Conn.). ¶ Information courtesy Dr. Elliot A. P. Evans, who cites: Frederick Clark Jewett, *The Jewett Family in America* (Rowley, Mass., 1908), II, 576; "Obituary," *Hartford Daily Courant,* Dec. 28, 1864; "Resolutions," Common Council Board, *ibid.,* Dec. 30, 1864; "Funeral Notice," *ibid.,* Jan. 2, 1865; Hartford CD 1840, 1854–63; *Commemorative Biographical Record of Hartford County, Conn.* (Chicago, 1901), I, 608; French, *Art and Artists in Connecticut,* 103–04; *Catalogue of the Works of Art Exhibited in the Alumni Building, Yale College, 1858* (New Haven, 1858), #161 (citation courtesy Miss Anna Wells Rutledge); Cowdrey, NAD; represented Hartford Club, Hartford. A "View of Simsbury," attributed to W. S. JEWETT in *Panorama,* IV, 51, is certainly by F. S. Jewett.

JEWETT, WILLIAM (1789/90–1874). A.N.A. Portrait, genre, and landscape painter, born in East Haddam (Conn.), January 14, 1789 or 1790. Before completing his apprenticeship to a coachmaker in New London (Conn.), he bought his release in 1812 in order to study portrait painting in NYC under SAMUEL LOVETT WALDO. By 1818 the latter had taken his pupil into partnership and, as WALDO & JEWETT, they collaborated until 1854, both at the same time also doing individual work. Jewett was elected an American Academician in 1825 and an Associate of the National Academy in 1847. In 1854 he retired to his farm in what is now Bergen (N.J.) and he died there on March 24, 1874. His son, WILLIAM SAMUEL LYON JEWETT, also was an artist. ¶ Information courtesy Dr. Elliot A. P. Evans, who cites: Ms. *Family Record;* death certificate and burial record, New York Bay Cemetery; Jewett, *Jewetts of America,* I, 331; Dunlap, *History;* Jersey City *Evening Journal,* March 25, 1874, obit.; inventory of Jewett estate, Superior Court of N.J.; NYCD 1820–55; Cowdrey, AA & AAU; Cowdrey, NAD; Cummings, *Historic Annals;* DAB; information courtesy Mrs. Edith Jewett Marvin Herrmann.

JEWETT, WILLIAM S. or SMITH (1812–1873). A.N.A. Portrait, religious, landscape, and genre painter; born August 6, 1812, at South Dover, Dutchess County (N.Y.). He was active as a portrait painter in NYC from 1833 to 1849, during which time he exhibited at the National Academy and the American Art-Union. From 1841 his studio was at New York University. He was elected an Associate of the National Academy in 1845. He evidently abandoned a promising career in NYC when he embarked with the "Hope" Company for San Francisco in May 1849. Though he may have intended to make his fortune in business or mining in California, he became instead California's first professional portrait painter. He maintained studios both in San Francisco (1850–69) and in Sacramento (1850–55) and turned out many landscapes and subject paintings as well as portraits. In September 1869 he returned to NYC, affluent and retired. The following year he married, returned briefly to California, and then went abroad. His only child, William Dunbar Jewett, who became a sculptor, landscape painter, and writer, was born in England in 1873. Soon after returning to the United States, Jewett died at Springfield (Mass.) on December 3, 1873. ¶ Information courtesy Dr. Elliot A. P. Evans, who cites: Preston-Jewett family Bible, Register of Births (owned by Mrs. L. B. Cleaver, Los Angeles); "Obituaries," Springfield (Mass.) *Republican,* Dec. 5, 1873; tombstone of W. S. Jewett in Springfield Cemetery; Cowdrey, NAD; Cowdrey, AA & AAU; NYCD 1833–37, 1845–49; San Francisco CD 1852–70; Sacramento (Cal.) *Union,* Sept. 10, 1851; Sacramento *Bee,* Oct. 21, 1885; Peters, *California on Stone;* Nelson, "The Jewetts, William and William S."; Nelson, "A Case of Confused Identity"; Van Nostrand and Coulter, *California Pictorial,* 116; Elliot Evans, "Some Letters of W. S. Jewett"; Elliot Evans, "William S. and William D. Jewett"; San Francisco *Alta California,* Jan. 13, 1876; paintings and letters owned by descendants. Represented NAD, De Young Museum (San Francisco), Sutter's Fort and State Capitol (Sacramento), Bowers Memorial Museum (Santa Ana).

JEWETT, WILLIAM SAMUEL LYON (1834–1876). Portrait painter, newspaper illustrator, and engraver (?). The only child of WILLIAM and Mary Lyon Jewett, he was born in NYC in May 1834. He was working in NYC as early as 1854 but his home, at least after 1858, was in Bergen (N.J.). As a correspondent for *Leslie's Illustrated Newspaper* he gained notoriety in 1859 during the trial of John Brown when he was expelled from Charleston (Va., now W. Va.) under suspicion of being a correspondent for the *New York Tribune.* Engravings and sketches, signed W. S. L. J. or W. J., appeared in *Harper's Weekly* and *Leslie's* from 1859 to 1876 and at least twenty of the portraits in *Harper's History of the Great Rebellion* were drawn by him. His only known oil portraits, mainly dating from his student days, are owned by his descendants. Although he came into an estate of about $150,000 on the death of his parents in 1874, Jewett's last years were marked by periods of worry and depression. He died of a pistol wound at his home in Bergen on July 23, 1876, and was survived by his wife, Mary Sikes Bliss Jewett (1834–1891) and three daughters. ¶ Information courtesy Dr. Elliot A. P. Evans, who cites: "Obituary," Jersey City *Evening Journal,* July 24, 1876; "Death Record," Bureau of Vital Statistics, Department of Health, N.J.; inventory of W. S. L. Jewett estate, No. 26701, Superior Court of N.J.; repros. in *Harper's Weekly,* Jan. 13, 1866 (portrait of Edwin Booth), and July 13, 1876 ("Waiting, a Scene in the Brooklyn Old Ladies' Home"); Milton Kaplan, comp., *Pictorial Americana . . .* (Library of Congress, 1945), p. 10, repro. of drawing by W. S. L. Jewett; *New York Tribune,* Nov. 17, 1859, p. 3, col. 4 (John Brown incident); information courtesy Mrs. Edith Jewett Marvin Herrmann of Brooklyn (N.Y.); NYBD 1854; Jersey City CD 1858; NYCD 1870; *Harper's History of the Great Rebellion* (N.Y., 1866).

JEWITT, W. J., is WILLIAM S. JEWETT.

JOB, LEON. Portrait and figure painter, pastellist, and lithographer. He was listed at a NYC address in 1857 when he exhibited at the National Academy. ¶ Cowdrey, NAD.

JOCELIN & MUNGER. Copperplate engravers at New Haven (Conn.) *c.* 1816. The firm was composed of NATHANIEL JOCELYN and GEORGE MUNGER. ¶ *American Collector* (March 1941), 7, repro.

JOCELIN, SIMEON (1746–1823). Engraver and clockmaker; father of NATHANIEL JOCELYN. He was born October 22, 1746, in New Haven (Conn.) and worked there from about 1768 until his death on June 5, 1823. His work as an engraver included the plates for the *Chorister's Song Books,* published between 1782 and 1791 by Jocelin alone and with AMOS DOOLITTLE. ¶ Rice, "Life of Nathaniel Jocelyn."

JOCELYN, ALBERT H. Wood engraver, active in NYC 1849–60. He was associated with the following firms: CHILDS & JOCELYN (1849–50), JOCELYN & PURCELL (1851), WHITNEY, JOCELYN & ANNIN (1853–54), and WHITNEY & JOCELYN (1856–58). ¶ NYCD 1849–60; Hamilton, 209, 220.

JOCELYN, DRAPER, WELSH & CO. Banknote engravers, NYC, 1854–58, also known as American Bank Note Company. This was the NYC branch of DRAPER, WELSH & Co. of Philadelphia. It was formed in 1854 by NATHANIEL and SIMEON STARR JOCELYN and in 1858 joined the new AMERICAN BANK NOTE COMPANY. ¶ Toppan, *100 Years of Bank-Note Engraving,* 12; Rice,

"Life of Nathaniel Jocelyn"; NYCD 1856–58.

JOCELYN, NATHANIEL (1796–1881). N.A. Engraver, portrait and miniature painter. Born January 31, 1796, at New Haven (Conn.), Nathaniel Jocelyn (or Jocelin) was the son of SIMEON JOCELIN, clockmaker and engraver. He was apprenticed to a clockmaker but about 1813 took up engraving under GEORGE MUNGER. About 1816 they published at least one print under the name JOCELIN & MUNGER. Jocelyn was next associated with the HARTFORD GRAPHIC & BANK NOTE ENGRAVING CO. In 1818 he and his brother SIMEON SMITH JOCELYN went into partnership as N. & S. S. JOCELYN, a collaboration which continued until 1843. From 1820 to 1822 Nathaniel was in Savannah (Ga.) and on his return to New Haven he established himself as a portrait painter. In 1829 he visited England and France. He had a portrait studio in NYC from 1843 to 1847, but after the burning of his New Haven studio in 1849 he gave up painting and joined the NYC banknote engraving firm of TOPPAN, CARPENTER & CO. With his nephew, SIMEON STARR JOCELYN, he founded in 1854 the firm of JOCELYN, DRAPER, WELSH & CO., New York branch of DRAPER, WELSH & CO. of Philadelphia. Both Jocelyns went with this firm into the AMERICAN BANK NOTE COMPANY in 1858. Nathaniel retired in 1864 and died at New Haven on January 13, 1881. ¶ Foster W. Rice, "Life of Nathaniel Jocelyn, 1796–1881, and the Jocelyn Engravers," MS, cited courtesy of the author; Sherman, "Nathaniel Jocelyn, Engraver and Portrait Painter"; Rice, "Nathaniel Jocelyn, Painter and Engraver"; DAB; Cowdrey, NAD; Cowdrey, AA & AAU; Stauffer; obit., Boston *Transcript,* Jan. 17, 1881; NYBD 1844–46; NYCD 1852–58.

JOCELYN, N. & S. S. Banknote engravers of New Haven (Conn.), 1818–43. The brothers NATHANIEL and SIMEON SMITH JOCELYN worked together as an independent company and as agents for FAIRMAN, DRAPER, UNDERWOOD & CO. (1822–29), for BALCH, STILES & CO. (1829–30), for DRAPER, UNDERWOOD, BALD & SPENCER (1830–40), and for RAWDON, CLARK & CO. A branch of N. & S. S. Jocelyn was established in NYC about 1834. The partnership was dissolved in 1843. ¶ Rice, "Life of Nathaniel Jocelyn."

JOCELYN & PURCELL. Wood engravers in NYC, 1850–51. The partners were ALBERT H. JOCELYN and, probably, EDWARD PURCELL. ¶ NYBD 1851; Hamilton, 209.

JOCELYN, SIMEON SMITH (1799–1879). Banknote and general engraver; son of SIMEON JOCELIN and younger brother of NATHANIEL JOCELYN; born on November 21, 1799, at New Haven (Conn.). He was working as an engraver as early as 1817 and the following year went into partnership with his brother as N. & S. S. JOCELYN, the collaboration continuing until about 1843. S. S. Jocelyn engraved a number of portraits painted by his brother. During the 1840's and early 1850's he was associated with the following banknote engraving firms: DRAPER, TOPPAN & CO. (1840–44), TOPPAN, CARPENTER & CO. (after 1844), and TOPPAN, CARPENTER, CASILEAR & CO. (*c.* 1850–53). In 1853 he gave up engraving to become secretary of the American Missionary Society and to take a more active role in the antislavery movement, in which he had been interested since 1831. He died at Tarrytown (N.Y.) on August 17, 1879. ¶ Rice, "Life of Nathaniel Jocelyn"; Stauffer; obit., *New York Herald,* Aug. 19, 1879; Cowdrey, NAD; New Haven CD 1834–43; NYCD 1844–60.

JOCELYN, SIMEON STARR. Banknote engraver. Simeon Starr Jocelyn, also known as Simeon S. Jocelyn, Jr., was the son of SIMEON SMITH JOCELYN. He entered the firm of TOPPAN, CARPENTER, CASILEAR & CO. in 1852 as a clerk. The following year he joined with his uncle, NATHANIEL JOCELYN, to establish the firm of JOCELYN, DRAPER, WELSH & CO., New York branch of DRAPER, WELSH & CO. of Philadelphia. From 1858 to 1864, he was a member of the AMERICAN BANK NOTE COMPANY. ¶ Rice, "Life of Nathaniel Jocelyn"; NYCD 1852–60.

JOHN, AUGUSTUS. Landscape painter and teacher of drawing, at Baltimore, 1849–50. He was a native of Prussia, born about 1821. He exhibited at the Maryland Historical Society in 1849. ¶ 7 Census (1850), Md., V, 642; Rutledge, MHS.

JOHN, CH. A. Painter of a portrait of Charles Stockton, owned (1940) by Albert Stockton of Pleasantville (N.J.). The painting is inscribed: "Ch. A. John, Painted 1847." *Cf.* AUGUSTUS JOHN and Charles John, artist, listed in NYC business directory for 1884–85. ¶ WPA (N.J.), Historical Records Survey; NYBD 1884–85.

JOHNS, CHRISTIAN. Wall painter in imitation

of paper, in oils or watercolors, at Philadelphia in 1823. ¶ Phila. *Columbian Observer,* May 28, 1823 (citation courtesy Helen McKearin).

JOHNS, JOSEPH W. Landscape and genre painter of Philadelphia; exhibitor, Pennsylvania Academy 1858–69. ¶ Rutledge, PA.

JOHNS, WILLIAM. Artist of Boston, in partnership with THOMAS C. SAVORY in 1837. ¶ Boston CD 1837.

JOHNSON, ——. Artist of Charleston (S.C.) who exhibited at Savannah (Ga.) in December 1858 mechanical and painted dioramas of naval battles. ¶ Savannah *Republican,* Dec. 15, 1858 (courtesy J. Earl Arrington).

JOHNSON, Mrs. ——. Figure painter of NYC who exhibited "Hebe" at the National Academy in 1837. ¶ Cowdrey, NAD.

JOHNSON, ANN. Watercolor painter working in Connecticut *c.* 1810–25. ¶ *American Folk Art,* no. 101 (repro. p. 29); Lipman and Winchester, 175.

JOHNSON, BENJAMIN, see BENJAMIN JOHNSTON.

JOHNSON, C. A. Amateur topographical artist of Blooming Grove (Wis.). His "First House Built in Madison" was hung in the Wisconsin Historical Society between 1857 and 1859. ¶ Butts, *Art in Wisconsin,* 95.

JOHNSON, CHARLES E. Engraver of SPIEGLE & JOHNSON, Philadelphia, 1855–57. ¶ Phila. CD and BD 1855–57.

JOHNSON, CHARLES F. Engraver at Philadelphia, 1850–60 and after. He was born in Pennsylvania about 1827 and had his residence in Camden (N.J.) from 1853. ¶ 7 Census (1850), Pa., LIII, 435; Phila. CD 1852–60+; Camden CD 1853–60+.

JOHNSON, DAVID (1827–1908). N.A. Landscape painter. He was born in NYC on May 10, 1827, studied under CROPSEY, and first exhibited at the National Academy and the American Art-Union in 1849. His professional life was spent chiefly in NYC, though he made numerous sketching trips into New England and up-state New York. He was made a National Academician in 1861. He died January 30, 1908, at Walden (N.Y.). He was a brother of JOSEPH HOFFMAN JOHNSON. ¶ *Art Annual,* VII, obit.; Clement and Hutton; Cowdrey, NAD; Cowdrey, AA & AAU; Born, *American Landscape Painting,* fig. 41, 66; Champlin and Perkins; 8 Census (1860), N.Y., LVII, 272.

JOHNSON, DAVID G. Portrait painter and engraver at NYC, 1831–35, 1843–45. ¶ Stauffer; NYCD 1831–35, 1843, 1845.

JOHNSON, EASTMAN (1824–1906). N.A. Genre and portrait painter. Jonathan Eastman Johnson (he rarely used his first name) was born in Lowell (Me.) in August 1824 and spent much of his boyhood in Augusta, his father being Secretary of State of Maine. At 16 he went to Boston and for about a year was employed in BUFFORD's lithographic shop. Dissatified with lithography, he took up crayon portraiture and with great success; from 1841 to 1849 he worked as a portraitist in Augusta (Me.), Cambridge (Mass.), Newport (R.I.), and Washington (D.C.). In 1849 he went to Europe. After two years with LEUTZE at Düsseldorf and visits to France and Italy, he studied for almost four years at The Hague where he was known as the "American Rembrandt" and was offered the post of Court Painter. Returning to the United States in 1855, Eastman Johnson painted in Wisconsin for two seasons (1856, 1857), in Cincinnati (1858), and in Washington (D.C.) before settling permanently in NYC about 1859. His well-known "The Old Kentucky Home" was painted in Washington and won him election to the National Academy, as an Associate in 1859 and an Academician in 1860. He began to visit Nantucket, the source of many of his best rural genre paintings, early in the 1870's. After the 1880's he painted few genre pictures, though his successful career as a portrait painter continued to the very end of his life. He died in NYC on April 5, 1906. ¶ John I. H. Baur, *An American Genre Painter: Eastman Johnson, 1824–1906,* includes a biographical sketch, exhibition catalogue and 42 plates; Johnson's work in Nantucket is detailed in Everett U. Crosby, *Eastman Johnson at Nantucket,* with checklist and numerous plates. See also: DAB; Karolik Cat.; Swan, BA; Cowdrey, NAD; Cowdrey, AA & AAU; Rutledge, PA; Baur, "Eastman Johnson, Artist-Reporter"; Heilbron, "A Pioneer Artist on Lake Superior."

JOHNSON, EDW. Engraver born in Pennsylvania, age 36, residing in Philadelphia in July 1860, with his wife Annie and three sons: Charles (12), Francis (8) and Theodore (4). ¶ 8 Census (1860), Pa., LIV, 310.

JOHNSON, FROST, see SAMUEL FROST JOHNSON.

JOHNSON, GUY (*c.* 1740–1788). Topographical artist. A native of Ireland, Guy Johnson came to America as early as 1756 and assisted his uncle, Sir William Johnson, as secretary and deputy agent for Indian affairs during the French and Indian War. It was at this time that he drew a view of Fort Johnson (N.Y.) later engraved and published in London as "A North View of Fort Johnson drawn on the spot by Mr. Guy Johnson, in Oct. 1759." After marrying Sir William's daughter and settling near Amsterdam (N.Y.), he became Superintendent of the Northern Department in 1774. He was loyal to the Crown in the Revolution and at its conclusion returned to England. He died in London on March 5, 1788. ¶ DAB; DNB; *Portfolio* (Feb. 1952), 137, repro.

JOHNSON, HAMLIN. Portrait painter in watercolors, active *c.* 1845 at Litchfield (Conn.). ¶ Lipman and Winchester, 175.

JOHNSON, HENRY. Drawing master from Hamburg (Germany), age 30, at San Francisco in July 1860. His property was valued at $6,000 in realty and $1,000 in personalty. His wife Ellen was Irish and their two-year-old daughter was born in California. ¶ 8 Census (1860), Cal., VII, 115; San Francisco CD 1861.

JOHNSON, HORACE CHAUNCEY. Portrait painter, born February 1, 1820, at Oxford (Conn.). He studied in Hartford with A. H. EMMONS, in NYC with S. F. B. MORSE and at the National Academy, and from 1856 to 1858 with WILLIAM PAGE in Rome. After his return from Italy, he settled in Waterbury (Conn.) where he was active as late as 1886. ¶ CAB; Clement and Hutton; French, 123; Hartford CD 1851; Fielding.

JOHNSON, J. E., is EASTMAN JOHNSON.

JOHNSON, JAMES. Lithographer associated with JACOBS & JOHNSON of NYC, 1859–61. ¶ NYBD 1859–61; NYCD 1860.

JOHNSON, JAMES. Maryland engraver, age 21, living in Baltimore in 1860. ¶ 8 Census (1860), Md., III, 230; Baltimore CD 1859.

JOHNSON, JAMES. Irish lithographer, age 26, living in Philadelphia in June 1860. He owned personal property valued at $6,000. ¶ 8 Census (1860), Pa., LIX, 107.

JOHNSON, JOHN. Artist from Baden (Germany), age 28, living in Boston in June 1860. ¶ 8 Census (1860), Mass., XXV, 14.

JOHNSON, JOHN, see JOHN JOHNSTON.

JOHNSON, JOHN R., see JOHN R. JOHNSTON.

JOHNSON, JONATHAN EASTMAN, see EASTMAN JOHNSON.

JOHNSON, JOSEPH HOFFMAN (1821–1890). Portrait painter, born in New York, working in NYC from the early 1840's to 1890. He exhibited at the American Institute in 1847. DAVID JOHNSON was his brother. ¶ Fielding; NYCD 1843–90; Am. Inst. Cat., 1847; repro. of two fire-engine panels in *Antiques* (Nov. 1937), 246–47; 8 Census (1860), N.Y., LVII, 272.

JOHNSON, LAURENCE. Wood engraver and stereotype founder. He had a stereotype foundery in Philadelphia from 1825 to 1847. In the latter year he formed the firm of L. Johnson & Co. In 1860 and after the firm was listed as wood engravers. ¶ Phila. CD 1847–60+.

JOHNSON, LYTLE W. Engraver, 33, a native of New York, at NYC in 1860. ¶ 8 Census (1860), N.Y., LIV, 442; NYCD 1863.

JOHNSON, NEVILLE. English wood engraver, born about 1808. He was working in Baltimore as early as 1836, in Philadelphia in 1838, again in Baltimore during the 1850's and in Philadelphia in 1860. His wife and two children were born in Maryland, the children about 1836. ¶ 7 Census (1850), Md., IV, 269; Phila. BD 1838, 1860; Baltimore BD 1852, 1857–58.

JOHNSON, S. D. Amateur landscape painter in water colors, active *c.* 1820. ¶ Lipman and Winchester, 175.

JOHNSON, SAMUEL. Painter at Philadelphia in 1717. ¶ Weiss, "The Growth of the Graphic Arts in Philadelphia 1663–1820," 77.

JOHNSON, SAMUEL FROST (1835–?). Still life, portrait, genre, and religious painter, born in NYC on November 9, 1835. After study in Milwaukee (Wis.) and at the National Academy in NYC, Frost Johnson went to Europe in 1859 for further study at Düsseldorf, Antwerp, and Paris. He subsequently had a studio in London for some years but returned to the United States in the 1870's to become professor of art and science at Fordham and at the Metropolitan Museum of Art in NYC. ¶ CAB; Clement and Hutton.

JOHNSON, THOMAS, see THOMAS JOHNSTON.

JOHNSON, WILLIAM. Engraver at Philadelphia, 1808–10: at NYC, 1810–17. ¶ Brown and Brown; NYCD 1810–17 (cited by McKay).

JOHNSON, WILLIAM. German lithographer, 40, at NYC in 1850. He was married and had a daughter, aged 12, who was born in New York. ¶ 7 Census (1850), N.Y., LI, 67.

JOHNSON, WILLIAM. Engraver and die-sinker at Covington (Ky.) in 1860. ¶ Cincinnati BD 1860.

JOHNSON, WILLIAM B. Steel plate engraver at Hartford (Conn.), 1849–60. ¶ Hartford CD 1849–60.

JOHNSON, WILLIAM T. (or W. T.). Engraver and/or watercolorist. W. T. Johnson was listed by Stauffer as engraver of subject plates for *Sartain's Magazine, c.* 1850. This may have been the William T. Johnson of Philadelphia who exhibited a water color drawing at the American Institute in 1849. ¶ Stauffer; Fielding; Am. Inst. Cat., 1849.

JOHNSTON (or Johnson), BENJAMIN (1740–1818). Portrait [?] and heraldic painter, japanner. Benjamin, son of THOMAS JOHNSTON, was born in Boston on September 7, 1740, and apparently trained by his versatile father. By 1775 he had moved to Newburyport, where he lived until his death on August 30, 1818. Benjamin Johnston was probably the artist and engraver of the 1775 "North East View of the Town and Harbour of Newbury Port" and Coburn suggests that many portraits in the lower Merrimack Valley may have been painted by him. ¶ Coburn, "The Johnstons of Boston," Part II, 133.

JOHNSTON, Mrs. D. Miniaturist and art teacher. The daughter of an English miniaturist, Mrs. D. Johnston opened a studio in Milwaukee (Wis.) in 1851 and taught at Milwaukee College. Her daughter, Mrs. James T. Kavanagh, studied with her and began her career as a portrait painter in 1865. ¶ Butts, *Art in Wisconsin,* 126–27.

JOHNSTON, DAVID CLAYPOOLE (1799–1865). Comic illustrator, engraver, and lithographer. He was born in March 1799 in Philadelphia and was apprenticed in 1815 to the engraver FRANCIS KEARNEY. At the conclusion of his apprenticeship he set up his own establishment in Philadelphia and produced a number of satirical prints which aroused considerable resentment in the city. Temporarily abandoning the burin, Johnson went on the stage in 1821, but about 1826, having meanwhile moved to Boston, he resumed his artistic career. He quickly became popular as a book illustrator, engraver, and lithographer, and won the title of "the American Cruikshank," after the English illustrator by whom he was greatly influenced. The latter half of Johnston's career was passed in Boston and he died at Dorchester on November 8, 1865. His son, THOMAS MURPHY JOHNSTON, a crayon portraitist, survived his father by only four years. ¶ DAB; Nevins and Weitenkampf, *A Century of Political Cartoons;* Stauffer; Peters, *America on Stone;* Swan, BA; Cowdrey, AA & AAU; Rutledge, PA; Cowdrey, NAD; Boston BD 1841–60; Thieme-Becker; 7 Census (1850), Mass., XXV, 567.

JOHNSTON, HENRIETTA (?–1728/29). Pastel portraitist, active in Charleston (S.C.) *c.* 1707–29. Henrietta Johnston, the first American pastellist and probably the first woman artist to work in America, came to Charleston about 1707 as the wife of the Reverend Mr. Gideon Johnston, Commissary of the Bishop of London in South Carolina and Rector of St. Philip's in Charleston. Mrs. Johnston eked out the family income by executing pastel portraits of the local aristocracy and made at least one trip to New York about 1725 for the same purpose. She died in Charleston on March 9, 1728/29. ¶ Rutledge, "Who Was Henrietta Johnston"; Rutledge, *Artists in the Life of Charleston,* 111; Keyes, "Coincidence and Henrietta Johnston"; Willis, "Henrietta Johnston, South Carolina Pastellist"; DAB; Bolton, *Crayon Draftsmen.*

JOHNSTON (or Johnson), JOHN (1753–1818). Portrait painter, pastellist, and figure painter. A son of THOMAS JOHNSTON, John was born in Boston (Mass.) in 1753, worked there as a painter *c.* 1789–1809, and died there on June 29, 1818. ¶ Coburn, "The Johnstons of Boston," Parts I and II, with repros. and checklist; Boston CD 1789–1809; Dresser, "The Thwing Likenesses"; CAB; Fielding; Swan, BA; Dunlap, *History.*

JOHNSTON, JOHN M. Engraver, 17, a native of New York, at NYC in 1850. ¶ 7 Census (1850), N.Y., XLVII, 493.

JOHNSTON (or Johnson), JOHN R. Portrait, historical, and landscape painter, sculptor, born in Ohio in the early 1820's. He was living in Cincinnati as early as 1842, assisted HENRY LEWIS with the latter's Mississippi panorama in 1848–49, and was still in Cincinnati as late as 1853. By 1857 he had moved to Baltimore where he was active until 1872. ¶ 7 Census (1850), Ohio, XX, 656; 8 Census (1860), Md., V, 504; Cincinnati CD 1850–53;

Cist, *Cincinnati in 1851;* Arrington, "Nauvoo Temple," Chap. 8; Baltimore CD 1858–72; Pleasants, *250 Years of Painting in Maryland,* 11; *Antiques,* 32 (Aug. 1937), 84, repro.; represented at MHS (Rutledge).

JOHNSTON (or Johnson), JOSHUA. Portrait painter working in Baltimore, 1796–1824. A Negro, Joshua Johnston was the first of his race known to have practised portrait painting in the United States. ¶ Pleasants, *An Early Baltimore Negro Portrait Painter, Joshua Johnston;* Hunter, "Joshua Johnston: 18th Century Negro Artist," six repros.; Lafferty; *Life,* IX (Dec. 9, 1940), 76; Pleasants, *250 Years of Painting in Maryland,* 35; represented MHS (Rutledge).

JOHNSTON (or Johnson), THOMAS (*c.* 1708–1767). Portrait and heraldic painter, japanner, and engraver. Born in Boston *c.* 1708, and worked there until his death on May 8, 1767. His earliest signed work is a map of Boston *c.* 1727–29. He was best known as a topographical, map, and music engraver and japanner, though he also built organs and is thought to have painted some portraits. In Johnston's shop JOHN GREENWOOD received his first training, as did Johnston's own sons—BENJAMIN, JOHN, WILLIAM, and THOMAS, JR., and his son-in-law DANIEL REA, JR. Still another son, Samuel, apparently gave up painting to become a master mariner. ¶ Coburn, "The Johnstons of Boston," especially Part I; DAB; Tuckerman; Stauffer; *American Processional,* 51.

JOHNSTON, THOMAS, JR. (1731–?). Painter and japanner, born in Boston on July 4, 1731. He was a son of THOMAS JOHNSTON the engraver and worked in Boston as a painter, japanner, and organ builder. He served on the Canada expedition of 1759. ¶ Coburn, "The Johnstons of Boston," Part II, 132.

JOHNSTON, THOMAS MURPHY (1834–1869). Crayon and oil portraitist. A son of the noted illustrator DAVID CLAYPOOLE JOHNSTON, he was born in Boston in 1834 and studied drawing there under his father, WILLIAM MORRIS HUNT, and SAMUEL ROWSE. In 1860 he was commissioned to do a crayon portrait of Lincoln in Springfield (Ill.). He did some lithographic work, then turned to landscape and religious painting. In 1868 he went to France for further study, but he died in Paris on February 28, 1869, at the age of 33. ¶ Wilson, *Lincoln in Portraiture,* 103–05; 7 Census (1850), Mass., XXV, 567; Swan, BA; Rutledge, PA; represented American Antiquarian Society.

JOHNSTON, WALTER R. A portrait by this artist is (1947) in the basement of the Executive Mansion, Albany (N.Y.). Information on the artist would be appreciated by the New York State Archivist. ¶ Hugh M. Flick to George C. Groce, March 4, 1947.

JOHNSTON, WILLIAM (1732–1772). Portrait painter, born December 30, 1732, in Boston, where his father, THOMAS JOHNSTON, was a well-known japanner and organbuilder. He was trained in his father's shop and began his career as a portrait painter in the 1750's. He is known to have worked at Portsmouth (N.H.) about 1759–61 and in 1762, at New London (Conn.) in 1762–63, and at Hartford, New Haven, and other central Connecticut towns in 1763–64. He was married at Boston in 1766, but some time before 1770 he went to the island of Barbados. He died at Bridge Town on August 14 or 15, 1772. ¶ Lyman, "William Johnston (1732–1772), a Forgotten Portrait Painter of New England"; Sawitzky, "The Portraits of William Johnston, a Preliminary Checklist"; Thomas, "William Johnston, Colonial Portrait Painter"; [Harlow], "William Johnston, Portrait Painter, 1732–1772" and "Some Comments on William Johnston."

JOHNSTON, WILLIAM L. Architect of Philadelphia who exhibited watercolor views and designs at the Artists' Fund Society in the early 1840's. ¶ Rutledge, PA; Phila. CD 1841–47.

JOHNSTON, WILLIAM M. (1821–1907). Portrait and landscape painter. A native of NYC, he was working there as early as 1849 and died in Brooklyn on April 30, 1907. In 1856 he was at Boston. ¶ *Art Annual,* VI (1907/08), 110, obit.; NYCD 1849; New England BD 1856.

JOINER, JOHN J. Engraver of NYC, 1852–54. ¶ NYBD 1852–54.

JONES, ——. Portrait painter at NYC in 1818. ¶ NYCD 1818.

JONES, A. L., see W. S. LAWRENCE.

JONES, ALFRED (1819–1900). N.A. Line engraver, portrait and genre painter. He was born April 7, 1819, in Liverpool (England) and came to America as a young man. After serving his apprenticeship with the banknote engraving firm of RAWDON,

WRIGHT, HATCH & EDSON, first in Albany, then in NYC, Jones embarked on a highly successful career as a vignette engraver. Though he worked chiefly for banknote engravers, he was well-known for his engravings after American artists. He was also an amateur painter and a National Academician and officer of the Academy. He spent his entire career, except for a visit to Europe in the mid-1840's, in NYC and he died there on April 28, 1900. ¶ DAB; Stauffer; Clement and Hutton; Thieme-Becker; *Art Annual,* III, obit.; Cowdrey, NAD; Cowdrey, AA & AAU; NYCD 1847 and after; 7 Census (1850), N.Y., LII, 212.

JONES, ANTHONY W. Carver and sculptor of NYC, active 1818–61. He was listed as a sculptor only after 1850. He exhibited a plaster bust of Gen. James Tallmadge at the 1844 Fair of the American Institute. ¶ NYCD 1818–61; Am. Inst. Cat., 1844.

JONES, BENJAMIN. Engraver of Philadelphia. He was most active from 1798 to 1815, but was apparently living as late as 1837. ¶ Stauffer; Dunlap, *History;* Phila. CD 1837; Fielding.

JONES, EDWARD. Lithographer of NYC, 1844–49. He was associated with the firms of JONES & PALMER (1844) and JONES & NEWMAN (1847–48). ¶ NYCD and BD 1844–49; Peters, *America on Stone.*

JONES, EDWARD C. Designer of medals for the Charleston (S.C.) Volunteers in 1849. The dies were cut by C. C. WRIGHT. ¶ Rutledge, *Artists in the Life of Charleston.*

JONES, EMERY. Ship figurehead carver of Newcastle and South Freeport (Me.), 1856–60. In 1856 he was with the firm of SOUTHWORTH & JONES. His figure of Samuel Skolfield is reproduced in Pinckney. ¶ Pinckney, *American Figureheads,* opp. 109, 194, 201.

JONES, EMANUEL. Topographical, scene, and decorative painter. A native of Frankfurt (Germany); working in Charleston (S.C.) from 1806 until his death in 1822. He worked as scene painter at the Charleston Theatre and at his death was keeper of the Charleston Academy of Fine Arts. ¶ Rutledge, *Artists in the Life of Charleston.*

JONES, F. P. Itinerant silhouettist of early 19th century New England. *Cf.* —— JONES, portrait painter at NYC in 1818, and T. P. JONES, silhouettist at Schenectady (N.Y.) in 1808. ¶ Carrick, *Shades of Our Ancestors,* 120.

JONES, FITZ EDWIN (or Fitz Edward). Portrait and subject engraver in mezzotint and stipple. Originally a printer at Carlisle (Pa.), he was listed as a copperplate printer in NYC in the 1840's and by 1854 was in business as an engraver and printer at Cincinnati. He also worked for the Methodist Book Concern of Cincinnati. ¶ Stauffer; NYCD 1840–53; Cincinnati CD 1856–60; Cist, *Cincinnati in 1859.*

JONES, FREDERICK. Engraver, 26, a native of England, living with GEORGE E. JONES in NYC in 1850. ¶ 7 Census (1850), N.Y., XLI, 40.

JONES, GEORGE. Engraver of NYC, 1838–45. Probably the George E. Jones, engraver, 36, a native of England, in the 1850 Census. FREDERICK JONES was of the same family. ¶ NYCD 1838–45; 7 Census (1850), N.Y., XLI, 40.

JONES, GEORGE EDWIN (1824–1870). Lithographer. He did a view of Lord and Taylor's building in NYC in 1860. In 1865 he was listed as a lithographer in Boston and in 1871–72 he exhibited at the Boston Athenaeum. ¶ Swan, BA; *Portfolio* (Feb. 1942), 22; Boston CD 1865.

JONES, GEORGE T. Engraver, born in Pennsylvania about 1818, but working in Cincinnati from 1849 to 1859 as agent for RAWDON, WRIGHT, HATCH & EDSON and the AMERICAN BANK NOTE COMPANY. ¶ 7 Census (1850), Ohio, XX, 813; Cincinnati CD 1849–59.

JONES & HORLOR. Engravers at NYC in 1858. The partners were JAMES P. JONES and HENRY P. HORLOR and possibly EDWARD C. HORLOR. ¶ NYBD 1858; NYCD 1858–59.

JONES, JAMES. English engraver, age 22, living in Cleveland (Ohio) in August 1850. ¶ 7 Census (1850), Ohio, XI, 415.

JONES, JAMES C. Maryland landscape painter who exhibited at the Maryland Historical Society in 1849. ¶ Rutledge, MHS.

JONES, JAMES P. Engraver of NYC, 1844–60. He was associated with the following firms: JONES & HORLOR (1858–59) and JONES, OVERBAUGH & JONES (1860). ¶ NYBD 1844–56; NYCD 1860.

JONES, JOHN. Maryland artist, born *c.* 1802, living in Baltimore in 1860 with his wife and four children, all born in Maryland. ¶ 8 Census (1860), Md., VI, 858.

JONES, JOHN. Engraver at Roxbury (Mass.) in 1849. ¶ New England BD 1849.

JONES, JOHN J. Engraver, of JONES, OVERBAUGH & JONES, NYC, 1860. ¶ NYCD 1860.

JONES, MARY. Landscape painter at Brooklyn (N.Y.), 1843. ¶ Brooklyn CD 1843.

JONES & NEWMAN. Lithographers of NYC, 1847–49. The partners were EDWARD JONES and GEORGE W. NEWMAN. They exhibited at the American Institute in 1847. ¶ Peters, *America on Stone;* NYCD 1847–49; Am. Inst. Cat., 1847.

JONES, OVERBAUGH & JONES. Engravers at NYC, 1860. The firm was composed of JAMES P. and JOHN J. JONES and ABRAM W. OVERBAUGH. ¶ NYBD and CD 1860.

JONES & PALMER. Lithographers at NYC in 1844. The partners were EDWARD JONES and E. S. PALMER. ¶ NYBD 1844.

JONES, ROBERT. Theatrical scene painter, active 1822–48. An Englishman, he was employed as a scene painter in NYC from 1822 to 1832 and by H. HANINGTON as a dioramist in 1836. After 1832 he worked chiefly in Boston, painting scenery and panoramas. He exhibited at the Boston Athenaeum and the Pennsylvania Academy. ¶ Odell, *Annals of the New York Stage,* Vol. III; NYCD 1822–30; Boston CD 1832–48; Swan, BA; Rutledge, PA; Rutledge, *Artists in the Life of Charleston;* N. Y. *Evening Post,* Aug. 21, 1826, Nov. 28, 1828, and Jan. 13, 1830; *Guide to Hanington's Moving Dioramas;* Boston *Evening Transcript,* March 29, 1833, March 16, 1839, Feb. 3, 1840, April 25, 1841, May 24, 1848 (citations courtesy J. E. Arrington).

JONES, ROBERT S. Engraver, working in NYC 1849–58. He exhibited at the American Institute in 1849 and 1856. Stauffer lists a line engraver, R. S. Jones, at Boston in 1873. ¶ NYBD 1854–58; Am. Inst. Cat., 1849, 1856; Stauffer; Fielding.

JONES, S. Artist of a view of the burning of the Masonic Hall, Philadelphia, on March 9, 1819, known through an engraving by JOHN HILL. *Cf.* SAMUEL JONES. ¶ Stauffer.

JONES, S. K. Portrait painter, born in February 1825 at Clinton (Conn.). After studying in NYC under ALVAN FISHER for a few months in 1846, he became an itinerant portrait painter. In 1861 he settled in New Haven (Conn.) where he was still active in 1879. ¶ French, *Art and Artists in Connecticut,* 123; Fielding. This is probably the Jones of Connecticut listed by Lipman and Winchester, 175.

JONES, SAMUEL (?–1818). Listed as an American painter (died in 1818) in the Pennsylvania Academy for 1827, when two of his scenes from Shakespeare's *Merry Wives of Windsor* were exhibited. This may be the —— Jones who exhibited landscapes and figure paintings at the Academy in 1816. A Mrs. Jones exhibited Welsh scenes at the Academy in 1812 and 1813. *Cf.* also, S. JONES, above. ¶ Rutledge, PA.

JONES, SAMUEL B. Portrait painter at NYC, 1860. He was a native of Massachusetts, born about 1827, and resided with Bradford Jones, deputy sheriff. ¶ NYBD 1860; 8 Census (1860), N.Y., LVII, 569.

JONES, T. P. Silhouettist working in the vicinity of Schenectady (N.Y.) in 1808. *Cf.* F. P. JONES. ¶ Baker, "The Story of Two Silhouettes," repro.

JONES, THEODORE. Wood engraver and designer at Cincinnati, 1856–59. ¶ Cincinnati CD and BD 1856–59.

JONES, THOMAS DOW (1811–1881). A.N.A. Portrait sculptor and medallionist, born December 11, 1811, in Oneida County (N.Y.). He moved to Ohio in the 1830's, worked in Cincinnati as a stonemason, and about 1842 began to produce portrait busts. During the next four decades he worked mainly in Ohio, but also in NYC, Nashville (Tenn.), Detroit, and Boston. His best known works are a bust of Lincoln (1861) and one of Salmon P. Chase (1876), the latter for the Supreme Court room of the U. S. Capitol at Washington. Jones died in Columbus (Ohio) on February 27, 1881. ¶ Boston *Transcript,* Feb. 28, 1881, obit.; *American Art Review,* II (1880), Part I, 256, obit.; Fairman, *Art and Artists of the U. S. Capitol,* 358–59; Clark, *Ohio Art and Artists,* 470; date of birth courtesy Mrs. J. E. Clark, letter to FARL, June 27, 1941; Cowdrey, NAD; NYBD 1855–57; Wilson, *Lincoln in Portraiture;* Rutledge, PA; represented at Md. Hist. Soc. and American Antiquarian Society.

JONES, THOMAS R. English artist, age 37, living in Philadelphia in 1850. He came to America between 1837 and 1841, apparently settled first in Connecticut, but was in Philadelphia by 1843. ¶ 7 Census (1850), Pa., LII, 635; Phila. CD 1850–52.

JONES, WILLIAM. Sculptor, 35, a native of South Carolina, at NYC in 1850. ¶ 7 Census (1850), N.Y., XLVI, 295.

JONES, WILLIAM FOSTER. Portrait, miniature and historical painter, and crayon artist. He was born in Pennsylvania about 1815 and was active as an artist in Philadelphia from 1836 at least until 1869, exhibiting frequently at the Academy and the Artists' Fund Society. In 1860 his property, real and personal, was valued at over $23,000. ¶ 7 Census (1850), Pa., LII, 574; 8 Census (1860), Pa., LV, 272; Phila. CD 1844–60+; Rutledge, PA.

JONES, WILLIAM R. Stipple engraver, who worked in Philadelphia from 1810 to 1824. He exhibited at the Society of Artists and Pennsylvania Academy. ¶ Stauffer; Rutledge, PA; Fielding; Thieme-Becker.

JONGH, JAMES DE. Portrait painter at NYC, 1835–36; exhibited at the National Academy 1836. ¶ NYCD 1835–36; Cowdrey, NAD.

JORDAN, HENRY. Line engraver of landscapes. An Englishman who came to America about 1836 and was for a time employed by ALFRED JONES in NYC. He later worked with FREDERICK or JOHN HALPIN. He returned to England for a time but eventually settled permanently in the United States. A steel engraving by him appeared in *Homes of American Authors* (1853). ¶ Stauffer; Hamilton, 394; Cowdrey, AA & AAU; Thieme-Becker; Fielding.

JORDAN (or Jordon), SAMUEL. Portrait painter of New York State, *c.* 1830. ¶ *American Provincial Painting,* No. 52; Lipman and Winchester, 175; Garbisch Collection, Catalogue, 66, repro.

JOSEPH, SAMUEL. Banknote engraver, age 23, at Philadelphia in 1860. He was a native of the city and owned property valued at $3,500. ¶ 8 Census (1860), Pa., LI, 254.

JOUETT, MATTHEW HARRIS (1787/88–1827). Portrait painter, born near Harrodsburg (Ky.) on April 22, either in 1787 (Jonas) or in 1788 (Martin, and Wilson). Though largely self-taught, he spent a few months with GILBERT STUART in Boston (Mass.) in 1816 and was one of that master's most distinguished pupils. Throughout his brief career Jouett was associated chiefly with his native state, though during the latter part of his life he spent his winters in Louisiana. He died near Lexington (Ky.) on August 10, 1827. The name Jouett, derived from the French Jouet, is pronounced in Kentucky as if spelled Jewett. ¶ The chief study of Jouett's work is Edward A. Jonas, *Matthew Harris Jouett* (Louisville: 1938), which is supplemented by Mrs. William H. Martin, *Catalogue of All Known Paintings by Matthew Harris Jouett* (Louisville, 1939), and Samuel M. Wilson, "Matthew Harris Jouett: Kentucky Portrait Painter; A Review," and "Additional Notes on Matthew Harris Jouett," *The Filson Club History Quarterly,* XIII (1939), 75–96, XIV (1940), 1–16, 65–102. See also: Morgan, *Gilbert Stuart and His Pupils;* Price, *Old Masters of the Blue Grass;* DAB; CAB; Thieme-Becker; New Orleans CD 1823–24 (cited by Delgado-WPA); WPA Guide, *Kentucky;* Flexner, *The Light of Distant Skies.*

JOUVENAL, JACQUES (1829–1905). Portrait sculptor; born March 18, 1829, of French Huguenot parents in Pinache (Germany). About 1845 he began his art studies in Stuttgart. After his arrival in the United States in 1853, he spent two years in NYC, then moved to Washington (D.C.) where he was employed until 1861 in finishing the capitals of the columns of the Capitol. He later took up portrait work and is represented in the Capitol by a bust of Aaron Burr. He lived in Washington until his death on March 8, 1905. ¶ Fairman, *Art and Artists of the Capitol,* 329.

JOYCE, JAMES. Engraver from Massachusetts, 19, at NYC in 1860. ¶ 8 Census (1860), N.Y., LI, 216.

JOYE, JOHN (1790–?). Profilist; baptized at Salem (Mass.) on March 14, 1790; working there as a profilist about 1812. ¶ Belknap, *Artists and Craftsmen of Essex County,* 21; Jackson, *Silhouette,* 121; Carrick, *Shades of Our Ancestors,* 115–16.

JUDKINS, ELIZA MARIA (1809–1887). Crayon portraitist who exhibited at the Boston Athenaeum in 1855 and 1859. Her portrait of Francis Sales (1777–1854) is at Harvard University. ¶ Swan, BA; Bolton, *Crayon Draftsmen.*

JUDSON, CHARLES H. Portrait painter at Rome and Utica (N.Y.) in 1859–60. ¶ Rome CD 1859; N. Y. State BD 1859–60.

JUMAN, H. Portrait and landscape draftsman. In 1831 he exhibited at the Pennsylvania Academy a sepia drawing of DeWitt Clinton and a black lead drawing of Claverack Falls, Columbia County (N.Y.). ¶ Rutledge, PA.

JUMP, EDWARD. Portrait painter and caricaturist. Born in France about 1831, Jump came to California about 1860 and worked in San Francisco until about 1868. Moving to Washington (D.C.), he enjoyed success there as a portrait painter, then moved on to NYC where he was employed as a comic illustrator for *Leslie's* and other papers. In the early 1870's he went west again, to St. Louis. Peters states that he committed suicide. ¶ 8 Census (1860), Cal., VII, 717; Peters, *California on Stone.*

JUMPELLO, SIMON. Listed in the 1860 Census of Boston as "panorama," possibly a painter of panoramas. He was 24 years of age and a native of Turkey. ¶ 8 Census (1860), Mass., XXVIII, 143.

JUNCA, MOUSX. Marine painter, and first bass at the New Orleans Theatre, New Orleans, 1857. ¶ Delgado-WPA cites *Picayune,* April 17, 1857.

JUNJEL & BARRET. Marble and stone sculptors at New Orleans, 1850–51. The partners were BARTHOL JUNJEL and ANTHONY BARRET. ¶ New Orleans CD 1850–51 (cited by Delgado-WPA).

JUNJEL, BARTHOL. Marble and stone sculptor, of JUNJEL & BARRET, at New Orleans, 1850–51. ¶ New Orleans CD 1851.

JUST, WILLIAM. French sculptor, 30, at NYC in 1850. ¶ 7 Census (1850), N.Y., XLVI, 170.

JUSTH, ——. Lithographer at San Francisco, 1851. He published prints under the name of Justh & Co., and Justh, Quirot & Co. ¶ Peters, *California on Stone.*

JUSTICE, JOSEPH. Engraver working with SCOLES in NYC in 1804, and in Philadelphia from 1810 to 1833. ¶ Stauffer; Fielding; Thieme-Becker.

K

KAEHRLE, GABRIEL. Wood engraver of NYC, 1856–58. ¶ NYCD 1856–58; NYBD 1858.

KAHL, GEORGE F. Artist of Baltimore, 1858 and after. ¶ Lafferty cites Baltimore CD 1858–59, 1868–71, 1874–75.

KAIN, FRANCIS (*c.* 1786–1844). Marble cutter and "sculptor" active in NYC from 1811 to 1839. He was with NORRIS & KAIN from 1811 to 1818 and with his brother, JAMES KAIN, from about 1827 to 1838. Francis and James Kain cut the NYC milestones of 1822–23 and erected the monuments over the graves of John Paulding, one of André's captors, and of Thomas Addis Emmet (1764–1827). They also had a branch in New Orleans in 1829–32. They are not known to have done any work that could be classed as sculpture, however. Francis moved to Eastchester (N.Y.) after James's death in 1838 and died there on June 11, 1844. ¶ Koke, "Milestones along the Old Highways of New York City," 189–92; NYCD 1811–18 (McKay), 1819–39 (Koke); Delgado-WPA cites *Argus,* Dec. 24, 1829, and New Orleans CD 1832.

KAIN, JAMES (?–1838). Marble cutter and "sculptor" active in NYC from about 1827 to 1838. He was in the marble business with his brother, FRANCIS KAIN. In 1829 he opened a branch in New Orleans and he was there again in 1832. He died in NYC on April 23, 1838. ¶ Koke, "Milestones along the Old Highways of New York City," 189–91; NYCD 1827, 1829, 1831; Delgado-WPA cites *Argus,* December 24, 1829, and New Orleans CD 1832.

KALBER, EDW. German lithographer, 50, at NYC in 1860. His wife also was a native of Germany, but their children were born in New York between 1851 and 1854. ¶ 8 Census (1860), N.Y., XLII, 633.

KANE, PAUL (1810–1871). Landscape and Indian genre painter. He was born in Toronto (Ont.) in 1810 and studied there at Upper Canada College. He came to the United States in 1836 and worked there as an artist until 1840, when he left for European study. Returning to Canada in 1845, he spent the next three years sketching in the Canadian West. His experiences, illustrated by his own pen, appeared in Kane's *Wanderings of an Artist among the Indians of North America* (London, 1859). He died in Toronto in 1871. ¶ CAB.

KANN, ALEXANDER and MORITZ. Lithographers living together in NYC in 1860. Both were born in Prussia, Alexander about 1828 and Moritz about 1826. In 1863 Alexander was listed as a writer and Moritz as "cards." ¶ 8 Census (1860), N.Y., XLV, 914; NYCD 1863.

KARST, JOHN (1836–1922). Wood engraver, born in 1836 at Bingen (Germany) and brought to the United States in infancy. Hamilton lists several books illustrated by him, the earliest dated 1855. He died at De Bruce (N.Y.) in the summer of 1922. ¶ *Art Annual,* XIX, obit.; Hamilton, 524; Fielding; Cowdrey, *Winslow Homer, Illustrator,* nos. 124 A and B, 125, 130, 148.

KAUFMANN, THEODOR (1814–?). Historical painter. Born December 18, 1814, at Nelsen, Hanover (Germany); studied painting in Hamburg and Munich. He came to America about 1850, having taken part in the Revolution of 1848. His studio was in NYC until the Civil War, in which he saw active service, but after the war he settled permanently in Boston. Best known for his Civil War paintings, he was still living in 1887. ¶ CAB; Clement and Hutton; NYBD 1854; Cowdrey, NAD; Thieme-Becker.

KAUTH, FRANCIS. Lithographer, 17, at NYC in 1860. He was born in New York and was living with his widowed mother, Monica Kauth. ¶ 8 Census (1860), N.Y., LIV, 1000.

KAWDEN, HENRY. Portrait painter at Baltimore in 1845. ¶ Lafferty.

KAY, WILLIAM. Engraver of NYC, 1854–58. ¶ NYBD 1854–58.

KAYFLICK, HENRY. Prussian-born lithographer, age 22, at Philadelphia in 1860. ¶ 8 Census (1860), Pa., L, 556.

KAYSER, see KEYSER.

KEALY, MINRATH. Swiss lithographer, 43, at NYC in 1860 with his wife Minerva and four children born in Switzerland before 1850. ¶ 8 Census (1860), N.Y., LIV, 25.

KEARNEY, FRANCIS (1785–1837). Engraver and lithographer. He was born in Perth Amboy (N.J.) on July 23, 1785, studied drawing at the Columbian Academy in NYC, and served his apprenticeship under the noted engraver PETER R. MAVERICK. After working independently in NYC for a few years, he moved to Philadelphia in 1810 and followed his profession there until 1833, when he returned to Perth Amboy. He died on September 1, 1837. While in Philadelphia, Kearney was a member of the banknote engraving firms of TANNER, KEARNEY & TIEBOUT and TANNER, VALLANCE, KEARNEY & CO., and for a short time in 1829–30 with the lithographic firm of PENDLETON, KEARNEY & CHILDS. Among the engravers who worked under Kearney were DAVID C. JOHNSTON, GEORGE B. ELLIS, and WILLIAM E. TUCKER. ¶ DAB; Stauffer; NYCD 1807–10; Phila. CD 1811–31; Rutledge, PA; Peters, *America on Stone. The Cabinet of Genius . . .* (N.Y., Thomas Powers, 1808) contains nine plates by Kearney.

KEATING, CHARLES. Irish engraver, age 45, living in Philadelphia in 1850 with EDWARD KEATING. ¶ 7 Census (1850), Pa., LII, 919.

KEATING (or Keatinge), EDWARD. Irish engraver, age 24, living in Philadelphia in 1850 with CHARLES KEATING, probably his father. Edward Keatinge was listed as a portrait, historical, and landscape engraver in NYC in 1860. ¶ 7 Census (1850), Pa., LII, 919; NYBD 1860.

KEEF, JOHN. English painter who arrived in Williamsburg (Va.) shortly before April 18, 1751. He advertised as a landscape, herald, and house painter. ¶ *Virginia Gazette,* April 18, 1751.

KEELER, JOHN, JR. Marble engraver from Germany, age 21, living in Cleveland (Ohio) in August 1850. ¶ 7 Census (1850), Ohio, II, 308.

KEELMANN, CHARLES. Portrait painter from France, age 60, living in Philadelphia in 1860. He was listed in city directories as early as 1855 and exhibited at the Pennsylvania Academy in 1856. ¶ 8 Census (1860), Pa., LIV, 79; Phila. CD 1855–60+; Rutledge, PA.

KEELY, ISAAC H. (or J. H.) (1817–1891). Portrait painter; possibly a native of Haverhill (Mass.). He was working in Bradford (Mass.) in the 1850's. Two of his portraits have been found in Boston and Pownall (Vt.). ¶ Letter of Mrs. C. Nichols Greene, Boston, to FARL, 1947; WPA (Mass.), *Portraits Found in Vt.*

KEEN, WILLIAM C. Sculptor in NYC, 1855–57. ¶ NYBD 1855, 1857.

KEENAN, WILLIAM. Engraver and lithographer; born in Charleston (S.C.) about 1810 and commenced his career there about 1828. From 1830 to 1833 he worked in Philadelphia, but from 1835 until 1855 he was in Charleston. His work included landscapes and portraits, book and magazine illustrations, medals, and engraving on silver. ¶ Stauffer; 7 Census (1850), S.C., II, 433; Rutledge, *Artists in the Life of Charleston;* Peters, *America on Stone;* Thieme-Becker; *Art News* (June 1, 1940), 12, repro.

KEFFER, J. L. Artist of a DUVAL naval print, 1839. The artist may have lived in Philadelphia. ¶ Peters, *America on Stone.*

KEHRWEIDER, CHARLES. Artist, at Philadelphia in 1860. A native of Mecklenburg (Germany), he was 27 years old and lived with his father WILLIAM, SR., and brothers WILLIAM, JR., and OTTO KEHRWEIDER, all artists. ¶ 8 Census (1860), Pa., LIV, 514; Phila. CD 1860.

KEHRWEIDER, OTTO. Artist, age 25, from Mecklenburg (Germany), living in Philadelphia in 1860. WILLIAM KEHRWEIDER, SR., was his father; CHARLES and WILLIAM, JR., his brothers. ¶ 8 Census (1860), Pa., LIV; Phila. CD 1860.

KEHRWEIDER, WILLIAM, SR. Artist from Mecklenburg (Germany), where he was born *c.* 1795. Kehrweider came to Philadelphia about 1857 and lived there in 1860 with his wife Johanna and sons CHARLES, OTTO, and WILLIAM, JR. ¶ 8 Census (1860), Pa., LIV, 514; Phila. CD 1857–60; Phila. BD 1859 as M. Kernweider.

KEHRWEIDER, WILLIAM, JR. Artist, age 30, from Mecklenburg (Germany), living in Philadelphia in 1860. His two children, twins aged two years, were born in Philadelphia, where Kehrweider lived with his father and brothers (see above), also artists. ¶ 8 Census (1860), Pa., LIV, 514; Phila. CD 1860+.

KEIL, VALENTINE. Lithographer of NYC, 1853–58. In 1856–57 he was with the firm of DUMCKE & KEIL. ¶ NYCD 1853–58.

KEIM, JOHN. Engraver, 33, born in Wittemburg [sic] (Germany), at NYC in 1860. His wife also was German, but their two children, aged 3 and 7, were born in New York. ¶ 8 Census (1860), N.Y., LVII, 748; NYCD 1863.

KEINES, SIMON. German engraver, 28, at NYC in 1860. ¶ 8 Census (1860), N.Y., LII, 422.

KEINHART, FRANCIS. Portrait painter at Baltimore in 1817. ¶ Lafferty.

KEINLEY, AUGUSTUS. German engraver, age 25, living in Southwark, a suburb of Philadelphia in August 1850. ¶ 7 Census (1850), Pa., LV, 130.

KEITH, DAVID. Engraver at Philadelphia in 1860. ¶ Phila. CD 1860.

KEITH, GEORGE A. Artist from New York State, age 26, boarding in New Orleans in October 1850. ¶ 7 Census (1850), La., IV(1), 597.

KEITH, WILLIAM (1839–1911). Landscape and portrait painter, engraver. Keith was born on November 21, 1839, at Old Meldrum, Aberdeenshire (Scotland) and was brought to the United States in boyhood. He began his professional career as an engraver for Harper's in NYC, but in 1859 he moved to California where he took up landscape painting and was for a time employed by the Northern Pacific Railroad to paint scenes along its route. He studied in Europe from 1869 to 1871 and again in 1893. During the 1880's he spent several years in New Orleans. He was a leader in California art until his death at Berkeley on April 13, 1911. ¶ WPA (Cal.), *Introduction to California Art Research,* Vol. II, contains a documented account. See also: DAB; Davisson, "William Keith"; Fielding; Cowdrey, NAD (1870/71). Represented at Corcoran Gallery, Washington (D.C.).

KELLEN, ROBERT. Portrait painter at Boston, 1844–45. ¶ Boston BD 1844–45.

KELLER, ADAM. Engraver with FISCHER & KELLER, New York City, 1858. ¶ NYBD & CD 1858.

KELLER, FRANCIS. Lithographer at Philadelphia, 1858–60. ¶ Phila. CD 1858, 1860.

KELLER, Mrs. J. Portrait painter at NYC, 1855; exhibitor at the National Academy. ¶ Cowdrey, NAD.

KELLER, WALLACE. Artist at Buffalo (N.Y.), 1857–60. ¶ Buffalo BD 1857–60.

KELLER, WILLIAM J. Copperplate and steel engraver at Philadelphia, 1857. ¶ Phila. CD 1857.

KELLEY, JOSEPH. Lithographer at Hartford (Conn.), 1857–59. He was associated with the firm of BINGHAM & KELLEY. ¶ Hartford CD 1857–59.

KELLINGER, JOHN A. Canadian engraver, 28, at NYC in 1850. ¶ 7 Census (1850), N.Y., XLIV, 200.

KELLOGG, CHARLES EDMUND. Lithographer of Hartford (Conn.). A son of EDMUND B. KELLOGG, he entered the lithographic firm of E. B. & E. C. KELLOGG in 1860 and continued with the business after its name was changed in 1867 to Kellogg & Bulkeley. ¶ Hartford CD 1860+; Peters, *America on Stone.*

KELLOGG & COMPANY. Lithographers and engravers of Hartford (Conn.), 1848. The firm was composed of JARVIS G. KELLOGG and GEORGE G. GRATACAP. ¶ Hartford CD 1848; Conn. Hist. Soc., *Cat. of Exhibition of Kellogg Prints.*

KELLOGG, D. W., & COMPANY. Lithographers of Hartford (Conn.). Established by DANIEL WRIGHT KELLOGG in 1830, the firm retained his name until 1842, although after 1836, when Kellogg went out west, the work was done mainly by his brothers and other employees. In 1842 the business was taken over formally by Daniel's younger brothers, E. B. & E. C. KELLOGG. ¶ Conn. Hist. Soc., *Cat. of Exhibition of Kellogg Prints;* Hartford CD 1838–41.

KELLOGG, DANIEL WRIGHT (1807–1874). Lithographer and engraver. Born July 21, 1807, at Tolland (Conn.), he studied lithography in Boston, then settled in Hartford (Conn.) about 1830 and established the firm of D. W. KELLOGG & Co. Although he is said to have gone out west in 1836, the firm retained his name until 1842, when it became E. B. & E. C. KELLOGG. D. W. Kellogg was listed in Hartford directories from 1842 to 1854 and again from 1864 to 1869, but he died in Jefferson (Wis.) on December 28, 1874. ¶ Conn. Hist. Soc., *Cat. of Exhibition of Kellogg Prints;* Knittle, "The Kelloggs, Hartford Lithographers"; Hartford CD 1842–54, 1864–69; Peters, *America on Stone.*

KELLOGG, E. B. & E. C. Lithographers of Hartford (Conn.) and NYC, 1842–48, 1855–67. Established in 1842 at Hartford by EDMUND BURKE and ELIJAH CHAPMAN KELLOGG, succeeding D. W. KELLOGG & Co. In 1848 the firm was joined by JOHN C. COMSTOCK and the name changed to KELLOGGS & COMSTOCK, but this association was dissolved in 1850. E. B. and E. C. Kellogg resumed their partnership in 1855 and carried on until the formation of Kellogg & Bulkeley in 1867. The Kelloggs rivalled CURRIER & IVES in the quantity and character of their work. ¶ Conn. Hist. Soc., *Cat. of Exhibition of Kellogg Prints;* Hartford CD 1842–48, 1855–67; NYCD 1847, 1849, 1855–56; *Richmond Portraits,* no. 102; Peters, *America on Stone.*

KELLOGG, EDMUND BURKE (1809–1872).

Printer and lithographer. Born May 27, 1809, at Tolland (Conn.), E. B. Kellogg was a printer by trade and worked on newspapers in New London and Stonington (Conn.) and Toronto (Canada) before taking up lithographic work in Hartford about 1832. At first employed by his brother DANIEL W. KELLOGG, in 1842 E. B. joined with another brother, ELIJAH CHAPMAN KELLOGG, in the firm of E. B. & E. C. KELLOGG. This became KELLOGGS & COMSTOCK in 1848, but the following year E. B. Kellogg went into business on his own. In 1855 the partnership of E. B. & E. C. KELLOGG was reorganized and both brothers were associated with it until the formation of Kellogg & Bulkeley in 1867. E. B. Kellogg died in Hartford on March 26, 1872. ¶ Conn. Hist. Soc., *Cat. of Exhibition of Kellogg Prints;* Knittle, "The Kelloggs, Hartford Lithographers"; Hartford CD 1842–67; NYBD 1846, 1857; Peters, *America on Stone.*

KELLOGG, ELIJAH CHAPMAN (1811–1881). Lithographer and engraver. The youngest of the Kellogg brothers of Hartford, he was born at Tolland (Conn.) on June 13, 1811. He studied engraving under JARVIS G. KELLOGG and first worked as a lithographer in his elder brother's establishment at Hartford, D. W. KELLOGG & Co. From 1842 to 1848 he and his brother EDMUND worked in partnership as E. B. & E. C. KELLOGG, and from 1848 to 1850 with JOHN C. COMSTOCK as KELLOGGS & COMSTOCK. After working independently for several years, E. C. and E. B. Kellogg resumed their partnership which lasted until the formation of its successor, Kellogg & Bulkeley, in 1867. E. C. Kellogg was a noted fish breeder and made a trip to Europe in 1860 as agent for Col. Samuel Colt, whose ponds were stocked under Kellogg's direction. He died in Hartford on December 14, 1881. ¶ Conn. Hist. Soc., *Cat. of Exhibition of Kellogg Prints;* Knittle, "The Kelloggs, Hartford Lithographers"; Hartford CD 1842–81; NYCD 1848–59; Peters, *America on Stone.*

KELLOGG & HANMER. Lithographers of Hartford (Conn.), 1845. The partners were JARVIS G. KELLOGG and the printer Samuel Hanmer, Jr. ¶ Conn. Hist. Soc., *Cat. of Exhibition of Kellogg Prints.*

KELLOGG, JARVIS GRIGGS (1805–1873). Engraver and lithographer. Born October 1 or 5, 1805, at Tolland (Conn.), he trained as a steel engraver under OLIVER PELTON in Boston. About 1841 he settled in Hartford (Conn.) and worked there until 1862, chiefly independently, but with KELLOGG & HANMER in 1845 and KELLOGG & Co. (with GEO. G. GRATACAP) in 1848. From 1862 to about 1870 he worked in Boston, but the last three years of his life were spent in Hartford where he died on July 24, 1873. ¶ Conn. Hist. Soc., *Cat. of Exhibition of Kellogg Prints;* Knittle, "The Kelloggs, Hartford Lithographers"; Hartford CD 1841–62, 1870–73; Boston CD 1862–72; Peters, *America on Stone;* Stauffer; Fielding; Thieme-Becker.

KELLOGG, MINER KILBOURNE (1814–1889). Painter of portraits, miniatures, and oriental scenes. He was born August 22, 1814, at Manlius Square (N.Y.) and began his artistic career in 1840 at Cincinnati. From 1841 to 1845 he was studying in Italy. He was at NYC in 1851, again in Europe from 1854 to 1858, and from 1867 to 1870 at Baltimore. He became an Honorary Member, National Academy in 1851. ¶ Hopkins, *The Kelloggs in the Old World and the New,* I, 479, II, 1132; Cist, *Cincinnati in 1841;* Cowdrey, NAD; Rutledge, PA; Lafferty; Swan, BA; Tuckerman; Clark, *Ohio Art and Artists;* Bolton, *Miniature Painters;* Thieme-Becker; represented MHS. Kellogg's journal and sketch books are owned by Mrs. Henry J. Butler of Clayton (Mo.).

KELLOGG, NOAH J. Landscape and portrait painter of NYC, 1844–55; of Ithaca (N.Y.), 1856–59. ¶ Cowdrey, NAD; Cowdrey, AA & AAU; Rutledge, PA; NYBD 1850.

KELLOGGS & COMSTOCK. Lithographers of Hartford (Conn.) and NYC, 1848–50. The firm consisted of E. B. & E. C. KELLOGG and JOHN C. COMSTOCK. E. B. Kellogg left the firm before 1850. ¶ Hartford CD 1848–50; NYCD 1848–50; Peters, *America on Stone.*

KELLOGGS & THAYER. Lithographers of NYC, 1846–47. The firm consisted of E. B. & E. C. KELLOGG of Hartford and Horace Thayer, map and print dealer of NYC. ¶ Conn. Hist. Soc., *Cat. of Exhibition of Kellogg Prints;* NYCD 1846–47.

KELLY, AUGUSTUS. Artist from New York, age 33, boarding in Philadelphia in June 1860. ¶ 8 Census (1860), Pa., LV, 272.

KELLY, JAMES. Sculptor at NYC, 1855. ¶ NYBD 1855.

KELLY, JOSEPH. Engraver of NYC, 1844–60. ¶ NYBD 1844, 1851–52, 1856–59; NYCD

1853, 1856, 1858, 1860; Stauffer (as J. Kelly); Fielding.

KELLY, MICHAEL. Irish lithographer, 25, at NYC in 1860. His wife also was Irish, but their children were born in New York after 1856. ¶ 8 Census (1860), N.Y., XLIV, 856.

KELLY, T. J. Wood engraver at Philadelphia in 1849. ¶ Phila. BD 1849.

KELLY, THOMAS (*c.* 1795–*c.* 1841). Line and stipple engraver of portraits and views. He was born in Ireland about 1795, attended the Dublin Society's School in 1802–03, and worked in Dublin until 1827. During the 1830's he worked in Boston, Philadelphia, and NYC, chiefly for book and magazine publishers. He died in a NYC almshouse about 1841. ¶ Stauffer; Strickland, *Dictionary of Irish Artists;* Rutledge, PA; Thieme-Becker; Fielding; repro. in *Art in America* (Dec. 1951), 169.

KELLY, THOMAS. Irish lithographer, 19, at NYC in 1850. ¶ 7 Census (1850), N.Y., XLVIII, 332.

KELLY, WILLIAM F. Lithographer, age 27, born in Pennsylvania, boarding in Philadelphia in July 1860. ¶ 8 Census (1860), Pa., LII, 442.

KELLY, WILLIAM J. Lithographer. He was born in Pennsylvania about 1838, the son of James Kelly, an Irish-born tailor, and began his career as a lithographer and lithographic printer in Philadelphia in 1860. ¶ 8 Census (1860), Pa., LIV, 395; Phila. CD 1860+.

KELSEY, C. Portrait painter, active about 1850. A portrait by him is owned by James Thomas Flexner of NYC. ¶ Information courtesy Mr. Flexner.

KELTER, WILLIAM J. General engraver of Rock Island (Ill.), 1858. ¶ Davenport, Moline, and Rock Island BD 1858.

KELTON, SAMUEL. Portrait painter at Pittsburgh (Pa.) in 1837. ¶ Bolton, "Portrait Painters in Oil."

KEMB, CHARLES. German lithographer, 25, at NYC in 1850. ¶ 7 Census (1850), N.Y., XLII, 148.

KEMBLE, WILLIAM. Engraver of NYC, 1844–59. ¶ NYBD 1844, 1859.

KEMMELMEYER, FREDERICK. Portrait, miniature, and historical painter, teacher; working in Baltimore from about 1788 to 1803. He is best known for a scene depicting Washington reviewing the troops at Fort Cumberland (Md.) on October 18, 1794, now in the Garbisch Collection. ¶ Prime, II, 17, 51; Mayo cites Baltimore CD 1796, 1800–03; Lafferty; Morgan and Fielding, *Life Portraits of Washington,* 199; *American Processional,* 238; *Antiques* (April 1954), 291, repro.

KEMP, WILLIAM. French engraver, 33, at NYC in 1860. His wife and children, the latter aged 2 and 6 years, were also natives of France. ¶ 8 Census (1860), N.Y., LIII, 100.

KEMPER, HENRY W. Portrait and landscape painter at Cincinnati, 1859. ¶ Cincinnati CD 1859; Ohio BD 1859.

KEMPSON, Mrs. JULIE (HART) BEERS (1835–1913). Landscape painter, sister of JAMES and WILLIAM HART. Born in Pittsfield (Mass.), she came to NYC in the mid-1850's with her brothers. As Mrs. Julie Hart Beers she exhibited at the National Academy in 1867 and at the Boston Athenaeum in 1867–68. She later married a Mr. Kempson and lived in Metuchen (N.J.). She died at Trenton (N.J.) on August 13, 1913. ¶ *Art Annual,* XI, obit.; Swan, BA; Thieme-Becker; Cowdrey, NAD (as Mrs. Julie Hart Beers).

KENNEDY, DAVID, see KENNEDY & LUCAS.

KENNEDY, D. J. Painter of Scottish and Irish landscapes shown at the Artists' Fund Society, Philadelphia, in 1841. He was listed as residing in Philadelphia. ¶ Rutledge, PA.

KENNEDY, JAMES. Engraver in line and stipple. He was working for a New York publisher in 1797 and remained in that city until about 1812, when he moved to Philadelphia. This may be the J. Kennedy who exhibited two India-ink drawings at the Society of Artists in 1813. ¶ Stauffer; NYCD 1808–11; Thieme-Becker; Fielding; Rutledge, PA.

KENNEDY, JOHN. Irish engraver, 32, at NYC in 1860. ¶ 8 Census (1860), N.Y., XLIII, 32.

KENNEDY & LUCAS. Lithographers of Philadelphia, 1829–35. This firm illustrated Thomas Earle's *Treatise on Railroads and Internal Communications* (1830) and J. F. Watson's *Annals of Philadelphia* (1830), and work for *The Floral Magazine and Botanical Repository.* In the directories, however, the firm was listed as a looking glass store. The partners were David Kennedy and William B. Lucas. ¶ Peters, *America on Stone;* McClinton, "American Flower Lithographs," 361; Phila. CD 1829–23.

KENNEDY, S. Engraver associated with WILLIAM CHARLES in Philadelphia about 1813. *Cf.* JAMES KENNEDY, engraver working in Philadelphia after 1812. There was also a Samuel Kennedy in Philadelphia from about 1813 to 1825, listed variously as looking glass maker, carver, and gilder; in 1819 his store was listed as the place where exhibitions of the Society of Artists were held. Samuel Kennedy and Samuel H. West were also print publishers for the Society that year, but there is no direct evidence that Samuel Kennedy was an engraver. ¶ Fielding; Dunlap, *History* (1918), III, 312; Phila. CD 1813–25; Brown and Brown cites *Aurora,* April 13, 1819.

KENNEDY, T. J. Painter of an allegory in oils, Auburn (N.Y.), about 1820. ¶ Lipman and Winchester, 175.

KENNEDY, WILLIAM W. Portrait painter. He was born in Massachusetts about 1817 and worked in Baltimore from 1851 to 1871. ¶ 8 Census (1860), Md., IV, 141; Lafferty.

KENNEY, BENJAMIN HARRIS. Sculptor. His marble bust of Lincoln, executed in the early 1850's, is owned by Mrs. Alvah Billings of Rutland (Vt.). ¶ WPA (Mass.), *Portraits Found in Vt.*

KENNICOTT, Mrs. J. A. (née Marie Antoinette Fiske). Teacher of painting and drawing, watercolorist, portraitist in pastel, crayon, and oil. A native of NYC, she began her teaching career at the age of 13 in Auburn (N.Y.), also taught in Aurora, Skaneateles, and Troy (N.Y.), and in 1851 moved to Chicago. She continued to paint and teach there as late as 1885, spending her vacations in New York and Washington. ¶ Andreas, *History of Chicago,* II, 560 (citation courtesy H. Maxson Holloway, Chicago Historical Society); Cowdrey, NAD (1883–85, as Mrs. M. A. Kennicott).

KENSETT, JOHN FREDERICK (1816–1872). N.A. Landscape painter, engraver; born March 22, 1816, at Cheshire (Conn.); received his first instruction in engraving from his father, THOMAS KENSETT. After the latter's death in 1829 the younger Kensett continued his studies under his uncle, ALFRED DAGGETT of New Haven, until about 1838 when he went to work for a banknote engraver in NYC. In 1840 he went to Europe with ASHER B. DURAND, J. W. CASILEAR, and T. P. ROSSITER to study painting. Kensett remained in Europe for seven years, travelling and studying in England, France, Germany, and Italy. Returning to NYC in 1847, he was soon regarded as one of America's leading landscape painters and was elected to the National Academy in 1849. Though he made his home in NYC, Kensett spent much time on painting trips to the mountains of New York and New England, to the New England coast, and even to Colorado (1866). He died in NYC on December 14, 1872. ¶ Cowdrey, "The Return of John Frederick Kensett," illus.; DAB; Clement and Hutton; Tuckerman; Karolik Cat.; Cowdrey, NAD; Cowdrey, AA & AAU; Rutledge, PA; Rutledge, MHS; Swan, BA; Sweet, *Hudson River School;* obit., N. Y. *Tribune,* Dec. 16, 1872.

KENSETT, THOMAS (1786–1829). Engraver. He was born August 17, 1786, at Hampton Court (Middlesex, England), but had emigrated to America and settled at New Haven (Conn.) by 1806, when he engraved an early map of the town. In 1812 he entered the firm of Shelton & Kensett, map and print publishers, and the following year married a sister of the engraver ALFRED DAGGETT. Their second son, JOHN FREDERICK KENSETT, studied engraving with his father and uncle and later won fame as a landscape painter. Thomas Kensett died in Cheshire (Conn.) on June 16, 1829. ¶ Fielding, *Supplement to Stauffer;* DAB (under J. F. Kensett); Swan, BA.

KENT, HENRY. Artist at Philadelphia in 1860. From 1857 to 1859 he was listed as a button manufacturer. ¶ Phila. CD 1857–60.

KENT, Miss M. E. Miniaturist, of NYC. In 1842 she exhibited at the American Institute a miniature in oil of Dr. Adam Clarke. ¶ Am. Inst. Cat., 1842.

KEOGH, MICHAEL. Lithographer; born in Ireland about 1821–23; working in England about 1848; in Washington (D.C.) 1850–52; in NYC from mid-fifties at least to 1863. ¶ 7 Census (1850), D.C., I, 183; 8 Census (1860), N.Y., LIV, 841; NYCD 1863.

KERCHE, VAN DER, see VAN DER KERCHE.

KERDER, AUGUST. Prussian artist, 36, at NYC in 1860. ¶ 8 Census (1860), N.Y., XLV, 89.

KERN, BENJAMIN JORDAN (1818–1849). Topographical draftsman, elder brother of EDWARD M. and RICHARD H. KERN. He was born in Philadelphia on August 3, 1818 and became a doctor. He accompanied FRÉMONT's fourth expedition to the Rockies in 1848 and was killed by Indians on March 14, 1849. ¶ Taft, *Artists and Illustrators of the Old West,* 258.

KERN, EDWARD MEYER (1823–1863). Landscapes and figure studies in watercolor, pencil, and oils. Born October 26, 1823, in Philadelphia, he showed an early interest in art and exhibited for the first time at the Artists' Fund Society in 1841. From 1845 to 1847 he served as topographer with FRÉMONT's third expedition to the Southwest and during the war with Mexico he served under Frémont's command in California. During the fall and winter of 1848–49 he and his two older brothers, BENJAMIN and RICHARD KERN, were with Frémont's fourth expedition to the Colorado Rockies in which Benjamin lost his life. In 1849 Edward served as topographer with Simpson's expedition into the Navajo country and from 1853 to 1856 he was official artist to the Ringgold exploring and surveying expedition in the North Pacific. After a short time in Washington, he joined the U. S. Navy's expedition to survey a route from California to China (1858–60). He served under Frémont's command during the first year of the Civil War, but was discharged in November 1861 along with Frémont's other appointees. Returning to Philadelphia in 1862, he died there on November 25, 1863. ¶ Information courtesy Josephine M. Bever, who cites: Information courtesy Henry E. Huntington Library, San Marino, Cal.; obit., Phila. *Public Ledger and Daily Transcript,* Nov. 26, 1863; Artists' Fund Society Cat., 1841; Phila. CD 1845–53 (as drawing teacher); Frémont, *Memoirs,* I, 424; information courtesy Office of the Adjutant General, Dept. of the Army; Bancroft, *History of the Pacific States of North America, California,* V, 298–99; Nevins, *Frémont, Pathmaker of the West,* 349, 627; Johnston, *Reports of the Secretary of War with Reconnaissances of Routes from San Antonio to El Paso,* and *Report of J. H. Simpson of an Expedition into the Navajo Country,* 31st Cong., 1st Sess., Senate Document 64 (1850); Schoolcraft, *Information Respecting the History, Conditions & Prospects of the Indian Tribes of the United States,* Part V, 649; information courtesy Office of Naval Records and Library, Dept. of the Navy; information courtesy National Collection of Fine Arts, Smithsonian Institution; Simpson, *Report of Explorations across the Great Basin,* Appendix Q, 478; Taft, *Artists and Illustrators of the Old West,* 358–59. Represented: The Museum, U. S. Naval Academy, Annapolis, Md.; National Collection of Fine Arts, Smithsonian Institution; Naval Records and Library Dept. of the Navy; U. S. Navy, Cartographic Records Section, National Archives; Henry E. Huntington Library and Art Gallery, San Marino, Cal.; private collection, Mrs. Edward M. East, Santa Barbara, Cal.

KERN, JOHN. Teacher of drawing. A native Pennsylvanian, he was 43 years old in 1850 and resided in Philadelphia with his wife and three children, all born in Pennsylvania. He was also listed there in 1851 and 1852, at the same address as EDWARD and RICHARD KERN. ¶ 7 Census (1850), Pa., LIII, 59; Phila. CD 1851–52.

KERN, RICHARD HOVENDEN (1821–1853). Landscape and figure studies in pencil and watercolor. He was born in Philadelphia on April 11, 1821, first exhibited at the Artists' Fund Society in 1840, and taught drawing there in the mid-1840's. In 1848–49 Richard, along with his brothers BENJAMIN and EDWARD KERN, served as a topographical draftsman with FRÉMONT's fourth expedition to the Southwest. In August and September 1849 he was with Simpson's expedition into the Navajo country. In 1851 he accompanied Sitgreaves' expedition down the Zuni and Colorado Rivers. He was in Washington in January 1853, but by May had joined Gunnison's exploration of a route for the Pacific Railroad. On October 26, 1853, he and several other members of the party were killed by Indians near Sevier Lake (Utah). ¶ Information courtesy Josephine M. Bever, who cites: Information courtesy Henry E. Huntington Library; Beckwith, *Report of Exploration of a Route for the Pacific Railroad from the Mouth of the Kansas to Sevier River into the Great Basin,* 33rd Cong., 1st Sess., House Doc. 129, 2; Artists' Fund Soc. Cat., 1840, 1841; Phila. CD 1845–53; Nevins, *Frémont, Pathmaker of the West,* 349; Johnston, *Reports of the Secretary of War with Reconnaissances of Routes from San Antonio to El Paso* and *Report of J. H. Simpson of an Expedition into the Navajo Country,* 31st Cong., 1st Sess., Senate Doc. 64; Sitgreaves, *Report of an Expedition down the Zuni and Colorado Rivers,* 32nd Cong., 2nd Sess., Senate Ex. Doc. 59; Cleland, *A History of California, the American Period,* Appendix D, 496; Taft, *Artists and Illustrators of the Old*

West, 259–61. Represented in Henry E. Huntington Library and Art Gallery, San Marino (Cal.).

KERNEY, see KEARNEY.

KERNWEIDER, M., see WILLIAM KEHRWEIDER, SR.

KERR, JAMES. Philadelphia engraver, 1860. ¶ Phila. CD 1860.

KERR, J. W. Ship painter of Pittsburgh (Pa.). His painting of the Pittsburgh and Cincinnati Steam Packet *Hibernia, No. 2,* was drawn on stone by C. PARSONS and published in the late 1840's by G. & W. ENDICOTT of NYC. ¶ *Portfolio* (Jan. 1948), 77, repro.

KERR, ROBERT. Lithographer and architect. In 1844 he drew and lithographed a design for a Washington Memorial for NYC. Other prints by him are known. ¶ Peters, *America on Stone;* Stokes, *Icon.,* III, 881, and pl. A-26-b.

KERSHAW, FREDERICK. Philadelphia engraver, 1860. ¶ Phila. CD 1860.

KERSHAW, JAMES M. Engraver of St. Louis, 1850's. ¶ Stauffer; St. Louis BD 1854, 1859.

KESLER (or Kessler), FREDERICK. Engraver from Saxony, age 30, living in Philadelphia in 1860 with his Swiss wife and three children born in Pennsylvania, the eldest five years of age. ¶ 8 Census (1860), Pa., LIX, 283; Phila. CD 1860.

KESSLER, ERNEST H. Engraver and die sinker at NYC, 1858. ¶ NYBD 1858.

KETT, EMIL. Landscape painter. Born in Bavaria about 1828, came to the U.S. and settled in Baltimore about 1850, was active there until 1880. His work was shown at the Maryland Historical Society. ¶ 8 Census (1860), Md., V, 108; Lafferty; Rutledge, MHS.

KETTELL, see KITTELL.

KETTERLINUS, EUGENE. Lithographer working in Philadelphia from 1843 to 1876. He had a large business, chiefly commercial work, which was continued after his retirement in 1876 by J. L. Ketterlinus. The firm was still in existence in 1931. ¶ Peters, *America on Stone;* Phila. CD 1843–60+.

KEY, FRANCIS SCOTT (?). Wood engraver. Mrs. Jessie Benton Frémont states in her discussion of the plates for FRÉMONT'S *Memoirs of My Life* that the engravings on wood of views taken on his 1853 expedition were done "by an artist young then, a namesake and grandson of Frank Key, the author of the 'Star Spangled Banner.'" This may have been JOHN ROSS KEY. ¶ Rasmussen, "Artists of the Explorations Overland, 1840–1860," 57.

KEY, FREDERICK C. Engraver and die sinker of NYC, 1844–46; at Philadelphia about 1850. ¶ NYBD 1844, 1846; Stauffer.

KEY, HENRY. Sculptor of Philadelphia, who exhibited at the Pennsylvania Academy in 1859. ¶ Rutledge, PA.

KEY, JOHN ROSS (1832–1920). Landscape painter and illustrator, born July 16, 1832, at Hagerstown (Md.), grandson of the author of "The Star Spangled Banner." He studied art in Munich and Paris and later painted for some years in Boston. In 1863 he was serving with the Corps of Engineers at Charleston (S.C.), recording pictorially the course of the Federal siege of the Confederate city. During the period immediately after the war he worked in NYC and Boston and exhibited at the National Academy, the Pennsylvania Academy and the Boston Athenaeum. He died in Baltimore on March 24, 1920. *Cf.* FRANCIS SCOTT KEY. ¶ *Art Annual,* XVII, obit.; CAB; Clement and Hutton; Fielding; Thieme-Becker; Rutledge, PA; Cowdrey, NAD; Rutledge, *Artists in the Life of Charleston;* represented Corcoran Gallery.

KEYES, CAROLINE (1810–?). Amateur watercolorist, living *c.* 1830 at Salisbury (Conn.). ¶ Information courtesy Mrs. Jean Lipman, correcting Lipman and Winchester, 175, which gives 1810 as her date of death.

KEYS, JANE. Teacher of painting, Troy (N.Y.), 1825. ¶ Lipman and Winchester, 175.

KEYSER, CONSTANTINE. Artist from Baden (Germany), age 38, living in Philadelphia in 1860 with his German wife and two children born in Pennsylvania, the elder nine years of age. Though listed in the Census as an artist, Keyser appears in the 1860 city directory as a commission merchant. His name does not appear before or after that year. ¶ 8 Census (1860), Pa., LII, 575; Phila. CD 1860.

KEYSER, PETER. Portrait painter of Philadelphia, whose lost portrait of ROBERT STREET, painted *c.* 1807, is known through an engraving by SARTAIN. This may be the Kayser who exhibited "an old head" at the Pennsylvania Academy in 1819 and a small full-length portrait in 1847. Peter Keyser appears in Philadelphia directories throughout this period as a lumber merchant. ¶ *American Collector* (June 1945), 6; Rutledge, PA; Phila. CD.

KIDD, ——. Silhouettist at Cincinnati in 1807. ¶ *Antiques* (March 1932), 152.

KIDD, J. Animal painter, NYC; exhibited at the National Academy in 1857. ¶ Cowdrey, NAD.

KIDD, J. B. Landscape painter and lithographer in NYC, *c.* 1836–37. In the latter year he showed a number of views in the British Isles at the National Academy. ¶ Cowdrey, NAD; Peters, *America on Stone.*

KIDDER, JAMES. Landscape artist, engraver, and aquatintist of Boston. As a youth Kidder produced an aquatint view of Boston Common which was published in the *Polyanthus* for June 1813. About 1823 he was working for ABEL BOWEN. Several views in Boston, as well as views of the White Mountains and the Massachusetts coast, date from the 1830's and Kidder was still working in Boston as late as 1840. He exhibited at the Boston Athenaeum. ¶ Stauffer; Swan, BA; Gage; Stokes, *Historic Prints,* 73–74.

KIDDER, JOHN C. Wood engraver from Maine, aged 24, at NYC in 1860. ¶ 8 Census (1860), N.Y., XLIII, 52.

KIDDER, WILLIAM. Artist, 40, a native of Massachusetts, at NYC in 1850. ¶ 7 Census (1850), N.Y., LVI, 359.

KIDNEY, WILLIAM F. Artist, 20, a native of New York, at NYC in 1860. He was married and had one child, aged 4 months. ¶ 8 Census (1860), N.Y., XLIV, 846; NYCD 1863.

KIEFFER, LOUIS. Landscape painter of NYC; exhibitor at the National Academy, 1858–64. ¶ Cowdrey, NAD; NYBD 1858.

KIENTZLE, see KINSLER.

KIESLING, CHARLES. Bavarian engraver, 45, at NYC in 1860. ¶ 8 Census (1860), N.Y., LV, 619; NYCD 1863 as clerk.

KIESSLING, CHRISTOPHER. Engraver at NYC, 1859. ¶ NYBD 1859.

KIGHLEY, JOHN. Painter of a small watercolor of the Forbes house, Newark (N.J.), probably about 1820. ¶ Information courtesy William H. Gerdts, Jr., Newark Museum.

KILBOURNE, SAMUEL A. (1836–1881). Fish and landscape painter. A native of Bridgetown (Me.), he studied landscape painting until about 1858 when he took up the painting of fish, in which he was patronized both by scientists and sportsmen. At the time of his death (May 10, 1881) he had just completed a series of illustrations for a book on *Game Fish of the United States.* ¶ *American Art Review,* II (1881), Part II, 90; Thieme-Becker; Cowdrey NAD (1861).

KILBURN (or Kilbrun), LAWRENCE (1720–1775). Portrait and miniature painter, fancy painter, teacher, and dealer in paint supplies, who arrived in New York from London in 1754 and worked there until his death on June 28, 1775, except for a brief residence in Albany in the spring of 1761. ¶ Moravian Church Records, NYC; Gottesman, *Arts and Crafts in New York,* I, 3–6; Groce, "New York Painting before 1800"; Barker, *American Painting,* 93; Kelby, *Notes on American Artists,* 1–3.

KILBURN & MALLORY. Engravers of Boston, 1852–65. The firm consisted of SAMUEL S. KILBURN, JR., and RICHARD P. MALLORY. ¶ Boston CD 1852; BD 1853–60+; Ford, "Some Trade Cards and Broadsides," 12.

KILBURN, SAMUEL S., JR. Boston engraver. He studied wood engraving under ABEL BOWEN in the 1830's and from 1852 to 1865 was associated with the firm of KILBURN & MALLORY. He did some work for book publishers. ¶ Ford, "Some Trade Cards and Broadsides," 12; Boston CD 1852–60+; Hamilton, 348, 524.

KILDEA, JOHN. Engraver, age 35, born in Pennsylvania, living in Philadelphia with his wife Emily in September 1850. ¶ 7 Census (1850), Pa., LV, 193.

KIMBALL, ——, see MANN & KIMBALL.

KIMBALL, ASA F. Engraver, 55, a native of New Hampshire, at NYC in 1860. In 1850 he was listed as a coffee-roaster. ¶ 8 Census (1860), N.Y., LI, 90; NYCD 1850, 1863.

KIMBALL, CHARLES FREDERICK (1835–1907). Landscape painter and etcher. Born in October 1835 at Monmouth (Me.), he moved to Portland at the age of eight and spent most of his life there. He studied briefly with CHARLES OCTAVIUS COLE, but worked as an amateur only until the 1880's. His first efforts in etching were highly praised in 1881. He died January 28, 1907. ¶ *American Art Review,* II (1881), Part I, 244; Thieme-Becker; Mallett; Cowdrey, NAD. "Maine Artists" gives place and date of birth as Bowdoin (Me.), 1836.

KIMBALL, H. C., & COMPANY. Landscape painters at Chicago in 1858. ¶ Chicago CD 1858.

KIMBALL, MRS. HORACE, see MARY E. LA LANNE.

KIMBALL, MARY ANN. Memorial painting on

velvet, Pennsylvania, *c.* 1825. ¶ Lipman and Winchester, 175.

KIMBALL, WILLIAM HAZEN (1817–92). Miniature painter. Born April 6, 1817, at Goffstown (N.H.), Kimball studied miniature painting in Boston and practised in Manchester (N.H.), Lowell (Mass.), and Philadelphia. Returning to Manchester, he edited a newspaper for two years before taking up daguerreotypy in 1844. He settled in Concord (N.H.) about 1860 and from 1867 to 1890 served as State Librarian of New Hampshire. He died in Concord on March 10, 1892. One of his sons, Edward Wyatt Kimball (born 1852), became a professional painter. ¶ Morrison and Sharples, *History of the Kimball Family in America,* II, 653–54; "Art and Artists in Manchester," 114; *Granite Monthly,* XIV (1892), 125–26; Manchester CD 1844; Concord CD 1860, 1876.

KIMBERLY, DENISON (1814–63). Engraver and portrait painter. Born in Guilford (Conn.), Kimberly studied engraving under ASAPH WILLARD of Hartford and worked chiefly in Boston during the 1840's. In 1858 he abandoned engraving for painting, studied in Boston, and in 1862 opened studios in Hartford and Manchester (Conn.). He died the following year. ¶ French, *Art and Artists in Connecticut,* 88; Stauffer; Grolier Club, *The United States Navy, 1776 to 1815,* 39; Boston CD 1841–50; BD 1842–49; Swan, BA; Bolton, *Crayon Draftsmen;* Thieme-Becker; Fielding.

KIMBERLY, JAMES H. Miniaturist of NYC, 1841–42. ¶ NYCD 1841–42; Bolton, *Miniature Painters;* Fielding.

KIMBERLY, JOSEPH A. Portrait painter. In 1775 he painted a portrait of Paul Revere. ¶ *Art News* (Oct. 15, 1947), 18; *Art Quarterly,* X, No. 3 (1947), 225.

KIMBLE (Kimball or Kemble), COLBY. Portrait painter. An itinerant artist who arrived in Rochester (N.Y.) about 1835 in charge of an exhibition of pictures at the Court House. He remained in Rochester at least until 1867 and by 1854 had completed 67 portraits of Rochester's pioneer settlers. *Cf.* COLBY BILMER. ¶ Little, "Itinerant Painting in America, 1750–1850," 214; Ulp, "Art and Artists in Rochester," 214; Rochester CD 1841–67; Cowdrey, NAD.

KIMMEL BROTHERS. Engravers of NYC, 1860. The partners were FREDERICK K. and JOHN D. KIMMEL. In 1861 they were joined by Margaret A. Kimmel. ¶ NYCD 1860–61.

KIMMEL, CHRISTOPHER. Engraver, lithographer, and printer; born in Germany about 1830; active in NYC from 1850 to 1876. He was with CAPEWELL & KIMMEL from 1853 to 1860, and later with Kimmel & Forster and Kimmel & Voight. ¶ 7 Census (1850), N.Y., XLI, 416 [as Kimbal]; NYCD 1853–76.

KIMMEL, FREDERICK K. (erroneously as P. K.). Engraver of vignettes and portraits, active in NYC, 1856–84. He was with KIMMEL BROTHERS in 1860. His widow, Elizabeth, was listed in 1887. ¶ NYCD 1856–87; Am. Inst. Cat., 1856. Stauffer lists P. K. Kimmel and gives information properly relating to CHRISTOPHER KIMMEL.

KIMMEL, JOHN D. Engraver, NYC, 1860 and after. He was with KIMMEL BROTHERS in 1860, and in 1861 was listed as selling cards. ¶ NYCD 1860+.

KIMMEL, P. K., see FREDERICK K. KIMMEL.

KINDLER, GEORGE. Irish artist, age 53, living in Philadelphia in 1860 with his wife and six children, of whom only the youngest, age 8, was born in Pennsylvania. ¶ 8 Census (1860), Pa., LIV, 515.

KING, CHARLES. Portrait painter working in Maine about 1850. ¶ Lipman and Winchester, 175.

KING, CHARLES. English artist, 34, at NYC in 1850. He was married and had two children, one born in England about 1847 and one born in New York about 1848. ¶ 7 Census (1850), N.Y., XLIII, 6.

KING, CHARLES BIRD (1785–1862). Portrait painter. Born in Newport (R.I.), C. B. King first studied under EDWARD SAVAGE in NYC, then in London under BENJAMIN WEST from 1805 to 1812. Returning to America, he spent several years in Philadelphia and Baltimore before settling in Washington, where he made his home until his death, March 18, 1862. He was particularly noted for his portraits of Indians and was made an Honorary Member, National Academy. ¶ Ewers, "Charles Bird King, Painter of Indian Visitors to the Nation's Capital"; CAB; Dunlap, *History;* Cummings, *Historic Annals,* 306; Rutledge, PA; Swan, BA; Cowdrey, NAD; Cowdrey, AA & AAU; Rutledge, MHS; *Richmond Portraits;* Tuckerman; Fielding; Born, "Notes on Still-life Painting in America," 159.

KING, EDWIN F. Artist, age 27, living in

Washington (D.C.) in 1860. He was a native of the city and lived with his father, James S. King, clerk. ¶ 8 Census (1860), D.C., II, 132; Washington CD 1860 (as "M. A.").

KING, FREDERICK. Map engraver of Paterson (N.J.), 1859. ¶ Paterson CD 1859.

KING, GEORGE B. Line engraver of portraits and book illustrations, working in NYC from 1817 to 1834. ¶ NYCD 1817–33; Stauffer; Fielding.

KING, JAMES S. Line engraver. Stauffer records him as engraver of subject plates for the *Ladies Repository* (Cincinnati, 1852). ¶ Stauffer.

KING, JAMES W., see JOHN WILLIAM KING.

KING, JOHN. Lithographer, age 28, living in Baltimore in June 1860. He was from New York; his wife Emilie, from Germany. ¶ 8 Census (1860), Md., IV, 739.

KING, JOHN CROOKSHANKS (1806–1882). Sculptor. Born October 11, 1806, in Kilwinning (Ayrshire, Scotland); came to America in 1829 and worked as a machinist in New Orleans, Louisville, and Cincinnati until about 1833. In Cincinnati he met HIRAM POWERS who encouraged him to take up sculpture. After several years in New Orleans and Louisville, he moved about 1840 to Boston, where he lived for the rest of his life. His work was chiefly portraiture, both marble busts and cameos. He died in Boston on April 22, 1882. ¶ Fairman, *Art and Artists of the Capitol,* 448; Gardner, *Yankee Stonecutters;* Lee, *Familiar Sketches;* CAB; Cist, *Cincinnati in 1841;* New Orleans *Commercial Bulletin,* April 9, 1841 (cited by Delgado-WPA); Swan, BA; Rutledge, PA; Cowdrey, NAD; Cowdrey, AA & AAU; Boston CD 1843–55; Cincinnati BD 1860; Hart, "Life Portraits of Daniel Webster"; Peters, *America on Stone* (as delineator of a Boston harbor scene, 1844).

KING, JOHN WILLIAM (erroneously as James W.). Portrait painter of New Haven (Conn.), 1855–58. ¶ New Haven CD 1855–58; New England BD 1856.

KING, JOSIAH BROWN (1831–1889). Miniature painter. Born December 16, 1831, at Florida (Mass.), King was paralyzed as a child but managed to lead a fairly normal and varied life. From about 1848 to 1863 he worked as an itinerant miniaturist in Massachusetts. After his marriage in the early 1860's he became a prison overseer at Windsor (Vt.) for a few years, then joined a cutlery firm in Shelburne Falls (Mass.) where he worked until his death in 1889. His work has been confused with that of JAMES SANFORD ELLSWORTH. ¶ Snow, "King versus Ellsworth."

KING, M. A., see EDWIN F. KING.

KING, MYRON. Copperplate engraver of Troy (N.Y.), 1850's. ¶ Troy BD 1852, 1857–58; N. Y. State BD 1859.

KING, SAMUEL (1748/49–1819). Portrait and miniature painter, mathematical instrument maker. He was born January 24, 1748/49, at Newport (R.I.) and spent most of his life there, except for a brief residence in Salem (Mass.) in 1771–72. He is best known as the teacher of GILBERT STUART, EDWARD GREENE MALBONE, and WASHINGTON ALLSTON. He died in Newport on December 30, 1819. ¶ DAB; CAB; Bolton, *Miniature Painters;* Fielding; Sherman, "American Miniatures of Revolutionary Times," repro.; *Antiques* (May 1947), 341.

KING, WILLIAM. Profilist. A native of Salem (Mass.), where he worked as a cabinet maker and ivory turner from about 1785 to 1804, King began taking profiles with the aid of a machine about 1804. During the next two years he took profiles in Salem and Boston (Mass.), Hanover and Portsmouth (N.H.), and Halifax (N.S.). He is said to have left his family in 1809 and gone to the South. ¶ Homer Eaton Keyes, notes on William King, *Antiques* (Sept. 1927), 201–03; Carrick, *Shades of Our Ancestors,* 45; Martin, "Some American Profiles and Their Makers," 88, 92; Jackson, *Silhouette,* 122–23; letter of Donald C. Mackay, Principal, Nova Scotia College of Art, to Mrs. McCook Knox of Washington, Feb. 24, 1950, citing Halifax *Royal Gazette,* Sept. 11 and Oct. 14, 1806, and Halifax *Weekly Chronicle,* Sept. 13 and Oct. 17, 1806 (citation courtesy Mrs. McCook Knox).

KING, WILLIAM J. English artist, age 32, living in Philadelphia in June 1860. Possibly the William J. King, printer, listed in the 1860 directory. ¶ 8 Census (1860), Pa., LII, 215; Phila. CD 1860.

KINGSLEY, DWIGHT. Landscape painter of NYC, 1850. ¶ NYBD 1850.

KINGSLEY, NORMAN WILLIAM (1829–1913). Dentist; amateur sculptor, portrait painter, and engraver. He was born October 26, 1829, in Stockholm (N.Y.) and practised dentistry in Elmira and Troy (N.Y.) before moving to NYC in 1852. His best known work is a bust of Whitelaw Reid at the Lotos Club, NYC. He exhibited at the National Academy 1859–1880. ¶ DAB; Cowdrey, NAD.

KINGSMORE, C. H. Portrait painter. A native of Abbeville District (S.C.), he went to Italy to study early in 1853. ¶ Rutledge, *Artists in the Life of Charleston.*

KINKADE, CHARLES. Engraver, age 24, born in Pennsylvania; living in Philadelphia in 1860. In 1861 he was listed as a machinist. ¶ 8 Census (1860), Pa., LVII, 465; Phila. CD 1861.

KINNERSLEY, AUGUSTUS F. Wood engraver working in NYC from 1845 to 1851. He was born about 1822 and was a brother of HENRY KINNERSLEY. He exhibited at the National Academy and the American Institute. ¶ 7 Census (1850), N.Y., LV, 842; Hamilton, *Early American Book Illustrators and Wood Engravers,* 524; NYCD 1848–50; Am. Inst. Cat., 1848–50; Cowdrey, NAD.

KINNERSLEY (Kinnersly), HENRY. Wood engraver, brother of AUGUSTUS F. KINNERSLEY. He learned wood engraving from SHUBAL D. CHILDS, probably in NYC during the early 1830's and practised there during the 1840's. ¶ Linton, *History of Wood Engraving in America,* 24; NYBD 1844, 1846–47; Cowdrey, NAD.

KINNEY, BENJAMIN HARRIS (1821–1888). Sculptor. He was born in Massachusetts on February 7, 1821, but spent his childhood at Sunderland (Vt.). By 1843 he was established in Worcester (Mass.) as a marble cutter and sculptor and he worked there until his death in December 1888. In August 1850 he was at Rutland (Vt.). ¶ Obituary newspaper clipping at American Antiquarian Society; 7 Census (1850), Vt., IX, 56; Worcester CD 1843; Mass. BD 1853; New England BD 1856–60; Swan, BA; represented Am. Antiq. Soc.

KINNEY, H. E. Portrait painter working in Worcester (Mass.). His portrait of Moses Brown (1783–1836) is at the Rhode Island Historical Society. ¶ C. K. Bolton, "Workers with Line and Color in New England."

KINSEY, NATHANIEL. Engraver of Cincinnati, 1850–59. He was born in Delaware about 1829. In 1850 he was associated with TOPPAN, CARPENTER & COMPANY, banknote engravers, and in 1854–55 with the Methodist Book Concern. ¶ 7 Census (1850), Ohio, XXI, 647; Cincinnati CD 1850–59; Stauffer.

KINSLER (or Kientzle), ALEXANDER. Portrait painter of Philadelphia, 1858 and after. EVERS & KIENTZLE were listed as portrait painters in 1860 and as photographers in 1861. ¶ Phila. CD 1858–61+.

KIPPS, ARTHUR. English landscape painter, age 26, living in Boston in July 1860. LOUIS PRANG lithographed a portrait of Nathaniel P. Banks signed "A. R. Kipps," *c.* 1860. ¶ 8 Census (1860), Mass., XXVII, 479; Havemeyer Collection, NYHS.

KIRCHBAUM, JOSEPH (*c.* 1831–1926). Amateur artist, born in Germany *c.* 1831. He came to Nauvoo (Ill.) soon after the Mormon exodus in 1846 and is said to have made several drawings of the Temple before its destruction in 1848. His earliest dated drawings, however, were done in the 1860's. He died in Nauvoo at the age of 95. His drawings were still owned by the family in 1947. ¶ Arrington, "Nauvoo Temple," Chap. 8.

KIRK, JOHN (*c.* 1823–*c.* 1862). Line engraver, born in England about 1823, came to America about 1841. He was employed in NYC by Putnams and other publishers and engravers and died in the United States about 1862. ¶ Stauffer; *Home Book of the Picturesque;* Thieme-Becker; 7 Census (1850), N.Y., LII, 205.

KIRKBY, THOMAS. Portrait painter. Sherman reported finding in New York a portrait of Edward Powers inscribed "Painted by Thomas Kirkby 1836." ¶ Sherman, "Unrecorded Early American Portrait Painters" (1933), 31.

KIRKHAM, SAMUEL R. Engraver in NYC, 1857–60. He was born in England about 1833 or 1836. ¶ NYBD 1857; 8 Census (1860), N.Y., XLIX, 804 [age 27]; 8 Census (1860), N.Y., LI, 243 [age 24].

KITCHELL, JOHN. Drawing and painting and music teacher at Charleston (S.C.) in 1831. ¶ Rutledge, *Artists in the Life of Charleston.*

KITTELL, NICHOLAS BIDDLE (1822–1894). Portrait and landscape painter. Kittell exhibited at the National Academy in 1847 as a resident of Norwich (Chenango County, N.Y.) and in 1857–69 as of NYC. He died in NYC on June 25, 1894. ¶ NYHS Cat. (1941), no. 525; N. Y. *Tribune,* June 28, 1894, obit.; Cowdrey, NAD; NYBD 1857–60. The year of his birth is here given as 1822 on the strength of the statement in his death certificate (NYC Dept. of Health) that he was aged 72 at the time of his death; other sources give his age as 80 (information courtesy Miss Helen Burr Smith).

KLAEBISCH, LOUIS. Engraver and die sinker of NYC, 1856–59. ¶ NYBD 1856, 1858–59.

KLAUDER, JACOB. Lithographer of Philadelphia, 1860. ¶ Phila. CD 1860.

KLAUPRECH & MENZEL. Lithographers of Cincinnati, 1840–59. The senior partner, Emil Klauprech, was editor of the Cincinnati *German Republican;* the other partner, ADOLPHUS MENZEL, was the chief lithographer. ¶ Cincinnati BD 1850–59; CD 1840–59; Peters, *America on Stone.*

KLEIN, AUGUST. French landscape painter, 50, at NYC in 1860. His wife was from Baden; two children, aged 9 and 11, were born in Pennsylvania; two children, aged 2 months and one year, were born in New York. ¶ 8 Census (1860), N.Y., LV, 657; NYCD 1863 as painter.

KLEINOFEN, HENRY. Landscape painter, of KLEINOFEN & RASMUSSEN, Chicago, 1859. ¶ Chicago CD 1859.

KLEINOFEN & RASMUSSEN. Landscape painters of Chicago, 1859. The partners were HENRY KLEINOFEN and NILS RASMUSSEN. ¶ Chicago CD 1859.

KLEINPETER & COMPANY. Boston engravers, 1858. Kleinpeter is otherwise unknown. ¶ *Boston Almanac* 1858.

KLINCKOWSTRÖM, AXEL LEONHARD (1775–1837). Amateur artist. Friherre Klinckowström, a Swedish nobleman, travelled in America in 1818–20 and published an account of the journey, *Bref om de Fôrenta Staterna . . .* (Stockholm, 1824). The accompanying atlas contained lithographs after his own drawings of American views. ¶ Union Catalogue, Library of Congress.

KLING, PHILIP. German "lithographist," age 25, living in Louisville (Ky.) in 1850. ¶ 7 Census (1850), Ky., XI, 538.

KLUMPP, WILLIAM. Engraver from Württemberg, born about 1828, working in San Francisco from 1852 to after 1860. ¶ 8 Census (1860), Cal., VII, 289; San Francisco CD 1852–61.

KNAPP, CHARLES W. (1823–1900). Landscape painter, born in Philadelphia. He was at NYC in 1859–61, when he exhibited at the National Academy. He died in Philadelphia on May 15, 1900. ¶ *Art Annual,* II, obit.; Cowdrey, NAD; NYBD 1859.

KNAPP, GEORGE KASSON (1833–1910). Portrait painter and banknote engraver. He was working in NYC as an engraver and die sinker in the late 1850's. He died in Syracuse (N.Y.) on May 9, 1910. ¶ *Art Annual,* VIII, obit.; NYBD 1856–59.

KNAPP, JOSEPH F. Lithographer. During the late 1840's he exhibited pencil and crayon drawings at the American Institute. He was working in NYC as a lithographer by 1856 and the following year was taken in to the firm of SARONY & MAJOR, which was known as SARONY, MAJOR & KNAPP until 1867. After Sarony's retirement from the firm in 1867, Major & Knapp continued to operate until 1871. ¶ Peters, *America on Stone;* Am. Inst. Cat., 1847–49; NYCD 1858+.

KNAPP, WILLIAM, JR. Engraver, 19, born in Massachusetts, at NYC in 1860. ¶ 8 Census (1860), N.Y., XLIII, 32.

KNEASS & DELLEKER. Philadelphia engravers, 1817. The firm was composed of WILLIAM KNEASS and GEORGE DELLEKER. ¶ Brown and Brown.

KNEASS, SAMUEL HONEYMAN (1806–58). Topographical draftsman, civil engineer, and architect. A son of WILLIAM KNEASS the engraver, he was born in Philadelphia November 5, 1806. About 1821 he was apprenticed to WILLIAM STRICKLAND. Kneass accompanied the latter to England in 1825 on a survey of English canals, railways, and roads and made the drawings to illustrate Strickland's *Reports* (Philadelphia, 1826). He became a noted railroad and canal engineer. He died in Philadelphia February 15, 1858. ¶ DAB.

KNEASS, WILLIAM (1780–1840). Engraver in line, stipple, and aquatint; die sinker. Born September 25, 1780, at Lancaster (Pa.); studied engraving in Philadelphia and went into business there in 1804. He was a member of the firms of KNEASS & DELLEKER and KNEASS, YOUNG & CO. In January 1824 he was appointed engraver and die sinker at the U. S. Mint, a position which he held until his death, August 27, 1840. His sons, SAMUEL HONEYMAN KNEASS and Strickland Kneass, became noted railroad and canal engineers. ¶ DAB; Stauffer; Phila. CD 1805–40; Fielding; Thieme-Becker; Society of Artists Cat., 1813–14.

KNEASS, YOUNG & COMPANY. Philadelphia engravers, 1818–20. The partners were WILLIAM KNEASS and JAMES H. YOUNG. Stauffer lists them as Young, Kneass & Co. ¶ Brown and Brown; Stauffer; DAB.

KNEELAND, HORACE (*c.* 1808–*c.* 1860). Sculptor; born in New York about 1808; working in NYC 1839–51; died about 1860. He exhibited at the National Academy and the American Art-Union.

¶ Thieme-Becker; Cowdrey, AA & AAU; Cowdrey, NAD; NYBD 1846; 7 Census (1850), N.Y., LVII, 347.

KNEIPP, G. Still life painter at Philadelphia, 1854–55; exhibitor at the Pennsylvania Academy, 1854. *Cf.* George Knieppe (1793–1862), German landscape painter. ¶ Phila. CD 1854–55; Rutledge, PA; Thieme-Becker.

KNEIVIH, OT. Philadelphia lithographer, 1860. Possibly the same as OTTO KNIRSCH, lithographer working in Philadelphia at this time. ¶ Phila. CD 1860–61.

KNICKERBOCKER, CHARLES E. Engraver of Albany (N.Y.), 1854–60. He was associated during this time with ABRAM J. HOFFMAN (in 1855–57 as HOFFMAN & KNICKERBOCKER). ¶ Albany CD 1854–60.

KNIGHT, CHARLES. Miniaturist of Philadelphia, active 1803–17. ¶ Phila. CD 1803–17; Rutledge, PA; Bolton, *Miniature Painters;* Fielding.

KNIGHT, CHARLES A. Boston engraver, 1854–after 1860. From 1857 he was with the firm of SMITH & KNIGHT. ¶ Boston CD 1854–60+.

KNIGHT, DANIEL RIDGWAY (1840–1924). Genre and figure painter. Born March 15, 1840, in Philadelphia, Knight studied at the Pennsylvania Academy, exhibiting there for the first time in 1858. In 1872 he went abroad to study under Gleyre and Meissonier in Paris. Most of his career was spent in France, though he exhibited frequently in his native country. During the First World War he served the French war effort as a pictorial propagandist. He died at his home in Rolleboise-par-Bonniers (Seine-et-Oise) on March 9, 1924. ¶ DAB; *Art Annual,* XXI, obit. (gives 1839 as year of birth); CAB; Clement and Hutton; Thieme-Becker; Rutledge, PA; Swan, BA; Cowdrey, NAD (1869–78).

KNIGHT, EDWARD. English engraver, 26, at NYC in 1850. ¶ 7 Census (1850), N.Y., XLVI, 191.

KNIGHT, GEORGE. Engraver, 25, born in New York, at NYC in 1850. ¶ 7 Census (1850), N.Y., XLVI, 626.

KNIGHT, HENRY. Engraver, born in Pennsylvania about 1830, son of JOHN KNIGHT. He was working in Washington from 1850 into the 1860's. ¶ 7 Census (1850), D.C., II, 235; 8 Census (1860), D.C., II, 733; Washington CD 1860, 1864.

KNIGHT, J. LEE. Engraver at Delphi (Ind.), 1858. ¶ Indiana BD 1858.

KNIGHT, JOHN. Engraver, born in Delaware about 1802. The dates and places of birth of his numerous progeny indicate that Knight was working in Pennsylvania about 1827 to 1835, in New Jersey about 1838–41, again in Pennsylvania about 1845, and in Washington from 1847 into the 1860's. Two of his sons, HENRY and ROBERT, also were engravers. ¶ 7 Census (1850), D.C., II, 235; 8 Census (1860), D.C., II, 733; Washington CD 1850–64.

KNIGHT, JOHN A. Marine and scenic painter. Born in Maine about 1825, he worked in Boston from the late 1840's into the 1860's. His real property was valued in 1860 at $6,000. ¶ 8 Census (1860), Mass., XXVIII, 296; Swan, BA; Boston CD 1850–60+.

KNIGHT, ROBERT T. Engraver, born in Pennsylvania about 1827, son of JOHN KNIGHT. He and his wife Harriet (born in New York) were living with his parents in Washington in 1850, but by 1860 they had settled in Philadelphia. ¶ 7 Census (1850), D.C., II, 235; Phila. CD 1860+.

KNIGHT, T. Engraver in line and stipple, Boston, 1856 and possibly earlier. Stauffer calls him a partner in SMITH, KNIGHT & TAPPAN, which suggests that this may be CHARLES A. KNIGHT. T. Knight does not appear in Boston directories. ¶ Stauffer.

KNIPERS, W. Primitive portrait painter in oils, active about 1860. ¶ Lipman and Winchester, 175.

KNIRSCH, OTTO. Lithographer. About 1853 he was living in Hoboken (N.J.) and working for CURRIER & IVES of New York. From 1858 into the 1860's he worked in Philadelphia. He is said to have been a native of Dresden (Germany). *Cf.* KNEIVIH. ¶ Peters, *America on Stone;* Peters, *Currier and Ives,* pl. 94; Phila. CD 1858, 1860+; *American Collector* (Dec. 1936), 2, repro.

KNOEDLER, CYRIAK. Wood engraver, 31, born in Württemberg, at NYC in 1860. His wife and children, ages 1 to 6, were born in New York. ¶ 8 Census (1860), N.Y., LVII, 464; NYCD 1863.

KNORR, GEORGE. Engraver at Philadelphia, 1860. ¶ Phila. CD 1860.

KNOWLES, W. L. Portrait painter, active about 1860, represented in the collection of Mr. James Thomas Flexner of NYC. ¶ Information courtesy Mr. Flexner.

KNOWLTON, HELEN MARY (1832–1918). Portrait painter and teacher. Born August 16, 1832, at Littleton (Mass.), Miss Knowlton studied under WILLIAM MOR-

RIS HUNT and had a studio in Boston from the mid-1860's. Her writings on art included: *Talks on Art by W. M. Hunt* (1879); *Hints for Pupils in Drawing and Painting* (1879); and *Art Life of William Morris Hunt* (1899). ¶ CAB; Smith; Union Catalogue, Library of Congress; Thieme-Becker; Cowdrey, NAD (1881).

KNOWLTON, J. H. Portrait painter at Manchester (N.H.), 1844. ¶ Manchester CD 1844.

KNOX, JOSEPH B. Engraver and die sinker of KNOX & LANG, Worcester (Mass.), 1858–60. ¶ Worcester CD 1858–60; New England BD 1860.

KNOX & LANG. Engravers and die sinkers of Worcester (Mass.), 1858–60. The partners were JOSEPH B. KNOX and CHARLES LANG. ¶ Worcester CD 1858–60; New England BD 1860.

KNOX, W. P. Delineator of a view of the New Orleans Orphan Asylum, known through an engraving by JOHN HILL (1770–1850). ¶ Stauffer.

KOCH, GEORGE. Portrait painter at Cleveland (Ohio), 1857–59. ¶ Cleveland BD 1857; Ohio BD 1859.

KOCK, J. C. Genre painter, known only for an American farm scene *c.* 1852. ¶ *Panorama* (Jan. 1846), 47.

KOEHLER, FRANCIS X. (1818–1886). Medallist, engraver, die sinker, jeweler. Born August 10, 1818, at Gmünd (Württemberg), he came to America in 1850 and settled in Baltimore. ¶ Thieme-Becker; 7 Census (1850), Md., V, 736; 8 Census (1860), Md., V, 104; Baltimore CD 1856–60.

KOEHLER, JOSEPH. Lithographer at NYC, 1857. ¶ NYBD 1857.

KÖHLER, KARL. Amateur artist. A German who visited America in the early 1850's and published an account, *Briefe aus Amerika* (Darmstadt, 1854), which was illustrated from his own drawings. ¶ Union Catalogue, Library of Congress.

KOEHLER (or Kohler), OTTO. Lithographer of Philadelphia, 1856–70 and after. ¶ Phila. CD 1856–71.

KOEHLER, see also KOHLER.

KÖHNER, WILLIAM (1816–1876). Portrait painter. A native of Berlin (Germany), he settled in Hartford (Conn.) in 1853. In 1866 he moved to Warehousepoint (Conn.) where he died ten years later. ¶ French, *Art and Artists in Connecticut,* 90.

KÖLLNER, AUGUSTUS (1813–?). Lithographer and engraver, **landscape painter in** water colors. Köllner was born in 1813 in Düsseldorf (Germany), studied painting and lithography there and at Frankfurt, and emigrated to the United States in 1839 or 1840. Settling in Philadelphia he was soon working on military prints for HUDDY & DUVAL's *U. S. Military Magazine.* During the 1840's he seems to have travelled widely in the United States, making watercolor views of American scenes which were lithographed and published by Goupil, Vibert of Paris in 1848–51 as *Views of American Cities,* fifty-four in all. Köllner was active in Philadelphia at least until the 1870's. ¶ Peters, *America on Stone;* Todd, "Huddy & Duval Prints"; Phila. CD 1850–60+; 7 Census (1850), Pa., LII, 135; *Portfolio* (May 1944), 195–203, repros.; Rutledge, PA; Stokes, *Historic Prints.* There was a Köllner exhibition at the Free Library of Phila. in February 1947.

KOEMPEL, HENRY. Historical painter. In 1840 he and GERHARDT MUELLER opened a studio in Cincinnati. Some of their work is said still to exist in the old Catholic churches of that city. ¶ Burnet, *Art and Artists of Indiana,* 65; Cincinnati CD 1850.

KOETH, THEO. Primitive genre painter in oils, active about 1860. ¶ Lipman and Winchester, 175.

KOFFNER, J. Painter of a water color of Valley Forge (Pa.) showing part of the City Troop of Philadelphia, 1844. *Cf.* AUGUSTUS KÖLLNER. ¶ *Antiques* (July 1931), 61, repro.

KOHL (or Cohle), ORTELIA (?). Lithographer, age 25, living in Philadelphia in July 1860. He (or she) was a native Pennsylvanian. No person of this name is listed in the directories. ¶ 8 Census (1860), Pa., LIX, 1023.

KOHLBECK, PETER. Portrait painter of NYC. He was painting portraits in the latter half of the 1850's, then turned to taking ambrotypes and photographs. He was active until 1878. ¶ NYBD 1856–61; NYCD 1860–78; NYHS Cat. (1941), nos. 164–65, 258 (repro.).

KOHLER, ROBERT. Artist, 48, a native of Saxony, at NYC in 1850. His wife and two children were born in Saxony before 1838. He was still active in NYC in 1863. ¶ 7 Census (1850), N.Y., XLVI, 736, as Kohelar; NYCD 1863.

KOHN, JULIUS. Artist of Baltimore, 1855–59. ¶ Lafferty.

KOHN, PHILIPPE. Engraver at NYC, 1851. ¶ NYBD 1851.

KOLLMER, HUBER. German engraver, age 22, at Cincinnati in August 1850. ¶ 7 Census (1850), Ohio, XXII, 115.

KOLLNER, see KÖLLNER.

KOLLOCK, MARY (1840–1911). Landscape, still life, and portrait painter; sculptor. Born in Norfolk (Va.) in 1840 (the *Artists Year Book* says August 20, 1832), she studied at the Pennsylvania Academy, the Art Students' League, and in Paris, and began exhibiting at the Pennsylvania Academy in 1864, and at the National Academy in 1866. The greater part of her life was spent in NYC, where she died on January 12, 1911. ¶ *Art Annual,* IX, obit.; *Artists Year Book,* 109; CAB; Clement and Hutton; Bénézit; Fielding; Rutledge, PA; Cowdrey, NAD (1866–87).

KOLUWSKY, HERMINIAS. Artist, age 37, from Poland. In June 1860 she was living in Philadelphia. ¶ 8 Census (1860), Pa., XLIX, 275.

KONGER, HENRY. German lithographer, 22, living in NYC in 1850 with JOHN SINGER. ¶ 7 Census (1850), N.Y., XLVIII, 130.

KOONS, JAMES. Philadelphia artist, 1860. ¶ Phila. CD 1860.

KOPPEL, CHARLES. "Assistant civil engineer and artist" of the California railroad survey party under Lt. R. S. Williamson, which sailed from NYC in May 1853. Williamson's report was illustrated with 21 lithographs and 26 wood-cuts after Koppel's sketches in the field, of which the best known is his view of Los Angeles in November 1853. Of Koppel's subsequent career nothing is known, except that his bust portrait of Jefferson Davis was published as a lithographic print in 1865. ¶ Taft, *Artists and Illustrators of the Old West,* 266–67; Peters, *America on Stone;* Van Nostrand and Coulter, *California Pictorial,* 152–53.

KORFF BROTHERS. Lithographers of NYC, 1852–60. The brothers were HERMAN and LOUIS KORFF. In 1856 they exhibited at the American Institute examples of their work in diplomas, stocks and bonds, checks, and other business paper. ¶ NYCD 1852–60; Am. Inst. Cat., 1856.

KORFF, HERMAN. Lithographer of NYC, 1849–60. Of MAYER & KORFF, 1849–51; of KORFF BROTHERS, 1852–60. ¶ Am. Inst. Cat., 1849–50; NYCD 1850–60.

KORFF, LOUIS. Lithographer of KORFF BROTHERS, NYC, 1852–60. ¶ NYCD 1852–60.

KORN, GEORGE. Engraver and die sinker at NYC, 1854. ¶ NYBD 1854.

KORN, JOSEPH. Engraver, 30, at NYC in 1860. Korn, his wife Eliza, and their two children, aged 8 and 10, were all born in Germany. ¶ 8 Census (1860), N.Y., XLI, 482.

KOSCIATOWSKI, NAPOLEON. Drawing master at Albany (N.Y.), 1835. ¶ Albany CD 1835.

KOSCIUSZKO, TADEUS A. B. (1746–1817). Amateur portrait artist in oils and crayons. Born February 12, 1746, in the Polish section of Lithuania, Kosciuszko came to America in 1776, joined the Continental Army, and served with distinction throughout the Revolution. In 1784 he returned to Europe and during the next two decades led several abortive revolutions aimed at freeing Poland. He revisited the United States in 1797–98. His latter years were spent in retirement at Solothurn (Switzerland) where he died on October 15, 1817. ¶ DAB; CAB; Bolton, *Crayon Draftsmen;* Fielding; Thieme-Becker; Swan, BA.

KOSKY, PURRE (?). Polish portrait painter, age 42, at New Orleans in September 1850. Of his three children, two were born in Scotland between 1839 and 1843 and the youngest in Connecticut about 1845. ¶ 7 Census (1850), La., V, 703.

KRAEMER, PETER, see PETER KRAMER.

KRAETZER, GUSTAV. Lithographer at NYC, 1857. ¶ NYBD 1857.

KRAFT, LEWIS. German lithographer, age 39, at Philadelphia in 1850. He came to America between 1845 and 1849. ¶ 7 Census (1850), Pa., L, 542.

KRAHLENG, CHARLES. Engraver at NYC, 1850. ¶ NYBD 1850.

KRAITSIR, see KREITSER.

KRAMER, CHARLES. Boston lithographer in 1856. ¶ Boston CD 1856.

KRAMER, JOHN MATTHIAS. Artist and teacher of music at Philadelphia in 1775. ¶ Brown and Brown.

KRAMER (Kraemer), PETER (1823–1907). Painter and lithographer. He was born July 24, 1823, at Zweibrücken (Bavaria) and came to the United States in 1848. He was employed by P. S. DUVAL in Philadelphia until 1857, then with the ROSENTHALS. In 1858 he returned to Germany, setting up a business in Stuttgart, but he was later exiled for caricaturing the king of Bavaria. He returned to America and established his studio in NYC. He died in Brooklyn on July 30, 1907. His son and grandson, both namesakes, also were artists. ¶ Thieme-Becker; Peters, *America on Stone;* Phila. CD 1852–59; 7 Census (1850), Pa., LI, 923; Perry, *Expedition to Japan.*

KRAMER, SEBASTIAN, & COMPANY. Lithographers at Boston in 1856. CHARLES KRAMER may have been connected with this firm, since he and Sebastian Kramer lived at the same address. ¶ Boston CD and BD 1856.

KRAMM, GUSTAVUS. German lithographer working in Philadelphia, 1843–54. His age in 1850 was 42 years. ¶ Phila. CD 1843–54; 7 Census (1850), Pa., LII, 907, listed as Gustavus Krim.

KRAMP, WILLIAM C. Lithographer and architect of NYC, 1836–42. ¶ Peters, *America on Stone;* NYCD 1836–41.

KRANS, OLAF (1838–1916). Primitive portrait and genre painter. Born Olaf Olson on November 2, 1838, at Selja (Vestmanland, Sweden), he accompanied his parents to America in 1850 and grew up in the Swedish religious colony at Bishop Hill (Ill.). After service in the Civil War, when he changed his name to Krans, he moved to Galesburg (Ill.) and became a house, sign, and decorative painter there and, after 1867, in Galva (Ill.). In his later years Krans amused himself by painting from memory scenes of pioneer life at Bishop Hill, many of which now hang in the old Colony Church at Bishop Hill. He died in Altoona (Ill.) in January 1916. ¶ Jacobson, "Olaf Krans," in Lipman and Winchester, 139–48, with 4 repros.; *Life* (Jan. 31, 1944), 10–12, illus.; *American Processional,* 136.

KRAUSE, HENRY. Portrait painter of NYC, 1856–60; born in Hamburg (Germany) about 1820. ¶ NYBD 1856–59; 8 Census (1860), N.Y., LIV, 846.

KRAUSS, STEPHEN. Portrait painter of NYC, 1854–60; in 1860, of MILLER, HILLYER & KRAUSS. ¶ NYBD 1854, 1857–60.

KREBS, ADOLPH K. Lithographer at Pittsburgh (Pa.), 1858–64; at Cincinnati in 1870 with PETER EHRGOTT. ¶ Peters, *America on Stone.*

KREEL, JOHN. Hessian engraver, age 36, at Philadelphia in 1860. He was there as early as 1852 when his first child was born. ¶ 8 Census (1860), Pa., 231.

KREITSER, H. Portrait painter at Philadelphia, 1860. ¶ Phila. CD 1860; BD 1860, as H. Kraitsir.

KRIEGHOFF, CORNELIUS (1812–1872). Portrait and genre painter. He was of Dutch parentage and had worked as an itinerant artist in Europe before emigrating to the United States in 1837. He was married in NYC to a French-Canadian and spent the rest of his life in Canada, where he was well known for his paintings of Indian and *habitan* life. ¶ *American Processional,* 242; *Panorama* (Oct.–Nov. 1949), 23; *Art News* (Nov. 1949), 35; Rutledge, PA.

KRIMMEL, JOHN LEWIS (1789–1821). Portrait and genre painter. A native of Ebingen (Württemberg), Krimmel emigrated to the United States in 1810, settling in Philadelphia, where he painted portraits, miniatures, and gently satiric street and domestic scenes. He returned to Germany in 1817 but was back in Philadelphia by 1819. Early in 1821 he was elected President of the Association of American Artists, but on July 15 of the same year he was accidentally drowned near Germantown. ¶ Jackson, "Krimmel, 'The American Hogarth' "; DAB; catalogue of a sale at Doggett's Repository of Arts, Phila., Nov. 22, 1821 (at FARL); Henderson, *Penna. Academy;* Rutledge, PA; Swan, BA; Cowdrey, AA & AAU; Thieme-Becker; *Analectic Magazine,* XVI (1820), 421; *Art in America* (Dec. 1922), 57–58; Dunlap, *History.*

KROUSE, CHARLES. Lithographer at Philadelphia, 1860. ¶ Phila. CD 1860.

KRUGER, FERDINAND. Portrait painter at NYC, 1848–49. ¶ NYBD 1848–49.

KUCHEL, CHARLES CONRAD. Lithographer, born in 1820 at Zweibrücken (Switzerland). He was in Philadelphia by 1846, employed by P. S. DUVAL. By 1853 he had moved to San Francisco where the firm of KUCHEL & DRESEL was prominent until after 1860. ¶ Peters, *America on Stone;* Peters, *California on Stone;* Phila. BD 1846; San Francisco CD 1856, BD 1858–60; Howell, "Pictorial Californiana," 63.

KUCHEL & DRESEL. San Francisco lithographers, 1853–65. CHARLES C. KUCHEL and EMIL DRESEL were the partners. Between 1855 and 1860 they issued a series of *Pacific Views,* showing towns of California and Oregon. ¶ Peters, *California on Stone;* San Francisco CD 1856, BD 1858–60; Ramsay, "The American Scene in Lithograph, The Album," 183; Stokes, *Historic Prints,* pl. 96-b; Jackson, *Gold Rush Album;* Rasmussen, "Art and Artists in Oregon" (citation courtesy David C. Duniway, Oregon State Archivist).

KUCHEL, JACOB. German artist, age 32, at

Philadelphia in September 1850. ¶ 7 Census (1850), Pa., LI, 924.

KÜHN, JUSTUS ENGLEHARDT (?–1717). Portrait painter. A German, Kühn settled at Annapolis (Md.) sometime before December 1708 and worked there until his death in November 1717. At least eleven works from his hand have been identified. Pleasants, "Justus Englehardt Kühn," with ten repros.; Pleasants, *250 Years of Painting in Maryland,* nos. 1–3; represented at MHS and Peabody Institute, Baltimore.

KÜNER, ALBERT (1819–1906). Engraver and die-sinker. George Ferdinand Albert (known in America as Albert) Küner was born October 10, 1819, at Lindau (Bavaria). In 1848 he emigrated to California and settled in San Francisco, where he made his home until his death on January 23, 1906. ¶ Thieme-Becker; 8 Census (1860), Cal., VII, 289; San Francisco CD 1852–56, BD 1858–60.

KUHL, FREDERICK. Lithographer working in Philadelphia, 1844–50; at San Francisco in 1856. ¶ Phila. BD 1844–50; San Francisco BD and CD 1856.

KUHN, ROBERT. Portrait painter at NYC, 1857. ¶ NYBD 1857.

KUMMER, JULIUS HERMANN (1817–after 1869). Landscape painter and lithographer. Born in Dresden (Saxony), studied at the Dresden Academy, 1832–35, and practised painting and lithography there until the Revolution of 1848. He came to America in 1849 and first worked in NYC and Brooklyn, then in Boston, and finally, after 1860, moved to St. Louis. He painted views on the Plains and in the Rocky Mountains during the 1860's. ¶ Powell, "Three Artists of the Frontier," 35, 41–43; Cowdrey, NAD; Cowdrey, AA & AAU; NYBD 1850–54; Cambridge BD 1860; Stokes, *Historic Prints,* pl. 97-a.

KUNKELY, JULIUS. Landscape painter, NYC, 1853. ¶ NYCD 1853.

KUNKERLEY, EDWARD. Portrait painter at Rome (N.Y.), 1859–60. ¶ Rome CD 1859; N. Y. State BD 1859.

KUNTZE, EDWARD J. (1826–1870). Sculptor and etcher. A native of Pomerania (Germany), who came to America in 1852, worked in Philadelphia in the mid-1850's and in NYC from 1857 until his death, except for a three year residence in London from 1860 to 1863. He was an Associate of the National Academy, 1869–70. ¶ Thieme-Becker; *Art Journal* (1861), 62; N. Y. *Home Journal,* April 13, 1870, obit.; Hamilton, 351; Rutledge, PA; Wilson, *Lincoln in Portraiture;* Clement and Hutton; CAB; Graves; Gardner, *Yankee Stonecutters;* Cowdrey, NAD.

KUONY, VICTOR. Artist, Baltimore, 1856. ¶ Baltimore CD 1856.

KUONY, VICTOR, JR. Artist, Baltimore, 1856. ¶ Baltimore CD 1856.

KURTZ, HENRY. Engraver, portrait and landscape painter. The son of a German baker, Kurtz was born in Massachusetts about 1822, worked as an engraver and painter in Boston from 1844 into the 1860's, and exhibited at the Boston Athenaeum. He was with NICHOLS & KURTZ in 1846. ¶ 7 Census (1850), Mass., XX, 698; Boston CD 1844–60+; Swan, BA.

KURTZ, HORATIO J. Lithographic artist at Philadelphia, 1859–60. ¶ Phila. CD 1859–60.

KURTZ, WILLIAM (1833–1904). Crayon portraitist and photographer. Probably German by birth, he came to the United States before 1861 and exhibited at the National Academy, 1865–82. He died at Far Rockaway (N.Y.) on December 5, 1904. ¶ *Art Annual,* V (1905), 121, obit.; represented at NYHS.

KURZ, EMIL (*Album of American Battle Art,* 272), is LOUIS KURZ.

KURZ, FRIEDRICH (originally Rudolph Friedrich) (1818–1871). Portrait, animal, and landscape painter; teacher. Born January 18, 1818, in Bern (Switzerland), studied art there. From 1846 to 1852 he was in the United States, travelling along the Mississippi and upper Missouri Rivers from New Orleans to St. Louis and Fort Union. His sketchbooks from these travels are now in the Bern Historical Museum. From 1855 to his death in 1871 Kurz was a teacher of design in the cantonal schools at Bern and founder and first director of its school of art. ¶ Bushnell, "Friedrich Kurz, Artist-Explorer"; Kurz, "Journal"; Thieme-Becker; *Museum Graphic* (Summer 1952), fourteen repros.

KURZ, LOUIS (1833–1921). Lithographer; mural and scene painter. A native of Austria, Kurz was brought to America in 1848. In 1852 he moved with his family to Chicago, where he began his career as a scene painter. He began to do lithographic work during the 1850's in Milwaukee (Wis.) and was associated there with HENRY SEIFERT. After service with the Union Army during the early part of the Civil War, he returned to Chicago and founded the Chicago Lithographic Company (1863–71). During the 1870's he headed the American Oleograph Company in Milwaukee. In 1878 he returned to Chicago and two years later entered into partnership with Alexander Allison, the firm producing chromolithographs at least until 1899. Kurz died in Chicago on March 21, 1921. His best known work was a series of views for Jevne and Almini's *Chicago Illustrated* (1866). ¶ Kent, "Early Commercial Lithography in Wisconsin," 249–50; Angle, "Jevne and Almini," 313–16; Peters, *America on Stone; Art Annual,* XVIII, obit.; Thieme-Becker; *Album of American Battle Art,* 272 (as Emil Kurz).

KUTTS, JOHN. Architect of Philadelphia, 1842–44, who exhibited water color designs for public buildings at the Artists' Fund Society. ¶ Rutledge, PA; Phila. CD 1843.

KYLE, JOHN. Artist, NYC, 1850. *Cf.* JOSEPH KYLE. ¶ NYCD 1850.

KYLE, JOSEPH (1815–1863). A.N.A. Panoramist; portrait and figure painter. A native of Ohio, Kyle studied in Philadelphia under SULLY and OTIS and came to NYC about 1846. He was a steady exhibitor at the Pennsylvania Academy, Artists' Fund Society, American Art-Union, and National Academy, and became an Associate of the National in 1849. In 1848 he advertised for sale his panorama of the Mississippi and during the next decade he collaborated with other artists on many other panoramas. He died in NYC in 1863. ¶ Smith; Rutledge, PA; Cowdrey, NAD; Thieme-Becker; Cowdrey, AA & AAU; information courtesy J. E. Arrington; repro. in Met. Mus., *Life in America;* 7 Census (1850), N.Y., LII, 272.

L

L——, A——. Exhibitor of a "composition" at the National Academy in 1842; a resident of NYC. *Cf.* ANNA LESLIE. ¶ Cowdrey, NAD.

LABASTE or LABARTE, JOHN B. Drawing master at Philadelphia, 1800–04. ¶ Brown and Brown.

LABATUT, ISADOR. Painter of portraits, miniatures, and transparencies; teacher of drawing. He was married at Charleston (S.C.) in May 1798 and worked there at least until 1825. He painted a miniature of Washington before July 1799. ¶ Rutledge, *Artists in the Life of Charleston,* 126, 205; Charleston CD 1825; Prime, II, 51–52; Bolton, *Miniature Painters.*

LABATUT, J. or T. Portrait painter, teacher of drawing at Charleston (S.C.), 1836–48. In 1841 his portrait of President Harrison was bought by the City Council. He also advertised as a public writer and translator. ¶ Rutledge, *Artists in the Life of Charleston,* 205–06.

LABORN or LABOM, ADOLPHE. Ohio-born lithographer, age 25, living in Philadelphia in 1860. FRANCIS DEVANNIE, sculptor, and NICHOLAS SHIPS and CHARLES SCHILCOCK, lithographers, lived at the same address. ¶ 8 Census (1860), Pa., LII, 432.

LACLOTTE, HYACINTHE (or Hethe). Architect, engraver, teacher of drawing and painting, scene painter. He worked in New Orleans between 1811 and 1815 as a scene painter and teacher, and in 1815 made a panoramic drawing of the Battle of New Orleans. He returned to France in 1817, had the battle scene engraved in Paris, and had it published in Philadelphia in 1818. That same year he was listed in Philadelphia as Hethe Laclotte, engraver and architect. Saunier's history of Bordeaux lists a late 18th-century architect by this name who may have been the same man. ¶ Delgado-WPA cites *La. Courier,* Sept. 19, 1811, and March 10, 1813, *Moniteur,* March 20 and July 29, 1813, *L'Ami des Lois,* July 27, 1813, and *La. Courier,* Oct. 27, 1817; Todd, "Huddy and Duval Prints"; *Album of American Battle Art,* plate 47; Brown and Brown; Saunier, *Bordeaux.*

LACOUR, PETER (or Pierre). Artist and teacher of drawing, who worked in NYC from 1785 to 1799, advertising himself as a "Scholar of the Royal Academy of Painting at Paris." His view of Washington's inauguration at Federal Hall in 1789 is known through an engraving by AMOS DOOLITTLE. ¶ NYCD 1789–99; Kelby, *Notes on American Artists,* 25; Gottesman, II, 342–43; Stokes, *Icon.,* III, 537–39, plate 8; Stokes, *Historic Prints,* frontis.

LACROIX, PAUL. Landscape painter at NYC, 1858. ¶ NYBD 1858.

LADD, B. F. Portrait and miniature painter, restorer, at Charleston (S.C.) 1828–29. ¶ Rutledge, *Artists in the Life of Charleston.*

LADD, Mrs. B. F. Teacher of "Poonah" or theorem painting on velvet and paper, as well as embroidery, bead, wax, and shell work, etc. At Charleston (S.C.) 1828–29. ¶ Rutledge, *Artists in the Life of Charleston.*

LADD, FRANKLIN BACON (1815–1898). Portrait and landscape painter, born September 10, 1815, at Augusta (Maine). He was exhibiting at the National Academy as early as 1837. In 1841 he was at New Orleans, in 1845 at NYC, in 1847 at Philadelphia, and in 1853 at Augusta. He later settled in Brooklyn (N.Y.) where he painted portraits of a number of its mayors. His last years were spent in the Home for the Aged, Brooklyn, where he died on April 9, 1898. ¶ North, *History of Augusta;* Cowdrey, NAD; Cowdrey, AA & AAU; Delgado-WPA cites New Orleans *Picayune,* March 27, 1841; Stokes, *Historic Prints,* pl. 90a; Rutledge, PA; obit., Boston *Transcript,* April 14, 1898; repro., *Art Digest,* July 1948, 6.

LADD, JAMES M. Amateur marine artist known only for his sketch of the bombardment of Vera Cruz (Mexico) during the Mexican War. A native of Maine, Ladd served in the U. S. Navy as a midshipman during that war and died on November 26, 1847, at the Naval Hospital in Norfolk (Va.). ¶ *Album of American Battle Art,* 137, pl. 63.

LAER, FERDINAND VON. Painter and lithographer. Von Laer worked in Berlin from 1828 until after 1846, then emigrated to America and settled at Cincinnati about 1850. He was still there in 1860. ¶ Thieme-

Becker; Peters, *America on Stone;* Cincinnati BD and CD 1850–60; repro., *Portfolio* (May 1951), 201.

LAFARGE, JOHN (1835–1910). N.A. Mural, still life, and landscape painter, designer of stained glass. Born in NYC on March 31, 1835, LaFarge graduated from Mount St. Mary's College in Maryland and studied law briefly before going to Europe in 1856. For two years he studied painting, then returned to America and studied for a short time with WILLIAM MORRIS HUNT at Newport (R.I.). About 1876 he turned from landscapes and flower studies to mural painting and the designing of stained glass, in both of which he was preeminent among the American artists of the day. LaFarge was also noted as a painter of scenes in the South Seas and as a writer of travel books and art criticism. He died at Providence (R.I.) on November 14, 1910. ¶ The principal biography of LaFarge, published the year after his death, is Royal Cortissoz's *John LaFarge: A Memoir and a Study.* E. A. Park's *Mural Painters in America,* Part I, has a long bibliography on LaFarge. See also repro. in McCausland, "American Still-life Paintings."

LAGURANE. Three brothers of this name, all born in Italy, were employed as figure makers by S. TREAGA of Philadelphia in August 1850. They were John (20), Peter (17), and Santonio (19). ¶ 7 Census (1850), Pa., L, 859.

LAIDLAW, JAMES B. (*c.* 1822–1854). Scene painter. An Englishman, who came to America probably in the mid-1840's. In 1848–49 he assisted HENRY LEWIS in painting the latter's Mississippi panorama at Cincinnati, and he was still there in 1850. He subsequently moved to St. Louis and was employed as scene painter at the theater there when he was murdered on May 5, 1854. ¶ 7 Census (1850), Ohio, XX, 129; Arrington, "Nauvoo Temple," Chap. 8; St. Louis *Missouri Republican,* May 6–8, 1854; Trenton (N.J.) *State Gazette,* May 15, 1854.

LAIDLER, THOMAS. Limner and drawing master at Charleston (S.C.) in 1768. ¶ Prime, I, 5; Rutledge, *Artists in the Life of Charleston.*

LAING, JOSEPH, & COMPANY. Lithographers of NYC, 1851–60. In 1858 his home was in Brooklyn. ¶ NYCD and BD 1851–60.

LAKEMAN, NATHANIEL (1756–after 1830). Portrait painter of Salem (Mass.). He exhibited at the Boston Athenaeum in 1830. ¶ Swan, BA; Fielding; Dunlap, *History* (1918), III, 313.

LAKEY, Mrs. EMILY JANE (1837–1896). Genre painter. Born June 22, 1837, at Quincy (N.Y.), Emily Jane Jackson was brought up there and taught school in Tennessee and Ohio before her marriage in 1864 to Dr. Charles D. Lakey. She first exhibited in Chicago and in 1873 was represented in the National Academy exhibition. She studied in France in 1877–78. She died at Cranford (N.J.) on October 24, 1896. ¶ CAB, supplement; Smith; Fielding.

LA LANNE, MARY E. Miniaturist of Boston; exhibited at the Athenaeum in 1833. She married Dr. Horace Kimball. *Cf.* Miss —— LELAND. ¶ Swan, BA, 186, 246; Bolton, *Miniature Painters;* Fielding.

LALL, JAMES. Portrait painter at NYC, 1848. ¶ NYBD 1848.

LAMARTIS, ——. Scene painter who assisted DELAMANO in painting a panorama of the Crystal Palace, shown in NYC in December 1851. ¶ N. Y. *Herald,* Dec. 2, 1851 (citation courtesy J. E. Arrington).

LAMB, JOHN. General engraver, at NYC in March 1756. ¶ Gottesman, I, 13.

LAMB, JOSEPH (1833–1898). Painter specializing in ecclesiastical and memorial work. A native of England, he passed most of his career in America where he died on December 13, 1898. ¶ *Art Annual,* I (supp.), obit.

LAMB, K. A. Primitive genre painter, said to have worked in New England about 1850. ¶ Lipman and Winchester, 176.

LAMBDIN, GEORGE COCHRAN (1830–1896). N.A. Portrait, genre, and flower painter. The eldest son of JAMES REID LAMBDIN, George was born at Pittsburgh (Pa.) in 1830 but was taken to Philadelphia at the age of eight. He studied with his father and began exhibiting at the Pennsylvania Academy in 1848. Except for visits to Europe in 1855 and 1870 and two years in NYC, 1868–70, he passed most of his professional career in Philadelphia, where he died on January 28, 1896. He was best known for sentimental genre and children's portraits and was elected a National Academician in 1868. ¶ Bolton, *Crayon Draftsmen;* Karolik Cat.; Rutledge; PA; Phila. CD 1852–60+; Rutledge, MHS; Swan, BA; Cowdrey, NAD; represented at Maryland Historical Society and Peabody Institute.

LAMBDIN, J. HARRISON. Painter. A son of JAMES REID LAMBDIN, born probably in

Philadelphia about 1841. Between 1859 and 1862 he exhibited a number of "studies from life and nature" at the Pennsylvania Academy and the Historical Society of Pennsylvania owns his copy in oil of a drawing by JOHN WATSON. ¶ Rutledge, PA; Sawitzky, *Hist. Soc. of Pa. Cat.*

LAMBDIN, JAMES REID (1807–1889). Portrait and miniature painter; born May 10, 1807, at Pittsburgh (Pa.). In 1823 he went to Philadelphia to study for a year or two under EDWARD MILES and THOMAS SULLY, after which he returned to Pittsburgh as a portrait painter and proprietor of a museum and gallery of art. About 1832 he moved to Louisville (Ky.) and thence in 1837 to Philadelphia, where he spent the rest of his life. Lambdin was for many years an officer in both the Artists' Fund Society and the Pennsylvania Academy and an Honorary Member of the National Academy. His sitters included many national figures, including Presidents Lincoln and Grant. Among his pupils were WILLIAM RUSSELL SMITH and his own sons, GEORGE COCHRAN and J. HARRISON LAMBDIN. He died in Philadelphia on January 31, 1889. ¶ DAB; Anderson, "Intellectual Life of Pittsburgh: Painting," 289, 291–92; Rutledge, PA; Phila. CD 1839–60+; O'Connor, "Reviving a Forgotten Artist"; Swan, BA; Cowdrey, NAD; Cowdrey, AA & AAU; Rutledge, MHS; Wilson, *Lincoln in Portraiture;* 7 Census (1850), Pa., LVI, 514; represented at Maryland Historical Society, University of Pennsylvania, Peabody Institute, and NYHS.

LAMBERT, CHARLES (1816–1892). Stonecutter who carved some of the sun-face capitals of the Nauvoo Temple of the Latter Day Saints at Nauvoo (Ill.) about 1844. He was born in Kirk Deighton, Yorkshire, on August 30, 1816; joined the Mormons in 1843 and came to Nauvoo the following year; settled in Utah in 1849; died in Salt Lake City on May 2, 1892. ¶ Arrington, "Nauvoo Temple."

LAMBERT, JOHN. Amateur artist. An Englishman who travelled in North America between 1806 and 1808, he later published an account of his journey, illustrated with aquatints after his own sketches. ¶ Lambert, *Travels Through Canada and the United States* (London, 1813).

LAMITH, JOSEPH. Image-maker at NYC, 1800. ¶ NYCD 1800.

LAMONT, DANIEL G. Portrait, miniature, and historical painter. He was at Concord (N.H.) in 1837–39, at Philadelphia in 1840 (exhibiting at the Academy in that and the following year), and at NYC from 1846 to 1850. ¶ WPA (N.H.), Historical Records Survey cites ads in *N. H. Patriot and Gazette;* Rutledge, PA; NYBD 1846, 1850; Bolton, *Miniature Painters;* repro., *American Collector* (Jan. 1945), 7.

LAMONT, FREDERICK. French "artist," age 22, at Philadelphia in July 1860. ¶ 8 Census (1860), Pa., LII, 42.

LA MONTAGNE or LA MONTAGUE, WALTER E. (1839–1915). Painter. He was listed as Lamontagne at Buffalo (N.Y.) in 1856 and 1858. By 1867 he had moved to Detroit where he apparently lived until his death on June 30, 1915. In the *Art Annual* obituary notice the name is given as La Montague, while in the Detroit directories he was listed sometimes as La Montague and sometimes as La Montagne. ¶ *Art Annual,* XII, obit.; Buffalo CD 1856, 1858; Detroit CD 1867, 1876, 1885, 1895.

LAMOR, ANTONY. Portrait and decorative painter at Philadelphia, 1856–60 and after. He was born in Hungary about 1824 and came to America before 1847, all his children having been born in Pennsylvania after that date. ¶ 8 Census (1860), Pa., LII, 495; Phila. CD 1856–60+.

LAMSON, J. Itinerant artist. A resident of Sebec (Maine), Lamson went to California with the "Gold Rush," returned East in 1852, and made a second California visit from 1856 to 1860. Though he tried his hand at mining and storekeeping, he was chiefly an itinerant artist who earned his way by executing drawings of mining claims and the homes of successful immigrants. His manuscript journal and a portfolio of sketches are in the California Historical Society. ¶ Van Nostrand and Coulter, *California Pictorial,* 94–95, 130–31.

LAMSON, JOSEPH. Tombstone carver of Charlestown (Mass.) early in the 18th century. His work included representations of faces and figures. ¶ Allen, "Winged Skull and Weeping Willow," 252.

LANCELIN, JOHN L. (?–1822). Portrait and miniature painter, scene painter and comedian. He was at New Orleans from 1819 until his death in October 1822, while still a young man. ¶ New Orleans CD 1822; Delgado-WPA cites *La. Cour-*

ier, Dec. 1819, and Jan. 1821, and obit. in *La. Gazette,* Oct. 11, 1822.

LANDER, LOUISA (1826–1923). Portrait sculptor; born September 1, 1826, at Salem (Mass.). After studying under THOMAS CRAWFORD in Rome about 1855, Miss Lander established her studio in Washington (D.C.). She died in Washington on November 14, 1923. ¶ Belknap, *Artists and Craftsmen of Essex County,* 18; Gardner, *Yankee Stonecutters;* CAB; Swan, BA.

LANDIS, JOHN. Portrait, historical, and religious painter, lithographer. Born October 15, 1805, at Lancaster (Pa.), he was active from 1830 to 1851. ¶ Lancaster County Hist. Soc. *Papers,* XVI (1912), 179–85; Peters, *America on Stone.*

LANDMANN, ——. Steel engraver at New Orleans in 1851. ¶ Delgado-WPA cites New Orleans CD 1851.

LANE, ALONZO. Artist, 23, a native of New York, at NYC in 1860 with his wife Hannah and son David. ¶ 8 Census (1860), N.Y., LX, 1024.

LANE, CHARLES (1790–1854). Portrait painter at Hingham (Mass.) during the 1840's and an exhibitor at the Boston Athenaeum. ¶ Swan, BA.

LANE, FITZ HUGH (1804–1865). Landscape and marine painter; lithographer. Nathaniel Rogers Lane, as he was christened, was born at Gloucester (Mass.) on December 18, 1804. About 1832 he went to Boston to learn lithography under PENDLETON and from 1837 to about 1845 he was employed by the Boston publishers Keith & Moore. From 1845 to 1847 he was in partnership with JOHN W. A. SCOTT. Returning to Gloucester in 1849, he lived there until his death, devoting himself to painting and making summer trips to Maine and possibly to Porto Rico. He died in Gloucester on August 13, 1865. ¶ McCormick, "Fitz Hugh Lane, Gloucester Artist"; Baur, "Unknown American Painters," 277–82; Brooks, "Fitz Lane's Drawings"; Karolik Cat.; Swan, BA; Cowdrey, NAD; Cowdrey, AA & AAU; Peters, *America on Stone;* Stokes, *Historic Prints.*

LANE, JOHN. Artist, 36, a native of New York, at NYC in 1860. ¶ 8 Census (1860), N.Y., XLVI, 238; NYCD 1863.

LANE & SCOTT. Lithographers of Boston, *c.* 1845–47. The firm consisted of FITZ HUGH LANE and JOHN W. A. SCOTT. ¶ Peters, *America on Stone;* Boston CD 1847, BD 1848.

LANE, SUSAN MINOT (1832–1893). Landscape painter of Cambridge (Mass.). ¶ Boston Museum of Fine Arts, *Cat.;* Fielding.

LANE, THOMAS HENRY (1815–1900). Miniature and portrait painter. Born February 24, 1815, in Philadelphia, he began his painting career there in the early 1840's. About 1845 he was associated with Poe on the staff of the *Broadway Journal* in NYC. He died in Elizabeth (N.J.) September 27, 1900. ¶ *Art Annual,* IV, 142, obit.; Phila. CD 1841–44; Rutledge, PA; Thieme-Becker.

LANE, WILLIAM JARED (1789–1867). Amateur miniaturist. He was born October 13, 1789, at New Milford (Conn.), studied law, and was for many years cashier of the Fulton Bank in NYC. He died at New Milford May 8, 1867. ¶ Sherman, "American Miniaturists of the Early 19th Century," 81 (repro.), 83.

LANG, CHARLES. Engraver of Worcester (Mass.), 1858–60; of KNOX & LANG. ¶ Worcester CD 1858–60; New England BD 1860.

LANG, CHARLES. Lithographer, 28, born in Bavaria, at NYC in 1860 with his wife Eliza. ¶ 8 Census (1860), N.Y., XLV, 14.

LANG, GEORGE. Portrait and landscape painter of Cincinnati, 1853–60. ¶ Cincinnati CD 1853–60.

LANG, GEORGE S. (1799–?). Line-engraver, born in 1799 in Chester County (Pa.). He is said to have been a pupil of GEORGE MURRAY in 1815. He worked in Philadelphia until about 1833, then apparently gave up engraving. He was still living in Delaware County in 1883. ¶ Stauffer.

LANG, LOUIS (1814–1893). N.A. Portrait, miniature, and genre painter. Born March 29, 1814, in Württemberg, he was studying in Paris in 1834 and emigrated to America in 1838. After a few years in Philadelphia, he went to Italy for several years, and on returning in 1847 settled in NYC where he was a well-known artist until his death on May 6, 1893. ¶ Thieme-Becker; Rutledge, PA; Cowdrey, NAD; Cowdrey, AA & AAU; Swan, BA; Rutledge, MHS; minutes of NYHS, May 1893; repro., NYHS *Quarterly* (April 1945), 71.

LANG, PH. Portrait painter who came from Germany probably in the late 1840's, spent a few years at Cincinnati, then moved to Rockport (Ind.) about 1852.

¶ Goss, *Cincinnati, the Queen City;* Peat, *Pioneer Painters of Indiana.*

LANG, WILLIAM. Lithographer; born in Scotland about 1825; working in NYC from 1849. He exhibited at the American Institute in 1849. ¶ 7 Census (1850), N.Y., XLI, 494; Am. Inst. Cat., 1849; NYCD and NYBD 1859.

LANGDELL, GILES. New Hampshire artist, age 35, living at Boston in 1850. His wife and daughter (5) were both born in Massachusetts. He was listed without occupation in 1853. ¶ 7 Census (1850), Mass., XXVI, 40; Boston CD 1853.

LANGDON, CHAUNCEY. Topographical artist. A Vermonter, Langdon went to California in 1851 and worked as a miner at Ophir, later as a farmer at Rohnerville, Humboldt County. While at Ophir he was engaged to make sketches of Gregory's express depots there and at Auburn, lithographs of which were used as letterheads. ¶ Van Nostrand and Coulter, *California Pictorial,* 112–13, repro.

LANGENBAHN, AUGUST A. (1831–1907). Sculptor; born in Germany on August 28, 1831, and came to America about 1852. He settled in Buffalo (N.Y.) about 1885 and died there June 7, 1907. ¶ *Art Annual,* VI, 111, obit. (erroneously as Langebahn); Thieme-Becker; represented: NYHS.

LANGENDERFER or LANGENDOEFFER, JOHN J. Portrait painter and crayon artist. He was listed at a Philadelphia address in 1836 when he exhibited at the Artists' Fund Society. In 1850 his crayon portrait of Martin Van Buren was shown at the Pennsylvania Academy. *Cf.* Johann Langenderfer, German portrait painter active about 1830. ¶ Rutledge, PA; Thieme-Becker.

LANGLOIS DE BARNVILLE, ——. Drawing instructor. He was proprietor of a French School at Charleston (S.C.) in 1803. He or his wife and daughter continued to give instruction in the polite arts to the young ladies of Charleston and Cannonsborough into the 1840's. After Mrs. Langlois' death in December 1844, the Academy was run by Miss Langlois at least until 1848. ¶ Rutledge, *Artists in the Life of Charleston,* 206.

LANGLUM, ——. "Lithographist" at New Orleans in April 1837. ¶ Delgado-WPA cites *Bee,* April 5, 1837.

LANGRIDGE, JAMES L. Wood engraver; born in England about 1837; exhibited at the American Institute in NYC in 1850 and 1851; working in NYC as an engraver for book publishers until about 1880. ¶ 8 Census (1860), N.Y., LIII, 1005; Am. Inst. Cat., 1850–51; Hamilton, *Early American Book Illustrators and Wood Engravers,* 524.

LANING or LANNING, WILLIAM M. (L., J., or S.). Genre and still life painter, decorator, and commercial artist. He was working in Charleston (S.C.) in 1837–38 with GIOVANNI CHIZZOLA; in Philadelphia, 1841–49, with R. G. Laning, as sign and house painters; in Baltimore, 1851–60, as block letterer and ornamental painter. He is presumed to be the Lanning, W. S. Laning, and W. L. Laning who exhibited genre and still life paintings at the Maryland Historical Society in 1853 and 1856. ¶ Rutledge, *Artists in the Life of Charleston,* 206; Phila. CD 1841–49; Baltimore CD 1851–60; Rutledge, MHS.

LANMAN, CHARLES (1819–1895). A.N.A. Landscape painter; born June 14, 1819, at Monroe (Mich.). After studying at Plymouth Academy, Norwich (Mass.), he worked from 1836 to 1845 in the East India mercantile house in NYC. During these years he studied engraving with ASHER B. DURAND and exhibited paintings at the National Academy and American Art-Union, and in 1846 he was elected an Associate of the Academy. After several years as a journalist in Michigan, Ohio, and NYC, he settled in Washington (D.C.), where he held a number of government posts and pursued a literary career. He is chiefly remembered for his *Dictionary of the United States Congress,* published in 1859. He died in Georgetown (D.C.) on March 4, 1895. ¶ DAB; French, *Art and Artists of Connecticut,* 104–06; Cowdrey, AA & AAU; Cowdrey, NAD; 8 Census (1860), D.C., I, 91; Washington Art Assoc. Cat., 1857, 1859; represented: Corcoran Gallery. His papers are in the Library of Congress.

LANNEAU, CHARLES H. Portrait painter of Charleston (S.C.), 1836–43. ¶ Rutledge, *Artists in the Life of Charleston,* 206.

LANNEAU, F. Amateur artist who showed four pen sketches of military evolutions at Charleston (S.C.) in 1850. ¶ Rutledge, *Artists in the Life of Charleston,* 206.

LANSING, ALFRED A. Wood engraver, son of GARRET LANSING. He practised in NYC from 1840 to 1858 and is said by Lossing to have been the first to engrave large pictures for circus and theater bills. He was also a comic actor. ¶ Lossing, *Me-*

morial of Alexander Anderson, 74; NYCD 1840–58.

LANSING, GARRET or GERRET. Wood engraver. A native of Albany (N.Y.), Lansing was in 1804 the first pupil of ALEXANDER ANDERSON and one of the earliest American engravers on wood. He worked in Albany and Boston for a number of years after 1804, but later settled in NYC where he was active in the late 1830's. His son, ALFRED A. LANSING, also became a wood engraver. ¶ Lossing, *Memorial of Alexander Anderson,* 74; Linton, *History of Wood Engraving in America,* 10; Hamilton, 355–58; NYCD 1837–40.

LANSOT, A. D. Portrait, miniature, and landscape painter and restorer at New Orleans, 1834–46. *Cf.* L. LANSOT. ¶ Delgado-WPA cites *Courier,* May 20, 1834, *Bee,* Nov. 22, 1837; New Orleans CD 1837–46.

LANSOT, L. Portrait and miniature painter and restorer, teacher, at New Orleans in 1835 and 1840. *Cf.* A. D. LANSOT. ¶ Delgado-WPA.

LANTZ, A. Crayon portraitist and genre painter. He was at Philadelphia in 1845, at NYC 1848–51. He exhibited at the National Academy, 1848–51. ¶ Phila. CD 1845; NYCD 1848–50; Cowdrey, NAD.

LAPHAM, J. M. Landscape artist working in California, 1852–58, for the lithograph trade. ¶ Peters, *America on Stone;* Peters, *California on Stone.*

LAPHAME, J. P. Engraver at New Orleans, 1860. ¶ Delgado-WPA cites CD 1860.

LAPLACE, CYRILLE PIERRE THEODORE (1793–1875). Topographical artist. A French naval officer, Laplace visited California in 1839 in the course of a circumnavigation of the world, the second such expedition conducted under his command. An engraving after his sketch of the San Carlos Mission, Carmel, appears in Laplace's account of this voyage, *Campagne de Circumnavigation de la Frégate l'Artémise* (Paris, 1841–44, 3 vols.). Laplace later became vice-admiral of the French fleet. ¶ Van Nostrand and Coulter, *California Pictorial,* 32–33, repro.

LARKIN, CHARLES HENRY. Engraver, 21, a native of New York, at NYC in 1860. ¶ 8 Census (1860), N.Y., LV, 892.

LARMANDE & BOURLIER. Sculptors at NYC, 1854–56; LEO J. LARMANDE and ALFRED J. B. BOURLIER. ¶ NYBD 1854, 1856.

LARMANDE or LARMANDO, LEO J. Sculptor, NYC, 1854–56; of LARMANDE & BOURLIER. ¶ NYBD and CD 1854, 1856.

LATHAM, JOHN. Engraver at New Orleans, 1842. ¶ New Orleans CD 1842.

LATHROP, BETSY B. Amateur painter in gouache and in watercolors on silk. She was active in New York State about 1810–12. Her subjects were historical and biblical scenes. ¶ *American Folk Art,* No. 106; Lipman and Winchester, 176.

LATHROP, JOHN D. Engraver at NYC, 1857–58; of LATHROP & POOLE. ¶ NYBD and CD 1857–58.

LATHROP & POOLE. General engravers and manufacturing jewellers, NYC, 1857–58. The partners were JOHN D. LATHROP and WILLIAM H. POOLE. ¶ NYBD and CD 1857–58.

LATILLA, EUGENIO HONORIUS (1808–1861). Figure and portrait painter. Latilla began exhibiting in London in 1828 and was elected a member of the Society of British Artists in 1838. He went to Rome in 1842, spent 1847–48 in Florence, and returned to London in 1849. He left for America in 1851 and worked in NYC until 1859. He was an Honorary Member, Professional, of the National Academy from 1847. He died at his home in Chappaqua (N.Y.) on October 30, 1861. ¶ Weitenkampf, "An Artist of Ante-Bellum Times"; Cummings, *Historic Annals,* 304; Graves; Redgrave; Thieme-Becker; Cowdrey, NAD; Tuckerman.

LATIMER BROTHERS & SEYMOUR. Engravers and die sinkers, lithographers, NYC, 1856–59. The firm was composed of JAMES M. and WILLIAM LATIMER and J. O. SEYMOUR. ¶ NYBD 1856–59; NYCD 1858–59.

LATIMER, JAMES M., see LATIMER BROTHERS & SEYMOUR.

LATIMER, WILLIAM T., see LATIMER BROTHERS & SEYMOUR.

LATIZAR, FERDINAND. Portrait painter in Louisiana during the 1790's. ¶ Van Ravenswaay, "The Forgotten Arts and Crafts of Colonial Louisiana," 195.

LATOUR, ARSENE LACARRIERE. Architect and teacher of drawing and coloring. He was a partner of HYACINTHE LACLOTTE at New Orleans from 1811 to 1813. ¶ Delgado-WPA cites *Courier,* Sept. 19, 1811, and March 10, 1813.

LATROBE, BENJAMIN HENRY (1764–1820). Architect; landscape and topographical painter. Born May 1, 1764, at Fulneck, Yorkshire, Latrobe was educated in Germany and studied engineering and architecture in London from 1786 to 1789. On the death of his first wife, he gave up a promising career in England to come to America, arriving in Norfolk (Va.) in March 1796. The next three years he spent in Virginia, chiefly at Richmond, but in 1798 he was called to Philadelphia to be the architect of the Bank of Pennsylvania and a year or so later of the Philadelphia water supply system. From 1803 to 1811, and again from 1815 to 1817, Latrobe was chief architect of the public buildings at the national capital, and his designs played an important part in the evolution of the present Capitol. He was also the architect of the great Roman Catholic Cathedral at Baltimore, as well as many other public and private buildings. Latrobe died in New Orleans on September 3, 1820, while working on a water system for that city. His notebooks and journals testify to his activity and ability, not only as an architect, but as a landscape painter and writer as well. ¶ Hamlin, *Benjamin Henry Latrobe,* is the definitive biography. The bulk of Latrobe's papers are in the Library of Congress and the Maryland Historical Society. The chief published sources are *The Journal of Latrobe* (1905) and *Impressions Respecting New Orleans,* edited by Samuel Wilson, Jr. (1951). See also: Hamlin, "Benjamin Henry Latrobe: The Man and the Architect" and Hamlin, "Benjamin Henry Latrobe, 1764–1820"; DAB; Rutledge, PA.

LATROBE, JOHN HAZLEHURST BONEVAL (1803–1891). Amateur landscape painter. A son of BENJAMIN H. LATROBE by his second wife, J. H. B. Latrobe was born in Philadelphia on May 4, 1803. After attending West Point from 1818 to 1821, he studied law in Baltimore and became one of the leaders of the bar of that city, particularly associated with the Baltimore & Ohio Rail Road. He was also active in the establishment of the Republic of Liberia. A founder of the Maryland Historical Society in 1844, he served as its President from 1871 until his death. Painting was his avocation and he was instrumental in establishing the gallery of art of the Historical Society. He died in Baltimore on September 11, 1891. ¶ Semmes, *John H. B. Latrobe and His Times, 1803–1891,* contains a number of repros. of his paintings and sketches. See also: DAB; Rutledge, MHS; represented: Md. Hist. Soc.

LATROBE, Miss MARY. Watercolorist who exhibited landscapes and nature studies at the Society of Artists in 1812. ¶ Rutledge, PA.

LATY, MICHAEL (1826–1848). Portrait and figure painter. A Baltimore artist who painted likenesses of Stephen A. Douglas and other well-known men. He died of typhoid at the age of twenty-two. ¶ Pleasants, *250 Years of Painting in Maryland,* 60; represented: Maryland Hist. Soc. (*Maryland History Notes,* VI, Nov. 1948).

LAUBENHEIMER, RUDOLPH. Engraver and diesinker at NYC, 1859. ¶ NYBD 1859.

LAUCK, JOHN. Sculptor. Though listed as a saloon keeper and barber in NYC, 1855–57, he exhibited a marble bas-relief at the American Institute in 1856. ¶ NYCD 1855–57; Am. Inst. Cat., 1856.

LAUD, HENRY S. Engraver. A resident of NYC, he exhibited a mezzotint, "Victoria," at the American Institute Fair in 1846. ¶ Am. Inst. Cat., 1846.

LAUDER, CHARLES. Engraver, 50, a native of New York, at NYC in 1860. ¶ 8 Census (1860), N.Y., XLV, 85.

LAUDER, ISAAC. Artist; born in Scotland about 1830; working in NYC from about 1858. ¶ 8 Census (1860), N.Y., L, 645; NYCD 1863, as "marble."

LAUDER, JAMES. Sculptor; born in New Jersey about 1825; working in NYC from 1846 to 1861 as a partner in BOYLE & LAUDER. Listed either as James or James, Jr. ¶ 7 Census (1850), N.Y., XLVII, 168; NYCD 1846–47 (James), 1848 (both James and James, Jr.), 1849–51 (James, Jr.), 1852–54 (James), 1855–61 (James, Jr.).

LAUDER, JOHN. Lithographer of NYC, 1847–55. His widow, Mary, was listed in 1863. ¶ NYCD 1847–55, 1863.

LAUDER, JOHN, JR. Engraver of NYC, 1842–60 and after. He is listed as Jr. only from 1847 to 1851. ¶ NYCD 1842–60+.

LAUDER, WILLIAM. Engraver of NYC, 1854–55; lithographer, 1856–60 and after. ¶ NYCD 1854–60+.

LAUDERBACH, see LOUDERBACH.

LAUNITZ, ROBERT EBERHARD SCHMIDT VON DER (1806–1870). N.A. Sculptor. Born in Riga (Latvia) on November 4, 1806, Launitz studied sculpture in Rome under an uncle and under Thorwaldsen. In 1828 he emigrated to the United States and found employment in NYC in the marble shop of JOHN FRAZEE. In 1831 the partnership of FRAZEE & LAUNITZ was formed. After 1839 the shop was taken over by Launitz alone. He trained a number of American sculptors, including THOMAS CRAWFORD, and played an important part in the development of this branch of art in America. His own work was chiefly for mantels and gravestones, though he executed a number of military and portrait monuments as well. He died in NYC on December 13, 1870. ¶ DAB; Cowdrey, NAD; Cowdrey, AA & AAU; Clement and Hutton; CAB; NYCD 1831–60+.

LAURENCE, JOHN, see JOHN LAWRENCE.

LAURENCE, SAMUEL (1812–1884). Portrait painter. A native of Guildford, Surrey (England), Laurence began exhibiting in London in 1834. He enjoyed a successful career as a portrait artist, being especially noted for his portraits of literary figures. On the suggestion of Thackeray, he came to the United States early in 1854. After a few months in Newport (R.I.) and a visit to Longfellow's home in Cambridge (Mass.), he settled in NYC, remaining there until about 1861. He then returned to England, continued exhibiting at the Royal Academy until 1882, and died in London on February 28, 1884. ¶ DNB; information courtesy Frank Miles, London; Bolton, *Crayon Draftsmen;* Cowdrey, NAD; Rutledge, PA; Swan, BA; NYCD 1856–61; Graves; repro., *Connoisseur* (Sept. 1947), 28.

LAURIE, A., see ALEXANDER LAWRIE.

LAURIER, ——. Painter and actor at Memphis (Tenn.) in 1855. ¶ *Trenton* (N.J.) *State Gazette,* Nov. 19, 1855.

LAUTZ, WILLIAM (1838–1915). Sculptor and actor who was born April 20, 1838, at Unstadt (Germany), came to America in 1854, and settled in Buffalo (N.Y.), where he died on June 24, 1915. ¶ *Art Annual,* XII, obit.; represented: Buffalo Hist. Soc.

LAVENDER, Mrs. CHARLES, née Eugénie Etienette Aubanel (1817–1898). Religious painter. Mlle. Aubanel studied in Paris under Delaroche and Scheffer. In 1851 she and her husband, with their two children, emigrated to America, settling first at Waco and later at Corpus Christi (Texas). One of her paintings was hung in the cathedral at Corpus Christi. ¶ Barker, *American Painting,* 455.

LAVENDER, CHRIST. Portrait painter at Waco (Texas) about 1840. He painted likenesses of Capt. and Mrs. Shapley P. Ross, owned in 1940 by Mrs. M. H. Lane of Waco. ¶ Courtesy WPA (Texas), Hist. Records Survey.

LAVERGNE, ANTOINE. Artist at New Orleans in 1827 and 1830. ¶ Delgado-WPA cites CD 1827, 1830.

LAVIGNE, ——. Engraver. A few plates in stipple by him were published in the *Polyanthus* at Boston in 1814. ¶ Stauffer.

LAW, Mrs. ——. Proprietress of painting and drawing academy at New Orleans, 1840–41. ¶ Delgado-WPA cites *Picayune,* Dec. 30, 1840, and New Orleans CD 1841.

LAWMAN, JASPER HOLMAN (1825–1906). Landscape and portrait painter; born in Ohio, either at Xenia (Clement and Hutton) or at Cleveland (*Art Annual*). He began painting in 1839 at Cincinnati, but made his home at Pittsburgh (Pa.) from 1846 until his death on April 4, 1906, except for a year's study in France in 1859–60. ¶ Clement and Hutton; *Art Annual,* VI, obit.; repro., *Antiques* (June 1935), 228.

LAWRENCE, A. A. Painter of "Race between Harvard Boat Clubs in Boston Harbor," painted in 1852 and now in the Karolik Collection. The artist may have been Amos Adams Lawrence, of Boston, who graduated at Harvard in 1835 and died in 1886. ¶ Karolik Cat., 416, repro. 417; Met. Mus., *Life in America.*

LAWRENCE & CAMERON. NYC lithographers, 1859. The partners were HENRY LAWRENCE and JOHN CAMERON. ¶ Peters, *America on Stone.*

LAWRENCE, CHARLES B. Portrait and landscape painter. He was born near Bordentown (N.J.), and is said to have studied with REMBRANDT PEALE and GILBERT STUART. He first exhibited at Philadelphia in 1813 and was active there as a portrait painter until about 1837. From 1840 to 1842 he was employed as a clerk in the Bank of Penn Township and from 1844 to 1856 as a plumber in Philadelphia. Although Dunlap stated that his work was without merit, the Pennsylvania Academy exhibited his copy of David's "Napoleon Crossing the Alps" regularly from 1831 to 1870. ¶ Dunlap, *History,* 254–55; Rutledge, PA; Phila. CD 1818–56; Egbert, *Princeton Portraits.*

LAWRENCE, HENRY. Lithographer of NYC, 1852–60; in 1859 of LAWRENCE & CAMERON. ¶ NYCD and BD 1852–60.

LAWRENCE, JOHN. Drawing master at NYC in 1783. ¶ Kelby, *Notes on American Artists;* Gottesman, II, No. 16.

LAWRENCE, JOHN. Lithographer and print colorer, NYC, 1834–58. Though listed only as a colorer in city directories, Lawrence is credited by Peters with at least one lithograph. ¶ NYCD 1834–58; Peters, *America on Stone.*

LAWRENCE, SAMUEL, see SAMUEL LAURENCE.

LAWRENCE, W. S. Landscape engraver. He was apprenticed to ALFRED JONES of NYC in 1840 and was doing work for NYC publishers in 1846. Stauffer states that plates signed A. L. Jones are the work of Lawrence, finished by his master Jones. Lawrence later gave up engraving to engage in the flour and grain business in NYC. ¶ Stauffer.

LAWRENCE, WILLIAM RODERICK (1829–1856). Figure painter. Born March 3, 1829, at Hartford (Conn.), W. R. Lawrence spent his entire life there except for two winters of study at the National Academy (1848 and 1849), and died of consumption on October 9, 1856. He received a medical education and illustrated a treatise on circulation of the blood. He also illustrated Lydia Sigourney's *Poems of the Sea* and painted a number of historical canvases. ¶ French, *Art and Artists of Connecticut,* 140–41; Hartford BD 1851–56.

LAWRIE (Lourie), ALEXANDER (1828–1917). A.N.A. Portrait, landscape, and genre painter, crayon artist, and engraver. Born in NYC on February 25, 1828, Lawrie was apprenticed to an engraver and studied drawing at the National Academy. From 1850 to 1854 he was at Philadelphia, where he exhibited at the Pennsylvania Academy. In 1854 he went to Europe to study at Düsseldorf, Paris, and Florence, returning to Philadelphia in 1858. He served during the Civil War, went abroad again about 1865, and had a studio in NYC from 1866 to 1876, winning election as an Associate of the National Academy in 1868. In 1896 he was living in Chalmers (Ind.) and in 1902 he was admitted to the Indiana State Soldiers' Home at Lafayette where he died on February 15, 1917. During his last years Lawrie painted a series of 158 portraits of Civil War Generals. ¶ DAB; Phila. BD 1849–64; Rutledge, PA; 7 Census (1850), Pa., LIV, 695; Owen, *Report on Wisconsin, Iowa, and Minnesota;* Swan, BA; Cowdrey, NAD; *Portfolio* (April 1942), 13, 16, repro.

LAWSON, ALEXANDER. (1773–1846). Engraver. Born December 19, 1773, near Ravenstruther, Lanarkshire (Scotland), Lawson emigrated to America in 1794 and found employment in Philadelphia with the engravers THACKARA & VALLANCE. Three years later he set up in business independently and he was active until a few days before his death on August 22, 1846. Lawson won international recognition for his work on the plates for ALEXANDER WILSON's *American Ornithology* (1808–14) and its supplement by Charles Lucien Bonaparte (1825–33). Two of his children, HELEN E. and OSCAR A. LAWSON, also became engravers. ¶ DAB; Stauffer; CAB; Rutledge, PA; Dunlap, *History,* I, 443–44; *Antiques* (July 1926), 26, and (July 1946), 43, repros.

LAWSON, HELEN E. Portrait and decorative painter, engraver. A daughter of the engraver ALEXANDER LAWSON, she exhibited in Philadelphia from 1830 to 1842. ¶ Fielding; Rutledge, PA.

LAWSON, OSCAR A. (1813–1854). Portrait and landscape painter, engraver. A son of ALEXANDER LAWSON, he was born in Philadelphia on August 7, 1813. In 1835 he exhibited some drawings at the Artists' Fund Society. He joined the U. S. Coast Survey at Washington about 1840 and worked there until ill health forced his return to Philadelphia in 1851. He died there three years later on September 6, 1854. He was an engraver of bookplates. ¶ CAB; Fielding; Rutledge, PA; 7 Census (1850), D.C., II, 198.

LAWSON, PERCIVAL P. Portrait painter; born in England about 1815; active in NYC from 1840 to 1851. He exhibited at the Apollo Association and the National Academy. ¶ 7 Census (1850), N.Y., XLVI, 244; NYBD 1840–51; Cowdrey, AA & AAU; Cowdrey, NAD.

LAWSON, THOMAS. Portrait painter from Pennsylvania, age 30, living in New Orleans in 1860 with his Louisiana-born wife and three-year-old son Cornelius. ¶ 8 Census (1860), La., VII, 609.

LAWSON, THOMAS BAYLEY (1807–1888). Portrait and miniature painter; born January 13, 1807, at Newburyport (Mass.) and first employed as a clerk in Boston. By 1829 he had established his own business there, but about 1841 he moved to Lowell and became a professional artist. Although he had a studio at Newburyport in 1858, he apparently made Lowell his home until his death on January 4, 1888. ¶ Coburn, *Thomas Bayley Lawson—Portrait Painter of Newburyport and Lowell, Mass.;* Belknap, *Artists and Craftsmen of*

Essex County, 10; Lowell BD 1848+; Swan, BA.

LAWTON, FRANCIS. Pennsylvania-born lithographer, age 25, living in Philadelphia in 1860. ¶ 8 Census (1860), Pa., LIV, 893.

LAWTON, RICHARD C. Engraver and die-sinker of NYC, 1849. ¶ NYBD 1849.

LAY, A. W. Wood engraver who executed three wood cuts for the 1792 Connecticut edition of Noah Webster's *American Spelling Book.* ¶ Hamilton, 14, 73–74.

LAY, FRED. L. Bavarian portrait painter, born about 1836, working in Boston in 1859–60. ¶ Boston BD 1859–60; CD 1860; 8 Census (1860), Mass., XXVII, 716 (as John Lay, but at same address as Fred L. Lay in directory).

LAYMAN, E. Portrait painter at New Orleans in 1838. ¶ New Orleans CD 1838.

LAYMAN, JAMES H. Wood engraver at Cincinnati, 1856–60. ¶ Cincinnati CD 1856–59; BD 1860.

LAZAREE or LAZZAREE, JOSEPH. Sculptor at NYC, 1843–50. He apparently died in 1850 or 1851, as his widow is listed in 1851. ¶ NYCD 1843–51. NYBD 1846 lists Joseph Lazzarino, sculptor, at the same address.

LAZARUS, JACOB HART (1822–1891). A.N.A. Portrait and figure painter. He was born in NYC, apparently spent his entire career there, and died there in 1891. He began exhibiting in 1841 at the National Academy, of which he became an Associate in 1850, and later exhibited also at the Boston Athenaeum and the Pennsylvania Academy. ¶ Smith; Cowdrey, NAD; Swan, BA; Rutledge, PA; NYBD 1844–60+; repro., Met. Mus., *Life in America,* and *Antiques* (Jan. 1933), 13.

LAZARUS, LEWIS. Engraver at NYC, 1854–59. ¶ NYBD 1854, 1859.

LEACH, A. Painter, Oshkosh (Wis.), 1849–85. In 1849 he painted the portrait of an early logger of Oshkosh and in 1885 a picture of a steamboat, both now in the Oshkosh Museum. ¶ Butts, *Art in Wisconsin,* 84 (repro.), 85.

LEACH, S. W. Artist at NYC, 1852–53. ¶ NYCD 1852–53.

LEACH, SAMUEL. Engraver from London at Philadelphia in December 1741. ¶ Prime, I, 19; Stauffer.

LEADLEY, DAVID. Engraver of Rochester (N.Y.), 1853–59. From 1855 he was with the firm of LEADLEY, MILLER & MIX. ¶ Rochester CD 1853–57; N. Y. State BD 1859.

LEADLEY, MILLER & MIX. Engravers of Rochester (N.Y.), 1855–59. The partners were DAVID LEADLEY, JOHN MILLER, and LUCIUS C. MIX. ¶ Rochester CD 1855–57; N. Y. State BD 1859.

LEAK, JOHN F. Engraver of Philadelphia, 1850–60 and after. A native of Pennsylvania, he was in 1850, at the age of 16, an apprentice to MARTIN LEANS. Ten years later he was in business for himself, married, with two children. ¶ 7 Census (1850), Pa., LV, 587; 8 Census (1860), Pa., LVIII, 52; Phila. CD 1858–60+.

LEAKE, Mrs. S. C. Portrait painter who exhibited at the Pennsylvania Academy in 1849. ¶ Rutledge, PA.

LEAMING, R. W. Philadelphia artist who exhibited a landscape at the Pennsylvania Academy in 1859. ¶ Rutledge, PA.

LEANS, MARTIN. Engraver of Philadelphia, 1843–60 and after. He was born in Pennsylvania about 1817. In 1850 JOHN F. LEAK was living in Leans' home, presumably as an apprentice. ¶ 7 Census (1850), Pa., LV, 25; Phila. CD 1843–60+.

LEARY, MICHAEL. Lithographer, age 22, at Boston in 1860. ¶ 8 Census (1860), Mass., XXVII, 351.

LEARY, NICHOLAS. Irish copperplate engraver, 25, at NYC in 1850. ¶ 7 Census (1850), N.Y., XLII, 471.

LEAVITT, GEORGE H. Engraver, 34, a native of Pennsylvania, at NYC in 1860 with his wife Martha. He owned real estate valued at $7,000. ¶ 8 Census (1860), N.Y., LVIII, 46.

LEAVITT, JOSEPH. "Profile-cutter" at Lowell (Mass.) in 1834. *Cf.* JOSEPH WARREN LEAVITT. ¶ Belknap, *Artists and Craftsmen of Essex County,* 21; Lowell CD 1834.

LEAVITT, JOSEPH WARREN (1804–1838). Primitive watercolorist, born in Chichester (N.H.) May 16, 1804; died August 11, 1838. He is known only as the painter of a watercolor showing the interior of a farmhouse at Loudon (N.H.) in 1825. Possibly this is the JOSEPH LEAVITT who was cutting profiles at Lowell (Mass.) in 1834. ¶ Noyes, *Leavitt: Descendants of Thomas Leavitt, the Immigrant,* 74; Little, "An Unusual Painting," repro.

LEBCKE or LEBEKE, CHARLES. Lithographer at Chicago, 1854–55. ¶ Chicago CD 1854 (Lebcke), 1855 (Lebeke).

LEBLANC, WILLIAM. Sculptor at New Orleans, 1849–51. ¶ Delgado-WPA cites New Orleans CD 1849–51.

LEBLOND, FRANCIS. Portrait painter, at Philadelphia in 1850 and NYC in 1851. This is presumably the "Prof. LeBlond" who between 1849 and 1851 exhibited in Philadelphia and NYC a panorama of a voyage to Europe, painted during "a few years residence in England." ¶ Phila. CD 1850 (as LeBland); NYCD 1851 (as LeBlond); information courtesy J. E. Arrington, who cites Phila. *Public Ledger,* Dec. 14, 1849, May 7 and 13, 1850, and N. Y. *Herald,* Nov. 13, 1851.

LE BLOND, ROBERT (1816–1863). Engraver and copperplate printer. He was born August 4, 1816, in London and established his own business there in 1840. The same year he visited America, leaving his business in the hands of his brother Abraham. Returning shortly to England, worked as an engraver in London until 1856 when he again left for America. He settled at Cincinnati and remained there until 1863. He went to England in 1863 and died there on October 18. His sons remained in the United States. ¶ Arrington, "Nauvoo Temple," Chap. 8.

LE BOUTEUX, JEAN-MICHEL. Topographical artist. He was among the first group of French settlers on John Law's concession at New Biloxi, Province de Louisianne (now Miss.). On December 10, 1720, a month or two after his arrival, Le Bouteux sketched a view of the new settlement, the original of which is now in the Ayer Collection, Newberry Library, Chicago. ¶ *Portfolio* (Feb. 1947), 142; *Art Quarterly* (Winter 1951), 348.

LE BRETON, WILLIAM. Engraver at Philadelphia, 1832. ¶ *Am. Adv. Directory,* 1832.

LEBRETTON, JULES. Cameo-cutter at New Orleans, 1860. ¶ Delgado-WPA cites BD 1860.

LE CLEAR, THOMAS (1818–1882). N.A. Portrait and genre painter. Le Clear was born at Owego (N.Y.) on March 11, 1818, and began to paint as a child. At the age of 12 he was already selling copies of his own work and he was employed as a portrait and decorative painter from about the age of 14. Le Clear's family moved in 1832 to London (Ont.), and he worked there and in Goderich (Ont.) until 1834. After several years' wanderings in western New York and as far west as Green Bay (Wis.), he settled in NYC in 1839. After his marriage in 1844 he moved to Buffalo, but he returned to NYC in 1860 and there spent the rest of his career. He was elected a National Academician in 1863. Le Clear died November 26, 1882, at his home in Rutherford Park (N.J.). ¶ DAB; Clement and Hutton; Champlin and Perkins; Ulp, "Art and Artists in Rochester," 32; CAB; Cowdrey, NAD; Cowdrey, AA & AAU; Swan, BA; Rutledge, PA; Buffalo BD 1855–60; Boston *Transcript,* Nov. 27, 1882, obit.; represented: Md. Hist. Soc. and Corcoran Gallery.

LEDBETTER, THOMAS. Engraver at NYC, 1857. ¶ NYBD 1857.

LEDLETON, T. Engraver at Boston, 1846. ¶ Boston BD 1846.

LEE & CLASSEN. Engravers at NYC, 1844. The partners were JOHN N. LEE and JAMES M. CLASSEN. ¶ NYBD 1844.

LEE, ELIJAH. Maryland-born artist, age 49, living in Baltimore in 1860. ¶ 8 Census (1860), Md., III, 972.

LEE, ELMINA BENNETT (1821–1908). Landscape painter. She was born at Westmoreland (N.H.), studied in Boston under WILLIAM MORRIS HUNT, exhibited frequently between 1840 and 1860, and taught painting to a number of pupils, among whom was her grandson, the portrait painter Cuthbert Lee. In 1848 Miss Bennett was married to the Rev. Dr. John Stebbins Lee, first president of St. Lawrence University, Canton (N.Y.). ¶ Information courtesy Cuthbert Lee.

LEE, G. M. Landscape painter who depicted the steamboat *Washington* on the Ohio River near Cincinnati in 1816. *Cf.* SAMUEL M. LEE. ¶ *American Collector* (April 1943), 17.

LEE, JAMES D., JR. Artist at New Orleans, 1859–66. ¶ Delgado-WPA cites CD 1859, 1861, 1866.

LEE, JOHN N. Engraver of NYC, 1840–44; in 1844 of LEE & CLASSEN. ¶ NYBD 1840–41, 1844; NYCD 1843.

LEE, SAMUEL M. (?–1841). Scene, landscape, and portrait painter. He was at Cincinnati in 1826 and in 1835 he exhibited a panorama, "The Destruction of Sodom and Gommorah," at New Orleans. About 1837/38 he painted the Fire Scene from Dante's *Inferno* for the Western Museum at Cincinnati. He was at Louisville (Ky.) in 1838–39 and was scene painter at the St. Charles Theatre at New Orleans when he died on August 2, 1841. ¶ Delgado-WPA cites *Picayune,* Aug. 21, 1841, and *Courier,* July 1, 1833; Cist, *Cincinnati in 1841,* 139; information courtesy Mrs. W. H. Whitley and J. E. Arrington.

LEECH, THOMAS. Landscape painter who arrived at Charleston from London in the fall of 1773. The following year he exhibited his "View of Charleston" which was shortly after sent to England and engraved there. ¶ Rutledge, *Artists in the Life of Charleston.*

LEEDS, JOHN WATTEY. Engraver, 20, a native of England, at NYC in 1850. ¶ 7 Census (1850), N.Y., LIV, 260.

LEEFE, GEORGE E. Lithographer at NYC, 1849–58. In 1849–50 he was listed as a printer with the lithographic firm of RISSO & LEEFE; in 1852–53 he was with MICHELIN & LEEFE. ¶ NYCD 1849–58; Peters, *America on Stone.*

LEEFE, JULIUS. Lithographer at NYC, 1855. He was at the same address as GEORGE E. LEEFE. ¶ NYCD 1855.

LEGARÉ, JAMES MATHEWES (1823–1859). Poet, short story writer, and amateur painter. Born November 26, 1823, in Charleston (S.C.), he studied painting at Saint Mary's College in Baltimore and exhibited several landscapes in Charleston in 1843 and 1856. In 1847 he was employed as drawing master in a private home in Augusta (Ga.). A volume of his poems, *Orta-Undis, and Other Poems,* was published in 1848. From about 1847 until his death on May 30, 1859, his home was in Aiken (S.C.). ¶ Davis, "The Several-Sided James Mathewes Legaré"; Davis, "Poet, Painter, and Inventor: Some Letters by James Mathewes Legaré"; Davis, "Fops, Frenchmen, Hidalgos, and Aztecs."

LEGARÉ, MARY S. (Mrs. William Bullen). Landscape painter of Charleston (S.C.). She was born in 1792 and was a sister of the writer and statesman, Hugh Swinton Legaré. During the 1840's she exhibited in Charleston, NYC, and Philadelphia. ¶ Rutledge, *Artists in the Life of Charleston;* Cowdrey, AA & AAU; Rutledge, PA.

LEGGETT, CATHARINE S. Copperplate engraver at Albany (N.Y.), 1859. ¶ Albany CD 1859.

LEGGETT, ROBERT. Engraver; born in Ireland about 1826; at NYC 1850–56. ¶ 7 Census (1850), N.Y., XLV, 255; NYBD 1856.

LE GRAND, ——. Landscape painter living in NYC in 1853, when he exhibited at the National Academy a number of views in Belgium, Scotland, and Spain. *Cf.* HENRY, JULES, and W. LE GRAND, and J. LE GRANDE. ¶ Cowdrey, NAD.

LE GRAND, HENRY. Portrait and landscape painter of NYC, exhibited at the National Academy in 1858–59 portraits and Dutch and Italian views. ¶ Cowdrey, NAD.

LEGRAND, JULES. Mural painter from the northern states who visited New Orleans in the early spring of 1857. *Cf.* J. LE GRANDE. ¶ Delgado-WPA cites *Bee,* March 21, 1857.

LE GRAND, W. Landscape painter of NYC, who exhibited at the National Academy in 1854. ¶ Cowdrey, NAD.

LE GRANDE, J. Landscape painter, address not given, who sold a number of Belgian and American views to the American Art-Union in 1850 and 1852. *Cf.* JULES LEGRAND. ¶ Cowdrey, AA & AAU.

LEGRANGE, VINCENT. French artist, 49, at NYC in 1850. ¶ 7 Census (1850), N.Y., XLI, 568.

LE HARDY, C. Teacher of landscape drawing and painting in water colors and oil, and of languages and sciences. He was at Charleston from 1853 to 1857. ¶ Rutledge, *Artists in the Life of Charleston.*

LEHMAN, B. B. Portrait painter at Philadelphia in 1842. ¶ Phila. CD 1842.

LEHMAN & DUVAL. Lithographers at Philadelphia, 1835–37; GEORGE LEHMAN and P. S. DUVAL. ¶ Phila. CD 1835, 1837; Peters, *America on Stone.*

LEHMAN, GEORGE (?–1870). Landscape painter, lithographer, and engraver. Born in Lancaster County (Pa.), Lehman exhibited Swiss and Pennsylvania views at the Pennsylvania Academy between 1825 and 1831. About 1831 he took up lithography and was employed for two years by CHILDS & INMAN. In 1835 he was taken into partnership by CEPHAS G. CHILDS, but the same year Lehman formed a partnership with P. S. DUVAL which lasted until 1837. He continued to work in Philadelphia as an aquatintist and designer for engravers and later formed the print-publishing firm of Lehman & Baldwin. He died in Philadelphia in 1870. ¶ Peters, *America on Stone;* Stauffer; Rutledge, PA; Stokes, *Historic Prints,* pl. 49a; Phila. CD 1830–44; Swan, BA.

LEHMAN, THOMAS E. or F. Portrait and genre painter. T. Lehman exhibited at the Apollo Gallery in NYC in 1838 and was listed as T. F. Lehman, portrait painter, in the city directories for 1838–39. Thomas E. Lehman, artist, was at New Orleans in 1849. ¶ Cowdrey, AA & AAU; NYCD 1838–39; Delgado-WPA cites New Orleans CD 1849.

LEHR, CHARLES. Scene painter. In 1836 he was working for the dioramist HANINGTON in NYC, and in 1839 his drop scene, "View in Spain," was shown in Cincinnati. In 1840 and 1841 he was employed as a scene painter at the Chestnut and Walnut Street Theatres in Philadelphia. He was a brother of JOHN H. LEHR. In 1851 he worked with DALLAS on a California panorama. ¶ J. E. Arrington cites: N. Y. *Herald,* Dec. 7 and 22, 1836, Cincinnati *Daily Gazette,* July 12, 1839, Philadelphia *Public Ledger,* Nov. 6, 1841, and Aug. 30, 1851; Rutledge, *Artists in the Life of Charleston;* Phila. CD 1842.

LEHR, JOHN H. (?–1841). Portrait painter, brother of CHARLES LEHR. He was working in Philadelphia in 1838 and in Charleston in 1840. He committed suicide in NYC in August 1841. ¶ Phila. BD 1838; Rutledge, *Artists in the Life of Charleston,* 166.

LEICHTERKOST, MARTIN. Lithographer at NYC, 1859. ¶ NYBD 1859.

LEICHTWEIS & HORTER. Engravers and diesinkers of NYC, 1856–58; LOUIS LEICHTWEIS and CHARLES HORTER. ¶ NYCD 1856–58.

LEICHTWEIS, LOUIS. Engraver; born in Germany about 1824; working in NYC from 1850 to 1860 and after. ¶ 8 Census (1860), N.Y., XLIV, 292; NYCD 1850–63.

LEIDY, WILLIAM B. Engraver, age 41, living in Philadelphia in 1850. He was a native of Pennsylvania, as were his wife and four children. ¶ 7 Census (1850), Pa., LI, 18.

LEIGHTON, GEORGE A. Portrait painter (of LEIGHTON & RYERSON) at Roxbury (Mass.) in 1860. ¶ Roxbury CD 1860; New England BD 1860.

LEIGHTON & RYERSON. Portrait painters of Roxbury (Mass.) in 1860. The firm was composed of GEORGE A. LEIGHTON and LUTHER L. RYERSON. ¶ Roxbury CD 1860; New England BD 1860.

LEISER, CHRISTIAN. Engraver, age 30, from Württemberg, living in Philadelphia in 1860. Of his three children, Charles (6) and Amelia (4) were born in New Jersey and William (2) in Pennsylvania. ¶ 8 Census (1860), Pa., LVI, 550.

LEITZ, LOUIS. Lithographer, age 36, from Hanover (Germany), at Philadelphia in 1860. He was listed in the 1860 directory as a "foreman." His wife was from Bavaria, but their children (ages 1 to 14) were born in Pennsylvania. Leitz owned real and personal property totalling $1,500. ¶ 8 Census (1860), Pa., XLIX, 458; Phila. CD 1860.

LE LANNE, see LA LANNE.

LELAND, Miss ——. Painter of a miniature on ivory of Sarah Ann Hyde, St. Albans (Vt.), March 1831. *Cf.* MARY E. LA LANNE. ¶ WPA (Mass.), *Portraits Found in Vt.*

LEMERE, ALEXIS. Landscape painter at NYC, 1844–46. ¶ NYBD 1844, 1846.

LEMERLE, AUGUSTUS E., JR. Engraver, age 22, living in Washington (D.C.) in July 1860. He and his mother were both born in Connecticut, but the father was French. ¶ 8 Census (1860), D.C., I, 817.

LEMET, LOUIS (*c.* 1779–1832). Crayon portraitist and engraver. At one time a partner of ST. MEMIN, Lemet was at Philadelphia in 1804, in NYC the following year, and by November 1805 in Albany (N.Y.), where he worked until about 1828. He was in NYC again in 1831–32 and died there on September 30, 1832. He is said to have worked in the manner of St. Memin. ¶ N. Y. *American,* Oct. 1, 1832, obit.; Stauffer; Bolton, *Crayon Draftsmen;* Albany *Balance* and *N. Y. State Journal,* March 7, 1809; Albany CD 1815–28; NYCD 1831–32.

LEMME, WILLIAM. Seal and metal engraver, Boston, 1850–52. ¶ Boston BD 1850–52, CD 1851.

LEMON, WILLIAM C. Amateur wood carver and tobacconist of NYC, who exhibited a statute of "Metamora" at the American Institute in 1849. ¶ Am. Inst. Cat., 1849; NYCD 1848.

LEMOSEY or LEMOSY, FRANCIS WILLIAM. Portrait painter who was at New Orleans in January 1839 and at Richmond in July of the same year. ¶ Delgado-WPA cites *Picayune,* Jan. 9, 1839; *Richmond Portraits,* 242.

LE MOYNE, JACQUES DE MORGUES (*d.* 1588). Watercolorist, the earliest artist known to have visited what is now the continental United States. He accompanied Laudonnière's expedition to Florida, Georgia, and the Carolinas in 1564, and was one of the few survivors of the ill-fated Huguenot settlement on the St. Johns River (Florida) which was destroyed by the Spanish in 1565. Le Moyne's watercolor views of American scenes and natural curiosities were engraved and published in Frankfort-am-Main by Theodore de Bry along with Le Moyne's narrative of the expedition. Le Moyne subsequently settled in London, produced a number of watercolors of English flora and fauna, and died there in 1588. ¶ Thieme-Becker; *American Processional,* 23–24; Lorant, *The New World,* repro.; represented: Victoria and Albert Museum.

LENEY, WILLIAM SATCHWELL (1769–1831). Engraver; born in London, January 16, 1769, and trained there by the English engraver Peltro W. Tompkins. He worked in London until 1805 when he emigrated to America and settled in NYC. Leney was one of the most successful engravers of the period in America, working in line and stipple on portrait, landscape, and subject plates as well as banknotes. He retired about 1820 to a farm near Montreal, but continued to do some engraving, including a series of views of the French-Canadian city and the first notes issued by the Bank of Montreal. He died November 26, 1831, at Longue Pointe, near Montreal. ¶ Stauffer; DAB; Cowdrey, AA & AAU; DNB; Rutledge, PA; NYCD 1806–18; Thieme-Becker.

LENGHI, MOSES G. Sculptor. Though listed only as a marble worker in the city directory, Lenghi exhibited statuary and a marble mantel at the American Institute in 1849. ¶ Am. Inst. Cat., 1849; NYCD 1848–49.

LENHARD, AUGUSTUS. German lithographer, 21, at NYC in 1860. ¶ 8 Census (1860), N.Y., LI, 333.

LENT, ABRAHAM E. Copperplate and steel engraver and printer, Philadelphia, 1851–60 and after. ¶ Phila. CD 1851–60+.

LENT, LOUIS P. Artist; born in New York about 1820; working in NYC as an engraver in 1850 and as an artist in 1860. His wife Mary and son Louis, born about 1853, were born in New York; two other children, born about 1855 and 1857, were born in Pennsylvania. ¶ 8 Census (1860), N.Y., LVI, 550; NYCD 1850.

LEONARD, ANTON. Prussian lithographer, 38, at NYC in 1860 with his wife Wilhelmina and two children born in New York in 1855 and 1857. ¶ 8 Census (1860), N.Y., LV, 632.

LEONARD, GEORGE M. Pennsylvania-born artist, 24, at NYC in 1850. ¶ 7 Census (1850), N.Y., LI, 479.

LEONARD, JAMES. Portrait painter working in Jefferson County (Va.) in 1820. ¶ Willis, "Jefferson County Portraits."

LEONHARD, CHARLES. Engraver at NYC, 1856–57. ¶ NYBD and CD 1856–57.

LEONHARDT, THEODORE (1818–1877). Lithographer and engraver. A native of Bautzen (Saxony), he served his apprenticeship under a lithographer in Leipzig and worked in Saxony until the Revolution of 1848 ruined his business and induced his emigration to America. Arriving in NYC in 1849, the next year he settled permanently in Philadelphia, finding employment first with TRAUBEL, SCHNABEL & FINKELDY, and then setting up his own business. He died in Philadelphia in 1877. ¶ Peters, *America on Stone;* Phila. CD 1854–60+.

LEONHARDT, THOMAS. Engraver at Philadelphia, 1859–60. ¶ Phila. CD 1859–60.

LEONORI, R. G. L. Landscape and still life painter who exhibited annually at the American Art-Union, 1846–52. His home was in NYC in 1847–48 and his subjects were mainly in the Hudson Valley and Catskill regions of New York State. ¶ Cowdrey, AA & AAU; *Panorama* (March 1947), 80, repro.

LEOPOLD, FRANCIS. Portrait painter at Newark (N.J.), 1859. ¶ Essex, Hudson, and Union Counties BD 1859.

LEOTTI, GEORGE. English artist, 35, at NYC in 1850. ¶ 7 Census (1850), N.Y., LI, 220.

LEPAGE, MICHEL. Artist at New Orleans, 1830. ¶ Delgado-WPA cites New Orleans CD 1830.

LE PAGE DU PRATZ, see DU PRATZ.

LEPELLETIER, MICHAEL. Engraver of NYC, active 1806–14. ¶ NYCD 1806, 1812–14 (cited by McKay); Stauffer.

LE ROUX, CHARLES. Engraver of paper currency for the Province of New York, 1715. ¶ Vail, *Knickerbocker Birthday,* 303.

LEROUX, L. Wood carver and sculptor at New Orleans, 1834. ¶ New Orleans CD 1834 (cited by Delgado-WPA).

LEROY, Mrs. ELIZABETH EMMET (1794–1878). Pastel and oil portraitist, active *c.* 1814–34. She was a cousin of ROBERT FULTON, whose portrait she painted in 1814, and the wife of William LeRoy. ¶ Information courtesy FARL; repro., Am. Antiq. Soc. *Proceedings,* 1946, opp. 94; *Art Digest* (Oct. 15, 1936), 28; represented: Am. Antiq. Soc.

LE SERRURIER, Mme. JACQUES (neé Elizabeth Leger). Amateur portrait painter. Mme. Le Serrurier was a French Huguenot who lived in Charleston (S.C.) from 1684 to about 1717. She is thought to have painted a self-portrait in oils, now owned by Dr. W. Jervey Ravenel of Charleston. ¶ Rutledge, *Artists in the Life of Charleston,* fig. 3; Barker, *American Painting,* 66.

LESLIE, ANNE (or Ann M. L.) 1792–after 1860). Portrait painter and copyist. Anne, sister of ELIZA and CHARLES ROBERT LESLIE, was born in Philadelphia shortly before the family moved to London in 1793. After their return in 1800 she lived in Philadelphia until 1822, when she joined her artist brother in London. While in England she made numerous copies after the work of her brother and other artists, as well as a few original portraits, and she began to exhibit in America after her return in 1825. In 1829 she went to England for another visit of several years' duration. During the 1830's and part of the 1840's she made her home in Philadelphia with her brother-in-law and sister, Mr. and Mrs. Henry Carey. About 1844 she established herself in NYC as a portrait painter and she worked there, with occasional periods in Philadelphia, until the mid-1850's. From 1856 to 1860 she was listed in NYC directories without occupation or as a boarding-house keeper. ¶ Dunlap, *History* (1918), III, 196; Cowdrey, AA & AAU; Cowdrey, NAD; Swan, BA; Rutledge, PA; NYCD 1844, 1848–49, 1851–54, 1856–58, 1860.

LESLIE, CHARLES ROBERT (1794–1859). Literary genre, historical, and portrait painter; lecturer and writer on painting. He was born in London October 19, 1794, of American parents, spent his childhood in Philadelphia where he was apprenticed to a bookseller, and returned to England in 1811 to study painting under WEST and ALLSTON. He met with early and continued success in England, especially as a painter of scenes from English literature and history, and was elected to the Royal Academy. In 1833 Leslie accepted an appointment as professor of drawing at the U. S. Military Academy, but he resigned after a few months and returned to England where he spent the rest of his life. He was Professor of Painting in the Royal Academy for a time and the author of several books, including *A Handbook for Young Painters* (1855) and lives of Reynolds and Constable. His *Autobiographical Recollections,* edited by Tom Taylor, was published the year after Leslie's death, which occurred in London on May 5, 1859. ¶ The most complete account is found in Leslie's *Autobiographical Recollections.* See also: Pierre Irving, *Life and Letters of Washington Irving;* Flagg, *Life and Letters of Washington Allston; Crayon,* VI (1859), 185, obit.; DAB; Bolton, *Miniature Painters;* Thieme-Becker; Rutledge, PA; Rutledge, MHS; Swan, BA; Cowdrey, AA & AAU; Cowdrey, NAD; Graves; Ophia D. Smith, "Charles and Eliza Leslie"; Flexner, *The Light of Distant Skies;* Dunlap, *History.*

LESLIE, ELIZA (1787–1858). Portrait and figure painter; author. Eliza, born November 15, 1787, at Philadelphia, was the older sister of ANNE and CHARLES ROBERT LESLIE and like them took up painting at an early age. In 1812 she exhibited at the Society of Artists in Philadelphia a copy after Salvator Rosa. Later, however, she turned to writing as her career and produced a large number of books on domestic economy, stories, and one novel. She died at Gloucester (N.J.) on January 1, 1858. ¶ DAB; Ophia D. Smith, "Charles and Eliza Leslie"; Bolton, *Crayon Draftsmen;* Fielding.

LESLIE, FRANK (1821–1880). Wood engraver, publisher. Born March 29, 1821, at Ipswich (England), Henry Carter (as he was christened) was apprenticed to a wood engraver and by 1842 was working for the *Illustrated London News.* He emigrated to America in 1848, changed his name to Frank Leslie, and worked as an engraver in NYC and Boston until 1854. In January 1854 he entered the periodical publishing business and in December 1855 appeared the first issue of *Frank Leslie's Illustrated Newspaper,* the best known of his publications. During the next quarter-century Leslie was one of the country's most spectacularly successful publishers. He died in NYC on January 10, 1880, his publishing interests being carried on by his widow who had her name legally changed to Frank Leslie. ¶ DAB; NYCD 1849–80; Boston CD 1852, BD 1853; Am. Inst. Cat., 1849; Thieme-Becker (as Henry Carter).

LESLIE & HOOPER. Wood engravers, active about 1856. Possibly FRANK LESLIE and EDWARD HOOPER. ¶ Hamilton, 474.

LESLIE, JOHN. Engraver at Riverdale (Ind.) in 1860. ¶ Indiana BD 1860.

LESLIE, JOHN L. Scene and panorama painter. He was employed as a scene painter at the Bowery Theatre, NYC, in 1828 and 1830. By 1840 he had moved to Ohio and was scene painter for the National

Theatre, Cincinnati, from then until 1855. In 1848–49 he assisted HENRY LEWIS with the latter's Mississippi panorama, and in 1853 he exhibited in Cincinnati a moving panorama and revolving cartoons of *Uncle Tom's Cabin.* John E. Leslie, scenic artist at the National Theatre from 1860 to 1870 may have been the same man or his son. ¶ Odell, *Annals,* III, 407; N. Y. *Evening Post,* Nov. 28, 1828, and Jan. 13, 1830, and Cincinnati *Daily Gazette,* July 1, 1853 (cited by J. E. Arrington); Cincinnati CD 1840–70; Arrington, "Nauvoo Temple," Chap. 8.

LESLIE, R. C. Landscape painter who exhibited a view of Niagara Falls at the National Academy in 1847. His address was London. This was probably CHARLES ROBERT LESLIE. ¶ Cowdrey, NAD.

LESLIE & TRAVERS. Wood engravers, NYC, 1848–50; FRANK LESLIE and JOHN A. TRAVERS. ¶ Hamilton, 208–09, 220, 307; NYCD 1849.

LESSEN, FERDINAND. German artist, age 27, at Philadelphia in September 1850. ¶ 7 Census (1850), Pa., LI, 924.

LESSLEY, WILLIAM JAMES. Miniaturist, painter on china and silk, teacher of drawing and painting. He was working at Charleston (S.C.) in 1770–71 and 1774–75. ¶ Rutledge, *Artists in the Life of Charleston.*

LESSNER, FREDERICK. Ohio-born fancy painter, age 35, at Cincinnati in July 1850. ¶ 7 Census (1850), Ohio, XXI, 241.

LESUEUR, CHARLES ALEXANDRE (1778–1846). Watercolorist, illustrator of scientific works, engraver, and lithographer. Born January 1, 1778, at Le Havre (France), Lesueur began his career as a naturalist-artist in 1800 when he was appointed a member of a French expedition to explore the coasts of Australia. After his return from this expedition in 1804, he spent the next decade in France, chiefly working on the reports of the Australian discoveries. He left France in 1815 with the geologist William Maclure, visited the West Indies, and arrived in the United States early in 1816. After traveling through the northeastern part of the country for a year, Lesueur settled in Philadelphia. There he remained for nine years, doing some engraving of his own scientific plates, teaching drawing and painting, and serving as curator of the Academy of Natural Sciences from 1817 to 1825. In the latter year he moved to New Harmony (Ind.) where for the next twelve years he taught drawing and engraved scientific plates for the noted conchologist Thomas Say, as well as making numerous trips to New Orleans and the upper South. In 1837 Lesueur returned to France. After eight years in Paris, where he took up lithography, he was made first Director of the Museum of Natural History in his native city, and he held that position at the time of his death, December 12, 1846, at Le Havre. The bulk of his papers and sketch books are now in the Museum at Le Havre, while some of his American sketch books are in the American Antiquarian Society, Worcester (Mass.). ¶ DAB; Vail, "American Sketch Books of a French Naturalist, 1816–1837," with illus., biblio., and geographical index of localities pictured in the Lesueur Collection at the Am. Antiq. Soc. See also: Rutledge, PA; Peat, *Pioneer Painters of Indiana.*

LETMATE, FREDERICK W. Engraver and lithographer, active in NYC from 1855 until after 1870. ¶ NYCD 1855–70+.

LETTON, RALPH. Wax modeler and taker of mechanical profiles, active in New England in 1808. From 1819 to 1836 he had a museum in Cincinnati. ¶ Jackson, *Silhouette,* 124; Carrick, *Shades of Our Ancestors;* repro. of broadside, *Antiques* (Oct. 1928), 326; information courtesy Edward H. Dwight, Cincinnati Art Museum.

LEUTZE, EMANUEL GOTTLIEB (1816–1868). N.A. Historical and portrait painter. Born May 24, 1816, in Gmünd (Württemberg), he was brought to America as a child and brought up in Philadelphia. He studied painting there under JOHN RUBENS SMITH and was painting portraits at Churchtown (Pa.) at the age of twenty. In 1840 he was enabled to go to Europe to study under Lessing at Düsseldorf, as well as at Munich, Venice, and Rome. He married and made his home in Düsseldorf for almost twenty years before returning to the United States in 1859 to paint "Westward the Course of Empire," an allegorical-historical mural for the House of Representatives in Washington. During the last decade of his life Leutze divided his time between NYC and Washington, dying in the latter city on July 18, 1868. He is remembered today chiefly as the painter of "Washington Crossing the Delaware." ¶ DAB; Cowdrey, "A Note on Emanuel Leutze," illus.; Champlin

panorama and model of Niagara Falls. He was a resident of NYC in 1847–48 and in 1849 he made a trip to California by the overland route, which he recorded in another panorama. In 1857 and 1858 Lewis was back in Boston, collaborating with several other artists on scenes from a stage version of Kane's Arctic voyages. He also exhibited at the American Art-Union in 1851–52. He was in NYC in June 1860. ¶ Information courtesy J. E. Arrington, who cites contemporary newspapers; NYCD 1847–48; Cowdrey, AA & AAU; 8 Census (1860), N.Y., LX, 87.

LEWIS, SAMUEL. Writing and drawing master of Philadelphia who exhibited landscapes, *trompe l'oeil* still lifes, and water color drawings from 1795 to 1814. In 1817, at the age of 60, he exhibited at the Pennsylvania Academy a sample of his calligraphic work. ¶ Columbianum Cat., 1795; Rutledge, PA.

LEWIS, W. D., JR. Painter of two landscapes, owned by W. D. Lewis, presumably his father, which were shown at the Pennsylvania Academy in 1847. ¶ Rutledge, PA.

LEWIS, WILLIAM (1788–?). Portrait and miniature painter, born in 1788 at Salem (Mass.). He was active in Salem in 1812 and until 1824, and exhibited at the Boston Athenaeum. ¶ Swan, BA, 187, 249; Belknap, *Artists and Craftsmen of Essex County*, 10; Stauffer, no. 75; repro., *Antiques* (Aug. 1925), 97.

LEWIS, WILLIAM. Lithographer. A native of Pennsylvania, age 26, he lived in Philadelphia with GEORGE THOMAS and WILLIAM KELLY, also lithographers, in July 1860. ¶ 8 Census (1860), Pa., LII, 442.

LEWIS, YARDLEY. Limner, surveyor, and mapmaker who advertised in the *Boston Weekly Journal*, December 13, 1737. He had come to Boston from London, via Ireland, and offered to draw "family pictures by the life," as well as survey and draw maps. ¶ Dunlap, *History* (1918), III, 315.

LIAUTAUD, B. A. Artist at New Orleans, 1859–61. ¶ Delgado-WPA cites CD 1859–61.

LIBBEY (Libby), WALTER. Portrait and genre painter of Brooklyn (N.Y.) who exhibited at the National Academy and the American Art-Union from 1845 to 1851. He is said to have died young. ¶ Cowdrey, NAD; Cowdrey, AA & AAU; repro., *Panorama* (Jan. 1949), 59.

LIBBY, EDWARD W. Boston engraver, active 1850–60 and after. ¶ Boston CD 1850–60+.

LIBENAU, see LIEBENAU.

LIBHART (Liebhart), JOHN JAY (1806–?). Portrait, miniature, landscape, historical, and still life painter; engraver; modeller in clay. Born in 1806 in York County (Pa.), Libhart grew up in Marietta, on the Susquehanna, and spent most of his life there. He received some instruction in painting from ARTHUR ARMSTRONG and as a young man painted portraits in Marietta, Harrisburg, Lebanon, Lancaster, and other central Pennsylvania towns. He also dabbled in other kinds of painting, modelled in clay, did professional engraving, collected natural curiosities, invented, taught school, and served in many public offices in Marietta and Lancaster County. He died after 1860. ¶ Libhart, "John Jay Libhart, Artist"; Lancaster Co. Hist. Soc., *Portraiture in Lancaster Co.*, 129.

LIBOLT, Mrs. S. H. Miniaturist, wife of Adam Libolt, M.D., of NYC. She exhibited at the National Academy in 1838 (listed erroneously as Sibolt), 1839, and 1841. ¶ Cowdrey, NAD; NYCD 1838–41.

LIDDLE, JAMES W. Philadelphia-born engraver, age 20, living with his family in Philadelphia, August 1850. ¶ 7 Census (1850), Pa., LV, 554.

LIEBENAU, HENRY. Landscape, standard, and banner painter; born in New York about 1802; active in NYC from 1833 to 1850. His wife and son, born about 1834, were natives of Pennsylvania, according to the 1850 Census. ¶ 7 Census (1850), N.Y., LVII, 187; NYCD 1833–49.

LIEBHART, see LIBHART.

LIEBLER, THEODORE AUGUST (1830–1890). Landscape painter, engraver, lithographer. Born February 22, 1830, at Constanz (Baden), Liebler is said to have come to America in 1848. He found employment as a lithographer in NYC (SCHEDLER & LIEBLER, 1854) and was also employed as an engraver by the AMERICAN BANK NOTE COMPANY, whose trademark eagle is said to have been designed and engraved by Liebler. He died in Brooklyn (N.Y.) on August 10, 1890. Members of the family own many of his oils and watercolors. ¶ Information courtesy Theodore A. Liebler, Jr., grandson of the artist; NYCD 1853–54.

LIGHTNER, ADAM MORTIMER. Portrait painter of Lancaster (Pa.), active *c.* 1838–40. He exhibited at the Pennsylvania Academy a number of copies after landscapes by

JOSHUA SHAW. ¶ Rutledge, PA; Lancaster Co. Hist. Soc., *Portraiture in Lancaster Co.,* 129–30, repro.; Lancaster Co. Hist. Soc., *Papers and Addresses* (1913).

LILLIS, ANT. [*sic*]. Irish artist, age 48, in the New Orleans work house, July 20, 1860. ¶ 8 Census (1860), La., VI, 529.

LIMBURG, FRANCIS. Prussian lithographer, 40, at NYC in 1860. His wife Julia and their two children, ages 12 and 15, were also born in Prussia. ¶ 8 Census (1860), N.Y., LIV, 971.

LIMOËLAN, see CLORIVIÈRE.

LINCOLN, HENRY. Engraver, age 18, born in Pennsylvania; living in Philadelphia in August 1850. ¶ 7 Census (1850), Pa., XLIX, 215.

LINCOLN, JAMES SULLIVAN (1811–1888). Portrait painter and engraver. He was born May 13, 1811, in Taunton (Mass.), but was apprenticed at the age of 14 to an engraver at Providence (R.I.). After 1837 he devoted himself to portrait painting in Providence. He was the first president of the Providence Art Club. His death occurred in Providence on January 18, 1888 (not 1887 as stated by Stauffer, or 1904 as stated by Arnold). ¶ Stauffer; Arnold, *Art and Artists in Rhode Island; Providence, Births, Marriages and Deaths Recorded in:* Deaths, 1881–1890; Providence CD 1847+; represented: Am. Antiq. Soc.

LIND & FIX. Engravers in NYC, 1854–55; LEWIS LIND and LOUIS FIX. ¶ NYBD 1854–55.

LIND, LEWIS. Engraver, NYC, 1853–55; of LIND & FIX, 1854–55. In 1855 his home address was given as Massachusetts. ¶ NYCD 1853–55.

LINDENMEYR, PHILIP. Artist, 36, a native of Hesse Cassel, at NYC in 1860. His wife Emily and their four children, ages 2 to 10, were born in New York. ¶ 8 Census (1860), N.Y., LX, 360.

LINDMARK, WINTER. Wood carver, NYC, 1842–70. In 1842 he and WILLETT (or William) MORRELL exhibited a full-size carving of a woman at the American Institute. ¶ Am. Inst. Cat., 1842; NYCD 1842–70; Pinckney, *American Figureheads,* 195.

LINDSAY, ANDREW JACKSON (?–1895). Topographical draftsman. Lindsay attended West Point, 1839–41, as a cadet from Alabama and Mississippi, but resigned to join the army in 1841. In 1846 he was appointed 1st Lt. in the Mounted Rifle Regiment and he served in the West until 1861. Resigning in the latter year, he joined the Confederate Army and fought with the South throughout the Civil War. To Lt. Lindsay have been ascribed a series of drawings illustrating the Mounted Rifles' expedition from Fort Leavenworth to Oregon in 1849, although these may have been the work of GEORGE GIBBS, another member of the expedition. ¶ Schafer, "Trailing a Trail Artist of 1849"; Brown, *Fort Hall on the Oregon Trail,* repros. pp. 126, 209, 215, 221.

LINDSAY, LIZZIE. Panoramist at Charleston (S.C.) in 1854. One of her works was a panorama of NYC. ¶ Rutledge, *Artists in the Life of Charleston.*

LINDSAY, THOMAS C. Landscape painter of Cincinnati, active from 1860. ¶ Information courtesy Edward H. Dwight, Cincinnati Art Museum.

LINDSAY, WILLIAM. Wood carver of Boston, active 1859. He carved the figurehead of the New Orleans clipper packet *Dione.* ¶ Pinckney, *American Figureheads,* 195, 314.

LINEN (or Linnen), GEORGE (1802–1888). Portrait painter, born in Greenlaw (Scotland), studied painting at the Royal Scottish Academy in Edinburgh. He emigrated to America in 1834 and worked mainly in NYC and New Jersey, though he traveled as far afield as Richmond and Baltimore in the 1850's and Terre Haute (Ind.) in the 1860's. He exhibited in NYC and Philadelphia. Linen died in 1888 either in NYC (Peat and Pleasants) or on a farm near Bloomsdale, N.J. (*Richmond Portraits*). JOHN LINEN was his brother. ¶ Thieme-Becker; *Richmond Portraits;* Pleasants, *250 Years of Painting in Maryland;* Peat, *Pioneer Painters of Indiana;* Cowdrey, NAD; Cowdrey, AA & AAU; Rutledge, PA; Thorpe, "New York Painters Fifty Years Ago," 575; represented at Md. Hist. Soc.

LINEN (or Linnen), JOHN. Portrait and figure painter, born in Scotland about 1800, brother of GEORGE LINEN. He was active in NYC from 1837 to 1860 and exhibited at the National Academy, the Apollo Association, and the American Institute. ¶ 8 Census (1860), N.Y., LVIII, 787; Cowdrey, NAD; Cowdrey, AA & AAU; NYBD 1844–60; Am. Inst. Cat., 1856.

LINES, AUGUSTUS E. Engraver, born in Connecticut about 1823, working in New Haven, 1850–60. ¶ 7 Census (1850),

Conn., VIII, 581; New Haven CD 1856–58; New England BD 1856, 1860.

LION, JULES. Portrait and miniature painter, lithographer, and first daguerreotypist of New Orleans. He was a native of France, born about 1816, who came to New Orleans as early as 1837 and worked there till 1865. According to the 1851 directory he was a "free man of color." He painted a portrait of JOHN JAMES AUDUBON. ¶ 7 Census (1850), La., V, 760 [as Lyon]; Peters, *America on Stone;* New Orleans *Bee,* March 14, Nov. 5, 1840, and New Orleans CD 1837–65 (courtesy Delgado-WPA); Thompson, *La. Writers Native and Resident; Report of U. S. National Museum,* Part II (1897), pl. 3 (courtesy Print Division, Library of Congress).

LION, P. P. Artist of New Orleans, 1841–42, listed at a different address from that of JULES LION. ¶ New Orleans CD 1841–42.

LIPER, JOHN. German lithographer, 19, at NYC in 1850. ¶ 7 Census (1850), N.Y., XLI, 591.

LIPMAN, LOUIS. Lithographer of Milwaukee (Wis.). In 1857 he went into partnership with WILLIAM R. RIDDLE. During the 1860's he worked independently. ¶ Kent, "Early Commercial Lithography in Wisconsin," 249.

LIPPENCOTT, EDWARD. Artist from Pennsylvania, age 25, at the City Hotel, Cincinnati in September 1850. ¶ 7 Census (1850), Ohio, XX, 349.

LIPPETT, SARA WICHES (1789–1847). Amateur painter, of Boston, who exhibited at the Athenaeum between 1834 and 1855. In 1834 she showed a copy of Leonardo's "John the Baptist." ¶ Swan, BA; BA Cat., 1834.

LIPPIATT & SCHUREMAN. Engravers of NYC, 1854–57; THOMAS LIPPIATT and ALPHONSO B. SCHUREMAN. ¶ NYCD 1854–57.

LIPPIATT, THOMAS. Engraver; born in New York about 1832; exhibited at the American Institute in 1846; living with and probably apprenticed to GEORGE M. SHEPHERD of NYC in 1850; in partnership with A. B. SCHUREMAN from 1854 to 1857 and with Ellsworth P. Maltby in 1870. ¶ 7 Census (1850), N.Y., XLIII, 398, and XLVI, 359; Am. Inst. Cat., 1846; NYCD 1853–77.

LISPENARD, GEORGE. Engraver, 27, a native of New York, at NYC in 1860. ¶ 8 Census (1860), N.Y., LI, 436.

LISSAUTE, PIERRE. Portrait painter and teacher at New Orleans, 1822. ¶ New Orleans CD 1822; Thompson, *La. Writers, Native and Resident.*

LITTLE, ANN. Primitive landscape painter, working in Massachusetts about 1820. ¶ Lipman and Winchester, 176.

LITTLEFIELD BROTHERS. Ship carvers at Portland (Me.), 1858–1870's. The brothers were Charles H. and Francis A., sons of NAHUM LITTLEFIELD. Their work included the figurehead of the *Ocean King* (1874). ¶ Pinckney, *American Figureheads,* 139, 196.

LITTLEFIELD, CHARLES H., see LITTLEFIELD BROTHERS.

LITTLEFIELD, FRANCIS A., see LITTLEFIELD BROTHERS.

LITTLEFIELD, NAHUM. Ship carver of Portland (Me.), active 1830's. He was the father of Charles and Francis Littlefield, who carried on the family carving business as LITTLEFIELD BROTHERS. ¶ Pinckney, *American Figureheads,* 196.

LIVASSE, WILLIAM. Lithographer, 50, a native of the District of Columbia, living in Philadelphia in 1860 in the same house with CHARLES R. WELLS, designer. ¶ 8 Census (1860), Pa., LII, 951.

LIVERMORE, Mrs. MARY SPEAR (MASON) (1806–?). Miniaturist of Boston; exhibited at the Boston Athenaeum in 1846 and at the American Institute, NYC, in 1847. ¶ Swan, BA, 187, 249; Boston BD 1844–49; Am. Inst. Cat., 1847.

LIVINGSTON, Dr. EDWARD. Painter of several American landscapes shown at the National Academy in 1839 and 1843. ¶ Cowdrey, NAD.

LIVINGSTON, HARRIET (1786–1824). Amateur miniaturist; daughter of Walter Livingston; married the artist-inventor ROBERT FULTON in 1808. After his death in 1815 she married Charles G. Dale. ¶ Van Rensselaer, *The Livingston Family in America,* 115; Bolton, *Miniature Painters.*

LIVINGSTON, HENRY. Landscape artist, active in New York State during the 1790's. Six views on the Hudson and Mohawk Rivers by him were engraved by CORNELIUS TIEBOUT. ¶ Weitenkampf, "Early American Landscape Prints," 50–51; Stauffer (see Gage's *Index of Artists*); *Connoisseur* (Sept. 1944), 46, repro.

LIVINGSTON, MONTGOMERY (1816–?). A.N.A. Landscape painter, born August 31, 1816, probably at Clermont (N.Y.), the home of his father, Robert L. Livingston. He apparently visited Europe in his youth, for his first pictures at the National Academy (1838) were Swiss scenes. He later exhibited New York and New England scenes at the Academy, as well as at the Art-Union and the Pennsylvania Academy. His address in 1838 was Clermont, in 1842 NYC, and from 1843 to 1852 Tivoli (N.Y.). He was an Associate of the National Academy 1843–44, and an Honorary Member, Professional, 1848–60, though he did not exhibit after 1852. ¶ Van Rensselaer, *The Livingston Family in America,* 114; Cowdrey, NAD; Cowdrey, AA & AAU; Rutledge, PA.

LIVINGSTONE, M. L. Designer of a medallion of Washington Irving, patented in 1860. ¶ Gardner, *Yankee Stonecutters,* 68.

LLOYD, JOHN W. Engraver from Connecticut, age 23, at Philadelphia in 1860. In 1871 he was listed as a silver chaser. ¶ 8 Census (1860), Pa., LXII, 522; Phila. CD 1871.

LLOYD, Mrs. WILLIAM H. Painter of a "Madonna" sold to the Art-Union in 1848; she was from Newark (N.J.). ¶ Cowdrey, AA & AAU.

LOCK, F. W. Landscape and portrait artist in watercolors and pastels. Sherman reported finding in Manchester (Vt.) a pastel portrait so signed, dated 1849. Orrin E. Dunlap owns a watercolor of Niagara Falls, signed and dated 1856. ¶ Sherman, "Newly Discovered American Portrait Painters"; letter, Orrin E. Dunlap to NYHS, Oct. 28, 1945.

LOCKINGTON, CHARLES, & COMPANY. Engravers in NYC, 1852. ¶ NYBD and CD 1852.

LOCKWOOD, EDWARD. Engraver, 30, a native of New York, at NYC in 1860 with his wife Nellie and three children. ¶ 8 Census (1860), N.Y., L, 497.

LOCKWOOD, JOSHUA. Engraver, 31, a native of New York, at NYC in 1850. In the 1850 directory he was listed as a measurer. ¶ 7 Census (1850), N.Y., LI, 18; NYCD 1850.

LOCKWOOD, REMBRANDT. Landscape, portrait, miniature, and figure painter, active 1840–55. He was in NYC in 1840, possibly visited Warren County (Ky.) the same year, painted portraits and miniatures in Richmond (Va.) in 1841 and 1843–44, and was living in Newark (N.J.) from 1848 to 1858. He exhibited at the National Academy, the American Art-Union, and the Pennsylvania Academy, and in 1855 was reported to have sold his "Last Judgment" to the Roman Catholic Cathedral in Philadelphia for $12,000. ¶ NYBD 1840; information courtesy Mrs. W. H. Whitley, Paris (Ky.); *Richmond Portraits,* 242; Cowdrey, NAD; Cowdrey, AA & AAU; Rutledge, PA; Chicago *Daily Press,* March 1, 1855; Newark CD 1848–58 (courtesy Newark Public Library).

LOCQUIST, ——. Artist "just arrived" in New Orleans, October 1851. ¶ Delgado-WPA cites *Bee,* Oct. 8, 1851.

LOEFFLER, CHARLES. Portrait painter at Brooklyn (N.Y.) in 1857. ¶ Brooklyn BD 1857.

LOEKLE, CHARLES. Seal engraver in NYC, 1858–60. ¶ NYBD 1858, 1860.

LOEWENBERG (or Loevenberg), HENRY. Pastel portraitist at Philadelphia, 1859–60. He exhibited at the Pennsylvania Academy in 1859. ¶ Rutledge, PA; Phila. CD and BD 1860.

LOFT, P. Landscape painter in watercolors, active 1860. He was a New Englander who migrated to California about 1861 and became a gold miner. Two views, dated August 27, 1860, have been tentatively identified as scenes near Rowley (Mass.). ¶ Lipman, "American Townscapes," 340–41, two repros.

LOGAN, —— C. Irish artist, age 55, living in Philadelphia in June 1860 with his English wife and three children, all natives of Pennsylvania and the eldest 20 years old. His personal property was valued at $2,200. ¶ 8 Census (1860), Pa., LX, 763.

LOGAN, JAMES. Engraver, 25, a native of New York, at NYC in 1860 with his wife Susan. ¶ 8 Census (1860), N.Y., LX, 249.

LOGHUER, HENRY. Swiss lithographer, 36, at NYC in 1850. ¶ 7 Census (1850), N.Y., XLI, 229.

LOGUE, JOHN JAMES. Portrait and still life painter, born in Pennsylvania about 1810, exhibiting in Philadelphia from 1840 to 1864. He was married and had one daughter, KATE LOGUE, who also painted. His real and personal property were valued in 1860 at $2,800. ¶ 8 Census (1860), Pa., LV, 750; Rutledge, PA; Phila. BD 1858.

LOGUE, KATE. Still life in watercolors. Kate, daughter of JOHN J. and Maria Logue of Philadelphia, was born about 1825. She exhibited at the Pennsylvania Academy only in 1853. ¶ 8 Census (1860), Pa., LV, 750; Rutledge, PA.

LOMBARD, Mrs. CATHERINE B. Portrait painter and teacher, born in Massachusetts about 1810, active in Boston, 1852–60.

¶ 8 Census (1860), Mass., XXVII, 52; Swan, BA; Boston BD 1853–57.

LONATI, NICHOLA. Italian artist, 60, at NYC in 1850. ¶ 7 Census (1850), N.Y., XLII, 151.

LONERGAN, JAMES. Engraver and lithographer at New Orleans, 1857–61. ¶ Delgado-WPA cites *Picayune,* April 2, 1857, New Orleans CD 1860–61.

LONG, ARTHUR. Portrait painter at New Orleans during the winter of 1853–54. His sitters included Edmond Forstall and daughter and a Mr. Tuyes, Sr. ¶ Delgado-WPA cites *Bee,* Jan. 26, 1854.

LONG, E. D. Botanical draftsman. He was one of the artists who worked on T. SINCLAIR's flower lithographs for *The North American Sylva,* published in Philadelphia in 1846. ¶ McClinton, "American Flower Lithographs," 362.

LONG, FREDERICK. Engraver and die-sinker, NYC, 1856–57. ¶ NYBD 1856–57.

LONG, SAMUEL P. Landscape painter of Portsmouth (N.H.) and Boston. He exhibited between 1833 and 1874 at the Boston Athenaeum and in 1850 at the Pennsylvania Academy. ¶ Swan, BA; Rutledge, PA.

LONGACRE, ANDREW. Engraver, son of JAMES B. LONGACRE. He was born in Philadelphia about 1831 and was listed as an engraver in the 1850 Census. He was then living with his parents. ¶ 7 Census (1850), Pa., LIII, 268.

LONGACRE, JAMES BARTON (1794–1869). Line and stipple engraver; portrait painter. Born August 11, 1794, in Delaware County (Pa.), Longacre was first apprenticed to John F. Watson, bookseller and historian of Philadelphia, and later to the engraver GEORGE MURRAY. In 1819 he established his own business and quickly won national fame by his engravings for such works as Sanderson's *Biography of the Signers of the Declaration of Independence* (1820–). He was also known as a painter of sepia and watercolor portraits. His major accomplishment was *The National Portrait Gallery of Distinguished Americans* which he published in collaboration with JAMES HERRING between 1834 and 1839 and to which he contributed a number of original portraits and engravings. On September 16, 1844, Longacre succeeded CHRISTIAN GOBRECHT as chief engraver at the U. S. Mint, Philadelphia, a position which he held until his death on January 1, 1869. ¶ DAB; Stauffer; Phila. CD 1825–60+; Rutledge, PA; 7 Census (1850), Pa., LIII, 266; 8 Census (1860), Pa., LVIII, 448; extracts from his diary, 1825, in *Pa. Mag. of Hist. and Biog.,* XXIX (April, 1905), 134–42. See also: DRAPER, TOPPAN, LONGACRE & CO.; —— LONGAXE.

LONGACRE, MATTHIAS REIFF (1836–?). Wood engraver and draftsman; born June 6, 1836, in Montgomery County (Pa.). At the age of 17 he was apprenticed to a Philadelphia wood engraver and two years later he went out to Cincinnati for a year. He then went to NYC, worked a short time for Harper's and Leslie's magazines, and about 1858 established his own business. During the Civil War he was military storekeeper at Baton Rouge (La.). After the war he had an engraving and lithography business in Philadelphia for some years, but later he became a plumber and made drawings of industrial plants. ¶ Autobiographical sketch and genealogy in *History of the Longacre-Longaker-Longenecker Family,* 109–25.

LONGAXE, ——. "Young artist of Philadelphia" who was exhibiting portraits at New Orleans in November 1824. This may well have been JAMES B. LONGACRE, engraver and portrait painter from Philadelphia, who was 30 in 1824 and later named one of his sons Orleans. ¶ Delgado-WPA cites *Gazette,* Nov. 20, 1824.

LONGFELLOW, WILLIAM PITT PREBLE (1836–1913). Architect, landscape, and decorative painter. A nephew of the poet, he was born October 25, 1836, at Portland (Me.), graduated from Harvard in 1855, and became an architect in Boston a few years later. For a time in the 1870's he was director of the newly opened school of drawing and painting of the Boston Museum of Fine Arts. He was noted as a writer on architecture and as an amateur composer. He died August 3, 1913, at East Gloucester (Mass.). ¶ DAB; represented in Boston Museum of Fine Arts.

LONGSTRETH, EDWARD (1839–1905). Draftsman. Born in Hatboro (Pa.) on June 22, 1839, Longstreth entered the Baldwin Locomotive Works in Philadelphia in 1857 and soon after made several pencil and wash drawings of Baldwin locomotive engines which have been reproduced. He was employed as a machinist until 1868, when he became Superintendent. Two years later he became a partner in the locomotive firm of M. Baird & Co. and in 1874 of Burnham, Parry, Williams & Co., with whom he remained until his retirement in 1886. He died in Philadelphia on February 24, 1905. ¶ Taylor, *The Longstreth Family Records,* 289–91; *Portfolio* (Feb. 1954), 139; Phila. CD 1862–94.

LONGWORTH, MONTREVILLE. Artist, 37, a native of New York, at NYC in 1850. ¶ 7 Census (1850), N.Y., XLVIII, 525.

LOOF, Monsieur A. Portrait painter at New Orleans for a short time in 1841. ¶ Delgado-WPA cites *Picayune,* April 1, 1841.

LOOKER, SILAS. Sign and ornamental painter at Cincinnati in 1819. ¶ Knittle, *Early Ohio Taverns,* 43.

LOOMIS & ANNIN. Wood engravers of NYC, 1858–59; PASCAL LOOMIS and PHINEAS F. ANNIN. ¶ NYBD 1858, CD 1859.

LOOMIS, CASPAR. Engraver, 24, born in Connecticut, at NYC in 1850 with his wife and one child. This may be an error for PASCAL LOOMIS. ¶ 7 Census (1850), N.Y., XLVI, 135.

LOOMIS, JAMES M. Engraver at Springfield (Mass.) in 1849. ¶ New England BD 1849.

LOOMIS, OSBERT BURR. Portrait, landscape, and panorama painter, born July 30, 1813, at Windsor (Conn.). He graduated from Yale in 1835 and immediately began his career as an artist, painting portraits in NYC and Charleston in 1836 and 1837, in NYC in 1843. Between 1843 and 1850 he spent six years in Cuba. His panorama of the island, painted from sketches made on the spot, was exhibited in Charleston, NYC, New Orleans, and Cincinnati, and offered for sale in NYC in 1853. Loomis exhibited at the National Academy sporadically until 1858. ¶ Loomis, *Descendants of Joseph Loomis in America,* 218; Cowdrey, NAD; NYCD 1843, 1856; Rutledge, *Artists in the Life of Charleston;* information courtesy J. E. Arrington.

LOOMIS, PASCAL (1826–1878). Wood engraver. Born July 24, 1826, at Hartford (Conn.), he worked as a wood engraver in NYC from 1848 to 1859, and in San Francisco from 1860 until his death, January 3, 1878. He was associated with the firms of LOOMIS & ANNIN (NYC, 1858–59), HEWET & LOOMIS (NYC, 1859), and EASTMAN & LOOMIS (San Francisco, 1860 and after). ¶ Loomis, *Descendants of Joseph Loomis in America,* 475; NYBD 1848, 1858, CD 1859; San Francisco BD 1860, CD 1861; Am. Inst. Cat., 1849. *Cf.* CASPAR LOOMIS and PARKER LUMAS.

LOOP, HENRY AUGUSTUS (1831–1895). N.A. Portrait and figure painter, born September 9, 1831, at Hillsdale (N.Y.). After a year's instruction from HENRY PETERS GRAY and several years' practice of his profession in NYC, Loop went to Paris in 1856 to study under Couture. After two years in France and Italy he returned to NYC. He was married in 1865 to Jennette Shepherd Harrison (see JENNETTE SHEPHERD HARRISON LOOP), one of his pupils, and with her he went to Europe again in 1867 for about eighteen months. The rest of his career was spent in NYC. He was elected a National Academician in 1861. Loop died October 20, 1895, at Lake George (N.Y.). ¶ DAB; Clement and Hutton; French, *Art and Artists in Conn.,* 142–43; Cowdrey, NAD; Rutledge, PA; Swan, BA; represented: Princeton Univ. and the Merchants' House, NYC; repro., *Mag. of Art* (Nov. 1947), 282; 7 Census (1850), N.Y., XLI, 674.

LOOP, JENNETTE SHEPHERD HARRISON (1840–1909). A.N.A. Portrait and figure painter, wife of HENRY AUGUSTUS LOOP. She was born March 5, 1840, at New Haven (Conn.) and received her first art training from LOUIS BAIL, WALES HOTCHKISS, and GEORGE DURRIE, all of New Haven. In 1863 she went to NYC to study further under HENRY A. LOOP, to whom she was married in 1865. They visited Europe in 1867–68, but the rest of her career was spent in the United States, chiefly in NYC. She was particularly noted as a portrayer of children. Mrs. Loop died April 17, 1909, at Saratoga (N.Y.). Her daughter, Edith Loop, was also a portrait painter. ¶ Clement and Hutton; CAB; French, *Art and Artists in Conn.,* 170–71; *Art Annual,* VII (1909/10), 79, obit.; represented: Yale Univ. Art Gallery and Merchants' House, NYC.

LOPAZE, D. Lithographer employed by JOHN PENDLETON of NYC, about 1831. *Cf.* —— LOPEZ. ¶ Landauer, *My City 'Tis of Thee,* frontis. and p. 17.

LOPEZ, ——. Lithographer employed by WILLIAM PENDLETON at Boston, about 1831. *Cf.* D. LOPAZE. ¶ Peters, *America on Stone.*

LORD, CHARLES M. Lithographer, 19, a native of Rhode Island, at NYC in 1850. ¶ 7 Census (1850), N.Y., LV, 497.

LORD, MARY. Amateur painter in water colors on silk, Litchfield (Conn.), about 1800. ¶ Lipman and Winchester, 176.

LORD, PHILIP (1814–88). Profilist, born at Newburyport (Mass.) and active from Maine to Massachusetts during the 1830's and 1840's. ¶ Carrick, "Silhouettes," 342, repro.; Carrick, *Shades of Our Ancestors,* 122; Jackson, *Silhouette,* 125.

LORD, PHOEBE GRIFFIN (1831–75). Miniaturist. She was a native of Connecticut and lived at Lyme. ¶ Bolton, *Miniature Painters;* Fielding.

LORD, THOMAS. Engraver working at Louisville (Ky.) in 1848 and at Philadelphia in 1850. ¶ Louisville CD 1848; Phila. CD 1850.

LORENZ, ALEXANDER. Portrait painter; born in Prussia about 1808; living in Baden about 1842–43; living in NYC from 1852 to 1863. ¶ 8 Census (1860), N.Y., LIV, 978; NYBD 1852, 1857–58; NYCD 1863.

LORIA, SAM F. Engraver, age 34, native of Pennsylvania; at Philadelphia in 1850. ¶ 7 Census (1850), Pa., LII, 238.

LORIO, PETER. Austrian lithographer, age 40, living in Philadelphia in 1860. His three-year-old son was born in Pennsylvania. ¶ 8 Census (1860), Pa., LII, 243.

LORING, FRANCIS WILLIAM (1838–1905). Landscape painter. He was born in Boston and died at Meran (Austria). ¶ Boston Museum of Fine Arts, *Catalogue;* Fielding; Smith.

LORTON, RICHARD. Miniature painter at Richmond (Va.), 1817–19. He and JAMES WARRELL founded the Virginia Museum in 1817; Lorton withdrew from its management in 1819. ¶ *Richmond Portraits,* 238.

LOSSING & BARRITT. Wood engravers of NYC, 1847–69; BENSON J. LOSSING and WILLIAM BARRITT. ¶ Hamilton, 525; NYCD 1847–69.

LOSSING, BENSON JOHN (1813–91). Wood engraver. Born February 12, 1813, at Beekman, Dutchess County (N.Y.), Lossing was apprenticed to a watchmaker in Poughkeepsie (N.Y.) but at the age of 22 became joint editor of a newspaper and literary magazine published there. He learned wood engraving from JOSEPH ALEXANDER ADAMS in Poughkeepsie and, in 1838, established himself in NYC as an engraver. From 1846 to 1869 he was associated in the engraving business with WILLIAM BARRITT. In 1848 Lossing commenced working on his *Pictorial Field-Book of the Revolution* (published in parts, 1850–52) and during the next 35 years he turned out a great many works of American history and biography, including *A Memorial of Dr. Alexander Anderson* (1872). Lossing died at his home in Dover Plains (N.Y.) on June 3, 1891. ¶ DAB; Am. Inst. Cat., 1842; repro., *American Collector* (Oct. 1947), 13, 43; NYCD 1841–69; 7 Census (1850), N.Y., LVI, 688.

LOSTINE, HENRY. Prussian sculptor, age 46, at New Orleans in June 1860. ¶ 8 Census (1860), La., V, 928.

LOTICHIUS, ERNEST. Animal, landscape, and genre painter. He was working in Düsseldorf and Munich about 1841, but by 1858 had settled in NYC, exhibiting in that year at the National Academy a hunting scene and a view in the Catskills. ¶ Thieme-Becker; Cowdrey, NAD.

LOTTA, L. Sculptor and portrait painter at New Orleans in 1842. ¶ Seebold, *Old Louisiana Plantation Homes and Family Trees,* I, 23.

LOTTER, MATTHEW ALBERT. Engraver at Philadelphia in 1777. ¶ Brown and Brown.

LOTZ, FREDERICK. German fresco painter, age 31, at Pittsburgh (Pa.) in August 1850. ¶ 7 Census (1850), Pa., III, 96.

LOUD, Mrs. H. C. Crayon portraitist of Philadelphia; exhibitor, Pennsylvania Academy, 1850. ¶ Rutledge, PA; Bolton, *Crayon Draftsmen.*

LOUDERBACH & HOFFMAN. Wood engravers and designers, Philadelphia, 1853–60; JAMES W. LOUDERBACH and GUSTAVUS A. HOFFMAN. ¶ Phila. CD 1853–60; Hamilton, 524.

LOUDERBACH (Louderback, or Lauderbach), JAMES W. Wood engraver of Philadelphia, 1852–60. ¶ Phila. CD 1853–60; Hamilton, 524; 8 Census (1860), Pa., LVII, 102.

LOUIS, C., see C. LOVIS.

LOUIS, JOHN F. Philadelphia landscape painter who exhibited at the Pennsylvania Academy in 1857 and 1862. ¶ Rutledge, PA.

LOURIE, ALEXANDER, see ALEXANDER LAWRIE.

LOUTERBURG, W., see A. C. H. DE LOUTHERBOURG.

LOUTHERBOURG, ANNIBALE CHRISTIAN HENRY DE (1765–1813). Miniaturist, son of the celebrated Anglo-French landscape painter, P. J. de Loutherbourg. The son was born in Paris in 1765, and accompanied his father to England, where he himself exhibited at the Royal Academy in 1793. In 1794 he came to America and established himself as a miniaturist in Philadelphia. In 1796, however, his occupation was given as soap-boiler. In 1798 he was listed as a limner and in that year he probably executed a sketch of George Washington on the occasion of the latter's farewell to Congress, although Jackson lists the artist as W. Louterburg. When de Loutherbourg returned to England is not known. He died in London in 1813. ¶ Thieme-Becker; Prime, II, 6; Phila. CD 1796, 1798; Jackson, *Silhouette,* 125.

LOVE, G. Engraver of frontispiece to Watts, *Divine Songs* (Philadelphia, 1807). ¶ Stauffer.

LOVEJOY, JOHN H. Wood engraver, Cincinnati, 1840–44. ¶ Cincinnati CD 1840–44 (courtesy Edward H. Dwight, Cincinnati Art Museum).

LOVELL, ANTONA [*sic*]. French lithographer, age 36, living with his Swiss wife in Boston, August 1850. ¶ 7 Census (1850), Mass., XXIV, 667.

LOVELL & BARRET. Sign and ornamental painters at Cincinnati, 1819. *Cf.* O. LOVELL & SON. ¶ Knittle, *Early Ohio Taverns,* 43.

LOVELL, O., & SON. Sign painters, Cincinnati, 1840. *Cf.* LOVELL & BARRET. ¶ Knittle, *Early Ohio Taverns,* 43.

LOVERIDGE, C. Landscape painter of Albany (N.Y.), 1857–60. ¶ Albany CD 1857–60.

LOVETT, GEORGE H. (1824–1894). Engraver and die sinker, born February 14, 1824, in Philadelphia, the son of ROBERT LOVETT. The family moved to NYC about 1826 and George was listed there as an engraver from 1847 until the early 1890's. He died in Brooklyn on January 28, 1894. ¶ Thieme-Becker; 7 Census (1850), N.Y., XLVII, 851; NYCD 1847+.

LOVETT, JOHN D. Engraver and die sinker, probably a son of ROBERT LOVETT. He worked in NYC from 1842 to 1896. ¶ NYCD 1842–96.

LOVETT, ROBERT. Engraver; born in New York about 1796–97; working in Philadelphia from about 1816 to 1825 and in NYC from 1826 to 1874. He was the father of ROBERT, GEORGE, THOMAS, and probably JOHN D. LOVETT, all engravers. ¶ 7 Census (1850), N.Y., XLVII, 851; 8 Census (1860), N.Y., XLVII, 657; Phila. CD 1818–24; NYCD 1826–74; Stauffer; Cowdrey, AA & AAU.

LOVETT, ROBERT, JR. Seal engraver and die sinker of Philadelphia, a son of ROBERT LOVETT. He was born either in England (1850 Census) or in Philadelphia (1860 Census) between 1817 and 1820; Philadelphia seems more probable since the elder Lovett was working there from 1816. Robert, Jr., began engraving about 1839 and was active until after 1860. ROBERT K. LOVETT, his son, was also an engraver. ¶ 7 Census (1850), Pa., LII, 613; 8 Census (1860), Pa., LVIII, 177; Phila. CD 1839–62+.

LOVETT, ROBERT K. Seal engraver, Philadelphia, 1860 and after. He was born in Philadelphia about 1841 or 1842 and was the son of ROBERT LOVETT, JR. ¶ 7 Census (1850), Pa., LII, 613; 8 Census (1860), Pa., LVIII, 177; Phila. CD 1862+.

LOVETT, THOMAS (*c.* 1820 1856). Engraver, son of ROBERT LOVETT. He worked in NYC as an engraver from 1844 to 1848, as a policeman from 1849 to 1852, and again as an engraver from 1853 until his death in NYC on November 10, 1856, at the age of 36. ¶ NYCD 1844–56; Barber, "Deaths Taken from the N. Y. *Evening Post,*" XXXIII.

LOVETT, WILLIAM (1773–1801). Portrait and miniature painter. He was born in Boston, worked there during the 1790's, and died there on June 29, 1801. ¶ Bolton, *Miniature Painters;* Prime, II, 17; Boston *Columbian Centinel,* March 28, 1798 (citation courtesy C. S. Brigham, Am. Antiq. Soc.); Belknap, *Artists and Craftsmen of Essex County,* 10; repros., *Worcester Art Museum Bulletin* (Oct. 1944), p. [1].

LOVIE & BAUERLE [& BRUEN]. Wood engravers and designers at Cincinnati, 1856–57. The original partners were HENRI LOVIE and CHARLES BAUERLE; they were joined in 1857 by JOHN C. BRUEN. ¶ Cincinnati CD and BD 1856–57.

LOVIE, HENRI. Portrait and landscape painter, designer, and illustrator. He was associated with the Cincinnati firms of LOVIE & BAUERLE and LOVIE, BAUERLE & BRUEN in 1856–57 and remained in Cincinnati at least until 1859, when he was listed as a portrait and landscape painter. During the Civil War he was a field illustrator for *Leslie's.* ¶ Cincinnati CD 1856–59; Ohio BD 1859; Taft, *Artists and Illustrators of the Old West,* 296.

LOVING, JOSEPH. Artist from New Hampshire, age 24, at Boston in September

1850. ¶ 7 Census (1850), Mass., XXVI, 440.

LOVIS, C. Landscape pencil drawing, *c.* 1818. ¶ Lipman and Winchester, 176, misprinted as Louis (information courtesy Jean Lipman).

LOW, ANDREW. Engraver in NYC, 1848. ¶ NYBD 1848.

LOW, see also LOWE.

LOWBER, J. B. S. Portrait painter, Philadelphia, 1850. ¶ Phila. BD 1850.

LOWE, EDWARD. English artist, 47, at NYC in 1850. Listed as a signpainter in the 1850 directory. ¶ 7 Census (1850), N.Y., L, 343; NYCD 1850.

LOWE, F. Engraver of eleven wood-cuts for *Sketches of Rochester* (Rochester, N.Y., 1838). ¶ Hamilton, 101.

LOWE, J. Engraver at New Orleans, 1837. See SAMUEL R. MAVERICK. ¶ Delgado-WPA cites CD 1837.

LOWE, JOHN. Engraver at Charleston (S.C.), 1804. He did hair-work, engraving, and gold and silversmith's work. ¶ Rutledge, *Artists in the Life of Charleston.*

LOWE, ROBERT. Engraver. He was working in NYC from 1832 to 1841 and at Worcester (Mass.) from 1849 to 1851. ¶ *Am. Adv. Directory* 1832; NYBD 1837, 1841; Worcester CD 1849–51; New England BD 1849.

LOWE (or LOW), SAMUEL W. Engraver on copper and steel, die sinker, and embosser, Philadelphia, 1844–60 and after. ¶ Phila. CD 1844–60+.

LOWELL, JOHN ADAMS. Engraver, of EASTMAN & LOWELL, Boston, 1859 and after. He was 23 years of age in 1860. ¶ Boston CD 1859–60+; 8 Census (1860), Mass., XXVIII, 49.

LOWENBERG, VICTOR. Lithographer, age 21, born in Pennsylvania, living in Philadelphia in 1860. In 1863 he was listed as a printer. His father, Louis Lowenberg, was a Prussian cap-maker and his mother an Italian. ¶ 8 Census (1860), Pa., LII, 674; Phila. CD 1863.

LOWNES, CALEB. Engraver, die sinker, and seal cutter, who worked in Philadelphia from the 1770's to 1790's. His engraved plan of Boston Harbor appeared in the *Pennsylvania Magazine* for June 1775. He is known to have engraved a seal for the Board of Admiralty in 1779, and possibly the wood-cut Coat of Arms of Pennsylvania (*c.* 1786). In 1797 Lownes was on the Philadelphia Board of Health. ¶ Middlebrook, "A Few of the New England Engravers," 362; Stauffer.

LUCAS, J. Painter of "Autumnal Landscape" (copy), shown in Charleston (S.C.), April 1822. ¶ Rutledge, *Artists in the Life of Charleston,* 242.

LUCAS, JEAN. Engraver on marble, New Orleans, 1822. ¶ New Orleans CD 1822.

LUCAS, WILLIAM B., see KENNEDY & LUCAS.

LUCCEARINI, ANDREW. Italian statue moulder, age 32, living with his brother JOHN LUCCEARINI in Washington (D.C.), June 1860. ¶ 8 Census (1860), D.C., I, 459.

LUCCEARINI, JOHN. Italian statue moulder, age 30, living with his brother ANDREW LUCCEARINI in Washington (D.C.), June 1860. ¶ 8 Census (1860), D.C., I, 459.

LUCECK, G. Hungarian artist, age 44, living in New Orleans in June 1860. ¶ 8 Census (1860), La., VII, 32.

LUCKENBACH, REUBEN O. (1818–1880). Landscape painter, painting, and drawing teacher. A native of Bethlehem (Pa.), where his father was a maker of tin and copper, Reuben was active in the Moravian Church as early as 1850. He studied art under GUSTAVUS GRUNEWALD at Bethlehem and succeeded him as drawing and painting master at the Young Ladies Seminary in 1866. He exhibited at the Pennsylvania Academy in 1863. ¶ Rutledge, PA; Levering, *History of Bethlehem,* 595, 690, 710.

LUDLOW, C. A. Watercolorist. A New Yorker and reputed pupil of ARCHIBALD ROBERTSON, Ludlow in 1802 painted a scene at Bethlehem (Pa.). ¶ Repro., *Panorama* (Aug.–Sept. 1946), 4.

LUDLOW, EDWARD HUNTER (1810–1884). Amateur marine painter. A younger brother of GABRIEL AUGUSTUS LUDLOW, he was born in NYC in 1810, studied medicine, and practiced for a year in Westchester County. In 1831 he opened a real estate office in NYC and devoted the rest of his life to business, being for many years president of the New York Real Estate Exchange. He died November 27, 1884. He had exhibited at the National Academy and the Apollo Association in 1841. ¶ Cowdrey, AA & AAU; Gordon, "Gabriel Ludlow and His Descendants."

LUDLOW, GABRIEL AUGUSTUS (1800–1838). Marine painter, elder brother of EDWARD HUNTER LUDLOW. He exhibited marine views at the National Academy in 1828, 1835–38. ¶ Cowdrey, NAD; Gordon, "Gabriel Ludlow and His Descendants."

LUDLOW, GULIAN (1764–1826). Pencil profilist. Born January 1, 1764, at Hyde

Park, near Hempstead, Long Island (N.Y.), Gulian Ludlow became a merchant in NYC. His only known work is a pencil profile of his son Gulian, Jr., taken shortly before the latter's death in October 1821. The elder Ludlow died on October 14, 1826. ¶ Sherman, "American Miniatures by Minor Artists," 422–23; Gordon, "Gabriel Ludlow and His Descendants."

LUDWIG, CHARLES L. Early lithographer of Richmond (Va.). ¶ Peters, *America on Stone.*

LUDWIG, HENRY. Xylographic (wood) engraver, NYC, 1841. ¶ NYBD 1841.

LUDWIG, WILLIAM. Lithographer from Brunswick (Germany), age 26, at Philadelphia in 1860. His wife was also German, but their three children, the eldest age 4, were born in Pennsylvania. ¶ 8 Census (1860), Pa., LII, 575.

LÜBBERS, T. C. Miniaturist. The New York Historical Society owns miniatures of Mr. and Mrs. James Madison by this artist, one signed. GIMBREDE made an engraving *c.* 1816 after Lübbers' miniature of an unidentified man. ¶ NYHS Catalogue (1941), nos. 517, 519; Stauffer, no. 1106.

LUFFMAN, JOHN. Engraver, NYC, 1819. ¶ NYCD 1819.

LUGENBUSH, JULIUS L. Landscape and marine painter at New Orleans, 1859. ¶ Delgado-WPA cites CD 1859.

LUKE, WILLIAM (1790–?). Figurehead carver of Portsmouth (Va.). He was born in 1790 and active in 1822. His figure of "Tamanend" has been reproduced. Luke is said to have been a joiner in the Gosport Navy Yard and to have carved for many ships of the Navy. ¶ Pinckney, *American Figureheads and their Carvers,* opp. 81, 96–97, 196.

LUM, CHARLES M. Artist from New York, age 33, at Detroit in 1860. ¶ 8 Census (1860), Mich., XX, 100; Detroit CD 1861.

LUMAS, PARKER. Engraver, 35, at NYC in 1860 with his wife and three children, ages 4 to 11. This may be an error for PASCAL LOOMIS. ¶ 8 Census (1860), N.Y., XLVI, 110.

LUMLEY, ARTHUR (*c.* 1837–1912). Painter and illustrator. A native of Dublin, Lumley came to America before 1840 and made his home in Brooklyn (N.Y.). He died September 27, 1912, at Mt. Vernon (N.Y.). ¶ *Art Annual,* X, obit.; Thieme-Becker; Hamilton, 367–68.

LUND, THEODORE. Miniaturist, working in NYC, 1836–43. He exhibited at the National Academy, Apollo Association, and American Institute. ¶ Cowdrey, NAD; Cowdrey, AA & AAU; Am. Inst. Cat., 1842; NYCD 1836–43.

LUNDBERY, PETER. Limner, sign, and general painter, at Charleston (S.C.), 1782. ¶ Rutledge, *Artists in the Life of Charleston.*

LUNDIE, ——. Topographical artist whose views of the New York Navy Yard and Youle's Shot Tower were engraved by DICK for Theodore Fay's *Views in New York* (1831). ¶ Fay, *Views in New York;* Stokes, *Icon.,* III, 599–603, pl. 102a.

LUNGKWITZ, HERMANN (1813–1891). Landscape painter. He was born March 14 or 15, 1813, at Halle (Germany), studied under L. Richter at Dresden, and married the sister of RICHARD PETRI. After the Dresden revolution of 1848 Lungkwitz and Petri brought their families to America, settling in 1850 at Fredericksburg (Texas). After the Civil War Lungkwitz moved to San Antonio and set up a photographic establishment with CARL G. VON IWONSKI, but continued to paint for amusement. He later moved to Austin, where he died in 1891. ¶ Thieme-Becker; Gideon, "Two Pioneer Artists of Texas"; "Texas in Pictures," 456, 458, three repros.

LUOLIE, PETER. Painter at Philadelphia, 1717. ¶ Weiss, "The Growth of the Graphic Arts in Phila., 1663–1820," 77.

LUPTON, Mrs. FRANCES PLATT TOWNSEND. A.N.A. Sculptor, miniaturist, and landscape painter. Frances Platt Townsend married Lancaster Lupton in NYC on March 27, 1803. As Mrs. Lupton she exhibited at the National Academy in 1828, 1829, and 1831, and in 1829 she presented to the City of New York her bust of Governor Throop. ¶ N. Y. *Evening Post,* April 8, 1803; Cowdrey, NAD; Stokes, *Icon.*

LUSBY, JAMES. English artist, age 34, at Washington (D.C.) in June 1860. ¶ 8 Census (1860), D.C., II, 513.

LUSCOMB, WILLIAM HENRY (1805–1866). Marine artist. A native of Ballston (N.Y.), he worked in Salem (Mass.), painting and sketching the packets and clippers of the 1840's and 1850's. ¶ Robinson and Dow, I, 62; Peters, "Paintings of the Old 'Wind-Jammer,' " 32.

LUSSAN, AUGUST. Artist at New Orleans, 1841–42. ¶ New Orleans CD 1841–42.

LUTZ, CONRAD. Wood engraver, 24, a native of Hesse-Darmstadt, at NYC in 1860 with his wife Catherine and a daughter one month old. ¶ 8 Census (1860), N.Y., LVII, 584.

LUTZ, JACOB. Lithographer, born in Germany about 1831. He was in NYC by August 1850, at the age of 19, and in 1851 he lithographed a frontispiece for *The New York Journal of Medicine and the Collateral Sciences,* VI (1851). ¶ 7 Census (1850), N.Y., LV, 643; Peters, *America on Stone* [as J. Lutz].

LUTZ, JACOB. Primitive, known only for a crude watercolor drawing of George Washington on horseback, painted in 1799. Probably a Pennsylvania-German. ¶ *Antiques* (July 1947), cover and p. 23.

LUX, RUDOLPH. Porcelain painter from Germany, at New Orleans 1858–60. He was 45 years of age in 1860, and had a son, age 5, born in Louisiana. ¶ 8 Census (1860), La., VI, 473; New Orleans CD 1858.

LUZADA, SAMUEL. Landscape painter in NYC, 1797. ¶ NYCD 1797 (cited by McKay).

LYBRAND, JACOB. Engraver of Philadelphia, 1828–29. This may be the J. Lybrand mentioned by Stauffer as a Philadelphia line engraver active about 1820. ¶ Phila. CD 1828–29; Stauffer.

LYCTSTON, F. A., see FRANCIS A. LYDSTON.

LYDSTON, FRANCIS A. (1819–?). Miniature and fresco painter, born in Massachusetts in 1819. He was working as a fancy or fresco painter in Boston, 1841–43, and in 1846 painted a miniature of a dead child, which has been reproduced. In the early sixties he moved to Milwaukee, painted some portraits including a self-portrait now in the Milwaukee Public Museum, and eventually turned to glass painting. ¶ Butts, *Art in Wisconsin,* 97; Boston CD 1841–43; *Antiques* (Jan. 1933), 13, repro. (as F. A. Lyctston).

LYDSTON, WILLIAM, JR. Portrait, miniature, and fancy painter of Boston, active 1835–60. A native of Massachusetts, born about 1813, and probably an elder brother of FRANCIS A. LYDSTON. ¶ 7 Census (1850), Mass., XXVI, 55; 8 Census (1860), Mass., XXVII, 764; Boston CD 1835–60.

LYMAN, ——. Landscape artist who, in collaboration with THOMAS BEHAN, drew and published in 1807 a view of the falls of the Passaic, Paterson (N.J.). ¶ Stauffer (cited by Gage).

LYMAN, ALBERT. Topographical artist who in 1849 sketched a view of Mormon Island (Calif.). ¶ Van Nostrand and Coulter, *California Pictorial,* 124.

LYMAN, H. Instructress in painting, Connecticut, 1820. ¶ Lipman and Winchester, 176.

LYMAN, SYLVESTER S. (1813–after 1878). Portrait and landscape painter, born September 24, 1813, at Easthampton (Mass.). He studied under HEWINS and EDWIN WHITE in Hartford (Conn.) and was still painting there, chiefly landscapes, in 1878. ¶ French, *Art and Artists in Connecticut,* 84; Hartford CD 1860.

LYNCH, Miss ANNA. Crayon drawing, Charleston (S.C.), 1853. ¶ Rutledge, *Artists in the Life of Charleston.*

LYNN, WILLIAM. His drawing of the frigate *Constitution* was engraved *c.* 1815 by ABEL BOWEN and published in Boston by the artist, who may have been the William Lynn listed as a rigger in the 1818 directory. ¶ *Portfolio* (Dec. 1951), 80; Boston CD 1818.

LYON, ALFRED. Engraver at Newark (N.J.), 1850. ¶ N. J. BD 1850.

LYON, EDWIN. Sculptor of Natchez (Miss.). In 1848 he exhibited at the Pennsylvania Academy busts of Gen. Zachary Taylor and the artist J. R. LAMBDIN, and in 1853 a medallion of Gen. Taylor. ¶ Rutledge, PA.

LYON, J. B. Miniaturist, age 29, native of Pennsylvania, living in a hotel at Pittsburgh (Pa.) in August 1850. ¶ 7 Census (1850), Pa., III (part 2), 125.

LYON, JULES, see JULES LION.

LYON, M. W. Miniaturist working in the neighborhood of Bridgeport (Conn.) in the 1840's and 1850's. ¶ Sherman, "Some Recently Discovered Early American Portrait Miniaturists," 293, repro.

LYONS, SIDNEY S. Portrait painter who came to Cincinnati in 1826 after studying in Europe and remained in Cincinnati at least until 1859. He also worked in Louisville (Ky.). ¶ Cist, *Cincinnati in 1841,* 140; Cist, *Cincinnati in 1859,* 202; information courtesy Mrs. W. H. Whitley, Paris (Ky.).

M

M., J. Engraver, age 14, of a portrait of Frederick the Great, published in Hugh Gaine's *New York Almanac* for 1759, and sold by J. Turner of Philadelphia. Stauffer suggests that the young engraver may have been an apprentice of JAMES TURNER, engraver then working in Philadephia. ¶ Stauffer.

M., P. J. Miniaturist at Albany (N.Y.) in 1796; probably PETER J. MEANCE. ¶ Prime, II, 18.

MAAS, CHARLES E. Philadelphia engraver, born in Pennsylvania about 1827, active 1848 to after 1860. He was associated with the firms of J. & C. E. Maas in 1854 and MAAS, PERCIVAL & MAAS from 1855 to 1857. He was probably a son of JACOB MAAS. ¶ 7 Census (1850), Pa., L, 391; Phila. CD 1848–71.

MAAS, JACOB. Wood engraver of Philadelphia, born in Pennsylvania about 1800, active 1825–60 and after. In collaboration with his son (?), CHARLES E. MAAS, he organized in 1855 the firm of MAAS, PERCIVAL & MAAS. ¶ 7 Census (1850), Pa., L, 507; 8 Census (1860), Pa., LX, 831; Phila. CD 1825–60+ (his widow listed in 1871).

MAAS, PERCIVAL & MAAS. Engravers, Philadelphia, 1855–57; JACOB MAAS, HENRY PERCIVAL, and CHARLES E. MAAS. ¶ Phila. CD 1855–57.

MAAS & VOGDES. Fancy printers and engravers, Philadelphia, 1860 and after. The partners, William A. Maas and Joseph Vogdes, were listed separately as printers. ¶ Phila. CD 1860+.

MAAS, WILLIAM A., see MAAS & VOGDES.

MAAS, see also MASS.

MCABEE, JOHN W. Portrait, genre, and still life painter. He was at Louisville (Ky.) in 1848–49 and in NYC from 1857 to 1861. Exhibited at the National Academy. ¶ Information courtesy Mrs. W. H. Whitley, Paris (Ky.); Cowdrey, NAD; NYBD 1857, CD 1860.

MCALLISTER, JAMES C. Engraver of New Orleans, active 1842–59. In 1854 he executed an engraving after MOISE's portrait of the race horse "La Compte." ¶ New Orleans CD 1842–56, BD 1859; Delgado-WPA cites *Courier,* July 28, 1854, and *Crescent,* Nov. 9, 1854.

MCALLISTER, JOHN. Artist at Baltimore, 1851. ¶ Baltimore CD 1851.

MCARDLE, HARRY ARTHUR (1836–1908). Historical painter and teacher, born June 9, 1836, in Belfast (Ireland). He came to America in 1847 and grew up in Maryland. During the Civil War he was at Richmond (Va.) and after the war he settled at Independence (Texas). He died February 16, 1908. ¶ Fisk, *Texas Artists.*

MCARDLE, JAMES. Irish lithographer, 28, at NYC in 1860. ¶ 8 Census (1860), N.Y., XLIII, 48.

MACARTHY, J. Artist of a pen-and-sepia drawing of NYC, drawn on October 9, 1801. ¶ Information courtesy David Carter, Dep't of Paintings, Metropolitan Museum of Art.

MCAULIFFE, J. Genre painter on velvet, active 1830–70. ¶ Lipman and Winchester, 176.

MACAULY, JOHN. Artist at Albany (N.Y.), 1813–15. ¶ Albany CD 1813–15; Bolton and Cortelyou, *Ezra Ames,* 28–29.

MACBRAIR, ARCHIBALD. Lithographer, copperplate engraver, and printer of Cincinnati, 1850's; occasionally as McBriar. ¶ Cincinnati BD 1850–59, CD 1856–59.

MCCABE, E. Vignette engraver working in NYC about 1855. ¶ Stauffer.

MCCAFFERTY, HENRY. Wood engraver, age 23, born in Pennsylvania; living in Philadelphia in 1860. ¶ 8 Census (1860), Pa., L, 304.

MCCALLUM, GILBERT. Steel engraver, 25, a native of New York, at NYC in 1860. ¶ 8 Census (1860), N.Y., XLV, 69.

MCCANN, H. D. G. Portrait painter, exhibited at the Maryland Historical Society in 1850. *Cf.* HENRY G. MCCANN. ¶ Rutledge, MHS.

MCCANN, HENRY G. Portrait, genre, and marine painter, active in Baltimore, 1847–60. He was born in England about 1808 and came to America before 1840. A daughter was born in NYC about 1839 and a son in Baltimore about 1846. He exhibited at the Maryland Historical Society during the 1850's. Miss MARY A. MCCANN was probably one of his elder daughters and J. MCCANN may also have been of the same family. *Cf.* H. D. G. MCCANN. ¶ 7 Census (1850), Md., V, 187; Baltimore CD 1847–60; Rutledge, MHS.

MCCANN, J. Pastel portraitist who exhibited at the Maryland Historical Society in

1858. He was probably a member of the family of HENRY G. McCANN of Baltimore. ¶ Rutledge, MHS.

McCANN, Miss MARY A. Portrait and genre painter, Baltimore, 1850–56. She exhibited at the Maryland Historical Society and was probably a daughter of HENRY G. McCANN. ¶ Rutledge, MHS; Baltimore CD 1853.

McCANN & VAUGHAN. Engravers, NYC, 1850; WILLIAM McCANN and HECTOR W. VAUGHAN. ¶ NYBD and CD 1850.

McCANN, WILLIAM. Engraver and die sinker of NYC, 1850's; in 1850 of McCANN & VAUGHAN. ¶ NYBD 1850–58, CD 1851.

McCARTER, WILLIAM. Engraver, Philadelphia, 1850. ¶ Phila. CD 1850.

McCARTHY, ——. Line engraver of portraits, employed by J. C. BUTTRE, NYC, 1860–65. ¶ Stauffer.

M'CARTHY (or M'Carty), EDWARD. Copperplate and steel engraver, Philadelphia, 1852–58. In 1852 he was associated with the firm of McCARTHY & CRAP. ¶ Phila. CD 1852–58.

McCARTHY & CRAP. Philadelphia engravers, 1852; EDWARD M'CARTHY and CHARLES F. CRAP. ¶ Phila. CD 1852.

McCARTHY, see also MACARTHY and McCARTY.

McCARTNEY, HENRY. Pennsylvania-born lithographer, 20, at NYC in 1860. ¶ 8 Census (1860), N.Y., XLVI, 419.

McCARTNEY, MARY ELIZABETH MAXWELL (1814–1893). Amateur landscape painter in watercolors. She was born April 21, 1814, probably in New Jersey, and married Washington McCartney of Easton (Pa.). During the early 1840's she sketched and painted a number of views in and around Easton, many of which are now owned by the Northampton County Historical and Genealogical Society. Some were used to illustrate Condit's *History of Easton* (1885). Mrs. McCartney died on Christmas Day, 1893. ¶ Information courtesy Mrs. Charles P. Maxwell, Easton (Pa.) and Douglas Maxwell Moffatt, NYC, grandson of the artist.

McCARTNEY, NAPOLEON. Engraver, age 17, living in Philadelphia in 1850. His father was Irish, but he was a native Philadelphian. ¶ 7 Census (1850), Pa., LI, 389.

McCARTY, ALEXANDER E. Apprentice plate engraver, Philadelphia, 1860. He was the son of JAMES McCARTY. They were working together in 1871 as James McCarty & Son. ¶ 8 Census (1860), Pa., LV, 320; Phila. CD 1871.

McCARTY, DANIEL. Sign and ornamental painter at Zanesville (Ohio) from before 1813 into the 1830's. ¶ Knittle, *Early Ohio Taverns,* 43.

McCARTY, EDWARD, see EDWARD M'CARTHY.

McCARTY, JAMES. Plate engraver, born in Pennsylvania about 1820, working in Philadelphia in 1860 and with his son, ALEXANDER E., in 1871. ¶ 8 Census (1860), Pa., LV, 320; Phila. CD 1871.

McCARTY, J. J. Engraver at Boston, 1856. ¶ Boston BD 1856.

McCHESNEY, WILLIAM J. Artist, age 41, born in New Jersey, living in Philadelphia in June 1860. ¶ 8 Census (1860), Pa., XLIX, 183.

McCLAIN, FRANCIS. Lithographer, age 22, born in Pennsylvania, living in Philadelphia in July 1860. ¶ 8 Census (1860), Pa., L, 319.

McCLAIN, see also McLANE and McLEAN.

McCLEAN, J. A. Portrait and miniature painter at Pittsburgh (Pa.) during the 1850's. ¶ Fleming, *History of Pittsburgh,* III, 626.

McCLEAN, JOHN. He exhibited in 1860 at the National Academy two pen-and-ink sketches of NYC scenes. His address was Harper Brothers, by whom he may have been employed as an illustrator. ¶ Cowdrey, NAD.

McCLEAN, see also McLEAN and McLANE.

McCLELAND (or McClelland), THOMAS. Portrait painter. A native of NYC, he painted portraits in 1821 and 1822 of Dr. Samuel Bard and Dr. John Bowden, the former for the Medical College of NYC and the latter for Columbia College. Both are now owned by Columbia University. ¶ N. Y. *Evening Post,* April 4, 1822, p. 4; WPA (Mass.), *Portraits Found in N.Y.*

McCLELLAND, DAVID. Engraver, age 39, living in Washington (D.C.) in 1860. He and all his family were born in the District of Columbia and he owned real and personal property valued at $12,000. ¶ 8 Census (1860), D.C., II, 59.

McCLELLAND, see also McLELLAN.

M'CLEMENT, A. & G. Engravers, die sinkers, and envelope manufacturers, Philadelphia, 1856–60 and after; Alexander and George M'Clement. ¶ Phila. CD 1856–60+.

McCLEUEN, DAVID. Scottish artist, 25, at NYC in 1850 with JAMES McCLEUEN. ¶ 7 Census (1850), N.Y., XLI, 494.

McCLEUEN, JAMES. Lithographer, 29, born in England, living in NYC in 1850 with

David McCleuen. ¶ 7 Census (1850), N.Y., XLI, 494.

McClory, Peter. Landscape painter who opened a studio in Pittsburgh (Pa.) in the 1840's. He was noted for a view of Passaic Falls (N.J.). ¶ Fleming, *History of Pittsburgh,* III, 626.

M'Cloud, ——. Landscape painter of Washington (D.C.), exhibited at the Artists' Fund Society, Philadelphia, in 1843. ¶ Artists' Fund Soc. Cat., 1843.

McClurg, Trevor (1816–93). Portrait, genre, and historical painter. He was painting in Pittsburgh (Pa.) from the mid-1840's until about 1859, when he moved to NYC. Exhibited at the Pennsylvania Academy, Artists' Fund Society, American Art-Union, and National Academy. ¶ Rutledge, PA; Cowdrey, AA & AAU; Cowdrey, NAD; Fleming, *History of Pittsburgh,* III, 626.

McCluskey, William. Steel engraver, NYC, 1842–44. ¶ NYCD 1842–43, BD 1844; Stauffer.

McComb, John (1763–1853). Architect and architectural draftsman. A native of NYC, born October 17, 1763, McComb was one of the leading designers of buildings in the City between 1790 and about 1820. Among his most notable works were the City Hall, Castle Garden, Government House, and St. John's Chapel. He was also prominent in the affairs of the American Academy, as an Academician, Director and, from 1820 to 1824, Treasurer. ¶ DAB; Cowdrey, AA & AAU; Stokes, *Icon.,* III, 869–71.

McConachy, John. Profilist working with L. Remouit at Richmond (Va.) in August 1807. ¶ *Richmond Portraits,* 242.

McConkey, Benjamin M. Landscape painter, born in Maryland about 1821. He settled in Cincinnati in the early forties and began sending pictures east for exhibition in 1846, many of them views in New Hampshire and New York. In 1851 he was studying at Düsseldorf. ¶ 7 Census (1850), Ohio, XX, 897; Cist, *Cincinnati in 1851;* Cowdrey, AA & AAU; Cowdrey, NAD.

McConkey, William. Landscape painter, exhibited Swiss scenes at the American Art-Union in 1850. ¶ Cowdrey, AA & AAU.

McConnell, James. Wood engraver, age 17, living in Philadelphia in 1860. He was the son of Samuel McConnell and, like his father, a native of Ireland. ¶ 8 Census (1860), Pa., LIII, 312.

McConnell, Samuel. Irish wood engraver, age 43, living in Philadelphia in 1860 with his wife and son, James, also a wood engraver. ¶ 8 Census (1860), Pa., LIII, 312.

McCoole, Michael. Irish engraver, 35, at NYC in 1850. His wife and one child were born in Ireland, the latter about 1834, while four other children, ages 1 to 8, were born in New York. A Michael McCoole, compositor, was listed in the 1850 directory. ¶ 7 Census (1850), N.Y., XLVII, 894–95; NYCD 1850.

McCormick, Alexander A. Engraver, age 34, native of Pennsylvania, living in Philadelphia in 1860 with his wife and four children. ¶ 8 Census (1860), Pa., LI, 450.

McCormick, James. Artist at Baltimore, 1860. ¶ Baltimore CD 1860.

McCreight, Patrick. Landscape and panorama painter, born in Ireland about 1825. He worked in Cincinnati from 1849 to 1851, then moved to St. Louis where by October 1851 he had completed a panorama of the New Testament. In 1852 he was working in St. Louis with a Charles Harrington. ¶ 7 Census (1850), Ohio XX, 294; Cist, *Cincinnati in 1851;* St. Louis *Daily Intelligencer,* Oct. 2, 1851 (citation courtesy J. E. Arrington); St. Louis CD 1852.

McCulloh, James H. (1781–1869). Caricaturist. Born December 4, 1781, he graduated from the University of Pennsylvania Medical School and served as a surgeon during the War of 1812. For 28 years he was Deputy Collector of Customs at Baltimore, where he died in December 1869. He was also Treasurer of the Delphian Club of Baltimore whose minutes, now at the Maryland Historical Society, he illustrated with lively watercolor caricatures of the members. ¶ Rutledge, "Another American Caricaturist," *Gazette des Beaux Arts,* April 1955, 221–26, illus.

McCullough, Davis. Painted wood panel portraits of pioneers in Fayette County (Ky.) before 1845. ¶ Information courtesy Mrs. W. H. Whitley, Paris (Ky.).

McCully, Henry. Engraver, age 22, living in Philadelphia with his father, George H. McCully, watchmaker, 1850. This may be the Henry V. McCully, jeweler of Philadelphia, who in 1869 exhibited a landscape at the Pennsylvania Academy. ¶ 7 Census (1850), Pa., LII, 720; Phila. CD 1861–69; Rutledge, PA.

McDermott, Bernard. Irish lithographer,

age 22, living in Philadelphia in 1860. ¶ 8 Census (1860), Pa., LV, 1.

McDermott, John. Irish lithographer, 27, at NYC in 1860 with his Scottish wife and one son, aged 3, born in New York. ¶ 8 Census (1860), N.Y., XLII, 846.

McDevitt, Patrick. Portrait painter at Brooklyn (N.Y.), 1857. This is presumably the P. McDevitt who was working in Baltimore in 1845–48. ¶ Brooklyn BD 1857; Lafferty cites Baltimore *Saturday Visitor,* March 22, 1845, and Baltimore CD 1847–48.

MacDonald, James Wilson Alexander (1824–1908). Sculptor and painter. Born August 25, 1824, at Steubenville (Ohio), MacDonald left home about the age of 16, went to work for a publishing firm in St. Louis, and studied art with Alfred Waugh, executing his first clay bust in 1845. He gave up business in 1854 to devote himself wholly to sculpture and won attention by a marble bust of Senator Benton. After the Civil War MacDonald moved to NYC and there enjoyed a successful career as a portrait sculptor. He also painted some portraits and landscapes. He died August 14, 1908, at Yonkers (N.Y.). ¶ DAB; *Art Annual,* VII (1909/10), 79; CAB; Thieme-Becker.

MacDonald, John. Teacher of drawing, flower and miniature painting, at Charleston (S.C.), 1848–51. ¶ Rutledge, *Artists in the Life of Charleston.*

McDonald, John D. Engraver, NYC, 1850–52. ¶ NYBD 1850–52.

McDonnell, E. Banner and decorative painter, Charleston (S.C.), 1860. ¶ Rutledge, *Artists in the Life of Charleston.*

McDonnough (or MacDonough), James. Banknote engraver, landscape painter. He was a prominent banknote engraver in NYC from 1845 until near the end of the century, serving as president of the American Bank Note Company from 1887 to 1896. Between 1849 and 1851 he exhibited landscapes at the National Academy and American Art-Union, one a Nicaraguan coastal scene. ¶ Toppan, *100 Years of Bank Note Engraving,* 13; NYCD 1851+; Cowdrey, NAD; Cowdrey, AA & AAU.

McDonough, Henry. Engraver, age 24, born in Pennsylvania, living in Philadelphia in 1860. ¶ 8 Census (1860), Pa., LV, 662.

McDougal, James Alexander, see John Alexander McDougall.

McDougal, John. Engraver from England, born about 1827–29, working in Philadelphia 1850–60. ¶ 7 Census (1850), Pa., XLVII, 141 (age 21); 8 Census (1860), Pa., LIX, 132 (age 33).

MacDougal, W. H., see W. H. Dougal.

M'Dougall, John. Glass cutter and engraver, NYC, 1804–05. ¶ NYCD 1804–05.

McDougall, John Alexander (1810/11–94). Miniaturist and portrait painter. A native of Livingston (N.J.), he spent most of his career in Newark (N.J.). He visited New Orleans in 1839 and at other times he practised his art in Charleston (S.C.) and Saratoga Springs (N.Y.). During the 1840's and 1850's he also had a studio in NYC and exhibited at the National Academy, the American Art-Union, the American Institute (winning the first prize for miniatures in 1845, 1847, and 1848), and the Artists' Fund Society of Philadelphia. ¶ Wehle and Bolton, *American Miniatures;* Delgado-WPA cites *Picayune,* Dec. 20, 1839; Newark CD 1835–59; NYCD 1841–50; Cowdrey, NAD; Cowdrey, AA & AAU; Rutledge, PA; Am. Inst. Cat., 1842, 1844, 1845, 1847, 1848; Am. Inst. *Transactions,* 1845, 1847, 1848.

McDowell, E. G. Landscape painter, exhibited at the Maryland Historical Society in 1858. ¶ Rutledge, MHS.

McDowell, James. Portrait and genre painter of Philadelphia, exhibited at the Artists' Fund Society, 1837–40. ¶ Rutledge, PA; Phila. BD 1838.

M'Dowell (or MacDowell), William H. Engraver, Philadelphia, 1844–60 and after. ¶ Phila. CD 1844–60+.

McEglaw, ——. Exhibitor of a Catskill Mt. landscape, National Academy, 1857. ¶ Cowdrey, NAD.

McEllerow, Charles. Irish artist, age 30, at Charleston (S.C.) in November 1850. ¶ 7 Census (1850), S.C., II, 565.

McEntee, Jervis (1828–91). N.A. Landscape painter. Born July 14, 1828, at Rondout (N.Y.), McEntee had his early schooling in Clinton (N.Y.) and studied painting in NYC under Frederick E. Church. He did not become a professional artist, however, until 1858, when he opened a studio in NYC. He made the customary European tour in 1859 in company with Sanford R. Gifford and was elected an Academician of the National Academy in 1861. A popular member of the "Hudson River School," he spent much of his time at Rondout and in the nearby Catskills. He died at Rondout on

January 27, 1891. ¶ DAB; Tuckerman; Cowdrey, NAD; Cowdrey, AA & AAU; Rutledge, PA; Rutledge, MHS; Swan, BA; represented: Corcoran Gallery and Peabody Institute.

McEUEN, Mrs. ANNE MIDDLETON (IZARD). Amateur watercolor portraitist of South Carolina. The New-York Historical Society owns her 1835 watercolor portrait of her mother, Elizabeth Middleton Izard (1787–1822). ¶ NYHS Catalogue (1941), no. 537.

McEVOY, HENRY N. or HARRY (1828–1914). Portrait painter. A native of Birmingham (England), McEvoy was working at Indianapolis (Ind.) by 1860. He also worked at Hamilton (Ont.) and NYC. He died April 21, 1914, at Detroit. ¶ *Art Annual,* XI, obit.; Indianapolis BD 1860; Peat, *Pioneer Painters of Indiana.*

McEWAN, WILLIAM. Genre and landscape painter of NYC and Brooklyn, active 1859–69. He exhibited at the National Academy and Pennsylvania Academy. ¶ Cowdrey, NAD; Rutledge, PA.

McFADDEN, JOHN B. Portrait painter, NYC, 1854–56; exhibitor, National Academy. ¶ NYBD 1854; Cowdrey, NAD.

M'FARLAN, THOMAS. Painter and drawing teacher in NYC, 1815–17. ¶ NYCD 1815–17.

McFARLAND, LUCY, see LUCY McFARLAND SHERMAN.

MACFARLAND, ROBERT. Painter of ships, 1850's and 1860's. His "Ship *South America* of the Black Ball Line" has been reproduced. ¶ Peters, "Paintings of the Old "Wind-Jammer,'" 30, 32.

McFARLANE, D. Painter of ships, active during the 1850's and 1860's, probably in New England. Several of his paintings are extant. ¶ Peters, "Paintings of the Old 'Wind-Jammer,'" 32; *American Processional,* 246; *Portfolio* (April 1947), 182, repro.

McFARLANE, R. Portrait painter active about 1843, probably in New England. ¶ Sears, *Some American Primitives,* 228.

MACFARREN, JOHN. Landscape painter, who exhibited several paintings at the American Art-Union in 1847 and 1848. He was then living in NYC. ¶ Cowdrey, AA & AAU.

M'GAHEY, ——. Engraver. In 1844 he exhibited at Nauvoo (Ill.) his drawing of "Joseph Smith Addressing the Indians." He had earlier made a series of folio engravings after CATLIN's Indian sketches. ¶ Arrington, "Nauvoo Temple," Chap. 8.

McGANN, JOHN C. Engraver's apprentice, age 18, living with his mother in Boston, 1860. ¶ 8 Census (1860), Mass., XXIX, 253.

McGAURAN, PATRICK. Engraver of NYC, 1850's; in 1858, of HARRIS & McGAURAN. *Cf.* McGOWRAN. ¶ NYCD 1853, 1856–59; NYBD 1854, 1858.

M'GEE, JOHN L. Artist, 26, a native of New York, at NYC in 1850. His wife Julia was from Pennsylvania. ¶ 7 Census (1850), N.Y., XLIV, 194.

McGEE, Miss JULIA. Painter in oils and watercolors, Charleston (S.C.), July 1853. ¶ Rutledge, *Artists in the Life of Charleston.*

McGEORGE, THOMAS. Portrait painter of Brooklyn (N.Y.), 1838–42. He exhibited at the National Academy and the American Institute. ¶ Cowdrey, NAD; Am. Inst. Cat., 1842.

McGIBBON, JAMES. Portrait and miniature painter, active 1800–27. He was at Boston from 1800 at least to 1810 and at Baltimore from 1812 to 1827. He also visited Richmond (Va.) in 1823. He was listed variously as portrait painter, painter, and gilder. ¶ Boston CD 1800-10; Lafferty cites Baltimore *American,* Feb. 12, 1812; Mayo cites Baltimore CD 1814–19; Baltimore CD 1827 (as —— McGibbon, portrait painter); *Richmond Portraits,* 242.

McGILLIVRAY, A. C. Crayon artist at Charleston (S.C.) in 1857. ¶ Rutledge, *Artists in the Life of Charleston.*

M'GINNIS, ——, see H. MAGENIS.

McGITTERGAN, THOMAS, JR. Artist, age 24, son of a custom house employee. He was a native of Pennsylvania and resided in Philadelphia in 1860. ¶ 8 Census (1860), Pa., LII, 198.

McGOEY, THOMAS. Engraver, age 19, Philadelphia, 1850. He was born in Pennsylvania of an Irish family. ¶ 7 Census (1850), Pa., L, 841.

McGOFFIN, JOHN. Engraver and miniaturist, born in Philadelphia in 1813. He was a pupil of JAMES W. STEELE for whom he was working in 1834. He continued to engrave at least until 1876 and was still living in 1883. He is said also to have painted miniatures. ¶ Stauffer; 8 Census (1860), Pa., LIV, 552.

McGONIGLE, WILLIAM, JR. Irish-born apprentice engraver, age 17, living in Philadelphia in 1860 with his father, a stonecutter. ¶ 8 Census (1860), Pa., XLIX, 453.

MacGowan, Edward. Lithographer in NYC, 1851–52. ¶ NYBD 1851–52.

McGowran, ——. Engraver, of Greene & McGowran, NYC, 1837. *Cf.* Patrick McGauran. ¶ NYCD 1837.

McGrath, James. Lithographer, 22, a native of New York, at NYC in 1860. ¶ 8 Census (1860), N.Y., XLII, 973.

McGregor, Edward. Portrait and landscape painter of Baltimore, 1853–72. He exhibited at the Maryland Historical Society in 1856. ¶ Lafferty; Baltimore CD 1871–72; Rutledge, MHS.

McGuigan, James. Lithographer, born in Pennsylvania about 1819, active in Philadelphia 1844–65. In 1844–45 he was with the firm of Pinkerton, Wagner & McGuigan, and from 1846 to 1858 with its successor, Wagner & McGuigan. ¶ 7 Census (1850), Pa., L, 890; Peters, *America on Stone;* Phila. CD 1846–60+.

McGuire, John. Engraver, age 20, born in Pennsylvania; boarding in Philadelphia in 1860. ¶ 8 Census (1860), Pa., LV, 269.

McGus, ——. Portrait painter, working probably in Virginia about 1800. One signed portrait is extant. ¶ Information courtesy Wilbur D. Peat, Indianapolis.

McHenry, Isaac. Portrait painter, age 21, born in Pennsylvania; living in Pittsburgh (Pa.) with his Irish father, a bricklayer, in 1850. ¶ 7 Census (1850), Pa., III (part 2), 447.

McHugh, Isaac. Portrait painter at Boston in September 1850. Isaac, age 26, and John McHugh, with whom he was living, were both Canadians. ¶ 7 Census (1850), Mass., XXV, 339.

McHugh, John. Portrait painter, age 25, living in Boston with Isaac McHugh in September 1850. Both were from the British Provinces (Canada). ¶ 7 Census (1850), Mass., XXV, 339.

McIlvaine, William, Jr. (1813–1867). Landscape painter, born in Philadelphia June 5, 1813. After graduation from the University of Pennsylvania in 1832, McIlvaine toured Europe, studying art, and for a number of years was in business in Philadelphia with his father, Joseph Bloomfield McIlvaine. He took up art professionally about 1845. In 1849 he visited the California gold fields and the following year was published his *Sketches of Scenery and Notes of Personal Adventures in California and Mexico,* containing sixteen plates after his own views. A panorama based on McIlvaine's sketches was painted by Russell Smith and shown in Philadelphia in 1850 and Baltimore in 1851. McIlvaine moved to NYC about 1856 and worked there until the Civil War, in which he served as a member of the N. Y. 5th Regiment of Volunteers. After the war he lived in Brooklyn where he died on June 16, 1867. ¶ Univ. of Penna., *Biographical Catalogue of the Matriculates of the College,* 86; Van Nostrand and Coulter, *California Pictorial,* 96–97; Phila. CD 1839–55; NYCD 1857–65; Brooklyn CD 1867; 7 Census (1850), Pa., L, 820; Rutledge, PA; Cowdrey, NAD; Phila. *Public Ledger,* Aug. 23, 1850, and Baltimore *Sun,* May 7, 1851 (citations courtesy J. E. Arrington); Jackson, *Gold Rush Album,* repros.; represented: NYHS.

McIlworth, Thomas. Portrait painter, active in the Province of New York, 1757–67. He was at NYC from 1757 to 1762, then moved to Schenectady where he lived until 1767. In that year he went to Montreal and he is thought to have died in the winter of 1769/70. His sitters included many prominent landowners of NYC, the Hudson Valley, and the Albany area. ¶ Sawitzky, "Thomas McIlworth," repros., checklist, and chronology.

McIntire, John. Scottish engraver, 41, at NYC in 1860. His wife Henrietta was also a native Scot, but their four children were born in New York between 1845 and 1857. ¶ 8 Census (1860), N.Y., LIII, 1009.

McIntire, Samuel (1757–1811). Architect, carver, sculptor in wood. A native of Salem (Mass.), where he was baptized on January 16, 1757, Samuel McIntire spent his entire life in or near Salem. From the 1780's until his death he was the designer and builder of most of its important houses, a proficient carver, and in his later years a portrait sculptor in wood. He died on February 6, 1811, leaving his business to be carried on by his son Samuel Field McIntire. ¶ Kimball, *Mr. Samuel McIntire, Carver, the Architect of Salem,* sums up all that is known of his career. Many of his drawings and papers are at the Essex Institute, Salem.

McIntire, Samuel Field (1780–1819). Carver, son of Samuel McIntire. He was born in Salem and baptized there in November 1780, worked with his father, and succeeded to the business in 1811. He died on September 27, 1819. ¶ Kimball, *Mr. Samuel McIntire, Carver, the Architect of Salem,* 7, 26–27; Kimball, "Furniture Carvings by Samuel Field McIntire."

MACK, Mr. ——. Miniaturist, NYC, 1834. ¶ Bolton, *Miniature Painters.*

MACK, DIXON & COMPANY. Lithographers of book illustrations, New Bedford (Mass.) about 1834. ¶ Peters, *America on Stone.*

MACK, EBENEZER. Limner and miniature painter working in Philadelphia in 1785 and 1788 and in NYC from 1791 to 1808. ¶ Prime, I, 5, and II, 18; NYCD 1791–1808 (cited by McKay).

MCKAY (or Mackay), ——. Portrait painter, active 1788–91. ¶ Repros., Met. Museum, *Life in America; Art News* (Jan. 15, 1945), 16; *American Collector* (Oct. 1937), 2; represented: American Antiq. Soc.

MCKAY, see also MACKEY.

MCKEEN, WILLIAM. Irish portrait engraver, 48, at NYC in 1860. His wife May and three children born between 1841 and 1849 were also born in Ireland. ¶ 8 Census (1860), N.Y., LXII, 608.

MCKENNA, P., & COMPANY. Lithographers, NYC, 1846. ¶ NYBD 1846.

MCKENNEY, HENRIETTA FOXHALL (1825–1887). Landscape painter. She was born in Georgetown (D.C.) on November 11, 1825, the daughter of Samuel and Mary Ann (Foxhall) McKenney and granddaughter of the famous ironmaster Henry Foxhall (1750–1823). Her known canvases include a view of Harper's Ferry (1841), a harbor scene (1845) and two foreign scenes, owned by Mrs. McCook Knox of Washington, and a view of Mt. Vernon (1840), owned by Mrs. John S. Moses of Andover (Mass.). Miss McKenney married a man named Cragin and died on February 2, 1887. ¶ Information courtesy Mrs. Katharine McCook Knox and Mrs. John S. Moses.

MCKENZIE, CALEB. Artist at Baltimore, 1812. ¶ Lafferty.

MCKENZIE, DONALD. A minor, residing in NYC, who won a prize for 2 crayon drawings exhibited at the American Institute in 1851. ¶ Am. Inst. Cat. and *Trans.*, 1851.

MACKENZIE, E. Stipple engraver who came to America from England about 1833 to engrave portraits for LONGACRE and HERRING's *National Portrait Gallery.* He was later employed by the Methodist Book Concern in NYC. ¶ Stauffer.

M'KENZIE, J. Carver or sculptor, Charleston (S.C.), 1846. ¶ Rutledge, *Artists in the Life of Charleston.*

MCKEON, THOMAS. Wood engraver, of ROBINSON & MCKEON, Troy (N.Y.), 1857. ¶ Troy BD and CD 1857.

MCKEON, WILLIAM. Scottish artist, age 30, at New Orleans in 1850. ¶ 7 Census (1850), La., VI, 317.

MACKEY, JAMES. Lithographer, 64, a native of Connecticut, living in NYC in 1860. He owned real estate valued at $50,000. His sons, James, Jr. (31) and William (37), both born in New York, were listed as artists. ¶ 8 Census (1860), N.Y., XLIX, 744.

MACKEY, JAMES, JR., see JAMES MACKEY, above.

MCKEY, MARTIN. Irish artist, 28, at NYC in 1860. His wife Ann also was born in Ireland, but their four children were born in New York between 1853 and 1860. ¶ 8 Census (1860), N.Y., XLVI, 763.

MACKEY or MACKIE, MATTHEW. Pennsylvania-born engraver, age 32, living in Philadelphia with his wife and four children in 1860. He was still there in 1871. ¶ 8 Census (1860), Pa., LVIII, 397; Phila. CD 1871.

MACKEY, WILLIAM, see JAMES MACKEY.

MACKINTOSH, Miss S. B. Exhibited a miniature copy of Domenichino's "St. John" at the Pennsylvania Academy in 1850. ¶ Rutledge, PA; Bolton, *Miniature Painters.*

MCKITTRICK, JOHN. Lithographer, of HART, MAPOTHER & COMPANY, Louisville (Ky.), 1859. ¶ Louisville BD 1859.

MACKLOW, J. Engraver of WOLLASTON's portrait of Martha Washington, published in the *Christian Family Annual* about 1835. ¶ Stauffer.

MCKNIGHT, DAVID. Irish engraver, age 19, brother of JOHN MCKNIGHT; living in Philadelphia in 1850. ¶ 7 Census (1850), Pa., LI, 709.

MCKNIGHT, JOHN. Irish engraver, age 21, brother of DAVID MCKNIGHT; living in Philadelphia in 1850. ¶ 7 Census (1850), Pa., LI, 709.

MCKOY, ROBERT. Copperplate and steel engraver, stamp cutter, Philadelphia, 1858–60. His widow is listed in 1861. ¶ Phila. CD 1858–61.

MACKWITZ, WILLIAM (1831–1919). German wood engraver who came to America about 1856 and established in St. Louis an engraving firm which was active until 1916. Mackwitz died there August 6, 1919. The Missouri Historical Society owns a scrapbook containing samples of his work, chiefly commercial. ¶ "William Mackwitz, Wood Engraver," with eleven repros.

McLANE, WILLIAM. Scottish engraver, age 27, living in Boston in 1850 with his Connecticut wife and three children, five years and younger, born in New York. ¶ 7 Census (1850), Mass., XXVI, 128.

McLAUGHLIN, GEORGE. Irish engraver, 55, at NYC in 1860. His wife Eliza and two sons, ages 21 and 23, were also born in Ireland. ¶ 8 Census (1860), N.Y., LXII, 302; NYCD 1862 as "pictures."

McLAUGHLIN, GEORGE. Sculptor, Cincinnati, 1849. ¶ Cincinnati CD 1849 (courtesy Edward H. Dwight, Cincinnati Art Museum).

McLEAN, ALEXANDER. Lithographer and engraver, born in Scotland about 1823. He was at Philadelphia in 1849, Louisville in 1850, and St. Louis from 1851 until the seventies. His work appeared in Taylor's *Sketch Book of St. Louis* (1858). After 1860 he was joined in the business by his son Alexander, Jr. ¶ 7 Census (1850), Ky., XI, 586; Phila. CD 1849; St. Louis CD 1851–72; Peters, *America on Stone*.

McLEAN, ALEXANDER C. Portrait painter working around Boston between 1831 and 1835. His known works include portraits of Francis Kittridge, Charlestown, 1831, and eight-year-old Adaline F. Pierce, South Boston, 1835. ¶ Information courtesy Harry Stone, NYC, and Mildred Deyo, Newburgh, N.Y.

McLEAN, see also McCLEAN and McCLAIN.

McLEES, ARCHIBALD (*c.* 1817–1890). Engraver, born in England, son of JOHN McLEES. He was active in NYC from 1841 until after 1860, much of that time in association with his father and with his brothers, JAMES, DANIEL, and MICHAEL. In 1863 he was one of the original corps of engravers employed at the Bureau of Engraving and Printing at Washington. He died in Rutherford (N.J.) on February 11, 1890, in his seventy-third year. ¶ Boston *Transcript,* Feb. 12, 1890, obit.; NYBD 1841–58; NYCD 1841–63; 8 Census (1860), N.Y., XLIX, 976.

McLEES, DANIEL. Engraver, 28, a native of New York, at NYC in 1850. He was a son of Archibald McLees, blacksmith. ¶ 7 Census (1850), N.Y., LV, 858.

McLEES, DANIEL. Engraver, born in New York about 1836, son of JOHN McLEES. He was active in NYC from about 1855 and from 1856 was with the wood engraving firm of McLEES & SHUGG. ¶ 8 Census (1860), N.Y., XLIX, 976; NYCD 1855–58.

McLEES, JAMES. Engraver, 26, a native of New York, at NYC in 1850. He was a son of Archibald McLees, blacksmith. ¶ 7 Census (1850), N.Y., LV, 858.

McLEES, JAMES. Engraver, born in New York about 1830, son of JOHN McLEES. He was active in NYC from 1848 into the sixties. From 1848 to 1850 he was associated with his father and his brother ARCHIBALD. ¶ 8 Census (1860), N.Y., XLIX, 976; NYBD 1848, 1850, 1854; NYCD 1850, 1858–59, 1863.

McLEES, JOHN. Engraver, born in Scotland about 1790. He came to NYC sometime in the 1820's and was still living there in 1860. Four of his sons were engravers also: ARCHIBALD, JAMES, MICHAEL, and DANIEL. ¶ 8 Census (1860), N.Y., XLIX, 976; NYCD 1847–59.

McLEES, JOHN. Engraver, 22, a native of New York, at NYC in 1850. He was a son of Archibald McLees, blacksmith. By 1860 he was married; his wife and one child, aged 4, were born in Pennsylvania; two younger children were born in New York. ¶ 7 Census (1850), N.Y., LV, 858; 8 Census (1860), N.Y., XLIX, 857.

McLEES, MICHAEL. Engraver, born in New York about 1833, son of JOHN McLEES. He was listed as an engraver in the 1860 Census. ¶ 8 Census (1860), N.Y., XLIX, 976.

McLEES & SHUGG. Wood engravers, NYC, 1856–59. DANIEL McLEES and RICHARD SHUGG. ¶ NYCD 1856–58; Hamilton, no. 525.

McLELLAN, DAVID. Lithographer, born in Scotland about 1825, son of JAMES McLELLAN. He was active in NYC from 1851. From 1859 to 1864 he was associated with his father and thereafter with his brothers. ¶ 8 Census (1860), N.Y., XLVII, 752; NYBD 1851–60+; Peters, *America on Stone*.

McLELLAN, DAVID. Lithographer, 17, a native of Scotland, living in NYC in 1860 with JAMES and DAVID McLELLAN. ¶ 8 Census (1860), N.Y., XLVII, 753.

McLELLAN, H. B. Stipple engraver of portraits at Boston about 1860. ¶ Stauffer.

McLELLAN, JAMES. Lithographer, born in Scotland about 1798. His six children were born in Scotland before 1850 and in 1860 four of them were listed as lithographers: JAMES, JR., DAVID, ROBERT, and JOHN. ¶ 8 Census (1860), N.Y.,

XLVII, 752; NYCD 1859–60; Peters, *America on Stone.*

McLELLAN, JAMES, JR. Lithographer, born in Scotland about 1828, son of JAMES McLELLAN. He was in partnership with his brother DAVID after 1864. ¶ 8 Census (1860), N.Y., XLVII, 752; Peters, *America on Stone.*

McLELLAN, JOHN. Lithographer, born in Scotland about 1841, son of JAMES McLELLAN. Presumably with the firm of David McLellan & Brothers, 1864–67. ¶ 8 Census (1860), N.Y., XLVII, 753; Peters, *America on Stone.*

McLELLAN, ROBERT. Lithographer, born in Scotland about 1843, son of JAMES McLELLAN. Presumably with the firm of David McLellan & Brothers, 1864–67. He was still in NYC in 1880. ¶ 8 Census (1860), N.Y., XLVII, 752; Peters, *America on Stone;* NYCD 1880.

McLENAN, JOHN (1827–1866). Illustrator and comic draftsman. A native of Pennsylvania, McLenan was working in a pork-packing plant at Cincinnati and drawing for amusement when he was discovered by the illustrator DEWITT C. HITCHCOCK about 1850. McLenan soon moved to NYC and became one of the most prolific of the early illustrators. Hamilton lists 52 books published between 1852 and 1866 containing his work. ¶ 7 Census (1850), Ohio, XX, 185; Hamilton, 382–91; Cowdrey, NAD; NYCD 1855–59.

McLEOD (or MacLeod), WILLIAM. Landscape painter. He was living in NYC in 1848 when he first exhibited at the American Art-Union but his subjects show that he had worked in Washington (D.C.), on the Delaware and Hudson Rivers, in New England, and in the Scottish Highlands. NYC was still his headquarters in 1852–53, when he exhibited at the National Academy, but by 1857 he had moved to Washington (D.C.). ¶ Cowdrey, AA & AAU; Cowdrey, NAD; Washington Art Assoc. Cat., 1857, 1859.

MACLIN, BENOIT. Engraver, NYC, 1858–59. ¶ NYBD 1858–59.

McMANNUS, JAMES. Irish lithographer, 31, at NYC in 1860. His wife and six children, ages 3 months to 10 years, were born in New York. ¶ 8 Census (1860), N.Y., LI, 130.

McMASTER, WILLIAM E. (1823–after 1860). Portrait and figure painter, born May 23, 1823, at Ballston Spa (N.Y.). He worked chiefly in NYC from 1845 to 1859, though he visited Chicago in 1855 and exhibited a number of pictures at the Illinois State Fair in October of that year. He is last heard of as the painter of a portrait of Calhoun at Charleston (S.C.) in March 1860. ¶ Champlin and Perkins, IV (Supp.); Thieme-Becker; Cowdrey, NAD; NYBD 1848, 1859; Chicago BD 1855; Chicago *Daily Press,* October 11 and 13, 1855; Rutledge, *Artists in the Life of Charleston.*

McMURTRIE, JAMES, JR. Portrait painter and art collector, who lived in Philadelphia and exhibited at the Pennsylvania Academy and the Artists' Fund Society between 1843 and 1864. ¶ Information courtesy Theodore Bolton; Rutledge, PA; represented: Univ. of Penna.

McMURTRIE, WILLIAM B. (or P.). Portrait and landscape painter. A Philadelphia artist, McMurtrie exhibited at the Artists' Fund Society from 1837 to 1844 and sold at least one of his landscapes to the Pennsylvania Academy. He appears to have been related to Henry McMurtrie, M.D., of Philadelphia. He went to California in 1849/50 and in April 1850 executed a view of San Francisco from Telegraph Hill which was published by N. CURRIER the following year; this print identifies the artist as "Draftsman of the U. S. Surveying Expedition." ¶ Rutledge, PA; Phila. CD 1844–45; Cowdrey, AA & AAU; Peters, *Calif. on Stone.*

McNAB or McNABB, RICHARD. Engraver; born in Ireland; working in NYC from 1850 to 1860. In 1850 his age was given as 18 and in 1860 as 25. ¶ 7 Census (1850), N.Y., XLII, 392; 8 Census (1860), N.Y., XLII, 787; NYBD 1856–59.

McNAIR, see McNEIR.

McNAUGHTON, ——. Portrait painter at NYC, 1832; exhibited at the National Academy. Perhaps this is the Robert McNaughton listed by Lipman and Winchester as a primitive portrait painter at Schoharie (N.Y.) about 1820. ¶ Cowdrey, NAD; Lipman and Winchester, 177.

McNAUGHTON, DONALD. Portrait painter, Cincinnati, 1843–44. ¶ Cincinnati CD 1843–44 (courtesy Edward H. Dwight, Cincinnati Art Museum).

MACNEIR (or McNAIR), ANDREW E. Portrait painter, born in Philadelphia about 1828 and active there as an artist from 1850 to 1862. He exhibited at the Pennsylvania Academy between 1855 and 1862. ¶ 7 Census (1850), Pa., LIII, 531 [age 24]; 8 Census (1860), Pa., LVIII, 177 [age 30]; Phila. BD 1852–60+; Rutledge, PA.

McNEVIN, JOHN. Historical painter, illustrator. He began illustrating books as early as 1856, contributed to *Harper's Weekly* in 1859 and 1860, and in 1859 exhibited in NYC a series of 24 paintings of Revolutionary War scenes. His home was in Brooklyn. ¶ Hamilton, 392; Brooklyn CD 1857–63; N. Y. *Herald*, Feb. 18, 1859 (citation courtesy J. E. Arrington).

McNIDER, ALEXANDER. Portrait painter, NYC, 1846. ¶ NYBD 1846.

McNULTY, P. M. Irish steel engraver, 24, at NYC in 1860. His wife also was Irish, and they had one child, aged 2, born in New York. ¶ 8 Census (1860), N.Y., XLII, 140.

MACOMBER, WILLIAM. Engraver, Providence (R.I.), 1850–57. ¶ Providence CD 1850–57.

MACOUGTRY, JAMES. Portrait painter working in Virginia and what is now West Virginia between 1828 and 1834. ¶ Willis, "Jefferson County Portraits."

McPHERSON, JOHN. Engraver and die sinker, Philadelphia, 1846–60 and after. ¶ Phila. CD 1846–60+.

McPHERSON, ROBERT A. Artist, born in Pennsylvania about 1812, working in Baltimore in 1849–50. ¶ 7 Census (1850), Md., V, 878; Lafferty.

McPHERSON, W. J. Miniaturist, Boston, 1846–47. His miniature of Henry Clay was engraved by STEEL. ¶ Boston BD 1846–47; Stauffer, no. 3002; Bolton, *Miniature Painters.*

McQUAY, WILLIAM. Itinerant portrait painter from Scotland, working in the United States early in the 19th century. In 1809 he painted a small portrait of Lloyd Mifflin, Sr. (1786–1878). McQuay was said to have been a friend of the poet Robert Burns. ¶ Information courtesy the late William Sawitzky; Sherman, "Unrecorded Early American Portrait Painters" (1933).

McRAE (or McRea), JOHN C. Engraver and print publisher, NYC, 1850–80. He worked in line and stipple. ¶ Stauffer; NYBD 1850–51; NYCD 1856–60+; Cowdrey, NAD; repros. in *Portfolio* (Nov. 1942), frontis., and (Feb. 1954), 127.

McSPEDON & BAKER. Lithographers, NYC, 1853. This firm, composed of Thomas McSpedon and Charles W. Baker, was primarily concerned with stationery, envelope-making, and the like, from the 1840's to 1860's. Peters lists one pamphlet illustrated by them. ¶ Peters, *America on Stone;* NYCD 1848–62.

MACY (or Macey), REUBEN. Portrait painter at Georgetown (Ky.) in 1848. ¶ Information courtesy FARL and Mrs. W. H. Whitley, Paris (Ky.).

MADAULE, L. Artist of the French Theatre, New Orleans, 1852–56. ¶ New Orleans CD 1852–56.

MADDEN, EDWARD. English engraver (in 1860 age 37), at NYC in 1859 and at Philadelphia in 1860. ¶ NYBD; 1859; 8 Census (1860), Pa., LI, 543.

MADDOCK, GEORGE C. Engraver at Philadelphia, 1854. ¶ Penna. BD 1854.

MADDOCK, WILLIAM A. Engraver, born in Pennsylvania about 1830, working in Philadelphia in 1854 and 1860. ¶ 8 Census (1860), Pa., L, 463; Penna. BD 1854.

MADEIRA, DANIEL. Painter working at Chillicothe (Ohio) probably during the early 1820's. ¶ *Antiques* (March 1932), 152.

MAENTLE, Dr. JACOB (1763–1863). Portrait painter. A native of Cassel (Germany), who was trained as a physician and is said to have served as secretary to Napoleon, Maentle came to America in the 1830's and settled in New Harmony (Ind.), where he painted a few portraits. He died in New Harmony in 1863, shortly before his hundredth birthday. ¶ Peat, *Pioneer Painters of Indiana,* 36–37.

MAFFEY, ——. Artist, inventor, mechanic, and proprietor of the "picturesque, mechanical, and maritime Theatre," which included a view of St. Helena, shown in NYC in June 1818. ¶ J. E. Arrington cites N. Y. *Evening Post,* June 17 and 23, 1818.

MAGEE, JOHN L. Lithographer and cartoonist. After serving his apprenticeship with ACKERMAN (James ?), Magee worked for lithographers in NYC from 1844 to 1847, then opened his own establishment in Philadelphia in 1850. He was working as late as 1867. He exhibited genre paintings at the American Art-Union and the National Academy. ¶ NYCD 1844–46; Peters, *America on Stone;* Cowdrey, NAD; Cowdrey, AA & AAU; Phila. CD 1855–60+; Stokes, *Icon.*, III, 882, and pl. A-26-c; Nevins and Weitenkampf, *A Century of Political Cartoons.*

MAGEE, RICHARD. Lithographer and bookseller, Philadelphia, 1856. ¶ Peters, *America on Stone,* pl. 94; Phila. CD 1856.

MAGENIS, H. Portrait painter at Philadelphia, 1817–19. He exhibited at the Pennsylvania Academy in 1818 a copy after Reynolds' "Holy Family" and a portrait of Lord Byron. He apparently went back to England, for in 1828 H. Magenis exhibited a portrait at the Suffolk Street Exhibition in London. ¶ Brown and Brown cite *U. S. Gazette,* Oct. 4, 1817; Rutledge, PA; Phila. CD 1819 (as M'Ginnis); Graves, *Dictionary.*

MAGER, DANIEL, see DANIEL MAJOR.

MAGGINNI, JOSEPH. Swiss "ornamental figure maker," age 60, at Cincinnati in 1850. His wife was from New Jersey, a son Joseph was born in Pennsylvania about 1826, and a daughter, age 12, in Ohio. ¶ 7 Census (1850), Ohio, XX, 210.

MAGNER, DAVID. Carver or sculptor, age 25, born in Massachusets, living in Boston in July 1860. ¶ 8 Census (1860), Mass., XXVII, 83 [as sculptor]; Boston CD 1860 [as carver].

MAGNUS, CHARLES. Lithographer, particularly of letterheads. Magnus had a large business in NYC and Washington from about 1854 into the seventies. Peters records a great number of views and ephemeral "news" prints turned out by him. ¶ NYBD 1854; Peters, *America on Stone,* pl. 95 and text.

MAGNUS, LEONARD. Engraver and lithographer, Cincinnati, 1860. ¶ Cincinnati BD 1860.

MAGNY, RISSO (1798–1850). Artist, brother of XAVIER MAGNY. He was a native of Thore, Vaucluse (France) and presumably came to America with his brother about 1848. He died in New Orleans on June 24, 1850. ¶ Delgado-WPA cites *Courier,* June 24, 1850.

MAGNY, XAVIER. Lithographer and dial maker, print publisher. A native of France, he came to New Orleans about 1849 and worked there until 1855. RISSO MAGNY, his brother, died in New Orleans in 1850. ¶ Delgado-WPA cites New Orleans CD 1849–55; Peters, *America on Stone; Antiques* (May 1936), 203, repro.

MAGRAGH, GEORGE. Wood carver of Philadelphia, who exhibited at the Pennsylvania Academy in 1811 and 1813. ¶ Rutledge, PA.

MAGRATH, WILLIAM (1838–1918). N.A. Genre and landscape painter, born March 20, 1838, in Cork (Ireland). He came to America in 1855 and established a studio in NYC about 1868. He was elected an Academician of the National Academy in 1876. In 1879 Magrath (pronounced Ma-graw') went to live in England but he returned to the United States in 1883 and settled in Washington (D.C.). By 1889 he had returned to NYC and in 1918, at the time of his death, he was living at Brighton (N.Y.). He was best known for his scenes of Irish life. ¶ CAB; *Who's Who in America,* 1899–1900; Clement and Hutton; Champlin and Perkins; NYCD 1868+; Smith; represented: Peabody Institute.

MAGUIRE, MARY M. (?–1910). Portrait and miniature painter. She was living at Hartford (Conn.) when she exhibited at the National Academy in 1849. By 1867, when she exhibited at the Pennsylvania Academy, she had settled in Baltimore where she lived until her death in 1910. ¶ Sherman, "Unrecorded Early American Painters," (1934), 146; Cowdrey, NAD; Rutledge, PA.

MAHAN, FRANCIS. Lithographer, publisher, and fashion designer. He worked in Philadelphia, 1829–71. ¶ *Album of American Battle Art,* 121, pl. 53.

MAHL, MAX. German engraver, 22, at NYC in 1850. ¶ 7 Census (1850), N.Y., XLI, 546.

MAIER, J. Exhibited oil paintings in Charleston (S.C.) in November 1850. ¶ Rutledge, *Artists in the Life of Charleston.*

MAIN, WILLIAM (1796–1876). N.A. Engraver. A native of NYC, Main went to Italy in 1817 as the pupil of MAURO GANDOLFI. They soon parted, however, and Main spent the next three years studying under the famous Italian engraver Raphael Morghen. He returned to NYC in 1820 and opened a studio there. In 1826 he was one of the founders of the National Academy, of which he was a Member from 1826 to 1836 and an Associate from 1837 to 1838. He left NYC about 1833 but continued to engrave at least until 1837. He died in NYC in 1876. ¶ Stauffer; NYCD 1821–33; Cowdrey, NAD; Cowdrey, AA & AAU; Thieme-Becker.

MAINE, GEORGE DE L. Artist, age 41, at Boston in October 1850. ¶ 7 Census (1850), Mass., XXIV, 405.

MAINS, J. R. Artist, age 27, from Maine, at Sacramento (Cal.) in 1860. ¶ 8 Census (1860), Cal., V, 22.

MAIR, C. H. Miniaturist, New Orleans, 1834. ¶ Delgado-WPA cites *Courier,* July 12, 1834.

MAJOR, DANIEL. Lithographer; born in Ireland about 1815; active in NYC from about 1840 to 1853. From 1850 he was associated with JOHN MAJOR. ¶ 7 Census (1850), N.Y., LII, 281; NYCD 1850–53; Peters, *America on Stone.*

MAJOR, HENRY B. Lithographer, NYC, 1844–54; of SARONY & MAJOR. Perhaps father of RICHARD MAJOR, who succeeded him in 1855 in the company. He seems also to have been related to JAMES P. MAJOR (see CD 1847). ¶ NYCD 1844–54; Peters, *America on Stone.*

MAJOR, J. & D., see JOHN and DANIEL MAJOR.

MAJOR, JAMES PARSONS (1818–1900). Engraver. Born at Frome, Somerset (England), he came to America in 1830 and settled in Brooklyn (N.Y.). He was employed by the AMERICAN BANK NOTE COMPANY for over half a century. He moved to Somerville (N.J.) after 1872 and died there October 17, 1900. He was apparently related to HENRY B. MAJOR (see NYCD 1847). ¶ Stauffer; NYCD 1850+.

MAJOR, JOHN. Lithographer, NYC, 1839–53. In 1850–53 he was working with DANIEL MAJOR, possibly his son. ¶ Peters, *America on Stone;* NYCD 1850–53.

MAJOR & KORFF, see MAYER & KORFF.

MAJOR, RICHARD C. Wood engraver, NYC, 1845–68. Probably a son of HENRY B. MAJOR, whom he succeeded in SARONY & MAJOR in 1855. From 1857 to 1867 he was with SARONY, MAJOR & KNAPP and from 1864 to 1868 with Major & Knapp. He exhibited at the American Institute in 1845 and 1847. ¶ Am. Inst. Cat., 1845, 1847; NYBD 1848–54; Peters, *America on Stone.*

MAJOR, WILLIAM WARNER (1804–1854). Portrait and landscape painter, born January 27, 1804, in Bristol (England). After joining the Church of Latter Day Saints in England in 1842, Major emigrated to America in 1844. He was an artist by profession. At Nauvoo (Ill.) in 1845 he exhibited his painting of the assassination of Joseph Smith; at that time he was engaged in a series of paintings to illustrate the sufferings of the Mormons. Major accompanied the Mormon trek to Utah in 1846–48, making sketches of the Indians and the Western scenery, and worked in Salt Lake City from 1848 to 1853. He returned to England in December 1853 and died there on September 2, 1854. ¶ Information courtesy J. E. Arrington and FARL.

MALAMBRE, JOHN A. Portrait artist of Dayton (Ohio), active 1850–70. *Cf.* JOHN MALMORE. ¶ Information courtesy Paul H. North, Jr., Columbus (Ohio).

MALBONE, EDWARD GREENE (1777–1807). Probably America's best known miniature painter, Malbone was born in Newport (R.I.) in August 1777. His career as an artist began in Providence in 1794 and from then until 1807 he moved about the country painting hundreds of miniatures in Providence, Newport, Boston, New York, Philadelphia, Charleston, and Savannah. In 1801 he made a brief visit to England in company with WASHINGTON ALLSTON. Late in 1806 he went to Jamaica for his health and on his return in January 1807 stopped at Savannah (Ga.), where he died on May 7. ¶ The fullest account of Malbone's life and catalogue of his works is found in the late Ruel P. Tolman's *Life of Edward Greene Malbone,* soon to be published by the New-York Historical Society. His work is represented in many museums.

MALCOLM, JAMES PELLER (1767–1815). Engraver and landscape draftsman. Born in Philadelphia in August 1767, Malcolm was educated in Quaker schools at Philadelphia and Pottstown (Pa.) during the Revolution. About 1784 he began the study of art and as early as 1786 engraved the plates for John Parke's edition of *The Lyric Works of Horace.* A year or two later, under the patronage of the Rev. Jacob Duché and others, he went to England and for three years studied landscape and historical painting at the Royal Academy, exhibiting there in 1791. Receiving little encouragement he returned to engraving, doing plates for the *Gentleman's Magazine* and others as well as illustrating such works as Lyson's *Environs of London.* He was also an avid antiquarian and wrote a number of books on English local history, with illustrations designed and engraved by himself. Among these were *Londinium Redivivum* (1803–07), *Excursions in the Counties of Kent, Gloucester, Hereford, Monmouth, and Somerset* (1807), and *Historical Sketch of the Art of Caricaturing* (1813). Malcolm died in London, after a long illness, on April 5, 1815. ¶ "Memoirs of James Peller Malcolm, F. S. A.," *Gentleman's Magazine,* May 1815, 467–69; Stauffer; DAB.

MALLET, F. Miniature painter at Baltimore, 1805. ¶ Lafferty cites Baltimore *Evening Post,* Sept. 18, 1805.

MALLORY, RICHARD P. Wood engraver and artist, Boston, 1830's to 1860's. Mallory was a pupil of ABEL BOWEN in the early 1830's. He was associated with the firms of CHANDLER, WRIGHT & MALLORY (1836–39), WRIGHT & MALLORY (1839–52), and KILBURN & MALLORY (1852–65). In 1848 he drew a panoramic view of Boston from Bunker Hill Monument which was engraved by JAMES SMILLIE. ¶ Boston CD 1836–60+; Ford, "Some Trade Cards and Broadsides"; Hamilton, 141, 191, 230; Phila. *Public Ledger,* June 13, 1848 (cited by J. E. Arrington).

MALMORE, JOHN. Portrait and/or landscape painter, Dayton (Ohio), 1859. *Cf.* JOHN A. MALAMBRE. ¶ Ohio BD 1859.

MALONEY, WILLIAM M. Irish portrait painter, born between 1815 and 1818, who was at New Orleans from 1848 to 1867. The name also appears as Molony. ¶ 7 Census (1850), La., V, 11; 8 Census (1860), La., V, 962; New Orleans CD 1854, 1859–67 (Delgado-WPA); Thompson, *La. Writers.*

MALUS, ALEX. Engraver, age 19, born in Louisiana. He resided in New Orleans in 1860 with his father François Malus, a native of France. ¶ 8 Census (1860), La., VII, 139.

MANCHESTER, M. M. Painter, active about 1820–30. The Memorial Art Gallery, Rochester (N.Y.), owns a large signed painting of a man and woman seated on a sofa with a scenic background. ¶ Information courtesy B. H. Leffingwell.

MANCINI, JOHN. Sculptor, NYC, 1841–57. ¶ NYBD 1841–57.

MANGER, CHARLES. Artist, age 28, born in Maryland, at Philadelphia in 1860. ¶ 8 Census (1860), Pa., LVI, 834; Phila. CD 1871.

MANGER, HEINRICH (Henry). Sculptor, born in 1833. He was active in Philadelphia from about 1862 to 1871 and exhibited a bust of Lincoln at the Pennsylvania Academy, 1865–67. ¶ Gardner, *Yankee Stonecutters,* 74; Phila. CD 1862–71; Rutledge, PA.

MANIC, PETER. Miniature painter at Philadelphia, 1809–10. *Cf.* PETER J. MEANCE. ¶ Brown and Brown.

MANIM, Sr. ——. Painted portrait of Merriwether Lewis in frontier garb against a mountainous background, known only through an engraving. ¶ *Analectic Magazine,* VII (1816), opp. p. 329. *Cf.* ST. MEMIN.

MANLEY, JANE HELENA. Amateur crayon artist, Kingston (N.Y.), 1843. ¶ Lipman and Winchester, 176.

MANLEY, WILLIAM T. English engraver, 18, at NYC in 1860, in the home of THOMAS NEALE. ¶ 8 Census (1860), N.Y., LI, 225.

MANLY, ——. Portrait painter working in Virginia about 1772. ¶ Dunlap, *History,* I, 145.

MANLY, JAMES. Irish engraver and miniaturist, formerly resident in London, who came to America about 1789. In March 1790 he was at Philadelphia, advertising a medal of George Washington. By June 1793, after a visit to the West Indies, he had opened a studio in NYC for miniature and profile painting and hair work. ¶ Prime, II, 70–71; Gottesman, II, 8.

MANN & KIMBALL. Dioramic artists who exhibited "The Battle of Tippecanoe" and scenes at North Bend (Ind.) in Boston, November 1840. ¶ Boston *Evening Transcript,* Nov. 23, 1840 (cited by J. E. Arrington).

MANNING & BROWN. Designers, Boston, 1856; JOHN H. MANNING and SAMUEL E. BROWN. ¶ Boston CD 1856.

MANNING, JOHN H. Wood engraver and designer of Boston, active 1841–59. He was a native of Massachusetts, born about 1820. In 1856 he was senior partner in MANNING & BROWN. ¶ Boston CD 1842–59; Hamilton, 370; 7 Census (1850), Mass., XXIII, 506.

MANNING, PIERRE. French artist, 24, at NYC in 1860 with his wife Louisa. ¶ 8 Census (1860), N.Y., XLVI, 288.

MANOOG, JOHN M. Wood engraver, NYC, 1856; exhibitor at the American Institute. ¶ NYBD 1856; Am. Inst. Cat., 1856.

MANOUVRIER, JULES. Lithographer, New Orleans, 1841–70. From 1841 to 1853, of MANOUVRIER & SNELL, and after 1860 in partnership with DIONIS (or Dennis) SIMON. ¶ New Orleans CD 1841–70.

MANOUVRIER & SNELL. Lithographers, New Orleans, 1841–53; JULES MANOUVRIER and P. SNELL. ¶ New Orleans CD 1841–53.

MANSAN, Mrs. ——. Teacher of drawing and painting, monochromatic painting, and fancy needlework; Charleston (S.C.), 1847. ¶ Rutledge, *Artists in the Life of Charleston.*

MANSURE, CHARLES. Lithographer, born in Pennsylvania about 1832, working in Philadelphia from 1850 to about 1860; brother of JOHN and ROBERT MANSURE. ¶ 7 Census (1850), Pa., LV, 601; Phila. CD 1854–60.

MANSURE, JOHN J. Lithographer, born in

Pennsylvania about 1834, working in Philadelphia from 1850 to about 1865; brother of CHARLES and ROBERT MANSURE. ¶ 7 Census (1850), Pa., LV, 601; Phila. CD 1857–65.

MANSURE, ROBERT. Lithographer, Philadelphia, 1857–59. He was of the same family as CHARLES and JOHN J. MANSURE, probably a brother. Robert Mansure, the father, was born in Delaware about 1804, and was listed as a carpenter in Philadelphia in the early fifties. ¶ 7 Census (1850), Pa., LV, 601; Phila. CD 1850–59.

MAPES, JAMES JAY (1806–66). Amateur miniature painter. Born May 29, 1806, at Maspeth, Long Island (N.Y.), Mapes became widely known as a chemical analyst in NYC and later as an experimental farmer and editor of *The Working Farmer* (1849–63). An amateur miniaturist, he exhibited at the National Academy during the 1830's and 1840's and also lectured at the Academy on the chemistry of colors. He was an Honorary Member, Amateur, from 1833 to 1860. Mapes died in NYC on January 19, 1866. ¶ DAB; Bolton, *Miniature Painters;* Cowdrey, NAD; Rutledge, PA.

MAPLES, THOMAS. Sculptor, Philadelphia, 1850–70's. He was born in England about 1803 and came to America with his family about 1850. ¶ 7 Census (1850), Pa., LIII, 554; Phila. CD 1851–70+.

MAPOTHER, DILLON H. Lithographer, of HART, MAPOTHER & COMPANY of Louisville (Ky.) and St. Louis (Mo.), 1855–70. ¶ Louisville CD 1855–70; St. Louis BD 1858–59.

MARAS, see MARRAS.

MARCELLE, VITO. Dioramic artist exhibiting at NYC in 1848. ¶ N. Y. *Herald,* July 3, 1848 (cited by J. E. Arrington).

MARCEY, WILLIAM. Artist, 25, a native of Massachusetts, at NYC in 1860. ¶ 8 Census (1860), N.Y., LVI, 510.

MARCH, GIOVANNI. Italian plaster image maker, age 17, living with and presumably employed by LORENZO HARDIE at Philadelphia, June 1860. ¶ 8 Census (1860), Pa., LXII, 106.

MARCHAIS DES GENTILS, JULES. French landscape, marine, and portrait painter, who came to Charleston (S.C.) about 1832 and taught drawing and painting. In 1841 he married a local widow and with her opened a French and English school for young ladies which was still open in 1847. ¶ Rutledge, *Artists in the Life of Charleston,* 159, 208–09, 243.

MARCHAND, DAVID. Engraver, 43, at NYC in 1860. His wife and one child, aged 9, were born in France; another child, aged 5, was born in New York. ¶ 8 Census (1860), N.Y., XLVI, 196.

MARCHAND, JULES. Engraver and die sinker, NYC, 1848–58. ¶ NYBD 1848–58.

MARCHANT, EDWARD DALTON (1806–87). A.N.A. Portrait and miniature painter, born December 16, 1806, at Edgartown (Mass.). He had begun his professional career by 1827–28 when he advertised in Charleston (S.C.). He first exhibited at the National Academy in 1832 and for the next five years or so seems to have had a studio in NYC. About 1838 he went west, visiting New Orleans and Ohio, where his son, HENRY A. MARCHANT, was born about 1839. By 1841 he had returned to NYC, but a few years later he moved to Nashville (Tenn.). He visited New Orleans again in 1849. Marchant was again in NYC in 1850 and 1852, but by 1854 he had settled in Philadelphia and he was still there in 1860. He died at Asbury Park (N.J.) on August 15, 1887. Marchant was an Associate of the National Academy from 1833 until his death. ¶ CAB; Rutledge, *Artists in the Life of Charleston,* 209; Cowdrey, NAD; 8 Census (1860), Pa., LIV, 146; Fielding; Delgado-WPA cites New Orleans *Picayune,* Dec. 4, 1839, Oct. 14, 1840, and Jan. 5, 1849; Cowdrey, AA & AAU; NYCD 1852; Phila. CD 1854–60; Rutledge, PA; represented: Univ. of Penna.

MARCHANT, G. W., see GEORGE W. MERCHANT.

MARCHANT, HENRY A. Miniature painter, son of EDWARD DALTON MARCHANT. He was born in Ohio about 1839 and in 1860 was living with his parents in Philadelphia. ¶ 8 Census (1860), Pa., LIV, 146.

MARCHINO, FREDERICK. Sculptor, of PROTIN & MARCHINO, NYC, 1850. ¶ NYBD and CD 1850.

MARCON or MARCOU, LUCIEN. Wax figure maker, New Orleans, 1858–59. ¶ Delgado-WPA cites New Orleans BD 1858–59.

MARE, JOHN (*c.* 1739–?). Portrait painter. Born in NYC, probably early in 1739, Mare was painting portraits in Albany as early as 1759. He worked in NYC from about 1760 to 1772, painting many prominent residents of the city and Hudson Valley landowners. In 1766 he painted a portrait of George III for the City. Mare went to Albany in 1772 and then disappears from sight until 1795 when he appears to have sold some property in NYC. ¶ Helen Burr Smith, "John Mare."

MARE, see also DE MARE.

MARFORD, MIRIBLE (1814–1827). Amateur watercolorist, of Eatontown (N.J.). ¶ Lipman and Winchester, 176.

MARGOT, AUGUSTUS P. Engraver, Boston, 1858–60 and after. ¶ Boston CD 1858–60+.

MARGRAFF, FRANCIS. German engraver, 32, at NYC in 1850. His wife and three older children were born in Germany before 1845 and one was born in New York about 1848. ¶ 7 Census (1850), N.Y., XLI, 754.

MARIO, ALESSANDRO E. Landscape and portrait painter, New Jersey and New York, 1858–68. He advertised as a portrait painter at Mt. Holly (N.J.) in July 1858, and in 1868 painted a view of NYC now owned by the New-York Historical Society. Miss Mary E. Bunce of Bayonne (N.J.), who owns Mario's painting of her great-grandmother's home on Long Island, reports a family tradition that the artist was an exile from Russia who painted the picture out of gratitude to Miss Bunce's great-uncle, a New York lawyer who had befriended him. Mario also exhibited at the Pennsylvania Academy in 1868. ¶ *N. J. Mirror and Burlington County Advertiser,* July 8 and 15, 1858; Rutledge, PA; information courtesy Miss Mary E. Bunce.

MARK, GEORGE WASHINGTON (?–1879). Portrait, fresco, landscape, and historical painter who lived in Greenfield (Conn.), having come there from Charleston (N.H.) in 1817. In addition to painting pictures, Mark painted or stenciled furniture and maintained a gallery of art in his home. The New-York Historical Society owns several of his primitive historical canvases. He died in Greenfield on July 27, 1879. ¶ Dods, "Connecticut Valley Painters," 208.

MARK, JAMES. Engraver and counterfeiter, New York, 1713. ¶ Dow, *The Arts and Crafts in New England, 1704–1775.*

MARKHAM, CHARLES C. (1837–1907). Genre and still life painter, living in Brooklyn (N.Y.) in 1859 when he first exhibited at the National Academy. ¶ Cowdrey, NAD.

MARKLAND, JAMES. Artist, Baltimore, 1853–54. ¶ Lafferty.

MARKOE, FRANCIS, JR. Amateur painter. He was a clerk in the State Department at Washington during the 1830's and 1840's and a friend of G. P. A. HEALY. ¶ de Mare, *G. P. A. Healy,* 157.

MARKS, ——. German artist who exhibited at Columbus (Ohio), in person, his North American Panorama, which included scenes in California, Italy, France, and England, and illustrations of the song "Ben Bolt." ¶ Columbus, *Ohio State Journal,* May 6, 8, and June 8, 1850 (courtesy J. Earl Arrington).

MARLING, JACOB (1774–1833). Portrait and landscape painter who settled at Raleigh (N.C.) about 1813 and lived there until his death on December 18, 1833. The State Library at Raleigh owns his view of the old State Capitol, painted before 1820. This may be the Marling whose miniature of the Rev. Anthony Forster of Charles Town (Va., now W. Va.) was engraved by GOODMAN & PIGGOT before 1822. ¶ "Jacob Marling," *N. C. Booklet X* (1910), 196–99; Stauffer, no. 1135.

MARLING, MRS. JACOB. Teacher of painting on silk, velvet, and glass at Raleigh (N.C.) before the Civil War. She later became a milliner. ¶ "Jacob Marling," *N. C. Booklet X* (1910), 199.

MAROT, SAMUEL. Engraver, Philadelphia, 1854–after 1870. He was born in Pennsylvania about 1835. ¶ Phila. CD 1854–71; 8 Census (1860), Pa., LVI, 150.

MARQUIS, ALEXANDER (1811–1884). Portrait painter, born in Glasgow (Scotland). He came to America about 1850, settled in Milwaukee (Wis.), and painted over three hundred portraits there during the next thirty years. In 1882 he moved to Denver (Col.) where he died two years later. ¶ Butts, *Art in Wisconsin,* 81–82.

MARRAS, JOHN. French miniaturist who advertised in NYC in September 1808. This may be the M. Maras whom DUNLAP described as a poor miniaturist who painted in NYC in 1801–02 and later turned up in Constantinople as court painter to the Sultan. One Maras also exhibited a miniature at the Pennsylvania Academy in 1820. ¶ Stokes, *Icon.,* V, 1495–96; NYCD 1808; Dunlap, *History,* II, 142; Rutledge, PA.

MARRIAS, ——. Miniaturist, Richmond (Va.), 1841. ¶ *Richmond Portraits,* 242.

MARROLIM, S. Painter of an oil portrait of

Holmes Prentice (1784–1861) of Cooperstown (N.Y.) about 1850–60. ¶ Information courtesy Clifford L. Lord, State Historical Society of Wisconsin.

MARRYAT, FRANCIS SAMUEL (1826–1855). Topographical artist. "Frank" Marryat, son of the English novelist, Captain Frederick Marryat, was born in London on April 18, 1826. He entered the Royal Navy at the age of fourteen and served for eight years. In the fall of 1849 he came to California, settled in San Francisco the following year, and remained there until his return to England in the spring of 1852. He returned to California in the fall and stayed another year before going back to England for the last time. He died in London at the age of twenty-nine. In the year of his death Marryat published *Mountains and Molehills,* an account of California illustrated with engravings after the author's sketches. Others of his sketches were lithographed by Hanharts of London. ¶ Marryat, *Mountains and Molehills;* Van Nostrand and Coulter, *California Pictorial,* 148–49; Howell, "Pictorial Californiana," 63; Jackson, *Gold Rush Album,* repros

MARSAC, HARVEY. Engraver, NYC, 1834. ¶ Stauffer.

MARSCHALL, NICOLA (1829–1917). Portrait painter, teacher of painting. Born March 16, 1829, in Germany, he emigrated to America in 1849, arriving in New Orleans and settling at Mobile (Ala.). He taught painting, music, and modern languages at the Marion (Ala.) Seminary for some years. From 1857 to 1859 he studied art at Munich and in Italy. On the outbreak of the Civil War, Marschall provided the design for the Confederate flag and for the uniform adopted by the Confederate Army, in which he served. He moved to Louisville (Ky.) in 1873 and died there on February 24, 1917. ¶ Hume, "Nicola Marschall"; Alabama Dept. of Archives and History, *Alabama Legislature Declares Nicola Marschall Designer First Confederate Flag.*

MARSDEN, THEODORE. Sporting artist best known for his *American Field Sports,* a series of four lithographs published in 1857, and for his horse prints. He has been listed as J., Thomas, and William, as well as Theodore. ¶ Peters, *America on Stone; Panorama* (Feb. 1948), back cover, and (May–June 1949), 102, repros.

MARSH, ANNIE. English artist, age 24, residing in the home of JOHN NEAGLE at Philadelphia in August 1860. ¶ 8 Census (1860), Pa., LII, 507.

MARSH, GEORGE. Artist, 26, a native of New York, at NYC in 1860. ¶ 8 Census (1860), N.Y., XLIV, 748.

MARSH, HENRY. Wood engraver, Boston, 1848–after 1860. In 1848 he was with HITCHCOCK & MARSH. ¶ Boston CD 1848–60+; Hamilton, 401; Linton, *History of Wood Engraving in America,* 35.

MARSH, JOHN. Engraver from England, Philadelphia, September 1850. ¶ 7 Census (1850), Pa., LII, 978.

MARSH, JOSEPH Y. Painter, NYC, 1840's. In 1848 he exhibited at the American Institute a painting on Hose Cart No. 5. ¶ NYCD 1847–49; Am. Inst. Cat., 1848.

MARSH, WILLIAM. Marine painter, exhibitor at the National Academy between 1844 and 1858. He was at Boston from 1844 to 1846, at Brooklyn in 1847, and in NYC in 1858. ¶ Cowdrey, NAD; Boston CD 1844–46.

MARSH, WILLIAM R. Engraver of vignettes, cards, etc.; born in New Jersey about 1810. He was active in NYC from 1833 until after 1860. ¶ 7 Census (1850), N.Y., LVI, 64; NYCD 1833–60+; Stauffer.

MARSHALL, ——. Engraver of one of the maps in John Marshall's *Life of Washington* (Phila., 1804–07). The engraving is signed "Marshall Sct.," but it may be that the map was drawn by the author and engraved by someone else. ¶ Stauffer.

MARSHALL, ELIJAH D. General and calico print engraver, Philadelphia, 1856–57. ¶ Phila. BD 1856–57.

MARSHALL, EMILY. Amateur watercolorist, White Plains (N.Y.), about 1810. ¶ Lipman and Winchester, 176.

MARSHALL, MATTHEW. Amateur engraver, exhibited at the American Institute in 1844 and 1845. He was a maker or retailer of glasses in NYC. ¶ Am. Inst. Cat., 1844–45; NYCD 1843–46.

MARSHALL, WILLIAM EDGAR (1837–1906). Portrait painter and engraver. Born in NYC on June 30, 1837, Marshall began engraving in a watch-case factory at the age of seventeen. Encouraged by CYRUS DURAND, he attempted portrait engraving about 1856, with such success that two years later he was employed as a vignette engraver by the AMERICAN BANK NOTE COMPANY. He was also interested in painting and from 1863 to 1865 studied portraiture in Paris under Couture. Returning to America in 1865, he painted and engraved a portrait of the late President Lincoln which had a wide circulation. In 1866 he opened a studio in NYC and for many years he painted portraits of distinguished Americans. He died in NYC on August 29, 1906. ¶ DAB; *Art Annual,* VI (1907/08), 112; Swan, BA; represented: NYHS.

MARSIGLIA, GHERLANDO (1792–1850). N.A. Portrait, landscape, and historical painter, art dealer. A native of Italy, Marsiglia came to NYC about 1817 and commenced exhibiting at the American Academy in 1824. In 1826 he was one of the founders and charter members of the National Academy of Design and from then until his death he was a frequent exhibitor in its gallery. He also exhibited at the Pennsylvania Academy and the Boston Athenaeum. He died in NYC on September 4, 1850. ¶ Cummings, *Historic Annals,* 224; Cowdrey, AA & AAU; Cowdrey, NAD; Rutledge, PA; Swan, BA; *Appleton's Journal,* May 25, 1872, 572; 7 Census (1850), N.Y., XLIII, 277; Dunlap, *History,* II, 296.

MARSIGLIA, M. Portrait painter, NYC, 1846; probably merely a misprint for G. MARSIGLIA, above. ¶ NYBD 1846 (same address as Gherlando Marsiglia in NYCD 1846).

MARSTON, J. B. Portrait painter at Boston, about 1807. ¶ Dunlap, *History* (1918), III, 316.

MARTEN, ——. Wood engraver who came to NYC from Sheffield (England) about 1796 and died of yellow fever about 1798. *Cf.* DAVID MARTIN. ¶ Dunlap, *History,* II, 47.

MARTENS, G. Portrait painter, active about 1840. ¶ Lipman and Winchester, 176.

MARTENS, JOHN W. Landscape painter. He was in NYC in 1836–37 when he exhibited views of the Brooklyn Navy Yards and the Mohawk Valley at the National Academy, and in Brooklyn in 1846 when he exhibited at the American Institute. ¶ Cowdrey, NAD; Am. Inst. Cat., 1846.

MARTER, JOHN. Italian artist, age 22, at Baltimore in 1860. ¶ 8 Census (1860), Md., III, 915.

MARTIN, ANGELIQUE MARIE, see LILLY MARTIN SPENCER.

MARTIN, CHARLES. Portrait painter, Philadelphia, 1817–20. ¶ Brown and Brown.

MARTIN, CHARLES (1820–1906). Portrait and landscape painter. He was at Charleston (S.C.) from 1846 to 1848, painting portraits and doing pastel portraits. When he exhibited at the National Academy in 1851 he was living at Bristol (R.I.). He died in London on April 5, 1906. ¶ Thieme-Becker; Rutledge, *Artists in the Life of Charleston,* 209; Cowdrey, NAD; *Art News,* April 1906, obit.

MARTIN, CHARLES. Lithographer, age 27, at Philadelphia in 1860. He was a native of Pennsylvania, as were his two children; his wife was from Delaware. ¶ 8 Census (1860), Pa., XLIX, 179.

MARTIN, DAVID. Engraver of NYC, 1796. He engraved one portrait and several maps for the *Monthly Military Repository,* published in NYC in that year. *Cf.* David Martin (1737–98), Scottish portrait painter and engraver, although the latter is not known to have come to America. *Cf.* also —— MARTEN. ¶ Stauffer; NYCD 1796; DNB.

MARTIN, E. Engraver for Cincinnati publishers, 1826. ¶ Stauffer.

MARTIN, E. HALL. Portrait and landscape painter. Cist states that Martin began to paint about 1831. He was in NYC in 1847–48 and exhibited at the American Art-Union, one of his paintings being a view of the Castle of San Juan d'Ulloa at the entrance to the harbor of Vera Cruz (Mexico). In 1851 he was residing in California. ¶ Cist, *Cincinnati in 1851,* 124; NYCD 1847; NYBD 1848; Cowdrey, AA & AAU.

MARTIN, E. O. Portrait painter, NYC, 1837. He exhibited at the National Academy in that year, giving New York University as his address. ¶ Cowdrey, NAD.

MARTIN, ERNEST F. Engraver and die sinker, NYC, 1859. ¶ NYBD 1859.

MARTIN, FERDINAND. German lithographer, age 23, living in Baltimore with his American wife, July 1860. ¶ 8 Census (1860), Md., VI, 257.

MARTIN, HOMER DODGE (1836–1897). N.A. Landscape painter and illustrator. Born October 28, 1836, in Albany (N.Y.), Homer Martin grew up there, tried his hand unsuccessfully at several trades, and finally in the mid-fifties turned to painting under encouragement from the Albany sculptor ERASTUS DOW PALMER. He moved to NYC in 1862 and made his home there for the next thirty years. He made several trips to England and France, notably his extended visit from 1881 to 1886, spent chiefly in Normandy and out of which grew some of his best known paintings, including "The Harp of the Wind." In 1893 Martin and his wife moved to St. Paul (Minn.) where, in spite of growing blindness and ill health, the artist produced some of his finest landscapes. He died in St. Paul on February 12, 1897. ¶ Mather, *Homer Martin, Poet in Landscape* and Mrs. Martin's *Homer Martin: A Reminiscence* are the chief biographical studies, while Dana H. Carroll's *Fifty-eight Paintings by Homer D. Martin* reproduces a representative selection of his work. See also: Hamilton, "Homer Martin as Illustrator"; Cowdrey, NAD; Rutledge, PA; Albany CD 1858–60+.

MARTIN, J. A. Landscape painter whose view of the Valley of Keene (N.H.) was shown at the American Art-Union in 1851 and 1852. ¶ Cowdrey, AA & AAU.

MARTIN, JAMES. Pastel and crayon portraits and miniatures. Martin came to America about 1794, advertised in New Jersey in September 1795 as "from New York, late of Fleet Street, London," and worked in NYC from 1797 until about 1820. His success, in spite of incompetence, is said to have inspired JOHN WESLEY JARVIS to take up portrait painting. ¶ *N. J. Journal,* Sept. 23, 1795 (quoted in *American Collector,* August 1934, 5); NYCD 1797–99, 1802–10, 1820 (cited by McKay); Dunlap, *History,* II, 47; Dickson, *John Wesley Jarvis,* 87.

MARTIN, JOHN A. LEE. Artist who was at Mormon Island (Cal.) in January 1850. ¶ Van Nostrand and Coulter, *California Pictorial,* 124.

MARTIN, JOHN BLENNERHASSETT (1797–1857). Portrait and miniature painter, engraver and lithographer, born September 5, 1797, at Bandon, County Cork (Ireland). He came to NYC about 1815, studied engraving there, and two years later moved to Richmond (Va.) where he made his home until his death on October 22, 1857. He worked as an engraver and lithographer as late as 1852 but for many years devoted himself chiefly to portrait painting. In his later years he visited other cities in search of commissions. Martin was also prominent in the Presbyterian Church at Richmond, of which he was a ruling elder from 1834 until his death. ¶ *Richmond Portraits,* 119–20; Fairman, *Art and Artists of the Capitol,* 365; Stauffer; Peters, *America on Stone.* His portrait of John Marshall hangs in the Supreme Court Building, Washington (D.C.).

MARTIN, JULIET. Painter of a watercolor view of Paterson (N.J.), signed and dated at New York in July 1797. ¶ Information courtesy Alexander J. Wall, Jr., Director, New Jersey Historical Society.

MARTIN, LILLY, see LILLY MARTIN SPENCER.

MARTIN, MARIA (?–1863). Painter of birds, flowers, and insects. A sister-in-law of the Rev. John Bachman of Charleston (S.C.), Miss Martin assisted JOHN JAMES AUDUBON by painting backgrounds for many of his series of American birds. In 1849 she married Bachman and she died in Charleston the day after Christmas, 1863. ¶ Herrick, *Audubon the Naturalist,* 6–7; 281; C. L. Bachman, *John Bachman,* 375.

MARTIN, ROBERT. Steel engraver from Scotland, aged 35, at NYC in 1860. He engraved the illustrations for an edition of J. F. Cooper's works published that year. ¶ 8 Census (1860), N.Y., LX, 928; Stauffer.

MARTIN, ROBERT. Artist, 40, a native of New Jersey, at NYC in 1860. His wife Mary, who ran a boarding house, and their three children, ages 15 to 24, were born in New York. ¶ 8 Census (1860), N.Y., XLIV, 905.

MARTIN, SOLOMON. Amateur watercolorist, probably in the Pennsylvania-German section of Pennsylvania, who painted a primitive vase of flowers in the summer of 1840. ¶ *Antiques* (May 1931), cover and p. 359.

MARTIN, THOMAS. Irish lithographer, age 35, living in Philadelphia in 1860. His wife was also a native of Ireland but all the children were born in Pennsylvania, the eldest about 1850. ¶ 8 Census (1860), Pa., LII, 297.

MARTIN, WILLIAM A. K. (1817–1867). Landscape, marine, and historical painter who was born and died in Philadelphia and apparently spent most of his career there, although his "Palermo," shown at the Pennsylvania Academy in 1853, may indicate that he had been to Europe. He also exhibited at the Artists' Fund Society and the Maryland Historical Society. ¶ Fielding; Rutledge, PA; Rutledge, MHS; Phila. CD 1850–60; 7 Census (1850), Pa., LI; *Portfolio* (April 1945), 212, and (June–July 1945), 5.

MARTIN, WILLIAM D. Painter of "A Storm at Sea," shown in Charleston (S.C.) in 1860. ¶ Rutledge, *Artists in the Life of Charleston.*

MARTINI, ——. Engraver of a plate of Bunker Hill Monument, about 1855.

¶ Dana, *The United States Illustrated,* Vol. I.

MARTINI, PIETRO. Painter and drawing teacher at Charleston (S.C.) in 1846–47. In February 1847 Signor Martini, "well known as an artist in Charleston," exhibited his cosmographic view of the ruins of Pompeii. ¶ Rutledge, *Artists in the Life of Charleston,* 209.

MARTY, BENJAMIN. Irish engraver, 32, at NYC in 1860. His wife Ann and their three oldest children were born in Ireland before 1856, while one child, aged 3, was born in New York. ¶ 8 Census (1860), N.Y., LXII, 561.

MARVIN, C. Painter of an oil, "Vigilantes, California, 1849." ¶ *Portfolio* (May 1951), 210.

MARVIN, J. L. Panoramist. His panorama of California was shown in NYC, Albany, Cincinnati, and St. Louis before it reached New Orleans in April 1851 and Boston in March 1852. ¶ New Orleans *Picayune,* April 8, 1851, and Boston *Evening Transcript,* March 27, 1852 (citations courtesy J. E. Arrington).

MARX, JOSEPH. Portrait painter, NYC, 1859. ¶ NYBD 1859.

MASON, ABRAHAM JOHN (1794–?). A.N.A. Wood engraver, born in Goswell Road, London, April 4, 1794. After serving as apprentice and assistant to Robert Branston from 1808 to 1820, Mason set up as a wood engraver in London and quickly won a prominent place in the profession. In 1829 he gave a series of public lectures on wood engraving. In November of the same year he sailed for America with his family, reached New York in December, and established himself in business there. He was elected an Associate of the National Academy in 1830, lectured there in 1831 and 1832, and in the latter year was appointed Professor of Wood Engraving in the Academy. His treatise on wood engraving was published in DUNLAP's *History of the Arts of Design* (1834). Mason returned to England in 1839. ¶ Dunlap, *History,* II, 445–47; Cowdrey, NAD; Cowdrey, AA & AAU; Rutledge, PA; Hamilton; Linton; Graves.

MASON, ALVA. Engraver on brass and maker of philosophical instruments, Philadelphia, 1817–59; from 1817 to 1830 with W. & A. MASON. ¶ Phila. CD 1818–59; Stauffer.

MASON, ASA. Wood engraver, Philadelphia, 1816–17; in 1817 with WILLIAM MASON. ¶ Phila. CD 1816–17.

MASON, BENJAMIN FRANKLIN (1804–1871). Portrait painter, born March 31, 1804, at Pomfret (Vt.). Crippled from the age of nine, Mason taught school for a few years but turned professional artist in 1825. In 1831 at Burlington (Vt.), he met and studied under J. G. COLE. As an itinerant artist, Mason painted in many towns of Vermont and New Hampshire, Boston (Mass.), Troy and Buffalo (N.Y.), Sheboygan and Milwaukee (Wis.), before taking up more or less permanent residence in Woodstock (Vt.) in 1861. He died there January 15, 1871. ¶ Frankenstein and Healy, "Two Journeymen Painters," 7–43, twenty-eight repros., checklist, bibliography.

MASON, C. D. Sculptor; born in France in 1830; died at Mineola, Long Island (N.Y.), in July 1915. ¶ *Art Annual,* XII, obit.

MASON, CHARLES. German lithographer, 50, at NYC in 1860. His wife Louisa and daughter, aged 14, were born in Hesse-Darmstadt. ¶ 8 Census (1860), N.Y., LV, 861.

MASON, DAVID. Painter, japanner, and gilder, Boston, 1758. He had served three years with the military forces on the frontier at Fort William Henry. He offered to paint coats of arms, make drawings on satin or canvas for embroidery, as well as general painting. ¶ Dow, *Arts and Crafts in New England,* 267.

MASON, DAVID H. Engraver, Philadelphia, 1805–30. He did music engraving, a few vignettes for MURRAY, DRAPER, FAIRMAN & Co. (1816), and in 1811 was listed as a wood engraver with WILLIAM MASON. In 1830 he signed a certificate as "architect and engraver." ¶ Stauffer; Phila. CD 1811–28.

MASON, GEORGE (?–1773). Crayon portraitist working at Boston in 1768. He died there in July (?) 1773. ¶ Dow, *Arts and Crafts in New England,* 2.

MASON, GEORGE CHAMPLIN (1820–1894). Landscape and architectural painter. Born July 17, 1820, at Newport (R.I.), he apparently went to Europe in his early twenties and on his return exhibited views in Italy, as well as Newport, at the National Academy between 1844 and 1848. He was again in Rome in 1858 when he exhibited at the National Academy a view of the Campagna. Most of Mason's career was spent as an architect in Newport. He was also a writer on art and architecture, his works in these fields including *The Application of Art to Manufactures*

(1858) and *The Life and Works of Gilbert Stuart* (1879). His *Newport Illustrated* (1854) was illustrated from his own drawings. Died in Philadelphia, January 30, 1894. ¶ CAB; Cowdrey, NAD; Cowdrey, AA & AAU; Washington Art Assoc. Cat., 1859.

MASON, JAMES L. Portrait painter, age 38, born in Massachusetts; living in a Philadelphia hotel in August 1850. ¶ 7 Census (1850), Pa., LII, 359.

MASON, JOHN W. Carver, Boston, 1836–1850's. He served his apprenticeship under LABAN BEECHER and did much figurehead and other carving on the clipper ships. ¶ Pinckney, *American Figureheads.*

MASON, JONATHAN, JR. (*c.* 1795–1884). Portrait and figure painter. He exhibited at the Boston Athenaeum in 1827–28 and in 1833–34 as of Boston. ¶ Swan, BA; Dunlap, *History* (1918), III, 316–17.

MASON, JOSEPH R. (1808–1842). Portrait painter. He was born in Camden (Del.) in 1808 and, according to Cist, commenced painting portraits in 1822. He exhibited at the Pennsylvania Academy in 1823. In 1832 he was one of the founders of the Last Man's Club of Cincinnati. In 1841 Cist stated that Mason was living in Michigan, but the artist died in Cincinnati on October 8, 1842. ¶ Shepard, "Last Man's Club," 27; Cist, *Cincinnati in 1841,* 139; Cincinnati CD 1834; Rutledge, PA.

MASON, RICHARD. Wood engraver, Cincinnati, 1856–60. ¶ Cincinnati CD 1856; BD 1859–60.

MASON, SAMUEL. Artist, Philadelphia, 1857–58. ¶ Phila. CD 1857–58.

MASON, SANFORD (*c.* 1798–after 1862). Portrait painter, born in Rhode Island. He began his career in Providence as a sign painter, turning to portrait work about 1824. About 1826 he moved to Boston, opened a studio, and exhibited at the Athenaeum in 1827–28, but the latter year he returned to Providence. During the 1830's he spent most of his time in Boston and Lowell (Mass.). From 1842 to 1845 he was at Philadelphia, where his son WILLIAM SANFORD MASON began his career. By 1847 he was back in Providence and thereafter he seems to have shuttled back and forth between Boston and Philadelphia. He is last heard of in Philadelphia in 1862. ¶ 8 Census (1860), Mass., XXVIII, 107; Karolik Cat., 418; Boston CD 1826–27, 1834–39, 1850, 1854, 1860; Providence CD 1828, 1847, 1850; Phila. CD 1842–45, 1852–53, 1856–59, 1862; Lowell CD 1833.

MASON, W. & A. Engravers of brass ornaments for book-binding, charter and patent medicine seals, embossed plates. Active Philadelphia, 1817–30; WILLIAM and ALVA MASON. ¶ Phila. CD 1817–30; Stauffer.

MASON, W. & D. H. Wood engravers, Philadelphia, 1811–16; WILLIAM and DAVID H. MASON. ¶ Phila. CD 1811–16.

MASON, WALTER G. Engraver of two plates in *Benjamin Franklin: His Autobiography* (N.Y.: 1849). ¶ Hamilton, 172.

MASON, WILLIAM. Engraver on wood, copper, and brass; landscape and still life painter; drawing teacher; active 1808–44. A native of Connecticut, Mason served his apprenticeship under the Hartford engraver ABNER REED from about 1804 to 1810. In 1808 he made his first efforts at wood engraving, and in 1810 he moved to Philadelphia, apparently in company with DAVID H. and possibly ALVA MASON. As W. & D. H. MASON, William and David did wood engraving until 1816, and during this period GEORGE GILBERT served his apprenticeship to William. In 1817 the firm became W. & A. MASON, engravers on brass, while David went into business independently. William seems to have given up engraving about 1830 and become a drawing teacher. He had exhibited landscapes at the Society of Artists in 1814 and between 1830 and 1841 he showed several landscapes and still lifes at the Pennsylvania Academy and the Artists' Fund Society. THOMAS H. HINCKLEY studied under him about this time. Mason appears in the directories as a drawing master from 1829 to 1835, as an engraver again in 1837 and 1839, and as a drawing teacher from 1841 until his name disappears altogether after 1844. The presence in Philadelphia at the same time of several other William Masons (see WILLIAM MASON, active 1823–24; WILLIAM G. MASON, active 1822–60+; and WILLIAM SANFORD MASON, active 1844–66) is confusing, but comparison of addresses in the directories and exhibition records indicates that these are all to be distinguished from the present William Mason. ¶ Dunlap, *History,* II, 228; Phila. CD 1811–45; Rutledge, PA; Karolik Cat., 354; Hamilton, 375–76. Dunlap erroneously gives 1804 as the year of his birth.

MASON, WILLIAM. Engraver, Philadelphia,

1823–24. This William Mason is distinguished from the above because they are listed simultaneously in the city directories with different business and home addresses. WILLIAM G. MASON, also engraving in Philadelphia at this time according to Stauffer, was not listed in the directory before 1829. Whether the present William can be equated with either of his contemporaries is an open question. ¶ Phila. CD 1823–24.

MASON, WILLIAM G. Engraver, particularly of buildings; landscape painter. Stauffer states that William G. Mason was active in Philadelphia as early as 1822, but he is first listed in the directory for 1829 and thereafter until after 1860. He may well have been the William Mason who drew several views of buildings for CEPHAS G. CHILDS' *Views of Philadelphia from Original Views Taken in 1827–1830*, and he executed the illustrations for JOSHUA SHAW's *United States Architecture*. In 1843 he exhibited a landscape at the Pennsylvania Academy. ¶ Stauffer; Phila. CD 1829–60+; Rutledge, PA; Doughty, "Thomas Doughty," 30–31.

MASON, WILLIAM SANFORD (1824–1864). Portrait, landscape, genre, literary, and historical painter. The son of SANFORD MASON, with whom he has often been confused, William Sanford Mason was born in Providence (R.I.) in 1824 and made his artistic debut in Philadelphia in 1843. Though he painted in a wide variety of genre, he was best known for his subject pictures from ancient and modern literature. He exhibited at the Artists' Fund Society, Pennsylvania Academy, American Art-Union, and Boston Athenaeum. Except for a visit to Boston in 1854 and painting trips into the country, he spent most of his career in Philadelphia and died there in 1864, although his name appears in the directories for 1865 and 1866. ¶ Lancaster Co. Hist. Soc., *Proceedings,* XVI (1912), 277; Karolik Cat., 418–21, two repros.; Cowdrey, AA & AAU; Rutledge, PA; Swan, BA; Phila. CD 1844–66; Boston CD 1854–55; Washington Art Assoc. Cat. 1859.

MASPERO, PIERRE ANTOINE (?–1822). Silhouette and profile cutter, print seller, advertised in Charleston (S.C.) in 1805 and 1806. He died there in October 1822. ¶ Rutledge, *Artists in the Life of Charleston,* 209

MASS, CHARLES, see CHARLES MAAS.

MASS, GOTFRIED or GODFREY. Engraver, seal engraver, and die sinker. Gotfried was working in NYC from 1840 to 1847 as an engraver and from 1850 to 1853 as a straw hat maker and French milliner. Godfrey was an engraver at Philadelphia in 1857–58. The two are presumed to be one. ¶ NYCD 1840–53; Phila. CD 1856–57.

MASS, JACOB, see JACOB MAAS.

MASSABO, JUSTIN. French sculptor, age 21, at NYC in September 1850. ¶ 7 Census (1850), N.Y., LI, 280.

MASSARD or MASSARO, VICTOR. Italian "artist," age 40, at Cincinnati in September 1850. There were Massards in Cincinnati at the time, but Victor is not listed in the directories. ¶ 7 Census (1850), Ohio, XX, 916.

MASSETT, J. W. Portrait painter, NYC, 1854. ¶ NYBD 1854.

MASSEY, ALBERT. Engraver, Philadelphia, 1858–60. Albert, born in Pennsylvania about 1837, was the son of Lemuel Massey, grocer, and older brother of AUGUSTUS MASSEY, engraver. Two other brothers were jewelers. ¶ Phila. CD 1858–59; 8 Census (1860), Pa., L, 144.

MASSEY, AUGUSTUS. Engraver, age 21, born in Pennsylvania and living in Philadelphia, 1860. He was a brother of ALBERT MASSEY. ¶ 8 Census (1860), Pa., L, 144.

MASSEY, JOSEPH. Engraver. A Charleston (S.C.) gunsmith, Massey engraved the first South Carolina paper currency. He died in May 1736. ¶ Rutledge, *Artists in the Life of Charleston,* 209.

MASSEY (or Massy), Miss MARIE L. Portrait painter, New Orleans, 1857–65. ¶ New Orleans CD, cited by Delgado-WPA.

MASSLENSON, T. W. G. Artist from Massachusetts, age 40, boarding in New Haven (Conn.) in October 1850. ¶ 7 Census (1850), Conn., VIII, 533.

MASSON, EMILE. Crayon portraitist, Boston, 1854–56. ¶ Boston BD 1854–56; Bolton, *Miniature Painters.*

MASSY, see MASSEY.

MASTINI, SILVAIN. Artist, age 32, born in the island of Madeira, living in Philadelphia in 1850 with his wife Catherine, a native of New Jersey. ¶ 7 Census (1850), Pa., LII, 953.

MATCH, AUGUSTUS. Portrait painter, Jersey City (N.J.), 1858–59. ¶ Jersey City CD, 1858–59, 122.

MATEL, ADOLPH. German engraver, age 53, living in Washington (D.C.) in 1860. All his family were born in Germany, including the youngest child, age 12. ¶ 8 Census (1860), D.C., I, 228.

MATESON, see MATTESON.

MATHEDI, ANGELO. Plaster image maker, age 24, from Tuscany, at Philadelphia in 1860. He lived with and was presumably employed by LORENZO HARDIE. ¶ 8 Census (1860), Pa., LXII, 106.

MATHER, WILLIAM. English lithographer, age 33, living in NYC in August 1860. ¶ 8 Census (1860), N.Y., LI, 419.

MATHES, ROBERT. Portrait painter at Milton (N.H.) about 1830. ¶ Lipman and Winchester, 176.

MATHEWS, ALFRED EDWARD (1831–1874). Topographical artist, landscape and panorama painter, lithographer. Born June 24, 1831, in Bristol (England), A. E. Mathews was brought to America at the age of two and grew up in Rochester (Ohio). Before the Civil War he traveled in the northern and southern states as a bookseller and artist. He served with the Federal forces during the war and produced numerous battle sketches and a panorama of the campaigns in the South from Vicksburg to Savannah. Immediately after the war he went west, made his headquarters at Denver, and devoted himself for several years to producing lithographs of the western scene. Many of these were issued separately, others in his now scarce books: *Pencil Sketches of Colorado* (1866), *Pencil Sketches of Montana* (1868), and *Gems of Rocky Mountain Scenery* (1869). From 1869 to 1872 he was chiefly engaged in promoting the settlement of Cañon City (Colo.). He visited southern California in 1872 and 1873. His death occurred October 30, 1874, on his ranch near Longmont (Colo.). ¶ Taft, *Artists and Illustrators of the Old West,* 72–85.

MATHEWS, CHARLES. Ohio-born artist, age 25, living in NYC in August 1850. ¶ 7 Census (1850), N.Y., XLVIII, 554.

MATHEWS, E. P. Still life painter who exhibited at the National Academy in 1851. The address listed is the same as that of GEORGE V. COOPER. ¶ Cowdrey, NAD; NYBD 1851.

MATHEWS, GEORGE H. Portrait painter, Auburn (N.Y.), 1859. ¶ N. Y. State BD 1859

MATHEWS, SAMUEL. Sculptor and scagliola artist, NYC, 1846–51. ¶ NYBD 1846–51.

MATHEWS, WILLIAM T. (1821–1905). Portrait painter, brother of ALFRED E. MATHEWS. Born May 7, 1821, in Bristol (England), he accompanied his family to Rochester (Ohio) about 1833 and began his painting career in Ohio during the forties. By 1850 he had gone to NYC where he had his studio until the late sixties. Much of his work was done in Washington, including portraits of Presidents Lincoln, Hayes, Garfield, Harrison, and McKinley. His later years were spent in obscurity and poverty. He died in Washington, January 11, 1905. ¶ Taft, *Artists and Illustrators of the Old West,* 303; Thieme-Becker; Washington *Post,* Jan. 13, 1905; Washington *Times,* Feb. 16, 1908; Cowdrey, NAD; Rutledge, PA; Swan, BA; Washington Art Assoc. Cat., 1857, 1859.

MATHEWS, see also MATTHEWS.

MATHEWSON, GEORGE BOWEN (1804–1877). Portrait painter, an example of whose work is reproduced in C. W. Bowen's *History of Woodstock* (Vt.), II, 221. ¶ Citation courtesy the late William Sawitzky.

MATHEWSON, THOMAS (*c.* 1815–1862). Portrait painter. He was active in Providence (R.I.) from 1852 to 1857 and in 1858 exhibited at the National Academy as a resident of Brooklyn (N.Y.). Mayo states that he died May 13, 1862, at East Greenwich (R.I.). ¶ Mayo; Providence CD 1852–57; Cowdrey, NAD.

MATHIES, J. L. D. Portrait painter. At Canandaigua (N.Y.) in 1816. About 1825 he and WILLIAM PAGE established a short-lived art gallery at Rochester (N.Y.). Page left for NYC a year later, but Mathies stayed on as a grocer, patent agent, and finally hotelkeeper. Sometime before 1838 he painted a portrait of Red Jacket which hung in the Clinton Hotel, of which the artist was proprietor. It is possible that he later moved to NYC, for a view on the East River by J. L. D. Mathies was exhibited in 1848 at the National Academy. This may, however, have been the work of the young wood engraver of the same name, listed below. The two may well have been related. ¶ Ulp, "Art and Artists of Rochester," 30, 40; Cowdrey, NAD; Rochester CD 1827, 1834, not in 1838 or after; Rev. Peter Stryker, "Diary," Aug. 9, 1816 (typescript at NYHS); represented: Ontario Co. Hist. Soc., Canandaigua, N.Y.

MATHIES (Mathus), J. L. D. (or John L. L. Matthews). Wood engraver. In 1848 J. L. D. Mathies or Mathus, a minor apparently apprenticed to NATHANIEL ORR, won a prize for a wood engraving shown at the American Institute. This is presumably the John L. L. Matthews, also of Orr's establishment in Nassau Street, who exhibited a wood engraving at the Institute in 1849. The J. L. D. Mathies who exhibited a landscape at the National Academy in 1848 may have been this or the previous artist of the same name. ¶ Am. Inst. Cat., 1848, 1849; Am. Inst. *Trans.,* 1848; NYBD 1849; Cowdrey, NAD.

MATHIEU, ANTOINE. Portrait painter at Salem (Mass.) in 1816. ¶ Belknap, *Artists and Craftsmen of Essex County,* 11.

MATHIEU, J. B. Portrait painter and hair-worker, Charleston (S.C.), 1806. ¶ Rutledge, *Artists in the Life of Charleston,* 209.

MATHIEU, PIERRE. French artist, born about 1804, working in New Orleans from 1859 to 1865. ¶ 8 Census (1860), La., VI, 790; Delgado-WPA cites New Orleans CD 1859–65.

MATHUS, see MATHIES.

MATLICK, WILLIAM. Primitive watercolor genre painter, New Jersey, about 1800. ¶ Lipman and Winchester, 176.

MATRAT, J. B. Professor of arts and sciences, New Orleans, 1843–44. ¶ New Orleans CD 1843–44.

MATTEI, MATTIS. Sculptor, Buffalo (N.Y.), 1855. ¶ Buffalo BD 1855.

MATTELL, ——. Portrait painter, Baltimore, 1807–08. ¶ Mayo; Lafferty.

MATTESON, TOMPKINS HARRISON (1813–1884). A.N.A. Historical, genre, and portrait painter, born May 9, 1813, at Peterboro (N.Y.). After studying briefly at the National Academy in NYC, Matteson married and established himself as a portrait painter in Sherburne and Auburn (N.Y.). In 1841 he moved to NYC, opened a studio, and made his reputation by paintings of patriotic subjects, such as "The Spirit of '76." In 1850 he returned to Sherburne where he spent the remainder of his life, dying there on February 2, 1884. Among his many pupils was ELIHU VEDDER. ¶ DAB; Clement and Hutton; NYBD 1844, 1846, 1848; Cowdrey, NAD; Cowdrey, AA & AAU; Swan, BA.

MATTHEWS, GEORGE H. Engraver, 22, a native of Massachusetts, at NYC in 1850. He was listed as "books" in the directories, 1856–63. ¶ 8 Census (1850), N.Y., XLIV, 1; NYCD 1856–63.

MATTHEWS, HENRY P. Artist, age 31, from Ohio, at NYC in June 1860. Perhaps a member of the family of ALFRED E. and WILLIAM T. MATHEWS. ¶ 8 Census (1860), N.Y., XLIII, 67.

MATTHEWS, JOHN L. L., see J. L. D. MATHIES (Mathus).

MATTHEWS, PETER B. or V. Artist, age 39, from New York, at Philadelphia in 1850. His wife and three children were born in Pennsylvania. Matthews was still in Philadelphia in 1852. ¶ 7 Census (1850), Pa., L, 347; Phila. CD (as Peter V. Matthews) 1850–52.

MATTHEWS, see also MATHEWS.

MATTHIAS, BENJAMIN. Lithographer, Philadelphia, 1856–60. Of WORLEY, BRACHER & MATTHIAS (1859–60). ¶ Phila. CD and BD 1856–60.

MAUCH, MAX. Sculptor who died at Chicago in 1864. ¶ Fielding.

MAUDE, JOHN. English gentleman who resided in the United States from 1797 to 1803. His journal of a visit to Niagara Falls in 1800, illustrated with engravings after his own sketches, was published in London in 1826. ¶ [John Maude], *Visit to the Falls of Niagara in 1800.*

MAUDSLEY, SUTCLIFFE. English designer and profilist who visited Nauvoo (Ill.) in 1844. He drew a profile of Joseph Smith and a view of the Mormon Temple; the latter was engraved and published in London in 1847. ¶ Josephson, "What Did the Prophet Joseph Smith Look Like?"; Arrington, *Nauvoo Temple,* Chap. 8.

MAULEVRIER, see COLBERT.

MAURER, LOUIS (1832–1932). Lithographer and painter. Maurer was born February 21, 1832, in Biebrich-on-the Rhine (Germany) and studied art at Mayence. In 1851 he emigrated with his parents to America, finding work first with T. W. STRONG and a few months later with CURRIER & IVES, with whom he remained for eight years. In 1860 or 1861 he went to work for Major & Knapp. From 1872 to 1884 he headed the commercial lithography firm of Maurer & Heppenheimer. After his retirement in 1884 Maurer devoted himself to a number of avocations, among which painting was his particular love. He lived in NYC until his death, at the age of 100 and a few months, on July 19, 1932. His son, Alfred H. Maurer (1868–1932), was a well-known painter. ¶ Peters, *Currier and Ives,* 63–70; N. Y. *Times,* July 20, 1932, obit.; Stokes, *Historic Prints,* pl. 143-a and -b;

Nevins and Weitenkampf; McCausland, *A. H. Maurer.*

MAURY, EDWARD. Landscape painter, active in NYC, about 1835–40. JASPER F. CROPSEY studied under him. ¶ *Panorama* (May 1946), 88; DAB, under Cropsey.

MAUVAIS, A. Portrait and miniature painter, Savannah (Ga.), 1776. ¶ Dunlap, *History* (1918), III, 317; represented at Essex Institute, Salem (Mass.).

MAVERICK, AARON HOWELL (1809–1846). Engraver, NYC, 1830; son of SAMUEL MAVERICK; born August 11, 1809, and died July 19, 1846. ¶ Stephens, *The Mavericks,* 183; *Minutes of the Common Council,* XIX (1830–31), 243.

MAVERICK, ANDREW (1782–1826). Copperplate engraver (?) and printer, born May 26, 1782. He was a son of PETER R. and brother of PETER and SAMUEL MAVERICK, and at one time a partner of CORNELIUS TIEBOUT. It is doubtful whether he ever did any engraving. He died in the spring of 1826. ¶ Stephens, *The Mavericks;* Ford, "Some Trade Cards and Broadsides," 11.

MAVERICK, ANDREW RUSHTON (*c.* 1809–*c.* 1835). Engraver and copperplate printer, NYC, 1829–30; son of ANDREW MAVERICK; husband of ANN (ANDERSON) MAVERICK. ¶ Stephens, *The Mavericks,* 73, 183.

MAVERICK, ANN (ANDERSON) (*c.* 1810–1863). Engraver; daughter of Dr. ALEXANDER ANDERSON, from whom she learned the art of engraving on wood. She married ANDREW R. MAVERICK about 1836 and a few years later, on his death, became a professional engraver. She followed the trade in NYC for almost thirty years, until her death in the fall of 1863. In 1842 Mrs. Maverick was married to one Joseph Riley of Boston, but the marriage was dissolved a few years later when she discovered that Mr. Riley had another wife, and she resumed the name of Maverick. ¶ Stephens, *The Mavericks;* NYCD 1848–58; Am. Inst. Cat., 1850, 1851.

MAVERICK, BREWSTER (*c.* 1830–1898). Lithographer and engraver, son of SAMUEL MAVERICK. He worked in NYC, at first as an engraver, but from about 1856 until his death as a lithographer. In 1866 he formed a partnership with Louis Stephan and in 1878 joined with J. G. Wissinger to establish the firm of Maverick & Wissinger, still in existence in NYC. ¶ Stephens, *The Mavericks;* NYCD 1846.

MAVERICK, CATHARINE (1811–1887). Lithographer, teacher of drawing and painting; daughter of PETER MAVERICK; born in Newark (N.J.) February 7, 1811. Trained in lithography by her father, she worked with her sister OCTAVIA as early as 1834. From 1847 to 1862 she taught drawing and painting at the Troy Female Seminary (now Emma Willard School). She died January 11, 1887. ¶ Stephens, *The Mavericks;* represented Newark Public Library.

MAVERICK, DURAND & COMPANY. Engravers, NYC and Newark (N.J.), 1817–20. On completion of his apprenticeship, A. B. DURAND was taken into partnership by PETER MAVERICK and went to NYC to open an office there. The following year CYRUS and possibly JOHN DURAND joined the partnership to make it a company. Disagreements between Maverick and A. B. Durand over the division of commissions led to the dissolution of the company in 1820. ¶ Stephens, *The Mavericks,* 51–55.

MAVERICK, EMILY (1803–1850). A.N.A. Engraver and lithographer. Born April 3, 1803, in NYC, Emily learned engraving from her father, PETER MAVERICK, and later took up lithography also. Before 1830 she and her sister MARIA ANN MAVERICK did a series of engravings for an edition of Shakespeare. In January 1830 Emily was married to Tobias A. Stoutenburgh of Johnstown (N.Y.). She died, presumably at Johnstown, in 1850. She was an Associate of the National Academy. ¶ Stephens, *The Mavericks;* Stauffer.

MAVERICK & HARRIS. Engravers, NYC, 1835; probably SAMUEL MAVERICK and JAMES HARRIS. ¶ NYCD 1835.

MAVERICK, MARIA ANN (1805–1832). A.N.A. Engraver and lithographer, daughter of PETER MAVERICK. Born in NYC on May 15, 1805, she worked in her father's shop and with her sister EMILY produced a series of illustrations for an edition of Shakespeare published in the mid-twenties. In 1828 she became the wife of John Franklin Townsend. She died in NYC a little over three years later, on January 12, 1832. She was an Associate of the National Academy. ¶ Stephens, *The Mavericks;* Stauffer.

MAVERICK, OCTAVIA (1814–1882). Lithographer, art teacher; daughter of PETER MAVERICK. Born in Newark (N.J.) on September 17, 1814, Octavia learned lithography in her father's shop and was working with her sister CATHARINE as early as 1834. In 1846 she married Edwin Spafard, a teacher, and she herself taught drawing and painting at the Packer Institute in Brooklyn from 1855 to 1863. She died June 23, 1882. ¶ Stephens, *The Mavericks;* represented Newark Public Library.

MAVERICK, PETER (1780–1831). N.A. Engraver and lithographer, son of PETER RUSHTON MAVERICK. Born in New York State on October 22, 1780, Peter studied engraving in his father's shop and published his first work at the age of nine. After his marriage in 1802 he established his own business in NYC where he lived until 1809. From 1809 to 1820 he lived and worked in Newark (N.J.), though maintaining an office in NYC most of the time. During this period he had ASHER B. DURAND as apprentice and, from 1817 to 1820, as partner. Returning to NYC in 1820 Maverick took up lithography and worked there until his death on June 7, 1831. Among his other pupils were ROBERT C. BRUEN and JOHN W. CASILEAR, as well as his own children: PETER, JR., CATHARINE, EMILY, MARIA ANN, and OCTAVIA MAVERICK. SAMUEL and ANDREW MAVERICK were his brothers, SAMUEL R., ANDREW R., and AARON HOWELL MAVERICK his nephews, and ANN (ANDERSON) MAVERICK his niece by marriage. He was a member of the National Academy from its founding. ¶ Stephens, *The Mavericks;* Stauffer; DAB; Cowdrey, NAD; Cowdrey, AA & AAU.

MAVERICK, PETER, JR. (1809–1845). Engraver and lithographer, son of PETER MAVERICK. Born October 26, 1809, in NYC or Newark (N.J.), the younger Peter learned engraving and lithography in his father's shops in NYC and Newark and practised in NYC from 1832 until his death on September 6, 1845. His only important work is the Reinagle-Maverick view of Wall Street, 1834. ¶ Stephens, *The Mavericks;* NYCD 1832–43; Stokes, *Icon.*, III, plate 3 and p. 615; Peters, *America on Stone.*

MAVERICK, PETER RUSHTON (1755–1811). Engraver, seal cutter, printer, and silversmith. Born April 11, 1755, in NYC, Peter Rushton Maverick was established in NYC as a silversmith by 1775. He was absent from the city during the British occupation, but by 1784 had returned to ply his trade as an engraver. During the next quarter-century he produced many illustrations for magazines and books, as well as the usual commercial work, bookplates, diplomas, etc. Among his pupils were WILLIAM DUNLAP, FRANCIS KEARNEY, and his own sons, PETER, ANDREW, and SAMUEL. The elder Maverick died in NYC on December 12, 1811. ¶ Stephens, *The Mavericks;* Stauffer; NYCD 1786–1811.

MAVERICK, SAMUEL (1789–1845). Engraver and copperplate printer, book auctioneer. Born June 5, 1789, in NYC, Samuel learned his trade as an engraver and printer under his father, PETER RUSHTON MAVERICK, though for a time he was an apprentice mariner. After his marriage in 1808 he established himself as an engraver in NYC, where he worked until his death, December 4, 1845. Before 1838 he also worked as an auctioneer. After his death his engraving business was carried on for several years by his widow. Samuel Maverick was the brother of ANDREW and PETER and the father of AARON H., BREWSTER, and SAMUEL R. MAVERICK. ¶ Stephens, *The Mavericks;* Stauffer; NYCD 1809–47; Roden, "Seventy Years of Book Auctions in New-York"; Am. Inst. Cat., 1844.

MAVERICK, SAMUEL R. (1812–1839). Engraver and copperplate printer, second son of SAMUEL MAVERICK. Born February 19, 1812, presumably in NYC, Samuel R. was working in NYC in 1833 but had moved to New Orleans by 1837. There he was employed by J. LOWE, engraver, and D. G. Johnson, printer. He died in New Orleans on August 24, 1839. ¶ Information courtesy S. D. Stephens; NYCD 1833; letter of Samuel R. to Samuel Maverick, March 26, 1838, MS in NYHS; New Orleans CD 1837.

MAVERICK, W. Wood carver, NYC; exhibited at the American Institute in 1846. ¶ Am. Inst. Cat., 1846.

MAXON, CHARLES. Engraver, NYC, 1833. ¶ Stauffer.

MAY, Miss CAROLINE. Landscape painter. Probably the daughter of the New York lawyer, Charles A. May, she exhibited at the National Academy in 1859. ¶ Cowdrey, NAD; NYCD 1859.

MAY, EDWARD. Artist, age 30, born in New York, living in NYC in September 1850. This is probably EDWARD HARRISON MAY, despite the discrepancies in date and place of birth. ¶ 7 Census (1850), N.Y., LII, 496.

MAY, EDWARD HARRISON (1824–1887).

A.N.A. Historical, genre, and portrait painter, born in 1824 at Croydon (England). He was brought to America at the age of ten, his father having been called to a pastorate in NYC. Trained at first for a career in engineering, he turned to painting in his early twenties and studied under DANIEL HUNTINGTON. He began exhibiting at the National Academy in 1844, at the American Art-Union in 1845, his early works being chiefly portraits. About 1851 he went to Paris to study in the salon of Couture and turned his talents to genre and historical painting, in which he was a great popular success. He made his home in Paris until his death, May 17, 1887. May was an Associate Member of the National Academy from 1850. ¶ DAB; Cowdrey, NAD; Cowdrey, AA & AAU; Rutledge, PA; Swan, BA; Rutledge, MHS; Washington Art Assoc. Cat., 1857, 1859; represented: Pennsylvania Academy, Metropolitan Museum of Art.

MAY, GEORGE W. Engraver, NYC, 1837–60. He was a member of the following firms: BALE & SMITH (1843–48), BALE & MAY (1848–51), and MAY & GLAUBRECHT (1852–60). ¶ NYCD 1837–60.

MAY & GLAUBRECHT. Engravers and die sinkers, NYC, 1852–60; GEORGE W. MAY and GEORGE J. GLAUBRECHT. The firm succeeded BALE & MAY. ¶ NYCD 1852–60.

MAY, Mrs. MARIA B. Portrait and miniature painter working in Baltimore between 1847 and 1857. ¶ Lafferty.

MAY, MICHAEL. Irish-born artist, age 18, living in Boston with his father, a mason, in July 1860. ¶ 8 Census (1860), Mass., XXVII, 965.

MAY, WILLIAM H. Philadelphia artist who exhibited two landscapes at the Artists' Fund Society in 1844. ¶ Rutledge, PA.

MAYALL, ELIZA MCLELLAN (or McClellan). Portrait painter, born June 22, 1822. She painted a portrait of her grandfather, Joseph Hicks (1747–1844) of North Yarmouth (Me.), when he was past his ninetieth year. ¶ Maine Historical Society, Catalogue; WPA (Mass.), *Portraits Found in Maine;* Lipman and Winchester, 176.

MAYBE, Mrs. EMMELINE (ANDERSON). Artist, daughter of ALEXANDER ANDERSON and sister of ANN (ANDERSON) MAVERICK. Mrs. Maybe is said to have been a skilled draftsman who did professional work, such as designing ball cards for the New York Caledonian Society. She was born before 1812. ¶ Lossing, *Memorial of Alexander Anderson,* 88, 100.

MAYBERRY, JAMES. Lithographer, born in Pennsylvania about 1841, working in Philadelphia in 1860. His brothers John and David were printers. They lived with their mother, Sarah Mayberry. ¶ 8 Census (1860), Pa., LI, 1084.

MAYCALL, JOHN. Sculptor, born in Massachusetts about 1842, living in Boston with his parents in 1860. ¶ 8 Census (1860), Mass., XXVIII, 261.

MAYER, C. W. Artist, Philadelphia, 1857. ¶ Phila. CD 1857.

MAYER, CONSTANT (1829–1911). A.N.A. Genre and portrait painter, born October 3, 1829, at Besançon (France). Mayer studied at the Ecole des Beaux Arts in Paris and worked in the French capital until 1857 when he emigrated to America. Settling in NYC, he became a citizen of the United States and an Associate of the National Academy. His work was popular on both sides of the Atlantic. He revisited France several times and in 1895 returned to spend his last years in Paris, where he died on May 12, 1911. ¶ DAB; Thieme-Becker; Bénézit; Rutledge, PA; Cowdrey, NAD.

MAYER or MEYER, FERDINAND. Lithographer, born in Germany about 1817. He worked in NYC from 1845 until about 1877. He was associated with NAGEL & MAYER (1846), MAYER & KORFF (1849–51), and Ferdinand Mayer & Sons (1854–*c.* 1877). He was the lithographer of some important mid-century views of NYC. ¶ 7 Census (1850), N.Y., XLIV, 194; NYCD 1845–60+; NYBD 1846–52; Peters, *America on Stone.*

MAYER, FRANCIS BLACKWELL (1827–1899). Historical, genre, ethnological, and portrait painter, born December 27, 1827, at Baltimore. A student of ALFRED J. MILLER in Baltimore and of Gleyre and Brion in Paris, Mayer was best known in his own day as a painter of Colonial subjects but today he is remembered as a painter of the Plains Indians and small genre pieces and landscapes. He visited Minnesota in 1851 and made many sketches, some of which were reproduced in his *With Pen and Pencil on the Frontier.* From 1864 to 1870 he was in Paris. The rest of his career was spent chiefly in Baltimore and Annapolis, where he died July 28, 1899. ¶ Mayer, *With Pen and Pencil on the Frontier;* Mayer, *Drawings and Paintings . . .* (1872); Pleasants, *250 Years of Painting in Maryland;* Clement and Hutton; CAB; Rutledge, PA; Rutledge, MHS; represented at Corcoran Gallery, Peabody Institute, and Newberry Library.

MAYER, JOSEPH. Irish lithographer, age 33, living in Boston in August 1850. His wife was Irish, their three oldest children (ages 16 to 2) were born in England, and the youngest (6 months) in Massachusetts. ¶ 7 Census (1850), Mass., XXV, 356.

MAYER, JULIUS. Lithographer, Boston, 1857–72. He was with PRANG & MAYER (1857–60), Mayer & Stetfield (1861–62), and J. Mayer & Co. (1863–72). His work includes views around Boston and Portland (Me.). ¶ Peters, *America on Stone;* Boston CD 1857–60+.

MAYER & KORFF. Lithographers, NYC, 1849–51; FERDINAND MAYER and HERMAN KORFF. They exhibited at the American Institute in 1849. ¶ Peters, *America on Stone;* NYCD and BD 1851; Am. Inst. Cat., 1849.

MAYERS, ANDREW. Limner, coach and sign painter working in Philadelphia between 1802 and 1820. ¶ Brown and Brown.

MAYHEW, WILLIAM C. Cameo-cutter of Buffalo (N.Y.) who exhibited at the American Institute in 1844. ¶ Am. Inst. Cat., 1844.

MAYO, J. E. An oil portrait by this artist of David Lawrence Morrill (1772–1849) is located in the State House, Concord (N.H.). ¶ WPA (Mass.), *Portraits Found in N.H.,* 15.

MAYR, CHRISTIAN (*c.* 1805–1851). N.A. Portrait and genre painter, designer, daguerreotypist. A native of Germany, Mayr appeared in NYC about 1834, when he first exhibited at the National Academy. He went to Boston in 1839 and the following year to Charleston (S.C.) where he made his headquarters until 1843. In 1844 he visited New Orleans and by 1845 he had returned to NYC where he made his home on Lispenard Street until his death, October 19, 1851. He was an Associate of the National Academy from 1836 to 1849 and was elected an Academician in 1849. ¶ 7 Census (1850), N.Y., XLIII, 16; Cowdrey, NAD; Cowdrey, AA & AAU; Swan, BA; Rutledge, *Artists in the Life of Charleston;* Delgado-WPA cites New Orleans *Commercial Bulletin,* Jan. 24, 1844; membership book of the Century Club (citation courtesy Mary Bartlett Cowdrey).

MAZARIN, JOHN. French engraver, age 38, living in NYC in August 1850. ¶ 7 Census (1850), N.Y., LI, 91.

MAZŸCK, ISAAC. Amateur miniaturist and topographical artist. A son-in-law of ELIZABETH LE SERRURIER, Mazÿck came to South Carolina from France with a group of Huguenots prior to 1685. His miniature self-portrait and some sketches and drawings of French fortifications have been preserved. ¶ Rutledge, *Artists in the Life of Charleston;* Barker, *American Painting,* 66.

MAZZARA, see MEZZERA.

MC, see MAC.

MEAD, HENRY E. Artist, born in Massachusetts about 1832, living in a Philadelphia hotel in July 1860. CHARLES WALLEN and JAMES G. BOILEAU were at the same hotel. ¶ 8 Census (1860), Pa., LII, 696.

MEAD, ELINOR GERTRUDE (1837–1910). Amateur artist. She was born in Brattleboro (Vt.) May 1, 1837, and was a sister of LARKIN G. MEAD, the sculptor, and William Rutherford Mead, the architect. In 1862 she married William Dean Howells, the writer. Mrs. Howells died May 6, 1910. ¶ Cabot, *Annals of Brattleboro,* I, 543; Howells, *Life in Letters of William Dean Howells,* I, 10, II, 284.

MEAD, LARKIN GOLDSMITH (1835–1910). Sculptor, born January 3, 1835, at Chesterfield (N.H.). Mead grew up in Brattleboro (Vt.) and studied sculpture under HENRY KIRKE BROWN from 1853 to 1855. After working in Brattleboro for a few years and serving for a short time as an artist-correspondent for *Harper's Weekly* in 1861, he left for Italy in 1862, accompanying his sister ELINOR to Paris where she was married to the novelist William Dean Howells. The young sculptor settled in Florence, married an Italian, and spent most of his life in Italy. On one of his numerous visits to the United States he was awarded a commission to design the Lincoln Memorial at Springfield (Ill.). He also designed sculptural decorations for the Agricultural Building at the Columbian Exposition, of which his younger brother, William Rutherford Mead (of McKim, Mead & White) was one of the architects. Died in Florence on October 15, 1910. ¶ DAB; Sartain, *Reminiscences,* 237–40; CAB; Fairman, *Art and Artists of the Capitol;* Thieme-Becker.

MEADE, FRANCIS. Portrait painter, born in Pennsylvania about 1814. He was active in Philadelphia between 1837 and 1860 and exhibited at both the Artists' Fund Society and the Pennsylvania Academy. ¶ 8 Census (1860), Pa., LXII, 109; Phila. CD 1837–60; Rutledge, PA.

MEADOWS, CHRISTIAN. Engraver, born in England about 1814. He came to America during the thirties, was married in Boston in 1839, and worked there until 1849. While in the employ of the Boston printer and engraver WILLIAM W. WILSON, Meadows became involved in a counterfeiting plot, was caught and convicted, and sentenced to prison at Windsor (Vt.). During his three years in prison, he was employed to engrave a view of Dartmouth College and also a vignette for the diploma of the New Hampshire State Society for the Advancement of Agriculture, Manufactures, Science and the Arts. In recognition of his ability and good conduct, Meadows was pardoned and released from prison on Independence Day, 1853. He was set up in business in Windsor and worked there as an engraver at least until 1859. At the time of his arrest for counterfeiting Meadows was considered one of the best engravers in New England. ¶ Ormsbee, "Christian Meadows, Engraver and Counterfeiter," with 10 repros.; Stauffer; Boston CD 1841–49; 7 Census (1850), Vt., III, 471.

MEADOWS, R. M. Stipple engraver of portraits of Edward Jenner, M.D. (1817) and Bishop Francis Asbury, both published in America. Stauffer expresses uncertainty whether they were engraved in America. It seems probable that they are the work of Robert Mitchell Meadows, English stipple engraver who was active during the late 18th and early 19th century. He died before 1812 and is not known to have worked in America. ¶ Stauffer; Redgrave; Thieme-Becker.

MEANCE, Miss ——. Exhibited a portrait of a young lady, stated to be her first attempt at portraiture, at the Society of Artists, Philadelphia, in 1811. ¶ Rutledge, PA.

MEANCE, PETER J. or I. French miniaturist working in NYC from 1793 to 1798. He also operated a drawing and painting academy. He may have visited Albany in 1796. *Cf.* PETER MANIC of Philadelphia, 1809–10. ¶ Gottesman, II, 8–9; NYCD 1794–98 (McKay); Prime, II, 18.

MEARES, JOHN (1756?–1809). English traveler, author, amateur artist. He visited the northwestern coast of the present United States in 1788–89 and made a number of topographical sketches upon which were based illustrations in his *Voyages.* ¶ Rasmussen, "Art and Artists in Oregon," cited by David C. Duniway; DNB; Meares, *Voyages Made in the Years 1788 and 1789, from China to the Northwest Coast of America* (London, 1790).

MEARS, CATHARINE (Mrs. Charles T.). Teacher of drawing and painting, NYC, 1835–77. At the Apollo Association in 1839 were exhibited "specimens of flower painting" and "specimen drawing in black lead," both "as taught by Mrs. Mears." She was listed as an artist and artist-teacher until the forties when she apparently opened a boarding and day school. Mrs. Mears' school on Madison Avenue was still flourishing when she retired or died about 1877 and it continued under the direction of Louisa Mears, probably her daughter. ¶ NYCD 1835–77; Cowdrey, AA & AAU.

MECHAU, ——. Fresco, ornamental, and portrait painter working with —— FARRAS at Richmond (Va.) in December 1847. ¶ *Richmond Portraits,* 241.

MECHESI, ——. Panorama painter, assistant to DELAMANO in the painting of the latter's "grand moving picture of the Crystal Palace," first shown in NYC in December 1851. ¶ N. Y. *Herald,* Dec. 2, 1851 (citation courtesy J. E. Arrington).

MECKEL, MAX. German lithographer, age 34, living in NYC in July 1850. ¶ 7 Census (1850), N.Y., XLVIII, 58.

MECORD, HENRY E. Swiss engraver, age 31, living in Philadelphia in July 1860. His wife was a native of Belgium, while their daughter Emilie was born in New York about 1852 and son Emile was born in Pennsylvania about 1857. Mecord's personal property was valued at $2,000. ¶ 8 Census (1860), Pa., XLIX, 341.

MEDAIRY, ALEXANDER R. Engraver, Baltimore, 1849–58. ¶ Baltimore CD 1849–58.

MEDAIRY & BANNERMAN. Engravers, Baltimore, 1827–31; JOHN MEDAIRY and WILLIAM BANNERMAN. ¶ Baltimore CD 1827–31; Stauffer.

MEDAIRY, CHARLES E. Engraver, Baltimore, 1850. Born in Maryland about 1834, he was the son of JOHN MEDAIRY and presumably was employed in his father's shop. ¶ 7 Census (1850), Md., VI, 129.

MEDAIRY, JOHN. Engraver, born in Maryland about 1798, active in Baltimore between 1827 and 1857. He worked with WILLIAM W. BANNERMAN in 1827–31. In 1850 his 16-year-old son CHARLES E. MEDAIRY was also listed as an engraver. ¶ 7 Census (1850), Md., VI, 129; Baltimore CD 1827–57.

MEDICI, COSMO. Portrait painter working in Virginia in 1772. Possibly the Cosmo Medici who served as a North Carolina cavalry officer in the Revolution, but more probably COSMO ALEXANDER, who painted in the South in 1770 or 1771. ¶ *Virginia Historical Portraiture,* 422; Flexner, *Gilbert Stuart,* 18.

MEEHAN, JOSEPH. Italian sculptor, age 26, living in NYC in August 1850. ¶ 7 Census (1850), N.Y., XLVIII, 246.

MEEKER, JOSEPH RUSLING (1827–?). Portrait and landscape painter, born April 21, 1827, at Newark (N.J.). He studied at the National Academy in NYC in 1845–46, painted for several years at Buffalo (N.Y.) and at Louisville (Ky.) from 1852–59. He then settled in St. Louis where he was still living in the seventies. During the Civil War he served with the Federal forces in the South. He was particularly noted for his Louisiana landscapes. ¶ *National Cyclopedia of American Biography,* XII, 52; CAB; NYBD 1844, 1846; Louisville CD 1859; Cowdrey, AA & AAU; Born, *American Landscape Painting,* fig. 49; *American Heritage* (Autumn 1950), 54.

MEEKS, J. R. Landscape painter who exhibited at the Pennsylvania Academy in 1862. This might be JOSEPH RUSLING MEEKER. ¶ Rutledge, PA.

MEER, JOHN, SR. Japanner, painter on glass and enamel, engraver on stone. Meer was active in Philadelphia as early as 1795 when he exhibited at the Columbianum. He had a varied career; in addition to his work as an artist and engraver he served as keeper of weights and measures for the city in 1817–18, was an inventor and manufacturer of razor strops and "Columbia hones," and operated a tavern. He was one of the earliest experimenters in engraving on stone (1824). His name appears in the directory for the last time in 1830 and in that year he exhibited engravings for the last time at the Pennsylvania Academy. His widow is listed in 1835. JOHN MEER, JR., was presumably his son. ¶ Columbianum Cat., 1795; Phila. CD 1810–30; Society of Artists Cat., 1812–13; Penna. Acad. Cat., 1817, 1829–30; Eckhardt, "Early Lithography in Philadelphia."

MEER, JOHN, JR. Artist, Philadelphia, 1819–25; presumably son of the above. ¶ Phila. CD 1819–25.

MEERBACH, see MEHRBACH.

MEFFERT, J. B. Lithographer, active between 1852 and 1861. He did illustrations for Perry's *Expedition to Japan* and other books. ¶ Perry, *Expedition to Japan;* Hamilton, 393.

MEGAREY, JOHN or HENRY J. (1818–1845). A.N.A. Portrait and landscape painter. He was at New Orleans in April 1841 to take a view of the city for his projected "Views of the Cities of the United States," which does not appear to have been published. From 1841 to 1845 he resided in NYC and exhibited portraits at the National Academy of which he was elected an Associate in 1844. He died in NYC on May 14, 1845. ¶ Cowdrey, NAD; Cummings, *Historic Annals,* 186; Delgado-WPA cites *Picayune,* April 14, 1841.

MEHRBACH or MEERBACH, PHILIP. Engraver from Hanover (Germany), age 28, at NYC in July 1860. This might be Philip Mehrboth, jeweller, in the 1860 directory. ¶ 8 Census (1860), N.Y., XLIV, 370; NYCD 1860.

MEIGNELLE, JAMES. Banknote engraver, Philadelphia, 1854–60. ¶ Phila. CD 1854–56, 1860.

MEINELL, WILLIAM. Artist, print cutter, drawer, Philadelphia, 1811–18. ¶ Brown and Brown.

MEINUNG, A. Landscape painter who exhibited Blue Ridge Mountains views at the Pennsylvania Academy in 1860. ¶ Rutledge, PA.

MEISEL, AUGUSTUS. Lithographer, Boston, 1856–71. From 1857 to 1861 he was associated with his brother BERTHOLD in the firm of MEISEL BROTHERS. ¶ Peters, *America on Stone;* Boston CD 1856–60+.

MEISEL, BERTHOLD. Lithographer, Boston, 1856–61. From 1857 to 1861 he was with the firm of MEISEL BROTHERS. In 1856 he was listed as a brass finisher. ¶ Peters, *America on Stone;* Boston CD 1856–61.

MEISEL BROTHERS. Lithographers of technical prints, Boston, 1857–61; AUGUSTUS and BERTHOLD MEISEL. ¶ Peters, *America on Stone;* Boston CD 1857–60.

MEISTER, FRED. Prussian artist, age 60, at Baltimore in 1860. He was still there in 1864. ¶ 8 Census (1860), Md., IV, 428; Baltimore CD 1864.

MELBERT, JAMES, see JACQUES MILBERT.

MELBOURNE, C., see C. MILBOURNE.

MELCHERS, JULIUS THEODORE (1830–1903). Wood carver and sculptor, born in Soest (Prussia). Emigrating to America after the 1848 Revolution, Melchers settled in 1855 at Detroit. He did some stone work and more wood carving, but is chiefly noted as the teacher of many Detroit artists of the post-Civil War period, among them his more famous son, Gari Melchers (1860–1932). ¶ Burroughs, "Painting and Sculpture in Michigan," 404; WPA Guide, *Michigan,* 138.

MELLEN, F. Genre painter of Portland (Me.), exhibited "The Organist" at the Boston Athenaeum in 1833. ¶ Swan, BA; BA Cat., 1833.

MELLIS, Mr. ——. Artist, age 33, born in Michigan, living in Detroit in July 1860 with ISAAC MELLIS. ¶ 8 Census (1860), Mich., XX, 117.

MELLIS, ISAAC. Artist, age 35, born in Michigan, living in Detroit in July 1860 with —— MELLIS, apparently a younger brother. Isaac owned realty valued at $5,000 and personalty of $5,000 value. ¶ 8 Census (1860), Mich., XX, 117.

MELLOR, GEORGE. Engraver, Lowell (Mass.), 1834. ¶ Belknap, *Artists and Craftsmen of Essex County,* 4.

MELOGAN, ALEXANDER. Lithographer, NYC, 1850. ¶ NYBD 1850.

MELROSE, ANDREW [W.] (1836–1901). Landscape painter. His studio was at West Hoboken and Guttenberg (N.J.) during the 1870's and 1880's, but his subjects include views in North Carolina, the Hudson Valley, the Berkshire Hills, New York City, Cornwall (England), Lake Killarney (Ireland), and the Tyrolese Alps. He died February 23, 1901, at West New York (N.J.). ¶ N. Y. *Herald,* Feb. 26, 1901, obit.; information courtesy Mrs. Victor Spark who cites a letter in the NYPL from Mr. Watson, Melrose's son-in-law, dated Feb. 11, 1935; NAD Cats., 1872, 1875, 1879–83; information courtesy Chicago Art Institute; represented at NYHS, Allen Memorial Art Museum (Oberlin College), collection of Mr. Norton Asner (Baltimore); repro., NYHS *Quarterly Bulletin* (April 1941), 51.

MELROSE, KENNETH. English engraver, 17, who was an inmate of the NYC Penitentiary in July 1860, serving a term for grand larceny. ¶ 8 Census (1860), N.Y., LXI, 182.

MEMIN, see SAINT MEMIN.

MENCHILLI, GEORGE G. Plaster bust maker from Italy, age 50, living at Louisville (Ky.) in 1850. His sons—Achille (24) and Francisco (19), and daughter Nicodema (16) were employed in his shop. ¶ 7 Census (1850), Ky., XI, 839.

MENDEL, EDWARD. Engraver and lithographer at Chicago, 1854–58. ¶ Chicago BD 1854–56, 1858.

MENDENHALL, J. Z. Portrait painter known only for his portrait of the nonagenarian Revolutionary veteran William Harrington, painted in 1850. There was a J. B. Mendenhall at Indianapolis in 1871–72. ¶ Picture caption by Lincoln Kirstein, *Magazine of Art* (April 1944), 146; Peat, *Pioneer Painters of Indiana,* 235.

MENG, JOHN. Portrait painter, born in 1734 at Germantown (Pa.), died about 1754 in the West Indies. His self-portrait is at the Historical Society of Pennsylvania. ¶ Sawitzky, *Hist. Soc. of Penna. Catalogue;* Fielding; Thieme-Becker.

MENGER, EDWARD. Artist, born in New York about 1832, working there in 1860. ¶ 8 Census (1860), N.Y., XLIII, 478.

MENKER, SAMUEL. German engraver, born about 1820, working in NYC from about 1853. ¶ 8 Census (1860), N.Y., XLII, 369.

MENZEL, ADOLPHUS. Lithographer of Cincinnati, 1840–59. He was associated with KLAUPRECH & MENZEL (1840–53) and Menzel & Company (1856–59). His relationship to the other Menzels here listed is not known. ¶ Cincinnati CD 1840–59.

MENZEL, CHARLES. German lithographer, born about 1822 and working in Cincinnati from 1842 to 1850. Possibly a brother of ADOLPHUS MENZEL. ¶ 7 Census (1850), Ohio, XX, 337; Cincinnati CD 1842–44.

MENZEL, GUSTAVUS A. Lithographer of Cincinnati, 1859 and after, in partnership with HERMAN G. MENZEL. ¶ Cist, *Cincinnati in 1859,* repro. opp. 238; Cincinnati CD 1860 and after.

MENZEL, HERMAN G. Lithographer of Cincinnati, 1859 and after, in partnership with GUSTAVUS A. MENZEL. ¶ Cincinnati CD 1860; Cist, *Cincinnati in 1859,* opp. 238.

MENZEL, WILLIAM. Lithographer of NYC, 1854. ¶ NYBD 1854.

MEORES, GEORGE. Italian artist, age 34, living in Philadelphia in August 1850. ¶ 7 Census (1850), Pa., L, 627.

MERCER, WILLIAM (1773–1850). Portrait, miniature, and historical painter. William, deaf-mute son of General Hugh Mercer of Fredericksburg (Va.), studied painting under CHARLES WILLSON PEALE in Philadelphia from 1783 to 1786 and pursued his profession for many years in Virginia. He is best known for his painting of the Battle of Princeton, owned by the Historical Society of Pennsylvania. ¶ Bolton, *Miniature Painters;* Sellers, *Charles Willson Peale,* I, 224, 248; *American Processional,* 236–37, repro. 73; Flexner, *The Light of Distant Skies.*

MERCHANT, BIDDLE. Engraver and painter of Albany (N.Y.), 1829–60 and after. ¶ Albany CD 1829, 1833–35, 1837–38, 1840–48, 1850–60 and after.

MERCHANT, GEORGE W. Engraver and printer, painter, of Albany (N.Y.), 1826–43. ¶ Albany CD 1826–27, 1831, 1835, 1837–38, 1841–43; Dunlap, *History* (1918), III, 316 [as Marchant].

MERINE, A. Portrait painter at South Bend (Ind.) in December 1841. *Cf.* J. C. MERINE and J. A. MOREIN. ¶ Peat, *Pioneer Painters of Indiana,* 139–40.

MERINE, J. C. Portrait painter active in Kentucky in 1848–49 and 1871. ¶ Information courtesy Mrs. W. H. Whitley, Paris (Ky.). *Cf.* A. MERINE and J. A. MOREIN.

MERINSKY, S. Lithographer at NYC, 1859. ¶ NYBD 1859.

MERKLE, AUGUSTUS. German lithographer, age 22, at NYC in August 1850. ¶ 7 Census (1850), N.Y., XLIV, 194.

MERLINI, G. Portrait carver, Philadelphia, 1813. ¶ Scharf and Westcott, *History of Philadelphia,* II, 1067.

MERMILLIOD, CHARLES. General engraver at Philadelphia in 1860. ¶ Phila. CD 1860.

MERRELL, B. S. Lithographer at Utica (N.Y.) in 1860. ¶ Rome BD 1860.

MERRELL, J. M. Artist, born in New York State about 1833, living in Dalles, Wasco County (Oregon) in 1860. ¶ 8 Census (1860), Oregon, citation courtesy David C. Duniway, Oregon State Archivist.

MERRETT, SUSAN. Watercolor painter of genre subjects, active in the 1840's at South Weymouth (Mass.). ¶ *Antiques* (July 1943), 27, repro.; Lipman and Winchester, 177; Born, *American Landscape Painting,* fig. 82.

MERRIAM, ANN PAGE. Watercolor painter active about 1820. Erroneously as Merridan. ¶ Information courtesy Mrs. Jean Lipman, correcting Lipman and Winchester, 177.

MERRIDAN, ANN PAGE, see ANN PAGE MERRIAM.

MERRIKEN, FRANCIS M. Engraver at Baltimore, 1858–60. ¶ Baltimore CD 1858–60.

MERRILL, ALONZO. French artist, age 30, at NYC in August 1850. ¶ 7 Census (1850), N.Y., XLVII, 597.

MERRILL, F. C. Portrait painter at Warren (Ohio) in 1853. ¶ Ohio BD 1853.

MERRILL, GARDNER B. Wood engraver at Lowell (Mass.), 1856–60. ¶ New England BD 1856, 1860.

MERRILL, JOHN P. Portrait and genre painter of Philadelphia, active from 1836 to 1847. He exhibited at the Artists' Fund Society, the Pennsylvania Academy, and the Apollo Association. ¶ Rutledge, PA; Cowdrey, AA & AAU.

MERRILL, M. W. Portrait and landscape painter of Pittsfield (Mass.), 1860. ¶ New England BD 1860.

MERRILL, SARAH. Watercolor painter of memorial pieces, active about 1815. ¶ Lipman and Winchester, 177.

MERRITT, E. Painter of a primitive watercolor of a ship, about 1850. ¶ Lipman and Winchester, 177.

MERVING, CHRISTOPHER. German-born artist, age 27, at New Orleans in August 1850. ¶ 7 Census (1850), La., V, 82.

MESIER, EDWARD S. Lithographer of NYC, 1832–51, possibly a brother of PETER MESIER. Edward did work for the *Cabinet of Natural History and American Rural Sports* in 1832 and with Peter produced a great many sheet music covers as well as other prints. ¶ Peters, *America on Stone;* Doughty, "Thomas Doughty," 40.

MESIER, PETER. Lithographer, NYC, 1835–36. Before and after these years he was listed as a bookseller and stationer at the same address as EDWARD S. MESIER. ¶ Peters, *America on Stone.*

MESSO, DOMINICK. French sculptor, age 33, at Philadelphia in August 1860. ¶ 8 Census (1860), Pa., LII, 575.

METCALF, ELIAB (1785–1834). Portrait and miniature painter, silhouette cutter. Born February 5, 1785, at Franklin (Mass.), Metcalf visited Guadeloupe in 1807–08 and Halifax (N.S.) in 1810. He then came to NYC to study painting and began to work there professionally several years later. In 1819 he went to New Orleans for his health and during the next few years he divided his time between that city and New York. During this period he was an exhibitor at the American Academy. About 1824 he went to Cuba and he made his home in Havana for the rest of his life. He died in NYC on January 15, 1834, during one of his annual visits to the city. ¶ Bolton, *Miniature Painters;* Piers, "Artists in Nova Scotia"; NYCD 1814–20; Cowdrey, AA & AAU; Delgado-WPA cites New Orleans *Gazette,* Jan. 27, 1820, June 13, 1820, and Jan. 2, 1821, and CD 1822; Cowdrey, NAD; Kelby, *Notes on American Artists,* 52; N. Y. *Evening Post,* May 31, 1814, p. 3; represented at NYHS.

METCALF, JOHN. Artist, age 24, born in Pennsylvania, living in NYC in July 1860. ¶ 8 Census (1860), N.Y., XLIII, 465.

METFORD, SAMUEL (1810–1896). Profile cutter. A native of Glastonbury (Somerset), Metford emigrated to America as a young man, worked in NYC and Charleston (S.C.) in the early 1840's, and returned to England in 1844. Except for a second visit to America (1865–67), he spent the rest of his life in England and died at Weston-super-Mare in 1896. ¶ *Connoisseur,* Vol. 74 (1926), p. 94, and Vol. 75 (1926), p. 44; Carrick, *Shades of Our Ancestors,* 111–13; Jackson, *Silhouette,* 127; Rutledge, *Artists in the Life of Charleston.*

METZ, A. F. Portrait painter, age 45, from Saxony, living in NYC in June 1860. His wife was also from Germany, but their two children, ages 5 and 2, were born in New York. ¶ 8 Census (1860), N.Y., XLIV, 305.

MEUCCI, ANTHONY. Portrait, miniature, and figure painter. Meucci and his wife NINA came to America from Rome in 1818. After some time in New Orleans they moved to Charleston and there opened an academy for drawing and painting (1821–22). By 1823 they were in NYC, in 1825 at Salem (Mass.), and in 1826 again in NYC. They are last heard of at New Orleans during the winter of 1826–27, Meucci at that time being employed in painting scenery for the New Orleans Theatre. ¶ Delgado-WPA cites *La. Courier,* Aug. 17 and Nov. 13, 1818, and New Orleans *Advertiser,* Nov. 13, 1826, and Feb. 2, 1827; Rutledge, *Artists in the Life of Charleston;* NYCD 1823–24, 1826; Belknap, *Artists and Craftsmen of Essex County,* 11; Charleston CD 1822; Cowdrey, AA & AAU; *Art in America,* April 1928, 131 (repro.); represented at La. State Museum, Essex Institute, and NYHS.

MEUCCI, NINA (Mrs. Anthony). Portrait and miniature painter. A native of Spain, she accompanied her husband to America in 1818 and worked with him in New Orleans, Charleston, NYC, and Salem (Mass.) until 1827, when both disappear from sight. While in Charleston she and ANTHONY opened an academy of drawing and painting. ¶ For sources, see under ANTHONY MEUCCI.

MEWSE, THOMAS. English miniaturist working in Baltimore in 1784. ¶ Prime, I, 5–6.

MEYER, CHRISTIAN (1838–1907). Landscape painter who came from Germany to America as a young man and was active as an artist after 1880. He died in Brooklyn on April 15, 1907. ¶ *Art Annual,* VI, obit.; Fielding.

MEYER, ELIZABETH. Primitive watercolorist of Pennsylvania about 1830. ¶ Lipman and Winchester, 177.

MEYER, FERDINAND, see FERDINAND MAYER.

MEYER, FRITZ. Lithographer of some views of West Point about 1857. This may be the same as FERDINAND MAYER (Meyer). ¶ Stokes, *Historic Prints,* pl. 94-b.

MEYER, GOTTLIEB. Lithographer, age 24, from Württemberg, living in Philadelphia in 1860 with his wife and child, the latter born in Pennsylvania the previous year. ¶ 8 Census (1860), Pa., LV, 629.

MEYER, H. E., see H. ED. MYER.

MEYER, HENRY HOPPNER (*c.* 1782–1847). Engraver, portrait painter, and draftsman. A nephew of the noted English painter John Hoppner, he was born in England and studied under the engraver Bartolozzi. He exhibited at the Royal Academy from 1821 to 1833 and also at the Society of British Artists, of which he was a founder and a president (1828–29). Meyer turned from engraving to painting and drawing portraits and, according to Bolton, came to America in 1830. As Hoppner Meyer he exhibited at the Artists' Fund Society in Philadelphia (1835–37, 1840) and the Pennsylvania Academy (1847). He returned to England probably in the early 1840's and died in London on May 28, 1847. ¶ DNB; Bolton, *Miniature Painters;* Redgrave, *Dictionary of Artists of the English School;* Rutledge, PA; Thieme-Becker.

MEYER, HOPPNER, see HENRY HOPPNER MEYER.

MEYER or MEYHER, JOHN. Maker or seller of statuary, NYC, 1811–16. ¶ NYCD 1811–12, 1815–16.

MEYER, JOSEPH. Engraver, NYC, 1859. ¶ NYBD 1859.

MEYER & KORFF, see MAYER & KORFF.

MEYER, WILLIAM H., see WILLIAM H. MEYERS.

MEYER, see also MAYER and MYER.

MEYERS or MYERS, WILLIAM H. Amateur watercolorist. A gunner on the U. S. sloop-of-war *Dale,* Meyers kept a sketchbook, now owned by the Franklin D. Roosevelt Library, in which he recorded in watercolors scenes of the American conquest of California in 1847. Two years later THOMAS B. GLESSING of Philadelphia painted a panorama of a voyage to California based on sketches taken by Meyers during sixteen years in the Pacific and in California. ¶ *American Processional,* 26–27, 243; Van Nostrand and Coulter, *California Pictorial,* 51; Taft, *Artists and Illustrators of the Old West,* 253; N. Y. *Herald,* Sept. 12, 1849, and March 5, 1850 (citations courtesy J. E. Arrington).

MEYERS, see also MYERS.

MEYERSTEIN or MOYERSTEIN, BENJAMIN. Portrait painter working in NYC in the 1850's. ¶ NYBD 1854 as Moyerstein; NYCD and BD 1858 as Meyerstein.

MEYHER, JOHN, see JOHN MEYER.

MEYNIAC, Mrs. M. R. Proprietress of an academy in Charleston (S.C.) in 1822–23. One of her specialties was painting on velvet. In 1823 she announced that she was closing her school and going abroad for her health, but expected to return. ¶ Rutledge, *Artists in the Life of Charleston.*

MEYR, see MAYR.

MEYRE, ——. Miniature painter working near Trenton (N.J.) in 1768. He did a portrait of Joseph Reed. ¶ Esther De Berdt to Joseph Reed, Feb. 15, 1768, Reed Papers, NYHS.

MEYRICK, RICHARD. Engraver working in Philadelphia in 1729. ¶ Stauffer; Brown and Brown; Weiss, "The Growth of the Graphic Arts in Philadelphia, 1663–1820," 78.

MEZARRA or MAZZARA or MEZZERA, FRANCIS. Portrait painter who exhibited at the American Academy in 1817 and the same year was convicted of libel for painting asses ears on the portrait of a gentleman who had rejected the likeness. *Cf.* M. MEZZERA. ¶ Cowdrey, AA & AAU; Kelby, *Notes on American Artists,* 52.

MEZZARA, ANGELICA (?–1868). Pastel miniaturist. Born in Paris, she began her career there about 1833. She was apparently in Philadelphia in 1844 when she exhibited at the Artists' Fund Society. She died in Paris in September 1868. ¶ Thieme-Becker; Rutledge, PA.

MEZZERA, M. Portrait painter at Philadelphia in 1823, exhibitor at the Pennsylvania Academy. *Cf.* FRANCIS MEZARRA. ¶ Rutledge, PA.

MEZZERER, PETER. French artist, age 35, living in San Francisco in June 1860. ¶ 8 Census (1860), Cal., VII, 1292.

MICHELIN & CREIFIELD. Lithographers, NYC, 1844; FRANCIS MICHELIN and —— CREIFIELD. ¶ Peters, *America on Stone* (under Michelin).

MICHELIN & CUIPERS. Lithographers, NYC, 1844–45; FRANCIS MICHELIN and PETER CUIPERS. ¶ Peters, *America on Stone;* NYCD 1844.

MICHELIN, FRANCIS. Lithographer. He first appears as a partner in SHARP, MICHELIN & CO. in Boston in 1840–41, but from 1844 he was located in NYC, working there independently or in various partnerships until 1858. He specialized in views. His partnerships included: SHARP, MICHELIN & CO. (1840–41); MICHELIN & CREIFIELD (1844); MICHELIN & CUIPERS (1844–45); MICHELIN & LEEFE (1852–53); MICHELIN & SHATTUCK (1853–54); and BOELL & MICHELIN (1856–58). ¶ Peters, *America on Stone;* NYCD 1844–58; *Portfolio* (Oct. 1942), frontis.

MICHELIN & LEEFE. Lithographers, NYC, 1852–53; FRANCIS MICHELIN and GEORGE E. B. LEEFE. ¶ Peters, *America on Stone.*

MICHELIN & SHATTUCK. Lithographers, NYC, 1853–54; FRANCIS MICHELIN and J. L. SHATTUCK. ¶ NYCD 1853; Peters, *America on Stone.*

MIDDLETON, ELIJAH C. Senior partner in the engraving, lithographing, and printing establishments of MIDDLETON, WALLACE & CO. (1855–58) and MIDDLETON, STROBRIDGE & CO. (1859–64) of Cincinnati. Middleton himself was listed as early as 1850 as a steel and copperplate printer and as a bookseller and stationer. ¶ Peters *America on Stone;* Cincinnati CD 1850–60.

MIDDLETON, GEORGE. Irish artist, age 26, at NYC in October 1850. ¶ 7 Census (1850), N.Y., XLVI, 823.

MIDDLETON, JOHN IZARD (1785–1849). Landscape painter and draftsman. Born August 13, 1785, at "Middleton Place," near Charleston (S.C.), he was educated in England and spent most of his adult life in France and Italy. He was a talented amateur landscape painter and archaeologist. Many of his accurate and detailed drawings were published in his chief work, *Grecian Remains in Italy, a Description of Cyclopian Walls and of Roman Antiquities with Topographical and Picturesque Views of Ancient Latium* (1812). Middleton died in Paris on October 5, 1849, and is buried at "Middleton Place." ¶ DAB; Rutledge, *Artists in the Life of Charleston.*

MIDDLETON, STROBRIDGE & COMPANY. Engravers and lithographers, Cincinnati, 1859–64. The partners were ELIJAH C. MIDDLETON, HINES STROBRIDGE, MARTIN B. EWING, and DOMINIQUE C. FABRONIUS. The firm was succeeded in 1864 by Strobridge, Gerlach & Wagner and in 1867 by Strobridge & Co. ¶ Peters, *America on Stone;* Cincinnati CD and BD 1859–60; *Antiques,* Vol. 50, 108 (repro.).

MIDDLETON, THOMAS (1797–1863). Amateur portrait and topographical painter of the same family as JOHN IZARD MIDDLETON. Thomas was born at Fanclure (Scotland) and died September 27, 1863, at Charleston (S.C.). He is best known for his view (1836) of the interior of St. Philip's, Charleston. ¶ Rutledge, *Artists in the Life of Charleston; American Processional,* 121; Stauffer, I, 180; Thieme-Becker.

MIDDLETON, WALLACE & COMPANY. Engravers and lithographers, Cincinnati, 1855–59. In 1855 the company was founded by ELIJAH C. MIDDLETON, WILLIAM R. WALLACE, and HINES STROBRIDGE, and in 1857 MARTIN B. EWING joined the firm. In 1859 Wallace dropped out and the firm became MIDDLETON, STROBRIDGE & CO. ¶ Peters, *America on Stone;* Cincinnati CD 1856–58, BD 1856–59.

MIESSE, GABRIEL (1807–?). Engraver. Born in 1807 at Reading (Pa.), Miesse settled in Greenville (Ohio) at the age of twenty and there spent the rest of his life. In addition to his engraving, he practiced "sympathetic healing" and dabbled in real estate and politics. ¶ Drepperd, "New Delvings in Old Fields—Found: A 'New' Early American Engraver," with 4 repros.

MIFFLIN, JOHN HOUSTON (1807–1888). Portrait and miniature painter. A native of Pennsylvania, Mifflin studied painting at the Pennsylvania Academy and began exhibiting there in 1832. He was a pupil of SULLY. In 1836–37 he was in Europe for further study, along with G. P. A. HEALY and several others. On his return to America, Mifflin worked in Philadelphia and also in Georgia. He gave up painting professionally about 1846, just about the time of the birth of his more famous son, the artist and poet Lloyd Mifflin. The elder Mifflin died in 1888 at Columbia (Pa.). ¶ Information courtesy the late William Sawitzky; Rutledge, PA; Bolton, *Miniature Painters;* Lancaster Co. Hist. Soc., *Portraiture in Lancaster County,* 131.

MIGHELS, HENRY. Artist, Cincinnati, 1849–50. ¶ Cincinnati CD 1849–50 (courtesy Edward H. Dwight, Cincinnati Art Museum).

MIGNOT, LOUIS REMY (1831–1870). N.A. Landscape painter. Mignot was born in Charleston (S.C.), studied drawing there, and in 1851 went to Holland for further study. Returning to America in 1855, he set up his studio in NYC where he remained, except for an important trip to Ecuador with FREDERIC CHURCH in 1857, until the outbreak of the Civil War. In 1862 Mignot went to England and there he made his home until his death at Brighton on September 22, 1870. He had been a member of the National Academy since 1858. ¶ DAB; Rutledge, *Artists in the Life of Charleston;* Cowdrey, NAD; Cowdrey, AA & AAU; Rutledge, PA; Rutledge, MHS; Swan, BA; Washington Art Assoc. Cat., 1857, 1859.

MILBERT, JACQUES GÉRARD (1766–1840). Landscape, portrait, and miniature painter and draftsman. Milbert, born in Paris on November 18, 1766, was a member of several scientific expeditions sent out by the French government. It was on such a mission that he came to America in 1815 to make a survey of American flora and fauna. Milbert remained in the United States for nine years, during which time he made his headquarters in NYC. The year after his return to France appeared Milbert's *Picturesque Views of North America* (1825) and three years later his *Itinéraire Pittoresque du Fleuve Hudson et des Parties Laterales* (1828–29), both illustrated by the author. During his stay in America, also, Milbert had exhibited several landscapes and figure paintings at the American Academy. He died in Paris on June 5, 1840. ¶ Thieme-Becker; NYCD 1818–21; Cowdrey, AA & AAU; Snow, "Delineators of the Adams-Jackson American Views," Part IV, 20–21; *Portfolio* (Jan. 1948), 80–81, four repros.; Stokes, *Historic Prints.*

MILBOURN, CHARLES C. Artist, NYC, 1814–16. *Cf.* C. MILBOURNE and COTTON MILBOURNE. ¶ NYCD 1814–16.

MILBOURNE, C. Water color artist who did a view of Government House, NYC, in 1797, the original of which is owned by NYHS. This is probably the same man as C. Melbourne, landscape painter in NYC, to whom PAUL SVININ referred in his *Picturesque Voyage in North America* (St. Petersburg, 1815). It seems probable also that C. Milbourne was the same as COTTON MILBOURNE, active in Philadelphia about 1794–95, that he was the otherwise unidentified Milbourne of NYC who exhibited at the Philadelphia Society of Artists in 1811, and that he was the CHARLES C. MILBOURN listed in the NYC directories for 1814–16. Odell records a Milbourne who was painting stage scenery in NYC between 1797 and 1811. ¶ Stokes, *Iconography,* I, 443–45, and pl. 66; Yarmolinsky, *Picturesque United States of America, 1811, 1812, 1813, Being a Memoir on Paul Svinin,* 41; Rutledge, PA; NYCD 1814–16; Odell, *Annals of the New York Stage,* I, 463; II, 40, 295–96, 313, 335.

MILBOURNE, COTTON. Landscape painter from England, working in Philadelphia in 1794–95. He painted stage scenery showing Philadelphia views, was one of the founders of the Columbianum, and was also one of the group of English artists who seceded from the Columbianum shortly after its establishment. He apparently then moved to NYC. *Cf.* C. MILBOURNE and CHARLES C. MILBOURN. ¶ Barker, *American Painting,* 289; Sellers, *Charles Willson Peale,* II, 69, 73.

MILBURN, JOHN. English artist, age 48, living in NYC in 1850. His wife was also English, but their children, ages 4 and 8, were born in New York. JOSIAH HOWARD, artist, resided with the Milburns. ¶ 7 Census (1850), N.Y., LIII, 260; NYCD 1850.

MILES, EDWARD (1752–1828). Portrait and miniature painter, crayon artist, drawing master. Born October 14, 1752, at Yarmouth (England), Miles went to London about 1771 and became a successful miniature painter. In 1794 he was appointed miniature painter to H. M. Queen Charlotte and he held that position until 1797, when he went to St. Petersburg to become court painter to Czar Paul and later to Czar Alexander I. Miles left Russia in 1807 and came to America, settling permanently in Philadelphia. During the latter part of his career he did little portrait work, confining himself chiefly to teaching drawing in the Academy at Philadelphia, of which he had been a founder. He died in Philadelphia on March 7, 1828. ¶ DAB; Scharf and Westcott, *History of Philadelphia,* II, 1051; Rutledge, PA; Thieme-Becker; DNB; Bolton, *Miniature Painters;* Bolton, *Crayon Draftsmen.*

MILES, GEORGE D. (*c.* 1827–1881). Artist; died in NYC on January 29, 1881. ¶ *American Art Review,* II, 218.

MILLEKEN, see MILLIKEN.

MILLER, A. Lithographer, age 23, native of New York, living in NYC in July 1850 with JOHN W. CROCKER and JOSEPH DUNN. ¶ 7 Census (1850), N.Y., XLVIII, 351.

MILLER, ALFRED JACOB (1810–1874). Landscape and portrait painter, especially noted for his studies of the Indians of the Rocky Mountain area. Born January 2, 1810, in Baltimore, Miller studied painting with THOMAS SULLY in 1831–32 and in Europe in 1833–34. After working for a few years in Baltimore, he moved to New Orleans in 1837. There he met Captain William Drummond Stewart, whom he accompanied as artist on an expedition into the Rocky Mountains. Miller made over a hundred on-the-spot sketches of Indian life which he later elaborated in his studio in Baltimore and during a visit to Stewart in Scotland in 1840–42. Miller returned to Baltimore in the latter year and there passed the rest of his life as a successful portrait painter. He died in Baltimore on June 26, 1874. ¶ Ross, *The West of Alfred Jacob Miller;* De Voto, *Across the Wide Missouri;* Hunter, *Alfred Jacob Miller, Artist of Baltimore and the West;* [Brunet], *Descriptive Catalogue of a Collection of Water-Colour Drawings by Alfred Jacob Miller (1810–1874) in the Public Archives of Canada;* Ross, "A List of Portraits and Paintings from Alfred Jacob Miller's *Account Book";* Baltimore CD 1833–74; Rutledge, PA; Rutledge, MHS; Cowdrey, AA & AAU; Washington Art Association Cat., 1857.

MILLER & BOYLE. Lithographers, NYC, 1851–60; PETER MILLER and JAMES A. BOYLE. ¶ NYCD 1851–60.

MILLER, C. G. Artist from Germany, born about 1800, working in Louisville (Ky.)

in the early 1850's. His son Fred was born in Kentucky about 1839. ¶ 7 Census (1850), Ky., XI, 395; Louisville CD 1852.

MILLER, CHARLES. Danish artist, 34, at NYC in 1860. ¶ 8 Census (1860), N.Y., LIV, 841.

MILLER, CHARLES, see CHARLES MÜLLER.

MILLER, CHARLES F. Lithographer from Baden (Germany), age 18, living in Philadelphia in June 1860. ¶ 8 Census (1860), Pa., XLIX, 194.

MILLER, CHARLES HENRY (1842–1922). Landscape painter and etcher. Born in NYC on March 20, 1842, he first exhibited at the National Academy in 1860. He received the degree of M.D. in 1863 and shortly after visited Europe. On his return Miller gave up medicine to become a painter and in 1867 went to Europe again to study art for three years at Munich and elsewhere. About 1870 he established a studio in NYC. He was elected to the National Academy in 1875. He was best known for his paintings and etchings of Long Island scenes. In 1885 he published, under the pseudonym Carl De Muldor, *The Philosophy of Art in America*. Miller died in NYC on January 21, 1922. ¶ DAB; Cowdrey, NAD.

MILLER & COMPANY, see PETER MILLER.

MILLER, EDWARD. Lithographer, age 29, living in Philadelphia in 1860. He and his wife were from Prussia, two of their children (ages 5 and 3) were born in Maryland, and the baby in Pennsylvania. ¶ 8 Census (1860), Pa., XLIX, 340.

MILLER, EDWARD A. Sign and banner painter, of ACKERMAN & MILLER, NYC, 1832–74. ¶ NYCD 1832–74.

MILLER, ELEAZER HUTCHINSON (1831–1921). Portrait painter, illustrator, and etcher. A native of Shepherdstown (Va., now W. Va.), Miller went to Washington in 1848 and studied under R. GIBSON. In 1855 he set up his own studio in Washington, where he spent the rest of his career. He died on April 4, 1921. ¶ Trotter, "Eleazer Hutchinson Miller"; *Art Annual,* XXV (1928), necrology; 8 Census (1860), D.C., I, 498.

MILLER, EMIL. Artist, age 31, at NYC in August 1850. He was from Germany, but his wife and daughter were both born in Hungary, the latter about 1846. ¶ 7 Census (1850), N.Y., XLIV, 170.

MILLER, GEORGE. A.N.A. Landscape painter. An English artist, Miller was in NYC about 1833–34, exhibited at the National Academy, and was an Associate of the Academy from 1833 to 1838. Several of his paintings were of the Abbey Church at Bath (England). This is almost certainly the George Miller of Bath who exhibited landscapes at the Suffolk Street exhibitions in London in 1827 and 1853. ¶ NYCD 1833–34; Cowdrey, NAD; Graves, *Dictionary*.

MILLER, GEORGE. German lithographer, age 25, at Baltimore in October 1860. ¶ 8 Census (1860), Md., III, 981.

MILLER, GEORGE. Engraver from Massachusetts, age 22, living with his father, JOHN MILLER, in NYC in July 1860. ¶ 8 Census (1860), N.Y., LXII, 642.

MILLER, GEORGE H. Engraver, born in Massachusetts about 1844, living with his father, Allen Miller, in Boston in 1860. ¶ 8 Census (1860), Mass., XXIV, 628.

MILLER, GEORGE M. (?–1819). Wax portraitist. A native of Scotland, Miller came to America in the late 1790's. In 1798, probably at Philadelphia, he modelled a wax portrait of Washington. Between 1810 and 1812 he appears to have been in Baltimore, where he was listed merely as George Miller, artist. He was back in Philadelphia by 1813 and exhibited at the Pennsylvania Academy from 1813 to 1815. He died in 1819. Two years later his widow exhibited a cast of his bust of Bishop White. His other known works include a wax portrait of Jefferson and a wax "Venus" which JAMES R. LAMBDIN exhibited at Pittsburgh in 1827. ¶ Rutledge, PA; Morgan and Fielding, *Life Portraits of Washington;* E. S. Bolton, *American Wax Portraits,* 42; Lafferty; Hart, "Life Portraits of Thomas Jefferson"; Anderson, "Intellectual Life of Pittsburgh: Painting," 291; repros., *Antiques* (Nov. 1941), 316.

MILLER, GOTTFRIED. Portrait and miniature painter of NYC, 1841–87. He appears in the 1850 Census as Godfrey Miller, 30, a native of New York, and in 1860 as Guthrie Miller, 46, a native of Germany. In NYC directories he is listed variously as Gottfried, Godfred, and Godfrey. His wife Catherina and their eldest child, born about 1844, were natives of New Jersey. ¶ Bolton, *Miniature Painters;* NYBD 1841, CD 1851 and after; 7 Census (1850), N.Y., XLVII, 869; 8 Census (1860), N.Y., XLVII, 72.

MILLER, HAMMOND. Engraver on ivory, age 33, from Baden (Germany), living in Philadelphia in 1860 with his Prussian wife and mother-in-law. ¶ 8 Census (1860), Pa., LVI, 829.

MILLER, HENRY. Topographical artist who made sketches of California towns and missions during a visit in 1856–57. He had previously traveled in the West Indies, Mexico, and South America. *Cf.* HENRY MULLER. ¶ Information courtesy Edith M. Coulter, University of California.

MILLER, HENRY, & COMPANY. Wood engravers at Louisville (Ky.) in 1859. ¶ Louisville CD 1859.

MILLER & HILLYER. Portrait and miniature painters, NYC, 1846–58; as Miller, Hillyer & Krauss, 1859–60. The partners were WILLIAM H. MILLER, WILLIAM HILLYER, and after 1859, STEPHEN KRAUSS. In 1846 Miller & Hillyer exhibited 17 oil portraits at the American Institute and won a 2nd prize. After 1860 they turned to photography. ¶ NYBD and CD 1846–64; Am. Inst. Cat. and *Trans.*, 1846.

MILLER, HILLYER & KRAUSS, see MILLER & HILLYER.

MILLER, ISAAC. Portrait and miniature painter of NYC, active 1816–38. L. Miller, widow of Isaac, is listed in 1839. *Cf.* J. MILLER. ¶ NYCD 1816–39.

MILLER, J. Portrait painter, NYC, 1813. *Cf.* ISAAC MILLER. ¶ NYCD 1813.

MILLER, J. C. Artist whose "The *Milwaukee* Bound up Lake Erie, Passing the Light at Buffalo" was engraved by W. J. BENNETT about 1838. ¶ Stauffer.

MILLER, JOHN. Engraver at Rochester (N.Y.) with LEADLEY, MILLER & MIX, 1855–59. ¶ Rochester CD 1855–57; N. Y. State BD 1859.

MILLER, JOHN. Engraver from Massachusetts, age 50, living in NYC in 1860. His eldest son, George, 22, was born in Massachusetts, but the other children, 17 to 9, were born in New York. GEORGE MILLER, the eldest son, was an engraver, and Henry, 17, was an apprentice engraver. John Miller apparently died a year later as his widow is listed in the directory for 1862. ¶ 8 Census (1860), N.Y., LXII, 642; NYCD 1862.

MILLER, JOHN. Engraver, 23, born at sea, living in San Francisco in June 1860. Possibly the John Miller, jeweler, listed in the 1861 directory as an employee of the Robert B. Gray Co. ¶ 8 Census (1860), Cal., VII, 1364; San Francisco CD 1861.

MILLER, JOSEPH. Landscape painter. Joseph Miller was an artist at Staindrop, County Durham (England) in 1818 when his more famous son, WILLIAM RICKARBY MILLER, was born. He followed his son to America in 1851 and settled at Cleveland (Ohio). ¶ Carlock, "William Rickarby Miller," 200–02.

MILLER, LEWIS (1795–1882). Carpenter and amateur artist whose diaries and sketch books are at the York (Pa.) Historical Society. Miller's home was in York, but he traveled in Pennsylvania, to Baltimore and to NYC (1842 and 1859), and even to Europe (1840). ¶ Nolan, "A Pennsylvania Artist in Old New York."

MILLER, LOUISA F. Amateur painter of watercolor memorials on silk, New Lebanon (N.Y.) about 1830. ¶ Lipman and Winchester, 177.

MILLER, PETER. Lithographer of NYC, 1834–60. From 1834 to 1838 he operated under the name of Miller & Co. or Peter Miller & Co., and from 1851 to 1860 as MILLER & BOYLE. ¶ NYCD 1834–60; NYBD 1840–60.

MILLER, ROBERT. Copperplate engraver and printer, lithographer, NYC, 1830–43. ¶ NYCD 1830–43.

MILLER, THOMAS, JR. Engraver from Germany, age 30, living in Philadelphia in 1850 with his father. ¶ 7 Census (1850), Pa., LIV, 661.

MILLER, WILLIAM (1835?–1907). Miniature painter, Cincinnati, 1847–57. So listed by Cist and in the Cincinnati directories, though he appears as William J. Miller, age 23, born in Pennsylvania, in the 1850 Cincinnati census. Clark states that he was born May 27, 1835, at Lexington (Ky.), worked in Cincinnati about 1847, and died in NYC on April 27, 1907. This birth date seems questionable, however, since it would make him only 12 at the time of his professional debut, while both the date and place of birth differ from those recorded in the census. To further confuse the story, Burnet states that William Miller was the son of GERHARDT MUELLER, a German artist who came to Cincinnati about 1840, that he worked in Indianapolis about 1846–48, as well as in Cincinnati, and later in NYC. All these accounts appear to refer to the same man (unless there has been some confusion with the NYC miniaturist WILLIAM H. MILLER), but some contradictions remain to be resolved. ¶ Cist, *Cincinnati in 1859;* Cincinnati CD 1850–57; 7 Census (1850), Ohio, XX, 140; Clark, *Ohio Art and Artists,* 479; Burnet,

Art and Artists of Indiana, 64–65; Peat, *Pioneer Painters of Indiana,* 162.

MILLER, WILLIAM. Engraver, NYC, 1847–48, 1854. ¶ NYCD 1847–48, 1854.

MILLER, WILLIAM H. Portrait and miniature painter, born in England about 1820, active in NYC from 1836 to after 1860. After 1854 he made his home in Brooklyn. From 1846 to 1860 he worked in partnership with WILLIAM HILLYER and STEPHEN KRAUSS (1859–60). MILLER & HILLYER exhibited 17 portraits at the American Institute in 1846 and Miller exhibited independently in 1847 and 1849. ¶ 7 Census (1850), N.Y., XLIII, 277; NYCD 1836–60+; Am. Inst. Cat., 1846, 1847, 1849; Bolton, *Miniature Painters;* repro., *Antiques* (Jan. 1933), 14; represented at NYHS.

MILLER, WILLIAM J., see WILLIAM MILLER, miniaturist.

MILLER, WILLIAM M. Copperplate printer and engraver, Boston, 1857–60+. From 1859 he was in partnership with MATTHEW WILSON under the name of William M. Miller & Co. ¶ Boston CD 1857–60+.

MILLER, WILLIAM RICKARBY (1818–1893). Landscape painter; son of JOSEPH MILLER; born May 20, 1818, at Staindrop, County Durham (England). Probably trained by his artist father, he had been sketching and painting for about eight years before his emigration to America in the winter of 1844–45. Except for a brief stay in Buffalo soon after his arrival, Miller made his home in NYC until the time of his death, in July 1893. During these years he produced hundreds of American views in watercolors and oils, as well as many illustrations for books and periodicals. From 1873 he was chiefly occupied in making pen-and-ink sketches for his projected *1,000 Gems* of American landscape, which was never published. ¶ Carlock, "William Rickarby Miller (1818–1893)"; Shelley, "Addendum: William R. Miller"; Cowdrey, NAD; Cowdrey, AA & AAU; Shelley, "William R. Miller, Forgotten 19th Century Artist."

MILLIGAN, Miss ELIZABETH. Miniature painter, Cincinnati, 1840. ¶ Cincinnati CD 1840 (courtesy Edward H. Dwight, Cincinnati Art Museum).

MILLIKAN, RHODA HOUGHTON (1838–1903). Painter and art teacher. Born in December 1838 at Marlboro (Vt.), she spent her mature life as a teacher at Piqua (Ohio) and Greenfield (Ind.) and died October 2, 1903, at Indianapolis. ¶ Burnet, *Art and Artists of Indiana,* 384; Peat, *Pioneer Painters of Indiana,* 235.

MILLIKEN, GEORGE. Portrait painter who exhibited at the Pennsylvania Academy in 1856 and 1858. Possibly the linen merchant of that name listed in the Philadelphia directories from 1856 to 1860. ¶ Rutledge, PA; Phila. CD 1856–60.

MILLINGTON, THOMAS CHARLES. Artist of a view of William and Mary College, Williamsburgh (Va.) about 1839, known through a lithograph published in 1840. He was the son of John Millington (1779–1868), a professor at the college from about 1835 to 1848. ¶ Stokes, *Historic Prints,* 88 and pl. 67a.

MILLON, SOLIDOR. Italian artist, 63, at NYC in 1850. ¶ 7 Census (1850), N.Y., XLIII, 39.

MILLS, CHARLES. Lithographer, NYC, 1845–60 and after. He exhibited at the American Institute in 1845 and from 1852 was with the firm of ENDICOTT & COMPANY. ¶ Am. Inst. Cat., 1845; NYCD 1852–60+.

MILLS, CLARK (1810–1883). Sculptor and pioneer bronze founder. Born near Syracuse (N.Y.) on December 13, 1810, Mills ran away from home at the age of 13 and worked at various jobs in Syracuse and New Orleans before settling in Charleston (S.C.) in the early 1830's. He began to model in clay about 1835, found employment as a maker of life masks and soon of portraits in marble. With the help of patrons in South Carolina he had a chance to see the works of other sculptors at Washington and Richmond and received his first major commission, for an equestrian statue of Andrew Jackson (now in Lafayette Square, Washington, D.C.). The success of this work won for him other commissions, including those from the Federal Government for an equestrian Washington and for a bronze cast of CRAWFORD's "Freedom" for the Capitol dome. From the 1850's his home was in Washington, where he died on January 12, 1883. Two of his sons, THEODORE A. and THEOPHILUS MILLS, became sculptors. ¶ DAB; Rutledge, *Artists in the Life of Charleston;* Rutledge, "Cogdell and Mills, Charleston Sculptors"; Fairman, *Art and Artists of the Capitol;* Taft, *History of American Sculpture;* Delgado-WPA cites New Orleans *Bee,* January 17 and 24, and Dec. 27, 1855, *Courier,* Jan. 6, 1856; 8 Census (1860), D.C., II, 95.

MILLS, GEORGE W. Engraver, 60, a native of New Jersey, at NYC in 1860. ¶ 8 Census (1860), N.Y., XLIII, 98.

MILLS, ROBERT (1781–1855). Architect, engineer, and watercolorist. Robert Mills, said to be America's first native professional architect, was born August 12, 1781, at Charleston (S.C.). He received his training in architecture from James Hoban and BENJAMIN LATROBE at Washington between 1800 and 1808 and was a practising architect in Philadelphia (1808–17), Baltimore (1817–20), Charleston (1820–30), and Washington (1830–55). From 1836 to 1851 he was Architect of Public Buildings, and it was during this period that he produced the winning design for the Washington Monument. His work as an artist was limited to water color drawings of architectural subjects. In 1810 he was a founder and first Secretary of the Society of Artists in Philadelphia. He died at Washington on March 3, 1855. ¶ DAB; Cohen, "Robert Mills, Architect of South Carolina"; Rutledge, PA; Gallagher, "Robert Mills, 1781–1855, America's First Native Architect"; Evans, "Letters from Robert Mills."

MILLS, THEODORE AUGUSTUS (1839–1916). Sculptor. A son of CLARK MILLS, he was born in Charleston (S.C.) but worked mainly in Washington (D.C.). He made a life mask of Lincoln and was noted for his Indian groups. He died in December 1916 at Pittsburgh (Pa.). ¶ *Art Annual*, XIV, obit.; 8 Census (1860), D.C., II, 95.

MILLS, THEOPHILUS. Sculptor. Second son of CLARK MILLS, born in Charleston (S.C.) about 1842. In 1860 he was listed by the Washington (D.C.) census-taker as a sculptor, age 18, residing with his father and brothers. ¶ 8 Census (1860), D.C., II, 95.

MILLSPAUGH, E. T. Still life painter of NYC who exhibited at the American Art-Union in 1847. ¶ Cowdrey, AA & AAU.

MILNE, A. Watercolorist who painted a view of Smithtown (Long Island) before 1860. ¶ Comstock, "American Water Colors before 1860," 5.

MILNE & BRUDER. Lithographers, Louisville (Ky.), 1848–50; COLIN R. MILNE and CHARLES BRUDER. ¶ Louisville CD 1848, 1852; BD 1850.

MILNE, COLIN R. Lithographer from Scotland, born about 1817, working in Louisville (Ky.) as the partner of CHARLES BRUDER from 1848 to 1852. ¶ 7 Census (1850), Ky., XI, 670; Louisville CD 1848, 1852.

MIMEE, E. W. Lithographer, NYC, 1847. ¶ Peters, *America on Stone*.

MINER, Mrs. ——. Painter of a primitive colonial scene, in oils, about 1850. ¶ Lipman and Winchester, 177.

MINES, JAMES H. Engraver, born in Ireland about 1825, working in Philadelphia from 1850 until after 1860. ¶ 7 Census (1850), Pa. (Phila.), 285; Phila. CD 1854–60+.

MINGEAU, FRANÇOIS. Engraver and stonecutter, New Orleans, 1841–42. ¶ New Orleans CD 1841–42.

MINGLE, ELIZABETH. Artist, born in Pennsylvania about 1835, the daughter of William Mingle, sea captain, with whom she was living in Philadelphia in 1860. ¶ 8 Census (1860), Pa., L, 176.

MINGLE, JOSEPH (1839–1903). Landscape and marine painter, born in Philadelphia June 13, 1839, died there September 14, 1903. ¶ *Art Annual*, IV, obit.

MINIFIE, WILLIAM (1805–1880). Professor of drawing, architect, and bookseller. Minifie was born August 14, 1805, in Devonshire (England) and emigrated to the United States in 1828. During the 1840's and 1850's he published a number of books on drawing. He made his home in Baltimore where he was curator of the Maryland Academy of Sciences and professor of drawing in the Maryland Institute's art school. He died in Baltimore on October 24, 1880. ¶ CAB; Baltimore CD 1851+; Union Catalogue, Library of Congress, lists his *Text Book of Geometrical Drawing* (Baltimore, 1849), *Essay on the Theory of Color* (Baltimore, 1854), and *Popular Lectures on Drawing and Design* (Baltimore, 1854).

MINOR, ROBERT CRANNELL (1839–1904). N.A. Landscape painter, born in NYC on April 30, 1839. Studied in NYC under ALFRED C. HOWLAND and then spent about ten years in Europe, studying in Antwerp, Paris, and Barbizon, and painting landscapes in England. He returned to America in the mid-1870's and had a studio in NYC. He was made a National Academician in 1897. Much of his work was done in the Adirondacks and around Waterford (Conn.), where he died on August 3, 1904. Minor was one of the chief American exponents of the Barbizon school. ¶ DAB; Thieme-Becker; Fielding.

MINOT, ——. Wood, steel, and copperplate

engraver. He apparently got his start in Boston with the BOSTON BEWICK COMPANY to whose *American Magazine of Useful and Entertaining Knowledge* he contributed a number of wood engavings in 1835. In 1842 he was working with WILLIAM CROOME in Philadelphia. Although Minot's work appears in numerous books and periodicals published in Philadelphia, NYC, and Cincinnati between 1839 and 1855, nothing further is known of his career, not even his Christian name. ¶ Hamilton, *Early American Book Illustrators and Wood Engravers;* Phila. CD 1842, under Croome & Minot.

MINOTT, ——. Painter of two views of Niagara Falls, dated 1818. ¶ Belknap Collection, NYHS.

MINTON, JOHN. Engraver, NYC, 1851. ¶ NYBD 1851.

MITCHELL, Miss AGNES. Landscape painter, Brooklyn, 1845–47. She exhibited at the National Academy views near Buffalo, Jersey City, and Staten Island, and a number of drawings of insects. ¶ Cowdrey, NAD.

MITCHELL, BENJAMIN T. (1816–1880). Stonecutter who cut the first capital for the Mormon Temple at Nauvoo (Ill.) about 1844. He was a native of Muncy (Pa.), born January 12, 1816; joined the Mormons at Akron (Ohio) in 1836; settled in Nauvoo in 1841; moved to Utah in 1848; died at Salt Lake City on March 9, 1880. ¶ Arrington, "Nauvoo Temple."

MITCHELL, E. English bookplate engraver who worked in the United States about 1790. ¶ Dunlap, *History* (1918); Fielding.

MITCHELL & COMPANY, F. N. & H. Seal engravers and die sinkers, Boston, 1859 and after; FRANCIS N. and HENRY MITCHELL. ¶ Boston CD 1859–60+.

MITCHELL, FRANCIS N. Seal engraver and die sinker, Boston, 1841–60+. He exhibited at the American Institute in NYC in 1847. After 1859 he was associated with his brother or son, HENRY MITCHELL. ¶ Boston BD 1841–42; CD 1843–60+; Am. Inst. Cat., 1847.

MITCHELL, FRANK. French historical painter, age 30, living in Cincinnati in 1850. His wife Polina was from Indiana, and their 5-months-old daughter was born in Ohio. ¶ 7 Census (1850), Ohio, XX, 201.

MITCHELL, GEORGE. English artist, born between 1820 and 1825, living in NYC 1850–60. ¶ 7 Census (1850), N.Y., LV, 788; 8 Census (1860), N.Y., LX, 119.

MITCHELL, HARVEY (*c.* 1801–*c.* 1863/4). Portrait painter, said to have been born about 1801 at the family home on the James River, opposite Lynchburg (Va.). He is reported to have been at Charleston (S.C.) about 1830 and to have died during the Civil War, about 1863/4. Twenty-three portraits have been attributed to him. ¶ Bowyer, *Harvey Mitchell, Virginia Painter;* Smith; Fielding; Dunlap, *History* (1918).

MITCHELL, HENRY. Seal engraver and die sinker, of F. N. & H. MITCHELL & Co., Boston, 1859–60 and after. ¶ Boston CD 1858–60+.

MITCHELL, J. Painter of a portrait of Samuel Adams of Boston, published at Newport (R.I.) in 1775. ¶ Stauffer, no. 2370.

MITCHELL, JOHN (1811–1866). Portrait painter, born at Hartford (Conn.). He worked principally in Hartford, although he was at New London (Conn.) in 1857–58. He died in NYC. ¶ French, *Art and Artists in Connecticut,* 78; Fielding.

MITCHELL, JUDITH (1793–1837). Amateur silhouettist, born November 18, 1793, on Nantucket (Mass.). Her married life was spent at De Ruyter (N.Y.). Her silhouettes were cut exclusively for friends and family. She died August 20, 1837. ¶ *Antiques* (Aug. 1932), 48, four repros.

MITCHELL, Miss MARIAN (1840–1885). Painter of Bangor (Me.). ¶ Simpson, *Leaflets of Artists.*

MITCHELL, MINA. Negro engraver, age 39, a native of Delaware, living in Philadelphia in 1850 with his wife and six children, ages 16 to 6, all born in Pennsylvania. ¶ 7 Census (1850), Pa., L, 791.

MITCHELL, PHOEBE. Primitive watercolorist, landscapes, New York State, about 1800–10. ¶ Lipman and Winchester, 177.

MITCHELL, WILLIAM J. Wood engraver at Buffalo (N.Y.), 1859–60. ¶ Buffalo BD 1859–60.

MITZSCHERLING, GUSTAVE. Engraver, born in Württemberg about 1823, living in San Francisco from 1856. ¶ 8 Census (1860), Cal., VII, 1320; San Francisco CD 1856–60.

MIX, LUCIUS C. Engraver, Rochester (N.Y.), 1855–60 and after. From 1855 to 1859 he was with LEADLEY, MILLER & MIX. ¶ Rochester CD 1855–60+.

MOALE, JOHN (1731–1798). Amateur landscape and portrait painter. Col. Moale was a prominent merchant and landowner of Baltimore, a member of the Maryland Assembly, Presiding Justice of the Baltimore County Court, and during the Revolution colonel of the Baltimore militia. His view of Baltimore before 1752 was presented in 1854 to the Maryland Historical Society, which also owns his wash drawing of John Knox. ¶ Pleasants, *250 Years of Painting in Md.*, 26; Stokes, *Historic Prints;* Rutledge, MHS; Rutledge, "Portraits in Varied Media."

MOELLER or MOLLER, CHARLES. Portrait and decorative painter, NYC, late 1850's. In 1857 he was probably the partner of JACOB W. FRANCK in FRANCK & MOELLER. Charles Moeller was also probably the father of Louis Charles Moeller (1855–1930), genre painter, who studied under his father, a NYC decorative painter, before going to Munich in the 1870's. ¶ NYCD 1857–58; NYBD 1857; CAB; Mallett.

MÖLLHAUSEN, HEINRICH BALDUIN (1825–1905). Topographical artist, born near Bonn (Germany) on January 27, 1825. He made three trips to America, in 1849–52, 1853–54, and 1857–58. During the first he lived at Belleville (Ill.) and accompanied the Rocky Mountain expedition of Prince Paul of Württemberg; during the second he was topographer and draftsman to Lt. A. W. Whipple's surveying expedition along the 35th parallel from Arkansas to California; and during the third he was a member of Lt. J. C. IVES's expedition to explore the Colorado River. Some of Möllhausen's sketches were lithographed for the official reports of these expeditions, while many more appeared as illustrations in his *Diary of a Journey from the Mississippi to the Coasts of the Pacific* (London: 1858) and *Reisen in die Felsenbirge Nord-Amerikas . . .* (Leipzig: 1861). Möllhausen also wrote many novels and short stories which have been compared with those of Fenimore Cooper. He spent his later years in Germany and died there in 1905. ¶ Taft, *Artists and Illustrators of the Old West,* 22 et seq.; Barba, *Balduin Möllhausen, the German Cooper;* U. S. War Dep't, *Reports of Explorations and Surveys,* 1855–60, Vol. III; Ives, *Report on the Colorado River;* Stokes, *Historic Prints.*

MOFFET, THOMAS. Steel, copper, brass, and wood engraver, Chicago, 1859. ¶ Chicago CD 1859.

MOFFITT, JOHN M. (1837–1887). Sculptor. He was born in England and served his apprenticeship to a London sculptor before coming to America just before the Civil War. His work was chiefly for cemeteries, churches, and military memorials. He returned to England in the 1880's and died in London on September 15, 1887. ¶ CAB; Fielding.

MOIRE, THOMAS. Portrait painter, New Orleans, 1842. *Cf.* THEODORE MOÏSE. ¶ New Orleans CD 1842.

MOISE, CHARLES W. Engraver, 27, born in Connecticut, living in NYC in 1850 with his wealthy father, Sydney E. Moise, editor. ¶ 7 Census (1850), N.Y., LVI, 481.

MOÏSE, THEODORE SYDNEY (1806–1883). Portrait and animal painter, born in Charleston (S.C.). In 1835–36 he was still at Charleston, advertising in those years as a portrait painter, restorer, and ornamental penman. By 1842 he had moved to New Orleans where he was associated with TREVOR THOMAS FOWLER. Moïse remained in New Orleans at least until the 1870's and died at Natchitoches (La.) in 1883. ¶ Wehle, "A Portrait of Henry Clay, Reattributed"; New Orleans CD 1850–70; Rutledge, *Artists in the Life of Charleston;* Delgado-WPA cites *Commercial Bulletin* (Feb. 14, 1842), *Picayune* (March 27, 1842, April 10, 1856), *Daily Topic* (Feb. 27, 1844), *Delta* (June 20, 1854).

MOLINI, RAFFAEL. Artist, NYC, 1850–63. Born in Italy about 1814 and had been in New York at least a year in 1850. His house was next door to that of NICOLINO CALYO. ¶ 7 Census (1850), N.Y., LVI, 1; NYCD 1850, 1863.

MOLLINARI, JOHN. Italian image maker, born about 1814, who worked in NYC from about 1845 to 1860. He was probably the father of JOSEPH MOLLINARI. ¶ NYCD 1850; 8 Census (1860), N.Y., XLIV, 159.

MOLLINARI, JOSEPH. Italian image maker, 20, living in NYC in 1860. Probably a son of JOHN MOLLINARI. ¶ 8 Census (1860), N.Y., XLIV, 159.

MOLONY, WILLIAM, see WILLIAM MALONEY.

MOLYNEUX, ——. Portrait engraver active about 1831, probably at Pittsburgh (Pa.). ¶ Stauffer, I, 180–81.

MOMBERGER, WILLIAM (1829–?). Landscape painter, lithographer, and illustrator. Born June 7, 1829, in Frankfort-on-Main (Germany), Momberger studied painting and lithography there. In 1848 he emigrated to the United States, settling in NYC. He first worked as a lithographer (COUGHEY & MOMBERGER, 1852), but later became a well-known illustrator of books and newspapers and a designer of banknotes.

He was employed to illustrate Duyckinck's *Cyclopedia of American Literature* and the *Gallery of American Landscape Artists.* He also traveled in the Midwest and published an illustrated account of the region in 1865. After the Civil War he had a studio at Morrisania (N.Y.) where he was working at least until 1888. ¶ CAB; 7 Census (1850), N.Y., LI, 425; NYBD 1852–59; Peat, *Pioneer Painters of Indiana.*

MONACHAISE, see NICOLA MONACHESI.

MONACHESI, F. Fresco and ornamental painter, Philadelphia, 1832–35. He exhibited at the Pennsylvania Academy and Artists' Fund Society. In 1832 he had the same address as NICOLA MONACHESI. ¶ Rutledge, PA.

MONACHESI, NICOLA (1795–1851). Portrait, historical, and decorative painter. He was born at Tolentino (Italy) in 1795 and came to America before 1832, when he first exhibited at the Pennsylvania Academy. He worked in Philadelphia until 1851. His address in 1832 was the same as that of F. MONACHESI, possibly his son. ¶ Champlin & Perkins; Rutledge, PA; Dunlap, *History,* II, 471, as Monachise; Fielding, as Monachaise; 7 Census (1850), Pa., LII, 869–70.

MONACHISE, see NICOLA MONACHESI.

MONÇEAU, see MONSSEAU.

MONDELLI, ANTOINE. Scene and ornamental painter, New Orleans, 1821–56. From 1824 to 1832 he was chief scene painter at Camp's Theatre in New Orleans. About 1830 he was the first teacher of LEON POMAREDE, later Mondelli's son-in-law. ¶ Kendall, *Golden Age of the New Orleans Theater,* 76 (courtesy J. E. Arrington); Delgado-WPA cites New Orleans CD 1822–56, *La. Courier* (Oct. 29, 1821, April 2, 1829, Oct. 1, 1835), *Gazette* (Oct. 22, 1822, Jan. 3 and Dec. 27, 1823, Jan. 7, 1824), and *Bee* (May 14, 1836); McDermott, "Leon Pomarede"; Arrington, "Leon Pomarede."

MONKS, CHARLES. Engraver, NYC, 1856–59. ¶ NYBD 1856–59.

MONMONIER, WILLIAM B. Lithographer who worked in many of the California mining towns about 1856–58. He specialized in letterhead views. ¶ Peters, *California on Stone.*

MONNIER, FRANCE X. (1831–1912). Sculptor. He was born in Belfort (France) and studied in France during the 1850's. Shortly before the Civil War he came to NYC to decorate the home of Commodore Vanderbilt. He later moved to Detroit where he died on April 5, 1912. ¶ *Art Annual,* X, obit.

MONSSEAU or MONÇEAU, P. H. Sculptor, New Orleans, 1838–1860's. In the late 1850's and 1860's he advertised himself as proprietor of a marble yard. ¶ New Orleans CD 1838–67.

MONTALANT, JULIUS O. Landscape painter. Between 1851 and 1861 he exhibited American, French, Italian, and Greek views at the Pennsylvania Academy. His addresses were: 1852–56, Philadelphia; 1858, Europe; 1859, Rome; 1861, Italy. ¶ Rutledge, PA.

MONTGOMERY, ——. Artist, of WINTERS & MONTGOMERY, Philadelphia, October 1761. ¶ Brown and Brown cite *Pa. Gazette,* Oct. 29, 1761.

MONTPENSIER, ANTOINE PHILIPPE D'ORLEANS, DUC DE (1775–1807). Amateur landscape painter. Montpensier, second son of Philippe "Egalité," duc d'Orleans (1747–1793), was born July 3, 1775, in the Palais Royal. After his father's execution in 1793 and several years of imprisonment Montpensier and his brothers, the future King Louis Philippe and the duc de BEAUJOLAIS, were permitted to go to America. After touring the United States thoroughly from February 1797 to 1798 they sailed for England, via Cuba, the Bahamas, and Halifax. Finding asylum in England, the brothers settled in a mansion at Twickenham and there Montpensier pursued his interest in the fine arts. From this period dates his oil painting of Niagara Falls, now owned by the New-York Historical Society. Montpensier died of consumption on May 18, 1807, and was buried in Westminster Abbey. ¶ Taylor, *Memoirs of the House of Orleans; Antiques* (Dec. 1950), 497, repro.

MONTPREVILLE or MONTREVILLE, CYRILLE or CYRUS DE. Lithographer, born in France about 1819, living in San Francisco from about 1853. ¶ 8 Census (1860), Cal., VII, 465; San Francisco CD and BD 1856–62.

MONTULÉ, EDOUARD DE. French amateur artist and lithographer who visited America in 1817 and four years later published an illustrated book on his travels. ¶ Scharff, "Collecting Views of Natchez," 217–19, repro.

MOODY, DAVID WILLIAM. Topographical artist and lithographer who worked in NYC from 1844 to 1851 and lived in Williamsburg, now Brooklyn. ¶ Peters, *America on*

Stone; Stokes, *Historic Prints;* Keyes, "'The Bottle' and Its American Refills"; repro., *Portfolio* (Nov. 1945), 54, and *Antiques* (June 1946), 363.

MOODY, EDWIN. Lithographer, San Francisco, about 1850 to 1860. ¶ Peters, *California on Stone,* repros.; San Francisco CD 1861.

MOODY, JOHN E. Engraver, Boston, 1840–42; of B. W. THAYER & Co., 1841–42. ¶ Boston CD 1840–42.

MOOERS, JACOB B. Painter of oil portraits on academy board, Deerfield (N.H.), 1840's. *Cf.* JACOB BAILEY MOORE. ¶ Lipman and Winchester, 177.

MOON, SAMUEL (1805–1860). Portrait painter who was working at Catawissa (Pa.) about 1831 and at Easton (Pa.) in 1834. He exhibited at the Pennsylvania Academy. ¶ Rutledge, PA; Ford, *Edward Hicks,* 83–84.

MOON, WILLIAM. English sculptor, 25, at Philadelphia in July 1850. ¶ 7 Census (1850), Pa., L, 852.

MOONEY & BUELL. Engravers and lithographers, Buffalo (N.Y.), 1852; LAWRENCE MOONEY and CHARLES W. BUELL. ¶ Buffalo CD 1852.

MOONEY & CHOWING. Engravers and lithographers, Buffalo (N.Y.), 1854; LAWRENCE MOONEY and HENRY C. CHOWING, JR. ¶ Buffalo CD 1854.

MOONEY, EDWARD LUDLOW (1813–1887). N.A. Portrait painter, born in NYC on March 25, 1813. Studied under INMAN and PAGE and spent most of his professional life in his native city, though he spent several winters working in Georgia. He was made a National Academician in 1840. He died in NYC in July 1887. ¶ CAB; Clement and Hutton; Cowdrey, AA & AAU; Cowdrey, NAD; NYCD 1846+; Swan, BA; Rutledge, PA; represented by 20 portraits at Princeton University (Egbert).

MOONEY, LAWRENCE. Engraver and lithographer, Buffalo (N.Y.), 1851–60. He was with MOONEY & BUELL in 1852 and with MOONEY & CHOWING in 1856, and for some years with HALL & MOONEY. ¶ Buffalo CD 1851–60; Peters, *America on Stone.*

MOORE, A. E. Primitive oil portraitist, active about 1830. *Cf.* ABEL BUEL MOORE. ¶ Lipman and Winchester, 177.

MOORE, ABEL BUEL (1806–1879). Portrait painter. A native of Rupert (Vt.), he studied under JOHN QUIDOR and worked mainly in Troy (N.Y.) from 1823 to 1875, although in 1858 he was in NYC and from 1858 to 1860 at Albany. He exhibited at the National Academy in 1835–36. ¶ Hayner, *Troy and Rensselaer County,* II, 357; Cowdrey, NAD; Albany CD 1858–60; NYBD 1858; Todd, "Huddy & Duval Prints"; represented at NYHS.

MOORE, BENJAMIN. Lithographer, NYC, 1859. ¶ NYBD 1859.

MOORE, CHARLES HERBERT (1840–1930). A.N.A. Landscape painter, lecturer and writer on the fine arts. He was born April 10, 1840, in NYC and received his early training in landscape there before the Civil War, exhibiting at the National Academy for the first time in 1858. After living for a number of years at Catskill (N.Y.), Moore was appointed drawing and watercolor instructor at the Lawrence Scientific School of Harvard in 1871. Three years later he joined the staff of Harvard College as instructor in principles of the fine arts. He taught there until his retirement in 1909 and from 1896 was also director of the Fogg Art Museum. Moore was much influenced by the ideas of John Ruskin, under whom he studied in Italy in 1876–77. After his retirement from Harvard, Moore built a house at Hartfield, Hampshire (England) and lived there until his death, February 15, 1930. He was especially noted as an authority on medieval architecture. ¶ DAB; Cowdrey, NAD; Sweet, *The Hudson River School;* Swan, BA; Gilman, "Studies in the Art of Drawing and Painting. . . ."

MOORE & CROSBY. Printers, engravers, lithographers, Boston, 1852–56; EMERY N. MOORE and CHARLES H. CROSBY. ¶ Boston CD 1852–56.

MOORE, E. English engraver, 33, at Philadelphia in July 1850. ¶ 7 Census (1850), Pa., LI, 245.

MOORE, EMERY N. (1816–1890). Engraver, lithographer, and printer. A native of Ellsworth (Me.), Moore came to Boston as a youth and spent his life there in the printing business. He was the senior partner in MOORE & CROSBY (1852–56), printers, engravers, and lithographers. He died in Boston on August 30, 1890. ¶ Boston *Transcript,* Sept. 2, 1890, obit.; Boston CD 1842–60+.

MOORE, EMERY N., & COMPANY. Printers, engravers, and lithographers, Boston, 1857–60+; EMERY N. MOORE and WILLIAM H. SUMNER. ¶ Boston CD 1857–60+.

MOORE, EMILY S. Landscape in charcoal, about 1855. ¶ Lipman and Winchester, 177.

MOORE, GEORGE. Engraver, 27, from New Jersey, at NYC in August 1850. ¶ 7 Census (1850), N.Y., XLI, 685.

MOORE, GEORGE. Artist, 18, living with his family, chiefly farmers, at West Fairlee (Vt.) in 1850. ¶ 7 Census (1850), Vt., VII, 122.

MOORE, Miss H. N. Painter of a miniature dated 1836 and signed, probably done near Richmond (Va.). ¶ Information courtesy Dr. H. W. Williams, Jr., Corcoran Gallery.

MOORE, ISAAC W. Engraver, Philadelphia, 1831–33. *Cf.* ISAAC W. MOORE, portrait and landscape painter. ¶ Phila. CD 1831–33; Stauffer.

MOORE, ISAAC W. Portrait and landscape painter, Philadelphia, 1846–58. In 1846 and 1847 he exhibited at the American Art-Union several views, including scenes at Newport (R.I.). In the Philadelphia directories he was listed as a portrait painter, once as a landscape painter, and from 1853 to 1855 as a surveyor. ¶ Cowdrey, AA & AAU; Rutledge, PA; Phila. CD 1848–58, BD 1850.

MOORE, JACOB BAILEY (1815–1893). Portrait painter. A native of Candia (N.H.), Moore left home at 15 to work for a number of years, chiefly as a clerk, in Lowell, Boston, and Lynn (Mass.). By 1846 he had returned to New Hampshire, settling in Manchester where he worked as an artist, journalist, and phrenologist until his death. Art was his mainstay until after 1860 when he became a newspaper editor. His *History of Candia* (Manchester, 1893) contains an autobiographical sketch. *Cf.* JACOB B. MOOERS. ¶ Spinney, "J. Bailey Moore"; Manchester BD 1856 and after; represented at Manchester Historic Association, Fitts Museum (Candia), and Griffin Museum (Auburn, N.H.).

MOORE, JAMES. Engraver, 20, a native of NYC and living there in 1850. ¶ 7 Census (1850), N.Y., XLV, 456.

MOORE, JOHN. Sign and ornamental painter, Cincinnati, 1819. ¶ Knittle, *Early Ohio Taverns.*

MOORE, JOHN. Engraver and die sinker, born in New York about 1810, working in NYC 1849–60. ¶ 8 Census (1860), N.Y., LXII, 678; NYCD 1850, BD 1849–50.

MOORE, JOHN. Engraver, 24, a native of Pennsylvania, living in Philadelphia in 1850. ¶ 7 Census (1850), Pa., L, 833.

MOORE, JOSEPH THOITS (1796–1854). Portrait painter, born March 8, 1796, at North Yarmouth (Me.). He was painting near Portland (Me.) in 1825, at New Orleans in 1837, and between 1828 and 1842 at Montgomery (Ala.). He died October 17, 1854, at Montgomery. ¶ Information courtesy Miss Lucharlle Wilson, via FARL; *Art in America* (Dec. 1933), 31; Delgado-WPA cites New Orleans CD 1837; letter, Ala. Dept. of Archives and History, Jan. 8, 1942.

MOORE, MORRIS. Engraver, 19, a native of South Carolina, boarding in Philadelphia in August 1850. ¶ 7 Census (1850), Pa., LII, 605.

MOORE, NELSON AUGUSTUS (1824–1902). Landscape and portrait painter. He was born August 2, 1824, at Kensington (Conn.), studied under THOMAS CUMMINGS and DANIEL HUNTINGTON in NYC, and spent most of his life in Kensington. In his later years he specialized in landscapes. ¶ French, *Art and Artists in Conn.*, 122–23; Corcoran Gallery, *Catalogue; Art Digest* (Oct. 1, 1934), 5, repro.

MOORE, THOMAS. English lithographer, Boston, 1835–41, successor to PENDLETON. ¶ Peters, *America on Stone.*

MOORE, WILLIAM (1790–1851). Portrait painter, said to be an American by birth, who painted on copper a likeness of Fanny Kemble, 1838. ¶ Sherman, "Unrecorded Early American Painters" (1934), 149.

MOORE, WILLIAM. Irish engraver working in NYC from 1849 to after 1860; from 1854 his home was in Jersey City (N.J.). He was about 23 in 1850. ¶ NYCD 1849–60+; 7 Census (1850), N.Y., XLVII, 461.

MOOREHEAD, SCIPIO. Artist, Boston, about 1773. He was a Negro servant of the Rev. John Moorehead. ¶ Porter, *Modern Negro Art,* 18.

MORAN, Mr. ——. Miniaturist, Charleston (S.C.), 1849. *Cf.* J. AUGUSTUS MOREIN. ¶ Rutledge, *Artists in the Life of Charleston.*

MORAN, C. Painter of a scene from *Lalla Rookh,* exhibited at the Pennsylvania Academy in 1858. This was probably an error for EDWARD MORAN. ¶ Rutledge, PA.

MORAN, E. & T. Artists, Philadelphia, 1857–60; EDWARD and THOMAS MORAN. ¶ Phila. CD 1857, 1860.

Moran, Edward (1829–1901). A.N.A. Marine and historical painter, born August 19, 1829, at Bolton, Lancashire (England). He began life as a weaver, but some years after the family's removal to Maryland in 1844 studied painting in Philadelphia with Paul Weber and James Hamilton. By 1857 he was established as an artist in Philadelphia, along with his younger brother Thomas. In 1862 Edward and Thomas went to England for further study. Edward moved from Philadelphia to NYC in 1872 and spent the rest of his career there, except for a visit to Paris in 1879–80. He was particularly noted for his Turner-esque seascapes and his paintings of American history. He died in NYC on June 9, 1901. ¶ DAB; Phila. CD 1857–60+; Cowdrey, NAD; Swan, BA; Rutledge, PA; Peters, *America on Stone; American Processional,* 217.

Moran, J. Portrait painter, Charles Town (Mass.), about 1832. ¶ Sears, *Some American Primitives,* 287; Lipman and Winchester, 177 (as J. Moron).

Moran, John. Artist, 29, at Philadelphia in 1860. A brother of Edward, Peter, and Thomas Moran; born presumably at Bolton, Lancashire, and brought to America in 1844. In 1871 he was a photographer in Philadelphia. ¶ 8 Census (1860), Pa., LXII, 219; Phila. CD 1871.

Moran, Peter (1841–1914). Animal painter and etcher, born March 4, 1841, at Bolton, Lancashire (England) and brought to America in 1844. Taught by his older brothers, Edward and Thomas, Peter Moran became a noted painter and etcher of animals. Except for a visit to England in 1863, he passed most of his career in Philadelphia. His wife, formerly Emily Kelley of Dublin (Ireland), also was an artist. He died in Philadelphia on November 9, 1914. ¶ DAB; 8 Census (1860), Pa., LXII, 219; Rutledge, PA.

Moran, Thomas (1837–1926). N.A. Landscape painter, etcher, engraver, lithographer. Born January 12, 1837, at Bolton, Lancashire (England), accompanied his family to Maryland in 1844, and studied painting with his brother Edward in Philadelphia during the mid-1850's. In 1862 the two Morans went to England for further study and came under the influence of Turner. Thomas visited Europe again in the same decade and several times in later years. His fame rests largely on his large paintings of scenes in the Far West, including Yellowstone Park, Yosemite, and the Grand Canyon of the Colorado. His home was in Philadelphia until 1872 when he moved to Newark (N.J.) and shortly after to NYC. In 1916 he moved to Santa Barbara (Cal.) where he died on August 26, 1926. ¶ DAB; Phila. CD 1857–60+; 8 Census (1860), Pa., LXII, 219; Rutledge, PA; Sweet, *The Hudson River School;* Born, *American Landscape Painting.*

Morange or Moranges, Etienne (Stephen). Miniaturist, Baltimore, 1795–1803. ¶ Bolton, *Miniature Painters;* Mayo; Lafferty.

Moras, Ferdinand (1821–1908). Lithographer, born in Rhenish Prussia. After working in Germany, Belgium, France, Scotland, and England, Moras came to Philadelphia in 1853 and continued in business there until the 1890's. ¶ Peters, *America on Stone;* Phila. BD 1857, CD 1858–60+.

More, Thomas. Ship carver. He was at Portsmouth (N.H.) in 1707, at Kittery (Me.) in 1720 when he carved a lion figurehead, and later lived in Boston with his son Samuel, also a carver. ¶ Pinckney, *American Figureheads and Their Carvers,* 46, 197.

Morein, J. Augustus. Portrait painter and miniaturist, born in the West Indies about 1810. He was at Charleston (S.C.) in 1835–36, at NYC 1841–44, again at Charleston in 1850, and NYC in 1854. He exhibited at the National Academy in 1841–42 and 1844. ¶ 7 Census (1850), S.C., II, 195; Rutledge, *Artists in the Life of Charleston;* Cowdrey, NAD; NYBD 1841, 1854; Bolton, *Miniature Painters.*

Morel, ——. Portrait painter, New Orleans, 1834. *Cf.* —— Morel, miniaturist; W. de Morrill; S. Mores. ¶ Delgado-WPA cites New Orleans CD 1834.

Morel, ——. Miniaturist at Richmond (Va.) in 1845, working with George Saunders. *Cf.* —— Morel, above; W. D. Morell. ¶ *Richmond Portraits,* 242.

Moreland, Augustus. Virginia-born engraver, 17, at Cincinnati in 1850. Augustus Moreland, carpenter and builder, was listed in Cincinnati directories from 1850 to 1858. ¶ 7 Census (1850), Ohio, XX, 827; Cincinnati CD 1850–58.

Moreley, James. Irish artist, 22, living in NYC in 1850 with James Bailey. ¶ 7 Census (1850), N.Y., L, 81.

Mores, S. Portrait painter, New Orleans, 1849. *Cf.* —— Morel. ¶ Delgado-WPA cites New Orleans CD 1849.

MOREWOOD, GEORGE. Engraver, 41, native of Rhode Island, living in NYC in 1860. ¶ 8 Census (1860), N.Y., XLIII, 59.

MOREY, EDWARD. Landscape and figure painter, NYC, 1836. He exhibited at the National Academy a view in the English Lake District. ¶ Cowdrey, NAD; NYCD 1836.

MORGAN, A. W. Engraver, Cleveland (Ohio), 1853. ¶ Cleveland BD 1853.

MORGAN, DAVID P. Lithographer, 22, a native of Washington (D.C.), living there in 1860 with his father, Jno. B., and brother, JOHN B. MORGAN, JR. ¶ 8 Census (1860), D.C., I, 591.

MORGAN, GRIFFITH. Portrait painter, born in Wales about 1819, working in NYC from the mid-1840's to after 1860. After 1856 his home was in Brooklyn. ¶ 7 Census (1850), N.Y., XLVIII, 257; NYBD 1846–50; Brooklyn CD 1856–60+; *Antiques* (Dec. 1950), repro. of his scene in the Brooklyn Central Bank.

MORGAN, JOHN B., JR. Apprentice lithographer, 20, born in Washington (D.C.) and living there in 1860 with his father and brother, John B. and DAVID P. MORGAN. ¶ 8 Census (1860), D.C., I, 591.

MORGAN, LOUIS M. (1814–1852). Portrait painter, born November 21, 1814, at Mt. Pleasant (Pa.). Soon after his family's removal to Pittsburgh about 1830 Morgan took up portrait painting. Sometime during the thirties he was commissioned to paint a portrait of Simon Kenton of Ohio for JAMES HERRING and JAMES B. LONGACRE's *National Portrait Gallery*. During the forties he worked chiefly in Kentucky, at Louisville, Frankfort, and Lexington. He moved to Tennessee shortly before his death in Montgomery County in the fall of 1852. ¶ Price, *Old Masters of the Blue Grass,* 125–44; Rutledge, PA.

MORGAN, THOMAS W. Portrait painter working in Indiana about 1821 and in Louisville in 1839 and 1841. ¶ Information courtesy Edward H. Dwight, Cincinnati Art Museum; Peat, *Pioneer Painters of Indiana,* 57.

MORGAN, TARQUATO (?). Engraver, 20, a native of Ohio, living in Cincinnati in 1850 with his father, David B. Morgan, miller. ¶ 7 Census (1850), Ohio, XX, 64.

MORGAN, WILLIAM (1826–1900). A.N.A. Portrait and figure painter, born in London (England) in 1826 (CAB) or 1830 (*Who's Who*). He was living in Brooklyn as early as 1851, at which time he was a student in the National Academy of Design. He also studied at Le Havre (France). Most of his artistic career was spent in NYC. He was made an Associate of the National Academy in 1865. ¶ *Art Annual,* IV, obit.; CAB; Clement and Hutton; *Who's Who in America,* 1899–1900; Cowdrey, NAD; Brooklyn CD 1851; NYCD 1855+; represented at Peabody Institute.

MORGAN, WILLIAM. Portrait painter, Orange (N.J.), 1859. ¶ Essex, Hudson, and Union Counties BD 1859.

MORGAN, WILLIAM P. Wood engraver of NYC, active 1811 to about 1872. Morgan was one of ALEXANDER ANDERSON's pupils and designed many of the wood cuts prepared by Anderson. His name appears intermittently in NYC directories from 1811 to 1838 and in Brooklyn directories from 1849 to 1858. Hamilton lists examples of his work dating from 1817 to 1872. ¶ NYCD 1811–13, 1815–16, 1818, 1824–31, 1833–34, 1836, 1838; Brooklyn CD 1849, 1851, 1854–58; Hamilton, *Early American Book Illustrators and Wood Engravers,* 408–10; Linton, *History of Wood Engraving in America,* 10; Lossing, *Memorial of Alexander Anderson,* 74–75.

MORHART, ADAM. Portrait painter from Bavaria, born about 1819. From the dates and place of birth of his children, it appears that he had come to NYC about 1853. ¶ 8 Census (1860), N.Y., XLVIII, 913.

MORIARTY, ALBERT P. Painter of fire engines and hose carriages, NYC, 1847–56. He exhibited at the American Institute in 1848, 1851, and 1856. ¶ NYCD 1847–56; Am. Inst. Cat., 1847, 1851, 1856.

MORIARTY, JOHN J. Apprentice lithographer, 19, born in Pennsylvania, living in Boston in 1860 with his mother, Mary Moriarty, tailoress. ¶ 8 Census (1860), Mass., XXIX, 382.

MORIN, ALEXANDER C. Seal engraver, die sinker, chaser, and jeweler, working in Philadelphia, 1821–60 and after. He was first listed as an engraver in 1855. ¶ Phila. CD 1821–60+.

MORIN, ANTHONY C. Seal engraver, die sinker, and chaser, Philadelphia, 1849–60. ¶ Phila. CD 1849–60.

MORIN, JOHN F. Engraver working in NYC from about 1825 to 1840. His widow is listed in 1841. ¶ Stauffer; NYCD 1828–41.

MORINE, HENRY. Lithographer, 31, a native of Pennsylvania, living in Philadelphia in 1860. His father, John Morine, was a shoemaker; a younger brother, WILLIAM, also was a lithographer. ¶ 8 Census (1860), Pa., LIX, 18.

MORINE, WILLIAM. Lithographer, 21, a native of Pennsylvania, living in Philadelphia. He was a younger brother of HENRY MORINE. ¶ 8 Census (1860), Pa., LIX, 18.

MORLEY, BRORHER & MATTHIAS. Lithographers, Philadelphia, 1859. This was actually WORLEY, BRACHER & MATTHIAS. ¶ Phila. BD 1859.

MORNS, F. Lithographer, Philadelphia, 1860. ¶ Phila. BD 1860.

MORON, J., see J. MORAN.

MORRELL, BENJAMIN. Engraver, 22, born in New York, living in Cincinnati in August 1850. ¶ 7 Census (1850), Ohio, XX, 748.

MORRELL, W. D. Portrait painter at Meriden Village, Plainfield (N.H.), 1849. *Cf.* —— MOREL; W. DE MORRILL. ¶ New England BD 1849.

MORRELL, WILLETT H. Shipcarver, NYC, 1842–51. In 1842 he and WINTER LINDMARK exhibited at the American Institute a full size wood carving of a woman. ¶ NYCD 1842–51; Am. Inst. Cat., 1842 (as William Morrell, but at Willett's address, so presumably the same).

MORRELL, WILLIAM, see WILLETT H. MORRELL.

MORRILL, D. Primitive genre in oils, Connecticut, 1860. ¶ Lipman and Winchester, 177.

MORRILL, W. DE. Painting and drawing teacher at New Orleans in 1844. *Cf.* W. D. MORRELL, —— MOREL. ¶ Delgado-WPA cites *Daily Topics,* May 21, 1844.

MORRIS, Mrs. ——. Painting and drawing teacher, Philadelphia, 1810–14. In 1828 she exhibited at the Pennsylvania Academy a sea view after Wright of Pimlico, who was stated to be her father. ¶ Brown and Brown; Rutledge, PA.

MORRIS, ANDREW. Portrait painter at NYC, 1848–52. In 1848 he showed at the American Art-Union a pair of portraits of a Scotch piper and a Highland drover. ¶ Cowdrey, AA & AAU; NYBD 1852.

MORRIS, DANIEL C. Engraver, Bangor (Me.), 1860. ¶ New England BD 1860.

MORRIS, DAVID. Sculptor, 33, from Wales, living in Philadelphia in August 1850. The directory indicates that he worked in plaster. ¶ 7 Census (1850), Pa., L, 40; Phila. CD 1850–51.

MORRIS, HENRY. Lithographer, 21, a native Pennsylvanian, in 1850 living with his father, a shoemaker, in Northern Liberties, Philadelphia. ¶ 7 Census (1850), Pa., XLIX, 952.

MORRIS, JONATHAN. Painter at Cincinnati (Ohio) in 1819. ¶ *Antiques* (March 1932), 152.

MORRIS, JONES FAWSON. Portrait painter at Sterling (Mass.) about 1835–40. ¶ Sears, *Some American Primitives,* 62 (repro.), 78.

MORRIS, LEWIS. Engraver, 25, born in Pennsylvania, living in Northern Liberties, Philadelphia, in August 1850. ¶ 7 Census (1850), Pa., XLIX, 327.

MORRIS, MARIA. Artist, 40, a native of Prussia, living in NYC in June 1860. ¶ 8 Census (1860), N.Y., XLV, 9.

MORRIS, RICHARD. Lithographer, 23, born in Ireland, living in NYC in June 1860. ¶ 8 Census (1860), N.Y., LI, 119.

MORRIS, WILLIAM V. Mural, fresco, and scene painter who emigrated from Wales to Utah in 1852 and opened the first art store in the territory. He did the art work for Brigham Young's Bee-Hive and Lion Houses, was the first scene painter for the Salt Lake Theater, a founder of the Deseret Academy of Arts in the sixties, and painter of the Assembly Hall frescoes in 1880. He died before 1887. ¶ Arrington, "Nauvoo Temple," Chap. 8.

MORRISON & CROWTHER, see JOSEPH M. MORRISON.

MORRISON, GEORGE W. (1820–1893). Portrait painter. A native of Maryland, Morrison started his career in Baltimore but moved out to Indiana about 1840 and spent most of his life in New Albany. ¶ Burnet, *Art and Artists of Indiana,* 384; Peat, *Pioneer Painters of Indiana,* 52–53, 235; Lafferty; information courtesy Katharine Woodward, Middleburg (Va.); *Antiques* (Nov. 1950), 394, repro.

MORRISON, JOSEPH M. General and banknote engraver, partner of HENRY CROWTHER in Morrison & Crowther, Cincinnati, 1853–60. ¶ Cincinnati CD 1853, 1856–59, BD 1860.

MORRISON, M. Wax portraitist, NYC, 1838; exhibited at the National Academy. ¶ Cowdrey, NAD.

MORRISON, WELLMAN or WILLIAM. Portrait painter, Boston, 1846–57; exhibitor at the Boston Athenaeum. ¶ Boston BD and CD 1846–57, as Wellman or William Morrison; Swan, BA.

MORSE, ALPHEUS CAREY (1818–1893). Portrait painter, Boston, 1847 and after. He exhibited at the Athenaeum in 1847. ¶ Swan, BA; Boston BD 1847–50.

MORSE, GEORGE FREDERICK (1834–?). Landscapes, marine views, and pencil sketches of vessels in Portland (Me.). He was living in Portland in 1858. ¶ Robinson and Dow, *Sailing Ships of New England,* I, 62.

MORSE, GEORGE HAZEN (1821–1885). Engraver of Boston, active from 1842. He was for many years associated with the firm of MORSE & TUTTLE. The earlier silversmith and engraver HAZEN MORSE probably was his father. ¶ Boston *Transcript,* Jan. 2, 1885, obit.; Boston CD 1842–60+.

MORSE, HAZEN. Silversmith and engraver, Boston, 1818–43. In 1830 he was with the SENEFELDER LITHOGRAPHIC COMPANY and from 1837 to 1843 headed the firm of MORSE & TUTTLE. He probably was the father of GEORGE HAZEN MORSE who joined the latter firm in 1842. ¶ Boston CD 1818–43; Stauffer; Whitmore, "Abel Bowen," 41.

MORSE, HENRY DUTTON (1826–1888). Amateur landscape and animal painter. A son of HAZEN MORSE, born in Boston on April 20, 1826. He learned engraving from his father, but soon turned to jewelry making and eventually to diamond-cutting. He was the first American to practice that trade and his improvements are said to have revolutionized it. Morse painted for amusement, but exhibited at the Athenaeum during the 1850's and 1860's. He died at Jamaica Plain (Mass.) on January 2, 1888. ¶ DAB; Swan, BA.

MORSE, JAMES H. Engraver, Westfield (Mass.), 1860. ¶ New England BD 1860.

MORSE, JOSEPH W. Wood engraver. He learned engraving from SHUBAEL D. CHILDS during the 1830's in NYC and practiced there from about 1840 to 1860. ¶ Linton, *History of Wood Engraving in America,* 20, 24; NYBD 1840–60.

MORSE, MOSES. Sign and ornamental painter, Marietta (Ohio), 1789. ¶ Knittle, *Early Ohio Taverns.*

MORSE, NATHANIEL (1688–1748). Engraver and silversmith who died at Boston on June 17, 1748. Known chiefly as a silversmith, he also engraved paper money for the colony of Massachusetts and at least one portrait. ¶ Stauffer, I, 183, and II, 374; *American Collector* (July 1947), 18, repro.

MORSE, SAMUEL FINLEY BREESE (1791–1872). N.A. Portrait, miniature, and historical painter; inventor. A son of Jedidiah Morse, the "father of American Geography," born in Charlestown (Mass.) on April 27, 1791. After attending Yale College, he decided to devote himself to painting and in 1811 went to London to study under BENJAMIN WEST. Returning to America in 1815 he spent the next few years painting portraits in New England and in Charleston (S.C.). In 1823 he settled in NYC and three years later was a leader in the formation of the National Academy of Design, of which he was the first President. From 1829 to 1833 Morse was in Europe. After his return to NYC he devoted increasingly less time to painting and more to the perfection of the electric telegraph with which his name is now almost exclusively associated. His later years were embittered by disputes and intrigues over the history and administration of the telegraph. Morse died in NYC on April 2, 1872. ¶ The most complete life is Mabee, *The American Leonardo;* see also Larkin, *Samuel F. B. Morse and American Democratic Art;* E. L. Morse, *Samuel F. B. Morse, His Letters and Journals;* Cowdrey, NAD; Cowdrey, AA & AAU; Rutledge, PA; Flexner, *The Light of Distant Skies.*

MORSE & TUTTLE. Engravers, Boston, 1837–60. Established in 1837 by HAZEN MORSE and JOSEPH W. TUTTLE, the firm became Morse, Tuttle & Co. in 1842 with the addition to the partnership of GEORGE HAZEN MORSE. After the elder Morse's retirement or death in 1843 the firm was again known as Morse & Tuttle. ¶ Boston CD 1837–60.

MORSE, W. H. Engraver whose work appeared in books published between *c.* 1851 and 1879. ¶ Hamilton, *American Book Illustrators and Wood Engravers,* 526.

MORTIMER, GEORGE D. or T. or F. Sculptor, NYC, exhibitor at the National Academy and Apollo Association between 1838 and 1842. ¶ Cowdrey, AA & AAU; Cowdrey, NAD; Gardner, *Yankee Stonecutters.*

MORTON, EDMUND. Miniaturist working in NYC in 1827–29 and 1845, and about 1861 at Cincinnati. He exhibited at the National Academy. He was living with HENRY J. and JOHN L. MORTON in 1828. ¶ Cowdrey, NAD; information courtesy Mrs. W. H. Whitley who cites Miss Grace Donaldson of Paris (Ky.).

MORTON, HENRY JACKSON. A.N.A. Portrait and genre painter. In 1828 he was living in NYC with EDMUND and JOHN L.

MORTON. He exhibited at the National Academy between 1827 and 1838. ¶ Cowdrey, NAD.

MORTON, J. N. Engraver, 50, born in New York, living in NYC in 1860. ¶ 8 Census (1860), N.Y., LVI, 490.

MORTON, JOHN LUDLOW (1792–1871). N.A. Portrait, historical, and landscape painter. He was active as early as 1815 when his view of the Susquehanna was engraved for the December *Port Folio.* From 1827 to 1860 he lived in NYC and exhibited frequently at the National Academy, of which he was a full member from 1831, and at the American Art-Union. John L., EDMUND, and HENRY J. MORTON were evidently close relatives, as they were all living together in 1828. John L. Morton died in NYC on August 1, 1871. ¶ Thieme-Becker; obit., N. Y. *Daily Tribune,* Aug. 3, 1871; *Port Folio,* XXIV (Dec. 1815), frontis.; Cowdrey, NAD; Cowdrey, AA & AAU; *American Collector* (July 1948), 8, repro.

MORVILLE, ROBERT W. Engraver, Lowell (Mass.), 1835–37. ¶ Belknap, *Artists and Craftsmen of Essex County,* 4.

MORVILLER, JOSEPH. Landscape painter, Boston, 1855–70. He exhibited at the Athenaeum between 1855 and 1864 and PRANG published some lithographs after his paintings. He also exhibited at the Pennsylvania Academy in 1859. ¶ Swan, BA; *Panorama* (Dec. 1945), 32; Rutledge, PA.

MOSELY, EDWARD. Map engraver at Charleston (S.C.), 1735. ¶ Rutledge, *Artists in the Life of Charleston.*

MOSES, B. and G. Portrait painters, New Orleans, 1859. ¶ New Orleans BD 1859; Thompson, *Louisiana Writers.*

MOSES, MORRIS. Daguerreotypist, Trenton (N.J.), 1857–65. This was probably the Mr. Moses who in 1859 advertised in Trenton that he executed crayon pictures. ¶ Trenton CD 1857, 1865; WPA (N.J.), Hist. Rec. Survey cites Trenton *Daily Gazette,* Dec. 22, 1859.

MOSES, SAMUEL C. Portrait and miniature painter, born in New Hampshire about 1818, the son of THOMAS P. MOSES of Portsmouth. Samuel was in Boston between 1841 and 1845 and exhibited at the Athenaeum. In August 1850 he was living in Portsmouth with his father. ¶ 7 Census (1850), N.H., II (1), 48; Swan, BA; Boston BD 1844–45.

MOSES, THOMAS P. Amateur painter of sailing ships. Born in New Hampshire about 1774, he was a tailor by trade and apparently spent most of his life in Portsmouth (N.H.). He was living there in 1850, as was also his artist son, SAMUEL C. MOSES. ¶ 7 Census (1850), N.H., II (1), 48; Lipman and Winchester, 177.

MOSIER, J., see JOSEPH MOZIER.

MOSLER, GUSTAVUS. Lithographer, Cincinnati, 1853. In 1856–57 he was listed as a tobacconist. ¶ Cincinnati CD 1853–57.

MOSLER, HENRY, JR. Genre and portrait painter, designer, and engraver. Born and brought up in Richmond (Ind.), he painted his first pictures there about 1858 but soon after moved to Cincinnati where he worked as an engraver and teacher of painting. One of his pupils was ELIZABETH NICHOLSON. ¶ Burnet, *Art and Artists of Indiana,* 75, 113, 271; Peat, *Pioneer Painters of Indiana;* Indiana BD 1858; Cincinnati CD 1858.

MOSS, EDWARD. Banknote engraver, 36, a native of Pennsylvania, living in NYC in 1860. He had apparently moved there from Pennsylvania only a year or two before. ¶ 8 Census (1860), N.Y., LIII, 174.

MOSS, FRANK (1838–after 1905). Figure painter, born May 9, 1838, in Philadelphia. He studied in Paris under Bonnat and exhibited after 1860 in the National Academy and Pennsylvania Academy. In 1905 he was living in Washington (D.C.). ¶ *Artists Year Book,* 137.

MOTE, ALDEN (1840–1917). Portrait and landscape painter, nephew of MARCUS MOTE. He was born August 27, 1840, at West Milton (Ohio) and died January 13, 1917, at Richmond (Ind.). ¶ Burnet, *Art and Artists of Indiana,* 276, 384; *Art Annual,* XIV, obit.; Peat, *Pioneer Painters of Indiana.*

MOTE, MARCUS (1817–1898). Portrait and religious painter. Born June 19, 1817, near West Milton (Ohio), Mote became a painter in spite of opposition from his Quaker family and friends. Lebanon (Ohio) was the center of his activity as a portrait painter. He also painted coaches for a company in Waynesville, designed election posters and newspaper advertisements, did some lithographic work, and took daguerreotypes and photographs. During 1853 and 1854 he painted a panorama of *Uncle Tom's Cabin* and several others on religious subjects. About 1866 Mote moved to Richmond (Ind.) where he taught in the public and Sunday schools and had a drawing academy. He died in Richmond February 26, 1898. ALDEN

MOTE, a nephew, was also a painter. ¶ Phillips, "Marcus Mote, Quaker Artist"; Thornburg, "The Panoramas of Marcus Mote"; Burnet, *Art and Artists of Indiana,* 385; Peat, *Pioneer Painters of Indiana.*

MOTT, B. H. Wood engraver, Philadelphia, 1860. ¶ Phila. BD 1860.

MOTTRAM, C. Engraver of JOHN W. HILL's view of NYC from Brooklyn in 1855, published in NYC in the same year. ¶ Stauffer.

MOULD, J. B. Stipple engraver of a number of portraits of foreigners, published in NYC about 1830. It is not known whether the engravings were done here or abroad. ¶ Stauffer.

MOULSON, DEBORAH. Drawing teacher of Philadelphia, 1825–33; exhibited in 1827 at the Pennsylvania Academy. ¶ Phila. CD 1825–33; Rutledge, PA.

MOULTHROP, REUBEN (1763–1814). Portrait and miniature painter, modeller in wax; active in New Haven (Conn.) as early as 1793 and in NYC in 1794. He appears to have painted only in Connecticut, but his wax works were exhibited from Boston to Harrisburg (Pa.) around the turn of the century. Moulthrop died at East Haven (Conn.) on July 29, 1814. ¶ Sawitzky, "Portraits by Reuben Moulthrop"; Information courtesy Helen McKearin who cites *Connecticut Journal,* Sept. 4, 1793, and Harrisburg, *Oracle of Dauphin County,* May 19, 1800; Gottesman, *Arts and Crafts in New York,* II, nos. 1281, 1287; New York *Evening Post,* Aug. 3, 1814, obit.; NYCD 1794; E. S. Bolton, *American Wax Portraits;* repro., *Art News* (Jan. 1953), 40; Flexner, *The Light of Distant Skies.*

MOUNT, HENRY SMITH (1802–1841). A.N.A. Figure, still life, animal, and landscape painter in oils; brother of SHEPARD ALONZO and WILLIAM SIDNEY MOUNT. He was born October 9, 1802, at Stony Brook, Long Island (N.Y.) and served his apprenticeship with the NYC sign painter, LEWIS CHILD, beginning in 1819. During the twenties and thirties he worked in NYC as a sign and ornamental painter. He began exhibiting at the National Academy in 1827 and was elected an Associate in 1828. He died January 20, 1841, at Setauket, Long Island. ¶ Cowdrey, *The Three Mount Brothers;* Cowdrey and Williams, *William Sidney Mount;* Cowdrey, NAD.

MOUNT, SHEPARD ALONZO (1804–1868). N.A. Portrait, landscape, and animal painter in oils; brother of HENRY SMITH and WILLIAM SIDNEY MOUNT. Born July 17, 1804, at Setauket, Long Island (N.Y.), he studied at the school of the National Academy in 1826 and worked chiefly in NYC during the next fifteen years. In 1837 he married a sister of the prominent portrait painter CHARLES LORING ELLIOTT. From 1841 until near the end of his life he lived at Stony Brook, Long Island. He died at Setauket on September 18, 1868. He was an Associate of the National Academy 1833–42 and an Academician 1842–68. ¶ A. D. Smith, *Shepard Alonzo Mount;* Cowdrey, *The Three Mount Brothers;* Cowdrey and Williams, *William Sidney Mount;* Cowdrey, NAD; Cowdrey, AA & AAU; 8 Census (1860), N.Y., XLV, 422.

MOUNT, WILLIAM SIDNEY (1807–1868). N.A. Genre, portrait, landscape, still life, and animal painter; brother of HENRY SMITH and SHEPARD ALONZO MOUNT. He was born November 26, 1807, at Setauket, Long Island (N.Y.) and spent most of his boyhood at Stony Brook, Long Island. In 1824 he was apprenticed to his brother Henry, a sign and ornamental painter in NYC, and two years later he entered the school of the National Academy. He returned to his home in 1827, but from 1829 to about 1836 he worked principally in NYC. From 1837, except for short trips, he lived at Stony Brook. Though his principal support came from portrait painting, Mount's reputation rests mainly on his genre paintings. His best work was done during the thirties. He was elected an Academician of the National Academy in 1832 and exhibited there frequently, as well as elsewhere. He died at Setauket on November 19, 1868. ¶ Cowdrey and Williams, *William Sidney Mount;* Cowdrey, *The Three Mount Brothers;* Cowdrey, NAD; Cowdrey, AA & AAU; Rutledge, MHS; Rutledge, PA.

MOYERSTEIN, see MEYERSTEIN.

MOZIER, JOSEPH (1812–1870). Sculptor. Born August 22, 1812, at Burlington (Vt.), Mozier became a successful merchant in NYC. In 1845 he abandoned his business career to become a sculptor, went to Rome, and there spent the rest of his life, except for a few short visits to America. His work was chiefly "ideal" and religious, though he also did some genre groups. He died October 3, 1870, at Faido (Switzerland). ¶ DAB; Taft, *His-*

tory of American Sculpture, 109; NYCD 1834–44; Cowdrey, NAD; Sheirr, "Joseph Mozier and His Handiwork"; Cowdrey, AA & AAU.

MUCHLEN, THOMAS. Lithographer, 35, from Germany, at Philadelphia in August 1850. ¶ 7 Census (1850), Pa., L, 627.

MUDGE, JOSEPH B. Author and illustrator of *The American Drawing Book,* published in Boston in 1843. The illustrations were views in the Hudson Valley. ¶ Peters, *America on Stone.*

MUDGE, ZACHARIAH. Topographical artist. He was an officer on the British ship *Discovery* on Vancouver's voyage of discovery in the north Pacific, 1790–95. One of the illustrations in Vancouver's account of the voyage (London, 1798) was based on a sketch by Mudge, off the coast of Oregon. ¶ Rasmussen, "Art and Artists of Oregon" (citation courtesy David C. Duniway).

MÜLLER or MILLER, CHARLES. Sculptor in bronze and marble. He was a native of Germany, born about 1820, who worked in NYC from about 1856 into the sixties. He exhibited at the National Academy and at the American Institute. ¶ 8 Census (1860), N.Y., LX, 257; Cowdrey, NAD; Am. Inst. Cat., 1856; NYBD 1857–60, CD 1862.

MUELLER, FREDERICK. German artist, 42, at Philadelphia in August 1850. ¶ 7 Census (1850), Pa., LII, 893.

MUELLER, GERHARDT. German historical painter who came to Cincinnati from Munich about 1840 and opened a studio with HENRY KOEMPEL. Examples of their work are said still to exist in the old Catholic churches of Cincinnati. Gerhardt Mueller was the father of WILLIAM MILLER. ¶ Burnet, *Art and Artists of Indiana,* 65.

MÜLLER, HENRY. Landscape painter who exhibited at the National Academy between 1850 and 1852 and also at the American Art-Union. His address in 1851–52 was in NYC. The subjects of his paintings suggest that he had worked in Europe and had visited Niagara and Trenton Falls in New York State. ¶ Cowdrey, NAD; Cowdrey, AA & AAU; NYCD 1851.

MÜLLER, JOHANN MICHAEL ENZING, see ENZING-MÜLLER.

MUELLER or MULLER, JOHN. Lithographic artist who in the fall of 1850 executed a view of Cleveland (Ohio), published in 1851. ¶ WPA (Ohio) *Annals of Cleveland,* Nov. 1850, Sept. 1851; Stokes, *Historical Prints,* 107; Peters, *America on Stone.*

MUELLER, JOHN JACOB (?–1781). Portrait painter of Nuremberg (Germany) who joined the Moravian Church in 1740 and served as secretary to Count Zinzendorf during the latter's 1741–43 visit to America. At this time he is said to have painted "Christ Bearing the Cross" for the chapel of the Community House at Bethlehem (Pa.). He returned to Europe in 1743, was ordained in 1760, and died at Nisky (Prussia) in 1781. ¶ Levering, *History of Bethlehem,* 73, 145.

MUELLER, see also MILLER and MULER.

MUGFORD, WILLIAM. Early American crayon portraitist thought to have worked in New England. ¶ Fielding.

MULER (Muller or Mueller), HECTOR B. Portrait, miniature, and landscape painter working in NYC from 1828 to 1853. Bailey and Goodspeed listed him as H. Muller, the NYC directories as Hector or Hector B. Muler, and the Boston Athenaeum as Mueller of NYC. ¶ NYCD 1830–53; Dunlap, *History* (1918), III, 320; Cowdrey, NAD; Swan, BA.

MULHOLLAND, ST. CLAIR. Landscape painter, 20, a native Pennsylvanian, living in Philadelphia in June 1860 in the home of SAMUEL SCARLETT. ¶ 8 Census (1860), Pa., L, 139.

MULLEN, E. F. or E. J. Illustrator for *Vanity Fair, c.* 1860, and for books published in the sixties. ¶ Hamilton, *Early American Book Illustrators and Wood Engravers,* 412; Murrell, *History of Amercan Graphic Humor,* 211, 215.

MULLER, see MILLER, MUELLER (Müller), and MULER.

MULLIKEN, JONATHAN (1746–1782). Engraver and clock maker who died at Newburyport (Mass.) on June 19, 1782. He engraved a facsimile of PAUL REVERE's Boston Massacre print. ¶ Belknap, *Artists and Craftsmen of Essex County,* 4.

MULLIN, PATRICK. Irish engraver, 36, at NYC in 1850. ¶ 7 Census (1850), N.Y., XLI, 789.

MUMFORD, ——. Engraver of a view of Lockport on the Erie Canal (N.Y.). *Cf.* EDWARD W. MUMFORD. ¶ *Ariel,* V (June 11, 1831), opp. 49.

MUMFORD, EDWARD WILLIAM (1812–1858). Oil and crayon portraitist, engraver, teacher of drawing. Born in 1812, probably in Newport (R.I.), moved to Philadelphia as early as 1835, and worked there the rest of his life. In 1852 he formed a partnership with his brother, THOMAS H. MUMFORD, to do electrotyping. Edward exhibited at the Artists' Fund Society and Pennsylvania Academy from 1837 to 1857 and died in 1858, presumably in Philadelphia. ¶ Mumford, *Mumford Memoirs,* 74; Phila. CD 1835–59; Rutledge, PA; Stauffer.

MUMFORD, THOMAS HOWLAND (1816–?). Wood engraver and electrotypist. He was probably born in Newport (R.I.), but from 1840 until after 1860 he was a resident of Philadelphia. In 1852 he and his brother EDWARD W. MUMFORD opened an electrotyping business. ¶ Mumford, *Mumford Memoirs,* 74; Phila. CD 1840–60+; Hamilton, *Early American Book Illustrators and Wood Engravers,* 414; 7 Census (1850), Pa., L, 391.

MUMLER, ANDREW C. Engraver, Boston, 1854–60 and after; in 1857 with WILLIAM H. MUMLER. ¶ Boston CD 1854–60+.

MUMLER, W. & A. Engravers, Boston, 1857; WILLIAM H. and ANDREW C. MUMLER. ¶ Boston BD 1857.

MUMLER, WILLIAM H. (1832–1884). Engraver. He was born in Boston, spent his whole life there, and died there May 16, 1884. Beginning about 1854 he worked as an engraver for 20 years. He invented a photo-electric plate and became treasurer of the company which produced them. In 1857 he was associated with ANDREW C. MUMLER. ¶ Boston *Transcript,* May 17, 1884, obit.; Boston CD 1854–60+.

MUNDSEN, SARAH H. Winner of a prize for monochromatic painting, Illinois State Fair, October 1855. ¶ Chicago *Daily Press,* Oct. 15, 1855.

MUNDY, JOHNSON MARCHANT (1831–1897). Sculptor and portrait painter, born May 13, 1831, at New Brunswick (N.J.) or Geneva (N.Y.). After serving a seven year apprenticeship with HENRY KIRKE BROWN, he opened a studio in Rochester (N.Y.) where for 20 years he was engaged chiefly in portrait painting. He later moved to Tarrytown (N.Y.), where he died in 1897. His most important piece of sculpture was a statue of Washington Irving. ¶ Mundy, *Nicholas Mundy and Descendants,* 11, 14; Gardner, *Yankee Stonecutters,* [74].

MUNGER, CAROLINE (1808–1892). Miniaturist; daughter of GEORGE MUNGER. She was born at East Guilford (Conn.) on May 15, 1808, married Horace B. Washburn in 1831, spent most of her life at East River (Conn.), and died at Madison (Conn.) on January 4, 1892. ¶ Munger, *The Munger Book,* 119; Bolton, *Miniature Painters;* Cowdrey, NAD; French, *Art and Artists in Connecticut,* 175.

MUNGER, CLARISSA (1806–1889). Flower painter; daughter of GEORGE MUNGER. Born May 20, 1806, at East Guilford (Conn.), she married the Rev. Milton Badger in 1828 and spent her married life in Andover (Mass.), NYC, and Madison (Conn.). Her flower paintings were well known through reproductions. She died December 14, 1889. ¶ Munger, *The Munger Book,* 118; French, *Art and Artists in Connecticut,* 175.

MUNGER, GEORGE (1781–1825). Portrait and miniature painter; engraver; born in Guilford (Conn.) on February 17, 1781. He became a professional artist about 1815, after a number of years in teaching, and worked in New Haven until his death, July 2, 1825. He was a cousin of ANSON DICKINSON, the teacher of NATHANIEL JOCELYN, and the father of CAROLINE, CLARISSA, and GEORGE NICHOLAS MUNGER, all of whom did some painting. ¶ Munger, *The Munger Book,* 62; Bolton, *Miniature Painters;* French, *Art and Artists in Connecticut,* 45 (dates erroneously given as 1783–1824; the error is repeated in Stauffer, Fielding, and Thieme-Becker); Cowdrey, AA & AAU; Rice, "Life of Nathaniel Jocelyn."

MUNGER, GEORGE NICHOLAS (1803–1882). Landscape painter; son of GEORGE MUNGER. Born September 23, 1803, at East Guilford (Conn.), he became a prominent mechanic and instrument maker in New Haven, and died at Madison (Conn.) on August 7, 1882. Painting was his avocation. ¶ Munger, *The Munger Book,* 118; information courtesy Foster W. Rice via FARL.

MUNGER, GILBERT DAVIS (1837–1903). Engraver and landscape painter, born in Madison (Conn.) on April 14, 1837. He worked as an engraver in Washington (D.C.) in the fifties (in 1860 living with WILLIAM H. DOUGAL.) He later became well-known here and abroad for his paintings of Niagara Falls, Venice, and the Barbizon country. He lived for many years in Paris. He died January 27, 1903, in Washington. ¶ *Art Annual,* IV (1903), obit.; Munger, *The Munger Book,* 158; 8 Census (1860), D.C., II, 28.

MUNN, JOHN D. Engraver, Louisville (Ky.), 1840's and 1850's. ¶ Louisville CD 1848, 1859.

MUNROE, NATHAN WINSHIP (1789–?). Portrait painter, born August 5, 1789, at Lexington (Mass.). Said to have been a pupil of GILBERT STUART. He was working in Boston in 1813 but died in his youth. ¶ Hudson, *History of the Town of Lexington,* II, 464; Boston CD 1813.

MUNSON, JAMES H. Engraver, Cincinnati, 1840. He was from Connecticut. ¶ Cincinnati CD 1840 (courtesy Edward H. Dwight, Cincinnati Art Museum).

MUNSON, LUCIUS (1796–1823). Portrait painter, born December 15, 1796, at New Haven (Conn.). He studied in NYC about 1818, worked for a year in New Haven, then in South Carolina, and again in New Haven. He went to Bermuda for his health about 1822, and died July 27, 1823, while visiting Turk's Island in the West Indies. ¶ French, *Art and Artists in Connecticut,* 59; represented in Bermuda Historical Society, *Loan Exhibition of Portraits,* 1935.

MUNSON, SAMUEL B. (1806–1880). Engraver, born May 29, 1806, probably in New Haven (Conn.). Soon after 1830 he settled in Cincinnati. He was with DOOLITTLE & MUNSON from 1831 to 1849 and agent for DANFORTH, WRIGHT & Co. from 1856 to 1859. He died on April 6, 1880. ¶ Munson, *The Munson Record,* II, 718; Stauffer; Cincinnati CD 1849, BD 1850–59; Hamilton, *Early American Book Illustrators and Wood Engravers,* 96.

MUNSON, WILLIAM GILES (1801–1878). Amateur landscape and flower painter, born February 28, 1801, probably in New Haven (Conn.). A dentist by profession, he painted many local scenes, some of which are now in the Yale University Art Gallery and the New Haven Colony Historical Society. He died September 27, 1878. ¶ Munson, *The Munson Record,* II, 716–17; *American Processional,* 109 (repro.), 240.

MURCHISON, WILLIAM. Lithographer, 26, a native of Pennsylvania, living in Philadelphia in 1850. ¶ 7 Census (1850), Pa., LII, 917.

MURDOCH, JOHN (1836–1923). Architect and civil engineer working in Baltimore from just after the Civil War. The Maryland Historical Society owns two watercolor drawings by him, one showing a proposed bridge (1867) and the other a Baltimore residence (1868). He died in Baltimore on November 16, 1923. ¶ *Maryland History Notes,* VI (Nov. 1948).

MURDOCK, JOHN. Portrait painter working at St. Louis in 1854 and at San Francisco in 1856. ¶ St. Louis BD 1854; San Francisco BD 1856; Peters, *California on Stone.*

MURIN, ——. French artist, 35, at San Francisco in 1860. ¶ 8 Census (1860), Cal., VII, 466.

MURINGER, CASPAR. Lithographer, 44, from France, living with his family in Philadelphia in 1850–52. His son Emile, 16, also was a lithographer. Probably the father-in-law of CHRISTIAN SCHUSSELE. ¶ 7 Census (1850), Pa., LI, 923; DAB, under Schussele.

MURPHY, JAMES. Irish lithographer, 20, in NYC in 1860. He lived with MICHAEL MURPHY, presumably a relative. ¶ 8 Census (1860), N.Y., XLII, 855.

MURPHY, JOHN A. Portrait painter living in NYC who exhibited a portrait of General Zachary Taylor at the 1851 fair of the American Institute. ¶ Am. Inst. Cat., 1851.

MURPHY, JOHN B. Apprentice engraver, 17, born in Pennsylvania, living in Philadelphia in 1860 with his father, William C. Murphy, carpenter. ¶ 8 Census (1860), Pa., XLIX, 271.

MURPHY, JOHN M. Irish engraver, 24, living at Dallas, Wasco County (Ore.) in 1860. ¶ 8 Census (1860), Oregon, cited by David C. Duniway, Oregon State Archivist.

MURPHY, JOHN R. Delineator of a view of New York Hospital, about 1811. ¶ Stokes, *Icon.,* III, 569 and pl. 88.

MURPHY, MICHAEL. Irish lithographer, 25, living in NYC in 1860 with JAMES MURPHY, presumably a relative. ¶ 8 Census (1860), N.Y., XLII, 855.

MURPHY, PETER. Irish sculptor or marble worker, 35, living in San Francisco in 1860. Three of his children were born in Massachusetts between about 1846 and 1852 and three others in California after 1855. ¶ 8 Census (1860), Cal., VII, 738; San Francisco CD 1861.

MURPHY, THOMAS J. Lithographer, Boston, 1860. ¶ Boston CD 1860.

MURPHY, WILLIAM. Architect; designer of a widely reproduced view of the Mormon Temple, Nauvoo (Ill.), first published at St. Louis in 1868. He came from the East and settled in Nauvoo probably before

1848. His view of the Temple was made sometime in the fifties. Murphy designed the Roman Catholic Church at Nauvoo in the sixties and spent his latter years in St. Louis. ¶ Arrington, "Nauvoo Temple," Chap. 8.

MURPHY, WILLIAM. General and wood engraver, die sinker, and lithographer, NYC, 1850's. ¶ NYBD 1852–60.

MURPHY, WILLIAM D. (1834–?). Portrait painter, born March 11, 1834, on a plantation in Madison County (Ala.). After graduating from Cumberland University, Lebanon (Tenn.), Murphy taught for a number of years and then became a photographer. He received his first instruction in painting from WILLIAM COOPER of Nashville. Murphy continued to work as a photographer in several Southern cities until 1876 when he moved to Philadelphia. He moved to NYC in 1883 and four years later married an artist, Harriet Anderson. Together Mr. and Mrs. Murphy painted portraits of many prominent men of the late 19th and early 20th century. ¶ Fairman, *Art and Artists of the Capitol,* 460; Thieme-Becker; Fielding.

MURPHY, WILLIAM F., & SONS. Lithographers, stationers, and printers, Philadelphia, 1859 and after. The firm consisted of William F., Harry F., and Charles S. Murphy. None of these was listed individually as a lithographer. ¶ Phila. CD 1859–60.

MURRAY, DRAPER, FAIRMAN & COMPANY. Banknote engravers, Philadelphia, 1810 or 1811 to 1818. The firm originally consisted of GEORGE MURRAY, JOHN DRAPER, and GIDEON FAIRMAN. Later members included JACOB PERKINS, ASA SPENCER, and CHRISTIAN GOBRECHT. With the withdrawal in 1818 of Draper, the firm became MURRAY, FAIRMAN & CO. ¶ Toppan, *100 Years of Bank Note Engraving,* 7–10; Brown and Brown.

MURRAY, EDWARD H. Sign and ornamental painter, Philadelphia, 1855–60 and after. He was listed as "artist" in 1857. ¶ Phila. CD 1857.

MURRAY, ELENOR. Painter of a romantic scene in watercolors; her home was at Red Bank (N.J.) about 1820. ¶ Lipman and Winchester, 177.

MURRAY, ELIZA. Painter of a watercolor memorial, New England, about 1810. ¶ Lipman and Winchester, 177.

MURRAY, Mrs. ELIZABETH HEAPHY (1815–1882). Landscape painter. She lived in Philadelphia between 1856 and 1861 and in Boston in 1868, and exhibited at the Pennsylvania Academy. Her husband was John M. Murray. ¶ Rutledge, PA; Thieme-Becker; Bénézit.

MURRAY, FAIRMAN & COMPANY. Banknote engravers, Philadelphia, 1819–21; GEORGE MURRAY and GIDEON FAIRMAN. This firm succeeded MURRAY, DRAPER, FAIRMAN & Co. and presumably came to an end in 1822 with Murray's death. Its successor was FAIRMAN, DRAPER & CO. ¶ Brown and Brown; Pa. Acad. Cat., 1821.

MURRAY, GEORGE (?–1822). Banknote and general engraver. A native of Scotland, he came to Philadelphia from the southern United States about 1800. About 1810 or 1811 he joined with several others to establish the banknote engraving firm of MURRAY, DRAPER, FAIRMAN & CO. and, after its dissolution in 1818, its successor MURRAY, FAIRMAN & CO. He died in Philadelphia on July 2, 1822. ¶ Stauffer; Toppan, *100 Years of Bank Note Engraving,* 7; catalogues of the Society of Artists (1812–14) and the Pennsylvania Academy (1817–20).

MURRAY, GEORGE J. Engraver, of GORY & MURRAY, Louisville (Ky.), 1859. ¶ Louisville CD 1859.

MURRAY, JAMES. Engraver from Scotland, 39, at Baltimore in 1860. His wife and two children, 8 and 5, were also natives of Scotland, indicating that he emigrated after 1855. ¶ 8 Census (1860), Md., IV, 189.

MURRAY, JOHN. Engraver of the 52d [British] Regiment at NYC in 1778. He was from Edinburgh. His advertisement emphasized engraving of coats of arms on copper and fancy engraving on gold and silver. ¶ Kelby, *Notes on American Artists,* 14.

MURRAY, JOHN ROBERT (1774–1851). Amateur artist and lithographer from NYC, known for a view of "Woodlawn," country seat of Lawrence Lewis near Mt. Vernon (Va.), done about 1824 during Lafayette's visit to America. ¶ *Antiques* (March 1952), 259, repro.

MURRAY, MARY. Portraitist in watercolor, oil, and crayon, NYC, 1834. ¶ Dunlap, *History,* II, 472.

MURRY, T. Ornamental penman and engraver, NYC, 1837. ¶ NYBD 1837.

MURTY, FRANK. Engraver, 23, a native of Pennsylvania, at Philadelphia in 1860. ¶ 8 Census (1860), Pa., LIV, 671.

MUSE, AARON. Italian sculptor, 20, in NYC in 1850. ¶ 7 Census (1850), N.Y., XLIII, 40.

MUSSEY, I. or J. OSGOOD. Landscape painter, born in New Hampshire about 1818. By 1848 the family had moved to Cincinnati and two years later the father, a physician, owned real estate in Cincinnati valued at $25,000. Osgood Mussey exhibited at the American Art-Union in 1848. ¶ 7 Census (1850), Ohio, XXII, 499; Cowdrey, AA & AAU.

MUZZY, C. B. Landscape and portrait painter, New Orleans, 1858. ¶ Delgado-WPA cites New Orleans BD 1858.

MYER, FELIX. German lithographer, 27, in the New York City Lunatic Asylum, October 1850. ¶ 7 Census (1850), N.Y., LVII, 429.

MYER, H. ED. Wood engraver, designer, and draftsman with FAXON & MYER, Buffalo (N.Y.), 1858–59. ¶ Buffalo CD 1858–59.

MYER, HENRY. Lithographer, 27, born in Württemberg, living in NYC in 1860. Also in the same house was George Myer, 14, apprentice lithographer. ¶ 8 Census (1860), N.Y., XLVI, 875.

MYER, see also MAYER and MEYER.

MYERS, W. Painter of a series of 12 scenes from the life of Christ which were shown in Cincinnati, where Myers lived, in 1851. This might be Warner Myers or Meyers, painter (1850 CD). ¶ Cincinnati *Daily Gazette,* April 12, 1851 (citation courtesy J. E. Arrington); Cincinnati CD 1850.

MYERS, WILLIAM BARKSDALE. Portrait and historical painter of ante-bellum Richmond (Va.). He was the son of a prominent lawyer, Gustavus A. Myers (1801–1869), and a member of the artistic circle which centered around the VALENTINE family. Myers exhibited at the Washington Art Association in 1857. ¶ *Richmond Portraits,* 142, 218; Washington Art Assoc. Cat., 1857.

MYERS, see also MEYERS.

MYNARTS, H. Miniaturist and portrait painter, profilist and silhouettist, at Charleston (S.C.) in 1821. ¶ Rutledge, *Artists in the Life of Charleston.*

MYNERTS, W. E. Portrait and miniature painter and teacher, New Orleans, 1840. ¶ Delgado-WPA cites *Picayune,* July 14, 1840, and *Commercial Bulletin,* Dec. 2, 1840.

N

Nachtrieb, Michael Strieby (1835–1916). Portrait, landscape, still life, and ornamental painter, born August 25, 1835, at Wooster (Ohio). Nachtrieb studied in NYC, did decorative painting in Ohio and on Mississippi River steamboats, and painted portraits of Lincoln, Edwin Booth, the College of Bishops of the Episcopal Church, and the founders and early presidents of Wooster College. He was at Cleveland in 1857. He died in Wooster on December 27, 1916. ¶ Clark, *Ohio Art and Artists,* 481; WPA (Ohio), *Annals of Cleveland.*

Nagel, Louis. Lithographer, born in Germany about 1817. He was working in NYC as early as 1844, exhibited at the American Institute in 1846 and 1847, and formed at least two partnerships: Nagel & Mayer (1846) and Nagel & Weingaertner (1849–56). After 1857 he was at San Francisco. ¶ 7 Census (1850), N.Y., XLVII, 443; NYBD 1844, CD 1845–56; San Francisco BD 1858–60; Am. Inst. Cat., 1846, 1847; *Portfolio* (June–July 1945), 226; Peters, *America on Stone.*

Nagel & Mayer. Lithographers, NYC, 1846; Louis Nagel and Ferdinand Mayer. ¶ NYBD 1846; Peters, *America on Stone.*

Nagel & Weingaertner. Lithographers, NYC, 1849–56; Louis Nagel and Adam Weingaertner. They exhibited at the American Institute in 1850. ¶ NYCD 1849–56; Am. Inst. Cat., 1850; Peters, *America on Stone.*

Nagle, James Frederick. Wood engraver, born in Pennsylvania about 1833, working in Philadelphia from 1850. In 1860 and after he was with Noble & Nagle. ¶ 7 Census (1850), Pa., L, 937; Phila. CD 1856–60+.

Nagle, see also Neagle.

Nahl, Arthur, see Hugo Wilhelm Arthur Nahl.

Nahl, Charles Christian (1818–1878). Portrait, historical, landscape, genre, and animal painter; engraver, lithographer, illustrator. Born October 13, 1818, at Cassel (Germany), Charles Nahl was the son and grandson of artists. He and his half-brother, Hugo W. A. Nahl, were at Paris in 1848 and emigrated to America the following year. After a brief stay in NYC they went on to California in 1850 and worked in the gold fields for a few months, but soon resumed their profession in San Francisco. Between 1850 and 1867 they worked chiefly as photographers and commercial artists, but also produced some paintings of historical interest. In 1867 Charles secured the patronage of Judge E. B. Crocker, for whom he did a number of large paintings, and during the seventies his pictures enjoyed quite a local vogue. At the time of his death, March 1, 1878, he was hailed as one of the leading painters of pioneer life in California. ¶ Van Nostrand and Coulter, *California Pictorial,* 66, 72, 110; 8 Census (1860), Cal., VII, 813; Cowdrey, AA & AAU; San Francisco BD 1856+; Jackson, *Gold Rush Album,* repros.; WPA (Cal.), *Introduction to California Art Research,* I; Peters, *America on Stone;* Gudde, "Carl Nahl, California's Pioneer of Painting."

Nahl, Hugo Wilhelm Arthur (1820–1889). Painter, crayon and charcoal artist, engraver, illustrator, designer of California state seal. Born in Cassel (Germany), Arthur (as he was usually known) was a student in Paris at the time of the 1848 Revolution which precipitated his emigration to America the following year. He and his half-brother Charles C. Nahl arrived in NYC in 1849 and a few months later moved on to the California gold fields. They soon resumed their profession, however, and worked in San Francisco as photographers and commercial artists from the mid-fifties until the late sixties. Arthur was a frequent exhibitor at the San Francisco Art Association during the 1870's and in 1888 won a silver medal at the California State Fair for his pictures in crayon and charcoal. He visited Europe in 1881. He died in San Francisco on April 1, 1889. ¶ Van Nostrand and Coulter, *California Pictorial,* 140–41; WPA (Cal.), *Introduction to California Art Research,* I; 8 Census (1860), Cal., VII, 813; Cowdrey, AA & AAU; Peters, *America on Stone.*

Nairn, Mrs. ——. Portrait and miniature painter, Baltimore, 1842–45. ¶ Baltimore CD 1842–45.

Nanon, Louis. Young portrait painter at New Orleans in 1854, said to have studied in Europe; he exhibited a biblical painting. ¶ Delgado-WPA cites *Bee,* Feb. 16 and Dec. 8, 1854.

NAPIER, GEORGE. Amateur artist who was in California during the Gold Rush and sent home to England a sketch of "Gold Washing at the Diggings," which was published in the *Illustrated London News* on November 17, 1849. ¶ Van Nostrand and Coulter, *California Pictorial,* 98–99.

NARINE, JAMES. Of Narine & Company, engravers, lithographers, and printers, NYC, 1839–60. ¶ NYCD 1839–60; Peters, *America on Stone.*

NARJOT, ERNESTE ETIENNE DE FRANCHEVILLE (1827–1898). Artist who was in California during the 1850's. Several of his oil paintings of the California scene are known, including two illustrating the U. S. Army's attempt to use camels on a march from Texas to California about 1857. ¶ *American Processional,* 27, 143 (repro.), 160 (repro.), 244–45.

NASH, J. F. Engraver from England, 24, at Boston in 1860. ¶ 8 Census (1860), Mass., XXVI, 481.

NASH, R. H. Artist of a series of tableaux, "The Onward March of American Freedom," shown in NYC in April 1854. ¶ N. Y. *Herald,* April 6, 1854 (citation courtesy J. E. Arrington).

NASON, DANIEL W. Amateur artist. A resident of Epping (N.H.), he sailed for California in 1849 as a member of the New England Pioneer Association of Boston. He stayed in the California gold fields until 1852, at intervals sending East sketches of life in the mines. Some of these appeared in Gleason's *Pictorial and Drawing-Room Companion* in 1851. In 1891 Nason gave a portfolio of his drawings to the New England Association of California Pioneers in Boston, of which he was a member. ¶ Van Nostrand and Coulter, *California Pictorial,* 70–71, repro.

NAST, THOMAS (1840–1902). Cartoonist and illustrator. Born September 27, 1840, at Landau (Germany), Nast was brought to this country in 1846 and grew up in NYC. After some study with THEODOR KAUFMANN and ALFRED FREDERICKS, and in the National Academy school, he was engaged as an illustrator for *Frank Leslie's Illustrated Newspaper* about 1855. In 1859 he joined the staff of the *New York Illustrated News.* In 1862 he became a staff artist for *Harper's Weekly* and his nearly 25 years' association with the magazine were the most fruitful of his career. He soon turned from pictorial reporting to the cartoon, his most noted work in this field being a series of cartoons exposing the "Tweed Ring." After leaving *Harper's* Nast contributed to a number of other periodicals and for a time published his own, *Nast's Weekly* (1892–93). He was appointed Consul at Guayaquil (Ecuador) in May 1902, but died on December 7, shortly after reaching his post. ¶ A. B. Paine, *Th. Nast: His Period and His Pictures* (1904); Kouwenhoven, "Thomas Nast as We Don't Know Him"; Cowdrey, NAD; DAB.

NATHANS, JOSEPH. English artist, 28, living in Philadelphia in 1860. ¶ 8 Census (1860), Pa., LIV, 265.

NATT, JOSEPH S. Wood engraver, Philadelphia, 1854, according to the Pennsylvania Business Directory for that year. Philadelphia directories from 1841 to 1871 list him as a merchant or "looking glasses." He was probably a brother of THOMAS J. NATT. ¶ Penna. BD 1854; Phila. CD 1842–71.

NATT, THOMAS J. Portrait painter and lithographer, Philadelphia, who exhibited at the Pennsylvania Academy in 1824 and 1829 and at the Artists' Fund Society in 1840. A portrait of Rev. Nath. Porter, painted and drawn on stone by Natt, was published in Philadelphia about 1832. This may also be the artist Natt referred to by John Neal in an article about Americans in London in the 1820's. He was the son of Thomas Natt, a carver, gilder, looking glass maker and print seller in Philadelphia from 1809 to 1843, and Thomas J. Natt also sold looking glasses and prints from 1835 to 1858 and coal in 1858–59. There is no record of him after 1859. His niece (?), Phebe D. Natt, was an artist in Philadelphia from 1878 to 1894; she was the daughter of Rev. George W. Natt who resided at the same address as Thomas J. Natt in 1855. ¶ Rutledge, PA; Peters, *America on Stone;* Dickson, *John Neal's Observations on American Art,* 53, 57; Phila. CD 1809–1894.

NAVARRE, BISYNTHE. Engraver, New Orleans, 1841–42. ¶ New Orleans CD 1841–42.

NAYLOR, CHARLES J. and HENRY L. Apprentice lithographers, Philadelphia, 1860. Charles, 18, and Henry, 15, were the Pennsylvania-born sons of Sampson Naylor, a master carpenter from England. ¶ 8 Census (1860), Pa., XLIX, 217.

NAYLOR, WILLIAM RIGBY. Teacher of architectural drawing, Charleston (S.C.), 1772. ¶ Rutledge, *Artists in the Life of Charleston.*

NEAGLE, Miss E. Flower and landscape painter of Philadelphia who exhibited at the Pennsylvania Academy in 1819, 1821, and 1822. ¶ Rutledge, PA.

NEAGLE, JAMES (*c.* 1769–1822). Engraver who worked in Philadelphia from about 1819 until his death, June 24, 1822, at the age of 53. ¶ Stauffer; Phila. CD 1819–24 [sic]; Pa. Acad. Cat., 1819, 1822.

NEAGLE, JOHN (1796–1865). Portrait painter; born November 4, 1796, while his parents were visiting in Boston, but grew up in Philadelphia. He received his first instruction in painting from PIETRO ANCORA, THOMAS WILSON, and BASS OTIS. He began to paint professionally in 1818 and, except for a brief excursion to Kentucky and New Orleans at the commencement of his career, he spent almost his entire life in Philadelphia. His reputation was established about 1826 with the famous portrait of Pat Lyon at his forge. Neagle was married in 1826 to a stepdaughter of THOMAS SULLY. He died in Philadelphia on September 17, 1865. ¶ Patrick, "John Neagle, Portrait Painter, and Pat Lyon, Blacksmith" (Mr. Patrick is preparing a biography of the artist); Lynch, "John Neagle's 'Diary' "; DAB; Rutledge, PA; Cowdrey, AA & AAU; Cowdrey, NAD; Rutledge, MHS; Swan, BA; Phila. CD 1818–60+; 8 Census (1860), Pa., LII, 507; Flexner, *The Light of Distant Skies,* biblio., 263.

NEAGLE, JOHN B. (*c.* 1796–1866). Engraver. A native of England, possibly the son of the English engraver John Neagle. He was working in Philadelphia as early as 1815–18, according to Stauffer, though he is not listed in the directories until 1825. He worked in Philadelphia until his death in 1866. A son, LEWIS NEAGLE, was also an engraver. ¶ Stauffer; 7 Census (1850), Pa., LII, 497; 8 Census (1860), Pa., LV, 306 (this census lists him as age 55, *i.e.* born about 1805); CAB; see also data in the Print Room of the New York Public Library.

NEAGLE, LEWIS. Wood engraver; son of JOHN B. NEAGLE. Born in Pennsylvania about 1837 and working with his father in Philadelphia in 1860. ¶ 8 Census (1860), Pa., LV, 307; Phila. CD 1866.

NEAGLE, see also NAGEL and NAGLE.

NEAL, DAVID DALHOFF (1838–1915). A.N.A. Historical and portrait painter, born October 20, 1838. He spent his boyhood in Lowell (Mass.) and Andover (N.H.) and went to California several years before the Civil War. His initial efforts in drawing and painting won the attention of a California patron who in 1861 enabled Neal to go to Europe. He entered the art school at Munich, married the daughter of one of his teachers, and made Munich his home until his death, May 2, 1915. His earlier work was chiefly historical in character, but in later years he specialized in portrait work which brought him frequently to America. ¶ DAB; CAB; Thieme-Becker; *Art Annual,* XII (1915), 261.

NEAL, JOHN (1793–1876). Drawing teacher and the first important commentator on American art. He was born August 25, 1793, at Portland (Me.) and during his early manhood taught penmanship and drawing in Maine and Baltimore. About 1815 he took up the study of law and began to write poems and novels. From 1823 to 1827 he was in England and contributed many articles to *Blackwood's Edinburgh Magazine,* including his views on American literature and art. After his return to America in 1827 Neal settled permanently in Portland and spent his life writing, editing, and promoting various political and social reforms. He died in Portland on June 20, 1876. ¶ DAB; Dickson, *Observations on American Art by John Neal.*

NEAL, LUCINDA. Amateur painter, Lancaster County (Pa.), 1848. ¶ Information courtesy David C. Duniway, Oregon State Archivist, who owns a signed and dated example of her work.

NEAL, WILLIAM. Engraver, 37, a native of New York, living in Cincinnati in 1850. All his children, ages 3 to 7, were born in Ohio. ¶ 7 Census (1850), Ohio, XX, 919.

NEALE, CHARLES. Engraver, NYC, 1843–51; of NEALE & WHITE (1843) and NEALE & PATE (1844). In 1851 he was listed as a plate printer. ¶ NYCD 1843–51; NYBD 1844.

NEALE, JOHN. Printer and engraver, NYC, who exhibited at the American Institute in 1844. ¶ NYCD 1844–45; Am. Inst. Cat., 1844.

NEALE & PATE. Engravers, NYC, 1844; CHARLES NEALE and WILLIAM PATE. ¶ NYBD 1844.

NEALE, THOMAS. Engraver, born in New York about 1826, working in NYC from

1850. He was apparently quite successful, since in 1860 he owned realty valued at $16,000. ¶ 7 Census (1850), N.Y., XLVIII, 285; 8 Census (1860), N.Y., LI, 225; NYCD 1851–60+.

NEALE & WHITE. Engravers, NYC, 1843; CHARLES NEALE and WILLIAM G. WHITE. ¶ NYCD 1843.

NEBEL, CARL. Artist of a series of battle scenes in *The War between the United States and Mexico* (Phila., 1851). ¶ Peters, *America on Stone.*

NED. Negro carver of Charleston (S.C.), 1859. His carvings on a hearse were described as representing "the weeping willow, encircled with appropriate drapery, surmounting which is an urn, and underneath a quiver. . . ." ¶ Rutledge, *Artists in the Life of Charleston.*

NEEDHAM, D. Lithographer (?). He was the Buffalo (N.Y.) agent for KELLOGG & THAYER and KELLOGGS & COMSTOCK, *c.* 1846–52. ¶ Peters, *America on Stone.*

NEELEY, O. Delineator of a view of Matawan (N.Y.) about 1832. ¶ Stauffer (Gage's index of artists).

NEELY, C. Painter of a portrait, signed and dated 1810, owned in 1941 by Sara H. Andrews of NYC. ¶ Information courtesy James Thomas Flexner.

NEFFENSPERGER, J. D. Watercolor-and-ink scene, Pennsylvania, about 1840. ¶ Lipman and Winchester, 177.

NEFFLEN or NIFFLIN, P. Portrait painter, Boston, 1859–60. ¶ Boston BD 1859–60.

NEGHLE, WILLIAM. Lithographer, 17, born in Massachusetts, living in Boston in 1860. His father, Charles Neghle, a machinist, was from Bavaria. ¶ 8 Census (1860), Mass., XXVIII, 725.

NEGUS, CAROLINE (1814–1867). Miniaturist and crayon artist, Boston, 1844–56. She was a daughter of JOEL NEGUS, a sister of NATHAN and JOSEPH NEGUS, and an aunt of GEORGE and AUGUSTUS FULLER. She married Richard Hildreth (1807–1865), the noted historian. She exhibited at the National Academy and the Boston Athenaeum. ¶ Swan, BA; Bolton, *Crayon Draftsmen;* Cowdrey, NAD; Boston BD 1854–56; DAB, under Hildreth.

NEGUS, JOEL. Sign painter, surveyor, and schoolmaster, Connecticut Valley, early 19th century. He was the father of NATHAN, JOSEPH, and CAROLINE NEGUS. ¶ Dods, "Connecticut Valley Painters," 208.

NEGUS, JOSEPH (?–1823). Scene, sign, and Masonic painter who worked as an itinerant in New England and the South between about 1815 and his death in 1823, somewhere in the South. He was the son of JOEL and brother of NATHAN and CAROLINE NEGUS. ¶ Dods, "Connecticut Valley Painters," 208; also *Antiques* (Sept. 1950), 194.

NEGUS, NATHAN (1801–1825). Itinerant portrait painter; son of JOEL and brother of JOSEPH and CAROLINE NEGUS. He was born March 20, 1801, at Petersham (Mass.). In 1815 he studied in Boston under ETHAN ALLEN GREENWOOD and JOHN PENNIMAN and four years later he exhibited in Boston a transparency of the Exchange fire. During 1820 he worked in a number of towns of Massachusetts, New Hampshire and Vermont. In November 1820 he went south with his brother JOSEPH, with whom he painted signs, Masonic emblems, and theater scenery at Savannah and other Georgia towns, and later in Alabama, Louisiana, and Florida. He returned to Petersham in 1825 and died there four days after his arrival. ¶ Dods, in *Antiques* (Sept. 1950), 194; Fuller, "Nathan Negus, 1801–1825," unpublished; Dods, "Connecticut Valley Painters," 208; *Somebody's Ancestors.*

NEHLIG, VICTOR (1830–1909). N.A. Historical, portrait, and genre painter. Born in Paris, came to America about 1856 after some time in Cuba, and worked mainly in NYC. He was elected an Academician of the National Academy in 1870. ¶ Rutledge, PA; Clement and Hutton; Thieme-Becker; *Art Annual,* VII (1909/10), 170; Fielding.

NEIDER, GUSTAVE. Sculptor, 43, a native of Bavaria, at Baltimore in 1860. ¶ 8 Census (1860), Md., IV, 727.

NEILL, HARVEY GORDON. Portrait painter who came to Little Rock (Ark.) from Shelbyville (Ky.) about 1819. He is said to have brought his family from Kentucky in 1823. ¶ WPA (Ark.), Hist. Records Survey cites *Arkansas Gazette,* May 6, 1934, 14.

NEILL, RICHARD. Copperplate engraver, 38, born in England, at Philadelphia in 1850. ¶ 7 Census (1850), Pa., LI, 169.

NEILSON, J. Delineator of a view of Weehawken (N.J.), engraved by G. B. ELLIS between 1825 and 1837. ¶ Stauffer (Gage's index of artists).

NEIMEYER, JOHN H., see JOHN HENRY NIEMEYER.

NELDER, A. Sculptor, New Orleans, 1846–56. ¶ New Orleans CD 1846, 1852–56.

NELLIS, SAUNDERS K. G. Armless silhouettist who worked with his toes. He was at Salem (Mass.) in 1836 and at Providence (R.I.) 1860–62. ¶ Carrick, *Shades of Our Ancestors;* Providence CD 1860–62; Jackson, *Silhouette,* 132.

NELSON, ——. Portrait and sign painter, Pittsburgh (Pa.), *c.* 1816–28. ¶ Dunlap, *History,* II, 274; Bolton, *Miniature Painters;* Anderson, "Intellectual Life of Pittsburgh: Painting," 291.

NELSON, Mrs. and Miss. Proprietors of a school for young ladies, Charleston (S.C.), 1825. Among other things they taught painting in oils and watercolors and painting on velvet. ¶ Rutledge, *Artists in the Life of Charleston.*

NELSON, EDWARD D. (?–1871). Landscape painter, NYC, 1849–60. He was a pupil of ASHER B. DURAND and exhibited at the National Academy, of which he was an Honorary Member, Amateur. ¶ Cowdrey, NAD; Durand, *Life and Times of Asher B. Durand,* 184; Clark, *History of the NAD,* 265.

NELSON, MORTIMER. Portrait painter, NYC, 1855–57. ¶ NYBD 1855, 1857.

NELSON, WILLIAM. Artist, 25, a native of New York, living in NYC in August 1850. ¶ 7 Census (1850), N.Y., XLVIII, 554.

NENDZNYSKI, J. A. Portrait painter, NYC, who exhibited at the National Academy in 1844. ¶ Cowdrey, NAD.

NESBITT, GEORGE F. Lithographer, stationer, and printer, NYC, 1840's and 1850's. ¶ NYCD 1840, 1850; NYBD 1844; Peters, *California on Stone;* Peters, *America on Stone.*

NESMITH, J. H. Engraver. He did work for Bradford's *Encyclopedia* (Phila., 1805–18), was associated with JAMES B. LONGACRE in 1824, and worked for New Haven (Conn.) publishers about 1828. ¶ Stauffer; Shaw's Phila. CD 1823.

NESSIG, PETER. Engraver, 44, from Hanover (Germany), at NYC in 1860. All his children were born in Germany before 1854. ¶ 8 Census (1860), N.Y., XLII, 371.

NETHERELIST, ——. Printer and lithographer (?) of HUGH REINAGLE's view of the American Theatre, New Orleans, *c.* 1832–33. ¶ Peters, *America on Stone.*

NETZ, ALEXANDER. Portrait painter, NYC, 1859–60. ¶ NYBD 1859–60.

NEUNABER, see NEYNABOR.

NEUPERT, CHARLES. Picture colorer, 23, from Germany, at Baltimore in 1850. ¶ 7 Census (1850), Md., V, 171.

NEUSER, L. A. W. (1837–1902). Portrait, landscape, and banner painter. He was born in Germany and came to New Orleans in the winter of 1855–56. He apparently settled there permanently. He died September 30, 1902, at New Orleans. ¶ New Orleans *Times-Democrat,* Oct. 1, 1902; Delgado-WPA cites *Creole,* Jan. 23 and 26, 1856, and New Orleans BD and CD 1856, 1861.

NEUVILLE, see HYDE DE NEUVILLE.

NEVERS, RODERICK. Copperplate engraver and printer, Hartford (Conn.), 1851. ¶ Hartford BD 1851.

NEVILLE, EDGAR N. Engraver, NYC, 1846–60. ¶ NYBD 1846–60.

NEVILLE, JAMES. Sculptor and carver, Charleston (S.C.), 1822. He was described as having long held a high rank among native carvers in wood and now sculpturing in marble. ¶ Rutledge, *Artists in the Life of Charleston.*

NEW ENGLAND BANK NOTE COMPANY. Banknote engravers, Boston, 1837–56. NATHANIEL PERKINS was listed as their agent 1837–47 and ISAAC CARY 1848–49. ¶ Boston CD 1841–56; Boston CD 1837–43.

NEW ORLEANS LITHOGRAPHIC OFFICE. Lithographers, New Orleans, 1838. ¶ Peters, *America on Stone.*

NEWBERRY, JOHN STRONG (1822–1892). Topographical artist. J. S. Newberry was born in Windsor (Conn.), studied medicine at Cleveland (Ohio) and in Paris, and practised in Cleveland during the early fifties. Between 1855 and 1859 he accompanied three exploring expeditions in the Far West as surgeon and naturalist. Some of his sketches made on the last of these appeared in Macomb's *Report of the Exploring Expedition from Santa Fe, New Mexico, to the Great Colorado of the West in 1859* (Washington, 1876). Newberry later served with the U. S. Sanitary Commission during the Civil War and as professor of geology and paleontology at Columbia College from 1866 until his death, December 7, 1892, at New Haven (Conn.). ¶ DAB; Macomb, *Report. . . .*

NEWBERY, EDWARD. English artist, 36, at NYC in 1850. His wife ROSE, also an artist, was from Ireland; their three children were born in New York between 1840 and 1850. ¶ 7 Census (1850), N.Y., LIII, 276; NYCD 1850.

NEWBERY, ROSE. Artist, 34, born in Ireland, living in NYC in 1850 with her artist husband, EDWARD NEWBERY, and three children born in New York after about 1840. ¶ 7 Census (1850), N.Y., LIII, 276; NYCD 1850.

NEWCOMB, D. Engraver, probably at Boston, 1820. ¶ Stauffer.

NEWCOMBE, GEORGE W. (1799–1845). A.N.A. Portrait and miniature painter, born September 22, 1799, in England. He was working in NYC as early as 1829 and died there February 10, 1845. He exhibited at the National Academy, of which he was an Associate from 1832, at the Artists' Fund Society of Philadelphia and at the Boston Athenaeum. ¶ Cummings, *Historic Annals,* 185; Cowdrey, NAD; NYCD 1834–44; Swan, BA; Rutledge, PA; Bolton, *Miniature Painters.*

NEWCOMMER, ABRAHAM. Portrait painter at Carlisle (Pa.) in April 1811. ¶ Carlisle *Gazette,* April 12, 1811 (citation courtesy Clarence S. Brigham).

NEWELL, HUGH (1830–1915). Portrait, genre, and landscape painter, born October 4, 1830, near Belfast (Ireland). He came to America about 1851, worked in Baltimore until about 1860, then for some years in Pittsburgh (Pa.), and again in Baltimore from 1879 to 1892. He died at Bloomfield (N.J.) in 1915. Newell exhibited at the Maryland Historical Society (1853–58), the Pennsylvania Academy, the Washington Art Association (1857), and the National Academy. ¶ CAB; Pleasants, *250 Years of Painting in Maryland,* 62; Cowdrey, NAD; Rutledge, MHS; Rutledge, PA; Washington Art Assoc. Cat., 1857; Baltimore CD 1853–58; represented at Peabody Institute.

NEWELL, J. P. Lithographic artist, probably from Rhode Island, active about 1858–66. He did Rhode Island and Massachusetts views for JOHN H. BUFFORD, ENDICOTT & COMPANY, and ROBERTSON, SEIBERT & SHEARMAN. He exhibited at the Pennsylvania Academy in 1866. ¶ Peters, *America on Stone;* Stokes, *Historical Prints,* pl. 98a and 100c; Rutledge, PA.

NEWHALL, JOHN BAILEY (1806–1849). Topographical artist; born in Lynn (Mass.) and settled in Burlington (Iowa) in the 1830's. In 1843 he visited Nauvoo (Ill.) and made a drawing of the Mormon Temple which he exhibited at Salem (Mass.) the same year in connection with a lecture promoting emigration. In 1843–44 he visited England and the Continent to promote the same cause. On his return to America he published *A Glimpse of Iowa in 1846* and continued to lecture and show his paintings, including some done in Europe. He died of cholera at Independence (Mo.), May 7, 1849. ¶ Arrington, "Nauvoo Temple," Chap. 8.

NEWMAN, A. G. Engraver and die sinker, NYC, 1852. ¶ NYBD 1852.

NEWMAN, B. Landscape engraver, NYC, 1860. ¶ Stauffer.

NEWMAN, BARTAS P. Engraver, 36, a native of Philadelphia where he was living in 1860 with his wife and three children. ¶ 8 Census (1860), Pa., LI, 430.

NEWMAN, GEORGE W. Lithographer, NYC, 1846–49; of JONES & NEWMAN (1847–49). ¶ NYBD 1846; Peters, *America on Stone.*

NEWMAN, HENRY RODERICK (?–1917/18). Architectural and flower painter. He was born at Easton (N.Y.) either about 1833 (CAB and *Art Annual*) or about 1843 (DAB) and brought up in Easton and NYC. During the 1860's he had a studio in NYC, but spent much time at Stockbridge (Mass.) and in the Green Mountains of Vermont. In 1869 he went to France and studied for some months under Thomas Couture and in the following year he went to Florence, where he made his home for the rest of his life. Newman was an intimate of Ruskin and the Brownings. He died in Florence during the winter of 1917/18. ¶ DAB; CAB; *Art Annual,* XV (1918).

NEWMAN, JOHN. Exhibited a sheet copper statue of Washington at the American Institute in 1856; his address was 43 Carmine St., NYC. ¶ Am. Inst. Cat., 1856.

NEWMAN, ROBERT LOFTIN (1827–1912). Painter of religious and literary subjects. He was born in Richmond (Va.) in 1827, spent his childhood there and after 1833 in Tennessee, and went to Paris in 1850 to study painting under Thomas Couture. He made a second trip to Paris in 1854. Newman served in the Confederate Army during the Civil War, but after the war established his studio in New York City. A man of rather retiring disposition, he received little recognition until 1894 when a group of his friends organized a Newman exhibition. He died in NYC on March 31, 1912. ¶ Sherman, "Robert Loftin Newman"; Sherman, "Robert Loftin Newman: An American Colorist"; Landgren, "Robert Loftin Newman"; *Art Annual,* X, obit.

NEWPORT, JAMES W. Miniaturist, Philadelphia, exhibitor at the Artists' Fund Society in 1845 and at the Pennsylvania

Academy from 1847 to 1868. He is listed in the city directories from 1845 to 1872 as a clerk; from 1859 at the Bank of North America. ¶ Rutledge, PA; Phila. CD 1845–72; Bolton, *Miniature Painters.*

NEWSAM, ALBERT (1809–1864). Lithographer and engraver. Newsam, a deaf-mute, was born at Steubenville (Ohio), May 20, 1809. In 1820 he was taken to Philadelphia where he was admitted to the new Asylum for the Deaf and Dumb. His talent for drawing was encouraged during the seven years he spent in the Asylum and in 1827 he was apprenticed to the engraver CEPHAS G. CHILDS, but he soon turned to lithography which he learned from P. S. DUVAL, then an employee of Childs. His career as a lithographer lasted until about 1859 when he began to go blind and suffered a paralytic stroke. His last years were spent in hospitals and nursing homes. He died November 20, 1864, near Wilmington (Del.). ¶ DAB; CAB; Stauffer; Peters, *America on Stone;* Phila. CD 1856–59; Rutledge, PA; Am. Inst. Cat., 1849; 7 Census (1850), Pa., L, 217; Bolton, *Crayon Draftsmen;* Todd, "Huddy and Duval Prints."

NEWSWANGER, GEORGE. Engraver, 18, born in Pennsylvania, at Philadelphia in 1850 in the home of his father, Edgar Newswanger. ¶ 7 Census (1850), Pa., LIII, 340.

NEWTON, Mrs. ——. Flower painter in watercolor, Roxborough (Pa.), exhibited at the Artists' Fund Society in 1841–43. ¶ Rutledge, PA.

NEWTON & DUNN. Stencil plate engravers, NYC, 1852; MARK NEWTON and LEVERETT H. DUNN. ¶ NYBD and CD 1852.

NEWTON, G. S. Lithographer of a "Mother and Child" published at Pittsburgh (Pa.) about 1835. One other print by him has been recorded. ¶ *American Collector* (Dec. 1948), 14, repro. It is possible that these are merely prints after works of GILBERT STUART NEWTON.

NEWTON, GILBERT STUART (1794–1835). Historical and portrait painter, born September 20, 1794, at Halifax (N.S.). On the death of his father in 1803, Newton was brought to Cambridge (Mass.). He lived there and in Boston until 1817 and during this period studied under his famous uncle, GILBERT STUART. In 1817 Newton visited Italy, met CHARLES R. LESLIE there and accompanied him to London, where he spent the rest of his life. He became a very popular painter of historical and literary subjects and did some portraits as well. In 1832 he returned to Boston to be married, but soon after his return to England went insane. He died at Chelsea on August 5, 1835. ¶ DNB; *Gentleman's Magazine* (Oct. 1835), 438–39; Morgan, *Gilbert Stuart and His Pupils;* Swan, BA; Rutledge, MHS; Cowdrey, AA & AAU; Cowdrey, NAD; repros.: *Antiques* (Aug. 1943), 52, and *American Collector* (Oct. 1947), 8; Dunlap, *History;* Flexner, *The Light of Distant Skies.*

NEWTON, JOHN O. Artist, NYC, 1852–53. ¶ NYCD 1852–53.

NEWTON, MARK. Engraver, of NEWTON & DUNN, NYC, 1852. ¶ NYBD and CD 1852.

NEWTON, MARTIN. English engraver, 35, at NYC in August 1850. ¶ 7 Census (1850), N.Y., LI, 490.

NEWTON, P. STEWART. Teacher of drawing and painting, New Orleans, 1821–22. ¶ Delgado-WPA cites *Gazette,* Nov. 26, 1821; New Orleans CD 1822.

NEWTON, WILLIAM G. or J. Engraver, born in Ohio about 1817 (1850 Census) or about 1804 (1860 Census), working in Washington (D.C.) 1850–64. In 1864 he was listed as a clerk in the Paymaster General's Office. ¶ 7 Census (1850), D.C., I, 315; 8 Census (1860), D.C., II, 210; Washington CD 1860–64.

NEYAL, VINCENT. Marine painter, advertised at Charleston (S.C.) in 1843. ¶ Rutledge, *Artists in the Life of Charleston.*

NEYNABOR, AUGUSTUS (?–1887). Landscape, flower, and mural painter who lived in Honey Brook, Chester County (Pa.) during the middle of the 19th century. He also worked in Lancaster County and at Rockville (1860). ¶ Andes, "Augustus Neynabor, Chester County Folk Artist"; Penna. BD 1860 (as Neunaber).

NIBLO, WILLIAM, JR. Deaf-and-dumb artist, son of William Niblo (1789–1878), well known proprietor of New York's Niblo's Garden. The younger Niblo exhibited paintings at the American Academy in 1835 and the National Academy in 1836. ¶ Cowdrey, AA & AAU; Cowdrey, NAD.

NICHOL, HENRY H. Engraver, 24, from Connecticut, living in NYC in 1860. ¶ 8 Census (1860), N.Y., LVII, 960.

NICHOLS, ABEL (1815–1860). Portrait and landscape painter, born June 4, 1815, at Danvers (Mass.). Encouraged by an aunt, Mrs. ANDREW NICHOLS, Abel took lessons in painting with her brother-in-law CHARLES OSGOOD and with CHESTER HARDING in the early 1830's. In 1836 he began his career in Charleston (S.C.), working there until his marriage in 1838, when he moved to Savannah (Ga.). The following year his wife died, and Nichols returned to Danvers after a trip to Cincinnati to do a portrait of William Henry Harrison. In 1841 he went to Italy for the first time. Returning to America he married again in 1843, worked for a time in Buffalo (N.Y.), and in 1849 again went to Italy. He lived with his family in Florence until 1858 and during this period painted chiefly landscapes and copies of the Old Masters. Nichols returned to Danvers in 1858 and died there two years later. SARAH NICHOLS was his sister. ¶ Nichols, "Abel Nichols, Artist," repro. and checklist; Cowdrey, NAD; Rutledge, *Artists in the Life of Charleston.*

NICHOLS, Mrs. ANDREW, see MARY HOLYOKE WARD.

NICHOLS, CHARLES. Portrait painter working in Lancaster County (Pa.) in 1847 at the age of nineteen. ¶ Lancaster County Hist. Soc., *Portraiture in Lancaster County,* 132.

NICHOLS, DAVID (1829–1911). Wood engraver born at Newburgh (N.Y.). He was working in NYC by 1850 and died in Brooklyn. ¶ Smith; 7 Census (1850), N.Y., L, 333; 8 Census (1860), N.Y., XLVIII, 232; Hamilton, *Early American Book Illustrators and Wood Engravers,* 526.

NICHOLS, EDWARD W. (1819–1871). A.N.A. Landscape painter. Born April 23, 1819, at Orford (N.H.), he became a lawyer but later took up painting professionally. After study in NYC with JASPER CROPSEY in 1848 and abroad in 1853, he married and settled at Hartford (Conn.). He died at Peekskill (N.Y.) on September 20, 1871. He was an Associate of the National Academy. ¶ French, *Art and Artists in Connecticut,* 106; Swan, BA; Rutledge, PA; NYBD 1857; Cowdrey, NAD.

NICHOLS, ELEANOR. Amateur landscape painter in water colors, Bridgeport (Conn.), about 1840. ¶ Lipman and Winchester, 177.

NICHOLS, FREDERICK B. (1824–after 1906). Engraver. A native of Bridgeport (Conn.), Nichols learned his trade in the firm of RAWDON, WRIGHT, HATCH & SMILLIE of NYC, and went into business for himself in the mid-forties. In 1848 he invented a process for relief engraving. He gave up engraving in 1858 to work on some inventions and in 1865 went to Nova Scotia as a mining engineer. He also taught chemistry and geology for a time in Canada. Returning to NYC in 1884 Nichols resumed engraving for a year with WILLIAM WELLSTOOD. In 1906 he was living in retirement at Bridgeport. ¶ Stauffer.

NICHOLS, GEORGE A. Marine painter, Boston, 1851–52. ¶ Boston CD 1851, BD 1852.

NICHOLS, HENRY. Wood engraver; born in Massachusetts about 1816/17 and active in Boston from 1844 until after 1860. In 1846 he was with NICHOLS & KURTZ. ¶ 7 Census (1850), Mass., XXV, 697; 8 Census (1860), Mass., XXVII, 874; Boston CD 1844–60+.

NICHOLS & KURTZ. Engravers, Boston, 1846; HENRY NICHOLS and HENRY KURTZ. ¶ Boston CD 1846.

NICHOLS, MARY HOLYOKE WARD, see MARY HOLYOKE WARD.

NICHOLS, MARY P. (1836–after 1905). Sculptor, born July 15, 1836, at Vernon (Ohio). She studied under Preston Powers, exhibited at the Chicago World's Fair in 1893, and in 1905 was living in Denver (Col.). ¶ *Artists Year Book,* 141–42.

NICHOLS, NICHOLAS. Engraver, 28, a native of New York, living in NYC in 1860. ¶ 8 Census (1860), N.Y., LXII, 369.

NICHOLS, SARAH. Amateur portrait, landscape, flower, and still life painter. A sister of ABEL NICHOLS and niece of MARY HOLYOKE WARD (Mrs. Andrew Nichols), Sarah spent most of her life in Danvers (Mass.). During the 1850's she lived for a time in Italy with her brother and his family. She was married twice, to a Mr. Page and a Mr. Berry. ¶ Nichols, "Abel Nichols, Artist," 16.

NICHOLS, W. D. Engraver of NYC, who exhibited at the National Academy in 1848. ¶ Cowdrey, NAD.

NICHOLSON, ——. Portrait, miniature, and ornamental painter at Troy (Ohio) in 1832. ¶ Knittle, *Early Ohio Taverns.*

NICHOLSON, ELIZABETH (1833–1926). Landscape, portrait, and china painter, born in Clinton County, Ohio (Burnet) or Indianapolis, Ind. (Peat). She studied art at the McMicken School of Design in Cincinnati, watercolor painting in Paris, china painting in Philadelphia, and portrait painting under THOMAS NOBLE and HENRY MOSLER. She taught art at the

Ohio Female College, College Hill (Ohio), at Kenwood Seminary in Chicago, and privately in Indianapolis, where she died April 26, 1926. ¶ Burnet, *Art and Artists of Indiana,* 74–75; Peat, *Pioneer Painters of Indiana.*

NICHOLSON, GEORGE W. (1832–1912). Landscape painter, born October 17, 1832. His career was spent chiefly in Philadelphia. In 1867 he exhibited at the Pennsylvania Academy a sketch from nature of Windsor Castle. He died October 19, 1912, at Hammonton (N.J.). ¶ *Art Annual,* X (1911–12), obit.; Rutledge, PA.

NICHOLSON, HENRY S. Painter of oil portraits of Mr. and Mrs. Stephen Dewey of Bennington (Vt.) about 1838. ¶ WPA (Mass.), *Portraits Found in Vt.*

NICHOLSON, JOHN (1825–1893). Portrait and sign painter, photographer, born July 12, 1825, in Jefferson County (Ind.). He was working at Columbus (Ind.) in 1847, from 1850 to 1860 at Franklin, and later at Crawfordsville, where he died. ¶ Beckwith, *History of Montgomery County, Indiana,* 315–16; Peat, *Pioneer Painters of Indiana.*

NICHOLSON, SUSAN FAUNTLEROY QUARLES. Portrait painter, Baltimore, about 1820. ¶ *American Provincial Painting,* no. 62.

NICHOLSONS, ——. Engraver or engravers of an illustration (p. 27) for Abbott's *Rollo on the Rhine* (Boston, 1855). ¶ Hamilton, *Early American Book Illustrators and Wood Engravers,* 234.

NICKERSON, REUBEN. Sculptor, 26, a native of Massachusetts, at Boston in June 1860. He owned realty valued at $2,000 and personalty at $100. ¶ 8 Census (1860), Mass., XXVI, 396.

NICKLIN, JOHN. Lithographer, NYC, 1851. ¶ NYBD 1851.

NICOLAI, A. T. Portrait painter, NYC, 1858. ¶ NYBD 1858.

NICOLE, PIERRE (?–1784). Topographical draftsman in water colors and ink. A native of Switzerland, he served as a British captain of engineers and as confidential agent to the Pennsylvania Loyalists. Several of his drawings and a map of Philadelphia have been recorded. ¶ *Album of American Battle Art,* 32–34, pl. 19–20. The map of Philadelphia is in the Library of Congress.

NICOUD & GARDIN. Engravers, NYC, 1854; HENRY E. NICOUD and FRANCIS GARDIN. ¶ NYBD 1854.

NICOUD, HENRY E. Engraver, NYC, 1854–56; in 1854 of NICOUD & GARDIN. ¶ NYBD 1854, 1856.

NIEMEYER, JOHN HENRY (1839–1932). Portrait and figure painter, teacher of drawing. Niemeyer was born June 25, 1839, at Bremen (Germany) but was brought to America in 1843 and grew up in Cincinnati. By 1858 he was at Indianapolis working as a sign painter. In 1860 he moved to NYC and taught for a few years before going abroad for study. From 1866 to 1870 he studied art in Paris. In 1871 he was appointed professor of drawing at Yale, a position which he filled with great distinction until 1908. After his retirement Niemeyer spent a good part of his time in Europe. He died in New Haven December 7, 1932. Among his many pupils were Augustus Saint-Gaudens and FREDERIC REMINGTON. ¶ DAB; Burnet, *Art and Artists of Indiana,* 385; CAB; Peat, *Pioneer Painters of Indiana,* 169.

NIERIKER, Mme. ERNEST, see MAY ALCOTT.

NIFFLIN, P., see P. NEFFLEN.

NILIS, PIERRE. Still life and portrait artist, NYC; exhibitor at the American Art-Union 1848–50. The directories list him as teacher. ¶ Cowdrey, AA & AAU; NYCD 1848.

NIMBS, AREUNA B. Portrait painter and photographer, Buffalo (N.Y.), 1856–60. ¶ Buffalo BD 1856–60.

NIMS, JEREMIAH (?–1842). A.N.A. Portrait painter, who lived in NYC and exhibited at the National Academy in 1839–41. He was made an Associate of the Academy in 1841. He died March 6, 1842, at Kingston (Jamaica). ¶ Thieme-Becker; Cowdrey, NAD; NYBD 1840. Mallett gives 1814 as his year of birth; Cowdrey gives it as *c.* 1818.

NIMS, MARY ALTHA. Watercolor romantic scenes, Bennington (Vt.), 1840. ¶ Lipman and Winchester, 177.

NIMS, THEODORE S. Crayon artist who exhibited at the American Institute in 1846 and 1851. He was a minor, possibly a son of Theodore S. Nims, lawyer of NYC. ¶ Am. Inst. Cat., 1846, 1851; NYCD 1845–46.

NIXON, CHARLES L. Portrait painter, Boston, 1852–70; exhibitor at the Athenaeum. ¶ Swan, BA; Boston BD 1853–56.

NIXON, D. Scene painter at the New Theatre, Charleston (S.C.), in 1837. ¶ Rutledge, *Artists in the Life of Charleston.*

NIXON, JAMES M. Artist, 28, a native of

New York, living in NYC in 1850. ¶ 7 Census (1850), N.Y., XLVIII, 380.

NIXON, JOHN B. Lithographer, NYC, 1856. ¶ Peters, *America on Stone.*

NIXON, T. Profile painter in watercolor, at Salem (Mass.) in 1810. He was also associated with WILLIAM BACHE, 1809–10. ¶ Belknap, *Artists and Craftsmen of Essex County,* 21; Jackson, *Silhouette,* 133; Carrick, "The Profiles of William Bache."

NOBLE, Miss ——. Portrait painter at Cincinnati in 1853; painting teacher at Cleveland in 1855. ¶ Ohio BD 1853; WPA (Ohio), *Annals of Cleveland.*

NOBLE, CHARLES F. Engraver, born in Pennsylvania about 1833, working in Philadelphia 1850 and after. He was with SCATTERGOOD & NOBLE in 1859 and NOBLE & NAGLE in 1860 and after. In 1871 he was employed by V. H. Earl & Company, jewellers. ¶ 7 Census (1850), Pa., LIV, 772; 8 Census (1860), Pa., LXII, 305; Phila. CD 1859–71.

NOBLE & NAGLE. General and wood engravers, Philadelphia, 1860 and after; CHARLES F. NOBLE and J. FREDERICK NAGLE. ¶ Phila. CD 1860+.

NOBLE, THOMAS SATTERWHITE (1835–1907). A.N.A. Historical and portrait painter, teacher of painting. Born May 29, 1835, at Lexington (Ky.), Noble grew up on a plantation. While still in his teens he went to NYC and later to Paris to study painting. He was a pupil of Thomas Couture. He returned to America just before the Civil War, went to New Orleans, and served during the war as a captain in the Confederate Army. After the war he opened a studio in NYC and established his reputation as a historical painter. In 1869 he was appointed professor of art and principal of the School of Design of McMicken University in Cincinnati, a position he held until his retirement in 1904. He was made an Associate of the National Academy in 1867. After his retirement Noble lived in NYC until his death, April 27, 1907. ¶ Garretson, "Thomas S. Noble and His Paintings"; Rutledge, PA; *Art Annual,* VI, obit.

NOELLE, see NOVELLE.

NOLEN, HENRY S. Artist, 50, born in Massachusetts, living in Philadelphia in 1860. ¶ 8 Census (1860), Pa., LV, 240.

NOLTE, EMIL F. Artist, 25, from Germany, at Boston in June 1860. ¶ 8 Census (1860), Mass., XXVIII, 77.

NOON, T. F. Portrait painter, New Orleans, 1838. ¶ New Orleans CD 1838.

NORMAN, Misses ——. Teachers of drawing and painting, as well as other branches of an English education, at Charleston (S.C.), 1837. They exhibited portraits in Charleston in 1843 and 1849. ¶ Rutledge, *Artists in the Life of Charleston.*

NORMAN & BEDWELL. Engravers and publishers, Philadelphia, 1779; JOHN NORMAN and THOMAS BEDWELL. ¶ Prime, I, 26, 30.

NORMAN, JOHN (*c.* 1748–1817). Engraver who came to Philadelphia from London about 1774. He worked there until about 1780 and then transferred his activity to Boston. In addition to engraving buildings, portraits, and landscapes for various publishers, Norman was one of the publishers of the *Boston Magazine* (1783–84) and brought out Boston's first directory in 1789. He died June 8, 1817, in Boston. ¶ DAB; Stauffer; Prime, I, 4, 19–26, 30, and II, 7; repro., *American Collector* (Sept. 1943), 7. See also: WALTERS & NORMAN; NORMAN & BEDWELL; NORMAN & WARD.

NORMAN & WARD. Engravers, Philadelphia, 1774; JOHN NORMAN and —— WARD, both from England. ¶ Prime, I, 20.

NORMAN, WILLIAM T. Wood engraver at NYC in 1850 and at Cincinnati 1856 and after. ¶ NYBD 1850; Cincinnati CD 1856–60+.

NORRIS, EDWARD. Stonecutter, of NORRIS & KAIN, NYC, 1811–18. Norris died during the winter of 1818–19 and letters of administration were granted to his widow, Mary A. Norris, on January 28, 1819. ¶ NYCD 1811–18; Barber, "Index of Letters of Administration, New York County, 1743–1875."

NORRIS, ETHELBERT. Sculptor, 21, a native of Maryland, living in Cincinnati in September 1850. ¶ 7 Census (1850), Ohio, XX, 813.

NORRIS & KAIN. Sculptors and marble yard, NYC, 1811–18; EDWARD NORRIS and FRANCIS KAIN. ¶ NYCD 1811–18.

NORTH & GALLAGHER. Engravers, NYC, 1838–1848; WILLIAM B. NORTH and FERDINAND H. GALLAGHER. They were at first listed as calico engravers. ¶ NYCD 1838–48.

NORTH, Mrs. MARY. Drawing teacher and still life painter, Philadelphia, 1829–40. She exhibited at the Pennsylvania Academy in 1828 and at the Artists' Fund Society in 1840. The 1830 and 1831 directories list two Mary Norths, both artists and at different addresses. ¶ Rutledge, PA; Phila. CD 1829–33.

NORTH, NOAH. Portrait painter working in Kentucky and at Cincinnati in the 1830's. ¶ *Antiques* (March 1932), 152; *Antiques* (Dec. 1951), 547, repro.

NORTH, WILLIAM B. Engraver, of NORTH & GALLAGHER, NYC, 1838–48; his home was in New Jersey. ¶ NYCD 1838–48.

NORTHCOTE, HENRY. Landscape painter, working with his brother (?) JAMES in NYC in 1859 and after. They came from England about 1858 and made their home in Brooklyn. ¶ NYCD and BD 1859–60.

NORTHCOTE, JAMES (1822–1904). Landscape and figure painter. He was a native of Hammerston (England) and came to the United States in 1858. In 1859 and after he was working in NYC and living in Brooklyn, in partnership with HENRY NORTHCOTE, probably a brother. James died in Brooklyn February 4, 1904. ¶ *Art Annual,* IV (1905/06), 123; Thieme-Becker; NYCD 1859–60.

NORTHERMAN, GEORGE. Engraver, NYC, 1848. ¶ NYBD 1848.

NORTON, LUCY KING. Painter of a water color family register, probably copied after the work of RICHARD BRUNTON in the 1790's. She lived at Suffield (Conn.). ¶ Warren, "Richard Brunton," 77–78, repro.

NORTON, W. H. Portrait painter, Boston, 1859–60. ¶ Boston BD 1859–60.

NOTAIRE, JOSEPH DESSAUX. Artist, New Orleans, 1841–42. Possibly the Joseph Notaire who was listed in 1822 as a "comedian" and in 1827 as an "artiste." The word artist in this instance may mean "actor." ¶ New Orleans CD 1841–42; Delgado-WPA cites New Orleans CD 1822, 1827.

NOTT, CHARLES. Lithographer, 31, a native of Bavaria, at NYC in 1860. ¶ 8 Census (1860), N.Y., XLV, 543.

NOTT, THOMAS J., see THOMAS J. NATT.

NOVELLE or NOELLE, FREDERICK. Portrait painter, NYC, 1854–57. ¶ NYBD 1854–57.

NOYES, F. A. Artist, Buffalo (N.Y.), 1858. ¶ Buffalo BD 1858.

NUMAN, BENJAMIN. Engraver, 30, from New Jersey, living in Philadelphia in 1860. ¶ 8 Census (1860), Pa., LX, 193.

NUMYER, FREDERICK. Engraver, 32, born in Germany, at Baltimore in 1850. All his children were born in Maryland after 1843. ¶ 7 Census (1850), Md., V, 733.

NUNES, ABRAHAM I. Portrait, landscape, and still life painter and drawing master, Philadelphia, 1810–14. He was an Associate of the Society of Artists and exhibited in their 1811 exhibition. ¶ Rutledge, PA; Scharf and Westcott, *History of Philadelphia,* II, 1051.

NUNES, J. B. Exhibitor of crayon portraits at the Pennsylvania Academy 1813–14. ¶ Rutledge, PA.

NUTTALL, THOMAS (1786–1859). Naturalist and amateur artist, born January 5, 1786, in the West Riding of Yorkshire. He came to the United States in 1807 and remained for 35 years. One of the leading botanists of his day, he traveled all over the United States in search of specimens and from 1822 to 1834 was professor of natural history at Harvard. He returned to England in 1842 and settled at Nutgrove, near St. Helens, Lancashire, where he died September 10, 1859. At least one of his books, *Travels into the Arkansas Territory* (Phila., 1821), was illustrated by Nuttall himself. ¶ DNB; Thwaites, *Early Western Travels,* XIII, 16–18.

NUTTING, BENJAMIN F. (?–1887). Portrait and landscape painter, lithographer, writer of drawing books. A native of New Hampshire, born between 1801 (1860 Census) and 1813 (Lipman and Winchester), Nutting was a fellow apprentice with NATHANIEL CURRIER at PENDLETON'S lithographic establishment in Boston *c.* 1828–33. By 1831 he was exhibiting paintings at the Boston Athenaeum and he continued to do so until 1865. He was the author of several drawing books and sets of "Teachers'-Aid Drawing Cards" published between 1849 and 1883. ¶ 8 Census (1860), Mass., XXVIII, 285; Lipman and Winchester, 177; Swan, BA; Peters, *America on Stone;* Boston BD 1844–60; Sears, *Some American Primitives,* 61 (repro.); *Antiques* (July 1936), 27 (repro.).

NUTTING, Miss EMILY. Miniature painter, Boston, 1835. She exhibited at the Boston Athenaeum and designed at least one portrait for ANNIN & SMITH, the Boston engravers and lithographers. ¶ Swan, BA; Peters, *America on Stone.*

NYE, E. Profilist at Newark (N.J.) in January 1809; portrait painter at Burlington (N.J.) in March 1811. ¶ Dunlap, *History* (1918), III, 321; Fielding; card in Bella C. Landauer Collection, NYHS.

O

Oakes, Mrs. A. T. Landscape painter, exhibitor at the National Academy. She was living in NYC in 1852 and in Boston in 1854. This may be the M. Oaks, female artist, 34, living in San Francisco in 1860; both she and her son Archy were born in New York. Van Nostrand states that Mrs. A. T. Oakes was in California about 1850. ¶ Cowdrey, NAD; 7 Census (1860), Cal., VII, 437; information courtesy Mrs. J. J. Van Nostrand, Berkeley.

Oakley, Edward. Lithographer, NYC, 1857. ¶ NYBD 1857.

Oakely, Frank F. Engraver and lithographer, Boston, 1848–60 and after. As early as 1848 he lithographed Isaac Sprague's illustrations for William Oakes' *Scenery of the White Mountains* and in 1856 he was described as successor to S. W. Chandler. ¶ Oakes, *Scenery of the White Mountains;* Boston CD 1856–57, BD 1857–60+; *Portfolio* (Jan. 1942), 15.

Oakley, George (1793–1869). A.N.A. Landscape, portrait, and genre painter. Apparently an English artist, probably a brother of Octavius Oakley. Came to America in the early 1820's, exhibiting at the American Academy as early as 1822. In 1827 he was made an Artist of the National Academy and in 1828 an Associate Member. Many of his paintings of English and American subjects were exhibited at the National Academy and the Apollo Association. Georgina and Juliana Oakley, his daughters, also painted, and a granddaughter, Violet Oakley, became a noted artist in Pennsylvania. ¶ Thieme-Becker; Cowdrey, AA & AAU; Cowdrey, NAD.

Oakley, Georgina. Still life painter, exhibitor at the National Academy in 1859. She lived in West Brooklyn (N.Y.) and was a daughter of George and sister of Juliana Oakley. She also exhibited at the Washington Art Association. ¶ Cowdrey, NAD; Washington Art Association Cat., 1859.

Oakley, Juliana. Genre, portrait, and still life painter. A daughter of George and sister of Georgina Oakley, Juliana lived in West Brooklyn (N.Y.) and exhibited at the National Academy and Pennsylvania Academy between 1859 and 1868. She married Count Michel de Tarnowsky, a Russian emigré, and spent most of her life in Nice (France), where she was living in 1912. ¶ Cowdrey, NAD; Rutledge, PA; information courtesy Miss Edith Emerson, Woodmere Art Gallery, Germantown (Pa.).

Oakley, Octavius (1800–1867). Genre, portrait, and landscape painter. The son of a London wool merchant, he was born April 27, 1800. He studied painting in London, worked in several provincial towns during the twenties and thirties, and in 1841 settled in London. He was frequently referred to as "Gipsy Oakley" because of his many watercolors of English gipsies. In 1835 he exhibited at the National Academy with a NYC address, the same as that of George Oakley who was probably an older brother. If Octavius did visit this country at that time, he soon went back and spent the rest of his career in England. He died in Bayswater, London, March 1, 1867. ¶ DNB; Thieme-Becker; Cowdrey, NAD.

Oaks, see Oakes.

Obe, ——. Genre painter, oil on wood, New Hampshire, about 1850. ¶ Lipman and Winchester, 177.

Obeno, see Aubineau.

O'Boyle, Michael. Wood engraver, NYC, 1860. ¶ NYBD 1860.

O'Brien & Brother. Engravers, NYC, 1859–60; Martin and Christopher O'Brien. ¶ NYBD 1859, CD 1860.

O'Brien, Christopher W. Engraver, of O'Brien & Brother, NYC, 1859–60. ¶ NYBD 1859, CD 1860.

O'Brien, Daniel. Sculptor working with John G. Draddy at Cincinnati in 1860. ¶ Cincinnati BD 1860.

O'Brien, James. Engraver, Detroit, 1859. ¶ Detroit CD 1859.

O'Brien, John (1834–1904). Sculptor. A native of Ireland, he was selected in 1860 to execute a monument to Commodore Perry at Cleveland (Ohio). He moved to Galveston (Texas) in 1882 and died there December 20, 1904. ¶ *Art Annual,* IV (1905–06), 122.

O'Brien, John W. Animal and landscape painter of Chicago who won a prize at the Illinois State Fair in 1855. ¶ Chicago *Daily News,* Oct. 12 and 15, 1855.

O'Brien, Martin. Engraver, NYC, 1855–60. In 1859–60 he was working with his brother, CHRISTOPHER O'BRIEN. ¶ NYCD 1855–60.

O'BRIEN, ROBERT. Engraver, NYC, 1848–57. ¶ NYBD 1848–51, CD 1856–57; Stauffer; Hamilton, *Early American Book Illustrators and Wood Engravers,* 265.

OCHS, GEORGE, JR. Engraver, 25, born in Philadelphia, living there in 1860 with his English-born father and brother, plate and case makers respectively. ¶ 8 Census (1860), Pa., LVIII, 100.

O'CONNOR, ——. Lithographer of one plate in the first volume of the *United States Military Magazine* (1839–40). ¶ Peters, *America on Stone.*

ODDIE, WALTER M. (*c.* 1808–1865). A.N.A. Landscape painter, Associate Member of the National Academy 1833–65. Oddie lived during these years at Bedford, Bushwick, and Brooklyn on Long Island, as well as in NYC. His landscapes were chiefly of Long Island, Hudson Valley, and New England scenes, though he ranged as far west as the Allegheny Mountains in what is now West Virginia. He was a frequent exhibitor at the National Academy, Apollo Association and American Art-Union, and in Philadelphia, Boston, and Washington. He was the earliest teacher of EDWARD LAMSON HENRY, about 1855. ¶ Smith; Cowdrey, NAD; Cowdrey, AA & AAU; Rutledge, PA; Rutledge, MHS; Swan, BA; McCausland, *Edward Lamson Henry;* Washington Art Assoc. Cat., 1859; *Panorama* (Dec. 1947), 46–47 (repros.).

ODELL, T. J. Portrait painter, formerly of Nashville (Tenn.), who committed suicide July 13, 1849, at Monroe (La.). ¶ Delgado-WPA cites New Orleans *Commercial Bulletin,* July 25, 1849.

ODELL, THOMAS. Engraver and counterfeiter who worked at Boston, in Rhode Island, and in Pennsylvania about 1705. ¶ Dow, *The Arts and Crafts in New England.*

O'DONNELL, JOHN. Irish lithographer, 30, working in NYC in August 1850. ¶ 7 Census (1850), N.Y., XLII, 471.

OELSCHLAGER, GUSTAVUS. Engraver, 27, a native of Canada, living in Philadelphia in 1860. His father, James C. Oelschlager, was a professor of languages from Hamburg (Germany) who had gone to Newfoundland sometime before 1830, married a Newfoundlander, and had a son Julius born there. Gustavus, the second son, was born in Canada about 1833, and James, the youngest, was born in Pennsylvania about 1853. ¶ 8 Census (1860), Pa., LIV, 210.

OERTEL, JOHANNES ADAM SIMON (1823–1909). A.N.A. Religious and portrait painter, engraver, and Episcopal clergyman. Born November 3, 1823, at Fürth (Bavaria), Oertel studied painting and engraving in Munich under J. M. ENZING-MÜLLER. He emigrated to America in 1848, settling in Newark (N.J.). During the next two decades he earned his way by teaching drawing, painting portraits, engraving banknotes, and designing ceiling decorations for the House of Representatives in Washington (1857–58). In 1871 he became a priest of the Protestant Episcopal Church and for over twenty years he served parishes in North and South Carolina, District of Columbia, Tennessee, Missouri, and Maryland. After his retirement in 1895 he was able to realize his ambition to paint a series of pictures illustrating the Redemption, as well as many other paintings on religious subjects. He spent his last years at Vienna (Va.) and died there on December 9, 1909. ¶ DAB cites J. F. Oertel, *A Vision Realized: A Life Story of Rev. J. A. Oertel* (1912); Cowdrey, NAD; Swan, BA; Cowdrey, AA & AAU; Rutledge, PA. His work is represented at the University of the South and in many churches, including the National Cathedral at Washington.

OESINGER, Mrs. S. Miniaturist, Philadelphia, 1856. ¶ Rutledge, PA.

OFFICER, THOMAS S. (*c.* 1810–1859). Miniaturist and portrait painter. Born in Carlisle (Pa.), he began his career in Philadelphia about 1834 and worked there until 1845. He was at Mobile (Ala.) in May 1837, at Richmond (Va.) in April 1845, and worked in NYC from 1846 to 1849. Bolton states that he visited Mexico and Australia. By 1856 he was at San Francisco, where he died during the latter part of 1859. ¶ Information courtesy Charles Coleman Sellers, Dickinson College, who cites obit. in *Carlisle* (Pa.) *Herald,* Jan. 1860; Bolton, *Miniature Painters;* Phila. BD 1838; Rutledge, PA; *Richmond Portraits;* Cowdrey, NAD; Cowdrey, AA & AAU; San Francisco BD 1856–59; represented: Dickinson College, Carlisle (Pa.); FARL photo. file.

O'FLYNN, EDWARD. Seal and general engraver, NYC, 1854–59. ¶ NYBD 1854–59.

OGILBY, R. E. Topographical artist working in California in 1852. Several of his views were lithographed and published in San Francisco. ¶ Peters, *California on Stone; Portfolio* (Nov. 1948), 59 (repro.).

OGILVIE, CLINTON (1838–1900). A.N.A. Landscape painter, born in NYC. He was a pupil of JAMES HART and exhibited after 1860 at the Boston Athenaeum and the Pennsylvania Academy. He died in NYC, November 29, 1900. ¶ *Art Annual,* IV, obit.; Swan, BA; Rutledge, PA; Clark, *History of the NAD,* 266.

OGLETON, JAMES. Engraver, 21, a native of New York, working in Georgetown (D.C.) in June 1860. ¶ 8 Census (1860), D.C., I, 50.

O'GRADY, PATRICK. Engraver, 34, from Ireland, at NYC in 1860. His wife and two children (9 and 10) were born in Ireland; a third child, age seven months, was born in NYC. ¶ 8 Census (1860), N.Y., LXII, 506.

O'GRADY, W. H. Artist for lithographers, San Francisco, 1854–57. ¶ Peters, *California on Stone;* Peters, *America on Stone,* pl. 80.

O'HALLORAN, PATRICK. Engraver, 60, from Ireland, working in NYC in 1860. ¶ 8 Census (1860), N.Y., LX, 776; the 1860 directory lists him as a stonecutter.

O'HARA, Miss SUSAN. Miniaturist, NYC, 1834–35. She exhibited at the National Academy. ¶ Bolton, *Miniature Painters;* Cowdrey, NAD; Dunlap, *History,* II, 470.

O'KEEFFE, MARY CATHERINE. Painter of fruit and flower pieces about 1840. She was the grandmother of the later artists Georgia, Ida, and Catherine O'Keeffe. ¶ *Art Digest* (April 1, 1933), 27.

OKEY, SAMUEL. British mezzotint engraver who won premiums from the Society of Artists in London in 1765 and 1767; later came to Newport (R.I.) where he and Charles Reak published portraits between 1773 and 1780. ¶ Stauffer; DNB; *Antiques* (July 1953), 45 (repro.).

OLAND, CHARLES. Italian sculptor, 50, at NYC in 1850. ¶ 7 Census (1850), N.Y., XLVIII, 246.

OLIPHANT, DAVID, JR. Drawing and painting teacher, coach and scene painter, Charleston (S.C.), 1784, 1794–95. ¶ Prime, I, 6; Rutledge, *Artists in the Life of Charleston.*

OLIVER, Miss EMMA SOPHIA (1819–1885). Amateur painter, exhibited a watercolor at the Pennsylvania Academy in 1858. ¶ Rutledge, PA.

OLIVER, GEORGE. Artist, 42, a Frenchman, in NYC in August 1850. ¶ 7 Census (1850), N.Y., XLII, 145.

OLIVER, HENRY. Engraver and stationer, born in New York about 1836, working in NYC 1860 and after. ¶ 8 Census (1860), N.Y., XLIII, 749; NYCD 1863.

OLIVER, JOHN. Artist and picture dealer, NYC, 1850–60 and after. He was a native of Scotland, born about 1807 or 1808. He came to NYC from Upper Canada (present Ontario) sometime after 1835. ¶ 7 Census (1850), N.Y., XLIII, 117; 8 Census (1860), N.Y., XLVI, 280; NYCD 1850, 1863.

OLIVER, L. Exhibitor of a plaster medallion at the National Academy in 1859. ¶ Cowdrey, NAD.

OLIVER, ROBIN. Engraver, 35, native of Pennsylvania, living in New Orleans in 1860. ¶ 8 Census (1860), La., V, 758.

OLIVER, WILLIAM. Engraver, 22, native of New York, living in NYC in 1860 with his father, Alexander Oliver, banknote printer. ¶ 8 Census (1860), N.Y., LVII, 1024.

OLMSTEAD, JOHN A. Engraver, NYC, 1850's. ¶ NYBD 1851–59.

O'MALLEY, JAMES. Painter of "Napoleon" and "Nativity," shown at the American Institute in 1851, and "Tear of Sorrow," shown at the American Art-Union in 1851. He was a resident of NYC. ¶ Am. Inst. Cat., 1851; Cowdrey, AA & AAU.

OMAN, JAMES. Heraldic painter, Philadelphia, 1816–17; probably JAMES O'MEARA. ¶ Brown and Brown.

O'MEARA, JAMES. Heraldic painter, Philadelphia, 1812–14. He exhibited at the Society of Artists in 1812. His widow was listed in 1818 and 1823. *Cf.* JAMES OMAN. ¶ Society of Artists Cat., 1812; Phila. CD 1814, 1818, 1823.

O'MEARA, PATRICK. Heraldic and other painting, Baltimore, 1792. ¶ Prime, II, 302.

O'MULLIN, WILLIAM. Engraver, 23, a native of New York, working in NYC in 1860. ¶ 8 Census (1860), N.Y., XLIX, 872.

O'NEAL, JAMES. Lithographer, 17, born in New York, working in NYC in 1850. ¶ 7 Census (1850), N.Y., LI, 183.

O'NEIL, ——. Wood engraver, 23, from Pennsylvania, at NYC in 1860. ¶ 8 Census (1860), N.Y., XLVII, 120.

O'NEIL, WILLIAM. Engraver, 26, from Connecticut, at NYC in 1860. His five children were all born in New York. *Cf.* WILLIAM A. and WILLIAM W. O'NEIL. ¶ 8 Census (1860), N.Y., LVI, 817.

O'NEIL, WILLIAM A. Engraver, NYC, 1854–

56; his home address was different from that of WILLIAM W. O'NEIL. *Cf.* WILLIAM O'NEIL. ¶ NYCD 1854, 1856.

O'NEIL, WILLIAM W. Wood engraver, NYC, 1850–56; different home address from WILLIAM A. O'NEIL. *Cf.* WILLIAM O'NEIL. ¶ NYBD 1850, 1854; NYCD 1854, 1856.

O'NEILL, JAMES. Painter of a panorama of Ireland shown in Chicago and Detroit in 1860–61. ¶ Chicago *Times,* Sept. 1 and 10, 1860, Detroit *Free Press,* Nov. 22, 1860, Dec. 28, 1861 (courtesy J. Earl Arrington).

O'NEILL or O'NEEL, JOHN. Engraver, 15, born in England, living in Philadelphia in 1850 with his father, Peter O'Neill or O'Neel, a copperplate printer from Ireland. ¶ 7 Census (1850), Pa., L, 348 and 394.

O'NEILL, JOHN A. New Jersey-born engraver on steel and wood who worked principally in NYC after 1857. He was elected mayor of Hoboken (N.J.) in 1876 and served as chief engraver in the U. S. Treasury Department under President Grover Cleveland. ¶ Stauffer; NYBD 1857–58; *Richmond Portraits,* 76 (repro.).

O'NEILL, ROBERT J. Engraver, Philadelphia, 1854. ¶ Phila. CD 1854.

ONKEN, OTTO. Lithographer, born in Germany about 1815, working in Cincinnati from about 1848 to 1860. ¶ 7 Census (1850), Ohio, XX, 313; Cincinnati BD and CD 1850–60; Peters, *America on Stone.*

ONTHANK, NAHUM BALL (1823–1888). Portrait and landscape painter. A native of Massachusetts; worked in Boston. He exhibited at the Boston Athenaeum between 1853 and 1872 and at the National Academy in 1848 and 1850. ¶ Swan, BA; New England BD 1856; Boston BD 1854–60; Cowdrey, NAD; 7 Census (1850), Mass., XXV, 796.

OPPERMAN, AUGUST. Engraver and jeweller, Washington (D.C.), 1860. ¶ Washington CD 1860.

OPPITZ, WILLIAM. Engraver, NYC, 1854–59. ¶ NYBD 1854, 1859.

ORAM, Miss ELIZABETH. Artist who exhibited "A Little Weary Girl" and a sketch after GEORGE LINEN at the Apollo Association in 1839. She was a teacher in NYC from 1815 to 1847. ¶ Cowdrey, AA & AAU; NYCD 1815–47.

ORD, JOSEPH BIAYS (1805–1865). Portrait, still life, and religious painter and picture restorer. A native of Philadelphia, he began exhibiting at the Pennsylvania Academy in 1824 and later showed his paintings at the Apollo Association, the Art-Union, the National Academy, and the Maryland Historical Society. In 1850 he was living with his father, George Ord, "Gentleman." He died in Philadelphia in 1865. ¶ Mallett; Rutledge, PA; Rutledge, MHS; Cowdrey, NAD; Cowdrey, AA & AAU; Phila. CD 1835–60+ (variously as Joseph, John and James); *Antiques* (Sept. 1946), 159 (repro.); 7 Census (1850), Pa., LV, 68.

ORD, P. Artist, New Orleans, 1844. ¶ Delgado-WPA cites New Orleans CD 1844.

ORDWAY, ALFRED T. (1819–1897). Portrait painter who worked mainly in Boston. He exhibited at the Athenaeum between 1855 and 1864. He died in Boston November 17, 1897. ¶ *Art Annual,* I, obit.; Boston BD 1846–60+; Lowell CD 1848; Swan, BA; Champney, *Sixty Years Memories,* 103.

O'REGAN, C. Engraver and die sinker, New Orleans, 1856. ¶ New Orleans CD 1856.

O'REGAN, JAMES. Engraver and die sinker, New Orleans, 1852–70. ¶ New Orleans CD 1852–56; information courtesy Delgado-WPA.

O'REILLY, PATRICK. Sculptor, 28, from Ireland, at NYC in 1860. ¶ 8 Census (1860), N.Y., LIII, 790.

ORLEANS, ANTOINE PHILIPPE D', see MONTPENSIER.

ORLEANS, LOUIS CHARLES D', see BEAUJOLAIS.

ORMSBY, ROBERT. Banknote engraver, NYC, 1841. ¶ NYBD 1841.

ORMSBY, WATERMAN LILLY (1809–1883). Banknote and general engraver. A native of Hampton (Conn.), he was apprenticed to an engraver, studied for a year at the National Academy (1829), and worked for a number of years in Rochester and Albany (N.Y.) and Lancaster (Mass.). He settled in NYC in the early 1840's and became a leading banknote engraver and inventor of engraving machines, proprietor of the New York Bank Note Company and a founder of the Continental Bank Note Company. Author of *Cycloidal Configurations, or the Harvest of Counterfeitors* (n.d.) and *A Description of the Present System of Banknote Engraving* (1852). He died in Brooklyn November 1, 1883. ¶ DAB; Stauffer; NYBD 1844–59; Hamilton, *Early American Book Illustrators and Wood Engravers,* 133, 467.

O'ROOKE (O'ROURKE ?), MICHAEL. Lithographer, 28, from Ireland, at NYC in 1850. ¶ 7 Census (1850), N.Y., XLI, 500.

ORR, HECTOR. Wood engraver, Philadelphia, 1860 and after. He was listed as a printer from 1837 to 1859. ¶ Phila. CD 1837–60+.

ORR, J. W. & N. Wood engravers, NYC, 1844–46; JOHN WILLIAM and NATHANIEL ORR. ¶ NYCD 1844–46.

ORR, JOHN WILLIAM (1815–1887). Wood engraver. Orr was born March 31, 1815, in Ireland, brought to America in infancy, and brought up at Buffalo (N.Y.). In 1836 he studied in NYC with WILLIAM REDFIELD; the following year he set up in business in Buffalo. He moved to Albany in 1842 and finally settled in NYC two years later. From 1844 to 1846 he and his brother NATHANIEL were in business together as J. W. & N. ORR. The Orrs were much in demand as book and magazine illustrators and had one of the largest engraving plants in the city. From 1862 to 1871 John was also the editor and publisher of the *American Odd Fellow.* He died March 4, 1887, in Jersey City (N.J.). ¶ CAB; NYCD and BD 1845–60+; Hamilton, *Early American Book Illustrators and Wood Engravers;* Am. Inst. Cat., 1844, 1848, 1849, 1856.

ORR, NATHANIEL. Wood engraver, probably a younger brother of JOHN WILLIAM ORR. Nathaniel and his brother got their start in NYC in 1844 and worked together at least until 1846. In 1848 Nathaniel was in partnership with JAMES H. RICHARDSON, but thereafter he worked independently. During the fifties he was one of the leading wood engravers in the country and his work appeared in many books and periodicals of the time. ¶ NYCD 1846–60; Hamilton, *Early American Book Illustrators and Wood Engravers;* Am. Inst. Cat., 1844–45, 1849–51.

ORR & RICHARDSON. Wood engravers, NYC, 1848; NATHANIEL ORR and JAMES H. RICHARDSON. ¶ NYCD and BD 1848.

ORR, see also TOWNSEND & ORR.

ORSOLLINI, THEODORE. French artist, 26, at Philadelphia in 1860. Possibly related to Adrien Orsilini of Philadelphia who exhibited a medallion and a model of a bust of Lincoln at the Pennsylvania Academy in 1861. ¶ 8 Census (1860), Pa., LIV, 263.

OSBORN, JAMES. Primitive watercolor portrait, about 1800. ¶ Lipman and Winchester, 178.

OSBORN, JOHN. Portrait and landscape painter at Cleveland in the winter of 1850–51. *Cf.* J. O. OSBORNE. ¶ WPA (Ohio), *Annals of Cleveland.*

OSBORN, M. Stipple engraver working in Baltimore about 1812 and in Philadelphia about 1820. Not the same as MILO OSBORNE. ¶ Stauffer.

OSBORN, MILO, see MILO OSBORNE.

OSBORN, NATHANIEL B. Portrait painter at Salem (Mass.) in 1853. ¶ Belknap, *Artists and Craftsmen of Essex County,* 11.

OSBORNE, ——. Miniaturist, New Orleans, 1841. ¶ Delgado-WPA cites *Bee,* July 27, 1841.

OSBORNE, J. O. Primitive landscape painter at Masillon (Ohio) in 1854. *Cf.* JOHN OSBORN. ¶ Information courtesy Albert Hise.

OSBORNE or OSBORN, MILO. Engraver and townscape artist, born in Massachusetts about 1810. The earliest mention of him is as one of the artists and engravers for Fay's *Views in New York and Its Environs* (1831–34). He continued in NYC until 1849 and is said later to have worked for Philadelphia publishers. In June 1860 he was living in Sacramento (Cal.). ¶ 8 Census (1860), Cal., V, 21; Stauffer; Stokes, *Historical Prints;* NYCD 1835–49; Am. Inst. Cat., 1848.

OSGOOD, CHARLES (1809–1890). Portrait and miniature painter, born at Salem (Mass.) February 25, 1809. A resident of Salem during most of his career, he also worked in Boston and Roxbury (Mass.) and in NYC. His wife was a sister of the artist MARY HOLYOKE WARD, whose nephew ABEL NICHOLS received his earliest training under Osgood. Osgood died in Salem in 1890. ¶ Belknap, *Artists and Craftsmen of Essex County,* 11; Salem CD 1837–60+; Swan, BA; repros., *Essex Institute Historical Collections,* LXXXV (Jan. 1949), opp. 12, and LXXXVI (April 1950), opp. 104 and 160; represented at Essex Inst., American Antiquarian Soc., and Mass. Hist. Soc.

OSGOOD, HENRY H. (1813–?). Portrait painter, born in Boston January 14, 1813; working there in 1841; died in early manhood. He was a younger brother of JOHN B. and SAMUEL S. OSGOOD. ¶ Osgood, *Genealogy of the Descendants of John, Christopher and William Osgood,* 100; Boston BD 1841.

OSGOOD, JOHN B. (1806–?). Sign painter, elder brother of HENRY H. and SAMUEL S. OSGOOD. He was born October 3, 1806, in Boston. From the mid-1850's he made his home at Indianapolis. JOHN H. NIEMEYER worked under him at the start of his career. ¶ Osgood, *Genealogy of the Descendants of John, Christopher and William Osgood,* 191; Burnet, *Art and Artists of Indiana,* 91; Peat, *Pioneer Painters of Indiana,* 169.

OSGOOD, SAMUEL STILLMAN (1808–1885). A.N.A. Portrait and historical painter; born June 9, 1808, possibly in New Haven (see French), although his brothers JOHN B. and HENRY H. OSGOOD were born in Boston. He grew up in Boston and studied painting there. After a visit to Charleston (S.C.) during the winter of 1829–30, he returned to Boston. In 1835 he married the noted poetess Frances S. Locke and with her went to Europe where Samuel studied for several years. After their return to America in 1839, the Osgoods visited Charleston and Boston and then settled in NYC. Here they lived until Mrs. Osgood's death in 1851 (except for a residence in Philadelphia between 1847 and 1849). After her death Samuel made a second trip to Europe and also went to New Orleans several times. He subsequently remarried and was living in NYC as late as 1869. He eventually moved to California and died there in 1885. Osgood was an Associate Member of the National Academy and exhibited frequently in NYC, Boston, and Philadelphia. ¶ Osgood, *Genealogy of the Descendants of John, Christopher and William Osgood,* 191–92; death date courtesy Donald A. Shelley; Rutledge, *Artists in the Life of Charleston;* French, *Art and Artists in Connecticut,* 60; Swan, BA; Cowdrey, NAD; Cowdrey, AA & AAU; Rutledge, PA; NYCD 1849+; Delgado-WP cites *Commercial Bulletin* (Feb. 22, Dec. 22, 1853), *Courier* (May 18, 1853), and *Picayune* (May 25, 1855).

O'SHANNESSY, J. J. Banknote and general engraver, Chicago, 1856–59. ¶ Chicago BD 1856, CD 1858–59.

OSLER, WILBUR. Engraver, 22, born in Pennsylvania, living in Philadelphia in 1860 with his father, Harman Osler, tailor. A younger brother, John (18), was also an engraver. In 1871 Wilbur was a photographer. ¶ 8 Census (1860), Pa., LXI, 584; Phila. CD 1871.

OSTERBURG, HERMAN. Engraver and die sinker, NYC, 1854. ¶ NYBD 1854.

OSTINELLE, L. Landscape painter. He exhibited a view of Madison Falls (N.Y.) at the American Art-Union in 1849. ¶ Cowdrey, AA & AAU.

OSTNER, CHARLES HINKLEY. Sculptor and carver, San Francisco, 1856–59. ¶ San Francisco CD 1856, BD 1858–59.

OSTRANDER, PHILIP. Engraver said to have been working in NYC and Cincinnati during the early 1850's. He was at Syracuse (N.Y.) in 1859. ¶ Stauffer; New York State BD 1859.

OTIS, BASS (1784–1861). Portrait painter and lithographer, born July 17, 1784, at Bridgewater (Mass.). Although apprenticed to a scythemaker, Otis managed to acquire the rudiments of an artistic training and appeared in NYC in 1808 as a professional portrait painter. He moved to Philadelphia in 1812, exhibiting for the first time that year at the Society of Artists. In 1818 or 1819 he produced the first lithograph executed in America. He continued to live in Philadelphia until 1845, then moved to NYC and a year or two later to Boston. He returned to Philadelphia in 1858 and died there November 3, 1861. ¶ DAB; Rutledge, PA; Phila. CD 1813–45, 1858–61; Swan, BA; Boston BD 1847–57; Cowdrey, NAD; Cowdrey, AA & AAU; Peters, *America on Stone.*

OTIS, FESSENDEN NOTT (1825–1900). Teacher of perspective and landscape drawing, topographical draftsman. Born March 6, 1825, at Ballston Springs (N.Y.), he took up the study of drawing after an accident in 1843 interrupted his studies. One of his books on the subject, *Easy Lectures in Landscape,* had run to five editions by 1856. He studied medicine in NYC, receiving his degree in 1852, and in 1853 became a ship's surgeon on the Panama route to California. It was during this period that he executed a view of San Francisco (1855), known through a lithograph by C. PARSONS. In 1860 Otis opened his practice in NYC, serving from 1861 to 1871 as police surgeon. He became an authority on genito-urinary diseases. In addition to a number of medical works, he published an *Illustrated History of the Panama Railroad* (1861). He died May 24, 1900, at New Orleans. ¶ DAB; *Portfolio* (Jan. 1952), 101 (repro.), 119; Van Nostrand and Coulter, *California Pictorial,* 154–55; Jackson, *Gold Rush Album,* 112, 119.

OTIS, LEWIS W. Wood engraver, NYC, 1860. ¶ NYBD 1860.

O'TOOLE, LAWRENCE J. Engraver with DEMPSEY & O'TOOLE, Washington (D.C.), 1860. ¶ Washington CD 1860.

OTT, PHILIP. Portrait painter in miniature and enamel, NYC, 1855–57; exhibitor, National Academy. ¶ Cowdrey, NAD; NYBD 1857.

OTTER, T. J. Genre painter, Philadelphia, exhibited at the National Academy in 1860. *Cf.* THOMAS P. OTTER. ¶ Cowdrey, NAD.

OTTER, THOMAS P. Artist and engraver, Philadelphia, 1855–67. He exhibited at the Boston Athenaeum and the Pennsylvania Academy. *Cf.* T. J. OTTER. ¶ Rutledge, PA; Swan, BA; Phila. CD 1857–60; Hamilton, *Early American Book Illustrators and Wood Engravers,* 464.

OTTO, WILLIAM. Lithographer, St. Louis, 1854. ¶ St. Louis BD 1854.

OURDAN, JOSEPH JAMES PROSPER (1803–1874). Engraver, born in March 1803 at Marseilles (France). He was working in NYC as early as 1821, later moved to Philadelphia, and from 1866 until his death was employed as a letter engraver in the U. S. Treasury Department at Washington. He died October 25, 1874. JOSEPH PROSPER OURDAN was his son. ¶ Stauffer; 8 Census (1860), Pa., LXII, 359.

OURDAN, JOSEPH PROSPER (1828–1881). Engraver and book illustrator, born February 16, 1828, in NYC, the son of JOSEPH JAMES PROSPER OURDAN. He worked in NYC, Philadelphia, and Washington, and was the head of the Bureau of Engraving and Printing at the time of his death, May 10, 1881. He was a partner of RAWSON PACKARD in 1850. ¶ Stauffer; 7 Census (1850), N.Y., XLIII, 143; NYHS *Annual Report* for 1954.

OURLAC, JEAN NICOLAS (1789–1821). Landscape painter. A native of New Orleans, Ourlac went to Paris to study under David. About 1815–17 he executed a number of views of NYC, Baltimore, Boston, and New Orleans. He died in Paris in 1821. ¶ CAB; Fielding.

OVERBAUGH, ABRAM W. Engraver, of JONES, OVERBAUGH & JONES at NYC in 1860. ¶ NYBD 1860.

OWEN, DAVID DALE (1807–1860). Topographical draftsman, portrait and landscape painter. The fourth son of the Scottish industrialist-reformer Robert Owen, David Dale Owen was born June 24, 1807, at New Lanark (Scotland). He came to America in 1827 and settled with his father and brothers, including RICHARD OWEN, at New Harmony (Ind.). He first took up printing and lithography there and in NYC, where another brother was an editor, but gave them up to study chemistry in London, 1831–32. Returning to New Harmony in 1833, he studied medicine for a time in Cincinnati. In 1837 he began the serious study of geology and the rest of his life was spent in making geological surveys of Indiana and other areas of the Middle and South West. His reports were largely illustrated by himself and he also painted portraits and landscapes as an amateur. He died in New Harmony November 13, 1860. ¶ Hendrickson, *David Dale Owen;* DAB; Peat, *Pioneer Painters of Indiana.*

OWEN, GEORGE. Lithographer, 30, at New Orleans in 1860. ¶ 8 Census (1860), La., VI, 354.

OWEN or OWENS, GEORGE, JR. Landscape painter who exhibited in NYC, Boston, and Philadelphia, 1858–77. He was in NYC between 1858 and 1867 and subsequently at Boston and Providence. New England scenes predominated in his work. ¶ Cowdrey, NAD; Swan, BA; Rutledge, PA.

OWEN, RICHARD. Landscape painter and draftsman. A brother of DAVID DALE OWEN, Richard was probably born at New Lanark (Scotland) during the first decade of the 19th century. He came to America in 1827 and settled at New Harmony (Ind.), then under the direction of his father Robert Owen, the Scottish manufacturer and reformer. He later became a professor at Indiana University and helped illustrate some of the geological works of David Dale Owen. ¶ Hendrickson, *David Dale Owen;* Owen, *Report on Indiana;* Peat, *Pioneer Painters of Indiana.*

OWENS, ——. Landscape painter at Cleveland (Ohio) in 1857. ¶ WPA (Ohio), *Annals of Cleveland.*

OWENS or OWEN, GRIFFITH. Artist, 28, born in Wales, living in Philadelphia in 1860. The father, Griffith J. Owens, was an inventor; all his children were born in Wales before about 1848. ¶ 8 Census (1860), Pa., LX, 573.

OZANNE, PIERRE (1737–1813). Marine painter. A native of Brest (France), Ozanne studied painting under his brother Nicolas Marie Ozanne, a well-known marine painter. Between May 1778 and October 1779 he served as official artist to the French fleet which came to the aid of America under command of the Comte d'Estaing. A portfolio of 22 water color drawings by Ozanne, now in the Library of Congress, portray the principal events of this expedition in American waters. Ozanne later served as a marine engineer at the French port of Toulon. He died at Brest in 1813. ¶ Thieme-Becker; *American Processional,* 76 (repro.), 237; information courtesy Library of Congress.

P

PABODIE, CHARLES A. Engraver of Providence (R.I.), active 1847–60. In 1857–58 he was with PABODIE & PARKHURST. ¶ Providence CD 1847–60; New England BD 1849–60.

PABODIE, EDWIN A. Engraver, Providence (R.I.), 1850. ¶ Providence CD 1850.

PABODIE & PARKHURST. Engravers, Providence (R.I.), 1857–58, CHARLES A. PABODIE and DANIEL S. PARKHURST. ¶ Providence CD 1857–58.

PACKARD, RAWSON ("Ross"). Engraver, born in New York State about 1813. He was a resident of Albany between 1837 and 1846, but moved to NYC by 1848 and was still there in 1851. In 1850 he was in partnership with JOSEPH PROSPER OURDAN. ¶ 7 Census (1850), N.Y., XLVII, 774; Albany CD 1837–46; NYBD 1848–51; NYHS *Annual Report* for 1954.

PADUANI (Paduane or Paduany), LOUIS. Miniaturist, landscape painter, and drawing teacher. He was at NYC in 1819, Richmond (Va.) in 1821, and Charleston (S.C.) in 1824. ¶ NYCD 1819; *Richmond Portraits;* Rutledge, *Artists in the Life of Charleston.*

PAGANINI, CHRISTOPHANI. Portrait and miniature painter, pastellist; at New Orleans in 1830. ¶ Delgado-WPA cites *Bee,* July 20, 1830.

PAGE, ALBY. Engraver, 22, born in Massachusetts, at Boston in 1860. ¶ 8 Census (1860), Mass., XXIX, 31.

PAGE, CHARLES. English artist, 32, at Spring Garden, Philadelphia, in 1850. His wife was a Pennsylvanian. ¶ 7 Census (1850), Pa., LIV, 657.

PAGE, H. Profile cutter active 1816, location unknown. Only one example of his work has been recorded, a profile of "Gen. Harris." ¶ Gillingham, "Notes on Philadelphia Profilists," 518 (repro.).

PAGE, H. Illustrator of *The Life of Rev. David Brainard* (N.Y., *c.* 1833). His landscape designs for this work were engraved by ALEXANDER ANDERSON. ¶ Hamilton, *Early American Book Illustrators and Wood Engravers,* 99, 427.

PAGE, H. C. Marble cutter, carver, and engraver; Charleston (S.C.), 1830. ¶ Rutledge, *Artists in the Life of Charleston.*

PAGE, SAMUEL (1823–1852). Portrait painter; born November 29, 1823, at Newburyport (Mass.); died there in 1852. ¶ Belknap, *Artists and Craftsmen of Essex County,* 11.

PAGE, Mrs. SARAH NICHOLS, see SARAH NICHOLS.

PAGE, S. P. Winner of a prize for pencil drawing at the Illinois State Fair, 1855. ¶ Chicago *Daily Press,* Oct. 15, 1855.

PAGE, WILLIAM (1811–1885). N.A. Portrait and figure painter. Born January 23, 1811, at Albany (N.Y.) but brought up in NYC, Page received his early training from JAMES HERRING and SAMUEL F. B. MORSE during the mid-1820's. Between 1829 and 1832 he worked in NYC, Northampton (Mass.), Albany and Rochester (N.Y.), but from 1833 to 1843 he was settled in NYC. He moved to Boston in 1844 and worked there until his departure for Italy in 1849. He remained in Italy until 1860, working mainly in Rome, where he was a prominent member of the Anglo-American colony. Returning to America in 1860, he lived for several years near GEORGE INNESS at Eagleswood (N.J.), but in 1866 he moved to Tottenville, Staten Island (N.Y.) where he lived until his death, October 1, 1885. Page was elected a member of the National Academy in 1837 and he was President of the Academy from 1871 to 1873. He is remembered today chiefly as a colorist and leading exponent of figure painting among the American Romantics. ¶ Richardson, "Two Portraits by William Page," contains an account of his life, bibliography, catalogue, and two repros.; DAB; Cowdrey, NAD; Cowdrey, AA & AAU; Rutledge, PA; Swan, BA.

PAGETT, Mrs. ——. Teacher of drawing and painting in watercolors, as well as needlework, at her husband's school in Charleston (S.C.) in 1794. ¶ Rutledge, *Artists in the Life of Charleston.*

PAGGATT, L. French engraver, 28, at San Francisco in 1860. ¶ 8 Census (1860), Cal., VII, 934.

PAIGE, J. F. Engraver, San Francisco, 1859. ¶ San Francisco CD 1859.

PAIN, A. Landscape painter who exhibited at the Pennsylvania Academy in 1854 and 1857. One of his pictures was a "view near Pottsville [Pa.]." ¶ Rutledge, PA.

PAIN, JACOB. Engraver, Philadelphia, 1793. ¶ Brown and Brown.

PAINE, ——. Decorative wall painter said

to have worked near Parsonfield (Me.) during the 1830's, possibly in collaboration with JONATHAN POOR. His "signature" was an uprooted dead tree falling between the branches of another ¶ *Art in America* (Oct. 1950), 165–66, 194 (repro.).

PAINE, SUSANNAH or SUSAN (1792–1862). Portrait and landscape painter; born June 9, 1792, at Rehoboth (Mass.); worked in Massachusetts, Connecticut, and Rhode Island. Her home was in Providence from the mid-forties until her death, November 10, 1862. ¶ C. K. Bolton, "Workers with Line and Color in New England"; Providence CD 1847–60.

PAINE, T. O. Sculptor; born in Maine about 1825; living in Bangor in 1850 and in Boston in 1852. ¶ 7 Census (1850), Maine, XIII, 307; Boston BD 1852.

PAINE, W. Primitive portraitist in oil on cardboard, at New Bedford (Mass.), about 1845. ¶ Lipman and Winchester, 178.

PAJOT, LOUIS E. Steel and medal engraver, NYC, 1817–22. He cut the seal of the New-York Historical Society in 1821. The name also appears as Pigot and Parjeaux. ¶ NYCD 1817–22; Vail, *Knickerbocker Birthday,* 62.

PALDI, ANGE. Battle artist who depicted the battles of Resaca de la Palma and Palo Alto during the Mexican War. He was with the 5th Infantry Regiment, U. S. Army. ¶ *Album of American Battle Art,* 129, pl. 55.

PALISSARD, LOUIS. Engraver, New Orleans, 1842. ¶ New Orleans CD 1842.

PALLENLIEF, ANDREW. Swiss sculptor, 36, at San Francisco in July 1860. His wife was also Swiss, but their five-month-old daughter was born in California. ¶ 8 Census (1860), Cal., VII, 756.

PALMATARY, JAMES T. Townscape artist who made views of Indianapolis (1854) and Washington (D.C.), and published a proposal to do a view of Columbus (Ohio) in 1854. ¶ Burnet, *Art and Artists of Indiana,* 65–66; Columbus, *Ohio Statesman,* Dec. 27, 1854 (courtesy J. Earl Arrington).

PALMER, ADALINE OSBURN (1817–1906). Portrait and miniature painter and teacher. A native of Rippon (Va., now W. Va.), she married John P. Palmer, a Richmond journalist who died in 1879. Mrs. Palmer lived in Fauquier County (Va.), Mobile (Ala.), and in Richmond. She died in her native town in 1906. ¶ Willis, "Jefferson County Portraits and Portrait Painters."

PALMER, ARTHUR C. English artist, 29, at NYC in 1850. Though listed as an artist in the census, he was listed in the directory as a decorator. ¶ 7 Census (1850), N.Y., XLIII, 129.

PALMER, BENJAMIN C. Portrait and townscape painter, who had a studio at New York University in 1845 and exhibited at the National Academy yearly from 1845 to 1849. Four views of Norwalk (Conn.) by B. C. Palmer, presumably the same man, were lithographed by JONES & NEWMAN about 1848. ¶ Cowdrey, NAD; NYCD 1845; *Portfolio* (Feb. 1951), 130 (repros.).

PALMER, C. H. Pennsylvania portrait painter about 1825. *Cf.* CH. B. R. PALMER. ¶ Lipman and Winchester, 178.

PALMER, C. K. Portrait and miniature painter working probably in Connecticut, about 1840–42. ¶ Sherman, "Some Recently Discovered Early American Portrait Miniaturists," 295 (repro.); NYHS Cat. (1941); information courtesy Mrs. T. Webster Nock, NYC.

PALMER, CH. B. R. Portrait painter working in Pennsylvania in 1826. *Cf.* C. H. PALMER. ¶ *American Folk Art,* no. 17 and repro. p. 15.

PALMER, EDWARD S. Lithographer, husband of FANNY PALMER. Edward and Fanny arrived in NYC in the early 1840's from Leicester (England). Although he worked for several years as a lithographer, the burden of supporting the family fell chiefly on Mrs. Palmer, who was employed as an artist by CURRIER & IVES. He died March 7, 1859, from a fall. ¶ Peters, *Currier & Ives,* 110–15; NYCD 1844–45; *cf.* SEYMOUR PALMER.

PALMER, ERASTUS DOW (1817–1904). Sculptor, born April 2, 1817, at Pompey, near Syracuse (N.Y.). He was apprenticed to a carpenter and followed the trade until after his marriage. While living in Utica he attempted cameo-cutting with considerable success and a few years later turned to modelling in clay. In 1851 he exhibited for the first time at the National Academy, of which he was an Honorary Member, Professional. Palmer moved to Albany in 1846 and had a studio there for over twenty-five years. His most popular work was "The White Captive," though he was also known for his portrait busts, reliefs, and memorials Palmer, unlike most of his American con temporaries in sculpture, did not visit Europe until late in his career and he stayed only a few months. Of his own pupils at Albany, LAUNT THOMPSON was probably the best known. Palmer died in Albany on March 9, 1904. ¶ DAB; Clement and Hutton; Gardner, *Yankee Stonecutters;* Cowdrey, NAD; Cowdrey, AA & AAU; Rutledge, PA; Swan, BA.

PALMER, F. & S. Lithographers, artists, and draftsmen, NYC, 1846–49; FANNY and SEYMOUR PALMER. They exhibited lithographs at the American Institute in 1848. ¶ NYCD 1846–49; Am. Inst. Cat., 1848.

PALMER, FANNY, née Frances Flora Bond (*c.* 1812–1876). Landscape and townscape painter, artist for CURRIER & IVES. Mrs. Palmer and her husband, EDWARD S. PALMER, came to NYC from Leicester (England) in the early 1840's. He did some lithographic work after their arrival but was rather irresponsible, and the burden of supporting the family rested chiefly on Mrs. Palmer who was for many years employed as an artist by the firm of CURRIER & IVES. The Palmers lived in Brooklyn, as did Fanny's sister and brother, MARIA and ROBERT BOND. Edward Palmer died in 1859 and Fanny on August 20, 1876. ¶ Peters, *Currier & Ives,* 110–15; Peters, *America on Stone;* Cowdrey, NAD; Am. Inst. Cat., 1846–48; NYCD 1846+. See also: SEYMOUR PALMER.

PALMER, J. Engraver of illustrations for an edition of *The Bible* published in NYC in 1826. ¶ Stauffer.

PALMER, JANE. Genre painting in water colors, about 1780. ¶ Lipman and Winchester, 178.

PALMER, JULIA ANN. Genre painting in watercolors, Hallowell (Me.), 1820. ¶ Lipman and Winchester, 178.

PALMER, R. D. Portrait painter, NYC (?), 1841. ¶ FARL to George C. Groce, Jan. 6, 1948.

PALMER, RANDOLPH. Portrait painter working at Auburn (N.Y.) from 1839 to 1843; also worked in Albany and Seneca Falls. Although Charles W. Jenkins of NYC, writing in 1878, said that Palmer died in 1842, a signed and dated portrait of the grandfather of Laurence B. Goodrich (who owned it in 1948) shows the artist to have been living in February 1843. ¶ Information courtesy FARL.

PALMER, SEYMOUR. Lithographic artist and draftsman working with FANNY PALMER in NYC, 1846–49. He exhibited independently at the American Institute in 1846 and with Fanny in 1848. Peters makes no mention of a Seymour Palmer in his discussion of the family in his *Currier & Ives,* but it is possible that Seymour was the middle name of Fanny's husband, EDWARD S. PALMER. ¶ NYCD 1846–47; NYBD 1846, 1848; Am. Inst. Cat., 1846, 1848.

PALMER, SYLVANUS. Portrait painter, Albany (N.Y.), 1844–54. He was the artist of a lithographed portrait of his father, Rev. Sylvanus Palmer, dated March 1844. ¶ Peters, *America on Stone;* Albany CD 1847–54.

PALMER, THERESA. Portrait painter, New Orleans, 1846. ¶ New Orleans CD 1846.

PALTENGHI, A. Sculptor; at New Orleans, 1854–56; at San Francisco, 1856–60. ¶ New Orleans CD 1854–56; San Francisco CD 1858–60.

PANTON, HENRY. Landscape painter, active 1850–60. He exhibited at the American Art-Union and at the National Academy, of which he was an Honorary Member, Amateur. His address in 1860 was NYC. ¶ Cowdrey, AA & AAU; Cowdrey, NAD.

PAOLI, J. Wax portraitist, Philadelphia, 1858. ¶ Phila. BD 1858.

PAPPRILL, HENRY. Aquatint engraver of two views of NYC, 1846 and 1848. ¶ Stokes, *Historical Prints;* Stauffer.

PAQUET, ANTHONY C. (1814–1882). Engraver on wood, copper, and steel. Born in Hamburg (Germany) in 1814, Paquet came to America in 1848. He worked in Philadelphia from 1850 to 1855, in NYC from 1856 to 1858, and then settled permanently in Philadelphia. He was an assistant engraver at the U. S. Mint from 1857 to 1864 and engraved the first Congressional Medal of Honor. He exhibited medals at the Pennsylvania Academy during the Civil War. He died in Philadelphia in 1882. ¶ Stauffer; Thieme-Becker; Phila. BD 1851–55; NYBD 1856–58; Rutledge, PA; Loubat, *Medallic History of the U. S.,* plates 70, 72–73, 75–76; information courtesy John R. Sinnot, Chief Engraver, U. S. Mint (1945); 7 Census (1850), Pa., L, 627 (as J. C. Paquet).

PARADISE, JOHN (1783–1833). N.A. Portrait painter, born October 24, 1783, in Hunterdon County (N.J.). After a brief period of training in Philadelphia under VOLOZAN, he set up as a professional painter about 1803. In 1810 he moved to NYC where he spent the rest of his career. He died November 26, 1833, at the home of his sister in Springfield (N.J.). He was one of the founders of the National Academy. His son, JOHN WESLEY PARADISE, was a portrait painter and engraver. ¶ Dunlap, *History,* II, 204–05; N. Y. *Evening Post,* Dec. 2, 1833, obit.; NYCD 1812–30; Cowdrey, NAD; Cummings, *Historic Annals of the NAD,* 133 (death date erroneously given as June 16, 1834).

PARADISE, JOHN WESLEY (1809–1862). A.N.A. Engraver and portrait painter, son of JOHN PARADISE. Born in New Jersey, he studied engraving with ASHER B. DURAND in NYC and followed the profession there from about 1828 until his death, August 17, 1862. He also exhibited frequently at the National Academy of which he was an Associate Member from 1833. ¶ Cummings, *Historic Annals of the NAD,* 308; Stauffer; Cowdrey, NAD; NYCD 1831–60; Durand, *Life and Times of A. B. Durand,* 90; Hamilton, *Early American Book Illustrators and Wood Engravers,* 96; 8 Census (1860), N.Y., LIII, 160.

PARDE[E?], PHINEAS. Connecticut-born artist, 31, at the Assembly House Hotel, New Haven (Conn.), August 10, 1850. ¶ 7 Census (1850), Conn., VIII, 277.

PARDO, AMBROISE. Portrait painter in Louisiana during the 1790's. ¶ Van Ravenswaay, "The Forgotten Arts and Crafts in Colonial Louisiana," 195.

PARDOE, JOHN. Portrait painter of NYC, who exhibited at the American Institute in 1848. ¶ Am. Inst. Cat., 1848; NYCD 1848–49, as "painter."

PARENTZ, ERNEST. French artist, 28, at NYC in September 1850. ¶ 7 Census (1850), N.Y., XLIV, 574.

PARISEN, Mr. ——. Teacher of drawing and wax modelling, Charleston (S.C.), 1837. ¶ Rutledge, *Artists in the Life of Charleston.*

PARISEN or PARRISEN, J. N.A. Portrait painter, founding member of the National Academy. He exhibited at the American Academy in 1821, 1823, 1827 and 1828, and at the National Academy in 1827. Both J. and WILLIAM D. PARISEN lived on William Street in 1827 and it may be that J. was William's brother Julian, mentioned in the will of PHILIP PARISEN in 1818. Neither J. nor Julian Parisen was mentioned in the NYC directories. J. Parisen painted the portrait of Samuel Latham Mitchill mentioned by DUNLAP. ¶ Cummings, *Historic Annals of the NAD,* 28; Cowdrey, AA & AAU; Cowdrey, NAD; lithographed copy of will of Philip Parisen, Liber 57, pp. 414–15, at NYHS; NYCD 1827; Dunlap, *History,* I, 160.

PARISEN, OTTO (1723–1811). Miniaturist, goldsmith, ornamental hairworker. A native of Berlin (Germany), Parisen came to NYC in the early 1760's and worked there, DUNLAP says, for about forty years. During his last years he lived at New Rochelle, where he died January 17, 1811, at the age of 88. He was the father of PHILIP and grandfather of J. and WILLIAM D. PARISEN. ¶ Kelby, *Notes on American Artists,* 49; Gottesman, *Arts and Crafts in New York,* I and II; Dunlap, *History,* I, 160.

PARISEN, PHILIP (?–1822). Miniature painter, silhouettist, hairworker, and silversmith. A son of OTTO PARISEN, Philip was active in NYC from 1790 to 1811 and visited Charleston (S.C.) as a drawing teacher in 1795. His will, dated 1818, was proved in 1822, presumably the year of his death. Among his children were a William and Julian who were probably the artists J. and WILLIAM D. PARISEN. ¶ N. Y. *Daily Gazette,* April 2, 1790 (citation courtesy Helen McKearin); Gottesman, *Arts and Crafts in New York,* II; NYCD 1797–1811; Rutledge, *Artists in the Life of Charleston;* Prime, II, 18–19; Dunlap, *History,* I, 160.

PARISEN, WILLIAM D. (1800–1832). Portrait and miniature painter and drawing teacher. A son of PHILIP PARISEN, William was born in February 1800, probably in NYC, and began exhibiting at the American Academy as early as 1816. In 1818–19 he was in Charleston (S.C.), in the latter year running a drawing academy with a Mr. HINCKLEY. The rest of his career was spent in NYC, where he mixed painting with money-brokerage and, DUNLAP says, failed in both, though he continued to exhibit occasionally at the American and National Academies. He died April 9, 1832, at the age of 32 years and 2 months, and was buried at New Rochelle. J. PARISEN was probably William's younger brother Julian; they were both living in William Street in 1827. ¶ N. Y. *Evening Post,* April 9, 1832, cited in Barber, "Deaths Taken from the N. Y. Evening Post"; Cowdrey, AA & AAU; Cowdrey, NAD; NYCD 1819–31; Rutledge, *Artists in the Life of Charleston;* Dunlap, *History,* I, 160.

PARISH, see PARRISH.

PARISIEN, see PARISEN.

PARJEAUX, see PAJOT.

PARKISEN, see PARISEN.

PARK, A. Portrait painter who advertised in Cincinnati in April 1820. *Cf.* ASA PARK. ¶ Courtesy Wilbur D. Peat, who cites *Liberty Hall and Cincinnati Gazette,* April 20, 1820.

PARK, ASA (?–1827). Portrait and still life painter who died at Lexington (Ky.) in 1827. He was a Virginian, had settled in Lexington before 1800, and was a close friend of the artist WILLIAM WEST of Lexington. *Cf.* A. PARK. ¶ Price, *Old Masters of the Bluegrass,* 4–5.

PARK, L. W. Engraver, Boston, 1847. ¶ Boston CD and BD 1847.

PARK, LINTON (1826–?). Primitive genre painter. A lumberman by trade, Park painted a number of logging and farm scenes in Clearfield and Indiana Counties (Pa.), probably in the late 1840's and 1850's. His painting of a flax-scutching party on a western Pennsylvania farm about 1860 is one of the best known American primitives. ¶ "A Pennsylvania Primitive Painter," *Antiques* (Feb. 1939), 84–86, with 6 repros.; Lipman and Winchester, 178. There is on deposit at Pennsylvania State University a thesis by Kathryn M. Royer, "Narrative Painting in Nineteenth Century America," in which Park is discussed.

PARK, RICHARD HENRY (1832–after 1890). Sculptor. A native of NYC, he was working in Florence (Italy) in 1890 and is represented in the Metropolitan Museum of Art, NYC. ¶ Gardner, *Yankee Stonecutters,* [74]; Thieme-Becker; Smith.

PARK, S. Engraver, Rockport (Ind.), 1860. ¶ Indiana BD 1860.

PARK, WILLAM. Stone, seal, and cameo engraver, NYC, 1858. ¶ NYBD 1858.

PARKE, MARY. Primitive watercolors of religious subjects, about 1825. ¶ Lipman and Winchester, 178.

PARKER, Mr. ——. Artist, born in Maine about 1822, living in Boston in 1850. ¶ 7 Census (1850), Mass., XXIV, 349.

PARKER, A. Owner and exhibitor, though not necessarily the painter, of a temperance panorama shown at Davenport (Iowa) in December 1858. Parker's two brothers were residents of Davenport. ¶ Schick, *The Early Theatres of Eastern Iowa,* 279 (citation courtesy J. E. Arrington).

PARKER, C. R. Portrait and historical painter who paid professional visits to New Orleans in 1826, 1832, 1838, and 1845–46. In 1826 his portraits of Washington, Jefferson, Lafayette, and Franklin were unveiled in the state legislative hall of Louisiana. In 1832 he had "lately returned from Europe." ¶ Delgado-WPA cites *Argus,* Dec. 2, 1826, *Advertiser,* April 11, 1832, *True American,* July 2, 1838, *Picayune,* Dec. 4, 1845, and Feb. 3, 1846, and New Orleans CD 1846.

PARKER, CHARLES H. (*c.* 1795–1819). Script, map, and ornamental engraver, born in Salem (Mass.). He studied under GIDEON FAIRMAN and worked in Philadelphia between 1812 and 1819. ¶ Stauffer.

PARKER, EDGAR (1840–?). Portrait painter. A native of Framingham (Mass.), he spent most of his career in Boston. Among his prominent sitters were Nathaniel Hawthorne, J. G. Whittier, and Theodore Sedgwick. He died after 1875. ¶ Fairman, *Art and Artists of the Capitol,* 280; Clement and Hutton; Thieme-Becker; represented at Faneuil Hall and U. S. Capitol.

PARKER, GEORGE (?–1868). Engraver. An Englishman, working in London in 1832, Parker came to the United States about 1834 to work on LONGACRE and HERRING's *National Portrait Gallery.* During the late forties and fifties he worked in Boston. ¶ Stauffer; Boston CD 1847–55.

PARKER, JOHN, JR. Made a survey and map of Portsmouth (N.H.) in 1778 and also painted miniatures. ¶ Lyman, "William Johnston," 70.

PARKER, JOHN ADAMS, JR. (1827 or 1829–about 1905). A.N.A. Landscape painter. Born November 29, 1829 (CAB) or November 27, 1827 (*Who's Who*) in NYC, Parker graduated from New York University and from 1850 to 1857 worked as a merchant. Turning to the study of painting, he exhibited for the first time at the NAD in 1858 and was elected an Associate Member in 1864. He specialized in views of the Adirondack, Catskill, and White Mountains. ¶ CAB; *Who's Who in America,* 1903–05; *Artists Year Book,* 148; Cowdrey, NAD.

PARKER, JOSEPH. Artist, Baltimore, 1856–57. ¶ Lafferty.

PARKER, LIFE, JR. (*c.* 1822–?). Sculptor, marble and stone engraver working in Lowell (Mass.) between 1837 and 1847. He was married to Hannah Lowe on February 8, 1845; their twin sons, Pliny and Preston, were born in Salem on March 17, 1846. He is also said to have painted portraits. ¶ *Vital Records of Lowell;* Belknap, *Artists and Craftsmen of Essex County,* 19; Lowell CD 1847; Lipman and Winchester, 178.

PARKER, M. S. Portrait painter at Philadelphia, 1835–46. He exhibited at the Apollo Association in NYC in 1838. Two watercolor portraits of Judge Richard Peters and his son Richard, presented to the Historical Society of Pennsylvania in 1939, were done in 1843 by an M. Parker, possibly the same as M. S. Parker. Likewise an 1843 watercolor portrait reproduced in *Antiques* (Jan. 1939) as the work of M. J. [S.?] Parker. *Cf.* W. S. PARKER. ¶ Rutledge, PA; Phila. CD 1839–46; information courtesy the late William Sawitzky; *Antiques* (Jan. 1939), repro.

PARKER, MATTHEW. Engraver, Chicago, 1858. ¶ Chicago CD 1858.

PARKER, NATHANIEL (1802–?). Decorative wall painter, born at North Weare (N.H.), said to have decorated the Buchman house in Antrim (N.H.). ¶ Little, *American Decorative Wall Painting,* 101, 133.

PARKER, THOMAS H. (1801–?). Miniaturist, born in 1801 at Sag Harbor, Long Island (N.Y.). After studying in NYC with MATTHEW ROGERS, he settled in Hartford (Conn.) and lived there for many years. He and one of his pupils, C. W. ELDRIDGE, are said to have worked in partnership in the manner of WALDO & JEWETT. Parker died after 1851. ¶ French, *Art and Artists in Connecticut,* 66; Bolton, *Miniature Painters;* Fielding.

PARKER, W. S. Portrait painter. His oil portrait of W. C. Anderson, painted in 1830 probably at Pittsburgh (Pa.), is now owned by the Pennsylvania Academy of the Fine Arts. *Cf.* M. S. PARKER. ¶ WPA (Pa.), Hist. Records Survey, "Catalogue of the Early American Portraits in the Penna. Acad."

PARKES, W. Painter of a view of Washington's birthplace, exhibited in Cincinnati in 1857. ¶ Cincinnati *Daily Gazette,* May 29, 1857 (citation courtesy J. E. Arrington).

PARKHURST, DANIEL S. Engraver, of Providence (R.I.), 1852–59; of PABODIE & PARKHURST in 1857–58. ¶ Providence CD 1852–59.

PARKINS, SIR J. Exhibited a view of Philadelphia at the Pennsylvania Academy in 1828. ¶ Rutledge, PA.

PARKINSON, RICHARD. Portrait painter at Richmond (Va.) in 1832. ¶ *Antiques* (Nov. 1929), 428, repro.

PARKS, ALONZO. Portrait painter at Corning (N.Y.), 1817 and after. ¶ Sherman, "Unrecorded Early American Portrait Painters" (1933), 31.

PARKS, ASA. Portrait painter, Boston, 1858–59. ¶ Boston BD 1858–59.

PARKS, FREDERICK. Engraver, Belleville (N.J.), 1850. *Cf.* RICHARD PARKS. ¶ N. J. BD 1850.

PARKS, J. Oil portraitist, Mohawk Valley (N.Y.), about 1830. ¶ Lipman and Winchester, 178.

PARKS, RICHARD. Steel plate engraver, Belleville (N.J.), 1859–60. *Cf.* FREDERICK PARKS. ¶ Essex, Hudson and Union Counties BD 1859; N. J. BD 1860.

PARKS, SAMUEL AUGUSTUS (1822–1877). Artist, son of Elisha Parks, merchant of Winchendon and Boston (Mass.). Samuel apparently spent his life in Boston. He died there on June 20, 1877. ¶ Parks, *Parks Records,* III, 129; 7 Census (1850), Mass., XXVI, 575; 8 Census (1860), Mass., XXVII, 3; Boston CD 1851, 1860.

PARKYNS, GEORGE ISHAM (*c.* 1749/50–*c.* 1820). Landscape and portrait painter, engraver. A native of Nottingham (England), Parkyns exhibited engravings and landscapes at London exhibitions from 1772 to 1813, and published *Monastic Remains and Ancient Castles in Great Britain.* About 1794 he came to the United States and, in association with James Harrison of NYC, published proposals to issue a series of 24 aquatints showing the principal cities and scenery of the United States. In January 1796 several of his drawings for this series, including the earliest view of the Federal City, were on view at Harrison's in NYC and at Parkyns' residence in Brooklyn. ¶ Thieme-Becker; Stauffer; Gottesman, *Arts and Crafts in New York,* II, nos. 119–20; Dunlap, *History,* II, 469; Stokes, *Historical Prints,* pl. 30a; *Antiques* (Feb. 1945), 103 (repro.).

PARMELEE, CHARLES N. Wood engraver, born in Connecticut about 1805, working in Philadelphia between 1837 and 1854. ¶ 7 Census (1850), Pa., L, 825; Phila. CD 1837–54; Hamilton, *Early American Book Illustrators and Wood Engravers,* 280, 398.

PARMELEE, ELMER EUGENE (1839–1861). Portrait and landscape painter, born June 12, 1839, at Middletown (Vt.), the son of Daniel S. and Syrena S. Parmelee. His father was a Baptist preacher. Elmer Parmelee studied painting in NYC and began exhibiting at the National Academy in 1857. In 1860 he was an instructor in drawing and painting in the Grammar School of New York University, along with BENJAMIN H. COE. He died October 31, 1861, in Brandon (Vt.), at the age of 22. Examples of his work are preserved in the family. ¶ Information courtesy Mr. Cullen W. Parmelee, Urbana (Ill.), nephew of the artist; Cowdrey, NAD; 8 Census (1860), N.Y., LX, 149.

PARRISEN or PARRISIEN, see PARISEN.

PARRISH, ANNE. Painted a portrait of Edward Parrish (1822–1872), first President of Swarthmore College. The artist may have been his sister, Ann Cox Parrish (1824–1844). The portrait is now owned by Swarthmore College. ¶ Information courtesy FARL, citing Mrs. George Huntington Barker, Altadena (Cal.), a descendant of Edward Parrish.

PARRISH, CHARLES LOUIS (?–1902). Townscape artist. A native of New York, Parrish went to California in 1850 to seek gold, later settled in Jackson and manufactured rock crushers and quartz mills and carried on other businesses. About 1865 he moved to Oakland. His work as an artist apparently was limited to views of California towns, such as Jackson, Volcano, and Mokelumne Hill, done about 1854. At least one was lithographed by BRITTON & REY. Parrish died in 1902 while on a visit to the East Coast. ¶ Van Nostrand and Coulter, *California Pictorial,* 138–39; *Antiques* (Jan. 1954), 41–42 (repros.).

PARSELL, ABRAHAM. Miniaturist born in New Jersey about 1792, working in NYC from 1820 to 1856. Presumably the father of JOHN H. PARSELL. ¶ 7 Census (1850), N.Y., XLVI, 644; NYCD 1820–56.

PARSELL, JOHN H. Miniaturist working in NYC, at the same address as ABRAHAM PARSELL, 1844–48. ¶ NYBD 1844, 1846; CD 1847–48.

PARSONS, ——. Wood engraver. An example of his work appeared in *The Annals of San Francisco* (N.Y., 1855). Possibly DANIEL PARSONS. ¶ Hamilton, *Early American Book Illustrators and Wood Engravers,* 238.

PARSONS, CHARLES (1821–1910). A.N.A. Lithographer, marine and landscape painter in watercolors. Born May 8, 1821, at Rowland's Castle, Hampshire (England), he was brought to America at the age of nine and grew up in NYC. At twelve he was apprenticed to GEORGE ENDICOTT, but two years later he was taken on as a regular employee of ENDICOTT & COMPANY, with whom he was associated until about 1861. During these years he executed many lithographs for CURRIER & IVES. In 1861 Parsons became the head of the art department of Harper & Brothers and he held that position until his retirement in 1889. An accomplished painter as well as lithographer, Parsons was elected an Associate of the National Academy in 1862 and he was also an active member of the American Watercolor Society. He died at his home in Brooklyn on November 9, 1910, in his ninetieth year. ¶ Peters, *Currier & Ives,* 130–32; Peters, *America on Stone;* CAB; Clement and Hutton; Alden, "Charles Parsons"; Cowdrey, NAD; Cowdrey, AA & AAU.

PARSONS, DANIEL. Engraver, NYC, 1851. This is probably the Mr. Parsons, 21, listed as an English-born engraver in NYC in the 1850 census of NYC. *Cf.* —— PARSONS, engraver for *The Annals of San Francisco* (N.Y., 1855). ¶ NYCD 1851; 7 Census (1850), N.Y., XLI, 422.

PARSONS, DAVID. Artist, NYC, 1854. ¶ NYCD 1854.

PARSONS, JAMES HERBERT (1831–1905). Artist, medallist, and engraver for Tiffany & Company of NYC. He died at West New Brighton, Staten Island (N.Y.) on Christmas Day, 1905. ¶ *Art Annual,* VI, obit.

PARTRIDGE, JOSEPH. Miniaturist. He was at Halifax (N.S.) from 1819 to 1822, but may also have worked in Providence (R.I.) since he did a miniature of the Rev. Stephen Gano of that city. ¶ Bolton, *Miniature Painters;* Stauffer, nos. 92 and 2443.

PARTRIDGE, NEHEMIAH. Limner, NYC, 1717–18. He advertised in Boston in 1713 as a japanner and paint seller and in 1715 as proprietor of "The Italian Matchean, or moving Picture," which may have been a mechanical toy rather than a forerunner of the panorama. Partridge was admitted a freeman of NYC on April 22, 1718. ¶ Dow, *Arts and Crafts in New England,* 302; NYHS *Collections,* XLII, 122; Kelby, *Notes on American Artists,* 1; Flexner, *First Flowers,* 66; Barker, *American Painting,* 73.

PATANIA, G. F. B. Portrait painter, NYC, 1859–60; exhibited, National Academy. ¶ Cowdrey, NAD; NYBD 1860.

PATCH, SAMUEL, JR. Artist, 30, a native of Massachusetts, at Weathersfield (Vt.) August 22, 1850. He was staying at a hotel. ¶ 7 Census (1850), Vt., XII, 730.

PATE, WILLIAM. Engraver, of NEAL & PATE, NYC, 1844. In 1854 he printed the GOLLMAN-DONEY engraving, "Distinguished Americans at a Meeting of The New-York Historical Society." ¶ NYBD 1844; Vail, *Knickerbocker Birthday,* 107.

PATON, A. R. Wax portraitist listed in E. S. Bolton's *American Wax Portraits.* This was probably Amelia R. Paton of Dunfermline (Scotland) who married the Scottish historical painter and photographer David Octavius Hill. She was a sculptor and, though she did at least one bust of an American, is not known to have visited the United States. ¶ E. S. Bolton, *American Wax Portraits,* 45; Clement and Hutton.

PATTEN, ZEBULON S. Engraver and designer, Bangor (Maine), 1855–60. ¶ *Maine Register,* 1855–56; New England BD 1860.

PATTERSON, EDWARD P. Engraver, Lowell (Mass.), 1834. ¶ Belknap, *Artists and Craftsmen of Essex County,* 4.

PATTERSON, H. Engraver of color plates of fish for the report of Matthew C. Perry's expedition to Japan. ¶ Perry, *Expedition to Japan.*

PATTERSON, JAMES S. (1832–1916). Wood engraver working in NYC from about 1858. He died April 15, 1916, at Hackensack (N.J.). ¶ *Art Annual,* XIII, obit.; NYBD 1858; Smith.

PATTERSON, JOSEPH. Drawing master, New Orleans, 1822. ¶ New Orleans CD 1822.

PATTERSON, WILLIAM. Caricaturist, born in Madison Parish (La.) about 1820, living in New Orleans in 1849–50. ¶ 7 Census (1850), La., VI, 61; Delgado-WPA cites *Delta,* July 22, 1849.

PATTI, P. Italian sculptor, 50, in NYC in June 1860. ¶ 8 Census (1860), N.Y., LVI, 723.

PATTISON, ROBERT J. (1838–1903). Landscape painter. He was born in NYC and began exhibiting there as early as 1858. He died September 13, 1903, in Brooklyn. ¶ *Art Annual,* IV; Cowdrey, NAD.

PATTON, WILLIAM. Lithographer, born in Pennsylvania about 1824, living in Philadelphia in 1850–52. ¶ 7 Census (1850), Pa., XLIX, 5; Phila. CD 1850–52.

PAUL, EUGÈNE. Mezzotint engraver, born in France about 1830. In 1855 he engraved a portrait of Henry Clay. In 1860 he was living in New Orleans with his wife Marguerite, a native Louisianian; in the same house was J. H. FROBUS. ¶ 8 Census (1860), La., VIII, 5; Stauffer.

PAUL-FREDÉRIC-WILLIAM, duke of Württemberg (1797–1860). Topographical artist. Born at Carlsruhe and brought up at Stuttgart, he gave up a military career to devote himself to travel and the study of natural history. He visited the Western Hemisphere four times: 1822–24, Mississippi and Missouri Valleys and Cuba; 1829–32, Mexico; 1849–56, North, Central, and South America, including Oregon and Florida; 1857, Mississippi Valley. His only published work was an account of his first voyage (Stuttgart, 1835). Stokes lists a lithograph of Balize at the mouth of the Mississippi after a drawing by the Herzog Paul von Württemberg. ¶ Larousse, *Grand Dictionnaire Universel du XIXème Siecle;* Stokes, *Historical Prints.*

PAUL, J. W. S. Theorem painting in watercolors, about 1840. ¶ Lipman and Winchester, 178.

PAUL, JEREMIAH, JR. (?–1820). Portrait, figure, and animal painter. Probably the son of a Quaker school teacher of Philadelphia, Paul first appears as one of the founders of the Columbianum at Philadelphia in 1795. He was a fellow-pupil with REMBRANDT PEALE. In 1796 Paul joined with several other Philadelphia artists under the name of PRATT, RUTTER & Co. Pratt dropped out after a few months and the firm became PAUL, RUTTER & CLARKE. Paul was still in Philadelphia in 1800, but during the winter of 1803 he was painting miniatures and tracing profiles at Charleston (S.C.). From 1806 to 1808 he was in Baltimore and in 1811 he exhibited "Venus and Cupid" in Philadelphia. In 1814 he was at Pittsburgh, painting portraits and signs. In his last years Paul is said to have painted theatrical scenery in the West. He died near St. Louis (Mo.) on July 13, 1820. ¶ Sellers, *Charles Willson Peale,* II; Columbianum Cat.; Dunlap, *History;* Prime, II, 19, 31; Dickson, "A Note on Jeremiah Paul"; Rutledge, *Artists in the Life of Charleston;* Baltimore CD 1806–08; Rutledge, PA; *Connoisseur* (Jan. 1954), 184–85, repro.; Flexner, *The Light of Distant Skies,* biblio., 263.

PAUL, JOHN. Artist, 44, a native Pennsylvanian, living at Frankford, near Philadelphia, in 1850. ¶ 7 Census (1850), Pa., LVI, 355.

PAUL, RUTTER & CLARKE. Portrait, sign, and ornamental painters, Philadelphia, 1796. The partners were JEREMIAH PAUL, GEORGE RUTTER, and WILLIAM CLARKE.

Earlier in the same year the firm had been organized as PRATT, RUTTER & Co., but MATTHEW PRATT dropped out after only a few months. ¶ Prime, II, 19; Dickson, "A Note on Jeremiah Paul."

PAULDING, RICHARD A. Portrait and landscape painter, NYC, 1841–54. He exhibited at the National Academy. ¶ Cowdrey, NAD; NYCD 1842, 1852; NYBD 1854.

PAULIN, THOMAS. Engraver, Newark (N.J.), 1859. ¶ Essex, Hudson, and Union Counties BD 1859.

PAULING, ——. Miniaturist at Albany (N.Y.) in 1820. ¶ Sherman, "Some Recently Discovered Early American Portrait Miniaturists," 294 (repro.).

PAWLEY, JAMES, SR. Landscape and marine painter, teacher of painting at Baltimore from 1842 to 1857. He exhibited a number of times at the Maryland Historical Society. In 1858 Mrs. James and James Pawley, Jr., were listed, the elder James Pawley presumably having died in 1857 or 1858. ¶ Baltimore CD 1842–56; Rutledge, MHS.

PAXTON, ELIZA. Still life painter in water colors, Philadelphia, 1814–16. ¶ Lipman and Winchester, 178.

PAYNE, ALFRED (*c.* 1815–1893). Portrait painter who studied under CHRISTOPHER P. CRANCH and worked in Ohio, Wisconsin, and elsewhere for over forty years. ¶ Barker, *American Painting,* 403.

PAYNE, CHARLES. Engraver of PAYNE & TAYLOR, Pawtucket (R.I.), 1857. ¶ Pawtucket and Woonsocket BD 1857.

PAYNE, ELOISA R. One of the first American woman engravers, active in the early years of the 19th century. ¶ Stephens, *The Mavericks,* 58.

PAYNE, HENRY. Crayon artist, NYC, 1844–48. He exhibited at the American Institute in 1844. ¶ Am. Inst. Cat., 1844; NYCD 1847–48.

PAYNE, JAMES. Engraver, Lowell (Mass.), 1834–37. ¶ Belknap, *Artists and Craftsmen of Essex County,* 4.

PAYNE, JOHN M. English artist, 31, at NYC in June 1860. ¶ 8 Census (1860), N.Y., XLVIII, 72.

PAYNE & TAYLOR. Engravers, Pawtucket (R.I.), 1857; CHARLES PAYNE and JUDE TAYLOR. ¶ Pawtucket and Woonsocket BD 1857.

PEABODY, FRANKLIN WINCHESTER (1826–?). Engraver and cameo cutter. Born August 21, 1826, at Whitehall (N.Y.), he exhibited cameos at the Pennsylvania Academy in 1851 and the same year was married in Blackwoodtown (N.J.). His children were born at Camden (N.J.), 1852; Kingston (Ont.), 1854 and 1856; Springmills (N.J.), 1858; Woodbury (N.J.), 1861; Kingston (Ont.), 1863; Wilton (Ont.), 1868; and Toledo (Ohio), 1870. He served with the New Jersey Volunteers in the Civil War and was wounded at the siege of Richmond. ¶ Peabody, *Peabody (Paybody, Pabody, Pabodie) Genealogy,* 348–49; Rutledge, PA.

PEABODY, Mrs. JAMES, see EMMA CLARA PEALE.

PEABODY, M. M. Stipple engraver at Utica (N.Y.) in 1835. ¶ Stauffer.

PEABODY, Mrs. MARY JANE, see MARY JANE DERBY.

PEABODY, SOPHIA AMELIA (1811–1871). Painter. Sophia, youngest of the famous Peabody sisters of Salem (Mass.), was born September 21, 1811. An invalid during early life, she took up painting as a diversion and later as a means of helping support her family. In 1842 she married Nathaniel Hawthorne. She died in England February 26, 1871. ¶ Tharp, *The Peabody Sisters of Salem;* Hawthorne, *Nathaniel Hawthorne and His Wife;* Swan, BA.

PEACE, ——. Engraver of one illustration in *A Universal History of the United States of America* (Buffalo, 1833). *Cf.* PEASE. ¶ Hamilton, *Early American Book Illustrators and Wood Engravers,* 114.

PEACHEY, Mrs. ——. Teacher of the art of "imitating Flowers &c in Wax," at Charleston (S.C.) in 1837. ¶ Rutledge, *Artists in the Life of Charleston.*

PEACOCK, ——. Portrait painter working in New England in the 18th century. ¶ Fielding.

PEACOCK, JOHN. An English convict servant who twice ran away from Elk-Ridge, Anne Arundel County (Md.) in 1775. Though a shoemaker by trade, he was described as "very officious in showing his skill in drawing pictures and making print letters, pretends to understand the painting business. . . ." ¶ *Maryland Gazette,* March 30 and Sept. 21, 1775 (cited in "Sill Abstracts").

PEALE, ANNA CLAYPOOLE (1791–1878). Miniaturist and still life painter, daughter of JAMES PEALE and granddaughter of JAMES CLAYPOOLE. She was born in Philadelphia March 6, 1791 and was twice married, in 1829 to the Rev. Dr. William Staughton, and in 1841 to General William Duncan. Her home was in Philadelphia and she was a frequent exhibitor at the Pennsylvania Academy between 1811 and 1842. She died in Philadelphia December 25, 1878. ¶ DAB; Sellers, *Charles Willson Peale,* II, 416; Rutledge, PA; Swan, BA; Rutledge, MHS; Born, "Female Peales"; Pleasants, *250 Years of Painting in Md.,* 25.

PEALE, CHARLES WILLSON (1741–1827). Portrait and miniature painter, engraver, museum proprietor, scientist, and inventor. Born April 15, 1741, in Queen Anne's County (Md.), he served his apprenticeship to a saddler and wood carver in Annapolis and in 1762 went into the saddling trade on his own. Shortly after, he received his first lessons in painting from JOHN HESSELIUS. In 1767 he went to London to study under BENJAMIN WEST. He returned to Annapolis in 1769 and made his home there until 1775, although painting commissions carried him as far afield as Baltimore, Philadelphia, Williamsburg, and in 1772 Mount Vernon, where he painted his first life portrait of Washington. After three years' service with the Continental Army, in 1778 Peale settled permanently in Philadelphia. In 1782 he opened a painting gallery and in 1786 he established the famous Peale Museum in Independence Hall. Although he continued to paint, Peale's time in later years was devoted principally to his museum and his interest in natural history and science. He was married three times, in 1762 to Rachel Brewer, in 1791 to Elizabeth DePeyster, and in 1805 to Hannah Moore, and was the father of 17 children, including RAPHAELLE, REMBRANDT, RUBENS, FRANKLIN, and TITIAN RAMSAY PEALE, all of whom became well-known artists. He died in Philadelphia February 22, 1827. ¶ The definitive study is Charles Coleman Sellers, *Charles Willson Peale,* in 2 volumes (Phila., American Philosophical Society, 1947), which is supplemented by Mr. Sellers' 1952 checklist, *Portraits and Miniatures by Charles Willson Peale,* published as Volume 42, Part 1, of the *Transactions* of the American Philosophical Society. Recent exhibitions of the work of the Peale family have been held at the Century Association (1953) and the Cincinnati Museum of Art (1954). See also: Flexner, *America's Old Masters* and *The Light of Distant Skies.*

PEALE, EMMA CLARA (1814–?). Painter, daughter of REMBRANDT PEALE. She was born in November 1814, married James A. Peabody in 1838 and Caleb D. Barton in 1845. She exhibited at the American Academy in 1835 and the Artists' Fund Society in 1840. ¶ Sellers, *Charles Willson Peale,* II, 419; Cowdrey, AA & AAU; Rutledge, PA.

PEALE, FRANKLIN (1795–1870). Medallist, son of CHARLES WILLSON PEALE. He was born October 15, 1795, in Philadelphia, and was named Benjamin Franklin Peale, though he was later known as Franklin. Trained as a mechanic, he operated a cotton mill near Philadelphia after the War of 1812 and for a number of years assisted his father and brothers at the Peale Museum. In 1833 he resigned as Manager of the Museum to take a position in the U. S. Mint and from 1840 to 1854 he was Chief Coiner. It was during this period that he executed President Polk's Indian medal, reproduced in Loubat. In his later years Franklin Peale served as President of the Hazleton Coal and Railroad Company, the Musical Fund Society, and the Pennsylvania Institution for Instruction of the Blind. He died in Philadelphia on May 5, 1870. ¶ Sellers, *Charles Willson Peale,* II, 382–83, 415; Loubat, *Medallic History of the U.S.,* plate 59.

PEALE, Miss J. M., see SARAH MIRIAM PEALE.

PEALE, JAMES (1749–1831). Miniature, portrait, and still life painter. A younger brother of CHARLES WILLSON PEALE, James was a cabinetmaker before he learned to paint under instruction from his brother in the early 1770's. After serving with the Continental Army during the Revolution, he settled in Philadelphia and specialized in miniature painting until his eyes began to fail about 1818. He was married in 1782 to Mary, daughter of the painter JAMES CLAYPOOLE; of their seven children at least five are known to have painted: MARIA, JAMES, ANNA CLAYPOOLE, MARGARETTA ANGELICA, and SARAH MIRIAM. James Peale died in Philadelphia May 24, 1831. ¶ Sellers, *Charles Willson Peale;* DAB; Rutledge, PA; Rutledge, MHS; Swan, BA; Brockway, "The Miniatures of James Peale," contains a checklist and 14 repros.; Sherman, "Two Recently Discovered Portraits in Oils by James Peale," with 4 repros. and checklist of oil portraits; Baur, "The Peales and the Development of American Still

Life"; exhibition catalogues of the Peale exhibitions at the Penna. Academy (1923), Century Association (1953), and Cincinnati Museum of Art (1954); Flexner, *The Light of Distant Skies.*

PEALE, JAMES, JR. (1789–1876). Landscape, marine, and still life painter, son of JAMES PEALE. Born in Philadelphia March 6, 1789, the younger James Peale became a bank employee, but exhibited paintings at the Pennsylvania Academy between 1825 and 1847. In 1822 he married SOPHONISBA, daughter of RAPHAELLE PEALE. He died in Philadelphia October 27, 1876. ¶ CAB; Sellers, *Charles Willson Peale,* 338, 344, 416; Rutledge, PA.

PEALE, MARGARETTA ANGELICA (1795–1882). Still life and portrait painter, daughter of JAMES PEALE. She was born in Philadelphia October 1, 1795, and died there January 17, 1882. Her work was shown at the Pennsylvania Academy and the Artists' Fund Society. ¶ Sellers, *Charles Willson Peale,* II, 416; Rutledge, PA; Phila. BD 1838; Born, "Female Peales: Their Art and Its Tradition"; McCausland, "American Still-life Paintings," repro.

PEALE, MARIA (1787–1866). Still life painter, daughter of JAMES PEALE. Exhibited at the Pennsylvania Academy in 1811. She died unmarried, March 27, 1866, at Philadelphia. ¶ Sellers, *Charles Willson Peale,* II, 416; Rutledge, PA.

PEALE, MARY JANE (1827–1902). Portrait and still life painter, daughter of RUBENS PEALE. Born February 16, 1827, in NYC, she spent most of her life in Philadelphia and was a professional portrait painter. She never married. She died at Pottsville (Pa.) in November 1902. ¶ Sellers, *Charles Willson Peale,* II, 420; Born, "Female Peales: Their Art and Its Tradition"; represented at Univ. of Penna.

PEALE, RAPHAELLE (1774–1825). Still life, portrait, and miniature painter. Born in Annapolis (Md.) February 17, 1774, RAPHAELLE was the eldest son of CHARLES WILLSON PEALE. During the 1790's he helped with the Peale Museum in Philadelphia and collaborated with his brother REMBRANDT on many portraits, notably the famous "Staircase Group" shown at the Columbianum exhibition in 1795. From 1797 to 1800 Raphaelle and Rembrandt conducted a museum in Baltimore. Returning to Philadelphia in 1800 Raphaelle became his father's chief assistant. Three years later he went into the profile-cutting business which carried him over much of the South and New England during the next two years. During his remaining years Raphaelle began to drink heavily, gradually abandoned portrait painting for still life, especially "deceptions" in which he displayed much skill and wit. He died in Philadelphia March 5, 1825, at the age of 51. ¶ Sellers, *Charles Willson Peale;* Bury, "Raphaelle Peale (1774–1825) Miniature Painter," with 8 repros. and checklist; Baur, "The Peales and the Development of American Still Life"; Rutledge, PA; Cowdrey, AA & AAU; Rutledge, *Artists in the Life of Charleston; Richmond Portraits;* DAB; McCausland, "American Still-life Paintings," repro.; Flexner, *The Light of Distant Skies.*

PEALE, REMBRANDT (1778–1860). N.A. Portrait, miniature and historical painter, son of CHARLES WILLSON PEALE. Born February 22, 1778, on a farm in Bucks County (Pa.), Rembrandt painted his first portrait in 1791. In 1795 he did the first of his Washington portraits. With his elder brother RAPHAELLE he visited Charleston (S.C.) during the winter of 1795–96; in 1797 they opened a museum in Baltimore. In 1802–03 Rembrandt was in England exhibiting the skeleton of a mastadon and studying at the Royal Academy. Returning to America late in 1803 he spent some months in Charleston and Baltimore before settling down in Philadelphia. Rembrandt was again in Europe in 1808 and 1809–10, chiefly at Paris, where he was inspired to take up historical painting. In 1814 he again opened a museum at Baltimore. His most ambitious historical work, *The Court of Death,* was painted in 1820. Rembrandt moved to NYC in 1822 and was a founder of the National Academy in 1826. He revisited Europe in 1829–30, and again in 1831, after which he settled permanently in Philadelphia. The latter part of his life was devoted principally to fostering the Washington cult through lectures illustrated with his own paintings. He died in Philadelphia October 3, 1860, shortly after the publication of his memoirs in *The Crayon.* ¶ Sellers, *Charles Willson Peale;* DAB; Rutledge, PA; Rutledge, MHS; Cowdrey, AA & AAU; Cowdrey, NAD; Swan, BA; Rutledge, *Artists in the Life of Charleston;* 7 Census (1850), Pa., LI, 686; 8 Census (1860), Pa., LV, 793; Peale, "Reminiscences";

Flexner, *The Light of Distant Skies,* biblio., 264.

PEALE, Mrs. REMBRANDT (*c.* 1800–1869). Painter. Born Harriet Cany, she married REMBRANDT PEALE in November 1840. Before and after her marriage she exhibited portraits, still lifes, and copies at the Artists' Fund Society and the Pennsylvania Academy. Mrs. Peale survived her husband by almost nine years, dying on January 12, 1869. ¶ 7 Census (1850), Pa., LI, 686 [age 50]; 8 Census (1860), Pa., LV, 793 [age 61]; Rutledge, PA; Sellers, *Charles Willson Peale,* II, 419; Born, "Female Peales: Their Art and Its Tradition"; *American Collector* (Dec. 1941), 3, repro.

PEALE, ROSALBA CARRIERA (1799–1874). Copyist, daughter of REMBRANDT PEALE. She was born July 28, 1799; married John A. Underwood in 1860; and died November 15, 1874. An Italian sunset, copied by her, was shown at the Artists' Fund Society in 1840. She was an Artist (1827) and Honorary Member, Professional (1828) of the National Academy. ¶ Sellers, *Charles Willson Peale,* II, 419; Rutledge, PA; Clark, *History of the NAD,* 266.

PEALE, RUBENS (1784–1865). Still life and animal painter, son of CHARLES WILLSON PEALE. Born May 4, 1784, in Philadelphia, Rubens grew up with weak eyes which prevented his becoming a professional painter. Museum management was his chief activity. From 1810 to 1822 he was in charge of the Philadelphia Museum founded by his father, from 1822 to 1825 he had a museum in Baltimore, and from 1825 to 1837 he managed the Peale Museum in NYC. Ruined by the panic of 1837 he retired to his father-in-law's property near Schuylkill Haven (Pa.) and there spent his latter years as a country gentleman. He died July 17, 1865. ¶ Sellers, *Charles Willson Peale;* Karolik Cat., 446–48; Detroit Institute *Bulletin* (April 1944), 58.

PEALE, SARAH MIRIAM (1800–1885). Portrait and still life painter, daughter of JAMES PEALE. Born May 19, 1800, in Philadelphia, she worked mainly in Philadelphia until 1831 when she moved to Baltimore. She worked there until about 1845 and then apparently moved to St. Louis. Returning to Philadelphia about 1877 she spent her last years there and died there February 4, 1885. She never married. ¶ Sellers, *Charles Willson Peale;* Born, "Female Peales: Their Art and Its Tradition"; Rutledge, PA; Rutledge, MHS; Phila. CD 1828; Baltimore CD 1831–45; St. Louis BD 1854; *Richmond Portraits;* Pleasants, *250 Years of Painting in Maryland.*

PEALE, TITIAN RAMSAY (1799–1885). Naturalist and illustrator of works on natural history, son of CHARLES WILLSON PEALE. He was born in Philadelphia November 17, 1799, shortly after the death of his older brother of the same name. After serving as artist-naturalist with Long's exploring expedition to the Upper Mississippi (1818–21), he became assistant manager of the Peale Museum in Philadelphia. He succeeded his brother FRANKLIN PEALE as manager in 1833. From 1838 to 1841 he was with Charles Wilkes' expedition to the Pacific. In 1844 he went to Washington and from 1849 to 1873 he worked in the Patent Office. His last years were spent in Philadelphia where he died March 13, 1885, shortly before completion of his important work on American entomology. ¶ Sellers, *Charles Willson Peale;* DAB; Rutledge, *Artists in the Life of Charleston;* McDermott, "Early Sketches of T. R. Peale"; Rutledge, PA.

PEALE, WASHINGTON (1825–1868). Landscape painter, son of JAMES PEALE, JR. He was born February 9, 1825. In 1860 he was living in NYC and exhibited at the National Academy a scene on the Delaware River. ¶ Sellers, *Charles Willson Peale,* II, 416; Cowdrey, NAD; NYCD 1860.

PEARCE, HART L. Engraver at Chicago in 1858–59 and in NYC in 1859. ¶ Chicago BD 1858–59; NYBD 1859. *Cf.* HARTELL PIERCE.

PEARCE, WILLIAM, see WILLIAM PIERCE, JR.

PEARL, SARAH WOOD. Painted in 1819 a watercolor portrait of Park Wood, owned in 1941 by Henry Clement of Rutland (Vt.). ¶ WPA (Mass.), *Portraits Found in Vt.*

PEARSON, HARRY. English engraver, 36, at NYC in June 1860. His wife and children were all born in England or Scotland, the youngest about 1856. ¶ 8 Census (1860), N.Y., LVII, 883.

PEARSON, JOSEPH. Artist, NYC, 1848. ¶ NYBD 1848.

PEARSON, ROBERT (?–1891). Landscape painter. He exhibited at the National Academy in 1860 a view of New York Bay and was at that time a resident of the city. This is probably the Robert Pearson who died at Malden (Mass.) February 12, 1891, and was described as an "artist of much repute" and a well-known resident of Malden. WILLIAM PEARSON was probably a relative. ¶ Cowdrey, NAD; Boston *Transcript,* Feb. 12, 1891.

PEARSON, WILLIAM. Landscape painter who exhibited New Hampshire and up-state New York views at the National Academy between 1857–60. In 1860 his address in NYC was the same as that given for ROBERT PEARSON. ¶ Cowdrey, NAD; Mrs. Alice E. Ferris, Watertown (Mass.), owns an Ulster County (N.Y.) landscape signed "W. Pearson—1837," possibly by this artist (letter to NYHS, July 31, 1955).

PEASE, ALONZO. Portrait and landscape painter at Cleveland (Ohio) in 1859, and at Detroit (Mich.) in 1860–61. ¶ WPA (Ohio), *Annals of Cleveland;* information courtesy Donald MacKenzie, Wooster College.

PEASE & BAKER. Engravers whose work appeared in a book published in NYC in 1846. Pease was BENJAMIN F. PEASE; Baker has not been identified. ¶ Hamilton, *Early American Book Illustrators and Wood Engravers,* 204.

PEASE, BENJAMIN F. (1822–?). Wood engraver, born November 17, 1822, in Poughkeepsie (N.Y.). He was working in NYC between 1845 and 1847, in 1846 with PEASE & BAKER. Sometime during the fifties he went to Lima (Peru) where he married and was still living in 1869. ¶ Pease, *A Genealogical and Historical Record of the Descendants of John Pease,* 206; NYCD and NYBD 1846; Am. Inst. Cat., 1845–46; Hamilton, *Early American Book Illustrators and Wood Engravers,* 204, 207.

PEASE, C. W. Miniaturist, Providence (R.I.), 1844. ¶ Providence *Almanac,* 1844; Bolton, *Miniature Painters.*

PEASE, HENRY or HARRY E. Lithographer, engraver, and stationer, Albany (N.Y.), 1856–60. In 1856–57 he was employed by ABRAM J. HOFFMAN. He was a son of RICHARD H. PEASE. ¶ Albany CD 1856–60; Pease, *A Genealogical and Historical Record of the Descendants of John Pease . . . ,* 211.

PEASE, JOSEPH IVES (1809–1883). Line engraver, watercolor and crayon artist; born August 9, 1809, at Norfolk (Conn.). He learned engraving under OLIVER PELTON at New Haven, worked briefly with his younger brother RICHARD H. PEASE in Albany 1834 and Philadelphia 1835, and remained in Philadelphia until 1850. He was noted as an engraver for the annuals and for Godey's. In 1850 he moved to Stockbridge (Mass.) and later to a farm near Salisbury (Conn.) where he died July 2, 1883. ¶ DAB; Stauffer; French, *Art and Artists in Conn.;* Rutledge, PA; Albany CD 1834; *Antiques* (April 1951), 301 (repro.); Pease, *A Genealogical and Historical Record of the Descendants of John Pease . . . ,* 209–10 and plates.

PEASE, RICHARD H. (1813–1869). Wood engraver and lithographer, born February 19, 1813, at Norfolk (Conn.). A younger brother of JOSEPH I. PEASE, Richard received his training in engraving in Connecticut, worked in Albany in 1834, and then for a short time in Philadelphia, where he was married in 1835. He returned to Albany, however, and lived there until about 1862. He was living in 1869. HARRY E. PEASE, his son, was working with him in the late 1850's. ¶ Peters, *America on Stone;* Stauffer; Hamilton, *Early American Book Illustrators,* 100, 204, 207; Albany CD 1834–62; McClinton, "American Flower Lithographs," 363; Pease, *A Genealogical and Historical Record of the Descendants of John Pease . . . ,* 211.

PEASE & WARREN. Engravers and lithographers, Albany, 1853; RICHARD H. PEASE and GEORGE W. WARREN. ¶ Albany CD 1853.

PEASLEY, A. M. Map and portrait engraver, Newburyport (Mass.), 1804. ¶ Belknap, *Artists and Craftsmen of Essex County,* 4; Stauffer.

PEAT, see PITT.

PEBBLES, FRANK M. (1839–?). Portrait painter, born October 16, 1839, in Wyoming County (N.Y.). He made his first attempts at portrait painting at 17 at Monroe (Wis.) and studied briefly under THEODORE B. CATLIN, but until after the Civil War did mostly sign and ornamental work. In the late 1860's he studied for a year in NYC, worked in Chicago, Detroit, San Francisco, and other Western cities, and eventually settled permanently in Chicago, where he became known as "the gubernatorial and judicial portrait painter." He was still active in Oak Park (Ill.) as late as 1905. ¶ Andreas, *History of Chicago,* II, 561; *Artists Year Book,* 151; represented at Chicago Historical Society (information courtesy H. Maxson Holloway).

PECK, JOHN. Portrait, miniature, and landscape painter, working in NYC from 1839 to 1850. He exhibited at the Apollo Association, the American Institute, and the National Academy. ¶ Cowdrey, NAD; Cowdrey, AA & AAU; Am. Inst. Cat., 1842; NYCD 1840, 1846; NYBD 1849–50.

PECK, NATHANIEL. Primitive genre painter, a resident of Long Island (N.Y.), active about 1827–30. ¶ Lipman and Winchester, 178; *Notes Hispanic* (1945), 25 (repro.).

PECK, SHELDON. Painter of oil portraits on wood of Mr. and Mrs. Alanson Peck of Cornwall (Vt.), 1824, owned in 1941 by Miss Georgiana Peck of Burlington. ¶ WPA (Mass.), *Portraits Found in Vermont.*

PECKARD, WILLIAM. English engraver, 35, at Philadelphia in 1860. His wife and children were all born in England before 1848. ¶ 8 Census (1860), Pa., LIII, 290.

PECKHAM, LEWIS or LOUIS (1788–1822). Portrait painter, born September 19, 1788, at Newport (R.I.). After studying in Boston about 1810, he went to Vincennes (Ind.) and worked there until his death, September 8, 1822. ¶ Peckham, *Peckham Genealogy;* Burnet, *Art and Artists of Indiana,* 387; Peat, *Pioneer Painters of Indiana.*

PECKHAM, ROBERT (1785–1877). Portrait painter, born September 10, 1785, probably at Westminster (Mass.). After his marriage he worked for a time at Northampton and Bolton (Mass.) but about 1821 he settled permanently in Winchester. He was well known locally as a portrait painter and a leader in the Congregational Church, especially in the temperance and abolition movements. He died at Westminister, June 29, 1877. ¶ Peckham, *Peckham Genealogy,* 399–400; Heywood, *History of Westminster,* 821–22.

PECKHAM, WILLIAM F. Wood engraver, NYC, 1838–48. ¶ NYCD 1838–48; Hamilton, *Early American Book Illustrators and Wood Engravers,* 172.

PEEIFFER, see VERHAEGEN & PEEIFFER.

PEEK, G. Engraver, Rockport (Ind.), 1860. ¶ Indiana BD 1860.

PEELE, JOHN THOMAS (1822–1897). A.N.A. Genre and portrait painter, born April 11, 1822, at Peterborough (England) and brought to the United States as a child. After a visit to England between 1841 and 1844 Peele opened a studio in NYC. He was made an Associate of the National Academy in 1846. He returned to England about 1852 and made his home there until his death on May 19, 1897, at London, although he continued to exhibit in America and may have visited there a number of times. ¶ CAB; Cowdrey, NAD; Cowdrey, AA & AAU; Rutledge, PA.

PEETSCH, CHARLES. Painter on glass, NYC, 1855. He offered for sale dissolving views and other kinds of paintings on glass, "on hand, or made to order." ¶ N. Y. *Herald,* March 23, 1855 (citation courtesy J. E. Arrington). *Cf.* CARL P. PFETSCH.

PEINT, GIRAULT. Portrait painter, NYC, 1797. ¶ NYCD 1797 (cited by McKay).

PEIRCE, Miss H. T. Boston artist who exhibited at the Athenaeum in 1859. ¶ Swan, BA.

PEIRCE, JOSHUA H. Miniaturist and lithographic artist. He was working in NYC in 1841–42; exhibited a frame of miniatures at the Boston Athenaeum in 1843 as a resident of Boston; was with SHARP & PEIRCE in Boston, 1846–49; turned up in San Francisco about 1850 and was active there as an artist for lithographers throughout the fifties. ¶ NYBD 1841–42; Swan, BA [as John H.]; Peters, *America on Stone;* Peters, *California on Stone.* The dates (*c.* 1801–1849) given in Swan are those of a John H. Peirce, laborer, who died at Chelsea (Mass.) in 1849.

PEIRCE, see also PEARCE and PIERCE.

PEIS, see PISE.

PEKENINO, MICHELE. Italian stipple engraver who was employed by ASHER B. DURAND in NYC about 1820. He soon after moved to Philadelphia, whence he returned to Italy, having raised money, it is said, by selling an engraved portrait of Durand as a portrait of Simon Bolivar. ¶ Durand, *Life and Works of Asher B. Durand,* 36; Stauffer.

PELBY, Mrs. ——. Wax modeller? Mrs. Pelby's collection of scriptural wax statuary was shown in NYC in 1848, in Boston in 1849, and in Philadelphia in 1851. ¶ N. Y. *Herald,* Jan. 4, 1848; Boston *Evening Transcript,* June 4, 1849; Phila. *Public Ledger,* Nov. 24, 1851 (citations courtesy J. E. Arrington).

PELHAM, HENRY (1749–1806). Portrait and miniature painter, engraver, map-maker; youngest son of PETER PELHAM and half-brother of JOHN SINGLETON COPLEY. Born in Boston February 14, 1749 (New Style), he presumably studied painting with his half-brother. A Loyalist, he left Boston in 1776 and rejoined the Copleys in London. He exhibited at the Royal Academy in 1777 and 1778. He later went to Ireland as an engineer and map-maker, served as estate agent for Lord Lansdowne, and was drowned in the Kenmare River in 1806. ¶ DAB; DNB; Stauffer; *Letters & Papers of John Singleton Copley and Henry Pelham* (Mass. Hist. Soc., 1914); Slade, "Henry Pelham"; *Antiques* (Feb. 1942), 141 (repro.).

PELHAM, PETER (1697–1751). Mezzotint engraver, portrait painter, schoolmaster. Born in London, he was apprenticed in 1713 to John Simon, one of the leading engravers in mezzotint of London. Between 1720 and 1726 he produced at least 25 mezzotint portraits of prominent persons. In 1727 he emigrated to America, settling in Boston where he made his debut as America's first mezzotintist with a portrait of Cotton Mather. After the death of his first wife in 1734, Pelham remarried and moved to Newport (R.I.), but he had returned to Boston by 1737 and there spent the rest of his life as a schoolmaster, though he continued to do some engraving. In 1748 he took as his third wife the widowed mother of JOHN SINGLETON COPLEY; they became the parents the following year of HENRY PELHAM. Pelham was a close associate of JOHN SMIBERT and undoubtedly influenced the young Copley to become a painter. He died in Boston in December 1751. ¶ Allison, "Peter Pelham—Engraver in Mezzotinto"; DAB; DNB; Coburn, "More Notes on Peter Pelham"; Stauffer; Flexner, *John Singleton Copley*.

PELLEGRIN, FRANCIS. Engraver, NYC, 1852. ¶ NYBD 1852.

PELTON, OLIVER (1798–1882). Banknote and general engraver, born August 31, 1798, at Portland (Conn.). He worked principally in Boston and died at East Hartford (Conn.) August 15, 1882. With TERRY, PELTON & Co. in 1836–37. ¶ Fielding, *Supplement to Stauffer;* Boston CD 1829–56.

PENABERT, F. Portrait painter, Philadelphia, 1856; exhibitor, Pennsylvania Academy. ¶ Rutledge, PA.

PENDERGAST, see PRENDERGAST.

PENDLETON, JOHN B. (1798–1866). Lithographer, born in NYC of English parents. He and his brother WILLIAM S. PENDLETON were employed in 1816 to rig up a system of gas lighting for the Peale Museums in Philadelphia and Baltimore and in 1820 they were in charge of the travelling exhibition of REMBRANDT PEALE's "Court of Death." John later went to France as agent for a bookseller and learned the new art of lithography which he introduced in Boston in 1825. He worked there with his brother until about 1828, then spent a short time in Philadelphia (PENDLETON, KEARNEY & CHILDS), and from 1829 to 1834 practised lithography in NYC. In 1834 he sold out to a former pupil, NATHANIEL CURRIER, and apparently abandoned lithography, as he was listed from 1835 to 1851 as a carpenter and proprietor of a planing mill. He died March 10, 1866. Peters regards John B. and William S. Pendleton as the real founders of lithography in America because of the great number of artists and lithographers who were introduced to the art by them. ¶ Peters, *America on Stone;* Pendleton, *Brian Pendleton and His Descendants,* 750.

PENDLETON, KEARNEY & CHILDS. Lithographers, Philadelphia, 1829–30; JOHN B. PENDLETON, FRANCIS KEARNEY, and CEPHAS G. CHILDS. ¶ Peters, *America on Stone;* Eckhardt, "Early Lithography in Philadelphia," 252.

PENDLETON, WILLIAM. Artist, 28, a native of New York, living in NYC in 1860. Both JOHN B. and WILLIAM S. PENDLETON had sons of this name, but they are not known to have been artists. ¶ 8 Census (1860), N.Y., XLII, 955; Pendleton, *Brian Pendleton and His Descendants,* 750–51.

PENDLETON, WILLIAM S. (1795–1879). Engraver and lithographer, born in NYC January 27, 1795, of English parents. With his younger brother JOHN B. PENDLETON he was employed to install gas fixtures in the Peale Museums at Philadelphia and Baltimore in 1816 and in 1820 to exhibit REMBRANT PEALE's "Court of Death" in various cities and towns. By 1825 he was working as an engraver in Boston in partnership with ABEL BOWEN, but the following year he joined his brother in lithographic work. He remained in Boston after John's departure in 1829 and continued as a lithographer until 1836, when he sold out to THOMAS MOORE, his bookkeeper. Subsequently William did banknote engraving and engaged in the hardware business in Philadelphia. After the Civil War he settled in Staten Island (N.Y.) and he died there January 22,

1879. ¶ Peters, *America on Stone;* Pendleton, *Brian Pendleton and His Descendants,* 750; Baldwin, *Diary,* 331.

PENÉLON, HENRI. French artist who painted some of the important *rancheros* of early California. ¶ *Antiques* (Nov. 1953), 368 (repro.), 369.

PENFIELD, see PAUL EMERT.

PENFOLD, WILLIAM. Portrait painter, Lockport (N.Y.), 1859. ¶ N.Y. State BD 1859.

PENHALLOW, BENJAMIN H. Lithographer and printer, Lowell (Mass.), 1859. ¶ Lowell CD 1859.

PENMORK, ——. Lithographer of a view of the entrance of the First Congregational Church, Broadway, NYC, in 1845. Peters lists him as Penwork. ¶ Copy of the lithograph at LC; Peters, *America on Stone.*

PENNEY, L. P. Portrait painter, Boston, 1845. ¶ Boston BD 1845; Bolton, *Miniature Painters.*

PENNIMAN, JOHN (*c.* 1817–1850). Lithographer, artist. He was at Baltimore from 1835 to 1840 and in NYC from 1842 until his death on February 25, 1850. ¶ N. Y. *Spectator,* Feb. 28, 1850, obit.; Peters, *America on Stone;* Baltimore CD 1835–40; NYCD 1842–49; Stokes, *Iconography,* I, 432–33; Swan, "John Ritto Penniman," 248.

PENNIMAN, JOHN RITTO (1783–?). Portrait and ornamental painter, lithographer. Born January 30, 1783, at Milford (Mass.), Penniman was married to Susannah Bartlett in Boston in September 1805 and worked there as a painter until 1827. He was apparently on close terms with GILBERT STUART and may have studied with him. In 1825 he began to work for WILLIAM S. and JOHN B. PENDLETON, pioneer lithographers of Boston. In 1830 he was in the House of Correction at Boston and, according to a fellow inmate (William J. Shelling, author of *The Rat-Trap,* 1837), agreed to serve as a draftsman on the frigate *Independence* for the next three years. WILLIAM DUNLAP, writing in 1833–34 states that Pennyman [sic] was already dead. He was the teacher of several early artists, including ALVAN FISHER, NATHAN NEGUS, and CHARLES BULLARD. ¶ Morgan, *Gilbert Stuart and His Pupils,* 33–34; Swan, "John Ritto Penniman"; Dunlap, *History,* II, 260; Boston CD 1805–27.

PENNY, CHARLES H. Engraver, 35, a native of New York, at NYC in 1850 with his wife and three children. ¶ 7 Census (1850), N.Y., XLV, 494.

PENNY, EDWARD (1714–1791). Portrait painter "of historical significance only." ¶ Neuhaus, *History and Ideals of American Art,* 14.

PENWORK, see PENMORK.

PEPITE, ——. Scene painter at a New Orleans theater, 1828–34; he was a pupil of FOGLIARDI. ¶ Delgado-WPA cites *La. Courier,* April 18, 1832, and New Orleans CD 1830, 1832, 1834.

PEPPER, EDWARD. Engraver, 22, a native Pennsylvanian, at Philadelphia in 1850. ¶ 7 Census (1850), Pa., XLIX, 195.

PEPPER, MARY. Early American wax portraitist. ¶ Bolton, *American Wax Portraits,* 45.

PERALLI, see PERELLI.

PERATEE, SEBASTIAN. Image maker, NYC, 1819. ¶ NYCD 1819 (McKay).

PERCEL, Mme. DE. Portrait painter, recently arrived from Paris, at New Orleans in March 1837. ¶ Delgado-WPA cites *Bee,* March 30, 1837, and *Courier,* April 6, 1837.

PERCELL, JOHN. Lithographer, Philadelphia, 1855. ¶ Phila. CD 1855.

PERCIVAL, EDWIN (1793–?). Portrait, historical, and landscape painter. A native of Kensington (Conn.), Percival was a brother of James Gates Percival, poet and scholar. In 1830 he began the study of art at Hartford (Conn.) and three years later he went to Albany (N.Y.) in partnership with HENRY BRYANT. He later went to Troy (N.Y.) and there, in a fit of melancholy, is said literally to have starved himself to death. ¶ French, *Art and Artists in Connecticut,* 55; Rutledge, PA; Fielding, *Supplement to Stauffer,* no. 509.

PERCIVAL, HENRY. English engraver and die sinker, born about 1810, working in Philadelphia from about 1854. His eldest child was born in New York about 1851. ¶ 8 Census (1860), Pa., LIII, 588; Phila. CD 1854–60+.

PEREGOY, CHARLES E. Lithographer at San Francisco in the early 1850's; associate of C. J. POLLARD. ¶ Peters, *California on Stone.*

PERELLI, ACHILLE (1822–1891). Sculptor, fish and game painter. A native of Milan (Italy), Perelli studied at the Academy of Arts there. After serving with Garibaldi he came to America and settled at New Orleans, becoming Louisiana's first sculptor in bronze. He died in New Orleans October 9, 1891. ¶ New Orleans *Daily Picayune,* Oct. 10, 1891, obit.; Delgado-

WPA cites New Orleans CD 1852–54, 1858, 1867–91, *La. Courier,* May 5, 1851, obits. in *Times Democrat* and *Daily Item,* Oct. 10, 1891; represented in Delgado Museum and Louisiana State Museum.

PERELLI, CESAR. Sculptor associated with ACHILLE PERELLI at New Orleans in 1853. ¶ New Orleans CD 1853 (as Peralli).

PERINE, GEORGE EDWARD (1837–1885). Portrait engraver whose work was done mainly in NYC. He was born July 9, 1837, at South Orange (N.J.) and died in Brooklyn (N.Y.) February 3, 1885. ¶ Stauffer.

PERINE & DEXTER. Engravers, plate printers, and stencil cutters, Indianapolis, 1858. T. B. PERINE was the engraver of the company. ¶ Indiana BD 1858.

PERINE, T. B. Engraver and plate printer, Indianapolis, 1855–59; in 1858 of PERINE & DEXTER. ¶ Indianapolis CD 1855, 1858–59; Indiana BD 1858.

PERING, CORNELIUS (1806–1881). Landscape, portrait, and miniature painter, born November 5, 1806, in England. In 1832 he established a "female seminary" at Bloomington (Ind.) and in 1849 he moved to Louisville (Ky.) where he founded an art school. He died in Louisville November 28, 1881. ¶ Peat, *Pioneer Painters of Indiana.*

PERINOR, Mr. ——. Portrait artist in oils and pastels, New Orleans, 1825. Purportedly a former pupil at the Royal School of Fine Arts in Paris, he came to New Orleans from Richmond (Va.). ¶ Delgado-WPA cites *La. Gazette,* April 5, 1825.

PERKINS, Miss ——. Pastel portraitist, Connecticut, about 1790. ¶ Bolton, *Crayon Draftsmen.*

PERKINS, ABRAHAM (1768–1839). Engraver and goldsmith, brother of JACOB and father of NATHANIEL PERKINS. Born May 4, 1768, at Newburyport (Mass.), he appears to have spent his whole life there. He died April 2, 1839. ¶ Perkins, *The Family of John Perkins,* III, 51; Belknap, *Artists and Craftsmen of Essex County,* 5.

PERKINS, CHARLES CALLAHAN (1823–1886). Etcher and amateur painter, writer and lecturer on art. A native of Boston, he studied in France under Ary Scheffer and others and exhibited at the Boston Athenaeum. He was the author of books on Tuscan and Italian sculptors and a critical essay on Raphael and Michelangelo, president of the Boston Art Club, and an Honorary Director of the Boston Museum of Fine Arts. The plates in his books were etched by Perkins mainly from his own drawings. ¶ Swan, BA; Clement and Hutton.

PERKINS & COMPANY. Engravers, NYC, 1850; S. LEE PERKINS. ¶ NYBD 1850.

PERKINS, E. G. Engraver of a portrait published in 1831 at Providence (R.I.). JACOB PERKINS had a son named Ebenezer Greenleaf Perkins (born 1797, died 1842), but it is not known whether he also did engraving. ¶ Stauffer; Perkins, *The Family of John Perkins,* III, 51.

PERKINS, FREDERICK STANTON (1832–1899). Portrait and landscape painter, born December 6, 1832, at Trenton (N.Y.). He studied in NYC and exhibited at the National Academy and the Pennsylvania Academy after 1855. In 1862 he moved to Wisconsin, settling first in Milwaukee and later at Burlington where he lived until his death in 1899. ¶ Perkins, *The Family of John Perkins,* III, 158; Cowdrey, NAD; Rutledge, PA; NYBD 1857–60; Butts, *Art in Wisconsin,* 99; 8 Census (1860), N.Y., XLIII, 286.

PERKINS, GRANVILLE (1830–1895). Scenery painter, book illustrator, born October 16, 1830, in Baltimore. He worked in Baltimore, Richmond, Philadelphia, and NYC, exhibited at the National Academy after 1860, and was a member of the Water Color Society. He died April 18, 1895, in NYC. ¶ CAB; Rutledge, PA; Hamilton, *Early American Book Illustrators,* 431–32.

PERKINS, HENRY (1803–?). Banknote engraver. Born November 15, 1803, at Salem (Mass.), he clerked in his brother's store in Hanover (N.H.) and in Utica (N.Y.), sold drugs in NYC, and finally settled permanently in Philadelphia before his marriage in 1835. In Philadelphia he was at first in the book trade, but about 1858 he became a member of the firm of DANFORTH, PERKINS & COMPANY and subsequently treasurer of the AMERICAN BANK NOTE COMPANY. He was active in a number of charitable and religious organizations. ¶ Perkins, *The Family of John Perkins,* I, 110; Phila. CD 1859+; 8 Census (1860), Pa., LIII, 269.

PERKINS, HORACE, JR. Engraver, 27, a native of New York, at NYC in 1860. ¶ 8 Census (1860), N.Y., LVII, 960.

PERKINS, JACOB (1766–1849). Banknote engraver, die-cutter, and inventor. Born July 9, 1766, at Newburyport (Mass.), he was apprenticed to a goldsmith, and learned also the art of engraving and sinking dies. He was associated with GIDEON FAIRMAN in Newburyport and again in Philadelphia from 1816 to 1819. In 1819 he went to England with Fairman and others to seek a contract for banknote engraving from the Bank of England. The plan failed but Perkins remained in England and prospered as an inventor. Among the inventions credited to him are a machine for making nails, stereotyping, and a propeller-driven steam boat. He died in London July 11, 1849. ABRAHAM PERKINS was a brother; E. G. PERKINS may have been his son Ebenezer Greenleaf Perkins. ¶ Perkins, *The Family of John Perkins,* III, 49–51; Toppan, *100 Years of Bank Note Engraving,* 8–10; Stauffer; Bathe, *Jacob Perkins.*

PERKINS, J. R. Landscape painter residing in NYC in 1855 when he exhibited at the National Academy; he also exhibited at the Maryland Historical Society in 1856. ¶ Cowdrey, NAD; Rutledge, MHS.

PERKINS, JOSEPH (1788–1842). Banknote and letter engraver. He was born August 19, 1788, at Unity (N.H.) and graduated in 1814 from Williams College. Soon after he went to Philadelphia, but from 1826 until his death April 27, 1842, he was a resident of NYC. From 1828 to 1831 he was in partnership with ASHER B. DURAND as DURAND, PERKINS & CO. He left one son (possibly the JOSEPH PERKINS listed below) and after his death the family is said to have moved to California. ¶ Stauffer; Perkins, *The Family of John Perkins,* II, 66; Rutledge, PA; NYCD 1826–42.

PERKINS, JOSEPH. Lithographer, NYC, 1851–53; exhibited at the American Institute. Possibly the son of JOSEPH PERKINS, above. ¶ NYCD 1851–53; Am. Inst. Cat., 1851.

PERKINS, LEE, see S. LEE PERKINS.

PERKINS, NATHANIEL (1803–1847). Engraver born April 18, 1803, at Newburyport (Mass.), a son of ABRAHAM PERKINS. He worked in Boston from 1836 until his death at Newburyport, November 29, 1847. He was an agent of the NEW ENGLAND BANK NOTE COMPANY from 1837 to 1847. ¶ Belknap, *Artists and Craftsmen of Essex County,* 5; Perkins, *The Family of John Perkins,* III, 51; Boston CD 1836–47.

PERKINS, S. LEE. Lithographer, NYC, 1848–56; from 1848 to 1852 with HENRY SERRELL, in whose house he was living in 1850. The 1850 Census gives his age as 23 and birthplace as Connecticut. This may be Lee Perkins, son of Timothy Pitkin Perkins of West Hartford (Conn.); he was born in the mid-1820's and was mortally wounded in the second battle of Bull Run in 1862. ¶ NYCD 1848–56; 7 Census (1850), N.Y., LIV, 583; Perkins, *The Family of John Perkins,* III, 77.

PERL, A. Sculptor, New Orleans, 1857. ¶ Delgado-WPA cites New Orleans CD 1857.

PERO, LORENZO. Plaster image maker, 23, a native of Tuscany, working and living with LORENZO HARDIE at Philadelphia in 1860. ¶ 8 Census (1860), Pa., LXII, 106.

PEROVANI, JOSEPH (?–1835). Portrait, historical, and landscape painter. He came to Philadelphia with JACINT COCCHI in 1795; both were from Venice and stated that they had worked in Rome as well as other Italian cities. Perovani was in Cuba in 1801 and died in Mexico in 1835. ¶ Thieme-Becker; Prime, II, 26.

PERRET, ANDREW. Senior partner in PERRET & BROTHER, engravers and "engine turners," Newark (N.J.), 1860 and after. ¶ Newark CD 1860–70; New Jersey BD 1860.

PERRET & BROTHER. Engravers and engine turners, Newark (N.J.), 1860 and after; ANDREW and HENRY PERRET. ¶ Newark CD 1860–70; New Jersey BD 1860.

PERRET, CHARLES E. Engraver and die sinker, NYC, 1856–59. ¶ NYBD 1856–59.

PERRET, HENRY. Junior partner in PERRET & BROTHER, engravers and "engine turners," Newark (N.J.), 1860 and after. ¶ Newark CD 1860–70; New Jersey BD 1860.

PERRET, PAULIN. Engraver, New Orleans, 1841–42. ¶ New Orleans CD 1841–42.

PERRIN, BERANGER. Artist, New Orleans, 1837. ¶ Delgado-WPA cites New Orleans CD 1837.

PERRY, C. H. Wood engraver, Cincinnati, 1853. ¶ Ohio BD 1853.

PERRY, EDWARD. Exhibited a frame of wood engravings at the American Institute in 1845; his address was 11 Spruce Street, NYC. ¶ Am. Inst. Cat., 1845.

PERRY, ENOCH WOOD, JR. (1831–1915). N.A. Genre, portrait, and landscape painter, born in Boston July 31, 1831. After clerking in a New Orleans store from 1848 to 1852, Perry went abroad to study painting. He was with LEUTZE in Düsseldorf for over two years, then with Couture in Paris, and he also visited Rome and

Venice, serving as U. S. Consul in the latter city from 1856 to 1858. Returning to America, he settled briefly in Philadelphia and New Orleans, but in 1862 set off on his travels once more, during the next four years painting in California, Hawaii, and Utah. In 1866 he opened a studio in NYC and he remained there, aside from later trips to California and Europe, until his death, December 14, 1915. He became a National Academician in 1869 and achieved wide popularity through his American genre pictures. ¶ Cowdrey, "The Discovery of Enoch Wood Perry," with 9 repros.; DAB; CAB; Clement and Hutton; Cowdrey, NAD; Rutledge, PA; Cline, "Art and Artists in New Orleans"; Swan, BA.

PERRY, FRANKLIN. Engraver, 24, a native of Vermont, at Boston in July 1860. ¶ 8 Census (1860), Mass., XXVII, 522.

PERRY, GEORGE F. Artist, Cincinnati, 1850. ¶ Cincinnati CD 1850 (courtesy Edward H. Dwight, Cincinnati Art Museum).

PERRY, IONE (1839–?). Figure painter, especially literary subjects. She was born in NYC and studied at the Cooper Institute and with HENRY LOOP. Her professional life was spent in NYC. Some of her paintings were reproduced in lithographs and widely circulated. ¶ Clement and Hutton.

PERSAC, ADRIAN. Landscape painter active in Louisiana between 1857 and 1872. The State Museum owns his "Olivier Plantation," painted about 1861. ¶ *American Processional,* 246.

PERSICO, E. LUIGI (1791–1860). Sculptor, miniature and portrait painter, who came to America from Naples, his birthplace, in 1818. In 1819 and 1820 he was at Lancaster, Harrisburg, and Philadelphia (Pa.). He was at Philadelphia again in 1824–25. In 1825 he was engaged to execute several pieces of sculpture for the U. S. Capitol at Washington, particularly the colossal "War" and "Peace" for the east portico. These were completed and delivered in 1834. Persico seems to have done the marble work in Italy. Between 1834 and 1855 Persico's work was exhibited at the Boston Athenaeum and the Artists' Fund Society of Philadelphia. His latter years apparently were spent in Europe and he died in 1860 at Marseilles. GENNARO PERSICO was his brother. ¶ Thieme-Becker; Lancaster County (Pa.) Hist. Soc., *Papers,* XVI, 67–107; Scharf and Westcott, *History of Philadelphia,* II, 1067; Fairman, *Art and Artists of the Capitol,* 48, 77–78; Nagler, *Neues Allgemeines Künstler-Lexikon,* II, 131; Rutledge, PA; Swan, BA.

PERSICO, GENNARO (?–*c.* 1859). Miniaturist and crayon artist, teacher of drawing and painting. A brother of E. LUIGI PERSICO, he came to America from Naples about 1820, worked in Lancaster, Philadelphia, and Reading (Pa.) during the 1820's, and in 1823 married the daughter of John McKnight, a Reading banker. During the 1830's he had an "English and French Academy for young ladies" at Richmond (Va.) and from 1837 to 1840 he was a vestryman of an Episcopal church in Richmond. After his wife's death in 1842 he attempted to carry on his school but apparently failed and returned to Naples. He was back in Richmond in 1852 and worked as an artist there until about 1859. He is said to have died at sea. ¶ *Richmond Portraits,* 226–28; Montgomery, *Berks County,* 808; Lancaster County Hist. Soc., *Papers,* XVI, 93–94; Rutledge, PA; Rutledge, MHS; Swan, BA.

PERUANI, JOSEPH, see JOSEPH PEROVANI.

PERUL, Mme. DE, see Mme. DE PERCEL.

PESSOU, LOUIS. Lithographer, New Orleans, 1853–66; 1855 and after, of PESSOU & SIMON. In 1870 he was registrar of births and deaths. ¶ Delgado-WPA cites New Orleans CD 1853–66; CD 1870.

PESSOU & SIMON. Lithographers, New Orleans, 1855–60; LOUIS PESSOU and BENEDICT SIMON. ¶ Delgado-WPA cites New Orleans CD 1855–60.

PETERS, C. Primitive watercolor memorials, Massachusetts, about 1835. ¶ Lipman and Winchester, 178.

PETERS, J. Primitive genre subjects in oils, Vermont, 1840. ¶ Lipman and Winchester, 178.

PETERS, J. Cartoonist, Philadelphia, 1843. ¶ Peters, *America on Stone.*

PETERS, J., SR. Painter of a landscape with Mennonite figures, probably in the Delaware Water Gap (Pa.) in the early 19th century. ¶ Born, *American Landscape Painting,* 126, fig. 84; *Antiques* (May 1941), 259.

PETERS, JOHN E. Fresco painter, 33, a native of Osnabruck (Germany), living in Washington (D.C.) in 1860. His wife was from Virginia; John S., 6, was born in Maryland, and Mary L., 3, in Washington. ¶ 8 Census (1860), D.C., I, 823.

PETERS, Miss S. A., see Mrs. SARA GROZELIER.

PETERS, W. T. Artist "from nature" of

several Yokohama scenes for Matthew C. Perry's report on his expedition to Japan in 1853–54. ¶ Perry, *Expedition,* I, list of illustrations.

PETERS, WILLIAM. Engraver, 29, a native Pennsylvanian, living in Philadelphia in 1860 with his wife and two children, also born in Pennsylvania. ¶ 8 Census (1860), Pa., L, 608.

PETERS, WILLIAM THOMPSON, JR. (1828–?). Engraver, born in Cheshire (Conn.) February 2, 1828. He was a son of William Thompson Peters (1805–1885) and Etha L. Town (1809–1871), daughter of the New Haven architect Ithiel Town. Young Peters was living with his parents in New Haven in 1850, as was a younger brother, Ithiel Town Peters, 16, listed as a painter. William, Jr., is said to have died in a Soldiers' Home in New York State. ¶ Peters, *Peters of New England,* 165–66; 7 Census (1850), Conn., VIII, 391.

PETERSON, A. H. M. Engraver, New Orleans, 1860. ¶ Delgado-WPA cites New Orleans CD 1860.

PETERSON, C., see NISS C. PETERSON.

PETERSON, H. Painter of portraits of Col. Joseph Wentworth (1818–1901) and his wife (1823–1897) of Sandwich (N.H.). The Wentworths were married about 1845. ¶ WPA (Mass.), *Portraits Found in N.H.,* 26.

PETERSON, NISS C. Landscape painter, NYC, 1859–60. The name is variously given as Niss C. Peterson, Ness C. Pettersen, C. Petersen, and simply Peterson. ¶ NYCD and NYBD 1859–60.

PETICOLAS, ARTHUR EDWARD. Painter, son of EDWARD F. and JANE PITFIELD BRADDICK PETICOLAS. He was probably born in Richmond (Va.) during the 1820's and in 1847 exhibited some oils in that city. He later turned to medicine and became professor of anatomy at the Medical College of Virginia. ¶ *Richmond Portraits,* 151.

PETICOLAS, EDWARD F. (1793–*c.* 1853). Portrait, miniature, and landscape painter, son of PHILIPPE ABRAHAM PETICOLAS. Born in Pennsylvania in 1793, he was brought to Richmond (Va.) by his parents in 1804 and was taking miniature likenesses there as early as 1807, having already received some instruction from THOMAS SULLY. About 1815 he made the first of three trips abroad and spent about four years in England, France, and Italy. He returned to Virginia in 1820, married Jane Pitfield Braddick (see Mrs. JANE PITFIELD BRADDICK PETICOLAS) in 1822, made a second trip to Europe about 1825 and a third in 1830–33. After 1840 he suffered from acute rheumatism which led to his giving up painting about 1845. He probably died in 1853. ARTHUR EDWARD PETICOLAS was his only son. ¶ *Richmond Portraits,* 150–51, 228–30; Swan, BA.

PETICOLAS, EDWARD F. Wood engraver at Cincinnati from 1857 to 1861. In 1863 he was listed as assistant librarian of the Young Men's Mercantile Library Association. He may have been a son of T. V. PETICOLAS who was working in Cincinnati in the 1830's and early 1840's. ¶ Cincinnati CD 1857–63.

PETICOLAS, Mrs. JANE PITFIELD BRADDICK (1791–1852). Portrait copyist. Probably of Scottish birth, she was living in Richmond (Va.) when she married EDWARD F. PETICOLAS in 1822. She died November 10, 1852, survived by her husband and one son, ARTHUR EDWARD PETICOLAS. ¶ *Richmond Portraits,* 229–30.

PETICOLAS, PHILIPPE ABRAHAM (1760–1841). Miniature painter, teacher of drawing and music. A native of Meziers (France), he had served eight years in the army of the King of Bavaria before coming to St. Domingo about the time of the slave insurrections in 1790. He left the island shortly after the birth of his first son Augustus and came to Philadelphia where he lived for a few years as a miniature painter and print seller. He later moved to Lancaster (Pa.) and remained there until his removal to Richmond (Va.) in 1804. There he taught music and painted until about 1820. He died at the home of a son in Petersburg (Va.) in August 1841. Of his four sons, two were artists: EDWARD F. and THEODORE V. PETICOLAS. ¶ *Richmond Portraits,* 228–29; Prime, II, 26, 52; Lancaster County Hist. Soc., *Papers,* XVI, 69; *Antiques* (Dec. 1942), 277, repro. of his miniature of Washington.

PETICOLAS, THEODORE V. (1797–?). Miniature and portrait painter, drawing teacher. The youngest son of PHILIPPE ABRAHAM PETICOLAS, he was born in Pennsylvania, probably at Lancaster, but was brought up in Richmond (Va.). After trying shopkeeping in Lancaster and miniature painting in Richmond (1819–20), he is said to have gone to the West. In 1833 he was painting in Huntsville (Ala.). From 1836 to 1842 he was at Cincinnati, though he exhibited at the Philadelphia Artists' Fund Society in 1840 as a Philadelphia resident. In 1851 Cist gives his residence as Clermont (Ohio). The Cincinnati engraver EDWARD F. PETICOLAS may have been his son or a nephew. ¶ *Richmond Portraits,* 229; WPA (Ala.) Hist. Records Survey cites Huntsville *Southern Advocate,* July 2, 1833; Cincinnati CD 1836–42 [as T. V. or Thomas V. Peticolas]; Rutledge, PA; Cist, *Cincinnati in 1841* and *Cincinnati in 1851.*

PETIGRU, CAROLINE (1819–?). Portrait and miniature painter, born May 24, 1819, at Charleston (S.C.). Her father was James Lewis Petigru (1789–1863), noted lawyer and Unionist of Charleston. Caroline studied painting in her native city, married William A. Carson in 1840, and moved to NYC in 1860 because of her Unionist sympathies. During the 1880's she spent some time in Rome. ¶ CAB; Carolina Art Association Catalogues, 1935, 1936.

PETRI, RICHARD (1824–1857). Portrait and figure painter. A native of Dresden (Germany), Petri studied painting at the Academy there. After the 1848 Revolution he and his brother-in-law HERMANN LUNGKWITZ came to America and settled for a time near the town of Fredericksburg (Texas). Petri shortly moved to Austin where he spent the remainder of his life. ¶ "Texas in Pictures," 456 (repros.); Gideon, "Two Pioneer Artists of Texas."

PETT, JOHN. Painter on glass, 1772, of a picture of the death of General Wolfe. ¶ Signed and dated painting on consignment at NYHS, 1950.

PETTERSON, NESS C., see NISS C. PETERSON.

PETTIBONE, DANIEL. Artist and edge-tool maker, Philadelphia, 1811–20. ¶ Brown and Brown.

PETTIS, see PITTIS.

PETTRICH, FERDINAND or FREDERICK AUGUST FERDINAND (1798–1872). Sculptor, born December 3, 1798, at Dresden (Germany). He was working in the United States by 1838 when his models for statues for the west front of the U. S. Capitol at Washington were rejected. He exhibited at the Pennsylvania Academy between 1843 and 1870. In 1847 he was listed as residing in Rio de Janeiro (Brazil). Rowland Petrich, 52, sculptor, listed in the Philadelphia census of 1850, was probably Ferdinand Pettrich. He died at Rome (Italy) February 14, 1872. ¶ Thieme-Becker; Holmes, *Catalogue of the National Gallery of Art;* Fairman, *Art and Artists of the Capitol,* 76; Rutledge, PA; 7 Census (1850), Pa., Phila., p. 893; *Antiques* (Aug. 1948), 100 (repro.).

PEW, JAMES. Artist, 28, from England, in the Charity Hospital of Orleans Parish (La.), in December 1850. ¶ 7 Census (1850), La., IV, 719.

PFAU, GUSTAVUS. Topographical artist for lithographers. Born in Germany about 1800, Pfau came to America about 1848 and was working in NYC and Boston from 1848 to 1850. ¶ 7 Census (1850), Mass., XXV, 88; *Album of American Battle Art,* pl. 64; Stokes, *Historical Prints,* 106; NYCD 1848–50.

PFEFFER, F. Landscape painter, exhibited at the American Institute in 1848 a view of Castle "Stoltzerfels," presumably in Germany. He had a NYC address. ¶ Am. Inst. Cat., 1848.

PFEIFFER, JACOB. French lithographer, 34, at Philadelphia in 1850. ¶ 7 Census (1850), Pa., L, 627.

PFEIFFER, see VERHAEGEN & PEEIFFER.

PFENNINGER, JACOB. Portrait painter, Cleveland (Ohio), 1857–59. ¶ Cleveland BD 1857; Ohio BD 1859.

PFETSCH (or Fetsch), CARL P. (1817–1898). Portrait and genre painter. A native of Blankenburg (Germany), Pfetsch came to America soon after 1848 and worked in NYC until about 1855. He then went west, first to Cincinnati, then to New Albany (Ind.) where he lived from 1856 to 1870. From 1870 until his death his home was at Indianapolis. ¶ Peat, *Pioneer Painters of Indiana* [as Fetsch]; NYBD 1850–55; Cowdrey, NAD. *Cf.* CHARLES PEETSCH.

PHELAN, CHARLES T. Landscape painter born in NYC in 1840. ¶ Champlin and Perkins.

PHELPS, E. Engraver at Northampton (Mass.), 1849–56. ¶ New England BD 1849, 1856.

PHILIP, FREDERICK WILLIAM (1814–1841). A.N.A. Portrait painter born November 17, 1814, in Brooklyn (N.Y.). He exhibited at the American and National Academies in 1833 while studying in Europe and in the same year became an Associate Member of the National Academy. He again exhibited at the National Academy and at the Apollo Association in 1840. He died on March 29, 1841. ¶ Thieme-Becker; Cummings, *Historic*

Annals, 168; NYBD 1840; Cowdrey, NAD; Cowdrey, AA & AAU.

PHILIP, WILLIAM H. Sculptor, NYC, 1858–59. ¶ NYCD 1858–59; NYBD 1858.

PHILIPPOTEAUX, PAUL DOMINICK. Historical and genre painter who came to Louisiana probably not long after the French Revolution of 1848. In February 1850 his "Proclamation of the French Republic" was on exhibition in New Orleans. A cotton picking scene painted before the Civil War is also known. ¶ New Orleans *Daily Picayune,* Feb. 5, 1850 (citation courtesy J. E. Arrington); *Antiques* (April 1944), 161 (repro.).

PHILIPS, ——. Painter of a portrait of Anna Noxon, September 1837. *Cf.* AMMI PHILLIPS. ¶ Sherman, "Unrecorded Early American Painters" (1934), 149.

PHILIPSE, MARY (1730–1825). Amateur artist. Mary Philipse was born July 3, 1730, at Philipse Manor (N.Y.) and married Roger Morris of NYC in 1765. For ten years they lived in what is now known as the Jumel Mansion in NYC. During the Revolution they emigrated to England and settled in Yorkshire where Mary lived until her death, July 18, 1825. Her self-portrait hangs in the Octagon Room of the Jumel Mansion. ¶ *Antiques* (March 1951), 217 (repro.); DAB under Roger Morris.

PHILLENE, FERDINAND J. Engraver, 26, from Jamaica, living in Philadelphia in 1860. ¶ 8 Census (1860), Pa., LII, 87.

PHILLIBROWNE, THOMAS. Engraver, born in London and working there in the 1830's. He came to the United States before 1851 when he engraved a portrait of Kossuth for a Boston firm. He was working in NYC from 1856. ¶ Stauffer; NYCD 1856–60; Am. Inst. Cat., 1856.

PHILLIPS, ——. Portrait painter who executed likenesses of a number of members of the Ten Broeck family of New York State between 1832 and 1834. This may be AMMI PHILLIPS. ¶ Runk, *Ten Broeck Genealogy,* 112, 155, 187, 189–90; WPA (Mass.), *Portraits Found in New York.*

PHILLIPS, Mrs. ——. Teacher of embroidery, music, drawing and painting, etc., Charleston (S.C.), 1795. ¶ Rutledge, *Artists in the Life of Charleston.*

PHILLIPS, AMMI (1787/88–1865). Portrait painter. A native of Berkshire County (Mass.), he lived for some time in Dutchess County (N.Y.) and is known to have painted portraits at Troy and Claverack (N.Y.). *Cf.* —— PHILIPS and —— PHILLIPS. ¶ Information courtesy Ralph D. Phillips, NYC.

PHILLIPS, BENJAMIN R. Artist, 39, a native New Yorker, at NYC in 1860. In 1863 he was listed as a photographer. ¶ 8 Census (1860), N.Y., XLIV, 417.

PHILLIPS, CHARLES. English-born engraver who was working in NYC in 1842. He exhibited at the National Academy. ¶ Stauffer; Cowdrey, NAD.

PHILLIPS, CHARLES C. Engraver, 20, at Philadelphia in 1850. ¶ 7 Census (1850), Pa., LV, 220.

PHILLIPS, GEORGE W. Portrait and landscape painter, born in the District of Columbia about 1822; living in Cincinnati in the 1850's and in Louisville (Ky.) in the late 1860's. ¶ 7 Census (1850), Ohio, XXI, 314; Cincinnati CD 1850–60; information courtesy Mrs. W. H. Whitley, Paris (Ky.).

PHILLIPS, HENRY J. Engraver, NYC, 1854–57. ¶ NYBD 1854–57.

PHILLIPS, JOHN (1822–?). Portrait painter, born May 8, 1822, at Paisley (Scotland). He emigrated to America about 1837 and took up portrait painting about 1842. In 1847 he was at Albany (N.Y.) painting the governor and many legislators. About 1849 he went to Porto Rico and from there in 1852 to Europe to study for two years in Spain, Italy, and France. Returning to America in 1854 he opened a studio in NYC. In 1858–59 he was in Cuba and in 1861 he went to Montreal. After an unsuccessful venture in the oil fields, he moved to Chicago in 1868 and there resumed his painting. He made occasional trips to New York State but Chicago remained his home at least into the mid-1880's. ¶ Andreas, *History of Chicago,* II, 561–62; Ulp, "Art and Artists in Rochester"; NYCD 1853–60; Cowdrey, NAD; Rutledge, PA; represented at Chicago Hist. Soc.

PHILLIPS, S. J. Sign and ornamental painter, Cleveland, 1840. ¶ Knittle, *Early Ohio Taverns,* 43.

PHILP, WILLIAM H. Portrait and ornamental painter working in NYC in the 1850's. He painted panels for Hose Co. No. 3's fire engine depicting the battle of Bunker Hill and Washington at the battle of Monmouth. This engine was exhibited at the American Institute in 1850. ¶ NYCD 1850–60; Smith, "Painted Fire Engine Panels," 246.

PHINNEY, DEIDAMIA. Drawing teacher, Philadelphia, 1818. ¶ Brown and Brown.

PHIPPEN, JOHN. Painter of ship pictures, Salem (Mass.), 1790. ¶ Robinson and Dow, *Sailing Ships of New England,* I, 62.

PHIPPS, G. W. Artist, 45, a native of Massachusetts, living in New Haven (Conn.) in 1850. ¶ 7 Census (1850), Conn., VIII, 279.

PHIPPS, WILLIAM C. Engraver, Washington (D.C.), 1855–60. ¶ Washington and Georgetown CD 1855, 1858, 1860.

PHYSICK, W. Lithographer of S. WALTER's painting of the New York packet ship *Roscius,* launched in 1839, lost in the Atlantic in 1860. The artists are presumed to be American. ¶ *Portfolio* (Feb. 1947), 138 (repro.).

PIATTI, ANTHONY. Sculptor, NYC, 1849–57; exhibited at the National Academy in 1850. ¶ NYBD 1849–57; Cowdrey, NAD.

PIATTI, PATRIZIO. Sculptor, NYC, 1857–60. ¶ NYBD 1857–60.

PICARD, PETER. Engraver, Philadelphia, 1816–17. ¶ Brown and Brown.

PICARD, PETER M., JR. Engraver, Philadelphia, 1818–19. ¶ Brown and Brown.

PICCHI, FREDERICK. Sculptor, New Orleans, 1860–61. ¶ Delgado-WPA cites New Orleans CD 1860–61.

PICKEN, A. Lithographer, NYC, about 1835. ¶ Peters, *America on Stone.*

PICKIL, ALEXANDER (?–*c.* 1840). Negro artist of New Orleans who destroyed all or nearly all his paintings because of "disillusionment with his environment and the attitude of critics and friends toward his art." ¶ Porter, "Versatile Interests of the Early Negro Artist," 21.

PICOT, see CLORIVIÈRE.

PIENOVI, ——. Scenic artist "from the Academy of Rome" who painted a drop curtain showing NYC scenes for a NYC theater, 1811. ¶ N. Y. *Evening Post,* Aug. 1, 1811 (citation courtesy J. E. Arrington).

PIERCE, ——. Portrait painter who advertised at Portsmouth (N.H.) in February 1819. ¶ *Antiques* (Sept. 1944), 158.

PIERCE, ——. Portrait painter whose 1821 likenesses of Mr. and Mrs. Matthew Perkins were owned in 1941 by Dr. Henry F. Perkins of Burlington (Vt.). ¶ WPA (Mass.), *Portraits Found in Vt.*

PIERCE, DAVID. Portrait painter, 41, a native of Massachusetts, at Detroit (Mich.) in 1860. In 1861 he was listed as a daguerreotypist. ¶ 8 Census (1860), Mich., XX, 919; Detroit CD 1861.

PIERCE, HARTELL (?). Engraver, 28, a native of New York, living in NYC in 1860 with his Irish wife and two children. *Cf.* HART L. PEARCE. ¶ 8 Census (1860), N.Y., LIV, 1.

PIERCE, JOSHUA, see JOSHUA H. PEIRCE.

PIERCE, NICHOLAS. Artist at Newburyport (Mass.) in 1850. ¶ Belknap, *Artists and Craftsmen of Essex County,* 11.

PIERCE, W. J. Wood engraver, NYC, exhibitor at the 1847 Fair of the American Institute. Possibly WILLIAM J. PIERCE, Boston engraver after 1850. ¶ Am. Inst. Cat., 1847.

PIERCE or PEARCE, WILLIAM, JR. Portrait painter from Virginia who studied under CHARLES WILLSON PEALE at Annapolis and Baltimore in 1774–75 and returned to Virginia in August 1775. ¶ Sellers, *Charles Willson Peale,* I, 119–20; *Virginia Gazette,* August 11, 1775 (cited in *William and Mary Quarterly,* II (1893–94), 35).

PIERCE, WILLIAM J. Engraver, 22, a native of Vermont, living in Burlington (Vt.) in 1850 with his father, a merchant. ¶ 7 Census (1850), Vt., IV, 597.

PIERCE or PEIRCE, WILLIAM J. Wood engraver at Boston from 1851 until about 1870. He was with WORCESTER & PIERCE in 1851 and 1852. ¶ Boston CD 1851–60+; Hamilton, *Early American Book Illustrators.*

PIERCY, FREDERICK (1830–?). Portrait and landscape painter, born January 27, 1830, at Portsmouth (England). He began painting portraits in England about 1848. In 1853 he made a trip from Liverpool to Salt Lake City, via New Orleans, St. Louis, and Nauvoo (Ill.), sketching scenes and portraits along the way. After his return to England in 1854 he wrote and illustrated an account of his journey, *Route from Liverpool to Great Salt Lake Valley* (1855). Piercy continued to exhibit portraits in London as late as 1880. ¶ Arrington, *Nauvoo Temple,* Chapter 8; Piercy, *Route from Liverpool to the Great Salt Lake Valley;* Jackson, *Gold Rush Album,* repros.; Powell, "Three Artists of the Frontier."

PIERRIE or PIERIE, WILLIAM. Landscape and townscape painter, officer in the Royal Artillery stationed in America. In 1768 as Lt. Pierie he drew a view of Niagara Falls and in 1774 another view of the Falls by Pierie, after a painting by a Mr. WILSON, was published. He did views of NYC and Boston in 1775 and 1776. He was promoted to Captain some time after 1768. ¶ Dow, *Niagara Falls,* I, 80; Stokes,

Historical Prints; Stokes, *Iconography,* VI, pl. 88a; Kelby, *Notes on American Artists,* 11.

PIERSON, PAUL R. B. Engraver, Boston, 1855–58; in 1855–56 of SMITH & PIERSON. ¶ Boston CD 1855–58, BD 1855–56.

PIERSON, SARAH. Genre painter. Her "Fulton Street, New York, 1821" was shown at the Corcoran Gallery in 1950. ¶ *American Processional,* 240.

PIGAL or PIGALLE, ——. Engraver from France working in NYC in 1795. ¶ NYCD 1795 (McKay); Dunlap, *History* (1918), II, 199, and III, 327.

PIGGOT, ROBERT (1795–1887). Stipple engraver. Born May 20, 1795, in NYC, Piggot was apprenticed to the Philadelphia engraver DAVID EDWIN. About 1816 he went into partnership with a fellow pupil, CHARLES GOODMAN, and the two did considerable work for periodicals and annuals until the early twenties. Piggot became an Episcopal deacon in 1823 and was ordained two years later. He continued to do a little engraving after his ordination. After holding charges in Pennsylvania and Delaware, Piggot became rector of Christ Church, Sykesville (Md.) in 1869. He died July 23, 1887, at Sykesville. ¶ DAB; Stauffer; Baker, *American Engravers.*

PIGOT, see PAJOT.

PIKE, JOS[EPH]. Lithographer, 23, native of Pennsylvania, living in Philadelphia in 1860 with his father, David Pike, merchant. ¶ 8 Census (1860), Pa., LVII, 489.

PIKE, S. Illustrator of *Lessons for Children* (Phila., 1818); the cuts were engraved by ALEXANDER ANDERSON. ¶ Hamilton, *Early American Book Illustrators,* 434.

PILBROW, EDWARD. Engraver, NYC, 1829–36; of ILLMAN & PILBROW, 1829–33. ¶ NYCD 1829–36.

PILGRIM, JAMES. Artist, 42, a native of England, living in Philadelphia in 1860. His wife was also English; their two children, 5 and 2, were born in Massachusetts. ¶ 8 Census (1860), Pa., L, 358.

PILIE, J. Teacher of figure, landscape, and flower painting, New Orleans, 1808. ¶ Delgado-WPA cites *Moniteur,* March 26, 1808.

PILKINGTON, ADAM (1810–1856). Amateur artist. A native of Lancaster (England), Pilkington worked as a bleacher in England before emigrating to America in the early 1840's. He settled in Nauvoo (Ill.) and helped build the Mormon Temple, of which he made a drawing some time before his death, February 14, 1856. ¶ Arrington, "Nauvoo Temple," Chapter 8.

PILKINGTON, JAMES E. Engraver and die sinker at Albany (N.Y.) with TRUE & PILKINGTON, 1856–57; at Baltimore in 1858. ¶ Albany CD 1856–57; Baltimore CD 1858.

PILLINER, C. A. Landscape in oils on tin, Cambridge (Mass.), 1860. ¶ Lipman and Winchester, 178.

PILLINER, FREDERICK J. Lithographer and wood engraver. He was at Boston in 1853–54 as junior partner in SCHENCK & PILLINER, and at Philadelphia 1856–60 and after. The name occasionally appears as Pillner or Pittner, though Pilliner is most common. ¶ Boston CD 1853–54; Phila. CD 1856–60+; Hamilton, *Early American Book Illustrators,* 216.

PILLNER, GEORGE. Lithographer, Philadelphia, 1860. ¶ Phila. CD 1860.

PILLOW, GEORGE. Lithographer of HAYWARD & PILLOW, NYC, 1837. ¶ NYCD and BD 1837.

PIMAT, P. MIGNON. Oil portraits, Massachusetts, 1810. ¶ Lipman and Winchester, 178.

PINE, JAMES. Portrait painter. He was a frequent exhibitor at the National Academy. Pine was working in NYC from 1834 to 1845, at Newark (N.J.) 1846–50, in NYC and at Sing Sing (N.Y.) from 1852 to 1857, and in Philadelphia in 1859. Between 1852 and 1858 he worked with his son, THEODORE PINE. ¶ Cowdrey, NAD; NYBD 1844–57; N. J. BD 1850; Rutledge, PA; Stillwell, "Some 19th Century Painters," 85–86.

PINE, ROBERT EDGE (1730?–1788). Portrait and historical painter. Pine was born in London, a son of the engraver John Pine and brother of Simon Pine, miniature painter; Alexander Cozens, the landscape painter, was his brother-in-law. Robert E. Pine was painting in London as early as 1749 and was well known as a painter of theatrical portraits and historical pictures. From 1772 to about 1777 he lived at Bath. In 1784 Pine emigrated to America with the idea of painting historical pictures on American revolutionary themes and he did several life portraits of Washington, as well as other well-known Americans. He died November 19, 1788, in Philadelphia, before completing his first American historical painting, "Congress Voting Independence," which was finished by Edward Savage and now hangs in Independence Hall. Pine's paintings were sold by lottery and were exhibited for a number of years in Philadelphia, NYC, and Boston by DANIEL BOWEN. ¶ DAB; DNB; Whitley, *Artists and Their Friends in England;* Prime, I, 7, and II, 26–29; Morgan and Fielding, *Life Portraits of Washington,* 83–88; Peale, "Reminiscences"; Dunlap, *History;* Flexner, *The Light of Distant Skies.*

PINE, THEODORE E. (1828–1905). Portrait painter and engraver, son of JAMES PINE. From 1847, when he first exhibited at the National Academy, until 1860, Theodore Pine worked in and around NYC, his home being in Newark until about 1855 and then at Sing Sing, now Ossining (N.Y.). In 1860 he appears to have gone abroad to study in Paris, Rome, and Munich. During the last third of the century he lived and worked in NYC, Chicago, St. Louis, Manitou (Colo.), and Asheville (N.C.). He died June 10, 1905, at Ogdensburg (N.Y.). ¶ *Art Annual,* V, obit.; Cowdrey, NAD; NYBD 1850–60; Stillwell, "Some 19th Century Painters," 88–93; information courtesy H. Maxson Holloway, Chicago Historical Society.

PINKERTON, E. J. Lithographer and polychrome engraver, Philadelphia, 1840–46; 1844–45 with PINKERTON, WAGNER & McGUIGAN. His work was published in the *U. S. Military Magazine* in 1840. ¶ Peters, *America on Stone;* Todd, "Huddy & Duval Prints"; *American Collector* (July 1946), 12 (repro.).

PINKERTON, WAGNER & McGUIGAN. Lithographers, Philadelphia, 1844–45; E. J. PINKERTON, THOMAS WAGNER, and JAMES McGUIGAN. In 1846 it became WAGNER & McGUIGAN. ¶ Phila. CD 1844–46; Peters, *America on Stone.*

PINKNEY, EDWARD J. Wood engraver, NYC, 1854. ¶ NYBD 1854.

PINKNEY, SAMUEL J. Wood engraver, NYC, 1848–65. He exhibited at the American Institute in 1848 as S. J. and in 1850 as J. J. Pinkney and was listed in the business directories as Samuel Pinkney, Jr. His home was in Brooklyn. ¶ Am. Inst. Cat., 1848, 1850; NYBD 1854, 1858; NYCD 1853–65; advertisement in Print Collection, Cooper Union (courtesy Miss Elizabeth Marting).

PINNEY, EUNICE (1770–1849). Primitive watercolorist in all genre. Born Eunice Griswold at Simsbury (Conn.) in 1770, she was married twice, first to a Mr. Holcombe and second to a Mr. Pinney. She took up painting about 1809 and continued until about 1826, most of her work being done at Windsor and Simsbury (Conn.). Her 54 recorded works include genre scenes, landscapes and buildings, figure pieces, memorials, allegories, religious, historical, and literary scenes. ¶ Lipman, "Eunice Pinney—An Early Connecticut Water-Colorist," with checklist and 5 repros.; Lipman and Winchester, chapter III, 4 repros.; Warren, "Richard Brunton" (1953).

PINOLI, Signor A. Portrait painter at New Orleans, 1838, 1841–42; in 1838 of CERESA & PINOLI. The 1838 directory lists him as Pirroli. ¶ New Orleans CD 1838, 1841–42; Delgado-WPA cites *Commercial Bulletin,* April 5, 1841.

PINT, JOSEPH. Engraver and die sinker, NYC, 1858. ¶ NYBD 1858.

PIRROLI, see PINOLI.

PIRRSON, JAMES W. Landscape painter, NYC, 1856–60; exhibited at the National Academy 1859–60. ¶ NYCD 1856; NYBD 1857; Cowdrey, NAD.

PISANI BROTHERS (F. and C.). Sculptors, San Francisco, 1860. ¶ San Francisco BD 1860.

PISE or PEIS, LEWIS. Miniaturist from Italy, working at Philadelphia in 1795 and 1797, and at Baltimore in 1800–01 and 1807–08. ¶ Prime, II, 29; Baltimore CD 1800–01, 1807–08 (Mayo).

PISHBOURNE, see FISHBOURNE.

PITMAN, THOMAS. Ship pictures, Marblehead (Mass.), about 1850. ¶ Robinson and Dow, *Sailing Ships of New England,* I, 62; F. J. Peters, "Paintings of the Old 'Wind-Jammer,'" 32.

PITT or PEAT, Miss ——. Portrait painter and copyist at Newport (R.I.) whose talents much impressed the Russian traveler PAUL SVININ during his visit to America, 1811–13. He spoke of her as a young girl. ¶ Yarmolinsky, *Picturesque United States of America,* 38.

PITT, JOSEPH B. Engraver, NYC, 1859. ¶ NYBD 1859.

PITTFIELD, WILLIAM. Engraver, 25, a native of France, at Philadelphia in 1850. ¶ 7 Census (1850), Pa., LII, 906.

PITTIS BROTHERS, see HENRY and THOMAS PITTIS.

PITTIS, HENRY. Engraver of NYC, working with his brother THOMAS PITTIS from 1844 to 1849. They exhibited jointly at the American Institute 1844–47. ¶ NYCD 1844–49; Am. Inst. Cat., 1844–47.

PITTIS, THOMAS. Engraver, NYC, 1842–68. He was born in the Isle of Wight (England) about 1807. From 1844 to 1849 he was in partnership with his brother HENRY PITTIS. He exhibited stencil engravings at the American Institute from 1844 to 1851. ¶ 8 Census (1860), N.Y., LVI, 995 [as Thomas Pettis]; NYCD 1842–68; Am. Inst. Cat., 1844–51.

PITTNER, F. J., see FREDERICK J. PILLINER.

PLAIN, BARTHOLOMEW. "Picture maker," NYC, 1802–18. ¶ NYCD 1802–18.

PLANTOU, Mme. ANTHONY. Historical and religious, landscape and portrait painter of Philadelphia, 1818–25. She was the wife of a Philadelphia dentist and is said to have studied under the French artist Renaud. Her European training is further indicated by the subjects of some of her works exhibited in Philadelphia in 1818 and 1820, which included a view near Paris, a miniature of Pius VII, and copies after Mignard and Raphael, done in 1802. In America she was noted for her painting of the Treaty of Ghent, first exhibited at Washington in 1817. With her husband and this painting, Mme. Plantou visited New Orleans and Washington in 1819–20. She was also in Charleston (S.C.) in the spring of 1823. Mme. Plantou was still in Philadelphia in 1825. ¶ Scharf and Westcott, *History of Philadelphia,* II, 1053; Rutledge, PA; Phila. CD 1818; Delgado-WPA cites *La. Gazette,* Jan. 20 and 29, 1819; Dunlap, *History;* Rutledge, *Artists in the Life of Charleston;* Washington *Daily National Intelligencer,* Dec. 13 and 23, 1817 (courtesy J. Earl Arrington).

PLASSMANN, ERNST (1823–1877). Sculptor and wood carver, born June 14, 1823, at Sondern, Westphalia (Germany). After studying in Germany and Paris for several years, Plassmann emigrated to America in 1853 and the following year he established in NYC an art school which he conducted until his death, November 28, 1877. He executed many statues and monuments for public and private patrons, especially in NYC, and he was the author of two books: *Modern Gothic Ornaments* (1875) and *Designs for Furniture* (1877). ¶ CAB; NYBD 1856–60+.

PLATEN, C. Lithographer, Charleston (S.C.), 1853. ¶ Rutledge, *Artists in the Life of Charleston.*

PLATT, Mrs., see ELIZABETH WRIGHT.

PLATT, GEORGE. Artist, NYC, 1846–48. ¶ NYBD 1846, 1848.

PLATT, GEORGE W. (1839–1899). Still life, landscape, and portrait painter, born July 16, 1839, in Rochester (N.Y.). After graduating from the University of Rochester about 1860, he spent several years in the West as draftsman with John Wesley Powell's geological surveys. He then studied for five years at the Pennsylvania Academy and subsequently in Italy and at Munich. During the 1880's he was in Chicago and during the 1890's at Denver (Col.) where he died September 16, 1899. ¶ Frankenstein, *After the Hunt,* 128–31, plates 71, 113, 116.

PLATT, H. Engraver and/or painter of a portrait published in Boston in 1832. ¶ Stauffer.

PLATT, JAMES C. (?–1882). Portrait, landscape, and still life painter. He worked in or near NYC and Brooklyn from about 1850 until his death, which occurred in Brooklyn on Christmas Eve 1882. He advertised in Charleston (S.C.) in 1846 and was at Chicago in 1859. He exhibited at the Pennsylvania Academy in 1869 as a resident of NYC. ¶ Thieme-Becker; Cowdrey, NAD; NYBD 1854–60; Rutledge, *Artists in the Life of Charleston;* Rutledge, PA; Chicago BD 1859.

PLATTENBERGER, ——. Biblical scene in oils, Pennsylvania, about 1860. ¶ Lipman and Winchester, 178.

PLEASANTS, ALBERT C. Artist of a view of Richmond (Va.) erroneously dated 1798. He was the son of Archibald and Mary (Brend) Pleasants who were married in Richmond in November 1812. He was living in Richmond in 1836. The family were Quakers. ¶ Information courtesy Mrs. Ralph Catterall, Valentine Museum, Richmond.

PLECKER, D. A. Artist of "A Correct View of the Mammoth Tree Grove" in California, lithographed by R. W. FISHBOURNE and published in 1855. ¶ Peters, *California on Stone.*

PLICATOR, FRANK. Engraver, 22, a native of New Orleans where he was living in 1860. ¶ 8 Census (1860), La., VI, 847.

PLOCHER, JACOB J. (?–1820). Engraver working in Philadelphia from 1815 until his death there on December 27, 1820. ¶ Stauffer.

PLUMB, ——. Painter of a portrait of Francis Thomas of Maryland which was engraved by ALFRED SEALEY (died *c.* 1860). ¶ Stauffer.

PLUMER, HARRISON LORENZO (1814–?). Portrait and genre painter. He was born March 2, 1814, at Haverhill (Mass.) and exhibited at the Boston Athenaeum in

1837. From 1837 to 1845 he was in London (England) and exhibited at the Royal Academy as H. L. Plummer. In 1859 at New Orleans he advertised that he could paint an oil portrait in five hours. ¶ Perley, *The Plumer Genealogy,* 185; Swan, BA; Graves, *Dictionary;* Delgado-WPA cites *Bee,* March 2, 1859.

PLUMER, JACOB P. Engraver, Boston, 1855–60 and after; in 1855–56 in partnership with NATHANIEL EVANS, JR. Possibly Jacob P. Plumer, son of Avery and Elizabeth (Paul) Plumer, born March 26, 1819. ¶ Boston CD 1855–60+; Perley, *The Plumer Genealogy,* 157.

PLUMMER, ADRIAN. Portrait painter, Boston, 1837; exhibited at the Athenaeum. ¶ Boston Athenaeum Cat., 1837.

PLUMMER, EDWARD. Watercolor miniature, Connecticut, about 1850. ¶ Lipman and Winchester, 178.

PLUMMER, EDWIN. Portrait painter at Salem (Mass.) in 1828 and at Boston 1841–46. ¶ Belknap, *Artists and Craftsmen of Essex County,* 12; Boston BD 1841, 1844, 1846.

PLUMMER, R. Landscape in oils, Maine, about 1860. ¶ Lipman and Winchester, 178.

PLUMMER, WILLIAM. Painter of miniature profiles in watercolors working in Massachusetts during the first quarter of the 19th century. He is said to have studied under ALLSTON. ¶ Sherman, "American Miniatures by Minor Artists."

PODESTA, STEPHEN. Plaster image maker from Italy, aged 50, living in Boston in 1860 with his Irish wife and four children born in Massachusetts since 1843. PETER GROPPO boarded with the family. ¶ 8 Census (1860), Mass., XXVI, 402.

POHL, EDWARD. Engraver, 19, born in Pennsylvania, living in Philadelphia in 1860 with his father, Paul Pohl, a customs house inspector from South Carolina. ¶ 8 Census (1860), Pa., LIII, 202.

POINCY, A. Young portrait painter from France who was at New Orleans in January 1859. ¶ Delgado-WPA cites *Bee,* Jan. 18, 1859.

POINCY, PAUL (1833–1909). Portrait, religious, and genre painter, born in New Orleans March 11, 1833. After studying at the École des Beaux Arts in Paris, he worked chiefly in New Orleans, specializing in children's portraits. He saw service with the Confederate Army. He also did some painting in Alabama (1859). ¶ Delgado-WPA file; WPA (Ala.), Hist. Records Survey; Cline, "Art and Artists in New Orleans."

POINDEXTER, JAMES THOMAS (1832–1891). Portrait painter. Born June 6, 1832, in Christian County (Ky.), he was painting portraits at Evansville (Ind.) as early as 1852. During the Civil War he was a telegraph operator. He died June 10, 1891, at Eddyville (Ky.). His work is represented in the Evansville Art Gallery and the New Harmony (Ind.) Library. ¶ Peat, *Pioneer Painters of Indiana;* Burnet, *Art and Artists of Indiana.*

POINT, Father NICHOLAS, S. J. Topographical artist. Father Point went out West in 1841 with Father de Smet, designed and built a mission among the Coeur d'Alene Indians in 1842, and in 1845 founded a mission among the Blackfeet. The Jesuit Provincial House at St. Louis owns over 100 of Father Point's sketches, while others formed the basis for lithographs illustrating Father de Smet's *Oregon Missions and Travels over the Rocky Mountains in 1845–46.* ¶ Rasmussen, "Art and Artists in Oregon, 1500–1900," cites also Cody, *History of the Coeur d'Alene Mission of the Sacred Heart* and Wagner, *The Plains and the Rockies.*

POINTEL, J. B. Portrait painter, New Orleans, 1838. ¶ New Orleans CD 1838.

POISSON, JULIEN. Teacher of drawing, Richmond (Va.), 1810. ¶ *Richmond Portraits.*

POLDEMAN, WILLIAM F. Artist, 33, a native of Baden (Germany), at NYC in 1860 with his wife and son, age 12, both born in Germany. ¶ 8 Census (1860), N.Y., XLIV, 356.

POLK, CHARLES PEALE (1767–1822). Portrait and general painter, nephew of CHARLES WILLSON PEALE. Born March 17, 1767, in Maryland, Polk was orphaned in 1777 and grew up in the home of his artist uncle. Trained by Peale, he first advertised as a portrait painter in Baltimore in 1785. In 1787 he advertised in Philadelphia as a house, ship, and sign painter, but from 1791 to 1793 he was again offering to paint portraits in Baltimore, as well as copies of his portraits of Washington, Franklin, and Lafayette. He was at Richmond during the winter of 1799–1800. Polk later painted a portrait of Jefferson. By 1818 he was settled in a government clerkship in Washington. He died in 1822. ¶ Sellers, *Charles Willson Peale;* Prime, I, 7, and II, 29–31, 52; Kimball, "Life Portraits of Jefferson"; Morgan and Fielding, *Life Portraits of Washington;*

Richmond Portraits; Pleasants, *250 Years of Painting in Maryland;* represented at Md. Hist. Soc., Am. Antiq. Soc., and Corcoran Gallery.

POLLARD & BRITTON. Lithographers, San Francisco, 1852; C. J. POLLARD and JOSEPH BRITTON (?). ¶ Peters, *California on Stone.*

POLLARD, C. J. Lithographer, San Francisco, 1850–52; worked with JOSHUA H. PEIRCE, CHARLES E. PEREGOY and JOSEPH BRITTON. ¶ Peters, *California on Stone;* San Francisco BD 1850.

POLLARD, CALVIN (1797–1850). Architect and draftsman, born June 14, 1797, at New Braintree (Mass.). He was an older brother of JOHN POLLARD. He was a prominent architect and builder in NYC from 1818 until his death, August 31, 1850. There is a watercolor by him of the residence of Henry Remsen, NYC, in the Belknap Collection at the NYHS. ¶ Underwood, *The Ancestry and Descendants of Jonathan Pollard,* 12–13; *Catalogue of the Belknap Collection.*

POLLARD, HENRY. Engraver, Boston, 1849. ¶ Boston CD 1849.

POLLARD, HENRY G., see BALL & POLLARD.

POLLARD, JOHN (1802–1885). Painter, especially of flower pieces. Born August 27, 1802, at New Braintree (Mass.), he was trained as a carver and worked at that trade in Albany (N.Y.) during the 1820's. Ill health forced him to go south where he met the English girl whom he married in 1831 at Philadelphia. Pollard lived in NYC until 1835, then moved to a farm at East Wilson, Niagara County (N.Y.) where he spent the rest of his life. He worked in pencil, oils, and watercolors. He died July 22, 1885. CALVIN POLLARD was his brother. ¶ Underwood, *The Ancestry and Descendants of Jonathan Pollard,* 14.

POLLARD, LUKE. Portrait painter at Harvard (Mass.) in 1845. ¶ Lipman and Winchester, 178; Sears, *Some American Primitives,* 5–7, 14–15 (repros.).

POLLARD, WILLIAM. Ship picture, 1851. ¶ F. J. Peters, "Paintings of the Old 'Wind-Jammer,'" 32 (repro.).

POLLOCK & DOTY. Engravers, NYC, 1841; THOMAS POLLOCK and WARREN S. DOTY. ¶ NYCD 1841.

POLLOCK & SMITH. Engravers, NYC, 1840; THOMAS POLLOCK was the senior partner. ¶ NYBD and CD 1840.

POLLOCK, THOMAS. Engraver. In 1833 he was at New Orleans; 1834–35, at Boston; 1839, at Providence (R.I.); 1840–57, at NYC. He was senior partner in the firms of POLLOCK & SMITH (1840) and POLLOCK & DOTY (1841). ¶ Delgado-WPA cites *Bee,* Jan. 7, 1833; Stauffer; Boston CD 1835; NYCD 1840–41; NYBD 1840–57.

POLLOCK & WILSON. Engravers, Boston, 1834; probably THOMAS POLLOCK and WILLIAM W. WILSON. ¶ Stauffer.

POLTER, see SAMUEL POTTER.

POMAREDE, EDWARDS. Portrait painter, New Orleans, 1859–61. ¶ Delgado-WPA cites New Orleans CD 1859–61.

POMAREDE, LEON (*c.* 1807–1892). Panoramist, landscape painter, miniaturist, and religious mural painter. Born about 1807 at Tarbes (France), Pomarede probably studied in Europe before coming to America in 1830. Settling in New Orleans he received further instruction from the theatrical painters MONDELLI and DEVELLE and married the daughter of the former. In 1832 he moved up to St. Louis, painted a view of the town and decorated the Cathedral. He returned to New Orleans and opened a studio there in 1837 and in 1841 painted three religious pictures for St. Patrick's Church. By 1843 he had gone back to St. Louis and gone into partnership with T. E. COURTENAY. In 1848 Pomarede collaborated for a short time with HENRY LEWIS on a panorama of the Mississippi but the association soon was broken and each produced his own version, Pomarede being assisted by his former partner Courtenay. Pomarede's "Panorama of the Mississippi River and Indian Life" was first shown in St. Louis in the fall of 1849, and subsequently in New Orleans and on the eastern seaboard until its destruction by fire at Newark (N.J.) in November 1850. After this loss Pomarede returned to St. Louis, reopened his studio and spent the rest of his life painting religious and genre pictures and murals for churches, theaters, and public buildings. He died in St. Louis in 1892 at the age of 85, from injuries received in a fall from a scaffold in a church he was decorating at Hannibal (Mo.). ¶ McDermott, "Leon Pomarede, 'Our Parisian Knight of the Easel,'" with seven repros.; Arrington, "Leon D. Pomarede's Panorama of the Mississippi River"; Arrington, "Nauvoo Temple," Chapter 8; Delgado-WPA cites *Courier,* Nov. 9, 1841, and *Daily Picayune,* Nov. 27, 1849.

POMEROY, Mrs. LAURA SKEEL (1833–1911). Sculptor; born in NYC in 1833; died there August 23, 1911. Vassar College has her bust of the founder, Matthew Vassar. ¶ *Art Annual,* IX, obit.

POMMAYRAC, ——. Miniaturist, New Orleans, 1833–35. ¶ Delgado-WPA cites *Courier,* Dec. 5, 1833, and New Orleans CD 1834–35.

PONCHON, ANTHONY. Landscape artist, born in France about 1820, living in NYC during the 1850's. ¶ 7 Census (1850), N.Y., XLIII, 2; NYBD 1858–59.

PONCIA, ANTONIO. Statuary and moulder, born in Italy about 1793, working in Baltimore in 1859–60. ¶ Baltimore CD 1859; 8 Census (1860), Md., III, 915.

POND, DAVID F. Crayon artist, Hartford (Conn.), 1851. ¶ Hartford BD 1851.

PONTELLI, M. L. DE. Portrait painter and teacher at New Orleans, 1842–44. ¶ Delgado-WPA cites *Bee,* Dec. 10, 1842, and New Orleans CD 1843–44. *Cf.* M. PONTEL DU PORTAIL.

POOLE, WILLIAM H. Engraver, born in New York about 1830, working there 1857 and after. He was with LATHROP & POOLE 1857–58. ¶ NYBD 1857–59; 8 Census (1860), N.Y., XLV, 841.

POOLEY, A. Painter who advertised in October 1752 at Annapolis (Md.). He was prepared to paint "either in the Limning Way, History, Altar Pieces for Churches, Landskips, Views of their own Houses and Estates, signs or any other Way of Painting and also Gilding. . . ." ¶ *Maryland Gazette,* Oct. 12, 1752, cited by Prime, I, 7.

POOR, JONATHAN D. Wall painter, active in Maine and eastern Massachusetts during the 1830's. He was a nephew of RUFUS PORTER, with whose work Poor's has marked similarities. ¶ Little, *American Decorative Wall Painting,* 127, 132; *Art in America* (Oct. 1950), 164–65, 173–78, 194 (repro.).

POPE, Mrs. ——. Portrait painter at Milwaukee (Wis.) in September 1847. ¶ Butts, *Art in Wisconsin,* 84–85.

POPE, JOHN (1820–1880). A.N.A. Portrait, landscape, and genre painter. Born March 2, 1820, at Gardiner (Me.), Pope was brought up as a farmer but went to Boston about 1836 to study painting. He began exhibiting at the Athenaeum in 1843. In 1849 he joined the rush to California, stayed a few years, returned to Boston briefly, and then went to Europe to study for several years in Rome and Paris. By 1857 he had established himself in NYC, where he maintained a studio until the time of his death, December 29, 1880. He was made an Associate of the National Academy in 1859. His best known work was a full length of Webster, painted for the town of Charlestown (Mass.). ¶ Pope, *A History of the Dorchester Pope Family,* 221–22; *American Art Review,* II, Part I (1881), 169, obit.; Swan, BA; Boston BD 1844–49, 1853+; Cowdrey, NAD; Rutledge, PA; Hart, "Life Portraits of Daniel Webster."

POPE, SARAH. Artist, 40, a native of Massachusetts, at Philadelphia in 1860. Possibly the Miss Pope who exhibited crayon portraits of dogs at the Pennsylvania Academy in 1851. ¶ 8 Census (1860), Pa., LVI, 494; Rutledge, PA.

POPE, THOMAS. Architect, artist, and engineer of Philadelphia, 1813–17. He exhibited at the Society of Artists. ¶ Brown and Brown; Rutledge, PA; Yarmolinsky, *Picturesque United States of America,* 41.

POPE, THOMAS BENJAMIN (?–1891). Landscape, genre, and still life painter. Born in New York or New Jersey, Pope was a liquor dealer in Newburgh (N.Y.) before he became a painter. He exhibited several crayon drawings at the American Institute in 1845 and 1849. After service in the Civil War, in which he was wounded, he returned to Newburgh where he painted landscapes and fruit pieces from which color advertisements were made. He was killed by a train at Fishkill Landing (N.Y.) in 1891. ¶ Information courtesy Mrs. Katharine McCook Knox, Washington (D.C.), who owns three of his paintings; Am. Inst. Cat., 1845, 1849; represented in the collection of the late Oscar T. Barck, Brooklyn, N.Y.

POPENOT, ——. Painting and dancing master, Baltimore, 1786. ¶ Prime, II, 52.

POPPEL, JOHN. Engraver of two illustrations for Dana's *United States Illustrated* (c. 1855). ¶ Dana, *The United States Illustrated.*

PORCHER, Miss ——. Advertised oil paintings at Charleston (S.C.) in 1850. ¶ Rutledge, *Artists in the Life of Charleston.*

PORTAIL, M. PONTEL DU. Portrait painter, teacher, and lithographer, said to have been a pupil of David in Paris. He was at New Orleans from 1836 to 1844. *Cf.* PONTELLI and POINTEL. ¶ Delgado-WPA cites *Bee,* Nov. 11, 1836, Nov. 22, 1837, and Feb. 11, 1840, and *Picayune,* Jan. 14, 1844.

PORTE CRAYON, see H. D. STROTHER.

PORTER, DAVID (1780–1843). Amateur artist. Born February 1, 1780, in Boston, David Porter entered the U. S. Navy as a midshipman in 1798, served with distinction as captain of several ships during the War of 1812, and resigned from the service in 1826 to become Commander-in-Chief of the Mexican navy. In 1830 he was named U. S. Consul at Algiers; a little over a year later he became American Chargé d'Affaires at Constantinople and in 1839 Minister to Turkey. He died in Constantinople March 3, 1843. Sketches by Porter were used to illustrate his *Journal of A Cruise Made in the Pacific Ocean in the Years 1812, 1813 and 1814*. ¶ DAB; rare books, Library of Congress; Stauffer (under William Strickland).

PORTER, J. T. Engraver, Middletown (Conn.), 1815. ¶ Stauffer.

PORTER, JOHN. Portrait painter, 1853, probably in Virginia. ¶ Willis, "Jefferson County Portraits and Portrait Painters."

PORTER, JOHN J. Landscape painter who exhibited at the National Academy and the American Art-Union between 1848 and 1850. His address in 1848 was given as NYC and one of his pictures was a scene in Schoharie County (N.Y.). ¶ Cowdrey, NAD; Cowdrey, AA & AAU.

PORTER, JOHN S. Miniaturist working in Boston from 1822 to 1833 and at Lowell (Mass.) in 1834. He exhibited at the Athenaeum in 1833. Possibly the John Porter of Massachusetts in Lipman and Winchester. ¶ Swan, BA; Belknap, *Artists and Craftsmen of Essex County*, 12; Bolton, *Miniature Painters; cf. Antiques*, XXIII, 13–14.

PORTER, M. Painter of a portrait of Philip Crosby Tucker (1800–1861) of Vergennes (Vt.), dated 1830. ¶ WPA (Mass.), *Portraits Found in Vermont.*

PORTER, RUFUS (1792–1884). Portrait and mural painter, silhouettist. Born May 1, 1792, at West Boxford (Mass.), he was brought up in Maine and began his career there as a house and sign painter. In 1816 he took up portrait painting and from then until about 1823 traveled throughout New England and the Middle States, and as far south as Virginia. In 1823 he began to cut silhouettes and paint landscapes and from 1824 to 1845 he worked primarily as an itinerant painter of mural decorations in New England. After 1845 he apparently gave up painting to edit the *Scientific American,* which he had founded in NYC. He was also an inventor and the author of several books, including *A Select Collection of Valuable and Curious Arts and Interesting Experiments.* Porter died August 13, 1884, while visiting a son at New Haven (Conn.). STEPHEN TWOMBLY PORTER was a son of Rufus, and JONATHAN D. POOR was his nephew. ¶ Lipman, *Rufus Porter, Yankee Wall Painter,* contains a checklist and 25 repros.; see also: Lipman and Winchester, 57–66; Little, *American Decorative Wall Painting,* 132; DAB.

PORTER, STEPHEN TWOMBLY (1816–1850). Wall painter, son of RUFUS PORTER. He was born at Portland (Me.) August 16, 1816 and worked with his father as a wall painter and later (1841–42) on the *New York Mechanic,* a magazine edited in NYC by Rufus. Stephen died October 6, 1850, at Billerica (Mass.). ¶ Little, *American Decorative Wall Painting,* 132.

PORTER, WILLIAM E. Engraver, Warren (Ohio), 1853. ¶ Ohio BD 1853.

PORTLOCK, NATHANIEL (1748?–1817). British naval officer who visited the northwest coast of the present United States in 1786–87 and made some sketches which were used to illustrate *A Voyage Round the World; But More Particularly to the North-West Coast of America: Performed in 1785, 1786, 1787, and 1788, in the King George and Queen Charlotte, Captains Portlock and Dixon.* ¶ Rasmussen, "Art and Artists in Oregon," cited by David C. Duniway; DNB.

PORTNER, EDWARD. Engraver, born in Pennsylvania about 1835, working in Philadelphia in 1850 and 1860. ¶ 7 Census (1850), Pa., LV, 100; 8 Census (1860), Pa., LI, 44.

POSSELWHITE, GEORGE W. (*c.* 1822–?). English-born engraver who came to America in 1850 and worked mainly in NYC and Philadelphia. He was living in New York in 1899. ¶ Stauffer.

POST, EDWARD C. Landscape painter who exhibited at the National and Pennsylvania Academies before 1860. In 1853 he was at NYC; 1855–56, in the Catskills; 1860, at Düsseldorf (Germany). ¶ Cowdrey, NAD; Rutledge, PA.

POTTER, CROWELL. Painter of miniatures of Cornelius Leverich Brower and John J. Brower of NYC, about 1825. ¶ WPA (Mass.), *Portraits Found in N.Y.;* FARL Photo Negatives 19191, 19193.

POTTER, EDWARD CLARK (1800–1826). N.A. Portrait painter and a founding member of the National Academy of Design. He died in NYC on December 4, 1826 at the age of 26. ¶ N. Y. *Evening Post,* December 5, 1826, obit.; Cummings, *Historic Annals,* 28, 76; Cowdrey, AA & AAU; Cowdrey, NAD.

POTTER, EDWARD TUCKERMAN. Architect, exhibited at the Pennsylvania Academy 1860–62. He was a son of Alonzo Potter, Protestant Episcopal Bishop of Pennsylvania. ¶ Rutledge, PA.

POTTER, HENRY. Portrait painter, Brooklyn (N.Y.), 1857. ¶ Brooklyn BD 1857.

POTTER or POLTER, SAMUEL. Engraver, 30, a native of Pennsylvania, living in the Northern Liberties of Philadelphia in 1850. ¶ 7 Census (1850), Pa., XLIX, 266.

POTTER, W. C. Landscape painter at Elmira (N.Y.) who exhibited at the National Academy in 1856. ¶ Cowdrey, NAD.

POTTS, WILLIAM STEPHENS (1802–1852). Engraver. Born October 13, 1802, probably near the present Bloomfield (Pa.), and brought up in Trenton (N.J.), Potts was apprenticed to a Philadelphia printer and possibly to PETER MAVERICK, engraver of Newark (N.J.). In 1824 he was working in NYC with WILLIAM CHAPIN. He entered Princeton Theological Seminary in 1825 and in 1828 took charge of a church at St. Louis. In 1837 he became president of Marion College in Missouri and from 1839 to 1852 he was pastor of the Second Presbyterian Church in St. Louis. He died March 28, 1852. ¶ Potts, *Historical Collections Relating to the Potts Family,* 175; Fielding; Stephens, *The Mavericks,* 42.

POUPARD, JAMES. Portrait painter and engraver, jeweller and goldsmith. Poupard came from Martinique and had been an actor in early life. He was at Philadelphia from 1769 to 1807 and at NYC in 1814. ¶ Hamilton, *Early American Book Illustrators;* Stauffer; Prime, I, 26–27; Brown and Brown; *Portfolio* (Jan. 1952), 117 (repro.).

POWELL, H. M. T. Townscape and portrait painter working in California in the 1850's. His *Santa Fe Trail to California* was edited and published in 1931. ¶ Taft, *Artists and Illustrators of the Old West,* 267; *American Processional,* 158.

POWELL, J. T. Lithographer, 27, living in Boston in 1850 with DANIEL BARRY, THOMAS BARRY, and —— COMRI. He was a native of one of the British Provinces (Canada). ¶ 7 Census (1850), Mass., XXV, 311.

POWELL, SAMUEL. Silhouettist whose portrait of Washington is owned by the Historical Society of Pennsylvania. This is SAMUEL FOLWELL. ¶ Jackson, *Silhouette,* 136–37; Sawitzky, *Hist. Soc. of Pa. Catalogue.*

POWELL, WILLIAM HENRY (1823–1879). A.N.A. Portrait and historical painter. Born in NYC February 14, 1823, Powell was taken to Cincinnati as an infant and grew up there. He received his first instruction in painting from JAMES H. BEARD. About 1840 he went to NYC to study under HENRY INMAN, and in 1842 he was at New Orleans. In 1847 he recived the commission to fill the last panel of the Rotunda of the Capitol and from 1848 to 1853 he worked in Paris on this painting, the discovery of the Mississippi River by De Soto. After several years in Washington Powell was commissioned by the State of Ohio to paint Perry's victory on Lake Erie during the War of 1812. Powell's studio for many years was in NYC where he died October 6, 1879. ¶ DAB; Cowdrey, AA & AAU; Cowdrey, NAD; New Orleans CD 1842; NYCD 1852, 1854; Cist, *Cincinnati in 1841* and *Cincinnati in 1859;* Delgado-WPA cites New Orleans *Bee,* Jan. 7, 1842, and *Commercial Bulletin,* Feb. 18, 1842; Fairman, *Art and Artists of the Capitol;* 7 Census (1850), N.Y., LII, 398.

POWER, JOHN. Lithographer, 30, a native of Prussia, at Baltimore in 1860. ¶ 8 Census (1860), Md., V, 510.

POWERS, A. G. Portrait and historical painter. At Baton Rouge (La.) in 1848 he painted an equestrian portrait of Gen. Zachary Taylor. From 1849 to 1854 he was at New Orleans. He left in June 1854 for study in Europe and did not return until December 1856. He was in New Orleans until at least 1861. ¶ Delgado-WPA cites the following: *Picayune,* Nov. 2, 1848; New Orleans CD 1849, 1851, 1853–54, 1858, 1860–61; *Delta,* March 12 and May 17, 1854; *Picayune,* June 27, 1854, March 25, 1856, and Jan. 4, 1859; and *Commercial Bulletin,* Dec. 22, 1856.

POWERS, ASAHEL L. (1813–?). Portrait painter, born February 23, 1813, at Springfield (Vt.). A pair of portraits by this artist, dated October 1839, were found in Ogdensburg (N.Y.) and a child's portrait of about 1850 was found in New Jersey. ¶ Powers, *The Powers Family,* 88; Sherman, "Unrecorded Early American Painters" (1934), 149; information courtesy Harry Stone Galleries; Lipman and Winchester, 178.

POWERS, HIRAM (1805–1873). Sculptor. Powers was born July 29, 1805, on a farm near Woodstock (Vt.), but during his childhood the family moved westward to New York State and later to Ohio where his father died. At 17 Hiram went to work in a clock and organ factory in Cincinnati. Six years later he was put in charge of the mechanical department of Dorfeuille's Western Museum in Cincinnati and he began his career as a sculptor by modelling wax figures for a representation of Dante's Inferno. Encouraged by his success at this and in taking likenesses in wax, Powers moved to Washington in 1834 and for several years did portrait busts there. In 1837 he sailed for Italy with his family and, after a few months in Paris, settled in Florence, where he was to spend the rest of his life. The international success of his "Greek Slave," completed in 1843, established Powers as the leading American sculptor of his day, though later critics have preferred his many portraits of men to the ideal female figures for which he was most popular. He died in Florence June 27, 1873. ¶ DAB; Taft, *History of American Sculpture;* Gardner, *Yankee Stonecutters;* Swan, BA; Rutledge, PA; Cowdrey, NAD; Lee, *Familiar Sketches of Sculpture and Sculptors;* Rutledge, MHS.

POWERS, J. Portrait painter, 45, a native of Philadelphia, at New Orleans in 1860. ¶ 8 Census (1860), La., VIII, 37.

POWERS, JAMES T. Lithographer and engraver, Boston, 1852–60 and after; of POWERS & WELLER. Probably of SWETT & POWERS, 1851. ¶ Boston CD 1852–60+.

POWERS, OLIVER. Sign and ornamental painter, Warren (Ohio), 1820. ¶ Knittle, *Early Ohio Taverns.*

POWERS, ROBERT A. Landscape painter of Brooklyn (N.Y.); exhibitor at the National Academy, Apollo Association, and American Art-Union between 1840 and 1849. He painted scenes in various parts of New York State. ¶ Cowdrey, AA & AAU; Cowdrey, NAD, NYCD 1840–45.

POWERS, S. Artist, 30, a native of New York, living in New Orleans in 1850. ¶ 7 Census (1850), La., V, 8.

POWERS & WELLER. Lithographers and engravers, Boston, 1852–60 and after; JAMES T. POWERS and EDWIN J. WELLER. The firm was known 1852–53 as J. T. Powers & Company. ¶ Boston CD 1852–60+; BD 1852–60.

POWNALL, THOMAS (1722–1805). Topographical artist. Born in Lincoln (England) in 1722, Pownall graduated from Cambridge in 1743 and in 1753 came to America as private secretary to Sir Danvers Osborn, Governor of New York. From 1757 to 1759 he was himself Governor of Massachusetts. After his return to England in 1760 Pownall was active in Parliament during the Revolution. He died at Bath February 25, 1805. A number of his American views were engraved and published in England. ¶ DNB; DAB; *Portfolio* (March 1948), 152; *Art Quarterly* (1945), 41.

PRADOS, Mme. ——. Miniaturist, New Orleans, about 1800. ¶ Fielding.

PRALL, ROBERT M., see ROBERT M. PRATT.

PRANG, LOUIS (1824–1909). Lithographer and wood engraver. The son of a calico printer of Breslau (Germany), Prang was born March 12, 1824, and was brought up to the same trade, which he practised in Germany, Austria, France and England until 1848. Suspected of implication in the Revolution of 1848, he was forced to flee first to Bohemia, then to Switzerland, and finally to America, landing in NYC on April 5, 1850. He settled in Boston, taught himself wood engraving and worked at it until 1856 when he went into the lithographic business in Boston with JULIUS MAYER. After the dissolution of the partnership in 1860 Prang carried on independently and built up a very successful business. Soon after the Civil War he began printing chromo lithographs; during the 1870's he introduced the Christmas Card and began to issue color reproductions of famous paintings. He was also a well-known dealer in artists' supplies and he published a number of very popular drawing books. He retired in 1899 and died ten years later, June 15, 1909, in a Los Angeles (Cal.) sanatorium. ¶ Rushford, "Lewis Prang"; DAB; *Art Annual,* VII, obit.; Peters, *America on Stone;* Boston CD 1852 and after.

PRANG & MAYER. Lithographers, Boston, 1856–60; LOUIS PRANG and JULIUS MAYER. After 1860 Mayer established the firm of Mayer & Stetfield and Prang continued as Louis Prang & Co. ¶ Boston CD 1856–60; Rushford, "Lewis Prang."

PRATT, CHARLES H. Engraver, 24, a native of Vermont, at Boston in 1860. ¶ 8 Census (1860), Mass., XXVI, 862.

PRATT, HENRY CHEEVER (1803–1880). Portrait and miniature, landscape and panorama painter. Born June 13, 1803, at Orford (N.H.), Pratt was working on a New Hampshire farm when his artistic talent was discovered by S. F. B. MORSE about 1817. Morse brought him to Boston, taught him to paint, and employed him as an assistant for a number of years, taking him to Charleston in 1819, to Washington in 1821, and again to Charleston in 1822. By 1827 Pratt was established in his own studio in Boston. His home was in Charlestown until 1860 when he moved to Montrose, part of Wakefield (Mass.). He was a friend of THOMAS COLE and went to Maine on a painting expedition with him in 1845. From 1851 to 1853 he was with JOHN RUSSELL BARTLETT's expedition to explore the Mexican boundary. He died at Wakefield November 27, 1880. ¶ Karolik Cat., 449–51; Mabee, *The American Leonardo;* Larkin, *Samuel F. B. Morse and American Democratic Art;* Rutledge, *Artists in the Life of Charleston;* Boston BD 1841–60+; Swan, BA; Cowdrey, NAD; Rutledge, PA; Boston *Transcript,* Nov. 30, 1880, obit.; Boston *Transcript,* June 5, 1849, and March 1, 1850, and Baltimore *Sun,* July 12, 1852 (citations courtesy J. E. Arrington); *American Processional,* 149; *Panorama* (Jan. 1949), 53, 55.

PRATT, J. Exhibited a view of Boston Common at the American Academy in 1825. ¶ Cowdrey, AA & AAU.

PRATT, MATTHEW (1734–1805). Portrait painter, born in Philadelphia September 23, 1734. From 1749 to 1755 he served his apprenticeship with his uncle, JAMES CLAYPOOLE, limner and general painter, and in 1758 he began his career as a portrait painter in Philadelphia. From 1764 to 1766 he studied under BENJAMIN WEST in London and the following year and a half he spent in Bristol. After his return to America in 1768 Pratt spent most of his time in Philadelphia, though he is known to have visited England and Ireland in 1770, NYC in 1772, and Virginia in 1773. During the 1780's he added sign painting to his repertory. He died in Philadelphia January 9, 1805. ¶ Sawitzky, *Matthew Pratt, 1734–1805,* chronology and checklist, 43 plates; Flexner, *The Light of Distant Skies,* biblio., 265.

PRATT, ROBERT M. (1811–1880). N.A. Portrait, figure, and flower painter. A native of Binghamton (N.Y.), he first exhibited at the National Academy in 1833 while still at Binghamton. From 1845 to 1858 he was in NYC; he became an Associate of the Academy in 1849 and a Member in 1851. In 1859 he was studying in Paris. He returned to NYC before 1867 and died there August 31, 1880. ¶ *American Art Review,* I (1880), 552, obit.; Cowdrey, NAD; Swan, BA; Rutledge, PA; NYCD 1845+; *Stranger's Guide* to NYC, 1847 (as Robert M. Prall).

PRATT, RUTTER & COMPANY. Portrait and ornamental painters, Philadelphia, 1796; the firm was composed of MATTHEW PRATT, GEORGE RUTTER, WILLIAM CLARKE and JEREMIAH PAUL. ¶ Prime, II, 31.

PRATVIEL, LOUIS. Portrait painter, St. Louis, 1854–59. ¶ St. Louis BD 1854, 1859.

PRECOUR, Mme. PETER. Drawing teacher and fan-painter, Charleston (S.C.), 1732. ¶ Rutledge, *Artists in the Life of Charleston.*

PREDLOVE, see **PRETLOVE.**

PRENDERGAST, JOHN. Amateur painter of California scenes, active between 1848 and 1851. He was an Englishman who came to San Francisco from Hawaii in July 1848. Several of his paintings and drawings survive, while others were used to illustrate several early books on California. ¶ Van Nostrand and Coulter, *California Pictorial,* 150–51; Peters, *California on Stone;* Jackson, *Gold Rush Album,* 118 (as Pendergast).

PRENTICE, GEORGE W. Ornamental painter, 37, a native of Rhode Island, living in Philadelphia in 1850 with his wife, a native of Massachusetts, and three children, ages 1 to 6, all born in Pennsylvania. ¶ 7 Census (1850), Pa., LIII, 26.

PRENTISS, ADDISON. Wood engraver of Worcester (Mass.), 1852–60. ¶ Worcester CD 1852–60.

PRENTISS, NATHANIEL SMITH. Engraver [?], of WRIGHT & PRENTISS, xylographic (wood) and copperplate engravers and printers, NYC, 1835–38. Prentiss is listed as a perfumer in NYC directories from 1818 to 1838, but from 1835 to 1838 he seems to have been associated with CHARLES CUSHING WRIGHT in the engraving business. ¶ NYCD 1818–38.

PRENTISS, SARAH J. Flower, figure, and still life painter; born November 29, 1823, at Paris (Me.); died October 21, 1877, at Elmbank (Me.). ¶ Simpson, *Leaflets of Artists.*

PRESCOTT, PLUMER (1833–1881). Portrait painter, born August 4, 1833, at Franklin

(N.H.); working in Buffalo (N.Y.) in 1855; died at Springfield (Ill.) in 1881. ¶ Runnels, *History of Sanbornton, N. H.*, II, 591; Buffalo BD 1855.

PRETLOVE, DAVID. Engraver of cylinders for embossing, NYC, 1846–48. He exhibited at the American Institute in 1846 and 1847. The name appears also as Predlove and Prestlove. ¶ NYCD 1846–48; NYBD 1847–48; Am. Inst. Cat., 1846, 1847.

PREUSS, CHARLES. Artist and map-maker on several early western surveys, including one of FRÉMONT's expeditions. His sketch of Ft. Laramie (Wyo.) and other western scenes are in Frémont's 1845 *Report.* Preuss was living in Washington (D.C.) in 1850 and 1853 and Jessie Benton Frémont stated that he committed suicide near Washington, probably about 1853. ¶ Frémont, *Report;* information courtesy Robert Taft, Lawrence (Kans.); Washington CD 1850, 1853.

PREVOST, VICTOR (1820–?). French lithographer who came to America about 1847/48 and was employed in NYC by SARONY & MAJOR. He later returned to France for further study and there developed a wax film which he used successfully as a photographer in NYC. He also worked as a chemist and a teacher. ¶ Van Nostrand and Coulter, *California Pictorial,* 54; Stokes, *Iconography,* III, 710–11, pl. 142a and 142b; NYBD 1850–51.

PREVOST, WILLIAM S. Artist, 25, a native of New Jersey, at Philadelphia in 1860. ¶ 8 Census (1860), Pa., LV, 56.

PRICE, GEORGE (1826–?). English engraver working in NYC in 1860 and after. ¶ Stauffer; 8 Census (1860), N.Y., XLVII, 311.

PRICE, JOHN. Portrait painter of NYC, exhibitor at the National Academy in 1844. ¶ Cowdrey, NAD.

PRICE, ROBERT. Wood engraver and lithographer, Albany (N.Y.), 1859. ¶ Albany CD 1859.

PRICE, SAMUEL WOODSON (1828–1918). Portrait and figure painter. Born August 5, 1828, at Nicholasville (Ky.), Price studied painting there in 1847 under WILLIAM READING and at Lexington under OLIVER FRAZER. After a brief period of study in NYC he returned to Kentucky and painted portraits there and in Tennessee until the outbreak of the Civil War. He served as Colonel in the Union Army during the war and was wounded at the battle of Kennesaw Mountain; he was brevetted Brigadier General in 1865. After the war he painted portraits for a time in Washington, served as postmaster at Lexington from 1869 to 1876, and continued to paint portraits and figure paintings until he went blind in 1881. He made his home at Louisville from 1878 to 1906, moved to St. Louis, and died there January 22, 1918. In 1902 the Filson Club of Louisville published Price's *Old Masters of the Bluegrass,* containing biographical accounts of Kentucky's painters dictated by the blind artist. ¶ Coleman, "Samuel Woodson Price, Kentucky Portrait Painter," with checklist; information courtesy Mrs. W. H. Whitley, Paris (Ky.).

PRIDHAM, HENRY. House and sign painter, glass stainer, Cincinnati, 1850. This may be the Pridham of WICHER & PRIDHAM, sign, ornamental, and steamboat painters at Cincinnati in 1844. ¶ Cincinnati CD 1850; Knittle, *Early Ohio Taverns.*

PRIEST, FRANCIS I. Sign and ornamental painter at Steubenville (Ohio) in 1830. ¶ Knittle, *Early Ohio Taverns.*

PRIEST, JOSEPH. English artist, 30, at NYC in 1850. His wife and one-year-old son were also born in England. ¶ 7 Census (1850), N.Y., XLVIII, 279.

PRIEST, JOSEPH. Virginia-born artist, 28, at NYC in 1860. ¶ 8 Census (1860), N.Y., LIV, 445.

PRIEST, WILLIAM. Engraver and publisher at Philadelphia, 1794–95. Possibly the same William Priest who advertised in Baltimore in 1796 "paintings in imitation of paper hangings by a mechanical process," as well as "laying plain grounds in distemper, with plain or festoon borders." ¶ Brown and Brown; Little, "Itinerant Painting in America, 1750–1850," 208.

PRIME, H. F. Portrait painter of Hudson (N.Y.) who exhibited at the National Academy in 1839 and 1840. ¶ Cowdrey, NAD.

PRIMUS, NELSON A. (1843–?). Negro portrait and religious painter, born at Hartford (Conn.) in 1843. He was apprenticed to GEORGE FRANCIS in 1858 and received instruction from him and from Mrs. ELIZABETH GILBERT JEROME. In 1864 he moved to Boston and established himself as a portrait and carriage painter. He was still in Boston as late as 1895. ¶ Porter, *Modern Negro Art,* 52–53; French, *Art and Artists in Connecticut,* 155.

PRINCE, LUKE, JR. Portrait painter, Haverhill (Mass.), about 1840. ¶ Lipman and Winchester, 179.

PRINGLE, JAMES FULTON (1788–1847). Marine painter, born January 7, 1788, at Sydenham, Kent (England). He came to America about 1832 and settled in Brooklyn (N.Y.). His work was exhibited at the National Academy and the Apollo Association. He died April 1, 1847. ¶ Information courtesy Miss M. L. Pringle, granddaughter of the artist; Cowdrey, NAD; Cowdrey, AA & AAU; Brooklyn CD 1833–46; *American Processional,* 120 (repro.); *Portfolio* (March 1943), frontis.; *American Collector* (Aug. 1943), frontis.

PRINGLE, JOSEPH. Marine painter, active 1849–1860's. ¶ Peters, "Paintings of the Old 'Wind-Jammer,'" 32.

PRINGLE, WILLIAM. Engraver, 28, a native of New York, at NYC in 1860 with his wife and son Edward (4). ¶ 8 Census (1860), N.Y., LVIII, 812.

PRINGLE, WILLIAM, JR. Journeyman engraver, 26, a native of New York, living in NYC in 1860 with his father William Pringle, Sr., whose property was valued at $35,000. ¶ 8 Census (1860), N.Y., LIX, 284; NYCD 1862.

PRIOR, M. B. According to F. F. Sherman, a native portrait painter who painted likenesses of a Mr. and Mrs. Ford of South Paris (Me.) in 1834. ¶ *Art in America* (March 1935), 82.

PRIOR, W. H. Illustrator of *Our World, or, The Slaveholder's Daughter,* an anti-slavery novel published in NYC in 1855. ¶ Hamilton, *Early American Book Illustrators,* 437.

PRIOR, WILLIAM MATTHEW (1806–1873). Portrait and landscape painter, born May 16, 1806, at Bath (Me.). His earliest known portrait was painted in 1824 at Portland (Me.). He lived in Portland from about 1831 to about 1840, part of the time with his brothers-in-law, the HAMBLENS. By 1841 he was settled in Boston and he maintained a studio there until 1846 and thereafter in East Boston. As an itinerant painter he also visited New Bedford (Mass.), Newport (R.I.) and Baltimore. He made many copies of Stuart's Athenaeum portrait of Washington, painted on glass. In his later years he was assisted by his sons Gilbert and Matthew Prior. He was the author of several religious books. Prior died in Boston in January 1873. ¶ Little, "William Matthew Prior," in Lipman and Winchester, 80–89; Little, "William Matthew Prior, Traveling Artist, and His In-Laws, the Painting Hamblens"; Lyman, "William Matthew Prior, the 'Painting Garret' Artist"; Karolik Cat., 452–55; Sears, *Some American Primitives,* 32–49; 7 Census (1850), Mass., XXIV, 203; Swan, BA; Flexner, *The Light of Distant Skies.*

PRITCHARD, CASPAR. Shade painter, 25, a native of Philadelphia where he was living in 1860. ¶ 8 Census (1860), Pa., LI, 311.

PROBASCO, ——. Reputed to have painted a "portrait" of "Uncle Sam" in 1816. ¶ San Francisco *Chronicle,* May 11, 1902 (citation courtesy Clarence S. Brigham, American Antiquarian Society).

PROBASCO, EDWIN A. Engraver, 21, a native of Pennsylvania, living in Philadelphia in 1860. ¶ 8 Census (1860), Pa., LVI, 563.

PROBST, JOHN. Lithographer, born in Germany about 1805, working in NYC from about 1838 to 1850. In 1844 he was with WILLIS & PROBST. ¶ 7 Census (1850), N.Y., XLIV, 424; NYCD 1844–50.

PROCTOR, JOSEPH. Negro artist, 74, born in Maryland, living in NYC in 1860 with his wife. ¶ 8 Census (1860), N.Y., LI, 166.

PROCTOR, WILLIAM JAMES. Draftsman. In 1814 he executed watercolor drawings of NYC fortifications. ¶ Stokes, *Iconography,* III, 551, and pl. 82a.

PROSPER, ——. Sculptor, marble cutter, engraver, and teacher; at New Orleans in 1825 and 1837. ¶ Delgado-WPA cites *La. Gazette,* June 13, 1825, and New Orleans CD 1837.

PROSPER, HENRI. Portrait painter of NYC, exhibited at the National Academy in 1857 and 1858. ¶ Cowdrey, NAD.

PROTIN & MARCHINO. Sculptors and carvers, NYC, 1850; VICTOR PROTIN and FREDERICK MARCHINO. ¶ NYCD and BD 1850.

PROTIN, VICTOR, see PROTIN & MARCHINO.

PROUDMAN, WILLIAM (1826–?). Engraver. Born in 1826 at Dover (N.H.), he later settled in Manchester (N.H.). He was married in 1849 at Lynn (Mass.). ¶ Belknap, *Artists and Craftsmen of Essex County,* 5.

PROUT, V. A. Painter of "chromatrope views" for a performance of *Uncle Tom's Cabin* at Ordway Hall, Boston, in January 1853. ¶ Boston *Evening Transcript,* Jan. 10, 1853 (citation courtesy J. E. Arrington).

PRUDEN, DANIEL R. Engraver of Boston, 1852–55. ¶ Boston BD and CD 1852–55.

PRUD'HOMME, JOHN FRANCIS EUGENE (1800–1892). N.A. Engraver. Prud'homme was born October 4, 1800, on the island of St. Thomas in the West Indies and was brought to NYC by his parents in 1807. About 1814 he was apprenticed to his brother-in-law, the engraver THOMAS GIMBREDE. By 1821 he was engraving under his own name and until 1852 he was a popular engraver of portraits and illustrations for books and periodicals. Elected an Associate of the National Academy in 1838 and an Academician in 1846, Prud'homme served as Curator of the Academy from 1845 to 1853. From 1852 to 1869 he was designer and engraver for a NYC banknote firm and from 1869 until his retirement in 1885 he was employed in the same capacity by the Bureau of Engraving and Printing in Washington (D.C.). He died June 22, 1892, in Georgetown (D.C.). ¶ DAB; NYCD 1819–52; Cowdrey, NAD; Cowdrey, AA & AAU; Stauffer; Hamilton, *Early American Book Illustrators,* 233; Cummings, *Historic Annals.*

PRURNACKÉ, CHARLES. Artist at New Orleans in 1838. ¶ New Orleans CD 1838.

PRYOR, GEORGE. English engraver, 26, living in Frankford, near Philadelphia, in 1850; his wife and infant son were born in Pennsylvania. ¶ 7 Census (1850), Pa., LVI, 302.

PUDOR, H. Family group portraits in oil, Lawville (N.Y.), about 1860. ¶ Lipman and Winchester, 179.

PUGNI, LOUIS. Italian artist, 33, at Washington (D.C.) in 1860. In 1862 he was listed as a grocer. ¶ 8 Census (1860), D.C., I, 703.

PUNDERSON, E. M. Exhibited monochromatic paintings ("Fancy Piece" and "Scene on the Ohio") at the Maryland Historical Society in 1850. ¶ Rutledge, MHS.

PUNDERSON, LEMUEL S. Engraver working in NYC during the early 1850's and thereafter in New Haven (Conn.). ¶ Stauffer; New England BD 1856–60; New Haven CD 1859.

PURCELL, EDWARD B. Painter, wood engraver, and designer of NYC and Brooklyn, 1835–70. He exhibited religious, historical, landscape, and genre paintings at the National Academy between 1835 and 1844 but during the fifties and sixties was primarily a designer and engraver on wood. He also published several art textbooks. This may be the miniaturist Edward Purcell who exhibited in Dublin (Ireland) in 1812 and 1815 and returned to Dublin from England in 1831 as a professor of drawing; nothing is known of his subsequent career. ¶ NYCD 1835–70; Cowdrey, NAD; Stokes, *Historical Prints;* Drepperd, "American Drawing Books"; Am. Inst. Cat., 1842, 1844, 1845; Hamilton, *Early American Book Illustrators,* 438; Strickland, *Dictionary of Irish Artists.*

PURCELL, EDWARD B., JR. Exhibitor of "Hector Dragged by Achilles Round the Walls of Troy," National Academy, 1836. His address in NYC was the same as that of EDWARD B. PURCELL, presumably his father. ¶ Cowdrey, NAD.

PURCELL, HENRY. Engraver who advertised in NYC in 1774 and 1775. In 1783–84 he was advertising in Philadelphia as Henry D. Pursell. These two are presumed to be the same man. ¶ Gottesman, *Arts and Crafts in New York,* I, 13; Kelby, *Notes on American Artists,* 12–13; Prime, I, 27.

PURCELL, ROSANNA. Landscape or genre painter at the same address as EDWARD B. PURCELL in 1836 when she exhibited at the National Academy. ¶ Cowdrey, NAD.

PURDIN, WILLIAM A. Artist of NYC who painted Olin's "Grand Moving Panorama of the Laying of the Atlantic Cable," 1858. ¶ Indianapolis, *Indiana State Sentinel,* Oct. 4, 1858 (courtesy J. Earl Arrington).

PURDY, ALBERT J. (*c.* 1835–1909). Portrait painter who died August 5, 1909, at Ithaca (N.Y.). ¶ *Art Annual,* VII, obit.

PURRINGTON, CALEB P. Panoramist? He appears to have collaborated with BENJAMIN RUSSELL on a panorama of a whaling voyage, shown in Boston in 1849, and subsequently, without mention of Purrington, at NYC and Cincinnati. ¶ Boston *Evening Transcript,* Jan. 3, 1849; information courtesy J. E. Arrington.

PURRINGTON, HENRY J. (1825–?). Ship carver, born at Mattapoisett (Mass.) and employed at New Bedford (Mass.) from 1848 to 1900. He was also a musician and amateur actor. He was still living in the 1920's. ¶ Pinckney, *American Figureheads and Their Carvers,* 147–50, pl. 28.

PURRINGTON (or Purinton), J. Miniaturist of NYC who advertised at Salem (Mass.) in 1802. He was listed in NYC in 1807. At Salem he was apparently associated with WILLIAM VERSTILLE. ¶ Belknap, *Artists and Craftsmen of Essex County,* 12; NYCD 1807; Felt, *Annals of Salem,* II, 79; Bolton, *Miniature Painters.*

PURSELL, HENRY D., see HENRY PURCELL.

PUTNAM, DAVID A. (*c.* 1816–1840). Portrait painter who died at Pernambuco (Brazil) on April 10, 1840. He was an adopted son of David Putnam of Salem (Mass.). ¶ Belknap, *Artists and Craftsmen of Essex County,* 12.

PUTNAM, EDMUND. Engraver, born in Massachusetts about 1800, active in Boston from about 1843 to 1860. ¶ 8 Census (1860), Mass., XXVI, 639; Boston CD 1843–60.

PUTNAM, GEORGE W. (*c.* 1812–?). Portrait painter, son of Joseph and Mary Putnam of Salem (Mass.). He exhibited at the Boston Athenaeum in 1841 and at the time of his marriage in 1844 was a resident of Nashua (N.H.). ¶ Belknap, *Artists and Craftsmen of Essex County,* 12; Swan, BA.

PYNE, R. L. or R. S. Landscape painter of NYC, 1856–60. He exhibited views of the Catskills and Berkshires of New York and Massachusetts at the National Academy. ¶ Cowdrey, NAD; NYBD 1859–60.

Q

Quarré, Frederick or Ferdinand. Steel and aquatint engraver. He was working in NYC as early as 1839 as an engraver for *Godey's Lady's Book* and other fashion magazines and in 1842 he edited and published his own magazine, *Artist*. He subsequently moved to Philadelphia where he was active as an engraver and lampshade maker until about 1849. His decorated shades were exhibited at the Franklin Institute in 1849. Quarré's most distinctive productions were flower aquatints embellished with engraved white lace, in the manner of the later valentine. ¶ Waite, "Pioneer Color Printer: F. Quarré."

Quartley, Arthur (1839–1886). N.A. Marine painter. Arthur, son of Frederick William Quartley, was born in Paris on May 24, 1839, and spent his childhood in France and England. In 1851 his mother died and shortly thereafter he was taken to America by his father, who settled in Peekskill (N.Y.) and found employment as an engraver. Arthur was apprenticed to a sign-painter in NYC and from 1862 to 1875 he was associated with the decorating firm Emmart & Quartley of Baltimore. In the meantime he had begun to paint marines and in 1875 he moved to NYC and opened a studio there. His summers were spent on the Isle of Shoals, off the coast of New Hampshire. He was elected an Associate of the National Academy in 1879 and an Academician in 1886. His promising career was cut short by his death in NYC on May 19, 1886, soon after his return from a year's visit to Europe. ¶ DAB; CAB; Clement and Hutton; represented at Peabody Institute.

Quartley, Frederick William (1808–1874). Engraver and landscape painter. Born July 5, 1808, at Bath (England), he took up wood engraving at the age of 16 and studied in Wales and Paris. After the death of his wife in 1851 he emigrated to America with his son, Arthur Quartley, and settled at Peekskill (N.Y.). He was a popular engraver for several publishers, his best known work being the illustrations for *Picturesque America* (1872) and *Picturesque Europe* (1875). He died in NYC on April 5, 1874. ¶ CAB; Clement and Hutton; Hamilton, *Early American Book Illustrators.*

Quaw, John C. Portrait painter at Albany (N.Y.) in 1852. ¶ Troy and Albany BD 1852.

Queby (or Quely), John. Sculptor, 42, a native of Florida, at NYC in 1850. ¶ 7 Census (1850), N.Y., XLIII, 22.

Queen, James (1824–*c.* 1877). Lithographer. A native of Philadelphia, Queen learned lithography under Wagner & McGuigan and did much work for P. S. Duval. A number of the illustrations for the *U. S. Military Magazine* (1840–42) were drawn and lithographed by him. ¶ Peters, *America on Stone;* Todd, "Huddy & Duval Prints"; Stokes, *Historical Prints; American Collector* (June 1942), 14 (repro.); Perry, *Expedition to Japan;* 7 Census (1850), Pa., LV, 194.

Quesenbury, William (1822–1888). Portrait and topographical painter, cartoonist. Quesenbury (pronounced Cushenbury) was a life-long resident of Fayetteville (Ark.). He was well known throughout the state as an editor of the *Arkansian* to which he also contributed cartoons under the name of "Bill Cush." A number of his portraits and views of Fayetteville buildings are still in existence. ¶ WPA Guide, *Arkansas*, 313.

Quesnay, Alexandre-Marie (1755–1820). Teacher of painting and drawing. Born November 23, 1755, at Saint-Germain-en-Viry (France), Quesnay was of noble birth and as a young man entered the *Gendarmes de la Garde du Roi.* In April 1777 he arrived in Virginia to assist the Continental Army, but in the fall of 1778 he had to retire because of ill health. He spent the next two years in Gloucester County (Va.) at the home of John Peyton. In 1780 he went to Philadelphia and conducted a school there for four years. In 1784 he moved to NYC where he advertised as a teacher of French, drawing, and dancing. In 1785 he returned to Virginia, opened a school in Richmond, and conceived the plan of an Academy of Arts and Sciences to be established there with branches in other American cities. He went back to France in 1786 to promote this project but his efforts were without positive results. Quesnay spent the remainder of his life in France, except for a brief exile during the French Revolution, and he died at Saint Maurice (Seine) on February 8, 1820. ¶ DAB; Kelby, *Notes on American Artists,* 18–24.

QUICK, H. B. Engraver at New Orleans in 1856. ¶ Delgado-WPA cites New Orleans CD 1856.

QUICK, ISAAC. Painter of a portrait of Jacob Throckmorton owned in 1940 by Verdi Throckmorton of Watchung (N.J.). ¶ WPA (N.J.), Historical Records Survey.

QUICK, ISRAEL. Portrait painter, 16, born in New York and living in NYC in 1850. He exhibited in Cincinnati in 1866. ¶ 7 Census (1850), N.Y., L, 381; information courtesy Edward H. Dwight, Cincinnati Art Museum.

QUICK, WILLIAM. Wood engraver, 17, born in New York and living in NYC in 1860. ¶ 8 Census (1860), N.Y., XLVIII, 1063.

QUIDOR, GEORGE W. Engraver and music publisher, born in New York about 1817, working in NYC in the early 1850's. ¶ 7 Census (1850), N.Y., LV, 891; NYBD 1854; Peters, *America on Stone.*

QUIDOR, JOHN (1801–1881). Figure painter, particularly of scenes from Cooper and Irving. Born January 26, 1801, at Tappan (N.Y.), Quidor grew up there and in NYC. He studied under JOHN WESLEY JARVIS for a short time. His career as an artist, extending from the mid-twenties into the 1860's, was not a very successful one; Quidor's romantic treatment of his literary themes did not meet the taste of the times, though he is today ranked high among his contemporaries. Except for a brief residence in Quincy (Ill.) during the mid-forties, he spent his career in NYC. In 1868 he retired to his daughter's home in Jersey City, where he died December 13, 1881. ¶ Baur, *John Quidor,* is the standard account of the artist; it contains also many illustrations and a catalogue of his work. See also: Cowdrey, NAD; Cowdrey, AA & AAU; Rutledge, PA; Swan, BA; 7 Census (1850), N.Y., L, 653.

QUILLIAM, J. Engraver, New Orleans, 1859. ¶ Delgado-WPA cites New Orleans CD 1859.

QUINER, JOANNA (1801–1873). Portrait sculptor of Beverly (Mass.). She exhibited at the Boston Athenaeum in 1846–48. ¶ Swan, BA.

QUINT, LOUIS H. Engraver, 26, from Maine, at Philadelphia in 1850 with his wife, also from Maine, and infant son, Silas H., born in Pennsylvania. ¶ 7 Census (1850), Pa., LI, 836.

QUINTIN, D. S. Lithographer, pupil of A. HOFFY at Philadelphia about 1841. ¶ Peters, *America on Stone.*

QUINTON, ——. Miniaturist, reputed to have painted a Mrs. Burroughs, aged 92, in 1804. ¶ Sherman, "Some Recently Discovered Early American Portrait Miniaturists," 294.

QUIROT, ——. Lithographer of San Francisco in the early 1850's. He was with JUSTH, QUIROT & Co. in 1851 and from 1851 to 1853 had his own company. ¶ Peters, *California on Stone.*

R

Raab, Ferdinand. Portrait painter, NYC, 1850–62. This may be the Frederick Raab who exhibited "The Shepherd Boy" at the American Art-Union in 1849. ¶ NYCD 1850–62; Cowdrey, AA & AAU; represented in the collection of Mrs. Wendell P. Colton, NYC.

Raab, Francis. Lithographer, born in Germany about 1813, living in NYC 1848–54. ¶ 7 Census (1850), N.Y., XLIV, 251; NYBD 1848–54.

Rabbeth, James, Jr. (1824–*c.* 1858). Painter of a view of Curtisville, now Naubuc, part of Glastonbury (Conn.), *c.* 1855. Rabbeth was a native of London (England). He died soon after his marriage in 1858 at Glastonbury. ¶ Conn. Hist. Soc. *Bulletin* (April 1947), 12–13.

Rabillon, Léonce (1814–1886). Sculptor of Baltimore (Md.). For many years a teacher of modern languages at Baltimore, Rabillon executed two portrait busts for the Peabody Institute in the early seventies. ¶ Peabody Institute Cat. (1949), 3; Baltimore CD 1856+.

Rabineau, Francis. Miniaturist, crayon portraitist, and job painter at NYC in 1791–92 and at Newark and New Brunswick (N.J.) in 1795–96. In 1795 he also painted standards and colors for the New Jersey militia regiments. ¶ NYCD 1791–92; Gottesman, II, nos. 36–37; Prime, II, 32; *The Guardian, or New Brunswick Advertiser,* May 19, 1795 (courtesy Donald A. Sinclair, Rutgers Univ. Library); *American Collector,* Aug. 23, 1934, 5.

Rabuski, Theodore. Portrait, landscape, and decorative painter, drawing teacher, painter on glass, and lithographer. A native of Posen (Poland), Rabuski studied under C. W. Wach in Berlin and was for a time professor of drawing at the Military Academy of Posen, according to his advertisement. He turned up in Charleston (S.C.) in 1848–49 and again in 1853 as an artist in varied media and in 1856 he was working in NYC as a lithographer and publisher of prints. ¶ Thieme-Becker; Rutledge, *Artists in the Life of Charleston;* Peters, *America on Stone;* Hamilton, *Early American Book Illustrators; Portfolio* (March 1948), 160 (repro.).

Radbourne, William H. (1838–1914). Painter; born September 11, 1838, in Brooklyn (N.Y.); lived in Brooklyn until 1905; died July 23, 1914, at Orleans (N.Y.). ¶ *Art Annual,* XI, obit.

Radcliffe, Charles (*c.* 1777–1807). Portrait and vignette engraver. He was working at Philadelphia in 1805 and was buried April 9, 1807, at Salem (Mass.). He claimed to be the son of the English novelist, Mrs. Ann Radcliffe. ¶ Belknap, *Artists and Craftsmen of Essex County,* 5; Stauffer.

Radcliffe, T. B. Still life painter of Philadelphia who exhibited at the Pennsylvania Academy in 1849. ¶ Rutledge, PA.

Radden, Thomas M. Lithographer, 19, a native of Massachusetts and living in Boston in 1850. ¶ 7 Census (1850), Mass., XXV, 415.

Ragusa, Signor ——. Italian artist who exhibited at Mobile (Ala.) in 1844 sixteen European views. ¶ Mobile *Register and Journal,* Nov. 26–Dec. 25, 1844 (courtesy J. Earl Arrington).

Rain or Raen, Isaac. Artist, 34, born in Pennsylvania, living in Philadelphia in 1850 with his wife and six children. ¶ 7 Census (1850), Pa., LIV, 780.

Rainsford, Miss ——. Landscape artist of NYC who exhibited at the National Academy in 1843 and 1844 several English views and pencil drawings. The Misses Rainsford, one of them named Lydia, kept a school for young ladies in NYC at that time. ¶ Cowdrey, NAD; NYCD 1842–54.

Ralph, John A. Engraver, 52, born in England, living in NYC in 1850 with his wife and two children born in England before about 1833. ¶ 7 Census (1850), N.Y., LVI, 4.

Ralph, W. Engraver of Philadelphia, active 1794–1808. ¶ Stauffer.

Ralston, George Washington (1819–1843). Portrait painter whose early years were spent at Strasburg, Lancaster County (Pa.) and who later lived at Columbia (Pa.). ¶ Letter of Jack Willson to FARL, Dec. 8, 1946.

Ralston, Robert. Engraver, Providence (R.I.), 1856. He was with Wood & Ralston, engravers to calico printers. ¶ Providence CD 1856.

Ramage, John (*c.* 1748–1802). Miniaturist. A native of Ireland, Ramage entered the

Dublin School of Artists in 1763. When he left Ireland is not known. He was a resident of Halifax (N.S.) in 1772 and 1774 and he was known as a miniaturist in Boston before the Revolution. A Loyalist, he left Boston in April 1776 and returned to Halifax. From there he moved, probably in 1777, to NYC where he remained until 1794 and enjoyed considerable success as a miniaturist. Financial difficulties forced him in 1794, however, to flee to Montreal where he spent his remaining years. He died there October 24, 1802. ¶ Morgan, *A Sketch of the Life of John Ramage, Miniature Painter;* Morgan and Fielding, *Life Portraits of Washington,* 139–42.

RAMÉE, JOSEPH JACQUES (1764–1842). Architect and landscape architect. Born April 18, 1764, at Charlemont (France), Ramée was trained as an architect in France. He came to America in 1811, worked in Philadelphia and Baltimore, and designed Union College and its grounds at Schenectady (N.Y.), and then returned to Europe. After working in Belgium and Germany he settled in Paris in 1823. He died at Beaurains, near Noyons, on May 18, 1842. While in America he exhibited architectural drawings at the Society of Artists in Philadelphia (1814). ¶ DAB; Rutledge, PA; *Architectural Review* (Feb. 1947), 57–62.

RAMSAY, DAVID. Engraver, NYC, 1854. ¶ NYBD 1854.

RAMSEY, Miss RACHEL. Amateur painter of Albany (N.Y.), aged 17, who exhibited a volume of paintings of flowers and other subjects at the American Institute in 1849. ¶ Am. Inst. Cat., 1849.

RANCON, VICTOR. Artist at New Orleans in 1824. ¶ Delgado-WPA cites New Orleans CD 1824.

RAND, F. Portrait painter of Boston who exhibited at the Athenaeum in 1829. This may have been JOHN GOFFE RAND who was in Boston at this time. ¶ Boston Athen. Cat., 1829.

RAND, JOHN GOFFE (1801–1873). A.N.A. Portrait painter. Rand was born in Bedford (N.H.) and was apprenticed to a furniture painter. He took up portraiture about 1825 and received some instruction from SAMUEL F. B. MORSE, then working in the vicinity of Manchester (N.H.). Rand then went to Boston where he exhibited at the Athenaeum in 1828 and 1829. In March and April 1831 he was at Charleston (S.C.). He moved to NYC about 1833, exhibited several works at the National Academy and was made an Associate Member in the same year. The following year he went abroad, settled in London for a number of years, exhibited at least once at the Royal Academy (1840), and there developed the screw-top compressible paint tube. Rand was back in NYC in 1840, but appears to have made a second visit to England in the forties. He returned to NYC about 1848 and established himself as a portrait painter. His home was at Roslyn, Long Island, where he died January 21, 1873. ¶ "Art and Artists in Manchester," 110–11; Swan, BA; Cowdrey, NAD; NYBD 1840, 1851; Rutledge, *Artists in the Life of Charleston; cf.* Lipman and Winchester, 179; Barber, "Deaths Taken from the N. Y. Evening Post."

RANDALL, GEORGE. Scene painter for *Uncle Tom's Cabin,* presented at Ordway Hall, Boston, in January 1853. ¶ Boston *Evening Transcript,* Jan. 10, 1853 (citation courtesy J. E. Arrington).

RANDELL, ABRAHAM R. Wood engraver of NYC, 1844–58; he was born in New York State about 1822. ¶ 7 Census (1850), N.Y., XLV, 43; NYBD 1844, 1858.

RANDELL or RANDEL, ELIAS, JR. Engraver, 22, a native of New York State, at NYC in 1850. ¶ 7 Census (1850), N.Y., L, 753 [as Randell]; NYCD 1850 lists an Elias Randel without occupation, possibly the engraver's father.

RANDOLPH, EDWARD WASHBURN. Painter of a portrait in oils, dated 1855, owned in 1941 by Mrs. Freda Lodd Smith of Barre (Vt.). ¶ WPA (Mass.), *Portraits Found in Vt.*

RANDOLPH, INNES (1837–1887). Portrait sculptor; born October 25, 1837; died April 28, 1887. He was a resident of Baltimore and about 1873 modelled a bust of George Peabody, founder of the Peabody Institute. ¶ Randolph, *The Randolphs of Virginia,* 25; Peabody Institute Cat. (1949).

RANDOLPH, JAMES THOMPSON (1817–1874). Wood carver and portrait sculptor. A native of Bound Brook (N.J.), he spent most of his life in Baltimore. In 1839 he was with the firm of HAROLD & RANDOLPH, ship carvers, and from 1853 to 1860 he headed the firm of RANDOLPH & SEWARD. Randolph executed a bust of John T. Randolph in 1858 and the McDonough Monument in Greenmount Cemetery in 1865. ¶ Gardner, *Yankee*

Stonecutters, 70; Pinckney, *American Figureheads,* 120–21, 199; Baltimore CD 1842–60.

RANDOLPH, JOSEPH FITZ, see WHITE & RANDOLPH.

RANDOLPH & SEWARD. Ship carvers, Baltimore, 1853–60; JAMES T. RANDOLPH and WILLIAM E. SEWARD. ¶ Pinckney, *American Figureheads,* 121, 199; Baltimore CD 1853–60.

RANNEY, WILLIAM TYLEE (1813–1857). A.N.A. Historical, genre, and portrait painter. Born May 9, 1813, at Middletown (Conn.), Ranney spent his childhood there but at the age of 13 was apprenticed to a tinsmith in Fayetteville (N.C.). By 1833 he was in Brooklyn (N.Y.) studying drawing and he had a portrait studio in NYC from 1843 to 1847. After seeing service in the Southwest during the Mexican War, Ranney married and settled in West Hoboken (N.J.). During the last eight years of his life he devoted himself chiefly to historical paintings and western scenes. He died November 18, 1857. ¶ DAB; Cowdrey, NAD; Cowdrey, AA & AAU; NYCD 1843; NYBD 1844–50; Rutledge, PA; Rutledge, MHS; Karolik Cat., 462–64; *Crayon,* V (1858), 26, obit. A study of Ranney's life and work is being made by his grandson, Claude J. Ranney, of Malvern (Pa.).

RANSOM, ALEXANDER. Portrait painter. He was working in Boston and Lowell (Mass.) in the 1840's, in London in 1850, in Boston in 1851–52, in NYC from 1853 to 1855, and again in Boston from 1856 at least until 1865. He exhibited at the National Academy, the Boston Athenaeum, and the Pennsylvania Academy. ¶ Swan, BA; Boston BD 1844–46, 1851–52, 1857–60; Lowell *Courier,* April 23, 1845, Jan. 3 or 31, 1850 (citations courtesy C. C. Leach); Lowell BD 1848; Cowdrey, NAD; Rutledge, PA.

RANSOM, CAROLINE L. ORMES (1838–1910). Portrait and landscape painter, born in Newark (Ohio). A graduate of Oberlin College and for several years a member of its faculty, Miss Ransom studied in NYC under DURAND and HUNTINGTON and in Munich under Kaulbach. In 1858–60 she was at Sandusky (Ohio) and later she had studios in Cleveland and NYC. She finally settled in Washington (D.C.) where she had a studio for many years. She was a founder of the Daughters of the American Revolution and of the Classical Club of Washington. Several of her portraits are in the U. S. Capitol. Miss Ransom died in Washington on February 12, 1910. ¶ Fairman, *Art and Artists of the Capitol,* 251; Cowdrey, NAD; Sandusky CD 1858; *Museum Echoes* (March 1951), cover.

RANSOM, LOUIS LISCOLM (1831–1926/27). Portrait, historical, and religious painter, born January 23, 1831, at Salisbury Corners (N.Y.). He studied under HENRY PETERS GRAY of NYC in 1851 and during the late 1850's and early 1860's worked chiefly in Utica, Rome, Lansingburg, and other up-state New York towns. In 1884 he was at Akron (Ohio) and he died in Cuyahoga Falls (Ohio). He is best known for his "John Brown on His Way to the Scaffold." ¶ Information courtesy Mr. Fordan Ransom of Washingtonville (N.Y.), son of the artist; Fletcher, "Ransom's John Brown Painting"; Rome CD 1859.

RAOUL, LOUIS. Miniaturist, physician, and author at Charleston (S.C.) in 1816. ¶ Carolina Art Assoc. Cat. (1935).

RAPER, B. W. Xylographic (wood) engraver, NYC, 1841. ¶ NYBD 1841.

RAPPÉ, MARY. Schoolgirl painter in watercolors, aged 14, of eastern Ohio about 1790. ¶ Lipman and Winchester, 179.

RASMUSSEN, NILS. Landscape painter, of KLEINOFEN & RASMUSSEN, Chicago, 1859. ¶ Chicago CD 1859.

RASSAU, J. H. First lithographer of Charleston (S.C.), 1845. ¶ Rutledge, *Artists in the Life of Charleston,* 167 and fig. 43.

RASZENSKI OR RASZEWSKI, ALEXANDRE. Miniaturist at NYC, 1853–54; exhibited at the National Academy. ¶ Cowdrey, NAD; NYBD 1854.

RATELLIER, FRANCIS. Lithographer, NYC, 1859. ¶ NYBD 1859.

RATHBUN, D. R. Portrait painter at Berlin (N.Y.) in 1859. ¶ N. Y. State BD 1859.

RAU, JACOB. Engraver, born in Holstein about 1821, living in NYC from about 1851. Until 1858 he was listed as a printer. ¶ 8 Census (1860), N.Y., LI, 285; NYCD 1851–60; NYBD 1859.

RAUCH, WILLIAM. Artist, 43, a native of Bavaria, at NYC in 1860 with his wife and three children, the oldest 6 years, all born in New York. ¶ 8 Census (1860), N.Y., LVII, 206.

RAUSCHNER, HENRY. Wax miniaturist "from the northward" who advertised in Charleston (S.C.) in November 1810 and April 1811. This may have been JOHN CHRISTIAN RAUSCHNER who was working in

Massachusetts and Pennsylvania in these years and is known to have traveled as far south as Virginia making wax portraits. ¶ Rutledge, *Artists in the Life of Charleston,* 128, 216.

RAUSCHNER, JOHN CHRISTIAN (1760–?). Wax portraitist, born in Frankfurt (Germany), the son of Christian Benjamin Rauschner, modeler and stucco worker. His name, originally Johann Christoph, became John Christian in America, and possibly even Henry (see HENRY RAUSCHNER). Although Rauschner maintained a NYC address from 1799 to 1808, he traveled widely in his search for sitters from Massachusetts south to Virginia and possibly South Carolina. He was certainly at Philadelphia in 1801 and again in 1810–11 and at Boston and Salem in 1809–10. Nothing is heard of him after 1811. ¶ Bolton, *American Wax Portraits,* 24–29, 46–60 (checklist); NYCD 1799–1808; notes by Homer Eaton Keyes in *Antiques* (Sept. 1936), 100, and (1937), 186–87; Brown and Brown [as Rawschnor]; represented at Essex Institute, NYHS, Am. Antiq. Soc., and Md. Hist. Soc.

RAVELLI, Father. Carver and painter whose work is found in St. Mary's Mission at Stephensville (Mont.). He was active about 1850. ¶ WPA Guide, *Montana.*

RAW, JACOB, is JACOB RAU.

RAWDON, CLARK & COMPANY. Engravers of Albany (N.Y.), 1826–34; RALPH RAWDON and ASAHEL CLARK. This was the immediate predecessor in Albany of the important banknote engraving company, RAWDON, WRIGHT, HATCH & EDSON, of which Rawdon was a founder. ¶ Albany CD 1826–34.

RAWDON, FREEMAN (*c.* 1801–1859). Engraver, brother of RALPH RAWDON. A native of Tolland (Conn.) according to Stauffer or of Pennsylvania according to the 1850 Census, Freeman Rawdon was active as an engraver and businessman in NYC from 1833 to 1859. During most of this time he was connected with the firm of RAWDON, WRIGHT & HATCH [& EDSON after 1847]. He died in NYC September 21, 1859, aged 58 years. He was the father of HENRY M. RAWDON. ¶ NYCD 1833–60; N. Y. *Evening Post,* Sept. 22, 1859, obit. (cited in Barber, "Deaths Taken from the N. Y. Evening Post"); Stauffer; 7 Census (1850), N.Y., LV, 434.

RAWDON, HENRY M. Engraver, 17, born in NYC, at NYC in 1850. He was a son of FREEMAN RAWDON. He was listed in 1863 and 1865 as a clerk. ¶ 7 Census (1850), N.Y., LV, 434; NYCD 1863, 1865.

RAWDON, RALPH. Engraver, brother of FREEMAN RAWDON. A native of Tolland (Conn.) according to Bowditch, Ralph Rawdon was associated with THOMAS KENSETT at Cheshire (Conn.) as early as 1813 and in 1816 was working with ASAPH WILLARD at Albany (N.Y.). In 1822 he was a partner in BALCH, RAWDON & Co. at Albany and from 1826 to 1834 he headed the firm of RAWDON, CLARK & Co., also at Albany. In 1828 he founded the NYC firm of RAWDON, WRIGHT & Co., but he apparently did not locate permanently in the city until 1835. For the next three years he was in mercantile business with Warren S. Kellogg, but by 1841 he had rejoined his brother FREEMAN in RAWDON, WRIGHT & HATCH, with which firm and its successor, RAWDON, WRIGHT, HATCH & EDSON, he remained until its merger with the AMERICAN BANK NOTE COMPANY in 1858. Rawdon continued his career as an engraver and made his home in Brooklyn at least until 1877. ¶ Stauffer; Grolier Club, *The United States Navy, 1776–1815,* 82; Bowditch, notes on American engravers of coats of arms; Albany CD 1816–34; NYCD 1828–32, 1835–46, 1850–55, 1857–62, 1864–66; Brooklyn CD 1860–77.

RAWDON, WRIGHT & COMPANY. Engravers, NYC, 1828–31; RALPH RAWDON and NEZIAH WRIGHT. Forerunner of the following. ¶ NYCD 1828–31.

RAWDON, WRIGHT & HATCH [& COMPANY]. Banknote engravers, NYC, 1832–34, 1836–46; RALPH and FREEMAN RAWDON, NEZIAH WRIGHT, and GEORGE W. HATCH. In 1835 and after 1847 this firm was known as RAWDON, WRIGHT, HATCH & EDSON. There was a branch at Albany in 1835 and at Boston from 1843 to 1847. The company exhibited specimens of banknote engraving at the American Academy in 1833. ¶ NYCD 1832–46; Albany CD 1835; Boston CD 1843–47; Cowdrey, AA & AAU.

RAWDON, WRIGHT, HATCH & EDSON. Banknote engravers, NYC, 1835, 1847–58; FREEMAN and, after 1850, RALPH RAWDON, NEZIAH WRIGHT, GEORGE W. HATCH, and TRACY R. EDSON. The firm had branches at Albany, Boston, Cincinnati, and New Orleans. In 1858 it was merged with the newly-formed AMERICAN BANK NOTE COMPANY. ¶ NYCD 1835, 1847–58; Albany CD 1835; Boston CD 1848–49; Cincinnati BD 1850–59; New Orleans BD 1859; Toppan, *100 Years of Bank Note Engraving,* 12.

RAWDON, WRIGHT, HATCH & SMILLIE. Banknote engravers, NYC, 1842; RAWDON, WRIGHT & HATCH plus JAMES SMILLIE. ¶ NYCD 1842.

RAWDON-HASTINGS, FRANCIS (1754–1826), 1st Marquis of Hastings and 2nd Earl of Moira. Born in England on December 9, 1754, Rawdon, as he was then known, came to America as a lieutenant of foot in 1773 and saw service during most of the American Revolution. Several watercolors from his own collection, later dispersed, are believed to be his work; they portray scenes of the Revolution around NYC. After his return to England in 1781 he served in Parliament, both in England and Ireland; rose to the rank of general; served as commander-in-chief of the forces in Scotland; and climaxed his career by his ten years (1813–1823) as Governor-General of India. Lord Hastings died at sea off Naples on November 28, 1826. ¶ DNB; Stokes, *Iconography,* I, 362–63, pl. 49.

RAWLINGS, HENRY. Die sinker, 30, from England, at Philadelphia in 1860. LEWIS TOMKINS, lithographer, lived in the same house. ¶ 8 Census (1860), Pa., LII, 252.

RAWSCHNOR, is RAUSCHNER.

RAWSON, ALBERT LEIGHTON (1829–1902). Landscape painter and engraver, author, and philologist. Born October 15, 1829, at Chester (Vt.), Rawson traveled extensively in the United States, Latin America, and the Orient. He exhibited at the National Academy in 1858, his address then being Weedsport (N.Y.). He died in NYC in November 1902. ¶ *Art Annual,* IV, obit.; Cowdrey, NAD.

RAWSON, E. M. Engraver, die sinker, and stencil cutter at Troy (N.Y.) in 1859. ¶ Troy CD 1859.

RAWSON, ELEANOR. Genre scenes in watercolor, Vermont, about 1820. ¶ Lipman and Winchester, 179.

RAWSTORNE, EDWARD or EDWIN. Landscape painter of NYC, 1858–60; exhibited at the National Academy. ¶ NYBD 1858; Cowdrey, NAD.

RAYMOND, GEORGE H. Lithographer, 25, a native New Yorker, at NYC in 1850. ¶ 7 Census (1850), N.Y., XLVIII, 433.

RAYNER, ROBERT J. Portrait and landscape painter, engraver, and lithographer of NYC, 1844–1856 and Newark (N.J.), 1859. He was born in England about 1818. In 1848 he was listed with THOMAS W. RAYNER, as a lithographer. ¶ 7 Census (1850), N.Y., LII, 433 [as engraver]; NYBD 1844–50; NYCD 1856; Essex, Hudson & Union Counties BD 1859; Cowdrey, NAD; Stokes, *Historical Prints,* pl. 71b.

RAYNER, THOMAS W. Lithographer with ROBERT J. RAYNER at NYC in 1848. ¶ NYCD and BD 1848.

REA, DANIEL, JR. (1743–?). Painter at Boston from about 1768 to 1803, brother-in-law and partner of JOHN JOHNSTON. He was chiefly a house, ship, and sign painter, but may also have done some portrait work. He learned his trade in the shop of his father-in-law THOMAS JOHNSTON. ¶ Coburn, "The Johnstons of Boston," Part II, 132–36; Boston CD 1789.

READ & BROTHER. Engravers, NYC, 1848; JAMES A. and DONALD F. READ. ¶ NYBD and CD 1848; Hamilton, *Early American Book Illustrators,* 295–96; J. A. and D. F. Read, *Journey to the Gold-Diggins by Jeremiah Saddlebags.*

READ, DONALD F. Wood engraver, artist, working in NYC between 1845 and 1860. He and his brother JAMES A. READ worked together as illustrators for a number of magazines, especially *Yankee Doodle,* but they are remembered principally for their comic *Journey to the Gold-Diggins by Jeremiah Saddlebags* (1849), republished in facsimile in 1950 with an introduction by Joseph Henry Jackson. ¶ J. A. and D. F. Read, *op. cit.;* Am. Inst. Cat., 1845–47; NYCD 1848, 1851–52.

READ, GEORGE. Irish engraver, 50, at New Haven (Conn.) in September 1850. Of his six sons, the eldest (19) was born in New York, the second (17) in Ireland, and the rest (13 to 1) in Connecticut. ¶ 7 Census (1850), Conn., VIII, 398.

READ, JAMES ALEXANDER. Wood engraver, artist, working in NYC between 1845 and 1860. With his brother DONALD F. READ James did engraving and illustrating for several magazines, especially *Yankee Doodle,* but he is best known for the comic *Journey to the Gold-Diggins by Jeremiah Saddlebags* (1849), illustrated by the brothers Read. ¶ J. A. and D. F. Read, *op. cit.;* NYCD 1845–49; Am. Inst. Cat., 1847.

READ, JAMES B. Portrait painter, artist, born in Pennsylvania about 1803. He was at NYC in 1849–50 and at Philadelphia from 1859 at least until 1870. ¶ 7 Census (1850), N.Y., XLVIII, 302; NYCD 1849–50; Phila. CD 1859–70.

READ or REID, JOHN. Engraver, NYC, 1855–56. ¶ NYCD 1855–56.

READ, NICHOLAS. Engraver, born in Pennsylvania about 1841, working in Philadelphia in 1860 and 1871. ¶ 8 Census (1860), Pa., LIX, 493.

READ, THOMAS BUCHANAN (1822–1872). Portrait and historical painter. Born March 12, 1822, on a farm in Chester County (Pa.), Read was apprenticed to a tailor about 1835 but soon after ran off to Philadelphia and then to Cincinnati where he became a ship and sign painter. For a short time he was SHOBAL V. CLEVENGER's assistant and by 1840 he was sufficiently known as a painter to win a commission for a portrait of William Henry Harrison. In 1841 Read went to Boston, where he made friends with ALLSTON and Longfellow, and in 1846 he moved to Philadelphia. By this time he was becoming known as a poet as well as an artist. In 1850 Read made the first of several trips to Europe where he spent much of his time during the next two decades. During the Civil War, however, he worked hard for the Union cause, serving on the staff of General Lew Wallace as a lecturer and propagandist. Read returned to Italy after the war and made his home in Rome and Florence until 1872. He died May 11, 1872, in NYC, just a week after his arrival from Europe. At the time of his death Read was regarded on both sides of the Atlantic as one of America's leading poets. ¶ Keller, "Thomas Buchanan Read"; Pleasants, *Four Great Artists of Chester County;* Borneman, "Thomas Buchanan Read"; DAB; Swan, BA; Rutledge, PA; Cowdrey, NAD; Boston BD 1842–46; Phila. CD 1850; Rutledge, MHS; Cowdrey, AA & AAU.

READ, WILLIAM (1607–1679). Portrait painter (?). A native of Batcombe (England), Read settled at Weymouth (Mass.) in 1635, moved to Boston in 1646, moved to Norwich (Conn.) in 1674, and died there in 1679. He is known to have drawn maps and is claimed to have painted the earliest portrait in America, that of Governor Bellingham in 1641. The late William Sawitzky considered this portrait English in origin and its attribution to Read "most doubtful." ¶ Sawitzky, Lecture III, 1–2; Fielding.

READ, see also REED and REID.

READER, GEORGE W. Engraver, born in Pennsylvania in the mid-1820's, working in Philadelphia in 1850 and 1860. ¶ 7 Census (1850), Pa., XLIX, 285; 8 Census (1860), Pa., LIV, 874.

READER, SAMUEL J. Amateur sketcher who illustrated a diary he kept at North Topeka (Kans.) from 1855 to 1909. ¶ WPA Guide, *Kansas,* 137.

READING or REDDING, WILLIAM. Portrait painter of Louisville (Ky.) who was painting at Nicholasville (Ky.) in the fall of 1847 and gave lessons to young SAMUEL W. PRICE. *Cf.* WILLIAM H. REDIN. ¶ Coleman, "Samuel Woodson Price, Kentucky Portrait Painter," 6.

READY, ——. Architect and draftsman who showed a design for a memorial tablet at Charleston (S.C.) in 1822. ¶ Rutledge, *Artists in the Life of Charleston.*

REAM, CARDUCIUS PLANTAGENET (*c.* 1836–1917). Painter and illustrator; born at Lancaster (Ohio); died June 20, 1917, at Chicago. ¶ *Art Annual,* XIV, obit.

REASE, WILLIAM H. Lithographer, born in Pennsylvania about 1818, working in Philadelphia from 1844 until after 1860. ¶ 7 Census (1850), Pa., LII, 171; Phila. CD 1844–60+; Peters, *America on Stone.*

REASON, HENRY J. Engraver, NYC, 1856. ¶ NYBD 1856.

REASON, PATRICK HENRY (1817–?). Negro engraver working in NYC from 1837 to 1866. Stauffer, who gives the name as Philip H., states that Reason was a clever engraver of portraits in stipple but that race prejudice forced him to give up engraving for other work in the 1850's. ¶ Porter, *Modern Negro Art,* 35–38; NYCD 1845–66; Stauffer; *Art in America* (1936), repro. opp. p. 22.

REASON, PHILIP H., is PATRICK HENRY REASON.

REBETY, VICTOR. Artist at New Orleans, 1860–65. ¶ Delgado-WPA cites New Orleans CD 1860–61, 1865.

REBICHON, EMILE. Designer, 23, born in France; living in Frankford, near Philadelphia, in 1850 with his father, THEODORUS REBICHON, engraver. ¶ 7 Census (1850), Pa., LVI, 316.

REBICHON, THEODORUS. French engraver, 49, living in Frankford, near Philadelphia, in 1850. He was the father of EMILE REBICHON. ¶ 7 Census (1850), Pa., LVI, 316.

REBISSO, LOUIS T. (1837–1899). Sculptor. A native of Genoa (Italy), Rebisso came to America and settled at Boston in 1857. He later went to Cincinnati where he was associated with THOMAS DOW JONES. Rebisso died there May 3, 1899. ¶ *Art Annual,* I (Supp.), obit.; Boston *Transcript,* May 4, 1899, obit.; Gardner, *Yankee Stonecutters.*

REBOLE, HENRY. German fresco painter, 29, at Pittsburgh (Pa.) in 1850 with his wife and FREDERICK LOTZ. ¶ 7 Census (1850), Pa., III, 96.

RECOLEY (?), JULIUS. German artist, 24, at Philadelphia in 1850. ¶ 7 Census (1850), Pa., LI, 149.

REDDING, ——. Portrait painter active in 1833. *Cf.* WILLIAM H. REDIN, W. REDING, and WILLIAM READING. ¶ FARL question file.

REDDING, Mr. ——. Landscape painter of Charleston (S.C.), active in 1851. Several of his views of Cannonsborough and vicinity were sold at a benefit fair. ¶ Rutledge, *Artists in the Life of Charleston.*

REDDING, WILLIAM. Engraver, 20, born in Maryland, at Baltimore in 1860 with his father, William Redding, oyster packer. ¶ 8 Census (1860), Md., V, 304.

REDFIELD, WILLIAM D. Engraver of NYC who exhibited at the National Academy in 1836 and did work for a number of books published in the early 1850's. ¶ Cowdrey, NAD; Hamilton, *Early American Book Illustrators.*

REDIN, WILLIAM H. Portrait painter who exhibited at the National Academy in 1848–49 as a NYC resident. In 1843 he was working as a brewery clerk in Louisville (Ky.) and he returned to Louisville in the late 1850's. In 1865 he was a photographer and in 1870 an architect. *Cf.* WILLIAM READING, —— REDDING, and W. REDING. ¶ Cowdrey, NAD; NYCD 1849; Louisville CD 1843, 1848, 1859, 1865, 1870.

REDING, W. Portrait painter of NYC who exhibited at the National Academy in 1852. *Cf.* WILLIAM H. REDIN. ¶ Cowdrey, NAD.

REDMAN, WILLIAM H. Lithographer and wood engraver, born in Ireland about 1833. He exhibited pencil and crayon drawings at the American Institute in 1850 and 1851 and was working in NYC from 1858. ¶ 8 Census (1860), N.Y., XLVI, 305; Am. Inst. Cat., 1850–51; NYBD 1858, 1860.

REDMAYNE, ROBERT. Military draftsman and map maker, born in Yorkshire (England) about 1826. He enlisted in the U. S. Army at Philadelphia on September 27, 1853, was assigned to Battery I, 32 U. S. Artillery, and was discharged at Benecia (Cal.) on October 11, 1856. In March 1856 he made some pen-and-ink maps and views of the military camp at Benecia. ¶ Adjutant-General's office, Dept. of the Army; Cartographic Records, National Archives.

REED, ABNER (1771–1866). Engraver, painter, and printer. A native of East Windsor (Conn.), Reed was working in NYC in 1797, at Hartford (Conn.) from 1803 to 1808 and with SAMUEL STILES in Hartford from 1821 to 1824. He subsequently worked in NYC and published a penmanship book illustrated with his own plates. He died at Toledo (Ohio) February 25, 1866. WILLIAM MASON was his pupil. ¶ Fielding's supplement to Stauffer; Swan, "Early Sign Painters," 403; Grolier Club, *The United States Navy, 1776 to 1815,* 78; Toppan, *100 Years of Bank Note Engraving,* 10; Dunlap, *History,* II, 47; Fielding.

REED, EDWIN O. Map and general engraver, born in Ohio about 1824, working at Cincinnati during the 1850's. He was a son of Samuel and Jane Reed. ¶ 7 Census (1850), Ohio, XXI, 295; Cincinnati CD and BD 1850–56.

REED, ERASTUS R. Engraver, 23, born in Ohio, living at Cincinnati in 1850 with his brother EDWIN and other members of the family. ¶ 7 Census (1850), Ohio, XXI, 295.

REED, FISHE P., see PETER FISHE REED.

REED, IZAH B. Artist, 35, born in Philadelphia and living there in 1860. ¶ 8 Census (1860), Pa., LII, 131.

REED (Read, Reede, or Reid), JOHN, see JOHN REID.

REED, JOHN B. Artist and sign painter at Lancaster (Ohio) in 1817. ¶ Knittle, *Early Ohio Taverns.*

REED, JOHN S. Engraver, 29, born in Pennsylvania and living in Philadelphia in 1860 with his parents, Mr. and Mrs. Elias Reed. The father was a cabinetmaker and the mother ran a boarding house. ¶ 8 Census (1860), Pa., LIV, 257.

REED, P. Portrait painter at Leominster (Mass.) about 1840. ¶ Sears, *Some Ameri-*

can Primitives, 287; Lipman and Winchester, 179.

REED, PETER FISHE (1817–1887). Landscape and figure painter, teacher of painting and drawing. He was born May 5, 1817, at Boston. About 1850 he went out to Indiana, settling first at Vernon and after 1860 in Indianapolis and Centerville, where he was professor of English and teacher of painting and drawing in White Water College. Reed later went to live in Chicago and also made frequent sketching trips to New England, particularly Vermont. He died at the home of a son in Burlington (Iowa) in 1887. ¶ Burnet, *Art and Artists of Indiana,* 104–08; Peat, *Pioneer Painters of Indiana.*

REED, SAMUEL. Painter at Cincinnati in 1819. ¶ *Antiques* (March 1932), 152.

REED, STILES & COMPANY. Engravers at Hartford (Conn.) from 1821 to 1824; ABNER REED and SAMUEL STILES. ¶ Grolier Club, *The United States Navy, 1776 to 1815,* 78; Hamilton, *Early American Book Illustrators and Wood Engravers,* 94.

REED, see also READ and REID.

REEDER, ALEXANDER, see ALEXANDER RIDER.

REEDER, BENJAMIN F. Artist-decorator, born in Pennsylvania about 1834, living in NYC in 1860. ¶ 8 Census (1860), N.Y., L, 323.

REEDER, J. H. Portrait painter, Cincinnati, 1850. ¶ Cincinnati CD 1850 (courtesy Edward H. Dwight, Cincinnati Art Museum).

REEN, CHARLES. Artist and lithographer, born in Germany about 1827. In 1850 Reen and his wife shared a house in Philadelphia with Mr. and Mrs. LEE ELLIOTT and MORRIS LEVLY. In 1857 Reen was in partnership with CHARLES SHOBER and the following year REEN & SHOBER were in Chicago. ¶ 7 Census (1850), Pa., LI, 657; Phila. CD 1856–57; Chicago CD 1858. *Cf.* CHARLES RUEN.

REEN & SHOBER. Engravers and lithographers at Philadelphia in 1857 and at Chicago in 1858. The partners were CHARLES REEN and CHARLES SHOBER. ¶ Phila. CD 1857; Chicago CD 1858.

REES, Mrs. LEWIS. Hair painter at Philadelphia in 1857. She was the wife of Lewis Rees, professor of classics. ¶ Phila. CD 1857.

REEVES, W. H. English artist, 27, living in Orleans Parish (La.) in 1850. His wife was also English, but their year-old son was born in Massachusetts. ¶ 7 Census (1850), La., IV(1), 660.

REHN, ISAAC. Philadelphia painter (1845–48), photographer (1849–59), and lithographer (1860 and after). ¶ Phila. CD 1845–60+.

REHN, JOHN. Pennsylvania-born artist, 24, living at Philadelphia in 1860 with his wife Elizabeth and son William, aged 1 year. ¶ 8 Census (1860), Pa., LIX, 475.

REHN, MICHAEL. German artist, 30, boarding in New Orleans in 1850. ¶ 7 Census (1850), La., V, 82.

REICH, JOHN or JOHANN MATHIAS (1768–1833). Die-sinker and medallist, born in Furth (Bavaria), the son of the German die-sinker Johann Christian Reich. He studied and worked in Germany for some years, but about 1800 came to Philadelphia. Between 1801 and 1813 he executed several fine medals for the U. S. Government and in 1807 he was made Assistant Engraver at the Mint. Reich was one of the founders of the Society of Artists in 1811 and one of the first group of Pennsylvania Academicians (1812). He is said to have gone West for his health soon after 1813, but he died in Albany (N.Y.) in 1833. ¶ Chamberlain, "John Reich, Assistant Engraver to the United States Mint"; Loubat, *Medallic History of the U. S.,* 133 ff. and plates XXII–XXV; Stauffer; Dunlap, *History,* II, 469; Phila. CD 1803–08; Scharf and Westcott, *History of Philadelphia,* II, 1064; Rutledge, PA.

REICHARDT, FERDINAND, see FERDINAND RICHARDT.

REICHARDT, JOHN (or S.). Landscape painter of NYC who exhibited at the National Academy in 1858. *Cf.* FERD. RICHARDT. ¶ Cowdrey, NAD; NYCD 1857, 1860.

REICHE, F. or J. F. Wood engraver working in Philadelphia between 1794 and 1804. His woodcuts appeared chiefly in German books published in Philadelphia and Maryland. The Philadelphia directories list him as Frederick Richie in 1794, as Frederick Reiche or Reicke in 1795–96, and as Francis Reiche in 1798, while his woodcuts are signed F. or J. F. Reiche. ¶ Phila. CD 1794–96, 1798; Stauffer; Hamilton, *Early American Book Illustrators and Wood Engravers,* 71, 440.

REICHEL, WILLIAM CORNELIUS (1824–1876). Painter who studied at Bethlehem (Pa.) under GRUNEWALD. A native of Salem (N.C.), Reichel became a Moravian minister and taught in Moravian schools at Bethlehem and Lititz (Pa.). He was also noted as a historian and naturalist. ¶ Levering, *History of Bethlehem.*

REID, J. J. Portrait painter at NYC in 1846. ¶ NYBD 1846.

REID or READ, JOHN. Engraver at NYC in 1855–56. ¶ NYCD 1855–56.

REID (Read, Reed, or Reede), JOHN. Portrait and genre painter; born in Ireland about 1832; working in NYC from 1858 to 1862 and possibly in Washington (D.C.) in 1872. He exhibited at the National Academy in 1858. In 1872 he published in Washington a lithograph by Duval & Hunter of his painting, "St. Patrick's Day in America." ¶ 8 Census (1860), N.Y., LI, 699 [as Reed]; Cowdrey, NAD [as Reed or Reede]; N. Y. State BD 1859 [as Read]; NYBD 1859 and NYCD 1860–62 [as Reid]; *Portfolio* (March 1952), 159 [as Reid].

REID, see also READ and REED.

REIGART, HENRY. Painter of a miniature of John Landis (1776–1850) of Lancaster (Pa.) [?]. ¶ Lancaster County Hist. Soc., *Portraiture in Lancaster County,* 135.

REILY, JOSEPH. Artist at Hamilton (Ohio) in 1841. ¶ Information courtesy Edward H. Dwight, Cincinnati Art Museum.

REINAGLE, HUGH (*c.* 1788–1834). N.A. Scene painter, landscape, historical, and portrait painter, and drawing teacher. A son of the noted musician and composer Alexander Reinagle (1756–1809), Hugh was born in Philadelphia probably about 1788. A few years later his father became musical director of the New Theater in Philadelphia, a position he held until his death in 1809, and it was there that Hugh presumably learned the art of scenery painting. By 1807 he was employed as a scene painter at the New Theatre in NYC and he appears to have remained in NYC until about 1813. From 1815 to 1817 he was at Albany painting scenery and running a drawing academy and in 1818 he opened an academy in Philadelphia. During the twenties Reinagle was chief scene painter at the Park Theatre, NYC. In 1826 he was a founding member of the National Academy. Reinagle's large painting of "Belshazzar's Feast" or "Daniel Interpreting the Handwriting on the Wall" was exhibited at Peale's Museum in NYC in 1830 and he took it to New Orleans to exhibit it during the winter and spring of 1833–34. He died in New Orleans of cholera on May 23, 1834. ¶ New Orleans *Bee* and *Argus,* May 24, 1834, obituaries (cited by Delgado-WPA); DAB [under Alexander Reinagle]; Odell, *Annals of the New York Stage;* NYCD 1813, 1826–33; Rutledge, PA; Albany CD 1815–16; Cowdrey, AA & AAU; Prime, II, 32; Cummings, *Historic Annals;* Cowdrey, NAD; Kendall, *The Golden Age of the New Orleans Theater,* 76; *Harper's Magazine,* LX (May 1883), 861; New Orleans *Bee,* Jan. 14 and May 17, 1834 (cited by Delgado-WPA); Peters, *America on Stone,* pl. 107; Stokes, *Historical Prints;* Stokes, *Iconography.*

REINAGLE, T. Scene painter at the Park Theatre, NYC, in 1826. This may have been HUGH REINAGLE's brother Thomas. ¶ Odell, *Annals of the New York Stage,* III, 231; DAB [under Alexander Reinagle].

REINBERGER, JOSEPH. A German who settled at Nauvoo (Ill.) in 1850 and made a drawing of the ruined city the following year. This was owned in 1947 by Marie Nasberg of Nauvoo. ¶ Arrington, "Nauvoo Temple," Chap. 8.

REINHART, BENJAMIN FRANKLIN (1829–1885). A.N.A. Portrait, historical, genre, and landscape painter, born August 29, 1829, near Waynesburg (Pa.). After receiving a few lessons in Pittsburgh about 1844, Reinhart went to NYC in 1847 and entered the school of the National Academy. Three years later he went abroad for three years' further study in Düsseldorf, Paris, and Rome. Returning to America in 1853 he opened a studio in NYC, but made a number of extensive painting trips into the Middle West and South. In 1861 he went to England and for the next seven years enjoyed considerable success there as a portrait painter. He returned to NYC in 1868 and spent most of his remaining years there, though he died in Philadelphia, on May 3, 1885. He was elected an Associate of the National Academy in 1871. The later Pittsburgh artist, Charles Stanley Reinhart (1844–1896), was his nephew. ¶ DAB; CAB; Clement and Hutton; Cowdrey, NAD; Ohio BD 1859; New Orleans CD 1860–61 (cited by Delgado-WPA); Rutledge, PA; Graves, *Dictionary;* Fleming, *History of Pittsburgh,* III, 626.

REINHOLD, CASPAR. Die sinker and engraver, NYC, 1829–32. ¶ NYCD 1829–32; *Am. Advertising Directory,* 1832, p. 147.

REINHOLD, RUDOLPH. Of HIERONIMUS & REINHOLD, lithographers, NYC, 1859. ¶ NYBD and CD 1859.

REINKE, AMADEUS ABRAHAM (1822–1889).

Amateur artist. Amadeus, son of SAMUEL REINKE, was born at Lancaster (Pa.) on March 11, 1822. After attending and teaching in the Moravian schools at Nazareth and Bethlehem from 1830 to 1844 and three years as a missionary in Jamaica, Reinke was ordained in 1848. His ministry was spent at Salem (N.C.), Graceham (Md.), Staten Island (N.Y.), Philadelphia, and after 1865 in NYC. He was made a bishop of the Moravian Church in 1870 and died at Herrnhut (Germany) August 10, 1889. He was the artist of a view of Bethlehem (Pa.) about 1853. ¶ Rice, *In Memoriam: Amadeus Abraham Reinke;* Levering, *History of Bethlehem,* 648, 700, 710.

REINKE, SAMUEL (*c.* 1790–?). Portrait painter in his youth, subsequently a minister and bishop of the Moravian Church. After graduating from Moravian College in Bethlehem about 1811, Reinke taught school in Bethlehem, Lancaster, and Lititz. From 1844 to 1847 and 1853–54 he was pastor of a church in Bethlehem. He was still living in 1870 at the age of 80. AMADEUS A. REINKE was his son. ¶ Levering, *History of Bethlehem,* 588, 602–03, 676, 689, 709; Rice, *In Memoriam: Amadeus Abraham Reinke.*

REISNER or REISSNER, MARTIN A. Landscape, panorama, and scenery painter who came to America about 1848 after having been for some years in charge of scene painting at the Imperial Theatre in St. Petersburg (Russia). In 1848 his panorama of Taylor's campaigns in Mexico was shown at Philadelphia. The next year he sold a landscape to the American Art-Union. In 1850 he exhibited at the National Academy from Brooklyn (N.Y.) and in 1859 at the Pennsylvania Academy from Germantown (Pa.). ¶ Phila. *Public Ledger,* July 3 and 13, Nov. 27, Dec. 2, 1848, and Jan. 18, 1849 (cited by J. E. Arrington); Cowdrey, AA & AAU; Cowdrey, NAD; Rutledge, PA.

REITMAN, JOSEPH. Lithographer, 30, from Bavaria, living in Philadelphia in 1860. ¶ 8 Census (1860), Pa., LXII, 323.

REMICK, CHRISTIAN (1726–?). Marine and townscape painter in watercolors, born April 8, 1726, at Eastham (Mass.). A master mariner and amateur artist, Remick was apparently at Boston in the fall of 1768 when he executed several views of the harbor and the Common, showing the landing and the encampment of the British regiments quartered on the town. In October 1769 he was again in Boston, lately from Spain and prepared to make pictures "to the life." Remick is known to have done some heraldic painting. He is said to have lived on Cape Cod after the Revolution. ¶ Cunningham, *Christian Remick;* Bowditch, "Early Water-Color Paintings of New England Coats of Arms," 183–84 and fig. 5; Dow, *Arts and Crafts in New England,* 2; Stokes, *Historical Prints,* 23.

REMECKE, ADOLPHE. German artist, 27, at Philadelphia in 1850. ¶ 7 Census (1850), Pa., LII, 893.

REMENEYE, EDWARD. Hungarian artist, 18, at NYC in 1850. ¶ 7 Census (1850), N.Y., XLI, 494.

REMINGTON, ELIZABETH (1825–1917). Painter. She was working in NYC about 1885 and died at Flushing (N.Y.) on January 22, 1917. ¶ *Art Annual,* XIV, obit.

REMMEY, CHARLES H. Engraver, NYC, 1844–58. ¶ NYBD 1844–58.

REMOUIT, L. Miniaturist and profilist. He visited Richmond (Va.) in the summer of 1807 with JOHN M'CONACHY. Remouit turned up in Charleston (S.C.) in November 1808. ¶ *Richmond Portraits;* Rutledge, *Artists in the Life of Charleston.*

REMUS, PETER. Sculptor, 26, a native of France, living in Pittsburgh (Pa.) with his English wife in September 1850. ¶ 7 Census (1850), Pa., III(2), 208.

RENAUD, see RENAULT.

RENAULT, ANTOINE (Anthony or Antonio). Painter, gilder, and varnisher from Paris; working in NYC from 1794 to about 1801 and at New Orleans in 1822–23. ¶ Gottesman, *Arts and Crafts in New York,* II, nos. 453–54; NYCD 1799–1801; New Orleans CD 1822–23.

RENAULT, JOHN FRANCIS. Allegorical and historical painter who claimed to have been at the Battle of Yorktown in 1781 as assistant secretary to Count de Grasse and Engineer to the French Army. His "Triumph of Liberty" was advertised in NYC in 1795 by D. F. LAUNY and again in 1797 by Renault and VERGER. An engraving of the British officers surrendering their arms to Washington at Yorktown was published by Renault in 1819, at which time he described himself as a citizen of the U.S. ¶ *Album of American Battle Art,* 47; Gottesman, *Arts and Crafts in New York,* II, nos. 99–101; copy of "The Triumph of Liberty" at NYHS.

RENIERS, PETER. Sculptor of a small bust of

Elisha Kent Kane (1820–1857), signed and dated at Philadelphia 1857. ¶ NYHS, *Catalogue of American Portraits.*

RENOIR, ALEXANDER. Artist and engraver, New Orleans, 1819–30. In 1819 he was listed as a portraitist in plaster, seal engraver, and painting restorer; in 1822, as a jeweller, engraver, and keeper of the Commercial Coffee-House and Museum; in 1827, as an engraver; and in 1830, as an engraver and proprietor of an art school. ¶ Delgado-WPA cites *La. Gazette,* Oct. 27, 1819, New Orleans CD 1822, 1827, 1830, and New Orleans *Bee,* July 29, 1830.

RENWICK, JAMES (1792–1863). Landscape painter, amateur. Born May 30, 1792, in Liverpool (England), Renwick was brought to America as a child and graduated from Columbia College in 1807. He traveled in Europe with Washington Irving and was in business in NYC for several years. From 1820 to 1853 he was professor of natural philosophy and experimental chemistry at Columbia and a widely respected consulting engineer. A member of the Board of Directors of the American Academy from 1817 to 1820 and Member of the Academy in 1825, Renwick exhibited a frame of English and American views there in 1820 [as I. Renwick]. He was also an Honorary Member, Amateur, of the National Academy from 1842 to 1860. Renwick died in NYC January 12, 1863. He was the father of James Renwick, the architect. ¶ DAB; Cowdrey, AA & AAU; Cowdrey, NAD.

RESTEIN, EDMUND P. or B. (1837–1891). Lithographer. A native of France, Restein came to America about 1852 and settled in Philadelphia. His father, James Restein [Reston in 1860 Census], was a "fancy card maker." Edmund and his younger brother LUDWIG were employed for a time by P. S. DUVAL, but in 1868 they went into business for themselves. Edmund died in 1891. ¶ Peters, *America on Stone;* 8 Census (1860), Pa., L, 252; *Portfolio* (Feb. 1954), 126 (repro.).

RESTEIN, LUDWIG (*c.* 1838–?). Lithographer. Born in France and brought to Philadelphia about 1852, Ludwig was first employed by DUVAL but after 1868 worked with his older brother, EDMUND RESTEIN. ¶ 8 Census (1860), Pa., L, 252; Peters, *America on Stone; Portfolio* (Feb. 1954), 126 (repro.).

RETZSCH, FREDERICK AUGUST MORITZ (1779–1857). A German painter, much admired for his illustrations of the works of Goethe, Schiller, and Shakespeare, Retzsch was born at Dresden and died near there in 1857. He has erroneously been listed as an American artist because T. S. Cummings gave the place of his death as New Dresden, which has wrongly been assumed to be in New York. Though Retzsch was an Honorary Member of the National Academy, he never visited the United States. ¶ Larousse, *Grand Dictionnaire Universel du XIXe Siècle; Art Journal,* Aug. 1, 1857, 252, obit.; Cummings, *Historic Annals,* 262; Cowdrey, NAD; Cowdrey, AA & AAU; Swan, BA; Thieme-Becker; Fielding.

REUSSNER, ROBERT. Engraver, NYC, 1859. ¶ NYBD 1859.

REVERE, C. H. Landscape painter, San Francisco, 1859. ¶ San Francisco BD 1859.

REVERE, JOSEPH WARREN (1812–1880). Topographical artist, grandson of PAUL REVERE. Born in Boston May 17, 1812, Revere entered the Navy as a midshipman in 1812 and rose to lieutenant before his retirement in 1850. From 1845 to 1848 he was assigned to California and he was in command of the party which raised the American flag at Sonoma in July 1846. Revere's *Tour of Duty in California* (1849) is illustrated by a number of California views from sketches by the author. Revere later served as a colonel and brigadier-general in the New Jersey Volunteers during the Civil War. His later years were spent in retirement and travel. He died at Hoboken (N.J.) April 20, 1880. ¶ DAB; Van Nostrand and Coulter, *California Pictorial,* 52–53; Jackson, *Gold Rush Album,* 4–7.

REVERE, PAUL (1735–1818). Engraver, silversmith, and cartoonist, born in Boston January 1, 1735. Though trained as a silversmith by his father, Paul Revere was a craftsman in many fields. About 1765 he began to engrave on copper; he was also a political cartoonist, copper worker, bell caster, and watercolorist. Before and during the Revolution he was an active patriot, performing particularly valuable service as a courier for the Massachusetts Committee of Correspondence. Revere spent his whole life in Boston and died there May 10, 1818. ¶ Goss, *The Life of Colonel Paul Revere;* Forbes, *Paul Revere and the World He Lived In.* For the definitive work on Revere's engravings see Dr.

Clarence S. Brigham's handsomely illustrated *Paul Revere's Engravings* (Worcester, 1954).

REVEREND, T. or J. Sculptor of Philadelphia who exhibited at the Pennsylvania Academy in 1859. ¶ Rutledge, PA.

REVIERE, ——. Scene painter at Wallack's Theatre, NYC, in 1858. He executed a number of Utah scenes for the production of *Deseret Deserted, or the Last Days of Brigham Young*. This was probably EDWARD RIVIERE. ¶ N. Y. *Herald,* May 24, 1858 (citation courtesy J. E. Arrington).

REY, JACQUES JOSEPH (1820–?). Lithographer born at Bouxviller (Alsace). He studied art and lithography in France and as a young man went to Russia as companion, secretary, and interpreter to a nobleman. About 1850 he emigrated to California and for the next three decades was associated in lithography with his brother-in-law JOSEPH BRITTON, except for the period 1859–64 when he was working as a gasfitter and maker of billiard tables. He is said to have died before Britton who died in 1901. ¶ Peters, *California on Stone;* 8 Census (1860), Cal., VII, 587; San Francisco BD 1856, 1858; Howells, *California in the Fifties.*

REYNES, Mrs. JOSEPH (1805–?). Miniaturist working at New Orleans in 1831. ¶ Represented at Delgado Museum, New Orleans (Delgado-WPA).

REYNOLDS, CATHERINE (*c.* 1782–1864). Amateur landscape artist in pencil, crayon, sepia wash, and watercolors. Born in Detroit (Mich.) about 1782, while her father was British Commissary there, she lived there until 1796 and thereafter at Amherstburg (Ont.), where her father was Deputy Commissary until his death in 1810. Miss Reynolds lived with her brother Robert in Amherstburg until her death September 17, 1864. Thirty existing works have been attributed to her, chiefly landscapes and scenes along the Detroit River and Lake Erie. ¶ Robinson, "Early Houses on the Detroit River and Lake Erie in Watercolors by Catherine Reynolds."

REYNOLDS, EMANUEL. Portrait and miniature painter working in NYC in 1836–37. He exhibited at the National Academy. ¶ Cowdrey, NAD; NYCD 1836–37; Sherman, "Unrecorded Early American Portrait Painters" (1933), 29, repro.

REYNOLDS, JOHN. Engraver and copperplate printer, 24, at Boston in 1850. ¶ 7 Census (1850), Mass., XXV, 83; Boston CD 1851–52.

REYNOLDS, JOHN. Of CRASKE & REYNOLDS, seal engravers of NYC, who exhibited specimens of a "new process of seal engraving" at the American Institute in 1851. ¶ Am. Inst. Cat., 1851; NYCD 1852.

REYNOLDS, JOSHUA W. Engraver, 25, born in Boston and living there with his widowed mother in 1860. ¶ 8 Census (1860), Mass., XXIX, 8; Boston CD 1860.

REYNOLDS, RICHARD (1827–1918). Painter; born in England; died January 1918 at Cincinnati (Ohio). ¶ *Art Annual,* XV, obit.

REYNOLDS, ROBERT F. Portrait painter and lithographer, born about 1818; active in Philadelphia from 1841 until after 1860. In 1841 he exhibited at the Artists' Fund Society a portrait after INMAN. ¶ 7 Census (1850), Pa., LII, 725; Rutledge, PA; Phila. CD 1843–60+.

REYNOLDS, THOMAS. Stone seal engraver and heraldic engraver from London and Dublin who opened a seal manufactory in Philadelphia in 1785 and was there until about 1788. He turns up again in NYC in 1804–05. ¶ Prime, II, 72; Gottesman, *Arts and Crafts in New York,* II, nos. 238–39; Kelby, *Notes on American Artists;* Phila. CD 1785; NYCD 1804 (McKay), 1805.

RHIND, C. An Erie Canal sketch by this artist appears in Colden's *Memoir* (1825) on the Canal. ¶ Colden, *Memoir.*

RHINEDESBACHER, see RINDISBACHER.

RHINELANDER, W. H. Artist at Baltimore in 1858. ¶ Baltimore BD 1858.

RHOADES, WILLIAM H. Artist at Philadelphia, 1860 and after. This may have been the William Rhoads, 22-year-old portrait painter born in Pennsylvania, who was at Pittsburgh (Pa.) in 1850. *Cf.* WILLIAM H. RHODES. ¶ Phila. CD 1860+; 7 Census (1850), Pa., III, 257.

RHOADS, WILLIAM, see WILLIAM H. RHOADES.

RHODES, GEORGE F. Engraver and die sinker at Cincinnati. In 1857 he headed the firm of G. F. Rhodes & Co.; in 1858–59 he was with the Cincinnati Type Foundry. ¶ Cincinnati CD 1857–59, BD 1857.

RHODES, WILLIAM H. Artist, 18, from Pennsylvania, living in Cincinnati in June 1860. He was a near neighbor of the Negro artist ROBERT DUNCANSON but was not himself listed as colored. *Cf.* WILLIAM H. RHOADES. ¶ 8 Census (1860), Ohio, XXV, 255.

RIAL, JOHN. Engraver, 50, from England, living at Frankford, near Philadelphia, in 1850. ¶ 7 Census (1850), Pa., LVI, 271.

RIBONI, GIACINTO. Portrait and figure painter. He was born in Piacenza (Italy) and was working in Rome between 1819 and 1828. By 1835 he had settled in Philadelphia. Thieme-Becker states that he died in 1838 but the Historical Society of Pennsylvania owns four portraits by him of the Boker family, one of which is signed and dated 1839. ¶ Thieme-Becker; Rutledge, PA; information courtesy the late William Sawitzky; Phila. BD 1838, CD 1839.

RICARBY, GEORGE. Engraver from England, 22, at New Orleans in 1850. ¶ 7 Census (1850), La., V, 91.

RICARDO, Mrs. R. J. Music and drawing teacher at Charleston (S.C.) in 1810. ¶ Rutledge, *Artists in the Life of Charleston.*

RICE & BUTTRE. Engravers, NYC, 1849–50. The junior partner in this firm was JOHN CHESTER BUTTRE; Rice has not been identified, though it may have been W. W. RICE who was working for RAWDON, WRIGHT, HATCH & Co. about this time. ¶ NYBD 1849–50; Stauffer [under Buttre].

RICE, CALVIN L. Engraver at Worcester (Mass.), 1859–60. ¶ Worcester CD 1859; New England BD 1860.

RICE, E. A. Portrait engraver in mezzotint working for Baltimore engravers about 1845. ¶ Stauffer.

RICE, EMERY. Decorator working in and around Hancock (N.H.) before 1850. ¶ Little, "Itinerant Painting in America, 1750–1850," 209.

RICE, JAMES R. (1824–?). Line engraver, born at Syracuse (N.Y.). He studied under his brother W. W. RICE in NYC and settled in Philadelphia in 1851. He was active as late as 1876. ¶ Stauffer; Phila. CD 1856–60+.

RICE, JOHN E. Made sketches in Kansas before the Civil War. ¶ WPA Guide, *Kansas.*

RICE, JOSEPH R. Engraver, Philadelphia, 1859. *Cf.* JAMES R. RICE. ¶ Phila. CD 1859.

RICE, ROBERT. Steel engraver, 27, a native of Vermont, at Boston in 1860. ¶ 8 Census (1860), Mass., XXVI, 304.

RICE, W. W. Line engraver employed by RAWDON, WRIGHT, HATCH & Co. of NYC in 1846 and after. He was engraving over his own name as late as 1860. JAMES R. RICE was his brother and pupil. *Cf.* RICE & BUTTRE. ¶ Stauffer.

RICE, WILLIAM. Sign painter of Hartford (Conn.) in 1844. ¶ *Magazine of Art* (April 1943), 129, repro. of tavern sign.

RICH, A. H. Engraver of a print of F. O. C. DARLEY's painting of the Battle of Concord. ¶ *American Collector* (April 1943), cover

RICH, HARVEY J. Artist of NYC who exhibited at the American Institute in 1849 and 1850, in the latter year "Moonlight View." ¶ Am. Inst. Cat., 1849–50.

RICHARD or RICHARDS, JOHN H. Draftsman, lithographer, and engraver, born in Germany about 1807. Between 1841 and and 1843 John H. Richards, in collaboration with P. S. DUVAL of Philadelphia, made experiments in "lithotinting," the result of which was "Grandpapa's Pet," said to be the first true lithotint produced in America, published in *Miss Leslie's Magazine* in April 1843. Richards was listed as an engraver in Philadelphia in 1843 and 1844, as an artist in the 1850 Census, and as an employee at the U. S. Mint in 1851–52. Between 1852 and 1855 J. H. Richard was employed at the Smithsonian Institution to make drawings of specimens of mammals, fish, and reptiles collected by western surveying expeditions, engravings of which appeared in the official reports published between 1855 and 1860. Richard also contributed drawings for DUVAL's series of turtle prints and eight steel plates for T. W. Harris's *Treatise on Some of the Insects Injurious to Vegetation* (Boston, 1862). J. Richards contributed the drawing for at least one of JOHN HART's 1868 prints of Germantown (Pa.). John H. Richards, J. H. Richard, John Richard or Richards, and J. Richard are believed to have been one artist. ¶ 7 Census (1850), Pa., LIII, 217 [as John Richards]; "The New Art of Lithotint," *Miss Leslie's Magazine,* April 1843, 113–14 [as Richards]; Peters, *America on Stone,* under Duval; Waite, "Beginnings of American Color Printing," 15 [as John C. Richards]; Phila. CD 1843–44 [as John Richards], 1851–52 [as John Richard]; Marcy, *Exploration of the Red River of Louisiana;* U. S. War Dept., *Reports of Explorations and Surveys,* vols. VI–VIII, X, XII; Hamilton, *Early American Book Illustrators and Wood Engrav-*

ers, 401; Peters, *America on Stone,* under J. Richards.

RICHARD, STEPHEN. Artist, 31, born in Maryland and living in Baltimore in 1850 with V. P. Richard, M.D., 25. ¶ 7 Census (1850), Md., IV, 236.

RICHARDS, BENJAMIN. Landscape painter at Philadelphia in 1860. ¶ Phila. CD 1860.

RICHARDS, DAVID (1828–1897). Portrait and genre sculptor, portrait painter in oils and crayon. Born in Abergwynolwyn (Wales) in 1828, Richards came to the United States about 1847 and found employment as a stone cutter at Utica (N.Y.). He later studied for seven years in NYC and exhibited at the National Academy in 1859–60. He also worked at Chicago (Ill.) and Woodside, Long Island (N.Y.). He died in Utica November 28, 1897. ¶ Utica *Daily Press,* Nov. 29, 1897, obit.; *Art Annual,* I (1898), 28, obit.; Cowdrey, NAD; NYCD 1859–60; information courtesy R. A. Hug, grandson of the artist. There is a collection of data on the artist and his work at the New York Public Library.

RICHARDS, FREDERICK DEBOURG. Landscape painter at NYC (1844–45), Philadelphia (1848–66), and Paris (1868). Before 1856 he exhibited chiefly Pennsylvania views; in 1856 and after he exhibited several Italian and one Welsh scene. His work was shown at the Pennsylvania Academy, the American Institute, the American Art-Union, and the National Academy. ¶ Am. Inst. Cat., 1844; Cowdrey, AA & AAU; Cowdrey, NAD; Rutledge, PA; Phila. BD 1850, 1853; *Portfolio* (Dec. 1946), 92, repro.

RICHARDS, J. R. Itinerant portrait painter at Logansport and other Indiana towns between 1837 and 1845 and perhaps into the fifties. ¶ Peat, *Pioneer Painters of Indiana;* Burnet, *Art and Artists of Indiana,* 389 [as —— Richards].

RICHARDS, JOHN (1831–1889). Primitive painter whose "Battle of Gettysburg," painted about 1870, is owned by Nelson A. Rockefeller. ¶ *American Processional,* 177, 246–47.

RICHARDS, JOHN H., see JOHN H. RICHARD.

RICHARDS, N. Stone cutter and sculptor, New Orleans, 1841–46. ¶ New Orleans CD 1841–42, 1846.

RICHARDS, THOMAS ADDISON (1820–1900). N.A. Landscape and portrait painter, teacher and illustrator. Born December 3, 1820, in London, Richards was brought to America in 1831 and grew up in Hudson (N.Y.) and in Penfield (Ga.). A precocious artist, he published his first book, an illustrated guide to flower painting, at the age of 18. In 1843–44 he was painting and teaching at Charleston (S.C.) and later in 1844 he went north to NYC to study for two years in the National Academy school. He was made an Associate of the Academy in 1848, an Academician in 1851, and in 1852 its Corresponding Secretary, an office he held for forty years. Richards was best known as a landscape painter of the Hudson River School. He traveled much in the United States and Europe and in 1857 published an illustrated handbook of American travel. He also contributed illustrated travel articles to several American magazines and was professor of art at New York University from 1867 to 1887. Richards died at Annapolis (Md.) June 28, 1900, and was buried at Providence (R.I.). ¶ DAB; *Art Annual,* II, obit.; Rutledge, *Artists in the Life of Charleston;* NYCD 1845, 1860; Cowdrey, NAD; Rutledge, PA; 8 Census (1860), N.Y., XLIX, 1038; Peters, *America on Stone; Home Authors and Home Artists.*

RICHARDS, THOMAS W. Architect and painter of Philadelphia and Baltimore who exhibited architectural studies and paintings of Oriental and Moorish scenes at the Pennsylvania Academy, 1854–62. ¶ Rutledge, PA; Phila. CD 1858.

RICHARDS, WILLIAM TROST (1833–1905). N.A. Marine, landscape, still life, and portrait painter, born in Philadelphia November 14, 1833. At first a designer of gas fixtures, he became interested in painting and went abroad in 1853 for three years of study in Florence, Rome, and Paris. After his return in 1856 he married and settled in Germantown (Pa.). He was preoccupied with landscapes and still life until about 1867 when he began to specialize in marine paintings, for which he is now chiefly known. In 1874 he began to summer at Newport and he settled there permanently in 1890. During his later years Richards made frequent trips to the British Isles and the Channel Islands. He died at Newport November 8, 1905. ¶ Morris, *Masterpieces of the Sea: William T. Richards, a Brief Outline of His Life and Art;* DAB; *Art Annual,* VI, obit.; Rutledge, PA; Cowdrey, NAD; Rutledge, MHS; Phila. CD 1854–60+; *Portfolio* (April 1945), 190–91.

RICHARDSON, ANDREW (1799–1876). N.A. Landscape painter. A Scotsman who came to NYC about 1831 and exhibited frequently at the American and National Academies and later at the Apollo Association and American Art-Union. He was elected an Associate of the National Academy in 1832 and an Academician in 1833, but retired from membership in 1858. Richardson apparently returned to Scotland about 1841 and was there in 1844, but by 1848 he was again in NYC. In 1852 he was back in Scotland. His exhibited works were chiefly Scottish, English, and New York or Pennsylvania scenes, though there were also a few copies after paintings in the Louvre. He died in New York in 1876. ¶ Cowdrey, NAD; Cowdrey, AA & AAU; Smith; Mallet; Thieme-Becker; Fielding.

RICHARDSON, BENJAMIN (1835–1926). Etcher and photographer, born in London in 1835, brought to Brooklyn (N.Y.) as a child. He died in Brooklyn February 28, 1926. ¶ *Art Annual,* XXIII, obit.

RICHARDSON & COX. Wood engravers of NYC, 1853–59; JAMES H. RICHARDSON and THOMAS COX, JR. ¶ NYCD 1853–59; Hamilton, *Early American Book Illustrators and Wood Engravers,* 528.

RICHARDSON, FREDERICK. English artist, 38, living with RICHARD RICHARDSON and family in Philadelphia, July 1860. He owned real estate valued at $30,000. ¶ 8 Census (1860), Pa., LII, 64.

RICHARDSON, GEORGE. Painter of a watercolor view of the East River with a distant view of the seat of Joshua Waddington, Esq., NYC, 1824. ¶ *Antiques,* May 1942, 308 (repro.).

RICHARDSON, HENRY. Engraver, 33, born in New York and living in NYC in 1850 with a wife and three children, all born in New York. ¶ 7 Census (1850), N.Y., XLVI, 614.

RICHARDSON, J. F. Wood engraver, Portland (Me.), 1860. ¶ Portland BD 1860.

RICHARDSON, JAMES H. Wood engraver of NYC, 1848–80. He was connected with the firms ORR & RICHARDSON (1848) and RICHARDSON & COX (1853–59). ¶ NYCD 1848–59; Hamilton, *Early American Book Illustrators and Wood Engravers,* 527.

RICHARDSON, L. C. Painter of oil portraits of Jacob Sheafe (1754–1829) and Mrs. Jacob Sheafe (1751–1833), now in the Wentworth Gardiner House, Portsmouth (N.H.). ¶ WPA (Mass.), *Portraits Found in N.H.,* 20.

RICHARDSON, RICHARD. English artist, 33, living in Philadelphia in 1860 with his English wife and brother (?), FREDERICK RICHARDSON, and a daughter Ellen, 3, born in Pennsylvania. ¶ 8 Census (1860), Pa., LII, 64.

RICHARDSON, S. Bookplate engraver, active about 1795, probably in America. ¶ Stauffer.

RICHARDSON, Mrs. SAMUEL or T. M., see CAROLINE SCHETKY.

RICHARDSON & WATSON. Portrait and fancy painters at New Orleans in 1836–37. ¶ Delgado-WPA cites New Orleans *Commercial Bulletin,* Dec. 12, 1836, and New Orleans CD 1837.

RICHARDT or REICHARDT, FERDINAND. Danish landscape painter; born at Brede in 1819; working in NYC between 1856 and 1859; died in Oakland (Cal.) in 1895. He was especially noted for his paintings of Niagara Falls. The New York State Historical Association owns fourteen of his paintings, and others are at the New York Public Library and in Copenhagen. *Cf.* JOHN (or S.) REICHARDT who exhibited at the NAD in 1858. ¶ Information courtesy Janet R. MacFarlane, Director, Albany Institute; N. Y. *Herald,* Nov. 19, 1856, and Jan. 11, 1859 (courtesy J. Earl Arrington); *Art Journal,* 1863.

RICHES, [W.?]. Of FELCH & RICHES, copper, steel, and seal engravers of Columbus (Ohio), 1856–57. ¶ Columbus BD 1856; Ohio BD 1857.

RICHMOND & WHITTLE. Painters of a sign at Barnstable (Mass.), the reverse of which shows a harbor with a steam packet and three-masted schooner. ¶ *American Collector* (March 6, 1934), 3.

RICHTER, RICHARD. Drew in colored charcoal a view of Naubuc (then Curtisville), Conn., in 1855 or 1856. ¶ Conn. Hist. Soc. *Bulletin* (April 1947), 9.

RICKERT, J. Drew a view of Nazareth (Pa.) which was engraved about 1831 by E. W. MUMFORD. ¶ Stauffer.

RICKET, THOMAS. Engraver, Philadephia, 1805. ¶ Brown and Brown.

RICKETSON, WALTON. Sculptor born May 27, 1839, at New Bedford (Mass.). ¶ *Art Annual,* XX, "Who's Who in Art"; Gardner, *Yankee Stonecutters,* 74.

RICKNER, LOUIS. German lithographer, 24, at Pittsburgh (Pa.) in August 1850. ¶ 7 Census (1850), Pa., III(2), 75.

RIDDLE, WILLIAM R. Lithographer working with LOUIS LIPMAN at Milwaukee (Wis.) in 1857. ¶ Kent, "Early Commercial Lithography in Wisconsin," 249.

RIDER, ALEXANDER. Portrait, miniature,

landscape, and figure painter who came to Philadelphia from Germany with KRIMMEL in 1810 and worked there until 1834. He also visited Charleston (S.C.) in 1819 and Washington (D.C.) in 1814. He exhibited frequently at the Pennsylvania Academy. ¶ Bolton, *Miniature Painter;* Rutledge, PA; Scharf and Westcott, *History of Philadelphia;* Rutledge, *Artists in the Life of Charleston;* Dunlap, *Diary,* III, 705, 714, 760.

RIDGWAY, W. Line engraver of NYC, 1854 and after. ¶ Stauffer.

RIDLEY, ESSEX. Painter of a profile of a daughter of John Jay, 1797. ¶ Jackson, *Silhouette,* 139.

RIEKARTS, FREDERICK. German engraver, 19, at Philadelphia in 1850. ¶ 7 Census (1850), Pa., L, 860.

RIFFINBURG, WILLIAM. German artist, 30, at Philadelphia in 1850. ¶ 7 Census (1850), Pa., LII, 970.

RIGALI, G. Sculptor, NYC, 1856. ¶ NYBD 1856.

RILEY, JEREMIAH H. Engraver and die sinker, NYC, 1854–59. ¶ NYBD 1854–59.

RILEY, JOHN. Irish artist, 30, at NYC in 1860. ¶ 8 Census (1860), N.Y., LX, 1046.

RIMMER, WILLIAM (1816–1879). Sculptor, portrait and figure painter, teacher and writer on art, born February 20, 1816, in Liverpool (England). Rimmer was taken to Nova Scotia at the age of two and to Boston in 1826. At the age of 15 he began to assist his family by painting portraits and signs. He also worked briefly in a lithographic office and tried his hand at making statuettes in gypsum. After his marriage in 1840 he spent several years as an itinerant portrait painter in and around Boston, but settled in Randolph (Mass.) in 1845 and for the next ten years supported his family by making shoes and painting portraits, miniatures, religious, and ideal pictures. In his spare time he studied medicine which he practised from about 1855 to 1863 in the village of East Milton. During these years he began his career as a sculptor, working first in granite, later in clay and marble. As his reputation spread, he was invited to give lectures on art anatomy in Boston and Lowell and from 1864 to 1866, his home then being in Chelsea, he conducted a school of drawing and modelling in Boston. From 1866 to 1870 he served as Director of the School for Design for Women at the Cooper Institute in NYC. Rimmer returned to Boston in 1870, reopened his school and taught there until 1876, and during the last three years of his life taught in the art school of the Boston Museum of Fine Arts. He died at South Milford (Mass.) on August 20, 1879. ¶ The most complete account of Rimmer's life and work is Truman H. Bartlett's *The Art Life of William Rimmer* (1882). His own writings on art include: *Elements of Design* and *Art Anatomy.* See also: DAB; Gardner, "Hiram Powers and William Rimmer"; Kirstein, "Rediscovery of Rimmer."

RIMPRECHT, JOHN or JOHANN BAPTIST (1801–1877). Genre and portrait painter, born June 19, 1801, at Triberg (Germany). He came to America in 1843, was working at Brooklyn (N.Y.) in 1857, but returned to Triberg after the Civil War. He died June 27, 1877. ¶ Thieme-Becker; Brooklyn BD 1857.

RINCK, A. D. Portrait and miniature painter at New Orleans from 1840 to 1871. ¶ Delgado-WPA cites *Bee,* Dec. 9, 1840, Jan. 8, 1842, Jan. 3, 1843, March 30, 1858, Feb. 17, 1871, *Picayune,* Jan. 9, 1851, and New Orleans CD 1841–42, 1846; *cf.* Seebold, *Old Louisiana Plantation Homes and Family Trees,* I, 23.

RINDISBACHER, PETER (1806–1834). Genre, landscape, animal, and miniature painter, born in Upper Emmenthal, Canton Bern (Switzerland) in 1806. He received some training in Switzerland before he accompanied his family in 1821 to the Earl of Selkirk's Red River colony in western Canada. During their five years in this frontier settlement Peter contributed to the family's support by the sale of drawings and watercolors of scenes of prairie life. The Rindisbachers moved south into Wisconsin in 1826 and Peter continued to paint what he saw about him. In 1829 he settled permanently in St. Louis, began to contribute sporting scenes to *The American Turf Register,* and was making a considerable reputation for his pictures of Indian and animal life in the West when he died August 13, 1834, in his 28th year. ¶ McDermott, "Peter Rindisbacher: Frontier Reporter," 10 repros., biblio.; Nute, "Peter Rindisbacher, Artist" and "Rindisbacher's Minnesota Water Colors"; Alice E. Smith, "Peter Rindisbacher: A Communication."

RINEHART, WILLIAM HENRY (1825–1874). Sculptor, born September 13, 1825, near Union Bridge (Md.). Apprenticed to a

Baltimore firm of stonecutters at the age of 21, Rinehart had his own studio within two years and was exhibiting portrait busts in Baltimore as early as 1853. He went to Italy in 1855 and studied there for two years. After an unsuccessful attempt to maintain a studio in Baltimore he returned to Italy in 1858 and made his home there until his death, revisiting the United States briefly in 1866 and 1872. He died in Rome on October 28, 1874. The last important representative of the classical school of American sculptors, Rinehart is today chiefly remembered for his "Clytie" (at the Peabody Institute in Baltimore) and "Latona and Her Daughters" (at the Metropolitan in NYC). ¶ The standard life is William S. Rusk's *William Henry Rinehart* (Baltimore, 1939), illus., catalogue of his works. See also: DAB; Gardner, *Yankee Stonecutters;* Taft, *History of American Sculpture;* "New Rinehart Letters," *Maryland Historical Magazine,* XXXI, 225–42.

RING, DAVID. Of RUTHVEN & RING, engravers, Baltimore, 1856–57. ¶ Baltimore CD 1856, BD 1857.

RINGGOLD, CADWALADER (1802–1867). Topographical draftsman and cartographer. A native of Maryland, Ringgold entered the U. S. Navy as a midshipman in 1819, retired in 1864 as a commodore, and was made a rear-admiral, retired, the year before his death. In 1849–50, as Commander Ringgold, he commanded a surveying expedition to the California coast. A sketch of the entrance to San Francisco Bay, made at this time, appeared in Ringgold's *Series of Charts, with Sailing Directions . . .* (1852). ¶ DAB; Peters, *California on Stone.*

RINK, JOHN J. Portrait painter, NYC, 1857. ¶ NYBD 1857.

RIOS, see DE LAS RIOS.

RISDON, RICHARD P. Wood engraver, NYC, 1858–60. ¶ NYBD 1858–60.

RISLEY, H. S. English artist who came to NYC in 1852 to exhibit a panorama of the River Thames, painted by several English artists from sketches by Risley and others. ¶ N. Y. *Herald,* Dec. 21, 1852, Jan. 4 and 26, 1853 (citations courtesy J. E. Arrington).

RISSO & BROWNE. Lithographers, NYC, 1832–38; CHARLES RISSO and WILLIAM R. BROWNE. ¶ NYCD 1833–35; Peters, *America on Stone.*

RISSO, CHARLES. Lithographer. He was in partnership with WILLIAM R. BROWNE in NYC from 1832 to 1836 and 1838, though in 1837 he apparently moved to New Orleans. His employer there, D. THEURET, called Risso the "oldest lithographer in the Union" and stated that he could speak English, French, Spanish, and Portuguese. Risso remained in New Orleans until 1846, then returned to NYC and went into a partnership with GEORGE E. LEEFE which lasted until about 1850. ¶ Peters, *America on Stone;* NYCD 1833–36, 1849; NYBD 1850; Delgado-WPA cites *Courier,* April 6, 1837, New Orleans CD 1838, 1841–42.

RISSO & LEEFE. Lithographers, NYC, 1849–50; CHARLES RISSO and GEORGE E. LEEFE. ¶ NYCD 1849, BD 1850; Peters, *America on Stone.*

RITCHIE, ALEXANDER HAY (1822–1895). N.A. Engraver; genre, portrait, and figure painter; born January 14, 1822, in Glasgow (Scotland). After studying in Edinburgh under Sir William Allan, Ritchie emigrated to America in 1841, worked for a few years in Canada, and settled in NYC about 1847. He established a prosperous engraving business and also became well known as a painter, winning election to the National Academy in 1871. During his last years he lived in New Haven (Conn.) where he died September 19, 1895. ¶ DAB; Cowdrey, NAD; Rutledge, PA; NYCD 1847+; Clement and Hutton.

RITCHIE, ANDREW, JR. (1782–1862). Painter of landscapes and battle pieces who was at Boston in 1836 and exhibited at the Athenaeum. ¶ Swan, BA.

RITCHIE, JOHN M. Portrait painter, NYC, 1844. ¶ NYBD 1844.

RIVE, LEON. Portrait painter, born in France about 1809. He was at New Orleans in 1849 and 1850, and also at Louisville (Ky.) in 1850. ¶ 7 Census (1850), Ky., XI, 160; New Orleans CD 1849–50.

RIVERS, JAMES. Made a drawing of the Academy and Congregational Church at Thomaston (Me.) for a map of 1855. ¶ *Journal of the Society of Architectural Historians,* X (Dec. 1951), 27.

RIVIERE, EDWARD. Artist, born in France about 1804, working in NYC 1858–60. This was probably the scene painter, REVIERE, at Wallack's Theatre in 1858, who designed scenery for *Deseret Deserted, or the Last Days of Brigham Young.* ¶ 8 Census (1860), N.Y., LIII, 507; NYCD 1858–59; N. Y. *Herald,* May 24, 1858 (courtesy J. Earl Arrington).

RIVIERE, PETER. Miniaturist, Philadelphia, 1784. ¶ Prime, I, 8.

RIXINGER, FRANCIS. Lithographer, NYC, 1859. ¶ NYBD 1859.

ROBBINS, ELLEN (1828–1905). American watercolorist represented at the Worcester (Mass.) Art Museum. ¶ Worcester Art Museum, *Catalogue;* Fielding.

ROBBINS, HORACE WOLCOTT, JR. (1842–1904). N.A. Landscape painter, born October 21, 1842, at Mobile (Ala.). After graduation from a college in Baltimore, he studied painting under JAMES M. HART in NYC and the following year, 1860, he opened his own studio there. In 1864 he was made an Associate of the National Academy; full membership came in 1878. In 1864 he went to Jamaica with F. E. CHURCH, then on to England and France. After two years of study in Paris and a sketching trip in Switzerland, he returned to NYC in 1867. He was best known for his watercolors. ¶ Cowdrey, NAD; Rutledge, PA; French, *Art and Artists in Connecticut,* 153–55; Century Association, *Yearbooks,* 1894–1904.

ROBBINS, MARVIN S. Portrait painter, born in Middlefield (Mass.) April 15, 1813; active in Middlefield and Beckett until about 1872. ¶ Sears, *Some American Primitives,* 290; *Vital Records of Middlefield:* Births.

ROBERT, ALEXANDER. Prussian lithographer, 28, living in NYC in 1860 with his French wife. ¶ 8 Census (1860), N.Y., XLIII, 618.

ROBERTS, ADAM. French artist, 24, at Baltimore in 1860. ¶ 8 Census (1860), Md., III, 981.

ROBERTS, ALLEN. Engraver, 22, a native of New York, living in NYC in 1850 in the home of ROBERT ROBERTS. ¶ 7 Census (1850), N.Y., XLVI, 555.

ROBERTS, BISHOP (?–1739). Painter and engraver working in Charleston (S.C.) from 1735 to 1739. He advertised his readiness to undertake portrait painting and engraving, heraldry and house painting, landscapes for chimney pieces, draughts of houses in colors or india ink, and instruction in drawing. Roberts' only known work is a view of Charleston about 1737–38, of which the original watercolor exists, as well as the engraving after it by W. H. Toms of London. Roberts died in Charleston in October 1739. His widow, MARY ROBERTS, for several years carried on his business. ¶ Rutledge, "Charleston's First Artistic Couple"; Wilson, "Art and Artists of Provincial South Carolina," 139; Prime, I, 8; Stokes, *Historical Prints,* pl. 14a.

ROBERTS, H. K. Engraver, NYC, 1832. ¶ NYCD 1832; *Am. Adv. Directory,* 1832, 148.

ROBERTS, J. H. or I. H. Portrait and landscape painter. "Painted by I. H. Roberts 1850" is inscribed on the back of a portrait owned in 1938 by Miss Margaret Weisinger of Richmond (Va.). This may be the same as J. H. Roberts, portrait painter at Springfield (Ohio) in 1853, portrait and landscape painter at Woodstock (Ohio) in 1859. ¶ FARL question file; Ohio BD 1853, 1859.

ROBERTS, JAMES. English copper engraver, 29, at Philadelphia in 1860. ¶ 8 Census (1860), Pa., LX, 709.

ROBERTS, JOHN (1768–1803). Portrait and miniature painter, engraver. A native of Scotland, he came to America about 1793 and settled in NYC, where he was active as an artist, engraver, inventor, and amateur musician until his death in 1803. He also visited Charleston (S.C.) in the winter of 1796–97 and possibly Portsmouth (N.H.) in March 1801. DUNLAP states that Roberts was a man of remarkable talents as an artist, musician, mechanic, and mathematician, but too unstable and intemperate to make good use of them. ¶ Dunlap, *History,* I, 427–29; Bolton, *Miniature Painters;* NYCD 1795–1803; Rutledge, *Artists in the Life of Charleston;* Prime, II, 32; Hamilton, *Early American Book Illustrators and Wood Engravers,* 86; *Antiques* (Sept. 1944), 158.

ROBERTS, MARVIN S., see MARVIN S. ROBBINS.

ROBERTS, MARY (?–1761). "Face painter" and copperplate printer at Charleston (S.C.). After the death in 1739 of her husband, BISHOP ROBERTS, Mary attempted to carry on as a limner and copperplate printer. By 1746, however, she had given up the printing side of the business. She died in Charleston and was buried in St. Philip's Parish on October 24, 1761. ¶ Rutledge, "Charleston's First Artistic Couple"; Prime, I, 8.

ROBERTS, NATHAN B. Exhibited pencil portraits at the American Institute in 1856; he was a resident of NYC. ¶ Am. Inst. Cat., 1856.

ROBERTS, ROBERT. Wood engraver, born in Wales about 1821, working in NYC from

1841 to 1850. He is said to have been a pupil of JOSEPH ALEXANDER ADAMS. In 1850 he lived with ALLEN ROBERTS, probably his brother. ¶ 7 Census (1850), N.Y., XLVI, 555; NYCD 1841–49; Am. Inst. Cat., 1842; Hamilton, *Early American Book Illustrators and Wood Engravers,* 78.

ROBERTS, W. Delineator of a view of Natural Bridge (Va.), engraved by WILLIAM MAIN who was working in NYC between 1820 and 1837. ¶ Stauffer.

ROBERTS, WILLIAM. Wood engraver, born in New York about 1829, active in NYC from 1846 to 1876. In 1846 he was with BUTLER & ROBERTS and from 1846 to 1851 he exhibited at the American Institute. ¶ NYCD 1846–76; NYBD 1846; Am. Inst. Cat., 1846–49, 1851; Sears, *Description of the U.S.,* frontis.; Hamilton, *Early American Book Illustrators and Wood Engravers,* 446, 528; 7 Census (1850), N.Y., XLVIII, 232 [as William E.].

ROBERTS, WILLIAM. Engraver at Philadelphia from about 1839 to 1860. According to the 1850 Census he was born in England about 1809, while the 1860 Census states that he was born in Germany about 1811. His wife was English and their two children were born in Pennsylvania about 1839 and 1845. ¶ 7 Census (1850), Pa., LII, 273; 8 Census (1860), Pa., LII, 898; Phila. CD 1851–52.

ROBERTS, WILLIAM J. Portrait painter at Newark (N.J.), 1857–60. ¶ Newark CD 1857, 1860.

ROBERTSON, ALEXANDER (1772–1841). Miniaturist and landscape painter, teacher of painting. A younger brother of ARCHIBALD (1765–1835), he was born at Aberdeen (Scotland), May 13, 1772, studied in London, and followed his brother to America in 1792. Both established themselves in NYC where for many years they conducted the Columbian Academy of Painting. Alexander was better known as a teacher than as a painter, though he exhibited regularly at the American Academy. A member of the Academy from 1817, he served as its Secretary from 1817 to 1825 and Keeper from 1820 to 1835. He died in NYC in 1841. ¶ Robertson, *Letters and Papers of Andrew Robertson,* 1, 2, 9, 285; Bolton, *Miniature Painters;* Cowdrey, AA & AAU; NYCD 1793+; Stokes, *Historical Prints;* Flexner, *The Light of Distant Skies,* biblio., 265.

ROBERTSON, ALEXANDER. Lithographer, NYC, 1852–60; of ROBINSON & SEIBERT (1854–57), of ROBERTSON, SEIBERT & SHEARMAN (1859–60). ¶ NYCD 1852–58; NYBD 1854, 1857–60.

ROBERTSON, ARCHIBALD (*c.* 1745–1813). Topographical draftsman. Entering the British army in 1759, he served at the siege of Havana in 1762 and in America during most of the Revolution (1775–80), as an officer of the Royal Engineers and Deputy Quartermaster General. A portfolio of 54 drawings made by him in Cuba and North America between 1762 and 1780 is owned by the New York Public Library and has been published, along with Robertson's diaries. After retirement from the service in 1786, Major (later Lt. General) Robertson spent the rest of his life on his estate, "Lawers," near Comrie, Perthshire (Scotland), where he died Feb. 12, 1813. ¶ Robertson, *Archibald Robertson, . . . His Diaries and Sketches in America;* Stokes, *Iconography,* V, 994.

ROBERTSON, ARCHIBALD (1765–1835). Miniature and portrait painter, teacher of painting. The son of a Scottish architect and draftsman, he was born at Moneymusk May 8, 1765 and grew up in Aberdeen. Trained as a painter in Aberdeen, Edinburgh, and London, he emigrated in 1791 and settled in NYC where for the next thirty years he enjoyed a successful career as a miniaturist and, with his brother ALEXANDER, proprietor of the Columbian Academy of Painting. His wife, the former ELIZA ABRAMSE of NYC, was also an artist of talent. Robertson was a member and Director of the American Academy. He retired in 1821 and died in NYC December 6, 1835. ¶ DAB; Robertson, *Letters and Papers of Andrew Robertson,* 1, 9, 11–16, 21–40, 285; Stillwell, "Archibald Robertson, Miniaturist"; Morgan and Fielding, *Life Portraits of Washington;* Dunlap, *History;* Flexner, *The Light of Distant Skies,* biblio., 265–66.

ROBERTSON, Mrs. ARCHIBALD, see ELIZA ABRAMSE.

ROBERTSON, GEORGE J. Portrait, landscape, and townscape painter, teacher of painting. A Scotsman, he studied at the Royal Academy in London and exhibited there from 1827 to 1836. By September 1845 he was at Cleveland (Ohio) and the following year he arrived in Milwaukee (Wis.). A view of Milwaukee, drawn by Robertson and lithographed by D. W.

Moody, was published in NYC in 1854. Robertson later went to teach at the Rockford (Ill.) Young Ladies Seminary. ¶ Butts, *Art in Wisconsin,* 80; Graves, *Dictionary; Portfolio* (Jan. 1952), 100.

Robertson, John. Ship picture in oils and watercolors on paper, *c.* 1845. ¶ Lipman and Winchester, 179.

Robertson, John Ewart (1820–1879). Portrait painter, exhibitor at the Pennsylvania Academy. He was at Liverpool (England) in 1853, Baltimore in 1860, and NYC in 1869. *Cf.* John Roy Robertson. Graves lists a John Robertson of Liverpool, who exhibited figure paintings at the Royal Academy, 1844–67. ¶ Rutledge, PA; Graves, *Dictionary*.

Robertson, John Roy. Portrait and figure painter of Baltimore, active *c.* 1857–69. He exhibited at the National Academy in 1859; also exhibited at the Maryland Historical Society which now owns two of his works. In 1863 he painted the portrait of Jefferson Davis. *Cf.* John Ewart Robertson. Graves lists J. R. and L. Roy Robertson of London, who exhibited figure paintings in London in 1866. Washington Art Association catalogues list J. Robertson of Washington in 1857 and of Baltimore in 1859. ¶ FARL cites Dr. J. Hall Pleasants of Baltimore; Cowdrey, NAD; Baltimore BD 1859; Lafferty; Rutledge, MHS; Graves, *Dictionary;* repro., Met, Mus., *Life in America,* no. 199; Washington Art Association Cat., 1857, 1859; represented at Md. Hist. Soc. and Chicago Hist. Soc.

Robertson & Seibert. Lithographers, NYC, 1854–57; Alexander Robertson and Henry Seibert. Succeeded by Robertson, Seibert & Shearman. ¶ NYBD 1854, 1857.

Robertson, Seibert & Shearman. Lithographers, NYC, 1859–60, succeeding Robertson & Seibert; the partners were Alexander Robertson, Henry Seibert, and James A. Shearman. ¶ NYBD 1859–60.

Robertson, Thomas. Of NYC, exhibited "Pleasure Yacht" at the American Art-Union, 1847. ¶ Cowdrey, AA & AAU.

Robertson, Walter (*c.* 1750–1802). Miniature painter. A native of Dublin (Ireland) and elder brother of the noted Irish miniaturist, Charles Robertson, Walter studied and worked in Dublin from about 1765 to 1784, then in London from 1784 to 1792. Returning to Dublin a bankrupt, he decided to go to America and in 1793 sailed in company with his friend, Gilbert Stuart. After about a year in NYC he moved with Stuart to Philadelphia. During the year 1795 he lived in Philadelphia with J. J. Barralet and Robert Field and was chiefly occupied with making miniature copies of Stuart portraits, though he also painted miniatures from life of Washington. He left America toward the end of 1795, went to India, and died at Futtehpore in 1802. ¶ Strickland, *Dictionary of Irish Artists;* Cone, "The American Miniatures of Walter Robertson"; NYCD 1795–96; Morgan and Fielding, *Life Portraits of Washington,* 195–98; Dunlap, *History;* Thieme-Becker.

Robertson, William or William R. Engraver (possibly two, since their addresses are different), NYC, 1832. ¶ *Am. Advt. Directory* 1832, p. 148; NYCD 1832.

Robin, Augustus. Portrait, historical, and landscape engraver, NYC, 1846; said to have been an employee of J. C. Buttre for about 40 years. ¶ NYBD 1846; Stauffer.

Robin, Edward, see Edward Robyn.

Robineau, Berthaut & Company. Engravers, NYC, 1860. Robineau is not listed separately in the directories; Berthaut is Tony Berthaut, engraver and die sinker, 1856–59. ¶ NYBD 1860; NYCD 1856–60.

Robineau, Francis, see Francis Rabineau.

Robins, John L. Artist, NYC, 1818–21. *Cf.* Luke Robins. ¶ NYCD 1818–21.

Robins or Robbins, Luke. Scene painter, teacher of painting. In July 1796 was announced Robins' appointment as scene painter at a new theater to be opened in Petersburg (Va.). He had previously been scene painter at the New Theatre in Philadelphia and was reported to be engaged for the future in Richmond and Norfolk (Va.). He later returned to Philadelphia where he taught landscape, architectural, and flower painting (1810). *Cf.* John L. Robins. ¶ Prime, II, 33; Brown and Brown.

Robinson, Alfred (1806–1895). Amateur sketcher. A native of Massachusetts, he went to California in 1829 and remained for eight years as agent for Bryant & Sturgis, Boston merchants. In 1837 he returned to the East with his wife, but he was in California again in 1840–42 as agent for Bryant & Sturgis, and after 1849 as representative of the Pacific Mail Steamship Company. In 1846 he published anonymously *Life in California,* containing seven lithographs based on his own sketches made between 1829 and 1842. ¶ Van Nostrand and Coulter, *California Pictorial,* 36.

ROBINSON & BATES. Portrait and landscape painters, Bellefontaine (Ohio), 1859. ¶ Ohio BD 1859.

ROBINSON, FRANK. Ship picture in watercolors and pencil, about 1860. ¶ Lipman and Winchester, 179.

ROBINSON, HENRY R. Caricaturist and lithographer of NYC. He was listed as a carver and gilder in 1833–34, caricaturist 1836–43, lithographer and print publisher 1843–51. He exhibited at the American Institute. ¶ Peters, *America on Stone;* NYCD 1836–51; Am. Inst. Cat., 1842, 1847; *Portfolio* (Jan. 1954), 116, repro.; *Antiques* (Sept. 1940), 120, and (July 1945), 34, repros.

ROBINSON, J. C. Painter of portraits of an old man and an old woman, 1848. ¶ Garbisch Collection catalogue, 94–95, repros.

ROBINSON, JOHN (?–1829). Portrait and miniature painter of Philadelphia, who exhibited at the Pennsylvania Academy 1816–24. He was an Englishman and exhibited portraits of BENJAMIN WEST and an English lady. In February 1818 appeared Robinson's *A Description of and Critical Remarks on the Picture of Christ Healing the Sick in the Temple Painted by Benjamin West, Esq.* He died in Philadelphia about 1829. ¶ Rutledge, PA; Robinson, *op. cit.;* Scharf and Westcott, *History of Philadelphia,* II, 1053; Dunlap, *History*

ROBINSON, JOHN. Engraver and die sinker, born in New York about 1832, working in NYC from about 1856. ¶ 8 Census (1860), N.Y., XLIX, 1028; NYBD 1856–59

ROBINSON, JOHN. Wood engraver, 25, a native of the United States, working in Boston in 1860. ¶ 8 Census (1860), Mass., XXVIII, 100.

ROBINSON & MCKEON. Wood engravers, Troy (N.Y.), 1857; THOMAS ROBINSON and THOMAS MCKEON. ¶ Troy BD and CD 1857.

ROBINSON, Mrs. PAULINE. Artist at New Orleans in 1846. ¶ Delgado-WPA cites New Orleans CD 1846.

ROBINSON, SNOWDEN. Lithographer, 22, a native of Maryland, at Washington in 1850. ¶ 7 Census (1850), D.C., I, 234.

ROBINSON, THOMAS. Of ROBINSON & MCKEON, wood engravers, Troy (N.Y.), 1857. ¶ Troy BD and CD 1857.

ROBINSON, THOMAS (1834–1888). Landscape, genre, and animal painter, born August 23, 1834, in Pictou (N.S.). He was working in NYC by 1856 and thereafter divided his time between NYC and Providence (R.I.), where he died March 1, 1888. He exhibited at the National Academy and the Boston Athenaeum and is represented at the Worcester Art Museum. ¶ Arnold, *Art and Artists of Rhode Island;* Cowdrey, NAD; Swan, BA; NYCD 1856; *Antiques* (March 1942), 170, repro.; Worcester Art Museum Cat.

ROBINSON, WILLIAM. Engraver, Philadelphia, *c.* 1815–18. He was probably the Robinson who engraved the illustrations for Parson Weems' *Life of Washington* (Phila. 1815). ¶ Brown and Brown.

ROBINSON, WILLIAM. Engraver, 40, a native of New York, at NYC in 1850. This might be the William Robinson who exhibited pencil drawings and crayon sketches at the American Institute in 1844 and 1845. ¶ 8 Census (1860), N.Y., XLI, 623; Am. Inst. Cat., 1844, 1845.

ROBYN, CHARLES. Lithographer with his brother EDWARD at St. Louis, 1850–57. ¶ Missouri Hist. Soc., *Bulletin,* IV (Jan. 1948), 103, and VI (Oct. 1949), 102.

ROBYN, EDWARD (1820–1862). Lithographer, engraver, portrait and landscape painter. A native of Emmerich (Prussia), he was working as a lithographer in Philadelphia from 1848 to 1850 (DRESER & ROBYN). In 1850 he moved to St. Louis (Mo.), where he and his brother CHARLES had a lithographic business until 1857, when it was bought out by THEODOR SCHRADER. Robyn's self-portrait, a sketch-book and ledger, and his panorama of the Eastern and Western Hemispheres are owned by the Missouri Historical Society. He moved to a farm near Hermann (Mo.) about 1856 and died there in 1862. ¶ Missouri Hist. Soc., *Bulletin,* III (Oct. 1946), 27; *ibid.,* IV (Jan. 1948), 103; *ibid.,* VI (Oct. 1949), 102; *ibid.,* VII (April 1951), 382–83; Phila. CD 1848–50; St. Louis CD 1853, BD 1854; WPA Guide, *Missouri;* letter of Charles van Ravenswaay to J. Earl Arrington, Jan. 12, 1955.

ROCHE, DAVID. Lithographer, 25, a native of Pennsylvania, at Philadelphia in 1860. ¶ 8 Census (1860), Pa., LV, 111.

ROCHON, JULIUS. Executed a wax portrait of Washington based on the work of other artists. It is not known whether he actually visited America. ¶ Bolton, *American Wax Portraits,* 60.

ROCKER, NICHOLAS. Image maker, 48, living in NYC in 1860 with JOHN MOLLINARI. ¶ 8 Census (1860), N.Y., XLIV, 159.

ROCKEY, ABRAHAM B. (1799–?). Portrait painter, born in Mifflinsburg (Pa.). He was active in Philadelphia from about 1828 until after 1860, and also painted some portraits in Delaware. He exhibited at the Artists' Fund Society and the Pennsylvania Academy. ¶ Smith; Rutledge, PA; Phila. CD 1829–60+; *Portraits in Delaware, 1700–1850,* 63, 64; 7 Census (1850), Pa., L, 254 [aged 48].

ROCKWELL, AUGUSTUS. Landscape painter at Buffalo (N.Y.), 1855–60+. His "Valley of the Au Sable [N.Y.]," painted in 1866, is owned by Beloit College, Beloit (Wis.). ¶ Buffalo BD 1855–60; information courtesy Philip B. Whitehead, Beloit College.

ROCKWELL, HORACE (1811–1877). Portrait painter, born July 6, 1811, possibly in Philadelphia where he exhibited at the Artists' Fund Society in 1835. He settled in Fort Wayne (Ind.) about 1836 and lived there and later in Roanoke (Ind.) until his death on January 9, 1877. He also painted scriptural pictures and experimented with a flying machine. ¶ Peat, *Pioneer Painters of Indiana,* 109–11, 237; Rutledge, PA; *Antiques* (Nov. 1950), 383.

RODDEN, H. Portrait painter, Warren (Ohio), 1853. ¶ Ohio BD 1853.

RODGERS, ——. Painter of a portrait of Joseph Rodman Drake (1795–1820), engraved by T. KELLY. The artist may have been NATHANIEL ROGERS. ¶ Stauffer, II, no. 1600.

RODGERS, JOSHUA. Artist, 21, born in Pennsylvania; living with his father, Samuel Rodgers, importer, at Philadelphia in 1860. ¶ 8 Census (1860), Pa., LV, 794.

RODWAY, ——. Partner in ACHESON & RODWAY, lithographers and engravers, Chicago, 1853. ¶ Chicago CD 1853.

ROE, NICHOLAS. Artist, 31, a native New Yorker, living in NYC in 1850. ¶ 7 Census (1850), N.Y., XLI, 539.

ROEHNER, WILHELM. Portrait and genre painter at NYC in 1854 and Newark (N.J.) in 1859. Possibly the Wilhelm Roehner who worked in Vienna, 1839–42, and Berlin, 1842–46. *Cf.* —— ROHNER. ¶ NYBD 1854; Newark CD 1859; Thieme-Becker.

ROESEN, SEVERIN (?–*c.* 1871). Still life painter and porcelain and enamel painter of Cologne (Germany), where he exhibited in 1847, who emigrated to America about 1848. In 1848–50 he sold eleven still lifes to the American Art-Union and he was listed in NYC directories from 1850 to 1857. From about 1858 to 1870 he lived in Williamsport (Pa.) and he is said to have died in 1871 in a Philadelphia almshouse. Of his more than 80 known paintings, most are still owned in Williamsport and Lycoming County. Roesen exhibited at the Pennsylvania Academy in 1863. ¶ Maurice A. Mook, "S. Roesen, 'The Williamsport Painter,'" Allentown (Pa.) *Morning Call,* Dec. 3, 1955; Thieme-Becker; Cowdrey, AA & AAU; R. B. Stone, "Not Quite Forgotten, A Study of the Williamsport Painter, S. Roesen," Lycoming Co. Hist. Soc., *Proceedings and Papers,* No. 9, 1951; NYCD 1850–1857; Born, *Still Life Painting in America;* Frankenstein, *After the Hunt,* 32 and pl. 30; *Portfolio* (Aug. 1944), cover and p. 15; *ibid.* (Jan. 1954), 118; *Williamsport Sun and Banner,* June 27, 1895.

ROETTER, PAULUS (1806–1894). Landscape and botanical painter, born January 4, 1806, at Nuremberg (Germany) or Thun (Switzerland). After studying art in Nuremberg, Düsseldorf, Munich, and possibly Paris, Roetter went to Switzerland in 1825 and for the next twenty years painted miniature landscapes for tourists and taught at Thun and Interlaken. He emigrated to America in 1845 to found a communistic colony, but settled in St. Louis, where he became an Evangelical pastor, school teacher, and first instructor in drawing at Washington University. Roetter made the drawings to illustrate Engelmann's "The Cactaceae of the Boundary" in *Report of the U. S. and Mexican Boundary Survey* (1859). After serving with the Home Guard during the Civil War, Roetter became an associate of Louis Agassiz at Harvard. He returned to St. Louis in 1884 and died ten years later. ¶ Powell, "Three Artists of the Frontier," 38–41; WPA Guide, *Missouri; Gazette des Beaux Arts* (Oct. 1946), 303, repro.; Thieme-Becker.

ROGERS, ——. Exhibited specimens of bird and flower painting in Charleston (S.C.) in November 1835. ¶ Rutledge, *Artists in the Life of Charleston.*

ROGERS, ——. Painter of a Mississippi River panorama for a production of *Uncle Tom's Cabin* at the National Theatre, NYC, March 1854. *Cf.* CHARLES ROGERS, scene painter at San Francisco. ¶ N. Y.

Herald, March 22, 1854 (citation courtesy J. E. Arrington).

ROGERS, CHARLES. Miniaturist at Boston, 1844–46. ¶ Boston BD 1844; Bolton, *Miniature Painters.*

ROGERS, CHARLES. Scene painter, working in San Francisco from about 1856 at least to 1872. In 1856 he was associated with JOHN W. FAIRCHILD, artist at the American Theatre, in preparing a panorama of scenes of the California Vigilance Committee. In 1859 he was at the Lyceum Theater. Later he was listed simply as "artist." After 1880 Charles A. Rogers, artist, is listed until 1902, but this may be a different man from the earlier Charles. *Cf.* also, —— ROGERS, scene painter in NYC in 1854. ¶ MacMinn, *The Theatre of the Golden Era in California,* 226 (citation courtesy J. E. Arrington); San Francisco CD 1859–1902.

ROGERS, D. Painted profile portraits of Joseph and Hyram Smith, Mormon leaders, at Nauvoo (Ill.) in 1842. ¶ Josephson, "What Did the Prophet Joseph Smith Look Like?", 313–14.

ROGERS, DAVID. Portrait painter active in NYC from 1829, when he first exhibited at the National Academy, at least until 1858. ¶ Cowdrey, NAD; NYCD 1829–58.

ROGERS, EDWARD. Wood engraver, Philadelphia, 1855–60 and after. ¶ Phila. CD 1855–60+.

ROGERS, GEORGE H. Artist, 24, a native of Connecticut, at New London (Conn.) in 1850. ¶ 7 Census (1850), Conn., X, 236.

ROGERS, HENRY W. Portrait and miniature painter at Salem (Mass.) in October 1782. ¶ Belknap, *Artists and Craftsmen of Essex County,* 12; Bolton, *Miniature Painters.*

ROGERS, HENRY WHITTINGHAM (1824–1855). Portrait and miniature painter who exhibited a drawing at the Boston Athenaeum in 1833 at the age of eight and worked as an artist in Salem from 1846 to 1855. He was the son of Nathaniel L. Rogers, merchant of Salem. ¶ Swan, BA; BA Cat., 1833; Salem CD 1846–56; Belknap, *Artists and Craftsmen of Essex County,* 12.

ROGERS, JOHN (*c.* 1808–*c.* 1888). English engraver who came to NYC about 1850 and was chiefly employed by book publishers. ¶ Stauffer; NYBD 1856+; Hamilton, *Early American Book Illustrators and Wood Engravers,* 133.

ROGERS, JOHN (1829–1904). N.A. Sculptor, particularly noted for his small genre and literary "groups." Born October 30, 1829, at Salem (Mass.), he spent his childhood in Cincinnati (Ohio) and Northampton and Roxbury (Mass.) and went to work at 16 as clerk in a Boston dry-goods store. From 1848 to 1857 he was employed as a draftsman and mechanic in Cochituate (Mass.), Manchester (N.H.), New York City, and Hannibal (Mo.). Although he began to model in clay as early as 1849, it was not until 1858 that he decided to become a professional sculptor. In the fall of 1858 he went abroad to study, first in Paris, then in Rome, but he found the neo-classical style of his teachers distasteful and returned to Roxbury after less than a year. Renouncing sculpture as a profession, he took a drafting job in Chicago, but within a few months he had won such notice there as a modeller of humorous genre subjects that he again decided to make sculpture his life work. Moving to NYC in the fall of 1859, he opened a studio and began a remarkably successful career. During the next thirty-five years he produced over 80 groups, casts of which achieved an estimated total sale of 80,000. Although he also did some portrait busts and monumental statues, his continuing reputation rests on the "Rogers Groups." He was elected to the National Academy in 1863. After his retirement in 1894, Rogers lived with his family in New Canaan (Conn.), where he died July 26, 1904. ¶ Smith, *Rogers Groups;* Barck, "John Rogers"; DAB. An almost complete collection of Rogers' published work is at the NYHS, which also owns his papers, from which a biography of the artist is being written by David H. Wallace.

ROGERS, MICHAEL G. (*c.* 1805–1832). Portrait painter. A native of Ohio, he was painting portraits at Indianapolis (Ind.) in 1831 and died there the following year on January 8. ¶ Peat, *Pioneer Painters of Indiana,* 149–50; Burnet, *Art and Artists of Indiana,* 61.

ROGERS, NATHANIEL (1788–1844). N.A. Miniature painter, born at Bridgehampton, Long Island (N.Y.) in 1788. He was painting miniatures in Connecticut probably before he went to NYC in 1811 to take lessons from JOSEPH WOOD. He had a studio in NYC from 1811 to 1839 and was a member of both the American and National Academies, and a founder of the latter. He died at Bridgehampton December 6, 1844. ¶ [Sherman,] "Nathaniel Rogers and His Miniatures," five repros. and checklist; NYCD 1812–39; Cowdrey, AA & AAU; Cowdrey, NAD; Cummings, *Historic Annals;* Bolton, *Miniature Painters;* represented at MHS.

ROGERS, RALPH. Three unsigned portraits, painted about 1800, at the Sheldon Museum and Middlebury College, Middlebury (Vt.), have been attributed to this artist, who is said to have been the son of a portrait painter of the same name. It is believed that these portraits may have been painted by RALPH E. W. EARL (*c.* 1785–1838), son of RALPH EARL (1751–1801), and that the two Ralph Rogerses never existed. ¶ Frankenstein and Healy, "Two Journeyman Painters," 15.

ROGERS, RANDOLPH (1825–1892). Sculptor. Born July 6, 1825, at Waterloo (N.Y.), spent most of his childhood and youth in Ann Arbor (Mich.). About 1843 he went to NYC and worked for five years as a clerk in Stewart's dry-goods store, during which time he took up modelling portrait busts. In 1848, with the help of his employers, he went to Italy to study for three years at Florence and two at Rome, where he worked on his well-known statue, "Nydia." Returning to the United States in 1853, he received several important commissions, including that for the bronze "Columbus" doors of the U. S. Capitol, and in 1855 he went back to Italy to execute them. Rome was his home for the rest of his life, though he made numerous professional visits to his native country. Rogers did some ideal figures in the neo-classical style, but he was chiefly occupied with portrait busts, funereal and military monuments. Before his death he shipped the casts of most of his works to the University of Michigan. Long the center of the American colony at Rome, he died there January 15, 1892. ¶ DAB; Taft, *History of American Sculpture;* Fairman, *Art and Artists of the Capitol.*

ROGERS, ROBERT. Engraver and die sinker, NYC, 1854–59. ¶ NYBD 1854, 1856–59.

ROGERS, SARAH (Sally). Armless painter who was exhibited as a prodigy in NYC in 1807 and Charleston (with MARTHA ANNE HONEYWELL) in 1808. Using her mouth only, Miss Rogers is said to have painted flowers and landscapes, cut paper and cloth with scissors, and threaded a needle. Examples of her painting were shown at the Pennsylvania Academy in 1811 and 1813. ¶ Jackson, *Silhouette,* 139; Rutledge, *Artists in the Life of Charleston;* Rutledge, PA.

ROHDE, WILLIAM F. Artist or painter, NYC, 1859–69. ¶ NYCD 1859–69.

ROHNER, Mr. ——. Artist at Hartford (Conn.) in 1860. *Cf.* WILHELM ROEHNER. ¶ Hartford CD 1860.

ROLAND, JOHN, see JOHN RUHLAND.

ROLFE or ROLF, Miss EMMA. Exhibited a portrait and a landscape sketch at the Apollo Gallery in 1839. Her address was Brooklyn. She was probably a daughter or sister of JOHN A. ROLPH or ROLFE. ¶ Cowdrey, AA & AAU.

ROLFE, JOHN, see JOHN A. ROLPH.

ROLLE, ALBERT. Engraver, 44, born in Prussia, living in Washington (D.C.) in 1860. He was employed in the Coast Survey. ¶ 8 Census (1860), D.C., II, 428.

ROLLINSON, CHARLES (*c.* 1793–1833). Engraver of NYC who died in Boston, January 19, 1833. He was probably a son of WILLIAM ROLLINSON, with whom he worked from about 1808 to 1832. In 1846 Charles's widow, Maria, was living at the same address as S. O. ROLLINSON and Joseph R. Rollinson, merchant. ¶ Sawyer, "Deaths Published in The Christian Intelligencer," Jan. 26, 1833; Stauffer; NYCD 1816–33, 1846.

ROLLINSON, S. O. Exhibited pencil sketches at the American Institute in 1846. He or she lived at the same NYC address as Joseph R. Rollinson and the widow of CHARLES ROLLINSON. ¶ Am. Inst. Cat., 1846.

ROLLINSON, WILLIAM (1762–1842). Engraver and miniaturist. Rollinson was born April 15, 1762, at Dudley (England) and emigrated to America in 1788, arriving in NYC February 15, 1789. One of his first jobs in America was the chasing of silver buttons for Washington's inaugural suit. About 1791 he took up copper engraving and he continued in the business until his death, which occurred September 21, 1842. His work appeared in books published in the 1790's and after and he also did considerable banknote work in collaboration with WILLIAM S. LENEY. CHARLES ROLLINSON, probably a son of William, was also an engraver; another Charles, great-grandson of William, was a noted illuminator of the late 19th and early 20th centuries in NYC. ¶ DAB; Reid and Rollinson, *William Rollinson, Engraver;* Decatur, "William Rollinson, Engraver"; NYCD 1790–1842; Stokes, *Historical Prints;* Dunlap, *History.*

ROLOFF, LOUIS. Engraver, NYC, 1852–60 and after. ¶ NYCD 1852–60+.

ROLPH or ROLFE, JOHN A. (1799–1862). Engraver and painter. A native of Essex (England), Rolph came to NYC about 1839. As John Rolph or Rolfe he exhibited portraits, historical compositions, landscapes, and engravings at the Apollo Association and the National Academy between 1839 and 1844. In the NYC directories his occupation is variously given: 1839, baskets; 1840–52, engraver; 1853, toys; 1854, fancy store; 1855, varieties; 1856, toys; 1857–60 [Brooklyn CD], engraver; 1861–62 [Brooklyn and NYC], engraver. In 1864 his widow, Emma, is listed as "toys" in NYC. *Cf.* EMMA ROLFE of Brooklyn, 1839. ¶ Smith; Cowdrey, NAD; Cowdrey, AA & AAU; NYCD 1839–64; Brooklyn CD 1857–61; Stokes, *Iconography,* III, 628–29; Stauffer.

ROMANS, BERNARD (*c.* 1720–1784). Engraver, mapmaker, botanist, and engineer. Born in Holland, Romans received his education in England and came to America in 1755 as a surveyor and botanist. He was employed for some time in Florida and in 1775 he published a work on the natural history of that region. On the outbreak of the Revolution he joined the colonists and was present at the battle of Bunker Hill. In September 1775 he published at Philadelphia an engraving of the battle of Charlestown. Romans planned and partially built one of the forts at West Point and from 1776 to 1778 he was captain of a Pennsylvania artillery company. He is said to have been captured and taken to England where he resumed his profession. He disappared on a voyage from England to the United States in 1784 and is said to have been murdered. ¶ Stauffer; *Portfolio* (Aug.–Sept. 1947), 11–13, and (Feb. 1954), 124.

ROMEGAR, ——. Portrait and landscape painter working in Louisiana, 1772. ¶ Thompson, *Louisiana Writers.*

ROMEIN, PETER DE H. Painter of a portrait, dated 1844, of one John Miller, owned by Howard S. Mott, NYC. ¶ Information courtesy Howard S. Mott.

ROMNEY, MILES (1806–1877). One of the chief wood carvers employed in the building of the Mormon Temple at Nauvoo (Ill.) in the mid-1840's. He was born July 13, 1806, at Dalton, Lancashire; joined the Mormon Church in England in 1837; came to Nauvoo in 1841; moved to Utah in 1850; and died at St. George (Utah) in May 1877. ¶ Arrington, "Nauvoo Temple."

RONALDS, GEORGE L. Portrait painter, NYC, 1860. ¶ NYBD 1860.

RONALDSON, DOUGLASS S. Engraver, born in England about 1835, working in Philadelphia from 1858. His parents came to Philadelphia before 1840; Archibald Ronaldson, the father, was listed as a gentleman. ¶ 8 Census (1860), Pa., LIV, 166; Phila. CD 1858–60+.

RONDEL, FREDERICK (1826–1892). A.N.A. Landscape painter who exhibited at the National and Pennsylvania Academies and the Boston Athenaeum between 1855 and 1870. In 1855 and 1857 he was at Boston, in 1858 at South Malden (Mass.), in 1859–60 at NYC, in 1862 in Europe, and in 1868 at NYC. ¶ Swan, BA; Cowdrey, NAD; Rutledge, PA; NYBD 1859.

ROOD, STEPHEN. Engraver, 43, a native of England, living in NYC in 1850. His daughter, aged 4, was born in NYC. ¶ 7 Census (1850), N.Y., LVII, 128.

ROOKER, SAMUEL SAFFEL (*c.* 1800–*c.* 1875). House and sign painter who painted a few portraits. Born near Knoxville (Tenn.), he settled in Indianapolis (Ind.) in 1821 and lived there until after 1865. His last years were spent in Mooresville and Martinsville (Ind.). None of his work is known to have survived. ¶ Peat, *Pioneer Painters of Indiana,* 146–48, 237; Burnet, *Art and Artists of Indiana,* 58–59.

ROOS, JOHN FREDERICK FITZGERALD. Amateur artist and traveler. Lithographs based on his sketches illustrated his *Personal Narrative of Travels in the United States and Canada* (1827). ¶ Roos, *Personal Narrative,* copy in Library of Congress.

ROOS, LEONARD HENRIK (1787–1827). Miniaturist and etcher, born December 22, 1787, in Hjalleskate (Sweden). After studying in Sweden, Rome, and France, he went to England in 1824 and thence to the United States. He exhibited at the Pennsylvania Academy in 1825–26 as an American artist. He died in Colombia in 1827. ¶ Thieme-Becker; Rutledge, PA.

ROOT, ELMIRA. Watercolor and pin-prick portrait, *c.* 1840, found in Ashley (Ohio). ¶ Lipman and Winchester, 179; *Antiques* (Jan. 1946), 34, repro.

ROOT, RUSSELL C., & COMPANY. Lithographers and stationers, NYC, 1846. ¶ NYBD and CD 1846.

ROPES, GEORGE (1788–1819). Marine, landscape, carriage, and sign painter, born

May 15, 1788, at Salem (Mass.). Deaf and dumb from birth, Ropes studied painting under MICHELE FELICE CORNÉ about 1802 and worked in Salem until his death, January 24, 1819. ¶ Belknap, *Artists and Craftsmen of Essex County,* 12; Robinson and Dow, *Sailing Ships of New England,* I, 63; Swan and Kerr, "Early Marine Painters of Salem"; *Antiques* (Jan. 1930), frontis.; *Panorama* (March 1946), 62.

ROPES, GEORGE. Marine painter, Salem (Mass.), 1835–50. Possibly the same as the foregoing. ¶ Lipman and Winchester, 179 [corrected by letter of Jean Lipman, 12/6/50].

ROPES, JOSEPH (1812–1885). Landscape, miniature, and crayon artist and drawing teacher. Born at Salem (Mass.) in 1812, he did not seriously study painting until in his mid-thirties when he took lessons from JOHN R. SMITH and at the National Academy. He exhibited at the Academy in 1848. From 1851 to 1865 he had a studio in Hartford (Conn.). In 1865 he went abroad for eleven years; on his return he settled in Philadelphia. He died in NYC in 1885. Ropes was the author of *Linear Perspective* (1850) and *Progressive Steps in Landscape Drawing* (1853). ¶ French, *Art and Artists in Connecticut,* 79; Bolton, *Miniature Painters;* Cowdrey, NAD; Swan, BA; Hartford CD 1855; Tuckerman, *Book of the Artists.*

ROQUEN, AUGUST. French lithographer, 35, at NYC in 1860. His wife and fourteen-year-old daughter were born in France. ¶ 8 Census (1860), N.Y., XLIII, 766.

ROSE, ELIHU, see ROSE & HOWE.

ROSE & HOWE. Painters of NYC, who exhibited a bronze statuette at the American Institute in 1846. The partners were Elihu Rose and Joseph C. Howe. ¶ NYCD 1846–47; Am. Inst. Cat., 1846.

ROSE, JOHN. Amateur watercolorist. Deacon John Rose, of Dorchester, some miles up the river from Charleston (S.C.), was an amateur musician and painter in the early part of the 19th century, or possibly earlier. ¶ Rutledge, *Artists in the Life of Charleston,* 151.

ROSE, GEORGE P. Engraver and jeweler at Elmira (N.Y.), 1857. ¶ Elmira BD 1857.

ROSENBERG, CHARLES G. Landscape, portrait and figure painter, working in NYC from about 1857 to 1863 and at Philadelphia in 1866. He exhibited at the National and Pennsylvania Academies. His "Wall Street, Half Past 2 O'Clock, October 13, 1857," painted in collaboration with JAMES H. CAFFERTY, is owned by the Museum of the City of New York. ¶ Cowdrey, NAD; Rutledge, PA; NYBD 1859–60; *American Processional,* 245.

ROSENTHAL, LOUIS N. Lithographer and miniaturist. Born in Russian Poland, Louis Rosenthal was sent at 13 to a rabbinical school in Berlin. He came to America about 1850 and settled in Philadelphia. With his brother MAX and later MORRIS and SIMON, he was active there as a lithographer, printer, and publisher until about 1875. His last years were spent in Chicago. He was one of the pioneers in chromo-lithography in America. In later life he also painted some miniatures. ¶ Peters, *America on Stone;* Waite, "Beginnings of American Color Printing"; Phila. CD 1852–60+; 8 Census (1860), Pa., LII, 910.

ROSENTHAL, MAX (1833–1918). Lithographer, etcher, mezzotint engraver, and portrait painter, born November 23, 1833, in Russian Poland. At the age of 13 he was sent to Paris to study lithography under MARTIN THURWANGER and in 1849 or 1850 he emigrated to America. He settled in Philadelphia and was active as a lithographer there until his retirement in 1884, working during much of that time with his older brothers LOUIS N., MORRIS, and SIMON ROSENTHAL. After his retirement from business, Rosenthal devoted himself to teaching, mezzotint engraving, and oil painting. He is best known for a series of over 500 portraits—etchings, lithographs, and mezzotints—executed in collaboration with his son Albert. He died in Philadelphia, August 8, 1918. ¶ Peters, *America on Stone;* Stauffer; Phila. CD 1852–60+; *Art Annual,* XV, obit.; *Artists Year Book;* Rutledge, PA; 8 Census (1860), Pa., LIX, 492.

ROSENTHAL, MORRIS. Lithographer, working with his brothers LOUIS, MAX, and SIMON in Philadelphia for several years around 1860. He had served his apprenticeship with a lithographic printer in London and came to America in the late 1850's. He later abandoned lithography. ¶ Peters, *America on Stone.*

ROSENTHAL, SIMON. Lithographer, brother of LOUIS N., MAX and MORRIS ROSENTHAL. Born in Russian Poland and trained as a lithographer in London from the age of 13, Simon emigrated to America in the late 1850's and was for a number of years associated with his brothers in lithography at Philadelphia. He later gave up lithography. ¶ Peters, *America on Stone;* Phila. CD 1857–60+.

ROSIENKIEWICZ, MARTIN. Artist and teacher at Cincinnati, 1846–50. ¶ Cincinnati CD 1846–50, courtesy Edward H. Dwight, Cincinnati Art Museum.

ROSS, Miss ——. Exhibited a copy of Reynolds' "Sleeping Girl" at the 1826 Pennsylvania Academy show. Her name appears in neither of the indices of the catalogue, foreign and American artists. *Cf.* Miss M. Ross. ¶ PA Cat., 1826.

ROSS, Mr. or Mrs. ——. Exhibited a view in Cumberland (England) at the National Academy in 1835; address, 279 Pearl Street, NYC. Listed in the catalogue as Mrs. and in the index as Mr. Ross. ¶ Cowdrey, NAD; no Ross at this address in NYCD 1834–36.

ROSS, CHARLES. Lithographer, 20, born in Pennsylvania, living in Philadelphia in 1860. ¶ 8 Census (1860), Pa., LIV, 1051.

ROSS, GEORGE GATES (1814–1856). Portrait painter, born April 10, 1814, at Springfield (N.J.). He was active in Newark (N.J.) from 1835 to 1856 and exhibited at the National Academy and the Apollo Association. He died in Newark August 17, 1856. ¶ Information courtesy Mrs. Grace P. Smith of Maplewood (N.J.), who cites: *Newarker* (April 1936), Newark *Daily Advertiser,* April 5, 1847, June 5, 1850, Dec. 3, 1852, Dec. 11, 1854, and obit., Aug. 18 and 19, 1856; Newark CD 1835–56; Cowdrey, NAD; Cowdrey, AA & AAU; *American Collector* (Jan. 1948), 6–7.

ROSS, Miss M. Exhibited "Morning" and "Evening" at the Boston Athenaeum in 1836; address, 16 Hancock Street, Boston. *Cf.* Miss —— Ross and Mrs. EDWIN DALTON. ¶ BA Cat., 1836; not listed in Boston CD 1835–37.

ROSS, ROBERT. Portrait painter of New Orleans, 1830–32. ¶ Delgado-WPA cites New Orleans CD 1830, 1832.

ROSSE, CHRIST. Engraver, 21, a native of Germany, at Philadelphia in 1860. ¶ 8 Census (1860), Pa., LII, 911.

ROSSE, LEON. Portrait painter from Paris. He was at Halifax (N.S.) in 1835 and at Philadelphia in 1842 when he exhibited at the Artists' Fund Society. He also exhibited at the Pennsylvania Academy in 1836, address not given. ¶ Piers, "Artists in Nova Scotia," 146; Rutledge, PA.

ROSSET, JOSEPH. Swiss engraver, 28, at NYC in 1860. ¶ 8 Census (1860), N.Y., XLIII, 605; NYCD 1863.

ROSSETTI or ROSSETTE, JOHN BAPTISTE (?–1797). Italian portrait and miniature painter. He was at NYC in 1794–95. In January 1797 he advertised in Charleston (S.C.) and his death there was announced on September 15 of the same year. ¶ NYCD 1794–95; Rutledge, *Artists in the Life of Charleston.*

ROSSI, JEAN. Artist of New Orleans, 1859–65. ¶ Delgado-WPA cites CD 1859–60, 1865.

ROSSI, Signor TOBIAS. Portrait, historical, and landscape painter at Cincinnati, 1857–60. ¶ Cincinnati CD 1857–59, BD 1859–60; Ohio BD 1859.

ROSSITER, JOSEPH PYNCHON (1789–1826). Profile painter, born September 12, 1789, at Guilford (Conn.). After graduating from Yale College in 1810, he practised law for a short time in Salina (N.Y.). In 1818 he was living at Adams (Mass.). He later moved to Detroit and was accidentally drowned there June 10, 1826. ¶ Dexter, *Biographical Sketches of the Graduates of Yale College,* VI, 358–59; Carrick, *Shades of Our Ancestors,* 14; Carrick, "Profiles, Real and Spurious," five repros.

ROSSITER, THOMAS PRICHARD (1818–1871). N.A. Historical, religious, and portrait painter, born September 29, 1818, at New Haven (Conn.). He began his studies under NATHANIEL JOCELYN at New Haven and had a portrait studio of his own by the time he was twenty. In 1840 he went to Europe with DURAND, KENSETT, and CASILEAR and spent the next six years studying in Paris, London, and Rome, and travelling in Italy, Germany, and Switzerland. On his return to America in 1846, he took a studio in NYC with KENSETT and LOUIS LANG. In 1853 he went to Europe again for three years' study in Paris. Returning to NYC in 1856 he began to devote himself chiefly to historical and religious painting. In 1860 he built a home at Cold Spring, on the Hudson, where he lived until his death, May 17, 1871. ¶ DAB; Cowdrey, NAD; Cowdrey, AA & AAU; Rutledge, PA; Clement and Hutton; Tuckerman; CAB.

ROST, CHRISTIAN. Engraver, born in Germany. He studied in Paris and London and about 1851 designed and engraved illustrations for a book on the Crystal Palace exhibition in London. By 1860 he was in NYC where he was later employed by the AMERICAN BANK NOTE COMPANY. Stauffer, writing in 1907, stated that Rost had died several years before at Mount Vernon (N.Y.). ¶ Stauffer; NYCD 1860+. Smith gives the date of birth as 1766, obviously an error.

ROSTAING, A. Cameo portraitist at Cincinnati, 1835–44. He was a Frenchman. ¶ Cist, *Cincinnati in 1841,* 141; information courtesy Edward H. Dwight, Cincinnati Art Museum.

ROSTAN, L. Portrait painter, Boston, 1845. ¶ Boston BD 1845.

ROSTER, D. Portrait painter working in Illinois, 1853–55; represented by portraits of Mr. and Mrs. George Flower at the Chicago Historical Society. ¶ *American Primitive Painting,* nos. 9 and 10; *Antiques* (Nov. 1950), 393.

ROTH, GEORGE J. Portrait painter at Buffalo (N.Y.) 1859–60. Sherman records a portrait painted by G. J. Roth, 1870, found at Schuylerville (N.Y.). ¶ Buffalo BD 1859–60; Sherman, "Unrecorded Early American Portrait Painters" (1933), 31.

ROTHAS, JACOB. Teacher of architecture and drawing, New Orleans, 1835. ¶ Delgado-WPA cites *Bee,* Nov. 21, 1835.

ROTHERMEL, PETER FREDERICK (1817–1895). Historical and portrait painter, born July 8, 1817, at Nescopeck (Pa.). After receiving instruction from JOHN R. SMITH and BASS OTIS, and at the Pennsylvania Academy in Philadelphia, Rothermel worked for a time as a portrait painter but made his first real success with a historical work, "De Soto Discovering the Mississippi." From 1847 to 1855 he was a director of the Pennsylvania Academy and chairman of its education committee. He went to Europe in 1856 and resided in Rome for two years, returning to Philadelphia in 1859. After the Civil War he devoted almost five years to his most ambitious work, "The Battle of Gettysburg," now in the State Capitol, Harrisburg (Pa.). In 1877 he moved to his home, "Grassmere," near Linfield (Pa.), where he lived until his death, August 15, 1895. ¶ DAB; Cowdrey, NAD; Cowdrey, AA & AAU; Rutledge, PA; Tuckerman; Clement and Hutton; Swan, BA; Washington Art Assoc. Cat., 1857, 1859; 7 Census (1850), Pa., LIII, 264; 8 Census (1860), Pa., LV, 953; Sartain, *Reminiscences,* 185, 265.

ROTHWELL, J. Engraver working in NYC in 1841. ¶ Stauffer.

ROTTMAN, AD. Engraver of a California scene, showing golddiggings on the Mokelumne River, *c.* 1850. ¶ Dana, *United States Illustrated,* II, opp. 150.

ROUANEZ, P. P. Artist and teacher, Philadelphia, 1807–19. ¶ Brown and Brown.

ROUARD, JOHN. Sculptor, San Francisco, 1856–58. ¶ San Francisco CD 1856, BD 1858

ROUGUT, (Rouget?), MICHAEL. French lithographer, 31, at Philadelphia in 1860. ¶ 8 Census (1860), Pa., LII, 42.

ROULERY, REUBEN. Portrait painter at Albany (N.Y.) who was the instructor of PHILIP HEWINS about 1832. Probably the same as REUBEN ROWLEY. ¶ French, *Art and Artists in Connecticut,* 72.

ROUNDING, WILLIAM. English engraver, 28, at Philadelphia in 1850. ¶ 7 Census (1850), Pa., LII, 978.

ROUPEL, GEORGE. Botanical draftsman and caricaturist. Roupel had a position in the post office at Charleston (S.C.) before the Revolution. He illustrated some botanical papers which Alexander Garden sent to the Royal Society and at least one caricature which has been preserved. During or after the Revolution he went to England, leaving his wife and daughter in Charleston. His portrait by COPLEY was exhibited at the Royal Academy in 1780. ¶ Rutledge, *Artists in the Life of Charleston,* 118, 119, 173 (repro.).

ROUSE, G. Supposed modeler of wax portraits of Washington, dated 1797. These were forgeries made in London about 1924. There is no reason to believe that there ever was an artist of this name. ¶ Wall, "Wax Portraiture," 22–24; Bolton, *American Wax Portraits,* 60.

ROUSSEAU, EDME. Miniature and portrait painter working in NYC between 1826 and 1830 and in 1843. He exhibited at the National Academy in the latter year. ¶ NYCD 1826–30, 1843; Cowdrey, NAD.

ROUSSEAU, THEODORE (1812–1867). Portrait painter at Boston in 1858–59 and at Charleston (S.C.) in May 1859. He was represented in the Boston Athenaeum exhibition of 1868. ¶ Swan, BA; Boston CD 1858, BD 1859; Rutledge, *Artists in the Life of Charleston.*

ROUX, FRANCIS. Lithographer, 30, a native of France, at Philadelphia in 1860 with his wife, an artificial flower maker, and two-year-old daughter, also born in France. ¶ 8 Census (1860), Pa., LVIII, 375.

ROVER, HENRY. Artist and artists' supplier, NYC, 1848. ¶ NYBD and CD 1848.

ROWAND, WILLIAM. Portrait and miniature

painter from Glasgow (Scotland) who advertised in NYC in December 1777. He also offered to teach drawing and had for sale a painting in oils emblematic of the times. ¶ Kelby, *Notes on American Artists,* 14; Gottesman, *Arts and Crafts in New York,* II, no. 43.

ROWE, E. R. Artist at Benecia (Cal.) in 1850. ¶ Peters, *California on Stone.*

ROWE, L. K. Painter of an oil portrait, Salem (Mass.), 1860. ¶ Lipman and Winchester, 179.

ROWELL, SAMUEL (1815–?). Portrait painter, born at Amesbury (Mass.), August 22, 1815. He was living in Amesbury at least until 1841, the year of his marriage. ¶ Belknap, *Artists and Craftsmen of Essex County,* 12.

ROWLAND, HENRY. Engraver, 21, a native of New York, at NYC in 1860. ¶ 8 Census (1860), N.Y., XLVI, 820.

ROWLAND, JAMES S. Engraver, 27, born in Massachusetts, living in Boston in 1850. His brother William was doorkeeper at the Athenaeum. ¶ 7 Census (1850), Mass., XXV, 752; Boston CD 1850–52 (as plate printer).

ROWLEY, REUBEN. Portrait and miniature painter. He was an itinerant artist, working in the Chenango and Susquehanna Valley towns of New York State in the mid-1820's. About 1832 he was at Albany, where he was probably the instructor of PHILIP HEWINS. From 1834 to 1838 Rowley was at Boston; he exhibited at the Athenaeum in 1834 and 1835. ¶ Rathbone, "Itinerant Portraiture," 20; French, *Art and Artists in Connecticut,* 72 [as REUBEN ROULERY]; Boston CD 1834–38; Swan, BA; Lipman and Winchester, 179 [erroneously as of Amesbury, Mass.]; *Antiques* (Aug. 1925), 96, repro.

ROWSE, J. B. Of SHERER & ROWSE, lithographers at Cincinnati, 1847. ¶ Peters, *America on Stone.*

ROWSE, SAMUEL. Lithographer, Cincinnati, 1845–48. ¶ Peters, *America on Stone.*

ROWSE, SAMUEL WORCESTER (1822–1901). Crayon portraitist, engraver, and lithographer. Born January 29, 1822, at Bath (Me.) and brought up in Augusta (Me.), Rowse was first apprenticed to a wood engraver in Augusta and then went to work in Boston, probably with the lithographic firm of TAPPAN & BRADFORD. He later became widely known as a crayon portraitist and had a studio in Boston for many years. He visited England in 1872 and in 1880 moved to NYC. His last years were spent in Morristown (N.J.), where he died May 24, 1901. He never married. ¶ DAB; *Art Annual,* IV, obit.; Boston BD 1844+; Cowdrey, NAD; NYCD 1858; Swan, BA; Peters, *America on Stone;* "Maine Artists."

ROXBOROUGH, ALEXANDER. Scottish engraver at Philadelphia between 1850 and 1860. His age in 1850 was given as 44, in 1860 as 50. Of his four children, two were born in England, including WILLIAM ROXBOROUGH; the last two were born in Rhode Island in the early 1840's. ¶ 7 Census (1850), Pa., LVI, 331; 8 Census (1860), Pa., LX, 709.

ROXBOROUGH, WILLIAM. Engraver, born in England about 1829, the son of ALEXANDER ROXBOROUGH. He was working as an engraver at Philadelphia from 1850 into the 1870's. His oldest child was born in New Jersey about 1854; two younger ones were born in Philadelphia. ¶ 7 Census (1850), Pa., LVI, 331; 8 Census (1860), Pa., LX, 701; Phila. CD 1871.

RUBINA, Signor ——. Artist of a panorama of the Hungarian War shown at Louisville (Ky.) in 1859. ¶ Louisville *Daily Democrat,* Feb. 25, 1859 (citation courtesy J. E. Arrington).

RUBLER, LOUIS. French artist, 35, at NYC in 1850. ¶ 7 Census (1850), N.Y., XLIII, 285.

RUCKDESCHEL, CHARLES or J. CHARLES. General engraver, Philadelphia, 1858–60 and after. ¶ Phila. CD 1858, 1860+.

RUCKER, ——. Portrait painter at Richmond (Va.) in February 1846. ¶ *Richmond Portraits.*

RUCKLE, THOMAS (1776–1853). House and sign painter, amateur artist. In the early decades of the 19th century he executed a number of Baltimore views and scenes of the War of 1812 around Baltimore. He was the father of THOMAS COKE RUCKLE. ¶ Pleasants, *250 Years of Painting in Maryland,* 39.

RUCKLE, THOMAS COKE (1811–1891). Portrait, landscape, genre, and panorama painter, son of THOMAS RUCKLE. He was active in Baltimore as early as 1833 and apparently spent most of his life there, though he died at Catonsville (Md.) in 1891. Ruckle exhibited at the Maryland Historical Society, the Apollo Association, and the Royal Academy (1839–40). ¶ Pleasants, *250 Years of Painting in Maryland,* 39; Baltimore CD 1835–68; Cowdrey, AA & AAU; Rutledge, MHS; 7 Census (1850), Md., V, 674; Baltimore

Sun, Sept. 27 and Oct. 14, 1858 (citations courtesy J. E. Arrington); Graves, *Dictionary.*

RUDD, NATHANIEL. Wood engraver, Boston, 1857–60 and after. ¶ Boston CD 1857–60+.

RUDIGER, AUGUST E. Engraver and die sinker, born in Germany about 1818, working in NYC in 1850 and after. ¶ 7 Census (1850), N.Y., LI, 15; NYBD 1854, 1856.

RUDOLPH, ERNEST. Artist, 36, a native of Massachusetts, living in Baltimore in 1860. AMEL FAGLER was also at the same address. ¶ 8 Census (1860), Md., VII, 193.

RUEN, CHARLES. Swiss lithographer, 37, at Philadelphia in 1860. ¶ 8 Census (1860), Pa., LII, 664. *Cf.* CHARLES REEN.

RUGER, WASHINGTON. Portrait and landscape painter, Binghamton (N.Y.), 1856–59. ¶ Binghamton CD 1857–59.

RUGGLES, E., JR. Engraver of one known New England bookplate, *c.* 1790–1800. ¶ Stauffer.

RUGGLES, EDWARD. Amateur landscape and marine painter of New York who exhibited several Italian and French views at the National Academy and American Art-Union between 1851 and 1860. He was a physician and an Honorary Member of the National Academy. ¶ Cowdrey, NAD; Cowdrey, AA & AAU.

RUGGLES, Mrs. MARY. Landscape painter, address not given; exhibited at the National Academy in 1859–60. One of her paintings was entitled "Roman Ruins." Possibly the wife of EDWARD RUGGLES. ¶ Cowdrey, NAD.

RUHLAND (or Roland), JOHN. Portrait and general painter at Buffalo (N.Y.), 1850's. ¶ Buffalo CD and BD 1855–60.

RUMBLE, Mrs. STEPHEN. Amateur landscape painter who filled her mansion, "Rosalie," at Natchez (Miss.) in the 1850's with examples of her own work. She had studied at a boarding school in New York. ¶ Barker, *American Painting,* 525.

RUMFORD, COUNT, see BENJAMIN THOMPSON.

RUMPLER, WILLIAM. Artist at New Orleans in 1853 and 1859; represented in the Louisiana State Museum. ¶ New Orleans CD 1853, 1859; Thompson, *Louisiana Writers;* Delgado-WPA.

RUMSEY, HIRAM. Virginia-born artist, 29, at Philadelphia in 1850. ¶ 7 Census (1850), Pa., LI, 83.

RUNGE, JOHN. Artist, 39, a native of Bremen (Germany), living in NYC in 1860 with his English wife and two children (3 and 1), both born in New York. ¶ 8 Census (1860), N.Y., LX, 1014.

RUPP, CHRISTIAN. Of SEILER & RUPP, engravers and die sinkers, NYC, 1850. ¶ NYCD 1850.

RUSBATCH, SAMUEL. Decorative, heraldic, and general painter, trained in England, who advertised in Annapolis (Md.) in January 1774. He was under the "direction" of Joseph Horatio Anderson, Annapolis architect. ¶ Prime, I, 293; Barker, *American Painting,* 178.

RUSH, Miss ——. Teacher of drawing and painting on paper, velvet, satin, and ivory, at Charleston (S.C.) in 1819. ¶ Rutledge, *Artists in the Life of Charleston.*

RUSH, IRA or J. Portrait painter, 28, from Ohio, at New Orleans in 1850. ¶ 7 Census (1850), La., VI, 489.

RUSH, Mrs. JACOB, see POLLY WRENCH.

RUSH, JOHN (1782–1853). Figurehead carver. He was the eldest son of WILLIAM RUSH, with whom he worked until the latter's death. John was active in Philadelphia until his death, January 2, 1853. ¶ Marceau, *William Rush,* genealogical table opp. 7; Pinckney, *American Figureheads and Their Carvers,* 58, 62–63, 199.

RUSH, WILLIAM (1756–1833). Sculptor in wood, born July 4, 1756, at Philadelphia. Rush learned ship carving in the shop of EDWARD CUTBUSH before the Revolution. After serving with the Continental Army, he set up his own shop in Philadelphia. Although his income was derived mainly from ship carving, Rush also carved portrait busts, anatomical models, and ideal figures such as the well-known "Nymph of the Schuylkill." He was a promoter of the Columbianum and the Pennsylvania Academy. Among his pupils were his son, JOHN RUSH, and DANIEL N. TRAIN. William Rush died in Philadelphia January 17, 1833. ¶ Marceau, *William Rush,* catalogue raisonnée, illus.; DAB; Pinckney, *American Figureheads and Their Carvers,* 56–71; Rutledge, PA; Dunlap, *History;* Taft, *History of American Sculpture.*

RUSS, JOHN. Engraver, 30, a native of France, at Philadelphia in July 1860. Possibly the John Russ, engraver, at NYC from 1856 to 1860. ¶ 8 Census (1860), Pa., LII, 94; NYBD 1856–60.

RUSSELL, ALBERT CUYP (1838–1917). Engraver and illustrator who died at Roxbury (Mass.) in December 1917. He was a son of MOSES B. RUSSELL and in 1860 was apprenticed to LEOPOLD GROZELIER of Boston. ¶ *Art Annual,* XV, obit.; 8 Census (1860), Mass., XXVIII, 103.

RUSSELL, BENJAMIN (1804–1885). Marine painter, specializing in whaling scenes. A native of New Bedford (Mass.), he spent four years on a whaler in the 1840's and thereafter devoted himself to painting watercolor marines. His panorama of a whaling voyage around the world was first exhibited in Boston in January 1849 and was subsequently shown in Cincinnati, Louisville, St. Louis, Baltimore, and NYC. He also worked with A. VAN BEEST and ROBERT S. GIFFORD. He was active until the 1870's. ¶ Childs, "Thar She Blows"; information courtesy J. E. Arrington; NYBD 1854 [as engraver]; Peters, *America on Stone.*

RUSSELL, DAVID. Engraver and plate printer, Boston, 1840's. ¶ Boston CD 1842–48.

RUSSELL, H. Miniaturist, Boston, about 1860. ¶ Sherman, "Some Recently Discovered Early American Portrait Miniaturists," 294, 295 (repro.).

RUSSELL, JOSEPH SHOEMAKER (1795–?). Amateur watercolorist. A native of New Bedford (Mass.), he moved to Philadelphia in 1818 and had a lamp oil store there. A number of his watercolors have been preserved, chiefly views of buildings and interiors in Philadelphia and New Bedford. ¶ Little, "Joseph Shoemaker Russell and His Water Color Views," seven repros.

RUSSELL, LYDIA SMITH. Painter of a portrait of Abigail (Smith) Adams, signed and dated 1804. ¶ WPA (Mass.), *Portraits Found in Mass.,* no. 6.

RUSSELL, MOSES B. (*c.* 1810–1884). Portrait, miniature, and figure painter, born either in New Hampshire (1850 Census) or Massachusetts (1860 Census). He was active in Boston from 1834 to 1850, in NYC during the late fifties, and at Philadelphia in 1860. He exhibited at the Boston Athenaeum and the American Institute. His wife was also a miniaturist and their son, ALBERT CUYP RUSSELL, became an engraver and illustrator. ¶ Swan, BA; 7 Census (1850), Mass., XXV, 646; 8 Census (1860), Pa., LIV, 266; Boston BD 1841–50; NYBD 1856–59; Am. Inst. Cat., 1856; Bolton, *Miniature Painters;* Jackson, *Ancestors in Silhouette,* 222; Lipman and Winchester [as N. B. Russell].

RUSSELL, Mrs. MOSES B. Miniaturist, born in Massachusetts about 1810; her Christian name was Clarissa. Mrs. Russell was at Boston from about 1842 to 1854 and exhibited at the Athenaeum. She was the mother of ALBERT CUYP RUSSELL. ¶ 7 Census (1850), Mass., XXV, 646; Swan, BA; Boston BD 1851–54; Jackson, *Ancestors in Silhouette,* 220.

RUSSELL, STEPHEN S. C. (or L. S.). Wood engraver and designer, born in Maine about 1836. In 1860 he was living in Boston in the home of his father, Edward T. Russell, and was in partnership with HENRY BRICHER. ¶ 8 Census (1860), Mass., XXVIII, 928; Boston CD 1858–60+.

RUSSELL, W. C. Miniaturist and portrait painter at NYC in 1837; exhibited at the National Academy. ¶ Cowdrey, NAD; Bolton, *Miniature Painters.*

RUTHERFORD, ALEXANDER W. (1826–1851). Genre, portrait, and still life painter. A native of Vermont, he studied in NYC under HUNTINGTON about 1847 and was patronized by the American Art-Union in 1848 and after. In 1850 he went to Europe to continue his studies but he died in London the following year at the age of 26. ¶ *Panorama* (Jan. 1949), 56–57, back cover; Cowdrey, AA & AAU; Cowdrey, NAD; Tuckerman, *Book of the Artists; American Collector* (Dec. 1948), 17.

RUTHERFORD, J. C. Painter of a portrait of John Calvin Bingham (1816–1870), owned in 1941 by Miss Catherine Bingham of St. Johnsbury (Vt.). ¶ WPA (Mass.), *Portraits Found in Vermont.*

RUTHERFORD, JOHN. Portrait painter at Cincinnati in 1818. ¶ Information courtesy Edward H. Dwight, Cincinnati Art Museum.

RUTHVEN, EDWIN C. Engraver at Baltimore in 1856 and at Philadelphia in 1860. ¶ Baltimore CD 1856; Phila. CD 1860.

RUTTER, GEORGE. Heraldic and ornamental painter working in Philadelphia in the 1780's and 1790's. In 1796 he was associated with JEREMIAH PAUL, MATTHEW PRATT, and WILLIAM CLARKE. ¶ Scharf and Westcott, *History of Philadelphia,* II, 1040; Prime, I, 19, and II, 3–14; Dickson, "A Note on Jeremiah Paul," 393.

RYAN, JAMES L. Lithographer's apprentice, 15, born in Massachusetts of an Irish mother, living in Boston in 1860. ¶ 8 Census (1860), Mass., XXVII, 254.

RYAN, JOHN. Engraver, 17, born in Pennsylvania of an Irish family, living in Philadelphia in 1850. His father, James

Ryan, was a tavernkeeper. ¶ 7 Census (1850), Pa., L, 941.

RYAN, WILLIAM REDMOND. Artist. A native of England, he lived for some years in America before 1847, when he went to California with a group of volunteers for the Mexican War. He remained in California until 1849 and did some gold-mining. After his return to England he published *Personal Adventures in Upper and Lower California, in 1848–49* (London, 1850), illustrated with 23 plates after his own sketches. ¶ CAB; NYCD 1847 [as artist]; Jackson, *Gold Rush Album;* Peters, *California on Stone.*

RYDER, J. F. Portrait painter at Cleveland (Ohio) in 1860. ¶ WPA (Mass.), *Portraits Found in Vt.*

RYDER, PLATT POWELL (1821–1896). A.N.A. Genre and portrait painter, born June 11, 1821, in Brooklyn (N.Y.). He began exhibiting at the National Academy in 1850 and was elected an Associate of the Academy in 1868. In 1869–70 he studied in Paris and London. His home was in Brooklyn and he was active in the founding of the Brooklyn Academy of Design. Ryder died July 15, 1896, at Saratoga Springs (N.Y.). ¶ CAB; Cowdrey, NAD; Rutledge, PA; Boston *Transcript,* July 17, 1896.

RYERSON, LUTHER L. Of LEIGHTON & RYERSON, portrait painters, Roxbury (Mass.), 1860. ¶ Roxbury CD 1860; New England BD 1860.

RYKER, EDWARD. Engraver, 24, born in New Jersey, living in NYC in 1850. ¶ 7 Census (1850), N.Y., XLV, 14.

RYLAND, MARK. Engraver, 27, born in New Jersey, living in NYC in 1860. ¶ 8 Census (1860), N.Y., LX, 655.

S

SACHEVERELL, JOHN. Engraver on gold, silver, brass, copper, and steel; active in Philadelphia in 1732–33. ¶ Hamilton, *Early American Book Illustrators and Wood Engravers,* 48; Brown and Brown.

SACHS, BERNARD. General and stencil engraver, Philadelphia, 1857 and after. ¶ Phila. CD 1857–60+.

SACHS, FREDERICK. German lithographer, 33, living in Philadelphia in 1850. His wife and three older children were also born in Germany; the youngest child, aged 2, was born in Pennsylvania. ¶ 7 Census (1850), Pa., L, 345; Phila. CD 1850.

SACHS, LAMBERT. Portrait and historical painter, teacher of drawing and painting, at Philadelphia in the 1850's. He exhibited at the Pennsylvania Academy in 1854. ¶ Rutledge, PA; Phila. CD 1855, BD 1860; repro., Garbisch Collection, *Catalogue,* 105.

SACHSE, AUGUST. Engraver, 50, a native of Germany, at Baltimore in 1860 with his wife Catherine and sons August, born in Germany about 1839, and Arthur, born in Maryland about 1854. He may have been a brother of the Baltimore lithographers, EDWARD and THEODORE SACHSE. The name is spelt Sase in the Census. August, Jr., was also an engraver. ¶ 8 Census (1860), Md., VI, 35.

SACHSE & COMPANY. Lithographers, Baltimore, 1851–1870 and after; EDWARD, THEODORE, and, in 1860, WILLIAM SACHSE. ¶ Baltimore CD 1851–74; *Portfolio* (Dec. 1948), 93; Peters, *America on Stone.*

SACHSE, EDWARD (1804–1873). Lithographer and painter. A native of Gorlitz, near Breslau (Germany), Sachse came to America in the late 1840's, accompanied by his family and his brother THEODORE. They settled in Baltimore where the firm of SACHSE & COMPANY, lithographers, was active until the 1870's. Edward also exhibited at the Maryland Historical Society. ¶ Pleasants, *250 Years of Painting in Maryland,* 51; Baltimore CD 1851–74; Peters, *America on Stone;* Stokes, *Historical Prints;* Rutledge, MHS.

SACHSE, JOHN HENRY DAVID. Miniaturist at Philadelphia about 1830. ¶ Information courtesy Mrs. Joseph Carson.

SACHSE, THEODORE. Lithographer, born in Germany about 1815. He came to America after 1847, settled in Baltimore, and there carried on a lithographic business with his older brother, EDWARD SACHSE, until the 1870's. ¶ 8 Census (1860), Md., VI, 52; Pleasants, *250 Years of Painting in Maryland,* 51; Baltimore CD 1851–74 [under SACHSE & Co.]. CD 1856 lists a Thomas Sachse, lithographer, probably an error for Theodore.

SACHSE, WILLIAM. Lithographer, of SACHSE & COMPANY, Baltimore, 1860. ¶ Baltimore CD 1860.

SACKETT, ESTHER. Watercolor still life, New York State, about 1840. ¶ Lipman and Winchester, 179.

SADD, HENRY S. English mezzotint engraver who came to America about 1840 and worked in NYC for about ten years, after which he went to Australia. He exhibited in London in 1832 and at the National Academy between 1840 and 1849. ¶ Stauffer; Thieme-Becker; Graves, *Dictionary;* Cowdrey, NAD; NYCD 1843–49; *Portfolio* (Feb. 1954), 127.

SADLER, RUPERT or RUFUS. Portrait painter and picture restorer, born in Cork (Ireland) about 1816, working in Boston after 1848. ¶ 8 Census (1860), Mass., XXV, 294 [as Rufus Saddler]; New England BD 1849 and Boston BD 1852 [as R. Sadler]; Boston CD 1851 [as Rupert Sadler].

SAENZ, MANUEL. Miniaturist at New Orleans in October 1842. He claimed a connection with the Madrid Academy of Painting and the Valladolid Society of Arts. ¶ Delgado-WPA cites *Courier,* Oct. 10, 1842.

SAGE, LETITIA, see Mrs. HENRY BENBRIDGE.

SAGE & SONS. Lithographers and music dealers at Buffalo (N.Y.), 1856–60. The firm consisted of John Sage and his sons Henry H., John B., and William Sage. ¶ Peters, *America on Stone;* Buffalo BD 1856–60.

SAGER, JOSEPH. Artist, Cincinnati, 1850. ¶ Cincinnati CD 1850 (courtesy Edward H. Dwight, Cincinnati Art Museum).

ST. ALARY, E. Pastel portraitist who came to Chicago in 1855 from Detroit and exhibited at the Illinois State Fair. He was said to have traveled all over the world. ¶ Chicago *Daily Press,* Oct. 4 and 11, 1855.

SAINT ARMAND, DREUX. Scene painter at a

New Orleans theater in 1838. ¶ Delgado-WPA cites *Courier,* Sept. 14, 1838.

SAINT-AULAIRE, FELIX ACHILLE DE BEAUPOIL, Marquis de (1801–?). Landscape painter and lithographer. He was a French nobleman who studied under the Garnerays in Paris and exhibited at the Salon in 1827 and 1838. In 1821 he visited the United States and traveled as far west as Guyandotte on the Ohio River, of which he made a watercolor view still extant. He also executed several lithographs of American views in 1832 in France. ¶ *Portfolio* (June 1948), 220–21; Davidson, *Life in America,* I, 179.

SAINT GES, ——. Artist and drawing master, New Orleans, 1816. ¶ Delgado-WPA cites *Ami des Lois,* June 7, 1816.

ST. JOHN, Mrs. SUSAN HELY (1833–1913). Painter. She studied under G. P. A. HEALY in Chicago and had a studio in Boston, where she died October 25, 1913. ¶ *Art Annual,* XI, obit.

ST. JOHN, ——. Flower painter, NYC, exhibited at the National Academy in 1839. ¶ Cowdrey, NAD.

SAINT-MÉMIN, CHARLES BALTHAZAR JULIEN FEVRET DE (1770–1852). Profilist, crayon and watercolor portraitist, landscape painter, and engraver. Born March 12, 1770, at Dijon (France), Saint-Mémin was intended for a military career but the outbreak of the French Revolution caused his family's emigration to Switzerland and thence to America about 1793. To assist his impoverished parents, he turned professional artist in 1796. His first productions were landscapes but he soon turned to the more lucrative branch of portraiture. With the aid of a physionotrace he took accurate profiles, many of which he reduced to miniature size and engraved himself. From NYC he moved in 1798 to Burlington (N.J.), then to Philadelphia. From 1804 to 1809 he worked in Baltimore, Annapolis, Washington, Richmond, and Charleston, and in 1810 he returned to France. Saint-Mémin was back in NYC in 1812 and remained for two years, painting portraits and landscapes. After his final return to Dijon in 1814 he served as director of the local museum until his death, June 23, 1852. ¶ There is one biography of Saint-Mémin: Guignard, *Notice Historique sur la Vie . . . de Saint-Mémin* (1853), as well as numerous monographs and articles on various aspects of his work, chief among them being the following: Norfleet, *Saint-Mémin in Virginia;* Pleasants, *Saint-Mémin Water Color Miniatures;* Bolton, "Saint-Mémin's Crayon Portraits"; and Rice, "An Album of Saint-Mémin Portraits," with a useful bibliography. Represented at Maryland Historical Society, the Corcoran Gallery, and NYHS. See also: DAB; *Richmond Portraits;* Stokes, *Iconography.*

SAINT REMY, Mme. DE. Portrait painter, NYC, exhibited at the National Academy in 1844. ¶ Cowdrey, NAD.

SAINTIN, JULES ÉMILE (1829–1894). A.N.A. Portrait, genre, and landscape painter, born April 14, 1829, at Leme (Aisne), France. He was working in NYC by 1856 and was an Associate Member of the National Academy from 1859. He exhibited at the Academy and at the Boston Athenaeum. He died in Paris July 14, 1894, when he was remembered chiefly for his "Pony Express" and a portrait of Stephen A. Douglas. ¶ N. Y. *Times,* July 16, 1894, obit.; NYBD 1856–60; Cowdrey, NAD; Swan, BA.

SALAZAR, FRANCISCO. Portrait painter in Louisiana during the 1790's. *Cf.* JOSÉ DE SALAZAR. ¶ Van Ravenswaay, "The Forgotten Arts and Crafts of Colonial Louisiana," 195.

SALAZAR, JOSÉ DE. Portrait (?) painter working in Louisiana and the United States between 1792 and 1801. *Cf.* FRANCISCO SALAZAR. ¶ Information courtesy the late William Sawitzky, who identified a number of paintings by this artist.

SALISBURY, C. B. Portrait painter at Albany (N.Y.) in 1852. ¶ Albany BD 1852.

SALMON, J. Landscape painter from Boston who exhibited at the Pennsylvania Academy in 1852. ¶ Rutledge, PA.

SALMON, ROBERT (*c.* 1775–*c.* 1842). Marine painter. Of Scottish descent, if not birth, Salmon was working in England as early as 1800; he was at Liverpool from 1806 to 1812 and at Greenock (Scotland) from 1812 to 1821, and later at North Shields. In 1828 he emigrated to America and settled in Boston where he had a flourishing business as a marine and ship painter until 1841. He probably died soon after the latter date. The Boston Public Library owns Salmon's diary, 1828–41, and many examples of his work are in museums and private homes in and around Boston. ¶ Childs, "Robert Salmon," with 15 repros.; Karolik Cat.; Boston CD 1831–40; Cowdrey, NAD; Swan, BA; Cowdrey, AA & AAU; Rutledge, PA;

Rutledge, MHS; Tolman, "Salmon's View of Boston."

SALOMON, WILLIAM. Engraver, born in Louisiana about 1823, active in New Orleans from 1841 to 1850. ¶ 7 Census (1850), La., VI, 173; New Orleans CD 1841–42, 1846.

SALTER, ANN ELIZABETH. Memorial painting on velvet, Massachusetts, about 1810. ¶ Lipman and Winchester, 179.

SALTZMANN, JOHN C. Engraver, New Orleans, 1827–32. The name also is given as Salzmann. ¶ Delgado-WPA cites New Orleans CD 1827, 1830, 1832.

SALVIGNAC, JEAN. Portrait painter, New Orleans, 1830. ¶ Delgado-WPA cites New Orleans CD 1830.

SAMOURI, CLAUDE. Engraver, New Orleans, 1850–51. ¶ Delgado-WPA cites New Orleans CD 1850–51.

SAMPSON, JOHN. Lithographer, 24, a native of Maryland, at Baltimore in 1850. ¶ 7 Census (1850), Md., V, 66.

SAMUELS, W. G. M. Amateur painter. He was an early sheriff of San Antonio (Tex.). The Witte Museum owns his four views of the main plaza of the city, dated 1849. ¶ *Antiques* (June 1948), 457; Lipman and Winchester, 179.

SAMYN, ——. Lithographer of ten plates in John Delafield's *Inquiry into the Origins of the Antiquities of America* (N.Y., 1839). ¶ Copy at Library of Congress.

SANCAN, J. Portrait painter, New Orleans, 1854. ¶ New Orleans CD 1854.

SAND, JOHN F. Portrait painter, NYC, 1840–43; exhibitor at the National Academy and the Apollo Association. *Cf.* Master SANDS; JOHN SANDS. ¶ Cowdrey, NAD; Cowdrey, AA & AAU.

SANDERS, ANDREW. Canadian engraver, 25, at NYC in 1860. ¶ 8 Census (1860), N.Y., XLII, 787.

SANDERS & BROTHERS. Varnishers and japanners, NYC, exhibited a painting at the American Institute in 1844. The firm consisted of James, Thomas W., and Walter Sanders. ¶ Am. Inst. Cat., 1844; NYCD 1845.

SANDERS, F. Artist, NYC, 1850. ¶ NYCD 1850.

SANDERS or SAUNDERS, W. C. Portrait, figure, and landscape painter. He first exhibited at the National Academy in 1838, after which he appears to have gone to Italy. He was exhibiting at the National Academy and the American Art-Union between 1845 and 1849, his address being Florence in 1847 and Mobile (Ala.) in 1847–48. In 1852 he also exhibited at the Pennsylvania Academy, giving Rome as his address. ¶ Cowdrey, NAD; Cowdrey, AA & AAU; Rutledge, PA.

SANDERS, see also SAUNDERS.

SANDERSON, ——. Painter or proprietor of a panorama of the Crimean War, shown in Baltimore in 1857 and Savannah (Ga.) in 1858. ¶ Baltimore *Sun,* Dec. 25, 1857, and Savannah *Republican,* April 8, 1858 (citations courtesy J. E. Arrington).

SANDERSON, CHARLES WESLEY (1838–1905). Landscape painter in oils and watercolors, born at Brandon (Vt.) in 1838. Though he became a music teacher by profession, he also studied painting and drawing, first in Vermont with JAMES HOPE, then with SAMUEL L. GERRY in Boston, and later in Paris and England. He made his home in Boston and died there March 8, 1905. ¶ Clement and Hutton; *Art Annual,* V, obit.

SANDERSON, GEORGE. English engraver, 15, living with GEORGE GIBSON in Cincinnati in 1850. He was presumably Gibson's apprentice. ¶ 7 Census (1850), Ohio, XXII, 438.

SANDERSON, HENRY (1808–1880). Portrait, historical, landscape, and genre painter; born in Philadelphia on August 24, 1808. He settled in New Brunswick (N.J.) about 1830 and spent the rest of his life there, except for a period of study in London about 1841. He exhibited at the National Academy 1841–44 and in 1868 sold at auction in New Brunswick ten of his paintings. His copy of LEUTZE's "Washington Crossing the Delaware" and one of his sketch books are at Rutgers University. Sanderson was also active in local affairs, serving on the Board of Education and from 1853 to 1861 as postmaster of New Brunswick. He died in New Brunswick on December 23 or 24, 1880. ¶ Tombstone, First Baptist Cemetery, New Brunswick; New Brunswick *Weekly Advertiser,* Dec. 30, 1880, obit.; New Brunswick *Fredonian,* Dec. 24, 1868 (citations courtesy Donald A. Sinclair, Rutgers Univ. Library); Cowdrey, NAD.

SANDMEYER, JACQUES. Lithographer, NYC, 1857–59. ¶ NYBD 1857, 1859.

SANDS, Master ——. Painter, pupil of J. H. SHEGOGUE. He exhibited at the Apollo Association in 1839 a copy of a genre painting by "Owen." ¶ Cowdrey, AA & AAU

SANDS, ALFRED R. Portrait painter, NYC, 1844. ¶ NYBD 1844.

SANDS, JOHN. Exhibited an oil painting at the American Institute in 1844. He was a resident of NYC. *Cf.* JOHN F. SAND. ¶ Am. Inst. Cat., 1844.

SANDS, RICHARD. Artist, NYC, 1847–48. ¶ NYCD 1847–48.

SANDYS, EDWIN. Engraver, Baltimore, 1859–60. ¶ Baltimore BD 1859, CD 1860.

SANFORD, ——. Painter (?) of a panorama of the Mississippi River, shown in NYC in 1853. ¶ N. Y. *Herald,* Jan. 28, March 21, June 1, 1853 (citations courtesy J. E. Arrington).

SANFORD, G. P. Landscape painter, NYC, exhibited at the National Academy in 1842. *Cf.* GEORGE T. SANFORD. ¶ Cowdrey, NAD.

SANFORD, GEORGE T. Lithographer and artist, NYC, 1843–46. *Cf.* G. P. SANFORD. ¶ NYCD 1843–44, 1846.

SANFORD, ISAAC. Engraver and occasional portrait and miniature painter who was active in Hartford (Conn.) from about 1783 to 1822. He was also an inventor and spent some years in England between 1799 and 1808 trying to push his inventions. He later settled in Philadelphia, where he died about 1842. Family miniatures by him are in the Wadsworth Athenaeum and his papers are preserved in the Connecticut Historical Society. ¶ Brainard, "Isaac Sanford"; Stauffer; Bolton, *Miniature Painters.*

SANFORD, J. Profilist and silhouettist, South Carolina, 1807. *Cf.* ISAAC SANFORD. ¶ Information courtesy Miss Anna Wells Rutledge.

SANFORD, LOCKWOOD. Wood engraver, born in Connecticut about 1817, active in New Haven in 1850 and after. ¶ 7 Census (1850), Conn., II; New England BD 1856, 1860; New Haven CD 1856–58; Hamilton, *Early American Book Illustrators and Wood Engravers,* 265, 329.

SANFORD, M. M. Battle scene in oils, primitive, about 1850. ¶ Lipman and Winchester, 179.

SANGER, ANTHONY. Sculptor, 25, a native of Württemberg, living in Boston in 1860 with WENDOLIN SANGER, presumably a younger brother. ¶ 8 Census (1860), Mass., XXVII, 365.

SANGER, HENRY L. Engraver, Boston, 1860. ¶ Boston CD 1860.

SANGER, WENDOLIN. Sculptor, 22, a native of Württemberg, living in Boston in 1860 with ANTHONY SANGER, presumably an older brother. ¶ 8 Census (1860), Mass., XXVII, 365.

SANGSTER, ——. Carver. A Cleveland (Ohio) newspaper in July 1846 spoke of this 14-year-old as having whittled his way to fame at Buffalo (N.Y.) by his carving of the Lord's Supper. ¶ WPA (Ohio), *Annals of Cleveland.*

SANGTELLER, see SENGTELLER.

SANSAY, Mme. ——. Of Hamilton (Pa.), exhibited artificial flowers at the Society of Artists in Philadelphia in 1813. *Cf.* Mrs. L. SARAZIN. ¶ Society of Artists Cat., 1813.

SANSOM, JOSEPH. Amateur landscape draftsman. A Philadelphian, noted in the early years of the 19th century as a traveler and author. In 1811 he contributed to *Port Folio* an account of Nantucket, illustrated by a view of Sherburne after his own sketch. ¶ *Panorama* (Feb. 1947), cover and p. 64; Stokes, *Historical Prints,* pl. 42a.

SANTELLA or SANTELLO, see SENGTELLER.

SARAZIN, Mrs. L. Drawing teacher, Hamilton (Pa.), who exhibited watercolors and crayon drawings at the Society of Artists and Pennsylvania Academy between 1813 and 1827. *Cf.* Mme. SANSAY. ¶ Rutledge, PA.

SARGENT, Mrs. CHRISTIANA KEADIE SWAN (Mrs. I. T.) (1777–1867). Landscape painter, who exhibited at the Boston Athenaeum in 1828 and 1837. ¶ Swan, BA.

SARGENT, HENRY (1770–1845). Portrait, historical, religious, and genre painter. A native of Gloucester (Mass.), where he was baptized November 25, 1770, Sargent spent his childhood there and in Boston. Though brought up to a commercial career, he chose instead to be a painter and in 1793 went to England to study under WEST. He returned to Boston about 1797 and there spent the rest of his life. For some years he was more active as a militia officer and politician than as a painter, and in later years he also devoted much time to mechanical invention. He continued to paint into old age, however, and in 1840 became an Honorary Member of the National Academy. In 1845, the year of his death, he was elected first president of the Artists' Association of Boston. Sargent died in Boston February 21, 1845. ¶ DAB; Addison, "Henry Sargent, a Boston Painter"; Dunlap, *History;* Dickson, *Observations on American Art by John Neal,* 7–8; Belknap, *Artists and Craftsmen of Essex County,* 12; Swan, BA; Flexner, *The Light of Distant Skies.*

SARGENT, Mrs. I. T., see Mrs. CHRISTIANA KEADIE SWAN SARGENT.

SARONY, HECTOR. Exhibited lithographs and a pencil drawing at the American Institute in 1848 and 1849. He was listed at the same address as NAPOLEON SARONY. ¶ Am. Inst. Cat., 1848, 1849.

SARONY & MAJOR. Lithographers, NYC, 1846–57. The firm was established in 1846 by NAPOLEON SARONY and HENRY B. MAJOR, former employees of NATHANIEL CURRIER. In 1857 it became SARONY, MAJOR & KNAPP. ¶ Peters, *America on Stone;* Am. Inst. Cat., 1847–49.

SARONY, MAJOR & KNAPP. Lithographers, NYC, 1857–67. The firm was established when JOSEPH F. KNAPP joined forces with SARONY & MAJOR in 1857. After Sarony's retirement from the company in 1867, the name was changed to Major & Knapp. ¶ Peters, *America on Stone.*

SARONY, NAPOLEON (1821–1896). Lithographer, photographer, charcoal portraitist. Born March 9, 1821, in Quebec, Sarony came to NYC about 1836, studied drawing with a Mr. ROBERTSON, probably ALEXANDER, and was employed as a lithographer by HENRY R. ROBINSON and NATHANIEL CURRIER. In 1846 he joined forces with HENRY B. MAJOR to form the firm of SARONY & MAJOR, later expanded to SARONY, MAJOR & KNAPP. Sarony left the firm about 1867, visited Cuba for his health, and then went to Europe for six years, during which time he did some lithographic work in Germany, France, and England. After a brief visit to NYC he again went abroad and opened a photographic studio in Birmingham, where he achieved a high reputation for artistic photography. Sarony eventually returned to NYC and was a successful photographer there for some years before his death. In later years he also did charcoal portraits. He died in NYC November 9, 1896. ¶ Peters, *America on Stone;* Peters, *Currier & Ives,* I, 120–29; NYBD 1846 and after; Am. Inst. Cat., 1850; *Antiques* (Feb. 1927), 108–09; represented at Princeton University by pastel portrait of Grover Cleveland (information courtesy Donald Egbert).

SARTAIN, HENRY (1833–*c.* 1895). Engraver, architectural draftsman, portrait and religious painter. Henry, second son of JOHN SARTAIN, was born in Philadelphia July 14, 1833. He was trained as an engraver by his father and probably also studied painting and drawing at the Pennsylvania Academy, where he exhibited between 1852 and 1861. In 1866 he gave up engraving to take charge of the printing establishment which handled his father's plates. ¶ Stauffer; Rutledge, PA; Phila. CD 1856+; 8 Census (1860), Pa., LIV, 260.

SARTAIN, JOHN (1808–1897). Engraver, portrait and miniature painter, born October 24, 1808, in London. In 1823 he was apprenticed to a London engraver, whose daughter he married on the completion of his term in 1830. Later the same year he emigrated to America and settled in Philadelphia. During the next two decades he was principally employed as an engraver for and publisher of magazines, including his own *Union Magazine of Literature and Art* (1849–52). After 1850 he did general engraving, including bank-note work, and also some portrait and miniature painting. He was very active in the art life of Philadelphia, serving as an officer of the Pennsylvania Academy, the Artists' Fund Society, and the Philadelphia School of Design for Women. He was in charge of the art department of the Centennial Exposition in 1876 and also represented this country at several European expositions. Of his eight children, four became engravers or painters: SAMUEL (1830–1906), HENRY (1833–*c.* 1895), Emily (1841–1927), and William (1843–1924). John Sartain died in Philadelphia October 25, 1897, shortly after finishing his autobiography, which was published two years later. ¶ Sartain, *Reminiscences of a Very Old Man;* DAB; Stauffer; Rutledge, PA; Phila. CD 1831+; Cowdrey, NAD; Cowdrey, AA & AAU; 7 Census (1850), Pa., L, 251; 8 Census (1860), Pa., LIV, 260.

SARTAIN, SAMUEL (1830–1906). Engraver. Samuel, born in Philadelphia on October 8, 1830, was the eldest son of JOHN SARTAIN, under whom he was trained as an engraver. He also studied painting at the Pennsylvania Academy, where he exhibited portraits and genre between 1848 and 1866. He established his own engraving business in 1851. During the latter part of his life he served as manager and treasurer of the Franklin Institute. He died in Philadelphia December 20, 1906. ¶ DAB; Stauffer; Rutledge, PA; Phila. CD 1853+; 8 Census (1860), Pa., LIV, 260.

SARTORI, GIOVANNI. Sculptor, working in Italy from about 1774 to 1793, and in Philadelphia about 1794. ¶ Thieme-Becker; Gardner, *Yankee Stonecutters.*

SASE, see SACHSE.

SASSMAN, JOHN C. or G. C. Engraver and seal engraver at New Orleans from 1807 to 1822; as G. C. Sassman in 1822 only. ¶ Delgado-WPA cites *Moniteur,* Oct. 17, 1807; New Orleans CD 1809; *Ami des Lois,* Aug. 26, 1813, and Nov. 10, 1817; *Gazette,* Oct. 15, 1822.

SATCHELL, JAMES. Engraver, 16, born in England, living with THOMAS NEALE in NYC in 1850; presumably an apprentice. ¶ 7 Census (1850), N.Y., XLVIII, 285.

SATTLER, HUBERT (1817–1904). Panorama and landscape painter, born in Vienna on January 27, 1817. He studied in Vienna and travelled widely in Europe, the Near East, North Africa, and North America, visiting NYC and Boston in 1850–51 with a collection of European and Asiatic views. He died in Vienna April 3, 1904. ¶ Thieme-Becker; Cowdrey, NAD; N. Y. *Herald,* Dec. 11 and 12, 1850, and April 13, 1851, and Boston *Transcript,* July 7 and 12, Sept. 30, Nov. 11, and Dec. 29, 1851 (courtesy J. Earl Arrington).

SAUERWEIN, CHARLES D. (1839–1918). Portrait and genre painter. He had a studio in Baltimore in 1857–58, but in 1860 went to Europe to study, married there, and remained for ten years. In 1870 he returned to Baltimore and in 1880 he moved to Red Bank (N.J.). He died in 1918 and was buried in Baltimore. ¶ Pleasants, *250 Years of Painting in Maryland,* 64; represented in Peabody Institute.

SAULNIER, HENRY E. Engraver with TOPPAN, CARPENTER & COMPANY of Philadelphia from about 1846 to 1860. ¶ Phila. CD 1846–60.

SAUNDERS, ——. Painter of a portrait of Florence and Elizabeth Crump of Waco (Tex.), 1843. ¶ WPA (Texas), Historical Records Survey.

SAUNDERS, GEORGE LETHBRIDGE (1807–1863). Miniaturist. An English artist, not to be confused with George Sanders or Saunders (1774–1846). He exhibited in London between 1829 and 1839 and again in 1851 and 1853. In 1840 he apparently came to the United States, as he exhibited in that year at the Apollo Association (as of NYC) and at the Artists' Fund Society (as of Philadelphia). When he exhibited at the Artists' Fund Society in 1841 his address was given as London. Sully met him in Philadelphia in 1843, shortly before Saunders again went to England. Saunders was at Richmond (Va.) in May 1845 and at Columbia (S.C.) in 1848; he is known to have worked also in Baltimore, Charleston, and Savannah. After his return to London, where he exhibited again in 1851 and 1853, nothing further is known of him until his death at Bristol on August 25, 1863. ¶ DNB [under George Sanders]; Cowdrey, AA & AAU; Rutledge, PA; Graves, *Dictionary;* Rutledge, *Artists in the Life of Charleston,* 167; *Richmond Portraits,* 242; represented at MHS. Redgrave, *Dictionary,* and *Antiques* (Dec. 1930), 481–82, confuse George Sanders and George L. Saunders.

SAUNDERS, HENRY DMOCHOWSKI (1810–1863). Sculptor, born October 14, 1810, at Vilna (Lithuania). His original name was Henry Dmochowski, the Saunders having been added after his coming to America. Educated in Vilna, then a part of Russian Poland, he fled to France after the unsuccessful Revolution of 1830. He studied sculpture in Paris about 1846 and subsequently lived for a time in London before coming to America. From 1853 to 1857 he lived in Philadelphia and exhibited at the Pennsylvania Academy. In 1857 he went to Washington and sold to the United States his busts of Kosciuszko and Pulaski, now in the Capitol. He was living in Washington in 1860. The sculptor soon after returned to Poland and died fighting for the liberation of his country in 1863. ¶ Fairman, *Art and Artists of the Capitol,* 161–62; Rutledge, PA; Phila. CD 1854–60; Washington CD 1860; Washington Art Assoc. Cat., 1857.

SAUNDERS, SOPHIA. Miniaturist, NYC, 1851–52. ¶ NYBD 1851–52; Bolton, *Miniature Painters.*

SAVAGE, A. J. Portrait painter, active 1845, probably in Ohio. Represented in Cincinnati Museum. ¶ *Antiques* (Jan. 1943), 37, repro.

SAVAGE, EDWARD (1761–1817). Portrait and historical painter and engraver. Born November 26, 1761 at Princeton (Mass.), he began his career as a painter in Boston about 1785. In 1789 he went to NYC to paint portraits of President Washington and his family and remained until 1791 when he left for England. After two years in London Savage returned to America, was married in Boston in October 1794, and in 1795 settled in Philadelphia.

During the next six years he was busy painting, engraving and selling prints (assisted by DAVID EDWIN and JOHN WESLEY JARVIS), and running a picture gallery and museum. During the yellow fever epidemic of 1798 he moved his business to Burlington (N.J.) for a few months. From 1801 to 1810 Savage was in NYC as a painter and proprietor of the Columbian Gallery, his interest in engraving having ceased. In 1811 or 1812 he moved his museum to Boston where he remained until shortly before his death, which took place at Princeton on July 6, 1817. ¶ Dresser, "Edward Savage"; DAB; Dickson, *John Wesley Jarvis,* 35–57; Morgan and Fielding, *Life Portraits of Washington,* 177–86; Stauffer.

SAVER, JOHN S. Of GREGSON & SAVER, engravers and lithographers, Cincinnati, 1860. ¶ Cincinnati BD 1860.

SAVORY, THOMAS C. Ornamental and fancy painter of Boston, active 1837–52. His painting of "The National Lancers on Boston Common, 1838," was exhibited at the Corcoran Gallery in 1950. ¶ Boston CD 1837–52; *American Processional,* 242.

SAWIN, EDWARD D. Engraver, NYC, 1846–50. He was a native of Rhode Island, born about 1822. ¶ 7 Census (1850), N.Y., XLIV, 223; NYBD 1846.

SAWIN, J. W. Landscape painter, Springfield (Mass.), 1850. ¶ Lipman and Winchester, 179.

SAWIN, WEALTHY O. Still life in watercolors, Massachusetts, about 1820. ¶ Lipman and Winchester, 179.

SAWKINS, JAMES G. Portrait and genre painter of Baltimore, who exhibited at the National Academy and the Artists' Fund Society in 1840. He may have been the young artist Sawkins who visited New Orleans in the winter of 1831 with JOSEPH H. BUSH. ¶ Cowdrey, NAD; Rutledge, PA; Delgado-WPA cites *Bee,* Dec. 9, 1831.

SAWYER, A. R. Portrait painter, Boston, 1859. ¶ Boston BD 1859.

SAWYER, BELINDA A. Theorem painter, active about 1820. ¶ *Antiques* (Feb. 1933), 61, repro.; Lipman and Winchester, 179.

SAWYER, JAMES J. (1813–1888). Portrait and landscape painter. He was living in NYC between 1840 and 1847 and exhibited at the National Academy and the American Institute. In 1856 he was living in Putnam (Conn.). ¶ Birth and death dates courtesy the late William Sawitzky; Cowdrey, NAD; NYCD 1840–47; NYBD 1846 [both as Sawyer and Sayer, at his business and home address respectively]; Am. Inst. Cat., 1842, 1845, 1846; New England BD 1856.

SAWYER, THOMAS H. Portrait painter, Boston, 1858–60. He was born in Connecticut about 1825. ¶ Boston BD 1858–60; 8 Census (1860), Mass., XXVIII, 79.

SAY, LUCY WAY SISTARE (Mrs. Thomas) (1801–1886). Drawings and engravings of shells. She was born October 14, 1801, in New London (Conn.) and in 1827 married Thomas Say, the noted naturalist, for whose *American Conchology* Mrs. Say provided some of the illustrations. Between 1833 and 1841 the Says lived at New Harmony (Ind.). Mrs. Say became the first woman member of the Academy of Natural Sciences of Philadelphia in 1841. After 1842 she lived in NYC, Newburgh, and West New Brighton (N.Y.). She died November 15, 1886, at Lexington (Mass.), aged 85. ¶ Weiss and Zeigler, *Thomas Say, Early American Naturalist,* Chap. XVI; Weiss and Zeigler, "Mrs. Thomas Say"; Peat, *Pioneer Painters of Indiana.*

SCACKI, FRANCISCO. Engraver of one plate depicting the Battle of New Orleans, published in 1815. He is not known to have made any other engravings. ¶ Drepperd, "Three Battles of New Orleans."

SCANDBERGER, AUGUST. Engraver, 19, from Württemberg, at Philadelphia in 1860. ¶ 8 Census (1860), Pa., LIV, 278.

SCARBOROUGH, JOHN. Listed as a portrait and miniature painter of Charleston by F. F. Sherman in *Antiques* (Dec. 1933), pages 27–29. This was in error for WILLIAM HARRISON SCARBOROUGH, as Sherman himself stated in *Antiques* (Oct. 1934), page 149.

SCARBOROUGH, WILLIAM HARRISON (1812–1871). Portrait and miniature painter, born November 7, 1812, at Dover (Tenn.). After studying art and medicine in Cincinnati and working as a portraitist for a few years in Tennessee, Scarborough moved to South Carolina in 1830. In 1836 he married into a prominent family there and he lived in Darlington District for several years before settling in 1843 at Columbia, where he made his home for the rest of his life. He enjoyed considerable success as a painter of portraits and miniatures in North and South Carolina and Georgia, and also made frequent visits to NYC, though he never had a studio in the North. In 1857 he went abroad for a year of European study. Scarborough died in Columbia on August 16, 1871. His sketchbooks, diaries, and many examples of his portrait work are owned by descendants in South Carolina. ¶ Hennig, *William Harrison Scarborough,* contains an account of the artist's life and a checklist of his work.

SCARLETT, SAMUEL (*c.* 1775–?). Landscape painter, picture restorer. A native of Staffordshire, Scarlett studied painting in London about 1795 and later practiced at Bath. He emigrated to America about 1817 and settled in Philadelphia where he was still living, at the age of 85, in 1860. From 1829 to 1846 he was curator or custodian of the Pennsylvania Academy. He exhibited at the Academy and at the Boston Athenaeum. ¶ 8 Census (1860), Pa., L, 139; Dunlap, *History;* Phila. CD 1820–60; Rutledge, PA; Swan, BA.

SCATTERGOOD, DAVID. Wood engraver and bookseller of Philadelphia, 1848–60. During the 1850's he did engraving in association with ROBERT TELFER, CHARLES F. NOBLE, and NICHOLAS SOLLIN. ¶ Phila. BD 1848–60, CD 1849–59; Hamilton, *Early American Book Illustrators and Wood Engravers,* 230, 238, 387.

SCATTERGOOD & NOBLE. Wood engravers, Philadelphia, 1859; DAVID SCATTERGOOD and CHARLES F. NOBLE. ¶ Phila. CD 1859.

SCATTERGOOD-SOLLIN. Wood engravers, Philadelphia, 1855; DAVID SCATTERGOOD and NICHOLAS SOLLIN. ¶ Hamilton, *Early American Book Illustrators and Wood Engravers,* 238, 387; Phila. CD 1855.

SCATTERGOOD & TELFER. Wood engravers, Philadelphia, 1852–54; DAVID SCATTERGOOD and ROBERT TELFER. ¶ Hamilton, *Early American Book Illustrators and Wood Engravers,* 230; Penna. BD 1854; Phila. CD 1852–54.

SCHAEFER, ANTHONY. Engraver and die sinker, NYC, 1857–59. ¶ NYBD 1857–59.

SCHAEFFER, JOHN SIMON. Artist of Brooklyn (N.Y.), active from 1859 to 1901. He exhibited at the National Academy in 1859. ¶ Cowdrey, NAD; Brooklyn CD 1859–1901.

SCHAEFFER, see also SCHEIFER, SCHIEFFER, SHAFFER.

SCHAERFF, CHARLES and J. W. Lithographers, St. Louis, 1854, operating under the name of Schaerff Brothers. ¶ St. Louis BD 1854.

SCHEDLER, JOSEPH. Lithographer, NYC, 1852–54; in 1854 with THEODORE LIEBLER. ¶ NYBD 1852, CD 1854.

SCHEDLER & LIEBLER. Lithographers, NYC, 1854; JOSEPH SCHEDLER and THEODORE A. LIEBLER. ¶ NYCD 1854.

SCHEIBLE, WILLIAM F. Engraver, die sinker, stencil cutter, seal press and awning manufacturer of Philadelphia, 1855 and after. ¶ Phila. CD 1855–60+.

SCHEIFER, H. Engraver and die sinker, NYC, 1851. This is either HENRY SCHIEFER or HERMAN SCHIEFFER, who may themselves have been one and the same. ¶ NYBD 1851.

SCHELL, FRANCIS H. (1834–1909). Newspaper illustrator, lithographer. A native of Pennsylvania, working as a lithographer in Philadelphia as early as 1850. During the Civil War he was one of the staff artists for *Frank Leslie's Illustrated Newspaper* and after the war he was in charge of Leslie's art department. He died March 31, 1909, at Germantown (Pa.). ¶ *Art Annual,* VIII, obit.; 7 Census (1850), Pa., XLIX, 423; Phila. CD 1856; Taft, *Artists and Illustrators of the Old West,* 296–97; *Portfolio* (Nov. 1944), cover.

SCHELL, FREDERICK A. Artist, born in Philadelphia about 1838, the son of Charles Schell, bookkeeper. He was active in the 1860's and 1870's. ¶ 8 Census (1860), Pa., LVIII, 349; Phila. CD 1871.

SCHELL, JOHN J. Lithographer, Philadelphia, 1856–59, with JACOBUS & SCHELL. ¶ Phila. CD 1856–59.

SCHELLENEN, C. Drew a crayon portrait about 1840 of Mrs. Edward Mayer, owned in Ferrisburg (Vt.) in 1941. ¶ WPA (Mass.), *Portraits Found in Vt.*

SCHENCK, JAMES R. Engraver (?) and copperplate printer, Charleston (S.C.), 1819. ¶ Rutledge, *Artists in the Life of Charleston.*

SCHENCK, JOHN H. Wood engraver, Boston, 1852–56; in 1854 of SCHENCK & PILLINER. ¶ Boston CD 1852–56.

SCHENCK & PILLINER. Engravers, Boston, 1854; JOHN H. SCHENCK and FREDERICK J. PILLINER. ¶ Boston CD 1854.

SCHERBONNIER, HENRY. French lithographer, 40, at Philadelphia in 1850. His wife was also French, but their nine children, aged 19 to 2, were born in Philadelphia. ¶ 7 Census (1850), Pa., LI, 432.

SCHERON, WILLIAM. German engraver, 23, at Philadelphia in 1850. ¶ 7 Census (1850), Pa., LII, 919.

SCHETKY, CAROLINE, Mrs. Samuel Richardson (1790–1852). Miniature, portrait, landscape, and still life painter. Miss Schetky, born in Edinburgh (Scotland)

March 3, 1790, was a daughter of the musician Johann Georg Christoph Schetky and a younger sister of JOHN CHRISTIAN SCHETKY. She came to Philadelphia about 1818 and lived there with another brother, the musician George Schetky, until her marriage in 1825 to Samuel Richardson of Boston. She was a regular exhibitor at the Pennsylvania Academy from 1818 to 1826. After her marriage she lived in Boston until her death on March 14, 1852. She was a frequent exhibitor at the Athenaeum and was for some years organist of the Brattle Street Church. ¶ Schetky, *The Schetky Family;* Vinton, *The Richardson Memorial,* 125–26; Phila. CD 1820–28; Rutledge, PA; Swan, BA; repro., *Analectic Magazine,* XIV (1819), frontis.

SCHETKY, JOHN CHRISTIAN (1778–1874). Marine painter. An elder brother of CAROLINE SCHETKY, J. C. Schetky exhibited at the Pennsylvania Academy in 1821, but probably did not himself visit America. He was for many years professor of drawing at the Royal Naval College at Portsmouth (England) and also Marine Painter in Ordinary to George IV, William IV, and Victoria. ¶ Rutledge, PA; DNB.

SCHEUERMANN, JOSEPH. Portrait painter, NYC, 1854–57. ¶ NYBD 1854, 1857.

SCHIEFER, HENRY. Engraver, NYC, 1851. Probably the same as H. SCHEIFER and HERMAN SCHIEFFER. ¶ NYCD 1851.

SCHIEFFER, HERMAN. Engraver, NYC, 1851. Probably the same as H. SCHEIFER and HENRY SCHIEFFER. ¶ NYCD 1851.

SCHIEFFER, PAUL. German lithographer, 32, at NYC in 1850. ¶ 7 Census (1850), N.Y., XLI, 495.

SCHIEFFER, see also SHAFFER.

SCHILCOCK, CHARLES. Lithographer, 30, a native of Ohio, living in Philadelphia in 1860. He was in the same boarding house with FRANCIS DEVANNIE, sculptor, and NICHOLAS SHIPS and ADOLPHE LABORN, lithographers. ¶ 8 Census (1860), Pa., LII, 432.

SCHILLER, GOTTFRIED. Engraver, Newark (N.J.), 1860. ¶ New Jersey BD 1860.

SCHIMONSKY or TZSCHUMANSKY, STANISLAS. Painter of Indian scenes in Nebraska, 1854. ¶ WPA Guide, *Nebraska;* Turner, "Early Artists."

SCHINOTTI, C. A. Professor of painting, Baltimore, 1842. ¶ Lafferty.

SCHINOTTI, E. Portrait and ornamental painter, New Orleans, 1846. ¶ New Orleans CD 1846.

SCHIPPER, GERRITT (1775–*c.* 1830). Miniaturist and crayon portraitist, born in September 1775 at Amsterdam (Holland). He studied art in Paris during the 1790's and came to America early in 1803. In April of that year he was at Charleston (S.C.); from October to December 1803, at Boston; June to August 1804, at Salem and Worcester (Mass.); and at Hartford (Conn.) in 1805. He was married at Amsterdam (N.Y.) in October 1806 and soon after he went to England where he spent the rest of his life. ¶ Hyer, "Gerritt Schipper, Miniaturist and Crayon Portraitist"; repro., NYHS *Annual Report* for 1948, page 8.

SCHLAGER[s], ——. Engraver of illustrations for *The Annals of San Francisco* (N.Y., 1855) and *Seven Years' Street Preaching in San Francisco* (N.Y., *c.* 1856). One cut is signed "Schlagers" and another "Genl. Schlager." ¶ Hamilton, *Early American Book Illustrators and Wood Engravers,* 238, 387.

SCHLEGEL, FRIDOLIN. A.N.A. Painter who exhibited portraits, still lifes, genre, and religious paintings at the National Academy, American Art-Union, and Pennsylvania Academy. He was living in NYC in 1848, in Newark (N.J.) in 1850, and in NYC from 1853 to 1861. ¶ Cowdrey, AA & AAU; Cowdrey, NAD; Rutledge, PA; New Jersey BD 1850; NYCD 1855–56, BD 1857–60; represented at NYHS.

SCHLEICH, CHARLES F. Of WETZEL & SCHLEICH, engravers, NYC, 1852–58. ¶ NYBD 1852–58.

SCHLEY, GEORGE. Artist; born August 21, 1795; died February 14, 1846. He was said to have studied under one of the PEALE family. ¶ Lafferty.

SCHMIDT, AUGUST. Sculptor from Germany, 41, living at Philadelphia in 1850. ¶ 7 Census (1850), Pa., LII, 893.

SCHMIDT, FREDERICK. Architect, NYC, 1830's to 1870's. He was the delineator of an 1834 view of the Park Hotel, lithographed and published by GEORGE ENDICOTT. ¶ NYCD 1837–70+; Stokes, *Iconography,* III, 878.

SCHMIDT, FREDERICK. Sculptor at Richmond (Va.) in January 1838. *Cf.* FREDERICK SMITH. ¶ *Richmond Portraits,* 242.

SCHMIDT, FREDERICK. Lithographer and lithographic printer of New Orleans, 1849–67. Listed in 1849 as Frederick Smith, otherwise as Schmidt. ¶ New Orleans CD 1849, 1852–55, 1860–61, 1865–67.

SCHMIDT, FREDERICK. Lithographer, NYC,

1856–60 and after. He was born in Saxony about 1826; his wife was a native of Saxe-Cobourg; their two sons were born in NYC about 1850 and 1854. ¶ 8 Census (1860), N.Y., XLV, 62; NYCD 1856–63.

SCHMIDT, PETER (1822–1867). Portrait painter. He was a native of Germany and was at New Orleans from 1859 until his death, April 28, 1867. ¶ Cline, "Art and Artists in New Orleans," 42; New Orleans CD 1859–67.

SCHMIDT, SOLOMON (*c.* 1806–?). General and banknote engraver who came to New Orleans from Baden (Germany) about 1840. He became the local agent for RAWDON, WRIGHT, HATCH & EDSON and later for the AMERICAN BANK NOTE COMPANY. He was active at least until 1870. ¶ 7 Census (1850), La., V, 458–59 [under the name of Henry Schmidt, though Solomon seems intended]; 8 Census (1860), La., VI, 930 [as S. Schmidt]; New Orleans CD 1843–70.

SCHMIDT, see also SMITH.

SCHMITT, JULIUS. German lithographer, 29, employed by and living with AUGUST HOEN of Baltimore in 1850. ¶ 7 Census (1850), Md., V, 418.

SCHMITZ, M. S. Artist and drawing master, Philadelphia, 1856–60. Probably Matthew Schmitz, music teacher at Philadelphia in the early fifties and after 1860. ¶ Phila. CD 1853–70; Phila. BD 1853 as M. Smitz, lithographer.

SCHMOLZE, KARL HEINRICH (or HERMANN) (1823–1861). Portrait, genre, and historical painter; engraver; illustrator. Born in Zweibrücken (Germany), he came to America in 1849 and settled in Philadelphia. He exhibited at the Pennsylvania Academy, which still owns his portrait of Washington, and at the Washington Art Association. Schmolze died in Philadelphia in 1861. ¶ Thieme-Becker; Rutledge, PA; Washington Art Assoc. Cat., 1859; WPA (Pa.), MS cat., of PA.

SCHNABEL, EDWARD. German-born lithographer, 31, at Philadelphia in 1850. With TRAUBEL, SCHNABEL & FINKELDEY in 1850. In 1857 he was associated with JOHN F. FINKELDEY and WILLIAM DEMME, and thereafter with FINKELDEY until after 1860. ¶ 7 Census (1850), Pa., L, 227; Peters, *America on Stone;* Phila. CD 1853–60+.

SCHNABEL & FINKELDEY. Lithographers, Philadelphia, 1857–60 and after. The firm was established in 1857 as Schnabel, Finkeldey & Demme, but Demme withdrew the same year. The partners were EDWARD SCHNABEL, JOHN FREDERICK FINKELDEY, and WILLIAM DEMME. ¶ Phila. CD 1857–60+; see also TRAUBEL, SCHNABEL & FINKELDEY.

SCHNARR, D. Portrait painter. So listed in NYC business directory for 1854. Daniel Schnarr, at the same address, is listed as a "hatter" in city directories from 1855 to 1860. ¶ NYBD 1854; NYCD 1855–60.

SCHNEIDER, CHARLES B. Engraver, born in Pennsylvania about 1821, active in Philadelphia from 1849. ¶ 8 Census (1860), Pa., LI, 654; Phila. BD 1849, CD 1854–60+.

SCHOENER, JACOB B. (1805–*c.* 1846). Miniature and portrait painter. Born in Reading (Pa.), he learned miniature painting from GENNARO PERSICO and also studied at the Pennsylvania Academy. He exhibited at the Pennsylvania Academy in 1826–28 and at the Boston Athenaeum in 1832. Schoener lived in Reading until about 1845 when he moved to Boston. He died not long after. ¶ Montgomery, *Berks County,* 808; Rutledge, PA; Swan, BA.

SCHOFF, STEPHEN ALONZO (1818–1904). A.N.A. Banknote and steel engraver, born January 16, 1818, in Danville (Vt.). At 16 he was apprenticed to OLIVER PELTON, Boston engraver, but after three years he left Pelton and studied under JOSEPH ANDREWS. With Andrews he went abroad in 1839/40 and studied mainly in Paris until his return to America in 1842. Thereafter he devoted himself mainly to banknote work, though he achieved a considerable reputation for his steel engravings and etchings of portraits, historical, and other paintings. Schoff worked in Boston during the fifties and sixties, but later made his home at various times in Washington, New York, Newtonville (Mass.), Brandon (Vt.), and finally in Norfolk (Conn.), where he died May 6, 1904. He was an Associate of the National Academy from 1844 to 1884. ¶ DAB; Stauffer; Thieme-Becker; Boston BD 1850–60+; Cowdrey, AA & AAU; Cowdrey, NAD; Clark, *History of the NAD,* 269.

SCHOLL, GUSTAVE. Engraver, 41, from Hamburg (Germany), at NYC in 1860. ¶ 8 Census (1860), N.Y., LI, 435.

SCHONBERG, CHARLES L. Lithographer of NYC, working with DAVID L. SCHONBERG, 1857–60. ¶ NYBD 1857, CD 1858–60.

SCHONBERG, DAVID L. Lithographer working

with CHARLES L. SCHONBERG in NYC, 1857–60. ¶ NYBD 1857, CD 1858–60.

SCHONBERG, JAMES. Artist, 28, from Hanover (Germany), at Philadelphia in 1860 with his wife, also from Hanover, and an infant born in Philadelphia. ¶ 8 Census (1860), Pa., LIV, 244.

SCHOOLCRAFT, HENRY ROWE (1793–1864). Topographical artist. Born March 28, 1793, in Albany County (N.Y.), Schoolcraft attended Union and Middlebury Colleges and was preparing to follow his father in the glass-making industry when he made his first visit to the frontier in 1818. In 1820 he accompanied Lewis Cass's expedition to the source of the Mississippi and became interested in the Indians of the region around Lake Superior, for whom he was appointed agent in 1822. On a second trip to the upper Mississippi, Schoolcraft discovered the headwaters of the river. From the 1830's Schoolcraft devoted himself to ethnological studies, the results of which were eventually embodied in his six-volume *Historical and Statistical Information Respecting the History, Condition, and Prospects of the Indian Tribes of the United States* (1851–57). Schoolcraft died in Washington (D.C.), December 10, 1864. ¶ DAB; *Encyclopedia Britannica* (11th ed.); examples of his work as an artist, in his *Scenes and Adventures in the Semi-Alpine Region of the Ozark Mountains of Missouri and Arkansas* (1853).

SCHOTT, ARTHUR (*c.* 1813–1875). Topographical artist with the U.S.–Mexico Boundary Survey expedition of 1849–55. Several engravings after his sketches appear in the *Report* of this survey. Schott was a resident of Washington for many years and died there or in Georgetown on July 26, 1875, at the age of 62. He was an ardent naturalist, engineer, physician, and professor of German and music. ¶ Taft, *Artists and Illustrators of the Old West,* 277; Emory, *Report on the U.S.–Mexican Boundary Survey;* Stokes, *Historical Prints.*

SCHOYER, RAPHAEL. Working at Baltimore in 1824 as a copperplate printer and at NYC in 1826 as a portrait engraver. ¶ Stauffer.

SCHRADER, THEODORE. Lithographer, St. Louis, 1859. ¶ St. Louis BD 1859.

SCHRADER, see also SHRADER.

SCHREINER, Mrs. T. Delineator of a view of the burning of the Cumberland Rail Road Bridge, Harrisburg (Pa.), December 4, 1844. ¶ Peters, *America on Stone.*

SCHROEDER, C. Portrait and miniature painter at NYC between 1811 and 1826. He visited Richmond (Va.) in December 1818. ¶ NYCD 1811–20 (McKay), 1826; *Richmond Portraits,* 243.

SCHROEDER, DAVID R. Engraver at New Orleans, 1853–54. ¶ New Orleans CD 1853–54.

SCHROEDER, JOHN. Designer of a view of Nauvoo (Ill.) and the Mormon Temple on a map of Hancock County (Ill.), 1859. ¶ Arrington, "Nauvoo Temple," Chap. 8.

SCHUCHARD, CARL (1827–1883). Topographical artist. Born in Germany in 1827, Schuchard came to California in 1849 as a mining engineer. He later became a surveyor and draftsman, his chief work in this line being the illustrations for Gray's survey of a railway route along the 32d parallel. Though he lived for a number of years in Texas, Schuchard spent the greater part of his life in Mexico where he died May 4, 1883. ¶ Taft, *Artists and Illustrators of the Old West,* 269.

SCHUCKMAN, GEORGE and WILLIAM. Lithographers, aged 14 and 26 respectively, natives of Germany, boarding together at Pittsburgh (Pa.) in 1850. ¶ 7 Census (1850), Pa., III (part 2), 75.

SCHULLER, JOHN D. Seal engraver, NYC, 1860. ¶ NYBD 1860.

SCHULTHEIS, CHRISTIAN. Engraver and die sinker, NYC, 1848–51. ¶ NYBD 1848, 1851.

SCHULTZ, FREDERICK. German engraver, 37, living in NYC in 1860. His wife was also a native of Germany, but their two children, ages 6 and 3, were born in NYC. ¶ 7 Census (1850), N.Y., XLI, 842.

SCHULTZ, WILLIAM. Portrait painter, Boston, 1856–57. ¶ New England BD 1856; Boston BD 1857.

SCHULTZ, see also SHULTZ.

SCHUREMAN, ALFRED. Engraver, born in Ohio, aged 16, in NYC in 1850. *Cf.* ALPHONSO B. SCHUREMAN. ¶ 7 Census (1850), N.Y., XLIX, 235.

SCHUREMAN, ALPHONSO B. Engraver, NYC, 1850's. He exhibited pencil sketches at the American Institute as early as 1849. From 1854 to 1857 he was associated with THOMAS LIPPIATT. *Cf.* ALFRED SCHUREMAN. ¶ NYCD 1854–60; Am. Inst. Cat., 1849.

SCHUSSELE, CHRISTIAN (1824 or 1826–1879).

Historical, genre, portrait, and landscape painter, lithographer, and teacher of painting and drawing. Schussele was born in Alsace on April 16, 1826, according to the DAB, although Rutledge and the censuses give 1824 as the year of his birth. After studying at Strasbourg and Paris and working as a chromolithographer in the latter city for a number of years, Schussele emigrated to America in 1848 and settled in Philadelphia, where he soon married the daughter of CASPAR MURINGER. Although he was obliged to support himself by chromolithographic work and designing for wood engravers, Schussele preferred to paint. In 1854 he made a popular success with a historical painting which was engraved by JOHN SARTAIN and thereafter he devoted himself entirely to painting. He was for several years president of the Artists' Fund Society and from 1868 until his death he was Professor of Drawing and Painting at the Pennsylvania Academy. From about 1863 Schussele was afflicted with palsy, but he continued to do some painting until the time of his death, which occurred August 21, 1879, at the home of his son-in-law at Merchantville (N.J.). ¶ DAB; Rutledge, PA; 7 Census (1850), Pa., LI, 924; 8 Census (1860), Pa., LV, 468; Sartain, *Reminiscences,* 249–51; Swan, BA; Thieme-Becker; *Connoisseur,* June 1947, 116; *American Collector,* July 1946, 13; *Portfolio,* Feb. 1952, 140.

SCHUSTER or SHUSTER, ARNAULD. Portrait painter at NYC in 1852, formerly a student at the Munich Academy. ¶ NYBD 1852; Thieme-Becker.

SCHUSTER or SHUSTER, SIGISMUND (1807–?). Miniaturist, pastellist, lithographer, landscape painter, and teacher. Born in Germany in 1807, he came to NYC about 1851 and was active there at least until 1860. In 1853 he published his *Practical Drawing Book*. He exhibited at the American Institute in 1851 and at the National Academy from 1853 to 1859. ¶ Thieme-Becker; Cowdrey, NAD; Am. Inst. Cat., 1851; NYCD 1851–60; Union Catalogue, LC.

SCHUTZ, J. Lithographic artist, employed by CURRIER about 1849–50, who did mostly lettering but also a few prints. ¶ *Portfolio* (April 1943), cover and p. 171; *American Collector* (Aug. 1945), 5.

SCHWAN, PHI[LIP?]. German artist, 26, boarding in New Orleans in 1850 with six other German artists; MERVING, REHN, and the four HEILLS. ¶ 7 Census (1850), La., V, 82.

SCHWARTZ, C. Stipple engraver working at Baltimore about 1814. ¶ Stauffer.

SCHWARTZ, CHRISTIAN. Engraver working in NYC and living in Jersey City, 1859. ¶ NYCD and BD 1859.

SCHWARTZ, FREDERICK. Portrait painter, NYC, 1841. ¶ NYBD 1841.

SCHWARTZE, JOHAN GEORG (1814/15–1874). Portrait and religious painter who exhibited frequently at Philadelphia between 1837 and 1858. His address in 1837 was Kensington (Pa.); in 1838, Philadelphia; 1844–1847, Düsseldorf; and 1847–58, Amsterdam. ¶ Rutledge, PA.

SCHWEBEL, LEWIS. Portrait painter, 48, a native of France, at Cincinnati in 1850 with his wife, a Frenchwoman, and six children born in Germany before 1846. One son, LEWIS SCHWEBEL, JR., was also a portrait painter. ¶ 7 Census (1850), Ohio, XXII, 143.

SCHWEBEL, LEWIS, JR. Portrait painter, 17, a native of Germany, at Cincinnati in 1850 with his father, LEWIS SCHWEBEL, also a portrait painter. ¶ 7 Census (1850), Ohio, XXII, 143.

SCHWINDT, ROBERT, is ROBERT GSCHWINDT.

SCHWITTER BROTHERS. Engravers, NYC, 1859; FRIDOLIN, GEORGE, and JOSEPH SCHWITTER. ¶ NYBD 1859.

SCHWITTER, FRIDOLIN. Engraver, NYC, 1857–60; in 1859 of SCHWITTER BROTHERS. ¶ NYCD 1857, 1860; NYBD 1859.

SCHWITTER, GEORGE. Engraver, NYC, 1859–60; in 1859 of SCHWITTER BROTHERS. ¶ NYBD 1859; NYCD 1860.

SCHWITTER, JOSEPH. Engraver, NYC, 1859–60; in 1859 of SCHWITTER BROTHERS. ¶ NYBD 1859; NYCD 1860.

SCHWODE, ANDREA. Portrait painter, 35, from Bavaria, at New Orleans in 1860. ¶ 8 Census (1860), La., VI, 761.

SCOLES, JOHN. Engraver working in NYC between 1793 and 1844; best known for his views of NYC buildings and his landscape prints. ¶ NYCD 1794–1820 (McKay), 1821–44 (after 1844 as "late engraver"); Stokes, *Iconography;* Weitenkampf, "Early American Landscape Prints"; *Portfolio* (Jan. 1943), 102.

SCOLLAY, Miss CATHERINE (?–1863). Landscape and figure painter of Boston. She exhibited at the Athenaeum between 1827 and 1848. A series of six views of Trenton Falls, drawn by Miss Scollay, was lithographed by JOHN PENDLETON. ¶ Swan, BA; Ramsay, "The American Scene in Lithograph, The Album," 181.

SCOT, ——. Artist, possibly an amateur, of Boston; in 1803 he painted a copy of the State House portrait of the Rev. John Wheelwright (1594–1679). ¶ Weis, *Checklist of the Portraits . . . in the American Antiquarian Society,* 116.

SCOT (or Scott), ROBERT. An English engraver and watchmaker who settled in Philadelphia in 1781; he described himself as "late engraver to the State of Virginia." He did general engraving for a number of years, but in 1793 began his long connection with the U. S. Mint at Philadelphia where he held the position of die-sinker at least until 1820. ¶ Prime, I, 27, and II, 73; Phila. CD 1796–1820; Stauffer; Dunlap, *History.*

SCOTT, EDWARD. Lithographer, New Orleans, 1854. ¶ New Orleans CD 1854.

SCOTT, JAMES B. Of JAMISON & SCOTT, lithographers of Buffalo (N.Y.), 1856. ¶ Buffalo CD 1856.

SCOTT, JOHN WHITE ALLEN (1815–1907). Portrait, landscape, and marine painter; lithographer and engraver. He was born in Roxbury (Mass.), served his apprenticeship under the Boston lithographer WILLIAM S. PENDLETON at the same time as NATHANIEL CURRIER, and spent his whole career in and around Boston. In the mid-forties he was in partnership with FITZ HUGH LANE. Scott exhibited at the Athenaeum. He died March 4, 1907, at Cambridge (Mass.). ¶ *Art Annual,* VI, obit.; Peters, *America on Stone;* Boston CD 1844–57; Swan, BA; 7 Census (1850), Mass., XXIII, 727.

SCOTT, JOSEPH T. Engraver at Philadelphia, 1793–96. He was chiefly a designer and engraver of maps. ¶ Stauffer; Brown and Brown.

SCOTT, THOMAS S. Artist working for the lithographer P. S. DUVAL at Philadelphia about 1852. ¶ Peters, *America on Stone.*

SCUDDER, Mrs. A. M. Painted in 1845 "A Vision of the Northeast Corner of Beaver and Broad Streets [in NYC] in the 1600's." ¶ *Antiques* (May 1934), 188, repro.

SCUDDER, JAMES LONG (1836–1881). Still life, portrait, landscape, genre, and animal painter, born April 17, 1836, at East Neck, Long Island (N.Y.). He became an artist after working as a house and sign painter. His entire life was passed on Long Island and he died at Huntington May 5, 1881. He exhibited at the National Academy in 1859. Scudder married Lydia E. Kelcey and had two sons, one of whom, Thomas Lessing Scudder, became an artist and lived in Santa Anna (Cal.). Most of Scudder's paintings are still in the family or at the Huntington Historical Society. ¶ Mrs. Martha K. Hall, "James Long Scudder, Artist," *The Long Island Forum,* XVIII, March 1955, 43–44, 56; Cowdrey, NAD.

SEABRING, ANDREW T. Engraver, NYC, 1857. ¶ NYBD 1857.

SEAGER, ——. Portraits in bronze. He was working at New Bedford and Salem (Mass.) in March 1834. In 1840 one Seager of London (and lately of the United States) advertised in Halifax (N.S.) that he painted portraits and miniatures and executed portraits in bronze; this was probably the same artist. ¶ Belknap, *Artists and Craftsmen of Essex County,* 22; Piers, "Artists in Nova Scotia," 146–47.

SEAGER, Miss ——. Portrait and miniature painter who exhibited at the National Academy between 1833 and 1840. From 1833 to 1836 she lived in NYC and in 1839–40 at Utica (N.Y.); her address was the same in both places as that of Mrs. SARAH SEAGER, probably her mother. ¶ Cowdrey, NAD; Dunlap, *History.*

SEAGER, EDWARD (*c.* 1809–1886). Portrait painter of Boston, 1840's. In 1844 he became drawing master at the English High School, where the sculptor JOHN ROGERS was one of his pupils. He also exhibited at the Athenaeum in 1847–48. ¶ Swan, BA; Boston CD 1845–50; *Catalogue of the Past and Present Members of the English High School of Boston,* [3].

SEAGER, Mrs. SARAH. Miniature and portrait painter of NYC (1833–36) and Utica (1839–40); exhibitor at the National Academy. This may be the Mrs. Seager of London who exhibited at the Royal Academy in 1827. Miss —— SEAGER, presumably her daughter, lived with her in NYC and Utica. ¶ NYCD 1833–36; Cowdrey, NAD; Utica CD 1839; Graves, *Dictionary.*

SEAGER, WILLIAM S., see WILLIAM S. SEGAR.

SEALEY (or Sealy), ALFRED (*c.* 1815–*c.* 1868). Line engraver, born in New York State, and active in NYC from 1838 to 1868. About 1858–60 he was with the firm of SEALEY & SMITH, of which his brother Benjamin T. Sealey was agent. After 1860 Alfred was with the AMERICAN

Bank Note Company. Although Stauffer reports that Sealey is said to have died in Canada about 1862, he was listed in NYC directories until 1868. ¶ 8 Census (1860), N.Y., LXI, 771; NYCD 1838–68; Cowdrey, NAD; Stauffer; Rice, "Life of Nathaniel Jocelyn."

Sealey & Smith. Engravers, NYC, 1858–60; Alfred Sealey and Charles H. Smith, engravers, and Benjamin T. Sealey, agent. ¶ NYBD and CD 1858; Stauffer.

Seaman, Charles. Portrait and miniature painter, who came to NYC about 1831, stayed for about two years, and then moved on to Albany (1834–35), Chambersburg (Pa.), and in 1839 to Maysville (Ky.), where he is thought to have died sometime before 1870. A cripple from birth, he is said to have worked with his toes as well as with his hands. ¶ Information courtesy Georgia M. Palmer, West Chester (Pa.), great-great-granddaughter of the artist; NYCD 1831–33; Albany CD 1834–35; Bolton, *Miniature Painters.*

Seaman, Emery. Portrait painter at Boston between 1849 and 1853 and at NYC from 1857 to 1859. ¶ Boston BD 1849, 1853; NYBD 1857–59.

Seaman, Henry. Artist, 36, a native of New York, at NYC in 1860 with his wife and two children under 10, also born in New York. ¶ 8 Census (1860), N.Y., LXII, 213.

Searle, Cyril. Music teacher and amateur artist who made a view of Augusta (Me.) in 1823. ¶ North, *History of Augusta,* frontis. and 445.

Searle, George (*c.* 1751–1796). Heraldic painter at Newburyport (Mass.). He was a nephew of John Gore and cousin of Samuel Gore and probably worked with Edward Bass, who succeeded to Searle's business. ¶ Bowditch, "Early Water-Color Paintings of New England Coats of Arms," 185–87, figs. 7 and 8.

Searle, Helen R. Still life painter at Rochester (N.Y.) about 1843. ¶ Ulp, "Art and Artists in Rochester."

Searle, John. Artist of a watercolor view of the interior of the Park Theatre in NYC during a performance in November 1822, with portraits of noted citizens. This may have been the John Searle listed as a wine merchant in NYC directories for 1822 and 1823. ¶ Stokes, *Iconography,* III, 576; NYCD 1822–23.

Sears, Ed. Wood engraver whose work appeared in books published in NYC between 1859 and 1879. ¶ Hamilton, *Early American Book Illustrators and Wood Engravers,* 248, 337, 475.

Seavey, Thomas. Figurehead carver of Bangor (Me.) during the first half of the 19th century. By 1843 he was working in partnership with his son, William L. Seavey. ¶ Harris, "American Ship Figureheads," 11; Pinckney, *American Figureheads and Their Carvers,* 142, 200.

Seavey, William L. Figurehead carver working with his father, Thomas Seavey, at Bangor (Me.) in 1843. ¶ Pinckney, *American Figureheads and Their Carvers,* 200.

Sebald, Hobarth. Engraver, 34, from Germany, at Philadelphia in 1860. His wife and two children, 6 and 2 years of age, were all born in Pennsylvania. *Cf.* Hugo Sebald. ¶ 8 Census (1860), Pa., LVI, 10.

Sebald, Hugo. Wood engraver and designer, Philadelphia, 1855–71. *Cf.* Hobarth Sebald. ¶ Phila. CD 1855–71.

Sebron, Hyppolite Victor Valentin (1801–1897). Diorama and landscape painter, born in Caudebec (France) August 21, 1801. He spent the years 1849 to 1855 in the United States, principally as a painter of dioramas. In 1851–52 he was at New Orleans and in 1854 he was in NYC. He died in Paris September 1, 1897. ¶ Thieme-Becker; Delgado-WPA cites *Courier,* May 12, 1852, and *Bee,* May 11, 1852; NYBD 1854; Cowdrey, NAD.

Seckel, Joshua C. Painter of small portraits and miniatures, Philadelphia, 1838 to 1850. ¶ Gillingham, "Notes on Philadelphia Profilists," 516; Phila. BD 1850.

Secor, David Pell (1824–1909). Artist, critic, and collector; born in Brooklyn (N.Y.); died March 30, 1909, at Bridgeport (Conn.). ¶ *Art Annual,* VII, obit.

Sedgwick, Susan Anne Livingston Ridley (*c.* 1789–1867). Painter of a miniature of a liberated slave, 1811. Susan Ridley was married in 1808 at Albany to Theodore Sedgwick (1780–1839). After practising law in Albany until 1821, Sedgwick retired to Stockbridge (Mass.) and there spent the rest of his life. Mrs. Sedgwick was known for her charm and intellectual interests, and was the author of a number of books for children and young people. She died January 20, 1867. ¶ WPA (Mass.), *Portraits Found in Mass.,* no. 1446; DAB, under Theodore Sedgwick.

See, Salvator. Artist, 28, a native of England, living in NYC in 1850. Of his children, John (4) was born in Maryland,

Steven (2) in England, and Rosina (9 months) in New York. ¶ 7 Census (1850), N.Y., LI, 54.

SEGAR (or Seager), WILLIAM S. (1823–1887). Portrait, landscape, sign, and ornamental painter; born in New York, Feb. 16, 1823. He began his career as a windowshade painter at Utica (N.Y.) about 1844, in association with J. Wesley Segar, his father or brother. William moved to Syracuse about 1852 and by the sixties was advertising as a copier of photographs, crayon portraitist, landscape, sign, and ornamental painter. He left Syracuse for Indiana about 1878 and died at Covington (Ind.), August 14, 1887. Possibly related to Mrs. SARAH SEAGER. ¶ Peat, *Pioneer Painters of Indiana,* 129, 238; Utica CD 1844–51; Syracuse CD 1853–78.

SEIBERT, EDWARD. Sculptor, NYC, 1856. ¶ NYCD 1856.

SEIBERT, HENRY. Lithographer, NYC, 1852–60; of ROBERTSON & SEIBERT and ROBERTSON, SEIBERT & SHEARMAN. ¶ NYCD 1852–58; NYBD 1854–60.

SEIBERT, JACOB. Lithographer, NYC, 1859–60; of SEIBERT & WETZLER. ¶ NYBD 1859; NYCD 1860.

SEIBERT & WETZLER. Lithographers, NYC, 1859–60; JACOB SEIBERT and ERNEST WETZLER. ¶ NYCD 1859–60.

SEIBERT, see also SIEBERT.

SEIDEL, CHARLES FREDERICK. Amateur artist who sketched the first house in Bethlehem (Pa.) shortly before its destruction in 1823. Seidel was a Moravian minister who came to America in 1806 and served as pastor at Salem (N.C.) from 1806–09, as pastor and school principal at Nazareth (Pa.), 1809–17, and pastor and school principal at Bethlehem (Pa.) from 1817 to 1861. ¶ Levering, *History of Bethlehem.*

SEIDEL, FREDERICK. Landscape painter, NYC, 1858–59. ¶ NYBD 1858–59.

SEIFERT, F. Portrait painter at Mobile (Ala.) in 1859. ¶ WPA (Ala.), Hist. Records Survey cites Mobile *Daily Register,* Feb. 4, 1859.

SEIFERT, HENRY (1824–1911). Lithographer. A native of Saxony, he came to America in 1852 as a trained lithographer and settled at Milwaukee (Wis.), where he was a leading lithographer until his retirement in 1898. He died in Milwaukee March 10, 1911. ¶ Kent, "Early Commercial Lithography in Wisconsin," 249.

SEILE, SIMEON B. Engraver, NYC, 1856. ¶ NYCD 1856.

SEILER, FREDERICK. Engraver and die sinker, NYC, 1850–54; of SEILER & RUPP in 1850. ¶ NYCD 1850, 1853–54; NYBD 1850, 1851, 1854.

SEILER & RUPP. Engravers and die sinkers, NYC, 1850; FREDERICK SEILER and CHRISTIAN RUPP. ¶ NYBD and NYCD 1850.

SEITZ, JOHN. Engraver, 42, at Philadelphia in 1850. Seitz, his wife, and their daughter (9) were all born in Germany. ¶ 7 Census (1850), Pa., LII, 100.

SEL, B. Theatrical scene painter and drawing master at New Orleans in 1813–14 and 1817. Possibly the same as JOHN B. SEL. ¶ Delgado-WPA cites *Moniteur,* July 29, 1813, *Ami des Lois,* Oct. 22, 1814, and *La. Courier,* Feb. 10, 1817.

SEL, JOHN (or Jean) B. (?–1832). Portrait and miniature painter at New Orleans from 1822 to his death on January 28, 1832. He also visited Alabama in 1825. Possibly the same as B. SEL. ¶ Delgado-WPA cites *La. Courier,* Jan. 28, 1832, obit.; New Orleans CD 1822–24, 1827, 1830; WPA (Ala.), Hist. Records Survey; Cline, "Art and Artists in New Orleans."

SELBY, F. Drew a pen and colored crayon sketch of Fort Crook, Shasta County (Cal.) in 1852. The artist was a member of Co. C, California Volunteer Cavalry. ¶ *Childs Gallery Bulletin* (Feb. 1952), back.

SELLERS, GEORGE ESCOL (1808–1899). Amateur artist, grandson of CHARLES WILLSON PEALE. Born November 26, 1808, Escol Sellers helped in his grandfather's museum as a boy, but did not become a professional artist. He was an inventor of note and established a manufacturing community in Hardin County (Ill.) about 1854, calling it Seller's Landing. The venture was not very successful and Sellers spent his latter years in Pennsylvania. He died January 1, 1899. ¶ Sellers, "Sellers Papers in the Peale-Sellers Collection," repro. of sketch on the Ohio River *c.* 1854; Sellers, *Charles Willson Peale,* II, 354, 420.

SELLSTEDT, LARS GUSTAF (1819–1911). N.A. Portrait, landscape, and marine painter, born April 30, 1819, at Sundsvall (Sweden). He went to sea at the age of 11 and worked as a merchant seaman until 1845 when he settled at Buffalo (N.Y.) and began a new career as a portrait painter. Except for several visits to Europe he spent the rest of his life in Buffalo where he was active in organizing the Buffalo Fine Arts Academy. He was made a National Academician in 1875. His autobiography was published in 1904, his *Art in Buffalo* in 1911, and his *Life and Works of William John Wilgus* in 1912. Sellstedt died in Buffalo on June 4, 1911. ¶ Sprague, "Lars Gustaf Sellstedt"; DAB; Sellstedt, *From Forecastle to Academy;* Cowdrey, NAD; Rutledge, PA.

SELWIN, ——. Assistant scene painter at the Boston Theatre in April 1856. ¶ Boston *Evening Transcript,* April 14, 1856 (courtesy J. E. Arrington).

SENCE & FLAGELLA. Sculptors, NYC, 1848–50; LEONARD SENCE and VICTOR FLAGELLA. They exhibited plaster statuary at the American Institute in 1848 and 1849, winning a diploma in 1848. ¶ Am. Inst. Cat. and *Proceedings,* 1848, 1849; NYBD 1849–50.

SENCE, LEONARD. Sculptor in plaster and marble, NYC, 1848–52. He was working with VICTOR FLAGELLA from 1848 to 1850. His widow was listed in 1856. ¶ Am. Inst. Cat., 1848–49; NYBD 1849–50; NYCD 1851–52, 1856.

SENCE, LEONARD. Engraver working in NYC from 1856 to 1859; his home was at Hoboken (N.J.). ¶ NYCD 1856–59.

SENDORF, REINHARDT. Engraver, 29, a native of Germany, at Philadelphia in 1860. ¶ 8 Census (1860), Pa., LVI, 861.

SENEFELDER LITHOGRAPHIC COMPANY. Of Boston, 1830. The partners in this enterprise, named after the European discoverer of the art of lithography, were HAZEN MORSE, THOMAS EDWARDS, WILLIAM B. ANNIN, GEORGE G. SMITH, and JOHN CHORLEY. ¶ Boston CD 1830 (adv.); Whitmore, "Abel Bowen."

SENGTELLER (Santello or Santella), ALEXANDER. Engraver with the U. S. Coast and Geodetic Survey, Washington (D.C.), 1858–71. He was born in France about 1813. ¶ Washington CD 1858–71; 8 Census (1860), D.C., II, 132.

SENIOR, C. F. Primitive genre painting in oils, Reading (Pa.), about 1780. ¶ Lipman and Winchester, 179.

SENNETT, JOHN T. Portrait painter, Elmira (N.Y.), 1859. ¶ N. Y. State BD 1859.

SERA, J. Painter of theatrical scenery, transparencies, landscapes, and fancy paintings, teacher of drawing and music. He was active in Charleston (S.C.) from 1824 until his death in December 1837. ¶ Rutledge, *Artists in the Life of Charleston.*

SERRELL, HENRY R. Lithographer of NYC, 1848–54; until 1852 of SERRELL & PERKINS. He exhibited in 1848 at the American Institute. He was born in England about 1817 but came to New York before 1838. ¶ NYBD 1848–52; NYCD 1848–54; Am. Inst. Cat., 1848; Peters, *America on Stone;* 7 Census (1850), N.Y., LIV, 583.

SERRELL & PERKINS. Lithographers, NYC, 1848–52; HENRY R. SERRELL and S. LEE PERKINS. ¶ NYBD 1848–52; Peters, *America on Stone.*

SERZ, JOHN. Engraver, born in Bavaria about 1810. He apparently left Germany about 1848, as he was working in NYC in 1849–50 and thereafter in Philadelphia, where he did banknote, portrait, landscape, and historical engraving. ¶ 8 Census (1860), Pa., LVI, 881; NYCD 1849–50; Phila. CD 1851–60+.

SETTY, see LOUIS CITTI.

SEVERANCE, BENJAMIN J. General and fancy painter who settled at Northfield (Mass.) in 1823. His fancy work included Masonic painting, carriages, signs, portraits, overmantels, and landscapes. ¶ Dods, "Connecticut Valley Painters," 207; Lipman and Winchester, 179.

SEVERYN or SEVERIN, CHARLES. Lithographer, born in Poland between 1808 and 1820. He was working in NYC by 1845 and continued at least into the sixties. He was occasionally employed by CURRIER & IVES, and he was also a partner of ELIPHALET BROWN (*c.* 1851–53) and of GEORGE W. HATCH (1853–54), but for the most part Severyn worked on his own. ¶ 7 Census (1850), N.Y., LVI, 1 [aged 30]; 8 Census (1860), N.Y., LVI, 14 [aged 52]; Peters, *Currier & Ives,* I, 119; Peters, *America on Stone.*

SEWARD, JAMES. Engraver, born in New York about 1832, working in NYC in 1858 and after. ¶ 8 Census (1860), N.Y., XLVI, 906; NYBD 1858.

SEWELL, H. Artist and lithographer working for HENRY and WILLIAM J. HANINGTON, the dioramists, in NYC in the mid-thirties. ¶ Peters, *America on Stone;* Fred J. Peters, *Clipper Ship Prints;* N. Y. *Herald,* Dec. 7 and 22, 1836, and Boston *Transcript,* Sept. 10, 1838 (courtesy J. E. Arrington).

SEWELL, HARRIET. Genre painting in watercolors, *c.* 1810. ¶ Lipman and Winchester, 179.

SEXTON, SAMUEL H. Portrait and landscape painter of Schenectady (N.Y.), 1839–60. He exhibited at the National Academy and the American Art-Union. ¶ Cowdrey,

NAD; Cowdrey, AA & AAU; Schenectady CD 1857, 1860; N. Y. State BD 1859; Stauffer, no. 2557; represented in N. Y. State Museum. Mrs. Margaret F. Eden of Los Angeles, Cal., owns a portrait signed and dated, "S. H. Sexton, Schenectady, March 1839" (letter, NYHS, April 8, 1956).

SEXTON, WILLIAM. Sculptor, 36, a native of Ireland, at NYC in 1860. ¶ 8 Census (1860), N.Y., LVII, 768.

SEYBOLD, HENRY. Lithographer, 28, from Frankfort (Germany), at NYC in 1860. His wife was Irish and their children, the oldest aged 6, were all born in New York. ¶ 8 Census (1860), N.Y., XLIII, 631.

SEYMOUR, J. O. Of LATIMER BROTHERS & SEYMOUR, engravers, die sinkers, lithographers, and stationers of NYC, 1856–59. ¶ NYBD 1856–59; NYCD 1856–59.

SEYMOUR, JOHN B. Wood engraver; at NYC in 1852; at Cincinnati, 1853–55. ¶ NYCD 1852; Cincinnati BD and CD 1853, 1855.

SEYMOUR, JOHN F. Engraver and printer, NYC, 1850's. ¶ NYCD 1856 [as printer]; 1857 [as engraver]; 1858 [as printer].

SEYMOUR, JOSEPH H. Engraver. He was employed by ISAIAH THOMAS at Worcester (Mass.) between 1791 and 1795; from about 1796 to 1822 he was established in Philadelphia. Joseph H. and SAMUEL SEYMOUR probably were related, since both had the same address in 1819–20. ¶ Stauffer; Fielding, *Supplement to Stauffer;* Phila. CD 1803–20.

SEYMOUR, SAMUEL. Engraver and landscape painter of Philadelphia, 1796–1823. In 1819–20 and 1823 he served as draftsman with S. H. Long's exploring expeditions, first to the Rocky Mountains and second to the upper reaches of the Mississippi, the published accounts of which are illustrated with Seymour's drawings. While he was absent in the West, Samuel was listed in the Philadelphia directories at the same address as JOSEPH H. SEYMOUR, presumably a close relative. Dunlap states that he was born in England. ¶ Stauffer; Fielding, *Supplement to Stauffer;* Phila. CD 1808–20; Butts, *Art in Wisconsin,* 24; James, *Account of an Expedition from Pittsburgh to the Rocky Mountains;* Keating, *Narrative of an Expedition to the Source of St. Peter's River;* Rutledge, PA; Stokes, *Iconography,* I, 468–69; Taft, *Artists and Illustrators of the Old West,* 379; McDermott, "Samuel Seymour: Pioneer Artist of the Plains and the Rockies," 16 plates.

SEYPPEL, FERDINAND. Wood engraver at Cincinnati, 1853–56. ¶ Ohio BD 1853; Cincinnati CD 1856.

SHACKLEFORD, W. S. Portrait painter active in Greencastle and Bloomington (Ind.) from the 1830's to 1860's. ¶ Peat, *Pioneer Painters of Indiana.*

SHAFER, SAMUEL C. Pen-and-ink group portrait, Ohio, about 1810. ¶ Lipman and Winchester, 179; *Antiques* (Jan. 1946), 35.

SHAFFER, HENRY. Delineator of a portrait of the Rev. Alfred Brunson, missionary to the Sioux Indians, engraved in 1837 by J. W. PARADISE. ¶ Stauffer, no. 2390.

SHAFFER, JOHN. Engraver, 35, a native of Pennsylvania, living in Philadelphia in 1860. ¶ 8 Census (1860), Pa., LVI, 747.

SHAFFER, see also SCHAEFFER, SCHEIFER, and SCHIEFFER.

SHAFTEBERG, LEWIS. Miniaturist at Baltimore in 1783. ¶ Prime, I, 8; Bolton, *Miniature Painters.*

SHALLUS, FRANCIS (1774–1821). Engraver, born in Philadelphia, the son of a Revolutionary officer. Though active as an engraver in Philadelphia from 1797 to 1821, Shallus was better known as the author of *The Chronological Tables for Every Day in the Year,* published in 1817. He also operated a circulating library and was active in politics and militia affairs. He died in Philadelphia November 12, 1821. ¶ Stauffer.

SHANKS, ——. Political cartoonist active in NYC in 1838. ¶ Peters, *America on Stone.*

SHANNON, W. Sculptor, San Francisco, 1858. ¶ San Francisco BD 1858.

SHARP, Mr. ——. Portrait painter at New Orleans in May 1838. ¶ Delgado-WPA cites *Commercial Bulletin,* May 12, 1838.

SHARP, EDWIN V. Lithographer, possibly from Georgia. His drawing of the Macon Volunteers appeared in the *U. S. Military Magazine* in 1842 and sometime in the 1850's F. HEPPENHEIMER lithographed Sharp's view of Stone Mountain in Georgia. ¶ Todd, "Huddy & Duval Prints"; Peters, *America on Stone; Portfolio* (Nov. 1945), 54.

SHARP, ELIZA MARY (1829–?). Artist, exhibited at the Boston Athenaeum in 1848. She was born in England on May 24, 1829, the daughter of WILLIAM and Emma Sharp, with whom she was living in Dorchester (Mass.) in 1848. ¶ *Vital Records of Dorchester,* 68; Swan, BA.

SHARP, GEORGE HENRY (1834–?). Lithographer, son of WILLIAM and Emma Sharp, born October 2, 1834, in England. He was working in Boston from about 1857 to 1862. ¶ *Vital Records of Dorchester,* 68; 8 Census (1860), Mass., XXIX, 583; Boston CD 1857–62.

SHARP, JAMES. Boston artist who exhibited "Simple Cottage Scene" at the Athenaeum in 1831. Possibly JAMES C. SHARP, who was only 13 at the time. ¶ BA Cat., 1831.

SHARP, JAMES CLEMENT (1818–1897). Lithographer and teacher of science. Born February 22, 1818, in Dorchester (Mass.), James C. was the son of Edward and Mary Sharp and elder brother of WILLIAM C. SHARP. He worked as a lithographer in Boston in the early 1840's, but apparently soon gave it up. His name is absent from the Boston directories until 1866; from then until the 1880's he is listed as a teacher of natural sciences. He died on April 9, 1897. ¶ *Dorchester Births,* 308; Boston CD 1842–97; Boston BD 1842–45; date of death in Boston CD 1897; Peters, *America on Stone.*

SHARP, MICHELIN & COMPANY. Lithographers, Boston, 1840–41; WILLIAM SHARP and FRANCIS MICHELIN. ¶ Boston BD 1841; Peters, *America on Stone.*

SHARP, PEIRCE & COMPANY. Lithographers, Boston, 1846–49. The firm was established by WILLIAM C. SHARP, JOSHUA H. PEIRCE, and H. CLAPP, but Clapp dropped out about 1848 and in its last year the firm was called simply Sharp & Peirce. ¶ Peters, *America on Stone;* Boston CD 1847–48, BD 1848–49.

SHARP, PHILIP THOMAS (1831–?). Lithographer and photographer, born in England January 27, 1831, the son of WILLIAM and Emma Sharp. Brought to Boston at the age of nine, he grew up there and began working as a lithographer with his father, who took him into partnership in 1852 (SHARP & SON). Philip later turned to photography and was active in Boston until about 1862. ¶ *Vital Records of Dorchester,* 68; 8 Census (1860), Mass., XXIX, 583; Boston CD 1852–62; Peters, *America on Stone* [erroneously as Philip P.].

SHARP & SON. Chromo-lithographers, Boston, 1852–53; WILLIAM and PHILIP T. SHARP. ¶ Boston CD 1852, BD 1853; Peters, *America on Stone.*

SHARP, W. & J. C. Lithographers, Boston, 1842. Though thus listed together, at 17 Tremont Row, in the business directory, WILLIAM and JAMES C. SHARP are listed separately in the city directory at 17 Tremont Row and 16 Franklin Street, respectively. ¶ Boston BD 1842, CD 1842–43.

SHARP, WILLIAM (*c.* 1802–?). Pioneer color lithographer, portrait and landscape painter, drawing teacher. Born at Ramsey, near Peterborough (England), Sharp was working as a lithographer in London by 1832 and possibly earlier, if he was the William Sharp who exhibited engravings at the Royal Academy between 1819 and 1831. He emigrated to America in 1838 or 1839 and settled in Boston. Although he exhibited portraits and landscapes at the Athenaeum several times between 1839 and 1872, Sharp was primarily a lithographer. One of the first American lithographers to experiment with color, he was particularly noted for his illustrations of fruit and flowers in *Fruits of America,* 1847–52. Between 1840 and 1862 Sharp had various partners, including EPHRAIM W. BOUVÉ, FRANCIS MICHELIN, and his own son PHILIP T. SHARP. Another son, GEORGE HENRY SHARP, also was a lithographer. None of the family are listed after 1862. William Sharp is to be distinguished from WILLIAM C. SHARP, also a lithographer in Boston at that time. ¶ 8 Census (1860), Mass., XXIX, 583 [aged 58]; Karolik Cat., 474–76 [erroneously as William C. Sharp]; Graves, *Dictionary;* Waite, "Beginnings of American Color Printing," 13, 18; *Portfolio* (Aug. 1946), 10–13; Swan, BA; Boston CD 1840–62; Peters, *America on Stone; Vital Records of Dorchester,* 67–68 [children of William and Emma Sharp].

SHARP, WILLIAM, & COMPANY. Lithographers, working in association with Charles Bradlee & Company, music publishers, Boston, 1845–47. ¶ Boston CD 1845–46, BD 1846–47.

SHARP, WILLIAM COMELY (1822–1897). Lithographer, born September 5, 1822, at Dorchester (Mass.), son of Edward and Mary and younger brother of JAMES C. SHARP. He worked as a lithographer in Boston from about 1844 into the 1880's and had his home in Dorchester. From 1846 to 1849 he was with the firm of SHARP, PEIRCE & COMPANY. He died August 1, 1897. ¶ *Dorchester Births,* 316; Boston CD 1844–98; death date in Boston CD 1898; Peters, *America on Stone.* Not to be confused with WILLIAM SHARP (*c.* 1802–?), also a Boston lithographer.

SHARPE, CHARLES W. (?–1875/76). Engraver and artist working in Newark (N.J.) from 1845 to 1875. His widow is listed in 1876. This may be the C. W. Sharpe mentioned by Stauffer as being at Philadelphia in 1850. Another Charles W. Sharpe, of London, exhibited four engravings at the Royal Academy between 1858 and 1883. ¶ Newark CD 1845–76; Stauffer; Graves, *Dictionary*.

SHARPE, CORNELIUS N. (?–1828). Ship carver of NYC; of SHARPE & ELLIS, 1810–12; of DODGE & SHARPE, 1814–28. ¶ Pinckney, 92, 200; NYCD 1814–30.

SHARPE & ELLIS. Ship carvers, NYC, 1810–12; CORNELIUS N. SHARPE and JOHN ELLIS. ¶ Pinckney, 200; NYCD 1810–12.

SHARPLES, ELLEN WALLACE (1769–1849). Pastel and watercolor portraitist, born March 4, 1769, possibly at Birmingham (England). Ellen Wallace studied drawing under JAMES SHARPLES at Bath and in 1787 became his third wife; they had two children, JAMES, JR., and ROLINDA, both of whom became professional artists. During the early years of their marriage James and Ellen Sharples lived in England, but about 1793 they came to America and settled at Philadelphia and four years later in NYC. During this time Ellen also became a professional artist, employed chiefly in executing copies of her husband's popular pastel portraits. She was also an expert fancy needleworker. The family returned to England in 1801 and remained there until 1809 when they once again settled in NYC. After James's death in February 1811 Mrs. Sharples and her children went back to England and settled permanently in Bristol. Mrs. Sharples survived all her children and died March 14, 1849, at the age of eighty. Her substantial estate was left to the Bristol Fine Arts Academy (now the Royal West of England Academy) which she had founded several years earlier with a gift of £2,000. Mrs. Sharples' diary and many examples of the work of the family are owned by the Academy. ¶ Knox, *The Sharples;* Bolton, *Crayon Draftsmen.*

SHARPLES, FELIX THOMAS (*c.* 1786–after 1824). Pastel portraitist, son of JAMES SHARPLES by his second wife. Felix spent his childhood partly in England and partly in America. He studied portraiture under his father and began his independent career in 1806 when he came to America for the second time, in company with his half-brother, JAMES SHARPLES, JR. The rest of the family came over in 1809 and settled in NYC, but Felix worked chiefly in the South. When his widowed stepmother returned to England in 1811, accompanied by her children, Felix remained in America. He worked in Virginia and North Carolina at least until 1824, after which date nothing is known of him. ¶ Knox, *The Sharples; Richmond Portraits,* 231; Fielding [gives dates as 1789–1844]; Bolton, *Miniature Painters.*

SHARPLES, JAMES (*c.* 1751–1811). Pastel and oil portraitist, inventor, born about 1751 in Lancashire (England). A pupil of Romney, according to Bolton, Sharples first exhibited at the Royal Academy in 1779 when he was living at Cambridge. In 1781 he was at Bath and Bristol and in 1783 and 1785 at London, again exhibiting portraits at the Royal Academy. In 1787 he took as his third wife (the first two having died) Ellen Wallace of Bath, who had been his pupil (see ELLEN WALLACE SHARPLES). Their two children, JAMES, JR., and ROLINDA, as well as a son FELIX by his second wife, also became artists. After several years in Liverpool and Bath, Sharples brought his family to America about 1793 and for the next eight years he worked in Philadelphia and NYC as a pastel artist. In 1801 they returned to England and settled down in Bath. In 1806 the two sons went to America as professional artists and the rest of the family followed in 1809. They established themselves in NYC, but James's health soon failed and he died there February 26, 1811. Soon after his death all the family except Felix returned to England. ¶ Knox, *The Sharples;* Bolton, "James Sharples"; N. Y. *Public Advertiser,* Feb. 28, 1811, obit.; Graves, *Dictionary;* DAB; Morgan and Fielding, *Life Portraits of Washington;* DNB.

SHARPLES, JAMES, JR. (*c.* 1788–1839). Pastel portraits, still life, watercolors. James, son of JAMES and ELLEN WALLACE SHARPLES, was born about 1788, probably in Liverpool, and spent his childhood in England and America. He was trained by his father and began his professional career in England at the age of 15. In 1806 he came to America with his half-brother FELIX SHARPLES; they were joined by the rest of the family in 1809. After the elder Sharples' death in 1811, James went back to England with his mother and sister, with whom he lived in Bristol until his death on August 10,

1839. ¶ Knox, *The Sharples;* Bolton, "James Sharples."

SHARPLES, ROLINDA (*c.* 1793–1838). Portrait, genre, and historical painter in oils and watercolors, pastellist, and watercolorist. The daughter of JAMES and ELLEN WALLACE SHARPLES, Rolinda was born either in Bath (England) shortly before the family came to America (Knox) or in NYC in 1794 shortly after their arrival (Bolton). She was already painting when the family made its second American stay in 1809–11 and after their final return to England in 1811 she devoted herself entirely to art. She lived in Bristol with her mother and brother for the rest of her life, exhibiting occasionally at the Royal Academy. She was made an Honorary Member of the Society of British Artists in 1827. She died in Bristol February 10, 1838. ¶ Knox, *The Sharples;* Bolton, "James Sharples"; Graves, *Dictionary.*

SHARRON, JOHN. Engraver from Bavaria, 37, at Philadelphia in 1860. ¶ 8 Census (1860), Pa., LIV, 795.

SHATTUCK, AARON DRAPER (1832–1928). N.A. Landscape, portrait, and animal painter, born March 9, 1832, at Francestown (N.H.). He studied in Boston in 1851 under ALEXANDER RANSOM and subsequently at the National Academy in NYC. In 1860 he married the sister of SAMUEL COLMAN, landscape painter, and in 1861 he was elected a Member of the National Academy. Shattuck painted during the summers in New England and after 1868 he settled permanently on a farm near Granby (Conn.), where he died July 30, 1928. ¶ DAB; French, *Art and Artists in Connecticut,* 144; Tuckerman, *Book of the Artists,* 560–61; Cowdrey, NAD; Swan, BA; Rutledge, MHS; Rutledge, PA; Washington Art Assoc. Cat., 1857.

SHATTUCK, J. L. Of MICHELIN & SHATTUCK, lithographers, NYC, 1853; his home was in Brooklyn. ¶ NYCD 1853.

SHAVER, A. G. Monochromatic artist who exhibited at the American Institute in 1856 and was located at Hartford (Conn.) in 1858–59. ¶ Am. Inst. Cat., 1856 [nos. 537–39, as A. G. Sharer; no. 2035, as A. G. Shaw; no. 2079, as A. G. Shaver]; Hartford CD 1858–59.

SHAVER, SAMUEL M. (*c.* 1816–1878). Portrait, miniature, and landscape painter, born near Kingsport (Tenn.). In 1845 he was married at Rogersville (Tenn.) to the daughter of Congressman Samuel Powel (1776–1841). He lived there until 1852, serving at least one year as professor of drawing and painting at the Odd Fellows' Female Institute and painting many portraits in Eastern Tennessee. His whereabouts are unknown from 1852 until the death of his wife in January 1856 when he returned to Rogersville. In 1859 Shaver moved to Knoxville and in 1863 he moved again to Russellville (Tenn.). In 1867 or 1868 he rejoined his wife's family at Jerseyville (Ill.), opposite St. Louis, and he made his home there until his death on June 21, 1878. ¶ Price, "Samuel Shaver: Portrait Painter," two repros., and checklist.

SHAVER, V. PAYSON. Portrait and miniature painter who exhibited at the National Academy in 1837 and 1840. In 1840 he was living in Albany (N.Y.). ¶ Cowdrey, NAD.

SHAW, ——. Teacher of flower and ornamental painting at New Orleans in March 1832; he was said to be from Boston. ¶ Delgado-WPA cites *Courier,* March 24, 1832.

SHAW, JAMES. English engraver, 30, at Philadelphia in 1860. His wife Sarah was also English, but their two-month-old son James was born in Pennsylvania. Sarah, widow of James, is listed in 1871. ¶ 8 Census (1860), Pa., LXII, 597; Phila. CD 1871.

SHAW, J. Portrait painter at Cincinnati (Ohio) in 1853. His address was the same as that of Dr. John Logan in the city directory for that year. ¶ Ohio BD 1853; Cincinnati CD 1853.

SHAW, JOSEPH. Artist, Philadelphia, 1819–24; probably JOSHUA SHAW. ¶ Phila. CD 1819–20, 1823–24.

SHAW, JOSHUA (*c.* 1777–1860). Landscape painter and inventor, born at Bellingborough, Lincolnshire. He was apprenticed to a sign-painter and followed his trade at Manchester, at the same time pursuing his studies until he won recognition as a painter of portraits, flowers, still life, landscapes, and cattle pieces. He began exhibiting at the Royal Academy and other London galleries in 1802, his address then being Bath. In 1817 he emigrated to America and settled in Philadelphia. DUNLAP met him in Norfolk (Va.) in 1819 and 1820 while Shaw was travelling through the South making sketches and taking subscriptions for a series of American views which were engraved by JOHN HILL and published in

Philadelphia in 1819 and 1820. Shaw resided in Philadelphia until about 1843 and was active in the formation of the Artists' Fund Society; he also exhibited frequently in Philadelphia, New York, Boston, and Baltimore and during the same period made a number of important improvements in firearms for which he later received substantial awards from the American and Russian governments. About 1843 Shaw moved to Bordentown (N.J.) and he continued to exhibit landscapes until 1853 when he was stricken with paralysis. He died on September 8, 1860, at Burlington (N.J.) at the age of 83. ¶ Cummings, *Historic Annals,* 288–89; obit., *The Christian Intelligencer,* Sept. 20, 1860 (cited in Sawyer, "Deaths Published in The Christian Intelligencer"); Dunlap, *History;* Dunlap, *Diary;* Graves, *Dictionary;* Rutledge, PA; Rutledge, MHS; Cowdrey, NAD; Cowdrey, AA & AAU; Swan, BA; Dickson, *John Wesley Jarvis;* Karolik Cat., repro.; Sartain, *Reminiscences;* Phila. CD 1819–24 [as Joseph Shaw], 1825–42; Stokes, *Iconography;* Flexner, *The Light of Distant Skies.* Shaw's own works include *A New and Original Drawing Book* (1816); *Picturesque Views of American Scenery* (2d ed., 1820, at NYHS); and *United States Directory for the Use of Travellers and Merchants* (1822). Some account of his inventions is found in *Documents, Official and Unofficial, Relating to the Claim of Joshua Shaw, the Inventor of the Percussion Caps and Locks for Small Arms . . .* (Washington, 1847). He is represented in the Karolik Collection and the Victoria and Albert Museum.

SHAW, STEPHEN WILLIAM (1817–1900). Portrait painter, born December 15, 1817, at Windsor (Vt.). He went to California in 1849, via New Orleans and Panama, and had a successful career as a portrait painter in San Francisco. From 1850 he was artist to the Masons of California and he is said to have painted over 200 portraits of Masonic officers, as well as of many western notables. He also took part in the expedition which discovered Humboldt Bay in New Guinea. He died in San Francisco February 12, 1900. ¶ *Art Annual,* III (1900), 60; *Antiques* (July 1946), 59; Delgado-WPA cites New Orleans *Picayune,* Jan. 10, 1849; San Francisco CD 1856+.

SHEA, JOHN. Irish lithographer, 20, at NYC in 1860. ¶ 8 Census (1860), N.Y., XLIII, 24.

SHEARER, CHRISTOPHER H. (1840–1926) Landscape painter of Reading (Pa.); died there April 29, 1926. ¶ *Art Annual,* XXIII, obit.

SHEARER, see also SHERER.

SHEARMAN, JAMES A. Lithographer, of ROBERTSON, SEIBERT & SHEARMAN, NYC, 1859–61. He later headed the firm of Shearman & Hart. ¶ Peters, *America on Stone;* NYBD 1859–60.

SHECKER, HERMAN. Lithographer. He was a butterfly collector at Reading (Pa.) about 1860 and made drawings on stone to illustrate his own publications. ¶ Peters, *America on Stone.*

SHEDWICK, JOHN. English engraver, 34, living in West Philadelphia in 1850; his wife and four children (10 to 2 years) were born in England. His real property was valued at $11,000. In 1852 Shedwick was listed as a pattern cutter. ¶ 7 Census (1850), Pa., LV, 1154; Phila. CD 1852.

SHEETS, JOHN. Artist, 48, a native of Prussia, at Philadelphia in 1860. His wife and two older children (ages 10 and 6) were born in Prussia, while a third child (3) was born in New York. ¶ 8 Census (1860), Pa., LIV, 373.

SHEFFIELD, ISAAC (1798–1845). Portrait and miniature painter. He was a native of Guilford (Conn.) who settled in New London about 1833 and worked there until his death in 1845. ¶ French, *Art and Artists in Conn.,* 60; Sherman, "Unrecorded Early American Portrait Painters" (Dec. 1933); *Art in America* (April 1936), 81, repro.

SHEGOGUE, ALFRED M. Exhibited a fruit piece at the National Academy in 1858. He was listed at the same address as JAMES H. SHEGOGUE, probably his father. ¶ Cowdrey, NAD.

SHEGOGUE, JAMES HAMILTON (1806–1872). N.A. Portrait, genre, historical, and landscape painter, born February 22, 1806, at Charleston (S.C.). He began his professional career in NYC about 1833, when he first exhibited at the American Academy and, except for several trips to Europe, he worked in NYC until his removal to Warrenville (Conn.) in 1862. Shegogue was elected an Associate of the National Academy in 1841 and an Academician two years later; he also served as its Corresponding Secretary for a time. Shegogue resided in Warrenville from

1862 until his death on April 7, 1872. ¶ French, *Art and Artists in Conn.*, 71; CAB and Fielding [erroneously as James Henry Shegogue]; Cowdrey, AA & AAU; Cowdrey, NAD; NYCD 1834+; 7 Census (1850), N.Y., LII, 323; Thieme-Becker; represented NYHS and Brooklyn Museum.

SHELDON, JOSHUA. Landscape painter at Newburyport (Mass.) in 1849 and at Salem (Mass.) in 1857. ¶ Belknap, *Artists and Craftsmen of Essex County,* 13.

SHELDON, LUCY (1788–1889). Amateur painter; born June 27, 1788, at Litchfield (Conn.); married Theron Beach in 1832; died in Litchfield, April 7, 1889. As a pupil at Miss Peirce's School in Litchfield about 1802–03, she painted several genre pictures which have been preserved and reproduced. ¶ Vanderpoel, *Chronicles of a Pioneer School,* 43–66.

SHELDON, WILLIAM HENRY (1840–1912). Painter and illustrator; born September 4, 1840, at Allen's Hill (N.Y.); died March 15, 1912, at Morristown (N.J.). ¶ *Art Annual,* X, obit.

SHEPARD, DANIEL M. Portrait and fresco painter at Salem (Mass.) in 1850. ¶ Belknap, *Artists and Craftsmen of Essex County,* 13.

SHEPHEART, FREDERICK. Artist, 37, at Philadelphia in 1850; he and his wife and their children (ages 9 to 3) were all born in Germany. ¶ 7 Census (1850), Pa., LI, 47.

SHEPHERD, FITCH. Engraver, 45, a native of New York, living in NYC in 1850. ¶ 7 Census (1850), N.Y., LII, 406.

SHEPHERD, G. S. Exhibited "View at Hempstead" [Long Island?] at the National Academy in 1847. *Cf.* N. G. SHEPHERD. ¶ Cowdrey, NAD.

SHEPHERD, GEORGE M. Engraver on copper and steel, born in England about 1823. He was working in NYC by 1846 and remained there, except for three years in Philadelphia (1854–57), until after 1860. ¶ 7 Census (1850), N.Y., XLIII, 398; NYCD 1846–53, 1857–60+; Phila. CD 1854–57.

SHEPHERD, N. G. Landscape painter of NYC, exhibitor at the National Academy in 1856. *Cf.* G. S. SHEPHERD. ¶ Cowdrey, NAD.

SHEPHERD, THOMAS S. Miniaturist, portrait painter, and draftsman working in NYC in the 1840's. He exhibited a specimen of print coloring at the American Institute in 1847. ¶ NYCD 1843–47; Am. Inst. Cat., 1847; Bolton, *Miniature Painters.*

SHEPPARD, EDWARD or EDWIN W. Painter of birds at Philadelphia in 1858–59 and Washington in 1860. ¶ Rutledge, PA; Washington Art Association Cat., 1859.

SHEPPARD, RICHARD H. Portrait, miniature, sign and ornamental painter of Baltimore, active 1840's and 1850's. ¶ Lafferty; Pleasants, *250 Years of Painting in Md.,* 55.

SHEPPARD, WILLIAM LUDLOW (1833–1912). Watercolorist, illustrator, and sculptor. A native of Richmond (Va.), he made a series of watercolors showing army life in the Civil War, now at the Confederate Museum in Richmond. He died March 27, 1912, at Richmond. ¶ *Art Annual,* X, obit.; Barker, *American Painting,* 553; Hamilton, *Early American Book Illustrators and Wood Engravers,* 455–57.

SHERER, JOHN. Lithographer and publisher, Cincinnati, 1847–59. In 1847 he was of SHERER & ROWSE, lithographers; in 1859 he was listed as a Masonic publisher. ¶ Peters, *America on Stone;* Cincinnati BD 1850, CD 1851, 1856–59.

SHERER & ROWSE. Lithographers, Cincinnati, 1847; JOHN SHERER and J. B. ROWSE. ¶ Peters, *America on Stone.*

SHERLOCK, ——. Artist at New Orleans in 1823. ¶ Delgado-WPA cites CD 1823.

SHERMAN, EDWIN ALLEN (1829–1914). Amateur artist, born August 25, 1829, at North Bridgewater (Mass.). Enlisting in the U. S. Army in 1845, he served in Mexico during the Mexican War and then joined the gold rush to California, arriving in May 1849. Soon after, he made a sketch of Sutter's Fort. After a year in the gold fields, he settled down in Sonoma and in 1852 became city clerk. A retrospective drawing of the raising of the American flag in Sonoma in 1846 dates from this period. Sherman revisited Massachusetts in 1854 but returned to California the same year and spent the rest of his life there. During his latter years he lived in Oakland where he died on March 17, 1914. ¶ Van Nostrand and Coulter, *California Pictorial,* 60–61.

SHERMAN, GEORGE E. Engraver, born in Connecticut about 1810/11. He was active as an engraver in NYC from 1840 at least until 1860; from 1840 to 1853 in partnership with JOHN CALVIN SMITH. In 1850 CHARLES SMITH and family were living in the same house with the Shermans. ¶ 7 Census (1850), N.Y., XLII, 160; 8 Census (1860), N.Y., XLIII, 623; NYCD 1840–58.

SHERMAN, JOHN H. Artist, 25, a native of Massachusetts, at Philadelphia in 1860. ¶ 8 Census (1860), Pa., LV, 271.

SHERMAN, LUCY MCFARLAND (1838–1878). Amateur watercolorist. Lucy McFarland was born June 14, 1838; married John Dempster Sherman in 1857; died March 14, 1878. She was the mother of Frank Dempster Sherman, born at Peekskill (N.Y.) in 1860 and Professor in the Columbia University School of Architecture from 1886 until his death in 1916. ¶ Sherman, *Sherman Genealogy,* 15–16; Lipman and Winchester, 180.

SHERMAN, Mrs. P. A. Exhibited fruit and flower pieces at the National Academy in 1860; her address was in NYC. ¶ Cowdrey, NAD.

SHERMAN & SMITH. Engravers, NYC, 1840–53; GEORGE E. SHERMAN and JOHN CALVIN SMITH. ¶ NYCD 1840–53.

SHERWIN, JOHN H. (1834–?). Lithographer and painter, born at Bellows Falls (Vt.). He studied first for the ministry but in 1851–52 he took up lithography in NYC under MORAWSKI. During the next ten years he worked in Philadelphia for the ROSENTHALS, then in NYC and Boston. He exhibited at the Pennsylvania Academy in 1860. After an unsuccessful painting venture in Boston, according to Peters, Sherwin retrieved his fortunes by marrying a rich widow. ¶ Peters, *America on Stone;* Rutledge, PA; *Antiques* (Feb. 1926), 83.

SHERWIN, THOMAS. Engraver at Wilmington (Del.) in 1857–59. ¶ Wilmington BD 1857; Delaware BD 1859.

SHERWOOD, A. Portrait painter, 27, a native of New York, at Cincinnati in 1850. ¶ 7 Census (1850), Ohio, XX, 257.

SHERWOOD, HENRY. Exhibited a landscape drawing at the American Academy in 1818, as a pupil of J. I. [J.] HOLLAND. ¶ Cowdrey, AA & AAU.

SHERWOOD, HENRY J. Artist, 55, a native of New York, living in NYC in 1850. ¶ 7 Census (1850), N.Y., XLVIII, 269. NYCD 1850 lists only Henry J. Sherwood, hardware. *Cf.* HENRY SHERWOOD.

SHERWOOD, J. P. Portrait and historical painter. The NYHS owns four portraits by this artist, probably painted in the mid-1830's; they represent Rev. and Mrs. Adiel Sherwood and Col. and Mrs. T. A. Sherwood. The NYHS also owns a portrait of J. P. Sherwood by JOHN VANDERLYN, JR. Vanderlyn and Sherwood advertised together in Charleston (S.C.) in 1836. ¶ NYHS artist file; Rutledge, *Artists in the Life of Charleston.*

SHEUE, ——. Miniaturist and landscape painter. A native of Prussia, where he is said to have been the tutor of a Count Feltenstine, Sheue taught German and painted miniatures at Pittsburgh and later painted miniatures, portraits, and landscapes in St. Louis, probably before 1860. ¶ Breckenridge, *Recollections of Persons and Places in the West,* 96–97, 233.

SHEYS or SHAYS, WILLIAM P. Portrait and miniature painter who studied under JOHN WESLEY JARVIS and was active in NYC in 1813 and 1820. Dunlap states that he sank to "vicious courses" and died a common sailor in a foreign land. ¶ NYCD 1813, 1820; Dickson, *John Wesley Jarvis;* Dunlap, *History.*

SHIELDS, ——. Engraver, 35, a native of Pennsylvania, at Boston in 1850. ¶ 7 Census (1850), Mass., XXIV, 354.

SHIELDS, CHARLES. Engraver and decorative painter, NYC, 1840–60; also printer. ¶ NYCD 1840–60.

SHIELDS & COLLINS. Copperplate engravers, New Orleans, 1842; THOMAS H. SHIELDS and CHARLES COLLINS. ¶ New Orleans CD 1842.

SHIELDS, THOMAS H. Wood and copperplate engraver of New Orleans, 1836–56; in 1842 of SHIELDS & COLLINS. ¶ Delgado-WPA cites *Picayune,* Jan. 9, 1836, and New Orleans CD 1841–42, 1844, 1849–56.

SHIELS or SHIELDS, WILLIAM. Portrait painter at NYC in 1817–18, when he exhibited at the American Academy, and at Charleston (S.C.) 1820–22. In 1821 he was a director of the South Carolina Academy of Fine Arts. Possibly the William Shiels (1785–1857) who was a member of the Royal Scottish Academy and exhibited domestic pictures at the Royal Academy in London between 1808 and 1852. ¶ Cowdrey, AA & AAU; Rutledge, *Artists in the Life of Charleston;* Swan, BA; Graves, *Dictionary;* Dunlap, *Diary,* 527.

SHIGG, WILLIAM. Wood engraver, 19, from England, at NYC in 1850. ¶ 7 Census (1850), N.Y., XLIX, 720.

SHIMONSKY, see SCHIMONSKY.

SHINDLER, A. ZENO. Painter of pastel portraits and landscapes; born in Germany about 1813. Shindler was a drawing teacher in Philadelphia during the 1850's and later he exhibited at the Pennsylvania Academy between 1852 and 1863 pastel portraits and scenes in Paris and London, as well as Pennsylvania, New Hampshire and Virginia. Stokes credits to him a view of Reading (Pa.) of about 1834. He is said later to have become a painter of Indian life. ¶ Rutledge, PA; Phila. CD 1853–60+; *Panorama* (Aug. 1946), 10; Stokes, *Historical Prints;* 7 Census (1850), Pa., LIII, 217.

SHIPLEY, HENRY H. Engraver; born in New York about 1830; active in Cincinnati from about 1850 to after 1860. He was associated with his brother WILLIAM SHIPLEY and in 1853 with GEORGE K. STILLMAN. ¶ 8 Census (1860), Ohio, XXV, 244; Cincinnati BD 1850–56, CD 1853–59.

SHIPLEY & STILLMAN. Wood engravers, Cincinnati, 1853; HENRY H. and WILLIAM SHIPLEY and GEORGE K. STILLMAN. ¶ Ohio BD 1853; Cincinnati CD 1853.

SHIPLEY, WILLIAM. Engraver, associated with his brother HENRY in Cincinnati, 1853–60. ¶ Cincinnati CD 1853–60.

SHIPPER, NICHOLAS L. Engraver, NYC, 1848–58. ¶ NYBD 1848–58.

SHIPPER, see also SCHIPPER.

SHIPS, NICHOLAS. Lithographer, 30, a native of Pennsylvania, boarding in Philadelphia in 1860 in the same house as FRANCIS DEVANNIE, sculptor, CHARLES SCHILCOCKS and ADOLPHE LABORN, lithographers. ¶ 8 Census (1860), Pa., LII, 432.

SHIRLAW, WALTER (1838–1909). N.A. Genre, mural, and portrait painter, illustrator, and banknote engraver. Born August 6, 1838, in Paisley (Scotland) and brought to America at the age of three, Shirlaw grew up in NYC and was apprenticed in the early 1850's to a firm of banknote engravers. After five years he turned to painting and exhibited for the first time at the National and Pennsylvania Academies in 1861. A few years later he was obliged to return to engraving and from 1865 to 1870 he worked for the Western Bank Note and Engraving Company of Chicago, during which time he was also active in the founding of the Art Institute of Chicago. From 1870 to 1877 he studied painting and drawing in Munich. After his return to America in 1877 he settled in NYC. He was a founder and the first president of the Society of American Artists and became a National Academician in 1888. During the latter part of his career Shirlaw painted murals, designed stained glass windows, and contributed charcoal illustrations to popular periodicals. He died in Madrid (Spain) on December 26, 1909. ¶ DAB; Dreier, "Walter Shirlaw," with 5 repros.; N. Y. *Times,* Dec. 30, 1909; *Art Annual,* VIII, obit.; Rutledge, PA; Graves, *Dictionary*.

SHIRVINGTON, J. Miniature portraits in water colors, Charlottesville (Va.), about 1840. ¶ Lipman and Winchester, 180.

SHNYDORE, IGNATIUS. Painting in all its branches. In June 1788 Shnydore advertised in NYC that he had resigned as scene painter to the Old American Company of Comedians, desired to become a citizen, and offered his services in every variety of painting, gilding, and glazing. He was still working in NYC in 1794. ¶ Gottesman, *Arts and Crafts in New York,* II, no. 1150; NYCD 1790–94 (McKay).

SHOBER, CHARLES. Lithographer. He was working in Philadelphia in 1856–57, but soon after moved to Chicago where he was active from about 1858 to 1883. In 1857–58 his partner was CHARLES REEN; after 1860 he and one Carqueville formed the Chicago Lithographic Company which flourished until it was burned out in 1883. ¶ Phila. CD 1856–57; Chicago CD 1858–59; Peters, *America on Stone;* Arrington, "Nauvoo Temple," Chap. 8.

SHOBERT, ALONZO. Lithographer of an illustration in *The Horticulturalist,* V (1855), probably at Philadelphia. ¶ Peters, *America on Stone.*

SHOCKLEIDGE, R. Portrait painter working in Connecticut in 1856. ¶ Information from signed and dated portrait, courtesy Thomas D. Williams, Litchfield (Conn.).

SHOEMAKER, ANDREW. Engraver, 32, at Philadelphia in 1860. He, his wife, and one child aged 9 were born in Bavaria; two younger children were born in Pennsylvania. ¶ 8 Census (1860), Pa., LV, 477.

SHOEMAKER, GOTTLIEB. Lithographer, 30, a native of Germany, at Philadelphia in 1850 with his German wife and three children under 7 born in Pennsylvania. He was listed in the directories during the early 1850's. ¶ 7 Census (1850), Pa., XLIX, 1073; Phila. CD 1850–52.

SHOTWELL, H. C. Wood engraver at Cincinnati in 1853. ¶ Stauffer.

SHOURDS, GEORGE WASHINGTON. Engraver, 17, a native Pennsylvanian, at Philadelphia in 1850. He was listed in the directories in 1854 and after and in 1855 contributed one engraving to *The Annals of San Francisco* (N.Y., 1855). ¶ 7 Census (1850), Pa., LV, 5; Phila. CD 1854–60+; Hamilton, *Early American Book Illustrators and Wood Engravers,* 331.

SHOURDS, JOHN. Lithographer, 22, a native Pennsylvanian, at Philadelphia in 1860, living with his father, William H. Shourds, constable. ¶ 8 Census (1860), Pa., LIV, 927; Phila. CD 1861.

SHRADER, ALFRED. Lithographer from Darmstadt (Germany), aged 37, living in Philadelphia in 1860 with his wife and son, aged 2, the latter born in Pennsylvania. ¶ 8 Census (1860), Pa., LII, 256.

SHRANK, WILLIAM. German artist, 43, an inmate of the Philadelphia Alms House in September 1850. ¶ 7 Census (1850), Pa., LVI, 122.

SHREEVE or SHREEVES, JOHN. Portrait painter of Philadelphia, 1845–after 1870. He was born in Pennsylvania about 1823. He may have been the John Shreeves of 80 Green St., Philadelphia, who executed two silhouettes reproduced in *Antiques* in September 1922. These silhouettes are assigned the date *c.* 1810, but as John Shreeves, the portrait painter, was living on Green St. between 1850 and 1854, it is possible that he was the artist and that the silhouettes have been wrongly dated. ¶ 8 Census (1860), Pa., LIV, 981; Phila. CD 1845–54, 1859–70+; *Antiques* (Sept. 1922), 131.

SHUGG, RICHARD. Wood engraver, NYC, 1858–60; in 1858 with MCLEES & SHUGG. ¶ NYBD 1858, 1860.

SHULTZ, CHARLES. Lithographer, 19, a native of Württemberg, living with his parents in Philadelphia in 1860. ¶ 8 Census (1860), Pa., LVIII, 396.

SHUMWAY, HENRY COLTON (1807–1884). N.A. Miniaturist and portrait painter, born July 4, 1807, at Middletown (Conn.). He entered the school of the National Academy in 1828 and after two years of study established himself as a miniature painter in NYC. Except for professional visits to Washington and Hartford, and summers at Middletown, his entire career was spent in NYC. Until the advent of the photograph he was highly successful as a miniaturist; after 1860 he devoted himself chiefly to coloring photographs. He was elected a National Academician in 1832. Shumway was for over fifty years prominent in the 7th New York Regiment of the State Militia. He died in NYC May 6, 1884. ¶ Bolton, *Miniature Painters;* Clement and Hutton; French, *Art and Artists in Connecticut,* 73–74; Cowdrey, NAD; Cowdrey, AA & AAU; NYCD 1834–60+; 8 Census (1860), N.Y., LVII, 365; Swan, BA; Rutledge, PA.

SHURTLEFF, ROSWELL MORSE (1838–1915). N.A. Landscape and animal painter, illustrator, lithographer. He was born at Rindge (N.H.) on June 14, 1838, attended but did not graduate from Dartmouth College, and went to work in 1857 as an architect's assistant in Manchester (N.H.). He worked for a lithographer in Buffalo (N.Y.) in 1858–59, then moved to Boston where he did drawing for the engraver JOHN ANDREW and studied nights at Lowell Institute. In 1860–61 he worked in NYC as a magazine illustrator and studied at the National Academy. Responding to the call for volunteers in 1861, he was wounded in July and spent eight months in a Southern prison, after which he returned to NYC and his work as a magazine illustrator. After his marriage in 1867, he settled in Hartford (Conn.) but he returned to NYC in 1875 and there made his home during the rest of his life. He turned to oil painting in 1870 and first exhibited at the National Academy in 1872. His first paintings were of animal subjects but about 1870 he turned to the forest landscapes for which he is chiefly noted, many of them painted at his summer home in the Adirondacks. He was elected a National Academician in 1890. He died in NYC on January 6, 1915. ¶ DAB; CAB; French, *Art and Artists in Connecticut,* 146; *Art Annual,* XII.

SHUSTER, see SCHUSTER.

SHUTE, Mrs. R. W. Portrait painter active in New Hampshire and Vermont (?), 1834–36. She was at Concord (N.H.) in 1836. ¶ WPA (Mass.), *Portraits Found in Vt.;* WPA (Mass.), *Portraits Found in N.H.*

SIBOLT, see LIBOLT.

SIEBERT, SELMAR (1808–?). Copper engraver, born September 4, 1808, at Lehnin (Prussia). He was trained in Germany and worked there until his emigration to America between 1840 and 1843. He settled in Washington (D.C.) and was working there in 1860. ¶ Thieme-Becker; Washington CD 1858–60; 8 Census (1860), D.C., II, 539.

SIEBERT, see also SEIBERT.

SIEGLER, ——. Painter or proprietor of a panorama of a voyage from New York to

California via Cape Horn, exhibited at Louisville (Ky.) in June 1850. ¶ Louisville *Morning Courier,* June 5, 1850 (citation courtesy J. E. Arrington).

SIEGNARS [?], CHARLES. Artist, 30, a native of Ohio, at Cincinnati in 1850. Not found in the Cincinnati Directory, though there is a Mrs. Mary Signar in the 1853 directory. ¶ 7 Census (1850), Ohio, XX, 731; Cincinnati CD 1850, 1853.

SIETZ, LEWIS. Artist, 33, from Württemberg, at NYC in 1860. His wife was from Baden and they had a son, 11 months old, born in NYC. ¶ 8 Census (1860), N.Y., LIV, 926; NYCD 1863.

SIGEL, EMIL. Engraver and die sinker, NYC, 1856–58. ¶ NYBD 1856, 1858.

SILL, EBENEZER ENOCH (1822–?). Artist, born September 14, 1822, in Moreau (N.Y.). He was living in NYC in 1854 when he was married to Beatris Weatherspoon. ¶ *Genealogy of the Descendants of John Sill,* 38.

SILL, JOSEPH. Portrait painter; born in Carlisle (England), 1801; died in Philadelphia, 1854. In 1837 he exhibited at the Artists' Fund Society a copy of a portrait by THOMAS SULLY. ¶ Information courtesy Mrs. Harold M. Sill, Philadelphia; Rutledge, PA.

SILSBURY, GEORGE M. Artist, 34, a native of Maine, at Portland in 1850. ¶ 7 Census (1850), Me., IV, 432.

SILVA, FRANCIS A. (1835–1886). Marine painter. As a schoolboy in NYC he exhibited pen drawings at the American Institute in 1848, 1849, and 1850. He took up art as his career after service during the Civil War and became known for his paintings of marine subjects from Chesapeake Bay to the coast of New England. He became a member of the Water Color Society in 1872. ¶ Am. Inst. Cat., 1848–50; *Panorama* (Aug. 1948), 9; *Portfolio* (May 1955), 216, repro.

SILVEIRA, JOSEPH N. Artist, Philadelphia, 1856. ¶ Phila. BD 1856.

SIMES, MARY JANE (1807–1872). Miniaturist, born in Baltimore April 1, 1807. She was a granddaughter of JAMES PEALE. Miniatures by her were exhibited in Philadelphia and Baltimore between 1825 and 1835. She later married Dr. John Floyd Yeates and she died May 16, 1872. ¶ Sellers, *Charles Willson Peale,* II, 423; Rutledge, PA; Rutledge, MHS; Lafferty.

SIMITIÈRE, see DU SIMITIÈRE.

SIMMONE, see SIMONNE.

SIMMONS, ABRAHAM. Engraver, NYC, 1814–15. ¶ NYCD 1814–15.

SIMMONS, FRANKLIN (1839–1913). Sculptor, born January 11, 1839, at Lisbon (Me.). He spent his boyhood in Bath (Me.) and took up modelling while employed in a mill at Lewiston (Me.). After study in Boston under JOHN ADAMS JACKSON, Simmons opened a studio in Lewiston but he soon turned itinerant, working in Waterville, Brunswick, and Portland before 1860. By 1865 he was sufficiently successful to go to Washington and model busts of a number of prominent national figures. In 1867 he went to Italy to work on a statue of Roger Williams and, except for visits to America, he made his home in Italy for the rest of his life. His work included many portrait busts, ideal figures, and Civil War monuments. Simmons died in Rome December 6, 1913, leaving his estate to the Portland (Me.) Society of Art which exhibits a collection of his work as the Franklin Simmons Memorial. ¶ DAB; *Art Annual,* XI, obit.; Fairman, *Art and Artists of the Capitol;* Clement and Hutton; New England BD 1860 [at Lewiston, Me.].

SIMMONS, S. Banner painter at Charleston (S.C.) in 1860. ¶ Rutledge, *Artists in the Life of Charleston.*

SIMON, AUGUST. Artist, 35, from Wittenberg or Württemberg [census record not clear], at NYC in 1860 with his wife, a native of Württemberg. ¶ 8 Census (1860), N.Y., XLV, 513.

SIMON, AUGUSTUS D. Miniaturist and portrait painter, teacher of drawing and miniature painting. He advertised in Salem (Mass.) in early September 1820 as Augustus D. Symon. Augustus D. or A. D. Simon also advertised in Charleston (S.C.) in November 1820 and 1821. ¶ Belknap, *Artists and Craftsmen of Essex County,* 13; Rutledge, *Artists in the Life of Charleston.*

SIMON, BENEDICT. Lithographer, born in Baden (Germany) between 1824 and 1829, working in New Orleans between 1850 and 1870. 1855–60 he was with PESSOU & SIMON and in 1860 two younger lithographers from Baden, AUGUST BERCOLI and HENRY FLICON, were living with Simon and his wife. ¶ 8 Census (1860), La., VIII, 14; 7 Census (1850), La., V, 84; New Orleans CD 1853–60.

SIMON, DENNIS or DIONIS. Lithographer, born in Baden (Germany) about 1830, working in New Orleans between 1857 and 1870. In 1860 he and his family resided with his partner JEAN TOLTI; in 1870 he was in partnership with JULES MANOUVRIER. ¶ 8 Census (1860), La., VIII, 15; *Creole,* March 26, 1857 (courtesy Delgado-WPA); New Orleans CD 1858–70.

SIMOND, LOUIS (1767–1831). Amateur painter. Simond left his native France in 1792 and settled in NYC where he was a merchant and auctioneer until his return to France in 1815. He was elected a member of the New-York Historical Society in 1812 and designed the vignette of Hudson's *Half Moon* which was later engraved for the Society's membership diploma by A. B. DURAND. His drawing of "Moses Rescued by Pharaoh's Daughter" was engraved by LENEY and PETER MAVERICK in 1816. Simond was the author of three travel books on England, Switzerland, and Italy, published between 1815 and 1828. He was also known as a distinguished amateur painter and art critic. He died in Geneva (Switzerland) in July 1831. ¶ *Biographie Universelle, Supplement* (1849); NYCD 1793–1814; Vail, *Knickerbocker Birthday,* 62–64, including repro. of a water color portrait of Simond by the Baroness HYDE DE NEUVILLE, owned by NYHS; Stephens, *The Mavericks,* 110.

SIMONDS, GEORGE W. Lithographic engraver, 22, a native of New York, at Boston in 1860, boarding at the same house as WILLARD C. VANDERLIP. ¶ 8 Census (1860), Mass., XXVII, 890.

SIMONI, ANTONIO. Artist, 29, from Italy, at Boston in 1860; LOUIS BERNETT boarded with him. ¶ 8 Census (1860), Mass., XXV. 32.

SIMONIN, D. Miniaturist at New Orleans before 1860. ¶ Carolina Art Assoc. Cat., 1935.

SIMONNE, T. Engraver working in NYC between 1814 and 1816; he did work for the publishers Longworth and T. C. Fay. Possibly the same as Thomas Simonne, teacher of French (1819) and Theodore Simonne, teacher of languages (1822–23). ¶ Stauffer [as T. Simmone]; NYCD 1815–20 [engraving by Simonne of Stollenwerck's Mechanical Panorama]; NYCD 1819, 1822–23.

SIMONS, the Misses. Teachers of drawing and painting, music, French, and other accomplishments, Charleston (S.C.), 1820. In 1822 only one Miss Simons advertised. They may have been related to CHARLES SIMONS, the Charleston engraver. ¶ Rutledge, *Artists in the Life of Charleston.*

SIMONS, CHARLES. Copperplate, die, and seal engraver working in Charleston (S.C.) between 1820 and 1835. ¶ Rutledge, *Artists in the Life of Charleston.*

SIMONS, FRANCIS X. Wood engraver, Philadelphia, 1855. ¶ Phila. CD 1855.

SIMONS, GEORGE (1834–1917). Painter of Western scenes, portrait painter, born January 22, 1834, at Streeter (Ill.). He was one of the earliest artists to visit the territory of Nebraska (1854) and an early settler of Council Bluffs (Iowa) where he was active as an artist into the 1890's. He died in 1917 in Long Beach (Cal.). ¶ *Art Annual,* XII, obit.; WPA Guide, *Nebraska;* Council Bluffs CD 1889, 1894; represented in Council Bluffs Public Library.

SIMONS, JOHN P. Lithographer, 16, a native of New York, at NYC in 1850. ¶ 7 Census (1850), N.Y., LIII, 275.

SIMONS, JOSEPH. Heraldic engraver on stone, steel, silver, and other metals who advertised in NYC in May 1763; he was from Berlin (Germany). ¶ Gottesman, *Arts and Crafts in New York,* I, 13–14; Stephens, *The Mavericks,* 16.

SIMONS, MILTON E. Portrait painter of NYC, 1835–37; exhibited at the National Academy. ¶ NYCD 1835; Cowdrey, NAD.

SIMPS, JAMES C., is JAMES C. SIMPSON.

SIMPSON, J. J. or I. Engraver, 21, a native of Pennsylvania, at Philadelphia in 1850. Possibly JOHN G. SIMPSON. ¶ 7 Census (1850), Pa., L, 672.

SIMPSON, JAMES ALEXANDER (1775–1848). Portrait painter, active in 1838. This may be the James Alexander Simpson below, who was active in Georgetown (D.C.) and Baltimore between 1850 and 1880, in which case the birth and death dates are wrong. ¶ FARL question file.

SIMPSON, JAMES ALEXANDER. Portrait painter at Georgetown (D.C.) from 1850 to 1864 and at Baltimore from 1865 to 1880. He was born in Georgetown about 1813, according to the 1850 Census, or about 1805, according to the 1860 Census. Possibly the same as James Alexander Simpson above. ¶ Washington and Georgetown CD 1853–64; Baltimore CD and Lafferty, 1865–80; 7 Census (1850), D.C., II, 460 [as J. Simpson]; 8 Census (1860), D.C., I, 46 [as J. R. Simpson].

SIMPSON, JAMES C. Engraver and die sinker, designer, and landscape painter in watercolors. He was working as an engraver and die sinker in NYC between 1847 and 1849 and exhibited at the National Academy in 1848. From 1851 to 1867 he was listed as a designer or artist in Philadelphia directories and he exhibited at the Pennsylvania Academy in 1856. ¶ NYCD 1847–49; NYBD 1849 [as James C. Simps]; Cowdrey, NAD; Phila. CD 1851–67; Rutledge, PA.

SIMPSON, JOHN. Artist, NYC, 1850. ¶ NYCD 1850.

SIMPSON, JOHN G. Engraver, Philadelphia, 1858–63. Possibly the same as J. J. SIMPSON. ¶ Phila. CD 1858, 1860, 1863.

SIMPSON, JOSEPH. Lapidary and seal engraver active in Baltimore from 1842 to about 1856. He was born in Hungary about 1794. ¶ Baltimore BD 1842, 1844, 1848, CD 1850, 1856; 7 Census (1850), Md., V, 168.

SIMPSON, JOSEPH. Engraver and stencil cutter, NYC, 1843–60 and after. ¶ NYCD 1843–60+.

SIMPSON, SOLOMON L. Amateur artist who exhibited drawings, including one of the steamship *Great Britain,* at the American Institute in 1845 and 1848. He was probably the son of Lissack H. Simpson, distiller and importer, and he himself had gone into the import trade by 1853. ¶ Am. Inst. Cat., 1845, 1848; NYCD 1845, 1853.

SIMPSON, WILLIAM H. (?–1872). Negro portrait painter who was born and brought up in Buffalo (N.Y.), served his apprenticeship there and in Boston under MATTHEW WILSON, and worked in Boston until his death in 1872. ¶ Brown, *The Rising Sun,* 478–81; Porter, *Modern Negro Art,* 51–52; Porter, "Versatile Interests of the Early Negro Artist," 2 repros.; Boston CD 1858–65.

SIMPSON, WILLIAM R. Portrait painter, born in St. Louis about 1826. He studied in NYC, probably under DANIEL HUNTINGTON, a portrait of whom he exhibited at the National Academy in 1849. He was still in NYC in July 1850 but soon after returned to St. Louis where he was working at least until 1854. In the latter year he was living in the home of Robert Simpson, treasurer of the Boatmen's Saving Institution. ¶ Cowdrey, NAD; NYCD 1850 [as William H. Simpson]; St. Louis CD 1851–54; FARL question file lists a portrait owned by J. H. Collyer, Jr., in 1938; 7 Census (1850), N.Y., LVI, 435.

SIMS, Miss, see MARY JANE SIMES.

SIMS (Simms or Syms), SAMUEL. Plaster modeler, NYC, 1844–46. He exhibited a plaster medallion of Andrew Jackson at the American Institute in 1845–46 and an unidentified plaster bust in 1844. The address given for him is that of Hannah, widow of Palin Sims, carpenter. ¶ Am. Inst. Cat., 1844–46; NYCD 1838, 1845.

SIMSON, R. Engraver of a map of the Raritan River of New Jersey in 1683, said to be the earliest known American engraving on copper. ¶ Weiss, "The Number of Persons and Firms . . . ," 4.

SINCLAIR, L. [?]. Lithographer, 19, a native of Pennsylvania, at Washington in 1850. ¶ 7 Census (1850), D.C., I, 304.

SINCLAIR, PETER. Painter of a panorama of the effects of intemperance, shown at Davenport (Iowa) in 1860. ¶ Schick, *The Early Theater of Eastern Iowa,* 301 (citation courtesy J. E. Arrington).

SINCLAIR, THOMAS S. (*c.* 1805–1881). Lithographer. A native of the Orkney Islands, Sinclair learned lithography in Edinburgh and other European cities and settled in America about 1830. Except for a few years in NYC in the mid-thirties, he was a resident of Philadelphia until his death in 1881. From about 1850 he was assisted by his sons WILLIAM and THOMAS, JR. The firm of Thomas Sinclair & Son, established in 1870, continued until 1889. ¶ Peters, *America on Stone;* 7 Census (1850), Pa., LV, 679; Phila. CD 1839–60+; Waite, "Beginnings of American Color Printing," 18; Am. Inst. Cat., 1849.

SINCLAIR, THOMAS, JR. Artist, born in Pennsylvania about 1832, a son of THOMAS SINCLAIR, the Philadelphia lithographer, with whom he lived in 1850. ¶ 7 Census (1850), Pa., LV, 679.

SINCLAIR, WILLIAM. Lithographer, born in Scotland about 1827/28, the eldest son of THOMAS SINCLAIR. William was brought to America as a child and grew up in NYC and Philadelphia. He was listed as a lithographer as early as 1850 and seems to have worked for his father until the latter's death in 1881. William carried on the business until 1889 and then sold out. ¶ 7 Census (1850), Pa., LV, 679; 8 Census (1860), Pa., XLIX, 198; Phila. CD 1855–60+; Peters, *America on Stone.*

SINGER, JOHN. German artist, 30, at NYC in 1850 at the same house as HENRY KONGER. ¶ 7 Census (1850), N.Y., XLVIII, 130; NYCD 1850.

SINGLE, J. F. Engraver at Painesville (Ohio) in 1853. ¶ Ohio BD 1853.

SINGLETON, Mr. ——. Painter of miniatures and perspective views of gentlemen's estates; advertised at Charleston (S.C.) in February 1784. ¶ Prime, I, 8; Rutledge, *Artists in the Life of Charleston.*

SINNETT, FRANCIS. Artist at Elmira (N.Y.) in 1857. ¶ Elmira BD 1857.

SINTZENICH, EUGENE. Landscape and portrait painter. He was living in England in 1833 when several of his views of Niagara Falls, Upper Canada, and New York State, painted during a visit to America in 1831, were shown in London. By 1841 he had returned to America and was painting portraits and more Niagara views in Rochester (N.Y.). From 1844 to 1848 he was at Albany and NYC and in 1849 he exhibited a watercolor at the American Institute. He also painted a view of NYC after the great fire of December 1845. In 1851 he was once again in Rochester, listed as a professor of drawing. He may have been dead by 1857 when Mrs. Esther Sintzenich was listed in the Rochester directory, along with Eugene M. Sintzenich, daguerreotypist. ¶ London *Times,* Jan. 7 and March 26, 1833 (courtesy J. Earl Arrington); Ulp, "Art and Artists in Rochester," 32; Rochester CD 1841, 1851, 1857; Albany CD 1844, 1845, 1848; NYBD 1846; Am. Inst. Cat., 1849; Peters, *America on Stone;* Smith, "New York's Fire of 1845 in Lithography," 120; *Portfolio* (Jan. 1942), 5; NYHS *Quarterly Bulletin* (Jan. 1945), 29.

SITGREAVES, W. K. Exhibited at the Pennsylvania Academy in 1813 a sepia drawing, from nature, of a view on the Delaware River. ¶ Rutledge, PA.

SIVRAJ, J. A painting entitled "Musidora" was exhibited at the Society of Artists in 1814 under the name of this artist, who was in all probability the well-known New York artist and wit JOHN WESLEY JARVIS. ¶ Rutledge, PA.

SKILLIN & DODGE. Ship carvers, NYC, 1810; probably CHARLES DODGE and SIMEON SKILLIN. ¶ NYCD 1810; Pinckney, *American Figureheads and Their Carvers,* 200.

SKILLIN, JOHN (1746–1800). Ship carver of Boston, son of SIMEON SKILLIN, SR. After serving his apprenticeship John worked as a carver in Boston from about 1767 until his death on January 24, 1800. In 1778 he carved the figurehead for the *Confederacy,* a Continental frigate, and from about 1780 he was in partnership with his brother, SIMEON SKILLIN, JR. ¶ Thwing, "The Four Carving Skillins," 326–28; Swan, "A Revised Estimate of McIntire," 340–43; Swan, "Boston's Carvers and Joiners, Part I," 199–200; Pinckney, *American Figureheads and Their Carvers,* 45–55.

SKILLIN, SAMUEL (?–*c.* 1816). Ship carver, probably a son of SIMEON SKILLIN, SR. He was active as a carver in Boston from about 1780 to 1816. ¶ Thwing, "The Four Carving Skillins," 326–28; Pinckney, *American Figureheads and Their Carvers,* 45–55.

SKILLIN, SIMEON, SR. (1716–1778). Ship carver of Boston, active from about 1738 to 1778. In 1777 he was commissioned to carve a figurehead for the brig *Hazard,* one of the first armed ships of the Revolution. He was the father of SIMEON, JR., JOHN, and SAMUEL SKILLIN. ¶ Swan, "Simeon Skillin, Senior, the First American Sculptor"; Thwing, "The Four Carving Skillins"; Swan, "Boston's Carvers and Joiners, Part I"; Pinckney, *American Figureheads and Their Carvers,* 45–55.

SKILLIN, SIMEON, JR. (1756/57–1806). Ship carver, son of SIMEON SKILLIN, SR. He was active in Boston from about 1776–1806 and worked with his brother JOHN during much of that time. The first figurehead of the U. S. *Constitution* was his work, as were a bust of Milton and four figures carved for the garden of Elias Hasket Derby of Salem in the late 1790's. ¶ Swan, "A Revised Estimate of McIntire"; Thwing, "The Four Carving Skillins"; Pinckney, *American Figureheads and Their Carvers;* Lipman, *American Folk Art,* repro. 180.

SKILLIN, SIMEON, 3d (1766–1830). Ship carver of Boston and Charlestown (Mass.), probably a son of SAMUEL SKILLIN. He was working in Charlestown in 1829. ¶ Swan, "Boston's Carvers and Joiners, Part II," 285; Thwing, "The Four Carving Skillins," 326–28.

SKILLIN, SIMEON. Ship carver of NYC, active 1799–1822; after 1822, a dealer in crockery and earthenware. His relationship, if any, to the Boston Skillins has not been established. In 1810 he was in partnership with CHARLES DODGE. ¶ NYCD 1799–1830.

SKINNER, JOHN R. M. (or M. R.). Portrait and landscape painter who exhibited at the National Academy in 1844 and 1846. In 1844 he was listed as a resident of Norwich (Conn.) and in 1846 as of NYC. ¶ Cowdrey, NAD.

SKINNER, WILLIAM. Albany (N.Y.) artist who exhibited a painting entitled "The Last Chance" at the American Institute in 1850. ¶ Am. Inst. Cat., 1850.

SKIPWORTH, ——. Painter of gouache portraits, dated 1804, of Ebenezer Storr, Treasurer of Harvard College, and Mrs. Storr. ¶ Information courtesy Israel Sack, NYC.

SKIRVING, JOHN. Marine painter and architectural designer in watercolors. He exhibited at the Artists' Fund Society and the Pennsylvania Academy between 1838 and 1865, his addresses being given as Philadelphia (1838–41), Washington (1853), Philadelphia (1858), and Germantown (1861–65). In 1849 he exhibited in Boston his panorama of Frémont's overland journey to California, painted from sketches by FRÉMONT and others. ¶ Rutledge, PA; Boston *Evening Transcript,* Sept. 26, and Oct. 4, 1849 (citation courtesy J. E. Arrington).

SLACK, ABRAHAM or ABRAM. Engraver, die sinker, and printer, born in Pennsylvania about 1811 and active in Philadelphia from the mid-fifties. He was the father of ROBERT M. and WILLIAM SLACK. ¶ 8 Census (1860), Pa., XLIX, 283; Phila. CD 1855–60+.

SLACK, ROBERT M. Engraver, born in Pennsylvania about 1842, son of ABRAHAM SLACK, with whom he was living in Philadelphia in 1860. ¶ 8 Census (1860), Pa., XLIX, 283.

SLACK, WILLIAM J. Lithographic printer, 16, a native of Pennsylvania, living in Philadelphia in 1860 with his father, ABRAHAM SLACK. ¶ 8 Census (1860), Pa., XLIX, 283.

SLADE, S. V. Engraver whose work appeared in *Our World: or, The Slaveholder's Daughter* (N.Y., 1855). ¶ Hamilton, *Early American Book Illustrators and Wood Engravers,* 437.

SLAFTER, ALONZO (1801–1864). Portrait and still life painter, born October 14, 1801, in Norwich (Vt.), the son of Edmund Farwell and Clarissa (Tolman) Slafter. He studied law but turned artist and poet and lived alone on a farm at Bradford (Vt.) until his death February 8, 1864. Some of his paintings are privately owned in Vermont and New Hampshire. Slafter was a pupil of Mrs. ABIGAIL HENDERSON in Newbury (Vt.). ¶ Information courtesy Mrs. Katharine McCook Knox, who cites Rev. Edmund Farwell Slafter, *Slafter Memorial . . . of John Slafter, with a Genealogical Account of His Descendants, Including Eight Generations* (Boston, 1869), 49; see also 7 Census (1850), Vt., VII, 353; WPA (Mass.), *Portraits Found in N.H.,* 22.

SLANEY, JOHN. Historical and portrait engraver, Philadelphia, 1846–48. ¶ Phila. BD 1846, 1848.

SLATER, ——. Exhibited a miniature portrait of a lady at the Boston Athenaeum in 1830. Swan suggests that this might be Josiah or J. W. Slater, a British miniaturist of this period. *Cf.* also S. M. SLATER. ¶ Swan, BA.

SLATER, ——. Delineator of a portrait of the Rev. Legh Richmond engraved for the American Sunday School Union at Philadelphia by JAMES B. LONGACRE. ¶ Stauffer, no. 2079.

SLATER, S. M. Painter of a miniature of a lady, signed and dated January 27, 1823, No. 3 State Street, New York. The name does not appear in the NYC directories, although John Slater, Jr., merchant, was at 8 State Street in 1823. ¶ *Antiques* (Aug. 1925), 99; NYCD 1823.

SLATTERY, ——. A young "genius at painting" of New Orleans for whose benefit a fund for European study was sought in March 1851. ¶ Delgado-WPA cites *Orleanian,* March 12, 1851.

SLATTERY, MICHAEL. Engraver and die sinker, NYC, 1852. ¶ NYBD 1852.

SLAUGHTER, ROBERT K. English artist, 24, at NYC in 1850. ¶ 7 Census (1850), N.Y., XLVIII, 71.

SLAUGHTON, Mrs. ——. Miniature painter, Philadelphia, 1835. This is ANNA CLAYPOOLE PEALE (Mrs. William Staughton). ¶ Phila. CD 1835.

SLEEPER, CHARLES FREDERICK. Architect of Boston, 1851–70; exhibited an architectural drawing at the Athenaeum in 1856. ¶ Swan, BA.

SLEEPER, JOHN, see JOHN STEEPER.

SLINGLANDT, JACOB. Music engraver, born in New Jersey about 1813; working in New York State about 1842 and in Louisville (Ky.) from about 1845 to 1870. His sons, Edgar and Benjamin F., worked with him after 1860. ¶ 7 Census (1850), Ky., XI, 387½; Louisville CD 1852–70.

SLOAN, JUNIUS R. (1827–1900). Landscape and portrait painter, born March 10, 1827, at Kingsville (Ohio). He started as an itinerant portrait painter at Ashtabula (Ohio) and Erie (Pa.) in 1848 and during the next few years worked in Ohio, Pennsylvania, up-state New York, and

Vermont, spending the winters in Erie and Cincinnati. He was at Princeton (Ill.) from 1855 to 1857 and at NYC during the winter of 1857–58. After his marriage in 1858 he settled in Erie where he remained, except for summer visits to NYC and the Catskills, until 1863. From 1863 to 1867 he had a studio in Chicago where he became well known as a landscape painter. From 1867 to 1873 he lived and painted in NYC and the Hudson Valley. After 1873 his home was in Chicago, although he made frequent trips to the East and through the Middle West. He died at Redlands (Cal.) in August 1900. ¶ Webster, "Junius R. Sloan," 15 repros.; Sweet, *Hudson River School;* NYBD 1858; represented at Chicago Hist. Soc. and Minn. Hist. Soc.

SLOAN, SAMUEL (1815–1884). Architect of Philadelphia; exhibited architectural drawings at the Pennsylvania Academy in 1852. ¶ Rutledge, PA.

SLOANE, A. B. Artist, 40, a native of South Carolina, at Charleston in 1850. ¶ 7 Census (1850), S.C., II, 330.

SLOCOMB, EDWIN PLINY (1823–1865). Portrait and landscape painter and miniaturist, born March 7, 1823, at Sutton (Mass.). He worked in Worcester (Mass.), Charleston (S.C.), Baltimore (Md.), Wilmington (Del.), and during the latter part of his life in and around NYC. He was married in Wilmington in 1859. A vegetarian and opponent of vaccination, he died of small pox in Morrisania (N.Y.) on December 31, 1865. ¶ Slocum, *History of the Slocums, Slocumbs and Slocombs of America,* I, 537; information courtesy Mrs. Leonard W. Edwards.

SLOOP, JACOB H. Landscape painter, Cincinnati, 1850–51. ¶ Cist, *Cincinnati in 1851.*

SMALL, GEORGE G. Portrait and landscape painter, 32, at Boston in 1850. He was at Charlestown, a suburb of Boston, in 1860. ¶ 7 Census (1850), Mass., XXIV, 38; New England BD 1860.

SMALLWOOD, WILLIAM. Artist at Indianapolis in 1860. ¶ Indianapolis BD 1860.

SMART, JOHN. Engraver, 50, a native of New York, at NYC in 1860. He owned property valued at $6,100. His son Robert, 18, was an apprentice engraver. ¶ 8 Census (1860), N.Y., LXII, 672.

SMET, Father PIERRE-JEAN DE, S.J. (1801–1873). Sketches of Western and Indian scenes. De Smet was born January 30, 1801, in Termonde (Belgium) and emigrated to America in 1821. He entered the Jesuit order in Maryland and in 1823 was sent to the new novitiate near St. Louis. In 1838 he began the missionary work among the Western Indians with which his name is associated. His chief missionary activity fell between 1840 and 1844, although he later acted on several occasions as a mediator between the Indians and the U. S. Government. Out of his experiences among the Indians Father de Smet wrote several books of travel, with illustrations based on his own sketches. He died in St. Louis on May 23, 1873. ¶ The most complete work on Father de Smet is the *Life, Letters and Travels,* by Hiram M. Chittenden and Alfred T. Richardson (1905) in 4 volumes; brief sketches of his life appear in DAB; Walsh, *American Jesuits;* and Garraghan, *The Jesuits of the Middle United States.*

SMIBERT, JOHN (1688–1751). Portrait painter. Born March 24, 1688, in Edinburgh (Scotland), Smibert was apprenticed to a house painter. At the age of 21 he went to London, found employment as a coach painter and copyist, and attended a drawing academy. After a brief return visit to Edinburgh in 1717, he went to Italy, remaining three years. From 1720 to 1728 he worked in London. In the latter year he accompanied his friend George Berkeley, later Bishop of Cloyne, to Newport (R.I.), but a few months later Smibert left Berkeley's party and went to Boston, where he spent the rest of his life. To supplement his income as a portrait painter, he also had a paint shop. Smibert died in Boston on April 2, 1751, leaving his wife and two sons, one of whom was NATHANIEL SMIBERT, also an artist. ¶ The standard life is Henry Wilder Foote's *John Smibert, Painter* (1950), which also contains a descriptive catalogue of his works and a bibliography.

SMIBERT, NATHANIEL (1735–1756). Portrait painter. Nathaniel, son of JOHN SMIBERT, was born in Boston on January 20, 1735 (New Style), painted portraits in Boston between 1750 and 1756, and died there on November 3, 1756, at the age of 22. ¶ Foote, *John Smibert, Painter,* 257–74, with catalogue of his work; Burroughs, "Paintings by Nathaniel Smibert."

SMILLIE, GEORGE HENRY (1840–1921). N.A. Landscape painter, son of JAMES SMILLIE. He was born in NYC December

29, 1840, studied engraving under his father and painting under JAMES MACDOUGAL HART, and spent his professional life in NYC, although he made painting trips which took him to all parts of the country. In 1881 he married Nellie Sheldon Jacobs, a pupil of JAMES D. SMILLIE, with whom they subsequently shared a studio in NYC. George H. Smillie was elected to the National Academy in 1882 and served as its Recording Secretary from 1892 to 1902; he was also an officer of the American Watercolor Society. He died at his home in Bronxville on November 10, 1921. ¶ DAB; CAB; *Art Annual,* XVIII; Rutledge, PA.

SMILLIE, JAMES (1807–1885). N.A. Engraver, born November 23, 1807, in Edinburgh (Scotland). He was apprenticed to an engraver and after the family's removal to Quebec in 1821 he worked with his father, a jeweler, and brother, WILLIAM C. SMILLIE, engraver. In 1827 he returned to Britain, but in 1829 he finally settled in NYC. During most of his career his chief income came from banknote engraving, though he was widely known for his fine steel engravings of landscapes and figure pieces by well-known artists, especially COLE's "Voyage of Life" series. He was elected to the National Academy in 1851. Three of his sons, JAMES DAVID, GEORGE HENRY, and William Main, were also noted artists. He died at Poughkeepsie (N.Y.) on December 4, 1885. ¶ DAB; Cowdrey, NAD; NYCD 1834–60+; Stokes, *Iconography,* pl. 136; Stauffer; Cowdrey, AA & AAU.

SMILLIE, JAMES DAVID (1833–1909). N.A. Landscape painter, engraver, etcher, and lithographer. James David, son of JAMES SMILLIE, was born in NYC January 16, 1833, and learned engraving from his father, with whom he collaborated until about 1864. From that time he devoted himself more to landscape painting, particularly mountain scenes, and to work in etching, dry point, aquatint, and lithography. He was a founder and officer of the American Watercolor Society, the New York Etching Club, and an officer of the National Academy. He died in NYC September 14, 1909. ¶ DAB; *Art Annual,* VII, obit.; Cowdrey, NAD; Swan, BA; Rutledge, PA; *Antiques* (June 1948), 457, repro.

SMILLIE, WILLIAM CUMMING (1813–?). Engraver, born September 23, 1813, in Edinburgh (Scotland). A brother of JAMES SMILLIE. He went to Quebec in 1821 with his father and learned engraving there. In 1830 he joined his brother in NYC and spent the rest of his professional life there as a banknote engraver. He was still living in 1899. ¶ Stauffer; NYCD 1832–58+; 7 Census (1850), N.Y., LIII, 252.

SMIRKE, ——. Engraver whose work appeared in Hinton's *History and Topography of the United States* (Boston, 1857). ¶ Hinton, *op. cit.*

SMITH, —— (*c.* 1747–after 1834). Portrait painter. WILLIAM DUNLAP, in his diary under date of June 2, 1834, mentions hearing from SAMUEL F. B. MORSE and James Fenimore Cooper of an old American artist, then residing in Florence, who was born about 1747 in New York or on Long Island and went to Italy in 1764, remaining there for the rest of his life. He did not excell as an artist and was thought to have been a picture dealer. In his *History* Dunlap expanded and changed this account of Smith, adding that he was the uncle of Col. William [Stephens] Smith, son-in-law of John Adams, and changing his year of birth to 1718, on the basis of somebody's assertion that in 1834 Smith was 116 years old! ¶ Dunlap, *Diary,* III, 790; Dunlap, *History,* I, 145.

SMITH, Mr. ——. Miniaturist and drawing teacher at Charleston (S.C.) in 1816. The following year Mr. and Mrs. Smith advertised as teachers of drawing and French. This was probably JOHN L. SMITH. ¶ Rutledge, *Artists in the Life of Charleston.*

SMITH, Messrs. ——. Exhibited and offered for sale at the Pennsylvania Academy in 1850 their "Picture of Philadelphia." *Cf.* BENJAMIN F. SMITH. ¶ Rutledge, PA.

SMITH, Miss A. Of Baltimore, exhibited at the Boston Athenaeum in 1829. ¶ Swan, BA.

SMITH, A. C. Miniaturist and portrait painter. He was at Baltimore most of the time between 1831 and 1837, though he also advertised at Charleston in January 1834. He was a resident of Philadelphia in 1844 when he exhibited at the Artists' Fund Society. And from 1852 to 1856 he was working in Clark County (Ky.). ¶ Baltimore CD 1831, 1837; Lafferty; Rutledge, *Artists in the Life of Charleston;* Rutledge, PA; Phila. CD 1844; information courtesy Mrs. W. H. Whitley, Paris (Ky.).

SMITH, ADOLPHUS. Artist, born in New York about 1828, son of WILLIAM D. SMITH, engraver. ¶ 7 Census (1850), N.Y., XLIII, 529.

SMITH, ALBERT. Itinerant portrait painter working in Morristown (N.J.) about 1804. ¶ N. Y. *Sunday Mirror,* Jan. 2, 1949, "Magazine Section," p. 18.

SMITH, ALBERT. Engraver, 18, a native of Pennsylvania, at Philadelphia with his family in 1850. ¶ 7 Census (1850), Pa., LIII, 553.

SMITH, ALLEN, JR. (1810–1890). A.N.A. Portrait and genre painter, born in Rhode Island in 1810. He came to NYC soon after 1830 and was elected an Associate of the National Academy in 1833. He exhibited regularly in NYC until 1842 when he moved to Cleveland (Ohio). There he lived until his death in 1890. ¶ Mallett; Cowdrey, NAD; Cowdrey, AA & AAU; Clark, *History of the NAD;* WPA (Ohio), *Annals of Cleveland;* 7 Census (1850), Ohio, XI, 249; Cleveland BD 1857; Ohio BD 1859.

SMITH, ARCHIBALD CAREY (1837–1911). Marine painter and yacht designer. Born in NYC on September 4, 1837, he learned the shipwright's trade and practised it in NYC until the mid-sixties. From about 1867 to 1877 he devoted himself mainly to marine painting, which he had studied under MAURITZ F. H. DE HAAS. After 1877 he did little painting, devoting himself almost entirely to the designing of yachts and other craft. He died at Bayonne (N.J.) on December 8, 1911. ¶ DAB; Swan, BA; Rutledge, PA; Clement and Hutton; *Art Annual,* X, obit.

SMITH, BENJAMIN F. (1830–1927). Lithographer, born at South Freedom (Me.). From 1848 to 1857 he and his brothers—George Warren, Francis, and David Clifford Smith—were in the print publishing business in Boston and NYC. Benjamin did some of the art work, though most of it was done by JOHN W. HILL, FANNY PALMER, and CHARLES PARSONS. In 1860 Benjamin went to Omaha (Neb.) where he went into banking. In the 1880's he and his brothers retired to Maine. ¶ *Portfolio* (Jan. 1954), 99–102; Stokes, *Historical Prints;* Stokes, *Iconography,* pl. 145.

SMITH, BLOOMFIELD. Engraver, NYC, 1856. ¶ NYBD 1856.

SMITH, CATHERINE N. Fancy wax worker, 75, a native of Philadelphia where she was living in 1860. ¶ 8 Census (1860), Pa., LVIII, 226.

SMITH, CHARLES. Engraver, 33, a native of Connecticut, at NYC in 1850 with his wife and two children, living with GEORGE SHERMAN. Smith's children, aged 7 years and 5 months respectively, were born in Connecticut. ¶ 7 Census (1850), N.Y., XLII, 160.

SMITH, CHARLES. Engraver, 29, born in New York, living in NYC in 1860 with his wife Emeline and four children, all born in New York. ¶ 8 Census (1860), N.Y., LIV, 655.

SMITH, CHARLES C. Engraver, NYC, 1836–59. He was listed as a geographer in 1854–55 and publisher in 1856–57. ¶ NYCD 1836–59.

SMITH, CHARLES H. Engraver, NYC, 1844–60; in 1858–60, with SEALEY & SMITH. His home was in Brooklyn and Bedford, Long Island. ¶ NYBD and CD 1844–60.

SMITH, CHARLES L. Panoramic artist, born in New York State about 1812, working in New Orleans from about 1830 to 1857. He painted panoramas of Texas and California, the Creation, and Perry's expedition to Japan. In 1850 three of his sons—James (19), William (16), and Charles (13)—were also listed as artists in the census. ¶ 7 Census (1850), La., IV (1), 423; Delgado-WPA cites *Bee,* May 1, 1852, and June 5, 1857, and *Crescent,* June 5, 1857; Arrington cites *Picayune,* April 29, 1852, and June 4, 1857.

SMITH, CHARLES W. Music engraver, born in Massachusetts about 1822, working in Boston 1850–53. ¶ 7 Census (1850), Mass., XXIV; Boston CD 1850–53.

SMITH, CHARLES W. Of BOURKE & SMITH, engravers, NYC, 1857–58; his home was in Brooklyn. ¶ NYCD 1857–58.

SMITH, Mrs. CREAGH. Portrait and religious painter of Philadelphia who exhibited at the Pennsylvania Academy in 1860–62. Probably the wife or mother of Creigh Smith, Jr., jeweler. ¶ Rutledge, PA; Phila. CD 1860.

SMITH, D. R. Artist who established the Pittsburgh (Pa.) Academy for Instruction in Drawing and Painting in 1855. *Cf.* ROBERT SMITH. ¶ Fleming, *History of Pittsburgh,* III, 626.

SMITH & DAMOREAU. Wood engravers and designers, Boston, 1860. The partners were DANIEL T. SMITH and probably CHARLES F. DAMOREAU. ¶ Boston Almanac 1860.

SMITH, DANIEL. Engraver, 35, a native of

England, at NYC in 1860. His wife and eldest child were born in Ireland; five younger children, ages 13 to 3, were born in New York. ¶ 8 Census (1860), N.Y., XLII, 975.

SMITH, DANIEL T. Wood engraver, active in NYC from 1846 to 1850 and in Boston from 1852 to after 1860. He exhibited at the American Institute in 1846 and 1847. In Boston he was associated with BAKER & SMITH, 1852–54; SMITH & PIERSON, 1855–56; SMITH & HILL, 1858; and SMITH & DAMOREAU, 1860. ¶ NYCD 1847–50; Am. Inst. Cat., 1846, 1847; Boston CD 1852–60+; Hamilton, *Early American Book Illustrators and Wood Engravers,* 134.

SMITH, DANIEL W. Engraver and copperplate printer at Charleston (S.C.), 1816–18. ¶ Rutledge, *Artists in the Life of Charleston.*

SMITH, DAVID (?–1841). Portrait painter of New Orleans who was convicted of petit larceny and died in jail in 1841. ¶ Delgado-WPA cites *Picayune,* March 4, 1841.

SMITH, DAVID. Lithographer, Philadelphia, 1858–59. ¶ Phila. CD 1858–59.

SMITH, DAVID H. (1844–1904). Amateur artist, born November 18, 1844, at Nauvoo (Ill.), the posthumous son of the Mormon leader Joseph Smith. As early as 1853 he made some drawings of the ruins of Nauvoo which have been preserved and reproduced, and in 1863 he painted an idealized picture of the same subject. He later became a leader of the Reorganized Church in Utah and a well-known hymn writer. He died at Elgin (Ill.) on August 27, 1904. ¶ Arrington, "Nauvoo Temple," Chap. 8.

SMITH, DAVID V. Miniaturist at Philadelphia in 1832 and Baltimore in 1833. In the former year he exhibited at the Pennsylvania Academy two miniatures after British artists. ¶ Rutledge, PA; Lafferty.

SMITH, E. P. German lithographer, 38, at NYC in 1860. His wife and two older children (16 and 7) were born in Germany; two younger children (4 and 2) were born in New York. ¶ 8 Census (1860), N.Y., XLII, 692.

SMITH, EDMUND REUEL (1829–1911). Landscape painter who was living at Skaneateles (N.Y.) when he exhibited at the National Academy in 1859. One of the views he showed was a scene in the vicinity of Düsseldorf (Germany). ¶ Cowdrey, NAD.

SMITH, EDWARD. Portrait, genre, and still life painter of Philadelphia who exhibited there in 1832, 1834, and 1844. ¶ Rutledge, PA.

SMITH, EDWIN B. Portrait and historical painter. Cist states that he began his career in Cincinnati in 1815 and was at New Orleans in 1841. Knittle locates him at Troy (Ohio) in 1832. ¶ Cist, *Cincinnati in 1841,* 139; Knittle, *Early Ohio Taverns;* Clark, *Ohio Art and Artists,* 73, 491.

SMITH, FRANCIS HOPKINSON (1838–1915). Landscape and portrait artist, born October 23, 1838, at Baltimore. An engineer by profession, he painted as a hobby until the 1880's when he gave up engineering to paint, travel, write, and lecture. He was particularly noted for his watercolors and charcoal drawings, many of which appeared in his books of travel. He died in NYC on April 7, 1915. ¶ DAB; CAB; *Art Annual,* XII, obit.

SMITH, FREDERIC AUGUSTUS (?–1852). Designer of the reverse of the medal struck in honor of General Zachary Taylor's victory at Buena Vista in 1847. Smith was a graduate of West Point in 1833; he was promoted to captain in 1838; died at Washington (D.C.) October 16, 1852. ¶ Loubat, *Medallic History of the U.S.,* pl. 64.

SMITH, FREDERICK, see FREDERICK SCHMIDT.

SMITH, FREDERICK. Sculptor, born in Germany about 1807, active in Washington (D.C.) from 1850 to 1855. ¶ 7 Census (1850), D.C., I, 185; Washington CD 1853, 1855.

SMITH, FREDERICK B. Engraver and die sinker, NYC, 1835–60 and after; from 1835 to 1847 of BALE & SMITH; 1850–59 of SMITH & HARTMANN. ¶ NYCD 1835–60+.

SMITH, G. G. A NYC artist who exhibited at the National Academy in 1833 a scene from Cooper's *The Water Witch. Cf.* GEORGE GIRDLER SMITH. ¶ Cowdrey, NAD.

SMITH, GEORGE. Engraver, NYC, 1778. He was from London. ¶ Kelby, *Notes on American Artists.*

SMITH, GEORGE. English engraver, 28, at Frankford, near Philadelphia, in 1850. ¶ 7 Census (1850), Pa., LVI, 329.

SMITH, GEORGE F. Designer, Philadelphia, 1851–52. ¶ Phila. CD 1851–52.

SMITH, GEORGE GIRDLER (1795–1878). Portrait and banknote engraver, lithographer, born September 8, 1795, at Danvers

(Mass.). He was probably a pupil of ABEL BOWEN, for whom he was working as early as 1815. From about 1820 to 1833 he was in partnership with WILLIAM B. ANNIN and in 1830 he was a member of the SENEFELDER LITHOGRAPHIC COMPANY. He later worked with TERRY, PELTON & Co. and with CHARLES A. KNIGHT and GEORGE H. TAPPAN. He died in Boston on December 18, 1878 [not 1858 as several authorities have it]. ¶ *Danvers Vital Records;* death date in Boston CD 1879; 7 Census (1850), Mass., XXV, 154; 8 Census (1860), Mass., XXVIII, 229; Stauffer; Belknap, *Artists and Craftsmen of Essex County,* 5; Boston CD 1820–79; Whitmore, "Abel Bowen," 41. Some of his watercolor drawings and mss. are in J. R. Smith's "Old Boston" (1857) at the Boston Public Library.

SMITH & HARTMANN. Die sinkers, NYC, 1850–59; FREDERICK B. SMITH and HERMAN HARTMANN. ¶ NYCD and BD 1850–59.

SMITH, HENRY. Engraver, 28, born in Pennsylvania, at Philadelphia in 1860 with his wife Anna and sons Frederick and William. ¶ 8 Census (1860), Pa., LVIII, 464.

SMITH, HENRY FEW, see FEWSMITH.

SMITH, HENRY S. Engraver, NYC, 1850–52. ¶ NYBD 1850–52.

SMITH, HENRY W. Engraver, Boston, 1851. Probably the Henry Smith, engraver, 28, born in New York, listed in the 1850 Boston census. ¶ Boston CD 1851; 7 Census (1850), Mass., XXV, 616.

SMITH, HEZEKIAH WRIGHT (1828–?). Engraver in line and stipple. Born in Edinburgh (Scotland), he was brought to America at the age of 5 and grew up in NYC. He studied engraving with THOMAS DONEY and in 1850 was working in Boston with JOSEPH ANDREWS. He worked in NYC from 1870 to 1877 and in Philadelphia from 1877 to April 1879, when he suddenly gave up his business, sold his belongings, and disappeared. ¶ Stauffer; Boston CD 1860.

SMITH & HILL. Engravers, Boston, 1858; DANIEL T. SMITH and GEORGE W. HILL. ¶ Boston BD 1858.

SMITH, I. B., see JOSEPH B. SMITH.

SMITH, Mrs. J. Exhibited "The Belle of Philadelphia" at the Maryland Historical Society in 1850. ¶ Rutledge, MHS.

SMITH, JACOB, JR. Wood engraver, NYC, 1854. ¶ NYBD 1854.

SMITH, JAMES, see CHARLES L. SMITH.

SMITH, JAMES E. Engraver, 22, a native of Ohio, at Cincinnati in 1850. His father, Thomas Smith, was Collector, his brother Stephen a lawyer and George W. a manufacturer of white lead. James worked in Cincinnati at least until 1853; in 1859 he was at Louisville (Ky.). ¶ 7 Census (1850), Ohio, XXI, 952; Cincinnati BD, 1850–53; Louisville CD 1859.

SMITH, JAMES P. (*c.* 1803–1888). Miniature and portrait painter whose professional career was spent in Philadelphia. He exhibited at the Pennsylvania Academy from 1824 to 1850. ¶ Smith; Rutledge, PA; Phila. CD 1829–60+; *Art in America* (April 1923), 160, repro. [dates given as 1808–1888].

SMITH, JOHN. Image maker, NYC, 1792. ¶ NYCD 1792 (McKay).

SMITH, JOHN. Artist, Philadelphia, 1798–1804. ¶ Brown and Brown.

SMITH, JOHN. Sculptor, 45, from Ireland, at NYC in 1850. His wife was also Irish, but their six children, ages 19 to 2, were born in New York. John Smith, stonecutter, appears in the 1863 directory. ¶ 7 Census (1850), N.Y., LVI, 386; NYCD 1863.

SMITH, JOHN, JR. Lithographer, 18, a native of New York, at NYC in 1850. ¶ 7 Census (1850), N.Y., LV, 274.

SMITH, JOHN A., see JOHN RUBENS SMITH.

SMITH, JOHN B. Lithographer, 25, a native of Pennsylvania, at Philadelphia in 1860. ¶ 8 Census (1860), Pa., LII, 648.

SMITH, JOHN CALVIN. Engraver of NYC, 1835–53; 1840–53, of SHERMAN & SMITH. ¶ NYCD 1835–53.

SMITH, Mrs. JOHN CALVIN. Exhibited a framed painting on velvet at the American Institute in 1842. ¶ Am. Inst. Cat., 1842, as Mrs. J. C. Smith; her address was the same as that of John Calvin Smith in the NYCD 1842.

SMITH, JOHN F. Engraver, 17, a native of Massachusetts, at Boston in 1850. ¶ 7 Census (1850), Mass., XXVI, 130.

SMITH, JOHN L. Profilist and miniaturist at Charleston from 1816 to 1819. *Cf.* Mr. —— SMITH. ¶ Rutledge, *Artists in the Life of Charleston;* Charleston CD 1819.

SMITH, JOHN LOCKHART. Portrait painter at St. Louis in 1852–53. ¶ St. Louis CD 1852–53.

SMITH, JOHN ROWSON (1810–1864). Scenic and panoramic artist, born May 11, 1810, at Boston, son of JOHN RUBENS SMITH. After studying with his father in Brooklyn and Philadelphia, J. R. Smith, Jr., as he was sometimes called, became a scene painter, working after 1832 in Philadelphia, New Orleans, St. Louis, and other cities. Toward the end of the thirties he took up panorama painting and in 1844 he completed a panorama of the Mississippi which was exhibited successfully in this country and in Europe. After his European tour in 1848 Smith made his home on a farm at Carlstadt (N.J.) but continued to paint scenery for theaters in NYC and other cities, especially in the South, until his death in Philadelphia on March 21, 1864. ¶ DAB; Rutledge, PA; McDermott, "Newsreel—Old Style."

SMITH, JOHN RUBENS (1775–1849). Portrait, miniature, and topographical painter; engraver and lithographer; teacher of drawing. He was born in London on January 23, 1775, a son of John Raphael Smith, mezzotint engraver, and grandson of Thomas Smith of Derby, landscape painter. He studied under his father and exhibited many portraits at the Royal Academy between 1796 and 1811. By April 1809 he had emigrated to America and was established as an artist in Boston. He moved to Brooklyn (N.Y.) about 1814 and there established a drawing academy; among his pupils were ELIAB METCALF, ANTHONY DEROSE, THOMAS SEIR CUMMINGS, and FREDERICK S. AGATE. During the 1830's he had a similar school at Philadelphia, where EMANUEL LEUTZE was one of his students. He also published several books of instruction in drawing. During his last years he lived in NYC where he died August 21, 1849. His son, JOHN ROWSON SMITH, was a well-known panoramic and scenic artist. ¶ DAB; Graves, *Dictionary;* NYCD 1814–26, 1846–47; Phila. CD 1834, 1841–43; Cowdrey, AA & AAU; Cowdrey, NAD; Rutledge, PA; Swan, BA; E. S. Smith, "John Rubens Smith," 9 repros.; Stauffer; Peters, *America on Stone;* Rutledge, *Artists in the Life of Charleston.*

SMITH, JOSEPH B. (1798–1876). Marine and townscape painter. A native of NYC and a life-long resident of NYC and Brooklyn, he is now chiefly remembered for his view of John Street Methodist Church, NYC, painted in 1824 and published in lithographic prints of 1844 and 1868. Smith also published views of other churches and a view of the Sing Sing Camp Meeting (1838) and painted ship portraits and marine scenes in partnership with his son, WILLIAM S. SMITH. P. C. SMITH probably was his brother. ¶ Howell, "Joseph B. Smith, Painter"; Stokes, *Iconography,* I, 344; NYCD 1824–28; Brooklyn CD 1852–61; *Portfolio* (June 1952), 232–33, and (July 1943), 262; Dunshee, *As You Pass By,* plate V.

SMITH & KNIGHT and SMITH, KNIGHT & TAPPAN. Engravers, Boston, 1857–60. From 1857 to 1859 the partners were GEORGE G. SMITH, CHARLES A. KNIGHT, and GEORGE H. TAPPAN; in 1860 Tappan was no longer with the firm. ¶ Boston CD 1857–60.

SMITH, LOCHLAN, see THOMAS LOCHLAN SMITH.

SMITH, MARY (1842–1878). Flower, animal, and landscape painter; born at Rockhill, near Philadelphia, September 25, 1842; died June 6, 1878. The daughter of RUSSELL and MARY PRISCILLA WILSON SMITH, she lived at Jenkintown (Pa.) and exhibited at the Pennsylvania Academy between 1859 and 1869. ¶ DAB, under Russell Smith; *A Brief Sketch of the Life of Mary Smith, the Painter;* Rutledge, PA.

SMITH, MARY A. Portrait painter at Rome (N.Y.) in 1859 and Utica (N.Y.) in 1860. ¶ Rome CD 1859, BD 1860.

SMITH, MARY PRISCILLA WILSON (Mrs. Russell Smith). Flower and landscape painter who in 1838 married RUSSELL SMITH. She had been a teacher of Latin and French. After their marriage the Smiths lived for a time in Philadelphia, then moved out to Jenkintown. Mrs. Smith exhibited at the Pennsylvania Academy and the Apollo Association and had at least one of her flower drawings reproduced in *The Florist and Horticultural Journal.* She was the mother of MARY C. and XANTHUS R. SMITH, also artists. ¶ DAB [under Russell Smith]; Rutledge, PA; Cowdrey, AA & AAU; McClinton, "American Flower Lithographs," 362.

SMITH, P. C. With JOSEPH B. SMITH in 1824 he drew a view of the John Street Methodist Church in NYC. This was probably the Peter C. Smith listed as a printer and book seller at the same address as Joseph B. Smith in 1828. ¶ Stokes, *Iconography,* I, 344; NYCD 1824, 1828.

SMITH & PIERSON. Engravers, Boston, 1855–56; DANIEL T. SMITH and PAUL R. B. PIERSON. ¶ Boston CD 1855, BD 1855–56.

SMITH & PLUMER. Engravers, Boston, 1855–56. Plumer was probably JACOB P. PLUMER; Smith could be HENRY W., GEORGE G., or DANIEL T. ¶ Boston CD 1855, BD 1855–56.

SMITH, R. K. Engraver of a stipple portrait of the Rev. John Flavel used as frontispiece to a book by Flavel published at Richmond (Va.) in 1824. ¶ Stauffer.

SMITH, R. P. Of F. BOURQUIN & COMPANY, Philadelphia lithographers, 1858–60 and after. This may be Robert Pearsall Smith, map publisher, although the addresses are different. ¶ Phila. CD 1858–60+.

SMITH, RAE. Engraver, NYC, 1859. ¶ NYBD 1859.

SMITH, RICHARD SOMERS (?–1877). Amateur artist. A graduate of West Point in 1829, he exhibited at the Pennsylvania Academy in 1849 and 1853 as Lt. R. S. Smith of West Point. In 1849 he showed "Mathematical Abstraction" and in 1853 "Peveril of the Peak." He died January 23, 1877. ¶ Rutledge, PA; Heitman, *Historical Register.*

SMITH, ROBERT. Delivered recitations and exhibited transparencies of Columbus, Washington, Jefferson, Madison, and Monroe at Pittsburgh in September 1826. In 1832 and 1839 he "photographed in oil" two Pittsburgh scenes. *Cf.* RUSSELL SMITH and D. R. SMITH. ¶ Anderson, "Intellectual Life of Pittsburgh: Painting," 290.

SMITH, ROBERT B. Portrait painter at Rochester (N.Y.) in the 1840's. ¶ Rochester CD 1844; Ulp, "Art and Artists in Rochester," 32.

SMITH, ROSWELL T. Portrait painter. A cripple from childhood, who became an itinerant painter in his youth and in the late 1850's worked around Nashua and Hollis (N.H.) and in Massachusetts. After his marriage he settled down in Nashua where for many years he had a book store. He was also an inventor. ¶ Sears, *Some American Primitives,* 91–109.

SMITH, RUSSELL (1812–1896). Scenic and panoramic artist, portrait and landscape painter, born in Glasgow (Scotland) April 26, 1812. His parents emigrated to western Pennsylvania in 1819 and finally located at Pittsburgh in 1824. Russell (he was baptized William Thompson Russell Smith) studied there under JAMES REID LAMBDIN and in 1833 began a distinguished career as a scene and panorama painter. Most of his professional work was done in Philadelphia, Baltimore, Washington, and Boston. In 1851–52 he visited Europe to paint a panorama of the Holy Land. His wife (MARY PRISCILLA WILSON SMITH) and both his children, MARY and XANTHUS R. SMITH, also were painters. He died at Glenside, near Philadelphia, November 8, 1896. ¶ DAB; Rutledge, PA; Cowdrey, AA & AAU; Sweet, *Hudson River School;* obits., N. Y. *Herald* and Boston *Transcript,* Nov. 9, 1896.

SMITH, SAMUEL. Artist and drawing master at Baltimore from 1824 to 1851. He was born in England about 1786; his wife and a daughter born about 1825 were also born in England. Three younger children, born between 1826 and 1829 were born in Maryland. ¶ Lafferty; 7 Census (1850), Md., V, 835.

SMITH, SAMUEL, JR. (?–1812). Miniaturist who studied in London and advertised at Charleston (S.C.) in 1801. He is thought to have died on October 23, 1812, at Charleston. ¶ Rutledge, *Artists in the Life of Charleston.*

SMITH, SAMUEL P. Miniature painter, 46, a native of Philadelphia, living there in 1850 with his wife and seven children. ¶ 7 Census (1850), Pa., L, 284.

SMITH, T. J. Exhibited a wood engraving at the American Institute in 1847. His address was 71 Nassau Street, NYC. He may have been an apprentice of BUTLER & ROBERTS, wood engravers at that address. ¶ Am. Inst. Cat., 1847; NYBD 1846.

SMITH, Master T. M. Exhibited india ink and chalk drawings, including a copy after one of the PEALE family, at the Pennsylvania Academy in 1827 and 1829. ¶ Rutledge, PA.

SMITH, THOMAS. Portrait painter. A "Major Thomas Smith" was paid four guineas by Harvard College in June 1680 for "drawing Dr. Ames's effigies." Although positive proof is lacking, this Thomas Smith is believed to be the same as a Captain Thomas Smith who came to Boston from Bermuda in 1650. And on that identification is based the attribution to Thomas Smith of a group of portraits of the last quarter of the 17th century, including his own portrait and that of his daughter, both at the Worcester Art Museum. ¶ The problem is discussed most fully in Louisa Dresser's *XVIIth Century Painting in New England.*

SMITH, THOMAS. Engraver at Lowell (Mass.) in 1834–35. ¶ Belknap, *Artists and Craftsmen of Essex County,* 5.

SMITH, THOMAS A. or H. Painter of a panorama entitled "California on Canvas," based on drawings by THOMAS A. AYRES. Possibly the same as THOMAS H. SMITH, below. ¶ Van Nostrand and Coulter, *California Pictorial,* 136 [as Thomas A.]; San Francisco *Daily Alta California,* Aug. 11 and 14, 1854, and N. Y. *Herald,* Feb. 5, 1856 [as Thomas H.], citations courtesy J. E. Arrington.

SMITH, THOMAS H. Portrait, figure, and flower painter of NYC, exhibitor at the National Academy and American Art-Union between 1843 and 1849. Possibly the painter of the panorama "California on Canvas" mentioned above under THOMAS A. or H. SMITH. ¶ Cowdrey, NAD; Cowdrey, AA & AAU; NYCD 1847.

SMITH, THOMAS LOCHLAN (1835–1884). A.N.A. Landscape painter, especially winter scenes. Born December 2, 1835, in Glasgow (Scotland), he came to America at an early age and studied painting under GEORGE H. BOUGHTON at Albany (N.Y.) where he opened a studio in 1859. He moved to NYC three years later and was elected an Associate Member of the National Academy in 1869. He died in NYC on November 5, 1884. ¶ CAB; Cowdrey, NAD; Swan, BA; Rutledge, PA; Albany CD 1859–60.

SMITH, Mrs. TRYPHENA GOLDSBURY (1801–1836). Amateur painter of watercolors and mural frescoes, wife of the Rev. Preserved Smith of Warwick (Mass.). ¶ Dods, "Connecticut Valley Painters," 209.

SMITH, VON, see VON SMITH.

SMITH, W. Painter of "Spanish Armada" and "Fire of London," exhibited by him in NYC in January 1810. ¶ N. Y. *Evening Post,* Jan. 3, 1810 (citation courtesy J. E. Arrington).

SMITH, WILLIAM. Modeler of a wax portrait of John Paul Jones; presumed to be American. ¶ E. S. Bolton, *American Wax Portraits,* 61.

SMITH, WILLIAM. Engraver at Washington (D.C.) from about 1835 to after 1860. He was born in England about 1811; his wife and children in Washington. ¶ 7 Census (1850), D.C., I, 204; 8 Census (1860), D.C., II, 741; Washington CD 1843–64.

SMITH, WILLIAM, see CHARLES L. SMITH.

SMITH, WILLIAM. Engraver, Philadelphia, 1858–60. ¶ Phila. BD 1858, 1860.

SMITH, WILLIAM C. Engraver, NYC, 1852. ¶ NYCD 1852.

SMITH, WILLIAM D. Engraver born in New York about 1800 and active in NYC from 1822 to after 1860. During part of this time he lived in Newark (N.J.). His son ADOLPHUS was listed as an artist in the 1850 census. ¶ 7 Census (1850), N.Y., XLIII, 529; Stauffer; *Portfolio* (May 1946), 198.

SMITH, WILLIAM E. Landscape painter of Philadelphia, exhibitor at the Artists' Fund Society in 1840–41. His subjects included English, Dutch, and Greek views. ¶ Rutledge, PA.

SMITH, WILLIAM GOOD. Portrait and miniature painter, NYC, 1842–44; exhibited an india ink drawing at the American Institute in 1842. ¶ Am. Inst. Cat., 1842; NYBD 1844; Bolton, *Miniature Painters.*

SMITH, WILLIAM O. Engraver, NYC, 1846. ¶ NYCD 1846.

SMITH, WILLIAM R. Still life and figure painter, NYC, exhibitor at the National Academy in 1836 and the Apollo Association in 1838. ¶ Cowdrey, NAD; Cowdrey, AA & AAU; NYCD 1838.

SMITH, WILLIAM R. Engraver, NYC, 1852–60. ¶ NYBD 1852–58, CD 1854–60.

SMITH, WILLIAM S. (1821–?). Marine painter, Brooklyn (N.Y.), 1853–60; son and partner of JOSEPH B. SMITH. He exhibited at the National Academy in 1860. ¶ Howell, "Joseph B Smith, Painter"; Brooklyn CD 1853–60; Cowdrey, NAD.

SMITH, WILLIAM THOMPSON RUSSELL, see RUSSELL SMITH.

SMITH, XANTHUS RUSSELL (1839–1929). Marine, landscape, portrait, and historical painter. Xanthus, son of RUSSELL and MARY PRISCILLA (WILSON) SMITH, was born at Philadelphia on February 26, 1839. He studied medicine at the University of Pennsylvania from 1856 to 1858, during which period he also began exhibiting landscapes at the Pennsylvania Academy. He studied painting at the Academy in Philadelphia, and at the Royal Academy in London. During the Civil War he saw active service in the South and painted many naval and land battles. After the war he devoted himself chiefly to marines and landscapes until his later years when he turned to portraits. For many years he had a summer home at Casco Bay (Me.); his winters were spent at Edgehill, near Philadelphia. He died at Edgehill on December 2, 1929. ¶ DAB; Rutledge, PA; Washington Art Assoc. Cat., 1859; *Antiques* (Nov. 1951), 39; *American Collector* (Oct. 1945), 11.

SMITHER, JAMES (?–1797). Engraver and seal cutter. He worked in Philadelphia from 1768 to 1778, when he was accused of treason and left with the British troops for NYC. By 1786 he had returned to Philadelphia and he died there in September 1797. ¶ Prime, I, 28, II, 73; Gottesman, II, no. 107; Weiss, "The Growth of the Graphic Arts in Phila.," 78.

SMITHER, JAMES, JR. Engraver, Philadelphia, 1794–1824; son of JAMES SMITHER. ¶ Brown and Brown; Phila. CD 1823–24 [as James Smithers].

SMITZ, M., see M. S. SCHMITZ.

SMYTH, WILLIAM (?–1877). British naval officer and topographical artist. He accompanied Captain Frederick Beechey's expedition to explore the Bering Strait in 1825. The expedition wintered in San Francisco and Monterey bays in 1826 and 1827 and Smyth painted at least eight California scenes. He later retired with the rank of Rear Admiral and died at Tunbridge Wells on September 25, 1877. ¶ Van Nostrand and Coulter, *California Pictorial,* 22–27; Peters, *California on Stone.*

SMYTHE, ROBERT L. Sculptor, 30, from Ireland, at NYC in 1850. ¶ 7 Census (1850), N.Y., LI, 575.

SNAËR, JONATHAN. Lithographer, 20, a native of Louisiana, at New Orleans in 1850. His father, Francis Snaër, was from the West Indies. ¶ 7 Census (1850), La., V, 409.

SNELL & BAKER. Lithographers, New Orleans, 1841; P. SNELL and GEORGE J. BAKER. ¶ Delgado-WPA cites New Orleans CD 1841.

SNELL & FISHBOURNE. Lithographers, New Orleans, 1842–44; P. SNELL and R. W. FISHBOURNE. ¶ Delgado-WPA cites New Orleans CD 1842–44.

SNELL, P. Lithographer, New Orleans, 1837–52. He was a partner in SNELL & BAKER (1841), SNELL & FISHBOURNE (1842–44), and MANOUVRIER & SNELL (1846–52). ¶ Delgado-WPA cites New Orleans CD 1837, 1841–44, 1846, 1851–52.

SNELL, WILLIAM R. Engraver, 23, a native of Pennsylvania, at Philadelphia in 1860. He was the son of Lewis Snell, weigher. ¶ 8 Census (1860), Pa., LVI, 78.

SNIDER, GEORGE. Lithographer, 20, a native of France, at Philadelphia in 1850. His parents, Michael and Sarah Snider, were French; of their four children only the youngest, aged 11, was born in the United States. The Sniders lived with the family of JOHN HENRY CAMP. ¶ 7 Census (1850), Pa., XLIX, 257.

SNOW, JENNY EMILY. Landscapes and biblical scenes in oils, Hinsdale (Mass.), about 1845. ¶ Lipman and Winchester, 180.

SNYDER & BLACK. Lithographers, NYC, 1850–53; GEORGE SNYDER and JAMES BLACK. ¶ NYCD 1850–53.

SNYDER, BLACK & STURN. Lithographers, NYC, 1854–72; GEORGE SNYDER, JAMES BLACK, and HERMANN STURN. ¶ NYCD 1854–72.

SNYDER, GEORGE. Lithographer, NYC, 1845–72; of SNYDER & BLACK and SNYDER, BLACK & STURN. He was born in New York about 1820. In 1860 he owned property to the value of $10,000. ¶ NYCD 1845–72; 8 Census (1860), N.Y., XLV, 868.

SNYDER, GEORGE. Lithographer, 48, from Germany, at NYC in 1850. ¶ 7 Census (1850), N.Y., XLIX, 935.

SNYDER, HENRY M. Wood engraver and designer, Philadelphia, 1852–71; 1853 and after, with VAN INGEN & SNYDER. ¶ Phila. CD 1852–71; Hamilton, *Early American Book Illustrators and Wood Engravers,* 432, 456, 483.

SNYDER, HENRY W. Stipple engraver who is said to have worked in NYC from 1797 to 1805, although his name does not appear in the directories. His work also appeared in books published in Boston between 1807 and 1816. He was an engraver at Albany (N.Y.) in 1813–15. From about 1822 to 1832 he was Chamberlain or Treasurer of the City of Albany and he also designed the Albany Alms House. ¶ Stauffer; Albany CD 1813–15, 1822, 1826, 1828, 1831, 1832; Munsell, *Annals of Albany; Antiques* (Feb. 1935), 51, repro.

SNYDER, PHILIP. Primitive painter in oils, Schoharie (N.Y.), about 1830. ¶ Lipman and Winchester, 180.

SNYDER, ROBERT. Engraver, 45, a native of Pennsylvania, at Philadelphia in 1860. His widow, Jane Snyder, was listed in 1871. ¶ 8 Census (1860), Pa., LVIII, 316; Phila. CD 1871.

SNYDER, WILLIAM HENRY (1829–1910). Landscape painter. He was a native of Brooklyn (N.Y.), a member of the Brooklyn Art Club at the time of his death on October 4, 1910. ¶ *Art Annual,* IX, obit.

SOBIESKE, THADDEUS. Crayon artist at Richmond (Va.) in May 1814. ¶ *Richmond Portraits,* 243.

SOHON, GUSTAVUS (1825–1903). Topographical and portrait draftsman. Born December 10, 1825, at Tilsit (East Prussia), Sohon came to America at the age of 17 and worked in Brooklyn as a bookbinder until his enlistment in the army in July 1852. During his five years in the army he served as artist on several Western exploring expeditions and from 1858 to 1862 he acted as guide and interpreter for a military road-building expedition in the extreme Northwest. In 1862 he went to Washington to assist with the official report of this last, which is illustrated with lithographs after Sohon's drawings. From 1863 to 1865 Sohon had a photographic studio in San Francisco, but in 1865 or 1866 he returned to Washington and for the rest of his life operated a show business there. He died in Washington on September 3, 1903. ¶ Ewers, "Gustavus Sohon's Portraits of Flathead and Pend D'Oreille Indians, 1854"; Draper, "John Mix Stanley"; Taft, *Artists and Illustrators of the Old West,* 276; represented in U. S. National Museum.

SOLOMON, J. Portrait painter at Charleston (S.C.) in 1845. ¶ Sherman, "Unrecorded Early American Painters" (Oct. 1934), 149.

SOLON, C. Delineator of a view of the Great Falls of the Missouri, lithographed by J. T. BOWEN of Philadelphia in the mid-1850's. The artist was probably GUSTAVUS SOHON whose view of these falls was lithographed by SARONY, MAJOR & KNAPP and published in Vol. XII, Part I, of the War Department's *Reports of Explorations and Surveys . . .* (1860). ¶ Peters, *America on Stone.*

SOMERBY, FREDERIC THOMAS (1814–*c.* 1870). Portrait and fancy painter, born January 4, 1814, at Newburyport (Mass.). As early as 1832 he painted a "deception" in oils on wood. The Somerby family, which also included HORATIO G. and LORENZO, moved to Boston about 1834. Frederic was listed as a portrait painter in 1838–39, an artist 1841–44, and a fancy painter from 1845 to 1870 when his name disappears from the directories. ¶ *Vital Records of Newburyport;* Lipman and Winchester, 180; Boston CD 1838–70.

SOMERBY, HORATIO GATES (1805–?). Fancy painter, born December 24, 1805, at Newburyport (Mass.). He was an older brother of FREDERIC T. and LORENZO SOMERBY and was active in Boston from 1834 into the 1840's. ¶ *Vital Records of Newburyport;* Boston CD 1834+.

SOMERBY, LORENZO (1816–1883). Portrait and banner painter, born August 9, 1816, at Newburyport (Mass.), younger brother of FREDERIC T. and HORATIO G. SOMERBY. The Somerby family moved to Boston about 1834 and Lorenzo was active there as a painter from 1838 to 1883. In his early days he did some portraits and from about 1870 he was called a banner painter. He died March 6, 1883. ¶ Sears, *Some American Primitives,* 94 (repro.), 109–10; *Vital Records of Newburyport;* Boston CD 1838–1883 [date of death in 1883 CD].

SOMERVILLE, M. Miniature and watercolor painter at NYC in 1841 when he exhibited at the Apollo Association a miniature of Lord Byron and watercolors entitled "Adoration" and "Parthenon." ¶ Cowdrey, AA & AAU.

SONNTAG (or Sontag), WILLIAM LOUIS (1822–1900). N.A. Landscape painter, born March 2, 1822, at East Liberty, now part of Pittsburgh (Pa.). He began his artistic career in Cincinnati about 1842 and worked there until he went to Italy in 1855 or 1856. After about a year of study in Florence, he returned to America and established himself in NYC where he made his home until his death, January 22, 1900. Early in his career Sonntag (with JOHN C. WOLFE) painted a panorama of Milton's *Paradise Lost* and *Paradise Regained,* but he was better known for his romantic American and Italian landscapes. He was a National Academician from 1861 and exhibited in many cities. ¶ *Art Annual,* II, obit.; CAB; Clement and Hutton; Cist, *Cincinnati in 1851;* Ohio BD 1853; Cowdrey, NAD; Cowdrey, AA & AAU; Rutledge, PA; Rutledge, MHS; Swan, BA; N. Y. *Herald,* May 5, 1851 (citation courtesy J. E. Arrington); Clark, *Ohio Art and Artists,* 78, repro.; *Art in America* (Oct. 1951), 104, repro.; represented at Corcoran Gallery and Peabody Institute.

SONREL, ANTOINE. Engraver at Woburn (Mass.), 1853–56. He also made drawings of insects which were engraved for *A Treatise on Some of the Insects Injurious to Vegetation* (Boston, 1862). ¶ Mass. BD 1853; New England BD 1856; Hamilton, *Early American Book Illustrators and Wood Engravers,* 401.

SOPER, RICHARD F. (*c.* 1810–*c.* 1862). Stipple engraver, born in England about 1810. He was working for NYC publishers as early as 1831, according to Stauffer, and later worked mainly for J. C. BUTTRE. His widow, Isabella Soper, was listed in the 1863 directory. ¶ 8 Census (1860), N.Y., XLIII, 625; Stauffer; NYCD 1863.

SOREN, JOHN JOHNSTON (?–1889). Landscape and marine painter of Boston, who exhibited at the Athenaeum between 1831 and 1846 and at the Apollo Association in 1841. From about 1826 to 1847 he was teller of the Washington Bank and from 1848 to 1875 cashier of the Boylston Bank. He died February 20, 1889. ¶ Swan, BA; Cowdrey, AA & AAU; Boston CD 1826–89.

SOTTA, ——. Portrait painter at New Orleans in 1842. ¶ New Orleans CD 1842.

SOUDER, GEORGE B. Made an on-the-spot drawing of the burning of the U. S. Steam Frigate "Missouri" at Gibraltar on August 26, 1843. It is not known whether Souder was a member of the crew or even an American. ¶ *Military Affairs,* XI (1947), 166, repro.

SOUFERT, ——. Executed a cameo portrait of General Taylor at New Orleans in 1849. *Cf.* SEIFERT. ¶ Delgado-WPA cites *Picayune,* Jan. 24, 1849.

SOULE, CHARLES, SR. (1809–1869). Portrait and job painter, born in Freeport (Me.). He was brought to Dayton (Ohio) at the age of two and began painting signs, carriages, etc., there and at Greenfield (Ohio) in his teens. He eventually turned to portraits and painted in several Ohio cities in the mid-thirties and later. He was at Cincinnati in 1849–51. He subsequently spent several years in NYC, but in 1856 returned to Ohio. He died in Dayton in 1869. He had two daughters and a son who were artists: CLARA, OCTAVIA, and CHARLES SOULE, JR. ¶ Clark, *Ohio Art and Artists,* 110–11; Cincinnati CD 1849–51; Cist, *Cincinnati in 1859; The Museum* (July 1949), 9; Knittle, *Early Ohio Taverns.*

SOULE, CHARLES, JR. Portrait painter at Dayton (Ohio) in 1859. He was the son of CHARLES SOULE, SR. ¶ Ohio BD 1859; Clark, *Ohio Art and Artists,* 111.

SOULE, CLARA. Portrait painter at Dayton (Ohio) in 1859. She was a daughter of CHARLES SOULE, SR., and later married a man named Medlar. ¶ Ohio BD 1859; Clark, *Ohio Art and Artists,* 111.

SOULE, OCTAVIA. Painter in watercolors and on porcelain, daughter of CHARLES SOULE, SR. She later became Mrs. Gottschall. ¶ Clark, *Ohio Art and Artists,* 111.

SOUTHGATE, JOHN FREDERICK (1831–1858). Copperplate engraver, born June 13, 1831, at Leicester (Mass.). His father, John P. Southgate, moved to Worcester about 1834 and John F. was active as an engraver there from 1851 until his death in 1858. ¶ Crane, *Historic Homes and Institutions . . . of Worcester County,* I, 256; Worcester CD 1851–58; Mass. BD 1853; New England BD 1856.

SOUTHGATE, WILLIAM (1782–1811). Portrait and heraldic painter of Leicester (Mass.). He is said to have received instruction from RALPH EARL, to whom he was remotely related, and GILBERT STUART. ¶ Crane, *Historic Homes and Institutions . . . of Worcester County,* I, 255; Bowditch, "Early Water-Color Paintings of New England Coats of Arms," 198.

SOUTHWARD, GEORGE (1803–1876). Portrait and miniature painter of Salem (Mass.). He was born in Salem in April 1803 and died there February 19, 1876. ¶ Belknap, *Artists and Craftsmen of Essex County,* 13; Salem BD 1851, 1853, 1855, 1857, 1859, 1861; Bolton, *Miniature Painters;* represented at American Antiquarian Society.

SOUTHWORTH, NATHANIEL (1806–1858). Miniaturist, born January 8, 1806, at Scituate (Mass.). He worked in Boston from about 1836 to 1848, then went to Europe, and on his return worked chiefly in NYC and Philadelphia. He exhibited at the Boston Athenaeum and the Pennsylvania Academy. He died April 25, 1858, at Dorchester (Mass.). ¶ CAB; *Scituate Vital Records;* Swan, BA; Boston BD 1842–50; Rutledge, PA; Bolton, *Miniature Painters.*

SPAFARD, Mrs. EDWIN, see OCTAVIA MAVERICK.

SPAFFORD, ELIZABETH H. Teacher of landscape drawing at the Albany Female Academy in 1835. ¶ Albany CD 1835.

SPAINHOUR, Mrs., see SELINA SPENCER.

SPALDING, ELIZA HART (1807–1851). Amateur watercolorist. Eliza Hart was born August 11, 1807, at Berlin (Conn.) and spent her childhood there and in Oneida County (N.Y.). In 1833 she married the Rev. Henry Harmon Spalding of Bath (N.Y.) and three years later they went out to Oregon Territory as missionaries of the Presbyterian Church. Mrs. Spalding died January 7, 1851, at Brownsville (Ore.). ¶ Rasmussen, "Art and Artists in Oregon"; Spaulding, *The Spalding Memorial,* 455; Warren, *Memoirs of the West, The Spaldings* (cited by Rasmussen); represented at Oregon Historical Society. This may be the E. Spalding, watercolor landscapist, listed in Lipman and Winchester, 180.

SPANG, O. S. Portrait painter, Philadelphia, 1860. ¶ Penna. BD 1860.

SPANGENBERG, FERDINAND T. Portrait painter, born in Prussia about 1820. He was working in NYC in the 1850's and at Richmond (Va.) in 1859. In 1860 he resided in NYC with his wife and three children (ages 2 to 6 years, born in New York) and owned realty valued at $6,000. By 1866 he had returned to Germany. ¶ 8 Census (1860), N.Y., L, 290; NYBD 1860; *Richmond Portraits;* letter of Edward V. Valentine to Sarah B. Valentine, Richmond, Sept. 3, 1866 (Valentine Museum, citation courtesy Mrs. Ralph Catterall).

SPARKS, EDWARD. Irish engraver, 19, at NYC in 1850. ¶ 7 Census (1850), N.Y., XLI, 379.

SPARROW, THOMAS (*c.* 1746–?). Engraver on wood and copper. In 1759 he left his home at Annapolis (Md.) to learn silversmithing in Philadelphia. He returned to Annapolis in September 1764 and worked there as a goldsmith, silversmith, engraver, and jeweler at least until 1784. His engravings include title pages and tail pieces for books, bookplates, paper money, and newspaper advertisements. ¶ Arthur, "Thomas Sparrow, an Early Maryland Engraver"; Hamilton, *Early American Book Illustrators and Wood Engravers,* 49; Stauffer.

SPATES, JOHN. Artist, 36, a native of Virginia, at Baltimore in 1860. His wife and children (12 and 9) were also born in Virginia. GEORGE CROSS and family lived with the Spates family. ¶ 8 Census (1860), Md., VII, 189.

SPEAKMAN, Miss ESTHER. Portrait painter and copyist, Philadelphia; exhibitor at the Artists' Fund Society in 1843 and the Pennsylvania Academy in 1843 and 1850. ¶ Rutledge, PA; Thieme-Becker.

SPEAR, JOSEPH. Engraver, 31, a native of New Jersey, at NYC in 1860. ¶ 8 Census (1860), N.Y., LVIII, 51.

SPEAR, THOMAS TRUMAN (1803–*c.* 1882). Portrait, miniature, and historical painter. He was a native of Massachusetts and worked in Boston principally, though he made frequent visits to Charleston (S.C.) between 1833 and 1851. He made copies of Stuart's Washington and Allston's "Belshazzar's Feast." ¶ Swan, BA; 7 Census (1850), Mass., XXV, 597 [aged 50]; Rutledge, *Artists in the Life of Charleston;* Boston BD 1841–60+.

SPEAR, WILLIAM F. Engraver, 18, from Nova Scotia, at Boston in 1860. His father, Robert Spear, was a tailor. ¶ 8 Census (1860), Mass., XXVIII, 537.

SPEARING, THOMAS P. Wood engraver, print colorer, and print seller of NYC in the 1840's. He was a partner of HENRY A. HAVELL with whom he exhibited samples of print coloring at the American Institute in 1844. Spearing was listed as a wood engraver only in 1841. ¶ NYBD 1841; NYCD 1844–45; Am. Inst. Cat., 1844.

SPENCER, ASA. Banknote engraver, born in Pennsylvania about 1805 and active in Philadelphia from about 1825 to 1850. He was probably trained by GIDEON FAIRMAN or JOHN DRAPER. He was associated with the following firms: FAIRMAN, DRAPER, UNDERWOOD & Co. (1825–27); probably DRAPER, UNDERWOOD & Co. (1827–31); DRAPER, UNDERWOOD, BALD & SPENCER (1833); UNDERWOOD, BALD & SPENCER (1835); UNDERWOOD, BALD, SPENCER & HUFTY (1837–43); DANFORTH, BALD, SPENCER & HUFTY (1843); and SPENCER, HUFTY & DANFORTH (1844–47). Spencer was listed in the 1850 Census, but his name does not appear in Philadelphia directories after 1849. ¶ 7 Census (1850), Pa., LI, 925; Phila. CD 1825–49; Toppan, *100 Years of Bank Note Engraving,* 8–11.

SPENCER, ASA, JR. Banknote engraver working in Philadelphia from 1841 to 1844; he was employed by UNDERWOOD, BALD, SPENCER & HUFTY and SPENCER, HUFTY & DANFORTH, in both of which firms his father was a partner. ¶ Phila. CD 1841–44.

SPENCER, BENJAMIN R. Artist, NYC, 1850's. ¶ NYCD 1850–57.

SPENCER, FREDERICK R. (1806–1875). N.A. Portrait and genre painter, born June 7, 1806, in Lennox (N.Y.). After studying at the National Academy, he settled in NYC and worked there from about 1831 to 1857. He was a member of the Board of Directors of the American Academy 1833–35, Associate of the National Academy 1837–46, Academician 1846–58, and Corresponding Secretary of the National Academy 1849–50. In 1858 he retired to up-state New York and he died at Wampoville on April 3, 1875. ¶ Dunlap, *History,* II, 436; CAB; Cowdrey, NAD; Cowdrey, AA & AAU; NYCD 1831–56;

NYBD 1841–57; Swan, BA; Stauffer, nos. 605, 2397.

SPENCER, G. P. Engraver or sculptor, St. Johnsbury (Vt.), 1849. ¶ New England BD 1849.

SPENCER, HUFTY & DANFORTH, see DANFORTH, SPENCER & HUFTY.

SPENCER, J. C. Portrait painter, Phelps (N.Y.), 1859. ¶ N. Y. State BD 1859.

SPENCER, JOB B. (1829–?). Fruit and flower, animal and landscape painter, born in Salisbury (Conn.). Trained as a house painter, he later studied for several years in NYC and in 1858 he exhibited at the National Academy. He subsequently settled in Scranton (Pa.) where he was still active in the 1870's. ¶ French, *Art and Artists in Connecticut,* 141; Cowdrey, NAD; Fielding [as Joseph B.].

SPENCER, JOSEPH B., see JOB B. SPENCER.

SPENCER, LILY MARTIN (1822–1902). Portrait and genre painter. Angelique Marie Martin was born November 26, 1822, in England where her French parents had a school. The family emigrated to America in 1830 and in 1833 moved out to Marietta (Ohio). Lily (or Lilli) began painting in her teens and received some instruction from CHARLES SULLIVAN and SALA BOSWORTH. She had an exhibition in Marietta in 1841 and the same year she went to Cincinnati. After her marriage to Mr. Spencer, she moved to NYC in 1847 and for many years she enjoyed great popularity as a painter of children and dogs. She continued to paint up to the time of her death at Crum's Elbow (N.Y.) on May 22, 1902. She was an Honorary Member, Professional, of the National Academy. ¶ Reiter, "Lily Martin Spencer"; Cowdrey, "Lilly Martin Spencer"; information courtesy Mrs. Pierre Spencer, daughter-in-law of the artist; Cowdrey, NAD; Newark CD 1858; Essex, Hudson, and Union Counties BD 1859; Clark, *Ohio Art and Artists,* 106; Swan, BA; *Art Digest* (Jan. 15, 1945), 30.

SPENCER, LYMAN POTTER (1840–?). Amateur artist, born May 11, 1840, at Geneva (Ohio). He was a son of Platt R. Spencer, originator of the "Spencerian System" of penmanship, and a brother-in-law of the artist JUNIUS R. SLOAN. He was studying art as early as 1854. During the Civil War he served with the army and the family has preserved his illustrated letters and sketchbooks of that period. He was later a publisher and a noted penman. He was living in Washington (D.C.) in 1878 and at Newark (N.J.) in 1889. ¶ Webster, "Junius R. Sloan," 116, 145; Williams, *History of Ashtabula County, Ohio,* 110; Spencer, *Spencer Family History and Genealogy.*

SPENCER, Miss MARY (1835–1923). Still life painter; came to Cincinnati in 1858. ¶ Information courtesy Edward H. Dwight, Cincinnati Art Museum.

SPENCER, SELINA. Portrait painter at Statesville (N.C.), 1847–60. She married a Mr. Spainhour. ¶ Information courtesy Dr. H. W. Williams, Jr., Corcoran Gallery.

SPENCER, W. H. Engraver, NYC, 1825. ¶ Dunlap, *History* (1918); Fielding.

SPENCER, WILLIAM. Engraver, 26, from England, at NYC in 1860 with his English wife and three children (3 years to 2 months old) born in New York. ¶ 8 Census (1860), N.Y., L, 771.

SPERONI, JOHN L. Of GRIFFIN & SPERONI, engravers, NYC, 1860–62. ¶ NYCD 1860–62.

SPERRY, THEODORE S. (1822–?). Landscape painter, born in 1822 at Bozrahville (Conn.). He studied medicine in Boston and was for a time a practising physician. About 1844 he began to paint and later in life he gave himself almost entirely to painting. He made his home in Hartford and was noted especially for his Connecticut Valley scenes. Dr. Spencer died of a fall in Allyn Hall, Hartford, where he was painting scenery, sometime before 1878. ¶ French, *Art and Artists in Connecticut,* 111.

SPIEGLE, CHARLES. Wood engraver, born in Pennsylvania about 1831. He was working in Philadelphia as early as 1850 and from 1855 to 1857 he headed the firm of SPIEGLE & JOHNSON there. Sometime between 1857 and 1863 he settled in Brooklyn (N.Y.) and for the next twenty years he worked in NYC. In 1885, the last year he was listed in the NYC directory, his home was in Passaic (N.J.). At that time two other members of the family, Frederick M. and Charles, Jr., also were working as engravers or designers in NYC. Charles Spiegle, Jr., was killed in 1905 as he stepped off a train near his home in Passaic. ¶ 7 Census (1850), Pa., XLIX, 827; Phila. CD 1854–57; Brooklyn CD 1863, 1866, 1867; NYCD 1868–85; *Art Annual,* V, obit.; Smith; Hamilton, *Early American Book Illustrators and Wood Engravers,* 223, 238.

SPIEGLE & JOHNSON. Wood engravers, Philadelphia, 1855–57; CHARLES SPIEGLE and

CHARLES E. JOHNSON. ¶ Phila. CD 1855–57; Hamilton, *Early American Book Illustrators and Wood Engravers,* 180, 354.

SPIELER, GEORGE. Miniaturist, Philadelphia, 1839–40. ¶ Phila. CD 1839–40.

SPIELER, WILLIAM F. Portrait painter and photographer, Philadelphia, 1844–60 and after. ¶ Phila. CD 1844–60+.

SPINDLER, JOHN. Teacher of drawing, crayon drawing, and oil painting, at Richmond (Va.) in January and February 1805. ¶ *Richmond Portraits,* 243.

SPINNING, ALFRED A. Landscape painter of Cincinnati, 1849–59. He lived with Jonathan Spinning, bricklayer, probably his father. *Cf.* C. S. SPINNING. ¶ Cincinnati CD 1849, 1853, 1857, 1859.

SPINNING, C. S. Landscape painter, Cincinnati, 1847–51. *Cf.* ALFRED A. SPINNING. ¶ Cist, *Cincinnati in 1851.*

SPITTALL, JOHN. Wood engraver, born in England about 1811, active in Philadelphia from 1837 to 1860 and after. ¶ 7 Census (1850), Pa., LIV, 1005; Phila. CD 1837–60+.

SPOHN, GEORGE. Lithographer, 27, a native of France, at Philadelphia in 1850. His wife was German, but their children (7 to 2 years) were born in Pennsylvania. ¶ 7 Census (1850), Pa., XLIX, 14; Phila. CD 1850.

"SPOODLYKS." Cartoonist and designer of sheet music covers published in NYC about 1843. ¶ *American Collector* (Aug. 1947), 13, repros.; represented by cover of "Knickerbocker Quadrille" in Bella C. Landauer Collection, NYHS.

SPOONER, CHARLES H. (1836–1901). Landscape painter; born in Philadelphia; died there March 4, 1901. He exhibited views in Pennsylvania and Nicaragua at the Pennsylvania Academy between 1863 and 1867. His address in 1864–65 was Germantown. ¶ *Art Annual,* IV, obit.; Rutledge, PA.

SPOONER, JANE E. Exhibited two oil paintings and one "Shell Church" at the American Institute in 1845. Born Jane E. Foot, she married first Allen Darrow and second SHEARJASHUB SPOONER. The Spooners were living in NYC during the forties and fifties. ¶ Am. Inst. Cat., 1845; DAB [under Shearjashub Spooner].

SPOONER, SHEARJASHUB (1809–1859). Engraver (?) and writer on art. Born in Orwell (Vt.) December 3, 1809, Spooner studied medicine at Montreal and in 1833 took up the study of dentistry in NYC. For a number of years he enjoyed a good dental practice in NYC, but sometime before 1842 he gave up dentistry to devote himself to the promotion of art in America. His first project was the republication, from the original plates, of Boydell's *Shakespeare Gallery.* His interest in this work may explain why he was listed in the 1850 business directory as an engraver. In 1850 Spooner published his three-volume *Anecdotes of Painters, Engravers, Sculptors and Architects* and three years later appeared his *Biographical and Critical Dictionary of Painters, Engravers, Sculptors and Architects.* He died March 14, 1859, at Plainfield (N.J.). ¶ DAB; NYBD 1850.

SPRAGUE, ISAAC (1811–1895). Landscape painter, born September 5, 1811, at Hingham (Mass.). In 1843 he served as artist-assistant to JOHN JAMES AUDUBON on an ornithological expedition up the Missouri River. By 1846 he had settled at Cambridge (Mass.), where he remained until his removal to Grantville, near Needham, in the mid-sixties. Sprague contributed several landscapes for Oakes' *Scenery of the White Mountains* (1848). He died, presumably at Grantville, in 1895. ¶ Sprague, *Sprague Families in America,* 307; Audubon, *Audubon and His Journals;* Oakes, *Scenery of the White Mountains; Cambridge* CD 1848–63.

SPRAGUE, MARTIN. Reputed to have worked in Boston as a portrait painter and engraver during the Colonial period. ¶ Bayley, *Little Known Early American Portrait Painters,* No. 3.

SPRATLEY, HENRY. Lithographer, NYC, 1850. ¶ NYBD 1850.

SPRING, EDWARD ADOLPHUS (1837–?). Sculptor and modeler, born in NYC in 1837. After studying in America under HENRY K. BROWN, JOHN Q. A. WARD, and WILLIAM RIMMER, as well as in England and France, Spring opened a studio at Eagleswood (N.J.) in the 1860's. In 1868 he turned his attention particularly to work in terra-cotta, establishing in 1877 the Eagleswood Art Pottery Company. He was also a popular lecturer and teacher. ¶ Clement and Hutton; Thieme-Becker.

SPRING, JOHN. Miniaturist at Charleston (S.C.) about 1796. ¶ Sherman, "Some Recently Discovered Early American Portrait Miniaturists."

SPROUL, JOHN. Architect of Philadelphia who exhibited drawings at the Columbianum in 1795. ¶ Columbianum Cat.

SPRUOR or SPROUR, JOHN. "Lithograph

grinder" of New Orleans, 1859–66. ¶ New Orleans 1859–66.

SQUIRES, S. A. NYC painter who exhibited a picture of the steamer *Cornelius Vanderbilt* at the American Institute in 1847. ¶ Am. Inst. Cat., 1847.

STACKER, ANTOINE. Lithographer, 36, a native of Germany, at Boston in 1850. His wife was also German, but their children, ages 4 years to 6 months, were born in Massachusetts. ¶ 7 Census (1850), Mass., XXV, 772.

STACKPOLE, PATRICK M. Engraver, NYC, 1852–54. ¶ NYBD 1852, 1854.

STADTFELD, see STATFELD.

STAEL, ——. Portrait painter at NYC in 1764. ¶ Groce, *William Samuel Johnson,* 196. *Cf.* —— STEELE.

STAFFORD, JOHN M. Wood engraver, NYC, 1847–48. In 1847 he exhibited "Specimen American Scenery" at the American Institute. ¶ Am. Inst. Cat., 1847; NYBD 1848.

STAGER, EMIL. Engraver, 22, a native of France, at Philadelphia in 1860. ¶ 8 Census (1860), Pa., LX, 709.

STAGI, PIETRO. Italian sculptor who worked in Carrara and Leghorn between 1783 and 1793 and in Philadelphia from 1795 to 1799. ¶ Gardner, *Yankee Stonecutters,* 59; Thieme-Becker.

STAIGER, Monsieur ——. Architect, teacher of architecture and drawing, at Charleston (S.C.) in March 1843. ¶ Rutledge, *Artists in the Life of Charleston.*

STAIGG, RICHARD MORELL (1817–1881). N.A. Portrait, miniature, genre, and landscape painter, born September 7, 1817, in Leeds (England). In 1831 his family came to America, eventually settling at Newport (R.I.), where Richard received his first instruction in painting from JANE STUART. He subsequently studied under WASHINGTON ALLSTON. He first exhibited in Boston in 1841 and most of his career was spent in that city, although he was working in Baltimore in 1845, in NYC much of the time in the 1850's, and occasionally in Newport. He gave up miniature painting about 1862 to devote himself to oil and crayon portraits; in later life he also painted landscapes and genre. He was elected an Associate of the National Academy in 1856 and a full member in 1861. He died in Newport October 11, 1881. ¶ Decatur, "Richard Morell Staigg," 6 repros.; CAB; Clement and Hutton; Tuckerman; Swan, BA; Cowdrey, NAD; Baltimore CD 1845; Boston BD 1849–53, 1858, 1860; NYBD 1858–60; Newport CD 1863, BD 1858.

STALKER, E. Engraver, probably at Philadelphia in 1815; he is thought to have been English. ¶ Stauffer; Brown and Brown.

STANCLIFF, J. W. (1814–?). Marine painter, born in Chatham (Conn.) in 1814. Trained as a carriage painter and copperplate engraver, he studied oil painting with ALEXANDER H. EMMONS and JARED B. FLAGG and watercolor painting with BENJAMIN H. COE. His studio was in Hartford for many years and in 1878 he was President of the Connecticut School of Design. ¶ French, *Art and Artists in Connecticut,* 84–85.

STANDISH, HENRY or H. P. Lithographer, NYC, 1860. The 1860 Census lists Henry Standish, 29, a native of England, lithographer, and H. P. Standish, 28, a native of England, lithographer. These may or may not be the same man. ¶ 8 Census (1860), N.Y., LVI, 601, and LVII, 589.

STANFIELD & COOPER. Transparency painters, NYC, 1843; F. W. STANFIELD and B. S. COOPER. ¶ NYCD 1843.

STANFIELD or STANSFIELD, F. W. Exhibited an oil painting at the American Institute in 1842. In 1843 he was connected with STANFIELD & COOPER, transparency painters. ¶ Am. Inst. Cat., 1842; NYCD 1843.

STANLEY, ABRAM R. Portrait painter, born in New York State in 1816. He received instruction from an Italian artist about 1830. In 1856 he painted a portrait of a resident of Shullsburg (Wis.) where Stanley had been postmaster for ten years. ¶ Butts, *Art in Wisconsin,* 97; repro., Garbisch Collection, Catalogue, 90.

STANLEY, HARVEY. One of the stonecutters employed on the sun-face capitals of the Mormon Temple at Nauvoo (Ill.) in the mid-1840's. He was a native of Vermont, born in December 1811, and went to Nauvoo as a Mormon convert soon after 1840. He did not join the trek to Utah in 1848, but spent the rest of his life in Missouri and Iowa. ¶ Arrington, "Nauvoo Temple."

STANLEY, JOHN MIX (1814–1872). Portrait and landscape painter who specialized in scenes of Indian life in the West. He was born January 17, 1814, at Canandaigua (N.Y.). Soon after moving to Detroit in 1834 he took up portrait painting and for the next few years worked there, at Fort Snelling (Minn.), and Galena and Chicago (Ill.). In 1840 he returned to the East to spend the next two years as a portrait artist at Troy (N.Y.), Philadelphia, and Baltimore. His career as an interpreter of the West began in 1842 when he went to Ft. Gibson in Arkansas Territory. By 1845 he was in Cincinnati completing a series of 85 Western scenes for exhibition. In 1846 he went to Santa Fe (N.M.) and thence with Kearny's military expedition to California. During 1847–48 he worked in California and Oregon, then sailed for Hawaii where he remained until 1850. Returning to the United States in 1850, he exhibited his Indian gallery in several Eastern cities and deposited it at the Smithsonian in Washington in hopes that it would be purchased by the Federal Government. Although this hope was not realized, Stanley remained in Washington for the next decade. About 1864 he retired to Detroit, where he died April 10, 1872. His last years were saddened by the almost total destruction of his valuable Indian paintings in the Smithsonian fire of 1865. ¶ This account is based chiefly on Taft, *Artists and Illustrators of the Old West,* but see also: Kinietz, *John Mix Stanley and His Indian Paintings;* Draper, "John Mix Stanley, Pioneer Painter"; Pipes, "John Mix Stanley"; Bushnell, "John Mix Stanley"; DAB; Rutledge, PA; 8 Census (1860), D.C., I, 743; Washington Art Assoc. Cat., 1857, 1859; Stanley, "Portraits of North American Indians."

STANSBURY, ARTHUR J. (1781–*c.* 1845). Artist of several NYC views in the 1820's and a flower print in *The Grammar of Botany;* illustrator of children's books. Stansbury was a native of New York, where he was licensed as a preacher in 1810. He was best known for his "Plan of the Floor of the House of Representatives Showing the Seat of Each Member" (1823). ¶ Peters, *America on Stone;* Stokes, *Iconography,* VI, pl. 96-a; *Antiques* (June 1946), 361.

STANTON, CHARLES. Painter of a group portrait at Stonington (Conn.) in 1853. ¶ FARL question file.

STANTON, G. E., & Co. Of Sing Sing (N.Y.), exhibited two oil paintings at the American Institute in 1849. ¶ Am. Inst. Cat., 1849.

STANTON, PHINEAS, JR. (1817–1867). Portrait and miniature painter, born September 23, 1817, probably at Wyoming (N.Y.), the son of General Phineas Stanton. He was working in NYC as early as 1841, at Charleston (S.C.) in 1844, in NYC again in 1845. He visited New Orleans in 1847 and the same year was married at Le Roy (N.Y.) to Emily Ingham. He was at New Orleans again in 1853. During the Civil War he was wounded and a few years later, on September 5, 1867, he died at Quito (Ecuador) while serving as artist on an expedition sponsored by Williams College and the Smithsonian Institution. ¶ Stanton, *A Record . . . of Thomas Stanton, of Connecticut, and His Descendants,* 521–22; Cowdrey, AA & AAU; Cowdrey, NAD; NYCD 1841, 1845; Rutledge, *Artists in the Life of Charleston;* Delgado-WPA cites *Bee,* April 16, 1847, and *Picayune,* April 4, 1847, and Jan. 26, 1853.

STANWOOD, A. Painter of a primitive scene in oils, about 1850. ¶ Lipman and Winchester, 180.

STARBIRD, MARY ANN. Artist, 30, a native of Maine, living in NYC in 1860 with her father, Solomon P. Starbird, "gentleman." In 1863 she was listed as Anne Starbird, artist. ¶ 8 Census (1860), N.Y., LIV, 598; NYCD 1863.

STARKENBORGH, JACOBUS NICOLAUS, Baron TJARDA VAN (1822–1895). Landscape and marine painter, born in Wehl, Groningen (Holland). With WILLIAM T. VAN STARKENBORGH, possibly his brother, he was at Philadelphia in 1850 and 1852 and exhibited at the Pennsylvania Academy. Later catalogues give his address as Germany (1855) and Düsseldorf (1858–61). In addition to European views, he exhibited views in Pennsylvania and New Jersey. He died August 4, 1895, at Wiesbaden (Germany). ¶ Thieme-Becker; Rutledge, PA; Phila. CD 1852.

STARKENBORGH, WILLIAM T. VAN. Landscape, marine, and animal painter, probably a brother of JACOBUS NICOLAUS TJARDA VAN STARKENBORGH. As W. T., W. F., or W. S. van Starkenborgh he exhibited at the Pennsylvania Academy between 1850 and 1862. His addresses were The Hague (1850), Philadelphia (1852–56), and Holland (1859). He was also listed in Philadelphia directories for 1852, 1856, and 1857, and exhibited as of Philadelphia at the Washington Art Association in 1857 and 1859. Besides European views, he showed several views in Pennsylvania, New Hampshire, New Jersey and New York. ¶ Rutledge, PA; Phila. CD 1852–57 [as Starkenborgh, Van Starkenburgh, or Van Starkbougher]; Washington Art Assoc. Cat., 1857, 1859.

STARKEY, ——. Portrait painter and silhouettist at Charleston (S.C.) in 1834. ¶ Information courtesy Miss Anna Wells Rutledge.

STARKEY, JAMES. Artist, 21, born in Pennsylvania, at Philadelphia in 1860. His father, Nathan Starkey, was a well-to-do manufacturer of medicine chests. ¶ 8 Census (1860), Pa., LIV, 266.

STARKWEATHER, Miss J. M. Landscape painter of Chicago who exhibited at the Illinois State Fair in 1855. ¶ Chicago *Daily Press,* Oct. 15, 1855.

STARR, ——. Exhibited "diaphanous paintings" in Boston in 1847. ¶ Boston *Evening Transcript,* Feb. 11, 1847 (citation courtesy J. E. Arrington).

STARR, ELIZA ALLEN (1824–1901). Art teacher and painter, born August 29, 1824, at Deerfield (Mass.). After studying with CAROLINE NEGUS (Mrs. Richard Hildreth), Miss Starr practiced in Boston for several years, but left in 1854 to teach art in private schools in Philadelphia and Brooklyn and in a private family at Natchez (Miss.). In 1856 she finally settled in Chicago. During the next two decades she was well known as a teacher and as a lecturer on art. After the loss of her studio in the great fire of 1871, she left Chicago to organize an art department at St. Mary's Academy in South Bend (Ind.). She later gained a national reputation as a lecturer on art and writer-illustrator of Catholic devotional books. She died at the home of a brother in Durand (Ill.) on September 7, 1901. ¶ DAB; Swan, BA.

STARR, N. B. Portrait painter, Cincinnati, 1841. ¶ Information courtesy Edward H. Dwight, Cincinnati Art Museum.

STARR, WILLIAM. Engraver, 25, a native of New York, at NYC in 1850. ¶ 7 Census (1850), N.Y., XLI, 494.

STARUP, EDWARD. Artist, 31, from Norway, at Boston in 1860. ¶ 8 Census (1860), Mass., XXVI, 400.

STATFELD, MORITZ. Artist, 30, of German birth, at NYC in 1860; property valued at $3,000. In 1863 he was listed as a photographer. ¶ 8 Census (1860), N.Y., LIII, 973; NYCD 1863.

STATTLER, GEORGE. Ship carver of Charleston (S.C.) who in 1798 carved a figurehead of General Charles C. Pinckney. ¶ Pinckney, *American Figureheads and Their Carvers,* 82, 201.

STAUCH, ALFRED. Sculptor of Philadelphia who exhibited at the Pennsylvania Academy between 1860 and 1869. He was born in Saxe-Coburg (Germany) about 1836 and probably was a younger brother of EDWARD STAUCH, with whom he was living in 1860. In 1866 he was in Europe, but he was back in Philadelphia by 1868. ¶ Rutledge, PA; 8 Census (1860), Pa., LV, 613.

STAUCH, EDWARD. Sculptor, born in Saxe-Coburg (Germany) about 1830, active in Philadelphia in the late fifties and sixties. He exhibited at the Pennsylvania Academy. ALFRED STAUCH, presumably his brother, was at the same address in 1860. ¶ 8 Census (1860), Pa., LV, 613; Rutledge, PA; Phila. CD 1854–60+.

STAUFFER, JACOB (1808–1880). Artist, as well as general storekeeper, job printer, pharmacist, lawyer, botanist, and photographer. From 1839 to 1858 he lived at Richland, now Mount Joy (Pa.), where his son Jacob McNeely Stauffer, author of *American Engravers upon Copper and Steel,* was born in 1845. In 1858 Jacob Stauffer moved to Lancaster (Pa.) and became librarian of the Lancaster Athenaeum. ¶ Kieffer, "David McNeely Stauffer."

STAUGHTON, see ANNA CLAYPOOLE PEALE.

STAUNTON, see STANTON.

STEAG, JACOB. Engraver, 26, born in Pennsylvania, at Philadelphia in 1860. ¶ 8 Census (1860), Pa., LX, 49.

STEARNS, JUNIUS BRUTUS (1810–1885). N.A. Portrait, genre, and historical painter, born July 2, 1810, at Arlington (Vt.). He was a student at the National Academy of Design, probably about 1838 when he first exhibited there and at the Apollo Association. In 1848 he was elected an Associate of the Academy and in 1849 he became an Academician. In 1849 he went abroad to study in Paris and London. Soon after his return he was elected Recording Secretary of the National Academy, an office he held from 1851 to 1865. Though he painted portraits chiefly, Stearns was also known for his historical subjects, especially a series on George Washington. He died in Brooklyn on September 17, 1885. ¶ CAB; Cowdrey, NAD; Cowdrey, AA & AAU; Clark, *History of the NAD,* 271; Swan, BA; NYCD 1838+; Rutledge, PA; several repros. listed in *Art Index.*

STEARNS, MARY ANN H. Watercolor still life, done at Billerica (Mass.) in 1827. ¶ Lipman and Winchester, 180.

STEARNS, WILLIAM. Still life on velvet, done

in Massachusetts or Maine about 1825. ¶ Lipman and Winchester, 180.

STEBBINS, CARLOS. Portrait painter working in western New York in the 1830's. His portrait of Mary Jemison is in the Museum in Letchworth State Park, Portage (N.Y.). ¶ Merrill, *The White Woman and Her Valley* (Rochester, 1955), 134, repro. opp. 22.

STEBBINS, EMMA (1815–1882). A.N.A. Portrait and monumental sculptor, portrait artist in oils, watercolors, crayon, and pastel. Born in NYC on September 1, 1815, Miss Stebbins worked with the brush and pencil until she was in her forties, exhibiting occasionally at the Pennsylvania and National Academies. She became interested in sculpture during a visit to Rome in 1857 and to it she devoted herself for the rest of her life. She remained in Rome until 1870 and thereafter worked in NYC. Her work included portrait busts and statues, several ideal subjects, and a figure for a fountain in Central Park. She died in NYC on October 25, 1882. ¶ CAB; Clement and Hutton; Taft, *History of American Sculpture,* 211; Rutledge, PA; Cowdrey, NAD; Gardner, *Yankee Stonecutters;* Tuckerman, *Book of the Artists,* 602–03.

STEEL, ALFRED B. Engraver, 32, born in Pennsylvania, at Philadelphia in 1860. He lived with his father, the engraver JAMES W. STEEL. ¶ 8 Census (1860), Pa., LI, 620.

STEEL, JAMES W. (1799–1879). Engraver. A native and life-long resident of Philadelphia, he was a pupil of BENJAMIN TANNER and GEORGE MURRAY and worked for a time for TANNER, VALLANCE, KEARNEY & Co. He did much portrait, historical, and landscape engraving, but later became a banknote engraver. He was still active in 1860 and died June 30, 1879. ALFRED B. STEEL, engraver, was his son. ¶ Stauffer; Phila. CD 1825–60; 8 Census (1860), Pa., LI, 620; Penna. Acad. Cat., 1832; *Antiques* (Aug. 1928), 131, repro.; NYHS *Quarterly Bulletin* (Oct. 1944), 121, repro.; Dunlap, *History,* II, 379.

STEEL or STEELS, JOHN. Lithographer, NYC, 1850–60; born in Germany about 1825. ¶ NYBD 1851–52, 1854, and NYCD 1851–52, 1858–60, as John Steel; NYBD 1856–59 and NYCD 1856–57, as John Steels; 7 Census (1850), N.Y., XLII, 348, as John Steel.

STEELE, Mr. ——. Portrait painter whom C. W. PEALE met in Philadelphia in 1762 or 1763. He is said to have been of a good Maryland family and to have studied in Italy, but Peale thought him a poor artist and slightly mad. ¶ Sellers, *Charles Willson Peale,* 50–52. *Cf.* —— STAEL.

STEELE, Mrs. A. Miniaturist at NYC in 1848 when she exhibited at the National Academy. Possibly the same as Mrs. DANIEL STEELE. ¶ Cowdrey, NAD.

STEELE, DANIEL. Portrait painter who began his career about 1830, probably at Cincinnati, and was at Rochester (N.Y.) in 1834. Possibly the husband of Mrs. DANIEL STEELE, below. ¶ Cist, *Cincinnati in 1841,* 140; Rochester CD 1834; Ulp, "Art and Artists in Rochester," 30.

STEELE, Mrs. DANIEL. Miniaturist and portrait painter. She advertised in Charleston (S.C.) in January 1841 and Richmond (Va.) in October 1842. She exhibited at the National Academy in 1843 as of NYC and in 1844 as of Syracuse (N.Y.). She may have been the wife of DANIEL STEELE, above, and the same as Mrs. A. STEELE, who exhibited at the National Academy in 1848 as of NYC. ¶ Rutledge, *Artists in the Life of Charleston; Richmond Portraits;* Cowdrey, NAD.

STEELE, WILLIAM PORTER (1817–1864). Painter of portraits, animals, and scenes from Shakespeare's plays. Born November 4, 1817, at Harmony Hall, Lancaster County (Pa.), he graduated from Rutgers College in New Jersey and studied law at Lancaster (Pa.). He later moved to NYC, where he died November 28, 1864. ¶ Lancaster County Historical Society, *Papers,* XVI (1912), 278.

STEEPER, JOHN. Engraver of Philadelphia, active 1755–62. In 1755 he collaborated with HENRY DAWKINS on an engraving entitled "Southeast Prospect of the Pennsylvania Hospital." ¶ Stauffer; Prime, I, 27 [erroneously as Sleeper]; *Penna. Gazette,* March 25, 1762; Hamilton, *Early American Book Illustrators and Wood Engravers,* 48.

STEERE or STEERS, ARNOLD (1792–1832). Portrait painter, born at Smithfield, now Woonsocket (R.I.). He worked in Woonsocket and Philadelphia between 1815 and 1832 and exhibited at the American and National Academies in 1828. ¶ Sears, *Some American Primitives,* 290, as Steere; Cowdrey, NAD, as Steers; Cowdrey, AA & AAU, as F. Steere.

STEFFAN, EDWARD. Apprentice lithographer, 18, born in Pennsylvania, at Philadelphia in 1860. He was listed in 1871 as a lithographer. ¶ 8 Census (1860), Pa., LX, 342; Phila. CD 1871.

STEFFAN, EUGENE. Swiss engraver, 21, at NYC in 1860. ¶ 8 Census (1860), N.Y., XLIII, 90.

STEGAGNINI or STEGNANI, LOUIS. Ornamental sculptor or marble mason, working in Philadelphia between 1823 and 1840. ¶ Phila. CD 1823–40, as Stegagnini; Scharf and Westcott, *History of Philadelphia,* as Stegnani.

STEIN, ——. Portrait painter who came to Steubenville (Ohio) about 1820 and encouraged young THOMAS COLE to take up painting. He is said to have been a native of Washington (Va.) and to have died young. ¶ Dunlap, *History,* II, 260.

STEIN, A. Landscape painter. He was at Munich in 1850, when he exhibited a copy after Murillo at the Pennsylvania Academy. When he again exhibited in 1855 he gave a Philadelphia address. ¶ Rutledge, PA.

STEIN, CHARLES. Portrait painter, NYC, 1854–57. ¶ NYBD 1854–57.

STEIN, JACOB. Engraver from Bavaria, 49, at NYC in 1860. Jacob Stein, machinist, was listed in 1863. ¶ 8 Census (1860), N.Y., XLVIII, 914; NYCD 1863.

STEINECKE, HENRY F. Engraver, seal engraver, and die sinker, NYC, 1858–59. ¶ NYBD 1858–59.

STEINEGGER, HENRY. Lithographer, born in Switzerland about 1831; working in San Francisco from 1859 to 1880 as an employee of JOSEPH BRITTON and JACQUES J. REY. ¶ 8 Census (1860), Cal., VII, 1312; Peters, *California on Stone.*

STELLWAGEN, CHARLES K. Philadelphia artist who exhibited portraits, landscapes, and animal subjects at the Artists' Fund Society in 1838, 1841, and 1843. Born in Pennsylvania about 1818, he moved to Washington sometime between 1847 and 1850 and was employed there in 1850 as a draftsman. *Cf.* STILLWAGON. ¶ Rutledge, PA; 7 Census (1850), D.C., II, 199.

STEPHENS, ——. Portrait painter active in Indiana in 1835. ¶ Burnet, *Art and Artists of Indiana,* 398.

STEPHENS, HENRY LOUIS (1824–1882). Illustrator and caricaturist, born February 11, 1824, at Philadelphia. He worked in Philadelphia during the fifties, but moved to NYC about 1859 to work for FRANK LESLIE. A few years later he became an illustrator for Harper Brothers. Best known as a caricaturist and illustrator of books and magazines, he also painted in watercolors. He died at Bayonne (N.J.) December 13, 1882. ¶ CAB; Thieme-Becker; Phila. CD 1852+; NYCD 1860+; Hamilton, *Early American Book Illustrators and Wood Engravers,* 463–66.

STEPHENS or STEVENS, LUTHER. Engraver and plate printer, 60, at Boston in 1850. His son, WILLIAM STEPHENS, also was an engraver. ¶ 7 Census (1850), Mass., XXIV, 698 [as Stephens, engraver]; Boston CD 1850–53 [as Stevens, plate printer].

STEPHENS, THOMAS. Engraver, NYC, 1858. ¶ NYBD 1858.

STEPHENS or STEVENS, WILLIAM. Engraver, 18, at Boston with his father LUTHER STEPHENS, engraver, in 1850. ¶ 7 Census (1850), Mass., XXIV, 698.

STEPHENS, see also STEVENS.

STEPHENSON, PETER (1823–*c.* 1860). Sculptor and cameo portraitist. Born in Yorkshire (England) on August 19, 1823, Stephenson came to America with his parents in 1827 and lived on farms in New York and Michigan until he was old enough to be apprenticed to a watchmaker in Buffalo (N.Y.). He soon turned to cutting cameo portraits and carving busts and in 1843 went to Boston. In two years he had earned enough to go to Rome for two years. After his return to Boston in 1847 Stephenson continued to specialize in cameos, though he also did some portrait busts and ideal figures. He exhibited frequently at the Boston Athenaeum. He died in 1860 or early in 1861; his widow is listed in the 1861 directory. ¶ Lee, *Familiar Sketches of Sculpture and Sculptors,* 191–94, contains an autobiographical account of the artist; Gardner, *Yankee Stonecutters,* 72; Boston CD 1847–61; Swan, BA; Washington Art Assoc. Cat., 1857, 1859; 7 Census (1850), Mass., XXV, 731; *Antiques* (Sept. 1946), 170, repro.; represented at American Antiquarian Society.

STEPHENSON, THOMAS. Engraver, 46, a native of Ohio, at Philadelphia in 1860. His wife was also from Ohio, but their children (ages 20 to 16) were born in Philadelphia. ¶ 8 Census (1860), Pa., LVIII, 323.

STEPHENSON, see also STEVENSON.

STERLING, MARY E. Amateur painter in oils, Painesville (Ohio), about 1860. ¶ Lipman and Winchester, 180.

STERLING, see also STIRLING.

STERN, GERSON. Engraver from Bavaria, 36, at NYC in 1860. His children (5 to 1) were born in New York. He was still in NYC in 1863. ¶ 8 Census (1860), N.Y., LIV, [930]; NYCD 1863.

STERRY, THOMAS N. Engraver at Norwich (Conn.) in 1860. ¶ New England BD 1860.

STETCHER, KARL (1831/32–1924). Portrait painter and craftsman. Born in Germany, he came to NYC at an early age. He died in January 1924 at Wichita (Kans.). ¶ *Art Annual,* XXI, obit.

STETTINIUS, SAMUEL ENREDY (1768–1815). Portrait painter in watercolors and oils. Born May 21, 1768, at Friedrichgratz, German Silesia, he emigrated to America in 1791, lived for some years in Hanover (Pa.), and died at Baltimore, August 5, 1815. He also published the first newspaper in Hanover. ¶ Millar, "Stettinius, Pennsylvania Portrait Painter."

STEVENS, AMBROSE. Lawyer and amateur artist of NYC, exhibited paintings of a horse and a cow at the American Institute in 1847. ¶ Am. Inst. Cat., 1847, 1849; NYCD 1846–49.

STEVENS, AMELIA (Mrs. Eugene Translot). Made a drawing of the ruins of the Mormon Temple at Nauvoo (Ill.) about 1857. ¶ Arrington, "Nauvoo Temple," Chap. 8.

STEVENS, CHARLES J. Engraver, born in New York State about 1822, active in New Orleans 1852–60. ¶ 8 Census (1860), La., VIII, 200; New Orleans CD 1852–56, 1859.

STEVENS, DANIEL. Engraver of Hartford (Conn.), 1854–60. ¶ Hartford CD 1854–60.

STEVENS, GEORGE. Engraver, born in London (England) about 1815, at NYC in 1860. His children, ages 4 to 20 years, were born in New York. ¶ 8 Census (1860), N.Y., XLII, 993.

STEVENS, GEORGE W. Miniaturist, Boston, 1840–42; thereafter as upholsterer and chairmaker. ¶ Boston CD 1840–58; Bolton, *Miniature Painters.*

STEVENS, JOHN (1819–1879). Panorama painter. A native of Utica (N.Y.), Stevens settled as a farmer at Rochester (Minn.) in 1853. In 1858 he turned to house and sign painting. Probably about 1863 he painted the first of several versions of his panorama of the Sioux Massacre of 1862; other versions, brought up to date with scenes of current interest, followed in 1868, 1870, and 1874, and Stevens made a handsome profit from their exhibition in the Middle West. He died in 1879. Two versions of his panorama are known to have survived; one at the Minnesota Historical Society, the other in the Gilcrease Museum at Tulsa (Okla.). ¶ Heilbron, "Documentary Panorama"; Heilbron, "The Sioux War Panorama of John Stevens"; *American Processional,* 246; *The New Yorker,* March 6, 1943, 13.

STEVENS, LUTHER and WILLIAM, see under STEPHENS.

STEVENS, WILLIAM. Lithographer, 28, a native of Hamburg (Germany), at NYC in 1860. His wife was Irish and their children, the oldest aged 5, were all born in New York. ¶ 8 Census (1860), N.Y., XLV, 790–91.

STEVENS, ZELETUS. Engraver, 22, a native of Vermont, at Northfield (Vt.) in 1850. ¶ 7 Census (1850), Vt., X, 133.

STEVENS, see also STEPHENS.

STEVENSON, ——. Portrait painter at Pittsburgh (Pa.) in 1813. ¶ FARL question file.

STEVENSON, A. MAY. Landscape painter of Philadelphia, exhibited chiefly southeastern Pennsylvania scenes at the Pennsylvania Academy between 1853 and 1861. ¶ Rutledge, PA.

STEVENSON, HAMILTON. Limner who, with his brother JOHN STEVENSON, opened a drawing and painting academy in Charleston (S.C.) in November 1774. He was in Jamaica in 1780, but returned to Charleston by June 1782. ¶ Prime, I, 8–10; Rutledge, *Artists in the Life of Charleston.*

STEVENSON, JAMES. Engraver, 16, born in Ireland, at Philadelphia in 1850. His mother was Irish, with real property valued at $10,000; her four daughters, aged 19 to 25, were born in Germany. ¶ 7 Census (1850), Pa., XLIX, 764.

STEVENSON, JOHN. Limner who first advertised at Charleston (S.C.) in September 1773. The following year he and his brother, HAMILTON STEVENSON, opened a drawing and painting academy in Charleston. Both were in Jamaica in 1780, but apparently only Hamilton returned to Charleston in 1782. John's repertory included history, landscape, portrait, and miniature painting, family and conversation pieces, etc. ¶ Prime, I, 9–10; Rutledge, *Artists in the Life of Charleston.*

STEVENSON, THOMAS H. Landscape and miniature painter, teacher of painting. T. H. Stevenson was a miniature painter and teacher at Cleveland (Ohio) from 1841 to 1845. This is probably the Thomas H. Stevenson who appeared at Madison and Milwaukee (Wis.) in 1855. During the next three years he worked in partnership with SAMUEL M. BROOKES. Their joint work included a series of ten views on the Fox and Wisconsin Rivers, now in the Wisconsin Historical Society, and three views of Indian battlegrounds, now in the State Museum. ¶ WPA (Ohio), *Annals of Cleveland;* Butts, *Art in Wisconsin,* 74–75; Milwaukee CD 1856, BD 1858.

STEVENSON, see also STEPHENSON.

STEWARD, ALFRED. Engraver, 35, a native of New York, at NYC in 1860 with his wife Paulina. ¶ 8 Census (1860), N.Y., LIV, 31.

STEWARD, JOSEPH (1753–1822). Portrait painter and silhouettist, born July 6, 1753, at Upton (Mass.). After graduating from Dartmouth in 1780, Steward entered the ministry. He was married in 1789 at Hampton (Conn.), where he made his home until 1796. Ill health forced him to give up preaching and he turned to painting about 1793. He opened a portrait studio at Hartford in 1796 and the following year opened a museum in the State House. He continued to paint as late as 1815; in his later years he also resumed preaching. He died April 22, 1822. ¶ "Joseph Steward and The Hartford Museum," Connecticut Historical Society *Bulletin,* XVIII (Jan.–April 1953), 13 repros.; French, *Art and Artists in Connecticut;* WPA (Mass.), *Portraits Found in N.H.,* 27; WPA (Mass.), *Portraits Found in Mass.,* nos. 2040–41; Stauffer, nos. 2522, 2657; Flexner, *The Light of Distant Skies.*

STEWART, Mrs. A. E. Of Chicago (Ill.), won a prize for flower painting exhibited at the Illinois State Fair in 1855. ¶ Chicago *Daily Press,* Oct. 15, 1855.

STEWART, ALEXANDER. Landscape, marine, and ornamental painter, who advertised in Philadelphia in 1769. He was a Scot and had studied in Glasgow and Edinburgh. ¶ Prime, I, 9.

STEWART, CHARLES. Engraver of portraits in mezzotint, probably at NYC, 1841. ¶ Fielding's supplement to Stauffer, 38.

STEWART, JOHN A. Portrait painter, NYC, 1851; exhibited at the National Academy. ¶ Cowdrey, NAD.

STEWART, S. Landscape painter. A "Landscape. Carriage Fording a River. By the late S. Stewart of Boston" was shown at the American Academy in 1820. ¶ Cowdrey, AA & AAU.

STEWART, WILLIAM H. Artist, Philadelphia, 1850–54. Listed in the 1850 Census as William Stuart, 21, born in New Brunswick; his wife was Catherine, 29, a native of Pennsylvania. *Cf.* WILLIAM H. STEWART, the engraver. ¶ 7 Census (1850), Pa., LIII, 326; Phila. CD 1851–54.

STEWART, WILLIAM H. Engraver, Philadelphia, 1856–60 and after. Listed in the 1860 Census as aged 29, a native of England; his wife, Catherine, was 28, a native of Ireland; they had five children, ages 8 years to 7 months, all born in Pennsylvania. *Cf.* WILLIAM H. STEWART, the artist. ¶ 8 Census (1860), Pa., LII, 655; Phila. CD 1856 [as William F.], 1858–60+.

STEWEL or STEIVEL, GUSTAV. Lithographer, 18, a native of Germany, at Baltimore in 1850. He lived with, and was probably employed by, AUGUST HOEN. ¶ 7 Census (1850), Md., V, 418.

STICKNEY, MEHITABEL. Memorial painting, 1825. ¶ Lipman and Winchester, 180.

STIDOLPH, ——. Engraver, Boston, 1842. ¶ Boston BD 1842.

STIDUN, JAMES. Mid-19th century Negro portrait painter whose portraits of Stephen Smith (1795–1873) and Mrs. Smith (née Harriet Lee) are owned by the Historical Society of Pennsylvania. ¶ Information courtesy the late William Sawitzky.

STIEBEL, AUGUSTUS. German-born lithographer, 28, at Baltimore in 1860. ¶ 8 Census (1860), Md., IV, 642.

STIEFFEL, HERMANN (1826–1882). Amateur landscape and battle painter who served for 25 years (1857–82) as a private in Company K, 5th U. S. Infantry. The Smithsonian Institution owns his watercolors of "The Attack on General Marcy's Train near Pawnee Fort, Kansas, September 23, 1867" and "A view of Fort Keogh in the Montana Territory," about 1879. ¶ *American Processional,* 26, 249, 250.

STIFFT, M. Engraver, 38, a native of Poland, at New Orleans in 1860. His wife Bertha was from Prussia; Solomon, age 4, was born in Ohio; Wolff, age 2, in Louisiana. In 1870 he was listed as a watchmaker. ¶ 8 Census (1860), La., VI, 70; New Orleans CD 1870.

STILES & COMPANY. Engravers, NYC, 1833–

35. Formed by SAMUEL STILES when he left BALCH, STILES, WRIGHT & CO. ¶ NYCD 1833–35.

STILES, JEREMIAH (1771–1826). Portrait and animal painter, civil engineer and surveyor, born May 21, 1771, at Keene (N.H.). ¶ Worcester (Mass.) Society of Antiquity, *Collections,* VI (1885), 169–70, 205–06; Stiles, "Jeremiah Stiles, Jr."

STILES, SAMUEL (1796–1861). Portrait painter and banknote engraver, born July 15, 1796, at East Windsor (Conn.). He was active as an engraver in NYC from about 1828; with BALCH, STILES & CO. (1828–30), BALCH, STILES, WRIGHT & CO. (1831–32), and STILES & COMPANY (1833–35). Died in NYC April 3, 1861. ¶ Bolton, "Workers with Line and Color in New England"; Stauffer; NYCD 1828–59; 7 Census (1850), N.Y., XLVII, 327.

STILES, WILLIAM M. Engraver, Philadelphia, 1850. ¶ Phila. BD 1850.

STILLMAN, GEORGE K. Wood engraver, Cincinnati, 1840–60. He was born in Massachusetts about 1821; his wife Mary was a native of Georgia. In 1850 they had two children, ages 4 and 1, both born in Ohio. ¶ 7 Census (1850), Ohio, XXII, 56; Cincinnati CD and BD 1840–60.

STILLMAN, WILLIAM JAMES (1828–1901). A.N.A. Landscape painter, born June 1, 1828, at Schenectady (N.Y.). After graduating from Union College in 1848, he studied landscape painting under FREDERIC E. CHURCH for a year, then visited England, where he began a long friendship with Ruskin. After participating in Kossuth's rebellion in Hungary about 1851, Stillman returned to America and opened a studio in NYC. In 1855 he founded the art magazine *Crayon,* but he retired from its direction after a year and moved to Cambridge (Mass.) where he continued to paint until 1860. He was in Europe when the Civil War broke out and soon after was appointed American Consul at Rome, which post he held until 1865. After three more years in a consular post in Crete, he settled in England. Much of his later life was spent in Rome as a special correspondent of the London *Times* and he also wrote many books on art, archaeology, and contemporary events. He retired to Surrey in 1898 and died there July 6, 1901. His *Autobiography of a Journalist* was published the same year. ¶ DAB; Cowdrey, NAD; Cowdrey, AA & AAU; Rutledge, PA; Swan, BA; Washington Art Assoc. Cat., 1857; Graves, *Dictionary;* repro., Met. Mus., *Life in America.*

STILLWAGON, G. B. Teacher of "mezzotint painting" and landscape painting, advertised in Indianapolis in 1845. At Bowling Green in 1868. *Cf.* STELLWAGEN. ¶ Peat, *Pioneer Painters of Indiana,* 239.

STINER, LOUIS. Engraver, 36, born in Germany, inmate of the NYC penitentiary on July 10, 1860, for petit larceny. ¶ 8 Census (1860), N.Y., LXI, 186.

STINSON, WILLIAM H. Engraver, lithographer, and plate printer, Boston, 1853–59; 1855–58, of HOLLAND & STINSON. ¶ Boston BD and CD 1853–59.

STIRLING, WILLIAM ARTHUR. Painter of a self-portrait, about 1800, now owned by the Sheldon Museum at Middlebury (Vt.). This may be the William Arthur Sterling who married Maria Ducoster Barrett at Boston, April 25, 1802. ¶ WPA (Mass.), *Portraits Found in Vt.;* Sterling, *The Sterling Genealogy,* 1248.

STIRLING, see also STERLING.

STITES, JOHN RANDOLPH (1836–?). Portrait, genre, and landscape painter. A native of Buffalo (N.Y.), he worked principally in Chicago (1870–80) and NYC (1883–87). Three portraits by him are at the Chicago Historical Society. ¶ Champlin and Perkins; information courtesy H. Maxson Holloway, Chicago Hist. Soc.; NYCD 1883–87.

STOCK, JOSEPH WHITING (1815–1855). Portrait painter, born January 30, 1815, at Springfield (Mass.). Crippled by an accident at the age of 11, Stock took up painting when he was about 17 and worked principally in Springfield, though at various times he traveled as far afield as New Bedford (Mass.), New Haven (Conn.), and Warren, Bristol, and Providence (R.I.). He also painted miniatures, landscapes, and even marines on occasion. His diary records over 900 portraits painted between 1842 and 1845. He died at Springfield on June 28, 1855. ¶ Clarke, "Joseph Whiting Stock," in Lipman and Winchester, 113–20; Museum of Modern Art, *American Folk Art,* 29–30; Rockefeller Folk Art Coll., *American Folk Art;* Springfield CD 1852.

STOCKER, FRANK ANTHONY. Lithographer, Boston, *c.* 1846–60. He was born about 1812 in Prussia; his wife also was a native of Prussia; but their children were born in Massachusetts. ¶ 8 Census (1860),

Mass., XXVIII, 373; Boston CD 1850, 1860.

STOCKTON, FRANCIS RICHARD (1834–1902). Wood engraver and illustrator, better known as a writer. Born April 5, 1834, at Philadelphia. On graduating from high school at 18, worked as a wood engraver in Philadelphia and NYC until about 1866, when he gave up engraving to write stories for *Riverside Magazine* and others. From 1873 to 1881 he was assistant editor of *St. Nicholas.* Stockton was the author of many humorous novels, including *Rudder Grange* and *The Casting Away of Mrs. Lecks and Mrs. Aleshines,* and stories, of which the best known is "The Lady or the Tiger?" His home for many years was in New Jersey, but three years before his death he moved to West Virginia, near Harper's Ferry. He died there April 20, 1902. ¶ DAB; CAB; Phila. CD 1856–60; Hamilton, *Early American Book Illustrators and Wood Engravers,* 320.

STOCKTON, JOHN DREAN (1836–1877). Steel and copperplate engraver. A brother of FRANCIS R. STOCKTON, born in Philadelphia April 26, 1836. He went to work as an engraver about 1859, but soon turned to journalism. He was manager of the *Philadelphia Press* for a time, associated with the *New York Tribune* in 1866, editor of the *Philadelphia Post* from 1867 to 1872. From 1873 until his death he was drama and music critic for the *New York Herald.* He died in Philadelphia November 3, 1877. ¶ CAB; DAB, under Frank R. Stockton; Phila. CD 1859–60.

STOCKWELL, FRANCIS F. Engraver, Boston, 1859–60 and after. ¶ Boston CD 1859–60+.

STOCKWELL, SAMUEL B. (1813–1854). Scene and panorama painter, born in Boston. The son of an actor, Stockwell was first an actor, then scene painter at Boston's Tremont Theatre, during the 1830's. He also painted scenery at Charleston (1841), Mobile (1843), and New Orleans (1843, 1846). Probably sometime after 1842 he settled in St. Louis, where his daughter Missouri was born in 1845. Stockwell worked for a time with HENRY LEWIS on a panorama of the Mississippi, but the partnership was dissolved and both completed separate versions in 1848. After exhibiting his panorama with great success in St. Louis, New Orleans, and Charleston, Stockwell brought it to Boston, where he remained for several years. In 1852–53 he was back in St. Louis painting scenes for the theater. From there he went to Savannah (Ga.), where he died of yellow fever on September 23, 1854. ¶ Arrington, "Samuel B. Stockwell and His Mississippi Panorama," manuscript; Arrington, "The Story of Stockwell's Panorama"; Delgado-WPA cites *Picayune,* Dec. 16, 1843, Dec. 3, 1848, and *Courier,* Jan. 2, 1849; Rutledge, *Artists in the Life of Charleston;* 7 Census (1850), Mass., XXV, 751.

STODART, ADAM. Lithographer, NYC, 1835; NATHANIEL CURRIER's first partner. Before and after 1835 Stodart was in the music business. ¶ Peters, *Currier & Ives,* I, 19–20; Peters, *America on Stone;* NYCD 1835–60.

STODART, G. Engraver of a stipple portrait of David Stoner, published in America in 1835, and a portrait of Washington, published in London. This may be George Stodart, an English stipple engraver who did reproductions of sculpture for the *Art Journal* for about 30 years until his death, December 28, 1884. It is not known whether he ever worked in America. ¶ Stauffer; *Art Journal* (1885), 64; Thieme-Becker.

STOKES, JOSEPH F. Engraver, Philadelphia, 1860–61. He was born in Philadelphia about 1842 and was the son of John Stokes, tailor, a native of Ireland. ¶ Phila. CD 1860 [as John F.], 1861 [as Joseph F.]; 8 Census (1860), Pa., LI, 231 [as Joseph].

STONE, BENJAMIN, JR. Engraver and music printer, Boston, 1852–60 and after. ¶ Boston CD 1852–60+.

STONE, BENJAMIN BELLOWS GRANT (1829–1906). Landscape artist, born January 21, 1829, at Watertown, now Belmont (Mass.). He studied with BENJAMIN CHAMPNEY and JASPER F. CROPSEY and exhibited at the National Academy and Boston Athenaeum. He served as an army officer during the Civil War. After the war he lived at Catskill (N.Y.) and devoted himself to painting, journalism, and politics. He was particularly noted for his charcoal landscapes. He died in Catskill on August 11, 1906. ¶ Bartlett, *Simon Stone Genealogy,* 313; Boston CD 1850–52, BD 1853; Cowdrey, NAD; Swan, BA; *Art News,* Aug. 18, 1906, obit.

STONE, ELIZABETH (1811–1872). Portrait painter at NYC in 1868 when two of her works were shown at the Pennsylvania Academy. ¶ Rutledge, PA.

STONE, EDMUND. Sailor of Beverly (Mass.)

who painted many pictures of the ship *George* of Salem about 1820. ¶ Robinson and Dow, *The Sailing Ships of New England,* I, 64.

STONE, FRED. Artist, born in Massachusetts about 1835, at NYC in 1860. Possibly Frederick Stone, varnisher, in 1860 directory. ¶ 8 Census (1860), N.Y., LI, 703; NYCD 1860.

STONE, GEORGE. Wood engraver and carver, Philadelphia, 1850–59. He was born in New York State about 1811; his wife was a native of Pennsylvania; a son Henry was born about 1842 in Maryland and a daughter Caroline in New York about 1846. ¶ 7 Census (1850), Pa., LII, 823; Phila. CD 1850–55, BD 1854, 1856.

STONE, HENRY. Pioneer lithographer, engraver, and portrait painter, active in Washington (D.C.) from about 1822 to 1846. He was born in England and brought to America as a boy. The family settled in Elizabethtown (N.J.), but moved to Washington about 1818. Stone introduced lithography in Washington in 1822. From 1837 to 1846 he was employed in the Patent Office, first as draftsman, then as assistant examiner. Probably related to WILLIAM J. STONE. ¶ Wright and McDevitt, "Henry Stone, Lithographer," repros. and checklist; Stauffer; Stokes, *Historical Prints.*

STONE, HORATIO (1808–1875). Sculptor, born December 25, 1808, at Jackson, Washington County (N.Y.). He was brought up to be a farmer but left home and became a physician, practising in NYC from 1841 to 1847. His chief interest, however, was sculpture to which he turned as a professional when he moved to Washington (D.C.) in 1848. He was a founder and in 1857 President of the Washington Art Association and a prime mover in the establishment of the National Gallery of Art. He served as a surgeon during the Civil War. After the war he made at least two visits to Italy and he died at Carrara on August 25, 1875. Several of his works are in the U. S. Capitol at Washington. ¶ DAB; Fairman, *Art and Artists of the Capitol;* Clement and Hutton; Cowdrey, NAD; Washington Art Assoc. Cat., 1857, 1859.

STONE, MARGARET. Artist, 45, a native of Massachusetts, at NYC in 1860. Possibly the Margaret Stone, "maps," in 1860 directory. ¶ 8 Census (1860), N.Y., LIII, 889; NYCD 1860.

STONE, N. Genre painting in oils, Prattsville (N.Y.), about 1830. ¶ Lipman and Winchester, 180.

STONE, WILLIAM J. (1798–1865). Engraver and lithographer. Born in London, he was brought to America by an uncle in 1804 and educated at Holmesburg (Pa.). After learning to engrave under PETER MAVERICK he settled in Washington (D.C.) in 1815 and there spent the rest of his life. His work included several maps of Washington and the 1823 facsimile of the Declaration of Independence. His wife also engraved maps. Stone died in January 1865. HENRY STONE was probably a brother or cousin. ¶ Peters, *America on Stone;* Stauffer; Washington *Star,* Jan. 19, 1865, obit.

STONE, WILLIAM OLIVER (1830–1875). N.A. Portrait painter, born September 26, 1830, at Derby (Conn.). After studying under NATHANIEL JOCELYN, he had a studio in New Haven for several years. In 1851 he moved to NYC where he became a successful painter of portraits, especially of women and children. He died at Newport (R.I.) on September 15, 1875. ¶ DAB; CAB; Clement and Hutton; NYBD 1854–60+; Cowdrey, NAD; Rutledge, PA; *Art in America* (April 1925), 156, 158, and (Jan. 1939), 44–46.

STOPER, FRANK. Lithographer, 40, a native of Austria, at Philadelphia in 1860. His wife and three children were also born in Austria, before 1853. ¶ 8 Census (1860), Pa., LII, 418.

STORER, Miss CATHERINE. Landscape painter of Albany (N.Y.) who exhibited at the Boston Athenaeum in 1833. A Miss Storer, address not given, exhibited landscapes at the American Academy in 1835 and at the American Art-Union in 1846 and 1849. ¶ Swan, BA; Cowdrey, AA & AAU.

STORM, G. F. Stipple engraver and etcher who came to Philadelphia from England about 1834 and engraved a number of portraits. His stay in America is said to have been brief. G. F. Storm of London exhibited a portrait in London in 1828. ¶ Stauffer; Graves, *Dictionary.*

STORM, GEORGE (1830–1913). Portrait painter. A native of Johnstown (Pa.), he spent the greater part of his career at Harrisburg (Pa.), where he painted portraits of many state officials. He died July 6, 1913, at Lancaster (Pa). ¶ *Art Annual,* XI, obit.

STORMS, CHRISTIAN S. Saddler and amateur artist of NYC who exhibited at the

American Institute in 1842 (watercolor painting) and 1844 (framed drawing of the New York State Arsenal). ¶ Am. Inst. Cat., 1842 (as C. C. Storms), 1844; NYCD 1844.

STORMS, JOHN. Genre painter at NYC in 1835 when he exhibited at the American Academy. ¶ Cowdrey, AA & AAU; NYCD 1835 only.

STORY, ——. Painter of a portrait of William Paterson (1793–1871), owned by the New Jersey Historical Society. *Cf.* GEORGE HENRY STORY. ¶ N. J. Hist. Soc., *Proceedings,* X (April 1925), 154.

STORY & ATWOOD. Portrait, historical, and landscape engravers, NYC, 1844; THOMAS C. STORY and JOHN M. ATWOOD. ¶ NYBD 1844.

STORY, GEORGE HENRY (1835–1923). A.N.A. Portrait and genre painter, born January 22, 1835, at New Haven (Conn.). He began studying at New Haven under LOUIS BAIL and CHARLES HINES and then went to Europe for a year. In 1858 he was at Portland (Me.). After two years in Washington (D.C.) and a year in Cuba, he settled in NYC. He was elected an Associate of the National Academy in 1875. He died in NYC on November 24, 1923. ¶ *Art Annual,* XX, obit.; Clement and Hutton.

STORY, THOMAS C. Portrait and historical engraver, NYC, 1837–44; in 1844, of STORY & ATWOOD. ¶ Stauffer; NYBD 1844.

STORY, WILLIAM WETMORE (1819–1895). Sculptor. Born February 12, 1819, at Salem (Mass.), the son of Associate Justice Joseph Story of the U. S. Supreme Court, William Wetmore Story grew up in the literary atmosphere of Cambridge, graduated from Harvard in 1838, took his law degree two years later, and practised in Boston for about five years. An amateur painter, modeler, and musician, in 1847 he was commissioned to design a memorial to his father and went to Italy to receive additional training in sculpture. After his return to Boston, he resumed his law practice, but in 1856 he decided to devote himself to sculpture, settled in Rome, and there spent the rest of his life, except for occasional visits to America. Highly regarded as a sculptor both in Europe and America, Story was also known as a poet and essayist and numbered among his close friends many of the leading literary figures of the day, including the Brownings, Lowell, and Henry James, his biographer. Story died October 7, 1895, at Vallombrosa (Italy). His two sons, Julian Russell and Thomas Waldo Story, also became artists of note. ¶ James, *William Wetmore Story and His Friends,* is the only biography of the artist; for brief accounts of his life see DAB; Fairman, *Art and Artists of the Capitol;* CAB; Clement and Hutton; Taft, *History of American Sculpture;* Swan, BA; 7 Census (1850), Mass., XXV, 583.

STOTE, THEODORE. Engraver, 54, born in Germany, at NYC in 1860. His wife and three older children (25 to 13) were born in Germany, while three younger children (10 to 4) were born in New York. ¶ 8 Census (1860), N.Y., LXII, 596.

STOTHARD, JAMES. Signpainter of 12 Madison Street, NYC, exhibited a flower painting in watercolors at the American Institute in 1847. James Stothard, Jr., of the same address, exhibited two watercolors at the Institute in 1846, and R. Stothard, of 14 Madison Street, exhibited an oil painting in 1847. ¶ NYCD 1845–46; Am. Inst. Cat., 1846, 1847.

STOTHARD, R., see JAMES STOTHARD.

STOTT, JOHN H. Stone, seal, and gem engraver, Boston, 1836–49. This is probably the John Stott, English heraldic artist at Boston about 1850, listed by Bowditch. ¶ Boston CD 1836–49, BD 1841–49; Bowditch, "Early Water-Color Paintings of New England Coats of Arms," 206.

STOTT or STOTTS, WILLIAM. Engraver, Philadelphia, 1849–53. ¶ Phila. BD 1849–53.

STOUGHTON, Mrs., see ANNA CLAYPOOLE PEALE.

STOUT, FRANKLIN. Artist or draftsman, born in Philadelphia about 1825, the son of George Stout, whipmaker. He was listed as an artist in the 1850 and 1860 Philadelphia censuses and as a draftsman in the 1871 directory. ¶ 7 Census (1850), Pa., XLIX, 170; 8 Census (1860), Pa., LVIII, 75; Phila. CD 1871.

STOUT, GEORGE H. (1807–1852). Engraver, born in NYC in 1807, a son of JAMES DEFOREST STOUT. He was active as an engraver from 1831 until his death, February 26, 1852, at which time he was in partnership with JACOB HYATT. ¶ Stout, *Stout and Allied Families,* 181; NYCD 1831–51; NYBD 1837–51; obit., Barber, "Deaths Taken from the N. Y. Evening Post."

STOUT & HEGEMAN. Engravers. NYC, 1859–60; WILLIAM C. STOUT and GEORGE HEGEMAN. ¶ NYBD 1859–60, CD 1859.

STOUT & HYATT. Engravers, NYC, 1850–52; GEORGE H. STOUT and JACOB HYATT. The partnership ended with Stout's death in February 1852. ¶ NYBD and CD 1850–51.

STOUT, JAMES. Engraver, Philadelphia, 1811. ¶ Brown and Brown.

STOUT, JAMES DEFOREST (1783–1868). Engraver and seal cutter, born in NYC July 22, 1783. He was active in NYC from about 1804 to 1840 and died there July 8, 1868. Except for 1833–34 when he was in the partnership of STOUT & WARNER, Stout seems to have worked independently or with his engraver sons: JOHN B., GEORGE H., JAMES V., and WILLIAM C. STOUT. He was also an uncle of Andrew Varick Stout (1812–83), teacher and banker of NYC. ¶ Stout, *Stout and Allied Families,* 181, 292; NYCD 1804–40, 1850, as engraver, 1853–57, as late engraver.

STOUT, JAMES VARICK (1809–1860). Engraver and die sinker, born in NYC in 1809, a son of JAMES DEFOREST STOUT. Stauffer states that he was active in NYC in the mid-thirties, but his name is absent from the directories. He died in NYC on April 26, 1860. ¶ Stout, *Stout and Allied Families,* 181; Stauffer; Barber, "Deaths Taken from the N. Y. Evening Post."

STOUT, JOHN BENJAMIN (1805–1877). Engraver and seal cutter, born in NYC on May 11, 1805, the eldest son of JAMES DEFOREST STOUT. John B. Stout & Co., engravers and seal sinkers, was listed in NYC directories from 1829 to 1831, but Stout soon after became a physician and surgeon. He died November 26, 1877, at Bridgeport (Ky.). ¶ Stout, *Stout and Allied Families,* 181, 293; NYCD 1829–31.

STOUT, WILLIAM. Ohio-born artist, 39, at NYC in 1850. ¶ 7 Census (1850), N.Y., XLVIII, 380.

STOUT, WILLIAM. English lithographer, 35, at Philadelphia in 1860. ¶ 8 Census (1860), Pa., LV, 536.

STOUT, WILLIAM CILL (1820–?). Engraver and artist, born in NYC in 1820, a son of JAMES DEFOREST STOUT. He was active in NYC from the forties at least until 1868, when he was granted letters of administration for his father's estate. Of STOUT & HEGEMAN in 1859–60. He later moved to California. ¶ Stout, *Stout and Allied Families,* 181; NYCD 1849; NYBD 1851–60; Barber, "Index of Letters of Administration of New York County, 1743–1875"; 7 Census (1850), N.Y., XLI, 827.

STOUTENBURGH, Mrs., see EMILY MAVERICK.

STOW, JOHN. Designer of the fire-mark of the Insurance Company of North America, cast iron on wood, Philadelphia, 1774. ¶ Lipman, *American Folk Art,* 17, repro. 85.

STRAHAN, CHARLES. Engraver, Philadelphia, 1818–19. ¶ Brown and Brown.

STRAIDY, ——. Portrait painter working in NYC about 1845. He is said to have been a jeweler. Possibly the Charles Straede, watchmaker, in NYC directories, 1842–51. ¶ *Art Digest* (Oct. 1, 1932), 16; NYCD 1842–51.

STRANGE, JOSEPH W. Designer and engraver at Bangor (Me.), 1855–56. ¶ *Maine Register,* 1855–56.

STRASBURGER, CHRISTOPHER. Sculptor, Troy (N.Y.), 1859. ¶ N. Y. State BD 1859.

STRASSER or STROSSER, ——. Painter of miniatures on enamel who exhibited at the Pennsylvania Academy in 1847 (as Strosser) and at the Maryland Historical Society in 1848 (as Strasser). The only persons of this name listed in Philadelphia between 1846 and 1850 are M. Strasser, tobacconist, and John Strosser, machinist. ¶ Rutledge, PA; Rutledge, MHS; Phila. CD 1846–50.

STRASSER, FREDERICK. Portrait painter, NYC, 1858. ¶ NYBD 1858.

STRATTON, WILLIAM D. (?–1892). Designer, engraver, and draftsman working in Boston from 1850; exhibited at the Athenaeum in 1859–60. ¶ Swan, BA; Boston CD 1850–60+.

STRATTON, WILLIAM F. Engraver and writing instructor of Boston. He was listed as an engraver from 1827 to 1833, as proprietor of a writing academy 1836–37, 1839, and again as an engraver 1841–44. ¶ Boston CD 1827–44.

STRAUSS, MOSES or MORRIS. Lithographer, Boston, 1853–56. ¶ Boston CD 1853–54 as Moses, 1855 as Morris; BD 1855–56.

STRAUSS, RAPHAEL. Portrait painter of Cincinnati, active 1859–97. ¶ Cincinnati CD 1859–97.

STRAUTHER, D. H., see DAVID HUNTER STROTHER.

STRECKER, HERMAN (1836–1901). Sculptor, naturalist, and author; born March 24, 1836, at Philadelphia; died November 30, 1901, at Reading (Pa.). ¶ *Art Annual,* IV, obit.

STREET, AUSTIN. Portrait and landscape painter, born in the District of Columbia about 1824 (1850 Census), a son of ROBERT STREET. He lived in Philadelphia and exhibited at the Artists' Fund Society and the Pennsylvania Academy between 1843 and 1861. Semon states that his name was Austin Del Sarto Street and that he was born in 1829. ¶ 7 Census (1850), Pa., LIII, 199; Rutledge, PA; Phila. CD 1849–60+; Semon, "Who was Robert Street?"

STREET, CLAUDE LORRAIN (1834–?). Portrait painter, born probably in Philadelphia, a son of ROBERT STREET. He was painting professionally in 1858. ¶ Semon, "Who Was Robert Street?"; 7 Census (1850), Pa., LIII, 460; Phila. BD 1858.

STREET, FRANKLIN. Artist, 34, a native of Pennsylvania, at Philadelphia in 1850. ¶ 7 Census (1850), Pa., LV, 398.

STREET, RUBENS or REUBEN C. (1826–?). Portrait painter, born probably in Philadelphia, a son of ROBERT STREET. Semon gives his full name as Rubens Correggio Street. He was working in Philadelphia during the 1840's and exhibited at the Artist's Fund Society and Pennsylvania Academy. In 1850 he was living with his father. ¶ Semon, "Who Was Robert Street?"; 7 Census (1850), Pa., LIII, 406; Rutledge, PA; Stauffer, no. 423.

STREET, ROBERT (1796–1865). Portrait, historical, religious, and landscape painter, born January 17, 1796, at Germantown (Pa.). He began exhibiting in Philadelphia in 1815. In 1824 he held an exhibition in Washington and painted a portrait of Andrew Jackson. Most of his career was spent in Philadelphia. In 1840 he held an exhibition of over 200 of his own paintings and "old masters" at the Artists' Fund Hall. Of his six children by three wives, at least four were artists: AUSTIN, CLAUDE L., RUBENS C., and THEOPHILUS. ¶ Street, *The Street Genealogy,* 378; death date courtesy the late William Sawitzky; Semon, "Who Was Robert Street?"; Karolik Cat.; 7 Census (1850), PA; Cowdrey, AA & AAU; Phila. BD 1838–53; Anderson, "Intellectual Life in Pittsburgh: Painting," 291.

STREET, THEOPHILUS. Portrait painter, born probably in Philadelphia about 1829, a son of ROBERT STREET. He was living with his father in 1850. ¶ 7 Census (1850), Pa., LIII, 460; Semon, "Who Was Robert Street?"

STREETER, LEANDER R. Miniature painter who was at Baltimore and Richmond in 1835 and at Lowell (Mass.) from 1848 to 1861. After 1848 he was listed as "agent." This is probably Leander Richardson Streeter, born August 1812 at Haverhill (Mass.), son of the Rev. Sebastian Streeter, later minister of the First Universalist Church of Boston. ¶ Lafferty (as Streeler); *Richmond Portraits;* Lowell BD 1848, CD 1849–61; Streeter, *Genealogical History of the Descendants of Stephen and Ursula Streeter,* 129–30.

STRICKLAND, GEORGE (1797–1851). Landscape and architectural draftsman, born in Philadelphia in 1797, a younger brother of WILLIAM STRICKLAND, under whom he studied drawing, painting, and engraving. He exhibited a scene from Scott's *Marmion* at the Pennsylvania Academy at the age of 17; in 1826 he exhibited sepia drawings of Philadelphia scenes, then being engraved for Childs' *Picturesque Views.* Unsuccessful in his attempt to become an architect, he taught drawing for a while at the Franklin Institute, but sometime in the thirties moved to Washington and became a Patent Office clerk. He was buried in Washington in April 1851. ¶ Gilchrist, *William Strickland,* 1, 137; Rutledge, PA; *Analectic Magazine,* XI (1818), opp. 23; *Portfolio* (June 1946), 232; *American Collector* (March 1941), 7; letter, A. R. Johnson, Congressional Cemetery, to Miss Anna Wells Rutledge, December 22, 1952 (NYHS files).

STRICKLAND, WILLIAM (1788–1854). Architect, engraver, painter, and draftsman. Born in November 1788 at Navesink (N.J.), Strickland was apprenticed in 1803 to the architect BENJAMIN H. LATROBE, with whom he remained about two years. After a season of scene painting at the Park Theatre in NYC, Strickland began his independent career as an architect in Philadelphia in 1809, though for a number of years he supplemented his income by surveying, engraving, and painting. His first important architectural commission came in 1818, the 2nd Bank of the United States, and many others followed during the next two decades. Although he employed various styles, Strickland is generally associated with the Greek Revival in America. From 1819 to 1846 he was also a Director of the Pennsylvania Academy. He visited Europe with his family in 1838, making many watercolor sketches which have been preserved. In 1845 Strickland moved to Nashville (Tenn.) and was engaged as architect of the Tennessee State Capitol there until his death, April 6, 1854. ¶ Gilchrist, *William Strickland, Architect and Engineer, 1788–1854,* contains the best account of his life, a checklist of his work, and many illustrations. See also: DAB; Stauffer; Stokes, *Iconography,* pl. 80; Rutledge, PA.

STROBEL, LOUISA CATHERINE (1803–1883). Amateur miniature painter, born in Liverpool (England) of American parents. She was brought to the United States for the first time in 1812, but from 1815 to 1830 she lived in Bordeaux (France), where her father was American Consul. Miss Strobel studied miniature painting in Bordeaux, but apparently never worked professionally. After her return to America in 1830, she married the Rev. Benjamin Martin who had charges in Washington, New Hampshire, Albany (N.Y.), and after 1852 in NYC, where Mrs. Martin died April 3, 1883. ¶ Information courtesy Mrs. Wilson Noyes of Savannah (Ga.), who cites the Carolina Art Association and an article on Mrs. Martin by her son, Dr. Daniel Strobel Martin, read at an Educational Association in Albany after her death (copy at Carolina Art Association).

STROBEL, MAX. Topographical draftsman who served briefly as artist of the Stevens Pacific Railroad Survey of 1853 and later the same year joined Frémont's expedition. He made a number of sketches in Minnesota, including a view of St. Paul in 1853. ¶ Taft, *Artists and Illustrators of the Old West,* 273; Stokes, *Historical Prints,* pl. 85a.

STROBRIDGE, HINES. Engraver and/or lithographer, Cincinnati, 1856–60 and after. He was with MIDDLETON, WALLACE & CO., 1856–58; MIDDLETON, STROBRIDGE & CO., 1859–64; Strobridge, Gerlacher & Wagner, 1864–67; and Strobridge & Co., 1867–? ¶ Cincinnati CD 1856–60; Peters, *America on Stone.*

STRONG, GEORGE H. Engraver on copper and wood, Buffalo (N.Y.), 1858–60. ¶ Buffalo BD 1858–60.

STRONG, HOWARD. Chicago artist, 1858–60, who exhibited at the Chicago Art Union's first show in the spring of 1859. ¶ Andreas, *History of Chicago,* II, 556–57 (citation courtesy H. Maxson Holloway, Chicago Hist. Soc.).

STRONG, THOMAS W. Wood engraver and lithographer, NYC, 1842–51; thereafter listed as publisher. He exhibited two frames of wood engravings at the American Institute in 1842. In 1844–45 he was doing work for the *New York Herald.* ¶ Am. Inst. Cat., 1842; NYBD 1844, 1846, 1848; NYCD 1851–57; Peters, *America on Stone;* Hamilton, *Early American Book Illustrators and Wood Engravers;* Arrington, "Nauvoo Temple," Chap. 8; *Antiques* (July 1945), 33; *Portfolio* (Aug. 1948), 18.

STRONG, WALTER. Artist, 28, born in New York, at NYC in 1850. ¶ 7 Census (1850), N.Y., L, 550.

STROOBANT, L. Color lithographs for *The Florist and Horticultural Journal,* published in Philadelphia, 1853–55. ¶ McClinton, "American Flower Lithographs," 362.

STROSSER, see STRASSER.

STROTHER, DAVID HUNTER (1816–1888). Illustrator; portrait and landscape draftsman. Strother was born September 26, 1816, at Martinsburg (Va., now W. Va.), graduated from Jefferson College, studied art in Philadelphia, and continued his art studies in France and Italy from 1840 to 1844. After his return to the United States he became an illustrator for various magazines and books. In 1853 he began publishing in *Harper's* a series of illustrated articles on Southern life, under the pseudonym "Porte Crayon." Many of these sketches were reprinted in a volume entitled *Virginia Illustrated* (1857). Strother served in the Union army during the Civil War and at its close was brevetted brigadier-general. After 1865 he made his home at Berkeley Springs (W. Va.) and continued to write for *Harper's.* From 1879 to 1885 he was U. S. Consul-General at Mexico City. He retired to Charleston (W. Va.) and died there March 8, 1888. ¶ DAB; Willis, "Jefferson County Portraits"; Cowdrey, NAD; Rutledge, PA; Rutledge, MHS; obit., Boston *Transcript,* March 9, 1888.

STROUD, THOMAS. Artist, 33, a native of Pennsylvania, at Philadelphia in 1850. The only person of this name listed between 1848 and 1854 is Thomas Stroud, locksmith, in 1851. ¶ 7 Census (1850), Pa., LI, 150; Phila. CD 1848–54.

STROUSE, RAPHAEL, see RAPHAEL STRAUSS.

STRYCKER, JACOBUS GERRITSEN (1619–1687). Long-believed to be the painter of a "self-portrait" at the Metropolitan Museum of Art. Research by the late Alexander J. Wall, Director of the New-York Historical Society, failed to uncover any contemporary reference to Strycker as a limner or painter, and the portrait of Strycker at the Metropolitan is no longer attributed to him. ¶ George C. Groce, based on information furnished by Alexander J. Wall, John Hill Morgan, and Harry B. Wehle. *Cf.* Groce, "New York Painting before 1800."

STRYPE, FREDERICK C. Of BUTLER & STRYPE, wood engravers, NYC, 1848; also listed as a draftsman. ¶ NYBD 1848; NYCD 1848.

STUART or STEWART, ALBERT F. Engraver, born in Pennsylvania in 1824, working in Philadelphia from 1845 to 1860 and after as junior partner in WAGNER & STUART. ¶ 7 Census (1850), Pa., LIII, 168; 8 Census (1860), Pa., LIV, 617; Phila. CD 1845–60+.

STUART, ALEXANDER. Polish artist, 28, at NYC in 1860. His wife Dora was a Texan, but their two children, aged 2 years and 3 months, were born in New York. He was still there in 1863. ¶ 8 Census (1860), N.Y., XLV, 25; NYCD 1863.

STUART, CHARLES GILBERT (*c.* 1787–1813). Landscape, portrait, and genre painter, son of GILBERT STUART. Probably a pupil of his famous father, although DUNLAP states that Stuart refused to teach his son. Died in Boston on March 10, 1813, at the age of 26. He had exhibited at the Pennsylvania Academy in 1811 and another of his works was shown at the Boston Athenaeum in 1827. ¶ Morgan, *Gilbert Stuart and His Pupils,* 46–48; Swan, "Gilbert Stuart in Boston," 66; Rutledge, PA; Swan, BA; Flexner, *The Light of Distant Skies.*

STUART & FOWLER. Engravers, Boston, 1855; FREDERICK G. STUART and EDWARD W. FOWLER. ¶ Boston CD and BD 1855.

STUART, FREDERICK D. Artist and engraver, born in New York about 1816. He went on one of the early exploring expeditions to the Pacific Northwest and contributed some illustrations to the 1844 *Narrative of the U. S. Exploring Expedition.* He moved to Washington (D.C.) from New York State soon after 1850 and was living there as late as 1871. In the 1860 census he was listed as an engraver. In 1862 he was off on another exploring expedition, from 1864 to 1866 he was in the Navy, and from 1867 he was listed as a hydrographer. ¶ 8 Census (1860), D.C., II, 423; Rasmussen, "Artists of the Explorations Overland," 58; Washington CD 1853–71 (as Stuart or Stewart).

STUART, FREDERICK G. Of STUART & FOWLER, engravers, Boston, 1855. *Cf.* FREDERICK T. STUART. ¶ Boston CD and BD 1855.

STUART, FREDERICK T. (1837–1913). Engraver and painter; active in Boston as an engraver from 1857; died at Brookline (Mass.), October 8, 1913. ¶ *Art Annual,* XI, obit.; Stauffer; Boston CD 1857–60+; 8 Census (1860), Mass., XXVII, 53 (as Stewart). *Cf.* FREDERICK G. STUART.

STUART, GILBERT (1755–1828). Portrait painter, born December 3, 1755, in the Township of North Kingstown (R.I.). The family moved in 1761 to Newport and there in 1769 or 1770 Gilbert became acquainted with the Scottish artist, COSMO ALEXANDER, his first teacher. In 1772 he went to Scotland with his teacher, who died in Edinburgh the same year; Stuart remained in Edinburgh for a short time but returned to his home in 1773. In 1775 he left Newport for London, attempted to make his way as a painter for several years with little success, and from 1777 to 1782 worked in the studio of BENJAMIN WEST. Setting up his own studio in 1782, Stuart enjoyed considerable success in London until 1787, then moved to Dublin where he remained for about five years. In 1792 he returned to the United States; he worked in NYC in 1793–94, in Philadelphia and Germantown 1794–1803 (during which period he painted three life portraits of Washington), in Washington 1803–05, at Bordentown (N.J.) in 1805, and the rest of his life in Boston, where he died on July 9, 1828. ¶ The most recent biographies are Whitley, *Gilbert Stuart* (1932) and Flexner, *Gilbert Stuart* (1955), and the standard checklist of his work, in four volumes and profusely illustrated, is Park, *Gilbert Stuart, an Illustrated Descriptive Catalogue* (1926). For extensive bibliographies see Flexner, *America's Old Masters* and *The Light of Distant Skies;* for Stuart's pupils see Morgan, *Gilbert Stuart and His Pupils.*

STUART, JAMES REEVE (1834–1915). Portrait painter and teacher. Born in Beaufort (S.C.) in 1834, he attended the University of Virginia and Harvard College and in Boston studied under JOSEPH AMES. He went to Germany for further study, entering the Royal Academy at Munich in 1860. After the Civil War he worked for a time in Savannah (Ga.) and Memphis (Tenn.), spent three years in St. Louis, and in 1872 settled permanently at Madison (Wis.). Although he taught at Milwaukee College and the University of Wisconsin for a few years, Stuart was best known as a portrait painter; thirty-five of his portraits hang in the Wisconsin State Historical Museum alone. He died in Madison in 1915. ¶ Butts, *Art in Wisconsin,* 116–19 (repro. p. 115); Karolik Cat.

STUART, JANE (1812–1888). Portrait painter, born in Boston in 1812, the youngest child of GILBERT STUART, from whom she received her early training. After her father's death in 1828, Jane and her mother and three sisters moved to Newport (R.I.) and there she spent most of her life, although she also maintained a Boston studio for some time during the fifties. Miss Stuart is remembered chiefly for her copies of her father's portraits of Washington. She died in Newport on April 27, 1888. ¶ Powel, "Miss Jane Stuart, 1812–1888"; Morgan, *Gilbert Stuart and His Pupils,* 49–51; 8 Census (1860), Mass., XXVIII, 58; Cowdrey, AA & AAU; Cowdrey, NAD; Swan, BA; Rutledge, PA; Rutledge, MHS; Boston *Transcript,* April 30, 1888, obit.

STUART or STEWART, OLIVER J. Engraver, 24, a native of New York, at NYC in 1850. He was still there in 1859. ¶ 7 Census (1850), N.Y., L, 376; NYBD 1859.

STUART or STEWART, PYTHIAS. Lithographer, 20, a native of Georgia, at Philadelphia in 1860. A Pythias D. Stewart, photographer, was at Philadelphia in 1871. ¶ 8 Census (1860), Pa., LVI, 821; Phila. CD 1871.

STUBBS, WILLIAM P. Painter of a genre scene at North Buckport (Me.) about 1855. ¶ *Old-Time New England* (Jan.–Mar. 1952), 68; *Art in America* (Feb. 1951), 16.

STUBENRAUCH, AUGUSTUS. Engraver and die sinker, NYC, 1860. Probably a brother of CHARLES STUBENRAUCH and his partner in the fifties. ¶ NYCD 1860; NYBD 1854–57.

STUBENRAUCH, CHARLES. Engraver and die sinker, NYC, 1854–58; St. Louis, 1859. AUGUSTUS STUBENRAUCH probably was his brother and partner in NYC. ¶ NYBD 1854–58; St. Louis CD and BD 1859.

STUCKEN, FERDINAND (?–1878). Portrait and historical painter; at Düsseldorf (Germany) in 1848; at NYC 1856 and after; exhibited at the National Academy. ¶ Thieme-Becker; Cowdrey, NAD; NYBD 1856–60.

STURDEVANT, S. Portrait engraver, active about 1822, possibly at Lexington (Ky.). ¶ Fielding's supplement to Stauffer.

STURDEVANT, THOMAS. Artist, 22, a native of Pennsylvania, at Philadelphia in 1860; apparently the son of Elizabeth and the late Joseph Sturdevant. Listed only in 1861 directory. ¶ 8 Census (1860), Pa., LI, 555; Phila. CD 1861.

STURDIVANT, H. M. Seal engraver, Philadelphia, 1857–60; in 1857 of STURDIVANT & MAAS. ¶ Phila. CD 1857–60; BD 1858–59, as M. M. Sturdivant.

STURDIVANT & MAAS. Engravers, Philadelphia, 1857; probably H. M. STURDIVANT and the printer WILLIAM MAAS. ¶ Phila. CD 1857.

STURGEON, J. V. Miniaturist at NYC in 1833, when he exhibited at the American Academy, and at Charleston in 1835 and 1836. ¶ Cowdrey, AA & AAU; Rutledge, *Artists in the Life of Charleston.*

STURN, HERMANN. Of SNYDER, BLACK & STURN, lithographers, NYC, 1854–72. ¶ NYCD 1854–72.

STYLES, D. Portrait and landscape painter at NYC, exhibited at the National Academy between 1848 and 1852. ¶ Cowdrey, NAD.

SUAW, see DU SUAW.

SULLIVAN, CHARLES (1794–1867). Portrait, landscape, and historical painter, born August 16, 1794, at Frankford (Pa.). After studying under THOMAS SULLY, Sullivan painted in and around Philadelphia and spent several winters in Georgia and Tennessee. In 1827 he moved to Wheeling (Va., now W. Va.) and in 1833 he settled permanently in Marietta (Ohio), where he died on November 26, 1867. ¶ Reiter, "Charles Sullivan (1794–1867)"; Clark, *Ohio Art and Artists,* 104–06; Rutledge, PA.

SULLIVAN, JOHN. Artist, 26, born in Germany, at NYC in 1850. ¶ 7 Census (1850), N.Y., XLVI, 823.

SULLIVAN, OWEN (?–1756). Engraver; had his ears cropped and cheeks branded for counterfeiting at Providence (R.I.) in 1752; hanged at NYC in May 1756 for a repetition of the same offense. ¶ Dow, *Arts and Crafts in New England,* 13.

SULLY, ALFRED (1820–1879). Amateur watercolorist, born in Philadelphia May 22, 1820, a son of THOMAS SULLY. He graduated from West Point in 1841 and had a long and distinguished military career which included service during both the Mexican and Civil Wars, as Quartermaster at Monterey (Cal.) from 1848 to 1852, and as commander of an expedition against the Indians in the Northwest in 1865. His known works include a view of Monterey in 1847 and a series of views of forts in Minnesota in the fifties. He died April 27, 1879. ¶ Hart, *Register of Portraits,* 14; Van Nostrand and Coulter, *California Pictorial,* 50–51; information courtesy Bertha Heilbron, Minn. Hist. Soc.

SULLY, BLANCHE (1814–1898). Amateur painter and sketcher, born in Philadelphia August 13, 1814, a daughter of THOMAS SULLY. She was her father's companion on several of his painting trips, notably on his trip to England in 1838 to paint the portrait of Queen Victoria. She was also with him at Charleston in 1841, when she made some sketches of Charleston scenes. Miss Sully spent most of her life in Philadelphia and died April 30, 1898. ¶ Hart, *Register of Portraits,* 13; Biddle and Fielding, *Life and Works of Thomas Sully,* 49–52; Rutledge, *Artists in the Life of Charleston,* 151, 163.

SULLY, ELLEN OLDMIXON (1816–1896). Amateur painter, born January 22, 1816, at Philadelphia, a daughter of THOMAS SULLY. She was married in 1836 to John Hill Wheeler and died August 6, 1896. The Historical Society of Pennsylvania owns her copies of her father's portraits of Charles Carroll of Carrollton and Bishop William White. ¶ Hart, *Register of Portraits,* 14; Sawitzky, *Hist. Soc. of Pa. Cat.*

SULLY, JANE COOPER, see JANE COOPER (SULLY) DARLEY.

SULLY, LAWRENCE (1769–1804). Miniaturist and fancy painter, born December 28, 1769, in Kilkenny (Ireland), elder brother of THOMAS SULLY. Trained as a miniaturist in England, he accompanied his parents to America in 1792 and established himself at Richmond (Va.). There he remained, except for a brief residence in Norfolk (1801–02) and occasional visits to Annapolis and Philadelphia, until his death in the summer or fall of 1804. His brother Thomas, who had studied under Lawrence for a time, married his widow and brought up his brother's children, including Mary Chester Sully who married JOHN NEAGLE. ¶ *Richmond Portraits,* 232–33; Hart, *Register of Portraits,* 11; Prime, II, 33.

SULLY, ROBERT MATTHEW (1803–1855). Portrait and miniature painter, born July 17, 1803, at Petersburg (Va.) a nephew of THOMAS SULLY. He studied under his uncle and later in England, where he exhibited at the Royal Academy (1825–27). In 1831–32 he was working in Philadelphia, Richmond, and Washington, but thereafter he seems to have worked mainly in Richmond; his work was exhibited in Philadelphia, Boston, and New York. He died in Buffalo (N.Y.), October 16, 1855, on his way to Madison (Wis.). ¶ Hart, *Register of Portraits,* 11; Bolton, *Miniature Painters;* Graves, *Dictionary;* Rutledge, PA; Cowdrey, NAD; Cowdrey, AA & AAU; Swan, BA; Wisconsin State Hist. Soc., *Historical Collections,* II, 68 (citation courtesy Benton H. Wilcox, Librarian).

SULLY, ROSALIE KEMBLE (1818–1847). Amateur miniaturist, born in Philadelphia June 3, 1818, a daughter of THOMAS SULLY. Exhibited five landscapes at the Apollo Association in 1839. She died July 8, 1847, at Philadelphia. ¶ Hart, *Register of Portraits,* 14; Bolton, *Miniature Painters;* Cowdrey, AA & AAU.

SULLY, THOMAS (1783–1872). Portrait, miniature, and figure painter, born June 19, 1783, at Horncastle, Lincolnshire (England), the youngest son of Matthew and Sarah Chester Sully, actors. He was brought by them to Charleston in 1792 and there he grew up. Receiving his first lessons in painting from his brother-in-law JEAN BELZONS and his own brother LAWRENCE SULLY, he began his independent career at Norfolk and Richmond (Va.) in 1801. In 1805 he married his brother's widow and moved from Richmond to NYC. Two years later he moved on to Hartford and Boston, but in 1808 he settled permanently in Philadelphia. After a year's study in London under WEST (1809–10), Sully quickly became the leading portrait painter of Philadelphia and he held that position until his death. In 1838 he went to England again to paint a portrait of the young Queen Victoria; he also made occasional professional visits to Baltimore, Boston, Washington, Charleston, Providence, and Richmond. He died in Philadelphia on November 5, 1872, in his ninetieth year. Of his nine children, six survived infancy and all were either amateur or professional artists, while one of his step-daughters married the portrait painter JOHN NEAGLE. ¶ Hart, *A Register of Portraits Painted by Thomas Sully;* Biddle and Fielding, *Life and Works of Thomas Sully;* Rutledge, PA; Graves, *Dictionary;* Cowdrey, NAD;

Rutledge, MHS; Swan, BA; Cowdrey, AA & AAU; *Richmond Portraits;* Karolik Cat.; Penna. Acad., *Catalogue of Memorial Exhibition of Portraits by Thomas Sully;* Sully, "Recollections of an Old Painter"; Flexner, *The Light of Distant Skies;* Ormsbee, "The Sully Portraits at West Point."

SULLY, THOMAS WILCOCKS (1811–1847). Portrait and miniature painter, born at Philadelphia January 3, 1811, a son of THOMAS SULLY. Active in Philadelphia during the thirties and forties, sometimes known as Thomas Sully, Jr. was an exhibitor at the Pennsylvania Academy and Artists' Fund Society. He died in Philadelphia April 18, 1847. ¶ Hart, *Register of Portraits,* 13; Rutledge, PA; Phila. CD 1841–47; Bolton, *Miniature Painters;* Thieme-Becker.

SUMMERVILLE, STEPHEN. Engraver; born in England about 1814; left England after 1841; at NYC in 1850; at Boston 1855–56; at Philadelphia 1860–71. ¶ 7 Census (1850), N.Y., XLI, 692; 8 Census (1860), Pa., LXII, 339; NYBD 1850; Boston CD 1855, BD 1855–56; Phila. CD 1871.

SUMNER, WILLIAM H. Of EMERY N. MOORE & COMPANY, printers, engravers, and lithographers at Boston, 1857–58. ¶ Boston CD 1857–58.

SUPLEE, ANDREW CALLENDER. Engraver, born in Philadelphia about 1829, the son of Jonas Suplee, carpenter. He was active from 1850 and listed variously as watch engraver, copperplate and steel engraver, letter and ornamental engraver, and general engraver. ¶ 7 Census (1860), Pa., LI, 76; 8 Census (1860), Pa., LXII, 319; Phila. CD 1850–60+.

SURIA, TOMAS. Artist on the Malaspina expedition which visited California in September 1791. A sketch of the Presidio at Monterey, now in the Naval Museum at Madrid, may be his work. ¶ *Antiques* (Nov. 1953), 371.

SURVILLIERS, Comtesse de, see CHARLOTTE BONAPARTE.

SUTLIPP, HENRY. English engraver, 36, at NYC in 1850. His wife was French; their three children (10 to 1) were born in New York. ¶ 7 Census (1850), N.Y., LVII, 124.

SUTTON, W. Painter of a portrait of a girl with a music book, about 1820. Lipman and Winchester list two artists by this name, both portrait painters, one active about 1840 and the other about 1850. ¶ Information courtesy Harry Stone of NYC; Lipman and Winchester, 180.

SUYDAM, HENRY. Landscape painter, brother of JAMES A. SUYDAM. He lived in NYC and exhibited at the Washington Art Association in 1859. A number of his canvases are owned by members of the family. ¶ Baur, "A Tonal Realist: James Suydam," 226; Washington Art Assoc. Cat., 1859.

SUYDAM, JAMES AUGUSTUS (1819–1865). N.A. Landscape painter, born in NYC March 27, 1819. He turned to painting after a decade in business with his brother John R. Suydam, studied under MINOR C. KELLOGG, and accompanied his teacher on a tour of Greece and Asia Minor probably in the mid-fifties. After his return Suydam was a frequent exhibitor at the National Academy, a Member from 1861, and Treasurer at the time of his death, which occurred September 15, 1865, at North Conway (N.H.). Suydam left to the Academy $50,000 and his collection of paintings by American and European artists. ¶ Baur, "A Tonal Realist: James Suydam"; Tuckerman, *Book of the Artists;* Clement and Hutton; CAB; Cowdrey, NAD; Swan, BA; N. Y. *Evening Post,* Sept. 16, 18, 1865; NYCD 1843–65.

SVININ, PAVEL PETROVITCH (1787/88–1839). Genre, landscape, and portrait painter in watercolors. Born in Russia either June 8, 1787 (Yarmolinsky) or June 19, 1788 (White), Svinin was educated at a school for the nobility in Moscow and studied drawing at the Academy of Fine Arts of St. Petersburg, of which he later was elected an Academician. He entered the service of the Foreign Office and in 1811 came to America as secretary to the Russian Consul-General, with headquarters at Philadelphia. During his two years in the United States Svinin traveled much from Maine to Virginia and made over fifty watercolors of American scenes, now owned by the Metropolitan Museum of Art. After his return to Russia Svinin published his *A Picturesque Voyage in North America,* as well as books on the Mediterranean and England. From 1818 to 1830 he was also the editor of a patriotic magazine, traveled widely in Russia, and wrote on many subjects. He died in St. Petersburg on April 21, 1839. ¶ A sketch of his life by Abraham Yarmolinsky, as well as reproductions of Svinin's American watercolors, are included in Yarmolinsky, ed., *Picturesque United States of America,*

1811, 1812, 1813 (New York, 1930). A more recent account of Svinin is White, "A Russian Sketches Philadelphia, 1811–1813." See also Rutledge, PA; *American Processional.*

SWAIM & CLARK. Portrait painters, South Bend (Ind.), 1860; CURRAN SWAIM and —— CLARK. ¶ Indiana BD 1860.

SWAIM, CURRAN (1826–1897). Portrait painter, born February 3, 1826, in Randolph County (N.C.). He was active at South Bend (Ind.) from 1856 to 1869 and in McHenry County (Ill.) from 1869 to 1878, and died September 1, 1897, in Jasper County (Mo.). Of SWAIM & CLARK, South Bend, 1860. ¶ Peat, *Pioneer Painters of Indiana;* Indiana BD 1860.

SWAIN, ——. Engraver whose work appeared in *Our World: or, The Slaveholder's Daughter* (N.Y., 1855). ¶ Hamilton, *Early American Book Illustrators and Wood Engravers,* 437.

SWAIN, Miss C. Exhibited a crayon portrait and other portraits at the Boston Athenaeum between 1860 and 1865. ¶ Swan, BA.

SWAIN, HARRIET. Portrait painter in watercolors, Nantucket (Mass.), 1830. Possibly related to WILLIAM SWAIN who was at Nantucket in 1828. ¶ Lipman and Winchester, 180.

SWAIN, ROLAND T. Delineator of the ship *Phebe,* January 23, 1835, for Orin A. Beebe, Greenport, Long Island (N.Y.). ¶ Taylor Collection of Ship Portraits in the Peabody Museum of Salem, *Catalogue,* no. 97.

SWAIN, WILLIAM (1803–1847). A.N.A. Portrait painter, born December 27, 1803. He was working in Nantucket in 1828, at New Bedford and Newburyport (Mass.) in 1830, and in NYC from 1833 to 1839. In 1836 he was elected an Associate of the National Academy. He was at Norfolk (Va.) in 1841 but went abroad the same year. After his return he was in NYC from 1844 to 1846 and he died in Norfolk on February 18, 1847. He was the grandfather of the noted Pennsylvania artist, Violet Oakley. ¶ Belknap, *Artists and Craftsmen of Essex County,* 13; Boston Athenaeum Cat., 1828; Cowdrey, NAD; NYCD 1834, 1837, 1839; NYBD 1846.

SWASEY, WILLIAM F. Amateur artist known only for a drawing of San Francisco made in the 1840's and lithographed in 1886. He was a native of Maine who went to California in 1845 and worked for Sutter and Thomas Larkin. After service in California during the Mexican War he settled in San Francisco and was elected secretary to the Town Council. ¶ Van Nostrand and Coulter, *California Pictorial,* 48; Peters, *California on Stone.*

SWAYNE, WILLIAM MARSHALL (1828–1918). Sculptor. Born December 1, 1828, in Pennsbury Township, Chester County (Pa.); modeled his first bust in 1850. He moved to Washington (D.C.) in 1859 and executed busts of Lincoln and others before returning to Chester County about 1862. He died in Chester County in 1918. ¶ Pleasants, *Yesterday in Chester County Art;* "Works by William Marshall Swayne," in *Chester County Collections,* XVI (1939), 503–04; 8 Census (1860), D.C., II, 375.

SWEENEY, DENNIS. Irish engraver, 28, at Boston in 1850. ¶ 7 Census (1850), Mass., XXV, 539; Boston CD 1851.

SWEENEY, THOMAS T. Engraver, NYC, 1854. ¶ NYBD 1854.

SWEENY, ROBERT O. (1831–1902). Artist of a number of scenes in Minnesota about 1852. Possibly the R. O. Sweeny, portrait painter, listed in Philadelphia in 1860. ¶ Information courtesy Bertha L. Heilbron, Minnesota Historical Society; Phila. CD 1860; Heilbron, "Pioneer Homemaker," two repros. of St. Paul scenes.

SWEET, SILAS A. Engraver, 33, a native of Maine, at Boston in 1850 with his wife and four children. ¶ 7 Census (1850), Mass., XXVI, 43.

SWEET, SIMEON. Ohio-born portrait painter, 24, at Cincinnati in 1850. ¶ 7 Census (1850), Ohio, XXI, 1027.

SWEET, WILLIAM. Portrait painter who worked at Urbana (Ohio) and died in 1840. Possibly the same as the young portrait painter named Sweet who is said to have died at Springfield (Ohio) in 1843. ¶ *Antiques* (March 1932), 152; Martin, "The City of Springfield," 493.

SWEEZEY, NELSON. Sculptor and designer of monuments, NYC, 1849–52. ¶ NYBD 1849–52.

SWETT, CYRUS A. Engraver; at Portland (Me.) in 1839; at Boston, 1849–after 1860. ¶ Stauffer; Fielding's supplement to Stauffer; Boston BD and CD 1849–60+.

SWETT, MOSES. Lithographer. He began in Boston in 1826 and worked there with the PENDLETONS and ANNIN & SMITH and in 1828–29 as superintendent of the SENEFELDER LITHOGRAPHIC CO. From 1830 to 1836 he was in NYC, working chiefly with GEORGE ENDICOTT. In 1837 he was working at Washington (D.C.). ¶ Peters, *America on Stone;* NYCD 1832–36; *Portfolio* (Aug. 1948), 6–7, and (Dec. 1948), back cover.

SWETT & POWERS. Engravers and lithographers, Boston, 1851; probably CYRUS A. SWETT and JAMES T. POWERS. ¶ Boston BD 1851.

SWIFT, ANN WATERMAN. Painter of a romantic scene in watercolors, Poughkeepsie (N.Y.), about 1810. ¶ Lipman and Winchester, 181.

SWINTON, ALFRED (1826–1920). Wood engraver, painter, and illustrator. A native of England, Swinton was working in NYC as early as 1851; the following year he was in partnership with AUGUSTUS FAY. Best known for his Civil War subjects. Died October 3, 1920, at Hackensack (N.J.). ¶ *Art Annual,* XVIII, obit.; Am. Inst. Cat., 1851; NYCD 1852–54.

SWINTON & FAY. Wood engravers, NYC, 1852–55; ALFRED SWINTON and AUGUSTUS FAY. ¶ NYCD 1852–53; Hamilton, *Early American Book Illustrators and Wood Engravers,* 233, 383.

SWINTON, FREDERICK. Of Staten Island (N.Y.), exhibited four watercolor drawings at the American Institute in 1842. Probably the same as: F. J. Swinton of Staten Island, who exhibited still life and animal paintings at the National Academy in 1837 and the Apollo Association in 1839; F. I. Swinton, lithographer of two caricatures after J. MAZE BURBANK about 1840; and F. Swinton of NYC or Albany who lithographed some of the plates in the ENDICOTTS' "Life in California" (1846). For this last, *American Processional* gives the dates (1821–1910). ¶ Am. Inst. Cat., 1842; Cowdrey, NAD; Cowdrey, AA & AAU; *Portfolio* (Jan. 1954), 104; Peters, *California on Stone; American Processional,* 242.

SWIRE, O. L. Painter of a portrait of an unidentified girl, owned by the Pennsylvania Academy. ¶ WPA (Pa.), "Cat. of Portraits in the Penna. Acad."

SWORD, JAMES BRADE (1839–1915). Portrait painter, born October 11, 1839, in Philadelphia. After leaving high school in Philadelphia in 1855, he took up civil engineering and worked on various canal and tunnel projects until he turned professional artist about 1863. He was prominent in several artistic organizations in Philadelphia, where most of his career was spent. He died in Philadelphia on December 1, 1915. ¶ Fairman, *Art and Artists of the Capitol,* 466; *Art Annual,* XIII, obit.; *American Collector* (Oct. 1945), 14; represented in U. S. Capitol and University of Pennsylvania.

SWYNEY, JOHN. Delineator of a locomotive engine built at the Globe Locomotive Works in Boston in 1854, lithographed by J. H. BUFFORD. ¶ *Portfolio* (Jan. 1945), 104.

SYKES, JOHN (1773–1858). Topographical artist. Born in England, Sykes entered the Royal Navy as a boy and in 1792 served as artist on Vancouver's voyage of discovery in the North Pacific, 1792–94. His sketches are in the possession of the Hydrographic Office of the Admiralty; three of his California views appeared in Vancouver's 1798 report. Sykes later saw action in the Napoleonic wars, was made rear admiral in 1838, and admiral shortly before his death in 1858. ¶ Van Nostrand and Coulter, *California Pictorial,* 8–10; Rasmussen, "Art and Artists in Oregon" (citation courtesy David C. Duniway).

SYKES, LYMAN R. Artist, 30, born in Massachusetts, at New London (Conn.) in 1850; his mother and 18-year-old brother were natives of Vermont. ¶ 7 Census (1850), Conn., X, 259.

SYMES, JOHN (?–1888). Landscape and portrait painter who settled at Niagara Falls (N.Y.) in 1847 and had a studio there for many years. He was also deputy postmaster for a time and captain of the excursion steamer *Maid of the Mist.* He died at Suspension Bridge, now part of Niagara Falls, on April 28, 1888. ¶ Information courtesy Orrin E. Dunlap (letter to NYHS, Oct. 28, 1945).

SYMMES, PEYTON S. Profiles in pencil, Cincinnati, 1840. ¶ Information courtesy Edward H. Dwight, Cincinnati Art Museum.

SYMON, see SIMON.

T

Taber, ——. Ornamental, sign, and house painter, Charleston (S.C.), 1837. ¶ Rutledge, *Artists in the Life of Charleston.*

Taggart, John G. Portrait and historical painter; at Albany (N.Y.), 1846–49; at Saratoga Springs (N.Y.), 1852; at NYC, 1853–64. ¶ Albany CD 1846–48; Cowdrey, NAD; NYCD 1853–60; NYHS Cat. (1941).

Tailor, Stephen. Exhibited a painting of the steamship *Atlantic* at the American Institute in 1847; his address was Pier 1, North River, NYC. ¶ Am. Inst. Cat., 1847.

Tailor, see also Taylor.

Tait, Arthur Fitzwilliam (1819–1905). N.A. Painter of sporting scenes and animals. Born August 5, 1819, at Livesey Hall, near Liverpool (England), Tait went to work in a picture store in Manchester as a boy and studied art on the side. In 1850 he emigrated to America and settled in NYC. Most of his summers were spent at his camp in the Adirondacks. His paintings of sporting scenes were very popular and many were lithographed by Currier & Ives. Tait was elected to full membership in the National Academy in 1858. He died April 28, 1905, at his home in Yonkers (N.Y.). ¶ DAB; Peters, *Currier & Ives,* I, 99–110; Keyes, "A. F. Tait in Painting and Lithograph"; Cowdrey, "Arthur Fitzwilliam Tait"; Cowdrey, NAD; Swan, BA; Cowdrey, AA & AAU; Rutledge, PA; Washington Art Assoc. Cat., 1859.

Tait, John Robinson (1834–1909). Landscape painter, born January 14, 1834, at Cincinnati (Ohio). After graduating from Bethany College (Va.) in 1852, he went to Europe for three years to write and sketch as an amateur. He went to Europe again in 1859 to study painting at Düsseldorf and remained for twelve years; in 1873 he made a third visit to Germany. In 1876 he settled permanently at Baltimore (Md.), where he died July 29, 1909. ¶ CAB; *Art Annual,* VII, obit.; Rutledge, PA; Clark, *Ohio Art and Artists,* 494; represented at Peabody Institute, Baltimore.

Taite, Augustus. Portrait in oils, Albany (N.Y.), about 1840. ¶ Lipman and Winchester, 181.

Talbot, Jesse (1806–1879). A.N.A. Landscape, portrait, and figure painter, born in 1806 (Bénézit) or 1807 (Smith). He began to exhibit in NYC in 1838 and was active at least until 1860; in 1842 he was elected an Associate Member of the National Academy. His address was NYC during most of this period, except for 1844–47 when he was living in Paterson (N.J.). His landscapes were scenes chiefly in New York, New Jersey, and New England. ¶ Bénézit; Smith; Cowdrey, NAD; Cowdrey, AA & AAU; Rutledge, PA; Hinton, *History and Topography; Home Book of the Picturesque.*

Talbot, Marshall. Exhibited crayon portraits at the Pennsylvania Academy in 1856; address, Philadelphia. ¶ Rutledge, PA.

Talcott, William. Portrait painter working in Massachusetts between 1820 and 1846. ¶ WPA (Mass.), *Portraits Found in Mass.,* II, 543; represented at American Antiquarian Society (Weis).

Talen, W. A. Sculptor and carver at New Orleans from 1858 to 1866. ¶ New Orleans CD 1858, 1860–61, 1866.

Tannen, ——. Copperplate engraver whose work appeared in *The Pleasures of Memory and Other Poems* (N.Y., 1802). Probably Benjamin Tanner. ¶ Hamilton, *Early American Book Illustrators and Wood Engravers,* 86.

Tanner, Benjamin (1775–1848). Engraver, born March 27, 1775, in NYC. After serving his apprenticeship under Peter C. Verger, he worked in NYC until 1799, then moved to Philadelphia where he lived until shortly before his death. He was the teacher of Henry S. Tanner, his younger brother, and also established two engraving firms: Tanner, Kearney & Tiebout, banknote engravers, 1817–24, and Tanner, Vallance, Kearney & Co., general engravers, 1818–20. In 1835 he gave up general engraving to produce check and note blanks by a process he had invented and called stereographing. He retired in 1845 and died in Baltimore on November 14, 1848. ¶ DAB; NYCD 1794–99; Phila. CD 1800–45; Rutledge, PA; Stauffer; Dunlap, *History,* II, 47; *American Collector* (April 1942), 3; *Panorama* (Feb. 1947), cover.

Tanner, Henry Schenck (1786–1858). Engraver and mapmaker, born in NYC in

1786, a younger brother of BENJAMIN TANNER, from whom he learned engraving. He was active in Philadelphia from about 1811 to 1850, did some general engraving, but was best known for his excellent work as a cartographer. His *New American Atlas,* published in five parts between 1818 and 1823, is still regarded as a model. He retired to New York in 1850 and died in Brooklyn on May 17, 1858. ¶ DAB; N. Y. *Evening Post,* May 18, 1858; Phila. CD 1811–43; Dunlap, *History* (1918).

TANNER, JESSE. Engraver, Philadelphia, 1803. This may be a printer's error for BENJAMIN TANNER. ¶ Phila. CD 1803.

TANNER, KEARNEY & TIEBOUT. Banknote engravers, Philadelphia, 1817–24; BENJAMIN and HENRY S. TANNER, FRANCIS KEARNEY, and CORNELIUS TIEBOUT. ¶ Phila. CD 1817–20; DAB, under Benjamin Tanner.

TANNER, VALLANCE, KEARNEY & COMPANY. General engravers, Philadelphia, 1817–19; BENJAMIN and HENRY S. TANNER, JOHN VALLANCE, and FRANCIS KEARNEY. Vallance apparently dropped out about 1819 and the firm was listed the following year as Tanner, Kearny & Co. ¶ Phila. CD 1818–19; Brown and Brown; DAB, under Benjamin Tanner.

TANSSEN, T. Painter of an 1831 view of Baltimore, owned by the Enoch Pratt Free Library of Baltimore. The painting was bought in Australia. ¶ Pleasants, *250 Years of Painting in Maryland,* 50–51.

TANTURIER, ——. Miniaturist from Paris at Philadelphia in 1794. ¶ Prime, II, 35.

TAPPAN & BRADFORD. Engravers and lithographers, Boston, 1849–54; EBENEZER TAPPAN and LODOWICK BRADFORD. ¶ Boston CD 1849–54.

TAPPAN, EBENEZER (1815–1854). Boston engraver, 1838–54; with the BOSTON BANK NOTE COMPANY, 1841–42, and TAPPAN & BRADFORD, 1849–54. He was born in Manchester (Mass.) September 11, 1815, and died January 25, 1854. He was a brother of GEORGE H. and WILLIAM H. TAPPAN. ¶ Tappan, *Tappan-Toppan Genealogy,* 49; Boston CD 1838–54.

TAPPAN, GEORGE HOOPER (1833–1865). Boston engraver, 1855–65; with SMITH & KNIGHT, 1857–59. He was born in Manchester (Mass.) on November 10, 1833, and died May 11, 1865. EBENEZER and WILLIAM H. TAPPAN were his brothers. ¶ Tappan, *Tappan-Toppan Genealogy,* 49; Boston CD 1855–59.

TAPPAN, WILLIAM HENRY (1821–1907). Topographical artist and engraver, born in Manchester (Mass.), October 30, 1821. After working in Boston during the early 1840's, he went out to Lake Superior in 1848 as a member of Louis Agassiz's expedition and the following year he went to Oregon. Fifty drawings made by him on this trip are now in the Wisconsin Historical Society. He settled in Clark County in the present state of Washington and in 1854 served on the first Territorial Council. Tappan returned to his native Manchester in 1876. He served in the Massachusetts Legislature and Senate during the eighties and was the author of a history of Manchester. He died on January 22, 1907. ¶ Tappan, *Tappan-Toppan Genealogy,* 49–50; Settle, *The March of the Mounted Riflemen,* foreword; Boston BD 1844–47; Rasmussen, "Artists of the Explorations Overland, 1840–1860," 61. Stauffer confuses W. H. Tappan with his brother GEORGE H. TAPPAN; EBENEZER TAPPAN also was his brother.

TARBELL, EDMUND N. Wood engraver, born in New York about 1831. He was working in NYC in 1854 and in Boston from 1857 to 1860. In 1860 he was a boarder in the house of HAMMATT BILLINGS. ¶ 8 Census (1860), Mass., XXVIII, 645; NYBD 1854; Boston BD 1857–60.

TATNALL, HENRY LEA (1829–1885). Landscape and marine painter, born December 31, 1829, at Brandywine Village (Del.). At first a farmer and lumber merchant, he moved to Wilmington in 1856 and soon after opened a studio there, where he painted marines and landscapes which met with great popular success. Tatnall was called the father of Delaware art and was elected first President of the Delaware Artists' Association. He died in Wilmington September 26, 1885. ¶ CAB.

TATTERSALL, GEORGE (1817–1849). Landscape and animal painter, architect. Born June 13, 1817, at Hyde Park Corner, London, he was a son of the founder of Tattersall's, London's famous horse-auction house. George was a talented draftsman and watercolorist and became an architect. At the age of 18 he illustrated a guide to the English Lakes. In 1836 he visited America and filled a portfolio with watercolor sketches of American scenes; this portfolio was owned by the Old Print Shop in 1948. Under the penname, "Wildrake," he subsequently became a well-known writer and illustrator of books on sporting architecture, horses, and hunting. He died in London in 1849. ¶ DNB; information courtesy Old Print Shop.

TAYLER, JOHN. Engraver, NYC, 1843–44, 1847–48. ¶ NYCD 1843–44, 1847–48; NYBD 1844.

TAYLOR, ——. Miniaturist at Philadelphia in 1760. ¶ Bolton, *Miniature Painters.*

TAYLOR, ——. Painter of "An American Slave Market," dated 1852. ¶ Met. Mus., *Life in America.*

TAYLOR, A. M. Watercolor landscape, New York State, about 1825. ¶ Lipman and Winchester, 181.

TAYLOR & ADAMS. Wood engravers and designers, Boston, 1850–60 and after; JAMES L. TAYLOR and THOMAS W. ADAMS. ¶ Boston CD 1850–60+.

TAYLOR, ALEXANDER H. Portrait painter, NYC, 1849–50. An artist by this name exhibited two genre paintings at the Artists' Fund Society in Philadelphia in 1840. He was born in England about 1820. ¶ NYBD 1849–50; Rutledge, PA; 7 Census (1850), N.Y., XLI, 230.

TAYLOR, BAKER. Wood engraver and job printer of Albany (N.Y.), 1855–60. ¶ Ford, "Some Trade Cards and Broadsides," 12, repro.

TAYLOR, BAYARD (1825–1878). Landscape painter; best known as an author and traveler. Born January 11, 1825, at Kennett Square (Pa.), he was apprenticed to a printer, but at the age of 19 published a first volume of poems and bought his remaining time in order to become a journalist. In 1844 he made his first visit to Europe as a traveling correspondent for several newspapers; on subsequent travels he visited and wrote articles and books about California, the Near and Far East, Africa, Russia, etc. His books were sometimes illustrated with his own landscape sketches, some of which he also exhibited at the National Academy. He also published many volumes of verse, novels, and a very successful translation of Goethe's *Faust.* Taylor was named Minister to Germany in 1878, but died in Germany on December 19, 1878. ¶ DAB cites several biographies; Cowdrey, NAD; *Yesterday in Chester County Art;* Perry, *Expedition to Japan;* Van Nostrand and Coulter, *California Pictorial,* 122; *Art in America* (April 1940), 76.

TAYLOR, CHARLES RYALL. Painter in oils, about 1860. ¶ Lipman and Winchester, 181.

TAYLOR, ELIZA ANN. Shaker artist, New Lebanon (N.Y.), 1845. ¶ Lipman and Winchester, 181.

TAYLOR, H. M. Pencil drawing of a schoolhouse in Delaware, about 1850. ¶ Lipman and Winchester, 181.

TAYLOR, JAMES. Artist, 24, a native of Wales, at NYC in 1860. ¶ 8 Census (1860), N.Y., LVI, 959.

TAYLOR, JAMES EARL (1839–1901). Painter and illustrator of the West, born December 12, 1839, at Cincinnati. He graduated from Notre Dame at the age of 16, painted a Revolutionary War panorama two years later, and in 1861 joined the Union Army. In 1863 he became an artist-correspondent for *Leslie's.* After the Civil War he went West on many occasions to portray the Indians and frontier life on the Great Plains. He left *Leslie's* in 1883 to work independently as an illustrator and watercolorist. He died June 22, 1901, in NYC. ¶ Taft, *Artists and Illustrators of the Old West,* 297; *Art Annual,* IV, obit.

TAYLOR, JAMES L. Wood engraver and designer, born in Massachusetts about 1831; active in Boston from 1850 to after 1860 as a member of the firm of TAYLOR & ADAMS. ¶ Boston CD 1850–60+; 7 Census (1850), Mass., XXIV, 436.

TAYLOR, JOHN (*c.* 1745–1806). Landscape painter of Bath (England) who was described in 1783 in a Philadelphia newspaper as "a native of this city." English sources give Bath as Taylor's birthplace. He studied in London and was popular for his landscapes with figures and cattle. He died in Bath, November 8, 1806. ¶ Prime, I, 10; DNB; Redgrave, *Dictionary of Artists of the English School.*

TAYLOR, JUDE. Of PAYNE & TAYLOR, engravers at Pawtucket (R.I.) in 1857. ¶ Pawtucket and Woonsocket BD 1857.

TAYLOR, N. H. Engraver, Chillicothe (Ohio), 1853. ¶ Ohio BD 1853.

TAYLOR, PETER. Engraver, Lowell (Mass.), 1834–37. ¶ Belknap, *Artists and Craftsmen of Essex County,* 5.

TAYLOR, T. Engraver of landscapes published in NYC in 1860. ¶ Stauffer.

TAYLOR, THOMAS. Artist, 43, a native of New York, at NYC in 1860. This may be the Thomas Taylor listed in city directories as "flowers" or "art flowers." ¶ 8 Census (1860), N.Y., LVIII, 274; NYCD 1855–63.

TAYLOR, W. H. Painter of a view, about 1850, of the Manning homestead near New Brunswick (N.J.). The painting is now in the possession of the New Brunswick chapter of the D.A.R. ¶ Information courtesy Donald A. Sinclair, Rutgers University.

TAYLOR, WALTER R. or S. Designer, born in England about 1813, active in Boston from 1848 to 1881. From 1867 to 1877 he was agent for a china and glass decorating factory. ¶ 7 Census (1850), Mass., XXV, 405; Boston CD 1848–81.

TAYLOR, WILLIAM (1764–1841). Miniature and landscape painter, born March 20, 1764. A graduate of Yale College, he taught school at New Milford (Conn.) and then became a merchant. He was an amateur artist; his 1790 portrait by RALPH EARL shows him sitting at an easel at work on a landscape. He died February 24, 1841. ¶ *Antiques* (Jan. 1933), 13; Dexter, *Yale Biographies and Annals, 1778–92* (citation courtesy the late William Sawitzky); *American Collector* (Nov. 1945), 12.

TAYLOR, WILLIAM. Ornamental painter, 21, a native of Ohio, at Pittsburgh (Pa.) in 1850. ¶ 7 Census (1850), Pa., III, 64.

TEEL, E. Engraver of portraits and landscapes, born in the United States about 1830. After working for NYC publishers he was employed in Cincinnati about 1854 and died before 1860 at Hoboken (N.J.). ¶ Stauffer.

TEISSEIRE, ARMAND. Portrait painter and teacher, San Francisco, 1856–78. ¶ San Francisco CD 1856–78.

TEJADA, M. S. DE. Miniaturist, New Orleans, 1843–44. ¶ Delgado-WPA cites New Orleans CD 1843–44.

TELFER, JOHN R. Wood engraver and designer, Cincinnati, 1850–58. ¶ Cincinnati CD 1850–58.

TELFER & LAWRIE. Engravers, Philadelphia, 1849; ROBERT TELFER and ALEXANDER LAWRIE. ¶ Phila. CD 1849.

TELFER, ROBERT. Wood engraver, Philadelphia, 1849–57; of TELFER & LAWRIE, 1849, and SCATTERGOOD & TELFER, 1852–54. ¶ Phila. CD 1849–57; Hamilton, *Early American Book Illustrators and Wood Engravers,* 151.

TEN BROECK, ALBERTINA (1760–1840). Cut and shaded silhouettes showing her father's "bouwerie" in Columbia County (N.Y.), probably in the 1770's or 1780's. She later married John Sanders of Scotia (N.Y.). ¶ Runk, *Ten Broeck Genealogy,* 68, 111–113, repros. on p. 26, 66.

TEN EYCK, RICHARD. Wood engraver, NYC, 1846–54; 1855–66 as "president" of unnamed company. He exhibited engravings at the American Institute. ¶ NYCD 1846–66; Am. Inst. Cat., 1846, 1850, 1851.

TEN EYCK, RICHARD, JR. Wood engraver, NYC, 1856–1903. ¶ NYCD 1856–1903; Am. Inst. Cat., 1847–48, possibly intended for RICHARD TEN EYCK, above.

TENNENT, W. Delineator of a view of Nassau Hall, Princeton (N.J.) in 1763, known through an engraving by HENRY DAWKINS. The artist may have been William Mackay Tennent (?–1810), a graduate of Princeton in 1763 and trustee from 1785 to 1808. ¶ Stokes, *Historical Prints,* pl. 19a; Princeton University, *General Catalogue, 1746–1906.*

TENNEY, ADNA (1810–1900). Portrait and miniature painter, born February 26, 1810, at Hanover (N.H.). Tenney was a farmer who turned to painting in his thirties, received a few weeks of training from FRANCIS ALEXANDER in Boston (1844), and worked as an itinerant artist in New Hampshire, as well as in NYC, Baltimore, and along the Mississippi (about 1856). He later moved to Winona (Minn.) and spent his last years at Oberlin (Ohio), where he died August 17, 1900. Examples of his work are at Dartmouth College and the State House, Concord (N.H.). ¶ Tenney, *The Tenney Family,* 230, repro. preceding 281; Boston BD 1857; New England BD 1860 (Concord, N.H.); information courtesy Mrs. Rowland M. Cross, NYC, grand-daughter of the artist.

TENNEY, M. B. Portrait painter in New England about 1840. ¶ Sears, *Some American Primitives,* 288.

TENNEY, ULYSSES DOW (1826–?). Portrait painter, born April 8, 1826, at Hanover (N.H.). After studying briefly under ADNA TENNEY (his uncle), ROSWELL T. SMITH, and FRANCIS ALEXANDER, he settled in Manchester (N.H.) in 1849 and remained there until 1864, with brief residences at nearby Concord and Hanover. After 1864 he resided in New Haven (Conn.), though he continued to do much of his work in New Hampshire. He was living in 1904. ¶ Tenney, *The Tenney Family,* 432–33; Manchester BD 1854–60.

TERIGGI or TERRIGGI, A. M., F. M., or A. F. Miniaturist and chalk artist who exhibited at the Pennsylvania Academy between 1820 and 1826; his address was given as Philadelphia only in 1824, when he exhibited a miniature portrait of the Comtesse de Survilliers (CHARLOTTE BONAPARTE). ¶ Rutledge, PA.

TERN, C. H. Landscape frescoes, Stoddard

(N.H.), about 1825. ¶ Lipman and Winchester, 181.

TERRELL or TERRYLL, RICHARD. Portrait painter working in Lexington (Ky.) in 1795 and later in Indiana. In 1825, at Madison he painted a life portrait of Lafayette. In 1828 he arrived in Indianapolis, where he was prepared to paint signs and banners as well as portraits. A few portraits survive. Nothing is known of his career after 1828. ¶ Peat, *Pioneer Painters of Indiana,* 57–58, 148–49, 239, repro. pl. 63; Burnet, *Art and Artists of Indiana,* 60.

TERRY, CLARISSA. Amateur painter in watercolors who lived at East Windsor (Conn.) and painted two views of Stafford Springs (Conn.) in 1816. ¶ *Portfolio* (April 1945), 188–89, repros.

TERRY, ELIPHALET (1826–1896). Animal and landscape painter, born July 2, 1826, in Hartford (Conn.). After studying in Rome under his cousin LUTHER TERRY (1846–47), he had a studio in Hartford for several years, but moved to NYC about 1851. He exhibited at the American Art-Union and the National Academy. ¶ Terry, *Notes of Terry Families,* 79; French, *Art and Artists in Connecticut,* 163; Cowdrey, NAD; Cowdrey, AA & AAU; NYBD 1851.

TERRY, LUTHER (1813–1869). Portrait and figure painter, born July 18, 1813, at Enfield (Conn.). A pupil of PHILIP HEWINS of Hartford, Terry went to Italy in 1837 and settled permanently in Rome the following year. He was an exhibitor at the American Art-Union, the Boston Athenaeum, and the National Academy and was elected an Honorary Member, Professional, of the latter in 1846. In 1861 he married the widow of THOMAS CRAWFORD, the sculptor. ¶ CAB; Cowdrey, NAD; Cowdrey, AA & AAU; Swan, BA; NYBD and CD 1846; Sherman, "Some Recently Discovered Early American Portrait Miniaturists," 294, 296 (repro.); represented at NYHS and MHS.

TERRY, PELTON & COMPANY. Banknote engravers, Boston, 1836–37; WILLIAM D. TERRY, OLIVER PELTON, and (in 1836) GEORGE G. SMITH. ¶ Boston CD 1836–37.

TERRY, WILLIAM D. Banknote engraver. He was working in Providence (R.I.) from 1830 to 1836; in 1836 he organized the Boston firm of TERRY, PELTON & CO., which lasted only until the next year; from 1838 to 1842 his whereabouts are unknown; and from 1843 to 1858 he was again working in Boston. Mrs. Terry is listed in 1859, which suggests that Terry died in the latter part of 1858 or early 1859. ¶ Providence CD 1830, 1832, 1836; Boston CD 1836–37, 1843–59; Stauffer.

TESCHMAKER, F. Artist of one of the ENDICOTTS' "Life in California" prints, published in 1846. Peters identifies the artist with Henry F. Teschemacher, who came to California about 1846 as a ship's clerk and remained to become a ship agent, real estate agent, and "capitalist." ¶ Peters, *California on Stone;* San Francisco CD 1854–82.

TESSIN, GERMAIN. French sculptor, 31, at New Orleans in 1860. ¶ 8 Census (1860), La., VI, 902.

TETLEY, WILLIAM BIRCHALL. Portrait and miniature painter; teacher of painting, drawing, and dancing. He came to NYC in 1774 from London. ¶ Gottesman, *Arts and Crafts in New York City,* I, 6–7.

TEUBNER, GEORGE W. Engraver, NYC, 1840–44. ¶ NYBD 1840–44.

TEUIL, VAL. Dutch artist who came to America about 1793 and worked in New Jersey for a few years before returning to Holland. His crayon portrait of Gerrit Boon of Trenton is at the Oneida Historical Society, Utica (N.Y.). ¶ WPA (Mass.), *Portraits Found in New York.*

TEULON, EDWARD A. Engraver, born in Nova Scotia about 1826, working in Boston from 1849 until after 1860. ¶ 7 Census (1850), Mass., XXV, 31; Boston CD 1849–60+.

TEULON, MATTHEW H. Engraver and printer, Boston, 1860 and after. ¶ Boston BD 1860 [as engraver]; Boston CD 1863 [as printer].

TEW, DAVID. Engraver, Philadelphia, 1785. ¶ Brown and Brown.

THACKARA, JAMES (1767–1848). Engraver and stationer of Philadelphia, born there March 12, 1767. From 1791 to about 1797 he was in partnership with JOHN VALLANCE. Later he worked with his son WILLIAM THACKARA. He was also Keeper of the Pennsylvania Academy after 1826. He died in Philadelphia August 15, 1848. ¶ Stauffer; Phila. CD 1791–1846; Hamilton, *Early American Book Illustrators and Wood Engravers,* 529.

THACKARA & VALLANCE. Engravers, Philadelphia, 1791–1797; JAMES THACKARA and JOHN VALLANCE. ¶ Phila. CD 1791–94; Prime, II, 74; Brown and Brown.

THACKARA, WILLIAM (1791–1839). Engraver, born in Philadelphia February 9, 1791, son of JAMES THACKARA. He was active as an engraver in Philadelphia from 1818 to 1824, part of that time in association with his father; after 1824 he was listed as a conveyancer. He died April 19, 1839. ¶ Stauffer; Phila. CD 1818–40.

THATCHER, GEORGE W. Wood engraver, born in New York about 1833. He exhibited at the American Institute in 1851, was listed as a wood engraver in 1854, and as an artist in the 1860 census. His personal property in 1860 was valued at $20,000. ¶ 8 Census (1860), N.Y., LVI, 697; Am. Inst. Cat., 1851; NYBD 1854.

THAYER, BENJAMIN W. Lithographer and engraver, Boston, 1841–53; his associates in Benjamin W. Thayer & Co. were JOHN H. BUFFORD and JOHN E. MOODY. In 1854 Thayer's occupation was given as broker. ¶ Boston CD 1841–54; Peters, *America on Stone.*

THAYER, HORACE (1811–?). Lithographer? Born June 29, 1811, in Hartwick (N.Y.), he came to NYC in 1845 from Warsaw (N.Y.) to become a partner of the KELLOGGS. The partnership was dissolved after about a year and Thayer went into the map-publishing business. In 1854 he went back to Warsaw where he had established a map-roller manufactory. In 1859 he returned to map-publishing in NYC but by 1864 was again in Warsaw. In 1866 he moved to the nearby village of Johnsonburg and he was still there in 1874. ¶ Young, *History of the Town of Warsaw,* 376; Thayer, *Memorial of the Thayer Name,* 240, 242; NYCD 1846–54, 1858–65; Peters, *America on Stone.*

THAYER, SANFORD (1820–1880). Portrait and genre painter; born July 19, 1820, at Cato (N.Y.); working in NYC in 1844, Syracuse in 1845, and Brooklyn in 1848; married in 1850 and settled in Syracuse where he lived until his death in December 1880. ¶ Thayer, *Memorial of the Thayer Name,* 490; Cowdrey, NAD; information courtesy Mr. Julian Denton Smith; Syracuse CD 1855+; *American Art Review,* I (1881), 169.

THEMMEN, CHARLES. Landscape painter at Springfield (Mass.) in 1856. Possibly the same as C. Themmer who had three paintings in the American Art-Union sale in 1852, two of them French scenes. ¶ New England BD 1856; Cowdrey, AA & AAU.

THEMMER, C., see CHARLES THEMMEN.

THETFORD, WILLIAM E. (1813–1903). Painter and art collector; born in London; came to the United States in 1836; died in Brooklyn November 23, 1903. ¶ *Art Annual,* V, obit.

THETEY, AUGUST. Portrait painter, 44, a native of Italy, at Cincinnati in 1850. ¶ 7 Census (1850), Ohio, XXII, 317.

THEURET, DOMINIQUE. Lithographer; born in France about 1812; active in New Orleans in 1837 and from 1849 to 1854. ¶ 7 Census (1850), La., V, 85; New Orleans CD 1837, 1849–54 (Delgado-WPA).

THEUS, JEREMIAH (*c.* 1719–1774). Portrait painter. Probably a native of Canton Grison (Switzerland), Theus came to South Carolina with his parents about 1735, settled in Charleston about 1739, and worked there as a limner and decorative painter until his death on May 17, 1774. Many of his portraits have been preserved. ¶ Middleton, *Jeremiah Theus, Colonial Artist of Charles Town,* is the standard study and contains a checklist and many illustrations.

THEW, ROBERT. English landscape engraver who came to America about 1850 and worked in NYC and Cincinnati until about 1860, when he returned to England. ¶ Stauffer.

THIBAULT, AIMÉE (1780–1868). A French miniaturist, born in Paris, who exhibited at the Salon from 1804 to 1810. She came to America about 1834 and worked for a short time in NYC, where she was known to the family of LOUIS F. BINSSE. She subsequently returned to France and died there in 1868. Several of her miniatures of New Yorkers are at the New-York Historical Society. ¶ Thieme-Becker; Bénézit; Dunlap, *History;* information courtesy Henry B. Binsse of Washington (D.C.); *Catalogue of the Belknap Collection.*

THIELCKE, HENRY D. Portrait painter. He was at NYC in 1842 when he exhibited at the National Academy and copied INMAN's portrait of John Watts, II (1749–1836). From 1855 to 1866 he was working in Chicago; his widow, Rebecca, was listed in 1878. ¶ Cowdrey, NAD; information courtesy Harry M. Allice, Montreal; Chicago BD 1855, CD 1855–66, 1878.

THIELE, CHARLES F. Engraver at Cleveland (Ohio) in 1857. ¶ Cleveland BD 1857.

THIERY BROTHERS (Charles and Edward). Engravers, San Francisco, 1858. Charles was listed as a jeweler in 1860 and enameler in 1868. ¶ San Francisco BD 1858; CD 1860, 1868.

THIERY, GUSTAVE. Wood engraver and/or

comedian, San Francisco, 1858. ¶ San Francisco BD and CD 1858.

THODE, C. C. Miniaturist and drawing master at Charleston (S.C.) in 1806. ¶ Rutledge, *Artists in the Life of Charleston.*

THOLEY, ——. Painter, pastel artist, engraver, and lithographer. He came to Philadelphia from Alsace-Lorraine in 1848, accompanied by his sons CHARLES and AUGUSTUS, who had been trained by him. They were employed by Philadelphia publishers and did some banknote work for the U. S. Government. The father may have been the Michael Tholey, painter, listed in directories from 1851 to 1856. ¶ Peters, *America on Stone;* Phila. CD 1851–56.

THOLEY, AUGUSTUS. Lithographer and pastel portraitist, son of the above. He came to Philadelphia in 1848 and worked there as a lithographer mainly, though he and his brother CHARLES later specialized in pastel portraits. Augustus died before 1898. ¶ Peters, *America on Stone.*

THOLEY, CHARLES P. (?–1898). Lithographer and pastel portraitist, son of —— THOLEY and brother of AUGUSTUS. He was working as a lithographer in Philadelphia at least by 1860; later he and Augustus gave up lithography to do portraits in pastels. ¶ Peters, *America on Stone;* Phila. CD 1860, 1870.

THOM, JAMES (1799–1850). Sculptor. A native of Ayrshire (Scotland), Thom exhibited at the British Institute in London as early as 1815. By 1834 he was in the United States, working in New Orleans, and after 1836 he made his home at Newark (N.J.) until he settled on a farm near Ramapo (N.J.). He died in NYC on April 17, 1850. His group illustrating Burns's "Tam O'Shanter" was owned by the Franklin Institute in Philadelphia and exhibited at the Pennsylvania Academy from 1850 to 1870. JAMES CRAWFORD THOM was his son. ¶ Bénézit; Graves, *Dictionary;* New Orleans *Courier,* March 22 and Oct. 7, 1834, and *Merchants' Daily News,* Feb. 27, 1834 (citations courtesy Delgado-WPA); Gardner, *Yankee Stonecutters;* Rutledge, PA.

THOM, JAMES CRAWFORD (1835–1898). Portrait, landscape, and genre painter, born in NYC, a son of JAMES THOM, the sculptor. He was active in NYC as early as 1857, when he first exhibited at the National Academy. From 1864 to 1873 he exhibited at the Royal Academy, his address given as Brentford (England). He also exhibited at the Boston Athenaeum and the Pennsylvania Academy. He died February 16, 1898, at Atlantic Highlands (N.J.). ¶ Smith; Thieme-Becker; Cowdrey, NAD; NYCD 1858–59; Graves, *Dictionary;* Swan, BA; Rutledge, PA.

THOMAS, AL. Painter of a portrait of Benjamin Hutton Devereux, about 1835, now at the Historical Society of Pennsylvania. ¶ Sawitzky, *Hist. Soc. of Pa. Cat.*

THOMAS, CHARLES. Engraver, 33, a native of Rhode Island, at NYC in 1850. ¶ 7 Census (1850), N.Y., XLVIII, 35.

THOMAS, CHARLES H. Portrait and miniature painter at NYC in 1838–39; exhibited at the National Academy and the Apollo Association. ¶ Cowdrey, NAD; Cowdrey, AA & AAU; Bolton, *Miniature Painters.*

THOMAS, DANIEL W. Engraver, 24, a native of New York, at NYC in 1860. ¶ 8 Census (1860), N.Y., LX, 965; NYCD 1862.

THOMAS, GEORGE. Engraver, born in Germany about 1815; at New Orleans in 1844 as a stencil and wood engraver; at Philadelphia, 1844–50, as a wood engraver; at Louisville (Ky.) in 1859, of THOMAS & GERMAN, wood engravers and lithographers. ¶ 7 Census (1850), Pa., L, 916; New Orleans *Picayune,* Jan. 30, 1844 (cited by Delgado-WPA); Phila. BD 1844, 1849–50; Louisville BD 1859–60.

THOMAS, GEORGE. Engraver, 45, a native of Scotland, at NYC in 1860. His wife was also Scottish, but their daughter Salinia was born in New York about 1840. ¶ 8 Census (1860), N.Y., LX, 852.

THOMAS, GEORGE. Lithographer, 24, a native of Pennsylvania, at Philadelphia in 1860. ¶ 8 Census (1860), Pa., LII, 442.

THOMAS, GEORGE H. (1824–1868). Wood engraver and designer. After serving his apprenticeship in London and working for some time in Paris, he came to NYC about 1846 and worked there for two years as an engraver and illustrator for one of the pictorial magazines. He returned to Europe in 1848, studied for a time in Italy, and later did pictorial reporting for the *Illustrated London News.* He became well known for his paintings of royal occasions and as a book illustrator. ¶ Clement and Hutton.

THOMAS & GERMAN. Wood engravers and lithographers, Louisville (Ky.), 1859; GEORGE THOMAS and CHARLES W. GERMAN. ¶ Louisville BD 1859.

THOMAS, HENRY. Portrait painter of Philadelphia; in 1832 he exhibited a portrait of Junius Brutus Booth as Richard III and in 1838 a copy of JOHN NEAGLE's "Pat Lyon at the Forge." ¶ Rutledge, PA; Fielding.

THOMAS, HENRY. Engraver, 39, a native of New York, at NYC in 1860. ¶ 8 Census (1860), N.Y., LVI, 975.

THOMAS, HENRY ATWELL (1834–1904). Lithographer and portrait artist, particularly noted for his theatrical portraits. He was a native of NYC and died November 12, 1904, in Brooklyn. ¶ *Art Annual,* V, obit.; Peters, *America on Stone.*

THOMAS, ISAIAH (1749–1831). Engraver of a few cuts in *The History of the Holy Jesus* (Boston, *c.* 1770). Born in Boston on January 19, 1749, Thomas was apprenticed to a printer and by the age of 17 was already considered one of the finest printers in America. He worked chiefly in Boston until 1775 and thereafter at Worcester (Mass.). After his retirement in 1802, he wrote *The History of Printing in America;* he was also the founder and first president of the American Antiquarian Society. He died at Worcester April 4, 1831. ¶ DAB; Fielding's supplement to Stauffer.

THOMAS, J. J. (or I. I.). Delineator of views of Aurora Village and Skaneateles (N.Y.), published *c.* 1830. ¶ *Portfolio* (Feb. 1951), 128, repros.

THOMAS, JOHN. Engraver, 36, a native of Pennsylvania, at Philadelphia in 1860. His wife Emma and children Marie and Samuel were also born in Pennsylvania. In the same house, though listed as a separate family unit, were MARIE, Susan, and Thomas Thomas. ¶ 8 Census (1860), Pa., LIV, 208.

THOMAS, JOSEPH F. Wood engraver, NYC, 1832–46. ¶ Am. Adv. Directory, 1832; NYBD 1846.

THOMAS, MARIE. Artist, 34, born in Pennsylvania, living in Philadelphia in 1860 with Susan, gentlewoman, and Thomas Thomas, clerk. In the same house lived the family of JOHN THOMAS, engraver, probably Marie's brother. ¶ 8 Census (1860), Pa., LIV, 208.

THOMAS, MICHAEL. Artist, 26, born in Pennsylvania, living in a theatrical boarding house in Philadelphia in 1860. ¶ 8 Census (1860), Pa., LII, 64.

THOMPSON, ——. Portrait painter of Troy (N.Y.) who exhibited at the National Academy in 1835. ¶ Cowdrey, NAD.

THOMPSON, Miss A. C. Portrait painter of NYC who exhibited at the National Academy in 1859. ¶ Cowdrey, NAD.

THOMPSON, [A. E. ?]. Painter of a view of Wetumpka Bridge (Ala.), 1847. ¶ Karolik Cat., 495–97, repro.

THOMPSON, ALFRED WORDSWORTH (1840–1896). N.A. Landscape, historical, and portrait painter. Born in Baltimore May 26, 1840, he was educated there and intended for a law career, but shortly before the Civil War he decided to become an artist and opened a studio in Baltimore. After serving as a war illustrator during the first year of the war, he went to France in 1861 for further study and it was not until 1868 that he returned to America. Thereafter his studio was in NYC, but he made several more trips to France and to the Mediterranean lands. He was elected a National Academician in 1875. He died in Summit (N.J.) August 28, 1896. ¶ DAB; Clement and Hutton; CAB; Rutledge, PA; diaries owned by NYHS.

THOMPSON, ALMERIN D. Portrait painter, 31, a native of Massachusetts, at Philadelphia in 1850. ¶ 7 Census (1850), Pa., LIII, 633; Phila. CD 1850.

THOMPSON, ARAD (1786–1843). Portrait painter. A younger brother of CEPHAS THOMPSON, Arad was born December 30, 1786, at Middleboro (Mass.), graduated from Dartmouth in 1807, and practiced medicine in Middleboro until his death, April 23, 1843. He is said to have painted portraits about 1808–10. ¶ Weston, *History of the Town of Middleboro,* 240; Fielding.

THOMPSON, BENJAMIN, Count Rumford (1753–1814). Amateur artist. Born in Woburn (Mass.), studied medicine in Boston before the Revolution. His notebook of that period, filled with drawings and caricatures, is now at the New Hampshire Historical Society. A Loyalist, he left for England in 1775 and served in civil and military offices during the Revolution. Later he was knighted by George III and created Count Rumford of the Holy Roman Empire for services rendered to the Elector of Bavaria. Count Rumford was an important pioneer physicist, noted particularly for his experiments on heat and light and for his inventions of heating and cooking stoves. His latter years were spent at Auteuil, near Paris, and he died there in 1814. ¶ DAB; *Historical New Hampshire* (Nov. 1948), 1–19; Allen, *Early American Book Plates.*

THOMPSON, CEPHAS (1775–1856). Portrait painter, born July 1, 1775, at Middleboro

(Mass.). Largely self-taught, Thompson had a successful career as a portraitist and was particularly well known in the South where he wintered for many years. There are records of his being at Baltimore in 1804, at Charleston in 1804, 1818, and 1822, at Richmond in 1809–10, and at New Orleans in 1816. After 1825 he lived in Middleboro until his death, November 6, 1856. His three children—CEPHAS GIOVANNI, JEROME B., and MARIETTA—also were artists, and his brother ARAD THOMPSON is said to have painted portraits. ¶ CAB; *Richmond Portraits,* 233–34; Weston, *History of the Town of Middleboro,* 389–90; Lafferty; Rutledge, *Artists in the Life of Charleston;* Delgado-WPA; Swan, BA; WPA (Mass.), *Portraits Found in Maine,* no. 320.

THOMPSON, CEPHAS GIOVANNI (1809–1888). A.N.A. Portrait and genre painter, son of CEPHAS THOMPSON. Born August 3, 1809, in Middleboro (Mass.), he studied under his father and DAVID C. JOHNSTON and commenced his career at Plymouth in 1827. Before settling in NYC in 1837 he had worked in Boston, Bristol (R.I.), and Philadelphia. From 1849 to 1852 he was at Boston. In 1852 he went abroad with his family and spent seven years in Italy where he became a friend of Hawthorne. Returning to NYC in 1859, he lived there until his death, January 5, 1888. He was made an Associate Member of the National Academy in 1861. ¶ DAB; CAB; Karolik Cat., 489; Swan, BA; Cowdrey, NAD; Cowdrey, AA & AAU; Rutledge, PA; Boston BD 1849–52; Rutledge, MHS; *Antiques* (Feb. 1942), 110; 7 Census (1850), Mass., XXV, 703.

THOMPSON, CHARLES A. Landscape painter of NYC, 1852–55; exhibited at the National Academy. ¶ Cowdrey, NAD, as C. A.; NYCD 1854, as Charles A.

THOMPSON, CHARLES W. Engraver. Listed in NYC directories from 1841 to 1847 as painter, jeweler, lumber, and engraver; from 1850 as engraver. Possibly the same as Charles W. Thompson, of GROSVENOR & THOMPSON, wood engravers at Cincinnati in 1849–50. ¶ NYCD 1841–47, 1850–60; Cincinnati CD and BD 1849–50.

THOMPSON & CROSBY. Wood engravers, Providence (R.I.), 1852–54; JOHN C. THOMPSON and JAMES CROSBY. ¶ Providence CD 1852, 1854.

THOMPSON, D. GEORGE (?–*c.* 1870). Watercolorist, portrait and landscape engraver. He was working in NYC in 1856 and died there about 1870. Stauffer says that he was born in England and spent his early years in India. ¶ Stauffer; Hinton, *History and Topography of the U.S.,* repro.; *American Collector* (Oct. 1947), 43, and (Dec. 1947), 3, repros.

THOMPSON, DOLLY S. Artist, 60, a native of England, at Baltimore in 1850. She was still there in 1853–54. ¶ 7 Census (1850), Md., V, 915; Lafferty.

THOMPSON, FRANCIS (1838–1905). Painter; born in Maine; died in California [?]. Eight of his paintings are in the Santa Barbara (Cal.) Historical Society. ¶ Information courtesy Katharine Hastings, Santa Barbara Hist. Soc.

THOMPSON, HARRY IVES (1840–1906). Portrait and figure painter, born January 31, 1840, at West Haven (Conn.). Originally a storekeeper, he decided to become an artist in 1861 and studied for a time under BENJAMIN H. COE. From about 1864 to 1867 he taught drawing in New Haven; subsequently he gained a local reputation as a portrait painter. He died at West Haven in 1906. ¶ French, *Art and Artists in Connecticut,* 147–48; Smith.

THOMPSON, HENRY. Irish artist, 60, at NYC in 1860. ¶ 8 Census (1860), N.Y., XLV, 513.

THOMPSON or THOMSON, JAMES. Portrait painter from Scotland who sailed from Belfast (Ireland) in October 1826 and was advertising in Charleston (S.C.) in January 1827. He had relatives at Pawtucket (R.I.). ¶ Rutledge, *Artists in the Life of Charleston,* 133.

THOMPSON, JARED D. Portrait painter and line engraver who studied under NATHANIEL JOCELYN at New Haven in 1850, exhibited at the National Academy in 1852–53, and was working in NYC in 1852 and later. ¶ Rice, "Life of Nathaniel Jocelyn"; Cowdrey, NAD; NYCD 1852; Stauffer.

THOMPSON, JEROME B. (1814–1886). A.N.A. Portrait, landscape, and genre painter, born January 30, 1814, at Middleboro (Mass.), a son of CEPHAS THOMPSON. He began his artistic career at Barnstable (Mass.) before he came of age and opened a studio in NYC in 1835. Elected an Associate of the National Academy in 1851, he went to England in 1852 for several years of study. On his return he settled on a farm at Mineola, Long Island, later moving to a farm at Glen Gardner (N.J.) where he died May 1, 1886. He was best known for his sentimental genre scenes, many of which were lithographed. ¶ DAB;

Karolik Cat., 492–93; Cowdrey, NAD; Cowdrey, AA & AAU; NYCD 1837–53; Swan, BA; Rutledge, PA.

THOMPSON or THOMSON, JOHN. Portrait and miniature painter, silhouettist. He worked in NYC from 1803 to 1805; at Halifax (N.S.) in 1809; at Kingston (Jamaica); and in 1810 at Charleston (S.C.), where he advertised himself as prepared to do portraits, miniatures, profiles, figures for rings and lockets, transparencies, views of estates, coats of arms, antiquities for antiquarians, landscapes, birds, flowers, and patterns for ladies to draw or work, etc. ¶ NYCD 1803–05; Piers, "Artists in Nova Scotia," 119–20; Rutledge, *Artists in the Life of Charleston.*

THOMPSON, JOHN. Irish wood engraver, 56, at Philadelphia in 1860. ¶ 8 Census (1860), Pa., LX, 643.

THOMPSON, JOHN C. Wood engraver at Providence (R.I.), 1852–60. ¶ Providence CD 1852, 1854–60; New England BD 1856, 1860.

THOMPSON, LAUNT (1833–1894). N.A. Sculptor, born February 8, 1833, at Abbeyleix, County Queens (Ireland). Brought to America in 1847, he grew up in Albany (N.Y.) and worked there under ERASTUS DOW PALMER for nine years. In 1857 he moved to NYC, where he became a successful portrait and ideal sculptor. He was elected a National Academician in 1862. In 1867 he spent a few months in Rome and he returned to Italy in 1875 for a six year stay. He died at Middletown (N.Y.), September 26, 1894. ¶ DAB; Taft, *History of American Sculpture;* Cowdrey, NAD.

THOMPSON, MARIETTA (1803–?). Miniaturist, daughter of CEPHAS and sister of CEPHAS G. and JEROME B. THOMPSON. She was born at Middleboro (Mass.) February 27, 1803. Their artistic leanings discouraged by their father, Marietta and Jerome left home in the early thirties and, after working a short time in Barnstable (Mass.), settled in NYC in 1835. Marietta is said to have been quite successful as a miniaturist. ¶ Thompson, *A Genealogy of Descendants of John Thomson, of Plymouth,* 75; DAB, under Jerome B. Thompson.

THOMPSON, MARTIN E. (*c.* 1786–1877). N.A. Architect. Starting as a carpenter in NYC early in the 19th century, Thompson made his name as an architect with his designs for the 2nd Bank of the United States and the Merchants' Exchange. In 1826 he was a founder of the National Academy, at which he exhibited many of his drawings. From 1827 he was in partnership with Ithiel Town. He retired in 1864 to spend the rest of his life at Glen Cove, Long Island, where he died July 24, 1877. ¶ DAB; Cowdrey, NAD; NYCD 1823–52.

THOMPSON, THOMAS (1775/6–1852). A.N.A. Landscape, marine, and portrait painter, lithographer. A native of England who is said to have come to America as early as 1813, Thomas Thompson was active in and around NYC from about 1828 until the time of his death, November 15, 1852. He was an Associate of the National Academy from 1834. His exhibited work included English and Irish views as well as New England and Hudson River landscapes and marines. ¶ Little, "Thomas Thompson, Artist-Observer of the American Scene," six repros.; Cummings, *Historic Annals,* 235; Stokes, *Iconography,* III, 593; Cowdrey, NAD; Cowdrey, AA & AAU; Rutledge, PA; Brooklyn CD 1841–47; Thieme-Becker.

THOMPSON, WILLIAM. Portrait and wall [?] painter working at Worcester (Mass.) in 1837 and Harvard (Mass.) in 1841. ¶ Sears, *Some American Primitives,* 3–5; information courtesy Clarence S. Brigham, Am. Antiq. Soc.

THOMPSON, WILLIAM JOHN (1771–1845). Portrait, miniature, and genre painter. A native of Savannah (Ga.), he went to England and began exhibiting at the Royal Academy in 1796. In 1812 he moved from London to Edinburgh, where he lived until his death in 1845. In 1829 he was made an Academician of the Royal Scottish Academy. ¶ Bolton, *Miniature Painters;* Graves, *Dictionary.*

THOMPSON, WILLIAM M. Engraver active in NYC from 1833 to 1860. In the 1830's he was listed both as Thompson and Tompson. He was also an importer of English refined steel and copper plates for engravers. ¶ NYCD 1833–60; Am. Inst. Cat., 1850.

THOMSON, ——. Delineator of engraved portraits of Bishop Alexander V. Griswold and the Rev. Thomas F. Sargent. ¶ Stauffer, nos. 1992, 2716.

THOMSON, ——. Engraver whose work appeared in *The Pictorial History of the American Navy* (N.Y., *c.* 1845). ¶ Hamilton, *Early American Book Illustrators and Wood Engravers,* 280.

THOMSON, CAMPBELL. Herald and coach

painter, landscape painter, and gilder, at Williamsburg (Va.) in April 1774. ¶ *Virginia Gazette,* April 14, 1774.

THOMSON, JAMES P. Of DAVENPORT & THOMSON, wood engravers, Cincinnati, 1859–60. ¶ Cincinnati CD 1859, BD 1860.

THOMSON, SARAH. Portraits in oil, Massachusetts, about 1800. ¶ Lipman and Winchester, 181.

THORAME, JEAN PIERRE. Professor of painting in Orleans College, New Orleans, 1822–32. ¶ Delgado-WPA cites CD 1822, 1827, 1830, 1832, and *Courier,* Sept. 27, 1824, Jan. 17, 1832.

THOREAU, SOPHIA (1819–1876). Amateur artist, youngest sister of Henry David Thoreau. She was born in Concord (Mass.) and spent almost all her life there, moving to Bangor (Me.) only a few years before her death. She painted in 1839 the only known life portrait of her brother, and she also made a drawing of his cabin by Walden Pond. ¶ Sanborn, *Henry David Thoreau* (1892), 10, (1917), 338; *Art Digest* (Dec. 1, 1932), 16, repro.

THORN, J. C. (1835–1898). Painter of a landscape entitled "The Locks," sold in Philadelphia in 1938. ¶ Sherman, "Unrecorded Early American Painters" (Oct. 1943).

THORN or THORNE, LINTON. Wood engraver of NYC who exhibited at the National Academy in 1835 and by 1838 was dead. ¶ Cowdrey, NAD; Lossing, *Memorial of Alexander Anderson,* 80.

THORNDIKE, GEORGE QUINCY (1825–1886/7). A.N.A. Landscape painter. A native of Boston, Thorndike graduated from Harvard in 1847 and went abroad to study art in Paris. On his return he settled in Newport (R.I.). From 1857 to 1863 he was at NYC, exhibiting at the National Academy, of which he was elected an Associate Member in 1861, and at the Pennsylvania Academy and the Boston Athenaeum. He died in Boston either in 1886 or in 1887. ¶ CAB; Thieme-Becker; Clement and Hutton; Harvard University, *Quinquennial Catalogue* (1890); Cowdrey, NAD; Rutledge, PA; Swan, BA.

THORNDIKE, JOHN JAMES. Engraver, Boston, 1850–52; he was born in Massachusetts about 1829 and lived with Nathaniel R. Thorndike, oil manufacturer. ¶ 7 Census (1850), Mass., XXVI, 327; Boston CD 1850–52.

THORNE, HENRY VANE. Landscape painter and teacher, a son of the English Lady Vane. He came to America and settled in Milwaukee in 1847, before he had reached his 21st birthday, and was doing very well as a drawing teacher when he died a few years later. ¶ Butts, *Art in Wisconsin,* 81.

THORNE, JOHN. Scenic and panoramic artist at NYC in 1859. Probably the same as the English artist, aged 24, of the same name, who was at NYC in 1850. ¶ NYBD 1859; 7 Census (1850), N.Y., XLVI, 170.

THORNTON, WILLIAM (1759–1828). Architect, draftsman, and painter. Born May 20, 1759, on the island of Jost Van Dyke, Virgin Islands, and educated in Scotland, Thornton settled in America in 1787 and became a citizen the following year. From 1788 to 1794 he lived in Philadelphia; during these years he designed the Library Company building there and was associated with JOHN FITCH in experiments in steam navigation. After the acceptance of his design for the U. S. Capitol at Washington in 1793, Thornton moved to the national capital, where he spent the rest of his life. From 1794 to 1802 he was one of the Commissioners for the District of Columbia and from 1802 to 1828 he was in charge of the Patent Office. He also found time to write novels and scientific treatises, design private homes and public buildings, and draw and paint "with facility." He died in Washington March 28, 1828. His wife, born ANNA MARIA BRODEAU, painted miniatures. ¶ DAB; Stauffer; Bolton, *Miniature Painters;* White, *The Jeffersonians,* 208–10.

THORP, ZEPHANIAH. Engraver, NYC, 1855–58. ¶ NYCD 1855–58.

THORPE, GEORGE H. Engraver and copperplate printer, St. Louis, 1853–59. ¶ St. Louis CD 1853 (p. 36); BD 1854, 1859.

THORPE, T. W. Of NYC, exhibited a specimen of painting on a fire engine (No. 48), at the American Institute in 1856. ¶ Am. Inst. Cat., 1856.

THORPE, THOMAS BANGS (1815–1878). Landscape and portrait painter, author, and journalist. Born March 1, 1815, at Westfield (Mass.). He showed an early interest in painting, exhibiting at the American Academy as early as 1833. In 1836 he left college to go to Louisiana, where he remained until 1854, dividing his time between painting and writing and editing. Returning to the East in 1854 he settled in NYC, practiced law for a short time, edited a newspaper, and served as an officer in the Civil War. After the war he became city surveyor of NYC and in 1869 an officer in the Customs House. He died September 20, 1878. Thorpe was the author of several articles on American artists, including CHARLES LORING ELLIOTT. ¶ DAB; Cowdrey, AA & AAU; Cowdrey, NAD; NYCD 1854–60; information courtesy Milton Rickels, Porterville (Cal.), who is writing a biography of Thorpe.

THRALL, A. N. Artist at New Harmony (Ind.) in 1850. ¶ Posey County BD 1850 (citation courtesy Wilbur D. Peat).

THRESHER or THRASHER, GEORGE. Marine painter, teacher of drawing and painting. He was active in NYC from 1806 to 1812, then moved to Philadelphia where he opened an academy for writing, drawing, painting, and book-keeping. He was said to have taught previously in Europe. ¶ *Antiques* (Oct. 1945), 230+; NYCD 1809 (McKay); information courtesy Clarence S. Brigham, Am. Antiq. Soc.

THROOP, BENJAMIN F. Engraver and plate printer, born in Washington (D.C.) about 1837/8, a son of JOHN PETER VAN NESS THROOP. He was active in Washington from about 1858 and in the late sixties he was employed by the Treasury. ¶ 8 Census (1860), D.C., II, 392, 585; Washington CD 1858–71.

THROOP, DANIEL SCROPE (1800–?). Engraver, born January 14, 1800, at Oxford (N.Y.), younger brother of JOHN P. V. N. and ORRAMEL H. THROOP. He was working at Utica in 1824 and at Hamilton (N.Y.) in 1830. He later moved to Elgin (Ill.) and died there. ¶ Fielding's supplement to Stauffer; Hamilton, *Early American Book Illustrators and Wood Engravers,* 397.

THROOP, Mrs. GEORGE ADDISON, see DEBORAH GOLDSMITH.

THROOP, JOHN PETER VAN NESS (1794–*c.* 1861). Copperplate and general engraver and lithographer, born April 15, 1794, at Oxford (N.Y.), older brother of ORRAMEL H. and DANIEL S. THROOP. He did work for Baltimore and NYC publishers, but settled in Washington (D.C.) about 1830 and worked there until his death, between 1860 and 1862. He was listed as J. V. or J. V. N. Throop in Washington. Sherman states that he also painted miniatures. BENJAMIN F. THROOP was his son. ¶ Fielding's supplement to Stauffer; Peters, *America on Stone;* Washington CD 1834–62; 7 Census (1850), D.C., I, 447; 8 Census (1860), D.C., II, 392; Sherman, "Unrecorded American Miniaturists."

THROOP, ORRAMEL HINCKLEY (1798–?). Engraver, born 1798 at Oxford (N.Y.), probably a brother of JOHN P. V. N. and DANIEL S. THROOP. He was working in NYC in 1825 and in New Orleans in 1831–32. ¶ Fielding's supplement to Stauffer; Delgado-WPA cites *La. Advertiser,* March 24, 1831, *Courier,* June 1, 1832, and *Emporium,* Sept. 28, 1832.

THURBER, GEORGE W. Engraver, 23, a native of New York, in NYC in 1850. ¶ 7 Census (1850), N.Y., XLVIII, 36; NYCD 1850.

THURLO, FRANK (1828–1913). Landscape painter; born at Newburyport (Mass.); died there December 25, 1913. ¶ *Art Annual,* XI, obit.

THURSTON, B. Engraver and designer at Portland (Me.) in 1855–56. ¶ *Maine Register,* 1855–56.

THURSTON, ELIZABETH. Memorial painting in watercolors on silk, Canaan (Conn.), 1820. ¶ Lipman and Winchester, 181.

THURSTON, NEPTUNE. Negro slave at Newport (R.I.), about 1765–70, whose sketches on barrel heads are said to have interested GILBERT STUART as a boy. ¶ Porter, *Modern Negro Art,* 16–17.

THURSTON, PERIS G. Drawing teacher. She was a student at Mount Holyoke Female Seminary from 1841 to 1845 and taught drawing there the next two years. She also made a view of the seminary which was lithographed. ¶ *American Collector* (Feb. 1945), 7.

THURWANGER, CHARLES. Lithographer, 19, born in New York, son of Mme. VENERIA THURWANGER, with whom he was living in Philadelphia in 1860. ¶ 8 Census (1860), Pa., LIV, 515.

THURWANGER, JOHN. Lithographer, son of Mme. VENERIA THURWANGER, with whom he was living in Philadelphia in 1860. ¶ 8 Census (1860), Pa., LIV, 515; not listed in Phila. CD.

THURWANGER, JOSEPH. Lithographer, 24, born in New York, son of Mme. VENERIA THURWANGER, with whom he was living in Philadelphia in 1860. Still there in 1870. ¶ 8 Census (1860), Pa., LIV, 515; Phila. CD 1861–70.

THURWANGER, MARTIN T. (?–1890). Lithographer; born in Mulhausen (Alsace); studied art and lithography in Paris and was in business there with a brother. Sometime about 1848–50 he was brought to America by the Smithsonian Institution and he worked for about 18 months in

Philadelphia, but he returned to Paris and worked there until his death in 1890. ¶ Peters, *America on Stone; Portfolio* (Feb. 1954), 131, repro.

THURWANGER, Mme. VENERIA or VERENA. Portrait, genre, and religious painter, born in Germany about 1813. She married Francis Thurwanger sometime in the early thirties. Her husband sold liquors in NYC during the 1840's, then moved to Philadelphia where he was listed as a trimmer in 1854–56 and as "pictures" in 1857. Mrs. Thurwanger, who had exhibited at the Pennsylvania Academy in 1852–53, was listed as his widow after 1857 and until 1863. Her three sons—CHARLES, JOHN, and JOSEPH—were lithographers. ¶ 8 Census (1860), Pa., LIV, 515; NYCD 1841–48; Phila. CD 1854–64; Rutledge, PA.

THWAITES, WILLIAM H. Landscape painter, engraver, and designer, NYC, 1854–60; exhibited English and Welsh views at the National Academy. ¶ Cowdrey, NAD; Hamilton, *Early American Book Illustrators and Wood Engravers,* 474–75.

THYSSENS, FRANCIS. Portrait painter at Evansville (Ind.) in 1860. ¶ Evansville CD 1860 (citation courtesy Wilbur D. Peat); Indiana BD 1860.

TIBBETS or TIBBETTS, GEORGE W. Wood engraver, born in New York about 1830, working in Cleveland (Ohio) in the 1850's. ¶ 7 Census (1850), Ohio, XI, 258; Cleveland CD 1857.

TICE, CHARLES WINFIELD (1810–1870). Portrait, landscape, and still life painter, born October 11, 1810, at Montgomery, near Newburgh (N.Y.). He spent most of his life in Newburgh and died there on August 9, 1870. He exhibited at the National Academy between 1837 and 1849. ¶ Letter of Miss Mary V. Rogers, President of the Historical Society of Newburgh Bay and the Highlands, to D. H. Wallace, May 22, 1955; Cowdrey, NAD; represented at Newburgh Bay Hist. Soc.

TICKNOR, GEORGE (1791–1871). Boston-born author, teacher, and amateur artist. He was professor of Romance languages and belles-lettres at Harvard (1819–35); a founder of the Boston Public Library; and author of *History of Spanish Literature* and *Life of William Hickling Prescott.* His 1803 watercolor of Dartmouth College has been reproduced. ¶ DAB; *Antiques* (Sept. 1944), frontis. and 127.

TIDBALL, JOHN CALDWELL (1825–1906). Topographical artist. Born January 25, 1825, in Ohio County (Va., now W. Va.); graduated from West Point in 1848. In 1853–54 he was with Lt. Whipple's survey along the 35th parallel; four of the illustrations in Whipple's report were by Tidball and there are four of his original sketches in the Oklahoma Historical Society. He later served with distinction in the Civil War. He died May 15, 1906. ¶ DAB; Taft, *Artists and Illustrators of the Old West,* 256–57.

TIDD, MARSHALL M. Lithographer working in Boston from 1853 to 1870. He probably was English. ¶ Peters, *America on Stone;* Mass. BD 1853; Boston BD 1854–60+.

TIDOLDI, JOHN C. Artist, 33, a native of Italy, living in Philadelphia in 1850. His wife was Irish, one son, aged 3, was born in New York, and a six-month-old son was born in Philadelphia. ¶ 7 Census (1850), Pa., LIII, 1012.

TIEBOUT, Mlle., see AIMÉE THIBAULT.

TIEBOUT, CORNELIUS (*c.* 1773–1832). Engraver; born in New York City, probably about 1773, although DAB gives 1777. He was apprenticed to a silversmith, under whom he learned to engrave, and his earliest known work is dated 1789. In 1793 he went to London to study under James Heath for three years. He returned to NYC in 1796, but in 1799 he moved to Philadelphia where he was active for a quarter-century. From 1817 to 1824 he was a member of the banknote engraving firm of TANNER, KEARNEY & TIEBOUT. During the winter of 1825–26 Tiebout and his daughter Caroline went to New Harmony (Ind.) and for the next seven years Tiebout taught engraving in the New Harmony school and did much of the engraving for Thomas Say's volumes on shells and insects; Caroline Tiebout was employed to color these engravings. Cornelius died at New Harmony in 1832. ¶ Stauffer; DAB; NYCD 1792–1800; Phila. CD 1802–25; Stokes, *Historical Prints;* Stokes, *Iconography;* Lockridge, *The Old Fauntleroy Home,* 79–80; *Richmond Portraits;* Burnet, *Art and Artists of Indiana,* 23.

TIERNAN, MICHAEL. Irish artist, 18, at New Orleans in 1850. ¶ 7 Census (1850), La., V, 5.

TIERS, MONTGOMERY C. Portrait painter at NYC in 1851–52; exhibited at the National Academy. ¶ Cowdrey, NAD; NYBD 1852.

TIFFAN, WILLIAM H. Artist born in New York State about 1820, living in Washington County (Ore.) in 1850. ¶ 7 Census (1850), Ore. (courtesy David C. Duniway, Oregon State Archivist).

TIFFANY, WILLIAM SHAW (1824–1907). Portrait and landscape painter. He was working in Boston in 1846, but later moved to Baltimore and exhibited at the Maryland Historical Society between 1856 and 1893. He died in NYC on September 27, 1907. ¶ *Art Annual,* VI, obit.; Boston BD 1846; Lafferty; Rutledge, MHS; Swan, BA.

TILESIUS VON TILENAU, WILHELM GOTTLIEF (1769–1857). Artist and naturalist, a native of Mülhausen (Alsace). He was with the Krusenstern expedition sent out by Czar Alexander I of Russia in 1803 to inspect Russian colonies in the North Pacific. He made many sketches, including some of California scenes in 1806, and they were used to illustrate Langsdorff's *Bemerkungen auf einer Reise um die Welt* (1812). ¶ Van Nostrand and Coulter, *California Pictorial,* 12–15.

TILLER, FREDERICK. Engraver, Philadelphia, 1831–35. Frederick W. Tiller, printer, was listed 1836–39 and 1847–50. ¶ Phila. CD 1831–50.

TILLER, ROBERT. Landscape engraver, Philadelphia, 1818–24; father of ROBERT TILLER, JR. ¶ Phila. CD 1818–24; Stauffer.

TILLER, ROBERT, JR. Engraver of portraits in stipple and subjects in line, Philadelphia, 1825–35; son of ROBERT TILLER. ¶ Phila. CD 1825–35; Stauffer.

TILLOU, ELIZABETH. Still life in watercolors, Brooklyn (N.Y.), about 1830. ¶ Lipman and Winchester, 181.

TILTON, BENJAMIN W. Of WATERS & TILTON, engravers, NYC, 1859. ¶ NYCD 1859.

TILTON, JOHN ROLLIN (1828–1888). Landscape painter, chiefly in watercolors. Born June 8, 1828, in Loudon (N.H.), he went to Italy in 1852 and lived in Rome until his death on March 22, 1888. He was a neighbor and close friend of WILLIAM WETMORE STORY. He travelled in Italy, Switzerland, Germany, Greece, and Egypt. He exhibited at the Pennsylvania Academy and the Boston Athenaeum. ¶ DAB; CAB; Clement and Hutton; Swan, BA; Rutledge, PA; James, *William Wetmore Story.*

TILYARD, PHILIP THOMAS COKE (1785–1830). Portrait painter, born in Baltimore, January 10, 1785. Trained as a sign and ornamental painter, he took up portraiture in Baltimore about 1814. After an unfortunate business venture, he resumed portrait work in 1822 and was embarked on a successful career when he died December 21, 1830. ¶ Hunter, "Philip Tilyard," 14 repros.; Municipal Museum of Baltimore, *The Paintings of Philip Tilyard,* catalogue of exhibition at Peale Museum, Jan.–Feb. 1949; Pleasants, *250 Years of Painting in Maryland,* 44.

TIMONTE, ALPHONSE. Sculptor at Buffalo (N.Y.) in 1858. ¶ Buffalo BD 1858.

TIMME, E. A. Engraver at Chicago in 1859. ¶ Chicago BD 1859.

TINKHAM, FOSTER. Engraver, NYC, 1846. ¶ NYBD 1846.

TINSLEY, CHARLES, indentured servant of. Tinsley, a resident of Newcastle (Va.), advertised in the *Virginia Gazette* of October 21, 1773, that he had "got" a man who was "a good Limner, Landscape Painter &c and an excellent Hand at Painting all Sorts of Signs, Coats of Arms, and Ciphers on Carriages." ¶ Williamsburg, *Virginia Gazette,* Oct. 21, 1773.

TINSLEY, WILLIAM. Portrait painter, Albany (N.Y.), 1852. ¶ Albany BD 1852.

TIRRELL, JOHN. Artist, 34, a native of Massachusetts, at Sacramento (Cal.) in 1860. His personal property was valued at $40,000 and he was connected in some way with one T. J. Hagemann. ¶ 8 Census (1860), Cal., V, 15.

TISDALE, ELKANAH (1771–?). Miniature painter, designer, and engraver. Born in Lebanon (Conn.) about 1771, he worked as an engraver and illustrator and miniature painter in NYC from 1794 to 1798 and in 1809–10, visited Albany with BENJAMIN TROTT about 1798, and later settled in Hartford (Conn.). He was a founder of the HARTFORD GRAPHIC AND BANK NOTE ENGRAVING COMPANY, and designed vignettes for them, but appears to have done no engraving in that connection. He left Hartford in the late 1820's, probably for his native town of Lebanon, and was living in 1834. ¶ French, *Art and Artists in Connecticut,* 37–38; NYCD 1794–95, 1798, 1809–10; Bolton, "Benjamin Trott," 262; Cowdrey, AA & AAU; Stauffer.

TISDALE, JOHN B. Portrait painter, born about 1822, probably in Mobile (Ala.). Early in 1844 Tisdale became acquainted with ALFRED S. WAUGH in Mobile. They worked together there for nearly a year, then moved on to New Orleans and St. Louis. They hoped to join Frémont's Third Expedition as artists but were turned down and from July 1845 to May 1846 they divided their time between Independence and Lexington (Mo.). From June 1846 to June 1847 Tisdale served as a private in Doniphan's Regiment, Missouri Mounted Volunteers, seeing service in New Mexico and California. A sketch of "The Volunteer," which appeared in Hughes' account of the Doniphan Expedition with the signature: J. D. Tisdell, was undoubtedly the work of Tisdale. By 1855 Tisdale was back in Mobile where he seems to have spent the rest of his life. In later years he served as deputy sheriff and county assessor. His name disappears from the Mobile directory after 1885. ¶ McDermott, *Travels in Search of the Elephant,* xii–xiii, 1 ff.; Hughes, *Doniphan's Expedition;* information from records in the Adjutant General's Office, Dept. of the Army, National Archives.

TITCOMB, WILLIAM H. (1824–1888). Painter and teacher; born September 24, 1824, in Raymond (N.H.). He took up painting after trying his hand at the dry goods trade and from about 1860 was a successful teacher in Cambridge and Boston. He died in Boston February 11, 1888. ¶ Boston *Transcript,* Feb. 11, 1888; Swan, BA; Cambridge BD 1860.

TITUS, FRANCIS or FRANZ M. Sculptor and carver; born in Bavaria about 1829; working in NYC from about 1854 to 1860. His widow, Gertrude, was listed in the 1863 directory. GOTTFRIED TITUS was very likely a brother. ¶ 8 Census (1860), N.Y., LIV, 1003; NYCD 1855–63.

TITUS, GOTTFRIED. Artist (painter). Working in NYC from 1858. His address in 1863 was the same as that of FRANCIS TITUS in 1857, suggesting that they were related. ¶ NYCD 1857–63.

TOBEY, SAMUEL. Copperplate and steel engraver, Philadelphia, 1858–59. Before and after those years he was listed variously as bookkeeper, agent, and envelope manufacturer. ¶ Phila. CD 1850–60+.

TOBIN, FREDERICK. Painter of six oils depicting California scenes in 1850, including a view of San Francisco. "The only clue to the artist's identity is contained in a dealer's note in an auction catalogue which reads: 'The following statement was pencilled on the back of one of the old frames from which this and the following four paintings were taken: "Painted by Fred Tobin, 1850, recently Secretary to the Society of Foreign Artists."' A search through contemporary San Francisco directories and art catalogues has failed to turn up any further information about this artist." ¶ Van Nostrand and Coulter, *California Pictorial,* 78–79.

TODD, ——. Of GRAY & TODD, engravers of astronomical plates published in Philadelphia in 1817. Possibly the same as A. TODD. ¶ Stauffer.

TODD, A. Engraver of a small bust portrait of Washington, published in 1812 for the Washington Benevolent Society, Concord (N.H.). ¶ Stauffer.

TODD, GEORGE [?]. Profilist who was working in Charleston (S.C.) from January to July 1807 and in Baltimore about 1810. ¶ Rutledge, *Artists in the Life of Charleston,* simply as Todd; Carrick, *Shades of Our Ancestors,* 41, as George [?]; represented MHS.

TODD, PAMELA. Profilist, NYC, 1812–21. She was the widow of Isaac Todd, M.D. (last listed 1811). She also ran a boardinghouse from 1819 to 1821. From 1822 to 1827 she was listed without occupation. ¶ NYCD 1812–27.

TODD, WILLIAM. Painter of a watercolor view of Mobile (Ala.), which was engraved by WILLIAM JAMES BENNETT and published in 1841. He may have been the Todd whose panorama of an overland trip to California was exhibited in New Orleans in 1857. ¶ Stokes, *Historical Prints;* New Orleans *Picayune,* April 14, 1857 (courtesy J. Earl Arrington).

TOIRY, P. Portrait painter at New Orleans in 1830. ¶ New Orleans CD 1830 (Delgado-WPA).

TOLAND, P. Landscape painter of Reading (Pa.) who exhibited at the Artists' Fund Society in 1841. ¶ Rutledge, PA.

TOLLE or TOLLEY, AUGUSTUS. Engraver and lithographer, of A. J. HOFFMAN & Co., Albany (N.Y.), 1856–57; alone, 1858–60. ¶ Albany CD 1856–60.

TOLMAN, JOHN, JR. Itinerant portrait painter who was working in Salem and Boston (Mass.) from December 1815 to July 1816, in Charleston (S.C.) in November 1816, and in Richmond (Va.) in December 1818. ¶ Belknap, *Artists and Craftsmen of Essex County,* 13; Rutledge, *Artists in the Life of Charleston; Richmond Portraits,* 243.

TOLMAN, L. A. Portrait painter, Boston, 1858–60. ¶ Boston BD 1858–60.

TOLTI & CARNAHAN. Lithographers and engravers, New Orleans, 1856–59; JOHN (Jean) TOLTI and CHARLES CARNAHAN. ¶ New Orleans CD 1856–59 (Delgado-WPA).

TOLTI, JOHN (Jean). Lithographer; born in

Italy about 1822; working in New Orleans from about 1849 to the 1860's. From 1856 to 1859 he was in partnership with CHARLES CARNAHAN and in 1860 with DENNIS or DIONIS SIMON. ¶ New Orleans *Bee,* Dec. 20, 1849 (Delgado-WPA); 7 Census (1850), La., V, 55 [as T. Tolti]; 8 Census (1860), La., VIII, 15 [as Jean Tolti]; New Orleans CD 1856–60 (Delgado-WPA).

TOLTI & SIMON. Lithographers, New Orleans, 1860; JOHN (Jean) TOLTI and DENNIS or DIONIS SIMON. ¶ New Orleans CD 1860 (Delgado-WPA).

TOMB, ROBERT. Irish-born engraver, 18, living in Northern Liberties, Philadelphia, 1850. ¶ 7 Census (1850), Pa., XLIX, 164.

TOMKINS, LEWIS. English lithographer, 19, living in Philadelphia in 1860 in the same house as HENRY RAWLINGS, die sinker. ¶ 8 Census (1860), Pa., LII, 252.

TOMLINSON, FRANK. Artist, 21, a native of Connecticut, living in NYC in 1860 with his father, WILLIAM A. TOMLINSON. ¶ 8 Census (1860), N.Y., LXI, 378.

TOMLINSON, WILLIAM Engraver, 27, a native of Pennsylvania, living in Philadelphia in 1860. ¶ 8 Census (1860), Pa., L, 426.

TOMLINSON, WILLIAM A. Artist, 50, a native of Connecticut, living in NYC in 1860; his property was valued at $20,800. FRANK TOMLINSON was his son. ¶ 8 Census (1860), N.Y., LXI, 378.

TOMPSON, WILLIAM M., see WILLIAM M. THOMPSON.

TONIERE, GAETANO. Figure maker at Boston in 1850. ¶ Boston CD 1850.

TONNELLIER, FRANCOIS. Wood engraver, 23, a native of France, living in Boston in 1850. ¶ 7 Census (1850), Mass., XXV, 54.

TOOKER, EDWARD B. Brassfounder of NYC, exhibited a portrait in oil at the American Institute in 1842. ¶ Am. Inst. Cat., 1842.

TOOLEY, JAMES, JR. (1816–1844). Miniature, portrait, and landscape painter, born August 8, 1816. A view of Natchez (Miss.) after a sketch by Tooley was lithographed by RISSO & BROWNE of NYC about 1835. In 1842 he was in Philadelphia; the following year, at Natchez, he painted a miniature of THOMAS SULLY. AUGUSTE EDOUART cut Tooley's silhouette in Philadelphia in December 1843 and in Natchez in April 1844. He died August 10, 1844. ¶ Sherman, "Newly Discovered American Miniaturists," 98; Stokes, *Historical Prints;* Rutledge, PA; Jackson, *Ancestors in Silhouette.*

TOPPAN, CARPENTER & CO. Banknote engravers. Organized by CHARLES TOPPAN of Philadelphia in 1845, with SAMUEL H. CARPENTER and others; became TOPPAN, CARPENTER, CASILEAR & CO. (1850–55); again as Toppan, Carpenter & Co. from 1856 to 1861. The headquarters were in Philadelphia, with a branch in NYC. This firm was one of the components of the AMERICAN BANK NOTE COMPANY after 1858. ¶ Phila. CD 1845–61; Stauffer; Toppan, *100 Years of Bank Note Engraving,* 12.

TOPPAN, CARPENTER, CASILEAR & CO. Banknote engravers. Formed in 1850 when JOHN W. CASILEAR joined TOPPAN, CARPENTER & CO. Other members of the firm included WILLIAM C. SMILLIE, HENRY E. SAULNIER, and the three JOCELYNS—NATHANIEL, SIMEON SMITH, and SIMEON STARR. After Casilear left the company in 1855 it was again known as TOPPAN, CARPENTER & CO. The head office was in Philadelphia and there were branches in NYC and Cincinnati. ¶ Phila. CD 1851–55; Rice, "Life of Nathaniel Jocelyn"; Cincinnati CD 1853; NYCD 1851–55.

TOPPAN, CHARLES (1796–1874). Banknote engraver, born February 10, 1796, in Newburyport (Mass.). A pupil of GIDEON FAIRMAN at Philadelphia as early as 1814, he was employed by MURRAY, DRAPER, FAIRMAN & CO. and other banknote engraving firms in Philadelphia until about 1835 when he became a partner in DRAPER, TOPPAN, LONGACRE & CO. From 1819 to about 1822 he was in England with FAIRMAN and JACOB PERKINS. From 1835 to his retirement about 1860 Toppan was a partner in the following banknote firms: DRAPER, TOPPAN, LONGACRE & CO. (1835–39); DRAPER, TOPPAN & CO. (1840–44); TOPPAN, CARPENTER & CO. (1845–50); TOPPAN, CARPENTER, CASILEAR & CO. (1851–55); and TOPPAN, CARPENTER & CO. (1856–61). About 1855 he moved from Philadelphia to NYC and there was a leader in the founding of the AMERICAN BANK NOTE CO., of which he was the first president (1858–60). He died in Florence (Italy) on November 20, 1874. ¶ Belknap, *Artists and Craftsmen of Essex County,* 5; Stauffer; Toppan, *100 Years of Bank Note Engraving,* 3–4, 8–10; Phila. CD 1830–61; NYCD 1856–62; 7 Census (1850), Pa., LI, 232. Charles Toppan was the author of a brief "History and Progress of Banknote Engraving," which appeared in *Crayon,* I (1855), 116–17.

TOPPAN, CHARLES, JR. Engraver, son of CHARLES TOPPAN; born in Connecticut about 1826; working in Philadelphia in 1850. ¶ 7 Census (1850), Pa., LI, 232.

TOPPAN, HARRIET. Engraver, daughter of CHARLES TOPPAN; born in Philadelphia about 1834; listed as an engraver, aged 16, in the 1850 Census. ¶ 7 Census (1850), Pa., LI, 232.

TORBETT, CHARLES W. Engraver, Boston, 1836–42. ¶ Boston CD 1836–42.

TORRANS, ROSELLA. Landscape painter active in Charleston (S.C.) about 1808. Ramsay's *History of South Carolina* (1809) speaks of her and her sister, Mrs. ELIZA COCHRAN, as the leading female artists of South Carolina. ¶ Rutledge, *Artists in the Life of Charleston;* Ramsay, *History of South Carolina,* II, 269–70. Dunlap, *History,* II, 472, mistakenly gives her name as Rosalba Torrens.

TORRENS, ROSALBA, see ROSELLA TORRANS.

TORREY, CHARLES CUTLER (1799–1827). Engraver, born July 9, 1799, in Beverly or Salem (Mass.), brother of MANASSEH CUTLER TORREY. He was working in Salem in 1820, moved to Nashville (Tenn.) in 1823, and died there February 9, 1827. ¶ Torrey, *The Torrey Families,* I, 210; Belknap, *Artists and Craftsmen of Essex County,* 5; Stauffer; *American Collector* (Nov. 1944), 17.

TORREY, FRANKLIN (1830–1912). Sculptor; born October 25, 1830, probably in Scituate (Mass.), son of David (1787–1877) and Vesta Howard Torrey (1790–1866). He spent over fifty years in Italy and died at Florence November 16, 1912. ¶ Torrey, *Torrey Families,* I, 193, 280; *Art Annual,* X, obit.

TORREY, HIRAM DWIGHT (1820–1900). Landscape and still life painter; born June 24, 1820, at New Lebanon (N.Y.). After his first marriage in 1849, he moved out to Milwaukee (Wis.) where he had a studio in 1851. From about 1853 to 1862 he lived in Reading (Pa.). In 1855 he exhibited at the Pennsylvania Academy. After his second marriage in 1862 he apparently took his family abroad, for a son was born in Glasgow (Scotland) in 1870. Torrey died August 11, 1900, at Delanco (N.J.). ¶ Torrey, *Torrey Families,* I, 237, and II, 237; Butts, *Art in Wisconsin,* 102; Rutledge, PA; letter, Earl L. Poole, Director, Reading Public Museum and Art Gallery, to Miss Anna Wells Rutledge, Jan. 8, 1953 (NYHS files).

TORREY, JULIETTE E. Still life painter, Philadelphia, 1832. ¶ Rutledge, PA.

TORREY, MANASSEH CUTLER (1807–1837). A.N.A. Portrait and miniature painter, born May 7, 1807, in Salem (Mass.), a younger brother of CHARLES CUTLER TORREY. A pupil of HENRY INMAN, he exhibited at the National Academy in 1833 and was made an Associate Member the same year. Between 1831 and 1837, however, he worked principally in Salem, exhibiting frequently at the Boston Athenaeum. He died September 24, 1837, at Pelham (Vt.). ¶ Torrey, *Torrey Families,* II, 73; Bolton, "Manasseh Cutler Torrey"; Swan, BA; Cowdrey, NAD; Clark, *History of the NAD;* Belknap, *Artists and Craftsmen of Essex County,* 14; repro., *Essex Institute Hist. Coll.,* 86 (April 1950), 164.

TORSCH, JOHN W. Wood engraver, 28, a native of Maryland, living in Baltimore with his parents in 1860. ¶ 8 Census (1860), Md., V, 302 [three months later he was boarding out, see III, 956]; Baltimore CD 1858–60.

TOWER, F. B. Author and illustrator of a book on the Croton Aqueduct, built in the 1840's to bring water to NYC. Tower may have been one of the engineers employed in its construction. ¶ Tower, *Illustrations of the Croton Aqueduct* (New York, 1843); Stokes, *Iconography,* III, 875–76.

TOWERS, J. Watercolor portraits, upper New York State, about 1850. ¶ Lipman and Winchester, 181.

TOWLE, EUNICE MAKEPEACE. Painter of a portrait of Martin Van Buren (1782–1862), now in Avery Hall, Columbia University, NYC. Her father was Van Buren's physician. ¶ Information courtesy Professor Vanderpool, Columbia University.

TOWNE, ANN SOPHIA, see Mrs. ANN SOPHIA TOWNE DARRAH.

TOWNE, ROSALBA (Rosa) M. (1827–?). Flower painter, born June 15, 1827, daughter of John and Sarah Robinson Towne. Her parents lived in Pittsburgh, Boston (1833–40), and Philadelphia (1840–51). She was living in Philadelphia from 1860 to 1866 and in Shoemakertown (Pa.) from 1868 to 1869, the years she exhibited at the Pennsylvania Academy. A sister, ANN SOPHIA, married Robert K. Darrah and was an artist; a brother, John Henry Towne (1818–1875) was a Philadelphia merchant who endowed the Towne Scientific School of the University of

Pennsylvania. ¶ Towne, *The Descendants of William Towne,* 106–07; Rutledge, PA.

TOWNSEND, CHARLES (1836–1894). Amateur painter, son of William H. and Cornelia Maverick Townsend, grandson of PETER MAVERICK. An accountant by profession, he exhibited once at the National Academy (1859). His home was at Arrochar, Staten Island (N.Y.) and he died April 7, 1894. ¶ Stephens, *The Mavericks;* Cowdrey, NAD.

TOWNSEND, CHARLES E. Engraver and lithographer, NYC, 1832. ¶ NYCD 1832; *Am. Adv. Directory,* 1832.

TOWNSEND, CHARLOTTE. Artist, 36, born in New Jersey, living in Philadelphia in 1860 as a boarder in the home of the portrait painter JOHN NEAGLE. ¶ 8 Census (1860), Pa., LII, 507.

TOWNSEND, GEORGE. Artist, 26, born in New York State, living in NYC in 1850. ¶ 7 Census (1850), N.Y., XLVI, 611.

TOWNSEND, HENRY L. L. Engraver, 27, a native of Connecticut, living in NYC in 1850. ¶ 7 Census (1850), N.Y., XLVIII, 70; NYCD 1850.

TOWNSEND, Mrs. JOHN F., see MARIA ANN MAVERICK.

TOWNSEND & ORR. Proprietors and, possibly, painters of a panorama of the Hudson River, shown in NYC in 1849. ¶ Odell, *Annals of the New York Stage,* V, 499–500.

TOWNSEND, WILLIAM H. Artist, 27, living with his father, William Townsend, at New Haven (Conn.) in 1850. ¶ 7 Census (1850), Conn., VIII, 582.

TRACY, S. or G. P. Landscape painter of Chicago who exhibited at the Chicago Art Union in the winter of 1859–60. Possibly the Simon P. Tracy, Senior 2d Lieutenant of Battery 2, 2d Illinois Light Artillery, who died in service on September 9, 1863. ¶ Andreas, *History of Chicago,* II, 276–7, 556–7 (courtesy H. Maxson Holloway, Chicago Hist. Soc.); repro., *Chicago History* (Spring 1951), 323.

TRAIN, DANIEL N. Ship carver, pupil of WILLIAM RUSH. He worked in NYC from 1799 to about 1811 and is known to have done the carving for the war ships *Adams* and *Trumbull* in 1799. ¶ Marceau, *William Rush,* 14; Pinckney, *American Figurehead Carvers,* 80, 202; NYCD 1799–1811.

TRANSLOT, Mrs. EUGENE, see AMELIA STEVENS.

TRAPP, AUGUST. German lithographer, 20, at NYC in 1860. ¶ 8 Census (1860), N.Y., XLII, 692.

TRAQUAIR, JAMES (1756–1811). Stonecutter and portrait sculptor working in Philadelphia from about 1802 until his death, April 5, 1811. ¶ Scharf and Westcott, *History of Philadelphia,* II, 1066.

TRAUBEL, M. (Morris or Martin) H. (1820–1897). Lithographer. Born in Frankfurt-am-Maine (Germany) and trained in Germany, Traubel came to Philadelphia about 1850 and established the firm of TRAUBEL, SCHNABEL & FINKELDEY. From 1853 to 1869 he headed the firm of M. H. Traubel & Co. He committed suicide in 1897. ¶ Peters, *America on Stone* [as Morris]; 7 Census (1850), Pa., L, 227 [as Martin, aged 25]; Phila. CD 1854+.

TRAUTWINE, JOHN CRESSON (1810–1883). Architect of Philadelphia, exhibited designs for a monument and a fountain at the Artists' Fund Society in 1844. ¶ Rutledge, PA; Phila. CD 1844.

TRAVIS, WILLIAM D. T. (1839–1916). Religious painter, illustrator, Civil War combat artist. His home was in Burlington (N.J.) where he died July 24, 1916. ¶ *Art Annual,* XIII, obit.

TREADWELL, JONA. Portrait painter working at Readfield (Me.) in 1840, active in New England (probably Maine) at least until 1851. ¶ Lipman and Winchester, 181; WPA (Mass.), *Portraits Found in Maine,* 223–24.

TREAGA, GENOZA. Italian figure maker, 36, living in Philadelphia in 1850 with his brother [?] SANTONIO TREAGA and four other figure makers. ¶ 7 Census (1850), Pa., L, 859.

TREAGA, SANTONIO. Italian figure maker, 40, living in Philadelphia in 1850 with his brother [?] GENOZA TREAGA and four other figure makers—LOUIS JAMACIE and the three LAGURANE brothers. ¶ 7 Census (1850), Pa., L, 859.

TREGO, JONATHAN K. (1817–*c.* 1868). Portrait, genre, and animal painter, born March 11, 1817, of a Quaker family of Bucks County (Pa.). He was living in Philadelphia from 1852 to 1855, at Yardleyville, Bucks County, 1858–59, and again in Philadelphia, 1865–68. During these years he exhibited western genre scenes and portraits at the Pennsylvania Academy, one done in collaboration with ISAAC L. WILLIAMS. Jonathan's crippled son, William T. Trego (1858–?), also was an artist of note in Detroit and Philadelphia in the seventies and eighties;

he was known as "the boy artist." ¶ Shertzer, *Historical Account of the Trego Family,* 70–76; Rutledge, PA; Phila. CD 1852–55, 1865–68.

TREMBLEY, RALPH. Lithographer; born in New York State about 1817; married a New Yorker, but their first four children were born in Pennsylvania between about 1839 and about 1847. He was working as a lithographer in NYC from about 1848 to 1851 and as a clerk in 1863. ¶ 7 Census (1850), N.Y., LV, 137; NYBD 1850–51, 1863; repro., *Portfolio* (March 1948), 150.

TRENCHARD, EDWARD C. (*c.* 1777–1824). Engraver. Born in Salem (N.J.), he studied engraving as a boy with his uncle JAMES TRENCHARD of Philadelphia. In 1793, at the age of 16, he went to England, returning the same year to Philadelphia in company with the young English engraver GILBERT FOX. In 1794 Edward and James were among the founders of the short-lived Columbianum and in 1796–98 Edward was engraving in Boston. In April 1800 he entered the U. S. Navy as a midshipman; he saw service in the War of 1812, in the Mediterranean, and off the African coast, and eventually rose to the rank of captain. In 1814 he married a daughter of Joshua Sands of Brooklyn. He died in Brooklyn on November 3, 1824. ¶ Sellers, *Charles Willson Peale,* II, 74–75; Maclay, *Reminiscences of the Old Navy,* 2–4 [he gives 1785 as Trenchard's birth year, but other evidence suggests that he must have been born about 1777]; Stauffer; CAB; Boston CD 1798 [as Trenchard & Dixon]; Hamilton, *Early American Book Illustrators and Wood Engravers,* 72.

TRENCHARD & HALLBERG. Drawing masters in Baltimore in 1788. ¶ Prime, II, 52–53.

TRENCHARD, JAMES (1747–?). Engraver, die sinker, and seal cutter; born in Penns Neck, Salem County (N.J.). He came to Philadelphia as early as 1777 and learned engraving from JAMES SMITHER. He was a founder and for some years editor of the *Columbian Magazine* and in 1794 a founder of the Columbianum. His nephew, EDWARD C. TRENCHARD, and JAMES THACKARA were among his pupils in engraving. Trenchard went to England in the mid-nineties and is said to have remained there for the rest of his life. ¶ Smith; Stauffer; Phila. CD 1785–93; Sellers, *Charles Willson Peale,* II, 75; *Portfolio* (Aug. 1947), 20, repro.; Prime, I, 29.

TRENCHARD & WESTON. Engravers, Philadelphia, 1800. Possibly EDWARD C. TRENCHARD and HENRY W. WESTON. ¶ Brown and Brown.

TRENHOLM, PORTIA ASHE, née Burden (*c.* 1812–1892). Amateur painter active in and around Charleston (S.C.) in the 1840's or 1850's. She was the wife of Charles L. Trenholm and died in Nashville (Tenn.) on March 23, 1892, in her 80th year. ¶ Information from her tombstone in Magnolia Cemetery, Charleston, copied by a descendant and forwarded to D. H. Wallace by Mrs. Nina Fletcher Little, May 12, 1955; Cahill, "Artisan and Amateur in American Folk Art," 210 (repro.), 211.

TRESTED, RICHARD. Engraver and die sinker, NYC, 1820. ¶ NYCD 1820 (McKay).

TRICHON, ——. Engraver whose work appeared in *Faggots for the Fireside . . .* (New York, 1855); one plate was also signed V. FOULQUIER. ¶ Hamilton, *Early American Book Illustrators and Wood Engravers,* 180.

TRINCHARD, J. B. Sculptor, New Orleans, 1841–42, 1846. ¶ New Orleans CD 1841–42, 1846.

TRIST, T. J. Landscape painter of NYC, exhibited at the National Academy in 1852. ¶ Cowdrey, NAD.

TROENDLE, JOSEPH F. Artist employed by a firm of photographers in Louisville (Ky.) in 1859. Possibly the J. F. Troendle who exhibited at the National Academy in 1858 several portraits and landscapes. ¶ Louisville CD 1859; Cowdrey, NAD.

TRONDLE or TROENDLE. Portrait painter working in NYC between 1856 and 1860. He was variously listed: Karl J. Trondle (1856); Conrad J. Trondle (1857); Charles J. Trondle (1858); John Troendle and Joachim Troendle (1859); John Troendle and Jacob Trondle (1860). ¶ NYCD 1856–60; NYBD 1859–60.

TROTT, BENJAMIN (*c.* 1770–1843). Miniature and portrait painter, born in Boston, about 1770. He was working in NYC in 1793–94, in Philadelphia from 1794 to 1797, visited Albany and Philadelphia in 1798, and was again in NYC 1798–99. He was at Philadelphia in 1804, went out to Kentucky the following year, but settled in Philadelphia in 1806, remaining there until 1819. During this period he lived with THOMAS SULLY and was a member of the Society of Artists. In 1819–20 he went south to Norfolk (Va.) and Charleston (S.C.). He returned to Philadelphia about

1823 but soon after moved to Newark (N.J.). From 1829 to 1833 he was living in NYC; in 1833–34 he was at Boston; from 1838 to 1841 he was in Baltimore. He died in Washington (D.C.) on November 27, 1843. ¶ Bolton, "Benjamin Trott"; Dunlap, *Diary;* Dunlap, *History;* DAB; Bolton and Tolman, "Catalogue of Miniatures by or Attributed to Benjamin Trott"; Rutledge, PA; Cowdrey, AA & AAU; obit., Washington *National Intelligencer,* Nov. 29, 1843 (courtesy Miss Anna Wells Rutledge).

TROTTER, NEWBOLD HOUGH (1827–1898). Animal and landscape painter, born in and a life-long resident of Philadelphia. He exhibited at the Pennsylvania Academy from 1858 and also at the Boston Athenaeum. He died February 21, 1898. ¶ *Art Annual,* I, obit.; CAB; Rutledge, PA; Swan, BA; Met. Mus., *Life in America,* repro.; *Portfolio* (May 1951), 213, repro.

TROUARD, ——. Sculptor. A young, self-taught native of Louisiana, he was working in New Orleans in 1848 and at Paris in 1850. *Cf.* JUSTINIAN TRUDEAU. ¶ Delgado-WPA cites *Courier,* July 6, 1848, and *Bee,* Dec. 28, 1850.

TROUCHE, AUGUSTE PAUL (?–1846). Landscape painter; born in Charleston; working there from 1835 until his death in 1846. ¶ Rutledge, *Artists in the Life of Charleston.*

TROUVELOT, L. Lithographer, Boston, 1860. ¶ Boston BD 1860.

TROWBRIDGE, N. C. Artist, 30, born in Massachusetts, at New Orleans in 1860. ¶ 8 Census (1860), La., VI, 491.

TROYE, EDWARD (1808–1874). Animal, portrait, and figure painter, born near Geneva (Switzerland), the son of a French artist, Jean-Baptiste de Troy. Troye came to America via the West Indies in 1828 and settled in Philadelphia where he did work for *Sartain's Magazine.* He visited Charleston (S.C.) in 1833 and from 1835 to 1874 he spent most of his time in Kentucky, specializing in portraits of race horses. From 1849 to 1855, however, he was teacher of painting at Spring Hill College, Mobile (Ala.). He also visited New Orleans in 1844, 1853, and 1857. He died in Georgetown (Ky.) July 25, 1874. ¶ DAB; Fairman, *Art and Artists of the Capitol,* 319–20; *Panorama* (Oct. 1945), 12; Rutledge, *Artists in the Life of Charleston;* Rutledge, PA; Cowdrey, AA & AAU; WPA Guide, *Alabama;* Delgado-WPA cites *Picayune,* Dec. 18, 1844, *Courier,* Jan. 19, 1853, and *Orleanian,* April 2, 1857; Met. Mus., *Life in America.*

TRUDEAU, JUSTINIAN. Sculptor; born in Louisiana about 1827; active in New Orleans from 1849 to 1854. In 1850 he exhibited his self-portrait. *Cf.* —— TROUARD. ¶ 7 Census (1850), La., VII, 309; Delgado-WPA cites *Courier,* June 27, 1849, *Bee,* Aug. 24, 1850, and New Orleans CD 1851–54.

TRUE, BENJAMIN C. Engraver, seal engraver, and die sinker, Cincinnati, 1850–60. ¶ Cincinnati CD 1850–60.

TRUE, DANIEL. Die sinker and seal engraver, Albany (N.Y.), 1853–60; of TRUE & PILKINGTON in 1856–57. ¶ Albany CD 1853–60.

TRUE & PILKINGTON. Seal engravers and die sinkers, Albany (N.Y.), 1856–57; DANIEL TRUE and JAMES E. PILKINGTON. ¶ Albany CD 1856–57.

TRUIST, SIGMUND. German engraver, 28, at Philadelphia in 1850. ¶ 7 Census (1850), Pa., XLIX, 657.

TRUMAN, EDWARD. Painter of a portrait, 1741, of Governor Thomas Hutchinson of Massachusetts, now at the Massachusetts Historical Society. The National Gallery owns his portrait of Jonathan Sewell. ¶ Burroughs, *Limners and Likenesses;* Smithsonian Institution, *Annual Report,* 1948.

TRUMBULL, JOHN (1756–1843). Historical, portrait, miniature (invariably oil on wood), religious, and landscape painter, amateur architect and cartographer, soldier, and diplomat. He was born June 6, 1756, at Lebanon (Conn.), the youngest son of Jonathan Trumbull, Revolutionary Governor of Connecticut. Graduating from Harvard in 1773, he taught school and dabbled in painting until the outbreak of the Revolution. From 1775 to 1777 he served as an officer in the Continental Army, but he resigned his commission over a fancied slight and returned to Lebanon to paint. In 1790 he went to London to study under WEST, only to be imprisoned in retaliation for the hanging of JOHN ANDRÉ. After his release, Trumbull returned to America, but in 1784 he was back in West's studio in London where he worked until 1789. During this period he also visited Paris, coming under the influence of David and Vigee-LeBrun, and began work on his series of scenes of the American Revolution. From 1789 to 1794 he was in America, making studies of the participants in the Revolution, as well as other portraits and miniatures. In 1794 he went to London a third time, as secretary to John Jay, and he remained in England until 1804 as one of the commissioners under the Jay Treaty. From 1804 to 1808 Trumbull had a studio in NYC, but in 1808 he returned to England for a fourth visit which extended until 1816. During his long residence in NYC, from 1816 to 1837, Trumbull received an important commission for four large historical paintings for the Capitol Rotunda; he was prominent in the affairs of the American Academy of Fine Arts as its President from 1816 to 1835; and in 1831 he sold to Yale College, for an annuity, his collection of his own works, the nucleus of the Yale University Art Gallery. In 1841 was published Trumbull's *Autobiography* and two years later, November 10, 1843, he died in NYC. ¶ Practically all that is known of Trumbull and his work has been assembled into the 1953 edition of his *Autobiography*, edited and supplemented by Theodore Sizer, and *The Works of Colonel John Trumbull*, an illustrated, descriptive catalogue, also compiled by Professor Sizer. See also: Flexner, *The Light of Distant Skies*.

TRUMBULL, Mrs. JOHN (1774–1824). Amateur fruit and flower painter. Born near London on April 1, 1774, Sarah Hope Harvey married JOHN TRUMBULL in London in 1800. She exhibited at the American Academy in 1816 and 1817 and at the Pennsylvania Academy in 1818. She died in NYC on April 12, 1824. Mrs. Trumbull was a great beauty but addicted to drink and her husband's reticence about her has given rise to much speculation about her origin. ¶ Sizer, *The Autobiography of Colonel John Trumbull*, 350–65 ("Who Was the Colonel's Lady?"); Cowdrey, AA & AAU; Rutledge, PA.

TRUNG, F. German artist, 23, at NYC in 1850. ¶ 7 Census (1850), N.Y., XLII, 147.

TRYON, BENJAMIN F. (1824–1896). Landscape painter who was born in NYC but worked principally in Boston. He was a pupil of RICHARD BENGOUGH and JAMES H. CAFFERTY. ¶ Swan, BA; Clement and Hutton.

TRYON, Mrs. BROWN. Portrait painter of Hoboken (N.J.) who exhibited at the National Academy in 1858–59. Probably the same as Mrs. E. A. TRYON and MARGARET B. TRYON. ¶ Cowdrey, NAD.

TRYON, Mrs. E. A. Portrait painter who exhibited at the National Academy; probably the same as MARGARET B. and Mrs. BROWN TRYON. ¶ Cowdrey, NAD.

TRYON, HORATIO L. Sculptor or marble-worker; born in New York State about 1826; active in NYC from 1852. ¶ 8 Census (1860), N.Y., LX, 823 and 1171; NYCD 1852–62.

TRYON, JOHN. Artist; born in New York about 1801; active in NYC from 1845 to 1851. ¶ 7 Census (1850), N.Y., XLVIII, 324; NYCD 1845–51.

TRYON, MARGARET B. Portrait painter, NYC, 1860–61. Exhibited at the National Academy in 1857 as M. P. Tryon of Hoboken (N.J.). Listed as Margaret T. B. Tryon, artist, in 1861 Hoboken directory. Probably the same as Mrs. BROWN TRYON and Mrs. E. A. TRYON. ¶ NYBD 1860–61; Cowdrey, NAD; Jersey City and Hoboken CD 1861.

TUBBY, JOSEPH (1821–1896). Landscape and portrait painter, born in Tottenham (England), August 25, 1821, to a Quaker family who emigrated to America and settled in Kingston (N.Y.) in 1832. He studied art briefly with a portrait painter named Black and did decorative painting in Kingston, as well as landscapes and a few portraits. He exhibited at the National Academy between 1851 and 1860 and was an intimate friend of JERVIS MCENTEE. He spent the last seven years of his life in Brooklyn and New Jersey, dying in Montclair (N.J.) on August 6, 1896. ¶ Senate House Museum, "Exhibition of Paintings by Joseph Tubby"; Cowdrey, NAD

TUBESING, HENRY. Wood engraver, Buffalo (N.Y.), 1855–59. ¶ Buffalo BD 1855–58; N. Y. State BD 1859.

TUCKER, ALICE. Flower painter in water colors, New Bedford (Mass.), 1807. ¶ Lipman and Winchester, 181.

TUCKER, BENJAMIN (1768–?). Portrait and job painter; born November 13, 1768, in Newburyport (Mass.); working there in 1796. ¶ Belknap, *Artists and Craftsmen of Essex County*, 14.

TUCKER, JOHN J. Portrait painter at Cincinnati in 1841; he had previously worked in Texas. ¶ Cist, *Cincinnati in 1841*, 140.

TUCKER, MARY B. Portraits in watercolors, Concord and Sudbury (Mass.), about 1840. ¶ Lipman and Winchester, 181.

TUCKER, WILLIAM E. (1801–1857). Engraver of portraits, landscapes, and subject plates and banknotes. A native and life-long resident of Philadelphia, he learned engraving from FRANCIS KEARNEY, and was active as an engraver from the early

1820's. ¶ Stauffer; Phila. CD 1823–57; DAB, under Kearney; 7 Census (1850), Pa., LII, 991.

TUCKERMAN, STEPHEN SALISBURY (1830–1904). Marine and landscape painter, teacher of drawing. Born in Boston, December 8, 1830, he first went into business. After studying drawing in Birmingham (England), however, he returned to Boston to head the New England School of Design. He went abroad again in 1860 and studied in Paris for a year, after which he taught drawing in Boston until 1864 when he turned to painting. After 1872 he spent most of his time in Europe, and he died in Standsford (England) in March 1904. ¶ CAB; *Art Annual,* V, obit.

TUDOR, ROBERT M. Portrait painter working in Philadelphia from 1858 to 1869. ¶ Rutledge, PA; Philadelphia CD 1858–60+.

TULLY, CHRISTOPHER. Engraver of Philadelphia, 1775, who also invented a wool-spinning machine. ¶ Fielding.

TUQUA, EDWARD. Portrait painter at Westport (Conn.) about 1830. ¶ Sherman, "Newly Discovered American Portrait Painters."

TURK, FRANCIS H. Landscape painter of NYC, who exhibited at the National Academy in 1842–43. He was listed in the directories as a clerk in the post office (1844–47) and a lawyer (1848). ¶ Cowdrey, NAD; NYCD 1844–48.

TURNER, Miss E. Exhibited at the Pennsylvania Academy in 1813 a drawing or water color entitled "The Lady of the Lake." ¶ Rutledge, PA.

TURNER & FISHER. Wood engravers and stationers, Philadelphia, 1840's; Frederick Turner and Abraham Fisher were the partners. The firm was listed under wood engravers only in 1844. ¶ Phila. BD 1844; Phila. CD 1843–49.

TURNER, HENRY. Portrait painter working in Rappahannock County (Va.) in 1845. ¶ Willis, "Jefferson County Portraits."

TURNER, L. or J. L. Portrait, landscape, and genre painter, living in Brooklyn (N.Y.) from 1832 to 1844. As L. Turner, portrait painter, 1832–33; as J. L. Turner, artist, 1834–44. Presumably the Turner of Brooklyn who exhibited as the Apollo Association in 1839. ¶ Brooklyn CD 1832–44; Cowdrey, AA & AAU.

TURNER, J. T. Portrait painter from New York who came to Pittsburgh (Pa.) in October 1811 and stayed about a year. In 1814 he was working in Cincinnati. He may have been the Turner at Maysville (Ky.) who was the teacher of AARON H. CORWINE about 1818–20. ¶ Anderson, "Intellectual Life of Pittsburgh: Painting," 288; Knittle, *Early Ohio Taverns,* 44; information courtesy R. E. Banta and Edward H. Dwight.

TURNER, JAMES. Engraver and silversmith who was working in Boston between 1744 and 1748; his woodcut view of Boston appeared on the cover of *The American Magazine* in 1744 and 1745. He was in Philadelphia by 1758 and died there of small pox in December 1759. Possibly the same as JAMES TURNER, below, although Bowditch thinks they are to be distinguished. ¶ Stauffer; Hamilton, *Early American Book Illustrators and Wood Engravers,* 12, 43; Dow, *Arts and Crafts in New England,* cites obit. in Boston *Evening Post,* Dec. 10, 1759; Prime, I, 29; Bowditch, notes on heraldic painters and engravers.

TURNER, JAMES. Heraldic engraver? At Marblehead (Mass.) in May and June 1752 he made or painted escutcheons and engraved a coffin plate for the funeral of William Lynde. Bowditch thinks he is to be distinguished from JAMES TURNER above. ¶ Bowditch, manuscript notes on American engravers of coats of arms.

TURNER, MARIA. Author and illustrator [?] of *The Young Ladies' Assistant in Drawing and Painting* (Cincinnati, 1833) and *Rudiments of Drawing and Shadowing Flowers* (n.p., n.d.). ¶ LC, Union Cat.; Drepperd, "American Drawing Books."

TURNER, W. Landscape painter of NYC, exhibited at the National Academy in 1828. ¶ Cowdrey, NAD.

TURNER, W. A. Engraver, New Orleans, 1856. ¶ New Orleans CD 1856 (Delgado-WPA).

TURNER, WILLIAM GREENE (*c.* 1832–1917). Sculptor and medallist; died December 22, 1917, at Newport (R.I.). ¶ *Art Annual,* XV, obit.; Thieme-Becker.

TURNEY, DENNIS. Lithographer, 22, a native of Pennsylvania, at NYC in 1850. *Cf.* DENNIS TWOMY. ¶ 7 Census (1850), N.Y., XLIII, 78.

TURPIN, JAMES. Engraver and die sinker, NYC, 1849. ¶ NYBD 1849.

TURTAZ, LEWIS. Miniature painter and teacher of drawing who advertised in Charleston (S.C.) in 1767; he was from Lausanne (Switzerland). ¶ Rutledge, *Artists in the Life of Charleston,* 118; Prime, II, 11.

TUTHILL, ABRAHAM G. D. (1776–1843). Portrait painter. Born at Oyster Pond,

Long Island (N.Y.), he studied under WEST in England at the end of the century and had a year in Paris also. After returning to America he moved about a good deal; he is known to have been in NYC in 1808 and 1810, in Pomfret (Vt.) about 1815, in Utica or Plattsburgh (N.Y.) about 1819–20, in Buffalo (N.Y.) in 1822, Detroit (Mich.) in 1825, Rochester (N.Y.) about 1827, Cincinnati in 1831, and Buffalo from 1837 to 1840. His last years were spent in the home of a sister in Montpelier (Vt.) where he died June 12, 1843. ¶ Frankenstein and Healy, *Two Journeyman Painters,* 46–63, with 18 repros. and checklist; Ulp, "Art and Artists in Rochester," 30; Cist, *Cincinnati in 1841,* 140 [as Tuttle]; Cincinnati CD 1831.

TUTHILL, DANIEL. Engraver, 25, a native of New York, at NYC in 1860. ¶ 8 Census (1860), N.Y., XLIII, 266.

TUTHILL, WILLIAM H. Engraver and lithographer of NYC, active 1825–after 1830. ¶ Stauffer; Peters, *America on Stone;* NYCD 1830–32.

TUTTLE, DAVID H. Wood engraver, NYC, 1858–60. ¶ NYBD 1858, 1860.

TUTTLE, GEORGE W. Dealer in "patent elastic baby jumpers" and fancy goods, NYC, 1840's and 1850's. In 1851 he exhibited at the American Institute a bust or statutette of Jenny Lind in wax and some "lithophanes" or transparent pictures. ¶ NYCD 1847–54; Am. Inst. Cat., 1851.

TUTTLE, HUDSON. Panorama painter who exhibited his panorama of Creation at NYC in 1855. There was a Hudson Tuthill, shipwright, active in NYC from 1825 to 1831. ¶ N. Y. *Herald,* Oct. 8, 1855 (cited by J. Earl Arrington); NYCD 1825–31.

TUTTLE, JOSEPH W. Of MORSE & TUTTLE, engravers, Boston, 1837–60. ¶ Boston CD 1837–60.

TUTTLE, OTIS P. Engraver, Boston, 1841–44. ¶ Boston CD 1841–43, BD 1842, 1844.

TWIBILL, GEORGE W. (*c.* 1806–1836). N.A. Portrait painter. Born in Lampeter, Lancaster County (Pa.), he studied under HENRY INMAN and was elected a National Academician in 1833. His promising career was cut short by his death in NYC on February 15, 1836. ¶ CAB; Cowdrey, NAD; Cowdrey, AA & AAU; represented at NYHS and NAD.

TWIGG, MRS. WILLIAM ALBERT, see VIRGINIA P. DUPALAIS.

TWITCHEL, THOMAS. Engraver, 35, from New York State, at Cincinnati in 1850. ¶ 7 Census (1850), Ohio, XXI, 599.

TWITCHELL, ASA WESTON (1820–1904). Portrait painter, born January 1, 1820, at Swanzey (N.H.). He spent most of his life in the neighborhood of Albany (N.Y.) and his work was exhibited in NYC at the National Academy and the American Art-Union. He died at Slingerlands, near Albany, April 26, 1904. ¶ Twitchell, *Genealogy of the Twitchell Family,* 290–91; Cowdrey, NAD; Cowdrey, AA & AAU; Albany CD 1848–60+.

TWOMBLY, MISS H. M. Artist in partnership with Miss A. H. DENNETT at Boston in 1860. ¶ Boston BD 1860.

TWOMY (?), DENNIS. Lithographer, 25, a native of Pennsylvania, at NYC in 1860. *Cf.* DENNIS TURNEY. ¶ 8 Census (1860), N.Y., XLIII, 740.

TYLER, BENJAMIN OWEN. Engraver or lithographer of a print of General William Henry Harrison, 1840. According to his own description it was "one of the most splendid prints ever published in this or any other country containing all the principal events in the life of Gen. Harrison." He threatened to turn the print into Van Buren propaganda if the Whigs failed to subsidize him. This may be the Benjamin Owen Tyler, born in Buckland (Mass.) September 24, 1789, who made a facsimile of the Declaration of Independence. ¶ NYHS owns three letters from Tyler to Luther Bradish, dated New York, June 27, June 27, and July 1, 1840; Brigham, *The Tyler Genealogy,* I, 366.

TYLER, EDWARD. Artist, 17, a native of New York, at NYC in 1850. ¶ 7 Census (1850), N.Y., LV, 420.

TYLER, GEORGE WASHINGTON (1803 or 1805–1833). A.N.A. Portrait painter. He was born in NYC, worked there in the early 1830's, and died there May 13, 1833. He was made an Associate of the National Academy in 1832. ¶ Bolton, *Portrait Painters in Oil;* Cowdrey, NAD; NYCD 1830–32; Clark, *History of the NAD,* 272.

TYLER, RALPH. Engraver, Lowell (Mass.), 1837. ¶ Belknap, *Artists and Craftsmen of Essex County,* 5.

TYLER, THOMAS. Sign and ornamental painter at Columbus (Ohio) in 1826. ¶ Knittle, *Early Ohio Taverns,* 44.

TYLER, WILLIAM H. Wood engraver, 21, a native of Massachusetts, living with his parents in Boston in June 1860. By September 1860 he was in NYC. ¶ 8 Census (1860), Mass., XXVII, 764; 8 Census (1860), N.Y., XLIII, 51.

TZSCHUMANSKY, see SCHIMONSKY.

U

UHL, WILLIAM. Portrait, theatrical scene painter, and teacher of drawing and painting. He was working in Charleston (S.C.) in 1844. ¶ Rutledge, *Artists in the Life of Charleston.*

UHLE, BERNARD. Painter of "An Election Day Bonfire, 5th and Chestnut Streets, Philadelphia," 1854, owned by the Atwater Kent Museum. ¶ *American Processional,* 245, repro. 158.

UHLE, G. ANTON. Portrait painter, Philadelphia, 1856–60+. ¶ Phila. CD 1856–60+.

ULBERTI, JOSEPH. Artist, 52, a native of Sardinia, living in Philadelphia in 1860. ¶ 8 Census (1860), Pa., LI, 508.

ULKE, HENRY (1821–1910). Portrait painter, born in Frankenstein (Germany) on January 29, 1821. He studied painting in Berlin but joined the revolutionary party, was wounded, captured and imprisoned during the 1848 uprising. On his release in 1849 Ulke came to America. After working in NYC as a designer and illustrator for a time, he moved to Washington where he spent the rest of his life. He painted many portraits of high government officials. Ulke died February 17, 1910. ¶ Fairman, *Art and Artists of the Capitol,* 356; *Art Annual,* VIII, 401; NYBD 1854–57.

UNDERWOOD, BALD & SPENCER. Banknote engravers, Philadelphia and NYC, 1835–36. The firm was composed of THOMAS UNDERWOOD, ROBERT BALD, and ASA SPENCER. After SAMUEL HUFTY joined the firm, about 1836, its name was changed to Underwood, Bald, Spencer & Hufty and so continued until 1843, when it became DANFORTH, BALD, SPENCER & HUFTY. ¶ Phila. CD 1835–43; NYCD 1835–43.

UNDERWOOD, Lt. J. A. Contributor of some illustrations in *Narrative of the United States Exploring Expedition* (1844). ¶ Rasmussen, "Artists of the Explorations Overland, 1840–1860."

UNDERWOOD, THOMAS (1795–1849). Banknote engraver working in Philadelphia from about 1825 to 1843. He was a partner in the following firms: FAIRMAN, DRAPER & UNDERWOOD (1825–27), DRAPER, UNDERWOOD & CO. (1827–33), DRAPER, UNDERWOOD, BALD & SPENCER (1833–35), UNDERWOOD, BALD & SPENCER [& Hufty] (1835–43), and DANFORTH, UNDERWOOD & CO. (1839–42). Underwood died in Lafayette (Ind.) July 13, 1849. ¶ Stauffer; Phila. CD 1825–43; NYCD 1835–43.

UNGER, ——. Miniature painter at Montrose (Pa.) in 1845. ¶ Carolina Art Assoc. Cat., 1936.

UNKART, Mrs. E. Portrait and figure painter of NYC and Brooklyn, exhibited at the National Academy in 1837 (as a pupil of CHRISTIAN MAYR) and the Apollo Association in 1840. ¶ Cowdrey, NAD; Cowdrey, AA & AAU.

UNTENREITH, L., see LOUIS AUTENRIETH.

UNTHANK, WILLIAM S. (1813–1892). Portrait painter. He was born in Richmond (Ind.); worked in Richmond, Centerville, Indianapolis, and Port Royal (Ind.) and Cincinnati (Ohio); spent his last years in Council Bluffs (Iowa) where he died July 22, 1892. ¶ Peat, *Pioneer Painters of Indiana,* 164–65, 239.

UPHAM & COLBURN. Lithographers, Boston, 1853; HERVEY UPHAM and CHARLES H. COLBURN. ¶ Boston CD 1853.

UPHAM, HERVEY. Lithographer (?) and printer, Boston, 1853–60 and after. In 1853 he was in the firm of UPHAM & COLBURN. ¶ Boston CD 1853–60+ [as a lithographer only in 1853].

UPJOHN, RICHARD (1802–1878). Architect and amateur landscape painter, born January 22, 1802, at Shaftesbury (England). Trained as a draftsman, he worked in Shaftesbury and London until 1829 when he came to America. He first settled in New Bedford (Mass.), where he worked as a draftsman and teacher of drawing until he decided to become an architect and moved to Boston in 1834. His first important commission was to design the new Trinity Church in NYC, one of the most important American examples of Gothic Revival. From that time until his retirement in 1876 Upjohn, assisted by his son Richard M. Upjohn, was one of the leading architects in America. He was a founder and first president (1857–76) of the American Institute of Architects. He was also very fond of landscape painting. Upjohn died August 17, 1878, at Garrison (N.Y.). ¶ DAB; Stokes, *Iconography,* III, 694; NYCD 1845–76.

UPSON, JEFFERSON T. Artist, Buffalo (N.Y.), 1860. ¶ Buffalo BD 1860.

URBANI, F. Sculptor and carver who was working in Charleston (S.C.) in 1850. He offered to repair marble statues, model busts and statues, and do bronzing and imitation iron work. ¶ Rutledge, *Artists in the Life of Charleston.*

URWILER, BENJAMIN. Lithographer, 30, a native of Pennsylvania, living in Philadelphia in 1860. Next door was John Urwiler, 31, lithographic printer. ¶ 8 Census (1860), Pa., LXI, 465.

UTLEY, Col. WILLIAM L. Portrait painter working in Ohio about 1830. ¶ Frary, "Ohio Discovers Its Primitives," 41.

V

VACHON, ACHILLE, see VACHON & GIRON.

VACHON & GIRON. Engravers, San Francisco, 1858; ACHILLE VACHON and MARC GIRON. ¶ San Francisco CD and BD 1858.

VAIL, ARAMENTA DIANTHE. Miniaturist, active 1837–47. She lived in Newark (N.J.) in 1837–38 and in NYC from 1839 to 1845. She exhibited at the National Academy, the Apollo Association, and the American Institute. ¶ Newark CD 1837–38; Cowdrey, AA & AAU; Cowdrey, NAD; Am. Inst. Cat., 1845; Bolton, *Miniature Painters.*

VAIL, JOSEPH. Chairmaker and amateur artist of NYC who exhibited a "landscape in bronze" at the American Institute in 1846. ¶ NYCD 1845–46; Am. Inst. Cat., 1846.

VAILLANT, Mme. ——. Miniaturist at NYC in 1825. ¶ Bolton, *Miniature Painters.*

VALAPERTA, GIUSEPPE (?–1817?). Sculptor. A native of Milan, Valaperta worked in Genoa; in Madrid for Joseph Bonaparte, King of Spain; and in France at the palace of Malmaison before Napoleon's downfall in 1815. He arrived in Washington (D.C.) in the fall of 1815 and for two years was employed as a sculptor at the National Capitol, where his eagle can still be seen on the frieze of the south wall of Statuary Hall. He also carved in ivory and modelled red wax portraits of Jefferson, Gallatin, Madison, Monroe, and Jackson, and was recommended by WILLIAM THORNTON and BENJAMIN LATROBE for the Washington statue commissioned by North Carolina and later executed by Canova. Valaperta disappeared from his Washington boarding house in March 1817, leaving a will, and is thought to have committed suicide, as he was never heard of again. ¶ Wall, "Joseph Valaperta"; Fairman, *Art and Artists of the Capitol,* 31–32, 452; Washington *National Intelligencer,* Nov. 4, 1815 (citation courtesy Miss Anna Wells Rutledge).

VALDENUIT, THOMAS BLUGET DE (1763–1846). Engraver and crayon portraitist. An ex-officer of the French army, Valdenuit came to America and opened a drawing school in Baltimore with one BOUCHÉ in November 1795. The following year he moved to NYC and became the partner of C. B. F. J. DE SAINT-MÉMIN in the profile and portrait engraving business. Valdenuit is said to have returned to France sometime after February 1797. ¶ Pleasants, *250 Years of Painting in Maryland,* 31; Norfleet, *Saint-Mémin in Virginia,* 14–16; Rice, "An Album of Saint-Mémin Portraits," 24–25; *Art Quarterly* (Winter 1951), 349, 352; Stauffer; Fielding's supplement to Stauffer.

VALENCIN, Signor ——. Spanish artist who was in NYC in December 1830 exhibiting "Fantocini" and "Chinese views," including views in Europe and a Goddess of Liberty. ¶ N. Y. *Evening Post,* Dec. 7, 1830 (courtesy J. Earl Arrington).

VALENTINE, CHARLES M. Portrait and miniature painter; at Germantown (Pa.) in 1836; at Philadelphia in 1838 and 1840. ¶ Rutledge, PA; Phila. BD 1838, CD 1840.

VALENTINE, EDWARD VIRGINIUS (1838–1930). Sculptor, born in Richmond (Va.) on November 12, 1838. Although intended for a business career, Valentine studied painting under WILLIAM JAMES HUBARD and began modelling portrait busts before he was 20. In 1859 he went to Paris to study painting under Thomas Couture, but in 1861 he went to Rome and began to study sculpture. Later the same year he went to Berlin and until 1865 he studied under the German sculptor, August Kiss. Returning to Richmond in 1865 he was soon busy making busts and statues of Confederate heroes. His last important work was done about 1908. He was also prominent in local historical studies and was president of the Valentine Museum in Richmond. He died October 19, 1930. ¶ *Richmond Portraits,* 234–35; Fairman, *Art and Artists of the Capitol;* DAB; CAB.

VALENTINE, ELIAS. Portrait and general engraver, NYC, 1810–18. ¶ Stauffer.

VALENTINE, JOHN. English artist, 50, in NYC in 1860. ¶ 8 Census (1860), N.Y., LIII, 376.

VALENTINE, JULIUS. Portrait painter, 33, born in Germany, at Baltimore in 1850. ¶ 7 Census (1850), Md., IV, 676.

VALENTINE, SAMUEL. Engraver, NYC, 1840. ¶ NYBD 1840.

VALENTINE, WILLIAM WINSTON. Painter. An older brother of EDWARD V. VALENTINE, he worked in the family store for a while, then turned painter, and finally became a teacher and philologist. ¶ *Richmond Portraits,* 199.

VALETTE, see VALLETTE.

VALFRAMBERT, Mlle. ——. Teacher of grammar and drawing who arrived in New Orleans from France in the spring of 1822. She was formerly drawing teacher at the "Royal House of St. Denis" and a pupil of "the late Imperial Castle of Ecouen." ¶ Delgado-WPA cites *Courier,* May 8, 1822.

VALLANCE, JOHN (*c.* 1770–1823). Engraver. A native of Scotland, active in Philadelphia from 1791 until his death there, June 14, 1823. From 1791 to 1797 he was with THACKARA & VALLANCE and from 1817 to 1819 with TANNER, VALLANCE, KEARNEY & Co. He was also associated with the Pennsylvania Academy from 1811 to 1817. ¶ Philadelphia *National Gazette and Literary Register,* June 16, 1823, obit.; Phila. CD 1791–1824; Society of Artists and Penna. Acad. Cats., 1811–23; Prime, II, 74; Stauffer; Hamilton, *Early American Book Illustrators and Wood Engravers,* 476.

VALLÉE, JEAN FRANCOIS DE (or John Francis Vallee or Valley). French miniaturist and silhouettist. In 1785 discussed with Jefferson the possibility of coming to America. By 1794 he was in Philadelphia, listed as a boardinghouse keeper in that year and in 1798. He was at Charleston (S.C.) in 1803, 1805, and 1806; in 1810 and 1815 he was at New Orleans, where he painted a miniature of Jackson. He cut a silhouette of Washington in 1795. ¶ Jefferson, *Writings* (Monticello ed.), V, 131–32; Phila. CD 1794, 1798; Rutledge, *Artists in the Life of Charleston;* Hart, "Life Portraits of Andrew Jackson," 799; Hart, "Life Portraits of Washington," 303; American-Anderson Art Galleries, Sales Cat., April 2–3, 1937; Jackson, *Silhouette,* 150; Bassett, *Correspondence of Andrew Jackson,* II, 209, 262, VI, 462, 468.

VALLEE, P. R. Miniaturist, New Orleans, 1810. Possibly the same as JEAN FRANCOIS DE VALLÉE. ¶ Delgado-WPA cites *La. Courier,* Oct. 10, 1810; Rutledge, *Artists in the Life of Charleston,* 126, cites the same issue of the *Courier* in reference to J. F. de Vallée.

VALLETTE, EDWIN F. (or Edward Valette). Letter, ornamental, and general engraver; born in Pennsylvania about 1829; working in Philadelphia from 1848 to after 1860. His brother JAMES also was an engraver. ¶ 7 Census (1850), Pa., LIII, 53; Phila. CD 1848–60+.

VALLETTE, JAMES. Engraver, 19, a native of Pennsylvania, at Philadelphia in 1850 with his mother Sarah and brother EDWIN VALLETTE. ¶ 7 Census (1850), Pa., LIII, 53.

VALOIS, EDWARD. Lithographer working in NYC from the 1840's into the 1860's. He worked with G. W. FASEL and others. ¶ Peters, *America on Stone;* NYCD 1856–60; *Portfolio* (March 1943), 158; *Portfolio* (June 1945), 231; Am. Inst. Cat., 1851.

VALUE, Miss ——. Miniature painter, teacher of drawing and painting, at Richmond (Va.) in 1830 and 1832. ¶ *Richmond Portraits,* 243.

VAN ALSTYNE, ARCHIBALD C. Steel engraver at Albany (N.Y.), 1857–59. ¶ Albany CD 1857–59.

VAN ALSTYNE, MARY. Still life on velvet, Massachusetts, about 1825. ¶ Lipman and Winchester, 168.

VANARDEN, GEORGE. English artist (picture cleaner in the directory), 54, at Baltimore in 1860. ¶ 8 Census (1860), Md., III, 980; Baltimore CD 1859.

VANARTSDALEN, JAMES. Engraver; born in Pennsylvania about 1811; working in Philadelphia from about 1849 to after 1860. ¶ 8 Census (1860), Pa., LXII, 78 [as Vanassdelen]; Phila. CD 1849–60+.

VANAUCHI, see VANNUCHI.

VAN BEEST, see BEEST.

VAN BRUNT, R. Landscape painter in watercolors, active in Brooklyn (N.Y.) and elsewhere on Long Island between 1857 and 1876. Some of his sketches are at the Long Island Historical Society. ¶ *Portfolio* (June 1945), 21–22, repro.

VAN DE CASTELLE (or Casteele), XAVIER. Lithographer with BRITTON & COMPANY, San Francisco, in 1860–61. He was born in Belgium about 1817. ¶ Peters, *California on Stone;* 8 Census (1860), Cal., VII, 1323; San Francisco CD 1861.

VANDECHAMP, see VAUDECHAMP.

VANDERBECK, JOHN HENRY. Lithographer, 23, a native of New York, living in NYC in 1860. ¶ 8 Census (1860), N.Y., LV, 832.

VANDERHOEF or VANDEROEF, JOHN J. Of WHITE & VANDER[H]OEF, engravers, NYC, 1857. ¶ NYBD and CD 1857.

VAN DER KERCHE, ——. Painter of a portrait of Mrs. John Drew, the actress, in 1857, possibly at Philadelphia. ¶ Mayo cites Smithsonian Institution morgue.

VANDERLIP, WILLARD C. Lithographer, 23, a native of Massachusetts, boarding in Boston in 1860 at the same house as GEORGE

W. Simonds. ¶ 8 Census (1860), Mass., XXVII, 890; Boston CD 1860.

Vanderlippe, D. J. Carriage, sign, and general painter at Charleston (S.C.) in 1844. ¶ Rutledge, *Artists in the Life of Charleston.*

Vanderlyn, John (1775–1852). N.A. Portrait, historical, and landscape painter, born October 15, 1775, in Kingston (N.Y.), son of Nicholas and grandson of Pieter Vanderlyn. He studied drawing under Archibald Robertson for three years and had a few months of training under Gilbert Stuart before being sent to Paris in 1796 by his patron, Aaron Burr. He remained in Paris for five years, returning to NYC in 1801. Two years later he again went abroad and he remained in Europe for almost twelve years, of which two were spent in Rome and the rest in Paris. It was during this period that he produced his best work, notably his *Marius amid the Ruins of Carthage* and the famous *Ariadne.* After his return to America in 1815 Vanderlyn painted portraits and for some years exhibited his panoramas in a specially constructed building in NYC. In 1837 he was commissioned to paint *The Landing of Columbus* for the Capitol Rotunda in Washington and again went to Paris for several years. Embittered by public indifference and artistic rivalries, Vanderlyn finally returned to his native town and died there in poverty on September 23, 1852. ¶ The NYHS owns two versions of a manuscript biography of Vanderlyn by Robert Gosman. See also: Flexner, *The Light of Distant Skies,* which contains a selective bibliography; DAB; Dunlap, *History;* Tuckerman, *Book of the Artists;* Schoonmaker, *John Vanderlyn, Artist, 1775–1852,* a 19th century biography first published in 1950 by the Senate House Association, Kingston, N.Y.

Vanderlyn, John, Jr. or 2d (1805–1876). Portrait painter, nephew and godson of John Vanderlyn. He was at Savannah (Ga.) in 1833 and possibly at Charleston (S.C.) in 1836, working with J. P. Sherwood, of whom Vanderlyn painted a portrait now at the NYHS. In 1859 he was at Kingston (N.Y.). ¶ Hastings, "Pieter Vanderlyn," 298; information courtesy Harold E. Dickson; N. Y. State BD 1859; Rutledge, *Artists in the Life of Charleston.*

Vanderlyn, Nicholas. House, sign, and portrait painter who was working in Kingston (N.Y.) in 1766. He was a son of Pieter, father of John, and grandfather of John, 2d. ¶ FARL, photo of signed portrait, dated 1741; *Ecclesiastical Records, State of New York,* I, 404; Schoonmaker, *History of Kingston,* 491; Hastings, "Pieter Vanderlyn," 296–99.

Vanderlyn, Pieter (1687–1778). Portrait painter? A native of Holland, Vanderlyn came to the Province of New York about 1718, lived in Albany during the 1720's, and then settled in Kingston, where he lived until shortly before his death. Although contemporary records do not mention him as a limner, it was believed by his grandson, John Vanderlyn, that Pieter Vanderlyn painted portraits. On the strength of this tradition, several early New York portraits have been attributed to this artist, although the question remains unsettled. ¶ Hastings, "Pieter Vanderlyn"; Harris, "Pieter Vanderlyn"; *Colonial Laws of New York,* I, 1034, and II, 375.

Vanderpool, James (1765–1799). Amateur portrait painter, brother of John Vanderpool. In 1787 he painted a portrait of his uncle James Van Dyke (1740–1828), now owned by the Newark (N.J.) Museum. ¶ *The Museum* (July 1949), 7–8; Vanderpoel, *Genealogy of the Vanderpoel Family,* 168–69.

Vanderpool, John. Portrait, banner, and transparency painter, NYC, late 18th and early 19th century. He was born sometime in the 1760's and was a brother of James Vanderpool. His portrait of his aunt, Mrs. James Van Dyke, painted in 1787, is owned by the Newark (N.J.) Museum. ¶ *The Museum* (July 1949), 7–8 and cover; Vanderpoel, *Genealogy of the Vanderpoel Family,* 168–69.

Vandevelde, Petro. Sculptor, NYC, who exhibited "Slave in Revolt" at the American Institute in 1850. ¶ Am. Inst. Cat., 1850; NYCD 1851.

Van Doort, M. Portrait painter, Massachusetts, about 1825. ¶ Lipman and Winchester, 181.

Vanduzee & Barton. Wood engravers, Buffalo (N.Y.), 1853–59; Benjamin C. Vanduzee and L. H. Barton. ¶ Buffalo CD 1853–59; Hamilton, *Early American Book Illustrators and Wood Engravers,* 180.

Vanduzee, Benjamin C. Wood engraver and designer, Buffalo (N.Y.), 1849–60 and after; of Vanduzee & Barton from 1853 to 1859. ¶ Buffalo CD 1849–60+.

Van Dyck, James. Portrait and miniature painter working in NYC in 1834–36 and

1843. He painted a portrait of Aaron Burr and exhibited at the National and American Academies. ¶ NYCD 1834–36, 1843; Cowdrey, NAD; Cowdrey, AA & AAU; Bolton, *Miniature Painters;* NYHS Cat. of Portraits.

VAN FAVOREN, J. H. Painted a portrait of Alexis Coquillard at South Bend (Ind.) in 1847, now owned by Notre Dame University. *Cf.* VAN STAVOREN. ¶ Peat, *Pioneer Painters of Indiana,* 139.

VANGELDERIN, GEORGE. Portrait painter, NYC, 1859. ¶ NYBD 1859.

VAN HASE, DAVID. Engraver, 17, a native of New York, at NYC in 1850. ¶ 7 Census (1850), N.Y., XLIX, 935.

VAN HOUTEANO, ——. Did colored lithographs for *The Florist and Horticultural Journal,* published in Philadelphia, 1853–55. ¶ McClinton, "American Flower Lithographs," 362.

VAN HUSEN, JOHN. Limner and glazier, apprenticed to RAPHAEL GOELET, NYC, 1726. ¶ Groce, "New York Painting Before 1800."

VAN INGEN, HENRY A. (1833–1899). Genre painter; born in Holland November 12, 1833; working in NYC in 1860 and after; died in the United States November 17, 1899. ¶ *Art Annual,* I, obit.; Cowdrey, NAD; Rutledge, PA.

VAN INGEN & SNYDER. Wood engravers and designers, Philadelphia, 1853–after 1860; WILLIAM H. VAN INGEN and HENRY M. SNYDER. ¶ Hamilton, *Early American Book Illustrators and Wood Engravers;* Phila. CD 1856–71.

VAN INGEN, WILLIAM H. Wood engraver and designer; born in New York about 1831; apprenticed to JOSEPH and WILLIAM HOWLAND in NYC about 1847–50, when he exhibited at the American Institute; settled in Philadelphia about 1853 and was in partnership there with HENRY M. SNYDER at least until 1871. ¶ 8 Census (1860), Pa., LV, 854; Am. Inst. Cat., 1847–50; Hamilton, *Early American Book Illustrators and Wood Engravers;* Phila. CD 1854–71

VAN LOO, PIERRE (1837–1858). Scene painter at the New Orleans Theatre at the time of his death, February 1858. He was a native of Ghent (Belgium). ¶ Delgado-WPA cites *Bee,* Feb. 13, 1858.

VAN NAME, GEORGE W. Portrait painter, Cincinnati, 1850–53. ¶ Cincinnati CD 1850; Ohio BD 1853.

VAN NORDEN, JOHN H. Landscape painter of Waterford (N.Y.) who exhibited at the National Academy in 1853 and 1859. ¶ Cowdrey, NAD.

VAN NORMAN, Mrs. D. C. Portrait painter who exhibited at the National Academy in 1857–58. Her husband was a minister. ¶ Cowdrey, NAD; NYCD 1859.

VAN NOSTRAND, HENRY. Wood engraver who exhibited at the American Institute in 1847–49. In 1847 he was an apprentice or employee of the HOWLANDS. ¶ Am. Inst. Cat., 1847–49.

VANNUCHI, F. or S. Wax modeller, born in Italy about 1800. He was in Charleston (S.C.) in 1845 with an exhibition of wax figures. In 1847 he exhibited in NYC and Philadelphia his "cosmorama" or collection of paintings of American views and historical scenes. By 1852 he had settled in New Orleans where he opened the American Museum and Waxworks; it was still flourishing in 1860, when Vannuchi's personal property was valued at $25,000. ¶ 8 Census (1860), La., VI, 202; Rutledge, *Artists in the Life of Charleston;* N. Y. *Herald,* June 15, 1847, and Phila. *Public Ledger,* Aug. 13, 1847 (courtesy J. Earl Arrington); *Orleanian,* Nov. 23, 1852, *Bee,* Jan. 3, 1853, and *Courier,* March 4, 1856 (courtesy Delgado-WPA); New Orleans CD 1855, 1858–59.

VANOSTEN, JOSEPH. Pennsylvania-born artist, 28, at Baltimore in 1860. ¶ 8 Census (1860), Md., III, 956.

VANSAUN, PETER D. Of HORLOR & VANSAUN, engravers, NYC, 1859–60. ¶ NYCD 1859–60.

VAN SCHOICK, J. A. Portrait painter, Philadelphia, active 1834–37. ¶ Rutledge, PA; Phila. CD 1837.

VAN SICKLE, ADOLPHUS (1835–?). Artist and photographer, born in Delaware County (Ohio) December 6, 1835, son of SELAH VAN SICKLE. His childhood was spent in Ohio, Illinois, and Michigan, but he was married in November 1871 at Elkhart (Ind.). Two years later he moved to Kalamazoo (Mich.) where he was in business as a photographer at least until 1880. ¶ Van Sickle, *A History of the Van Sickle Family,* 228; information courtesy Wilbur D. Peat who cites Bartholomew's *History of Elkhart, Indiana* (1930).

VAN SICKLE, J. N. Portrait painter at Xenia (Ohio) in 1855. ¶ Information courtesy Edward H. Dwight, Cincinnati Art Museum.

VAN SICKLE, SELAH (1812–?). Portrait and panorama painter. Born in Cayuga, now Tompkins, County (N.Y.) on June 8,

1812, he was taken by his parents to central Ohio in 1817. He was married in 1834 in Delaware County (Ohio) and he lived there until 1845 when he moved to Nauvoo (Ill.). There he painted a portrait of Brigham Young. In 1846 he moved to St. Joseph County (Mich.). A signed and dated portrait in the La Porte Historical Museum indicates that Van Sickle visited that Indiana town in 1849. In 1851 he moved back to Delaware County (Ohio) and in 1853–54 he painted a panorama of the life of Christ. He later turned to farming for his livelihood, working in Morrow County (Ohio) from 1857 to 1863, Clinton County (Mich.) 1863–73, Marshall County (Iowa) 1873–76, and again in Clinton County (Mich.) where he was living in 1880. ¶ Van Sickle, *A History of the Van Sickle Family,* 207–09; information courtesy Wilbur D. Peat.

VAN STARKENBORGH, see STARKENBORGH.

VAN STAVOREN, ——. Portrait painter, Cincinnati, 1846. *Cf.* VAN FAVOREN. ¶ Cincinnati CD 1846 (courtesy Edward H. Dwight, Cincinnati Art Museum).

VANSTRYDONCK, CHARLES. Of VERELST & VANSTRYDONCK, lithographers, NYC, 1859. ¶ NYCD 1859.

VANURANKEN, JOHN. Engraver, NYC, 1846–54. ¶ NYBD 1846, 1854.

VANUCHI, see VANNUCHI.

VAN VLECK, DURBIN. Wood engraver. As a boy he exhibited at the American Institute in 1851. By 1856 he was in business in San Francisco where he was active at least until 1867. ¶ Am. Inst. Cat., 1851; San Francisco CD 1856, BD 1858–59; Hamilton, *Early American Book Illustrators and Wood Engravers,* 345, 416.

VAN WILLIS, see EDMUND A. WILLIS.

VAN ZANDT, THOMAS K. Portrait and animal painter active in Albany from about 1844 until after 1860. ¶ Cowdrey, NAD; Albany CD 1846–60+; *Panorama* (Dec. 1946), 45.

VAN ZANDT, W. THOMPSON. Amateur portrait and genre painter active in NYC in 1844–45. He was a merchant. ¶ Cowdrey, NAD; Cowdrey, AA & AAU; NYCD 1845.

VARLEY, JOHN. Swedish engraver, 34, at NYC in 1850. ¶ 7 Census (1850), N.Y., XLIII, 279.

VASSEUR, HERMANN. Engraver, NYC, 1850–52. ¶ NYBD 1850–52.

VATEL, JOHN. "Picture maker," NYC, 1790. ¶ NYCD 1790.

VAUDECHAMP, JEAN JOSEPH (1790–1866). Portrait painter. A native of France, Vaudechamp spent the winters of 1832–36 in New Orleans and then returned to France, where he died in 1866. WILLIAM DUNLAP in May 1834 reported that he had made $30,000 in three winters in New Orleans. ¶ Cline, "Art and Artists in New Orleans"; Dunlap, *Diary,* III, 785; Delgado-WPA cites *Courier,* Nov. 28, 1832, and Dec. 26, 1833, and *Bee,* Dec. 28, 1833, Jan. 3, 1834, Nov. 30 and Dec. 1, 1836.

VAUDRICOURT, A. DE. Lithographer, topographical draftsman, drawing and piano teacher. He was at New Orleans in 1835, did work for BOUVÉ & SHARP in Boston in 1844, did lithographic work in NYC in 1845–46. In 1850 he served for about a year as artist with the boundary survey in Texas; at this time he drew a view of the Plaza of El Paso which was published. ¶ Delgado-WPA cites *Courier,* Feb. 16, 1835; Peters, *America on Stone;* NYBD 1846; Taft, *Artists and Illustrators of the Old West,* 277–78; Stokes, *Historical Prints; Antiques,* June 1948, 459, repro.

VAUGHAN, CHARLES A. Portrait painter in oils who was active in Cincinnati from 1844 to 1856 and in St. Louis in 1859. He also worked in Kentucky. He exhibited at the Boston Athenaeum. ¶ Cincinnati BD 1844, 1856; Swan, BA; St. Louis BD 1859.

VAUGHAN, HECTOR W. Of MCCANN & VAUGHAN, engravers, NYC, 1850. ¶ NYCD 1850.

VAUGHAN, JAMES W. Engraver and painter, NYC, 1851–54. ¶ NYCD 1851–54.

VAUGHAN, N. J. Still life in watercolors, American, about 1825. ¶ Lipman and Winchester, 181.

VAUTIN, N. Portrait painter, Boston, 1845–46. ¶ Boston BD 1845–46.

VEASEY or VESEY, THOMAS. Landscape painter. Thomas Veasey exhibited a view of Passaic Falls (N.J.) at the National Academy in 1846. Thomas Vesey, artist, 30, a native of Maine, was living in NYC in 1850. ¶ Cowdrey, NAD; 7 Census (1850), N.Y., LI, 17.

VEDDER, ELIHU (1836–1923). N.A. Figure and mural painter. Born February 26, 1836, in NYC, he spent much of his childhood in Schenectady (N.Y.) and began to study art at 12. He received some instruction from TOMPKINS H. MATTESON at Sherburne (N.Y.). In 1856 Vedder went to France and thence to Italy for several years. He returned to NYC in 1861 and spent the war years there. He was elected to the National Academy in 1865 and the same year he again went abroad to settle permanently in Italy. Although he made frequent visits to America, Vedder made his home in Rome, spending his summers on the Isle of Capri. Though perhaps best known for his illustrations for *The Rubaiyat of Omar Khayyam,* Vedder was primarily a painter of ideal figures of a rather mystical quality; in his later years he also painted a number of large murals. In 1910 his autobiography appeared under the title of *The Digressions of V.* He died in Rome, January 29, 1923. ¶ DAB; Tuckerman, *Book of the Artists;* Park, *Mural Painters in America.*

VEILER, JOSEPH. Sculptor, New Orleans, 1840's. J. H. Veilex, sculptor at New Orleans in 1838, is presumed to be the same man. ¶ New Orleans CD 1838, 1841–44, 1849

VEILLERET (?), PIERRE. Italian engraver, 25, at NYC in 1860. ¶ 8 Census (1860), N.Y., XLII, 422.

VELLUTO, ——. Assistant to DELAMANO in painting the panorama of the Crystal Palace, first exhibited in NYC in December 1851. ¶ N. Y. *Herald,* Dec. 2, 1851 (courtesy J. Earl Arrington).

VENINO, FRANCIS. Painter and lithographer active in NYC during the 1850's. In 1852 his lithograph of TRUMBULL's "Surrender of Cornwallis" was published by N. CURRIER. In 1856 Venino was listed as a photographer; in 1858–59 as an artist. In 1858 he exhibited "The Destruction of Carthage" at the National Academy. ¶ *Portfolio* (Feb. 1942), 7; NYCD 1856, 1858–59; Cowdrey, NAD.

VENNE, JUS. Artist, 32, a native of Maine, at the Tremont Hotel in New Orleans in October 1850. ¶ 7 Census (1850), La., IV (1), 614.

VERBRICK, RICHARD. Miniature and portrait painter, Cincinnati, 1825 and 1831. ¶ Cincinnati CD 1825, 1831 (courtesy Edward H. Dwight, Cincinnati Art Museum).

VER BRYCK, CORNELIUS (1813–1844). N.A. Landscape, historical, and portrait painter, born January 1, 1813, at Yaugh Paugh (N.J.). He began painting professionally about 1835 in NYC and worked there until his death, except for visits to Alabama in 1837–38, to England and France in 1839, and a second visit to England in 1843. He was the brother-in-law of DANIEL HUNTINGTON and a close friend of HENRY PETERS GRAY. He died in Brooklyn (N.Y.) on May 31, 1844. ¶ Sketch of "The Late Mr. Ver Bryck" by THOMAS COLE in Cummings, *Historic Annals of the NAD,* 182–84; Cowdrey, NAD; Cowdrey, AA & AAU; CAB.

VER BRYCK, WILLIAM (1823–1899). Portrait painter; born in NYC; studied at the National Academy and began painting professionally in NYC about 1851. After 1860 he made a number of professional visits to Milwaukee and he finally settled there in 1881. He died June 21, 1899. ¶ *Art Annual,* II (1899, supp.), 84, obit.; Cowdrey, NAD; Cowdrey, AA & AAU; Butts, *Art in Wisconsin,* 97.

VERDI, CLAUDIUS. Engraver, 35, born in Florence (Italy), in the New York State penitentiary in NYC for grand larceny, July 1860. ¶ 8 Census (1860), N.Y., LXI, 187.

VERELST, FRANCIS. Of VERELST & VANSTRYDONCK, lithographers, NYC, 1859. ¶ NYCD 1859.

VERELST & VANSTRYDONCK. Lithographers, NYC, 1859; FRANCIS VERELST and CHARLES VANSTRYDONCK. ¶ NYBD and CD 1859.

VERGER, PETER C. Sculptor, engraver, and hair worker from Paris who was active in NYC from 1795 to 1797 and at Paris in 1806. He was associated with JOHN FRANCIS RENAULT in the publication of the latter's "Triumph of Liberty" print. ¶ Gottesman, *Arts and Crafts in NYC, 1777–99,* no. 100–01, 111; NYCD 1796–97; Stauffer; Thieme-Becker.

VERGRIES, M. Teacher of drawing, mathematics, French, and piano at Charleston (S.C.) in 1846. ¶ Rutledge, *Artists in the Life of Charleston.*

VERHAEGEN, LOUIS. Sculptor, NYC, 1851–60. Exhibited plaster figure of Tom Thumb and a marble bust of Daniel Webster at the American Institute in 1856. In 1851 he was with VERHAEGEN & PEEIFFER. ¶ NYBD and CD 1851–60; Am. Inst. Cat., 1856.

VERHAGEN & PEEIFFER [*sic*]. Sculptors, NYC, 1851; LOUIS VERHAEGEN and an unidentified Peeiffer or Pfeiffer. ¶ NYBD 1851.

VERLEGER or VERLIGER, CHARLES FREDERICK. Artist and carver, Baltimore. As carver, 1851–54; as artist, 1855–57; as veterinary surgeon, 1858–59; and as herb doctor, 1860. ¶ Lafferty; Baltimore CD 1851–60

VERMONNET, ——. Miniature and portrait

painter who arrived in NYC about July 1792 and was at Baltimore from December 1792 to October 1793. ¶ N. Y. *Daily Advertiser,* July 23, 1792 (courtesy Miss Helen McKearin); Prime, II, 37.

VERNELLE, BERNARD. Portrait painter at New Orleans 1852–53. ¶ New Orleans CD 1852–53.

VERNERT, LEON JOB. Portrait, genre, and landscape painter, who exhibited at the Pennsylvania Academy in 1858 as of Paris and in 1860 as of Philadelphia. ¶ Rutledge, PA.

VERNET, CHARLES. Artist, 30, a native of France, at New Orleans in 1850. He left France between 1846 and 1849. ¶ 7 Census (1850), La., V, 227.

VERNIER, WESLEY. Ohio artist, 30, at NYC in 1850. ¶ 7 Census (1850), N.Y., XLVIII, 554.

VERNON, THOMAS (*c.* 1824 1872). Line engraver. A native of Staffordshire (England), he studied engraving in Paris and London and did art reproductions for the London *Art Journal.* He came to America about 1853 and for about three years was employed in NYC chiefly on banknote work. He returned to England about 1856 and died in London January 23, 1872. ¶ *Art Journal,* XXIV, March 1, 1872, 75, obit.; Stauffer; Cowdrey, NAD; Clement and Hutton.

VERRICK, WILLIAM. Prussian-born artist, 34, at San Francisco in 1860. His wife was also German, but their children were born in California after 1855. ¶ 8 Census (1850), Cal., VII, 1305.

VERSTILLE, WILLIAM (*c.* 1755–1803). Miniaturist and portrait painter. He was at Philadelphia in 1782 and 1783, at NYC in 1784, at Salem (Mass.) in 1802; he died in Boston on December 6, 1803. Sometime during the 1790's he also worked in Connecticut. ¶ Belknap, *Artists and Craftsmen of Essex County,* 14; Prime, II, 11; Gottesman, *Arts and Crafts in NYC,* II, no. 55; Felt, *Annals of Salem,* II, 79; Lipman, "William Verstille's Connecticut Miniatures," 7 repros.

VERVOORT, V. Painter of a portrait of Captain Ward Chipman of Salem (Mass.) about 1819. ¶ Sherman, "Unrecorded Early American Painters" (Oct. 1934), 150.

VESEY, THOMAS, see THOMAS VEASEY.

VETHAKE, ADRIANA. Landscapes and buildings in watercolors. She was a pupil of ARCHIBALD ROBERTSON of NYC and was active around NYC and Boston from 1795 to 1801. ¶ *Portfolio* (Aug. 1950), 2–6; *Antiques* (Oct. 1950), 271.

VEUDUCOURT, see VAUDRICOURT.

VEYRIER, JOSEPH. Portrait and miniature painter of Philadelphia, active 1813–17. The name is variously spelled: Veyrier, Verier, Verree, Veyreer. ¶ Phila. CD 1813–14, 1816–17; information courtesy Norris S. Oliver of East Orange (N.J.) who owns a portrait by Veyrier.

VIANDEN, HEINRICH (1814–1899). Landscape painter. Born in Poppelsdorf (Germany), Vianden was trained in steel engraving, etching, and lithography, as well as in painting at Munich and Antwerp. He left his home in Cologne in 1849 and settled with his family in Milwaukee where he was the leading landscape painter for the next fifty years. His students included many of the best known Wisconsin artists of the latter 19th century. ¶ Butts, *Art in Wisconsin,* 109–13; Thieme-Becker.

VICTOR, MICHAEL. Lithographer, 27, a native of France, living in Philadelphia in 1860 in the home of AUGUSTUS KOELLNER. ¶ 8 Census (1860), Pa., LII, 135.

VIEDER, ALFRED. Artist, 35, born in New York, at NYC in 1860. ¶ 8 Census (1860), N.Y., XLVI, 128.

VIGNIER, A. Landscape painter who exhibited at the Pennsylvania Academy and the Society of Artists between 1811 and 1828. He was listed as a resident of Philadelphia from 1811 to 1814. One of his landscapes was a Swiss scene. ¶ Rutledge, PA; Dunlap, *History,* II, 472.

VIGNOLES, CHARLES BLACKER (1793–1875). Topographical draftsman, surveyor, and civil engineer. An English army officer who served briefly with Bolivar in South America, Vignoles came to Charleston (S.C.) in 1817 and soon after was appointed Assistant Surveyor-General of South Carolina. He also did considerable private work there and in Florida and sometime before his departure in 1823 he drew a view of Charleston which was engraved in aquatint by WILLIAM KEENAN and published in Charleston about 1835. Vignoles returned to England in 1823 and became a prominent civil engineer, specializing in railroad construction. He was the author of *Observations upon the Floridas.* ¶ Stokes, *Historical Prints,* 59, cites O. J. Vignoles, *Life of Charles Blacker Vignoles* (London, 1889); Rutledge, *Artists in the Life of Charleston.*

VILMER, COLBY. Portrait painter at Rochester (N.Y.) in 1842. Undoubtedly the same as COLBY KIMBLE. ¶ FARL cites letter of Mrs. M. Perkins Donnell, Nov. 10, 1941.

VINCENTI, FRANCIS. Italian sculptor who was employed at the Capitol in Washington from 1853 to 1858. He modelled several busts of visiting Indians and supplied anatomical models for other Capitol sculptors. After leaving Washington he worked for EDWARD V. VALENTINE in Richmond for a time, then returned to Europe and was last heard of in Paris. ¶ Fairman, *Art and Artists of the Capitol,* 168–69.

VINCKLEBACK, WILLIAM. German artist, 26, at NYC in 1850. ¶ 7 Census (1850), N.Y., XLIII, 146.

VINTON, E. P. Painter of a portrait of John Wheeler (1798–1862), owned by Dartmouth College, Hanover (N.H.). ¶ WPA (Mass.), *Portraits Found in N.H.,* 27.

VIOGET, JEAN JACQUES (1799–1855). Amateur watercolorist. A native of Switzerland, Vioget served briefly in the French army and was apprenticed to a naval engineer. He came to California in 1837 and went into business at Yerba Buena (San Francisco) as a hotel keeper. He also made some surveys and maps for General Sutter. In 1843 he moved to the vicinity of San Jose, where he lived until his death in 1855. His watercolor of Yerba Buena in 1837 has been reproduced. ¶ Van Nostrand and Coulter, *California Pictorial,* 30–31; Peters, *California on Stone.*

VISCHER, EDWARD (1809–1879). Landscape artist. Born in Bavaria, Vischer went to Mexico at the age of 19 and spent fourteen years there in business. After several years of travel in Europe and Asia, he finally settled in California at the time of the Gold Rush and established himself as a merchant and agent in San Francisco. He took up sketching about 1852 and produced a great many California views which he published in several volumes, notably the *Pictorial of California* (1870). ¶ Peters, *California on Stone,* cites Francis P. Farquhar, *Edward Vischer: His Pictorial of California* (San Francisco, 1932).

VISSCHER, MAX. Engraver, Albany (N.Y.), 1852. ¶ Albany BD, 1852.

VOGDES, JOSEPH, see MAAS & VOGDES.

VOGEL, EMIL. Artist of Baltimore, 1858–80. ¶ Lafferty.

VOGLER, E. A. Lithographer of a view of the Square in Old Salem (N.C.), about 1845. ¶ *Antiques* (June 1951), 469, repro.

VOGLER, JOHN (1783–1881). Silhouettist, cabinetmaker, clockmaker, and silversmith of Salem (N.C.). The Wachovia Museum in Salem has a Vogler Room devoted to the various works of this craftsman, including his silhouettes of himself and his wife and the machine by which he took them. ¶ Swan, "Moravian Cabinetmakers of a Piedmont Craft Center," 458, repro.

VOIGHT, LEWIS TOWSON. Portrait and miniature painter, fashion artist, and poet. He was working in Baltimore and elsewhere in Maryland between 1839 and 1845. After 1845 he moved to NYC where he continued his portrait work and did fashion drawings for *Godey's Lady's Book* for about twenty years. ¶ Pleasants, *250 Years of Painting in Maryland,* 53; NYBD 1850–59.

VOLCK, ADALBERT JOHN (1828–1912). Caricaturist, painter, worker in bronze and silver. Born April 14, 1828, in Augsburg (Germany), Volck studied in Nürnberg and Munich but had to flee Germany because of his revolutionary activity in 1848. Coming to America, he spent a few years in St. Louis and in California before settling permanently in Baltimore, where he practised as a dentist for many years. During the Civil War he was active as a Confederate cartoonist, signing his work "V. Blada," but after the war he gave up political art for portraits and work in bronze and silver. He was prominent in the social and artistic life of Baltimore. He died March 26, 1912. FREDERICK VOLCK, the sculptor, was his brother. ¶ DAB; Pleasants, *250 Years of Painting in Maryland,* 62; Met. Mus., *Life in America;* Rutledge, MHS; 8 Census (1860), Md., IV, 588.

VOLCK, FREDERICK (1833–1891). Sculptor, younger brother of ADALBERT J. VOLCK. Born in Bavaria, he was living with his brother's family in Baltimore in 1860. During the Civil War he is said to have designed the head of Jefferson Davis for the Confederate ten cent stamp. He was active in Baltimore after the war and is represented in the Peabody Institute collections. ¶ Information courtesy Anna Wells Rutledge; 8 Census (1860), Md., IV, 588; DAB, under Adalbert J. Volck.

VOLK, LEONARD WELLS (1828–1895). Sculptor. Born November 7, 1828, in Wellstown (now Wells, N.Y.), he spent his boyhood on a farm and at 16 began to learn marble cutting from his father. After working in Bethany, Batavia, and Buffalo (N.Y.), he went out to St. Louis and began to learn drawing and modeling. In 1852 he married and the next few years were spent in Illinois and St. Louis. In 1855, with the help of his wife's cousin, Stephen A. Douglas, Volk went to Rome to study for two years. On his return to America he opened a studio in Chicago where he spent the rest of his life, except for two more European visits and occasional American trips. He was best known for his portraits and war monuments; of his portraits, the most admired were those of Douglas and Lincoln, based on studies made during the famous debates of 1858. Volk died August 19, 1895, while on a summer visit to Osceola (Wis.). His son, Douglas Volk (1856–1935), was a painter. ¶ DAB; Taft, *History of American Sculpture;* Clement and Hutton; Gardner, *Yankee Stonecutters;* Chicago BD 1858+; Wilson, *Lincoln in Portraiture.*

VOLKMAR, CHARLES. Portrait and landscape painter. He was born in Germany about 1809 and settled permanently in Baltimore about 1842. He exhibited at the Maryland Historical Society and the Washington Art Association and was active at least until 1880. ¶ 7 Census (1850), Md., V, 167; Baltimore CD 1842–60+; Lafferty; Rutledge, MHS; Washington Art Assoc. Cat., 1857; represented at Peabody Institute.

VOLLEEN, FRANK. English artist, 30, living in NYC in 1860 with his wife and a six-year-old child born in New York. ¶ 8 Census (1860), N.Y., XLVII, 165.

VOLLMERING, JOSEPH (1810–1887). A.N.A. Portrait and landscape painter, born in Anhalt (Germany). He came to NYC in 1847 and worked there until his death in 1887, exhibiting both at the National Academy and at the American Art-Union. ¶ Fielding; 7 Census (1850), N.Y., XLIII, 144; Cowdrey, NAD; Cowdrey, AA & AAU.

VOLLUM, EDWARD P. Exhibited wood engravings at the American Institute in NYC in 1846. ¶ Am. Inst. Cat., 1846.

VOLOZAN, DENIS A. Artist working in Philadelphia between 1806 and 1819 and possibly later. He exhibited frequently at the Pennsylvania Academy, chiefly historical and figure paintings, landscapes and a few portraits. Dunlap states that he was a Frenchman who worked principally in crayon, taught drawing, and was the first instructor of JOHN PARADISE. ¶ Rutledge, PA; Dunlap, *History,* II, 263.

VON BECKH, H. V. A. Artist with Simpson's expedition to the Great Basin of Utah in 1859. ¶ Simpson, *Report of Explorations across the Great Basin;* Taft, *Artists and Illustrators of the Old West,* 268.

VON BRANDES, W. F. Painter of military subjects. He was in NYC in 1847–48 when he exhibited at the American Art-Union. ¶ Cowdrey, AA & AAU.

VON IWONSKI, see IWONSKI.

VON PHUL, ANNA MARIA (1786–1823). Amateur artist of Lexington (Ky.) and St. Louis (Mo.). Born May 17, 1786, in Philadelphia, she lived in Lexington from 1800 to 1821 and studied there with GEORGE and MARY BECK. On a visit to St. Louis in 1818 she made a number of genre and landscape sketches which have been preserved. She lived in St. Louis during her last years, though she died at the home of a sister in Edwardsville (Ill.) on July 28, 1823. ¶ Van Ravenswaay, "Anna Maria Von Phul"; also repros. in *Antiques* (Sept. 1953), 195.

VON SMITH, AUGUSTUS A. Portrait painter who lived in Vincennes (Ind.) from about 1835 to about 1842. Burnet states that he was foreign-born and had a son who also was an artist. One of them was at New Orleans in 1842 in the firm of BRAMMER & VON SMITH. ¶ Peat, *Pioneer Painters of Indiana,* 24, 240; Burnet, *Art and Artists of Indiana,* 11, 400; New Orleans CD 1842.

VON TILENAU, see TILESIUS VON TILENAU.

VON WEBBER, ——. New York artist who exhibited a landscape painting at the American Art-Union in 1848. ¶ Cowdrey, AA & AAU.

VON WITTKAMP, ANDREW L. Physician and amateur artist of Philadelphia in the 1850's. His painting of a black cat in a chair is in the Karolik Collection. ¶ Karolik Cat., 522–23; *Art News* (Oct. 1951), 5, and cover.

VOTEY, CHARLES A. Exhibited wood engravings at the American Institute in 1847; a resident of NYC. ¶ Am. Inst. Cat., 1847.

VOYER, JANE. Teacher of drawing, embroidery, and French at Charleston (S.C.) in 1739–40. ¶ Rutledge, *Artists in the Life of Charleston.*

VULTEE, FREDERICK L. Portrait painter, NYC, 1830–38; exhibited at the Apollo Association. After 1835 he was variously listed in the directories as a broker, boarding house, deputy sheriff, porter, lawyer, under sheriff, and secretary. ¶ Cowdrey, AA & AAU; NYCD 1830–69.

W

WACHTER, MILEUS. Artist, 70, a native of Saxony, living in the home of Mrs. Leland Balch, NYC, in 1860. ¶ 8 Census (1860), N.Y., XLIV, 416.

WADE, H. (possibly K. or W.). Lithographer of a sheet music cover, "The Texas Quick Step," published in NYC in 1841. *Cf.* WILLIAM WADE. ¶ John Mayfield Collection, Washington (D.C.).

WADE, HANNAH C. Artist, 40, a native of Pennsylvania, who was an inmate of the Philadelphia Hospital for the Insane in June 1860. ¶ 8 Census (1860), Pa., LX, 799.

WADE, J. H. Portrait painter working in Cleveland (Ohio) and through the South between 1810 and 1823. ¶ Fielding.

WADE, JOHN C. Engraver; born in New York about 1827; working in NYC from about 1850 to 1860. ¶ 7 Census (1850), N.Y., XLVIII, 127; NYBD 1854–60.

WADE, SAMUEL. Engraver; born in Maryland about 1820; working in NYC from about 1848 to 1860. In 1860 his fifteen-year-old son John was listed as an apprentice engraver. ¶ 8 Census (1860), N.Y., LXII, 637.

WADE, WILLIAM. Engraver, designer, and draftsman working in NYC from about 1844 to 1852. In 1844 he published an engraved panorama of the Hudson River from New York to Albany; he also exhibited this panorama at the American Institute in 1846. *Cf.* H. WADE. ¶ Stokes, *Historical Prints;* NYCD 1845–52; Am. Inst. Cat., 1846.

WADLOW, CHARLES E., & COMPANY. Lithographers, NYC, 1854. ¶ NYBD 1854.

WADSWORTH, DANIEL (1771–1848). Amateur artist and collector. A Hartford merchant and nephew by marriage of JOHN TRUMBULL, Wadsworth is remembered chiefly as the founder of the Wadsworth Athenaeum Gallery in Hartford in 1844. His own work in watercolors included sketches made on a trip to Quebec in 1819, some of which were engraved to illustrate his published account of the trip, and two views of his own mansion, "Monte Video," near Hartford, now in the Connecticut Historical Society. ¶ Conn. Hist. Soc. *Bulletin,* XIX (Jan. 1954), 22–25; French, *Art and Artists in Connecticut,* 9–11.

WADSWORTH, W. Engraver at San Francisco in 1858. Two years later he was one of the proprietors of the magazine *California Culturist.* ¶ San Francisco CD 1858, 1860.

WADSWORTH, WILLIAM. Wood engraver and designer of Hartford (Conn.) whose work appeared in Noah Webster's *American Spelling Book* (*c.* 1798) and *The Cannibal's Progress* (1798). ¶ Hamilton, *Early American Book Illustrators and Wood Engravers,* 14, 73.

WAESCHE, METTA HENRIETTA (1806–1900). Amateur artist of Baltimore whose crayon and watercolor view of the Repold-Waesche House in 1822 is now owned by the Maryland Historical Society. ¶ Pleasants, *250 Years of Painting in Maryland,* 51, 52 (repro.).

WAGANER, ANTHONY. Statuary, NYC, 1834–35. ¶ NYCD 1834–35.

WAGEMAN, MICHAEL. Portrait painter at Newark (N.J.), 1857–59. ¶ Newark CD 1857; Essex, Hudson, and Union Counties BD 1859.

WAGGONER, WILLIAM W. Wood engraver of Cincinnati, 1853–59. ¶ Cincinnati CD 1853–59.

WAGNER, ——. Seal engraver of NYC who exhibited at the Pennsylvania Academy in 1834. ¶ Penna. Acad. Cat., 1834.

WAGNER, ANDREW. Wood engraver and lithographer of Cincinnati, 1856–60. He worked for ADOLPHUS MENZEL. ¶ Cincinnati CD 1856–60.

WAGNER, DANIEL (1802–1888). Miniature, portrait, and landscape painter. Born April 14, 1802, in Leyden (Mass.), he spent most of his boyhood in Norwich (N.Y.). He was crippled by an accident in childhood and took up portrait and miniature painting which he practised successfully for many years in collaboration with his sister, MARIA LOUISA WAGNER. Together they worked in the Chenango Valley (N.Y.) during the late thirties, visiting Binghamton, Utica, Whitestown, and Ithaca; from about 1842 to about 1860 they had a studio in Albany; and from 1862 to 1868 they were in NYC. After 1868 they resided in Norwich and turned more to landscape painting. Daniel exhibited at the National Academy and at the Centennial Exhibition in Philadelphia. He died in Norwich on January

21, 1888. Among his works were portraits of Erastus Corning, Martin Van Buren, Silas Wright, Millard Fillmore, and Daniel Webster. ¶ Norwich *Semi-Weekly Telegraph,* Jan. 25, 1888, obit. (courtesy Anna Wells Rutledge); Albany CD 1843–44, 1857; Cowdrey, NAD; NYCD 1862–68; *Antiques* (Jan. 1933), 12.

WAGNER, HENRY S. Portrait engraver active in Philadelphia from 1849 to 1858. ¶ Phila. CD 1849–58; Stauffer.

WAGNER, J. F. or E. Landscape and topographical painter of Nashville (Tenn.), active *c.* 1840–1860. ¶ *Portfolio* (Jan. 1943), 114, and (Feb. 1954), 141, repros.; Nashville CD 1860.

WAGNER & M'GUIGAN. Lithographers, Philadelphia, 1846–58; THOMAS S. WAGNER and JAMES M'GUIGAN. This firm succeeded PINKERTON, WAGNER & M'GUIGAN. ¶ Phila. CD 1846–58.

WAGNER, MARIA LOUISA. Miniature, portrait, genre, and landscape painter, sister of DANIEL WAGNER. For thirty years she and her crippled brother worked together as artists in the Chenango Valley (N.Y.), Albany, and NYC. In 1868 they retired to Norwich (N.Y.) and Maria Louisa survived her brother at his death in 1888. She exhibited between 1839 and 1868 at the National Academy, the Boston Athenaeum, the American Art-Union, and the Pennsylvania Academy. ¶ Norwich *Semi-Weekly Telegraph,* Jan. 25, 1888, obit. of Daniel Wagner (courtesy Anna Wells Rutledge); Cowdrey, NAD; Swan, BA; Cowdrey, AA & AAU; Rutledge, PA; *Antiques* (Jan. 1933), 12.

WAGNER, PHILIP. German lithographer, born about 1811, working in NYC about 1843–49 and in Boston in 1850–53. ¶ 7 Census (1850), Mass., XXVI, 95; Boston CD 1852–53.

WAGNER, RUDOLPH. Lithographer, 24, a native of Prussia, living in Philadelphia in 1860. His father, Joseph, was a hotel keeper who had come to Philadelphia before 1842. ¶ 8 Census (1860), Pa., LXII, 19.

WAGNER & STUART. General engravers, lithographic engravers, and die sinkers, Philadelphia, 1845–after 1860; WILLIAM W. WAGNER and ALBERT STUART. ¶ Phila. CD 1845–60+.

WAGNER, THOMAS S. Lithographer active in Philadelphia from 1840 to about 1865, most of that time as a partner in PINKERTON, WAGNER & M'GUIGAN (1844–45) and WAGNER & M'GUIGAN (1846–58). ¶ Phila. CD 1840–60+; Peters, *America on Stone.*

WAGNER, W. A. Engraver of one illustration in *Our World: or, The Slaveholder's Daughter* (N.Y., 1855). ¶ Hamilton, *Early American Book Illustrators and Wood Engravers,* 437.

WAGNER, WILLIAM. Engraver of York (Pa.), active about 1820–60. His view of York Springs appeared in *Port Folio* in 1827. ¶ Stauffer; *Port Folio,* XLVII (1827), opp. 177; Penna. BD 1860.

WAGNER, WILLIAM W. Engraver; born in Pennsylvania about 1817; active in Philadelphia from 1845 to after 1860 in the firm of WAGNER & STUART. ¶ 7 Census (1850), Pa., LV, 615; Phila. CD 1845–60+.

WAGONER, CHARLES. Lithographer, 26, a native of Germany, at Pittsburgh (Pa.) in 1850. *Cf.* WEGNER & BUECHNER. ¶ 7 Census (1850), Pa., III, 74.

WAGSTAFF, CHARLES EDWARD (1808–?). Portrait engraver on copper. A native of London, he came to Boston about 1840 and worked there into the fifties, part of the time in association with JOSEPH ANDREWS. ¶ Stauffer; Boston CD 1851–52.

WAGSTAFF, JOHN C. Exhibited a miniature on ivory at the American Institute in 1845; he was a resident of NYC. ¶ Am. Inst. Cat., 1845.

WAHLMANN, FREDERICK. Engraver and die sinker, NYC, 1849–54. ¶ NYBD 1849, 1854.

WAITE, LUCRETIA ANN, see Mrs. JOSEPH GOODHUE CHANDLER.

WAITES, EDWARD P. Engraver, NYC, 1847–54. ¶ Am. Inst. Cat., 1847; NYBD 1854.

WAITT or WAITE, BENJAMIN FRANKLIN (1817–?). Wood engraver and sculptor; born March 3, 1817, at Malden (Mass.); active in Philadelphia from about 1845 to 1884. He was listed as a sculptor in the 1860 Census and the 1860 and 1862 directories; otherwise as an engraver and (1870) lithographer. ¶ Corey, *The Waite Family of Malden, Mass.,* 67; Phila. CD 1845–84; 8 Census (1860), Pa., L, 498; Hamilton, *Early American Book Illustrators and Wood Engravers,* 530; 7 Census (1850), Pa., LII, 793, as Benjamin F. Watt, sculptor.

WAKELAW, FREDERICK. English engraver, 21, at Cincinnati in 1850 with his father, WILLIAM J. WAKELAW. ¶ 7 Census (1850), Ohio, XXI, 662.

WAKELAW, WILLIAM J. English engraver, 53, at Cincinnati in 1850. All of his children, ages 11 to 21, were born in England. His eldest son, FREDERICK, was also an engraver. ¶ 7 Census (1850), Ohio, XXI, 662.

WAKEMAN, THOMAS (1812–1878). English watercolorist who visited America about 1850 and painted over forty views of cities and towns from Boston south to Washington. Stokes states that Wakeman was a scene painter by profession. He died in Rome. ¶ Mallett, supplement; Stokes, *Historical Prints; Antiques* (Oct. 1936), 174; Sotheby & Co., auction catalogue, June 18–21, 1951, pp. 12–14.

WALCUTT, DAVID BRODERICK (1825–?). Portrait and landscape painter, brother of GEORGE and WILLIAM WALCUTT. Born in Columbus (Ohio), he was working in Cincinnati as early as 1846. In 1850 he was in NYC, where he exhibited at the American Institute. He was back in Cincinnati by 1858 and later worked in St. Louis. ¶ Clark, *Ohio Art and Artists,* 114, 498; Cist, *Cincinnati in 1851;* NYBD 1850; Am. Inst. Cat., 1850; Cincinnati CD 1858, BD 1859.

WALCUTT, GEORGE (1825–?). Portrait and landscape painter, brother of DAVID B. and WILLIAM WALCUTT. He was born in Columbus (Ohio) and spent the early part of his career there, later moving to Kentucky. ¶ Clark, *Ohio Art and Artists,* 114, 498; *Antiques* (March 1932), 152.

WALCUTT, WILLIAM (1819–1882 or 1895). Sculptor and portrait painter, brother of DAVID B. and GEORGE WALCUTT. Born in Columbus (Ohio), he began his artistic career as a portrait painter there in the early forties and studied in Columbus, NYC, and Washington. In 1852 he went abroad for three years, to study sculpture in London and Paris. On his return he opened a studio in NYC. In 1859–60 he was at Cleveland (Ohio) working on his notable monument to Oliver Hazard Perry. His death date has been given as 1882 by Clark and 1895 by Gardner. ¶ Gardner, *Yankee Stonecutters,* 73; Clark, *Ohio Art and Artists,* 114, 139–40, 498; *Antiques* (March 1932), 152; Cist, *Cincinnati in 1851,* 204; Cowdrey, NAD; WPA (Ohio), *Annals of Cleveland;* Hamilton, *Early American Book Illustrators and Wood Engravers; Art Digest* (Jan. 15, 1935), 17.

WALDO & JEWETT. Portrait painters of NYC from 1820 to 1854. This was a highly successful partnership between SAMUEL L. WALDO and his former pupil WILLIAM JEWETT. They painted the portraits of many prominent New Yorkers during their thirty-odd years of activity; Waldo is said to have specialized in heads and hands and Jewett in costumes and backgrounds. Their work was exhibited at the American Academy, the Apollo Association, the National Academy, and the Artists' Fund Society of Philadelphia. ¶ NYCD 1820–54; Sherman, "Samuel L. Waldo and William Jewett"; Karolik Cat.; Cowdrey, AA & AAU; Cowdrey, NAD; Rutledge, PA; Vail, *Knickerbocker Birthday,* frontis.

WALDO, SAMUEL LOVETT (1783–1861). N.A. Portrait painter, born April 6, 1783, in Windham (Conn.). Waldo received his first instruction in painting from JOSEPH STEWARD of Hartford about 1799. He opened his own studio in Hartford in 1803 but soon after left for Litchfield (Conn.) and Charleston (S.C.), where he spent three years. From 1806 to 1808 he worked and studied in London and on his return to America early in 1809 he opened a studio in NYC. In 1820 he took into partnership his pupil WILLIAM JEWETT and the firm of WALDO & JEWETT flourished for over thirty years, until 1854. Waldo died in NYC on February 16, 1861. He was one of the founders of the National Academy. ¶ DAB; Sherman, "Samuel L. Waldo and William Jewett"; Rutledge, *Artists in the Life of Charleston;* Graves, *Dictionary;* NYCD 1811–60; Rutledge, PA; Cowdrey, AA & AAU; Cowdrey, NAD; Swan, BA; Dunlap, *History;* Karolik Cat.; N. Y. *Evening Post,* Feb. 18, 1861, and *The Crayon,* VII (1861), 98–99, obits.

WALDRON, Mrs. ADELIA. "Oil painter," 35, a native of Kentucky, living in San Francisco in 1860 with her Vermont-born husband, Henry Waldron, merchant. ¶ 8 Census (1860), Cal., VII, 1400.

WALE, T. Portraits in oil on wood, White River Junction (Vt.), 1820. ¶ Lipman and Winchester, 181.

WALES, N. F. Portrait painter. About 1810 he painted portraits of Capt. and Mrs. Nathan Sage of Redfield (N.Y.). He was at Charleston (S.C.) in 1815. ¶ Information courtesy Miss Mildred Steinbach, FARL; Rutledge, *Artists in the Life of Charleston.*

WALKE, HENRY (1808–1896). Naval combat artist. Born in Virginia on December 24, 1808, Walke entered the U. S. Navy in 1827 and retired with the rank of rear-admiral in 1871. His Mexican and Civil

War sketches were lithographed and published in *Naval Scenes in the Mexican War* (1847–48) and *Naval Scenes and Reminiscences of the Civil War* (1877). He died in Brooklyn (N.Y.) on March 8, 1896. ¶ *Album of American Battle Art,* 137–38; Perry, *Expedition to Japan;* Ramsay, "The American Scene in Lithograph, The Album," 183; *Magazine of Art* (March 1944), 108.

WALKER, ——. Scene painter at the Park Theatre in the 1827–28 and 1829–30 seasons and at the Olympic Theatre, NYC, in 1837. He also painted three scenes for HANINGTON in 1836–37. ¶ Odell, *Annals of the New York Stage;* N. Y. *Herald,* Dec. 7 and 22, 1836, and March 28, 1837 (courtesy J. Earl Arrington).

WALKER FAMILY. Gravestone sculptors active in Charleston (S.C.) from the 1790's to the 1830's. The founder of the family was Thomas Walker, a stonecutter who came to Charleston from Edinburgh about 1793. He was active until 1836 and died in 1838, leaving the business to be continued by his sons James E., Robert D. W., and William S. Walker. Two other members of the family, possibly also sons of Thomas, were A. W. and C. S. Walker, apprentices of Thomas in 1831. ¶ Ravenel, "Here Lyes Buried," 194–95; Rutledge, *Artists in the Life of Charleston.*

WALKER, Miss [?] A. M. Marine and landscape painter of Philadelphia, 1840–44. This artist exhibited at the Artists' Fund Society and the Apollo Association views in Pennsylvania, New Jersey, and NYC and a number of pictures of American naval vessels in the Mediterranean and American waters. Her address in 1840–42 was the same as that of Miss E. WALKER and Samuel G. Walker, secretary of the Fire and Inland Insurance Company. A. M. Walker, "gent.," is listed in Philadelphia directories, 1845–47. ¶ Rutledge, PA [as Miss A. M. Walker]; Cowdrey, AA & AAU [as A. M. Walker]; *American Collector* (June 1948), frontis.; Phila. CD 1840–46.

WALKER, A. W., see WALKER FAMILY, above.

WALKER & BOWEN. Portrait painters, Boston, 1845–46; SIMEON WALKER and GEORGE P. BOWEN. ¶ Boston CD 1845, BD 1846 [as Walker & Bower].

WALKER, C. S., see WALKER FAMILY, above.

WALKER, C. W. Engraver on copper and wood, Buffalo (N.Y.), 1858. ¶ Buffalo BD 1858.

WALKER, DANIEL. Scottish engraver, 33, at NYC in 1860; personal property valued at $2,000. ¶ 8 Census (1860), N.Y., XLIII, 405.

WALKER, Miss E. Philadelphia artist who exhibited a landscape after JOSHUA SHAW at the Artists' Fund Society in 1840. She lived at the same address as A. M. WALKER and Samuel G. Walker, secretary of the Fire and Inland Insurance Company. ¶ Artists' Fund Society Cat., 1840; Rutledge, PA [as Miss Elizabeth L. Walker].

WALKER, E. L. Lithographic engraver, Philadelphia, 1856. ¶ Phila. BD 1856.

WALKER, ELIZABETH L. Watercolor romantic scene, Massachusetts, 1840. ¶ Lipman and Winchester, 181.

WALKER, EVELINE. Artist, 33, a native of Massachusetts, at NYC in 1860. ¶ 8 Census (1860), N.Y., LI, 703.

WALKER, JAMES (1819–1889). Historical painter, born in England on June 3, 1819. He was brought to NYC as a child and spent the greater part of his life there. As a young man he went to New Orleans and then to Mexico City where he was living at the time of the outbreak of the Mexican War. After his escape from the city he joined the American forces as an interpreter and was present at the capture of the capital city and during its occupation. He returned to NYC in 1848 and, after a visit to South America, established a studio there. In 1857–62 he was in Washington painting his "Battle of Chapultepec" for the U. S. Capitol. This was followed by many other historical canvases, mainly picturing battles of the Civil War. Walker left NYC for California in 1884 and died at the home of a brother in Watsonville on August 29, 1889. ¶ Fairman, *Art and Artists of the Capitol,* 212; Taft, *Artists and Illustrators of the Old West,* 303; 8 Census (1860), D.C., II, 375; Cowdrey, NAD; CAB; San Francisco *Morning Call,* Sept. 4, 1889, obit.; *Album of American Battle Art; Art Digest* (Oct. 1, 1944), 1; *Magazine of Art* (May 1944), 186; represented at the U. S. War Department Building, Washington, by twelve Mexican War scenes.

WALKER, JAMES. Engraver, 21, a native of New York, in NYC in 1860. Possibly the J. M. Walker who exhibited a wood engraving at the American Institute in 1856. ¶ 8 Census (1860), N.Y., LVIII, 262; Am. Inst. Cat., 1856.

WALKER, JAMES, & SON. Copper and steel engravers and die sinkers, Philadelphia,

1858–60 and after. The son was WILLIAM WALKER. ¶ Phila. BD 1858–60+.

WALKER, JAMES E., see WALKER FAMILY, above.

WALKER, JAMES L. Figure and ornamental painter at Baltimore in 1792. In August of that year he opened a school where he taught figure and ornamental painting and architectural drawing. ¶ Prime, II, 37–38; folio broadside in LC (Evans, *American Bibliography,* VIII, no. 24979).

WALKER, M. Primitive genre painter in watercolors, active about 1835. ¶ Lipman and Winchester, 181.

WALKER, ROBERT D. W., see WALKER FAMILY.

WALKER, SAMUEL. Portrait, figure, and marine painter. There was an artist by this name at London in 1850–52, when he exhibited at the Royal Academy; at Brooklyn and NYC in 1853–54, when he exhibited at the National Academy; at New Orleans in 1860–61; and at Philadelphia 1865–68, when he exhibited at the Pennsylvania Academy. It is uncertain whether all these references are to one man. ¶ Graves, *Dictionary;* Cowdrey, NAD; Brooklyn CD 1853; New Orleans CD 1860–61; Rutledge, PA; Phila. CD 1866–68.

WALKER, SAMUEL SWAN (1806–1848). Portrait painter, born in Butler County (Ohio) February 17, 1806. He was trained as a physician but gave up his practice in 1836 to become a portrait and miniature painter. He worked principally in Cincinnati, but in 1841 he visited Richmond (Ind.) and there became a pupil and close friend of J. INSCO WILLIAMS. Walker died in Cincinnati on May 15, 1848. ¶ Peat, *Pioneer Painters of Indiana,* 91, 240.

WALKER, SIMEON. Portrait painter, of WALKER & BOWEN, Boston, 1845–46. ¶ Boston CD 1845, BD 1846.

WALKER, THOMAS, see WALKER FAMILY, above.

WALKER, WILLIAM. Engraver, son of JAMES WALKER the Philadelphia engraver; they were working together as J. Walker & Son 1858 and after. ¶ Phila. CD 1858–60+.

WALKER, WILLIAM AIKEN (*c.* 1838–1921). Genre and portrait painter. A native of Charleston, he first exhibited there at the age of 12 in 1850. He subsequently studied at Düsseldorf. Though he spent most of his life in Charleston, he also did some work in Louisiana and Florida which was lithographed by CURRIER & IVES in the 1880's. Walker died in Charleston January 3, 1921. ¶ Bland Galleries, *Exhibition of Southern Genre Paintings by William Aiken Walker,* catalogue; Rutledge, *Artists in the Life of Charleston;* Karolik Cat.; *Portfolio* (April 1946), 186–87; *Art News* (Oct. 1949), 40; *American Heritage* (Autumn 1950), 55.

WALKER, WILLIAM F. Of GREENE & WALKER, music and plate engravers of Boston, 1857–60. Earlier he was listed as a music engraver. ¶ Boston CD 1854–60.

WALL, ALFRED S. (1809–1896). Landscape painter. Born in England, he and his brother, WILLIAM COVENTRY WALL, came to America in the 1840's and settled in Pittsburgh (Pa.). Alfred exhibited at the Pittsburgh Art Association in 1859 and 1860 and at the Pennsylvania Academy in 1867. He was a trustee of the Carnegie Institute. He died in Pittsburgh on June 6, 1896. ¶ Letter, Rose Demorest, Carnegie Library of Pittsburgh, to Anna Wells Rutledge, Oct. 31, 1950 (NYHS files); Fleming, *History of Pittsburgh,* III, 626; Rutledge, PA; *Antiques* (Sept. 1945), 156; Smith.

WALL, WILLIAM ALLEN (1801–1885). Portrait and landscape painter of New Bedford (Mass.), where he was born on May 19, 1801. He was apprenticed to a watchmaker but turned to painting and studied under THOMAS SULLY. In 1831 he went abroad to study for the next two years in England, France, and Italy. On his return he settled permanently in New Bedford. He was particularly noted for his paintings of early 19th-century New Bedford scenes. He died September 6, 1885. ¶ Robinson, "William Allen Wall of New Bedford," six repros.; Childs, " 'Thar She Blows,' " cites the supplement to the 100th anniversary edition of the *New Bedford Mercury;* Cowdrey, NAD; Swan, BA; Boston BD 1847; Stokes, *Historical Prints.*

WALL, WILLIAM ARCHIBALD (1828–after 1875). Landscape painter, son of WILLIAM GUY WALL. He was born in NYC and in 1860 had a studio in Newburgh (N.Y.). ¶ Shelley, "William Guy Wall . . . ," 25 fn.

WALL, WILLIAM COVENTRY (1810–1886). Landscape and portait painter of Pittsburgh (Pa.). He was born in England and came to Pittsburgh, probably in the early forties, with his brother ALFRED S. WALL, also an artist. He was noted for his views of Pittsburgh and vicinity, and particularly for his views of the city after the fire of 1845. He also made picture frames. He died in Pittsburgh, November 19, 1886. ¶ Glassburn, "Artist Reports on the Fire of 1845"; *Antiques* (Sept. 1945), 156; *Panorama* (Dec. 1946), 43; Rutledge, PA; Fleming, *History of Pittsburgh,* III, 626; letter, Rose Demorest, Carnegie Library of Pittsburgh, to Miss Anna Wells Rutledge, Oct. 31, 1950 (NYHS files).

WALL, WILLIAM GUY (1792–after 1864). Landscape painter in watercolors. Wall was born in Dublin (Ireland) and married there in 1812. He arrived in NYC on September 1, 1818, already a well-trained artist. For the next ten years he lived in NYC and won wide recognition by his views of the Hudson River and NYC. Twenty of these were engraved and published in the popular *Hudson River Portfolio,* which went through several editions between 1820 and 1828. Wall also exhibited at the National Academy, of which he was one of the founders, and later at the Pennsylvania Academy and the Apollo Association. His son, WILLIAM ARCHIBALD WALL, was born in NYC in 1828. After 1828 Wall moved to Newport (R.I.), remaining there until about 1834; in August 1834 he was at New Haven (Conn.); and in 1836 he was living in Brooklyn. He then returned to Ireland, settling in Dublin, where he became associated with Master HUBARD, the silhouettist, for whom Wall painted pictorial backgrounds. During the forties and fifties Wall continued to exhibit in Dublin, once in London, and in several American galleries. In 1856 he returned to America and settled in Newburgh where he was still active as late as July 1862. Soon after he went back to Dublin and was living there in 1864. The date and place of his death are not known. ¶ Shelley, "William Guy Wall and His Watercolors for the Historic *Hudson River Portfolio,*" summarizes the known facts of Wall's life, reproduces several of his original watercolors owned by the NYHS, and contains a catalogue of his work. For additional bibliography see Flexner, *The Light of Distant Skies.*

WALLACE, ——. Assistant scene painter at Wallack's Theatre, NYC, 1857–59. ¶ Odell, *Annals of the New York Stage;* N. Y. *Herald,* June 16, 1858 (courtesy J. Earl Arrington).

WALLACE, A. H. Portrait painter, Brooklyn (N.Y.), 1837. ¶ NYBD 1837.

WALLACE, BENJAMIN A. Portrait and miniature painter and writing master, active in NYC from 1824 to 1830. ¶ NYCD 1824–30; NYHS *Quarterly Bulletin* (July 1926), 60, 62; represented at NYHS.

WALLACE, JAMES. Sculptor in marble, New Orleans, 1852–56. ¶ New Orleans CD 1852–56.

WALLACE, LEWIS (1827–1905). Amateur painter. Best known as the author of *Ben Hur,* "Lew" Wallace was a lawyer by profession, a prominent Civil War general, governor of New Mexico (1878–81), minister to Turkey (1881–85), and man of letters. His boyhood was spent in Indianapolis, where he worked for the painter JACOB COX as color-grinder for a time. Although his father prevented him from taking up art as a profession, in later life Wallace painted as an amateur and occasionally exhibited, *e.g.* "The Dead Line at Andersonville," shown in Indianapolis in 1878. His last years were spent in Crawfordsville (Ind.) where he died February 15, 1905. *Lew Wallace, an Autobiography* appeared the following year. ¶ DAB; Peat, *Pioneer Artists of Indiana;* Burnet, *Art and Artists of Indiana.*

WALLACE, OSCAR J. Artist, Cincinnati, 1856. ¶ Cincinnati CD 1856.

WALLACE, THOMAS J. Sculptor, Troy (N.Y.), 1858–60. From 1854 to 1857 he was listed as a music teacher. ¶ Troy CD 1854–60; N. Y. State BD 1859.

WALLACE, WILLIAM H. Amateur landscape painter in watercolors and etcher. An employee of a NYC insurance firm for many years, Wallace made hundreds of topographical drawings of NYC scenes from the 1850's to the 1880's; he also etched about eighty plates from his own drawings. Many of these are now at the New York Public Library. ¶ Stokes, *Historical Prints,* 101; *Portfolio* (Feb. 1945), 140–41, repros.

WALLACE, WILLIAM R. Of MIDDLETON, WALLACE & COMPANY, engravers and lithographers, Cincinnati, 1855–59. Wallace dropped out in 1859 and the firm became MIDDLETON, STROBRIDGE & COMPANY. ¶ Cincinnati CD 1856–58; Peters, *America on Stone.*

WALLESTEIN, JULIUS. Portrait painter, Baltimore, 1849–50. ¶ Baltimore CD 1849–50; Lafferty.

WALLER, EDWARD L. Lithographer, Philadelphia, 1855–58. ¶ Peters, *America on Stone.*

WALLER, JOHN. Engraver, Chicago, 1853–54. ¶ Chicago BD 1853–54.

WALLIN, SAMUEL. Engraver and draftsman

active in NYC from 1838 to 1851. He exhibited several drawings at the National Academy in 1843 and did some illustrations for *The Parthenon* (1851). SAMUEL WALLIN, JR., engraver, was working with him in 1846. ¶ NYCD 1838–50; Cowdrey, NAD; NYPL Print Room catalogue.

WALLIN, SAMUEL, JR. Engraver working with and presumably the son of SAMUEL WALLIN, above, in NYC in 1846. ¶ NYBD 1846.

WALLING, HENRY F. Lithographer, Boston, 1854. So listed only in the business directory; in the city directories he was listed as an engineer. ¶ Boston BD 1854; Boston CD 1852–55.

WALLIS, FREDERICK I. Portrait painter, Chicago, 1859. ¶ Chicago BD 1859.

WALSH & BAKER. Wood engravers of NYC who exhibited at the American Institute in 1846. Their address was the same as that of DANIEL T. SMITH and WILLIAM ROBERTS. Baker was probably WILLIAM JAY BAKER, later a partner of DANIEL T. SMITH; Walsh is otherwise unknown. ¶ Am. Inst. Cat., 1846; NYCD 1846.

WALSH, DAVID. Lithographer, 23, at NYC in 1860. ¶ 8 Census (1860), N.Y., XLII, 900; NYCD 1858, 1860.

WALSH, EDWARD. Topographical painter in watercolors. He was a surgeon attached to the 49th Regiment of the British Army, stationed near Niagara Falls for several years before the War of 1812. He made a number of watercolor views of Lake Erie and Buffalo Creek (N.Y.), one of which was engraved in aquatint and published in London in 1811. ¶ Stokes, *Historical Prints,* 53.

WALSH, FRANCIS. Canadian engraver, 25, at Philadelphia in 1850. ¶ 7 Census (1850), Pa., LIV, 695.

WALSH, JAMES. Irish engraver, 40, at NYC in 1860. His wife and children, ages 6 to 13, were born in New York. ¶ 8 Census (1860), N.Y., XLII, 370.

WALSH, JEREMIAH. Landscape painter, NYC, 1859. ¶ NYBD 1859.

WALSH, JOSEPH W. Lithographer; born in New York about 1828; active from about 1850. He may have been the artist of this name who exhibited a portrait painting at the American Institute in 1842, although he would have been in his early teens at that time. ¶ 7 Census (1850), N.Y., L, 771; 8 Census (1860), N.Y., XLIV, 851; NYCD 1854–60; Am. Inst. Cat., 1842.

WALTER, ADAM B. (1820–1875). Engraver, chiefly in mezzotint. He was a native of Philadelphia and was active there from the early forties until his death, October 14, 1875. ¶ Stauffer; 7 Census (1850), Pa., LVI, 784; 8 Census (1860), Pa., LIV, 1026; Phila. CD 1843–60+.

WALTER, JOHN. Engraver and miniaturist, see JOHN WALTERS.

WALTER, JOHN. Sculptor, New Orleans, 1846. ¶ New Orleans CD 1846.

WALTER, JOSEPH (1783–1856). Marine artist of Bristol (England) who depicted the departure of the steamship *Great Western* from Bristol and her arrival off Tompkinsville, Staten Island (N.Y.) in 1838. It is not known whether Walter ever came to America. ¶ *American Processional,* 131, 242; Stokes, *Historical Prints;* Stokes, *Iconography,* repros.

WALTER, JOSEPH SAUNDERS. Amateur artist, son of THOMAS USTICK WALTER. In 1840 he exhibited at the Artists' Fund Society an Italian view, a Swiss scene after Stanfield, and "Grace Darling." He had probably accompanied his father on his visit to Europe in 1838. The younger Walter died of fever at La Guaira (Venezuela) while assisting his father in the construction of a breakwater there. ¶ Rutledge, PA; DAB, under Thomas U. Walter.

WALTER, THOMAS USTICK (1804–1887). Architect and architectural draftsman in watercolors. Born in Philadelphia on September 4, 1804, Walter learned the bricklayer's trade from his father and studied architecture under WILLIAM STRICKLAND. He began his independent career in Philadelphia in 1830 and was very successful. He visited Europe with his son, JOSEPH S., in 1838. From 1851 to 1865 he was in charge of construction of the wings and dome of the U. S. Capitol and other government buildings in Washington. He returned to Philadelphia in 1865 and spent the rest of his life there in semi-retirement. He was the second President of the American Institute of Architects (1876–1887). Many of his designs for buildings were exhibited at the Pennsylvania Academy, the Artists' Fund Society, and the Apollo Association. He died in Philadelphia on October 30, 1887. ¶ DAB; Rutledge, PA; Cowdrey, AA & AAU.

WALTERS, JAMES L., see JAMES L. WATTLES.

WALTERS, JOHN. Engraver and miniature painter of Philadelphia. In 1779 he was engraving and publishing in partnership with JOHN NORMAN; the partnership was dissolved the same year and Walters became involved in a newspaper dispute with Norman and THOMAS BEDWELL. By 1782 Walters and Bedwell were in partnership as miniature and landscape painters, copyists, and heraldic artists. In 1784 Walters had added hair work and jewelery making to his repertory. ¶ Prime, I, 11–13, 26, 29–31; Bolton, *Miniature Painters.*

WALTERS, JOSEPHINE. Amateur artist who studied with ASHER B. DURAND in NYC. ¶ Durand, *Life and Times of Asher B. Durand,* 184.

WALTERS & NORMAN. Engravers and printers, Philadelphia, 1779; JOHN WALTERS and JOHN NORMAN. The partnership was dissolved the same year and the former partners became involved in a newspaper dispute over the ownership of certain plates. ¶ Prime, I, 26, 29–31.

WALTERS, SUSANE. Painter of a child's memorial portrait, 1852. ¶ Garbisch Collection catalogue, 97, repro.

WALTHER, HENRY. Prussian-born fresco painter, 30, at Washington (D.C.) in 1860. ¶ 8 Census (1860), D.C., I, 799.

WALTON, HENRY. Portrait, miniature, and landscape painter and lithographer, known chiefly for his lithographed views of upstate New York towns between 1836 and 1850. He is thought to have been an Englishman. His studio was in Ithaca from 1836 to 1846. At some time he also lithographed buildings for PENDLETONS of Boston. *Cf.* N. WALTON. ¶ *Portfolio* (Oct. 1945), 40–44; Peters, *America on Stone;* N. Y. *World-Telegram and Sun,* Dec. 29, 1950, repro. of view of Watkins Glen (N.Y.); *Antiques* (Nov. 1937), cover and 227; *Antiques* (June 1938), 311; Stokes, *Historical Prints.*

WALTON, N. Delineator of a view of Congress Hall, Saratoga (N.Y.), engraved by RAWDON, WRIGHT & Co. of NYC, 1828–31. Probably HENRY WALTON. ¶ Fielding, supplement to Stauffer, no. 1260.

WALTON, WILLIAM E. Artist, NYC, 1859–62; thereafter as tailor. He was born in New Jersey about 1824, married a Connecticut girl, and had two sons born in Connecticut about 1846–48. ¶ NYCD 1859–66; 8 Census (1860), N.Y., LX, 1055.

WANDESFORDE, JUAN (or James) B. Portrait, genre, and landscape painter. He was a Scotsman who came to NYC in the early 1850's and worked there until after 1860. In 1858 he was living at Centerport, Long Island. He was the teacher of Mrs. CORNELIA FASSETT. He later moved to California and in 1869 he illustrated *The Golden Gate,* published in San Francisco. ¶ Cowdrey, NAD; Cowdrey, AA & AAU; DAB, under Cornelia Fassett; NYCD 1858–60; Hamilton, *Early American Book Illustrators and Wood Engravers,* 481; represented in the Belknap Collection, NYHS.

WAPPENSTEIN, JOSEPH. Engraver. He was at Sandusky (Ohio) in 1853, but by 1859 had moved to Cincinnati where he specialized in banknote engraving. ¶ Ohio BD 1853; Cincinnati CD 1859–60.

WARBOURG, DANIEL. Negro engraver and stone mason, St. Louis, 1854. He was a brother of the sculptor EUGENE WARBOURG. ¶ Porter, *Modern Negro Art,* 46–47.

WARBOURG, EUGENE (1825–1859). Sculptor. A free-born Negro of New Orleans, who had a studio there in the forties and early fifties where he executed busts and cemetery sculpture. In 1850 his "Ganymede Offering a Cup of Nectar to Jupiter" was raffled in New Orleans for $500. In 1852 Warbourg went to Europe. He was patronized by the Duchess of Sutherland who commissioned a series of bas-reliefs based on *Uncle Tom's Cabin.* After visiting France and Belgium, Warbourg settled in Rome where he died January 12, 1859. DANIEL WARBOURG was his brother. ¶ Porter, *Modern Negro Art,* 46–47; Porter, "Versatile Interests of the Early Negro Artist"; New Orleans *Bee,* Dec. 13, 1850, and obit., March 9, 1859; New Orleans CD 1852–53.

WARBRICK, JOHN. Engraver, Philadelphia, 1860. He was born in England about 1836, the son of George Warbrick, machinist, and brother of WILLIAM WARBRICK, also an engraver. ¶ Phila. CD 1860; 8 Census (1860), Pa., LVIII, 2.

WARBRICK, WILLIAM. Engraver, 20, a native of England, at Philadelphia in 1860. He was a younger brother of JOHN WARBRICK, engraver. ¶ 8 Census (1860), Pa., LVIII, 2.

WARBURTON, JAMES (1827–1898). Engraver who died at Pawtucket (R.I.) July 15, 1898. ¶ *Art Annual,* I, obit.

WARD, ——. Of NORMAN & WARD, engravers, Philadelphia, 1774. Both men were from England. They also sold prints and taught drawing. ¶ Prime, I, 20.

WARD, The Misses. Teachers of drawing and painting who opened a seminary in Charleston (S.C.) in 1842. One or both exhibited landscapes and fancy pieces at the Apprentices' Library in 1843. ¶ Rutledge, *Artists in the Life of Charleston.*

WARD, ALFRED R. Exhibited at the National Academy in 1855; probably a misprint for ALFRED R. WAUD. ¶ Cowdrey, NAD.

WARD, CALEB. Painter, father of JACOB C. and CHARLES V. WARD. He was a native of Bloomfield (N.J.) and worked in NYC from 1826 to 1833. He may have been the engraver, C. Ward, of Jacob C. Ward's view of the scene of the Hamilton-Burr duel at Weehawken (N.J.), published about 1830. ¶ Folsom, *Bloomfield, Old and New,* 21; Folsom, "Jacob C. Ward"; Stokes, *Historical Prints;* NYCD 1826–33.

WARD, CHARLES CALEB (*c.* 1831–1896). Genre, landscape, and portrait painter, born in St. John (N.B.) where his grandfather had gone from NYC as a Loyalist. As a young man he was sent to London to learn the family business, but he took up painting instead, studying under William Henry Hunt. In 1850–51 he was in NYC and exhibited landscapes at the National Academy. By 1856 he was back in New Brunswick where he passed most of his life. From 1868 to 1872 he had a studio in NYC and again was an exhibitor at the National Academy. In 1882 he settled permanently at Rothesay (N.B.) where he died February 24, 1896 at the age of 65. ¶ Green, "Charles Caleb Ward, the Painter of the 'Circus is Coming,'" eight repros., checklist; Cowdrey, NAD; obit., Boston *Transcript,* Feb. 26, 1896.

WARD, CHARLES V. Landscape painter and daguerreotypist. He was a native of Bloomfield (N.J.), the son of CALEB and brother of JACOB C. WARD. He exhibited landscapes at the National Academy in 1829 and 1830, at which time he was a resident of NYC. From 1845 to 1847 he and his brother were itinerant daguerreotypists in South America, working in Santiago and Valparaiso (Chile), La Paz (Bolivia), Lima (Peru), and Panama, returning to New Jersey in 1847 or 1848 with a small fortune. Of his subsequent career nothing is known. ¶ Folsom, "Jacob C. Ward"; Folsom, *Bloomfield, Old and New,* 21; Cowdrey, NAD; Dunlap, *History,* II, 379–80; Met. Mus. *Bulletin* (1931), 165, repro.

WARD, DAVID B. Engraver and designer, Bangor (Me.), 1855–56. ¶ *Maine Register* 1855–56.

WARD, EDGAR MELVILLE (1839–1915). N.A. Genre and landscape painter, born February 24, 1839, at Urbana (Ohio), younger brother of the sculptor JOHN QUINCY ADAMS WARD. He studied at the National Academy in NYC in 1870–71 and then went to Paris to study for two years under Alexandre Cabanel. His professional life was spent mainly in NYC, though he also spent some time in Europe. He was made a National Academician in 1883 and in 1889 became instructor in drawing in its school. He died in NYC May 15, 1915. ¶ CAB; *Art Annual,* XII, obit.; Clark, *History of the NAD,* 139; Graves, *Dictionary;* Clement and Hutton.

WARD, G. M. Illustrator of volumes of poetry published in NYC in 1860 and 1867. ¶ Hamilton, *Early American Book Illustrators and Wood Engravers,* 482.

WARD, H. Painter of a watercolor scene, Youngstown (Ohio), 1840. ¶ Lipman and Winchester, 181.

WARD, JACOB C. (1809–1891). Landscape and still life painter, pioneer daguerreotypist. Born in Bloomfield (N.J.), the son of CALEB WARD, he began his career as an artist in NYC about 1829, exhibiting several times at the National and American Academies, the Apollo Association, and American Art-Union between 1829 and 1852. About 1830 he painted a view of the scene of the Hamilton-Burr duel at Weehawken (N.J.), engraved by C. Ward, possibly his father. In 1845 he joined his brother, CHARLES V. WARD, in Chile and for three years they took daguerreotype likenesses and sketched scenery in Chile, Bolivia, Peru, and Panama, returning to New Jersey in 1847 or 1848 via Jamaica and Cuba. In 1852 he exhibited at the National Academy as of London. The rest of his life was spent in Bloomfield where he died in 1891. ¶ Folsom, "Jacob C. Ward, an Old-time Landscape Painter"; Cowdrey, NAD; Cowdrey, AA & AAU; Stokes, *Historical Prints;* Met. Mus. *Bulletin* (1931), 165; Dunlap, *History,* II, 379–80.

WARD, JAMES C. Made a sketch of San Francisco in November 1848 which appeared in Bayard Taylor's *El Dorado, or Adventures in the Path of Empire* (1850). ¶ Van Nostrand and Coulter, *California Pictorial,* 122; Jackson, *Gold Rush Album,* 10; Peters, *California on Stone.*

WARD, JOHN F. Engraver, 32, at NYC in 1860. He was a native of New York State. ¶ 8 Census (1860), N.Y., XLIX, 600.

WARD, JOHN QUINCY ADAMS (1830–1910). N.A. Sculptor, born June 29, 1830, at

Urbana (Ohio). He spent his boyhood on a farm and was intended for a medical career, but at the age of 19 he entered the studio of Henry Kirke Brown in Brooklyn to learn sculpture. He remained with Brown seven years as pupil and assistant and helped him with the casting of the Union Square "Washington." From 1857 to 1860 Ward was working in Washington as a portrait sculptor. In 1861 he opened a studio in NYC where he worked for the next fifty years. His first important work was the statue of the "Indian Hunter" in Central Park, which was followed by many important monuments and portrait works. He has been called the "sculptor-laureate" of the latter 19th century and "the first native sculptor to create, without benefit of foreign training, an impressive body of good work." Ward was elected a National Academician in 1863 and served as President of the Academy in 1873–74. He died in NYC on May 1, 1910. ¶ Adams, *John Quincy Adams Ward;* DAB; Taft, *History of American Sculpture;* 8 Census (1860), D.C., II, 375; Clark, *History of the NAD.*

Ward, Joseph. Lithographer and print and frame seller, Boston, 1848–49. ¶ Boston CD 1848–49; Peters, *America on Stone.*

Ward, Mary Holyoke (1800–1880). Portrait painter and copyist, born in Salem (Mass.), May 2, 1800. She is known to have made copies after Copley and Frothingham. In 1833 she married Dr. Andrew Nichols; she was a sister-in-law of Charles Osgood and aunt of Abel Nichols. She died April 15, 1880. ¶ Belknap, *Artists and Craftsmen of Essex County,* 14; Nichols, "Abel Nichols, Artist."

Ward, William. English sculptor from Leicester who settled in Utah in 1852. He carved Utah's stone for the Washington Monument in Washington (D.C.), a lion for Brigham Young's house, and a bust of Shakespeare. He was also assistant architect of the Mormon Temple in Salt Lake City. He later left the church and went to St. Louis. In 1892 he returned to Salt Lake City to teach drawing at the University of Utah. ¶ Arrington, "Nauvoo Temple."

Ward, William. Painter of ship pictures, Salem (Mass.), 1799–1800. ¶ Robinson and Dow, *The Sailing Ships of New England,* I, 64.

Wardell, S. R., see Warwell.

Warden, Miss C. A. Miniaturist who exhibited at the Artists' Fund Society in 1842 as a Philadelphia resident. ¶ Rutledge, PA.

Wardle, Richard C. Portrait and historical engraver, NYC, 1848–49. ¶ NYBD 1848–49.

Wardrope, William S. Lithographer, 37, a native of Scotland, at NYC in 1860. His wife was English; one child, 10, was born in Scotland; a second child, 4, was born in New York. ¶ 8 Census (1860), N.Y., XLVIII, 1.

Ware, Joseph (1827–?). Sculptor. In 1846, at the age of 19, he exhibited at the Boston Athenaeum his first work, a bas-relief in marble of St. John. ¶ Boston Athen. Cat., 1846; Swan, BA.

Waren (Warren?), ——. Engraver, 36, a native of Philadelphia where he was living in 1860 with his wife Sarah and five children, all born in Pennsylvania. ¶ 8 Census (1860), Pa., XLIX, 680.

Warfel, Jacob Eshleman (1826–1855). Portrait painter, born July 21, 1826, in Paradise Township (Pa.). He worked chiefly in Lancaster County (Pa.), though he was in Richmond (Va.) in October 1846. He is known to have painted one still life. He died June 2, 1855, of consumption. ¶ Lancaster County Hist. Soc., *Papers,* XVI (1912), 251–52; *Richmond Portraits,* 243.

Warin, Joseph. Made a pen-and-ink wash drawing of Pittsburgh (Pa.) in 1796. He was a travelling companion of General Victor Collot, a French officer, who made a journey through the western part of the United States from March to December 1796 for the purpose of gathering information for the French Minister at Philadelphia. ¶ Stokes, *Historical Prints,* 42, pl. 34a.

Waring, Sophia F. Malbone (1787–1823). Amateur miniaturist, wife of Dr. Edmund T. Waring of Newport (R.I.) and Charleston (S.C.). ¶ Carolina Art Assoc. Cat., 1935.

Warne, Thomas. Engraver, 30, a native of Pennsylvania, at Philadelphia in 1860 with his wife Emma and children, Daniel and William. This may be the Thomas A. Warne, jeweler, listed in the 1866 directory. ¶ 8 Census (1860), Pa., XLIX, 207; Phila. CD 1866.

Warner, Alfred. General and seal engraver, NYC, 1836–60. From 1836 to 1841 he was in partnership with Charles Warner. This may be the Alfred Warren [*sic*], engraver, aged 40 and a native New Yorker, listed in the 1860 Census. ¶ NYCD 1836–60; 8 Census (1860), N.Y., XLVII, 187.

WARNER, C. J. Engraver in stipple of a portrait published in NYC in 1796. Possibly the same as George J. Warner, watchmaker of NYC, 1795–1811. ¶ Stauffer; NYCD 1795, 1799–1811.

WARNER, CATHERINE TOWNSEND. Memorial painting in watercolors on silk, Rhode Island, 1810. ¶ Lipman and Winchester, 181.

WARNER, CHARLES. Engraver, NYC, 1835–41; with ALFRED WARNER from 1836. ¶ NYCD 1835–41.

WARNER, GEORGE D. Engraver of a botanical plate for the *New York Magazine,* December 1791. ¶ Stauffer.

WARNER, J. H. Mural landscape painter active at Fitchburg (Mass.) about 1840. ¶ Winchester, "A Painted Wall," repro.; Lipman and Winchester, 181.

WARNER, LEON. French artist, 38, at NYC in 1860 with his wife Emma, also French. ¶ 8 Census (1860), N.Y., LIV, 649.

WARNER, RALPH N. "Mezzotint grainer," Philadelphia, 1848. ¶ Phila. BD 1848, under historical and portrait engravers.

WARNER, WILLIAM, JR. (*c.* 1813–1848). Painter and mezzotint engraver who was born in Philadelphia and worked there from about 1836 until his death. He exhibited portraits and miniatures, landscapes and literary subjects at the Artists' Fund Society, Pennsylvania Academy, and Apollo Association. ¶ Stauffer; Rutledge, PA; Cowdrey, AA & AAU; Phila. BD 1838–39, 1846, 1849.

WARNICK or WARNICKE, JOHN G. (?–1818). Engraver who worked in Philadelphia from 1811 until his death on December 29, 1818. There was another John Warnick, engraver, listed in the 1811 directory at a different address, but this may have been a printer's error. ¶ Stauffer; Phila. CD 1811; repro., *Connoisseur* (March 1948), 48.

WARR, JOHN. Engraver, born in Scotland about 1798/99, active in Philadelphia at least from 1828 to 1860. His eldest son, WILLIAM WARR, also was an engraver. ¶ 7 Census (1850), Pa., LIII, 179; 8 Census (1860), Pa., LVIII, 570; Phila. CD 1860.

WARR, WILLIAM. Engraver; born in Pennsylvania about 1828, the son of JOHN WARR, engraver; active in 1850. ¶ 7 Census (1850), Pa., LIII, 179.

WARRE, Sir HENRY JAMES (1819–1898). Topographical artist. In 1845–46 he made a military reconnaissance of the Oregon country for the British Government, taking many sketches on the spot which were later engraved to illustrate his *Sketches in North America and the Oregon Territory* (1848). The originals of Warre's views in Oregon and Washington are now in the American Antiquarian Society. Warre later served as colonel of the Wiltshire regiment in the Crimean and New Zealand wars and retired with the rank of General. ¶ DNB; Rasmussen, "Artists of the Explorations Overland, 1840–1860," 59–60; *American Heritage* (Summer 1953), 58–59, repros.; *American Processional,* 134; Stokes, *Historical Prints.*

WARRELL, JAMES (*c.* 1780–before 1854). Portrait and historical painter, scenic artist. Warrell's parents were actors who emigrated to America in 1793; he himself made his stage debut the following year in Philadelphia, but by 1799 he had opened a dancing school in Richmond (Va.). In 1808 he suffered a leg injury which ended his dancing career, whereupon he turned to painting. Although he painted stage scenery and drop curtains as far afield as Providence (R.I.), most of his time was spent in Richmond and Petersburg (Va.) where he also painted many portraits and historical subjects. In 1817 he and his brother-in-law, Richard Lorton, opened Richmond's first museum, which struggled along for almost twenty years before finally expiring in 1836. Warrell gave up its management sometime in the twenties and left Richmond for a time. In 1825 and 1826–27 he spent some time in New Orleans and from 1829 to 1831 he was in NYC. Between 1831 and 1839 he seems to have divided his time between Richmond and NYC and after 1839 nothing is heard of him. It is not known when or where he died, though it was certainly before 1854, when his widow disposed of some property in Richmond. ¶ *Richmond Portraits,* 235–39; Rutledge, *Artists in the Life of Charleston;* Rutledge, PA; Cowdrey, NAD; Delgado-WPA cites *La. Gazette,* Feb. 21, 1825, *Courier,* March 10, 1826, and New Orleans CD 1827; NYCD 1829–31, 1833–34, 1839.

WARREN, ANDREW W. (?–1873). A.N.A. Marine and landscape painter born in Coventry (N.Y.). After studying under T. H. MATTESON at Sherburne (N.Y.), he shipped as cabinboy on a ship bound for South America in order to study the sea. In 1855 and 1857 he was at Coventry and 1858–60 at NYC, but much of his time was spent on Mt. Desert Island (Me.). He made a trip to Central America about 1867. He died in 1873, probably in NYC. ¶ Fielding; Tuckerman, *Book of the Artists,* 552; Cowdrey, NAD; NYBD 1858–59; Rutledge, PA; Swan, BA; *Portfolio* (May 1943), 208, repro.

WARREN, ASA. Portrait and miniature painter, father of ASA COOLIDGE WARREN. The elder Warren was listed as a painter only in the Boston directories (business) for 1846 and 1847; in the city directories he was listed as a musician during the 1830's and 1840's. ¶ Boston BD 1846–47; Boston CD 1830–50; Bolton, *Miniature Painters.*

WARREN, ASA COOLIDGE (1819–1904). Engraver and illustrator, who also painted some portraits and landscapes. A son of ASA WARREN, miniature painter and musician, he was born March 25, 1819, in Boston. He served his apprenticeship under the Boston engraver, GEORGE GIRDLER SMITH, and later worked for JOSEPH ANDREWS, the NEW ENGLAND BANK NOTE COMPANY, and the Boston publishers Ticknor & Field. Eye trouble forced him to give up engraving for five years, during which time he drew designs on wood for other engravers. In 1863 he went to NYC as an engraver of banknote vignettes and book illustrations and later he was employed in the Government Printing Office at Washington. During his last years he took up landscape painting. He died in NYC on November 22, 1904. ¶ Stauffer; *Art Annual,* V, 124, obit.; Boston BD 1842–60.

WARREN & BUELL. Lithographers, Buffalo (N.Y.), 1856; HENRY WARREN and CHARLES W. BUELL. ¶ Buffalo CD 1856–57.

WARREN, HENRY. Limner who advertised at Williamsburg (Va.) in February 1769; he offered to paint "night pieces" and "family pieces," "or anything of the like (landscapes excepted). . . ." ¶ *Virginia Gazette,* Feb. 23, 1769.

WARREN, HENRY. Landscape, marine, and figure painter; born in England about 1793; active in Philadelphia from about 1822 at least until 1860. He may have been working in America as early as 1815, for a view of the Washington Monument in Baltimore was engraved about that time by W. H. FREEMAN after a drawing by "H. Warren." He exhibited British and American views, as well as literary and religious paintings, at the Pennsylvania Academy, Artists' Fund Society, and the Apollo Association. ¶ 7 Census (1850), Pa., LI, 912; Phila. CD 1823–60; Rutledge, PA; Cowdrey, AA & AAU; Gage, *Artists' Index to Stauffer.*

WARREN, HENRY. Lithographer, Buffalo (N.Y.), 1856–57; in 1856 of WARREN & BUELL. ¶ Buffalo CD 1856–57.

WARREN, GEORGE W. Of PEASE & WARREN, engravers and lithographers at Albany (N.Y.) in 1853. In 1854 he was listed as a music teacher. ¶ Albany CD 1853–54.

WARREN, J. Miniaturist at Boston in January 1830. ¶ Sherman, "Newly Discovered American Miniaturists," 98–99, repro.

WARREN, M., JR. Portrait painter in watercolors, working at White Plains (N.Y.) in 1830. ¶ Lipman and Winchester, 181; *American Provincial Painting,* no. 74.

WARREN, THOMAS. Heraldic painter from Boston who advertised at Portsmouth (N.H.) in 1775. ¶ Bowditch, "Early Water-Color Paintings of New England Coats of Arms," 206.

WARTZ, MICHAEL. Lithographer, 30, a native of Darmstadt (Germany), at Philadelphia in 1860 with his German-born wife and two children, ages 3 and 1, both born in Pennsylvania. ¶ 8 Census (1860), Pa., LII, 244.

WARWELL, —— (?–1767). Limner from London who arrived in Charleston (S.C.) with his wife MARIA in October 1765 and died there May 29, 1767. He advertised his readiness to paint history pieces, heraldry, altar pieces, coaches, landscapes, window blinds, sea pieces, chimney blinds, flowers, screens, fruit, scenery, "deceptive triumphal arches, ruins, obelisks, statues &c for groves and gardens." He also did gilding, picture cleaning, copying, and restoring, and wall painting. ¶ Rutledge, *Artists in the Life of Charleston,* 118, 223; Prime, I, 18. Listed as S. R. Wardell in Neuhaus, *History and Ideals of American Art,* 14.

WARWELL, Mrs. MARIA. Restorer of china and statuary. She came from London to Charleston (S.C.) in 1765 with her husband, the painter Mr. WARWELL. After his death in 1767 she advertised her skill in mending useful and ornamental china and statues in china, glass, plaster, bronze, or marble; if a piece was missing, she was ready to "substitute a composition in its room, and copy the pattern as nigh as possible. . . ." ¶ Rutledge, *Artists in the Life of Charleston,* 224.

WASDELL, HENRY. Engraver, born in England about 1831, working in NYC from 1859. ¶ 8 Census (1860), N.Y., LVIII, 783; NYBD 1859; NYCD 1863.

WASHBURN, EDWARD PAYSON (1831–1860). Portrait and genre painter, born November 17, 1831, in New Dwight in the Cherokee Nation, now Oklahoma. The family moved to Arkansas in 1840 and Edward began painting portraits at Fort Smith in 1851. After studying for eighteen months in NYC under CHARLES L. ELLIOTT and at the National Academy, he returned to Arkansas and settled in Norristown. In 1858 he painted his best-known work, "The Arkansas Traveler." ¶ Reynolds, "Papers and Documents of Eminent Arkansans," 239; Brown, "Two Versions of the Arkansas Traveler," repro.; NYBD 1854.

WASHBURN, Mrs. HORACE B., see CAROLINE MUNGER.

WASHBURN, WILLIAM. Engraver, 19, born in Vermont and working in NYC in 1850. ¶ 7 Census (1850), N.Y., XLIII, 96.

WASHINGTON, WILLIAM DE HARTBURN (1834–1870). Portrait and historical painter. He was a native of Virginia and worked in Washington (D.C.), 1856–60, and NYC, 1868. He exhibited at the Pennsylvania Academy and the Washington Art Association. ¶ Rutledge, PA; 8 Census (1860), D.C., I, 474; Washington CD 1858, 1860; Washington Art Assoc. Cat., 1857, 1859.

WATERMAN, MARCUS (Mark) A. (1834–1914). A.N.A. Landscape and figure painter born in Providence (R.I.) on September 1, 1834. After graduating from Brown University, he went to NYC where he had his studio from 1857 to 1874. He exhibited at the National Academy and was elected an Associate Member in 1861. After 1874 he made his home in Boston, but spent much time in Vermont and Cape Cod and made at least two visits to Europe and North Africa. In 1900 he went to Europe to stay and he died in Moderno (Italy) on April 2, 1914. He was best known for his New England forest scenes, Cape Cod marines, and a series of scenes from the Arabian Nights, based on his Algerian experiences. ¶ *Art Annual,* XII (1915), 498, obit.; *Art News* (April 11, 1914), 4, obit.; Downes, "An American Painter: Mark Waterman," six repros.; Clark, *History of the NAD,* 273; Cowdrey, NAD; Rutledge, PA; CAB.

WATERS, ALMIRA. Still life, watercolors, painted at Portland (Me.) about 1830. ¶ Lipman and Winchester, 181.

WATERS, CHARLES J. B. Engraver, NYC, 1858–60. He was with the following firms: BRIGHTLY, WATERS & Co. and C. J. B. Waters & Co. in 1858; WATERS & TILTON, 1859; and WATERS & SON, 1860. JOHN W. WATERS was his son. ¶ NYCD 1858–60.

WATERS, D. E. Painter of a watercolor, 1840. ¶ Lipman and Winchester, 181.

WATERS, E. A. Painter of a literary subject, watercolors, 1840. ¶ Lipman and Winchester, 181.

WATERS, GEORGE W. (1832–1912). Landscape and portrait painter. He was born in Coventry (N.Y.), studied art in NYC and later in Dresden and Munich (Germany), and was for many years director of the art department at Elmira College, Elmira (N.Y.). He died in Elmira. ¶ Fielding; Cowdrey, NAD.

WATERS, JOHN P. Engraver, NYC, 1849–60. ¶ NYBD 1849–59; NYCD 1850–60.

WATERS, JOHN W. Of WATERS & SON, engravers of NYC, 1860. His father was CHARLES J. B. WATERS. ¶ NYBD 1860.

WATERS, MATTHEW. Engraver, NYC, 1846. ¶ NYBD 1846.

WATERS & SON. Wood engravers, NYC, 1860; CHARLES J. B. and JOHN W. WATERS. ¶ NYBD 1860.

WATERS & TILTON. Engravers, NYC, 1859; CHARLES J. B. WATERS and BENJAMIN W. TILTON. ¶ NYCD 1859.

WATERSTON or WATERSON, JAMES R. Landscape painter and draftsman at NYC, 1846–60, and Philadelphia, 1848. He exhibited at the American Institute in 1846–47, at the American Art-Union from 1847 to 1852, and at the National Academy from 1855 to 1859. His subjects were mainly Scottish, New York, and New Jersey scenes. ¶ Am. Inst. Cat., 1846, 1847; Cowdrey, AA & AAU; Cowdrey, NAD; NYBD 1854, 1856; NYCD 1860.

WATIES, JULIUS PRINGLE. Painter (amateur) of a miniature of William Waties (1797–1847), probably in South Carolina. ¶ Carolina Art Assoc. Cat., 1935.

WATKINS, WILLIAM. Miniaturist. He came with his parents to Ohio from England or Wales about 1840, began his career as an artist in Steubenville, and later worked in Cincinnati. ¶ Clark, *Ohio Art and Artists,* 102.

WATMOUGH, E. C. Philadelphia landscape painter who exhibited at the Pennsylvania Academy in 1847–48 and at the American Art-Union in 1846. He was also the artist of "Repulsion of the British at Fort Erie," lithographed and published in the *U. S. Military Magazine,* II, March 1841. Possibly he was the Edward C. Watmough, lawyer, listed in Philadelphia directories, 1825–37. ¶ Rutledge, PA; Cowdrey, AA & AAU; *Portfolio* (Dec. 1953), 93, repro.

WATRIN, T. T. Painter of a miniature (1836) of Obadiah Romney Van Benthuysen (1787–1845) of Albany (N.Y.). ¶ Information courtesy Dr. H. W. Williams, Jr., Corcoran Gallery.

WATSON, C. A. Lithographer, partner of JOHN FRAMPTON WATSON at Philadelphia in 1835. ¶ Phila. CD 1835.

WATSON, J. R. British naval officer and amateur watercolorist who visited the United States and took several watercolor views, probably shortly before 1820. The Tomb of Washington and the Falls of St. Anthony (Minn.) in JOSHUA SHAW'S *Picturesque Views of American Scenery* (1819) were after paintings by Captain Watson, R.N. A view of the Schuylkill River near Philadelphia after Captain J. R. Watson appeared in CEPHAS G. CHILDS' *Views of Philadelphia from Original Views Taken in 1827–1830* (1830), while Captain Watson, R.N., also was represented in the Pennsylvania Academy exhibition of 1829 by a view on the Schuylkill and a view of Exeter (England). The artist may have been Joshua Rowley Watson, born 1772, commissioned post-captain in the Royal Navy in 1798, and on active service at least until 1818. ¶ Shaw, *Picturesque Views;* Childs, *Views of Philadelphia;* Rutledge, PA; DNB [under Rundle Burges Watson]; Admiralty-Office, *List of the Flag Officers . . . ,* 1818.

WATSON, JOHN (1685–1768). Portrait painter and draftsman who was born in Scotland, probably at Dumfries, on July 28, 1685. He settled in Perth Amboy (N.J.) as early as 1714 and resided there until his death on August 22, 1768. In 1726 he did some portraits in NYC, both oils and plumbago drawings. Watson made a trip to Scotland in 1730 and brought back to New Jersey his niece and nephew, as well as a collection of paintings which he displayed in his house. He was the owner of much property in Perth Amboy. ¶ The most recent summary of the artist's career is Bolton, "John Watson of Perth Amboy, Artist," which contains a bibliography of earlier writings on Watson. The largest collection of Watson's work is at the New Jersey Historical Society; other examples are at the NYHS.

WATSON, JOHN. Scottish lithographer, 34, at NYC in 1850. ¶ 7 Census (1850), N.Y., XLIII, 88.

WATSON, JOHN FRAMPTON. Lithographer working in Philadelphia from about 1833 until after 1860. He was also listed as a daguerreotypist in 1841. In 1835 he was in partnership with C. A. WATSON. He was a native Pennsylvanian, born about 1805, according to the 1850 Census. ¶ Phila. CD 1833–60+; Peters, *America on Stone;* 7 Census (1850), Pa., LII, 997.

WATSON, JOHN W. General and wood engraver, NYC, 1840's and 1850's. ¶ NYBD 1846, 1857.

WATSON, RICHARD. Exhibited a plaster bust of the NYC architect, David Jardine, at the 1856 fair of the American Institute. He was listed as a NYC resident. ¶ Am. Inst. Cat., 1856.

WATSON, STEWART (Stuart). A.N.A. Portrait, animal, and historical painter who began exhibiting at the National Academy in 1834 and was elected an Associate Member in 1836. He went abroad about 1837 and apparently studied in France and Italy from about 1838 to 1841 and then settled in London, exhibiting at the Royal Academy and other galleries from 1843 to 1847. In 1858, when he was made an Honorary Member, Professional, of the National Academy, he was listed as a resident of Edinburgh (Scotland). ¶ Cowdrey, NAD; NYCD 1835–36; Clark, *History of the NAD,* 273; Cowdrey, AA & AAU; *American Collector* (Nov. 1942), 8, repro.; Graves, *Dictionary.*

WATTLES, ANDREW D. Portrait and landscape painter working in Philadelphia from 1848 to 1853. ¶ Phila. BD 1848–53; Rutledge, PA.

WATTLES, J. HENRY. Portrait painter at Baltimore in 1842, possibly the son of JAMES L. WATTLES. ¶ Baltimore CD 1842.

WATTLES, JAMES L. Portrait painter, originally from Wilmington (Del.), who was working in Philadelphia in 1825 and in Baltimore from about 1829 to 1854. He is said to have been a rival of ALFRED JACOB MILLER in Indian portraiture. He had a son who also was a portrait painter, possibly J. HENRY WATTLES. ¶ Pleasants, *250 Years of Painting in Maryland,* 49; Baltimore CD 1829–54 (Lafferty); Rutledge, PA; represented at the Md. Hist. Soc.

WATTLES, W. Painter of a portrait (about 1821) of William Poultney Farquhar (1781–1831), owned by J. Harris Lippincott of Atlantic City (N.J.). ¶ Information courtesy WPA (N.J.), Hist. Records Survey.

WATTS, JAMES W. (?–1895). Banknote, landscape, and portrait engraver who worked for the AMERICAN BANK NOTE COMPANY for many years. He began his career as an engraver in Boston about 1848 and died at West Medford (Mass.) on March 13, 1895. ¶ Boston *Transcript,* March 14, 1895, obit.; Boston BD 1848–60; Stauffer.

WAUD, ALFRED R. (1828–1891). Civil War and Western illustrator. Born in London (England) October 2, 1828, he and his brother WILLIAM came to the United States about 1858. Alfred almost immediately became a staff artist for *Harper's Weekly* and during the Civil War was one of the magazine's most prolific artist-correspondents. After the war he toured the South and West for *Harper's* and he also contributed many illustrations to Bryant's *Picturesque America* (1872). After 1882 his activity was curtailed by ill health. He died April 6, 1891, in Marietta (Ga.). ¶ Taft, *Artists and Illustrators of the Old West,* 58–62; *Album of American Battle Art,* 166–67, and 16 repros.; represented in LC.

WAUD, WILLIAM (?–1878). Civil War illustrator for *Leslie's Illustrated Weekly* and *Harper's Weekly.* A brother of ALFRED R. WAUD, he was born in England and trained as an architect, assisting Sir Joseph Paxton in the designing of the London Crystal Palace about 1851. He probably came to the United States with his brother about 1858 and was employed as an illustrator during the Civil War. He died in Jersey City (N.J.) on November 10, 1878. ¶ Taft, *Artists and Illustrators of the Old West,* 296; *Harper's Weekly,* Nov. 30, 1878; Rutledge, *Artists in the Life of Charleston.*

WAUGH, ALFRED S. (?–1856). Portrait sculptor, portrait and miniature painter, profilist, writer and lecturer on the fine arts. A native of Ireland, Waugh studied modelling in Dublin in 1827, then went on a tour of the Continent. By 1833 he was in Baltimore and in 1838 he modelled several busts at Raleigh (N.C.). He was in Alabama by July 1842, at Pensacola (Fla.) in the summer of 1843, and at Mobile (Ala.) in 1844. There he joined forces with JOHN B. TISDALE, a young artist just beginning his career, and together they went to Missouri in 1845 and worked principally at Jefferson City, Independence, and Lexington for about a year. In 1846 Waugh made a trip to Santa Fe (N.M.), after which he painted portraits and miniatures in Boonville (Mo.) for a year. He moved to St. Louis in 1848 and there spent the rest of his life. During his eight years in St. Louis, Waugh turned out a number of busts and portraits, wrote several articles on the fine arts for the *Western Journal* and lectured on the same subject, and wrote an autobiography entitled *Travels in Search of the Elephant,* of which only the first part survives in manuscript. He died in St. Louis on March 18, 1856. ¶ McDermott, ed., *Travels in Search of the Elephant: The Wanderings of Alfred S. Waugh, Artist, in Louisiana, Missouri, and Santa Fe, in 1845–1846.*

WAUGH, MARY ELIZA (YOUNG). Miniaturist and wife of the panoramist SAMUEL B. WAUGH. ¶ Fielding; Neuhaus, *History and Ideals of American Art,* 300.

WAUGH, HENRY W. Landscape, panorama, and scenery painter and nephew of the panoramist SAMUEL B. WAUGH. He arrived in Indianapolis (Ind.) in 1853 when he was 18 or 20 years old and a member of a theatrical troupe. During the winter of 1853–54 he assisted JACOB COX of Indianapolis in painting a 30-scene temperance panorama. While in Indianapolis Waugh also did scene and banner painting and exhibited some landscapes. In order to earn money for study abroad he became a circus clown, under the name of "Dilly Fay." Eventually he went to Rome for six years, but he died of consumption in England on his way home. He was still at Rome in 1862 when he exhibited at the Pennsylvania Academy. ¶ Burnet, *Art and Artists of Indiana,* 93–97; Peat, *Pioneer Painters of Indiana,* 156–57; Rutledge, PA.

WAUGH, SAMUEL BELL (1814–1885). A.N.A. Portrait and landscape painter, best known for his panorama of Italy. A native of Mercer (Pa.), he spent eight years in Italy before 1841. After that date he spent most of his time in Philadelphia, though he was in NYC in 1844–45 and at Bordentown (N.J.) in 1853. His Italian panorama was first shown in Philadelphia in 1849 and was still being exhibited as late as 1855. A second series, entitled "Italia," was shown from 1854 to 1858.

He was made an Associate of the National Academy in 1845 and an Honorary Member, Professional, in 1847. He died at Janesville (Wis.) in 1885. Other artists in his family included his wife, MARY ELIZA (YOUNG) WAUGH, their son Frederick Judd Waugh (1861–1940), their daughter Ida Waugh (?–1919), and a nephew, HENRY W. WAUGH. ¶ Smith; Graves, *Dictionary;* Rutledge, PA; Cowdrey, NAD; Cowdrey, AA & AAU; Clark, *History of the NAD,* 273; Phila. CD 1846–53; Swan, BA; Washington Art Association Cat., 1857, 1859; Phila. *Public Ledger,* Oct. 2, 1849, Sept. 12, 1854, Baltimore *Sun,* March 28, 1855, and New Orleans *Daily Picayune,* March 6, 1858 (courtesy J. Earl Arrington); *Art Annual,* XVI, obit.; *American Collector* (May 1941), 10, repro.; represented at Univ. of Penna.

WAUGH, WILLIAM. Artist, 40, a native of Philadelphia, at Philadelphia in 1850 with his wife Mary and daughter Fanny. ¶ 7 Census (1850), Pa., LI, 123; not listed in Phila. CD 1848–54.

WAY, ANDREW JOHN HENRY (1826–1888). Still life, portrait, and landscape painter, born April 27, 1826, in Washington (D.C.). After studying in Cincinnati with JOHN P. FRANKENSTEIN and in Baltimore with ALFRED J. MILLER, Way went to Paris in 1850 for four years' further study there and at Florence. On his return he settled in Baltimore where he lived until his death, February 7, 1888. At first a portrait painter, he later became well known as a painter of still life, especially grapes. His son, George Brevitt Way (1854–?), also was a painter. ¶ CAB; Pleasants, *250 Years of Painting in Maryland,* 60–61; Baltimore CD 1858–60+; 8 Census (1860), Md., VII, 584; Rutledge, MHS; Washington Art Assoc. Cat., 1857; *Gazette des Beaux Arts* (May 1946), 316, repro.; represented at Peabody Institute, Baltimore.

WAY, Miss MARY. Miniature painter and drawing mistress from New London (Conn.) who was active in NYC from 1811 to 1819 and exhibited at the American Academy in 1818. ¶ Kelby, *Notes on American Artists,* 50–51; NYCD 1814–19 (McKay); Cowdrey, AA & AAU.

WAY, WILLIAM. Artist, Baltimore, 1859. ¶ Baltimore BD 1859.

WEATHERBY, J. A., see ISAAC AUGUSTUS WETHERBY.

WEAVER. Portrait painter in oils on tin who was at NYC about 1797 and painted a portrait of Alexander Hamilton; probably English (Dunlap). This was probably the Joseph Weaver, painter and japanner, who painted allegorical decorations on a musical clock exhibited at Baker's New Museum in NYC in 1794 (Gottesman). Later references to apparently the same artist include: I. Weaver, miniaturist, at NYC in 1796 (NYCD); John Weaver, portrait painter on tin and wood, at Halifax (N.S.) in 1797–98 (Piers); William J. Weaver, portrait painter, at Charleston (S.C.) in 1806 when he advertised his portrait of Hamilton (Rutledge); W. J. Weaver, portrait painter on tin, who planned a professional visit to Salem (Mass.) in 1809 (Belknap); and P. T. Weaver, whom Fielding identified as the Weaver mentioned by Dunlap. Engravings after William J. Weaver's portraits of Dr. George Buist of Charleston and Dr. S. L. Mitchill of NYC were mentioned in Charleston in 1808–11 and 1823, respectively. ¶ Dunlap, *History,* II, 64; NYCD 1794; Gottesman, *Arts and Crafts in New York,* II, no. 1302; NYCD 1796 (McKay); Piers, *Robert Field,* 144; Rutledge, *Artists in the Life of Charleston,* 128, 224, 238; Belknap, *Artists and Craftsmen of Essex County,* 14; Fielding.

WEAVER, GEORGE M. Painter of a panorama of the overland route to California from sketches made by himself. By 1858 he had added the Isthmus of Panama route and eighty California scenes. ¶ MacMinn, *The Theater of the Golden Era in California,* 226 (courtesy J. Earl Arrington).

WEAVER, LEWIS. German-born engraver, 30, at Philadelphia in 1860. He and his German wife had one child, born in Pennsylvania about 1858. ¶ 8 Census (1860), Pa., LII, 960.

WEBB, EBENEZER R. Of WELLS & WEBB, wood engravers, NYC, 1846. ¶ NYBD 1846.

WEBB, EDWARD J. Architect of NYC who exhibited watercolors at the American Institute in 1842. ¶ Am. Inst. Cat., 1842; NYCD 1842.

WEBB, H. T. Portrait painter, Wilton (Conn.), 1840. ¶ Lipman and Winchester, 181.

WEBB, JAMES. English engraver, 40, at Philadelphia in 1850. ¶ 7 Census (1850), Pa., LII, 978.

WEBB, JAMES. English engraver, 43, a pauper in the NYC Alms House in July 1860. ¶ 8 Census (1860), N.Y., LXI, 156.

WEBB, WILLIAM N. Shade painter in partnership with CHARLES ELLENWOOD at Boston in 1850. ¶ Boston CD 1850.

WEBBER, Mrs. ——. Drew on stone a view of Bellows Falls (Vt.) which was published by the PENDLETONS of Boston, probably sometime in the 1830's. ¶ Peters, *America on Stone.*

WEBBER, CHARLES T. (1825–1911). Portrait, historical, and landscape painter; sculptor. Born December 31, 1825, on the east shore of Cayuga Lake (N.Y.), Webber moved to Springfield (Ohio) in 1844 and thence in 1858 to Cincinnati where he spent the rest of his life. He was a leader in Cincinnati art circles during the latter half of the 19th century, organizer in 1869 of the McMickin School of Art and Design, and a charter member of the Sketch Club (1860) and the Art Club (1890). Aside from his numerous portraits, he was best known for his historical painting, "The Underground Railroad," and his group portrait of Major Daniel McCook and his nine sons. ¶ Rodabaugh, "Charles T. Webber"; Cincinnati CD 1860+.

WEBBER, JOHN (*c.* 1750–1793). Landscape painter born in London, the son of a Swiss sculptor. He spent much of his childhood in Bern (Switzerland) and studied painting there and at Paris. After his return to England he was employed as a decorative painter, but in 1776 he went as artist on Captain James Cook's last voyage to the Pacific. During this four year voyage, Webber made many sketches, including some on the coast of the present states of Washington and Oregon, and after his return to England in 1780 he developed them into paintings which were used to illustrate the report of the expedition. Subsequently Webber painted landscapes in Great Britain, Switzerland, and Italy and published between 1787 and 1792 sixteen views of places he had visited with Cook, etched and colored by himself. He was made a Royal Academician in 1791 and died two years later, April 29, 1793, in London. ¶ DNB; Rasmussen, "Art and Artists in Oregon" (courtesy David C. Duniway); *American Processional,* 237; Gould, *Beyond the Shining Mountains,* opp. 54, 59.

WEBER, CAROLINE. Artist and teacher of painting at Buffalo (N.Y.) in 1857. ¶ Buffalo BD 1857.

WEBER, EDWARD. Lithographer of Baltimore, active from about 1835 to about 1851. He was probably a native of Germany. The brothers HOEN were his nephews and AUGUST HOEN was his partner for some years before 1848 when Hoen set up his own lithographic business. ¶ Peters, *America on Stone;* Baltimore CD 1837–51. Examples of Weber's work are found in Abert, *Journal;* Owen, *Report of a Geological Exploration of Part of Iowa, Wisconsin, and Illinois;* Cross, *Journey from Fort Leavenworth to Fort Vancouver;* and Frémont, *Report.*

WEBER, JOHN S. Engraver, St. Louis, 1859. ¶ St. Louis BD 1859.

WEBER, PAUL (1823–1916). Landscape and portrait painter born at Darmstadt (Germany) in 1823. After studying in Frankfort, he came to the United States in 1848 and settled in Philadelphia where he was a frequent exhibitor at the Pennsylvania Academy from 1849. In 1857 he toured Scotland and Germany and in 1860 he returned to Darmstadt where he was appointed court painter. Later he returned to the United States and he died in Philadelphia in 1916. ¶ Clement and Hutton; Fielding; Rutledge, PA; Swan, BA; Rutledge, MHS; Cowdrey, NAD; Cowdrey, AA & AAU; NYBD 1856–60; 8 Census (1860), Pa., LIV, 261; Washington Art Assoc. Cat., 1857, 1859; represented in Corcoran Gallery.

WEBSTER, IRA. Lithographer (?) of "Confiding Monkeys Crossing a Stream," entered by him at Hartford (Conn.) in 1844. ¶ Peters, *America on Stone.*

WEBSTER, DANIEL C. Copper and steel engraver, Boston, 1844–after 1860. ¶ Boston CD and BD 1844–60+.

WEBSTER, WALTER. Wood engraver, 24, a native of Massachusetts, at Boston in 1860. ¶ 8 Census (1860), Mass., XXVII, 432.

WEDDERBURN, ALEXANDER. Engraver at Lowell (Mass.), 1835–37. ¶ Belknap, *Artists and Craftsmen of Essex County,* 5.

WEED, EDWIN A. Wood engraver; born in New York State about 1828; working in NYC from about 1850 at least until 1860. ¶ 7 Census (1850), N.Y., L, 690; 8 Census (1860), N.Y., XLIV, 543; NYCD 1850; NYBD 1854, 1860.

WEEDING, NATHANIEL. Of NYC, exhibited a painting of a dog's head at the American Institute in 1849. ¶ Am. Inst. Cat., 1849.

WEEKES or WEEKS, STEPHEN. Wood engraver active in NYC from 1844 to about 1855. He exhibited at the American Institute,

1844–45 and 1847. ¶ NYCD 1844–48; Am. Inst. Cat., 1844–45, 1847; Hamilton, *Early American Book Illustrators and Wood Engravers,* 109.

WEEKS, WILLIAM (1813–1900). Architect, stone and wood carver. Born April 11, 1813, on Martha's Vineyard (Mass.), he became a builder and after various wanderings in the Middle West joined the Mormon Church and settled in Nauvoo (Ill.) about 1841. He was the chief architect of the Mormon Temple there and did some of the ornamental carving for it. He joined the trek to Utah in 1847 but broke with the church in 1848. He eventually settled in California and died in Los Angeles on March 8, 1900. His architectural drawings are preserved in the Historian's Office of the Mormon Church, Salt Lake City. ¶ Arrington, "Nauvoo Temple."

WEGNER & BUECHNER. Lithographers working in Pittsburgh (Pa.) sometime before 1859. *Cf.* CHARLES WAGONER. ¶ Drepperd, "Pictures with a Past," 96.

WEHNERE [?], EDWARD. Artist, 40, a native of Maryland, at Baltimore in 1850. No artist of this name appears in the Baltimore directories, but there was an EDWARD WELLMORE, portrait and miniature painter, possibly the same man. ¶ 7 Census (1850), Md., V, 474; Baltimore CD 1837–67.

WEIDENBACH, AUGUSTUS. Landscape painter who exhibited at the Maryland Historical Society as early as 1853 and was listed in Baltimore directories from 1858 to 1869. His view of Harper's Ferry (W. Va.) was lithographed by EDWARD SACHSE & Co. between 1860 and 1863. ¶ Lafferty; Rutledge, MHS; Stokes, *Historical Prints.*

WEIL, ALEXANDER. Lithographer, born in Baden about 1818, working in NYC from about 1854. He was associated with DAVID WEIL in 1857. ¶ 8 Census (1860), N.Y., XLIX, 137; NYBD 1857, 1859; NYCD 1863.

WEIL, DAVID. Lithographer working in NYC in 1857–59; in 1857 associated with ALEXANDER WEIL. ¶ NYBD 1857, 1859.

WEIL, JOHN. Artist, 40, a native of New York State, at NYC in 1850. ¶ 7 Census (1850), N.Y., LII, 263.

WEINEDEL, CARL (1795–1845). A.N.A. Portrait and miniature painter. He advertised in Richmond (Va.) as early as 1821 and was in NYC from 1834 until the time of his death, May 11, 1845. In 1839 he was elected an Associate of the National Academy. ¶ Cummings, *Historic Annals of the NAD,* 186; Cowdrey, NAD; Bolton, *Miniature Painters; Richmond Portraits,* 243; Stauffer, no. 2041.

WEINGAERTNER, ADAM. Of NAGEL & WEINGAERTNER, lithographers, NYC, 1849–56. ¶ NYCD 1849–56.

WEINMANN, R. Lithographer, New Orleans, 1854–59. In 1857, because of illness, he offered for sale his three-press lithographic plant. ¶ New Orleans CD 1854–56, BD 1858–59; Delgado-WPA cites *Bee,* Jan. 1, 1857.

WEIR, CHARLES E. (*c.* 1823–1845). Portrait and genre painter, brother of ROBERT W. WEIR. He was exhibiting as early as 1841 at the National Academy and the American Art-Union. He died in NYC on June 20, 1845, at the age of 22. ¶ Cummings, *Historic Annals of the NAD,* 188; N. Y. *Evening Post,* June 21, 1845 (Barber); Cowdrey, NAD; Cowdrey, AA & AAU.

WEIR, ROBERT WALTER (1803–1889). N.A. Landscape, portrait, and genre painter and illustrator, born June 18, 1803, in NYC, not New Rochelle, as frequently stated. The family moved to New Rochelle in 1811, but was back in NYC by 1817. Weir had his earliest art training from JOHN WESLEY JARVIS and an English heraldic artist, ROBERT COX. He became a professional artist about 1821 and in 1824 he went to Italy for three years of study at Florence. On his return he opened a studio in NYC. He was elected a National Academician in 1829. In 1834 he was named instructor of drawing at West Point to succeed CHARLES R. LESLIE and in 1846 he was made professor. After his retirement in 1876 he had a studio in NYC until his death, May 1, 1889. Two of Weir's children also became well-known artists, John F. (1841–1926) and Julian Alden Weir (1852–1919). ¶ The only biography of Weir is *Robert W. Weir, Artist,* by his grand-daughter Irene Weir. See also: DAB; CAB; Clement and Hutton; Dunlap, *History;* Tuckerman, *Book of the Artists;* Webber, "The Birthplace of Robert Weir"; Cowdrey, NAD; Cowdrey, AA & AAU; Swan, BA; Rutledge, PA; Rutledge, MHS; Karolik Cat.; Met. Mus., *Life in America.* Weir's best-known work, "The Embarkation of the Pilgrims," is in the Rotunda of the Capitol at Washington.

WEIS, GEORGE. Sculptor and gilder at New Orleans in 1830. There was also a George Weis, artist, at Baltimore from 1830 to

1835. ¶ Delgado-WPA cites *Courier,* Nov. 20, 1830; Lafferty.

WEISMAN, JOSEPH. Portrait painter. He exhibited a self-portrait at the Pennsylvania Academy in 1822 and in 1824 he was at Easton (Pa.). ¶ Rutledge, PA; Easton *Gazette,* Dec. 11, 1824.

WEISS, JACOB. Lithographer and engraver, Philadelphia, 1859 and after. ¶ Phila. CD 1859–60+.

WEISS, JOHN E., see JOHN E. WEYSS.

WEISS, RUDOLPH. Landscape painter; born about 1826 in Hesse-Cassel (Germany); living in Philadelphia at least from 1855. He may have been the artist of two marines by "Weiss" exhibited at the Pennsylvania Academy in 1851. ¶ 8 Census (1860), Pa., LII, 245; Rutledge, PA.

WEISSENBORN, G. Lithographer working with HENRY BRUCKNER in NYC, 1861. ¶ *Portfolio* (Feb. 1954), 126.

WEISTER, JACOB. French lithographer, 40, living in Southwark, a suburb of Philadelphia, in 1850. His wife and children were also born in France, all before 1843. ¶ 7 Census (1850), Pa., LV, 409.

WEITH, SIMON. French lithographer, 25, at Philadelphia in 1860. He lived with his father, Joseph, and brother, STEPHEN WEITH. ¶ 8 Census (1860), Pa., LII, 437.

WEITH, STEPHEN. French lithographer, 23, at Philadelphia. He lived with his father, Joseph, and brother, SIMON WEITH. ¶ 8 Census (1860), Pa., LII, 437.

WELBY, ADLARD. Amateur sketcher. An English gentleman of South Rauceby (Lincolnshire) who visited the United States from May 1819 to May 1820 and published a rather unfavorable account of his experiences and observations in 1821. The book was illustrated with views of the places he visited, presumably based on his own sketches. ¶ Welby, *A Visit to North America and the English Settlements in Illinois. . . .*

WELCH, JOHN (1711–1789). Boston carver; born in Boston August 19, 1711; died there February 9, 1789. He is believed to have carved the Codfish which still hangs in the House of Representatives, Old State House, Boston. He was a very successful ship and ornamental carver and chairmaker. ¶ Brown, "John Welch, Carver," repros.; Swan, "Boston's Carvers and Joiners, Part I," 198–99.

WELCH, JOHN. Portrait painter at Baltimore in 1849. ¶ Baltimore CD 1849.

WELCH, JOHN T. Engraver at NYC, 1856–59. ¶ NYBD 1856–59.

WELCH, JOSEPH. Wood engraver and designer, Utica (N.Y.), 1859. ¶ N. Y. State BD 1859.

WELCH, L. T. Engraver at Bainbridge (Ind.) in 1860. ¶ Indiana BD 1860.

WELCH, THOMAS B. (1814–1874). Engraver and portrait painter who was born in Charleston (S.C.) but passed most of his life in Philadelphia. Beginning in 1832, he exhibited portraits and ideal subjects at the Pennsylvania Academy and Artists' Fund Society and at the American Academy and Apollo Association. He died in Paris on November 5, 1874. ¶ Stauffer; Rutledge, PA; Rutledge, *Artists in the Life of Charleston;* Cowdrey, AA & AAU; Phila. CD 1837–60+; 7 Census (1850), Pa., LI, 486; 8 Census (1860), Pa., LXII, 343.

WELCH, W. H. Engraver, NYC, 1850–51. ¶ NYBD 1850–51.

WELCH, see also WELSCH and WELSH.

WELCHER, F. German-born artist at St. Louis in 1854 when he assisted EDWARD ROBYN in the painting of a panorama of the Eastern Hemisphere. ¶ Letter of Charles van Ravenswaay, St. Louis, to J. Earl Arrington, Jan. 12, 1955 (courtesy J. Earl Arrington).

WELD, ISAAC (1774–1856). Topographical artist and writer, born March 15, 1774, in Dublin (Ireland). Weld traveled in the United States (from New York to Virginia) and the Canadas during the years 1795–97 and published an account of his experiences in 1799, illustrated with engravings after his own sketches. In 1807 appeared his *Illustrations of the Scenery of Killarney,* also illustrated by himself. Most of his life was spent in Dublin, where he was prominent in the Royal Dublin Society, though in his later years he spent much time in Rome. He died August 4, 1856, at Ravenswell, near Bray (Ireland). ¶ DNB; Weld, *Travels Through the United States. . . .*

WELDING, HENRY. Engraver, 19, a native Pennsylvanian, living in Philadelphia in 1860 with his father, Charles Welding, alderman. ¶ 8 Census (1860), Pa., LII, 633.

WELFARE, DANIEL (1796–1841). Portrait and still life painter, born in North Carolina. He studied under THOMAS SULLY in Philadelphia and exhibited at the Pennsylvania Academy in 1825. He died at Salem (N.C.) in 1841. ¶ Fielding; Rutledge, PA.

WELL, DAVID. San Francisco lithographer,

1858. *Cf.* DAVID WEIL. ¶ San Francisco BD 1858.

WELLAND, THOMAS. Engraver and die sinker, NYC, 1850–59. According to the 1850 census, he was born in England about 1806. His wife also was English, but their children were born in the United States, one in Massachusetts about 1836, two in New Jersey about 1842–43, and two in Pennsylvania between 1844 and 1847. Welland was first listed as a calico printer and paper embosser (1851) and subsequently simply as an engraver. ¶ 7 Census (1850), N.Y., LIII, 181; NYBD 1851; NYCD 1851–59.

WELLER, EDWIN J. (or John E.). Lithographer and engraver of Boston, active 1848 until after 1860. With WELLER & GREEN[E] in 1852 and POWERS & WELLER from 1852. According to the 1850 census he was born in New York State about 1822, but the 1860 census gives his birthplace as Philadelphia. ¶ Boston CD 1848 [as John E.], 1849–60+ [as Edwin J.]; 7 Census (1850), Mass., XXIV, 615; 8 Census (1860), Mass., XXVII, 456.

WELLER & GREEN[E]. Engravers, Boston, 1852; probably EDWIN J. WELLER and HENRY F. GREENE. ¶ Boston BD and CD 1852.

WELLING, WILLIAM. Engraver, 22, a native of New York State, at NYC in 1850. ¶ 7 Census (1850), N.Y., L, 794.

WELLMAN, BETSY. Painter of a watercolor equestrian portrait about 1840. ¶ Lipman and Winchester, 182.

WELLMORE or WILLMORE, EDWARD. Engraver, portrait and miniature painter, and crayon portraitist. He learned engraving under JAMES B. LONGACRE of Philadelphia and engraved several plates for Longacre's *National Portrait Gallery* (1834–35). From 1837 to 1867 he was in Baltimore as a portrait and miniature painter. Stauffer states that he later worked in NYC and is thought to have become a clergyman. *Cf.* EDWARD WEHNERE [?]. ¶ Stauffer; Baltimore CD 1837–67; Dunlap, *History;* represented at Maryland Historical Society.

WELLS, CHARLES R. Designer, 28, born in Pennsylvania, at Philadelphia in 1860. He lived in the same house with WILLIAM LIVASSE, lithographer. ¶ 8 Census (1860), Pa., LII, 951.

WELLS, DARIUS. Of WELLS & WEBB, wood engravers and printers' furnishing warehouse, NYC, 1846. ¶ NYBD and NYCD 1846.

WELLS or WELL, HENRY. Ship carver of Norfolk (Va.) who carved figureheads for the brigs *Norfolk* and *Tetsworth.* He was active from 1748 to 1800. ¶ Pinckney, *American Figureheads and Their Carvers,* 82, 202.

WELLS, J. W. Said to have painted a portrait of James Buchanan in 1856. ¶ Courtesy Harry Stone, NYC.

WELLS, JACOB. Artist and draftsman, NYC, 1851–58, thereafter as bookseller. He may have been the J. Wells who designed three illustrations for the *American Missionary Memorial* (New York, 1853). ¶ NYCD 1851–60+; Hamilton, *Early American Book Illustrators and Wood Engravers,* 491.

WELLS, JOHN. Engraver, 30, at Philadelphia in 1850; he was a native of Pennsylvania. ¶ 7 Census (1850), Pa., LV, 542.

WELLS, JOSEPH R. Engraver, 29, a native of Pennsylvania, at Philadelphia in 1850. ¶ 7 Census (1850), Pa., LII, 662.

WELLS, LEWIS I. B. Artist, "operative," chemist; Philadelphia, 1814–20. ¶ Brown and Brown.

WELLS, MORRIS. Engraver, 21, a native of Washington (D.C.), where he was living in 1860 with his father, Thomas Wells, police officer. ¶ 8 Census (1860), D.C., II, 427.

WELLS, RACHEL. Wax portraitist, sister of PATIENCE LOVELL WRIGHT. The Lovells lived in Bordentown (N.J.), but after her marriage Rachel moved to Philadelphia. Her only known work in wax was a full-length figure of the Rev. George Whitefield, modelled before his death in 1770 and later given to Bethesda College (Ga.). It was soon after destroyed in a fire. ¶ Bolton, *American Wax Portraits,* 22, 61.

WELLS & WEBB. Wood engravers and printers' furnishings warehouse, NYC, 1846; DARIUS WELLS and EBENEZER R. WEBB. ¶ NYBD and NYCD 1846.

WELLSTOOD, BENSON & HANKS. Banknote engravers, NYC, 1848–51. The partners were JOHN G. WELLSTOOD, BENJAMIN W. BENSON, and OWEN G. HANKS. After 1851 the name was changed to WELLSTOOD, HANKS, HAY & WHITING. ¶ NYCD 1848–51.

WELLSTOOD, HANKS, HAY & WHITING. Banknote engravers, NYC, 1852–55; JOHN G. WELLSTOOD, OWEN G. HANKS, DE WITT CLINTON HAY, and WILLIAM H. WHITING. After 1855 it became WELLSTOOD, HAY & WHITING. ¶ NYCD 1852–55.

WELLSTOOD, HAY & WHITING. Banknote engravers, NYC, 1856–58; JOHN G. WELLSTOOD, DE WITT CLINTON HAY, and WILLIAM H. WHITING. One of the firms which merged in 1858 to form the AMERICAN BANK NOTE COMPANY. ¶ NYCD 1856–58; Toppan, *100 Years of Bank Note Engraving,* 12.

WELLSTOOD, JOHN GEIKIE (1813–1893). Banknote engraver. Born in Edinburgh (Scotland) on January 18, 1813, he came to America in 1830 with his family and went to work for RAWDON, WRIGHT & COMPANY. In 1847 he left to form his own banknote firm which was active in NYC for a decade under the names, WELLSTOOD, BENSON & HANKS; WELLSTOOD, HANKS, HAY & WHITING; and WELLSTOOD, HAY & WHITING. In 1858 Wellstood was one of the leaders in the formation of the AMERICAN BANK NOTE COMPANY and he remained with the new firm until 1871 when he left to establish the Columbian Bank Note Company in Washington (D.C.). He returned to the American in 1879 and was still active as late as 1889. He died four years later, on January 21, 1893, at Greenwich (Conn.). WILLIAM WELLSTOOD was his brother. ¶ CAB; Fielding; Smith; NYCD 1836–60+.

WELLSTOOD & PETERS. Portrait, historical, and landscape engravers, NYC, 1854; WILLIAM WELLSTOOD, engraver, and Henry Peters, plate printer. ¶ NYBD and NYCD 1854.

WELLSTOOD, WILLIAM (1819–1900). Portrait, historical, and landscape engraver and etcher, and brother of the banknote engraver JOHN G. WELLSTOOD. He was born in Edinburgh (Scotland) on December 19, 1819 and brought to NYC by his parents at the age of eleven. He began his career with the Western Methodist Book Concern in the early forties and also did some work for NYC publishers, but he was best known for his landscape engravings. His home was in NYC from the mid-forties probably until his death on September 19, 1900. His son James (1855–1880) also was an engraver. ¶ Stauffer; CAB; NYCD 1847+.

WELMORE, see WELLMORE.

WELMORE, J. Philadelphia artist who exhibited a copy in miniature of an unidentified portrait of George Washington at the Artists' Fund Society in 1835. ¶ Rutledge, PA.

WELSCH, ——. Artist, New Orleans, 1837. ¶ New Orleans CD 1837 (Delgado-WPA).

WELSCH, THEODORE or THOMAS C. Landscape and genre painter who exhibited at the National Academy in 1858 (address: Syracuse, N.Y.) and 1860 (address: Cincinnati). ¶ Cowdrey, NAD.

WELSCH, see also WELCH and WELSH.

WELSH, CHARLES. Banknote engraver of Philadelphia, active from about 1841 to after 1860. In 1851 he joined the firm of DRAPER, WELSH & COMPANY which was absorbed into the AMERICAN BANK NOTE COMPANY in 1858. Welsh was a native of Pennsylvania, born about 1812 (1850 Census) or 1817 (1860 Census). ¶ Phila. CD 1841–60+; 7 Census (1850), Pa., LV, 593; 8 Census (1860), Pa., LI, 211.

WELSH, EDWARD. Irish-born engraver, 46, at NYC in 1860. One of his children was born in Ireland about 1833 and two were born in NYC about 1838 and 1840. ¶ 8 Census (1860), N.Y., XLV, 933.

WELSH, ISAAC. English engraver, 37, at NYC in 1860. ¶ 8 Census (1860), N.Y., XLV, 906.

WELSH, see also WELCH and WELSCH.

WEMMEL, CHARLES W. (*c.* 1839–1916). Artist and collector; born in Brooklyn (N.Y.) about 1839; died there March 31, 1916. ¶ *Art Annual,* XIII, obit.

WEMMER, N. J. Artist, Philadelphia, 1850–52. ¶ Phila. CD 1850–52.

WENDEROTH, AUGUST (1825–?). Historical, animal, landscape, and portrait painter; lithographer. He was born in Cassel (Germany), the son of the painter Carl Wenderoth, and studied art at the Cassel Academy. In 1845 he went to Paris and also visited Algeria. He came to America about 1848 and lived in Brooklyn (N.Y.) for several years. By 1854 he was in San Francisco in partnership with the lithographer and painter CHARLES C. NAHL, also from Cassel. Wenderoth soon returned east, however, and was at Philadelphia in 1858. He was active at least until 1863, since he painted a picture of the Battle of Gettysburg, but his subsequent history is unknown. ¶ Peters, *America on Stone;* Met. Mus., *Life in America,* no. 150; Nägler; Cowdrey, AA & AAU; San Francisco CD 1854; Peters, *California on Stone;* Phila. BD 1858; *Magazine of Art* (May 1944), 188, repro. *Cf.* FREDERICK A. WENDEROTH.

WENDEROTH & BOLLES, see FREDERICK A. WENDEROTH and JESSE BOLLES.

WENDEROTH, FREDERICK A. "Artist, painter, and photographer" who was at Charleston (S.C.) in 1857 with JESSE BOLLES and at Philadelphia in 1860 and after. *Cf.* AUGUST WENDEROTH. ¶ Rutledge, *Artists in the Life of Charleston,* 165, 224; Phila. CD 1860+.

WENGLER, JOHN B. An Austrian landscape artist who visited Wisconsin about 1850–51 and exhibited at the American Art-Union in 1851. He returned to Austria and is represented in the museum at Linz. ¶ Butts, *Art In Wisconsin,* 63–64; Cowdrey, AA & AAU.

WENIGE, G. Lithographer at Boston in 1860. ¶ New England BD 1860.

WENNER, WILLIAM E., see WILLIAM E. WINNER.

WENTWORTH, CLAUDE. Landscape painter of NYC who exhibited at the National Academy in 1859. ¶ Cowdrey, NAD.

WENTWORTH, JEROME BLACKMAN (1820–1893. Artist, probably amateur, who exhibited at the Boston Athenaeum in 1842. He was born August 17, 1820; married Catherine Rogers Motley Clapp in 1848; and died February 17, 1893, in Boston. ¶ Swan, BA; Watkins, *The Residuary Legatees of the Will of Mrs. Eliza Ann (Blackman) Colburn,* 12, 14; Wentworth, *The Wentworth Genealogy,* gives the date of birth as December 18, 1818.

WENTWORTH, THOMAS HANFORD (1781–1849). Portrait, miniature, and landscape painter; profilist; aquatint engraver and lithographer. Born March 15, 1781, in Norwalk (Conn.), he was sent as a youth to an uncle in St. John's (N.B.) for business experience and in 1805 to England. On his return in 1806 he settled at Oswego (N.Y.) where he made his home until his death, although he travelled as far afield as Connecticut and NYC as an itinerant portraitist. He also published several lithographs of Niagara Falls. He died at Oswego on December 18, 1849. WILLIAM HENRY WENTWORTH was his son. ¶ Wentworth, *The Wentworth Genealogy,* II, 21–22; Bolton, *Miniature Painters;* Sherman, "American Miniatures by Minor Artists," 424; Vanderpoel, *Chronicles of a Pioneer School,* opp. 220, 224, 228; *Antiques* (Jan. 1937), 10, (June 1937), 291, (July 1937), 7–8.

WENTWORTH, WILLIAM HENRY (1813–?). Portrait painter, son of THOMAS HANFORD WENTWORTH of Oswego (N.Y.). He was born in Oswego on November 29, 1813, and was living there in 1859. ¶ Wentworth, *The Wentworth Genealogy,* II, 22; N. Y. State BD 1859.

WENZEL, EDWARD (Edouard). Engraver, San Francisco, 1859 and after. ¶ San Francisco CD 1859–64.

WENZEL, WILLIAM. Lithographer, San Francisco, 1860 and after. ¶ San Francisco CD 1860–64.

WENZLAWSKI, HENRY C. Portrait painter, NYC, 1854. ¶ NYBD and NYCD 1854.

WENZLER, ANTHON HENRY (Henry, Jr., or Henry Antonio, Jr.) (?–1871). N.A. Portrait, miniature, still life, genre, and landscape painter. He was active in NYC from 1838 until after 1860 and died in 1871. He exhibited at the Apollo Association, the Pennsylvania Academy, and the National Academy and was an Associate of the last-named from 1848 to 1860 and an Academician from 1860. ¶ Cowdrey, NAD; Cowdrey, AA & AAU; Rutledge, PA; NYCD 1838–40, 1845–48, 1851–53, 1855–60+; Bolton, *Miniature Painters;* Clark, *History of the NAD,* 274; Washington Art Assoc. Cat., 1859.

WENZLER, H. WILHELMINA (?–*c.* 1871). Still life painter of NYC who exhibited at the National Academy in 1860, the Boston Athenaeum 1864–68, and the Pennsylvania Academy 1868–69. ¶ Swan, BA; Cowdrey, NAD; Rutledge, PA [as S. W. Wenzler].

WENZLER, JOHN HENRY. Artist, NYC, 1846–53. ¶ NYCD 1846–47 as Henry, 1849 and 1851–53 as John Henry.

WENZLER, WILLIAM. Artist, NYC, 1843. ¶ NYCD 1843.

WERNER, ERNEST. Fresco painter from Saxony, aged 39, living in Philadelphia in 1860. His wife was from Maryland, while one child (16) was born in Saxony and the other (10) in Maryland. ¶ 8 Census (1860), Pa., LIII, 507.

WERNER, OTTO. Prussian-born lithographer, 27, living in Baltimore in 1860 with his wife Dora, a native of Hanover. ¶ 8 Census (1860), Md., V, 802.

WERNER, REINHOLD. Engraver and die sinker, NYC, 1857–59. ¶ NYBD 1857–59.

WERNIGK, REINHART. Winner of first prize for flower painting, Illinois State Fair, Chicago, 1855. ¶ Chicago *Daily Press,* Oct. 15, 1855.

WERTEMBERGER, GODFREY S. Sign and ornamental painter of Springfield (Ohio) about 1840; later a portrait painter and cycloramist at Cincinnati. ¶ Knittle, *Early Ohio Taverns,* 44.

WERTMÜLLER, ADOLPH ULRICH (1751–1811). Portrait, miniature, historical, and figure painter, born February 18, 1751, in Stockholm (Sweden). He studied painting in Stockholm, Paris, and Rome. From 1783 to 1788 he had a studio in Paris, after which he moved to Bordeaux. In 1794 he came to Philadelphia where he remained for a little over two years, returning in 1796 to Sweden. Four years later he settled permanently in America on a farm, "Claymont," in Newcastle County (Del.), where he died October 5, 1811. His best-known works were his *Danae* and *Ariadne;* he also painted a portrait of Washington. ¶ Bolton, *Miniature Painters;* Benisovich, "Roslin and Wertmüller"; Benisovich, "The Sale of the Studio of Adolph Ulrich Wertmüller"; Cowdrey, AA & AAU; Rutledge, PA; CAB; Morgan and Fielding, *Life Portraits of Washington,* 203–06; *Portraits in Delaware, 1700–1850,* 119; Flexner, *The Light of Distant Skies.* The Library of Congress has a photostat of his diary; most of his personal papers are in Stockholm.

WESCOTT, P. B. Memorial painting in watercolors, Greenfield (Mass.), 1835. ¶ Lipman and Winchester, 182.

WESSEL, HENRY. Wood engraver, NYC, 1848. ¶ NYBD 1848.

WEST, Mrs. ——. Portrait painter at Attleborough (Mass.) about 1820. ¶ Fielding.

WEST, BENJAMIN (1738–1820). Historical, portrait, religious, genre, and landscape painter; born October 10, 1738, in Springfield (Pa.), now the campus of Swarthmore College; died March 10, 1820, in London. Encouraged in his earliest attempts at portrait and historical painting by cultured gentlemen of Philadelphia and Lancaster, West went to Italy in 1760 and studied the Renaissance and Baroque Masters for three years before establishing himself in London in 1763. Within a short time he had gained the front rank among British artists and in 1772 he was appointed historical painter to King George III. A charter member of the Royal Academy, he served as its President, with only one year's interruption, from 1792 until his death in 1820. His subject matter was of the widest variety: portraiture, mythology, The Bible, ancient and modern history, landscape, and genre, reflecting the aesthetic ideas of Gavin Hamilton, Shaftesbury, Burke, and Payne Knight and the demands of his patrons: King George III, Sir George Beaumont, Archbishop Drummond, Alderman Beckford, Lord Elgin and others. Some of his more important paintings are: *Death of Socrates* (1757, owned by Mrs. Thomas H. A. Stites, Nazareth, Pa.); *Agrippina at Brundisium* (1769, Yale University); *Hannibal at the Altar* and *Regulus* (both at Kensington Palace, London); *Self Portrait* (National Gallery, Washington); *Kosciusko* (Oberlin College); *Death on the Pale Horse,* sketch (Philadelphia Museum of Art); *Una and the Lion* (Wadsworth Athenaeum); *Sheep Washing* (Rutgers University); *Woodcutters in Windsor Park* (Herron Institute, Indianapolis); *The Conversion of St. Paul and two other subjects* (Smith College Museum of Art, Northampton, Mass.); *Death of General Wolfe* (National Gallery of Canada, Ottawa); *Penn's Treaty with the Indians* (Independence Hall, Philadelphia). Besides those mentioned in Thieme-Becker, there are portraits of his American period at the Historical Society of Pennsylvania and the Pennsylvania Academy. Large collections of his drawings are owned by the Boston Museum of Fine Arts, the Historical Society of Pennsylvania, Swarthmore College, and Mr. H. Margary, Bagshot, Surrey, England.

West married Elizabeth Shewell in 1764. His two children, RAPHAEL LAMARR and Benjamin, Jr., both were pupils of their father. Among his American pupils were MATTHEW PRATT, CHARLES WILLSON PEALE, REMBRANDT PEALE, GILBERT STUART, SAMUEL F. B. MORSE, ROBERT FULTON, WASHINGTON ALLSTON, JOHN TRUMBULL, and JOHN SINGLETON COPLEY. His influence extended also to France where prints after his paintings were well known amongst both the neo-classics and the romantics. ¶ Courtesy Helmut von Erffa, Rutgers University, who cites: Farington, *The Farington Diary,* 8 vols. (London, 1922–28); Flexner, *America's Old Masters* (important for bibliography); Flexner, *The Light of Distant Skies;* Galt, *Life, Studies and Works of Benjamin West,* 2 vols. (London, 1820), based on West's own account, but inaccurate; Moses, *The Gallery of Pictures Painted by Benjamin West* (London, 1811); Phila. Museum of Art, *Catalogue of Benjamin West Exhibition* (Phila., 1938); Robins, *A Catalogue Raisonné . . . of Historical Pictures . . . by Benjamin West to be sold at Auction . . .* (London, 1829); Waterhouse, *Painting in Britain 1530–1790* (London, 1953); von Erffa, "West's Washing of Sheep," *Art Quarterly,* XV (1952), 160–65; Flexner, "Benjamin

West's American Neo-Classicism," *NYHS Quarterly,* XXXVI (1952), 5–41; Mitchell, "Benjamin West's Death of General Wolfe," *Journal of Warburg and Courtauld Institutes,* VII (1944), 20–33; Sawitzky, "The American Work of Benjamin West," *Pa. Mag. of Hist. and Biog.,* LXII (1938), 433–62; Grose Evans, "Benjamin West's Development and the Sources of His Style," thesis, Johns Hopkins University, 1953; Joseph T. Burke, "A Biographical and Critical Study of Benjamin West, 1738–92, with a Supplementary Chapter on His Circle," MA thesis, Yale University, 1937; von Erffa, "An Oil Sketch by Benjamin West," *The Register of the Museum of Art of the University of Kansas,* May 1956, 1–8.

WEST, BENJAMIN FRANKLIN (1818–1854). Marine and ship painter, born June 15, 1818, at Salem (Mass.); died there in 1854. His copy of Hogarth's "Columbus and the Egg" is at the Essex Institute and a whaling scene is in the Peabody Museum. ¶ Belknap, *Artists and Craftsmen of Essex County,* 14; letter from the Marine Society of Salem to FARL, Jan. 27, 1940; Robinson and Dow, *Sailing Ships of New England,* I, 64; *American Processional,* 126; *Antiques* (Oct. 1922), 162.

WEST, FREDERICK. German-born engraver, 35, living in Washington (D.C.) in 1860. His wife was from Pennsylvania and their one-year-old son Frederick was born in Maryland. ¶ 8 Census (1860), D.C., I, 867.

WEST, G. One of the artists of THOMAS SINCLAIR's lithographs illustrating *The North American Sylva,* 1846. ¶ McClinton, "American Flower Lithographs," 362.

WEST, GEORGE R. Topographical artist who assisted WILLIAM HEINE in painting the panorama of China and Japan which was exhibited in NYC in 1856. Several of his paintings of Oriental scenes were exhibited in 1857 by the Washington Art Association; he was then listed as a resident of Washington. ¶ N. Y. *Herald,* Jan. 27, 1856 (courtesy J. Earl Arrington); Washington Art Association Cat., 1857.

WEST, GEORGE WILLIAM (1770–1795). Portrait and miniature painter, born January 22, 1770 in St. Andrew's Parish, St. Mary's County (Md.). His father, the Rev. William West was then rector of that parish, but in 1779 he became rector of St. Paul's in Baltimore. The son began painting portraits before he was fifteen and in 1788 he went to London to study under BENJAMIN WEST (not a relative). Having contracted tuberculosis, young West returned to his Baltimore home early in 1790. During the next few years he continued to paint portraits but his career was cut short in his twenty-sixth year. He died August 1, 1795. ¶ Pleasants, "George William West—A Baltimore Student of Benjamin West," with checklist and 14 repros.; Pleasants, *250 Years of Painting in Maryland,* 37; Prime, II, 38; represented at MHS.

WEST, JOHN B. Miniaturist of Lexington (Ky.) who exhibited at the Pennsylvania Academy in 1814. ¶ Rutledge, PA.

WEST, RAPHAEL LAMARR (1769–1850). Painter and lithographer. The elder son of BENJAMIN WEST, Raphael was born in London in 1769 and studied under his father. He was an intimate friend of WILLIAM DUNLAP while the latter was studying in London. He was well known for his painting of Orlando rescuing his brother from the lioness in *As You Like It* published in Boydell's *Shakespeare Gallery* and for his skill in drawing trees and figures. He came to America in 1800, intending to settle in western New York, but returned to England two years later. In his later years he did some lithographic work. He died May 22, 1850, in England. ¶ Dunlap, *History;* Thieme-Becker.

WEST, R. C. Engraver of two illustrations in *Benjamin Franklin: His Autobiography* (New York, 1849). ¶ Hamilton, *Early American Book Illustrators and Wood Engravers,* 172.

WEST, SAMUEL S. Portrait painter of Philadelphia who exhibited at the Pennsylvania Academy in 1818 and 1829–30. ¶ Rutledge, PA.

WEST, Mrs. SOPHIE (1825–1914). Landscape painter; born in Paris; died at the home of a son in Pittsburgh (Pa.) on May 12, 1914. She came to America at the age of twenty. *Cf.* Mrs. SOPHIE ANDERSON. ¶ *Art Annual,* XI, obit.

WEST, W. R. Philadelphia artist who exhibited at the Artists' Fund Society in 1841 a landscape after THOMAS DOUGHTY. This might be the WILLIAM WEST, artist, of the 1841 directory or the William R. West, carpenter, of the 1840 and 1843 directories. ¶ Rutledge, PA; Phila. CD 1840–43.

WEST, WILLIAM. Portrait and landscape painter of Philadelphia who exhibited a few portraits and watercolor landscapes, including views of Durham Cathedral,

Sterling Castle, and a Welsh scene, at the Pennsylvania Academy in 1827 and 1829. His address was given as 32 North 4th Street. The directory for 1823 lists William and John West, painters and glaziers, at 30 North 4th and that for 1825 lists William alone at the same address. From 1829 to 1833 William was listed at 1 Loxley Court. There was a William West, artist, listed in 1841 and the same year a W. R. West of Philadelphia exhibited at the Artists' Fund Society a landscape after THOMAS DOUGHTY. ¶ Rutledge, PA [included in the entry for WILLIAM EDWARD WEST, who was in London from 1825 to 1838]; Phila. CD 1820–33.

WEST, WILLIAM EDWARD (1788–1857). Portrait and figure painter, born December 10, 1788 in Lexington (Ky.). After studying in Philadelphia under THOMAS SULLY about 1807, he worked in Philadelphia until about 1818, then went to Natchez (Miss.), and thence in 1819 to Italy. He stayed in Italy for about four years, during which time he painted his well-known portraits of Byron, the Countess Guiccioli, Shelley, and Trelawney. In 1824 he went to Paris and from 1825 to 1838 he had a studio in London. In the latter year, having lost his money in an unfortunate investment, West returned to America and opened a studio in Baltimore, moving to NYC in 1841 and remaining there until 1855. His last years were spent in Nashville (Tenn.) where he died November 2, 1857. ¶ DAB; Dunn, "Unknown Pictures of Shelley"; Dunn, "An Artist of the Past"; Richardson, "E. J. Trelawney by William Edward West"; Rutledge, PA; Brown and Brown; Graves, *Dictionary;* Cowdrey, NAD; Cowdrey, AA & AAU; Swan, BA; NYCD 1840–52; *Album of American Battle Art.*

WESTBROOK, Lieutenant ——. A view of the NYC fire of 1835, sketched by Lt. Westbrook, was lithographed by A. PICKEN. ¶ Peters, *America on Stone.*

WESTERL, ROBERT. Engraver at Lowell (Mass.), 1834–35. ¶ Belknap, *Artists and Craftsmen of Essex County,* 6.

WESTERN, A. S. Landscape in oils, painted at Boston about 1820. ¶ Lipman and Winchester, 182.

WESTERN, THEODORE B. English sign and ornamental painter at Cincinnati in the 1840's. He is said to have painted banners and badges for the Harrison campaign in 1840. ¶ Knittle, *Early Ohio Taverns,* 44; Cincinnati CD 1840–44.

WESTLAVER (Westover?), ——. Pennsylvania-born engraver, 24, living in Philadelphia in 1860 with his father, John A. Westlaver, jeweler. ¶ 8 Census (1860), Pa., L, 598.

WESTON, H. Landscape in oils, painted in Virginia about 1850. ¶ Lipman and Winchester, 182.

WESTON, HENRY W. Engraver working in Philadelphia from 1800 to 1806. In 1800 he was a partner of EDWARD C. TRENCHARD. ¶ Stauffer; Brown and Brown.

WESTON, J. G. Engraver of woodcut frontispiece (from an English original) of a story in *The Children's Miscellany* (Boston, 1796). ¶ Hamilton, *Early American Book Illustrators and Wood Engravers,* 72.

WESTON, JAMES. Wood and seal engraver, NYC, 1858–60. ¶ NYBD 1858, 1860.

WESTON, Mrs. MARY PILLSBURY (1817–1894). Portrait and landscape painter. The daughter of a Baptist minister, Mary B. Pillsbury was born January 5, 1817, in Hebron (N.H.). As a young woman she is said to have run away from home to study painting in Hartford (Conn.). Her early work was in miniature, but she later turned to oil portraits, landscapes, and religious subjects. She married Valentine W. Weston and went to live in NYC, where he had a looking glass business in the early forties. She exhibited at the National Academy in 1842. Mr. Weston died in 1863 but Mrs. Weston survived him by over thirty years, dying in Lawrence (Kans.) in May 1894. ¶ Pilsbury and Getchell, *The Pillsbury Family,* 163; French, *Art and Artists in Connecticut,* 175–76; Bolton, *Miniature Painters;* Cowdrey, NAD; NYCD 1842; Lipman and Winchester, 182.

WETHERALD, SAMUEL B. Portrait artist who exhibited at the Maryland Historical Society in 1848 heads of J. C. Jones and G. B. Cook, medium not indicated. The same society owns his wash drawing of Thomas McKean, after STUART, and his iron bas-relief of Zachary Taylor. Samuel B. Wetherald, of Resin & Wetherald, was in the Baltimore directories for 1853 and 1855, but the nature of his business was not given. ¶ Rutledge, MHS; Rutledge, "Portraits in Varied Media"; Baltimore CD 1853, 1855.

WETHERALL, SAMUEL H. Engraver, 26, a native of Maryland, at Baltimore in 1860. ¶ 8 Census (1860), Md., VI, 393; Baltimore CD 1860.

WETHERBY, ISAAC AUGUSTUS (1819–1904). Portrait and ornamental painter; photographer. Born December 6, 1819, in Providence (R.I.), he was educated in Charlestown and Stow (Mass.) and began his career as a portrait painter at Norway (Me.) in 1834. From 1835 to 1846 he had his studio in Boston, although he made a trip to Louisville (Ky.) in 1844. After his marriage in 1846, he moved to Roxbury and in 1848 to Milton (Mass.). In 1854 he went out to Iowa and set up a daguerreotype studio in Iowa City, but after a few months he went to Rockford (Ill.) where he had a daguerreotype studio until 1857. After two years at Eureka (Iowa), Wetherby and his family finally settled in Iowa City. He retired from his photographic business in 1874 but lived until February 23, 1904. ¶ Holloway, "Isaac Augustus Wetherby (1819–1904) and His Account Books"; WPA (Mass.), *Portraits Found in N.H.,* 28 [as J. A. Weatherby].

WETHERBY, JEREMIAH WOOD. Portrait painter born April 29, 1780 at Stow (Mass.). ¶ Sears, *Some American Primitives,* 285; *Vital Records of Boxborough.*

WETMORE, C. F. (or J.). Portrait painter at Providence (R.I.) in 1824 and at Boston in 1829. *Cf.* C. G. WETMORE. ¶ Swan, BA.

WETMORE, C. G. Portrait and miniature painter at Charleston (S.C.) in 1822. He was also agent for the Baltimore Floor Cloth Manufactory. *Cf.* C. F. (or J.) WETMORE. ¶ Rutledge, *Artists in the Life of Charleston.*

WETZEL, CHARLES. Of WETZEL & SCHLEICH, engravers at NYC, 1852–58. ¶ NYBD 1852–58.

WETZEL & SCHLEICH. Engravers, NYC, 1852–58; CHARLES WETZEL and CHARLES SCHLEICH. ¶ NYBD 1852–58.

WETZLER, ERNEST. Lithographer, NYC, 1857–60; of SEIBERT & WETZLER, 1859–60. ¶ NYBD 1857–60.

WEVER, ADOLPH. Artist who proposed to take four views of Cleveland (Ohio) in May 1844 for the purpose of lithographing and selling them. ¶ WPA (Ohio), *Annals of Cleveland.*

WEVIL or WEVILL, GEORGE, JR. Wood engraver who worked in Philadelphia from 1850 to 1857 and in Cincinnati in 1859–60. ¶ Phila. CD 1852–57; Phila. BD 1850–56; Ohio BD 1859; Cincinnati BD 1859–60; Hamilton, *Early American Book Illustrators and Wood Engravers,* 464.

WEYL, MAX (1837–1914). Landscape painter born December 1, 1837 in Mühlen-on-Neckar (Germany). He came to America in 1853 and settled in Washington (D.C.). He died in Washington July 6, 1914. ¶ *Art Annual,* XI, obit.; CAB; represented in Corcoran Gallery.

WEYMAN, Miss ——. Teacher of monochromatic painting in a young ladies' seminary at Charleston (S.C.), 1844–45, 1847–48. ¶ Rutledge, *Artists in the Life of Charleston.*

WEYSS, JOHN (*c.* 1820–1903). Topographical artist who served with Emory's Mexican Boundary Survey from 1849 to 1855 and contributed many illustrations to his three-volume report (1857–59). He subsequently served as a major in the Union Army and after the war was again connected with Western surveys. He died in Washington (D.C.) on June 24, 1903, at the age of 83. ¶ Taft, *Artists and Illustrators of the Old West,* 277; Jackson, *Gold Rush Album,* 81–82.

WHAITES, EDWARD P. Engraver of NYC, active 1837–after 1860. In 1850 he had the same business address as JOHN L. WHAITES. ¶ NYCD 1837–60+.

WHAITES, JOHN A. Engraver, NYC, 1850. ¶ NYCD 1850.

WHAITES, JOHN L. Engraver and printer of NYC, active 1827–50; listed as "late engraver" in 1852–53. His business address in 1850 was the same as EDWARD P. WHAITES's. ¶ NYCD 1827–52.

WHAITES, WILLIAM. Engraver, NYC, 1852; probably the same as William C. Whaites, printer active from 1826 to 1850; last listed, without occupation, in 1853. ¶ NYCD 1826–53.

WHAITES, WILLIAM N. Lithographer, NYC, 1853. In 1845 he was listed as a printer at the same address as William C. Whaites (see WILLIAM WHAITES, above). ¶ NYCD 1845, 1853.

WHALTER, R. Painter of oil portraits of James Madison and Col. John Armstrong about 1800. ¶ Courtesy Robert B. Campbell, Boston.

WHARTON, JOSEPH. Engraver, 17, a native of Pennsylvania, living in Philadelphia in 1850. He lived with his mother, Margaret Wharton, and was the eldest of seven children. ¶ 7 Census (1850), Pa., LIV, 688.

WHARTON, THOMAS KELAH (1814–1862). Landscape painter and lithographer, born April 17, 1814, in Hull (England). He came to America with his parents in 1830 and settled in Ohio. In 1832 he entered the office of the NYC architect MARTIN E. THOMPSON and in 1834–35 he exhibited landscapes at the National Academy, two of them scenes in the Hudson Highlands around West Point. About 1838 he drew and lithographed a view of Reading (Pa.) and he was also the artist of two pencil views of Natchez (Miss.) about 1850, now in the Stokes Collection at the New York Public Library. The Library also owns two of his diaries (1830–34, 1853–54) and a sketch book. Wharton died in New Orleans in 1862. ¶ Stokes, *Historical Prints,* 86, 107; Cowdrey, NAD.

WHATELEY, H. Delineator of a view of Mount Vernon, the home of Washington, lithographed by THOMAS SINCLAIR and published in 1859. ¶ Stokes, *Historical Prints,* 123.

WHEATON, DANIEL. Portrait painter working in Greenville (S.C.) in 1827. ¶ Courtesy Miss Anna Wells Rutledge.

WHEATON, MILES K. Engraver, NYC, 1851. ¶ NYBD 1851.

WHEELER, ASA H. Writing teacher and amateur artist who exhibited monochromatic paintings at the American Institute in NYC in 1848, 1849, and 1850. ¶ NYCD 1847–50; Am. Inst. Cat., 1848–50.

WHEELER, CANDACE THURBER (Mrs. Thomas M.). Designer and writer on household decoration. Born in Delhi (N.Y.) in 1828, she married Thomas M. Wheeler of NYC in 1846. She became a well-known authority on home decoration, founded the Society of Decorative Arts, and was director of the Woman's Building at the World's Columbian Exposition, Chicago, 1893. She died August 5, 1923. Her daughter, Dora Wheeler, born in 1858, was also an artist and designer. ¶ *Art Annual,* XX, obit.; *Who's Who in America* (1922).

WHEELER, GERVASE. Philadelphia artist, probably an amateur, who exhibited a view near Tarrytown (N.Y.) at the Pennsylvania Academy in 1850. ¶ Rutledge, PA; not listed in Phila. CD 1849–55.

WHEELER, Mrs. JOHN HILL, see ELLEN OLDMIXON SULLY.

WHEELER, N. Miniature painter at Boston in 1809 and Portsmouth (N.H.) in April 1810. *Cf.* NATHAN W. WHEELER. ¶ Boston CD 1809; *Antiques* (Sept. 1944), 158.

WHEELER, NATHAN W. Portrait painter at Cincinnati in 1831, and at New Orleans in 1844. He was a veteran of the War of 1812 according to the 1844 newspaper notice. His work is known only through an engraving of his portrait of Sam Houston, President of Texas. *Cf.* N. WHEELER, above. ¶ *Antiques* (March 1932), 152; Delgado-WPA cites *Courier,* Jan. 24, 1844; Fielding's supplement to Stauffer, no. 1176.

WHEELER, SYLVIA A. A fire screen of about 1830 has a drawing of the Baltimore Battle Monument, with the inscription: "Drawn by Sylvia A. Wheeler." ¶ *Antiques* (July 1934), cover and p. 5.

WHEELER, WILLIAM R. (1832–*c.* 1894). Portrait and miniature painter who was born in Scio (Mich.) of a Connecticut family and received his first instruction from an itinerant miniaturist in Michigan. He started painting professionally at the age of fifteen (1847). About 1850 he studied for a year in Detroit under ALVAH BRADISH. He moved to Hartford (Conn.) about 1862 and had a studio there until 1893. His specialty was children's portraits, though in later life he also did some landscape studies. He died between 1893 and 1896, when his widow was listed in the Hartford directory. ¶ French, *Art and Artists in Connecticut,* 143; Hartford CD 1862–96; Bolton, *Miniature Painters.*

WHEELOCK, MERRILL G. (1822–1866). Portrait and landscape painter in watercolors; architect. Born in Calais (Vt.) in 1822, he was working in Boston as an architect in 1853 and as a portrait painter in watercolors from 1858 to 1861. He probably was the Wheelock who illustrated Thomas Starr King's *The White Hills,* published in Boston in 1860. ¶ Waite, *The Wheelock Family of Calais, Vermont,* 97; Boston CD 1858–61; King, *The White Hills.*

WHEELOCK, WALTER W. Portrait painter, NYC, 1842–43; exhibited at the National Academy. ¶ Cowdrey, NAD; NYCD 1843.

WHEELWRIGHT, EDWARD (1824–1900). An American painter who exhibited at the Boston Athenaeum in 1858. ¶ Swan, BA.

WHELPLEY, PHILIP M. Engraver and landscape painter of NYC, active 1845–52. He exhibited landscapes at the American Art-Union and engraved mezzotint portraits of William H. Seward, Robert Toombs, and Richard Yeadon for *The Whig Portrait Gallery* (1852). ¶ Stauffer; *The Whig Portrait Gallery;* Cowdrey, AA & AAU.

WHELPLEY, THOMAS. Delineator of two views of Cleveland (Ohio) in 1833, engraved by M. OSBORNE and published in 1834 by Whelpley, a resident of Cleveland. ¶ Stokes, *Historical Prints,* 75.

WHETSTONE, JOHN S. Portrait sculptor working in Cincinnati (Ohio), 1837–41. ¶ Cist, *Cincinnati in 1841,* 141.

WHETTING, JOHN. German born artist, 38, at Cincinnati in 1850. ¶ 7 Census (1850), Ohio, XX, 766.

WHIPPLE, ——. Proprietor and possibly the artist of a series of dissolving views shown in Baltimore in 1851. ¶ Baltimore *Sun,* Jan. 26, 1851 (courtesy J. Earl Arrington).

WHISTLER, GEORGE WASHINGTON (1800–1849). Drawing teacher. Born May 19, 1800, at Fort Wayne (Ind.), he entered West Point in 1814, graduated in 1819, and served as assistant professor of drawing at the Academy during the winter of 1821–22. He became a prominent civil engineer, helping to build the Baltimore and Ohio and other railroads. Retiring from the army in 1833, he settled in Lowell (Mass.), where his famous son, JAMES ABBOTT MCNEILL WHISTLER, was born in 1834. In 1842 the elder Whistler went to Russia to build a railroad between St. Petersburg and Moscow for the Russian Government. He died in St. Petersburg April 7, 1849. ¶ DAB; Pennell, *The Life of James McNeill Whistler.*

WHISTLER, JAMES ABBOTT MCNEILL (1834–1903). Portrait, figure, and landscape painter; etcher; lithographer. Born July 10, 1834, in Lowell (Mass.), the son of GEORGE WASHINGTON WHISTLER, he spent his childhood in the United States and Russia (1842–49). In 1851 he entered the Military Academy at West Point, but he left in 1854 without graduating and was employed for a year in the Coast and Geodetic Survey as a draftsman. In 1855 Whistler went to Paris to study art. After five years in France he settled permanently in London. Although he made many visits to the Continent, Whistler never revisited his native country. In London his sharp tongue and unorthodox paintings, which reflected the influence of the Japanese print and the French impressionists, won for Whistler a notoriety which he celebrated in his book, *The Gentle Art of Making Enemies.* In his later years, however, he was generally recognized as one of the leading painters and etchers of the day. He died in London on July 17, 1903. ¶ The chief biography is *The Life of James McNeill Whistler* by Elizabeth R. and Joseph Pennell, first published in 1908. Extensive bibliographies are found in Park, *Mural Painters in America,* Part I, and in Lane's *Whistler,* which also contains many reproductions of his work. For brief notices, see DAB and DNB.

WHITAKER, CHARLES. Of BINGLEY & WHITAKER, engravers, NYC, 1842. ¶ NYCD 1842.

WHITAKER, EDWARD H. Painter born in New Hampshire about 1808. He exhibited still lifes at the Boston Athenaeum in 1830 and 1831 and was listed as a fresco painter in Boston in the 1850 Census. Swan states that he was active until 1862. ¶ Swan, BA; BA Cat., 1831; 7 Census (1850), Mass., XXVI, 705.

WHITCOMB, SUSAN. Amateur artist of Brandon (Vt.) who in 1842 painted a view of Mount Vernon, Washington's home, after A. Robertson (probably ARCHIBALD ROBERTSON). ¶ *Antiques* (July 1946), 41.

WHITE, AMOS. Portrait painter at Hanover (N.Y.) in 1859. ¶ N. Y. State BD 1859.

WHITE, BENJAMIN. Philadelphia artist, born in Ireland about 1828, who exhibited a landscape at the Pennsylvania Academy in 1850. He was listed in the 1850 directory as a sculptor. ¶ 7 Census (1850), Pa., LI, 376; Rutledge, PA; Phila. CD 1850.

WHITE, DUKE. Scenery painter at the Bowery Theatre, NYC, from 1828 to 1832. In 1836 he painted a drop-scene of Mount Vernon for the dioramists HENRY and WILLIAM J. HANINGTON. ¶ N. Y. *Evening Post,* Nov. 28, 1828, and Jan. 13, 1830, and N. Y. *Herald,* Dec. 7 and 22, 1836 (citations courtesy J. Earl Arrington); Odell, *Annals of the New York Stage,* III, 571.

WHITE, EBENEZER BAKER (1806–1888). Portrait painter. He was born February 16, 1806 in Sutton (Mass.); worked in Boston in the late thirties, exhibiting at the Athenaeum in 1837; settled in Providence (R.I.) about 1844; and lived there until his death, February 3, 1888. ¶ *Vital Records of Sutton, Mass.;* Swan, BA; Boston CD 1839; Providence CD 1844–88; *Providence, Births, Marriages and Deaths;* Sears, *Some American Primitives,* 113; Lipman and Winchester, 182.

WHITE, EDWARD B. Designer of the membership certificate of the Washington Light Infantry of Charleston (S.C.), of which he was apparently colonel. The certificate was engraved in 1857 by

THOMAS B. WELCH. ¶ Rutledge, *Artists in the Life of Charleston.*

WHITE, EDWIN (1817–1877). N.A. Genre, historical, and portrait painter. Born May 21, 1817, in South Hadley (Mass.), he began to paint at the age of twelve and first exhibited at the National Academy in 1840 when he was living in Bridgeport (Conn.). During the forties he lived in NYC and he was elected to the National Academy in 1848 as an Associate and in 1849 as an Academician. He was in Europe from 1850 to 1858, studying at Düsseldorf, Paris, Rome, and Florence, and he went abroad again in 1869. He was particularly noted for his historical works, many of which were exhibited at the National and Pennsylvania Academies, the American Art-Union, the Boston Athenaeum, and the Washington Art Association. White died at Saratoga Springs (N.Y.) on June 7, 1877. ¶ Smith; N. Y. *Herald,* June 9, 1877, obit.; Clement and Hutton; Tuckerman; CAB; Cowdrey, NAD; Cowdrey, AA & AAU; Swan, BA; Rutledge, PA; Washington Art Association Cat., 1857, 1859; Providence *Almanac* 1849; *Portfolio* (March 1955), 166, repro.

WHITE, FRANKLIN. Sculptor, Philadelphia, 1852. ¶ Phila. CD 1852.

WHITE, GEORGE. Drawing master, Philadelphia, 1807–09. ¶ Brown and Brown.

WHITE, GEORGE. Engraver, Philadelphia, 1839. *Cf.* GEORGE I., GEORGE R., or GEORGE T. WHITE. ¶ Phila. CD 1839.

WHITE, GEORGE GORGAS (?–1898). Wood engraver and illustrator who was a pupil of JOHN CASSIN and was working in Philadelphia from 1854 to 1861. He died in NYC February 24, 1898. ¶ *Art Annual,* I, obit.; Phila. CD 1854, 1856, 1860–61; Hamilton, *Early American Book Illustrators and Wood Engravers,* 493–94.

WHITE, GEORGE IRWINE. Engraver working in Philadelphia from 1850 to 1855 and possibly in 1861. *Cf.* GEORGE, GEORGE R., and GEORGE T. WHITE. ¶ Phila. CD 1850–55 [as G. Irwine White], 1861 [as George I. White, artist]; Stauffer.

WHITE, GEORGE R. Engraver working in Philadelphia from 1848 to 1860. He was a native of Pennsylvania, born between 1811 and 1815. In 1860 he owned real property valued at $25,000 and personal property to the value of $1,500. *Cf.* GEORGE, GEORGE I., and GEORGE T. WHITE. ¶ 7 Census (1850), Pa., LIII, 265; 8 Census (1860), Pa., LXII, 311; Phila. CD 1848.

WHITE, GEORGE T. Artist, Philadelphia, 1846. *Cf.* GEORGE, GEORGE I., and GEORGE R. WHITE. ¶ Phila. CD 1846.

WHITE, GEORGE W. Engraver, NYC, 1843–58; of WHITE & VANDER[H]OEF, 1857. ¶ NYCD 1843–58.

WHITE, GEORGE W. (1826–1890). Portrait, figure, and landscape painter. Born in Oxford (Ohio), November 8, 1826, he received his first art lessons from SAMUEL SWAN WALKER about 1840. He went to Cincinnati in 1843 intending to open a studio but met with little encouragement. For the next few years he travelled with a minstrel show as a blackface singer. Returning to Cincinnati, in 1847 he resumed his painting career and shared a studio with the landscape painter, WILLIAM L. SONNTAG. His first real success came in 1848 when he painted two views of POWERS' statue, *The Greek Slave.* Until 1857 White worked in Cincinnati and lived in Covington (Ky.), except for a year in NYC. In 1857 he moved to Hamilton (Ohio) where he spent the rest of his life, except for the Civil War years when he lived in Cincinnati. He died in Hamilton in 1890. ¶ *History and Biographical Encyclopedia of Butler County, Ohio,* 364–65; Bartlow *et al., Centennial History of Butler County,* 921–22; Cist, *Cincinnati in 1851,* 127; Cincinnati BD 1848; Ohio BD 1859; Hamilton CD 1873.

WHITE, HENRY F. Genre and still life painter, NYC, exhibited at the National Academy 1857–59. ¶ Cowdrey, NAD.

WHITE, J. Amateur painter of Flemington (N.J.?) who in 1788 made a copy in oils of an engraving after a painting by the English animal painter George Stubbs (1724–1806). ¶ *Antiques* (March 1939), 150, repro.; *Antiques* (May 1940), 258.

WHITE, JOHN. English watercolorist who went to Sir Walter Raleigh's colony on Roanoke Island in 1585 to record the natural and aboriginal curiosities of Virginia. In 1587 he returned as the second governor of the colony, along with his married daughter who soon after gave birth to Virginia Dare, the first English child born in America. White went back to England later in 1587 and did not see Virginia again until 1590 when he returned to find no trace of "the lost colony." Of his later life nothing is known except that he was living in Newtowne in Kylmore, Ireland, in February 1593.

Twenty-three of his Virginia views were engraved by the German engraver Theodore De Bry and published in the latter's *A Briefe and True Report of the New Found Land of Virginia* (Frankfurt-am-Main, 1590). Over seventy of White's original watercolors are now in the British Museum. ¶ DAB; Lorant, *The New World; the First Pictures of America . . .*, reproduces many of White's watercolors in color. See also, Bushnell, "John White . . ."

WHITE, JOHN. Landscape in oils, Cheshire (Conn.), 1850. ¶ Lipman and Winchester, 182.

WHITE, JOHN BLAKE (1781–1859). Historical, portrait, and miniature painter. Born September 2, 1781, near Eutaw Springs (S.C.), he went to London in 1800 and studied for three years under BENJAMIN WEST. On his return to America in 1803 he painted portraits in Charleston and Boston (1804), but meeting with little success, turned to the study of law and began to practice in Charleston in 1808. Except for a brief residence at Columbia (S.C.) about 1831, he spent the rest of his life in Charleston. He continued to paint in his leisure, specializing in scenes from American history, four examples of which are in the Capitol at Washington. He was a director of the South Carolina Academy of Fine Arts. White also wrote a number of plays which were performed in Charleston and elsewhere. He was elected an Honorary Member of the National Academy in 1837 and exhibited there, as well as at the Boston Athenaeum and the Apollo Association. He died in Charleston August 24, 1859. ¶ DAB; Rutledge, *Artists in the Life of Charleston;* Clement and Hutton; White, "Journal"; Clark, *History of the NAD,* 274; Cowdrey, NAD; Cowdrey, AA & AAU; Swan, BA; Cummings, *Historic Annals of the NAD,* 143–44; Dunlap, *History; Portfolio* (Aug. 1947), 8.

WHITE, JOSEPH. Engraver, 16, a native of Pennsylvania, living in the home of JOSHUA BERING at Philadelphia in 1860. ¶ 8 Census (1860), Pa., LVIII, 429.

WHITE, JOSIAH. Artist, Philadelphia, 1811; as a wire manufacturer, 1813–20. ¶ Brown and Brown.

WHITE, LEMUEL. Portrait painter, Philadelphia, 1813–17, who exhibited profiles of ladies and several copies of figure paintings, Society of Artists, 1812–13. Philadelphia directories, 1819–33, list Lemuel White, professor of elocution, and 1837–39, Lemuel G. White, teacher. ¶ Rutledge, PA [erroneously as Lorenzo White]; Society of Artists, Cats. 1812 and 1813 [as L. White]; Phila. CD 1814–39.

WHITE, LORENZO (?–1834). Portrait painter of Boston who exhibited at the Athenaeum between 1829 and 1832. He was listed in the directories as a musician, 1829–32, and portrait painter, 1833–34. ¶ Swan, BA; Boston CD 1829–34.

WHITE, M. Portrait painter, Boston, 1847. ¶ Boston BD 1847.

WHITE, NATHAN F. Wood engraver, Troy (N.Y.), 1851–53. ¶ Troy CD 1851–53.

WHITE, ROSWELL N. Wood engraver working in NYC from 1832 to 1837 and in Chicago from 1846 to 1848. He may also have worked in Cincinnati about 1851, when a book containing some examples of his work was published there. There was a Roswell M. White, lumber dealer, in Cincinnati in the mid-fifties. ¶ NYCD 1832–37; Chicago CD 1846, BD 1848; Hamilton, *Early American Book Illustrators and Wood Engravers;* Cincinnati CD 1853+.

WHITE & VANDER[H]OEF. Engravers, NYC, 1857; GEORGE W. WHITE and JOHN J. VANDER[H]OEF. ¶ NYBD and NYCD 1857

WHITE, WILLIAM. Lithographer, 17, born in Pennsylvania, the son of John White, bricklayer, with whom he was living in Philadelphia in 1860. ¶ 8 Census (1860), Pa., LV, 567.

WHITE, WILLIAM. Artist, 17, a native of New York, living with his father John White, "shoefinder," in NYC, 1860. ¶ 8 Census (1860), N.Y., XLV, 8.

WHITE, WILLIAM G. Of NEALE & WHITE, engravers, NYC, 1843. ¶ NYCD 1843.

WHITE, WILLIAM JAMES. Engraver, lithographer, and seal cutter working in Chicago during the 1850's. ¶ Chicago BD 1852–53, CD 1855–59.

WHITECHURCH, ROBERT (1814–*c.* 1880). Portrait and banknote engraver. Born in London (England) in 1814, he did not take up engraving until he was about thirty. He emigrated to America in 1848, settled in Philadelphia, and was there until about 1872, after which he went to Washington to work for the Treasury Department. He probably died about 1880, as his widow was listed in the Philadelphia directory for 1881. ¶ Stauffer; Phila. CD 1850–72, 1881; Rutledge, PA.

WHITEFIELD, EDWIN (1816–1892). English

landscape and flower painter who came to the United States probably about 1840. In 1841–42 he was painting views of Hudson Valley estates and in 1844 he was in NYC. In 1845 appeared Emma C. Embury's *American Wild Flowers in Their Native Haunts* with illustrations by Whitefield and two years later he issued a series of views under the title, *North American Scenery*. From 1856 to 1859 he made several trips to Minnesota to promote his real estate interests there; from this period date a number of watercolor landscapes now in the Minnesota Historical Society. During the 1880's Whitefield lived in Boston and Reading (Mass.) and published three volumes of *The Homes of Our Forefathers,* showing early houses of New England. In 1888 he was planning a trip to England to promote English settlement in Minnesota. ¶ Information courtesy Bertha L. Heilbron, Minnesota Historical Society; Heilbron, "Edwin Whitefield's Minnesota Lakes"; NYCD 1844; McClinton, "American Flower Lithographs," 363; information courtesy Arthur Carlson, NYHS.

WHITEHORNE, JAMES A. (1803–1888). N.A. Portrait and miniature painter, born August 22, 1803 at Wallingford (Vt.). He studied at the National Academy about 1826, was elected an Associate Member in 1829 and an Academician in 1833, and served as Recording Secretary of the Academy from 1838 to 1844. He also exhibited at the American Academy, the Apollo Association, the Pennsylvania Academy, and the American Institute. He lived in NYC until his death, March 31, 1888. ¶ CAB; Cowdrey, NAD; Cowdrey, AA & AAU; Rutledge, PA; Am. Inst. Cat., 1856.

WHITEHOUSE, JAMES HORTON (1833–1902). Seal engraver and jewel cutter; born October 28, 1833, in Staffordshire (England); came to the United States in 1857 and worked for Tiffany, the NYC jeweler; died in Brooklyn, November 29, 1902. ¶ *Art Annual,* VI, obit.

WHITELOCK, SAMUEL WEST. Portrait and miniature painter working in Baltimore from 1831 to 1840. ¶ Lafferty.

WHITESIDE, ——. Painted a portrait of Mrs. John W. Forney of Philadelphia in 1850. ¶ Lancaster County Hist. Soc., *Portraiture in Lancaster County,* 141.

WHITFIELD, E. Artist, 30, a native of Massachusetts, at Philadelphia in 1850. ¶ 7 Census (1850), Pa., LII, 341.

WHITFIELD, JOHN S. (or W.). Portrait painter, sculptor, and cameo portraitist. He was at Cambridge (Mass.) in 1828, Philadelphia in 1829, Paterson (N.J.) in 1848, and NYC from 1849 to 1851. ¶ Swan, BA; Rutledge, PA; Cowdrey, NAD; NYBD 1849–50; NYCD 1851.

WHITING, DANIEL POWERS. Artist of F. SWINTON's lithograph, "The Heights of Monterey from the Saltillo Road Looking Towards the City, September 21, 1846." Whiting was an infantry captain who graduated from West Point in 1832 and was brevetted major for gallantry at the Battle of Cerro Gordo (Mexico) in 1847. He retired as a lieutenant colonel in 1863. He was a New Yorker. ¶ *American Processional,* 242; Heitman, *Historical Register of the U. S. Army,* 691; Jackson, *Gold Rush Album,* 124–25; Peters, *America on Stone* [as D. W. Whiting]; represented at NYHS.

WHITING, D. W., see DANIEL POWERS WHITING.

WHITING, F. H. (possibly Frances S.). American artist who exhibited at the Boston Athenaeum in 1859 and was active as late as 1883. ¶ Swan, BA.

WHITING, FABIUS (1792–1842). Portrait painter of Lancaster (Mass.), where he was born May 10, 1792, and died May 18, 1842. He was a pupil of GILBERT STUART but had only a brief career as an artist. He entered the U. S. Army in time to hold a lieutenant's commission during the War of 1812 and subsequently rose to the rank of brevet major (1829). Whiting is said to have been the first instructor of JAMES FROTHINGHAM. ¶ Morgan, *Gilbert Stuart and His Pupils,* 70–71.

WHITING, WILLIAM H. Banknote engraver who began his career in Albany (N.Y.) about 1835, but from 1837 worked in NYC. From 1852 to 1858 he was a partner in WELLSTOOD, HANKS, HAY & WHITING and WELLSTOOD, HAY & WHITING. He was one of the founders of the AMERICAN BANK NOTE COMPANY in 1858 and served as its secretary from 1860 to 1862. ¶ Albany CD 1835; NYCD 1837–62.

WHITLEY, THOMAS W. Landscape and figure painter. He was an Englishman who apparently settled in Paterson (N.J.) about 1835 and remained there until about 1839. From 1839 to 1842 he was living in NYC, after which he may have spent some time in Italy. In 1848 he went to Cincinnati and became superintendent of Edwin Forrest's farm at Covington (Ky.), across the river from Cincinnati. Having lost that job, in 1849 he returned to NYC where he became a writer on the arts and drama for the N. Y. *Herald*. He was the prime mover in the attack on the legality of the American Art-Union's lottery which resulted in the dissolution of that organization in the early fifties. Whitley exhibited at the National Academy from 1835 to 1863 and at the Apollo Association and the Art-Union in 1841 and 1848–49. ¶ Bloch, "The American Art-Union's Downfall"; Cowdrey, NAD; Cowdrey, AA & AAU; NYCD 1839–42; NYBD 1844, 1850–51, 1857; Essex, Hudson, and Union Counties (N.J.) BD 1859.

WHITMAN, JACOB (?–1798). Portrait and sign painter of Philadelphia (1792) and Reading (1795). He was one of the founders of the Columbianum in 1795. In 1827 his copy of WEST's *Penn's Treaty*, painted in 1790, was exhibited at the Pennsylvania Academy. He died in Philadelphia at the end of September 1798. ¶ Prime, II, 38–39; Columbianum Cat., 1795; Rutledge, PA [as Witman].

WHITMAR, JULIA. Artist, 30, a native of Pennsylvania, at Philadelphia in 1860. ¶ 8 Census (1860), Pa., LIV, 165.

WHITMORE, J. Wood engraver at Media (Ohio) in 1853. ¶ Ohio BD 1853.

WHITNEY, ANNE (1821–1915). Sculptor, born September 2, 1821, in Watertown (Mass.). She took up modeling in her middle thirties and opened a studio in Watertown in 1860. In 1872, after four or five years of study in Europe, she settled in Boston where she spent the rest of her life. Though best known for her portrait works, including a statue of Samuel Adams in the U. S. Capitol, she also executed a number of ideal figures. She died in Boston, January 23, 1915. ¶ DAB; Taft, *History of American Sculpture; *Gardner, *Yankee Stonecutters; Art Annual,* XII, obit.; Cowdrey, NAD; Rutledge, MHS.

WHITNEY & ANNIN. Wood engravers, NYC, 1852; ELIAS J. WHITNEY and PHINEAS F. ANNIN. The firm became WHITNEY, JOCELYN & ANNIN in 1853 and WHITNEY & JOCELYN in 1856. ¶ NYBD 1852; Hamilton, *Early American Book Illustrators and Wood Engravers.*

WHITNEY, ELIAS JAMES (1827–?). Wood engraver and genre painter, born in NYC on February 20, 1827. After his marriage in 1847 he moved to Brooklyn where he was living in 1874. He exhibited a pencil drawing at the American Institute as early as 1842 and during the fifties he exhibited wood engravings and genre paintings at the National Academy. From 1852 to 1857 he was associated with the firms of WHITNEY & ANNIN; WHITNEY, JOCELYN & ANNIN; and WHITNEY & JOCELYN. JOHN HENRY ELLSWORTH WHITNEY was his brother. ¶ Phoenix, *The Whitney Family of Connecticut,* I, 865; Am. Inst. Cat., 1842, 1845, 1848; Cowdrey, NAD; NYCD 1848–57; Linton, *History of Wood Engraving in America;* Hamilton, *Early American Book Illustrators and Wood Engravers,* 496–97.

WHITNEY, J. D. Topographical artist who assisted CHARLES T. JACKSON during the winter of 1840–41 in a geological survey of New Hampshire. Jackson's *Final Report* (1844) and his *Scenery and Views of New Hampshire* (1845) were illustrated with many views by Whitney. ¶ Jackson, *Final Report on the Geology and Mineralogy of the State of New Hampshire;* Jackson, *Views and Map Illustrative of the Scenery and Views of New Hampshire.*

WHITNEY, JOHN HENRY ELLSWORTH (1840–1891). Wood engraver, born in NYC on July 30, 1840, a younger brother of ELIAS JAMES WHITNEY. He enlisted in the Union Army in 1861, was wounded at Antietam, and was mustered out in 1863. He made his home in Brooklyn until 1870 when he moved to Chappaqua (N.Y.). He was the author of *The Hawkins Zouaves (Ninth N.Y.V.): Their Battles and Marches.* ¶ Phoenix, *The Whitney Family of Connecticut,* I, 866; Smith; Hamilton, *Early American Book Illustrators and Wood Engravers,* 457.

WHITNEY & JOCELYN. Wood engravers, NYC, 1856–58; ELIAS J. WHITNEY and ALBERT H. JOCELYN, successors to WHITNEY, JOCELYN & ANNIN. ¶ NYCD 1856–58; Am. Inst. Cat., 1856; Hamilton, *Early American Book Illustrators and Wood Engravers.*

WHITNEY, JOCELYN & ANNIN. Wood engravers, NYC, 1853–55. The partners were ELIAS J. WHITNEY, ALBERT H. JOCELYN, and PHINEAS F. ANNIN. The firm grew out of WHITNEY & ANNIN and in 1856 became WHITNEY & JOCELYN. ¶ NYCD 1853–54; Hamilton, *Early American Book Illustrators and Wood Engravers.*

WHITNEY, JOHN P. Engraver, Boston, 1854–after 1860. Possibly the John Whitney, engraver, 24, born in Maine, listed in the 1860 census. ¶ 8 Census (1860), Mass., XXVI, 403.

WHITNEY, THOMAS RICHARD (1807–1858). Engraver and author, born April 30, 1807 in Norwalk (Conn.). After his marriage in 1827 he settled in NYC. In 1830 he published *The Young Draftsman's Companion.* Later he became the editor of *The Republic* and *The Sunday Times,* a State Senator (1854–55), Congressman (1855–57), and the author of a volume of poetry. He died in NYC on April 12, 1858. ¶ Phoenix, *The Whitney Family of Connecticut,* I, 383; Union Cat., LC; NYCD 1828+.

WHITNEY, WILLIAM K. Engraver, 21, a native of Massachusetts, living in Boston in 1860 with his father, Nahum Whitney, undertaker. ¶ 8 Census (1860), Mass., XXVI, 520; Boston CD 1860.

WHITTAKER, JOHN BERNARD (1836–?). Portrait painter. He was born in Ireland and worked in Brooklyn (N.Y.) from 1857. He exhibited at the National Academy. ¶ Mallett; Brooklyn BD 1857–58; Cowdrey, NAD.

WHITTIER, WILLIAM. Plate engraver, 17, a native of Massachusetts, boarding in Boston in 1860. ¶ 8 Census (1860), Mass., XXVII, 433.

WHITTLE, B. Painter of a view of the Bloomingdale Flint Glass Works near NYC about 1837, owned by the New-York Historical Society. ¶ *American Collector* (Jan. 23, 1934), 3.

WHITTREDGE, THOMAS WORTHINGTON (1820–1910). N.A. Landscape painter. Born May 22, 1820, in Springfield (Ohio), he began his art career in Cincinnati about 1840, and worked there as a portrait painter until 1849, with a brief residence at Indianapolis in 1842. In 1849 he went abroad to study, spending five years at Düsseldorf and five more chiefly in Rome. On his return to America in 1859 he opened a studio in NYC where he stayed until 1880, after which he made his home in Summit (N.J.). In 1865–66 he made a trip to the Rocky Mountains in company with SANFORD R. GIFFORD and J. F. KENSETT, but he was best known for his New York and New England landscapes. Elected a National Academician in 1861, he served as president of the Academy in 1865 and from 1874 to 1877. He died February 25, 1910, in Summit (N.J.). ¶ Baur, ed., "Autobiography of Worthington Whittredge"; DAB; Karolik Cat., 509–19; Sweet, *Hudson River School;* Met. Mus., *Life in America;* Cowdrey, NAD; Cowdrey, AA & AAU; Rutledge, PA; Rutledge, MHS; Peat, *Pioneer Painters of Indiana,* 159–60.

WICHER & PRIDHAM. Sign, ornamental, and steamboat painters, Cincinnati, 1844. Possibly Lawrence S. Wicker (painter, 1846) and HENRY PRIDHAM. ¶ Knittle, *Early Ohio Taverns,* 44; Cincinnati CD 1846.

WICKER, AUGUST. Designer, 28, a native of France, living in Philadelphia in 1860. ¶ 8 Census (1860), Pa., LII, 42.

WICKERSHAM, THOMAS. Portrait painter at Cincinnati, 1858–60. Listed as W. Wickersham in the Ohio business directory for 1859. ¶ Cincinnati CD 1858, BD 1859–60; Ohio BD 1859.

WIDER, CHARLES. Prussian-born engraver, 32, at NYC in 1860. His eldest child, aged 9, was born in Germany, but three younger ones, aged 1 to 5, were born in NYC. ¶ 8 Census (1860), N.Y., LIV, 165.

WIDEVELD, see WYDEVELD.

WIGGIN, ALFRED J. Portrait painter at Cape Ann (Mass.), 1850. ¶ Lipman and Winchester, 182.

WIGGINS, SAMUEL A. Engraver, 26, a native of New Brunswick, at Detroit (Mich.) in 1860. ¶ 8 Census (1860), Mich., XX, 110; Detroit CD 1861.

WIGHT, MOSES (1827–1895). Portrait and genre painter, born in Boston on April 2, 1827. He started painting portraits in Boston about 1845 and went abroad to study for the first time in 1851. His first important work was a portrait of Alexander von Humboldt, 1852. Returning from Rome in 1854, he had a studio in Boston from then until 1873, although he made two trips to Paris, in 1860 and in 1865. In 1873 he settled permanently in Paris and began to specialize in interiors. ¶ Wight, *The Wights,* 191–92; Smith; Clement and Hutton; Tuckerman; Boston BD 1845–60; Swan, BA; represented at American Antiquarian Society.

WIGHT, W. Painter of a portrait of Richard Fletcher (1788–1869), now at Dartmouth College. Possibly MOSES WIGHT. ¶ WPA (Mass.), *Portraits Found in N.H.,* 8.

WIGHTMAN, GEORGE D. Wood engraver of Buffalo (N.Y.), active 1848–96. He may have been the George Wightman of 74 Fulton Street, NYC, who exhibited a wood engraving at the American Institute in 1847. ¶ Buffalo CD 1848–96; Am. Inst. Cat., 1847.

WIGHTMAN, N. Lithographer of a portrait of Bishop John Henry Hobart (1775–1830) of NYC. ¶ Peters, *America on Stone.*

WIGHTMAN, THOMAS. Engraver who came to Massachusetts from England probably shortly after 1800. He did 25 copperplate illustrations for Dean's *Analytical Guide to Penmanship,* published at Salem in 1802, and in 1806 he did some plates for two books published in Boston. In 1814 he was working for ABEL BOWEN. He was listed in Boston directories from 1805 to 1810 and possibly in 1818 (Thomas, Jr.). ¶ Fielding; Hamilton, *Early American Book Illustrators and Wood Engravers;* Boston CD 1805, 1809–10, 1818.

WIGHTMAN, THOMAS (1811–1888). A.N.A. Portrait and still life painter, possibly from Charleston (S.C.). He studied under HENRY INMAN in NYC and first exhibited at the National Academy in 1836. In June 1841 he left Charleston to complete his studies in NYC where he seems to have stayed, except for visits to Charleston in 1843 and 1844, until about the time of the Civil War when he returned to the South. He was made an Associate of the National Academy in 1849 and he exhibited there until 1854. Of his later career nothing is known, except that he had a son Horace who also was a painter. ¶ *Art Annual,* X, 402; Rutledge, *Artists in the Life of Charleston;* Cowdrey, NA; Brooklyn CD 1843–52; Stillwell, "Some Nineteenth Century Painters," 82, 84, 85 (repro.), 87 (repro.).

WILBUR, ISAAC E. Portrait painter at Rochester (N.Y.) in 1843. ¶ Ulp, "Art and Artists in Rochester," 32.

WILBUR, S. Wood engraver whose work appeared in *The Lumiere* (New York, 1831). ¶ Hamilton, *Early American Book Illustrators and Wood Engravers,* 97.

WILCOX, JOHN ANGEL JAMES (1835–?). Steel engraver and etcher; portrait painter. Born August 21, 1835, in Portage (N.Y.), he learned engraving in Hartford (Conn.) under JARVIS GRIGGS KELLOGG in the mid-fifties. In 1860 he moved to Boston where he was active as an engraver until 1913. He worked in line, stipple, and mezzotint, etched, and painted some portraits. ¶ Fielding's supplement to Stauffer; Hartford CD 1858–61; Boston CD 1866–1913; repro., *Ohio State Archaeological and Historical Quarterly* (Jan. 1948), opp. 4.

WILCOX, JOSEPH P. Sculptor and marble cutter of Newark (N.J.) who exhibited two marble reliefs and one bust at the American Institute in 1856 and the National Academy in 1859. ¶ Newark CD 1857–60; Am. Inst. Cat., 1856; Cowdrey, NAD.

WILCOX, W. H., see WILLIAM H. WILLCOX.

WILD, ALEXANDER. German lithographer, 46, in NYC in 1860. ¶ 8 Census (1860), N.Y., XLVIII, 949.

WILD & CHEVALIER. Lithographers, Philadelphia, 1838–39; JOHN CASPAR WILD and J. B. CHEVALIER. In 1838 they published twenty lithographed views of Philadelphia after drawings by Wild. ¶ *Portfolio* (Jan. 1946), 120; Phila. CD 1839; Drepperd, "Pictures with a Past," 96.

WILD, JOHN CASPAR (*c.* 1804–1846). Landscape painter and lithographer. A native of Zurich (Switzerland); came to the United States about 1830. He was at Philadelphia in 1831 and at Cincinnati from 1833 or 1835 until 1837. Back in Philadelphia, in 1838 he established a brief partnership with the lithographer J. B. CHEVALIER; their chief work was a set of twenty views of Philadelphia and vicinity after drawings by Wild. In 1839 Wild moved to St. Louis (Mo.) and in 1845 to Davenport (Iowa) where he died in August the following year. His work in the Midwest included *Views of St. Louis* (1840), *The Valley of the Mississippi Illustrated in a Series of Views* (1841), and numerous paintings and lithographs of towns and scenic spots in Illinois, Iowa, and Minnesota. ¶ McDermott, "J. C. Wild, Western Painter and Lithographer," 12 repros.; McDermott, "J. C. Wild and Fort Snelling," one repro.; Wilkie, *Davenport Past and Present,* 307–10; Phila. CD 1838; *Portfolio* (Jan. 1946), 120; *Antiques* (Aug. 1946), 109; Stokes, *Historical Prints;* Rutledge, PA (as C. Wild).

WILDE, DAVID. French engraver, 30, at San Francisco in 1860. ¶ 8 Census (1860), Cal., VII, 1374.

WILDE or WILD, HAMILTON GIBBS (1827–1884). Portrait, genre, and landscape painter of Boston, who studied in Europe in 1846 and again about 1859. His father, James C. Wilde or Wild, was a bank cashier. Exhibited at the Boston Athenaeum, the National Academy, and the Pennsylvania Academy. ¶ Swan, BA; 8 Census (1860), Mass., XXVI, 684; Champney, *Sixty Years' Memories of Art and Artists,* 79; Boston CD 1852–57,

BD 1853–54; Cowdrey, NAD; Rutledge, PA.

WILDER, EMIL. German portrait painter, 30, living in Boston in 1850 with his wife Nina. ¶ 7 Census (1850), Mass., XXV, 586.

WILDER, F. H. Itinerant portrait painter working in Fitchburg and Leominster (Mass.) in 1846. ¶ Sears, *Some American Primitives,* 287; Lipman and Winchester, 182.

WILDER, MATILDA. Amateur watercolorist, Massachusetts, 1820. ¶ Lipman and Winchester, 182.

WILES, LEMUEL MAYNARD (1826–1905). Landscape painter, born October 21, 1826, in Perry (N.Y.). Between 1848 and 1851 he studied with WILLIAM HART and J. F. CROPSEY, after which he taught and painted in Washington (D.C.), Albany (N.Y.), and Utica (N.Y.) until 1864. After that date he had a studio in NYC. In 1873–74 he visited Panama, California, and Colorado taking sketches upon which he based the larger works for which he was best known. His summers were spent at Ingham (N.Y.) where he conducted drawing classes. He died in NYC on January 28, 1905. ¶ Clement and Hutton; *Art Annual,* V, obit.; Rutledge, PA.

WILES, WILLIAM. Ornamental painter at Lebanon (Ohio) in 1813. ¶ Knittle, *Early Ohio Taverns,* 44.

WILGUS, WILLIAM JOHN (1819–1853). Portrait painter, born January 28, 1819, in Troy (N.Y.). From 1833 to 1836 he was a pupil of SAMUEL F. B. MORSE and he remained in NYC until about 1841. Thereafter he made his home in Buffalo, though he traveled as far afield as Georgia, Missouri, and the West Indies. He died in Buffalo on July 23, 1853. ¶ Sellstedt, *Life and Works of William John Wilgus;* Cowdrey, NAD; Swan, BA; Met. Mus., *Life in America;* Cummings, *Historic Annals of the NAD,* 233; represented at Corcoran Gallery and Yale University.

WILHELM, AUG[UST]. Wood engraver from Hesse (Germany), aged 23, at Philadelphia in 1860. ¶ 8 Census (1860), Pa., LV, 642.

WILKES, CHARLES (1798–1877). Topographical artist. Born in NYC on April 3, 1798, he went to sea at seventeen, and entered the U. S. Navy as a midshipman in 1818. From 1838 to 1842 he was in command of the U. S. Exploring Expedition which visited the Oregon coast, some of the Pacific islands, and the coast of Antarctica, and from 1843 to 1861 he was in Washington preparing for publication the various reports of the expedition. Wilkes's *Narrative* contains some illustrations after his own sketches. JOHN SKIRVING also used some of his drawings for a panorama of Frémont's overland journey to California (1849). Wilkes was on active service at sea during the early part of the Civil War but was placed on the retired list in 1863. He died in Washington, February 8, 1877. ¶ DAB; Rasmussen, "Artists of the Explorations Overland," 57–58; Boston *Evening Transcript,* Sept. 26, 1849 (courtesy J. Earl Arrington).

WILKIE, JOHN. Portrait painter who worked in the neighborhood of Schenectady (N.Y.) in 1840. Union College owns his portrait of DeWitt Clinton. His portrait of Moncrieff Livingston of Columbia County (N.Y.), painted in 1840, is owned by Mr. and Mrs. Laurence Barrington of Worcester (Mass.). ¶ Information courtesy Mrs. Laurence Barrington; Lipman and Winchester, 182.

WILKIE, ROBERT D. (1828–1903). Landscape, genre, still life, and bird painter. He was born in Halifax (N.S.) and began his artistic career there about 1849. By 1853 he had begun to contribute landscape views to *Gleason's Pictorial Drawing Room Companion* and in 1856 he was listed for the first time in the Boston directory. From then until 1902 he lived in Boston and Roxbury. In 1863–65 he was Boston artist-correspondent for *Frank Leslie's Illustrated Weekly;* in 1868 and later he was doing work for the Boston lithographer, LOUIS PRANG. During the seventies he made a number of painting trips to the White and Adirondack Mountains and taught painting in Boston. Probably between 1896 and 1899 he painted over a hundred watercolor scenes from Dickens' novels. His health failing, in 1902 he moved to Swampscott (Mass.) and the following year he died there at the home of his son. 120 of his paintings were exhibited at the Vose Galleries in Boston in 1948. ¶ Vose Galleries, "Robert D. Wilkie, 1828–1903, Rediscovery of a 19th Century Boston Painter," based on information from Miss Ruth K. Wilkie, the artist's granddaughter. The Vose Galleries published at the same time two catalogues, one of 98 Dickens scenes and the other of 22 miscellaneous oils and watercolors.

WILKIE, THOMAS. Portrait painter at Albany (N.Y.), 1859–60. ¶ Albany CD 1859–60.

WILKINS, GEORGE W. Portrait painter of NYC who exhibited at the National Academy in 1840. ¶ NYBD 1840; Cowdrey, NAD.

WILKINS, JAMES F. Portrait, miniature, and panorama painter. An Englishman, Wilkins studied at the Royal Academy and exhibited portraits there in 1835–36. In 1832–43 he was in New Orleans as a portrait and miniature painter. He settled in St. Louis about 1844 and in 1850–51 he exhibited a panorama of the overland route to California from sketches made by himself in 1849. ¶ Graves, *Dictionary;* New Orleans CD 1842; New Orleans *Picayune,* Jan. 27, 1843 (courtesy Delgado-WPA); St. Louis *Intelligencer,* Oct. 20, 1850, and March 6, 1851 (courtesy J. Earl Arrington); Butts, *Art in Wisconsin,* 54; McDermott, "Gold Rush Movies."

WILKINS, SARAH. Memorial painting in watercolors, Massachusetts, 1830. ¶ Lipman and Winchester, 182.

WILKINSON, ——. Engraver at Philadelphia in 1766. ¶ Prime, I, 31–32.

WILKINSON, Mrs. J. Teacher of drawing and languages, New Orleans, 1826. ¶ Delgado-WPA cites *La. Gazette,* April 18, 1826.

WILKINSON, JOHN. Exhibited at the National Academy in 1839 a view of Niagara Falls, a cattle piece after Jackson, and "Taking a Comfortable Nap." His address was New York. ¶ Cowdrey, NAD.

WILL, JOHN M. AUGUST (1834–1910). Crayon portraitist, landscape draftsman, and designer. A native of Weimar (Germany), Will was at NYC as early as 1855 when he made a pen-and-ink drawing of the NYC Post Office. His home was in Jersey City, where he died January 23, 1910. ¶ *Art News,* Jan. 29, 1910; Stokes, *Iconography,* pl. 28; Stokes, *Historical Prints;* NYCD 1857–60+.

WILLARD, ARCHIBALD M. (1836–1918). Painter, born August 22 or 26, 1836, in Bedford (Ohio). A carriage painter by trade, in 1873 he went to NYC to study art. His best-known work was "The Spirit of '76," of which he painted at least four versions. He lived in Cleveland most of his life and died there on October 11, 1918. ¶ Pope, *Willard Genealogy,* 567; Daywalt, "The Spirit of '76"; *Art Annual,* XVI, 225, obit.

WILLARD, ASAPH (1786–1880). Copperplate, steel, and wood engraver, born December 24, 1786, at Wethersfield (Conn.). He learned engraving from Deacon ABNER REED of East Windsor, was working at Albany (N.Y.) in 1816, and from 1817 to 1819 was a member of the HARTFORD GRAPHIC AND BANK NOTE ENGRAVING CO. He made his home in Hartford until his death, July 14, 1880, at the age of 93. JAMES D. WILLARD was his son. ¶ Pope, *Willard Genealogy,* 171; *American Art Review,* I (1880), 455; Stauffer; Rice, "Life of Nathaniel Jocelyn"; Dunlap, *History;* Hamilton, *Early American Book Illustrators and Wood Engravers,* 94; Peters. *America on Stone.*

WILLARD, F. W. Amateur artist of NYC who exhibited an oil painting of Pomona, Goddess of Fruit, at the American Institute in 1856. ¶ Am. Inst. Cat., 1856.

WILLARD, HENRY (1802–1855). Portrait, miniature, and genre painter of Boston, active from about 1833. Among his works exhibited at the Athenaeum between 1834 and 1842 was a self-portrait. He also exhibited at the National Academy in 1833 and the Washington Art Association in 1859. ¶ Swan, BA; Cowdrey, NAD; Washington Art Assoc. Cat., 1859; Boston CD 1833–56; Stauffer, no. 2508.

WILLARD, JAMES DANIEL (1817–?). Engraver, born October 31, 1817, probably in Hartford (Conn.). He was active in Hartford during the 1850's, in 1860 in association with his father, ASAPH WILLARD. ¶ Pope, *Willard Genealogy,* 171; Hartford BD 1851, 1857–60.

WILLARD, SOLOMON (1783–1861). Carver in stone and wood, architect, teacher of drawing and sculpture. Born June 26, 1783, at Petersham (Mass.), learned the carpenter's trade there and went to Boston in 1804. He took up wood carving in 1809 and began carving figureheads in 1813, his most notable work in this line being the figure for the frigate *Washington.* In 1817 he visited Richmond to study HOUDON's bust of Washington and designed one himself, intending to carve it in marble, but the clay model was accidentally destroyed and Willard never completed the project. After 1820 he became a leading architect in Boston, though he also taught drawing and sculpture. His chief occupation from 1825 to 1842 was the supervision of the erection of the Bunker Hill Monument, which he had designed. After its completion he retired to Quincy and spent the rest of his life as a gentleman farmer. He died in Quincy on February 27, 1861. ¶ DAB; Pickney, *American Figureheads and Their Carvers.*

WILLARD, WILLIAM (1819–1904). Portrait

painter; born March 24, 1819 at Sturbridge (Mass.); died there November 1, 1904. He was active in Boston during the 1850's and exhibited at the Athenaeum Gallery. The American Antiquarian Society owns his self-portrait and his portraits of Charles Sumner, Daniel Webster, and George Frisbie Hoar. He also painted a panorama of Boston from Bunker Hill. ¶ Weis, *Checklist of Portraits;* Boston CD 1851–60; Swan, BA; Boston *Evening Transcript,* May 2, 1849 (courtesy J. Earl Arrington).

WILLCOX or WILCOX, WILLIAM H. Landscape painter born in New York State about 1831. In 1849, when he was living in Williamsburgh, Long Island, he exhibited two pencil drawings at the American Institute and sold two landscapes to the American Art-Union. By 1850 he had moved with his parents to Philadelphia and he was active there at least until 1868, during which time he exhibited at the Pennsylvania Academy views in New Hampshire, Vermont, New York, and Pennsylvania. ¶ 7 Census (1850), Pa., LIII, 661; Am. Inst. Cat., 1849; Cowdrey, AA & AAU; Rutledge, PA; Phila. CD 1856.

WILLIAMS, ——. Pastellist of Monmouth and Middlesex Counties (N.J.), active about 1815–30. About 60 of his pastel portraits have been identified, including some previously attributed to HENRY CONOVER. Possibly the same as MICAH WILLIAMS. ¶ Cortelyou, "A Mysterious Pastellist Identified," with 7 repros.; Cortelyou, "Henry Conover: Sitter, Not Artist."

WILLIAMS, ——. Scene painter at the New Theatre, Charleston (S.C.) in 1837, along with J. SERA and D. NIXON. ¶ Rutledge, *Artists in the Life of Charleston.*

WILLIAMS, A. Oil painting of a ship *c.* 1850. ¶ Lipman and Winchester, 182.

WILLIAMS, ABIGAIL OSGOOD (1823–1913). Painter and drawing teacher, born in Boston in October 1823. She and her younger sister, MARY ELIZABETH WILLIAMS, spent most of their lives together in Salem and were teachers of drawing in the Salem schools. In 1860 they went to Rome to study painting for eighteen months. Mary Elizabeth died in 1902 and Abigail died on April 26, 1913. ¶ Belknap, *Artists and Craftsmen of Essex County,* 15–16; Swan, BA.

WILLIAMS, ALLEN. Wood engraver, NYC, 1860. ¶ NYBD 1860.

WILLIAMS, CHARLES. Ohio-born artist, 22, at Cincinnati in 1850. ¶ 7 Census (1850), Ohio, XX, 901.

WILLIAMS, E. Artist, New Orleans, 1849. ¶ Delgado-WPA cites New Orleans CD 1849.

WILLIAMS, E. F. or F. Pseudonym of FRANCIS W. EDMONDS.

WILLIAMS, FREDERICK DICKINSON (1829–1915). Portrait, landscape, and figure painter born in Boston. He was active in his native city during the 1850's and 1860's and taught drawing in the public schools, but in the mid-1870's he went to Paris for a number of years. He died in Brookline (Mass.), January 27, 1915. His wife (née Lunt), a native Bostonian, also was a painter and crayon artist. ¶ *Art Annual,* XII, obit.; Clement and Hutton; Boston BD 1856–60; 8 Census (1860), Mass., XXVIII, 876; Washington Art Assoc. Cat., 1859; Swan, BA.

WILLIAMS, GEORGE. Irish engraver, 16, at Philadelphia in 1850. ¶ 7 Census (1850), Pa., LIII, 828.

WILLIAMS, HENRY (1787–1830). Portrait and miniature painter, profile cutter, wax modeler, and engraver. He was born in Boston and lived there all his life. In 1814 he published *Elements of Drawing.* He died October 21, 1830, in Boston. ¶ Bolton, *Miniature Painters;* Stauffer; Jackson, *Silhouette,* 153; Boston *Independent Chronicle,* 1808, cited by Dr. Clarence L. Brigham; Drepperd, "American Drawing Books"; Swan, BA; Dunlap, *History;* WPA (Mass.), *Portraits Found in N. H.,* 14, 20; *Antiques* (Oct. 1928), 325–26, repros.; *Antiques* (Aug. 1940), 54, repro.; *Art in America* (July 1940), 120, repro.

WILLIAMS, ISAAC L. (1817–1895). Portrait, landscape, and figure painter, born June 24, 1817, in Philadelphia. A pupil of JOHN R. SMITH and JOHN NEAGLE, he began exhibiting in Philadelphia in 1837 and later exhibited also in NYC, Boston, Baltimore, and Washington. Until 1844 he painted chiefly portraits, but after that he became primarily a landscape painter. Most of his life was spent in Philadelphia, though he had a studio in Lancaster (Pa.) in 1854–55 and visited England, France, and Italy in 1866. He became a member of the Artists' Fund Society in 1860 and later served as its president. He died on April 23, 1895, in Philadelphia. ¶ Lancaster County Hist. Soc., *Papers,* XVI (1912), 261–69; Clement and Hutton; 8 Census (1860), Pa., LVIII, 133; Rutledge, PA; Rutledge, MHS; Cowdrey, NAD; Cowdrey, AA & AAU; Swan, BA; Washington Art Assoc. Cat., 1859; Phila. CD 1846, 1852, 1857.

WILLIAMS, J. Philadelphia artist who exhibited "Joan of Arc in Prison" and "The Sailor Boy's Return" at the Apollo Association in 1838–39. Possibly the same as JAMES W., ISAAC L., or JOHN C. WILLIAMS. ¶ Cowdrey, AA & AAU.

WILLIAMS, J. C. Portrait painter at San Francisco, 1860–65. He was a native of Pennsylvania, born about 1814. Possibly the same as JOHN C. WILLIAMS. ¶ 8 Census (1860), Cal., VII, 521; San Francisco CD 1860–61, 1865.

WILLIAMS, JAMES W. Portrait, miniature, and marine painter, born in England about 1787. He had settled in Philadelphia by 1823, when he was listed as a coach and sign painter. From 1825 to 1833 he appears as a sign and ornamental painter, but thereafter he is listed as miniature painter, artist, or "artists' emporium." Between 1837 and 1847 his name disappears from the Philadelphia directories; in February 1843 and December 1845 he was in New Orleans and in 1844 he visited Danville (Ky.). He was listed at Philadelphia again from 1847 to 1868. Between 1829 and 1844 he exhibited a number of marine paintings at the Pennsylvania Academy. *Cf.* J. WILLIAMS. ¶ 8 Census (1860), Pa., LII, 659; Phila. CD 1823–37, 1847–68; Rutledge, PA; Delgado-WPA cites *Picayune,* Feb. 10, 1843, and Dec. 9, 1845; information courtesy Mrs. W. H. Whitley, Paris (Ky.).

WILLIAMS, JAMES W. Engraver, 44, a native of Pennsylvania, living in Philadelphia in 1860. All his children, ages 7 to 16, were born in Pennsylvania. ¶ 8 Census (1860), Pa., LIV, 451.

WILLIAMS, JOHN. Lithographer, 25, a native of New York, at NYC in 1860. ¶ 8 Census (1860), N.Y., XLVI, 478.

WILLIAMS, JOHN C. Philadelphia artist who exhibited a portrait at the Artists' Fund Society in 1837. Possibly the same as J. C. WILLIAMS, portrait painter of San Francisco, 1860–65, who was a native of Pennsylvania. ¶ Rutledge, PA.

WILLIAMS, JOHN L. Artist, Philadelphia, 1853–58. The 1860 Census lists a John Williams, artist, born in England about 1822, living in Philadelphia with his wife and two children (11 and 9), all born in Maine. ¶ Phila. CD 1853–56, 1858; 8 Census (1860), Pa., LIV, 242.

WILLIAMS, JOHN INSCO (1813–1873). Portrait and panorama painter, born in 1813 at Oldtown (Ohio). After a brief apprenticeship to a carriage painter, he turned professional portrait painter about 1832 and worked as an itinerant in central Indiana for three years. He then spent three years in Philadelphia as a pupil of RUSSELL SMITH and THOMAS SULLY. By 1840 he was back in Indiana and soon after he settled in Cincinnati (Ohio) where he made his home until shortly before his death. In 1847 he again visited Indiana. In 1849 he completed a panorama of Biblical history from the Creation to the fall of Babylon, which was shown with great success in Cincinnati, Dayton, Baltimore, Washington, and Boston before its destruction by fire in Independence Hall, Philadelphia, in March 1851. A second version of this panorama was exhibited all over the country between 1856 and 1871. Williams died in the home of a son at Dayton (Ohio) in 1873. His wife and two daughters also were painters. ¶ Peat, *Pioneer Painters of Indiana,* 86–91; Clark, *Ohio Art and Artists,* 111; Rutledge, PA; Rutledge, MHS; information courtesy J. Earl Arrington.

WILLIAMS, Mrs. JOHN INSCO. Amateur painter. Born Mary Forman, about 1833, she was living with foster parents at Richmond (Ind.) in 1847 when she first met Williams. He took her to his parents' home in Dayton and two years later, when she was sixteen, married her. She painted ideal pictures, including a "Bleeding Kansas." ¶ Peat, *Pioneer Painters of Indiana,* 90; Clark, *Ohio Art and Artists,* 111.

WILLIAMS, MARY. Still life painter, probably a Philadelphia amateur, who exhibited at the Pennsylvania Academy in 1811 and 1814. ¶ Rutledge, PA.

WILLIAMS, MARY ELIZABETH (1825–1902). Painter and drawing teacher, younger sister of ABIGAIL OSGOOD WILLIAMS, with whom she lived in Salem (Mass.) almost all her life. They taught drawing in the Salem schools and in 1860–61 spent eighteen months studying art in Rome. She died September 15, 1902. ¶ Belknap, *Artists and Craftsmen of Essex County,* 15–16.

WILLIAMS, MICAH. Portrait painter who is said to have been working at New London (Conn.) and Peekskill (N.Y.) about 1790. It has been suggested that he may have been the pastellist, —— WILLIAMS, active in New Jersey between 1815 and 1830.

¶ *American Provincial Painting,* no. 12; Lipman and Winchester, 182; Cortelyou, "A Mysterious Pastellist Identified" and "Henry Conover: Sitter, Not Artist."

WILLIAMS, MICHAEL. Lithographer working in NYC from 1826 to 1834. ¶ Peters, *America on Stone; American Collector* (June 1942), 10.

WILLIAMS, MOSES. Philadelphia profile cutter, 1813–20. In 1819 he was listed as a Negro. ¶ Brown and Brown.

WILLIAMS, S. Engraver of one illustration in Harper's illustrated edition of Benjamin Franklin's *Autobiography* (New York, 1849). *Cf.* T. WILLIAMS. ¶ Hamilton, *Early American Book Illustrators and Wood Engravers,* 172.

WILLIAMS, T. Engraver of several illustrations in Harper's illustrated edition of Benjamin Franklin's *Autobiography* (New York, 1849). *Cf.* S. WILLIAMS. There was a Thomas Williams, engraver, working in NYC between 1869 and 1871; examples of his work have been found in books published as late as 1879. ¶ Hamilton, *Early American Book Illustrators and Wood Engravers,* 172–73, 237, 432, 501; NYCD 1869–71.

WILLIAMS, THOMAS. Professor of drawing and painting at New Orleans in 1835. ¶ Delgado-WPA cites *Courier,* Jan. 5, 1835.

WILLIAMS, VIRGIL (1830–1886). Landscape, genre, and portrait painter. A native of Taunton (Mass.), he went to Europe to study art about 1856, returning to Boston before 1862 when he again left, this time for San Francisco. He was back in Boston by 1865 but in 1871 he settled permanently in California. His wife was a daughter of the painter WILLIAM PAGE. Williams died on his ranch near Mt. St. Helena on December 18, 1886. ¶ WPA (Cal.), *Introduction to California Art Research,* II, 138–57, biblio., repros.; Rutledge, PA; *Antiques* (May 1947), 307, repro.; *Panorama* (Jan. 1946), 46, and (Aug. 1948), back cover.

WILLIAMS, WELLINGTON. Copperplate and steel engraver, Philadelphia, 1850–after 1860. ¶ Phila. CD 1850–60+. See also, Wellington Williams, *Appleton's Northern and Eastern Traveller's Guide . . .* (New York and Philadelphia, 1850).

WILLIAMS, WILLIAM. Portrait painter, decorative and scenic artist, drawing and music teacher, novelist. He was an Englishman who went to sea at an early age and after a series of adventures, later described in fictional form in his Defoesque novel, *The Journal of Llewellyn Penrose,* came to Philadelphia about 1747 and established himself as a portrait painter. Soon after, he gave the young BENJAMIN WEST his first instruction in painting. Williams was one of the builders of the first theater in Philadelphia in 1759 and also painted scenery for it. In 1763 he returned to Philadelphia from a visit to the West Indies. He was still painting in the Colonies as late as 1775, but by 1780 he had gone back to England, where he posed for a figure in WEST's "The Battle of La Hogue." Not long after, possibly as late as 1790, he died in an almshouse in Bristol, leaving to a patron the manuscript of his novel and an unpublished *Lives of the Painters.* ¶ Sawitzky, "William Williams" and "Further Light on . . . William Williams"; Flexner, "The Amazing William Williams" and "Benjamin West's American Neo-Classicism with Documents on West and William Williams"; Prime, II, 13; Gottesman, I, 7.

WILLIAMS, WILLIAM (1787–1850). Wood engraver, printer, bookseller. Born October 12, 1787, in Framingham (Mass.), he went to Utica (N.Y.) in 1800 and served as apprentice in a print shop until 1807 when he became a partner in the business. In 1835 he moved to Tonawanda (N.Y.). He died June 10, 1850, in Utica. Hamilton lists two books containing wood engravings by him. ¶ Williams, *An Oneida County Printer, William Williams;* Hamilton, *Early American Book Illustrators and Wood Engravers,* 502.

WILLIAMS, WILLIAM (1796–1874). Amateur sketcher. He was born December 6, 1796, in Westmoreland County (Pa.), where he spent the greater part of his life in business. In 1850 he went out to Iowa and established a provisions store at Fort Dodge, then a military installation, of which he made a drawing in 1852. When the troops were removed in 1854, Williams bought the military buildings and laid out the town of Fort Dodge. In 1869 he was elected first mayor of the incorporated city and he held the office for two years. He died in Fort Dodge on February 26, 1874. ¶ Pratt, *History of Fort Dodge and Webster County, Iowa,* I, 155, repros. opp. 72 and 82; *Iowa Journal of History* (April 1951), cover and 169.

WILLIAMS, WILLIAM, see also WILLIAM JOSEPH WILLIAMS.

WILLIAMS, WILLIAM GEORGE (1801–1846).

Topographical engineer and amateur portrait painter. He was born January 1, 1801, in Philadelphia and attended West Point, graduating in 1824. During the thirties and early forties he was employed by the U. S. Army on surveys of canal routes and harbor installations on the Great Lakes and elsewhere. He exhibited portraits at the National Academy in 1840, 1843–45. He was chief of engineers under General Taylor during the Mexican War and was killed at the Battle of Monterey on September 21, 1846. He was an Honorary Member of the National Academy. ¶ CAB; Cowdrey, NAD.

WILLIAMS, WILLIAM JOSEPH (1759–1823). Portrait and miniature painter, born November 17, 1759, in NYC and probably a nephew of the painter JOHN MARE. He was christened William Williams and used that name until his conversion to the Roman Catholic faith about 1821, when he adopted the Joseph. His career as an artist began in NYC in 1779 and he worked there until about 1792. In 1792 or 1793 he went to Virginia; from 1793 to 1797 he was in Philadelphia, where he painted a portrait of Washington as a Mason; in 1798 and 1804 he married his second and third wives in South Carolina (probably at Charleston); from 1804 to 1807 he was at Newbern (N.C.); from 1807 to 1817 he was in NYC; from 1817 until his death on November 30, 1823, he lived in Newbern. ¶ Williams, *William Joseph Williams and His Descendants;* Smith, "John Mare . . . with Notes on the Two William Williams," 375–85; Prime, II, 38; NYCD 1813–17; Morgan and Fielding, *Life Portraits of Washington,* 201; Rutledge, *Artists in the Life of Charleston.*

WILLIAMSON, ——. Painter (?) of a panorama of the bombardment of Vera Cruz during the Mexican War. It was exhibited at Louisville (Ky.) in June 1849, having previously been shown in NYC and Ohio. ¶ Louisville *Courier,* June 7 and 13, 1849 (courtesy J. Earl Arrington).

WILLIAMSON, CHARLES. Artist, 28, a native of New York, at NYC in 1850. ¶ 7 Census (1850), N.Y., XLIV, 583.

WILLIAMSON, JOHN (1826–1885). A.N.A. Landscape painter. Born April 10, 1826, at Toll Cross, near Glasgow (Scotland), he came to America as a child and spent most of his life in Brooklyn. He began exhibiting at the National Academy in 1850 and was elected an Associate Member in 1861; he also exhibited in Brooklyn, Washington, and Boston. His subjects were chiefly views in New England, New York, and Pennsylvania. He died May 28, 1885, in Glenwood-on-the-Hudson. ¶ CAB; Clement and Hutton; Cowdrey, NAD; Cowdrey, AA & AAU; Swan, BA; Washington Art Assoc. Cat., 1857; NYBD 1850+; *Art Digest* (May 1, 1945), 2, repro.

WILLIAMSON, WILLIAM. Pennsylvania-born engraver, 21, at Philadelphia in 1850. ¶ 7 Census (1850), Pa., LI, 504.

WILLIS, EDMUND AYLBURTON (1808–1899), also known as A. Van Willis. Landscape painter; born October 12, 1808, in Bristol (England); active in NYC and Brooklyn from about 1852; died in Brooklyn, February 3, 1899. He exhibited at the National Academy in the early fifties. ¶ *Art Annual,* 1899, obit.; Cowdrey, NAD; NYCD 1857, 1860.

WILLIS, FREDERICK. Artist, 36, at Philadelphia in 1860. He was English, but his wife Clarissa and son William, aged 2, were both born in Pennsylvania. ¶ 8 Census (1860), Pa., LX, 740.

WILLIS, JOHN. Artist, 50, a native of New Jersey, at NYC in 1860. ¶ 8 Census (1860), N.Y., LXI, 844.

WILLIS & PROBST. Lithographers, NYC, 1844; WILLIAM R. WILLIS and JOHN PROBST. ¶ NYBD and NYCD 1844.

WILLIS, WILLIAM H. Landscape painter of NYC who exhibited at the National Academy in 1847 and 1856. In 1847 his address was the same as the 1842–46 address of William Henry Willis, merchant, but there is no William H. Willis listed in the directories around 1856. ¶ Cowdrey, NAD; NYCD 1842–57.

WILLIS, WILLIAM R. Lithographer of NYC, active 1838–49. In 1844 he was with WILLIS & PROBST. ¶ NYCD 1838.

WILLMORE, EDWARD C., see EDWARD WELLMORE.

WILLITTS, S. C. Philadelphia artist who exhibited at the Artists' Fund Society in 1840 a "Portrait of an Artist." The painting was owned by the artist ROBERT STREET and Willitts may have been one of his pupils; both were living on Vine Street at the time. ¶ Rutledge, PA.

WILLOUGHBY, EDWARD C. H. Landscape painter at Chicago in 1859. ¶ Chicago CD 1859.

WILLS, J. R. Engraver at Philadelphia in 1849. ¶ Phila. BD 1849.

WILLSON (or WILSON), JOSEPH (1825–1857).

Cameo cutter, die sinker, and sculptor. He was born in Canton (N.Y.) and studied portrait painting there with SALATHIEL ELLIS. In 1842 he followed Ellis to NYC and there took up cameo cutting and die sinking. In 1848 he moved to Washington, where he was again associated with Ellis. He went to Italy in 1851 to study sculpture for three years and on his return settled in NYC, where he died September 8, 1857. ¶ Loubat, *Medallic History of the United States;* NYBD 1856–57; Cowdrey, NAD; Washington Art Assoc. Cat., 1857.

WILLSON, MARY ANN. Primitive watercolorist who came from one of the eastern states and settled in Greenville, Greene County (N.Y.) early in the 19th century. She lived there "for many years" with a friend, Miss Brundage, who managed the farm while Miss Willson painted her crude watercolors for sale. After Miss Brundage's death, Miss Willson left Greenville and was not heard of again. A portfolio containing twenty of her pictures was discovered in 1943 and exhibited at the Harry Stone Gallery in NYC. ¶ Lipman, "Miss Mary Ann Willson," three repros.; Lipman, "Miss Willson's Watercolors," five repros.; Lipman, "Mermaids in Folk Art."

WILMARTH, LEMUEL EVERETT (1835–1918). N.A. Genre painter, born March 11, 1835, in Attleborough (Mass.). After studying at the Pennsylvania Academy, in 1859 he went to Munich to study for three years under Kaulbach and in 1863 to Paris for four more years with Gérôme. On his return to America in 1867 he settled in NYC. In 1868 he became director of the schools of the Brooklyn Academy of Design and two years later he was appointed professor of the free schools of the National Academy. In 1871 he was made an Associate and in 1873 a Member of the Academy. He was in charge of the Academy's schools until 1890. He died in Brooklyn July 27, 1918. ¶ DAB; CAB; Clement and Hutton; *Art Annual,* XV, 284; Rutledge, PA; Swan, BA.

WILMER, WILLIAM A. Stipple engraver of portraits who died about 1855. He had been a pupil of JAMES B. LONGACRE of Philadelphia and did some engraving for Longacre's *National Portrait Gallery.* ¶ Stauffer.

WILMORE, EDWARD, see EDWARD WELLMORE.

WILSON, ——. Painter of a view of Niagara Falls, a copy of which by Lt. WILLIAM PIERRIE was engraved and published in 1774. ¶ Kelby, *Notes on American Artists,* 11.

WILSON, ——. Landscape painter of Boston who exhibited at the Maryland Historical Society in 1850. No artist of this name was listed in the Boston directories, 1849–51, and only WILLIAM F. WILSON, portrait painter, from 1852 to 1854. ¶ Rutledge, MHS; Boston CD 1849–51, BD 1852–54.

WILSON, Mrs. ——. Portrait sculptor active in Cincinnati in the early 1850's. Born near Cooperstown (N.Y.), she went to Cincinnati with her parents and there married a Dr. Wilson. Her interest in sculpture was aroused by a visit to a studio in Cincinnati and she began to model and to carve in stone for her own amusement. ¶ Lee, *Familiar Sketches of Sculpture and Sculptors,* 216–18; Gardner, *Yankee Stonecutters,* 73. The 1853 Cincinnati directory lists three doctors named Wilson: Israel, Singleton C., and T. Wilson.

WILSON, ——. Philadelphia painter who exhibited at the Washington Art Association in 1859. This might be JEREMY, STEPHEN D., or SAMUEL WILSON, portrait painters active in Philadelphia in the fifties. ¶ Washington Art Assoc. Cat., 1859.

WILSON, ——. Portrait painter boarding at the Hancock House in Boston on July 12, 1860. He was thirty-six years old, a native of Canada, deaf and dumb from birth. ¶ 8 Census (1860), Mass., XXVIII, 172.

WILSON, ALBERT (1828–1893). Ship and ornamental carver, son of JOSEPH WILSON. He was born in Newburyport (Mass.), June 29, 1828; worked there with his father and brother (JAMES WARNER WILSON) from about 1850 until his death, November 26, 1893. ¶ *Vital Records of Newburyport,* I, 416; Newburyport CD 1850–91, 1894 (date of death given); Pinckney, *American Figureheads and Their Carvers,* 141; Swan, "Ship Carvers of Newburyport," 81.

WILSON, ALEXANDER (1766–1813). Ornithologist and sketcher. Born July 6, 1766, near Paisley (Scotland), Wilson worked as a weaver and peddler in Scotland until 1794 when he emigrated to America. For about ten years he taught school in New Jersey and Pennsylvania, but in 1802, after meeting the naturalist WILLIAM BARTRAM, he began to collect material and make sketches for a work on American birds. The first volume of his classic *American Ornithology* appeared in 1808, with engravings by ALEXANDER LAWSON after Wilson's drawings, and the eighth volume was in the press at the time of Wilson's death, which occurred in Philadelphia on August 23, 1813. While working on his book Wilson had traveled widely throughout the United States, east of the Mississippi. In 1804 he made a sketch of Niagara Falls which was engraved for *Port Folio,* March 1810. Wilson also tried his hand at engraving and etching, but with little success. ¶ DAB; Stauffer; Weitenkampf, "Early American Landscape Prints," 42.

WILSON, ALFRED F. Pennsylvania-born portrait painter, aged 21, living in Philadelphia in 1850. ¶ 7 Census (1850), Pa., L, 607.

WILSON, CARRINGTON. Painter of NYC who exhibited "Landing of Columbus" at the National Academy in 1841. He was a sign painter by trade and worked in NYC from about 1840 to 1845. ¶ Cowdrey, NAD; NYCD 1840–45.

WILSON, D. W. Engraver of a ball ticket and a bookplate, Albany, about 1825–30. *Cf.* DAVID WEST WILSON. ¶ Stauffer.

WILSON, DAVID WEST (*c.* 1799–1827). N.A. Miniaturist of NYC who was a founder of the National Academy. He died in NYC, April 28, 1827. His miniature of Kosciuzko was stolen from the Academy. *Cf.* D. W. WILSON. ¶ N. Y. *Evening Post,* April 28, 1827, obit. (Barber); N. Y. *Mirror,* Dec. 24, 1825, p. 175 (courtesy Mary Bartlett Cowdrey); Cowdrey, AA & AAU.

WILSON, E. Itinerant portrait painter of the pre-1860 period; painted portraits of Rev. and Mrs. Frank Cooper of Antrim (N.H.). ¶ Sears, *Some American Primitives,* 286; Lipman and Winchester, 182.

WILSON, Miss E. Portrait painter, Chicago, 1855. ¶ *Chicago Almanac,* 1855.

WILSON, E. H. Sign and ornamental painter at Wooster (Ohio), 1820–50. ¶ Knittle, *Early Ohio Taverns,* 44.

WILSON, GEORGE W. Mulatto artist from Virginia, aged 30, residing with ROBERT DUNCANSON at Cincinnati in 1860. He had a photographic gallery there in 1861, but he may also have been a painting pupil of Duncanson. ¶ 8 Census (1860), Ohio, XXV, 255; Cincinnati CD 1861.

WILSON, H. & O. Second prize winners at the Illinois State Fair, October 1855, for animal painting in oils. Probably HENRY and OLIVER WILSON who had a marble works in Chicago at that time under the name of H. & O. Wilson. ¶ Chicago *Daily Press,* October 15, 1855; Chicago CD 1855.

WILSON, HENRY. Marble cutter of Chicago, active 1849–60. He was listed as a sculptor in 1851 and in 1855, with OLIVER WILSON, won a prize for animal painting in oils at the Illinois State Fair. ¶ Chicago CD 1849–60; Chicago *Daily Press,* Oct. 15, 1855.

WILSON, HENRY. Portrait painter, Brooklyn (N.Y.), 1857. ¶ Brooklyn BD 1857.

WILSON, HENRY. Pennsylvania-born artist, 25, at Philadelphia in 1860. ¶ 8 Census (1860), Pa., LV, 210.

WILSON, J. Portrait and miniature painter at NYC in 1844. *Cf.* JOHN WILSON (artist, 1850) and JOHN T. WILSON (portrait painter, 1860). ¶ NYBD 1844, 1860; NYCD 1850.

WILSON, J. B. Painted a portrait of James B. Richardson, Governor of South Carolina, 1802–04; signed and dated 1804. ¶ Information courtesy the late William Sawitzky.

WILSON, J. G. Portrait painter, New Orleans, 1838–42. ¶ New Orleans CD 1838, 1841–42.

WILSON, JAMES. Copperplate engraver of Bradford (Vt.), associated in 1813 with ISAAC EDDY of Wethersfield. ¶ Stauffer.

WILSON, JAMES. English artist, 34, living in NYC in 1860. His wife and three children (8 to 2) were born in New York. Possibly the same as JAMES CLAUDIUS WILSON. ¶ 8 Census (1860), N.Y., LIV, 361.

WILSON, JAMES CLAUDIUS. Marine painter. Born in Scotland, but brought to America at the age of ten by his father and uncle, who were employed as commercial copyists in NYC. He was listed as an artist from about 1855 and in 1856 exhibited an oil painting, "National Guard," at the American Institute. During the latter fifties and the sixties he painted pictures of ships in the NYC area. Possibly the same as JAMES WILSON, above. ¶ Peters, "Paintings of the Old 'Wind-Jammer,'" 31–32, repro.; NYCD 1855–57; Am. Inst. Cat., 1856.

WILSON, JAMES WARNER (1825–1893). Ship and ornamental carver, son of JOSEPH WILSON (1779–1857). He was born in Newburyport (Mass.) on July 2, 1825, worked there all his life, first with his father and later with his brother ALBERT, and died in Newburyport on October 19, 1893. ¶ *Vital Records of Newburyport,* I, 417; Newburyport CD 1850–91, death date in CD 1894; Swan, "Ship Carvers of Newburyport," 81; Pinckney, *American Figureheads and Their Carvers,* 141.

WILSON, JEREMY. Portrait and landscape painter who exhibited at the Pennsylvania Academy between 1853 and 1863. He was living in Philadelphia in 1853–56, Rome (Italy) in 1859, Philadelphia in 1861–62, and Harrisburg (Pa.) in 1863. ¶ Rutledge, PA.

WILSON, JOHN. Artist, NYC, 1850. *Cf.* J. WILSON and JOHN T. WILSON. ¶ NYCD 1850.

WILSON, JOHN. Engraver, St. Louis, 1859. ¶ St. Louis BD 1859.

WILSON, JOHN. Artist, 28, a native of Pennsylvania, at Philadelphia in 1860. ¶ 8 Census (1860), Pa., LIV, 333.

WILSON, JOHN. Irish-born engraver, 27, at Philadelphia in 1860. ¶ 8 Census (1860), Pa., LIV, 251.

WILSON, JOHN T. Negro engraver at NYC in 1856. ¶ NYCD 1856.

WILSON, JOHN T. Portrait painter and colorist at NYC, 1859–60. *Cf.* JOHN WILSON, artist, NYC, 1850. ¶ NYCD 1859–60; NYBD 1860.

WILSON, JOSEPH. Counterfeitor of banknotes who broke out of the Cecil County (Md.) jail, where he was awaiting execution, in November 1749. ¶ Prime, II, 32.

WILSON, JOSEPH (1779–1857). Ship and ornamental carver; born November 2, 1779, in Marblehead (Mass.); working in Chester (N.H.) in 1796–98 and thereafter at Newburyport (Mass.); died in Newburyport on March 25, 1857. He carved a number of portrait statues and animal figures for the grounds of "Lord" Timothy Dexter's house in Newbury, including figures of Washington, Adams, and Jefferson, Dexter himself, Napoleon and Lord Nelson, and other prominent persons, as well as four lions, an eagle, lamb, unicorn, dog, horse, Adam and Eve, Fame, and a traveling preacher. After about 1850 he was assisted by his sons, ALBERT and JAMES WARNER WILSON. ¶ Swan, "Ship Carvers of Newburyport," 78–81; Pinckney, *American Figureheads and Their Carvers,* 141; *Antiques* (Aug. 1945), 80, repro.

WILSON, JOSEPH (sculptor), see JOSEPH WILLSON.

WILSON, JOSEPH C. Lithographer, 15, at Philadelphia in 1860. He was a native of Pennsylvania, the son of William Wilson, a steamfitter of English birth. ¶ 8 Census (1860), Pa., XLIX, 217.

WILSON, L. D., see STEPHEN D. WILSON.

WILSON, MARY ANN, see MARY ANN WILLSON.

WILSON, MARY PRISCILLA, see MARY PRISCILLA WILSON SMITH (Mrs. Russell Smith).

WILSON, MARY R. Painter of a still life in watercolors, Massachusetts, 1820. ¶ Lipman and Winchester, 182.

WILSON, MATTHEW (1814–1892). A.N.A. Portrait and miniature painter, crayon and pastel portraitist. Born July 17, 1814, in London (England), he came to the United States in 1832, settled in Philadelphia, and became a pupil of HENRY INMAN. In 1835 he went to Paris to study under Dubufe. On his return he settled in Brooklyn (N.Y.) and sent a number of paintings to the National Academy, of which he became an Associate in 1843. He visited New Orleans in the spring of 1845. In 1847 he went to Baltimore for at least two years. In the early fifties, probably, he was in Ohio and from 1856 to 1860 in Boston. He then had a studio in Hartford (Conn.), 1861–63, after which he settled permanently in Brooklyn. During the Civil War he spent some time in Washington painting portraits of prominent men, including one of Lincoln two weeks before the latter's assassination. He died in Brooklyn February 23, 1892. ¶ CAB; Cowdrey, NAD; Brooklyn CD 1843–45; Swan, BA; Delgado-WPA cites New Orleans *Daily Topic,* May 15, 1845; Lafferty; Pleasants, *250 Years of Painting in Maryland,* 56; Rutledge, PA; New England BD 1856; Boston CD 1858–60; French, *Art and Artists in Connecticut,* 162; represented at Peabody Institute.

WILSON, MATTHEW. Copperplate printer and engraver at Boston, 1853–60. He was with the printing firm of Wilson & Daniels from 1853 to 1858 and with the engravers WILLIAM M. MILLER & Co. from 1859. ¶ Boston CD 1853–60+.

WILSON, OLIVER. Marble cutter in partnership with HENRY WILSON at Chicago in the 1850's. Together they won a prize for animal painting in oils at the Illinois State Fair in October 1855. ¶ Chicago CD 1853–55; Chicago *Daily Press,* Oct. 15, 1855.

WILSON, SAMUEL. Engraver of Holmesburg (Pa.), 1856–60+. ¶ Phila. CD 1856–60+.

WILSON, SAMUEL. Artist, Philadelphia, 1859. ¶ Phila. CD 1859.

WILSON, STEPHEN D. Portrait painter, born in Pennsylvania about 1825, working in

Philadelphia from 1847 until after 1860. ¶ 7 Census (1850), Pa., LII, 390; Phila. CD 1847–60+; Phila. BD 1850 [as L. D. Wilson].

WILSON, THOMAS. Coach and ornamental painter of Philadelphia under whom JOHN NEAGLE served his apprenticeship from about 1813 to 1818. During this time Wilson was himself taking lessons in painting from BASS OTIS. ¶ Dunlap, *History,* II, 372–73.

WILSON, WILLIAM (?–1850). Portrait painter born in Yorkshire (England). He was established in Charleston (S.C.) by 1840 and worked principally in Georgia and South Carolina for the next eleven years, although he was also in NYC in 1842–43 and at New Orleans in 1845. He died in Charleston on December 28, 1850. ¶ Rutledge, "Early Painter Rediscovered," with checklist and two repros.; Rutledge, *Artists in the Life of Charleston,* 167.

WILSON, WILLIAM. Engraver, NYC, 1850. ¶ NYCD 1850.

WILSON, WILLIAM F. Portrait painter, Boston, 1852–54. ¶ Boston BD 1852–54.

WILSON, WILLIAM W. Copperplate engraver and printer at Boston, 1832–after 1860. In 1834 he was a member of the firm of POLLOCK & WILSON. ¶ Boston CD 1832–60+, BD 1841–60; Stauffer.

WILTBERGER, AND[REW?]. Artist, 39, at Philadelphia in 1860. He was from Bavaria, but his wife and children were born in Pennsylvania, the latter between 1842 and 1850. ¶ 8 Census (1860), Pa., LIV, 688.

WILTON, BERNARD. An English painter working in Philadelphia in 1760 when he painted a sign for the Bull's Head Tavern, long attributed to BENJAMIN WEST. ¶ Barker, *American Painting,* 162; Scharf and Westcott, *History of Philadelphia.*

WILTZ, EMILE. Portrait painter at New Orleans in 1841–42. He was listed as a tax collector in 1846. ¶ New Orleans CD 1841–42, 1846.

WILTZ, LEONARD, JR. Marble sculptor, New Orleans, 1846–53. ¶ New Orleans CD 1846, 1852–53.

WIMAR, CHARLES or KARL FERDINAND (1828–1862). Painter of the Western Indians and buffalo; also portrait and historical painter. Born February 20, 1828, in Siegburg, near Bonn (Germany), he came to America at the age of 15, settling with his parents in St. Louis. About 1846 he became a pupil and assistant of LEON POMAREDE and in 1849 he accompanied his master on a trip up the Mississippi. After leaving Pomarede in 1851 he opened a painting shop in St. Louis, but a year later he was able to go to Düsseldorf, where he stayed four years and studied under EMANUEL LEUTZE. Wimar returned to St. Louis in 1856 and devoted himself mainly to paintings of the Indians and buffalo herds of the Great Plains. He made at least three trips to the headwaters of the Missouri in search of material. He also did some portrait painting and in 1861 executed the mural decorations in the rotunda of the St. Louis Court House. He died in St. Louis, of consumption, on November 28, 1862. ¶ Rathbone, "Charles Wimar," biographical sketch, bibliography, and illustrated catalogue of an exhibition at the City Art Museum of St. Louis in 1946.

WINANS, WILLIAM O. Wood engraver, born in New York State about 1830 and working in Cincinnati during the 1850's. ¶ 7 Census (1850), Ohio, XXII, 437; Cincinnati CD 1851–56.

WINDEAT, WILLIAM. Portrait painter of NYC who exhibited at the National Academy in 1849. ¶ Cowdrey, NAD.

WINN or WINNE, ALFRED. English glass-stainer, 37, at NYC in 1850. ¶ 7 Census (1850), N.Y., XLIII, 39; NYCD 1850.

WINNER, WILLIAM E. (*c.* 1815–1883). Portrait, genre, historical, and religious painter; born in Philadelphia and worked there from 1836 probably until his death in 1883. He also visited Charleston in 1848. He was a frequent exhibitor at the Pennsylvania Academy, Boston Athenaeum, Apollo Association and American Art-Union, and at the National Academy, of which he was an Honorary Member, Professional. ¶ 7 Census (1850), Pa., LI, 322, as Wenner; Rutledge, PA; Cowdrey, NAD; Swan, BA; Cowdrey, AA & AAU; Phila. CD 1839–60+; Rutledge, *Artists in the Life of Charleston; Portfolio* (Nov. 1944), 54, repro.

WINSHIP, W. W. Engraver at Georgetown (D.C.) in 1860; born in the District of Columbia about 1834. ¶ 8 Census (1860), D.C., I, 67.

WINSLOW, C. Made an early drawing of the Mormon Temple at Nauvoo (Ill.), probably about 1845. ¶ Arrington, "Nauvoo Temple," Chap. 8.

WINSLOW, HENRY J. Engraver and copperplate printer, NYC, 1832–40. ¶ *Am. Adv. Directory,* 1832; NYBD 1837, 1840.

WINSTANLEY, WILLIAM. Landscape and portrait painter. A young Englishman, he came to the United States sometime before April 1793 when he sold two Hudson River landscapes to President Washington. Soon after, he visited the newly-created District of Columbia to paint several views on the Potomac, two of which were also purchased by the President. From 1795 to 1799 Winstanley's headquarters were in NYC; during this time he exhibited two panoramas, of London (1795) and of Charleston (1797), and took up portrait painting. According to WILLIAM DUNLAP he made copies of a portrait of Washington by GILBERT STUART and palmed them off as originals, but the evidence of Winstanley's guilt in the matter is not wholly convincing (Pleasants). The Washington portrait in the White House is said to be one of these copies. In 1801 he published a play, *The Hypocrite Unmask't,* in NYC. The last record of his American activity is a prospectus of a series of eight American views, to be engraved in aquatint; the prospectus appeared in a Boston newspaper in November 1801, at which time Winstanley appears to have been living in Boston. Of his later activity, nothing is known except that he returned to England and exhibited several landscapes at the British Institution in London in 1806. ¶ Pleasants, *Four Late Eighteenth Century Anglo-American Landscape Painters,* 301–24, three repros. and checklist; NYCD 1795, 1798–99; Cowdrey, AA & AAU; Odell, *Annals of the New York Stage,* I, 443; Vail, "A Dinner at Mount Vernon," 79; Gottesman, *Arts and Crafts in New York,* II, nos. 58–60; Dunlap, *History;* Flexner, *The Light of Distant Skies,* biblio., 269.

WINTER, C. Philadelphia artist, active about 1840, whose painting of an early minstrel show scene is now in the Karolik Collection. ¶ Karolik Cat., 520, 521 (repro.).

WINTER, CHARLES. Portrait painter, 38, at NYC in 1860. He was a native of Louisiana, his wife was from New Jersey, one child (12) was born in Pennsylvania, and two others (5 and 9) were born in New York State. ¶ 8 Census (1860), N.Y., LIII, 168.

WINTER, GEORGE (1810–1876). Portrait and landscape painter, born June 10, 1810, in Portsea (England). At 16 he went to London to study art but received little formal training before he emigrated to America in 1830. Settling in NYC, he attended the schools of the Academy of Design for three years and did some work as a miniature painter, but about 1835 he moved west to Cincinnati and after a year there on to Logansport (Ind.). He lived in Logansport until 1851 and then moved to Lafayette (Ind.) where he lived until his death, February 1, 1876. The most important of Indiana's pioneer artists, Winter painted portraits of many early Indiana settlers and Indians, as well as landscapes. Many of his works have survived and also several of his journals. The best known of his pupils was JOHN INSCO WILLIAMS. ¶ The Indiana Historical Society published in 1948 a volume entitled *The Journals and Indian Paintings of George Winter 1837–1839,* which contains an essay on "Winter, the Artist" by Wilbur D. Peat and a "Biographical Sketch" by Gayle Thornbrough, along with his autobiography and journals and 31 repros. See also: Peat, *Pioneer Painters of Indiana;* Burnet, *Art and Artists of Indiana;* and *American Heritage* (August 1950), 34–39.

WINTER, JOHN. Painter of landscapes, coaches, coats of arms, and ornamental work of all kinds. He first advertised in Philadelphia in March 1739/40 and was still there in 1771. Sometime before 1755 he was in business with GUSTAVUS HESSELIUS. In 1761 he may have been one of the artists of a view of the Pennsylvania Hospital, by Winters and Montgomery, for the engraver ROBERT KENNEDY. ¶ Brown and Brown; Prime, I, 13.

WINTER, R. Painter of chemical dioramas, crystalline views, chromatropes and metamorphoses, which included European views and "The Death of Napoleon." Winter exhibited his work at NYC (Nov. 1843), St. Louis (Feb. 1845), Charleston (Nov. 1845), Richmond (March 1846), Nashville (April 1847), Philadelphia (June 1847), Baltimore (Oct.–Nov. 1847), Brooklyn (1847), Nashville (Feb.–March 1850), Cincinnati (Feb.–March 1853), Baltimore (December 1856), and Philadelphia (April 1857). *Cf.* ROBERT WINTER. ¶ Information courtesy J. Earl Arrington, based on newspaper notices and Odell, *Annals of the New York Stage,* V, 409.

WINTER, ROBERT. Portrait painter, Philadelphia, 1860. ¶ Phila. CD 1860.

WINTER, T. or J. A. German-born portrait painter, 29, at New Orleans in 1850. His wife Mary, 19, was a native of France. ¶ 7 Census (1850), La., VII, 331.

WINTER, WILLIAM. Miniature painter, Cincinnati, 1856. ¶ Cincinnati CD 1856.

WINTERHALDER, J. Portrait and landscape painter, New Orleans, 1852–56. From 1858 to 1866 the directories list J. Winterhalder, bakery, and J. Winterholder, wheelwright. ¶ New Orleans CD 1852–66.

WINTON, WILLIAM. Ohio-born artist, 20, at NYC in June 1860. ¶ 8 Census (1860), N.Y., XLVI, 397.

WIRTH, COLVERT and ROBERT. Prussian-born engravers living together in NYC in June 1860. Colvert was 29 and Robert 25. ¶ 8 Census (1860), N.Y., XLIV, 815.

WISE, C. Engraver of portraits in stipple. An Englishman, he came to the United States about 1850; was at Boston in 1852; later did work for publishers in NYC and Philadelphia; is thought to have died about 1889. ¶ Stauffer; Boston BD 1852.

WISE, GEORGE. Artist, Baltimore, 1849–50. ¶ Lafferty.

WISE, JAMES. Portrait and miniature painter who was working in New Orleans in May 1843 and at Charleston (S.C.) in 1844 and 1845. His portrait of John C. Calhoun was engraved by SARTAIN. He also worked in Virginia and at St. Joseph (Mo.). A James H. Wise, possibly the same man, was listed as a portrait painter at San Francisco from 1856 to 1860. ¶ Delgado-WPA cites N. O. *Picayune,* May 3, 1843; Rutledge, *Artists in the Life of Charleston;* Willis, "Jefferson County Portraits and Portrait Painters"; San Francisco BD 1856, 1858–60.

WISE, SAMUEL C. Engraver, 24, at NYC in July 1850. He was from Connecticut but his wife and daughter were both born in New York State. ¶ 7 Census (1850), N.Y., XLVIII, 128.

WISER or WIZAR, ANGELO. Artist; born in Pennsylvania about 1841; active in Philadelphia in 1860–61. ¶ 8 Census (1860), Pa., LIII, 172; Phila. CD 1861.

WISER, JOHN. Panorama and scenery painter, born in Pennsylvania about 1815. He may have studied in Europe, since he exhibited at the Artists' Fund Society in 1841 two landscapes, "Ruins of the Convent of the Carmelites at Bruges" and "Ruins of the Temple of Peace." In November 1841 he was a scene painter at the Walnut Street Theatre in Philadelphia, along with CHARLES LEHR and PETER GRAIN, JR. In April 1850 he was scene painter at the Chestnut Street Theatre and in 1849–50 and 1853 he exhibited in Philadelphia his panorama of the Creation, Paradise, and the Flood. He was still in Philadelphia in July 1860. ¶ 8 Census (1860), Pa., LII, 693; Rutledge, PA; Phila. CD 1841; Phila. *Public Ledger,* Nov. 6, 1841, Dec. 4 and 14, 1849, April 8, 1850, and April 25, 1853 (citations courtesy J. Earl Arrington).

WISONG, W. A. Painter of a portrait of Christian B. Herr of Lancaster County (Pa.) in 1852. ¶ Lancaster County Hist. Soc., *Portraiture in Lancaster County,* 142.

WISSLER, JACQUES (James) (1803–1887). Engraver and lithographer, portraitist in crayons and oils. A native of Strasbourg (Alsace), he was trained as a lithographer and engraver in Paris. He emigrated to America in 1849. In 1860 he was in NYC with the firm of DRESER & WISSLER, but when the Civil War broke out in 1861 he was working in Richmond. His services were commandeered by the Confederate Government to engrave the plates for the paper currency and bonds of the Confederate States. At the close of the war he moved to Macon (Miss.) and later to Camden (N.J.) where he died November 25, 1887. Though primarily an engraver, he was also a successful portrait artist. ¶ Stauffer; CAB; NYBD and NYCD 1860; Boston *Transcript,* Nov. 28, 1887, obit.

WITHERS, CAROLINE. Miniaturist active in Charleston (S.C.) before the Civil War. She was presumably one of the Misses Withers mentioned in Mrs. E. F. Ellet's *Women Artists in All Ages and Countries* (reviewed in *Russell's Magazine,* VI (Jan. 1860), 384). ¶ Carolina Art Assoc. Cat., 1935, 1936; Rutledge, *Artists in the Life of Charleston,* 167.

WITHERS, EBENEZER. Portrait painter active in NYC from 1835 to 1839 and an exhibitor at the National Academy and the Apollo Association. ¶ Cowdrey, NAD; Cowdrey, AA & AAU; NYCD 1837.

WITMAN, see WHITMAN.

WITT, Dr. CHRISTOPHER (1675–1765). Physician and amateur artist. An Englishman, Witt (or DeWitt) came to America in 1704 to join the little colony of Pietistic mystics at Germantown (Pa.) and the following year painted an oil portrait of the leader, Johannes Kelpius (1673–1708). Witt spent the rest of his life in Germantown, where he had a reputation as a sorcerer, and died there at the age of 90. The Kelpius portrait is now at the

Historical Society of Pennsylvania. ¶ Welsh, "Artists of Germantown," 235–36; Hocker, *Germantown 1683–1933,* 51; Pennypacker, *The Settlement of Germantown,* 226 (repro. opp.).

WITT, JOHN HENRY (1840–1901). A.N.A. Portrait painter, born May 18, 1840, in Dublin (Ind.). At eighteen he went to Cincinnati to study art with JOSEPH O. EATON and from 1862 to about 1879 he had a studio in Columbus (Ohio), where he painted portraits of a number of early Ohio governors as well as other prominent citizens. In 1873 he spent some time in Washington (D.C.). In 1879 he moved to NYC where he died on September 13, 1901. He was elected an Associate of the National Academy in 1885. Fairman, Burnet, and Clark (*History of the NAD*) give Harrison as the middle name, but he is listed as John Henry in *Museum Echoes* (May 1951) and as J. Henry in the Columbus directory for 1867. ¶ Fairman, *Art and Artists of the Capitol,* 353; *Museum Echoes* (May 1951), 37 and cover; Peat, *Pioneer Painters of Indiana,* 99–100; Clark, *Ohio Art and Artists,* 114; Clark, *History of the NAD,* 274; Columbus CD 1867–77; NYCD 1880–99; Borough of Manhattan, *Deaths Reported in 1901,* 401.

WITTENBERG, THEODORE C. Artist, 40, at NYC in 1860. He, his wife, and their three children were all born in New York State. ¶ 8 Census (1860), N.Y., XLIV, 357; NYCD 1863.

WIZAR, see WISER.

WOGRAM, FREDERICK. Lithographer, NYC, 1854–59. ¶ NYBD 1854, 1857, 1859.

WOISERI, see BOQUETA DE WOISERI.

WOLCOTT, JOSIAH. New England portrait painter active from 1835 to 1857. He exhibited at the Boston Athenaeum in 1837 and painted portraits of Mr. and Mrs. Abel Houghton, now owned (1941) by Theodore S. Houghton of St. Albans (Vt.). ¶ WPA (Mass.), *Portraits Found in Vt.;* Swan, BA.

WOLFE, JOHN C. Portrait, landscape, and panorama painter who worked in Cincinnati and Dayton (Ohio) between 1843 and 1851 and at Chicago in 1859. He was the artist of a panorama of *Pilgrim's Progress* and, with WILLIAM L. SONNTAG, of a panorama of *Paradise Lost.* ¶ Cincinnati CD 1843, 1851; Chillicothe *Daily Scioto Gazette,* April 24, 1850; Chicago CD 1859; Baltimore *Sun,* June 3, 1850 (courtesy J. Earl Arrington).

WOLFE, JOHN K. Painter and draftsman, born in Pennsylvania about 1835, the son of William B. and Mary K. Wolfe of Philadelphia, with whom he was living in 1860. His father was fairly well-to-do, owning personal property valued at $40,000. In 1861 the artist exhibited "Sleepy Hollow" at the Pennsylvania Academy. He was listed as "drawing" in the 1871 directory. ¶ 8 Census (1860), Pa., LX, 975; Rutledge, PA; Phila. CD 1871.

WOLFF, ——. NYC artist who exhibited several still lifes of birds and fruit at the National Academy in 1850. ¶ Cowdrey, NAD.

WOLFORD, CHARLES. Portrait painter at Louisville (Ky.), 1843–58. He was a native of Pennsylvania, born about 1811. From 1865 to 1867 he was a clerk in a Louisville stationery store and in 1870 he was listed as Capt. Charles Wolford, president of the Arctic Mining & Manufacturing Company. ¶ 7 Census (1850), Ky., XI, 346; Louisville CD 1843–70.

WOLGAMUTH, H. Sculptor, San Francisco, 1856. ¶ San Francisco BD 1856.

WOLLASTON, JOHN. Portrait painter. Probably a son of J. Woolaston [*sic*], a London artist of the early 18th century, the younger Wollaston was painting in London as early as 1736 and is said to have studied there under a noted drapery painter. He came to America in 1749 and remained for almost ten years, during which time he produced at least three hundred portraits in NYC (1749–52), Annapolis and elsewhere in Maryland (1753–54), Virginia (*c.* 1755–57), and Philadelphia (1758), and exerted a marked influence on his American contemporaries, including WEST, PRATT, MARE, and the elder HESSELIUS. Wollaston left the Colonies in 1758 to go to India as "writer" for the East India Company in Bengal, where he remained for about six years. In January 1767 he was again in the American Colonies, at Charleston, but he left for England in May of the same year. Of his later career nothing is known. ¶ Groce, "John Wollaston (fl. 1736–1767): A Cosmopolitan Painter in the British Colonies," is the most complete account; see also Bolton and Binsse, "Wollaston, An Early American Portrait Manufacturer"; Morgan, "Wollaston's Portraits of Brandt and Margaret Van Wyck Schuyler"; and Groce,

"John Wollaston's Portrait of Thomas Appleford, Dated 1746."

WOOD, CHARLES. Exhibited "specimens of lithography" at the American Institute in 1844; he was a resident of NYC. ¶ Am. Inst. Cat., 1844.

WOOD, CHARLES. Artist, 17, a native of New York State, at Cincinnati in September 1850. ¶ 7 Census (1850), Ohio, XX, 711.

WOOD, CHARLES. Massachusetts-born artist, 24, living with his parents, Mr. and Mrs. John H. Wood, in Boston in 1860. ¶ 8 Census (1860), Mass., XXVI, 214.

WOOD, CHARLES C. Painter of two water colors depicting the "perilous situation" of the U. S. Frigate *Macedonian* in a North Atlantic hurricane, September 27, 1818. Wood, who made drawings on the spot, may have been a member of the ship's company. ¶ *Portfolio* (June 1952), 235, repros.

WOOD, DANIEL. Artist, 29, from New Hampshire, at New Orleans in October 1850. ¶ 7 Census (1850), La., IV (1), 597.

WOOD, EZRA (1798–1841). Wood-turner and liquor seller of Buckland (Mass.) who also executed hollow-cut profiles. He was born in Buckland December 2, 1798, and died there June 12, 1841. ¶ Robinson, "Ezra Wood, Profile Cutter," 3 repros.

WOOD, GEORGE BACON, JR. (1832–1910). Landscape and genre painter, silhouettist. A native of Philadelphia, he worked and lived there or in nearby Germantown from the mid-1850's, exhibiting occasionally at the Pennsylvania Academy. ¶ Rutledge, PA; London, *Shades of My Forefathers,* 79, 185 (repro.).

WOOD, HENRY BILLINGS. Portrait painter at Boston in 1853. ¶ Boston BD 1853.

WOOD, J. Advertised in Richmond (Va.) as a miniaturist and profilist in October 1803 and as a teacher of drawing, painting, and mathematics in December 1804. *Cf.* JOHN WOOD. ¶ *Richmond Portraits,* 243.

WOOD, J. Engraver of aquatint views of Philadelphia and the penitentiary at Richmond (Va.) and a conchological plate for Rees' *Encyclopedia,* first decade of the 19th century. *Cf.* JAMES WOOD, and JOSEPH WOOD. ¶ Groce and Willet, "Joseph Wood," 154, 157.

WOOD, Mrs. J. G. Cincinnati artist, 1841–42. ¶ Information courtesy Edward H. Dwight, Cincinnati Art Museum.

WOOD, JAMES. Engraver of Charleston (S.C.), became a Director of the South Carolina Academy of Fine Arts in 1821. It was probably James rather than JOSEPH WOOD, who engraved a view of the South Carolina Medical College in 1826. In 1828 he made a plaster cast of the medal presented to Lafayette by the National Guards of Paris. ¶ Rutledge, *Artists in the Life of Charleston;* Groce and Willet, "Joseph Wood," 157–58.

WOOD, JAMES (*c.* 1803–1867). Engraver of Providence (R.I.), active 1847–67. He was employed chiefly in engraving for calico printers. In 1856 he was working with ROBERT RALSTON and from 1859 with his son, JAMES R. WOOD. James, Sr., died in Providence, January 17, 1867, at the age of 64. ¶ Providence CD 1847–67; *Providence, Births, Marriages and Deaths;* Vol. III: Deaths, 1851–70.

WOOD, JAMES R. (*c.* 1833–1887). Engraver of Providence (R.I.), active 1859–87. He was the son of JAMES WOOD and, like his father, was principally employed as a calico engraver. He died in Providence, March 16, 1887, at the age of 54. ¶ Providence CD 1859–87; *Providence, Births, Marriages and Deaths:* Deaths from 1881 to 1890.

WOOD, JOHN. Limner and teacher, NYC, 1801. He made a wash drawing of NYC from Long Island, which was engraved by WILLIAM ROLLINSON and published in 1801. *Cf.* the J. WOOD who was at Richmond (Va.) in 1803–04. ¶ McKay, "Register of Artists . . ."; Stokes, *Iconography,* pl. 74.

WOOD, JOSEPH (*c.* 1778–1830). Miniature and portrait painter. Born on a farm near Clarkstown (N.Y.), Wood left home at the age of 15 and went to NYC where he was apprenticed to a silversmith but practiced miniature painting on the side. He opened a studio in 1801 but the next year joined forces with JOHN WESLEY JARVIS. They worked together until about 1810, when Jarvis went south, and Wood continued in NYC on his own for three more years. He then moved to Philadelphia and from there, in 1816, to Washington where he spent most of his remaining years, except for occasional professional visits to Baltimore and Philadelphia. Though at one time held in high esteem for his miniatures, Wood was later reduced to making drawings for patent applications. He died in Washington on June 15, 1830. ¶ Groce and Willet, "Joseph Wood: A Brief Account of His Life and the First Catalogue of His Work"; Rutledge, PA; Cowdrey, AA &

AAU; Pleasants, *250 Years of Painting in Maryland,* 41.

WOOD, ORISON (1811–1842). Decorative wall painter who was working in West Auburn, Lewiston, and Webster Corner (Me.) about 1830. He is said to have learned the technique of painting on plaster from his father, SOLOMON WOOD, who was in the figure-making business in Boston. ¶ Little, *American Decorative Wall Painting,* 126 (repro.), 127, 132.

WOOD & RALSTON. Calico engravers, Providence (R.I.), 1856; JAMES WOOD and ROBERT RALSTON. ¶ Providence CD 1856.

WOOD, SAMUEL M. Wood engraver, 19, a native of Pennsylvania, at NYC in August 1850. ¶ 7 Census (1850), N.Y., XLIV, 222.

WOOD, SILAS (or S., Jr.). Landscape painter. He first appears at Cleveland (Ohio) in 1841 as a painting teacher; then at Charleston (S.C.) in 1848 as a landscape painter; at Cincinnati in 1850 as a monochromatic artist; and again at Cleveland in June 1851 as a teacher of landscape painting. From 1854 to 1860 he was in NYC, exhibiting landscapes and monochromatic paintings at the National Academy and the American Institute. SUSAN D. WOOD, who also exhibited a monochromatic painting at the Institute in 1856, lived at the same address and was probably the wife or daughter of Silas. ¶ WPA (Ohio), *Annals of Cleveland;* Rutledge, *Artists in the Life of Charleston;* Cincinnati CD 1850; Cowdrey, NAD; Am. Inst. Cat., 1856; NYCD 1859–60.

WOOD, SOLOMON. Plaster figuremaker who learned his trade from an Italian in Boston in the first quarter of the 19th century. His son, ORISON WOOD, was a wall painter at Auburn (Me.) about 1830 and is said to have learned from his father the technique of painting plaster. ¶ Little, *American Decorative Wall Painting,* 127.

WOOD, SUSAN D. Monochromatic painter who exhibited at the American Institute in 1856. Her address was the same as that of SILAS WOOD. ¶ Am. Inst. Cat., 1856.

WOOD, THOMAS. Lithographer, stationer, and publisher, active in NYC from 1843 to 1860. ¶ Peters, *America on Stone;* NYCD 1843–59; Am. Inst. Cat., 1844; *Antiques* (July 1945), 33 (repro.).

WOOD, THOMAS HOSMER (1798–1874). Amateur painter. A native of Massachusetts, he settled in Utica (N.Y.) about 1837 and became a prosperous merchant. He took an active part in forming the Utica Art Association and promoting its exhibitions, while some of his own paintings are said to have "adorned the homes of many citizens in the vicinity." He died in Paris in January 1878 while on a tour of the art centers of the Continent. ¶ Bagg, *Memorial History of Utica,* 233–34.

WOOD, THOMAS WATERMAN (1823–1903). N.A. Genre and portrait painter, born November 12, 1823, at Montpelier (Vt.). After studying under CHESTER HARDING at Boston, 1846–47, he worked for the next decade as a portrait painter in Quebec, Washington, NYC (1854–57), and Baltimore (1856–58). In 1858 he went abroad for further study, returning two years later. Until 1867 he worked in Nashville (Tenn.) and Louisville (Ky.) and in that year he settled permanently in NYC. During the rest of his career he was primarily a genre painter. He became prominent in the artistic life of NYC, serving as President of the Watercolor Society and of the National Academy, and helping to organize the New York Etching Club. He died in NYC on April 14, 1903. ¶ CAB; *Art Annual,* IV, obit.; Pleasants, *250 Years of Painting in Maryland,* 58; MacAgy, "Three Paintings . . ."; NYBD 1854–57; Lafferty; New England BD 1860; Cowdrey, NAD; *Art Digest* (April 1, 1935), 32 (repro.).

WOOD, WILLIAM F. English artist, 45, at Philadelphia in 1850. His wife and two oldest children (ages 18 and 16) were also born in England, but the four younger children were born in Pennsylvania between 1840 and 1847, except for one born in New York State about 1844. ¶ 7 Census (1850), Pa., LII, 237.

WOODBRIDGE, JOHN J. Artist, NYC, 1848–49. ¶ NYCD 1848–49.

WOODBURY, M. A. Engraver, Chicago, 1859. ¶ Chicago BD 1859.

WOODCOCK & HARVEY. Engravers and copperplate printers, Brooklyn (N.Y.), 1838–45. The partners were Frederick Woodcock, listed separately as a "print block cutter," and John Q. Harvey, copperplate printer. In 1845 the firm also included T. Woodcock, possibly the same as T. S. WOODCOCK. Frederick Woodcock had an oil cloth manufactory in Brooklyn from 1846 to 1859. ¶ Brooklyn CD 1838–59.

WOODCOCK, T. S. Engraver and inventor from Manchester (England) who came to America about 1830. He was working in Philadelphia in 1836 and in Brooklyn

(N.Y.) in 1842. He may have been connected with the firm of WOODCOCK & HARVEY in Brooklyn, although his address in 1842 was not the same as the firm's. He is said to have inherited money sometime in the forties and returned to England. ¶ Stauffer; Brooklyn CD 1842, 1844.

WOODIN, J. A. Watercolor portraits, Palmyra (N.Y.), 1830. ¶ Lipman and Winchester, 182.

WOODIN, THOMAS. Carver and cabinet maker of Charleston (S.C.) who also taught drawing, 1767. His daughter Rebecca taught young ladies "in the different branches of POLITE EDUCATION," presumably including the arts of design. She was still in Charleston in 1778. ¶ Rutledge, *Artists in the Life of Charleston,* 120.

WOODMAN, MRS. GEORGE. Amateur artist who exhibited a "Study from Nature" at the National Academy in 1859. Her husband was a lawyer of NYC. ¶ Cowdrey, NAD; NYCD 1859.

WOODRUFF, M. Pennsylvania-born artist, 28, living in Philadelphia in June 1860. ¶ 8 Census (1860), Pa., LV, 507.

WOODRUFF, S. He exhibited a portrait at the National Academy in 1844, address of the artist not given. In 1849 he exhibited "Crystallized Minerals, Sparta, N.J.," giving Sparta as his address. ¶ Cowdrey, NAD.

WOODRUFF, WILLIAM. Engraver and copperplate engraver who worked in Philadelphia, 1817–24, and Cincinnati, 1831–32. ¶ Stauffer; *Am. Adv. Directory,* 1831–32.

WOODRUFF, WILLIAM E. A. Kentucky-born artist, 23, at Louisville in 1850. Possibly the William E. Woodruff who was listed as a law student in 1852 and as an attorney-at-law in 1855. ¶ 7 Census (1850), Ky., XI, 447; Louisville CD 1852, 1855.

WOODS, IGNATIUS. Artist, 23 a native of Scotland, at Cincinnati in August 1850. ¶ 7 Census (1850), Ohio, XX, 743.

WOODSIDE, ABRAHAM (1819–1853). Portrait, historical, genre, and religious painter. The younger son of JOHN ARCHIBALD WOODSIDE, SR., Abraham was born in Philadelphia in 1819 and had his studio there from 1844 until his death, August 15, 1853. He exhibited at the Pennsylvania Academy, the Maryland Historical Society, and the American Art-Union. His best-known work was "Hagar and Ishmael in the Desert." ¶ Jackson, "John A. Woodside," 64–65; Trenton *State Gazette,* Aug. 17, 1853, obit.; Phila. CD 1844–54; Rutledge, PA; Rutledge, MHS; Cowdrey, AA & AAU.

WOODSIDE, JOHN ARCHIBALD, SR. (1781–1852). Sign and ornamental painter, who also did still life and animal pictures. Born in Philadelphia, he may have learned the trade of sign painting from MATTHEW PRATT. He had his shop in Philadelphia from 1805 until his death, February 26, 1852. His work was much admired by his contemporaries, including WILLIAM DUNLAP who wrote in his *History of the Rise and Progress of the Arts of Design in America* (1834) that Woodside "paints signs with talent beyond many who paint in higher branches." Woodside was a member of the Artists' Fund Society and exhibited at the Pennsylvania Academy between 1817 and 1836. His sons, ABRAHAM and JOHN A. WOODSIDE, JR., were also artists. ¶ Jackson, "John A. Woodside, Philadelphia's Glorified Signpainter"; Trenton *State Gazette,* March 1, 1852, obit.; Phila. CD 1805–52; Rutledge, PA; Swan, BA; Dunlap, *History,* II, 471; *Antiques* (Sept. 1946), 158, repro.; *Art Digest* (Aug. 1, 1950), 8, repro.; *Connoisseur* (April 1953), 68; Sherman, "Some Recently Discovered Early American Portrait Miniaturists," 295, repro.; McCausland, "American Still-life Paintings," repro.; Chamberlain, "A Woodside Still Life"; Flexner, *The Light of Distant Skies.*

WOODSIDE, JOHN ARCHIBALD, JR. Wood engraver of Philadelphia, elder son of JOHN A. WOODSIDE, SR. He was listed in Philadelphia only from 1837 to 1840, though his work has been found in a book published in 1852. ¶ Jackson, "John A. Woodside," 64; Phila. CD 1837–40; Hamilton, *Early American Book Illustrators and Wood Engravers,* 100, 151, 505.

WOODVILLE, RICHARD CATON (1825–1856). Genre painter born April 30, 1825, in Baltimore. He was educated in Baltimore and intended at first to become a doctor, but in 1845 he decided instead to devote himself to painting. He went to Düsseldorf in that year and remained there about six years, during which time he sent several paintings to American exhibitions. The Art-Union also had several engraved for distribution to its members. After 1851 Woodville lived chiefly in Paris and London. He died in London September 30, 1856, possibly from an overdose of laudanum. His son of the same name became a popular illustrator for the *Illustrated*

London News. ¶ Cowdrey, "Richard Caton Woodville"; Pleasants, *250 Years of Painting in Maryland;* Cowdrey, NAD; Cowdrey, AA & AAU; Rutledge, MHS; Rutledge, PA; *Antiques* (July 1941), 48, repro.; *Art Digest* (June 1, 1939), 42, repro.

WOODWARD, DAVID ACHESON (1823–1909). Portrait painter. He exhibited in 1842 at the Artists' Fund Society as a Philadelphian, but from 1849 he was a resident of Baltimore. ¶ Rutledge, PA; Baltimore CD 1849–60+; Rutledge, MHS; represented at Princeton University (Egbert).

WOODWARD, E. F. Engraver of maps and historical vignettes for a school atlas published at Hartford (Conn.) in 1839 and subsequently an engraver at Philadelphia, 1844–53. ¶ Stauffer; Phila. BD 1844, CD 1845–53.

WOODWARD, HENRY. Portrait painter of Worcester (Mass.), 1848–52. In 1857 he was listed as treasurer of the Mechanics' Savings Bank, Worcester. ¶ New England BD 1849; Worcester CD 1848–57.

WOODY, SOLOMON (1828–1901). Portrait and landscape painter born March 11, 1828, near Fountain City, Wayne County (Ind.). He got some informal art training in Cincinnati, where he worked as men's clothing salesman during the 1840's, and throughout his life painted for amusement, gaining his living from a general store he conducted in Fountain City. He died there November 30, 1901. ¶ Peat, *Pioneer Painters of Indiana,* 95–96, 241.

WOOLEY, JOSEPH. Engraver, 35, at Frankford (Pa.) in 1850. He, his wife, and their elder daughter, aged two, were born in England, but their younger daughter was born in Pennsylvania about September 1849. ¶ 7 Census (1850), Pa., LVI, 263.

WOOLEY, see also WOOLLEY.

WOOLLETT, WILLIAM. Portrait painter active in and around Philadelphia 1819–24. His portrait of President Ashbel Green (1762–1848) is owned by Princeton University. ¶ Phila. CD 1819–24; Egbert, *Princeton Portraits,* 56.

WOOLLEY, WILLIAM. Portrait painter and mezzotint engraver. He was an Englishman who came to America about 1797 and worked for a few years in NYC and Philadelphia, according to Dunlap. He painted and engraved portraits of George and Martha Washington which were published about 1800 by David Longworth of NYC and he may also have painted a portrait of the Rev. Ashbel Green, signed "Wooley," now owned by Princeton University, although this portrait has been dated *c.* 1825. ¶ Dunlap, *History,* II, 63; Stauffer; Egbert, *Princeton Portraits,* 56.

WOOLF, MICHAEL ANGELO (1837–1899). Actor, illustrator, and genre painter who was born in London (England) and brought to America as an infant. He was well known for his humorous illustrations in black-and-white. He died March 4, 1899. ¶ *Art Annual,* I, obit.; Bénézit; Muller, *Allgemeines Kunstler Lexikon.*

WOOLNOTH, T. Engraver of J. W. JARVIS's portrait of Daniel D. Tompkins for Herring and Longacre's *National Portrait Gallery* (1834). The engraving was exhibited at the American Academy in 1833. This is probably the English engraver Thomas Woolnoth (1785–?), noted for his theatrical portraits of which many were published in London between 1818 and 1833. ¶ Dunlap, *History,* II, 469; Cowdrey, AA & AAU; Redgrave, *Dictionary of Artists of the English School;* Hall, *Catalogue of Dramatic Portraits.*

WOOLSON, EZRA (1824–1845). Portrait painter of Fitzwilliam (N.H.), where he died January 15, 1845, at the age of 21. He was in Boston in 1843. ¶ Norton, *History of Fitzwilliam, N. H.,* 208 (repro.), 209; Lipman and Winchester, 182.

WOOLYDIE, M. German-born lithographer, 30, at NYC in 1850. He left Germany with his wife and two children after 1846. ¶ 7 Census (1850), N.Y., XLII, 15.

WORCESTER, FERNANDO E. Wood engraver, born in New Hampshire about 1817. He was active in Boston from about 1836 to 1852 and was connected with the firms of BROWN & WORCESTER (1846–47) and WORCESTER & PIERCE (1851–52). ¶ 7 Census (1850), Mass., XXVI, 305; Boston CD and BD 1842–52.

WORCESTER & PIERCE. Wood engravers, Boston, 1851–52; FERNANDO E. WORCESTER and WILLIAM J. PIERCE. ¶ Boston CD 1851–52.

WORLEY, BRACHER & MATTHIAS. Lithographers, Philadelphia, 1859–60; GEORGE WORLEY, WILLIAM BRACHER, and BENJAMIN MATTHIAS. The firm was known as Worley & Bracher after 1860. ¶ Phila. CD 1859–61.

WORLEY, GEORGE. Philadelphia lithographer, active 1846–after 1860. In 1846 he was one of the artists employed by THOMAS SINCLAIR to illustrate *The North American Sylva.* In 1859 he became senior partner in the firm of WORLEY, BRACHER &

MATTHIAS, later known as Worley & Bracher. ¶ McClinton, "American Flower Lithographs," 362; Phila. CD 1849–60+.

WORRALL, HENRY (1825–1902). Illustrator and painter. Born April 14, 1825, in Liverpool (England) and brought to America at the age of ten, Worrall spent his youth mainly in Buffalo and Cincinnati and became well known in the latter city during the 1850's as a professional musician. In the late sixties he moved to Topeka (Kans.) where he soon became prominent both as a musician and as an artist. Though he painted some portraits and gave humorous illustrated lectures, it was as a delineator of Western scenes that he made his greatest reputation. His work appeared in *Harper's Weekly* and *Frank Leslie's Illustrated Newspaper* between 1877 and 1893 and he also illustrated several books of Western history. He died in Topeka on June 20, 1902. ¶ Taft, *Artists and Illustrators of the Old West,* 117–28.

WORRELL, CHARLES (1819–?). Amateur artist who depicted the battle between the *Merrimac* and the *Monitor* in Hampton Roads (Va.) in November 1862. He was then a lieutenant in the 20th New York Volunteers, stationed at Fort Monroe (Va.). He resigned his commission December 29, 1863. ¶ *Album of American Battle Art,* 173–74, pl. 217; War Dept. records, Adjutant General's Office, at National Archives.

WORRELL, JAMES, see JAMES WARRELL.

WORRELL, JAMES. Engraver, 29, at Philadelphia in 1860. He was a native of Philadelphia, the son of Isaac, musician, and Eliza Worrell. An older brother, Francis, was listed as a painter. ¶ 8 Census (1860), Pa., LI, 355.

WORRELL or WARRALL, JOHN. An English scenery painter who was working in Providence (R.I.) about 1809 and in Boston about 1811–13. His view of Providence, used as a drop curtain at the old Providence Theatre, is now owned by the Rhode Island Historical Society. ¶ Yarmolinsky, *Picturesque United States of America,* 41; *Antiques* (Nov. 1943), 236, repro.

WORSHIP, ——. Engraver of plans for machinery, Philadelphia, 1815–20. ¶ Stauffer.

WORTH, DAVID G. Miniaturist and mechanical profilist working on the island of Nantucket (Mass.) in November 1826. ¶ Nantucket *Inquirer,* Nov. 18, 1826 (courtesy Miss Helen McKearin).

WORTH, THOMAS (1834–1917). Comic and genre artist. Born February 12, 1834, in NYC, Worth sold his first comic sketch to NATHANIEL CURRIER in 1855 and later became one of the most popular of the artists whose work was lithographed by CURRIER & IVES. Though best known for his comics, he also did many racing scenes. His home for many years was at Islip, Long Island, but in his later years he lived on Staten Island. He died December 29, 1917. ¶ CAB; Merritt, "Thomas Worth, Humorist to Currier & Ives"; Peters, *Currier & Ives,* I, 70–91; *Antiques* (Sept. 1946), 184.

WORTLEY, DAVID. Engraver and die sinker, NYC, 1856–59. ¶ NYBD 1856–59.

WOTHERSPOON, WILLIAM WALLACE (1821–1888). A.N.A. Landscape painter. From 1844, when he first exhibited at the National Academy and the American Art-Union, until 1848, his address was NYC and his subjects were drawn mainly from the White Mountains. In 1849 and 1850 he sent to the Academy several Scottish landscapes and in 1851 he was listed as resident in Rome. From 1852 to 1857 he was again in NYC, exhibiting Italian landscapes at the National and Pennsylvania Academies and a Scottish scene at the Washington Art Association. He was an Associate of the National Academy from 1848 until his death in 1888. ¶ Mallett; Muller, *Allgemeine Kunstler Lexikon;* Cowdrey, NAD; Cowdrey, AA & AAU; Rutledge, PA; Washington Art Assoc. Cat., 1857.

WRENCH, POLLY (Mary). Miniaturist, pupil of CHARLES WILLSON PEALE and sister-in-law of JAMES CLAYPOOLE. She was a native of the Eastern Shore of Maryland. In 1772, as a young woman, she supported her widowed mother and younger brother by painting miniatures in Philadelphia. She later married Jacob Rush, brother of Benjamin, and gave up painting. ¶ Sellers, *Charles Willson Peale,* I, 110–11; Bolton, *Miniature Painters;* Wharton, *Heirlooms in Miniatures.*

WRIGHT, ——. An oil portrait of one Seward of Hurdtown (Va.) is signed "Wright of Sparta" (owned in 1940 by W. P. Hill, dealer, of Richmond). ¶ Information courtesy H. W. Williams, Jr., Corcoran Gallery.

WRIGHT, ALMIRA KIDDER. Amateur painter in watercolors on silk. She was a resident of Vermont early in the 19th century. ¶ Lipman and Winchester, 182.

WRIGHT, AMBROSE. Connecticut-born engraver, 22, at NYC in June 1860. ¶ 8 Census (1860), N.Y., XLIV, 727.

WRIGHT & BALE. Engravers, NYC, 1829–33; CHARLES CUSHING WRIGHT and JAMES BALE. ¶ NYCD 1829–33.

WRIGHT, CHARLES CUSHING (1796–1854). N.A. Medallist and engraver, born May 1, 1796, in Damariscotta (Me.). He took up engraving while working for a silversmith in Utica (N.Y.) about 1817 and worked briefly in Albany and NYC before going to Savannah (Ga.) in 1819. In 1820, after losing all his possessions in the great fire at Savannah, he moved to Charleston (S.C.) where he remained for four years. In Charleston he married Lavinia Dorothy Simons (see Mrs. CHARLES CUSHING WRIGHT). In 1823 he moved to NYC and there spent the rest of his life. Though best known as a medallist, he was also a member of the following engraving firms: DURAND & WRIGHT (1826–27), BALE & WRIGHT (1829–33), and WRIGHT & PRENTISS (1835–38). He was a founder of the National Academy and exhibited there and at the American Art-Union. He died in NYC on June 7, 1854. His son, CHARLES WASHINGTON WRIGHT, also became an engraver. ¶ A manuscript biography of Charles Cushing and Lavinia Dorothy Wright by their great-grandson, Charles Lennox Wright II is at the NYHS. See also: Loubat, *Medallic History of the U. S.;* Stauffer; Cummings, *Historic Annals of the NAD,* 262; Dunlap, *History;* Cowdrey, NAD; Cowdrey, AA & AAU; NYCD 1826–53; Rutledge, *Artists in the Life of Charleston.*

WRIGHT, Mrs. CHARLES CUSHING (1805–1869). Amateur still life and portrait artist. Lavinia Dorothy Simons, born in Charleston (S.C.) on December 5, 1805, was married to the engraver CHARLES CUSHING WRIGHT at Charleston in 1820 and spent most of her life in NYC. She became an educator and pioneer advocate of women's rights. She died in NYC on May 15, 1869. ¶ Wright, "Charles Cushing Wright—Lavinia Dorothy Wright," manuscript biography at NYHS.

WRIGHT, CHARLES WASHINGTON (1824–1869). Medallist and wood engraver, son of CHARLES CUSHING and Lavinia Dorothy WRIGHT. He was born March 18, 1824, in Washington (D.C.) and was active as an engraver in NYC from about 1844 until his death, October 29, 1869. He did work for *Harper's* and *Frank Leslie's Illustrated Weekly.* His son, Charles Lennox Wright I (1852–1901) also became an engraver and was the pioneer of zinc etching, and his grandson is also an artist. ¶ Wright, "The Pioneer of Zinc Etching," 201; Wright, "Charles Cushing Wright—Lavina Dorothy Wright," 152; Am. Inst. Cat., 1844.

WRIGHT, CHAUNCY. Wood engraver, 26, a native of Connecticut, at NYC in 1860. ¶ 8 Census (1860), N.Y., XLIII, 51.

WRIGHT, EDWARD. Wood engraver of Boston, 1835–53. During most of this time he was connected with the firm of CHANDLER, WRIGHT & MALLORY and its successor WRIGHT & MALLORY. ¶ Boston CD 1835–53; Hamilton, *Early American Book Illustrators and Wood Engravers,* 171, 192.

WRIGHT, EDWARD HARLAND. Portrait painter, Norwich (Conn.), 1850. ¶ Lipman and Winchester, 182.

WRIGHT, ELIZABETH. Wax modeller. The eldest daughter of PATIENCE LOVELL WRIGHT, Elizabeth was presumably born in Bordentown (N.J.) in the early 1750's. In 1772 she was living in NYC but she later followed her mother to London and took up wax work. She married one Ebenezer Platt and lived in London until her death. Her younger brother JOSEPH WRIGHT was a noted portrait painter and one of her sisters, Phebe, married the English artist John Hoppner. ¶ Perrine, *The Wright Family of Oyster Bay,* 89–92.

WRIGHT, GEORGE. Portrait painter, Philadelphia, 1854–60. ¶ Rutledge, PA; Phila. CD 1860.

WRIGHT, GEORGE FREDERICK (1828–1881). Portrait painter, born December 19, 1828, in Washington (Conn.). After taking up painting professionally, he first settled in Wallingford (Conn.) and for a short time was custodian of the Wadsworth Atheneum Gallery at Hartford. After a year of study at the National Academy, about 1848, he returned to Hartford. About 1857 he went abroad for two years, studying in Baden and Rome. By 1860 he was back in the United States and in September of that year he went out to Springfield (Ill.) to paint the portrait of the Republican nominee for the presidency, Abraham Lincoln. He painted a second portrait of Lincoln at Washington later that year. Wright also worked in the South, but most of his time was spent in Hartford, where he died in 1881. ¶ French, *Art and Artists in Connecticut,* 137; Wilson, *Lincoln in Portraiture;* New England

BD 1849; Hartford BD 1851, CD 1855; Cowdrey, NAD; Met. Mus., *Life in America; Antiques* (Feb. 1948), 93, repro.; *Mag. of Art* (Feb. 1948), 71, repro.

WRIGHT, JAMES. Banknote engraver of NYC, with the firm of DANFORTH, WRIGHT & COMPANY, 1853–59. In 1857 his home was in Orange (N.J.). ¶ NYCD 1853–59.

WRIGHT, JAMES D. Portrait painter of Terre Haute (Ind.). He exhibited at the Indiana State Fair in 1857 and was listed at Terre Haute in 1860 and 1868. He also worked at Zionsville (Ind.) about 1860. ¶ Peat, *Pioneer Painters of Indiana,* 42; Indiana BD 1860.

WRIGHT, JAMES HENRY (1813–1883). Still life, landscape, marine, and portrait painter. The earliest notice of his activity was at New Orleans in July 1836, but from 1842 he was working in and around NYC. He was a native of New York State and died in Brooklyn. He was a frequent exhibitor at the National Academy and the American Art-Union. ¶ D'Otrange, "James H. Wright, 19th Century New York Painter," one repro.; Smith; Delgado-WPA cites *Bee,* July 6, 1836; 8 Census (1860), N.Y., XLIX, 984; Cowdrey, NAD; Cowdrey, AA & AAU; *Art Digest* (Sept. 1945), 12.

WRIGHT, JEFFERSON or T. JEFFERSON (1798–1846). Portrait painter who worked in Virginia (Culpeper, 1831–32), Kentucky, and Texas (Houston, 1837–42). He painted a portrait of Sam Houston in 1838. ¶ Willis, "Jefferson County Portraits and Portrait Painters"; O'Brien, *Art and Artists of Texas* (cited in Barker, *American Painting,* 454); Williams and Barber *Writings of Sam Houston,* II, 190–91, and III, 236.

WRIGHT, JOHN. Engraver, 42, born in New York State, at NYC in 1860. ¶ 8 Census (1860), N.Y., L, 183.

WRIGHT, JOSEPH (1756–1793). Portrait painter, modeler in clay and wax, medallist, die sinker and etcher. The only son of Joseph and PATIENCE LOVELL WRIGHT, Joseph was born at Bordentown (N.J.) on July 16, 1756. After his father's death in 1769, his mother moved to NYC and opened a waxworks and in 1772 she went to England, leaving Joseph in school in Philadelphia. Later, he and his sisters joined Mrs. Wright in London, where he learned to model under his mother and to paint under WEST and his brother-in-law John Hoppner. He exhibited at the Royal Academy in 1780 and in 1782, after a brief visit to Paris, returned to his native land. Soon after his arrival in America, Wright painted Washington's portrait at Princeton and later he made at least two other portraits from life as well as a clay bust. From 1783 to 1786 he was in Philadelphia and from 1786 until 1790 he was in NYC. The last three years of his life were spent in Philadelphia where he died during the yellow fever epidemic of 1793. ¶ DAB; Kimball, "Joseph Wright and His Portraits of Washington," ten repros.; Perrine, *The Wright Family of Oyster Bay,* 89–92; Loubat, *Medallic History of the U. S.,* pl. 6; Dunlap, *History;* Prime, II, 39; Gottesman, II, 60a, 108, 1286; Storer, "The Manly-Washington Medal"; Swan, BA; Rutledge, PA; Graves, *Dictionary;* Morgan and Fielding, *Life Portraits of Washington.*

WRIGHT & MALLORY. Wood engravers, Boston, 1840–52, successors to CHANDLER, WRIGHT & MALLORY. The partners were EDWARD WRIGHT and RICHARD P. MALLORY. ¶ Boston CD 1836–51, BD 1841–52.

WRIGHT, MOSES, see MOSES WIGHT.

WRIGHT, NEZIAH. Banknote engraver of NYC. He was with RAWDON, WRIGHT & COMPANY and its successors from 1828 to 1858 and then with the AMERICAN BANK NOTE COMPANY. He was born in New Hampshire about 1804. ¶ NYCD 1828–60; 7 Census (1850), N.Y., LV, 423.

WRIGHT, PATIENCE LOVELL (1725–1786). Wax modeller. Born in Bordentown (N.J.), Patience Lovell married Joseph Wright in 1748 and had four children: ELIZABETH, who became a wax modeller; JOSEPH, who became a modeller and painter; Phebe, who married the English artist John Hoppner; and Sarah. After her husband's death in 1769, Mrs. Wright opened a waxworks in NYC with her sister, RACHEL WELLS. In 1772 she went to England and opened a waxworks in London which became very popular. Her wax busts and figures were much admired and her wax statue of Lord Chatham was placed in Westminster Abbey. During the Revolution Mrs. Wright acted as a spy for the Americans. She died March 23, 1786. ¶ Lesley, "Patience Lovell Wright, America's First Sculptor," four repros.; DAB; Hart, "Patience Wright, Modeller in Wax"; Bolton, *American Wax Portraits;* Wall, "Wax Portraiture," 5–13.

WRIGHT & PRENTISS. "Xylographic" and copperplate engravers and printers, NYC, 1835–38. The partners were CHARLES CUSHING WRIGHT and, probably, NATHANIEL SMITH PRENTISS. ¶ NYCD 1835–38.

WRIGHT, RUFUS (1832–?). Portrait and figure painter. He was born in Cleveland (Ohio), studied at the school of the National Academy and under GEORGE AUGUSTUS BAKER, JR., in NYC. He apparently made a trip west during the fifties, for SARONY, MAJOR & KNAPP published in 1859 a view of Davenport (Iowa) drawn by Wright, and he seems also to have painted a panorama of the Mormons about this time. In 1860 he was living in NYC and most of his career was passed there, in Brooklyn, and in Washington (D.C.). ¶ CAB; *Portfolio* (Oct. 1946), 41; Schick, *Early Theatre in Eastern Iowa,* 270 (citation courtesy J. Earl Arrington); NYBD 1860.

WRIGHTSON, A. Landscape painter at NYC in 1857 when he exhibited at the National Academy. ¶ Cowdrey, NAD.

WRIT, R. W. Painter of an oil portrait of Sylvanus Thayer, owned by Dartmouth College, Hanover (N.H.). ¶ WPA (Mass.), *Portraits Found in N.H.,* 22.

WUESTE, LOUISE HEUSER (1803–1875). Portrait painter, born in Gummersbach-on-Rhine (Germany). She came to Texas with her husband, Leopold Wueste, and settled at San Antonio about 1852. She died at Eagle Pass (Tex.) in 1875. ¶ O'Brien, *Art and Artists of Texas,* 19.

WUNDER, ADALBERT (1827–?). Portraitist in oils, crayon, and india-ink. He was born in Berlin (Germany) on February 5, 1827, and began his art studies there at the age of sixteen, later spending two years at the Dresden Academy. He came to America in 1855 and settled in Hartford (Conn.) where he was well known for his portraits in crayon and ink. In 1869 he left Hartford for Hamilton (Ont.). ¶ French, *Art and Artists in Connecticut,* 136; Hartford CD 1856–57; Cowdrey, NAD; Bolton, *Crayon Draftsmen.*

WUNDERLICH, GEORGE. Landscape and historical painter, born in Pennsylvania about 1826. He was active in Philadelphia during the 1850's and 1860's, exhibiting at the Pennsylvania Academy frequently from 1853 to 1868. In 1854 he exhibited a series of moving paintings illustrative of American History. ¶ 7 Census (1850), Pa., LII, 609 [as George Wonderly]; Phila. CD 1852–61; Rutledge, PA; Phila. *Public Ledger,* Dec. 13 and 22, 1854 (citation courtesy J. Earl Arrington).

WURMS, GOTTLIEB. Engraver from Württemberg, aged 34, living in Philadelphia in 1860 with his German-born wife and three children (two to eight) born in Pennsylvania. ¶ 8 Census (1860), Pa., LIV, 306.

WURMSKI, General ——. Silhouettist, at Philadelphia in the 1840's. He is said to have been an emigré Polish patriot. ¶ *Antiques* (March 1949), 216, repros.

WURZBACH, W. Wood engraver, Boston, 1853–54, and NYC, 1858. Hamilton records examples of his work in books published between 1854 and 1881. ¶ Boston BD 1853–54; NYCD 1858; Hamilton, *Early American Book Illustrators and Wood Engravers,* 160, 179, 432, 487.

WUST, ALEXANDER (1837–1876). A.N.A. Landscape painter. A native of Dordrecht (Netherlands), Wust came to America in the late 1850's and had a studio in NYC from 1858 at least until 1869, during which time he exhibited views in the northeastern United States and Europe at the National and Pennsylvania Academies. He later returned to Europe and died at Antwerp (Belgium) in 1876. ¶ Mallett; NYBD 1858; Cowdrey, NAD; Rutledge, PA; represented by "Morning in the Catskills" in Pawtucket Club, Haverhill (Mass.).

WYAND, GEORGE. Pennsylvania-born engraver, 20, who was an inmate of the Pennsylvania Hospital for the Insane, Philadelphia, in October 1860. ¶ 8 Census (1860), Pa., LX, 796.

WYANT, ALEXANDER HELWIG (1836–1892). N.A. Landscape painter, born January 11, 1836, at Evans Creek, Tuscarawas County (Ohio). He was apprenticed to a harness maker but at the age of 21 decided to become a painter. On the advice of GEORGE INNESS, whom he went to see in NYC, he sought the patronage of Nicholas Longworth of Cincinnati and was enabled to study for a year at the National Academy and in 1865 at Düsseldorf. His stay in Germany was short, however, and he opened a studio in NYC. In 1873 he suffered a paralytic stroke which forced him to learn to paint with his left hand. During the remaining years of his life he worked during winter in NYC and in the summer at Keene Valley (N.Y.) and after 1889 at Arkville in the Catskills. He died in NYC on November 29, 1892. ¶ Clark, *Alexander Wyant;* DAB; Swan, BA; Rutledge, PA; *Panorama* (Jan. 1947), 55, repro.; *Magazine of Art* (Nov. 1946), 289, repro.; *Art Digest* (Aug. 1, 1936), 10, repro.

WYBRANT, ——. Portrait painter in watercolors, Gloucester (Mass.), about 1850. ¶ Lipman and Winchester, 182.

WYCKOFF, ISABEL DUNHAM. Flower painter, active about 1840. She was the maternal grandmother of the artists Ida, Catherine, and Georgia O'Keeffe. ¶ *Art Digest* (April 1, 1933), 27.

WYDEVELD, ARNOUD. Still life and genre painter working in NYC from 1855 to about 1862. He exhibited at the Washington Art Association in 1857 as Wydefield and in 1859 as Wydefeldt; at the National Academy in 1859 as Wideveld; and at the Pennsylvania Academy in 1862 as A. Wydevelde. ¶ NYCD 1855–58; Washington Art Assoc. Cat., 1857, 1859; Cowdrey, NAD; Rutledge, PA.

WYETH, FRANCIS. Lithographer, Boston, 1832–33. ¶ Peters, *America on Stone.*

WYETH, P. C. Portrait painter who was living in NYC in 1846 when he exhibited at the National Academy. From 1849 to 1851 he was at Cincinnati, and in 1852 he painted a group portrait of the children of Charles L. Shrewsbury at Madison (Ind.). The last record of him is in 1858 when he was living in Brooklyn and again exhibited at the National Academy. ¶ Cowdrey, NAD; Peat, *Pioneer Painters of Indiana,* 61 and pl. 23.

WYLIE, ROBERT (1839–1877). Genre painter and sculptor. Born on the Isle of Man (England) in 1839, he was brought to America as a child. From 1859 to 1862 he was a student at the Pennsylvania Academy, in whose exhibitions he exhibited work in ivory and clay. In 1863 he went to France where he spent the rest of his life. He was known chiefly as a painter of Breton peasant scenes. He died in Brittany on February 4, 1877. ¶ CAB; Clement and Hutton; Rutledge, PA; represented in Corcoran Gallery and Peabody Institute.

WYMAN, JOHN. Artist, 40, a native of New York State but living in Philadelphia in 1860. The Philadelphia directories list him as a ventriloquist (1852–54), daguerreotypist (1855), and artist (1856–61). ¶ 8 Census (1860), Pa., LVIII, 114; Phila. CD 1852–61.

WYSE, F. H. Engraver, NYC, 1846. Possibly the H. Wyse of Albany who exhibited two specimens of engraving at the American Institute in 1849. ¶ NYBD 1846; Am. Inst. Cat., 1849.

WYSZYNSKI, EUSTACE. Lithographer, NYC, 1845–52. In 1845–46, with RUDOLPH DOLANOWSKI. ¶ NYCD 1845–52; NYBD 1846.

WYTHE, J. Portrait painter of NYC who exhibited at the National Academy in 1852. ¶ Cowdrey, NAD.

X

XÁNTUS, JÁNOS (1825–1894). Topographical artist. Born October 5, 1825, in Csokonya (Hungary), Xántus studied law and served in the ill-fated Rebellion of 1848. Making his escape to the United States in 1851, he became a topographer with one of the Pacific Railroad Surveys in 1852 and again in 1855. He also served with the U. S. Coast Survey in California and commanded a Navy meteorological expedition in the Pacific and for several years after 1861 he was U. S. Consul at Manzanillo (Mexico). While he was in California he made important contributions to the study of Western birds and several new species were named for him. In 1864 Xántus returned to Hungary permanently and became keeper of the ethnographical division of the National Museum in Budapest, which position he held until his death on December 13, 1894. He published two books on his American experiences, illustrated with his own sketches: *Levelei Ejszakamerikából* (Pest, 1858) and *Utazás Kalifornia déli Részeiben* (Pest, 1860). ¶ DAB.

Y

YARNELL, D. F. "Fancy sign painter" at Shreve (Ohio) in 1847. ¶ Knittle, *Early Ohio Taverns,* 45.

YATES, Mrs. ——. Miniature painter of Philadelphia who exhibited several originals and copies at the Artists' Fund Society in 1835. ¶ Rutledge, PA.

YEAGER, EDWARD. Portrait, historical, and map engraver on copper, steel, and wood, active in Philadelphia during the 1840's and 1850's. ¶ Phila. CD 1840–59.

YEAGER, JOSEPH (*c.* 1792–1859). Engraver. Probably a native of Philadelphia, Yeager worked there as an engraver from about 1809 to about 1849. Half of his known work consists of etched portraits and the other half of line engraved views of scenery and buildings. He was also a printseller and publisher of children's books. In 1848 he became president of the Harrisburg & Lancaster Railroad, later absorbed into the Pennsylvania system. Yeager died in Philadelphia, June 9, 1859. ¶ DAB; Stauffer; Phila. CD 1816–47; *Antiques* (Aug. 1928), 130, repro.

YEARSLEY, JOSEPH. Delaware-born lithographer, 26, at Philadelphia in 1860. His wife and two small children were born in Pennsylvania. ¶ 8 Census (1860), Pa., XXVI, 221.

YENNI, see JOHANN HEINRICH JENNY.

YEOMANS, GEORGE. Delineator of a view of Williamstown (Mass.) lithographed by P. S. DUVAL & Co. at Philadelphia, about 1855–56. ¶ Stokes, *Historical Prints.*

YEWELL, GEORGE HENRY (1830–1923). N.A. Portrait and genre painter, born January 20, 1830, in Havre-de-Grace (Md.). Part of his childhood was spent in Iowa, but in 1851 he came east again to study at the National Academy for five years. In 1856 he went to Paris to study under Thomas Couture and he later married and settled in Rome. In 1875 he visited Egypt. Returning to NYC in 1878 he made his home there until his retirement to Lake George (N.Y.), where he died September 26, 1923. Although he painted genre and architectural subjects early in his career, he was best known as a portrait painter. He was an Associate of the National Academy from 1862 to 1880 when he became an Academician. ¶ Ness and Orwig, *Iowa Artists of the First Hundred Years,* 227; Cowdrey, NAD; Clark, *History of the NAD;* Swan, BA; Rutledge, PA.

YON or YOU, THOMAS. Engraver, gold- and silversmith, and jeweler working in Charleston (S.C.) 1764–68. He engraved views of St. Michael's Church and St. Philip's Church. ¶ Prime, I, 33 [as Yon]; Rutledge, *Artists in the Life of Charleston* [as You].

YONGE, ——. Painter of a miniature of a Mrs. Hopton, presumably of South Carolina, dated 1771. ¶ Carolina Art Assoc. Cat., 1935.

YOUNG, Rev. ——. Watercolor and ink portraitist said to have been active in Center County (Pa.) from about 1825 to 1840. ¶ Lipman and Winchester, 182.

YOUNG, Miss ——. Landscape painter, Chicago, 1856. A Miss Young from New York State, aged 18, was listed as an engraver in the 1850 Census of Cleveland (Ohio). ¶ Chicago CD 1856; 7 Census (1850), Ohio, XI, 450.

YOUNG, ALEXANDER. Terra cotta maker of NYC who exhibited "one figure, one corbel and Gothic cap [and] one full-trimmed Elizabethan window" at the American Institute in 1851. ¶ Am. Inst. Cat., 1851; NYCD 1851.

YOUNG, ANDREW. Apprentice lithographer, 20, a native of Pennsylvania, at Philadelphia in 1860. His parents, James and Mary Young, were both Irish. ¶ 8 Census (1860), Pa., LIV, 253.

YOUNG, AUGUST (1837–1913). Portrait and historical painter of Brooklyn (N.Y.). He was born July 8, 1837, either in NYC of German parents (Stiles) or in Germany (*Art Annual* and N. Y. *Times*). After studying with JUNIUS BRUTUS STEARNS and THEODORE KAUFMAN and at the National Academy, Young went to Europe about 1853. After three years in Munich and Paris he returned to NYC and took instruction in watercolors from J. B. WANDESFORDE. He settled in Brooklyn in 1860 and there spent the rest of his career. He died in Brooklyn on November 6, 1913. ¶ Stiles, *History of King's County,* II, 1160–61; *Art Annual,* XI, obit.; N. Y. *Times,* Nov. 9, 1913, obit.; Brooklyn *Eagle,* Nov. 7, 1913, obit.; Cowdrey, NAD; NYCD 1856, 1858; Brooklyn CD 1904.

YOUNG, B. Painter of a portrait of a hunter,

inscribed on the back: "J. G. Henry [?] by B. Young 1838." ¶ Sherman, "Newly Discovered American Portrait Painters," 235.

YOUNG & DELLEKER. Engravers, Philadelphia, 1822–23; JAMES H. YOUNG and GEORGE DELLEKER. Also known as Delleker & Young. ¶ Phila. CD 1822–23.

YOUNG, GUSTAV. Artist, Baltimore, 1812. ¶ Lafferty.

YOUNG, HARVEY B. (1840–1901). Landscape painter, born in Post Mills (Vt.). He went to Colorado in 1859 as a prospector and artist. During the seventies he studied in Paris under Carolus Duran, exhibiting at the Salon in 1878. Much of his professional career was spent in California. He died May 14, 1901, in Colorado Springs. ¶ *Art Annual,* IV, obit.; Clement and Hutton.

YOUNG, JAMES H. Engraver active in Philadelphia from 1817–66. He was associated in business with WILLIAM KNEASS (1818–20) and GEORGE DELLEKER (1822–23). ¶ Brown and Brown; Phila. CD 1817–66.

YOUNG, J. H. A. Engraver, 30, a native of Prussia, at Washington (D.C.) in 1860. His wife was from New York and their son John, aged 2, was born in Washington. ¶ 8 Census (1860), D.C., I, 599.

YOUNG, JAMES HARVEY (1830–1918). Portrait painter, born June 14, 1830, in Salem (Mass.). He studied architecture but as early as 1848 opened a portrait studio in Boston where he spent most of his life. He died in Brookline in 1918. Examples of his work are in the American Antiquarian Society and the Essex Institute, the latter owning a self-portrait. ¶ Essex Institute, *Cat. of Portraits,* 258; Swan, BA; Sears, *Some American Primitives,* 85–86, repro. p. 68; 8 Census (1860), Mass., XXVI, 488; Rutledge, PA; Boston BD 1858–60; Essex Institute *Historical Collections,* LXXXVI (April 1950), 172–74.

YOUNG, JOHN J. (*c.* 1830–1879). Topographical draftsman and painter who accompanied the Williamson-Abbot railroad survey of northern California and Oregon in 1855. The report of this expedition, Vol. VI of *Reports of Explorations and Surveys,* contains a number of illustrations from his drawings. He also illustrated, probably from the drawings of others, several other reports of surveys of the late fifties. During the sixties and seventies Young's name appears in Washington directories as draftsman for the War Department, topographical engineer, and engraver. He died in Washington on October 13, 1879, at the age of 49. ¶ Taft, *Artists and Illustrators of the Old West,* 267–68.

YOUNG, JOHN L. Lithographer, 29, at Baltimore in 1850. He was a native of Maryland. ¶ 7 Census (1850), Md., V, 832.

YOUNG, JOHN T. (*c.* 1814–1842). Landscape artist working in and around Rochester (N.Y.) from about 1835 to 1842. He illustrated Henry O'Reilly's *Sketches of Rochester* (1838) and also drew a view of the upper Genesee Falls which was lithographed. He died in Rochester on September 7, 1842, at the age of 28. ¶ Taft, *Artists and Illustrators of the Old West,* 268; Ulp, "Art and Artists of Rochester"; Stokes, *Historical Prints* and Peters, *America on Stone* list him as J. Young [not to be confused with JOHN J. YOUNG].

YOUNG, MARY ELIZA, see Mrs. ELIZA WAUGH.

YOUNG, PHILIP. Artist, Cincinnati, 1836. ¶ Cincinnati CD 1836 (courtesy Edward H. Dwight, Cincinnati Art Museum).

YOUNG, THOMAS. Portrait and miniature painter who painted likenesses of several prominent citizens of Providence (R.I.) between 1817 and 1840. ¶ Fielding; information courtesy Dr. H. W. Williams, Jr., Corcoran Gallery.

YOUNG, THOMAS A. (1837–1913). Landscape painter. A native of London (England), he had been a resident of Flatbush, Brooklyn (N.Y.) for over fifty years at the time of his death in November 14, 1913. Not to be confused with AUGUST YOUNG (1837–1913), also a Brooklyn artist. ¶ *Art Annual,* XI, obit.; Brooklyn CD 1890, 1904, 1912.

YOUNG, TOBIAS. Painter of two views in NYC about 1824. ¶ Stokes, *Iconography,* VI, pl. 96a-b.

YOUNGLOVE, ELBRIDGE G. Artist of Buffalo (N.Y.), 1856–59. ¶ Buffalo BD 1856, CD 1857–59.

Z

ZABRESKI, see ZAKRESKI.

ZACHRESKY, see ZAKRESKI.

ZAHN, EDWARD. Lithographer, NYC, 1854. ¶ NYBD 1854.

ZAHNER, RALPH. Artist from Prussia, 25, at NYC in August 1850. ¶ 7 Census (1850), N.Y., XLIV, 270.

ZAKRESKI (Zabreski, Zachresky), ALEXANDER. Lithographer and topographical draftsman working in San Francisco from 1850 to 1858. In 1850 he was associated with one Hartman, probably J. W. HARTMAN. In 1858 he was listed as a draftsman with the Surveyor General's Office. ¶ Peters, *California on Stone;* San Francisco CD 1850–58.

ZAVYTOWSKY, A. Polish artist, 24, at New Orleans in 1850 with his English wife and another couple, also English, Mr. and Mrs. B. DE BAR. ¶ 7 Census (1850), La., IV, 465.

ZELIFF, A. E. Painter of genre and still life, Essex County (N.J.), about 1850. ¶ Lipman and Winchester, 182; repro., Garbisch Collection, Catalogue, 103.

ZELL, CHRISTIAN. Lithographer, Philadelphia, 1859. ¶ Phila. BD 1859.

ZENON, GORA. Professor of drawing at Mandeville College, Louisiana, in 1844. ¶ New Orleans *Bee,* March 22, 1844 (Delgado-WPA).

ZIEGLER, GEORGE FREDERICK. Engraver, NYC, 1857–58. ¶ NYBD 1857–58.

ZIEGLER, H. Painter of watercolor portraits about 1840. ¶ Lipman and Winchester, 182.

ZIGLER, JOHN. Engraver, 23, a native of Pennsylvania, at Philadelphia in 1850. ¶ 7 Census (1850), Pa., XLIX, 583.

ZIMMER, ——. Of Zimmer & Droz, lithographers and engravers at New Orleans in 1833. Zimmer was the lithographer and A. DROZ the engraver. ¶ New Orleans *Courier,* Jan. 25, 1833, and *Bee,* June 3, 1833 (Delgado-WPA).

KEY TO CITATIONS OF SOURCES

INCLUDED in this key are all books (except directories), pamphlets, articles, periodicals, newspapers, and unpublished manuscripts cited as sources in the *Dictionary*. They are listed alphabetically *as cited.*

Directories of states, counties, cities, and towns have been used extensively but, with the exception of classified business directories, they have been combed systematically only for particular artists. In directory citations the abbreviations CD and BD following the name of the city or state (*e.g.*, Chicago CD, Boston BD) refer to City Directory (alphabetical by name) and Business Directory (alphabetical by business or trade). Since the titles of directories varied from year to year, they have not been listed in the Key to Citations. Directories for the following localities have been cited and are available for consultation at the Library of Congress, New York Public Library, or New-York Historical Society:

Albany, N.Y.; Baltimore, Md.; Boston, Mass.; Brooklyn, N.Y.; Buffalo, N.Y.; Cambridge, Mass.; Chicago, Ill.; Cincinnati, O.; Cleveland, O.; Council Bluffs, Ia.; Davenport, Ia., Moline and Rock Island, Ill.; Detroit, Mich.; Dover, N.H.; Elmira, N.Y.; Essex, Hudson, and Union Counties, N.J.; Fall River, Mass. and R.I.; Hamilton, O.; Hartford, Conn.; Indianapolis, Ind.; Lawrence, Mass.; Long Island, N.Y.; Louisville, Ky.; Lowell, Mass.; Madison, Wis.; Maine; Manchester, N.H.; Massachusetts; Milwaukee, Wis.; Mobile, Ala.; Montgomery, Ala.; Nashua, N.H.; Nashville, Tenn.; New Brunswick, N.J.; New England; New Haven, Conn.; New Jersey; New Orleans, La.; New York, N.Y.; New York State; Newark, N.J.; Newburyport, Mass.; Norristown, Pa.; Norwich, Conn.; Ohio; Oswego, N.Y.; Pawtucket and Woonsocket, R.I.; Pennsylvania; Philadelphia, Pa.; Pittsburgh, Pa.; Portland, Me.; Providence, R.I.; Rochester, N.Y.; Rome, N.Y.; Saco and Biddeford, Me.; St. Louis, Mo.; Sandusky, O.; San Francisco, Cal.; Schenectady, N.Y.; Springfield, Ill.; Springfield, Mass.; Springfield, O.; Syracuse, N.Y.; Taunton, Mass.; Troy, N.Y.; Utica, N.Y.; Washington and Georgetown, D.C.; Worcester, Mass.

Individuals who have contributed information used in the dictionary (cited as: Information courtesy of . . .) are included in the Acknowledgments.

In using all these sources, primary and secondary, the authors have in general relied on the accuracy of documented studies and checked wherever possible on undocumented work. It should be emphasized, however, that citation of a source does not imply a guarantee of its accuracy. The reader, like the authors, must exercise his own critical judgment in each case.

A

Abert, James William, "Journal . . . Aug. 9–Nov. 12, 1845," 29 Cong., 1 Sess., *Senate Exec. Doc.* 438.

Abraham, Evelyn, "David G. Blythe, American Painter and Woodcarver," *Antiques,* XXVII, May 1935, 180–3.

Adams, Adeline V., *John Quincy Adams Ward: An Appreciation . . . ,* New York, 1912.

Addison, Agnes, ed., *Portraits in the University of Pennsylvania,* Philadelphia, 1940.

Addison, Julia DeWolf, "Henry Sargent, a Boston Painter," *Art in America,* XVII, Oct. 1929, 279–84.

Admiralty-Office, *List of the Flag Officers and Other Commissioned Officers of His Majesty's Fleet . . . ,* London, 1818.

Agate, Grace B., "Joseph Jefferson, Painter of the Teche," *National Historical Magazine,* LXXII, Nov. 1938, 23–5.

Agricultural Intelligencer, Boston newspaper.

Alabama, Dep't of Archives and History, *Alabama Legislature Declares Nicola Marschall Designer First Confederate Flag . . . ,* Montgomery, 1931; Historical and Patriotic Series No. 12.

Albany Argus, newspaper.

[Albany] *The Balance and New York State Journal,* newspaper.

Albee, John, *Henry Dexter, Sculptor . . . ,* Cambridge, 1898.

Album of American Battle Art, 1755–1918, Washington, 1947.

Alden, H. M., "Charles Parsons," *Harper's Weekly;* LIV, Nov. 19, 1910, 21.

Alexander, Constance G., *Francesca Alexander . . . ,* Cambridge, 1927.

Allen, Charles Dexter, *A Classified List of Early American Book Plates . . . ,* New York, 1894.

Allen, Edward B., *Early American Wall Paintings, 1710–1850,* New Haven, 1926.

Allen, Virginia W., "Winged Skull and Weeping Willow," *Antiques,* XXIX, June 1936, 250–3.

Allen Memorial Art Museum Bulletin, Oberlin, O., 1944—.

Allison, Anne, "Peter Pelham, Engraver in Mezzotinto," *Antiques,* LII, Dec. 1947, 441–3.

American Academy of Fine Arts [New York], annual exhibition catalogues, 1816–35 [indexed in Cowdrey, *American Academy of Fine Arts and American Art-Union,* II].

American Advertising Directory, New York, 1831–32.

American-Anderson Art Galleries, Sales Cat., April 2–3, 1937. American Art Association-Anderson Galleries, Inc., Catalogue No. 4314, "American Furniture and Silver . . . Portraits . . . from the Collection of Herbert Lawton . . . ," New York, 1937.

American Art Review, Boston, 1880–81.

American Art-Union [New York] publications include the *Bulletin* (1848–53), the *Transactions* (1844–52), and annual exhibition catalogues (1844–52). These are listed in full in Cowdrey, *American Academy and American Art-Union,* I, 246–85, and the catalogues indexed in Vol. II of the same work.

American Battle Painting, 1776–1918. Catalogue, with text by Lincoln Kirstein, of an exhibition at the National Gallery of Art, Washington, and the Museum of Modern Art, New York, in 1944.

American Collector, New York, 1933–48.

American Folk Art; A Collection of Paintings and Sculpture . . . the Gift of Mrs. John D. Rockefeller, Jr., to Colonial Williamsburg . . . , Williamsburg, 1940.

American Heritage, American Association of State and Local History, 1947—.

American Institute of the City of the New York: catalogues of the annual fairs, New York, 1842, 1844–51, 1856; *Fifth Annual Report . . . ,* Albany, 1847; *List of Premiums Awarded by the Managers of the 24th Annual Fair . . . ,* New York, 1852; *Transactions . . . for the Year 1856,* Albany, 1857.

American Museum Journal, New York, American Museum of Natural History, 1900–18.

American Paintings in the Corcoran Gallery of Art, Handbook of the, comp. by E. B. Swenson, Washington, 1947.

American Primitive Painting, Nineteenth Century; The Chicago Historical Society's Collection, Chicago, 1950.

American Processional. U. S. National Capitol Sesquicentennial Commission, *American Processional, 1492–1900,* Washington, 1950.

American Provincial Paintings, 1680–1860, from the Collection of J. Stuart Halladay and Herrel George Thomas . . . , Pittsburgh, 1941.

Amesbury, Mass. *Vital Records of Amesbury, Mass., to the End of the Year 1849,* Topsfield, Mass., 1913.

Analectic Magazine, Philadelphia, 1813–20.

Anderson, Edward P., "The Intellectual Life of Pittsburgh, 1786–1836: VIII, Painting," *Western Pennsylvania Historical Magazine,* XIV, Oct. 1931, 288–93.

Andes, Martin L., "Augustus Neynabor, Chester County Folk Artist," *Chester County* [Pa.] *Collections,* No. 9, Jan. 1938, 335–6.

Andrews, Wayne, "The Baroness Was Never Bored: The Baroness Hyde de Neuville's Sketches of American Life 1807–1822," *New-York Historical Society Quarterly,* XXXVIII, April 1954, 105–17.

Angle, Paul M., "Jevne and Almini," *Chicago History,* I, Spring 1948, 313–16.

Annals of San Francisco, by Frank Soulé, John H. Gihon, and James Nisbet, New York, 1855.

Antiques, New York, 1922—.

Antiques Journal, Mount Vernon, O., 1946—.

Apollo; A Journal of the Arts, London, 1925—.

Apollo Association [New York], annual exhibition catalogues, 1839–43 [described and indexed in Cowdrey, *American Academy and American Art-Union*].

——— *Transactions,* 1839–43 [described in Cowdrey, *American Academy and American Art-Union,* I, 243–6].

Appleton's Journal of Literature, Science and Art, New York, 1869–79.

Architect and Engineer, San Francisco, 1905—.

Architectural Review, Boston, 1891–1921.

Ariel; A Semimonthly Literary and Miscellaneous Gazette, Philadelphia, 1827–32.

Arkansas Gazette, Little Rock newspaper.

Armstrong, David M., *Day Before Yesterday . . .* , New York, 1920.

Arnold, John N., *Art and Artists in Rhode Island,* Providence, 1905.

Arrington, J. Earl, "Leon D. Pomarede's Original Panorama of the Mississippi River," *Missouri Historical Society Bulletin,* IX, April 1953, 261–73.

——— "Nauvoo Temple," unpublished manuscript.

——— "Samuel A. Hudson's Panorama of the Ohio and Mississippi Rivers," unpublished manuscript.

——— "Samuel B. Stockwell and His Mississippi Panorama," unpublished manuscript.

——— "The Story of Stockwell's Panorama," *Minnesota History,* XXXIII, Autumn 1953, 284–90.

L'Art; Revue Illustrée, Paris, 1875–1907.

"Art and Artists in Manchester," *Manchester* [N.H.] *Historic Association Collections,* IV, Part I (1908), 109–28.

Art Annual. American Art Annual, Florence N. Levy, ed., Washington, 1898—.

Art Digest, New York, 1926—.

Art in America, New York, 1913—.

Art Index . . . , edited by Beatrice B. Rakestraw and Margaret Furlong, New York, 1929—.

Art Journal, London, 1849–1912.

Art News, New York, 1902—.

Art Quarterly, Detroit, 1938—.

Arthur, Helen, "Thomas Sparrow, an Early Maryland Engraver," *Antiques,* LV, Jan. 1949, 44–5.

Artists' Fund Society of Philadelphia, annual exhibition catalogues, 1835–45 [described and indexed in Rutledge, *Cumulative Record of Exhibition Catalogues . . .*].

Artists Year Book; A Handy Reference Book Wherein May Be Found Interesting Data Pertaining to Artists . . . , ed. by Arthur N. Hosking, Chicago, 1905.

Association of the Graduates of the U. S. Military Academy, *Annual Reunion,* 1896.

Audubon, John Woodhouse, *Audubon's Western Journal: 1849–50 . . .* , Cleveland, 1906.

Audubon, Maria Rebecca, *Audubon and His Journals . . .* , New York, 1897.

Aurora, Philadelphia newspaper.

Averill, Esther C., "Early Weather-vanes Made in Many Styles and Forms," *American Collector,* II, Aug. 9, 1934, 7.

Avery, Lillian Drake, *A Genealogy of the Ingersoll Family in America, 1629–1925 . . .* , New York, 1926.

B

Bachman, C. L., ed., *John Bachman . . . the Pastor of St. John's Lutheran Church, Charleston,* Charleston, 1888.

Bagg, M. M., ed., *Memorial History of Utica, N.Y.,* Syracuse, 1892.

Baker, C. H. Collins, "Notes on Joseph

Blackburn and Nathaniel Dance," *Huntington Library Quarterly,* IX, Nov. 1945, 33–47.
Baker, Charles E., "The Story of Two Silhouettes," *New-York Historical Society Quarterly,* XXXI, Oct. 1947, 218–28.
Baker, George Holbrook, "Records of a California Journey," *Society of California Pioneers Quarterly,* VII, Dec. 1930, 217–43.
——— "Records of a California Residence," *Society of California Pioneers Quarterly,* VIII, March 1931, 39–70.
Baker, Mary E., *Folklore of Springfield,* Springfield, Vt., 1922.
Baker, William S., *American Engravers and Their Works,* Philadelphia, 1875.
——— *The Engraved Portraits of Washington, with Notices of the Originals and Brief Biographical Sketches of the Painters,* Philadelphia, 1880.
Baldwin, Christopher Columbus, *Diary of Christopher Columbus Baldwin, Librarian of the American Antiquarian Society, 1829–1835,* Worcester, 1901.
Ball, Thomas, *My Three Score Years and Ten . . . ,* Boston, 1891.
Ballou, Adin, *An Elaborate History and Genealogy of the Ballous in America,* Providence, 1888.
Baltimore American, newspaper.
Baltimore Sun, newspaper.
Bancroft, Hubert Howe, *History of the Pacific States of North America,* Vol. XVII: *California, 1846–48,* San Francisco, 1886.
Bangor [Me.] *Historical Magazine,* Bangor, 1885–91; continued as *Maine Historical Magazine.*
Banvard; or, the Adventures of an Artist, Paternoster Road, London, n.d.
"Baptisms from 1639 to 1730 in the Reformed Dutch Church, N.Y.," *Collections of the New York Genealogical and Biographical Society,* II (1901), 228.
Barba, Preston A., *Balduin Möllhausen, the German Cooper,* Philadelphia, 1914.
Barber, Gertrude A., "Deaths Taken from the New York Evening Post, Nov. 16, 1801—Dec. 31, 1890," typed manuscript, 1933–47, a copy of which is in the library of the New-York Historical Society.
——— "Index of Letters of Administration of New York County from 1743 to 1875," typed manuscript, 1950–51, a copy of which is in the library of the New-York Historical Society.
Barber, John W., *The History and Antiquities of New England, New York, New Jersey, and Pennsylvania . . . ,* Hartford, 1856.
Barck, Dorothy C., "John Rogers, American Sculptor," *Old-Time New England,* XXIII, Jan. 1933, 99–114.
Barker, Virgil, *American Painting, History and Interpretation,* New York, 1950.
Barnouw, Adriaan Jacob, "A Life of Albertus Van Beest," *Rotterdam Year Book,* Rotterdam, Neth., 1919.
Barr, Lockwood, "William Faris, Annapolis Clockmaker," *Antiques,* XXXVII, April 1940, 174–6.
Bartholomew, George W., Jr., *Record of the Bartholomew Family,* Austin, 1885.
Bartholomew, Henry S. K., *Pioneer History of Elkhart, Ind.,* Goshen, 1930.
Bartlett, Joseph G., *Simon Stone Genealogy: Ancestry and Descendants of Deacon Simon Stone of Watertown, Mass., 1320–1926,* Boston, 1926.
Bartlett, John Russell, *Personal Narrative of Explorations and Incidents in Texas, New Mexico, California, Sonora, and Chihuahua . . . ,* New York and London, 1854.
Bartlett, Truman Howe, *The Art Life of William Rimmer, Sculptor, Painter and Physician,* Boston, 1882.
Bartlow, Bert S., and others, *Centennial History of Butler County, Ohio . . . ,* B. F. Bowen & Co., 1905.
Bassett, John Spencer, ed., *Correspondence of Andrew Jackson . . . ,* Washington, 1926–35.
Bates, Albert Carlos, *An Early Connecticut Engraver and His Work,* Hartford, 1906.
Bathe, Greville and Dorothy, *Jacob Perkins, His Inventions, His Times, and His Contemporaries,* Philadelphia, 1943.
Baur, John I. H., *An American Genre Painter: Eastman Johnson, 1824–1906,* Brooklyn Museum, 1940.
——— ed., "The Autobiography of Worthington Whittredge, 1820–1910," *Brooklyn Museum Journal,* I (1942), 5–68.
——— "Eastman Johnson, Artist-Reporter," *American Collector,* IX, Feb. 1940, 6–7.
——— *John Quidor, 1801–1881,* Brooklyn Museum, 1942.
——— "The Peales and the Development of American Still Life," *Art Quarterly,* III, Winter 1940, 81–92.
——— "A Romantic Impressionist: James Hamilton," *Brooklyn Museum Bulletin,* XII, Spring 1951, 1–9.
——— "A Tonal Realist: James Suydam," *Art Quarterly,* XIII, Summer 1950, 221–27.

——— "Unknown American Painters of the 19th Century," *College Art Journal,* VI, Summer 1947, 277–82.

Bayley, Frank W., "An Early New England Limner—Some Account of the Recently Discovered Portraits of Mr. and Mrs. Jeremiah Dummer, Painted by Him," *Old-Time New England,* XII, July 1921, 3–5.

——— *Little Known Early American Portrait Painters,* Boston, 1915–17; five pamphlets issued "with the compliments of the Copley Gallery, Boston."

Beardsley, Eben E., *Life and Times of William Samuel Johnson . . . ,* New York, 1876.

Beardsley, William A., "An Old New England Engraver and His Work: Amos Doolittle," *Papers of the New Haven Colony Historical Society,* VIII (1914), 132–50.

Beckwith, Lt. E. G., "Report of Exploration of a Route for the Pacific Railroad . . . from the Mouth of the Kansas to Sevier River, in the Great Basin," 33 Cong., 1 Sess., *House Exec. Doc.* 129.

Beckwith, Hiram Williams, *History of Montgomery County* [Ind.] . . . , Chicago, 1881.

Beers' *History of York County, Pa.,* by George R. Prowell, Chicago, J. H. Beers & Co., 1907.

Belknap, Henry W., *Artists and Craftsmen of Essex County, Mass.,* Salem, 1927.

Belknap, Waldron Phoenix, Jr., "The Identity of Robert Feke," *Art Bulletin,* XXIX, Sept. 1947, 201–7.

Bender, Horace, *see* Horatio Greenough.

Bénézit, Emmanuel, ed., *Dictionnaire Critique et Documentaire des Peintres, Sculpteurs, Dessinateurs et Graveurs . . . ,* Paris, 1911–23.

Benisovich, Michel N., "Roslin and Wertmüller, Some Unpublished Documents," *Gazette des Beaux Arts,* VI Ser., XXV, April 1944, 221–30.

——— "The Sale of the Studio of Adolph Ulrich Wertmüller," *Art Quarterly,* XVI, Spring 1953, 21–39.

Benjamin, Samuel G. W., "Fifty Years of American Art, 1828–1878," *Harper's New Monthly Magazine,* LIX, July 1879, 241–57; Sept. 1879, 481–96; Oct. 1879, 673–88.

——— *Our American Artists,* Boston, 1879.

Bennet, James O'Donnell, *The Mask of Fame; The Heritage of Historical Life Masks Made by John Browere, 1825 to 1833,* with Everett L. Millard, Highland Park, Ill., 1938.

Bennett, H. Selfe, "The Story of Two Old Prints," *Art in America,* VI, Aug. 1918, 240–8.

Bentley, William, *The Diary of William Bentley* [1784–1819], Salem, 1905–14.

Bermuda Historical Society, *Loan Exhibition of Portraits, XVII, XVIII, and XIX Centuries . . . ,* Hamilton, Bermuda, 1935.

Bernard du Hautcilly, Auguste, *Voyage Autour du Monde, Principalement à la Californie et aux Îles Sandwich, Pendant les Années 1826, 1827, 1828, et 1829,* Paris, 1834–35.

Biddle, Edward, and Mantle Fielding, *The Life and Works of Thomas Sully,* Philadelphia, 1921.

Bigot, Marie (Healy), *Life of George P. A. Healy, by His Daughter Mary (Madame Charles Bigot) followed by a Selection of His Letters* (n.p., n.d.).

Bingham, George Caleb, ". . . Letters of George Caleb Bingham to James S. Rollins," edited by C. B. Rollins, *Missouri Historical Review,* XXXII (1937–38), 3–34, 164–202, 340–77, 484–522; XXXIII (1938–39), 45–78, 203–29, 349–84, 499–526.

Biographical Record of Clark County, Ohio . . . , New York and Chicago, 1902.

Biographie Universelle, Paris, Mechaud Frères, 1811–62, 85 vols.

Bishop, Edith, *Oliver Tarbell Eddy 1799–1868. A Catalogue of His Works . . . in Connection with an Exhibition Shown at The Newark Museum, March 28–May 7, 1950, The Baltimore Museum of Art, May 28–June 25, 1950.*

Blanchard, Julian, "The Durand Engraving Companies," *Essay Proof Journal,* Nos. 26–8, April and July 1950, Jan. 1951.

Bland Galleries [New York], *Exhibition of Southern Genre Paintings by William Aiken Walker,* catalogue, Feb.–March 1940.

Bloch, E. Maurice, "The American Art-Union's Downfall," *New-York Historical Society Quarterly,* XXXVII, Oct. 1953, 331–59.

Bodley Book Shop, Catalogue No. 80: "Books with a Selection of Autograph Material" (1945).

Boggs, William E., *The Genealogical Record of the Boggs Family, the Descendants of Ezekiel Boggs,* Halifax, 1916.

Bolton, Charles Knowles, *The Founders;*

Portraits of Persons Born Abroad Who Came to the Colonies in North America before the Year 1701 . . . , Boston, 1919–26.

——— "Workers with Line and Color in New England," manuscript volume at the Boston Athenaeum.

Bolton, Ethel Stanwood, *American Wax Portraits,* Boston, 1929.

——— *Wax Portraits and Silhouettes,* Boston, 1914.

Bolton, Theodore, "Benjamin Trott," *Art Quarterly,* VII, Autumn 1944, 257–90.

——— "The Book Illustrations of F. O. C. Darley," *Proceedings of the American Antiquarian Society,* LXI, Part I, April 1951, 136–82.

——— "Charles Loring Elliott; An Account of his Life and Work" and "A Catalogue of the Portraits Painted by Charles Loring Elliott," *Art Quarterly,* V, Winter 1942, 59–96.

——— *Crayon Draftsmen.* Full title: *Early American Portrait Draughtsmen in Crayons,* New York, 1923.

——— "Henry Inman, an Account of His Life and Work" and "Catalogue of the Paintings of Henry Inman," *Art Quarterly,* III, Autumn 1940, 353–75, and Supplement, 401–18.

——— "James Sharples," *Art in America,* XI, April 1923, 137–43.

——— "John Hazlitt," *Essex Institute Historical Collections,* LVI, Oct. 1920, 293–6.

——— "John Watson of Perth Amboy, Artist," *Proceedings of the New Jersey Historical Society,* LXXII, Oct. 1954, 233–47.

——— "Manasseh Cutler Torrey," *Essex Institute Historical Collections,* LVII, April 1921, 148–9.

——— *Miniature Painters.* Full title: *Early American Portrait Painters in Miniature,* New York, 1921.

——— *Peale Family Exhibition, Century Association, 1953,* New York, 1953.

——— "Portrait Painters in Oil." Full title: "Early American Portrait Painters in Oil," unpublished manuscript at New-York Historical Society.

——— "Saint-Mémin's Crayon Portraits," *Art in America,* IX, June 1921, 160–7.

——— and Harry L. Binsse, "Robert Feke, First Painter to Colonial Aristocracy," *Antiquarian,* XV, Oct. 1930, 32–7, 74–82.

——— and Harry L. Binsse, "Wollaston, an Early American Portrait Manufacturer," *Antiquarian,* XVI, June 1931, 30–3, 50, 52.

——— and Irwin F. Cortelyou, *Ezra Ames of Albany, Portrait Painter, Craftsman, Royal Arch Mason, Banker, 1768–1836 . . . and a Catalogue of His Works,* New York, 1955.

——— and George C. Groce, "John Hesselius, an Account of His Life and the First Catalogue of His Portraits," *Art Quarterly,* II, Winter 1939, 77–91.

——— and George C. Groce, "John Wesley Jarvis, an Account of His Life and the First Catalogue of His Work," *Art Quarterly,* I, Autumn 1938, 299–321.

——— and Ruel P. Tolman, "Catalogue of Miniatures by or Attributed to Benjamin Trott," *Art Quarterly,* VII, Autumn 1944, 278–90.

Born, Wolfgang, *American Landscape Painting; An Interpretation,* New Haven, 1948.

——— "The Female Peales: Their Art and Its Tradition," *American Collector,* XV, Aug. 1946, 12–14.

——— "Notes on Still Life Painting in America," *Antiques,* L, Sept. 1946, 158–60.

——— *Still-Life Painting in America,* New York, 1947.

Borneman, Henry S., "Thomas Buchanan Read, The Odyssey of an Artist, 1822–1872," in *Yesterday in Chester County Art,* by Henry J. Pleasants and others, West Chester, Pa., 1936.

Borneman, Richard R., "Franzoni and Andrei: Italian Sculptors in Baltimore, 1808," *William and Mary Quarterly,* 3d Ser., X, Jan. 1953, 108–11.

Borough of Manhattan, *Deaths Reported in 1901,* New York, Dep't of Health, 1902.

Borthwick, J. D., *Three Years in California . . . ,* Edinburgh and London, 1857; republished in New York, 1927, as *The Gold Hunters,* ed. by Horace Kephart.

Boston Daily Advertiser, newspaper.

[Boston] *Agricultural Intelligencer,* newspaper.

Boston Athenaeum, annual exhibition catalogues, 1827–30, 1833–48, 1850–51, 1853, 1856–60.

[Boston] *Citizen,* newspaper.

Boston Evening Transcript, newspaper.

Boston Marriages, 1752–1809. Boston, Mass., Registry Dep't, . . . *Records Relating to the Early History of Boston,* Vol. XXX, Boston, 1903.

Boston. Museum of Fine Arts, *Catalogue of Paintings,* preliminary edition, Boston, 1921.

Boston Transcript, same as *Boston Evening Transcript.*

Bowditch, Harold, "Early Water-Color Paintings of New England Coats of Arms," *Publications of the Colonial Society of Massachusetts,* XXXV (Boston, 1951), 172–210.

——— "The Gore Roll of Arms," *Rhode Island Historical Society Collections,* XXIX (1936), 11–30, 51–64, 92–6, 121–8; XXX (1937), 28–32, 54–64, 88–96, 116–28; XXXI (1938), 24–32, 56–64, 90–6, 124–8.

——— "Heraldry and the American Collector," *Antiques,* LX, Dec. 1951, 538–41.

——— manuscript notes on American engravers of coats of arms, in the possession of Harold Bowditch.

Bowen, Clarence W., ed., *History of the Centennial Celebration of the Inauguration of George Washington . . . ,* New York, 1892.

Bowen, Clarence W., *History of Woodstock, Conn.,* Norwood, Mass., 1926–43.

Bowen, John T., *The United States Drawing Book . . . ,* Philadelphia, 1839.

Bowes, Frederick P., *The Culture of Early Charleston,* Chapel Hill, 1942.

Bowyer, Campbell T., *Harvey Mitchell, Virginia Painter,* Bedford Democrat, 1952.

Boxborough, Mass. *Vital Records of Boxborough, Mass., to the Year 1850,* Boston, 1915.

Brackenridge, H. M., *Recollections of Persons and Places in the West,* 2nd ed., Philadelphia, 1868.

Bradbury, Anna R., *History of the City of Hudson, New York . . . ,* Hudson, 1908.

Brainard, Newton C., "Isaac Sanford," *Connecticut Historical Society Bulletin,* XIX, Oct. 1954, 122.

"Brief Notes on Some Deceased Artists . . . ," *Publications of the Rhode Island Historical Society,* New Ser., III (1895), 107–11.

Brief Sketch of the Life of Mary Smith, the Painter . . . , Philadelphia, 1878.

Brigham, Clarence S., "Notes on the Thomas Family Portraits," *Proceedings of the American Antiquarian Society,* LVI (Worcester, 1947), 49–54.

——— *Paul Revere's Engravings,* Worcester, 1954.

Brigham, Willard I. T., *The Tyler Genealogy . . . ,* Plainfield, N.J., 1912.

Brinton, Christian, "Gustavus Hesselius," in Philadelphia Museum of Art, *Gustavus Hesselius, 1682–1755,* catalogue of an exhibition under the auspices of the Pennsylvania 300th Anniversary Commission, 1938.

Brockway, Jean Lambert, "The Miniatures of James Peale," *Antiques,* XXII, Oct. 1932, 130–4.

Brooklyn [N.Y.] *Eagle,* newspaper.

Brooks, Alfred M., "Fitz Lane's Drawings," *Essex Institute Historical Collections,* LXXXI, Jan. 1945, 83–6.

Brown, Alexander, *The Cabells and Their Kin,* Boston and New York, 1895.

Brown, Bruce, "Two Versions of the Arkansas Traveler," *American Collector,* VI, May 1937, 6.

Brown, Jennie Broughton, *Fort Hall on the Oregon Trail, a Historical Study . . . ,* Caldwell, Ida., 1932.

Brown, Mary Louise, "John Welch, Carver," *Antiques,* IX, Jan. 1926, 28–30.

Brown, Ralph Hall, *Mirror for Americans; Likeness of the Eastern Seaboard 1810,* New York, 1943.

Brown, Roscoe C. E., *Church of the Holy Trinity, Brooklyn Heights in the City of New York, 1847–1922 . . . ,* New York, 1922.

Brown, William Henry, *Portrait Gallery of Distinguished American Citizens . . . ,* Hartford, 1845; reissued at Troy, N.Y., in 1925 and at New York in 1931.

Brown, William Wells, *The Rising Sun; or, The Antecedents and Advancement of the Colored Race,* 13th ed., Boston, 1882.

Brown and Brown. H. Glenn Brown and Maude O. Brown, *A Directory of the Book-Arts and Book Trade in Philadelphia to 1820, Including Painters and Engravers,* New York, 1950; reprinted from *New York Public Library Bulletin,* May 1949–March 1950.

[Brunet, Pierre,] *Descriptive Catalogue of a Collection of Water-Colour Drawings by Alfred Jacob Miller (1810–1874) in the Public Archives of Canada,* Ottawa, 1951.

Bryan, Michael, *Bryan's Dictionary of Painters and Engravers,* ed. by George C. Williamson, London, 1903–05.

Buffet, Edward P., "William Sidney Mount, A Biography," published serially in *The Port Jefferson* [N.Y.] *Times,* 1923–24.

"Burial Records of Philadelphia Board of Health, 1807–1814," manuscript, Genealogical Society of Pennsylvania, Philadelphia.

"Burials in the Dutch Church, N.Y.," *Year Book of the Holland Society, 1899* (New York, 1899), 139–211.

Burke, Joseph T., "A Biographical and Critical Study of Benjamin West, 1738–

92, with a Supplementary Chapter on His Circle," Yale University Master's Essay, 1937, on deposit in Yale University Library.
Burke, William, *Mineral Springs of Western Virginia . . . with Remarks on Their Use . . .* , New York, 1842.
Burnaby, Andrew, *Travels Through the Middle Settlements in North-America, in the Years 1759 and 1760 . . .* , 3d ed., London, 1798.
Burnet, Mary Q., *Art and Artists of Indiana . . .* , New York, 1921.
Burnham, Roderick H., *The Burnham Family . . .* , Hartford, 1869.
Burr, Frederick M., *Life and Works of Alexander Anderson . . .* , New York, 1893.
Burroughs, Alan, *John Greenwood in America, 1745–1752,* Andover, Mass., 1943.
——— "A Letter from Alvan Fisher," *Art in America,* XXXII, July 1944, 117–26.
——— *Limners and Likenesses; Three Centuries of American Painting,* Cambridge, 1936.
——— "Paintings by Nathaniel Smibert," *Art in America,* XXXI, April 1943, 88–97.
Burroughs, Clyde H., "Painting and Sculpture in Michigan," *Michigan History Magazine,* XX, Autumn 1936, 395–409; XXI, Winter 1937, 39–54.
Burroughs, Louise, "An Inscription by John Hesselius on a Portrait in the Metropolitan Museum of Art," *Art Quarterly,* IV, Spring 1941, 110–14.
Bury, Edmund, "Raphaelle Peale (1774–1825), Miniature Painter," *American Collector,* XVII, Aug. 1948, 6–9.
Bushnell, David I., Jr., "Drawings by George Gibbs in the Far Northwest, 1849–1851," *Smithsonian Miscellaneous Collections,* XCVII, No. 8, Dec. 30, 1938.
——— "Friedrich Kurz, Artist-Explorer," Smithsonian Institution *Annual Report,* 1927 (Washington, 1928), 507–27.
——— "John Mix Stanley, Artist-Explorer," Smithsonian Institution *Annual Report,* 1924 (Washington, 1925), 507–12.
——— "John White; The First English Artist to Visit America, 1585," *The Virginia Magazine,* XXXV, Oct. 1927, 419–30; XXXVI, Jan. 1928, 17–26, April 1928, 124–34.
——— "Seth Eastman, Master Painter of the North American Indian," *Smithsonian Miscellaneous Collections,* LXXXVII, No. 3, April 1932.
Butts, Porter, *Art in Wisconsin,* Madison, 1936.
Bye, Arthur E., "Edward Hicks," *Art in America,* XXXIX, Feb. 1951, 25–35.
——— "Edward Hicks, Painter-Preacher," *Antiques,* XXIX, Jan. 1936, 13–16.

C

CAB. *Appleton's Cyclopaedia of American Biography,* ed. by James Grant Wilson and John Fiske, New York, 1887–89.
——— (rev. ed.). *Appleton's Cyclopaedia of American Biography,* edited by James Grant Wilson and John Fiske, rev. ed., New York, 1898–1900.
Cabinet of Genius Containing All the Theory and Practice of the Fine Arts, No. I, New York, 1808.
Cabot, Mary R., *Annals of Brattleboro, 1681–1895,* Brattleboro, Vt., 1921–22.
Cahill, Holger, "Artisan and Amateur in American Folk Art," *Antiques,* LIX, March 1951, 210–11.
Caldwell, Henry Bryan, "John Frazee, American Sculptor," Master's Thesis, New York University, Graduate School, 1951.
California Historical Society Quarterly, San Francisco, 1922—.
Campbell, Orson, *Treatise on Carriage, Sign and Ornamental Painting,* Scott, N.Y., and De Ruyter, N.Y., 1841.
Campbell, Patrick, *Travels in the Interior Inhabited Parts of North America in the Years 1791 and 1792 . . .* , Edinburgh, 1793; republished, with introduction and notes by H. H. Langton and W. F. Ganong, by The Champlain Society, Toronto, 1937.
Carlock, Grace Miller, "William Rickarby Miller (1818–1893)," *New-York Historical Society Quarterly,* XXXI, Oct. 1947, 199–209.
Carnegie Magazine, Carnegie Institute, Pittsburgh, Pa., 1927—.
Carolina Art Association, *Cat.* 1935. Carolina Art Association, *Exhibition of Miniatures from Charleston and Its Vicinity Painted Before the Year 1860,* Charleston, Gibbes Memorial Art Gallery, 1935.
——— *Cat.* 1936. Carolina Art Association, *An Exhibition of Miniatures Owned in South Carolina and Miniatures of South Carolinians Owned Elsewhere Painted Before the Year 1860,* Charleston, Gibbes Memorial Art Gallery, 1936.

——— *Catalogue with a Short Sketch of Charles Fraser and List of Miniatures Exhibited Jan./Feb. 1934,* Charleston, 1934.

——— manuscript on miniatures. Unpublished *catalogue raisonné* of American miniatures of South Carolinians, prepared by Anna Wells Rutledge for the Carolina Art Association.

Carpenter, Helen G., *The Reverend John Graham of Woodbury, Ct., and His Descendants,* Chicago, 1942.

Carr, Cornelia, ed., *Harriet Hosmer: Letters and Memories,* New York, 1912.

Carrick, Alice V. L., "Novelties in Old American Profiles," *Antiques,* XIV, Oct. 1928, 322–7.

——— "The Profiles of William Bache," *Antiques,* XIV, Sept. 1928, 220–4.

——— "Profiles Real and Spurious," *Antiques,* XVII, April 1930, 320–4.

——— *Shades of Our Ancestors; American Profiles and Profilists,* Boston, 1928.

——— "Silhouettes," *Antiques,* VI, Aug. 1924, 84–9; VIII, Dec. 1925, 341–4.

Carroll, Dana H., *Fifty-eight Paintings by Homer D. Martin . . . ,* New York, 1913.

Carvalho, Solomon N., *Incidents of Travel and Adventure in the Far West . . . ,* New York and Cincinnati, 1857.

Catalogue of the Belknap Collection. John Marshall Phillips, Barbara N. Parker, and Kathryn C. Buhler, eds., *The Waldron Phoenix Belknap, Jr., Collection of Portraits and Silver, with a Note on the Discoveries of Waldron Phoenix Belknap, Jr., Concerning the Influence of the English Mezzotint on Colonial Painting,* Cambridge, 1955.

Catalogue of the Works of Art Exhibited in the Alumni Building, Yale College, 1858, New Haven, 1858.

Catesby, Mark, *The Natural History of Carolina, Florida and the Bahama Islands,* London, 1731–43.

Catlin, George, *Letters and Notes on the Manners, Customs, and Condition of the North American Indians,* London, 1841.

Census records. Manuscript records of the 7th (1850) and 8th (1860) Census, in the National Archives, Washington. References are to state, volume, and page.

Century Association, *Yearbook,* New York, annual.

Chamberlain, Georgia S., "Bas-Relief Portraits by Salathiel Ellis," *Antiques Journal,* IX, Oct. 1954, 23, 39.

——— "John Reich, Assistant Engraver to the United States Mint," *The Numismatist,* LXVIII, March 1955, 242–9.

——— "Medals Made in America by Moritz Furst," *The Numismatist,* LXVII, Sept. 1954, 937–43; Oct. 1954, 1075–80.

——— "Moritz Furst, Die-Sinker and Artist," *The Numismatist,* LXVII, June 1954, 588–92.

——— "Salathiel Ellis: Cameo-Cutter, Sculptor, Artist of Nineteenth Century America," *Antiques Journal,* IX, Feb. 1954, 36–7.

——— "A Woodside Still Life," *Antiques,* LXVII, Feb. 1955, 149.

Chamberlain, George Walter, and Lucia Glidden Strong, *The Descendants of Charles Glidden of Portsmouth and Exeter, N.H.,* Boston, 1925.

Champlin, John D., and Charles C. Perkins, eds., *Cyclopedia of Painters and Paintings,* New York, 1886–87.

Champney, Benjamin, *Sixty Years' Memories of Art and Artists,* Woburn, Mass., 1900.

Chandler, George, *The Chandler Family; The Descendants of William and Annis Chandler . . . ,* Worcester, 1883.

Chapin, Howard M., *Cameo Portraiture in America,* Providence, 1918.

——— "George Oliver Annibale," *Rhode Island Historical Society Collections,* XXII, Oct. 1929, 119–28.

Charleston [S.C.] *Courier,* newspaper.

Chase, Mary Ellen, *Jonathan Fisher, Maine Parson, 1768–1847,* New York, 1948.

Chatterton, Elsie B., "A Vermont Sculptor," *News and Notes* (Vermont Historical Society), VII, Oct. 1955, 10–14.

Cheney, Ednah Dow, ed., *Louisa May Alcott, Her Life, Letters, and Journals,* Boston, 1889.

——— *Memoir of John Cheney, Engraver,* Boston, 1889.

——— *Memoir of Seth W. Cheney, Artist,* Boston, 1881.

Chicago Daily Press, newspaper.

Chicago History, Chicago Historical Society, 1945—.

Childs, Cephas G., *Views of Philadelphia from Original Drawings Taken in 1827–1830,* Philadelphia, 1827–30.

Childs, Charles D., "Robert Salmon, a Boston Painter of Ships and Views," *Old-Time New England,* XXVIII, Jan. 1938, 91–102.

——— "Thar She Blows: Some Notes on American Whaling Pictures," *Antiques,* XL, July 1941, 20–3.

Childs Gallery Bulletin, Boston, Mass.

Chinard, Gilbert, ed., *Houdon in America: A Collection of Documents in the Jeffer-*

son Papers in the Library of Congress, Baltimore, 1930.

Chittenden, Hiram M., and Alfred T. Richardson, *Life, Letters and Travels of Father Pierre-Jean De Smet, S.J. . . . ,* New York, 1905.

Christ-Janer, Albert, *George Caleb Bingham of Missouri, the Story of an Artist,* New York, 1940.

Cincinnati Daily Gazette, newspaper.

Cincinnati Miscellany; or, Antiquities of the West, Cincinnati, Oct. 1844–April 1846.

Cist, Charles, *Cincinnati in 1841 . . . ,* Cincinnati, 1841.

——— *Sketches and Statistics of Cincinnati in 1851,* Cincinnati, 1851.

——— *Sketches and Statistics of Cincinnati in 1859,* Cincinnati, 1859.

City Art Museum of St. Louis, Mo., *Charles Wimar, 1828–1862, Painter of the Indian Frontier,* exhibition catalogue, St. Louis, 1946.

Clark, Alvan, "Autobiography of Alvan Clark," communicated by Hon. Wm. A. Richardson, *New-England Historical and Genealogical Register,* CLXIX, Jan. 1889, 52–8.

Clark, Edna M., *Ohio Art and Artists,* Richmond, Va., 1932.

Clark, Eliot C., *Alexander Wyant,* New York, 1916.

——— *History of the National Academy of Design, 1825–1953,* New York, 1954.

Clarke, Hermann Frederick, and Henry Wilder Foote, *Jeremiah Dummer, Colonial Craftsman and Merchant, 1645–1718,* Boston, 1935.

Clarke, John Lee, Jr., "Joseph Whiting Stock," in Lipman and Winchester, *Primitive Painters in America, 1750–1950,* New York, 1950.

Clarke, Thomas Wood, *Emigrés in the Wilderness,* New York, 1941.

Cleland, Robert G., *A History of California; The American Period,* New York, 1922.

Clement, Clara Erskine, and Laurence Hutton, *Artists of the Nineteenth Century and Their Work . . . ,* Boston and New York, 1884.

Cline, Isaac M., "Art and Artists in New Orleans Since Colonial Times," in Louisiana State Museum, *Biennial Report of the Board of Curators for 1920–21,* 32–42.

Coad, Oral Sumner, *William Dunlap, a Study of His Life and Works and of His Place in Contemporary Culture,* New York, 1917.

Coburn, Frederick W., "The Johnstons of Boston," *Art in America,* XXI, Dec. 1932, 27–36; Oct. 1933, 132–8.

——— "Mather Brown," *Art in America,* XI, Autumn 1923, 252–60.

——— "More Notes on Peter Pelham," *Art in America,* XX, June–Aug. 1932, 143–54.

——— *Thomas Bayley Lawson; Portrait Painter of Newburyport and Lowell, Mass.,* Salem, 1947.

——— "Thomas Child, Limner," *American Magazine of Art,* XXI, June 1930, 326–8.

Cody, Edmund R., *History of the Coeur d'Alene Mission of the Sacred Heart . . . ,* Caldwell, Ida., 1930.

Coe, Benjamin, *Easy Lessons in Landscape Drawing . . . ,* Hartford, 1840.

Coffin, Charles C., *The History of Boscawen and Webster* [N.H.] *from 1733 to 1878,* Concord, N.H., 1878.

Cohen, Hennig, "Robert Mills, Architect of South Carolina," *Antiques,* LV, March 1949, 198–200.

Coke, Edward Thomas, *A Subaltern's Furlough, Descriptive of Scenes in Various Parts of the United States, Upper and Lower Canada, New Brunswick, and Nova Scotia, During the Summer and Autumn of 1832,* London, 1833.

Colbert, Edouard Charles Victurnien, comte de Maulevrier, *Voyage dans l'Intérieur des Etats-Unis et au Canada,* with introduction and notes by Gilbert Chinard, Baltimore, 1935.

Colden, Cadwallader D., *Memoir Prepared at the Request of the Committee of the Common Council of the City of New York and Presented to the Mayor of the City, at the Celebration of the Completion of the New York Canals,* New York, 1825.

Cole, Gertrude S., "Some American Cameo Portraitists," *Antiques,* L, Sept. 1946, 170–1.

Cole, Thomas, "The Late Mr. Ver Bryck," in Cummings, *Historic Annals of the National Academy of Design* (Philadelphia, 1865), 182–4.

Coleman, J. Winston, Jr., "Joel T. Hart; Kentucky Sculptor," *Antiques,* LII, Nov. 1947, 367.

——— "Samuel Woodson Price, Kentucky Portrait Painter," *The Filson Club Historical Quarterly,* XXIII, Jan. 1949, 5–24.

Colonial Laws of New York . . . , Albany, 1894.

Colton, Walter, *Three Years in California,* New York and Cincinnati, 1850.

Columbianum Cat. *Exhibition of the*

Columbianum, or American Academy of Painting, Sculpture and Architecture, &c., Established at Philadelphia, 1795, Philadelphia, 1795.

Commemorative Biographical Record of Hartford County, Conn. . . . , Chicago, 1901.

Comstock, Helen, "American Watercolors Before 1860," *Panorama,* II, Aug.–Sept. 1948, 3–12.

——— "The Complete Work of Robert Havell, Jr.," *Connoisseur,* CXXVI, Nov. 1950, 127.

——— "An 18th Century Audubon," *Antiques,* XXXVII, June 1940, 282–4.

——— "The Hoff Views of New York," *Antiques,* LI, April 1947, 250–2.

Cone, Bernard H., "The American Miniatures of Walter Robertson," *American Collector,* IX, April 1940, 6–7, 14, 20; May 1940, 24.

Connecticut Courant, Hartford newspaper.

Connecticut Historical Society, *Annual Report,* Hartford, May 1950.

Connecticut Historical Society Bulletin, Hartford, 1934—.

Connecticut Historical Society, *Kellogg Prints . . . ,* exhibition catalogue, Hartford, 1952.

Connecticut Journal and New-Haven Post Boy, newspaper.

Connoisseur, an Illustrated Magazine for Collectors, London, 1901—.

[Cooke, George,] "Sketches of Georgia," by G. C., *Southern Literary Messenger,* VI, 1840, 775–7.

——— manuscripts in the possession of Dr. J. Hall Pleasants, of Baltimore, Md., and the Valentine Museum, Richmond, Va.

Corcoran Cat. Corcoran Gallery of Art, *Handbook of the American Paintings in the Collection of the Corcoran Gallery of Art,* comp. by E. B. Swenson, Washington, 1947.

Corcoran Gallery of Art, *150th Anniversary of the Formation of the Constitution; Catalogue of a Loan Exhibition of Portraits . . . Nov. 27, 1937 to Feb. 1, 1938.*

Corey, Deloraine P., *The Waite Family of Malden, Mass.,* Malden, 1913.

Corning, A. Elwood, "Hoyle's Painting of Washington's Headquarters," Historical Society of Newburgh Bay and the Highlands, *Publication* No. XXX (1944), 17–18.

——— "Washington's Headquarters, Newburgh, N.Y.: A Painting," Historical Society of Newburgh Bay and the Highlands, *Publication* No. XXIX (1943), 5–7.

Cortelyou, Irwin F., "Henry Conover: Sitter, Not Artist," *Antiques,* LXVI, Dec. 1954, 481.

——— "A Mysterious Pastellist Identified," *Antiques,* LXVI, Aug. 1954, 122–4.

Cortissoz, Royal, *John LaFarge: A Memoir and a Study,* Boston and New York, 1911.

Cortland Academy [Homer, N.Y.], *Catalogue of the Trustees, Instructors and Students . . . ,* Homer, N.Y., 1836 and 1837.

Cowdrey, Mary Bartlett, *American Academy of Fine Arts and American Art-Union,* New York, 1953. Cited as Cowdrey, AA & AAU.

———"Arthur Fitzwilliam Tait, Master of the American Sporting Scene," *American Collector,* XIII, Jan. 1945, 5, 18.

——— "Asher Brown Durand, 1796–1886," *Panorama,* II, Oct. 1946, 13–23.

——— "The Discovery of Enoch Wood Perry," *Old Print Shop Portfolio,* IV, April 1945, 169–81.

——— "Edward Lamson Henry, An American Genre Painter," *American Collector,* XIV, July 1945, 6–7, 12, 16.

——— *George Henry Durrie, 1820–1863, Connecticut Painter of American Life, Special Loan Exhibition, March 12–April 13, 1947,* Hartford, Wadsworth Atheneum, 1947.

——— "Jasper F. Cropsey, 1823–1900, The Colorist of the Hudson River School," *Panorama,* I, May 1946, 85–94.

——— "Lilly Martin Spencer, 1822–1902, Painter of the American Sentimental Scene," *American Collector,* XIII, Aug. 1944, 6–7, 14, 19.

[———] *The Mount Brothers: An Exhibition,* Stony Brook, N.Y., Suffolk Museum, 1947.

[———] *National Academy of Design Exhibition Record, 1826–1860,* New York, 1943. Cited as Cowdrey, NAD.

——— "A Note on Emanuel Leutze," *Antiques,* XLIX, Feb. 1946, 110.

——— "The Return of John F. Kensett," *Old Print Shop Portfolio,* IV, Feb. 1945, 121–36.

——— "Richard Caton Woodville, An American Genre Painter," *American Collector,* XIII, April 1944, 6–7, 14, 20.

——— "Seth Eastman, Soldier and Painter, 1808–1875," *Panorama,* I, Feb. 1946, 50–6.

——— "The Stryker Sisters by Ralph Earl,"

Art in America, XXXVI, Jan. 1948, 55–7.
——— "William Henry Bartlett and the American Scene," *New York History,* XXII, Oct. 1941, 388–400.
——— *Winslow Homer: Illustrator . . . ,* Northampton, Mass., Smith College Museum of Art, 1951.
——— and Herman W. Williams, Jr., *William Sidney Mount, 1807–1868; An American Painter,* New York, 1944.
Cox, Kenyon, *Winslow Homer,* New York, 1914.
Cramer, Maurice B., "Henry FewSmith, Philadelphia Artist, 1821–1846," *Pennsylvania Magazine of History and Biography,* LXV, Jan. 1941, 31–55.
Crane, Ellery B., *Historic Homes and Institutions and Genealogical and Personal Memoirs of Worcester County, Mass. . . . ,* New York and Chicago, 1907.
The Crayon: A Journal Devoted to the Graphic Arts and the Literature Related to Them, New York, monthly, 1855–61.
Crosby, Everett U., *Eastman Johnson at Nantucket; His Paintings and Sketches of Nantucket People and Scenes,* Nantucket, 1944.
Cross, Osborne, "Journey from Ft. Leavenworth, Kansas, to Ft. Vancouver," 31 Cong., 2 Sess., *Senate Exec. Doc.* 1, 126–244; reprinted in Settle, *March of the Mounted Riflemen,* Glendale, Cal., 1940.
Crouse, Russel, *Mr. Currier and Mr. Ives, A Note on Their Lives and Times,* Garden City, 1930.
Cullum, George W., *Biographical Register of the Officers and Graduates of the U. S. Military Academy . . . from Its Establishment in 1802 to 1890 . . . ,* 3d ed., Boston and New York, 1891.
Cuming, Fortescue, *Cuming's Tour to the Western Country, 1807–09,* reprinted in Thwaites, *Early Western Travels* (Cleveland, 1904), Vol. IV.
Cummings, Thomas S., *Historic Annals of the National Academy of Design . . . ,* Philadelphia, 1865.
Cunningham, Henry W., *Christian Remick, An Early Boston Artist . . . ,* Boston, 1904.
Currier, John J., *History of Newburyport, Mass., 1764–1909,* Newburyport, 1906–09.

D

DAB. *Dictionary of American Biography,* ed. by Allen Johnson and Dumas Malone, New York, 1928–36.
Daingerfield, Elliott, *George Inness; The Man and His Art,* New York, 1911.
Dana, Charles A., ed., *The United States Illustrated; in Views of City and Country . . . ,* New York, *c.* 1855.
Danvers, Mass. *Vital Records of Danvers, Mass., to the End of the Year 1849 . . . ,* Salem, 1909–10.
Danvers [Mass.] Historical Society, *Historical Collections,* Danvers, 1913—.
Darrach, Charles G., "Christian Gobrecht, Artist and Inventor," *Pennsylvania Magazine of History and Biography,* XXX, July 1906, 355–8.
Dartmouth College, *General Catalogue of Dartmouth College and the Associated Schools, 1769–1900 . . . ,* Hanover, N.H., 1900.
Davidson, Marshall, *Life in America,* Boston, 1951.
Davis, Curtis Carroll, "Fops, Frenchmen, Hidalgos, and Aztecs; Being a Survey of the Prose Fiction of J. M. Legaré of South Carolina (1823–1859)," *North Carolina Historical Review,* XXX, Oct. 1953, 524–60.
——— "Poet, Painter, and Inventor: Some Letters by James Mathewes Legaré," *North Carolina Historical Review,* XXI, July 1944, 215–31.
——— "The Several-sided James Mathewes Legaré: Poet," *Transactions of the Huguenot Society of South Carolina,* No. 57 (Charleston, 1952), 5–12.
Davis, Edw. Morris III, *A Retrospective Exhibition of the Work of John Adams Elder 1833–1895,* Richmond, Virginia Museum of Fine Arts, 1947.
Davis, William W. H., *History of Doylestown, Old and New . . . 1745–1900,* Doylestown, Pa., *c.* 1904.
Davisson, G. D., "William Keith," *Bulletin of the California Palace of the Legion of Honor Museum,* III, July 1945, 34–9.
Daywalt, Alberta T., "The Spirit of '76," *Antiques,* XL, July 1941, 24.
Decatur, Stephen, "The Conflicting History of Henry Dawkins, Engraver," *American Collector,* VII, Jan. 1939, 6–7.
——— "Richard Morell Staigg," *American Collector,* IX, Aug. 1940, 8–9.

——— "William Rollinson, Engraver," *American Collector*, IX, Dec. 1940, 8–9.

DeKay, Charles, *Illustrated Catalogue of Oil Paintings by the Late Alfred Cornelius Howland, N.A., to be Sold . . .*, New York, 1910.

Delafield, John, *An Inquiry into the Origin of the Antiquities of America*, New York, 1839.

Delafield, John Ross, *Delafield, The Family History*, New York, 1945.

Delgado-WPA. Isaac Delgado Museum of Art [New Orleans], Delgado Art Museum Project, W.P.A., "New Orleans Artists Directory, 1805–1940," unpublished.

de Mare, Marie, *G. P. A. Healy, American Artist; an Intimate Chronicle of the Nineteenth Century*, New York, 1954.

Demuth, C.B., "Aaron Eshleman," *Historical Papers and Addresses of the Lancaster County* [Pa.] *Historical Society*, XVI (1912), 247–50.

Descriptive Catalogue of Paintings . . . with a Memoir of George Cooke, [Prattville, Ala.?] 1853.

"*Detroit Advertiser* Digest," Burton Historical Collection, Detroit Public Library.

Detroit Free Press, newspaper.

"*Detroit Free Press* Digest," Burton Historical Collection, Detroit Public Library.

Detroit Historical Society, *Bulletin*, Detroit, 1945—.

Detroit Institute of Arts, *Bulletin*, Detroit, 1919—.

——— *The French in America, 1520–1880 . . .*, Detroit, 1951.

De Voto, Bernard A., *Across the Wide Missouri . . .*, Boston, 1947.

Dexter, Arthur, "The Fine Arts in Boston," in Justin Winsor, *Memorial History of Boston . . .* (Boston, 1880–81), Vol. IV.

Dexter, Elizabeth W. A., *Career Women of America, 1776–1840*, Francestown, N.H., 1950.

Dexter, Franklin B., *Biographical Sketches of the Graduates of Yale College . . .*, New York, 1885–1912.

Dexter, Orrando P., *Dexter Genealogy, 1642–1904 . . .*, New York, 1904.

Dickinson, Henry W., *Robert Fulton, Engineer and Artist; His Life and Works*, London and New York, 1913.

Dickinson, Thomas A., "Rufus Alexander Grider," *Proceedings of the Worcester* [Mass.] *Society of Antiquity*, XVII, March–April 1900, 110–13.

Dickson, Harold E., "The Case Against Savage," *American Collector*, XIV, Jan. 1946, 6–7, 17.

——— *John Wesley Jarvis, American Painter, 1780–1840 . . .*, New York, 1949.

——— "A Misdated Episode in Dunlap," *Art Quarterly*, IX, Jan. 1946, 33–6.

——— "A Note on Jeremiah Paul, American Artist," *Antiques*, LI, June 1947, 392–3.

——— ed., *Observations on American Art; Selections from the Writings of John Neal*, State College, Pa., 1943.

Diers, Herman H., "The Strange Case of Alonzo Chappel," *Hobbies*, XLIX, Oct. 1944, 18–20, 28.

Dintruff, Emma J., "The American Scene a Century Ago," *Antiques*, XXXVIII, Dec. 1940, 279–81.

DNB. *Dictionary of National Biography*, London, 1921–22.

Dods, Agnes M., "A Check List of Portraits and Paintings by Erastus Salisbury Field," *Art in America*, XXXII, Jan. 1944, 32–40.

——— "Connecticut Valley Painters," *Antiques*, XLVI, Oct. 1944, 207–9.

——— "More About Jennys," *Art in America*, XXXIV, April 1946, 114–16.

——— "Nathan Negus," *Antiques*, LVIII, Sept. 1950, 194.

——— "Newly Discovered Portraits by J. William Jennys," *Art in America*, XXXIII, Jan. 1945, 5–12.

——— "Sarah Goodridge," *Antiques*, LI, May 1947, 328–9.

Doggett's Repository of Arts [Philadelphia], *Original Cabinet Paintings Now Arranged at . . . Nov. 22, 1821* [copy at Frick Art Reference Library, New York City].

Doolittle, William F., *The Doolittle Family in America . . .*, Cleveland, 1901–08.

Dorchester Births, Marriages, and Deaths. A Report of the Record Commissioners of the City of Boston, Containing Dorchester Births, Marriages, and Deaths to the End of 1825 . . ., Boston, 1890.

Dorchester, Mass. *Vital Records of the Town of Dorchester from 1826 to 1849*, Boston, 1905.

d'Otrange, Marie-Louise, "James H. Wright, 19th Century New York Painter," *American Collector*, XII, Feb. 1943, 5, 19.

Doughty, Howard N., "Life and Works of Thomas Doughty," unpublished manuscript in the possession of the New-York Historical Society.

Dow, Charles M., *Anthology and Bibliography of Niagara Falls*, Albany, 1921.

Dow, George F., "Old-Time Ship Pictures," *Antiques*, II, Oct. 1922, 161–4.

——— *The Arts and Crafts in New Eng-*

land, 1704–1775 . . . , Topsfield, Mass., 1927.

Downes, William H., "An American Painter: Mark Waterman," *Magazine of Art* (1895), 269–73.

——— "George Fuller's Pictures," *International Studio,* LXXV, July 1922, 265–73.

——— *The Life and Works of Winslow Homer,* Boston, 1911.

Draper, Benjamin P., "American Indians, Barbizon Style: The Collaborative Paintings of Millet and Bodmer," *Antiques,* XLIV, Sept. 1943, 108–10.

——— "John Mix Stanley, Pioneer Painter," *Antiques,* XLI, March 1942, 180–2.

——— "Karl Bodmer, an Artist Among the Indians," *Antiques,* XLV, May 1944, 242–4.

Drayton, John, *The Carolinian Florist of Governor John Drayton of South Carolina . . . with Water-Color Illustrations from the Author's Original Manuscript* . . . , edited by Margaret B. Meriwether, Columbia, S.C., 1943.

——— *Memoirs of the American Revolution* . . . , 2 vols., Charleston, 1821.

Dreier, Dorothea A., "Walter Shirlaw," *Art in America,* VII, Autumn 1919, 206–16.

Drepperd, Carl W., "American Drawing Books," *New York Public Library Bulletin,* XLIX, Nov. 1945, 795–812.

——— "New Delvings in Old Fields—Found: A 'New' Early American Engraver," *Antiques,* XLII, Oct. 1942, 204–5.

——— "Pictures with a Past," *American Collector,* IV, June 1927, 88–97.

——— "Rare American Prints, Drawn from a Drawing Book," *Antiques,* XVI, July 1929, 26–8.

——— "Three Battles of New Orleans," *Antiques,* XIV, Aug. 1928, 129–31.

Dresser, Louisa, "Christian Gullager; An Introduction to His Life and Some Representative Examples of His Work," *Art in America,* XXXVII, July 1949, 105–79.

——— "Edward Savage, 1761–1817," *Art in America,* XL, Autumn 1952, 157–212.

——— ed., *XVIIth Century Painting in New England* . . . , Worcester, Mass., 1935.

——— "The Thwing Likenesses, A Problem in Early American Portraiture," *Old-Time New England,* XXIX, Oct. 1938, 45–51.

Dumont de Montigny, Louis François Benjamin, "L'Etablissement de la Province de la Louisiane," Societé des Américanistes de Paris, *Journal,* New Ser. XXIII (1931), 273–440.

——— *Mémoires Historiques sur la Louisiane* . . . , Paris, 1753.

Dunlap, William, *Diary of William Dunlap (1766–1839)* . . . , edited by Dorothy C. Barck, New York, 1930.

——— *A History of the American Theatre,* New York, 1832.

——— *History of the Rise and Progress of the Arts of Design in the United States* (New York, 1834), [cited as Dunlap, *History*].

——— *History of the Rise and Progress of the Arts of Design in the United States,* edited by Frank W. Bayley and Charles E. Goodspeed (Boston, 1918) [cited as Dunlap, *History* (1918)].

Dunn, N. P., "An Artist of the Past: William Edward West and His Friends at Home and Abroad," *Putnam's Monthly,* II, Sept. 1907, 658–69.

——— "Unknown Pictures of Shelley," *The Century Magazine,* LXX, Oct. 1905, 909–17.

Dunshee, Kenneth H., *As You Pass By,* New York, 1952.

Durand, John, *The Life and Times of A. B. Durand,* New York, 1894.

Durrie, Mary C., "George Henry Durrie, Artist," *Antiques,* XXIV, July 1933, 13–15.

Dwight, Edward H., "Aaron Houghton Corwine: Cincinnati Artist," *Antiques,* LXVII, June 1955, 502–4.

——— "John P. Frankenstein," *Museum Echoes,* XXVII, July 1954, 51–3.

——— "Robert S. Duncanson," *Museum Echoes,* XXVII, June 1954, 43–5.

——— "Robert S. Duncanson," *Bulletin of the Historical and Philosophical Society of Ohio,* XIII, July 1955, 203–11.

E

Earle, Pliny, *The Earle Family; Ralph Earle and His Descendants,* Worcester, 1888.

Eastman, Mary H., *American Aboriginal Portfolio . . . Illustrated by S[eth] Eastman, U. S. Army,* Philadelphia, 1853.

[Easton] *Maryland Herald,* newspaper.

Eaton, Cyrus, *History of Thomaston, Rockland, and South Thomaston, Maine* . . . , Hallowell, Me., 1865.

Ecclesiastical Records, State of New York, Albany, 1901–16.

Eckhardt, George H., "Early Lithography in Philadelphia," *Antiques,* XXVIII, Dec. 1935, 249–52.

Eckstorm, Fannie Hardy, "Jeremiah Pearson Hardy: A Maine Portrait Painter," *Old-Time New England,* XXX, Oct. 1939, 41–66.

Edmonds, Francis W., "Frederick S. Agate," *The Knickerbocker or New-York Monthly Magazine,* XXIV, Aug. 1844, 157–63.

Edwards, Edward, *Anecdotes of Painters Who Have Resided or Been Born in England . . . ,* London, 1808.

Egbert, Donald D., *Princeton Portraits,* with the assistance of Diane Martindell Lee, Princeton, 1947.

Eisen, Gustavus A., "A Houdon Medallion," *Antiques,* XVII, Feb. 1930, 122–5.

Eldridge, Charles W., "Journal of a Tour Through Vermont to Montreal and Quebec in 1833," *Vermont Historical Society Proceedings,* New Ser. II, June 1931, 53–82.

[Elizabeth] *New Jersey Journal,* newspaper.

Ely, Lydia, "Art and Artists of Milwaukee," in Howard Louis Conard, ed., *History of Milwaukee County,* Chicago, 1898.

Elzas, Barnett A., *The Jews of South Carolina from the Earliest Times to the Present Day,* Philadelphia, 1905.

Emmet, Thomas Addis, *The Emmet Family . . . ,* New York, 1898.

Emory, William H., *United States and Mexican Boundary Survey, Report of William H. Emory . . . ,* Washington, 1857–59.

Emory University Quarterly, Atlanta, 1945—.

Encyclopedia Britannica, 11th ed., Cambridge, England, 1910–11.

Endicott, Frederic, ed., *Record of Births, Marriages and Deaths . . .* [in Stoughton, Canton and Dorchester, Mass.], Canton, Mass., 1896.

Erffa, Helmut von, "An Oil Sketch by Benjamin West," *The Register of the Museum of Art of the University of Kansas,* No. 7, May 1956, 1–8.

——— "West's Washing of Sheep," *Art Quarterly,* XV, Summer 1952, 160–5.

Essex Institute [Salem, Mass.], "Additions to the Catalogue of Portraits in the Essex Institute," *Essex Institute Historical Collections,* LXXXVI, April 1950, 155–74.

——— *Catalogue of Portraits in the Essex Institute . . . ,* Salem, 1936.

Essex Institute Historical Collections, Salem, Mass., 1859—.

Evans, Charles, *American Bibliography . . . ,* Chicago, 1903–34.

Evans, Elliot, "Some Letters of William S. Jewett," *California Historical Society Quarterly,* XXIII, June 1944, 149–77, and Sept. 1944, 227–46.

——— "William S. and William D. Jewett," *California Historical Society Quarterly,* XXXIII, Dec. 1954, 309–20.

Evans, Grose, "Benjamin West's Development and the Sources of His Style," unpublished thesis, Johns Hopkins University, 1953.

Evans, Richard X., ed., "Letters from Robert Mills," *South Carolina Historical and Genealogical Magazine,* XXXIX, July 1938, 110–24.

Ewers, John C., "Charles Bird King, Painter of Indian Visitors to the Nation's Capital," *Annual Report of the Board of Regents of the Smithsonian Institution . . . 1953,* 463–73.

——— "Gustavus Sohon's Portraits of Flathead and Pend d'Oreille Indians, 1854," *Smithsonian Miscellaneous Collections,* CX, No. 7, Nov. 1948.

F

Fagnani, Emma E., *The Art Life of a XIXth Century Portrait Painter, Joseph Fagnani . . . ,* Paris, 1930.

Fairman, Charles E., *Art and Artists of the Capitol of the United States of America,* Washington, 1927.

Farington, Joseph, *The Farington Diary,* ed. by James Greig, London, 1923–28.

FARL. Frick Art Reference Library, New York City.

Farmer, Silas, *The History of Detroit and Michigan . . . ,* Detroit, 1884.

Farquhar, Francis P., *Edward Vischer: His Pictorial of California,* San Francisco, 1932.

Fay, Theodore S., *Views in New York and Its Environs . . . ,* New York and London, 1831.

Felt, Joseph B., *Annals of Salem,* Salem and Boston, 1845–49.

Fenton, William N., "The Hyde de Neuville Portraits of New York Savages in 1807–1808," *New-York Historical Society Quarterly,* XXXVIII, April 1954, 119–37.

Fielding, Mantle, *American Engravers upon Copper and Steel . . . A Supplement to . . . Stauffer's American Engravers* (Philadelphia, 1917) [cited as Fielding, *Supplement to Stauffer*].

——— *Catalogue of the Engraved Work of David Edwin,* Philadelphia, 1905.

——— *Dictionary of American Painters,*

Sculptors, and Engravers, Philadelphia, 1926.

——— *Supplement to Stauffer,* see Fielding, *American Engravers.*

Fincham, Henry W., *Artists and Engravers of British and American Book Plates . . . ,* London, 1897.

Fine Arts Journal . . . , Chicago, 1899–1919.

Fine Arts Quarterly Review, London, 1863–67.

Finn, Matthew D., *The Theorematical System of Painting . . . ,* New York, 1830.

First Fifty Years of Cazenovia Seminary 1825–1875, Cazenovia, N.Y., 1877.

First German Reformed Church, New York City, records of, at New-York Historical Society.

Fisher, Philip A., *The Fisher Genealogy . . . ,* Everett, Mass., 1898.

Fisk, Frances B., *A History of Texas Artists and Sculptors,* Abilene, 1928.

Flagg, Jared B., *The Life and Letters of Washington Allston,* New York, 1892.

Flagg, Norman Gershom and Lucius C. S., *Family Records of the Descendants of Gershom Flagg . . . ,* Quincy, Ill., 1907.

Fleming, George Thornton, ed., *History of Pittsburgh and Environs . . . ,* New York and Chicago, 1922.

Fletcher, Edward H., *Fletcher Genealogy . . . ,* Boston, 1871.

Fletcher, Robert S., "Ransom's John Brown Painting," *Kansas Historical Quarterly,* IX, Nov. 1940, 343–6.

Flexner, James T., "The Amazing William Williams: Painter, Author, Teacher, Musician, Stage Designer, Castaway," *Magazine of Art,* XXXVII, Nov. 1944, 242–6, 276–8.

——— *America's Old Masters; First Artists of the New World,* New York, 1939.

——— "Benjamin West's American Neo-Classicism, with Documents on West and William Williams," *New-York Historical Society Quarterly,* XXXVI, Jan. 1952, 5–41.

——— *First Flowers of Our Wilderness,* Boston, 1947.

——— *Gilbert Stuart; A Great Life in Brief,* New York, 1955.

——— *John Singleton Copley,* Boston, 1948.

——— *The Light of Distant Skies, 1760–1835,* New York, 1954.

——— "Winthrop Chandler: An 18th-Century Artisan Painter," *Magazine of Art,* XL, Nov. 1947, 274–8.

Folsom, Elizabeth K., *Genealogy of the Folsom Family . . . ,* Rutland, Vt., 1938.

Folsom, Joseph F., ed., *Bloomfield, Old and New,* Bloomfield, N.J., 1912.

Folsom, Joseph F., "Jacob C. Ward, One of the Old-Time Landscape Painters," *Proceedings of the New Jersey Historical Society,* New Ser. III, April 1918, 83–93.

Foote, Abram W., *Foote Family . . . ,* Rutland, Vt., 1907.

Foote, Henry Wilder, "Charles Bridges: 'Sergeant-Painter of Virginia,' 1735–1740," *Virginia Magazine of History and Biography,* LX, Jan. 1952, 1–55.

——— *John Smibert, Painter . . . ,* Cambridge, 1950.

——— *Robert Feke, Colonial Portrait Painter,* Cambridge, 1930.

Forbes, Esther, *Paul Revere and the World He Lived In,* Boston, 1942.

Forbes, Harriette M., "Early Portrait Sculpture in New England," *Old-Time New England,* XIX, April 1929, 159–74.

Ford, Alice, *Edward Hicks, Painter of The Peaceable Kingdom,* Philadelphia, 1952.

——— *Pictorial Folk Art, New England to California,* New York, 1949.

Ford, Alice E., "Some Trade Cards and Broadsides," *American Collector,* XI, June 1942, 10–13.

Ford, Henry A. and Mrs. Kate B., *History of Cincinnati, Ohio,* Cleveland, 1881.

Ford, Worthington C., *British Officers Serving in the American Revolution 1774–1783,* Brooklyn, 1897.

——— "Broadsides, Ballads etc. Printed in Massachusetts 1639–1800," *Massachusetts Historical Society Collections,* LXXV, Boston, 1922.

Forrer, Leonard, *Biographical Dictionary of Medallists . . . ,* London, 1902–30.

1440 Early American Portrait Artists, see W.P.A. Historical Records Survey, New Jersey.

Frankenstein, Alfred V., *After the Hunt: William Harnett and Other American Still Life Painters, 1870–1900,* Berkeley and Los Angeles, 1953.

——— "J. F. Francis," *Antiques,* LIX, May 1951, 374–7, 390.

——— and Arthur K. D. Healy, *Two Journeymen Painters,* Sheldon Museum, Middlebury, Vt., 1950; reprinted from *Art in America,* XXXVIII, Feb. 1950.

Frankenstein, John, *American Art: Its Awful Altitude,* Cincinnati, 1864.

Frary, I. T., "Ohio Discovers Its Primitives," *Antiques,* XLIX, Jan. 1946, 40–1.

Fraser, Charles, *Reminiscences of Charleston . . . ,* Charleston, 1854.

Frazee, John, "The Autobiography of

Frazee, the Sculptor," *North American Magazine,* V, April 1835, 395–403; VI, July 1835, 1–22.

Frederick [Md.] *Herald,* newspaper.

[Fredericksburg, Va.] *Political Arena,* newspaper.

Freeman, James E., *Gatherings from an Artist's Portfolio,* New York, 1877.

——— *Gatherings from an Artist's Portfolio in Rome,* Boston, 1883.

Frémont, John Charles, *Memoirs of My Life . . . ,* New York, 1887.

——— *Report of the Exploring Expedition to the Rocky Mountains in the Year 1842, and to Oregon and North California in the Years 1843–'44 . . . ,* Washington, 1845.

French, Henry W., *Art and Artists in Connecticut,* Boston, 1879.

French, Hollis, *Jacob Hurd and His Sons, Nathaniel and Benjamin, Silversmiths, 1702–1781,* Cambridge, 1939.

From Colony to Nation: An Exhibition of American Painting, Silver and Architecture from 1650 to the War of 1812, Art Institute of Chicago, 1949.

Fulton, Eleanor J., "Robert Fulton as an Artist," *Papers of the Lancaster County* [Pa.] *Historical Society,* XLII, No. 3 (1938), 49–96.

G

Gage, Thomas H., *An Artist Index to Stauffer's American Engravers,* Worcester, 1921; reprinted from *Proceedings of the American Antiquarian Society,* 1921.

Gaillard, William, *The History and Pedigree of the House of Gaillard or Gaylord . . . ,* Cincinnati, 1872.

Gallagher, H. M. Pierce, "Robert Mills, 1781–1855, America's First Native Architect," *Architectural Record,* LXV, April 1929, 387–93; May 1929, 478–84; LXVI, July 1929, 67–72.

Galt, John, *The Life, Studies, and Works of Benjamin West . . . ,* London, 1820.

Garbisch Collection catalogue. U. S. National Gallery of Art, *American Primitive Paintings from the Collection of Edgar William and Bernice Chrysler Garbisch,* Washington, 1954.

Gardner, Albert T. E., "Fragment of a Lost Monument: Marble Bust of Washington," *Metropolitan Museum of Art Bulletin,* VI, March 1948, 189–97.

——— "Hiram Powers and William Rimmer, Two 19th Century American Sculptors," *Magazine of Art,* XXXVI, Feb. 1943, 43–7.

——— "Hudson River Idyl," *Metropolitan Museum of Art Bulletin,* VI, April 1948, 232–6.

——— "Ingham in Manhattan," *Metropolitan Museum of Art Bulletin,* X, May 1952, 245–53.

——— *Yankee Stonecutters; The First American School of Sculpture 1800–1850,* New York, 1944.

Garraghan, Gilbert J., *The Jesuits of the Middle United States,* New York, 1938.

Garretson, Mary N. W., "Thomas S. Noble and His Paintings," *New-York Historical Society Quarterly Bulletin,* XXIV, Oct. 1940, 113–23.

Gass, Patrick, *Gass's Journal of the Lewis and Clark Expedition . . . ,* Chicago, 1904.

Gazette des Beaux-Arts, Paris, 1859—.

Gegenheimer, Albert F., "Artist in Exile: The Story of Thomas Spence Duché," *Pennsylvania Magazine of History and Biography,* LXXIX, Jan. 1955, 3–26.

The Gem, or Fashionable Business Directory for the City of New York, New York, 1844.

Genealogy of the Descendants of John Sill . . . , Albany, 1859.

Genin, Sylvester, *Selections from the Works of the Late Sylvester Genin, Esq., in Poetry, Prose, and Historical Design, with a Biographical Sketch,* New York, 1855.

Gentleman's Magazine, London, 1731–1907.

Geske, Norman A., "A Pioneer Minnesota Artist," *Minnesota History,* XXXI, June 1950, 99–104.

Ghent, William J., *The Road to Oregon, a Chronicle of the Great Emigrant Trail,* London, 1929.

Gibbes, Robert W., *A Memoir of James De Veaux . . . ,* Columbia, S.C., 1846.

Gideon, Samuel E., "Two Pioneer Artists in Texas," *American Magazine of Art,* IX, Sept. 1918, 452–6.

Gilchrist, Agnes A., *William Strickland, Architect and Engineer, 1788–1854,* Philadelphia, 1950.

Gillingham, Harrold E., "Notes on Philadelphia Profilists," *Antiques,* XVII, June 1930, 516–18.

Gilman, Margaret E., "Studies in the Art of Drawing and Painting by Members of the

Dep't of Fine Arts," *Fogg Museum Bulletin*, X, March 1945, 74–80.

Girodie, André, *Un Peintre Alsacien de Transition; Clément Faller*, Strasbourg, 1907.

Gladding, Henry C., *The Gladding Book . . .* , Providence, 1901.

Glassburn, Dorothy E., "Artist Reports on the Fire of 1845; Two Paintings by William Coventry Wall," *Carnegie Magazine*, XVIII, March 1945, 300–2.

Goodrich, Lloyd, *American Watercolor and Winslow Homer*, Walker Art Center, Minneapolis, 1945.

——— "Ralph Earl," *Magazine of Art*, XXXIX, Jan. 1946, 2–8.

——— "Robert Feke," in *Robert Feke*, catalogue of an exhibition at the Whitney Museum, Heckscher Art Museum, and Boston Museum of Fine Arts, 1946.

——— *Winslow Homer*, New York, 1944.

Goodwin, Hermon C., *Pioneer History; or, Cortland County and the Border Wars of New York . . .* , New York, 1859.

Gordon, William S., "Gabriel Ludlow (1663–1736) and His Descendants," *New York Genealogical and Biographical Record*, L, Jan. and April 1919, 34–55, 134–56.

Gosman, Robert, "Life of John Vanderlyn," unpublished; two typed drafts at the New-York Historical Society.

Goss, Charles F., *Cincinnati, the Queen City, 1788–1912*, Chicago and Cincinnati, 1912.

Goss, Elbridge H., *The Life of Colonel Paul Revere*, Boston, 1891.

Gottesman, Rita S., *The Arts and Crafts in New York, 1726–1776 . . .* , New York, 1938; cited as Gottesman, I.

——— *The Arts and Crafts in New York, 1777–1799 . . .* , New York, 1954; cited as Gottesman, II.

Gould, Dorothy F., *Beyond the Shining Mountains*, Portland, Ore., 1938.

Graffenried, Thomas P. de, *History of the de Graffenried Family from 1191 A.D. to 1925*, Binghamton and New York, 1925.

Grande Encyclopedie, Inventaire Raisonné des Sciences, des Lettres et des Arts . . . , Paris, 1886–1902.

Granite Monthly, Manchester, N.H., 1877–1930.

Grant, Maurice H., *A Dictionary of British Landscape Painters from the 16th Century to the Early 20th Century*, Leigh-on-the-Sea, 1952.

Graves, Algernon, *A Dictionary of Artists Who Have Exhibited Works in the Principal London Exhibitions of Oil Paintings from 1760 to 1880*, London, 1884.

Green, Samuel Abbott, *John Foster, The Earliest American Engraver and the First Boston Printer*, Boston, 1909.

Green, Samuel M., "Uncovering the Connecticut School," *Art News*, LI, Jan. 1953, 38–41, 57.

——— "Charles Caleb Ward, the Painter of the 'Circus is Coming,'" *Art Quarterly*, XIV, Autumn 1951, 231–51.

Greenough, Frances Boott, ed., *Letters of Horatio Greenough to His Brother, Henry Greenough . . .* , Boston, 1887.

Greenough, Horatio [Horace Bender, pseud.], *The Travels, Observations, and Experience of a Yankee Stonecutter*, New York, 1852.

Greve, Charles T., *Centennial History of Cincinnati and Representative Citizens*, Chicago, 1904.

Griffin, Grace Gardner, *Writings on American History* [1906–40], Washington and New Haven, 1908–49.

Groce, George C., "John Wollaston (fl. 1736–1767): A Cosmopolitan Painter in the British Colonies," *Art Quarterly*, XV, Summer 1952, 133–48.

——— "John Wollaston's Portrait of Thomas Appleford, Dated 1746," *New-York Historical Society Quarterly*, XXXIV, Oct. 1950, 261–8.

——— "New York Painting before 1800," *New York History*, XIX, Jan. 1938, 44–57.

——— "Who Was J[ohn?] Cooper (b. *ca.* 1695–living 1754?)," *Art Quarterly*, XVIII, Spring 1955, 73–82.

——— "William John Coffee, Long-lost Sculptor," *American Collector*, XV, May 1946, 14–15, 19–20.

——— *William Samuel Johnson; A Maker of the Constitution*, New York, 1937.

——— and J. T. Chase Willet, "Joseph Wood: A Brief Account of His Life and the First Catalogue of His Work," *Art Quarterly*, III, Spring 1940, 149–61, and Supplement 1940, 393–418.

Grolier Club, *The United States Navy, 1776 to 1815, Depicted in an Exhibition of Prints . . .* , New York, 1942.

Gudde, Erwin G., "Carl Nahl, California's Pioneer of Painting," *American-German Review*, VII (1940), 18–20.

Guide to Hanington's Moving Dioramas, New York, 1837.

Guignard, Philippe, *Notice Historique sur la Vie et les Traveaux de M. Fevret de Saint-Mémin*, Dijon, 1853.

H

Haberly, Loyd, *Pursuit of the Horizon; A Life of George Catlin, Painter and Recorder of the American Indian,* New York, 1948.

Hain, Harry H., *History of Perry County, Pa. . . . ,* Harrisburg, 1922.

Hale, Edward Everett, "The Early Art of Thomas Cole," *Art in America,* IV, Dec. 1915, 22–40.

Hale, Susan, *Life and Letters of Thomas Gold Appleton,* New York, 1885.

Hall, Lillian A., *Catalogue of Dramatic Portraits in the Theatre Collection of the Harvard College Library,* Cambridge, 1930.

Hall, Martha K., "James Long Scudder, Artist," *The Long Island Forum,* XVIII, March 1955, 43–4, 56.

Hamersly, Thomas H. S., *General Register of the United States Navy and Marine Corps . . . ,* Washington, 1882.

Hamilton, Sinclair, *Early American Book Illustrators and Wood Engravers, 1670–1870 . . . ,* Princeton, 1950.

——— "Homer Martin as Illustrator," *New Colophon,* I, July 1948, 256–63.

Hamlin, Talbot, *Benjamin Henry Latrobe,* New York, 1955.

——— "Benjamin Henry Latrobe, 1764–1820," *Magazine of Art,* XLI, March 1948, 89–95.

——— "Benjamin Henry Latrobe: The Man and the Architect," *Maryland Historical Magazine,* XXXVII, Dec. 1942, 339–60.

Harding, Chester, *My Egotistography,* Boston, 1866.

Hardy, Harrison Claude and Rev. Edwin N., *Hardy and Hardie, Past and Present . . . ,* Syracuse, 1935.

Harlow, Alvin F., *The Serene Cincinnatians,* New York, 1950.

[Harlow, Thompson R.,] "William Johnston, Portrait Painter, 1732–1772," *Connecticut Historical Society Bulletin,* XIX, Oct. 1954, 97–100, 108.

[Harlow, Thompson R.,] "Some Comments on William Johnston, Painter, 1732–1772," *Connecticut Historical Society Bulletin,* XX, Jan. 1955, 25–32.

Harper's Magazine or *Harper's New Monthly Magazine,* New York, 1850—.

Harper's Weekly, New York, 1857–1916.

Harris, Charles E., "American Ship Figureheads," *American Collector,* VIII, May 1939, 11–12.

Harris, Charles X., "Henri Couturier, an Artist of New Netherland," *New-York Historical Society Quarterly Bulletin,* XI, July 1927, 45–52.

——— "Peter Vanderlyn, Portrait Painter," *New-York Historical Society Quarterly Bulletin,* V, Oct. 1921, 59–73.

Harris, Edward D., *A Genealogical Record of Thomas Bascom and His Descendants,* Boston, 1870.

Harshberger, John W., *The Botanists of Philadelphia and Their Work,* Philadelphia, 1899.

Hart, Charles H., *Browere's Life Masks of Great Americans,* New York, 1899.

——— "The Earliest Painter in America," *Harper's New Monthly Magazine,* XCVI, March 1898, 566–70.

——— "Gustavus Hesselius," *Pennsylvania Magazine of History and Biography,* XXIX, April 1905, 129–33.

——— "The Last of the Silhouettists," *Outlook,* LXVI, Oct. 1900, 329–35.

——— "Life Portraits of Andrew Jackson," *McClure's Magazine,* IX, July 1897, 795–804.

——— "Life Portraits of Daniel Webster," *McClure's Magazine,* IX, May 1897, 619–30.

——— "Life Portraits of George Washington," *McClure's Magazine,* VIII, Feb. 1897, 291–308.

——— "Life Portraits of Henry Clay," *McClure's Magazine,* IX, Sept. 1897, 939–48.

——— "Life Portraits of Thomas Jefferson," *McClure's Magazine,* XI, May 1898, 47–55.

——— "Patience Wright, Modeller in Wax," *Connoisseur,* XIX, Sept. 1907, 18–22.

——— "Portrait of John Grimes, Painted by Matthew Harris Jouett," *Art in America,* IV, April 1916, 175–6.

——— "Portrait of Thomas Dawson, Viscount Cremorne, Painted by Mather Brown," *Art in America,* V, Oct. 1917, 309–14.

——— ed., *A Register of Portraits Painted by Thomas Sully, 1801–1871,* Philadel*phia,* 1909.

——— "Unknown Life Masks of Great Americans," *McClure's Magazine,* IX, Oct. 1897, 1053–60.

——— and Edward Biddle, *Memoirs of the Life and Works of Jean Antoine Houdon, the Sculptor of Voltaire and of Washington,* Philadelphia, 1911.

[Hartford] *Connecticut Courant,* newspaper.

Hartford Daily Courant, newspaper.

Harvard University, *Harvard Tercentenary*

Exhibition Catalogue . . . , Cambridge, 1936.

——— *Quinquennial Catalogue of the Officers and Graduates . . . ,* Cambridge, 1890.

Harvey, George, *Harvey's Scenes of the Primitive Forest of America . . . ,* New York, 1841.

Hastings, George E., *The Life and Works of Francis Hopkinson,* Chicago, 1926.

Hastings, Mrs. Russell, "Pieter Vanderlyn, a Hudson River Portrait Painter (1687–1778)," *Antiques,* XLII, Dec. 1942, 296–9.

Hatch, John Davis, Jr., "Isaac Hutton, Silversmith," *Antiques,* XLVII, Jan. 1945, 32–5.

Havell, Harry P., "Robert Havell's 'View of the Hudson from Tarrytown Heights,'" *New-York Historical Society Quarterly,* XXXI, July 1947, 160–2.

Hawthorne, Julian, *Nathaniel Hawthorne and His Wife: A Biography,* Boston, 1885.

Hawthorne, Nathaniel, *Mosses from an Old Manse,* New York, 1846.

Hayner, Rutherford, *Troy and Rensselaer County, New York,* New York and Chicago, 1925.

Hazard, Samuel, ed., *The Register of Pennsylvania . . . ,* Philadelphia, 1828–35.

Healy, George P. A., *Reminiscences of a Portrait Painter,* Chicago, 1894.

Heilbron, Bertha L., "Documentary Panorama," *Minnesota History,* XXX, March 1949, 14–23.

——— "Edwin Whitefield's Minnesota Lakes," *Minnesota History,* XXXIII, Summer 1953, 247–51.

——— "Making a Motion Picture in 1848; Henry Lewis on the Upper Mississippi," *Minnesota History,* XVII (1936), 131–58, 288–301, 421–36.

——— "A Pioneer Artist on Lake Superior," *Minnesota History,* XXI, June 1940, 149–57.

——— "Pioneer Homemaker, Reminiscences of Mrs. Joseph Ullmann," *Minnesota History,* XXXIV, Autumn 1954, 96–105.

——— "Seth Eastman's Water Colors," *Minnesota History,* XIX, Dec. 1938, 419–23.

——— "The Sioux War Panorama of John Stevens," *Antiques,* LVIII, Sept. 1950, 184–6.

Heitman, Francis B., *Historical Register and Dictionary of the United States Army . . . ,* Washington, 1903.

Held, Julius S., "Edward Hicks and the Tradition," *Art Quarterly,* XIV, Summer 1951, 121–36.

Hemenway, Abby Maria, ed., *Vermont Historical Gazetteer . . . ,* Burlington, 1868–91.

Henderson, Helen W., *The Pennsylvania Academy of the Fine Arts and Other Collections of Philadelphia . . . ,* Boston, 1911.

Hendrickson, Walter B., *David Dale Owen, Pioneer Geologist of the Middle West,* Indianapolis, 1943.

Hennig, Helen K., *William Harrison Scarborough, Portraitist and Miniaturist . . . ,* Columbia, S.C., 1937.

Hensel, William U., "An Artistic Aftermath," *Lancaster County* [Pa.] *Historical Society Papers,* XVII (1913), 106–11.

——— "Jacob Eichholtz, Painter . . . ," *Lancaster County* [Pa.] *Historical Society Papers,* XVI (1912), Supp.

Heraldic Journal; Recording the Armorial Bearings and Genealogies of American Families, Boston, 1865–68.

Herberman, Charles G., *The Sulpicians in the United States,* New York, 1916.

Herrick, Francis H., *Audubon the Naturalist: A History of His Life and Time,* New York and London, 1917.

Herring, James, autobiography, manuscript at New-York Historical Society; a portion of it published as "'The World Was All Before Me': A New Jersey Village Schoolmaster, 1810," by Charles E. Baker, in *Proceedings of the New Jersey Historical Society,* LXXII, Jan. 1954.

Hewins, Amasa, *Hewins's Journal. A Boston Portrait-painter Visits Italy . . . ,* ed. by Francis H. Allen, Boston, 1931.

Heywood, William S., *History of Westminster, Mass. . . . ,* Lowell, 1893.

Hicks, Edward, *Memoirs of the Life and Religious Labors of Edward Hicks . . . Written by Himself,* Philadelphia, 1851.

Hicks, George A., "Thomas Hicks, Artist, a Native of Newtown," *Bucks County* [Pa.] *Historical Society Papers,* IV (1917), 89–92.

Hildeburn, Charles R., "Records of Christ Church, Philadelphia, Baptisms, 1709–1760," *Pennsylvania Magazine of History and Biography,* XIII (1889), 237–41.

Hill, John Henry, *John William Hill, An Artist's Memorial,* New York, 1888.

Hill, Nola, "Bellamy's Greatest Eagle," *Antiques,* LI, April 1947, 259.

Hillard, George S., "Thomas Crawford: A Eulogy," *Atlantic Monthly,* XXIV, July 1869, 40–54.

Hines, Harvey K., *An Illustrated History of the State of Oregon . . . ,* Chicago, 1893.

Hinton, John H., *The History and Topogra-*

phy of the United States of North America . . . , Boston, 1857.

Historic Minnesota, A Centennial Exhibition . . . , Minneapolis Institute of Arts, 1949.

Historical New Hampshire, occasional publication of the New Hampshire Historical Society.

History and Biographical Cyclopaedia of Butler County, Ohio . . . , Cincinnati, 1882.

History of Edwards, Lawrence and Wabash Counties, Ill. . . . , Philadelphia, 1883.

History of Monroe County, N.Y. . . . , Philadelphia, 1877.

History of the Longacre-Longaker-Longenecker Family, Philadelphia, *c.* 1902.

Hitchcock, Margaret R., "And There Were Women Too," *Amherst Graduate Quarterly,* XXVI (1937), 191–4.

Hocker, Edward W., *Germantown 1683–1933 . . .* , Germantown, Pa., 1933.

Holloway, H. Maxson, "Isaac Augustus Wetherby and His Account Books," *New-York Historical Society Quarterly Bulletin,* XXV, April 1941, 55–72.

Holmes, William H., *Smithsonian Institution, The National Gallery of Art, Catalogue of Collections,* Washington, 1922.

Home Authors and Home Artists; or, American Scenery, Art, and Literature . . . (New York, 1852); also known as *The Home Book of the Picturesque.*

Home Book of the Picturesque, see *Home Authors and Home Artists.*

Home Journal, New York, 1846–1901; continued as *Town and Country.*

[Hopkins, John Henry, Jr.,] *The Life of the Late Right Reverend John Henry Hopkins . . .* , New York, 1873.

Hopkins, Timothy, *The Kelloggs in the Old World and the New,* San Francisco, 1903.

Hosmer, Herbert H., Jr., "John G. Chandler," *Antiques,* LII, July 1947, 46–7.

Howe, Gilman Bigelow, *Genealogy of the Bigelow Family of America . . .* , Worcester, 1890.

Howell, Ethel, "Joseph B. Smith, Painter," *Antiques,* LXVII, Feb. 1955, 150–1.

Howell, Warren R., "Pictorial Californiana," *Antiques,* LXV, Jan. 1954, 62–5.

Howell's *California in the Fifties . . .* , ed. by Douglas S. Watson, San Francisco, John Howell, 1936.

Howells, Mildred, ed., *Life in Letters of William Dean Howells,* Garden City, 1928.

Howland, Garth A., "John Valentine Haidt, a Little Known 18th Century Painter," *Pennsylvania History,* VIII, Oct. 1941, 304–13.

Hubbard, Geraldine H., "The Hopkins Flower Prints," *Antiques,* LV, April 1949, 286–7.

Hudson, Charles, *History of the Town of Lexington, Middlesex County, Mass. . . .* , Boston and New York, 1913.

Hughes, John T., *Doniphan's Expedition . . .* , Cincinnati, 1848.

Hume, Edgar E., "Nicola Marschall . . . the German Artist Who Designed the Confederate Flag and Uniform," *American-German Review,* VI (1940), No. 6, 6–9, 39–40.

Hunter, Wilbur H., Jr., "The Battle of Baltimore Illustrated," *William and Mary Quarterly,* 3d Ser. VIII, April 1951, 235–7.

——— "Joshua Johnston: 18th Century Negro Artist," *American Collector,* XVII, Feb. 1948, 6–8.

——— *The Paintings of Alfred Jacob Miller, Artist of Baltimore and the West,* Baltimore, 1950.

——— "Philip Tilyard," *William and Mary Quarterly,* 3d Ser. VII, July 1950, 393–405.

[Huntsville, Ala.] *Southern Advocate,* newspaper.

Hyer, Richard, "Gerritt Schipper, Miniaturist and Crayon Portraitist," *New York Genealogical and Biographical Record,* LXXXIII, April 1952, 70–2.

I

Ide, John Jay, "A Discovery in Early American Portraiture," *Antiques,* XXV, March 1934, 99–100.

——— *The Portraits of John Jay . . .* , New York, 1938.

[Indianapolis] *Daily Indiana State Sentinel,* newspaper.

Innes, John H., *New Amsterdam and Its People . . .* , New York, 1902.

Inness, George, Jr., *Life, Art and Letters of George Inness,* New York, 1917.

International Studio, New York, 1897–1931.

Iowa Journal of History and Politics, Iowa City, 1903—.

Ireland, Joseph N., *Records of the New York Stage,* New York, 1866–67.

Irving, Pierre M., *Life and Letters of Washington Irving,* New York, 1864.

Irving, Washington, *Journals of Washington Irving,* ed. by William P. Trent and George S. Hellman, Boston, 1919.

Ives, Joseph C., *Report upon the Colorado River of the West Explored in 1857 and 1858,* Washington, 1861.

J

Jackson, Charles T., *Final Report on the Geology and Mineralogy of the State of New Hampshire . . . ,* Concord, 1844.

——— *Views and Map Illustrative of the Scenery and Geology of the State of New Hampshire,* Boston, 1845.

Jackson, Emily N., *Ancestors in Silhouette, Cut by August Edouart . . . ,* London and New York, 1921.

——— *Silhouette; Notes and Dictionary,* London, 1938.

Jackson, Joseph, "Krimmel, 'The American Hogarth,'" *International Studio,* XCIII, June 1929, 33–6, 86, 88.

——— "John A. Woodside, Philadelphia's Glorified Sign-Painter," *Pennsylvania Magazine of History and Biography,* LVII, Jan. 1933, 58–65.

Jackson, Joseph H., ed., *Gold Rush Album,* New York, 1949.

"Jacob Marling, an Early North Carolina Artist," *North Carolina Booklet* X, April 1910, 196–9.

Jacobson, Margaret E., "Olaf Krans," in Lipman and Winchester, *Primitive Painters in America, 1750–1950; An Anthology* (New York, 1950), 139–48.

James Eddy . . . Biographical Sketch, Providence, 1889.

James, Edwin, comp., *Account of an Expedition from Pittsburgh to the Rocky Mountains, Performed in the Years 1819, '20 . . . ,* London, 1823; reprinted in Thwaites, *Early Western Travels,* XIV–XVII.

James, Henry, *William Wetmore Story and His Friends, from Letters, Diaries, and Recollections,* Boston, 1903.

Jameson, Ephraim O., *The Jamesons in America, 1647–1900 . . . ,* Boston, Mass., and Concord, N.H., 1901.

Jefferson, Thomas, *The Writings of Thomas Jefferson,* Monticello Edition, Washington, 1904–05.

Jenkins, Lawrence W., "William Cook of Salem, Mass . . . ," *Proceedings of the American Antiquarian Society,* XXXIV, April 1924, 27–38.

[Jersey City] *Evening Journal,* newspaper.

Jewett, Frederick C., *History and Genealogy of the Jewetts of America . . . ,* New York, 1908.

Jewett Family Record, manuscript owned by Mrs. P. B. McLean.

Johnson, Charlotte B., "The European Tradition and Alvan Fisher," *Art in America,* XLI, Spring 1953, 79–87.

Johnson, Jane T., "William Dunlap and His Times," *Antiques,* XXXVII, Feb. 1940, 72–4.

Johnston, Joseph E., "Reports of the Secretary of War, with Reconnaissances of Routes from San Antonio to El Paso," 31 Cong., 1 Sess., *Senate Exec. Doc.* 64, 1850.

Jonas, Edward A., *Matthew Harris Jouett, Kentucky Portrait Painter,* Louisville, 1938.

Jones, Emma C. B., *The Brewster Genealogy, 1566–1907 . . . ,* New York, 1908.

Jones, J. Wesley, "Jones' Pantoscope of California," *California Historical Society Quarterly,* VI, June 1927, 109–29, and Sept. 1927, 238–53.

"Joseph Steward and The Hartford Museum," *Connecticut Historical Society Bulletin,* XVIII, Jan.–April 1953.

Josephson, Marba C., "What Did the Prophet Joseph Smith Look Like," *The Improvement Era,* May 1953, 311–13, 374.

Journal des Arts, Paris, 1879–1932.

Journal of the American Society of Architectural Historians, 1940—.

K

Kaplan, Milton, comp., *Pictorial Americana; a Select List of Photographic Negatives in the Prints and Photographs Division of the Library of Congress . . . ,* Washington, 1945.

Karolik Cat. *M. and M. Karolik Collection of American Paintings 1815 to 1865,* Cambridge, 1949.

Karr, Louise, "Paintings on Velvet," *Antiques,* XX, Sept. 1931, 162–5.

Katz, Irving I., "Jews in Detroit, Prior to and Including 1850," *Detroit Historical Society Bulletin,* VI, Feb. 1950, 4–10.

Keating, William H., *Narrative of an Expedition to the Source of St. Peter's River . . . in 1823 . . . ,* London, 1825.

Kelby, William, *Notes on American Artists 1754–1820 . . .*, New York, 1922.
Keller, I. C., "Thomas Buchanan Read," *Pennsylvania History,* VI, July 1939, 133–46.
Kellner, Sydney, "The Beginnings of Landscape Painting in America," *Art in America,* XXVI, Oct. 1938, 158–68.
Kendall, John S., *The Golden Age of the New Orleans Theater,* Baton Rouge, 1952.
Kende Galleries [New York], Catalogue No. 228, Feb. 9, 1946.
Kent, Alan E., "Early Commercial Lithography in Wisconsin," *Wisconsin Magazine of History,* XXXVI, Summer 1953, 247–51.
Kentucky Gazette, Lexington newspaper.
Kentucky Herald, Lexington newspaper.
Keyes, Homer E., "A. F. Tait in Painting and Lithograph," *Antiques,* XXIV, July 1933, 24–5.
——— "The Boston State House in Blue Staffordshire," *Antiques,* I, March 1922, 115–20.
——— " 'The Bottle' and Its American Refills," *Antiques,* XIX, May 1931, 386–8, 390.
——— "Coincidence and Henrietta Johnston," *Antiques,* XVI, Dec. 1929, 490–4.
——— "Doubts Regarding Hesselius," *Antiques,* XXXIV, Sept. 1938, 144–6.
Kidder, Mary H., *List of Miniatures Painted by Anson Dickinson, 1803–1851,* Hartford, 1937.
Kieffer, Elizabeth C., "David McNeely Stauffer," *Papers of the Lancaster County [Pa.] Historical Society,* LVI, No. 7 (1952), 161–75.
Kimball, Sidney Fiske, "Furniture Carvings by Samuel Field McIntire," *Antiques,* XXIII, Feb. 1933, 56–8.
——— "Joseph Wright and His Portraits of Washington," *Antiques,* XV, May 1929, 376–82; XVII, Jan. 1930, 35–9.
——— *The Life Portraits of Jefferson and Their Replicas,* Philadelphia, 1944; Vol. LXXXVIII of the *Proceedings of the American Philosophical Society.*
——— *Mr. Samuel McIntire, Carver, the Architect of Salem,* Portland, Me., 1940.
King, Thomas Starr, *The White Hills; Their Legends, Landscapes, and Poetry,* Boston, 1860.
Kinietz, William V., *John Mix Stanley and His Indian Paintings,* Ann Arbor, 1942.
Kingston, Mass. *Vital Records of Kingston, Massachusetts, to the Year 1850,* Boston, 1911.
Kirstein, Lincoln, "Rediscovery of William Rimmer," *Magazine of Art,* XL, March 1947, 94–5.
Knittle, Rhea M., *Early Ohio Taverns, Tavern-sign, Stage-coach, Barge, Banner, Chair and Settee Painters,* No. 1 of The Ohio Frontier Series, Aug. 1, 1937.
——— "The Kelloggs, Hartford Lithographers," *Antiques,* X, July 1926, 42–6.
Knoedler, M., and Company, *Life Masks of Noted Americans of 1825, by John I. H. Browere,* New York, Feb. 1940.
Knowlton, Helen M., *Art Life of William Morris Hunt,* Boston, 1899.
Knox, Dudley W., *A History of the U. S. Navy,* New York, 1936.
Knox, Katharine McCook, "A Note on Michel Felice Corné," *Antiques,* LVII, June 1950, 450–1.
——— *The Sharples . . .*, New Haven, 1930.
Knubel, Helen M., "Alexander Anderson; a Self Portrait," *Colophon,* New Graphic Series, I, No. 1 (New York, 1939), 8–11.
Köhler, Karl, *Briefe aus Amerika . . .*, Darmstadt, 1854.
Koehler, Sylvester R., *Catalogue of the Engraved and Lithographed Work of John Cheney and Seth Wells Cheney,* Boston, 1891.
Koke, Richard J., "Milestones Along the Old Highways of New York City," *New-York Historical Society Quarterly,* XXXIV, July 1950, 165–234.
Kouwenhoven, John A., *The Columbia Historical Portrait of New York . . .*, New York, 1953.
——— "Th. Nast as We Don't Know Him," *Colophon,* New Graphic Series, I, No. 2 (New York, 1939), 37–48.
Kunstchronik und Kunstmarkt, Leipzig, 1866–1926.
Kurz, Frederick, *Journal . . . 1846 to 1852,* Washington, 1937; Bulletin 115 of the Bureau of American Ethnology, Smithsonian Institution.

L

Ladies Garland and Family Wreath . . ., Philadelphia, 1837–50.
Lafferty, S. E., "Artists Who Have Worked in Baltimore, 1796–1880," unpublished manuscript compiled about 1934.
Lambert, John, *Travels Through Canada*

and the United States of North America in the Years 1806, 1807, and 1808 . . . , London, 1813.
Lancaster, Clay, "Primitive Mural Painter of Kentucky: Alfred Cohen," *American Collector,* XVII, Dec. 1948, 6–8, 19.
Lancaster County [Pa.] Historical Society, *Historical Papers and Addresses of the . . .* , Lancaster, 1896—.
——— *Loan Exhibition of Historical and Contemporary Portraits Illustrating the Evolution of Portraiture in Lancaster County . . . November 23 to December 13, 1912,* Lancaster, 1912.
Landauer, Bella C., *My City, 'Tis of Thee; New York City on Sheet-music Covers . . .* , New York, 1951.
Landgren, Marchal E., "Robert Loftin Newman," *American Magazine of Art,* XXVIII, March 1935, 134–40.
Lane, Gladys R., "Rhode Island's Earliest Engraver," *Antiques,* VII, March 1925, 133–7.
Lane, James Warren, *Whistler,* New York, 1942.
Lanman, Charles, *Haphazard Personalities; Chiefly of Noted Americans,* Boston and New York, 1886.
Larkin, Oliver W., *Samuel F. B. Morse and American Democratic Art,* Boston and Toronto, 1954.
Larousse, Pierre, *Grand Dictionnaire Universel du XIXème Siecle . . .* , Paris, 1866–90.
Larsen, Ellouise B., *American Historical Views on Staffordshire China,* New York, 1939.
Lassiter, William L., "James Eights and His Albany Views," *Antiques,* LIII, May 1948, 360–1.
Latrobe, Benjamin Henry, *Impressions Respecting New Orleans . . .* , ed. by Samuel Wilson, Jr., New York, 1951.
——— *The Journal of Latrobe,* with an introduction by J. H. B. Latrobe, New York, 1905.
Lee, Cuthbert, "John Smibert," *Antiques,* XVIII, Aug. 1930, 118–21.
[Lee, Hannah F.,] *Familiar Sketches of Sculpture and Sculptors,* Boston, 1854.
Leng, Charles W., and William T. Davis, *Staten Island and Its People, A History, 1609–1933,* New York, 1930–33.
Lesley, Everett Parker, "Patience Lovell Wright, America's First Sculptor," *Art in America,* XXIV, Oct. 1936, 148–54, 157.
——— "Some Clues to Thomas Cole," *Magazine of Art,* XLII, Feb. 1949, 42–8.
——— "Thomas Cole and the Romantic Sensibility," *Art Quarterly,* V, Summer 1942, 199–220.
Leslie, Charles R., *Autobiographical Recollections . . .* , Boston and London, 1860.
Lester, C. E., "Charles Loring Elliott," *Harper's New Monthly Magazine,* XXXVIII, Dec. 1868, 42–50.
Letters and Papers of John Singleton Copley and Henry Pelham, 1739–1776, Boston, 1914; Vol. LXXI of the *Collections* of the Massachusetts Historical Society.
Levering, Joseph M., *A History of Bethlehem, Pa., 1741–1892 . . .* , Bethlehem, 1903.
Levinge, Richard G. A., *Echoes from the Backwoods . . .* , London, 1846.
Lewis, Charles L., "Alonzo Chappell and His Naval Paintings," *Proceedings of the United States Naval Institute,* LXIII (1937), 359–62.
Lewis, Henry, "Journal of a Canoe Voyage from the Falls of St. Anthony to St. Louis," *Minnesota History,* XVII (1936), 149–58, 288–301, 421–36.
Lewis, James O., *The Aboriginal Portfolio . . .* , Philadelphia, 1835.
[Lexington] *Kentucky Gazette,* newspaper.
[———] *Kentucky Herald,* newspaper.
Libhart, Antonio C., "John Jay Libhart, Artist," *Historical Papers and Addresses of the Lancaster County* [Pa.] *Historical Society,* XVI (1912), 241–6.
Life, Chicago, 1936—.
Linton, William J., *The History of Wood Engraving in America,* Boston, 1882.
Lipman, Jean, *American Folk Art in Wood, Metal and Stone,* New York, 1948.
——— "American Townscapes," *Antiques,* XLVI, Dec. 1944, 340–1.
——— "Benjamin Greenleaf, New England Limner," *Antiques,* LII, Sept. 1947, 195–7.
——— "Deborah Goldsmith, Itinerant Portrait Painter," *Antiques,* XLIV, Nov. 1943, 227–9.
——— "Eunice Pinney, An Early Connecticut Water-colorist," *Art Quarterly,* VI, Summer 1943, 213–21.
——— "I. J. H. Bradley, Portrait Painter," *Art in America,* XXXIII, July 1945, 154–66.
——— "Joseph H. Hidley (1830–1872): His New York Townscapes," *American Collector,* XVI, June 1947, 10–11.
——— "Mary Ann Willson," in Lipman and Winchester, *Primitive Painters in America,* New York, 1950.
——— "Mermaids in Folk Art," *Antiques,* LIII, March 1948, 211–13.

——— "Miss Willson's Watercolors," *American Collector,* XIII, Feb. 1944, 8–9, 20.
——— "Peaceable Kingdoms by Three Pennsylvania Primitives," *American Collector,* XIV, Aug. 1945, 6–7, 16.
——— "Rufus Porter, Yankee Wall Painter," *Art in America,* XXXVIII, Oct. 1950, 135–200.
——— "William Verstille's Connecticut Miniatures," *Art in America,* XXIX, Oct. 1941, 229.
——— and Alice Winchester, *Primitive Painters in America, 1750–1850; An Anthology,* New York, 1950.
List of All the Officers of the Army and Royal Marines . . . , London, War Office, March 13, 1815.
"List of Portraits Painted by Ethan Allen Greenwood," *Proceedings of the American Antiquarian Society,* LVI, April 1946, 129–53.
Little, Nina Fletcher, *American Decorative Wall Painting, 1700–1850,* Sturbridge, 1952.
——— "An Unusual Painting," *Antiques,* XLIII, May 1943, 222.
——— "Dr. Rufus Hathaway, Physician and Painter of Duxbury, Mass., 1770–1822," *Art in America,* XLI, Summer 1953, 95–139.
——— "Earliest Signed Picture by T. Chambers . . . ," *Antiques,* LIII, April 1948, 285.
——— "Itinerant Painting in America, 1750–1850," *New York History,* XXX, April 1949, 204–16.
——— "J. S. Blunt, New England Landscape Painter," *Antiques,* LIV, Sept. 1948, 172–4.
——— "Joseph Shoemaker Russell and His Water Color Views," *Antiques,* LIX, Jan. 1951, 52–3.
——— "Recently Discovered Paintings by Winthrop Chandler," *Art in America,* XXXVI, April 1948, 81–97.
——— "T. Chambers, Man or Myth," *Antiques,* LIII, March 1948, 194–6.
——— "Thomas Thompson, Artist-Observer of the American Scene," *Antiques,* LV, Feb. 1949, 121–3.
——— "William Matthew Prior, the Traveling Artist, and His In-laws, the Painting Hamblens," *Antiques,* LIII, Jan. 1948, 44–8.
——— "Winthrop Chandler," *Art in America,* XXXV, April 1947, 77–168.
[Little Rock] *Arkansas Gazette,* newspaper.
Loan Exhibition of Historical and Contemporary Portraits Illustrating the Evolution of Portraiture in Lancaster County, Pa., Lancaster County Historical Society, 1912.
Locke, Alain LeRoy, *The Negro in Art . . . ,* Washington, 1940.
Lockley, Fred, *Oregon Trail Blazers,* New York, 1929.
Lockridge, Ross F., *The Old Fauntleroy House,* New Harmony, Ind., 1939.
London, Hannah R., *Portraits of Jews by Gilbert Stuart and Other Early American Artists,* New York, 1927.
——— *Shades of My Forefathers,* Springfield, Mass., 1941.
Longacre, James B., "Diary," *Pennsylvania Magazine of History and Biography,* XXIX, April 1905, 134–42.
Loomis, Elias and Elisha S., *Descendants of Joseph Loomis in America . . . ,* Beria, Ohio, 1909.
Looney, Ben Earl, "Historical Sketch of Art in Louisiana," *Louisiana Historical Quarterly,* XVIII (1935), 382–96.
Lorant, Stefan, *The New World; The First Pictures of America, Made by John White and Jacques Le Moyne and Engraved by Theodore De Bry . . . ,* New York, 1946.
Lord, Jeanette M., "Some Light on Hubard," *Antiques,* XIII, June 1928, 485.
Lossing, Benson J., "The National Academy of the Arts of Design and Its Surviving Founders," *Harper's New Monthly Magazine,* LXVI, May 1883, 852–63.
Loubat, Joseph F., *The Medallic History of the United States of America 1776–1876,* New York, 1878.
[Louisville, Ky.] *Focus,* newspaper.
Lovejoy, Edward D., "Poker Drawings of Ball-Hughes," *Antiques,* L, Sept. 1946, 175.
Lowell, Mass. *Vital Records of Lowell, Mass., to the End of the Year 1849,* Salem, 1930.
Lucas, Fielding, *Progressive Drawing Book . . . ,* Baltimore, 1827.
Lyman, Grace A., "William Matthew Prior, the 'Painting Garret' Artist," *Antiques,* XXVI, Nov. 1934, 180.
Lyman, Horace S., *History of Oregon . . . ,* New York, 1903.
Lyman, Lila Parrish, "William Johnston (1732–1772), a Forgotten Portrait Painter of New England," *New-York Historical Society Quarterly,* XXXIX, Jan. 1955, 63–78.
Lynch, Marguerite, "John Neagle's Diary," *Art in America,* XXXVII, April 1949, 79–99.

M

Mabee, Carleton, *The American Leonardo; A Life of Samuel F. B. Morse,* New York, 1943.

MacAgy, Jermayne, "Three Paintings by Thomas Waterman Wood (1823–1903)," *California Palace of the Legion of Honor Bulletin,* II, May 1944, 9–15.

McCausland, Elizabeth, *A. H. Maurer,* New York, 1951.

——— "American Still-life Paintings in the Collection of Paul Magriel," *Antiques,* LXVII, April 1955, 324–7.

——— "The Early Inness," *American Collector,* XV, May 1946, 6–8.

——— *George Inness, An American Landscape Painter, 1825–1894,* New York, 1946; catalogue of exhibition at Springfield, Mass.

——— *The Life and Work of Edward Lamson Henry . . . ,* Albany, 1945.

McClinton, Katharine, "American Flower Lithographs," *Antiques,* XLIX, June 1946, 361–3.

Macomb, John N., *Annual Report, Chief Topographical Engineer, 1860 and 1861. His Expedition from Santa Fé to the Portion of the Grand and Green Basin of the Colorado of the West, in 1859,* Washington, 1876.

McCormack, Helen G., "The Hubard Gallery Duplicate Book," *Antiques,* XLV, Feb. 1944, 68–9.

——— *William James Hubard, 1807–1862,* Valentine Museum, Richmond, Va., 1948.

McCormick, Gene E., "Fitz Hugh Lane, Gloucester Artist, 1804–1865," *Art Quarterly,* XV, Winter 1952, 291–306.

McCracken, Harold, *Portrait of the Old West . . . ,* New York, 1952.

McCreery, Emilie, "The French Architect of the Allegheny City Hall," *Western Pennsylvania Historical Magazine,* XIV, July 1931, 237–41.

McDermott, John F., "Charles Deas: Painter of the Frontier," *Art Quarterly,* XIII, Autumn 1950, 293–311.

——— "Early Sketches of T. R. Peale," *Nebraska History,* XXXIII, Sept. 1952, 186–9.

——— "Gold Rush Movies," *California Historical Society Quarterly,* XXXIII, March 1954, 29–38.

——— "Indian Portraits," *Antiques,* LI, May 1947, 320–2; LV, Jan. 1949, 61.

——— "J. C. Wild and Fort Snelling," *Minnesota History,* XXXII, Spring 1951, 12–14.

——— "J. C. Wild, Western Painter and Lithographer," *Ohio State Archaeological and Historical Quarterly,* LX, April 1951, 111–25.

——— "Leon Pomarede, 'Our Parisian Knight of the Easel,'" *Bulletin of the City Art Museum of St. Louis,* XXXIV, Winter 1949, 8–18.

——— "Likeness by Audubon," *Antiques,* LXVII, June 1955, 499–501.

——— ed., "Minnesota 100 Years Ago, Described and Pictured by Adolf Hoeffler," *Minnesota History,* XXXIII, Autumn 1952, 112–25.

——— "Newsreel—Old Style; or, Four Miles of Canvas," *Antiques,* XLIV, July 1943, 10–13.

——— "Peter Rindisbacher: Frontier Reporter," *Art Quarterly,* XII, Spring 1949, 129–45.

——— "Samuel Seymour: Pioneer Artist of the Plains and the Rockies," *Annual Report of the Smithsonian Institution,* 1950, 497–509.

——— ed., *Travels in Search of the Elephant: The Wanderings of Alfred S. Waugh, Artist, in Louisiana, Missouri, and Santa Fé, in 1845–1846,* St. Louis, 1951.

MacFarlane, Janet R., "Hedley, Headley, or Hidley, Painter," *New York History,* XXVIII, Jan. 1947, 74–5.

M'Ilvaine, William, Jr., *Sketches of Scenery and Notes of Personal Adventure in California and Mexico,* Philadelphia, 1850.

McIntyre, Robert G., *Martin Johnson Heade, 1819–1904* (New York, 1948).

McKay, George L., "A Register of Artists, Booksellers, Printers and Publishers in New York City," *New York Public Library Bulletin:* [1801–10], XLIII (1939), 711–24, 849–58; [1811–20], XLIV (1940), 351–7, 415–28, 475–87; [1781–1800], XLV (1941), 387–95, 483–99.

Maclay, Edgar S., *Reminiscences of the Old Navy from the Journals and Private Papers of Captain Edward Trenchard and Rear-Admiral Stephen Decatur Trenchard,* New York and London, 1898.

MacMinn, George R., *The Theater of the Golden Era in California,* Caldwell, Ida., 1941.

Magazine of Art, London and New York, 1878–1904.

——— Washington, American Federation of Arts, 1936—.

"Maine Artists," *Maine Library Bulletin,* XIII, July–Oct. 1927, 3–23.
Maine Historical Society [Portland], "Catalogue of Oil Portraits in the Library," typed manuscript (1938) at Frick Art Reference Library, New York.
Maine Register, for the Year 1855 . . . with a Complete Business Directory of the State, Boston, 1855.
Maine Register and Business Directory for the Year 1856 . . . , South Berwick, Me., 1856.
Mallett, Daniel T., *Mallett's Index of Artists . . . ,* New York, 1935.
——— *Supplement to Mallett's Index of Artists . . . ,* New York, 1940.
Manchester Historic Association, *Collections of the . . . ,* Manchester, N.H., 1897–1912.
Marblehead, Mass. *Vital Records of Marblehead, Mass., to the End of the Year 1849,* Salem, 1903–08.
Marceau, Henri, *William Rush, 1756–1833, the First Native American Sculptor,* Philadelphia, 1937.
Marcy, Randolph B., *Exploration of the Red River of Louisiana . . .* (Washington, 1853); also in 32 Cong., 2 Sess., *Senate Exec. Doc.* 54.
Markens, Isaac, *The Hebrews in America, a Series of Historical and Biographical Sketches,* New York, 1888.
Marryat, Francis S. ("Frank"), *Mountains and Molehills; or, Recollections of a Burnt Journal,* New York, 1855.
Martin, Elizabeth G., *Homer D. Martin, a Reminiscence,* New York, 1904.
Martin, Mary, "Profiles of Our Early American Forebears Painted on Glass," *House and Garden,* LVI, Dec. 1929, 82–3, 126, 130, 146.
——— "Some American Profiles and Their Makers," *Connoisseur,* LXXIV, Feb. 1926, 87–98.
Martin, Oscar T., "The City of Springfield: Fine Arts," in *The History of Clark County, Ohio,* Chicago, 1881, 489–96.
Martin, Mrs. William H., *Catalogue of All Known Paintings by Matthew Harris Jouett,* Louisville, 1939.
Marvin, Abijah P., *History of the Town of Lancaster, Mass. . . . 1643–1879,* Lancaster, 1879.
Maryland Herald, Easton newspaper.
Maryland History Notes, Maryland Historical Society, 1943—.
Mason, George C., *Reminiscences of Newport,* Newport, 1884.
Mason, J. Alden, "Grand Moving Diorama, a Special Feature," *Pennsylvania Archaeologist,* Jan. 1942, 14–16.
Massachusetts Historical Society, *Collections of the . . . ,* Boston, 1792—.
——— *Proceedings of the . . . ,* Boston, 1859—.
Masterson, James R., *Tall Tales of Arkansaw,* Boston, 1943.
Mather, Frank Jewett, Jr., *Homer Martin, Poet in Landscape,* New York, 1912.
Maude, John, *Visit to the Falls of Niagara in 1800,* London, 1826.
Mayer, Francis B., *Drawings and Paintings by Francis B. Mayer,* Baltimore, 1872.
——— *With Pen and Pencil on the Frontier in 1851; The Diary and Sketches of Frank Blackwell Mayer,* ed. by Bertha L. Heilbron, Publications of the Minnesota Historical Society, Narratives and Documents, Vol. I, St. Paul, 1932.
Mayo. Unpublished notes on Washington and Baltimore artists by the late J. F. H. Mayo of Washington, D.C., and Bethesda, Md.
Meares, John, *Voyages Made in the Years 1788 and 1789, from China to the Northwest Coast of America . . . ,* London, 1790.
"Memoirs of James Peller Malcolm, F.S.A.," *Gentleman's Magazine,* LXXXV, May 1815, 467–9.
Meredith, Roy, *Mr. Lincoln's Camera Man: Mathew B. Brady,* New York, 1946.
Merrill, Arch, *The White Woman and Her Valley,* Rochester, 1955.
Merritt, Jesse, "Thomas Worth, Humorist to Currier & Ives," *American Collector,* X, Aug. 1941, 8–9.
Metropolitan Museum of Art [New York] *Bulletin,* 1905—.
Metropolitan Museum of Art [New York], *Life in America . . . ,* New York, 1939.
——— *William Sidney Mount and His Circle,* New York, 1945.
Middlebrook, L. F., "A Few of the New England Engravers," *Essex Institute Historical Collections,* LXII, Oct. 1926, 359–63.
Middlefield, Mass. *Vital Records of Middlefield, Mass., to the Year 1850,* Boston, 1907.
Middleton, Margaret S., *Jeremiah Theus, Colonial Artist of Charles Town,* Columbia, S.C., 1953.
——— "Thomas Coram, Engraver and Painter," *Antiques,* XXIX, June 1936, 242–4.
Military Affairs, American Military Institute, Washington, 1937—.
Millar, Bruce, "Stettinius, Pennsylvania

Primitive Portraitist," *American Collector,* VIII, May 1939, 5.

Millard, Everett L., "The Browere Life Masks," *Art in America,* XXXVIII, April 1950, 69–80.

Miller, Dorothy, *The Life and Work of David G. Blythe,* Pittsburgh, 1950.

Miller, F. de Wolfe, *Christopher Pearse Cranch and His Caricatures of New England Transcendentalism,* Cambridge, 1951.

Miller, John, *A Twentieth-Century History of Erie County, Pa . . . ,* Chicago, 1909.

Millet, Josiah B., ed., *George Fuller, His Life and Works,* Boston and New York, 1886.

Miner, George L., *Angell's Lane: The History of a Little Street in Providence,* Providence, 1948.

Minick, Rachel, "Henry Ary, an Unknown Painter of the Hudson River School," *Brooklyn Museum Bulletin,* XI, Summer 1950, 14–24.

Minnesota History, St. Paul, Minnesota Historical Society, 1915—.

Minutes of the Common Council of the City of New York, 1784–1831, Vol. XIX, May 3, 1830, to May 9, 1831, New York, 1917.

Minutes of the Provincial Council of Pennsylvania . . . , Philadelphia and Harrisburg, 1852.

Missouri Democrat, St. Louis newspaper.

Missouri Historical Review, Columbia, State Historical Society of Missouri, 1906—.

Missouri Historical Society, *Bulletin of the . . . ,* St. Louis, 1944—.

Mitchell, C. H., "Benjamin West's Death of General Wolfe," *Journal of the Warburg and Courtauld Institutes,* VII (1944), 20–33.

Mitchell, Lucy B., "James Sanford Ellsworth, American Miniature Painter," *Art in America,* XLI, Autumn 1953, 151–84.

Monaghan, Frank, "The American Drawings of Baroness Hyde de Neuville," *Franco-American Review,* II, Spring 1938, 217–20.

Montgomery, Morton L., *History of Berks County in Pennsylvania,* Philadelphia, 1886.

Montgomery [Ala.] *Daily Advertiser,* newspaper.

——— *Weekly Mail,* newspaper.

Mook, Maurice A., "S. Roesen, 'The Williamsport Painter,'" *The Morning Call* [Allentown, Pa.], Dec. 3, 1955.

Moravian Church Records, New York City, 1744–1805. Births, deaths, etc. Photostatic copy at New-York Historical Society.

Morgan, Charles H., and Margaret C. Toole, "Benjamin West: His Times and His Influence," *Art in America,* XXXVIII, Dec. 1950, 205–78.

Morgan, John Hill, *Early American Painters . . . ,* New York, 1921.

——— *Gilbert Stuart and His Pupils,* New York, 1939.

——— "John Wollaston's Portraits of Brandt and Margaret Van Wyck Schuyler," *Antiques,* XXI, Jan. 1932, 20–2.

——— *A Sketch of the Life of John Ramage, Miniature Painter,* New York, 1930.

——— and Mantle Fielding, *The Life Portraits of Washington and Their Replicas,* Philadelphia, 1931.

——— and Henry W. Foote, "An Extension of Lawrence Park's Descriptive List of the Works of Joseph Blackburn," *Proceedings of the American Antiquarian Society,* XLVI, April 1936, 15–81.

Morman, John F., "The Painting Preacher: John Valentine Haidt," *Pennsylvania History,* XX, April 1953, 180–6.

Morris, Harrison S., *Masterpieces of the Sea: William T. Richards, a Brief Outline of His Life and Art,* Philadelphia and London, 1912.

Morrison, Leonard A., and Stephen P. Sharples, *History of the Kimball Family in America, from 1634 to 1897 . . . ,* Boston, 1897.

Morse, Edward L., *Samuel F. B. Morse, His Letters and Journals,* Boston and New York, 1914.

Moses, Henry, *The Gallery of Pictures Painted by Benjamin West,* London, 1811.

[Mount Holly,] *New Jersey Mirror and Burlington County Advertiser,* newspaper.

Müller, Hermann A., *Allgemeines Künstler-Lexikon . . . ,* Frankfurt-am-Main, 1895–1901.

Mulkearn, Lois, "Pittsburgh in 1806," *Carnegie Magazine,* XXII, May 1949, 322.

Mumford, James G., *Mumford Memoirs; Being the Story of the New England Mumfords from the Year 1655 to the Present Time,* Boston, 1900.

Mundy, Ezra F., *Nicholas Mundy and Descendants Who Settled in New Jersey in 1665,* Lawrence, Kans., 1907.

Munger, Jeremiah B., *The Munger Book . . . ,* New Haven, 1915.

Municipal Museum of Baltimore, *The Paint-*

ings of Philip Tilyard . . . , Baltimore, 1949.
Munsell, Joel, *The Annals of Albany,* Albany, 1850–59.
——— *Collections on the History of Albany . . . ,* Albany, 1865–71.
Munson, Myron A., *The Munson Record . . . ,* New Haven, 1895.
Murphy, Henry C., ed., *Journal of a Voyage to New York and a Tour in Several of the American Colonies in 1679–80, by Jaspar Dankers and Peter Sluyter . . . ,* Brooklyn, 1867.
Murrell, William, *A History of American Graphic Humor,* New York, 1933–38.
The Museum, Newark, N.J., Museum Association, 1917—.
Museum Echoes, Ohio State Museum, Ohio State Archaeological and Historical Society, Columbus, 1928—.
Museum Graphic, St. Joseph, Mo., Museum, 1949—.
Museum Notes, Rhode Island School of Design, Museum of Arts, Providence, 1943—.
Museum of the City of New York, *Bulletin,* 1937—.
Museum of Modern Art, *American Folk Art: The Art of the Common Man in America,* New York, 1932.

N

NAD Cat. Catalogues of annual exhibitions, National Academy of Design.
Nägler, Georg K., *Neues allgemeines Künstler-Lexikon . . . ,* Munich, 1835–52.
National Cyclopedia of American Biography . . . , New York, 1893—.
National Academy of Design, annual exhibition catalogues (New York, 1826–60); for a convenient index to these, see Cowdrey, *National Academy of Design.*
——— *Catalogue of the Permanent Collection,* New York, 1911.
National Gallery of Art, *American Battle Painting 1776–1918,* Washington, 1944.
Navy Register. Register of the Commissioned and Warrant Officers of the Navy of the United States . . . for the year . . . , Washington, 1859–61.
Nelson, Helen C., "A Case of Confused Identity; Two Jewetts Named William," *Antiques,* XLII, Nov. 1942, 251–3.
——— "The Jewetts, William and William S.," *International Studio,* LXXXIII, Jan. 1926, 39–42.
Nelson's Biographical Dictionary and Historical Reference Book of Erie County, Pa. . . . , Erie, 1896.
Nerney, Helen, "An Italian Painter Comes to Rhode Island," *Rhode Island History,* I, July 1942, 65–71.
Ness, Zenobia, and Louise Orwig, *Iowa Artists of the First Hundred Years,* Des Moines, 1939.
Neuhaus, Eugen, *The History and Ideals of American Art,* Stanford, Cal., 1931.
Nevins, Allan, *Frémont, Pathmaker of the West,* New York, 1939.
——— and Frank Weitenkampf, *A Century of Political Cartoons; Caricature in the United States from 1800 to 1900,* New York, 1944.
"The New Art of Lithotint," *Miss Leslie's Magazine,* April 1843, 113–14.
[New Brunswick, N.J.] *Fredonian,* newspaper.
New England Magazine, Boston, 1884–1917.
[New Haven] *Connecticut Journal and New-Haven Post Boy,* newspaper.
New Haven, Conn. *Vital Records of New Haven, 1649–1850,* Hartford, 1917.
New Jersey Historical Society, *Proceedings of the . . . ,* Newark, 1847—.
New Jersey Journal, Elizabeth newspaper.
New Jersey Mirror and Burlington County Advertiser, Mount Holly newspaper.
New Orleans Argus, newspaper.
New Orleans Bee, newspaper.
New Orleans Commercial Times, newspaper.
New Orleans Creole, newspaper.
New Orleans Crescent, newspaper.
[New Orleans] *Delta,* newspaper.
[———] *L'Ami des Lois et Journal du Soir,* newspaper.
[———] *Louisiana Courier,* newspaper.
[———] *Louisiana Gazette,* newspaper.
[———] *Mercantile Advertiser,* newspaper.
[———] *Moniteur du Sud,* newspaper.
[———] *Orleanian,* newspaper.
[———] *Picayune,* newspaper.
[———] *Times Democrat,* newspaper.
[———] *True Delta,* newspaper.
New York American, newspaper.
New York As It Is [date] . . . , New York, 1833–37.
New York Colonial Documents. E. B. O'Callaghan, ed., *Documents Relating to the Colonial History of the State of New York . . . ,* Albany, 1856–61.
[New York] *Commercial Advertiser,* newspaper.

[———] *Diary,* newspaper.
[———] *Evening Post,* newspaper.
New York Herald, newspaper.
New-York Historical Society, *Annual Report* [for 1944], New York, 1945.
——— *A Catalogue of American Portraits in The New-York Historical Society,* by Donald A. Shelley, New York, 1941.
——— *Collections,* I–IV (New York, 1809–29); 2d Ser., I–IV (New York, 1841–59); Publication Fund Series, I–LXXXI (New York, 1868–1948).
——— manuscript Minutes.
New-York Historical Society Quarterly, 1917—; as *Quarterly Bulletin* until 1945.
New York Home Journal, see *Home Journal.*
[New York] *Minerva,* newspaper.
New York Public Library, *Bulletin of the . . . ,* New York, 1897—.
New York State Historical Association, *Life Masks of Noted Americans of 1825, by John I. H. Browere* (New York, 1940), catalogue of an exhibition at M. Knoedler & Co., New York, Feb. 1940.
——— "List of American Paintings in the Fenimore House Collection," *Art in America,* XXXVIII, April 1950, 125–8.
[New York] *Time Piece,* newspaper.
New York Times, newspaper.
New York Tribune, newspaper.
[Newark, N.J.] *Daily Advertiser,* newspaper.
Newark [N.J.] *Daily Journal,* newspaper.
Newburyport, Mass. *Vital Records of Newburyport, Mass., to the End of the Year 1849,* Salem, 1911.
Nichols, Mary E., "Abel Nichols, Artist," *Historical Collections of the Danvers Historical Society,* XXIX (1941), 4–31.
Noble, Louis L., *The Course of Empire, Voyage of Life, and Other Pictures of Thomas Cole, N.A., with Selections from His Letters and Miscellaneous Writings, Illustrative of His Life, Character, and Genius,* New York, 1853.
Nolan, J. Bennet, "A Pennsylvania Artist in Old New York," *Antiques,* XXVIII (1935), 148–50.
Norfleet, Fillmore, *Saint-Mémin in Virginia . . . ,* Richmond, 1942.
North, James W., *History of Augusta . . . ,* Augusta, Me., 1870.
Norton, John F., *The History of Fitzwilliam, N.H., from 1752 to 1887,* New York, 1888.
[Norwich, N.Y.] *Chenango Semi-Weekly Telegraph,* newspaper.
Notes Hispanic, New York, Hispanic Society of America, 1941–45.
Now and Then, Muncy, Pa., Muncy Historical Society, 1868—.
Noyes, Emily L., *Leavitt, Vol. IV. Descendants of Thomas Leavitt, the Immigrant, 1616–1696, and Isabella Bland,* Tilton, N.H., 1953.
Nute, Grace Lee, "Peter Rindisbacher, Artist," *Minnesota History,* XIV, Sept. 1933, 283–7.
——— "Rindisbacher's Minnesota Water Colors," *Minnesota History,* XX, March 1939, 54–7.

O

Oakes, William, *Scenery of the White Mountains,* Boston, 1848.
O'Brien, Esse F., *Art and Artists of Texas,* Dallas, 1935.
O'Connor, John, Jr., "David Gilmour Blythe, 1815–1865," *Panorama,* I, Jan. 1946, 39–45.
——— "Reviving a Forgotten Artist; A Sketch of James Reid Lambdin, the Pittsburgh Painter of American Statesmen," *Carnegie Magazine,* XII (1938), 115–18.
Odell, George C. D., *Annals of the New York Stage,* New York, 1927–45.
Oertel, John F., *A Vision Realized: A Life Story of Rev. J. A. Oertel, D.D., Artist, Priest, Missionary,* Milwaukee, 1917.
Ohio State Archaeological and Historical Quarterly, Columbus, 1887—.
Old Family Portraits of Kennebunk, Kennebunk, Me., The Brick Store Museum, 1944.
Old Print Shop Portfolio (Old Print Shop, New York, 1941—); cited as *Portfolio.*
[Orange, N.J.] *Daily Chronicle,* newspaper.
Oregon Daily Journal, Portland newspaper.
Oregon Historical Quarterly, Salem, 1900—.
Ormsbee, Thomas H., "Christian Meadows, Engraver and Counterfeiter," *American Collector,* XIII, Jan. 1945, 6–9, 18.
——— "Robert Fulton, Artist and Inventor," *American Collector,* VII, Sept. 1938, 6–7, 16–17.
——— "The Sully Portraits at West Point," *American Collector,* IX, Sept. 1940, 6–7, 14, 20.
Osgood, Ira, and Eben Putnam, *A Genealogy of the Descendants of John, Christo-*

pher, and William Osgood . . . , Salem, Mass., 1894.

Owen, David Dale, *Report of a Geological Exploration of Part of Iowa, Wisconsin and Illinois . . . in Autumn 1839,* Washington, 1844.

——— *Report of a Geological Survey of Wisconsin, Iowa, and Minnesota . . .* , Philadelphia, 1852.

Owen, Hans C., "America's Youngest Engraver," *Antiques,* XXVI, Sept. 1934, 104–5.

——— "John Cheney, Connecticut Engraver," *Antiques,* XXV, May 1934, 172–5.

Owen, Richard, *Report of a Geological Reconnaissance of Indiana Made During the Years 1859 and 1860 . . .* , Indianapolis, 1862.

P

PA Cat., *see* Pennsylvania Academy.

Pageant of America, a Pictorial History of the United States, ed. by Ralph H. Gabriel, New Haven, 1925–29.

Paine, Albert Bigelow, *Th. Nast: His Period and His Pictures,* New York and London, 1904.

"Paintings of Grove S. Gilbert," *Rochester* [N.Y.] *Historical Society Fund Series,* XIV (1936), 54–60.

Panorama, New York, Harry Shaw Newman Gallery, 1945—.

Parish Register of St. Anne's Church, Lowell, Mass., Lowell, 1885.

Park, Esther A., *Mural Painters in America:* Part I, Pittsburg, Kans., 1949.

Park, Lawrence, "An Account of Joseph Badger, and a Descriptive List of His Work," *Proceedings of the Massachusetts Historical Society,* LI, Dec. 1917, 158–201.

——— *Gilbert Stuart, an Illustrated Descriptive List of His Works . . .* , ed. by William Sawitzky, New York, 1926.

——— "Joseph Badger of Boston, and His Portraits of Children," *Old-Time New England,* XIII, Jan. 1923, 99–109.

——— "Two Portraits by Blackburn," *Art in America,* VII, Feb. 1919, 70–9.

Parker, Barbara N., "The Dickinson Portraits by Otis A. Bullard," *Harvard Library Bulletin,* VI, Winter 1952, 133–7.

——— "George Harvey and His Atmospheric Landscapes," *Bulletin of the Museum of Fine Arts,* Boston, XLI, Feb. 1943, 7–9.

——— "The Identity of Robert Feke Reconsidered in the Light of W. Phoenix Belknap's Notes," *Art Bulletin,* XXXIII, Sept. 1951, 192–4.

——— and Anne B. Wheeler, *John Singleton Copley; American Portraits in Oil, Pastel, and Miniature . . .* , Boston, 1938.

Parks, Frank S., *Parks Records, Volume 3 . . .* , Washington, 1925.

Parrish, Philip H., *Historic Oregon,* New York, 1937.

Pasadena [Cal.] *Daily Evening Star,* newspaper.

[Passaic, N.J.] *Daily News,* newspaper.

Patrick, Ransom R., "John Neagle, Portrait Painter, and Pat Lyon, Blacksmith," *Art Bulletin,* XXXIII, Sept. 1951, 187–92.

Peabody, Robert S. and Francis G., *A New England Romance: The Story of Ephraim and Mary Jane Peabody . . .* , Boston and New York, 1920.

Peabody, Selim H., *Peabody (Paybody, Pabody, Pabodie) Genealogy,* Boston, 1909.

Peabody Institute [Baltimore], *List of Works of Art in the Collection of the . . .* , Baltimore, 1949.

Peabody Museum of Salem, Mass., *A Catalogue of the Charles H. Taylor Collection of Ship Portraits . . .* , comp. by Lawrence W. Jenkins, Salem, 1949.

[Peach, A. W., ed.,] "From Tunbridge, Vermont, to London, England: The Journal of James Guild . . . from 1818 to 1824," *Proceedings of the Vermont Historical Society,* New Ser. V, Sept. 1937, 249–314.

Peale, Rembrandt, "Reminiscences," *The Crayon,* I–III, 1855–56.

Pease, David, *A Genealogical and Historical Record of the Descendants of John Pease . . .* , Springfield, Mass., 1869.

Peat, Wilbur D., *Pioneer Painters of Indiana,* Indianapolis, 1954.

——— "Preliminary Notes on Early Indiana Portraits and Portrait Painters," *Indiana History Bulletin,* XVII, Feb. 1940, 77–93.

Peck, William F., *Semi-Centennial History of the City of Rochester . . .* , Syracuse, 1884.

Peckham, Stephen F., *Peckham Genealogy . . .* , New York, 1922.

Pendleton, Everett H., *Brian Pendleton and*

His Descendants . . . , East Orange, N.J., 1910.
Pennell, Elizabeth R. and Joseph, *The Life of James McNeill Whistler,* Philadelphia and London, 1908.
Pennsylvania Academy of the Fine Arts, catalogues of the annual exhibitions, 1812–60.
——— *Catalogue of the Memorial Exhibition of Portraits by Thomas Sully,* Philadelphia, 1922.
Pennsylvania Gazette, Philadelphia newspaper.
Pennsylvania History, Pennsylvania Historical Association, 1934—.
Pennsylvania Magazine of History and Biography, Philadelphia, Historical Society of Pennsylvania, 1877—.
"A Pennsylvania Primitive Painter," *Antiques,* XXXV, Feb. 1939, 84–6.
Pennypacker, Samuel W., *The Settlement of Germantown, Pa., and the Beginning of German Immigration to North America,* Lancaster, 1899.
Perkins, George A., *The Family of John Perkins of Ipswich, Mass.,* Salem, 1889.
Perley, Sidney, *History of Salem, Mass.,* Salem, 1928.
——— *The Plumer Genealogy . . .* , Salem, 1917.
Perrine, Howland D., *The Wright Family of Oyster Bay . . .* , New York, 1923.
Perry, Matthew Calbraith, *Narrative of the Expedition of an American Squadron to the China Seas and Japan . . .* , New York and London, 1856.
Peters, Edmond F. and Eleanor B., *Peters of New England, a Genealogy and Family History,* New York, 1903.
Peters, Fred J., *Clipper Ship Prints . . .* , New York, 1930.
——— "Paintings of the Old 'Wind-Jammer,' " *Antiques,* III, Jan. 1923, 30–2.
Peters, Harry T., *America on Stone . . .* , Garden City, 1931.
——— *California on Stone,* Garden City, 1935.
——— *Currier & Ives, Print Makers to the American People,* Garden City, 1929–31.
——— "George Henry Durrie, 1820–1863," *Panorama,* I, Dec. 1945, 27–9.
[Philadelphia] *Aurora,* newspaper.
[———] *Daily Pennsylvanian,* newspaper.
[———] *Democratic Press,* newspaper.
Philadelphia Museum of Art, *Benjamin West, 1738–1820,* Philadelphia, 1938.
[Philadelphia] *Pennsylvania Gazette,* newspaper.
[———] *Public Ledger,* newspaper.
Phillips, Hazel S., "Marcus Mote, Quaker Artist," *Museum Echoes,* XXVII, Feb. 1954, 11–14.
Phillips, John M., "Ralph Earl, Loyalist," *Art in America,* XXXVII, Oct. 1949, 187–9.
Phoenix, Stephen W., *The Whitney Family of Connecticut . . .* , New York, 1878.
Pictures, Rochester, N.Y., 1938—.
Pierce, Bessie L., *A History of Chicago,* New York and London, 1937–40.
Pierce, Catharine W., "Francis Alexander," *Old-Time New England,* XLIV, Oct.–Dec. 1953, 29–46.
Piercy, Frederick, *Route from Liverpool to Great Salt Lake Valley . . .* , Liverpool, 1855.
Piers, Harry, "Artists in Nova Scotia," *Nova Scotia Historical Society Collections,* XVIII (1914), 101–65.
Piers, Harry, *Robert Field, Portrait Painter in Oils, Miniature, and Water-Colours and Engraver,* New York, 1927.
Pilsbury, David B., and Emily A. Getchell, *The Pillsbury Family . . .* , Everett, Mass., 1898.
Pinckney, Pauline A., *American Figureheads and Their Carvers,* New York, 1940.
Pipes, Nellie B., "John Mix Stanley, Indian Painter," *Oregon Historical Quarterly,* XXXIII, Sept. 1932, 250–8.
Pleasants, Henry, Jr., *Four Great Artists of Chester County,* West Chester, Pa., 1936.
[Pleasants, Henry, Jr., and others], Chester County Art Association, *Yesterday in Chester County Art,* West Chester, Pa., 1936.
Pleasants, J. Hall, Boudet Transcripts: copies of contemporary newspaper articles, etc., concerning D. W. and N. V. Boudet, in the possession of Dr. Pleasants, Baltimore.
——— *An Early Baltimore Negro Portrait Painter, Joshua Johnston,* Windham, Conn., 1940.
——— "Four Late Eighteenth Century Anglo-American Landscape Painters," *Proceedings of the American Antiquarian Society,* LII, Oct. 1942, 187–324.
——— "Francis Guy, Painter of Gentlemen's Seats," *Antiques,* LXV, April 1954, 288–90.
——— "George Beck, an Early Baltimore Landscape Painter," *Maryland Historical Magazine,* XXXV (1940), 241–3.
——— "George William West, a Baltimore Student of Benjamin West," *Art in America,* XXXVII, Jan. 1949, 7–47.
——— "Justus Engelhardt Kühn, an Early

Eighteenth Century Maryland Portrait Painter," *Proceedings of the American Antiquarian Society,* XLVI, Oct. 1936, 243–80.
——— *Saint-Mémin Water Color Miniatures,* Portland, Me., 1947.
[———] *250 Years of Painting in Maryland,* Baltimore Museum of Art, 1945.
——— and Howard Sill, *Maryland Silversmiths 1715–1830 . . . ,* Baltimore, 1930.
Plowden, Helen H., *William Stanley Haseltine, Sea and Landscape Painter . . .* London, 1947.
Political Arena, Fredericksburg, Va., newspaper.
Pope, Charles H., *The Cheney Genealogy . . . ,* Boston, 1897.
——— *A History of the Dorchester Pope Family . . . ,* Boston, 1888.
——— ed., *Willard Genealogy, Sequel to Willard Memoir . . . ,* Boston, 1915.
Port Folio, Philadelphia, 1801–27.
Porter, Edward G., "The Ship Columbia and the Discovery of Oregon," *The New England Magazine,* New Series VI, Old Series XII, June 1892, 472–88.
Porter, James A., *Modern Negro Art,* New York, 1943.
——— "Robert S. Duncanson, Midwestern Romantic-Realist," *Art in America,* XXXIX, Oct. 1951, 99–154.
——— "Versatile Interests of the Early Negro Artist: A Neglected Chapter of American Art History," *Art in America,* XXIV, Jan. 1936, 16–27.
Portfolio. *Old Print Shop Portfolio,* Old Print Shop, New York, 1941—.
[Portland] *Oregon Daily Journal,* newspaper.
Portrait and Biographical Record of Western Oregon . . . , Chicago, 1904.
"Portraits Found in Vermont." WPA Historical Records Survey, Mass., *Portraits Found in Vermont.*
Portraits in Delaware, 1700–1850, a Check List, Wilmington, 1951.
[Portsmouth] *New Hampshire Gazette,* newspaper.
Potts, Thomas M., *Historical Collections Relating to the Potts Family . . . ,* Canonsburg, Pa., 1901.
Powel, Mary E., "Miss Jane Stuart . . . ," *Bulletin of the Newport* [R.I.] *Historical Society,* XXXI, Jan. 1920, 1–16.
Powell, Mary M., "Three Artists of the Frontier," *Bulletin of the Missouri Historical Society,* V, Oct. 1948, 34–43.
Powers, Amos H., *The Powers Family . . . ,* Chicago, 1884.
Pratt, Harlow M., *History of Fort Dodge and Webster County, Iowa,* Chicago, 1913.
Pratt, Waldo, *A Forgotten American Painter: Peter Baumgras* (n.p., n.d.).
Price, Prentiss, "Samuel Shaver: Portrait Painter," *The East Tennessee Historical Society's Publications,* No. 24 (1952), 92–105.
Price, Samuel W., *The Old Masters of the Bluegrass,* Louisville, Filson Club Publications, XVII, 1902.
Prime, Alfred C., *The Arts and Crafts in Philadelphia, Maryland, and South Carolina, 1721–1785* (Topsfield, Mass., 1929); cited as Prime, I.
——— *The Arts and Crafts in Philadelphia, Maryland, and South Carolina, 1786–1800* (Topsfield, Mass., 1932); cited as Prime, II.
Princeton Museum Record, Princeton Museum of Historic Art, 1942—.
Princeton University, *General Catalogue, 1746–1906,* Princeton, 1908.
Princeton University Library Chronicle, Friends of the Princeton Library, 1939—.
Pringle, Ashmead F., Jr., "Thomas Coram's Bible," *Antiques,* XXX, Nov. 1936, 226–7.
Providence, R.I. *Alphabetical Index of Births, Marriages, and Deaths Recorded in Providence . . . ,* Providence, 1879—.
Providence [R.I.] *Journal,* newspaper.

R

RA Cat. Annual exhibition catalogues of the Royal Academy, London.
Ramsay, David, *The History of South Carolina . . . ,* Charleston, 1809.
Ramsay, John, "The American Scene in Lithograph: The Album," *Antiques,* LX, Sept. 1951, 180–3.
Randall, Alice S., "Connecticut Artists and Their Work; Fidelia Bridges in Her Studio at Canaan . . . ," *Connecticut Magazine,* VII, No. 5, Feb.–March 1902, 583–8.
Randolph, Robert I., *The Randolphs of Virginia . . . ,* Chicago? 1936?
Les Raretés des Indes, "Codex Canadiensis," Album Manuscrit de la Fin du XVIIe Siecle Contenant 108 Dessins . . . , Paris, 1930.
Rasmussen, Louise, "Art and Artists of Oregon, 1500–1900," unpublished manuscript, Oregon State Library.
——— "Artists of the Explorations Overland, 1840–1860," *Oregon Historical*

Quarterly, XLIII, March 1942, 56–62.

Rathbone, Perry T., "Charles Wimar," in City Art Museum of St. Louis, *Charles Wimar 1828–1862, Painter of the Indian Frontier* (St. Louis, 1946), 8–30.

——— "Itinerant Portraiture in New York and New England," Master's Thesis, Harvard University, 1933, photostatic copy at Frick Art Reference Library, New York.

——— ed., *Mississippi Panorama . . . ,* City Art Museum of St. Louis, 1949.

Ravenel, Beatrice St. J., "Here Lyes Buried; Taste and Trade in Charleston Tombstones," *Antiques,* XLI, March 1942, 193–5.

Read, George W., and Ruth Gaines, ed., *Gold Rush: The Journals, Drawings, and Other Papers of J. Goldsborough Bruff . . . April 2, 1849–July 20, 1851,* New York, 1944.

Read, J. A. and D. F., *Journey to the Gold-Diggins by Jeremiah Saddlebags,* New York, 1849; reprinted in facsimile with introduction by Joseph Henry Jackson, Burlingame, Cal., 1950.

Réau, Louis, "A Great French Sculptor of the 18th Century, Jean-Antoine Houdon," *Connoisseur,* CXXI, June 1948, 74–7.

Recherches Historiques, Levis, Que., Société des Etudes Historiques, 1895–1925.

"Records of Christ Church Burials, 1785–1900," manuscript, Genealogical Society of Pennsylvania, Philadelphia.

Redgrave, Samuel, *A Dictionary of Artists of the English School . . . ,* London, 1878.

Reed Papers. Manuscript correspondence of General Joseph Reed, 1757–95, in 12 volumes, New-York Historical Society.

Reese, Albert, "A Newly Discovered Landscape by Ralph Earl," *Art in America,* XXXVI, Jan. 1948, 49–53.

Reichel, William C., *History of the Rise, Progress, and Present Condition of the Moravian Seminary for Young Ladies at Bethlehem, Pa.,* 2d ed., Philadelphia, 1874.

Reid, Robert R., *Washington Lodge, No. 21, F. and A.M., and Some of Its Members,* New York, 1911.

Reid, Robert W., "Some Early Masonic Engravers in America," *Transactions of the American Lodge of Research, Free and Accepted Masons,* III, No. 1 (1938–39), 97–125.

——— and Charles Rollinson, *William Rollinson, Engraver,* New York, 1931.

Reiter, Edith S., "Charles Sullivan (1794–1867)," *Museum Echoes,* XXVII, Jan. 1954, 3–5.

——— "Lily Martin Spencer," *Museum Echoes,* XXVII, May 1954, 35–8.

——— "Sala Bosworth," *Museum Echoes,* XXVII, March 1954, 19–21.

Remarks upon the Athenaeum Gallery of Paintings, for 1831, August 17, Boston, 1831.

Report of the United States National Museum . . . for the Year Ending June 30, 1897, Washington, 1899.

Revue Louisianaise, Société Littéraire et Typographique de la Nouvelle-Orleans, 1846–58.

Reynolds, John H., "Papers and Documents of Eminent Arkansans," *Publications of the Arkansas Historical Association,* I (1906), 230–52.

Reznikoff, Charles, and Uriah Z. Engelman, *The Jews of Charleston: A History of an American Jewish Community,* Philadelphia, 1950.

Rhode Island History, Rhode Island Historical Society, Providence, 1942—.

Rice, Foster W., "Life of Nathaniel Jocelyn," unpublished manuscript in the possession of the author.

——— "Nathaniel Jocelyn, Painter and Engraver," *American Collector,* XVI, Dec. 1947, 6–9.

Rice, Howard C., Jr., "An Album of Saint-Mémin Portraits," *Princeton University Library Chronicle,* XIII, Autumn 1951, 23–31.

Rice, William H., *In Memoriam: Amadeus Abraham Reinke,* New York, 1889.

Richardson, Edgar P., *American Romantic Painting,* New York, 1944.

——— "E. J. Trelawney by William Edward West," *Art Quarterly,* XIV, Summer 1951, 157–60.

——— "Gustavus Hesselius," *Art Quarterly,* XII, Summer 1949, 220–6.

——— "Portraits by Jacob Eichholtz," *Art in America,* XXVII, Jan. 1939, 14–22.

——— "Two Portraits by William Page," *Art Quarterly,* I, Spring 1938, 91–103.

——— *Washington Allston, a Study of the Romantic Artist in America,* Chicago, 1948.

——— "Winslow Homer's Drawings in *Harper's Weekly,*" *Art in America,* XIX, Dec. 1930, 38–47.

Richmond [Va.] *Dispatch,* newspaper.

——— *Enquirer,* newspaper.

Richmond Portraits in an Exhibition of

Makers of Richmond 1737–1860, Richmond, Valentine Museum, 1949.

Richmond [Va.] *Whig,* newspaper.

Rimmer, William, *Art Anatomy,* Boston, 1877.

——— *Elements of Design,* Boston, 1864.

Roberts, W., "Thomas Spence Duché," *Art in America,* VI, Oct. 1918, 273–4.

Robertson, Archibald, *Archibald Robertson, Lieutenant-General of Royal Engineers, His Diaries and Sketches in America, 1762–1780,* ed. by H. M. Lydenburg, New York, 1930.

Robertson, Emily, ed., *Letters and Papers of Andrew Robertson . . . ,* London, 1895?.

Robie, Virginia, "Waldo Portraits by Smibert and Blackburn," *American Society Legion of Honor Magazine,* XX, Spring 1949, 43–52.

Robins, George, *A Catalogue Raisonné . . . of Historical Pictures . . .* [by] *Benjamin West . . .* [to] *be Sold at Auction . . . ,* London, 1829.

Robinson, Francis W., "Early Houses on the Detroit River and Lake Erie in Watercolors by Catherine Reynolds," *Bulletin of the Detroit Institute of Arts,* XXXIII, No. 1 (1953–4), 17–20.

Robinson, Frederick B., "Erastus Salisbury Field," *Art in America,* XXX, Oct. 1942, 244–53.

Robinson, John, *A Description of and Critical Remarks on the Picture of Christ Healing the Sick in the Temple Painted by Benjamin West, Esq.,* Philadelphia, 1818.

Robinson, John, and George F. Dow, *The Sailing Ships of New England, 1607–1907,* Salem, 1922.

Robinson, Mary T., "William Allen Wall of New Bedford," *Magazine of Art,* XXX, Feb. 1937, 108–10, 128.

Robinson, Olive C., "Ezra Wood, Profile Cutter," *Antiques,* XLII, Aug. 1942, 69–70.

Rochester Historical Society, *Scrapbook,* Vol. I, 1950, Rochester, N.Y., 1950.

Rodabaugh, James H., "Charles T. Webber," *Museum Echoes,* XXVII, Aug. 1954, 59–62.

Roden, Robert F., "Seventy Years of Book Auctions in New York," *New York Times Book Review,* March 19, 1898 (also as a separate).

Roos, John Frederick Fitzgerald De, *Personal Narrative of Travels in the United States and Canada in 1826 . . . ,* London, 1827.

Root, Edward W., *Philip Hooker: A Contribution to the Study of the Renaissance in America,* New York, 1929.

Rosenthal, Albert, "Two American Painters: West and Fulton," *The Antiquarian,* XII, July 1929, 43.

Ross, Marvin C., "A List of Portraits and Paintings from Alfred Jacob Miller's *Account Book," Maryland Historical Magazine,* XLVIII, March 1953, 27–36.

——— *The West of Alfred Jacob Miller . . . ,* Norman, Okla., 1951.

——— "William Birch, Enamel Miniaturist," *American Collector,* IX, July 1940, 5, 20.

[Ross, Robert Budd,] "Detroit in 1837," a series of articles published in the [Detroit] *News Tribune,* Aug. 12, 1894–Sept. 15, 1895.

Rotterdam Year Book or *Rotterdamsch Jaarboek,* for 1919, Rotterdam, Neth., 1919.

Rowell, Hugh Grant, "Washington Irving the Artist," *American Collector,* XIV, April 1945, 6–7, 16, 19.

Royer, Kathryn M., "Narrative Painting in Nineteenth Century America," Master's Thesis, Pennsylvania State College, 1941.

Rudkin, W. Harley, "George Inness, American Landscape Painter," *Art in America,* XXXIV, April 1946, 109–14.

Runk, Emma Ten Broeck, *The Ten Broeck Genealogy . . . ,* New York, 1897.

Runnels, Moses T., *History of Sanbornton, N.H.,* Boston, 1881–82.

Runyan, Alice, "John André, the Artist," *American Collector,* XIV, June 1945, 5, 18.

Rushford, Edward A., "Lewis Prang, Engraver on Wood," *Antiques,* XXXVII, April 1940, 187–9.

Rusk, Fern H., *George Caleb Bingham, the Missouri Artist,* Jefferson City, 1917.

Rusk, William S., ed., "New Rinehart Letters," *Maryland Historical Magazine,* XXXI, Sept. 1946, 225–42.

Rusk, William S., *William Henry Rinehart, Sculptor,* Baltimore, 1939.

Rutledge, Anna Wells, "Another American Caricaturist," *Gazette des Beaux Arts,* XLVII, April 1955, 221–6.

——— *Artists in the Life of Charleston, through Colony and State from Restoration to Reconstruction,* Philadelphia, American Philosophical Society, *Transactions,* XXXIX, Part 2, Nov. 1949.

Rutledge, Anna Wells, "Charleston's First Artistic Couple," *Antiques,* LII, Aug. 1947, 100–2.

——— "Cogdell and Mills, Charleston Sculptors," *Antiques,* XLI, March 1942, 192–3, 205–7.

——— "A Cosmopolitan in Carolina," *William and Mary Quarterly,* 3d Ser., VI, Oct. 1949, 637–43.

——— *Cumulative Record of Exhibition Catalogues, The Pennsylvania Academy of the Fine Arts, 1807–1870, the Society of Artists, 1800–1814, the Artists' Fund Society, 1835–1845,* Philadelphia, American Philosophical Society, *Memoirs,* XXXVIII, 1955.

——— "Early Painter Rediscovered: William Wilson," *American Collector,* XV, April 1946, 8–9, 20–1.

——— "A French Priest, Painter, and Architect in the United States: Joseph-Pierre Picot de Limoëlan de Clorivière," *Gazette des Beaux Arts,* XXXIII, March 1948, 159–76.

——— "Handlist of Miniatures in the Collections of the Maryland Historical Society," *Maryland Historical Magazine,* XL, June 1945, 119–36.

——— "Henry Benbridge (1743–1812?) American Portrait Painter," *American Collector,* XVII, Oct. 1948, 8–10, 23; Nov. 1948, 9–11, 23.

——— "Henry Bounetheau (1797–1877), Charleston, S.C., Miniaturist," *American Collector,* XVII, July 1948, 12–15, 23.

——— "A Humorous Artist in Colonial Maryland," *American Collector,* XVI, Feb. 1947, 8–9, 14–15.

——— MHS. "Cross File of Maryland Historical Society Catalogues," unpublished manuscript by Anna Wells Rutledge.

——— PA, see Rutledge, Anna Wells, *Cumulative Record . . .*

——— "Portraits in Varied Media in the Collections of the Maryland Historical Society," *Maryland Historical Magazine,* XLI, Dec. 1946, 282–326.

——— "Portraits Painted Before 1900 in the Collections of the Maryland Historical Society," *Maryland Historical Magazine,* XLI, March 1946, 11–50.

——— "Who Was Henrietta Johnston?" *Antiques,* LI, March 1947, 183–5.

——— "William Henry Brown of Charleston," *Antiques,* LX, Dec. 1951, 532–3.

——— "William John Coffee as a Portrait Sculptor," *Gazette des Beaux Arts,* XXVIII, Nov. 1945, 297–312.

S

Safford, Victor, "John Haley Bellamy, the Woodcarver of Kittery Point," *Antiques,* XXVII, March 1935, 102–6.

[St. Louis] *Daily Missouri Democrat,* newspaper.

[St. Louis] *Missouri Republican,* newspaper.

Sanborn, Franklin B., *Henry David Thoreau,* New York and Boston, 1882.

——— "Thomas Leavitt and His Artist Friend James Akin," *Granite Monthly,* XXV, Oct. 1898, 224–34.

Sartain, John, *The Reminiscences of a Very Old Man, 1808–1897,* New York, 1899.

Saunier, Charles, *Bordeaux,* Paris, 1909.

Sawitzky, Susan, "The Portraits of William Johnston, a Preliminary Checklist," *New-York Historical Society Quarterly,* XXXIX, Jan. 1955, 79–89.

Sawitzky, William, "The American Work of Benjamin West," *Pennsylvania Magazine of History and Biography,* LXII, Oct. 1938, 433–62.

——— *Catalogue, Descriptive and Critical, of the Paintings and Miniatures in the Historical Society of Pennsylvania,* Philadelphia, 1942.

——— "Further Light on the Work of William Williams," *New-York Historical Society Quarterly Bulletin,* XXV, July 1941, 101–12.

——— "Further Notes on John Hesselius," *Art Quarterly,* V, Autumn 1942, 340–1.

——— "Lectures." Mimeographed syllabus, based on notes taken by Alice L. Moe, of thirteen lectures on Early American Painting delivered by Mr. Sawitzky in 1940–41 at The New-York Historical Society under the sponsorship of the Society and New York University under a grant from the Carnegie Foundation.

——— *Matthew Pratt, 1734–1805 . . .,* New York, 1942.

——— *Ralph Earl 1751–1801,* New York, 1945; catalogue of an exhibition at the Whitney Museum and the Worcester Art Museum.

——— "William Williams, First Instructor of Benjamin West," *Antiques,* XXXI, May 1937, 240–2.

——— and Susan, "Portraits by Reuben Moulthrop, a Checklist by William Sawitzky Supplemented and Edited by Susan Sawitzky," *New-York Historical Society Quarterly,* XXXIX, Oct. 1955, 385–404.

——— and Susan, "Thomas McIlworth . . . ," *New-York Historical Society Quarterly,* XXXV, April 1951, 117–39.

Sawyer, Ray C., "Deaths Published in The Christian Intelligencer of the Reformed Dutch Church from 1830 to 1871," typed manuscript in seven vols., New-York Historical Society.

Schafer, Joseph, "Trailing a Trail Artist of 1849," *Wisconsin Magazine of History,* XII, Sept. 1928, 97–108.

Scharf, John T., *The Chronicles of Baltimore . . . ,* Baltimore, 1874.

——— and Thompson Westcott, *History of Philadelphia 1609–1884,* Philadelphia, 1884.

Scharff, Maurice R., "Collecting Views of Natchez," *Antiques,* LXV, March 1954, 217–19.

Schetky, Lawrence O., *The Schetky Family . . . ,* Portland, Ore., 1942.

Schick, Joseph S., *The Early Theater in Eastern Iowa . . . ,* Chicago, 1939.

Schmitt, Evelyn L., "Two American Romantics: Thomas Cole and William Cullen Bryant," *Art in America,* XLI, Spring 1953, 61–8.

Schoolcraft, Henry R., *Information Respecting the History, Condition, and Prospects of the Indian Tribes of the United States . . . ,* Philadelphia, 1851–57.

——— *Scenes and Adventures in the Semi-Alpine Region of the Ozark Mountains of Missouri and Arkansas . . . ,* Philadelphia, 1853.

Schoonmaker, Marius, *The History of Kingston, N.Y. . . . ,* New York, 1888.

——— *John Vanderlyn, Artist, 1775–1852,* Kingston, N.Y., 1950.

Schutz, Géza, "Old New York in Switzerland," *Antiques,* XXXIII, May 1938, 260–1.

Scituate, Mass. *Vital Records of Scituate, Mass., to the Year 1850 . . . ,* Boston, 1909.

Scott, Kenneth, "Abijah Canfield of Connecticut," *Antiques,* LIX, March 1951, 212.

Scott, Leonora Cranch, *The Life and Letters of Christopher Pearse Cranch,* Boston and New York, 1917.

Scribners [New York], "Rare Books in Science and Thought, 1490–1940," Catalogue 138, 1952.

Sears, Clara E., *Highlights among the Hudson River Artists,* Boston, 1947.

——— *Some American Primitives . . . ,* Boston, 1941.

Sears, Robert, *A New and Popular Pictorial Description of the United States . . . ,* New York, 1848.

Seebold, Herman Boehm de Bachellé, *Old Louisiana Plantation Homes and Family Trees,* New Orleans, 1941.

Sellers, Charles Coleman, *Charles Willson Peale,* Philadelphia, 1947.

——— "James Claypoole: A Founder of the Art of Painting in Pennsylvania," *Pennsylvania History,* XVII, April 1950, 106–9.

——— *Portraits and Miniatures by Charles Willson Peale,* Philadelphia, 1952.

——— "Sellers Papers in the Peale-Sellers Collection," *Proceedings of the American Philosophical Society,* XCV, No. 3, June 12, 1951, 262–5.

Sellstedt, Lars G., *From Forecastle to Academy, Sailor and Artist; Autobiography by Lars Gustaf Sellstedt,* Buffalo, 1904.

——— *Life and Works of William John Wilgus, Artist, 1819–1853 . . . ,* Buffalo, 1912.

Semmes, John E., *John H. B. Latrobe and His Times, 1803–1891,* Baltimore, 1917.

Semon, Kurt M., "Who Was Robert Street?" *American Collector,* XIV, June 1945, 6–7, 19.

Senate House Museum, Kingston, N.Y., "Exhibition of Paintings by Joseph Tubby," mimeographed catalogue of exhibition, Dec. 1953–Jan. 1954.

Settle, Raymond W., ed., *The March of the Mounted Riflemen . . . ,* Glendale, Cal., 1940.

Sewall, Samuel, *Diary of Samuel Sewall,* Boston, Massachusetts Historical Society Collections, 5th Ser., V–VII, 1878–82.

Shannon, Martha A. S., *Boston Days of William Morris Hunt,* Boston, 1923.

Shapley, Fern Rusk, "Bingham's 'Jolly Flatboatmen,'" *Art Quarterly,* XVII, Winter 1954, 352–6.

Shaw, Joshua, *A New and Original Drawing Book,* Philadelphia, 1816.

[———] *Picturesque Views of American Scenery,* Philadelphia, 1820–21?.

——— *United States Directory for the Use of Travellers and Merchants . . . ,* Philadelphia, 1822.

Sheeler, Robert L., "The Strange and Cryptic Picture Diary of Charles DeWolf Brownell," [Providence, R.I.] *Sunday Journal,* June 8, 1947.

Sheirr, Rodman J., "Joseph Mozier and His Handiwork," *Potter's American Monthly,* VI, Jan. 1876, 24–8.

Shelley, Donald A., "Addendum: William

R. Miller," *New-York Historical Society Quarterly,* XXXI, Oct. 1947, 210–11.

——— "American Painting in Irving's Day," *American Collector,* XVI, Oct. 1947, 19–21, 50.

——— "Audubon to Date," *New-York Historical Society Quarterly,* XXX, July 1946, 168–73.

——— "George Harvey and His Atmospheric Landscapes of North America," *New-York Historical Society Quarterly,* XXXII, April 1948, 104–13.

——— "George Harvey, English Painter of Atmospheric Landscapes in America," *American Collector,* XVII, April 1948, 10–13.

——— "John James Audubon, Artist," *Magazine of Art,* XXXIX, May 1946, 171–5.

——— "William Guy Wall and His Watercolors for the Historic *Hudson River Portfolio,*" *New-York Historical Society Quarterly,* XXXI, Jan. 1947, 25–45.

——— "William R. Miller, Forgotten 19th Century Artist," *American Collector,* XVI, Nov. 1947, 16, 23.

Shepard, Lee, "Last Man's Society," *Bulletin of the Historical and Philosophical Society of Ohio,* V, Sept. 1947, 25–9.

Sherman, Frederic F., "American Miniatures by Minor Artists," *Antiques,* XVII, May 1930, 422–5.

——— "American Miniatures of Revolutionary Times," *Art in America,* XXIV, Jan. 1936, 39–43.

——— "American Miniaturists of the Early 19th Century," *Art in America,* XXIV, April 1936, 76–83.

——— "Asher B. Durand as a Portrait Painter," *Art in America,* XVIII, Oct. 1930, 309–16.

——— *Early American Painting,* New York, 1932.

——— "Four Figure Pictures by George Fuller," *Art in America,* VII, Feb. 1919, 84–91.

——— "James Sanford Ellsworth," in Lipman and Winchester, *Primitive Painters in America.*

——— "Nathaniel Jocelyn, Engraver and Portrait Painter," *Art in America,* XVIII, Aug. 1930, 251–8.

——— "Nathaniel Rogers and His Miniatures," *Art in America,* XXIII, Oct. 1935, 158–62.

——— "Newly Discovered American Miniaturists," *Antiques,* VIII, Aug. 1925, 96–99.

——— "Newly Discovered American Portrait Painters," *Art in America,* XXIX, Oct. 1941, 234–5.

——— "Pierre Henri's American Miniatures," *Art in America,* XXVIII, April 1940, 78, 81.

——— "The Portraits of Washington from Life," *Art in America,* XVIII, April 1930, 150–62.

——— "Ralph Earl, Biographical and Critical Notes," *Art in America,* XXIII, March 1935, 57–68.

——— "Samuel L. Waldo and William Jewett, Portrait Painters," *Art in America,* XVIII, Feb. 1930, 81–6.

——— *Richard Jennys, New England Portrait Painter,* Springfield, Mass., 1941.

——— "Robert Loftin Newman: An American Colorist," *Art in America,* IV, April 1916, 177–84.

——— "Robert Loftin Newman," *Art in America,* XXVII, April 1939, 73–5.

——— "Some Recently Discovered Early American Portrait Miniaturists," *Antiques,* XI, April 1927, 293–6.

——— "Three New England Miniatures," *Antiques,* IV, Dec. 1923, 275–6.

——— "Two Newly Discovered Watercolor Portraits by Robert Field," *Art in America,* XX, Feb. 1932, 85–6.

——— "Two Recently Discovered Portraits in Oils by James Peale," *Art in America,* XXI, Oct. 1933, 114–21.

——— "Unrecorded American Miniaturists," *Art in America,* XVI, April 1928, 130, 133.

——— "Unrecorded Early American Painters," *Art in America,* XXII, Oct. 1934, 145–50; XXXI, Oct. 1943, 208.

——— "Unrecorded Early American Portrait Painters," *Art in America,* XXII, Dec. 1933, 26–31.

Sherman, Thomas T., *Sherman Genealogy . . . ,* New York, 1920.

Shertzer, Abram Trego, *A Historical Account of the Trego Family,* Baltimore, 1884.

Shinn, Josiah H., *The History of the Shinn Family in Europe and America,* Chicago, 1903.

Shoemaker, Alfred L., "Reading's First Artist, a Painter of Butterflies," *Historical Review of Berks County* [Pa.], XIII, April 1948, 89–90.

Sieben-Morgan, Ruth, "Samuel Putnam Avery (1822–1904), Engraver on Wood; A Bio-Bibliographical Study," Master's Essay, Columbia University, 1940; revised, with additions, and reproduced from typewritten copy, 1942, Columbia University Library.

"Sill Abstracts." Howard Sill, comp., "Miscellaneous Abstracts from Maryland Gazette 1730–1775; Source Material Relating Chiefly to Craftsmen," typed transcripts, two volumes, New-York Historical Society.

Simkin, Colin, ed., *Currier & Ives' America: A Panorama of the Mid-Nineteenth Century Scene . . .*, New York, 1952.

Simpson, Corelli C. W., *Leaflets of Artists*, Bangor, Me., 1893.

Simpson, James H., *Report of Explorations Across the Great Basin . . .*, Washington, 1876.

——— "Report . . . of an Expedition into the Navajo Country," 31 Cong., 1 Sess., *Senate Exec. Doc.* 64 (Washington, 1850), 55–168.

Siple, Walter H., "A Romantic Episode in Cincinnati," *Bulletin of the Cincinnati Art Museum*, XI, April 1940, 42–52.

Sitgreaves, Lorenzo, "Report of an Expedition down the Zuni and Colorado Rivers," 32 Cong., 2 Sess., *Senate Exec. Doc.* 59, Washington, 1853.

Sizer, Theodore, ed., *The Autobiography of Colonel John Trumbull, Patriot-Artist, 1756–1843*, New Haven, 1953.

Sizer, Theodore, *The Works of Colonel John Trumbull, Artist of the American Revolution*, New Haven, 1950.

Slade, Denison R., "Henry Pelham, the Half-Brother of John Singleton Copley," *Publications of the Colonial Society of Massachusetts*, Vol. V, *Transactions, 1897, 1898* (Boston, 1902), 193–211.

Slafter, Edmund F., *Slafter Memorial of John Slafter, with a Genealogical Account of His Descendants . . .*, Boston, 1869.

Slocum, Charles E., *A Short History of the Slocums, Slocumbs and Slocombs of America . . .*, Vol. I, Syracuse, N.Y., 1882; Vol. II, Defiance, O., 1908.

Smet, Pierre Jean de, *Oregon Missions and Travels over the Rocky Mountains in 1845–46*, New York, 1847; reprinted in Thwaites, *Early Western Travels*, XXIX, 103–424.

Smith, Albert D., *A Loan Exhibition of the Works of Shepard Alonzo Mount, 1804–1868*, Heckscher Art Museum, Huntington, L.I., 1945.

Smith, Alice E., "Peter Rindisbacher: A Communication," *Minnesota History*, XX, June 1939, 173–5.

Smith, Alice R. H. and D. E. H., *Charles Fraser*, New York, 1924.

——— ed., *A Charleston Sketch Book, 1796–1806 . . .*, Charleston, 1940.

Smith, Mr. and Mrs. Chetwood, *Rogers Groups; Thought and Wrought by John Rogers*, Boston, 1934.

Smith, Edward S., "John Rubens Smith, an Anglo-American Artist," *Connoisseur*, LXXXV, May 1930, 300–7.

Smith, Helen Burr, "John Mare . . . New York Portrait Painter, with Notes on the Two William Williams," *New-York Historical Society Quarterly*, XXXV, Oct. 1951, 355–99.

Smith, Jerome I., "Cerracchi and His American Visit," *American Collector*, V, Aug. 1936, 3, 19.

——— "New York's Fire of 1845 in Lithography," *Antiques*, XXXVIII, Sept. 1940, 119–20.

——— "Painted Fire Engine Panels," *Antiques*, XXXII, Nov. 1937, 245–7.

Smith, John Chaloner, *British Mezzotint Portraits . . .*, London, 1883.

Smith, Olive C., and Addison J. Throop, ed., *Ancestral Charts of George Addison Throop, Deborah Goldsmith . . .*, East St. Louis, Ill., 1934.

Smith, Ophia D., "Charles and Eliza Leslie," *Pennsylvania Magazine of History and Biography*, LXXIV, Oct. 1950, 512–27.

——— "Frederick Eckstein, the Father of Cincinnati Art," *Bulletin of the Historical and Philosophical Society of Ohio*, IX, Oct. 1951, 266–82.

Smith, Ralph C., *A Biographical Index of American Artists*, Baltimore, 1930.

Smith, S. Winifred, "James Henry Beard," *Museum Echoes*, XXVII, April 1954, 27–30.

Smith, William Henry, *The History of the State of Indiana . . .*, Indianapolis, 1897.

Smithsonian Institution, *Carl Bodmer Paints the Indian Frontier; A Traveling Exhibition . . .*, Washington, 1954.

Sniffen, Harold S., "James and John Bard, Painters of Steamboat Portraits," *Art in America*, XXXVII, April 1949, 51–66.

Snow, Julia D. S., "Delineators of the Adams-Jackson American Views, Part I, Thomas Cole," *Antiques*, XXX, Nov. 1936, 214–19; ". . . Part II, Alexander Jackson Davis," *Antiques*, XXXI, Jan. 1937, 26–30; ". . . Part III, C. Burton and W. Goodacre, Jr.," *Antiques*, XXXII, July 1937, 22–6; ". . . Part IV, Miscel-

lany," *Antiques,* XXXVI, July 1939, 18–21.
——— "King *versus* Ellsworth," *Antiques,* XXI, March 1932, 118–21.
Society of Artists, annual exhibition catalogues, Philadelphia, 1811–14.
Society of California Pioneers Quarterly, San Francisco, 1924–33.
Solon, Louis M., *The Art of the Old English Potter,* London, 1883.
Somebody's Ancestors: Paintings by Primitive Artists of the Connecticut Valley, Springfield, Mass., Museum of Fine Arts, 1942.
Southern Advocate, Huntsville, Ala., newspaper.
Southwestern Baptist, Montgomery, Ala., 1851–65.
Spaulding, Charles W., *The Spalding Memorial . . . ,* Chicago, 1897.
Spencer, Robert C., *Spencer Family History and Genealogy,* Milwaukee, 1889.
Spendlove, F. St. George, "The Canadian Watercolours of James Pattison Cockburn . . . ," *Connoisseur,* CXXXIII, May 1954, 203–7.
Spieler, Gerhard G., "A Noted Artist in Early Colorado; The Story of Albert Bierstadt," *American-German Review,* XI, June 1945, 13–17.
Spielmann, M. H., "Francesca Alexander and 'The Roadside Songs of Tuscany,'" *Magazine of Art* (1895), 295–9.
Spinney, Frank O., "J. Bailey Moore," *Old-Time New England,* XLII, Jan.–March 1952, 57–62.
——— "Joseph H. Davis, New Hampshire Artist of the 1830's," *Antiques,* XLIV, Oct. 1943, 177–80.
——— "Joseph H. Davis," in Lipman and Winchester, *Primitive Painters in America,* 97–105.
——— "The Method of Joseph H. Davis," *Antiques,* XLVI, Aug. 1944, 73.
——— "William S. Gookins, Portrait Painter of Dover, N.H.," *Old-Time New England,* XXXIV, April 1944, 61–6.
Sprague, Henry W., "Lars Gustav Sellstedt," *Publications of the Buffalo Historical Society,* XVII (Buffalo, 1913), 37–74.
Sprague, Warren V., *Sprague Families in America,* Rutland, Vt., 1913.
Sprague's Journal of Maine History, Dover, Me., 1913–26.
Springfield [Mass.] *Republican,* newspaper.
Stackpole, Everett S., *History of Winthrop, Maine,* Auburn, Me., 1925.
Stanger, Frank M., ed., *Off for California; the Letters, Log, and Sketches of William H. Dougal, Gold Rush Artist,* Oakland, Cal., 1949.
Stanley, John Mix, "Portraits of North American Indians," *Smithsonian Miscellaneous Collections,* II, Washington, 1862.
Stansbury, Howard, *Exploration and Survey of the Valley of the Great Salt Lake . . . ,* Philadelphia, 1852.
Stanton, William A., *A Record . . . of Thomas Stanton of Connecticut and His Descendants,* Albany, 1891.
Stauffer, David McN., *American Engravers upon Copper and Steel,* New York, 1907.
Stechow, Wolfgang, "Another Signed Bradley Portrait," *Art in America,* XXXIV, Jan. 1946, 30–2.
Steinman, George, "Benjamin West Henry, a Lancaster Artist," *Historical Papers and Addresses of the Lancaster County Historical Society,* XVI, No. 9, Nov. 1, 1912, 270–2.
Stephens, Stephen D., *The Mavericks, American Engravers,* New Brunswick, N.J., 1950.
Sterling, Albert M., *The Sterling Genealogy,* New York, 1909.
Stern, Madeleine B., *Louisa May Alcott,* Norman, Okla., 1950.
Stiles, Frederick G., "Jeremiah Stiles, Jr.," *Collections of the Worcester Society of Antiquity,* VI, *Proceedings for 1884* (Worcester, 1885), 205–9.
Stiles, Henry R., ed., *The Civil, Political, Professional, and Ecclesiastical History . . . of the County of Kings and the City of Brooklyn, N.Y. . . . ,* New York, 1884.
——— *The History of Ancient Wethersfield, Conn.,* New York, 1904.
Stillman, William J., *The Autobiography of a Journalist,* Boston and New York, 1901.
Stillwell, John E., "Archibald Robertson, Miniaturist, 1765–1835," *New-York Historical Society Quarterly Bulletin,* XIII, April 1929, 1–33.
——— "Some 19th Century Painters," *New-York Historical Society Quarterly Bulletin,* XIV, Oct. 1930, 79–93.
Stokes, *Historic Prints.* I. N. Phelps Stokes and Daniel C. Haskell, *American Historical Prints; Early Views of American Cities, Etc., from the Phelps Stokes and Other Collections,* New York Public Library, 1933.
Stokes, I. N. Phelps, *The Iconography of Manhattan Island 1498–1909,* New York, 1915–28.
Stone, R. B., "Not Quite Forgotten, a Study

of the Williamsport Painter, S. Roesen," *Proceedings and Papers of the Lycoming County* [Pa.] *Historical Society,* No. 9, 1951.

Storer, Malcolm, "The Manly Washington Medal," *Proceedings of the Massachusetts Historical Society,* LII (1918–19), 6–7.

Stout, Herald F., *Stout and Allied Families,* Dover, O.? 1943.

Stowe, Lyman Beecher, "The First of the Beechers," *Atlantic Monthly,* CLII, Aug. 1933, 209–20.

Street, Mary E. A., *The Street Genealogy,* Exeter, N.H., 1895.

Streeter, Milford B., *A Genealogical History of the Descendants of Stephen and Ursula Streeter . . . ,* Salem, 1896.

Strickland, Walter G., *A Dictionary of Irish Artists,* Dublin and London, 1913.

Stryker, Peter, "Journal of Peter Stryker from New York City to Saratoga, 1788, and in New York State and New Jersey, 1815–1816," unpublished manuscript owned about 1940 by Paul Goodman of New York City; typed transcript at New-York Historical Society.

Sully, Thomas, "Recollections of an Old Painter," *Hours at Home,* X (Philadelphia, 1873), 69ff.

Sutton, Mass. *Vital Records of Sutton, Mass., to the End of the Year 1849,* Worcester, 1907.

Svin'in, Pavel Petrovich, *Picturesque United States of America, 1811–13,* ed. by Abraham Yarmolinsky, New York, 1930.

Swan, Mabel M., *The Athenaeum Gallery 1827–1873 . . .* (Boston, 1940); cited as Swan, BA.

——— "Boston's Carvers and Joiners, Part I, Pre-Revolutionary," *Antiques,* LIII, March 1948, 198–201; ". . . Part II, Post-Revolutionary," *Antiques,* LIII, April 1948, 281–5.

——— "Early Sign Painters," *Antiques,* XIII, May 1928, 402–5.

——— "The Goddard and Townsend Joiners," *Antiques,* XLIX, April 1946, 228–31.

——— "Gilbert Stuart in Boston," *Antiques,* XXIX, Feb. 1936, 65–7.

——— "John Ritto Penniman," *Antiques,* XXXIX, May 1941, 246–8.

——— "Master Hubard, Profilist and Painter," *Antiques,* XV, June 1929, 496–500.

——— "Moravian Cabinetmakers of a Piedmont Craft Center," *Antiques,* LIX, June 1951, 456–9.

——— "A Neglected Aspect of Hubard," *Antiques,* XX, Oct. 1931, 222–3.

——— "A Revised Estimate of McIntire," *Antiques,* XX, Dec. 1931, 338–43.

——— "Ship Carvers of Newburyport," *Antiques,* XLVIII, Aug. 1945, 78–81.

——— "Simeon Skillin, Senior, the First American Sculptor," *Antiques,* XLVI, July 1944, 21.

——— and Louise Karr, "Early Marine Painters of Salem," *Antiques,* XXXVIII, Aug. 1940, 63–5.

Sweet, Charles F., *A Champion of the Cross, Being the Life of John Henry Hopkins . . . ,* New York, 1894.

Sweet, Frederick A., "Asher B. Durand, Pioneer American Landscape Painter," *Art Quarterly,* VIII, Spring 1945, 140–60.

——— *The Hudson River School and the Early American Landscape Tradition,* Chicago, 1945; catalogue of exhibition at Art Institute of Chicago and Whitney Museum of American Art, New York.

T

Taft, Lorado, *The History of American Sculpture,* New York, 1925.

Taft, Robert, *Artists and Illustrators of the Old West, 1850–1900,* New York, 1953.

——— "The Pictorial Record of the Old West," fifteen articles in the *Kansas Historical Quarterly,* 1946 to 1952, subsequently revised and published as *Artists and Illustrators of the Old West, 1850–1900,* New York, 1953.

Tappan, Daniel L., *Tappan-Toppan Genealogy . . . ,* Arlington, Mass., 1915.

Taylor, Agnes L., *The Longstreth Family Records,* Philadelphia, 1909.

Taylor, William C., *Memoirs of the House of Orleans . . . ,* London, 1849.

Tenney, Martha J., *The Tenney Family . . . ,* Concord, N.H., 1904.

Terry, James, *Allyn Hyde of Ellington, Conn., Together with a Review of "An Early Connecticut Engraver and His Work,"* Hartford, 1906.

Terry, Stephen, *Notes of Terry Families in the United States . . . ,* Hartford, 1887.

"Texas in Pictures," *Antiques,* LIII, June 1948, 453–9.

Tharp, Louise H., *The Peabody Sisters of Salem,* Boston, 1950.

Thayer, Bezaleel, *Memorial of the Thayer Name . . . ,* Oswego, N.Y., 1874.

Thieme-Becker. Ulrich Thieme and

Felix Becker, *Allgemeines Lexikon der bildenden Künstler . . . ,* Leipzig, 1907—.

Thomas, Isaiah, *The History of Printing in America . . . ,* 2d ed., Albany, 1874.

Thomas, Milton H., ed., *Elias Boudinot's Journey to Boston in 1809,* Princeton, 1955.

Thomas, Ralph W., "William Johnston, Colonial Portrait Painter," *New Haven Colony Historical Society Journal,* IV, March 1955, 4–8.

Thomas, Stephen, "The American Career of Albert Van Beest," *Antiques,* XXXI, Jan. 1937, 14–18.

Thomas, W. Stephen, "George Catlin, Portrait Painter," *Antiques,* LIV, Aug. 1948, 96–7.

Thompson, Charles H., *A Genealogy of the Descendants of John Thompson, of Plymouth . . . ,* Lansing, Mich., 1890.

Thompson, Thomas P., *Louisiana Writers Native and Resident . . . to Which Is Added a List of Artists,* New Orleans, 1904.

Thornburg, Opal, "The Panoramas of Marcus Mote, 1853–1854," *Art in America,* XLI, Winter 1953, 22–35.

Thorne, Thomas, "America's Earliest Nude?" *William and Mary Quarterly,* 3d Ser., VI, Oct. 1949, 565–8.

Thorpe, Thomas B., "New York Artists Fifty Years Ago," *Appleton's Journal of Literature, Science, and Art,* VII, May 25, 1872, 572–5.

——— "Reminiscences of Charles L. Elliot, Artist," [New York] *Evening Post,* Sept. 30, Oct. 1, 1868; *Semi-Weekly Post,* Oct. 6, 1868.

Thwaites, Reuben Gold, ed., *Early Western Travels, 1748–1846 . . . ,* 32 vols., Cleveland, 1904–07.

Thwing, Leroy L., "The Four Carving Skillins," *Antiques,* XXXIII, June 1938, 326–8.

Todd, Frederick P., "Huddy & Duval Prints, an Adventure in Military Lithography," *Journal of the American Military Institute,* III (1939), 166–76.

Tolles, Frederick B., "A Contemporary Comment on Gustavus Hesselius," *Art Quarterly,* XVII, Autumn 1954, 271–3.

Tolman, Ruel P., "Attributing Miniatures," *Antiques,* XIV, Nov. 1928, 413–16; Dec. 1928, 523–6.

——— "Boston City and Harbor, 1839, Painted by Robert W. Salmon," *Art in America,* IX, Feb. 1921, 81–2.

——— *Life of Edward Greene Malbone,* New York, 1957.

——— "The Technique of Charles Fraser, Miniaturist," *Antiques,* XXVII, Jan. 1935, 19–22; Feb. 1935, 60–2.

[Toppan, Charles,] "History and Progress of Banknote Engraving," *The Crayon,* I, Feb. 21, 1855, 116–17.

Toppan, Robert N., *A Hundred Years of Bank Note Engraving in the United States,* New York, 1896.

Torrence, Robert M., *Torrence and Allied Families,* Philadelphia, 1938.

Torrey, Frederic C., *The Torrey Families and Their Children in America,* Lakehurst, N.J., 1924–29.

Tower, Fayette B., *Illustrations of the Croton Aqueduct,* New York, 1843.

Towne, Edwin E., *The Descendants of William Towne . . . ,* Newtonville, Mass., 1901.

Trenton [N.J.] *State Gazette,* newspaper.

Trollope, Frances M., *Domestic Manners of the Americans,* New York, 1832.

Trotter, Jessie, "E. Hutchinson Miller (1831–1921) the Artist," *Jefferson County* [W. Va.] *Historical Society Magazine,* V (1939), 38–40.

Tuckerman, Henry T., *Book of the Artists . . . ,* New York, 1867.

——— *A Memorial of Horatio Greenough . . . ,* New York, 1853.

Turner, Maria, "Early Artists in Nebraska," in *Nebraska Art and Artists,* ed. by Clarissa Bucklin, Lincoln, 1932.

Twitchell, Ralph E., *Genealogy of the Twitchell Family . . . ,* New York, 1929.

U

Ulp, Clifford McC., "Art and Artists in Rochester," *Rochester Historical Society Publication Fund Series,* XIV (1936), 29–60.

Underwood, Lucien M., *The Ancestry and Descendants of Jonathan Pollard . . . ,* Syracuse, 1891.

United States Exploring Expedition, see Wilkes, Charles.

United States, War Dep't, *Reports of Explorations and Surveys to Ascertain the Most Practicable and Economic Route for a Railroad from the Mississippi River to the Pacific Ocean,* 12 vols. in 13, Washington, 1855–60.

University of Pennsylvania, *Biographical Catalogue of the Matriculates of the College . , . 1749–1893,* Philadelphia, 1894.

V

Vail, Robert W. G., "The American Sketchbooks of a French Naturalist, 1816–1837, a Description of the Charles Alexandre Lesueur Collection, with a Brief Account of the Artist," *Proceedings of the American Antiquarian Society,* XLVIII, April 1938, 49–155.

——— "A Dinner at Mount Vernon, from the Unpublished Journal of Joshua Brookes (1773–1859)," *New-York Historical Society Quarterly,* XXXI, April 1947, 72–85.

——— *Gold Fever: A Catalogue of the California Gold Rush Centennial Exhibition,* New-York Historical Society, 1949.

——— *Knickerbocker Birthday: A Sesqui-Centennial History of The New-York Historical Society, 1804–1954,* New York, 1954.

——— "The Last Meeting of the Giants," *New-York Historical Society Quarterly,* XXXII, April 1948, 69–77.

——— "Report of the Board of Trustees," *Annual Report* of The New-York Historical Society for 1952 (New York, 1953), 17–37.

——— "Storied Windows Richly Dight," *New-York Historical Society Quarterly,* XXXVI, April 1952, 149–59.

Valentine, Elizabeth G., *Dawn to Twilight; Work of Edward V. Valentine,* Richmond, 1929.

Valentine, David T., comp., *Manual of the Corporation of the City of New York for 1860,* New York, 1860.

Vanderpoel, Emily N., comp., *Chronicles of a Pioneer School from 1782 to 1833 . . . ,* Cambridge, 1903.

Vanderpoel, George B., *Genealogy of the Vanderpoel Family . . . ,* New York, 1912.

Vann, Elizabeth C., and Margaret C. D. Dixon, *Denny Genealogy, Second Book,* Rutland, Vt., 1947.

Van Nostrand, Jeanne, "Thomas A. Ayres: Artist-Argonaut of California," *California Historical Society Quarterly,* XX, Sept. 1941, 275–9.

——— and Edith Coulter, *California Pictorial; A History in Contemporary Pictures, 1786–1859 . . . ,* Berkeley and Los Angeles, 1948.

Van Ravenswaay, Charles, "Anna Maria von Phul," *Missouri Historical Society Bulletin,* X, April 1954, 367–84.

——— "The Forgotten Arts and Crafts of Colonial Louisiana," *Antiques,* LXIV, Sept. 1953, 192–5.

Van Rensselaer, Florence, *The Livingston Family in America and Its Scottish Origins,* New York, 1949.

Van Sickle, John W., *A History of the Van Sickle Family in the United States . . . ,* Springfield, O., 1880.

Vedder, Elihu, *The Digressions of V,* Boston and New York, 1910.

Vermont, Edgar de Valcourt-, *America Heraldica, a Compilation of Coats of Arms, Crests, and Mottoes of Prominent American Families . . . ,* New York, 1886–89.

Vignoles, Olinthus J., *Life of Charles Blacker Vignoles . . . ,* London and New York, 1889.

Vinton, John A., *The Richardson Memorial . . . ,* Portland, Me., 1876.

Virginia Gazette, Williamsburg newspaper.

Virginia Historical Portraiture, 1585–1830, ed. by Alexander W. Weddell, Richmond, 1930.

Von Hagen, Victor W., "F. Catherwood, Archt.," *New-York Historical Society Quarterly,* XXX, Jan. 1946, 17–29.

——— *Frederick Catherwood, Archt.,* New York, 1950.

Vose Galleries [Boston], "Robert D. Wilkie, 1828–1903, Re-discovery of a 19th Century Boston Painter," chronology and two catalogues of Wilkie paintings exhibited at the Vose Galleries in November 1948.

W

Wadsworth Athenaeum [Hartford], *Bulletin* and *News Bulletin,* Hartford, 1922—.

——— *George Henry Durrie, 1820–1863, Connecticut Painter of American Life . . . ,* comp. by Mary Bartlett Cowdrey, Hartford, 1947.

Wagner, Henry R., and Charles L. Camp, *The Plains and the Rockies, a Bibliography . . . ,* 3d ed., Columbus, O., 1953.

Waite, Emma F., "Pioneer Color Printer: F. Quarré," *American Collector,* XV, Dec. 1946, 12–13, 20.

Waite, Marcus W., *The Wheelock Family of Calais, Vt. . . . ,* North Montpelier, Vt., 1940.

Walker Art Galleries [Minneapolis], *Illus-*

trated Catalogue of Indian Portraits . . . Painted by Henry H. Cross, Minneapolis, 1927.

Wall, Alexander J., "Joseph Valaperta, Sculptor," *New-York Historical Society Quarterly Bulletin,* XI, July 1927, 53–6.

——— "Wax Portraiture," *New-York Historical Society Quarterly Bulletin,* IX, April 1925, 3–26.

Walsh, James J., *American Jesuits,* New York, 1934.

Warren, Eliza S., *Memoirs of the West; The Spaldings,* Portland, Ore., 1916?.

Warren, William L., "A Checklist of Jennys Portraits," *Connecticut Historical Society Bulletin,* XXI, April 1956, 33–64.

——— "The Jennys Portraits," *Connecticut Historical Society Bulletin,* XX, Oct. 1955, 97–128.

——— "Mary Ann Hardy, an Appreciation," *Old-Time New England,* XLV, Winter 1955, 73–6.

——— "Richard Brunton, Itinerant Craftsman," *Art in America,* XXXIX, April 1951, 81–94; XLI, Spring 1953, 69–78.

Washbourn, John T., "The Work of David E. Cronin," *New-York Historical Society Quarterly Bulletin,* XXV, Jan. 1941, 17–25.

Washington, George, *The Diaries of George Washington, 1748–1799,* ed. by John C. Fitzpatrick, Boston and New York, 1925.

Washington [D.C.] Art Association, catalogues of the 1st to 4th annual exhibitions, 1857–60.

[Washington] *Evening Star,* newspaper.

[Washington] *National Intelligencer,* newspaper.

Washington Post, newspaper.

Washington Times, newspaper.

Waterhouse, Ellis K., *Painting in Britain 1530–1790,* London and Baltimore, 1953.

Watkins, Walter K., "John Coles, Heraldry Painter," *Old-Time New England,* XXI, Jan. 1931, 129–43.

——— *The Residuary Legatees of the Will of Mrs. Eliza Ann (Blackman) Colburn . . . ,* Boston, 1900.

Watlington, H. T., "The Incomplete Story of John Green, Artist and Judge," *Bermuda Historical Quarterly,* VI, May 1949, 65–76.

Watson, Douglas S., ed., *California in the Fifties . . . ,* San Francisco, 1936.

Watson, Forbes, *Winslow Homer,* New York, 1942.

Wayland, John W., *A History of Shenandoah County, Va.,* Strasburg, Va., 1927.

Weaks, Mabel C., "A Miniature of Herman Melville's Mother," *Antiques,* LIV, Oct. 1948, 259.

Webber, Richard, "The Birthplace of Robert Walter Weir, Artist," *New-York Historical Society Quarterly Bulletin,* XIV, Oct. 1930, 94.

Weber, Frederick P., *Medals and Medallions of the Nineteenth Century, Relating to England, by Foreign Artists,* London, 1894–1907.

Webster, J. Carson, "Junius R. Sloan, Self-taught Artist," *Art in America,* XL, Summer 1952, 103–52.

Wehle, Harry B., "A Portrait of Henry Clay, Reattributed," *Metropolitan Museum of Art Bulletin,* XX, Sept. 1925, 215–16.

——— and Theodore Bolton, *American Miniatures, 1730–1850 . . . ,* New York, 1927.

Weir, Irene, *Robert W. Weir, Artist,* New York, 1947.

Weis, Frederick L., *Check List of the Portraits in the Library of the American Antiquarian Society,* Worcester, 1947.

Weiss, Harry B., "The Growth of the Graphic Arts in Philadelphia 1663–1820," *Bulletin of the New York Public Library,* LVI, Feb. 1952, 76–83; March 1952, 139–45.

——— "The Number of Persons and Firms . . . Connected with the Graphic Arts in New York City, 1633–1820," *Bulletin of the New York Public Library,* L, Oct. 1946, 775–86.

——— and Grace M. Zeigler, "Mrs. Thomas Say," *Journal of the New York Entomological Society,* XLI, Dec. 1933.

——— *Thomas Say, Early American Naturalist,* Springfield, Ill., and Baltimore, 1931.

Weitenkampf, Frank, *American Graphic Art,* New York, 1912; rev. ed., 1924.

——— "An Artist of Ante-Bellum Times," *The Independent,* XLVI, March 29, 1894, 395.

——— "Early American Landscape Prints," *Art Quarterly,* VIII, Winter 1945, 40–67.

——— "F. O. C. Darley, American Illustrator," *Art Quarterly,* X, Spring 1947, 100–13.

——— "The Intimate Homer; Winslow Homer's Sketches," *Art Quarterly,* VI, Autumn 1943, 307–21.

——— "John Greenwood; An American-born Artist in 18th Century Europe, with a Checklist of His Etchings and Mezzotints," *Bulletin of the New York Public Library,* XXXI, Aug. 1927, 623–34.

——— "John Hill and American Landscapes in Aquatint," *American Collector,* XVII, July 1948, 6–8.

——— *Political Caricature in the United States in Separately Published Cartoons; An Annotated List,* New York, 1953.

——— "A Swiss Artist among the Indians," *Bulletin of the New York Public Library,* LII, Nov. 1948, 554–6.

Welby, Adlard, *A Visit to North America and the English Settlements in Illinois . . . ,* London, 1821; reprinted in Thwaites, *Early Western Travels,* XII.

Weld, Isaac, *Travels through the States of North America, and the Provinces of Upper and Lower Canada during the Years 1795, 1796, and 1797,* London, 1800.

Weld, Ralph F., *Brooklyn Village 1816–1834,* New York, 1938.

Weller, Allen, "A Note on Winslow Homer's Drawings in *Harper's Weekly,*" *Art in America,* XXII, March 1934, 76–8.

Welsh, Herbert, "Artists of Germantown," in *Germantown History* (Germantown Site and Relic Society, 1915), 233–47.

Wentworth, John, *The Wentworth Genealogy . . . ,* Boston, 1870.

West Stockbridge, Mass. *Vital Records of West Stockbridge, Mass., to the Year 1850,* Boston, 1907.

Western Reserve Historical Society, *Publications of the . . . ,* Cleveland, 1870–1929.

Weston, Thomas, *History of the Town of Middleboro, Mass.,* Boston and New York, 1906.

Wharton, Anne H., *Heirlooms in Miniatures,* Philadelphia, 1898.

——— *Salons Colonial and Republican,* Philadelphia, 1900.

Whig Portrait Gallery, New York, *c.* 1850.

White, D. Fedotoff, "A Russian Sketches Philadelphia, 1811–1813," *Pennsylvania Magazine of History and Biography,* LXXV, Jan. 1951, 3–24.

White, John Blake, "The Journal of John Blake White," ed. by Paul R. Weidner, *South Carolina Historical and Genealogical Magazine,* XLII (1941), 55–71, 99–117, 169–86; XLIII (1942), 34–46, 103–17, 161–74.

White, Leonard D., *The Jeffersonians; A Study in Administrative History, 1801–1829,* New York, 1951.

White, Margaret E., ed., *A Sketch of Chester Harding, Artist, Drawn by His Own Hand,* Boston, 1890; new ed., 1929.

White, Philip L., *The Beekmans of New York in Politics and Commerce, 1647–1877,* New York, 1956.

Whitehill, Walter M., "Portraits of American Ships," *American Collector,* X, April 1941, 6–8.

Whitley, William T., *Artists and Their Friends in England, 1700–1799,* London and Boston, 1928.

——— *Gilbert Stuart,* Cambridge, 1932.

Whitmore, William H., "Abel Bowen," *Bostonian Society Publications,* I (1886–88), 29–56.

——— *A Brief Genealogy of the Gore Family . . . ,* Boston, 1875.

——— *Notes Concerning Peter Pelham . . . and His Successors Prior to the Revolution,* Cambridge, 1867.

Who's Who in America . . . , Chicago, 1899—.

Wied-Neuwied, Maximilian Alexander Philipp, prince of, *Maximilian, Prince of Wied's Travels in the Interior of North America, 1832–1834,* Cleveland, 1906; vols. XXII–XXV of Thwaite, *Early Western Travels.*

Wight, William W., *The Wights . . . ,* Milwaukee, 1890.

Wilkes, Charles, *Narrative of the United States Exploring Expedition . . . ,* Philadelphia, 1844.

Wilkie, Franc B., *Davenport, Past and Present . . . ,* Davenport, Iowa, 1858.

William and Mary Quarterly, Williamsburg, Va., 1892—.

"William Mackwitz, Wood Engraver," *Missouri Historical Society Bulletin,* VIII, Jan. 1952, 176–9.

Williams, Amelia W., and Eugene C. Barber, ed., *The Writings of Sam Houston 1813–1863,* Austin, Tex., 1938–43.

Williams, John C., *An Oneida County Printer, William Williams . . . ,* New York, 1906.

Williams, John F., *William J. Williams, Portrait Painter, and His Descendants,* Buffalo, 1933.

Williams, Wellington, *Appleton's Northern and Eastern Traveller's Guide . . . ,* New York and Philadelphia, 1850.

Williams, William W., *History of Ashtabula County, Ohio . . . ,* Philadelphia, 1878.

[Williamsburg] *Virginia Gazette,* newspaper.

Willis, Eola, *The Charleston Stage in the 18th Century, with Social Settings of the Time,* Columbia, S.C., 1924.

——— "Henrietta Johnston, South Carolina Pastellist," *The Antiquarian,* XI, Sept. 1928, 46–7.

Willis, Patty, "Jefferson County Portraits and

Portrait Painters," *Magazine of the Jefferson County* [W. Va.] *Historical Society,* VI, Dec. 1940, 21–39.

Wilson, Erasmus, ed., *Standard History of Pittsburgh, Pa.,* Chicago, 1898.

Wilson, Francis, *Joseph Jefferson, Reminiscences of a Fellow Player,* New York, 1906.

Wilson, Robert, "Art and Artists in Provincial South Carolina," *Year Book, 1899, Charleston, South Carolina,* Appendix, 137–47.

Wilson, Rufus R., *Lincoln in Portraiture,* New York, 1935.

Wilson, Samuel M., "Matthew Harris Jouett, Kentucky Portrait Painter; A Review," *The Filson Club History Quarterly,* XIII, April 1939, 75–96; "Additional Notes . . . ," *ibid.,* XIV, 1940, 1–16, 65–102.

Winchester, Alice, "A Painted Wall," *Antiques,* XLIX, May 1946, 310–11.

Winn, David W. and Elizabeth J., *Ancestors and Descendants of John Quales Winn and His Wife Mary Liscome Jarvis . . . ,* Baltimore, 1932.

Winter, George, *The Journals and Indian Paintings of George Winter 1837–1839,* Indianapolis, 1948.

Winter, William, *The Jeffersons,* Boston, 1881.

Winwar, Frances, *American Giant: Walt Whitman and His Times,* New York, 1941.

Wisconsin Magazine of History, Madison, 1917—.

Wisconsin, State Historical Society of, *Historical Collections of the . . . ,* Madison, 1854—.

——— *Second Triennial Catalogue of the Portrait Gallery of the . . . ,* Madison, 1892.

Wiseman, Charles M. R., *Centennial History of Lancaster, Ohio, and Lancaster People . . . ,* Lancaster, 1898.

Wood, Edmund, "William Bradford," *Old Dartmouth Historical Sketches,* XXVI (1909), 6–8.

Woodward, E. M., and John M. Hageman, *History of Burlington and Mercer Counties, N.J. . . . ,* Philadelphia, 1883.

Woolsey, Theodore S., "The American Vasari," *Yale Review,* III, July 1914, 778–89.

Worcester Art Museum, *Bulletin* and *News Bulletin and Calendar,* Worcester, Mass., 1910—.

——— *Catalogue of Paintings and Drawings,* Worcester, Mass., 1922.

——— *Christian Gullager, 1759–1826, An Exhibition . . . ,* Worcester, Mass., 1949.

Worcester Society of Antiquity (later Worcester Historical Society), *Collections of the . . . ,* Worcester, Mass., 1881–1901.

"Works of William Marshall Swayne," *Chester County* [Pa.] *Collections,* XVI, Oct. 1939, 503–4.

W.P.A., American Guide Series, *Alabama, A Guide to the Deep South,* New York, 1941.

——— *California, A Guide to the Golden State,* New York, 1939.

——— *Georgia, A Guide to Its Towns and Countryside,* Athens, Ga., 1940.

——— *Kansas, A Guide to the Sunflower State,* New York, 1939.

——— *Kentucky, A Guide to the Bluegrass State,* New York, 1954.

——— *Maine, A Guide "Down East,"* Boston, 1937.

——— *Michigan, A Guide to the Wolverine State,* New York, 1941.

——— *Missouri, A Guide to the "Show Me" State,* New York, 1941.

——— *Montana, A State Guide Book,* New York, 1949.

——— *Nebraska, A Guide to the Cornhusker State,* New York, 1939.

——— *New Hampshire, A Guide to the Granite State,* Boston, 1938.

——— *Tennessee, A Guide to the State,* New York, 1949.

——— *Texas, A Guide to the Lone Star State,* New York, 1940.

——— *Wisconsin, A Guide to the Badger State,* New York, 1941.

W.P.A. (Ala.). Historical Records Survey, Alabama.

W.P.A. (Ark.). Historical Records Survey, Arkansas.

W.P.A. (Cal.), *Introduction to California Art Research,* I and II, San Francisco, 1936–37.

W.P.A. (Mass.), *Portraits Found in Maine.* W.P.A., Hisorical Records Survey (Mass.), *American Portraits (1645–1850) Found in the State of Maine* (Boston, 1941), mimeographed preliminary report.

——— *Portraits Found in Mass.* W.P.A., Historical Records Survey (Mass.), *American Portraits 1620–1825 Found in Massachusetts* (Boston, 1939), 2 vols., mimeographed.

——— *Portraits Found in N.H.* W.P.A., Historical Records Survey (Mass.), *Preliminary Checklist of American Portraits 1620–1860 Found in New Hampshire* (Boston, 1942), mimeographed.

——— *Portraits Found in N.Y.* W.P.A.,

Historical Records Survey (Mass.), "American Portraits Found in New York," manuscript volume, Library of Congress.

——— *Portraits Found in Vt.* W.P.A., Historical Records Survey (Mass.), "Portraits Found in Vermont," manuscript volume, Library of Congress.

W.P.A. (N.H.). Historical Records Survey, New Hampshire.

W.P.A. (N.J.). Historical Records Survey, New Jersey.

W.P.A., Historical Records Survey (New Jersey), *1440 Early American Portrait Artists,* Newark, 1940.

W.P.A., Historical Records Survey (Ohio), *Annals of Cleveland, 1818–1935* (Cleveland, 1936+).

W.P.A., Historical Records Survey (Pa.), "Catalogue of the Early American Portraits in the Pennsylvania Academy of the Fine Arts," manuscript volume, Library of Congress.

W.P.A., Historical Records Survey (Pa.), *Descriptive Catalogue of the Du Simitière Papers in the Library Company of Philadelphia,* Philadelphia, 1940.

W.P.A. (Texas). Historical Records Survey, Texas.

W.P.A. (Vt.). Historical Records Survey, Vermont.

Wright, Charles Lennox II, "Charles Cushing Wright—Lavinia Dorothy Wright—Their Life and Works," manuscript biography, New-York Historical Society.

——— "The Pioneer of Zinc Etching, Introduction to the Charles Lennox Wright I Collection," *New-York Historical Society Quarterly,* XXXVI, April 1952, 195–209.

Wright, Edith A., and Josephine A. McDevitt, "Henry Stone, Lithographer," *Antiques,* XXXIV, July 1938, 16–19.

Wright, Nathalia, "Horatio Greenough, Boston Sculptor," *Old-Time New England,* XLV, Jan.–March 1955, 55–60.

Wroth, Lawrence C., *Abel Buell of Connecticut, Silversmith, Type Founder, and Engraver,* New Haven, 1926.

Wynne, Nancy, and Beaumont Newhall, "Horatio Greenough: Herald of Functionalism," *Magazine of Art,* XXXII, Jan. 1934, 12–15.

Y

Yale Associates in Fine Arts, *Bulletin of the . . . ,* New Haven, 1926—.

Yale University Gallery of Fine Arts, *Connecticut Portraits by Ralph Earl, 1761–1801,* foreword by William Sawitzky, New Haven, 1935.

Yanaguana Society [San Antonio], *Catalogue* of a loan exhibition, San Antonio, Texas, December 1933.

Yancey, Rosa F., *Lynchburg and Its Neighbors,* Richmond, 1935.

Yarmolinsky, *see* Svin′in.

Yesterday in Chester County Art, see under Pleasants, Henry, Jr.

Young, Andrew W., *History of the Town of Warsaw, New York . . . ,* Buffalo, 1869.